MAP PAGES

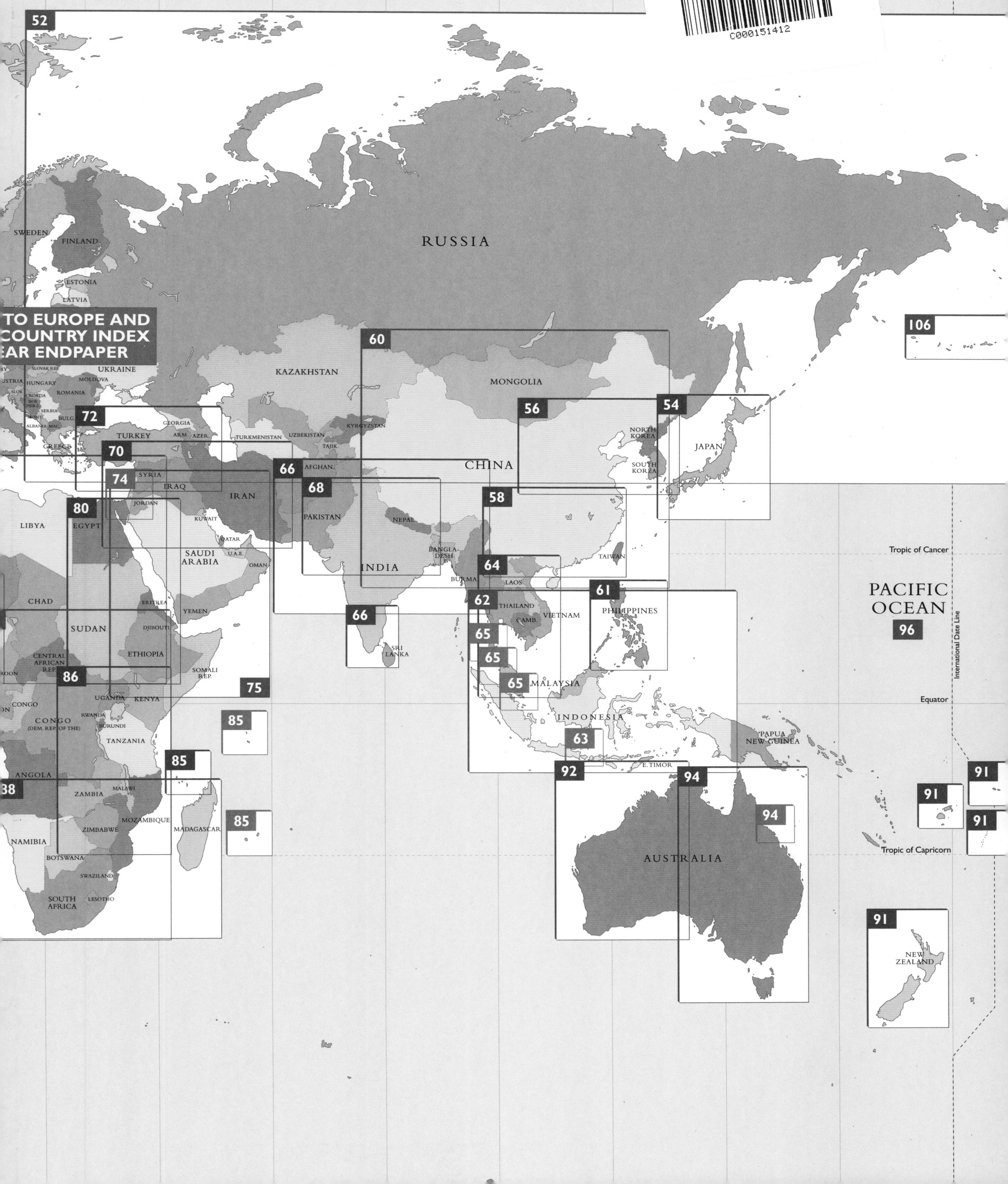

52

SWEDEN

FINLAND

ESTONIA

LATVIA

RUSSIA

TO EUROPE AND
COUNTRY INDEX
EAR ENDPAPER

KAZAKHSTAN

MONGOLIA

60

106

USTRIA   SLOVAK REP.   UKRAINE

SLOV.   HUNGARY   MOLDOVA

CROATIA   ROMANIA

BOS.   SERBIA

HERZ.

MONT.   BULG.

ALBANIA MAC.

GREECE

72

GEORGIA

TURKEY   ARM. AZER.   TURKMENISTAN   UZBEKISTAN

KYRGYZSTAN

TAJIK.

56

54

NORTH
KOREA

JAPAN

70

74   SYRIA

IRAQ

IRAN

66   AFGHAN.

68

CHINA

SOUTH
KOREA

58

80

JORDAN

PAKISTAN

NEPAL

BANGLA-
DESH

64

TAIWAN

LIBYA   EGYPT

KUWAIT

QATAR

U.A.E.

SAUDI
ARABIA

OMAN

INDIA

BURMA   LAOS

Tropic of Cancer

PACIFIC
OCEAN

96

CHAD

ERITREA

YEMEN

66

62   THAILAND

CAMB.

VIETNAM

PHILIPPINES

61

SUDAN

DJIBOUTI

ETHIOPIA

SRI
LANKA

65

65

SOMALI
REP.

75

65   MALAYSIA

CENTRAL
AFRICAN
REP.

UGANDA   KENYA

86

RWANDA

BURUNDI

85

INDONESIA

International Date Line

Equator

91

CONGO

CONGO
(DEM. REP. OF THE)

TANZANIA

85

63

PAPUA
NEW GUINEA

91

ANGOLA

85

E. TIMOR

92

94

91

38

ZAMBIA   MALAWI

MOZAMBIQUE

MADAGASCAR

85

94

NAMIBIA

ZIMBABWE

Tropic of Capricorn

BOTSWANA

AUSTRALIA

SWAZILAND

SOUTH
AFRICA   LESOTHO

91

NEW
ZEALAND

PHILIP'S

WORLD TRAVELLER'S ATLAS

PHILIP'S

WORLD TRAVELLER'S ATLAS

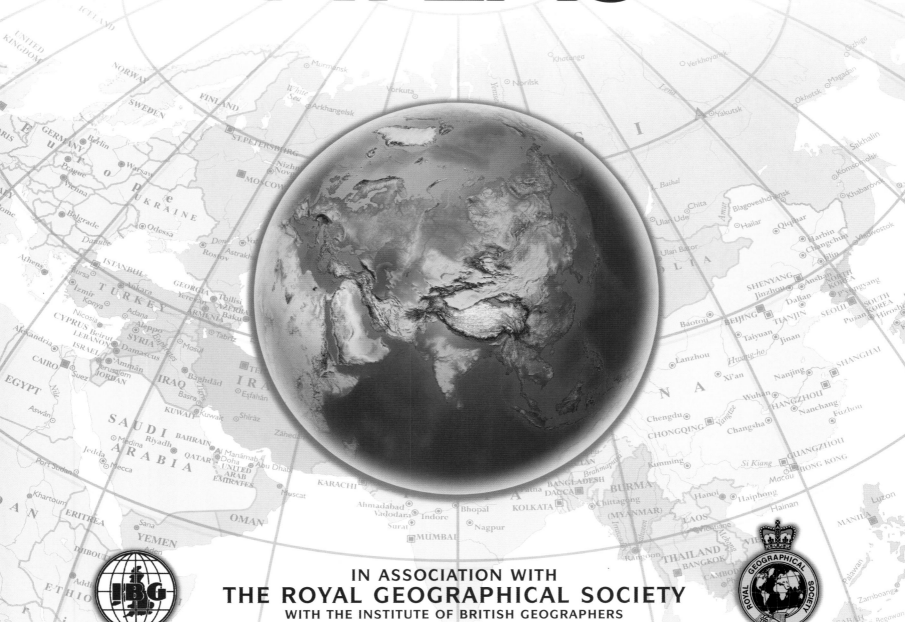

IN ASSOCIATION WITH
THE ROYAL GEOGRAPHICAL SOCIETY
WITH THE INSTITUTE OF BRITISH GEOGRAPHERS

PICTURE ACKNOWLEDGEMENTS

WORLD EXPLORER:

© *CORBIS* 26 bottom, 27 bottom, /Adam Woolfitt 5 centre right, 30 centre left, /AFP 24 top, 25 bottom, /Angelo Hornak 29 centre left, /Australian Picture Library 13 top, /Bob Krist 14 top, /Bob Winsett 20 top, /Brandon D. Cole 11 bottom, /Buddy Mays 26 centre, 22 bottom, /Catherine Karnow 19 bottom, /Charles and Josette Lenars 30 bottom right, /Charles O'Rear 23 left, /Clem Haagner; Gallo Images 10 centre, /Dave G. Houser 30 top, /David Muench 4 left, /Dean Conger 15 bottom, /Derek Hall; Frank Lane Picture Agency 3 centre, /Douglas Peebles 32 bottom, /Duomo 20 right, /Enzo and Paolo Ragazzini 16 bottom, /Galen Rowell 2 left, 9 bottom, 21 top, /George H. H. Huey 4 top, /George Lepp 12 bottom, /Hans Georg Roth 5 top, /Inge Yspeert 10 bottom right, /James Marshall 6 centre right, /John Dakers; Eye Ubiquitous 25 right, /Kevin Schafer 13 bottom, /Marc Muench 20 left, /Michael and Patricia Fogden 8 /Michael Busselle 3 top, /Michael S. Yamashita 22 top, /Milepost 92½ 15 top, /Mimmo Jodice 29 bottom, /Morton Beebe, S. F. 24 centre right, /Nik Wheeler 19 top, /O. Alamany and E. Vicens 5 bottom, /Patrick Ward 7 bottom, 16 centre right, /Peter Johnson 10 top, /Peter Wilson 28 bottom, /Premium Stock 28 top, /Quadrillion 31 bottom, /Raymond Gehman 2 top, 6 top, /Rick Doyle 23 bottom, /Robert Holmes 16 top, /Roger Ressmeyer 3 bottom, /Roger Tidman 9 left, /Stephanie Maze 24 bottom, /Stephen Frink 12 top, 13 centre, /Steve Kaufman 6 bottom, /Tim Thompson 14 centre right, 14 bottom, /Tiziana and Gianni Baldizzone 7 centre right, /Tom Bean 8 bottom, /Tom Brakefield 11 top, /Tom Nebbia 17 right, /Tony Arruza 23 top, /Vanni Archive 29 top, /W. Cody 18 right, 27 top, /Wild Country 26 top, /Wolfgang Kaehler 17 top, 18 top and bottom, 8 top.
© *ALTON TOWERS* 32 left.

CITY GAZETTEER:

© *CORBIS* /Bettmann 41 right, /Carmen Redondo 44 left, /Charles E. Rotkin 40 right, /Chris Lisle 47 centre, /Hubert Stadler 41 centre, /John Heseltine 42 centre, /Larry Lee 46 right, /Lindsay Hebberd 42 left, /Patrick Ward 44 right, /Paul A. Souders 47 right, /Richard T. Nowitz 43 centre, /Tim Thompson 41 left, /Todd Gipstein 44 centre, /Wolfgang Kaehler 45 right, /Yann Arthus-Bertrand 46 left.
© *MIKE MOULE* 40 left, 42 right, 43 right, 45 left, 46 centre, 48 centre and right.

CITY MAPS
Cartography by Philip's

PAGE 10, DUBLIN: The town plan of Dublin is based on Ordnance Survey Ireland by permission of the Government Permit Number 8186. © Ordnance Survey Ireland and Government of Ireland.

Ordnance Survey **PAGE 11, EDINBURGH, and PAGE 15, LONDON:** This product includes mapping data licensed from Ordnance Survey® with the permission of the Controller of Her Majesty's Stationery Office. © Crown copyright 2007. All rights reserved. Licence number 100011710.

VECTOR DATA: Courtesy of Gräfe and Unser Verlag GmbH, München, Germany (city-centre maps of Bangkok, Beijing, Cape Town, Jerusalem, Mexico City, Moscow, Singapore, Sydney, Tokyo and Washington D.C.)

The following city maps utilize base data supplied courtesy of MapQuest.com, Inc. (© MapQuest): Las Vegas, New Orleans, Orlando.

> **NOTE:**
> For reasons of safety or politics, there may be times when it is not advisable, or desirable, to visit one or more of the places described in the World Explorer and City Gazetteer sections. If in doubt, please check with the Foreign Office.

Published in Great Britain in 2007 by Philip's,
a division of Octopus Publishing Group Limited,
2–4 Heron Quays, London E14 4JP
An Hachette Livre UK Company

Copyright © 2007 Philip's

Cartography by Philip's

ISBN-13 978-0-540-09014-3
ISBN-10 0-540-09014-X

A CIP catalogue record for this book is available from the British Library.

Printed in Hong Kong

Details of other Philip's titles and services can be found on our website at:
www.philips-maps.co.uk

Philip's World Atlases are published in association with The Royal Geographical Society (with The Institute of British Geographers).

The Society was founded in 1830 and given a Royal Charter in 1859 for 'the advancement of geographical science'. It holds historical collections of national and international importance, many of which relate to the Society's association with and support for scientific exploration and research from the 19th century onwards. It was pivotal in establishing geography as a teaching and research discipline in British universities close to the turn of the century, and has played a key role in geographical and environmental education ever since.

Today the Society is a leading world centre for geographical learning – supporting education, teaching, research and expeditions, and promoting public understanding of the subject.

The Society welcomes those interested in geography as members. For further information, please visit the website at: www.rgs.org

USER GUIDE

The reference maps which form the main body of this atlas have been prepared in accordance with the highest standards of international cartography to provide an accurate and detailed representation of the Earth. The scales and projections used have been carefully chosen to give balanced coverage of the world, while emphasizing the most densely populated and economically significant regions. A hallmark of Philip's mapping is the use of hill shading and relief colouring to create a graphic impression of landforms: this makes the maps exceptionally easy to read. However, knowledge of the key features employed in the construction and presentation of the maps will enable the reader to derive the fullest benefit from the atlas.

MAP SEQUENCE

The atlas covers the Earth continent by continent: first Europe; then its land neighbour Asia (mapped north before south, in a clockwise sequence), then Africa, Australia and Oceania, North America and South America. This is the classic arrangement adopted by most cartographers since the 16th century. For each continent, there are maps at a variety of scales. First, physical relief and political maps

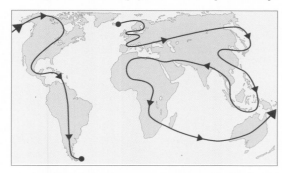

of the whole continent; then a series of larger-scale maps of the regions within the continent, each followed, where required, by still larger-scale maps of the most important or densely populated areas. The governing principle is that by turning the pages of the atlas, the reader moves steadily from north to south through each continent, with each map overlapping its neighbours.

MAP PRESENTATION

With very few exceptions (e.g. for the Arctic and Antarctica), the maps are drawn with north at the top, regardless of whether they are presented upright or sideways on the page. In the borders will be found the map title; a locator diagram showing the area covered; continuation arrows showing the page numbers for maps of adjacent areas; the scale; the projection used; the degrees of latitude and longitude; and the letters and figures used in the index for locating place names and geographical features. Physical relief maps also have a height reference panel identifying the colours used for each layer of contouring.

MAP SYMBOLS

Each map contains a vast amount of detail which can only be conveyed clearly and accurately by the use of symbols. Points and circles of varying sizes locate and identify the relative importance of towns and cities; different styles of type are employed for administrative, geographical and regional place names to aid identification. A variety of pictorial symbols denote landforms such as glaciers, marshes and coral reefs, and man-made structures including roads, railways, airports and canals. International borders are shown by red lines. Where neighbouring countries are in dispute, for example in parts of the Middle East, the maps show the *de facto* boundary between nations, regardless of the legal or historical situation. The symbols are explained on the first page of the World Maps section of the atlas.

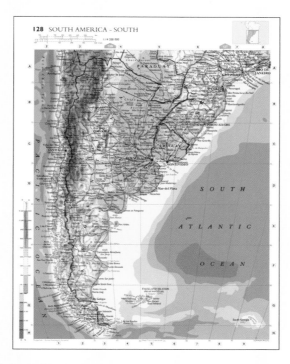

MAP SCALES

1:16 000 000
1 inch = 252 statute miles

The scale of each map is given in the numerical form known as the 'representative fraction'. The first figure is always one, signifying one unit of distance on the map; the second figure, usually in millions, is the number by which the map unit must be multiplied to give the equivalent distance on the Earth's surface. Calculations can easily be made in centimetres and kilometres, by dividing the Earth units figure by 100 000 (i.e. deleting the last five 0s). Thus 1:1 000 000 means 1 cm = 10 km. The calculation for inches and miles is more laborious, but 1 000 000 divided by 63 360 (the number of inches in a mile) shows that 1:1 000 000 means approximately 1 inch = 16 miles. The table below provides distance equivalents for scales down to 1:50 000 000.

LARGE SCALE		
1:1 000 000	1 cm = 10 km	1 inch = 16 miles
1:2 500 000	1 cm = 25 km	1 inch = 39.5 miles
1:5 000 000	1 cm = 50 km	1 inch = 79 miles
1:6 000 000	1 cm = 60 km	1 inch = 95 miles
1:8 000 000	1 cm = 80 km	1 inch = 126 miles
1:10 000 000	1 cm = 100 km	1 inch = 158 miles
1:15 000 000	1 cm = 150 km	1 inch = 237 miles
1:20 000 000	1 cm = 200 km	1 inch = 316 miles
1:50 000 000	1 cm = 500 km	1 inch = 790 miles
SMALL SCALE		

MEASURING DISTANCES

Although each map is accompanied by a scale bar, distances cannot always be measured with confidence because of the distortions involved in portraying the curved surface of the Earth on a flat page. As a general rule, the larger the map scale (i.e. the lower the number of Earth units in the representative fraction), the more accurate and reliable will be the distance measured. On small-scale maps such as those of the world and of entire continents, measurement may only

be accurate along the 'standard parallels', or central axes, and should not be attempted without considering the map projection.

MAP PROJECTIONS

Unlike a globe, no flat map can give a true scale representation of the world in terms of area, shape and position of every region. Each of the numerous systems that have been devised for projecting the curved surface of the Earth on to a flat page involves the sacrifice of accuracy in one or more of these elements. The variations in shape and position of landmasses such as Alaska, Greenland and Australia, for example, can be quite dramatic when different projections are compared.

For this atlas, the guiding principle has been to select projections that involve the least distortion of size and distance. The projection used for each map is noted in the border. Most fall into one of three categories – conic, azimuthal or cylindrical – whose basic concepts are shown above. Each involves plotting the forms of the Earth's surface on a grid of latitude and longitude lines, which may be shown as parallels, curves or radiating spokes.

LATITUDE AND LONGITUDE

Accurate positioning of individual points on the Earth's surface is made possible by reference to the geometrical system of latitude and longitude. Latitude *parallels* are drawn west–east around the Earth and numbered by degrees north and south of the Equator, which is designated 0° of latitude. Longitude *meridians* are drawn north–south and numbered by degrees east and west of the *prime meridian*, 0° of longitude, which passes through Greenwich in England. By referring to these co-ordinates and their subdivisions of minutes (1/60th of a degree) and seconds (1/60th of a minute), any place on Earth can be located to within a few hundred metres. Latitude and longitude are indicated by blue lines on the maps; they are straight or curved according to the projection employed. Reference to these lines is the easiest way of determining the relative positions of places on different maps, and for plotting compass directions.

NAME FORMS

For ease of reference, both English and local name forms appear in the atlas. Oceans, seas and countries are shown in English throughout the atlas; country names may be abbreviated to their commonly accepted form (e.g. Germany, not The Federal Republic of Germany). Conventional English forms are also used for place names on the smaller-scale maps of the continents. However, local name forms are used on all large-scale and regional maps, with the English form given in brackets only for important cities – the large-scale map of Russia and Central Asia thus shows Moskva (Moscow). For countries which do not use a Roman script, place names have been transcribed according to the systems adopted by the British and US Geographic Names Authorities. For China, the Pin Yin system has been used, with some more widely known forms appearing in brackets, as with Beijing (Peking). Both English and local names appear in the index, the English form being cross-referenced to the local form.

CONTENTS

WORLD STATISTICS

Countries	x
Cities	xi
Distances	xii
Climate	xiii
Physical Dimensions	xiv–xv
Regions in the News	xvi

WORLD EXPLORER

Mountains and volcanoes	2–3
Deserts and canyons	4–5
Lakes and waterfalls	6–7
Wildlife in the Americas and Europe	8–9
Wildlife in Africa, Asia and Australasia	10–11
Marine wildlife	12–13
Great railway journeys	14–15
River and canal journeys	16–17
Sea and ocean cruises	18–19
Winter sports	20–21
Great beaches	22–23
Festivals	24–25
Historic sites in the Americas	26–27
Historic sites in Europe	28–29
Historic sites in Africa, Asia and Australasia	30–31
Theme parks	32

WORLD CITIES

CITY MAPS

Amsterdam	2
Athens	2
Atlanta	3
Baghdad	3
Bangkok	3
Barcelona	4
Beijing	4
Berlin	5
Boston	6
Brussels	6
Budapest	7
Buenos Aires	7
Cairo	7
Cape Town	8
Copenhagen	8
Chicago	9
Delhi	10
Dublin	10
Edinburgh	11
Guangzhou (Canton)	11
Helsinki	11
Hong Kong	12
Istanbul	12
Jakarta	12
Jerusalem	13
Johannesburg	13
Karachi	13
Kolkata (Calcutta)	14
Lagos	14
Las Vegas	14
Lima	14
London	15
Lisbon	16
Los Angeles	16–17
Madrid	17
Manila	17
Melbourne	18
Mexico City	18
Miami	18
Milan	19
Moscow	19
Montréal	20
Mumbai (Bombay)	20
Munich	21
New Orleans	21
New York	22
Orlando	23
Osaka	23
Oslo	23
Paris	24
Prague	25
Rio de Janeiro	25
Rome	26
San Francisco	26
St Petersburg	27
Santiago	27
São Paulo	27
Seoul	27
Shanghai	28
Singapore	28
Stockholm	29
Sydney	29
Tokyo	30
Tehran	31
Toronto	31
Vienna	32
Warsaw	32
Washington	33
Wellington	33

INDEX TO CITY MAPS 34–39

CITY GAZETTEER

Accra, Ghana	40
Agra, India	40
Amsterdam, The Netherlands	40
Antwerp, Belgium	40
Athens, Greece	40
Atlanta, Georgia, USA	40
Auckland, New Zealand	40
Bangkok, Thailand	40
Barcelona, Spain	40
Beijing, China	40
Berlin, Germany	40
Boston, Massachusetts, USA	41
Brisbane, Queensland, Australia	41
Brussels, Belgium	41
Budapest, Hungary	41
Buenos Aires, Argentina	41
Cairo, Egypt	41
Cape Town, South Africa	41
Cartagena, Colombia	41
Chicago, Illinois, USA	41
Cologne, Germany	41
Copenhagen, Denmark	41
Delhi, India	42
Dublin, Ireland	42
Edinburgh, Scotland	42
Esfahan, Iran	42
Fès, Morocco	42
Florence, Italy	42
Geneva, Switzerland	42
Guangzhou (Canton), China	42
Hamburg, Germany	42
Hanoi, Vietnam	42
Havana, Cuba	42
Helsinki, Finland	43
Hong Kong, China	43
Istanbul, Turkey	43
Jaipur, India	43
Jakarta, Indonesia	43
Jerusalem, Israel	43
Johannesburg, South Africa	43
Kairouan, Tunisia	43
Karachi, Pakistan	43
Katmandu, Nepal	43
Kolkata (Calcutta), India	43
Kraków, Poland	43
Kuala Lumpur, Malaysia	44
Kyoto, Japan	44
Lagos, Nigeria	44
Lahore, Pakistan	44
Las Vegas, Nevada, USA	44
Lima, Peru	44
Lisbon, Portugal	44
London, England	44
Los Angeles, California, USA	44
Luxembourg City, Luxembourg	44
Madrid, Spain	44
Manila, Philippines	45
Marrakech, Morocco	45
Melbourne, Victoria, Australia	45
Mexico City, Mexico	45
Miami, Florida, USA	45
Milan, Italy	45
Montréal, Québec, Canada	45
Moscow, Russia	45
Mumbai (Bombay), India	45
Munich, Germany	45
Nairobi, Kenya	45
New Orleans, Louisiana, USA	45
New York, NY, USA	46
Orlando, Florida, USA	46
Osaka, Japan	46
Oslo, Norway	46
Paris, France	46
Perth, Western Australia, Australia	46
Prague, Czech Republic	46
Quito, Ecuador	46
Reykjavik, Iceland	46
Riga, Latvia	46
Rio de Janeiro, Brazil	46
Rome, Italy	46
St Petersburg, Russia	47
San Francisco, California, USA	47
Santiago, Chile	47
São Paulo, Brazil	47
Seattle, Washington, USA	47
Seoul, South Korea	47
Shanghai, China	47
Singapore City, Singapore	47
Stockholm, Sweden	47
Sydney, New South Wales, Australia	47
Tehran, Iran	47
Tianjin, China	48
Tokyo, Japan	48
Toronto, Ontario, Canada	48
Vancouver, British Columbia, Canada	48
Varanasi, India	48
Venice, Italy	48
Vienna, Austria	48
Warsaw, Poland	48
Washington, DC, USA	48
Wellington, New Zealand	48
Xi'an, China	48
Yangon (Rangoon), Burma (Myanmar)	48

WORLD MAPS

Map Symbols — 1

The World: Political
1:84 000 000 — 2–3

Arctic Ocean
1:31 100 000 — 4

Antarctica
1:31 100 000 — 5

Europe

Europe: Physical
1:17 800 000 — 6

Europe: Political
1:17 800 000 — 7

Scandinavia
1:5 300 000
Iceland 1:5 300 000
Færoe Islands 1:5 300 000 — 8–9

Denmark and Southern Sweden
1:2 200 000 — 10–11

Ireland
1:1 800 000 — 12

Scotland
1:1 800 000
Orkney Islands 1:1 800 000
Shetland Islands 1:1 800 000 — 13

England and Wales
1:1 800 000
Isles of Scilly 1:1 800 000 — 14–15

British Isles
1:4 400 000 — 16

Netherlands, Belgium and Luxembourg
1:2 200 000 — 17

Northern France
1:2 200 000 — 18–19

Southern France
1:2 200 000 — 20–21

Central Europe
1:4 400 000 — 22–23

Germany and Switzerland
1:2 200 000 — 24–25

Austria, Czech Republic and Slovak Republic
1:2 200 000 — 26–27

Hungary, Romania and the Lower Danube
1:2 200 000 — 28–29

Poland and the Southern Baltic
1:2 200 000 — 30–31

Baltic States, Belarus and Ukraine
1:4 400 000 — 32–33

The Volga Basin and the Caucasus
1:4 400 000 — 34–35

Western Spain and Portugal
1:2 200 000 — 36–37

Eastern Spain
1:2 200 000
Menorca 1:2 200 000 — 38–39

Northern Italy, Slovenia and Croatia
1:2 200 000 — 40–41

Southern Italy
1:2 200 000 — 42–43

The Balkans
1:2 200 000 — 44–45

Southern Greece and Western Turkey
1:2 200 000

46–47

The Balearics, the Canaries and Madeira
1:900 000 / 1:1 800 000

48

Malta, Crete, Corfu, Rhodes and Cyprus
1:900 000 / 1:1 200 000

49

Asia

Asia: Physical
1:44 400 000

50

Asia: Political
1:44 400 000

51

Russia and Central Asia
1:17 800 000

52–53

Japan
1:4 400 000
Ryukyu Islands 1:4 400 000

54–55

Northern China and Korea
1:5 300 000

56–57

Southern China
1:5 300 000

58–59

China
1:17 800 000

60

The Philippines
1:6 700 000

61

Indonesia and the Philippines
1:11 100 000
Java and Madura 1:6 700 000
Bali 1:1 800 000

62–63

Mainland South-east Asia
1:5 300 000
Ko Phuket 1:900 000
Ko Samui 1:900 000
Pinang 1:900 000
Singapore 1:900 000

64–65

South Asia
1:8 900 000

66–67

Northern India, Pakistan and Nepal
1:5 300 000
Jammu and Kashmir 1:5 300 000

68–69

The Middle East
1:6 200 000

70–71

Turkey and Transcaucasia
1:4 400 000

72–73

The Near East
1:2 200 000

74

Arabia and the Horn of Africa
1:13 300 000

75

Africa

Africa: Physical
1:37 300 000

76

Africa: Political
1: 37 300 000

77

Northern Africa
1:13 300 000
The Azores 1:13 300 000
Cape Verde Islands 1:8 900 000

78–79

The Nile Valley
1:7 100 000
The Nile Delta 1:3 600 000

80–81

West Africa
1:7 100 000

82–83

Central and Southern Africa
1:13 300 000
Seychelles 1:2 200 000
Réunion 1:2 200 000
Mauritius 1:2 200 000
Comoros 1:7 100 000

84–85

East Africa
1:7 100 000

86–87

Southern Africa
1:7 100 000
Madagascar 1:7 100 000

88–89

Australia and Oceania

Australia and Oceania:
Physical and Political
1:44 400 000   90

New Zealand
1:5 300 000
Fiji 1:5 300 000
Samoan Islands 1:5 300 000
Tonga 1:5 300 000
Tahiti and Moorea 1:1 100 000

91

Western Australia
1:7 100 000

92–93

Eastern Australia
1:7 100 000
Whitsunday Islands 1:2 200 000
Tasmania 1:7 100 000

94–95

Pacific Ocean
1:48 000 000   96–97

North America

North America: Physical
1:31 100 000   98

North America: Political
1:31 100 000   99

Canada
1:13 300 000

100–101

Western Canada
1:6 200 000

102–103

Eastern Canada
1:6 200 000

104–105

United States
1:10 700 000
Hawai'i 1:8 900 000
Alaska 1:26 650 000

106–107

United States – West
1:6 250 000

108–109

Central and Southern California
and Western Washington
1:2 200 000

110–111

United States Midwest and North-east
1:6 250 000

112–113

North-eastern United States
1:2 200 000

114–115

United States – South
1:6 250 000

116–117

Mexico
1:7 100 000

118–119

Central America and the West Indies
1:7 100 000
Jamaica 1:2 700 000
Guadeloupe 1:1 800 000
Martinique 1:1 800 000
Puerto Rico 1:2 700 000
Virgin Islands 1:1 800 000
St Lucia 1:890 000
Barbados 1:890 000

120–121

South America

South America: Physical
1:31 100 000   122

South America: Political
1:31 100 000   123

South America – North
1:14 200 000
Trinidad and Tobago 1:2 200 000

124–125

Central South America
1:7 100 000

126–127

South America – South
1:14 200 000

128

INDEX TO WORLD MAPS

129–224

WORLD STATISTICS: COUNTRIES

This alphabetical list includes all the countries and territories of the world. If a territory is not completely independent, the country it is associated with is named. The area figures give the total area of land, inland water and ice.

The population figures are 2006 estimates. The annual income is the Gross Domestic Product per capita in US dollars. The figures are the latest available, usually 2006 estimates.

Country/Territory	Area km² Thousands	Area miles² Thousands	Population Thousands	Capital	Annual Income US $
Afghanistan	652	252	31,057	Kabul	800
Albania	28.7	11.1	3,582	Tirana	5,600
Algeria	2,382	920	32,930	Algiers	7,700
American Samoa (US)	0.20	0.08	58	Pago Pago	5,800
Andorra	0.47	0.18	71	Andorra La Vella	38,800
Angola	1,247	481	12,127	Luanda	4,300
Anguilla (UK)	0.10	0.04	13	The Valley	8,800
Antigua & Barbuda	0.44	0.17	69	St John's	10,900
Argentina	2,780	1,074	39,922	Buenos Aires	15,000
Armenia	29.8	11.5	2,976	Yerevan	5,400
Aruba (Netherlands)	0.19	0.07	72	Oranjestad	21,800
Australia	7,741	2,989	20,264	Canberra	32,900
Austria	83.9	32.4	8,193	Vienna	35,500
Azerbaijan	86.6	33.4	7,962	Baku	7,300
Azores (Portugal)	2.2	0.86	236	Ponta Delgada	15,000
Bahamas	13.9	5.4	304	Nassau	21,300
Bahrain	0.69	0.27	699	Manama	25,300
Bangladesh	144	55.6	147,365	Dhaka	2,200
Barbados	0.43	0.17	280	Bridgetown	18,200
Belarus	208	80.2	10,293	Minsk	7,800
Belgium	30.5	11.8	10,379	Brussels	31,800
Belize	23.0	8.9	288	Belmopan	8,400
Benin	113	43.5	7,863	Porto-Novo	1,100
Bermuda (UK)	0.05	0.02	66	Hamilton	69,900
Bhutan	47.0	18.1	2,280	Thimphu	1,400
Bolivia	1,099	424	8,989	La Paz/Sucre	3,000
Bosnia-Herzegovina	51.2	19.8	4,499	Sarajevo	5,500
Botswana	582	225	1,640	Gaborone	11,400
Brazil	8,514	3,287	188,078	Brasília	8,600
Brunei	5.8	2.2	379	Bandar Seri Begawan	25,600
Bulgaria	111	42.8	7,385	Sofia	10,400
Burkina Faso	274	106	13,903	Ouagadougou	1,300
Burma (=Myanmar)	677	261	47,383	Rangoon/Naypyidaw	1,800
Burundi	27.8	10.7	8,090	Bujumbura	700
Cambodia	181	69.9	13,881	Phnom Penh	2,600
Cameroon	475	184	17,341	Yaoundé	2,400
Canada	9,971	3,850	33,099	Ottawa	35,200
Canary Is. (Spain)	7.2	2.8	1,682	Las Palmas/Santa Cruz	19,900
Cape Verde Is.	4.0	1.6	421	Praia	6,000
Cayman Is. (UK)	0.26	0.10	45	George Town	43,800
Central African Republic	623	241	4,303	Bangui	1,100
Chad	1,284	496	9,944	Ndjaména	1,500
Chile	757	292	16,134	Santiago	12,700
China	9,597	3,705	1,313,974	Beijing	7,600
Colombia	1,139	440	43,593	Bogotá	8,400
Comoros	2.2	0.86	691	Moroni	600
Congo	342	132	3,702	Brazzaville	1,300
Congo (Dem. Rep. of the)	2,345	905	62,661	Kinshasa	700
Cook Is. (NZ)	0.24	0.09	21	Avarua	9,100
Costa Rica	51.1	19.7	4,075	San José	12,000
Croatia	56.5	21.8	4,495	Zagreb	13,200
Cuba	111	42.8	11,383	Havana	3,900
Cyprus	9.3	3.6	784	Nicosia	22,700
Czech Republic	78.9	30.5	10,235	Prague	21,600
Denmark	43.1	16.6	5,451	Copenhagen	37,000
Djibouti	23.2	9.0	487	Djibouti	1,000
Dominica	0.75	0.29	69	Roseau	3,800
Dominican Republic	48.5	18.7	9,184	Santo Domingo	8,000
East Timor	14.9	5.7	1,063	Dili	800
Ecuador	284	109	13,548	Quito	4,500
Egypt	1,001	387	78,887	Cairo	4,200
El Salvador	21.0	8.1	6,822	San Salvador	4,900
Equatorial Guinea	28.1	10.8	540	Malabo	5,200
Eritrea	118	45.4	4,787	Asmara	1,000
Estonia	45.1	17.4	1,324	Tallinn	19,600
Ethiopia	1,104	426	74,778	Addis Ababa	1,000
Faroe Is. (Denmark)	1.4	0.54	47	Tórshavn	31,000
Fiji	18.3	7.1	906	Suva	6,100
Finland	338	131	5,231	Helsinki	32,800
France	552	213	60,876	Paris	30,100
French Guiana (France)	90.0	34.7	200	Cayenne	8,300
French Polynesia (France)	4.0	1.5	275	Papeete	17,500
Gabon	268	103	1,425	Libreville	7,200
Gambia, The	11.3	4.4	1,642	Banjul	2,000
Gaza Strip (OPT)*	0.36	0.14	1,429	–	1,500
Georgia	69.7	26.9	4,661	Tbilisi	3,800
Germany	357	138	82,422	Berlin	31,400
Ghana	239	92.1	22,410	Accra	2,600
Gibraltar (UK)	0.006	0.002	28	Gibraltar Town	27,900
Greece	132	50.9	10,668	Athens	23,500
Greenland (Denmark)	2,176	840	56	Nuuk	20,000
Grenada	0.34	0.13	90	St George's	3,900
Guadeloupe (France)	1.7	0.66	453	Basse-Terre	7,900
Guam (US)	0.55	0.21	171	Agana	15,000
Guatemala	109	42.0	12,294	Guatemala City	4,900
Guinea	246	94.9	9,690	Conakry	2,000
Guinea-Bissau	36.1	13.9	1,442	Bissau	900
Guyana	215	83.0	767	Georgetown	4,700
Haiti	27.8	10.7	8,309	Port-au-Prince	1,800
Honduras	112	43.3	7,326	Tegucigalpa	3,000
Hungary	93.0	35.9	9,981	Budapest	17,300
Iceland	103	39.8	299	Reykjavik	38,100
India	3,287	1,269	1,095,352	New Delhi	3,700
Indonesia	1,905	735	245,453	Jakarta	3,800
Iran	1,648	636	68,688	Tehran	8,900
Iraq	438	169	26,783	Baghdad	2,900
Ireland	70.3	27.1	4,062	Dublin	43,600
Israel	20.6	8.0	6,352	Jerusalem	26,200
Italy	301	116	58,134	Rome	29,700
Ivory Coast (=Côte d'Ivoire)	322	125	17,655	Yamoussoukro	1,600
Jamaica	11.0	4.2	2,758	Kingston	4,600
Japan	378	146	127,464	Tokyo	33,100
Jordan	89.3	34.5	5,907	Amman	4,900
Kazakhstan	2,725	1,052	15,233	Astana	9,100
Kenya	580	224	34,708	Nairobi	1,200
Kiribati	0.73	0.28	105	Tarawa	2,700
Korea, North	121	46.5	23,113	Pyŏngyang	1,800
Korea, South	99.3	38.3	48,847	Seoul	24,200
Kuwait	17.8	6.9	2,418	Kuwait City	21,600
Kyrgyzstan	200	77.2	5,214	Bishkek	2,000
Laos	237	91.4	6,368	Vientiane	2,100
Latvia	64.6	24.9	2,275	Riga	15,400
Lebanon	10.4	4.0	3,874	Beirut	5,500
Lesotho	30.4	11.7	2,022	Maseru	2,600
Liberia	111	43.0	3,042	Monrovia	1,000
Libya	1,760	679	5,901	Tripoli	12,700
Liechtenstein	0.16	0.06	34	Vaduz	25,000
Lithuania	65.2	25.2	3,586	Vilnius	15,100
Luxembourg	2.6	1.0	474	Luxembourg	68,800
Macedonia (FYROM)	25.7	9.9	2,051	Skopje	8,200
Madagascar	587	227	18,595	Antananarivo	900
Madeira (Portugal)	0.78	0.30	241	Funchal	22,700
Malawi	118	45.7	13,014	Lilongwe	600
Malaysia	330	127	24,386	Kuala Lumpur/Putrajaya	12,700
Maldives	0.30	0.12	359	Malé	3,900
Mali	1,240	479	11,717	Bamako	1,200
Malta	0.32	0.12	400	Valletta	20,300
Marshall Is.	0.18	0.07	60	Majuro	2,900
Martinique (France)	1.1	0.43	436	Fort-de-France	14,400
Mauritania	1,026	396	3,177	Nouakchott	2,600
Mauritius	2.0	0.79	1,241	Port Louis	13,500
Mayotte (France)	0.37	0.14	201	Mamoundzou	4,900
Mexico	1,958	756	107,450	Mexico City	10,600
Micronesia, Fed. States of	0.70	0.27	108	Palikir	2,300
Moldova	33.9	13.1	4,467	Chişinău	2,000
Monaco	0.001	0.0004	33	Monaco	30,000
Mongolia	1,567	605	2,832	Ulan Bator	2,000
Montenegro	14.0	5.4	631	Podgorica	3,800
Montserrat (UK)	0.10	0.04	9	Plymouth	3,400
Morocco	447	172	33,241	Rabat	4,400
Mozambique	802	309	19,687	Maputo	1,500
Namibia	824	318	2,044	Windhoek	7,400
Nauru	0.02	0.008	13	Yaren District	5,000
Nepal	147	56.8	28,287	Katmandu	1,500
Netherlands	41.5	16.0	16,491	Amsterdam/The Hague	31,700
Netherlands Antilles (Neths)	0.80	0.31	222	Willemstad	16,000
New Caledonia (France)	18.6	7.2	219	Nouméa	15,000
New Zealand	271	104	4,076	Wellington	26,000
Nicaragua	130	50.2	5,570	Managua	3,000
Niger	1,267	489	12,525	Niamey	1,000
Nigeria	924	357	131,860	Abuja	1,400
Northern Mariana Is. (US)	0.46	0.18	82	Saipan	12,500
Norway	324	125	4,611	Oslo	47,800
Oman	310	119	3,102	Muscat	14,100
Pakistan	796	307	165,804	Islamabad	2,600
Palau	0.46	0.18	21	Koror	7,600
Panama	75.5	29.2	3,191	Panamá	7,900
Papua New Guinea	463	179	5,671	Port Moresby	2,700
Paraguay	407	157	6,506	Asunción	4,700
Peru	1,285	496	28,303	Lima	6,400
Philippines	300	116	89,469	Manila	5,000
Poland	323	125	38,537	Warsaw	14,100
Portugal	88.8	34.3	10,606	Lisbon	19,100
Puerto Rico (US)	8.9	3.4	3,927	San Juan	19,100
Qatar	11.0	4.2	885	Doha	29,400
Réunion (France)	2.5	0.97	788	St-Denis	6,200
Romania	238	92.0	22,304	Bucharest	8,800
Russia	17,075	6,593	142,894	Moscow	12,100
Rwanda	26.3	10.2	8,648	Kigali	1,600
St Kitts & Nevis	0.26	0.10	39	Basseterre	8,200
St Lucia	0.54	0.21	168	Castries	4,800
St Vincent & Grenadines	0.39	0.15	118	Kingstown	3,600
Samoa	2.8	1.1	177	Apia	2,100
San Marino	0.06	0.02	29	San Marino	34,100
São Tomé & Príncipe	0.96	0.37	193	São Tomé	1,200
Saudi Arabia	2,150	830	27,020	Riyadh	13,800
Senegal	197	76.0	11,987	Dakar	1,800
Serbia	88.4	34.1	9,396	Belgrade	4,400
Seychelles	0.46	0.18	82	Victoria	7,800
Sierra Leone	71.7	27.7	6,005	Freetown	900
Singapore	0.68	0.26	4,492	Singapore City	30,900
Slovak Republic	49.0	18.9	5,439	Bratislava	17,700
Slovenia	20.3	7.8	2,010	Ljubljana	23,400
Solomon Is.	28.9	11.2	552	Honiara	600
Somalia	638	246	8,863	Mogadishu	600
South Africa	1,221	471	44,188	Cape Town/Pretoria	13,000
Spain	498	192	40,398	Madrid	27,000
Sri Lanka	65.6	25.3	20,222	Colombo	4,600
Sudan	2,506	967	41,236	Khartoum	2,300
Suriname	163	63.0	439	Paramaribo	7,100
Swaziland	17.4	6.7	1,136	Mbabane	5,500
Sweden	450	174	9,017	Stockholm	31,600
Switzerland	41.3	15.9	7,524	Bern	33,600
Syria	185	71.5	18,881	Damascus	4,000
Taiwan	36.0	13.9	23,036	Taipei	29,000
Tajikistan	143	55.3	7,321	Dushanbe	1,300
Tanzania	945	365	37,445	Dodoma	800
Thailand	513	198	64,632	Bangkok	9,100
Togo	56.8	21.9	5,549	Lomé	1,700
Tonga	0.65	0.25	115	Nuku'alofa	2,200
Trinidad & Tobago	5.1	2.0	1,066	Port of Spain	19,700
Tunisia	164	63.2	10,175	Tunis	8,600
Turkey	775	299	70,414	Ankara	8,900
Turkmenistan	488	188	5,043	Ashkhabad	8,900
Turks & Caicos Is. (UK)	0.43	0.17	21	Cockburn Town	11,500
Tuvalu	0.03	0.01	12	Fongafale	1,600
Uganda	241	93.1	28,196	Kampala	1,800
Ukraine	604	233	46,711	Kiev	7,600
United Arab Emirates	83.6	32.3	2,603	Abu Dhabi	49,700
United Kingdom	242	93.4	60,609	London	31,400
United States of America	9,629	3,718	301,139	Washington, DC	43,500
Uruguay	175	67.6	3,432	Montevideo	10,700
Uzbekistan	447	173	27,307	Tashkent	2,000
Vanuatu	12.2	4.7	209	Port-Vila	2,900
Venezuela	912	352	25,730	Caracas	6,900
Vietnam	332	128	84,403	Hanoi	3,100
Virgin Is. (UK)	0.15	0.06	23	Road Town	38,500
Virgin Is. (US)	0.35	0.13	109	Charlotte Amalie	14,500
Wallis & Futuna Is. (France)	0.20	0.08	16	Mata-Utu	3,800
West Bank (OPT)*	5.9	2.3	2,460	–	1,500
Western Sahara	266	103	273	El Aaiún	N/A
Yemen	528	204	21,456	Sana'	900
Zambia	753	291	11,502	Lusaka	1,000
Zimbabwe	391	151	12,237	Harare	2,000

*OPT = Occupied Palestinian Territory   N/A = Not available

WORLD STATISTICS: CITIES

This list shows the principal cities with more than 750,000 inhabitants. The figures are taken from the most recent census or estimate available, usually 2005, and as far as possible are the population of the metropolitan area or urban agglomeration (for example, greater New York, Mexico or Paris). All the figures are in thousands. Local name forms have been used for the smaller cities (for example, Thessaloniki).

AFGHANISTAN
Kabul 3,288
ALGERIA
Algiers 3,260
ANGOLA
Luanda 2,839
ARGENTINA
Buenos Aires 13,349
Córdoba 1,592
Rosario 1,312
Mendoza 1,072
San Miguel de Tucumán 837
ARMENIA
Yerevan 1,066
AUSTRALIA
Sydney 4,388
Melbourne 3,663
Brisbane 1,769
Perth 1,484
Adelaide 1,137
AUSTRIA
Vienna 2,190
AZERBAIJAN
Baku 1,830
BANGLADESH
Dhaka 12,560
Chittagong 4,171
Khulna 1,497
Rajshahi 1,035
BELARUS
Minsk 1,709
BELGIUM
Brussels 964
BOLIVIA
La Paz 1,533
Santa Cruz 1,352
Cochabamba 797
BRAZIL
São Paulo 18,333
Rio de Janeiro 11,469
Belo Horizonte 5,304
Pôrto Alegre 3,795
Recife 3,527
Brasília 3,341
Salvador 3,331
Fortaleza 3,261
Curitiba 2,871
Campinas 2,640
Belém 2,097
Goiânia 1,878
Manaus 1,673
Santos 1,634
Vitória 1,602
Maceió 1,137
Natal 1,049
São Luís 982
São José dos Campos 972
João Pessoa 931
Teresina 895
Campo Grande 821
BULGARIA
Sofia 1,045
BURKINA FASO
Ouagadougou 870
BURMA (MYANMAR)
Rangoon 4,082
Mandalay 927
CAMBODIA
Phnom Penh 1,174
CAMEROON
Douala 1,980
Yaoundé 1,727
CANADA
Toronto 5,060
Montréal 3,511
Vancouver 2,125
Ottawa 1,120
Calgary 1,074
Edmonton 1,005
CHILE
Santiago 5,623
CHINA
Shanghai 12,665
Beijing 10,849
Tianjin 9,346
Hong Kong 7,182
Wuhan 6,003
Chongqing 4,975
Shenyang 4,916
Guangzhou 3,881
Chengdu 3,478
Xi'an 3,256
Changchun 3,092
Harbin 2,898
Nanjing 2,806
Zibo 2,775
Dalian 2,709
Jinan 2,654
Taiyuan 2,516
Guiyang 2,467
Qingdao 2,431
Zhengzhou 2,250
Zaozhuang 2,189
Handan 2,120
Liupanshui 1,118
Changsha 2,051
Linyi 2,035
Lu'an 2,015
Wanxian 1,963
Hangzhou 1,955
Tianmen 1,948
Jinxi 1,850
Heze 1,847
Lanzhou 1,788
Tangshan 1,773
Xiantao 1,758
Kunming 1,748
Nanchang 1,742
Shijiazhuang 1,733
Yantai 1,707
Yulin 1,691
Yancheng 1,678
Xuzhou 1,662
Luoyang 1,594
Xinghua 1,587
Pingxiang 1,562
Ürümqi 1,562
Zhanjiang 1,562
Tai'an 1,550
Suining, Sichuan 1,520
Yiyang 1,510
Jilin 1,496
Changde 1,483
Wenzhou 1,475
Anshan 1,459
Qiqihar 1,452
Neijiang 1,449
Fushun 1,425
Huainan 1,422
Fuzhou 1,398
Nanning 1,395
Baotou 1,367
Weifang 1,360
Shantou 1,356
Xintai 1,334
Hefei 1,320
Huaian 1,297
Yueyang 1,286
Shenzhen 1,285
Tianshui 1,269
Suqian 1,258
Jingmen 1,228
Yuzhou 1,226
Zaoyang 1,210
Suzhou 1,201
Wuxi 1,192
Ningbo 1,188
Yongzhou 1,182
Mianyang 1,174
Leshan 1,172
Dongguan 1,150
Chifeng 1,140
Xiaoshan 1,130
Yixing 1,129
Zigong 1,123
Daqing 1,117
Datong 1,113
Huzhou 1,102
Jining, Shandong 1,101
Nanchong 1,072
Fuyu 1,068
Liuzhou 1,031
Xinyi, Jiangsu 1,022
Jixi 1,012
Linqing 1,009
Jiamusi 1,006
Hohhot 998
Xianyang 988
Changzhou 976
Zhangjiakou 973
Benxi 967
Xiangxiang 936
Zhangjiagang 936
Xinyu 932
Yichun, Heilongjiang 916
Yichun, Jiangxi 890
Jinzhou 888
Zhaotong 879
Yuyao 876
Anshun 864
Hengyang 853
Xuanzhou 851
Tongliao 847
Huaibei 830
Mudanjiang 827
Jiaxing 817
Kaifeng 810
Fuxin 807
Hunjiang 798
COLOMBIA
Bogotá 7,594
Medellín 3,236
Cali 2,583
Barranquilla 1,918
Bucaramanga 1,069
Cartagena 1,002
Cúcuta 883
CONGO
Brazzaville 1,153
CONGO (DEM. REP. OF THE)
Kinshasa 5,717
Lubumbashi 1,102
Mbuji-Mayi 806
COSTA RICA
San José 1,145
CROATIA
Zagreb 1,067
CUBA
Havana 2,192
CZECH REPUBLIC
Prague 1,164
DENMARK
Copenhagen 1,091
DOMINICAN REPUBLIC
Santo Domingo 2,563
Santiago de los Caballeros 804
ECUADOR
Guayaquil 2,387
Quito 1,514
EGYPT
Cairo 11,146
Alexandria 3,760
Shubrâ el Kheima 937
EL SALVADOR
San Salvador 1,472
ETHIOPIA
Addis Ababa 2,899
FINLAND
Helsinki 937
FRANCE
Paris 9,630
Lyons 1,353
Marseilles 1,290
Lille 991
Nice 889
Toulouse 761
Bordeaux 754
GEORGIA
Tbilisi 1,406
GERMANY
Berlin 3,387
Hamburg 1,705
Munich 1,195
Cologne 963
GHANA
Accra 1,970
Kumasi 862
GREECE
Athens 3,238
Thessaloniki 824
GUATEMALA
Guatemala City 3,242
GUINEA
Conakry 1,465
HAITI
Port-au-Prince 2,090
HONDURAS
Tegucigalpa 1,061
HUNGARY
Budapest 1,670
INDIA
Mumbai 18,336
Delhi 15,334
Kolkata 14,299
Chennai 6,915
Bangalore 6,532
Hyderabad 6,145
Ahmedabad 5,171
Pune 4,485
Surat 3,671
Kanpur 3,040
Jaipur 2,796
Lucknow 2,589
Nagpur 2,359
Patna 2,066
Indore 1,941
Vadodara 1,686
Bhopal 1,656
Coimbatore 1,628
Ludhiana 1,583
Agra 1,526
Visakhapatnam 1,468
Cochin 1,461
Nashik 1,408
Meerut 1,340
Faridabad 1,330
Varanasi 1,300
Ghaziabad 1,277
Asansol 1,272
Jamshedpur 1,246
Madurai 1,245
Jabalpur 1,234
Rajkot 1,205
Dhanbad 1,195
Amritsar 1,162
Allahabad 1,153
Vijayawada 1,093
Srinagar 1,093
Aurangabad 1,065
Bhilainagar-Durg 1,051
Solapur 1,012
Ranchi 999
Jodhpur 954
Guwahati 941
Gwalior 939
Trivandrum 918
Calicut 917
Tiruchchirapalli 913
Chandigarh 896
Hubli-Dharwad 854
Mysore 851
INDONESIA
Jakarta 13,194
Bandung 4,020
Surabaya 2,735
Medan 2,109
Palembang 1,675
Ujung Pandang 1,205
Bandar Lampung 915
Malang 898
Tegal 898
Semarang 816
Bogor 761
IRAN
Tehran 7,352
Mashhad 2,147
Esfahan 1,547
Tabriz 1,396
Karaj 1,235
Shiraz 1,230
Qom 1,045
Ahvaz 967
Bakhtaran 771
IRAQ
Baghdad 5,910
Mosul 1,236
Basra 1,187
Irbil 840
IRELAND
Dublin 985
ISRAEL
Tel Aviv-Yafo 3,025
Haifa 948
ITALY
Rome 2,649
Milan 1,183
Naples 993
Turin 857
Genoa 803
IVORY COAST
Abidjan 3,516
JAPAN
Tokyo 12,064
Yokohama 6,427
Osaka 2,599
Nagoya 2,172
Sapporo 1,922
Kobe 1,493
Kyoto 1,468
Fukuoka 1,341
Kawasaki 1,250
Hiroshima 1,126
Kitakyushu 1,011
Sendai 1,008
Chiba 887
Sakai 792
JORDAN
Amman 1,292
KAZAKHSTAN
Almaty 1,103
KENYA
Nairobi 2,818
KOREA, NORTH
Pyŏngyang 3,124
Hamhung 821
KOREA, SOUTH
Seoul 9,888
Pusan 3,830
Inch'on 2,884
Taegu 2,675
Taejŏn 1,522
Kwangju 1,379
Sŏngnam 1,353
Ulsan 1,340
Ansan 984
Puch'on 900
Suwŏn 876
P'ohang 790
KUWAIT
Kuwait City 879
KYRGYZSTAN
Bishkek 828
LATVIA
Riga 719
LEBANON
Beirut 2,070
LIBYA
Tripoli 1,733
Benghazi 829
MADAGASCAR
Antananarivo 1,808
MALAYSIA
Kuala Lumpur 1,392
MALI
Bamako 1,379
MEXICO
Mexico City 19,013
Guadalajara 3,905
Monterrey 3,517
Toluca 1,987
Puebla 1,880
Tijuana 1,570
Ciudad Juárez 1,469
León 1,438
Torreón 1,057
San Luis Potosí 927
Mérida 919
Querétaro 913
Mexicali 840
Culiacán 799
MONGOLIA
Ulan Bator 842
MOROCCO
Casablanca 3,743
Rabat 1,859
Fès 1,032
Marrakesh 951
MOZAMBIQUE
Maputo 1,316
NEPAL
Katmandu 1,176
NETHERLANDS
Amsterdam 1,157
Rotterdam 1,112
NEW ZEALAND
Auckland 1,152
NICARAGUA
Managua 1,159
NIGER
Niamey 997
NIGERIA
Lagos 11,135
Kano 2,884
Ibadan 2,375
Kaduna 1,329
Benin City 1,022
Ogbomosho 959
Port Harcourt 942
NORWAY
Oslo 808
PAKISTAN
Karachi 11,819
Lahore 6,373
Faisalabad 2,533
Rawalpindi 1,794
Gujranwala 1,466
Multan 1,459
Hyderabad 1,392
Peshawar 1,255
Islamabad 791
PANAMA
Panamá 1,173
PARAGUAY
Asunción 1,750
PERU
Lima 8,180
PHILIPPINES
Manila 10,677
Davao 1,326
POLAND
Warsaw 1,626
Łódź 815
PORTUGAL
Lisbon 1,977
Porto 1,303
PUERTO RICO
San Juan 2,357
ROMANIA
Bucharest 1,764
RUSSIA
Moscow 10,672
Saint Petersburg 5,315
Novosibirsk 1,425
Nizhniy Novgorod 1,288
Yekaterinburg 1,281
Samara 1,140
Omsk 1,132
Kazan 1,108
Rostov 1,081
Chelyabinsk 1,067
Ufa 1,035
Volgograd 1,016
Perm 1,014
Voronezh 918
Saratov 881
Simbirsk 864
Krasnoyarsk 840
Togliatti 771
SAUDI ARABIA
Riyadh 5,514
Jedda 3,807
Mecca 1,529
Medina 1,044
Dammam 920
SENEGAL
Dakar 2,313
SERBIA
Belgrade 1,116
SIERRA LEONE
Freetown 1,007
SINGAPORE
Singapore City 4,372
SOMALIA
Mogadishu 1,257
SOUTH AFRICA
Johannesburg 2,950
Cape Town 2,930
Durban / eThekwini 2,391
Pretoria / Tshwane 1,590
Port Elizabeth 1,006
SPAIN
Madrid 3,017
Barcelona 1,527
SUDAN
Khartoum 2,742
SWEDEN
Stockholm 1,729
Gothenburg 829
SWITZERLAND
Zürich 984
SYRIA
Aleppo 2,505
Damascus 2,317
Homs 915
TAIWAN
Taipei 2,473
Kaohsiung 1,506
T'aichung 1,066
TANZANIA
Dar es Salaam 2,683
THAILAND
Bangkok 6,604
TUNISIA
Tunis 2,063
TURKEY
Istanbul 8,953
Ankara 3,203
Izmir 2,250
Bursa 1,184
Adana 1,133
Gaziantep 862
Konya 761
UGANDA
Kampala 1,345
UKRAINE
Kiev 2,621
Kharkov 1,521
Dnepropetrovsk 1,122
Donetsk 1,065
Odessa 1,027
Zaporozhye 863
Lvov 794
UNITED ARAB EMIRATES
Abu Dhabi 928
Dubai 886
UNITED KINGDOM
London 8,089
Birmingham 2,373
Manchester 2,353
Liverpool 852
Glasgow 832
UNITED STATES OF AMERICA
New York 17,800
Los Angeles 11,789
Chicago 8,308
Philadelphia 5,149
Miami 4,919
Dallas–Fort Worth 4,146
Boston 4,032
Washington 3,934
Detroit 3,903
Houston 3,823
Atlanta 3,500
San Francisco 3,229
Phoenix 2,907
Seattle 2,712
San Diego 2,674
Minneapolis–St Paul 2,389
St Louis 2,078
Baltimore 2,076
Tampa–St Petersburg 2,062
Denver 1,985
Cleveland 1,787
Pittsburgh 1,753
Portland 1,583
San Jose 1,538
San Bernardino 1,507
Cincinnati 1,503
Norfolk–Virginia Beach 1,394
Sacramento 1,393
Kansas City 1,362
San Antonio 1,328
Las Vegas 1,314
Milwaukee 1,309
Indianapolis 1,219
Providence 1,175
Orlando 1,157
Columbus 1,133
New Orleans 1,009
Buffalo 977
Memphis 972
Austin 902
Stamford 889
Salt Lake City 888
Jacksonville 882
Louisville 864
Hartford 852
Richmond 819
Charlotte 759
URUGUAY
Montevideo 1,353
UZBEKISTAN
Tashkent 2,160
VENEZUELA
Caracas 3,276
Valencia 2,330
Maracaibo 2,182
Maracay 1,138
Ciudad Guayana 966
Barquisimeto 923
VIETNAM
Ho Chi Minh City 5,030
Hanoi 4,147
Haiphong 1,817
YEMEN
Sana' 1,621
ZAMBIA
Lusaka 1,450
ZIMBABWE
Harare 1,527
Bulawayo 824

WORLD STATISTICS: DISTANCES

The table shows air distances in miles and kilometres between 30 major cities. Known as 'Great Circle' distances, these measure the shortest routes between the cities, which aircraft use wherever possible. The maps show the world centred on six cities, and illustrate, for example, why direct flights from Japan to northern America and Europe are across the Arctic regions. The maps have been constructed on an Azimuthal Equidistant projection, on which all distances measured through the centre point are true to scale. The red lines are drawn at 5,000, 10,000 and 15,000 km from the central city.

Distances above the diagonal are in Kms; distances below the diagonal are in Miles.

	Beijing	Buenos Aires	Cairo	Caracas	Chicago	Hong Kong	Honolulu	Johannesburg	Kolkata	Lagos	London	Los Angeles	Mexico City	Moscow	Mumbai	Nairobi	New York	Paris	Rio de Janeiro	Rome	Singapore	Sydney	Tokyo	Wellington
Beijing	**Beijing**	11972	4688	8947	6588	1220	5070	7276	2031	7119	5057	6251	7742	3600	2956	5727	6828	5106	10773	5049	2783	5561	1304	6700
Buenos Aires	19268	**Buenos Aires**	7341	3167	5599	11481	7558	5025	10268	4919	6917	6122	4591	8374	9275	6463	5298	6867	1214	6929	9867	7332	11410	6202
Cairo	7544	11814	**Cairo**	6340	6127	5064	8838	3894	3541	2432	2180	7580	7687	1803	2706	2197	5605	1994	6149	1325	5137	8959	5947	10268
Caracas	14399	5096	10203	**Caracas**	2502	10166	6009	6847	9609	4810	4664	3612	2228	6175	9024	7173	2131	4738	2825	5196	11407	9534	8801	8154
Chicago	10603	9011	3206	4027	**Chicago**	7783	4247	8689	7978	5973	3949	1742	1694	4971	8048	8005	711	4132	5311	4809	9369	9243	6299	8358
Hong Kong	1963	18478	8150	16360	12526	**Hong Kong**	5543	6669	1653	7360	5980	7232	8775	4439	2683	5453	8047	5984	11001	5769	1615	4582	1786	5857
Honolulu	8160	12164	14223	9670	6836	8921	**Honolulu**	11934	7048	10133	7228	2558	3781	7036	8024	10739	4958	7437	8290	8026	6721	5075	3854	4669
Johannesburg	11710	8088	6267	11019	13984	10732	19206	**Johannesburg**	5256	2799	5637	10362	9063	5692	4334	1818	7979	5426	4420	4811	5381	6860	8418	7308
Kolkata	3269	16524	5699	15464	12839	2659	11343	8459	**Kolkata**	5727	4946	8152	9494	3438	1034	3839	7921	4883	9366	4486	1800	5678	3195	7055
Lagos	11457	7916	3915	7741	9612	11845	16308	4505	9216	**Lagos**	3118	7713	6879	3886	4730	2366	5268	2929	3750	2510	6925	9643	8376	9973
London	8138	11131	3508	7507	6356	9623	11632	9071	7961	5017	**London**	5442	5552	1552	4467	4237	3463	212	5778	889	6743	10558	5942	11691
Los Angeles	10060	9852	12200	5812	2804	11639	4117	16676	13120	12414	8758	**Los Angeles**	1549	6070	8700	9659	2446	5645	6310	6331	8776	7502	5475	6719
Mexico City	12460	7389	12372	3586	2726	14122	6085	14585	15280	11071	8936	2493	**Mexico City**	6664	9728	9207	2090	5717	4780	6365	10321	8058	7024	6897
Moscow	5794	13477	2902	9938	8000	7144	11323	9161	5534	6254	2498	9769	10724	**Moscow**	3126	3942	4666	1545	7184	1477	5237	9008	4651	10283
Mumbai	4757	14925	4355	14522	12953	4317	12914	6974	1664	7612	7190	14000	15656	5031	**Mumbai**	2816	7793	4356	8332	3837	2432	6313	4189	7686
Nairobi	9216	10402	3536	11544	12883	8776	17282	2927	6179	3807	6819	15544	14818	6344	4532	**Nairobi**	7358	4029	5548	3350	4635	7552	6996	8490
New York	10988	8526	9020	3430	1145	12950	7980	12841	12747	8477	5572	3936	3264	7510	12541	11842	**New York**	3626	4832	4280	9531	9935	6741	8951
Paris	8217	11051	3210	7625	6650	9630	11968	8732	7858	4714	342	9085	9200	2486	7010	6485	5836	**Paris**	5708	687	6671	10539	6038	11798
Rio de Janeiro	17338	1953	9896	4546	8547	17704	13342	7113	15073	6035	9299	10155	7693	11562	13409	8928	7777	9187	**Rio de Janeiro**	5725	9763	8389	11551	7367
Rome	8126	11151	2133	8363	7739	9284	12916	7743	7219	4039	1431	10188	10243	2376	6175	5391	6888	1105	9214	**Rome**	6229	10143	6127	11523
Singapore	4478	15879	8267	18359	15078	2599	10816	8660	2897	11145	10852	14123	16610	8428	3914	7460	15339	10737	15712	10025	**Singapore**	3915	3306	5298
Sydney	8949	11800	14418	15343	14875	7374	8168	11040	9138	15519	16992	12073	12969	14497	10160	12153	15989	16962	13501	16324	6300	**Sydney**	4861	1383
Tokyo	2099	18362	9571	14164	10137	2874	6202	13547	5141	13480	9562	8811	11304	7485	6742	11260	10849	9718	18589	9861	5321	7823	**Tokyo**	5762
Wellington	10782	9981	16524	13122	13451	9427	7513	11761	11354	16050	18814	10814	11100	16549	12370	13664	14405	18987	11855	18545	8526	2226	9273	**Wellington**

Northern Hemisphere

MEXICO CITY
19° 26'N 99° 04'W

LONDON
51° 28'N 00° 27'W

TOKYO
35° 33'N 139° 46'E

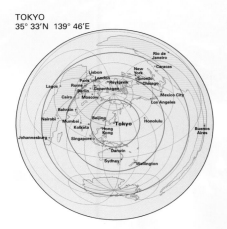

Southern Hemisphere

RIO DE JANEIRO
22° 50'S 43° 15'W

SINGAPORE
1° 21'N 103° 54'E

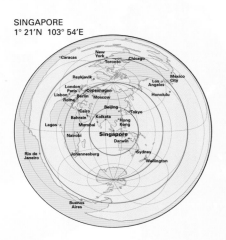

SYDNEY
33° 56'S 151° 10'E

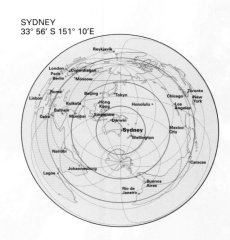

World Statistics: Climate

Rainfall and temperature figures are provided for more than 70 cities around the world. As climate is affected by altitude, the height of each city is shown in metres beneath its name. For each location, the top row of figures shows the total rainfall or snow in millimetres, and the bottom row the average temperature in degrees Celsius; the total annual rainfall and average annual temperature are at the end of the rows.

	Jan.	Feb.	Mar.	Apr.	May	June	July	Aug.	Sept.	Oct.	Nov.	Dec.	Year
EUROPE													
Athens, Greece	62	37	37	23	23	14	6	7	15	51	56	71	402
107 m	10	10	12	16	20	25	28	28	24	20	15	11	18
Berlin, Germany	46	40	33	42	49	65	73	69	48	49	46	43	603
55 m	–1	0	4	9	14	17	19	18	15	9	5	1	9
Istanbul, Turkey	109	92	72	46	38	34	34	30	58	81	103	119	816
14 m	5	6	7	11	16	20	23	23	20	16	12	8	14
Lisbon, Portugal	111	76	109	54	44	16	3	4	33	62	93	103	708
77 m	11	12	14	16	17	20	22	23	21	18	14	12	17
London, UK	54	40	37	37	46	45	57	59	49	57	64	48	593
5 m	4	5	7	9	12	16	18	17	15	11	8	5	11
Málaga, Spain	61	51	62	46	26	5	1	3	29	64	64	62	474
33 m	12	13	16	17	19	29	25	26	23	20	16	13	18
Moscow, Russia	39	38	36	37	53	58	88	71	58	45	47	54	624
156 m	–13	–10	–4	6	13	16	18	17	12	6	–1	–7	4
Odesa, Ukraine	57	62	30	21	34	34	42	37	37	13	35	71	473
64 m	–3	–1	2	9	15	20	22	22	18	12	9	1	10
Paris, France	56	46	35	42	57	54	59	64	55	50	51	50	619
75 m	3	4	8	11	15	18	20	19	17	12	7	4	12
Rome, Italy	71	62	57	51	46	37	15	21	63	99	129	93	744
17 m	8	9	11	14	18	22	25	25	22	17	13	10	16
Shannon, Irish Republic	94	67	56	53	61	57	77	79	86	86	96	117	929
2 m	5	5	7	9	12	14	16	16	14	11	8	6	10
Stockholm, Sweden	43	30	25	31	34	45	61	76	60	48	53	48	554
44 m	–3	–3	–1	5	10	15	18	17	12	7	3	0	7
ASIA													
Bahrain	8	18	13	8	<3	0	0	0	0	0	18	18	81
5 m	17	18	21	25	29	32	33	34	31	28	24	19	26
Bangkok, Thailand	8	20	36	58	198	160	160	175	305	206	66	5	1,397
2 m	26	28	29	30	29	29	28	28	28	28	26	25	28
Beirut, Lebanon	191	158	94	53	18	3	<3	<3	5	51	132	185	892
34 m	14	14	16	18	22	24	27	28	26	24	19	16	21
Colombo, Sri Lanka	89	69	147	231	371	224	135	109	160	348	315	147	2,365
7 m	26	26	27	28	28	27	27	27	27	27	26	26	27
Harbin, China	6	5	10	23	43	94	112	104	46	33	8	5	488
160 m	–18	–15	–5	6	13	19	22	21	14	4	–6	–16	3
Ho Chi Minh, Vietnam	15	3	13	43	221	330	315	269	335	269	114	56	1,984
9 m	26	27	29	30	29	28	28	28	27	27	27	26	28
Hong Kong, China	33	46	74	137	292	394	381	361	257	114	43	31	2,162
33 m	16	15	18	22	26	28	28	28	27	25	21	18	23
Jakarta, Indonesia	300	300	211	147	114	97	64	43	66	112	142	203	1,798
8 m	26	26	27	27	27	27	27	27	27	27	27	26	27
Kabul, Afghanistan	31	36	94	102	20	5	3	3	<3	15	20	10	338
1,815 m	–3	–1	6	13	18	22	25	24	20	14	7	3	12
Karachi, Pakistan	13	10	8	3	3	18	81	41	13	<3	3	5	196
4 m	19	20	24	28	30	31	30	29	28	28	24	20	26
Kazalinsk, Kazakhstan	10	10	13	13	15	5	5	8	8	10	13	15	125
63 m	–12	–11	–3	6	18	23	25	23	16	8	–1	–7	7
Kolkata (Calcutta), India	10	31	36	43	140	297	325	328	252	114	20	5	1,600
6 m	20	22	27	30	30	30	29	29	29	28	23	19	26
Mumbai (Bombay), India	3	3	3	<3	18	485	617	340	264	64	13	3	1,809
11 m	24	24	26	28	30	29	27	27	27	28	27	26	27
New Delhi, India	23	18	13	8	13	74	180	172	117	10	3	10	565
218 m	14	17	23	28	33	34	31	30	29	26	20	15	25
Omsk, Russia	15	8	8	13	31	51	51	51	28	25	18	20	318
85 m	–22	–19	–12	–1	10	16	18	16	10	1	–11	–18	–1
Shanghai, China	48	58	84	94	94	180	147	142	130	71	51	36	1,135
7 m	4	5	9	14	20	24	28	28	23	19	12	7	16
Singapore	252	173	193	188	173	173	170	196	178	208	254	257	2,413
10 m	26	27	28	28	28	28	28	27	27	27	27	27	27
Tehran, Iran	46	38	46	36	13	3	3	3	3	8	20	31	246
1,220 m	2	5	9	16	21	26	30	29	25	18	12	6	17
Tokyo, Japan	48	74	107	135	147	165	142	152	234	208	97	56	1,565
6 m	3	4	7	13	17	21	25	26	23	17	11	6	14
Ulan Bator, Mongolia	<3	<3	3	5	10	28	76	51	23	5	5	3	208
1,325 m	–26	–21	–13	–1	6	14	16	14	8	–1	–13	–22	–3
Verkhoyansk, Russia	5	5	3	5	8	23	28	25	13	8	8	5	134
100 m	–50	–45	–32	–15	0	12	14	9	2	–15	–38	–48	–17
AFRICA													
Addis Ababa, Ethiopia	<3	3	25	135	213	201	206	239	102	28	<3	0	1,151
2,450 m	19	20	20	20	19	18	18	19	21	22	21	20	20
Antananarivo, Madagas.	300	279	178	53	18	8	8	10	18	61	135	287	1,356
1,372 m	21	21	21	19	18	15	14	15	17	19	21	21	19
Cairo, Egypt	5	5	5	3	3	<3	0	0	<3	<3	3	5	28
116 m	13	15	18	21	25	28	28	28	26	24	20	15	22
Cape Town, S. Africa	15	8	18	48	79	84	89	66	43	31	18	10	508
17 m	21	21	20	17	14	13	12	13	14	16	18	19	17
Johannesburg, S. Africa	114	109	89	38	25	8	8	8	23	56	107	125	709
1,665 m	20	20	18	16	13	10	11	13	16	18	19	20	16
Khartoum, Sudan	<3	<3	<3	<3	3	8	53	71	18	5	<3	0	158
390 m	24	25	28	31	33	34	32	31	32	32	28	25	29
Kinshasa, Congo (D.R.)	135	145	196	196	158	8	3	3	31	119	221	142	1,354
325 m	26	26	27	27	26	24	23	24	25	26	26	26	25
Lagos, Nigeria	28	46	102	150	269	460	279	64	140	206	69	25	1,836
3 m	27	28	29	28	28	26	26	25	26	26	28	28	27
Lusaka, Zambia	231	191	142	18	3	<3	<3	0	<3	10	91	150	836
1,277 m	21	22	21	21	19	16	16	18	22	24	23	22	21
Monrovia, Liberia	31	56	97	216	516	973	996	373	744	772	236	130	5,138
23 m	26	26	27	27	26	25	24	25	25	25	26	26	26
Nairobi, Kenya	38	64	125	211	158	46	15	23	31	53	109	86	958
1,820 m	19	19	19	19	18	16	16	16	18	19	18	18	18
Timbuktu, Mali	<3	<3	3	<3	5	23	79	81	38	3	<3	<3	231
301 m	22	24	28	32	34	35	32	30	32	31	28	23	29
Tunis, Tunisia	64	51	41	36	18	8	3	8	33	51	48	61	419
66 m	10	11	13	16	19	23	26	27	25	20	16	11	18
Walvis Bay, Namibia	<3	5	8	3	3	<3	<3	3	<3	<3	<3	<3	23
7 m	19	19	19	18	17	16	15	14	14	15	17	18	18
AUSTRALIA, NEW ZEALAND AND ANTARCTICA													
Alice Springs, Australia	43	33	28	10	15	13	8	8	8	18	31	38	252
579 m	29	28	25	20	15	12	12	14	18	23	26	28	21
Christchurch, N. Zealand	56	43	48	48	66	66	69	48	46	43	48	56	638
10 m	16	16	14	12	9	6	6	7	9	12	14	16	11
Darwin, Australia	386	312	254	97	15	3	<3	3	13	51	119	239	1,491
30 m	29	29	29	29	28	26	25	26	28	29	30	29	28
Mawson, Antarctica	11	30	20	10	44	180	4	40	3	20	0	0	362
14 m	0	–5	–10	–14	–15	–16	–18	–18	–19	–13	–5	–1	–11
Perth, Australia	8	10	20	43	130	180	170	149	86	56	20	13	881
60 m	23	23	22	19	16	14	13	13	15	16	19	22	18
Sydney, Australia	89	102	127	135	127	117	117	76	73	71	73	73	1,181
42 m	22	22	21	18	15	13	12	13	15	18	19	21	17
NORTH AMERICA													
Anchorage, Alaska, USA	20	18	15	10	13	18	41	66	66	56	25	23	371
40 m	–11	–8	–5	2	7	12	14	13	9	2	–5	–11	2
Chicago, Illinois, USA	51	51	66	71	86	89	84	81	79	66	61	51	836
251 m	–4	–3	2	9	14	20	23	22	19	12	5	–1	10
Churchill, Man., Canada	15	13	18	23	32	44	46	58	51	43	39	21	402
13 m	–28	–26	–20	–10	–2	6	12	11	5	–2	–12	–22	–7
Edmonton, Alta., Canada	25	19	19	22	43	77	89	78	39	17	16	25	466
676 m	–15	–10	–5	4	11	15	17	16	11	6	–4	–10	3
Honolulu, Hawaii, USA	104	66	79	48	25	18	23	28	36	48	64	104	643
12 m	23	18	19	20	22	24	25	26	26	24	22	19	22
Houston, Texas, USA	89	76	84	91	119	117	99	99	104	94	89	109	1,171
12 m	12	13	17	21	24	27	28	29	26	22	16	12	21
Kingston, Jamaica	23	15	23	31	102	89	38	91	99	180	74	36	800
34 m	25	25	25	26	26	28	28	28	27	27	26	26	26
Los Angeles, Calif., USA	79	76	71	25	10	3	<3	<3	5	15	31	66	381
95 m	13	14	14	16	17	19	21	22	21	18	16	14	17
Mexico City, Mexico	13	5	10	20	53	119	170	152	130	51	18	8	747
2,309 m	12	13	16	18	19	19	17	18	18	16	14	13	16
Miami, Florida, USA	71	53	64	81	173	178	155	160	203	234	71	51	1,516
8 m	20	20	22	23	25	27	28	28	27	25	22	21	24
Montréal, Que., Canada	72	65	74	74	66	82	90	92	88	76	81	87	946
57 m	–10	–9	–3	6	13	18	21	20	15	9	2	–7	6
New York City, NY, USA	94	97	91	81	81	84	107	109	86	89	76	91	1,092
96 m	–1	–1	3	10	16	20	23	23	21	15	7	2	11
St Louis, Mo., USA	58	64	89	97	114	114	89	86	81	74	71	64	1,001
173 m	0	1	7	13	19	24	26	26	22	15	8	2	14
San José, Costa Rica	15	5	20	46	229	241	211	241	305	300	145	41	1,798
1,146 m	19	19	21	21	22	21	21	21	21	20	20	19	20
Vancouver, BC, Canada	154	115	101	60	52	45	32	41	67	114	150	182	1,113
14 m	3	5	6	9	12	15	17	17	14	10	6	4	10
Washington, DC, USA	86	76	91	84	94	99	112	109	94	74	66	79	1,064
22 m	1	2	7	12	18	23	25	24	20	14	8	3	13
SOUTH AMERICA													
Antofagasta, Chile	0	0	0	<3	<3	3	5	3	<3	3	<3	0	13
94 m	21	21	20	18	16	15	14	14	15	16	18	19	17
Buenos Aires, Argentina	79	71	109	89	76	61	56	61	79	86	84	99	950
27 m	23	23	21	17	13	9	10	11	13	15	19	22	16
Lima, Peru	3	<3	<3	<3	5	5	8	8	8	3	3	<3	41
120 m	23	24	24	22	19	17	17	16	17	18	19	21	20
Manaus, Brazil	249	231	262	221	170	84	58	38	46	107	142	203	1,811
44 m	28	28	28	27	28	28	28	28	29	29	29	28	28
Paraná, Brazil	287	236	239	102	13	<3	3	5	28	127	231	310	1,582
260 m	23	23	23	23	23	21	21	22	24	24	24	23	23
Rio de Janeiro, Brazil	125	122	130	107	79	53	41	43	66	79	104	137	1,082
61 m	26	26	25	24	22	21	21	21	21	22	23	25	23

WORLD STATISTICS: PHYSICAL DIMENSIONS

Each topic list is divided into continents and within a continent the items are listed in order of size. The bottom part of many of the lists is selective in order to give examples from as many different countries as possible. The order of the continents is as in the atlas, Europe through to South America. The world top ten are shown in square brackets; in the case of mountains this has not been done because the world top 30 are all in Asia. The figures are rounded as appropriate.

WORLD, CONTINENTS, OCEANS

THE WORLD	km²	miles²	%
The World	509,450,000	196,672,000	–
Land	149,450,000	57,688,000	29.3
Water	360,000,000	138,984,000	70.7
Asia	44,500,000	17,177,000	29.8
Africa	30,302,000	11,697,000	20.3
North America	24,241,000	9,357,000	16.2
South America	17,793,000	6,868,000	11.9
Antarctica	14,100,000	5,443,000	9.4
Europe	9,957,000	3,843,000	6.7
Australia & Oceania	8,557,000	3,303,000	5.7
Pacific Ocean	155,557,000	60,061,000	46.4
Atlantic Ocean	76,762,000	29,638,000	22.9
Indian Ocean	68,556,000	26,470,000	20.4
Southern Ocean	20,327,000	7,848,000	6.1
Arctic Ocean	14,056,000	5,427,000	4.2

SEAS

PACIFIC	km²	miles²
South China Sea	2,974,600	1,148,500
Bering Sea	2,268,000	875,000
Sea of Okhotsk	1,528,000	590,000
East China & Yellow	1,249,000	482,000
Sea of Japan	1,008,000	389,000
Gulf of California	162,000	62,500
Bass Strait	75,000	29,000

ATLANTIC	km²	miles²
Caribbean Sea	2,766,000	1,068,000
Mediterranean Sea	2,516,000	971,000
Gulf of Mexico	1,543,000	596,000
Hudson Bay	1,232,000	476,000
North Sea	575,000	223,000
Black Sea	462,000	178,000
Baltic Sea	422,170	163,000
Gulf of St Lawrence	238,000	92,000

INDIAN	km²	miles²
Red Sea	438,000	169,000
Persian Gulf	239,000	92,000

MOUNTAINS

EUROPE		m	ft
Elbrus	Russia	5,642	18,510
Mont Blanc	France/Italy	4,808	15,774
Monte Rosa	Italy/Switzerland	4,634	15,203
Dom	Switzerland	4,545	14,911
Liskamm	Switzerland	4,527	14,852
Weisshorn	Switzerland	4,505	14,780
Taschorn	Switzerland	4,490	14,730
Matterhorn/Cervino	Italy/Switzerland	4,478	14,691
Mont Maudit	France/Italy	4,465	14,649
Dent Blanche	Switzerland	4,356	14,291
Nadelhorn	Switzerland	4,327	14,196
Grandes Jorasses	France/Italy	4,208	13,806
Jungfrau	Switzerland	4,158	13,642
Barre des Ecrins	France	4,103	13,461
Gran Paradiso	Italy	4,061	13,323
Piz Bernina	Italy/Switzerland	4,049	13,284
Eiger	Switzerland	3,970	13,025
Monte Viso	Italy	3,841	12,602
Grossglockner	Austria	3,797	12,457
Wildspitze	Austria	3,772	12,382
Monte Disgrazia	Italy	3,678	12,066
Mulhacén	Spain	3,478	11,411
Pico de Aneto	Spain	3,404	11,168
Etna	Italy	3,340	10,958
Zugspitze	Germany	2,962	9,718
Musala	Bulgaria	2,925	9,596
Olympus	Greece	2,917	9,570
Triglav	Slovenia	2,863	9,393
Monte Cinto	France (Corsica)	2,710	8,891
Galdhøpiggen	Norway	2,469	8,100
Ben Nevis	UK	1,342	4,403

ASIA		m	ft
Everest	China/Nepal	8,850	29,035
K2 (Godwin Austen)	China/Kashmir	8,611	28,251
Kanchenjunga	India/Nepal	8,598	28,208
Lhotse	China/Nepal	8,516	27,939
Makalu	China/Nepal	8,481	27,824
Cho Oyu	China/Nepal	8,201	26,906
Dhaulagiri	Nepal	8,167	26,795
Manaslu	Nepal	8,156	26,758
Nanga Parbat	Kashmir	8,126	26,660
Annapurna	Nepal	8,078	26,502
Gasherbrum	China/Kashmir	8,068	26,469
Broad Peak	China/Kashmir	8,051	26,414
Xixabangma	China	8,012	26,286
Gayachung Kang	Nepal	7,897	25,909
Himalchuli	Nepal	7,893	25,896
Disteghil Sar	Kashmir	7,885	25,869
Nuptse	Nepal	7,879	25,849
Kangbachen	Nepal	7,858	25,781
Khunyang Chhish	Kashmir	7,852	25,761
Masherbrum	Kashmir	7,821	25,659
Nanda Devi	India	7,817	25,646
Rakaposhi	Kashmir	7,788	25,551
Batura	Kashmir	7,785	25,541
Namche Barwa	China	7,782	25,531
Kamet	India	7,756	25,447
Soltoro Kangri	Pakistan	7,742	25,400
Gurla Mandhata	China	7,728	25,354
Trivor	Pakistan	7,720	25,328
Kongur Shan	China	7,719	25,324
Jannu	Nepal	7,710	25,295
Tirich Mir	Pakistan	7,690	25,229
K'ula Shan	Bhutan/China	7,543	24,747
Pik Imeni Ismail Samani	Tajikistan	7,495	24,590
Demavend	Iran	5,604	18,386
Ararat	Turkey	5,165	16,945
Gunong Kinabalu	Malaysia (Borneo)	4,101	13,455
Yu Shan	Taiwan	3,997	13,113
Fuji-San	Japan	3,776	12,388

AFRICA		m	ft
Kilimanjaro	Tanzania	5,895	19,340
Mt Kenya	Kenya	5,199	17,057
Ruwenzori			
(Margherita)	Uganda/Congo (D.R.)	5,109	16,762
Meru	Tanzania	4,565	14,977
Ras Dashen	Ethiopia	4,533	14,872
Karisimbi	Rwanda/Congo (D.R.)	4,507	14,787
Mt Elgon	Kenya/Uganda	4,321	14,176
Batu	Ethiopia	4,307	14,130
Guna	Ethiopia	4,231	13,882
Toubkal	Morocco	4,165	13,665
Irhil Mgoun	Morocco	4,071	13,356
Mt Cameroun	Cameroon	4,070	13,353
Amba Ferit	Ethiopia	3,875	13,042
Pico del Teide	Spain (Tenerife)	3,718	12,198
Thabana Ntlenyana	Lesotho	3,482	11,424
Emi Koussi	Chad	3,415	11,204
Mt aux Sources	Lesotho/South Africa	3,282	10,768
Mt Piton	Réunion	3,069	10,069

OCEANIA		m	ft
Puncak Jaya	Indonesia	5,029	16,499
Puncak Trikora	Indonesia	4,730	15,518
Puncak Mandala	Indonesia	4,702	15,427
Mt Wilhelm	Papua New Guinea	4,508	14,790
Mauna Kea	USA (Hawai'i)	4,205	13,796
Mauna Loa	USA (Hawai'i)	4,169	13,678
Aoraki Mt Cook	New Zealand	3,753	12,313
Mt Balbi	Solomon Islands	2,439	8,002
Orohena	French Polynesia (Tahiti)	2,241	7,352
Mt Kosciuszko	Australia	2,230	7,316

NORTH AMERICA		m	ft
Mt McKinley			
(Denali)	USA (Alaska)	6,194	20,321
Mt Logan	Canada	5,959	19,551
Pico de Orizaba	Mexico	5,610	18,405
Mt St Elias	USA/Canada	5,489	18,008
Popocatépetl	Mexico	5,452	17,887

NORTH AMERICA (continued)		m	ft
Mt Foraker	USA (Alaska)	5,304	17,401
Iztaccihuatl	Mexico	5,286	17,343
Mt Lucania	Canada	5,226	17,146
Mt Steele	Canada	5,073	16,644
Mt Bona	USA (Alaska)	5,005	16,420
Mt Blackburn	USA (Alaska)	4,996	16,391
Mt Sanford	USA (Alaska)	4,940	16,207
Mt Wood	Canada	4,840	15,880
Nevado de Toluca	Mexico	4,670	15,321
Mt Fairweather	USA (Alaska)	4,663	15,298
Mt Hunter	USA (Alaska)	4,442	14,573
Mt Whitney	USA	4,418	14,495
Mt Elbert	USA	4,399	14,432
Mt Harvard	USA	4,395	14,419
Mt Rainier	USA	4,392	14,409
Blanca Peak	USA	4,372	14,344
Longs Peak	USA	4,345	14,255
Tajumulco	Guatemala	4,220	13,845
Grand Teton	USA	4,197	13,770
Mt Waddington	Canada	4,019	13,186
Mt Robson	Canada	3,959	12,989
Chirripó Grande	Costa Rica	3,837	12,589
Pico Duarte	Dominican Rep.	3,175	10,417

SOUTH AMERICA		m	ft
Aconcagua	Argentina	6,962	22,841
Bonete	Argentina	6,872	22,546
Ojos del Salado	Argentina/Chile	6,863	22,516
Pissis	Argentina	6,779	22,241
Mercedario	Argentina/Chile	6,770	22,211
Huascarán	Peru	6,768	22,205
Llullaillaco	Argentina/Chile	6,723	22,057
Nudo de Cachi	Argentina	6,720	22,047
Yerupaja	Peru	6,632	21,758
N. de Tres Cruces	Argentina/Chile	6,620	21,719
Incahuasi	Argentina/Chile	6,601	21,654
Cerro Galan	Argentina	6,600	21,654
Tupungato	Argentina/Chile	6,570	21,555
Sajama	Bolivia	6,520	21,391
Illimani	Bolivia	6,485	21,276
Coropuna	Peru	6,425	21,079
Ausangate	Peru	6,384	20,945
Cerro del Toro	Argentina	6,380	20,932
Siula Grande	Peru	6,356	20,853
Chimborazo	Ecuador	6,267	20,561
Alpamayo	Peru	5,947	19,511
Cotapaxi	Ecuador	5,896	19,344
Pico Cristóbal Colón	Colombia	5,800	19,029
Pico Bolivar	Venezuela	5,007	16,427

ANTARCTICA	m	ft
Vinson Massif	4,897	16,066
Mt Kirkpatrick	4,528	14,855
Mt Markham	4,349	14,268

OCEAN DEPTHS

ATLANTIC OCEAN	m	ft	
Puerto Rico (Milwaukee) Deep	9,220	30,249	[7]
Cayman Trench	7,680	25,197	[10]
Gulf of Mexico	5,203	17,070	
Mediterranean Sea	5,121	16,801	
Black Sea	2,211	7,254	
North Sea	660	2,165	
Baltic Sea	463	1,519	
Hudson Bay	258	846	

INDIAN OCEAN	m	ft
Java Trench	7,450	24,442
Red Sea	2,635	8,454
Persian Gulf	73	239

PACIFIC OCEAN	m	ft	
Mariana Trench	11,022	36,161	[1]
Tonga Trench	10,882	35,702	[2]
Japan Trench	10,554	34,626	[3]
Kuril Trench	10,542	34,587	[4]
Mindanao Trench	10,497	34,439	[5]
Kermadec Trench	10,047	32,962	[6]

PACIFIC OCEAN (continued)

	m	ft	
Peru–Chile Trench	8,050	26,410	[8]
Aleutian Trench	7,822	25,662	[9]

ARCTIC OCEAN

	m	ft
Molloy Deep	5,608	18,399

SOUTHERN OCEAN

	m	ft
South Sandwich Trench	7,235	23,737

LAND LOWS

		m	ft
Caspian Sea	Europe	−28	−92
Dead Sea	Asia	−418	−1,371
Lake Assal	Africa	−156	−512
Lake Eyre North	Oceania	−16	−52
Death Valley	North America	−86	−282
Valdés Peninsula	South America	−40	−131

RIVERS

EUROPE

		km	miles
Volga	Caspian Sea	3,700	2,300
Danube	Black Sea	2,850	1,770
Ural	Caspian Sea	2,535	1,575
Dnepr (Dnipro)	Black Sea	2,285	1,420
Kama	Volga	2,030	1,260
Don	Black Sea	1,990	1,240
Petchora	Arctic Ocean	1,790	1,110
Oka	Volga	1,480	920
Belaya	Kama	1,420	880
Dnister (Dniester)	Black Sea	1,400	870
Vyatka	Kama	1,370	850
Rhine	North Sea	1,320	820
N. Dvina	Arctic Ocean	1,290	800
Desna	Dnepr (Dnipro)	1,190	740
Elbe	North Sea	1,145	710
Wisla	Baltic Sea	1,090	675
Loire	Atlantic Ocean	1,020	635

ASIA

		km	miles	
Yangtze	Pacific Ocean	6,380	3,960	[3]
Yenisey–Angara	Arctic Ocean	5,550	3,445	[5]
Huang He	Pacific Ocean	5,464	3,395	[6]
Ob–Irtysh	Arctic Ocean	5,410	3,360	[7]
Mekong	Pacific Ocean	4,500	2,795	[9]
Amur	Pacific Ocean	4,442	2,760	[10]
Lena	Arctic Ocean	4,402	2,735	
Irtysh	Ob	4,250	2,640	
Yenisey	Arctic Ocean	4,090	2,540	
Ob	Arctic Ocean	3,680	2,285	
Indus	Indian Ocean	3,100	1,925	
Brahmaputra	Indian Ocean	2,900	1,800	
Syrdarya	Aral Sea	2,860	1,775	
Salween	Indian Ocean	2,800	1,740	
Euphrates	Indian Ocean	2,700	1,675	
Vilyuy	Lena	2,650	1,645	
Kolyma	Arctic Ocean	2,600	1,615	
Amudarya	Aral Sea	2,540	1,578	
Ural	Caspian Sea	2,535	1,575	
Ganges	Indian Ocean	2,510	1,560	
Si Kiang	Pacific Ocean	2,100	1,305	
Irrawaddy	Indian Ocean	2,010	1,250	
Tarim–Yarkand	Lop Nor	2,000	1,240	
Tigris	Indian Ocean	1,900	1,180	

AFRICA

		km	miles	
Nile	Mediterranean	6,695	4,180	[1]
Congo	Atlantic Ocean	4,670	2,900	[8]
Niger	Atlantic Ocean	4,180	2,595	
Zambezi	Indian Ocean	3,540	2,200	
Oubangi/Uele	Congo (D.R.)	2,250	1,400	
Kasai	Congo (D.R.)	1,950	1,210	
Shaballe	Indian Ocean	1,930	1,200	
Orange	Atlantic Ocean	1,860	1,155	
Cubango	Okavango Delta	1,800	1,120	
Limpopo	Indian Ocean	1,770	1,100	
Senegal	Atlantic Ocean	1,640	1,020	
Volta	Atlantic Ocean	1,500	930	

AUSTRALIA

		km	miles
Murray–Darling	Southern Ocean	3,750	2,330
Darling	Murray	3,070	1,905
Murray	Southern Ocean	2,575	1,600
Murrumbidgee	Murray	1,690	1,050

NORTH AMERICA

		km	miles	
Mississippi–Missouri	Gulf of Mexico	5,971	3,710	[4]
Mackenzie	Arctic Ocean	4,240	2,630	
Missouri	Mississippi	4,088	2,540	

NORTH AMERICA (continued)

		km	miles
Mississippi	Gulf of Mexico	3,782	2,350
Yukon	Pacific Ocean	3,185	1,980
Rio Grande	Gulf of Mexico	3,030	1,880
Arkansas	Mississippi	2,340	1,450
Colorado	Pacific Ocean	2,330	1,445
Red	Mississippi	2,040	1,270
Columbia	Pacific Ocean	1,950	1,210
Saskatchewan	Lake Winnipeg	1,940	1,205
Snake	Columbia	1,670	1,040
Churchill	Hudson Bay	1,600	990
Ohio	Mississippi	1,580	980
Brazos	Gulf of Mexico	1,400	870
St Lawrence	Atlantic Ocean	1,170	730

SOUTH AMERICA

		km	miles	
Amazon	Atlantic Ocean	6,450	4,010	[2]
Paraná–Plate	Atlantic Ocean	4,500	2,800	
Purus	Amazon	3,350	2,080	
Madeira	Amazon	3,200	1,990	
São Francisco	Atlantic Ocean	2,900	1,800	
Paraná	Plate	2,800	1,740	
Tocantins	Atlantic Ocean	2,750	1,710	
Orinoco	Atlantic Ocean	2,740	1,700	
Paraguay	Paraná	2,550	1,580	
Pilcomayo	Paraná	2,500	1,550	
Araguaia	Tocantins	2,250	1,400	
Juruá	Amazon	2,000	1,240	
Xingu	Amazon	1,980	1,230	
Ucayali	Amazon	1,900	1,180	
Uruguay	Plate	1,610	1,000	

LAKES

EUROPE

		km²	miles²
Lake Ladoga	Russia	17,700	6,800
Lake Onega	Russia	9,700	3,700
Saimaa system	Finland	8,000	3,100
Vänern	Sweden	5,500	2,100

ASIA

		km²	miles²	
Caspian Sea	Asia	371,000	143,000	[1]
Lake Baikal	Russia	30,500	11,780	[8]
Tonlé Sap	Cambodia	20,000	7,700	
Lake Balqash	Kazakhstan	18,500	7,100	
Aral Sea	Kazakhstan/Uzbekistan	17,160	6,625	
Lake Dongting	China	12,000	4,600	
Lake Ysyk	Kyrgyzstan	6,200	2,400	
Lake Orumiyeh	Iran	5,900	2,300	
Lake Koko	China	5,700	2,200	
Lake Poyang	China	5,000	1,900	
Lake Khanka	China/Russia	4,400	1,700	
Lake Van	Turkey	3,500	1,400	

AFRICA

		km²	miles²	
Lake Victoria	East Africa	68,000	26,300	[3]
Lake Tanganyika	Central Africa	33,000	13,000	[6]
Lake Malawi/Nyasa	East Africa	29,600	11,430	[9]
Lake Chad	Central Africa	25,000	9,700	
Lake Bangweulu	Zambia	9,840	3,800	
Lake Turkana	Ethiopia/Kenya	8,500	3,290	
Lake Volta	Ghana	8,480	3,270	
Lake Kariba	Zambia/Zimbabwe	5,580	2,150	
Lake Albert	Uganda/Congo (D.R.)	5,300	2,050	
Lake Nasser	Egypt/Sudan	5,250	2,030	
Lake Mweru	Zambia/Congo (D.R.)	4,920	1,900	
Lake Kyoga	Uganda	4,430	1,710	
Lake Tana	Ethiopia	3,620	1,400	
Lake Cabora Bassa	Mozambique	2,750	1,070	
Lake Rukwa	Tanzania	2,600	1,000	
Lake Mai-Ndombe	Congo (D.R.)	2,300	890	

AUSTRALIA

		km²	miles²
Lake Eyre	Australia	8,900	3,400
Lake Torrens	Australia	5,800	2,200
Lake Gairdner	Australia	4,800	1,900

NORTH AMERICA

		km²	miles²	
Lake Superior	Canada/USA	82,350	31,800	[2]
Lake Huron	Canada/USA	59,600	23,010	[4]
Lake Michigan	USA	58,000	22,400	[5]
Great Bear Lake	Canada	31,800	12,280	[7]
Great Slave Lake	Canada	28,500	11,000	[10]
Lake Erie	Canada/USA	25,700	9,900	
Lake Winnipeg	Canada	24,400	9,400	
Lake Ontario	Canada/USA	19,500	7,500	
Lake Nicaragua	Nicaragua	8,200	3,200	
Lake Athabasca	Canada	8,100	3,100	
Smallwood Reservoir	Canada	6,530	2,520	
Reindeer Lake	Canada	6,400	2,500	
Nettilling Lake	Canada	5,500	2,100	

SOUTH AMERICA

		km²	miles²
Lake Titicaca	Bolivia/Peru	8,300	3,200
Lake Poopo	Bolivia	2,800	1,100

ISLANDS

EUROPE

		km²	miles²	
Great Britain	UK	229,880	88,700	[8]
Iceland	Atlantic Ocean	103,000	39,800	
Ireland	Ireland/UK	84,400	32,600	
Novaya Zemlya (N.)	Russia	48,200	18,600	
W. Spitzbergen	Norway	39,000	15,100	
Novaya Zemlya (S.)	Russia	33,200	12,800	
Sicily	Italy	25,500	9,800	
Sardinia	Italy	24,000	9,300	
N. E. Spitzbergen	Norway	15,000	5,600	
Corsica	France	8,700	3,400	
Crete	Greece	8,350	3,200	
Zealand	Denmark	6,850	2,600	

ASIA

		km²	miles²	
Borneo	South-east Asia	744,360	287,400	[3]
Sumatra	Indonesia	473,600	182,860	[6]
Honshu	Japan	230,500	88,980	[7]
Sulawesi (Celebes)	Indonesia	189,000	73,000	
Java	Indonesia	126,700	48,900	
Luzon	Philippines	104,700	40,400	
Mindanao	Philippines	101,500	39,200	
Hokkaido	Japan	78,400	30,300	
Sakhalin	Russia	74,060	28,600	
Sri Lanka	Indian Ocean	65,600	25,300	
Taiwan	Pacific Ocean	36,000	13,900	
Kyushu	Japan	35,700	13,800	
Hainan	China	34,000	13,100	
Timor	Indonesia	33,600	13,000	
Shikoku	Japan	18,800	7,300	
Halmahera	Indonesia	18,000	6,900	
Ceram	Indonesia	17,150	6,600	
Sumbawa	Indonesia	15,450	6,000	
Flores	Indonesia	15,200	5,900	
Samar	Philippines	13,100	5,100	
Negros	Philippines	12,700	4,900	
Bangka	Indonesia	11,910	4,600	
Palawan	Philippines	11,790	4,550	
Panay	Philippines	11,500	4,400	
Sumba	Indonesia	11,100	4,300	
Mindoro	Philippines	9,750	3,800	

AFRICA

		km²	miles²	
Madagascar	Indian Ocean	587,040	226,660	[4]
Socotra	Indian Ocean	3,600	1,400	
Réunion	Indian Ocean	2,500	965	
Tenerife	Atlantic Ocean	2,350	900	
Mauritius	Indian Ocean	1,865	720	

OCEANIA

		km²	miles²	
New Guinea	Indonesia/Papua NG	821,030	317,000	[2]
New Zealand (S.)	Pacific Ocean	150,500	58,100	
New Zealand (N.)	Pacific Ocean	114,700	44,300	
Tasmania	Australia	67,800	26,200	
New Britain	Papua New Guinea	37,800	14,600	
New Caledonia	Pacific Ocean	19,100	7,400	
Viti Levu	Fiji	10,500	4,100	
Hawai'i	Pacific Ocean	10,450	4,000	
Bougainville	Papua New Guinea	9,600	3,700	
Guadalcanal	Solomon Islands	6,500	2,500	
Vanua Levu	Fiji	5,550	2,100	
New Ireland	Papua New Guinea	3,200	1,200	

NORTH AMERICA

		km²	miles²	
Greenland	Atlantic Ocean	2,175,600	839,800	[1]
Baffin Is.	Canada	508,000	196,100	[5]
Victoria Is.	Canada	212,200	81,900	[9]
Ellesmere Is.	Canada	212,000	81,800	[10]
Cuba	Caribbean Sea	110,860	42,800	
Newfoundland	Canada	110,680	42,700	
Hispaniola	Dominican Rep./Haiti	76,200	29,400	
Banks Is.	Canada	67,000	25,900	
Devon Is.	Canada	54,500	21,000	
Melville Is.	Canada	42,400	16,400	
Vancouver Is.	Canada	32,150	12,400	
Somerset Is.	Canada	24,300	9,400	
Jamaica	Caribbean Sea	11,400	4,400	
Puerto Rico	Atlantic Ocean	8,900	3,400	
Cape Breton Is.	Canada	4,000	1,500	

SOUTH AMERICA

		km²	miles²
Tierra del Fuego	Argentina/Chile	47,000	18,100
Falkland Is. (East)	Atlantic Ocean	6,800	2,600
South Georgia	Atlantic Ocean	4,200	1,600
Galapagos (Isabela)	Pacific Ocean	2,250	870

WORLD: REGIONS IN THE NEWS

KASHMIR

0   100   200 km

With the partition of India in 1947, war broke out between India and Pakistan for the control of Kashmir.

- Aksai Chin – Administered by China, claimed by India
- Shaksam Valley – Administered by China, claimed by India
- Azad Kashmir – Administered by Pakistan, claimed by India
- Northern Areas – Administered by Pakistan, claimed by India
- Siachen Glacier – Administered by India, claimed by Pakistan
- Jammu and Kashmir – Administered by India

- ·–·–· International boundaries
- ······ Disputed boundaries
- ·········· Line of Control
- ------ Province boundaries
- ■ Capital cities
- ● Main towns
- —— Roads

THE NEAR EAST

0   25   50 km

- ·–·–· 1949 Armistice Line
- ------ 1950 Armistice Line
- ------ 1974 Cease-fire Line
- Palestinian control
- Joint Israeli/ Palestinian control
- *Efrata* ● Main Jewish settlements
- Halhul Main Palestinian Arab towns
- —— Israeli security fence (April 2006)
- —— Israeli security fence subject to further ministerial examination

ISRAEL
POPULATION: 6,352,000 (inc. Israeli settlers in West Bank and Golan Heights)
INFANT MORTALITY: 6.7 deaths per 1,000 births
RELIGIONS: Jewish 76.4%, Muslim 16%, Christian 2.1%
GDP PER CAPITA: US$26,200 (2006)

WEST BANK
POPULATION: 2,460,000 (Muslim 75%, Jewish 17%)
INFANT MORTALITY: 18.7 deaths per 1,000 births
GDP PER CAPITA: US$1,100 (2003)

GAZA STRIP
POPULATION: 1,429,000 (Muslim 98.7% Christian 0.7%, Jewish 0.6%)
INFANT MORTALITY: 21.9 deaths per 1,000 births
GDP PER CAPITA: US$600 (2003)

JORDAN
POPULATION: 5,907,000 (Palestinian Arab 50%)

LEBANON
POPULATION: 3,874,000 (Palestinian Arab 11%)

IRAQ

0   100   200 km

- ·–·–· International boundaries
- ------ Province boundaries
- *Arbil* Underlined towns give their name to the administrative area in which they stand
- Oilfields
- —— Oil pipelines
- ///// Kurdish area
- ≡≡≡ Shi'ite area
- ■ Capital cities
- ● Main towns
- ∴ Archaeological sites
- —— Roads

AREA: 438,317 sq km [169,234 sq miles]
POPULATION: 26,783,000 (Arab 77%, Kurdish 19%, Assyrian and others 4%)
RELIGIONS: Islam 97% (Shi'ite Muslim 60%, Sunni Muslim 37%), others 3%
OIL RESERVES: Between 112 and 186 billion barrels (second in the world after Saudi Arabia)
CONFLICTS: Iran 1980–88, Kuwait invasion (Gulf War) 1990–91, US-led Coalition 2003
GDP PER CAPITA: US$2,900 (2006)

AFGHANISTAN

0   100   200 km

- ·–·–· International boundaries
- ------ Province boundaries
- ■ Capital cities
- ● Main towns
- Roads and road tunnel
- ///// Land over 3,000 m
- Mountain passes

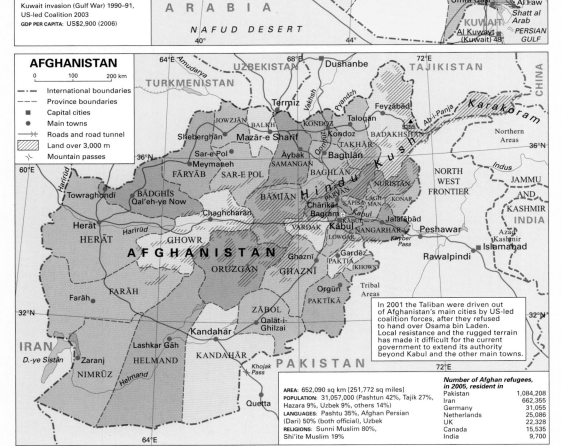

In 2001 the Taliban were driven out of Afghanistan's main cities by US-led coalition forces, after they refused to hand over Osama bin Laden. Local resistance and the rugged terrain has made it difficult for the current government to extend its authority beyond Kabul and the other main towns.

AREA: 652,090 sq km [251,772 sq miles]
POPULATION: 31,057,000 (Pashtun 42%, Tajik 27%, Hazara 9%, Uzbek 9%, others 14%)
LANGUAGES: Pashtu 35%, Afghan Persian (Dari) 50% (both official), Uzbek
RELIGIONS: Sunni Muslim 80%, Shi'ite Muslim 19%

Number of Afghan refugees, in 2005, resident in	
Pakistan	1,084,208
Iran	662,355
Germany	31,055
Netherlands	25,086
UK	22,328
Canada	15,535
India	9,700

SUDAN

0   250   500 km

- ● Refugee sites
- ● IDP sites (Internally Displaced Persons)
- Area of damaged/ destroyed villages
- ------ Regional boundaries
- ■ Capital cities
- ● Main towns

AREA: 2,505,813 sq km [967,494 sq miles]
POPULATION: 41,236,000 (Black 52%, Arab 39%, Beja 6%, others 3%)
RELIGIONS: Sunni Muslim 70% (mostly in the north), indigenous beliefs 25%, Christian 5% (mostly in the south)

Sudan has more internally displaced people than any other country (5.3 million in 2006) and there are 229,000 Sudanese refugees in neighbouring Chad. Up to 400,000 people are estimated to have been killed since conflict began in the Darfur region in early 2003.

WORLD EXPLORER

CONTENTS

Mountains and volcanoes	2–3	Sea and ocean cruises	18–19
Deserts and canyons	4–5	Winter sports	20–21
Lakes and waterfalls	6–7	Great beaches	22–23
Wildlife in the Americas and Europe	8–9	Festivals	24–25
Wildlife in Africa, Asia and Australasia	10–11	Historic sites in the Americas	26–27
Marine wildlife	12–13	Historic sites in Europe	28–29
Great railway journeys	14–15	Historic sites in Africa, Asia and Australasia	30–31
River and canal journeys	16–17	Theme parks	32

Mountains and volcanoes

The world's mountains provide a huge variety of magnificent scenery, ranging from the tree-covered Blue Mountains of Australia, little more than 1,070 m (3,500 ft) high, to the towering snow-covered Himalayan peaks of Nepal and China, several of which are over 8,000 m (26,000 ft) high. Many are accessible by road, or sometimes by train or cable car, but walking, even if only a short distance, is usually the best way to experience the breathtaking views that they offer.

◀ **Rocky Mountains, Banff National Park, Canada**
Pointed peaks and sheer cliffs contribute to a magnificent landscape. Over 1,600 km (1,000 miles) of trails pass by glaciers, turquoise lakes and forests of pine, fir and spruce. In the town of Banff a cable car rises to the top of Sulfur Mountain, 2,263 m (7,440 ft) high.
Best time to visit: June–September

THE AMERICAS

Mount McKinley, Denali National Park, Alaska, USA
The USA's highest mountain at 6,194 m (20,321 ft) is in a spectacular wilderness of snow-covered peaks and glaciers with wildlife that includes brown bears, caribou, moose and marmots. Activities include river rafting and sightseeing by plane.
Best time to visit: June–August

Popocatepetl Volcano ('Smoking Mountain'), Sierra Nevada, Mexico
A cloud of smoke often hovers above the massive crater of Popocatepetl, which is 5,452 m (17,887 ft) high. It is possible to climb and descend the mountain in one very long day with the aid of a guide.
Best time to climb: November–March

Cotopaxi and Chimborazo Volcanoes, Ecuador
The two highest active volcanoes in the world are in a country where the main road is known as the 'Avenue of the Volcanoes'. Non-mountaineers can climb Cotopaxi (5,896 m/19,344 ft) and get near to the top of Chimborazo (6,267 m/20,561 ft).
Best time to climb: January–April

Cordillera Blanca, Huascaran National Park, Peru
With 663 glaciers, the peaks of the Cordillera Blanca, more than 50 of which rise to heights of between 5,000 and 6,000 m (16,500 and 19,700 ft), are a great attraction for ice climbers. Huaraz is the main climbing centre. An alternative for those who prefer to trek is the richly glaciated Huayhuash range.
Best time to visit: July–September

EUROPE

Landmannalaugar, Iceland
A combination of volcanic and geothermal activity has produced a unique landscape in Landmannalaugar, where mountain peaks (little more than 1,070 m/3,500 ft high) rise above a landscape of convoluted lava fields and blue mountain lakes, and hot springs provide open-air baths.
Best time to visit: July–early September

Mount Vesuvius, Italy
The volcano of Vesuvius dominates the landscape around Naples. Although it lost its plume of smoke after erupting in 1944, it is still active. A bus from Pompeii goes to within 1.5 km (1 mile) of the summit (1,277 m/4,189 ft).
Time to visit: All seasons

AFRICA

Atlas Mountains, Morocco
Canyons with dramatic rock formations are to be found in these rugged mountains that rise to a height of over 3,900 m (13,000 ft). Organized treks pass by numerous isolated Berber villages, far from the road from Marrakech, which winds up to a mountain pass 2,275 m (7,467 ft) high.
Best time to visit: June–October

Mount Kilimanjaro, Tanzania
Africa's highest mountain rises majestically to 5,895 m (19,340 ft) above the plains of Amboseli National Park. It is possible to trek to the top for stunning views over Kenya and Tanzania, along

▲ **Sierra Nevada, Yosemite National Park, USA**
The Californian Yosemite National Park is famous for its sheer-sided granite domes, such as the Half Dome and the 2,307 m (7,569 ft) high El Capitan, which rise above forests and emerald lakes. Among the many species of flowers and trees to be found in the park are ancient giant sequoias over 60 m (200 ft) high, one of which is estimated to be 2,700 years old. An added attraction are the Yosemite Falls which, with a drop of 739 m (2,425 ft), are the highest in North America. Walkers can escape the summer crowds by using the 1,280 km (800 miles) of trails.
Best time to visit: May–September

• Town/city with major airport

▲ **Mont Blanc, Alps, France**
Europe's highest mountain rises to a height of 4,807 m (15,760 ft). A splendid view of it can be had from the peak of the Aiguille de Midi, a granite spear 3,840 m (12,600 ft) high, that is reached by a steep 3 km (2-mile) ascent in a cable car from Chamonix. Below Mont Blanc is the start of a long-distance ski and walking route, which passes ten of the 12 highest peaks in the Alps on its way to the Matterhorn in Switzerland and Italy.
Best time for walking: May–September

▼ **Mt Bromo, Java**
A crater within a vast outer crater, Bromo emits white smoke, as does Mount Semeru, seen here in the distance. Visitors usually stay over-night in a village at the rim of the outer crater, from where it is possible to walk to Bromo at dawn to watch the sun rise up over the outer crater.
Best time to visit: April–October

routes that pass through farmland and lush forest before reaching alpine-like vegetation and snow-covered rock.
Best time to climb: mid January–late February and late August–September

Drakensberg Mountains, South Africa
Vast pinnacles and blocks of basalt rise to a height of over 3,475 m (11,400 ft) in this range of mountains that also runs through Lesotho. Snowcapped in winter, many of the peaks are an enormous challenge for mountaineers. The Royal Natal National Park has numerous hiking trails.
Best time to visit: April–October

ASIA

Himalayas, Nepal
Within the Himalayas in Nepal are ten of the world's 14 peaks with a height of over 8,000 m (26,000 ft), including Everest (8,850 m/29,035 ft). Far below the snow-capped peaks are terraced hillsides dotted with villages, while above a height of about 2,700 m (9,000 ft) are forests in which rhododendrons bloom between February and April. The most popular base for exploring the mountains is Pokhara. The famous ten-day trek to the mountain town of Jomsom begins here, as does the three-to four-day Annapurna Skyline Trek which provides superb views while being easy enough to be undertaken with children.
Best time to visit: October–April

Karakorams, Pakistan
The jagged peaks of the Karakorams include K2, the world's second highest mountain (8,611 m/28,400 ft). A journey along the Karakoram Highway follows the route of the old Silk Road along the Indus Valley from Rawalpindi to Kashgar in China, sometimes clinging to cliff faces as it winds its way through the mountains up to the Khunjerab Pass at 4,934 m (16,280 ft).
Best time to visit: May–August

Great mountain treks
The following is a selection of great mountain treks that take four or more days. The months given are those in which it is best to undertake each trek.

Long Trail, Vermont, USA (424 km/265 miles; 16–21 days; May–Sept) Easily reached by road, the trail through Vermont's Green Mountains can be walked in sections. It is part of the 3,456 km (2,160-mile) long Appalachian Trail, whose most demanding section is through New Hampshire's White Mountains.
Inca Trail, Peru (4–5 days; April–Sept) By far the best way to approach the spectacular Inca site of Machu Picchu (see *Historic Sites of the Americas*), the Inca Trail begins some distance from Cuzco.
Mont Blanc Circuit, France and Switzerland (10 days; July–Sept) Possibly the finest walk in Europe, it usually starts from Chamonix. With an average altitude of 1,525 m (5,000 ft), it links the seven valleys surrounding Mont Blanc.

Annapurna Circuit, Nepal (17 days; Oct–Nov and March–April) Regarded as Nepal's classic trek, it goes through many types of landscape *(see picture below)*, and reaches a height of 5,416 m (17,765 ft), as well as providing superb views of Annapurna and Dhaulagiri.
Everest Trek, Nepal (14–16 days; Oct–Nov and March–April) A trek from Jiri to the Everest Base Camp on the Khumbu Glacier provides wonderful views of Everest. It is possible to fly back to Katmandu from Lukla, three days' walk away.
Milford Track, New Zealand (54 km/34 miles; 4 days; Oct–April) A walk that is regarded as a must by most New Zealanders ends at the breathtaking Milford Sound (see *Sea and ocean cruises*). The number of walkers is limited and booking well ahead is necessary.

Mayon Volcano, Philippines
Often described as the world's most perfect volcano cone, Mayon (2,462 m/8,075 ft) is still very active. An eruption in 1993 killed 70 people. It can be climbed in two days but it is essential to do so with a guide.
Best time to climb: December–May

Mt Kinabalu, Borneo, Malaysia
It is possible to walk rather than climb to the top of the highest mountain in South-east Asia (4,010 m/13,455 ft). It does, however, take two days and hiring a guide is compulsory. The view from the top sometimes stretches to the Philippines.
Best time to climb: April–September

Huangshan, China
The Chinese regard the 72-peak Huang-shan range as one of the great natural attractions of their country. Some 30 peaks rise to over 1,500 m (4,900 ft). There are two main walking routes up the side of the range, and an eight-minute cable-car ride from Yungusi to the top.
Best time to visit: spring and autumn

Mt Fuji, Japan
The perfectly symmetrical cone of Japan's highest mountain (3,776 m/12,388 ft), which last erupted in 1707, is climbed by people of all ages in the summer. A road goes to the fourth and fifth 'stations', from where it takes four or five hours to climb to the crater. This is best reached at dawn, before the clouds gather.
Best time to climb: July–August

AUSTRALASIA

Blue Mountains, New South Wales, Australia
Reaching a height of just over 1,070 m (3,500 ft), the Blue Mountains – with their densely forested slopes, sandstone chasms, dramatic rock formations and waterfalls – provide a beautiful environment in which to drive and walk. As well as a network of trails there are a number of interesting villages and towns, of which the largest, Katoomba, is served by a railway from Sydney just 80 km (50 miles) away.
Time to visit: All seasons

Cradle Mountain/Lake St Clair National Park, Tasmania, Australia
Australia's best mountain trails and rugged alpine scenery are to be found around Cradle Mountain. Jagged peaks, the highest of which is Mt Ossa (1,617 m/5,300 ft), rise above tarns and lakes in deep valleys.
Best time to visit: November–March

Deserts and canyons

For the adventurous traveller, the stunning landscapes of rock and sand which make up some of the world's most inhospitable environments offer a challenge not to be missed. From the vast sand seas of the Sahara Desert to the deep canyons and distinctive rock formations of the south-western United States, there is an extraordinary range of landforms to explore.

NORTH AMERICA

Bryce Canyon, Utah, USA

On a more human scale than the Grand Canyon, Bryce Canyon is not really a canyon at all but a natural amphitheatre filled with dazzling orange, red and pink rock pinnacles – known as 'hoodoos' – overlooking spectacularly colourful ravines. This surreal landscape can be explored on foot along a network of marked trails, or simply enjoyed from one of the viewpoints along the rim of the amphitheatre.

Monument Valley, Arizona, USA

With its majestic rock pillars towering over a barren, desert landscape, Monument Valley is an awe-inspiring sight. It has been made famous as a backdrop to numerous Hollywood westerns and is now part of the Navajo Reservation. A 27 km (17-mile) road tour of the valley takes two to three hours and offers stunning views of this unforgettable place.

Zion Canyon, Utah, USA

The road through the steep-sided Zion Canyon can become crowded in summer, and it is worth leaving the car to follow one of the short trails to the Emerald Pools or the hanging gardens at Weeping Rock. Longer trails lead from the canyon to the desert plateau above and offer spectacular views of the contrasting landscapes.

SOUTH AMERICA

Colca Canyon, Peru

High in the Andes the River Colca runs through a gorge which is twice the depth of the Grand Canyon, past ancient Inca granaries cut into the rock and green slopes covered by pre-Inca terracing. This astonishingly beautiful landscape, complete with smoking volcano in the background, is home to the Collagua and Cabana people, whose traditional way of life is punctuated with lively festivals.

Atacama Desert, Chile

Overlooked by a ruined pre-Inca fortress, the picturesque oasis village of San Pedro de Atacama, with its adobe buildings and excellent archeological museum, makes a good base for exploring the canyons, saltpans and stark landscapes of the surrounding desert. One of the most beautiful places to visit is the Valle de la Luna, where the multi-coloured desert formations are a magnet for photographers and filmmakers.

EUROPE

Almerían Desert, Spain

The setting for the film *Lawrence of Arabia* as well as many 'spaghetti westerns', the Almerían Desert is an extraordinary, almost lunar landscape of sand dunes dissected by dried-up river beds and littered with sandstone cones. Film sets are open to the public at Mini-Hollywood.

Timanfaya National Park, Lanzarote, Canary Islands

On an island where it rarely rains, a series of volcanic eruptions in the 1730s created an extraordinary apocalyptic landscape. Guided tours go to an area of solidified lava and volcanic cones, aptly called the Mountains of Fire, where a dry bush dropped into a crevice will burst into flames and meals at a solitary restaurant are barbecued on a volcano.

AFRICA

Draa Valley, the Sahara, Morocco

From the town of Ouarzazate, with its dramatic kasbah, the Draa river runs south-east through a rich landscape of dramatic gorges, agricultural land and kasbahs towards the Sahara. After around 160 km (100 miles), the river reaches the former frontier fort of Zagora, which makes a good base for exploring the desert.

▲ **Grand Canyon, Arizona, USA**
Carved by the Colorado River out of the multi-coloured rock of the Arizona Desert, the Grand Canyon is one of North America's most awe-inspiring natural features. Drives and trails around its rim – 443 km (277 miles) in length – provide stunning views. Visitors can walk or ride mules down one of the vertiginous trails to the valley floor, 1.7 km (1 mile) below, or try rafting on the river.

▲ **Sonoran Desert, USA/Mexico**
Almost encircling the Gulf of California and covering 310,000 sq km (120,00 sq miles), the Sonoran Desert is the hottest of North America's deserts. Tucson, Arizona, serves as a base for tours into the desert, including archaeological tours. Nearby are the excellent Arizona-Sonora Desert Museum and the protected desert habitat of Organ Pipe Cactus National Monument where visitors can see the giant saguaro and organ pipe cacti which have come to symbolize the area. There are good trails and scenic drives around the park, and plenty of desert wildlife to watch.

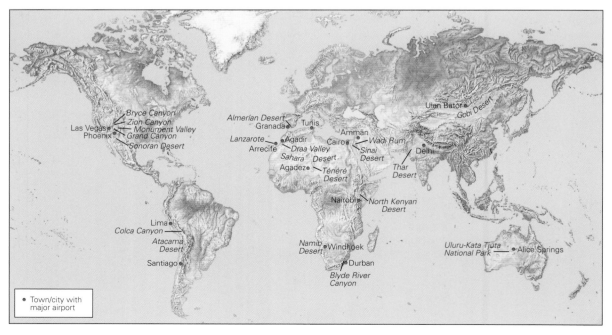

Bryce Canyon
Zion Canyon
Las Vegas• Monument Valley
Phoenix• Grand Canyon
Sonoran Desert

Almerían Desert
Granada• Tunis
Lanzarote• •Agadir
Arrecife •Draa Valley
Sahara Desert
Agadez• •Ténéré Desert

Amman•
Cairo• •Wadi Rum
Sinai Desert
•Delhi
Thar Desert

Ulan Bator•
Gobi Desert

Nairobi• •North Kenyan Desert

Lima•
Colca Canyon
Atacama Desert
Santiago•

Namib Desert •Windhoek
•Durban
Blyde River Canyon

Uluru-Kata Tjuta National Park •Alice Springs

● Town/city with major airport

Saharan oases, Tunisia
The shifting sand dunes around the town of Douz are an excellent example of the landscape popularly associated with the Sahara Desert. In fact the desert, which covers an area of 8,600,000 sq km (3,320,000 sq miles), has extensive stony plains, rock-strewn plateaux, mountains and large oasis depressions as well as seas of sand. Douz is a good base for camel safaris and for exploring the more isolated southern oases. To the north-west the town of Tozeur, with its beautiful 12th-century mosque, is set beside a vast oasis fed by over 200 springs. It serves as an excellent starting point for four-wheel-drive tours into the desert and to the nearby beautiful mountain oases, such as Tamerza, Mides and Chebika.

Guided expeditions of up to a week can include camel riding and stargazing under the immense Saharan sky.

Ténéré Desert, Niger
For desert purists the seemingly endless sea of sand that is the Ténéré Desert is perhaps the most beautiful part of the Sahara. A two-week round trip from the desert city of Agadez might pass through a massive dinosaur cemetery on the way to the classic oasis town of Bilma and the prehistoric cave paintings of the Djado Plateau. Crossing the Ténéré is notoriously challenging and often dangerous, but the experience is unforgettable.

Sinai Desert, Egypt
Inland from the coastal resorts of the Sinai Peninsula is a hot, desolate wilderness sprinkled with oases and ancient settlements. They include the 6th-century monastery of St Catherine, which stands at the foot of Mount Sinai, where Moses is said to have received the Ten Command-ments from God. Camel treks and jeep safaris take visitors into the aptly-named Wilderness of Wanderings, in the centre of the peninsula.

North Kenyan Desert
In sharp contrast to the developed south of Kenya, the North Kenyan Desert is a vast tract of scrubland inhabited by ancient nomadic tribes whose way of life has changed little over the centuries. A rich diversity of desert landscapes here includes scrub desert – which bursts into colour after rainfall – and lunar, volcanic areas. There are lush oases and river-cut canyons too, but the reason most people come here is to see the 'Jade Sea', Lake Turkana, with its profusion of birdlife, hippos and Nile crocodiles.

Namib Desert, Namibia
Stretching for 1,930 km (1,200 miles) down the length of the Namibian coastline to the mouth of the Orange River in South Africa, the Namib is a strip of desert with an average width of 110 km (70 miles). The highest sand dunes in the world – sometimes exceeding 244 m (800 ft) – are to be found at Sossus Vlei, in the Namib-Naukluft National Park. The northern section is known as Skeleton Coast because of the many shipwrecks that lie on the ocean bed nearby.

Blyde River Canyon, South Africa
The view over the canyon from the spot known as God's Window is one of the highlights of any visit to the beautiful Blyde River Nature Reserve, in the Drakensberg. There are two trails down into the canyon – which in some places is over 700 m (2,300 ft) deep – from Bourke's Luck Potholes, where strange natural rock formations can be seen.

ASIA AND AUSTRALASIA

Thar Desert, Rajasthan, India
Within the Rajasthan Desert National Park two areas of interest to tourists can be reached easily from the attractive city of Jaisalmer with its 12th-century fort. One is the Akal Fossil Park where the petrified trunks of 25 trees once covered by the sea lie on a bare hillside. The second is the 3 km (2-mile) long Sam Dunes, just 40 km (25 miles) from Jaisalmer. The dunes are usually crowded with tourists taking camel rides, but it is possible to escape the crowds and go on safaris of several days, by either jeep or camel.

Gobi Desert, Mongolia
For 70 years part of the Soviet Union, the Gobi Desert has only recently become accessible to western travellers. Its greatest attraction is the red sandstone Flaming Cliffs, 80 km (50 miles) north-west of Dalandzadgad, which became famous in the 1920s when the explorer and scientist Roy Chapman Andrews (on whom the character of Indiana Jones was based) discovered fossilized dinosaur remains there. Still rich in dinosaur fossils, the cliffs are just north of the vast Three Beauties National Park with a landscape of mountains, canyons, gravel and sand.

▼ **Wadi Rum, Jordan**
Soaring vertically from the desert floor of Wadi Rum are the massive rock form-ations known as jebels for which the area is famous. Vehicles and camels can be hired in the Bedouin settlement of Rum, but it is hard to beat the experience of walking through this extraordinary, silent landscape and sleeping out in the desert under the stars.

◀ **Uluru National Park, Northern Territory, Australia**
The largest sand-stone monolith in the world, Uluru (Ayers Rock) is a magnificent sight, particularly at sunset when it appears to burn from within. Some 40 km (25 miles) to the west are the Olgas – 36 enormous granite domes – which, like Uluru, are an important Aboriginal site. Access is restricted, but visitors can exper-ience their haunting beauty by following the trail through the Valley of the Winds.

Lakes and waterfalls

From the azure tranquillity of Lake Garda in Italy to the thundering roar of Zimbabwe's Victoria Falls, the great lakes and waterfalls of the world are set amidst dramatically beautiful scenery. Many resorts offer watersports as well as long-distance trails for ramblers and horse-riders.

► **Lake Maligne, Jasper National Park, Canada**
The glacier-fed Lake Maligne – shown here at dawn – is set among the snow-covered peaks of Jasper National Park, the biggest and wildest of Canada's four Rocky Mountain national parks at 10,400 sq km (4,000 sq miles). Boat and hiking tours, fishing, rafting and riding are available, while the independent explorer can hire a boat or walk along the excellent network of trails.

▼ **Angel Falls, Venezuela**
The world's highest waterfall with an uninterrupted drop of 2,650 ft (807 m), Angel Falls are 16 times the height of Niagara Falls. Although often shrouded in mist, the Falls are at their most spectacular during the rainy season (June–November) when the volume of water is greatest and when visitors can travel by motorized canoe along the river to Devil's Canyon at the foot of the Falls.

▼ **Lake Argentino, Argentina**

The south-western arm of Lake Argentino is periodically dammed by the Moreno Glacier, from which icebergs regularly break off and crash into the channel below. Visitors can see, hear and photograph the glacier in safety from a series of platforms and viewing points. The massive Upsala Glacier on the northern arm of the lake can be reached by boat from Puerto Bandera.

NORTH AMERICA

Niagara Falls, Canada/USA
The most-visited waterfall in the world, Niagara Falls has been developed as a tourist attraction offering every possible viewing experience, including cable cars, helicopter rides, viewing towers, boats and even tunnels in the rockface. Despite the commercialization, this massive, perpetual curtain of falling water lives up to its reputation as one of the wonders of the natural world.

Waterton-Glacier Park, Montana and Alberta, Canada/USA
Silver lakes are a major feature of the landscape of mountain peaks, waterfalls and hanging valleys, carved by glaciers 10,000 years ago, in the Waterton-Glacier Park. There are spectacular trails for walkers of all levels, and the Going-to-the-Sun Road through the park is considered to be one of the USA's driving highlights.

Lake Tahoe, California, USA
High in the Sierra Nevada mountains on the border between California and Nevada, Lake Tahoe is a popular year-round holiday destination. In winter the area is packed with skiers (see *Winter sports*) while summer brings people seeking the cooler temperatures of the mountains and the crystal waters and sandy beaches of the lake. On the California side, there is swimming, boating, fishing and walking, while the Nevada side offers a glittering nightlife of restaurants and casinos.

SOUTH AMERICA

Iguaçu Falls, Brazil
The torrential waters of the Iguaçu River plunge more than 75 m (250 ft) over a huge, crescent-shaped cliff into the gorge below in a series of some 275 separate waterfalls. Surrounded by lush rainforest, the 4 km (2.5-mile) wide cascades can be viewed from platforms and paths on both sides of the Falls.

Lake Titicaca, Bolivia
High in the Altiplano the clear blue waters of Lake Titicaca bring an oasis of life and colour to the parched landscape. At 8,340 sq km (3,220 sq miles), it is the largest lake in South America, with many lakeside settlements. Boat trips can be made to the floating reed islands inhabited by the Uros, and to ancient Inca ruins on the sacred islands of the Sun and Moon.

Lake Llanquihue, Chile
A reflection of the perfect cone of Volcano Osorno can be seen in this immense lake which lies amid gently rolling pastureland. Towns on the shore include Frutillar Bajo, a popular summer resort with black-sand beaches, and Puerto Varas, a centre for 'adventure' activities such as rafting, riding, hiking and climbing.

EUROPE

Lake Siljan, Sweden
In a land of around 96,000 lakes, Siljan is noted as a centre of Swedish folk tradition

and art. Locals and visitors arrive in boats reminiscent of Viking longships during midsummer celebrations at the lakeside church of Rättvik, and traditional mystery plays are performed annually in the open-air theatre at Leksand. Visitors can watch traditional painted wooden horses being made at Nusnäs, and visit the studio of the painter Anders Zorn, who lived in the lakeside town of Mora.

Lake District, England
Famous as the haunt of the Romantic Poets, the Lake District is a beautiful and varied landscape of hills, mountains, lakes and rivers, encompassing a wide range of scenery within a relatively small area. The southern lakes – including Windermere, Coniston and Grasmere – are surrounded by gentle green slopes and attract enormous numbers of visitors in summer.

The wilder north, with its sheer, forbidding crags is more spectacular and much less crowded. Boating is popular on the larger lakes, and a network of paths makes the area a haven for walkers and climbers.

Lake Lucerne, Switzerland
The picturesque medieval town of Lucerne with its famous Kapellbrücke bridge makes an excellent base for exploring this beautiful lake and its mountain surroundings. Visitors can go on a lake cruise and stop off at some of the peaceful villages along the shore, or take the oldest mountain railway in Europe to Mount Rigi for wonderful views of the Alpine scenery.

Lake Garda, Italy
The largest of Italy's lakes, Lake Garda is certainly one of its most beautiful. Sheltered from the north-east by the Dolomites, its climate is particularly gentle, with orange and lemon groves flourishing on its banks. Dotted around the lake are many attractive and historic resort towns – some dating back to Roman times – and romantic hillside villas.

AFRICA

Lake Bosumtwi, Ghana
Sacred to the Asante people, the crater lake of Bosumtwi is the deepest natural lake in Ghana, and its waters are still rising. Its beautiful setting among thickly wooded crater walls makes it a relaxing place to go fishing, boating and swimming. Motorboat trips across the lake are available, and walks around the shore can include visits to lakeside villages.

Murchison Falls, Uganda
The sheer force of the Nile as it shoots through a narrow cleft in the rocks and crashes over a 30 m (100 ft) precipice is what makes Murchison Falls so spectacular. A journey up the river from Paraa Camp to the base of the falls is also an excellent way to see some of the wildlife of the Murchison Falls National Park, including crocodiles, elephants, hippos, giraffes, buffalo, waterbucks and many bird species.

Lake Baringo, Kenya
Encircled by mountains and rich in bird and animal life, Lake Baringo is a fascinating and beautiful place to visit. The shoreline is home to crocodiles and herds of hippos and the area is famous for its hundreds of bird species, attracting birdwatchers from all over the world. A resident ornithologist offers guided walks, and there are also horse rides, camel rides and boat trips to the lake's islands.

ASIA

Lake Toba, Sumatra
Encircled by steep crags – once the rim of an enormous ancient volcano – Lake Toba is the largest crater lake in the world. The area is home to the Toba Batak people, whose brightly painted houses with distinctive crescent-shaped roofs can be seen around the lake. The beautiful island of Samosir is a popular tourist destination

with excellent trekking and rafting as well as interesting megalithic tombs to visit.

Lake Batur, Bali
The largest lake in Bali, Lake Batur is a crater lake and is sacred to the Balinese as the home of the goddess Dewi Danu. The hot springs at Toya Bungkah are said to have healing properties, and the lakeside temple of Pura Jati presides over a holy bathing place. From Toyah Bungkah there are trekking routes up to the summit of Gunung Batur, the soaring 1,717 m (5,630 ft) high volcano which dominates the lake.

Lake Karakul, Tajikistan
At a height of 3,600 m (11,800 ft) in the foothills of the Pamir mountains, Lake Karakul's setting is remote and beautiful. Flanked by the massive Mount Kongur to the north and the magnificent Mount Muztaghata to the south, Karakul is the home of the Kirgiz people and their herds of sheep, goats, horses and camels. It takes a day to walk around the lake, after which walkers can stay overnight in a traditional felt-covered *yurt* at the visitors' camp.

Lake Chuzenji-ko and Kegon Waterfall, Japan
Visitors to Lake Chuzenji-ko and the dramatic Kegon Waterfall are well provided for with cable cars and platforms from which to gaze at the spectacular view, especially popular in autumn when the

leaves are changing colour. Beside the lake is a colourful shrine after which both the town and lake are named.

AUSTRALASIA

Lake Rotorua, New Zealand
Bubbling hot springs, vertical jets of steam and scalding geysers make Rotorua an exciting place to visit. There are lakeside bath houses where visitors can sample the waters, as well as cruises and facilities for a wide range of watersports on the lake and nearby rivers. Maoris have lived beside the lake for around 700 years, and there are many cultural attractions on offer, some more authentic than others.

▲ **Keli Mutu, Flores, Indonesia**
An extinct volcano, Keli Mutu has three extraordinary crater lakes. Not only is each lake a different colour, but the colours change over decades from vivid green through to deep red and intense turquoise as mineral layers dissolve.

◄ **Victoria Falls, Zimbabwe**
The 1.7 km (1-mile) wide Victoria Falls are made up of five separate waterfalls which plummet more than 100 m (320 ft) into the gorge below. The Falls are a popular base for adrenaline-boosting activities, such as bungee jumping, white-water rafting and riverboarding, and tours of every description can be taken from operators based in Victoria Falls town.

7

Wildlife in the Americas and Europe

From the bears and moose of the Alaskan wilderness, to the jaguars and toucans of the Central American forests, to the condors and rheas of Patagonia, the Americas have an amazing variety of wildlife. Europe by contrast is famed for its seabirds, and the vast flocks of migrant wildfowl that gather in its wetlands.

▶ **Torres del Paine National Park, Chile**
An awe-inspiring landscape of forests, glaciers, shimmering lakes, thundering cascades and soaring granite pillars, Torres del Paine National Park in Patagonia is a haven for wildlife, including guanacos, rheas, flamingos, condors and the shy huemul (Chilean deer). There is an excellent network of short- and long-distance trails through the park.

▼ **Wrangell-St Elias National Park, Alaska, USA**
Of all the Alaskan national parks, Wrangell-St Elias is the best for wildlife watching. This vast landscape of mountains and glaciers is home to moose, wolves, wolverines, bears, beavers and herds of caribou. There are several campsites but few other facilities for visitors in this true wilderness park.

NORTH AMERICA

Wood Buffalo National Park, Alberta/NW Territories, Canada
Canada's largest national park, Wood Buffalo is famous for its free-roaming buffalo herd. Among other inhabitants are lynx, bears and hundreds of bird species, including a river rookery of rare white pelicans and the few remaining whooping cranes in the world. Fort Smith has some accommodation, but canoeing along the rivers and camping are perhaps the best ways to explore this wilderness of forest, marsh and grassland.

Yellowstone National Park, Wyoming, USA
Famous for its many geothermal geysers and hot springs, Yellowstone Park is also home to one of the largest and most diverse populations of mammals in North America. Inhabitants include bison, moose, elks, Bighorn sheep, beavers and marmots as well as lynx, bobcats, wolves and coyotes. Millions of visitors flock to Yellowstone every year, but despite the inevitable tourist development, most of the park is still a true wilderness.

Everglades National Park, Florida, USA
The largest sub-tropical wilderness on the North American mainland, Everglades National Park is a vast area of swamps, mangrove forests and grasslands. It is the only place in the world where alligators and crocodiles live side by side, and there are still a few panthers and black bears. Canoe trails and boat tours are the best way to view the abundant wildlife, which includes a huge variety of bird species.

CENTRAL AMERICA

Braulio Carrillo National Park, Costa Rica
Many different habitats exist in Braulio Carrillo, a large area of rainforest covering a range of altitudes from just above sea level to 3,000 m (9,850 ft). Each has its own distinct flora and fauna, although the astonishingly lush vegetation can make spotting animals such as tapirs, sloths, ocelots, jaguars and pumas difficult. The park's abundant birdlife includes toucans, quetzels, umbrella birds, guans and eagles.

Corcovado National Park, Costa Rica
Set on the remote Osa peninsula, Corcovado National Park encompasses coastal mangrove swamps, pristine cloud forests and rocky canyons. Many of Costa Rica's endangered species live here, including tapirs, caymans and jaguars, while crocodiles swim in its waters and turtles lay their eggs on the park's deserted beaches. Ranger stations provide simple accommodation and advice.

Darién National Park, Panama
More than 500 bird species have been seen in the pristine rainforest of Darién National Park, among them many endangered species such as the harpy eagle. Indeed, Cerro Pirre mountain is considered by many birdwatchers to be one of the best sites in the world. Boat trips and forest walks are ideal ways to view the abundant wildlife, although visitors should seek advice on when it is safe to travel because of possible paramilitary activity.

Cockscomb Basin Wildlife Sanctuary, Belize
Beneath the peaks of the Cockscomb mountain range, the dense rainforest of the Cockscomb Basin is home to around 600 jaguars as well as tapirs, anteaters, armadillos and otters. Nearly 300 bird species have been reported in this lush jungle, and a wide variety of reptiles and amphibians are readily visible. Excellent forest trails make this a very rewarding place for wildlife watchers.

SOUTH AMERICA

Podocarpus National Park, Ecuador
Encompassing a wide range of habitats at different altitudes, Podocarpus (near Loja) has many rare plant and animal species, such as the Andean fox, the Andean speckled bear and the mountain tapir. Birdlife is abundant, and it is easy to see many fascinating species. This is, however, a park in peril, with the authorities struggling to protect the environment from poachers, loggers and others. For visitors prepared to rough it, there is much to enjoy in this landscape of lakes, mountains and rainforest.

Manu Biosphere Reserve, Peru
Altitudes range from 200 m (650 ft) to over 4,000 m (13,000 ft) in this area of rainforest near Cuzco. An astonishing 850 bird species are found here, and mammals include jaguars, ocelots, otters and many primate species. The reserve is divided into zones, with restricted visitor access in some areas. A stay in the Reserved Zone, which is set aside for ecotourism and research, must be arranged in advance, but offers the best jungle experience.

▲ **Monteverde Cloud Forest Reserve, Costa Rica**
Festooned with bromeliads and orchids, the towering rainforest trees of Monteverde Cloud Forest provide shelter for an enormous variety of wildlife including tapirs, monkeys, coatimundis and armadillos, as well as more than 400 bird species. The reserve was established in 1950 by a group of Quakers, who have developed a range of unobtrusive facilities for visitors, including simple accommodation and excellent guided walks.

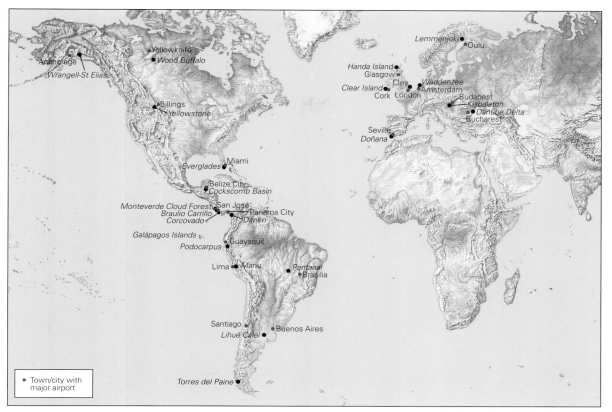

▶ Handa Island, Scotland

The sea cliffs of Handa Island are one of north-west Europe's largest seabird nesting sites, with the high cliff ledges attracting guillemots, razorbills and kittiwakes in enormous numbers. Fulmars, puffins and shags also nest here, while the island's moorland is home to great and Arctic skuas, red-throated divers, shelducks, ringed plovers, wheatears, meadow pipits and skylarks. The island can be visited for the day by boat from the mainland village of Tarbet, near Loch Laxford.

Pantanal, Brazil

A vast swamp covering an area the size of Great Britain, the Pantanal is perhaps the best place to see wildlife in the Americas. Animals wander freely around the wide open spaces, making it relatively easy for visitors to spot such creatures as alligators, jaguars and anacondas, and birds such as the giant red-necked stork. There are organized tours by boat or jeep and on horseback, with overnight accommodation at converted ranch houses.

Lihué Calel National Park, Argentina

An arid landscape of low, pink granite mountains and scrub forest, Lihué Calel (south-west of Santa Rosa) is home to several wild cat species and other mammals such as guanacos, Patagonian foxes, Patagonian hares and chinchillas. Birdlife is plentiful, too, and includes many species of birds of prey. The park has an excellent campsite and visitor centre.

EUROPE

Lemmenjoki National Park, Lappland, Finland

Lemmenjoki (near Inarijärvi) is one of the most extensive areas of uninhabited, forested wilderness in Europe (2,855 sq km/1,102 sq miles). Wide rivers flow through a landscape of peatland and spruce- and birch-forested hills, home to brown bears, golden eagles, foxes, lynx, wolverines and moose. There are also plenty of semi-domesticated reindeer.

Clear Island, Ireland

Ireland's southernmost inhabited island, tiny Clear Island is famous for its birds. It has breeding populations of chough, black guillemot and rock dove and is visited by many migrant species in August–October, including the rare bee-eater, little bittern, night and purple herons, and great reed warbler, as well as many seabirds. The Bird Observatory has a full-time bird-warden and offers simple accommodation.

Cley Marshes, Norfolk, England

One of Britain's leading birdwatching reserves, Cley Marshes (near Sheringham) has many thatched hides offering excellent views of thousands of water birds. Migrating waders stop in the area on their way to and from their Arctic breeding grounds, and in summer bitterns and avocets breed here. Wildfowl such as teals, widgeons and shovelers are plentiful in winter.

Waddenzee, The Netherlands

Regarded by birdwatchers as the most important intertidal area in Europe, Waddenzee has huge populations of waders and wildfowl. One of the best areas to see the birds is around Schiermonnikoog, particularly at high tide. Among the birds present in summer are avocets, godwits and ruffs, while in winter they include Bewick's swans, barnacle geese, marsh and hen harriers and white-tailed eagles.

Kisbalaton Reserve, Lake Balaton, Hungary

With its reed beds, the Kisbalaton Reserve provides the perfect environment for marsh birds to breed. Night, purple and squacco herons are all to be found here along with little and great white egrets, spoonbills, marsh harriers and several warblers. From October huge flocks of migrating ducks and geese stop in the reserve on their journey south.

Danube Delta, Romania

One of Europe's last unspoiled ecosystems, consisting of forest, lakes, reed beds and marshland, the Danube Delta is home to huge numbers of birds. Due to the lack of tourist facilities, it is probably best-visited in an organized group, ideally from late May–June. Species include bitterns, pygmy cormorants, white pelicans, night, purple and squacco herons, spoonbills, ruddy shelducks, honey buzzards, bee-eaters and white-tailed eagles.

Doñana National Park, Spain

Huge sand dunes and the seasonally flooded plains (*marismas*) behind them provide ideal conditions for a great variety of birdlife in one of Europe's most important wildlife habitats. Peregrines, stone-curlews and short-toed eagles are to be seen in the dunes, while the marismas are feeding grounds for white storks, spoonbills, night and purple herons and colonies of little and cattle egrets.

Galápagos Islands and ecotourism

Lying 960 km (600 miles) off the coast of Ecuador, the fragile wilderness of the Galápagos Islands provides a habitat for a surprising combination of penguins and corals as well as giant tortoises, land and marine iguanas, sperm whales, sea lions, fur seals, orca whales, sharks and a variety of tropical fish. Many of the species living here are found nowhere else in the world, making the Galápagos a vital laboratory for the study of animal and plant life. Access to the islands is strictly controlled and limited to 50 designated visitor sites. The development of ecotourism in the Galápagos Islands aims to ensure the preservation of the habitats and wildlife while enabling tourists to visit and learn about this unique environment.

Wildlife in Africa, Asia and Australasia

An African safari is one of the world's great wildlife-watching experiences. Vast stretches of open savanna are home to the 'big five' – lion, leopard, elephant, rhinoceros and buffalo – as well as herds of zebra and gazelle. The endangered Indian tiger and exotic komodo dragon are just two of the animals that attract visitors to Asia, while Australia has its own unique fauna, including kangaroo, koala and duck-billed platypus.

◀ **Masai Mara National Reserve, Kenya**
Kenya's greatest concentration of wildlife can be seen in Masai Mara, where cheetahs, hyenas, zebras, hartebeest, hippos and crocodiles share the territory with the 'big five'. During the summer enormous herds of wildebeest, zebras and gazelles arrive from the Serengeti on the first stage of their dramatic annual migration.

AFRICA

Abuko Nature Reserve, Gambia
In this small reserve, mangroves, gallery forest and savanna combine to attract over 270 bird species – including the world's largest and smallest kingfishers – making it one of the best birdwatching sites in West Africa. Abuko is also known for its troops of colobus, patas and vervet monkeys.

Niokolo-Koba National Park, Senegal
Some 80 mammal species, including lions, leopards, elephants, waterbucks, bush-bucks, baboons and chimpanzees live in Niokolo-Koba, along with around 350 bird species. The best time to see the animals is when they gather at waterholes during the hot season in April and May.

Tsavo (East and West), Kenya
Tsavo East and Tsavo West combine to make one of the world's biggest national parks, covering an area of 21,000 sq km (8,000 sq miles). As well as the 'big five', the animals include cheetahs, giraffes, zebras, crocodiles, hippos, porcupines and mongooses. Tsavo East is a popular safari destination while at Tsavo West the excellent facilities include underwater hides for hippo watching.

Ngorongoro Crater, Tanzania
Protected within a circle of thickly-forested crater walls, Ngorongoro Crater is an expanse of grassland and forest measuring 14 km (9 miles) across and teeming with wildlife. Elephants, leopards, hyenas, bushbucks, buffalo, wildebeest, elands, warthogs, gazelles and ostriches live alongside the rare black rhinoceros and the handsome black-maned lion, while Lake Makat is home to flocks of flamingos and other water birds.

Jozani Reserve, Zanzibar, Tanzania
The largest remaining area of indigenous forest on Zanzibar, Jozani Reserve is home to a variety of birds and butterflies, as well as a number of rare mammals, including the red colobus monkey, which can only be found here.

Bwindi National Park, Uganda
Half of all the world's endangered mountain gorillas live in Bwindi National Park, an area of hilly rainforest. The park supports a rich variety of animal life including chimpanzees, golden cats, civets, leopards, bushpigs and giant forest hogs. Small groups of visitors who have booked several months in advance can go on guided gorilla-tracking expeditions.

Chobe National Park, Botswana
Encompassing habitats that range from marshland to forest, Chobe is home to a great variety of wildlife, including the rare puku and red lechwe antelope. Other inhabitants include lions, cheetahs, buffalo, giraffes, elephants, zebras, jackals, warthogs, hippos, crocodiles, hyenas, antelopes and wildebeest, as well as an abundance of birdlife. The animals can be viewed from boats on the Chobe River.

Kruger National Park, South Africa
A vast game reserve covering almost 20,000 sq km (7,400 sq miles), Kruger Park is home to around 137 mammal species, including lions, elephants, rhinoceros, leopards, buffalo, zebras, giraffes, impalas, wildebeest, hippos and crocodiles, as well as the rare roan and sable antelopes and oribi. The northern part is especially noted for its birdlife, including the highest density of birds of prey anywhere in the world.

Bird Island, Seychelles
Huge colonies of seabirds nest on the tiny, coral Bird Island. The sooty tern, fairy tern and common noddy are everywhere, while passing migrants add to the interest for birdwatchers. The island is also home to large numbers of giant turtles.

▼ **Serengeti National Park, Tanzania**
Covering 14,763 sq km (5,700 sq miles) and including woodland and mountains, as well as huge tracts of open grassland, the Serengeti is home to the 'big five' plus cheetahs, hyenas, zebras, giraffes, gazelles and many others. It also has around 500 bird species. It is most famous for the spectacular summer migration of gazelles, wildebeest and zebras, when around 2 million animals set off on a 800 km (500-mile) trek to fresh feeding grounds.

▲ **Etosha National Park, Namibia**
One of the most important wildlife reserves in Africa, Etosha covers a vast 20,000 sq km (7,720 sq miles) of woodland and grassland surrounding the Etosha Pan – an immense saline desert. Animals living here include springboks, impalas, kudu, wildebeest, hartebeest, roan antelopes, elands, zebras, elephants and the rare white rhinoceros, as well as predators such as lions, leopards, cheetahs, caracals, jackals and hyenas. There are around 340 bird species, including eagles, ostriches and secretary birds. Accommodation to suit all budgets is available.

ASIA

Kaziranga National Park, Assam, India

Famous as the home of the rare one-horned Great Indian Rhinoceros – most of the surviving 1,500 are here – Kaziranga (east of Guwahati) also has tigers, bears, elephants, bison and many bird species. A good way to travel around the tall-grass and swampy terrain is on an elephant. The park is only open from November to April.

Keoladeo Ghana National Park, Rajasthan, India

Formerly known as the Bharatpur Bird Sanctuary, Keoladeo is famous for its breeding populations of native water birds as well as its thousands of migrating birds which arrive every year from China and Siberia, including herons, storks, snake birds and the rare Siberian crane. The best time to visit is from October to February, when the migratory birds are in residence.

Sundarbans Wildlife Sanctuary, India/Bangladesh

Home to one of the largest remaining tiger populations in India, the Sundarbans Wildlife Sanctuary covers 6,695 sq km (2,585 sq miles) of mangrove swamp in the vast Ganges delta. Tigers are not often spotted by visitors, but a boat excursion through the peaceful mangroves will reveal many other animals – monkeys, wild pigs, spotted deer, crocodiles and fishing cats, as well as a profusion of birdlife.

Kanha National Park, Madhya Pradesh, India

Kipling set his *Jungle Book* in this beautiful landscape of forests, rivers and grasslands (near Mandla). Kanha is the only home of the barasingha (swamp deer) and it also plays an important role in the preservation of the tiger, leopard, chital, sambar and gaur (Indian bison). The park is open November–May, with sightings increasing from March onwards as the hot weather brings out the animals in search of water. Excursions are available.

Khao Yai National Park, Thailand

Encompassing a variety of habitats, from mountains clad in evergreen forest to lowland scrub and grassland, Khao Yai (north-east of Bangkok) has an abundance of wildlife, including elephants, gibbons, porcupines, tigers, leopards, Indian munjaks, Malaysian sun bears and several species of deer and monkey. There are over 250 bird species here, too, including the great hornbill and many colourful parrots and parakeets. Visitors can venture deep into the forest on several excellent trails, some of which require guides.

Taman Negara, Malaysia

Covering 4,340 sq km (1,676 sq miles) of ancient tropical rainforest, Taman Negara is a haven for hundreds of species of birds and animals, while its vegetation includes some of the world's rarest orchids. Inhabitants include tapirs, bears, elephants and gibbons. The park, which is the most visited in Pahang, has an elevated canopy walkway, and jungle hides in the trees, where visitors can spend the night.

Komodo National Park, Indonesia

The world's largest lizard, the astonishing 3 m (10 ft) long Komodo dragon, is found only on Komodo and a few neighbouring small islands. Guided treks usually include visits to dragon feeding places, and allow visitors to see some of the other wildlife of the park, such as wild pigs, deer, monkeys, water buffalo and eagles.

Ujung Kulon National Park, Indonesia

The last remaining low-relief forest on Java, in the far west, Ujung Kulon National Park is the only home of the one-horned Javan rhinoceros. Other inhabitants include the Javan gibbon, Javan tiger, muntjac (barking deer), chevrotain (mouse deer), green sea turtle and crocodile.

AUSTRALASIA

Eungella National Park, Queensland, Australia

With its tall, ancient rainforest trees, rocky creeks and spectacular waterfalls, Eungella is an extraordinarily beautiful place to watch wildlife. Among its inhabitants are kangaroos, possums, feathertail gliders, pythons and the native Eungella honey-eater, but the star attraction is the shy duck-billed platypus, which can be seen around the riverbanks at dawn and dusk.

Otago Peninsula, New Zealand

A remarkable variety of wildlife is concentrated on the Otago Peninsula. Seals and other marine life can be seen along the rocky coastline, while the inlets and beaches shelter numerous waders and waterfowl. A protected albatross nesting-site at Taiaroa Head is open to the public once the eggs are laid, and yellow-eyed penguins can be seen at close quarters from an excellent conservation reserve.

Catlins Forest Park, New Zealand

Ancient rainforest runs down to the rocky inlets and estuaries of the coast, offering a variety of habitats for some of New Zealand's rarest plants and animals. There are colonies of Hooker's sea lion and yellow-eyed penguin, and much birdlife. Two- and four-day ecotours are available.

◄ **Royal Chitwan National Park, Nepal**
With its lush sub-tropical jungle and floodplain swamp, Chitwan National Park is a natural habitat for animals such as the tiger, Indian rhinoceros and leopard. Tours on foot, by jeep or on the back of an elephant are best undertaken between October and March.

▼ **Kakadu National Park, Northern Territory, Australia**
Australia's largest national park, Kakadu encompasses a spectacular collection of rainforest, ravines and wetlands along the South Alligator River. These varied habitats shelter a vast array of wildlife, including 1,500 species of butterflies and moths, 75 reptile species, including crocodiles, 25 species of frog and one third of all Australia's bird species. Mammals include kangaroos, wallabies, walleroos, dingoes and many species of bat.

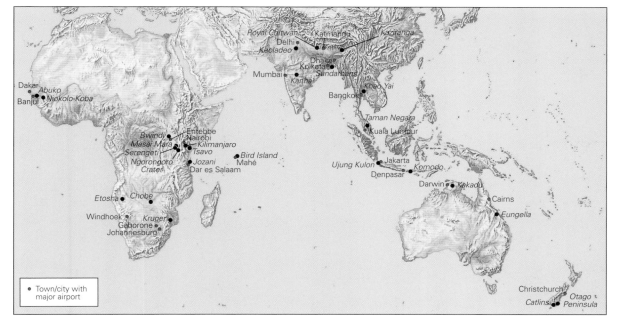

- Town/city with major airport

Marine wildlife

With whale numbers recovering strongly following the world ban on hunting, many seaports in North America, South Africa and Australasia offer boat trips to watch whales and other large fish and mammals. In the warm waters of the tropics, coral reefs teeming with vividly coloured sealife can be explored by scuba divers and snorkellers or viewed from the comfort of a glass-bottomed boat.

◀ **Florida Keys, USA**
Among many places in the Caribbean that serve as a base for viewing or swimming with dolphins is Florida Keys. Consisting of 45 islands surrounded by spectacular corals, Florida Keys also provides a perfect environment for scuba diving.

THE AMERICAS

Johnstone Strait, Canada
The sea between Vancouver Island and the mainland is one of the best places in the world to see orcas (killer whales), the largest and most powerful predators on earth, and minke whales.

Hudson Bay, Canada
Beluga whales can be seen in June, July and August in the bay's Arctic waters. Particularly large numbers spend these months in the Churchill River estuary, an area famous for its polar bears.

Cape Breton and Grand Manan Islands, Canada
Whale-watching boat trips take place around both islands. Off Grand Manan, in the Bay of Fundy, up to 20 whale species, including the rare northern right whale and the finback, can be seen.

Massachusetts Bay, USA
Stellwagen Bank in Massachusetts Bay is a feeding ground for humpback, finback and minke whales from April to October. It is a world-renowned whale-watching area, attracting around 1.5 million whale watchers a year. The coastal towns of New England offer a range of boat trips.

Caribbean Sea, Cayman Islands
The islands are famous among scuba divers for their exceptionally clear waters and deep diving with spectacular sponge colonies and a wide range of reef fish. Those interested in larger species can see dolphins, barracudas and sharks – including silky sharks – here.

Caribbean Sea, Belize
The barrier reef of Belize is the largest in the western hemisphere, and second only to Australia's in the world. Between the reef and the mainland lie more than 175 cays and atolls (coral islands and rings) offering some of the best diving opportunities in the world. The extraordinary Blue Hole at the centre of Lighthouse Reef is a circular shaft over 120 m (395 ft) deep which was once a cavern underneath the sea bed. Half Moon Caye offers one of Belize's most spectacular wall dives, with an almost sheer drop overhung with wonderful coral spurs, rich in marine life.

Caribbean Sea, Venezuela
There is good diving to be had around the offshore islands of Venezuela, especially in the archipelago of Los Roques with its white sand beaches and beautiful coral reefs. The Parque Nacional Morrocoy on the north-west coast of Venezuela is very popular for snorkelling.

Paracas National Park, Peru
A boat trip around the offshore islands within this national park provides an opportunity to see dolphins, seals and sea lions, as well as pelicans and the great Andean condors that inhabit the cliffs.

AFRICA AND THE INDIAN OCEAN

Canary Islands
The waters around the islands provide sheltered feeding grounds for pilot whales, not usually seen so close to shore, and there are many boat trips available from Tenerife. Unfortunately, whale watching is not properly regulated here and whales have been injured by the boats.

Red Sea, Egypt
Hurghada is a good base for snorkelling and diving around the coral reefs of the Red Sea. Jolanda Reef, at the tip of the Sinai Peninsula in the Ras Muhammad National Park, is a spectacular column of coral 800 m (2,625 ft) high. The park is best approached from the Sharm el Sheikh resort.

▲ **Point Reyes, California, USA**
Grey whales can be seen from Point Reyes, north of San Francisco, between October and January as they migrate down the coast of Canada and the USA to the Gulf of California. Between December and March they can be found at Guerrero Negro in Mexico, where they gather to calve.

Whale watching
Diving
Other

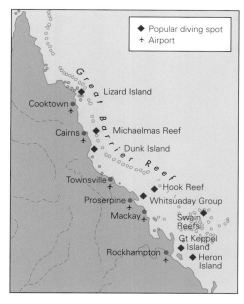

Pemba, Zanzibar and Mafia, Tanzania
The three main islands off the Tanzanian coast are surrounded by spectacular coral reefs which are home to a wide variety of marine species including bat fish, lion fish, turtles and rays. They offer some of the best diving opportunities in the world from August to December. Mafia Island is also a favourite breeding ground for giant turtles.

Cape of Good Hope, South Africa
In a country which has the strictest whale protection laws in the world, most whale watching takes place from the shore. The 'Whale Route' is a spectacularly scenic road along the coast from Cape Town, around the Cape of Good Hope, to the Indian Ocean, with many official whale-viewing sites. The town of Hermanus (the self-proclaimed 'whale capital' of South Africa) makes a good base. From June to October southern right whales, once hunted to near-extinction, can be seen swimming in these waters.

Seychelles
The outlying islands in particular offer world-class diving. The reef-ringed shores are a paradise for snorkellers, with over 150 species of tropical reef fish and 30 species of coral. Dophins, porpoises, sharks and barracudas can also be seen. There are four marine national parks and diving schools with good facilities.

Maldives
Without doubt the Maldives are the best place in the Indian Ocean for diving. There are hundreds of diving sites, with something for everyone from beginners to experts. The more adventurous can explore shipwrecks as well as spectacular caves and terraces of coral. There is also plenty of scope for snorkellers.

► **Tortuguero Park, Costa Rica**
In the company of a guide, limited numbers of visitors can watch green turtles at their largest nesting site in the western hemisphere. The turtles lay their eggs on the beach between July and October, the peak time being late August.

Australia's Great Barrier Reef
The Great Barrier Reef is the largest structure on earth made by living organisms. It is a chain of coral reefs 2,000 km (1,200 miles) long, encompassing more than 600 islands and cays. About 20 of these islands have resort facilities, with Heron Island and Lizard Island both especially popular with divers. There are around 2,000 species of fish living on the reef and the area is home to many marine mammals, including the rare dugong and several species of whale. The best time to visit the reef is between April and December. Cairns is the mainland base for most reef activities and offers all kinds of tours.

ASIA

Ang Thong National Marine Park, Thailand
Boat trips around 42 limestone islands, many eroded into fantastic shapes, provide opportunities for seeing a variety of wildlife – including dolphins, turtles and sea otters – and for snorkelling and diving.

Similan Islands, Thailand
The gently sloping coral reefs and deep gorges around the Similan Islands feature a huge variety of marine life, including turtles, manta rays and whale sharks.

Sipadan Island, Sabah, Malaysia
An amazing undersea 'wall', teeming with marine life that includes whale sharks, manta rays, turtles and tuna, makes Sipadan one of the world's great diving destinations. The island is the tip of an underwater mountain, making it possible to dive from the beach.

Bunaken Island, Sulawesi, Indonesia
Perhaps the most famous marine destination in Indonesia, Bunaken Island near Manado serves as the main base for exploring the stunning coral reefs known as the 'sea gardens of Sulawesi'.

AUSTRALASIA AND THE PACIFIC

Kaikoura, New Zealand
A world-famous whale-watching centre, Kaikoura caters for 30,000 whale watchers

a year. The deepwater canyons near the shore are home to sperm whales.

Hawaii, USA
The extraordinary song of the humpback whale can be heard in the waters around Hawaii from November to May, after which these rare animals return to their summer feeding grounds in the near-polar waters of the north Pacific. Whale watching is strictly regulated, but there are plenty of boat trips on offer. Hawaii also has coral reefs, though with fewer species than on other Indo-Pacific reefs. Diving is popular, with lessons being provided in the crater lake of the extinct Molokini volcano. Excursions in submarines down to a depth of 50 m (160 ft) offer superb views of the underwater world through portholes.

Rangiroa, Tuamotu Islands
Among many excellent diving sites in French Polynesia, this is possibly the best, with outstanding coral, sharks, dolphins, barracudas and rays.

Marquesas Islands
The oxygen-rich water around the islands, which is thick with plankton, supports a variety of marine creatures, including hammerhead and white-tipped sharks, leopard and manta rays, tuna and barracudas. There are around 20 dive sites, including some impressive caves.

▲ **Malindi and Wasini Island, Kenya**
One of a number of good diving and snorkelling spots in Kenya, Malindi also offers excursions in glass-bottomed boats to the nearby coral reef. The Kisite Marine National Park on Wasini Island, in the far south, provides spectacular diving safaris.

Great railway journeys

From the luxury of the Orient-Express to the spartan rigours of the Trans-Siberian Railway, the world's great train journeys exert an irresistible lure for many travellers, passing through spectacular landscapes. Journeys vary in length from a few hours to a fortnight, and the more sought-after trains must be booked well in advance.

NORTH AMERICA

Green Mountain Flyer, Vermont, USA
Distance: 21 km (13 miles)
A vintage train takes passengers through the beautiful Vermont countryside, running alongside the Connecticut River for part of the way. Largely a tourist service, the peak period is during October when the autumn colours are at their best.

Coast Starlight, USA
Distance: 2,235 km (1,389 miles)
A journey from Seattle to Los Angeles, through the magnificent landscapes of the west coast of the USA, includes amongst its highlights the mountains of the Oregon Cascades and the Californian Coast Range. South of Oakland the track runs along the edge of the Pacific Ocean, passing several of California's most popular beaches.

Los Mochis to Chihuahua, Mexico
Distance: 655 km (407 miles)
This 14-hour journey is one of contrasting landscapes, from the tropical Pacific coastlands to the high northern plateau by way of the magnificent Copper Canyon (Barranca del Cobre). Longer and deeper than Arizona's Grand Canyon, this is an area of steeply wooded gorges and spectacular mountain peaks.

SOUTH AMERICA

Guayaquil to Quito, Ecuador
Distance: 463 km (288 miles)
For those who relish danger as well as breathtaking scenery, this line – which has been called 'the world's greatest roller-

▶ **Palace on Wheels**
India's most luxurious train, originally hauled by the *Desert Queen*, takes passengers on a seven-day tour that begins and ends in Delhi. It includes Jaipur and the other major cities of Rajasthan, and Agra.

coaster' – is a must. It climbs high into the Andes, zigzagging perilously to an altitude of 3,609 m (11,840 ft) and passing directly under a waterfall. Trains are erratic and often break down.

Central Railway, Peru
Distance: 335 km (208 miles)
The highest railway in the world, this takes passengers on an eight- to nine-hour journey across the Andes, from Lima to Huancayo. Dizzy heights, sheer drops, zigzags, loops and tunnels abound.

EUROPE

Flåm Railway, Norway
Distance: 20 km (12 miles)
Dropping 865 m (2,838 ft) in just 20 km (12 miles), this is one of the steepest non-rack railways in the world. Beginning with a view over the Kjosfossen lake and waterfall, the train weaves its way from Myrdal towards Aurlands Fjord and Flåm through a series of tunnels, with spectacular views between tunnels and snow shelters.

◀ **Glacier Express, Switzerland**
Distance: 290 km (180 miles)
An exhilarating seven-and-a-half hour journey in the Swiss Alps, between the ski resorts of St Moritz and Zermatt, is provided by this train. Extraordinary feats of engineering are displayed as it weaves its way through the mountains, travelling through 91 tunnels, crossing 291 bridges and negotiating hairpin bends and steep ascents.

West Highland Line, Scotland
Distance: 264 km (164 miles)
Running between Glasgow and Mallaig, this line provides one of the most spectacular railway journeys in Britain. The route is particularly dramatic between Fort William and Mallaig, with a series of viaducts and tunnels through the mountains high above the Atlantic coast.

Venice Simplon-Orient-Express, Europe
Distance: 1,714 km (1,065 miles)
Passengers travel in style on a train that re-creates the romance of the golden age of rail as it crosses Europe from London to Venice, via Paris, Zürich, Innsbruck and Verona, in 32 hours. Orient-Express trains also run to Rome, and to Istanbul and Prague via a variety of routes that take in Budapest, Bucharest, Vienna, Kraków and Warsaw.

Andalusian Express, Spain
Distance: 740 km (460 miles)
The luxurious *Al Andalus* follows a circular route from Seville through the beautiful Andalusian countryside, with its citrus and olive groves, vineyards and hilltop villages. There are opportunities to stop off and see the sites at Jerez de la Frontera, Málaga, Granada and Córdoba.

▲ **Canadian, Canada**
Distance: 2,776 miles (4,4467 km)
On a 69-hour journey that begins in Toronto, this train passes through some of the most beautiful scenery on earth. The prairie lands of Manitoba and Saskatchewan give way to the cattle ranches of Alberta, from where the train climbs into the Rockies. Here it passes lakes, glaciers and the dramatic Fraser Canyon before reaching Vancouver.

Useful web addresses
all preceded by www.

Canadian trains:
viarail.ca

US trains:
amtrak.com

European trains:
raileurope.com

Orient-Express:
orient-expresstrains.com

Pride of Africa:
rovos.co.za

Palace on Wheels:
palaceonwheels.net

Eastern and Oriental Express:
orient-express.com/web/eoe/eoe_a2a_home.jsp

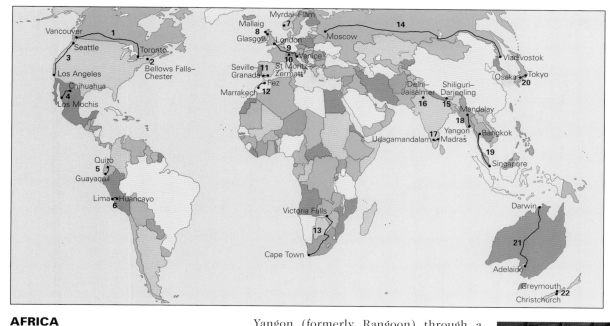

1 Canadian, Canada
2 Green Mountain Flyer, USA
3 Coast Starlight, USA
4 Los Mochis to Chihuahua, Mexico
5 Guayaquil to Quito, Ecuador
6 Central Railway, Peru
7 Flåm Railway, Norway
8 West Highland Line, Scotland
9 Venice Simplon-Orient-Express, Europe
10 Glacier Express, Switzerland
11 Andalusian Express, Spain
12 Marrakech Express, Morocco
13 Pride of Africa, Southern Africa
14 Trans-Siberian Railway, Russia
15 Darjeeling Himalayan Railway, India
16 Palace on Wheels, India
17 Madras to Udagamandalam, India
18 Mandalay Express, Burma (Myanmar)
19 Eastern and Oriental Express, Thailand and Malaysia
20 Tokyo to Osaka, Japan
21 The Ghan, Australia
22 TranzAlpine Express, New Zealand

AFRICA

Marrakech Express, Morocco
Distance: 583 km (362 miles)
Passing through Morocco's four imperial cities, this nine-hour journey begins in Marrakech, near the foot of the High Atlas Mountains, and travels north through the desert to Casablanca. From here the line follows the Atlantic coast to Rabat then gradually heads back inland through orchards and olive groves to Meknès and on to Fès.

Pride of Africa, Southern Africa
Distance: 3,2000 km (2,000 miles)
The journey from Cape Town in this luxurious train is full of romance and drama. In the early stages the train travels through a landscape of vineyards and farmland and across the Karoo Desert to Pretoria. Passengers can enjoy watching wildlife as the journey continues through the African bush across Botswana and Zimbabwe to the spectacular Victoria Falls on the Zambian border.

ASIA

Madras to Udagamandalam, India
Distance: 640 km (400 miles)
This 16-hour journey takes travellers from the plains of Madras through a colourful rural landscape and up into the beautiful Nilgiri hills to the famous hill station of Udagamandalam, formerly known as Ootacamund, or Ooty. The train passes through some of the most dramatic scenery India has to offer, climbing steeply on India's only rack railway to the gentler landscapes of the Deccan Plateau.

Darjeeling Himalayan Railway, India
Distance: 88 km (55 miles)
The tiny engine used on this railway, which is a UNESCO heritage site, takes passengers from Shiliguri on the hot Bengal plains to the mountain climate of Darjeeling in the Himalayas. The journey involves steep ascents and precipitous curves, climbing 2,164 m (7,100 ft). On the way the train passes through Ghoom, which is the second highest station in the world at 2,258 m (7,408 ft) above sea level.

Mandalay Express, Burma (Myanmar)
Distance: 616 km (385 miles)
By no means a tourist train, the Express offers the traveller a truly local experience as it makes its way slowly north from Yangon (formerly Rangoon) through a landscape of rice fields and golden-spired pagodas. The crowded train makes numerous – often unscheduled – stops along the way, making it an unpredictable and colourful journey. Best undertaken between November and February, the journey takes around 16 hours.

Eastern and Oriental Express, Thailand and Malaysia
Distance: 1,943 km (1,207 miles)
Starting in Bangkok, this train takes 52 hours to travel south through the terraced farmlands of Thailand and the rubber plantations and jungles of Malaysia to Singapore. It represents the height of luxury in train travel, while International Express trains that follow the same route provide a more down-to-earth experience.

AUSTRALASIA

The Ghan, Australia
Distance: 2,962 km (1,851 miles)
Named after the Afghan camel-drivers who once transported provisions along its route, the Ghan passenger train made its first journey from Adelaide to Darwin in February 2004. In 47 hours the train passes through vine-covered hills to the craggy mountains of the MacDonnell Ranges, the multi-coloured desert of central Australia and the woodland of the north, much to the delight of train enthusiasts who long campaigned for the line north of Alice Springs to be completed.

◄ **Tokyo to Osaka, Japan**
Distance: 518 km (322 miles)
The Nozomi Express – the fastest scheduled train service in the world – travels at speeds of up to 300 km/h (186 mph) along this line. Not quite as fast, the Hikari Express completes the journey in just over three hours. However, the scenery, which includes Mount Fuji, can best be appreciated from the slower 'bullet' trains.

TranzAlpine Express, New Zealand
Distance: 233 km (154 miles)
Travelling from Christchurch on the South Island's east coast to Greymouth on the west coast, the Express takes passengers on a four-and-a-half hour journey through a variety of landscapes. After crossing the farmlands of the Canterbury Plains it follows the Waimakariri River gorge into the mountainous Arthur's Pass National Park, where it enters the long Otira tunnel. From here the line descends through lush rainforest, passing lakes Poerua and Brunner, to Greymouth.

Trans-Siberian Railway, Russia
Distance: 9,297 km (5,776 miles)
The southern shore of Lake Baikal is on the route of the Trans-Siberian Railway, the world's longest, and possibly most famous, railway. The eight-day journey takes passengers from Moscow to Vladivostok via the Urals, the forested wilderness of Siberia, and the Transbaikalian Mountains.

In the early days of the railway, built between 1891 and 1916, a ferry was used in summer to carry the train across Lake Baikal, while in winter, when the lake froze, temporary rails were laid over the ice. The Siberian landscape is particularly beautiful in winter when it is covered with snow. In the spring there are carpets of wild flowers while in autumn there are the golden colours of the birch forests.

River and canal journeys

The world's great boat journeys give travellers a unique perspective on the countries through which they pass: rivers and canals were the highways of the past, and there are often opportunities to visit historic sites or natural habitats. Whether you are steaming down the Mississippi in a paddleboat, gliding through the French countryside past castles and vineyards or exploring the tributaries of the Amazon, the pace of the journey gives ample time to enjoy the beauty of the surroundings.

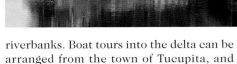

NORTH AMERICA

St Lawrence, Canada
From Kingston, where Lake Ontario flows into the majestic St Lawrence River, a six-night journey can be made on a replica steamboat to Montréal (see *World Cities*) and Québec (see *Historic sites in the Americas*). Just east of Kingston the river is dotted with literally a Thousand Islands, many of which have summer houses and opulent mansions set amid forests of yellow birch, silver maple and red and white trillium. In the spring the trillium trees are covered by white blossom.

Upper Mississippi, USA
In the summer months, seven-day cruises by paddleboat run between Minneapolis/St Paul and St Louis. There are also three-day cruises between St Louis and Memphis. The upper river, flowing through relatively flat countryside, is wide, slow moving and dotted with islands, but the stretch immediately below St Louis flows between rocky bluffs. Days spent cruising are alternated with sightseeing tours of such places as the boyhood home of Mark Twain, in Hannibal, Memphis, and a historic Native American site in Burlington, Iowa.

► St Petersburg to Moscow, Russia
This seven-day cruise passes through a network of rivers, lakes and canals in the richly wooded region of Southern Karelia, and down the upper reaches of the Volga River. Ports of call include the ancient town of Yaroslavl, the attractive Karelian capital of Petrozavodsk, and the Church of the Transfiguration on the island of Kizhi in Lake Onega, with its 22 wooden domes, constructed without a single nail.

CENTRAL AND SOUTH AMERICA

Amazon, Peru and Brazil
Cruises of between three and ten days along the Amazon River, starting from the remote but elegant Peruvian town of Iquitos, or from the brash and bustling Manaus in Brazil, are a relatively comfortable way to see the abundant wildlife of the rainforest. Many companies adopt an educational approach and include lectures on the local flora and fauna. Some include an opportunity to explore smaller tributaries by canoe. For the adventurous independent traveller who is prepared to rough it, a six-day journey by local riverboat from the Atlantic port of Belém to Manaus offers an unforgettable experience of local life and culture.

Orinoco Delta, Venezuela
The vast Orinoco Delta – a maze of channels running between countless forested islands – is one of Venezuela's wildest regions. The area is home to the indigenous Warao people, known for their skilled carving and basketwork, whose houses on stilts can be seen on the riverbanks. Boat tours into the delta can be arranged from the town of Tucupita, and usually last for between two and four days.

EUROPE

Shropshire Union Canal, UK
From Autherley, a 100 km (60-mile) journey can be taken on a slow-moving barge along the Shropshire Union Canal. Deep wooded cuttings, peaceful rural landscapes, medieval market towns and quiet villages are all passed at little more than walking pace. The ancient city of Chester, with its Roman ruins and medieval city walls, is a highlight of the journey. The canal ends at Ellesmere Port on the River Mersey, where there is an excellent boating museum.

Rhine, Switzerland, Germany and the Netherlands
A ten-day journey down the Rhine from Basel to Arnhem combines stunning scenery with a chance to visit the historic towns and cities along its banks. After flowing through the German Black Forest, the river passes romantic clifftop castles, sloping vineyards and picturesque villages on its way to the cities of the north: Bonn, Cologne and Düsseldorf. A detour up the River Neckar to the historic town of Heidelberg is often included.

◄ Lower Mississippi, USA
A seven-day cruise by paddleboat can be taken from Memphis to New Orleans. The Mississippi twists and turns on its way to the marshlands bordering the coast. There are opportunities to visit some of the historic sites of the Deep South, including the Civil War battlefields of Vicksburg, and the elegant mansion at Oak Alley Plantation, and to sample some of the local Creole and Cajun cuisine.

▲ The Burgundy Canal, France
Passing through a landscape of wooded valleys and sleepy villages, the six-day journey on a barge from Tonnere to Dijon along the Burgundy Canal provides an opportunity to see the beautiful 16th-century chateaux of Tanlay and Ancy le Franc and the 12th-century Cistercian Abbey of Fontenay. The region is famous for its *grand cru* vineyards and its robust cuisine, and there are plenty of opportunities to enjoy both along the way.

Douro, Portugal

Most cruises on the Douro are round trips of seven to nine days, beginning and ending in Porto. Once the boat leaves the coastal plain, it passes between spectacularly terraced vineyards, in an area unspoilt by major roads. Ports of call include the picturesque towns of Lamego and Vila Real. The region is the centre of Portugal's port wine production, and all cruises include a visit to a vineyard to sample the local produce.

Danube, Hungary, Slovak Republic, Austria and Germany

A Danube cruise of around eight days combines sightseeing tours of some of Central Europe's most historic towns and cities with an opportunity to relax on board, watching rich farmland and terraced slopes slip past. A cruise up-river from Budapest to Regensburg includes frequent stops, enabling passengers to explore Bratislava, Vienna, Linz and Passau, and to visit the sumptuous Baroque palace of Schönbrunn and the Benedictine Abbey in Melk. Since the boat berths overnight, passengers can also enjoy some nightlife ashore, and attend specially organized classical concerts.

AFRICA

River Gambia National Park, Gambia

A day trip on the river from Janjanbureh (Georgetown) or Kuntaur provides an opportunity to view crocodiles and hippos at close range. As the rice fields and coconut trees on the banks give way to dense forest, it may also be possible to glimpse monkeys, baboons and many species of birds.

Niger, Mali

A journey along the River Niger as it curves through the semi-desert of the Sahel is the classic way to see and experience the life of this area. Local passenger boats are scheduled to take seven days, but can take as long as 14 to travel between Gao and Koulikoro. The most popular section is the two days or so between Mopti and Korioumé, the stopping point for visits to the ancient desert city of Timbuktu. Also highly recommended is a detour up the River Bani to the beautiful old town of Djenné, where the mosque is a stunning example of construction using mud bricks and render.

ASIA AND AUSTRALASIA

Backwaters of Kerala, India

The eight-hour journey through the backwaters of Kerala, from Kollam (Quilon) to Alappuzha, is popular with tourists. Passengers are transported along a network of rivers, canals and lagoons, overhung with dense tropical foliage that every so often gives way to open paddy fields. Brightly coloured birds and ancient buildings can be glimpsed on the banks, and the Keralan people can be seen going about their daily lives.

Gorges of the Yangtze, China

Time is running out for those who want to experience the full splendour of a cruise along the Yangtze River as it passes between the rocky pinnacles of the Three Gorges. The controversial Three Gorges Dam project is due to be completed in 2009, and the flooding that will eventually create a 560 km (350-mile) long reservoir is well under way. The dam itself has become a tourist attraction. In the meantime, three- to four-day cruises from Chongqing to Wuhan, through the magnificent Qutang, Wuhang and Xiling gorges, continue to provide stunning views of a dramatic natural landscape. It is also possible to take a longer cruise from Shanghai to Chongqing.

Sepik, Papua New Guinea

The Sepik River twists and turns its way from the central mountains of Papua New Guinea through jungles, swamps and grasslands to the sea. Most cruises start from a remote inland location, to which passengers are transferred from Port Moresby by small plane. There is then a leisurely journey through the rainforest, with stops at riverside villages, some of which are on stilts. The people of the region are renowned for their woodcarving and traditional art, each village having its own distinctive style.

Murray, South Australia

A six-day cruise on a paddelboat, beginning and ending at Mannum, passes through colourful scenery, including verdant wetlands, brick-red plains, sandstone cliffs and deep blue lagoons. The cruise may also include a visit to the old river port of Morgan and an opportunity to hear about Aboriginal customs from elders at the Ngaut Ngaut Conservation Park.

◄ Nile, Egypt

A week-long cruise up the Nile from Luxor to Aswan and back combines visits to magnificent historic sites – such as the huge temple of Karnak and the tombs in the Valley of the Kings at Luxor – with periods of relaxation on board an air-conditioned riverboat. There are also opportunities to take camel rides into the desert that lies beyond the narrow fertile strip on either side of the river. From Aswan, where it is possible to sail on the river in a *felucca* (pictured here), a short flight takes passengers to the splendid temple of Abu Simbel, above the shores of Lake Nasser. Abu Simbel can also be reached by taking a luxury three-day cruise on the lake. Created by the building of the Aswan Dam, the lake itself is an impressive sight.

Useful web addresses
all preceded by www.
rivercruises.com
smallshipcruises.com
burgundy-canal.com
travelchinaguide.com/ cruise
majesticamericaline.com

▼ Li, China

The 80 km (50-mile) journey down the Li River from Guilin to the beautiful town of Yangshuo passes through a landscape of precipitous peaks, with names such as Paint Brush Hill and Five Tigers Catch a Goat Hill. Gliding past bamboo-lined riverbanks and picturesque villages, the trip and a bus-ride back to Guilin takes one day.

• Place of embarkation/ disembarkation

Sea and ocean cruises

Cruises attract all kinds of travellers and cater for an increasingly wide range of tastes. The steep-sided inlets of Alaska, Chile, Norway and New Zealand allow cruise liners to hug the coast, providing matchless views of these dramatic landscapes. Caribbean cruises allow almost daily shore visits, for shopping and exploring. Transatlantic cruises provide lavish on-board entertainment during the long sea passages. Cruise companies also vary in their appeal: some include lectures on the places they visit; others take a far less serious approach!

◀ The Caribbean
There are numerous variations on the Caribbean cruise, but virtually all have relatively short sea passages and a visit to a different island almost every day. There are organized trips to the rain-forests of Puerto Rico and sites of European colonial history. Some passengers, however, prefer to spend their time simply enjoying the islands' magnificent beaches.

NORTH AMERICA AND THE ATLANTIC

Alaska/British Columbia
The main attractions of a cruise in this area are the spectacular mountain scenery and the opportunity to see whales and seals, bears and birds of prey at close hand. Ships hug the coastline, entering steep-sided fjords and sailing close to the mouths of glaciers. Ports of call include Juneau, Alaska's capital, the 'gold rush' town of Skagway, and the Russian settlement of Sitka, with its onion domes.

Mexican Riviera
Mexico's west coast is becoming an increasingly popular area for relatively short cruises to catch the late-summer sunshine. For some tourists, the attractions are miles of unspoilt beaches fringed by jungle, such as those at Manzanillo and Zihuatanejo, and being able to go marlin fishing. For others they are the opportunities to experience Mexican culture and to visit the chic resort of Puerto Vallarta.

Atlantic Isles (Canaries, Madeira)
The Atlantic Isles are a popular cruise destination, particularly in winter and spring, when the lower mountain slopes are brilliant with flowers. Shore visits in Madeira usually include the novelty of a ride in a bullock cart or wicker sled on the mountain roads, while a trip to the summit of Tenerife's Mount Teide (3,718 m/12,000 ft) provides spectacular views of the surrounding islands.

Transatlantic cruises
Cruises link Europe with New York or Boston, with ports further south, such as Miami, and also with various Caribbean islands. The most direct, more northerly, route is for those wishing to enjoy the elaborate onboard entertainment, high standard of cuisine, and formal social life that are typical of the transatlantic liner. On ships plying more southerly waters, passengers can combine a luxury lifestyle with sunbathing, swimming and various other deck activities.

SOUTH AMERICA

Chilean fjords
Cruises along the most southern 1,000 km (625 miles) of Chile's coastline provide magnificent views of mountains and glaciers. The further south, the colder and less predictable the weather becomes, but for many the thrill of travelling the route of Darwin's *Beagle* and visiting Tierra del Fuego outweighs the risk of storms.

EUROPE

Norwegian fjords
Those cruising the fjords of Norway do so primarily to enjoy the majestic mountain scenery. Waterfalls, glaciers and wildlife can all be viewed from the comfort of the ship, while shore visits include a ride on a spectacular mountain railway from Flåm (see *Great railway journeys*). Some cruises extend as far as Europe's most northern point, where passengers can experience the midnight sun.

Western Mediterranean
One of the joys of a cruise in the Western Mediterranean is the opportunity to sample the local cuisine and wines. Most cruises include a day in the vibrant Spanish city of Barcelona. In Italy, there are brief organized trips to view the art treasures of Pisa and Florence, and the Roman remains of Pompeii (see *Historic sites in Europe*). There are also opportunities to enjoy the high-life in some of the fashionable resorts of the French Riviera, such as St Tropez, to visit the casinos of Monte Carlo, and to watch the Spanish flamenco dancers in Cartagena. Some cruises extend as far as the Adriatic, call in at the fortress town of Dubrovnik and include a day's sightseeing in Venice.

Eastern Mediterranean
A region rich in the remains of earlier civilizations, the Eastern Mediterranean provides much of historic interest, and many cruises have on-board experts to give background lectures. Some of the main sites visited include the Roman town of Ephesus in Turkey, the Ancient Greek ruins of Delos, the Crusader castle of Krak des Chevaliers in Syria, and the pyramids in Egypt (see *Historic sites in Africa*). Most cruises also include opportunities for swimming, snorkelling and sunbathing.

▲ North-east America
The north-eastern seaboard of America offers areas of great natural beauty such as Acadia National Park in Maine, whose fall colours are the focus of October cruises. There is also an opportunity to see the whales that frequent the waters of Stellwagen Bank off the coast of Massachusetts. Included in a wide variety of shore visits are the Canadian fishing town of Lunenburg, the popular US resort of Martha's Vineyard, and the cities of Boston and New York.

▼ Antarctica
Many of the 'expedition cruises' to the Antarctic use converted research ships or ice breakers, which offer less luxurious accommodation than other cruise ships. Passengers are taken ashore in small inflatable craft, and are thus able to get close to the teeming wildlife. There is always the chance of encountering whales in the surrounding seas, as well as sighting beautifully sculpted icebergs.

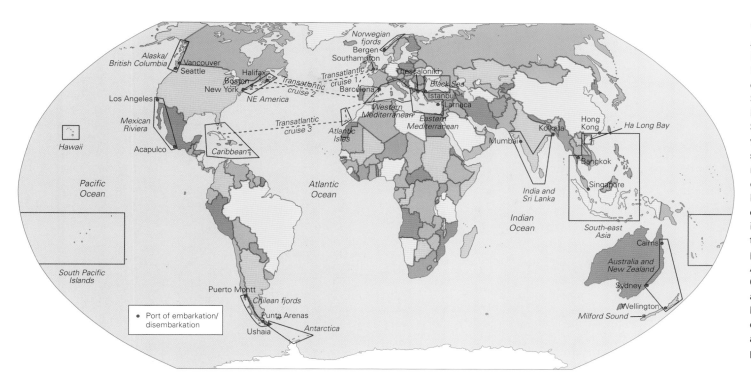

▼ **Black Sea**

A day in Istanbul (see *World Cities*) is included in most cruises of the Black Sea.
The countries bordering the Black Sea provide a rich variety of historic sites, from the medieval churches of Nesebúr in Bulgaria, to the 19th-century opera house in Ukrainian Odessa, the 18th-century palace of Tsar Alexander II on the Crimean peninsula, and the abandoned Byzantine monastery of Sumela, high above the Turkish port of Trabzon.

AFRICA, ASIA AND THE INDIAN OCEAN

India and Sri Lanka

Cruises around the Indian subcontinent provide an opportunity to visit a number of historic sites without the strain of overland travel. A day's sightseeing is followed by a day's relaxation in the relatively cool sea breezes. Many of the sites visited are from India's colonial past – the Dutch fort at Cochin, the former Portuguese colony of Goa, remnants of the British Raj in Madras – but there are also trips to some indigenous sites, such as the Hindu cave temples of Mumbai (Bombay).

South-east Asia

With such a wealth of possible sights and exciting ports of call, there are many varieties of the South-east Asian cruise, which is a popular option for the Christmas break. Most shore visits consist of whistle-stop tours of the port of call, but there are also more adventurous expeditions, such as a visit to an orang-utan sanctuary in Sarawak, or a trek to catch a glimpse of the famous 'Komodo dragon' (see *Wildlife in Asia*). Many of the cruises visit Bali, with its sandy beaches, terraced rice fields and ornate Hindu temples.

AUSTRALASIA AND THE PACIFIC

Australia and New Zealand

Most cruises of Australia's east coast provide more than one opportunity to stop on the 2,000 km (1,250-mile) long Great Barrier Reef (see *Marine wildlife*). By way of contrast, the natural wonders of New Zealand include the spouting geysers and boiling mud of Rotorua (see *Lakes and waterfalls*), and the dolphins, whales and penguins of the verdant Bay of Islands.

Milford Sound, New Zealand

Milford Sound is perfect for a cruise of just a few hours. It is possible to enjoy lunch while gazing out at towering granite peaks and glaciers, and, on the lower slopes, thick beech forests and waterfalls. There is always the chance of sighting the dolphins, seals, penguins and other sea birds that inhabit the sheltered inlet.

Hawaii, USA

The mountainous Hawaiian island chain was formed by a series of volcanoes, many of which are still active. Trips to Volcanoes National Park and the world's most active volcano usually include the memorable experience of getting as close as is safe to the actual lava flow. The lower slopes of the mountains are covered in rainforest, home to 20,000 species of orchid and echoing to the sound of waterfalls. Hawaii is a port of call for most Pacific cruises, but it is also possible to take a cruise exclusively of the islands, and so be able to enjoy some of the dramatic beaches and the local culture.

Where, when and for how long?		
	Main season	Duration of cruise (in days)
Alaska	May–Sept	7–14
NE America	Aug–Oct	7–14
Mexican Riviera	Sept–Oct	7–10
Atlantic Islands	Apr–Dec	9–14
Transatlantic	April and Sep–Nov	14
Caribbean	Oct–Dec	3–23
Chilean fjords	Oct–May	3–7
Antarctica	mid-Oct–early March	9–12
Norwegian fjords	May–July	7–14
Western Mediterranean	Apr–Nov	12–14
Eastern Mediterranean	Aug–Dec	10–14
Black Sea	Aug–Oct	14
India/Sri Lanka	Dec–Feb	14
South-east Asia	Dec–Feb	8–17
Ha Long, Vietnam	All year	1
Australia/New Zealand	Nov–Apr	14
Milford Sound	Nov–Apr	half day
Hawaii	Sept–Oct	7–14

Useful web addresses all preceded by www.

cruise.com

cruises.about.com

discover-cruises.co.uk

goway.com/cruises

cruiseweb.com

cruisein.co.uk

cruiseinformationservice. com

◀ **Ha Long Bay, Gulf of Tonkin, Vietnam**

'Ha Long' means 'where the dragon plunged into the sea', and the bay contains around 3,000 islands, famous for their sheer, limestone cliffs with honeycombs of caves. A day trip from Haiphong (by motorboat or slower junk) is included in the itineraries of long-distance cruises as well as being available to the independent traveller.

Winter sports

Mountain resorts all over the world are upgrading their facilities: constructing 'ski parks' for snowboarders, installing faster ski-lifts to cut queuing times, and using snow cannons to guarantee good conditions. Now that many of the top resorts can be reached by long-haul flights from either hemisphere, it is possible to enjoy 'winter sports' at any time of year.

◀ **Vail, Colorado, United States**
Vail has runs for all abilities and a special family skiing area. Snowboarders are provided with dedicated pistes, a half-pipe and two fun parks. Numerous winter sports are possible, including dog sledding and snowmobiling.

THE AMERICAS

Whistler, British Columbia, Canada
Considered one of the top ski resorts in the world, the resort provides access to two mountains with vertical drops of around 1,500 m (5,000 ft). As well as a wide variety of runs, Whistler's crowning glory is its five bowls, which provide plenty of scope for expert skiers and boarders, the latter being well catered for. The base village, which is pedestrian-only, has over 100 restaurants.

Banff, Alberta, Canada
The city of Banff is the gateway to three resorts that are linked by a shuttle bus and share a lift pass. **Lake Louise**, a particularly beautiful resort, is a good choice for families of mixed ability, with a beginners' run from the top of every chair lift. **Sunshine Village** includes 'Delirium Dive', one of the most challenging runs in North America. **Mt Norquay/Mystic Ridge** has a number of runs for the very best skiers and also offers night skiing.

Killington, Vermont, USA
The largest ski area in the eastern USA, Killington spreads over seven mountains. It caters for every level of skier, but is especially suitable for beginners, who have their own network of pistes, and for snowboarders who are provided with their own trail map. Snow cannons ensure good coverage throughout an extended season.

▼ **Jackson Hole, Wyoming, USA**
One of the most spectacular mountain resorts in the United States, Jackson Hole is most suited to the experienced skier or snowboarder. A 60-person cable car transports skiers from Teton Village to Mount Rendezvous, from where the skilled and intrepid can experience some of the most difficult piste skiing in the world. Other attractions include trips into Yellowstone Park, a swim at 2,460 m (8,000 ft) in the Granite Hot Springs, and sleigh rides to view a huge elk herd.

Lake Tahoe (Squaw Valley, Heavenly) California/Nevada, USA
Lake Tahoe is surrounded by ski resorts. **Squaw Valley** comprises six inter-linked mountain areas, some of which are still open in June. It has excellent facilities for children, including a family fun snow park. **Heavenly** has a spectacular setting, with something to suit skiers and snowboarders of all abilities. Snowboarders are further catered for by specially constructed mountainside features and by a dedicated fun park. A single ski pass is available for all resorts in the area.

Aspen, Colorado, USA
Long considered the smartest ski resort in the United States, Aspen provides an enormous range of facilities and entertainment, including opera. A linked ticket gives access to four mountains. Aspen Mountain and Aspen Highlands are most suitable for intermediates and experts, Buttermilk for beginners, and Snowmass for all levels. Snowboarding is allowed on all but Aspen Mountain.

Valle Nevado, Chile
A purpose-built resort in the Andes, at an altitude of 2,900 m (9,500 ft), Valle Nevado has wide, open pistes and spectacular views. It is also possible to heli-ski.

Gran Catedral (Bariloche), Argentina
Perched on Catedral Mountain, overlooking Lake Nahuel Huapi, Gran Catedral (formerly Bariloche) is Argentina's best-known and most extensive resort. Many visitors are attracted to the area in August for the National Snow Party.

EUROPE

Geilo, Norway
On the edge of the Hardanger plateau, Geilo provides uncomplicated downhill skiing as well as extensive cross-country trails. It is an excellent family resort, with ski schools giving tuition (in English) in snowboarding and cross-country skiing, as well as alpine skiing.

Soldeu/El Tarter, Andorra
For those on a budget, Andorra is a good option, and Soldeu/El Tarter the best of its resorts. Its reputable ski school and gentle slopes make it ideal for the beginner. A drag lift linking it with the neighbouring resorts of Pas de la Casa/Grau Roig has expanded the quality and quantity of runs available for the more experienced skier.

Three Valleys, France
The vast inter-linked ski area of the Three Valleys can be accessed from several resorts. **Courchevel** provides varied skiing, including wooded slopes, but intrepid skiers can also make their way across the whole Three Valleys system. **Méribel** is conveniently placed in the centre of the system. **Val Thorens**, which at 2,320 m (7,544 ft) is Europe's highest ski resort, has three lifts still open in summer.

Chamonix, France
Chamonix is an attractive town set in a steep-sided valley and dominated by Mont Blanc (see *Mountains and volcanoes*). There is extensive, varied skiing on both sides of the valley, linked by bus services. The most famous run, the Vallée Blanche, involves a cable-car ride up to the Aiguille du Midi, followed by a tough walk to the top of the glacier, and a 20 km (13-mile) run down to the valley. The Mont Blanc Ski Pass includes other resorts, giving access to 1,000 km (625 miles) of piste.

▲ **Val d'Isère/Tignes, France**
Snowboarders and off-piste skiiers are among those well catered for by the huge inter-linked system of L'Espace Killy. The system is served by a number of modern resorts. The largest is **Val d'Isère**, which is better suited to more advanced skiers than to beginners, since its easiest skiing is inconveniently located on the upper slopes. **Tignes**, a collection of villages clustered around a mountain lake, offers skiing for much of the year. The lift pass provides access to the whole Espace Killy, as well as a day's skiing at nearby Les Arcs or La Plagne.

Skiing and snowboarding resorts

Level: B = Beginner I = Intermediate A = Advanced Sb = Snowboarding

Resort	Main season	Skiable area or distance	Best-suited level(s)
THE AMERICAS			
Whistler	Nov–Apr	2,863 ha (7,071 acres)	I/A/Sb
Banff	Dec–Apr	3,059 ha (7,558 acres)	I
Killington	Oct–Apr	489 ha (1,209 acres)	B/Sb
Squaw Valley	Nov–May	1,600 ha (4,000 acres)	I/A/Sb
Heavenly	Nov–May	1,942 ha (4,800 acres)	I/A
Jackson Hole	Dec–Apr	1,011 ha (2,500 acres)	A
Aspen	late Nov–Apr	1,936 ha (4,785 acres)	all
Vail	early Nov–late May	2,140 ha (5,289 acres)	all
Valle Nevado	mid-June–mid-Oct	64 km (40 miles)	I/A
Gran Catedral	mid-June–end Sept	640 ha (1,600 acres)	I
EUROPE			
Geilo	Nov–May	25 km (16 miles) / 250 km (156 miles) cross-country	B/I
Soldeu/El Tarter	Dec–Mar	74 km (46 miles)	B/I
Three Valleys	Dec–Apr	600 km (374 miles)	all/Sb
Val d'Isère/Tignes	Dec–Apr	300 km (187 miles)	I/A/Sb
Chamonix	Dec–Apr	140 km (87 miles)	A/Sb
Zermatt	Dec–Apr	150 km (93 miles)	I/A
Cervinia	Dec–Mar	80 km (50 miles)	B/I
Wengen/Grindelwald	Dec–Mar	195 km (121 miles)	B/I
St Moritz	Dec–Mar	80 km (50 miles)	I
St Anton	Dec–Apr	170 km (106 miles)	I/A
Söll, Ski-Welt	Dec–Mar	250 km (156 miles)	B/I
Cortina	Dec–Mar	140 km (87 miles)	all
ASIA AND AUSTRALASIA			
Hakuba	Dec–Apr	c. 500 ha (1,250 acres)	all
Perisher Blue	June–Oct	1,250 ha (3,100 acres)	I
The Remarkables	June–Oct	220 ha (550 acres)	I
Coronet Peak	June–Oct	280 ha (700 acres)	I

◄ **Matterhorn (Zermatt, Cervinia), Switzerland/Italy**
The visitor to the Matterhorn area has the choice of staying in the expensive, car-free, Swiss resort of **Zermatt**, or the cheaper, more lively, Italian resort of **Cervinia**. The lift systems of the two resorts are linked. Zermatt provides a huge variety of skiing, from the wooded slopes immediately above the town to the steep runs below the Kleine Matterhorn. The sunny, south-facing slopes of Cervinia provide plenty of runs of intermediate standard. Summer skiing is possible on the highest slopes.

Jungfrau (Wengen, Grindelwald), Switzerland

The slopes of this famous mountain are served by two of Switzerland's best-known resorts. **Wengen**, which considers itself the 'birthplace of Alpine skiing', is an attractive town whose charm is enhanced by a lack of cars (a mountain railway providing the only access). **Grindelwald** is a larger, livelier town. The two are linked by a lift system that provides access to wonderfully varied skiing.

St Moritz, Switzerland

Famous in particular for its glamorous nightlife, St Moritz serves as a gateway to two major lift systems. Corvatsch/Furtshellas provides an opportunity for glacier skiing in both winter and summer. Corviglia provides varied skiing, interspersed by numerous restaurants in spectacular locations.

St Anton, Austria

St Anton attracts skiers from all over the world to its challenging ski runs, with cannon ensuring a good snow coverage. Dramatic off-piste skiing adds to its attraction for the experienced skier and boarder, but there is little for the beginner.

Söll, Ski-Welt, Austria

Söll provides good family skiing. It is ideal for the beginner and intermediate skier, but is not for the adventurous. Its low altitude results in a short season, although snow cannons have been installed.

Cortina, Italy

Surrounded by the distinctive rocky outcrops of the Dolomites, Cortina provides skiing in five main areas. There are runs for a range of skills, including a difficult descent from the Tofana bowl, and the gentle runs of the Socrepes–Pocol area. Cortina is the smartest of the Italian resorts, with a lively nightlife. Activities off the slopes include ice-skating.

ASIA AND AUSTRALASIA

Hakuba, Japan

The village of Hakuba (near Nagano) is the gateway to seven ski areas, providing runs for different standards of skiers, with beginners and intermediates best served by **Hakuba Goryu-Toomi**, and more advanced skiers by Happo'one (where night skiing is possible) and **Hakuba 47**.

Perisher Blue, Australia

This winter sports area comprises four resorts, spread over seven mountain peaks, accessed by an underground alpine railway and covered by one ski pass. There is a Nordic Ski Centre at Guthega, and 90 km (55 miles) of cross-country skiing. The main resort town is Jindabyne.

Queenstown (Coronet Peak, The Remarkables), New Zealand

Queenstown provides a residential base for two winter sports areas, The Remarkables and Coronet Peak, with shuttles operating between them. As well as good skiing, both areas offer facilities for snowboarders, including pipes and a terrain park. Families are well catered for, with good ski schools. Heli-skiing is also available.

● Town/city with major airport

Great beaches

▶ Negril, Jamaica

Negril beach is 11 km (7 miles) long and fringed by trees that hide low-rise hotels and restaurants. While definitely a tourist resort, it still retains a laid-back Jamaican character. Growing environmentalism has led to planning restrictions and active preservation of the surrounding area, including the creation of the Negril Marine Park. This encompasses the Great Morass swamp behind the beach, and the coral reef, cliffs and grottoes that make Negril so popular with scuba divers and snorkellers.

From California to the Caribbean to Australia, the lure of the beach still has a part in most holiday plans. The range is endless – chic and cosmopolitan in the Mediterranean, wild and rugged along the Atlantic shores or palm-fringed coral in the South Pacific. This small selection highlights some of the great beaches that can be linked into a round-the-world trip – whether for the exhilaration of surfing or sailing, or just to do absolutely nothing.

NORTH AMERICA

Venice Beach, Los Angeles, USA

Venice Beach is famous not so much for its wide stretch of sand as for its curving 'boardwalk'. Here, some of LA's more flamboyant citizens display themselves – on foot, skateboard, rollerblade and cycle. The area was originally developed to imitate its European namesake and, although there is no comparison, it is pleasant to stroll along its canals.

Assateague Island, Maryland/Virginia, USA

Assateague Island National Seashore on the Atlantic coast of the Chesapeake Peninsula consists of 60 km (37 miles) of pristine sandy beach, fringed by pine forest and salt marsh. Only a small area of it is accessible by car and the rest of the beach is deserted, except for the more intrepid campers, many of whom come for the fishing and birdwatching. Herds of wild ponies roam the island.

Sanibel Island, Florida, USA

Sanibel's 19 km (12 miles) of beaches are famous for their seashells. Visitors can be seen scouring the seashore or taking boat trips to more remote locations to find the best shells. Around 40% of the island, which can be toured on rented bicycles, is a wildlife preserve and it is also within striking distance of the Florida Everglades (see *Wildlife in the Americas*).

Puerto Escondido, Mexico

The resort of Puerto Escondido has a beach to suit every taste. 'Playa Zicatela' is considered one of the best surfing beaches in North America, but is suitable only for the strongest swimmers. 'Playa Principal' is a more urban beach, with pleasure craft and waterfront restaurants, while the small coves just out of town provide perfect swimming conditions.

THE CARIBBEAN AND SOUTH AMERICA

Magens Bay, St Thomas, US Virgin Islands

The heart-shaped Magens Bay contains a gently sloping sandy beach, surrounded by overhanging trees that provide welcome shade. Protected from the winds and currents, the bay is safe for bathing. Although nude bathing is not allowed on the main beach, it is permitted on the nearby Little Magens Beach. Interesting rock formations on the fringes of the bay are good for snorkelling. The beach is well served by restaurants and bars, carefully hidden among the trees.

Copacabana Beach, Rio de Janeiro, Brazil

Copacabana's 4 km (2.5 miles) of sand is fringed by a wavy black and white mosaic walkway. The beach is provided with modern amenities, such as public showers, kiosks and restaurants, and the shopping centre is only a short walk away. As well as attracting tourists, the beach is a meeting place for the citizens of Rio, and is the focus of the New Year celebrations. It is framed on one side by a huge granite headland and on the other by an imposing World War I fort, below which is an area from which local fishermen still operate.

Viña del Mar, Chile

Known as 'the Garden City' because of the luscious, tropical foliage that lines its boulevards, Viña del Mar also has a beautiful beach. Visitors who tire of the soft white sand and rolling surf can enjoy a tour of the town by horse-drawn carriage, visit the art museum and the extensive botanical gardens. Evening entertainment comes in the form of gourmet restaurants, casinos, discos and concerts.

▲ Oahu, Hawaiian Islands, USA

Most visitors to the island of Oahu flock to the string of connected beaches in the resort of Waikiki, just to the east of Honolulu, where the curving sand, studded with palm trees, is backed by a towering wall of high-rise hotels. Those looking for a more peaceful holiday, however, head further around the coast and seek out Waimanalo Beach (above), with its gently shelving, near-white sand and mountain backdrop. On the north coast the calm waters of Waimea Bay in summer also provide excellent swimming, but in winter months it is the centre of the surfing scene, as 10 m (30 ft) waves roll in across the Pacific.

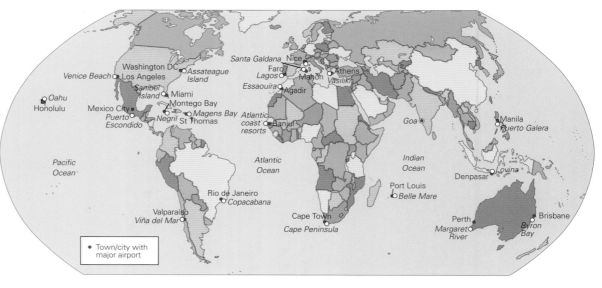

• Town/city with major airport

Lagos, Portugal

EUROPE

Nice, France
Nice is the largest town on the Côte d'Azur, renowned for the clarity of its light and the colour of its sea. Many famous artists have been inspired by the region, and some are represented in the town's art gallery. The long curved beach is rather pebbly, but its surroundings are attractive, with a wide esplanade on which 'to see and be seen'.

Santa Galdana, Menorca
The Balearic Island least affected by tourism, Menorca is famous for its beaches. The main beach at Santa Galdana can be very crowded in summer, but it is still possible to find relatively unspoilt coves nearby. Just a 1 km (0.5-mile) walk east is the wood-lined sandy beach of Cala Mirjana, where the favourite sport is to jump from rocks into crystal-clear water.

Vasiliki, Levkás, Greece
The small resort of Vasiliki is one of the foremost windsurfing and dinghy sailing centres in the eastern Mediterranean. Set in a bay that provides some shelter for the beginner, it is blessed with reliable winds. The lighter breezes of the morning are followed, after a brief lunchtime lull, by winds strong enough to delight the expert.

AFRICA AND THE INDIAN OCEAN

Essaouira, Morocco
The ancient town of Essaouira provides a fascinating backdrop to 3 km (2 miles) of

◀ **Lagos, Portugal**
Lagos is a busy fishing port and one of the Algarve's oldest settlements, with a long maritime tradition. To the east lie miles of sand dunes and the gently sloping Meia beach. West of the town, the dramatically eroded sandstone cliffs typical of the region form numerous small coves, some of which are only accessible from the sea. Lagos is an excellent base for surfers, who can travel the short distance to Portugal's west-facing beaches if local surf fails. The town provides plenty of interest, from seafood restaurants and bars to the curiosities of the local museum.

sandy shoreline. The commercial life of the town tends to spill over on to the beach, with fishermen offering to cook their catch and camel drivers selling rides, although it is possible to find more secluded areas. The town is the centre of the craft of wood inlay, the local Thuya trees providing the raw material.

Atlantic coast resorts, Gambia
The resorts of Kololi, Kotu, Fajara and Bakau, strung out along a 10 km (6-mile) coastal strip, provide a full range of amenities, including golf courses, equipment for water sports, and swimming pools. Although the sea is relatively safe, there are times when the conditions are unsuitable for all but the strongest swimmer. For those seeking a more authentic African experience, the market town of Serekunda is nearby.

Belle Mare, Mauritius
The coral reef that surrounds much of the island of Mauritius provides a natural breakwater, ensuring calm inshore waters. The beaches are all beautiful, although some have been over-developed or have areas cordoned off by hotels. However, Belle Mare, on the less-developed east coast, still has plenty of public areas. There are also the attractions of a mixed French, Indian and Chinese culture, evident in the island's architecture and cuisine.

ASIA

Goa, India
The dozens of beaches on Goa's 100 km (62-mile) coastline provide plenty of choice. Calangute and Colva, to which young people flocked in the 1970s, are now tourist resorts. However, at both the northern and southern ends of the Goan coast are many relatively unspoilt beaches, including Arambol and Palolem, where beach huts and tree houses provide the main accommodation. At Palolem visitors can take dolphin-watching boat trips.

Puerto Galera, Mindoro, Philippines
A resort area comprising 12 separate coastal districts, Puerto Galera is renowned for its pristine sandy coves, sheltered by a rugged, jungle-covered coastline. Accommodation ranges from

bamboo beach huts to air-conditioned bungalows and family-run hotels. The rich marine life of the area attracts scuba-divers, and equipment for underwater and other marine activities is available for hire.

Lovina, Bali
Although second in size only to Kuta, famous for its surf, Lovina manages to retain the relaxed atmosphere its larger rival has long since lost. Situated on Bali's rugged northern coast, the resort comprises six villages, dotted along 8 km (5 miles) of black-sand beach. Those who enjoy some lively nightlife make for the village of Kalibukbuk. Beach-centred activities include snorkelling and dolphin watching. Excursions can be made inland to nearby hot springs and a Buddhist temple, or further afield to the volcanic regions of Bedugul and Batur.

AUSTRALASIA

Byron Bay, New South Wales, Australia
Byron Bay offers a wide range of beaches. Main Beach is ideal for families, with a life-guard patrol and play equipment shaded by trees, while those wishing for more seclusion head for the smaller coves out on Cape Byron. The area also provides some good surfing and the opportunity to watch passing whales and dolphins. The town itself is less commercial, and better suited to those seeking an alternative lifestyle, than the popular resort of Gold Coast, 50 km (30 miles) to the north.

▼ **Margaret River, Western Australia**
Margaret River is among the best surfing areas in Australia, providing conditions to suit both beginners and experts. It also has much for the non-surfer to enjoy, including swimming beaches, river canoeing trips, and visits to local vineyards to taste some of Australia's best wines.

▲ **Cape Peninsula, South Africa**
Among the many beaches on the narrow peninsula south of Cape Town is Boulders Beach, so named because of the huge rocks that provide shelter from the wind. Here, visitors share the sands with a colony of jack-ass penguins. Other resorts on the peninsula, where the ocean water to the west is considerably colder than that of False Bay to the east, include some, such as Fish Hoek, which cater specifically for families, and some, such as the fashionable Clifton area, which attract the young and wealthy. Surfers head for the remote Long Beach at Kommetjie.

Festivals

Whether sacred or profane, festivals throughout the world bring thousands of participants and spectators out on to the streets with grand processions often featuring magnificent costumes and dazzling displays of music and dance, drama and sporting prowess.

THE AMERICAS

▼ Chinese New Year, San Francisco, California, USA

For Chinese communities everywhere, the New Year is a week-long festival. Many celebrations are family-based, but they lead up to a very public grand finale. Chinatown in San Francisco is taken over by the Golden Dragon Parade when hundreds of people, including drummers and other musicians, accompany a 23 m (75 ft) dragon through the streets. The Chinese follow a lunar calendar, which means that their New Year occurs in late January or early February.

Corn Dance Festival, Santa Domingo, New Mexico, USA

At Santa Domingo (near Albuquerque) the Pueblo people honour the harvest goddess, Iyatiko, in the Corn Dance Festival. Celebrants, known as the *koshare*, dress in cornhusks and animal skins to enact the history of their people on a day that is filled with drumming, dancing and feasting. The festival which, unlike many Pueblo ceremonies, is a public event, is always held on 4 August.

Heritage and Jazz Festival, New Orleans, Louisiana, USA

Jazz evolved in New Orleans during the late 19th and early 20th centuries, but the first jazz festival was not until 1968. A major event in the musical calendar and organized by the Heritage and Jazz Festival, it runs over two weekends in April or May. The devastating effects of Hurricane Katrina in 2005 have not stopped the festival being staged, and it continues to feature big-name musicians from all over the world.

Fisherman's Festival, Jamaica

29 June is Saint Peter's day. He is the patron saint of fishermen, and in the fishing ports of Jamaica boats are drawn up to the beach where the owners decorate them with shells and flowers. Long processions follow priests to the edge of the sea where they bless the boats, and the beaches become crowded with steel bands, dancers and family picnics.

Urkupina, Calvario Hill, Bolivia

Early in the 20th century a girl tending her sheep on Calvario Hill had a vision of the Virgin Mary. Now, on 15 August, thousands of pilgrims carrying candles and flowers, and accompanied by musicians, performers and vendors, climb the hill to pay homage to the Virgin. The festivities that follow last for three days.

National Rodeo Festival, Rancagua, Chile

Rodeos take place all over the country and, in late March, the best competitors go to the National Rodeo in Rancagua. This event celebrates the Chilean *huaso* or cowboy. Thousands come to watch as huasos, wearing traditional costume and the heavy spurs unique to Chile, provide exhibitions of horsemanship. The town is given over to feasts of cowboy food and *la cueca*, the erotic folk dance of Chile.

◄ Palio, Siena, Italy

Celebrated every year on 2 July and 16 August, the Palio is a bare-back horserace that dates from the 16th century. Ten horses, each representing one of Siena's *contrade*, or districts, race three times around the crowded central piazza, sometimes barging into each other and unseating their riders. Before the race there is a procession in which men dressed in medieval clothes whirl and twist the *palio*, or flag, of their *contrada*, to the accompaniment of drummers.

EUROPE

Puck Fair, Killorglin, Ireland

A billygoat, King Puck – adorned with ribbons and a crown – opens the three-day Puck Fair every year on 2 August. Musicians from all over Europe perform, and Romanies are among those who entertain the crowds with Irish jigs and stories. The billy is honoured because in the 17th century a herd of goats warned the village of an impending English attack.

Oktober Bierfest, Munich, Germany

The Oktober Bierfest has been an annual event since 1835. It is an important festival for most young visitors to the city and is a huge celebration in honour of beer. It runs for 16–18 days in September–October, and vast beer tents that each house 5,000 drinkers are erected. Food stalls and funfairs add to the festive atmosphere.

Lajkonic, Kraków, Poland

Every year, usually in June, a man dressed as a Tartar rides a mock horse through the streets, accompanied by trumpeters and citizens dressed in medieval costume. He does so in memory of Lajkonic, who in the 13th century killed a Tartar and put on the dead man's clothing before riding into the city to warn that the Tartars were about to attack. The resulting defeat of the Tartars is now celebrated with much pageantry.

San Fermin, Pamplona, Spain

Starting on 6 July and running for eight days, the festival is held in honour of Fermin, patron saint of bullfighters. Each day starts with the playing of drums and pipes, and an effigy of the saint is followed by a procession of matadors and horses, dressed and decorated for the occasion. A rocket signals the release of the bulls from their pen to race through the streets to the bullring. Men run and leap ahead of them, a practice that more than once has resulted in someone being killed. Bull fights and parties fill the evenings.

Mardi Gras Carnaval, Rio de Janeiro, Brazil

All over the Catholic Christian world, there are festivals at Mardi Gras, the last day before the 40 days of Lenten fasting. The Mardi Gras Carnaval in Rio de Janeiro is the most famous. Over the course of two nights the city's 14 main samba schools compete with each other by dancing and parading down the 1 km (0.5-mile) long Sambadrome, watched by thousands of spectators. Each school's parade consists of around 4,000 people in lavish, often extravagant, costumes, accompanied by enormous and elaborate floats, and a band of over 500 drummers. The judging takes place a few days later. Broadcast live on television, it is followed by great celebrations.

Aksu Black Sea Festival, Turkey

The origins of this July festival are very old, dating back to pre-Christian fertility rites. Cybele, the fertility goddess, wore a pebble in her crown and women still throw pebbles into the Black Sea in the hope that this will help them conceive. The highlight of the festival is a performance by male dancers dressed in black and silver, and other artists – musicians, potters, painters and weavers – flock to the site where they perform or sell their work.

AFRICA

Odwira, Ghana

The Asante calendar is filled with religious days and ceremonies, of which the Odwira, usually in August or September, is one of the most important. The high chiefs and priests are involved for some days in secret and sacred rituals, and then the roll of drums announces the start of feasting. It all ends with a grand procession, in which the chiefs are carried in splendid palanquins.

Abu El-Haggag, Luxor, Egypt

Among the ancient ruins of Luxor is a small mosque dedicated to a 12th-century Muslim saint, El-Haggag. Each year, in October or November, thousands of people crowd into Luxor for the saint's *mulid*, or festival, during which Sufis and floats parade the streets. Three model boats are carried about by groups of men, though whether this is in memory of the Ancient Egyptian journey into the Underworld, or of the time when the pilgrimage to Mecca involved a sea crossing, is uncertain.

Timket, Ethiopia

Ethiopian Christians celebrate the baptism of Christ for three days starting on 19 January. The priests, after all-night prayers, emerge from churches carrying holy tabots – caskets holding sacred texts – followed by singing children. Multi-coloured umbrellas, signifying high office and authority, are held above the priests. After this religious ceremony, a party mood takes over and there are huge communal meals, music, and excited horse races which sometimes lurch into the spectators.

▶ Ganesh Festival, Mumbai, India

Chowpatty Beach is crowded for ten days in August through to September. Families exchange gifts and women decorate shrines to Shiva, mother of the Hindu elephant-headed god Ganesh. On the tenth day a huge effigy of Ganesh is carried through the streets to be cast into the sea. Drummers and pipers announce its passage, which is followed by a large procession of people dancing and singing.

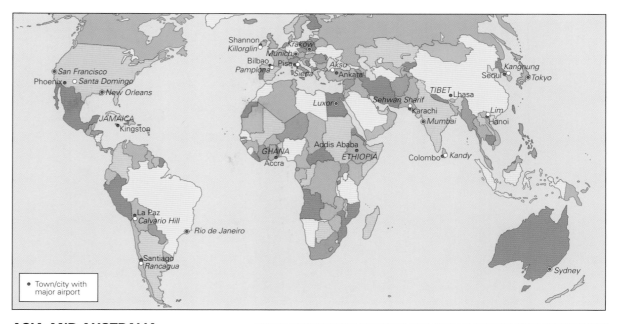

ASIA AND AUSTRALIA

Urs to Lal Shahbaz Qalandar, Sehwan Sharif, Pakistan

All over Pakistan, Muslims celebrate holy men with *urs*, or saints' days. One of the most popular, attracting many thousands of pilgrims, is held in Sehwan Sharif, around the tomb of the 12th-century Iranian scholar-poet Lal Shahbaz Qalandar. For three days, in October or November, Sufis perform their holy, trance-like dances, while drums and gongs beat hour after hour. The entire crowd dances and chants, and many offer votive offerings to the tomb.

Festival of the Tooth, Kandy, Sri Lanka

In the Esala Perhera temple in Kandy is the Tooth Relic of the Buddha. Usually in July, but occasionally in August, there is a spectacular festival in which there are festive meals and dances to celebrate the relic and Buddha. At the festival's climax a great procession of dancers, drummers, temple chieftains, and over 50 elephants in ceremonial attire, goes to the temple, followed by huge crowds of pilgrims.

Ho Lim, Lim, Vietnam

Singers from all over Vietnam pour into the village of Lim (near Bac Ninh) seven days after Tet, the Chinese New Year, in January or February. They participate in a folk-singing contest, and competition is fierce. The crowds who come to listen are also entertained by a circus, street performers, wrestling competitions, and chess games in which people play the parts of the pieces.

Losar, Tibet

The calendar in Tibet follows the lunar cycle. There are two 'New Year' days, but the significant one is Gyalpo Losar, the King's New Year, which is usually in April. People wear new, decorative clothing; the priests fill the temples with chanting, the beating of gongs and the ringing of bells, and new prayer flags are lifted above the temple roofs. Throughout the city, street theatres and musicians perform while people party and play dice in the parks.

Tano, Kangnung, South Korea

This spring festival, usually in April or May, traditionally involved displays of the Korean form of wrestling, *ssirum*, even in the most remote villages. Now, many Koreans spend the holiday watching *ssirum* on television, except in the village of Kangnung. Here they celebrate for five days, not only with wrestling matches but also with performances of the traditional dance called *nong-ak*. The huge crowds also enjoy a spring drink, *chehotang*.

Gay and Lesbian Mardi Gras, Sydney, Australia

Participants pride themselves on outrageous displays and flamboyant costumes during the annual Mardi Gras parade. The street procession comes at the end of a three- to four-week cultural festival in February–March, and ends in a huge party which is restricted to ticket holders. However, revellers throughout the city regard this as an opportunity to party until dawn and beyond.

▲ Sanja Matsuri, Tokyo, Japan

Matsuri – festivals where shrines, or *mikoshi*, believed to contain a god-spirit, are carried through towns and villages – take place all over Japan. However, the biggest event is in Tokyo in April or May. Here the *mikoshi* weigh about 1 tonne each, and 50 men are needed to hoist one through the streets to the Asakusa Temple. Groups of costumed figures, and musicians playing flutes and beating drums, accompany the *mikoshi* on its journey.

Historic sites in the Americas

Amid the rocky canyons of New Mexico, Arizona and Colorado, the dense jungle of Central America and the towering peaks of the Andes lie the spectacular ruins of civilizations that flourished long before 1500 and the arrival of the Europeans. Scattered throughout the continent are the mansions, churches, cathedrals and forts built by European settlers and their descendants since the 16th century.

Mesa Verde and the Anasazi

Mesa Verde National Park in Colorado, USA, contains the ruins of spectacular Anasazi complexes of multi-storey apartments constructed on natural or artificial platforms on the face of canyon cliffs. They are among the remains of hundreds of villages that were built by the Anasazi from the 8th century onwards in south-western USA. Called pueblos by the Spanish, they took various forms. In Chaco Canyon, for example, elaborate complexes of adjoining rooms surrounded circular subterranean ceremonial structures known as *kivas*. The Anasazi began to abandon their pueblos in the 15th century, eventually settling along the Rio Grande. There are many impressive sites worth visiting, but they are usually in remote locations.
Peak season: May–October
Nearest airports: Albuquerque, Santa Fe

▲ **Savannah, Georgia, USA**
The Cotton Exchange is just one of over 1,000 splendid 18th- and 19th-century buildings that have been restored in the historic downtown district of Savannah. Others include the US Customs House and the gold-domed City Hall. Near the city are the Civil War forts of Old Fort Jackson and Fort Pulaski.

NORTH AMERICA

Québec, Canada
Founded by the French in 1608 and now the only walled city in the Americas north of Mexico, Québec has several 17th- and 18th-century buildings. The area by the St Lawrence River has the general appearance of 1759, when the city was captured by the British. On the cliff-top above is the citadel of Cap Diamant, dating from 1820.

Plymouth Plantation, Massachusetts, USA
Costumed actors re-create the life and times of the first permanent colony and a Native American encampment in New England at Plymouth Plantation, a historical theme park. Visitors can go aboard the *Mayflower II*, a reconstruction of the ship that brought the original settlers from England in 1620.

Historic Triangle, Virginia, USA
The colonial towns of Williamsburg, Jamestown and Yorktown comprise the Historic Triangle. **Williamsburg**, Virginia's capital 1699–1780, has a large restored historic district of 17th- and 18th-century buildings with tours led by costumed guides. **Jamestown**, founded in 1607, has some 17th-century ruins, a reconstruction of the 1607 James Fort and full-scale replicas of 17th-century ships. **Yorktown**, the site of the last major battle (1781) in the American Revolution, and besieged during the Civil War, contains fortifications dating from both wars. Other historic sites in Virginia include Thomas Jefferson's house, **Monticello**, George Washington's house, **Mount Vernon**, the plantation house, **Shirley Plantation**, built in the 1660s, and Civil War sites in **Richmond**.

Pueblo de Taos, New Mexico, USA
The largest, multi-storied, adobe (sun-dried brick) structure in the USA, Pueblo de Taos dates from around 1450 and is still inhabited by 1,500 Native Americans. In the town of Taos is the home of Kit Carson, the famous 19th-century mountain man.

Chaco Culture National Historic Park, New Mexico, USA
Impressive Anasazi ruins are to be found in this remote park. Among them is the site of Pueblo Bonito, with remains of a massive plaza surrounded by a semi-circular, five-storey tiered complex of some 200 rooms which once housed up to 1,200 people.

Charleston, South Carolina, USA
A historic centre of Southern culture, Charleston has many colonial buildings. The military relics of the Battery overlook the harbour, while 5 km (3 miles) away is Fort Sumter where the first shot of the Civil War was fired.

San Miguel de Allende, Mexico
An almost totally colonial town, San Miguel de Allende has many attractive houses and churches dating from the 18th century. It is also an important artistic centre, where painting, pottery, sculpture, drama, music and literature all flourish.

Guanajuato, Mexico
A former silver-mining town, founded in the 16th century, Guanajuato has colonial buildings dating from the 17th and 18th centuries among its narrow streets with houses painted in bright colours.

Teotíhuacán, Mexico
Impressive ruins are all that remain of a city which in AD 500 was the sixth largest in the world, with a population of around

Chichén-Itzá and the Maya

Chichén-Itzá in Mexico is a particularly impressive Mayan site that is unique because it displays many features of the Toltecs who occupied the city in the 10th century. Among them is the reclining sculpture of the Toltec rain god. The magnificent remains of the literate Mayan civilization are scattered throughout southern Mexico, Guatemala, Belize and Honduras. Mayan cities expanded rapidly in the 7th and 8th centuries but were then abandoned between the 9th and 13th centuries. Their ruins often include stone-built pyramids crowned by temples and palaces, and courts used in a ritual ball game that involved the sacrifice of the losing team.

There are numerous Mayan sites worth visiting, and it is possible to spend two to three weeks following a route that links the most important in Mexico, Guatemala and Belize.
Peak season: November–April
Nearest airports: See map of 'Mayan Route'

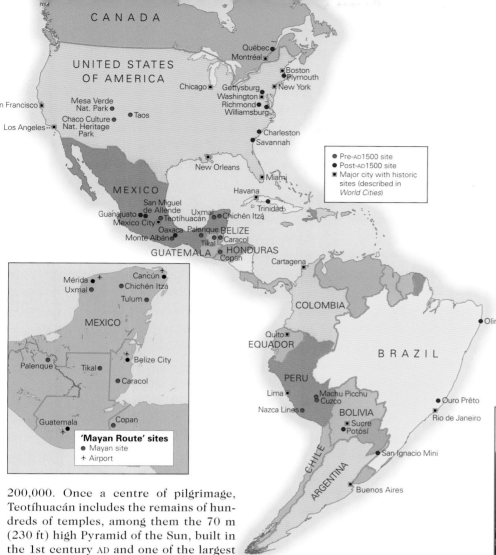

● Pre-AD1500 site
● Post-AD1500 site
■ Major city with historic sites (described in *World Cities*)

'Mayan Route' sites
● Mayan site
✈ Airport

▲ Gettysburg National Cemetery, Pennsylvania, USA
The burial place of 979 Union soldiers killed in the Civil War battle of 1863 is also the site of President Lincoln's famous Gettysburg Address. Tours include the 91 m (300 ft) National Tower and the Cyclorama Centre, where a film about the battle is shown.

Machu Picchu and the Incas
Machu Picchu in Peru is the most spectacular of many Inca sites in the Andes. Tier upon tier of houses, palaces, temples and defensive walls rise up the side of a high mountain ridge overlooked by the granite pinnacle of Huayana Picchu. The Spaniards failed to find the site in the 16th century, and it was mysteriously abandoned and forgotten until the early 20th century. The Incas developed an enormous empire between the 14th and 15th centuries that extended from modern Ecuador, through Peru to southern Chile. It was conquered by the Spaniards in the 1530s.
Peak season: April–October
Nearest airport: Lima

200,000. Once a centre of pilgrimage, Teotíhuacán includes the remains of hundreds of temples, among them the 70 m (230 ft) high Pyramid of the Sun, built in the 1st century AD and one of the largest buildings in the New World before 1500.

Oaxaca and Monte Albán, Mexico
Oaxaca is a well-preserved colonial town with a cathedral and many other buildings dating from the 16th century onwards. Just 10 km (6 miles) away are the impressive ruins of Monte Albán, which from the 7th century BC served as a centre of worship for many different peoples, including the Maya. Surrounding a huge man-made plateau are the remains of pyramids, a ball court, burial chambers with beautiful murals, and carvings of dancers.

Palenque, Mexico
A Mayan site in a clearing in the jungle, Palenque has numerous buildings with particularly beautiful decoration. They include the Temple of Inscriptions, a stepped pyramid with a 25 m (80 ft) tunnel that leads to a crypt containing the sarcophagus of a 7th-century Mayan king.

Uxmal, Mexico
One of the most beautiful pre-1500 sites in Mexico, Uxmal has Classical Maya architecture. The chief building is the smooth-sided El Adivino, or Pyramid of the Soothsayer, up which there is an almost vertical climb to the 35 m (115 ft) high summit that is crowned by a temple. Nearby is the Governor's Palace, which features a frieze with 103 masks.

CENTRAL AMERICA AND THE CARIBBEAN

Caracol, Belize
An amazing Mayan site deep in the rainforest, Caracol is still being excavated. The ruins, whose full extent has only recently become apparent, include a pyramid 42 m (140 ft) high.

Tikal, Guatemala
Possibly the greatest Mayan site, Tikal is surrounded on all sides by jungle. The remains of 3,000 buildings can be seen, some with painted carvings. The pyramid-like Temple of the Great Jaguar, built in AD 700, is considered the world's best example of Mayan temple construction.

Trinidad, Cuba
Cuba's best-preserved colonial town, Trinidad has many buildings that reflect the town's prosperity as a centre of the sugar trade in the 18th and 19th centuries.

SOUTH AMERICA

Cuzco and the Urubumba Valley, Peru
Former capital of the Incas high in the Andes, Cuzco contains extensive Inca ruins mixed with colonial churches, palaces, houses and a 17th-century cathedral. An attractive and lively town, it is the main starting point for people visiting Machu Picchu (by train or a four-day trek) and other Inca ruins in the Urubumba Valley.

Nazca Lines, Peru
People of the Nazca culture (375 BC–AD 650) created gigantic lines by removing stones to expose the desert soil beneath. The lines, which depict geometrical shapes, birds – one with a wing-span of over 100 m (328 ft) – and animals, are best seen from the air, in a local plane.

Potosí, Bolivia
Founded in 1545 as a silver-mining town, Potosí was the largest city in the Americas in the early 17th century. Today it has over 2,000 colonial buildings, including several 18th-century Baroque churches.

Olinda, Brazil
One of the best-preserved colonial cities in Brazil, on a hill overlooking the Atlantic, Olinda has many 16th- to 18th-century buildings. It is a major cultural centre, with art galleries, music and festivals.

Ouro Prêto, Brazil
A beautiful colonial town founded in 1711, Ouro Prêto has cobblestone roads, statues, fountains, churches, a palace and a theatre. It also serves as a base for exploring other colonial towns in Minas Gerais province, such as Diamantina.

San Ignacio Mini, Argentina
The most impressive of the ruins of Jesuit mission villages in the Misiones region, San Ignacio Mini had 4,356 Guarani inhabitants before the Jesuits were expelled from Spanish territory in 1767. The ruins of only three other missions indicate their former splendour: Sao Miguel in Brazil, and Jesús and Trinidad in Paraguay.

Major cities with historic sites
(see *World Cities*)
• Boston
• Buenos Aires
• Cartagena
• Chicago
• Havana
• Lima
• Los Angeles
• Miami
• Mexico City
• Montréal
• New Orleans
• New York
• Quito
• Rio de Janeiro
• San Francisco
• Sucre
• Washington

Historic sites in Europe

There is a huge variety of historic sites in Europe, ranging from prehistoric monuments over 5,000 years old to 19th-century castles. Ruins of the architectural achievements of the Classical Greek and Roman civilizations contrast with what are often perfectly preserved cathedrals, churches, monasteries, castles, palaces and civic buildings dating from the 11th century onwards.

◀ **Neuschwanstein Castle, Germany**
The ultimate fairytale castle, Neuschwanstein (near Fussen) was built in 1869–86 and is the most famous of Ludwig II's castles inspired by Wagner's vision of medieval Germany. It has a wide range of architectural styles, and its tall white marble towers topped by cone-shaped pinnacles, which have been copied by Disneyworld, are instantly recognizable.

Rock of Cashel, Ireland
Poised dramatically above the town of Cashel in County Tipparary stands a limestone outcrop, 109 m (358 ft) high, known as the Rock of Cashel. It is topped by a group of medieval ecclesiastical ruins, which include a bishop's palace, the 13th-century St Patrick's Cathedral, and the adjoining 12th-century Romanesque St Cormac's chapel.

Caernarfon Castle, Wales
Considered to be the finest of the castles built by Edward I of England after his conquest of Wales in 1283, Caernarfon Castle is exceptionally well preserved. Constructed as a royal palace as well as a military stronghold, it dominates the surrounding walled town, which was also founded by Edward.

Stonehenge, England
The most famous prehistoric monument in Europe, Stonehenge is a circular arrangement of massive standing stones, surrounded by earthworks, whose function is a subject of controversy. Built in stages between c. 3100 BC and c. 1000 BC, it may have been an astronomical observatory, a temple or a secular ceremonial centre. Its distinctive stone trilithons – pairs of uprights topped with horizontal lintels – are an impressive landmark on the Salisbury Plain.

▼ **Meteora, Greece**
Perched on top of natural rock pinnacles which rise hundreds of metres from the flat plain of Thessaly, near Tríkkala, is a group of Greek orthodox monasteries, some of which are still inhabited today. The highest of these – at 533 m (1,749 ft) is Great Meteoron, which was built from 1356 with a domed church added in the 16th century.

Bruges, Belgium
Once one of Europe's greatest trading centres, Bruges is a well-preserved medieval city with narrow streets and canals spanned by picturesque bridges. Within its 13th-century walls are many historic buildings, including the magnificent Gothic Town Hall and the medieval Cloth Hall. The Groeninge Museum contains paintings by the 15th-century Flemish masters.

Mont-St-Michel, France
Rising dramatically out of the Bay of St-Michel is a steep, rocky island with a medieval abbey on its summit. Buildings and fortifications have been added since the 11th century, resulting in a mixture of styles and shapes which culminate in the 19th-century spire of the church.

Versailles, France
Built for Louis XIV, the 'Sun King', the vast Baroque palace of Versailles was the envy of all Europe in the 17th century. Today, visitors flock to see the Hall of Mirrors – where the Treaty of Versailles was signed at the end of World War I – and to wander between the elaborate fountains in the magnificent formal gardens.

Heidelberg, Germany
Majestically set on the banks of the River Neckar and dominated by the romantic ruins of the castle, Heidelberg is one of Germany's most beautiful and best preserved historic towns, with many fascinating buildings. Its 600-year-old university provides a youthful atmosphere on the streets, especially in the evenings.

Petrodvorets, Russia
An imperial palace in the Baroque style, Petrodvorets was built by Peter the Great after he had visited Versailles. It is set in beautiful parkland interwoven by a system of fountains, cascades and waterways connected to the sea.

- ● Pre-AD 500 site
- ● Post-AD 500 site
- ■ Major city with historic sites (described in *World Cities*)

Salzburg, Austria

Set in a magnificent subalpine landscape, Salzburg is a picturesque city with many fine Baroque churches and a grand Italianate cathedral, the first of its kind to be built north of the Alps. The simple apartment where Mozart was born is a place of pilgrimage for music lovers.

Český Krumlov, Czech Republic

One of Europe's most picturesque towns, Český Krumlov has hardly changed since the 18th century. Its beautiful medieval and Renaissance buildings are almost

▲ **Chartres Cathedral, France**
Built in the middle of the 13th century, and almost unaltered since, the great cathedral of Notre Dame at Chartres is an exceptionally fine example of high Gothic architecture, with its flying buttresses, vaulted ceilings, intricate stonework and beautifully detailed stained glass. A rare 13th-century labyrinth design on the floor, a Renaissance choir screen and the glowing stained glass of the rose window all add to the beauty and impact of the building.

encircled by the Vltava River and overlooked by a magnificent castle. Originally a Gothic fortress, Krumlov Castle was rebuilt in the 16th century as a fortified palace.

Évora, Portugal

An attractive city with a history dating back to Roman times, Évora has a walled medieval centre with a distinctly Moorish atmosphere, and many fine Renaissance buildings from its time as a royal residence. The church of São Francisco is a good example of the Portuguese Manueline style of architecture, combining Gothic and Moorish influences.

Toledo, Spain

An ancient city of steep, winding streets lined with elegant if sombre buildings, Toledo is a splendid monument to the many cultures that have flourished here in the past. Moorish, Jewish and Christian traditions are all represented, and parts of the city walls date from the 6th century, when the Visigoths made Toledo their capital. The cathedral is a particularly fine example of the Spanish Gothic.

Segovia, Spain

Set on a rock, Segovia is a delightful old town with a fairytale castle and a 1st-century Roman aqueduct. Other notable buildings include the palace of La Granja, the 16th-century Gothic cathedral and the 12-sided, 13th-century Templar church of Vera Cruz.

Pisa, Italy

The famous Leaning Tower of Pisa is just one of a quartet of ecclesiastical buildings which make up the beautiful Campo dei

Pompeii and the Romans

Pompeii is an exceptional historic site because, when the eruption of Vesuvius in AD 79 engulfed the city in volcanic debris, the life of the people, their homes and streets, public spaces and palaces were preserved as if frozen in time. Excavations have revealed a wealth of detailed information about the everyday life of citizens of the Roman Empire, including their public notices, graffiti, brothels, latrines, furnishings and food. At its greatest extent, in the 1st–4th centuries AD, the Roman Empire encircled the Mediterranean Sea, reaching north as far as Britain and south into Egypt. Remains of Roman theatres, temples, baths, arenas, villas and other buildings can be found at sites throughout Europe and north Africa.

Miracoli (Field of Miracles) in this medieval walled city. The black and white marble facades of the Duomo and Baptistery, decorated by a succession of distinguished sculptors, are perfect examples of the Pisan Romanesque style, while the cloistered cemetery of Camposanto contains 14th-century frescoes.

Siena, Italy

Surrounded by city walls, Siena's medieval centre, with its narrow, winding streets, fine buildings and palaces, is wonderfully preserved. It is dominated by the Piazza del Campo, a large, shell-shaped square where the spectacular horserace known as the Corsa del Palio is held (see *Festivals*).

Delphi, Greece

In a stunning location, at the foot of Mount Parnassós, lie the impressive ruins of a sanctuary dedicated to Apollo, whose oracle was the most important in Classical Greece. The ruins include the 4th-century BC Temple of Apollo, the Doric Treasury of Athens, a theatre restored by the Romans, and a well-preserved stadium where the Pythian games were held.

Knossós, Crete

The ruined palace of Knossós is one of the few remains of the Minoan civilization, which flourished c. 3000–1100 BC. The first palace at Knossós was built around 2000 BC, and was rebuilt after an earthquake in c. 1720 BC. Excavations have revealed workshops, storerooms, dwellings and ceremonial rooms, one of which contains a gypsum throne.

Dubrovnik, Croatia

The fortifications of the ancient port of Dubrovnik rise straight from the Adriatic, and the double line of city walls encompass two palaces, two monasteries and many churches and other historic buildings, mostly dating from the 15th and 16th centuries. The narrow, winding streets of the old city are free from motor vehicles.

Ephesus, Turkey

The extensive and well-preserved ruins of the ancient city of Ephesus are one of Turkey's most popular historic sites, containing buildings from ancient Greek, Roman and Byzantine times. Among those dating from the Roman period are several temples, a theatre, a library, terraced houses, public baths and latrines, as well as some fine mosaics and wall paintings.

▲ **The Alhambra, Granada, Spain**
The most splendid example of Moorish architecture in Spain is the hilltop Alhambra palace, which was built in the 13th–14th centuries. The unassuming fortress walls contain a richly decorated interior made up of many halls and courtyards, with fountains and pools throughout.

Major cities with historic sites
(see *World Cities*)
- Amsterdam
- Antwerp
- Athens
- Barcelona
- Berlin
- Brussels
- Budapest
- Copenhagen
- Dublin
- Edinburgh
- Florence
- Geneva
- Hamburg
- Helsinki
- Istanbul
- Kraków
- Lisbon
- London
- Luxembourg
- Madrid
- Milan
- Moscow
- Munich
- Oslo
- Paris
- Prague
- Reykjavik
- Riga
- Rome
- St Petersburg
- Stockholm
- Vienna
- Warsaw
- Venice

Historic sites in Africa, Asia and Australasia

Africa is the home of the imposing ruins of ancient Egypt – one of the world's first civilizations. With the Middle East, it also has historic sites that reflect the competing influences of Christianity and Islam. In Asia, vast temple complexes, often adorned with wonderful sculptures, are among the remains of great empires, while in Australia, Aboriginal rock paintings are evidence of a culture that flourished long before the Europeans arrived.

AFRICA AND THE MIDDLE EAST

Dogon cliffside villages, Mali
Built among the rocks at the foot of the Bandiagara escarpment are the picturesque traditional houses, temples, granaries and meeting places of the Dogon people, whose culture has survived since the 14th century. The area can be reached only on foot and conditions can be gruelling. The best time to visit is December, for the harvest celebrations.

Rock churches of Lalibela, Ethiopia
Carved out of the red volcanic rock of the central highlands are 11 extraordinary medieval churches containing rare and beautiful frescoes, elaborate carvings and bas-reliefs. A complex network of tunnels and passageways connects the churches, some of which are hidden in deep trenches while others have been cut into the cliff face. The best time to visit is the Ethiopian Christmas (7 January) and Easter.

Kilwa Kisiwani, Tanzania
Once an Islamic city-state, the island of Kilwa Kisiwani has extensive ruins, which include a 12th-century mosque, several palaces and grand houses, and a 15th-century Portuguese fort. The impressive 14th-century cliff-top palace of Husuni Kubwa has a 30 m (98 ft) high dome and over 100 rooms.

Zanzibar, Tanzania
The buildings of Zanzibar Town's 'old quarter', Stone Town, reflect its colourful history as an important trading centre, particularly in the 19th century. A maze of narrow streets contain a sultan's palace, an ochre-coloured Arab fort, and the home of the notorious slave trader Tippu Tip, as well as numerous bazaars.

Great Zimbabwe, Zimbabwe
The extensive ruins of a major medieval city dating from the 10th century onwards, Great Zimbabwe is made up of curved stone walls and enclosures which incorporate features of the landscape into their design. The Elliptical Building, with an unusual conical tower and a diameter of almost 100 m (328 ft), is the largest ancient structure in sub-Saharan Africa.

Akko, Israel
The ancient walled port of Akko contains many relics of its long and distinguished history, including the underground 12th-century Crusader vaults and halls, the Ottoman Turkish citadel, and the beautiful 18th-century El Jazzar mosque. A remarkable 18th-century Turkish bath-house has been sensitively restored.

Petra, Jordan
Carved out of red sandstone mountains, the majestic remains of the desert city of Petra include two theatres, the High Place of Sacrifice, a temple and many elaborate tombs. The majority date from the period c. 100 BC –AD 150, when Petra was at the height of its prosperity as an important centre of trade. It had strong links with the Greek Hellenistic world, which are reflected in the Classical facades of its tombs.

ASIA

Mohenjodaro, Pakistan
The excavated remains of a city, Mohenjodaro is the most impressive of all the sites relating to the civilization that flourished in the Indus Valley c. 2600–1800 BC. The site consists of a raised citadel, with public buildings that include an assembly hall and a Great Bath, and a lower town containing residential and industrial areas.

◄ **Angkor, Cambodia**
The magnificent ruins at Angkor, capital of the Khmer empire, merit more than one day of sight-seeing. The best-preserved of the buildings is the 12th-century sandstone temple of Angkor Wat, which symbolizes the Hindu universe. Surrounded by pools, it is lavishly decorated with statues and bas-reliefs that are the longest in the world. Around 1.5 km (1 mile) away is the temple complex of Angkor Thom, within which is the Buddhist temple of Bayon with reliefs depicting everyday life.

▼ **Ajanta and Ellora Caves, near Aurangabad, India**
Cut into a spectacular horseshoe-shaped cliff, the Buddhist temples and monasteries of Ajanta are decorated with wall-paintings which are among the greatest examples of early Indian art. The series of rock-cut temples at Ellora includes the 8th-century Hindu Kailasa temple which is renowned for its exceptional sculptures of gods and mythological figures.

The Pyramids and Ancient Egypt
Khafre's Sphinx, 73 m (240 ft) in length and carved from a limestone outcrop, stands near the three pyramids at Giza. The most famous of the Egyptian pyramids, they were built as spectacular royal tombs over 4,500 years ago, during the period of the Old Kingdom. The largest at Giza is nearly 150 m (500 ft) high. The last of the Old Kingdom dynasties collapsed c. 2180 BC, but central government was restored by the dynasties of the Middle Kingdom (c. 2055–1650 BC) and New Kingdom (c. 1550–1070 BC). In the era of the New Kingdom, vast temples and lavishly painted royal tombs were constructed, most notably those either side of the River Nile at Luxor and overlooking Lake Nasser at Abu Simbel (see *River and canal journeys*).

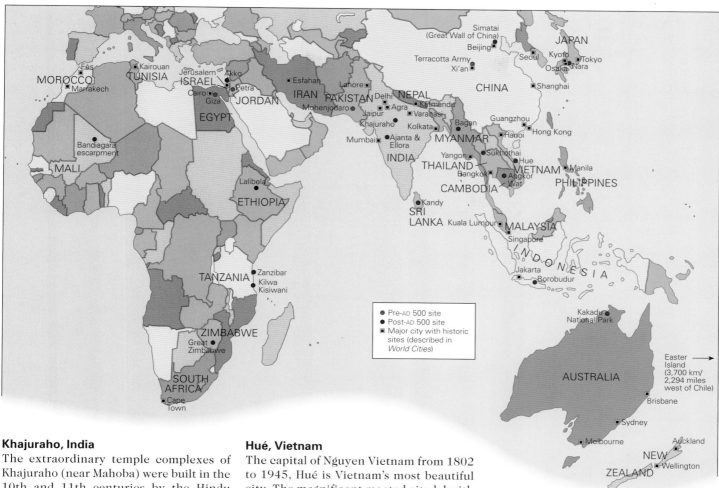

Major cities with historic sites
(see *World Cities*)

AFRICA
- Cairo
- Cape Town
- Fès
- Kairouan
- Marrakech

ASIA
- Agra
- Bangkok
- Beijing
- Delhi
- Esfahan
- Guangzhou (Canton)
- Hanoi
- Hong Kong
- Jaipur
- Jakarta
- Jerusalem
- Katmandu
- Kolkata (Calcutta)
- Kuala Lumpur
- Kyoto
- Lahore
- Manila
- Mumbai
- Osaka
- Seoul
- Singapore
- Tokyo
- Varanasi
- Xi'an
- Yangon

AUSTRALASIA
- Auckland
- Brisbane
- Melbourne
- Sydney
- Wellington

Khajuraho, India

The extraordinary temple complexes of Khajuraho (near Mahoba) were built in the 10th and 11th centuries by the Hindu Chandela dynasty, but were abandoned in the 14th century. Rediscovered in the jungle in 1838, they were carefully restored and are now famous for their sensual and erotic sculptures depicting human, divine, animal and mythological subjects.

Kandy and the Cultural Triangle, Sri Lanka

Famous for its temple and Festival of the Tooth (see *Festivals*), Kandy is one of three former Sinhalese capitals that together form a 'Cultural Triangle'. The other two are Anuradhapura, a huge site with the remains of palaces and temples dating back to the 3rd century BC, and the more compact and better-preserved Polonnaruwa, around 1,000 years old. Within the triangle is the 1st-century BC cave-temple of Dambulla, with 150 Buddha images, and the impressive 6th-century palace-fortress of Sigiriya. Built on top of 'Lion Rock', this is decorated with frescoes and includes a water garden.

Bagan, Burma (Myanmar)

Built between the 11th and the 13th centuries, Bagan (Pagan, near Pakkoku) became known as 'the city of 4 million pagodas', and was the capital of a vast realm. Today it is an important archeological site covering about 40 sq km (15 sq miles) with over 2,000 structures still standing. Among the most impressive are the Temple of Ananda and the Shwezigon Pagoda, with glazed plaques showing scenes from the life of Buddha.

Old Sukhothai, Thailand

The ruins of the 13th-century capital of the Sukhothai empire have been preserved as a 70 sq km (27 sq mile) historical park. They contain numerous temples set in a landscape of lakes, trees and lawns. The most impressive is Wat Mahathat, with fine stucco work and carved Buddhas.

Hué, Vietnam

The capital of Nguyen Vietnam from 1802 to 1945, Hué is Vietnam's most beautiful city. The magnificent moated citadel with its ten fortified gates contains a palace, a mandarin hall and a museum. In the hills to the south of the city there are seven elaborate royal tombs.

Borobudur, Java, Indonesia

Rising like a squat pyramid from the Kedu Plain, Borobudur (near Yogyakarta) is a colossal 9th-century Buddhist stupa (temple) built by the Sailendra dynasty. The largest monument in the southern hemisphere, it covers 200 sq m (2,153 sq ft) and includes over 500 shrines with seated Buddhas. The walls of the stupa, which has five square and four circular terraces, are decorated with bas-reliefs.

Great Wall of China, Simatai, China

Stretching from the Central Asian desert to the Yellow Sea, the Great Wall is over 2,240 km (1,400 miles) long, averages over 6 m (20 ft) in height, and has a central walkway nearly 4 m (13 ft) wide. Much of what exists today dates from the 14th–16th centuries. The Wall can be visited at Badaling, just 70 km (45 miles) from Beijing. However, a less crowded section is at Simatai, 110 km (68 miles) from Beijing, where there are wonderful views to the distant mountains.

Nara, Japan

The ancient city of Nara has many beautiful pagodas, shrines, gardens and temples, the most famous of which is the 8th-century Eastern Great Temple, the Tadai-Ji. Its Great Buddha Hall houses Japan's largest bronze statue of Buddha; the hall itself is the largest wooden building in the world.

AUSTRALASIA AND THE PACIFIC

Kakadu National Park, Australia

Thousands of Aboriginal rock paintings cover the walls of the caves and cliffs of the ancient Aboriginal lands in Kakadu National Park (see also *Wildlife in Australasia*). The paintings, some of which are estimated to be over 20,000 years old, provide a continuous link with the past for the several hundred Aboriginal people who still live there today.

Easter Island statues, Polynesia

The extraordinary stone statues of Easter Island are the legacy of a lost culture which flourished on the island between around AD 400 and 1600. More than 800 colossal stone heads were erected all around the island's coast. The volcanic crater from which the stone was quarried still contains hundreds of unfinished statues, including the 20 m (65 ft) high El Gigante.

◄ **Army of Terracotta Warriors, near Xi'an, China**
The massive underground mausoleum of China's first emperor, Shi Huang Di, who died in 210 BC, contains an army of around 7,500 life-size terracotta soldiers. Standing in military formation, they are a unique sight.

31

Theme parks

Inspired by the phenomenon of Disneyland Resort, Los Angeles, the top theme parks around the world are irresistible to children both young and old, as well as adults. The combination of charm and fantasy with white-knuckle rides and superb service guarantees a successful family visit, and since most are located near major cities it is easy to incorporate them into a longer itinerary.

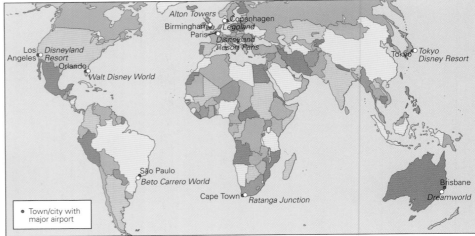

▲ Alton Towers, England

The combination of a ruined stately home, wooded parkland and over 100 rides means that Alton Towers (in Staffordshire) provides entertainment for all tastes. For younger visitors there are the attractions of Cariba Creek – a huge indoor lagoon – and rides such as Charlie and the Chocolate Factory and Squirrel Nutty. The more challenging rides have a much darker theme, with names such as Nemesis and Oblivion.

Useful web addresses
preceded by www.
themeparks.about.com
funguide.com/country
disney.co.uk

Disneyland Resort, Los Angeles, USA

Disneyland Resort, founded in 1955, is the original Disney theme park, and Mainstreet, Frontierland and Fantasyland – representations of American life and its dreams – have been duplicated in Disney theme parks around the world. Visitors are attracted not only by rides like the runaway train of Big Thunder Mountain, the parade of Disney characters and the famous nightly firework show, but also out of nostalgia and a desire to experience what is itself now a historic site.

Beto Carrero World, Santa Catarina, Brazil

The most extensive theme park in Brazil, Beto Carrero World (near Itajaí) combines thrilling rides, shows and a zoo. Its themed areas cover a range of cultures, including a German House complete with beer cellar, a Viking longboat and a Wild West area. Its shows are similarly wide-ranging and feature the legend of Excalibur. Its white-knuckle rides include the free-falling Tower of Terror, and Star World Mountain, with two 360-degree loops. The animal park includes African wildlife and a large collection of cobras.

Disneyland Resort Paris, France

Although based on the same formula as the Los Angeles theme park, the marketing for Disneyland Resort Paris emphasizes the educational element. There are 'Discovery rides', such as the 'Mississippi Steamboat' which provides information about life in frontier towns, while the Swiss Family Robinson tree-house demonstrates practical survival tips. Most visitors, however, go for the glamour of the shows and parades, and the thrill of the rides. These include being catapulted 'From the Earth to the Moon' on a Jules Verne style rocket.

Legoland, Billund, Denmark

Legoland, in which everything is built out of lego, is divided into themed areas, such as Pirateland and Castleland, where children recognize, and are able to interact with, their favourite lego characters. Although the park is aimed primarily at children, providing them with opportunities to play creatively, adults are also charmed by the intricate scale models of real, if somewhat idealized, scenes.

Ratanga Junction, Cape Town, South Africa

Africa's first theme park opened in the late 1990s. It takes as its theme the wildlife of Africa, with rides such as The Cobra, Monkey Falls, and Crocodile Gorge, in which visitors can experience white-water rafting in controlled conditions. A diamond mine is featured, with an underground runaway mine train providing the thrills. There are also less alarming rides for all the family, and 'interactive play areas' for young children.

Tokyo Disney Resort, Japan

With many of the same attractions as other Disney theme parks, Tokyo Disney Resort is unashamedly American in its culture. Rides range from the gentle Mark Twain Riverboat to the exciting Space Mountain. Around 200 Disney characters, from the earliest cartoons through to the present day, take part in the regular 'Disney's Dreams' parade.

Dreamworld, Queensland, Australia

Thrilling rides and shows are combined with a wildlife park and conservation zone in Dreamworld (near Gold Coast). The Tower of Terror roller coaster reaches speeds of 160 km (100 miles) per hour as it descends from a height of 115 m (375 ft). The Giant Drop uses the same structure to release passengers vertically so that they experience momentary weightlessness. In an 'interactive tiger exhibition' tigers swim with their trainers, while in the Koala Park visitors can handle koalas and watch other native Australian animals.

Walt Disney World, Orlando, Florida, USA

The massive Walt Disney World in Florida encompasses four separate theme parks. At Magic Kingdom there are rides graded for every taste, from those in Fantasyland aimed specifically at younger children, to the Space Mountain rocket trip, which is not for the faint-hearted. The Epcot Centre aims to re-create the atmosphere and architecture of different countries, including Norway, China and Italy. Visitors can eat food typical of the region, and enjoy themed rides, shows and videos. Disney MGM re-creates urban areas, such as New York Street and Hollywood Boulevard, and uses computer technology to enable visitors to come face to face with characters from recent films. The newest of the parks, Animal Kingdom, combines a safari park with typical Disney features, including thrilling rides, exhibitions and shows.

WORLD CITIES

CITY MAPS

Amsterdam	2	Copenhagen	8	Lagos	14	Mumbai	20	São Paulo	27
Athens	2	Chicago	9	Las Vegas	14	Munich	21	Seoul	27
Atlanta	3	Delhi	10	Lima	14	New Orleans	21	Shanghai	28
Baghdad	3	Dublin	10	London	15	New York	22	Singapore	28
Bangkok	3	Edinburgh	11	Lisbon	16	Orlando	23	Stockholm	29
Barcelona	4	Guangzhou	11	Los Angeles	16	Osaka	23	Sydney	29
Beijing	4	Helsinki	11	Madrid	17	Oslo	23	Tokyo	30
Berlin	5	Hong Kong	12	Manila	17	Paris	24	Tehran	31
Boston	6	Istanbul	12	Melbourne	18	Prague	25	Toronto	31
Brussels	6	Jakarta	12	Mexico City	18	Rio de Janeiro	25	Vienna	32
Budapest	7	Jerusalem	13	Miami	18	Rome	26	Warsaw	32
Buenos Aires	7	Johannesburg	13	Milan	19	San Francisco	26	Washington	33
Cairo	7	Karachi	13	Moscow	19	St Petersburg	27	Wellington	33
Cape Town	8	Kolkata	14	Montréal	20	Santiago	27	INDEX	34–39

CITY GAZETTEER 40–48

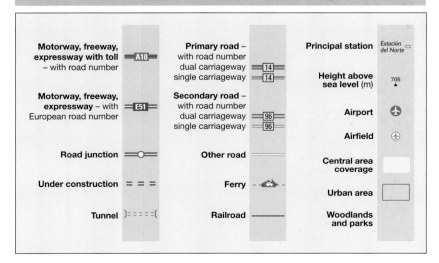

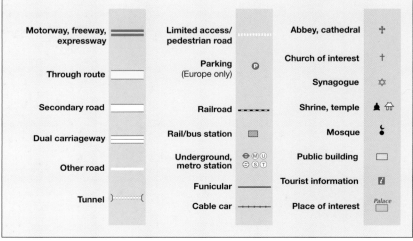

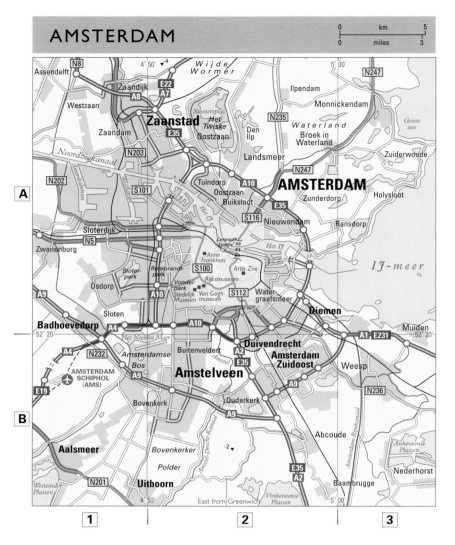

AMSTERDAM

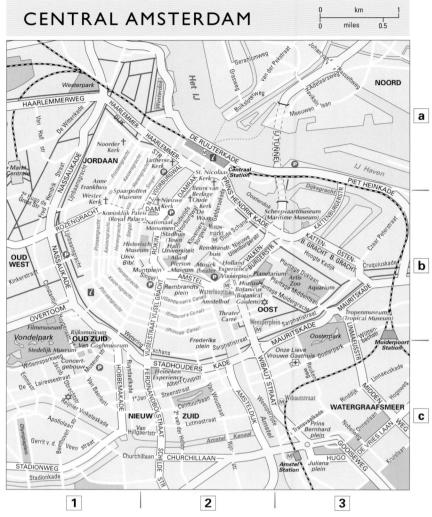

CENTRAL AMSTERDAM

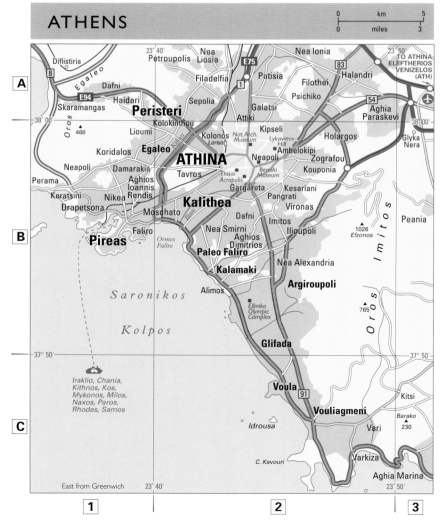

ATHENS

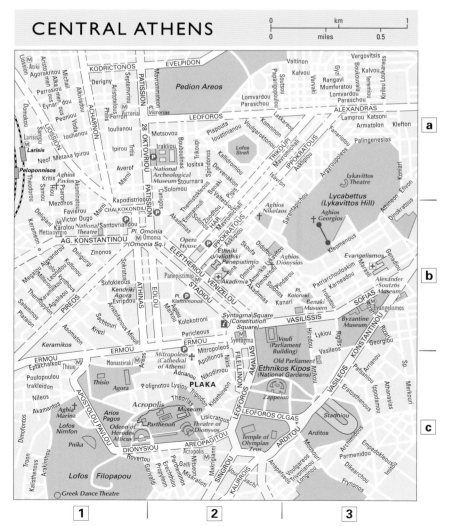

CENTRAL ATHENS

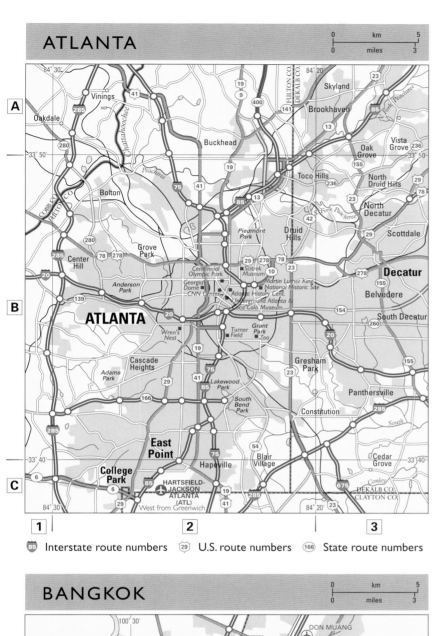

ATLANTA

km 0 — 5
miles 0 — 3

85 Interstate route numbers   29 U.S. route numbers   166 State route numbers

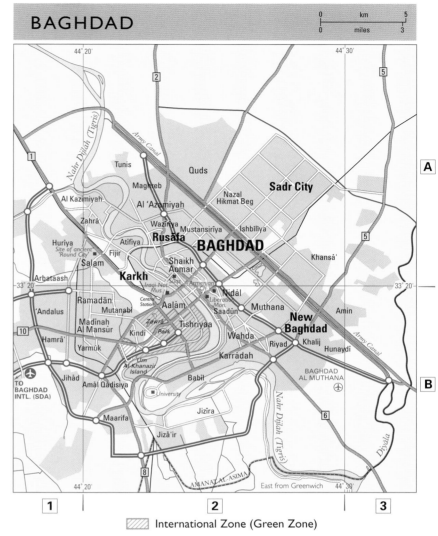

BAGHDAD

km 0 — 5
miles 0 — 3

International Zone (Green Zone)

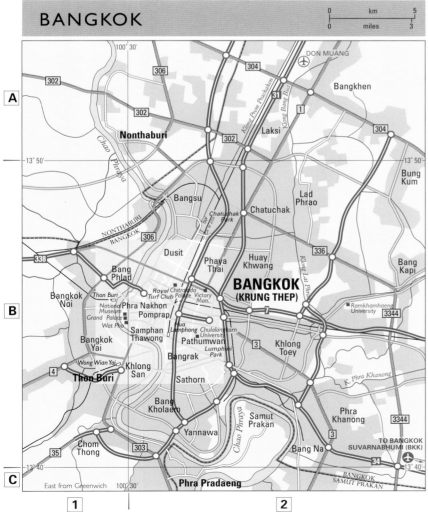

BANGKOK

km 0 — 5
miles 0 — 3

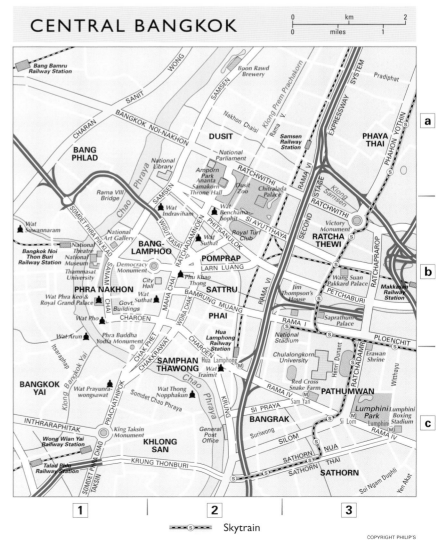

CENTRAL BANGKOK

km 0 — 2
miles 0 — 1

Skytrain

COPYRIGHT PHILIP'S

BARCELONA

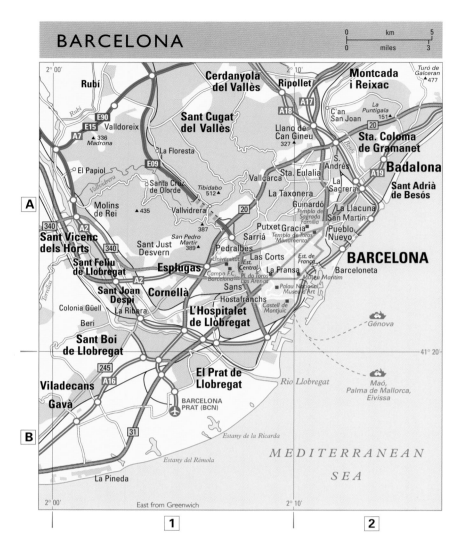

CENTRAL BARCELONA

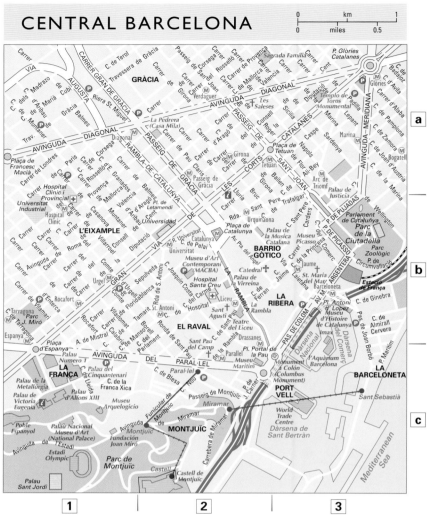

BEIJING

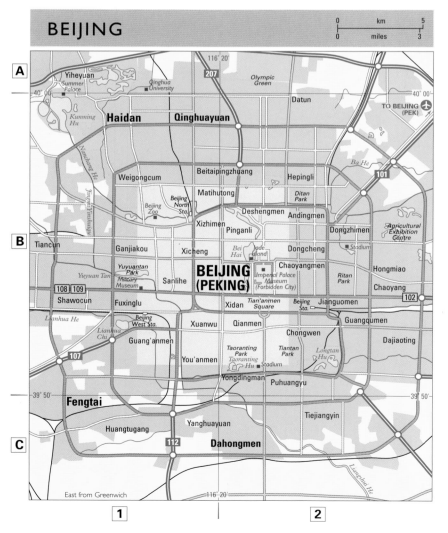

CENTRAL BEIJING

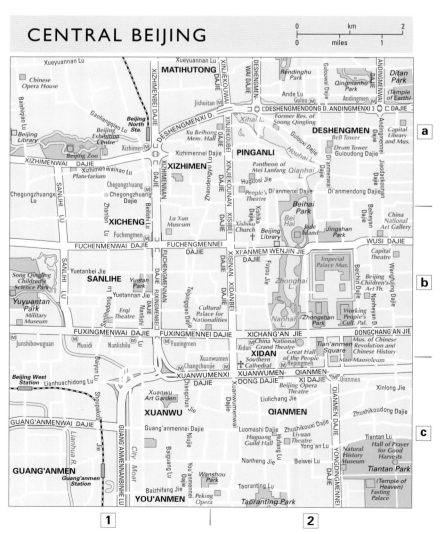

BERLIN

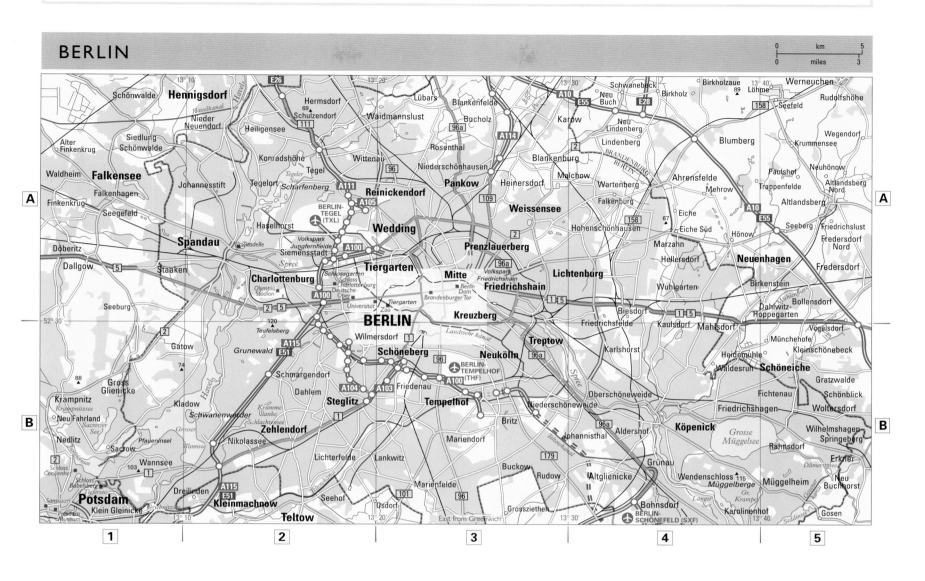

CENTRAL BERLIN

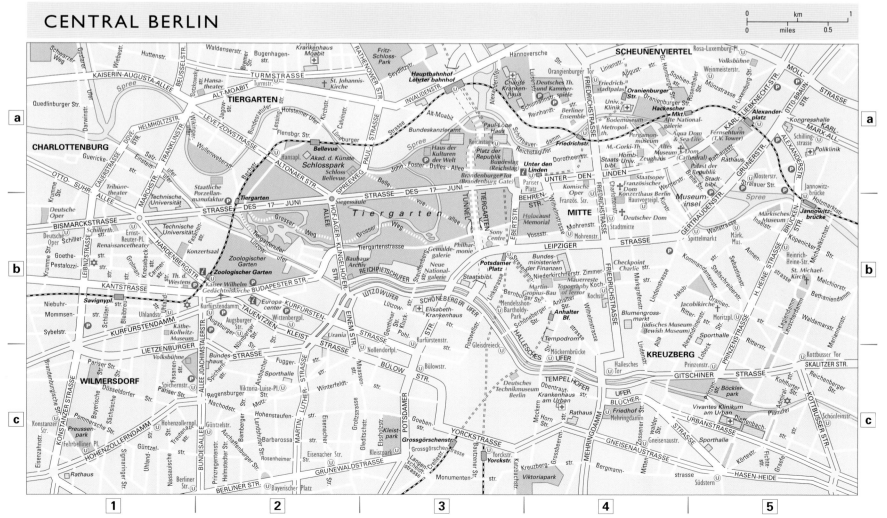

BOSTON

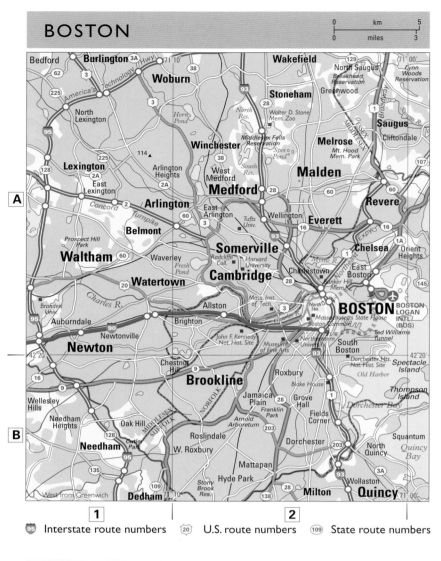

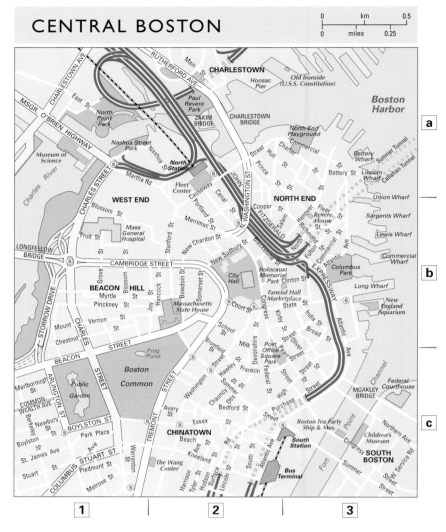

CENTRAL BOSTON

🛡️95 Interstate route numbers 〈20〉 U.S. route numbers 〈109〉 State route numbers

BRUSSELS

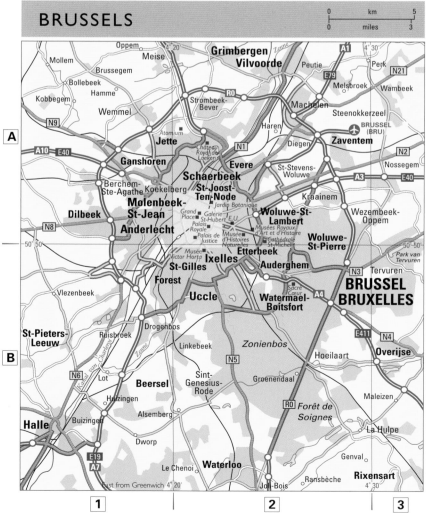

CENTRAL BRUSSELS

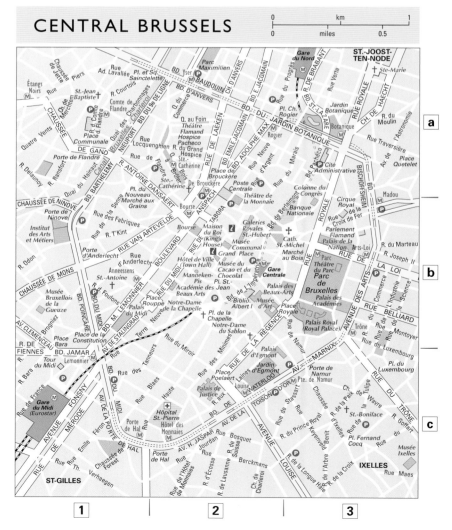

BUDAPEST

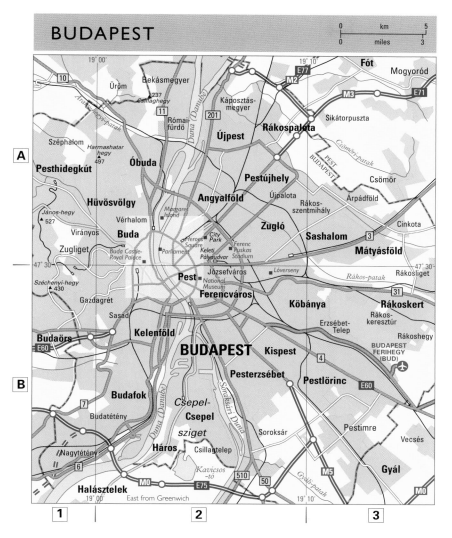

CENTRAL BUDAPEST

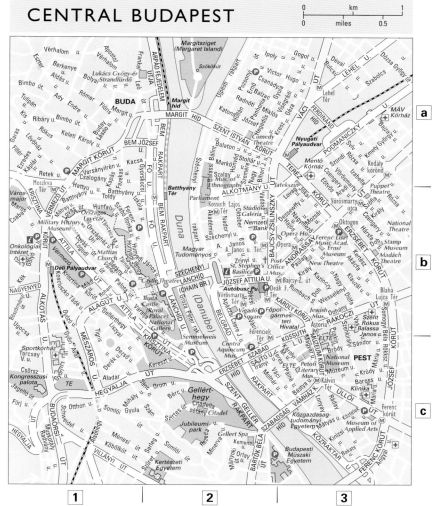

BUENOS AIRES

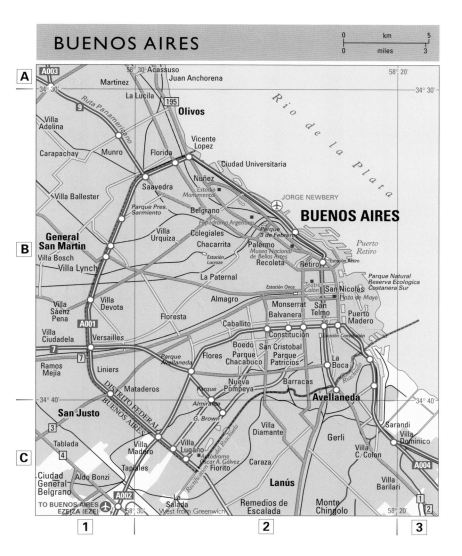

CAIRO

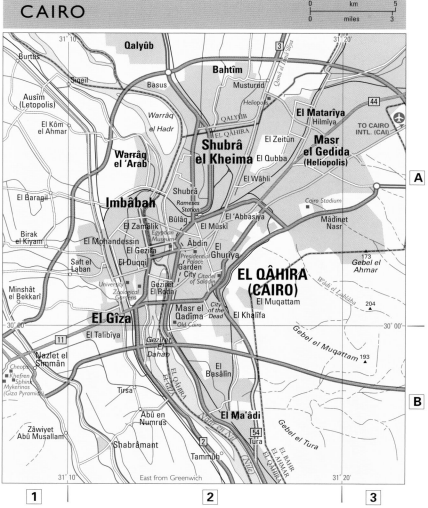

CAPE TOWN

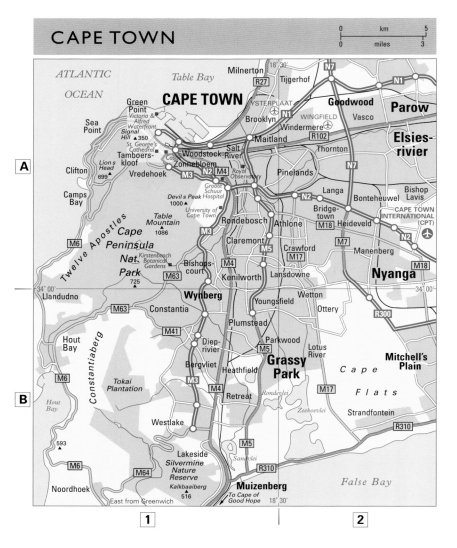

CENTRAL CAPE TOWN

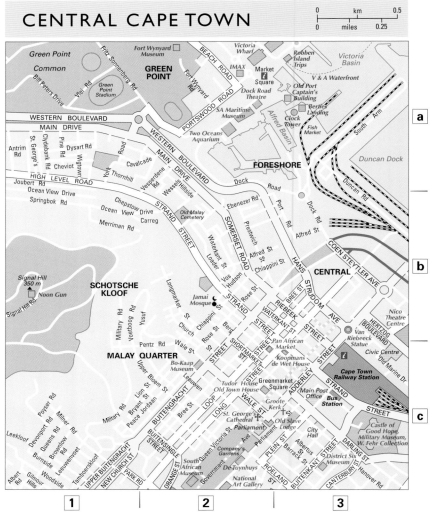

COPENHAGEN

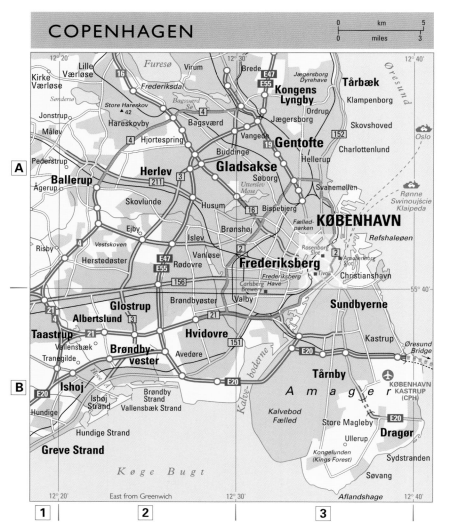

CENTRAL COPENHAGEN

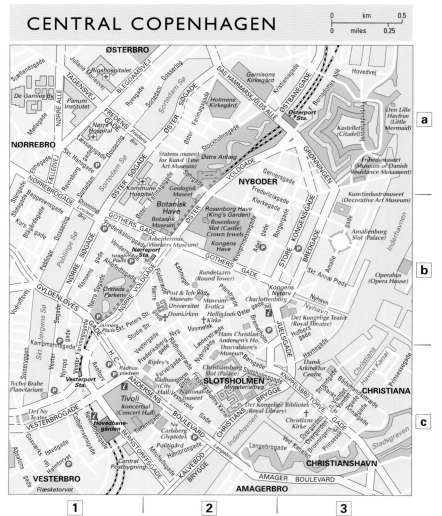

CHICAGO

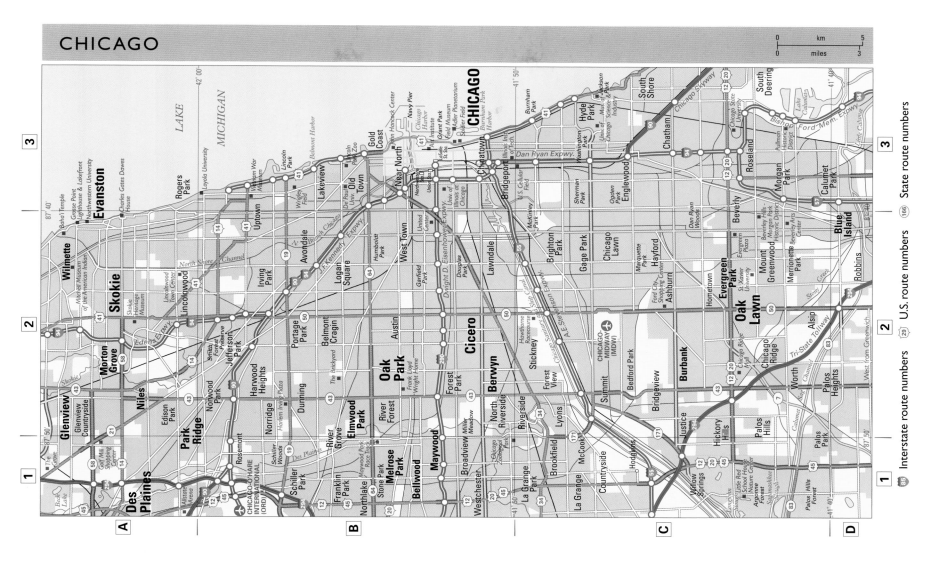

State route numbers (166)

U.S. route numbers (29)

Interstate route numbers

CENTRAL CHICAGO

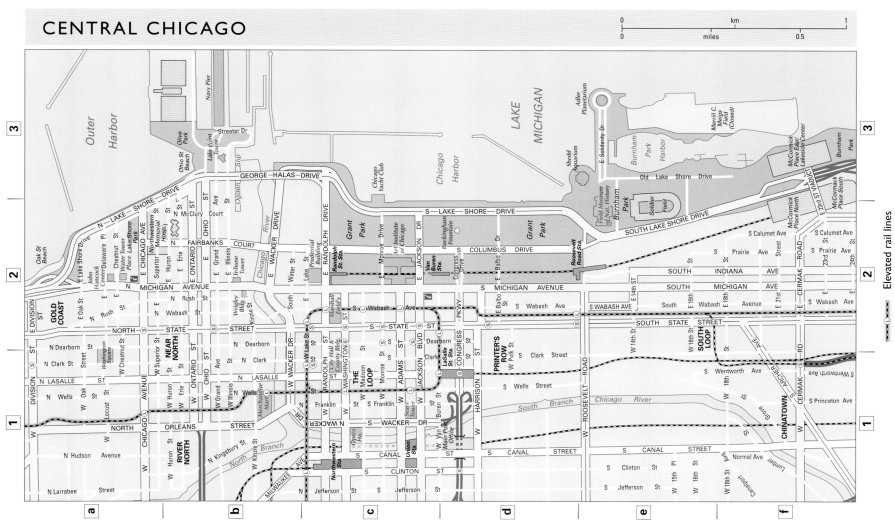

Elevated rail lines

DELHI

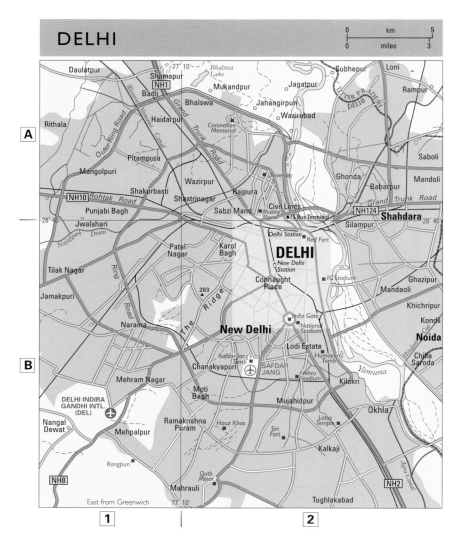

CENTRAL DELHI

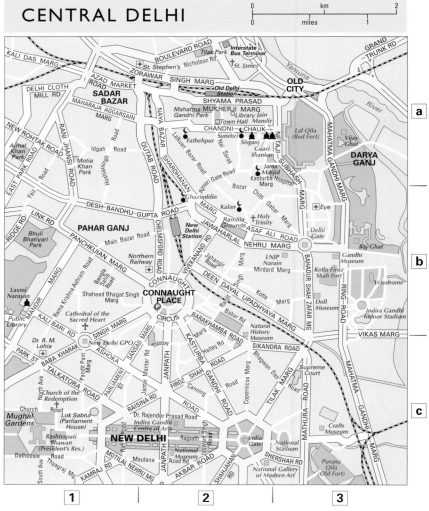

DUBLIN

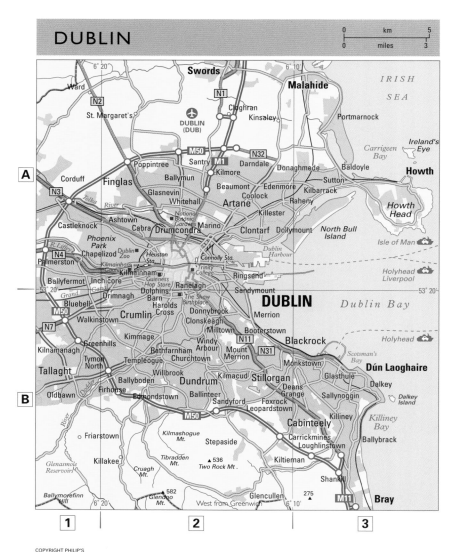

CENTRAL DUBLIN

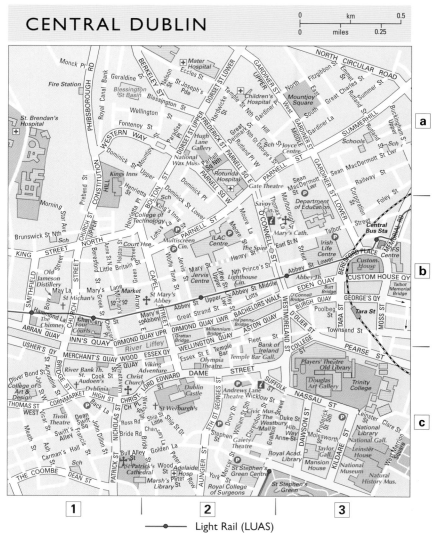

Light Rail (LUAS)

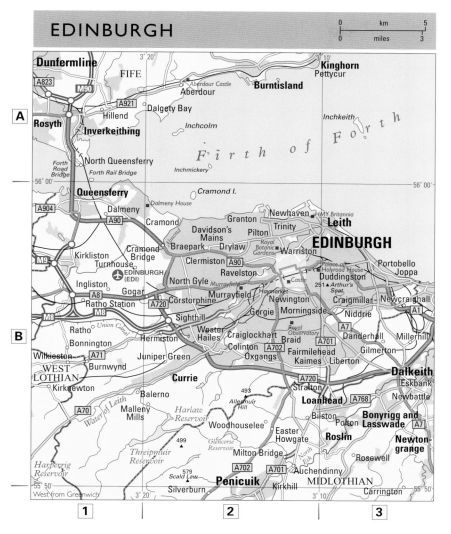

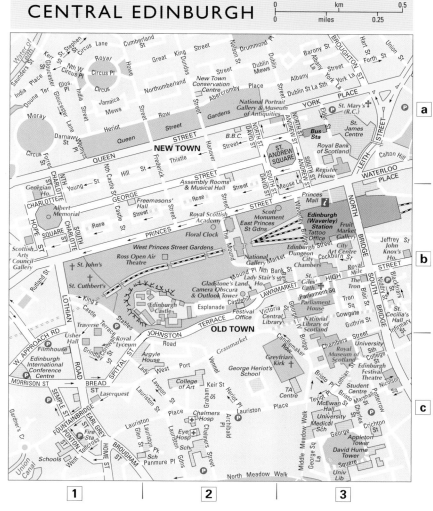

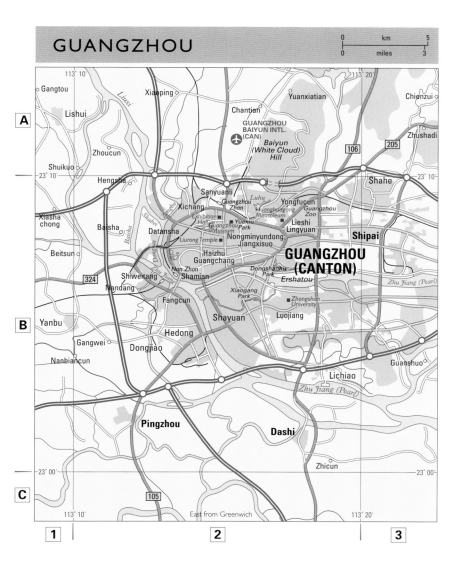

COPYRIGHT PHILIP'S

HONG KONG

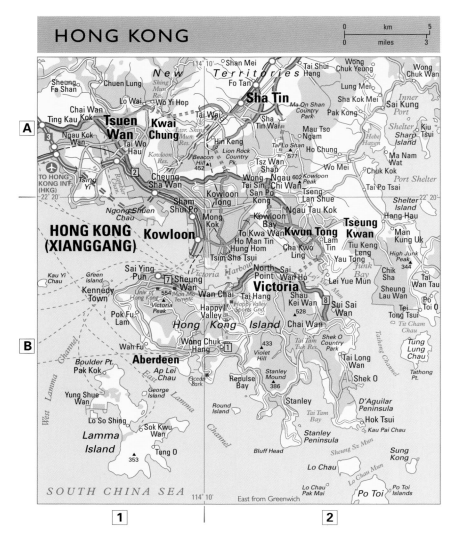

CENTRAL HONG KONG

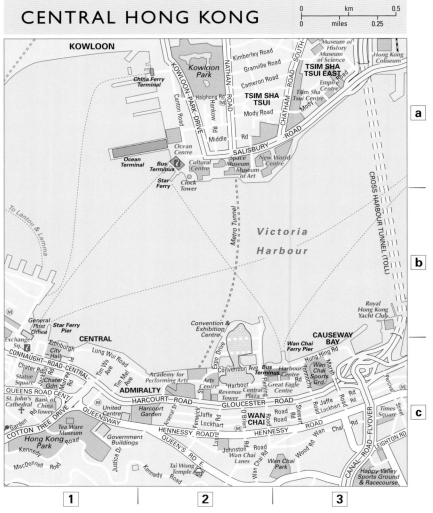

ISTANBUL

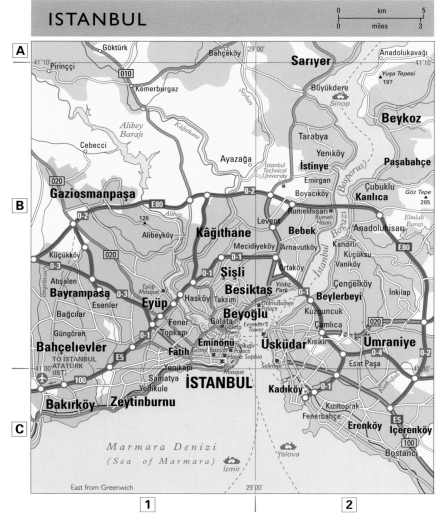

JAKARTA

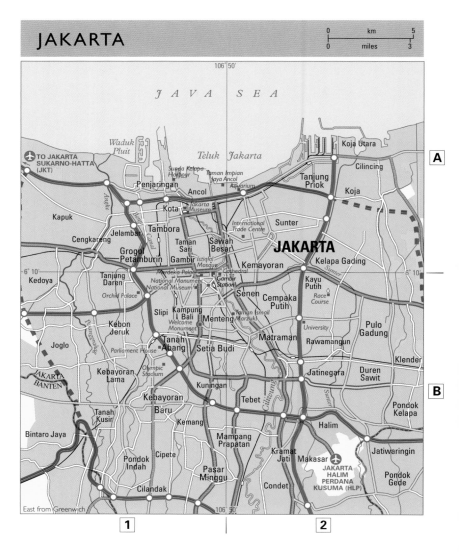

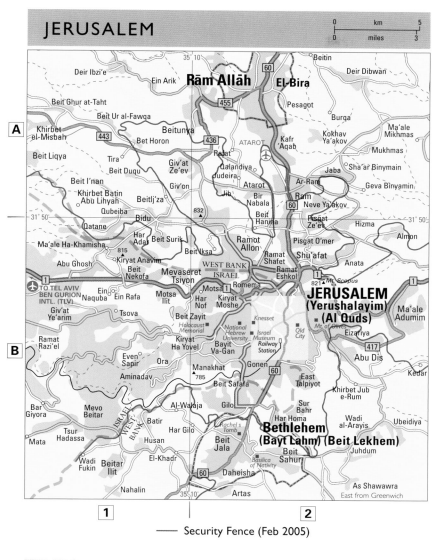

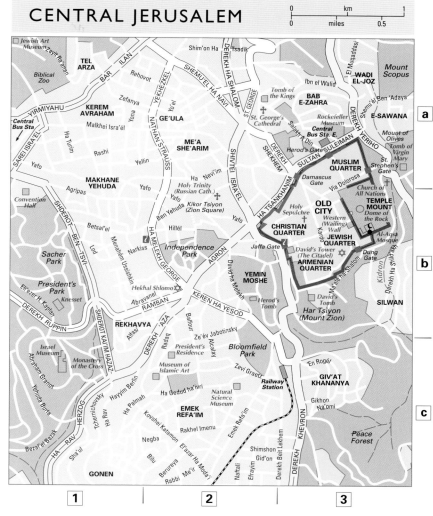

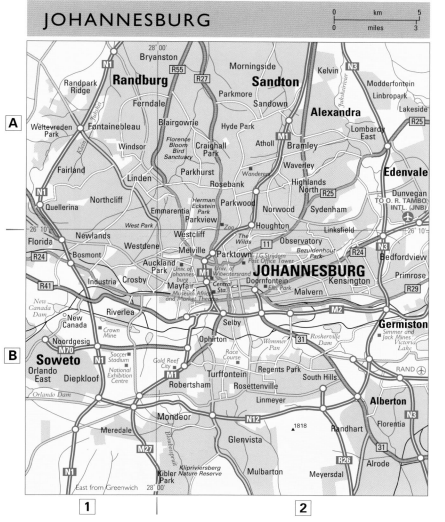

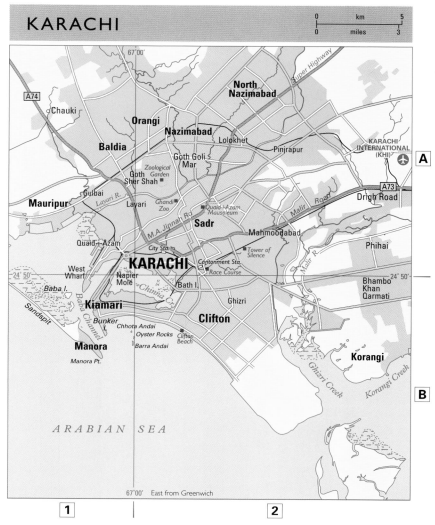

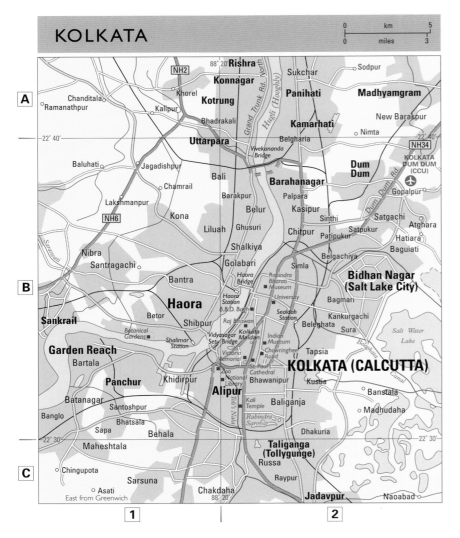

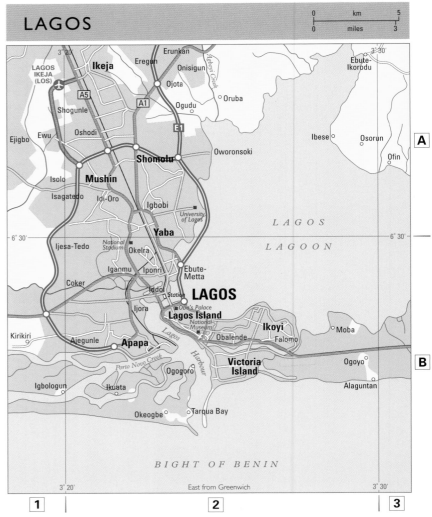

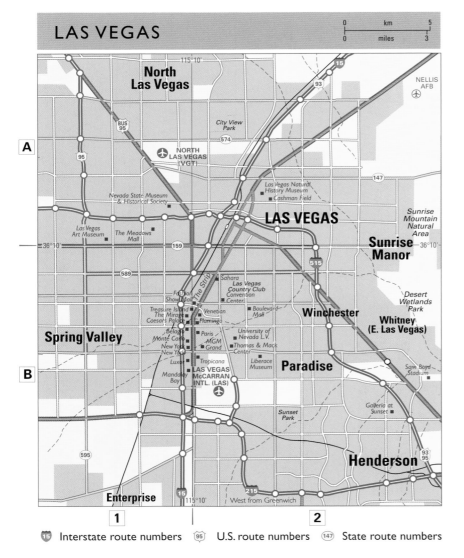

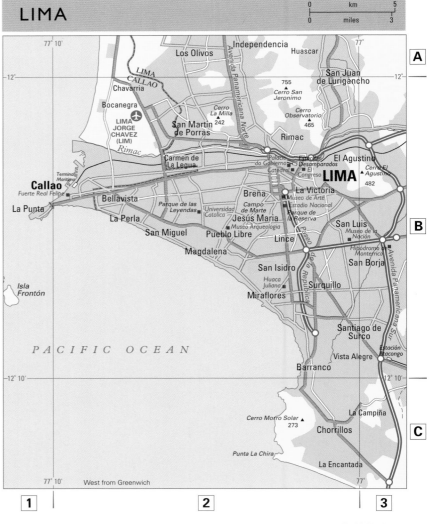

🛡15 Interstate route numbers   95 U.S. route numbers   147 State route numbers

LONDON

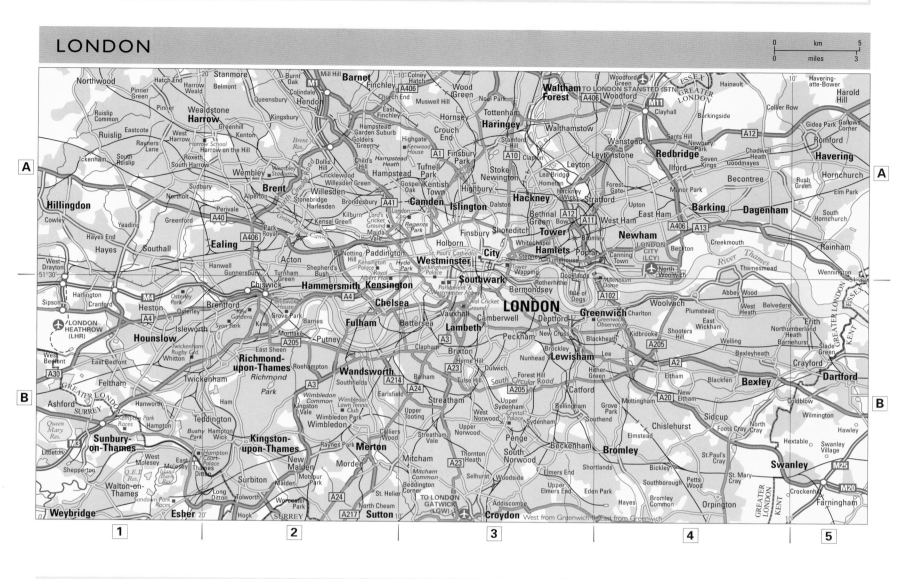

CENTRAL LONDON

— Congestion Charging Zone

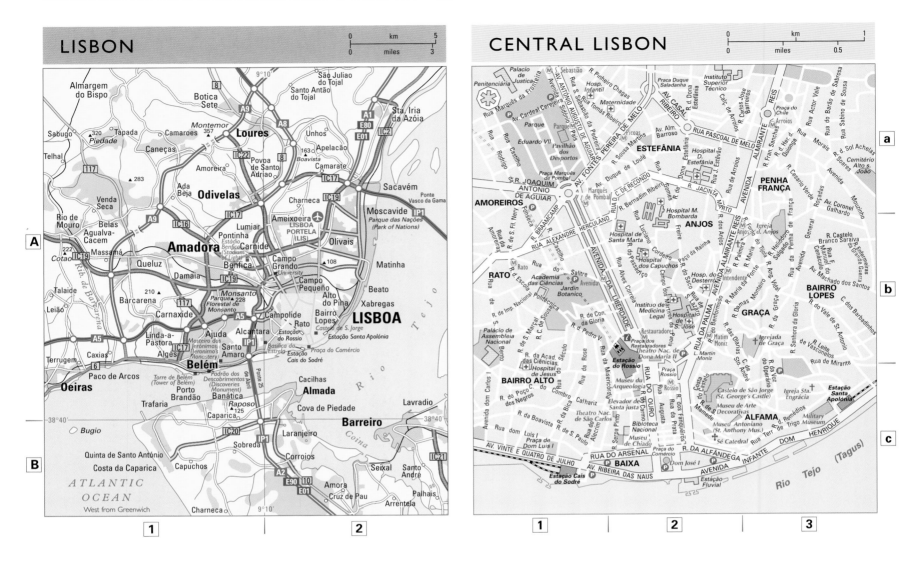

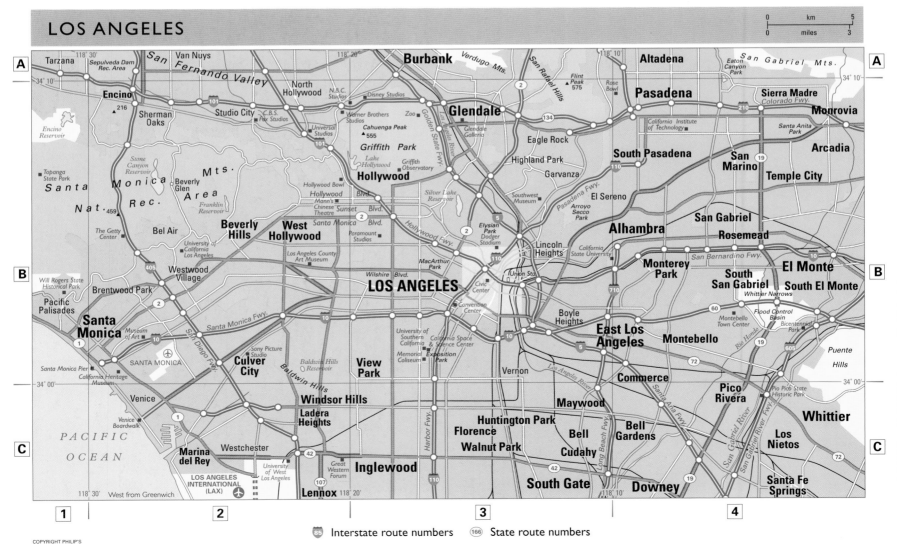

Interstate route numbers   State route numbers

COPYRIGHT PHILIP'S

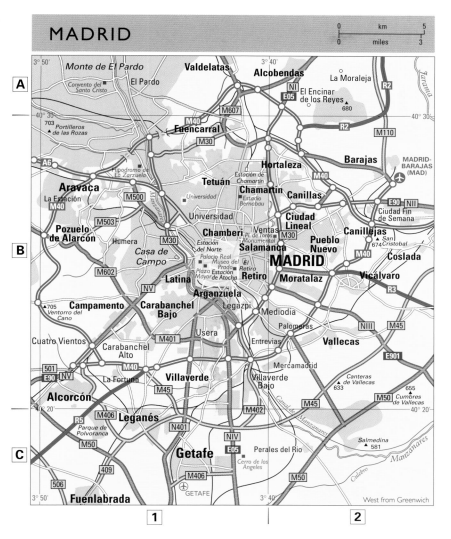

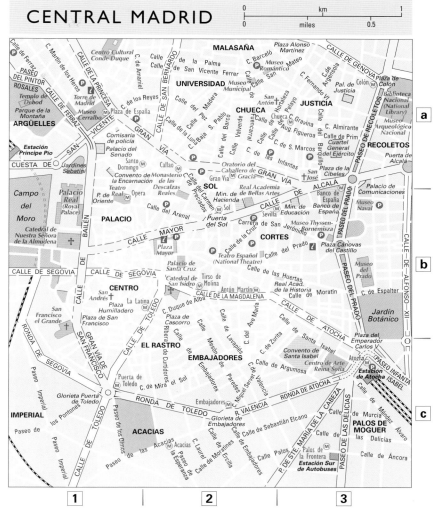

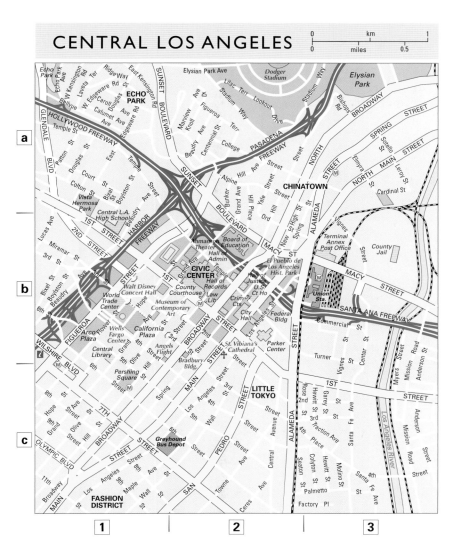

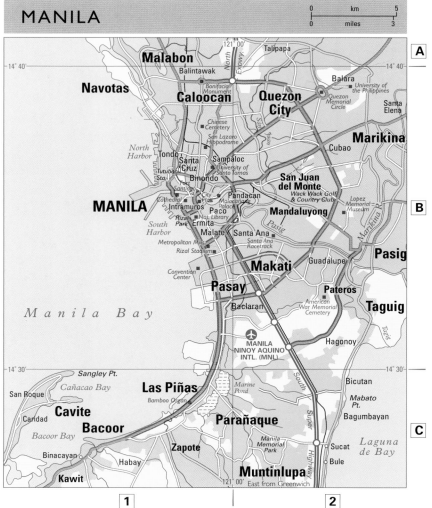

COPYRIGHT PHILIP'S

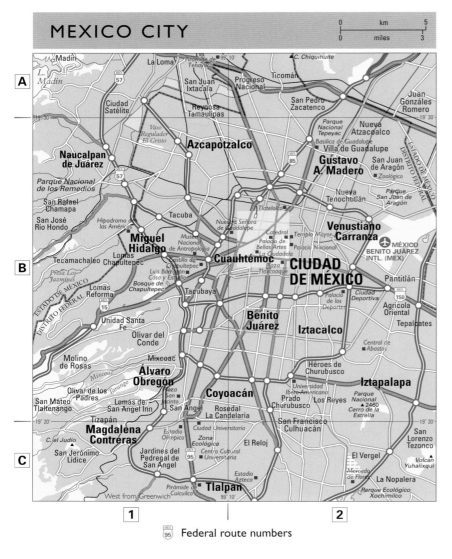

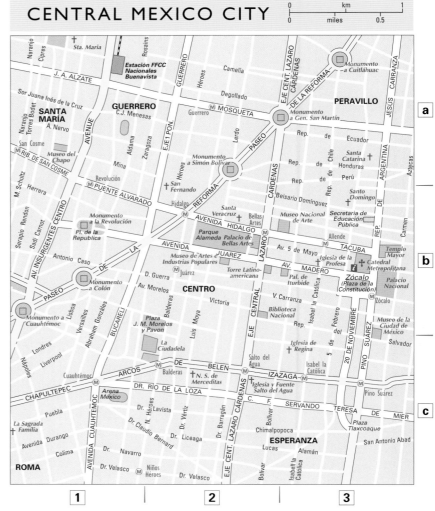

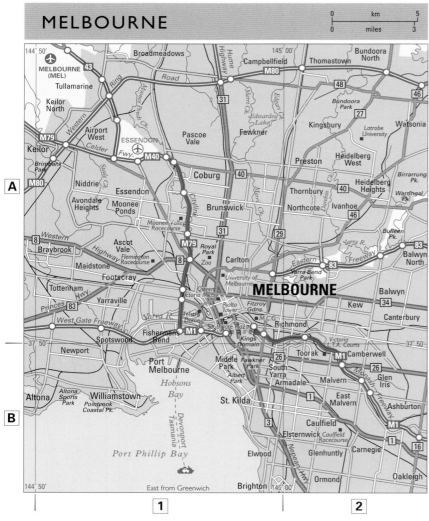

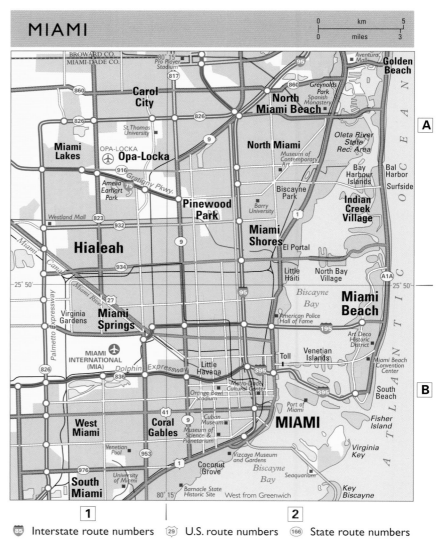

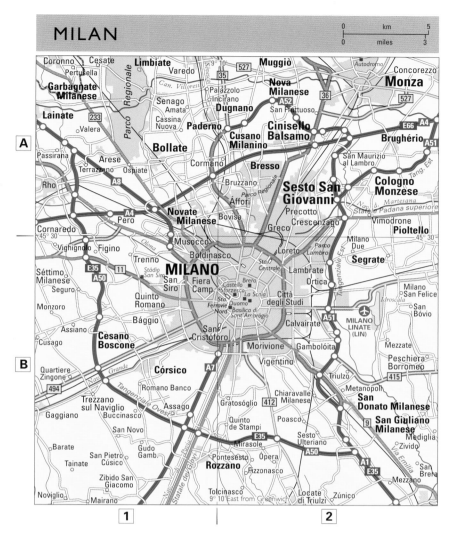

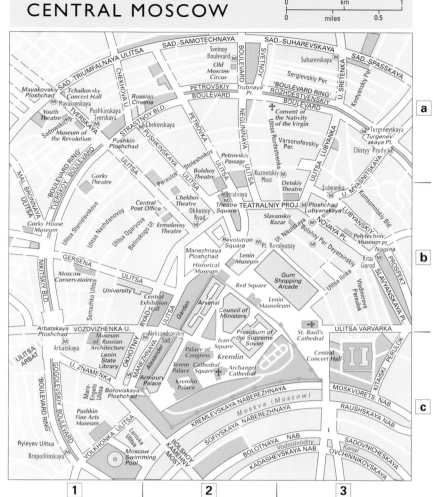

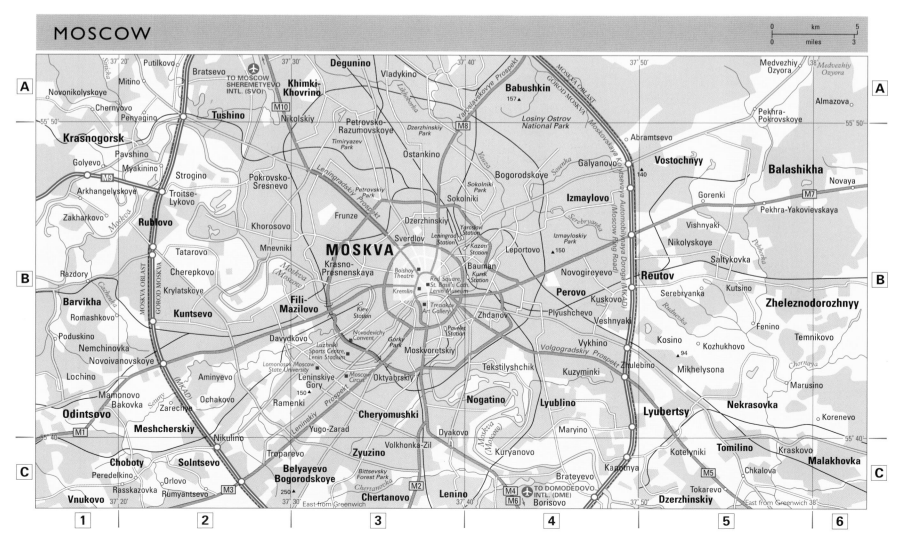

MONTRÉAL

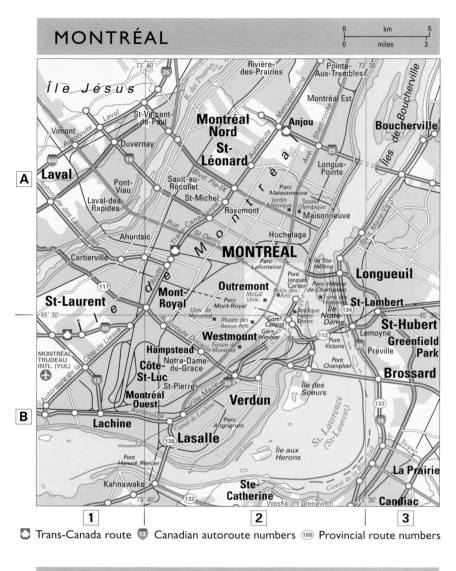

CENTRAL MONTRÉAL

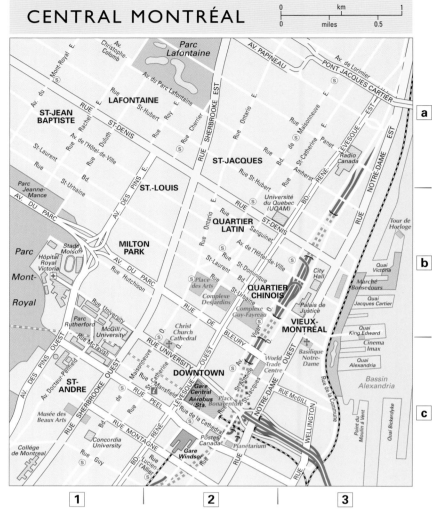

Trans-Canada route   Canadian autoroute numbers   Provincial route numbers

MUMBAI

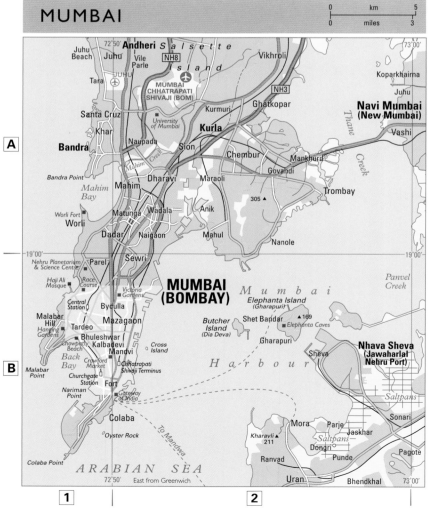

CENTRAL MUMBAI

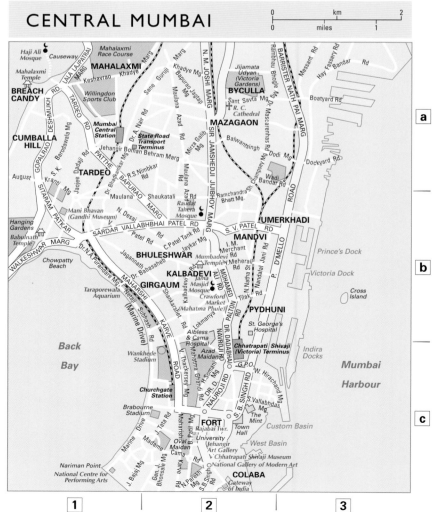

MUNICH

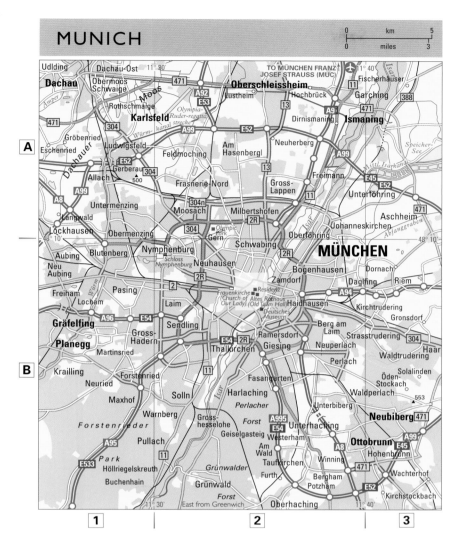

CENTRAL MUNICH

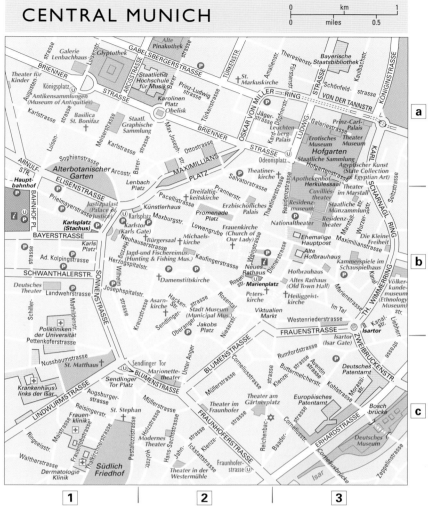

NEW ORLEANS

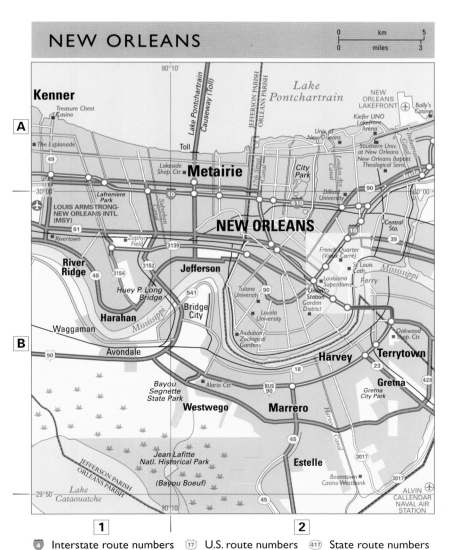

CENTRAL NEW ORLEANS

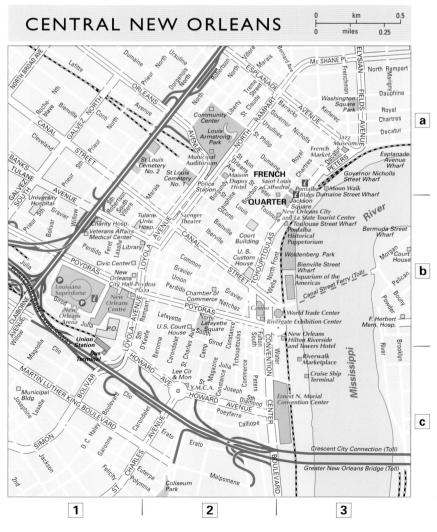

Interstate route numbers U.S. route numbers State route numbers

COPYRIGHT PHILIP'S

NEW YORK

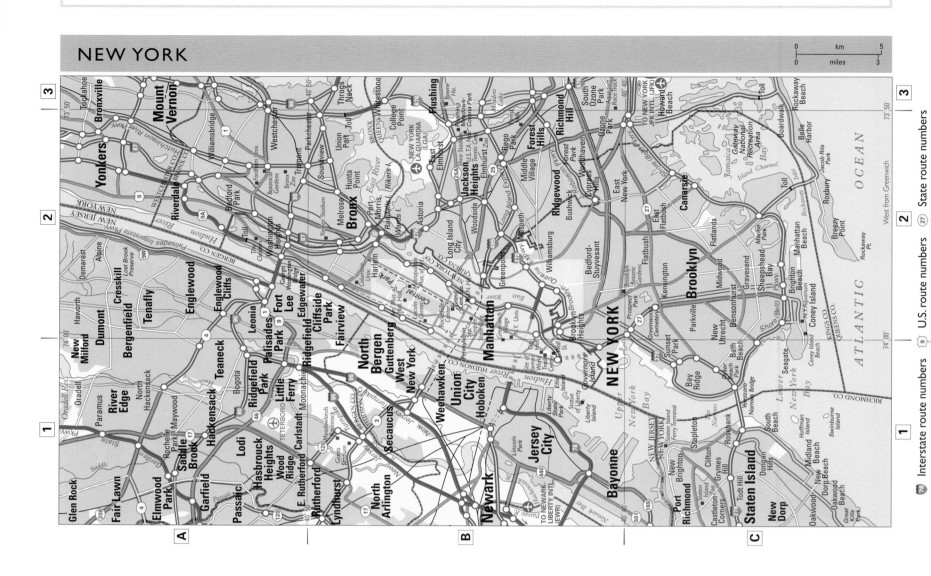

km 5
miles 3

CENTRAL NEW YORK

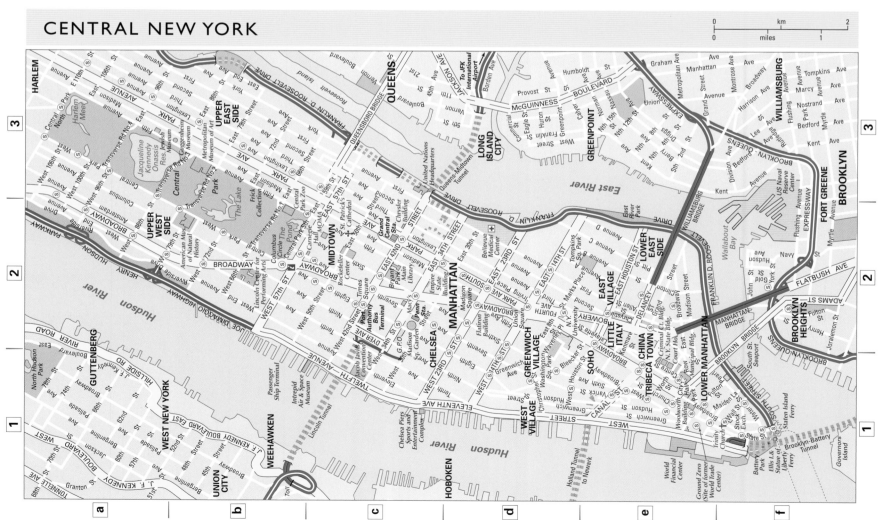

km 2
miles 1

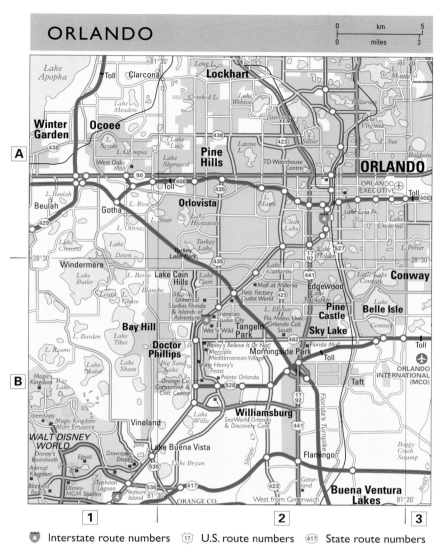

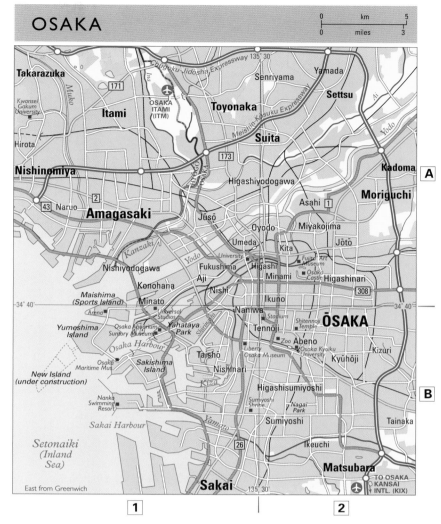

Interstate route numbers U.S. route numbers State route numbers

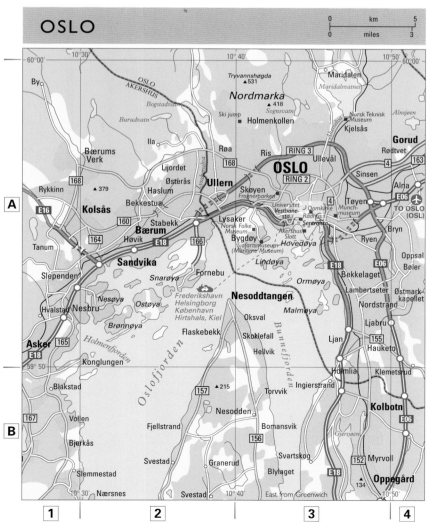

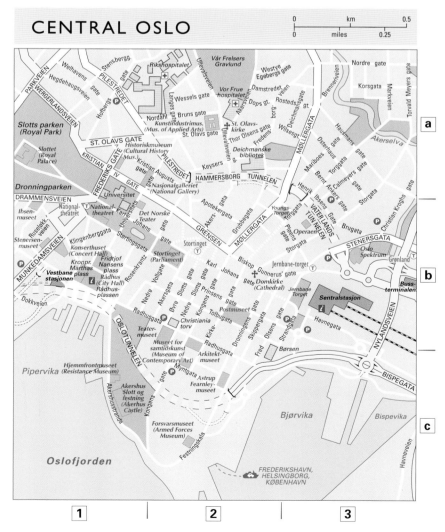

COPYRIGHT PHILIP'S

PARIS

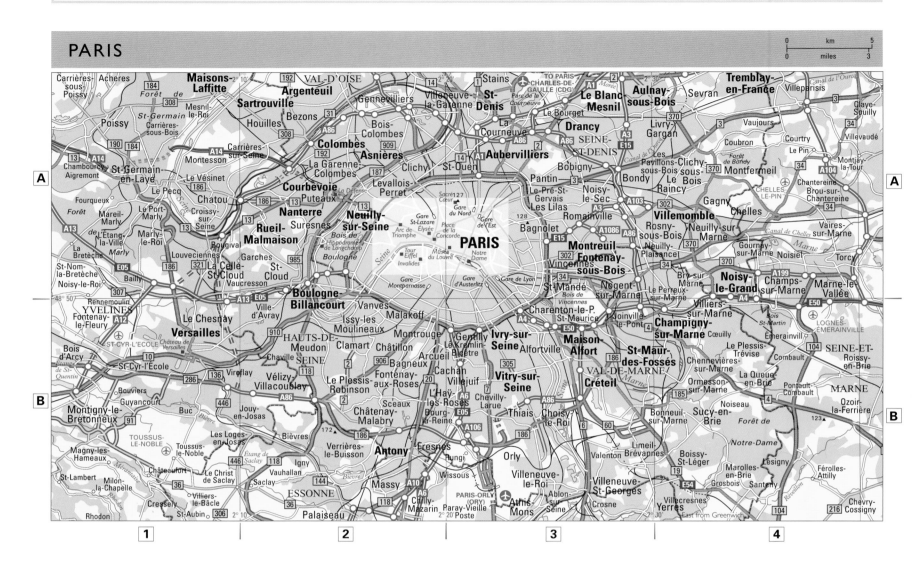

CENTRAL PARIS

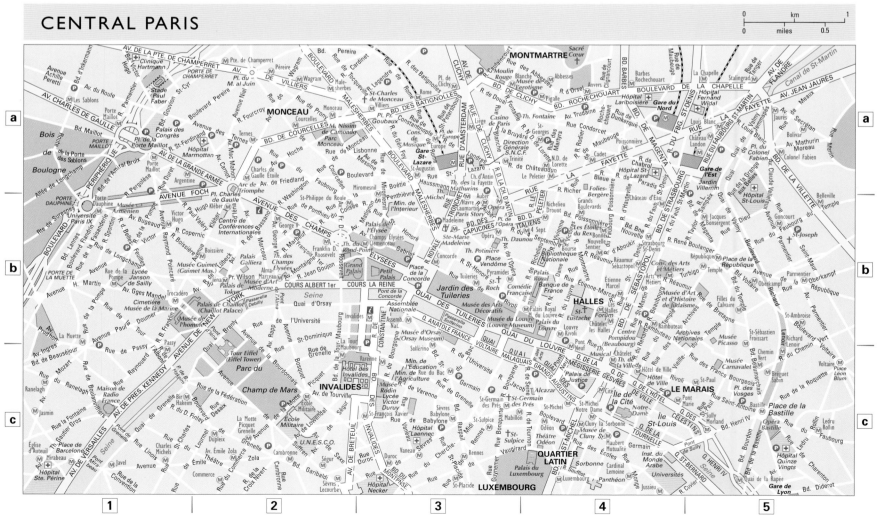

PRAGUE

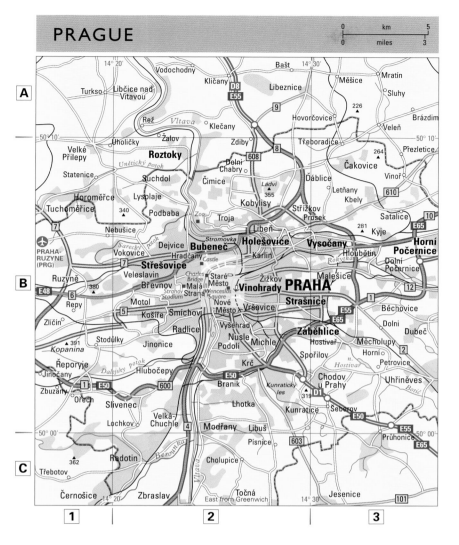

CENTRAL PRAGUE

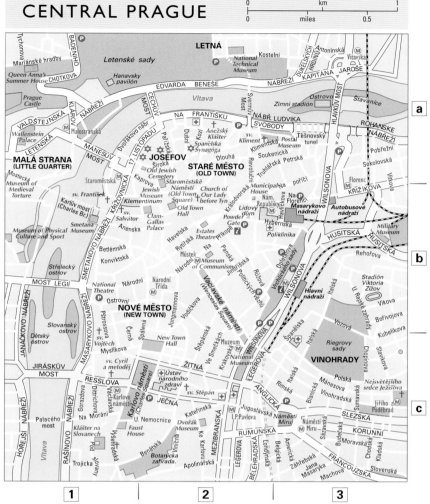

RIO DE JANEIRO

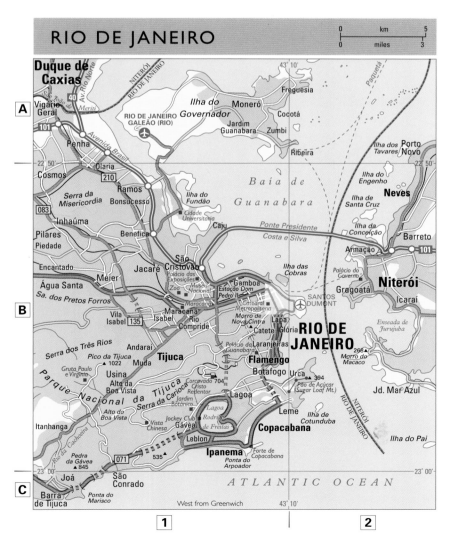

CENTRAL RIO DE JANEIRO

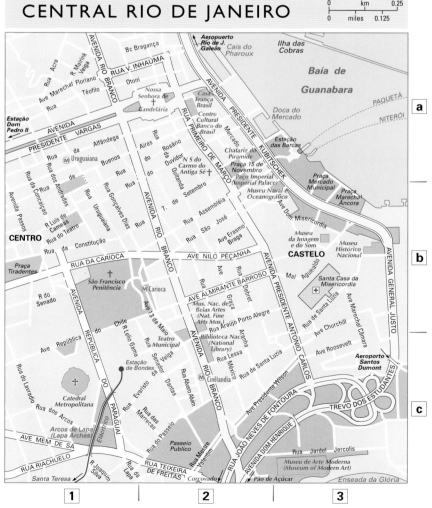

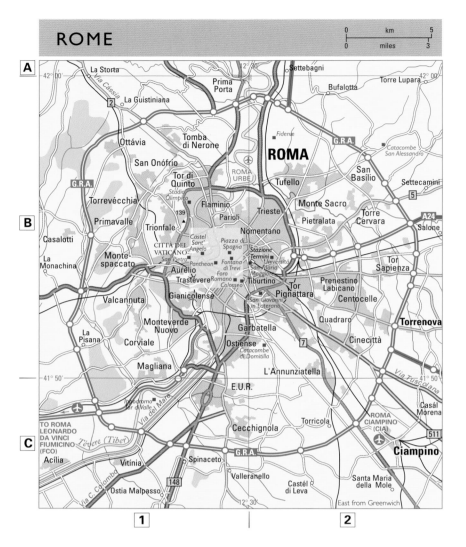

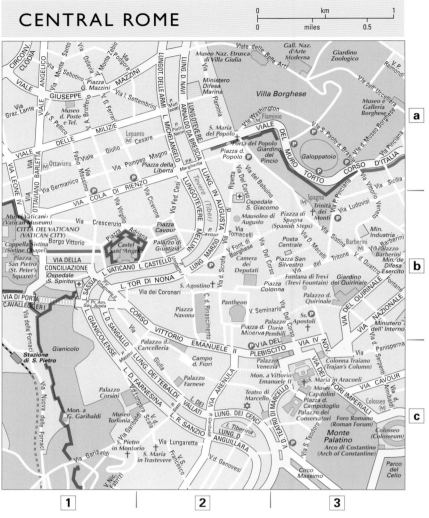

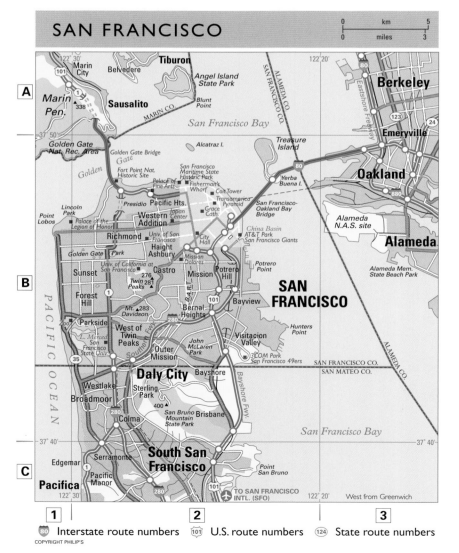

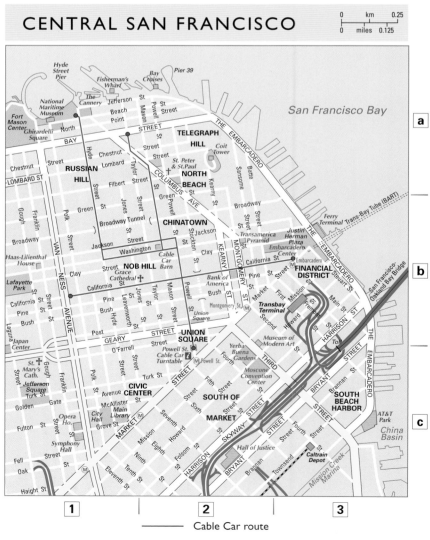

Interstate route numbers   U.S. route numbers   State route numbers

Cable Car route

COPYRIGHT PHILIP'S

ST PETERSBURG

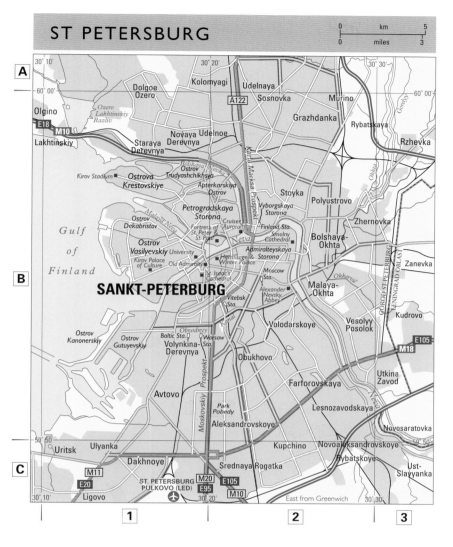

SANTIAGO

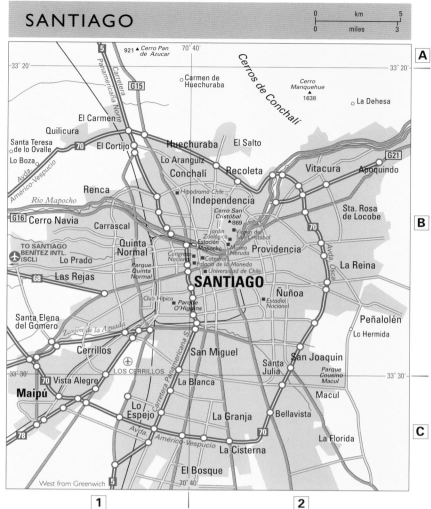

SÃO PAULO

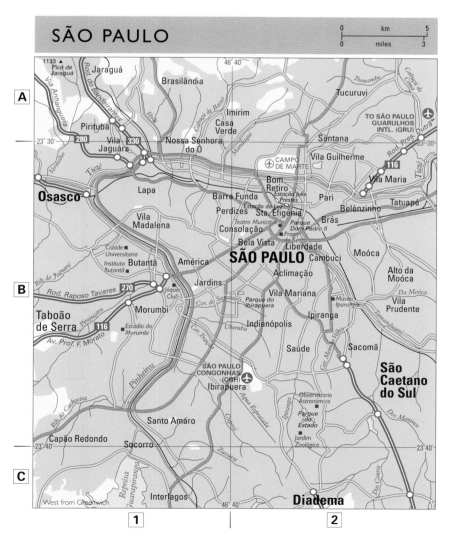

SEOUL

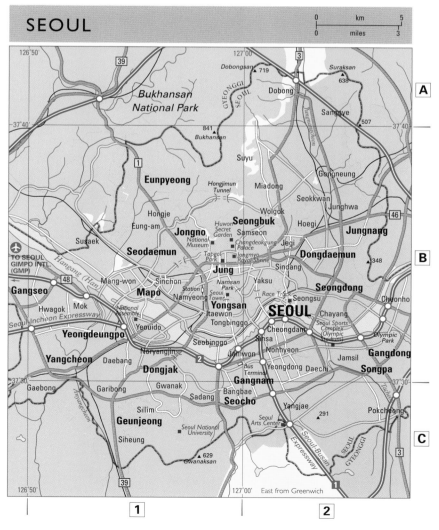

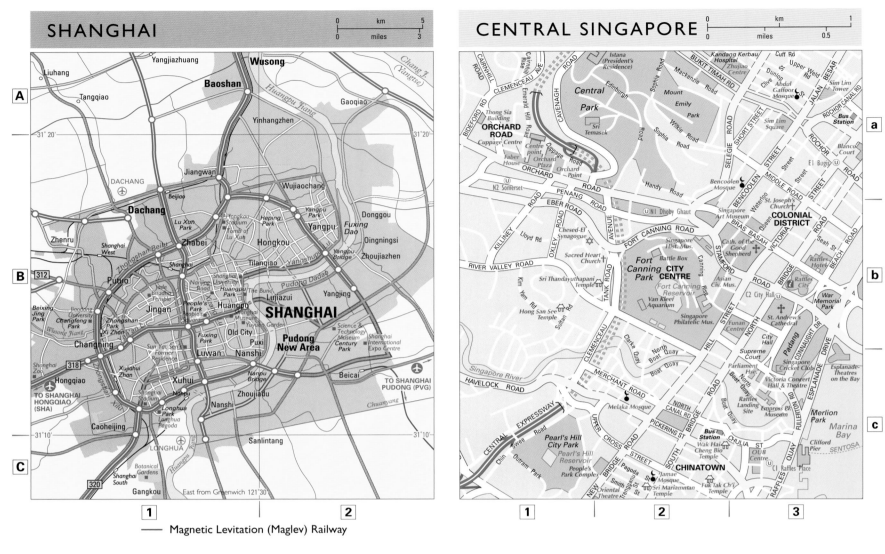

— Magnetic Levitation (Maglev) Railway

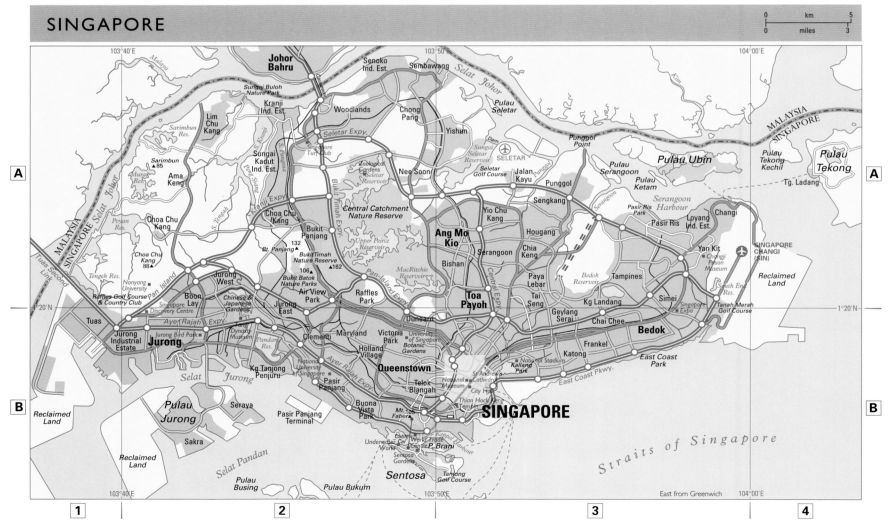

STOCKHOLM

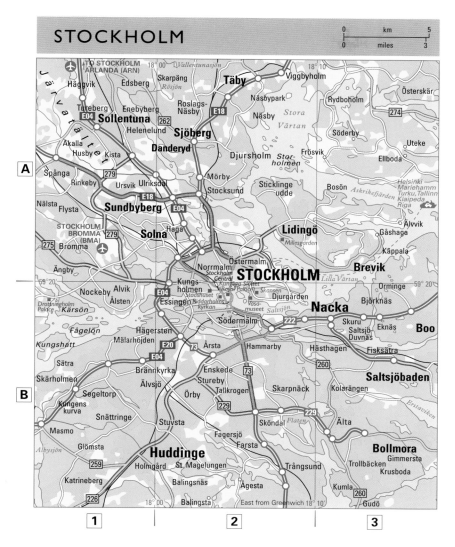

0 km 5
0 miles 3

	1	2	3

Järvafältet · TO STOCKHOLM ARLANDA (ARN) · Vallentunasjön · 18° 00 · 18° 10 · Skarpäng · Viggbyholm · Täby · Näsbypark · Österskär · Rydboholm · 274 · Häggvik · Edsberg · Rösjön · E04 · Tureberg · Enebyberg · Roslags-Näsby · Näsby · E18 · Sollentuna · Heleneund · 262 · Sjöberg · Stora Värtan · Söderby · Uteke · Akalla · Husby · Kista · Danderyd · Djursholm · Frösvik · Ellboda · Spånga · Rinkeby · 279 · Ursvik · Ulriksdal · Mörby · Starholmen · Helsinki Mariehamn Turku, Tallinn Klaipeda Riga · Nälsta · Flysta · Stocksund · Sticklinge udde · Bosön · Askrikefjärden
A · Sundbyberg · E04 · E18 · Haga · Lidingö · Gåshaga · Älvvik
Solna · STOCKHOLM BROMMA (BMA) · Millesgården · Brevik
275 · Bromma · Norrmalm Stockholm Central · Östermalm · Orminge · 59° 20 · Ängby · Kungs-holmen · Stadshuset Royal Palace · Skansen · Djurgården · Vasa-museet · Lilla Värtan · Nacka · Björknäs · Nockeby · Alvik · Ålsten · Essingen · Södermalm · Saltsjö-Duvnäs · Skuru · Eknäs · Boo
B · Drottningholm Palace · Kärsön · Hägersten · Mälarhöjden · 222 · Årsta · Hammarby · Hästhagen · Fisksätra · Fågelön · Kungshatt · E20 · 73 · Enskede · Stureby · Skarpnäck · 260 · Saltsjöbaden · Sätra · Skärholmen · E04 · Brännkyrka · Älvsjö · Örby · Tallkrogen · 73 · Kolarängen · Segeltorp · 229 · Kungens kurva · Snättringe · Stuvsta · 229 · Älta · Bollmora · Masmo · Sköndal · Fagersjö · Gimmersta · Huddinge · Farsta · Trollbäcken · Krusboda · 259 · Holmgård · St. Magelungen · Ågesta · Trångsund · Kumla · 260 · Katrineberg · Balingsnäs · Gudö · 226 · 18° 00 · Balingsta · Balingsta · East from Greenwich 18° 10

CENTRAL STOCKHOLM

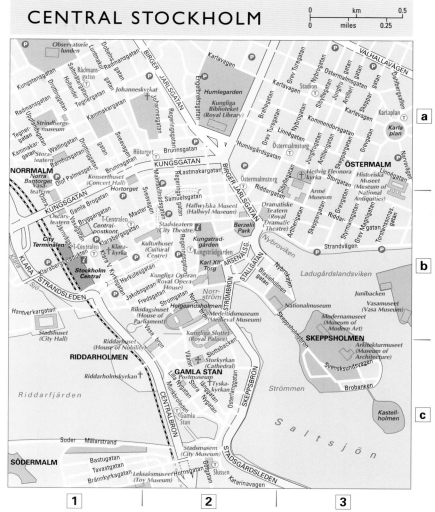

0 km 0.5
0 miles 0.25

	1	2	3

SYDNEY

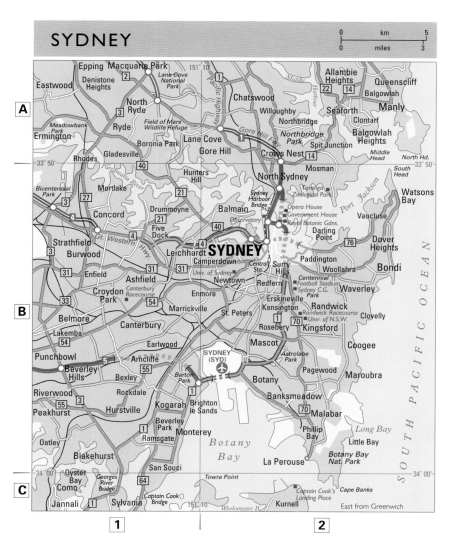

0 km 5
0 miles 3

	1	2

CENTRAL SYDNEY

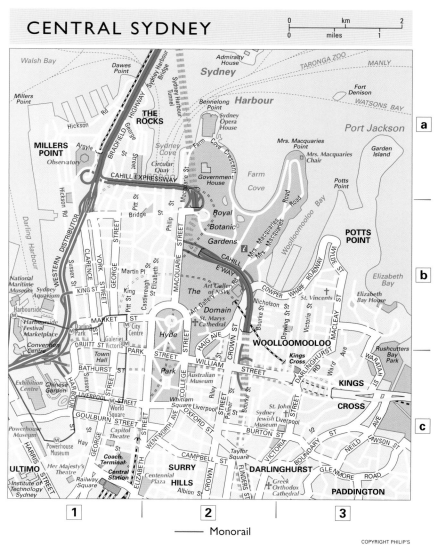

0 km 2
0 miles 1

	1	2	3

— Monorail

TOKYO

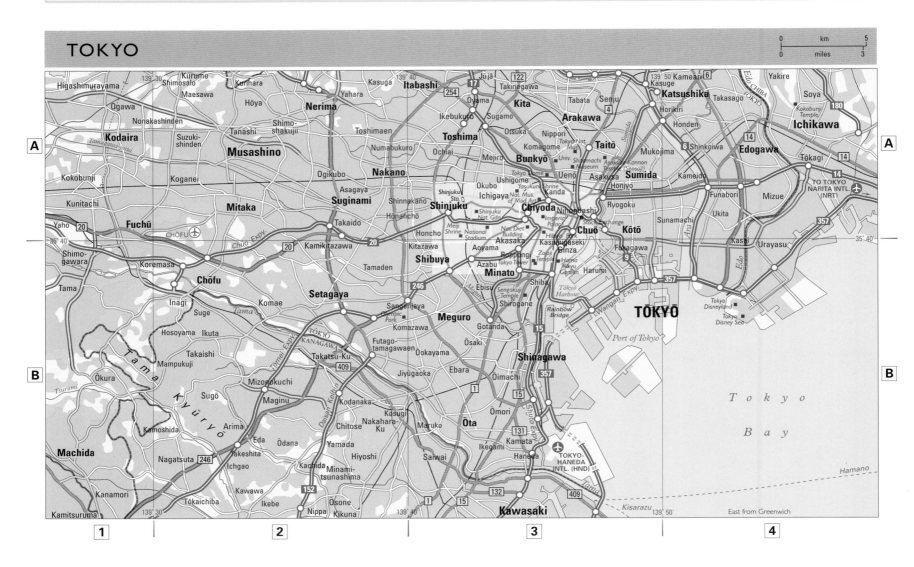

CENTRAL TOKYO

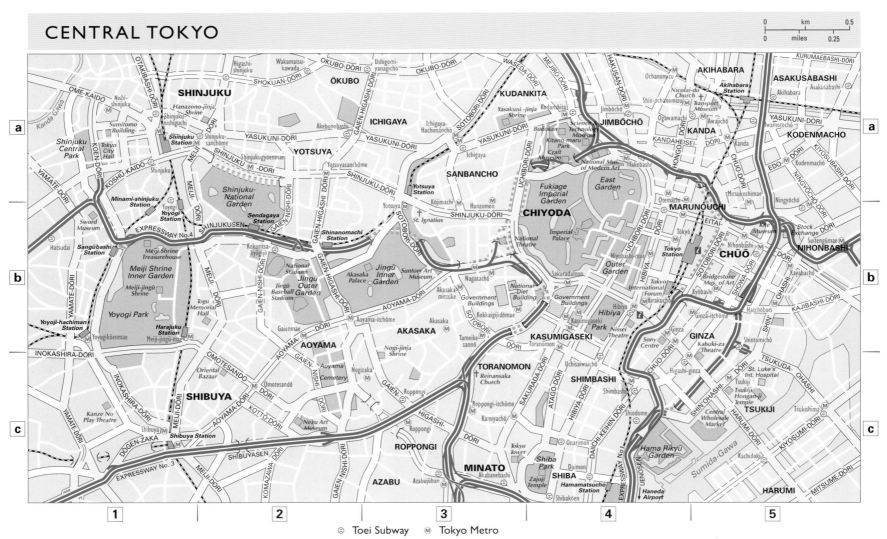

⊖ Toei Subway   Ⓜ Tokyo Metro

TEHRAN

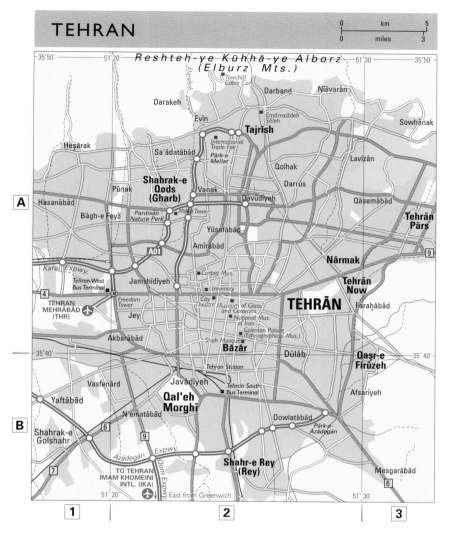

CENTRAL TORONTO

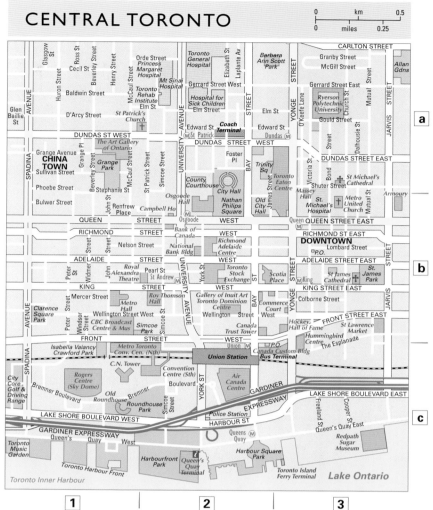

TORONTO

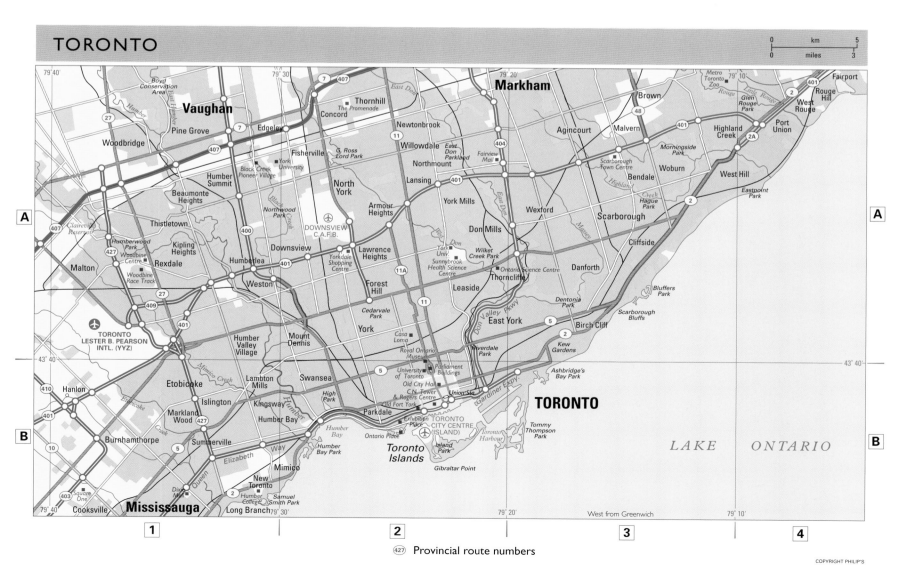

427 Provincial route numbers

VIENNA

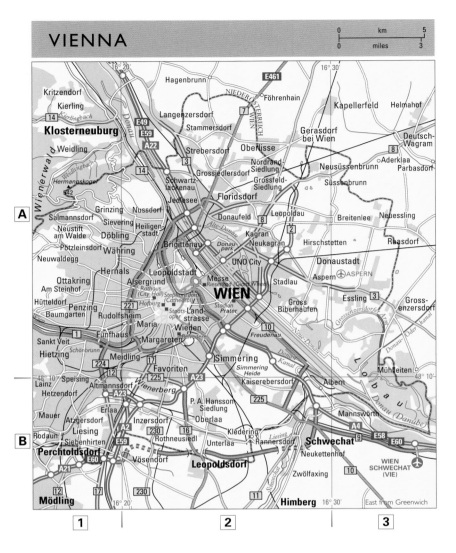

CENTRAL VIENNA

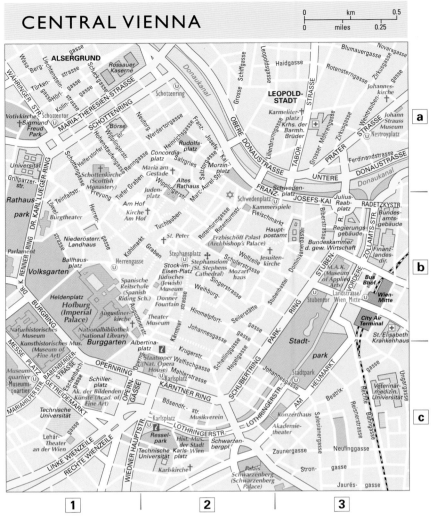

WARSAW

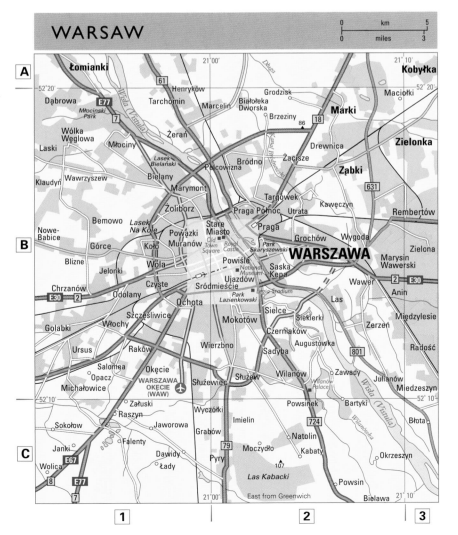

CENTRAL WARSAW

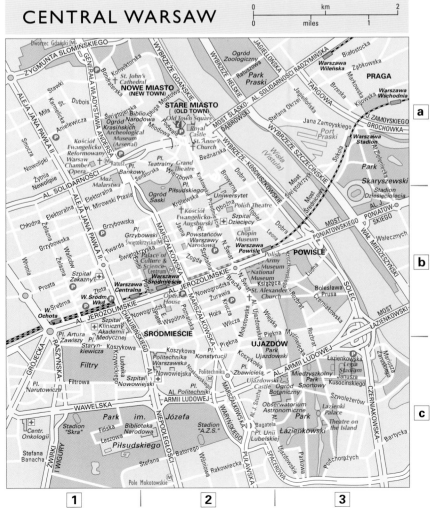

WASHINGTON

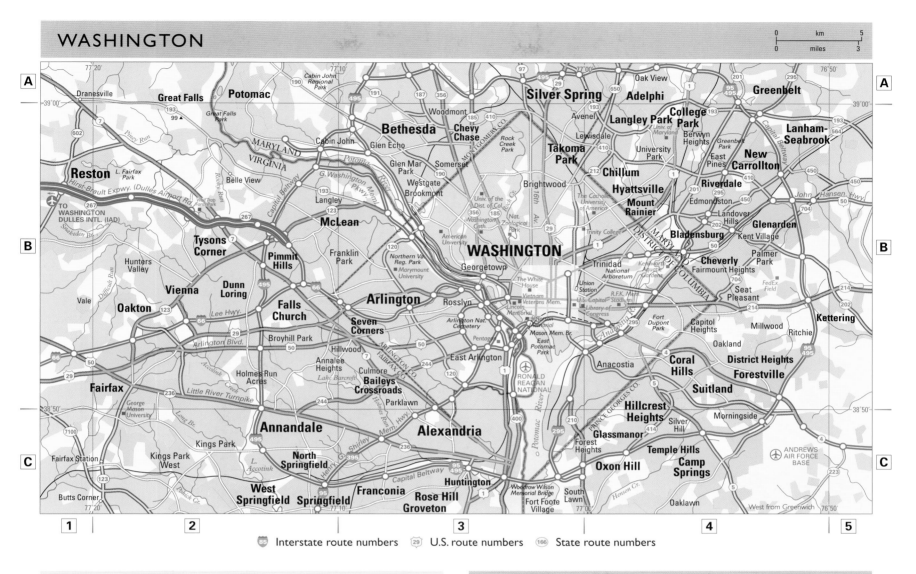

Interstate route numbers   U.S. route numbers   State route numbers

CENTRAL WASHINGTON

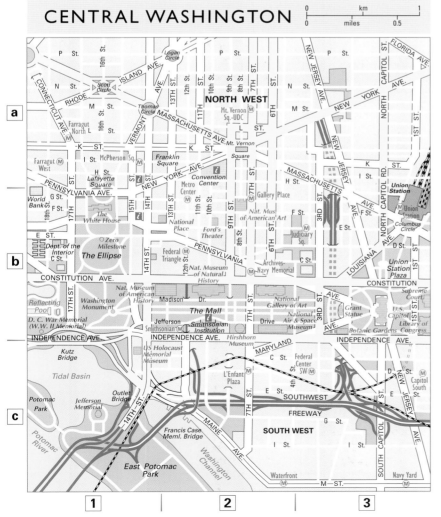

WELLINGTON

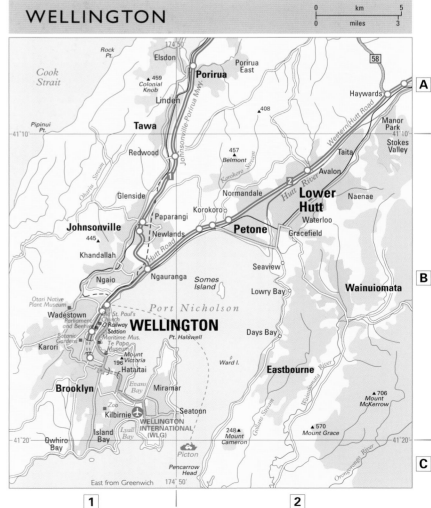

COPYRIGHT PHILIP'S

INDEX TO CITY MAPS

The index contains the names of all the principal places and features shown on the City Maps. Each name is followed by an additional entry in italics giving the name of the City Map within which it is located.

The number in bold type which follows each name refers to the number of the City Map page where that feature or place will be found.

The letter and figure which are immediately after the page number give the grid square on the map within which the feature or place is situated.

The letter represents the latitude and the figure the longitude. The full geographic reference is provided in the border of the City Maps.

The location given is the centre of the city, suburb or feature and is not necessarily the name. Rivers, canals and roads are indexed to their name. Rivers carry the symbol → after their name.

An explanation of the alphabetical order rules and a list of the abbreviations used are to be found at the beginning of the World Map Index.

A

Aalām *Baghdad* **3** B2
Abbey Wood *London* **15** B4
Abcoude *Amsterdam* **2** B2
Âbdin *Cairo* **7** A2
Abeno *Osaka* **23** B2
Aberdeen *Hong Kong* **12** B1
Aberdour *Edinburgh* **11** A2
Aberdour Castle *Edinburgh* **11** A2
Abfanggraben → *Munich* **21** A3
Ablon-sur-Seine *Paris* **24** B3
Abramtsevo *Moscow* **19** B3
Abu Dis *Jerusalem* **13** B2
Abû en Numrus *Cairo* **7** B2
Abu Ghosh *Jerusalem* **13** B1
Acassuso *Buenos Aires* **7** A1
Accotink, L. *Washington* **33** C2
Accotink Cr. → *Washington* **33** B2
Achères *Paris* **24** A1
Acilia *Rome* **26** C1
Aclimação *São Paulo* **27** B2
Acropolis *Athens* **2** B2
Acton *London* **15** A2
Açúcar, Pão de *Rio de Janeiro* **25** B2
Ada Beja *Lisbon* **16** A1
Adams Park *Atlanta* **3** B2
Addiscombe *London* **15** B3
Adelphi *Washington* **33** A4
Aderklaa *Vienna* **32** A3
Adler Planetarium *Chicago* **9** B3
Admiralteyskaya Storona *St. Petersburg* **27** B2
Åffori *Milan* **19** A2
Aflandshage *Copenhagen* **8** B3
Afsarīyeh *Tehran* **31** B2
Agboyi Cr. → *Lagos* **14** A2
Ågerup *Copenhagen* **8** A1
Ågesta *Stockholm* **29** B2
Aghia Marina *Athens* **2** C3
Aghia Paraskevi *Athens* **2** A2
Aghios Dimitrios *Athens* **2** B2
Aghios Ioannis Rendis *Athens* **2** B1
Agincourt *Toronto* **31** A3
Agra Canal *Delhi* **10** B2
Agricola Oriental *Mexico City* **18** B2
Agua Espraiada → *São Paulo* **27** B2
Agualva-Cacem *Lisbon* **16** A1
Agustino, Cerro El *Lima* **14** B3
Ahrensfelde *Berlin* **5** A4
Ahuntsic *Montreal* **20** A1
Ai → *Osaka* **23** A2
Aigremont *Paris* **24** A1
Air View Park *Singapore* **28** A2
Airport West *Melbourne* **18** A1
Ajegunle *Lagos* **14** B2
Aji *Osaka* **23** A1
Ajuda *Lisbon* **16** A1
Akalla *Stockholm* **29** A1
Akasaka *Tokyo* **30** A3
Akbarābād *Tehran* **31** A2
Akershus Castle = Akershus Slott *Oslo* **23** A3
Akershus Slott *Oslo* **23** A3
Al 'Azamīyah *Baghdad* **3** A2
Al Quds = Jerusalem *Jerusalem* **13** B2
Al-Walaja *Jerusalem* **13** B1
Alaguntan *Lagos* **14** B2
Alameda *San Francisco* **26** B3
Alameda Memorial State Beach Park *San Francisco* **26** B3
Albern *Vienna* **32** B2
Albert Park *Melbourne* **18** B1
Alberton *Johannesburg* **13** B2
Albertslund *Copenhagen* **8** B2
Albysjön *Stockholm* **29** B1
Alcantara *Lisbon* **16** A1
Alcatraz I. *San Francisco* **26** B2
Alcobendas *Madrid* **17** A2
Alcorcón *Madrid* **17** B1
Aldershof *Berlin* **5** B4
Aldo Bonzi *Buenos Aires* **7** C1
Aleksandrovskoye *St. Petersburg* **27** B2
Alexander Nevsky Abbey *St. Petersburg* **27** B2
Alexandra *Johannesburg* **13** A2
Alexandra *Singapore* **28** B2
Alexandria *Washington* **33** C3
Alfortville *Paris* **24** B3
Algés *Lisbon* **16** A1
Alhambra *Los Angeles* **16** B4
Alibey → *Istanbul* **12** B1
Alibey Barajı *Istanbul* **12** B1
Alibeyköy *Istanbul* **12** B1
Alimos *Athens* **2** B2
Alipur *Kolkata* **14** B1
Allach *Munich* **21** A1
Allambie Heights *Sydney* **29** A2
Allermuir Hill *Edinburgh* **11** B2
Allstate Arena *Chicago* **9** A1
Allston *Boston* **6** A2
Almada *Lisbon* **16** A2
Almagro *Buenos Aires* **7** B2
Almargem do Bispo *Lisbon* **16** A1
Almirante G. Brown, Parque *Buenos Aires* **7** C2
Almon *Jerusalem* **13** B2
Almond → *Edinburgh* **11** B2
Alna *Oslo* **23** A4
Alnsjøen *Oslo* **23** A4
Alperton *London* **15** A2
Alpine *New York* **22** A2
Alrode *Johannesburg* **13** B2
Alsemberg *Brussels* **6** B1
Alsergrund *Vienna* **32** A2
Alsip *Chicago* **9** C2
Ålsten *Stockholm* **29** B1
Älta *Stockholm* **29** B3
Altadena *Los Angeles* **16** A4
Alte-Donau → *Vienna* **32** A2
Alter Finkenkrug *Berlin* **5** A1
Altes Rathaus *Munich* **21** B2
Altglienicke *Berlin* **5** B4
Altlandsberg *Berlin* **5** A5
Altlandsberg Nord *Berlin* **5** A5
Altmannsdorf *Vienna* **32** B1
Alto da Boa Vista *Rio de Janeiro* **25** B1
Alto da Moóca *São Paulo* **27** B2
Alto do Pina *Lisbon* **16** A2
Altona *Melbourne* **18** B1
Alvik *Stockholm* **29** B1
Älvsjo *Stockholm* **29** B2
Älvvik *Stockholm* **29** A3
Am Hasenbergl *Munich* **21** A2
Am Steinhof *Vienna* **32** A1
Am Wald *Munich* **21** B2
Ama Keng *Singapore* **28** A2
Amadora *Lisbon* **16** A1
Amagasaki *Osaka* **23** A1
Amager *Copenhagen* **8** B3
Amāl Qādisiya *Baghdad* **3** B2
Amalienborg Slot *Copenhagen* **8** A3
Amata *Milan* **19** A1
Ambelokipi *Athens* **2** B2
Ameixoeira *Lisbon* **16** A2
América *São Paulo* **27** B1
American Police Hall of Fame *Miami* **18** B2
American University *Washington* **33** B3
Amin *Baghdad* **3** B2
Aminadav *Jerusalem* **13** B1
Amīrābād *Tehran* **31** A2
Amora *Lisbon* **16** B2
Amoreira *Lisbon* **16** A1
Amper → *Munich* **21** A1
Amstel-Drecht-Kanaal *Amsterdam* **2** B2
Amstelveen *Amsterdam* **2** B2
Amsterdam *Amsterdam* **2** A2
Amsterdam ✈ (AMS) *Amsterdam* **2** B1
Amsterdam-Rijnkanaal *Amsterdam* **2** B3
Amsterdam Zuidoost *Amsterdam* **2** B2
Amsterdamse Bos *Amsterdam* **2** B1
Anacosta → *Washington* **33** B4
Anacostia *Washington* **33** B4
Anadoluhisarı *Istanbul* **12** B2
Anadolukavağı *Istanbul* **12** A2
Anata *Jerusalem* **13** B2
Ancol *Jakarta* **12** A1
'Andalus *Baghdad* **3** B1
Andaraí *Rio de Janeiro* **25** B1
Anderlecht *Brussels* **6** A1
Anderson Park *Atlanta* **3** B2
Andingmen *Beijing* **4** B2
Ang Mo Kio *Singapore* **28** A3
Ängby *Stockholm* **29** A1
Angel I. *San Francisco* **26** A2
Angel Island State Park △ *San Francisco* **26** A2
Angke, Kali → *Jakarta* **12** A1
Angyalföld *Budapest* **7** A2
Anik *Mumbai* **20** A2
Anin *Warsaw* **32** B2
Anjou *Montreal* **20** A2
Annalee Heights *Washington* **33** B2
Annandale *Washington* **33** C2
Anne Frankhuis *Amsterdam* **2** A2
Antony *Paris* **24** B2
Aoyama *Tokyo* **30** B3
Ap Lei Chau *Hong Kong* **12** B1
Apapa *Lagos* **14** B2
Apelacão *Lisbon* **16** A2
Apopka, L. *Orlando* **23** A1
Apoquindo *Santiago* **27** B2
Apterkarskiy Ostrov *St. Petersburg* **27** B2
Ar Kazimiyah *Baghdad* **3** B1
Ar Ram *Jerusalem* **13** A2
Ara → *Tokyo* **30** A4
Arakawa *Tokyo* **30** A3
Arany-hegyi-patak → *Budapest* **7** A2
Aravaca *Madrid* **17** B1
Arbataash *Baghdad* **3** A1
Arc de Triomphe *Paris* **24** A2
Arcadia *Los Angeles* **16** B4
Arcueil *Paris* **24** B2
Arese *Milan* **19** A1
Arganzuela *Madrid* **17** B1
Argenteuil *Paris* **24** A2
Argiroupoli *Athens* **2** B2
Argonne Forest *Chicago* **9** C1
Arima *Tokyo* **30** B2
Arlanda ✈ (ARN) *Stockholm* **29** A1
Arlington *Boston* **6** A1
Arlington *Washington* **33** B3
Arlington Heights *Boston* **6** A1
Arlington Nat. Cemetery *Washington* **33** B3
Armação *Rio de Janeiro* **25** B2
Armadale *Melbourne* **18** B2
Armour Heights *Toronto* **31** A2
Arncliffe *Sydney* **29** B1
Arnold Arboretum *Boston* **6** B2
Árpádföld *Budapest* **7** A3
Arrentela *Lisbon* **16** B2
Arroyo Seco Park *Los Angeles* **16** B3
Årsta *Stockholm* **29** B2
Art Institute *Chicago* **9** B3
Artane *Dublin* **10** A2
Artas *Jerusalem* **13** B2
Arthur's Seat *Edinburgh* **11** B3
Arts, Place des *Montreal* **20** A2
As Shawawra *Jerusalem* **13** B2
Asagaya *Tokyo* **30** A2
Asahi *Osaka* **23** A2
Asakusa *Tokyo* **30** A3
Asati *Kolkata* **14** C1
Aschheim *Munich* **21** A3
Ascot Vale *Melbourne* **18** A1
Ashbridge's Bay Park *Toronto* **31** B3
Ashburn *Chicago* **9** C2
Ashburton *Melbourne* **18** B2
Ashfield *Sydney* **29** B1
Ashford *London* **15** B1
Ashtown *Dublin* **10** A2
Askisto *Helsinki* **11** B1
Askrikefjärden *Stockholm* **29** A3
Asnières *Paris* **24** A2
Aspern *Vienna* **32** A2
Aspern ✈ *Vienna* **32** A3
Assago *Milan* **19** B1
Assendelft *Amsterdam* **2** A1
Assiano *Milan* **19** B1
Astoria *New York* **22** B2
Astrolabe Park *Sydney* **29** B2
Atarot *Jerusalem* **13** A2
Atarot ✈ *Jerusalem* **13** A2
Atghara *Kolkata* **14** B2
Athens = Athina *Athens* **2** B2
Athina *Athens* **2** B2
Athina ✈ (ATH) *Athens* **2** A3
Athínai = Athina *Athens* **2** B2
Athis-Mons *Paris* **24** B3
Athlone *Cape Town* **8** A2
Atholl *Johannesburg* **13** A2
Atīfiya *Baghdad* **3** A2
Atişalen *Istanbul* **12** B1
Atlanta *Atlanta* **3** B2
Atlanta Hartsfield Int. ✈ (ATL) *Atlanta* **3** C2
Atlanta Zoo *Atlanta* **3** B2
Atomium *Brussels* **6** A2
Attiki *Athens* **2** A2
Atzgersdorf *Vienna* **32** B1
Aubervilliers *Paris* **24** A3
Aubing *Munich* **21** B1
Auburndale *Boston* **6** A1
Auchendinny *Edinburgh* **11** B2
Auckland Park *Johannesburg* **13** B2
Auderghem *Brussels* **6** B2
Augustówka *Warsaw* **32** B2
Aulnay-sous-Bois *Paris* **24** A3
Aurelio *Rome* **26** B1
Ausîm *Cairo* **7** A1
Austerlitz, Gare d' *Paris* **24** A3
Austin *Chicago* **9** B2
Avalon *Wellington* **33** B2
Avedøre *Copenhagen* **8** B2
Avellaneda *Buenos Aires* **7** C2
Avenel *Washington* **33** B4
Avondale *Chicago* **9** B2
Avondale Heights *Melbourne* **18** A1
Avtovo *St. Petersburg* **27** B1
Ayazağa *Istanbul* **12** B1
Ayer Chawan, Pulau *Singapore* **28** B2
Ayer Merbau, Pulau *Singapore* **28** B2
Azabu *Tokyo* **30** B3
Azcapotzalco *Mexico City* **18** B1
Azteca, Estadia *Mexico City* **18** C2
Azucar, Cerro Pan de *Santiago* **27** A1

B

Baambrugge *Amsterdam* **2** B2
Baba Ch. *Karachi* **13** B1
Baba I. *Karachi* **13** B1
Babarpur *Delhi* **10** A2
Babushkin *Moscow* **19** A3
Back B. *Mumbai* **20** B1
Baclaran *Manila* **17** B2
Bacoor *Manila* **17** C1
Bacoor B. *Manila* **17** C1
Badalona *Barcelona* **4** A2
Badhoevedorp *Amsterdam* **2** A1
Badli *Delhi* **10** A1
Bærum *Oslo* **23** A2
Bağcılar *Istanbul* **12** B1
Bággio *Milan* **19** B1
Bāgh-e-Feyz *Tehran* **31** A1
Baghdād *Baghdad* **3** A2
Baghdad al Muthana ✈ *Baghdad* **3** B2
Baghdad Int. ✈ (SDA) *Baghdad* **3** B1
Bagmari *Kolkata* **14** B2
Bagneux *Paris* **24** B2
Bagnolet *Paris* **24** A3
Bagsværd *Copenhagen* **8** A2
Bagsværd Sø *Copenhagen* **8** A2
Baguiati *Kolkata* **14** B2
Bagumbayan *Manila* **17** C2
Baha'i Temple *Chicago* **9** A2
Bahçeköy *Istanbul* **12** A1
Bahçelıevler *Istanbul* **12** B1
Bahtîm *Cairo* **7** A2
Baile Atha Cliath = Dublin *Dublin* **10** A2
Baileys Crossroads *Washington* **33** B3
Bailly *Paris* **24** A1
Bairro Lopes *Lisbon* **16** A2
Baisha *Guangzhou* **11** B2
Baiyun Hill *Guangzhou* **11** B2
Baiyun Int. ✈ (CAN) *Guangzhou* **11** A2
Bakırköy *Istanbul* **12** C1
Bal Harbor *Miami* **18** A2
Balara *Manila* **17** B2
Baldia *Karachi* **13** A1
Baldoyle *Dublin* **10** A3
Baldwin, L. *Orlando* **23** A3
Baldwin Hills *Los Angeles* **16** B2
Baldwin Hills Res. *Los Angeles* **16** B2
Balgowlah *Sydney* **29** A2
Balgowlah Heights *Sydney* **29** A2
Balham *London* **15** B3
Bali *Kolkata* **14** B1
Baliganja *Kolkata* **14** B2
Balingsnäs *Stockholm* **29** B2
Balingsta *Stockholm* **29** B2
Balintawak *Manila* **17** B1
Ballerup *Copenhagen* **8** A2
Ballinteer *Dublin* **10** B2
Ballyboden *Dublin* **10** B2
Ballybrack *Dublin* **10** B3
Ballyfermot *Dublin* **10** A1
Ballymorefinn Hill *Dublin* **10** B1
Ballymun *Dublin* **10** A2
Balmain *Sydney* **29** B2
Baluhati *Kolkata* **14** B1
Balvanera *Buenos Aires* **7** B2
Balwyn *Melbourne* **18** A2
Balwyn North *Melbourne* **18** A2
Banática *Lisbon* **16** A1
Bandra *Mumbai* **20** A1
Bandra Pt. *Mumbai* **20** A1
Bang Kapi *Bangkok* **3** B2
Bang Na *Bangkok* **3** B2
Bangbae *Seoul* **27** C1
Bangkhen *Bangkok* **3** A2
Bangkok *Bangkok* **3** B2
Bangkok Noi *Bangkok* **3** B1
Bangkok Yai *Bangkok* **3** B1
Banglo *Kolkata* **14** B1
Bangrak *Bangkok* **3** B2
Bangsu *Bangkok* **3** B2
Banks, C. *Sydney* **29** C2
Banksmeadow *Sydney* **29** B2
Banstala *Kolkata* **14** B2
Bantra *Kolkata* **14** B1
Baoshan *Shanghai* **28** A1
Bar Giyora *Jerusalem* **13** B1
Barahanagar *Kolkata* **14** B2
Barajas *Madrid* **17** B2
Barajas, Madrid ✈ (MAD) *Madrid* **17** B2
Barakpur *Kolkata* **14** A2
Barcarena *Lisbon* **16** A1
Barcarena, Rib. de → *Lisbon* **16** A1
Barcelona *Barcelona* **4** A2
Barcelona-Prat ✈ (BCN) *Barcelona* **4** B1
Barceloneta *Barcelona* **4** A2
Barcroft, L. *Washington* **33** B3
Barking *London* **15** A4
Barkingside *London* **15** A4
Barnes *London* **15** B2
Barnet *London* **15** A2
Barra Andai *Karachi* **13** B2
Barra Funda *São Paulo* **27** B2
Barracas *Buenos Aires* **7** B2
Barrackpur = Barakpur *Kolkata* **14** A2
Barranco *Lima* **14** B2
Barreiro *Lisbon* **16** B2
Barreto *Rio de Janeiro* **25** B2
Bartala *Kolkata* **14** B1
Barton Park *Sydney* **29** B1
Bartyki *Warsaw* **32** C2
Basus *Cairo* **7** A2
Batanagar *Kolkata* **14** B1
Bath Beach *New York* **22** C1
Bath I. *Karachi* **13** B2
Batir *Jerusalem* **13** B1
Batok, Bukit *Singapore* **28** A2
Battersea *London* **15** B3
Bauman *Moscow* **19** B3
Baumgarten *Vienna* **32** A1
Bay, L. *Orlando* **23** A2
Bay Harbour Islands *Miami* **18** A2
Bay Hill *Orlando* **23** B1
Bay Ridge *New York* **22** C1
Bayit Va-Gan *Jerusalem* **13** B2
Bayonne *New York* **22** B1
Bayrampaşa *Istanbul* **12** B1
Bayshore *San Francisco* **26** B2
Bayt Lahm *Jerusalem* **13** B2
Bayview *San Francisco* **26** B2
Bāzār *Tehran* **31** A2
Beacon Hill *Hong Kong* **12** A2
Beato *Lisbon* **16** A2
Beaumont *Dublin* **10** A2
Beaumonte Heights *Toronto* **31** A1
Bebek *Istanbul* **12** B2
Běchovice *Prague* **25** B3
Beck L. *Chicago* **9** A1
Beckenham *London* **15** B3
Beckton *London* **15** A4
Becontree *London* **15** A4
Beddington Corner *London* **15** B3
Bedford *Boston* **6** A1
Bedford Park *Chicago* **9** C2
Bedford Park *New York* **22** A2
Bedford Stuyvesant *New York* **22** B2
Bedford View *Johannesburg* **13** B2
Bedok *Singapore* **28** B3
Bedok, Res. *Singapore* **28** A3
Beersel *Brussels* **6** B1
Behala *Kolkata* **14** B1
Bei Hai *Beijing* **4** B2
Beicai *Shanghai* **28** B2
Beijing *Beijing* **4** B1
Beit Duqu *Jerusalem* **13** A1
Beit Ghur at-Taht *Jerusalem* **13** A1
Beit Ghur el-Fawqa *Jerusalem* **13** A1
Beit Hanina *Jerusalem* **13** B2
Beit Ij'za *Jerusalem* **13** A1
Beit Iksa *Jerusalem* **13** B2
Beit I'nan *Jerusalem* **13** A1
Beit Jala *Jerusalem* **13** B2
Beit Lekhem = Bayt Lahm *Jerusalem* **13** B2
Beit Liqya *Jerusalem* **13** A1
Beit Nekofa *Jerusalem* **13** B1
Beit Sahur *Jerusalem* **13** B2
Beit Sofafa *Jerusalem* **13** B2
Beit Surik *Jerusalem* **13** B1
Beit Ur al-Fawqa *Jerusalem* **13** A1
Beit Zayit *Jerusalem* **13** B1
Beitaipingzhuan *Beijing* **4** B1
Beitar Ilit *Jerusalem* **13** B1
Beitin *Jerusalem* **13** A2
Beitsun *Guangzhou* **11** B2
Beitunya *Jerusalem* **13** A2
Beixing Jing Park *Shanghai* **28** B1
Békásmegyer *Budapest* **7** A2
Bekkelaget *Oslo* **23** A3
Bekkestua *Oslo* **23** A2
Bel Air *Los Angeles* **16** B2
Bela Vista *São Paulo* **27** B2
Bélanger *Montreal* **20** A1
Belas *Lisbon* **16** A1
Beleghata *Kolkata* **14** B2
Belém *Lisbon* **16** A1
Belém, Torre de *Lisbon* **16** A1
Belènzinho *São Paulo* **27** B2
Belgachiya *Kolkata* **14** B2
Belgharia *Kolkata* **14** B2
Belgrano *Buenos Aires* **7** B2
Bell *Los Angeles* **16** C3
Bell Gardens *Los Angeles* **16** C4
Bellavista *Lima* **14** B2
Bellavista *Santiago* **27** C2
Belle Harbor *New York* **22** C2
Belle Isle *Orlando* **23** B2
Belle View *Washington* **33** B2
Bellingham *London* **15** B3
Bellwood *Chicago* **9** B1
Belmont *Boston* **6** A1
Belmont *London* **15** A2
Belmont, Mt. *Wellington* **33** B2
Belmont Cragin *Chicago* **9** B2
Belmont Harbor *Chicago* **9** B3
Belmore *Sydney* **29** B1
Belur *Kolkata* **14** B2
Belvedere *Atlanta* **3** B3
Belvedere *London* **15** B4
Belvedere *San Francisco* **26** A2
Belyayevo Bogorodskoye *Moscow* **19** C2
Bemowo *Warsaw* **32** B1
Benaki Museum *Athens* **2** B2
Bendale *Toronto* **31** A3
Benefica *Rio de Janeiro* **25** B1
Benfica *Lisbon* **16** A1
Benito Juárez *Mexico City* **18** B2
Benito Juárez, Int. ✈ (MEX) *Mexico City* **18** B2
Bensonhurst *New York* **22** C2
Berchem-Ste-Agathe *Brussels* **6** A1
Berg am Laim *Munich* **21** B2
Bergenfield *New York* **22** A2
Bergham *Munich* **21** B2
Bergvliet *Cape Town* **8** B1
Beri *Barcelona* **4** A1
Berkeley *San Francisco* **26** A3
Berlin *Berlin* **5** A3
Berlin Dom *Berlin* **5** A3
Berlin Tegel ✈ (TXL) *Berlin* **5** A2
Berlin Tempelhof ✈ (THF) *Berlin* **5** B3
Bermondsey *London* **15** B3
Bernabeu, Estadio *Madrid* **17** B1
Bernal Heights *San Francisco* **26** B2
Berwyn *Chicago* **9** B2
Berwyn Heights *Washington* **33** B4
Besiktas *Istanbul* **12** B2
Besós → *Barcelona* **4** A2
Bessie, L. *Orlando* **23** B1
Bet Horon *Jerusalem* **13** A1
Bethesda *Washington* **33** B3
Bethlehem = Bayt Lahm *Jerusalem* **13** B2
Bethnal Green *London* **15** A3
Betor *Kolkata* **14** B1
Beulah *Orlando* **23** A1
Beulah, L. *Orlando* **23** A1
Beverley Hills *Sydney* **29** B1
Beverley Park *Sydney* **29** B1
Beverly *Chicago* **9** C3
Beverly Arts Center *Chicago* **9** C2
Beverly Glen *Los Angeles* **16** B2
Beverly Hills *Los Angeles* **16** B2
Beverly Hills -Morgan Park Historic District *Chicago* **9** C2
Bexley *Sydney* **29** B1
Bexley □ *London* **15** B4
Bexleyheath *London* **15** B4
Beykoz *Istanbul* **12** B2
Beylerbeyi *Istanbul* **12** B2
Beyoğlu *Istanbul* **12** B1
Bezons *Paris* **24** A2
Bezuidenhout Park *Johannesburg* **13** B2
Bhadrakali *Kolkata* **14** A2
Bhalswa *Delhi* **10** A2
Bhambo Khan Qarmati *Karachi* **13** B2
Bhatsala *Kolkata* **14** B1
Bhawanipur *Kolkata* **14** B2
Bhendkhal *Mumbai* **20** B2
Bhuleshwar *Mumbai* **20** B1
Białołeka Dworska *Warsaw* **32** B2
Bicentennial Park *Los Angeles* **16** B4
Bicentennial Park *Sydney* **29** B1
Bickley *London* **15** B4
Bicutan *Manila* **17** C2
Bidhan Nagar *Kolkata* **14** B2
Bidu *Jerusalem* **13** B1
Bielany *Warsaw* **32** B1
Bielawa *Warsaw* **32** C2
Biesdorf *Berlin* **5** A4
Bièvre → *Paris* **24** B1
Bièvres *Paris* **24** B2
Big Sand Lake *Orlando* **23** B2
Bilston *Edinburgh* **11** B2
Binacayan *Manila* **17** C1
Binondo *Manila* **17** B1
Bintaro Jaya *Jakarta* **12** B1
Bir Nabala *Jerusalem* **13** A2
Birak el Kiyam *Cairo* **7** A1
Birch Cliff *Toronto* **31** A3
Birkenstein *Berlin* **5** A5
Birkholz *Berlin* **5** A4
Birkholzaue *Berlin* **5** A4
Birrarrung Park *Melbourne* **18** A2
Biscayne Park *Miami* **18** A2
Bishop Lavis *Cape Town* **8** A2
Bishopscourt *Cape Town* **8** A1
Bispebjerg *Copenhagen* **8** A3
Bittsevsky Forest Park *Moscow* **19** C2
Björknäs *Stockholm* **29** B3
Black Cr. → *Toronto* **31** A2
Black Creek Pioneer Village *Toronto* **31** A1
Blackfen *London* **15** B4
Blackheath *London* **15** B4
Blackrock *Dublin* **10** B2
Bladensburg *Washington* **33** B4
Blair Village *Atlanta* **3** C2
Blairgowrie *Johannesburg* **13** A2
Blake House *Boston* **6** B2
Blakehurst *Sydney* **29** B1
Blakstad *Oslo* **23** B1
Blanche, L. *Orlando* **23** B1
Blankenburg *Berlin* **5** A3
Blankenfelde *Berlin* **5** A3
Blizne *Warsaw* **32** B1
Blota *Warsaw* **32** C3
Blue Island *Chicago* **9** D2
Blue Mosque = Sultanahme Camil *Istanbul* **12** B1
Bluebell *Dublin* **10** B1
Bluff Hd. *Hong Kong* **12** B2
Bluffers Park *Toronto* **31** A3
Blumberg *Berlin* **5** A4
Blunt Pt. *San Francisco* **26** A2
Blutenberg *Munich* **21** B1
Blylaget *Oslo* **23** B3
Boa Vista, Alto do *Rio de Janeiro* **25** B1
Boardwalk *New York* **22** C3
Boavista *Lisbon* **16** A2
Bobigny *Paris* **24** A3
Bocanegra *Lima* **14** B2
Boedo *Buenos Aires* **7** B2
Bogenhausen *Munich* **21** B2
Boggy Creek Swamp *Orlando* **23** B2
Bogorodskoye *Moscow* **19** B3
Bogota *New York* **22** A1
Bogstadvatnet *Oslo* **23** A2
Bohnsdorf *Berlin* **5** B4
Bois-Colombes *Paris* **24** A2
Bois-d'Arcy *Paris* **24** B1
Boissy-St-Léger *Paris* **24** B4
Boldinasco *Milan* **19** B1
Bøler *Oslo* **23** A4
Bollate *Milan* **19** A1
Bollebeek *Brussels* **6** A1
Bollensdorf *Berlin* **5** A5
Bollmora *Stockholm* **29** B3
Bolshaya Okhta *St. Petersburg* **27** B2
Bolton *Atlanta* **3** B2
Bom Retiro *São Paulo* **27** B2
Bombay = Mumbai *Mumbai* **20** B2
Bondi *Sydney* **29** B2
Bondy *Paris* **24** A3
Bondy, Forêt de *Paris* **24** A4
Bonifacio Monument *Manila* **17** B1
Bonneuil-sur-Marne *Paris* **24** B4
Bonnington *Edinburgh* **11** B1
Bonnyrigg and Lasswade *Edinburgh* **11** B3
Bonsucesso *Rio de Janeiro* **25** B1
Bonteheuwel *Cape Town* **8** A2
Boo *Stockholm* **29** A3
Booterstown *Dublin* **10** B2
Borisovo *Moscow* **19** C3
Borle *Mumbai* **20** A2
Boronia Park *Sydney* **29** A1
Bosmont *Johannesburg* **13** B1
Bosön *Stockholm* **29** A3
Bosporus = İstanbul Boğazı *Istanbul* **12** B2
Bostancı *Istanbul* **12** C2
Boston *Boston* **6** A2
Boston Common *Boston* **6** A2
Boston Logan Int. ✈ (BOS) *Boston* **6** A2
Botafogo *Rio de Janeiro* **25** B1
Botany *Sydney* **29** B2
Botany B. *Sydney* **29** B2
Botany Bay Nat. Park △ *Sydney* **29** B2
Botič → *Prague* **25** B3
Botica Sete *Lisbon* **16** A1
Boucherville *Montreal* **20** A3
Boucherville, Îs. de *Montreal* **20** A3
Bougival *Paris* **24** A1
Boulder Pt. *Hong Kong* **12** B1
Boulogne, Bois de *Paris* **24** A2
Boulogne-Billancourt *Paris* **24** A2
Bourg-la-Reine *Paris* **24** B2
Bouviers *Paris* **24** B1
Bovenkerk *Amsterdam* **2** B2
Bovenkerker Polder *Amsterdam* **2** B2
Bovisa *Milan* **19** A2
Bow *London* **15** A3
Boyacıköy *Istanbul* **12** B2
Boyd Conservation Area *Toronto* **31** A1
Boyle Heights *Los Angeles* **16** B3
Braepark *Edinburgh* **11** B2
Braid *Edinburgh* **11** B2
Bramley *Johannesburg* **13** A2
Brandeis University *Boston* **6** A1
Brandenburger Tor *Berlin* **5** A3
Brani, Pulau *Singapore* **28** B3
Branik *Prague* **25** B2
Brännkyrka *Stockholm* **29** B2
Brás *São Paulo* **27** B2
Brasilândia *São Paulo* **27** A1
Brateyevo *Moscow* **19** C3
Braybrook *Melbourne* **18** A1
Brázdim *Prague* **25** A3
Breakheart Reservation *Boston* **6** A2
Brede *Copenhagen* **8** A3
Breezy Point *New York* **22** C2
Breitenlee *Vienna* **32** A3
Breña *Lima* **14** B2
Brent □ *London* **15** A2
Brent Res. *London* **15** A2
Brentford *London* **15** B2
Brentwood Park *Los Angeles* **16** B2
Brera *Milan* **19** B2
Bresso *Milan* **19** A2
Brevik *Stockholm* **29** A3
Břevnov *Prague* **25** B2
Brickyard, The *Chicago* **9** B2
Bridgeport *Chicago* **9** B3
Bridgetown *Cape Town* **8** A2
Bridgeview *Chicago* **9** C2
Brighton *Boston* **6** A2
Brighton *Melbourne* **18** B1
Brighton Beach *New York* **22** C2
Brighton le Sands *Sydney* **29** B1
Brighton Park *Chicago* **9** C2
Brightwood *Washington* **33** B3
Brigittenau *Vienna* **32** A2
Brimbank Park *Melbourne* **18** A1
Brisbane *San Francisco* **26** B2
Britz *Berlin* **5** B3
Brixton *London* **15** B3
Broadmeadows *Melbourne* **18** A1
Broadmoor *San Francisco* **26** B2
Broadview *Chicago* **9** B1
Brockley *London* **15** B3
Bródno *Warsaw* **32** B2
Bródnowski, Kanal *Warsaw* **32** B2
Broek *Amsterdam* **2** A2
Bromley □ *London* **15** B4
Bromley Common *London* **15** B4
Bromma *Stockholm* **29** A1
Bromma ✈ *Stockholm* **29** A1
Brøndby Strand *Copenhagen* **8** B2
Brøndbyøster *Copenhagen* **8** B2
Brøndbyvester *Copenhagen* **8** B2
Brondesbury *London* **15** A2
Brønnøya *Oslo* **23** A2
Brønshøj *Copenhagen* **8** A2
Bronxville *New York* **22** A3
Brookfield *Chicago* **9** C1
Brookhaven *Atlanta* **3** A2
Brookline *Boston* **6** B2
Brooklyn *Cape Town* **8** A1
Brooklyn *New York* **22** C2
Brooklyn *Wellington* **33** B1
Brooklyn Heights *New York* **22** B2
Brookmont *Washington* **33** B3
Brossard *Montreal* **20** B3
Brou-sur-Chantereine *Paris* **24** A4
Brown *Toronto* **31** A3
Broyhill Park *Washington* **33** B2
Brughério *Milan* **19** A2
Brunswick *Melbourne* **18** A1
Brussegem *Brussels* **6** A1
Brussel *Brussels* **6** A2
Brussel ✈ (BRU) *Brussels* **6** A2
Brussels = Brussel *Brussels* **6** A2
Bruxelles = Brussel *Brussels* **6** A2
Bruzzano *Milan* **19** A2
Bry-sur-Marne *Paris* **24** A4
Bryan, L. *Orlando* **23** B2
Bryanston *Johannesburg* **13** A1
Bryn *Oslo* **23** A1
Brzeziny *Warsaw* **32** B2
Bubeneč *Prague* **25** B2
Buc *Paris* **24** B1
Buchenhain *Munich* **21** B1
Buchholz *Berlin* **5** A3
Buckhead *Atlanta* **3** A2
Buckingham Palace *London* **15** A3
Buckow *Berlin* **5** B3
Buda *Budapest* **7** A2
Buda Castle = Budavāripalota *Budapest* **7** A2
Budafok *Budapest* **7** B2
Budaörs *Budapest* **7** B1
Budapest *Budapest* **7** B2
Budapest ✈ (BUD) *Budapest* **7** B3
Budatétény *Budapest* **7** B2
Budavāripalota *Budapest* **7** A2
Buddinge *Copenhagen* **8** A3
Buena Ventura Lakes *Orlando* **23** B2
Buena Vista *San Francisco* **26** B2
Buenos Aires *Buenos Aires* **7** B2
Bufalotta *Rome* **26** B2
Bugio *Lisbon* **16** B1
Buiksloot *Amsterdam* **2** A2
Buitenveldert *Amsterdam* **2** B2
Buizingen *Brussels* **6** B1
Bukhansan *Seoul* **27** B1
Bukit Panjang Nature Reserve *Singapore* **28** A2
Bukit Timah Nature Reserve *Singapore* **28** A2
Bukum, Pulau *Singapore* **28** B2
Bûlâq *Cairo* **7** A2
Bule *Manila* **17** C2
Bulim *Singapore* **28** A2
Bullen Park *Melbourne* **18** A2
Bund, The *Shanghai* **28** B1
Bundoora North *Melbourne* **18** A2
Bundoora Park *Melbourne* **18** A2
Bunker Hill Memorial *Boston* **6** A2
Bunker I. *Karachi* **13** B1
Bunkyō *Tokyo* **30** A3
Bunnefjorden *Oslo* **23** A3
Buona Vista Park *Singapore* **28** B2
Burbank *Chicago* **9** C2
Burbank *Los Angeles* **16** A3
Burden, L. *Orlando* **23** B1
Burlington *Boston* **6** A1
Burnham Park *Chicago* **9** C3
Burnham Park Harbor *Chicago* **9** B3
Burnhamthorpe *Toronto* **31** B1
Burnt Oak *London* **15** A2
Burntisland *Edinburgh* **11** A2
Burnwynd *Edinburgh* **11** B1
Burqa *Jerusalem* **13** A2
Burtus *Cairo* **7** A1
Burudvatn *Oslo* **23** A2
Burwood *Sydney* **29** B1
Bushwick *New York* **22** B2
Bushy Park *London* **15** B1
Butantã *São Paulo* **27** B1
Butcher I. *Mumbai* **20** B2
Butler, L. *Orlando* **23** B1
Butts Corner *Washington* **33** C2
Büyükdere *Istanbul* **12** B2
Byculla *Mumbai* **20** B2
Bygdøy *Oslo* **23** A3

C

C.B.S. Fox Studios *Los Angeles* **16** B2
C.N.N. Center *Atlanta* **3** B2
C.N. Tower *Toronto* **31** B2
Caballito *Buenos Aires* **7** B2
Cabin John *Washington* **33** B2
Cabin John Regional Park △ *Washington* **33** A2
Cabinteely *Dublin* **10** B3
Cabra *Dublin* **10** A2
Cabuçú de Baixo → *São Paulo* **27** A1
Cabuçú de Cima → *São Paulo* **27** A2
Cachan *Paris* **24** B2
Cachoeira, Rib. da → *São Paulo* **27** B1
Cacilhas *Lisbon* **16** A2

Golestan Palace 35

Cahuenga Park Los Angeles 16 B3
Cain, L. Orlando 23 B2
Cairo = El Qâhira Cairo 7 A2
Cairo Int. ✈ (CAI) Cairo 7 A3
Caju Rio de Janeiro 25 B1
Čakovice Prague 25 B3
Calcutta = Kolkata Kolkata 14 B2
California Inst. of Tech. Los Angeles 16 B4
California Los Angeles, University of Los Angeles 16 B2
California State University Los Angeles 16 B3
Callao Lima 14 B2
Caloocan Manila 17 B1
Calumet L. Chicago 9 C3
Calumet Park Chicago 9 C3
Calumet Sag Channel → Chicago 9 C2
Calvairate Milan 19 B2
Camarate Lisbon 16 A2
Camaroes Lisbon 16 A1
Camberwell London 15 B3
Camberwell Melbourne 18 B2
Cambridge Boston 6 A2
Cambuci São Paulo 27 B2
Camden □ London 15 A3
Cameron, Mt. Wellington 33 B2
Çamlıca Istanbul 12 B2
Camp Springs Washington 33 C4
Campamento Madrid 17 B1
Campbellfield Melbourne 18 A1
Camperdown Sydney 29 B2
Campo, Casa de Madrid 17 B1
Campo F.C. Barcelona Barcelona 4 A1
Campo Grando Lisbon 16 A2
Campo Pequeño Lisbon 16 A2
Campolide Lisbon 16 A2
Camps Bay Cape Town 8 A1
C'an San Joan Barcelona 4 A2
Cañacao B. Manila 17 C1
Canarsie New York 22 C2
Candiac Montreal 20 B3
Caneças Lisbon 16 A1
Canillas Madrid 17 B2
Canillejas Madrid 17 B2
Canning Town London 15 A4
Canteras de Vallecas Madrid 17 B2
Canterbury Melbourne 18 A2
Canterbury Sydney 29 B1
Canton = Guangzhou Guangzhou 11 B2
Caoheijing Shanghai 28 B1
Capão Redondo São Paulo 27 B1
Caparica Lisbon 16 A2
Caparica, Costa da Lisbon 16 B1
Cape Flats Cape Town 8 B2
Cape Peninsula △ Cape Town 8 A1
Cape Town Cape Town 8 A1
Cape Town Int. ✈ (CPT) Cape Town 8 A2
Capitol Heights Washington 33 B4
Captain Cook Bridge Sydney 29 C1
Captain Cook Landing Place Park Sydney 29 C2
Capuchos Lisbon 16 B1
Carabanchel Alto Madrid 17 B1
Carabanchel Bajo Madrid 17 B1
Carapachay Buenos Aires 7 B1
Caraza Buenos Aires 7 C2
Caridad Manila 17 C1
Carioca, Sa. da Rio de Janeiro 25 B1
Carlstadt New York 22 A1
Carlton Melbourne 18 A1
Carmen de Huechuraba Santiago 27 B1
Carmen de la Legua Lima 14 B2
Carnaxide Lisbon 16 A1
Carnegie Melbourne 18 B2
Carnide Lisbon 16 A1
Carol City Miami 18 A1
Carrascal Santiago 27 B1
Carrickmines Dublin 10 B3
Carrières-sous-Bois Paris 24 A1
Carrières-sous-Poissy Paris 24 A1
Carrières-sur-Seine Paris 24 A2
Carrigeen B. Dublin 10 A3
Cartierville Montreal 20 A1
Casa Loma Toronto 31 A2
Casa Verde São Paulo 27 A1
Casal Morena Rome 26 C2
Casalotti Rome 26 B1
Cascade Heights Atlanta 3 B2
Castel di Leva Rome 26 C2
Castel Sant'Angelo Rome 26 B1
Castleknock Dublin 10 A1
Castleton Corners New York 22 C1
Catete Rio de Janeiro 25 B1
Catford London 15 B3
Catherine, L. Orlando 23 B2
Caulfield Melbourne 18 B2
Cavite Manila 17 C1
Caxias Lisbon 16 A1
Çebecci Istanbul 12 B1
Cecchignola Rome 26 C2
Cecilienhof, Schloss Berlin 5 B1
Cedar Grove Atlanta 3 C3
Cedarvale Park Toronto 31 A2
Cempaka Putih Jakarta 12 B2
Çengelköy Istanbul 12 B2
Cengkareng Jakarta 12 A1
Centennial Olympic Park Atlanta 3 B2
Centennial Park Sydney 29 B2
Center Hill Atlanta 3 B2
Centocelle Rome 26 B2
Central, Gare Montreal 20 B2
Central Park New York 22 B2
Cerdanyola del Vallès Barcelona 4 A1
Cerillos Santiago 27 B1
Cerro de la Estrella, Parque Nacional △ Mexico City 18 B2
Cerro de los Angeles Madrid 17 C1
Cerro Navia Santiago 27 B1
Cesano Boscone Milan 19 B1
Cesate Milan 19 A1
Cha Kwo Ling Hong Kong 12 B2
Chacarrita Buenos Aires 7 B2
Chadwell Heath London 15 A4
Chai Chee Singapore 28 B3
Chai Wan Hong Kong 12 B2
Chai Wan Kok Hong Kong 12 A1
Chakdaha Kolkata 14 C1
Chamartín Madrid 17 B1
Chamberí Madrid 17 B1
Chambourcy Paris 24 A1
Champigny-sur-Marne Paris 24 B4
Champlain, Pont Montreal 20 B2
Champs-sur-Marne Paris 24 A4
Chamrail Kolkata 14 B1
Chanakyapuri Delhi 10 B2
Chanditala Kolkata 14 A1
Changfeng Park Shanghai 28 B1
Changhai = Shanghai Shanghai 28 B2
Changi Singapore 28 A3
Changi, Singapore ✈ (SIN) Singapore 28 A3
Changning Shanghai 28 B1
Chantereine Paris 24 A4
Chantian Guangzhou 11 A2
Chaoyang Beijing 4 B2
Chaoyangmen Beijing 4 B2
Chapelizod Dublin 10 A1
Chapultepec, Bosque de Mexico City 18 B1
Chapultepec, Castillo de Mexico City 18 B1
Charenton-le-Pont Paris 24 B3
Charleroi, Kanal de → Brussels 6 B1
Charles Bridge = Karlův most Prague 25 B2
Charles Gates Dawes House Chicago 9 A2
Charlestown Boston 6 A2
Charlottenburg Berlin 5 A2
Charlottenburg, Schloss Berlin 5 A2
Charlottenlund Copenhagen 8 A3
Charlton London 15 B4
Charneca Lisbon 16 A2
Chase, L. Orlando 23 B1
Châteaufort Paris 24 B1
Châtenay-Malabry Paris 24 B2
Chatham Chicago 9 C3
Châtillon Paris 24 B2
Chatou Paris 24 A1
Chatpur Kolkata 14 B2
Chatswood Sydney 29 A2
Chatuchak Bangkok 3 B2
Chatuchak Park Bangkok 3 B2
Chauki Karachi 13 A1
Chavarria Lima 14 B2
Chaville Paris 24 B2
Chayang Seoul 27 B2
Chelles Paris 24 A4
Chelles, Canal de Paris 24 A4
Chells-le-Pin ✈ Paris 24 A4
Chelsea Boston 6 A2
Chelsea London 15 B2
Chembur Mumbai 20 A2
Chennevières-sur-Marne Paris 24 B4
Cheongdam Seoul 27 B2
Cheonho Seoul 27 B2
Cheops Cairo 7 B1
Chertanovka → Moscow 19 C2
Chertanovo Moscow 19 C2
Cheryomushki Moscow 19 B2
Chestnut Hill Boston 6 B1
Cheung Sha Wan Hong Kong 12 A1
Cheverly Washington 33 B4
Chevilly-Larue Paris 24 B3
Chevry-Cossigny Paris 24 B4
Chevy Chase Washington 33 B3
Chhatrapati Shivaji, Mumbai ✈ (BOM) Mumbai 20 A2
China Keng Singapore 28 A3
Chiaravalle Milanese Milan 19 B2
Chicago Chicago 9 B3
Chicago, University of Chicago 9 C3
Chicago Harbor Chicago 9 B3
Chicago Lawn Chicago 9 C2
Chicago-Midway ✈ (MDW) Chicago 9 C2
Chicago O'Hare Int. ✈ (ORD) Chicago 9 B1
Chicago Ridge Chicago 9 C2
Chicago River, North Branch → Chicago 9 B2
Chicago Sanitary and Ship Canal Chicago 9 C2
Chicago State University Chicago 9 C3
Chicago Zoo Chicago 9 B1
Chienzui Guangzhou 11 A3
Chik Sha Hong Kong 12 B2
Child's Hill London 15 A2
Chilla Saroda Delhi 10 B2
Chillum Washington 33 B4
Chilly-Mazarin Paris 24 B2
China Basin San Francisco 26 B2
Chingupota Kolkata 14 C1
Chinna Cr. → Karachi 13 B2
Chiquihuite, Cerro Mexico City 18 A2
Chislehurst London 15 B4
Chiswick London 15 B2
Chiswick House London 15 B2
Chitose Tokyo 30 B2
Chitralada Palace Bangkok 3 B2
Chiyoda Tokyo 30 A3
Choa Chu Kang Singapore 28 A2
Chodov u Prahy Prague 25 B3
Chōfu Tokyo 30 B2
Choisy-le-Roi Paris 24 B3
Cholupice Prague 25 C2
Chom Thong Bangkok 3 B1
Chong Pang Singapore 28 A2
Chongwen Beijing 4 B2
Chorrillos Lima 14 C2
Chowpatty Beach Mumbai 20 B1
Christianshavn Copenhagen 8 A3
Chrzanów Warsaw 32 B1
Chuen Lung Hong Kong 12 A1
Chuk Kok Hong Kong 12 A2
Chulalongkorn Univ. Bangkok 3 B2
Chuō Tokyo 30 A3
Church End London 15 A2
Churchtown Dublin 10 B2
Ciampino Rome 26 C2
Ciampino ✈ Rome 26 C2
Cicero Chicago 9 B2
Cilandak Jakarta 12 B1
Cilincing Jakarta 12 A2
Ciliwung → Jakarta 12 B2
Čimice Prague 25 B2
Cinecittà Rome 26 B2
Cinisello Bálsamo Milan 19 A2
Cinkota Budapest 7 A3
Cipete Jakarta 12 B1
Città degli Studi Milan 19 B2
Città del Vaticano = Vatican City ■ Rome 26 B1
City, The London 15 A3
City of the Dead Cairo 7 A2
Ciudad de México Mexico City 18 B2
Ciudad Deportiva Mexico City 18 B2
Ciudad Fin de Semana Madrid 17 B2
Ciudad General Belgrano Buenos Aires 7 C1
Ciudad Lineál Madrid 17 B2
Ciudad Satélite Mexico City 18 A1
Ciudad Universitaria Buenos Aires 7 B2
Ciudad Universitaria Mexico City 18 C1
Claireville Res. Toronto 31 A1
Clamart Paris 24 B2
Clapham London 15 B3
Clapton London 15 A3
Claremont Cape Town 8 A1
Clayhall London 15 A4
Clear, L. Orlando 23 A2
Clermiston Edinburgh 11 B2
Clichy Paris 24 A2
Clichy-sous-Bois Paris 24 A4
Cliffside Toronto 31 A3
Cliffside Park New York 22 B2
Clifton Cape Town 8 A1
Clifton Karachi 13 B2
Clifton New York 22 C1
Clifton Beach Karachi 13 B2
Cliftondale Boston 6 A2
Clonskeagh Dublin 10 B2
Clontarf Dublin 10 A2
Clontarf Sydney 29 A2
Clovelly Sydney 29 B2
Cobras, I. das Rio de Janeiro 25 B2
Coburg Melbourne 18 A1
Cocotá Rio de Janeiro 25 A1
Cœuilly Paris 24 B4
Coina Lisbon 16 B2
Coker Lagos 14 B2
Colaba Mumbai 20 B1
Colaba Pt. Mumbai 20 B1
Colegiales Buenos Aires 7 B2
Colindale London 15 A2
Colinton Edinburgh 11 B2
College Park Atlanta 3 C2
College Park Washington 33 B4
College Point New York 22 B2
Collégien Paris 24 A4
Collier Row London 15 A4
Colliers Wood London 15 B2
Colma San Francisco 26 B2
Colney Hatch London 15 A3
Colognо Monzese Milan 19 A2
Colombes Paris 24 A2
Colonia Güell Barcelona 4 A1
Colonial Knob Wellington 33 A1
Colosseo Rome 26 B1
Colosseum = Colosseo Rome 26 B1
Combault Paris 24 B4
Comércio, Praça do Lisbon 16 A2
Commerce Los Angeles 16 B4
Como Sydney 29 C1
Conceição, I. da Rio de Janeiro 25 B2
Conchali Santiago 27 B2
Concord Sydney 29 B1
Concord Toronto 31 A2
Concorde, Place de la Paris 24 A2
Concorezzo Milan 19 A2
Condet Jakarta 12 A2
Coney Island New York 22 C2
Congonhas São Paulo ✈ (CGH) São Paulo 27 B2
Conley → Atlanta 3 C3
Connaught Place Delhi 10 B2
Consolação São Paulo 27 B2
Constantia Cape Town 8 B1
Constitución Buenos Aires 7 B2
Constitution Atlanta 3 B2
Convention Center Los Angeles 16 B3
Conway Orlando 23 B2
Conway, L. Orlando 23 B2
Coogee Sydney 29 B2
Cooksville Toronto 31 B1
Coolock Dublin 10 A2
Copacabana Rio de Janeiro 25 B1
Copenhagen = København Copenhagen 8 A2
Coral Gables Miami 18 B2
Coral Hills Washington 33 B4
Corcovado, Cristo Redentor Rio de Janeiro 25 B1
Corduff Dublin 10 A1
Cormano Milan 19 A2
Cornaredo Milan 19 A1
Còrsico Milan 19 B1
Corstorphine Edinburgh 11 B2
Corviale Rome 26 B1
Coslada Madrid 17 B2
Cossigny Paris 24 B4
Cotao Lisbon 16 A1
Côte-St-Luc Montreal 20 B2
Cotunduba, I. de Rio de Janeiro 25 B2
Coubron Paris 24 A4
Countryside Chicago 9 C1
County Art Museum Los Angeles 16 B2
Courbevoie Paris 24 A2
Courtry Paris 24 A4
Cowley London 15 A1
Coyoacán Mexico City 18 B2
Craighall Park Johannesburg 13 A2
Craiglockhart Edinburgh 11 B2
Craigmillar Edinburgh 11 B3
Cramond Edinburgh 11 B2
Cramond Bridge Edinburgh 11 B1
Cramond I. Edinburgh 11 B2
Cranford London 15 B1
Crawford Cape Town 8 A2
Crayford London 15 B5
Creekmouth London 15 A4
Crescent, L. Orlando 23 A1
Crescenzago Milan 19 A2
Cressely Paris 24 B1
Cresskill New York 22 A2
Créteil Paris 24 B3
Cricklewood London 15 A2
Cristo Redentor, Estatua do Rio de Janeiro 25 B1
Crockenhill London 15 B4
Croissy-Beaubourg Paris 24 B4
Croissy-sur-Seine Paris 24 A1
Crosby Johannesburg 13 B1
Crosne Paris 24 B3
Cross I. Mumbai 20 B2
Crouch End London 15 A3
Crown Mine Johannesburg 13 B1
Crows Nest Sydney 29 A2
Croydon London 15 B3
Croydon Park Sydney 29 B1
Cruagh Mt. Dublin 10 B2
Crumlin Dublin 10 B2
Cruz de Pau Lisbon 16 B2
Crystal Palace London 15 B3
Csepel Budapest 7 B2
Csepelsziget Budapest 7 B2
Csillaghegy Budapest 7 A2
Csillagtelep Budapest 7 B2
Csömör Budapest 7 A3
Csömöri-patak → Budapest 7 A3
Cuatro Vientos Madrid 17 B1
Cuauhtémoc Mexico City 18 B2
Cuban Museum Miami 18 B2
Cubao Manila 17 B2
Çubuklu Istanbul 12 B2
Cudahy Los Angeles 16 C3
Cuicuilco, Pirámido de Mexico City 18 C1
Culmore Washington 33 B3
Culver City Los Angeles 16 B2
Cumbres de Vallecas Madrid 17 B2
Cupecé São Paulo 27 B1
Currie Edinburgh 11 B2
Cusago Milan 19 B1
Cusano Milanino Milan 19 A2
Cutler Park Boston 6 B1
Çuvuşabaşi → Istanbul 12 B1
Cypress Hills New York 22 B2
Czerniaków Warsaw 32 B2
Czyste Warsaw 32 B1

D

Da Moóca → São Paulo 27 B2
Ďáblice Prague 25 B2
Dąbrowa Warsaw 32 B1
Dachang Shanghai 28 B1
Dachang ✈ Shanghai 28 B1
Dachau Munich 21 A1
Dachau-Ost Munich 21 A1
Dachauer Moos Munich 21 A1
Dadar Mumbai 20 A1
Daebang Seoul 27 B1
Daechi Seoul 27 B2
Dafni Athens 2 B2
Dagenham London 15 A4
Daglfing Munich 21 B2
Dahab, Gezîret el Cairo 7 B2
Daheisha Jerusalem 13 B2
Dahlem Berlin 5 B2
Dahlwitz-Hoppegarten Berlin 5 A5
Dahongmen Beijing 4 C2
Dajiaoting Beijing 4 B2
Dakhnoye St. Petersburg 27 C1
Dalejsky potok → Prague 25 B2
Dalgety Bay Edinburgh 11 A1
Dalkeith Edinburgh 11 B3
Dalkey Dublin 10 B3
Dalkey I. Dublin 10 B3
Dallgow Berlin 5 A1
Dalmeny Edinburgh 11 B1
Dalston London 15 A3
Daly City San Francisco 26 B2
Damaia Lisbon 16 A1
Damarakia Athens 2 B1
Dämeritzsee Berlin 5 B5
Dan Ryan Woods Chicago 9 C2
Danderhall Edinburgh 11 B3
Danderyd Stockholm 29 A2
Danforth Toronto 31 A3
Darakeh Tehran 31 A2
Darband Tehran 31 A2
Darling Point Sydney 29 B2
Darndale Dublin 10 A2
Darrūs Tehran 31 A2
Dartford London 15 B5
Dashi Guangzhou 11 B2
Datansha Guangzhou 11 B2
Datun Beijing 4 B2
Daulatpur Delhi 10 A1
Davidson, Mt. San Francisco 26 B2
Davidson's Mains Edinburgh 11 B2
Dāvūdiyeh Tehran 31 A2
Davydkovo Moscow 19 B1
Dawidy Warsaw 32 C1
Days Bay Wellington 33 B2
Decatur Atlanta 3 B3
Dedham Boston 6 B1
Degunino Moscow 19 A2
Deir Dibwan Jerusalem 13 A2
Deir Ibzi'e Jerusalem 13 A1
Dejvice Prague 25 B2
Dekabristov, Ostrov St. Petersburg 27 B1
Delhi Delhi 10 B2
Demarest New York 22 A2
Den Ilp Amsterdam 2 A2
Denistone Heights Sydney 29 A1
Dentonia Park Toronto 31 A3
DePaul University Chicago 9 B3
Deptford London 15 B3
Des Plaines Chicago 9 A1
Deshengmen Beijing 4 B2
Deutsch-Wagram Vienna 32 A3
Deutsche Oper Berlin 5 A2
Deutsches Museum Munich 21 B2
Devil's Peak Cape Town 8 A1
Dhakuria Kolkata 14 B2
Dharavi Mumbai 20 A2
Diadema São Paulo 27 C2
Diegem Brussels 6 A2
Diemen Amsterdam 2 A2
Diepkloof Johannesburg 13 B1
Dieprivier Cape Town 8 B1
Difficult Run → Washington 33 B2
Dilbeek Brussels 6 A1
Dilli = Delhi Delhi 10 B2
Dirnismaning Munich 21 A2
Disney-M.G.M. Studios Orlando 23 B1
Disney Studios Los Angeles 16 B3
District Heights Washington 33 B4
Djakarta = Jakarta Jakarta 12 A2
Djursholm Stockholm 29 A2
Döberitz Berlin 5 A1
Döbling Vienna 32 A2
Dobong Seoul 27 B2
Dobongsan Seoul 27 A2
Docklands London 15 A3
Doctor Phillips Orlando 23 B2
Dodder → Dublin 10 B1
Dodger Stadium Los Angeles 16 B3
Dogs, Isle of London 15 B3
Dolgoe Ozero St. Petersburg 27 A1
Dollis Hill London 15 A2
Dollymount Dublin 10 A2
Dolní Prague 25 B3
Dolni Chabry Prague 25 B2
Dolní Počernice Prague 25 B3
Dolphins Barn Dublin 10 B2
Dom Pedro II, Parque São Paulo 27 B2
Don Mills Toronto 31 A2
Don Muang Int. ✈ (BKK) Bangkok 3 A2
Donaghmede Dublin 10 A3
Donau-Oder Kanal Vienna 32 A3
Donaufeld Vienna 32 A2
Donaupark Vienna 32 A2
Donaustadt Vienna 32 A2
Dongan Hills New York 22 C1
Dongcheng Beijing 4 B2
Dongdaemung Seoul 27 B2
Donggou Shanghai 28 B2
Dongjak Seoul 27 B1
Dongjiao Guangzhou 11 B2
Dongri Mumbai 20 B2
Dongshanhu Park Guangzhou 11 B2
Dongzhimen Beijing 4 B2
Donnybrook Dublin 10 B2
Doornfontein Johannesburg 13 B2
Dorchester Boston 6 B2
Dorchester B. Boston 6 B2
Dorchester Heights Nat. Historical Site ⌂ Boston 6 B2
Dornach Munich 21 B3
Dorval Int., Montréal ✈ (YUL) Montreal 20 B1
Dos Couros → São Paulo 27 C2
Dos Moninos → São Paulo 27 C2
Douglas Park Chicago 9 B2
Dover Heights Sydney 29 B2
Dowlatābād Tehran 31 B2
Down, L. Orlando 23 A1
Downey Los Angeles 16 C4
Downsview Toronto 31 A1
Downsview C.A.F.B. ✈ Toronto 31 A2
Dragør Copenhagen 8 B3
Drancy Paris 24 A3
Dranesville Washington 33 A1
Drapetsona Athens 2 B1
Dreilinden Berlin 5 B2
Drewnica Warsaw 32 B2
Drigh Road Karachi 13 A2
Drimnagh Dublin 10 B2
Drogenbos Brussels 6 B1
Druid Hills Atlanta 3 B2
Drumcondra Dublin 10 A2
Drummoyne Sydney 29 B1
Drylaw Edinburgh 11 B2
Dubeč Prague 25 B3
Dublin Dublin 10 A2
Dublin ✈ (DUB) Dublin 10 A2
Dublin B. Dublin 10 B3
Dublin Harbour Dublin 10 A2
Duddingston Edinburgh 11 B3
Dugnano Milan 19 A2
Duivendrecht Amsterdam 2 B2
Dūlāb Tehran 31 B2
Dulwich London 15 B3
Dum Dum Kolkata 14 B2
Dum Dum Int. ✈ (CCU) Kolkata 14 B2
Dumont New York 22 A2
Dún Laoghaire Dublin 10 B3
Dundrum Dublin 10 B2
Dunearn Singapore 28 B2
Dúnleary = Dún Laoghaire Dublin 10 B3
Dunn Loring Washington 33 B2
Dunning Chicago 9 B2
Dunvegan Johannesburg 13 A2
Duomo Milan 19 B2
Duque de Caxias Rio de Janeiro 25 A1
Duren Sawit Jakarta 12 B2
Dusit Bangkok 3 B2
Dworp Brussels 6 B1
Dyakovo Moscow 19 B2
Dyker Beach Park New York 22 C1
Dzerzhinskiy Moscow 19 B2
Dzerzhinskiy Park Moscow 19 B2

E

E.U.R. = Esposizione Universale di Roma Rome 26 C1
Eagle Rock Los Angeles 16 B3
Ealing □ London 15 A2
Earlsfield London 15 B2
Earlwood Sydney 29 B1
East Arlington Boston 6 A2
East Arlington Washington 33 B3
East Bedfont London 15 B1
East Boston Boston 6 A2
East Don → Toronto 31 A2
East Don Parkland Toronto 31 A2
East Elmhurst New York 22 B2
East Finchley London 15 A2
East Flatbush New York 22 C2
East Ham London 15 A4
East Humber → Toronto 31 A1
East Lamma Channel Hong Kong 12 B1
East Lexington Boston 6 A1
East Los Angeles Los Angeles 16 B3
East Molesey London 15 B1
East New York New York 22 B2
East Pines Washington 33 B4
East Point Atlanta 3 B2
East Potomac Park Washington 33 B3
East River → New York 22 B2
East Rutherford New York 22 A1
East Sheen London 15 B2
East Talpiyot Jerusalem 13 B2
East Wickham London 15 B4
East York Toronto 31 A2
Eastbourne Wellington 33 B2
Eastcote London 15 A1
Easter Howgate Edinburgh 11 B2
Eastpoint Park Toronto 31 A4
Eastwood Sydney 29 A1
Eaton Canyon Park Los Angeles 16 A4
Ebara Tokyo 30 B3
Ebisu Tokyo 30 B3
Ebute-Ikorodu Lagos 14 A2
Ebute-Metta Lagos 14 B2
Eda Tokyo 30 B2
Edendale Johannesburg 13 A2
Edenmore Dublin 10 A2
Edgars Cr. → Melbourne 18 A1
Edgeley Toronto 31 A1
Edgemar San Francisco 26 C2
Edgewater New York 22 B2
Edgewood Orlando 23 B2
Edinburgh Edinburgh 11 B2
Edinburgh ✈ (EDI) Edinburgh 11 B1
Edinburgh Castle Edinburgh 11 B2
Edison Park Chicago 9 A2
Edmondston Washington 33 B4
Edmondstown Dublin 10 B2
Edo → Tokyo 30 B4
Edogawa Tokyo 30 A4
Edsberg Stockholm 29 A1
Edwards L. Melbourne 18 A1
Efzonos Athens 2 B2
Egaleo Athens 2 B1
Egaleo, Oros Athens 2 B1
Eiche Berlin 5 A4
Eiche Sud Berlin 5 A4
Eiffel, Tour Paris 24 A2
Ein Arik Jerusalem 13 A1
Ein Naquba Jerusalem 13 B1
Ein Rafa Jerusalem 13 B1
Eizariya Jerusalem 13 B2
Ejby Copenhagen 8 A2
Ejigbo Lagos 14 A1
Ekeberg Oslo 23 A3
Eknäs Stockholm 29 B3
El 'Abbasiya Cairo 7 A2
El Agustino Lima 14 B2
El Baragil Cairo 7 A1
El Basâtîn Cairo 7 B2
El Bira Jerusalem 13 A2
El Bosque Santiago 27 C2
El Carmen Santiago 27 B1
El Cortijo Santiago 27 B1
El Cristo, Vaso Regulador Mexico City 18 B1
El Duqqi Cairo 7 A2
El Encinar de los Reyes Madrid 17 A2
El Gezira Cairo 7 A2
El Ghuriya Cairo 7 A2
El Giza Cairo 7 A2
El Khadr Jerusalem 13 B1
El Khalīfa Cairo 7 A2
El Kôm el Ahmar Cairo 7 A2
El Ma'âdi Cairo 7 B2
El Matarîya Cairo 7 A2
El Mohandessin Cairo 7 A2
El Monte Los Angeles 16 B4
El Muqattam Cairo 7 A2
El Mûski Cairo 7 A2
El Pardo Madrid 17 A1
El Portal Miami 18 A2
El Prat de Llobregat Barcelona 4 B1
El Qâhira Cairo 7 A2
El Qubba Cairo 7 A2
El Reloj Mexico City 18 C2
El Retiro Madrid 17 B1
El Salto Santiago 27 B2
El Sereno Los Angeles 16 B3
El Talibîya Cairo 7 B2
El Vergel Mexico City 18 C2
El Wâhli Cairo 7 A2
El Zamâlik Cairo 7 A2
El Zeitûn Cairo 7 A2
Elephanta Caves Mumbai 20 B2
Elephanta I. Mumbai 20 B2
Ellboda Stockholm 29 A3
Ellenor, L. Orlando 23 B2
Elliniko Olympic Complex Athens 2 B2
Ellis I. New York 22 B1
Elm Park London 15 A5
Elmers End London 15 B3
Elmhurst New York 22 B2
Elmstead London 15 B4
Elmwood Park Chicago 9 B2
Elmwood Park New York 22 A1
Elsdon Wellington 33 A1
Elsiesrivier Cape Town 8 A2
Elsternwick Melbourne 18 B2
Eltham London 15 B4
Elwood Melbourne 18 B1
Élysée Paris 24 A2
Elysian Park Los Angeles 16 B3
Emāmzādeh Sāleh Tehran 31 A2
Émerainville Paris 24 B4
Emeryville San Francisco 26 A3
Eminönü Istanbul 12 B1
Emirgan Istanbul 12 B2
Emmarentia Johannesburg 13 A2
Empire State Building New York 22 B2
Encantado Rio de Janeiro 25 B1
Encino Los Angeles 16 B2
Encino Res. Los Angeles 16 B1
Enebyberg Stockholm 29 A1
Enfield Sydney 29 B1
Engenho, I. do Rio de Janeiro 25 B2
Englewood Chicago 9 C3
Englewood New York 22 A2
Englewood Cliffs New York 22 A2
Enmore Sydney 29 B2
Enskede Stockholm 29 B2
Entrevias Madrid 17 B1
Epcot Orlando 23 B1
Epping Sydney 29 A1
Eregun Lagos 14 A2
Erenköy Istanbul 12 C2
Erith London 15 B5
Erlaa Vienna 32 B1
Ermington Sydney 29 A1
Ermita Manila 17 B1
Ershatou Guangzhou 11 B2
Erskineville Sydney 29 B2
Erunkan Lagos 14 A2
Erzsébet-Telep Budapest 7 B3
Eschenried Munich 21 A1
Esenler Istanbul 12 B1
Esher London 15 B1
Eskbank Edinburgh 11 B3
Esplugas Barcelona 4 A1
Esposizione Universale di Roma Rome 26 C1
Essendon Melbourne 18 A1
Essendon ✈ (MEB) Melbourne 18 A1
Essingen Stockholm 29 B1
Essling Vienna 32 A3
Est, Gare de l' Paris 24 A3
Estado, Parque do São Paulo 27 B2
Estrela, Basilica da Lisbon 16 A2
Etobicoke Toronto 31 B1
Etobicoke Cr. → Toronto 31 B1
Etterbeek Brussels 6 B2
Eung-am Seoul 27 B1
Eunpyeong Seoul 27 B1
Evanston Chicago 9 A2
Even Sapir Jerusalem 13 B1
Evere Brussels 6 A2
Everett Boston 6 A2
Evergreen Park Chicago 9 C2
Evin Tehran 31 A2
Ewu Lagos 14 A1
Exhibition Place Toronto 31 B2
Exposições, Palácio das Rio de Janeiro 25 B1
Eyüp Istanbul 12 B1
Ezeiza ✈ (EZE) Buenos Aires 7 B2

F

Fabour, Mt. Singapore 28 B2
Fælledparken Copenhagen 8 A3
Fågelön Stockholm 29 B1
Fagersjö Stockholm 29 B2
Fair Lawn New York 22 A1
Fairfax Washington 33 B2
Fairfax Station Washington 33 C2
Fairland Johannesburg 13 A1
Fairmilehead Edinburgh 11 B2
Fairmount Heights Washington 33 B4
Fairport Toronto 31 A4
Fairview New York 22 B2
Fairview, L. Orlando 23 A2
Falenty Warsaw 32 C1
Faliro Athens 2 B1
Faliro, Ormos Athens 2 B2
Falkenburg Berlin 5 A4
Falkenhagen Berlin 5 A1
Falkensee Berlin 5 A1
Falls Church Washington 33 B2
Falomo Lagos 14 B2
False Bay Cape Town 8 B2
Fangcun Guangzhou 11 B2
Faraḥābād Tehran 31 A2
Farforovskaya St. Petersburg 27 B2
Farningham London 15 B5
Farsta Stockholm 29 B2
Fasanerie-Nord Munich 21 A2
Fasangarten Munich 21 B2
Fatih Istanbul 12 B1
Favoriten Vienna 32 B2
Fawkner Melbourne 18 A1
Fawkner Park Melbourne 18 B1
FedEx Stadium Washington 33 B4
Feijó Lisbon 16 B2
Feldkirchen Munich 21 B3
Feldmoching Munich 21 A2
Feltham London 15 B1
Fener Istanbul 12 B1
Fenerbahçe Istanbul 12 C2
Fengtai Beijing 4 C1
Ferencváros Budapest 7 B2
Ferihegy, Budapest ✈ (BUD) Budapest 7 B3
Ferndale Johannesburg 13 A2
Férolles-Attilly Paris 24 B4
Fichtenau Berlin 5 B5
Field Museum of Natural History Chicago 9 B3
Fields Corner Boston 6 B2
Fiera Camp Milan 19 B1
Figino Milan 19 B1
Fījīr Baghdad 3 A2
Filadelfia Athens 2 A2
Fili-Mazilovo Moscow 19 B1
Filothei Athens 2 A2
Finchley London 15 A2
Fine Arts, Museum of Boston 6 A2
Finglas Dublin 10 A2
Finsbury London 15 A3
Finsbury Park London 15 A3
Fiorito Buenos Aires 7 C2
Firhouse Dublin 10 B2
Fischerhäuser Munich 21 A3
Fisher Island Miami 18 B2
Fishermans Bend Melbourne 18 A1
Fisherville Toronto 31 A2
Fisksätra Stockholm 29 B3
Fitzroy Gardens Melbourne 18 A1
Five Dock Sydney 29 B1
Fjellstrand Oslo 23 B2
Flamengo Rio de Janeiro 25 B1
Flamingo Orlando 23 B2
Flaminio Rome 26 B1
Flaskebekk Oslo 23 A2
Flatbush New York 22 C2
Flaten Stockholm 29 B2
Flatlands New York 22 C2
Flemington Racecourse Melbourne 18 A1
Flint Pk. Los Angeles 16 B3
Florence Los Angeles 16 C3
Florence Bloom Bird Sanctuary ⌂ Johannesburg 13 A2
Florentia Johannesburg 13 B2
Flores Buenos Aires 7 B2
Flores, Mercado de Mexico City 18 C2
Floresta Buenos Aires 7 B2
Florida Buenos Aires 7 B2
Florida Johannesburg 13 B1
Floridsdorf Vienna 32 A2
Flushing New York 22 B3
Flushing Meadows Corona Park New York 22 B2
Flysta Stockholm 29 A1
Fo Tan Hong Kong 12 A2
Föhrenhain Vienna 32 A2
Fontainebleau Johannesburg 13 A1
Fontenay-aux-Roses Paris 24 B2
Fontenay-le-Fleury Paris 24 B1
Fontenay-sous-Bois Paris 24 A3
Foots Cray London 15 B4
Footscray Melbourne 18 A1
Forbidden City = Imperial Palace Museum Beijing 4 B2
Forest Brussels 6 B1
Forest Gate London 15 A4
Forest Heights Washington 33 C3
Forest Hill London 15 B3
Forest Hill Toronto 31 A2
Forest Hills New York 22 B2
Forest Park Chicago 9 B2
Forest Park New York 22 B2
Forest View Chicago 9 C2
Forestville Washington 33 B4
Fornebu Oslo 23 A2
Foro Romano Rome 26 B1
Forstenried Munich 21 B1
Forstenrieder Park Munich 21 B1
Fort Mumbai 20 B1
Fort Dupont Park Washington 33 B4
Fort Foote Village Washington 33 C3
Fort Lee New York 22 A2
Forth, Firth of Edinburgh 11 A2
Forth Rail Bridge Edinburgh 11 A1
Forth Road Bridge Edinburgh 11 A1
Fót Budapest 7 A3
Fourqueux Paris 24 A1
Foxrock Dublin 10 B2
Franconia Washington 33 C3
Frank Lloyd Wright Home Chicago 9 B2
Frankel Singapore 28 B3
Franklin Park Boston 6 B2
Franklin Park Chicago 9 B1
Franklin Park Washington 33 B3
Franklin Res. Los Angeles 16 B2
Frauenkirche Munich 21 B2
Frederiksberg Copenhagen 8 A3
Frederiksdal Copenhagen 8 A2
Fredersdorf Berlin 5 A5
Freguesia Rio de Janeiro 25 A1
Freidrichshain, Volkspark Berlin 5 A3
Freiham Munich 21 B1
Freimann Munich 21 A2
French Quarter New Orleans 21 B2
Fresh Pond Boston 6 A2
Fresnes Paris 24 B2
Freudenau Vienna 32 A2
Friarstown Dublin 10 B1
Friedenau Berlin 5 B3
Friedrichsfelde Berlin 5 B4
Friedrichshagen Berlin 5 B4
Friedrichshain Berlin 5 A3
Friedrichslust Berlin 5 A5
Friherrs Helsinki 11 B1
Frilufts Museum Helsinki 11 B2
Frontón, I. Lima 14 B1
Frunze Moscow 19 B2
Fūchū Tokyo 30 A1
Fuencarral Madrid 17 B1
Fuenlabrada Madrid 17 C1
Fukagawa Tokyo 30 B3
Fukushima Osaka 23 A1
Fulham London 15 B2
Funabori Tokyo 30 A4
Fundão, I. do Rio de Janeiro 25 B1
Fünfhaus Vienna 32 A2
Furesø Copenhagen 8 A2
Fürth Munich 21 B2
Futago-tamagawaen Tokyo 30 B2
Fuxing Dao Shanghai 28 B2
Fuxing Park Shanghai 28 B1
Fuxinglu Beijing 4 B1

G

G. Ross Lord Park Toronto 31 A2
Gaebong Seoul 27 C1
Gage Park Chicago 9 C2
Gagny Paris 24 A4
Galata Istanbul 12 B1
Galata Tower Istanbul 12 B1
Galatsi Athens 2 A2
Galeão, Int. de ✈ (GIG) Rio de Janeiro 25 A1
Galyanovo Moscow 19 B3
Gambir Jakarta 12 A1
Gamboa Rio de Janeiro 25 B1
Gamboloita Milan 19 B2
Gamlebyen Oslo 23 A3
Gangdong Seoul 27 B2
Gangnam Seoul 27 B1
Gangseo Seoul 27 B1
Gangtou Guangzhou 11 A1
Gangwei Guangzhou 11 B2
Ganjiakou Beijing 4 B1
Ganshoren Brussels 6 A1
Gants Hill London 15 A4
Gaoqiao Shanghai 28 A2
Garbagnate Milanese Milan 19 A1
Garbatella Rome 26 B2
Garches Paris 24 A2
Garching Munich 21 A3
Garden City Cairo 7 A2
Garden Reach Kolkata 14 B1
Garder Oslo 23 B2
Garfield New York 22 A1
Garfield Park Chicago 9 B2
Gargareta Athens 2 B2
Garibong Seoul 27 C1
Garvanza Los Angeles 16 B3
Gāshaga Stockholm 29 A3
Gateway ⌂ New York 22 C2
Gateway of India Mumbai 20 B2
Gatow Berlin 5 B1
Gavà Barcelona 4 B1
Gávea Rio de Janeiro 25 B1
Gávea, Pedra da Rio de Janeiro 25 B1
Gazdagrét Budapest 7 B1
Gaziosmanpaşa Istanbul 12 B1
Gebel el Ahmar Cairo 7 A3
Gebel el Muqattam Cairo 7 A2
Gebel el Tura Cairo 7 B2
Geiselgasteig Munich 21 B2
General San Martin Buenos Aires 7 B1
Gennevilliers Paris 24 A2
Gentilly Paris 24 B3
Gentofte Copenhagen 8 A3
Genval Brussels 6 B2
George I. Hong Kong 12 B1
Georges River Bridge Sydney 29 C1
Georgetown Washington 33 B3
Georgia Dome Atlanta 3 B2
Gerasdorf bei Wien Vienna 32 A2
Gerberau Munich 21 A1
Gerli Buenos Aires 7 C2
Germiston Johannesburg 13 B2
Gern Munich 21 B2
Getafe Madrid 17 C1
Getty Center, The Los Angeles 16 B2
Geunjeong Seoul 27 C1
Geva Binyamin Jerusalem 13 A2
Geylang Serai Singapore 28 B3
Gharapuri Mumbai 20 B2
Gharb = Shahrak-e Qods Tehran 31 A2
Ghatkopar Mumbai 20 A2
Ghazipur Delhi 10 B2
Ghizri Karachi 13 B2
Ghizri Cr. → Karachi 13 B2
Ghonda Delhi 10 A2
Ghusuri Kolkata 14 B2
Gianicolense Rome 26 B1
Giant Wheel = Riesenrad Vienna 32 A2
Gibraltar Pt. Toronto 31 B2
Gidea Park London 15 A5
Giesing Munich 21 B2
Gilmerton Edinburgh 11 B3
Gilo Jerusalem 13 B2
Gimmersta Stockholm 29 B3
Ginza Tokyo 30 B3
Giv'at Ram Jerusalem 13 B2
Giv'at Ye'arim Jerusalem 13 B1
Giv'at Ze'ev Jerusalem 13 A2
Giv'on Jerusalem 13 A2
Giza = El Giza Cairo 7 A2
Giza Pyramids Cairo 7 B1
Gjersjøen Oslo 23 B3
Gladesville Sydney 29 B1
Gladsakse Copenhagen 8 A2
Glasnevin Dublin 10 A2
Glassmanor Washington 33 C4
Glasthule Dublin 10 B3
Glen Iris Melbourne 18 B2
Glen Mar Park Washington 33 B3
Glen Rock New York 22 A1
Glen Rouge Park Toronto 31 A4
Glenarden Washington 33 B4
Glenasmole Reservoirs Dublin 10 B1
Glencorse Res. Edinburgh 11 B2
Glencullen Dublin 10 B2
Glendale Los Angeles 16 B3
Glendoo Mt. Dublin 10 B2
Glenhuntly Melbourne 18 B2
Glenside Wellington 33 B1
Glenview Chicago 9 A2
Glenview Countryside Chicago 9 A2
Glenvista Johannesburg 13 B2
Glifada Athens 2 B2
Glömsta Stockholm 29 B1
Glostrup Copenhagen 8 B2
Gogar Edinburgh 11 B2
Göktürk Istanbul 12 A1
Golabari Kolkata 14 B2
Golabki Warsaw 32 B1
Gold Coast Chicago 9 B3
Golden Gate San Francisco 26 B2
Golden Gate ⌂ San Francisco 26 A2
Golden Gate Bridge San Francisco 26 B2
Golden Gate Park San Francisco 26 B2
Golden Horn = Haliç Istanbul 12 B1
Golders Green London 15 A2
Golestan Palace Tehran 31 A2

Gollans Stream → *Wellington* 33 B2
Gonen *Jerusalem* 13 B2
Gongneung *Seoul* 27 B2
Goodmayes *London* 15 A4
Goodwood *Cape Town* 8 A2
Gopalpur *Kolkata* 14 B2
Gore Hill *Sydney* 29 A2
Gorelly → *St. Petersburg* 27 A3
Gorgie *Edinburgh* 11 B2
Gorky Park *Moscow* 19 B2
Gosen *Berlin* 5 B5
Gosener kanal *Berlin* 5 B5
Gospel Oak *London* 15 A3
Gotanda *Tokyo* 30 B3
Goth Goli Mar *Karachi* 13 A2
Goth Sher Shah *Karachi* 13 A1
Gotha *Orlando* 23 A1
Gournay-sur-Marne *Paris* 24 A4
Governador, I. do
   Rio de Janeiro 25 B1
Governors I. *New York* 22 B1
Grabów *Warsaw* 32 C1
Grace, Mt. *Wellington* 33 B2
Gracefield *Wellington* 33 B2
Gracia *Barcelona* 4 A2
Gräfelfing *Munich* 21 B1
Gragoatá *Rio de Janeiro* 25 B2
Grand Bazaar = Kapali
   Carsi *Istanbul* 12 B1
Grand Central Station
   New York 22 B2
Grand Palace *Bangkok* 3 B1
Grande Place *Brussels* 6 B2
Grankulla = Kauniainen
   Helsinki 11 B2
Grant Park *Chicago* 9 B3
Granton *Edinburgh* 11 B2
Grassy Park *Cape Town* 8 B2
Gratosóglio *Milan* 19 B2
Gratzwalde *Berlin* 5 B5
Gravesend *New York* 22 C2
Grazhdanka *St. Petersburg* 27 B2
Great Falls *Washington* 33 B2
Great Falls Park *Washington* 33 B2
Great Western Forum
   Los Angeles 16 C2
Greco *Milan* 19 A2
Green I. *Hong Kong* 12 B1
Green Point *Cape Town* 8 A1
Greenbelt *Washington* 33 A4
Greenbelt Park *Washington* 33 B4
Greenfield Park *Montreal* 20 B3
Greenford *London* 15 A1
Greenhill *London* 15 A2
Greenhills *Dublin* 10 B1
Greenpoint *New York* 22 B2
Greenwich □ *London* 15 B3
Greenwich Observatory
   London 15 B3
Greenwich Village *New York* 22 B2
Greenwood *Boston* 6 A2
Grefsen *Oslo* 23 A3
Gresham Park *Atlanta* 3 B2
Greve Strand *Copenhagen* 8 B1
Griebnitzsee *Berlin* 5 B2
Griffith Park *Los Angeles* 16 B3
Grimbergen *Brussels* 6 A2
Grinzing *Vienna* 32 A2
Gröbenried *Munich* 21 A1
Grochów *Warsaw* 32 B2
Grodzisk *Warsaw* 32 B2
Groenendaal *Brussels* 6 B2
Grogol Petamburin *Jakarta* 12 A1
Gronsdorf *Munich* 21 B3
Grorud *Oslo* 23 A4
Gross-Glienicke *Berlin* 5 B1
Gross-Hadern *Munich* 21 B1
Gross-Lappen *Munich* 21 A2
Grosse Krampe *Berlin* 5 B5
Grosse Müggelsee *Berlin* 5 B4
Grosse Point Lighthouse
   Chicago 9 A2
Grossensdorf *Vienna* 32 A3
Grossenzersdorfer Arm →
   Vienna 32 A3
Grosser Biberhaufen *Vienna* 32 A2
Grosser Wannsee *Berlin* 5 B2
Grossfeld-Siedlung *Vienna* 32 A2
Grosshesselohe *Munich* 21 B2
Grossjedlersdorf *Vienna* 32 A2
Grossziethen *Berlin* 5 B3
Ground Zero *New York* 22 B1
Grove, The *Chicago* 9 A1
Grove Hall *Boston* 6 B2
Grove Park *Atlanta* 3 B2
Grove Park *Hounslow, London* 15 B2
Grove Park *Lewisham, London* 15 B4
Groveton *Washington* 33 C3
Grünau *Berlin* 5 B4
Grunewald *Berlin* 5 B2
Grünwald *Munich* 21 B2
Grünwalder Forst *Munich* 21 B2
Grymes Hill *New York* 22 C1
Guadalupe *Manila* 17 B2
Guadalupe, Basilica de
   Mexico City 18 B2
Guanabara, B. de
   Rio de Janeiro 25 B1
Guanabara, Jardim
   Rio de Janeiro 25 B1
Guanabara, Palácio da
   Rio de Janeiro 25 B1
Guang'anmen *Beijing* 4 B1
Guangqumen *Beijing* 4 B2
Guangzhou *Guangzhou* 11 B2
Guanshuo *Guangzhou* 11 B3
Gudö *Stockholm* 29 B3
Güell, Parque de *Barcelona* 4 A2
Guinardó *Barcelona* 4 A2
Gulbai *Karachi* 13 A1
Güngören *Istanbul* 12 B1
Gunnersbury *London* 15 B2
Gustavo A. Madero
   Mexico City 18 A2
Gutenberg *New York* 22 B1
Gutuyevskiy, Ostrov
   St. Petersburg 27 B2
Guyancourt *Paris* 24 B1
Gwanak *Seoul* 27 C1
Gwanak *Seoul* 27 C1
Gyál *Budapest* 7 B3
Gyáli-patak → *Budapest* 7 B2

H

Haaga *Helsinki* 11 B2
Haar *Munich* 21 B3
Habay *Manila* 17 C1
Hackbridge *London* 15 B3
Hackensack *New York* 22 A1
Hackensack → *New York* 22 B1
Hackney □ *London* 15 A3
Hackney Wick *London* 15 A3

Hadr, Warrãq el *Cairo* 7 A2
Haga *Stockholm* 29 A2
Hägersten *Stockholm* 29 B1
Häggvik *Stockholm* 29 A1
Hagonoy *Manila* 17 B2
Hague Park *Toronto* 31 A3
Haidan *Beijing* 4 B1
Haidari *Athens* 2 A1
Haidarpur *Delhi* 10 A1
Haizhu Guangchang
   Guangzhou 11 B2
Hakunila *Helsinki* 11 B3
Halandri *Athens* 2 A2
Halásztelek *Budapest* 7 B1
Haliç *Istanbul* 12 B1
Halim Perdana Kusuma
   Int. ✈ (HLP) *Jakarta* 12 B2
Halle *Brussels* 6 B1
Haltiala *Helsinki* 11 B2
Haltiavuori *Helsinki* 11 B2
Ham *London* 15 B2
Hämeenkylä *Helsinki* 11 B1
Hammarby *Stockholm* 29 B2
Hamme *Brussels* 6 A1
Hammersmith *London* 15 A2
Hammersmith *London* 15 B2
Hampstead *Montreal* 20 B2
Hampstead *London* 15 A2
Hampstead Garden Suburb
   London 15 A2
Hampstead Heath *London* 15 A2
Hampton *London* 15 B1
Hampton Court Palace
   London 15 B1
Hampton Wick *London* 15 B2
Hamrã' *Baghdad* 3 B1
Hanala *Helsinki* 11 B3
Haneda *Tokyo* 30 B3
Haneda, Tōkyō ✈ (HND)
   Tokyo 30 B3
Hang Hau *Hong Kong* 12 B2
Hanging Gardens *Mumbai* 20 B1
Hanlon *Toronto* 31 A1
Hanwell *London* 15 A1
Hanworth *London* 15 B1
Haora *Kolkata* 14 B1
Hapeville *Atlanta* 3 C2
Happy Valley *Hong Kong* 12 B2
Har Adar *Jerusalem* 13 B1
Har Gilo *Jerusalem* 13 B2
Har Homa *Jerusalem* 13 B2
Har Nof *Jerusalem* 13 B2
Haren *Brussels* 6 A2
Hareskovby *Copenhagen* 8 A2
Haringey □ *London* 15 A3
Harjusuo *Helsinki* 11 B3
Harlaching *Munich* 21 B2
Harlaw Res. *Edinburgh* 11 B2
Harlem *New York* 22 B2
Harlesden *London* 15 A2
Harlington *London* 15 B1
Harmaja *Helsinki* 11 C2
Harmashatar hegy *Budapest* 7 A2
Harolds Cross *Dublin* 10 B2
Harperrig Res. *Edinburgh* 11 B1
Harrow □ *London* 15 A2
Harrow on the Hill *London* 15 A1
Harrow School *London* 15 A1
Harrow Weald *London* 15 A1
Hartsfield-Atlanta Int. ✈
   (ATL) *Atlanta* 3 C2
Harumi *Tokyo* 30 B3
Harvard University *Boston* 6 A2
Harwood Heights *Chicago* 9 B2
Hasanābād *Tehran* 31 A2
Hasbrouck Heights *New York* 22 A1
Haselhorst *Berlin* 5 A2
Hasköy *Istanbul* 12 B1
Hasle *Oslo* 23 A3
Haslum *Oslo* 23 A2
Hästhagen *Stockholm* 29 B2
Hatatiai *Wellington* 33 B1
Hatch End *London* 15 A1
Hatiara *Kolkata* 14 B2
Hauketo *Oslo* 23 A3
Hauz Khas *Delhi* 10 B2
Havel → *Berlin* 5 A2
Havelkanal *Berlin* 5 A2
Havering □ *London* 15 A5
Havering-atte-Bower *London* 15 A5
Haworth *New York* 22 A1
Hawthorne Racecourse
   Chicago 9 B2
Hayes *Bromley, London* 15 B4
Hayes *Hillingdon, London* 15 A1
Hayes End *London* 15 A1
Hayford *Chicago* 9 C2
Haywards *Wellington* 33 A2
Heathfield *Cape Town* 8 B1
Heathrow, London ✈ (LHR)
   London 15 B1
Hebe Haven *Hong Kong* 12 A2
Hedong *Guangzhou* 11 B2
Heidelberg Heights *Melbourne* 18 A2
Heidelberg West *Melbourne* 18 A2
Heidemühle *Berlin* 5 B5
Heideveld *Cape Town* 8 A2
Heiligensee *Berlin* 5 A2
Heiligenstadt *Vienna* 32 A2
Heinersdorf *Berlin* 5 A3
Hélène de Champlain,
   Parc de *Montreal* 20 A2
Helenelund *Stockholm* 29 A1
Heliopolis = Masr el Gedida
   Cairo 7 A2
Hellersdorf *Berlin* 5 A4
Hellerup *Copenhagen* 8 A2
Helmahof *Vienna* 32 A3
Helsingfors = Helsinki
   Helsinki 11 B2
Helsinki *Helsinki* 11 B2
Helsinki-Vantaa ✈ (HEL)
   Helsinki 11 B2
Hendon *London* 15 A2
Hengsha *Guangzhou* 11 B2
Hennigsdorf *Berlin* 5 A2
Henryków *Warsaw* 32 B1
Henson Cr. → *Washington* 33 C4
Henttaa *Helsinki* 11 B1
Heping Park *Shanghai* 28 B2
Hepingli *Beijing* 4 B2
Herlev *Copenhagen* 8 A2
Herman Eckstein Park
   Johannesburg 13 A2
Hermannskogel *Vienna* 32 A1
Hermiston *Edinburgh* 11 B2
Hermitage and Winter
   Palace *St. Petersburg* 27 B2
Hermsdorf *Berlin* 5 A2
Hernals *Vienna* 32 A2
Herne Hill *London* 15 B3

Héroes de Churubusco
   Mexico City 18 B2
Herons, Î. aux *Montreal* 20 B2
Herstedoster *Copenhagen* 8 A2
Herttoniemi *Helsinki* 11 B3
Ḩeşārak *Tehran* 31 A1
Heston *London* 15 B1
Hetzendorf *Vienna* 32 B2
Hextable *London* 15 B5
Hialeah *Miami* 18 A1
Hiawassa, L. *Orlando* 23 A2
Hickory Hills *Chicago* 9 C2
Hiekkaharju *Helsinki* 11 B3
Hietaniemi *Helsinki* 11 B2
Higashi *Osaka* 23 A2
Higashimurayama *Tokyo* 30 A1
Higashinari *Osaka* 23 A2
Higashiosayoshi *Osaka* 23 A2
Higashiyodogawa *Osaka* 23 A1
High Park *Toronto* 31 B2
Highbury *London* 15 A3
Highgate *London* 15 A3
Highland Cr. → *Toronto* 31 A3
Highland Creek *Toronto* 31 A3
Highland Park *Los Angeles* 16 B3
Highlands North *Johannesburg* 13 A2
Hillcrest Heights *Washington* 33 C4
Hillend *Edinburgh* 11 A1
Hillingdon □ *London* 15 A1
Hillwood *Washington* 33 B3
Hilmiya *Cairo* 7 A2
Hin Keng *Hong Kong* 12 A2
Hirota *Osaka* 23 A2
Hirschstetten *Vienna* 32 A2
History Centre *Atlanta* 3 B2
Hither Green *London* 15 B3
Hiyoshi *Tokyo* 30 B2
Hizma *Jerusalem* 13 B2
Hjortekær *Copenhagen* 8 A3
Hjortespring *Copenhagen* 8 A2
Hlubočepy *Prague* 25 B2
Ho Chung *Hong Kong* 12 A2
Ho Man Tin *Hong Kong* 12 B2
Hoboken *New York* 22 B1
Hobsons B. *Melbourne* 18 B1
Hochbrück *Munich* 21 A2
Hochelaga *Montreal* 20 A2
Hochkuglin *Osaka* 9 C1
Hoegi *Seoul* 27 B2
Hoeilaart *Brussels* 6 B2
Hofburg *Vienna* 32 A2
Hoffman I. *New York* 22 C1
Hohenbrunn *Munich* 21 B3
Hohenschönhausen *Berlin* 5 A4
Holargos *Athens* 2 A2
Holborn *London* 15 A3
Holden, L. *Orlando* 23 B2
Holešovice *Prague* 25 B2
Holland Village *Singapore* 28 B2
Höllriegelskreuth *Munich* 21 B1
Hollywood *Los Angeles* 16 B3
Hollywood Bowl *Los Angeles* 16 B2
Holmenkollen *Oslo* 23 A3
Holmes Run Acres
   Washington 33 B2
Holmgård *Stockholm* 29 B1
Holmlia *Oslo* 23 B4
Holocaust Memorial
   Jerusalem 13 B2
Holroyd House, Palace of
   Edinburgh 11 B3
Holysloot *Amsterdam* 2 A3
Homerton *London* 15 A3
Hometown *Chicago* 9 C2
Hōnanchō *Tokyo* 30 A2
Honcho *Tokyo* 30 A4
Honden *London* 15 A1
Hondo, Río → *Los Angeles* 16 B4
Hong Kong *Hong Kong* 12 B2
Hong Kong, Univ. of
   Hong Kong 12 B1
Hongje *Seoul* 27 B1
Hongjimun Tunnel *Seoul* 27 B1
Hongkou *Shanghai* 28 B1
Hongqiao *Shanghai* 28 B1
Honjyo *Tokyo* 30 A3
Honoré Mercier, Pont
   Montreal 20 B2
Hönow *Berlin* 5 A4
Hook *London* 15 B2
Horikiri *Tokyo* 30 A4
Horn Pond *Boston* 6 A1
Hornchurch *London* 15 A5
Horni *Prague* 25 B2
Horni Počernice *Prague* 25 B3
Hornsey *London* 15 A3
Horoměřice *Prague* 25 B2
Hortaleza *Madrid* 17 B2
Hosoyama *Tokyo* 30 B2
Hostafranchs *Barcelona* 4 A1
Hostivař *Prague* 25 B3
Houbětín *Prague* 25 B3
Houghton *Johannesburg* 13 A2
Houilles *Paris* 24 A2
Hounslow □ *London* 15 B1
Hout Bay *Cape Town* 8 B1
Hove Å → *Copenhagen* 8 A1
Hovedøya *Oslo* 23 A3
Høvik *Oslo* 23 A2
Hovorčovice *Prague* 25 A3
Howard Beach *New York* 22 C2
Howrah = Haora *Kolkata* 14 B1
Howth *Dublin* 10 A3
Howth Hd. *Dublin* 10 A3
Hōya *Tokyo* 30 A2
Hradčany *Prague* 25 B2
Huanghuagang
   Mausoleum *Guangzhou* 11 B2
Huangpu *Shanghai* 28 B2
Huangpu Jiang → *Shanghai* 28 B1
Huangpu Park *Shanghai* 28 B1
Huangtugang *Beijing* 4 C1
Huay Khwang *Bangkok* 3 B2
Huddinge *Stockholm* 29 B1
Huechuraba *Santiago* 27 B1
Huertas de San Beltran
   Barcelona 4 A1
Huizingen *Brussels* 6 B1
Humayun's Tomb *Delhi* 10 B2
Humber → *Toronto* 31 A2
Humber B. *Toronto* 31 B2
Humber Bay *Toronto* 31 B2
Humber Bay Park *Toronto* 31 B2
Humber College *Toronto* 31 A1
Humber Summit *Toronto* 31 A1
Humber Valley Village
   Toronto 31 A1
Humberlea *Toronto* 31 A1
Humberwood Park *Toronto* 31 A1
Humboldt Park *Chicago* 9 B2
Humera *Madrid* 17 B1

I

Ibese *Lagos* 14 A2
Ibirapuera *São Paulo* 27 B1
Ibirapuera, Parque do
   São Paulo 27 B2
Icaraí *Rio de Janeiro* 25 B2
Içerenköy *Istanbul* 12 C2
Ichgao *Tokyo* 30 B2
Ichigaya *Tokyo* 30 A3
Ichikawa *Tokyo* 30 A4
Ickenham *London* 15 A1
Iddo *Lagos* 14 B2
Idi-Oro *Lagos* 14 A2
Iganmu *Lagos* 14 B2
Igbobi *Lagos* 14 A2
Igbologun *Lagos* 14 B1
Igny *Paris* 24 B2
Ij, Het → *Amsterdam* 2 A2
IJ-meer *Amsterdam* 2 A3
IJesa-Tedo *Lagos* 14 B1
Ijora *Lagos* 14 B2
Ikebe *Tokyo* 30 B2
Ikebukuro *Tokyo* 30 A3
Ikegami *Tokyo* 30 B3
Ikeja *Lagos* 14 A2
Ikeuchi *Osaka* 23 B2
Ikoyi *Lagos* 14 B2
Ikuata *Lagos* 14 B2
Ikuno *Osaka* 23 A2
Ikuta *Tokyo* 30 B2
Ila *Oslo* 23 A2
Ilford *London* 15 A4
Ilioupoli *Athens* 2 B2
Illinois at Chicago,
   University of *Chicago* 9 B3
Illinois Institute of
   Technology *Chicago* 9 B3
Ilpendam *Amsterdam* 2 A2
Ilsos → *Athens* 2 B2
Imbābah *Cairo* 7 A2
Imielin *Warsaw* 32 C2
Imirim *São Paulo* 27 A1
Imitos *Athens* 2 B2
Imitos, Oros *Athens* 2 B2
Imperial Palace Museum
   Beijing 4 B2
Inagi *Tokyo* 30 B2
Incholm *Edinburgh* 11 A2
Inchicore *Dublin* 10 A1
Inchkeith *Edinburgh* 11 A3
Inchmickery *Edinburgh* 11 A2
Incirano *Milan* 19 A1
Independencia *Lima* 14 A2
Independencia *Santiago* 27 B2
India Gate *Delhi* 10 B2
Indian Creek Village *Miami* 18 A2
Indianópolis *São Paulo* 27 B1
Indira Gandhi Int. ✈ (DEL)
   Delhi 10 B1
Industria *Johannesburg* 13 B1
Ingierstrand *Oslo* 23 B3
Inglewood *Los Angeles* 16 C3
Ingliston *Edinburgh* 11 B1
Inhaúma *Rio de Janeiro* 25 B1
Inner Port Shelter *Hong Kong* 12 A2
Interlagos *São Paulo* 27 C1
Intramuros *Manila* 17 B1
Invalides *Paris* 24 A2
Inverkeithing *Edinburgh* 11 A1
Inzersdorf *Vienna* 32 B2
Ipanema *Rio de Janeiro* 25 B1
Ipiranga *São Paulo* 27 B2
Ipiranga → *São Paulo* 27 B2
Iponri *Lagos* 14 B2
Ireland's Eye *Dublin* 10 A3
Irving Park *Chicago* 9 B2
Isabel *Rio de Janeiro* 25 B1
Isagatedo *Lagos* 14 B1
Isar → *Munich* 21 B2
Ishbīlīya *Baghdad* 3 A2
Ishoj Strand *Copenhagen* 8 B2
Island Bay *Wellington* 33 B1
Island Park *Toronto* 31 B2
Islev *Copenhagen* 8 A2
Isleworth *London* 15 B2
Islington *Toronto* 31 B1
Islington □ *London* 15 A3
Ismaning *Munich* 21 A3
Ismayloskiy Park *Moscow* 19 B3
Isolo *Lagos* 14 A1
Issy-les-Moulineaux *Paris* 24 B2
Istanbul *Istanbul* 12 B1
İstanbul Boğazı *Istanbul* 12 B1
İstinye *Istanbul* 12 B2
Itä Hakkila *Helsinki* 11 B3
Itaewon *Seoul* 27 B1
Itami *Osaka* 23 A1
Itanhanga *Rio de Janeiro* 25 B1
Ivanhoe *Melbourne* 18 A2
Ivry-sur-Seine *Paris* 24 B3
Ixelles *Brussels* 6 B2
Izmaylovo *Moscow* 19 B3
Iztacalco *Mexico City* 18 B2
Iztapalapa *Mexico City* 18 B2

J

Jaba *Jerusalem* 13 A2
Jacaré *Rio de Janeiro* 25 B1
Jackson Heights *New York* 22 B2
Jackson Park *Chicago* 9 C3
Jacques-Cartier *Montreal* 20 A3

Hunaydi *Baghdad* 3 B2
Hundige *Copenhagen* 8 B1
Hundige Strand *Copenhagen* 8 B2
Hung Hom *Hong Kong* 12 B2
Hunters Hill *Sydney* 29 B1
Hunters Pt. *San Francisco* 26 B2
Hunters Valley *Washington* 33 B4
Huntington *Washington* 33 C3
Huntington Park *Los Angeles* 16 C3
Huríya *Baghdad* 3 A1
Hurstville *Sydney* 29 B1
Husan *Jerusalem* 13 B1
Husby *Stockholm* 29 A1
Husum *Copenhagen* 8 A2
Hutt → *Wellington* 33 B2
Hütteldorf *Vienna* 32 A1
Huvasina Plain *Boston* 6 B2
Hüvösvölgy *Budapest* 7 A2
Hvalstad *Oslo* 23 A1
Hvalstrand *Oslo* 23 A1
Hvidovre *Copenhagen* 8 B2
Hwagok *Seoul* 27 B1
Hyattsville *Washington* 33 B4
Hyde Park *Boston* 6 B2
Hyde Park *London* 15 A2
Hyde Park *Johannesburg* 13 A2
Hyde Park *Sydney* 29 B2

J (continued)

Jacques-Cartier, Pont
   Montreal 20 A2
Jade Buddha Temple *Shanghai* 28 B1
Jægersborg *Copenhagen* 8 A3
Jægersborg Dyrehave
   Copenhagen 8 A3
Jagadishpur *Kolkata* 14 B1
Jagatpur *Delhi* 10 A2
Jaguaré, Rib. do → *São Paulo* 27 B1
Jahangirpur *Delhi* 10 A1
Jakarta *Jakarta* 12 A1
Jakarta, Teluk *Jakarta* 12 A1
Jalan Kayu *Singapore* 28 A3
Jamaica B. *New York* 22 C3
Jamaica Plain *Boston* 6 B2
Jamakpuri *Delhi* 10 B1
Jamshidiyeh *Tehran* 31 A2
Jamsil *Seoul* 27 B2
Jamwon *Seoul* 27 B2
Janki *Warsaw* 32 C1
Jannali *Sydney* 29 C1
Jaraguá *São Paulo* 27 A1
Jaraguá, Pico de *São Paulo* 27 A1
Jardim Paulista *São Paulo* 27 B1
Järvätältet *Stockholm* 29 A1
Jaskhar *Mumbai* 20 B2
Jatinegara *Jakarta* 12 B2
Javādīyeh *Tehran* 31 B2
Jaworowa *Warsaw* 32 C1
Jedlesee *Vienna* 32 A2
Jefferson Memorial
   Washington 33 B3
Jefferson Park *Chicago* 9 B2
Jegi *Seoul* 27 B2
Jelambar *Jakarta* 12 A1
Jelonki *Warsaw* 32 B1
Jerónimos, Mosteiro dos
   Lisbon 16 A1
Jersey City *New York* 22 B1
Jerusalem *Jerusalem* 13 B2
Jessamine, L. *Orlando* 23 B2
Jésus, Î. *Montreal* 20 A1
Jesus Maria *Lima* 14 B2
Jette *Brussels* 6 A1
Jey *Tehran* 31 B2
Jianguomen *Beijing* 4 B2
Jiangwan *Shanghai* 28 B1
Jib *Jerusalem* 13 A2
Jihād *Baghdad* 3 B1
Jingan *Shanghai* 28 B1
Jinočany *Prague* 25 B2
Jinonice *Prague* 25 B2
Jiulong = Kowloon
   Hong Kong 12 B2
Jiyūgaoka *Tokyo* 30 B3
Jīzā'ir *Baghdad* 3 B2
Joãdo *Baghdad* 3 A2
Johannesburg *Johannesburg* 13 B2
Johannesburg, Univ. of
   Johannesburg 13 B2
Johanneskirchen *Munich* 21 A2
Johannesstift *Berlin* 5 A2
Johannisthal *Berlin* 5 B4
John F. Kennedy Int. ✈
   New York 22 C3
John McLaren Park
   San Francisco 26 B2
Johnsonville *Wellington* 33 B1
Joinville-le-Pont *Paris* 24 B3
Joli-Bois *Brussels* 6 B2
Jollas *Helsinki* 11 B3
Jongmyo Royal Shrine *Seoul* 27 B1
Jongno *Seoul* 27 B1
Jonstrup *Copenhagen* 8 A2
Joppa *Baghdad* 3 A1
Jorge Chavez, Int. ✈ (LIM)
   Lima 14 B2
Jorge Newbery ✈ *Buenos Aires* 7 B2
Jósefa Piłsudskiego Park
   Warsaw 32 B1
Jōtō *Osaka* 23 A2
Jouy-en-Josas *Paris* 24 B2
Juan Anchorena *Buenos Aires* 7 B2
Juan González Romero
   Mexico City 18 A2
Juárez Int. ✈ (MEX)
   Mexico City 18 B2
Judeira *Jerusalem* 13 A2
Juhdum *Jerusalem* 13 B2
Juhu *Mumbai* 20 A2
Jūjā *Tokyo* 30 A3
Jukskeirivier → *Johannesburg* 13 A2
Julianów *Warsaw* 32 B2
Jungfernheide, Volkspark
   Berlin 5 A2
Jungfernsee *Berlin* 5 B1
Junghwa *Seoul* 27 B2
Jungnang *Seoul* 27 B2
Jungnangcheon → *Seoul* 27 B1
Juniper Green *Edinburgh* 11 B2
Junk B. *Hong Kong* 12 B2
Jurong *Singapore* 28 B2
Jurong, Selat *Singapore* 28 B2
Jurong Industrial Estate
   Singapore 28 B1
Jurujuba, Enseada de
   Rio de Janeiro 25 B2
Jūsō *Osaka* 23 A1
Justice *Chicago* 9 C2
Jwalahari *Delhi* 10 B1

K

Kaapstad = Cape Town
   Cape Town 8 A1
Kabaty *Warsaw* 32 C2
Kadıköy *Istanbul* 12 C2
Kadoma *Osaka* 23 A2
Kafr 'Aqab *Jerusalem* 13 A2
Kāğıthane *Istanbul* 12 B1
Kāğıthane *Istanbul* 12 B1
Kagran *Vienna* 32 A2
Kahnawake *Montreal* 20 B1
Kaimes *Edinburgh* 11 B2
Kaivoksela *Helsinki* 11 B2
Kalamaki *Athens* 2 B2
Kalbadevi *Mumbai* 20 B2
Kalipur *Kolkata* 14 A1
Kalithea *Athens* 2 B2
Kalkaji *Delhi* 10 B2
Kalvebod Fælled *Copenhagen* 8 B3
Kalveboderne *Copenhagen* 8 B2
Kamariteli *Kolkata* 14 B2
Kamata *Tokyo* 30 B3
Kameari *Tokyo* 30 A4
Kamifukuoka *Tokyo* 30 A2
Kami-Itabashi *Tokyo* 30 A3
Kamikitazawa *Tokyo* 30 B3
Kamisuma *Tokyo* 30 B1
Kamoshida *Tokyo* 30 B2

Kampong Landang *Singapore* 28 A3
Kampong Tanjong Penjuru
   Singapore 28 B1
Kampung Bali *Jakarta* 12 B1
Kanamori *Tokyo* 30 B1
Kanda *Tokyo* 30 A3
Kandilli *Istanbul* 12 B2
Kankurgachi *Kolkata* 14 B2
Kanlıca *Istanbul* 12 B2
Kanonerskiy, Ostrov
   St. Petersburg 27 B1
Kanzaki → *Osaka* 23 A1
Kapali Carsi *Istanbul* 12 B1
Kapellerfeld *Vienna* 32 A2
Kapotnya *Moscow* 19 B3
Kapuk *Jakarta* 12 A1
Kāpylä *Helsinki* 11 B2
Karachi *Karachi* 13 B2
Karachi Int. ✈ (KHI) *Karachi* 13 A2
Karkh *Baghdad* 3 B1
Karlin *Prague* 25 B2
Karlsfeld *Munich* 21 A1
Karlshorst *Berlin* 5 B4
Karlův most *Prague* 25 B2
Karol Bagh *Delhi* 10 B2
Karolinenhof *Berlin* 5 B4
Karori *Wellington* 33 B1
Karow *Berlin* 5 A3
Karrādah *Baghdad* 3 B2
Kärsön *Stockholm* 29 B1
Kasai *Tokyo* 30 B4
Kasipur *Kolkata* 14 B2
Kastrup *Copenhagen* 8 B3
Kastrup, København ✈
   (CPH) *Copenhagen* 8 B3
Kasuga *Tokyo* 30 A3
Kasuge *Tokyo* 30 A3
Kasumigaseki *Tokyo* 30 B3
Katong *Singapore* 28 B3
Katrineberg *Stockholm* 29 B1
Katsushika *Tokyo* 30 A4
Kau Pai Chau *Hong Kong* 12 B2
Kau Yi Chau *Hong Kong* 12 B1
Kaulsdorf *Berlin* 5 B4
Kauniainen *Helsinki* 11 B1
Kawasaki *Tokyo* 30 B3
Kawawa *Tokyo* 30 B2
Kaya *Jakarta* 12 B2
Kayu Putih *Jakarta* 12 A2
Kbely *Prague* 25 B3
Kebayoran Baru *Jakarta* 12 B1
Kebayoran Lama *Jakarta* 12 B1
Kebon Jeruk *Jakarta* 12 B1
Kedar *Jerusalem* 13 B2
Kedoya *Jakarta* 12 A1
Keilor *Melbourne* 18 A1
Keilor North *Melbourne* 18 A1
Keimola *Helsinki* 11 A1
Kelapa Gading *Jakarta* 12 A2
Kelenföld *Budapest* 7 B2
Kelvin *Johannesburg* 13 A2
Kemang *Jakarta* 12 B1
Kemayoran *Jakarta* 12 B1
Kemerburgaz *Istanbul* 12 B1
Kempton Park Races *London* 15 B1
Kenilworth *Cape Town* 8 B2
Kennedy Town *Hong Kong* 12 B1
Kensal Green *London* 15 A2
Kensington *Johannesburg* 13 B2
Kensington *London* 15 A2
Kensington *New York* 22 C2
Kensington *Sydney* 29 B2
Kensington Palace *London* 15 A2
Kent Village *Washington* 33 B4
Kentish Town *London* 15 A3
Kenton *London* 15 A2
Kenwood House *London* 15 A3
Kepa *Warsaw* 32 B2
Keppel Harbour *Singapore* 28 B2
Kesariani *Athens* 2 B2
Kettering *Washington* 33 B5
Kew *London* 15 B2
Kew → *Melbourne* 18 A2
Kew Gardens *London* 15 B2
Kew Gardens *Toronto* 31 A3
Key Biscayne *Miami* 18 B2
Khalji *Baghdad* 3 B2
Khandallah *Wellington* 33 B1
Khansã' *Baghdad* 3 A2
Kharavli *Mumbai* 20 B2
Khefren *Cairo* 7 B1
Khichripur *Delhi* 10 B2
Khidirpur *Kolkata* 14 B1
Khimki-Khovrino *Moscow* 19 A2
Khirbat Batin Abu Lihyah
   Jerusalem 13 B1
Khirbet el-Misbah *Jerusalem* 13 A1
Khirbet Jub e-Rum *Jerusalem* 13 A2
Khlong San *Bangkok* 3 B2
Khlong Toey *Bangkok* 3 B2
Khorel *Kolkata* 14 B2
Khorosovo *Moscow* 19 B1
Kiamari *Karachi* 13 B1
Kierling *Vienna* 32 A1
Kierlingbach → *Vienna* 32 A1
Kifisos → *Athens* 2 A2
Kikuna *Tokyo* 30 B2
Kilbarrack *Dublin* 10 A3
Kilbirnie *Wellington* 33 B1
Kilburn *London* 15 A2
Kilkalee *Dublin* 10 A2
Killester *Dublin* 10 A2
Killiney *Dublin* 10 B3
Killiney B. *Dublin* 10 B3
Kilmacud *Dublin* 10 B2
Kilmainham *Dublin* 10 A2
Kilmainham Gaol *Dublin* 10 A2
Kilmashogue Mt. *Dublin* 10 B2
Kilmore *Dublin* 10 A2
Kilnamanagh *Dublin* 10 B1
Kilo *Helsinki* 11 B1
Kilo *Baghdad* 3 A2
Kitierman *Dublin* 10 B2
Kimmage *Dublin* 10 B2
Kindi *Baghdad* 3 B1
Kinghorn *Edinburgh* 11 A2
Kings Domain *Melbourne* 18 A1
Kings Forest =
   Kongelunden *Copenhagen* 8 B3
Kings Park *Johannesburg* 13 A2
Kings Park West *Washington* 33 C2
Kingsbury *Melbourne* 18 A2
Kingsbury *London* 15 A2
Kingsford *Sydney* 29 B2
Kingsford Smith, Sydney ✈
   (SYD) *Sydney* 29 B2
Kingston-upon-Thames □
   London 15 B2
Kingston Vale *London* 15 B2
Kingsway *Toronto* 31 B1
Kinsaley *Dublin* 10 A3
Kipling Heights *Toronto* 31 A1
Kipseli *Athens* 2 B1

Kirchstockbach *Munich* 21 B3
Kirchtrudering *Munich* 21 B3
Kirikiri *Lagos* 14 B2
Kirke Værlose *Copenhagen* 8 A1
Kirkhill *Edinburgh* 11 B2
Kirklisten *Edinburgh* 11 B2
Kirknewton *Edinburgh* 11 B1
Kirov Palace of Culture
   St. Petersburg 27 B2
Kiryat Anavim *Jerusalem* 13 B1
Kiryat Ha Yovel *Jerusalem* 13 B1
Kısıklı *Istanbul* 12 B2
Kispest *Budapest* 7 B2
Kista *Stockholm* 29 A1
Kita *Osaka* 23 A1
Kita *Tokyo* 30 A3
Kitazawa *Tokyo* 30 B3
Kiu Tsiu *Hong Kong* 12 A2
Kivistö *Helsinki* 11 A2
Kızıltoprak *Istanbul* 12 C2
Kızuri *Osaka* 23 B2
Kjelsås *Oslo* 23 A3
Kladow *Berlin* 5 B1
Klampenborg *Copenhagen* 8 A3
Klaudyn *Warsaw* 32 B1
Klečany *Prague* 25 A2
Kledering *Vienna* 32 B2
Klein Jukskei → *Johannesburg* 13 A1
Kleinmachnow *Berlin* 5 B2
Kleinschönebeck *Berlin* 5 B5
Klemetsrud *Oslo* 23 B4
Klender *Jakarta* 12 A2
Kličany *Prague* 25 A2
Klipriviersberg Nature
   Reserve *Johannesburg* 13 B2
Klosterneuburg *Vienna* 32 A1
Kōbánya *Budapest* 7 B2
Kobbegem *Brussels* 6 A1
København *Copenhagen* 8 A2
København ✈ (CPH)
   Copenhagen 8 B3
Kobylisy *Prague* 25 B2
Kobylka *Warsaw* 32 B3
Kodaira *Tokyo* 30 A1
Kodanaka *Tokyo* 30 B2
Koganei *Tokyo* 30 A2
Kogarah *Sydney* 29 B1
Koivupää *Helsinki* 11 B2
Koja *Jakarta* 12 A2
Koja Utara *Jakarta* 12 A2
Kokhav Ya'akov *Jerusalem* 13 A2
Kokobunji *Tokyo* 30 A1
Kokobunji-Temple *Tokyo* 30 A1
Kolarängen *Stockholm* 29 B3
Kolbotn *Oslo* 23 B3
Kolkata *Kolkata* 14 B2
Kolkata salah *Kolkata* 14 B1
Kolkata Dum Dum Int. ✈
   (CCU) *Kolkata* 14 A2
Kolkata Maidan *Kolkata* 14 B1
Kolo *Warsaw* 32 B1
Kolokinthou *Athens* 2 B1
Kolomosyagi *St. Petersburg* 27 B2
Kolomos *Athens* 2 B2
Kolsäs *Oslo* 23 A2
Komae *Tokyo* 30 B2
Komagome *Tokyo* 30 A3
Komazawa *Tokyo* 30 B3
Kona *Kolkata* 14 B1
Konala *Helsinki* 11 B2
Kondli *Delhi* 10 B2
Kongelunden *Copenhagen* 8 B3
Kongens Lyngby *Copenhagen* 8 A3
Kongo *Helsinki* 11 B2
Konnagar *Kolkata* 14 A2
Konohana *Osaka* 23 A1
Konradshöhe *Berlin* 5 A2
Kopanina *Prague* 25 B2
Koparkhairna *Mumbai* 20 A2
Köpenick *Berlin* 5 B4
Korangi *Karachi* 13 B2
Koremasa *Tokyo* 30 B1
Koridalos *Athens* 2 B1
Korokoro *Wellington* 33 B2
Korokoro Stream →
   Wellington 33 B2
Kosino *Moscow* 19 B3
Kosugi *Tokyo* 30 B4
Kota *Jakarta* 12 A1
Kōtō *Tokyo* 30 A3
Kotrung *Kolkata* 14 A2
Kouponia *Athens* 2 B2
Koukou *Hong Kong* 12 B1
Kowloon Peak *Hong Kong* 12 A2
Kowloon Res. *Hong Kong* 12 A1
Kowloon Tong *Hong Kong* 12 A2
Kraainem *Brussels* 6 A2
Krailling *Munich* 21 B1
Krampnitz *Berlin* 5 A1
Krampnitzsee *Berlin* 5 B1
Kranji, Sungei = *Singapore* 28 A2
Kranji Industrial Estate
   Singapore 28 A2
Krasno-Presnenskaya
   Moscow 19 B2
Krč *Prague* 25 B2
Kremlin *Moscow* 19 B2
Krestovskiy, Ostrov
   St. Petersburg 27 B1
Kreuzberg *Berlin* 5 A3
Kritzendorf *Vienna* 32 A1
Krumme Lanke *Berlin* 5 B2
Krummensee *Berlin* 5 A5
Krung Thep = Bangkok
   Bangkok 3 B2
Krusboda *Stockholm* 29 B3
Kuangchou = Guangzhou
   Guangzhou 11 B2
Küçükcköy *Istanbul* 12 B1
Küçüksu *Istanbul* 12 B2
Kudrovo *St. Petersburg* 27 B3
Kulosaari *Helsinki* 11 B3
Kumla *Stockholm* 29 B3
Kungens kurva *Stockholm* 29 B1
Kungliga Mottet *Stockholm* 29 B2
Kungshatt *Stockholm* 29 B1
Kungsholmen *Stockholm* 29 B2
Kuningan *Jakarta* 12 B1
Kunitachi *Tokyo* 30 A1
Kunming Hu *Beijing* 4 B1
Kunratice *Prague* 25 B2
Kupchino *St. Petersburg* 27 C2
Kurbağalı → *Istanbul* 12 C2
Kurla *Mumbai* 20 A2
Kurume *Tokyo* 30 A2
Kuryanovo *Moscow* 19 C3
Kuskovo *Moscow* 19 B3
Kustia *Kolkata* 14 B2
Kwangmyon *Seoul* 27 C1
Kwai Chung *Hong Kong* 12 A1
Kwangju = Guangzhou
   Guangzhou 11 B2

Kwun Tong *Hong Kong* 12 B2
Kyje *Prague* 25 B3
Kyūhōji *Osaka* 23 B2

L

La Blanca *Santiago* 27 C2
La Boca *Buenos Aires* 7 B2
La Bretèche *Paris* 24 A1
La Campiña *Lima* 14 C2
La Celle-St-Cloud *Paris* 24 A1
La Cisterna *Santiago* 27 C2
La Courneuve *Paris* 24 A3
La Dehesa *Santiago* 27 B2
La Encantada *Lima* 14 C2
La Estación *Madrid* 17 B1
La Florida *Barcelona* 4 A1
La Florida *Santiago* 27 C2
La Fortuna *Madrid* 17 B1
La Fransa *Barcelona* 4 A1
La Garenne-Colombes *Paris* 24 A2
La Giustiniana *Rome* 20 B1
La Grange *Chicago* 9 C1
La Grange Park *Chicago* 9 C1
La Granja *Santiago* 27 C2
La Guardia, New York ✈
   (LGA) *New York* 22 B2
La Hulpe *Brussels* 6 B2
La Llacuna *Barcelona* 4 A2
La Loma *Mexico City* 18 A1
La Lucila *Buenos Aires* 7 B2
La Maladrerie *Paris* 24 A1
La Milla, Cerro *Lima* 14 B2
La Monachina *Rome* 20 B1
La Moraleja *Madrid* 17 A2
La Nopalera *Mexico City* 18 C2
La Paternal *Buenos Aires* 7 B2
La Perla *Lima* 14 B2
La Perouse *Sydney* 29 B2
La Pineda *Barcelona* 4 B1
La Pisana *Rome* 20 B1
La Prairie *Montreal* 20 B3
La Punta *Lima* 14 B1
La Puntigala *Barcelona* 4 A2
La Queue-en-Brie *Paris* 24 B4
La Reina *Santiago* 27 B2
La Ribera *Barcelona* 4 A2
La Sagrera *Barcelona* 4 A2
La Salada *Buenos Aires* 7 C2
La Scala *Milan* 19 B2
La Storta *Rome* 20 B1
La Taxonera *Barcelona* 4 A2
La Victoria *Lima* 14 B2
Laajalahti *Helsinki* 11 B1
Laajasalo *Helsinki* 11 B3
Laaksolahti *Helsinki* 11 B1
Labláha, W. el → *Cairo* 7 A2
Lachine *Montreal* 20 B1
Lachine, Canal de *Montreal* 20 B2
Lad Phrao *Bangkok* 3 A2
Ladera Heights *Los Angeles* 16 C2
Lādví *Prague* 25 B2
Lady *Warsaw* 32 C1
Lafontaine, Parc *Montreal* 20 A2
Lagoa *Rio de Janeiro* 25 B1
Lagos *Lagos* 14 B2
Lagos Harbour *Lagos* 14 B2
Lagos-Ikeja ✈ (LOS) *Lagos* 14 A1
Lagos Island *Lagos* 14 B2
Lagos Lagoon *Lagos* 14 B2
Laguna de B. *Manila* 17 C2
Lainate *Milan* 19 A1
Lainz *Vienna* 32 A1
Lake Buena Vista *Orlando* 23 B1
Lake Cain Hills *Orlando* 23 B2
Lake Fairfax Park *Washington* 33 B2
Lakemba *Sydney* 29 B1
Lakeside *Cape Town* 8 B1
Lakeside *Johannesburg* 13 A2
Lakeview *Chicago* 9 B3
Lakewood Park *Atlanta* 3 B2
Lakhtinskiy Razliv, Oz.
   St. Petersburg 27 B1
Lakshmanpur *Kolkata* 14 B1
Laksi *Bangkok* 3 A2
Lal Qila *Delhi* 10 B2
Lam Tin *Hong Kong* 12 B2
Lambert *Oslo* 23 A3
Lambeth □ *London* 15 B3
Lambrate *Milan* 19 B2
Lambro, Parco *Milan* 19 B2
Lambton Mills *Toronto* 31 B1
Lamma I. *Hong Kong* 12 B1
Landauer Hills *Washington* 33 B4
Landower *Amsterdam* 2 A2
Landstrasse *Vienna* 32 A2
Landwehr kanal *Berlin* 5 B3
Lane Cove *Sydney* 29 A1
Lane Cove National Park △
   Sydney 29 A1
Langa *Cape Town* 8 A2
Langenzersdorf *Vienna* 32 A2
Langer See *Berlin* 5 B4
Langley *Washington* 33 A3
Langley Park *Washington* 33 B4
Langwald *Munich* 21 A1
Lanham *Washington* 33 B4
Lankwitz *Berlin* 5 B3
L'Annunziatella *Rome* 20 B2
Lansdowne *Cape Town* 8 A2
Lansing *Toronto* 31 A2
Lanus *Buenos Aires* 7 C2
Lapa *Rio de Janeiro* 25 B1
Laranjeiras *Rio de Janeiro* 25 B1
Las Warsaw* 32 B2
Las Corts *Barcelona* 4 A1
Las Kabacki *Warsaw* 32 C2
Las Pinas *Manila* 17 C1
Las Rejas *Santiago* 27 B1
LaSalle Street Station *Chicago* 9 B3
Lasek Bielański *Warsaw* 32 B1
Lasek Na Kole *Warsaw* 32 B1
Latina *Madrid* 17 B1
Lautasaari *Helsinki* 11 C2
Laval-des-Rapides *Montreal* 20 A1
Lavīzān *Tehran* 31 A2
Lawalon *Lisbon* 16 A2
Lawndale *Chicago* 9 B2
Lawrence Heights *Toronto* 31 A2
Layari *Karachi* 13 A1
Layari → *Karachi* 13 A1
Lazienkowski Park *Warsaw* 32 B1
Le Blanc-Mesnil *Paris* 24 A3
Le Bourget *Paris* 24 A3
Le Chenoi *Brussels* 6 B2
Le Chesnay *Paris* 24 B1
Le Christ de Saclay *Paris* 24 B1
Le Kremlin-Bicêtre *Paris* 24 B3
Le Mesnil-le-Roi *Paris* 24 A1

Le Pecq *Paris* **24** A1
Le Perreux *Paris* **24** A3
Le Pin *Paris* **24** A4
Le Plessis-Robinson *Paris* **24** B2
Le Plessis-Trévise *Paris* **24** B4
Le Port-Marly *Paris* **24** A1
Le Raincy *Paris* **24** A4
Le Vésinet *Paris* **24** A1
Lea Bridge *London* **15** A3
Leaside *Toronto* **31** A2
Leblon *Rio de Janeiro* **25** B1
Lee *London* **15** B4
Leganés *Madrid* **17** C1
Legazpi *Madrid* **17** B1
Lehtisaari *Helsinki* **11** B2
Lei Yue Mun *Hong Kong* **12** B2
Leião *Lisbon* **16** A1
Leichhardt *Sydney* **29** B1
Leith *Edinburgh* **11** B3
Leme *Rio de Janeiro* **25** B2
Lemoyne *Montreal* **20** B3
Lenin *Moscow* **19** B2
Lenino *Moscow* **19** C2
Leninskiye Gory *Moscow* **19** B2
Lennox *Los Angeles* **16** C2
Leonia *New York* **22** A2
Leopardstown *Dublin* **10** B2
Leopoldau *Vienna* **32** A2
Leopoldsdorf *Vienna* **32** B2
Leopoldstadt *Vienna* **32** A2
Leportovo *Moscow* **19** B3
Leppävaara *Helsinki* **11** B1
Les Lilas *Paris* **24** A3
Les Loges-en-Josas *Paris* **24** B1
Les Pavillons-sous-Bois *Paris* **24** A4
Lésigny *Paris* **24** B4
Lesnozavodskaya
    St. Petersburg **27** B2
Lhotka *Prague* **25** B2
Liangshui He → *Beijing* **4** C2
Lianhua Chi *Beijing* **4** B1
Lianhua He → *Beijing* **4** B1
Libčice nad Vltavou *Prague* **25** A2
Libeň *Prague* **25** B2
Liberdade *São Paulo* **27** B2
Liberton *Edinburgh* **11** B3
Liberty I. *New York* **22** B1
Liberty Osaka Museum
    Osaka **23** B2
Liberty State Park △
    New York **22** B1
Libeznice *Prague* **25** A2
Libuš *Prague* **25** B2
Lichiao *Guangzhou* **11** B2
Lichtenberg *Berlin* **5** A4
Lichterfelde *Berlin* **5** B2
Lidingö *Stockholm* **29** A2
Lieshi Lingyuan *Guangzhou* **11** B2
Liesing *Vienna* **32** B1
Liesing → *Vienna* **32** B2
Ligovo *St. Petersburg* **27** C1
Lijordet *Oslo* **23** A2
Likhoborka → *Moscow* **19** A2
Lilla Vártan *Stockholm* **29** A3
Lille Værløse *Copenhagen* **8** A2
Liluah *Kolkata* **14** B1
Lim Chu Kang *Singapore* **28** A2
Lima *Lima* **14** B2
Limbiate *Milan* **19** A1
Limehouse *London* **15** A3
Limeil-Brévannes *Paris* **24** B3
Linate, Milano ✕ (LIN) *Milan* **19** B2
Linbropark *Johannesburg* **13** A2
Lincoln Center for
    Performing Arts *New York* **22** B2
Lincoln Heights *Los Angeles* **16** B3
Lincoln Memorial *Washington* **33** B3
Lincoln Park *Chicago* **9** B2
Lincoln Park *New York* **22** B1
Lincoln Park *San Francisco* **26** B1
Lincoln Park Zoo *Chicago* **9** B2
Lincolnwood *Chicago* **9** A2
Linda-a-Pastora *Lisbon* **16** A1
Linden *Johannesburg* **13** A2
Linden *Wellington* **33** A1
Lindenberg *Berlin* **5** A4
Lindoya *Oslo* **23** A3
Liniers *Buenos Aires* **7** B1
Linkebeek *Brussels* **6** B2
Linksfield *Johannesburg* **13** A2
Linmeyer *Johannesburg* **13** B2
Linna *Helsinki* **11** A2
Lintuvaara *Helsinki* **11** B1
Lion Rock Country Park △
    Hong Kong **12** A2
Lion's Head *Cape Town* **8** A1
Lioumi *Athens* **2** B2
Lisboa *Lisbon* **16** A2
Lisboa ✕ (LIS) *Lisbon* **16** A2
Lisbon = Lisboa *Lisbon* **16** A2
Lishui *Guangzhou* **11** A1
Little B. *Sydney* **29** B2
Little Calumet → *Chicago* **9** D3
Little Ferry *New York* **22** A1
Little Lake Conway *Orlando* **23** B2
Little Red School House
    Nature Center *Chicago* **9** C1
Little Rouge → *Toronto* **31** A4
Liuhang *Shanghai* **28** A1
Liurong Temple *Guangzhou* **11** B2
Livry-Gargan *Paris* **24** A4
Ljan *Oslo* **23** A3
Llano de Can Gineu *Barcelona* **4** A2
Lo Aranguiz *Santiago* **27** B2
Lo Boza *Santiago* **27** B1
Lo Chau *Hong Kong* **12** B2
Lo Chau Pak Mai *Hong Kong* **12** B2
Lo Espejo *Santiago* **27** C1
Lo Hermida *Santiago* **27** B2
Lo Prado *Santiago* **27** B1
Lo So Shing *Hong Kong* **12** B1
Lo Wai *Hong Kong* **12** A1
Loanhead *Edinburgh* **11** B3
Lobau *Vienna* **32** A3
Lobos, Pt. *San Francisco* **26** B1
Lochkov *Prague* **25** B2
Lockhausen *Munich* **21** A1
Lodi *New York* **22** A1

Lodi Estate *Delhi* **10** B2
Logan Int., Boston ✕ (BOS)
    Boston **6** A2
Logan Square *Chicago* **9** B2
Lognes-Émerainville ✕ *Paris* **24** B4
Löhme *Berlin* **5** A5
Lolokhet *Karachi* **13** A2
Lomas Chapultepec
    Mexico City **18** B1
Lomas de San Angel Inn
    Mexico City **18** B1
Lombardy East *Johannesburg* **13** A2
Lomianki *Warsaw* **32** A1
Lomus Reforma *Mexico City* **18** B1
London *London* **15** B3
London City ✕ (LCY) *London* **15** A4
London Heathrow ✕ (LHR)
    London **15** B1
London Zoo *London* **15** A3
Long B. *Sydney* **29** B2
Long Branch *Toronto* **31** B1
Long Brook → *Washington* **33** C2
Long Ditton *London* **15** B2
Long Island City *New York* **22** B2
Longchamp, Hippodrome
    de *Paris* **24** A2
Longhua Pagoda *Shanghai* **28** B1
Longhua Park *Shanghai* **28** B1
Longjohn Slough *Chicago* **9** C1
Longtan Hu → *Beijing* **4** B2
Longue-Pointe *Montreal* **20** A2
Longueuil *Montreal* **20** A3
Longueuil-St-Hubert =
    St-Hubert *Montreal* **20** B3
Loni *Delhi* **10** A2
Loop, The *Chicago* **9** B3
Lord's Cricket Ground *London* **15** A2
Loreto *Milan* **19** B2
Los Angeles *Los Angeles* **16** B3
Los Angeles Int. ✕ (LAX)
    Los Angeles **16** C2
Los Cerrillos ✕ (ULC) *Santiago* **27** B1
Los Nietos *Los Angeles* **16** C4
Los Olivos *Lima* **14** A2
Los Reyes *Mexico City* **18** B2
Losiny Ostrov △ *Moscow* **19** A3
Lot *Brussels* **6** B1
Lotus River *Cape Town* **8** B2
Lotus Temple *Delhi* **10** B2
Loughlinstown *Dublin* **10** B3
Louise, L. *Orlando* **23** A2
Louisiana Superdome
    New Orleans **21** B2
Loures *Lisbon* **16** A1
Louveciennes *Paris* **24** A1
Louvre, Musée du *Paris* **24** A3
Lower B. *New York* **22** C1
Lower Hutt *Wellington* **33** B2
Lower New York B. =
    Lower B. *New York* **22** C1
Lower Shing Mun Res.
    Hong Kong **12** A1
Lowry Bay *Wellington* **33** B2
Loyola University *Chicago* **9** B3
Lu Xun, Tomb of *Shanghai* **28** B1
Lu Xun Park *Shanghai* **28** B1
Lúbars *Berlin* **5** A3
Lucy, L. *Orlando* **23** A2
Ludwigsfeld *Munich* **21** A1
Luhu *Guangzhou* **11** B2
Lumiar *Lisbon* **16** A2
Lundtofte *Copenhagen* **8** A3
Lung Mei *Hong Kong* **12** A2
Luojiang *Guangzhou* **11** B2
Lustheim *Munich* **21** A1
Luwan *Shanghai* **28** B1
Luzhniki Sports Centre
    Moscow **19** B2
Lyndhurst *New York* **22** B1
Lynn Woods Res. *Boston* **6** A2
Lyon, Gare de *Paris* **24** A3
Lyons *Chicago* **9** C2
Lysaker *Oslo* **23** A2
Lysakerselva → *Oslo* **23** A2
Lysolaje *Prague* **25** B2
Lyublino *Moscow* **19** B3

M

Ma Nam Wat *Hong Kong* **12** A2
Ma On Shan Country
    Park △ *Hong Kong* **12** A2
Ma'ale Adumim *Jerusalem* **13** B2
Ma'ale Ha Khamisha
    Jerusalem **13** B1
Ma'ale Mikhmas *Jerusalem* **13** A2
Maantiekylä *Helsinki* **11** A3
Maarifa *Baghdad* **3** B2
Mabato Pt. *Manila* **17** C2
Mabel, L. *Orlando* **23** A2
Macaco, Morro do
    Rio de Janeiro **25** B2
McCook *Chicago* **9** C2
McGill University *Montreal* **20** A2
Machelen *Brussels* **6** A2
Machida *Tokyo* **30** B1
Maciolki *Warsaw* **32** B2
McKerrow, Mt. *Wellington* **33** B2
McKinley Park *Chicago* **9** C2
McLean *Washington* **33** B2
Macopocho → *Santiago* **27** B1
MacRitchie Res. *Singapore* **28** A2
Macul *Santiago* **27** B2
Madhudaha *Kolkata* **14** B2
Madhyamgram *Kolkata* **14** A2
Madin *Mexico City* **18** A1
Madin, L. *Mexico City* **18** A1
Madinah Al Mansūr *Baghdad* **3** B2
Mādīnet Nasr *Cairo* **7** A2
Madrid *Madrid* **17** B1
Madrid Barajas ✕ (MAD)
    Madrid **17** B2
Madrona *Barcelona* **4** A1
Maesawa *Tokyo* **30** A2
Magdalena *Lima* **14** B2
Magdalena Contreras
    Mexico City **18** C1
Maghreb *Baghdad* **3** A2
Maginu *Tokyo* **30** B2
Magliana *Rome* **26** B1
Magny-les-Hameaux *Paris* **24** B1
Maheshtala *Kolkata* **14** C1
Mahim *Mumbai* **20** A2
Mahim B. *Mumbai* **20** A2
Mahlsdorf *Berlin* **5** A4
Mahmoodabad *Karachi* **13** A2
Mahrauli *Delhi* **10** B1
Mahul *Mumbai* **20** A2
Maida Vale *London* **15** A2
Maidstone *Melbourne* **18** A1
Maipú *Santiago* **27** B1
Maisonneuve, Parc *Montreal* **20** A2
Maisons-Alfort *Paris* **24** B3
Maisons-Laffitte *Paris* **24** A1

Maissoneuve *Montreal* **20** A2
Maitland *Cape Town* **8** A1
Makasar *Jakarta* **12** A2
Makati *Manila* **17** B2
Mäkiniitty *Helsinki* **11** A2
Malá Strana *Prague* **25** B2
Malabar *Sydney* **29** B2
Malabar Hill *Mumbai* **20** B1
Malabar Pt. *Mumbai* **20** B1
Malabon *Manila* **17** B1
Malacañang Palace *Manila* **17** B1
Malahide *Dublin* **10** A3
Malakoff *Paris* **24** B2
Målarhöjaen *Stockholm* **29** B1
Malate *Manila* **17** B1
Malaya Neva *St. Petersburg* **27** B1
Malaya Okhta *St. Petersburg* **27** B2
Malchow *Berlin* **5** A3
Malden *Boston* **6** A2
Malden *London* **15** B2
Maleizen *Brussels* **6** B3
Malešice *Prague* **25** B3
Malir → *Karachi* **13** B2
Malleny Mills *Edinburgh* **11** B2
Malmi *Helsinki* **11** B2
Malmoya *Oslo* **23** A3
Málov *Copenhagen* **8** A2
Malton *Toronto* **31** A1
Malvern *Johannesburg* **13** B2
Malvern *Melbourne* **18** B2
Malvern *Toronto* **31** A3
Mampang Prapatan *Jakarta* **12** B1
Mampukuji *Tokyo* **30** B2
Man Budrukh *Mumbai* **20** A2
Man Khurd *Mumbai* **20** A2
Manakhat *Jerusalem* **13** B2
Mandaluyong *Manila* **17** B2
Mandaoli *Delhi* **10** B2
Mandaqui → *São Paulo* **27** A2
Mandoli *Delhi* **10** A2
Mandvi *Mumbai* **20** B2
Manenberg *Cape Town* **8** A2
Mang Kung Uk *Hong Kong* **12** B2
Mang-won *Seoul* **27** B1
Mangolpuri *Delhi* **10** A1
Manguinhos ✕ *Rio de Janeiro* **25** B1
Manhattan *New York* **22** B2
Manhattan Beach *New York* **22** C2
Manila *Manila* **17** B1
Manila Ninoy Aquino
    Int. ✕ (MNL) *Manila* **17** B2
Mankkaa *Helsinki* **11** B1
Manly *Sydney* **29** A2
Mann, L. *Orlando* **23** A2
Mann's Chinese Theatre
    Los Angeles **16** B2
Mansworth *Vienna* **32** B3
Manuel Park *London* **15** A4
Manor Park *Wellington* **33** A2
Manora *Karachi* **13** B1
Manora Pt. *Karachi* **13** B1
Manquehue, L. *Santiago* **27** B2
Manzanares, Canal de *Madrid* **17** C2
Mapo *Seoul* **27** B1
Maracanã *Rio de Janeiro* **25** B1
Maraoli *Mumbai* **20** A2
Marcelin *Warsaw* **32** B1
Mareil-Marly *Paris* **24** A1
Margareten *Vienna* **32** A2
Maria *Vienna* **32** A2
Maridalen *Oslo* **23** A3
Maridalsvatnet *Oslo* **23** A3
Marienberg *Berlin* **5** B3
Marienfelde *Berlin* **5** B3
Marikina *Manila* **17** B2
Marikina → *Manila* **17** B2
Marin City *San Francisco* **26** A2
Marin Pen. *San Francisco* **26** A1
Marina del Rey *Los Angeles* **16** C2
Marino *Dublin* **10** A2
Marisco, Ponta de
    Rio de Janeiro **25** C1
Markham *Toronto* **31** A2
Marki *Warsaw* **32** A2
Markland Wood *Toronto* **31** B1
Marly, Forêt de *Paris* **24** A1
Marly-le-Roi *Paris* **24** A1
Marne-la-Vallée *Paris* **24** A4
Marolles-en-Brie *Paris* **24** B4
Maroubra *Sydney* **29** B2
Marquette Park *Chicago* **9** C2
Marrickville *Sydney* **29** B1
Marsfield *Sydney* **29** A1
Marsha, L. *Orlando* **23** A2
Marte, Campo de *São Paulo* **27** B2
Martesana, Naviglio della
    Milan **19** A2
Martin Luther King Nat.
    Historic Site △ *Atlanta* **3** B2
Martinez *Buenos Aires* **7** B1
Martinkylä *Helsinki* **11** B2
Martinried *Munich* **21** B1
Maruko *Tokyo* **30** B3
Maryino *Moscow* **19** B3
Maryfield *Edinburgh* **11** B2
Massy *Paris* **24** B2
Mata *Jerusalem* **13** B1
Matihutong *Beijing* **4** B1
Matinha *Lisbon* **16** A2
Matramam *Jakarta* **12** B1
Matsubara *Osaka* **23** B2
Mattapan *Boston* **6** B2
Mátyásföld *Budapest* **7** A3
Mau Tso Ngam *Hong Kong* **12** A2
Mauer *Vienna* **32** B2
Mauripur *Karachi* **13** A1
Maxhof *Munich* **21** B1
Mayfair *Johannesburg* **13** B2
Mayor, Plaza *Madrid* **17** B1
Maywood *Chicago* **9** B1
Maywood *Los Angeles* **16** C3
Maywood *New York* **22** A1
Maywood Park Race Track
    Chicago **9** B1
Mazagaon *Mumbai* **20** B2
Meadowbank Park *Sydney* **29** A1
Mêchoulap *Prague* **25** B3
Mêčice *Prague* **25** A2
Mecidiyeköy *Istanbul* **12** B1
Medford *Boston* **6** A2
Mediodia *Madrid* **17** B2
Meguro *Tokyo* **30** B3
Meguro → *Tokyo* **30** B3

Mehpalpur *Delhi* **10** B1
Mehrābād ✕ (THR) *Tehran* **31** A1
Mehram Nagar *Delhi* **10** B1
Mehrow *Berlin* **5** A4
Meidling *Vienna* **32** B2
Méier *Rio de Janeiro* **25** B1
Meiji Shrine *Tokyo* **30** A3
Meise *Brussels* **6** A1
Mejiro *Tokyo* **30** A3
Melbourne *Melbourne* **18** A1
Melbourne ✕ (MEL)
    Melbourne **18** A1
Melkki *Helsinki* **11** C2
Mellunkylä *Helsinki* **11** B3
Mellunmäki *Helsinki* **11** B3
Melrose *Boston* **6** A2
Melrose *New York* **22** B2
Melrose Park *Chicago* **9** B1
Melsbroek *Brussels* **6** A2
Melville *Johannesburg* **13** B2
Menteng *Jakarta* **12** B1
Mérantaise → *Paris* **24** B1
Mercamadrid *Madrid* **17** B2
Merced, L. *San Francisco* **26** B2
Meredale *Johannesburg* **13** B1
Merrilmau, Pulau *Singapore* **28** B2
Merri Cr. → *Melbourne* **18** A1
Merrion *Dublin* **10** B2
Merrionette Park *Chicago* **9** C2
Merton □ *London* **15** B2
Mesgarābād *Tehran* **31** B3
Messe *Vienna* **32** A2
Metanópoli *Milan* **19** B2
Metro-Dade Cultural
    Centre *Miami* **18** B2
Metro Toronto Zoo *Toronto* **31** A3
Metropolitan Museum of
    Art *New York* **22** B2
Meudon *Paris* **24** B2
Mevaseret Tsiyon *Jerusalem* **13** B1
Mevo Beitar *Jerusalem* **13** B1
México *Mexico City* **18** B2
México, Ciudad de
    Mexico City **18** B2
Mexico City Int. ✕ (MEX)
    Mexico City **18** B2
Meyersdal *Johannesburg* **13** B2
Mezzate *Milan* **19** B2
Miadong *Seoul* **27** B2
Miami *Miami* **18** B2
Miami Beach *Miami* **18** B2
Miami Canal *Miami* **18** A1
Miami Int. ✕ (MIA) *Miami* **18** B1
Miami Shores *Miami* **18** A2
Miami Springs *Miami* **18** B1
Miasto *Warsaw* **32** B1
Michalowice *Warsaw* **32** B1
Michle *Prague* **25** B2
Middle Harbour *Sydney* **29** A2
Middle Hd. *Sydney* **29** A2
Middle Park *Melbourne* **18** B1
Middle Village *New York* **22** B2
Middlesex Fells Reservation
    Boston **6** A2
Midland Beach *New York* **22** C1
Midtown *New York* **22** B2
Miedzeszyn *Warsaw* **32** B3
Międzylesie *Warsaw* **32** B3
Miessaari *Helsinki* **11** C1
Miguel Hidalgo *Mexico City* **18** B1
Milan = Milano *Milan* **19** B1
Milanese, Parco
    Regionale △ *Milan* **19** A1
Milano *Milan* **19** B1
Milano Due *Milan* **19** B2
Milano Linate ✕ (LIN) *Milan* **19** B2
Milano San Felice *Milan* **19** B2
Milbertshofen *Munich* **21** A2
Mill Hill *London* **15** A2
Millennium Dome *London* **15** A4
Miller Meadow *Chicago* **9** B1
Millerhill *Edinburgh* **11** B3
Milltown *Dublin* **10** B2
Millwood *Washington* **33** B4
Milnerton *Cape Town* **8** A1
Milon-la-Chapelle *Paris* **24** B1
Milton *Boston* **6** B2
Milton Bridge *Edinburgh* **11** B2
Mimico *Toronto* **31** B1
Mimico Creek → *Toronto* **31** B1
Minami *Osaka* **23** A2
Minamitsunashima *Tokyo* **30** B2
Minato *Osaka* **23** B1
Minato *Tokyo* **30** B3
Minshât el Bekkari *Cairo* **7** A1
Miraflores *Lima* **14** B2
Miramar *Wellington* **33** B1
Misericordia, Sa. da
    Rio de Janeiro **25** B2
Mission *San Francisco* **26** B2
Mississauga *Toronto* **31** B1
Mitaka *Tokyo* **30** A2
Mitcham *London* **15** B2
Mitcham Common *London* **15** B3
Mitchell Museum of the
    American Indian *Chicago* **9** A2
Mitchell's Plain *Cape Town* **8** B2
Mitte *Berlin* **5** A3
Mittel Isarkanal → *Munich* **21** A3
Mixcoac *Mexico City* **18** B1
Miyakojima *Osaka* **23** A1
Mizonokuchi *Tokyo* **30** B2
Mizue *Tokyo* **30** A4
Mlocinski Park *Warsaw* **32** A1
Mlociny *Warsaw* **32** A1
Mnevniki *Moscow* **19** B2
Moba *Lagos* **14** B2
Moczydlo *Warsaw* **32** C2
Modderfontein *Johannesburg* **13** A2
Modřany *Prague* **25** B2
Mogyoród *Budapest* **7** A3
Moinho Velho, Cr. →
    São Paulo **27** B2
Mok *Seoul* **27** B1
Mokótow *Warsaw* **32** B2
Molenbeek-St-Jean *Brussels* **6** A1
Molino de Rosas *Mexico City* **18** B1
Mollem *Brussels* **6** A1
Mollins de Rey *Barcelona* **4** A1
Mondeor *Johannesburg* **13** B2
Moneda, Palacio de la
    Santiago **27** B2
Monerö *Rio de Janeiro* **25** B2
Mong Kok *Hong Kong* **12** B2
Monkstown *Dublin* **10** B3
Monnickendam *Amsterdam* **2** A2
Monrovia *Los Angeles* **16** B4
Monsanto *Lisbon* **16** A1
Monsanto, Parque Florestal
    de *Lisbon* **16** A1
Mont-Royal *Montreal* **20** A2
Mont-Royal, Parc *Montreal* **20** A2
Montana de Montjuich
    Barcelona **4** A1
Mont *Mataك Tehran* **31** A1
Monte Chingolo *Buenos Aires* **7** C2

Montebello *Los Angeles* **16** B4
Montemor *Lisbon* **16** A1
Monterey Park *Los Angeles* **16** B4
Montespaccato *Rome* **26** B1
Montesson *Paris* **24** A1
Monteverde Nuovo *Rome* **26** B1
Montfermeil *Paris* **24** A4
Montigny-le-Bretonneux
    Paris **24** B1
Montjay-la-Tour *Paris* **24** A4
Montparnasse, Gare *Paris* **24** A2
Montréal *Montreal* **20** A2
Montréal, Î. de *Montreal* **20** A2
Montréal, Université de
    Montreal **20** B2
Montréal Est *Montreal* **20** A2
Montréal-Nord *Montreal* **20** A2
Montréal-Ouest *Montreal* **20** B1
Montréal Trudeau Int. ✕
    (YUL) *Montreal* **20** B1
Montreuil *Paris* **24** A3
Montrouge *Paris* **24** B2
Montserrat *Buenos Aires* **7** B2
Monza *Milan* **19** A2
Monzoro *Milan* **19** B1
Mooca *São Paulo* **27** B2
Moonachie *New York* **22** B1
Moonee Ponds *Melbourne* **18** A1
Moonee Valley Racecourse
    Melbourne **18** A1
Moosach *Munich* **21** A2
Mora *Mumbai* **20** B2
Moratalaz *Madrid* **17** B2
Mörby *Stockholm* **29** A2
Morden *London* **15** B2
Morée → *Paris* **24** A3
Morgan Park *Chicago* **9** C3
Moriguchi *Osaka* **23** A2
Morivione *Milan* **19** B2
Morningside *Edinburgh* **11** B2
Morningside *Johannesburg* **13** A2
Morningside *Washington* **33** C4
Morningside *Orlando* **23** A2
Morningside Park *Orlando* **23** A2
Morro Solar, Cerro *Lima* **14** C2
Mortlake *London* **15** B2
Mortlake *Sydney* **29** B1
Morton Grove *Chicago* **9** A2
Morumbi *São Paulo* **27** B1
Moscavide *Lisbon* **16** A2
Moschato *Athens* **2** B2
Moscow = Moskva *Moscow* **19** B2
Moskva *Moscow* **19** B2
Moskvoretskiy *Moscow* **19** B2
Mosman *Sydney* **29** B2
Móstoles *Madrid* **17** C1
Moti Bagh *Delhi* **10** B2
Motol *Prague* **25** B1
Motsa *Jerusalem* **13** B1
Motsa Ilit *Jerusalem* **13** B1
Motspur Park *London* **15** B2
Mottingham *London* **15** B4
Mount Dennis *Toronto* **31** A2
Mount Greenwood *Chicago* **9** C2
Mount Hood Memorial
    Park △ *Boston* **6** A2
Mount Merrion *Dublin* **10** B2
Mount Rainier *Washington* **33** B4
Mount Vernon *New York* **22** A3
Müggelberge *Berlin* **5** B4
Müggelheim *Berlin* **5** B5
Müggelsee *Berlin* **5** B4
Mühleiten *Vienna* **32** A3
Mühlenfliess → *Berlin* **5** A5
Muiden *Amsterdam* **2** A3
Muizenberg *Cape Town* **8** B1
Mujahidpur *Delhi* **10** B2
Mukandpur *Delhi* **10** A2
Mukhmas *Jerusalem* **13** A2
Muko → *Osaka* **23** A1
Mukojima *Tokyo* **30** A3
Mulbarton *Johannesburg* **13** B2
Mumbai *Mumbai* **20** B2
Mumbai Chhatrapati
    Shivaji Int. ✕ (BOM)
    Mumbai **20** A2
Mumbai Harbour *Mumbai* **20** B2
Munch Museum *Oslo* **23** A3
Münchehofe *Berlin* **5** B5
München *Munich* **21** B2
München Franz Josef
    Straus ✕ (MUC) *Munich* **21** A2
Munich = München *Munich* **21** B2
Munkkiniemi *Helsinki* **11** B2
Munro *Buenos Aires* **7** B1
Muntinlupa *Manila* **17** C2
Murai Res. *Singapore* **28** A1
Muranów *Warsaw* **32** B1
Murino *St. Petersburg* **27** B1
Musashino *Tokyo* **30** A2
Mushin *Lagos* **14** A2
Musocco *Milan* **19** B1
Mustansiríya *Baghdad* **3** A2
Musturud *Cairo* **7** A2
Mutanabi *Baghdad* **3** B2
Mutiara *Baghdad* **3** B2
Mykerinos *Cairo* **7** B1
Myllypuro *Helsinki* **11** B3
Mystic → *Boston* **6** A2

N

Nacka *Stockholm* **29** B3
Naenae *Wellington* **33** B2
Nærsnes *Oslo* **23** B1
Nagatsuta *Tokyo* **30** B2
Nagytétény *Budapest* **7** B2
Nahalin *Jerusalem* **13** B1
Najafgarh Drain → *Delhi* **10** B1
Nakahara *Tokyo* **30** B2
Nakano *Tokyo* **30** A2
Namsan Park *Seoul* **27** B1
Namyeong *Seoul* **27** B1
Nanbiancun *Guangzhou* **11** B1
Nanchang He → *Beijing* **4** B1
Nanchang *Guangzhou* **11** B2
Nanchang Dewat *Delhi* **10** B1
Naniwa *Osaka* **23** B1
Nanole *Mumbai* **20** A2
Nanpu Bridge *Shanghai* **28** B2
Nanterre *Paris* **24** A2
Naoabad *Kolkata* **14** C2
Napier Mole *Karachi* **13** B1
Naraina *Delhi* **10** B1
Narela *Delhi* **10** A1
Narimanabe → *Osaka* **23** A1
Narimam Pt. *Mumbai* **20** B1
Naruo *Osaka* **23** A1
Näsby *Stockholm* **29** A2

Näsbypark *Stockholm* **29** A2
National Arboretum
    Washington **33** B4
National Zoological Park
    Washington **33** B3
Nativity, Basilica of *Jerusalem* **13** B2
Natolin *Warsaw* **32** C2
Naucalpan de Juárez
    Mexico City **18** B1
Naupada *Mumbai* **20** A2
Navi Mumbai *Mumbai* **20** A2
Naviglio di Pavia *Milan* **19** B1
Naviglio Grande *Milan* **19** B1
Navotas *Manila* **17** B1
Nawaz Sharif *Karachi* **13** A1
Navy Pier *Chicago* **9** B3
Nazal Hikmat Beg *Baghdad* **3** A2
Nazimabad *Karachi* **13** A2
Nazlet el Simmân *Cairo* **7** B1
Nea Alexandria *Athens* **2** B1
Nea Erythraia *Athens* **2** B2
Nea Ionia *Athens* **2** A2
Nea Liosia *Athens* **2** A2
Nea Smirni *Athens* **2** B2
Near North *Chicago* **9** B3
Nebušice *Prague* **25** B1
Nederhorst *Amsterdam* **2** A3
Nedlitz *Berlin* **5** B1
Nee Soon *Singapore* **28** A2
Needham *Boston* **6** B1
Needham Heights *Boston* **6** B1
Nerima *Tokyo* **30** A3
Nesodden *Oslo* **23** B3
Nesoddtangen *Oslo* **23** B3
Nesoya *Oslo* **23** B2
Neu Aubing *Munich* **21** B1
Neu Buch *Berlin* **5** A4
Neu Buchhorst *Berlin* **5** B5
Neu Fahrland *Berlin* **5** B1
Neu Lindenberg *Berlin* **5** A4
Neubiberg *Munich* **21** B3
Neuenhagen *Berlin* **5** A4
Neuessling *Vienna* **32** A3
Neuhausen *Munich* **21** B2
Neuherberg *Munich* **21** A2
Neuhönow *Berlin* **5** A5
Neuilly-Plaisance *Paris* **24** A4
Neuilly-sur-Marne *Paris* **24** A4
Neuilly-sur-Seine *Paris* **24** A2
Neukagran *Vienna* **32** A2
Neukölln *Berlin* **5** B3
Neuperlach *Munich* **21** B2
Neuried *Munich* **21** B1
Neustift am Walde *Vienna* **32** A1
Neusüssenbrunn *Vienna* **32** A2
Neuwaldegg *Vienna* **32** A1
Neve Ya'akov *Jerusalem* **13** A2
Neves *Rio de Janeiro* **25** B2
New Baghdād *Baghdad* **3** B2
New Barakpur *Kolkata* **14** A2
New Brighton *New York* **22** C1
New Canada *Johannesburg* **13** B1
New Canada Dam
    Johannesburg **13** B1
New Carrollton *Washington* **33** B4
New Cross *London* **15** B3
New Delhi *Delhi* **10** B2
New Dorp *New York* **22** C1
New Dorp Beach *New York* **22** C1
New Malden *London* **15** B2
New Milford *New York* **22** A1
New Mumbai = Navi
    Mumbai *Mumbai* **20** A2
New Territories *Hong Kong* **12** A1
New Toronto *Toronto* **31** B1
New Utrecht *New York* **22** C2
New York *New York* **22** B3
New York La Guardia ✕
    (LGA) *New York* **22** B2
Newark B. *New York* **22** B1
Newbattle *Edinburgh* **11** B3
Newbury Park *London* **15** A4
Newcraighall *Edinburgh* **11** B3
Newham □ *London* **15** A4
Newhaven *Edinburgh* **11** B2
Newington *Edinburgh* **11** B2
Newlands *Johannesburg* **13** B1
Newlands *Wellington* **33** B1
Newport *Melbourne* **18** A1
Newton *Boston* **6** B1
Newtonbrook *Toronto* **31** A2
Newtongrange *Edinburgh* **11** B3
Newtonville *Boston* **6** A1
Newtown *Sydney* **29** B2
Ngaio *Wellington* **33** B1
Ngau Chi Wan *Hong Kong* **12** A2
Ngau Tau Kok *Hong Kong* **12** B2
Ngauranga *Wellington* **33** B1
Ngong Shuen Chau
    Hong Kong **12** B1
Ngua Kok Wan *Hong Kong* **12** A1
Nhava Sheva *Mumbai* **20** B2
Niävärän *Tehran* **31** A2
Nibra *Kolkata* **14** B1
Nidal *Baghdad* **3** B2
Niddrie *Edinburgh* **11** B3
Niddrie *Melbourne* **18** A1
Nieder Neuendorf *Berlin* **5** A2
Niederschöneweide *Berlin* **5** B3
Niederschönhausen *Berlin* **5** A3
Niemeyer *Rio de Janeiro* **25** B1
Nieuwendam *Amsterdam* **2** A2
Nihonbashi *Tokyo* **30** A3
Niipperi *Helsinki* **11** B1
Nikea *Athens* **2** B1
Nikolassee *Berlin* **5** B2
Nikolskiy *Moscow* **19** B1
Niles *Chicago* **9** A2
Nimta *Kolkata* **14** A2
Ninoy Aquino Int. ✕ (MNL)
    Manila **17** B2
Nippa *Tokyo* **30** B2
Nippori *Tokyo* **30** A3
Nishi *Osaka* **23** B1
Nishinari *Osaka* **23** B1
Nishinomiya *Osaka* **23** A1
Nishiyodogawa *Osaka* **23** A1
Niterói *Rio de Janeiro* **25** B2
Nockeby *Stockholm* **29** B1
Nogatino *Moscow* **19** B3
Nogent-sur-Marne *Paris* **24** A3
Noida *Delhi* **10** B2
Noisiel *Paris* **24** A4
Noisy-le-Roi *Paris* **24** A1
Noisy-le-Sec *Paris* **24** A3
Nokkala *Helsinki* **11** C1
Nomentano *Rome* **26** B1
Nonakashinden *Tokyo* **30** A2
Nongminyundong
    Jiangxisuo *Guangzhou* **11** B2
Nonhyeon *Seoul* **27** B2
Nonthaburi *Bangkok* **3** B1

Näsbypark *Stockholm* **29** A2

Ogikubo *Tokyo* **30** A2
Ogogoro *Lagos* **14** B2
Ogoyo *Lagos* **14** B2
Ogudu *Lagos* **14** A2
O'Hare Int., Chicago ✕
    (ORD) *Chicago* **9** B1
Ohariu Stream → *Wellington* **33** B1
O'Higgins, Parque *Santiago* **27** B2
Ōimachi *Tokyo* **30** B3
Ojota *Lagos* **14** A2
Okęcie *Warsaw* **32** B1
Okęcie, Warszawa ✕
    (WAW) *Warsaw* **32** B1
Okelra *Lagos* **14** B2
Okeogbe *Lagos* **14** B2
Okhla *Delhi* **10** B2
Okhta → *St. Petersburg* **27** B2
Okkervil → *St. Petersburg* **27** B2
Okrzeszyn *Warsaw* **32** C2
Oksval *Oslo* **23** A3
Oktyabrskiy *Moscow* **19** B2
Okubo *Tokyo* **30** A3
Ōkura *Tokyo* **30** B1
Olari *Helsinki* **11** B1
Olaria *Rio de Janeiro* **25** B1
Old City *Jerusalem* **13** B2
Old City *Shanghai* **28** B1
Old Fort York *Toronto* **31** B2
Old Fort York *Toronto* **31** B2
Old Harbor *Boston* **6** B2
Old Town *Chicago* **9** B3
Old Town Hall = Altes
    Rathaus *Munich* **21** B2
Oldbawn *Dublin* **10** B1
Olgino *St. Petersburg* **27** A1
Olimpico, Estadio *Mexico City* **18** C1
Olivais *Lisbon* **16** A2
Olivar de los Padres
    Mexico City **18** B1
Olivar del Conde *Mexico City* **18** B1
Olives, Mt. of *Jerusalem* **13** B2
Olivia, L. *Orlando* **23** A1
Olivos *Buenos Aires* **7** B2
Olona → *Milan* **19** B1
Olympia, L. *Orlando* **23** A1
Olympic Stadium = Turner
    Field *Atlanta* **3** B2
Olympic Stadium *Helsinki* **11** B2
Olympique, Stade *Montreal* **20** A2
Ōmori *Tokyo* **30** B3
Onisigun *Lagos* **14** A2
Ontario Science Centre
    Toronto **31** A2
Ōokayama *Tokyo* **30** B3
Oostzaan *Amsterdam* **2** A2
Opa-Locka *Miami* **18** A1
Opa-Locka ✕ (OPF) *Miami* **18** A1
Opacz *Warsaw* **32** B1
Ophirton *Johannesburg* **13** B2
Oppegård *Oslo* **23** B3
Oppem *Brussels* **6** A1
Oppsal *Oslo* **23** A4
Ora *Jerusalem* **13** B1
Oradell *New York* **22** A1
Oradell Res. *New York* **22** A1
Orange Bowl Stadium *Miami* **18** B2
Orangi *Karachi* **13** A2
Ordrup *Copenhagen* **8** A3
Orech *Prague* **25** B1
Orient Heights *Boston* **6** A3
Orlando *Orlando* **23** A2
Orlando Dam *Johannesburg* **13** B1
Orlando East *Johannesburg* **13** B1
Orlando Executive ✕ *Orlando* **23** A2
Orlando Int. ✕ (MCO)
    Orlando **23** B2
Orlovista *Orlando* **23** A2
Orly *Paris* **24** B3
Orly, Paris ✕ (ORY) *Paris* **24** B3
Ormesson-sur-Marne *Paris* **24** B4
Ormond *Melbourne* **18** B2
Ornoya *Oslo* **23** A3
Orpington *London* **15** B4
Ortaköy *Istanbul* **12** B2
Ortica *Milan* **19** B2
Oruba *Lagos* **14** A2
Ōsaka *Osaka* **23** B2
Osaka Castle *Osaka* **23** A2
Ōsaka Harbor *Osaka* **23** B1
Ōsaka Itami Int. ✕ (ITM)
    Osaka **23** A1
Ōsaka Kansai ✕ (KIX) *Osaka* **23** B2
Ōsone *Tokyo* **30** B2
Osorun *Lagos* **14** A2
Ospiate *Milan* **19** A1
Ostankino *Moscow* **19** B2
Osterley *London* **15** B1
Osterley Park *London* **15** B1
Östermalm *Stockholm* **29** A2
Österskär *Stockholm* **29** A3
Östia Malpasso *Rome* **26** C1
Ostense *Rome* **26** B1
Ostmarkkapellet *Oslo* **23** A4
Ostoya *Oslo* **23** A2
Østre Aker *Oslo* **23** A3
Ōta *Tokyo* **30** B3
Otaniemi *Helsinki* **11** B1
Otari Open Air Museum
    Wellington **33** B1
Otsuka *Tokyo* **30** A3
Ottakring *Vienna* **32** A1
Ottávia *Rome* **26** B1
Ottery *Cape Town* **8** B2
Ottobrunn *Munich* **21** B3
Ouderkerk *Amsterdam* **2** B2
Oulunkylä *Helsinki* **11** B2
Outer, Canal de l' *Paris* **24** A3
Outer Mission *San Francisco* **26** B2
Outremont *Montreal* **20** A2
Overijse *Brussels* **6** B3
Owhiro Bay *Wellington* **33** C1
Oworonsoki *Lagos* **14** A2
Oxgangs *Edinburgh* **11** B2
Oxon Hill *Washington* **33** C4
Oyodo *Osaka* **23** A1
Oyster B. *Sydney* **29** C1
Oyster Rocks *Karachi* **13** B2
Oyster Rocks *Karachi* **13** B2
Ozoir-la-Ferrière *Paris* **24** B4
Ozone Park *New York* **22** B2

P

Pacific Heights *San Francisco* **26** B2
Pacific Manor *San Francisco* **26** C2
Pacific Palisades *Los Angeles* **16** B1

Pacifica San Francisco 26 C2
Paco Manila 17 B1
Paco de Arcos Lisbon 16 A1
Paddington London 15 A2
Paddington Sydney 29 B2
Paderno Milan 19 A1
Pagewood Sydney 29 B2
Pagote Mumbai 20 B2
Pai, I. do Rio de Janeiro 25 B2
Pak Kok Hong Kong 12 B1
Pak Kong Hong Kong 12 A2
Pakila Helsinki 11 B2
Palacio Real Madrid 17 B1
Palaiseau Paris 24 B2
Palazzolo Milan 19 A1
Paleo Faliro Athens 2 B2
Palermo Buenos Aires 7 B2
Palhais Lisbon 16 B2
Palisades Park New York 22 A1
Palmer Park Washington 33 B4
Palmerston Dublin 10 A2
Paloheinä Helsinki 11 B2
Palomeras Madrid 17 B2
Palos Heights Chicago 9 D2
Palos Hills Chicago 9 C1
Palos Hills Forest Chicago 9 C1
Palos Park Chicago 9 C1
Palpara Kolkata 14 B2
Panchur Kolkata 14 B1
Pandacan Manila 17 B2
Pandan, Selat Singapore 28 B2
Pandan Res. Singapore 28 B2
Pangrati Athens 2 B2
Pangsua, Sungei → Singapore 28 A2
Panihati Kolkata 14 B2
Panjang, Bukit Singapore 28 A2
Panke → Berlin 5 A3
Pankow Berlin 5 A3
Pantheon Rome 26 B1
Panthersville Atlanta 3 B3
Pantin Paris 24 A3
Pantitlán Mexico City 18 B2
Panvel Cr. → Mumbai 20 B2
Paparangi Wellington 33 B1
Papiol Barcelona 4 A1
Paramount Studios Los Angeles 16 B3
Paramus New York 22 A1
Paranaque Manila 17 B1
Paray-Vieille-Poste Paris 24 B3
Pardisän Nature Park Tehran 31 A2
Parel Mumbai 20 B2
Pari São Paulo 27 B2
Parioli Rome 26 B1
Paris Paris 24 A3
Paris Orly ✈ (ORY) Paris 24 B3
Parje Mumbai 20 B2
Pärk = Äzädegän Tehran 31 B2
Pärk-e Mellat Tehran 31 A2
Park Ridge Chicago 9 A1
Park Royal London 15 A2
Parkchester New York 22 B2
Parkdale Toronto 31 B2
Parkhurst Johannesburg 13 A2
Parklawn Washington 33 C3
Parkmore Johannesburg 13 A2
Parkside San Francisco 26 B2
Parktown Johannesburg 13 B2
Parkview Johannesburg 13 A2
Parkville New York 22 C2
Parkwood Cape Town 8 B1
Parkwood Johannesburg 13 A2
Parow Cape Town 8 A2
Parque Chacabuco Buenos Aires 7 B2
Parque Patricios Buenos Aires 7 B2
Parramatta → Sydney 29 A1
Paşabahçe Istanbul 12 B2
Pasadena Los Angeles 16 B4
Pasar Minggu Jakarta 11 B1
Pasay Manila 17 B1
Pascoe Vale Melbourne 18 A1
Pasig Manila 17 B2
Pasig → Manila 17 B2
Pasila Helsinki 11 B2
Pasing Munich 21 B1
Pasir Panjang Singapore 28 B2
Pasir Ris Singapore 28 A3
Passaic New York 22 A1
Passaic → New York 22 B1
Passirana Milan 19 A1
Patel Nagar Delhi 10 B1
Pateros Manila 17 B2
Pathumwan Bangkok 3 B2
Patipukur Kolkata 14 B2
Patisia Athens 2 A2
Paulo E. Virginia, Gruta Rio de Janeiro 25 B2
Paulshof Berlin 5 A5
Paya Lebar Singapore 28 A3
Peakhurst Sydney 29 B1
Pearson Int. Toronto ✈ (YYZ) Toronto 31 A1
Peckham London 15 B3
Pederstrup Copenhagen 8 A2
Pedralbes Barcelona 4 A1
Pedregal de San Angel, Jardines del Mexico City 18 C1
Peip'ing = Beijing Beijing 4 B1
Peking = Beijing Beijing 4 B1
Pelcowizna Warsaw 32 B2
Peñalolén Santiago 27 B2
Pencarrow Hd. Wellington 33 C2
Peng Siang → Singapore 28 A2
Penge London 15 B3
Penha Rio de Janeiro 25 B2
Penicuik Edinburgh 11 B2
Penjaringan Jakarta 11 A1
Pentagon Washington 33 B3
Penzing Vienna 32 A1
People's Park Shanghai 28 B1
People's Square Shanghai 28 B1
Perales del Rio Madrid 17 C2
Perchtoldsdorf Vienna 32 B1
Perdizes São Paulo 27 B2
Peristeri Athens 2 A2
Perivale London 15 A2
Perk Brussels 6 A2
Perlach Munich 21 B2
Perlacher Forst Munich 21 B2
Pero Milan 19 A1
Peropok, Bukit Singapore 28 B2
Perovo Moscow 19 B3
Pertusella Milan 19 A1
Pesagot Jerusalem 13 B2
Pesanggrahan, Kali → Jakarta 11 B1
Peschiera Borromeo Milan 19 B2
Pesek, Pulau Singapore 28 B2
Pest Budapest 7 A2
Pestersébet Budapest 7 B2
Pesthidegkút Budapest 7 A1
Pestimre Budapest 7 B3
Pestlőrinc Budapest 7 B3

Pestújhely Budapest 7 A2
Petas Helsinki 11 B2
Petone Wellington 33 B2
Petrogradskaya Storona St. Petersburg 27 B2
Petroupoli Athens 2 A2
Petrovice Prague 25 B3
Petrovskiy Park Moscow 19 B2
Petrovsko-Razumovskoye Moscow 19 B2
Pettycur Edinburgh 11 A2
Peutie Brussels 6 A2
Pfaueninsel Berlin 5 B1
Phaya Thai Bangkok 3 B2
Phihai Karachi 13 A2
Phillip B. Sydney 29 B2
Phoenix Park Dublin 10 A2
Phra Khanong Bangkok 3 B2
Phra Nakhon Bangkok 3 B2
Phra Pradaeng Bangkok 3 C2
Phranakhon Bangkok 3 B1
Pico Rivera Los Angeles 16 C4
Piedade Lisbon 16 A1
Piedade Rio de Janeiro 25 B1
Piedade, Cova da Lisbon 16 A2
Piedmont Park Atlanta 3 B2
Pierre Elliott Trudeau ✈ (YUL) Montreal 20 B1
Pietralata Rome 26 B1
Pihlajamäki Helsinki 11 B2
Pihlajasaari Helsinki 11 C2
Pilares Rio de Janeiro 25 B1
Pilton Edinburgh 11 B2
Pimmit Hills Washington 33 B2
Pine Castle Orlando 23 B2
Pine Grove Toronto 31 A1
Pine Hills Orlando 23 A2
Pinewood Park Miami 18 A2
Piney Run → Washington 33 B2
Pinganli Beijing 4 B2
Pingzhou Guangzhou 11 B2
Pinheiros → São Paulo 27 B1
Pinjrapur Karachi 13 A1
Pinner London 15 A1
Pinner Green London 15 A1
Pioltello Milan 19 A2
Pipinui Pt. Wellington 33 A1
Piraeus = Piraias Athens 2 B1
Piraiévs = Piraias Athens 2 B1
Pirajuçara → São Paulo 27 B1
Pireas Athens 2 B1
Pirinçci Istanbul 12 B1
Pirituba São Paulo 27 B1
Pirkkola Helsinki 11 B2
Pisgat O'mer Jerusalem 13 A2
Pisgat Ze'ev Jerusalem 13 B2
Pisnice Prague 25 C2
Pitampura Delhi 10 A1
Pitkäjärvi Helsinki 11 B1
Planegg Munich 21 B1
Pleasure Island Orlando 23 B1
Plumstead Cape Town 8 B1
Plumstead London 15 B4
Plyushchevo Moscow 19 B3
Po Toi Hong Kong 12 B2
Po Toi O Hong Kong 12 B2
Poaseo Milan 19 B2
Podbaba Prague 25 B2
Podoli Prague 25 B2
Pohick Creek → Washington 33 C2
Pointe-Aux-Trembles Montreal 20 A2
Poissy Paris 24 A1
Pok Fu Lam Hong Kong 12 B1
Pokcheong Seoul 27 C2
Pokrovsko-Sresnevo Moscow 19 B1
Polton Edinburgh 11 B3
Polvoranca, Parque de Madrid 17 C1
Polyustrovo St. Petersburg 27 B2
Pomprap Bangkok 3 B2
Pondok Gede Jakarta 11 B2
Pondok Indah Jakarta 11 B1
Pont-Viau Montreal 20 A1
Pontault-Combault Paris 24 B4
Pontinha Lisbon 16 A1
Poplar London 15 A3
Poppintree Dublin 10 A2
Porirua Wellington 33 A2
Porirua East Wellington 33 A2
Port Melbourne Melbourne 18 A1
Port Nicholson Wellington 33 B2
Port Richmond New York 22 C1
Port Shelter Hong Kong 12 A2
Port Union Toronto 31 A4
Portage Park Chicago 9 B2
Portela, Lisboa ✈ (LIS) Lisbon 16 A2
Porter, L. Orlando 23 A3
Portmarnock Dublin 10 A3
Porto Brandão Lisbon 16 A1
Pôrto Novo Rio de Janeiro 25 A2
Porto Novo Cr. → Lagos 14 B2
Portobello Edinburgh 11 B3
Portrero San Francisco 26 B3
Potomac Washington 33 B2
Potrero Pt. San Francisco 26 B2
Potsdam Berlin 5 B1
Potzham Munich 21 B2
Pötzleinsdorf Vienna 32 A1
Povoa de Santo Adrião Lisbon 16 A2
Powązki Warsaw 32 B1
Powisle Warsaw 32 B2
Powsin Warsaw 32 C2
Powsinek Warsaw 32 C2
Poyan Res. Singapore 28 A2
Pozuelo de Alarcón Madrid 17 B1
Prado, Museo del Madrid 17 B1
Prado Churubusco Mexico City 18 B2
Praga Warsaw 32 B2
Prague = Praha Prague 25 B2
Praha Prague 25 B2
Praha ✈ (PRG) Prague 25 B1
Praires, R. des → Montreal 20 A2
Prater Vienna 32 A2
Precotto Milan 19 A2
Prenestino Labicano Rome 26 B1
Prenzlauerberg Berlin 5 A3
Preston Melbourne 18 A1
Pretos Forros, Sa. dos Rio de Janeiro 25 B1
Préville Montreal 20 B2
Přezletice Prague 25 B3
Prima Porta Rome 26 B1
Primavalle Rome 26 B1
Primrose Johannesburg 13 B2
Progreso Nacional Mexico City 18 B2
Prosek Prague 25 B3
Prospect Hill Park Boston 6 A1
Providencia Santiago 27 B2
Průhonice Prague 25 C3
Psichiko Athens 2 A2
Pudong New Area Shanghai 28 B2
Pueblo Libre Lima 14 B2

Pueblo Nuevo Barcelona 4 A2
Pueblo Nuevo Madrid 17 B2
Puerto Madero Buenos Aires 7 B2
Puhuangyu Beijing 4 B2
Puistola Helsinki 11 B3
Pukinmäki Helsinki 11 B2
Pulkovo Int. ✈ (LED) St. Petersburg 27 C1
Pullach Munich 21 B1
Pullman Historic District Chicago 9 C3
Pulo Gadung Jakarta 11 B2
Pünak Tehran 31 A2
Punchbowl Sydney 29 B1
Punde Mumbai 20 B2
Punggol Singapore 28 A3
Punggol, Sungei → Singapore 28 A3
Punggol Pt. Singapore 28 A3
Punjabi Bagh Delhi 10 A1
Puotila Helsinki 11 B3
Puteaux Paris 24 A2
Putney London 15 B2
Putuo Shanghai 28 B1
Putxet Barcelona 4 A1
Puxi Shanghai 28 B1
Pyramids Cairo 7 B1
Pyry Warsaw 32 C1

Q

Qalandiya Jerusalem 13 A2
Qal'eh Morghi Tehran 31 B2
Qanā el Ismā'īliya Cairo 7 A2
Qāsemābād Tehran 31 A2
Qasr-e Firūzeh Tehran 31 B3
Qatane Jerusalem 13 B1
Qianmen Beijing 4 B2
Qinghuayuan Beijing 4 B1
Qingningsi Shanghai 28 B2
Qolhak Tehran 31 A2
Quadraro Rome 26 B2
Quaid-i-Azam Karachi 13 A1
Quartiere Zingone Milan 19 B1
Qubeiba Jerusalem 13 A1
Quds Baghdad 3 A2
Queen Mary Res. London 15 B1
Queen Victoria Market Melbourne 18 A1
Queensbury London 15 A2
Queenscliffe Sydney 29 A2
Queensferry Edinburgh 11 B1
Queenstown Singapore 28 B2
Quellerina Johannesburg 13 A1
Quezon City Manila 17 B2
Quilicura Santiago 27 B1
Quincy Boston 6 B3
Quincy B. Boston 6 B3
Quinta Normal Santiago 27 B1
Quinto de Stampi Milan 19 B2
Quinto Romano Milan 19 A1
Quirinale Rome 26 B1

R

R.F.K. Memorial Stadium Washington 33 B4
Raasdorf Vienna 32 A3
Radcliffe College Boston 6 A2
Rådhus Oslo 23 A3
Radlice Prague 25 B2
Radość Warsaw 32 B3
Radotín Prague 25 C2
Rafat Jerusalem 13 A2
Raffles Park Singapore 28 B2
Raheny Dublin 10 A3
Rahnsdorf Berlin 5 B5
Rainham London 15 A5
Rajakylä Helsinki 11 B3
Rajpura Delhi 10 A2
Raszyn Warsaw 32 C1
Räm Allāh Jerusalem 13 A2
Ramadān Baghdad 3 B2
Ramakrishna Puram Delhi 10 B1
Rämällah = Räm Allāh Jerusalem 13 A2
Ramanathpur Kolkata 14 A1
Ramat Alton Jerusalem 13 B2
Ramat Eshkol Jerusalem 13 B2
Ramat Razi'el Jerusalem 13 B1
Ramat Shafet Jerusalem 13 B2
Rambler Channel Hong Kong 12 A1
Ramenki Moscow 19 B1
Ramersdorf Munich 21 B2
Rameses Station Cairo 7 A2
Ramos Rio de Janeiro 25 B1
Ramos Mejía Buenos Aires 7 B1
Ramot Jerusalem 13 A2
Ramsgate Sydney 29 B1
Rand ✈ (QRA) Johannesburg 13 B2
Randalls I. New York 22 B2
Randburg Johannesburg 13 A1
Randhart Johannesburg 13 B2
Randpark Ridge Johannesburg 13 A1
Randwick Sydney 29 B2
Ranelagh Dublin 10 A2
Rangpuri Delhi 10 B1
Rannersdorf Vienna 32 B2
Ransbèche Brussels 6 B2
Ransdorf Amsterdam 2 A2
Ranvad Mumbai 20 B2
Raposo Rio de Janeiro 25 A1
Rastaala Helsinki 11 B1
Rastila Helsinki 11 B3
Rathfarnham Dublin 10 B2
Ratho Edinburgh 11 B1
Ratho Station Edinburgh 11 B1
Ratton Lisbon 16 A2
Ravelston Edinburgh 11 B2
Rawamangun Jakarta 11 B2
Rayners Lane London 15 A1
Raynes Park London 15 B2
Raypur Kolkata 14 B2
Real Felipe, Fuerte Lima 14 B2
Reams, L. Orlando 23 B1
Recoleta Buenos Aires 7 B2
Recoleta Santiago 27 B2
Red Fort = Lal Qila Delhi 10 B2
Red Square Moscow 19 B2
Redbridge □ London 15 A4
Redfern Sydney 29 B2
Redwood Wellington 33 B1

Refshaleøen Copenhagen 8 A3
Regents Park Johannesburg 13 B2
Regent's Park London 15 A3
Rego Park New York 22 B2
Reinickendorf Berlin 5 A3
Rekola Helsinki 11 B3
Rembertów Warsaw 32 B2
Rembrandtpark Amsterdam 2 A2
Remedios, Parque Nacional de los △ Mexico City 18 B1
Remedios de Escalada Buenos Aires 7 C2
Rémola, Estany del Barcelona 4 B1
Renca Santiago 27 B1
Rennemoulin Paris 24 A1
Reporyje Prague 25 B1
Repulse Bay Hong Kong 12 B2
Repy Prague 25 B1
Residenz Munich 21 B2
Reston Washington 33 B2
Retiro Buenos Aires 7 B2
Retiro Madrid 17 B1
Retiro, Puerto Buenos Aires 7 B2
Retreat Cape Town 8 B1
Reutov Moscow 19 B4
Réveillon → Paris 24 B4
Revere Boston 6 A2
Rexdale Toronto 31 A1
Reynosa Tamaulipas Mexico City 18 A1
Rho Milan 19 A1
Rhodes Sydney 29 B1
Rhodon Paris 24 B1
Rhodon → Paris 24 B1
Rialto Towers Melbourne 18 A1
Ribeira Rio de Janeiro 25 A1
Ricarda, Estany de la Barcelona 4 B1
Richmond Melbourne 18 A2
Richmond San Francisco 26 B2
Richmond Hill New York 22 B2
Richmond Park London 15 B2
Richmond-upon-Thames □ London 15 B2
Ridge, The Delhi 10 A2
Ridgefield New York 22 B1
Ridgefield Park New York 22 A1
Ridgewood New York 22 B2
Riem Munich 21 B3
Riesenrad Vienna 32 A2
Rijksmuseum Amsterdam 2 A2
Rikers I. New York 22 B2
Rimac Lima 14 B2
Ringsend Dublin 10 A3
Rio Compride Rio de Janeiro 25 B1
Rio de Janeiro Rio de Janeiro 25 B1
Rio de Janeiro Galeão ✈ (GIG) Rio de Janeiro 25 A1
Rio de Mouro Lisbon 16 A1
Ripollet Barcelona 4 A1
Ris Oslo 23 A3
Risby Copenhagen 8 A1
Rishra Kolkata 14 A2
Ritchie Washington 33 B4
Rithala Delhi 10 A1
Rive Sud, Canal de la Barcelona 4 A2
River Edge New York 22 A1
River Forest Chicago 9 B1
River Grove Chicago 9 B1
Riverdale New York 22 A2
Riverdale Washington 33 B4
Riverdale Park Toronto 31 A2
Riverlea Johannesburg 13 B1
Riverside Johannesburg 13 A1
Riverwood Sydney 29 B1
Rivière-des-Praires Montreal 20 A2
Rixensart Brussels 6 B3
Riyad Baghdad 3 B2
Rizal Park Manila 17 B1
Rizal Stadium Manila 17 B1
Roa Oslo 23 A3
Robbins Chicago 9 C2
Robertsham Johannesburg 13 B2
Rochelle Park New York 22 A1
Rock Cr. → Washington 33 B3
Rock Creek Park Washington 33 B3
Rock Pt. Wellington 33 A2
Rockaway Beach New York 22 C3
Rockaway Pt. New York 22 C2
Rockdale Sydney 29 B1
Rockefeller Center New York 22 B2
Rocky Run → Washington 33 B2
Roda, Gezîret el Cairo 7 A2
Roda I. = Roda, Gezîret el Cairo 7 A2
Rodaon Vienna 32 B1
Rodovre Copenhagen 8 A2
Rodrigo de Freitas, L. Rio de Janeiro 25 B2
Roehampton London 15 B2
Rogers Park Chicago 9 B2
Roihuvuori Helsinki 11 B3
Roissy-en-Brie Paris 24 B4
Rokytka → Prague 25 B3
Roma Rome 26 B1
Roma Urbe ✈ Rome 26 B2
Római-Fürdő Budapest 7 A2
Romainville Paris 24 A3
Roman Forum = Foro Romano Rome 26 B1
Romano Banco Milan 19 B1
Rome = Roma Rome 26 B1
Romema Jerusalem 13 B2
Romford London 15 A5
Ronald Reagan National, Washington ✈ (DCA) Washington 33 B3
Rondebosch Cape Town 8 A1
Roppongi Tokyo 30 B3
Rose, L. Orlando 23 A1
Rose Bowl Los Angeles 16 B4
Rose Hill Washington 33 C3
Rosebank Johannesburg 13 A1
Rosebank New York 22 C1
Rosebery Sydney 29 B2
Rosedal La Candelaria Mexico City 18 B2
Roseland Chicago 9 C3
Rosemead Los Angeles 16 B4
Rosemont Chicago 9 B1
Rosemont Montreal 20 A2
Rosenborg Slot Copenhagen 8 A3
Rosenthal Berlin 5 A3
Rosettenville Johannesburg 13 B2
Rosewell Johannesburg 13 A1
Rosherville Dam Johannesburg 13 B2
Rösjön Stockholm 29 A2
Roslags-Näsby Stockholm 29 A2
Roslin Edinburgh 11 B3
Roslindale Boston 6 B3
Rosny-sous-Bois Paris 24 A4
Rosslyn Washington 33 B3
Rossmoyne Washington 33 B3
Rotherhithe London 15 B3

Rothneusiedl Vienna 32 B2
Rothschmaige Munich 21 A1
Rouge Hill Toronto 31 A4
Round I. Hong Kong 12 B2
Roxbury Boston 6 B2
Roxeth London 15 B1
Royal Botanic Gardens Edinburgh 11 B2
Royal Observatory Edinburgh 11 B2
Royal Palace = Kungliga Slottet Stockholm 29 B2
Royal Park Melbourne 18 A1
Röylä Helsinki 11 B1
Rozas, Portilleros de las Madrid 17 B1
Roztoky Prague 25 B2
Rozzano Milan 19 B1
Rubí → Barcelona 4 A1
Rudolfsheim Vienna 32 A2
Rudolfshöhe Berlin 5 A5
Rudow Berlin 5 B3
Rueil-Malmaison Paris 24 A1
Ruisbroek Brussels 6 B1
Ruislip London 15 A1
Rumelihisarı Istanbul 12 B2
Rungis Paris 24 B3
Rusäfa Baghdad 3 A2
Rush Green London 15 A5
Russa Kolkata 14 B2
Rutherford New York 22 B1
Ruzynė Prague 25 B1
Ruzyne, Praha ✈ (PRG) Prague 25 B1
Rybatskaya St. Petersburg 27 B2
Rydboholm Stockholm 29 A3
Ryde Sydney 29 A1
Ryogoku Tokyo 30 A3
Rzhevka St. Petersburg 27 B3

S

Sa'ādatābād Tehran 31 A2
Saadün Baghdad 3 B2
Saboli Delhi 10 A2
Sabugo Lisbon 16 A1
Sabzi Mand Delhi 10 A2
Sacavém Lisbon 16 A2
Saclay Paris 24 B1
Saclay, Étang de Paris 24 B1
Sacomã São Paulo 27 B2
Sacré Cœur Paris 24 A3
Sacrow Berlin 5 B1
Sacrower See Berlin 5 B1
Sadang Seoul 27 C1
Saddle → New York 22 A1
Saddle Brook New York 22 A1
Sadr Karachi 13 A2
Sadr City Baghdad 3 A2
Safa Baghdad 3 B2
Safdar Jang's Tomb Delhi 10 B2
Saft el Laban Cairo 7 A2
Saganashkee Slough Chicago 9 C1
Sagene Oslo 23 A3
Sagrada Familia, Templo de Barcelona 4 A2
Sahar, Mumbai ✈ (BOM) Mumbai 20 A2
Sai Kung Hong Kong 12 A2
Sai Wan Ho Hong Kong 12 B2
Sai Ying Pun Hong Kong 12 B1
St-Aubin Paris 24 B1
St-Cloud Paris 24 A2
St-Cyr-l'École Paris 24 B1
St-Cyr-l'École ✈ Paris 24 B1
St-Denis Paris 24 A3
St-Germain, Forêt de Paris 24 A1
St-Germain-en-Laye Paris 24 A1
St-Gilles Brussels 6 B2
St. Helier London 15 B2
St-Hubert Montreal 20 B3
St. Hubert, Galeries Royales Brussels 6 B2
St. Isaac's Cathedral St. Petersburg 27 B1
St-Jacques Montreal 20 B3
St-Joost-Ten-Node Brussels 6 A2
St. Kilda Melbourne 18 B1
St-Lambert Montreal 20 A3
St-Lambert Paris 24 B1
St-Laurent Montreal 20 A1
St-Léonard Montreal 20 A2
St. Magelungen Stockholm 29 B2
St-Mandé Paris 24 A3
St. Margaret's Dublin 10 A2
St-Martin, Bois Paris 24 B4
St. Mary Cray London 15 B4
St-Maur-des-Fossés Paris 24 B3
St-Maurice Paris 24 A3
St-Michel Montreal 20 A2
St. Nikolaus-Kirken Prague 25 B2
St-Ouen Paris 24 A3
St. Paul's Cray London 15 B4
St. Peters Sydney 29 B2
St. Petersburg = Sankt-Peterburg St. Petersburg 27 B1
St-Pierre Montreal 20 B2
St-Pieters Leew Brussels 6 B1
St-Quentin, Étang de Paris 24 B1
St-Stevens-Woluwe Brussels 6 A2
St-Vincent-de-Paul Montreal 20 A1
St. Xavier University Chicago 9 C2
Ste-Catherine Montreal 20 B2
Ste-Hélène, Î. Montreal 20 B2
Saiwai Tokyo 30 B3
Sakai Osaka 23 B1
Sakai Harbour Osaka 23 B1
Sakra, Pulau Singapore 28 B2
Salam Baghdad 3 A2
Salamanca Madrid 17 B1
Sallynoggin Dublin 10 B3
Salmannsdorf Vienna 32 A1
Salmedina Madrid 17 C2
Salomea Warsaw 32 B1
Salsette I. Mumbai 20 A2
Salt Lake City = Bidhan Nagar Kolkata 14 B2
Salt River Cape Town 8 A1
Salt Water I. Kolkata 14 B2
Saltsjö-Duvnäs Stockholm 29 B3
Samatya Istanbul 12 C1
Sampaloc Manila 17 B2
Samphan Thawong Bangkok 3 B2
Samseon Seoul 27 B1
Samuel Smith Park Toronto 31 B1
Samut Prakan Bangkok 3 C2
Samut Sakhon Bangkok 3 C1
San Andrés Barcelona 4 A2
San Basilio Rome 26 B2
San Bóvio Milan 19 B2
San Borja Lima 14 B3
San Bruno, Pt. San Francisco 26 C2
San Bruno Mountain State Park □ San Francisco 26 B2

San Cristobal Buenos Aires 7 B2
San Cristóbal Madrid 17 B2
San Cristóbal, Cerro Santiago 27 B2
San Cristoforo Milan 19 B1
San Donato Milanese Milan 19 B2
San Francisco San Francisco 26 B2
San Francisco de Sales San Francisco 26 B3
San Francisco Culhuacán Mexico City 18 C2
San Fruttuoso Milan 19 A2
San Gabriel Los Angeles 16 B4
San Gabriel → Los Angeles 16 C4
San Giuliano Milanese Milan 19 B2
San Isidro Lima 14 B2
San Jerónimo Lídice Mexico City 18 C1
San Joaquin Santiago 27 B2
San José Rio Hondo Los Angeles 16 B4
San Juan → Manila 17 B2
San Juan de Aragón, Parque Mexico City 18 B2
San Juan de Lurigancho Lima 14 A2
San Juan del Monte Manila 17 B2
San Juan Ixtacala Mexico City 18 A1
San Just Desvern Barcelona 4 A1
San Justo Buenos Aires 7 C1
San Lorenzo Tezonco Mexico City 18 C2
San Luis Lima 14 B2
San Marino Los Angeles 16 B4
San Martín Barcelona 4 A2
San Martin de Porras Lima 14 B2
San Mateo Tlaltenango Mexico City 18 B1
San Miguel Lima 14 B2
San Miguel Santiago 27 B2
San Nicolás Buenos Aires 7 B2
San Onófrio Rome 26 B1
San Pedro Martir Barcelona 4 A1
San Pedro Zacatenco Mexico City 18 A2
San Pietro, Piazza Rome 26 B1
San Po Kong Hong Kong 12 A2
San Rafael Chamapa Mexico City 18 B1
San Rafael Hills Los Angeles 16 A3
San Roque Manila 17 B2
San Siro Milan 19 A1
San Souci Sydney 29 B1
San Telmo Buenos Aires 7 B2
San Vicenc dels Horts Barcelona 4 A1
Sandown Johannesburg 13 A2
Sandown Park Races London 15 B1
Sandton Johannesburg 13 A2
Sandvika Oslo 23 A2
Sandyford Dublin 10 B2
Sandymount Dublin 10 A3
Sangenjaya Tokyo 30 B2
Sanggye Seoul 27 B2
Sangley Pt. Manila 17 C1
Sankrail Kolkata 14 B1
Sankt-Peterburg St. Petersburg 27 B1
Sankt Veit Vienna 32 A1
Sanlihe Beijing 4 B1
Sanlintang Shanghai 28 C1
Sans Barcelona 4 A1
Sanssouci Berlin 5 B1
Sant Ambrogio, Basilica di Milan 19 B2
Sant Boi de Llobregat Barcelona 4 A1
Sant Feliu de Llobregat Barcelona 4 A1
Sant Joan Despi Barcelona 4 A1
Santa Ana Manila 17 B2
Santa Anita Park Los Angeles 16 B4
Santa Coloma de Gramenet Barcelona 4 A2
Santa Cruz Manila 17 B2
Santa Cruz Mumbai 20 A1
Santa Cruz, I. de Rio de Janeiro 25 B1
Santa Cruz de Olorde Barcelona 4 A1
Santa Efigénia São Paulo 27 B1
Santa Elena Manila 17 B2
Santa Elena del Gomero Santiago 27 B1
Santa Eulalia Barcelona 4 A1
Santa Fe Springs Los Angeles 16 C4
Santa Iria da Azóia Lisbon 16 A2
Santa Julia Santiago 27 C2
Santa Monica Los Angeles 16 B2
Santa Monica Mts. Los Angeles 16 B2
Santa Rosa de Locobe Santiago 27 B2
Santa Teresa de la Ovalle Santiago 27 C1
Santahamina Helsinki 11 C3
Santana São Paulo 27 B1
Santiago Santiago 27 B2
Santiago Benítez ✈ (SCL) Santiago 27 B1
Santo Amaro Lisbon 16 A1
Santo Amaro São Paulo 27 C1
Santo Amaro São Paulo 27 B1
Santo André Lisbon 16 A2
Santo Antão do Tojal Lisbon 16 A2
Santo António, Qta. de Lisbon 16 B1
Santo Tomas, Univ. de Manila 17 B2
Santos Dumont ✈ (SDU) Rio de Janeiro 25 B2
Santoshpur Kolkata 14 B1
Santragachi Kolkata 14 B1
Santry Dublin 10 A2
Sanyuanli Guangzhou 11 B2
São Conrado Rio de Janeiro 25 C1
São Cristovão Rio de Janeiro 25 B1
São Jorge, Castelo de Lisbon 16 A2
São João do Tojal Lisbon 16 A2
São Paulo São Paulo 27 B2
São Paulo Congonhas ✈ (CGH) São Paulo 27 B2
Sapa Kolkata 14 B1
Sapateiro, Cor. do → São Paulo 27 B2
Sarandí Buenos Aires 7 C2
Saraswati → Kolkata 14 A1
Sarecky potok → Prague 25 B2
Saribumi Singapore 28 A2
Saribumi Res. Singapore 28 A2
Sariyer Istanbul 12 B2
Sarria Barcelona 4 A1
Sarsuna Kolkata 14 C1
Sartrouville Paris 24 A2
Sasad Budapest 7 B2
Sashalom Budapest 7 A3
Saska Kępa Warsaw 32 B2

Satalice Prague 25 B3
Satgachi Kolkata 14 B2
Satpukur Kolkata 14 B2
Sätra Stockholm 29 B1
Saúde São Paulo 27 B2
Saugus Boston 6 A2
Saugus → Boston 6 A1
Sault-au-Récollet Montreal 20 A2
Sausalito San Francisco 26 A2
Sawah Besar Jakarta 11 A1
Scald Law Edinburgh 11 B2
Scarborough Toronto 31 A3
Scarborough Bluffs Toronto 31 A3
Sceaux Paris 24 B2
Schaerbeek Brussels 6 A2
Scharfenberg Berlin 5 A2
Schiller Park Chicago 9 B1
Schiller Woods Chicago 9 B1
Schiphol, Amsterdam ✈ (AMS) Amsterdam 2 B1
Schlachtensee Berlin 5 B2
Schlossgarten Berlin 5 A2
Schmargendorf Berlin 5 B2
Schönblick Berlin 5 B5
Schönbrunn Vienna 32 A1
Schöneberg Berlin 5 B3
Schönefeld Berlin 5 B4
Schöneiche Berlin 5 B5
Schönwalde Berlin 5 A1
Schulzendorf Berlin 5 A2
Schwabing Munich 21 B2
Schwanebeck Berlin 5 A4
Schwanenwerder Berlin 5 B2
Schwarzlackenau Vienna 32 A2
Schwechat Vienna 32 B2
Schwechat, Wien ✈ (VIE) Vienna 32 B2
Science and Industry, Museum of Chicago 9 C3
Scitech Museum Atlanta 3 B2
Scopus, Mt. Jerusalem 13 B2
Scottdale Atlanta 3 B3
Seabrook Washington 33 B5
Seacliff San Francisco 26 B2
Seaforth Sydney 29 A2
Seagate New York 22 C1
Seat Pleasant Washington 33 B4
Seaview Wellington 33 B2
SeaWorld Orlando 23 B2
Šeberov Prague 25 C3
Secaucus New York 22 B1
Seddinsee Berlin 5 B5
Seeberg Berlin 5 A5
Seeburg Berlin 5 A1
Seefeld Berlin 5 A5
Segelfeld Berlin 5 B1
Seehof Berlin 5 B2
Segeltorp Stockholm 29 B1
Segrate Milan 19 A2
Seguro Milan 19 A1
Seixal Lisbon 16 B2
Selby Johannesburg 13 B2
Seletar Hills Singapore 28 A3
Seletar Res. Singapore 28 A2
Selhurst London 15 B3
Sembawang Singapore 28 A2
Senago Milan 19 A1
Sending Munich 21 B2
Senju Tokyo 30 A3
Sentryama Osaka 23 A2
Sentosa Singapore 28 B2
Seobinggo Seoul 27 B1
Seocho Seoul 27 C1
Seodaemun Seoul 27 B1
Seokkwan Seoul 27 B2
Seongbuk Seoul 27 B2
Seongdong Seoul 27 B2
Seongsu Seoul 27 B2
Seoul Seoul 27 B2
Seoul National University Seoul 27 C1
Seoul Tower Seoul 27 B1
Sepolia Athens 2 A2
Sepulveda Dam Rec. Area □ Los Angeles 16 A2
Serangoon Singapore 28 A3
Serangoon, Pulau Singapore 28 A3
Serangoon, Sungei → Singapore 28 A3
Serangoon Harbour Singapore 28 A3
Seraya, Pulau Singapore 28 B2
Serebryanka → Moscow 19 B3
Serramonte San Francisco 26 C2
Sesto San Giovanni Milan 19 A2
Sesto Ulteriano Milan 19 B2
Setagaya Tokyo 30 B2
Seter Oslo 23 A3
Setia Budi Jakarta 11 B1
Settebagni Rome 26 A2
Settecamini Rome 26 B2
Settimo Milanese Milan 19 B1
Settsu Osaka 23 A2
Seutula Helsinki 11 A2
Seven Corners Washington 33 B3
Seven Kings London 15 A4
Sèveco → Milan 19 A1
Sevran Paris 24 A4
Sewri Mumbai 20 B2
Sforzesco, Castello Milan 19 B2
Sha Kok Mei Hong Kong 12 A2
Sha Tin Hong Kong 12 A2
Sha Tin Wai Hong Kong 12 A2
Sha'ar Binyamin Jerusalem 13 A2
Shabrämänt Cairo 7 B1
Shah Mosque Tehran 31 B2
Shahdara Delhi 10 A2
Shahe Guangzhou 11 B2
Shahr-e Rey Tehran 31 B2
Shahrak-e Golshahr Tehran 31 B1
Shahrak-e Qods Tehran 31 A1
Shaikh Aomar Baghdad 3 A2
Shakurbasti Delhi 10 A1
Shalkiya Kolkata 14 B1
Shamapur Delhi 10 A1
Sham Shui Po Hong Kong 12 A1
Shamapur Delhi 10 A1
Shamian Guangzhou 11 B2
Shan Mei Hong Kong 12 A2
Shanghai Shanghai 28 B2
Shanghai Hongqiao ✈ (SHA) Shanghai 28 B1
Shanghai Pudong ✈ (PVG) Shanghai 28 B2
Shankill Dublin 10 B3
Sharp I. Hong Kong 12 A2
Shau Kei Wan Hong Kong 12 B2
Shawocun Beijing 4 B1
Shayuan Guangzhou 11 B2
Sheen, L. Orlando 23 B1
Sheepshead Bay New York 22 C2
Shek O Hong Kong 12 B2

Shelter I. Hong Kong 12 B2
Shepherds Bush London 15 A2
Shepperton London 15 B1
Sheremetyevo ✈ (SVO) Moscow 19 A2
Sherman Oaks Los Angeles 16 B2
Sherman Park Chicago 9 C2
Sherwood, L. Orlando 23 A2
Shet Bandar Mumbai 20 B2
Sheung Fa Shan Hong Kong 12 A1
Sheung Lau Wan Hong Kong 12 B2
Sheung Wan Hong Kong 12 B1
Sheva Mumbai 20 B2
Sheva Nhava Mumbai 20 B2
Shiba Tokyo 30 B3
Shibpur Kolkata 14 B1
Shibuya Tokyo 30 B3
Shimogawara Tokyo 30 A2
Shimosalo Tokyo 30 A2
Shimoshakujii Tokyo 30 A2
Shinagawa Tokyo 30 B3
Shing Mun Res. Hong Kong 12 A1
Shinjuku Tokyo 30 A3
Shinjuku National Garden Tokyo 30 A3
Shinkoiwa Tokyo 30 A4
Shinnakano Tokyo 30 A3
Shipai Guangzhou 11 B3
Shirinashi → Osaka 23 B1
Shirogane Tokyo 30 B3
Shitennoji Temple Osaka 23 B2
Shiweitang Guangzhou 11 B2
Shogunle Lagos 14 A2
Shomolu Lagos 14 A2
Shooters Hill London 15 B4
Shoreditch London 15 A3
Shortlands London 15 B4
Shu'afat Jerusalem 13 B2
Shubrâ Cairo 7 A2
Shubrâ el Kheima Cairo 7 A2
Shuikou Guangzhou 11 B1
Sidcup London 15 B4
Siebenhirten Vienna 32 B1
Siedlung Berlin 5 A1
Siekierki Warsaw 32 B2
Sielce Warsaw 32 B2
Siemensstadt Berlin 5 A2
Sierra Madre Los Angeles 16 B4
Sievering Vienna 32 A2
Sighthill Edinburgh 11 B2
Signal Hill Cape Town 8 A1
Siheung Seoul 27 C1
Sikátorpuszta Budapest 7 A3
Silampur Delhi 10 B2
Sillim Seoul 27 C1
Silver, L. Orlando 23 A2
Silver Hill Washington 33 C4
Silver Spring Washington 33 B3
Silvermine Nature Reserve Cape Town 8 B1
Silvolantekojärvi Helsinki 11 B2
Simei Singapore 28 A3
Simla Kolkata 14 B2
Simmering Vienna 32 A2
Simmering Heide Vienna 32 A3
Simonkylä Helsinki 11 B3
Sinchon Seoul 27 B1
Sindang Seoul 27 B1
Singapore ■ Singapore 28 B2
Singapore, Univ. of Singapore 28 B2
Singapore Changi ✈ (SIN) Singapore 28 A3
Sinki, Selat Singapore 28 B2
Sinsa Seoul 27 B2
Sint-Genesius-Rode Brussels 6 B2
Sion Mumbai 20 A2
Sipson London 15 B1
Siqeil Cairo 7 A2
Şişli Istanbul 12 B1
Site of Former World Trade Center = Ground Zero New York 22 B1
Skansen Stockholm 29 B2
Skärholmen Stockholm 29 B1
Skarpäng Stockholm 29 A2
Skarpnäck Stockholm 29 B2
Skaryszewski, Park Warsaw 32 B2
Skokie Chicago 9 A2
Skokie → Chicago 9 A2
Skokie Heritage Museum Chicago 9 A2
Skoklefall Oslo 23 A4
Sköndal Stockholm 29 B2
Skovlunde Copenhagen 8 A2
Skovshoved Copenhagen 8 A3
Skuru Oslo 23 A4
Sky Lake Orlando 23 B2
Skyland Atlanta 3 A2
Slade Green London 15 B5
Slemmestad Oslo 23 B1
Slipi Jakarta 11 B1
Slivenec Prague 25 B2
Sloten Amsterdam 2 A1
Sloterdijk Amsterdam 2 A1
Sloterpark Amsterdam 2 A1
Sluhy Prague 25 A3
Sluzew Warsaw 32 C2
Sluzewiec Warsaw 32 C2
Smichov Prague 25 B2
Smith Forest Preserve Chicago 9 B1
Smolny St. Petersburg 27 B2
Smolny Cathedral St. Petersburg 27 B2
Snake Creek Canal Miami 18 A2
Snakeden Branch → Washington 33 B2
Snarøya Oslo 23 A2
Snättringe Stockholm 29 B1
Soborg Copenhagen 8 A2
Sobreda Lisbon 16 B1
Söderby Stockholm 29 A2
Södermalm Stockholm 29 B2
Soeurs, I. des Montreal 20 B2
Sognsvatn Oslo 23 A3
Soignes, Forêt de Brussels 6 B2
Sok Kwu Wan Hong Kong 12 B1
Sokolniki Moscow 19 B3
Sokolniki Park Moscow 19 B3
Sokołów Warsaw 32 C1
Solalinden Munich 21 B3
Sollentuna Stockholm 29 A1
Solln Munich 21 B2
Solna Stockholm 29 A1
Somerset Washington 33 B3
Somerville Boston 6 A2
Somes I. Wellington 33 B2
Sonari Mumbai 20 B2
Søndersø Copenhagen 8 A2
Songpa Seoul 27 B2
Sony Picture Studio Los Angeles 16 B2
Soroksár Budapest 7 B2

Soroksári Duna → *Budapest* 7 B2
Sosenka → *Moscow* 19 B3
Sosnovka *St. Petersburg* 27 B2
Sŏul = Seoul *Seoul* 27 B2
Soundview *New York* 22 B2
South Beach *New York* 22 C1
South Bend Park *Atlanta* 3 B2
South Boston *Boston* 6 A2
South Decatur *Atlanta* 3 B3
South Deering *Chicago* 9 C3
South El Monte *Los Angeles* 16 B4
South Gate *Los Angeles* 16 C3
South Harbor *Manila* 17 B2
South Harrow *London* 15 A1
South Hd. *Sydney* 29 B2
South Hills *Johannesburg* 13 B2
South Hornchurch *London* 15 A5
South Lawn *Washington* 33 C2
South Miami *Miami* 18 B1
South Norwood *London* 15 B3
South of Market *San Francisco* 26 B2
South Ozone Park *New York* 22 B4
South Pasadena *Los Angeles* 16 B4
South Res. *Boston* 6 A2
South Ruislip *London* 15 A1
South San Francisco
  San Francisco 26 C2
South San Gabriel *Los Angeles* 16 B4
South Shore *Chicago* 9 C3
Southall *London* 15 A1
Southborough *London* 15 B4
Southend *London* 15 B3
Southern California,
  University of *Los Angeles* 16 B3
Southfields *London* 15 B2
Southwark □ *London* 15 B3
Southwest Museum
  Los Angeles 16 B3
Sovang *Copenhagen* 8 B3
Soweto *Johannesburg* 13 B1
Sowhānak *Tehran* 31 A3
Soya *Tokyo* 30 A4
Spandau *Berlin* 5 A1
Spånga *Stockholm* 29 A1
Spanish Monastery *Miami* 18 A2
Spectacle I. *Boston* 6 A2
Speicher-See *Munich* 21 A3
Speising *Vienna* 32 B1
Sphinx *Cairo* 7 B1
Spinaceto *Rome* 26 C1
Spit Junction *Sydney* 29 A2
Spořilov *Prague* 25 B3
Spot Pond *Boston* 6 A2
Spotswood *Melbourne* 18 B1
Springeberg *Berlin* 5 B5
Springfield *Washington* 33 C2
Squantum *Boston* 6 A2
Srednaya Rogatka
  St. Petersburg 27 C2
Śródmieście *Warsaw* 32 B2
Staaken *Berlin* 5 A1
Stabekk *Oslo* 23 A2
Stadlau *Vienna* 32 A2
Stadshuset *Stockholm* 29 B2
Stains *Paris* 24 A3
Stamford Hill *London* 15 A3
Stammersdorf *Vienna* 32 A2
Stanley *Hong Kong* 12 B2
Stanley Pen. *Hong Kong* 12 B2
Stanmore *London* 15 A2
Stapleton *New York* 22 C1
Staraya Derevnya
  St. Petersburg 27 B1
Staré Město *Prague* 25 B2
Stare Miasto *Warsaw* 32 B2
Starke, L. *Orlando* 23 A1
Staten Island Zoo *New York* 22 C1
Staten Islands Ferry
  Terminal *New York* 22 C1
Statenice *Prague* 25 B1
Stedelijk Museum *Amsterdam* 2 A2
Steele Creek *Melbourne* 18 A1
Steenokkerzeel *Brussels* 6 A2
Steer, L. *Orlando* 23 A2
Steglitz *Berlin* 5 B2
Stepaside *Dublin* 10 B2
Stephansdom *Vienna* 32 A2
Stepney *London* 15 A3
Sterling Park *San Francisco* 26 B2
Sticklinge udde *Stockholm* 29 A2
Stickney *Chicago* 9 C2
Stillorgan *Dublin* 10 B2
Stockholm *Stockholm* 29 B2
Stocksund *Stockholm* 29 A2
Stodůlky *Prague* 25 B1
Stoke Newington *London* 15 A3
Stokes Valley *Wellington* 33 B2
Stone Canyon Res.
  Los Angeles 16 B2
Stone Park *Chicago* 9 B1
Stonebridge *London* 15 A2
Stoneham *Boston* 6 A2
Stony Brook Res. *Boston* 6 B2
Stony Creek → *Chicago* 9 C2
Stora Värtan *Stockholm* 29 A2
Store Hareskov *Copenhagen* 8 A2
Store Magleby *Copenhagen* 8 B3
Storholmen *Stockholm* 29 A2
Stoyka *St. Petersburg* 27 B2
Straiton *Edinburgh* 11 B3
Strandfonteïn *Cape Town* 8 B2
Strašnice *Prague* 25 B2
Strasstrudering *Munich* 21 B3
Stratford *London* 15 A4
Strathfield *Sydney* 29 B1
Streatham *London* 15 B3
Streatham Vale *London* 15 B3
Strebersdorf *Vienna* 32 A2
Střešovice *Prague* 25 B2
Střížkov *Prague* 25 B2
Strombeek-Bever *Brussels* 6 A2
Stromovka *Prague* 25 B2
Studio City *Los Angeles* 16 B2
Stureby *Stockholm* 29 B2
Stuvsta *Stockholm* 29 B2
Subhepur *Delhi* 10 A2
Sucat *Manila* 17 C2
Suchdol *Prague* 25 B2
Sucy-en-Brie *Paris* 24 B4
Sue, L. *Orlando* 23 A2
Sugamo *Tokyo* 30 A3
Sugar Loaf Mt. = Açúcar,
  Pão de *Rio de Janeiro* 25 B2
Suge *Tokyo* 30 B2
Suginami *Tokyo* 30 A2
Sugō *Tokyo* 30 B2
Sui Sai Wan *Hong Kong* 12 B1
Suita *Osaka* 23 A2
Suitland *Washington* 33 B4
Sukchar *Kolkata* 14 A2
Sultanahme Camil *Istanbul* 12 B1
Sumida *Tokyo* 30 A3
Sumida → *Tokyo* 30 A3
Sumiyoshi *Osaka* 23 B1

Sumiyoshi Shrine *Osaka* 23 B1
Summerville *Toronto* 31 B1
Summit *Chicago* 9 C2
Sunamachi *Tokyo* 30 A4
Sunbury-on-Thames *London* 15 B1
Sundbyberg *Stockholm* 29 A1
Sundbyerne *Copenhagen* 8 B3
Sung Kong *Hong Kong* 12 B2
Sungei Kadut Industrial
  Estate *Singapore* 28 A2
Sungei Selatar Res. *Singapore* 28 A3
Sunset Park *New York* 22 C2
Sunter *Jakarta* 12 A2
Sunter, Kali → *Jakarta* 12 B2
Suomenlinna *Helsinki* 11 C2
Sur Bahr *Jerusalem* 13 B2
Sura *Kolkata* 14 B2
Suraksan *Seoul* 27 A2
Surbiton *London* 15 B2
Suresnes *Paris* 24 A2
Surfside *Miami* 18 A2
Surquillo *Lima* 14 B2
Surrey Hills *Sydney* 29 B2
Susaek *Seoul* 27 B1
Süssenbrunn *Vienna* 32 A2
Sutton *Dublin* 10 A3
Sutton *London* 15 B2
Suyu *Seoul* 27 B2
Suzukishinden *Tokyo* 30 A2
Svanemøllen *Copenhagen* 8 A3
Sveaborg = Suomenlinna
  Helsinki 11 C2
Sverdlov *Moscow* 19 B2
Svestad *Oslo* 23 A2
Svinö *Helsinki* 11 C1
Swanley *London* 15 B4
Swansea *Toronto* 31 B2
Swinburne I. *New York* 22 C1
Swords *Dublin* 10 A2
Sydenham *Johannesburg* 13 A2
Sydney *Sydney* 29 B2
Sydney, Univ. of *Sydney* 29 B2
Sydney Harbour Bridge
  Sydney 29 B2
Sydney Kingsford Smith ✈
  (SYD) *Sydney* 29 B2
Sydstranden *Copenhagen* 8 B3
Sylvania *Sydney* 29 C1
Syon Park *London* 15 B1
Szczęśliwice *Warsaw* 32 B1
Széchenyi-hegy *Budapest* 7 B1
Széphalom *Budapest* 7 A1

T

Taastrup *Copenhagen* 8 B1
Tabata *Tokyo* 30 A3
Tablada *Buenos Aires* 7 C1
Table B. *Cape Town* 8 A1
Table Mt. *Cape Town* 8 A1
Taboão da Serra *São Paulo* 27 B1
Täby *Stockholm* 29 A2
Tacuba *Mexico City* 18 B1
Tacubaya *Mexico City* 18 B1
Tafelbaai = Table B. *Cape Town* 8 A1
Taft *Orlando* 23 B2
Tagig → *Manila* 17 B2
Taguig *Manila* 17 B2
Tai Hang *Hong Kong* 12 B2
Tai Lo Shan *Hong Kong* 12 A2
Tai Po Tsai *Hong Kong* 12 A2
Tai Seng *Singapore* 28 A3
Tai Shui Hang *Hong Kong* 12 A2
Tai Tam B. *Hong Kong* 12 B2
Tai Tam Tuk Res. *Hong Kong* 12 B2
Tai Wai *Hong Kong* 12 A2
Tai Wan Tau *Hong Kong* 12 B2
Tai Wo Hau *Hong Kong* 12 A2
Tainaka *Osaka* 23 B2
Taishō *Osaka* 23 B1
Taita *Wellington* 33 B2
Tajrish *Tehran* 31 A2
Takaido *Tokyo* 30 A2
Takaishi *Tokyo* 30 B2
Takarazuka *Osaka* 23 A1
Takasago *Tokyo* 30 A4
Takatsu *Tokyo* 30 B2
Takeshita *Tokyo* 30 A2
Takinegawa *Tokyo* 30 A3
Takoma Park *Washington* 33 B3
Taksim *Istanbul* 12 B1
Talaide *Lisbon* 16 A1
Taliganga *Kolkata* 14 B2
Talipapa *Manila* 17 A2
Tallaght *Dublin* 10 B1
Tallkrogen *Stockholm* 29 B2
Tama *Tokyo* 30 B1
Tama → *Tokyo* 30 B2
Tama Kyūryō *Tokyo* 30 B2
Tamaden *Tokyo* 30 A2
Tamagawa-josui → *Tokyo* 30 A1
Taman Sari *Jakarta* 12 A1
Tamanduateí → *São Paulo* 27 B2
Tamboerskloof *Cape Town* 8 A1
Tambora *Jakarta* 12 A1
Tammisalo *Helsinki* 11 B3
Tammūn *Cairo* 7 B2
Tampines *Singapore* 28 A3
Tanah Abang *Jakarta* 12 B1
Tanah Kusir *Jakarta* 12 B1
Tangelo Park *Orlando* 23 B2
Tanjung Duren *Jakarta* 12 B1
Tanjung Priok *Jakarta* 12 A2
Tanum *Oslo* 23 A1
Tapada *Lisbon* 16 A1
Tapanila *Helsinki* 11 B3
Tapiales *Buenos Aires* 7 C1
Tapiola *Helsinki* 11 B1
Tapsia *Kolkata* 14 B2
Tara *Mumbai* 20 A1
Tarabya *Istanbul* 12 B2
Tårbæk *Copenhagen* 8 A3
Tarchomin *Warsaw* 32 B2
Tardeo *Mumbai* 20 B1
Targówek *Warsaw* 32 B2
Tárnby *Copenhagen* 8 B3
Tarqua Bay *Lagos* 14 B2
Tathong Channel *Hong Kong* 12 B2
Tatoio → *Athens* 2 A2
Tatuapé *São Paulo* 27 B2
Taufkirchen *Munich* 21 B2
Tavares, I. dos *Rio de Janeiro* 25 A2
Tavros *Athens* 2 B2
Tawa *Wellington* 33 A1
Te Papa Museum *Wellington* 33 B1
Teaneck *New York* 22 A1
Tebet *Jakarta* 12 B2
Tecamachalco *Mexico City* 18 B1
Ted Williams Tunnel *Boston* 6 A2
Teddington *London* 15 B1
Tegel *Berlin* 5 A2
Tegel, Berlin ✈ (TXL) *Berlin* 5 A2
Tegeler See *Berlin* 5 A2

Tegelort *Berlin* 5 A2
Teheran = Tehrān *Tehran* 31 A2
Teheran *Tehran* 31 A2
Tehrān *Tehran* 31 A2
Tehrān Pārs *Tehran* 31 A3
Tei Tong Tsui *Hong Kong* 12 B2
Tejo, Rio → *Lisbon* 16 A2
Tekstilyshchik *Moscow* 19 B3
Telhal *Lisbon* 16 A1
Telok Blangah *Singapore* 28 B2
Teltow *Berlin* 5 B2
Teltow kanal *Berlin* 5 B3
Tempelhof *Berlin* 5 B3
Tempelhof, Berlin ✈ (THF)
  Berlin 5 B3
Temple City *Los Angeles* 16 B4
Temple Hills *Washington* 33 C4
Templeogue *Dublin* 10 B2
Temppeliaukio Church
  Helsinki 11 B2
Tenafly *New York* 22 A2
Tenayuca, Pirámide de
  Mexico City 18 A1
Tengah → *Singapore* 28 A2
Tennoji *Osaka* 23 B2
Tepalcates *Mexico City* 18 B2
Tepeyac, Parque
  Nacional □ *Mexico City* 18 A1
Terrazzano *Milan* 19 A1
Terre des Indes *Montreal* 20 A2
Terrugem *Lisbon* 16 A1
Tervuren *Brussels* 6 B3
Tervuren, Park van *Brussels* 6 B3
Tetuán *Madrid* 17 B1
Teufelsberg *Berlin* 5 B2
Thalkirchen *Munich* 21 B2
Thames Ditton *London* 15 B1
Thamesmead *London* 15 A4
Thana Cr. → *Mumbai* 20 A2
Thisio *Athens* 2 B2
Thistletown *Toronto* 31 A1
Thomastown *Melbourne* 18 A2
Thompson I. *Boston* 6 A2
Thon Buri *Bangkok* 3 B1
Thornbury *Melbourne* 18 A2
Thorncliffe *Toronto* 31 A2
Thornhill *Toronto* 31 A2
Thornton *Cape Town* 8 A2
Thornton Heath *London* 15 B3
Threipmuir Res. *Edinburgh* 11 B2
Throgs Neck *New York* 22 B3
Tian'anmen Square *Beijing* 4 B2
Tiancun *Beijing* 4 B1
Tibet, L. *Orlando* 23 B1
Tibidabo *Barcelona* 4 A1
Tibradden Mt. *Dublin* 10 B2
Tiburon *San Francisco* 26 A2
Tiburtino *Rome* 26 B2
Ticomán *Mexico City* 18 A2
Tiefersee *Berlin* 5 A5
Tiejiangyin *Beijing* 4 C2
Tiergarten *Berlin* 5 A3
Tijgerhof *Cape Town* 8 A2
Tijuca *Rio de Janeiro* 25 B1
Tijuca, Pico da *Rio de Janeiro* 25 B1
Tijuca △ *Rio de Janeiro* 25 B1
Tikkurila *Helsinki* 11 B3
Tilak Nagar *Delhi* 10 B1
Tilanqiao *Shanghai* 28 B1
Timah, Bukit *Singapore* 28 A2
Timiryazev Park *Moscow* 19 B2
Ting Kau *Hong Kong* 12 A1
Tira *Jerusalem* 13 A1
Tirsa *Cairo* 7 B2
Tishrīyaa *Baghdad* 3 B2
Tiu Keng Leng *Hong Kong* 12 A2
Tizapán *Mexico City* 18 C1
Tlalnepantla → *Mexico City* 18 A1
Tlalpan *Mexico City* 18 C2
To Kwai Wan *Hong Kong* 12 B2
Toa Payoh *Singapore* 28 A3
Točná *Prague* 25 C2
Toco Hills *Atlanta* 3 B2
Todt Hill *New York* 22 C1
Tōkaichiba *Tokyo* 30 B2
Tōkaichiba *Tokyo* 30 B2
Tōkyō *Tokyo* 30 A3
Tōkyō B. = Tōkyō-Wan
  Tokyo 30 B3
Tōkyō Disneyland *Tokyo* 30 B4
Tōkyō Haneda ✈ (HND)
  Tokyo 30 B3
Tōkyō Harbour *Tokyo* 30 B3
Tōkyō-Wan *Tokyo* 30 B4
Tolka → *Dublin* 10 A2
Tollygunge = Taliganga
  Kolkata 14 B2
Tolworth *London* 15 B2
Tomba di Nerone *Rome* 26 B1
Tommy Thompson Park
  Toronto 31 B3
Tondo *Manila* 17 B1
Tongbinggo *Seoul* 27 B1
Tongqiao *Shanghai* 28 A1
Toorak *Melbourne* 18 B2
Topanga State Park △
  Los Angeles 16 B2
Topkapı *Istanbul* 12 B1
Topkapı Palace *Istanbul* 12 B1
Tor di Quinto *Rome* 26 B1
Tor Pignattara *Rome* 26 B2
Tor Sapienza *Rome* 26 B2
Torcy *Paris* 24 A4
Toronto *Toronto* 31 B2
Toronto, Univ. of *Toronto* 31 B2
Toronto City Centre ✈
  (YTZ) *Toronto* 31 B2
Toronto I. *Toronto* 31 B2
Toronto Lester B. Pearson
  Int. ✈ (YYZ) *Toronto* 31 A1
Torre Lupara *Rome* 26 B2
Torre Nova *Rome* 26 B2
Torrellas → *Barcelona* 4 A1
Torrevecchia *Rome* 26 B1
Toshima *Tokyo* 30 A2
Toshimaen *Tokyo* 30 A2
Tottenham *London* 15 A3
Tottenham *Melbourne* 18 B1
Toussus-le-Noble *Paris* 24 B1
Toussus-le-Noble ✈ *Paris* 24 B1
Towchāl Cable Car *Tehran* 31 A2
Tower Hamlets □ *London* 15 A3
Tower of London *London* 15 A3
Towra Pt. *Sydney* 29 C2
Tøyen *Oslo* 23 A3
Toyonaka *Osaka* 23 A1
Trafaria *Lisbon* 16 A1
Traição, Cor. → *São Paulo* 27 B2
Tranegilde *Copenhagen* 8 B2
Trångsund *Stockholm* 29 B3
Trappenfelde *Berlin* 5 A4
Trastévere *Rome* 26 B1

Treasure I. *San Francisco* 26 B2
Trěboradice *Prague* 25 B3
Třebotov *Prague* 25 C1
Tremblay-en-France *Paris* 24 A4
Tremembe → *São Paulo* 27 A2
Tremont *New York* 22 A2
Trenno *Milan* 19 B1
Treptow *Berlin* 5 B3
Três Rios, Sa. dos
  Rio de Janeiro 25 B1
Trevi, Fontana di *Rome* 26 B1
Trezzano sul Navíglio *Milan* 19 B1
Trieste *Rome* 26 B2
Trinidad *Washington* 33 B4
Trinity *Edinburgh* 11 B2
Trinity College *Dublin* 10 A2
Trionfale *Rome* 26 B1
Triulzo *Milan* 19 B2
Troja *Prague* 25 B2
Trollbäcken *Stockholm* 29 B3
Trombay *Mumbai* 20 A2
Troparevo *Moscow* 19 C1
Trudeau, Montréal ✈ (YUL)
  Montreal 20 A1
Trudyashchikhsya, Ostrov
  St. Petersburg 27 B1
Tryvasshøgda *Oslo* 23 A3
Tsang Lan Shue *Hong Kong* 12 A2
Tseung Kwan *Hong Kong* 12 A2
Tsim Sha Tsui *Hong Kong* 12 B2
Tsing Yi *Hong Kong* 12 A1
Tsova *Jerusalem* 13 B1
Tsuen Wan *Hong Kong* 12 A1
Tsur Hadassa *Jerusalem* 13 B1
Tsurumi → *Tokyo* 30 B3
Tsz Wan Shan *Hong Kong* 12 A2
Tuas *Singapore* 28 B1
Tuomarila *Helsinki* 11 B1
Tureberg *Stockholm* 29 A1
Turffontein *Johannesburg* 13 B2
Turkey L. *Orlando* 23 A2
Turkey Lake Park *Orlando* 23 A2
Turner Field *Atlanta* 3 B2
Turnham Green *London* 15 B2
Turnhouse *Edinburgh* 11 B1
Tuscolana, Via *Rome* 26 B2
Twelve Apostles *Cape Town* 8 A1
Twickenham *London* 15 B1
Twickenham Rugby
  Ground *London* 15 B1
Twin Peaks *San Francisco* 26 B2
Two Rock Mt. *Dublin* 10 B2
Tymon North *Dublin* 10 B1
Tysons Corner *Washington* 33 B2

U

U.S. Capitol *Washington* 33 B3
U.S. Cellular Field *Chicago* 9 C3
Ubeidiya *Jerusalem* 13 B2
Uberaba → *São Paulo* 27 B2
Ubin, Pulau *Singapore* 28 A3
Uccle *Brussels* 6 B2
Udelnaya *St. Petersburg* 27 A2
Udelnoe *St. Petersburg* 27 B1
Uddling *Munich* 21 A1
Ueno *Tokyo* 30 A3
Ůholíčky *Prague* 25 B1
Ûhříněves *Prague* 25 B3
Uithoorn *Amsterdam* 2 B1
Újpadov *Warsaw* 32 B2
Újpalota *Budapest* 7 A2
Újpest *Budapest* 7 A2
Ukita *Tokyo* 30 A4
Ullerup *Copenhagen* 8 B3
Ullevål *Oslo* 23 A3
Ulriksdal *Stockholm* 29 A1
Ulyanka *St. Petersburg* 27 B1
Um Al-Khanazir Island
  Baghdad 3 B2
Umeda *Osaka* 23 A1
Ůmraniye *Istanbul* 12 B2
Underground Atlanta *Atlanta* 3 B2
Underhill, L. *Orlando* 23 A3
Unětický potok → *Prague* 25 B2
Unhos *Lisbon* 16 A2
Unidad Santa Fe *Mexico City* 18 B1
Union City *New York* 22 B1
Union Port *New York* 22 B2
Union Station *Toronto* 31 B2
United Center *Chicago* 9 B2
United Nations
  Headquarters *New York* 22 B2
Universal Studios *Los Angeles* 16 B2
Universal Studios *Orlando* 23 B2
Universidad *Madrid* 17 B1
Universidad de Chile *Santiago* 27 B2
University Park *Washington* 33 B4
Unterföhring *Munich* 21 A2
Unterhaching *Munich* 21 B2
Unterlaa *Vienna* 32 B2
Untermenzing *Munich* 21 A1
Upper B. *New York* 22 C1
Upper Elmers End *London* 15 B3
Upper New York B. = Upper
  B. *New York* 22 C1
Upper Norwood *London* 15 B3
Upper Peirce Res. *Singapore* 28 A2
Upper Sydenham *London* 15 B3
Upper Tooting *London* 15 B2
Upton *London* 15 A4
Uptown *Chicago* 9 B2
Uran *Mumbai* 20 B2
Urayasu *Tokyo* 30 A4
Urbe ✈ *Rome* 26 B2
Úritsk *St. Petersburg* 27 C1
Ürömi *Budapest* 7 A2
Ursus *Warsaw* 32 B1
Ursvik *Stockholm* 29 A1
Usera *Madrid* 17 B1
Ushigome *Tokyo* 30 A3
Usina *Rio de Janeiro* 25 B1
Úsküdar *Istanbul* 12 B2
Ust-Slavyanka *St. Petersburg* 27 C3
Uteke *Stockholm* 29 A3
Utrata *Warsaw* 32 B1
Uttarpara *Kolkata* 14 B1
Uttersløv Mose *Copenhagen* 8 A2

V

Václavské námeští *Prague* 25 B2
Vadaul *Mumbai* 20 A2
Vaires-sur-Marne *Paris* 24 A4
Valby *Copenhagen* 8 B3
Valcannuta *Rome* 26 B1
Valdelatas *Madrid* 17 A1
Vale *Washington* 33 B2
Valenton *Paris* 24 B3
Valera *Milan* 19 A1
Vallcarca *Barcelona* 4 A1
Valldoreix *Barcelona* 4 A1
Vallecas *Madrid* 17 B2
Vallensbæk *Copenhagen* 8 B2
Vallensbæk Strand *Copenhagen* 8 B2
Vallentunasjön *Stockholm* 29 A2
Valleranello *Rome* 26 C1
Vallisaari *Helsinki* 11 C3
Vallvidrera *Barcelona* 4 A1
Valvidrera → *Barcelona* 4 A1
Vanak *Tehran* 31 A2
Vanda = Vantaa *Helsinki* 11 B2
Vangede *Copenhagen* 8 A3
Vaniköy *Istanbul* 12 B2
Vanløse *Copenhagen* 8 A2
Vantaa *Helsinki* 11 B2
Vantaankoski *Helsinki* 11 B2
Vantaanpuisto *Helsinki* 11 B2
Vanves *Paris* 24 B2
Varedo *Milan* 19 A1
Varkiza *Athens* 2 C2
Vartiokylä *Helsinki* 11 B3
Vartiosaari *Helsinki* 11 B3
Vasamuseet *Stockholm* 29 B2
Vasco *Cape Town* 8 A2
Vasfanärd *Tehran* 31 A2
Vashi *Mumbai* 20 A2
Vasilyevskiy, Ostrov
  St. Petersburg 27 B1
Vatican City ■ *Rome* 26 B1
Vaucluse *Sydney* 29 B2
Vaucresson *Paris* 24 A1
Vaughan *Toronto* 31 A1
Vauhallan *Paris* 24 B2
Vaujours *Paris* 24 A4
Vauxhall *London* 15 B3
Vecsés *Budapest* 7 B3
Veleň *Prague* 25 A3
Veleslavín *Prague* 25 B2
Vélizy-Villacoublay *Paris* 24 B2
Velká-Chuchle *Prague* 25 B2
Velké Přílepy *Prague* 25 B1
Venda Seca *Lisbon* 16 A1
Venetian Islands *Miami* 18 B2
Venice *Los Angeles* 16 C2
Ventas *Madrid* 17 B1
Ventorro del Cano *Madrid* 17 B1
Venustiano Carranza
  Mexico City 18 B2
Verdi *Paris* 24 B2
Verdugo Mts. *Los Angeles* 16 A2
Verdun *Montreal* 20 B2
Vérrheaom *Budapest* 7 B1
Vermelho → *São Paulo* 27 B1
Vernon *Los Angeles* 16 C3
Verrières-le-Buisson *Paris* 24 B2
Versailles *Buenos Aires* 7 B1
Versailles *Paris* 24 B1
Veshnyaki *Moscow* 19 B3
Vesoly Posolok *St. Petersburg* 27 B2
Vestra *Helsinki* 11 B2
Vestskoven *Copenhagen* 8 B2
Vicálvaro *Madrid* 17 B2
Vicente Lopez *Buenos Aires* 7 B2
Victoria *Hong Kong* 12 B1
Victoria, Mt. *Wellington* 33 B1
Victoria, Pont *Montreal* 20 B2
Victoria and Alfred
  Waterfront *Cape Town* 8 A1
Victoria Gardens *Mumbai* 20 B2
Victoria Harbour *Hong Kong* 12 B1
Victoria Island *Lagos* 14 B2
Victoria I. *Johannesburg* 13 B2
Victoria Lawn Tennis
  Courts *Melbourne* 18 B2
Victoria Park *Singapore* 28 B2
Victoria Peak *Hong Kong* 12 B1
Vienna = Wien *Vienna* 32 A2
Vienna *Washington* 33 B2
Vietnam Veterans
  Memorial *Washington* 33 B3
Vietnam War Museum
  Chicago 9 B3
View Park *Los Angeles* 16 C3
Vigário Geral *Rio de Janeiro* 25 B1
Vigentino *Milan* 19 B2
Viggbyholm *Stockholm* 29 A2
Vighignolo *Milan* 19 B1
Viikki *Helsinki* 11 B3
Vikhroli *Mumbai* 20 A2
Vila Guilherme *São Paulo* 27 B2
Vila Isabel *Rio de Janeiro* 25 B1
Vila Jaguára *São Paulo* 27 B1
Vila Madalena *São Paulo* 27 B1
Vila Maria *São Paulo* 27 B2
Vila Mariana *São Paulo* 27 B2
Vila Prudente *São Paulo* 27 B2
Viladecans *Barcelona* 4 B1
Vile Parle *Mumbai* 20 A2
Vila Adelina *Buenos Aires* 7 B1
Villa Barilari *Buenos Aires* 7 C2
Villa C. Colon *Buenos Aires* 7 C2
Villa Ciudadela *Buenos Aires* 7 B1
Villa de Guadalupe
  Mexico City 18 B2
Villa Devoto *Buenos Aires* 7 B1
Villa Diamante *Buenos Aires* 7 C2
Villa Dominico *Buenos Aires* 7 C3
Villa Lugano *Buenos Aires* 7 C2
Villa Lynch *Buenos Aires* 7 B1
Villa Madero *Buenos Aires* 7 C1
Villa Sáenz Pena *Buenos Aires* 7 B1
Villa Urquiza *Buenos Aires* 7 B1
Villaverde *Madrid* 17 B1
Villecresnes *Paris* 24 B4
Villejuif *Paris* 24 B3
Villemomble *Paris* 24 A4
Villeneuve-la-Garenne *Paris* 24 A2
Villeneuve-le-Roi *Paris* 24 B3
Villeneuve-St-Georges *Paris* 24 B3
Villeparisis *Paris* 24 A4
Villepinte *Paris* 24 A4
Villevaudé *Paris* 24 A4
Villiers-le-Bâcle *Paris* 24 B1
Villiers-sur-Marne *Paris* 24 B4
Villinki *Helsinki* 11 C3

Villoresi, Canale *Milan* 19 A1
Vilvoorde *Brussels* 6 A2
Vimodrone *Milan* 19 A2
Vimont *Montreal* 20 A1
Vincennes *Paris* 24 A3
Vincennes, Bois de *Paris* 24 B3
Vineland *Orlando* 23 B1
Vinings *Atlanta* 3 A1
Vinohrady *Prague* 25 B2
Vinoř *Prague* 25 B3
Violet Hill *Hong Kong* 12 B2
Virginia, L. *Orlando* 23 A2
Virginia Gardens *Miami* 18 B1
Virginia Key *Miami* 18 B2
Viroflay *Paris* 24 B2
Vironas *Athens* 2 B2
Virum *Copenhagen* 8 A2
Visitacion Valley
  San Francisco 26 B2
Vista Alegre *Lima* 14 B3
Vista Alegre *Santiago* 27 C1
Vista Grove *Atlanta* 3 A3
Vitacura *Santiago* 27 B2
Vitinia *Rome* 26 C1
Vitry-sur-Seine *Paris* 24 B3
Vizcaya Museum and
  Gardens *Miami* 18 B2
Vladykino *Moscow* 19 A2
Vlezenbeek *Brussels* 6 B1
Vokovice *Prague* 25 B2
Volders *Amsterdam* 2 A2
Vösendorf *Vienna* 32 B2
Voula *Athens* 2 C2
Vouliagmeni *Athens* 2 C2
Vredehoek *Cape Town* 8 A1
Vršovice *Prague* 25 B2
Vyborgskaya Storona
  St. Petersburg 27 B2
Vykhino *Moscow* 19 B3
Vyšehrad *Prague* 25 B2

W

Wachterhof *Munich* 21 B3
Wadala *Mumbai* 20 A2
Wadestown *Wellington* 33 B1
Wadi al-Arayis *Jerusalem* 13 B2
Wadi Fukin *Jerusalem* 13 B1
Waduk Pluit *Jakarta* 12 A1
Wah Fu *Hong Kong* 12 B1
Wahda *Baghdad* 3 B2
Währing *Vienna* 32 A2
Waidmannslust *Berlin* 5 A3
Wainuiomata *Wellington* 33 B2
Wainuiomata → *Wellington* 33 B2
Wakefield *Boston* 6 A2
Waldesruh *Berlin* 5 B4
Waldperlach *Munich* 21 B3
Waldtrudering *Munich* 21 B3
Walkinstown *Dublin* 10 B1
Wall Street *New York* 22 B1
Walt Disney World *Orlando* 23 B1
Walter D. Stone Memorial
  Zoo *Boston* 6 A1
Waltham *Boston* 6 A1
Walthamstow *London* 15 A3
Walton-on-Thames *London* 15 B1
Wambeek *Brussels* 6 A3
Wan Chai *Hong Kong* 12 B2
Wandsworth □ *London* 15 B2
Wannsee *Berlin* 5 B2
Wansdorf *Berlin* 5 A1
Wanstead *London* 15 A4
Wapping *London* 15 A3
Ward *Dublin* 10 A2
Ward I. *Wellington* 33 B2
Wards I. *New York* 22 B2
Warnberg *Munich* 21 B2
Warner Brothers Studios
  Los Angeles 16 B2
Warráq el 'Arab *Cairo* 7 A2
Warringal Park *Melbourne* 18 A2
Warriston *Edinburgh* 11 B2
Warsaw = Warszawa
  Warsaw 32 B2
Warszawa *Warsaw* 32 B2
Warszawa ✈ (WAW)
  Warsaw 32 B1
Wartenberg *Berlin* 5 A4
Washington *Washington* 33 B3
Washington Heights
  New York 22 A2
Washington Park *Chicago* 9 C3
Washington Ronald
  Reagan National ✈
  (DCA) *Washington* 33 B3
Wat Pho *Bangkok* 3 B1
Water of Leith → *Edinburgh* 11 B3
Watergraafsmeer *Amsterdam* 2 A2
Waterland *Amsterdam* 2 A2
Waterloo *Brussels* 6 B2
Waterloo *Wellington* 33 B2
Watermael-Boitsfort *Brussels* 6 B2
Watertown *Boston* 6 A1
Watsonia *Melbourne* 18 A2
Waverley *Johannesburg* 13 A2
Waverley *Sydney* 29 B2
Wawer *Warsaw* 32 B2
Wawrzyszew *Warsaw* 32 B1
Wazirabad *Delhi* 10 A2
Wazīrīya *Baghdad* 3 A2
Wazirpur *Delhi* 10 A2
Wealdstone *London* 15 A1
Wedding *Berlin* 5 A3
Weehawken *New York* 22 B1
Weesp *Amsterdam* 2 B2
Weidling *Vienna* 32 A1
Weidlingbach *Vienna* 32 A1
Weigongcun *Beijing* 4 B1
Weissensee *Berlin* 5 A3
Wellesley Hills *Boston* 6 B1
Welling *London* 15 B4
Wellington *Boston* 6 A2
Wellington *Wellington* 33 B1
Wellington Int. ✈ (WLE)
  Wellington 33 B1
Welvreden Park
  Johannesburg 13 A1
Wembley *London* 15 A2
Wemmel *Brussels* 6 A1
Wenceslas Square =
  Vaclavské námeští *Prague* 25 B2

Wendenschloss *Berlin* 5 B4
Wennington *London* 15 A5
Werneuchen *Berlin* 5 A5
West Don → *Toronto* 31 A2
West Drayton *London* 15 A1
West Ham *London* 15 A4
West Harrow *London* 15 A1
West Heath *London* 15 B4
West Hill *Toronto* 31 A3
West Hollywood *Los Angeles* 16 B2
West Lamma Channel
  Hong Kong 12 B1
West Los Angeles,
  University of *Los Angeles* 16 C2
West Medford *Boston* 6 A2
West Miami *Miami* 18 B1
West Molesey *London* 15 B1
West New York *New York* 22 B1
West of Twin Peaks
  San Francisco 26 B2
West Park *Johannesburg* 13 A1
West Rouge *Toronto* 31 A4
West Roxbury *Boston* 6 B2
West Springfield *Washington* 33 C2
West Town *Chicago* 9 B2
West Wharf *Karachi* 13 B1
Westchester *Chicago* 9 B1
Westchester *New York* 22 A2
Westcliff *Johannesburg* 13 B2
Westdene *Johannesburg* 13 B1
Westend *Helsinki* 11 C1
Wester Hailes *Edinburgh* 11 B2
Westerham *Munich* 21 B2
Western Addition
  San Francisco 26 B2
Westgate *Washington* 33 B3
Westlake *Cape Town* 8 B1
Westlake *San Francisco* 26 C2
Westminster *London* 15 A3
Westmont *Boston* 6 B1
Westmount *Montreal* 20 B2
Weston *Toronto* 31 A2
Westwood Village *Los Angeles* 16 B2
Westzaan *Amsterdam* 2 A1
Wetton *Cape Town* 8 B2
Wexford *Toronto* 31 A3
Weybridge *London* 15 B1
Wezembeek-Oppem *Brussels* 6 A2
White Cloud Hill = Baiyun
  Hill *Guangzhou* 11 B2
White House, The *Washington* 33 B3
Whitechapel *London* 15 A3
Whitehall *Dublin* 10 A2
Whittier *Los Angeles* 16 C4
Whitton *London* 15 B1
Wieden *Vienna* 32 A2
Wien *Vienna* 32 A2
Wien-Schwechat ✈ (VIE)
  Vienna 32 B3
Wienerberg *Vienna* 32 B2
Wierzbno *Warsaw* 32 B2
Wijde Wormer *Amsterdam* 2 A2
Wilanów *Warsaw* 32 B2
Wilanów → *Warsaw* 32 C2
Wilds, The *Johannesburg* 13 B2
Wilhelmshagen *Berlin* 5 B5
Wilket Creek Park *Toronto* 31 A2
Wilkieston *Edinburgh* 11 B1
Will Rogers State Historical
  Park △ *Los Angeles* 16 B1
Willbrook *Dublin* 10 B2
Willesden *London* 15 A2
Willesden Green *London* 15 A2
Williamsbridge *New York* 22 A2
Williamsburg *New York* 22 B2
Williamsburg *Orlando* 23 B2
Williamstown *Melbourne* 18 B1
Willoughby *Sydney* 29 A2
Willow Springs *Chicago* 9 C1
Willowdale *Toronto* 31 A2
Wilmersdorf *Berlin* 5 B2
Wilmette *Chicago* 9 A2
Wilmington *Boston* 6 A1
Wimbledon *London* 15 B2
Wimbledon Common *London* 15 B2
Wimbledon Tennis Ground
  London 15 B2
Winchester *Boston* 6 A1
Windermere *Cape Town* 8 A2
Windermere *Orlando* 23 B1
Windsor *Johannesburg* 13 A1
Windsor, Gare *Montreal* 20 B2
Windsor Hills *Los Angeles* 16 C2
Windy Arbour *Dublin* 10 B2
Winning *Munich* 21 A2
Wissous *Paris* 24 B2
Wittenau *Berlin* 5 A3
Witwatersrand, Univ. of
  Johannesburg 13 B2
Wlochy *Warsaw* 32 B1
Wo Mei *Hong Kong* 12 A2
Wo Yi Hop *Hong Kong* 12 A1
Woburn *Boston* 6 A1
Woburn *Toronto* 31 A3
Wola *Warsaw* 32 B1
Wolf Trap Farm Park
  Washington 33 B2
Wolgok *Seoul* 27 B2
Wolica *Warsaw* 32 C1
Wólka Węglowa *Warsaw* 32 B1
Wollaston *Boston* 6 B2
Woltersdorf *Berlin* 5 B5
Woluwe-St-Lambert *Brussels* 6 A2
Woluwe-St-Pierre *Brussels* 6 A2
Wong Chuk Hang *Hong Kong* 12 B2
Wong Chuk Wan *Hong Kong* 12 A2
Wong Chuk Yeung
  Hong Kong 12 A2
Wong Tai Sin *Hong Kong* 12 A2
Wood Green *London* 15 A3
Woodbine Race Track
  Toronto 31 A1
Woodbridge *Toronto* 31 A1
Woodford *London* 15 A4
Woodford Bridge *London* 15 A4
Woodford Green *London* 15 A4
Woodhaven *New York* 22 B2
Woodhouselee *Edinburgh* 11 B2
Woodlands *Singapore* 28 A2
Woodmont *Washington* 33 B3
Woodside *New York* 22 B2
Woodside *London* 15 B3
Woollahra *Sydney* 29 B2
Woolooware B. *Sydney* 29 C1
Woolwich *London* 15 A4
World Trade Center, site of
  former *New York* 22 B1
Worli *Mumbai* 20 A1
Worth *Chicago* 9 C2
Wren's Nest *Atlanta* 3 B1

Wrigley Field *Chicago* 9 B3
Wuhlgarten *Berlin* 5 A4
Wujiaochang *Shanghai* 28 B2
Würm → *Munich* 21 A1
Würm-kanal *Munich* 21 A1
Wusong *Shanghai* 28 B1
Wyczółki *Warsaw* 32 C1
Wygoda *Warsaw* 32 B2
Wynberg *Cape Town* 8 B1

X

Xabregas *Lisbon* 16 A2
Xianggang = Hong Kong
  Hong Kong 12 B1
Xiaogang Park *Guangzhou* 11 B2
Xiaoping *Guangzhou* 11 A2
Xiasha chong *Guangzhou* 11 B1
Xichang *Guangzhou* 11 A2
Xicheng *Beijing* 4 B1
Xidan *Beijing* 4 B2
Xizhimen *Beijing* 4 B1
Xochimilco, Parque
  Ecológico *Mexico City* 18 C2
Xuanwu *Beijing* 4 B2
Xuhui *Shanghai* 28 B1

Y

Yaba *Lagos* 14 A2
Yaftābād *Tehran* 31 A2
Yahara *Tokyo* 30 A2
Yaho *Tokyo* 30 A1
Yakire *Tokyo* 30 A4
Yaksu *Seoul* 27 B2
Yamada *Osaka* 23 A1
Yamada *Tokyo* 30 B2
Yamato → *Osaka* 23 B1
Yan Kit *Singapore* 28 A3
Yanbu *Guangzhou* 11 A2
Yangcheon *Seoul* 27 B1
Yanghuayuan *Beijing* 4 C1
Yangjae *Seoul* 27 C2
Yangjiazhuang *Shanghai* 28 A1
Yangjing *Shanghai* 28 B2
Yangpu *Shanghai* 28 B2
Yangpu Park *Shanghai* 28 B2
Yanmawa *Bangkok* 3 B2
Yannawa *Bangkok* 3 B2
Yarra Bend Park *Melbourne* 18 A2
Yarraville *Melbourne* 18 A1
Yau Tong *Hong Kong* 12 B2
Yauza → *Moscow* 19 A3
Yeading *London* 15 A1
Yedikule *Istanbul* 12 C1
Yenikapı *Istanbul* 12 C1
Yeniköy *Istanbul* 12 B2
Yeongdeungpo *Seoul* 27 B1
Yeongdong *Seoul* 27 B2
Yeouido *Seoul* 27 B1
Yerba Buena I. *San Francisco* 26 B2
Yerres *Paris* 24 B4
Yerushalayim = Jerusalem
  Jerusalem 13 B2
Yiheyuan *Beijing* 4 A1
Yıldız Park *Istanbul* 12 B2
Yinhangzhen *Shanghai* 28 A1
Yishun *Singapore* 28 A2
Ylästö *Helsinki* 11 B2
Yodo → *Osaka* 23 A2
Yongdingman *Beijing* 4 B2
Yongfucun *Guangzhou* 11 B2
Yongsan *Seoul* 27 B1
Yonkers *New York* 22 A2
York *Toronto* 31 A2
York Mills *Toronto* 31 A2
York University *Toronto* 31 A1
You'anmen *Beijing* 4 B1
Youngsfield *Cape Town* 8 B1
Yuanxiatian *Guangzhou* 11 A2
Yuexiu Park *Guangzhou* 11 B2
Yugo-Zarad *Moscow* 19 B2
Yuhalixqui, Volcan
  Mexico City 18 C2
Yung Shue Wan *Hong Kong* 12 B1
Yūsofābād *Tehran* 31 A2

Z

Zaandam *Amsterdam* 2 A1
Zaandijk *Amsterdam* 2 A1
Zaanstad *Amsterdam* 2 A1
Záběhlice *Prague* 25 B2
Zabki *Warsaw* 32 B2
Zacisze *Warsaw* 32 B2
Zahrā *Baghdad* 3 A1
Žalov *Prague* 25 B1
Zaluski *Warsaw* 32 C1
Zamdorf *Munich* 21 B2
Zanevka *St. Petersburg* 27 B3
Zapote *Manila* 17 C1
Zaventem *Brussels* 6 A2
Zawady *Warsaw* 32 B2
Zâwyet 'Abû Musallam *Cairo* 7 B1
Zawrá' Park *Baghdad* 3 B2
Zbraslav *Prague* 25 C2
Zbuzany *Prague* 25 B1
Zdiby *Prague* 25 B2
Zeekoevlei *Cape Town* 8 B2
Zehlendorf *Berlin* 5 B2
Zenne → *Brussels* 6 B1
Žeraň *Warsaw* 32 B2
Zerzeń *Warsaw* 32 B2
Zeytinburnu *Istanbul* 12 C1
Zhabei *Shanghai* 28 B1
Zhdanov *Moscow* 19 B3
Zhenru *Shanghai* 28 B1
Zhernovka *St. Petersburg* 27 B3
Zhongshan Park *Shanghai* 28 B1
Zhoucun *Guangzhou* 11 A2
Zhoujiadu *Shanghai* 28 B1
Zhoujiazhen *Shanghai* 28 A1
Zhulebino *Moscow* 19 B4
Zhushadi *Guangzhou* 11 A3
Zielona *Warsaw* 32 B3
Zielonka *Warsaw* 32 B3
Žižkov *Prague* 25 B2
Zličín *Prague* 25 B1
Zografou *Athens* 2 B2
Zoliborz *Warsaw* 32 B1
Zonnebloem *Cape Town* 8 A1
Zugliget *Budapest* 7 B1
Zugló *Budapest* 7 A2
Zuiderwoude *Amsterdam* 2 A3
Zumbi *Rio de Janeiro* 25 B2
Zunderdorp *Amsterdam* 2 A2
Zuvuvu → *São Paulo* 27 C1
Zwanenburg *Amsterdam* 2 A1
Zwölfaxing *Vienna* 32 B2

CITY GAZETTEER

The entries below provide information on places of interest in cities throughout the world that have particularly large numbers of visitors, whether in a business or tourist capacity. The map page reference at the start of an entry indicates that one or more relevant maps are included in the City Maps section.

Accra, Ghana

Accra is not the most beautiful city in West Africa, but its people are considered to be among the friendliest and best educated. It has several lively markets and a National Museum with displays of West African art and artefacts. Near the city are some beautiful sandy beaches, although visitors should be alert to the powerful undertow. Further along the coast are forts and castles that once served as slave-trading centres, including St George's Castle at Elmina, the oldest European structure in sub-Saharan Africa.

Agra, India

Agra is visited primarily for its architectural wonders, especially the 17th-century Taj Mahal. This magical building, a symbol of Mughal emperor Shah Jahan's love for his favourite wife, Mumtaz Mahal, captures the imagination even when crowded with tourists in the heat of the day. Agra's 16th-century Red Fort contains elaborately decorated royal apartments and gardens that give a vivid impression of life at the Mughal court. Just 40 km (25 miles) away is the Mughal 'ghost city' of Fatehpur Sikri which was abandoned almost immediately after it had been built in the 1570s.

Taj Mahal, Agra

Amsterdam, The Netherlands   *Map page 2*

In the centre of Amsterdam is a network of canals, crossed by around a thousand bridges and edged with tree-lined streets of 17th- and 18th-century gabled houses. Canal cruises are an excellent way to get to know the city, and visitors can also hire bicycles – a major form of transport in Amsterdam. Among the museums are the Rijksmuseum, with its famous art collection, the Van Gogh Museum, and the Stedelijk Museum, housing modern art. The heart of the city is Dam Square, with the royal palace and Anne Frank's house (now a museum) close by. Rembrandt's house can also be visited in an area full of bars, nightclubs and restaurants.

Antwerp, Belgium

A vibrant city with much to see, Antwerp – on the River Scheldt and Europe's second largest port – deserves to be a highly rated tourist destination. At the heart of its beautiful old town is the Great Market, with a 16th-century town hall. Nearby, among cobbled streets lined with bars, restaurants and shops, is the impressive Gothic cathedral with paintings by Rubens, the city's most famous artist. There is also much to attract those who want a really enjoyable night on the town.

Athens, Greece   *Map page 2*

Athens is a curious mixture of ancient and modern, where ugly concrete tower blocks rub shoulders with Classical monuments. Dominating the centre of the city are the ruins on the Acropolis, dating from the 5th century BC and crowned by the magnificent Parthenon. Other interesting ruins include the Temple of Olympian Zeus, the largest temple in Greece. The National Archaeological Museum houses gold artefacts from Mycenae and spectacular Minoan frescoes. Nestling beneath the Acropolis is the engaging Pláka quarter, with its small Byzantine churches and bustling tavernas. For most visitors the centre of Athens is Syntagma Square, with its large hotels, banks and open-air cafés. Ferries to the islands depart from the port of Piraeus, 10 km (6 miles) from the square.

Atlanta, Georgia, USA   *Map page 3*

Beneath the glittering high-rise buildings of Atlanta's modern financial centre lies 'Underground Atlanta' – the revitalized old centre, complete with cobbled, gas-lit streets and packed with shops and restaurants. The piazza above it is filled with street entertainers and flanked by the Coca-Cola Museum. Atlanta is most famously associated with Martin Luther King, and an area of the city is devoted to his memory and to the history of the civil rights movement. The Centennial Olympic Park, with its Fountain of Rings, is an entertaining outdoor venue, and the adjacent CNN Center provides an interesting studio tour.

Auckland, New Zealand

The heart of Auckland is the magnificent Waitemata Harbour, where sailing is a popular pastime. The city is not renowned for its nightlife, but it is pleasant to walk its streets, perhaps following the 13 km (8-mile) Coast-to-Coast Walkway from the Ferry Building to Manukau Harbour. On the route, in an area of parkland known as The Domain, is the Auckland Museum, with a unique collection of Maori and Pacific Island artefacts. Beyond is the inner suburb of Parnell, with its colonial buildings, east of which is Underwater World, a particularly impressive aquarium. There are several city beaches, and surfing beaches beyond the Waitakere Ranges.

Bangkok, Thailand   *Map page 3*

With its choking traffic, Bangkok can be both a daunting and an exhilarating city for short-stay visitors. Something of the old Siam can be uncovered by using the river-bus service to visit the Royal Grand Palace and the ornate Temple of the Emerald Buddha (Wat Phra Keo). Other Buddhist temples include the Temple of the Dawn (Wat Arun), whose 82 m (266 ft) high gilded stupa is best seen from the Chao Phraya River. At Jim Thompson's House there is an extraordinary private museum of Thai domestic architecture. The network of canals, with their floating markets, is well worth exploring, as are the shops for silk and other textiles, clothes, jewellery and handicrafts. Night-time entertainment includes traditional dancing and Thai boxing.

Floating market, Bangkok

Barcelona, Spain   *Map page 4*

The capital of Catalonia and Spain's second city, Barcelona is a major port with a fashionable, cosmopolitan cultural life. Particularly enjoyable is strolling along the Ramblas, a broad avenue which bisects central Barcelona, and has a vibrant street life. At the southern end is the renovated harbour area, with shops, restaurants and tapas bars. The district of greatest historic interest is the Barri Gòtic, where medieval houses cluster around the great Gothic cathedral, La Seu. Barcelona has over 50 museums and galleries, including world-class museums dedicated to the works of Picasso and Miró, but it is the buildings of Antonio Gaudí that are most often associated with the city. His incomplete Sagrada Família Cathedral has become a symbol for Barcelona, and is perhaps the most fantastic of all his eccentric creations.

Beijing, China   *Map page 4*

Despite Beijing's daunting scale, extreme climate and heavy traffic, its sights are well worth visiting. They include the massive Tiananmen Square, the Mao Mausoleum, the Great Hall of the People, the Imperial Palace (Forbidden City), the buildings of the Summer Palace along the shore of Kunming Lake, and the 15th-century Temple of Heaven. Beijing has many interesting parks, including Beihai Park with its historic buildings and exquisite Jade Island. However, perhaps the most famous attraction of all is the Great Wall, which can be visited at Badaling, just 70 km (40 miles) north-west of the city, on a trip that also takes in the Ming tombs in the Shisan Ling Valley.

Berlin, Germany   *Map page 5*

Since 1990, when West and East Berlin were united, intense building activity has transformed Mitte, the historic centre of this dynamic city. From the modern dome on the renovated Reichstag building there are fine views of the glittering new buildings, such as those of Potsdamer Platz. In contrast, to the east of the Brandenburg Gate is an area of grand old squares and streets containing Berlin's main museums, including the Pergamon, with archeological treasures that are not be missed. To the west is the landscaped Tiergarten park, with its famous zoo, and the wealthy heart of former West Berlin. To the south, in the Turkish district of Kreuzberg, is the extraordinary Jewish Museum. The city's youthful 'alternative' scene continues to thrive, as does its famous nightlife, most notably in the Scheunenviertel, north of the Spree River.

Boston, Massachusetts, USA   *Map page 6*

The oldest areas of Boston have a European feel, their street plan based on meandering farm tracks. The Beacon Hill district contains splendid 19th-century brick houses and narrow alleyways, and the Massachusetts State House. A 'Freedom Trail', marked by a line of red bricks, takes the visitor past 17th- and 18th-century buildings, some of which are associated with the American Revolution. There are also guided tours of the USA's oldest surviving battleship – the USS *Constitution*, built in 1797 – moored in Boston Harbour. Across the Charles River lies Cambridge, with Harvard University and Square. Boston is a relatively unthreatening city for visitors, with a lively intellectual and artistic life, and a 'necklace' of city parks and tree-lined streets within a compact central area.

Brisbane, Queensland, Australia

The relaxed atmosphere and compactness of its centre make Brisbane a pleasant place to stroll around. Its historic precinct, next to the Botanic Gardens, contains some fine 19th-century buildings, among them the Treasury. South of the River Brisbane is the State Art Gallery and the Cultural Centre, which includes two theatres and a superb concert hall. Day trips are possible to the beaches of the Gold and Sunshine Coasts.

Brussels, Belgium   *Map page 6*

The centre of government for the European Union, Brussels is renowned for its excellent restaurants and shops, with everything from flea markets to the designer boutiques in the Galéries St Hubert. The imposing Hôtel de Ville, the gilded 17th-century houses and the Maison du Roi make the Grand-Place one of the world's most beautiful central squares. To the east lies the Gothic cathedral, the Palais Royal and the Royal Art Museums, containing both ancient and modern art. The city is full of fine examples of Art Nouveau architecture, including the museum dedicated to the founder of the movement, Victor Horta. A popular tourist site is the irreverent 17th-century statue, Manneken Pis.

Budapest, Hungary   *Map page 7*

The Danube and Parliament building, Budapest

Formerly two cities, Buda and Pest, on opposite sides of the Danube, the capital of Hungary is a fascinating destination. The Castle Hill district of Buda includes the cobbled streets and medieval houses of the Old Town, and the Royal Palace (Budavári palota), containing the national art gallery and museum. The Fishermen's Bastion gives sweeping views over the city. A network of grand 19th-century boulevards forms the centre of the larger, more cosmopolitan Pest, with its imposing Parliament building (Orzágház).

There are many elegant spa baths (gyógyfürdo) dotted around the city, and extensive Roman remains, including an amphitheatre, at Óbuda and Rómaifürdo. Famous for its cafés, Budapest has excellent restaurants and offers a huge range of entertainment, including opera, jazz and discos.

Buenos Aires, Argentina   *Map page 7*

The centre of Buenos Aires is laid out on a grand scale, with wide boulevards, imposing 19th-century buildings, modern tower blocks, and spacious plazas. Around this area, however, are the more intimate districts (*barrios*), each with its distinctive character. San Telmo is the artists' quarter, while La Boca, with its brightly painted houses, is the city's port district. The most fashionable district, Recoleta, houses the National Museum of Art, but is best known for the ornate tombs of its cemetery.

La Boca, Buenos Aires

Cairo, Egypt   *Map page 7*

The largest city in Africa, Cairo is full of hooting taxis and bustling crowds. Modern buildings have risen next to the minarets of the old mosques, while a maze of markets provide potential bargains. The Pyramids of Giza are visible from the upper storeys of buildings all over the city. Famous worldwide for its unrivalled collection of antiquities, the Egyptian Museum houses the treasures of the Pharaoh Tutankhamun, and more than 100,000 other relics and antiquities from all periods of ancient Egyptian history. Experiences not to be missed include the *Son et Lumière* that takes place daily by the Sphinx at Giza, and drifting on the Nile in a *felucca* while watching the sun sink below the Cairo skyline.

Cape Town, South Africa   *Map page 8*

South Africa's oldest city, Cape Town has several buildings of historic interest, including the Castle of Good Hope, the Old Town House, the Tuynhuis and the Parliament building. Artefacts from all over Africa are sold at the Saturday market in Greenmarket Square. The city lies below the spectacular Table Mountain, accessible by cable car. There are numerous good beaches, such as those at Clifton and Camps Bay on the cold Atlantic Ocean, and at Muizenberg and Fishoek on the warmer Indian Ocean. The old docks have been developed as the Victoria and Alfred Waterfront, which boasts a range of restaurants. Boat trips run from here to the infamous Robben Island, where Nelson Mandela was imprisoned.

Cartagena, Colombia

Several impressive 16th-century forts overlook the channel leading to the bay of Cartagena, evidence of the city's origins as an imperial Spanish stronghold. Huge 17th- and 18th-century walls surround narrow streets, palaces, churches, monasteries and plazas. The Palace of the Inquisition is a fine example of colonial architecture, with its magnificent Baroque gateway.

Chicago, Illinois, USA   *Map page 9*

Built on the shore of Lake Michigan, Chicago played a key role in the economic development of the USA, serving as a railhead for the cattle trade of the Midwest. Its skyline includes skyscrapers dating from the 1890s, buildings in the International Style of the 1950s, and particularly fine examples of more recent architecture. The Sears Tower provides fantastic views of four states from its Space Deck. A closer view can be had on a boat trip up the Chicago River or from 'The Loop', an elevated railway that lends its name to the area it encircles. There are several important museums, including the vast Museum of Science and Industry and the Art Institute of Chicago. For outdoor pursuits, there is the extensive Grant Park, bordering the lake. The city is renowned for its rich musical life and, as well as a world-class symphony orchestra, there is a multitude of clubs offering blues, jazz, rock and folk music.

Skyline with Sears Tower, Chicago

Cologne, Germany

Despite the almost total destruction of central Cologne during World War II, many historic buildings have been restored to their former glory, including the massive and beautiful twin-towered Gothic cathedral (Dom). Among the museums and art galleries are the Roman-Germanic Museum and the Imhoff-Stollwek Museum of Chocolate. The city's unique beer, *kslsch*, can be sampled in the numerous beer halls. Short boat trips on the Rhine provide views of the impressive riverfront, while longer boat excursions go to, for example, Königswinter and Linz.

Copenhagen, Denmark   *Map page 8*

Scandinavia's largest and liveliest city, Copenhagen has excellent art collections, royal palaces, churches and other historic buildings as well as entertainment late into the night. Punctuated by parks, lakes, fountains and squares, the city is easily explored on foot or bicycle. The old harbour of Nyhavn, with its tall, brightly painted buildings, is packed with pavement cafés and bars, while the Latin Quarter is good for restaurants. From the top of the Round Tower (Rundee Taarn), Europe's oldest functioning observatory, there are magnificent views over the city. The famous Tivoli Gardens is a delightfully varied amusement park dating from 1843. A bridge now links Copenhagen to the attractive Swedish city of Malmö.

Delhi, India
Map page 10

Red Fort, Delhi

The capital of India, Delhi is a city with two centres: New Delhi, which was established by the British in 1911, and Old Delhi, whose present layout dates from the 17th century. The streets of the old town, and in particular Chandni Chauk, are famously frenetic. The massive walls of the Red Fort and the Lahore Gate enclose a host of palace buildings, although many have been stripped of their fine decoration. India's largest mosque, the Jama Masjid, is also in the old town. The new city, with its broad avenues and imposing marble buildings, contains some older sites, including the 16th-century tomb of Humayun and the 12th-century Qutb Minar tower.

Dublin, Ireland
Map page 10

Built on the River Liffey, Ireland's capital contains elegant 18th-century buildings, two Norman cathedrals, a castle, and some fine museums, three of them in Leinster House. One of the oldest books in the world, the 9th-century illuminated Book of Kells, is housed in Trinity College library, while the Writers' Museum pays homage to local literary figures such as W. B. Yeats, James Joyce and Oscar Wilde. Dublin has a relaxed, friendly atmosphere, and plenty of pubs and restaurants. In summer, outdoor events are often held in Phoenix Park. The famous Easter Uprising of 1916 is commemorated at Kilmainham Jail, where many heroes of Irish independence were once incarcerated.

Edinburgh, Scotland
Map page 11

Set on a dramatic rock that soars 76 m (250 ft) from the valley floor, the Old Town of Edinburgh is a collection of historic buildings, towering tenements and narrow passages huddling beneath a romantic castle. The Royal Mile, lined with 16th- and 17th-century buildings, leads from the castle to the royal residence of Holyrood. The Royal Museum lies to its south, as does the lively Grassmarket district with its bars and restaurants. The small but elegant National Gallery sits in Princes Street Gardens to the north. Beyond lie graceful Georgian squares, terraces and crescents of the New Town. Scotland's capital has a rich cultural life, including the world-famous International and Fringe festivals.

Esfahan, Iran

On the four sides of the vast central square of Esfahan, with its formal lawns and pool, are the delicately tiled façades of public buildings. These include the opulent Royal Mosque and the magnificent entrance to the bazaar, whose crowded streets twist and turn towards the steps of the Great Mosque, a complex of buildings spanning a 700-year period. Among other historic sites are the shrine of Imamzadeh Ahmad and several royal palaces. Esfahan's high altitude keeps it relatively cool, making it pleasant to stroll through the streets and parks, and sample the many teahouses.

Fès, Morocco

The old part of Fès – Fès el-Bali – is one of the largest living medieval cities in the world. A fascinating labyrinth of some 94,000 streets and lanes, its covered bazaars are crammed with every conceivable sort of craft workshop, restaurants and market stalls, as well as extensive dye pits and tanneries. On the edge of the old town, the Museum of Moroccan Arts houses a splendid collection of artefacts, including colourful tribal carpets and the city's famous blue pottery.

Florence, Italy

The pedestrianized streets in the beautiful centre of Florence enable visitors to wander about freely, visiting such well-known Renaissance sites as the cathedral, with its red-roofed dome, and the spacious Piazza della Signoria, dominated by the crenellated Palazzo Vecchio. Between the piazza and the River Arno is the Uffizi Gallery, containing famous works by Botticelli and Titian among many others. The 14th-century Ponte Vecchio bridge, lined on both sides with jewellery and gift shops, provides a route to the imposing Pitti Palace. The city's churches range in style from the exquisite San Miniato, through the austere Santo Croce to the classically inspired San Lorenzo. Of the many religious frescoes, those by Fra Angelico in the monastery of San Marco, and by Masaccio in the church of Santa Maria del Carmine, stand out. The Bargello has a fine collection of sculpture, while the Accademia houses Michelangelo's *David*.

Cathedral with Brunelleschi's dome, Florence

Geneva, Switzerland

Geneva enjoys one of the world's most dramatic locations, straddling the Rhône where it leaves Lake Geneva, and overlooked by the Alps on one side and the Jura mountains on the other. A cosmopolitan, French-speaking city, it is a world centre for banking and commerce as well as for international organizations, such as the Red Cross. South of the river, the oldest part has excellent museums, galleries and historic buildings, including St Peter's Cathedral, where John Calvin preached. Geneva lives up to its reputation for efficiency, cleanliness and safety, but all this comes at a price: restaurants, clubs and other entertainments are smart and expensive.

Guangzhou (Canton), China
Map page 11

An economic success but a planning disaster, Guangzhou holds more attraction for the business traveller than for those seeking historic sites. There are, however, numerous decaying French and British colonial buildings on Shamian Island, which provides a haven of peace from the bustle of Guangzhou's streets. A climb to the top of the 11th-century Temple of Six Banyan Trees (Liurong Temple) provides a fine view. Another way of seeing the city is to take a cruise on the Pearl River.

Hamburg, Germany

Germany's largest port (there are daily harbour tours from March to November), Hamburg combines its busy commercial life with a graceful, old-world charm. Situated on the River Elbe and criss-crossed by a network of canals, at its heart is the Alster lake, where boating is a popular pastime in the summer. The city has many extensive parks, stylish shopping arcades, elegant boulevards, museums and art galleries, among them the Kunsthalle with a fine collection of art spanning several centuries. There are numerous café-bars and all-night entertainment, most notably in the St Pauli Quarter, where The Beatles famously performed in the 1960s.

Hanoi, Vietnam

Built on the Red River, around several large lakes, Hanoi has both peaceful tree-lined avenues and parks, and a bustling old city where almost anything can be purchased, including silk, lacquerware, puppets and jewellery. Bikes are the main form of transport. The city's many religious buildings include the One-Pillar Pagoda and the 11th-century Temple of Literature. Ho Chi Minh's mausoleum provides a memorable experience, with visitors being escorted to view the embalmed body. A day trip can be made to the Perfume Pagoda – actually a complex of pagodas and Buddhist shrines carved out of limestone cliffs. A cruise from Haiphong around the limestone islands of Halong Bay is also recommended.

Havana, Cuba

Ironically for a country that is proud of its independence from imperialism, one of the main attractions of Cuba's capital is its colonial past. The vast open space of Plaza de la Revolución and the post-colonial buildings of the Vedado district are worth seeing, but it is the boulevards and squares of Old Havana that are most fascinating. The palaces surrounding the Plaza de Armas, the Baroque cathedral and the elegant thoroughfare 'The Paseo' are all fine examples of colonial architecture. There are few cars on the streets, but many bicycles. There are also many nightclubs, where salsa is the predominant dance style.

Capitol building and Grand Theatre, Havana

Helsinki, Finland
Map page 11

Helsinki is almost surrounded by water and is full of the sounds and scents of the sea. Among its architectural gems are the 19th-century Neo-classical buildings of Senate Square – which also contains the blue-domed Lutheran Cathedral – and the rock-hewn church of Temppeliauko (1969) where many concerts are held. Although its combination of attractive buildings, good restaurants and excellent art galleries and museums make it a year-round tourist destination, Helsinki really comes to life in summer, with open-air cafés, concerts, and boat trips to the ruined fortress on nearby Suomenlinna Island.

Hong Kong, China
Map page 12

Most visitors to Hong Kong take the short ferry ride from Kowloon across the harbour, with its spectacular view of the high-rise buildings on the waterfront of Hong Kong Island. A visit to the Man Mo temple, with its ornate interior, provides a complete contrast. A funicular goes to the top of Victoria Peak where there are shady paths through lush vegetation. The Tsim Sha Tsui area of Kowloon contains a group of modern exhibition buildings, including the Space Museum and the Hong Kong Museum of History, as well as air-conditioned shopping malls. A ferry goes to the islands of Lamma, where there are relatively uncrowded beaches, country walks and seafood restaurants. A hydrofoil goes to Macau.

Istanbul, Turkey
Map page 12

Formerly known as Constantinople, Istanbul has an imperial history dating back to the time of the Roman Empire. Its strategic position straddling the Bosporus Strait makes it both a European and an Asian city. Among the churches built in the 6th century by Emperor Constantine is the domed Hagia Sophia (Aya Sofya), which was converted into a mosque in 1453 and is now a museum. The 17th-century Blue Mosque (Sultanahmet Camii) is a masterpiece of Ottoman architecture, while the Topkapi Palace, with its imperial treasury stuffed with gold and jewels, is on every itinerary. In old Istanbul is the labyrinthine Kapali Carsi (the world's largest covered bazaar) where more than 4,000 shops and stalls sell carpets, jewellery, ceramics, brass and leatherware. A fascinating mixture of both the ancient and modern, Istanbul also has a renowned cuisine.

Jaipur, India

Known as the 'Pink City' because of the salmon-coloured wash applied to many of its buildings, Jaipur is the capital of the colourful state of Rajasthan. It is divided into areas dedicated to specialist activities, such as elephant-handling or the sale of textiles, silver or gems. Within the walled town are the Palace of Winds (Hawa Mahal), with its delicately screened windows, the City Palace – now a museum – and Jai Singh's extraordinary Observatory, with its huge angular stone instruments. Nearby is the hill town and Rajput palace complex of Amber.

Jakarta, Indonesia
Map page 12

Jakarta's glinting high-rise office blocks contrast sharply with the cobbled square at the heart of what was 18th-century Batavia (now known as Kota). Much can be discovered of this colonial period at the dock of Sunda Kelapa, where many magnificent schooners are moored and a maritime museum has been created in an old warehouse. The National Museum has excellent displays on Indonesia's ethnic groups. There is a theme park at Taman Impian Jaya Ancol, and Balinese dancing and traditional music at Taman Ismail Marzuki. Jakarta also offers a fine range of restaurants.

Jerusalem, Israel
Map page 13

Dome of the Rock, Jerusalem

The focus of most visits to Jerusalem is the Old City with its different quarters. The heart of the Christian quarter is the Church of the Holy Sepulchre, the site of Christ's crucifixion. This is reached along the Via Dolorosa, much of which passes through the Muslim quarter, with its impressive Mamluk architecture. The Western (Wailing) Wall is in the Jewish quarter, which also contains the multi-layered Temple Mount Excavations. The Armenian quarter, the centre of the Armenian Church, contains the impressive Citadel. Towering over all these is the golden Dome of the Rock, a sacred Muslim site in the Temple Mount compound.

Johannesburg, South Africa
Map page 13

The richest city in Africa, Johannesburg is also a lively centre of South African culture. Museum-Africa has collections relating to the history and art of all sections of the community, while the nearby Market Theatre Complex, which contains four theatres, is an attractive place in which to eat and drink, and listen to music. Visitors, however, should be aware of the high crime rate in the downtown area, and enjoy instead the restaurants and gardens of northern suburbs such as Rosebank and Melville. Outside the city is Soweto, the vast black township which has a lively music and theatre scene but is best visited on a guided tour.

Kairouan, Tunisia

An important centre for the Muslim faith, Tunisia's holy city has over 130 mosques, including the 9th-century Great Mosque, which once doubled as a fortress. A special permit is required to visit the holy sites. Kairouan's maze of buildings and narrow, winding streets is enclosed by ancient city walls, and it is a fascinating place in which to stroll. Artisans carry out the traditional trades of weaving and carpentry, and carpet sellers try to attract visitors to their stalls in the souk (bazaar).

Karachi, Pakistan
Map page 13

Developed as a city by the British from the 1840s, Karachi is a business rather than a tourist centre. It does, however, have many colourful bazaars in Sadr, the central district, which specialize in such products as jewellery, cloth, dried fruit and bottles. It also has a fascinating coastline which can be viewed on a traditional lateen-sailed boat trip from the harbour. Clifton Beach, with its camel rides and fairground, is well equipped for families, while other, rather less commercialized beaches are a short drive away.

Katmandu, Nepal

Katmandu is an intriguing mixture of modern buildings and narrow, traffic-clogged streets with intricately carved temples and shrines. Many of these ancient buildings are grouped around Durbar Square, including the Jaganath Temple, with its erotic carvings. The Old Royal Palace houses an interesting museum. Jochne, better known as 'Freak Street', is a focal point for many visitors, with its fascinating shops, cheap hotels and restaurants. Outside the city are three huge temples: the Hindu Pashupatinath complex, with its riverside ghats, and the Buddhist stupas of Boudhanath and Swayambunath.

Street scene, Katmandu

Kolkata (Calcutta), India
Map page 14

The capital of West Bengal, Kolkata (Calcutta) is regarded by many as the cultural and intellectual centre of India. It also has a reputation for extreme poverty and squalor. One of the great colonial cities of Asia, its main historic sites date from the days of the British Raj and include the white marble Victoria Memorial, the neo-Gothic St Paul's Cathedral, and the Indian Museum, with sculptures from all over India. These buildings are all in the vicinity of the Maidan, one of the largest city parks in the world, where hundreds of different interests – among them yoga, cricket and riding – are regularly pursued, and live entertainment is provided.

Kraków, Poland

Having come through World War II virtually unscathed, and with not a high-rise building in sight, Kraków's densely packed old centre is full of historic churches and picturesque streets and squares. The central market square, which is reputed to be the largest medieval town square in Europe, contains a number of interesting buildings, among them the largely 16th-century Cloth Hall. The square is also the focus of the city's vigorous cultural life. There are several jazz and cabaret clubs in the Old Town, as well as numerous attractive cafés, bars and restaurants. To the south are the castle and cathedral of Wawel, behind which lies Kazimierz, the gradually reviving Jewish district.

Kuala Lumpur, Malaysia

A city that has sprung up since the 1860s, Kuala Lumpur is short on historic sites but has plenty to offer the visitor. Its colonial, 19th-century heart is Merdeka Square. Nearby is the most spectacular of the city's mosques, Masjid Jamek. Chinatown and Little India provide much of interest, and Malaysian craftwork and antiques can be bought at the Art Deco Central Market. The 'Golden Triangle' business area includes the Petronas Twin Towers, one of the world's tallest buildings. The Lake Gardens contain a Bird Park, Orchid Garden and Butterfly Park. A half-hour drive outside the city are the Batu Caves, used as Hindu temples. Day trips can be made to the historic city of Malacca and the Genting Highlands Casino Complex.

Kyoto, Japan

Japan's capital for over 1,000 years, Kyoto has numerous Buddhist temples, Shinto shrines, palaces and gardens. Despite extensive modern development, there are still traditional wooden houses and craft shops in the back streets. A city that is particularly spectacular when clad in either cherry blossom or autumnal colours, its main sights include the 1,001 gilded statues of Buddha lined up in the Hall of the Thirty-Three Bays, the view from the temple of Kiyomizu-dera, and the intriguing gardens of Ginkaku-ji. Other famous gardens include the lake-garden of Kinkaku-ji, and the 500-year-old garden of Ryoan-ji. The city of Nara, 35 km (22 miles) south, contains the huge bronze Buddha of Todai-ji, and other fine examples of early Japanese art and architecture.

Temple of Kiyomizu-dera, Kyoto

Lagos, Nigeria   Map page 14

Although no longer the capital of Nigeria, Lagos is by far the largest city in West Africa. At its heart lies Lagos Island, a business centre whose skyline is spiked by skyscrapers. The National Museum provides a fascinating insight into the country's cultural heritage and includes works of art dating back 2,800 years, including beautiful Benin bronzes. The city's main attraction, however, is modern African music, and many of the country's best-known singers have nightclubs here.

Lahore, Pakistan

Lahore is renowned for its Mughal architecture. The most attractive of its many mosques is that of Wazir Kahn, covered in intricate glazed mosaic tiles, but the largest is the Badshahi Mosque. The massive walls of Lahore Fort surround a compound of elegant buildings. Away from the centre is Jahangir's tomb and the Shalimar Garden, with its geometrically arranged terraces, ponds, fountains and, in February and March, its spectacular flowers.

Las Vegas, Nevada, USA   Map page 14

A city whose population grew from 30 to half a million in just 90 years, Las Vegas is continually reinventing itself, with the casinos on The Strip providing ever bigger and better spectacles. The most famous is Caesar's Palace, with staff dressed as centurions and Cleopatra lookalikes. New York, New York entices with its replica skyscrapers and a Statue of Liberty. Treasure Island has a mock sea battle, Mirage an erupting volcano and Circus Circus live fire-eaters. Food and lodging are cheap, particularly midweek, with the real profits being made on the gambling tables and slot machines. Las Vegas is popular for outrageous weddings, with services being conducted in the most unlikely places – in a 'drive-through' chapel, the nearby Grand Canyon, or even in mid-air.

The Strip, Las Vegas

Lima, Peru   Map page 14

A once-beautiful city, Lima has suffered badly at the hands of modern developers. It is worth visiting primarily for its fine museums, which provide background information about Peru's Inca sites. It is also a useful base from which to explore the surrounding countryside, including the beautiful beaches to the south, over which towers the temple complex of Pachacamac.

Lisbon, Portugal   Map page 16

There are many hills to climb and much to see in Portugal's capital. Stretching north from the Rio Tejo, the Baixa district – rebuilt after the devastating earthquake of 1755 – contains many of the city's museums and theatres. The old Moorish area, the Alfama, survived the earthquake and its warren of narrow streets, stairways and squares leads up to the hilltop Castle of St George, with magnificent views. On the edge of the city the Belém area contains fine examples of 16th-century architecture, including the marvellous Jerônimos Monastery and the famous white Belém Tower. At night the haunting traditional *fado* music is played in bars in, for example, the Bairro Alto district. Day trips can be made to the hill town of Sintra or to the beaches on the Estoril coast.

London, England   Map page 15

Europe's largest city, London is a lively, cosmopolitan metropolis, offering a huge range of attractions to the visitor. From the grand squares of Knightsbridge and Belgravia to the business district of the City, central London is made up of a mosaic of areas, each with its own distinctive atmosphere and architectural style. Historic buildings include the Tower of London (containing the Crown Jewels), St Paul's Cathedral, Westminster Abbey, the Houses of Parliament and Buckingham Palace. Among the many art galleries are the Tate Modern, housed in a converted power station on the South Bank of the River Thames,

and The National Gallery, overlooking Trafalgar Square. The British Museum contains a monumental collection of Egyptian, Greek and Roman artefacts. Soho, Piccadilly and Covent Garden form the heart of the theatre district, with numerous restaurants, clubs and bars. Day excursions can be made to Hampton Court Palace, Windsor Castle, Canterbury Cathedral, the Royal Pavilion in Brighton, and the historic university towns of Oxford and Cambridge.

Los Angeles, California, USA   Map pages 16–17

Among the skyscrapers in Los Angeles' downtown area are some notable public buildings, including the Museum of Contemporary Art. To the southwest is Exposition Park, home to three museums, including the interactive California Space and Science Center. Most visitors, however, flock to Hollywood in search of film stars, although the big names have long since left for more salubrious neighbourhoods, such as Beverly Hills and elegant Bel Air. Other attractions include the Warner Bros. Studio Tour, and the thrilling rides at Universal Studios. On the coast, the long sandy beach linking Santa Monica and Venice is a magnet for Los Angeles' more colourful characters.

Luxembourg City, Luxembourg

The picturesque old walled city of Luxembourg perches above the Pétrusse and Alzette valleys, overlooked by the ruins of its ancient fortress with a labyrinth of defensive tunnels and underground chambers (the casemates), which is a UNESCO World Heritage Site. Running between the Citadelle du St Esprit, which provides spectacular views, and the Grand Ducal Palace is the elegant Chemin de la Corniche, one of Europe's most beautiful pedestrian promenades.

Madrid, Spain   Map page 17

Spain's capital is a huge metropolis with a remarkable collection of museums and art galleries, beautiful parks and a famously vibrant nightlife centred on Plaza de Santa Ana. The city is made up of a number of districts (*barrios*), each with its own distinct character. The area of most interest to visitors is around the 17th-century Plaza Mayor, with the elaborately decorated Royal Palace, the Royal Theatre (Teatro Real) and the famous Prado Museum all within easy reach. The city has a vivacious character and a buzzing street life. Tapas bars are everywhere, and shoppers can explore the busy Gran Via or the atmospheric Rastro flea market centred on Plaza de Cascorro. Excursions can be made to the austere monastery of El Escorial and to the historic towns of Toledo, Segovia, Avila and Aranjuez.

Plaza Mayor, Madrid

Manila, Philippines
Map page 17

Many people visit Manila purely for its bars and nightlife, and the city provides plenty to choose from in the business district of Makati and the streets behind Roxes Boulevard. The walled area known as Intramuros contains the most significant historic sites, including Fort Santiago and the imposing Romanesque cathedral. Rizal Park, projecting out into Manila Bay, contains a lagoon, a spectacular fountain, a replica of Beijing's Summer Palace, a Japanese Garden and planetarium. Manila's Chinatown (on the border of Santa Cruz and Binondo) is the place to go for silk, porcelain and Chinese dumplings.

Marrakech, Morocco

Famous for its lively street life, Marrakech is also known for the pink colour that dominates the city from the earth walls around the old town centre to the flat-roofed houses. Every evening in Djemaa El Fna, the old town's central square, acrobats, snake charmers and storytellers perform. Nearby is the labyrinthine souk (bazaar), with its hundreds of small shops selling jewellery, carpets, metalware and leather. There are several beautiful gardens, and the Museum of Arts contains a magnificent display of carpets. Just an hour's drive away are the spectacular High Atlas mountains.

The souk, Marrakech

Melbourne, Victoria, Australia
Map page 18

Central Melbourne, on the north bank of the River Yarra, is a striking blend of past and present. Ornate 19th-century buildings sit alongside towering skyscrapers, as in Collins Street where the 1980s Rialto Towers provide splendid views from an Observation Deck. Elsewhere, the Old Melbourne Gaol is a major historic attraction and there are many fine parks and gardens, including the outstanding Botanic Gardens. The city's multi-ethnic nature is apparent in the popular Queen Victoria Market and in the huge variety of restaurants. Outside the centre several inner suburbs, each with a distinct character, can be explored by tram. Places of interest nearby include the Yarra Valley with its wineries and wildlife sanctuaries, and Phillip Island with its penguins.

Mexico City, Mexico
Map page 18

It is worth braving the traffic and pollution of Mexico City to see the impressive architecture of the buildings surrounding the main square (Zócalo), including the National Palace, with its murals by Diego Rivera. Nearby are the fascinating excavations of an Aztec temple (Templo Mayor). Bosque de Chapultepec, with its boating lakes, gardens and zoo, provides some relief from the hectic street life. It is also home to the outstanding

Museo de Antropologia, whose indoor and outdoor exhibition spaces house the world's greatest collection of Mexican art and artefacts. Just 48 km (30 miles) away from the centre are the splendid ruins of the ancient city of Teotihuacán.

Miami, Florida, USA
Map page 18

Miami is spread out along the fragmented coast-line of Biscayne Bay. The Spanish language predominates and the downtown area, with its modern tower blocks, is greatly enlivened by the Latin American street life. Little Havana and Little Haiti are two areas worth visiting for their strong culture. The city's most elegant neighbourhood is Coral Gables, built as a 'model suburb' in the 1920s. Miami Beach, on an island linked to the mainland by causeways, has many fine examples of Art Deco buildings and miles of sandy beaches, hotels and bars.

Milan, Italy
Map page 19

Famous as a world centre for design and fashion, and for its grand opera house, La Scala, Milan has many historic buildings alongside its modern skyscrapers. The enormous Gothic cathedral dominates the main square, Piazza del Duomo, and the nearby convent of Santa Maria delle Grazie houses Leonardo da Vinci's fresco *The Last Supper*. Italy's most beautiful shopping arcade, the Galleria Vittorio Emanuele II, runs between the cathedral and La Scala. The Castello Sforzesco, a striking red-brick castle which was once the seat of the Dukes of Milan, houses the excellent municipal art collections. Excursions can be made to the old university town of Pavia and to the lake resorts such as Varenna and Bellagio on Lake Como, and Stresa on Lake Maggiore.

Montréal, Québec, Canada
Map page 20

Situated on the St Lawrence River, Montréal is Canada's second-largest city. The multi-ethnic nature of its population, of whom around 60% are French-speaking, is evident in the diversity of its cuisine and cultural festivals. The Parisian-style old city has numerous 17th-, 18th- and 19th-century buildings, among them the Neo-gothic Basilique Notre-Dame. By the river a public space has been created out of the old shipyards, complete with exhibitions and amusements. Boat trips can be taken up and down the St Lawrence, including one through the Lachine Rapids. The collection in the Art Museum is wide-ranging and includes a display of Inuit art. There are also particularly interesting Botanic Gardens.

Moscow, Russia
Map page 19

Moscow radiates outwards from the Kremlin in a series of rings, of which the innermost is of greatest interest to visitors and is small enough to be explored on foot. Among the buildings enclosed by the thick red-brick walls of the Kremlin are three imposing palaces and the Archangel Cathedral. Outside is Red Square, with the exotic, multi-coloured domes of St Basil's Cathedral, the Lenin Mausoleum, the Historical Museum and the magnificent 19th-century state department store, GUM, facing each other across the famous cobbled parade ground. There are also numerous literary museums and art galleries. The palatial metro system with its glittering chandeliers and fabulous marble architecture should not be missed.

St Basil's Cathedral, Moscow

Mumbai (Bombay), India
Map page 20

Home to India's thriving film industry, Mumbai also has the largest slum area of any city in Asia. The influence of the British colonial heritage is apparent in the Victorian Gothic buildings of the Fort district, the triumphal Gateway of India arch, and the red double-decker buses. The frenetic streets and bazaars are, however, pure India. Malabar Hill, with its Hanging Gardens, provides some relief from the crowds, as do the Mahatma Gandhi Museum and an impressive new National Gallery of Modern Art. Most visitors take a boat trip across the large harbour to Elephanta Island, to see the Hindu temples hewn out of the rock.

Munich, Germany
Map page 21

Munich is a cosmopolitan city, close to the Bavarian Alps, with many beautiful buildings and a wide variety of theatres, museums, galleries and restaurants. In the centre of the old town is the Marienplatz with its famous old town hall (Rathaus), and several historic churches. Many visitors shop in the glamorous Maximilianstrasse and spend an evening at the opera or drink in one of the city's many historic beer cellars, such as the famous Hofbräuhaus. Another attraction is the beer festival in October. Just outside the city is the Baroque palace of Nymphenburg.

Nairobi, Kenya

East Africa's most modern city has broad streets lined with jacaranda trees. The compact city centre can be walked in 20 minutes, but visitors should be aware that street robberies are a growing problem. The National Museum details the history of Kenyan tribal groups. Close to the city is the Bomas of Kenya, where traditional dances and songs are performed, and the Nairobi National Park where zebras, giraffes, lions, leopards and rhinos are among the animals that can be seen, particularly from July to September.

New Orleans, Louisiana, USA
Map page 21

Its fantastic mix of cultures – French, Spanish, Native American, African and Caribbean – has traditionally made New Orleans one of America's most stimulating cities. However, it is now only slowly recovering from the enormous damage inflicted by Hurricane Katrina in August 2005, and many neighbourhoods remain abandoned. These do not include the main tourist areas – in particular, the French Quarter, with its elegant architecture – where visitors can enjoy the Creole and Cajun cuisines, both variations on the French, and the music. Known as the 'cradle of jazz', the city continues to stage its annual Jazz Festival in April or May, as well as a Mardi Gras carnival in February or March.

New York, NY, USA
Map page 22

Manhattan and the Statue of Liberty, New York

New York is the ultimate destination for those who love cities, with most of its main attractions on Manhattan Island. However, its famous skyline was changed forever following the destruction of the twin towers of the World Trade Center on 11 September 2001; the 1930s Empire State Building is now the city's tallest building. The dozens of art galleries include the Metropolitan Museum of Art and the Guggenheim Museum of predominantly 20th-century art. The ferry to Staten Island provides panoramic views of Manhattan, while the Circle Line runs ferries across the harbour to the Statue of Liberty and Ellis Island. Districts to be toured on foot include Greenwich Village, with its cafés, SoHo, renowned for its art galleries and boutiques, and Little Italy. Some visitors are drawn to the city by stores such as Bloomingdales, others by its nightlife. Providing a haven from the big-city traffic is Central Park, where there is often live entertainment.

Orlando, Florida, USA
Map page 23

Surrounded by theme parks, and close to Cape Canaveral, Orlando is a thriving tourist centre. It has a lot more than its location to offer, including the excellent restaurants and shops on International Drive, the nightclubs on Orange Avenue, and the scenic boat tours and art museums in Winter Park. Downtown Orlando has a historic district dating from between 1880 and 1940, as well as several good arts centres and museums. The central Lake Eola Park provides a haven from the bustle of the city.

Osaka, Japan
Map page 23

The Japanese city most welcoming to foreign visitors, Osaka is enjoyed mainly for its lively nightlife and varied cuisine. It has some fine historic sites, such as the castle and the red-painted Sumiyoshi Shinto shrine to the gods of the sea. Its museums include the Liberty Osaka Museum of Human Rights and the Suntory Museum of 20th-century graphic art. The spectacular Osaka Aquarium is another attraction.

Oslo, Norway
Map page 23

The oldest of Scandinavia's capitals, Oslo is an attractive city situated at the head of Oslofjord. The impressive medieval Akershus castle contains grand staterooms, dungeons and the Norwegian Resistance Museum. The Munch Museum has over 5,000 drawings and paintings by Edvard Munch, while in the beautiful Vigeland Park, sculptures by Gustav Vigeland are on permanent display. Across the harbour is the Bygdøy peninsula with good beaches, an open-air folk museum and maritime museums containing Viking ships as well as Thor Heyerdahl's raft, *Kon-Tiki*.

Paris, France
Map page 24

Famously beautiful in springtime, Paris is fascinating at any time of year. Packed with historic buildings, world-famous art collections, fine restaurants and street cafés, it is one of the world's most elegant cities. Compact enough to explore on foot, the centre is made up of a number of distinct areas or *quartiers*, each with its own character. On a hill crowned by the basilica of Sacré-Coeur is Montmartre, with its village-like atmosphere, street artists, nearby flea markets and a splendid view over the city. The Notre Dame Cathedral and Sainte Chapelle are on the peaceful Île de la Cité, an island in the River Seine. The Picasso Museum is set among the beautiful old houses and courtyards of the Marais. The colourful Pompidou Centre looms above the galleries and cafés of the Beaubourg. The Louvre occupies a vast stretch of the Right Bank of the Seine, and there is a magnificent unbroken view through the Tuileries gardens and along the Champs Elysées to the Arc de Triomphe. Attractions on the Left Bank include the Musée d'Orsay – containing a huge collection of Impressionist art – and the Eiffel Tower. Excursions can be made to the royal palaces of Versailles and Fontainebleu, Monet's house at Giverney, and the beautiful cathedral at Chartres.

The Seine and Notre Dame, Paris

Perth, Western Australia, Australia

Situated on a sweep of the Swan River, Perth has lots of sunshine and an easy-going atmosphere. Its centre is relatively compact and dominated by skyscrapers, among which are scattered some Victorian buildings, such as the ornate Government House and the Old Flour Mill. A few miles to the west lie excellent sandy beaches and opportunities for surfing, while cruise companies offer dolphin- and whale-watching trips. The port of Fremantle, just 20 km (12 miles) away, is worth visiting, as is Rottnest Island.

Prague, Czech Republic
Map page 25

With a centre full of beautiful buildings covering 900 years of architecture it is easy to see why Prague, on the River Vitava, is one of Europe's top tourist attractions. Prague Castle (Prazsky Hrad), encompassing the 10th-century Church of St George and the Gothic St Vitus' Cathedral, is the focus of most visits to the city. Other architectural treasures include Baroque and Rococo palaces and the Neoclassical National Theatre (Náordní divadlo). The Old Jewish Quarter (Josefov) contains the Jewish Cemetery and several synagogues, including the Old-New Synagogue (Staranová). Prague's rich cultural life centres especially on its music – it is home to two fine orchestras. It is also arguably the beer-drinking capital of the world, and has several famous beer halls as well as numerous pubs and bars.

Quito, Ecuador

At a height of 2,850 m (9,350 ft), Quito escapes the oppressive temperature and pollution of many Latin American cities. The historic centre, with its whitewashed buildings and red roofs, is a UNESCO heritage site and includes a 16th-century monastery and cathedral, as well as a number of museums. There is also a new spectacular skytram that takes passengers up the flank of Volcán Pichincha to a height of 4,700 m (15,420 ft).

Reykjavik, Iceland

The world's northernmost capital, Reykjavik is a small modern city with colourful buildings, fashionable shops and a lively nightlife. The Arni Magnússon Institute houses a famous collection of Icelandic saga manuscripts, while the National Museum in the Old Town displays relics from the earliest days of settlement. The modern church of Hallgrímskirkja is built in the shape of a lava mountain and offers excellent views over the city from its 75 m (246 ft) high tower.

Riga, Latvia

A bustling industrial city, Riga also has a waterfront castle, a medieval centre and a lively cultural life. Places to visit include the cavernous Dome Cathedral, the Riga Motor Museum, an open-air ethnographical museum and St Peter's Church – with a view over Old Riga from the spire, which is reached by a lift. To the west, a string of resort towns known collectively as Jurmala stretches for 20 km (12 miles) along the coast, with peaceful beaches and good restaurants.

Rio de Janeiro, Brazil
Map page 25

With a spectacular location at the entrance to a bay, Rio has two famous landmarks that provide breathtaking views: Corcovado Mountain, topped by a huge statue of Christ, and Sugar Loaf Mountain. There are many museums, including the National Historical and the wide-ranging National. The city is best known, however, for its lively beaches, including Copacabana, and the more upmarket Ipanema. At night, the bars, clubs and discos of Rio resound to jazz and rock. There are samba shows primarily for tourists as well as more authentic dancehalls. A particularly popular time to visit is during the spectacular Mardi Gras Carnaval, in February or March.

View from Sugar Loaf Mountain, Rio de Janeiro

Rome, Italy
Map page 26

The historic capital of the Roman Empire, of Latin Christendom and now of Italy, Rome is exceptionally rich in treasures from many eras. Ancient buildings include the Colosseum, the Arch of Constantine, Trajan's Column, the Roman Forum

and the Pantheon. Among the early Christian sites are the famous catacombs and the basilicas of Santa Maria Maggiore and San Giovanni in Laterano (near the Colosseum). Michelangelo's Piazza del Campidoglio – bordered by three palaces – is a fine example of Renaissance town planning – but Rome is known more for its Baroque buildings and squares, and landmarks such as the Trevi Fountain and the Spanish Steps. In the centre of Rome, the Vatican City is the world's smallest independent state, containing St Peter's Square, St Peter's Basilica, the Sistine Chapel and ten museums. Increased pedestrianization of the centre has made it easier to enjoy the exuberant street life for which the city is famous.

St Petersburg, Russia   *Map page 27*

Situated in the Neva River delta, St Petersburg is a city of canals, bridges and elegant architecture. Founded in 1703 by Peter the Great, its oldest landmark is the massive Peter-Paul Fortress, with the slender spire of the Cathedral of St Peter and St Paul rising above it. At the heart of the city is Palace Square, dominated by the pastel-coloured façade of the Winter Palace. The palace is part of the Hermitage Museum, which contains one of the world's greatest collections of European art. Along the Nevsky Prospekt are the former homes of many famous Russians as well as several palaces, department stores, theatres, restaurants, churches and the richly decorated Kazan Cathedral. Day trips can be taken to several summer palaces, among them Pushkin and Petrodvorets.

San Francisco, California, USA   *Map page 26*

One of the USA's most spectacular cities, San Francisco's trademarks are its elegant suspension bridges (Golden Gate and Oakland Bay Bridge) and the street cars that service the steep streets. It is also famous as America's gay capital, the main focus of the gay community being the Castro district. The city has a thriving Chinatown, and its North Beach area (between Russian and Telegraph hills) has long been associated with alternative culture. The northern waterfront includes the famous and crowded Fisherman's Wharf development, with its numerous restaurants. The Golden Gate Park is home to several specialist gardens, art galleries and museums. A boat takes visitors to Alcatraz, the notorious island prison.

Santiago, Chile   *Map page 27*

Santiago is a sprawling city set on a wide plain at the foot of the Andes. However, its central area is relatively compact, and its tree-lined streets and landscaped parks are pleasant to explore on foot, with diversions to the Museum of Pre-Colombian Art in the Real Casa de Aduana and the Santiago Museum, close to the cathedral. A funicular goes to the peak of San Cristóbal and the Pablo Neruda Museum. Day trips can be made to the beaches of Valparaiso and the ski resort of Valle Nevado.

São Paulo, Brazil   *Map page 27*

Although much of São Paulo is modern, the area around the central square (Praça da Sé) contains several interesting old buildings, such as the whitewashed Palácio do Colégio, (a 19th-century replica of Baroque buildings), the Igreja de Santo Antônio and the Solar da Marquesa de Santos. The city has plenty of nightlife and a varied cuisine,

some of its best bars and restaurants being in the suburb known as the Jardins. The nearby Parque do Ibirapuera is a centre for sporting activities and home to several of the city's museums, as well as providing a haven of peace in its 'reading woods'.

Seattle, Washington, USA

The sparkling skyscrapers of downtown Seattle, including the trademark 'flying saucer' of the Space Needle, rise from the shores of Elliott Bay against the spectacular backdrop of the snowy peak of Mount Rainier. A recent surge in the city's prosperity (Seattle is home to the Microsoft Corporation) has led to much new building and the restoration of the historic centre. The city is a centre for contemporary arts and music, the embodiment of which is the high-tech Experience Music Project building. It also contains the headquarters of the Boeing Corporation, whose out-of-town Museum of Flight is a popular attraction.

Seoul, South Korea   *Map page 27*

Secret Garden of palace of Ch'angdok , Seoul

Selected as the site of the ruling dynasty's capital in 1394, Seoul today consists of a series of linked districts, each with its own centre. The National Assembly and financial institutions are on the small island of Youido. Spread around the old centre is a series of royal palaces, the best preserved of which is Ch'angdok, with its Secret Garden of wooded hills and ponds. T'apkol Park is a good place to meet the locals, while Namsan Park is home to the Botanic Gardens, and also to Seoul Tower, which provides a fine view of the city.

Shanghai, China   *Map page 28*

Rapidly regaining its status as a major trading and commercial centre, Shanghai's colonial past is clearly visible in the massive 1920s Neoclassical buildings of its waterfront trading area, famous as 'The Bund'. The maze of narrow streets in the Old City and the crowded bazaar of Yuyuan Park provide a complete contrast. Chinese culture is celebrated in the impressive collection of paintings, ceramics, calligraphy, and sculpture in the new Shanghai Museum. Just 80 km (50 miles) away are the famous city gardens of Suzhou, some of which are over 1,000 years old.

Singapore City, Singapore   *Map page 28*

Singapore is a popular 'stopover' city because it is relatively compact, has an efficient infrastructure and its shopping malls are a source of bargains. Amid the high-rise developments are colonial, Chinese, Malay and Indian enclaves that have retained their character, and some fine historic buildings, such as Coleman's Parliament building, the Buddhist Temple of Heavenly Happiness (Thian Hock Keng Temple) and the colourful Sri

Mariamman Hindu Temple. On the riverside are the restored old shops of Boat and Clarke Quays, both of which are relatively lively nightspots. To the south a cable car and causeway go to the island of Sentosa, which has beaches and attractions such as the impressive Underwater World, while to the north is the well-designed zoo, which features a night safari park. To the west attractions include the Jurong Bird Park and Tang Dynasty City.

Stockholm, Sweden   *Map page 29*

Built on 14 islands, between Lake Mälaren and the Baltic Sea, Stockholm is a beautiful city with numerous parks. It has an essentially modern feel, with many fine 20th-century buildings, although there is still a medieval Old Town (Gamla Stan), with narrow streets and a 15th-century cathedral (Storkyrkan). A ferry goes to Drottningholm – the royal family's island castle, complete with lakeside gardens and an 18th-century theatre. The island of Djurgarden is home to an open-air museum of Swedish vernacular architecture (Skansen) and the cathedral-like building that covers the *Vasa* – a beautifully restored 17th-century warship.

Sydney, NSW, Australia   *Map page 29*

Australia's oldest and largest city is built around a beautiful harbour that is both a major port and recreational area. Best known for its sail-shaped opera house and striking steel-arched harbour bridge, Sydney also has excellent beaches such as Manly, which can be reached by ferry, and the famous Bondi. In the centre, ferries and harbour cruises set out from Circular Quay, near which is The Rocks, with a restored historic quarter. Another area of waterside redevelopment is Darling Harbour, not far from which is the bustling Sydney Fish Market. Away from the harbour, inner suburbs worth visiting include Glebe, Newtown and Paddington, each with a distinct character and attractive 19th-century terraced houses. With an exciting mix of Asian and European cultures, the city offers a cosmopolitan choice of restaurants, theatres and music. The many museums and art galleries include the Australian Museum, which has a gallery devoted to Aboriginal history. A day trip can be made by train to the spectacular Blue Mountains only 80 km (50 miles) away.

Opera House, Sydney

Tehran, Iran   *Map page 31*

Most visitors to Tehran concentrate on its excellent museums. The National Museum and the Golestan Palace Museum house many ancient objects, including those taken from famous sites such as Persepolis. The Museum of Glass and Ceramics is well designed and organized, and the Reza Abbasis Museum displays Islamic art. For those willing to brave the heat and noise, Iran has an extensive bazaar.

Tianjin, China

The centre of Tianjin, for decades an important trading port, is a mixture of international architectural styles – British, French, German and Japanese – from the late 19th century. The Ancient Culture Street, a major draw for visitors, is an attempt to re-create the feel of ancient China. For a more authentic experience of Chinese culture, it is worth going to the Antiques Market and taking a walk through the Hai River Park.

Tokyo, Japan   Map page 30

Visitors to Tokyo, faced with a vast urban sprawl, normally work outwards from the Imperial Palace and the surrounding gardens, which contain the remains of Edo Castle. Immediately to the east is the downtown area, with a wide choice of restaurants and shops and some fine examples of modern architecture, including the Tokyo International Forum, with a 60 m (200 ft) high glass atrium. To the west is the Meijii Shrine, set in attractive gardens. The city centre has many art galleries, exhibiting both Japanese and European art. However, many of the largest museums, including the Tokyo National Museum, are further north, in Ueno. The adjacent Asakusa district reveals a more tranquil world of wooden houses, temples and shrines, including the magnificent temple of Senso-ji.

Toronto, Ontario, Canada   Map page 31

Standing on the shore of Lake Ontario, Toronto is Canada's leading commercial city. In its centre is the tallest free-standing structure in the world: the CN Tower. Glass-fronted lifts transport visitors to the Space Deck, 442 m (1,400 ft high), from where it is possible to see as far as Niagara Falls. The city's museums include the Royal Ontario Museum and the Gallery of Inuit Art. Along the waterfront an area of old warehouses has been developed as the Harbourfront Park, with hotels, theatres, shops and restaurants. Toronto's large immigrant population has helped create a vibrant city culture, with a thriving music scene.

Vancouver, British Columbia, Canada

Built around a natural harbour, Vancouver is a major port and city of inlets and green spaces, set against a mountain backdrop. The downtown area contains a cluster of sparkling, glass-fronted skyscrapers. Vancouver has a thriving Chinatown and a dynamic artistic and musical scene that encompasses classical, jazz and rock music. Of the many museums, the Museum of Anthropology is the finest. Stanley Park – a peninsula containing a large area of semi-wilderness – has three of Vancouver's many city beaches and the Vancouver Aquarium. Nearby is Vancouver Island, with its rainforest and glacial mountain peaks.

Varanasi, India

Built on the banks of the sacred River Ganges, Varanasi is famous for the flights of stone steps (ghats), lining 5 km (3 miles) of the river banks, where Hindu pilgrims bathe in the waters and cremate their dead. The old town consists of a maze of narrow alleyways at the heart of which is the Golden Temple, dedicated to the god Shiva. The city is also sacred for Buddhists, and at nearby Sarnath there is a collection of restored temples.

Venice, Italy

Distant view of Church of Santa Maria delle Salute, Venice

Built on a collection of islands and criss-crossed by 177 canals, Venice is a city like no other, where boats are the only means of transport. A journey by gondola or vaporetto along the Grand Canal passes many grand palaces, including the Gothic Ca' d'Oro and Ca' Foscari, the Renaissance Palazzo Grimani and the Baroque Rezzonico. The familiar landmark of the Rialto Bridge presides over the busiest shopping area in Venice. Around St Mark's Square is the stunning 11th-century Byzantine Basilica, the Pala d'Oro, and the Doge's Palace. A lift to the top of the towering Campanile provides exceptional views over the city and the lagoon, across which lies the Lido, with beaches and hotels. The Accademia contains the world's most comprehensive collection of Venetian art, including paintings by Titian, while the Peggy Guggenheim collection is one of the most important of 20th-century art outside the USA.

Vienna, Austria   Map page 32

Formerly the capital of the Habsburg and Austro-Hungarian empires, today's Vienna preserves an atmosphere of historic grandeur. A city of cafés, beer cellars, parks and elegant boulevards, it has a centre, the Innere Stadt, that is sufficiently compact to be explored on foot. It contains numerous Baroque churches and palaces, the magnificent Gothic St Stephen's Cathedral, and the Hofburg – the Habsburgs' imperial palace, which is now home to the famous Spanish Riding School. Among the city's many museums are the Kunsthistorisches (Art History Museum), with an unrivalled collection of paintings by Peter Breugel the Elder, and the fine 18th-century Belvedere palace complex which features paintings by Klimt and Schiele among others. Outside the centre is Schönbrunn, the Habsburgs' impressive summer palace, and the Prater (in Leopoldstadt), a vast park featuring Vienna's giant ferris wheel. To the north the hills of Kahlenberg and Leopoldsberg provide magnificent views over the city.

Warsaw, Poland   Map page 32

The old centre of Warsaw, on the left bank of the River Vistula, was reduced to rubble during World War II, but it has been meticulously rebuilt and is now a UNESCO World Heritage site. All the buildings appear to date from the 18th century or earlier. They include St John's Cathedral and the Renaissance and Baroque merchants' houses surrounding the Old Market Square (Rynek Starego Miasta). There is also the excellent Historical Museum of Warsaw, many lively cafés and some fine restaurants. Outside the Old Town is the beautiful Lazienki park and palace complex and, 6 km (4 miles) further south, the restored Baroque Wilanów park and palace.

Washington, DC, USA   Map page 33

The main public buildings of Washington, DC, are grouped on and around the National Mall – a broad swathe of parkland containing the Washington Monument, the Lincoln and Jefferson memorials, and the V-shaped polished black stone wall incised with thousands of names, which commemorates the Americans who fell in Vietnam. On the north side of the Mall is the White House, and over-looking all from the eastern end is the Capitol building, with its 55 m (180 ft) high rotunda. Home to the House of Representatives and the Senate, it is open to visitors. The National Gallery of Art and the National Air and Space Museum are two of the many museums. Central Washington, DC, can be dangerous at night. Georgetown is more relaxed, with its restaurants, bars and handsome streets. Within easy reach of the city are Chesapeake Bay and several Civil War battle sites.

Wellington, New Zealand   Map page 33

Overlooked by Mount Victoria, Wellington is the political and commercial capital of New Zealand. Wooden Victorian houses climb the steep hills surrounding the magnificent harbour of Port Nicholson, and a cable car provides a spectacular view of the city. Among the historic buildings in the centre are the Old Government Buildings, while the city's museums include the recently opened Museum of New Zealand (Te Papa). A lively, cosmopolitan city, Wellington has an exciting cultural scene, as evidenced in February and March by the annual Fringe Festival and the biennial International Festival of the Arts.

View over the harbour, Wellington

Xi'an, China

As well as being a base from which to visit the famous Army of Terracotta Warriors, Xi'an possesses its own historic sites. These include the impressive city walls that all but surround the old town, and the 64 m (200 ft) high Big Goose Pagoda. Xi'an also has a strong Islamic culture and its Great Mosque is the largest in China. The Shaanxi Provincial Museum presents a fascinating history of the Silk Road.

Yangon (Rangoon), Burma (Myanmar)

The star attraction of Yangon, the former capital of Burma, is the magnificent 90 m (290 ft) high Schwedagon stupa. Shaped like a bell, and completely covered in gold, it is surrounded by a host of smaller gilded stupas, statues, temples and pavilions. Of the many other Buddhist sites around the city, the huge reclining Buddha at Chaukhtatgyi Paya is the most impressive. Two large lakes provide areas of recreation, and the many tree-lined streets and areas of near-jungle give some parts an almost rural feel.

WORLD MAPS

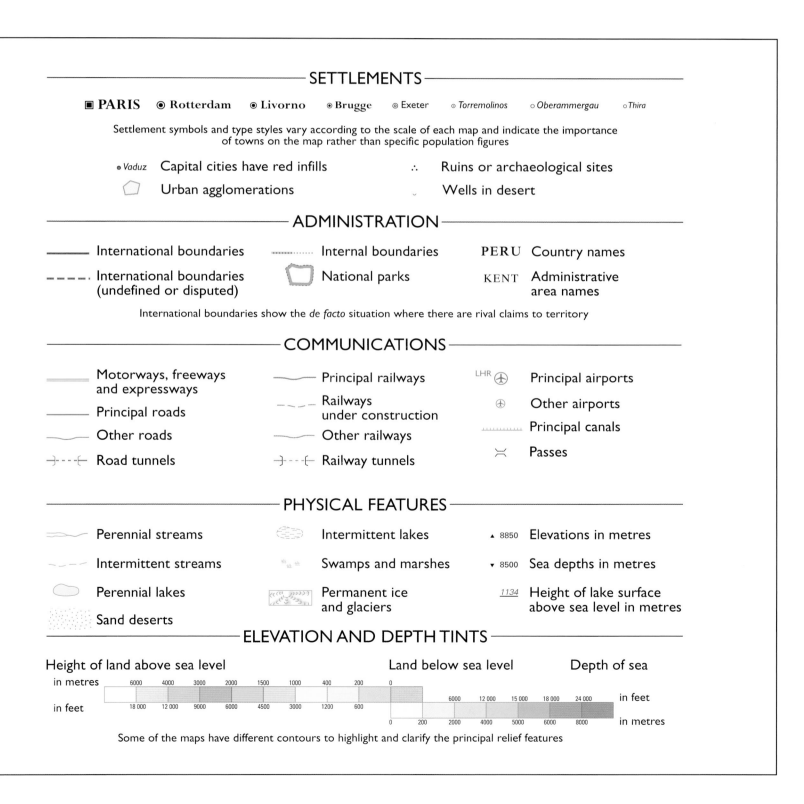

SETTLEMENTS

▣ **PARIS**   ◉ **Rotterdam**   ◉ **Livorno**   ◉ **Brugge**   ◎ Exeter   ∘ *Torremolinos*   ∘ *Oberammergau*   ∘ *Thira*

Settlement symbols and type styles vary according to the scale of each map and indicate the importance
of towns on the map rather than specific population figures

• *Vaduz*   Capital cities have red infills   ∴   Ruins or archaeological sites

⬠   Urban agglomerations   ˯   Wells in desert

ADMINISTRATION

——— International boundaries   ·········· Internal boundaries   **PERU**   Country names

– – – · International boundaries
(undefined or disputed)   ⬡ National parks   KENT   Administrative
area names

International boundaries show the *de facto* situation where there are rival claims to territory

COMMUNICATIONS

═══ Motorways, freeways
and expressways

——— Principal roads

——— Other roads

+–··–+ Road tunnels

——— Principal railways

– – – Railways
under construction

——— Other railways

+–··–+ Railway tunnels

LHR ✈   Principal airports

⊕   Other airports

············ Principal canals

⤄   Passes

PHYSICAL FEATURES

〜 Perennial streams

– – Intermittent streams

⬭ Perennial lakes

⬚ Sand deserts

⬯ Intermittent lakes

⸬ Swamps and marshes

⬭ Permanent ice
and glaciers

▲ 8850   Elevations in metres

▼ 8500   Sea depths in metres

1134   Height of lake surface
above sea level in metres

ELEVATION AND DEPTH TINTS

Height of land above sea level   Land below sea level   Depth of sea

in metres   6000 4000 3000 2000 1500 1000 400 200 0

6000 12 000 15 000 18 000 24 000   in feet

in feet   18 000 12 000 9000 6000 4500 3000 1200 600

0 200 2000 4000 5000 6000 8000   in metres

Some of the maps have different contours to highlight and clarify the principal relief features

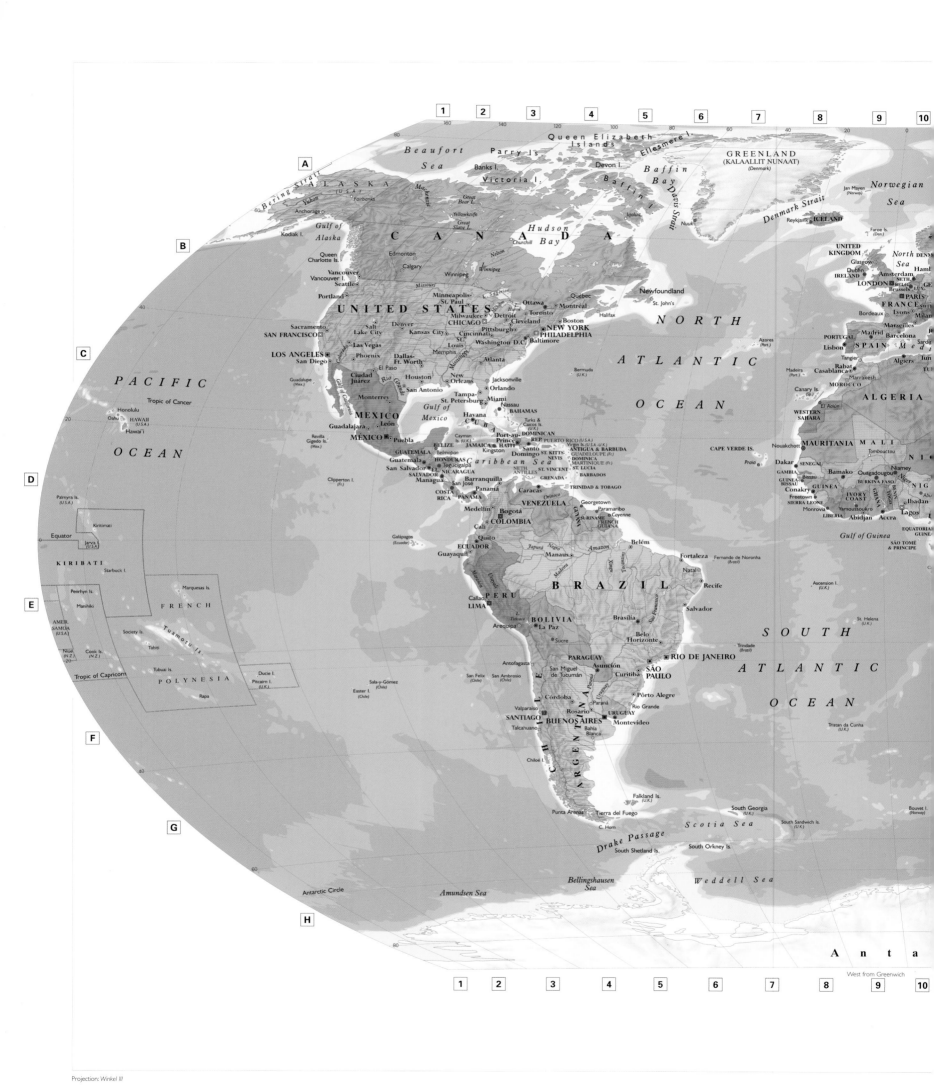

Projection: Winkel III

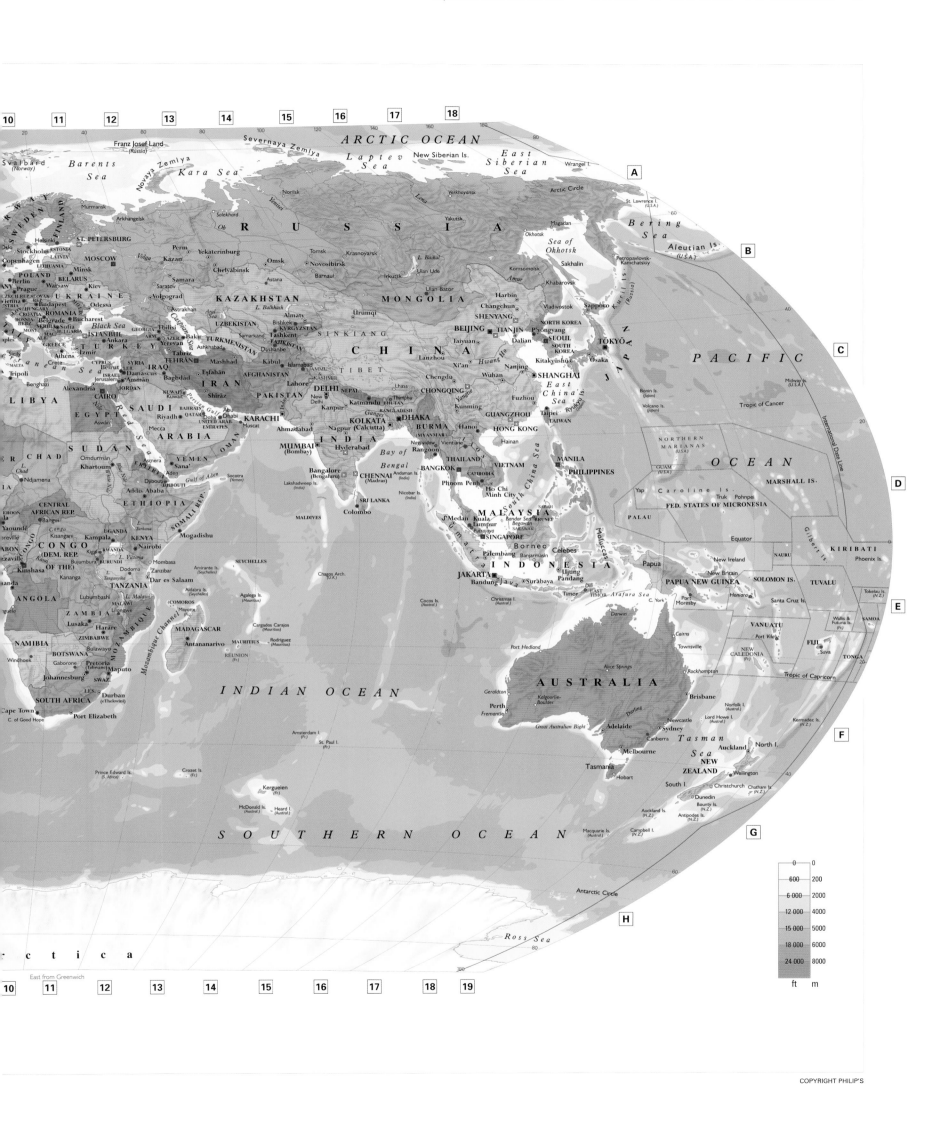

ARCTIC OCEAN

Franz Josef Land
(Russia)

Severnaya Zemlya

Laptev
Sea

New Siberian Is.

East
Siberian
Sea

Wrangel I.

Svalbard
(Norway)

Barents
Sea

Novaya Zemlya

Kara Sea

Norilsk

Yerkhoyansk

Arctic Circle

SWEDEN
FINLAND

Murmansk

Arkhangelsk

R   U   S   S   I   A

Lena

Yakutsk

Magadan

St. Lawrence I.
(U.S.A.)

Bering
Sea

NORWAY

Solekhard

Okhotsk

Petropavlovsk-
Kamchatskiy

Helsinki
ST. PETERSBURG

Perm

Yekaterinburg

Ob

Tomsk

Krasnoyarsk

Sea of
Okhotsk

Aleutian Is.
(U.S.A.)

Stockholm
ESTONIA

MOSCOW

Volga
Kazan

Omsk

Novosibirsk

L. Baikal

Irkutsk

Ulan Ude

Komsomolsk

Sakhalin

Copenhagen
LATVIA
LITHUANIA

Minsk

Samara

Saratov

Chelyabinsk

Astana

Barnaul

Amur

Khabarovsk

POLAND
BELARUS

Kiev

Volgograd

M   O   N   G   O   L   I   A

Ulan Bator

Harbin

Vladivostok

Sapporo

Berlin
Warsaw

UKRAINE

Odessa

Astrakhan

Aral
Sea

KAZAKHSTAN

L. Balkhash

Almaty

Ürümqi

Changchun

SHENYANG

NORTH KOREA

Pyongyang

SEOUL

TŌKYŌ

Prague
CZECH REPUBLIC SLOVAK

Bucharest

Black Sea

Georgia

Caspian Sea

Bishkek

Taiyuan

Ho

BEIJING
TIANJIN

Dalian

SOUTH
KOREA

Kitakyūshū

Osaka

Budapest
HUNGARY
ROMANIA

Belgrade

Tbilisi

UZBEKISTAN

Tashkent

KYRGYZSTAN

SINKIANG

Hwang

C   H   I   N   A

Nanjing

SHANGHAI

East
China's
Sea

Midway Is.
(U.S.A.)

 İSTANBUL

Baku

Samarkand

TURKMENISTAN

Dushanbe

TAJIKISTAN

Kābul

Lanzhou

Xi'an

Chengdu

Wuhan

CHONGQING

Yangtze

Bonin Is.
(Japan)

GREECE
Athens
İzmir

TURKEY

Yerevan

ARM

Tabrīz

Ashkhabad

Islamabad

T   I   B   E   T

Lhasa

Fuzhou

Volcano Is.
(Japan)

Beirut

SYRIA

TEHRĀN

Eşfahān

AFGHANISTAN

JAMMU & KASHMIR

Kunming

GUANGZHOU

HONG KONG

Taipei

Tropic of Cancer

IRAQ

Damascus

ISRAEL

Baghdad

I   R   A   N

Shīrāz

Lahore

DELHI

NEPAL

Katmandu

BHUTAN

BANGLADESH

TAIWAN

Jerusalem
Amman

JORDAN

KUWAIT
Kuwait

New
Delhi

Kanpur

Thimphu

DHAKA

BURMA
(MYANMAR)

Hainan

LIBYA

CAIRO

EGYPT

Red Sea

Aswān

SAUDI

Riyadh

QATAR

Abu
Dhabi

Muscat

KARACHI

PAKISTAN

Ahmadabad

Nagpur

I   N   D   I   A

Hyderabad

KOLKATA
(Calcutta)

Nagpur

Naypyidaw

Vientiane

THAILAND

Hanoi

Rangoon

NORTHERN
MARIANAS

GUAM
(U.S.A.)

PACIFIC

OCEAN

BAHRAIN
Doha
UNITED ARAB
EMIRATES

Mecca

ARABIA

OMAN

MUMBAI
(Bombay)

Bay of
Bengal

CHENNAI
(Madras)

Andaman Is.
(India)

BANGKOK

CAMBODIA

VIETNAM

MANILA

PHILIPPINES

CHAD

SUDAN

Omdurman
Khartoum

ERITREA

YEMEN

Sana'

Gulf of Aden

Socotra
(Yemen)

Lakshadweep Is.
(India)

Bangalore
(Bengaluru)

Nicobar Is.
(India)

Phnom Penh

Ho Chi
Minh City

South China Sea

FED. STATES OF MICRONESIA

MARSHALL IS.

Chad

Ndjamena

DJIBOUTI

Addis Ababa

ETHIOPIA

SOMALI REP.

SRI LANKA

Colombo

MALDIVES

MALAYSIA

Medan

Kuala
Lumpur

SABAH

Bandar Seri
Begawan

BRUNEI

SARAWAK

Yap

PALAU

Caroline Is.

Truk

Pohnpei

Equator

CENTRAL
AFRICAN REP.

Bangui

UGANDA

KENYA

Mogadishu

Putrajaya

SINGAPORE

Borneo

Celebes

Moluccas

NAURU

KIRIBATI

Phoenix Is.

CAMEROON

CONGO
(DEM. REP.
OF THE)

Kisangani

RWANDA

Kampala

L. Victoria

Nairobi

Palembang

Banjarmasin

I   N   D   O   N   E   S   I   A

Papua

New Ireland

New Britain

PAPUA NEW GUINEA

SOLOMON IS.

TUVALU

GABON
Libreville

Brazzaville

Kinshasa

Kigali
BURUNDI
Bujumbura

Kananga

TANZANIA

Dodoma

Dar es Salaam

Zanzibar

Aldabra Is.
(Seychelles)

SEYCHELLES

Amirante Is.
(Seychelles)

Chagos Arch.
(U.K.)

JAKARTA

Bandung

Java

Surabaya

Ujung
Pandang

Dili

EAST
TIMOR

Timor

Arafura Sea

Honiara

Port
Moresby

C. York

Santa Cruz Is.

Tokelau Is.
(N.Z.)

ANGOLA

Luanda

ZAMBIA

Lubumbashi

MALAWI

Lilongwe

L. Malawi

COMOROS

Mayotte
(Fr.)

MOZAMBIQUE CHANNEL

MADAGASCAR

Cargados Carajos
(Mauritius)

Cocos Is.
(Austral.)

Christmas I.
(Austral.)

Darwin

Cairns

Townsville

NEW
CALEDONIA
(Fr.)

VANUATU

Port Vila

Wallis &
Futuna Is.
(Fr.)

SAMOA

NAMIBIA

Windhoek

BOTSWANA

ZIMBABWE

Bulawayo

Harare

Lusaka

Antananarivo

MAURITIUS

Rodriguez
(Mauritius)

RÉUNION
(Fr.)

Agalega Is.
(Mauritius)

Port Hedland

Alice Springs

Geraldton

AUSTRALIA

Rockhampton

Brisbane

Port Vila

FIJI

Suva

TONGA

Gaborone

Pretoria

SWAZ.

LES.

Maputo

Johannesburg

Durban
(eThekwini)

SOUTH AFRICA

Cape Town

C. of Good Hope

Port Elizabeth

Amsterdam I.
(Fr.)

St. Paul I.
(Fr.)

INDIAN   OCEAN

Perth
Fremantle

Great Australian Bight

Kalgoorlie-
Boulder

Adelaide

Sydney

Canberra

Melbourne

Newcastle

Lord Howe I.
(Austral.)

Tasman
Sea

Norfolk I.
(Austral.)

Auckland

North I.

Kermadec Is.
(N.Z.)

Prince Edward Is.
(S. Africa)

Crozet Is.
(Fr.)

Kerguelen
(Fr.)

McDonald Is.
(Austral.)

Heard I.
(Austral.)

Tasmania

Hobart

NEW
ZEALAND

Wellington

South I.

Christchurch

Dunedin

Chatham Is.
(N.Z.)

SOUTHERN   OCEAN

Macquarie Is.
(Austral.)

Campbell I.
(N.Z.)

Auckland Is.
(N.Z.)

Bounty Is.
(N.Z.)

Antipodes Is.
(N.Z.)

Antarctic Circle

Ross Sea

Antarctica

East from Greenwich

A B C D E F G H

International Date Line

ft	m
0	0
600	200
6 000	2000
12 000	4000
15 000	5000
18 000	6000
24 000	8000

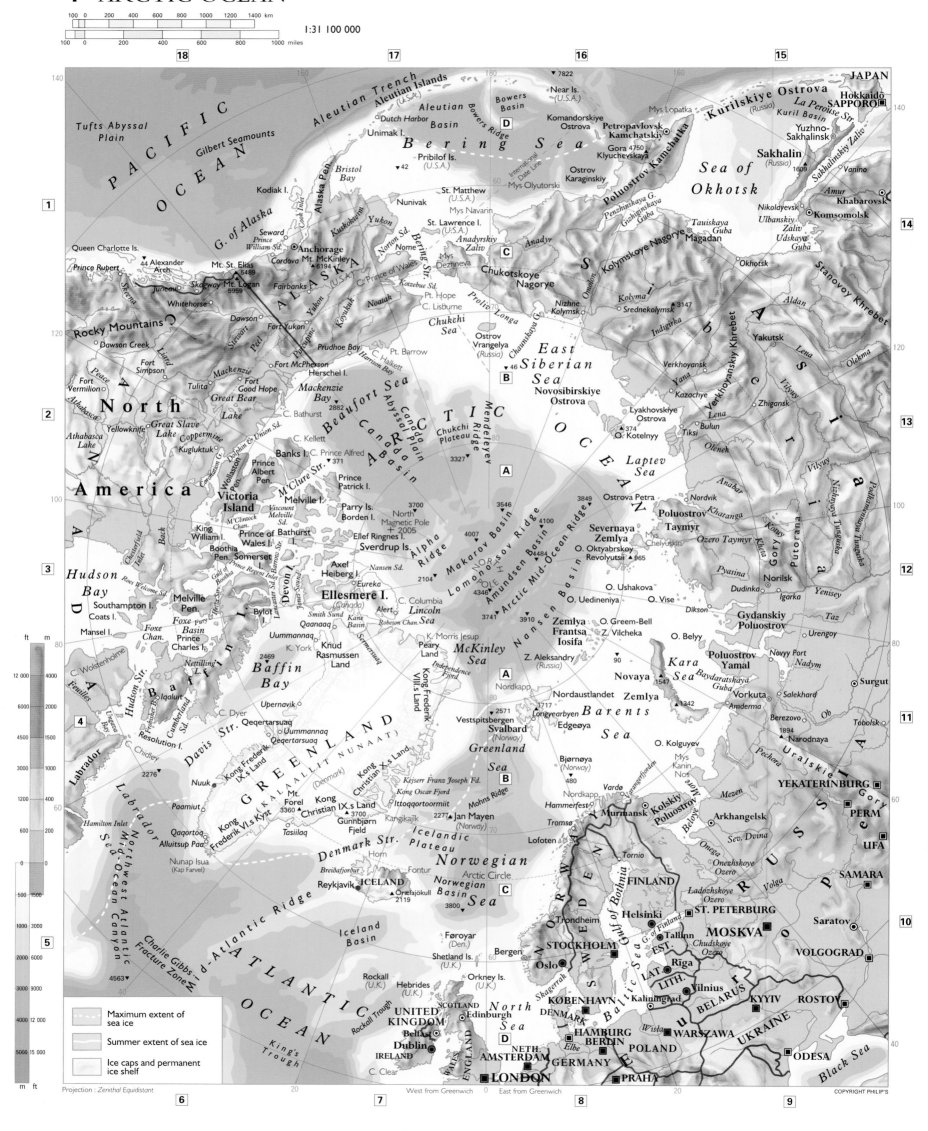

1:31 100 000

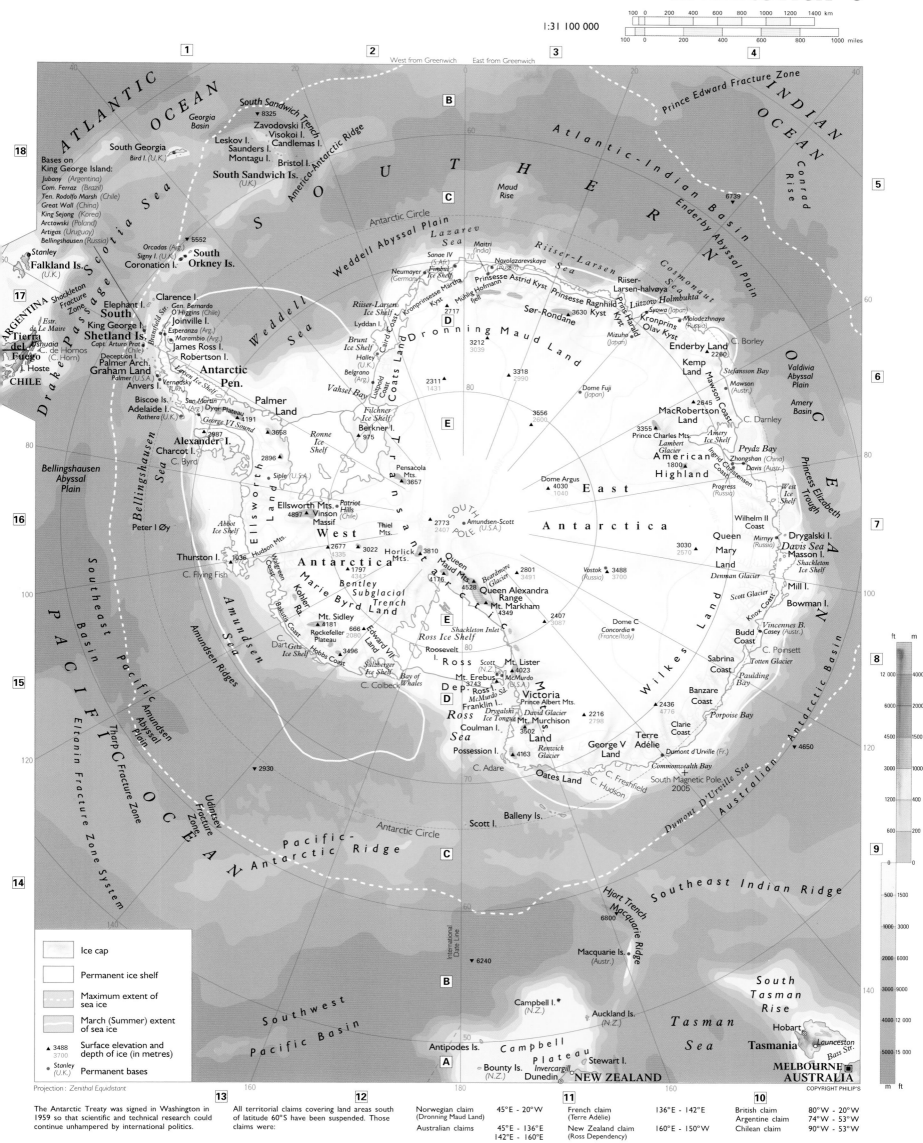

Bases on
King George Island:
Jubany (Argentina)
Com. Ferraz (Brazil)
Ten. Rodolfo Marsh (Chile)
Great Wall (China)
King Sejong (Korea)
Arctowski (Poland)
Artigas (Uruguay)
Bellingshausen (Russia)

Legend:
- Ice cap
- Permanent ice shelf
- Maximum extent of sea ice
- March (Summer) extent of sea ice
- ▲ 3488 / 3700 Surface elevation and depth of ice (in metres)
- • Stanley (U.K.) Permanent bases

Projection: Zenithal Equidistant

COPYRIGHT PHILIP'S

The Antarctic Treaty was signed in Washington in 1959 so that scientific and technical research could continue unhampered by international politics.

All territorial claims covering land areas south of latitude 60°S have been suspended. Those claims were:

Norwegian claim (Dronning Maud Land)	45°E - 20°W
Australian claims	45°E - 136°E
	142°E - 160°E
French claim (Terre Adélie)	136°E - 142°E
New Zealand claim (Ross Dependency)	160°E - 150°W
British claim	80°W - 20°W
Argentine claim	74°W - 53°W
Chilean claim	90°W - 53°W

1:17 800 000

Projection: Bonne

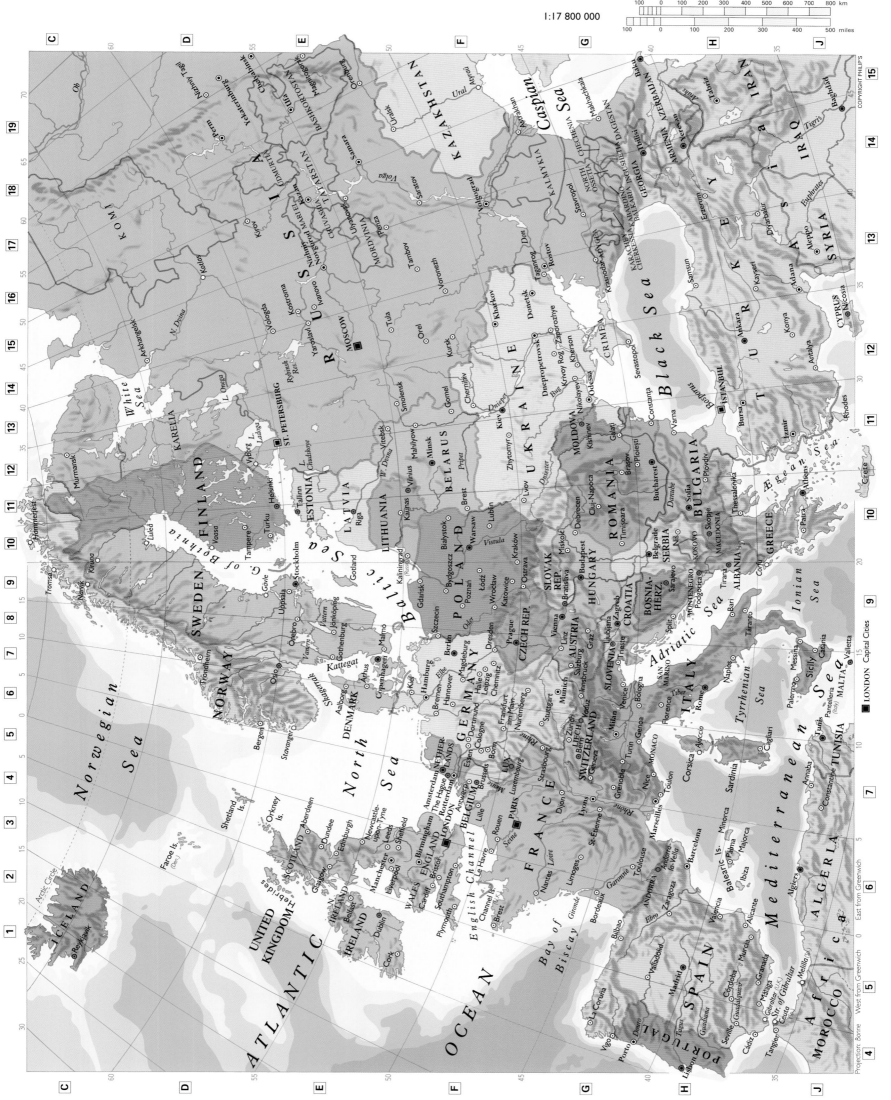

1:17 800 000

Projection: Bonne   West from Greenwich   East from Greenwich

■ LONDON Capital Cities

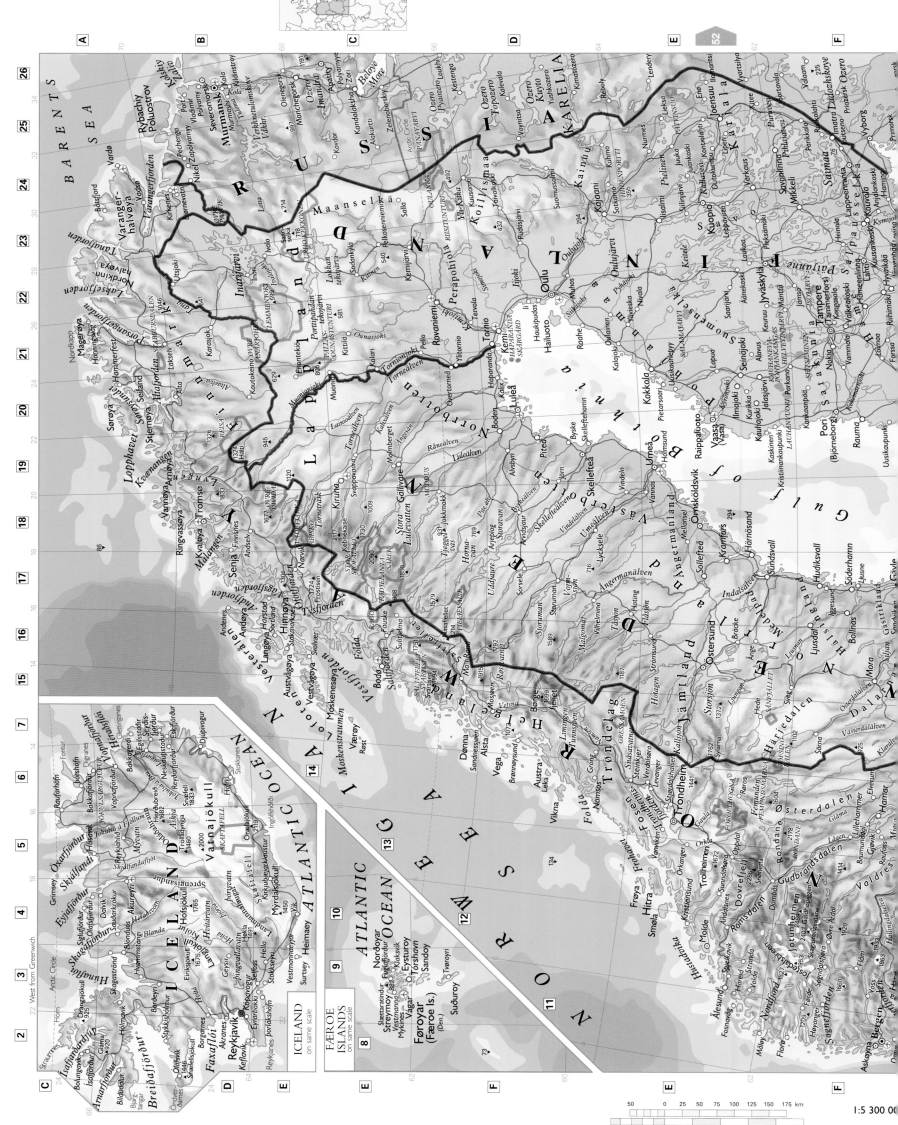

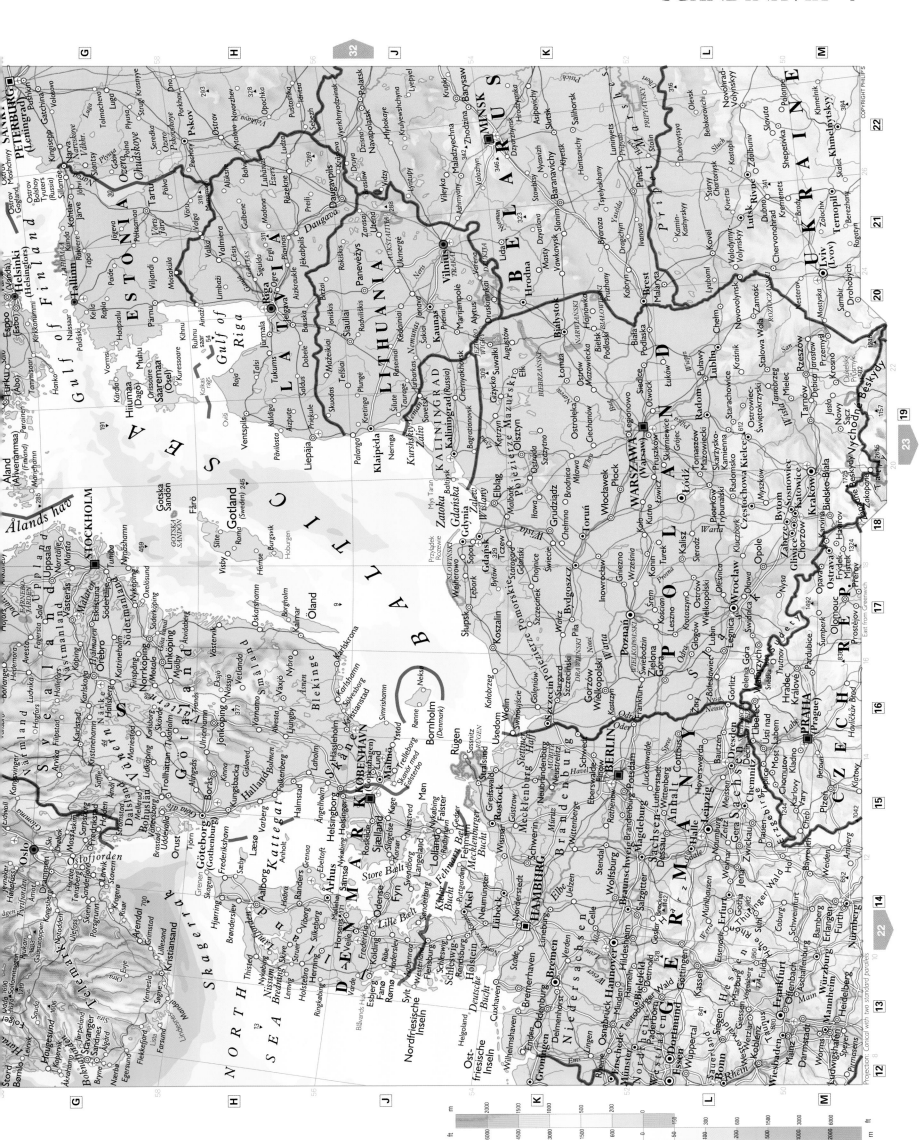

Projection: Conical with two standard parallels

East from Greenwich

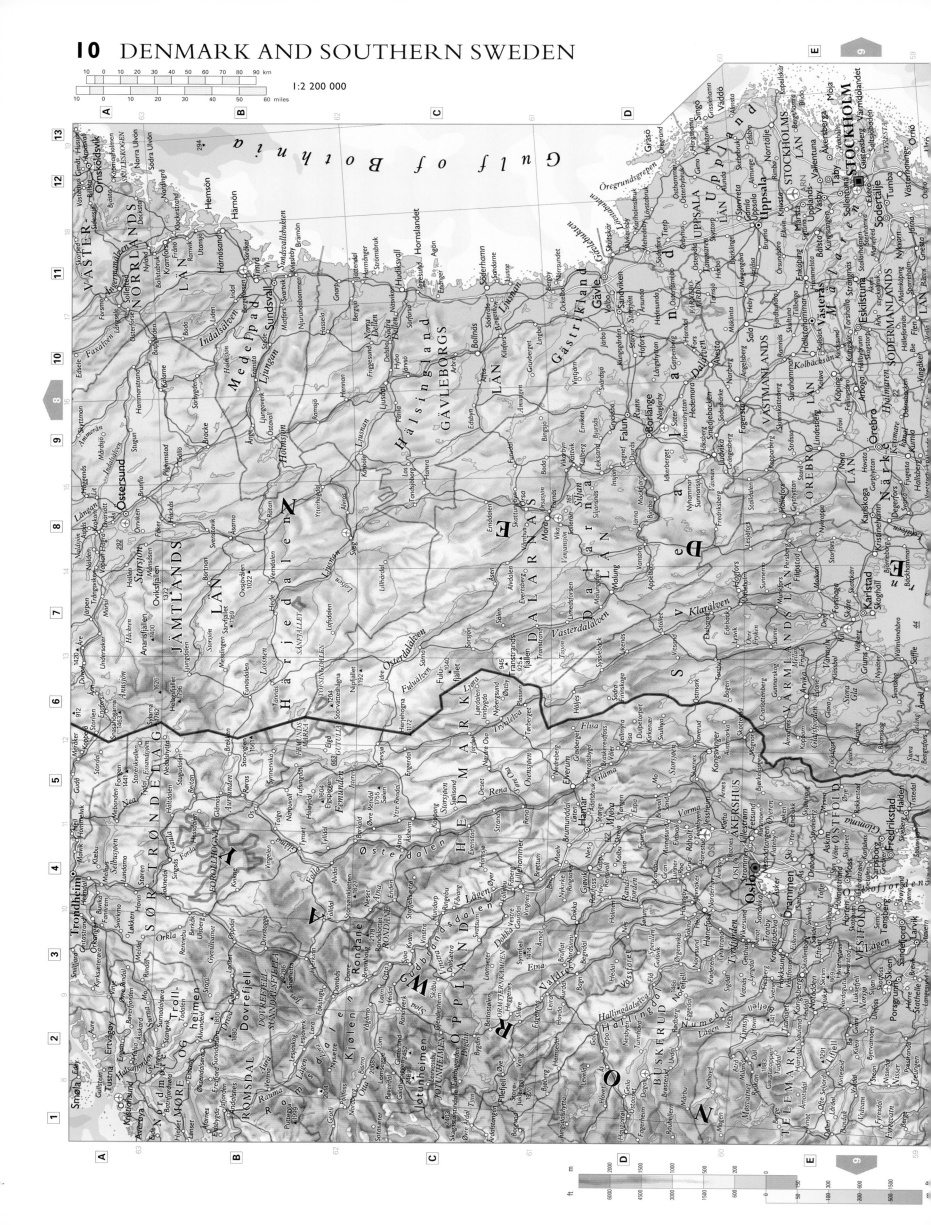

National Parks

Projection : Lambert's Conformal Conic

12 IRELAND

1:1 800 000

Projection : Lambert's Conformal Conic

West from Greenwich

COPYRIGHT PHILIP'S

National Parks

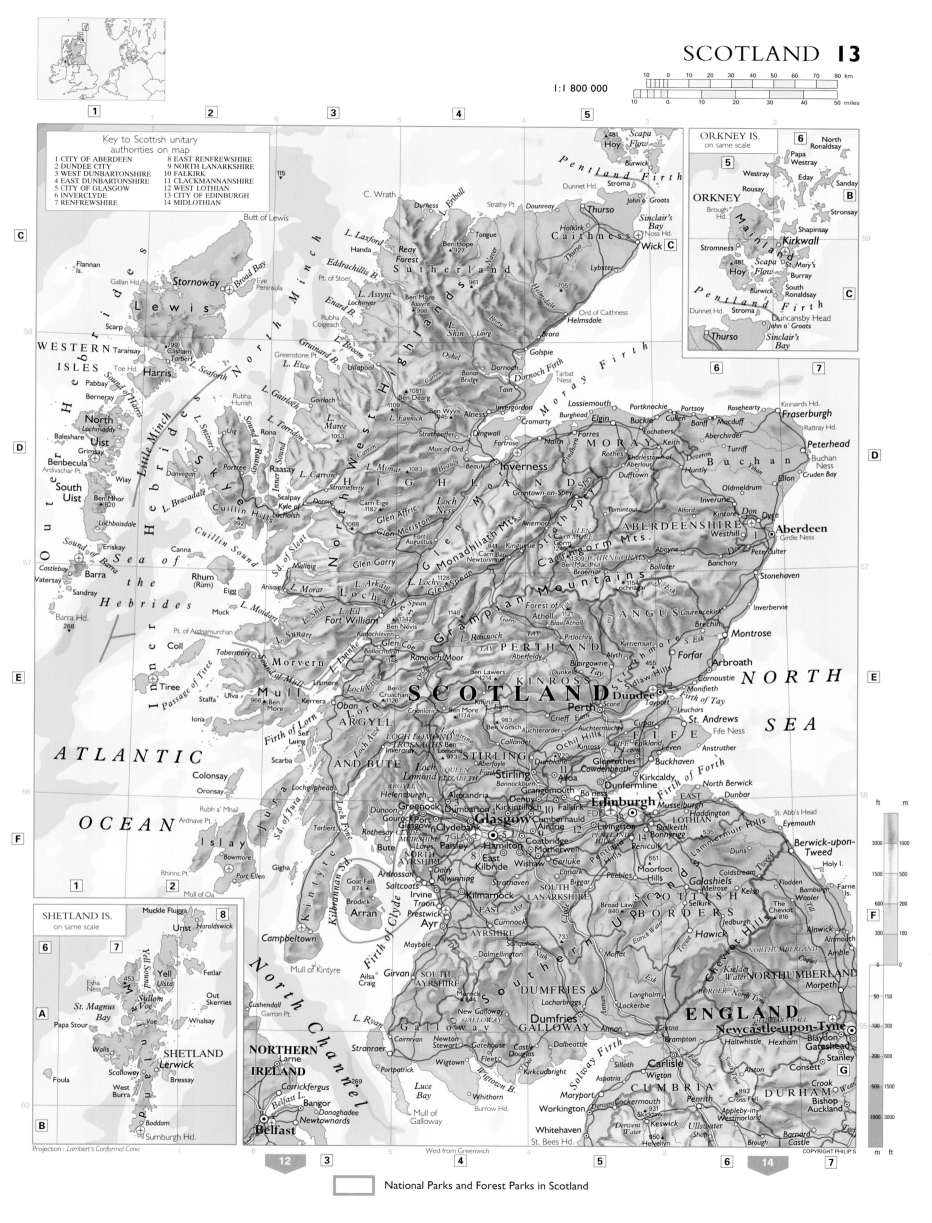

1:1 800 000

10 0 10 20 30 40 50 60 70 80 km
10 0 10 20 30 40 50 miles

Key to Scottish unitary authorities on map
1 CITY OF ABERDEEN
2 DUNDEE CITY
3 WEST DUNBARTONSHIRE
4 EAST DUNBARTONSHIRE
5 CITY OF GLASGOW
6 INVERCLYDE
7 RENFREWSHIRE
8 EAST RENFREWSHIRE
9 NORTH LANARKSHIRE
10 FALKIRK
11 CLACKMANNANSHIRE
12 WEST LOTHIAN
13 CITY OF EDINBURGH
14 MIDLOTHIAN

ORKNEY IS.
on same scale

ORKNEY

SHETLAND IS.
on same scale

SHETLAND

WESTERN ISLES

OUTER HEBRIDES

ATLANTIC OCEAN

NORTH SEA

SCOTLAND

HIGHLAND

Grampian Mountains

Inverness
Aberdeen
Dundee
Perth
Stirling
Glasgow
Edinburgh
Ayr

ENGLAND

NORTHERN IRELAND

Belfast

North Channel

Projection : Lambert's Conformal Conic

West from Greenwich

COPYRIGHT PHILIP'S

National Parks and Forest Parks in Scotland

10 0 10 20 30 40 50 60 70 80 km
10 0 10 20 30 40 50 miles

1:1 800 000

Key to English unitary authorities on map

25 HARTLEPOOL
26 DARLINGTON
27 STOCKTON-ON-TEES
28 MIDDLESBROUGH
29 REDCAR AND CLEVELAND
30 BLACKPOOL
31 BLACKBURN WITH DARWEN
32 HALTON
33 WARRINGTON
34 KINGSTON UPON HULL
35 NORTH EAST LINCOLNSHIRE
36 STOKE-ON-TRENT
37 TELFORD AND WREKIN
38 DERBY CITY
39 CITY OF NOTTINGHAM
40 LEICESTER CITY
41 RUTLAND
42 PETERBOROUGH
43 MILTON KEYNES
44 LUTON
45 NORTH SOMERSET
46 CITY OF BRISTOL
47 BATH AND NORTH EAST SOMERSET
48 SWINDON
49 READING
50 WOKINGHAM
51 WINDSOR AND MAIDENHEAD
52 SLOUGH
53 BRACKNELL FOREST
54 THURROCK
55 SOUTHEND-ON-SEA
56 MEDWAY
57 PLYMOUTH
58 TORBAY
59 POOLE
60 BOURNEMOUTH
61 SOUTHAMPTON
62 PORTSMOUTH
63 BRIGHTON AND HOVE

Key to Welsh unitary authorities on map

15 SWANSEA
16 NEATH PORT TALBOT
17 BRIDGEND
18 RHONDDA CYNON TAFF
19 MERTHYR TYDFIL
20 CAERPHILLY
21 BLAENAU GWENT
22 TORFAEN
23 CARDIFF
24 NEWPORT

NORTH SEA

IRISH SEA

North Channel

SCOTLAND

NORTHERN IRELAND

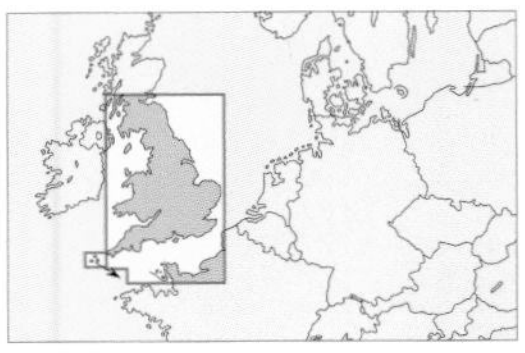

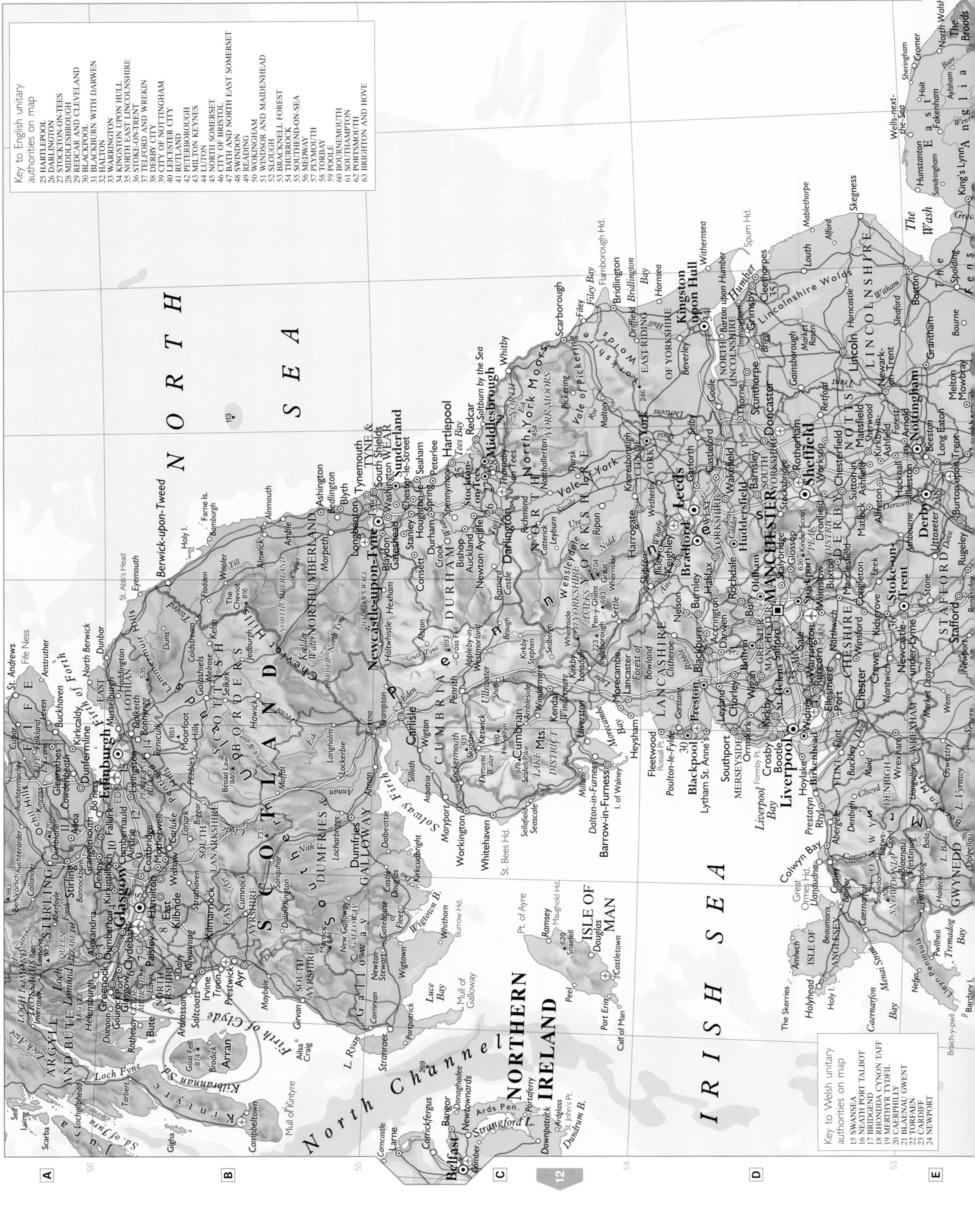

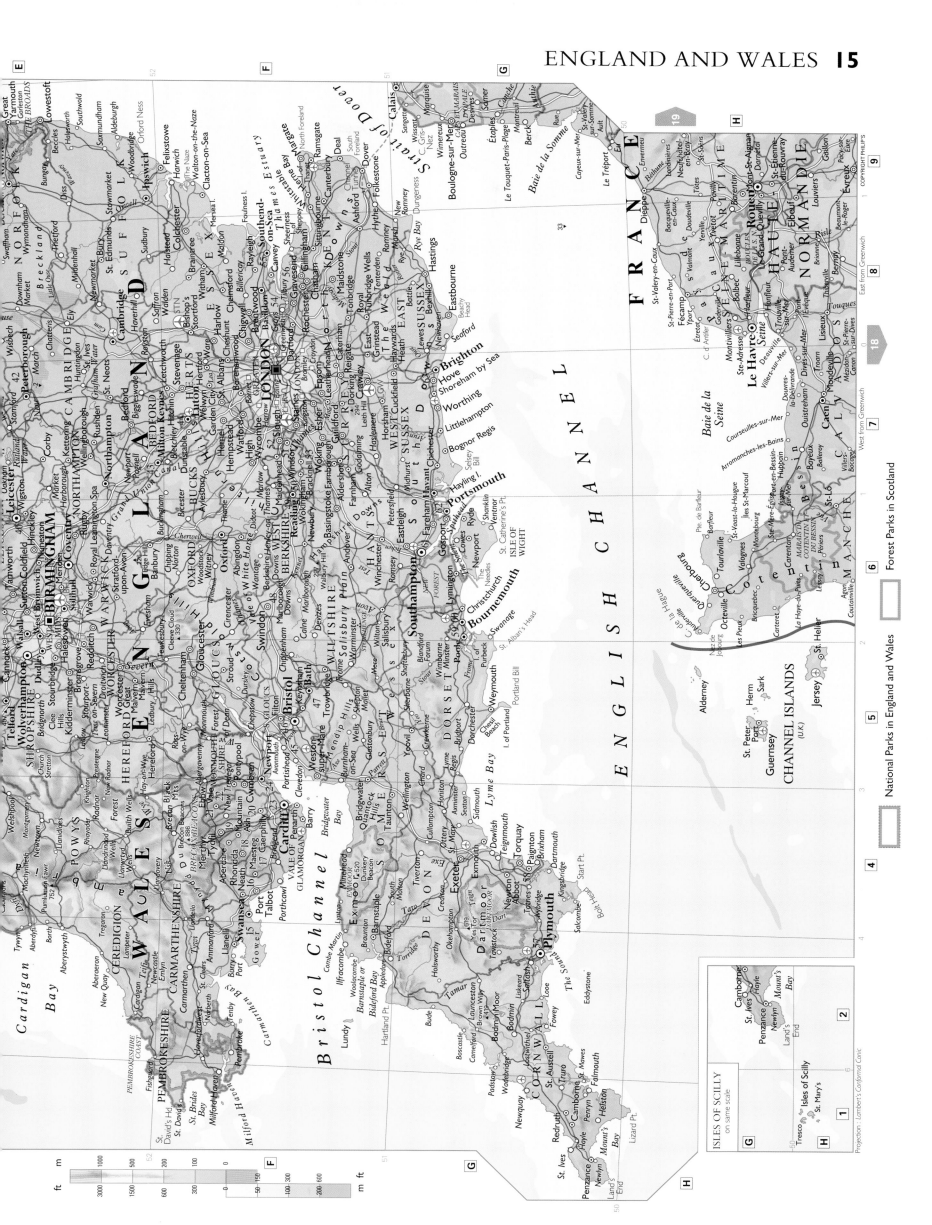

50 0 25 50 75 100 125 150 175 km
50 0 25 50 75 100 125 miles

1:4 400 000

1 2 3 4 5 6 7 8 9

NORWAY

Askøyna
Bergen
Osøyro
Stord
Bømlo
Leirvik
Haugesund
Kopervik
Åkrahamn
Boknafjord
Stavanger
Sandnes
Bryne
Nærbø

Shetland Is.
Yell
Unst
Fetlar
Foula
Mainland
Lerwick
Fair Isle

Orkney Is.
Westray
Sanday
Stronsay
Mainland
Kirkwall
Hoy
South Ronaldsay
C. Wrath
Pentland Firth

ATLANTIC OCEAN

316
1224

St. Kilda
Lewis
Stornoway
Harris
789
North Uist
Benbecula
South Uist
Barra

Outer Hebrides
North Minch
Inner Hebrides
Sea of the Hebrides

Thurso
Wick
Helmsdale
Lairg
Ullapool
Golspie
Tain
Invergordon
Dingwall
Inverness
Nairn
Elgin
Buckie
Banff
Fraserburgh
Peterhead
Huntly
Inverurie

Skye
Mallaig
1182
Portree
North West Highlands
Glen More
L. Ness
Aviemore
CAIRNGORMS Mts.
Don
Aberdeen
Rhum
Eigg
Ben Nevis
1342
Fort William
1311
Dee
Ballater
Stonehaven

SCOTLAND
Grampian Mts.

Coll
Tobermory
Tiree
Mull
Oban
Colonsay
1214
Tay
Forfar
Montrose
Arbroath

L. LOMOND & TROSSACHS
L. Awe
L. Lomond
973
Dundee
St. Andrews
Perth
Glenrothes
Kirkcaldy
Stirling
Dunfermline
Dunbar

Jura
Islay
L. Fyne
Dumbarton
Greenock
Paisley
Glasgow
Motherwell
East Kilbride
Hamilton
Edinburgh
Berwick-upon-Tweed

Arran
Campbeltown
Firth of Clyde
North Channel
Irvine
Kilmarnock
Ayr
Galashiels
Jedburgh
Southern Uplands
840
Hawick
816
Cheviot Hills
Alnwick

Malin Hd.
Buncrana
Aran I.
Letterkenny
Lifford
Coleraine
Ballymena
Larne
GLENVEAGH
Londonderry
Donegal
Omagh
Ulster
NORTHERN IRELAND
Antrim
Bangor
Belfast
Lisburn
Lurgan
Bundoran
Lower L. Erne
Lough Neagh
Portadown
Armagh
Newry
Sligo
Enniskillen
Leitrim
Cavan
Clones
Castleblaney
Dundalk
Drogheda

Girvan
Dumfries
Annan
893
Kirkcudbright
Stranraer
Workington
Mull of Galloway
Whitehaven
Carlisle
Hexham
Gateshead
Durham
Pennines
Newcastle-upon-Tyne
South Shields
Sunderland
Hartlepool
Redcar
NORTHUMBERLAND
Cumbrian Mts.
978
Lake District
Darlington
Middlesbrough
Stockton-on-Tees
16
N. YORK MOORS
Scarborough
Barrow-in-Furness
YORKSHIRE DALES

UNITED KINGDOM

Douglas
I. of Man
238
Lancaster
Bridlington

Achill I.
Ballina
Castlebar
Lough Mask
Lough Corrib
Connemara
Westport
Roscommon
Longford
Lough Ree
Athlone
Mullingar
Ballinasloe
Tullamore
Ceanannus Mor
Boyne

IRELAND

953
Galway B.
Galway
Aran Is.
BURREN
Ennis
Kilrush
Lough Derg
Nenagh
Thurles
Tullamore
Portlaoise
Athy
Carlow
Kilkenny
926
Wicklow Mts.
Arklow

Listowel
Tralee
Dingle
Carrauntoohill
1041
Macgillycuddy's Reeks
Valencia I.
Killarney
Mallow
Clonmel
Carrick-on-Suir
Waterford
Wexford
Rosslare

Shannon
Limerick
Tipperary
Blackwater
Dungarvan
Youghal
Cork
Cóbh
Bandon
Kinsale
Bantry
C. Clear
99

Dublin
Dun Laoghaire
Bray
Liffey

IRISH SEA

Holyhead
Anglesey
Bangor

Blackpool
Preston
Blackburn
Burnley
Halifax
Huddersfield
Bolton
MANCHESTER
Oldham
Stockport
Rotherham
Barnsley
Liverpool
Warrington
636
Sheffield
Keighley
Bradford
Leeds
York
Beverley
Kingston upon Hull
Harrogate
Scunthorpe
Grimsby
Humber
Louth
Skegness
Lincoln
Mansfield
Boston
The Wash
Chesterfield
Nottingham
Cromer
Grantham
Derby
Trent
THE BROADS
Great Yarmouth
Lowestoft
Norwich

Colwyn Bay
Chester
Crewe
Stoke-on-Trent
1085
PEAK DISTRICT
Wrexham
Snowdon
Stafford
Telford
Shrewsbury
Nuneaton
Leicester
Corby
Peterborough
Thetford
Ely
Bury St. Edmunds
Ipswich
Welshpool
Wolverhampton
Coventry
Rugby
Northampton
Cambridge
Felixstowe
Harwich
SNOWDONIA
Cambrian Mts.
BIRMINGHAM
Redditch
Royal Leamington Spa
Bedford
Milton Keynes
Stevenage
Colchester
Chelmsford

ENGLAND

Cardigan
Aberystwyth
Cardigan Bay
886
Worcester
Hereford
Cheltenham
Gloucester
Oxford
Luton
Harlow
Luton
Pwllheli

WALES
Carmarthen
BRECON BEACONS
Brecon
Merthyr Tydfil
Neath
Cwmbran
Newport
High Wycombe
Hemel Hempstead
Watford
Slough
LONDON
Southend-on-Sea
Margate
Fishguard
Haverfordwest
Milford Haven
Pembroke
PEMBROKESHIRE COAST
Llanelli
Swansea
Rhondda
Cardiff
Bristol
Bath
Swindon
Newbury
Reading
Reigate
Chatham
Canterbury
Dover
Port Talbot
Barry
Weston-super-Mare
Basingstoke
Guildford
Maidstone
Folkestone
Str. of Dover

St. George's Channel
Bristol Channel
EXMOOR
Exmoor
Barnstaple
Taunton
Yeovil
Salisbury
Winchester
Southampton
Fareham
Crawley
Hastings
Eastbourne
Worthing
Brighton
New Forest
Portsmouth
Havant
Bude
Newport
Isle of Wight
English Channel

CELTIC SEA

Newquay
618
DARTMOOR
Dartmoor
Exeter
Exmouth
Weymouth
Poole
Bournemouth
Truro
St. Austell
Torquay
Plymouth
Falmouth
Penzance
Land's End
Isles of Scilly

NORTH SEA

Texel
Den Helder
Alkmaar

Haarlem
NETHERLANDS
's-Gravenhage (Den Haag)
Hoek van Holland
ROTTERDAM
Dordrecht

Vlissingen
Oostende
Zeebrugge
Brugge
Gent
Mechelen
Antwerpen
BELGIUM
Brussel (Bruxelles)
Tournai

Calais
Dunkerque
St-Omer
Grisnez
Boulogne-sur-Mer
Le Touquet-Paris-Plage
33
Abbeville
Picardie
Lille
Tourcoing
Béthune
Lens
Bruay-la-Buissière
Villeneuve-d'Ascq
Valenciennes
Cambrai
St-Quentin

C. de la Hague
Pte. de Barfleur
Cherbourg
Alderney
St. Peter Port
Guernsey
Sark
Channel Is. (U.K.)
Jersey
St. Helier
Cotentin
Valognes
Bayeux
Caen
Lisieux
Elbeuf

Fécamp
Pays de Caux
Le Havre
Trouville-sur-Mer
Bolbec
Rouen
Seine
Le Tréport
Dieppe
Amiens
FRANCE
Laon

East from Greenwich
West from Greenwich
Projection: Conical with two standard parallels

ft m
3000 1000
1500 500
600 200
0 0
50 150
100 300
200 600
500 1500
1000 3000
2000 6000
m ft

COPYRIGHT PHILIP'S
18 19 17

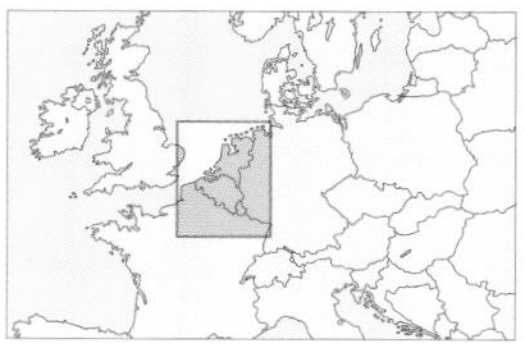

1:2 200 000

10 0 10 20 30 40 50 60 70 80 90 km
10 0 10 20 30 40 50 60 miles

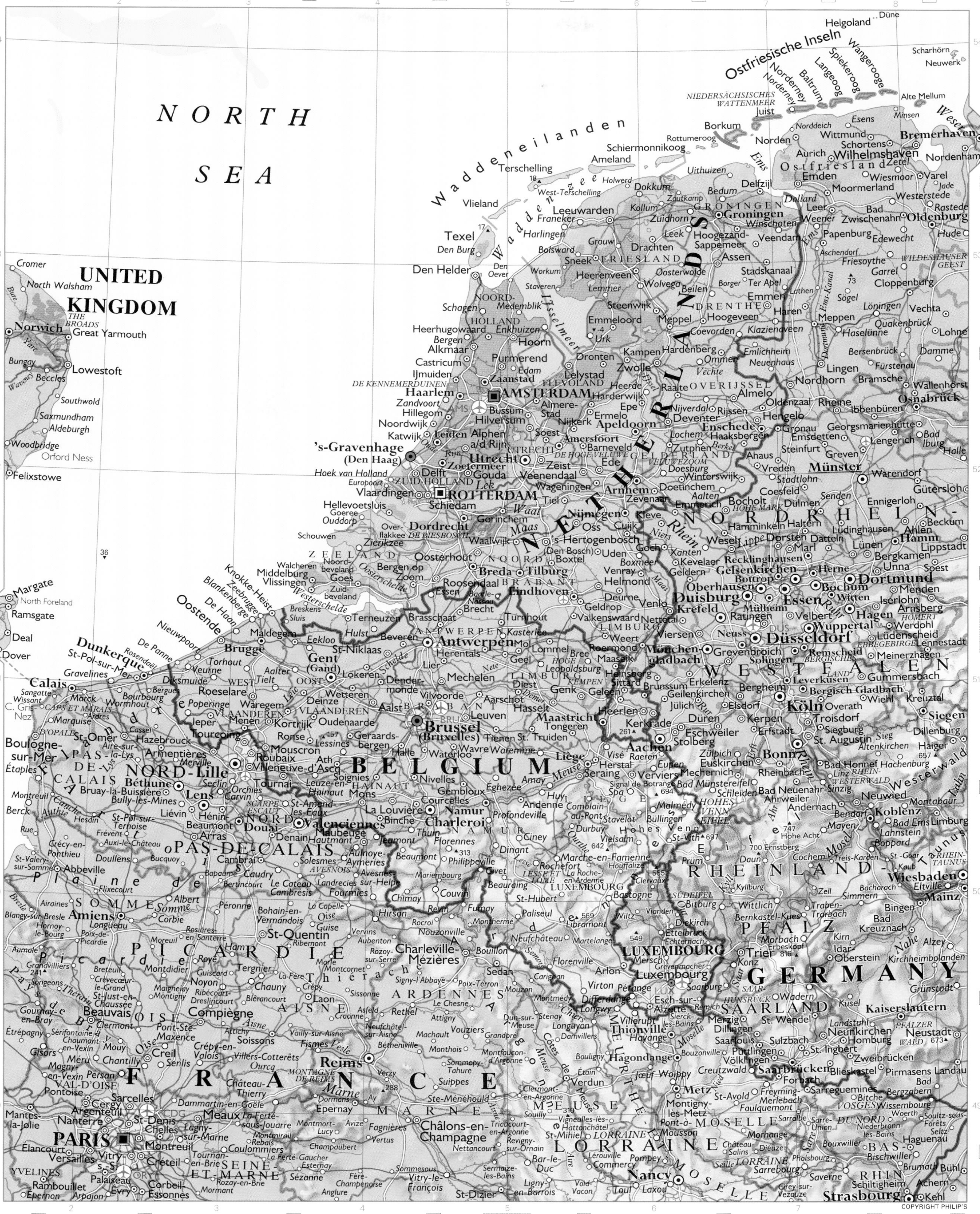

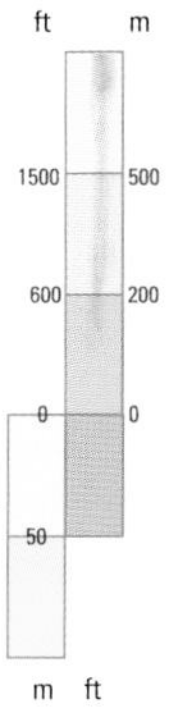

NORTH

SEA

UNITED
KINGDOM

NETHERLANDS

AMSTERDAM

's-Gravenhage
(Den Haag)

ROTTERDAM

Utrecht

BELGIUM

Brussel
(Bruxelles)

Antwerpen

Gent
(Gand)

NORD-Lille

Namur

Charleroi

Liège

Maastricht

Aachen

LUXEMBOURG

Luxembourg

GERMANY

Düsseldorf

Köln

Bonn

Dortmund

Essen

Duisburg

Münster

Bremerhaven

Oldenburg

Groningen

Wiesbaden

Mainz

Strasbourg

Nancy

Metz

Saarbrücken

Kaiserslautern

FRANCE

PARIS

Reims

Amiens

Paris

Calais

Dunkerque

Boulogne-sur-Mer

National Parks

Underlined towns give their name to the
administrative area in which they stand.

COPYRIGHT PHILIP'S

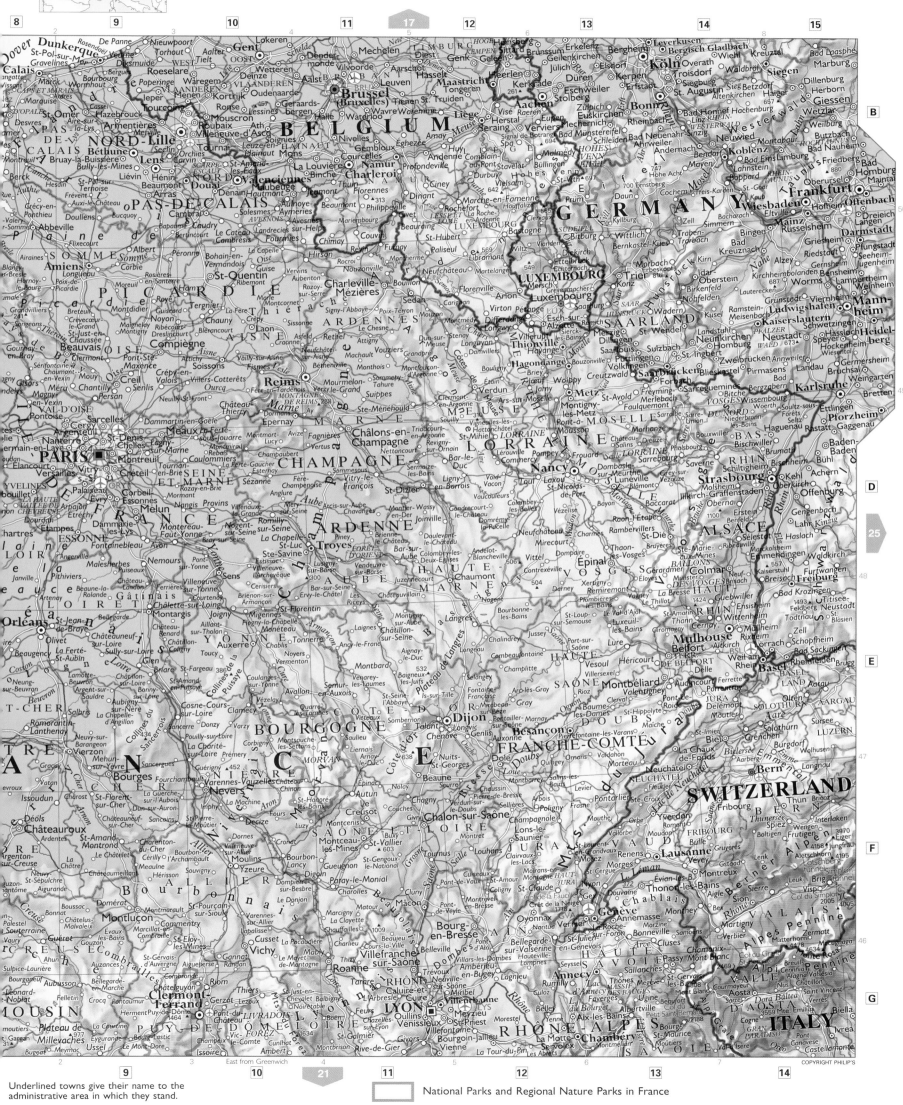

Underlined towns give their name to the
administrative area in which they stand.

National Parks and Regional Nature Parks in France

COPYRIGHT PHILIP'S

1:2 200 000

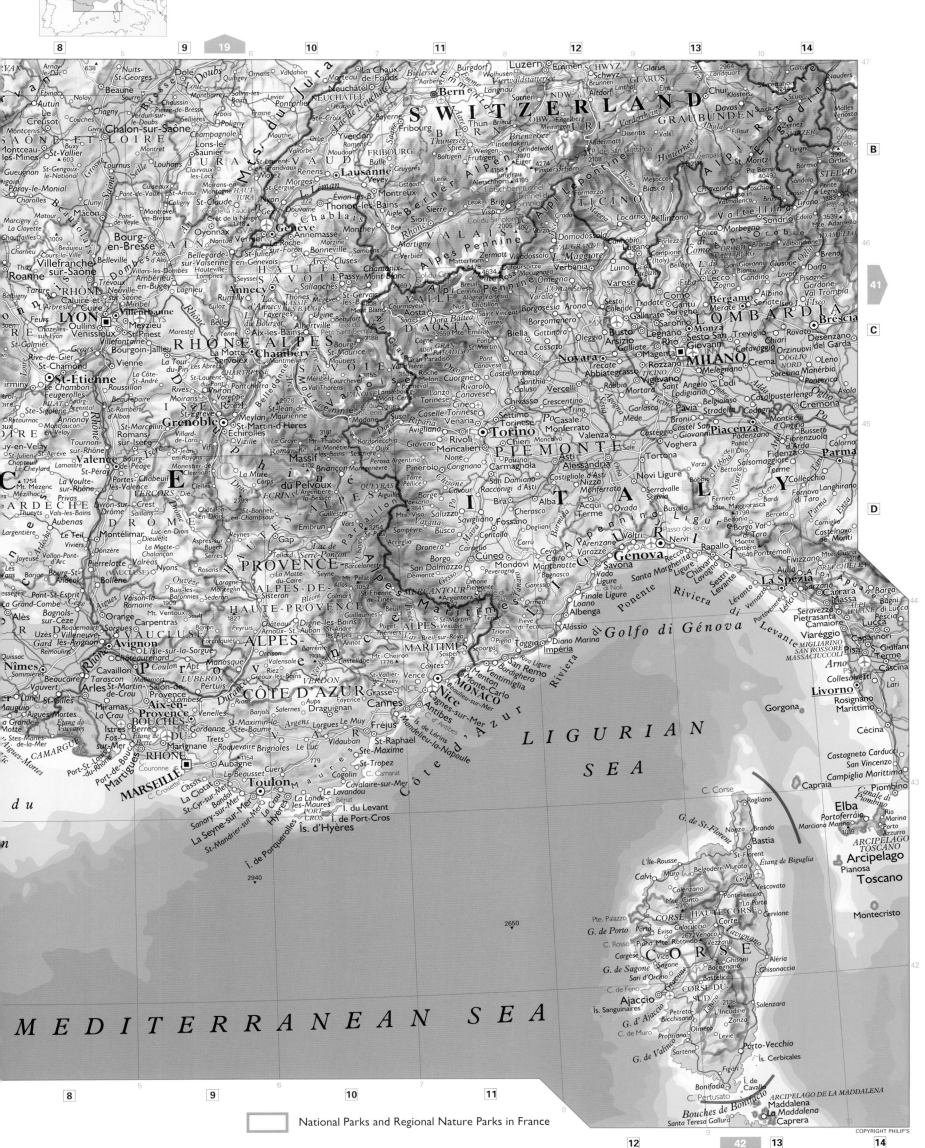

National Parks and Regional Nature Parks in France

1:4 400 000

50   0   25   50   75   100   125   150   175 km
50   0   25   50   75   100   125 miles

Countries / Seas

NORTH SEA

BALTIC SEA

ADRIATIC SEA

Golfo di Génova

Golfo di Venézia

UNITED KINGDOM

NETHERLANDS

BELGIUM

LUXEMBOURG

FRANCE

GERMANY

DENMARK

SWITZERLAND

AUSTRIA

ITALY

SLOVENIA

CZECH

Île-de-France

Picardie

Flandre

Niedersachsen

Nordrhein-Westfalen

Mecklenburg

Brandenburg

Sachsen-Anhalt

Sachsen

Thüringer Wald

Bayern

Baden-Württemberg

Schwäbische

Hessen

Rheinland-Pfalz

Tirol

Kärnten

Steiermark

Piemonte

Lombardia

Liguria

Massif Central

Cévennes

Provence

Cities (selected)

HAMBURG · BERLIN · Bremen · Hannover · Magdeburg · Potsdam · Leipzig · Dresden · Erfurt · Frankfurt · Wiesbaden · Mainz · Mannheim · Stuttgart · Nürnberg · MÜNCHEN (Munich) · Augsburg · Köln (Cologne) · Bonn · Düsseldorf · Dortmund · Essen · Duisburg · Münster · Bielefeld · Kiel · Lübeck · Rostock · Schwerin · Kassel · Göttingen · Braunschweig · Salzgitter · Osnabrück · Oldenburg · Bremerhaven · Flensburg · Freiburg · Ulm · Regensburg · Würzburg · Heidelberg · Karlsruhe · Saarbrücken · Trier · Koblenz

AMSTERDAM · 's-Gravenhage (Den Haag) · ROTTERDAM · Utrecht · Eindhoven · Groningen · Haarlem · Arnhem · Nijmegen · Maastricht

BRUSSEL (Bruxelles) · Antwerpen · Gent · Brugge · Liège · Charleroi · Namur · Mons

PARIS · Créteil · Lille · Amiens · Reims · Metz · Nancy · Strasbourg · Dijon · Lyon · Grenoble · Chambéry · Besançon · Mulhouse · Belfort · Nîmes · Avignon · Marseille · Toulon · Nice · Monaco · Monte-Carlo

PRAHA (Prague) · Plzeň · České Budějovice · Liberec · Karlovy Vary · Hradec Králové · Jihlava

Wien · Innsbruck · Salzburg · Graz · Klagenfurt · Linz · Wiener Neustadt

SWITZERLAND: Zürich · Bern · Basel · Genève · Lausanne · Luzern · Winterthur · St. Gallen · LIECHTENSTEIN · Vaduz

MILANO · Torino (Turin) · Génova · Verona · Venézia (Venice) · Pádova · Trieste · Bologna · Parma · Modena · Ferrara · Brescia · Bérgamo · Como · Trento · Bolzano · Piacenza

Ljubljana · ZAGREB · Maribor · Rijeka

København area: Svendborg · Nakskov · Rügen · Szczecin · Gorzów Wielkopolski · Zielona Góra

Physical features / elevation legend

ft   m
12000 4000
9000   3000
6000   2000
4500   1500
3000   1000
1500   500
600   200
0   0

m   ft
50   150
100   300
200   600
500   1500
1000   3000
2000   6000

Zugspitze 2963 · Grossglockner · Mont Blanc 4808 · Matterhorn 4478 · Monte Rosa · Gran Paradiso 4061 · Jungfrau 4158 · Piz Bernina 4049 · Ortles 3899 · Dolomiti · Karawanken

Projection: Conical with two standard parallels

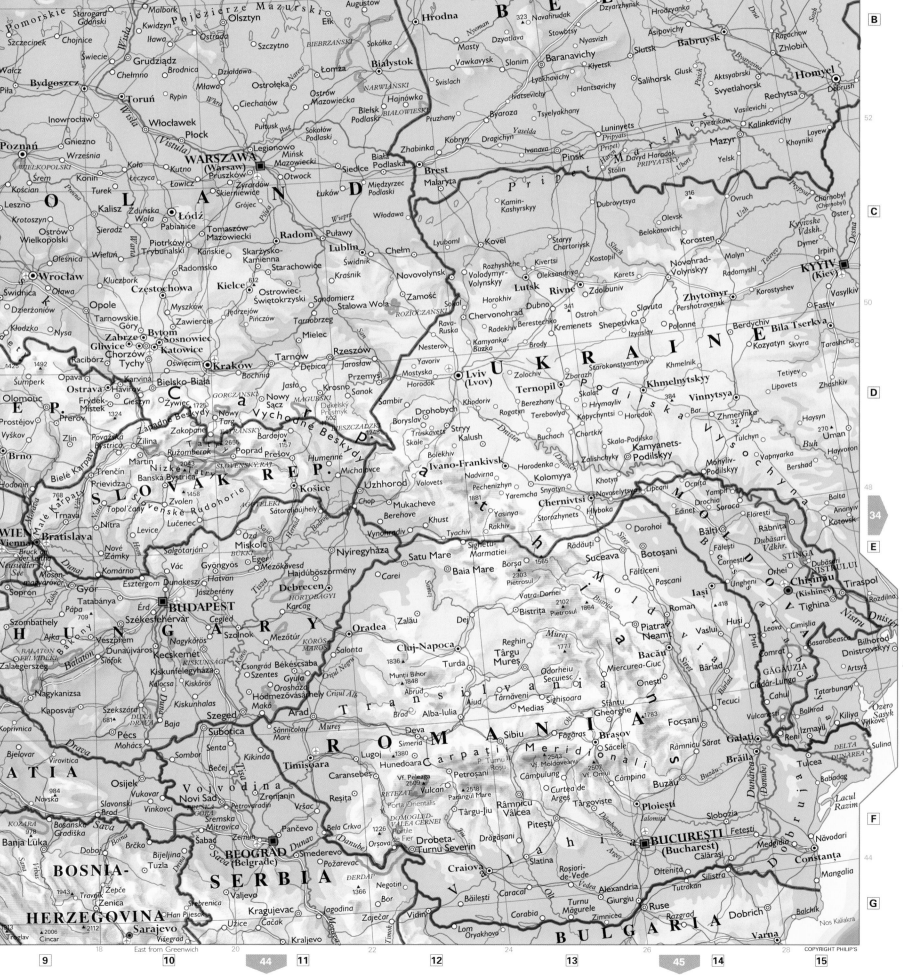

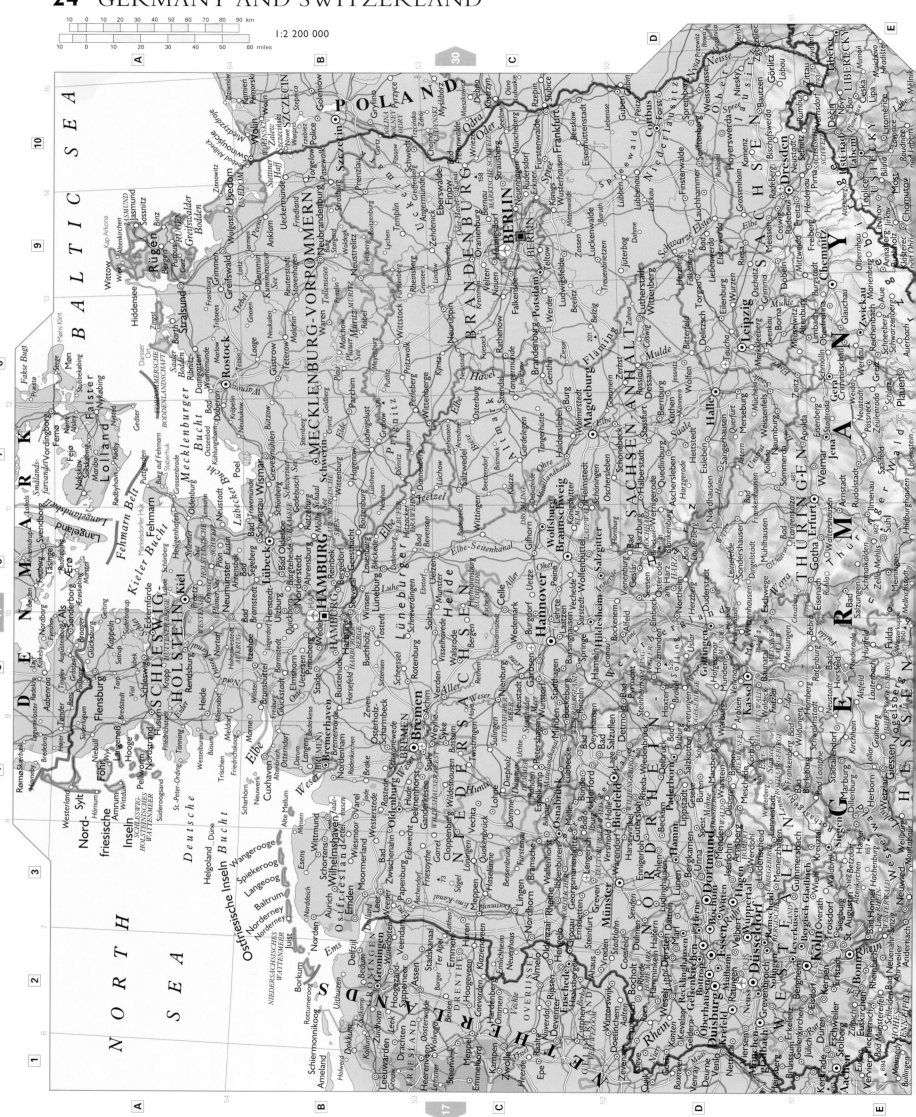

National Parks and Nature Parks in Germany

Underlined towns give their name to the administrative area in which they stand.

Projection: Lambert's Conformal Conic

East from Greenwich

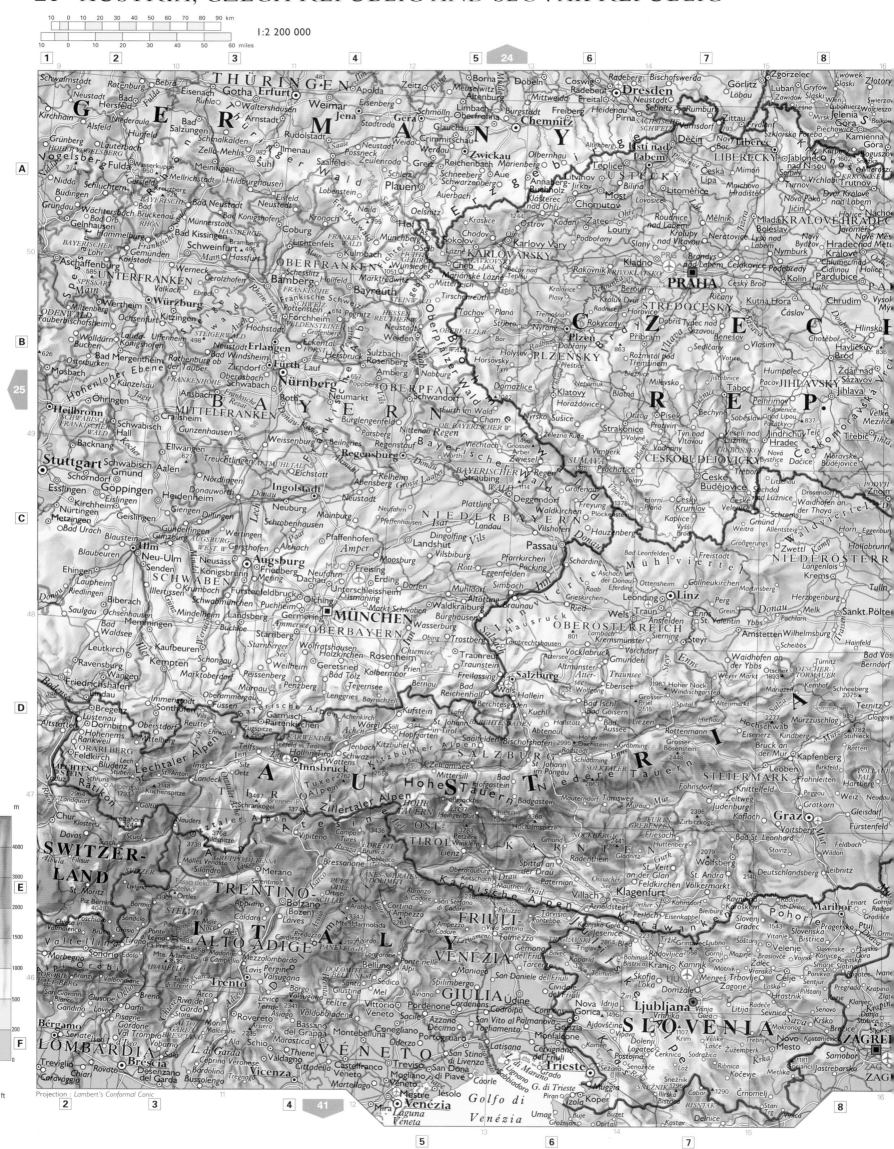

National Parks

Underlined towns give their name to the administrative area in which they stand.

1:2 200 000

Projection : Lambert's Conformal Conic

East from Greenwich

Administrative divisions in Croatia:
1 Brodsko-Posavska
2 Koprivničko-Križevačka
4 Medimurska
5 Osječko-Baranjska
6 Požeško-Slavonska
8 Virovitičko-Podravska
9 Vukovarsko-Srijemska

Inter-entity boundaries as agreed
at the 1995 Dayton Peace Agreement

National Parks

Underlined towns give their name to the
administrative area in which they stand.

COPYRIGHT PHILIP'S

1:2 200 000

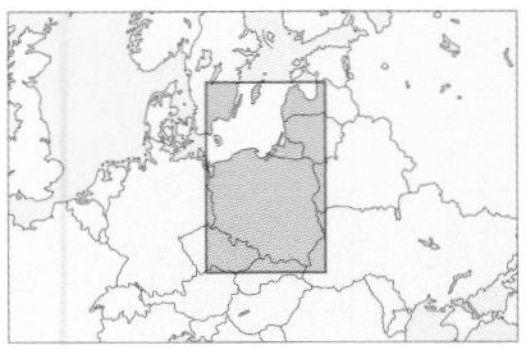

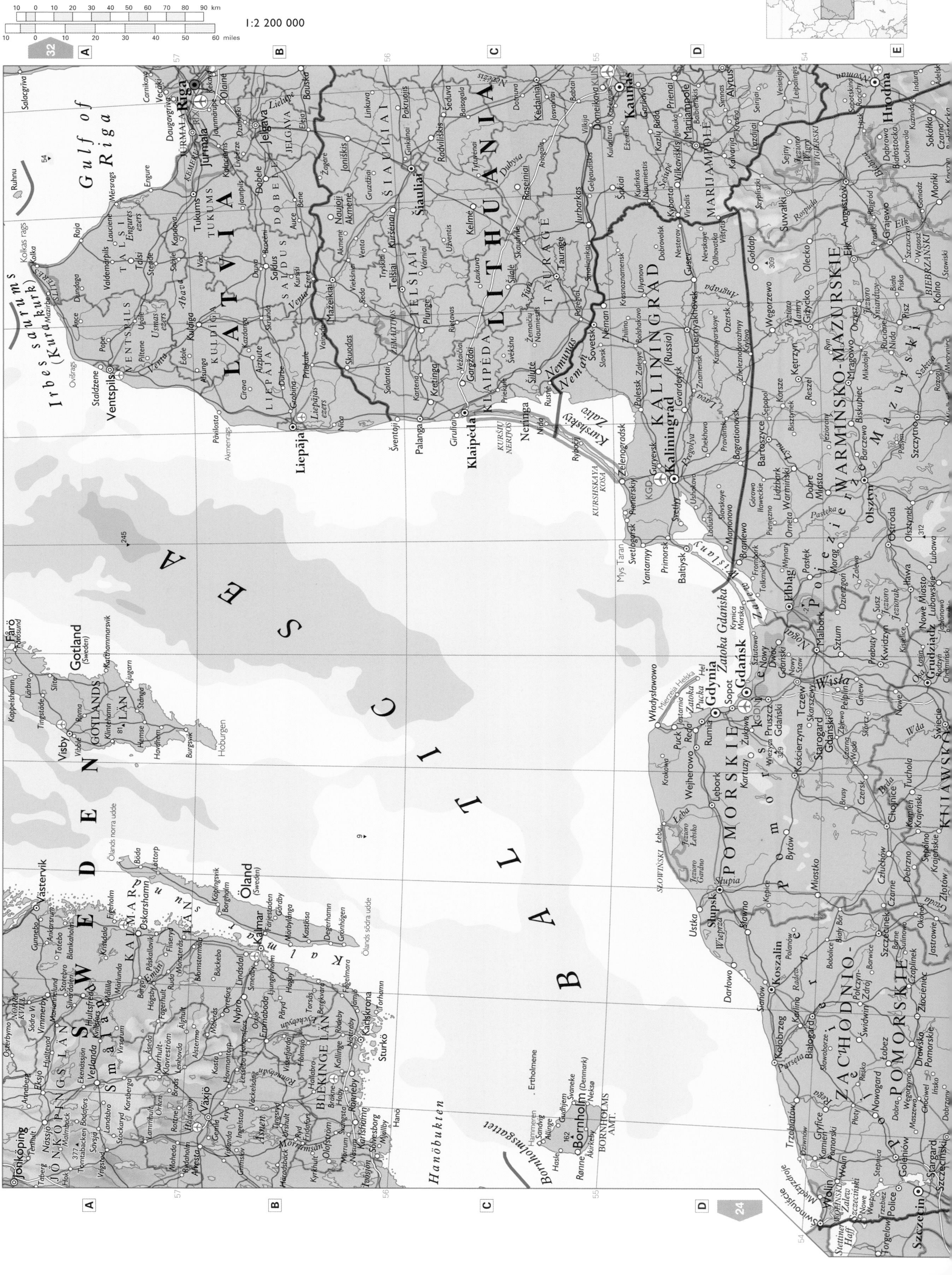

10 0 10 20 30 40 50 60 70 80 90 km
10 0 10 20 30 40 50 60 miles
32
11
24
A
B
C
D
E
1
2
3
4
5
6
7
8
9
10
11
LATVIA
LITHUANIA
SWEDEN
BALTIC SEA
Gulf of Riga
Irbes šaurums (Kura kurk)
KALININGRAD (Russia)
Kaliningrad
POMORSKIE
WARMIŃSKO-MAZURSKIE
ZACHODNIO-POMORSKIE
Pojezierze Mazurskie
Pomorze
Gotland (Sweden)
Öland (Sweden)
Bornholm (Denmark)
Hanöbukten
Bornholmsgattet
Kalmarsund
Zatoka Gdańska
Zalew Wiślany
Kurshskiy Zaliv
Riga
Jūrmala
Jelgava
Liepāja
Ventspils
Klaipėda
Šiauliai
Kaunas
Marijampolė
Alytus
Hrodna
Gdańsk
Gdynia
Sopot
Elbląg
Olsztyn
Koszalin
Słupsk
Szczecin
Kalmar
Karlskrona
Växjö
Jönköping
Visby
Rønne
Neman
Wisła
Nemunas
24

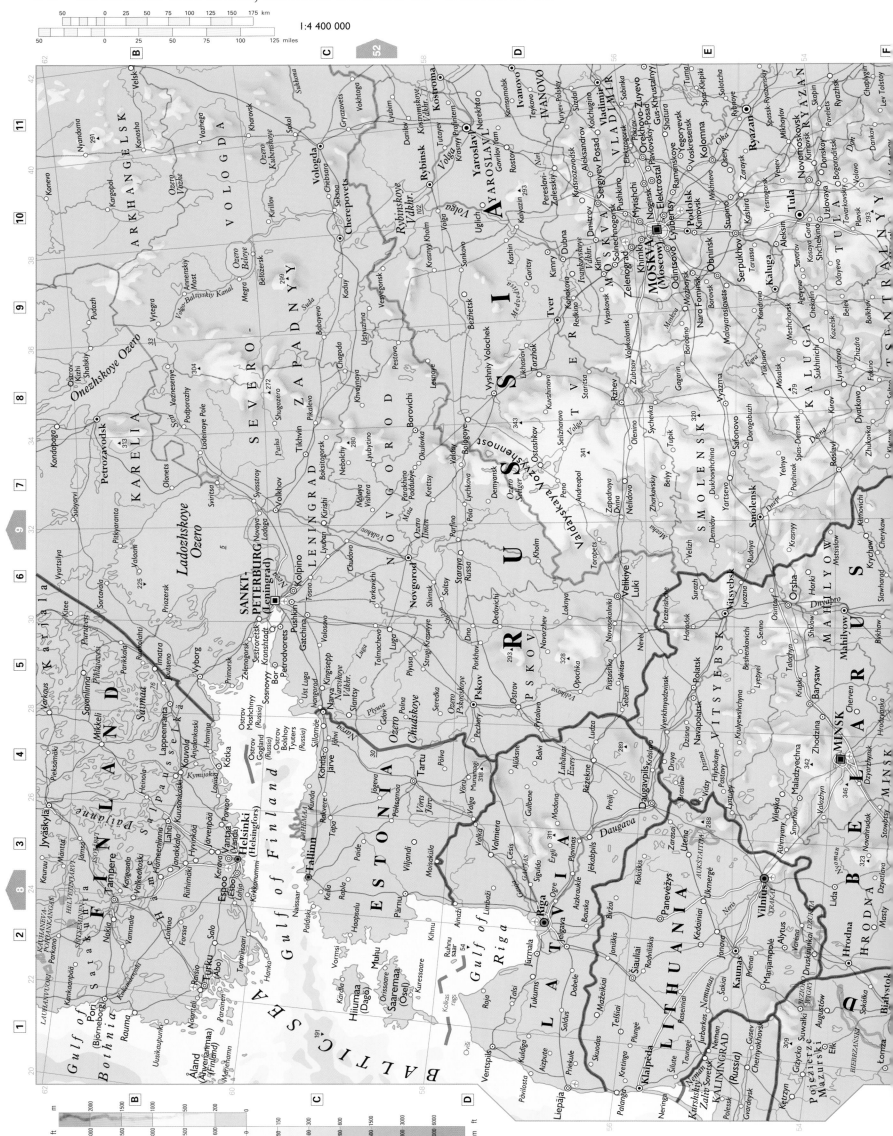

East from Greenwich

Projection: Conical with two standard parallels

Sea of Azov

BLACK SEA

Countries and regions:
LIPETSK · VORONEZH · OREL · KURSK · BRYANSK · BELOGOROD · KHARKIV · LUHANSK · ROSTOV · KRASNODAR · CRIMEA · SUMY · POLTAVA · CHERNIHIV · KYYIV · DNIPROPETROVSK · DONETSK · ZAPORIZHZHYA · KHERSON · MYKOLAYIV · KIROVOHRAD · CHERKASY · ZHYTOMYR · VINNYTSYA · KHMELNYTSKYY · TERNOPIL · LVIV · IVANO-FRANKIVSK · ZAKARPATTYA · CHERNIVTSI · RIVNE · VOLYN · BREST · HOMYEL · MAZOVIA · MOLDOVA · GAGAUZIA · ROMANIA · BULGARIA · HUNGARY · SLOVAK REP. · POLAND

Major cities:
Voronezh · Orel · Kursk · Belgorod · KHARKIV (Kharkov) · Luhansk · ROSTOV · Taganrog · Mariupol · DONETSK · DNIPROPETROVSK · Zaporizhzhya · Kherson · Mykolayiv · ODESA · Kirovohrad · Cherkasy · KYIV (Kiev) · Chernihiv · Sumy · Poltava · Kremenchuk · Kryvyy Rih · Simferopol · Sevastopol · Yalta · Feodosiya · Kerch · Chernivtsi · Ternopil · Lviv (Lvov) · Ivano-Frankivsk · Uzhgorod · Rivne · Lutsk · Brest · Pinsk · Babruysk · Homyel · Zhytomyr · Vinnytsya · Khmelnytskyy · CHIŞINĂU · Tiraspol · Tighina · BUCUREŞTI (Bucharest) · Galaţi · Braila · Constanţa · Ruse · Dobrich

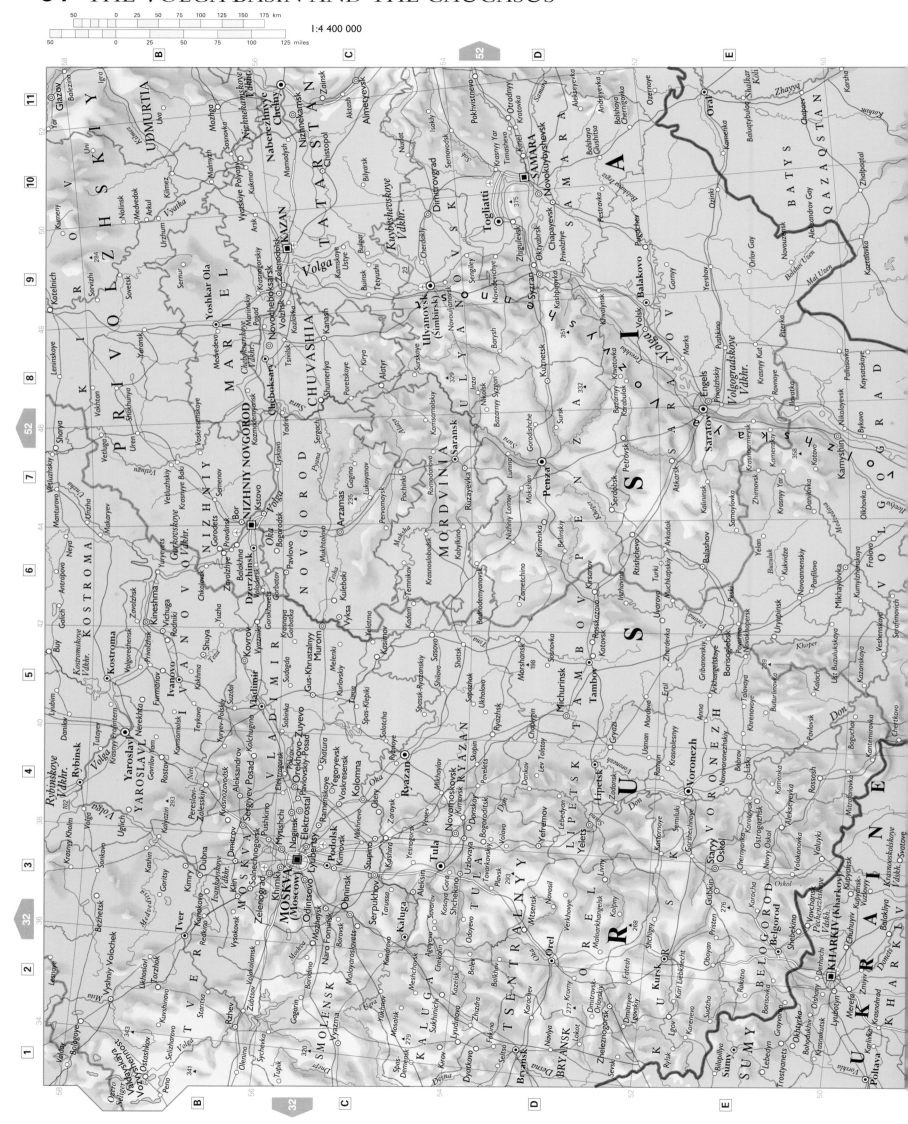

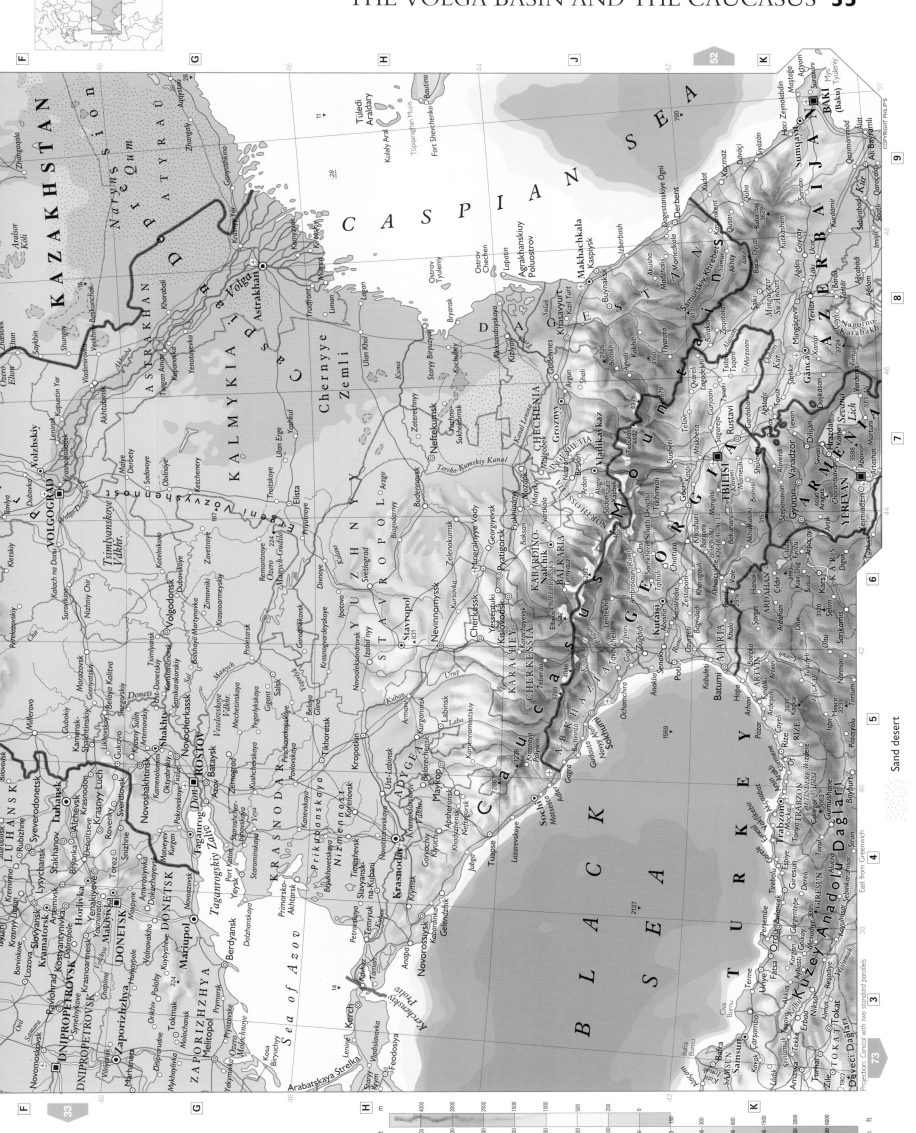

Sand desert

Projection: Conical with two standard parallels

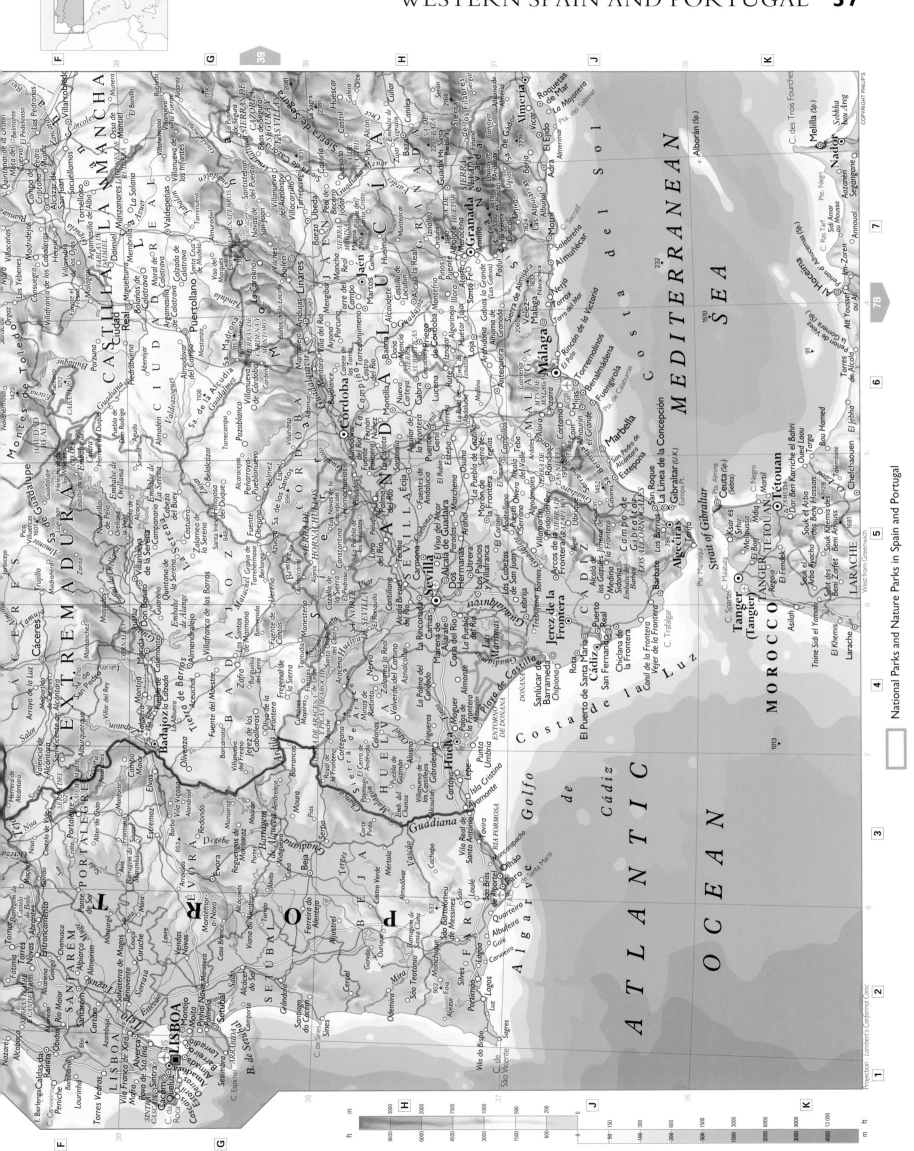

National Parks and Nature Parks in Spain and Portugal

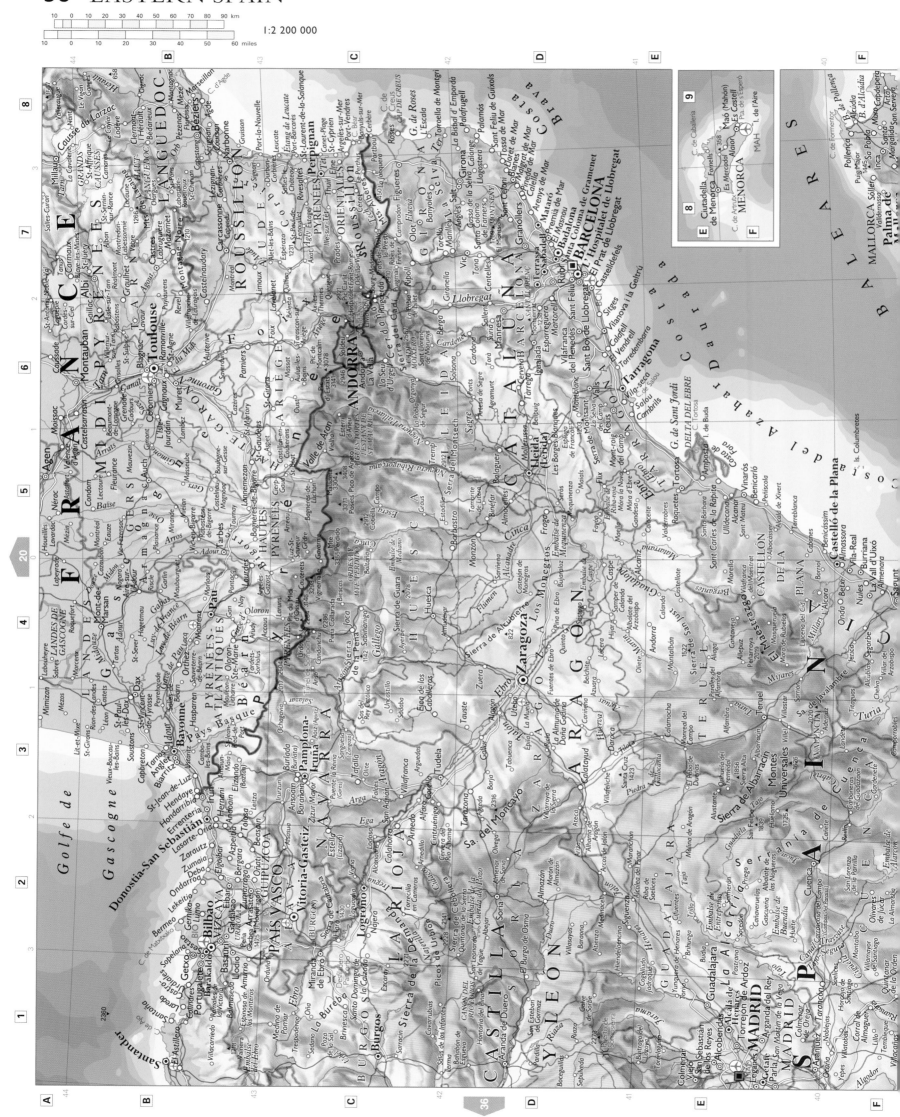

1:2 200 000

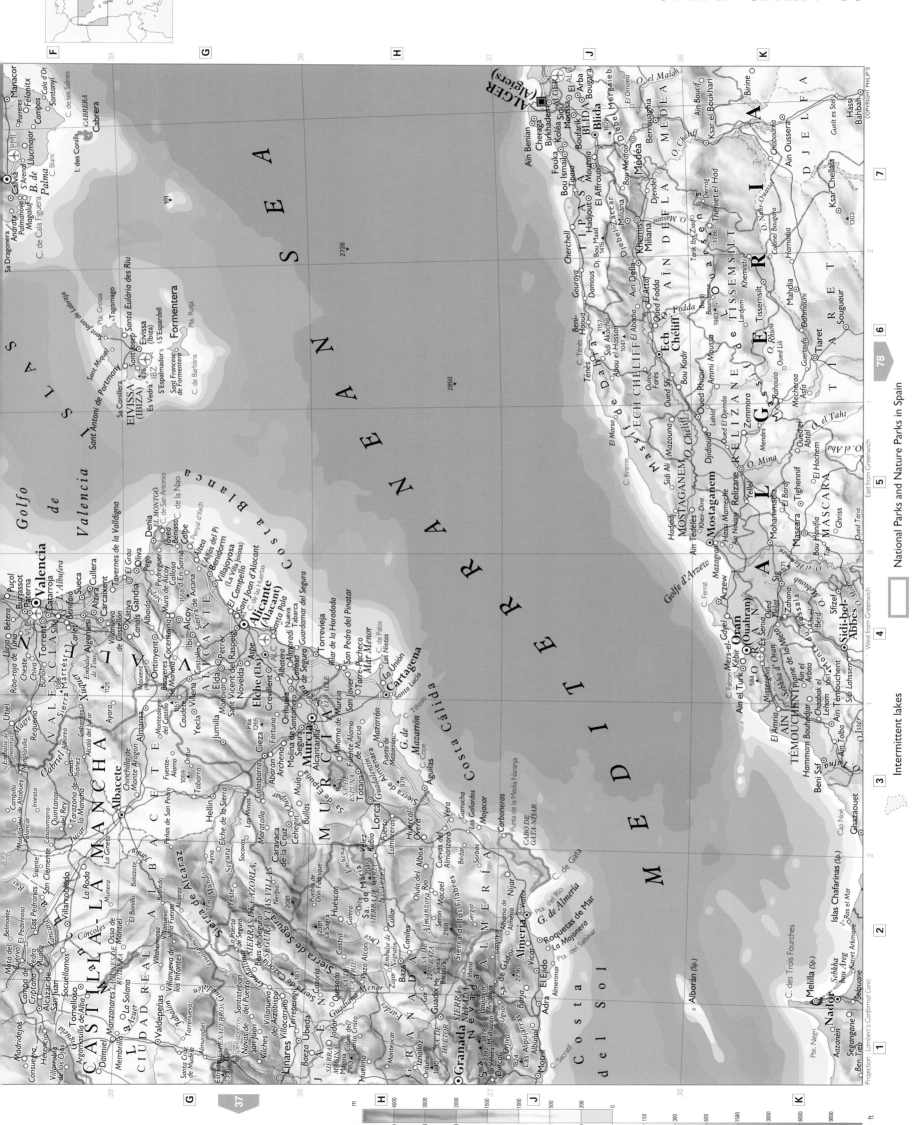

National Parks and Nature Parks in Spain

Intermittent lakes

1:2 200 000

Projection : Lambert's Conformal Conic

East from Greenwich

Underlined towns give their name to the
administrative area in which they stand.

Administrative divisions in Croatia:

Brodsko-Posavska	4 Medimurska	8 Virovitičko-Podravska
Koprivničko-Križevačka	6 Požeško-Slavonska	10 Zagreba čka
Krapinsko-Zagorska	7 Varaždinska	

National Parks and Nature Parks in Italy

Inter-entity boundaries as agreed at the 1995 Dayton Peace Agreement

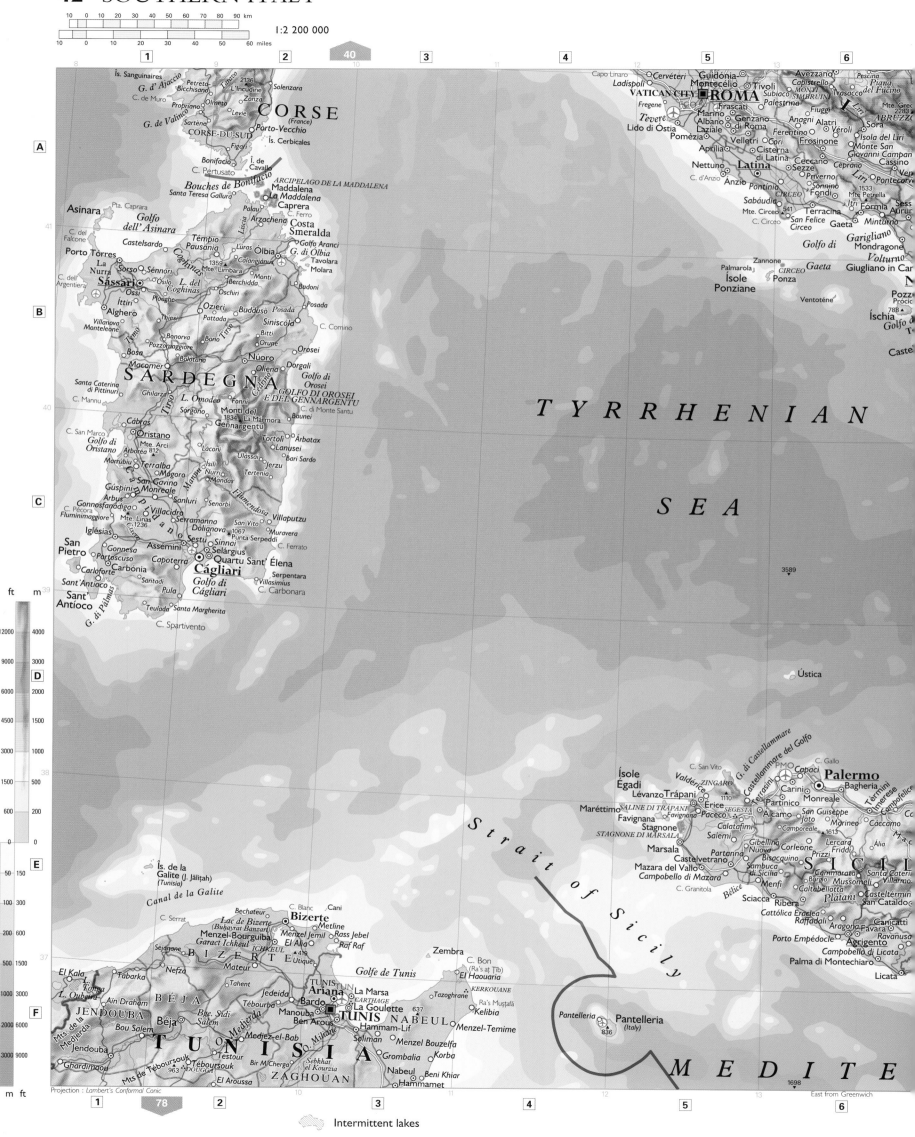

10 0 10 20 30 40 50 60 70 80 90 km

1:2 200 000

10 0 10 20 30 40 50 60 miles

CORSE
(France)
CORSE-DU-SUD

Ís. Sanguinaires
G. d'Ajaccio
Petretu
Bicchisano
Propriano
Olmeto
Sartène
Figari
Bonifacio
C. de Muro
Zonza
Levie
Tappu
L'Incudine 2136
Solenzara
C. Pertusato
Î. de Cavallu
Bouches de Bonifacio
Santa Teresa Gallura
Maddalena
La Maddalena
Caprera
C. Ferro
Palau
Arzachena
ARCIPELAGO DE LA MADDALENA
ARCIPELAGO DE LA MADDALENA
Costa Smeralda

Asinara
Pta. Caprara
C. del Falcone
Golfo dell' Asinara
Porto Tôrres
La Nurra
Sorso
Séņnori
Castelsardo
Tèmpio Pausânia
Lúras
Calangianus
Olbia
Golfo Aranci
G. di Olbia
Tavolara
Molara
C. dell'Argentiera
Alghero
Íttiri
Óssi
Òsilo
Ploaghe
Thiesi
Bonorva
Macomer
Bolótana
SÁSSARI
Monti
Berchidda
Oschiri
L. del Coghinas
Coghinas
Mte. Limbara 1359
Pattada
Budoni
Posada
Bòsa
Pozzomaggiore
Bono
Ozieri
Buddusò
Bitti
Orune
Posada
Villanova Monteleone
Tirso
Orosei
C. Comino
Santa Caterina di Pittinuri
C. Mannu
Ghilarza
L. Omodeo
Sòrgono
Fonni
Núoro
Oliena
Dorgali
Golfo di Orosei
GOLFO DI OROSEI E DEL GENNARGENTU
Baunei
C. di Monte Santu
Cábras
Oristano
Golfo di Oristano
C. San Marco
Arboréa 812
Mte. Arci
Làconi
Monti del Gennargentu
La Mármora 1834
Tortolì
Lanusei
Árbatax
Marrúbiu
Terralba
Mógoro
Isili
Nurri
Jerzu
Tertenia
Ulàssai
Bari Sardo
Gúspini
San Gavino Monreale
Sanluri
Senorbì
Mandas
Arbus
Gonnosfanádiga
Villacidro
Serramanna
Dòlianova
San Vito
1067 Punta Serpeddi
Muravera
C. Ferrato
C. Pécora
Fluminimaggiore
P. di Pula
Mte. Linas 1236
Iglésias
Assémini
Sestu
Sínnai
Selárgius
Quartu Sant' Élena
San Pietro
Gonnesa
Portoscuso
Carloforte
Carbónia
Santadi
Capoterra
CÁGLIARI
Golfo di Cágliari
Serpentara
Villasímius
C. Carbonara
Sant'Antíoco
Sant' Antíoco
Pula
Teulada
Santa Margherita
G. di Pálmas
C. Spartivento

SARDEGNA

Capo Linaro
Cervéteri
Ladispoli
Montecélio
Guidónia
Tivoli
Subiaco
Fregene
VATICAN CITY
ROMA
Frascati
Palestrina
Marino
Genzano di Roma
Albano
Lido di Óstia
Pomézia
Aprilia
Velletri
Nettuno
Cisterna di Latina
Cori
LATINA
Sezze
Priverno
Anzio
C. d'Anzio
Pontínia
Sabáudia
CIRCEO
Mte. Circeo 541
C. Circeo
San Felice Circeo
Terracina
Mte. Grec. 2283
ABRUZZO
Avezzano
Pescina
Piana del Fúcino
Trasacco
MONTI SIMBRUINI
Capistrello
Fiuggi
Ferentino
Anagni
Alatri
Véroli
Frosinone
Isola del Liri
Ceccano
Monte San Giovanni Campan
Ceprano
Cassino
Sonnino
Fondi
Itri
Formia
Gaeta
Minturno
Sabáudia
Pontecorv
Aurur
Sora
Liri
Gariglíano
Golfo di Gaeta
Mondragone
Volturno
Giugliano in Car
N
Pozz
Prócic
Íschia
788
Golfo di
Caste

Palmarola
Zannone
Ísole Ponziane
Ponza
Ventotène

TYRRHENIAN

SEA

3589

Ústica

G. di Castellammare del Golfo
C. San Vito
C. Gallo
Capaci
ZINGARO
Castellammare del Golfo
Ísole Égadi
Valdérici
Terrasini
Carini
Lévanzo
Trápani
Érice
Monreale
PMO
Palermo
Bagheria
Términi
Marèttimo
SALINE DI TRAPANI
1110
SEGESTA
Partinico
Bórgo
San Giuseppe Jato
Corleone
Monreale
Favignana
Paceco
Alcamo
Morineo
Cáccamo
Favignana
Calatafimi
Camporeale
1613
Campobello del
Marsala
STAGNONE DI MARSALA
Salemi
Gibellina Nuova
Partanna
Bisacquino
Prizzi
Lercara Friddi
Mazara del Vallo
Castelvetrano
Sambuca di Sicilia
Ália
Campobello di Mazara
Menfi
SICIL
Cammarata
Santa Catari
Villalm
Gibellina
Mussomeli
C. Granitola
Bélice
Sciacca
Ribera
Menfi
Caltabellotta
Castellterm
San Cataldo
Strait of Sicily
Cattólica Eraclea
Raffadali
Plátani
Aragona
Favara
Canicatti
Ravanusa
Porto Empédocle
Agrigento
Palma di Montechiaro
Campobello di Licata
Licata

Ís. de la Galite (J. Jâlitah) (Tunisia)
Canal de la Galite
C. Blanc
Cani
C. Serrat
Bechateur
Lac de Bizerte (Buḥayrat Banzart)
Zembra
Bizerte
Metline
Rass Jebel
C. Bon (Ra's aṭ Ṭīb)
El Haouaria
Pantelleria
Pantelleria (Italy)
836
El Kala
L. Tonga
L. Oubeira
Tabarka
Aïn Draham
Nefza
Menzel-Bourguiba
Menzel Jemil
El Alia
Raf Raf
Sejnane
Garaet Ichkeul
ICHKEUL
Utique
Tazoghrane
Kerkouane
Kelibia
Menzel-Temime
BÉJA
Mts. de la Medjerda
Medjerda
Bge. Sidi Salem
Mateur
Tahent
Jedeida
Manouba
TUNIS
Ariana
Bardo
La Marsa
CARTHAGE
La Goulette
637
Béja
JENDOUBA
Bou Salem
Béja
Téboursouk
Testour
Medjez-el-Bab
Ben Arous
TUNIS
Hammam-Lif
NABEUL
Menzel Bouzelfa
Korba
Soliman
Grombalia
Jendouba
Bir M'Cherga
Sebkhat el Kourzia
Nabeul
Beni Khiar
Ghardimaou
Mts de Téboursouk
963
DOUGGA
Testour
Soliman
El Aroussa
ZAGHOUAN
El Aroussa
Mikane
Hammamet
TUNISIA
1698
MEDITE

East from Greenwich

Projection : Lambert's Conformal Conic

Intermittent lakes

ft m
12000 4000
9000 3000
6000 2000
4500 1500
3000 1000
1500 500
600 200
0 0
50 150
100 300
200 600
500 1500
1000 3000
2000 6000
3000 9000
m ft

National Parks and Nature Parks in Italy

Underlined towns give their name to the administrative area in which they stand.

COPYRIGHT PHILIP'S

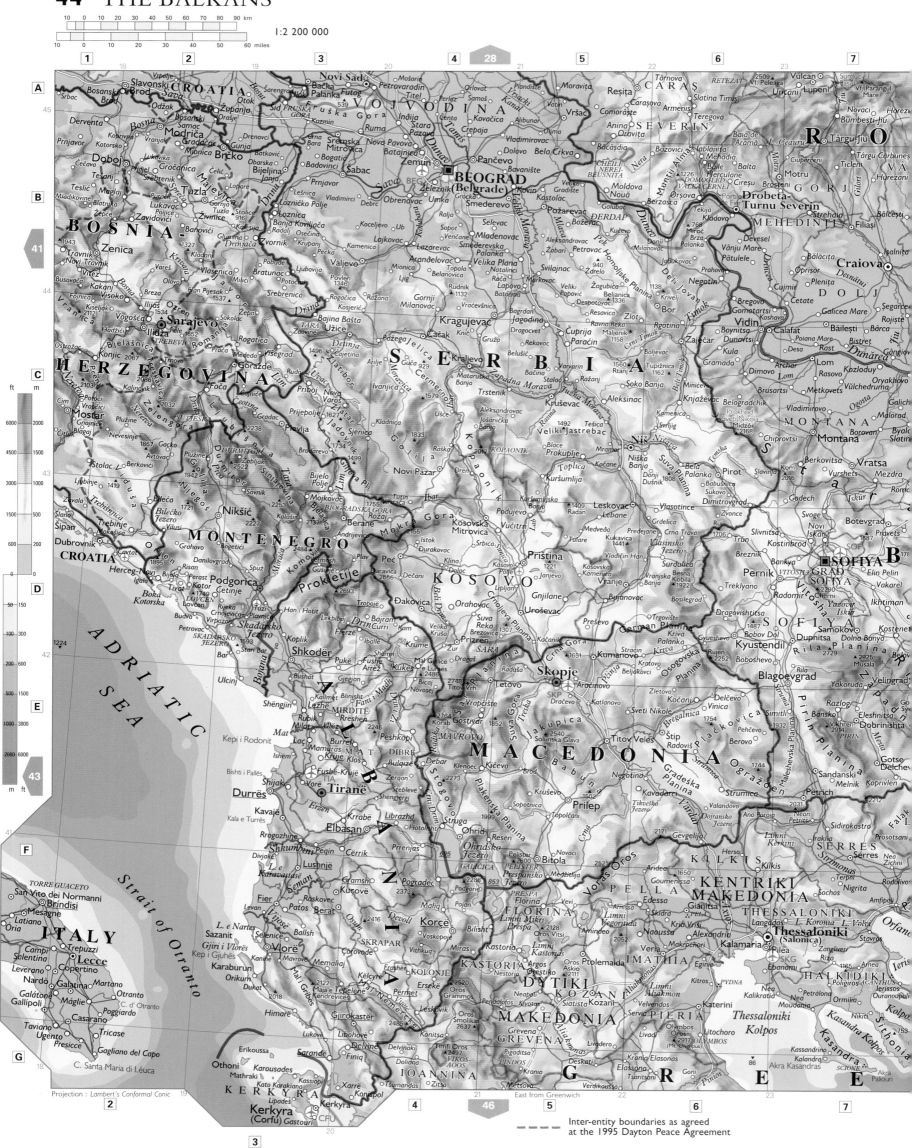

1:2 200 000

Projection : Lambert's Conformal Conic

Inter-entity boundaries as agreed
at the 1995 Dayton Peace Agreement

East from Greenwich

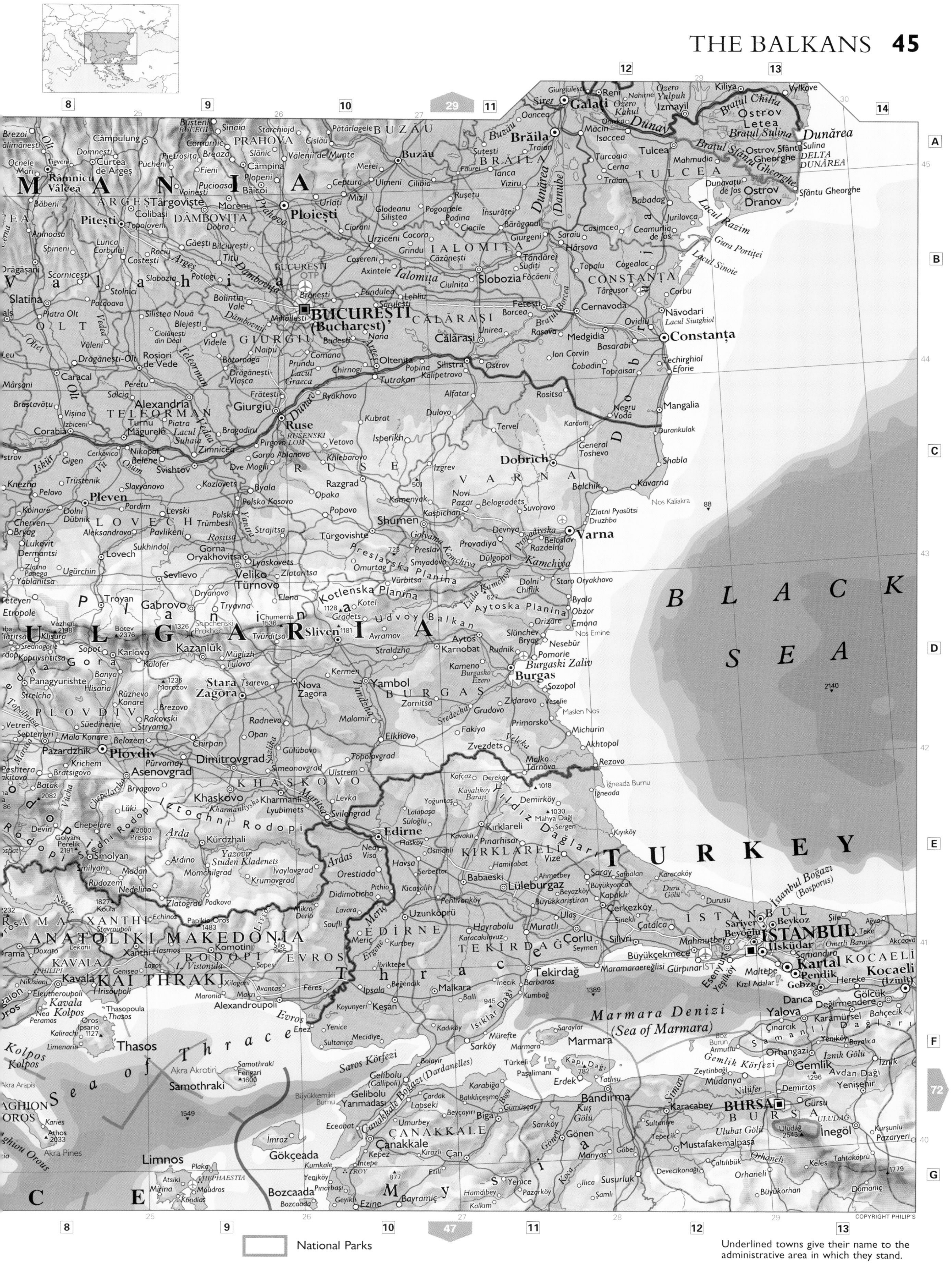

THE BALKANS

BLACK SEA

TURKEY

BULGARIA

ROMANIA

Marmara Denizi (Sea of Marmara)

Sea of Thrace

Major places:
BUCUREŞTI (Bucharest), Ploieşti, Piteşti, Braşov area, Galaţi, Brăila, Buzău, Constanţa, Călăraşi, Giurgiu, Ruse, Pleven, Veliko Tŭrnovo, Gabrovo, Stara Zagora, Sliven, Yambol, Burgas, Varna, Dobrich, Shumen, Plovdiv, Asenovgrad, Pazardzhik, Dimitrovgrad, Khaskovo, Kŭrdzhali, Smolyan, Edirne, Kırklareli, Lüleburgaz, Çorlu, Tekirdağ, İSTANBUL (Istanbul), Üsküdar, Kartal, Pendik, Gebze, Kocaeli (İzmit), BURSA, Çanakkale, Bandırma, Gökçeada, Limnos, Thasos, Samothraki, KAVALA, Xanthi, ANATOLIKI MAKEDONIA KAI THRAKI, Komotini, Alexandroupoli.

DELTA DUNĂREA

National Parks

Underlined towns give their name to the
administrative area in which they stand.

COPYRIGHT PHILIP'S

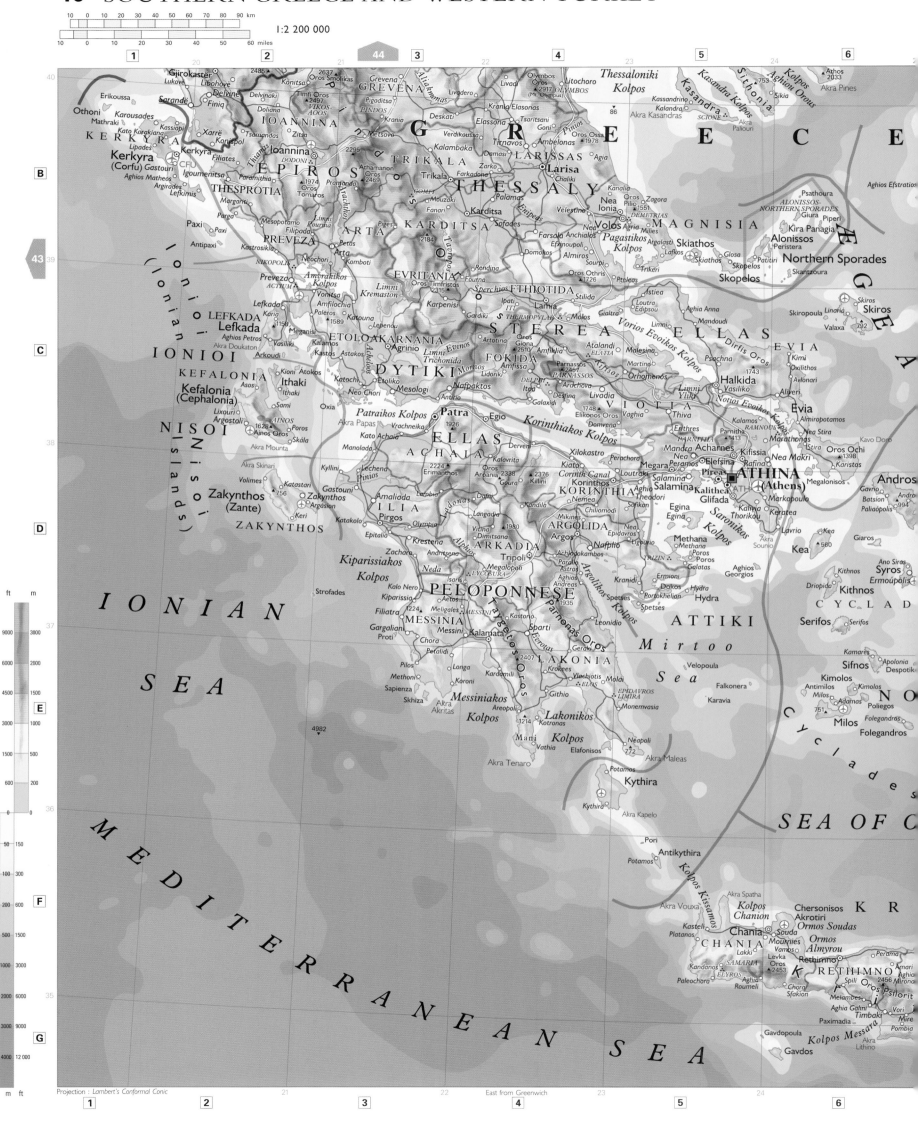

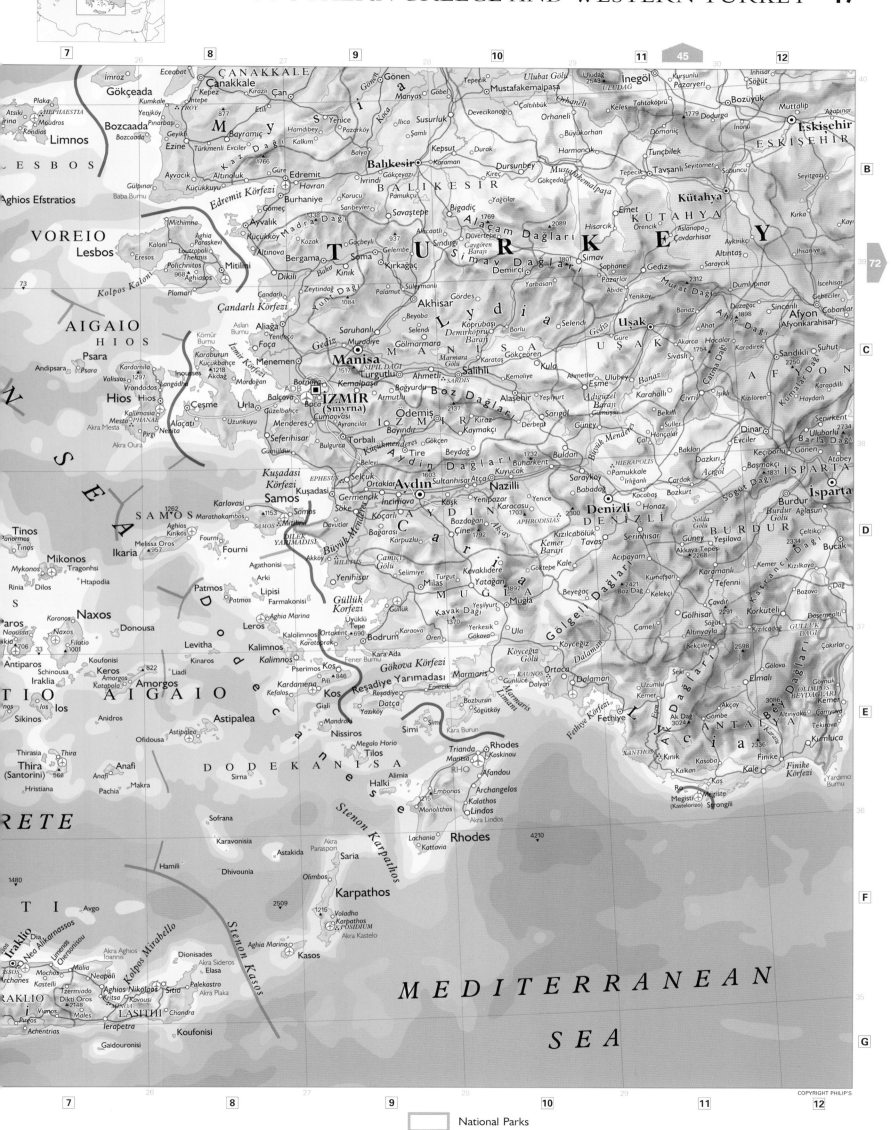

National Parks

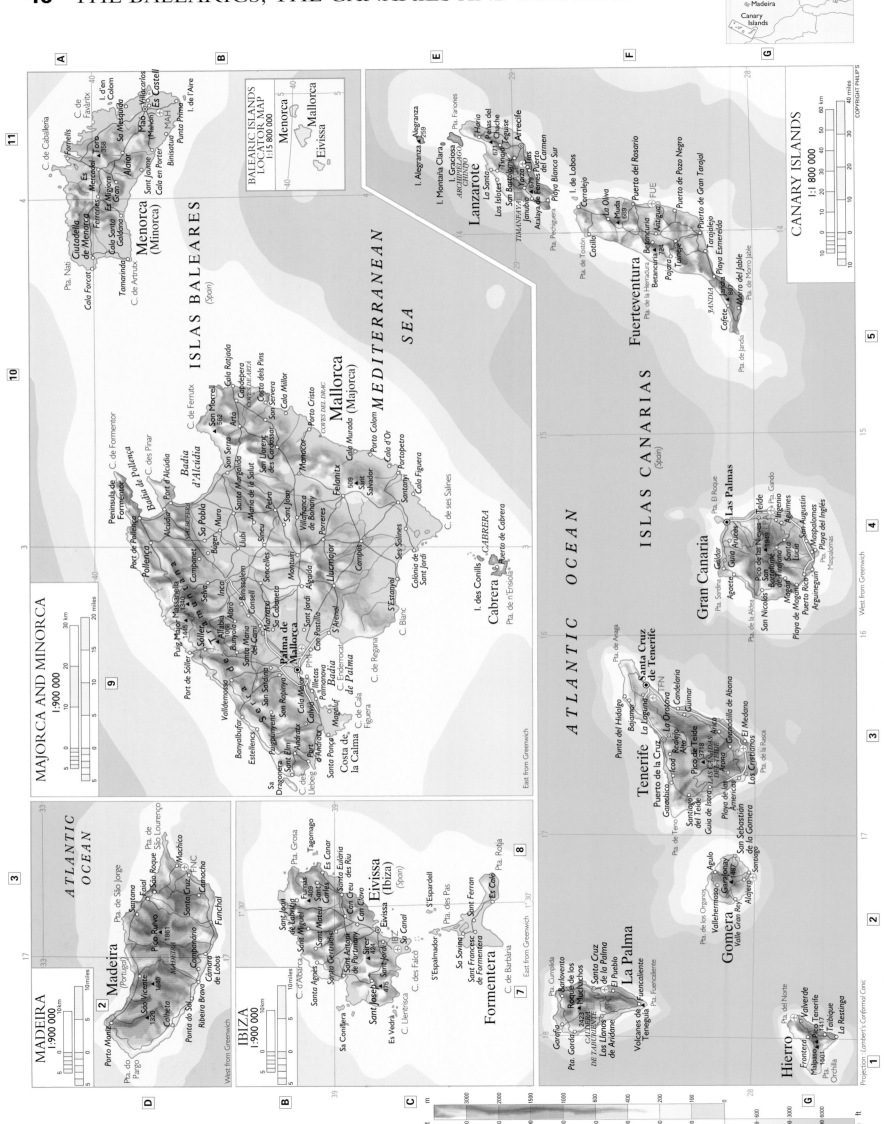

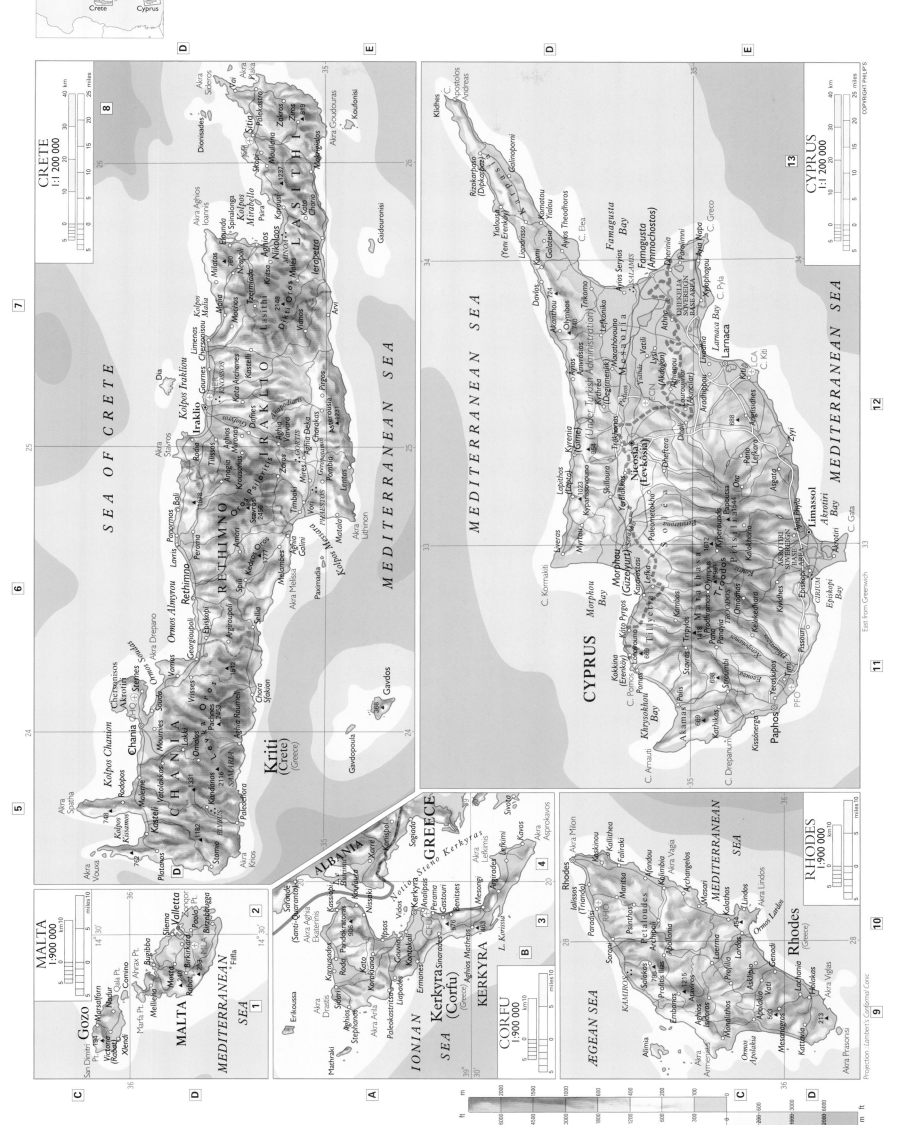

CRETE 1:1 200 000

CYPRUS 1:1 200 000

MALTA 1:900 000

CORFU 1:900 000

RHODES 1:900 000

SEA OF CRETE

Kriti
(Crete)
(Greece)

MEDITERRANEAN SEA

MEDITERRANEAN SEA

CYPRUS

MEDITERRANEAN SEA

IONIAN SEA

AEGEAN SEA

Rhodes
(Greece)

GREECE

ALBANIA

GOZO

MALTA

Kerkyra
(Corfu)
(Greece)

KERKYRA

Projection: Lambert's Conformal Conic

East from Greenwich

1:44 400 000

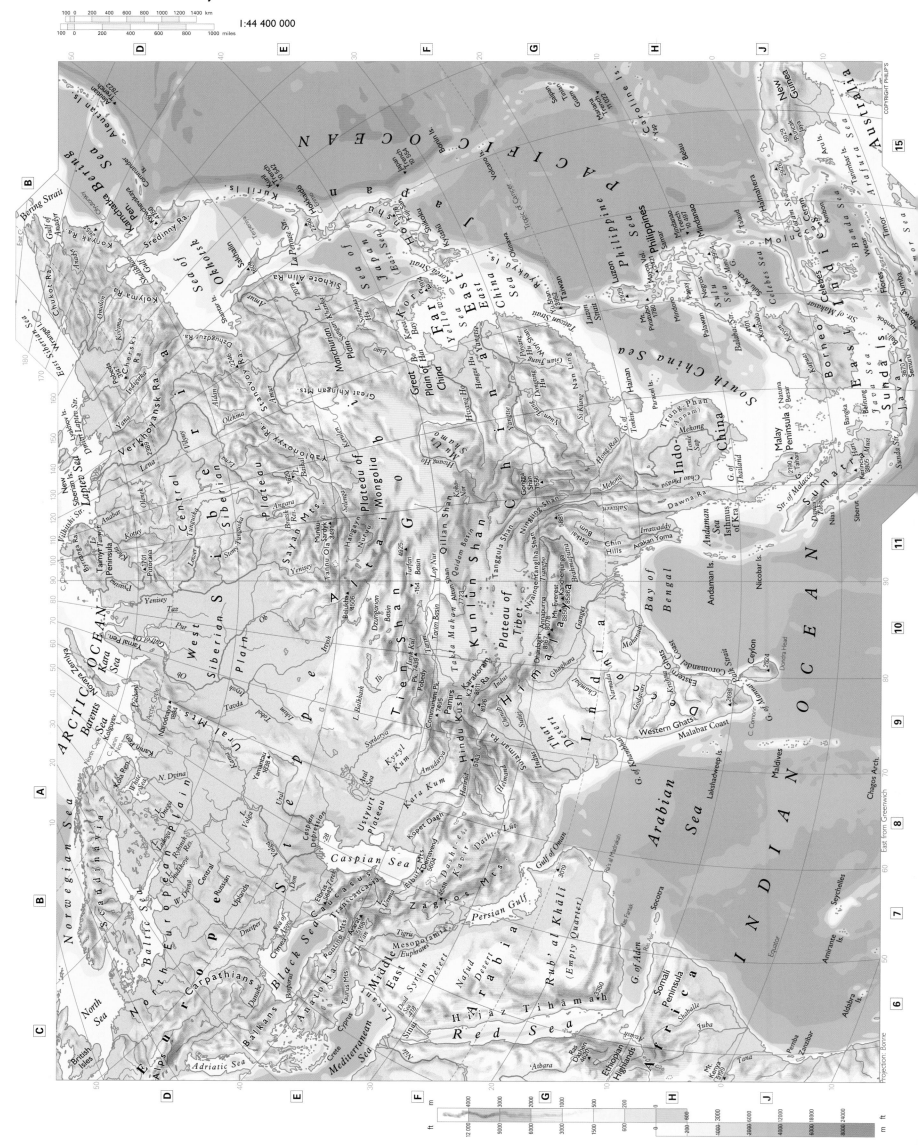

1:44 400 000

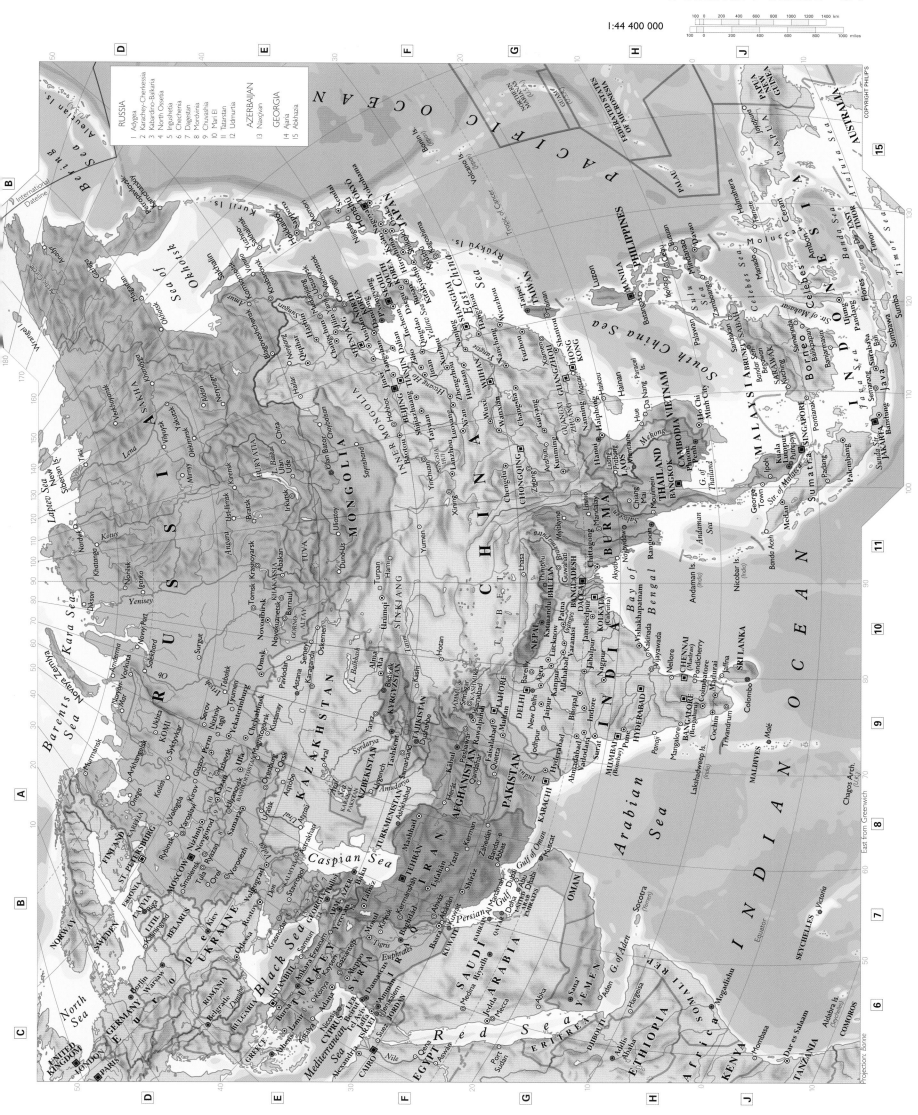

	RUSSIA
1	Adygea
2	Karachey-Cherkessia
3	Kabardino-Balkaria
4	North Ossetia
5	Ingushetia
6	Chechenia
7	Dagestan
8	Mordovina
9	Chuvashia
10	Mari El
11	Tatarstan
12	Udmurtia
	AZERBAIJAN
13	Naxçivan
	GEORGIA
14	Ajaria
15	Abkhazia

Projection: Bonne

1:17 800 000

RUSSIA
1 Adygea
2 Karachey-Cherkessia
3 Kabardino-Balkaria
4 North Ossetia
5 Ingushetia
6 Chechenia
7 Dagestan
8 Mordvinia
9 Chuvashia
10 Mari El
11 Tatarstan
12 Udmurtia
13 Khakassia
AZERBAIJAN
14 Naxçivan
GEORGIA   UKRAINE
15 Ajaria   17 Crimea
16 Abkhazia

Projection: Conical Orthomorphic with two standard parallels

East from Greenwich

1:4 400 000

50 0 25 50 75 100 125 150 175 km
50 0 25 50 75 100 125 miles

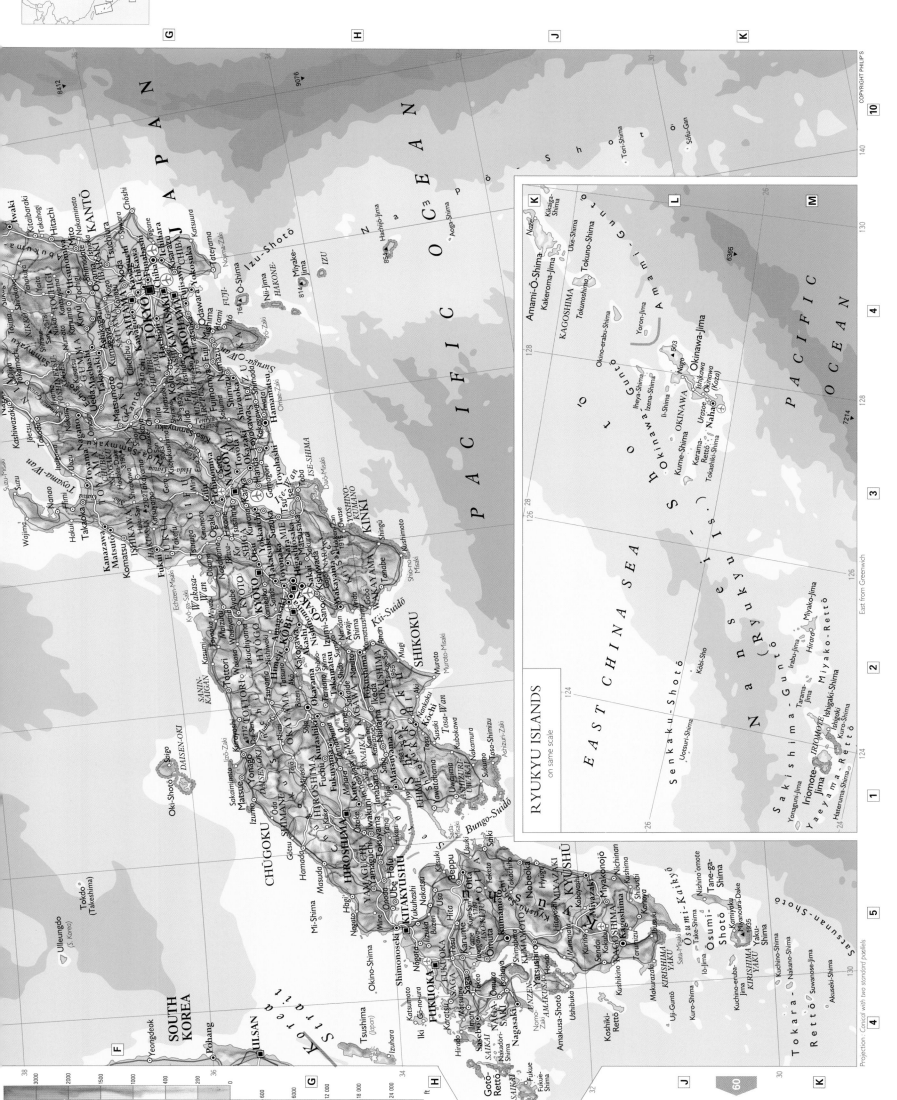

1:5 300 000

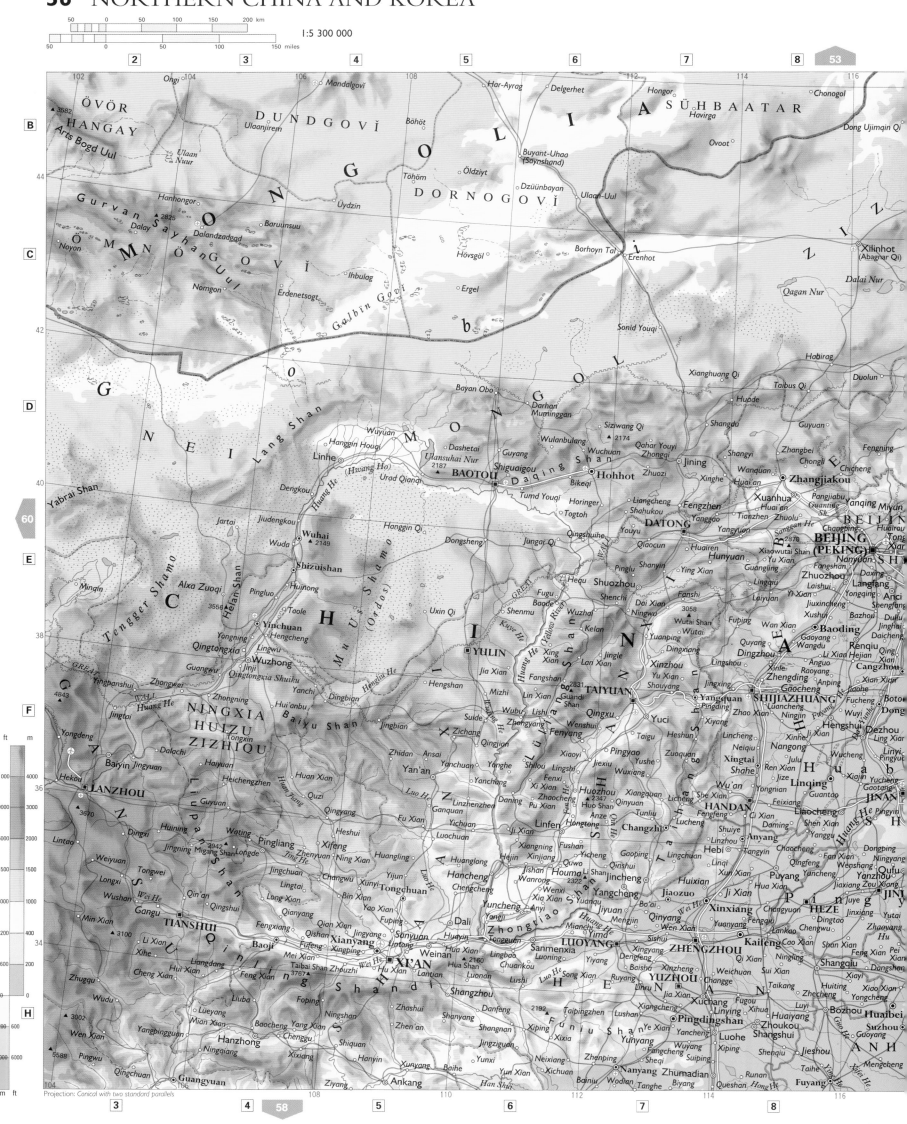

Sand deserts

B

118   120

Horqin Youyi Qianqi
(Ulanhot)

Huolin Gol
Huolin He

Zhenlai
Taoer He
Nen Jiang
Songhua Jiang
HARBIN   Bin Xian
Maoxing   Zhaoyuan   Shuangcheng   Acheng   Shangzhi
Yanshou

H I Q U

Baicheng   Da'an
Tuquan
Taonan
Anguang
Qagan
Nur Qian   Changchunling   H E I L O N G J I A N G
Linkou
Jixi
Turiy Rog   69

B

Hulin He
Tongyu
J Qian'an
Shenjingzi
FUYU
Beitaolaizhao
Sanchahe
Yushu   Shulan
Yimianpo
Wuchang
Hengdaohezi
Zhangguangcai Ling   Mudanjiang   Maqiaohe   Pogranichnyy   RUSSIA

Changling
Fulongquan
Dehui
1690   Hailin   Xiachengzi   Suifenhe
Nong'an   Jiutai
Muling   Muling   Suiyang

Jarud Qi
1949   Zhanyu
Beizhengzhen
CHANGCHUN   J   Ning'an   Dongjingcheng   Dongning   Ussuriysk   44

Horqin Zuoyi
Zhongqi   Huaidezhen   JILIN   Jiaohe   Emu   Luozigou   Razdolnoye   Artem

Xinkai He   Maolin
Fanjiatun
Xinzhan   Huangsongdian   Dunhua   Daxinggou   Chunyang   Tavrichanka

Kailu   Tonghua   Shuangliao   Gongzhuling   Yitong   Songhua   Hu   Wangqing   Shixian   Vladivostok   C

Bairin   Linxi
Zuoqi   Jargalang   Lishu   Siping   Liaoyuan   Panshi   Huadian   Mingyuegue   Tumen   Yanji   Hunchun   Slavyanka

2029   Hexigten Qi   Bamiancheng   Xifeng   Dongfeng   Huinan   Quanyang   Baishan   Longjing   Helong   Namyang   Kraskino   Posyet

Bairin Youqi
Xar Moron He   Zhangwu   Huifa   Jingyu   Fusong   Songjianghe   Changbai Shan   Antu   Baihe   1677   Hoeryong   Musan   Unggi   Najin   Sosura

Ongniud Qi
Kangping   Kaiyuan   Meihekou   Shanchengzhen   Liuhe   Jiangyuan   Shiren   Paektu-san   2744   Puryong   Nanam   Ch'ongjin   42

2020   Xiawa   WALL   Faku   Tiefa   Qingyuan   Hunjiang   Linjiang   Chunggang-up   Changbai   Pugodong

CHIFENG   Hure Qi   Fuxin   Zhangwu   Tieling   Tonghua   Xinbin   2541   Kyongsong

Heishui   WILLOW   Xinlitun   Xinmin   Piao'ertun   Huamen   1845   Ji'an   Kasan-dong   Hyesan   Odaejin   D

Weichang
Beipiao   Qinghemen   Heishan   SHENYANG   FUSHUN   Dongbei   Manp'o   Kanggye   Puksubaek-san   Kilchu   55

1885   Chaoyang   Ningcheng   Beizhen   Sujiatun   Liaozhong   Qinghecheng   Yalu   Huch'ang   Kasan-dong   Hapsu   Kapsan

Longhua   Lingyuan   Liaoyang   Benxi   Tianshifu   Ch'osan   2522   P'ungsan

Chengde   Pingquan   Jinzhou   Anping   LIAONING   Gongchangling   Lianshanguan   Kuandian   Wiwon   Pujon-ho   Tanch'on
Luanne   Jianchang   Shangbancheng   ANSHAN   Supung   Changjin-ho   Kwangdaeri   Iwon   D

Luanping
Kuancheng   JINXI   Tianzhuangtai   Haicheng   Shuiku   Pyoktong   Koin   Changhungni   Pukch'ong   Sinch'ang   40

Miyun   Xinglong   Shuku   Huludao   Niuzhuang   Dashiqiao   Fengcheng   Xiuyan   Sokchu   Taegwan   Pukchin   Sinhung   Hongwon

Shangbancheng   Xingcheng   Yingkou   Gaizhou   Xiuyan   Cao He   Uiju   Kusong   Kusong   Chongju   Pakch'on   Sinp'o

Sahhe   Liaodong   Wanfu   1131   Buyun Shan   Gushan   Donggou   Langtou   Sinuiju   Yongamp'o   Sonch'on   Taegwan   Tokch'on   Hamhung   Hungnam   E

Zunhua   Fengrun   Lulong   Qinhuangdao   Wan   Zhuanghe   Yalu Jiang   Sinmi-do   Anju   Munch'on   Wonsan

Yutian   Luan Xian   Changli   Bandao   Pikou   Changshan   Sukch'on   Anju   Oro   Hamju   Tongjoson   SEA OF

 Baodi   Luan He   Leting   Pulandian   Qundao   Kangdong   Tongyang   Anbyon   Man

TANGSHAN   Funing   Xinjian   Jinzhou   Jin Xian   Sunch'on   P'yongsong   Sunan   Kowon   JAPAN

TIANJIN SHI   Wafangdian   Koksan   Kosan   Wonsan

Wuqing   Yangliuqing   Lushun   DALIAN   Korea   P'YONGYANG   Chunghwa   Sepo-ri   Changdo-n   Gangseong
TIANJIN   Tanggu   (Luda)   Namp'o   Songnim   Pyonggang   Hwach'on   1638   Sokcho   (EAST SEA)

Dagu   Bo Hai   Bay   Sariwon   Suan   Cheorwon   Hwacheon   1708   Yang-yang   38

Oikou   Miaodao   Chaeryong   Sinmak   Nam-ch'on   Gimhwa   Chuncheon   Jumunjin

Huanghua   Qundao   Changyon   Sinch'on   Kumch'on   Cheorwon   Hongcheon   Donghae   Samcheok   Ulleungdo

Xincun   Penglai   Haeju   Kumch'on   Kaesong   Panmunjom   Ujeongbu   Hongseong   (S. Korea)

Yanshan   Longkou   Daxindian   Ongjin   Yonan   Munsan   SEOUL   SEONGNAM   Gangneung

Qingyun   Wudi   Zhanhua   Huang He   Laizhou   Huang   Weihai   Baengnyeongdo   Ganghwa   Bucheon   Hongcheon   F

guang   Huimin   Wan   Xian   Fushan   Muping   (S. Korea)   INCHEON   Anyang   Heungseong   Wonju   Yeong-wol   Uljin

Deping   Binzhou   Dongying   YANTAI   Chengshan Jiao   SUWON   Ansan   Icheon-yeoju   Jecheon   Yeongju

Qingcheng   Shanghe   Dajiawa   Zhaoyuan   Qixia   Wendeng   Pyeongtaek   Chungju   SOUTH   Yeongdeok

Wangcun   Gaoyuan   Guangrao   Shouguang   923   Rongcheng   Seosan   Cheonan   KOREA   Andong

Zhoucun   Huantai   Laiyang   Rushan   Shidao   Hongseong   Yesan   Cheongju   Yecheon   Heunghae

Mashang   ZIBO   Linzi   Shandong Bandao   Laixi   Nanhuang   Gongju   Seongju   Seonsan   Pohang

WEIFANG   Hongshan   Fangzi   Pingdu   Hoiyang   Anmyeondo   Nonsan   DAEJEON   Yeongdong   Gimcheon   Gumi   Gyeongju

Tai Shan   Boshan   Linqu   Laiwu   Lancun   Jimo   Ganggyeong   Iksan   Waegwan   Cheongdo   ULSAN

1524   TAI'AN   Anqiu   Gaomi   Chengyang   Gunsan   Gimje   Jeonju   DAEGU   Miryang   G

1108   XINTAI   Mengyin   Yishui   Wulian   Jiaozhou   QINGDAO   Jeong-eup   Buan   Geochang   Hamyang   Jinju   Masan   Ginhae   Dongnae

ANDONG   Pingyi   Zhucheng   Fushan Wan   Namwon   Jirisan   1915   Chang-won   BUSAN

NGuan   Fei Xian   Tengzhou   Liangcheng   Damyang   Hadong   Sacheon   Tong-yeong

LINYI   Ganyu   Rizhao   Shijiusuo   YELLOW SEA   GWANGJU   Suncheon   Masan   Korea Strait

Weishan   Hanzhuang   Haizhou   Andongwei   Naju   Hadong   Tsushima
ZAOZHUANG   Jiawang   Pizhou   Lianyungang   (Huang Hai)   Mokpo   Boseong   Beolgyo   Yeosu   (Japan)   Izuhara

Weishan Hu   Xinyi   Guanyun   Chenjiagang   Jangheung   Haenam   Heuksando   Jongheung   Jindo   (S. Korea)   34

XUZHOU   Yaowan   Guannan   Xiangshui   Jindo   Iki   Karatsu

Shuanggou   SUQIAN   Shuyang   Binhai   JAPAN   Kashima

Suining   Lianshui   Funing   Sheyang   Heuksando   Jeju   Jeju-do   (S. Korea)   Omura   Isahaya

Lingbi   Huaiyin   HUAI'AN   Baoying   Hallim   Hallasan   Namju   Nakadori-Shima   Nagasaki

Guzhen   Sixian   Hongze   Chuzhou   Liuzhuang   YANCHENG   Daejeong   Seogwipo   Namjeju   Kuchinotsu   H

Huaiyuan   Hu   XINGHUA   Dongtai   Fukue-Shima   Imari

Bengbu   Fengyang   Gaoyou Hu

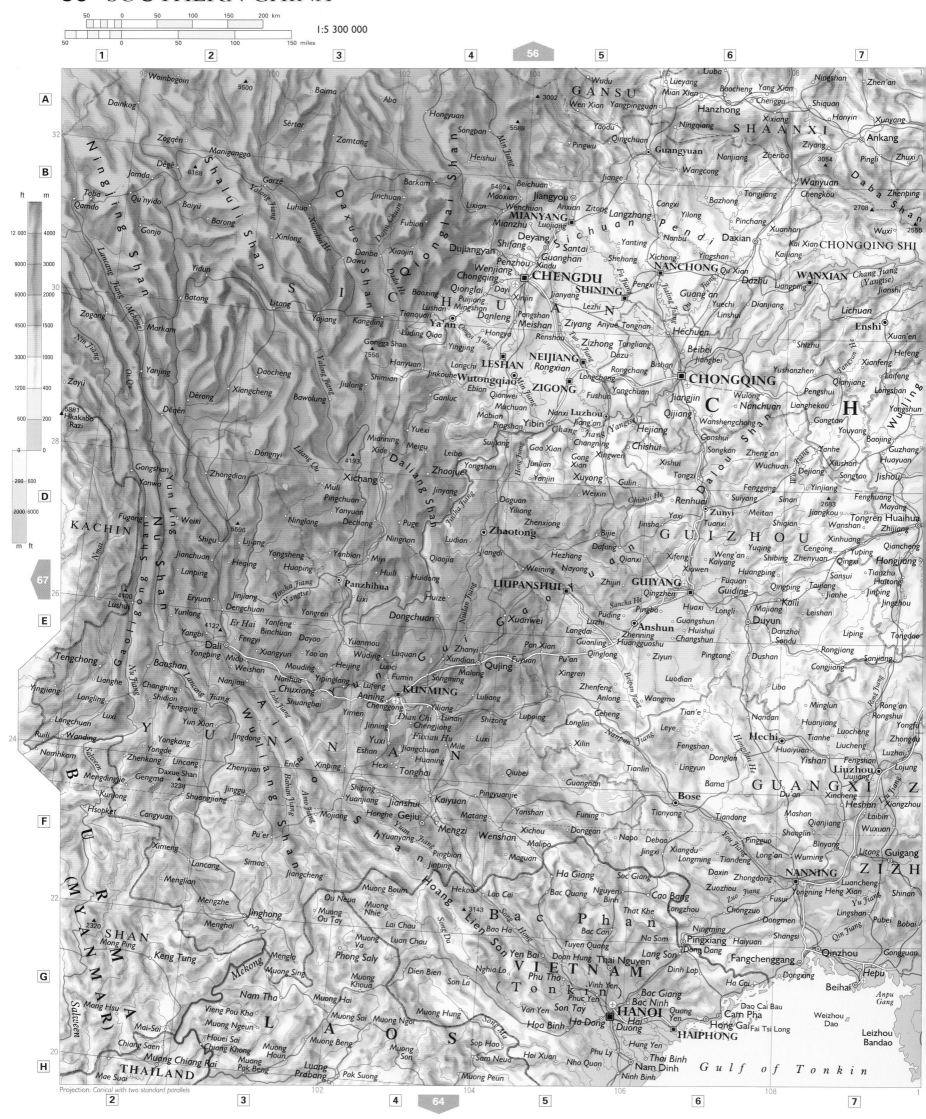

1:5 300 000

Projection: Conical with two standard parallels

1:17 800 000

100 0 100 200 300 400 500 600 700 800 km
100 0 100 200 300 400 500 miles

East from Greenwich

Projection: Bonne

RUSSIA

MONGOLIA

KAZAKHSTAN

KYRGYZSTAN

CHINA

NEI MONGOL ZIZHIQU

XINJIANG UYGUR ZIZHIQU

XIZANG ZIZHIQU (TIBET)

QINGHAI

SICHUAN

YUNNAN

GUIZHOU

HUNAN

HUBEI

HENAN

HEBEI

SHANDONG

JIANGSU

ANHUI

ZHEJIANG

JIANGXI

FUJIAN

GUANGDONG

GUANGXI ZIZHIQU

HAINAN

GANSU

NINGXIA

SHAANXI

SHANXI

HEILONGJIANG

JILIN

LIAONING

NORTH KOREA

SOUTH KOREA

JAPAN

VIETNAM

LAOS

THAILAND (SIAM)

MYANMAR (BURMA)

BANGLADESH

INDIA

NEPAL

BHUTAN

KASHMIR

PHILIPPINES

TAIWAN (FORMOSA)

YELLOW SEA

EAST CHINA SEA

SOUTH CHINA SEA

BAY OF BENGAL

Korea Bay

Bo Hai

Hangzhou Wan

Tropic of Cancer

BEIJING TIANJIN SHANGHAI HONG KONG (Xianggang) SEOUL PYONGYANG FUKUOKA HARBIN WUHAN CHONGQING CHENGDU GUANGZHOU SHENZHEN KUNMING HANOI DHAKA KOLKATA (Calcutta)

m / ft elevation scale

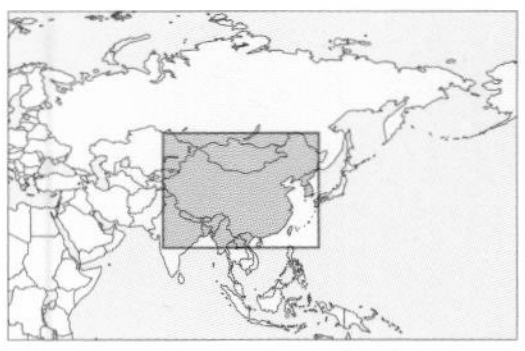

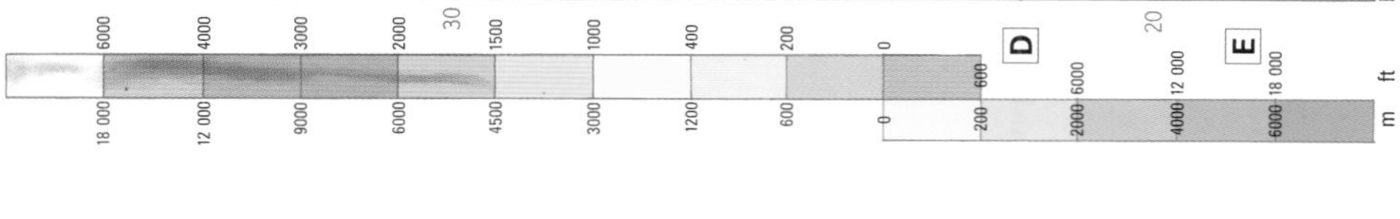

1:6 700 000

50 0 100 150 200 250 300 km
50 0 50 100 150 200 miles

PACIFIC

OCEAN

Dongsha Dao
(Pratas I.)

Itbayat I.
Batanes Is.
Batan I.

Luzon Strait

Balintang Channel

Calayan I.
Dalupiri I.
Babuyan
Islands
Fuga I.
Babuyan
Camiguin I.

Babuyan Channel

Mayraira Pt.
Bacarra Bangui Clayeria
San Nicolas Laoag Aparri Santa Ana
Batac Kabugao Gonzaga
Cabugao Tuao Tuguegarao Gattaran
Vigan Bangued
Santa Maria 2360
Candon Lubuagan
Bontoc Ilagan Mt. Cresta
Balaoan Roxas 1685
San Mateo Palanan Pt.
Santiago Palanan

Luzon

Cordillera Central
Mt. Data
San Fernando Mt. Pulog 2928
Lingayen Baguio Cordon
Bolinao Solano Bayombong
Alaminos HUNDRED ISLANDS Dagupan Rosario Mt. Anacuao 1852
Lingayen Gulf C. San Ildefonso
San Carlos San Manuel
Santa Cruz Bayambang San Jose Baler Bay
Camiling Cuyapo Victoria Baler
Masinloc Moncada AURORA MEMORIAL
Iba 2037 Tarlac La Paz Cabanatuan Dingalan
Concepcion Gapan
Mt. Pinatubo 1780 Angeles San Fernando
San Antonio Polillo Is.
Olongapo Patnanongan I.
BATAAN Malabon Jomalig I.
Orani Caloocan Quezon City
Manila Bay **MANILA**
Subic B. Cavite Pasay Santa Cruz Lumon Bay
Bataan Dasmariñas Lucban Paracale
Nasugbu Tagaytay Lucena Alabat I. Labo Pandan
Balayan San Pablo Atimonan Daet
Lemery Lipa Lopez Calauag Viga
Lubang Is. Batangas Lobo Catanauan BICOL Catanduanes
Verde I. Pass Tayabas Bay Calabanga San Andres
5245 C. Calavite Boac Mt. Isarog 1976 Virac
Marin- Naga Iriga Tabaco Rapu Rapu I.
Calapan Victorias duque 2421 Mayon Vol.
Mamburao Victoria Burias I. Ligao Sorsogon
Mindoro Mt. Baco 2487 Legazpi Donsol Gubat
Sablayan SIBUYAN Magallanes San Bernardino Str.
Pinamalayan Romblon Bulan
Bongabong Ticao I. Irosin Allen Laoang
Roxas Tablas I. Sibuyan I. Aroroy Mondragon Catarman Gamay
San Jose Odiongan SEA Masbate Milagros Arteche
Ilin I. Mandaon Masbate Calbayog Oras

Busuanga I.
Culion I. Calamian Placer Catbalogan Paranas **Samar**
Linapacan Str. Group Pandan Kalibo Roxas Bilinao I. Calbiga Santa Borongan
Linapacan I. Tibiao 2117 Dao Ajuy Bantayan Rita Basey General MacArthur
Cuyo West Pass Bugasong **Panay** Passi Cadiz Palompon **Leyte** Tacloban Guiuan
Taytay Cuyo Is. Pototan Sagay Bogo Ormoc Dulag
Cuyo East Pass Cuyo San Jose **Iloilo** Silay Victorias Tuburan Abuyog Homonhon I.
Dumaran I. Jordan **Bacolod** Danao Camotes Sogod Baybay
Palawan Guimaras San Carlos CENTRAL CEBU San Juan
ST. PAUL Himamaylan Binalbagan La 2450 **Mandaue** Bato Dinagat I. 10 497
1593 Carlota **Cebu** Maasin Dinagat
Irahuan Honda Bay Himamaylan Guihulngan Carcar Panaon I. Siargao I.
Puerto Princesa Kabankalan Cebu Sea Argao Bohol I. Surigao Placer
Sipalay Bais MT. Bucas Grande I.
1727 **Negros** Tanjay SIKATUNA Oslob Tagbilaran Carrascal
Cagayan Is. Siaton Dumaguete **Bohol** Siquijor I. Lanuza
Mt. Mantalingajan Bayawan Zamboanguita Camiguin I. Cabadbaran 2012 Jandag
2085 Dapitan Talisayan Tago
C. Buliluyan **SULU** 5576 Dipolog SEA Balingasag Gingoog **Butuan** Bayugan Marihatag
Bugsuk I. TUBBATAHA Manukan Iligan Opol Esperanza Talacogan Lianga
REEFS Oroquieta Bay **Cagayan de Oro** Hinatuan
SEA Sindangan Ozamiz Alubijid Malaybalay Bislig
Balabac I. Labason MT. **Iligan** 2938 Marawi City Valencia Cateel
Balabac Strait Liloy MALINDANG Tubod Bunawan
Siocon Kabasalan Pagadian 2815 Baganga
Balambangan Turtle Is. Sibuca **Mindanao** Tagum
Banggi Cagayan Sulu I. Margosatubig Illana Parang Panabo Pantukan Manay
Kudat Jambongan Sibuca Bay Midsayap Mt. Apo Davao Mati
Senaja Pilas Isabela Cotabato Pikit 2954 **Davao**
Kota Kinabalu Langkon Group Basilan I. Moro Gulf Datu Piang Kidapawan Digos Davao San Isidro
G. Kinabalu 4101 **Zamboanga** Talayan Gulf
Kota Belud Telok Samales Basilan Str. Lamitan Kalamansig Lebak Koronadal Malita
Papar Labuk Group Jolo Kiamba C. San Agustin
Sandakan Jolo 2083 **General Santos**
Keningau Pangutaran Jolo Parang Santos
SABAH Group Talipao Tinaca Pt. Sarangani Is.
MALAYSIA Kuamut Tapul Pata I. 5824 Kep. Talaud
Melalap Siasi I.
Borneo Tg. Labian Tapul **CELEBES**
Tawi-tawi Sulu Archipelago **SEA**
Teluk Darvel Group Sibutu Sibutu Group **INDONESIA**
Sibutu Passage

SOUTH

CHINA

SEA

PHILIPPINE

SEA

PHILIPPINES

VISAYAN SEA

Mindanao Trench

Banjaran Crocker

Banjaran Brassey

Projection: Lambert's Conformal Conic
East from Greenwich
COPYRIGHT PHILIP'S

National Parks

ft m
9000 3000
6000 2000
4500 1500
3000 1000
1200 400
600 200
0 0
200 600
4000 12 000
8000 24 000
m ft

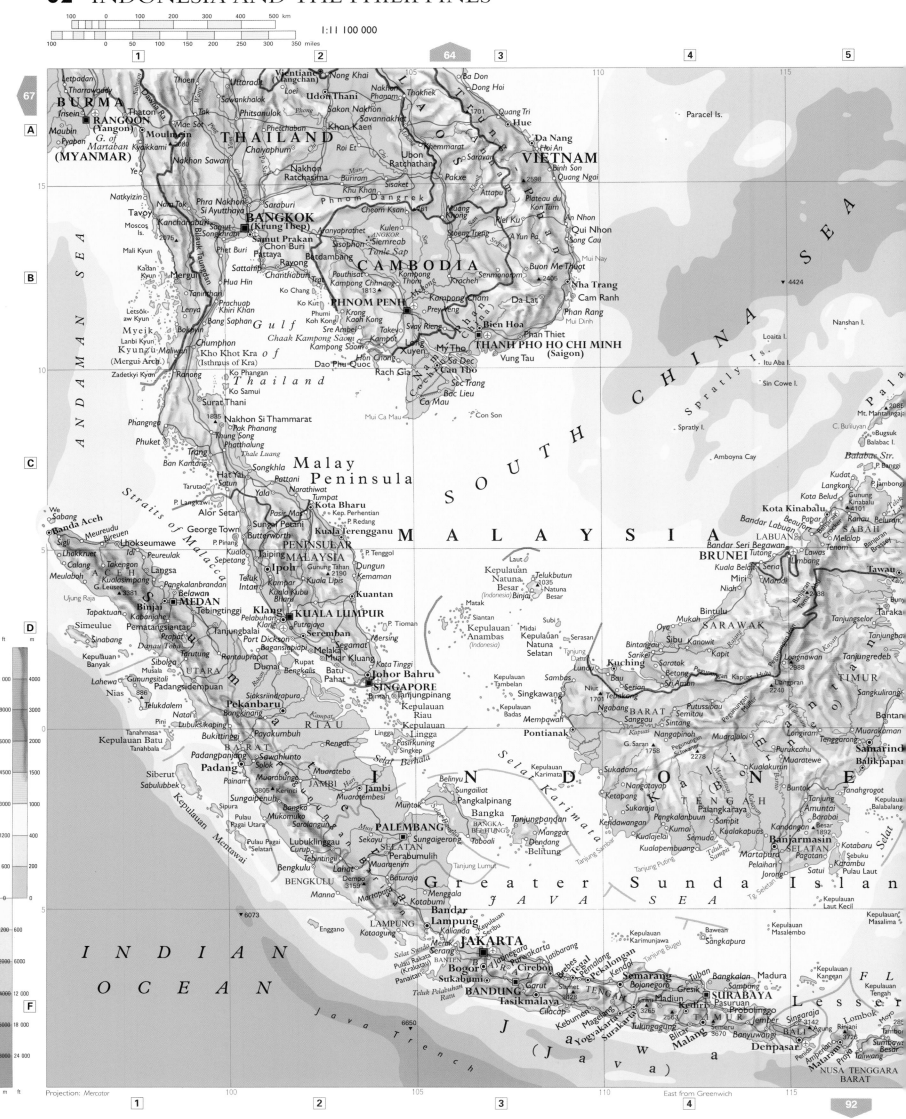

JAVA AND MADURA
1:6 700 000

50 0 50 100 150 200 250 300 km
50 0 50 100 150 200 miles

BALI
1:1 800 000

10 0 10 20 30 km
10 0 10 20 miles

PHILIPPINE SEA

Luzon
MANILA
Quezon City
Cebu
DAVAO
Mindanao

SULU SEA

CELEBES SEA

MOLUCCA SEA

PACIFIC OCEAN

Halmahera
Sulawesi (Celebes)
IRIAN JAYA BARAT
PAPUA
Pegunungan Maoke

BANDA SEA

CERAM SEA

FLORES SEA

Sunda Is.
Flores
Sumba
NUSA TENGGARA TIMUR
EAST TIMOR

ARAFURA SEA

PAPUA NEW GUINEA

JAKARTA
BANDUNG
Semarang
SURABAYA
Madura
Yogyakarta
Malang
TIMUR
TENGAH
BARAT
BANTEN

BALI SEA

Bali
Lombok
Denpasar
Mataram

INDIAN OCEAN

COPYRIGHT PHILIP'S

1:5 300 000

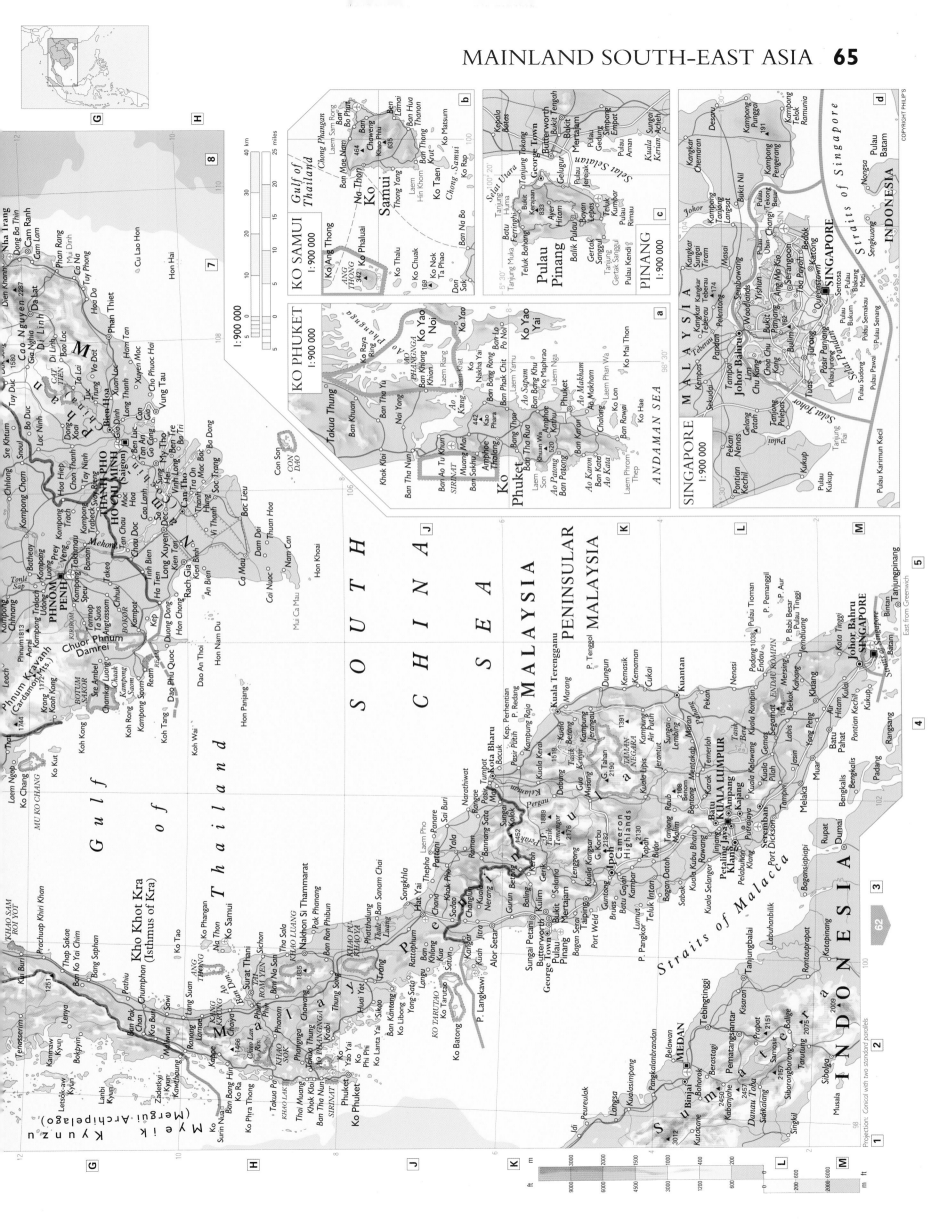

1:8 900 000

continuation southwards
on same scale

Projection: Conical with two standard parallels

Sand deserts   Intermittent lakes

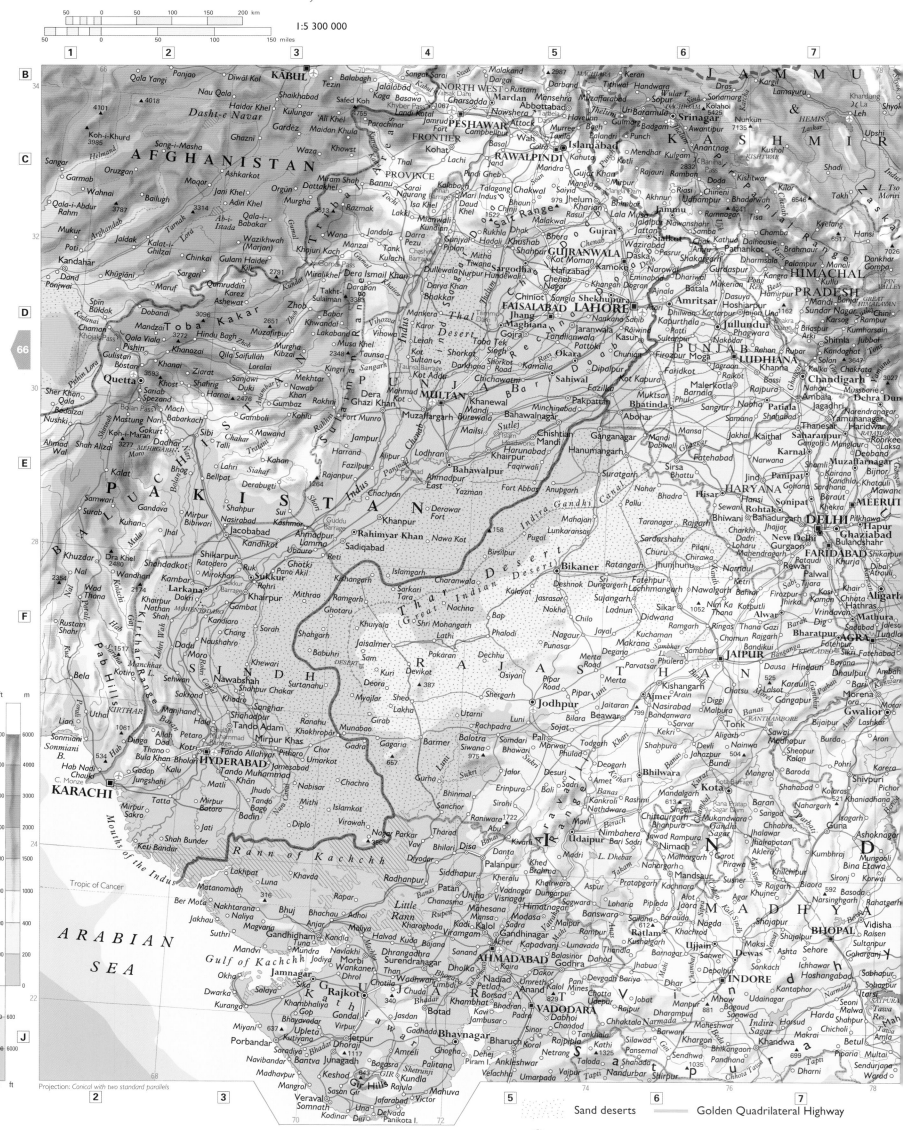

1:5 300 000

Projection: Conical with two standard parallels

Sand deserts Golden Quadrilateral Highway

Intermittent lakes

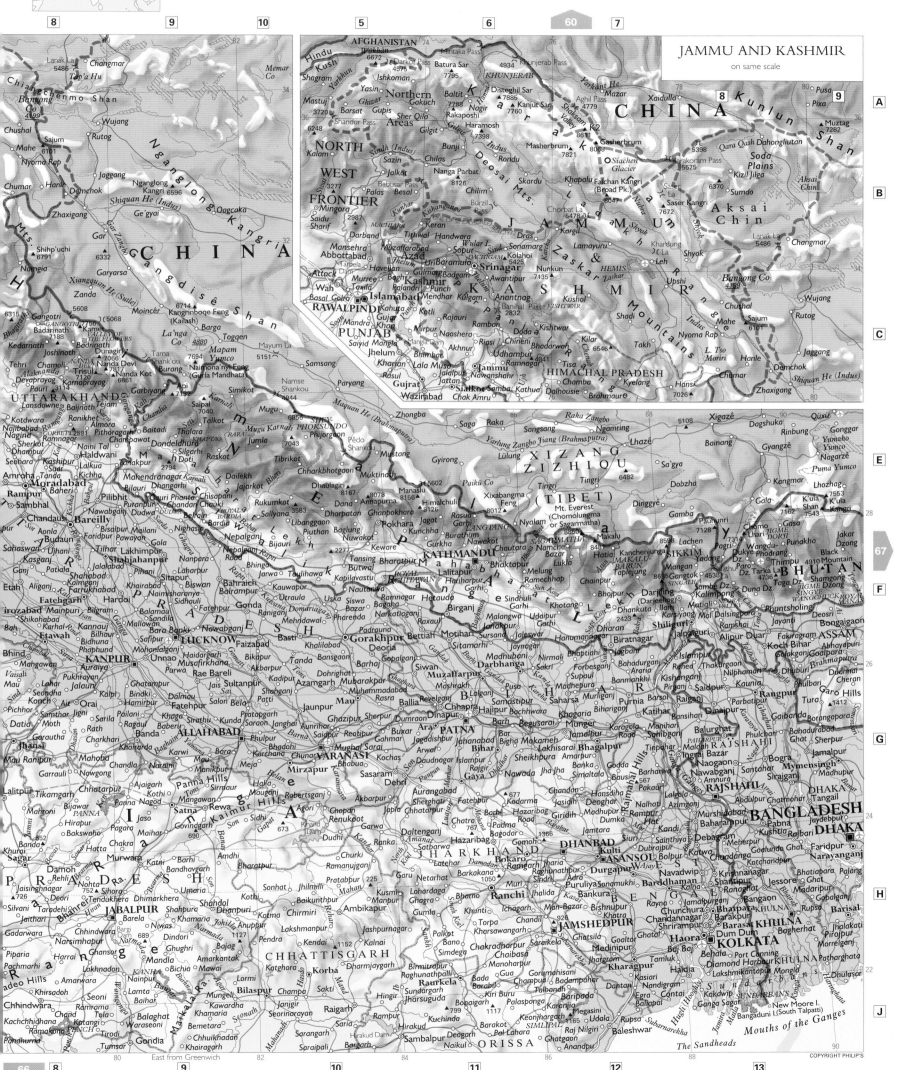

JAMMU AND KASHMIR
on same scale

COPYRIGHT PHILIP'S

1:6 200 000

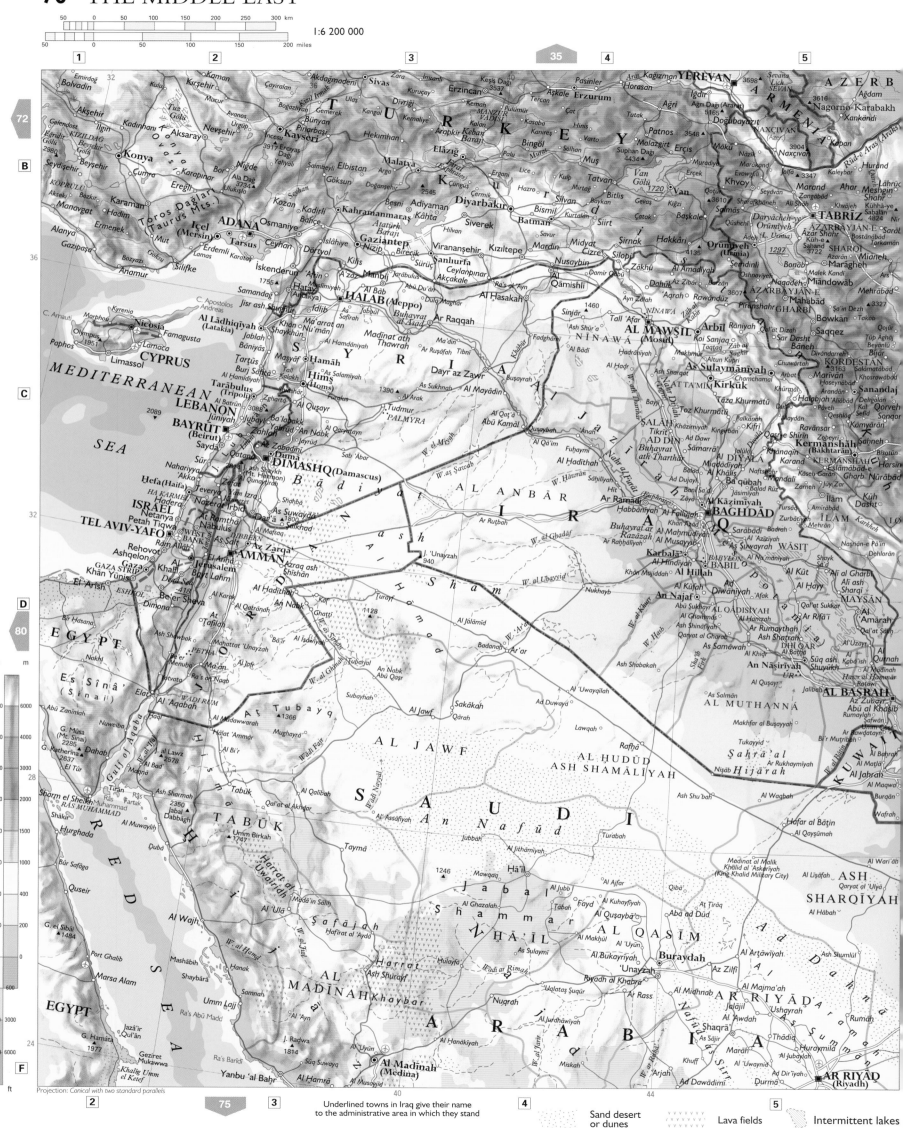

Projection: Conical with two standard parallels

Underlined towns in Iraq give their name
to the administrative area in which they stand

Sand desert
or dunes

Lava fields

Intermittent lakes

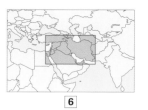

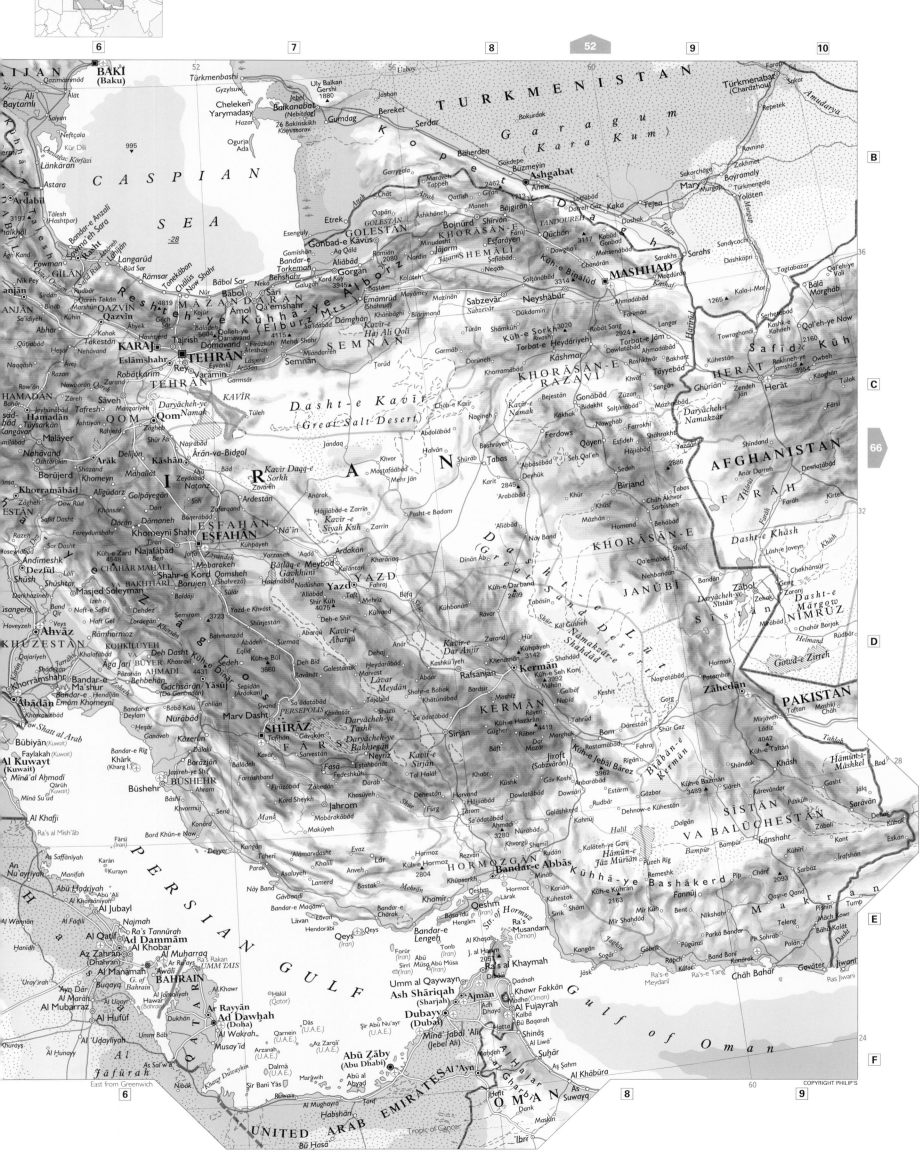

50 0 25 50 75 100 125 150 175 km
50 0 25 50 75 100 125 miles

1 : 4 400 000

BLACK SEA

BULGARIA

Stara Zagora
Yambol
Elkhovo
Aytos
Burgas
Michurin
Nos Emine
1830
2206

Kırklareli
Edirne
Pınarhisar
İğneada Burnu
İğneada
Demirköy
Orestiada
Arda
Yıldız Dağları
1018
Uzunköprü
Hayrabolu
Muratlı
Vize
Çerkezköy
Kilimli
Zonguldak
Çatalağzı
Ereğli
Devrek
Karabük
Safranbolu
Kastamonu
İnce Burnu
Kerempe Burnu
Sinop
İnebolu
Abana
Ayancık
Erfelek
Çatalzeytin
Küre
Küre Dağları
SINOP
Gerze
Bafra Burnu
SAMSUN
Samsun
Terme
Çarşamba
Ünye
Fatsa
Perşembe
Civa Burnu

İpsala
Keşan
Enez
Malkara
Tekirdağ
Şarköy
Büyükçekmece
Silivri
Çorlu
Çatalca
İSTANBUL
Kartal
Kocaeli
Sakarya
(İzmit) (Adapazarı)
Gebze
Darıca
Körfez
Karasu
Akçakoca
Düzce
Bolu
Gerede
Çerkeş
Kurşunlu
İlgaz
Çankırı
Çorum
Mecitözü
Amasya
Havza
Ladik
Tokat
Kavak
Taşköprü
Durağan
Vezirköprü
Altınkaya Barajı
Suluova
Merzifon
Gümüşhacıköy
Osmancık
İskilip
Kargı

Gökçeada
Samothraki
Gelibolu
Saros Körfezi
Çanakkale
TROY
Biga
Gönen
Bandırma
Erdek
Marmara
Kapı Dağı
Kuş Gölü
Karacabey
Mudanya
BURSA
Yenişehir
İznik
İznik Gölü
Geyve
Göynük
Mudurnu
Seben
Beypazarı
Ayaş
Sincan
Kızılcahamam
Kalecik
Elmadağ
Kırıkkale
Keskin
Delice
Sulakyurt
Boğazkale
Sungurlu
Ortaköy
Zile
Turhal
Reşadiye
Niksar
Almus
Deveci Dağları
Erbaa
Akkuş
Korgan
Kabataş
Aybastı

Marmara Denizi (Sea of Marmara)

İstanbul Boğazı (Bosporus)

Bozcaada
Ezine
Ayvacık
Baba Burnu
Edremit
Bayramiç
Balya
Mustafakemalpaşa
Uludağ
İnegöl
Bozüyük
Bilecik
Söğüt
Sakarya
Nallıhan
Sarıyar Barajı
Gölpazarı
Eskişehir
Mihalıççık
Alpu
Polatlı
Gölbaşı
ANKARA
Bala
Yerköy
Yozgat
Sorgun
Çekerek
Artova
Çırçır
Yıldızeli
Hafik
SİVAS
Sivas
Ak Dağ
2802
Kangal
Şarkışla
Gemerek
Gürün

Mitilini
Lesbos
Hios
Foça
Karaburun
Çeşme
İZMİR (Smyrna)
Menemen
Manisa
Turgutlu
Salihli
Akhisar
Kırkağaç
Soma
Bergama
Edremit Körfezi
Ayvalık
Burhaniye
Bigadiç
Sındırgı
Balıkesir
Susurluk
Dursunbey
Simav
Emet
Tavşanlı
Kütahya
Gediz
Altıntaş
Domaniç
Seyitgazi
Kırka
Çifteler
Sivrihisar
Haymana
Kulu
Tuz Gölü
899
Şereflikoçhisar
Aksaray
Ortaköy
Gülşehir
Nevşehir
Avanos
GÖREME
3370
Hacılar
KAYSERİ
Kayseri
Talas
Bünyan
Pınarbaşı
Sarız
Gürün
Darende
Akçadağ

Anadolu
ANATOLIA

Lydia
Phrygia
Pisidia
Pamphylia
Lycia
Cilicia
Konya Ovası
 Licaonia
Cappadocia
TURKEY

SARDIS
Menemen
Bozdağ
Ödemiş
Tire
Nazilli
Aydın
Söke
Kuşadası
Samos
Ikaria
Fourni
Patmos
DILEK YARIMADASI
EPHESUS
MILETUS
İncirliova
Karacasu
Çine
Bozdoğan
Yatağan
Muğla
Gökova Körfezi
Bodrum
Ören
Milas
Güllük
Kalimnos
Kos
Astipalea
Dodecanese
Karpathos
Kasos
Tilos
Simi
Rhodes (Rhodes)
Lindos
1215
4210

Buldan
Sarayköy
Denizli
Honaz Dağı
2528
Tavas
Kale
Acıpayam
Gölgeli Dağları
2421
Boz Dağ
Çameli
Tefenni
Korkuteli
Fethiye
3024
Ak Dağ
3070
XANTHOS
Kaş
Kalkan
Finike
Megiste
Kale
Kemer
BEYDAĞLARI OLİMPOS
Antalya
Serik
ASPENDOS
Manavgat
Alanya
Gazipaşa
Anamur
Anamur Burnu
İncekum Burnu

Uşak
Banaz
Murat Dağı
2224
Eşme
Güney
Çivril
Dinar
Sandıklı
2610
Çay
Şuhut
Bolvadin
Eber Gölü
Akşehir Gölü
Afyon (Afyonkarahisar)
Yunak
Emirdağ
Sultan Dağları
Akşehir
İlgın
Kadınhanı
Sarayönü
Cihanbeyli
Obruk
Karapınar
Ereğli
Ulukışla
Niğde
3134
Çamardı
Pozantı
Kozan
Kadirli
İmamoğlu
Ceyhan
Osmaniye
İslahiye
Gaziantep
Nizip
Oğuzeli

Burdur
Burdur Gölü
Isparta
Eğirdir
Eğirdir Gölü
974
Gelendost
Yalvaç
Şarkikaraağaç
Beyşehir
Beyşehir Gölü
1116
2980
Seydişehir
Bozkır
Hadım
2464
Taşkent
Ermenek
Mut
Gülnar
Silifke
Erdemli
İçel (Mersin)
Tarsus
ADANA
Dörtyol
İskenderun
İskenderun Körfezi
HATAY (Antakya)
Kırıkhan
Reyhanlı
Kilis

Konya
KONYA
Çumra
Karaman
KARAMAN
Göksu
Toros Dağları
KAHRAMANMARAŞ
Kahramanmaraş
Pazarcık
Araban
Halfeti
Yavuzeli

GREECE

Rhodes (Rhodes)

MEDITERRANEAN SEA

CYPRUS

Rizokarpaso
Apostolos Andreas
Kyrenia
Morphou
Nicosia
Famagusta
Polis
Paphos
Olympus
1951
Troodos
Episkopi
Limassol
Larnaca
Akrotiri

Al Lādhiqīyah (Latakia)
Jablah
Baniyās
Tartūs
Tarābulus (Tripoli)
Al Batrūn
Zgharta
Bsharri
3088
Jubayl
Jūniyah
BAYRŪT (Beirut)
Saydā
Jisr ash Shughūr
Idlib
Ma'arrat an Nu'mān
IDLIB
Khān Shaykhūn
1385
'Āṣī
Hamāh
HAMĀH
As Salamīyah
Ḥimṣ (Homs)
HIMṢ
Shinshār
Al Qaryatayn
Al Qusayr
Al Hirmil
Ba'labak
An Nabk
Yabrūd
Zabadānī
Zaḥlah
Dūma
DIMASHQ (Damascus)
Jaramānah
Qaṭanā

SYRIA
HALAB
HALAB (Aleppo)
As Sāfirah
Manbij
Al Bāb
'Azāz
Afrīn

LEBANON

ISRAEL
Hefa (Haifa)
HA KARMEL
'Akko
Nazerat
Hadera
Netanya
TEL AVIV-YAFO
Rehovot
Ashdod
Ashqelon
WEST BANK
Nābulus
Ramla
El Arīḥā
Jerusalem
AMMĀN
Az Zarqā
As Salt
Al Mafraq
JORDAN
Irbid
Dar'ā
Busra ash Sham
Salkhad
AS SUWAYDĀ'
As Suwaydā'
Shahbā
1800
Qiryat Shemona
Nahariyya
Zefat
Teverya
Yam Kinneret
Al Qunayṭirah

Projection: Conical with two standard parallels

Division between Greeks and Turks in Cyprus; Turks to the North.

80 3 4 5 74 7 6

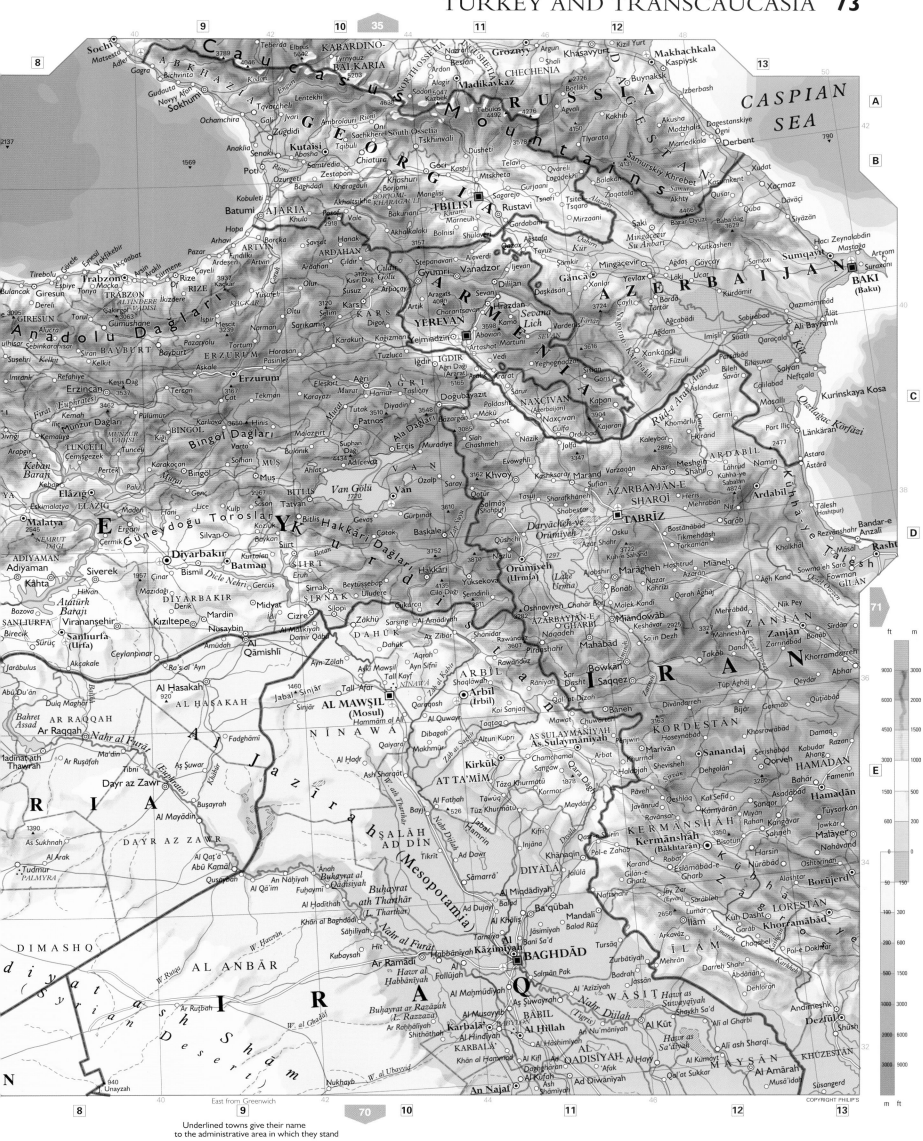

Underlined towns give their name
to the administrative area in which they stand

1:2 200 000

10 0 10 20 30 40 50 60 70 80 100 km
10 0 10 20 30 40 50 60 miles

CYPRUS

Paphos
Kividhes
Episkopi
Limassol
Akrotiri Bay
Episkopi Bay
C. Gata
Zyyi

MEDITERRANEAN SEA

2775
2089

Al Hamīdīyah · **Ḥimṣ** (Homs) · Shinshār · Furqlus
Tall Kalakh
Ḥalbā
ASH SHAMĀLS · Al Ḥirmil · Al Quṣayr · **ḤIMṢ**
Al Mīnā' · **Ṭarābulus** (Tripoli) · Zghartā · Qurnat as Sawdā' 3088
Al Batrūn · Bsharrī · Al Labwah · 2464 · Al Qaryatayn
Jubayl · Qarṭabā · Ba'labakk · An Nabk
Ibrāhīm · 2616 · Bi'r Ghadīr
Jūniyah · **BAYRŪT** (Beirut) · Bikfayyā · 2628 · J. Sannīn · Yabrūd
Alayh · Zaḥlah · Sirghāya · Khān Abū Shāmat
Ash Shuwayfāt · Ad Dāmūr · JABAL LUBNĀN · Az Zabadānī · Dumayr
LEBANON · 1942 · Ḥawsh Mūssā · Al Quṭayfah · Jayrūd
J. al Bārak · **DIMASHQ** (Damascus)
Saydā (Sidon) · Jazzīn · Darayyā · DAM · Jaramānah · Al Ḥājānah
An Nabaṭīyah at Taḥta · 2814 · Marj 'Uyūn · Al Kiswah · Burāq
AL JANŪB · Al Khiyām · O. Mas'ada
Sūr (Tyre) · Qiryat Shemona · 1197 · Al Qunayṭirah · As Sanamayn
Nahariyya · Me'ona · 1208 · Zefat · Yaʻar Kinneret · DAR'Ā · Shahbā
'Akko (Acre) · Qiryat Karmi'el · (Sea of Galilee) · Izra · Jabal Ad Durūz
Mifraz Hefa · Yam HAZAFON · Fiq · Shaykh Miskīn
Hefa (Haifa) · Qiryat Ata · Teverya (Tiberias) · -210 · Saham al Jawlān · As Suwaydā · 1800
Dāliyat el Karmel · HEFA KARMEL · Nazerat (Nazareth) · Ṭafīla · **AS SUWAYDĀ** · Ṣalāh
TEL MEGIDDO · Afula · Takiba Yarmūk · Dar'ā · Malaḥ
Umm el Fahm · Bet She'an · IRBID · At Ramthā
CAESAREA · Jenīn · 'AJLŪN · Buṣrá ash Shām · AL MAFRAQ
Ḥadera · SHŌMRŌN · J. Umm ad Daraj · Jarash · Umm al Qiṭṭayn
Hanna-Karkur · Ṭūbās · 4247 · JARASH
ISRAEL · Tulkarm · SAMARIA · Al Mafraq
Netanya · Nāblus · N. az Zarqā · Az Zarqā
HAMERKAZ · Ra'ananna · Az Zarqā
Herzliyya · Kefar Sava · SHILOH · AL BALQĀ'
Benē Beraq · Petah Tiqwa · As Salt · **'AMMĀN**
TEL AVIV-YAFO · Ramat Gan · Wādī as Sīr · AMM
Bat Yam · Lod · **WEST BANK** · Karama
Holon · Ramla · Ram Allah · Nā'ūr · AZ ZARQĀ
Rishon le Ziyyon · Yavne · El Arīḥā (Jericho) · Azraq ash Shīshān
Ashdod · Rehovot · -289 · Ma'daba
Qiryat Mal'akhi · Jerusalem (Yerushalayim) (Al Quds) · MA'DĀBA · 'AMMAN
Ashqelon · Bet Shemesh · Bayt Laḥm (Bethlehem) · Dhibān
Qiryat Gat · TEL LAKHISH · Al Khalīl (Hebron) · W. al Ḥaydān
Gaza · N. Shiqma · Zāhirīyah · Dead Sea · -418 · 'En Gedi
GAZA STRIP · Sederot · Arad · 1305
Khān Yūnis · Be'er Sheva (Beersheba) · Al Karak · AL KARAK
Rafaḥ · 'En Boqeq · Al Mazar
El Daheir · Bor Mashash · Sedom · -333
Bûr Sa'îd (Port Said) · Dimona · W. al Ḥasā · **JORDAN**
BÛR SA'ÎD · Khalîg el Tîna · HADAROM · At Ṭafīlah · Bā'ir
Râs Burûn · Sabkhet el Bardawîl · Qezi'ot · AT ṬAFĪLAH · J. ash Shawmari
Râmâni · El 'Arîsh · Birein · Dana · 1072
Bîr el 'Abd · Bîr el Garârât · W. el 'Arîsh · Sedé Boqér · Maḥaṭṭat 'Unayzah
El Qantara · Bîr Kaseiba · Muweilih · Ma'ān
Wâḥid · Bîr el Jafîr · Abu Aweigîla · Mizpe Ramon · Nijil · MA'ĀN
Bîr Madkûr · SHAMÂL SÎNÎ · El Quseima · 1736 · Al Jafr
892 · Rujm Tal'at al Jamā'ah · PETRA · Qa'el Jafr
Ismâ'ilîya · Bîr Ḥasapa · **Hanegev** (Negev Desert) · Wādī Mūsā
ISMÂ'ILÎYA · Talâta · Bîr Beidâ · N. Paran · Ma'ān
Khamsa · G. Yi 'Allaq 1094 · W. Qrâiya · N. Ḥiyyon · Bi'r al Mārī
El Buheirat el Murrat el Kubra (Great Bitter L.) · El 'Agrûd · N. Ḥiyyon
Gineifa · Bîr el Thamâda · W. el Brûk · W. Maḥaslem · Ra's an Naqb
EGYPT · Mamarr Mitlâ · W. Girâfi · El Kuntilla · MA'ĀN
El Suweis (Suez) · ES SÎNÎ (Sinai) · Yotvata · Mahaṭṭat ash Shīdīyah
Bûr Taufiq · Nakhl · W. Ruâq · 'En 'Avrona · SAUDI ARABIA
Adabiya · Ain Sudr · Bîr Abu Muḥammad · AL 'AQABAH
Uyûn Mûsa · 948 · Bîr al Buṭayyiḥāt · Bi'r al Qaṭṭār
Râs Sudr · G. el Kabrît · Gebel el Tîh · 'Ilai · 1592 · W. Rum 1754 · WADI RUM · Baṭn al Ghūl
Ghubbet el Bûs · 1272 · JANŪB SÎNÎ · Bîr el Biarât · Al 'Aqaba · Rum · Aṭ Ṭubayq
Bîr Abu Ṣandûs · Râs Matarma · W. Abu Ga'da · Bîr Ṭâba · Ra's an Naqb 1435
Bîr Wuseit · W. Abu el Gîn · Bîr el Heisi · Ḥaql · Al Mudawwarah · ARABIA
EL SUWEIS · 1165 · Gulf of Aqaba

ft m
9000 3000
6000 2000
4500 1500
3000 1000
1200 400
600 200
0 0
100 300
200 600
500 1500
1000 3000
2000 6000
m ft

Projection: Polyconic · East from Greenwich · COPYRIGHT PHILIP'S

– – – 1974 Cease Fire Lines

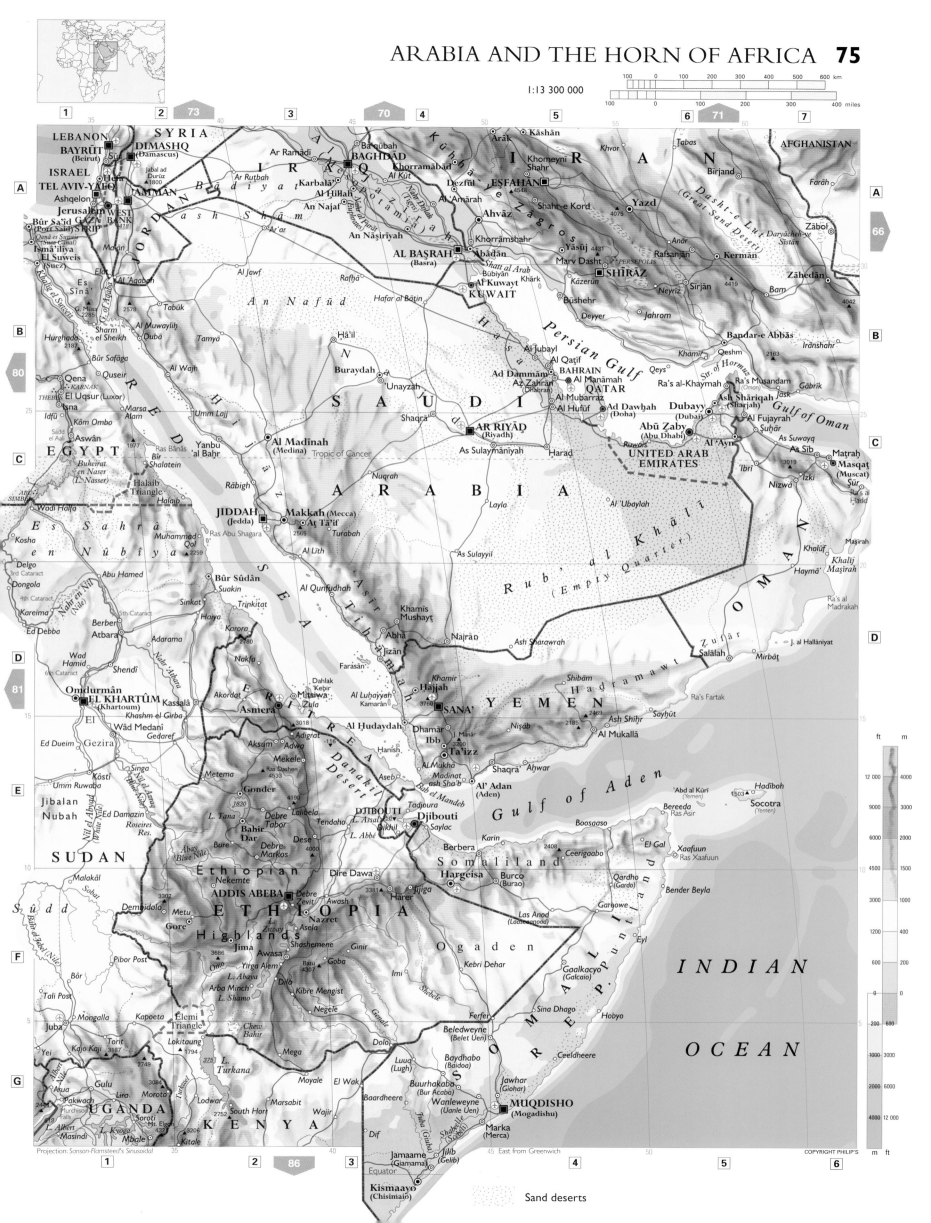

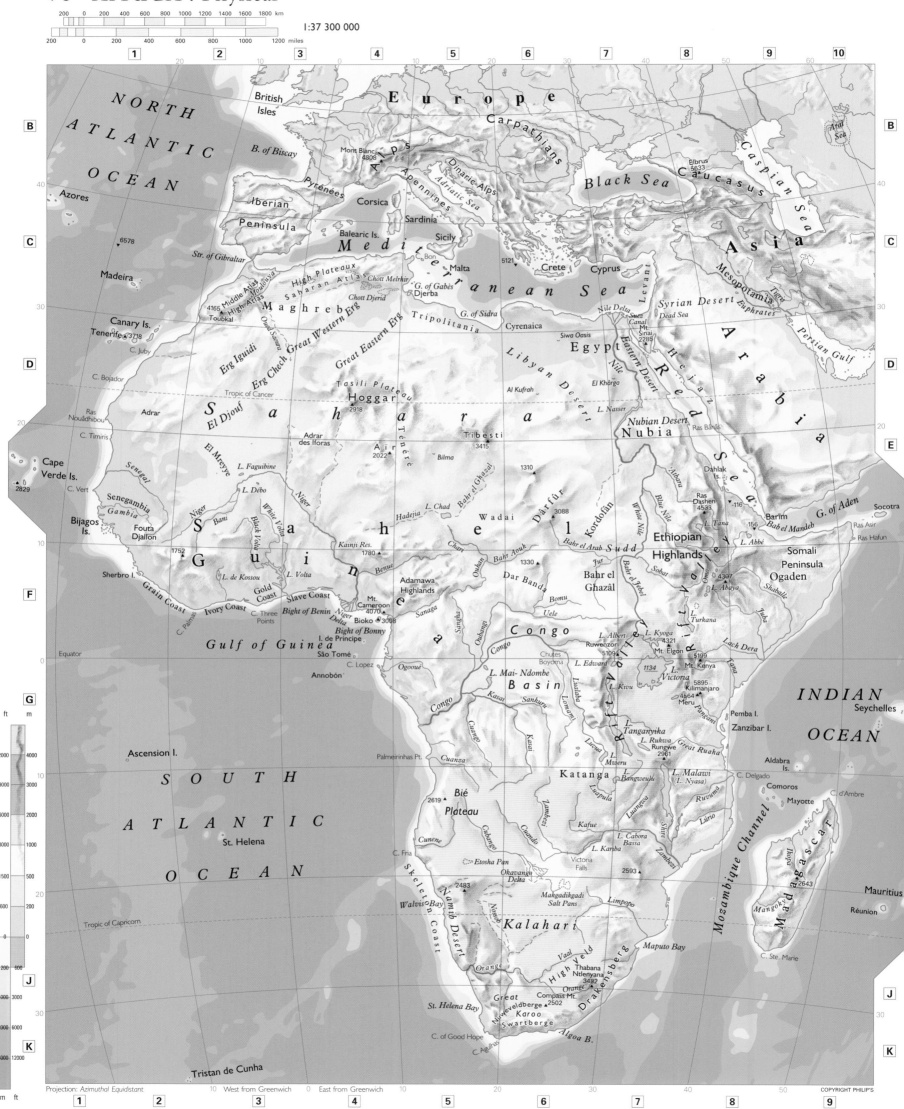

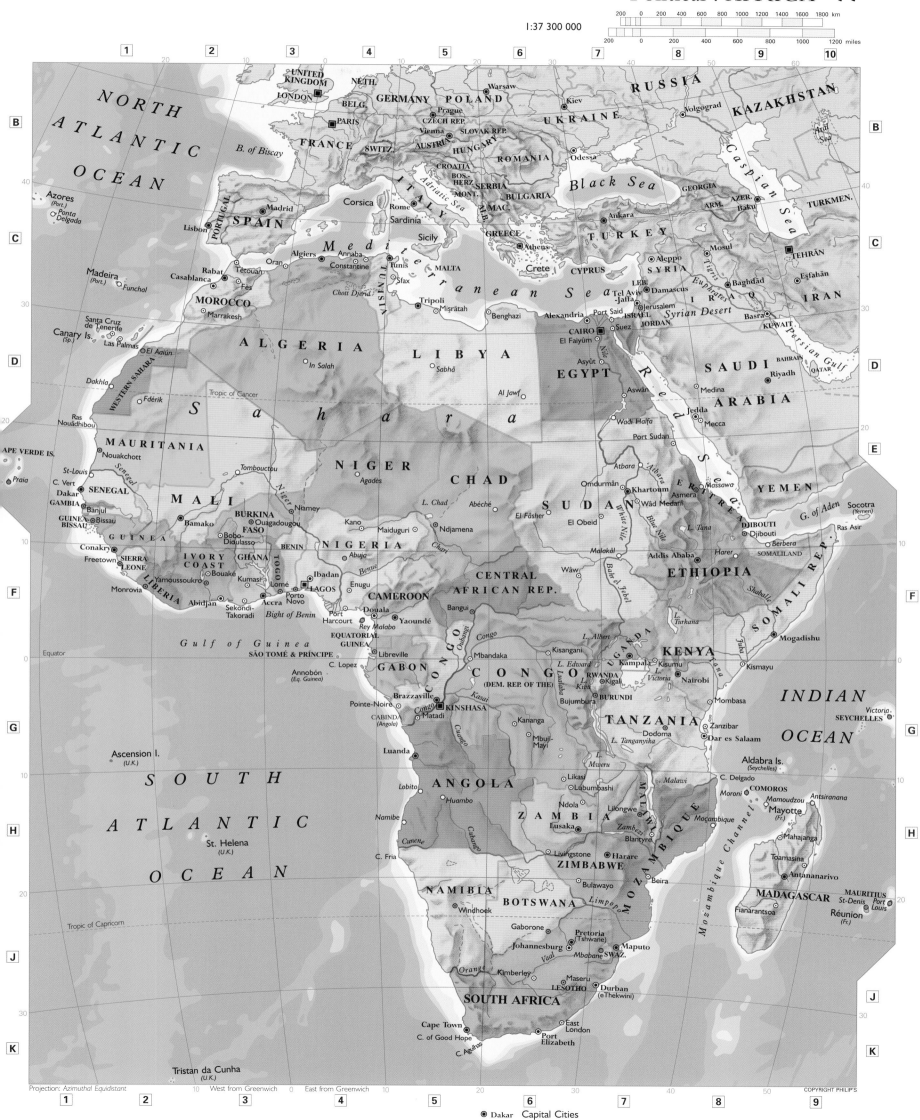

1:37 300 000

200 0 200 400 600 800 1000 1200 1400 1600 1800 km

200 0 200 400 600 800 1000 1200 miles

NORTH ATLANTIC OCEAN

UNITED KINGDOM
LONDON
NETH.
BELG.
GERMANY POLAND
Warsaw
Kiev
RUSSIA
KAZAKHSTAN
Aral Sea
PARIS
FRANCE
SWITZ.
CZECH REP.
Prague
Vienna
AUSTRIA HUNGARY
SLOVAK REP.
ROMANIA
Odessa
UKRAINE
Volgograd
B. of Biscay
CROATIA
BOS.-HERZ.
SERBIA
MONT.
N.MAC.
BULGARIA
Black Sea
GEORGIA
ARM. AZER.
Baku
Caspian Sea
TURKMEN.
PORTUGAL
SPAIN
Madrid
Corsica
Rome
ITALY
Adriatic Sea
GREECE
Athens
Ankara
TURKEY
Mosul
Tehrān
Eşfahān
Lisbon
Azores (Port.)
Ponta Delgada
Madeira (Port.)
Funchal
Algiers
Oran
Tétouan
Annaba
Constantine
Tunis
Sardinia
Sicily
MALTA
Mediterranean Sea
Crete
CYPRUS
Aleppo
SYRIA
Tigris
Baghdād
IRAQ
IRAN
Rabat
Fès
Casablanca
MOROCCO
Marrakesh
Tripoli
Mişrātah
Sfax
TUNISIA
Chott Djerid
Benghazi
Alexandria
Port Said
Tel Aviv -Jaffa
Damascus
Jerusalem
LEB.
ISRAEL
JORDAN
Syrian Desert
Euphrates
Basra
KUWAIT
Persian Gulf
Santa Cruz de Tenerife
Canary Is. (Sp.)
Las Palmas
El Aaiún
WESTERN SAHARA
ALGERIA
In Salah
Sabhā
LIBYA
EGYPT
CAIRO
El Faiyûm
Suez
Asyût
Aswân
Red Sea
SAUDI ARABIA
Riyadh
Medina
BAHRAIN
QATAR
Dakhla
Fdérik
Ras Nouâdhibou
Tropic of Cancer
S   a   h   a   r   a
Al Jawf
Wadi Halfa
Port Sudan
Jedda
Mecca
CAPE VERDE IS.
MAURITANIA
Nouakchott
NIGER
CHAD
Atbara
Atbara
Omdurmân
Khartoum
ERITREA
Massawa
Asmera
YEMEN
G. of Aden
Socotra (Yemen)
Praia
St-Louis
C. Vert
Dakar
GAMBIA
Banjul
GUINEA-BISSAU
Bissau
SENEGAL
Senegal
MALI
Tombouctou
Niger
Niamey
Agadès
Kano
Maiduguri
L. Chad
Abéché
Ndjamena
SUDAN
El Fâsher
El Obeid
Wâd Medani
White Nile
Blue Nile
L. Tana
DJIBOUTI
Djibouti
Berbera
SOMALILAND
Ras Asir
GUINEA
Conakry
Freetown
SIERRA LEONE
BURKINA FASO
Ouagadougou
Bobo-Dioulasso
Bamako
BENIN
NIGERIA
Abuja
Chari
Malakál
Wâw
Bahr el Jebel
Addis Ababa
Harer
ETHIOPIA
Shabelle
IVORY COAST
GHANA
Yamoussoukro
Bouaké
Kumasi
TOGO
Ibadan
Enugu
Benue
CENTRAL AFRICAN REP.
L. Turkana
Jubba
SOMALI REP.
LIBERIA
Monrovia
Abidjan
Sekondi-Takoradi
Accra
Lomé
Porto Novo
LAGOS
CAMEROON
Douala
Yaoundé
Bangui
Congo
UGANDA
L. Albert
Kisangani
Mogadishu
Bight of Benin
Port Harcourt
Rey Malabo
EQUATORIAL GUINEA
SÃO TOMÉ & PRÍNCIPE
Libreville
GABON
Congo
Ubangi
Mbandaka
Kampala
Kisumu
L. Victoria
Nairobi
KENYA
Kismayu
Gulf of Guinea
C. Lopez
Equator
Annobón (Eq. Guinea)
CONGO
CONGO (DEM. REP. OF THE)
Lualaba
L. Edward
RWANDA
Kigali
L. Kivu
BURUNDI
Bujumbura
Kasai
TANZANIA
Mombasa
INDIAN OCEAN
Victoria
SEYCHELLES
Brazzaville
Pointe-Noire
KINSHASA
Matadi
CABINDA (Angola)
Congo
Kananga
Mbuji-Mayi
Dodoma
Zanzibar
Dar es Salaam
L. Tanganyika
Ascension I. (U.K.)
Luanda
SOUTH ATLANTIC OCEAN
ANGOLA
Lobito
Huambo
Namibe
Cuanza
Likasi
Lubumbashi
Ndola
L. Mweru
ZAMBIA
Lusaka
Aldabra Is. (Seychelles)
C. Delgado
COMOROS
Moroni
Mamoudzou
Mayotte (Fr.)
Antsiranana
St. Helena (U.K.)
Cunene
Cubango
Lilongwe
MALAWI
Zambezi
Blantyre
MOZAMBIQUE
Moçambique
Mahajanga
NAMIBIA
Cunene
C. Fria
Livingstone
Harare
ZIMBABWE
Bulawayo
Beira
Mozambique Channel
Toamasina
Antananarivo
MADAGASCAR
MAURITIUS
St-Denis
Port Louis
Réunion (Fr.)
BOTSWANA
Limpopo
Fianarantsoa
Windhoek
Gaborone
Pretoria (Tshwane)
Johannesburg
Maputo
Mbabane
SWAZ.
Vaal
Orange
Kimberley
Maseru
LESOTHO
Durban (eThekwini)
SOUTH AFRICA
Cape Town
C. of Good Hope
East London
Port Elizabeth
C. Agulhas

Tristan da Cunha (U.K.)

● Dakar   Capital Cities

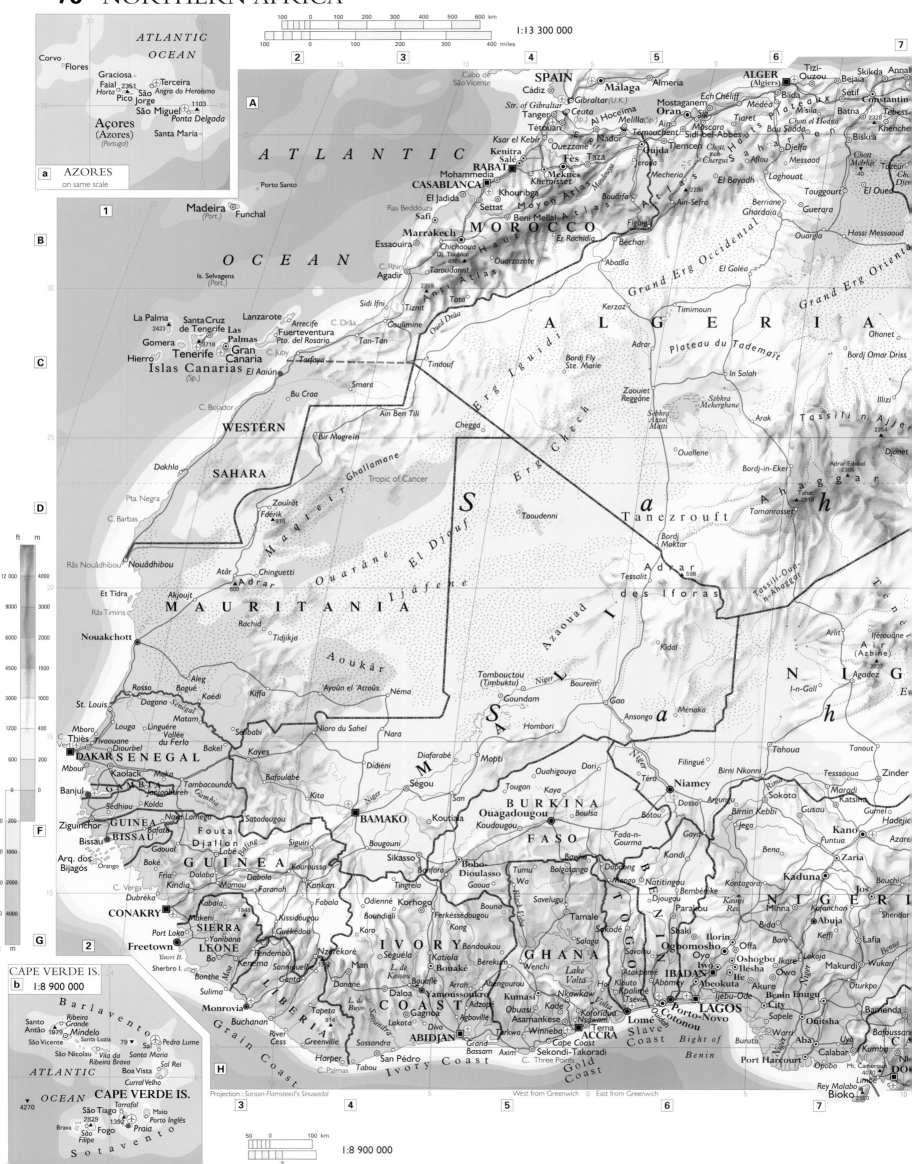

a
b

8 9 10 11 12 13 14

Bizerte
Ariana
CARTHAGE Ra's at Tib (C. Bon)
TUNIS Nabeul Pantelleria (It.)
El Kef Beja Sousse Monastir Valletta
Kairouan Msaken Mahdia MALTA
Sfax Lampedusa (It.)
Gafsa Îles Kerkenna
Gabès Golfe de Gabès
Médenine Djerba
Zarzis Ben Gardane
Dehibat Zuwarah TARĀBULUS (Tripoli)
Az Zāwiyah Al Khums
Gharyān Misrātah
Mizdah 968 LEPTIS MAGNA
Daraj

Sicilia ITALY
Peloponnese Cyclades
GREECE
Chania Rhodes Rhodes
Kriti

TURKEY ADANA
Antalya Alanya Sifke HALAB (Aleppo)
Anamur Hatay Nahr al Furāt (Euphrates)
Al Lādhiqīyah
CYPRUS Hamāh SYRIA
Nicosia
Paphos Limassol Tarābulus Himş
LEBANON Şūr
BAYRŪT (Beirut) DIMASHQ (Damascus)
Jabal ad Durūz 1800 IRAQ
ISRAEL Hefa Ar Rutbah
TEL AVIV-YAFO WEST AMMĀN Bādiyat
Ashqelon BANK
Jerusalem 418 ash Shām
GAZA STRIP Ma'ān

M E D I T E R R A N E A N   S E A

A
B
C
D
E
F
G
H

CYRENE
Marsá Sūsah
Al Bayda Darnah
Banghāzī Al Marj Khalij Bumbah
Suluq Tubruq
Surt Khalīj Surt Bardīyah Salûm
Ajdābiya Ed Déffa
Tarābulus (Tripolitania) Barqa (Cyrenaica)
Al Hamādah al al Ḥamrā' Dahra -47
Ghadāmis Hūn Al Jaghbūb
Awjilah
Birāk Marādah Siwa -133
Al Harūj al Aswad 1200 Zillah Munkhafed el Qattâra
Idehan Awbāri Sarīr Calanscio
Sabhā Es Sahrâ, el Gharbîya
Awbāri Tazerbo Qasr Farâfra
Marzūq Sahrâ' Lîbîya
W. Barjūj Marzûq Es Sahrâ
Fezzan Wāw al Kabīr Esh Shargîya
Ghāt 1428 Sahrâ' Rebiana El Wâhât el Dakhla
Al Qaṭrūn Al Jawf Al Kufrah El Khârga
Mût El Wâhât el Khârga

EL ISKANDARÏYA (Alexandria)
Marsâ Matrûh El Mahalla el Kubra Damanhur
El Alamein Dumyât Bûr Sa'îd (Port Said)
Tanta El Mansûra
Zagazig Ismâ'îliya Qanâ es Suweis (Suez Canal)
EL GÎZA El Suweis (Suez) Al Jawf
PYRAMIDS EL QÂHIRA (Cairo) El Faiyûm Khalîg el Suweis
Helwân Beni Suef Es Sînâ' Al 'Aqabah
El Minyâ Maghâgha G. Mûsâ 2285 Elat
Manfalût Es Sahrâ Sharm el Sheikh Tabūk
Asyût 2578 Al Muwayliḥ
Tahta Esh Shargîya Hurghada
Sohâg 2187 Bûr Safâga
Girga Qena Quseir Al Wajh
THEBES KARNAK Umm Lajj
El Uqsur (Luxor) Marsa Alam
Isna Ras Bânâs
Idfû Kôm Ombo
Aswân Yanbu al Bahr
1977 Bîr Shalatein Rābigh

SAUDI ARABIA

JORDAN

RED SEA

75

Ghât Ya'mad
El Wâhât el Dakhla
Hadabat el Gilf el Kebîr 1082
J. Uweinat 1893
El Wâhât el Selîma
Es Sahrâ en Nûbîya Muhammad Qol 2259
Ras Abu Shagara
Halaib Triangle
Halaib Ras Hadarba
Wâdi Halfa Kosha Buḥeirat en Naser (L. Nasser)
Toshka Lakes Delgo ABU SIMBEL
3rd Cataract Abu Hamed
Bākkū Bitti 2286 Dongola
Pic Toussidé 3265 3376 Kareima 4th Cataract Bûr Sûdân
Bardai Tarso Emissi Suakin
Aozou 2910 Ed Debba Nahr en Nîl (Nile) Trinkitat
Zouar Ma'tan as Sarra Berber 5th Cataract
Tibesti Emi Koussi 3415 Bir 'Atrun Atbara Haiya
Aozou Strip Karora 2180
Sarīr Tibastī Adarama Nakfa
ERITREA Akordat
Borkou Wad Hamid 4th Cataract
Ouninga Kébir Shendî
Grand Erg de Bilma Dépression du Mourdi El Khartûm Bahri
Bilma Faya-Largeau Fada Ennedi 1310 Omdurmân EL KHARTÛM (Khartoum)
Fachi Dépression du Bodélé Zagaoua Malha El Wuz Kassalâ
iu Ténéré Erg du Djourab Oum Chalouba 1954 Khashm el Girba
Ziguéy W. Hawar (Shâti) SUDAN El Gezira Gedaref
Boultoum Nguigmi Biltine Kutum Wâd Medanî
Bahr el Ghazal Abéché Al Junaynah El Fâsher Sodiri Metema
Kumagaman Mao Darfûr Umm Keddada Singa Gonder
Bosso Moussoro Oum Hadjer Zalingei J. Marrah 3088 En Nahud El Obeid Kôstî 1830
Gashua Geidam Ati Massakory Nyâlā Kordofân Er Rahad Nîl el Azraq (Blue Nile)
Nguru Lac Tchad 346 Bokoro Mongo Goz Beïda Umm Ruwaba Abû Zabad Jibalan Nubah 1325 Ed Damazin Roseires Res. L. Tana
Maiduguri Kousséri Bitkine Bahr el   Kâdugli Bahir Dar
Potiskum NDJAMENA Massenya Abou-Deïa El Odaiya Nîl el Abyad (White Nile) Abay Blue Nile
Goniri Bama CHAD Am Timan Birao Debre Markos
Bajoga Chibuk Chari Bousso Ed Dueim
Gombe Biu Maroua Bongor Harazé Mt. Toussoro 1330 Sa'îd Bundas Bahr el Ghazâl Malakâl Nekemte
Numan Guider Logone Laï Sarh Ndélé Jur 3202 Dembidolo
Yola Garoua Kélo Koumra Doba Massîf des Bongos Râga Sûdd Sobat ETHIOPIA
Jalingo Pala Moundou Goré Kaga Bandoro Gogriâl Wâw Tonj Metu Gore
2042 Rés. de Largô Baïbokoum Batangafo Bahr el Ghazâl Rumbêk Bôr Pibor Post Jima 3686
Gashaka 1960 Ngaoundéré Paoua Yalinga Toinya Tali Post Omo L. Abaya
2419 Rés. de Mbabou Meiganga Bossangoa Bria Bakouma Amadi Jûba Arba Minch L. Shamo
Massif de Adamaoua Tibat Bétaré Oya CENTRAL AFRICAN REPUBLIC Ippy Kotto Obo El Istiwa'îya Kapoeta Elemi Triangle
Fouman Yoko Bouar Bozoum Sibut Bambari Ouanga Bomu Yâmbiô Kajo Kaji Lokitaung Chew Bahir
gsamba Nanga-Eboko Bafia Bossembélé BANGUI Bimbo Zongo Bosobolo Mobayi Yei Torit 3187 L. Turkana
ALA YAOUNDÉ Abong-Mbang Berbérati Mbaïki Libenge Bondo Dungu Faradje 375

MEROON Sanaga Nanga-Eboko Batouri Oubangi Mobaye Ango Uele

84 9 10 11 12 13 86

1:7 100 000

THE NILE DELTA
1:3 600 000

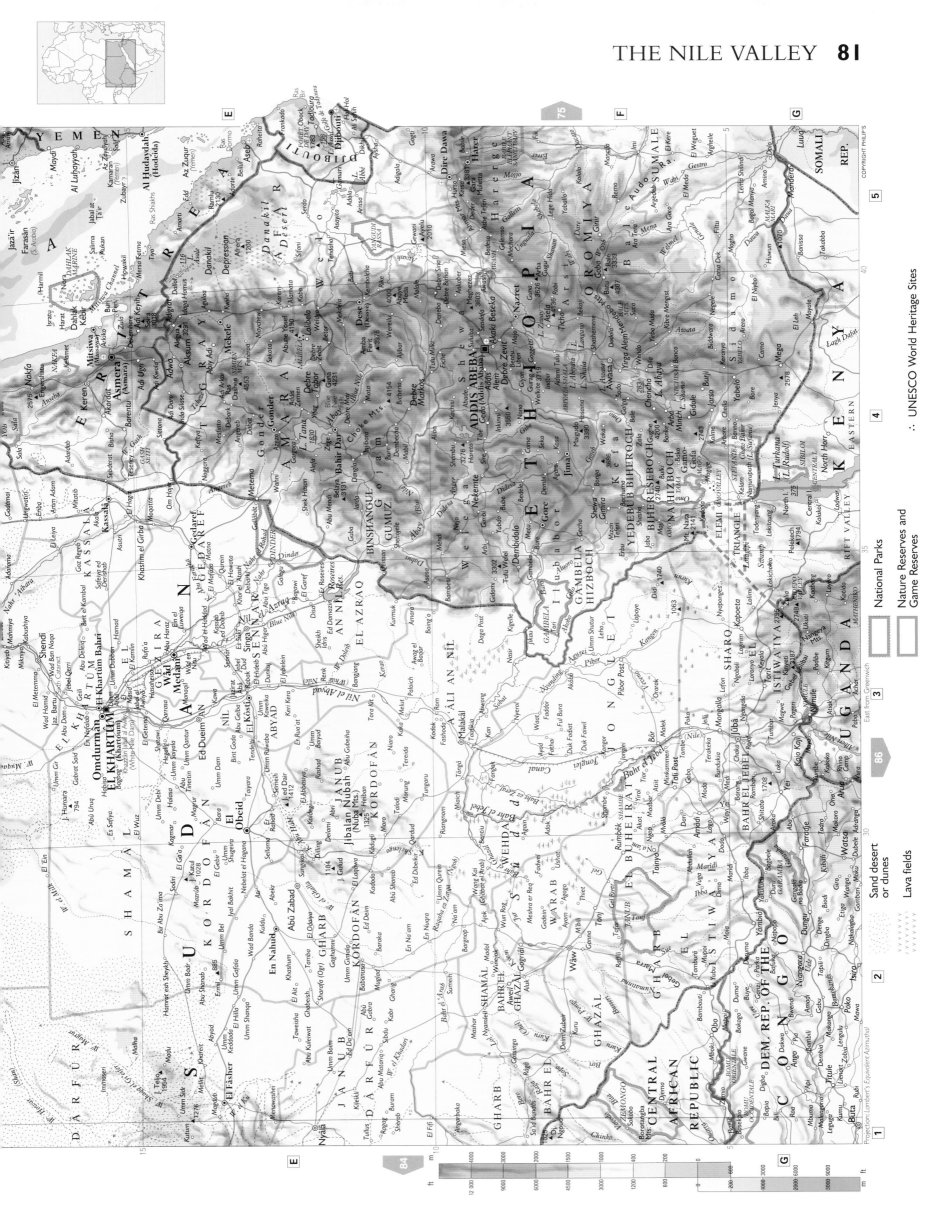

Projection : Lambert's Equivalent Azimuthal

Underlined towns give their name to the administrative area in which they stand.

West from Greenwich

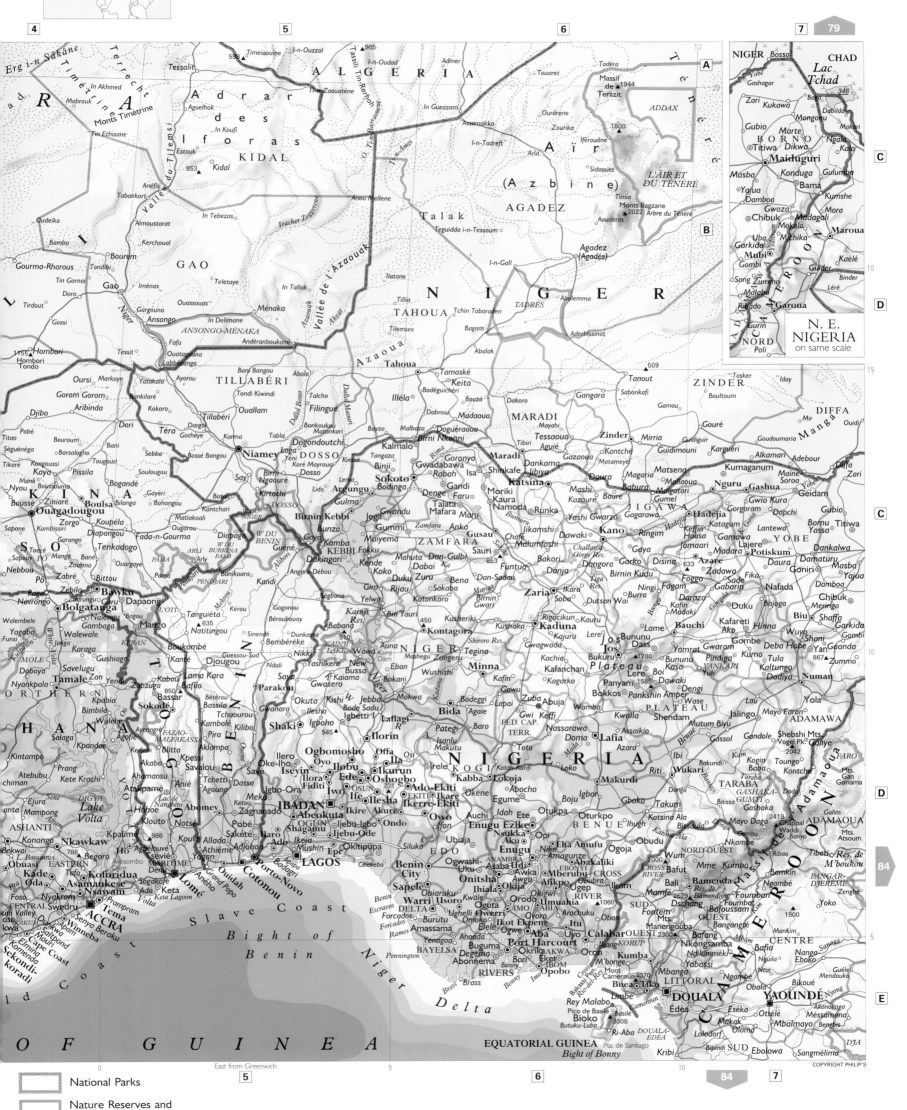

N. E.
NIGERIA
on same scale

☐ National Parks

☐ Nature Reserves and
Game Reserves

∴ UNESCO World Heritage Sites

COPYRIGHT PHILIP'S

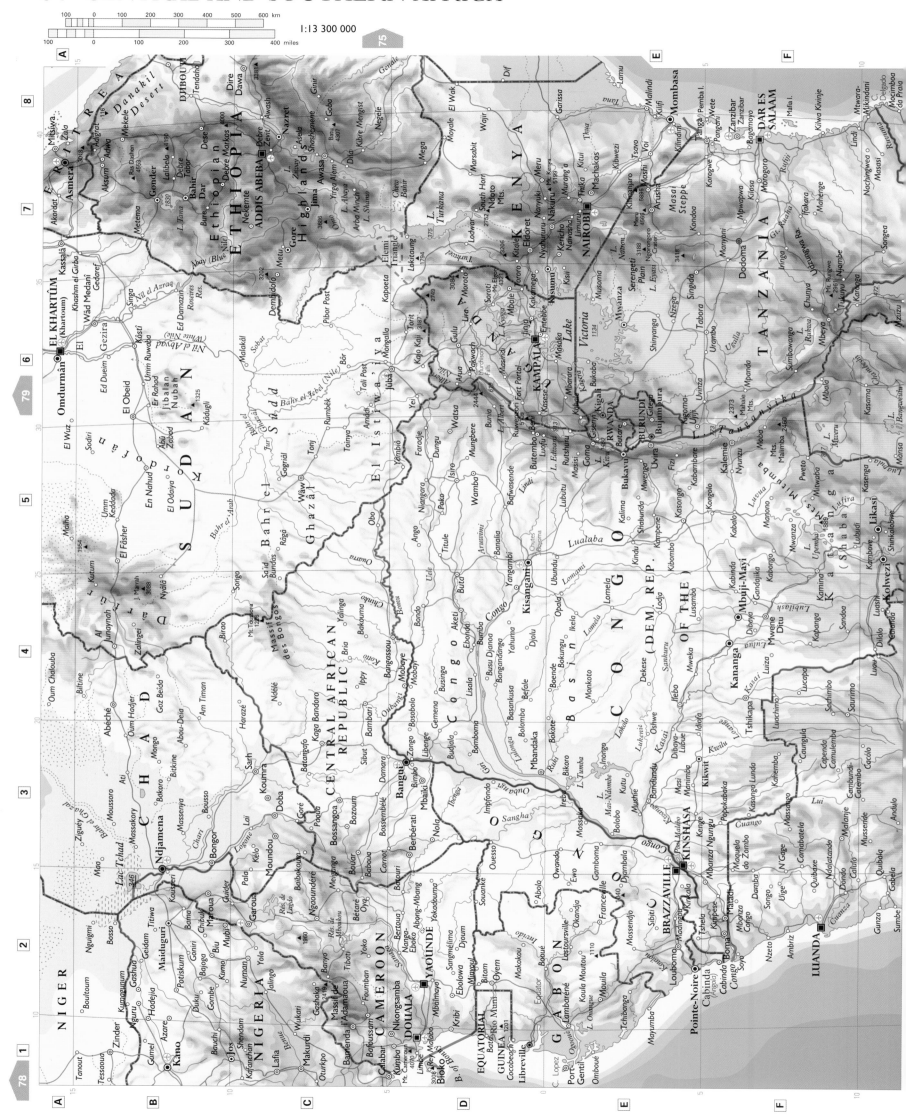

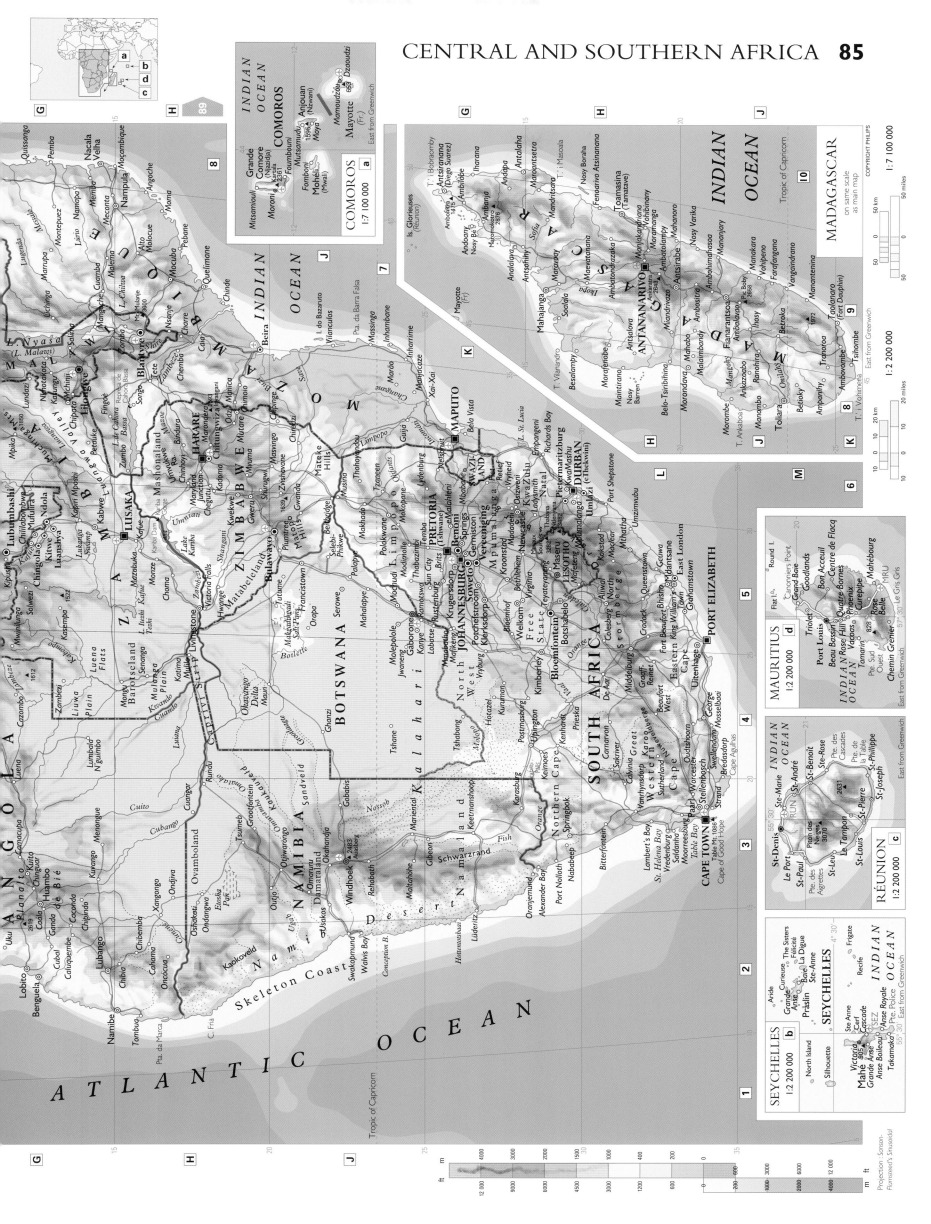

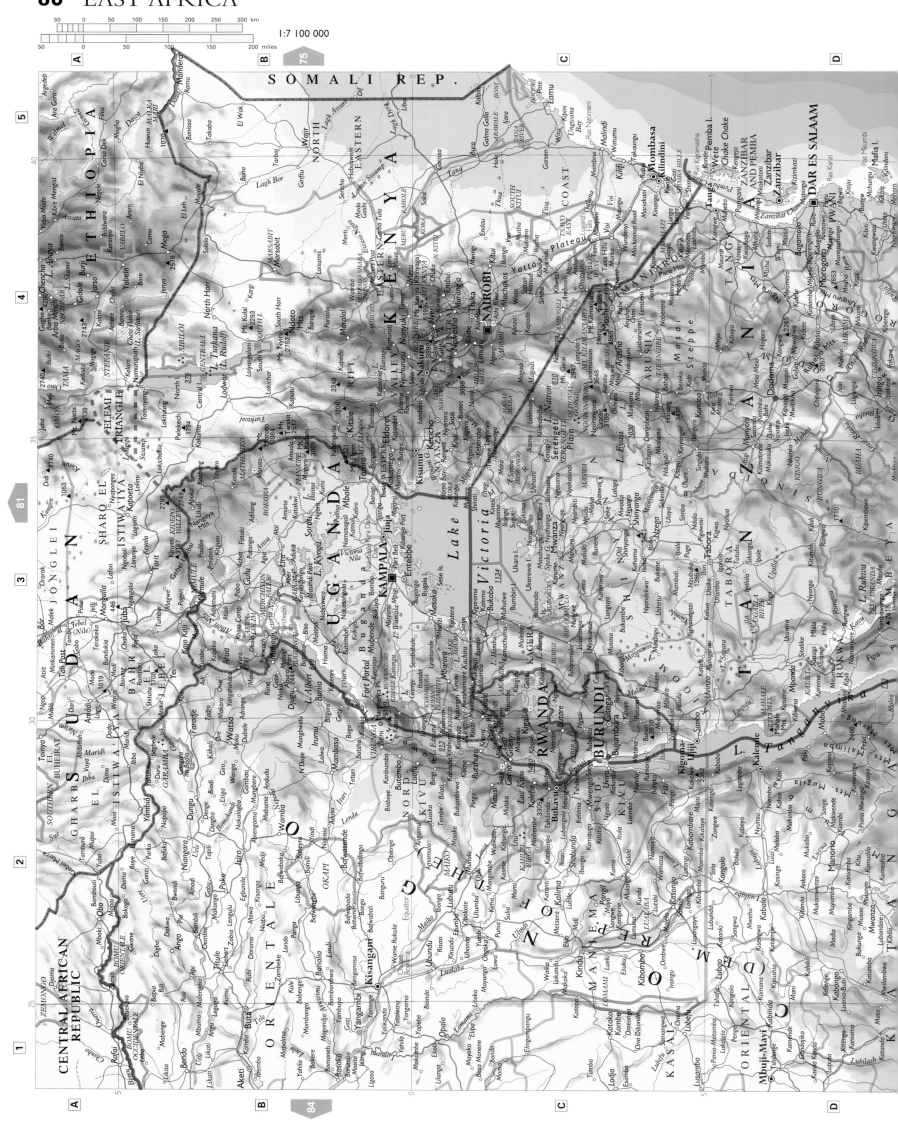

1:7 100 000

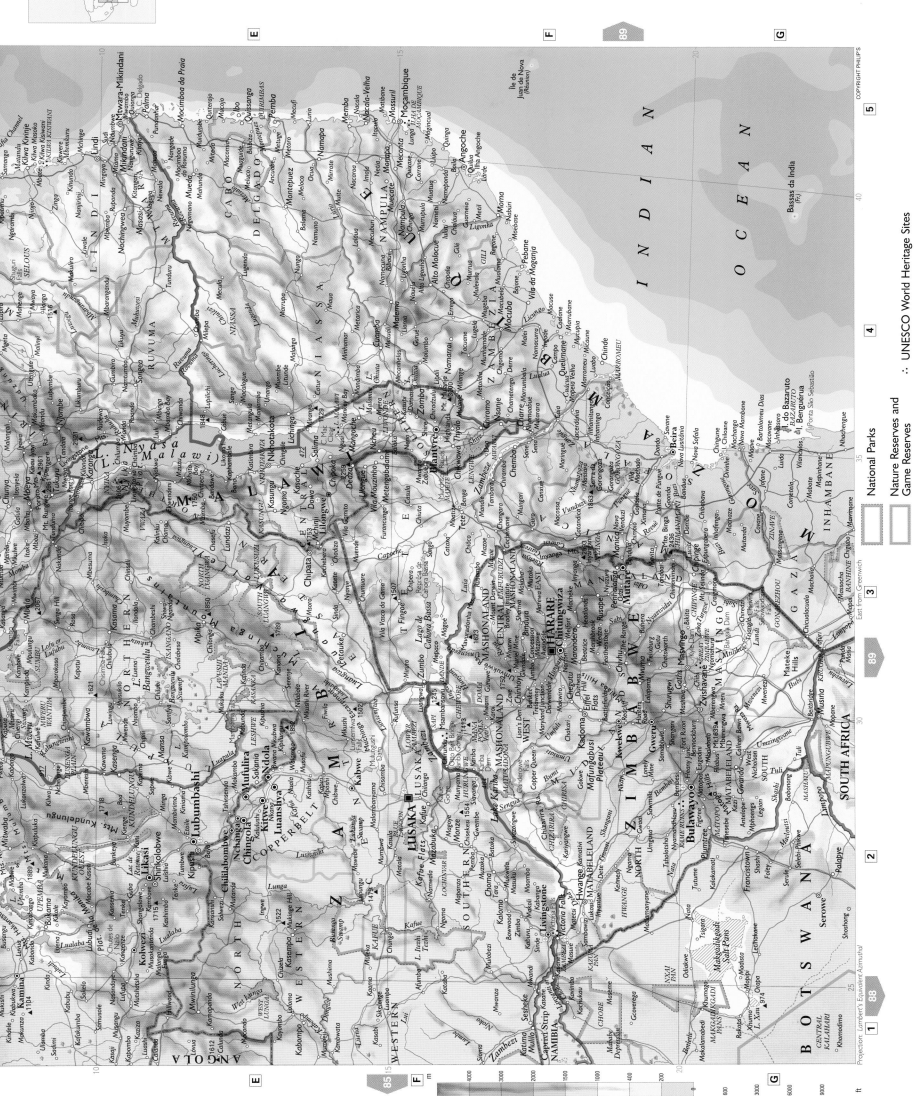

National Parks

:: UNESCO World Heritage Sites

Nature Reserves and
Game Reserves

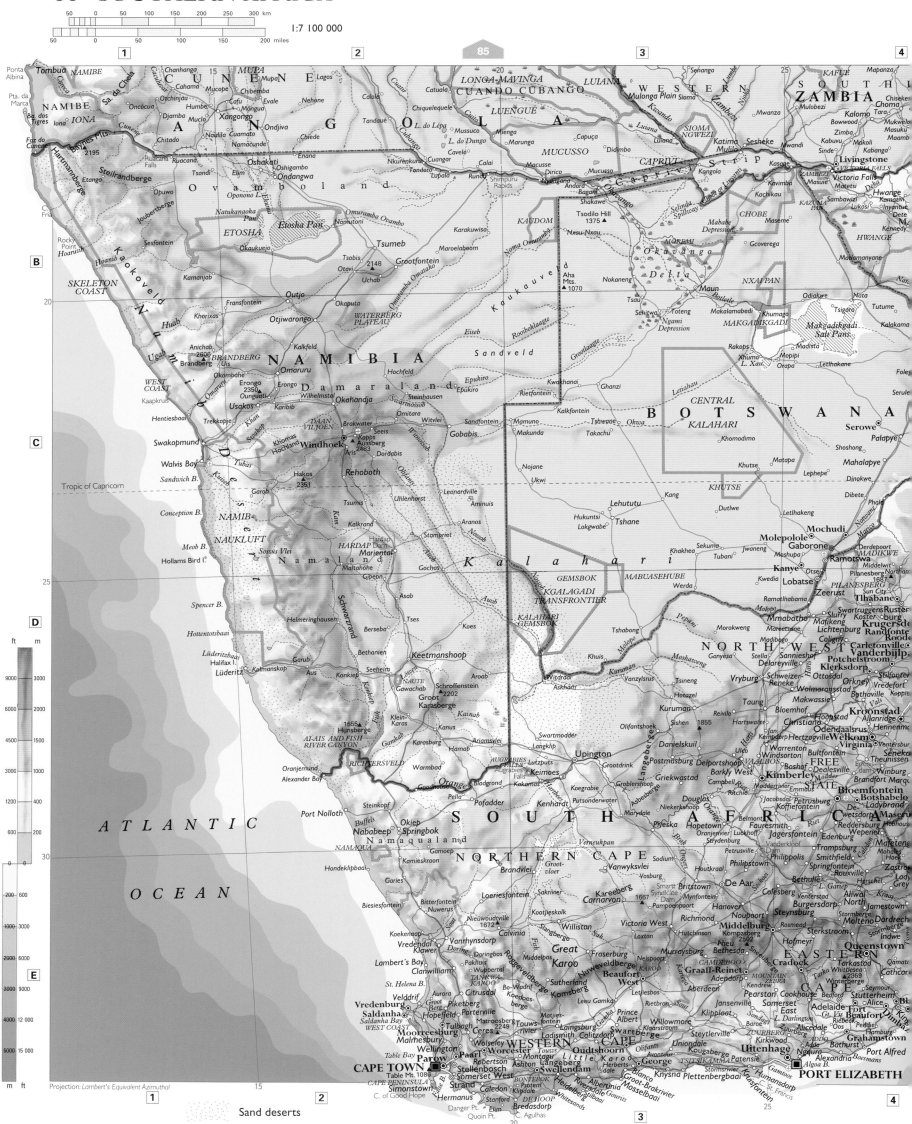

1:7 100 000

Projection: *Lambert's Equivalent Azimuthal*

Sand deserts

National Parks

Nature Reserves and
Game Reserves

⋄ UNESCO World Heritage Sites

MADAGASCAR
1:7 100 000

Projection: Lambert's Equivalent Azimuthal

COPYRIGHT PHILIP'S

East from Greenwich

East from Greenwich

INDIAN

OCEAN

Tropic of Capricorn

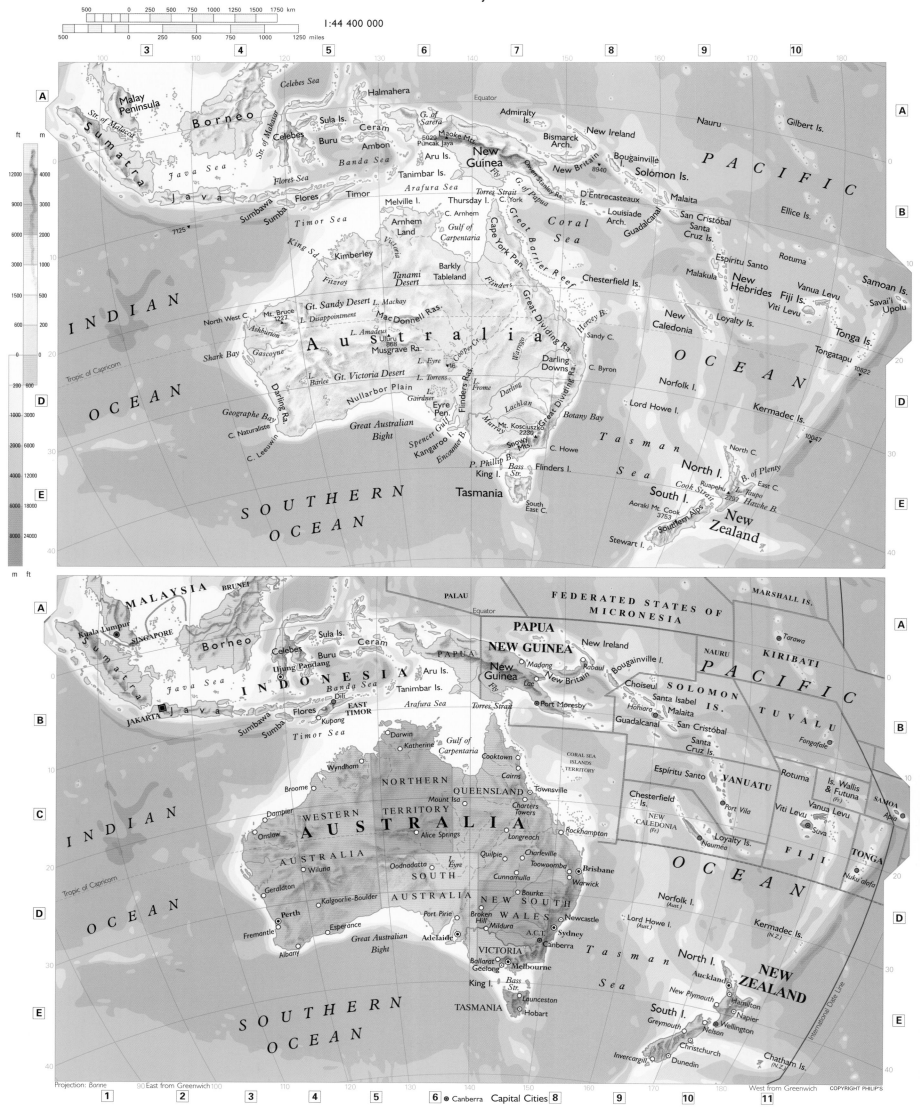

500   0   250   500   750   1000   1250   1500   1750 km

1:44 400 000

500   0   250   500   750   1000   1250 miles

Physical map (top)

3	4	5	6	7	8	9	10	

ft / m
12000 / 4000
9000 / 3000
6000 / 2000
3000 / 1000
1500 / 500
600 / 200
0 / 0
200 / 600
1000 / 3000
2000 / 6000
4000 / 12000
6000 / 18000
8000 / 24000
m / ft

Malay Peninsula
Str. of Malacca
Sumatra
Borneo
Celebes Sea
Halmahera
Str. of Makasar
Celebes
Sula Is.
Ceram
Ambon
Buru
Aru Is.
Banda Sea
Java Sea
Java
Flores Sea
Sumbawa
Sumba
Flores
Timor
Arafura Sea
Timor Sea
7125
Equator
Admiralty Is.
New Ireland
Bismarck Arch.
5029 Maoke Mts.
Puncak Jaya
New Guinea
Fly
G. of Sarera
G. of Papua
Owen Stanley Ra.
New Britain 8940
Bougainville I.
Solomon Is.
PACIFIC
Nauru
Gilbert Is.
D'Entrecasteaux Is.
Louisiade Arch.
Malaita
San Cristóbal
Guadalcanal
Santa Cruz Is.
Espíritu Santo
Rotuma
Ellice Is.
Samoan Is.
Coral Sea
Chesterfield Is.
New Caledonia
Malakula
New Hebrides
Fiji Is.
Vanua Levu
Viti Levu
Savai'i
Upolu
Loyalty Is.
Tonga Is.
Tongatapu
10822
INDIAN OCEAN
Melville I.
Thursday I.
Torres Strait
C. York
C. Arnhem
Arnhem Land
Gulf of Carpentaria
Victoria
Barkly Tableland
Cape York Pen.
Great Barrier Reef
Kimberley
King Sd.
Fitzroy
Tanami Desert
Flinders
Great Dividing Ra.
Hervey B.
North West C.
Mt. Bruce 1227
Gt. Sandy Desert
L. Mackay
L. Disappointment
MacDonnell Ras.
Ashburton
L. Amadeus
Uluru 868
Australia
Cooper Cr.
Warrego
Sandy C.
Shark Bay
Gascoyne
Musgrave Ra.
L. Eyre 16
Darling Downs
C. Byron
L. Barlee
Gt. Victoria Desert
L. Torrens
Darling
Norfolk I.
Nullarbor Plain
L. Gairdner
L. Frome
Lachlan
OCEAN
Eyre Pen.
Flinders Ras.
Murray
Botany Bay
Lord Howe I.
Kermadec Is.
10047
Geographe Bay
Darling Ra.
Great Australian Bight
Spencer Gulf
Mt. Kosciuszko 2230
Snowy Mts.
C. Naturaliste
Kangaroo I.
Encounter B.
Tasman Sea
North C.
North I.
B. of Plenty
East C.
C. Leeuwin
P. Phillip B.
King I.
Bass Str.
C. Howe
Flinders I.
Cook Strait
Ruapehu 2797
L. Taupo
Hawke B.
SOUTHERN OCEAN
Tasmania
South East C.
Aoraki Mt. Cook 3753
Southern Alps
South I.
New Zealand
Stewart I.

Political map (bottom)

1	2	3	4	5	6	7	8	9	10	11

MALAYSIA
BRUNEI
Kuala Lumpur
SINGAPORE
Sumatra
Borneo
Celebes
Buru
Ceram
Sula Is.
PALAU
Equator
FEDERATED STATES OF MICRONESIA
MARSHALL IS.
Ujung Pandang
PAPUA
INDONESIA
JAKARTA
Java
Banda Sea
Java Sea
Dili
Aru Is.
Tanimbar Is.
PAPUA NEW GUINEA
New Guinea
Madang
New Ireland
Rabaul
New Britain
Lae
Fly
Bougainville I.
Choiseul
Santa Isabel
SOLOMON IS.
NAURU
Tarawa
KIRIBATI
PACIFIC
EAST TIMOR
Kupang
Arafura Sea
Torres Strait
Port Moresby
Honiara
Guadalcanal
Malaita
San Cristóbal
TUVALU
Sumbawa
Sumba
Flores
Timor Sea
Darwin
Katherine
Gulf of Carpentaria
Cooktown
Santa Cruz Is.
Fongafale
Wyndham
NORTHERN TERRITORY
Cairns
Townsville
CORAL SEA ISLANDS TERRITORY
Espíritu Santo
VANUATU
Rotuma
Is. Wallis & Futuna (Fr.)
SAMOA
Broome
Dampier
WESTERN AUSTRALIA
Mount Isa
QUEENSLAND
Charters Towers
Chesterfield Is.
Port Vila
Viti Levu
Vanua Levu
Apia
INDIAN
Onslow
AUSTRALIA
Alice Springs
Longreach
Rockhampton
NEW CALEDONIA (Fr.)
Loyalty Is.
Nouméa
Suva
FIJI
OCEAN
Wiluna
L. Eyre
Quilpie
Charleville
Toowoomba
TONGA
Tropic of Capricorn
SOUTH
Oodnadatta
Cunnamulla
Brisbane
Warwick
Norfolk I. (Aust.)
Nuku'alofa
Geraldton
Kalgoorlie-Boulder
AUSTRALIA
Bourke
NEW SOUTH WALES
Lord Howe I. (Aust.)
OCEAN
Perth
Fremantle
Esperance
Port Pirie
Broken Hill
Mildura
Newcastle
A.C.T.
Sydney
Kermadec Is. (N.Z.)
Albany
Great Australian Bight
Adelaide
VICTORIA
Canberra
North I.
Ballarat
Melbourne
Geelong
Tasman Sea
Auckland
NEW ZEALAND
King I.
Bass Str.
New Plymouth
Hamilton
Napier
SOUTHERN OCEAN
TASMANIA
Launceston
Hobart
South I.
Greymouth
Wellington
Nelson
International Date Line
Invercargill
Christchurch
Dunedin
Chatham Is. (N.Z.)

Projection: Bonne
90 East from Greenwich 100
West from Greenwich
COPYRIGHT PHILIP'S

● Canberra Capital Cities

1:5 300 000

50 0 50 100 150 200 km
50 0 50 100 150 miles

4 96 **5** **6** **7**

FIJI *a*
on same scale

PACIFIC OCEAN

Great Sea Reef
Kia
Udu Pt.
Ringgold Is.
Yaqaga
Labasa
Natewa Bay
Rabi
Vanua Levu ▲1031
Buca
Yasawa Group
Yasawa
Yadua
Bua
Savusavu Bay
Somosomo
Qamea
Taveuni
BOUMA
Nacula
Nabouwalu
Naitaba
Viwa
Naviti
Namenalala
Kanacea
Vanua Balavu
Waya
Vatu Vara
Vatu
Vara
Northern Lau Group
Voma
Tavua
Rakiraki
Levuka
Wakaya
Cicia
Lautoka
Malolo
Navai ▲1323
KOROYANITU
Tomanivi
Lawaki
Ovalau
Batiki
Tuvuca
Nadi
Viti Levu
Keiyasi
Korovou
Nairai
Nayau
KORO SEA
Sigatoka
Korolevu
Navua
Nausori
Gau
Lakeba Passage
Lakeba
Tubou
Yanuca
Beqa
Moala
Oneata
Moce
Vatulele
Namuka-i-Lau
Yagasa Cluster
Kadavu Passage
Matuku
Fulaga
Ogea Levu
Kadavu
Ono
Tavuki
Vunisea
Totoya
Ogea Driki
18 S
FIJI
178 E
180
East from Greenwich
West from Greenwich

SAMOA
Asau
Safune
Falelima
▲1858
Pu'apu'a
Savai'i
Sataua itea
Salelologa
Taga
Manono
Falefa
Apia
Mulifanua
Falelatai
'Upolu
OLE PUPU PU'E
▲416
Amaile
Safata Bay
14 S

PACIFIC OCEAN

AMERICAN SAMOA (U.S.A.)
Ofu
Olosega
AMERICAN SAMOA
Ta'ū
Tutuila
Pago Pago
Luma
Manu'a Is.
Leone
Vaitogi
AMERICAN SAMOA

SAMOAN ISLANDS *b*
on same scale
170 W
172 W
West from Greenwich

TONGA *c*
on same scale
174 W

PACIFIC OCEAN

Fonualei
Toku
Vava'u
Neiafu
Vava'u Group
Late
Home Reef
Disney Reef
Ofolanga
Tofua
Kao
Foa
Ha'ano
Ha'apai Group
Lifuka
Uiha
Kotu Group
Fonuafo'ou
Oto Tolu Group
Nomuka Group
Mango Group
Tonumea
Hunga Ha'apai
18 S
20 S
174 W

TONGA
Nuku'alofa
Tongatapu
Tongatapu Group
Eua
West from Greenwich

1

PACIFIC OCEAN

C. Reinga
C. Maria van Diemen
North C.
Houhora Heads
Rangaunu B.
Doubtless B.
Mangonui
Whangaroa Harb.
Ahipara B.
Kaitaia
Okaihau
Waitangi
B. of Islands
C. Brett
Opua
Tauroa Pt.
Rawene
Kaikohe
Hikurangi
Hokianga Harbour
Kaikohe
Whangarei
Whangarei Harb.
Waipoua Forest
Waipu
Bream Hd.
Dargaville
Bream B.
Little Barrier I.
Warkworth
C. Rodney
Great Barrier I.
Kaipara Harbour
Helensville
C. Colville
Cuvier I.
Coromandel
Takapuna
Hauraki Gulf
Whitianga
AUCKLAND
Manukau
Papakura
Thames
Whangamata
North Island
Pukekohe
Waiuku
Mercer
Waihi
Mayor I.
Waikato
Huntly
Te Aroha
Tauranga Harb.
Whakatane
Morrinsville
Tauranga
Mount Maunganui
Whakaari (White I.)
Raglan
Hamilton
Cambridge
Te Puke
Runaway
Te Awamutu
Rotorua
Kawerau
East C.
Kawhia Harbour
Putaruru
L. Rotorua
Te Kuiti
Kinleith
L. Tarawera
Murupara
Raukumara Ra.
Otorohanga
Tokoroa
Hikurangi ▲1763
Waitomo Caves
Mokau
Wairakei
UREWERA
Taneatua
Mokau
Taupo
Motu
North Taranaki Bight
Ongarue
Rangipo Mts.
Tolaga Bay
Waitara
Taumarunui
Turangi
Waikaremoana
Waipiro
New Plymouth
Inglewood
WHANGANUI
Whangamomona
KAIMANAWA MTS.
Gisborne
Mt. Taranaki or Mt. Egmont
C. Egmont
▲2518
Stratford
Ōhakune
TONGARIRO
Ruahine Ra.
Wairoa
Poverty Bay
Opunake
Kapuni
Eltham
Raetihi
Waiouru
Waikokopu
Hawera
Mahia Pen.
Waverley
Mangaweka
Taihape
Napier
Bay View
Hawke Bay
South Taranaki Bight
Patea
Wanganui
Marton
Hunterville
Taihape
Hastings
C. Kidnappers
Bulls
Halcombe
Waipawa
Palmerston North
Feilding
Dannevirke
Waipukurau
Foxton
Woodville
Shannon
Pahiatua
C. Turnagain
Levin
Eketahuna
Otaki
Paraparaumu
Masterton
Kapiti I.
Carterton
Greytown
Upper Hutt
Featherston
Martinborough
Wairarapa
Petone
Lower Hutt
Eastbourne
Wellington
Cook Strait

C. Farewell
Golden B.
D'Urville I.
Collingwood
Takaka
ABEL TASMAN
Tasman B.
Motueka
Pelorus Sd.
KAHURANGI
Tasman Mts.
Motueka
Queen Charlotte Sd.
Karamea
Nelson
Havelock
Picton
Karamea Bight
Matiri Ra.
Tadmor
Richmond
Wakefield
Blenheim
Seddonville
Tadmor
Seddon
Granity
Lyell
Ward
Murchison
NELSON LAKES
Awatere
Westport
Inangahua
L. Rotoroa
PAPAROA
Reefton
Spenser Mts.
Kaikoura
Punakaiki
Blackball
Lewis Pass
Hanmer Springs
Runanga
Mt. Travers ▲2337
Waiau
Greymouth
Stillwater
Hanmer
Clarence
Kumara
L. Brunner
ARTHUR'S PASS
Waiau
Hokitika
Jacksons
Arthur's Pass
Waikari
Hurunui
Ross
Amberley
Waipara
Culverden
South Island
Oxford
Kaiapoi
Pegasus Bay
Westland Bight
Springfield
Rangiora
New Brighton
Abut Hd.
WESTLAND
Aoraki Mt. Cook ▲3753
Methven
Whitecliffs
Christchurch
Lyttelton
Staveley
Riccarton
Akaroa
Jackson B.
Okuru
Southern Alps
Tiritiri o te Moana
Lincoln
Banks Pen.
MT. COOK
Mount Cook
Rakaia
L. Tekapo
Little River
L. Ellesmere
Haast
L. Coleridge
Canterbury Plains
MOUNT ASPIRING
Mt. Aspiring ▲3033
L. Ohau
Fairlie
Southbridge
Mt. Earnslaw ▲2819
L. Wanaka
L. Pukaki
Geraldine
Ashburton Bight
Milford Sd.
Sutherland Falls
Mt. Aspiring
Temuka
Bligh Sound
L. Wakatipu
Timaru
George Sound
Arrowtown
Cromwell
St. Andrews
Secretary I.
Doubtful I.
Queenstown
Clyde
Waimate
Kingston
Alexandra
Kurow
Oamaru
FIORDLAND
Mossburn
Roxburgh
Maheno
Hampden
Manapouri
Lumsden
Naseby
Danback
Breaksea Sd.
Mt. Aspiring
Ranfurly
Palmerston
Resolution I.
L. Te Anau
OTAGO
Dusky Sd.
Edievale
Port Chalmers
Solander I.
Nightcaps
Kelso
Otago Harbour
Waikouaiti
Clifden
Winton
Clinton
Dunedin
C. Saunders
Tuatapere
Southland
Ohai
Milton
Orepuki
Gore
Mataura
Kaitangata
Te Waewae Bay
Riverton
Hedgehope
Lawrence
Balclutha
Owaka
Preservation Inlet
Invercargill
South Invercargill
Wyndham
Tokanui
Tahakopa
Chalky Inlet
Bluff
Ruapuke I.
Nugget Pt.
Foveaux Str.
Halfmoon Bay
Stewart I. (Rakiura)
RAKIURA
Port Pegasus
South West C.

TASMAN SEA

PACIFIC OCEAN

Moorea (France)
Papetoai
Pte. Aroa
Paopao
Pte. Vénus
B. de Matavai
Mahina
Papenoo
Haapiti
Mt. Tohiea ▲1207
Afareaitu
Arue
Pirae
Papeete
Tiarei
Tahiti (France)
Faaa
Hitiaa
Maharepa
Punaauia
Mt. Aorai ▲2060
Mt. Orohena ▲2241
Faaone
Paea
Mt. Tetufera ▲1799
Lac Vaihiria
Isthme de Taravao
Maraa
Papara
Taravao
Afaahiti
Pte. Tatatua
Atimaono
Mataiea
Pueu
Vairao
Mt. Rooniu ▲1332
Tautira
Teahupoo
Presqu'île de Taiarapu

TAHITI & MOOREA 1:900 000
COPYRIGHT PHILIP'S

Projection : Conical with two standard parallels
166 168 170 172 East from Greenwich

ft m
9000 3000
6000 2000
3000 1000
1200 400
600 200
0 0
200 600
2000 6000
4000 12 000
6000 18 000
m ft

10 0 10 km
10 0 10 miles
1:900 000

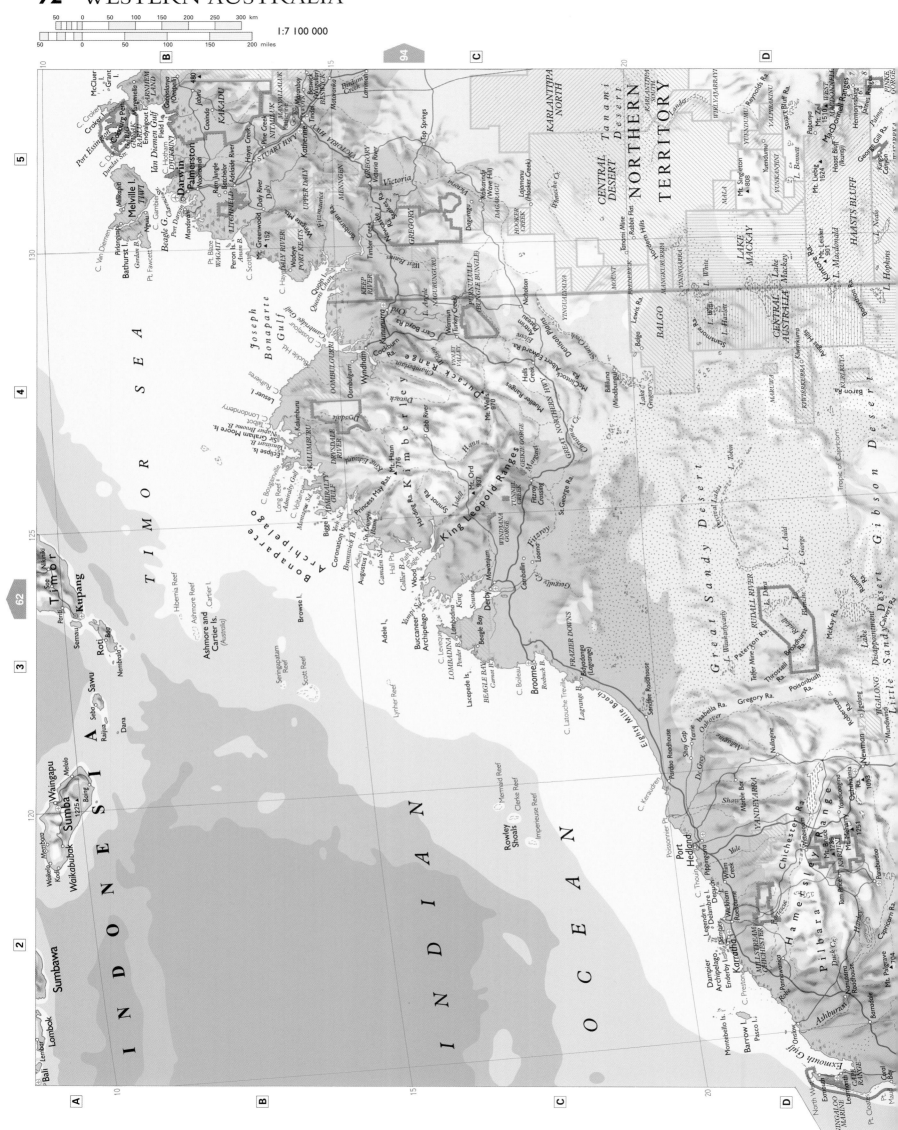

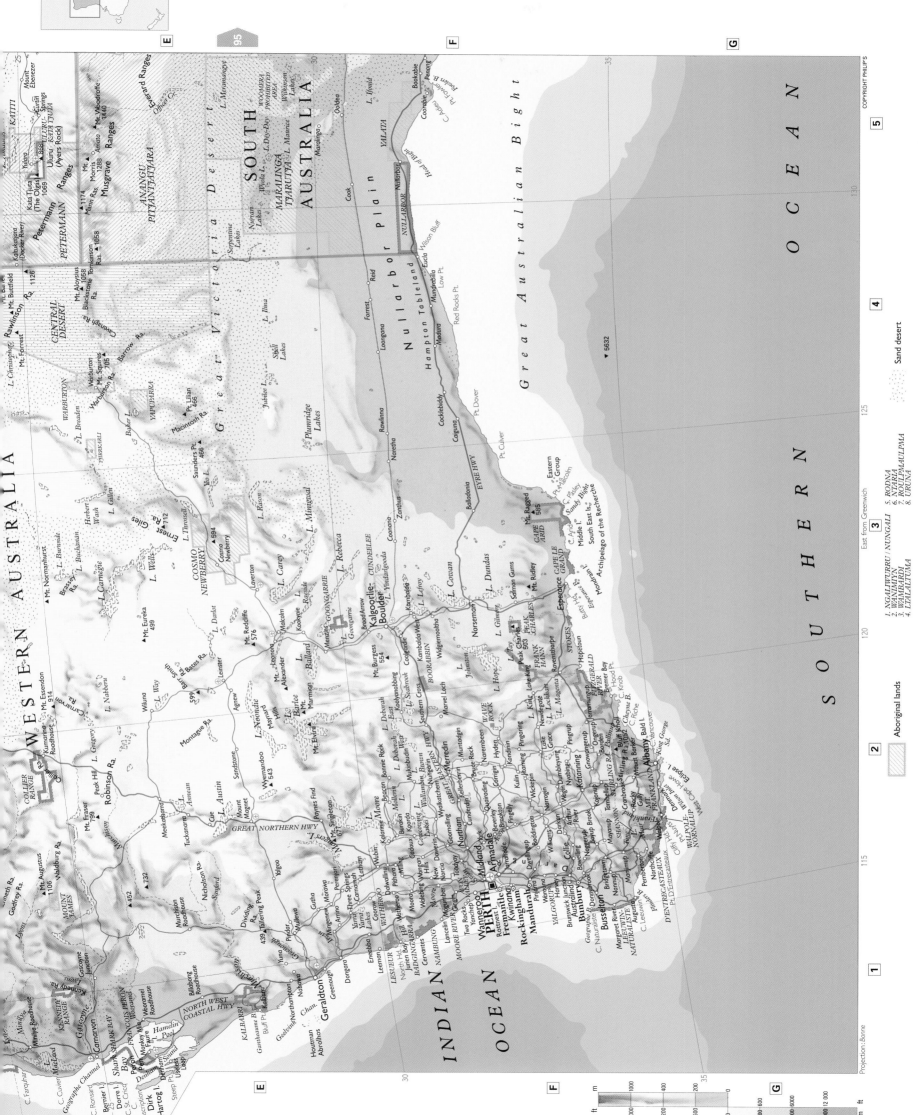

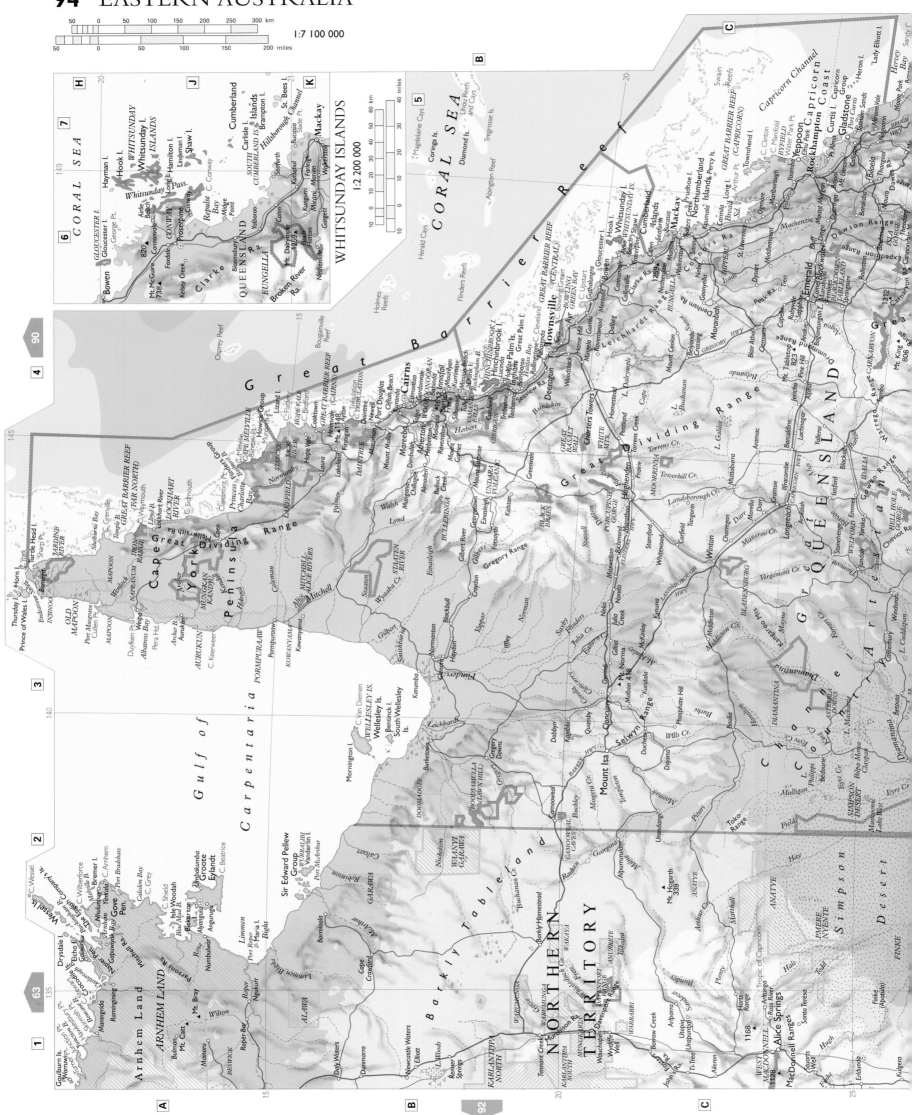

Map scale 1:7 100 000

50 0 50 100 150 200 250 300 km
50 0 50 100 150 200 miles

WHITSUNDAY ISLANDS 1:2 200 000

0 10 20 30 40 50 60 km
0 10 20 30 40 miles

CORAL SEA

GLOUCESTER I.
Gloucester I.
Bowen
WHITSUNDAY ISLANDS
Hayman I.
Hook I.
Whitsunday I.
Long I.
Hamilton I.
Lindeman I.
Shaw I.
Cumberland

Airlie Beach
Cannonvale
Proserpine
Foxdale
Kelsey Creek
Mt McGuire 738
Mt Dalrymple 1259
Broken River Ra.
QUEENSLAND
EUNGELLA
Clarke Ra.

SOUTH CUMBERLAND IS.
Carlisle I.
Brampton I.
St. Bees I.
Seaforth
Kutkabul
Bucasia
Farleigh
Slade Pt.
Mackay
Walkerston
Kunguri
Mirani, Marian
Gargett
Netherdale
Hatton

Repulse Bay
Midge Point
C. Conway
Yalboroo

GREAT BARRIER REEF

CORAL SEA

Magdelaine Cays
Coringa Is.
Lihou Reefs and Cays
Diamond Is.
Tregrosse Is.

Herald Cays
Holmes Reefs
Flinders Reefs
Abington Reef
Bougainville Reef
Osprey Reef

Lizard I.
Howick Group
C. Flattery
C. Bedford
Cooktown
GREAT BARRIER REEF (FAR NORTH)

Gulf of Carpentaria

ARNHEM LAND
Arnhem Land
Gove Pen.
Groote Eylandt

NORTHERN TERRITORY

QUEENSLAND

Great Dividing Range

Cape York Peninsula

Cairns
Townsville
Mackay
Rockhampton
Gladstone

Tropic of Capricorn

Alice Springs

SIMPSON DESERT

Mount Isa

Capricorn Coast

Barkly Tableland

Great Artesian Basin

Great Dividing Range

Channel Country

Diamantina

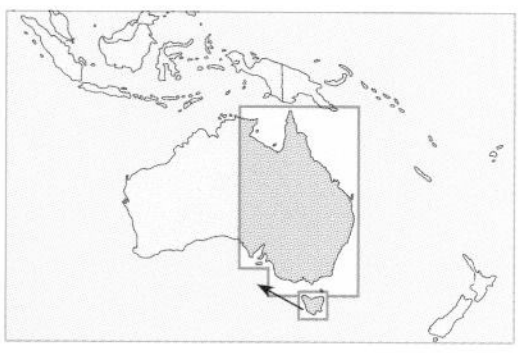

COPYRIGHT. GEORGE PHILIP LTD.

T A S M A N   S E A

SOUTH AUSTRALIA

NEW SOUTH WALES

VICTORIA

QUEENSLAND

TASMANIA

BRISBANE
SYDNEY
ADELAIDE
MELBOURNE
Canberra
Newcastle
Wollongong
Hobart
Launceston
Geelong
Ballarat
Bendigo

Great Dividing Range

Darling Downs

Barrier Range

Flinders Ranges

Lake Eyre
Lake Eyre (North)
Lake Eyre (South)
Lake Torrens
Lake Gairdner
Lake Frome
Lake Blanche

Sturt Stony Desert
Strzelecki Desert
Simpson Desert
Big Desert
Little Desert

Bass Strait
Flinders Island
Cape Barren I.
King Island
Furneaux Group
Kangaroo I.

Spencer Gulf
Gulf St. Vincent
Eyre Peninsula
Yorke Peninsula

Murray River
Darling River

Broken Hill

Aboriginal lands

Sand desert

East from Greenwich

on same scale

Projection: Bonne

ft   m   1500   1000   400   200   0   -200
m   ft   4500   3000   1200   600   0   -600
2000   6000
4000   12 000

R U S S I A

Yekaterinburg
Moskva
Volga
Tomsk
Ob'
Novosibirsk
Lena
Irkutsk
Oz. Baykal
Chita
Okhotsk
Sea of Okhotsk
Poluostrov Kamchatka
Shirshov Ridge
Aleutian Basin
Bering Sea

Astana (Aqmola)
Semey
KAZAKHSTAN
Balqash Köl
Altai
MONGOLIA
Ulaanbaatar
Blagoveshchensk
Amur
Khabarovsk
Sakhalin
Kurilskiye Ostrova (Russia)
Kuril-Kamchatka Trench
La Pérouse Str.
Petropavlovsk-Kamchatskiy
Komandorskiye Ostrova (Russia)
Near Is. (U.S.A.)
Andreanof Is. (U.S.A.)
7822

Aral Sea
Toshkent
Almaty
Ürümqi
KYRGYZSTAN
TAJIKISTAN
Harbin
Changchun
Shenyang
Vladivostok
Hakodate
Sapporo
Sea of Japan
10,542
Emperor Seamount Chain
Emperor Trough
N o r t h w e s t
Chinook Trough
Aleutian Trench
A l e u t i a n

AFGHANISTAN
Kabul
Srinagar
PAKISTAN
Indus
Lahore
Delhi
Kanpur
CHINA
Kunlun Shan
Lanzhou
Xi'an
Beijing
Tianjin
Taiyuan
Huang He
Dalian
Qingdao
NORTH KOREA
SOUTH KOREA
Seoul
Kyōto
Osaka
Nagoya
Yokohama
Tōkyō
Sendai
JAPAN
Fuji-San 3776
Shikoku
Kyūshū
10,554
Shatsky Rise
P a c i f i c
B a s i n
Midway Is. (U.S.A.)
Hawaii

XIZANG
Himalaya
Nepal
Mt. Everest 8850
Lhasa
Chongqing
Chengdu
Wuhan
Changsha
Nanjing
Hangzhou
Shanghai
East China Sea
Okinawa
Ryūkyū-rettō (Japan)
Japan Trench
Iwo-Jima (Japan)
Ogasawara Gunto (Japan)
Minami-Tori-Shima (Japan)
Kazan-Rettō (Japan)
Lisianski I. (U.S.A.)

INDIA
Hyderabad
Kolkata (Calcutta)
BANGLADESH
Dhaka
Ganga
Brahmaputra
BURMA
Mandalay
Irrawaddy
Kunming
Fuzhou
Guangzhou
Macau
Hong Kong
Taipei
TAIWAN
Taroko
Philippine Sea
Kyushu-Palau Ridge
Kyushu-Ozima Ridge
Sitito-Ozima Ridge
M i d - P a c i f i c
Wake I. (U.S.A.)
P A
Mount

Chennai (Madras)
Bay of Bengal
Rangoon
LAOS
Hanoi
Hainan
Salween
Mekong
Luzon
Paracel Is.
Manila
C. Engano
West Mariana Basin
NORTHERN MARIANAS (U.S.A.)
East Mariana Basin
Tinian
Saipan
MARSHALL IS.
International Date Line
P A

THAILAND
Bangkok
CAMBODIA
Phnom Penh
VIETNAM
PHILIPPINES
South China Sea
Mindoro
Samar
Palawan
GUAM (U.S.A.)
Mariana Trench
Challenger 11,022 Deep
10,497
M i c r o n e s i a
Yap
Caroline Is.
Chuuk
Enewetak Atoll
Bikini Atoll
Ralik Chain
Ratak Chain
Kwajalein
Majuro

SRI LANKA
Colombo
Andaman Is. (India)
Nicobar Is. (India)
G. of Thailand
Thanh Pho Ho Chi Minh
Sulu Sea
Mindanao
Davao
Mindanao Trench
Koror
PALAU
West Caroline Basin
Eauripik Rise
FED. STATES OF MICRONESIA
East Caroline Basin
Pohnpei
Palikir
Jaluit I.
Butaritari
Tarawa
Howland I. (U.S.A.)
Baker I. (U.S.A.)
Phoenix Is.
Abariringa Enderbury
Pacific
Central
K I

MALAYSIA
Kuala Lumpur
Singapore
PEN. MALAYSIA
SARAWAK
SABAH
BRUNEI
4101
Celebes Sea
Sumatera
Sunda Island
Borneo
Sulawesi
Ujung Pandang
Halmahera
Seram
Buru
Maluku
INDONESIA
Puncak Jaya 5029
PAPUA
PAPUA NEW GUINEA
Admiralty Is.
New Ireland
Bismarck Arch.
New Britain
Rabaul
Bougainville
Lae
New Guinea
8940
M e l a n e s i a
Solomon Rise
Melanesian Basin
Solomon Basin
NAURU
Banaba
Gilbert Is.
Fongafale
TUVALU
Tokelau Is. (N.Z.)

Palembang
Java Sea
Jakarta
Jawa
Surabaya
Bali
Sumbawa
Flores Sea
Flores
Banda Sea
7440
Dili
EAST TIMOR
Timor
Sumba
Arafura Sea
Torres Strait
C. York
Port Moresby
Louisiade Arch.
SOLOMON IS.
Honiara
Guadalcanal
Santa Cruz I. 9165
VANUATU
Espiritu Santo
Port Vila
Rotuma
Is. Wallis & Futuna (Fr.)
SAMOA
Apia
KIRIBATI

I N D I A N
Ninetyeast Ridge
Java Trench
Cocos Is. (Austral.)
Christmas I. (Austral.)
North Australian Basin
C. Arnhem
Darwin
Gulf of Carpentaria
Broome
Coral Sea Basin
Cairns
Coral Sea
Î. Chesterfield
Îs. Loyauté
Nouméa
NEW CALEDONIA (Fr.)
7570
Vanua Levu
Viti Levu
Suva
FIJI
West Fiji Basin
Nuku'alofa
TONGA
10,822
Tonga Trench

O C E A N
Wharton Basin
Exmouth Plateau
North West C.
Mount Isa
Great Barrier Reef
Great Dividing Ra.
Townsville
Rockhampton
Brisbane
Middleton Basin
Lord Howe Rise
Norfolk I. (Austral.)
New Caledonia Ridge
Lord Howe Trough
Norfolk Ridge
South Fiji Basin
Tonga Trench

Geraldton
AUSTRALIA
Alice Springs
L. Eyre
Darling
Perth Basin
Perth
Naturaliste Plateau
Albany
Great Australian Bight
Adelaide
Canberra
Sydney
Mt. Kosciuszko 2230
Murray
Lord Howe I. (Austral.)
10,047
Kermadec Is. (N.Z.)
Kermadec Trench 10,047
South Fiji Basin

Mid-Indian Ridge
Nouvelle Amsterdam (Fr.)
I. St. Paul (Fr.)
Broken Ridge
South Australian Basin
Melbourne
Bass Str.
Tasmania
Hobart
East Tasman Plateau
Tasman Sea
Aoraki Mt. Cook 3753
NEW ZEALAND
Auckland
Wellington
Cook Strait
Christchurch
Chatham Is. (N.Z.)
Chatham Rise
Dunedin
Bounty Trough
Bounty Is. (N.Z.)

Is. Crozet (Fr.)
Kerguelen (Fr.)
S O U T H E R N   O C E A N
Heard I. (Austral.)
South Tasman Rise
South Tasman Basin
Tasman Basin
Invercargill
Antipodes Is. (N.Z.)
Campbell I. (N.Z.)
Auckland Is. (N.Z.)
Campbell Plateau
Macquarie Is. (N.Z.)

ft   m
12 000   4000
9000   3000
6000   2000
3000   1000
1500   500
600   200
0   0
200   600
1000   3000
2000   6000
4000   12 000
6000   18 000
8000   24 000
m   ft

Arctic Circle

ALASKA
(U.S.A.)
Anchorage
5959

Bristol Bay
Gulf of Alaska
Juneau
Prince of Wales I.
(U.S.A.) Prince Rupert
Queen Charlotte Is.
(Canada)

Is. (U.S.A.)

ROCKY

CANADA

NORTH

Edmonton
L. Winnipeg
Newfoundland

Vancouver
Vancouver I.
Victoria
Seattle
Portland
Boise
Calgary
Regina
Winnipeg
St. Lawrence
Québec
St. John's
Montréal
Ottawa
Boston
Toronto
Detroit
Buffalo
L. Superior
L. Michigan
L. Huron
L. Ontario
L. Erie

Tufts
Abyssal
Plain
Snake

Northeast
Mendocino Fracture Zone C. Mendocino
Minneapolis
Missouri
Chicago
Pittsburgh
Cincinnati
New York
Philadelphia
Baltimore
Washington D.C.

Sacramento
San Francisco
6741
4418
Colorado
UNITED STATES
Denver
Kansas City
St. Louis
Memphis
Atlanta
ATLANTIC

Murray Fracture Zone
Oklahoma City
C. Hatteras

Los Angeles
San Diego
Phoenix
Dallas
Ciudad
Juárez
Houston
San Antonio
New
Orleans
Jacksonville
Bermuda
(U.K.)

Pacific
Guadalupe
(Mex.)
Baja California
Gulf of Mexico
Monterrey
Tampa
Miami
Sargasso Sea

Molokai Fracture Zone
MEXICO
BAHAMAS
OCEAN

Tropic of Cancer
Basin
C. San Lucas
La Habana
West Indies

Honolulu
Maui
HAWAIIAN IS.
(U.S.A.)
Kauai
Oahu
4205
Hilo
Hawaii
Golfo de California
Clarion Fracture Zone Is. Revilla Gigedo
(Mex.)
Guadalajara
Mexico
Puebla
Mérida
Canal de Yucatán
9200
CUBA
HAITI
DOMINICAN REP.
Leeward
Is.

Johnston I.
(U.S.A.)
CIFIC
Acapulco
GUATEMALA
BELIZE
7680
JAMAICA
Kingston
PUERTO
RICO
(U.S.A.)
BARBADOS

Middle America Trench
6610
HONDURAS
Guatemala
Caribbean Sea
Windward Is.

North West Christmas Ridge
Guatemala
Basin
6662
San Salvador
EL SALVADOR
NICARAGUA
Managua
San José
Barranquilla
San
Maracaibo

Palmyra Is.
(U.S.A.)
I. Clipperton
(Fr.)
COSTA
RICA
Colón
Panamá
Caracas
VENEZUELA

Basin
Cooper Ridge
Clipperton Fracture Zone
PANAMA
Panama
Basin
I. del Coco
(Costa Rica)
Medellín
Bogotá
COLOMBIA
Cali

OCEAN
Teraina
Tabuaeran
Kiritimati
Line Islands
Galápagos Fracture Zone
Galápagos
(Ecuador)
Carnegie Ridge
I. de Malpelo
(Colombia)
Quito
ECUADOR

Equator
Jarvis I.
(U.S.A.)
Malden I.
Starbuck I.
Guayaquil
C. Paliñas
Iquitos
BRAZIL
Amazonas

KIBATI
Penrhyn
(Tongareva)
Manihiki
Pukapuka
Plateau
Manihiki
Vostok I.
Caroline I.
(Millennium I.)
Nuku Hiva
Îs. Marquises
Hiva Oa
Marquesas Fracture Zone
Yupanqui
Basin
Mendaña
Fracture Zone
Trujillo

SAMER.
SAMOA
(U.S.A.)
Suwarrow Is.
Îs. de la
Société
Flint I.
Rangiroa
East Pacific Ridge
6369
PERU
Lima
Cuzco

Swains I.
Bora Bora
Huahine
Raiatéa
Papeete
Tahiti
Îs. Tuamotu
Galápagos Rise
Peru Basin
L. Titicaca
6550
Nevado Ancohuma
Arequipa
La Paz
BOLIVIA

Niue
(N.Z.)
Cook Is.
(N.Z.)
Aitutaki
Atiu
Australs Seamount Chain
FRENCH POLYNESIA
Îs. Gambier
6866
Peru-
Arica
Iquique
Chile

Rarotonga
Mangaia
Îs. Tubuaï
Mururoa
Tropic of Capricorn
Antofagasta
PARAGUAY

Chile Ridge
Oeno I.
Henderson I.
Pitcairn I.
(U.K.)
Ducie I.
Easter Fracture Zone
Sala y Gómez Ridge
Sala-y-Gómez
(Chile)
I. de Pascua
(Chile)
San Felix
(Chile)
San Ambrosio
(Chile)
8050
Trench
San Miguel
de Tucumán
Asunción
Córdoba
Pôrto
Alegre

Rapa
Roggeveen
Basin
Arch. de
Juan Fernández
(Chile)
Valparaíso
Aconcagua
6962
Rosario
URUGUAY
Montevideo

Southwest
Challenger Fracture Zone
Chile Rise
Santiago
Buenos
Aires
Río de la Plata

Pacific
Concepción
ARGENTINA
SOUTH

Basin
Pacific-Antarctic Ridge
East Pacific Rise
Menard Fracture Zone
ATLANTIC

OCEAN
6212

Falkland Is.
(U.K.)

Southeast
Pacific Basin
Punta Arenas
Est. de Magallanes
Tierra del Fuego
C. de Hornos
Drake Passage
South Georgia
(U.K.)

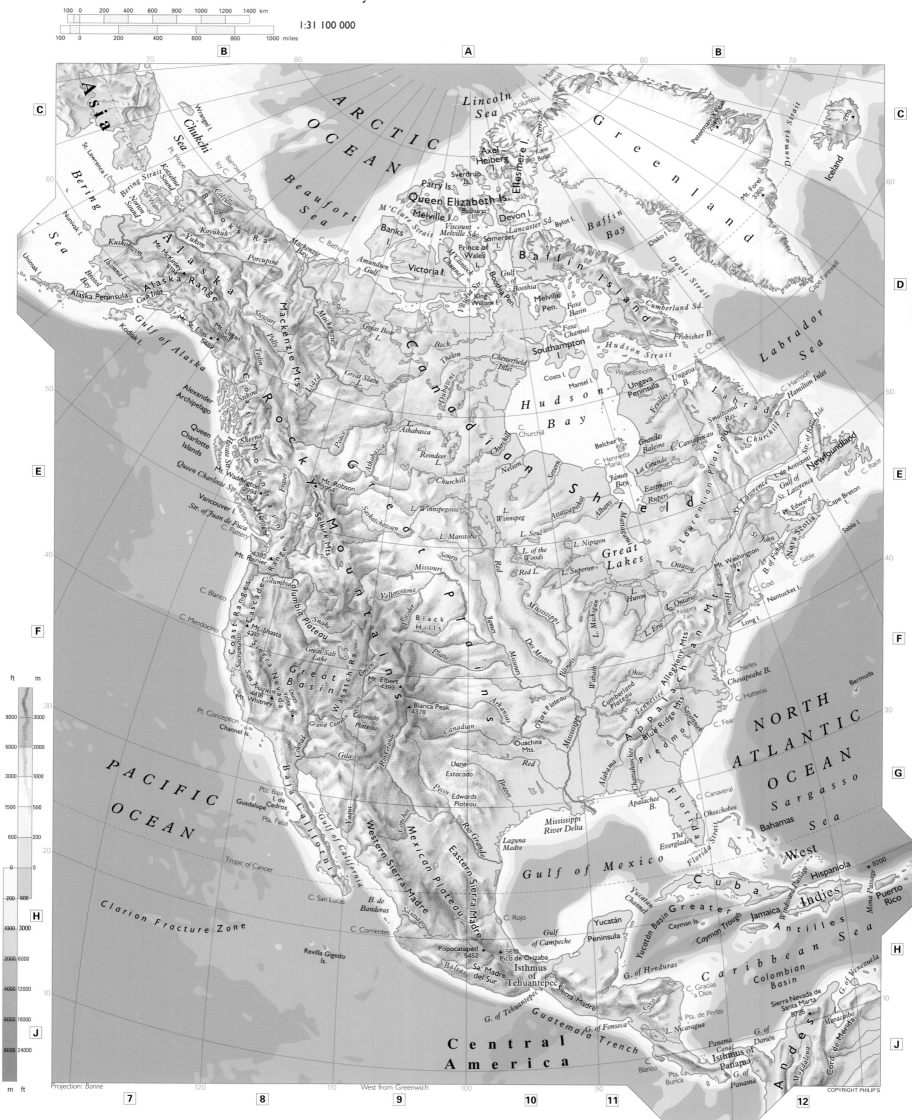

Projection: Bonne

West from Greenwich

COPYRIGHT PHILIP'S

1:31 100 000

1:31 100 000

100 0   200   400   600   800   1000 1200 1400 km

100 0   200   400   600   800   1000 miles

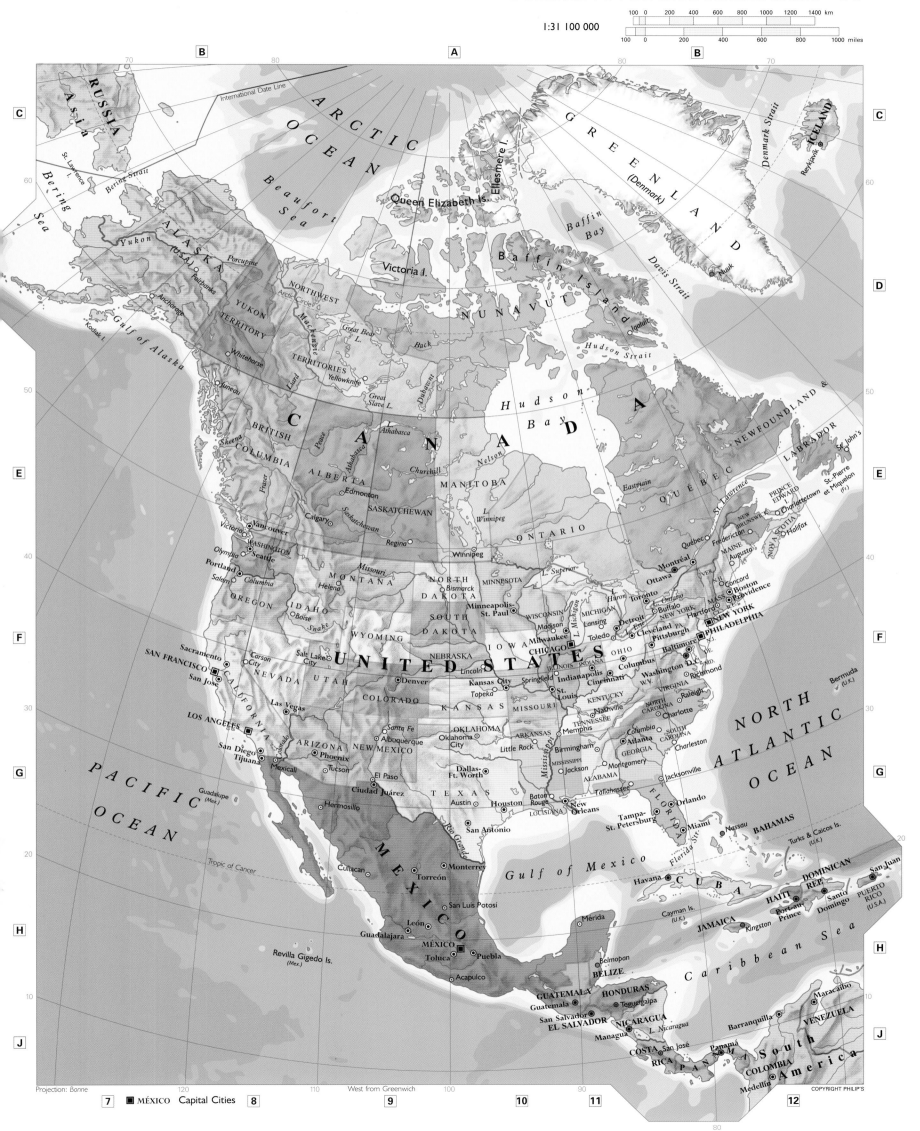

B   80   A   80   B

C   70   70   C

RUSSIA
Asia

ARCTIC OCEAN

International Date Line

St. Lawrence
I.

Bering Strait

60   60

Beaufort Sea

Bering Sea

Queen Elizabeth Is.

Ellesmere I.

GREENLAND
(Denmark)

Denmark Strait

ICELAND
Reykjavik

C

Baffin Bay

ALASKA
(USA)

Yukon
Porcupine

Fairbanks

Anchorage

Victoria I.

Baffin Island

Nuuk

D   D

Kodiak I.

Gulf of Alaska

Arctic Circle

Whitehorse

YUKON TERRITORY

NORTHWEST

Mackenzie

Great Bear L.

N U N A V U T

Hudson Strait

Iqaluit

Davis Strait

Juneau

Liard

TERRITORIES

Yellowknife

Dubawnt

Back

Great Slave L.

50   50

Skeena

BRITISH COLUMBIA

Peace

Athabasca

Athabasca

C   A   N   A   D   A

Churchill

Nelson

Hudson Bay

NEWFOUNDLAND &

LABRADOR

St. John's

Fraser

ALBERTA

Edmonton

Saskatchewan

MANITOBA

L. Winnipeg

Eastmain

QUÉBEC

St. Lawrence

E   E

Victoria

Vancouver

Calgary

SASKATCHEWAN

Regina

ONTARIO

Québec

PRINCE EDWARD

St-Pierre et Miquelon (Fr.)

WASHINGTON

Seattle

Winnipeg

NEW BRUNSWICK

Fredericton

NOVA SCOTIA

Charlottetown

Halifax

Olympia

40   40

Portland

Salem

Columbia

OREGON

Helena

MONTANA

Missouri

Bismarck

NORTH DAKOTA

MINNESOTA

L. Superior

L. Huron

Montréal

Ottawa

L. Ontario

VER.

MAINE

Augusta

N.H.

Concord

Boston

MASS.

Providence

F   F

Sacramento

SAN FRANCISCO

San Jose

Carson City

Salt Lake City

Boise

IDAHO

WYOMING

Snake

SOUTH DAKOTA

WISCONSIN

Madison

L. Michigan

MICHIGAN

Lansing

Toronto

Detroit

Buffalo

L. Erie

Cleveland

Toledo

PA

NEW YORK

Hartford

CT R.I.

NEW YORK

PHILADELPHIA

NEBRASKA

Lincoln

IOWA

CHICAGO

ILLINOIS

INDIANA

Pittsburgh

Baltimore

Washington D.C.

NEVADA

UTAH

U N I T E D   S T A T E S

Denver

Kansas City

Topeka

Springfield

St. Louis

Indianapolis

OHIO

Columbus

Cincinnati

W.V.

MD.

DEL.

Richmond

Las Vegas

LOS ANGELES

CALIFORNIA

San Diego

COLORADO

KANSAS

MISSOURI

KENTUCKY

Nashville

VIRGINIA

Raleigh

NORTH CAROLINA

Charlotte

G   G

Santa Fe

ARIZONA

NEW MEXICO

Oklahoma City

OKLAHOMA

ARKANSAS

Little Rock

Mississippi

Memphis

TENNESSEE

Birmingham

MISSISSIPPI

Jackson

ALABAMA

Montgomery

Atlanta

GEORGIA

Columbia

SOUTH CAROLINA

Charleston

NORTH ATLANTIC OCEAN

Bermuda (U.K.)

Phoenix

Tijuana

Mexicali

Tucson

El Paso

Dallas

Ft. Worth

Austin

TEXAS

Rio Grande

Houston

Baton Rouge

LOUISIANA

New Orleans

Tallahassee

Jacksonville

FLORIDA

Orlando

San Antonio

Guadalupe (Mex.)

PACIFIC OCEAN

Tropic of Cancer

Hermosillo

Culiacán

Torreón

Monterrey

Gulf of Mexico

Tampa-St. Petersburg

Miami

Florida Str.

Nassau

BAHAMAS

Turks & Caicos Is. (U.K.)

San Juan

H   H

M   É   X   I   C   O

San Luis Potosí

León

Guadalajara

Havana

CUBA

HAITI

DOMINICAN REP.

Port-au-Prince

Santo Domingo

PUERTO RICO
(U.S.A.)

Revilla Gigedo Is. (Mex.)

MÉXICO

Toluca

Puebla

Mérida

Cayman Is. (U.K.)

JAMAICA

Kingston

Caribbean Sea

Acapulco

BELIZE

Belmopan

GUATEMALA

Guatemala

HONDURAS

Tegucigalpa

Maracaibo

J   J

San Salvador

EL SALVADOR

Managua

NICARAGUA

L. Nicaragua

Barranquilla

VENEZUELA

COSTA RICA

San José

Panamá

PANAMA

COLOMBIA

Medellín

South America

Projection: Bonne

120   West from Greenwich   110   90   80

COPYRIGHT PHILIP'S

100 0 100 200 300 400 500 600 km
100 0 100 200 300 400 miles
1:13 300 000

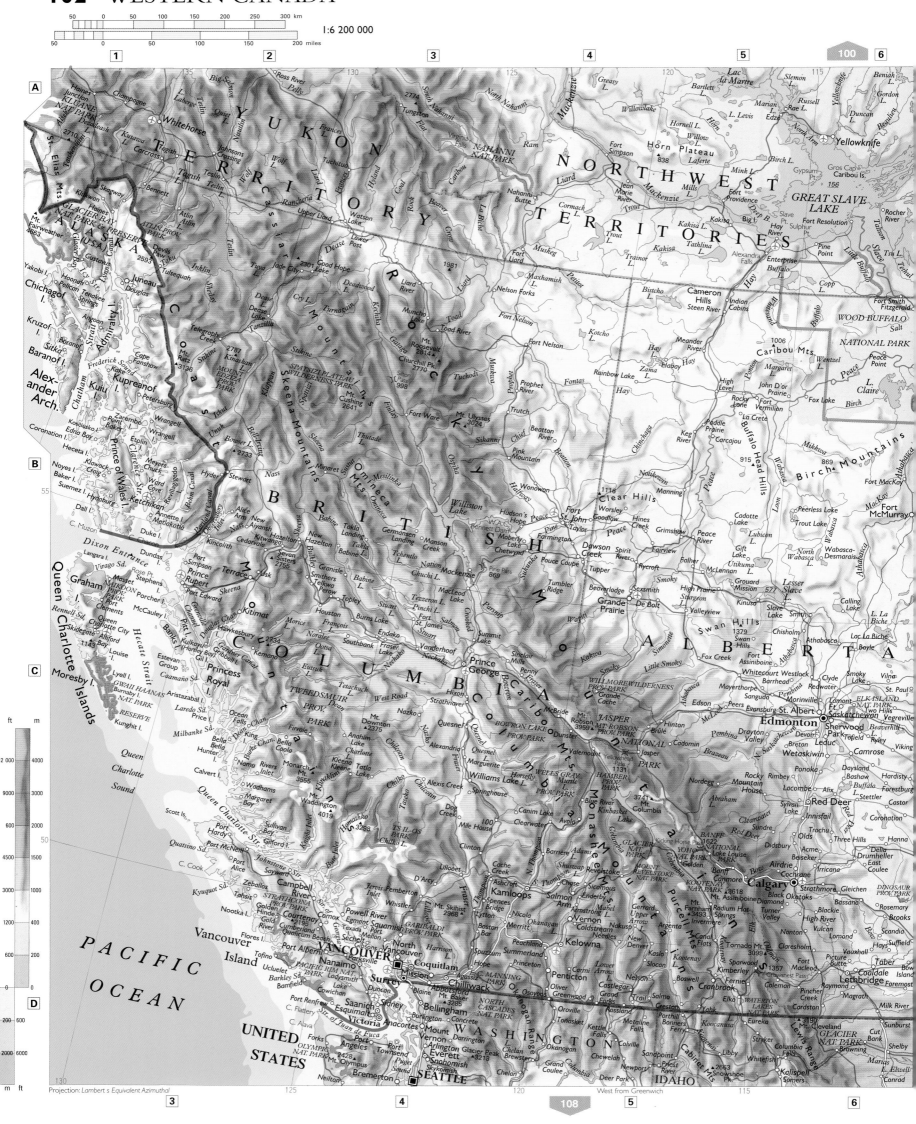

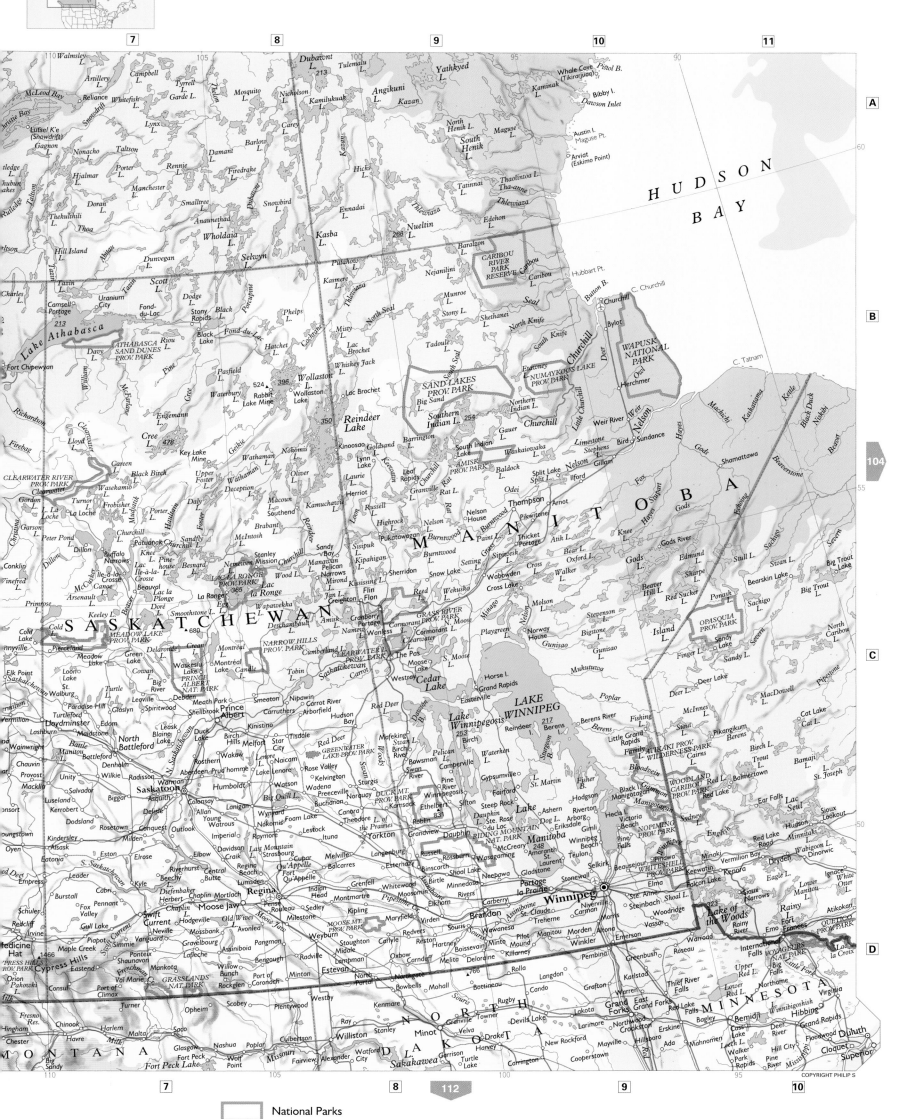

COPYRIGHT PHILIP'S

National Parks

1:6 200 000

Projection: Lambert's Equivalent Azimuthal

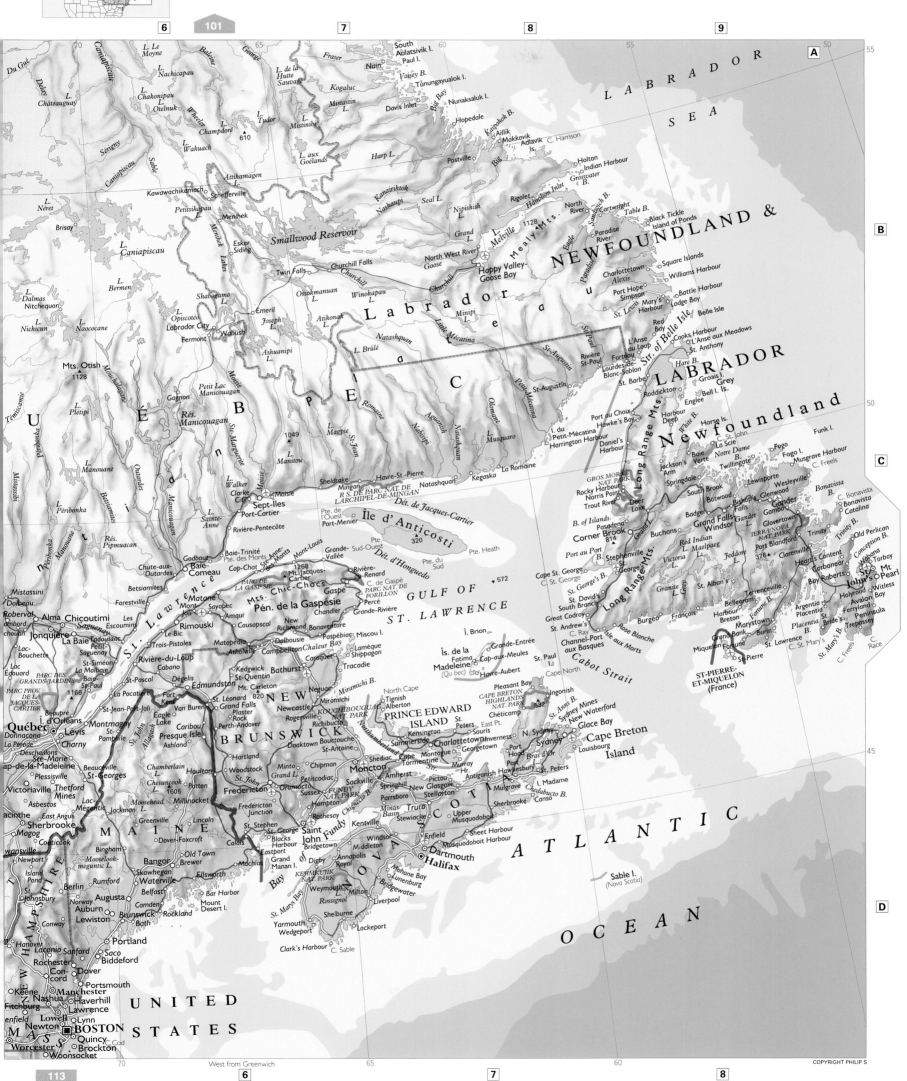

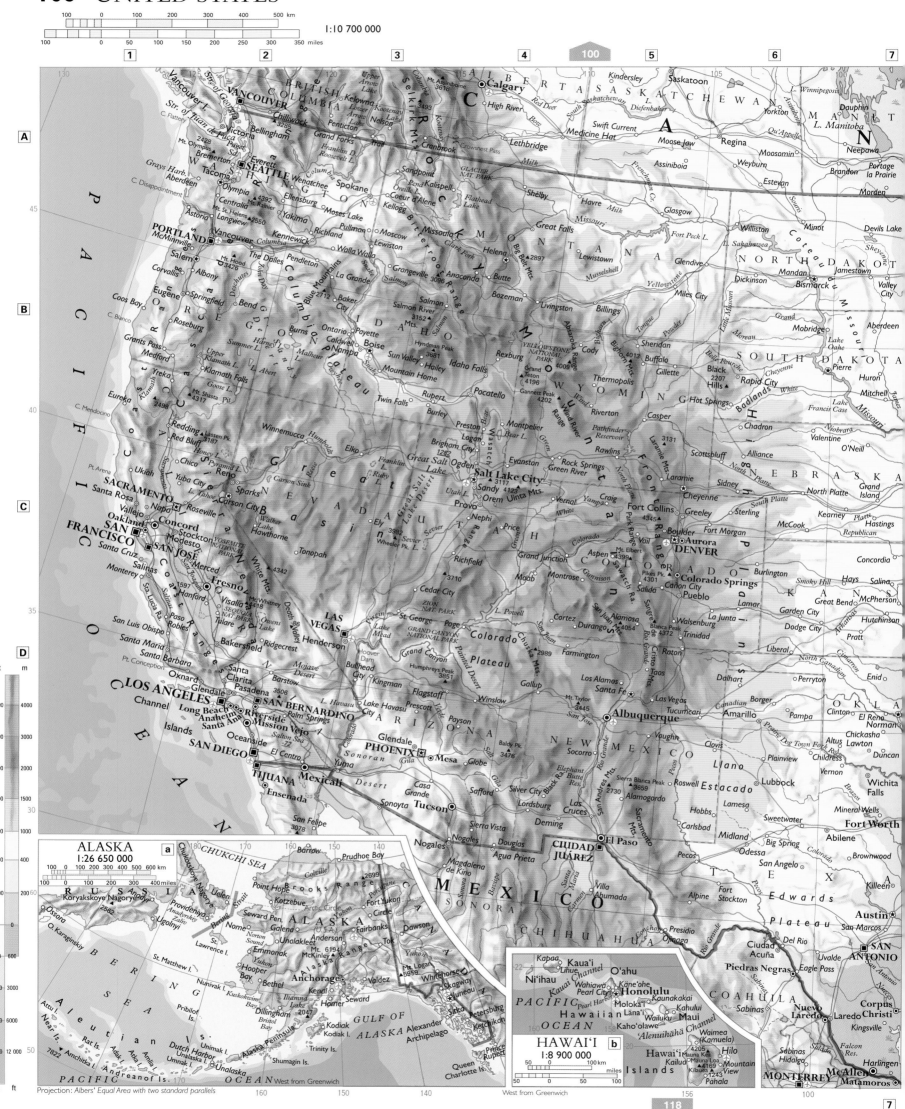

100   0   100   200   300   400   500 km
1:10 700 000
100   0   50   100   150   200   250   300   350 miles

1   **2**   **3**   **4**   **5**   **6**   **7**

A

B

C

D

E

ft   m
12 000   4000
9000   3000
6000   2000
4500   1500
3000   1000
1200   400
600   200
0   0
200   600
1000   3000
2000   6000
4000   12 000
m   ft

ALASKA
1:26 650 000
100   0   100   200   300   400   500   600 km
100   0   100   200   300   400 miles

HAWAI'I
1:8 900 000
50   0   50   100 km
50   0   50   100 miles

Projection: Albers' Equal Area with two standard parallels

West from Greenwich

118

Tallahassee ✶   U.S. state capitals

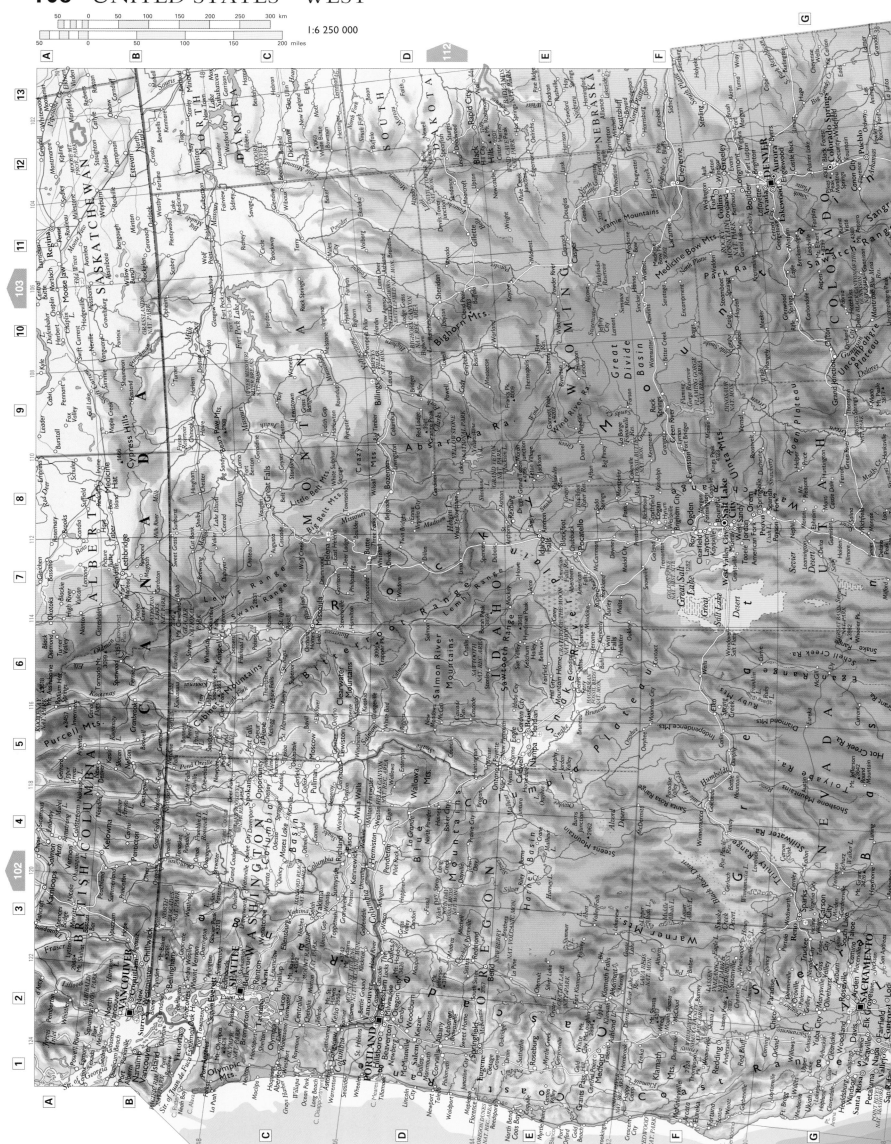

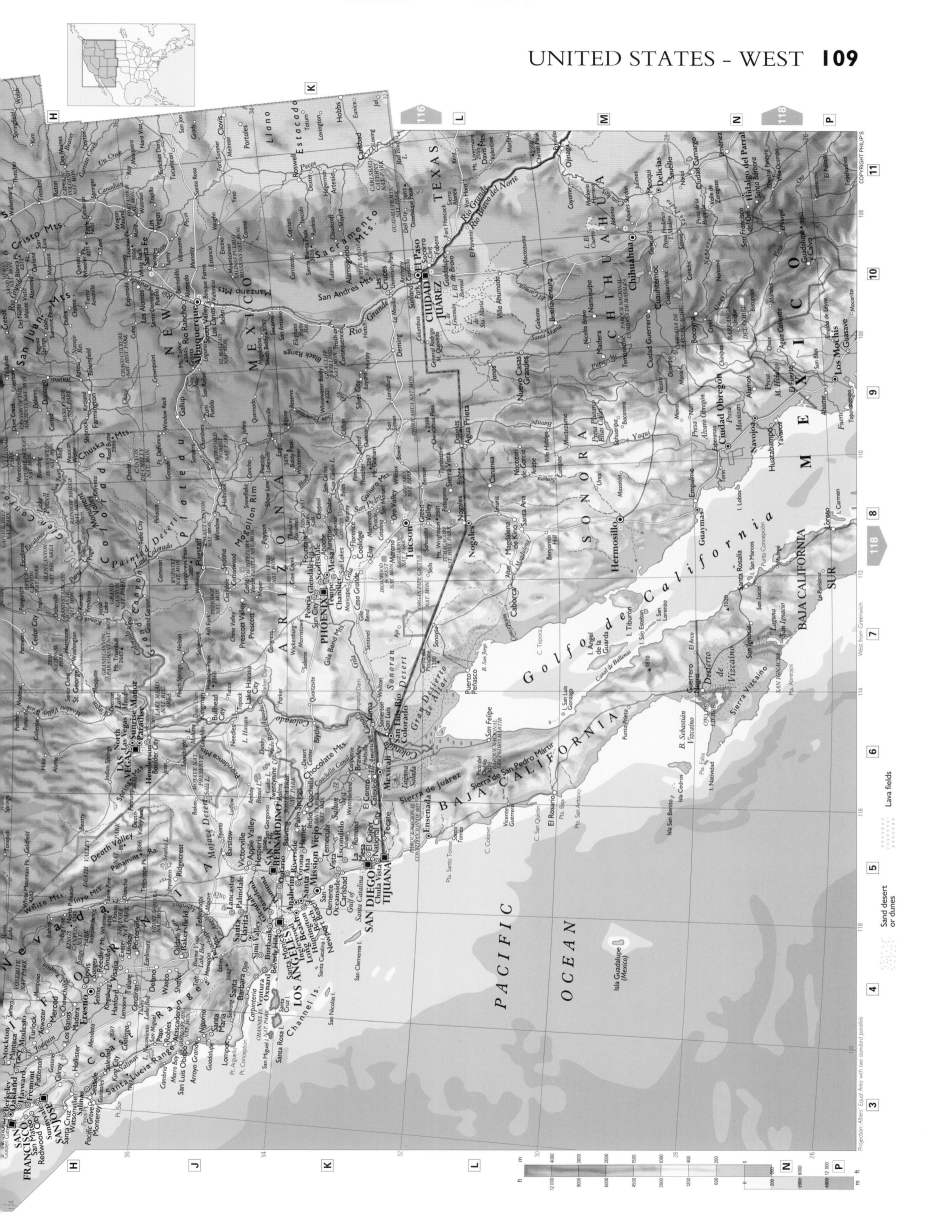

Projection: Albers' Equal Area with two standard parallels

Sand desert or dunes

Lava fields

1:2 200 000

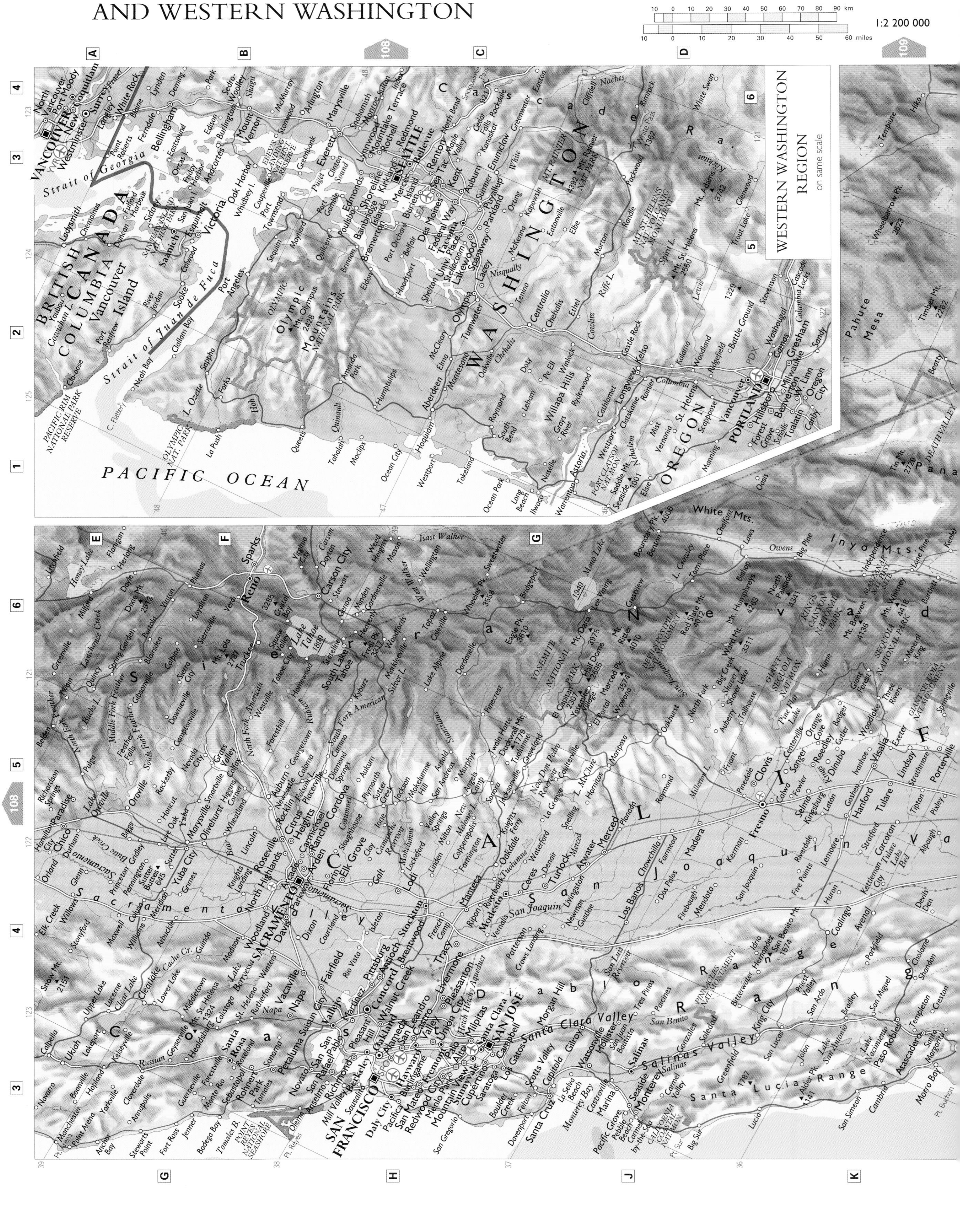

10 0 10 20 30 40 50 60 70 80 90 km
10 0 10 20 30 40 50 60 miles

WESTERN WASHINGTON REGION
on same scale

PACIFIC OCEAN

BRITISH COLUMBIA

Vancouver Island

Strait of Georgia

Strait of Juan de Fuca

OLYMPIC MOUNTAINS
Mt. Olympus 2428
OLYMPIC NATIONAL PARK

PACIFIC RIM NATIONAL PARK RESERVE

Victoria

Vancouver

Seattle

Tacoma

Olympia

WASHINGTON

Mt. Rainier 4392 Mt. Rainier Nat. Park

MT. ST. HELENS NAT. VOLCANIC MONUMENT
Mt. St. Helens 2550

Mt. Adams 3742

OREGON

Portland

PDX

Pahute Mesa

Inyo Mts.

Owens

White Mts.

KINGS CANYON NATIONAL PARK

SEQUOIA NATIONAL PARK

Mt. Whitney 4418

Mt. Williamson 4341

YOSEMITE NATIONAL PARK

El Capitan 2307

Half Dome

Mono Lake

Lake Tahoe 1899

Reno

Sparks

Carson City

SIERRA NEVADA

S a c r a m e n t o   V a l l e y

SACRAMENTO

Sacramento

San Joaquin Valley

Fresno

Visalia

Stockton

Modesto

Merced

SAN FRANCISCO

Oakland

SAN JOSE

Santa Clara Valley

Salinas Valley

Santa Lucia Range

Santa Rosa

Napa

Monterey

Santa Cruz

PINNACLES NATIONAL MONUMENT

DEATH VALLEY

Pana

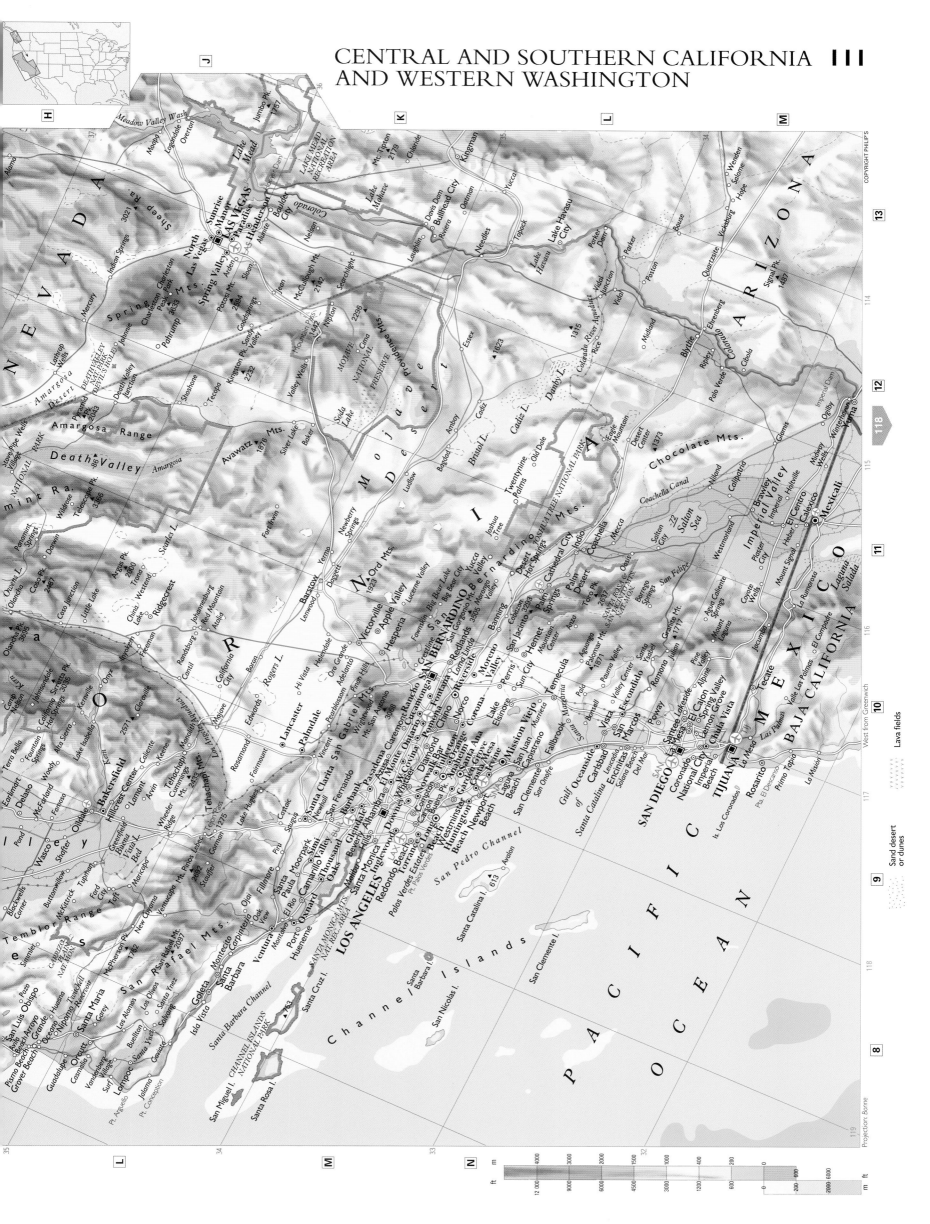

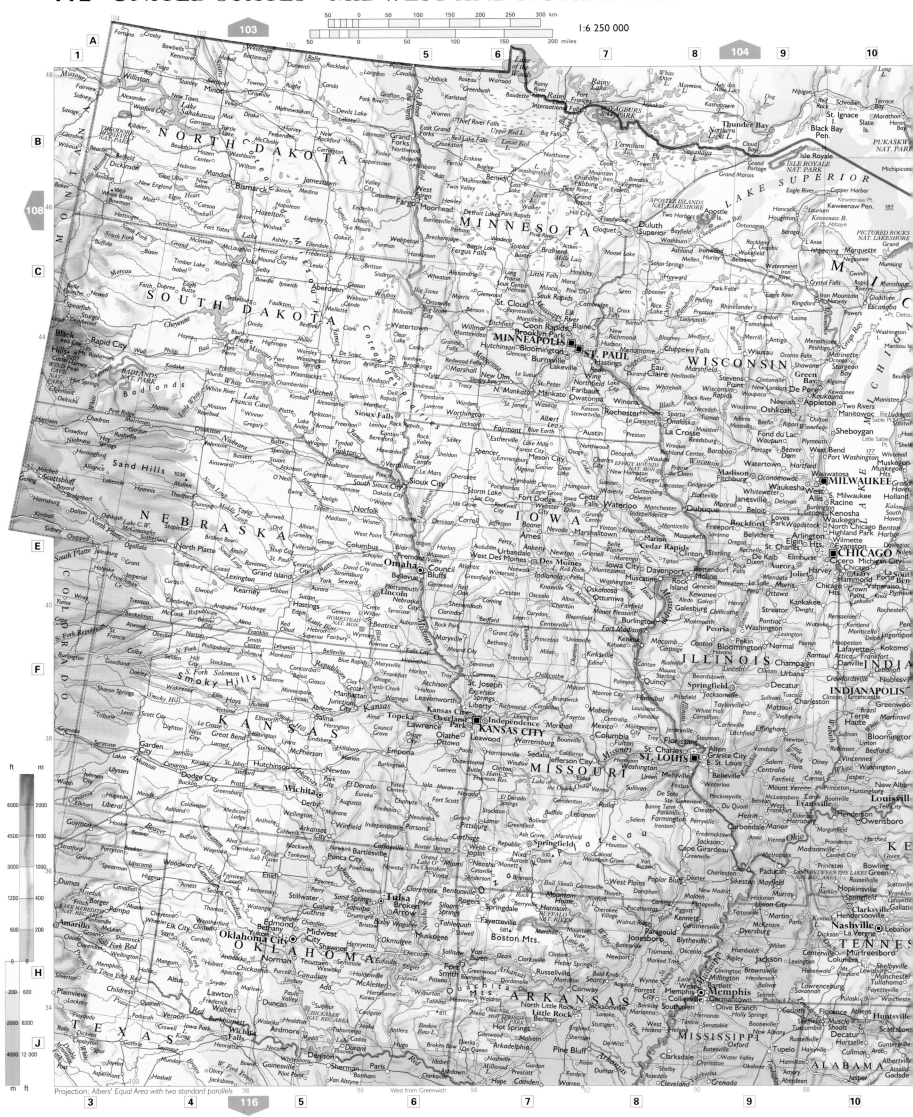

1:6 250 000

Projection: Albers' Equal Area with two standard parallels   West from Greenwich

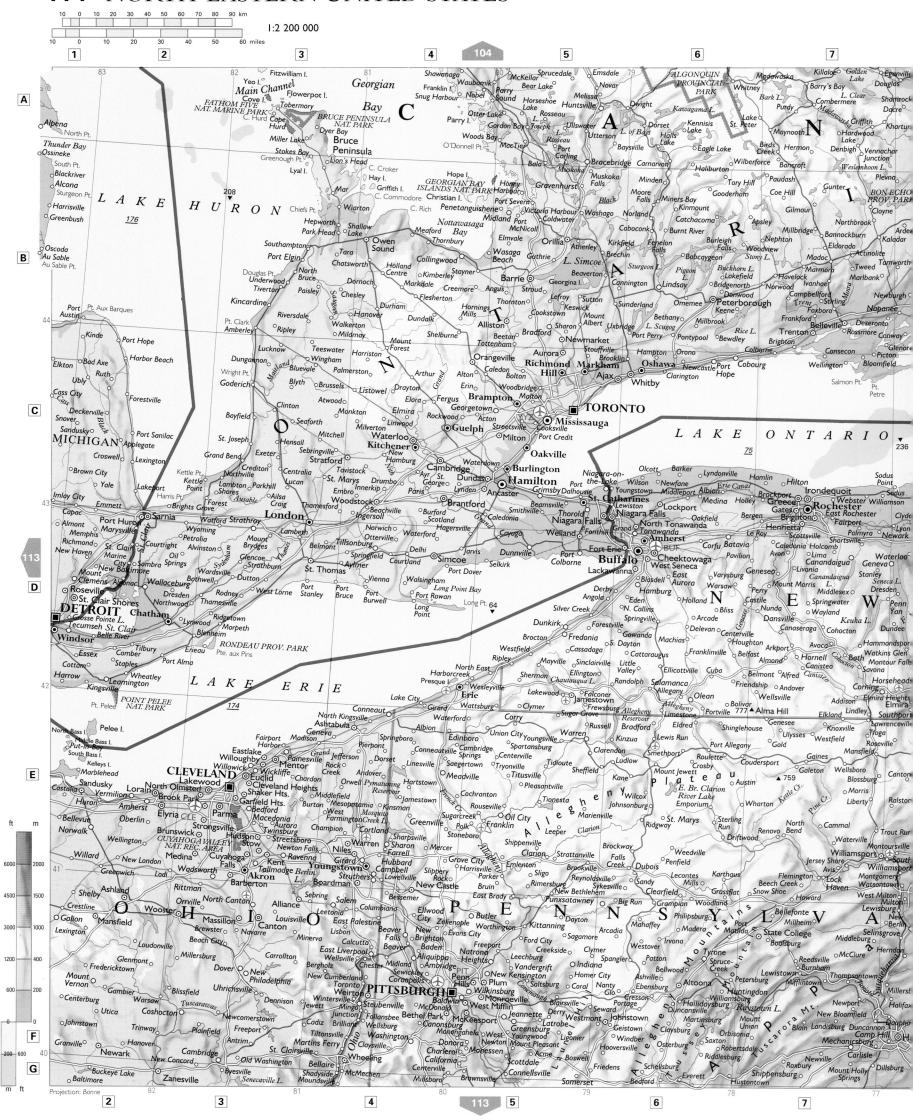

1:2 200 000

Projection: Bonne

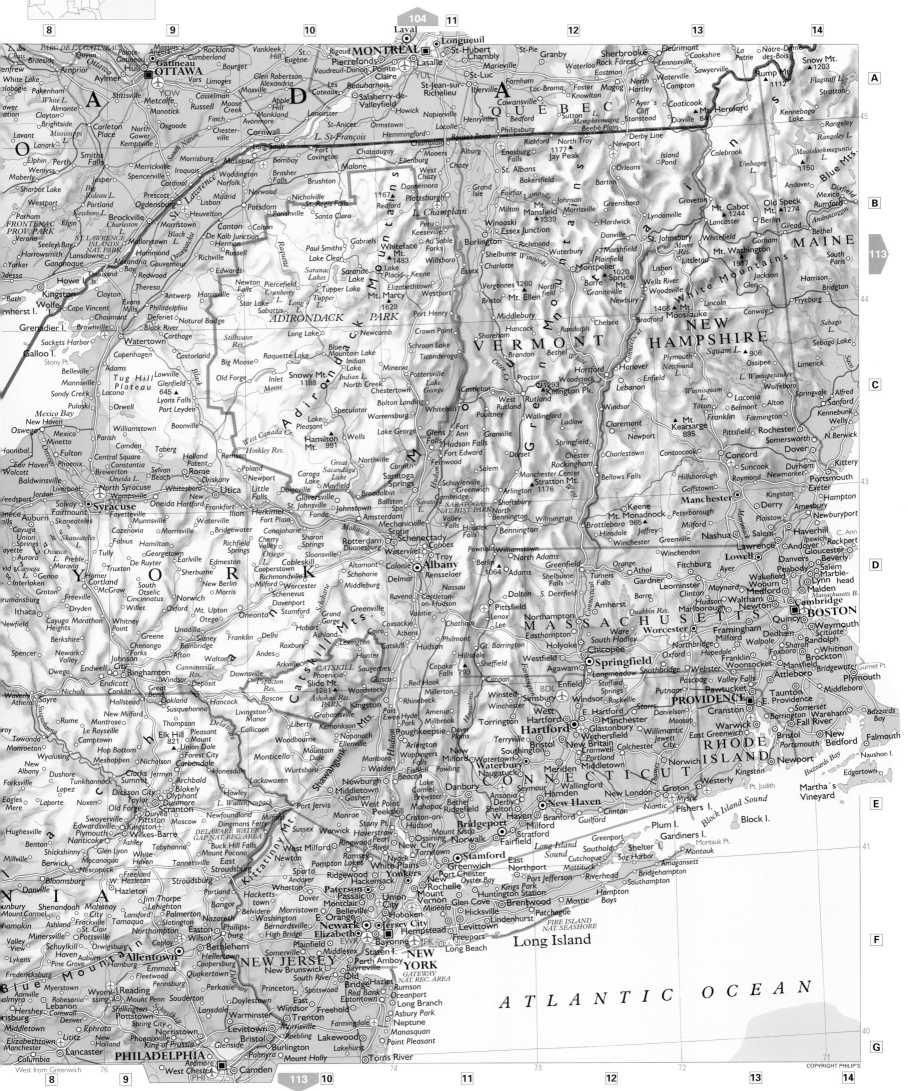

West from Greenwich

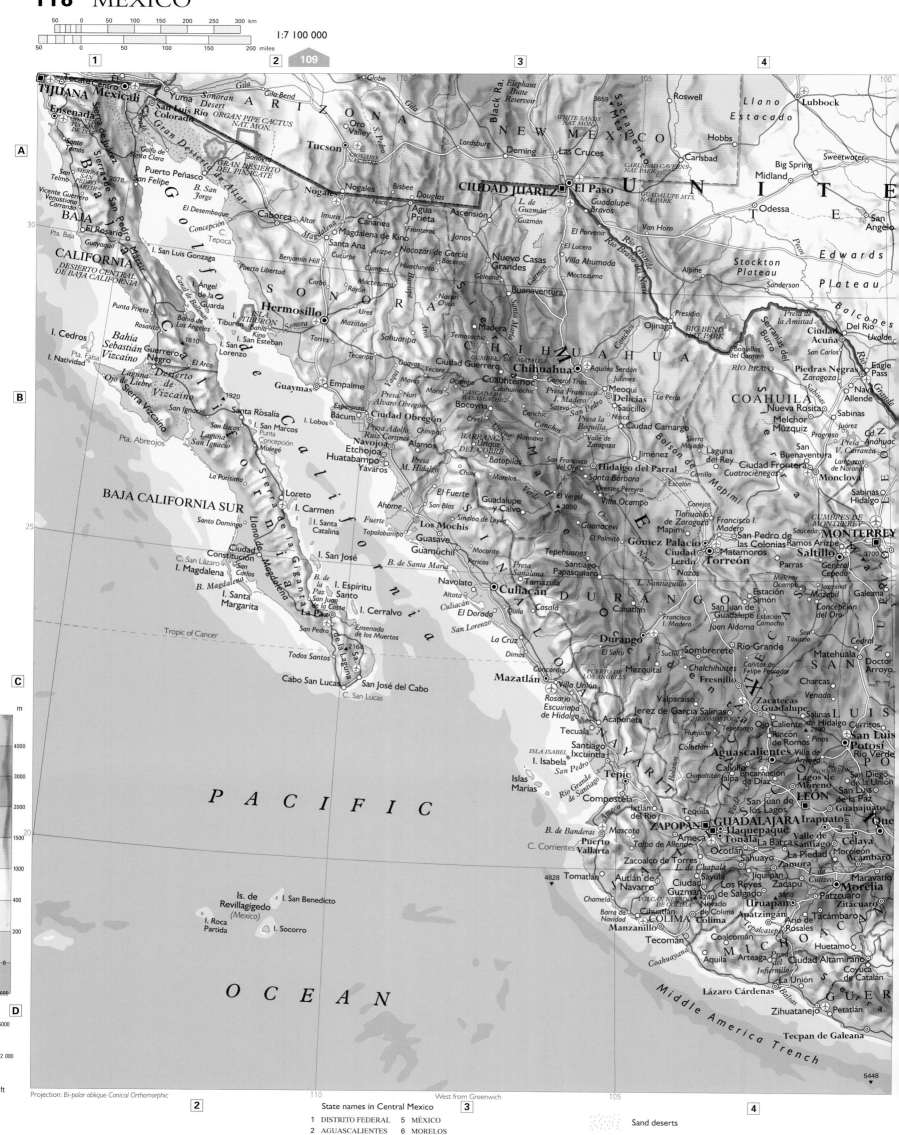

1:7 100 000

Projection: Bi-polar oblique Conical Orthomorphic

West from Greenwich

State names in Central Mexico

1 DISTRITO FEDERAL   5 MÉXICO
2 AGUASCALIENTES   6 MORELOS
3 GUANAJUATO   7 QUERÉTARO
4 HIDALGO   8 TLAXCALA

Sand deserts

5   **6**   117   **7**   **8**

Wichita
Falls
Denison
Sherman
Paris
Camden
Greenville
Tuscaloosa
Opelika
Columbus
Cordele
McRae
Denton
ARKANSAS
Texarkana
El Dorado
Greenville
Tombigbee
Phenix City
Columbus
Ozmulgee

Possum
Kingdom
Lake
Fort Worth
DALLAS
Cleburne
Longview
Monroe
Vicksburg
Meridian
Selma
Montgomery
Americus
Tifton
Waycross

Ranger
Hillsboro
Tyler
Marshall
Shreveport
MISSISSIPPI
Jackson
ALABAMA
Troy
GEORGIA

Abilene
Brownwood
Waco
Corsicana
Palestine
Toledo
Bend
Res.
Alexandria
Natchez
Laurel
Hattiesburg
Brewton
Dothan
Albany
Valdosta

A

Temple
Bryan
Lufkin
Nacogdoches
San
Rayburn
Reservoir
McComb
Bogalusa
Mobile
Pensacola
FLORIDA
Lake
City

HOUSTON
Huntsville
College Station
Baton
Rouge
Hammond
Biloxi
Gulfport
Panama City
Apalachee
Bay
Suwannee

B

San Antonio
Victoria
Beaumont
Port
Arthur
Lake Charles
Lafayette
NEW
ORLEANS
Bréton Sd.
C. San Blas

Dilley
Galveston
Rosenberg
Atchafalaya
Bay
Terrebonne Bay
Mississippi
River Delta
Clearwater

Nueces

GULF   **OF**

Corpus Christi

Laredo
Kingsville
Alice
PADRE ISLAND
NAT. SEASHORE

Nuevo Laredo
Zapata
Laguna Madre

MEXICO

Presa
Falcón
McAllen
Harlingen
Brownsville

General
Treviño
Camargo
Reynosa
China
Río Bravo
Matamoros

Cadereyta Jiménez
Valle Hermoso
Santa Teresa
Laguna Madre

C

Montemorelos
Villa de Méndez
Tropic of Cancer

Linares
San Fernando
Banco
Campeche

Villagrán
Santander Jiménez
I. Desterrada
I. Pérez
(Mexico)
CUBA
Guane
La Fé
La Esperanza

Villa
Hidalgo
Zaragoza
Soto la Marina
C. San Antonio
C. Corrientes

Ciudad
Victoria
Sierra de Tamaulipas
Pta.
Yalkubul
Río Lagartos
C. Catoche
Isla
Mujeres
Cancún

Llera de
Canales
Tula
Aldama
Pta. Jerez
Dzilam
de Bravo
Temax
El Cuyo

Ocampo
Canal de Yucatán

Tula
González
Progreso
Motul
Izamal
Espita
Tizimín
Puerto Morelos

Ciudad Mante
Altamira
Ciudad Madero
Dzibilchaltún
Maxcanú
Mérida
YUCATÁN
Chichén
Itzá
Valladolid
Playa del Carmen
Isla
Cozumel

Cárdenas
Ebano
Ciudad
Valles
Tampico
Pánuco
Mayapán
Ticul
Sotuta
Cozumel

TO SÍ
Ozuluama
L. de Tamiahua
Tekax
Peto
Tulum

Tantoyuca
C. Rojo
Teabo
Bolonchén

Jalpan
Tempoal
de Sánchez
Naranjos
Uxmal
D

Chicontepec
Tamazunchale
Tuxpan
Teyabo
Campeche
B. de la Ascensión
SIAN KA'AN
B. del Espíritu Santo

Zimapán
Zacualtipán
Poza Rica
Nautla
Edzná
Hopelchén
Felipe
Carrillo
Puerto
QUINTANA
ROO
Yucatan
Basin

retaro
San Juan del Río
Huauchinango
Misantla
Champotón
Xochob
Bacalar
Banco
Chinchorro

Tula
Pachuca
Zumpango
Tulancingo
Teziutlán
Papantla
Golfo
de
Campeche
Chetumal
B. de
Chetumal

El Oro
Teotihuacán
Apizaco
Coatepec
Xalapa
Zempoala
Veracruz
Ciudad del
Carmen
L. de
Términos
Escárcega
Corozal
Ambergris Cay

MÉXICO
Toluca
Ecatepec
Tlaxcala
Pico de Orizaba
Boca del Río
San Andrés
Tuxtla
Frontera
PANTANOS
DE CENTLA
Palizada
CAMPECHE
Orange Walk
San Pedro

Tenancingo
Amecameca
Popocatépetl
Córdoba
Orizaba
Alvarado
Tlacotalpan
Paraíso
Villahermosa
Balancán
CALAKMUL
BELIZE
Belize
City
Turneffe Is.
Barrier

PUEBLA
Tehuacán
Cosamaloapan
Tierra
Blanca
Comalcalco
TABASCO
Macuspana
LAGUNA
DEL TIGRE
MIRADOR
RÍO AZUL
Uaxactún
San Ignacio
Belmopan
Reef

Guernavaca
Taxco
Izúcar de
Matamoros
San Gabriel
Ajalpan
Tres Valles
Acayucan
Minatitlán
Cárdenas
Teapa
Palenque
Tenosique
SIERRA DE
LACANDÓN
TIKAL
Benque
Viejo
Victoria Pk.
Is. de
la Bahía

Iguala
Chiautla
Acatlán
Huajuapan
de León
Asunción
Nochixtlán
Miguel
Alemán
Tuxtepec
Valle Nacional
Jesús Carranza
Copainalá
Simojovel
Ocosingo
L. Petén Itzá
La Libertad
Flores
Dangriga
Roatán

RERO
Chilapa
Chilpancingo
Huautla
Tlaxiaco
Silacayoápan
Istmo
de
Tehuantepec
Chiapa de
Corzo
MONTES
AZULES
CHIQUIBUL
Playa Vista Ms.
Monkey River
Punta Gorda
La
Ceiba

Coyuca
de Benítez
Ayutla de los Libres
Ometepec
Oaxaca
MONTE ALBÁN
Tlacolula
San Jerónimo Ixtepec
Matías Romero
Tuxtla
Gutiérrez
San Cristóbal de
las Casas
La Independencia
Comitán de Domínguez
San Luis
San Antonio
Golfo de Honduras
Puerto
Barrios
Livingston
Puerto
Cortés
Choloma
San Pedro Sula
El Progreso

Acapulco
Santiago
Pinotepa Nacional
OAXACA
Ocotlán
San Jerónimo
Taviche
Ejutla
Juchitán de
Zaragoza
Tehuantepec
CAÑÓN DEL
SUMIDERO
Arriaga
Tonalá
CHIAPAS
Angostura
La Concordia
Cuilco
L. de Izabal
Zacapa
Gualán
Santa
Bárbara
L. de
Yojoa
Villanueva
Danlí
E

Punta
Maldonado
LAGUNAS DE
CHACAHUA
San Pedro
Tututepec
Barras de
Chacahua
3139
Salina Cruz
Puerto
Arista
Pijijiapan
Mapastepec
Sierra de los Cuchumatanes
Huehuetenango
Cobán
Jalapa
Chiquimula
Copán
Santa Rosa
de Copán
Siguatepeque
Comayagua
Catacamas

Puerto
Escondido
Puerto Ángel
Verde
Golfo de
Huatulco
Motozintla de
Mendoza
Huixtla
Tapachula
Retalhuleu
San Marcos
Totonicapán
Sololá
GUATEMALA
Antigua
Mazate-
nango
Amatitlán
ESCUINTLA
Jutiapa
HONDURAS
La Paz
TEGUCIGALPA

Tehuantepec
Puerto Madero
ATITLÁN
Yuscarán

5   **6**   **7**   **8**

120

120

COPYRIGHT PHILIP'S

5

PUERTO RICO **d**
1:2 700 000
10 0 10 20 30 40 50 km
10 0 10 20 30 miles

VIRGIN ISLANDS **e**
1:1 800 000
10 0 10 20 30 km
10 0 10 20 miles

ATLANTIC OCEAN

PUERTO RICO
(U.S.A.)

Pta. Agujereada
Aguadilla Isabela Barceloneta SAN JUAN
Arecibo Manati Vega Baja Bayamón Rio Grande Dewey
Mayagüez San Sebastian Utuado Carolina Sierra de Fajardo Culebra
San German Adjuntas Cordillera Central Caguas Luquillo Pta. Vieques
Yauco Mts. de Cerro Humacao Puerca Esperanza
San German Uroyan 1338 de Punta Cayey Yabucoa
Guanica Coamo Naguabo
Pta. Aguila Ponce Guayama
I. Caja de Muertos

Rufling Pt. The Settlement
Anegada East Pt.
Virgin Islands (U.K.)
Jost Van Guana I. Great Camanoe
Virgin Is. Dyke I. 521 Beef Virgin Gorda
(U.S.A.) Haas Lollik I. Tortola Road Town Spanish Town
Cruz Bay VIRGIN IS. Peter I.
Charlotte St. St. John I.
Amalie Thomas I.

ST. LUCIA **f**
1:890 000
5 0 10 km
5 0 5 10 miles

Cap Point
Gros Islet Pte. Hardy
Castries Esperance Bay
Girard Marquis
Anse la Raye
Canaries Millet Dennery
Soufrière Mt. Gimie
Soufrière 950 Trou Gras Pt.
Bay 750 Petit Piton Micoud
Gros Piton Pt. 796 Vierge Pt.
Choiseul Gros Piton
Laborie ST. LUCIA
Vieux Fort
C. Moule à Chique

6 **B** **7**

Crab Hill North Point ATLANTIC OCEAN
Fustic Spring Hall
Portland Boscobelle
Speightstown 245 Belleplaine
Westmoreland Bathsheba BARBADOS
Alleynes Bay Mt. Hillaby Hillcrest
Holetown 340 Martin's Bay
Jackson Bridgefield Massiah
Street
Black Rock Ellerton Six Cross Roads
Bridgetown Ivy Edey The Crane
Carlisle Bay Oistins St. Martins
Worthing BGI Chancery Lane
Oistins South Point
Bay

BARBADOS **g**
1:890 000
5 0 10 km
5 0 5 10 miles

AMAS

ATLANTIC OCEAN

Arthur's Town
New Bight
Cat I.
San Salvador I.
Conception I.
Rum Cay Tropic of Cancer
Long I.
Clarence Samana Cay
Town
Cay Verde Crooked I. Plana Cays
Albert Snug Mayaguana I.
Town Corner Acklins I.
Mira por vos Cay
Hogsty Reef
Cay Santa Little Inagua I.
Domingo Turks & Caicos Is.
INAGUA Caicos Is. (U.K.)
C. Lucrecia Lake Rose Cockburn Town
Moa Matthew Great Turks Is.
Mayari Town Inagua I.
Baracoa Silver Bank Passage Navidad Bank
Guantánamo Mouchoir Bank Silver Bank
Maisí
GUANTANAMO Pta. de Maisí
BAY (U.S.A.) Monte Puerto Rico Trench
Cap- Cristi Milwaukee
Haitien LA ISABELA Deep
Jérémie Port-de-Paix Puerto 9200
Jamaica Channel Paso de los Vientos Plata Santiago de
(Windward Passage) los Caballeros
Cap-à- Gonaïves La Vega San Francisco de Macoris
Foux Hinche Central Nagua Samana
St-Marc 3175 Sánchez Sabana de la Mar
HAITI DOMINICAN LOS Aguadilla Arecibo Bayamón SAN JUAN
PORT- Pico Duarte REP. Hato Mayor Carolina
AU-PRINCE HAITISES Higuey Virgin Gorda Anegada
San Juan C. Engaño Tortola Virgin Is. (U.K.) Sombrero (U.K.)
L. Enriquillo SANTO St. Thomas Road Town Anguilla (U.K.)
SIERRA DE DOMINGO Fajardo St-Martin (Fr.)
Les Cayes Aquin 2680 BAORUCO Mayagüez Ponce Culebra Charlotte Amalie St-Barthélemy (Fr.)
Jacmel Azua Bani Isla Guayama Vieques Virgin Is. Saba (Neth.) Barbuda
Pointe-à-Gravois Barahona Mona PUERTO (U.S.A.) St. Eustatius ANTIGUA
I. à Vache Pedernales Compostela RICO Christiansted (Neth.) St. Kitts & BARBUDA
C. Beata (U.S.A.) St. Croix Basseterre & NEVIS St. John's
C. Beata Frederiksted (U.S.A.) Nevis Antigua
Redonda Soufrière
Hispaniola Montserrat 914 Guadeloupe Passage
(U.K.)
Antilles Ste-Rose Le Moule La Désirade
GUADELOUPE Pointe-à-Pitre
(Fr.) 1467 Marie-Galante (Fr.)
Basse-Terre Grand-Bourg
(Fr.) I. des Saintes
Dominica Passage
Beata Ridge Portsmouth 1447 DOMINICA
Morne
CARIBBEAN Diablotin MORNE
Venezuelan Roseau TROIS PITONS
Martinique Passage
SEA Basin I. de Aves Mt. Pelée Ste-Marie
(Venezuela) 1397 Le François
Fort-de- Rivière-Pilote
COLOMBIAN France MARTINIQUE
BASIN St. Lucia Channel (Fr.)
Castries ST. LUCIA
Soufrière
Aves Ridge St. Vincent Passage
Colombian Soufrière 1234 St. Vincent
Basin Speightstown 340
Kingstown BARBADOS
Bridgetown
ABC Lesser Bequia ST. VINCENT
Islands Antilles The Grenadines & THE
Aruba Canouan GRENADINES
Oranjestad (Neth.) Curaçao Carriacou
C. San Román Bonaire St. George's 840 GRENADA
MACUIRA Pen. de Willemstad NETH.
Pta. Gallinas Paraguaná ANTILLES ARC. LOS I. Blanquilla (Ven.)
Pen. de la Punto Fijo Is. Las Aves ROQUES Is. Los Hermanos Tobago
COLOMBIA Guajira Pta. (Ven.) Is. Los Roques (Ven.) Is. Los Testigos Scarborough
Espada (Ven.) NUEVA (Ven.) Port of
Ríohacha Uribia Punta ESPARTA CERRO EL COPEY Spain Galera Pt.
Santa GUAJIRA Cardón Golfo de I. de Margarita 987 Trinidad
Marta ISLA DE San Venezuela La Asunción 940
ARRAN- TAYRONA SALAMANCA Rafael Coro La Vela MEDANOS DE CORO Porlamar Pen. de Paria Arima
QUILLA Ciénaga SA. NEVADA DE CUEVA DE LA Cumaná Carúpano Río Claro
Baranoa SANTA MARTA QUEBRADA HENRI Cariaco Güiria San
TLANTICO Sierra Nevada de Altagracia DEL TORO PITTIER MOCHIMA G. de Paria Fernando
Soledad Santa Marta Mene de Mauroa Tucacas Maiquetía La Guaira TRINIDAD
Sabanalarga 5775 FALCÓN Puerto MARACAY CARACAS Puerto Barcelona & TOBAGO
Fundación La Concepción Tocuyo Cabello VARGAS Higuerote La Cruz Caicara
Calamar Villa del MIRANDA Río Chico MARIUSA
Magdalena Rosario Cabimas LARA Turmero Los Teques Maturín
Plato Ciudad Carora VALENCIA Ocumare del Tuy DELTA
Zambrano Agustín Ojeda Barquisimeto Yaritagua CARABOBO San Juan MONAGAS
Codazzi YARACUY Villa de los Morros Anaco Tucupita
Mompós Machiques San Felipe de Cura Altagracia de Orituco Caripito
Corozal CÉSAR Lago de El Tocuyo San Carlos El Tigre
Magangué Maracaibo San Carlos COJEDES Aragua de AMACURO
El Banco ZULIA Mene Grande Barcelona MONAGAS Ciudad Guayana
Encontrados CIÉNAGAS DEL Acarigua El Sombrero Valle de ANZOATEGUI
Sahagún CATATUMBO El Guache la Pascua Pariaguán
San Carlos GUARICO Santa María El Callao
Planeta del Zulia Betijoque PORTUGUESA Calabozo de Ipire Los Barrancos
Ocaña Valera Guanare El Baúl Tumeremo
Ayapel CATATUMBO-BARI Trujillo Portuguesa Upata
OBA NORTE Barinas Ciudad Guasipati
Caucasia MERIDA Libertad Bolívar
Cúcuta MÉRIDA Barinas Embalse de Guri
SANTANDER TACHIRA Ciudad de Nutrias Orinoco
SIERRA NEVADA BARINAS San Fernando Caicara
Simití 2640 de Apure
Santa Ciudad Mapire
TACHIRA Bárbara Bolivia VENEZUELA Apure Guasipati
Bruzual Achaguas

75 West from Greenwich 70 65 60

4000 3000 2000 1500 1000 400 200 0 ft
12 000 9000 6000 4500 3000 1200 600 0 600 6000 12 000 18 000 24 000 ft
200 2000 4000 6000 8000 m

1:31 100 000

Projection: Lambert's Azimuthal Equal Area

COPYRIGHT PHILIP'S

1:31 100 000

| 100 | 0 | 200 | 400 | 600 | 800 | 1000 | 1200 | 1400 km |

| 100 | 0 | 200 | 400 | 600 | 800 | 1000 miles |

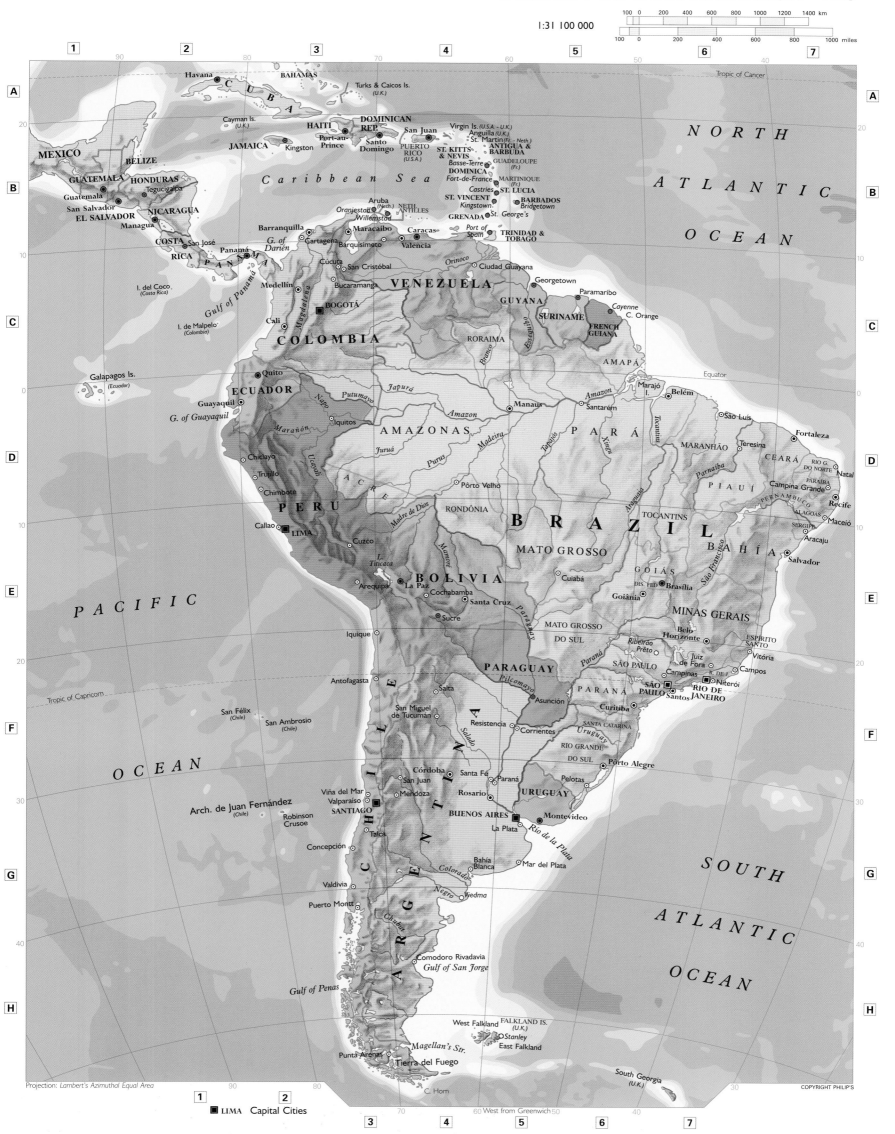

Projection: Lambert's Azimuthal Equal Area

COPYRIGHT PHILIP'S

■ LIMA Capital Cities

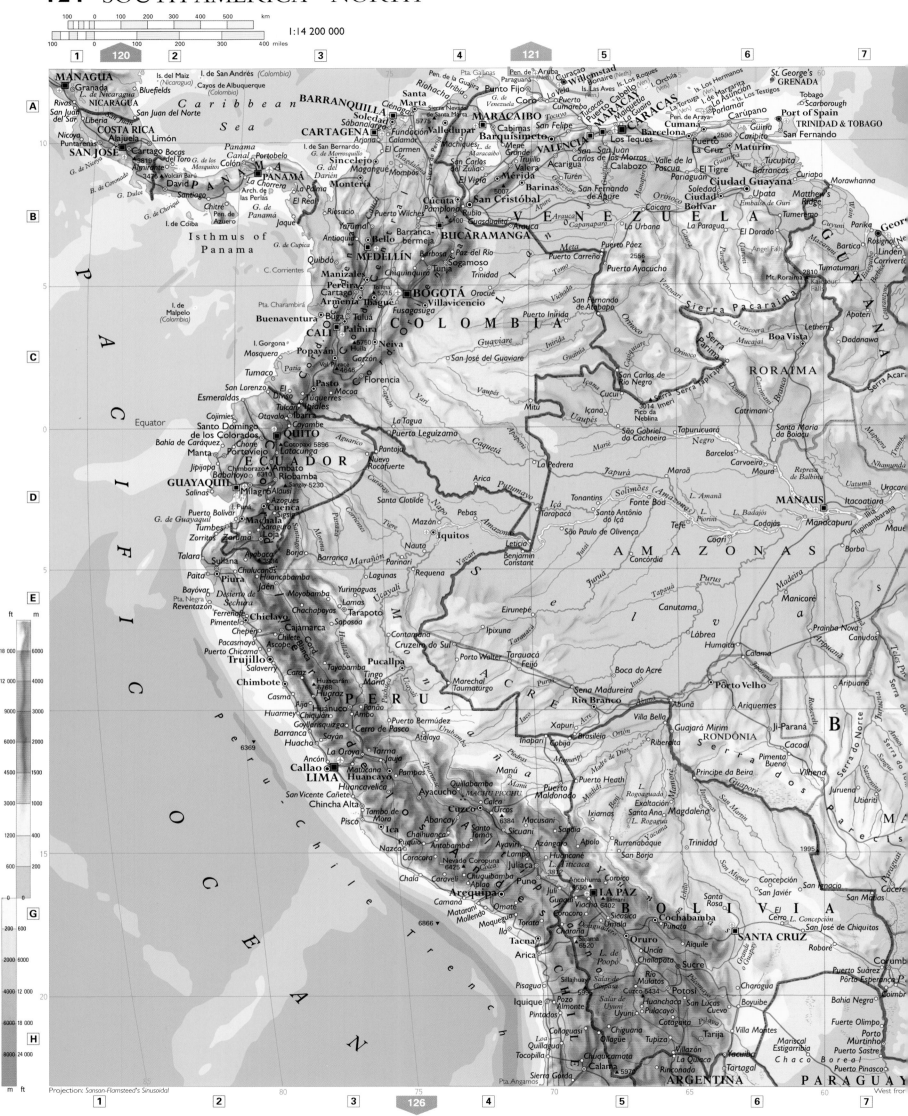

TRINIDAD AND TOBAGO
1:2 200 000

```
10    0    10   20   30   40   50 km
10    0    10        20        30 miles
```

West from Greenwich

A T L A N T I C

O C E A N

ATLANTIC
OCEAN

Tobago
Charlotteville
North Pt.
Castara
565
Ridge
Little
Tobago
Plymouth
Man
Roxborough
Buccoo Reef
Scarborough
Crown Pt.
Rockly Bay

VENEZUELA
Pen. de
Paria
Corozal
Pt.
Monos
Maraval
Macuro
936
940
Mt. Aripo
Tunapuna
Valencia
Northern Range
Salybia
Redhead
Galera Pt.
Toco

**Port
of Spain**
San
Juan
Arima
Sangre Grande
Matura
Bay
Upper Manzanilla
Nariva
Swamp
Cocos
Bay
Güiria

Chaguanas
Caroni
Talparo
Couva
Trinidad
Point Lisas
Otaheite Bay
Gasparillo
Rio Claro
Guaturo Pt.

Golfo de Paria
San Fernando
Brighton
La Brea
Princes Town
Pierreville
Mayaro Bay

Guapo Bay
Pitch
Lake
Penal
Basse Terre
Guayaguayare
Point Fortin
Cedros
Bay
Palo Seco
Siparia
Galeota Pt.

Bonasse
La Lune
304
Trinity
Hills
Icacos Pt.
Erin Pt.
Moruga

Serpent's Mouth
VENEZUELA
Pta. Bombedor

Ctown
Amsterdam
Nieuw Nickerie
Totness
Kwakoegron
Paramaribo
Albina
Nieuw Amsterdam
Moengo
Iracoubo
St-Laurent du Maroni
Kaw
Sinnamary
Kourou
Cayenne

W. J. van
Blommestein
Meer
C. Orange
St-Georges
Oiapoque

SURINAME
1230
Julianatop
**FRENCH
GUIANA**
Camopi

Serra Tumucumaque
Amapá
I. de Maracá

AMAPÁ
Araguari

Merirumã
Serra do
Navio

Macapá
I. Caviana
Mazagão
I. Mexiana
Afuá
C. Maguarinho
Chaves
Soure
Curuçá
Salinópolis
Equator
São Pedro &
São Paulo
(Braz.)

I. Grande
de Gurupá
Almeirim
Vigia
Bragança

Óbidos
Monte
Alegre
Porto de Moz
Breves
Marajó
BELÉM
Viseu

Faro
Alenquer
Gurupá
Castanhal
Turiaçu
Cururupu
Juruti
Santarém
Amazonas
Curralinho
Abaetetuba
São Luís
Barreirinhas
Parintins
Belterra
Aveiro
Cametá
Baião
Pinheiro
Viana
Rosário
Parnaíba
Luís Correia
Camocim
Granja
Itapipoca
Caucaia

Brasília Legal
Altamira
Santa Inês
Itapecuru-
Mirim
Brejo
Piracuruca
Sobral
Maranguape
Cascavel
FORTALEZA
Rocas
Fernando de Noronha
(Braz.)

Represa de
Tucuruí
Tucuruí
Bacabal
Codó
Caxias
Campo
Maior
Ipu
Quixadá
Aracati
Russas
Macau
Ceará-Mirim

Itaituba
Acailandia
Pedreiras
Oitica
Crateús
Areia Branca
NATAL

Maraba
Marabá
São João do
Araguaia
MARANHÃO
Barra
do Corda
Teresina
Senador
Pompeu
CEARÁ
RIO GRANDE
Mossoró
DO NORTE
Canguaretama
Mamanguape

Carajás
Imperatriz
Colinas
Amarante
Valença
do Piauí
Iguatu
Cedro
Sousa
Caraúbas
Caicó
Cabedelo
João Pessoa

Conceição do
Araguaia
Tocantinópolis
Estreito
Carolina
Floriano
Oeiras
Picos
Crato
Juàzeiro
Cajazeiras
Patos
Alagoa
Grande
Olinda
RECIFE

Araguacema
Araguaína
Loreto
Riachão
Nova Iorque
Uruçuí
PIAUÍ
Chapada do Araripe
do Norte
Ouricuri
PARAÍBA
**Campina
Grande
Caruaru**
Jaboatão

Pedro Afonso
São João
do Piauí
Santa
Filomena
Gurguéia
Paulistana
PERNAMBUCO
Pesqueira
Garanhuns
Vitória de Santo Antão

Palmas
Porto Nacional
Parnaguá
Caracol
Remanso
Casa Nova
Juàzeiro
Petrolina
Salgueiro
Palmares
Rio Largo
MACEIÓ

TOCANTINS
Barra
Xique-Xique
Mundo
Novo
Senhor-do-
Bonfim
Paulo Afonso
dos
Indios
Propriá
Penedo
ALAGOAS

R A Z I L
Porto
Nacional
Sono
Jacobina
Paulo Afonso
Arapiraca
6059

Apiacás
Santa Isabel
do Morro
Aruanã
Niquelândia
1678
Posse
Taguatinga
Barreiras
Ibotirama
Xique-Xique
Itaberaba
Queimadas
Capela
São Cristóvão
SERGIPE
Aracaju
Estância

Diamantino
Planalto do
Gurupi
São Domingos
Santa Maria
da Vitória
BAHIA
Bom Jesus
da Lápa
Serra do Sincorá
Castro
Alves
Santo Amaro
Nazaré

Cuiabá
Mato Grosso
Campos Belos
Januária
Carinhanha
Caetité
Brumado
**Feira de
Santana**
Cachoeira
SALVADOR

Santo Antonio
Barra do Garças
Goiás
Uruaçu
São Francisco
Condeúba
Jequié
Valença
B. de Todos os Santos

TO GROSSO
Rondonópolis
Anápolis
DIST.
FED.
Formosa
Monte Azul
Vitória da
Conquista
Itabuna
Ilhéus

Diamantino
Luziânia
Taguatinga
BRASÍLIA
São Francisco
Janaúba
Pedra Azul
Canavieiras

MATO GROSSO
GOIÂNIA
Vianópolis
Paracatu
Piraporá
Salinas
Jequitinhonha
Belmonte

GOIÁS
Morninhos
Ipameri
Montes
Claros
Araçuaí
Itamaraju
Porto Seguro

DO SUL
Alto Araguaia
Jataí
Rio Verde
Itumbiara
Catalão
Patos de
Minas
Corinto
Teófilo Otoni
Nanuque
Prado
Caravelas

Coxim
Quirinópolis
Araguari
Uberlândia
1340
Diamantina
Governador
Valadares
Mucuri
Banco dos
27

Taquari
**Campo
Grande**
Ituiutaba
Prata
Araxá
Ibiá
Patrocínio
Curvelo
Sête Lagoas
Ipatinga
Itabira
Colatina
São Mateus
Conceição da Barra
Abrolhos

Miranda
Aquidauana
Santa Fé do Sul
Uberaba
Frutal
BELO HORIZONTE
Sabará
Ouro
Prêto
Caratinga
Cariacica
VITÓRIA
Trindade
(Braz.)

Bela
Vista
Dourados
São José do
Rio Preto
Barretos
França
Divinópolis
Lima
Lafaiete
Nova
Ubá
Itapemirim
Vila Velha

Pedro Juan
Caballero
Ponta Porã
Andradina
Araçatuba
Catanduva
Araraquara
Poços de
São João
del Rei
Barbacena
Juiz de Fora
Cachoeiro de Itapemirim
Campos

Presidente
Epitácio
Penápolis
Marília
Jaú
São Carlos
Caldas
São Lourenço
Três Rios
Nova Friburgo

Presidente
Prudente
Assis
Bauru
Piracicaba
Limeira
Moji-Mirim
2787
Petrópolis
Cabo Frio

Botucatu
CAMPINAS
Volta
Redonda
RIO DE JANEIRO
Niterói

MINAS GERAIS
Igarapava
Ribeirão Prêto
São José do
Ituiutaba
Uberlândia

Greenwich
55
50
45
40
35
30

COPYRIGHT PHILIP'S

J
11
K
L
D
5
E
10
F
15
G
20
H

1:7 100 000

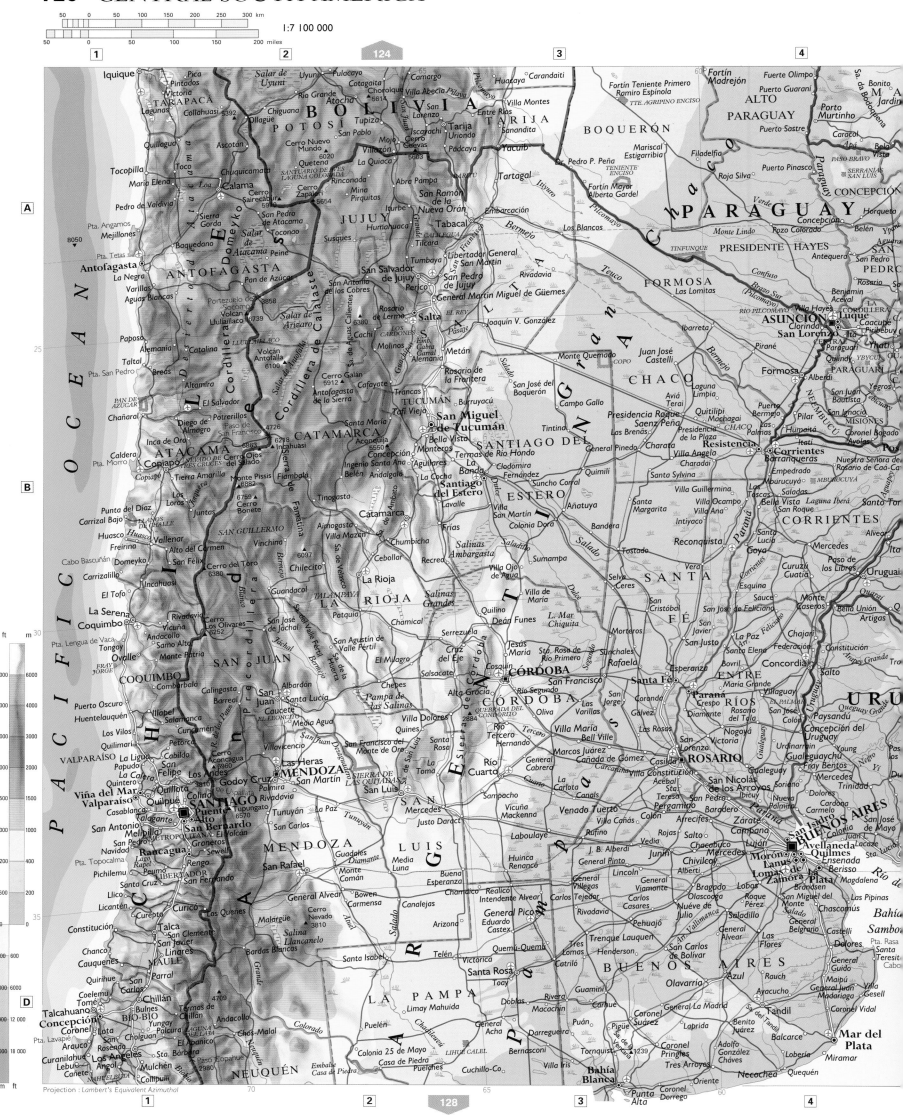

Projection : Lambert's Equivalent Azimuthal

VITÓRIA
BELO HORIZONTE
Betim Contagem
Itabirito
Vila Velha
Guarapari

Sidrolândia
Nioaque
TO GROSSO
Três Lagoas
Andradina
Mirasso
Olímpia
São José
do Rio Preto
Bebedouro
Passos
Batatais
São Sebastião
do Paraíso
Oliveira
Conselheir
Campo Belo
Ouro
Prêto
Ponte Nova
Carangola
Cachoeiro
de Itapemirim
Xavantina Mirandópolis
Araçatuba
Catanduva
Taquaritinga
Ribeirão
Prêto
Guaxupé
Lavras
Barbacena
Cataguases
Iaperuna
Castelo

DO SUL
Nova Alvorada
Panorama
Birigüi
Tupã
São Carlos
São
da Boa Vista
Araras
Moji-Guaçu
São João
del Rei
Ubá
Muriaé
Pico da
Bandeira
2880
Maracaju
Adamantina
SÃO PAULO
Poços de
Pousa
Alegre
Santos
Dumont
Leopoldina
Cambuci
São João
de Barra
Dourados
Presidente
Prudente
Marília
Bauru
Jaú Rio Claro
Limeira
Americana
Juiz de Fora
Três
Rios
Campos

CURITIBA
PORTO ALEGRE
FLORIANÓPOLIS
RIO DE JANEIRO
SÃO PAULO

BRAZIL

ATLANTIC

OCEAN

MONTEVIDEO

1:14 200 000

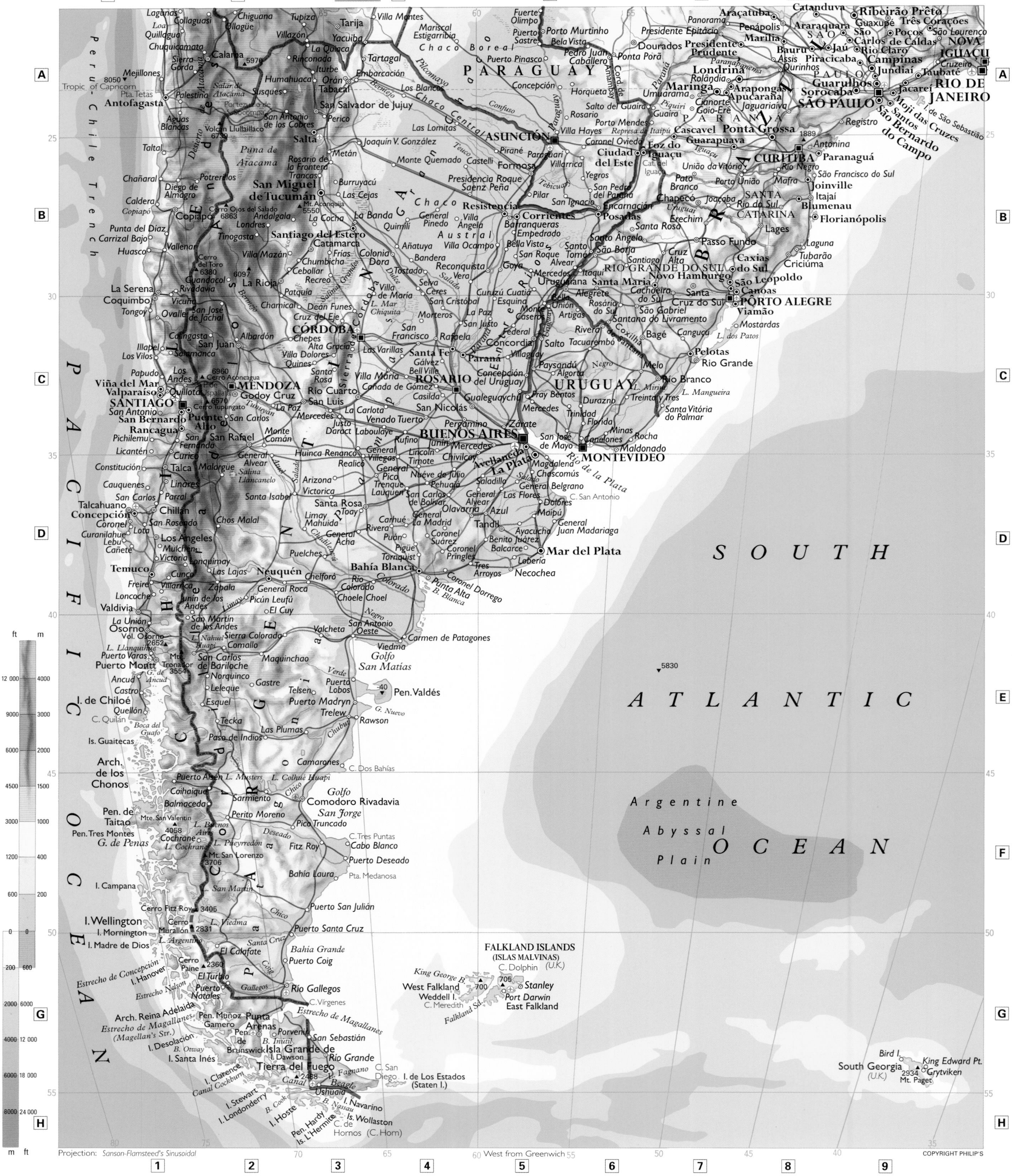

km

100 0 100 200 300 400 500

100 0 100 200 300 400 miles

126   127

PARAGUAY

BRASIL

SÃO PAULO

RIO DE JANEIRO

Ribeirão Prêto

NOVA IGUAÇU

Guarulhos

CURITIBA

PORTO ALEGRE

RIO GRANDE DO SUL

SANTA CATARINA

PARANÁ

Florianópolis

Blumenau

ASUNCIÓN

ARGENTINA

CÓRDOBA

ROSARIO

MENDOZA

SANTIAGO

CHILE

Valparaíso

BUENOS AIRES

LA PLATA

MONTEVIDEO

URUGUAY

Mar del Plata

Bahía Blanca

Neuquén

Puerto Montt

Valdivia

Temuco

Concepción

Talcahuano

Golfo San Matías

Pen. Valdés

Golfo San Jorge

Comodoro Rivadavia

Río Gallegos

Punta Arenas

Tierra del Fuego

Ushuaia

Isla Grande de Tierra del Fuego

Beagle

C. Horn (C. Horn)

SOUTH

ATLANTIC

OCEAN

Argentine Abyssal Plain

5830

FALKLAND ISLANDS
(ISLAS MALVINAS) (U.K.)

West Falkland

East Falkland

Stanley

Port Darwin

South Georgia
(U.K.)

Bird I.

King Edward Pt.

Grytviken

Mt. Paget 2934

PACIFIC OCEAN

Peru–Chile Trench

Tropic of Capricorn

Projection: Sanson-Flamsteed's Sinusoidal

West from Greenwich

COPYRIGHT PHILIP'S

ft   m

12 000   4000

9000   3000

6000   2000

4500   1500

1200   400

600   200

0   0

200   600

2000   6000

4000   12 000

6000   18 000

8000   24 000

m   ft

INDEX TO WORLD MAPS

How to use the index

The index contains the names of all the principal places and features shown on the World Maps. Each name is followed by an additional entry in italics giving the country or region within which it is located. The alphabetical order of names composed of two or more words is governed primarily by the first word and then by the second. This is an example of the rule:

Miquelon *St-P. &M.* **105** C8
Mir *Niger* **83** C7
Mīr Kūh *Iran* **71** E8
Mīr Shahdād *Iran* **71** E8
Mira *Italy* **41** C9

Physical features composed of a proper name (Erie) and a description (Lake) are positioned alphabetically by the proper name. The description is positioned after the proper name and is usually abbreviated:

Erie, L. *N. Amer.* **114** D4

Where a description forms part of a settlement or administrative name however, it is always written in full and put in its true alphabetic position:

Mount Morris *U.S.A.* **114** D7

Names beginning with M' and Mc are indexed as if they were spelled Mac. Names beginning St. are alphabetised under Saint, but Sankt, Sint, Sant', Santa and San are all spelt in full and are alphabetised accordingly. If the same place name occurs two or more times in the index and all are in the same country, each is followed by the name of the administrative subdivision in which it is located. For example:

Jackson *Ky., U.S.A.* **113** G12
Jackson *Mich., U.S.A.* **113** D11
Jackson *Minn., U.S.A.* **112** D6

The number in bold type which follows each name in the index refers to the number of the map page where that feature or place will be found. This is usually the largest scale at which the place or feature appears.

The letter and figure which are in bold type immediately after the page number give the grid square on the map page, within which the feature is situated. The letter represents the latitude and the figure the longitude. A lower case letter immediately after the page number refers to an inset map on that page.

In some cases the feature itself may fall within the specified square, while the name is outside. This is usually the case only with features which are larger than a grid square.

Rivers are indexed to their mouths or confluences, and carry the symbol ➔ after their names. The following symbols are also used in the index: ■ country, ☑ overseas territory or dependency, ☐ first order administrative area, △ national park, ⌒ other park (provincial park, nature reserve or game reserve), ✈ (LHR) principal airport (and location identifier).

How to pronounce place names

English-speaking people usually have no difficulty in reading and pronouncing correctly English place names. However, foreign place name pronunciations may present many problems. Such problems can be minimised by following some simple rules. However, these rules cannot be applied to all situations, and there will be many exceptions.

1. In general, stress each syllable equally, unless your experience suggests otherwise.
2. Pronounce the letter 'a' as a broad 'a' as in 'arm'.
3. Pronounce the letter 'e' as a short 'e' as in 'elm'.
4. Pronounce the letter 'i' as a cross between a short 'i' and long 'e', as the two 'i's in 'California'.
5. Pronounce the letter 'o' as an intermediate 'o' as in 'soft'.
6. Pronounce the letter 'u' as an intermediate 'u' as in 'sure'.
7. Pronounce consonants hard, except in the Romance-language areas where 'g's are likely to be pronounced softly like 'j' in 'jam'; 'j' itself may be pronounced as 'y'; and 'x's may be pronounced as 'h'.
8. For names in mainland China, pronounce 'q' like the 'ch' in 'chin', 'x' like the 'sh' in 'she', 'zh' like the 'j' in 'jam', and 'z' as if it were spelled 'dz'. In general pronounce 'a' as in 'father', 'e' as in 'but', 'i' as in 'keep', 'o' as in 'or', and 'u' as in 'rule'.

Moreover, English has no diacritical marks (accent and pronunciation signs), although some languages do. The following is a brief and general guide to the pronunciation of those most frequently used in the principal Western European languages.

		Pronunciation as in
French	é	day and shows that the e is to be pronounced; e.g. Orléans.
	è	mare
	î	used over any vowel and does not affect pronunciation; shows contraction of the name, usually omission of 's' following a vowel.
	ç	's' before 'a', 'o' and 'u'.
	ë, ï, ü	over 'e', 'i' and 'u' when they are used with another vowel and shows that each is to be pronounced.
German	ä	fate
	ö	fur
	ü	no English equivalent; like French 'tu'
Italian	à, é	over vowels and indicates stress.
Portuguese	ã, õ	vowels pronounced nasally.
	ç	boss
	á	shows stress
	ô	shows that a vowel has an 'i' or 'u' sound combined with it.
Spanish	ñ	canyon
	ü	pronounced as w and separately from adjoining vowels.
	á	usually indicates that this is a stressed vowel.

Abbreviations

A.C.T. – Australian Capital Territory
A.R. – Autonomous Region
Afghan. – Afghanistan
Afr. – Africa
Ala. – Alabama
Alta. – Alberta
Amer. – America(n)
Arch. – Archipelago
Ariz. – Arizona
Ark. – Arkansas
Atl. Oc. – Atlantic Ocean
B. – Baie, Bahía, Bay, Bucht, Bugt
B.C. – British Columbia
Bangla. – Bangladesh
Barr. – Barrage
Bos.-H. – Bosnia-Herzegovina
C. – Cabo, Cap, Cape, Coast
C.A.R. – Central African Republic
C. Prov. – Cape Province
Calif. – California
Cat. – Catarata
Cent. – Central
Chan. – Channel
Colo. – Colorado
Conn. – Connecticut
Cord. – Cordillera
Cr. – Creek
Czech. – Czech Republic
D.C. – District of Columbia
Del. – Delaware
Dem. – Democratic
Dep. – Dependency
Des. – Desert
Dét. – Détroit
Dist. – District
Dj. – Djebel
Domin. – Dominica
Dom. Rep. – Dominican Republic
E. – East

E. Salv. – El Salvador
Eq. Guin. – Equatorial Guinea
Est. – Estrecho
Falk. Is. – Falkland Is.
Fd. – Fjord
Fla. – Florida
Fr. – French
G. – Golfe, Golfo, Gulf, Guba, Gebel
Ga. – Georgia
Gt. – Great, Greater
Guinea-Biss. – Guinea-Bissau
H.K. – Hong Kong
H.P. – Himachal Pradesh
Hants. – Hampshire
Harb. – Harbor, Harbour
Hd. – Head
Hts. – Heights
I.(s). – Île, Ilha, Insel, Isla, Island, Isle
Ill. – Illinois
Ind. – Indiana
Ind. Oc. – Indian Ocean
Ivory C. – Ivory Coast
J. – Jabal, Jebel
Jaz. – Jazīrah
Junc. – Junction
K. – Kap, Kapp
Kans. – Kansas
Kep. – Kepulauan
Ky. – Kentucky
L. – Lac, Lacul, Lago, Lagoa, Lake, Limni, Loch, Lough
La. – Louisiana
Ld. – Land
Liech. – Liechtenstein
Lux. – Luxembourg
Mad. P. – Madhya Pradesh
Madag. – Madagascar
Man. – Manitoba

Mass. – Massachusetts
Md. – Maryland
Me. – Maine
Medit. S. – Mediterranean Sea
Mich. – Michigan
Minn. – Minnesota
Miss. – Mississippi
Mo. – Missouri
Mont. – Montana
Mozam. – Mozambique
Mt.(s) – Mont, Montaña, Mountain
Mte. – Monte
Mti. – Monti
N. – Nord, Norte, North, Northern, Nouveau
N.B. – New Brunswick
N.C. – North Carolina
N. Cal. – New Caledonia
N. Dak. – North Dakota
N.H. – New Hampshire
N.I. – North Island
N.J. – New Jersey
N. Mex. – New Mexico
N.S. – Nova Scotia
N.S.W. – New South Wales
N.W.T. – North West Territory
N.Y. – New York
N.Z. – New Zealand
Nac. – Nacional
Nat. – National
Nebr. – Nebraska
Neths. – Netherlands
Nev. – Nevada
Nfld. & L. – Newfoundland and Labrador
Nic. – Nicaragua
O. – Oued, Ouadi
Occ. – Occidentale
Okla. – Oklahoma

Ont. – Ontario
Or. – Orientale
Oreg. – Oregon
Os. – Ostrov
Oz. – Ozero
P. – Pass, Passo, Pasul, Pulau
P.E.I. – Prince Edward Island
Pa. – Pennsylvania
Pac. Oc. – Pacific Ocean
Papua N.G. – Papua New Guinea
Pass. – Passage
Peg. – Pegunungan
Pen. – Peninsula, Péninsule
Phil. – Philippines
Pk. – Peak
Plat. – Plateau
Prov. – Province, Provincial
Pt. – Point
Pta. – Ponta, Punta
Pte. – Pointe
Qué. – Québec
Queens. – Queensland
R. – Rio, River
R.I. – Rhode Island
Ra. – Range
Raj. – Rajasthan
Recr. – Recreational, Récréatif
Reg. – Region
Rep. – Republic
Res. – Reserve, Reservoir
Rhld-Pfz. – Rheinland-Pfalz
S. – South, Southern, Sur
Si. Arabia – Saudi Arabia
S.C. – South Carolina
S. Dak. – South Dakota
S.I. – South Island
S. Leone – Sierra Leone
Sa. – Serra, Sierra
Sask. – Saskatchewan

Scot. – Scotland
Sd. – Sound
Sev. – Severnaya
Sib. – Siberia
Sprs. – Springs
St. – Saint
Sta. – Santa
Ste. – Sainte
Sto. – Santo
Str. – Strait, Stretto
Switz. – Switzerland
Tas. – Tasmania
Tenn. – Tennessee
Terr. – Territory, Territoire
Tex. – Texas
Tg. – Tanjung
Trin. & Tob. – Trinidad & Tobago
U.A.E. – United Arab Emirates
U.K. – United Kingdom
U.S.A. – United States of America
Ut. P. – Uttar Pradesh
Va. – Virginia
Vdkhr. – Vodokhranilishche
Vdskh. – Vodoskhovyshche
Vf. – Vîrful
Vic. – Victoria
Vol. – Volcano
Vt. – Vermont
W. – Wadi, West
W. Va. – West Virginia
Wall. & F. Is. – Wallis and Futuna Is.
Wash. – Washington
Wis. – Wisconsin
Wlkp. – Wielkopolski
Wyo. – Wyoming
Yorks. – Yorkshire

A

A 'Âli an Nîl □ Sudan 81 F3
A Baña Spain 36 C2
A Cañiza Spain 36 C2
A Coruña Spain 36 B2
A Coruña □ Spain 36 B2
A Cruz do Incio Spain 36 C3
A Estrada Spain 36 C2
A Fonsagrada Spain 36 B3
A Guarda Spain 36 D2
A Gudiña Spain 36 C3
A Pobre Spain 36 C3
A Ramallosa Spain 36 C2
A Rúa Spain 36 C3
A Serra de Outes Spain 36 C2
Aabenraa Denmark 11 J3
Aabybro Denmark 11 G3
Aachen Germany 24 E2
Aalborg Denmark 11 G3
Aalborg Bugt Denmark 11 H4
Aalen Germany 25 G6
Aalestrup Denmark 11 H3
Aalst Belgium 17 D4
Aalten Neths. 17 C6
Aalter Belgium 17 C3
Äänekoski Finland 8 E21
Aarau Switz. 25 H4
Aarberg Switz. 25 H3
Aare → Switz. 25 H4
Aargau □ Switz. 25 H4
Aarhus = Århus Denmark 11 H4
Aars Denmark 11 H3
Aarschot Belgium 17 D4
Aba China 58 A3
Aba Dem. Rep. of the Congo 86 B3
Aba Nigeria 83 D6
Âbâ, Jazîrat Sudan 81 E3
Abaco I. Bahamas 120 A4
Abadab, J. Sudan 80 D4
Ābādān Iran 71 D6
Abade Ethiopia 81 F4
Ābādeh Iran 71 D7
Abadín Spain 36 B3
Abadla Algeria 78 B5
Abaetetuba Brazil 125 D9
Abagnar Qi = Xilinhot China 56 C9
Abah, Tanjung Indonesia 63 K18
Abai Paraguay 127 B4
Abak Nigeria 83 E6
Abakaliki Nigeria 83 D6
Abakan Russia 53 D10
Abala Niger 83 C5
Abalak Niger 83 B6
Abalemma Niger 83 B6
Abana Turkey 72 B6
Abancay Peru 124 F4
Abano Terme Italy 41 C8
Abarán Spain 39 G3
Abariringa Kiribati 96 H10
Abarqū Iran 71 D7
Abasha Georgia 35 J6
Abashiri Japan 54 B12
Abashiri-Wan Japan 54 C12
Abaújszántó Hungary 28 B6
Abava → Latvia 30 A8
Ābay = Nîl el Azraq → Sudan 81 D3
Abay Kazakhstan 52 E8
Abaya, L. Ethiopia 81 F4
Abaza Russia 52 D9
Abbadia di Fiastra ⌂ Italy 41 E10
Abbadia San Salvatore Italy 41 F8
'Abbāsābād Iran 71 C8
Abbay = Nîl el Azraq → Sudan 81 D3
Abbaye, Pt. U.S.A. 112 B9
Abbé, L. Ethiopia 81 E5
Abbeville France 19 B8
Abbeville Ala., U.S.A. 117 F12
Abbeville La., U.S.A. 116 G8
Abbeville S.C., U.S.A. 117 D13
Abbeyfeale Ireland 12 D2
Abbiategrasso Italy 40 C5
Abbot Ice Shelf Antarctica 5 D16
Abbotsford Canada 102 D4
Abbottabad Pakistan 68 B5
ABC Islands = Netherlands Antilles ☒ W. Indies 124 A5
Abd al Kūrī Yemen 75 E5
Ābdānān Iran 73 F12
Ābdar Iran 71 D7
'Abdolābād Iran 71 C8
Abdulpur Bangla. 69 G13
Abéché Chad 79 F10
Abejar Spain 38 D2
Abekr Sudan 81 E2
Abel Tasman △ N.Z. 91 D4
Abengourou Ivory C. 82 D4
Abenójar Spain 37 G6
Åbenrå = Aabenraa Denmark 11 J3
Abensberg Germany 25 G7
Abeokuta Nigeria 83 D5
Aber Uganda 86 B3
Aberaeron U.K. 15 E3
Aberayron = Aberaeron U.K. 15 E3
Aberchirder U.K. 13 D6
Abercorn Australia 95 D5
Aberdare U.K. 15 F4
Aberdare △ Kenya 86 C4
Aberdare Ra. Kenya 86 C4
Aberdeen Australia 95 E5
Aberdeen Canada 103 C7
Aberdeen S. Africa 88 E3
Aberdeen U.K. 13 D6
Aberdeen Idaho, U.S.A. 108 E7
Aberdeen Md., U.S.A. 113 F15
Aberdeen Miss., U.S.A. 117 E10
Aberdeen S. Dak., U.S.A. 112 C4
Aberdeen Wash., U.S.A. 110 D3
Aberdeen, City of □ U.K. 13 D6
Aberdeenshire □ U.K. 13 D6
Aberdovey = Aberdyfi U.K. 15 E3
Aberdyfi U.K. 15 E3
Aberfeldy U.K. 13 E5
Aberfoyle U.K. 13 E4
Abergavenny U.K. 15 F4
Abergele U.K. 14 D4
Abernathy U.S.A. 116 E4
Abert, L. U.S.A. 108 E3
Aberystwyth U.K. 15 E3
Abhā Si. Arabia 80 D5
Abhar Iran 73 D13
Abhayapuri India 69 F14
Abia □ Nigeria 83 D6
Abide Turkey 47 C11
Abidiya Sudan 80 D3
Abidjan Ivory C. 82 D4
Abilene Kans., U.S.A. 112 F5
Abilene Tex., U.S.A. 116 E5
Abingdon U.K. 15 F6
Abingdon U.S.A. 113 G13
Abington Reef Australia 94 B4
Abitau → Canada 103 B7
Abitibi → Canada 104 B3
Abitibi, L. Canada 104 C4
Abiy Adi Ethiopia 81 E4
Abiyata-Shala △ Ethiopia 81 F4
Abkhaz Republic = Abkhazia □ Georgia 35 J5
Abkhazia □ Georgia 35 J5
Abminga Australia 95 D1
Abnûb Egypt 80 B3
Åbo = Turku Finland 32 B2
Abocho Nigeria 83 D6
Abohar India 68 D6
Aboisso Ivory C. 82 D4
Abomey Benin 83 D5
Abong-Mbang Cameroon 84 D2
Abonnema Nigeria 83 E6
Abony Hungary 28 C5
Aboso Ghana 82 D4
Abou-Deïa Chad 79 F9
Abovian Armenia 35 K7
Aboyne U.K. 13 D6
Abra Pampa Argentina 126 A2
Abraham L. Canada 102 C5
Abrantes Portugal 37 F2
Abreojos, Pta. Mexico 118 B2
Abri Esh Shamâliya, Sudan 80 C3
Abri Janub Kordofân, Sudan 81 E3
Abrolhos, Banco dos Brazil 125 F11
Abrud Romania 28 D8
Abruzzo □ Italy 41 F10
Absaroka Range U.S.A. 108 D9
Abtenau Austria 26 D6
Abu India 68 G5
Abū al Abyad U.A.E. 71 E7
Abū al Khaṣīb Iraq 70 D5
Abū 'Alī Si. Arabia 71 E6
Abū 'Alī → Lebanon 74 A4
Abu Ballas Egypt 80 C2
Abu Deleiq Sudan 81 D3
Abu Dhabi = Abū Ẓāby U.A.E. 71 E7
Abu Dis Sudan 80 D3
Abu Dom Sudan 81 D3
Abū Du'ān Syria 73 D8
Abu el Gaīn, W. → Egypt 74 F2
Abu Fatma, Ras Sudan 80 C4
Abû Gabra Sudan 81 E2
Abu Ga'da, W. → Egypt 74 F1
Abu Gelba Sudan 81 E3
Abu Gubeiha Sudan 81 E3
Abu Habl, Khawr → Sudan 81 E3
Abū Ḥadrīyah Si. Arabia 71 E6
Abu Hamed Sudan 80 D3
Abu Haraz An Nîl el Azraq, Sudan 80 D3
Abu Haraz El Gezira, Sudan 81 E3
Abu Haraz Esh Shamâliya, Sudan 80 D3
Abû Higar Sudan 81 E3
Abū Kamāl Syria 73 E9
Abu Kuleiwat Sudan 81 E2
Abū Madd, Ra's Si. Arabia 70 E3
Abu Matariq Sudan 81 E2
Abu Mendi Ethiopia 81 E4
Abū Mūsā U.A.E. 71 E7
Abū Qaṣr Si. Arabia 70 D3
Abu Qir Egypt 80 H7
Abu Qireiya Egypt 80 C4
Abu Qurqâs Egypt 80 B3
Abu Shagara, Ras Sudan 80 C4
Abû Shanab Sudan 81 E2
Abu Simbel Egypt 80 C3
Abū Şukhayr Iraq 73 G11
Abu Sultân Egypt 80 H8
Abu Tabari Sudan 80 D2
Abu Tig Egypt 80 B3
Abu Tiga Sudan 81 E3
Abu Tineitin Sudan 81 E3
Abû Uruq Sudan 81 D3
Abû Zabad Sudan 81 E2
Abū Ẓāby U.A.E. 71 E7
Abū Zeydābād Iran 71 C6
Abuja Nigeria 83 D6
Abukuma-Gawa → Japan 54 E10
Abukuma-Sammyaku Japan 54 F10
Abunã Brazil 124 E5
Abunã → Brazil 124 E5
Abune Yosef Ethiopia 81 E4
Aburo Dem. Rep. of the Congo 86 B3
Abut Hd. N.Z. 91 E3
Abuye Meda Ethiopia 81 E4
Abwong Sudan 81 F3
Åby Sweden 11 F10
Aby, Lagune Ivory C. 82 D4
Abyad Sudan 81 E2
Ābyek Iran 71 B6
Acadia △ U.S.A. 113 C19
Açailândia Brazil 125 D9
Acajutla El Salv. 120 D2
Acámbaro Mexico 118 D4
Acanthus Greece 44 F7
Acaponeta Mexico 118 C3
Acapulco Mexico 119 D5
Acaraí, Serra Brazil 124 C7
Acarigua Venezuela 124 B5
Acatlán Mexico 119 D5
Acayucán Mexico 119 D6
Accéglio Italy 40 D4
Accomac U.S.A. 113 G16
Accous France 20 E3
Accra Ghana 83 D4
Accrington U.K. 14 D5
Acebal Argentina 126 C3
Aceh □ Indonesia 62 D1
Acerra Italy 43 B7
Aceuchal Spain 37 G4
Achaia □ Greece 46 C3
Achalpur India 66 J10
Acharnes Greece 46 C5
Acheloos → Greece 46 C3
Acheng China 57 B14
Achenkirch Austria 26 D4
Achensee Austria 26 D4
Achentrias Greece 47 G7
Acher India 68 H5
Achern Germany 25 G4
Achill Hd. Ireland 12 C1
Achill I. Ireland 12 C1
Achim Germany 24 B5
Achinsk Russia 53 D10
Achladokambos Greece 46 D4
Acıgöl Turkey 47 D11
Acıpayam Turkey 47 D11
Acireale Italy 43 E8
Ackerman U.S.A. 117 E10
Acklins I. Bahamas 121 B5
Acme Canada 102 C6
Acme U.S.A. 114 F5
Aconcagua, Cerro Argentina 126 C2
Aconquija, Mt. Argentina 126 B2
Açores, Is. dos Atl. Oc. 78 a
Acornhoek S. Africa 89 C5
Acquapendente Italy 41 F8
Acquasanta Terme Italy 41 F10
Acquasparta Italy 41 F9
Acquaviva delle Fonti Italy 43 B9
Ácqui Terme Italy 40 D5
Acraman, L. Australia 95 E2
Acre = 'Akko Israel 74 C4
Acre □ Brazil 124 E4
Acre → Brazil 124 E5
Acri Italy 43 C9
Acs Hungary 28 C3
Actinolite Canada 114 B7
Actium Greece 46 C2
Acton Canada 114 C4
Ad Dafinah Si. Arabia 80 C5
Ad Daghghāran Iraq 73 G11
Ad Dammām Si. Arabia 71 E6
Ad Dāmūr Lebanon 74 B4
Ad Dawādimī Si. Arabia 70 E5
Ad Dawḥah Qatar 71 E6
Ad Dawr Iraq 73 E10
Ad Dir'īyah Si. Arabia 70 E5
Ad Dīwānīyah Iraq 73 F11
Ad Dujayl Iraq 73 F11
Ad Duwayd Si. Arabia 70 D4
Ada Ghana 83 D5
Ada Serbia 28 E5
Ada Minn., U.S.A. 112 B5
Ada Okla., U.S.A. 116 D6
Adabiya Egypt 74 F1
Adair, C. Canada 101 B12
Adaja → Spain 36 D6
Adak I. U.S.A. 106 a
Adamaoua □ Cameroon 83 D7
Adamaoua, Massif de l' Cameroon 83 D7
Adamawa □ Nigeria 83 D7
Adamawa Highlands = Adamaoua, Massif de l' Cameroon 83 D7
Adamello, Mte. Italy 40 B7
Adamello ⌂ Italy 40 B7
Adami Tulu Ethiopia 81 F4
Adaminaby Australia 95 F4
Adams Mass., U.S.A. 115 D11
Adams N.Y., U.S.A. 115 C8
Adams Wis., U.S.A. 112 D9
Adams, Mt. U.S.A. 110 D5
Adam's Bridge Sri Lanka 66 Q11
Adams L. Canada 102 C5
Adam's Peak Sri Lanka 66 R12
Adamuz Spain 37 G6
Adana Turkey 72 D6
Adana □ Turkey 72 D6
Adanero Spain 36 E6
Adapazarı = Sakarya Turkey 72 B4
Adar Gwagwa, J. Sudan 80 C4
Adarama Sudan 81 D3
Adare, C. Antarctica 5 D11
Adarte Eritrea 81 E5
Adaut Indonesia 63 F8
Adavale Australia 95 D3
Adda → Italy 40 C6
Addis Ababa = Addis Abeba Ethiopia 81 F4
Addis Abeba Ethiopia 81 F4
Addis Alem Ethiopia 81 F4
Addis Zemen Ethiopia 81 E4
Addison U.S.A. 114 D7
Addo S. Africa 88 E4
Addo △ S. Africa 88 E4
Adebour Niger 83 C7
Ādeh Iran 70 B5
Adel U.S.A. 117 F13
Adelaide Australia 95 E2
Adelaide S. Africa 88 E4
Adelaide I. Antarctica 5 C17
Adelaide Pen. Canada 100 C10
Adelaide River Australia 92 B5
Adelaide Village Bahamas 120 A4
Adelanto U.S.A. 111 L9
Adele I. Australia 92 C3
Adélie, Terre Antarctica 5 C10
Adelie Land = Adélie, Terre Antarctica 5 C10
Adelsk Belarus 30 E10
Ademuz Spain 38 E3
Aden = Al 'Adan Yemen 75 E4
Aden, G. of Ind. Oc. 75 E4
Adendorp S. Africa 88 E3
Aderbissinat Niger 83 B6
Adh Dhayd U.A.E. 71 E7
Adhoi India 68 H4
Adi Indonesia 63 E8
Adi Arkai Ethiopia 81 E4
Adi Daro Ethiopia 81 E4
Adi Keyih Eritrea 81 E4
Adi Kwala Eritrea 81 E4
Adi Ugri Eritrea 81 E4
Adieu, C. Australia 93 F5
Adieu Pt. Australia 92 C3
Adigala Ethiopia 81 E5
Adige → Italy 41 C9
Adigrat Ethiopia 81 E4
Adıgüzel Barajı Turkey 47 C11
Adilabad India 66 K11
Adilcevaz Turkey 73 C10
Adirondack ⌂ U.S.A. 115 C10
Adirondack Mts. U.S.A. 115 C10
Adis Abeba = Addis Abeba Ethiopia 81 F4
Adıyaman Turkey 73 D8
Adıyaman □ Turkey 73 D8
Adjohon Benin 83 D5
Adjud Romania 29 D12
Adjumani Uganda 86 B3
Adjuntas Puerto Rico 121 d
Adlavik Is. Canada 105 B8
Adler Russia 35 J4
Admer Algeria 83 A6
Admiralty G. Australia 92 B4
Admiralty I. U.S.A. 102 B2
Admiralty Is. Papua N. G. 90 B7
Adnan Menderes, İzmir ✈ (ADB) Turkey 47 C9
Ado Nigeria 83 D5
Ado-Ekiti Nigeria 83 D6
Adok Sudan 81 F3
Adola Ethiopia 81 E5
Adolfo González Chaves Argentina 126 D3
Adolfo Ruiz Cortines, Presa Mexico 118 B3
Adonara Indonesia 63 F6
Adoni India 66 M10
Adony Hungary 28 C3
Adour → France 20 E2
Adra India 69 H12
Adra Spain 37 J7
Adrano Italy 43 E7
Adrar Algeria 78 C6
Adrar Mauritania 78 D3
Adrar □ Mauritania 82 A3
Adrar des Iforas Africa 83 B5
Ádria Italy 41 C9
Adrian Mich., U.S.A. 113 E11
Adrian Tex., U.S.A. 116 D3
Adriatic Sea Medit. S. 6 G9
Adua Indonesia 63 E7
Adwa Ethiopia 81 E4
Adygea □ Russia 35 H5
Adzhar Republic = Ajaria □ Georgia 35 K6
Adzopé Ivory C. 82 D4
Ægean Sea Medit. S. 47 C7
Aerhtai Shan Mongolia 60 B4
Ærø Denmark 11 K4
Ærøskøbing Denmark 11 K4
Aetos Greece 46 D3
Afaahiti Tahiti 91 d
'Afak Iraq 73 F11
Afandou Greece 49 C10
Afar □ Ethiopia 81 E5
Afareaitu Moorea 91 d
Afghanistan ■ Asia 66 C4
Afikpo Nigeria 83 D6
Aflou Algeria 78 B6
Afragóla Italy 43 B7
Afram → Ghana 83 D4
Afrera Ethiopia 81 E5
Africa 76 E6
'Afrīn Syria 72 D7
Afşin Turkey 72 C7
Afton N.Y., U.S.A. 115 D9
Afton Wyo., U.S.A. 108 E8
Afuá Brazil 125 D8
'Afula Israel 74 C4
Afyon Turkey 47 C12
Afyon □ Turkey 47 C12
Afyonkarahisar = Afyon Turkey 47 C12
Aga Egypt 80 H7
Āgā Jarī Iran 71 D6
Agadès = Agadez Niger 83 B6
Agadez Niger 83 B6
Agadir Morocco 78 B4
Agaete Canary Is. 48 F4
Agaie Nigeria 83 D6
Again Sudan 81 F2
Agalega Is. Mauritius 3 E12
Ağapınar Turkey 47 B12
Agar India 68 H7
Agaro Ethiopia 81 F4
Agartala India 67 H17
Agăş Romania 29 D11
Agassiz Canada 102 D4
Agats Indonesia 63 F9
Agawam U.S.A. 115 D12
Agbélouvé Togo 83 D5
Agboville Ivory C. 82 D4
Ağcabädi Azerbaijan 35 K8
Ağdam Azerbaijan 35 L8
Ağdaş Azerbaijan 35 K8
Agde France 20 E7
Agde, C. d' France 20 E7
Agdzhabedi = Ağcabädi Azerbaijan 35 K8
Agen France 20 D4
Agerbæk Denmark 11 J2
Agersø Denmark 11 J5
Ageyevo Russia 32 E9
Aggteleki △ Hungary 28 B5
Āgh Kand Iran 73 D13
Aghathonisi Greece 47 D8
Aghia Anna Greece 46 C5
Aghia Deka Greece 49 D6
Aghia Ekaterinis, Akra Greece 49 A3
Aghia Galini Greece 49 D6
Aghia Marina Kasos, Greece 47 F8
Aghia Marina Leros, Greece 47 D8
Aghia Paraskevi Greece 47 B8
Aghia Roumeli Greece 46 F5
Aghia Varvara Greece 49 D7
Aghiasos Greece 47 B8
Aghio Theodori Greece 46 D5
Aghion Oros □ Greece 45 F8
Aghios Andreas Greece 46 D4
Aghios Efstratios Greece 46 B6
Aghios Georgios Greece 46 D5
Aghios Ioannis, Akra Greece 49 D7
Aghios Isidoros Greece 49 C9
Aghios Kirikos Greece 47 D8
Aghios Matheos Greece 49 B3
Aghios Mironas Greece 47 F7
Aghios Nikolaos Greece 49 D7
Aghios Petros Greece 46 C2
Aghios Stephanos Greece 49 A3
Aghiou Orous, Kolpos Greece 44 F7
Aghireşu Romania 29 D8
Agia Greece 46 B4
Aginskoye Russia 53 D12
Ağlasun Turkey 47 D12
Agly → France 20 F7
Agnew Australia 93 E3
Agnibilékrou Ivory C. 82 D4
Agnita Romania 29 E9
Agnone Italy 41 G11
Agofie Ghana 83 D5
Agogna → Italy 40 C5
Agogo Sudan 81 F2
Agoitz = Aoiz Spain 38 C3
Agön Sweden 10 C11
Agon Coutainville France 18 C5
Ágordo Italy 41 B9
Agori India 69 G10
Agouna Benin 83 D5
Agout → France 20 E5
Agra India 68 F7
Agrakhanskiy Poluostrov Russia 35 J8
Agramunt Spain 38 D6
Ágreda Spain 38 D3
Ağri Turkey 73 C10
Ağri □ Turkey 73 C10
Agri → Italy 43 B9
Ağrı Dağı Turkey 73 C11
Ağri Karakose = Ağri Turkey 73 C10
Agria Greece 46 B5
Agrigento Italy 42 E6
Agrinio Greece 46 C3
Agrópoli Italy 43 B7
Ağstafa Azerbaijan 35 K7
Agua Caliente Mexico 111 N10
Agua Caliente Springs U.S.A. 111 N10
Água Clara Brazil 125 H8
Agua Fria ⌂ U.S.A. 109 J8
Agua Hechicera Mexico 111 N10
Agua Prieta Mexico 118 A3
Aguadilla Puerto Rico 121 d
Aguadulce Panama 120 E3
Aguanga U.S.A. 111 M10
Aguanish Canada 105 B7
Aguanish → Canada 105 B7
Aguapey → Argentina 126 B4
Aguaray Guazú → Paraguay 126 A4
Aguarico → Ecuador 124 D3
Aguaro-Guariquito △ Venezuela 121 E6
Aguas → Spain 38 D4
Aguas Blancas Chile 126 A2
Aguas Calientes, Sierra de Argentina 126 B2
Aguascalientes Mexico 118 C4
Aguascalientes □ Mexico 118 C4
Agudo Spain 37 G6
Águeda Portugal 36 E2
Agueda → Spain 36 D4
Aguelhok Mali 83 B5
Aguié Niger 83 C6
Aguila, Punta Puerto Rico 121 d
Aguilafuente Spain 36 D6
Aguilar de Campóo Spain 36 C6
Aguilar de la Frontera Spain 37 H6
Aguilares Argentina 126 B2
Águilas Spain 39 H3
Agüimes Canary Is. 48 G4
Aguja, C. de la Colombia 122 B3
Agujereada, Pta. Puerto Rico 121 d
Agulaa Ethiopia 81 E4
Agulhas, C. S. Africa 88 E3
Agulo Canary Is. 48 F2
Agung, Gunung Indonesia 63 J18
Agur Uganda 86 B3
Agusan → Phil. 61 G6
Ağva Turkey 45 E13
Agvali Russia 35 J8
Aha Mts. Botswana 88 B3
Ahaggar Algeria 78 D7
Ahamansu Ghana 83 D5
Ahar Iran 73 C12
Ahat Turkey 47 C11
Ahaus Germany 24 C2
Ahipara B. N.Z. 91 A4
Ahir Dağı Turkey 47 C12
Ahiri India 66 K12
Ahlat Turkey 73 C10
Ahlen Germany 24 D3
Ahmad Wal Pakistan 68 E1
Ahmadabad India 68 H5
Aḥmadābād Khorāsān, Iran 71 C9
Aḥmadābād Khorāsān, Iran 71 C8
Aḥmadī Iran 71 E8
Ahmadnagar India 66 K9
Ahmadpur East Pakistan 68 E4
Ahmadpur Lamma Pakistan 68 E4
Ahmar, Mts. Ethiopia 81 F5
Ahmedabad = Ahmadabad India 68 H5
Ahmednagar = Ahmadnagar India 66 K9
Ahmetbey Turkey 45 E11
Ahmetler Turkey 47 C11
Ahmetli Turkey 47 C9
Ahoada Nigeria 83 D6
Ahome Mexico 118 B3
Ahoskie U.S.A. 117 C16
Ahr → Germany 24 E3
Ahram Iran 71 D6
Ahrax Pt. Malta 49 D1
Ahrensbök Germany 24 A6
Ahrensburg Germany 24 B6
Ahuachapán El Salv. 120 D2
Ahun France 19 F9

Åhus *Sweden* 11 J8
Ahvāz *Iran* 71 D6
Ahvenanmaa = Åland
  Finland 9 F19
Aḥwar *Yemen* 75 E4
Ahzar → *Mali* 83 B5
Ai → *India* 69 F14
Ai-Ais *Namibia* 88 D2
Ai-Ais and Fish River
  Canyon △ *Namibia* 88 C2
Aichach *Germany* 25 G7
Aichi □ *Japan* 55 G8
Aigle *Switz.* 25 J2
Aignay-le-Duc *France* 19 E11
Aigoual, Mt. *France* 20 D7
Aigre *France* 20 C4
Aigrettes, Pte. des *Réunion* 85 c
Aiguá *Uruguay* 127 C5
Aigueperse *France* 19 F10
Aigues → *France* 21 D8
Aigues-Mortes *France* 21 E8
Aigues-Mortes, G. d' *France* 21 E8
Aigües-Tortes i Estany de
  St. Maurici △ *Spain* 38 C4
Aiguilles *France* 21 D10
Aiguillon *France* 20 D4
Aigurande *France* 19 F8
Aihui = Heihe *China* 53 D13
Aija *Peru* 124 E3
Aikawa *Japan* 54 E9
Aiken *U.S.A.* 117 E14
Ailao Shan *China* 58 F3
Aileron *Australia* 94 C1
Aillant-sur-Tholon *France* 19 E10
Aillik *Canada* 105 A8
Ailsa Craig *Canada* 114 C3
Ailsa Craig *U.K.* 13 F3
Aim *Russia* 53 D14
Aimere *Indonesia* 63 F6
Aimogasta *Argentina* 126 B2
Ain □ *France* 19 F12
Ain → *France* 21 C9
Aïn Ben Tili *Mauritania* 78 C4
Ain Dalla *Egypt* 80 B2
Ain el Mafki *Egypt* 80 B2
Ain Girba *Egypt* 80 B2
Ain Murr *Sudan* 80 C2
Ain Qeiqab *Egypt* 80 B1
Aïn Sefra *Algeria* 78 B5
Ain Sheikh Murzûk *Egypt* 80 B2
Ain Sudr *Egypt* 74 F2
Ain Sukhna *Egypt* 80 J8
Aïn Témouchent *Algeria* 78 A5
Ain Zeitûn *Egypt* 80 B2
Ainaži *Latvia* 32 D3
Ainos Oros *Greece* 46 C2
Ainsworth *U.S.A.* 112 D4
Aiquile *Bolivia* 124 G5
Aïr *Niger* 83 B6
Air Force I. *Canada* 101 C12
Air Hitam *Malaysia* 65 M4
Airaines *France* 19 C8
Airdrie *Canada* 102 C6
Airdrie *U.K.* 13 F5
Aire → *France* 19 C11
Aire → *U.K.* 14 D7
Aire, I. de l' *Spain* 48 B11
Aire-sur-la-Lys *France* 19 B9
Aire-sur-l'Adour *France* 20 E3
Airlie Beach *Australia* 94 J6
Airvault *France* 18 F6
Aisch → *Germany* 25 F6
Aisne □ *France* 19 C10
Aisne → *France* 19 C9
Ait *India* 69 G8
Aitana, Sierra de *Spain* 39 G4
Aitkin *U.S.A.* 112 B7
Aitutaki *Cook Is.* 97 J12
Aiud *Romania* 29 D8
Aix-en-Provence *France* 21 E9
Aix-la-Chapelle = Aachen
  Germany 24 E2
Aix-les-Bains *France* 21 C9
Aixe-sur-Vienne *France* 20 C5
Aíyina = Egina *Greece* 46 D5
Aizawl *India* 67 H18
Aizenay *France* 18 F5
Aizkraukle *Latvia* 32 D3
Aizpute *Latvia* 30 B8
Aizuwakamatsu *Japan* 54 F9
Ajabshir *Iran* 73 D11
Ajaccio *France* 21 G12
Ajaccio, G. d' *France* 21 G12
Ajai △ *Uganda* 86 B3
Ajaigarh *India* 69 G9
Ajalpan *Mexico* 119 D5
Ajanta Ra. *India* 66 J9
Ajari Rep. = Ajaria □
  Georgia 35 K6
Ajaria □ *Georgia* 35 K6
Ajax *Canada* 114 C5
Ajdābiyā *Libya* 79 B10
Ajdovščina *Slovenia* 41 C10
Ajibar *Ethiopia* 81 E4
Ajka *Hungary* 28 C2
'Ajlūn *Jordan* 74 C4
'Ajlūn □ *Jordan* 74 C4
'Ajmān *U.A.E.* 71 E7

Ajmer *India* 68 F6
Ajnala *India* 68 D6
Ajo *U.S.A.* 109 K7
Ajo, C. de *Spain* 36 B7
Ajok *Sudan* 81 F2
Ajuy *Phil.* 61 F5
Ak Dağ *Turkey* 47 E11
Ak Dağlar *Turkey* 72 C7
Ak Dağları *Turkey* 47 E11
Akaba *Togo* 83 D5
Akabira *Japan* 54 C11
Akagera △ *Rwanda* 86 C3
Akaki Beseka *Ethiopia* 81 F4
Akala *Sudan* 81 F2
Akamas *Cyprus* 49 D11
Akan △ *Japan* 54 C12
Akanthou *Cyprus* 49 D12
Akarca *Turkey* 47 C11
Akaroa *N.Z.* 91 E4
Akasha *Sudan* 80 C3
Akashi *Japan* 55 G7
Akbarpur *Bihar, India* 69 G10
Akbarpur *Ut. P., India* 69 F10
Akçaabat *Turkey* 73 B8
Akçadağ *Turkey* 72 C7
Akçakale *Turkey* 73 D8
Akçakoca *Turkey* 72 B4
Akçaova *Turkey* 45 E13
Akçay *Turkey* 47 E11
Akçay → *Turkey* 47 D10
Akdağ *Turkey* 47 C8
Akdağmadeni *Turkey* 72 C6
Akdoğan = Lysi *Cyprus* 49 D12
Akelamo *Indonesia* 63 D7
Aketi *Dem. Rep. of the Congo* 84 D4
Akhalkalaki *Georgia* 35 K6
Akhaltsikhe *Georgia* 35 K6
Akhisar *Turkey* 47 C9
Akhmîm *Egypt* 80 B3
Akhnur *India* 69 C6
Akhtopol *Bulgaria* 45 D11
Akhtuba → *Russia* 35 G8
Akhtubinsk *Russia* 35 F8
Akhty *Russia* 35 K8
Akhtyrka = Okhtyrka
  Ukraine 33 G8
Aki *Japan* 55 H6
Akimiski I. *Canada* 104 B3
Akimovka *Ukraine* 33 J8
Akıncı Burnu *Turkey* 72 D6
Akincilar = Louroujina
  Cyprus 49 E12
Åkirkeby *Denmark* 11 J8
Akita *Japan* 54 E10
Akita □ *Japan* 54 E10
Akjoujt *Mauritania* 82 B2
Akka *Mali* 82 B4
Akkaya Tepesi *Turkey* 47 D11
Akkeshi *Japan* 54 C12
'Akko *Israel* 74 C4
Akköy *Turkey* 47 D9
Akkuş *Turkey* 72 B7
Aklampa *Benin* 83 D5
Aklavik *Canada* 100 C6
Aklera *India* 68 G7
Akmenė *Lithuania* 30 B9
Akmenrags *Latvia* 30 B8
Akmonte = Almonte *Spain* 37 H4
Akō *Japan* 55 G7
Akobô *Sudan* 81 F3
Akobo → *Ethiopia* 81 F3
Akola *India* 66 J10
Akonolinga *Cameroon* 83 E7
Akor *Mali* 82 B4
Akordat *Eritrea* 81 D4
Akosombo Dam *Ghana* 83 D5
Akot *Sudan* 81 F3
Akoupé *Ivory C.* 82 D4
Akpatok I. *Canada* 101 C13
Åkrahamn *Norway* 9 G11
Akranes *Iceland* 8 D2
Akreïjit *Mauritania* 82 B3
Akritas, Akra *Greece* 46 E3
Akron *Colo., U.S.A.* 108 F12
Akron *Ohio, U.S.A.* 114 E3
Akrotiri *Cyprus* 49 E11
Akrotiri, Akra *Greece* 45 F9
Akrotiri Bay *Cyprus* 49 E12
Aksai Chin *China* 69 B8
Aksaray *Turkey* 72 C6
Aksaray □ *Turkey* 72 C5
Aksay = Aqsay *Kazakhstan* 52 D6
Akşehir *Turkey* 72 C4
Akşehir Gölü *Turkey* 72 C4
Akstafa = Ağstafa *Azerbaijan* 35 K7
Aksu *China* 60 B3
Aksu → *Turkey* 72 D4
Aksum *Ethiopia* 81 E4
Aktash *Russia* 34 C11
Aktsyabrski *Belarus* 23 B15
Aktyubinsk = Aqtöbe
  Kazakhstan 52 D6
Aku *Nigeria* 83 D6
Akure *Nigeria* 83 D6
Akureyri *Iceland* 8 D4

Akuseki-Shima *Japan* 55 K4
Akusha *Russia* 35 J8
Akwa-Ibom □ *Nigeria* 83 E6
Akyab = Sittwe *Burma* 67 J18
Akyazı *Turkey* 72 B4
Al 'Adan *Yemen* 75 E4
Al Aḥsā = Hasa *Si. Arabia* 71 E6
Al Ajfar *Si. Arabia* 70 E4
Al Amādīyah *Iraq* 73 D10
Al 'Amārah *Iraq* 73 G12
Al 'Anbār □ *Iraq* 70 C4
Al 'Aqabah *Jordan* 74 F4
Al 'Aqabah □ *Jordan* 74 F4
Al Arak *Syria* 73 E8
Al 'Aramah *Si. Arabia* 70 E5
Al 'Arṭāwiyah *Si. Arabia* 70 E5
Al 'Awdah *Si. Arabia* 70 E5
Al 'Ayn *Si. Arabia* 70 E3
Al 'Ayn *U.A.E.* 71 E7
Al 'Azīzīyah *Iraq* 73 F11
Al Bāb *Syria* 72 D7
Al Bad' *Si. Arabia* 70 D2
Al Bādī *Iraq* 70 C4
Al Baḥrah *Kuwait* 70 D5
Al Baḥral Mayyit = Dead
  Sea *Asia* 74 D4
Al Balqā' □ *Jordan* 74 C4
Al Bārūk, J. *Lebanon* 74 B4
Al Bāṣah *Si. Arabia* 80 C5
Al Baṣrah *Iraq* 70 D5
Al Baṭḥā *Iraq* 70 D5
Al Batrūn *Lebanon* 74 A4
Al Baydā *Libya* 79 B10
Al Biqā *Lebanon* 74 A5
Al Bi'r *Si. Arabia* 70 D3
Al Burayj *Syria* 74 A5
Al Bukayrīyah *Si. Arabia* 70 E4
Al Fādilī *Si. Arabia* 71 E6
Al Fallūjah *Iraq* 73 F10
Al Fatḥah *Iraq* 73 E10
Al Fāw *Iraq* 71 D6
Al Fujayrah *U.A.E.* 71 E8
Al Ghadaf, W. → *Jordan* 74 D5
Al Ghammās *Iraq* 70 D5
Al Ghazālah *Si. Arabia* 70 E4
Al Ḥadīthah *Iraq* 73 E10
Al Ḥadīthah *Si. Arabia* 74 D6
Al Hadr *Iraq* 73 E10
Al Ḥājānah *Syria* 74 B5
Al Ḥajar al Gharbī *Oman* 71 E8
Al Ḥāmad *Si. Arabia* 70 D3
Al Ḥamdānīyah *Syria* 70 C3
Al Ḥamīdīyah *Syria* 74 A4
Al Ḥammār *Iraq* 70 D5
Al Ḥamrā *Si. Arabia* 70 E3
Al Ḥamzah *Iraq* 70 D5
Al Ḥanākīyah *Si. Arabia* 70 E4
Al Ḥarūj al Aswad *Libya* 79 C9
Al Ḥasakah *Syria* 73 D9
Al Ḥasakah □ *Syria* 73 D9
Al Hāshimīyah *Iraq* 73 G11
Al Ḥayy *Iraq* 73 F12
Al Ḥijarah *Asia* 70 D4
Al Ḥillah *Iraq* 73 F11
Al Ḥillah *Si. Arabia* 75 B4
Al Hindīyah *Iraq* 73 F11
Al Hirmil *Lebanon* 74 A5
Al Hoceïma *Morocco* 78 A5
Al Ḥudaydah *Yemen* 75 E3
Al Ḥudūd ash
  Shamālīyah □ *Si. Arabia* 70 D4
Al Hufūf *Si. Arabia* 71 E6
Al Ḥumaydah *Si. Arabia* 70 D2
Al Ḥunayy *Si. Arabia* 71 E6
Al Īsāwīyah *Si. Arabia* 70 D3
Al Jafr *Jordan* 74 E5
Al Jāfūrah *Si. Arabia* 71 E7
Al Jaghbūb *Libya* 79 C10
Al Jahrah *Kuwait* 70 D5
Al Jalāmīd *Si. Arabia* 70 D3
Al Jamalīyah *Qatar* 71 E6
Al Janūb □ *Lebanon* 74 B4
Al Jawf *Libya* 79 D10
Al Jawf *Si. Arabia* 70 D3
Al Jawf □ *Si. Arabia* 70 D3
Al Jazair = Algeria ■ *Africa* 78 C6
Al Jazirah *Iraq* 73 E10
Al Jithāmīyah *Si. Arabia* 70 E4
Al Jubayl *Si. Arabia* 71 E6
Al Jubaylah *Si. Arabia* 70 E5
Al Jubb *Si. Arabia* 70 E4
Al Junaynah *Sudan* 79 F10
Al Kabā'ish *Iraq* 70 D5
Al Karak *Jordan* 74 D4
Al Karak □ *Jordan* 74 E5
Al Kāẓimīyah *Iraq* 73 F11
Al Khābūrah *Oman* 71 F8
Al Khafji *Si. Arabia* 71 E6
Al Khalīl *West Bank* 74 D4
Al Khāliṣ *Iraq* 73 F11
Al Kharsānīyah *Si. Arabia* 71 E6
Al Khaṣab *Oman* 71 E8
Al Khawr *Qatar* 71 E6
Al Khiḍr *Iraq* 70 D5
Al Khiyām *Lebanon* 74 B4

Al Khobar *Si. Arabia* 71 E6
Al Khums *Libya* 79 B8
Al Kifl *Iraq* 73 G11
Al Kiswah *Syria* 74 B5
Al Kūfah *Iraq* 73 F11
Al Kufrah *Libya* 79 D10
Al Kuhayfīyah *Si. Arabia* 70 E4
Al Kumayt *Iraq* 73 G12
Al Kūt *Iraq* 73 F11
Al Kuwayt *Kuwait* 70 D5
Al Labwah *Lebanon* 74 A5
Al Lādhiqīyah *Syria* 72 E6
Al Lādhiqīyah □ *Syria* 72 E6
Al Līth *Si. Arabia* 80 C5
Al Liwā' *Oman* 71 E8
Al Luḥayyah *Yemen* 75 D3
Al Madīnah *Iraq* 70 D5
Al Madīnah *Si. Arabia* 70 E3
Al Mafraq *Jordan* 74 C5
Al Mafraq □ *Jordan* 74 C5
Al Maghreb = Morocco ■
  N. Afr. 78 B4
Al Maḥmūdīyah *Iraq* 73 F11
Al Majma'ah *Si. Arabia* 70 E5
Al Makhruq, W. → *Jordan* 74 D6
Al Makhūl *Si. Arabia* 70 E4
Al Mālikīyah *Syria* 73 D10
Al Manāmah *Bahrain* 71 E6
Al Maqwa' *Kuwait* 70 D5
Al Marāḥ *Si. Arabia* 71 E6
Al Marj *Libya* 79 B10
Al Maṭla *Kuwait* 70 D5
Al Mawṣil *Iraq* 73 D10
Al Mayādin *Syria* 73 E9
Al Mazār *Jordan* 74 D4
Al Midhnab *Si. Arabia* 70 E5
Al Minā' *Lebanon* 74 A4
Al Miqdādīyah *Iraq* 73 E11
Al Mubarraz *Si. Arabia* 71 E6
Al Mudawwarah *Jordan* 74 F5
Al Mughayrā' *U.A.E.* 71 E7
Al Muḥarraq *Bahrain* 71 E6
Al Mukallā *Yemen* 75 E4
Al Mukhā *Yemen* 75 E3
Al Musayjīd *Si. Arabia* 70 E3
Al Musayyib *Iraq* 73 F11
Al Muthanná □ *Iraq* 70 D5
Al Muwayh *Si. Arabia* 80 C5
Al Muwayliḥ *Si. Arabia* 70 E2
Al Owuho = Otukpa *Nigeria* 83 D6
Al Qādisīyah □ *Iraq* 70 D5
Al Qā'im *Iraq* 73 E9
Al Qalībah *Si. Arabia* 70 D3
Al Qāmishlī *Syria* 73 D9
Al Qaryatayn *Syria* 74 A6
Al Qaşīm □ *Si. Arabia* 70 E4
Al Qaṭ'ā *Syria* 73 E9
Al Qaṭīf *Si. Arabia* 71 E6
Al Qaṭrānah *Jordan* 74 D5
Al Qaṭrūn *Libya* 79 D9
Al Qawz *Si. Arabia* 80 C5
Al Qayşūmah *Si. Arabia* 70 D5
Al Quds = Jerusalem
  Israel/West Bank 74 D4
Al Qunayṭirah *Syria* 74 C4
Al Qunfudhah *Si. Arabia* 80 D5
Al Qurnah *Iraq* 70 D5
Al Quşayr *Iraq* 70 D5
Al Quşayr *Syria* 74 A5
Al Qutayfah *Syria* 74 B5
Al Quwayr *Iraq* 73 D10
Al 'Ubaylah *Si. Arabia* 75 C5
Al 'Udaylīyah *Si. Arabia* 71 E6
Al 'Ulā *Si. Arabia* 70 E3
Al 'Uqayr *Si. Arabia* 71 E6
Al 'Uwaynid *Si. Arabia* 70 E5
Al 'Uwayqīlah *Si. Arabia* 70 D4
Al 'Uyūn *Ḥijāz, Si. Arabia* 70 E3
Al 'Uyūn *Najd, Si. Arabia* 70 E4
Al 'Uzayr *Iraq* 70 D5
Al Wajh *Si. Arabia* 70 E3
Al Wakrah *Qatar* 71 E6
Al Waqbah *Si. Arabia* 70 D5
Al Wari'āh *Si. Arabia* 70 E5
Al Yaman = Yemen ■ *Asia* 75 E3
Ala *Italy* 40 C8
Ala Dağ *Turkey* 70 B2
Ala Dağları *Turkey* 73 C10
Ala Tau *Asia* 52 E9
Alabama □ *U.S.A.* 117 E11
Alabama → *U.S.A.* 117 F11
Alabaster *U.S.A.* 117 E11
Alaca *Turkey* 72 B6
Alaçam *Turkey* 72 B6
Alaçam Dağları *Turkey* 47 B10
Alacant = Alicante *Spain* 39 G4
Alaçatı *Turkey* 47 C8
Alachua *U.S.A.* 117 G13
Alaejos *Spain* 36 D5
Alagir *Russia* 35 J7
Alagna Valsésia *Italy* 40 C4
Alagoa Grande *Brazil* 125 E11
Alagoas □ *Brazil* 125 E11
Alagoinhas *Brazil* 125 F11
Alagón *Spain* 38 D3
Alagón → *Spain* 36 F4
Alaior *Spain* 48 B11

Alajero *Canary Is.* 48 F2
Alajuela *Costa Rica* 120 D3
Alakamisy *Madag.* 89 C8
Alaknanda → *India* 69 D8
Alaköl *Kazakhstan* 60 B3
Alakurtti *Russia* 8 C24
Alamarvdasht *Iran* 71 E7
Alamata *Ethiopia* 81 E4
Alameda *Calif., U.S.A.* 110 H4
Alameda *N. Mex., U.S.A.* 109 J10
Alaminos *Phil.* 61 C3
Alamo *U.S.A.* 111 H11
Alamogordo *U.S.A.* 109 K11
Alamos *Mexico* 118 B3
Alamosa *U.S.A.* 109 H11
Åland *Finland* 9 F19
Alandroal *Portugal* 37 G3
Ålands hav *Europe* 9 G18
Alange, Embalse d' *Spain* 37 G4
Alania = North Ossetia □
  Russia 35 J7
Alanís *Spain* 37 G5
Alanya *Turkey* 72 D5
Alaotra, Farihin' *Madag.* 89 B8
Alapayevsk *Russia* 52 D7
Alappuzha = Alleppey *India*
  66 Q10
Alar del Rey *Spain* 36 C6
Alaraz *Spain* 36 E5
Alarcón, Embalse de *Spain* 38 F2
Alaró *Spain* 48 B9
Alarobia-Vohiposa *Madag.* 89 C8
Alaşehir *Turkey* 47 C10
Alashtar *Iran* 73 F13
Alaska □ *U.S.A.* 106 C1
Alaska, G. of *Pac. Oc.* 106 a
Alaska Peninsula *U.S.A.* 106 a
Alaska Range *U.S.A.* 106 a
Alássio *Italy* 40 D5
Älät *Azerbaijan* 35 L9
Alatau Shan = Ala Tau *Asia* 52 E9
Alatri *Italy* 41 G10
Alatyr *Russia* 34 C8
Alatyr → *Russia* 34 C8
Alausi *Ecuador* 124 D3
Álava □ *Spain* 38 C2
Alava, C. *U.S.A.* 108 B1
Alaverdi *Armenia* 35 K7
Alavo = Alavus *Finland* 8 E20
Alavus *Finland* 8 E20
'Alayh *Lebanon* 74 B4
Alazana → *Azerbaijan* 35 K8
Alazani → *Azerbaijan* 35 K8
Alba *Italy* 40 D5
Alba □ *Romania* 29 D8
Alba Adriática *Italy* 41 F10
Alba de Tormes *Spain* 36 E5
Alba-Iulia *Romania* 29 D8
Albac *Romania* 28 D7
Albacete *Spain* 39 F3
Albacete □ *Spain* 39 G3
Albacutya, L. *Australia* 95 F3
Ålbæk *Denmark* 11 G4
Ålbæk Bugt *Denmark* 11 G4
Albaida *Spain* 39 G4
Albalate de las Nogueras
  Spain 38 E2
Albalate del Arzobispo *Spain* 38 D4
Alban *France* 20 E6
Albanel, L. *Canada* 104 B5
Albania ■ *Europe* 44 E4
Albano Laziale *Italy* 41 G9
Albany *Australia* 93 G2
Albany *Ga., U.S.A.* 117 F12
Albany *N.Y., U.S.A.* 115 D11
Albany *Oreg., U.S.A.* 108 D2
Albany *Tex., U.S.A.* 116 E5
Albany → *Canada* 104 B3
Albarca, C. d' *Spain* 48 B7
Albardón *Argentina* 126 C2
Albarracín *Spain* 38 E3
Albarracín, Sierra de *Spain* 38 E3
Albatera *Spain* 39 G4
Albatross B. *Australia* 94 A3
Albemarle *U.S.A.* 117 D14
Albemarle Sd. *U.S.A.* 117 C16
Albenga *Italy* 40 D5
Alberche → *Spain* 36 F6
Alberdi *Paraguay* 126 B4
Albert, L. *Africa* 86 B3
Albert, L. *Australia* 95 F2
Albert Edward Ra. *Australia* 92 C4
Albert Lea *U.S.A.* 112 D7
Albert Nile → *Uganda* 86 B3
Albert Town *Bahamas* 121 B5
Alberta □ *Canada* 102 C6
Alberti *Argentina* 126 D3
Albertinia *S. Africa* 88 E3
Albertirsa *Hungary* 28 C4
Alberton *Canada* 105 C7
Albertville *France* 21 C10
Albertville *U.S.A.* 117 D11

Albi *France* 20 E6
Albia *U.S.A.* 112 E7
Albina *Suriname* 125 B8
Albina, Ponta *Angola* 88 B1
Albino *Italy* 40 C6
Albion *Mich., U.S.A.* 113 D11
Albion *Nebr., U.S.A.* 112 E4
Albion *Pa., U.S.A.* 114 E4
Alborán *Medit. S.* 37 K7
Alborea *Spain* 39 F3
Ålborg = Aalborg *Denmark* 11 G3
Ålborg Bugt = Aalborg
  Bugt *Denmark* 11 H4
Alborz, Reshteh-ye
  Kūhhā-ye *Iran* 71 C7
Albox *Spain* 39 H2
Albufeira *Portugal* 37 H2
Albula → *Switz.* 25 J5
Albuñol *Spain* 37 J7
Albuquerque *U.S.A.* 109 J10
Albuquerque, Cayos de
  Caribbean 120 D3
Alburg *U.S.A.* 115 B11
Alburno, Mte. *Italy* 43 B8
Alburquerque *Spain* 37 F4
Albury *Australia* 95 F4
Alcácer do Sal *Portugal* 37 G2
Alcáçovas *Portugal* 37 G2
Alcalá de Guadaira *Spain* 37 H5
Alcalá de Henares *Spain* 36 E7
Alcalá de los Gazules *Spain* 37 J5
Alcalá de Xivert *Spain* 38 E5
Alcalá del Júcar *Spain* 39 F3
Alcalá del Río *Spain* 37 H5
Alcalá del Valle *Spain* 37 J5
Alcalá la Real *Spain* 37 H7
Álcamo *Italy* 42 E5
Alcanadre *Spain* 38 C2
Alcanadre → *Spain* 38 D4
Alcanar *Spain* 38 E5
Alcanede *Portugal* 37 F2
Alcanena *Portugal* 37 F2
Alcañices *Spain* 36 D4
Alcañiz *Spain* 38 D4
Alcântara *Brazil* 125 D10
Alcántara *Spain* 37 F4
Alcántara, Embalse de *Spain* 36 F4
Alcantarilla *Spain* 39 H3
Alcaracejos *Spain* 37 G6
Alcaraz *Spain* 39 G2
Alcaraz, Sierra de *Spain* 39 G2
Alcaudete *Spain* 37 H6
Alcázar de San Juan *Spain* 37 F7
Alchevsk *Ukraine* 33 H10
Alcira = Alzira *Spain* 39 F4
Alcobaça *Portugal* 37 F2
Alcobendas *Spain* 36 E7
Alcolea del Pinar *Spain* 38 D2
Alcorcón *Spain* 36 E7
Alcoutim *Portugal* 37 H3
Alcova *U.S.A.* 108 E10
Alcoy *Spain* 39 G4
Alcubierre, Sierra de *Spain* 38 D4
Alcublas *Spain* 38 F4
Alcúdia *Spain* 48 B10
Alcúdia, B. d' *Spain* 48 B10
Alcúdia, Sierra de la *Spain* 37 G6
Aldabra Is. *Seychelles* 77 G8
Aldama *Mexico* 119 C5
Aldan *Russia* 53 D13
Aldan → *Russia* 53 C13
Aldea, Pta. de la *Canary Is.* 48 G4
Aldeburgh *U.K.* 15 E9
Alder Pk. *U.S.A.* 110 K5
Alderney *U.K.* 15 H5
Aldershot *U.K.* 15 F7
Åled *Sweden* 11 H6
Aledo *U.S.A.* 112 E8
Alefa *Ethiopia* 81 E4
Aleg *Mauritania* 82 B2
Alegranza *Canary Is.* 48 E6
Alegranza, I. *Canary Is.* 48 E6
Alegre *Brazil* 127 A7
Alegrete *Brazil* 127 B4
Aleksandriya =
  Oleksandriya *Kirovohrad,
  Ukraine* 33 H7
Aleksandriya =
  Oleksandriya *Rivne,
  Ukraine* 23 C14
Aleksandriyskaya *Russia* 35 J8
Aleksandrov *Russia* 32 D10
Aleksandrov Gay *Russia* 34 E9
Aleksandrovac *Serbia* 44 C5
Aleksandrovac *Serbia* 44 B5
Aleksandrovka =
  Oleksandrivka *Ukraine* 33 H7
Aleksandrovo *Bulgaria* 45 C8
Aleksandrovsk-
  Sakhalinskiy *Russia* 53 D15
Aleksandrów Kujawski
  Poland 31 B5
Aleksandrów Łódzki *Poland* 31 G6
Aleksandry, Zemlya *Russia* 52 A5
Alekseyevka *Samara, Russia* 34 D10
Alekseyevka *Voronezh,
  Russia* 33 G10

Aleksin *Russia* **32** E9
Aleksinac *Serbia* **44** C5
Além Paraíba *Brazil* **127** A7
Alemania *Argentina* **126** B2
Alemania *Chile* **126** B2
Alençon *France* **18** D7
Alenquer *Brazil* **125** D8
'Alenuihähä Channel *U.S.A.* **106** b
Aleppo = Ḥalab *Syria* **72** D7
Aléria *France* **21** F13
Alert *Canada* **101** A13
Alès *France* **21** D8
Aleşd *Romania* **28** C7
Alessándria *Italy* **40** D5
Ålesund *Norway* **8** E12
Alet-les-Bains *France* **20** F6
Aletschhorn *Switz.* **25** J4
Aleutian Basin *Pac. Oc.* **96** B9
Aleutian Is. *Pac. Oc.* **106** a
Aleutian Trench *Pac. Oc.* **4** D17
Alexander *U.S.A.* **112** B2
Alexander, Mt. *Australia* **93** E3
Alexander Arch. *U.S.A.* **100** D6
Alexander Bay *S. Africa* **88** D2
Alexander City *U.S.A.* **117** E12
Alexander I. *Antarctica* **5** C17
Alexandra *Australia* **95** F4
Alexandra *N.Z.* **91** F2
Alexandra Falls *Canada* **102** A5
Alexandria = El
  Iskandarîya *Egypt* **80** H7
Alexandria *B.C., Canada* **102** C4
Alexandria *Ont., Canada* **115** A10
Alexandria *Romania* **29** G10
Alexandria *S. Africa* **88** E4
Alexandria *U.K.* **13** F4
Alexandria *La., U.S.A.* **116** F8
Alexandria *Minn., U.S.A.* **112** C6
Alexandria *S. Dak., U.S.A.* **112** D5
Alexandria *Va., U.S.A.* **113** F15
Alexandria Bay *U.S.A.* **115** A8
Alexandrina, L. *Australia* **95** F2
Alexandroupoli *Greece* **45** F9
Alexis → *Canada* **105** B8
Alexis Creek *Canada* **102** C4
Aleysk *Russia* **52** D9
Alfabia *Spain* **48** B9
Alfambra *Spain* **38** E3
Alfaro *Spain* **38** C3
Alfatar *Bulgaria* **45** C11
Alfeld *Germany* **24** D5
Alfenas *Brazil* **127** A6
Alföld *Hungary* **28** D3
Alfonsine *Italy* **41** D9
Alford *Aberds., U.K.* **13** D6
Alford *Lincs., U.K.* **14** D8
Alfred *Maine, U.S.A.* **115** C14
Alfred *N.Y., U.S.A.* **114** D7
Alfreton *U.K.* **14** D6
Alfta *Sweden* **10** C10
Algaida *Spain* **48** B9
Algar *Spain* **37** J5
Ålgård *Norway* **9** G11
Algarinejo *Spain* **37** H6
Algarve *Portugal* **37** J2
Algeciras *Spain* **37** J5
Algemesí *Spain* **39** F4
Alger *Algeria* **78** A6
Alger □ *Algeria* **39** J8
Alger ✈ (ALG) *Algeria* **39** J8
Algeria ■ *Africa* **78** C6
Algha *Kazakhstan* **52** E6
Alghero *Italy* **42** B1
Älghult *Sweden* **11** G9
Algiers = Alger *Algeria* **78** A6
Algoa B. *S. Africa* **88** E4
Algodonales *Spain* **37** J5
Algodor → *Spain* **36** F7
Algoma *U.S.A.* **112** C10
Algona *U.S.A.* **112** D6
Algonac *U.S.A.* **114** D2
Algonquin △ *Canada* **104** C4
Algorta *Uruguay* **128** C5
Alhama de Almería *Spain* **37** J8
Alhama de Aragón *Spain* **38** D3
Alhama de Granada *Spain* **37** H7
Alhama de Murcia *Spain* **39** H3
Alhambra *U.S.A.* **111** L8
Alhaurín el Grande *Spain* **37** J6
Alhucemas = Al Hoceïma
  Morocco **78** A5
'Alī al Gharbī *Iraq* **73** F12
'Alī ash Sharqī *Iraq* **73** F12
Äli Bayramlı *Azerbaijan* **35** L9
'Alī Khēl *Afghan.* **68** C3
Alī Shāh *Iran* **70** B5
Ália *Italy* **42** E6
Alīābād *Iran* **71** B7
'Alīābād *Khorāsān, Iran* **71** C8
'Alīābād *Kordestān, Iran* **70** C5
'Alīābād *Yazd, Iran* **71** D7
Aliağa *Spain* **38** E4
Aliağa *Turkey* **47** C8
Aliakmonas → *Greece* **44** F6
Alibo *Ethiopia* **81** F4

Alibori → *Benin* **83** C5
Alibunar *Serbia* **28** E5
Alicante *Spain* **39** G4
Alicante □ *Spain* **39** G4
Alicante ✈ (ALC) *Spain* **39** G4
Alice *S. Africa* **88** E4
Alice *U.S.A.* **116** H5
Alice → *Queens., Australia* **94** C3
Alice → *Queens., Australia* **94** B3
Alice, Punta *Italy* **43** C10
Alice Arm *Canada* **102** B3
Alicedale *S. Africa* **88** E4
Aliceville *U.S.A.* **117** E10
Alicudi *Italy* **43** D7
Aliganj *India* **69** F8
Aligarh *Raj., India* **68** G7
Aligarh *Ut. P., India* **68** F8
Alīgūdarz *Iran* **71** C6
Alijó *Portugal* **36** D3
Alimia *Greece* **49** C9
Alingsås *Sweden* **11** G6
Alipur *Pakistan* **68** E4
Alipur Duar *India* **67** F16
Aliquippa *U.S.A.* **114** F4
Alishan *Taiwan* **59** F13
Aliste → *Spain* **36** D5
Aliveri *Greece* **46** C6
Aliwal North *S. Africa* **88** E4
Alix *Canada* **102** C6
Aljezur *Portugal* **37** H2
Aljustrel *Portugal* **37** H2
Alkamari *Niger* **83** C7
Alkmaar *Neths.* **17** B4
All American Canal *U.S.A.* **109** K6
Allada *Benin* **83** D5
Allagash → *U.S.A.* **113** B19
Allah Dad *Pakistan* **68** G2
Allahabad *India* **69** G9
Allan *Canada* **103** C7
Allanche *France* **20** C6
Allanridge *S. Africa* **88** D4
Allaqi, Wadi → *Egypt* **80** C3
Allariz *Spain* **36** C3
Allassac *France* **20** C5
Ålleberg *Sweden* **11** F7
Allegany *U.S.A.* **114** D6
Allegheny → *U.S.A.* **114** F5
Allegheny Mts. *U.S.A.* **113** F13
Allegheny Plateau *U.S.A.* **113** E14
Allegheny Res. *U.S.A.* **114** E6
Allègre *France* **20** C7
Allègre, Pte. *Guadeloupe* **120** b
Allen, Bog of *Ireland* **12** C5
Allen, L. *Ireland* **12** B3
Allendale *U.S.A.* **117** E14
Allende *Mexico* **118** B4
Allentown *U.S.A.* **115** F9
Allentsteig *Austria* **26** C8
Alleppey *India* **66** Q10
Allepuz *Spain* **38** E4
Aller → *Germany* **24** C5
Alleynes B. *Barbados* **121** g
Alliance *Nebr., U.S.A.* **112** D2
Alliance *Ohio, U.S.A.* **114** F3
Allier □ *France* **19** F9
Allier → *France* **19** F10
Alligator Bay *Canada* **102** C2
Alligator Pond *Jamaica* **120** a
Allinge *Denmark* **11** J8
Alliston *Canada* **114** B5
Alloa *U.K.* **13** E5
Allones *France* **18** D8
Allora *Australia* **95** D5
Allos *France* **21** D10
Alluitsup Paa *Greenland* **4** C5
Alma *Canada* **105** C5
Alma *Ga., U.S.A.* **117** F13
Alma *Kans., U.S.A.* **112** F5
Alma *Mich., U.S.A.* **113** D11
Alma *Nebr., U.S.A.* **112** E5
Alma *Wis., U.S.A.* **112** C8
Alma Ata = Almaty
  Kazakhstan **52** E8
Alma Hill *U.S.A.* **114** D7
Almacelles *Spain* **38** D5
Almada *Portugal* **37** G1
Almaden *Australia* **94** B3
Almadén *Spain* **37** G6
Almalyk = Olmaliq
  Uzbekistan **52** E7
Almanor, L. *U.S.A.* **108** F3
Almansa *Spain* **39** G3
Almanza *Spain* **36** C5
Almanzor, Pico *Spain* **36** E5
Almanzora → *Spain* **39** H3
Almaş, Munţii *Romania* **28** E7
Almassora *Spain* **38** E4
Almazán *Spain* **38** D2
Almeirim *Brazil* **125** D8
Almeirim *Portugal* **37** F2
Almelo *Neths.* **17** B6
Almenar de Soria *Spain* **38** D2
Almenara *Spain* **38** E4
Almenara, Sierra de *Spain* **39** H3
Almendra, Embalse de *Spain* **36** D4

Almendralejo *Spain* **37** G4
Almere-Stad *Neths.* **17** B5
Almería *Spain* **37** J8
Almería □ *Spain* **39** H2
Almería, G. de *Spain* **39** J2
Almetyevsk *Russia* **34** C11
Älmhult *Sweden* **11** H8
Almirante *Panama* **120** E3
Almiropotamos *Greece* **46** C6
Almiros *Greece* **46** B4
Almodôvar *Portugal* **37** H2
Almodóvar del Campo *Spain* **37** G6
Almodóvar del Río *Spain* **37** H5
Almond → *U.S.A.* **114** D7
Almont *U.S.A.* **114** D1
Almonte *Canada* **115** A8
Almonte *Spain* **37** H4
Almora *India* **69** E8
Almoradí *Spain* **39** G4
Almorox *Spain* **36** E6
Almoustarat *Mali* **83** B5
Almuñécar *Spain* **37** J7
Almunge *Sweden* **10** E12
Almuradiel *Spain* **37** G7
Almus *Turkey* **72** B7
Almyrou, Ormos *Greece* **49** D6
Alness *U.K.* **13** D4
Alnmouth *U.K.* **14** B6
Alnwick *U.K.* **14** B6
Aloi *Uganda* **86** B3
Alon *Burma* **67** H19
Alonissos *Greece* **46** B5
Alonissos-Northern
  Sporades △ *Greece* **46** B6
Alor *Indonesia* **63** F6
Alor Setar *Malaysia* **65** J3
Álora *Spain* **37** J6
Alosno *Spain* **37** H3
Alot *India* **68** H6
Aloysius, Mt. *Australia* **93** E4
Alpaugh *U.S.A.* **110** K7
Alpe Apuane △ *Italy* **40** D7
Alpedrinha *Portugal* **36** E3
Alpena *U.S.A.* **113** C12
Alpes-de-Haute-
  Provence □ *France* **21** D10
Alpes-Maritimes □ *France* **21** E11
Alpha *Australia* **94** C4
Alpha Ridge *Arctic* **4** A2
Alphen aan den Rijn *Neths.* **17** B4
Alphios → *Greece* **46** D3
Alpiarça *Portugal* **37** F2
Alpine *Ariz., U.S.A.* **109** K9
Alpine *Calif., U.S.A.* **111** N10
Alpine *Tex., U.S.A.* **116** F3
Alps *Europe* **22** E5
Alpu *Turkey* **72** C4
Alpurrurulam *Australia* **94** C2
Alqueta, Barragem do
  Portugal **37** G3
Alrø *Denmark* **11** J4
Als *Denmark* **11** K3
Alsace □ *France* **19** D14
Alsask *Canada* **103** C7
Alsasua *Spain* **38** C2
Alsek → *U.S.A.* **102** B1
Alsfeld *Germany* **24** E5
Alsta *Norway* **8** D15
Alstermo *Sweden* **11** H9
Alston *U.K.* **14** C5
Alta *Norway* **8** B20
Alta, Sierra *Spain* **38** E3
Alta Gracia *Argentina* **126** C3
Alta Sierra *U.S.A.* **111** K8
Altaelva → *Norway* **8** B20
Altafjorden *Norway* **8** A20
Altai = Aerhtai Shan
  Mongolia **60** B4
Altai = Gorno-Altay □
  Russia **52** D9
Altamaha → *U.S.A.* **117** F14
Altamira *Brazil* **125** D8
Altamira *Chile* **126** B2
Altamira *Mexico* **119** C5
Altamira, Cuevas de *Spain* **36** B6
Altamont *U.S.A.* **115** D10
Altamura *Italy* **43** B9
Altanbulag *Mongolia* **60** A5
Altar *Mexico* **118** A2
Altar, Gran Desierto de
  Mexico **118** B2
Altata *Mexico* **118** C3
Altavista *U.S.A.* **113** G14
Altay *China* **60** B3
Altdorf *Switz.* **25** J4
Alte Mellum *Germany* **24** B4
Altea *Spain* **39** G4
Altenberg *Germany* **24** E9
Altenbruch *Germany* **24** B4
Altenburg *Germany* **24** E8
Altenkirchen
  *Mecklenburg-Vorpommern,
  Germany* **24** A9
Altenkirchen *Rhld-Pfz.,
  Germany* **24** E3

Alter do Chão *Portugal* **37** F3
Altınkaya Barajı *Turkey* **72** B6
Altınoluk *Turkey* **47** B8
Altınova *Turkey* **47** B8
Altıntaş *Turkey* **47** B12
Altınyaka *Turkey* **47** E12
Altınyayla *Turkey* **47** D11
Altiplano *Bolivia* **124** G5
Altkirch *France* **19** E14
Altmark *Germany* **24** C7
Altmühl → *Germany* **25** G7
Altmühltal △ *Germany* **25** G7
Altmunster *Austria* **26** D6
Alto Adige = Trentino-Alto
  Adige □ *Italy* **41** B8
Alto Araguaia *Brazil* **125** G8
Alto Cuchumatanes =
  Cuchumatanes, Sierra
  de los *Guatemala* **120** C1
Alto del Carmen *Chile* **126** B1
Alto Garda Bresciano △
  Italy **40** C7
Alto Ligonha *Mozam.* **87** F4
Alto Molocue *Mozam.* **87** F4
Alto Paraguay □ *Paraguay* **126** A4
Alto Paraná □ *Paraguay* **127** B5
Alton *Canada* **114** C4
Alton *U.K.* **15** F7
Alton *Ill., U.S.A.* **112** F8
Alton *N.H., U.S.A.* **115** C13
Altona *Canada* **103** D9
Altoona *U.S.A.* **114** F6
Altötting *Germany* **25** G8
Altstätten *Switz.* **25** H5
Altun Kupri *Iraq* **73** E11
Altun Shan *China* **60** C3
Alturas *U.S.A.* **108** F3
Altus *U.S.A.* **116** D5
Alubijid *Phil.* **61** G6
Alucra *Turkey* **73** B8
Aluk *Sudan* **81** F2
Alūksne *Latvia* **32** D4
Alunda *Sweden* **10** D12
Alunite *U.S.A.* **111** K12
Aluoro → *Ethiopia* **81** F3
Alupka *Ukraine* **33** K8
Alushta *Ukraine* **33** K8
Alusi *Indonesia* **63** F8
Alustante *Spain* **38** E3
Alva *U.S.A.* **116** C5
Alvaiázere *Portugal* **36** F2
Älvängen *Sweden* **11** G6
Alvão △ *Portugal* **36** D3
Alvarado *Mexico* **119** D5
Alvarado *U.S.A.* **116** E6
Alvaro Obregón, Presa
  Mexico **118** B3
Älvdalen *Sweden* **10** C8
Alvear *Argentina* **126** B4
Alverca *Portugal* **37** G1
Alvesta *Sweden* **11** H8
Alvin *U.S.A.* **116** G7
Alvinston *Canada* **114** D3
Alvito *Portugal* **37** G3
Älvkarleby *Sweden* **10** D11
Alvord Desert *U.S.A.* **108** E4
Älvros *Sweden* **10** B8
Älvsbyn *Sweden* **8** D19
Alwar *India* **68** F7
Alxa Zuoqi *China* **56** E3
Alyangula *Australia* **94** A2
Alyata = Älät *Azerbaijan* **35** L9
Alyth *U.K.* **13** E5
Alytus *Lithuania* **32** E3
Alzada *U.S.A.* **108** D11
Alzamay *Russia* **53** D10
Alzey *Germany* **25** F4
Alzira *Spain* **39** F4
Am Timan *Chad* **79** F10
Amadeus, L. *Australia* **93** D5
Amadi *Dem. Rep. of the Congo* **86** B2
Amâdi *Sudan* **81** F3
Amadjuak L. *Canada* **101** C12
Amadora *Portugal* **37** G1
Amagansett *U.S.A.* **115** F12
Amagasaki *Japan* **55** G7
Amager *Denmark* **11** J6
Amagunze *Nigeria* **83** D6
Amahai *Indonesia* **63** E7
Amaile *Samoa* **91** b
Amakusa-Shotō *Japan* **55** H5
Åmål *Sweden* **10** E6
Amaliás *Italy* **41** F9
Amaliada *Greece* **46** D3
Amalner *India* **66** J9
Amamapare *Indonesia* **63** E9
Amambaí *Brazil* **127** A4
Amambaí → *Brazil* **127** A5
Amambay □ *Paraguay* **127** A4
Amambay, Cordillera de
  S. Amer. **127** B4
Amami-Guntō *Japan* **55** L4
Amami-Ō-Shima *Japan* **55** K4
Aman, Pulau *Malaysia* **65** c
Amaná, L. *Brazil* **124** D6
Amanat → *India* **69** G11
Amanda Park *U.S.A.* **110** C3

Amankeldi *Kazakhstan* **52** D7
Amantea *Italy* **43** C9
Amapá *Brazil* **125** C8
Amapá □ *Brazil* **125** C8
Amara *Sudan* **81** E3
Amara □ *Ethiopia* **81** E4
Amarante *Brazil* **125** E10
Amarante *Portugal* **36** D2
Amaranth *Canada* **103** C9
Amareleja *Portugal* **37** G3
Amargosa *Brazil* **125** F11
Amargosa → *U.S.A.* **111** J10
Amargosa Desert *U.S.A.* **111** J10
Amargosa Range *U.S.A.* **111** J10
Amari *Greece* **49** D6
Amârna, Tell el' *Sudan* **80** B3
Amaro, Mte. *Italy* **41** F11
Amarpur *India* **69** G12
Amarti *Eritrea* **81** E5
Amarwara *India* **69** H8
Amasra *Turkey* **72** B5
Amassama *Nigeria* **83** D6
Amasya *Turkey* **72** B6
Amasya □ *Turkey* **72** B6
Amata *Australia* **93** E5
Amatignak I. *U.S.A.* **106** b
Amatikulu *S. Africa* **89** D5
Amatitlán *Guatemala* **120** D1
Amatrice *Italy* **41** F10
Amay *Belgium* **17** D5
Amazon = Amazonas →
  S. Amer. **125** D8
Amazonas □ *Brazil* **124** E6
Amazonas → *S. Amer.* **125** D8
Amba Ferit *Ethiopia* **81** E4
Ambah *India* **68** F8
Ambahakily *Madag.* **89** C7
Ambahita *Madag.* **89** C8
Ambala *India* **68** D7
Ambalavao *Madag.* **89** C8
Ambanja *Madag.* **89** A8
Ambararata *Madag.* **89** C8
Ambarchik *Russia* **53** C17
Ambarijeby *Madag.* **89** A8
Ambaro, Helodranon'
  Madag. **89** A8
Ambato *Ecuador* **124** D3
Ambato *Madag.* **89** B8
Ambato, Sierra de *Argentina* **126** B2
Ambato Boeny *Madag.* **89** B8
Ambatofinandrahana
  Madag. **89** C8
Ambatolampy *Madag.* **89** B8
Ambatomainty *Madag.* **89** B8
Ambatomanoina *Madag.* **89** B8
Ambatondrazaka *Madag.* **89** B8
Ambatosoratra *Madag.* **89** B8
Ambelonas *Greece* **46** B4
Ambenja *Madag.* **89** B8
Amberg *Germany* **25** F7
Ambergris Cay *Belize* **119** D7
Ambérieu-en-Bugey *France* **21** C9
Amberley *Canada* **114** B3
Amberley *N.Z.* **91** E4
Ambert *France* **20** C7
Ambidédi *Mali* **82** C2
Ambikapur *India* **69** H10
Ambikol *Sudan* **80** C3
Ambilobé *Madag.* **89** A8
Ambinanindrano *Madag.* **89** C8
Ambinanitelo *Madag.* **89** B8
Ambinda *Madag.* **89** B8
Ambleside *U.K.* **14** C5
Ambo *Peru* **124** F3
Amboahangy *Madag.* **89** C8
Ambodifototra *Madag.* **89** B8
Ambodilazana *Madag.* **89** B8
Ambodiriana *Madag.* **89** B8
Ambohidratrimo *Madag.* **89** B8
Ambohidray *Madag.* **89** B8
Ambohimahamasina
  Madag. **89** C8
Ambohimahasoa *Madag.* **89** C8
Ambohimanga *Madag.* **89** C8
Ambohimitombo *Madag.* **89** C8
Ambohitra *Madag.* **89** A8
Amboise *France* **18** E8
Ambon *Indonesia* **63** E7
Ambondro *Madag.* **89** D8
Amboseli, L. *Kenya* **86** C4
Amboseli △ *Kenya* **86** C4
Ambositra *Madag.* **89** C8
Ambovombe *Madag.* **89** D8
Amboy *U.S.A.* **111** L11
Amboyna Cay *S. China Sea* **62** C4
Ambridge *U.S.A.* **114** F4
Ambriz *Angola* **84** F2
Ambrolauri *Georgia* **73** A10
Amchitka I. *U.S.A.* **106** a
Amderma *Russia* **52** C7
Amdhi *India* **69** H9
Amdo *China* **67** C17
Ameca *Mexico* **118** C4
Ameca → *Mexico* **118** C3
Amecameca de Juárez
  Mexico **119** D5
Ameland *Neths.* **17** A5

Amélia *Italy* **41** F9
Amendolara *Italy* **43** C9
Amenia *U.S.A.* **115** E11
America-Antarctica Ridge
  S. Ocean **5** B1
American Falls *U.S.A.* **108** E7
American Falls Res. *U.S.A.* **108** E7
American Fork *U.S.A.* **108** F8
American Highland
  Antarctica **5** D6
American Samoa ☑ *Pac. Oc.* **91** b
American Samoa △
  Amer. Samoa **91** b
Americana *Brazil* **127** A6
Americus *U.S.A.* **117** E12
Amerigo Vespucci,
  Firenze ✈ (FLR) *Italy* **41** E8
Amersfoort *Neths.* **17** B5
Amersfoort *S. Africa* **89** D4
Amery Basin *S. Ocean* **5** C6
Amery Ice Shelf *Antarctica* **5** C6
Ames = Bertamirans *Spain* **36** C2
Ames *U.S.A.* **112** D7
Amesbury *U.S.A.* **115** D14
Amet *India* **68** G5
Amfikleia *Greece* **46** C4
Amfilochia *Greece* **46** C3
Amfipoli *Greece* **44** F7
Amfissa *Greece* **46** C4
Amga *Russia* **53** C14
Amga → *Russia* **53** C14
Amgu *Russia* **54** B8
Amgun → *Russia* **53** D14
Amherst *Canada* **105** C7
Amherst *Mass., U.S.A.* **115** D12
Amherst *N.Y., U.S.A.* **114** D6
Amherst *Ohio, U.S.A.* **114** E2
Amherst I. *Canada* **115** B8
Amherstburg *Canada* **104** D3
Amiata, Mte. *Italy* **41** F8
Amidon *U.S.A.* **112** B2
Amiens *France* **19** C9
Amindeo *Greece* **44** F5
Åminne *Sweden* **11** G7
Amino *Ethiopia* **81** G5
Aminuis *Namibia* **88** C2
Amīrābād *Iran* **70** C5
Amirante Is. *Seychelles* **50** J7
Amisk → *Canada* **103** B9
Amisk L. *Canada* **103** C8
Amistad, Presa de la *Mexico* **118** B4
Amistad △ *U.S.A.* **116** G4
Amite *U.S.A.* **117** F9
Amla *India* **68** J8
Amlapura = Karangasem
  Indonesia **63** J18
Amlia I. *U.S.A.* **106** a
Amlwch *U.K.* **14** D3
Amm Adam *Sudan* **81** D4
'Ammān *Jordan* **74** D4
'Ammān □ *Jordan* **74** D5
'Ammān ✈ (AMM) *Jordan* **74** D4
Ammanford *U.K.* **15** F4
Ammassalik = Tasiilaq
  Greenland **4** C6
Ammerån → *Sweden* **10** A10
Ammersee *Germany* **25** G7
Ammochostos =
  Famagusta *Cyprus* **49** D12
Ammon *U.S.A.* **108** E8
Amnat Charoen *Thailand* **64** E5
Amnura *Bangla.* **69** G13
Amo Jiang → *China* **58** F3
Åmol *Iran* **71** B7
Amorgos *Greece* **47** E7
Amory *U.S.A.* **117** E10
Amos *Canada* **104** C4
Åmot *Norway* **9** G13
Åmotfors *Sweden* **10** E6
Amoy = Xiamen *China* **59** E12
Ampanavoana *Madag.* **89** B9
Ampang *Malaysia* **65** L3
Ampangalana,
  Lakandranon' *Madag.* **89** C8
Ampanihy *Madag.* **89** C7
Amparafaravola *Madag.* **89** B8
Amparo *Brazil* **127** A6
Ampasinambo *Madag.* **89** C8
Ampasindava,
  Helodranon' *Madag.* **89** A8
Ampasindava, Saikanosy
  Madag. **89** A8
Ampenan *Indonesia* **63** K18
Amper *Nigeria* **83** D6
Amper → *Germany* **25** G7
Ampezzo *Italy* **41** B9
Amphoe Kathu *Thailand* **65** a
Amphoe Thalang *Thailand* **65** a
Ampitsikinana *Madag.* **89** A8
Ampombiantambo *Madag.* **89** A8
Amposta *Spain* **38** E5
Ampotaka *Madag.* **89** D7
Ampoza *Madag.* **89** C7
Amqui *Canada* **105** C6
Amravati *India* **66** J10
Amreli *India* **68** J4
Amritsar *India* **68** D6
Amroha *India* **69** E8
Amrum *Germany* **24** A4

Amsterdam *Neths.* **17** B4
Amsterdam *U.S.A.* **115** D10
Amsterdam ✈ (AMS) *Neths.* **17** B4
Amsterdam, I. = Nouvelle
  Amsterdam, Î. *Ind. Oc.* **3** F13
Amstetten *Austria* **26** C7
'Amūdah *Syria* **73** D9
Amudarya → *Uzbekistan* **52** E6
Amund Ringnes I. *Canada* **101** B10
Amundsen Abyssal Plain
  S. Ocean **5** C14
Amundsen Basin *Arctic* **4** A
Amundsen Gulf *Canada* **100** B7
Amundsen Ridges *S. Ocean* **5** C14
Amundsen-Scott *Antarctica* **5** E
Amundsen Sea *Antarctica* **5** D15
Amungen *Sweden* **10** C9
Amuntai *Indonesia* **62** E5
Amur → *Russia* **53** D15
Amur, W. → *Sudan* **80** D3
Amurang *Indonesia* **63** D6
Amurrio *Spain* **38** B1
Amursk *Russia* **53** D14
Amusco *Spain* **36** C6
Amvrakikos Kolpos *Greece* **46** C2
Amvrosiyivka *Ukraine* **33** J10
Amyderya =
  Amudarya → *Uzbekistan* **52** E6
An Bien *Vietnam* **65** H5
An Hoa *Vietnam* **64** E7
An Nabaṭīyah at Tahta
  Lebanon **74** B4
An Nabk *Si. Arabia* **70** D3
An Nabk *Syria* **74** A5
An Nafūd *Si. Arabia* **70** D4
An Nāḩiyah *Iraq* **73** E9
An Najaf *Iraq* **73** G11
An Nāṣirīyah *Iraq* **70** D5
An Nhon *Vietnam* **64** F7
An Nîl □ *Sudan* **80** D3
An Nîl el Abyaḍ □ *Sudan* **81** E3
An Nîl el Azraq □ *Sudan* **81** E3
An Nu'ayrīyah *Si. Arabia* **71** E6
An Nu'mānīyah *Iraq* **73** F11
An Thoi, Dao *Vietnam* **65** H5
An Uaimh *Ireland* **12** C5
Anabar → *Russia* **53** B12
'Anabtā *West Bank* **74** C4
Anaconda *U.S.A.* **108** C7
Anacortes *U.S.A.* **110** B4
Anacuao, Mt. *Phil.* **61** C4
Anadarko *U.S.A.* **116** D5
Anadia *Portugal* **36** E2
Anadolu *Turkey* **72** C5
Anadyr *Russia* **53** C18
Anadyr → *Russia* **53** C18
Anadyrskiy Zaliv *Russia* **53** C19
Anafi *Greece* **47** E7
Anaga, Pta. de *Canary Is.* **48** F3
Anagni *Italy* **41** G10
'Ānah *Iraq* **73** E10
Anaheim *U.S.A.* **111** M9
Anahim Lake *Canada* **102** C3
Anakapalle *India* **67** L13
Anakie *Australia* **94** C4
Anaklia *Georgia* **35** J5
Analalava *Madag.* **89** A8
Analavoka *Madag.* **89** C8
Analipsis *Greece* **49** A3
Anambar → *Pakistan* **68** D3
Anambas, Kepulauan
  Indonesia **62** D3
Anambas Is. = Anambas,
  Kepulauan *Indonesia* **62** D3
Anambra □ *Nigeria* **83** D6
Anamosa *U.S.A.* **112** D8
Anamur *Turkey* **72** D5
Anamur Burnu *Turkey* **72** D5
Anan *Japan* **55** H7
Anand *India* **68** H5
Ananes *Greece* **46** E6
Anantapur *India* **66** M10
Anantnag *India* **69** C6
Ananyiv *Ukraine* **29** C14
Anapa *Russia* **33** K9
Anápolis *Brazil* **125** G9
Anapu → *Brazil* **125** D8
Anār *Iran* **71** D7
Anārak *Iran* **71** C7
Anarisfjällen *Sweden* **10** A7
Anas → *India* **68** H5
Anatolia = Anadolu *Turkey* **72** C5
Añatuya *Argentina* **126** B3
Anaunethad L. *Canada* **103** A8
Anbyŏn *N. Korea* **57** E14
Ancares, Sierra dos *Spain* **36** C4
Ancares △ *Spain* **36** C4
Ancaster *Canada* **114** C5
Ancenis *France* **18** E5
Anchor Bay *U.S.A.* **110** G3
Anchorage *U.S.A.* **100** C5
Anci *China* **56** E9
Ancohuma, Nevado *Bolivia* **124** G5
Ancón *Peru* **124** F3
Ancona *Italy* **41** E10
Ancud *Chile* **128** E2

Ancud, G. de *Chile* **128** E2
Ancy-le-Franc *France* **19** E11
Andacollo *Argentina* **126** D1
Andacollo *Chile* **126** C1
Andaingo *Madag.* **89** B8
Andalgalá *Argentina* **126** B2
Åndalsnes *Norway* **8** E12
Andalucía □ *Spain* **37** H6
Andalusia = Andalucía □
  Spain **37** H6
Andalusia *U.S.A.* **117** F11
Andaman Is. *Ind. Oc.* **51** G11
Andaman Sea *Ind. Oc.* **62** B1
Andamooka *Australia* **95** E2
Andapa *Madag.* **89** A8
Andara *Namibia* **88** B3
Andelot-Blancheville
  France **19** D12
Andenes *Norway* **8** B17
Andenne *Belgium* **17** D5
Andéranboukane *Mali* **83** B5
Andermatt *Switz.* **25** J4
Andernach *Germany* **24** E3
Andernos-les-Bains *France* **20** D2
Anderslöv *Sweden* **11** J7
Anderson *Alaska, U.S.A.* **106** a
Anderson *Calif., U.S.A.* **108** F2
Anderson *Ind., U.S.A.* **113** E11
Anderson *Mo., U.S.A.* **112** G6
Anderson *S.C., U.S.A.* **117** D13
Anderson → *Canada* **100** C7
Anderstorp *Sweden* **11** G7
Andes *U.S.A.* **115** D10
Andes, Cord. de los *S. Amer.* **124** H5
Andfjorden *Norway* **8** B17
Andhra Pradesh □ *India* **66** L11
Andijon *Uzbekistan* **52** E8
Andikíthira = Antikythira
  Greece **46** F5
Andilamena *Madag.* **89** B8
Andīmeshk *Iran* **73** F13
Andímilos = Antimilos
  Greece **46** E6
Andíparos = Antiparos
  Greece **47** D7
Andípaxoi = Antipaxi *Greece* **46** B2
Andipsara *Greece* **47** C7
Andizhan = Andijon
  Uzbekistan **52** E8
Andoain *Spain* **38** B2
Andoany *Madag.* **89** A8
Andohahela △ *Madag.* **89** C8
Andong *S. Korea* **57** F15
Andongwei *China* **57** G10
Andorra *Spain* **38** E4
Andorra ■ *Europe* **20** F5
Andorra La Vella *Andorra* **20** F5
Andover *U.K.* **15** F6
Andover *Maine, U.S.A.* **115** B14
Andover *Mass., U.S.A.* **115** D13
Andover *N.J., U.S.A.* **115** F10
Andover *N.Y., U.S.A.* **114** D7
Andover *Ohio, U.S.A.* **114** E4
Andoya *Norway* **8** B16
Andradina *Brazil* **125** H8
Andrahary *Madag.* **89** A8
Andramasina *Madag.* **89** B8
Andranopasy *Madag.* **89** C7
Andranovory *Madag.* **89** C7
Andratx *Spain* **48** B9
Andreanof Is. *U.S.A.* **106** a
Andreapol *Russia* **32** D7
Andrews *S.C., U.S.A.* **117** E15
Andrews *Tex., U.S.A.* **116** E3
Andreyevka *Russia* **34** D10
Ándria *Italy* **43** A9
Andriamena *Madag.* **89** B8
Andriandampy *Madag.* **89** C8
Andriba *Madag.* **89** B8
Andrijevica *Montenegro* **44** D3
Andringitra △ *Madag.* **89** C8
Andritsena *Greece* **46** D3
Androka *Madag.* **89** C7
Andros *Greece* **46** D6
Andros I. *Bahamas* **120** B4
Andros Town *Bahamas* **120** B4
Androscoggin → *U.S.A.* **115** C14
Andrychów *Poland* **31** J6
Andselv *Norway* **8** B18
Andújar *Spain* **37** G6
Andulo *Angola* **84** G3
Aneby *Sweden* **11** G8
Anéfis *Mali* **83** B5
Anegada *Br. Virgin Is.* **121** e
Anegada Passage *W. Indies* **121** C7
Aného *Togo* **83** D5
Anenni-Noi *Moldova* **29** D14
Aneto, Pico de *Spain* **38** C5
Anfu *China* **59** D10
Ang Mo Kio *Singapore* **65** d
Ang Thong *Thailand* **64** E3
Ang Thong, Ko *Thailand* **65** b
Ang Thong △ *Thailand* **65** b
Angamos, Punta *Chile* **126** A1
Angara → *Russia* **53** D10
Angarab *Sudan* **81** F1
Angarsk *Russia* **53** D11

Angas Hills *Australia* **92** D4
Angaston *Australia* **95** E2
Änge *Sweden* **10** B9
Ángel, Salto = Angel Falls
  Venezuela **124** B6
Ángel de la Guarda, I.
  Mexico **118** B2
Angel Falls *Venezuela* **124** B6
Angeles *Phil.* **61** D4
Ängelholm *Sweden* **11** H6
Angels Camp *U.S.A.* **110** G6
Ängelsberg *Sweden* **10** E10
Anger → *Ethiopia* **81** F4
Angereb *Ethiopia* **81** E4
Angereb → *Ethiopia* **81** E4
Ångermanälven → *Sweden* **10** A11
Ångermanland *Sweden* **8** E17
Angermünde *Germany* **24** B9
Angers *Canada* **115** A9
Angers *France* **18** E6
Angerville *France* **19** D9
Ängesån → *Sweden* **8** C20
Angikuni L. *Canada* **103** A9
Angkor *Cambodia* **64** F4
Anglès *Spain* **38** D7
Anglesey *U.K.* **14** D3
Anglesey, Isle of □ *U.K.* **14** D3
Anglet *France* **20** E2
Angleton *U.S.A.* **116** G7
Anglin → *France* **20** B4
Anglure *France* **19** D10
Angmagssalik = Tasiilaq
  Greenland **4** C6
Ango *Dem. Rep. of the Congo* **86** B2
Angoche *Mozam.* **87** F4
Angoche, I. *Mozam.* **87** F4
Angol *Chile* **126** D1
Angola *Ind., U.S.A.* **113** E11
Angola *N.Y., U.S.A.* **114** D5
Angola ■ *Africa* **85** G3
Angoulême *France* **20** C4
Angoumois *France* **20** C4
Angra do Heroismo *Azores* **78** a
Angra dos Reis *Brazil* **127** A7
Angrapa → *Russia* **30** D8
Angtassom *Cambodia* **65** G5
Angu *Dem. Rep. of the Congo* **86** B1
Anguang *China* **57** B12
Anguilla ☑ *W. Indies* **121** C7
Anguo *China* **56** E8
Angurugu *Australia* **94** A2
Angus *Canada* **114** B5
Angus □ *U.K.* **13** E6
Angwa → *Zimbabwe* **89** B5
Anhanduí → *Brazil* **127** A5
Anholt *Denmark* **11** H5
Anhua *China* **59** C8
Anhui □ *China* **59** B11
Anhwei = Anhui □ *China* **59** B11
Anichab *Namibia* **88** C1
Anidros *Greece* **47** E7
Anié *Togo* **83** D5
Animas → *U.S.A.* **109** H9
Anina *Romania* **28** E6
Aninoasa *Romania* **29** F9
Anivorano *Madag.* **89** B8
Anjalankoski *Finland* **32** B4
Anjar *India* **68** H4
Anji *China* **59** B12
Anjou *France* **18** E6
Anjouan *Comoros Is.* **85** a
Anjozorobe *Madag.* **89** B8
Anju *N. Korea* **57** E13
Anka *Nigeria* **83** C6
Ankaboa, Tanjona *Madag.* **89** C7
Ankang *China* **56** H5
Ankara *Turkey* **72** C5
Ankara □ *Turkey* **72** C5
Ankarafantsika △ *Madag.* **89** B8
Ankaramena *Madag.* **89** C8
Ankaratra *Madag.* **85** H9
Ankarsrum *Sweden* **11** G10
Ankasakasa *Madag.* **89** B7
Ankavandra *Madag.* **89** B8
Ankazoabo *Madag.* **89** C7
Ankazobe *Madag.* **89** B8
Ankeny *U.S.A.* **112** E7
Ankilimalinika *Madag.* **89** C7
Ankilizato *Madag.* **89** C8
Ankisabe *Madag.* **89** B8
Anklam *Germany* **24** B9
Ankober *Ethiopia* **81** F4
Ankoro *Dem. Rep. of the Congo* **86** D2
Ankororoka *Madag.* **89** D8
Anlong *China* **58** E5
Anlong Veng *Cambodia* **64** E5
Anlu *China* **59** B9
Anmyeondo *S. Korea* **57** F14
Ånn *Sweden* **10** A6
Ann, C. *U.S.A.* **115** D14
Ann Arbor *U.S.A.* **113** D12
Anna *Russia* **34** E5
Anna *U.S.A.* **112** G9
Annaba *Algeria* **78** A7
Annaberg-Buchholz
  Germany **24** E9
Annalee → *Ireland* **12** B4

Annam *Vietnam* **64** E7
Annamitique, Chaîne *Asia* **64** D6
Annan *U.K.* **13** G5
Annan → *U.K.* **13** G5
Annapolis *U.S.A.* **113** F15
Annapolis Royal *Canada* **105** D6
Annapurna *Nepal* **69** E10
Annean, L. *Australia* **93** E2
Anneberg *Sweden* **11** G8
Annecy *France* **21** C10
Annecy, Lac d' *France* **21** C10
Annemasse *France* **19** F13
Annette I. *U.S.A.* **102** B2
Anning *China* **58** E4
Anniston *U.S.A.* **117** E12
Annobón *Atl. Oc.* **77** G4
Annonay *France* **21** C8
Annot *France* **21** E10
Annotto B. *Jamaica* **120** a
Ánnsjön *Sweden* **10** A6
Annville *U.S.A.* **115** F8
Ano Poroia *Greece* **44** E7
Ano Siros *Greece* **46** D6
Anogia *Greece* **49** D6
Anorotsangana *Madag.* **89** A8
Anosibe *Madag.* **89** B8
Anou Mellene *Mali* **83** B5
Anoumaba *Ivory C.* **82** D4
Anping *Hebei, China* **56** E8
Anping *Liaoning, China* **57** D12
Anpu Gang *China* **58** G7
Anqing *China* **59** B11
Anqiu *China* **57** F10
Anren *China* **59** D9
Ansager *Denmark* **11** J2
Ansai *China* **56** F5
Ansan *S. Korea* **57** F14
Ansbach *Germany* **25** F6
Anse Boileau *Seychelles* **85** b
Anse Royale *Seychelles* **85** b
Anseba → *Eritrea* **81** D4
Ansfelden *Austria* **26** C7
Anshan *China* **57** D12
Anshun *China* **58** D5
Ansião *Portugal* **36** F2
Ansley *U.S.A.* **112** E4
Ansó *Spain* **38** C4
Ansoáin *Spain* **38** C3
Anson *U.S.A.* **116** E5
Anson B. *Australia* **92** B5
Ansongo *Mali* **83** B5
Ansongo-Ménaka △ *Mali* **83** B5
Ansonia *U.S.A.* **115** E11
Anstruther *U.K.* **13** E6
Ansudu *Indonesia* **63** E9
Antabamba *Peru* **124** F4
Antakya = Hatay *Turkey* **72** D7
Antalaha *Madag.* **89** A9
Antalya *Turkey* **72** D4
Antalya □ *Turkey* **47** E12
Antalya Körfezi *Turkey* **72** D4
Antambohobe *Madag.* **89** C8
Antanambao-
  Manampotsy *Madag.* **89** B8
Antanambe *Madag.* **89** B8
Antananarivo *Madag.* **89** B8
Antananarivo □ *Madag.* **89** B8
Antanifotsy *Madag.* **89** B8
Antanimbaribe *Madag.* **89** C7
Antanimora *Madag.* **89** C8
Antarctic Pen. *Antarctica* **5** C18
Antarctica **5** E3
Antelope *Zimbabwe* **87** G2
Antequera *Paraguay* **126** A4
Antequera *Spain* **37** H6
Antero, Mt. *U.S.A.* **108** G10
Antevamena *Madag.* **89** C7
Anthony *Kans., U.S.A.* **112** G4
Anthony *N. Mex., U.S.A.* **109** K10
Anti Atlas *Morocco* **78** C4
Anti-Lebanon = Sharqi, Al
  Jabal ash *Lebanon* **74** B5
Antibes *France* **21** E11
Antibes, C. d' *France* **21** E11
Anticosti, Î. d' *Canada* **105** C7
Antifer, C. d' *France* **18** C7
Antigo *U.S.A.* **112** C9
Antigonish *Canada* **105** C7
Antigua *Canary Is.* **48** F5
Antigua *Guatemala* **120** D1
Antigua *W. Indies* **121** C7
Antigua & Barbuda ■
  W. Indies **121** C7
Antikythira *Greece* **46** F5
Antilla *Cuba* **120** B4
Antilles = West Indies
  Cent. Amer. **121** D7
Antimilos *Greece* **46** E6
Antioch *U.S.A.* **110** G5
Antioche, Pertuis d' *France* **20** B2
Antioquia *Colombia* **124** B3
Antiparos *Greece* **47** D7
Antipaxi *Greece* **46** B2
Antipodes Is. *Pac. Oc.* **96** M9
Antipolo *Greece* **46** C3
Antlers *U.S.A.* **116** D7

Antoetra *Madag.* **89** C8
Apies → *S. Africa* **89** D4
Apizaco *Mexico* **119** D5
Aplao *Peru* **124** G4
Apo, Mt. *Phil.* **63** C7
Apolakia *Greece* **49** C9
Apolakia, Ormos *Greece* **49** C9
Apolda *Germany* **24** D7
Apollonia = Marsá Susah
  Libya **79** B10
Apollonia *Greece* **49** C9
Apolonia *Greece* **46** E6
Apopa *El Salv.* **120** D2
Aporé → *Brazil* **125** G8
Apostle Is. *U.S.A.* **112** B8
Apostle Islands ○ *U.S.A.* **112** B8
Apóstoles *Argentina* **127** B4
Apostolos Andreas, C.
  Cyprus **49** D13
Apostolovo *Ukraine* **33** J7
Apoteri *Guyana* **124** C7
Appalachian Mts. *U.S.A.* **113** G14
Äppelbo *Sweden* **10** D8
Appennini *Italy* **40** D7
Appennino Ligure *Italy* **40** D6
Appenzell-Ausser
  Rhoden □ *Switz.* **25** H5
Appenzell-Inner Rhoden □
  Switz. **25** H5
Appiano *Italy* **41** B8
Apple Hill *Canada* **115** A10
Apple Valley *U.S.A.* **111** L9
Appleby-in-Westmorland
  U.K. **14** C5
Appledore *U.K.* **15** F3
Appleton *U.S.A.* **112** C9
Approuague → *Fr. Guiana* **125** C8
Apricena *Italy* **41** G12
Aprília *Italy* **42** A5
Apsheronsk *Russia* **35** H4
Apsley *Canada* **114** B6
Apt *France* **21** E9
Apuane, Alpi *Italy* **40** D7
Apucarana *Brazil* **127** A5
Apulia = Púglia □ *Italy* **43** A9
Apure → *Venezuela* **124** B5
Apurimac → *Peru* **124** F4
Apuseni, Munţii *Romania* **28** D7
Āq Qālā *Iran* **71** B7
Aqaba = Al 'Aqabah *Jordan* **74** F4
'Aqabah, Khalīj al =
  Aqaba, G. of *Red Sea* **70** D2
'Aqdā *Iran* **71** C7
Aqiq *Sudan* **80** D4
Aqīq, Khalīg *Sudan* **80** D4
'Aqrah *Iraq* **73** D10
Aqsay *Kazakhstan* **52** D6
Aqtaū *Kazakhstan* **52** E6
Aqtoghay *Kazakhstan* **52** E8
Aqtöbe *Kazakhstan* **52** D6
Aqtoghay *Kazakhstan* **52** E8
Aquidauana *Brazil* **125** H7
Aquila *Mexico* **118** D4
Aquiles Serdán *Mexico* **118** B3
Aquin *Haiti* **121** C5
Aquitaine □ *France* **20** D3
Ar Rachidiya = Er
  Rachidia *Morocco* **78** B5
Ar Rafid *Syria* **74** C4
Ar Raḩḩālīyah *Iraq* **73** F10
Ar Ramādī *Iraq* **73** F10
Ar Ramthā *Jordan* **74** C5
Ar Raqqah *Syria* **73** E8
Ar Raqqah □ *Syria* **73** E8
Ar Rass *Si. Arabia* **70** E4
Ar Rayyān *Qatar* **71** E6
Ar Rifā'ī *Iraq* **70** D5
Ar Riyāḑ *Si. Arabia* **70** E5
Ar Ru'ays *Qatar* **71** E6
Ar Rukhaymīyah *Iraq* **70** D5
Ar Rumaythah *Iraq* **70** D5
Ar Ruṣāfah *Syria* **73** E8
Ar Ruṭbah *Iraq* **73** F9
Ara *India* **69** G11
Ara Goro *Ethiopia* **81** F5
Ara Tera *Ethiopia* **81** F5
Arab *U.S.A.* **117** D11
'Arab, Bahr el → *Sudan* **81** F2
Arab, Khalīg el *Egypt* **80** A2
Arab, Shatt al → *Asia* **71** D6
'Araba, W. → *Egypt* **80** J8
'Arabābād *Iran* **71** C8
Araban *Turkey* **72** D7
Arabatskaya Strelka *Ukraine* **33** K8
Arabba *Italy* **41** B8
Arabia *Asia* **50** F6
Arabian Desert = Es Sahrâ'
  Esh Sharqîya *Egypt* **80** B3
Arabian Gulf = Persian
  Gulf *Asia* **71** E6
Arabian Sea *Ind. Oc.* **50** G8
Araç *Turkey* **72** B5
Aracaju *Brazil* **125** F11
Aracati *Brazil* **125** D11
Araçatuba *Brazil* **127** A5
Aracena *Spain* **37** H4
Aracena, Sierra de *Spain* **37** H4

Apiacás, Serra dos *Brazil* **124** E7

Arachova *Greece* 46 C4
Arachthos → *Greece* 46 B3
Aračinovo *Macedonia* 44 D5
Araçuaí *Brazil* 125 G10
'Arad *Israel* 74 D4
Arad *Romania* 28 D6
Arad □ *Romania* 28 D6
Arādān *Iran* 71 C7
Aradhippou *Cyprus* 49 E12
Arafura Sea *E. Indies* 90 B6
Aragats *Armenia* 35 K7
Aragón □ *Spain* 38 D4
Aragón → *Spain* 38 C2
Aragona *Italy* 42 E6
Araguacema *Brazil* 125 E9
Araguaia → *Brazil* 125 E9
Araguaína *Brazil* 125 E9
Araguari *Brazil* 125 G9
Araguari → *Brazil* 125 C9
Arahal *Spain* 37 H5
Arain *India* 68 F6
Arak *Algeria* 78 C6
Arāk *Iran* 71 C6
Araka *Sudan* 81 G3
Arakan Coast *Burma* 67 K19
Arakan Yoma *Burma* 67 K19
Araklı *Turkey* 73 B9
Araks = Aras, Rūd-e →
  Asia 35 K9
Aral *Kazakhstan* 52 E7
Aral Sea *Asia* 52 E7
Aral Tengizi = Aral Sea *Asia* 52 E7
Aralık *Turkey* 73 C11
Aralsk = Aral *Kazakhstan* 52 E7
Aralskoye More = Aral
  Sea *Asia* 52 E7
Aralsor, Ozero = Aralsor
  Köli *Kazakhstan* 35 F9
Aralsor Köli *Kazakhstan* 35 F9
Aramac *Australia* 94 C4
Aran I. *Ireland* 12 A3
Aran Is. *Ireland* 12 C2
Aranda de Duero *Spain* 36 D7
Arandān *Iran* 70 C5
Aranđelovac *Serbia* 44 B4
Aranjuez *Spain* 36 E7
Aranos *Namibia* 88 C2
Aransas Pass *U.S.A.* 116 H6
Aranyaprathet *Thailand* 64 F4
Araouane *Mali* 82 B4
Arapahoe *U.S.A.* 112 E4
Arapey Grande → *Uruguay* 126 C4
Arapgir *Turkey* 73 C8
Arapiraca *Brazil* 125 E11
Arapis, Ákra *Greece* 45 F8
Arapongas *Brazil* 127 A5
Ar'ar *Si. Arabia* 70 D4
Araranguá *Brazil* 127 B6
Araraquara *Brazil* 125 H9
Ararás, Serra das *Brazil* 127 B5
Ararat *Armenia* 73 C11
Ararat *Australia* 95 F3
Ararat, Mt. = Ağrı Dağı
  Turkey 73 C11
Araria *India* 69 F12
Araripe, Chapada do *Brazil*
  125 E11
Aras, Rūd-e → *Asia* 35 K9
Aratāne *Mauritania* 82 B3
Arauca *Colombia* 124 B4
Arauca → *Venezuela* 124 B5
Arauco *Chile* 126 D1
Aravalli Range *India* 68 G5
Arawa *Ethiopia* 81 F5
Arawale △ *Kenya* 86 C5
Araxá *Brazil* 125 G9
Araya, Pen. de *Venezuela* 124 A6
Arba Gugu *Ethiopia* 81 F5
Arba Minch *Ethiopia* 81 F4
Arbat *Iraq* 73 E11
Árbatax *Italy* 42 C2
Arbi *Ethiopia* 81 F4
Arbīl *Iraq* 73 D11
Arbīl □ *Iraq* 73 D11
Arboga *Sweden* 10 E9
Arbois *France* 19 F12
Arbore *Ethiopia* 81 F4
Arboréa *Italy* 42 C1
Arborfield *Canada* 103 C8
Arborg *Canada* 103 C9
Arbre du Ténéré *Niger* 83 B7
Arbroath *U.K.* 13 E6
Arbuckle *U.S.A.* 110 F4
Arbus *Italy* 42 C1
Arc → *France* 21 C10
Arc-lès-Gray *France* 19 E12
Arcachon *France* 20 D2
Arcachon, Bassin d' *France* 20 D2
Arcade *U.S.A.* 114 D6
Arcadia *Fla., U.S.A.* 117 H14
Arcadia *La., U.S.A.* 116 E8
Arcadia *Pa., U.S.A.* 114 F6
Arcata *U.S.A.* 108 F1
Arcévia *Italy* 41 E9
Arcachnes *Greece* 47 F7
Archangel = Arkhangelsk
  Russia 52 C5

Archángelos *Greece* 49 C10
Archar *Bulgaria* 44 C6
Archbald *U.S.A.* 115 E9
Archena *Spain* 39 G3
Archer → *Australia* 94 A3
Archer B. *Australia* 94 A3
Archer Bend = Mungkan
  Kandju △ *Australia* 94 A3
Archers Post *Kenya* 86 B4
Arches △ *U.S.A.* 108 G9
Archidona *Spain* 37 H6
Archipel-de-Mingan △
  Canada 105 B7
Archipiélago Chinijo △
  Canary Is. 48 E6
Archipiélago Los Roques △
  Venezuela 121 D6
Arci, Mte. *Italy* 42 C1
Arcidosso *Italy* 41 F8
Arcipelago de la
  Maddalena △ *Italy* 42 A2
Arcipelago Toscano △ *Italy* 40 F7
Arcis-sur-Aube *France* 19 D11
Arckaringa Cr. → *Australia* 95 D2
Arco *Italy* 40 C7
Arco *U.S.A.* 108 E7
Arcos de Jalón *Spain* 38 D2
Arcos de la Frontera *Spain* 37 J5
Arcos de Valdevez *Portugal* 36 D2
Arcot *India* 66 N11
Arcozelo *Portugal* 36 E3
Arctic Bay *Canada* 101 B11
Arctic Mid-Ocean Ridge *Arctic* 4 A
Arctic Ocean *Arctic* 4 B18
Arctic Red River =
  Tsiigehtchic *Canada* 100 C6
Arctowski *Antarctica* 5 C18
Arda → *Bulgaria* 45 E10
Arda → *Italy* 40 C7
Ardabīl *Iran* 71 B6
Ardabīl □ *Iran* 71 B6
Ardahan *Turkey* 73 B10
Ardahan □ *Turkey* 73 B10
Ardakān = Sepīdān *Iran* 71 D7
Ardakān *Iran* 71 C7
Ardala *Sweden* 11 F7
Ardales *Spain* 37 J6
Ardara *Ireland* 12 B3
Ardas → *Greece* 45 E10
Ardèche □ *France* 21 D8
Ardèche → *France* 21 D8
Ardee *Ireland* 12 C5
Arden *Canada* 114 B8
Arden *Denmark* 11 H3
Arden *Calif., U.S.A.* 110 G5
Arden *Nev., U.S.A.* 111 J11
Ardenne *Belgium* 17 E5
Ardennes = Ardenne
  Belgium 17 E5
Ardennes □ *France* 19 C11
Ardentes *France* 19 F8
Arderin *Ireland* 12 C4
Ardeşen *Turkey* 73 B9
Ardestān *Iran* 71 C7
Ardfert *Ireland* 12 D2
Ardglass *U.K.* 12 B6
Ardhéa = Aridea *Greece* 44 F6
Ardila → *Portugal* 37 G3
Ardino *Bulgaria* 45 E9
Ardivachar Pt. *U.K.* 13 D1
Ardlethan *Australia* 95 E4
Ardmore *Okla., U.S.A.* 116 D6
Ardmore *Pa., U.S.A.* 115 F9
Ardnamurchan, Pt. of *U.K.* 13 E2
Ardnave Pt. *U.K.* 13 F2
Ardon *Russia* 35 J7
Ardore *Italy* 43 D9
Ardres *France* 19 B8
Ardrossan *Australia* 95 E2
Ardrossan *U.K.* 13 F4
Ards Pen. *U.K.* 12 B6
Arduan *Sudan* 80 D3
Ardud *Romania* 28 C7
Åre *Sweden* 10 A7
Arecibo *Puerto Rico* 121 d
Areia Branca *Brazil* 125 E11
Arena, Pt. *U.S.A.* 110 G3
Arenal *Honduras* 120 C2
Arenas = Las Arenas *Spain* 36 B6
Arenas de San Pedro *Spain* 36 E5
Arendal *Norway* 9 G13
Arendsee *Germany* 24 C7
Arenys de Mar *Spain* 38 D7
Arenzano *Italy* 40 D5
Areópoli *Greece* 46 E4
Arequipa *Peru* 124 G4
Arero *Ethiopia* 81 G4
Arès *France* 20 D2
Arévalo *Spain* 36 D6
Arezzo *Italy* 41 E8
Arga *Turkey* 70 B3
Arga → *Spain* 38 C3
Argalasti *Greece* 46 B5
Argamasilla de Alba *Spain* 37 F7
Argamasilla de Calatrava
  Spain 37 G6
Arganda del Rey *Spain* 36 E7
Arganil *Portugal* 36 E2

Argedeb *Ethiopia* 81 F5
Argelès-Gazost *France* 20 E3
Argelès-sur-Mer *France* 20 F7
Argens → *France* 21 E10
Argent-sur-Sauldre *France* 19 E9
Argenta *Canada* 102 C5
Argenta *Italy* 41 D8
Argentan *France* 18 D6
Argentário, Mte. *Italy* 41 F8
Argentat *France* 20 C5
Argentera *Italy* 40 D4
Argenteuil *France* 19 D9
Argentia *Canada* 105 C9
Argentiera, C. dell' *Italy* 42 B1
Argentina ■ *S. Amer.* 128 D3
Argentine Basin *Atl. Oc.* 128 F6
Argentino, L. *Argentina* 128 G2
Argenton-Château *France* 18 F6
Argenton-sur-Creuse *France* 19 F8
Argeş □ *Romania* 29 F9
Argeş → *Romania* 29 F11
Arghandab → *Afghan.* 68 D1
Argheile *Ethiopia* 81 F5
Argirades *Greece* 49 B3
Argiroúpoli *Greece* 49 D6
Argo *Sudan* 80 D3
Argolída □ *Greece* 46 D4
Argolikós Kólpos *Greece* 46 D4
Argonne *France* 19 C12
Argos *Greece* 46 D4
Árgos Orestikó *Greece* 44 F5
Argostóli *Greece* 46 C2
Arguedas *Spain* 38 C3
Arguello, Pt. *U.S.A.* 111 L6
Arguineguín *Canary Is.* 48 G4
Argun *Russia* 35 J7
Argun → *Russia* 53 D13
Argungu *Nigeria* 83 C5
Argus Pk. *U.S.A.* 111 K9
Argyle, L. *Australia* 92 C4
Argyll *U.K.* 13 E4
Argyll & Bute □ *U.K.* 13 E3
Arhavi *Turkey* 73 B9
Århus *Denmark* 11 H4
Ariadnoye *Russia* 54 B7
Ariamsvlei *Namibia* 88 D2
Ariana *Tunisia* 79 A8
Ariano Irpino *Italy* 43 A8
Aribinda *Burkina Faso* 83 C4
Arica *Chile* 124 G4
Arica *Colombia* 124 D4
Arico *Canary Is.* 48 F3
Arid, C. *Australia* 93 F3
Arida *Japan* 55 G7
Aridea *Greece* 44 F6
Ariège □ *France* 20 F5
Ariège → *France* 20 E5
Arieş → *Romania* 29 D8
Arīhā *Israel* 80 A4
Arīḥā *Syria* 72 B7
Arila, Ákra *Greece* 49 A3
Arilje *Serbia* 44 C4
Arima *Trin. & Tob.* 121 D7
Arinos → *Brazil* 124 F7
Ario de Rosales *Mexico* 118 D4
Ariogala *Lithuania* 30 C10
Aripo, Mt. *Trin. & Tob.* 125 K15
Aripuanã *Brazil* 124 E6
Aripuanã → *Brazil* 124 E6
Ariquemes *Brazil* 124 E6
Arisaig *U.K.* 13 E3
Arissa *Ethiopia* 81 E5
Aristazabal I. *Canada* 102 C3
Arivonimamo *Madag.* 89 B8
Ariza *Spain* 38 D2
Arizaro, Salar de *Argentina* 126 A2
Arizona *Argentina* 126 D2
Arizona □ *U.S.A.* 109 J8
Arizpe *Mexico* 118 A2
'Arjah *Si. Arabia* 70 E5
Arjäng *Sweden* 10 E6
Arjeplog *Sweden* 8 C17
Arjepluovve = Arjeplog
  Sweden 8 C17
Arjona *Colombia* 124 A3
Arjona *Spain* 37 H6
Arjuna *Indonesia* 63 G15
Arka *Russia* 53 C15
Arkadak *Russia* 34 E6
Arkadelphia *U.S.A.* 116 D8
Arkadía □ *Greece* 46 D4
Arkaig, L. *U.K.* 13 E3
Arkalyk = Arqalyk
  Kazakhstan 52 D7
Arkansas □ *U.S.A.* 116 D8
Arkansas → *U.S.A.* 116 E9
Arkansas City *U.S.A.* 112 G5
Arkaroola *Australia* 95 E2
Arkavaz *Iran* 73 F12
Arkhángelos *Russia* 52 C5
Arkhangelskoye *Russia* 34 E5
Arki *Greece* 47 D8
Arki *India* 68 D7
Arkiko *Eritrea* 81 D4
Arklow *Ireland* 12 D5
Arkona, Kap *Germany* 24 A9
Arkösund *Sweden* 11 F10

Arkoúdi *Greece* 46 C2
Arkport *U.S.A.* 114 D7
Arktícheskiy, Mys *Russia* 53 A10
Arkul *Russia* 34 B10
Arkville *U.S.A.* 115 D10
Årla *Sweden* 10 E10
Arlanda, Stockholm ✈
  (ARN) *Sweden* 10 E11
Arlanza → *Spain* 36 C6
Arlanzón → *Spain* 36 C6
Arlbergpass *Austria* 26 D3
Arles *France* 21 E8
Arli △ *Burkina Faso* 83 C5
Arli △ *Burkina Faso* 83 C5
Arlington *S. Africa* 89 D4
Arlington *N.Y., U.S.A.* 115 E11
Arlington *Oreg., U.S.A.* 108 D3
Arlington *S. Dak., U.S.A.* 112 C5
Arlington *Tex., U.S.A.* 116 E6
Arlington *Va., U.S.A.* 113 F15
Arlington *Vt., U.S.A.* 115 C11
Arlington *Wash., U.S.A.* 110 B4
Arlington Heights *U.S.A.* 112 D10
Arlit *Niger* 78 E7
Arlon *Belgium* 17 E5
Arlparra *Australia* 94 C1
Arltunga *Australia* 94 C1
Armadale *Australia* 93 F2
Armagh *U.K.* 12 B5
Armagh □ *U.K.* 12 B5
Armagnac *France* 20 E4
Armançon → *France* 19 E10
Armando Bermudez △
  Dom. Rep. 121 C5
Armavir *Russia* 35 H5
Armenia *Colombia* 124 C3
Armenia ■ *Asia* 35 K7
Armeniş *Romania* 28 E7
Armenistís, Ákra *Greece* 49 C9
Armentières *France* 19 B9
Armidale *Australia* 95 E5
Armilla *Spain* 37 H7
Armori *India* 66 J12
Armour *U.S.A.* 112 D4
Armstrong *B.C., Canada* 102 C5
Armstrong *Ont., Canada* 104 B2
Armstrong → *Australia* 94 C1
Armutlu *Bursa, Turkey* 45 F12
Armutlu *İzmir, Turkey* 47 C9
Arnarfjörður *Iceland* 8 D2
Arnaud → *Canada* 101 D13
Arnauti, C. *Cyprus* 49 D11
Arnay-le-Duc *France* 19 E11
Arnea *Greece* 44 F7
Arnedillo *Spain* 38 C2
Arnedo *Spain* 38 C2
Arnett *U.S.A.* 116 C5
Arnhem *Neths.* 17 C5
Arnhem, C. *Australia* 94 A2
Arnhem B. *Australia* 94 A2
Arnhem Land *Australia* 94 A1
Arnissa *Greece* 44 F5
Arno → *Italy* 40 E7
Arno Bay *Australia* 95 E2
Arnold *U.K.* 14 D6
Arnold *U.S.A.* 110 G6
Arnoldstein *Austria* 26 E6
Arnon → *France* 19 E9
Arnot *Canada* 103 B9
Arnøya *Norway* 8 A19
Arnprior *Canada* 115 A8
Arnsberg *Germany* 24 D4
Arnsberger Wald △
  Germany 24 D4
Arnstadt *Germany* 24 E6
Aroa, Pte. *Moorea* 91 d
Aroab *Namibia* 88 D2
Aroánia Óros *Greece* 46 D4
Aroche *Spain* 37 H4
Arochuku *Nigeria* 83 D6
Arolsen *Germany* 24 D5
Aron *India* 68 G6
Aron → *France* 19 F10
Arona *Canary Is.* 48 F3
Arona *Italy* 40 C5
Aroroy *Phil.* 61 E5
Aros → *Mexico* 118 B3
Arousa, Ría de → *Spain* 36 C2
Arpaçay *Turkey* 73 B10
Arpajon *France* 19 D9
Arpajon-sur-Cère *France* 20 D6
Arpaşu de Jos *Romania* 29 E9
Arqalyk *Kazakhstan* 52 D7
Arrah = Ara *India* 69 G11
Arran *U.K.* 13 F3
Arras *France* 19 B9
Arrasate *Spain* 38 B2
Arrats → *France* 20 D4
Arreau *France* 20 F4
Arrecife *Canary Is.* 48 F6
Arrecifes *Argentina* 126 C3
Arrée, Mts. d' *France* 18 D3
Arriaga *Mexico* 119 D6
Arribes del Duero △ *Spain* 36 D4
Arrilalah *Australia* 94 C3
Arrino *Australia* 93 E2

Arkoúdi *Greece* 46 C2
Arriondas *Spain* 36 B5
Arromanches-les-Bains
  France 18 C6
Arronches *Portugal* 37 F3
Arros → *France* 20 E3
Arrow, L. *Ireland* 12 B3
Arrowtown *N.Z.* 91 F2
Arroyo de la Luz *Spain* 37 F4
Arroyo Grande *U.S.A.* 111 K6
Ars *Iran* 70 B5
Ars-sur-Moselle *France* 19 C13
Arsenault L. *Canada* 103 B7
Arsenev *Russia* 54 B6
Arsi *Ethiopia* 81 F4
Arsiero *Italy* 41 C8
Arsin *Turkey* 73 B8
Arsk *Russia* 34 B9
Arta *Greece* 46 B3
Artà *Spain* 48 B10
Árta □ *Greece* 46 B3
Artà, Coves de *Spain* 48 B10
Artashat *Armenia* 73 B11
Arteaga *Mexico* 118 D4
Arteche *Phil.* 61 E6
Arteijo = Arteixo *Spain* 36 B2
Arteixo *Spain* 36 B2
Artem = Artyom *Azerbaijan* 35 K10
Artem *Russia* 54 C6
Artemovsk *Russia* 53 D10
Artemovsk *Ukraine* 33 H9
Artemovskiy *Russia* 35 G5
Artenay *France* 19 D8
Artern *Germany* 24 D7
Artesa de Segre *Spain* 38 D6
Artesia = Mosomane
  Botswana 88 C4
Artesia *U.S.A.* 109 K11
Arthington *Liberia* 82 D2
Arthur *Canada* 114 C4
Arthur → *Australia* 95 G3
Arthur Cr. → *Australia* 94 C2
Arthur Pt. *Australia* 94 C5
Arthur River *Australia* 93 F2
Arthur's Pass *N.Z.* 91 E3
Arthur's Pass △ *N.Z.* 91 E3
Arthur's Town *Bahamas* 121 B4
Artigas *Antarctica* 5 C18
Artigas *Uruguay* 126 C4
Artik *Armenia* 35 K6
Artillery L. *Canada* 103 A7
Artois *France* 19 B9
Artotina *Greece* 46 C4
Artova *Turkey* 72 B7
Artrutx, C. de *Spain* 48 B10
Artsyz *Ukraine* 29 D14
Artvin *Turkey* 73 B9
Artvin □ *Turkey* 73 B9
Artyk *Russia* 53 C15
Artyom *Azerbaijan* 35 K10
Aru, Kepulauan *Indonesia* 63 F8
Aru Is. = Aru, Kepulauan
  Indonesia 63 F8
Arua *Uganda* 86 B3
Aruanã *Brazil* 125 F8
Aruba ☒ *W. Indies* 121 D6
Arucas *Canary Is.* 48 F4
Arudy *France* 20 E3
Arué *Tahiti* 91 d
Arun → *Nepal* 69 F12
Arun → *U.K.* 15 G7
Arunachal Pradesh □ *India* 67 F19
Arusha *Tanzania* 86 C4
Arusha □ *Tanzania* 86 C4
Arusha △ *Tanzania* 86 C4
Arusha Chini *Tanzania* 86 C4
Aruwimi →
  Dem. Rep. of the Congo 86 B1
Arvada *Colo., U.S.A.* 108 G11
Arvada *Wyo., U.S.A.* 108 D10
Arvayheer *Mongolia* 53 E11
Arve → *France* 19 F13
Arvi *Greece* 49 E7
Arviat *Canada* 103 A10
Arvidsjaur *Sweden* 8 D18
Arvika *Sweden* 10 E6
Arvin *U.S.A.* 111 K8
Arwal *India* 69 G11
Arxan *China* 60 B6
Åryd *Sweden* 11 H8
Arys *Kazakhstan* 52 E7
Arzachena *Italy* 42 A2
Arzamas *Russia* 34 C6
Arzanah *U.A.E.* 71 E7
Arzew *Algeria* 78 A5
Arzgir *Russia* 35 H7
Arzignano *Italy* 41 C8
Arzúa *Spain* 36 C2
Aš *Czech Rep.* 26 A5
Ås *Sweden* 10 A8
As Pontes de García
  Rodríguez *Spain* 36 B3
Aş Şafā *Syria* 74 B6
As Saffānīyah *Si. Arabia* 71 E6
As Safīrah *Syria* 72 D7
Aş Şahm *Oman* 71 E8
As Sājir *Si. Arabia* 70 E5
As Salamīyah *Syria* 72 C7
As Salmān *Iraq* 70 D5

As Salt *Jordan* 74 C4
As Sal'w'a *Qatar* 71 E6
As Samāwah *Iraq* 70 D5
As Sanamayn *Syria* 74 B5
As Sohar = Şuḥār *Oman* 71 E8
As Sukhnah *Syria* 73 E8
As Sulaymānīyah *Iraq* 70 D5
As Sulaymānīyah □ *Iraq* 73 E11
As Sulaymī *Si. Arabia* 70 E4
As Sulayyil *Si. Arabia* 75 B4
As Summān *Si. Arabia* 70 E5
Aş Şuwar *Syria* 73 E9
As Suwaydā *Syria* 74 C4
As Suwaydā' □ *Syria* 74 C4
As Suwayq *Oman* 71 F8
Aş Şuwayrah *Iraq* 73 F11
Åsa *Sweden* 11 G6
Asab *Namibia* 88 D2
Asaba *Nigeria* 83 D6
Asad, Buḥayrat al *Syria* 73 D8
Asadābād *Iran* 73 E13
Asafo *Ghana* 82 D4
Asahi-Gawa → *Japan* 55 G6
Asahigawa *Japan* 54 C11
Asale, L. *Ethiopia* 81 E5
Asaluyeh *Iran* 71 E7
Asamankese *Ghana* 83 D4
Asan → *India* 69 F8
Asansol *India* 69 H12
Åsarna *Sweden* 10 B8
Asau *Samoa* 91 b
Asayita *Ethiopia* 81 E5
Asbe Teferi *Ethiopia* 81 F5
Asbesberge *S. Africa* 88 D3
Asbestos *Canada* 105 C5
Asbury Park *U.S.A.* 115 F10
Ascea *Italy* 43 B8
Ascensión *Mexico* 118 A3
Ascensión, B. de la *Mexico* 119 D7
Ascension I. *Atl. Oc.* 77 G2
Aschach an der Donau
  Austria 26 C7
Aschaffenburg *Germany* 25 F5
Aschendorf *Germany* 24 B3
Aschersleben *Germany* 24 D7
Asciano *Italy* 41 E8
Áscoli Piceno *Italy* 41 F10
Áscoli Satriano *Italy* 43 A8
Ascope *Peru* 124 E3
Ascotán *Chile* 126 A2
Aseb *Eritrea* 81 E5
Åseda *Sweden* 11 G9
Asela *Ethiopia* 81 F4
Åsen *Sweden* 10 C7
Asenovgrad *Bulgaria* 45 D8
Asfeld *France* 19 C11
Asfūn el Matā'na *Egypt* 80 B3
Aşgabat = Ashgabat
  Turkmenistan 71 B8
Asgata *Cyprus* 49 E12
Ash Fork *U.S.A.* 109 J7
Ash Grove *U.S.A.* 112 G7
Ash Shabakah *Iraq* 70 D5
Ash Shamāl □ *Lebanon* 74 A5
Ash Shāmīyah *Iraq* 73 G11
Ash Shāriqah *U.A.E.* 71 E7
Ash Sharmah *Si. Arabia* 70 D2
Ash Sharqāt *Iraq* 73 E10
Ash Shaţrah *Iraq* 70 D5
Ash Shawbak *Jordan* 70 D2
Ash Shiḥr *Yemen* 75 E4
Ash Shināfīyah *Iraq* 70 D5
Ash Shu'bah *Si. Arabia* 70 D5
Ash Shumlūl *Si. Arabia* 70 E5
Ash Shūr'ab *Si. Arabia* 70 E4
Ash Shurayf *Si. Arabia* 70 E4
Ash Shuwayfāt *Lebanon* 74 B4
Ashanti □ *Ghana* 83 D4
Ashau *Vietnam* 64 D6
Ashbourne *U.K.* 14 D6
Ashburn *U.S.A.* 117 F13
Ashburton *N.Z.* 91 E3
Ashburton → *Australia* 92 D1
Ashcroft *Canada* 102 C4
Ashdod *Israel* 74 D3
Ashdown *U.S.A.* 116 E7
Asheboro *U.S.A.* 117 D15
Ashern *Canada* 103 C9
Asherton *U.S.A.* 116 G5
Asheville *U.S.A.* 117 D13
Ashewat *Pakistan* 68 D3
Asheweig → *Canada* 104 B2
Ashford *Australia* 95 D5
Ashford *U.K.* 15 F8
Ashgabat *Turkmenistan* 71 B8
Ashibetsu *Japan* 54 C11
Ashikaga *Japan* 55 F9
Ashington *U.K.* 14 B6
Ashizuri-Uwakai △ *Japan* 55 H6
Ashizuri-Zaki *Japan* 55 H6
Ashkarkot *Afghan.* 68 C2
Ashkhabad = Ashgabat
  Turkmenistan 71 B8
Āshkhāneh *Iran* 71 B8
Ashland *Kans., U.S.A.* 112 G4
Ashland *Ky., U.S.A.* 113 F12
Ashland *Maine, U.S.A.* 113 B19
Ashland *Mont., U.S.A.* 108 D10

Ashland *Ohio, U.S.A.* **114** F2
Ashland *Oreg., U.S.A.* **108** E2
Ashland *Pa., U.S.A.* **115** F8
Ashland *Va., U.S.A.* **113** G15
Ashland *Wis., U.S.A.* **112** B8
Ashley *N. Dak., U.S.A.* **112** B4
Ashley *Pa., U.S.A.* **115** E9
Ashmore and Cartier Is. *Ind. Oc.* **92** B3
Ashmore Reef *Australia* **92** B3
Ashmûn *Egypt* **80** H7
Ashmyany *Belarus* **23** A13
Ashokan Res. *U.S.A.* **115** E10
Ashoknagar *India* **68** G7
Ashta *India* **68** H7
Ashtabula *U.S.A.* **114** E4
Ăshtiyān *Iran* **71** C6
Ashton *S. Africa* **88** E3
Ashton *U.S.A.* **108** D8
Ashuanipi, L. *Canada* **105** B6
Ashuapmushuan ➜ *Canada* **104** C5
Ashville *U.S.A.* **114** F6
'Āṣī ➜ *Asia* **72** D6
Asia **50** E9
Asia, Kepulauan *Indonesia* **63** D8
Asiago *Italy* **41** C8
Asifabad *India* **66** K11
Asino *Russia* **52** D9
Asipovichy *Belarus* **23** B15
'Asīr *Si. Arabia* **75** D3
Asir, Ras *Somali Rep.* **75** E5
Aşkale *Turkey* **73** C9
Askersund *Sweden* **11** F8
Askham *S. Africa* **88** D3
Askī Mawşil *Iraq* **73** D10
Askim *Norway* **9** G14
Askio, Oros *Greece* **44** F5
Askja *Iceland* **8** D5
Askøyna *Norway* **8** F11
Asl *Egypt* **80** B3
Aslan Burnu *Turkey* **47** C8
Aslanapa *Turkey* **47** B11
Asländuz *Iran* **73** C12
Asmara = Asmera *Eritrea* **81** D4
Asmera *Eritrea* **81** D4
Asnæs *Denmark* **11** J4
Åsnen *Sweden* **11** H8
Aso Kuju △ *Japan* **55** H5
Åsola *Italy* **40** C7
Asos *Greece* **46** C2
Asosa *Ethiopia* **81** E3
Asoteriba, Jebel *Sudan* **80** C4
Aspatria *U.K.* **14** C4
Aspe *Spain* **39** G4
Aspen *U.S.A.* **108** G10
Aspendos *Turkey* **72** D4
Aspermont *U.S.A.* **116** E4
Aspet *France* **20** E4
Aspiring, Mt. *N.Z.* **91** F2
Aspres-sur-Buëch *France* **21** D9
Asprokavos, Akra *Greece* **49** B4
Aspromonte △ *Italy* **43** D8
Aspur *India* **68** H6
Asquith *Canada* **103** C7
Assab = Aseb *Eritrea* **81** E5
Assâba □ *Mauritania* **82** B2
Assâba, Massif de l' *Mauritania* **82** B2
Assagny △ *Ivory C.* **82** D4
Assaikio *Nigeria* **83** D6
Assal, L. *Djibouti* **81** E5
Assam □ *India* **67** G18
Assamakka *Niger* **83** B6
Assateague Island △ *U.S.A.* **113** F16
Asse *Belgium* **17** D4
Assémini *Italy* **42** C1
Assen *Neths.* **17** A6
Assens *Denmark* **11** J3
Assini *Ivory C.* **82** D4
Assiniboia *Canada* **103** D7
Assiniboine ➜ *Canada* **103** D9
Assiniboine, Mt. *Canada* **102** C5
Assis *Brazil* **127** A5
Assisi *Italy* **41** E9
Assynt, L. *U.K.* **13** C3
Astaffort *France* **20** D4
Astakida *Greece* **47** F8
Astakos *Greece* **46** C3
Astana *Kazakhstan* **52** D8
Ăstăneh *Iran* **71** B6
Astara *Azerbaijan* **73** C13
Ăstārā *Iran* **73** C13
Astarabad = Gorgān *Iran* **71** B7
Asterousia *Greece* **49** E7
Asti *Italy* **40** D5
Astipalea *Greece* **47** E8
Astorga *Spain* **36** C4
Astoria *U.S.A.* **110** D3
Åstorp *Sweden* **11** H6
Astrakhan *Russia* **35** G8
Astrakhan □ *Russia* **35** G8
Astrebla Downs *Australia* **94** C3

Astudillo *Spain* **36** C6
Asturias □ *Spain* **36** B5
Asturias ✈ (OVD) *Spain* **36** B4
Asunción *Paraguay* **126** B4
Asunción Nochixtlán *Mexico* **119** D5
Åsunden *Sweden* **11** F9
Asutri *Sudan* **81** D4
Aswa ➜ *Uganda* **86** B3
Aswa-Lolim △ *Uganda* **86** B3
Aswad, Ra's al *Si. Arabia* **80** C4
Aswân *Egypt* **80** C3
Aswan High Dam = Sadd el Aali *Egypt* **80** C3
Asyût *Egypt* **80** B3
Asyûti, Wadi ➜ *Egypt* **80** B3
Aszód *Hungary* **28** C4
At Ṭafīlah *Jordan* **74** E4
At Ṭafīlah □ *Jordan* **74** E4
Aṭ Ṭā'if *Si. Arabia* **80** C5
At Ta'mīm □ *Iraq* **70** C5
Aṭ Ṭirāq *Si. Arabia* **70** E5
Aṭ Ṭubayq *Si. Arabia* **70** D3
Aṭ Ṭunayb *Jordan* **74** D4
Atabey *Turkey* **47** D12
Atacama □ *Chile* **126** B2
Atacama, Desierto de *Chile* **126** A2
Atacama, Salar de *Chile* **126** A2
Atakpamé *Togo* **83** D5
Atalandi *Greece* **46** C4
Atalaya *Peru* **124** F4
Atalaya de Femes *Canary Is.* **48** F6
Atami *Japan* **55** G9
Atamyrat *Turkmenistan* **52** F7
Atapupu *Indonesia* **63** F6
Atâr *Mauritania* **78** D3
Atarfe *Spain* **37** H7
Atari *Pakistan* **68** D6
Atascadero *U.S.A.* **110** K6
Atasū *Kazakhstan* **52** E8
Atatürk, İstanbul ✈ (IST) *Turkey* **45** F12
Atatürk Baraji *Turkey* **73** D8
Atauro *E. Timor* **63** F7
Ataviros *Greece* **49** C9
Atbara *Sudan* **80** D3
'Atbara, Nahr ➜ *Sudan* **80** D3
Atbasar *Kazakhstan* **52** D7
Atça *Turkey* **47** D10
Atchafalaya B. *U.S.A.* **116** G9
Atchison *U.S.A.* **112** F6
Atebubu *Ghana* **83** D4
Ateca *Spain* **38** D3
Aterno ➜ *Italy* **41** F10
Ăteshān *Iran* **71** C7
Atesine, Alpi *Italy* **41** B8
Atessa *Italy* **41** F11
Atfîh *Egypt* **80** J7
Ath *Belgium* **17** D3
Athabasca *Canada* **102** C6
Athabasca ➜ *Canada* **103** B6
Athabasca, L. *Canada* **103** B7
Athabasca Sand Dunes △ *Canada* **103** B7
Athamanon Oros *Greece* **46** B3
Athboy *Ireland* **12** C5
Athenry *Ireland* **12** C3
Athens = Athina *Greece* **46** D5
Athens *Ala., U.S.A.* **117** D11
Athens *Ga., U.S.A.* **117** E13
Athens *N.Y., U.S.A.* **115** D11
Athens *Ohio, U.S.A.* **114** F5
Athens *Pa., U.S.A.* **115** E8
Athens *Tenn., U.S.A.* **117** D12
Athens *Tex., U.S.A.* **116** E7
Atherley *Canada* **114** B5
Atherton *Australia* **94** B4
Athi River *Kenya* **86** C4
Athiéme *Benin* **83** D5
Athienou *Cyprus* **49** D12
Athina *Greece* **46** D5
Athina ✈ (ATH) *Greece* **46** D5
Athínai = Athina *Greece* **46** D5
Athlone *Ireland* **12** C4
Athna *Cyprus* **49** D12
Athol *U.S.A.* **115** D12
Athol, Forest of *U.K.* **13** E5
Atholville *Canada* **105** C6
Athos *Greece* **45** F8
Athy *Ireland* **12** C5
Ati *Chad* **79** F9
Ati *Sudan* **81** E2
Atiak *Uganda* **86** B3
Atienza *Spain* **38** D2
Atiit *Sudan* **81** F3
Atik L. *Canada* **103** B9
Atikaki △ *Canada* **103** C9
Atikameg ➜ *Canada* **104** B3
Atikokan *Canada* **104** C1
Atikonak L. *Canada* **105** B7
Atimaono *Tahiti* **91** d
Atimonan *Phil.* **61** E4
Atitlán △ *Cent. Amer.* **119** E6
Atiu *Cook Is.* **97** J12
Atka *Russia* **53** C16
Atka I. *U.S.A.* **106** a
Atkarsk *Russia* **34** E7
Atkinson *U.S.A.* **112** D4

Atlanta *Ga., U.S.A.* **117** E12
Atlanta *Tex., U.S.A.* **116** E7
Atlantic *U.S.A.* **112** E6
Atlantic City *U.S.A.* **113** F16
Atlantic-Indian Basin *Antarctica* **5** B4
Atlantic Ocean **2** D8
Atlas Mts. = Haut Atlas *Morocco* **78** B4
Atlin *Canada* **102** B2
Atlin, L. *Canada* **102** B2
Atlin △ *Canada* **102** B2
Atmore *U.S.A.* **117** F11
Atoka *U.S.A.* **116** D6
Atokos *Greece* **46** C2
Atolia *U.S.A.* **111** K9
Atrai ➜ *Bangla.* **69** G13
Atrak = Atrek ➜ *Turkmenistan* **71** B8
Ătran *Sweden* **11** G6
Ătran ➜ *Sweden* **11** H6
Atrauli *India* **68** E8
Atrek ➜ *Turkmenistan* **71** B8
Atri *Italy* **41** F10
Atsiki *Greece* **47** B7
Atsoum, Mts. *Cameroon* **83** D7
Atsuta *Japan* **54** C10
Attalla *U.S.A.* **117** D11
Attapu *Laos* **64** E6
Attawapiskat *Canada* **104** B3
Attawapiskat ➜ *Canada* **104** B3
Attawapiskat L. *Canada* **104** B2
Attersee *Austria* **26** D6
Attica *Ind., U.S.A.* **112** E10
Attica *Ohio, U.S.A.* **114** E2
Attichy *France* **19** C10
Attigny *France* **19** C11
Attika = Attiki □ *Greece* **46** D5
Attikamagen L. *Canada* **105** B6
Attiki □ *Greece* **46** D5
Attleboro *U.S.A.* **115** E13
Attock *Pakistan* **68** C5
Attopeu = Attapu *Laos* **64** E6
Attu I. *U.S.A.* **106** a
Attur *India* **66** P11
Atuel ➜ *Argentina* **126** D2
Åtvidaberg *Sweden* **11** F10
Atwater *U.S.A.* **110** H6
Atwood *Canada* **114** C3
Atwood *U.S.A.* **112** F4
Atyraū *Kazakhstan* **52** E6
Au Sable ➜ *U.S.A.* **113** C12
Au Sable Forks *U.S.A.* **115** B11
Au Sable Pt. *U.S.A.* **114** B1
Auas *Honduras* **120** C3
Auasberg *Namibia* **88** C2
Aubagne *France* **21** E9
Aube □ *France* **19** D11
Aube ➜ *France* **19** D10
Aubenas *France* **21** D8
Aubenton *France* **19** C11
Auberry *U.S.A.* **110** H7
Aubigny-sur-Nère *France* **19** E9
Aubin *France* **20** D6
Aubrac, Mts. d' *France* **20** D7
Auburn *Ala., U.S.A.* **117** E12
Auburn *Calif., U.S.A.* **110** G5
Auburn *Ind., U.S.A.* **113** E11
Auburn *Maine, U.S.A.* **113** C18
Auburn *N.Y., U.S.A.* **115** D8
Auburn *Nebr., U.S.A.* **112** E6
Auburn *Pa., U.S.A.* **115** F8
Auburn *Wash., U.S.A.* **110** C4
Auburn Ra. *Australia* **95** D5
Auburndale *U.S.A.* **117** G14
Aubusson *France* **20** C6
Auce *Latvia* **30** B9
Auch *France* **20** E4
Auchi *Nigeria* **83** D6
Auchterarder *U.K.* **13** E5
Auchtermuchty *U.K.* **13** E5
Auckland *N.Z.* **91** B5
Auckland Is. *Pac. Oc.* **96** N8
Aude □ *France* **20** E6
Aude ➜ *France* **20** E7
Auden *Canada* **104** B2
Auderville *France* **18** C5
Audierne *France* **18** D2
Audincourt *France* **19** E13
Audo Ra. *Ethiopia* **81** F5
Audubon *U.S.A.* **112** E6
Aue *Germany* **24** E8
Auerbach *Germany* **24** E8
Augathella *Australia* **95** D4
Aughnacloy *U.K.* **12** B5
Aughrim *Ireland* **12** C5
Augrabies Falls *S. Africa* **88** D3
Augrabies Falls △ *S. Africa* **88** D3
Augsburg *Germany* **25** G6
Augsburg-Westliche Wälder △ *Germany* **25** G6
Augusta *Australia* **93** F2
Augusta *Italy* **43** E8
Augusta *Ark., U.S.A.* **116** D9
Augusta *Ga., U.S.A.* **117** E14
Augusta *Kans., U.S.A.* **112** G5
Augusta *Maine, U.S.A.* **113** C19

Augusta *Mont., U.S.A.* **108** C7
Augustenborg *Denmark* **11** K3
Augustów *Poland* **30** E9
Augustus, Mt. *Australia* **93** D2
Augustus I. *Australia* **92** C3
Aujuittuq = Grise Fiord *Canada* **101** B11
Aukan *Eritrea* **81** D5
Aukrug △ *Germany* **24** A5
Aukštaitija △ *Lithuania* **9** J22
Aukum *U.S.A.* **110** G6
Auld, L. *Australia* **92** D3
Aulifeltet *Norway* **10** D5
Aulla *Italy* **40** D6
Aulnay *France* **20** B3
Aulne ➜ *France* **18** D3
Aulnoye-Aymeries *France* **19** B10
Ault *France* **18** B8
Ault *U.S.A.* **108** F11
Aulus-les-Bains *France* **20** F5
Aumale *France* **19** C8
Aumont-Aubrac *France* **20** D7
Auna *Nigeria* **83** C5
Auning *Denmark* **11** H4
Aunis *France* **20** B3
Aunu'u *Amer. Samoa* **91** b
Auponhia *Indonesia* **63** E7
Aups *France* **21** E10
Aur, Pulau *Malaysia* **65** L5
Auraiya *India* **69** F8
Aurangabad *Bihar, India* **69** G11
Aurangabad *Maharashtra, India* **66** K9
Auray *France* **18** E4
Aurich *Germany* **24** B3
Aurillac *France* **20** D6
Auronzo di Cadore *Italy* **41** B9
Aurora *Canada* **114** C5
Aurora *S. Africa* **88** E2
Aurora *Colo., U.S.A.* **108** G11
Aurora *Ill., U.S.A.* **112** E9
Aurora *Mo., U.S.A.* **112** G7
Aurora *N.Y., U.S.A.* **115** D8
Aurora *Nebr., U.S.A.* **112** E5
Aurora *Ohio, U.S.A.* **114** E3
Aurukun *Australia* **94** A3
Aus *Namibia* **88** D2
Ausable ➜ *Canada* **114** C3
Auschwitz = Oświęcim *Poland* **31** H6
Austerlitz = Slavkov u Brna *Czech Rep.* **27** B9
Austin *Minn., U.S.A.* **112** D8
Austin *Nev., U.S.A.* **108** G5
Austin *Pa., U.S.A.* **114** E6
Austin *Tex., U.S.A.* **116** F6
Austin, L. *Australia* **93** E2
Austin I. *Canada* **103** A10
Austra *Norway* **8** D14
Austral Is. = Tubuaï, Is. *French Polynesia* **97** K13
Austral Seamount Chain *Pac. Oc.* **97** K13
Australia ■ *Oceania* **90** D6
Australian-Antarctic Basin *S. Ocean* **5** C9
Australian Capital Territory □ *Australia* **95** F4
Australind *Australia* **93** F2
Austria ■ *Europe* **26** E7
Austvågøya *Norway* **8** B16
Auterive *France* **20** E5
Authie ➜ *France* **19** B8
Authon-du-Perche *France* **18** D7
Autlán de Navarro *Mexico* **118** D4
Autun *France* **19** F11
Auvergne □ *France* **20** C7
Auvergne, Mts. d' *France* **20** C7
Auvézère ➜ *France* **20** C4
Auxerre *France* **19** E10
Auxi-le-Château *France* **19** B9
Auxonne *France* **19** E12
Auzances *France* **19** F9
Av-Dovurak *Russia* **53** D10
Ava *U.S.A.* **112** G7
Avallon *France* **19** E10
Avalon *U.S.A.* **110** M8
Avalon Pen. *Canada* **105** C9
Avanos *Turkey* **72** C6
Avantas *Greece* **45** F9
Avaré *Brazil* **127** A6
Avawatz Mts. *U.S.A.* **111** K10
Avdan Dağları *Turkey* **45** F13
Avdan *U.S.A.* **115** D13
Avej *Iran* **71** C6
Avellaneda *Argentina* **126** C4
Avellino *Italy* **43** B7
Avenal *U.S.A.* **110** K6
Aversa *Italy* **43** B7
Avery *U.S.A.* **108** C6
Aves, I. de *W. Indies* **121** C7
Aves, Is. las *Venezuela* **121** D6
Avesnes-sur-Helpe *France* **19** B10
Avesnois △ *France* **19** B10
Avesta *Sweden* **10** D10
Aveyron □ *France* **20** D6

Aveyron ➜ *France* **20** D5
Avezzano *Italy* **41** F10
Avgo *Greece* **47** F7
Aviá Terai *Argentina* **126** B3
Aviano *Italy* **41** B9
Aviemore *U.K.* **13** D5
Avigliana *Italy* **40** C4
Avigliano *Italy* **43** B8
Avignon *France* **21** E8
Ávila *Spain* **36** E6
Ávila □ *Spain* **36** E6
Ávila, Sierra de *Spain* **36** E5
Avila Beach *U.S.A.* **111** K6
Avilés *Spain* **36** B5
Avintes *Portugal* **36** D2
Avis *Portugal* **37** F3
Avis *U.S.A.* **114** E7
Avíz = Avis *Portugal* **37** F3
Avize *France* **19** D11
Avlonari *Greece* **46** C6
Avlum *Denmark* **11** H2
Avoca ➜ *Australia* **95** F3
Avoca *Ireland* **12** D5
Avoca *U.S.A.* **114** D7
Avola *Canada* **102** C5
Avola *Italy* **43** F8
Avon ➜ *Australia* **93** F2
Avon ➜ *Bristol, U.K.* **15** F5
Avon ➜ *Dorset, U.K.* **15** G6
Avon ➜ *Warks., U.K.* **15** E5
Avon Park *U.S.A.* **117** H14
Avondale *Zimbabwe* **87** F3
Avonlea *Canada* **103** D8
Avonmore *Canada* **115** A10
Avonmouth *U.K.* **15** F5
Avramov *Bulgaria* **45** D10
Avranches *France* **18** D5
Avre ➜ *France* **18** D8
Avrig *Romania* **29** E9
Avrillé *France* **18** E6
Avtovac *Bos.-H.* **44** C2
Awa-Shima *Japan* **54** E9
Awag el Baqar *Sudan* **81** E3
A'waj ➜ *Syria* **74** B5
Awaji-Shima *Japan* **55** G7
'Awalī *Bahrain* **71** E6
Awantipur *India* **69** C6
Awasa *Ethiopia* **81** F4
Awasa, L. *Ethiopia* **81** F4
Awash *Ethiopia* **81** F5
Awash ➜ *Ethiopia* **81** E5
Awash △ *Ethiopia* **81** F5
Awaso *Ghana* **82** D4
Awatere ➜ *N.Z.* **91** D5
Awbārī *Libya* **79** C8
Awbārī, Idehan *Libya* **79** C8
Awe, L. *U.K.* **13** E3
Aweil *Sudan* **81** F2
Awgu *Nigeria* **83** D6
Awjilah *Libya* **79** C10
Awka *Nigeria* **83** D6
Ax-les-Thermes *France* **20** F5
Axat *France* **20** F6
Axe ➜ *U.K.* **15** F5
Axel Heiberg I. *Canada* **101** B11
Axim *Ghana* **82** E4
Axintele *Romania* **29** F11
Axios ➜ *Greece* **44** F6
Axminster *U.K.* **15** G4
Axvall *Sweden* **11** F7
Ay *France* **19** C11
Ayabaca *Peru* **124** D3
Ayabe *Japan* **55** G7
Ayacucho *Argentina* **126** D4
Ayacucho *Peru* **124** F4
Ayaguz = Ayaköz *Kazakhstan* **52** E9
Ayaköz *Kazakhstan* **52** E9
Ayamé *Ivory C.* **82** D4
Ayamonte *Spain* **37** H3
Ayan *Russia* **53** D14
Ayancık *Turkey* **72** B6
Ayas *Turkey* **72** B5
Ayaviri *Peru* **124** F4
Aybastı *Turkey* **72** B7
Aydın *Turkey* **72** D2
Aydın □ *Turkey* **47** D9
Aydın Dağları *Turkey* **47** D10
Ayelu *Ethiopia* **81** E5
Ayenngré *Togo* **83** D5
Ayer *U.S.A.* **115** D13
Ayer Hitam *Malaysia* **65** c
Ayer's Cliff *Canada* **115** A12
Ayers Rock = Uluru *Australia* **93** E5
Ayeyarwady = Irrawaddy ➜ *Burma* **67** M19
Áyia Napa *Cyprus* **49** E13
Áyia Phyla *Cyprus* **49** E12
Áyios Amvrósios *Cyprus* **49** D12
Áyios Seryios *Cyprus* **49** D12
Áyios Theodhoros *Cyprus* **49** D13
Áyios Yeóryios = Aghios Georgios *Greece* **46** C5
Aykhal *Russia* **53** C12

Aykirikçi *Turkey* **47** B12
Aylesbury *U.K.* **15** F7
Aylmer *Canada* **115** D8
Aylmer, L. *Canada* **100** C9
'Ayn, Wādī al *Oman* **71** F7
Ayn Dār *Si. Arabia* **71** E7
Ayn Sifnī *Iraq* **73** D10
Ayn Zālah *Iraq* **73** D10
Ayna *Spain* **39** G2
Ayod *Sudan* **81** F3
Ayolas *Paraguay* **126** B4
Ayom *Sudan* **81** F2
Ayon, Ostrov *Russia* **53** C17
Ayora *Spain* **39** F3
Ayorou *Niger* **83** C5
'Ayoûn el 'Atroûs *Mauritania* **82** B3
Ayr *Australia* **94** B4
Ayr *Canada* **114** C4
Ayr *U.K.* **13** F4
Ayr ➜ *U.K.* **13** F4
Ayrancı *Turkey* **72** D5
Ayrancılar *Turkey* **47** C9
Ayre, Pt. of *I. of Man* **14** C3
Aysha *Ethiopia* **81** E5
Ayton *Australia* **94** B4
Aytos *Bulgaria* **45** D11
Aytoska Planina *Bulgaria* **45** D11
Ayu, Kepulauan *Indonesia* **63** D8
Ayutla *Guatemala* **120** D1
Ayutla de los Libres *Mexico* **119** D5
Ayvacık *Turkey* **72** C2
Ayvalık *Turkey* **47** B8
Az Zabadānī *Syria* **74** B5
Aẕ Ẕāhirīyah *West Bank* **74** D3
Aẕ Ẕahrān *Si. Arabia* **71** E6
Az Zarqā *Jordan* **74** C5
Az Zarqā' *U.A.E.* **71** E7
Az Zarqā □ *Jordan* **74** C5
Az Zāwiyah *Libya* **79** B8
Az Zibār *Iraq* **73** D11
Az Zilfī *Si. Arabia* **70** E5
Az Zubayr *Iraq* **70** D5
Az Zuqur *Yemen* **81** E5
Azad Kashmir □ *Pakistan* **69** C5
Azambuja *Portugal* **37** F2
Azamgarh *India* **69** F10
Azangaro *Peru* **124** F4
Azaouad *Mali* **82** B4
Azaouak ➜ *Mali* **83** B5
Azaouak, Vallée de l' *Mali* **83** B5
Ăzar Shahr *Iran* **73** D11
Azara *Nigeria* **83** D6
Azarān *Iran* **73** D12
Ăzārbāyjān ■ Azerbaijan ■ *Asia* **35** K9
Ăzārbāyjān-e Gharbī □ *Iran* **70** B5
Ăzārbāyjān-e Sharqī □ *Iran* **70** B5
Azare *Nigeria* **83** C7
Azay-le-Rideau *France* **18** E7
A'zāz *Syria* **72** D7
Azbine = Aïr *Niger* **83** B6
Azerbaijan ■ *Asia* **35** K9
Azezo *Ethiopia* **81** E4
Azimganj *India* **69** G13
Aznalcóllar *Spain* **37** H4
Azogues *Ecuador* **124** D3
Azores = Açores, Is. dos *Atl. Oc.* **78** a
Azov *Russia* **35** G4
Azov, Sea of *Europe* **33** J9
Azovskoye More = Azov, Sea of *Europe* **33** J9
Azpeitia *Spain* **38** B2
Azraq ash Shīshān *Jordan* **74** D5
Aztec *U.S.A.* **109** H10
Azúa de Compostela *Dom. Rep.* **121** C5
Azuaga *Spain* **37** G5
Azuara *Spain* **38** D4
Azuer ➜ *Spain* **37** F7
Azuero, Pen. de *Panama* **120** E3
Azuga *Romania* **29** E10
Azul *Argentina* **126** D4
Azusa *U.S.A.* **111** L9
Azzano Décimo *Italy* **41** C9
Azzel Matti, Sebkra *Algeria* **78** C6

B

Ba Be △ *Vietnam* **64** A5
Ba Don *Vietnam* **64** D6
Ba Dong *Vietnam* **65** H6
Ba Ngoi = Cam Lam *Vietnam* **65** G7
Ba Tri *Vietnam* **65** G6
Ba Vi *Vietnam* **64** B5
Ba Xian = Bazhou *China* **56** E9
Baa *Indonesia* **63** F6
Baamonde *Spain* **36** B3
Baardheere *Somali Rep.* **75** G3
Baarle-Nassau *Belgium* **17** C4
Bab el Mandeb *Red Sea* **75** E3
Baba *Bulgaria* **44** E7
Bābā, Koh-i- *Afghan.* **66** B5
Baba Burnu *Turkey* **47** B8
Baba dag *Azerbaijan* **35** K9
Bābā Kalū *Iran* **71** D6
Babadag *Romania* **29** F13

Babadağ *Turkey* **47** D10
Babaeski *Turkey* **45** E11
Babahoyo *Ecuador* **124** D3
Babai = Sarju ➤ *India* **69** F9
Babana *Nigeria* **83** C5
Babanusa *Sudan* **81** E2
Babar *Indonesia* **63** F7
Babar *Pakistan* **68** D3
Babarkach *Pakistan* **68** E3
Babayevo *Russia* **32** C8
Babb *U.S.A.* **108** B7
Babenhausen *Germany* **25** F4
Băbeni *Romania* **29** F9
Baberu *India* **69** G9
Babi Besar, Pulau *Malaysia* **65** L4
Babia Gora *Europe* **31** J6
Babian Jiang ➤ *China* **58** F3
Bābil □ *Iraq* **70** C5
Babile *Ethiopia* **81** F5
Babimost *Poland* **31** F2
Babinda *Australia* **94** B4
Babine *Canada* **102** B3
Babine ➤ *Canada* **102** B3
Babine L. *Canada* **102** C3
Babiogórski △ *Poland* **31** J6
Babo *Indonesia* **63** E8
Babócsa *Hungary* **28** D2
Bābol *Iran* **71** B7
Bābol Sar *Iran* **71** B7
Baborów *Poland* **31** H5
Baboua *C.A.R.* **84** C2
Babruysk *Belarus* **23** B15
Babuhri *India* **68** F3
Babuna *Macedonia* **44** E5
Babura *Nigeria* **83** C6
Babusar Pass *Pakistan* **69** B5
Babušnica *Serbia* **44** C6
Babuyan Chan. *Phil.* **61** B4
Babylon *Iraq* **73** F11
Bač *Serbia* **28** E4
Bâc ➤ *Moldova* **29** D14
Bac Can *Vietnam* **58** F5
Bac Giang *Vietnam* **58** G6
Bac Lieu *Vietnam* **65** H5
Bac Ninh *Vietnam* **58** G6
Bac Phan *Vietnam* **58** G5
Bac Quang *Vietnam* **58** F5
Bacabal *Brazil* **125** D10
Bacalar *Mexico* **119** D7
Bacan, Kepulauan *Indonesia* **63** E7
Bacarra *Phil.* **61** B4
Bacău *Romania* **29** D11
Bacău □ *Romania* **29** D11
Baccarat *France* **19** D13
Bacerac *Mexico* **118** A3
Băceşti *Romania* **29** D11
Bach Long Vi, Dao *Vietnam* **64** B6
Bach Ma △ *Vietnam* **64** D6
Bacharach *Germany* **25** E3
Bachhwara *India* **69** G11
Bachuma *Ethiopia* **81** F4
Bačina *Serbia* **44** C5
Back ➤ *Canada* **100** C9
Bačka Palanka *Serbia* **28** E4
Bačka Topola *Serbia* **28** E4
Bäckebo *Sweden* **11** H10
Bäckefors *Sweden* **11** F6
Bäckhammar *Sweden* **10** E8
Bački Petrovac *Serbia* **28** E4
Backnang *Germany* **25** G5
Baco, Mt. *Phil.* **61** E4
Bacolod *Phil.* **61** F5
Bacqueville-en-Caux *France* **18** C8
Bács-Kiskun □ *Hungary* **28** D4
Bácsalmás *Hungary* **28** D4
Bacuag = Placer *Phil.* **61** G6
Bacuk *Malaysia* **65** J4
Bácum *Mexico* **118** B2
Bād *Iran* **71** C7
Bad ➤ *U.S.A.* **112** C3
Bad Aussee *Austria* **26** D6
Bad Axe *U.S.A.* **114** C2
Bad Bergzabern *Germany* **25** F3
Bad Berleburg *Germany* **24** D4
Bad Bevensen *Germany* **24** B6
Bad Bramstedt *Germany* **24** B5
Bad Brückenau *Germany* **25** E5
Bad Doberan *Germany* **24** A7
Bad Driburg *Germany* **24** D5
Bad Ems *Germany* **25** E3
Bad Frankenhausen
  Germany **24** D7
Bad Freienwalde *Germany* **24** C10
Bad Goisern *Austria* **26** D6
Bad Harzburg *Germany* **24** D6
Bad Hersfeld *Germany* **24** E5
Bad Hofgastein *Austria* **26** D6
Bad Homburg *Germany* **25** E4
Bad Honnef *Germany* **24** E3
Bad Iburg *Germany* **24** C4
Bad Ischl *Austria* **26** D6
Bad Kissingen *Germany* **25** E6
Bad Königshofen *Germany* **25** E6
Bad Kreuznach *Germany* **25** F3
Bad Krozingen *Germany* **25** H3
Bad Laasphe *Germany* **24** E4
Bad Langensalza *Germany* **24** D6
Bad Lauterberg *Germany* **24** D6

Bad Leonfelden *Austria* **26** C7
Bad Liebenwerda *Germany* **24** D9
Bad Mergentheim *Germany* **25** F5
Bad Münstereifel *Germany* **24** E2
Bad Nauheim *Germany* **25** E4
Bad Neuenahr-Ahrweiler
  Germany **24** E3
Bad Neustadt *Germany* **25** E6
Bad Oeynhausen *Germany* **24** C4
Bad Oldesloe *Germany* **24** B6
Bad Orb *Germany* **25** E5
Bad Pyrmont *Germany* **24** D5
Bad Reichenhall *Germany* **25** H8
Bad Säckingen *Germany* **25** H3
Bad St. Leonhard *Austria* **26** E7
Bad Salzuflen *Germany* **24** C4
Bad Salzungen *Germany* **24** E6
Bad Schwartau *Germany* **24** B6
Bad Segeberg *Germany* **24** B6
Bad Tölz *Germany* **25** H7
Bad Urach *Germany* **25** G5
Bad Vöslau *Austria* **27** D9
Bad Waldsee *Germany* **25** H5
Bad Wildungen *Germany* **24** D5
Bad Wimpfen *Germany* **25** F5
Bad Windsheim *Germany* **25** F6
Bad Zwischenahn *Germany* **24** B4
Bada Barabil *India* **69** H11
Badagara *India* **66** P9
Badagri *Nigeria* **83** D5
Badajós, L. *Brazil* **124** D6
Badajoz *Spain* **37** G4
Badajoz □ *Spain* **37** G4
Badalona *Spain* **38** D7
Badakhshān □ *Afghan.* **66** A7
Badalzai *Afghan.* **68** E1
Badampahar *India* **67** H15
Badanah *Si. Arabia* **70** D4
Badarinath *India* **69** D8
Badas, Kepulauan *Indonesia* **62** D3
Baddo ➤ *Pakistan* **66** F4
Bade *Indonesia* **63** F9
Badeggi *Nigeria* **83** D6
Badéguichéri *Niger* **83** C6
Baden *Austria* **27** C9
Baden *Switz.* **25** H4
Baden *U.S.A.* **114** F4
Baden-Baden *Germany* **25** G4
Baden-Württemberg □
  Germany **25** G4
Badgam *India* **69** B6
Badgastein *Austria* **26** D6
Badger *Canada* **105** C8
Badger *U.S.A.* **110** J7
Bādghīs □ *Afghan.* **66** B3
Badgingarra *Australia* **93** F2
Badia Polésine *Italy* **41** C8
Badiar △ *Guinea* **82** C2
Badin *Pakistan* **68** G3
Badinka △ *Mali* **82** C3
Badlands *U.S.A.* **112** D2
Badlands △ *U.S.A.* **112** D2
Badogo *Mali* **82** C3
Badoumbé *Mali* **82** C2
Badrah *Iraq* **73** F11
Badrinath *India* **69** D8
Badulla *Sri Lanka* **66** R12
Badung, Selat *Indonesia* **63** K18
Baena *Spain* **37** H6
Baengnyeongdo *S. Korea* **57** F13
Baeza *Spain* **37** H7
Bafang *Cameroon* **83** D7
Bafatá *Guinea-Biss.* **82** C2
Baffin B. *N. Amer.* **101** B13
Baffin I. *Canada* **101** C12
Bafia *Cameroon* **83** E7
Bafilo *Togo* **83** D5
Bafing ➤ *Mali* **82** C2
Bafing △ *Mali* **82** C2
Bafliyūn *Syria* **70** B3
Bafoulabé *Mali* **82** C2
Bafoussam *Cameroon* **83** D7
Bāfq *Iran* **71** D7
Bafra *Turkey* **72** B6
Bafra Burnu *Turkey* **72** B7
Bāft *Iran* **71** D8
Bafut *Cameroon* **83** D7
Bafwasende
  Dem. Rep. of the Congo **86** B2
Bagaha *India* **69** F11
Bagam *Niger* **83** B6
Bagamoyo *Tanzania* **86** D4
Bagan Datoh *Malaysia* **65** L3
Bagan Serai *Malaysia* **65** K3
Baganga *Phil.* **61** H7
Bagani *Namibia* **88** B3
Bagansiapiapi *Indonesia* **62** D2
Bagasra *India* **68** J4
Bagaud *India* **68** H6
Bagawi *Sudan* **81** E3
Bagbag *Sudan* **81** D3
Bagdad *U.S.A.* **111** L11
Bagdarin *Russia* **53** D12
Bagé *Brazil* **127** C5
Bagenalstown = Muine
  Bheag *Ireland* **12** D5
Baggs *U.S.A.* **108** F10
Bagh *Pakistan* **69** C5

Baghain ➤ *India* **69** G9
Baghdād *Iraq* **73** F11
Baghdadi *Georgia* **73** A10
Bagheria *Italy* **42** D6
Baghlān *Afghan.* **66** A6
Baghlān □ *Afghan.* **66** B6
Bagley *U.S.A.* **112** B6
Bagnara Cálabra *Italy* **43** D8
Bagnasco *Italy* **40** D5
Bagni di Lucca *Italy* **40** D7
Bagno di Romagna *Italy* **41** E8
Bagnoles-de-l'Orne *France* **18** D6
Bagnols-sur-Cèze *France* **21** D8
Bagnorégio *Italy* **41** F9
Bago = Pegu *Burma* **67** L20
Bagodar *India* **69** G11
Bagrationovsk *Russia* **30** D7
Bagrdan *Serbia* **44** B5
Baguio *Phil.* **61** C4
Bağyurdu *Turkey* **47** C9
Bagzane, Monts *Niger* **83** B6
Bah *India* **69** F8
Bahabón de Esgueva *Spain* **36** D7
Bahadurganj *India* **69** F12
Bahadurgarh *India* **68** E7
Bahama, Canal Viejo de
  W. Indies **120** B4
Bahamas ■ *N. Amer.* **121** B5
Bahār *Iran* **71** C6
Bahār *Iran* **73** E13
Baharampur *India* **69** G13
Baharîya, El Wâhât al *Egypt* **80** B2
Baharu Pandan = Pandan
  Malaysia **65** d
Bahawalnagar *Pakistan* **68** E5
Bahawalpur *Pakistan* **68** E4
Bahçe *Turkey* **72** D7
Bahçecik *Turkey* **45** F13
Bäherden *Turkmenistan* **71** B8
Baheri *India* **69** E8
Bahgul ➤ *India* **69** F8
Bahi *Tanzania* **86** D4
Bahi Swamp *Tanzania* **86** D4
Bahía = Salvador *Brazil* **125** F11
Bahía □ *Brazil* **125** F10
Bahía, Is. de la *Honduras* **120** C2
Bahía Blanca *Argentina* **126** D3
Bahía de Caráquez *Ecuador* **124** D2
Bahía Kino *Mexico* **118** B2
Bahía Laura *Argentina* **128** F3
Bahía Negra *Paraguay* **124** H7
Bahir Dar *Ethiopia* **81** E4
Bahmanzād *Iran* **71** D6
Bahr el Ahmar □ *Sudan* **80** D4
Bahr el Jabal □ *Sudan* **81** G3
Bahraich *India* **69** F9
Bahrain ■ *Asia* **71** E6
Bahror *India* **68** F7
Bāhū Kalāt *Iran* **71** E9
Bai *Mali* **82** C4
Bai Bung, Mui = Ca Mau,
  Mui *Vietnam* **65** H5
Bai Duc *Vietnam* **64** C5
Bai Thuong *Vietnam* **64** C5
Baia de Aramă *Romania* **28** E7
Baia Mare *Romania* **29** C8
Baia-Sprie *Romania* **29** C8
Baião *Brazil* **125** D9
Baïbokoum *Chad* **79** G9
Baicheng *China* **57** B12
Băicoi *Romania* **29** E10
Baidoa = Baydhabo
  Somali Rep. **75** G3
Baie-Comeau *Canada* **105** C6
Baie-St-Paul *Canada* **105** C5
Baie Ste-Anne *Seychelles* **85** b
Baie-Trinité *Canada* **105** C6
Baie Verte *Canada* **105** C8
Baignes-Ste-Radegonde
  France **20** C3
Baigneux-les-Juifs *France* **19** E11
Baihar *India* **69** H9
Baihe *China* **56** H6
Ba'ijī *Iraq* **73** E10
Baijnath *India* **69** E8
Baikal, L. = Baykal, Oz.
  Russia **53** D11
Baikonur = Bayqongyr
  Kazakhstan **52** E7
Baikunthpur *India* **69** H10
Baile Atha Cliath = Dublin
  Ireland **12** C5
Băile Govora *Romania* **29** E9
Băile Herculane *Romania* **28** F7
Băile Olăneşti *Romania* **29** E9
Băile Tuşnad *Romania* **29** D10
Bailén *Spain* **37** G7
Băileşti *Romania* **29** F8
Baima *China* **58** A3
Bain-de-Bretagne *France* **18** E5
Bainbridge, Ga., U.S.A. **117** F3
Bainbridge N.Y., U.S.A. **115** D9
Bainbridge Island *U.S.A.* **110** C4
Baing *Indonesia* **63** F6
Bainiu *China* **56** H7
Baiona *Spain* **36** C2

Bā'ir *Jordan* **74** E5
Bairiki = Tarawa *Kiribati* **96** G9
Bairin Youqi *China* **57** C10
Bairin Zuoqi *China* **57** C10
Bairnsdale *Australia* **95** F4
Baisha *China* **58** G7
Baissa *Nigeria* **83** D7
Baitadi *Nepal* **69** E9
Baiyin *China* **56** F3
Baiyü *China* **58** B2
Baiyu Shan *China* **56** F4
Baiyuda *Sudan* **80** D3
Baj Baj *India* **69** H13
Baja *Hungary* **28** D3
Baja, Pta. *Mexico* **118** B1
Baja California *Mexico* **118** A1
Baja California □ *Mexico* **118** B2
Baja California Sur □
  Mexico **118** B2
Bajag *India* **69** H9
Bajamar *Canary Is.* **48** F3
Bajana *India* **68** H4
Bajatrejo *Indonesia* **63** J17
Bajera *Indonesia* **63** J18
Bajgīrān *Iran* **71** B8
Bajimba, Mt. *Australia* **95** D5
Bajina Bašta *Serbia* **44** C3
Bajmok *Serbia* **28** E4
Bajo Boquete *Panama* **120** E3
Bajo Nuevo *Caribbean* **120** C4
Bajoga *Nigeria* **83** C7
Bajool *Australia* **94** C5
Bak *Hungary* **28** D1
Bakar *Croatia* **41** C11
Bakel *Senegal* **82** C2
Baker *Calif., U.S.A.* **111** K10
Baker *Mont., U.S.A.* **108** C11
Baker, L. *Canada* **100** C10
Baker, Mt. *U.S.A.* **108** B3
Baker City *U.S.A.* **108** D5
Baker I. *Pac. Oc.* **96** G10
Baker I. *U.S.A.* **102** B2
Baker I. *Australia* **93** E4
Baker Lake *Canada* **100** C10
Bakers Creek *Australia* **94** C4
Bakers Dozen Is. *Canada* **104** A4
Bakersfield *Calif., U.S.A.* **111** K8
Bakersfield *Vt., U.S.A.* **115** B12
Bakharden = Bäherden
  Turkmenistan **71** B8
Bakhchysaray *Ukraine* **33** K7
Bakhmach *Ukraine* **33** G7
Bākhtarān = Kermānshāh
  Iran **73** E12
Bākhtarān =
  Kermānshāh □ *Iran* **70** C5
Bakı *Azerbaijan* **35** K9
Bakır ➤ *Turkey* **47** C9
Bakırdağı *Turkey* **72** C6
Bakkafjörður *Iceland* **8** C6
Baklan *Turkey* **47** C11
Bako *Ethiopia* **81** F4
Bako *Ivory C.* **82** D3
Bakony *Hungary* **28** C2
Bakony Forest = Bakony
  Hungary **28** C2
Bakori *Nigeria* **83** C6
Bakouma *C.A.R.* **84** C4
Baksan *Russia* **35** J6
Bakswaho *India* **69** G8
Baku = Bakı *Azerbaijan* **35** K9
Bakundi *Nigeria* **83** D7
Bakuriani *Georgia* **73** B10
Bakutis Coast *Antarctica* **5** D15
Baky = Bakı *Azerbaijan* **35** K9
Bala *Canada* **114** A5
Bala *Senegal* **82** C2
Balâ *Turkey* **72** C5
Bala *U.K.* **14** E4
Bala, L. *U.K.* **14** E4
Balabac I. *Phil.* **62** C5
Balabac Str. *E. Indies* **62** C5
Balabagh *Afghan.* **68** B4
Ba'labakk *Lebanon* **74** B5
Balabalangan, Kepulauan
  Indonesia **62** E5
Bălăciţa *Romania* **29** F8
Balad *Iraq* **73** F11
Balad Rūz *Iraq* **73** F11
Bālādeh *Fārs, Iran* **71** D6
Bālādeh *Māzandaran, Iran* **71** B6
Balaghat *India* **66** J12
Balaghat Ra. *India* **66** K10
Balaguer *Spain* **38** D5
Balakän *Azerbaijan* **73** B12
Balakhna *Russia* **34** B6
Balaklava *Ukraine* **33** K7
Balakliya *Ukraine* **33** H9
Balakovo *Russia* **34** D8
Balamau *India* **69** F9
Bălan *Romania* **29** D10
Balancán *Mexico* **119** D6
Balashov *Russia* **34** E6

Balasinor *India* **68** H5
Balasore = Baleshwar *India* **67** J15
Balassagyarmat *Hungary* **28** B4
Balāt *Egypt* **80** B2
Balaton *Hungary* **28** D2
Balaton-Felvidéki △
  Hungary **28** D2
Balatonboglár *Hungary* **28** D2
Balatonfüred *Hungary* **28** D2
Balatonszentgyörgy
  Hungary **28** D2
Balayan *Phil.* **61** E4
Balazote *Spain* **39** G2
Balbieriškis *Lithuania* **30** D10
Balbigny *France* **21** C8
Balbina, Represa de *Brazil* **124** D7
Balboa *Panama* **120** E4
Balbriggan *Ireland* **12** C5
Balcarce *Argentina* **126** D4
Balcarres *Canada* **103** C8
Bălceşti *Romania* **29** F8
Balchik *Bulgaria* **45** C12
Balclutha *N.Z.* **91** G2
Balcones Escarpment
  U.S.A. **116** G5
Balçova *Turkey* **47** C9
Bald I. *Australia* **93** F2
Bald Knob *U.S.A.* **116** D9
Baldock L. *Canada* **103** B9
Baldwin *Mich., U.S.A.* **113** D11
Baldwin *Pa., U.S.A.* **114** F5
Baldwinsville *U.S.A.* **115** C8
Baldy Peak *U.S.A.* **109** K9
Bale *Croatia* **41** C10
Bale *Oromiya, Ethiopia* **81** F5
Bale *Oromiya, Ethiopia* **81** F5
Bale Mts. △ *Ethiopia* **81** F4
Baleares, Is. *Spain* **48** B10
Balearic Is. = Baleares, Is.
  Spain **48** B10
Baleine = Whale ➤ *Canada* **105** A6
Baleine, Petite R. de la ➤
  Canada **104** A4
Băleni *Romania* **29** E12
Baler *Phil.* **61** D4
Baler Bay *Phil.* **61** D4
Baleshare *U.K.* **13** D1
Baleshwar *India* **67** J15
Baley *Russia* **53** D12
Balezino *Russia* **34** B11
Balfate *Honduras* **120** C2
Balfour *S. Africa* **89** D4
Balfour Downs *Australia* **92** D3
Balgo *Australia* **92** D4
Bali *Cameroon* **83** D7
Bali *Greece* **49** D6
Bali *India* **68** G5
Bali □ *Indonesia* **63** J18
Bali □ *Indonesia* **63** J18
Bali, Selat *Indonesia* **63** J17
Bali Sea *Indonesia* **63** J17
Balia *S. Leone* **82** D2
Baliapal *India* **69** J12
Balige *Indonesia* **65** L2
Baligród *Poland* **31** J9
Balik Pulau *Malaysia* **65** c
Balikeşir *Turkey* **47** B9
Balıkeşir □ *Turkey* **47** B9
Balıkh ➤ *Syria* **73** E8
Balıklıçeşme *Turkey* **45** F11
Balikpapan *Indonesia* **62** E5
Balimbing *Phil.* **63** C5
Balingen *Germany* **25** G4
Balingian *Malaysia* **62** D4
Balint *Romania* **28** E6
Balintang Channel *Phil.* **61** B4
Balkan Mts. = Stara
  Planina *Bulgaria* **44** C7
Balkanabat *Turkmenistan* **71** B7
Balkhash = Balqash
  Kazakhstan **52** E8
Balkhash, Ozero = Balqash
  Köli *Kazakhstan* **52** E8
Ballachulish *U.K.* **13** E3
Balladonia *Australia* **93** F3
Ballaghaderreen *Ireland* **12** C3
Ballarat *Australia* **95** F3
Ballard, L. *Australia* **93** E3
Ballater *U.K.* **13** D5
Ballé *Mali* **82** B3
Ballenas, Canal de *Mexico* **118** B2
Balleny Is. *Antarctica* **5** C11
Balleroy *France* **18** C6
Ballerup *Denmark* **11** J6
Ballı *Turkey* **45** F11
Ballia *India* **69** G11
Ballina *Australia* **95** D5
Ballina *Ireland* **12** B2
Ballinasloe *Ireland* **12** C3
Ballinger *U.S.A.* **116** F5
Ballinrobe *Ireland* **12** C2
Ballinskelligs B. *Ireland* **12** E1
Ballon *France* **18** D7
Ballons des Vosges △
  France **19** E14
Ballsh *Albania* **44** F3
Ballston Spa *U.S.A.* **115** D11
Ballyboghil *Ireland* **12** C5
Ballybunion *Ireland* **12** D2
Ballycanew *Ireland* **12** D5

Ballycastle *U.K.* **12** A5
Ballyclare *U.K.* **12** B5
Ballydehob *Ireland* **12** E2
Ballygawley *U.K.* **12** B4
Ballyhaunis *Ireland* **12** C3
Ballyheige *Ireland* **12** D2
Ballymena *U.K.* **12** B5
Ballymoney *U.K.* **12** A5
Ballymote *Ireland* **12** B3
Ballynahinch *U.K.* **12** B6
Ballyquintin Pt. *U.K.* **12** B6
Ballyshannon *Ireland* **12** B3
Balmaceda *Chile* **128** F2
Balmaseda *Spain* **38** B1
Balmazújváros *Hungary* **28** C6
Balmertown *Canada* **103** C10
Balmoral *Australia* **95** F3
Balmoral *U.K.* **13** D5
Balmorhea *U.S.A.* **116** F3
Balochistan =
  Baluchistan □ *Pakistan* **66** F4
Balonne ➤ *Australia* **95** D4
Balotra *India* **68** G5
Balqash *Kazakhstan* **52** E8
Balqash Köli *Kazakhstan* **52** E8
Balrampur *India* **69** F10
Balranald *Australia* **95** E3
Balş *Romania* **29** F9
Balsas ➤ *Brazil* **125** E9
Balsas ➤ *Mexico* **118** D4
Balsas del Norte *Mexico* **119** D5
Bålsta *Sweden* **10** E11
Balta *Romania* **28** F7
Balta *Ukraine* **29** B14
Baltanás *Spain* **36** D6
Bălţi *Moldova* **29** C12
Baltic Sea *Europe* **9** H18
Baltîm *Egypt* **80** H7
Baltimore *Ireland* **12** E2
Baltimore *Md., U.S.A.* **113** F15
Baltimore *Ohio, U.S.A.* **114** G2
Baltinglass *Ireland* **12** D5
Baltit *Pakistan* **69** A6
Baltiysk *Russia* **30** D6
Baltrum *Germany* **24** B3
Baluchistan □ *Pakistan* **66** F4
Baluqtybulaq *Kazakhstan* **34** E10
Balurghat *India* **69** G13
Balvi *Latvia* **32** D4
Balya *Turkey* **47** B9
Bam *Iran* **71** D8
Bama *China* **58** E6
Bama *Nigeria* **83** C7
Bamaga *Australia* **94** A3
Bamaji L. *Canada* **104** B1
Bamako *Mali* **82** C3
Bamba *Mali* **83** B4
Bambara Maoundé *Mali* **82** B4
Bambari *C.A.R.* **84** C4
Bambaroo *Australia* **94** B4
Bambaya *Guinea* **82** D2
Bamberg *Germany* **25** F6
Bamberg *U.S.A.* **117** E14
Bambesi *Ethiopia* **81** F3
Bambey *Senegal* **82** C1
Bambili *Dem. Rep. of the Congo* **86** B2
Bamboi *Ghana* **82** D4
Bamburgh *U.K.* **14** B6
Bamenda *Cameroon* **83** D7
Bamendjing, Rés. de
  Cameroon **83** D7
Bamfield *Canada* **102** D3
Bāmīān □ *Afghan.* **66** B5
Bamiancheng *China* **57** C13
Bamkin *Cameroon* **83** D7
Bampūr *Iran* **71** E9
Bampūr ➤ *Iran* **71** E8
Ban *Burkina Faso* **82** C4
Ban Ao Tu Khun *Thailand* **65** a
Ban Ban *Laos* **64** C4
Ban Bang Hin *Thailand* **65** H2
Ban Bang Khu *Thailand* **65** a
Ban Bang Rong *Thailand* **65** a
Ban Bo Phut *Thailand* **65** b
Ban Chaweng *Thailand* **65** b
Ban Chiang Klang *Thailand* **64** C3
Ban Choho *Thailand* **64** E4
Ban Dan Lan Hoi *Thailand* **64** D2
Ban Don = Surat Thani
  Thailand **65** H2
Ban Don *Vietnam* **64** F6
Ban Don, Ao ➤ *Thailand* **65** H2
Ban Dong *Thailand* **64** C3
Ban Hong *Thailand* **64** C2
Ban Hua Thanon *Thailand* **65** b
Ban Kantang *Thailand* **65** J2
Ban Karon *Thailand* **65** a
Ban Kata *Thailand* **65** a
Ban Keun *Laos* **64** C4
Ban Khai *Thailand* **64** F3
Ban Kheun *Laos* **64** B3
Ban Khlong Khian *Thailand* **65** a
Ban Khlong Kua *Thailand* **65** J3
Ban Khuan *Thailand* **65** J2
Ban Khuan Mao *Thailand* **65** J2
Ban Ko Yai Chim *Thailand* **65** G2
Ban Laem *Thailand* **64** F2
Ban Lamai *Thailand* **65** b
Ban Lao Ngam *Laos* **64** E6

Ban Le Kathe *Thailand* **64** E2
Ban Lo Po Noi *Thailand* **65** a
Ban Mae Chedi *Thailand* **64** C2
Ban Mae Nam *Thailand* **65** b
Ban Mae Sariang *Thailand* **64** C1
Ban Mê Thuôt = Buon Ma
  Thuot *Vietnam* **64** F7
Ban Mi *Thailand* **64** E3
Ban Muong Mo *Laos* **64** C4
Ban Na Bo *Thailand* **65** b
Ban Na Mo *Laos* **64** D5
Ban Na San *Thailand* **65** H2
Ban Tha Song Yang *Thailand* **64** B3
Ban Tham Bac *Laos* **64** B4
Ban Nam Ma *Laos* **64** A3
Ban Ngang *Laos* **64** E6
Ban Nong Bok *Laos* **64** D5
Ban Nong Boua *Laos* **64** E6
Ban Nong Pling *Thailand* **64** E3
Ban Pak Chan *Thailand* **65** G2
Ban Patong *Thailand* **65** a
Ban Phai *Thailand* **64** D3
Ban Phak Chit *Thailand* **65** a
Ban Pong *Thailand* **64** F2
Ban Rawai *Thailand* **65** a
Ban Ron Phibun *Thailand* **65** H2
Ban Sakhu *Thailand* **65** a
Ban Sanam Chai *Thailand* **65** J3
Ban Sangkha *Thailand* **64** E4
Ban Tak *Thailand* **64** D2
Ban Tako *Thailand* **64** E4
Ban Tha Dua *Thailand* **64** D2
Ban Tha Nun *Thailand* **65** a
Ban Tha Rua *Thailand* **65** a
Ban Tha Yu *Thailand* **65** a
Ban Thahine *Laos* **64** E5
Ban Thong Krut *Thailand* **65** b
Ban Xien Kok *Laos* **64** B3
Ban Yen Nhan *Vietnam* **64** B6
Banaba *Kiribati* **96** H8
Banalia *Dem. Rep. of the Congo* **86** B2
Banam *Cambodia* **65** G5
Banamba *Mali* **82** C3
Banana Is. *S. Leone* **82** D2
Bananal, I. do *Brazil* **125** F8
Banas → *Gujarat, India* **68** H4
Banas → *Mad. P., India* **69** G9
Bânâs, Ras *Egypt* **80** C4
Banaz *Turkey* **47** C11
Banaz → *Turkey* **47** C11
Banbridge *U.K.* **12** B5
Banbury *U.K.* **15** E6
Banchory *U.K.* **13** D6
Banco *Ethiopia* **81** F4
Bancroft *Canada* **114** A7
Band *Romania* **29** D9
Band Bonī *Iran* **71** E8
Band Qīr *Iran* **71** D6
Banda *Ut. P., India* **69** G8
Banda *Mad. P., India* **69** G9
Banda, Kepulauan *Indonesia* **63** E7
Banda Aceh *Indonesia* **62** C1
Banda Banda, Mt. *Australia* **95** E5
Banda Elat *Indonesia* **63** F8
Banda Is. = Banda,
  Kepulauan *Indonesia* **63** E7
Banda Sea *Indonesia* **63** F8
Bandai-Asahi △ *Japan* **54** F10
Bandai-San *Japan* **54** F10
Bandama → *Ivory C.* **82** D3
Bandama Blanc → *Ivory C.* **82** D4
Bandama Rouge → *Ivory C.* **82** D4
Bandān *Iran* **71** D9
Bandanaira *Indonesia* **63** E7
Bandanwara *India* **68** F6
Bandar = Machilipatnam
  India **67** L12
Bandar-e Abbās *Iran* **71** E8
Bandar-e Anzalī *Iran* **73** D13
Bandar-e Bushehr =
  Būshehr *Iran* **71** D6
Bandar-e Chārak *Iran* **71** E7
Bandar-e Deylam *Iran* **71** D6
Bandar-e Emām
  Khomeyn *Iran* **71** D6
Bandar-e Lengeh *Iran* **71** E7
Bandar-e Maqām *Iran* **71** E7
Bandar-e Ma'shur *Iran* **71** D6
Bandar-e Rīg *Iran* **71** D6
Bandar-e Torkeman *Iran* **71** B7
Bandar Lampung *Indonesia* **62** F3
Bandar Maharani = Muar
  Malaysia **65** L4
Bandar Penggaram = Batu
  Pahat *Malaysia* **65** M4
Bandar Seri Begawan *Brunei* **62** D5
Bandawe *Malawi* **87** E3
Bande *Spain* **36** C3
Bandeira, Pico da *Brazil* **127** A7
Bandera *Argentina* **126** B3
Banderas, B. de *Mexico* **118** C3
Bandhavgarh *India* **69** H9
Bandi → *India* **68** F6
Bandiagara *Mali* **82** C4
Bandikui *India* **68** F7

Bandırma *Turkey* **45** F11
Bandjarmasin =
  Banjarmasin *Indonesia* **62** E4
Bandol *France* **21** E9
Bandon *Ireland* **12** E3
Bandon → *Ireland* **12** E3
Bandula *Mozam.* **87** F3
Bandundu
  Dem. Rep. of the Congo **84** E3
Bandung *Indonesia* **63** G12
Bané *Burkina Faso* **83** C4
Băneasa *Romania* **29** E12
Bāneh *Iran* **73** E11
Banes *Cuba* **121** B4
Banff *Canada* **102** C5
Banff *U.K.* **13** D6
Banff △ *Canada* **102** C5
Banfora *Burkina Faso* **82** C4
Bang Fai → *Laos* **64** D5
Bang Hieng → *Laos* **64** D5
Bang Krathum *Thailand* **64** D3
Bang Lamung *Thailand* **64** F3
Bang Mun Nak *Thailand* **64** D3
Bang Pa In *Thailand* **64** E3
Bang Rakam *Thailand* **64** D3
Bang Saphan *Thailand* **65** G2
Bang Thao *Thailand* **65** a
Bangaduni I. *India* **69** J13
Bangala Dam *Zimbabwe* **87** G3
Bangalore *India* **66** N10
Banganga → *India* **68** F6
Bangangté *Cameroon* **83** D7
Bangaon *India* **69** H13
Bangassou *C.A.R.* **84** D4
Banggai *Indonesia* **63** E6
Banggai, Kepulauan
  Indonesia **63** E6
Banggai Arch. = Banggai,
  Kepulauan *Indonesia* **63** E6
Banggi, Pulau *Malaysia* **62** C5
Banghāzī *Libya* **79** B10
Bangjang *Sudan* **81** E3
Bangka *Sulawesi, Indonesia* **63** D7
Bangka *Sumatera, Indonesia* **62** E3
Bangka, Selat *Indonesia* **62** E3
Bangka-Belitung □ *Indonesia* **62** E3
Bangkalan *Indonesia* **63** G15
Bangkinang *Indonesia* **62** D2
Bangko *Indonesia* **62** E2
Bangkok *Thailand* **64** F3
Bangladesh ■ *Asia* **67** H17
Bangli *Indonesia* **63** J18
Bangolo *Ivory C.* **82** D3
Bangong Co *China* **69** C8
Bangor *Down, U.K.* **12** B6
Bangor *Gwynedd, U.K.* **14** D3
Bangor *Maine, U.S.A.* **113** C19
Bangor *Pa., U.S.A.* **115** F9
Bangued *Phil.* **61** C4
Bangui *C.A.R.* **84** D3
Bangui *Phil.* **61** B4
Banguru
  Dem. Rep. of the Congo **86** B2
Bangweulu, L. *Zambia* **87** E3
Bangweulu Swamp *Zambia* **87** E3
Banhine △ *Mozam.* **89** C5
Bani *Burkina Faso* **83** C4
Baní *Dom. Rep.* **121** C5
Bani → *Mali* **82** C4
Bani Bangou *Niger* **83** B5
Banī Sa'd *Iraq* **73** F11
Bania *Ivory C.* **82** D4
Banihal Pass *India* **69** C6
Banikoara *Benin* **83** C5
Banissa *Kenya* **81** G5
Bāniyās *Syria* **72** C3
Banja Luka *Bos.-H.* **28** F2
Banjar *India* **68** D7
Banjar → *India* **69** H9
Banjarmasin *Indonesia* **62** E4
Banjul *Gambia* **82** C1
Banka *India* **69** G12
Bankas *Mali* **82** C4
Bankeryd *Sweden* **11** G8
Banket *Zimbabwe* **87** F3
Bankilaré *Niger* **83** C5
Bankipore *India* **67** G14
Banks I. *B.C., Canada* **102** C3
Banks I. *N.W.T., Canada* **100** B7
Banks Pen. *N.Z.* **91** E4
Banks Str. *Australia* **95** G4
Bankura *India* **69** H12
Banmankhi *India* **69** G12
Bann → *Armagh, U.K.* **12** B5
Bann → *L'derry., U.K.* **12** A5
Bannalec *France* **18** E3
Bannang Sata *Thailand* **65** J3
Banning *U.S.A.* **111** M10
Banno *Ethiopia* **81** G4
Bannockburn *Canada* **114** B7
Bannockburn *U.K.* **13** E5
Bannockburn *Zimbabwe* **87** G2
Bannu *Pakistan* **66** C7
Bano *India* **69** H11
Bañolas = Banyoles *Spain* **38** C7
Banon *France* **21** D9
Baños de la Encina *Spain* **37** G7

Baños de Molgas *Spain* **36** C3
Bánovce nad Bebravou
  Slovak Rep. **27** C11
Banovići *Bos.-H.* **28** F3
Bansgaon *India* **69** F10
Banská Bystrica *Slovak Rep.* **27** C12
Banská Štiavnica
  Slovak Rep. **27** C11
Bansko *Bulgaria* **44** E7
Banswara *India* **68** H6
Bantaeng *Indonesia* **63** F5
Bantaji *Nigeria* **83** D7
Bantayan *Phil.* **61** F5
Banten □ *Indonesia* **63** G11
Bantry *Ireland* **12** E2
Bantry B. *Ireland* **12** E2
Bantul *Indonesia* **63** G14
Bantva *India* **68** J4
Banya *Bulgaria* **45** D8
Banyak, Kepulauan
  Indonesia **62** D1
Banyalbufar *Spain* **48** B9
Banyeres de Mariola *Spain* **39** G4
Banyo *Cameroon* **83** D7
Banyoles *Spain* **38** C7
Banyuls-sur-Mer *France* **20** F7
Banyumas *Indonesia* **63** G13
Banyuwangi *Indonesia* **63** J17
Banzare Coast *Antarctica* **5** C9
Bao Ha *Vietnam* **58** F5
Bao Lac *Vietnam* **64** A5
Bao Loc *Vietnam* **65** G6
Bao'an = Shenzhen *China* **59** F10
Baocheng *China* **56** H4
Baode *China* **56** E6
Baodi *China* **57** E9
Baoding *China* **56** E8
Baoji *China* **56** G4
Baojing *China* **58** C7
Baokang *China* **59** B8
Baoshan *Shanghai, China* **59** B13
Baoshan *Yunnan, China* **58** E2
Baotou *China* **56** D6
Baoxing *China* **58** B4
Baoying *China* **57** H10
Baoyou = Ledong *China* **64** C7
Bap *India* **68** F5
Bapatla *India* **67** M12
Bapaume *France* **19** B9
Bāqerābād *Iran* **71** C6
Ba'qūbah *Iraq* **73** F11
Baquedano *Chile* **126** A2
Bar *Montenegro* **44** D3
Bar *Ukraine* **23** D14
Bar Bigha *India* **69** G11
Bar Harbor *U.S.A.* **113** C19
Bar-le-Duc *France* **19** D12
Bar-sur-Aube *France* **19** D11
Bar-sur-Seine *France* **19** D11
Bara *India* **69** G9
Bâra *Romania* **29** C12
Bara Banki *India* **69** F9
Barabai *Indonesia* **62** E5
Baraboo *U.S.A.* **112** D9
Baracoa *Cuba* **121** B5
Baradā → *Syria* **74** B5
Baradero *Argentina* **126** C4
Bărăganul *Romania* **29** F12
Baragoi *Kenya* **86** B4
Barah → *India* **68** F6
Barahona *Dom. Rep.* **121** C5
Barail Range *India* **67** G18
Barajas, Madrid ✈ (MAD)
  Spain **36** E7
Baraka → *Sudan* **81** D4
Baraka → *Sudan* **80** D4
Barakaldo *Spain* **38** B2
Barakar → *India* **69** G12
Barakot *India* **69** J11
Barakpur *India* **69** H13
Baralaba *Australia* **94** C4
Baralla *Spain* **36** C3
Baralzon L. *Canada* **103** B9
Barameiya *Sudan* **80** D4
Baramula *India* **69** B6
Baran *India* **68** G7
Baran → *Pakistan* **68** G3
Barañain *Spain* **38** C3
Baranavichy *Belarus* **23** B14
Barani *Burkina Faso* **82** C4
Baranof *U.S.A.* **102** B2
Baranof I. *U.S.A.* **100** D6
Baranów Sandomierski
  Poland **31** H8
Baranya □ *Hungary* **28** E3
Baraolt *Romania* **29** D10
Baraona *Spain* **38** D2
Barapasi *Indonesia* **63** E9
Barasat *India* **69** H13
Barat Daya, Kepulauan
  Indonesia **63** F7
Barataria B. *U.S.A.* **117** G10
Barauda *India* **68** H6
Baraut *India* **68** E7

Barbacena *Brazil* **127** A7
Barbados ■ *W. Indies* **121** g
Barban *Croatia* **41** C11
Barbária, C. de *Spain* **48** C7
Barbaros *Turkey* **45** F11
Barbas, C. *W. Sahara* **78** D2
Barbastro *Spain* **38** C5
Barbate *Spain* **37** J5
Barberino di Mugello *Italy* **41** E8
Barberton *S. Africa* **89** D5
Barberton *U.S.A.* **114** E3
Barbezieux-St-Hilaire *France* **20** C3
Barbosa *Colombia* **124** B4
Barbourville *U.S.A.* **113** G12
Barbuda *W. Indies* **121** C7
Bârca *Romania* **29** G8
Barcaldine *Australia* **94** C4
Barcarrota *Spain* **37** G4
Barcellona Pozzo di Gotto
  Italy **43** D7
Barcelona *Spain* **38** D7
Barcelona *Venezuela* **124** A6
Barcelona □ *Spain* **38** D7
Barcelona-Prat ✈ (BCN)
  Spain **38** D7
Barceloneta *Puerto Rico* **121** d
Barcelonette *France* **21** D10
Barcelos *Brazil* **124** D6
Barcin *Poland* **31** F4
Barclayville *Liberia* **82** E3
Barcoo → *Australia* **94** D3
Barcs *Hungary* **28** E2
Barczewo *Poland* **30** E7
Barda *India* **68** J3
Bardas Blancas *Argentina* **126** D2
Bardawīl, Sabkhet el *Egypt* **74** D2
Barddhaman *India* **69** H12
Bardejov *Slovak Rep.* **27** B14
Bardera = Baardheere
  Somali Rep. **75** G3
Bardi *Italy* **40** D6
Bardīyah *Libya* **79** B10
Bardolino *Italy* **40** C7
Bardonécchia *Italy* **40** C3
Bardsey I. *U.K.* **14** E3
Bardstown *U.S.A.* **113** G11
Bareilly *India* **69** E8
Barela *India* **69** H9
Barentin *France* **18** C7
Barenton *France* **18** D6
Barents Sea *Arctic* **4** B9
Barentu *Eritrea* **81** D4
Barfleur *France* **18** C5
Barfleur, Pte. de *France* **18** C5
Barga *Italy* **40** D7
Bargara *Australia* **94** C5
Bargas *Spain* **36** F6
Bargi Dam *India* **69** H9
Bargnop *Sudan* **81** F2
Bargteheide *Germany* **24** B6
Barguzin *Russia* **53** D11
Barh *India* **69** G11
Barhaj *India* **69** F10
Barharwa *India* **69** G12
Barhi *India* **69** G11
Bari *India* **68** F7
Bari *Italy* **43** A9
Bari Doab *Pakistan* **68** D5
Bari Sadri *India* **68** G6
Bari Sardo *Italy* **42** C2
Barīdī, Ra's *Si. Arabia* **70** E3
Barīm *Yemen* **75** E8
Barinas *Venezuela* **124** B4
Baring, C. *Canada* **100** C8
Baringo, L. *Kenya* **86** B4
Bâris *Egypt* **80** C3
Barisal *Bangla.* **67** H17
Barisal □ *Bangla.* **67** H17
Barisan, Pegunungan
  Indonesia **62** E2
Barito → *Indonesia* **62** E4
Baritú △ *Argentina* **126** A3
Barjac *France* **21** D8
Barjols *France* **21** E10
Barjūj, Wadi → *Libya* **79** C8
Bark L. *Canada* **114** A7
Barka = Baraka → *Sudan* **80** D4
Barkakana *India* **69** H11
Barkam *China* **58** B4
Barker *U.S.A.* **114** C6
Barkley, L. *U.S.A.* **117** C10
Barkley Sound *Canada* **102** D3
Barkly East *S. Africa* **88** E4
Barkly Homestead *Australia* **94** B2
Barkly Tableland *Australia* **94** B2
Barkly West *S. Africa* **88** D3
Barkol, Wadi → *Sudan* **80** D3
Barla Dağı *Turkey* **47** C12
Bârlad *Romania* **29** D12
Bârlad → *Romania* **29** E12
Barlee, L. *Australia* **93** E2
Barlee, Mt. *Australia* **93** D4
Barletta *Italy* **43** A9
Barlinek *Poland* **31** F2
Barlovento *Canary Is.* **48** F2

Barlovento *C. Verde Is.* **78** b
Barlow L. *Canada* **103** A8
Barmedman *Australia* **95** E4
Barmer *India* **68** G4
Barmera *Australia* **95** E3
Barmouth *U.K.* **14** E3
Barmstedt *Germany* **24** B5
Barna → *India* **69** G10
Barnagar *India* **68** H6
Barnala *India* **68** D6
Barnard Castle *U.K.* **14** C6
Barnaul *Russia* **52** D9
Barnesville *Ga., U.S.A.* **117** E12
Barnesville *Minn., U.S.A.* **112** B5
Barnet □ *U.K.* **15** F7
Barneveld *Neths.* **17** B5
Barneville-Carteret *France* **18** C5
Barnhart *U.S.A.* **116** F4
Barnsley *U.K.* **14** D6
Barnstable *U.S.A.* **113** E18
Barnstaple *U.K.* **15** F3
Barnstaple Bay = Bideford
  Bay *U.K.* **15** F3
Barnwell *U.S.A.* **117** E14
Baro *Nigeria* **83** D6
Baro → *Ethiopia* **81** F3
Baroda = Vadodara *India* **68** H5
Baroda *India* **68** G7
Baroe *S. Africa* **88** E3
Baron Ra. *Australia* **92** D4
Barong *China* **58** B2
Barotseland *Zambia* **85** H4
Barouéli *Mali* **82** C3
Barpeta *India* **67** F17
Barqa *Libya* **79** C10
Barques, Pt. Aux *U.S.A.* **114** B2
Barquísimeto *Venezuela* **124** A5
Barr *France* **19** D14
Barr, Ras el *Egypt* **80** H7
Barr Smith Range *Australia* **93** E3
Barra *Brazil* **125** F10
Barra *U.K.* **13** D1
Barra de Navidad *Mexico* **118** D4
Barra do Corda *Brazil* **125** E9
Barra do Garças *Brazil* **125** G8
Barra do Piraí *Brazil* **127** A7
Barra Falsa, Pta. da *Mozam.* **89** C6
Barra Hd. *U.K.* **13** E1
Barra Mansa *Brazil* **127** A7
Barraba *Australia* **95** E5
Barrackpur = Barakpur
  India **69** H13
Barradale *Australia* **92** D1
Barrafranca *Italy* **43** E7
Barraigh = Barra *U.K.* **13** E1
Barranca *Lima, Peru* **124** F3
Barranca *Loreto, Peru* **124** D3
Barranca del Cobre △
  Mexico **118** B3
Barrancabermeja *Colombia* **124** B4
Barrancas *Venezuela* **124** B6
Barrancos *Portugal* **37** G3
Barranqueras *Argentina* **126** B4
Barranquilla *Colombia* **124** A4
Barraute *Canada* **104** C4
Barre *Mass., U.S.A.* **115** D12
Barre *Vt., U.S.A.* **115** B12
Barreal *Argentina* **126** C2
Barreiras *Brazil* **125** F10
Barreirinhas *Brazil* **125** D10
Barreiro *Portugal* **37** G1
Barrême *France* **21** E10
Barren, Nosy *Madag.* **89** B7
Barretos *Brazil* **125** H9
Barrhead *Canada* **102** C6
Barrie *Canada* **114** B5
Barrier Ra. *Australia* **95** E3
Barrier Reef *Belize* **119** D7
Barrière *Canada* **102** C4
Barrington *U.S.A.* **115** E13
Barrington L. *Canada* **103** B8
Barrington Tops *Australia* **95** E5
Barringun *Australia* **95** D4
Barron *U.S.A.* **112** C8
Barrow *U.S.A.* **106** a
Barrow → *Ireland* **12** D5
Barrow, Pt. *U.S.A.* **98** B4
Barrow Creek *Australia* **94** C1
Barrow I. *Australia* **92** D2
Barrow-in-Furness *U.K.* **14** C4
Barrow Pt. *Australia* **94** A3
Barrow Ra. *Australia* **93** E4
Barrow Str. *Canada* **4** B3
Barruecopardo *Spain* **36** D4
Barruelo de Santullán *Spain* **36** C6
Barry *U.K.* **15** F4
Barry's Bay *Canada* **114** A7
Barsalogho *Burkina Faso* **83** C4
Barsat *Pakistan* **69** A5
Barsham *Syria* **73** E9
Barsi *India* **66** K9
Barsinghausen *Germany* **24** C5
Barsoi *India* **67** G15
Barstow *U.S.A.* **111** L9
Barth *Germany* **24** A8
Barthélemy, Col *Vietnam* **64** C5
Bartica *Guyana* **124** B7
Bartın *Turkey* **72** B5

Bartle Frere *Australia* **94** B4
Bartlesville *U.S.A.* **116** C7
Bartlett *Calif., U.S.A.* **110** J8
Bartlett *Tenn., U.S.A.* **117** H10
Bartlett, L. *Canada* **102** A5
Bartolomeu Dias *Mozam.* **87** G4
Barton *U.S.A.* **115** B12
Barton upon Humber *U.K.* **14** D7
Bartoszyce *Poland* **30** D7
Bartow *U.S.A.* **117** H14
Barú, Volcan *Panama* **120** E3
Barumba
  Dem. Rep. of the Congo **86** B1
Baruth *Germany* **24** C9
Baruun Urt *Mongolia* **53** E12
Baruunsuu *Mongolia* **56** C3
Barvinkove *Ukraine* **33** H9
Barwani *India* **68** H6
Barwice *Poland* **30** E3
Barycz → *Poland* **31** G3
Barysaw *Belarus* **23** A15
Barysh *Russia* **34** D8
Barzān *Iraq* **70** B5
Bârzava *Romania* **28** D6
Bas-Rhin □ *France* **19** D14
Bāsa'idū *Iran* **71** E7
Basal *Pakistan* **68** C5
Basankusa
  Dem. Rep. of the Congo **84** D3
Basarabeasca *Moldova* **29** D13
Basarabi *Romania* **29** F13
Basarabia = Bessarabiya
  Moldova **23** E15
Basauri *Spain* **38** B2
Basawa *Afghan.* **68** B4
Bascuñán, C. *Chile* **126** B1
Basel *Switz.* **25** H3
Basel, Euroairport ✈ (BSL)
  Europe **19** E14
Basel-Landschaft □ *Switz.* **25** H3
Basento → *Italy* **43** B9
Bashākerd, Kūhhā-ye *Iran* **71** E8
Bashaw *Canada* **102** C6
Bāshī *Iran* **71** D6
Bashkir Republic =
  Bashkortostan □ *Russia* **52** D6
Bashkortostan □ *Russia* **52** D6
Bashtanivka *Ukraine* **29** E14
Basibasy *Madag.* **89** C7
Basilan *Phil.* **61** H5
Basilan Str. *Phil.* **61** H5
Basildon *U.K.* **15** F8
Basilé Eq. Guin. **83** E6
Basilé, Pico de *Eq. Guin.* **83** E6
Basilicata □ *Italy* **43** B9
Basim = Washim *India* **66** J10
Basin *U.S.A.* **108** D9
Basingstoke *U.K.* **15** F6
Baška *Croatia* **41** D11
Başkale *Turkey* **73** C10
Baskatong, Rés. *Canada* **104** C4
Basle = Basel *Switz.* **25** H3
Başmakçı *Turkey* **47** D12
Basoda *India* **68** H7
Basodino *India* **66** K9
Basoko *Dem. Rep. of the Congo* **86** B1
Basque, Pays *France* **20** E2
Basque Provinces = País
  Vasco □ *Spain* **38** C2
Basra = Al Başrah *Iraq* **70** D5
Bass Str. *Australia* **95** F4
Bassano *Canada* **102** C6
Bassano del Grappa *Italy* **41** C8
Bassar *Togo* **83** D5
Bassas da India *Ind. Oc.* **87** G4
Basse-Normandie □ *France* **18** D6
Basse-Pointe *Martinique* **120** c
Basse Santa-Su *Gambia* **82** C2
Basse-Terre *Guadeloupe* **120** b
Basse Terre *Trin. & Tob.* **125** K15
Bassein *Burma* **67** L19
Basses, Pte. des *Guadeloupe* **120** b
Basseterre *St. Kitts & Nevis* **121** C7
Bassett *U.S.A.* **112** D5
Bassi *India* **68** D7
Bassigny *France* **19** E12
Bassikounou *Mauritania* **82** B3
Bassila *Benin* **83** D5
Bassum *Germany* **24** C4
Båstad *Sweden* **11** H6
Bastak *Iran* **71** E7
Baştām *Iran* **71** B7
Bastar *India* **67** K12
Bastelica *France* **21** F13
Basti *India* **69** F10
Bastia *France* **21** F13
Bastogne *Belgium* **17** D5
Bastrop *La., U.S.A.* **116** E9
Bastrop *Tex., U.S.A.* **116** F6
Basuo = Dongfang *China* **64** C7
Bat Yam *Israel* **74** C3
Bata *Eq. Guin.* **84** D1
Bata *Romania* **28** D7
Bataan □ *Phil.* **61** D4
Batabanó *Cuba* **120** B3
Batabanó, G. de *Cuba* **120** B3
Batac *Phil.* **61** B4
Batagai *Russia* **53** C14

Batajnica *Serbia* **44** B4
Batak *Bulgaria* **45** E8
Batala *India* **68** D6
Batalha *Portugal* **36** F2
Batama *Dem. Rep. of the Congo* **86** B2
Batamay *Russia* **53** C13
Batang *China* **58** B2
Batang *Indonesia* **63** G13
Batangafo *C.A.R.* **84** C3
Batangas *Phil.* **61** E4
Batanta *Indonesia* **63** E8
Batatais *Brazil* **127** A6
Batavia *U.S.A.* **114** D6
Bataysk *Russia* **33** J10
Batchelor *Australia* **92** B5
Batdambang *Cambodia* **64** F4
Batemans B. *Australia* **95** F5
Batemans Bay *Australia* **95** F5
Bates Ra. *Australia* **93** E3
Batesburg-Leesville *U.S.A.* **117** E14
Batesville *Ark., U.S.A.* **116** D9
Batesville *Miss., U.S.A.* **117** D10
Batesville *Tex., U.S.A.* **116** G5
Bath *Canada* **115** B8
Bath *U.K.* **15** F5
Bath *Maine, U.S.A.* **113** D19
Bath *N.Y., U.S.A.* **114** D7
Bath & North East
  Somerset □ *U.K.* **15** F5
Batheay *Cambodia* **65** G5
Bathurst *Australia* **95** E4
Bathurst *Canada* **105** C6
Bathurst *S. Africa* **88** E4
Bathurst, C. *Canada* **100** B7
Bathurst B. *Australia* **94** A3
Bathurst Harb. *Australia* **95** G4
Bathurst I. *Australia* **92** B5
Bathurst I. *Canada* **101** B11
Bathurst Inlet *Canada* **100** C9
Bati *Ethiopia* **81** E5
Batie *Burkina Faso* **82** D4
Batiki *Fiji* **91** a
Batlow *Australia* **95** F4
Batman *Turkey* **73** D9
Baṭn al Ghūl *Jordan* **74** F4
Batna *Algeria* **78** A7
Batobato = San Isidro *Phil.* **61** H7
Batočina *Serbia* **44** B5
Batoka *Zambia* **87** F2
Baton Rouge *U.S.A.* **116** F9
Batong, Ko *Thailand* **65** J2
Bátonyterenye *Hungary* **28** C4
Batopilas *Mexico* **118** B3
Batouri *Cameroon* **84** D2
Båtsfjord *Norway* **8** A23
Battambang =
  Batdambang *Cambodia* **64** F4
Batticaloa *Sri Lanka* **66** R12
Battipáglia *Italy* **43** B7
Battle *U.K.* **15** G8
Battle → *Canada* **103** C7
Battle Creek *U.S.A.* **113** D11
Battle Ground *U.S.A.* **110** E4
Battle Harbour *Canada* **105** B8
Battle Lake *U.S.A.* **112** B6
Battle Mountain *U.S.A.* **108** F5
Battlefields *Zimbabwe* **87** F2
Battleford *Canada* **103** C7
Battonya *Hungary* **28** D6
Batu *Ethiopia* **81** F4
Batu *Malaysia* **65** L3
Batu, Kepulauan *Indonesia* **62** E1
Batu Ferringhi *Malaysia* **65** c
Batu Gajah *Malaysia* **65** K3
Batu Is. = Batu,
  Kepulauan *Indonesia* **62** E1
Batu Pahat *Malaysia* **65** M4
Batuata *Indonesia* **63** F6
Batugondang, Tanjung
  Indonesia **63** J17
Batukau, Gunung *Indonesia* **63** J18
Batumi *Georgia* **35** K5
Batur *Indonesia* **63** J18
Batur, Danau *Indonesia* **63** J18
Batur, Gunung *Indonesia* **63** J18
Batura Sar *Pakistan* **69** A6
Baturaja *Indonesia* **62** E2
Baturité *Brazil* **125** D11
Baturiti *Indonesia* **63** J18
Bau *Malaysia* **62** D4
Baubau *Indonesia* **63** F6
Baucau *E. Timor* **63** F7
Bauchi *Nigeria* **83** C6
Bauchi □ *Nigeria* **83** C7
Baud *France* **18** E3
Baudette *U.S.A.* **112** A6
Bauer, C. *Australia* **95** E1
Bauhinia *Australia* **94** C4
Baukau = Baucau *E. Timor* **63** F7
Bauld, C. *Canada* **101** D14
Baume-les-Dames *France* **19** E13
Baunatal *Germany* **24** D5
Baunei *Italy* **42** B2
Baure *Nigeria* **83** C6
Bauru *Brazil* **127** A6
Bausi *India* **69** G12
Bauska *Latvia* **30** B11

Bautino *Kazakhstan* **35** H10
Bautzen *Germany* **24** D10
Bauya *S. Leone* **82** D2
Bavănāt *Iran* **71** D7
Bavaniște *Serbia* **28** F5
Bavaria = Bayern □
  Germany **25** G7
Båven *Sweden* **10** E10
Bavispe → *Mexico* **118** B3
Bawdwin *Burma* **67** H20
Bawean *Indonesia* **62** F4
Bawku *Ghana* **83** C4
Bawlake *Burma* **67** K20
Bawolung *China* **58** C3
Baxley *U.S.A.* **117** F13
Baxoi *China* **58** B1
Baxter *U.S.A.* **112** B6
Baxter Springs *U.S.A.* **112** G6
Baxter State △ *U.S.A.* **113** B19
Bay, L. de *Phil.* **61** D4
Bay City *Mich., U.S.A.* **113** D12
Bay City *Tex., U.S.A.* **116** G7
Bay Minette *U.S.A.* **117** F11
Bay Roberts *Canada* **105** C9
Bay St. Louis *U.S.A.* **117** F10
Bay Springs *U.S.A.* **117** F10
Bay View *N.Z.* **91** C6
Baya *Dem. Rep. of the Congo* **87** E2
Bayamo *Cuba* **120** B4
Bayamón *Puerto Rico* **121** d
Bayan Har Shan *China* **60** C4
Bayan Hot = Alxa Zuoqi
  China **56** E3
Bayan Lepas *Malaysia* **65** c
Bayan Obo *China* **56** D5
Bayan-Ovoo = Erdenetsogt
  Mongolia **56** C4
Bayana *India* **68** F7
Bayanaūyl *Kazakhstan* **52** D8
Bayandalay *Mongolia* **56** C2
Bayanhongor *Mongolia* **56** B3
Bayard *France* **19** F11
Bayard *N. Mex., U.S.A.* **109** K9
Bayard *Nebr., U.S.A.* **112** E2
Bayawan *Phil.* **61** G5
Baybay *Phil.* **61** F6
Bayburt *Turkey* **73** B9
Bayburt □ *Turkey* **73** B9
Baydaratskaya Guba *Russia* **52** C7
Baydhabo *Somali Rep.* **75** G3
Bayelsa □ *Nigeria* **83** E6
Bayerische Alpen *Germany* **25** H7
Bayerische Rhön △ *Germany* **25** E6
Bayerischer Spessart △
  Germany **25** F6
Bayerischer Wald *Germany* **25** G8
Bayern □ *Germany* **25** G7
Bayeux *France* **18** C6
Bayfield *Canada* **114** C3
Bayfield *U.S.A.* **112** B8
Bayındır *Turkey* **47** C9
Baykal, Oz. *Russia* **53** D11
Baykan *Turkey* **73** C9
Baynes Mts. *Namibia* **88** B1
Bayombong *Phil.* **61** C4
Bayon *France* **19** D13
Bayona = Baiona *Spain* **36** C2
Bayonne *France* **20** E2
Bayonne *U.S.A.* **115** F10
Bayovar *Peru* **124** E2
Bayqongyr *Kazakhstan* **52** E7
Bayram-Ali = Baýramaly
  Turkmenistan **71** B9
Baýramaly *Turkmenistan* **71** B9
Bayramiç *Turkey* **47** B8
Bayreuth *Germany* **25** F7
Bayrischzell *Germany* **25** H8
Bayrūt *Lebanon* **74** B4
Baytown *U.S.A.* **116** G7
Bayun *Indonesia* **63** J18
Bayzo *Niger* **83** C5
Baza *Spain* **37** H8
Bazar Dyuzi *Russia* **35** K8
Bazardüzü = Bazar Dyuzi
  Russia **35** K8
Bāzārgān *Iran* **73** C11
Bazarny Karabulak *Russia* **34** D8
Bazarnyy Syzgan *Russia* **34** D8
Bazaruto, Tanjung *Indonesia* **63** K18
Bazaruto △ *Mozam.* **89** C6
Bazas *France* **20** D3
Bazhong *China* **58** B6
Bazhou *China* **56** E9
Bazmān, Kūh-e *Iran* **71** D9
Baztan = Elizondo *Spain* **38** B3
Beach *U.S.A.* **112** B2
Beach City *U.S.A.* **114** F3
Beachport *Australia* **95** F3
Beachville *Canada* **114** C4
Beachy Hd. *U.K.* **15** G8
Beacon *Australia* **93** F2
Beacon *U.S.A.* **115** E11
Beaconsfield *Australia* **95** G4
Beagle, Canal *S. Amer.* **128** H3
Beagle Bay *Australia* **92** C3
Beagle G. *Australia* **92** B5

Bealanana *Madag.* **89** A8
Beals Cr. → *U.S.A.* **116** E4
Beamsville *Canada* **114** C5
Bear → *Calif., U.S.A.* **110** G5
Bear → *Utah, U.S.A.* **106** B4
Béar, C. *France* **20** F7
Bear I. *Ireland* **12** E2
Bear I. *Canada* **110** G5
Bear L. *Canada* **103** B9
Bear L. *U.S.A.* **108** F8
Bear Lake *Canada* **114** A5
Beardmore *Canada* **104** C2
Beardmore Glacier *Antarctica* **5** E11
Beardstown *U.S.A.* **112** E8
Bearma → *India* **69** G8
Béarn *France* **20** E3
Bearpaw Mts. *U.S.A.* **108** B9
Bearskin Lake *Canada* **104** B1
Beas → *India* **68** D6
Beas de Segura *Spain* **37** G8
Beasain *Spain* **38** B2
Beata, C. *Dom. Rep.* **121** C5
Beata, I. *Dom. Rep.* **121** C5
Beatrice *U.S.A.* **112** E5
Beatrice *Zimbabwe* **87** F3
Beatrice, C. *Australia* **94** A2
Beatton → *Canada* **102** B4
Beatton River *Canada* **102** B4
Beatty *U.S.A.* **110** J10
Beau Bassin *Mauritius* **85** d
Beaucaire *France* **21** E8
Beauce, Plaine de la *France* **19** D8
Beauceville *Canada* **105** C5
Beaudesert *Australia* **95** D5
Beaufort *France* **21** C10
Beaufort *Malaysia* **62** C5
Beaufort *N.C., U.S.A.* **117** D16
Beaufort *S.C., U.S.A.* **117** E14
Beaufort Sea *Arctic* **98** B5
Beaufort West *S. Africa* **88** E3
Beaugency *France* **19** E8
Beauharnois *Canada* **115** A11
Beaujeu *France* **19** F11
Beaujolais *France* **19** F11
Beaulieu → *Canada* **102** A6
Beaulieu-sur-Dordogne
  France **20** D5
Beaulieu-sur-Mer *France* **21** E11
Beauly *U.K.* **13** D4
Beauly → *U.K.* **13** D4
Beaumaris *U.K.* **14** D3
Beaumont *Belgium* **17** D4
Beaumont *France* **20** D4
Beaumont *U.S.A.* **116** F7
Beaumont-de-Lomagne
  France **20** E5
Beaumont-le-Roger *France* **18** C7
Beaumont-sur-Sarthe
  France **18** D7
Beaune *France* **19** E11
Beaune-la-Rolande *France* **19** D9
Beaupré *Canada* **105** C5
Beaupréau *France* **18** E6
Beauraing *Belgium* **17** D4
Beaurepaire *France* **21** C9
Beausejour *Canada* **103** C9
Beauvais *France* **19** C9
Beauval *Canada* **103** B7
Beauvoir-sur-Mer *France* **18** F4
Beauvoir-sur-Niort *France* **20** B3
Beaver *Okla., U.S.A.* **116** C4
Beaver *Pa., U.S.A.* **114** F4
Beaver *Utah, U.S.A.* **108** G7
Beaver → *B.C., Canada* **102** B4
Beaver → *Ont., Canada* **104** A2
Beaver → *Sask., Canada* **103** B7
Beaver → *U.S.A.* **116** C5
Beaver City *U.S.A.* **112** E4
Beaver Creek *Canada* **100** C5
Beaver Dam *U.S.A.* **112** D9
Beaver Falls *U.S.A.* **114** F4
Beaver Hill L. *Canada* **103** C10
Beaver I. *U.S.A.* **113** C11
Beavercreek *U.S.A.* **113** F11
Beaverhill L. *Canada* **102** C6
Beaverlodge *Canada* **102** B5
Beaverstone → *Canada* **104** B2
Beaverton *Canada* **114** B5
Beaverton *U.S.A.* **110** E4
Beawar *India* **68** F6
Bebedouro *Brazil* **127** A6
Bebera, Tanjung *Indonesia* **63** K18
Beboa *Madag.* **89** B7
Bebra *Germany* **24** E5
Becán *Mexico* **119** D7
Bécancour *Canada* **113** B17
Beccles *U.K.* **15** E9
Beceni *Romania* **29** E11
Becerreá *Spain* **36** C3
Béchar *Algeria* **78** B5
Bechyně *Czech Rep.* **26** B7
Beckley *U.S.A.* **113** G13
Beckum *Germany* **24** D4
Beclean *Romania* **29** C9
Bečov nad Teplou *Czech Rep.* **26** A5
Bečva → *Czech Rep.* **27** B10
Bédar *Spain* **39** H3
Bédarieux *France* **20** E7

Beddouza, Ras *Morocco* **78** B4
Bedele *Ethiopia* **81** F4
Bederkesa *Germany* **24** B4
Bedeso *Ethiopia* **81** F4
Bedford *Canada* **115** A12
Bedford *S. Africa* **88** E4
Bedford *U.K.* **15** E7
Bedford *Ind., U.S.A.* **112** F10
Bedford *Iowa, U.S.A.* **112** E6
Bedford *Ohio, U.S.A.* **114** E3
Bedford *Pa., U.S.A.* **114** F6
Bedford *Va., U.S.A.* **113** G14
Bedford, C. *Australia* **94** B4
Bedfordshire □ *U.K.* **15** E7
Będków *Poland* **31** G6
Bednja → *Croatia* **41** B13
Bednodemyanovsk *Russia* **34** D6
Bedok *Singapore* **65** d
Bedónia *Italy* **40** D6
Bedourie *Australia* **94** C2
Bedum *Neths.* **17** A6
Będzin *Poland* **31** H6
Beebe Plain *Canada* **115** A12
Beech Creek *U.S.A.* **114** E7
Beechy *Canada* **103** C7
Beechworth *Australia* **95** F4
Beef I. *Br. Virgin Is.* **121** e
Beelitz *Germany* **24** C8
Beenleigh *Australia* **95** D5
Be'er Menuha *Israel* **70** D2
Be'er Sheva *Israel* **74** D3
Beersheba = Be'er Sheva
  Israel **74** D3
Beeskow *Germany* **24** C10
Beestekraal *S. Africa* **89** D4
Beeston *U.K.* **14** E6
Beeton *Canada* **114** B5
Beetzendorf *Germany* **24** C7
Beeville *U.S.A.* **116** G6
Befale *Dem. Rep. of the Congo* **84** D4
Befandriana *Mahajanga,*
  Madag. **89** B8
Befandriana *Toliara, Madag.* **89** C7
Befasy *Madag.* **89** C7
Befotaka *Antsiranana, Madag.* **89** A8
Befotaka *Fianarantsoa,*
  Madag. **89** C8
Bega *Australia* **95** F4
Bega, Canalul *Romania* **28** E5
Bégard *France* **18** D3
Beğendik *Turkey* **45** F10
Begoro *Ghana* **83** D4
Begusarai *India* **69** G12
Behăbād *Iran* **71** C8
Behala *India* **69** H13
Behara *Madag.* **89** C8
Behbehān *Iran* **71** D6
Behm Canal *U.S.A.* **102** B2
Behshahr *Iran* **71** B7
Bei Jiang → *China* **59** F9
Bei'an *China* **60** B7
Beibei *China* **58** C6
Beihai *China* **58** G7
Beijing *China* **56** E9
Beijing □ *China* **56** E9
Beilen *Neths.* **17** B6
Beiliu *China* **59** F8
Beilngries *Germany* **25** F7
Beilpajah *Australia* **95** E3
Beilul *Eritrea* **81** E5
Beinn na Faoghla =
  Benbecula *U.K.* **13** D1
Beipan Jiang → *China* **58** E5
Beipiao *China* **57** D11
Beira *Mozam.* **87** F3
Beirut = Bayrūt *Lebanon* **74** B4
Beiseker *Canada* **102** C6
Beit Lekhem = Bayt Lahm
  West Bank **74** D4
Beitaolaizhao *China* **57** B13
Beitbridge *Zimbabwe* **87** G3
Beiuș *Romania* **28** D7
Beizhen = Binzhou *China* **57** F10
Beizhen *China* **57** D11
Beizhengzhen *China* **57** B12
Beja *Portugal* **37** G3
Béja *Tunisia* **79** A7
Beja □ *Portugal* **37** H3
Bejaïa *Algeria* **78** A7
Béjar *Spain* **36** E5
Bejestān *Iran* **71** C8
Bekaa Valley = Al Biqā
  Lebanon **74** A5
Bekçiler *Turkey* **47** E11
Békés *Hungary* **28** D6
Békés □ *Hungary* **28** D6
Békéscsaba *Hungary* **28** D6
Bekilli *Turkey* **47** C11
Bekily *Madag.* **89** C8
Bekisopa *Madag.* **89** C8
Bekitro *Madag.* **89** C8
Bekodoka *Madag.* **89** B8
Bekoji *Ethiopia* **81** F4
Bekok *Malaysia* **65** L4
Bekopaka *Madag.* **89** B7
Bekuli *Indonesia* **63** J17
Bekwai *Ghana* **83** D4
Bela *India* **69** G10

Bela *Pakistan* **68** F2
Bela Bela *S. Africa* **89** C4
Bela Crkva *Serbia* **28** F6
Bela Palanka *Serbia* **44** C5
Bela Vista *Brazil* **126** A4
Bela Vista *Mozam.* **89** D5
Bélâbre *France* **20** B5
Belalcázar *Spain* **37** G5
Belan → *India* **69** G9
Belanovica *Serbia* **44** B4
Belarus ■ *Europe* **23** B14
Belau = Palau ■ *Palau* **90** A6
Belavenona *Madag.* **89** C8
Belawan *Indonesia* **62** D1
Belaya *Ethiopia* **81** E4
Belaya Glina *Russia* **35** G5
Belaya Kalitva *Russia* **35** F5
Belaya Tserkov = Bila
  Tserkva *Ukraine* **23** D16
Belaya Zemlya, Ostrova
  Russia **52** A7
Belcești *Romania* **29** C12
Belchatów *Poland* **31** G6
Belcher Chan. *Canada* **101** B10
Belcher Is. *Canada* **104** A3
Belchite *Spain* **38** D4
Belden *U.S.A.* **110** E5
Beledweyne *Somali Rep.* **75** G4
Belém *Brazil* **125** D9
Belén *Argentina* **126** B2
Belén *Paraguay* **126** A4
Belen *Turkey* **72** D7
Belen *U.S.A.* **109** J10
Belene *Bulgaria* **45** C9
Bélesta *France* **20** F5
Belet Uen = Beledweyne
  Somali Rep. **75** G4
Belev *Russia* **32** F9
Belevi *Turkey* **47** C9
Belfair *U.S.A.* **110** C4
Belfast *S. Africa* **89** D5
Belfast *U.K.* **12** B6
Belfast *Maine, U.S.A.* **113** C19
Belfast *N.Y., U.S.A.* **114** D6
Belfast L. *U.K.* **12** B6
Belfield *U.S.A.* **112** B2
Belfort *France* **19** E13
Belfort, Territoire de □
  France **19** E13
Belfry *U.S.A.* **108** D9
Belgaum *India* **66** M9
Belgioioso *Italy* **40** C6
Belgium ■ *Europe* **17** D4
Belgodère *France* **21** F13
Belgorod *Russia* **33** G6
Belgorod □ *Russia* **33** G9
Belgorod-Dnestrovskiy =
  Bilhorod-Dnistrovskyy
  Ukraine **33** J6
Belgrade = Beograd *Serbia* **44** B4
Belgrade *U.S.A.* **108** D8
Belgrano *Antarctica* **5** D1
Belhaven *U.S.A.* **117** D16
Beli Drim → *Europe* **44** D4
Beli Manastir *Croatia* **28** E3
Beli Timok → *Serbia* **44** C6
Bélice → *Italy* **42** E5
Belimbing *Indonesia* **63** J18
Belinskiy *Russia* **34** D6
Belinyu *Indonesia* **62** E3
Beliton Is. = Belitung
  Indonesia **62** E3
Belitung *Indonesia* **62** E3
Beliu *Romania* **28** D6
Belize ■ *Cent. Amer.* **119** D7
Belize City *Belize* **119** D7
Beljakovci *Macedonia* **44** D5
Beljanica *Serbia* **44** B5
Belkovskiy, Ostrov *Russia* **53** B14
Bell → *Canada* **104** C4
Bell I. *Canada* **105** B8
Bell-Irving → *Canada* **102** B3
Bell Peninsula *Canada* **101** C11
Bell Ville *Argentina* **126** C3
Bella *Italy* **43** B8
Bella Bella *Canada* **102** C3
Bella Coola *Canada* **102** C3
Bella Unión *Uruguay* **126** C4
Bella Vista *Corrientes,*
  Argentina **126** B4
Bella Vista *Tucuman,*
  Argentina **126** B2
Bellac *France* **20** B5
Bellágio *Italy* **40** C6
Bellaire *U.S.A.* **114** F4
Bellária *Italy* **41** D9
Bellary *India* **66** M10
Bellata *Australia* **95** D4
Belle Fourche *U.S.A.* **112** C2
Belle Fourche → *U.S.A.* **106** B6
Belle Glade *U.S.A.* **117** H14
Belle-Île *France* **18** E3
Belle Isle *Canada* **105** B8
Belle Isle, Str. of *Canada* **105** B8
Belle Plaine *U.S.A.* **112** E7
Belle River *Canada* **114** D2
Belle Yella *Liberia* **82** D3
Belledonne *France* **21** C10

Bellefontaine *U.S.A.* **113** E12
Bellefonte *U.S.A.* **114** F7
Bellegarde *France* **19** E9
Bellegarde-en-Marche
  France **20** C6
Bellegarde-sur-Valserine
  France **19** F12
Bellême *France* **18** D7
Belleoram *Canada* **105** C8
Belleplaine *Barbados* **121** g
Belleville *Canada* **114** B7
Belleville *France* **19** F11
Belleville *Ill., U.S.A.* **112** F9
Belleville *Kans., U.S.A.* **112** F5
Belleville *N.J., U.S.A.* **115** F10
Belleville *N.Y., U.S.A.* **115** C8
Belleville-sur-Vie *France* **18** F5
Bellevue *Idaho, U.S.A.* **108** E6
Bellevue *Nebr., U.S.A.* **112** E6
Bellevue *Ohio, U.S.A.* **114** E2
Bellevue *Wash., U.S.A.* **110** C4
Belley *France* **21** C9
Bellin = Kangirsuk *Canada* **101** D13
Bellinge *Denmark* **11** J4
Bellingen *Australia* **95** E5
Bellingham *U.S.A.* **110** B4
Bellingshausen Abyssal
  Plain *S. Ocean* **5** C16
Bellingshausen Sea
  Antarctica **5** C17
Bellinzona *Switz.* **25** J5
Bello *Colombia* **124** B3
Bellows Falls *U.S.A.* **115** C12
Bellpat *Pakistan* **68** E3
Bellpuig *Spain* **38** D6
Belluno *Italy* **41** B9
Bellwood *U.S.A.* **114** F6
Bélmez *Spain* **37** G5
Belmont *Canada* **114** D3
Belmont *S. Africa* **88** D3
Belmont *U.S.A.* **114** D6
Belmonte *Brazil* **125** G11
Belmonte *Portugal* **36** E3
Belmonte *Spain* **39** F2
Belmopan *Belize* **119** D7
Belmullet *Ireland* **12** B2
Belo Horizonte *Brazil* **125** G10
Belo-sur-Mer *Madag.* **89** C7
Belo-Tsiribihina *Madag.* **89** B7
Belogorsk = Bilohirsk
  Ukraine **33** K8
Belogorsk *Russia* **53** D13
Belogradchik *Bulgaria* **44** C6
Belogradets *Bulgaria* **45** C11
Beloha *Madag.* **89** D8
Beloit *Kans., U.S.A.* **112** F4
Beloit *Wis., U.S.A.* **112** D9
Belokorovichi *Ukraine* **23** C15
Belomorsk *Russia* **52** C4
Belonia *India* **67** H17
Belopolye = Bilopillya
  Ukraine **33** G8
Belorechensk *Russia* **35** H4
Belorussia = Belarus ■
  Europe **23** B14
Beloslav *Bulgaria* **45** C11
Belovo *Bulgaria* **45** D8
Belovo *Russia* **52** D9
Belovodsk *Ukraine* **33** H10
Beloyarskiy *Russia* **52** C7
Beloye, Ozero *Russia* **32** B9
Beloye More *Russia* **8** C25
Belozem *Bulgaria* **45** D9
Belozersk *Russia* **32** B9
Belpasso *Italy* **43** E7
Belpre *U.S.A.* **113** F13
Belrain *India* **69** E9
Belt *U.S.A.* **108** C8
Beltana *Australia* **95** E2
Belterra *Brazil* **125** D8
Beltinci *Slovenia* **41** B13
Belton *U.S.A.* **116** F6
Belton L. *U.S.A.* **116** F6
Beltsy = Bălți *Moldova* **29** C12
Belturbet *Ireland* **12** B4
Belukha *Russia* **52** E9
Beluran *Malaysia* **62** C5
Beluša *Slovak Rep.* **27** B11
Belušić *Serbia* **44** C5
Belvedere Maríttimo *Italy* **43** C8
Belvès *France* **20** D5
Belvidere *Ill., U.S.A.* **112** D9
Belvidere *N.J., U.S.A.* **115** F9
Belvís de la Jara *Spain* **36** F6
Belyando → *Australia* **94** C4
Belyando Crossing *Australia* **94** C4
Belyy *Russia* **32** E7
Belyy, Ostrov *Russia* **52** B8
Belyy Yar *Russia* **52** D9
Belz *Ukraine* **31** H11
Bełżec *Poland* **31** H10
Belzig *Germany* **24** C8
Belzoni *U.S.A.* **117** E9
Bełżyce *Poland* **31** G9
Bemaraha, Lembalemban'
  i *Madag.* **89** B7
Bemarivo *Madag.* **89** C7
Bemarivo → *Antsiranana,*
  Madag. **89** A9

Bemarivo → Mahajanga, Madag. 89 B8
Bemavo Madag. 89 C8
Bembéréke Benin 83 C5
Bembesi Zimbabwe 87 G2
Bembesi → Zimbabwe 87 F2
Bembézar → Spain 37 H5
Bembibre Spain 36 C4
Bemetara India 69 J9
Bemidji U.S.A. 112 B6
Bemolanga Madag. 89 B8
Ben Iran 71 C6
Ben Cruachan U.K. 13 E3
Ben Dearg U.K. 13 D4
Ben En △ Vietnam 64 C5
Ben Gardane Tunisia 79 B8
Ben Hope U.K. 13 C4
Ben Lawers U.K. 13 E4
Ben Lomond N.S.W., Australia 95 E5
Ben Lomond Tas., Australia 95 G4
Ben Lomond U.K. 13 E4
Ben Lomond △ Australia 95 G4
Ben Luc Vietnam 65 G6
Ben Macdhui U.K. 13 D5
Ben Mhor U.K. 13 D1
Ben More Argyll & Bute, U.K. 13 E2
Ben More Stirling, U.K. 13 E4
Ben More Assynt U.K. 13 C4
Ben Nevis U.K. 13 E3
Ben Quang Vietnam 64 D6
Ben Tre Vietnam 65 G6
Ben Vorlich U.K. 13 E4
Ben Wyvis U.K. 13 D4
Bena Nigeria 83 C6
Benalla Australia 95 F4
Benalmádena Spain 37 J6
Benares = Varanasi India 69 G10
Bénat, C. France 21 E10
Benavente Portugal 37 G2
Benavente Spain 36 C5
Benavides U.S.A. 116 H5
Benavides de Órbigo Spain 36 C5
Benbecula U.K. 13 D1
Benbonyathe Hill Australia 95 E2
Bend U.S.A. 108 D3
Bender Beyla Somali Rep. 75 F5
Bendery = Tighina Moldova 29 D14
Bendigo Australia 95 F3
Bendorf Germany 24 E3
Benē Beraq Israel 74 C3
Bénéna Mali 82 C4
Benenitra Madag. 89 C8
Benešov Czech Rep. 26 B7
Benevento Italy 43 A7
Benfeld France 19 D14
Benga Mozam. 87 F3
Bengal, Bay of Ind. Oc. 67 M17
Bengaluru = Bangalore India 66 N10
Bengbis Cameroon 83 E7
Bengbu China 57 H9
Benghazi = Banghāzī Libya 79 B10
Bengkalis Indonesia 65 M4
Bengkulu Indonesia 62 E2
Bengkulu □ Indonesia 62 E2
Bengough Canada 103 D7
Bengtsfors Sweden 10 E6
Benguela Angola 85 G2
Benguérua, I. Mozam. 89 C6
Benha Egypt 80 H7
Beni → Bolivia 124 F5
Beni Mazâr Egypt 80 B3
Beni Mellal Morocco 78 B4
Beni Suef Egypt 80 J7
Beniah L. Canada 102 A6
Benicarló Spain 38 E5
Benicássim Spain 38 E5
Benidorm Spain 39 G4
Benin ■ Africa 83 D5
Benin → Nigeria 83 D6
Benin, Bight of W. Afr. 83 E5
Benin City Nigeria 83 D6
Benissa Spain 39 G5
Benito Juárez Argentina 126 D4
Benitses Greece 49 A3
Benjamin Aceval Paraguay 126 A4
Benjamin Constant Brazil 124 D4
Benjamín Hill Mexico 118 A2
Benkelman U.S.A. 112 E3
Benkovac Croatia 41 D12
Bennett Canada 102 B2
Bennett, L. Australia 92 D5
Bennetta, Ostrov Russia 53 B15
Bennettsville U.S.A. 117 D15
Bennichchâb Mauritania 82 B1
Bennington N.H., U.S.A. 115 D11
Bennington Vt., U.S.A. 115 D11
Bénodet France 18 E2
Benom Malaysia 65 L4
Benoni S. Africa 89 D4
Benque Viejo Belize 119 D7
Bensheim Germany 25 F4
Benson Ariz., U.S.A. 109 L8
Benson Minn., U.S.A. 112 C6
Bent Iran 71 E8
Benteng Indonesia 63 F6

Bentinck I. Australia 94 B2
Bentiu Sudan 81 F2
Bentley Subglacial Trench Antarctica 5 E15
Bento Gonçalves Brazil 127 B5
Benton Ark., U.S.A. 116 D8
Benton Calif., U.S.A. 110 H8
Benton Ill., U.S.A. 112 F9
Benton Pa., U.S.A. 115 E8
Benton Harbor U.S.A. 112 D10
Bentong Malaysia 65 L3
Bentonville U.S.A. 116 C7
Bentu Liben Ethiopia 81 F4
Benue □ Nigeria 83 D6
Benue → Nigeria 83 D6
Benxi China 57 D12
Beo Indonesia 63 D7
Beograd Serbia 44 B4
Beograd ✈ (BEG) Serbia 44 C4
Beolgyo S. Korea 57 G14
Beoumi Ivory C. 82 D3
Bepan Jiang → China 58 E6
Beppu Japan 55 H5
Beqa Fiji 91 a
Beqaa Valley = Al Biqā Lebanon 74 A5
Ber Mota India 68 H3
Bera, Tasik Malaysia 65 L4
Berach → India 68 G6
Beraketa Madag. 89 C7
Berane Montenegro 44 D3
Berastagi Indonesia 65 L2
Berat Albania 44 F3
Beravina Madag. 89 B8
Berber Sudan 80 D3
Berbera Somali Rep. 75 E4
Berbérati Cent. Afr. 84 D3
Berbice → Guyana 124 B7
Berceto Italy 40 D6
Berchidda Italy 42 B1
Berchtesgaden Germany 25 H8
Berchtesgaden △ Germany 25 H8
Berck France 19 B8
Berdichev = Berdychiv Ukraine 23 D15
Berdsk Russia 52 D9
Berdyansk Ukraine 33 J9
Berdychiv Ukraine 23 D15
Berea U.S.A. 113 G11
Berebere Indonesia 63 D7
Bereeda Somali Rep. 75 E5
Berehomet Ukraine 29 B10
Berehove Ukraine 28 B9
Bereket Turkmenistan 71 B7
Berekum Ghana 82 D4
Berenice Egypt 80 C4
Berens → Canada 103 C9
Berens I. Canada 103 C9
Berens River Canada 103 C9
Beresford U.S.A. 112 D5
Berestechko Ukraine 23 C13
Bereşti Romania 29 E12
Beretău → Romania 28 C6
Berettyó → Hungary 28 D6
Berettyóújfalu Hungary 28 D6
Berevo Mahajanga, Madag. 89 B7
Berevo Toliara, Madag. 89 B7
Bereza = Byaroza Belarus 23 B13
Berezhany Ukraine 23 D13
Berezina = Byarezina → Belarus 23 B16
Berezivka Ukraine 33 J6
Berezna Ukraine 33 G6
Bereznik Russia 52 C5
Berezniki Russia 52 C7
Berezovo Russia 52 C7
Berezyne Ukraine 29 D14
Berga Spain 38 C6
Berga Sweden 11 G10
Bergama Turkey 47 B9
Bérgamo Italy 40 C6
Bergara Spain 38 B2
Bergby Sweden 10 D11
Berge Norway 10 E2
Bergedorf Germany 24 B6
Bergeforsen Sweden 10 B11
Bergen Mecklenburg-Vorpommern, Germany 24 A9
Bergen Niedersachsen, Germany 24 C5
Bergen Neths. 17 B4
Bergen Norway 8 F11
Bergen U.S.A. 114 C7
Bergen op Zoom Neths. 17 C4
Bergerac France 20 D4
Bergheim Germany 24 E2
Bergholz U.S.A. 114 F4
Bergisch Gladbach Germany 17 D7
Bergisches Land □ Germany 24 E3
Bergkamen Germany 24 D3
Bergkvara Sweden 11 H10
Bergshamra Sweden 10 E12
Bergsjö Sweden 10 C11
Bergstrasse-Odenwald △ Germany 25 F1
Bergues France 19 B9

Bergviken Sweden 10 C10
Bergville S. Africa 89 D4
Berhala, Selat Indonesia 62 E2
Berhampore = Baharampur India 69 G13
Berhampur = Brahmapur India 67 K14
Berheci → Romania 29 E12
Bering Sea Pac. Oc. 106 a
Bering Strait Pac. Oc. 106 a
Beringovskiy Russia 53 C18
Berisso Argentina 126 C4
Berja Spain 37 J8
Berkeley U.S.A. 110 H4
Berkner I. Antarctica 5 D18
Berkovitsa Bulgaria 44 C7
Berkshire □ U.K. 15 D8
Berkshire Downs U.K. 15 F6
Berlanga Spain 37 G5
Berlenga, I. Portugal 37 F1
Berlin Germany 24 C9
Berlin Md., U.S.A. 113 F16
Berlin N.H., U.S.A. 115 B13
Berlin N.Y., U.S.A. 115 D11
Berlin Wis., U.S.A. 112 D9
Berlin □ Germany 24 C9
Berlin L. U.S.A. 114 E4
Berlin Tegel ✈ (TXL) Germany 24 C9
Bermeja, Sierra Spain 37 J5
Bermejo → Formosa, Argentina 126 B4
Bermejo → San Juan, Argentina 126 C2
Bermejo, Paso = Uspallata, P. de Argentina 126 C2
Bermen, L. Canada 105 B6
Bermeo Spain 38 B2
Bermillo de Sayago Spain 36 D4
Bermuda ☑ Atl. Oc. 99 F13
Bern Switz. 25 J3
Bern □ Switz. 25 J3
Bernalda Italy 43 B9
Bernalillo U.S.A. 109 J10
Bernardo de Irigoyen Argentina 127 B5
Bernardsville U.S.A. 115 F10
Bernasconi Argentina 126 D3
Bernau Bayern, Germany 25 H8
Bernau Brandenburg, Germany 24 C9
Bernay France 18 C7
Bernburg Germany 24 D7
Berndorf Austria 26 D9
Berne = Bern Switz. 25 J3
Berne → Bern □ Switz. 25 J3
Berner Alpen Switz. 25 J3
Berneray U.K. 13 D1
Bernier I. Australia 93 D1
Bernina, Piz Switz. 25 J5
Bernkastel-Kues Germany 25 F3
Beroroha Madag. 89 C8
Béroubouay Benin 83 C5
Beroun Czech Rep. 26 B7
Berounka → Czech Rep. 26 B7
Berovo Macedonia 44 E6
Berre, Étang de France 21 E9
Berre-l'Étang France 21 E9
Berri Australia 95 E3
Berriane Algeria 78 B6
Berry Australia 95 E5
Berry France 19 F8
Berry Is. Bahamas 120 A4
Berryessa, L. U.S.A. 110 G4
Berryville U.S.A. 116 C8
Berseba Namibia 88 D2
Bersenbrück Germany 24 C3
Bershad Ukraine 29 B14
Bertamirans Spain 36 C2
Berthold U.S.A. 112 A3
Berthoud U.S.A. 108 F11
Bertincourt France 19 B9
Bertoua Cameroon 84 D2
Bertraghboy B. Ireland 12 C2
Berwick U.S.A. 115 E8
Berwick-upon-Tweed U.K. 14 B6
Berwyn Mts. U.K. 14 E4
Beryslav Ukraine 33 J7
Berzasca Romania 28 F6
Berzence Hungary 28 D2
Besal Pakistan 69 B5
Besalampy Madag. 89 B7
Besançon France 19 E13
Besar Indonesia 62 E5
Beshenkovichi Belarus 32 E5
Beška Serbia 28 E5
Beslan Russia 35 J7
Besna Kobila Serbia 44 D6
Besnard L. Canada 103 B7
Besni Turkey 72 D7
Besor, N. → Egypt 74 D3
Bessarabia = Basarabeasca Moldova 29 D13
Bessarabka = Basarabeasca Moldova 29 D13
Bessèges France 21 D8
Bessemer Ala., U.S.A. 117 E11
Bessemer Mich., U.S.A. 112 B8
Bessemer Pa., U.S.A. 114 F4
Bessin France 18 C6

Bessines-sur-Gartempe France 20 B5
Beswick Australia 92 B5
Bet She'an Israel 74 C4
Bet Shemesh Israel 74 D4
Betafo Madag. 89 B8
Betancuria Canary Is. 48 F5
Betanzos Spain 36 B2
Bétaré Oya Cameroon 84 C2
Betatao Madag. 89 B8
Bétera Spain 39 F4
Bétérou Benin 83 D5
Bethal S. Africa 89 D4
Bethanien Namibia 88 D2
Bethany Canada 114 B6
Bethany Mo., U.S.A. 112 E6
Bethany Okla., U.S.A. 116 B6
Bethel Alaska, U.S.A. 106 a
Bethel Conn., U.S.A. 115 E11
Bethel Maine, U.S.A. 115 B14
Bethel Vt., U.S.A. 115 C12
Bethel Park U.S.A. 114 F4
Bethlehem = Bayt Lahm West Bank 74 D4
Bethlehem S. Africa 89 D4
Bethlehem U.S.A. 115 F9
Bethulie S. Africa 88 E4
Béthune France 19 B9
Béthune → France 18 C8
Betioky Madag. 89 C7
Betong Malaysia 65 K3
Betong Thailand 65 K3
Betoota Australia 94 D3
Betor Ethiopia 81 E4
Betroka Madag. 89 C8
Betsiamites Canada 105 C6
Betsiamites → Canada 105 C6
Betsiboka → Madag. 89 B8
Bettendorf U.S.A. 112 E8
Bettiah India 69 F11
Bettna Sweden 11 F10
Béttola Italy 40 D6
Betul India 66 J10
Betws-y-Coed U.K. 14 D4
Betxí Spain 38 F4
Betzdorf Germany 24 E3
Beuil France 21 D10
Beulah Mich., U.S.A. 112 C10
Beulah N. Dak., U.S.A. 112 B3
Beuvron → France 18 E8
Beveren Belgium 17 C4
Beverley Australia 93 F2
Beverley U.K. 14 D7
Beverly U.S.A. 115 D14
Beverly Hills Calif., U.S.A. 111 L8
Beverly Hills Fla., U.S.A. 117 G13
Beverungen Germany 24 D5
Bevoalavo Madag. 89 D7
Bewas → India 69 H8
Bewdley Canada 114 B6
Bex Switz. 25 J3
Bexhill U.K. 15 G8
Bey Dağları Turkey 47 E12
Beyānlū Iran 70 C5
Beyazköy Turkey 45 E11
Beyçayırı Turkey 45 F10
Beydağ Turkey 47 C10
Beyeğaç Turkey 47 D10
Beyin Ghana 82 D4
Beykoz Turkey 45 E13
Beyla Guinea 82 D3
Beynat France 20 C5
Beyneu Kazakhstan 52 E6
Beyoba Turkey 47 C9
Beyoğlu Turkey 45 E12
Beypazarı Turkey 72 B4
Beyşehir Turkey 72 D4
Beyşehir Gölü Turkey 72 D4
Beytüşşebap Turkey 73 D10
Bezdan Serbia 28 E3
Bezhetsk Russia 32 D9
Béziers France 20 E7
Bezwada = Vijayawada India 67 L12
Bhabua India 69 G10
Bhachau India 66 H7
Bhadar → Gujarat, India 68 H5
Bhadar → Gujarat, India 68 J3
Bhadarwah India 69 C6
Bhadgaon = Bhaktapur Nepal 69 F11
Bhadohi India 69 G10
Bhadra India 68 E6
Bhadrakh India 67 J15
Bhadran India 68 H5
Bhadravati India 66 N9
Bhag Pakistan 68 E2
Bhagalpur India 69 G12
Bhagirathi → Uttarakhand, India 69 D8
Bhagirathi → W. Bengal, India 69 H13
Bhakkar Pakistan 68 D4
Bhakra Dam India 68 D7
Bhaktapur Nepal 69 F11
Bhamo Burma 67 G20

Bhandara India 66 J11
Bhanpura India 68 G6
Bhanrer Ra. India 69 H8
Bhaptiahi India 69 F12
Bharat = India ■ Asia 66 K11
Bharatpur Chhattisgarh, India 69 H9
Bharatpur Raj., India 68 F7
Bharatpur Nepal 69 F11
Bharno India 69 H11
Bharuch India 66 J8
Bhatinda India 68 D6
Bhatpara India 69 H13
Bhattu India 68 E6
Bhaun Pakistan 68 C5
Bhaunagar = Bhavnagar India 66 J8
Bhavnagar India 66 J8
Bhawari India 68 G5
Bhayavadar India 68 J4
Bhera Pakistan 68 C5
Bhera India 69 F11
Bhikangaon India 68 J6
Bhilai = Bhilainagar-Durg India 67 J12
Bhilainagar-Durg India 67 J12
Bhilsa = Vidisha India 68 H7
Bhilwara India 68 G6
Bhima → India 66 L10
Bhimbar Pakistan 69 C6
Bhind India 69 F8
Bhinga India 69 F9
Bhinmal India 68 G5
Bhisho S. Africa 89 E4
Bhiwandi India 66 K8
Bhiwani India 68 E7
Bhogava → India 68 H5
Bhola Bangla. 67 H17
Bholari Pakistan 68 G3
Bhopal India 68 H7
Bhubaneshwar India 67 J14
Bhuj India 68 H3
Bhumiphol Res. Thailand 64 D2
Bhusawal India 66 J9
Bhutan ■ Asia 67 F17
Biafra, B. of = Bonny, Bight of Africa 83 E6
Biak Indonesia 63 E9
Biała Poland 31 H4
Biała → Poland 31 H7
Biała Piska Poland 30 E9
Biała Podlaska Poland 31 F10
Biała Rawska Poland 31 G7
Białobrzegi Poland 31 G7
Białogard Poland 30 D2
Białowieski △ Poland 31 F10
Białowieża Poland 31 F10
Biały Bór Poland 30 E3
Białystok Poland 31 E10
Biancavilla Italy 43 E7
Bianco Italy 43 D9
Biankouma Ivory C. 82 D3
Biaora India 68 H7
Biāra Indonesia 63 J18
Biasca Switz. 25 J4
Biba Egypt 80 J7
Bibai Japan 54 C10
Bibbiena Italy 41 E8
Bibby I. Canada 103 A10
Bibei → Spain 36 C3
Biberach Germany 25 G5
Bibiani Ghana 82 D4
Bibungwa Dem. Rep. of the Congo 86 C2
Bicaj Albania 44 E4
Bicaz Romania 29 D11
Bicazu Ardelean Romania 29 D10
Bíccari Italy 43 A8
Bicester U.K. 15 F6
Bichena Ethiopia 81 E4
Bicheno Australia 95 G4
Bichia India 69 H9
Bickerton I. Australia 94 A2
Bicske Hungary 28 C3
Bida Nigeria 83 D6
Bidar India 66 L10
Biddeford U.S.A. 113 D18
Biddwara Ethiopia 81 F4
Bideford U.K. 15 F3
Bideford Bay U.K. 15 F3
Bidhuna India 69 F8
Bīdokht Iran 71 C8
Bidor Malaysia 65 K3
Bidyadanga Australia 92 C3
Bie Sweden 10 E10
Bié, Planalto de Angola 85 G3
Bieber U.S.A. 108 F3
Biebrza → Poland 31 E9
Biebrzański △ Poland 30 E9
Biecz Poland 31 J8
Biel Switz. 25 H3
Bielawa Poland 31 H3
Bielefeld Germany 24 C4
Bielersee Switz. 25 H3
Biella Italy 40 C5
Bielsk Podlaski Poland 31 F10

Bielsko-Biała Poland 31 J6
Bien Hoa Vietnam 65 G6
Bienne = Biel Switz. 25 H3
Bienvenida Spain 37 G4
Bienville, L. Canada 104 A5
Bierné France 18 E6
Bierun Poland 31 H6
Bierutów Poland 31 G4
Biescas Spain 38 C4
Biese → Germany 24 C7
Biesiesfontein S. Africa 88 E2
Bieszczadzki △ Poland 31 J9
Bietigheim-Bissingen Germany 25 G5
Biferno → Italy 41 G12
Big → Canada 105 B8
Big B. Canada 105 A7
Big Bear City U.S.A. 111 L10
Big Bear Lake U.S.A. 111 L10
Big Belt Mts. U.S.A. 108 C8
Big Bend Swaziland 89 D5
Big Bend △ U.S.A. 116 G3
Big Black → U.S.A. 117 E9
Big Blue → U.S.A. 112 F5
Big Creek U.S.A. 110 H7
Big Cypress △ U.S.A. 117 H14
Big Desert Australia 95 F3
Big Falls U.S.A. 112 A7
Big Fork → U.S.A. 112 A7
Big Horn Mts. = Bighorn Mts. U.S.A. 108 D10
Big I. Canada 102 A5
Big Lake U.S.A. 116 F4
Big Moose U.S.A. 115 C10
Big Muddy Cr. → U.S.A. 108 B11
Big Pine U.S.A. 110 H8
Big Piney U.S.A. 108 E8
Big Quill L. Canada 103 C8
Big Rapids U.S.A. 113 D11
Big Rideau L. Canada 115 B8
Big River Canada 103 C7
Big Run U.S.A. 114 F6
Big Sable Pt. U.S.A. 112 C10
Big Salmon → Canada 102 A2
Big Sand L. Canada 103 B9
Big Sandy U.S.A. 108 B8
Big Sandy → U.S.A. 113 F12
Big Sandy Cr. = Sandy Cr. → U.S.A. 108 F9
Big Sandy Cr. → U.S.A. 108 G12
Big Sioux → U.S.A. 112 D5
Big South Fork △ U.S.A. 117 C12
Big Spring U.S.A. 116 E4
Big Stone City U.S.A. 112 C5
Big Stone Gap U.S.A. 113 G12
Big Stone L. U.S.A. 112 C5
Big Sur U.S.A. 110 J5
Big Timber U.S.A. 108 D9
Big Trout L. Canada 104 B2
Big Trout Lake Canada 104 B2
Biga Turkey 45 F11
Biga → Turkey 45 F11
Bigadiç Turkey 47 B10
Biganos France 20 D3
Biggar Canada 103 C7
Biggar U.K. 13 F5
Bigge I. Australia 92 B4
Biggenden Australia 95 D5
Biggleswade U.K. 15 E7
Biggs U.S.A. 110 F5
Bighorn U.S.A. 108 C10
Bighorn → U.S.A. 108 C10
Bighorn Canyon △ U.S.A. 108 D10
Bighorn L. U.S.A. 108 D9
Bighorn Mts. U.S.A. 108 D10
Bignona Senegal 82 C1
Bigorre France 20 E4
Bigstone L. Canada 103 C9
Biguglia, Étang de France 21 F13
Bigwa Tanzania 86 D4
Bihać Bos.-H. 41 D12
Bihar India 69 G11
Bihar □ India 69 G12
Biharamulo Tanzania 86 C3
Biharamulo △ Tanzania 86 C3
Bihariganj India 69 G12
Biharkeresztes Hungary 28 C6
Bihor □ Romania 28 D7
Bihor, Munții Romania 28 D7
Bijagós, Arquipélago dos Guinea-Biss. 82 C1
Bijaipur India 68 F7
Bijapur Chhattisgarh, India 67 K12
Bijapur Karnataka, India 66 L9
Bījār Iran 73 E12
Bijawar India 68 G8
Bijela Montenegro 44 D3
Bijeljina Bos.-H. 28 F4
Bijelo Polje Montenegro 44 C3
Bijie China 58 D5
Bijnor India 68 E8
Bikaner India 68 E5
Bikapur India 69 F10
Bikeqi China 56 D6
Bikfayyā Lebanon 74 B4
Bikin Russia 54 A7
Bikin → Russia 54 A7

Bikini Atoll *Marshall Is.* **96** F8
Bikita *Zimbabwe* **89** C5
Bīkkū Bīttī *Libya* **79** D9
Bikoué *Cameroon* **83** E7
Bila Tserkva *Ukraine* **23** D16
Bilara *India* **68** F5
Bilaspur *Chhattisgarh, India* **69** H10
Bilaspur *Punjab, India* **68** D7
Biläsuvar *Azerbaijan* **73** C13
Bilauk Taungdan *Thailand* **64** F2
Bilbao *Spain* **38** B2
Bilbao ✕ (BIO) *Spain* **38** B2
Bilbeis *Egypt* **80** H7
Bilbo = Bilbao *Spain* **38** B2
Bilbor *Romania* **29** C10
Bilche-Zolote *Ukraine* **29** B10
Bilciureşti *Romania* **29** F10
Bildudalur *Iceland* **8** D2
Bílé Karpaty *Europe* **27** B11
Bileća *Bos.-H.* **44** D2
Bilecik *Turkey* **72** B4
Bilecik □ *Turkey* **72** B3
Bilećko Jezero *Bos.-H.* **44** D2
Bileh Savār *Iran* **73** C13
Bilgoraj *Poland* **31** H9
Bilgram *India* **69** F9
Bilhaur *India* **69** F9
Bilhorod-Dnistrovskyy
    Ukraine **33** J6
Bilibino *Russia* **53** C17
Bilibiza *Mozam.* **87** E5
Bilisht *Albania* **44** F5
Billabong Roadhouse
    Australia **93** E2
Billdal *Sweden* **11** G5
Billiluna *Australia* **92** C4
Billings *U.S.A.* **108** D9
Billiton Is. = Belitung
    Indonesia **62** E3
Billsta *Sweden* **10** A12
Billund *Denmark* **11** J3
Bilma *Niger* **79** E8
Bilo Gora *Croatia* **28** E2
Biloela *Australia* **94** C5
Bilohirsk *Ukraine* **33** K8
Bilopillya *Ukraine* **33** G8
Biloxi *U.S.A.* **117** F10
Bilpa Morea Claypan
    Australia **94** D3
Biltine *Chad* **79** F10
Bilyarsk *Russia* **34** C10
Bima *Indonesia* **63** F5
Bimban *Egypt* **80** C3
Bimbila *Ghana* **83** D5
Bimbo *C.A.R.* **84** D3
Bimini Is. *Bahamas* **120** A4
Bin Xian *Heilongjiang, China* **57** B14
Bin Xian *Shaanxi, China* **56** G5
Bin Yauri *Nigeria* **83** C5
Bina-Etawah *India* **68** G4
Binalbagan *Phil.* **61** F5
Binalong *Australia* **95** E4
Bīnālūd, Kūh-e *Iran* **71** B8
Binatang = Bintangau
    Malaysia **62** D4
Binche *Belgium* **17** D4
Binchuan *China* **58** E3
Binder *Chad* **83** D7
Bindki *India* **69** F9
Bindslev *Denmark* **11** G4
Bindura *Zimbabwe* **87** F3
Binéfar *Spain* **38** D5
Bingara *Australia* **95** D5
Bingen *Germany* **25** F3
Bingerville *Ivory C.* **82** D4
Bingham *U.S.A.* **113** C19
Binghamton *U.S.A.* **115** D9
Bingöl *Turkey* **73** C9
Bingöl □ *Turkey* **73** C9
Bingöl Dağları *Turkey* **73** C9
Bingsjö *Sweden* **10** C9
Binh Dinh = An Nhon
    Vietnam **64** F7
Binh Khe *Vietnam* **64** F7
Binh Son *Vietnam* **64** E7
Binhai *China* **57** G10
Binic *France* **18** D4
Binisatua *Spain* **48** B11
Binissalem *Spain* **48** B9
Binjai *Indonesia* **62** D3
Binji *Nigeria* **83** C5
Binnaway *Australia* **95** E4
Binongko *Indonesia* **63** F6
Binscarth *Canada* **103** C8
Binshangul Gumuz □
    Ethiopia **81** E4
Bint Goda *Sudan* **81** E3
Bintan *Indonesia* **62** D2
Bintangau *Malaysia* **62** D4
Bintulu *Malaysia* **62** D4
Bintuni *Indonesia* **63** E8
Binyang *China* **58** F7
Binz *Germany* **24** A9
Binzert = Bizerte *Tunisia* **79** A7
Binzhou *China* **57** F10
Bío Bío □ *Chile* **126** D1
Bíobío → *Chile* **126** D1

Biograd na Moru *Croatia* **41** E12
Biogradska Gora △
    Montenegro **44** D3
Bioko *Eq. Guin.* **83** E6
Biokovo *Croatia* **41** E14
Bipindi *Cameroon* **83** E7
Bir *India* **66** K9
Bīr, Ras *Djibouti* **81** E5
Bîr Abu Hashim *Egypt* **80** C3
Bîr Abu Minqar *Egypt* **80** B2
Bîr Abu Muḩammad *Egypt* **74** F3
Bi'r ad Dabbāghāt *Jordan* **74** E4
Bîr Adal Deib *Sudan* **80** C4
Bi'r al Butayyihāt *Jordan* **74** F4
Bi'r al Mārī *Jordan* **74** E4
Bi'r al Qattār *Jordan* **74** F4
Bîr 'Asal *Egypt* **80** B3
Bîr Atrun *Sudan* **80** D2
Bîr Beiḑa *Egypt* **74** E3
Bîr Diqnash *Egypt* **80** A2
Bîr el 'Abd *Egypt* **74** D2
Bîr el Basur *Egypt* **80** B2
Bîr el Biarât *Egypt* **74** F3
Bîr el Duweidar *Egypt* **74** E1
Bîr el Garârât *Egypt* **74** D2
Bîr el Gellaz *Egypt* **80** A2
Bîr el Heisi *Egypt* **74** F3
Bîr el Jafir *Egypt* **74** E1
Bîr el Mâlḥi *Egypt* **74** E2
Bîr el Shaqqa *Egypt* **80** A2
Bîr el Thamâda *Egypt* **74** E2
Bîr Fuad *Egypt* **80** A2
Bîr Gebeil Ḥişn *Egypt* **74** E2
Bi'r Ghadīr *Syria* **74** A6
Bîr Haimur *Egypt* **80** C3
Bîr Ḥasana *Egypt* **74** E2
Bîr Hōōker *Egypt* **80** H7
Bîr Kanayis *Egypt* **80** C3
Bîr Kaseiba *Egypt* **74** E2
Bîr Kerawein *Egypt* **80** B2
Bîr Lahfân *Egypt* **74** E2
Bîr Madkûr *Egypt* **74** E1
Bîr Maql *Egypt* **80** C3
Bîr Mîneiga *Sudan* **80** C4
Bîr Misaha *Egypt* **80** C2
Bîr Mogreïn *Mauritania* **78** C3
Bîr Murr *Egypt* **80** C3
Bi'r Muţribah *Kuwait* **70** D5
Bîr Nakheila *Egypt* **80** C3
Bîr Qaţia *Egypt* **74** E1
Bîr Qatrani *Egypt* **80** A2
Bîr Ranga *Egypt* **80** C4
Bîr Sahara *Egypt* **80** C2
Bîr Seiyâla *Egypt* **80** C3
Bîr Shalatein *Egypt* **80** C4
Bîr Shebb *Egypt* **80** C2
Bîr Shût *Egypt* **80** C4
Bîr Terfawi *Egypt* **80** C2
Bîr Umm Qubûr *Egypt* **80** C3
Bîr Ungât *Egypt* **80** C3
Bîr Za'farâna *Egypt* **80** J8
Bîr Zeidûn *Egypt* **80** B3
Bīrāk *Libya* **79** C8
Biramféro *Guinea* **82** C3
Biratnagar *Nepal* **69** F12
Birawa *Dem. Rep. of the Congo* **86** C2
Birch → *Canada* **102** B6
Birch Hills *Canada* **103** C7
Birch I. *Canada* **103** C8
Birch L. *N.W.T., Canada* **102** A5
Birch L. *Ont., Canada* **104** B1
Birch Mts. *Canada* **102** B6
Birch River *Canada* **103** C8
Birchip *Australia* **95** F3
Birchiş *Romania* **28** E7
Bird *Canada* **103** B10
Bird I. = Aves, I. de
    W. Indies **121** C7
Bird I. *S. Georgia* **128** G9
Birds Creek *Canada* **114** A7
Birdsville *Australia* **94** D2
Birdum Cr. → *Australia* **92** C5
Birecik *Turkey* **73** D8
Birein *Israel* **74** E3
Bireuen *Indonesia* **62** C1
Biri → *Sudan* **81** F2
Birifo *Gambia* **82** C2
Birigüi *Brazil* **127** A5
Bīrjand *Iran* **71** C8
Birkenfeld *Germany* **25** F3
Birkenhead *U.K.* **14** D4
Birkerød *Denmark* **11** J6
Birket Qârûn *Egypt* **80** J7
Birkfeld *Austria* **26** D8
Bîrlad = Bârlad *Romania* **29** D12
Birmingham *U.K.* **15** E6
Birmingham Int. ✕ (BHX)
    U.K. **15** E6
Birmitrapur *India* **67** H14
Birni Ngaouré *Niger* **83** C5
Birni Nkonni *Niger* **83** C6
Birnin Gwari *Nigeria* **83** C6
Birnin Kebbi *Nigeria* **83** C5
Birnin Kudu *Nigeria* **83** C6
Birobidzhan *Russia* **53** E14
Birr *Ireland* **12** C4
Birrie → *Australia* **95** D4

Birsilpur *India* **68** E5
Birsk *Russia* **52** D6
Birštonas *Lithuania* **30** D11
Birtle *Canada* **103** C8
Birur *India* **66** N9
Biryuchiy *Ukraine* **33** J8
Biržai *Lithuania* **32** D3
Birzebbugga *Malta* **49** D2
Bisa *Indonesia* **63** E7
Bisáccia *Italy* **43** A8
Bisacquino *Italy* **42** E6
Bisalpur *India* **69** E8
Bisbee *U.S.A.* **109** L9
Biscarrosse *France* **20** D2
Biscarrosse et de Parentis,
    Étang de *France* **20** D2
Biscay, B. of *Atl. Oc.* **6** F5
Biscayne B. *U.S.A.* **117** J14
Biscéglie *Italy* **43** A9
Bischheim *France* **19** D14
Bischofshofen *Austria* **26** D6
Bischofswerda *Germany* **24** D10
Bischwiller *France* **19** D14
Biscoe Is. *Antarctica* **5** C17
Biscotasing *Canada* **104** C3
Biševo *Croatia* **41** F13
Bisha *Eritrea* **81** D4
Bishah, W. → *Si. Arabia* **80** C5
Bishan *China* **58** C6
Bishkek *Kyrgyzstan* **52** E8
Bishnupur *India* **69** H12
Bisho = Bhisho *S. Africa* **89** E4
Bishop *Calif., U.S.A.* **110** H8
Bishop *Tex., U.S.A.* **116** H6
Bishop Auckland *U.K.* **14** C6
Bishop's Falls *Canada* **105** C8
Bishop's Stortford *U.K.* **15** F8
Bisignano *Italy* **43** C9
Bisina, L. *Uganda* **86** B3
Biskra *Algeria* **78** B7
Biskupiec *Poland* **30** E7
Bismarck *U.S.A.* **112** B3
Bismarck Arch. *Papua N. G.* **90** B7
Bismark *Germany* **24** C7
Bismil *Turkey* **73** D9
Biso *Uganda* **86** B3
Bison *U.S.A.* **112** C2
Bīsotūn *Iran* **73** E12
Bispgården *Sweden* **10** A10
Bissagos = Bijagós,
    Arquipélago dos
    Guinea-Biss. **82** C1
Bissau *Guinea-Biss.* **82** C1
Bissaula *Nigeria* **83** D7
Bissikrima *Guinea* **82** C2
Bissorã *Guinea-Biss.* **82** C1
Bistcho L. *Canada* **102** B5
Bistreţ *Romania* **29** G8
Bistrica = Ilirska-Bistrica
    Slovenia **41** C11
Bistriţa *Romania* **29** C9
Bistriţa → *Romania* **29** D11
Bistriţa Năsăud □ *Romania* **29** C9
Bistriţei, Munţii *Romania* **29** C10
Biswan *India* **69** F9
Bisztynek *Poland* **30** D7
Bitam *Gabon* **84** D2
Bitburg *Germany* **25** F2
Bitche *France* **19** C14
Bithynia *Turkey* **72** B4
Bitkine *Chad* **79** F9
Bitlis *Turkey* **73** C10
Bitlis □ *Turkey* **73** C10
Bitola *Macedonia* **44** E5
Bitolj = Bitola *Macedonia* **44** E5
Bitonto *Italy* **43** A9
Bitter Creek *U.S.A.* **108** F9
Bitter L. = Buheirat-
    Murrat-el-Kubra *Egypt* **80** H8
Bitterfeld *Germany* **24** D8
Bitterfontein *S. Africa* **88** E2
Bitterroot → *U.S.A.* **108** C6
Bitterroot Range *U.S.A.* **108** C6
Bitterwater *U.S.A.* **110** J6
Bitti *Italy* **42** B2
Bittou *Burkina Faso* **83** C4
Biu *Nigeria* **83** C7
Biwa-Ko *Japan* **55** G8
Biwabik *U.S.A.* **112** B7
Bixad *Romania* **29** C8
Bixby *U.S.A.* **116** D7
Biyang *China* **56** H7
Biysk *Russia* **52** D9
Bizana *S. Africa* **89** E4
Bizen *Japan* **55** G7
Bizerte *Tunisia* **79** A7
Bjargtangar *Iceland* **8** D1
Bjärnum *Sweden* **11** H7
Bjästa *Sweden* **10** A12
Bjelašica *Montenegro* **44** D3
Bjelašnica *Bos.-H.* **28** G3
Bjelovar *Croatia* **41** C13
Bjerringbro *Denmark* **11** H3
Björbo *Sweden* **10** D8
Björklinge *Sweden* **10** D11
Björneborg = Pori *Finland* **32** B1

Björneborg *Sweden* **10** E8
Bjørnevatn *Norway* **8** B24
Bjørnøya *Arctic* **4** B8
Bjursås *Sweden* **10** D9
Bjuv *Sweden* **11** H6
Bla *Mali* **82** C3
Blace *Serbia* **44** C5
Blachownia *Poland* **31** H5
Black = Da → *Vietnam* **58** G5
Black → *Ariz., U.S.A.* **109** K8
Black → *Ark., U.S.A.* **116** D9
Black → *La., U.S.A.* **116** F9
Black → *Mich., U.S.A.* **114** D2
Black → *N.Y., U.S.A.* **115** C8
Black → *Wis., U.S.A.* **112** D9
Black Bay Pen. *Canada* **104** C2
Black Birch L. *Canada* **103** B7
Black Braes △ *Australia* **94** B3
Black Canyon of the
    Gunnison △ *U.S.A.* **108** G10
Black Diamond *Canada* **102** C6
Black Duck → *Canada* **104** A2
Black Forest =
    Schwarzwald *Germany* **25** G4
Black Forest *U.S.A.* **108** G11
Black Hd. *Ireland* **12** C2
Black Hills *U.S.A.* **112** D2
Black L. *Canada* **103** B7
Black L. *Mich., U.S.A.* **113** C11
Black L. *N.Y., U.S.A.* **115** B9
Black Lake *Canada* **103** B7
Black Mesa *U.S.A.* **116** C3
Black Mt. = Mynydd Du
    U.K. **15** F4
Black Range *U.S.A.* **109** K10
Black River *Jamaica* **120** a
Black River *U.S.A.* **115** C9
Black River Falls *U.S.A.* **112** C8
Black Rock *Barbados* **121** g
Black Rock Desert *U.S.A.* **108** F4
Black Sea *Eurasia* **6** G12
Black Tickle *Canada* **105** B8
Black Volta → *Africa* **82** D4
Black Warrior → *U.S.A.* **117** E11
Blackall *Australia* **94** C4
Blackball *N.Z.* **91** E3
Blackbull *Australia* **94** B3
Blackburn *U.K.* **14** D5
Blackburn with Darwen □
    U.K. **14** D5
Blackdown Tableland △
    Australia **94** C4
Blackfoot *U.S.A.* **108** E7
Blackfoot → *U.S.A.* **108** C7
Blackfoot Res. *U.S.A.* **108** E8
Blackpool *U.K.* **14** D4
Blackpool □ *U.K.* **14** D4
Blackriver *U.S.A.* **114** B1
Blacks Harbour *Canada* **105** C6
Blacksburg *U.S.A.* **113** G13
Blacksod B. *Ireland* **12** B1
Blackstairs Mt. *Ireland* **12** D5
Blackstone *U.S.A.* **113** G14
Blackstone Ra. *Australia* **93** E4
Blacktown *Australia* **95** E5
Blackwater → *West
    Road → Canada* **102** C4
Blackwater *Australia* **94** C4
Blackwater → *Meath, Ireland* **12** C4
Blackwater → *Waterford,
    Ireland* **12** D4
Blackwater → *U.K.* **12** B5
Blackwell *U.S.A.* **116** C6
Blackwells Corner *U.S.A.* **111** K7
Bladensburg △ *Australia* **94** C3
Blaenau Ffestiniog *U.K.* **14** E4
Blaenau Gwent □ *U.K.* **15** F4
Blagaj *Bos.-H.* **44** C1
Blagnac *France* **20** E5
Blagnac, Toulouse ✕ (TLS)
    France **20** E5
Blagodarnoye =
    Blagodarnyy *Russia* **35** H6
Blagodarnyy *Russia* **35** H6
Blagoevgrad *Bulgaria* **44** D7
Blagoveshchensk *Russia* **53** D13
Blahkiuh *Indonesia* **63** J18
Blain *France* **18** E5
Blain *U.S.A.* **114** F7
Blaine *Minn., U.S.A.* **112** C7
Blaine *Wash., U.S.A.* **110** B4
Blaine Lake *Canada* **103** C7
Blair *U.S.A.* **112** E5
Blair Athol *Australia* **94** C4
Blair Atholl *U.K.* **13** E5
Blairgowrie *U.K.* **13** E5
Blairsden *U.S.A.* **110** F6
Blairsville *U.S.A.* **114** F5
Blaj *Romania* **29** D8
Blakang Mati, Pulau =
    Sentosa *Singapore* **65** d
Blake Pt. *U.S.A.* **112** A9
Blakely *Ga., U.S.A.* **117** F12
Blakely *Pa., U.S.A.* **115** E9
Blâmont *France* **19** D13

Blanc, C. *Spain* **48** B9
Blanc, Mont *Europe* **21** C10
Blanca, B. *Argentina* **128** D4
Blanca, Cord. *Peru* **124** C2
Blanca Peak *U.S.A.* **109** H11
Blanche, C. *Australia* **95** E1
Blanche, L. *S. Austral.,
    Australia* **95** D2
Blanche, L. *W. Austral.,
    Australia* **92** D3
Blanchisseuse *Trin. & Tob.* **125** K15
Blanco *S. Africa* **88** E3
Blanco *U.S.A.* **116** F5
Blanco → *Argentina* **126** C2
Blanco, C. *Costa Rica* **120** E2
Blanco, C. *U.S.A.* **108** E1
Blanda → *Iceland* **8** D3
Blandford Forum *U.K.* **15** G5
Blanding *U.S.A.* **109** H9
Blanes *Spain* **38** D7
Blangy-sur-Bresle *France* **19** C8
Blanice *Czech Rep.* **26** B6
Blankaholm *Sweden* **11** G10
Blankenberge *Belgium* **17** C3
Blankenburg *Germany* **24** D6
Blanquefort *France* **20** D3
Blanquilla *Venezuela* **121** D7
Blanquillo *Uruguay* **127** C4
Blansko *Czech Rep.* **27** B9
Blantyre *Malawi* **87** F4
Blarney *Ireland* **12** E3
Blasdell *U.S.A.* **114** D6
Błaszki *Poland* **31** G5
Blatná *Czech Rep.* **26** B6
Blato *Croatia* **41** F13
Blaubeuren *Germany* **25** G5
Blaustein *Germany* **25** G5
Blåvands Huk *Denmark* **11** J2
Blaydon *U.K.* **14** C6
Blaye *France* **20** C3
Blaye-les-Mines *France* **20** D6
Blayney *Australia* **95** E4
Blaze, Pt. *Australia* **92** B5
Błażowa *Poland* **31** J9
Bleckede *Germany* **24** B6
Bled *Slovenia* **41** B11
Bleiburg *Austria* **26** E7
Blejeşti *Romania* **29** F10
Blekinge *Sweden* **9** H16
Blekinge län □ *Sweden* **11** H9
Blenheim *Canada* **114** D3
Blenheim *N.Z.* **91** D4
Bléone → *France* **21** D10
Blérancourt *France* **19** C10
Bletchley *U.K.* **15** F7
Blida *Algeria* **78** A6
Blidö *Sweden* **10** E12
Blidsberg *Sweden* **11** G7
Blieskastel *Germany* **25** F3
Bligh Sound *N.Z.* **91** F1
Bligh Water *Fiji* **91** a
Blind River *Canada* **104** C3
Blinisht *Albania* **44** E3
Bliss *Idaho, U.S.A.* **108** E6
Bliss *N.Y., U.S.A.* **114** D6
Blissfield *U.S.A.* **114** F3
Blitar *Indonesia* **63** H15
Blitta *Togo* **83** D5
Block I. *U.S.A.* **115** E13
Block Island Sd. *U.S.A.* **115** E13
Bloemfontein *S. Africa* **88** D4
Bloemhof *S. Africa* **88** D4
Blois *France* **18** E8
Blomskog *Sweden* **10** E6
Blomstermåla *Sweden* **11** H10
Blönduós *Iceland* **8** D3
Blongas *Indonesia* **63** K19
Blonie *Poland* **31** F7
Bloodvein → *Canada* **103** C9
Bloody Foreland *Ireland* **12** A3
Bloomer *U.S.A.* **112** C8
Bloomfield *Canada* **114** C7
Bloomfield *Iowa, U.S.A.* **112** E7
Bloomfield *N. Mex., U.S.A.* **109** H10
Bloomfield *Nebr., U.S.A.* **112** D5
Bloomington *Ill., U.S.A.* **112** E9
Bloomington *Ind., U.S.A.* **112** F10
Bloomington *Minn., U.S.A.* **112** C7
Bloomsburg *U.S.A.* **115** F8
Bloomsbury *Australia* **94** J6
Blora *Indonesia* **63** G14
Blossburg *U.S.A.* **114** E7
Blouberg *S. Africa* **89** C4
Blountstown *U.S.A.* **117** F12
Bludenz *Austria* **26** D2
Blue Earth *U.S.A.* **112** D6
Blue Hole △ *Belize* **120** C2
Blue Lagoon △ *Zambia* **87** F2
Blue Mesa Res. *U.S.A.* **108** G10
Blue Mountain Lake *U.S.A.*
    115 C10
Blue Mountain Pk. *Jamaica* **120** a
Blue Mt. *U.S.A.* **115** F8
Blue Mts. *Jamaica* **120** a
Blue Mts. *Maine, U.S.A.* **115** B14
Blue Mts. *Oreg., U.S.A.* **108** D4
Blue Mud B. *Australia* **94** A2
Blue Nile = Nîl el Azraq →
    Sudan **81** D3

Blue Nile Falls *Ethiopia* **81** E4
Blue Rapids *U.S.A.* **112** F5
Blue Ridge *U.S.A.* **113** G13
Blue River *Canada* **102** C5
Bluefield *U.S.A.* **113** G13
Bluefields *Nic.* **120** D3
Bluevale *Canada* **114** C3
Bluff *Australia* **94** C4
Bluff *N.Z.* **91** G2
Bluff *U.S.A.* **109** H9
Bluff Knoll *Australia* **93** F2
Bluffton *U.S.A.* **113** E11
Blumenau *Brazil* **127** B6
Blunt *U.S.A.* **112** C4
Bly *U.S.A.* **108** E3
Blyde River Canyon △
    S. Africa **89** C5
Blyth *Canada* **114** C3
Blyth *U.K.* **14** B6
Blythe *U.S.A.* **111** M12
Blytheville *U.S.A.* **117** D10
Bo *S. Leone* **82** D2
Bo Duc *Vietnam* **65** G6
Bo Hai *China* **57** E10
Bo Xian = Bozhou *China* **56** H8
Boa Vista *Brazil* **124** C6
Boa Vista *C. Verde Is.* **78** b
Boac *Phil.* **61** E5
Boaco *Nic.* **120** D2
Bo'ai *China* **56** G7
Boal *Spain* **36** B4
Boalsburg *U.S.A.* **114** F7
Boane *Mozam.* **89** D5
Boardman *U.S.A.* **114** E4
Bobadah *Australia* **95** E4
Bobai *China* **58** F7
Bobbili *India* **67** K13
Bóbbio *Italy* **40** D6
Bobcaygeon *Canada* **114** B6
Böblingen *Germany* **25** G5
Bobo-Dioulasso *Burkina Faso* **82** C4
Bobolice *Poland* **30** E3
Boboshevo *Bulgaria* **44** D7
Bobov Dol *Bulgaria* **44** D6
Bóbr → *Poland* **31** F2
Bobraomby, Tanjon' i
    Madag. **89** A8
Bobrinets *Ukraine* **33** H7
Bobrov *Russia* **34** E5
Bobrovitsa *Ukraine* **33** G6
Bobruysk = Babruysk
    Belarus **23** B15
Boby, Pic *Madag.* **85** J9
Boca del Río *Mexico* **119** D5
Boca do Acre *Brazil* **124** E5
Boca Raton *U.S.A.* **117** H14
Bocanda *Ivory C.* **82** D4
Bocas del Dragón *Venezuela*
    125 K15
Bocas del Toro *Panama* **120** E3
Boceguillas *Spain* **36** D7
Bochnianivka *Ukraine* **29** C14
Bochnia *Poland* **31** J7
Bocholt *Germany* **24** D2
Bochum *Germany* **24** D3
Bockenem *Germany* **24** C6
Boćki *Poland* **31** F10
Bocognano *France* **21** F13
Bocoyna *Mexico* **118** B3
Bocşa *Romania* **28** E6
Boda *Dalarna, Sweden* **10** C9
Böda *Kalmar, Sweden* **11** G11
Boda *Västernorrland, Sweden* **10** B10
Bodafors *Sweden* **11** G8
Bodaybo *Russia* **53** D12
Boddam *U.K.* **13** B7
Boddington *Australia* **93** F2
Bode Sadu *Nigeria* **83** D5
Boden *Sweden* **8** D19
Bodensee *Europe* **25** H5
Bodenteich *Germany* **24** C6
Bodhan *India* **66** K10
Bodinga *Nigeria* **83** C6
Bodmin *U.K.* **15** G3
Bodmin Moor *U.K.* **15** G3
Bodø *Norway* **8** C16
Bodrog → *Hungary* **28** B6
Bodrum *Turkey* **47** D9
Bódva → *Hungary* **28** B5
Boën *France* **21** C8
Boende *Dem. Rep. of the Congo* **84** E4
Boerne *U.S.A.* **116** E7
Boesmans → *S. Africa* **88** E4
Boffa *Guinea* **82** C2
Bogalusa *U.S.A.* **117** F10
Bogan → *Australia* **95** D4
Bogan Gate *Australia* **95** E4
Bogandé *Burkina Faso* **83** C4
Bogantungan *Australia* **94** C4
Bogata *U.S.A.* **116** E7
Bogatić *Serbia* **44** B3
Boğazkale *Turkey* **72** B6
Boğazlıyan *Turkey* **72** C6
Bogen *Sweden* **10** D6
Bogense *Denmark* **11** J4
Bogetići *Montenegro* **44** D2

Boggabilla *Australia* 95 D5
Boggabri *Australia* 95 E5
Boggeragh Mts. *Ireland* 12 D3
Boglan = Solhan *Turkey* 73 C9
Bognor Regis *U.K.* 15 G7
Bogo *Phil.* 61 F6
Bogodukhov =
Bohodukhiv *Ukraine* 33 G8
Bogol Manya *Ethiopia* 81 G5
Bogong, Mt. *Australia* 95 F4
Bogor *Indonesia* 63 G12
Bogoroditsk *Russia* 32 F10
Bogorodsk *Russia* 34 B6
Bogoso *Ghana* 82 D4
Bogotá *Colombia* 124 C4
Bogotol *Russia* 52 D9
Bogou *Togo* 83 C5
Bogra *Bangla.* 67 G16
Boguchany *Russia* 53 D10
Boguchar *Russia* 34 F5
Bogué *Mauritania* 82 B2
Boguslav *Ukraine* 33 H6
Boguszów-Gorce *Poland* 31 H3
Bohain-en-Vermandois
France 19 C10
Bohdan *Ukraine* 29 B9
Bohemian Forest =
Böhmerwald *Germany* 25 F9
Bohinjska Bistrica *Slovenia* 41 B11
Böhmerwald *Germany* 25 F9
Bohmte *Germany* 24 C4
Bohodukhiv *Ukraine* 33 G8
Bohol □ *Phil.* 61 G6
Bohol Sea *Phil.* 63 C6
Bohongou *Burkina Faso* 83 C5
Böhönye *Hungary* 28 D2
Bohorodchany *Ukraine* 29 B9
Bohorok *Indonesia* 65 L2
Bohuslän *Sweden* 11 F5
Boi *Nigeria* 83 D6
Boi, Pta. do *Brazil* 127 A6
Boiaçu *Brazil* 124 D6
Boileau, C. *Australia* 92 C3
Boing'o *Sudan* 81 F3
Boiro *Spain* 36 C2
Boise *U.S.A.* 108 E5
Boise City *U.S.A.* 116 C3
Boissevain *Canada* 103 D8
Bóite → *Italy* 41 B9
Boitzenburg *Germany* 24 B9
Boizenburg *Germany* 24 B6
Bojador, C. *W. Sahara* 78 C3
Bojana → *Albania* 44 E3
Bojano *Italy* 43 A7
Bojanowo *Poland* 31 G3
Bøjden *Denmark* 11 J4
Bojnürd *Iran* 71 B8
Bojonegoro *Indonesia* 63 G14
Boju *Nigeria* 83 D6
Boka *Serbia* 28 E5
Boka Kotorska *Montenegro* 44 D2
Bokala *Ivory C.* 82 D4
Bokani *Nigeria* 83 D6
Bokaro *India* 69 H11
Boké *Guinea* 82 C2
Bokhara → *Australia* 95 D4
Bokkos *Nigeria* 83 D6
Boknafjorden *Norway* 9 G11
Bokor △ *Cambodia* 65 G5
Bokora △ *Uganda* 86 B3
Bokoro *Chad* 79 F9
Bokpyin *Burma* 65 G2
Boksitogorsk *Russia* 32 C7
Bokungu
Dem. Rep. of the Congo 84 E4
Bol *Croatia* 41 E13
Bolama *Guinea-Biss.* 82 C1
Bolan → *Pakistan* 68 E2
Bolan Pass *Pakistan* 66 E5
Bolaños → *Mexico* 118 C4
Bolaños de Calatrava *Spain* 37 G7
Bolayir *Turkey* 45 F10
Bolbec *France* 18 C7
Boldājī *Iran* 71 D6
Boldești-Scăeni *Romania* 29 E11
Bole *China* 60 B3
Bole *Ethiopia* 81 F4
Bole *Ghana* 82 D4
Bolekhiv *Ukraine* 23 D12
Bolesławiec *Poland* 31 G2
Bolgatanga *Ghana* 83 C4
Bolgrad = Bolhrad *Ukraine* 29 E13
Bolhrad *Ukraine* 29 E13
Bolinao *Phil.* 61 C3
Bolintin-Vale *Romania* 29 F10
Bolivar *Mo., U.S.A.* 112 G7
Bolivar *N.Y., U.S.A.* 114 D6
Bolivar *Tenn., U.S.A.* 117 D10
Bolivia ■ *S. Amer.* 124 G6
Bolivian Plateau =
Altiplano *Bolivia* 124 G5
Boljevac *Serbia* 44 C5
Bolkhov *Russia* 32 F9
Bolków *Poland* 31 H3
Bollebygd *Sweden* 11 G6
Bollène *France* 21 D8
Bollnäs *Sweden* 10 C10
Bollon *Australia* 95 D4

Bollstabruk *Sweden* 10 B11
Bolmen *Sweden* 11 H7
Bolnisi *Georgia* 35 K7
Bolnisi *Georgia* 73 B11
Bolobo *Dem. Rep. of the Congo* 84 E3
Bologna *Italy* 41 D8
Bologna ✈ (BLQ) *Italy* 41 D8
Bologoye *Russia* 32 D8
Bolomba
Dem. Rep. of the Congo 84 D3
Bolon, Ozero *Russia* 60 B8
Bolonchén *Mexico* 119 D7
Bolótana *Italy* 42 B1
Boloven, Cao Nguyen *Laos* 64 E6
Bolpur *India* 69 H12
Bolsena *Italy* 41 F8
Bolsena, L. di *Italy* 41 F8
Bolshakovo *Russia* 30 D8
Bolshaya Chernigovka
Russia 34 D10
Bolshaya Glushitsa *Russia* 34 D10
Bolshaya Martynovka
Russia 35 G5
Bolshaya Vradiyevka
Ukraine 33 J6
Bolshevik, Ostrov *Russia* 53 B11
Bolshoy Anyuy → *Russia* 53 C17
Bolshoy Begichev, Ostrov
Russia 53 B12
Bolshoy Kamen *Russia* 54 C6
Bolshoy Kavkas =
Caucasus Mountains
Eurasia 35 J7
Bolshoy Lyakhovskiy,
Ostrov *Russia* 53 B15
Bolshoy Tyuters, Ostrov
Russia 32 C4
Bolsward *Neths.* 17 A5
Bolt Head *U.K.* 15 G4
Boltaña *Spain* 38 C5
Boltigen *Switz.* 25 J3
Bolton *Canada* 114 C5
Bolton *U.K.* 14 D5
Bolton Landing *U.S.A.* 115 C11
Bolu *Turkey* 72 B4
Bolu □ *Turkey* 72 B4
Bolungavík *Iceland* 8 C2
Boluo *China* 59 F10
Bolvadin *Turkey* 72 C4
Bolzano *Italy* 41 B8
Bom Jesus da Lapa *Brazil* 125 F10
Boma *Dem. Rep. of the Congo* 84 F2
Bombala *Australia* 95 F4
Bombarral *Portugal* 37 F1
Bombay = Mumbai *India* 66 K8
Bombay *U.S.A.* 115 B10
Bombedor, Pta. *Venezuela* 125 L15
Bomboma
Dem. Rep. of the Congo 84 D3
Bombombwa
Dem. Rep. of the Congo 86 B2
Bomi Hills *Liberia* 82 D2
Bomili *Dem. Rep. of the Congo* 86 B2
Bomlo *Norway* 9 G11
Bomokandi →
Dem. Rep. of the Congo 86 B2
Bomu → *C.A.R.* 84 D4
Bon, C. = Ra's at Tib *Tunisia* 76 C5
Bon Acceuil *Mauritius* 85 d
Bon Echo △ *Canada* 114 B7
Bon Sar Pa *Vietnam* 64 F6
Bonāb *Āzarbājān-e Sharqī,
Iran* 73 D12
Bonāb *Zanjān, Iran* 73 D13
Bonaigarh *India* 69 J11
Bonaire *Neth. Ant.* 121 D6
Bonampak *Mexico* 119 D6
Bonang *Australia* 95 F4
Bonanza *Nic.* 120 D3
Bonaparte Arch. *Australia* 92 B3
Boñar *Spain* 36 C5
Bonar Bridge *U.K.* 13 D4
Bonasse *Trin. & Tob.* 125 K15
Bonaventure *Canada* 105 C6
Bonavista *Canada* 105 C9
Bonavista, C. *Canada* 105 C7
Bonavista B. *Canada* 105 C9
Bondeno *Italy* 41 D8
Bondo *Dem. Rep. of the Congo* 86 B1
Bondoukou *Ivory C.* 82 D4
Bondowoso *Indonesia* 63 G15
Bonerate *Indonesia* 63 F6
Bonerate, Kepulauan
Indonesia 63 F6
Bo'ness *U.K.* 13 E5
Bonete, Cerro *Argentina* 126 B2
Bong Son = Hoai Nhon
Vietnam 64 E7
Bonga *Ethiopia* 81 F4
Bongabong *Phil.* 61 E4
Bongananga
Dem. Rep. of the Congo 84 D4
Bongor *Chad* 79 F9
Bongos, Massif des *C.A.R.* 84 C4
Bongouanou *Ivory C.* 82 D4
Bonham *U.S.A.* 116 E6
Boni *Mali* 82 B4

Boni △ *Kenya* 86 C5
Bonifacio *France* 21 G13
Bonifacio, Bouches de
Medit. S. 42 A2
Bonin Is. = Ogasawara
Gunto *Pac. Oc.* 51 F16
Bonke *Ethiopia* 81 F4
Bonkoukou *Niger* 83 C5
Bonn *Germany* 24 E3
Bonnat *France* 19 F8
Bonne Terre *U.S.A.* 112 G8
Bonners Ferry *U.S.A.* 108 B5
Bonnétable *France* 18 D7
Bonneval *France* 21 C11
Bonneval-sur-Arc *France* 18 D8
Bonneville *France* 19 F13
Bonney, L. *Australia* 95 F3
Bonnie Rock *Australia* 93 F2
Bonny *Nigeria* 83 E6
Bonny → *Nigeria* 83 E6
Bonny, Bight of *Africa* 83 E6
Bonny-sur-Loire *France* 19 E9
Bonnyrigg *U.K.* 13 F5
Bonnyville *Canada* 103 C6
Bono *Italy* 42 B2
Bonoi *Indonesia* 63 E9
Bonorva *Italy* 42 B1
Bonsall *U.S.A.* 111 M9
Bontang *Indonesia* 62 D5
Bontebok △ *S. Africa* 88 E3
Bonthe *S. Leone* 82 D2
Bontoc *Phil.* 61 C4
Bonyeri *Ghana* 82 D4
Bonyhád *Hungary* 28 D3
Bonython Ra. *Australia* 92 D4
Boodjamulla △ *Australia* 94 B2
Bookabie *Australia* 93 F5
Booker *U.S.A.* 116 C4
Boola *Guinea* 82 D3
Booligal *Australia* 95 E3
Boonah *Australia* 95 D5
Boone *Iowa, U.S.A.* 112 D7
Boone *N.C., U.S.A.* 117 C14
Booneville *Ark., U.S.A.* 116 D8
Booneville *Miss., U.S.A.* 117 D10
Boonville *Calif., U.S.A.* 110 F3
Boonville *Ind., U.S.A.* 112 F10
Boonville *Mo., U.S.A.* 112 F8
Boonville *N.Y., U.S.A.* 115 C9
Boorabbin △ *Australia* 93 F3
Boorindal *Australia* 95 E4
Boorowa *Australia* 95 E4
Boosaaso *Somali Rep.* 75 E4
Boothia, Gulf of *Canada* 101 B11
Boothia Pen. *Canada* 100 B10
Bootle *U.K.* 14 D4
Boou é *Gabon* 84 E2
Boppard *Germany* 25 E3
Boquilla, Presa de la *Mexico* 118 B3
Boquillas del Carmen
Mexico 118 B4
Bor *Czech Rep.* 26 B5
Bor *Russia* 34 B7
Bor *Serbia* 44 B6
Bôr *Sudan* 81 F3
Bor *Sweden* 11 G8
Bor *Turkey* 72 D6
Bor Mashash *Israel* 74 D3
Bora Bora *French Polynesia* 97 J12
Borah Peak *U.S.A.* 108 D7
Borang *Sudan* 81 G3
Borås *Sweden* 11 G6
Borāzjān *Iran* 71 D6
Borba *Brazil* 124 D7
Borba *Portugal* 37 G3
Borborema, Planalto da
Brazil 122 D7
Borcea *Romania* 29 F12
Borçka *Turkey* 73 B9
Bord Khûn-e Now *Iran* 71 D6
Borda, C. *Australia* 95 F2
Bordeaux *France* 20 D3
Bordeaux ✈ (BOD) *France* 20 D3
Borden *Australia* 93 F2
Borden-Carleton *Canada* 105 C7
Borden I. *Canada* 101 B8
Borden Pen. *Canada* 101 B11
Border Ranges △ *Australia* 95 D5
Borders = Scottish
Borders □ *U.K.* 13 F6
Bordertown *Australia* 95 F3
Borðeyri *Iceland* 8 D3
Bordighera *Italy* 40 E4
Bordj Fly Ste. Marie *Algeria* 78 C5
Bordj-in-Eker *Algeria* 78 D6
Bordj Moktar *Algeria* 78 D6
Bordj Omar Driss *Algeria* 78 C7
Bore *Ethiopia* 81 G4
Borehamwood *U.K.* 15 F7
Borek Wielkopolski *Poland* 31 G4
Borensberg *Sweden* 11 F9
Borgå = Porvoo *Finland* 32 B3
Borgarfjörður *Iceland* 8 D7
Borgarnes *Iceland* 8 D3
Børgefjellet *Norway* 8 D15
Borger *Neths.* 17 B6
Borger *U.S.A.* 116 D4
Borgholm *Sweden* 11 H10

Bórgia *Italy* 43 D9
Borgo San Dalmazzo *Italy* 40 D4
Borgo San Lorenzo *Italy* 41 E8
Borgo Val di Taro *Italy* 40 D6
Borgo Valsugana *Italy* 41 B8
Borgomanero *Italy* 40 C5
Borgorose *Italy* 41 F10
Borgosésia *Italy* 40 C5
Borhoyn Tal *Mongolia* 56 C6
Bori *Nigeria* 83 E6
Borikhane *Laos* 64 C4
Borisoglebsk *Russia* 34 E6
Borisov = Barysaw *Belarus* 23 A15
Borisovka *Russia* 33 G9
Borja *Peru* 124 D3
Borja *Spain* 38 D3
Borjas Blancas = Les
Borges Blanques *Spain* 38 D5
Borjomi *Georgia* 35 K6
Borkou *Chad* 79 E9
Borkum *Germany* 24 B2
Borlänge *Sweden* 10 D9
Borley, C. *Antarctica* 5 C5
Borlu *Turkey* 47 C10
Bormida → *Italy* 40 D5
Bórmio *Italy* 40 B7
Borna *Germany* 24 D8
Borne Sulinowo *Poland* 30 E3
Borneo *E. Indies* 62 D5
Bornholm *Denmark* 11 J8
Bornholmsgattet *Europe* 11 J8
Bornos *Spain* 37 J5
Bornova *Turkey* 47 C9
Bornu Yassa *Nigeria* 83 C7
Boro → *Sudan* 81 F2
Borodino *Russia* 32 E8
Borodino *Ukraine* 29 D14
Borogontsy *Russia* 53 C14
Boromo *Burkina Faso* 82 C4
Boron *U.S.A.* 111 L9
Borongan *Phil.* 61 F6
Borotangba Mts. *C.A.R.* 81 F2
Borotou *Ivory C.* 82 D3
Borovan *Bulgaria* 44 C7
Borovichi *Russia* 32 C7
Borovsk *Russia* 32 E9
Borrby *Sweden* 11 J8
Borrego Springs *U.S.A.* 111 M10
Borriol *Spain* 38 E4
Borrisokane *Ireland* 12 D3
Borroloola *Australia* 94 B2
Borşa *Cluj, Romania* 29 D8
Borşa *Maramureş, Romania* 29 C9
Borsad *India* 68 H5
Borsec *Romania* 29 D10
Borshchiv *Ukraine* 29 B11
Borsod-Abaúj-Zemplén □
Hungary 28 B6
Bort-les-Orgues *France* 20 C6
Borth *U.K.* 15 E3
Börtnan *Sweden* 10 B7
Borüjerd *Iran* 73 F13
Boryeong *S. Korea* 57 F14
Borynya *Ukraine* 31 J10
Boryslav *Ukraine* 31 J10
Boryspil *Ukraine* 33 G6
Borzhomi = Borjomi *Georgia* 35 K6
Borzna *Ukraine* 33 G7
Borzya *Russia* 53 D12
Bosa *Italy* 42 B1
Bosanska Dubica *Bos.-H.* 41 C13
Bosanska Gradiška *Bos.-H.* 28 E2
Bosanska Kostajnica
Bos.-H. 41 C13
Bosanska Krupa *Bos.-H.* 41 D13
Bosanski Brod *Bos.-H.* 28 E2
Bosanski Novi *Bos.-H.* 41 C13
Bosanski Petrovac *Bos.-H.* 41 D13
Bosanski Šamac *Bos.-H.* 28 E3
Bosansko Grahovo *Bos.-H.* 41 D13
Boscastle *U.K.* 15 G3
Boscobelle *Barbados* 121 g
Bose *China* 58 F6
Boseong *S. Korea* 57 G14
Boshan *China* 57 F9
Boshof *S. Africa* 88 D4
Boshrūyeh *Iran* 71 C8
Bosilegrad *Serbia* 44 D6
Bosna → *Bos.-H.* 28 E3
Bosna i Hercegovina =
Bosnia-Herzegovina ■
Europe 28 G2
Bosnia-Herzegovina ■
Europe 28 G2
Bosnik *Indonesia* 63 E9
Bosobolo
Dem. Rep. of the Congo 84 D3
Bosporus = İstanbul
Boğazı *Turkey* 45 E13
Bosque Farms *U.S.A.* 109 J10
Bossangoa *C.A.R.* 84 C3
Bossé Bangou *Niger* 83 C5
Bossier City *U.S.A.* 116 E8
Bosso *Niger* 83 C7
Bosso, Dallol → *Niger* 83 C5

Bostan *Pakistan* 68 D2
Bostānābād *Iran* 73 D12
Bosten Hu *China* 60 B3
Boston *U.K.* 14 E7
Boston *U.S.A.* 115 D13
Boston Bar *Canada* 102 D4
Boston Mts. *U.S.A.* 116 D8
Bosumtwi, L. *Ghana* 83 D4
Bosut → *Croatia* 28 E3
Boswell *Canada* 102 D5
Boswell *U.S.A.* 114 F5
Botad *India* 68 H4
Botan → *Turkey* 73 D10
Botany B. *Australia* 90 E8
Botene *Laos* 64 D3
Botev *Bulgaria* 45 D8
Botevgrad *Bulgaria* 44 D7
Bothaville *S. Africa* 88 D4
Bothnia, G. of *Europe* 8 F19
Bothwell *Australia* 95 G4
Bothwell *Canada* 114 D3
Boticas *Portugal* 36 D3
Botletle → *Botswana* 88 C3
Botlikh *Russia* 35 J8
Botna → *Moldova* 29 D14
Botoroaga *Romania* 29 F10
Botoşani *Romania* 29 C11
Botoşani □ *Romania* 29 C11
Botou *Burkina Faso* 83 C5
Botricello *Italy* 43 D9
Botro *Ivory C.* 82 D3
Botshabelo *S. Africa* 88 D4
Botswana ■ *Africa* 88 C3
Bottineau *U.S.A.* 112 A3
Bottnaryd *Sweden* 11 G7
Bottrop *Germany* 17 C6
Botucatu *Brazil* 127 A6
Botum Sakor △ *Cambodia* 65 G4
Botwood *Canada* 105 C8
Bou Djébéha *Mali* 82 B4
Boû Rjeïmât *Mauritania* 82 B1
Bou Saâda *Algeria* 78 A6
Bouaflé *Ivory C.* 82 D3
Bouaké *Ivory C.* 82 D3
Bouar *C.A.R.* 84 C3
Bouârfa *Morocco* 78 B5
Boucaut B. *Australia* 94 A1
Bouches-du-Rhône □ *France* 21 E9
Boucle de Baoulé △ *Mali* 82 C3
Boucles de la Seine
Normande △ *France* 18 C7
Bouctouche *Canada* 105 C7
Bougainville, C. *Australia* 92 B4
Bougainville I. *Papua N. G.* 90 B8
Bougainville Reef *Australia* 94 B4
Bougie = Bejaïa *Algeria* 78 A7
Bougouni *Mali* 82 C3
Bouillon *Belgium* 17 E5
Boukombé *Benin* 83 C5
Boulal *Mali* 82 B3
Boulazac *France* 20 C4
Boulder *Colo., U.S.A.* 108 F11
Boulder *Mont., U.S.A.* 108 C7
Boulder City *U.S.A.* 111 K12
Boulder Creek *U.S.A.* 110 H4
Boulder Dam = Hoover
Dam *U.S.A.* 111 K12
Bouli *Mauritania* 82 B2
Boulia *Australia* 94 C2
Bouligny *France* 19 C12
Boulogne → *France* 18 E5
Boulogne-sur-Gesse *France* 20 E4
Boulogne-sur-Mer *France* 19 B8
Bouloire *France* 18 E7
Boulouli *Mali* 82 B3
Boulsa *Burkina Faso* 83 C4
Boultoum *Niger* 83 C7
Bouma △ *Fiji* 91 a
Boûmdeïd *Mauritania* 82 B2
Boun Neua *Laos* 64 B3
Boun Tai *Laos* 64 B3
Bouna *Ivory C.* 82 D4
Boundary Peak *U.S.A.* 110 H8
Boundiali *Ivory C.* 82 D3
Bountiful *U.S.A.* 108 F8
Bounty Is. *Pac. Oc.* 96 M9
Bounty Trough *Pac. Oc.* 96 M9
Boura *Mali* 82 C4
Bourbon-Lancy *France* 19 F10
Bourbon-l'Archambault
France 19 F10
Bourbonnais *France* 19 F10
Bourbonne-les-Bains
France 19 E12
Bourbourg *France* 19 B9
Bourdel L. *Canada* 104 A5
Bourem *Mali* 83 B4
Bourg *France* 20 C3
Bourg-Argental *France* 21 C8
Bourg-de-Péage *France* 21 C9
Bourg-en-Bresse *France* 19 F12
Bourg-Lastic *France* 20 C6
Bourg-Madame *France* 20 F5
Bourg-St-Andéol *France* 21 D8
Bourg-St-Maurice *France* 21 C10
Bourganeuf *France* 20 C5
Bourgas = Burgas *Bulgaria* 45 D11
Bourges *France* 19 E9

Bourget *Canada* 115 A9
Bourget, Lac du *France* 21 C9
Bourgneuf, B. de *France* 18 E4
Bourgneuf-en-Retz *France* 18 E5
Bourgogne □ *France* 19 F11
Bourgoin-Jallieu *France* 21 C9
Bourgueil *France* 18 E7
Bourke *Australia* 95 E4
Bourne *U.K.* 14 E7
Bournemouth *U.K.* 15 G6
Bournemouth □ *U.K.* 15 G6
Bouroum *Burkina Faso* 83 C4
Bouse *U.S.A.* 111 M13
Boussac *France* 19 F9
Boussé *Burkina Faso* 83 C4
Bousso *Chad* 79 F9
Boussouma *Burkina Faso* 83 C4
Boutilimit *Mauritania* 82 B2
Boutonne → *France* 20 C3
Bouvet I. = Bouvetøya
Antarctica 2 G10
Bouvetøya *Antarctica* 2 G10
Bouxwiller *France* 19 D14
Bouza *Niger* 83 C6
Bouzonville *France* 19 C13
Bova Marina *Italy* 43 E8
Bovalino Marina *Italy* 43 D9
Bovec *Slovenia* 41 B10
Bovill *U.S.A.* 108 C5
Bovino *Italy* 43 A8
Bovril *Argentina* 126 C4
Bow → *Canada* 102 C6
Bow Island *Canada* 108 B8
Bowbells *U.S.A.* 112 A2
Bowdle *U.S.A.* 112 C4
Bowelling *Australia* 93 F2
Bowen *Argentina* 126 D2
Bowen *Australia* 94 J6
Bowen Mts. *Australia* 95 F4
Bowers Basin *Pac. Oc.* 4 D16
Bowers Ridge *Pac. Oc.* 4 D17
Bowie *Ariz., U.S.A.* 109 K9
Bowie *Tex., U.S.A.* 116 E6
Bowkān *Iran* 73 D12
Bowland, Forest of *U.K.* 14 D5
Bowling Green *Ky., U.S.A.* 112 G10
Bowling Green *Ohio, U.S.A.*
113 E12
Bowling Green, C. *Australia* 94 B4
Bowling Green Bay △
Australia 94 B4
Bowman *U.S.A.* 112 B2
Bowman I. *Antarctica* 5 C8
Bowmanville = Clarington
Canada 114 C6
Bowmore *U.K.* 13 F2
Bowral *Australia* 95 E5
Bowraville *Australia* 95 E5
Bowron → *Canada* 102 C4
Bowron Lake △ *Canada* 102 C4
Bowser L. *Canada* 102 B3
Bowsman *Canada* 103 C8
Bowwood *Zambia* 87 F2
Box Cr. → *Australia* 95 E3
Boxholm *Sweden* 11 F9
Boxmeer *Neths.* 17 C5
Boxtel *Neths.* 17 C5
Boyabat *Turkey* 72 B6
Boyalıca *Turkey* 45 F13
Boyang *China* 59 C11
Boyany *Ukraine* 29 B11
Boyce *U.S.A.* 116 F8
Boyd L. *Canada* 104 B4
Boyle *Canada* 102 C6
Boyle *Ireland* 12 C3
Boyne → *Ireland* 12 C5
Boyne City *U.S.A.* 113 C11
Boynitsa *Bulgaria* 44 C6
Boynton Beach *U.S.A.* 117 H14
Boyolali *Indonesia* 63 G14
Boysen Res. *U.S.A.* 108 E9
Boyuibe *Bolivia* 124 G6
Boyup Brook *Australia* 93 F2
Boz Burun *Turkey* 45 F12
Boz Dağ *Turkey* 47 D11
Boz Dağları *Turkey* 47 C10
Bozburun *Turkey* 47 E10
Bozcaada *Turkey* 72 C2
Bozdoğan *Turkey* 47 D10
Bozeman *U.S.A.* 108 D8
Bozen = Bolzano *Italy* 41 B8
Boževac *Serbia* 44 B5
Bozhou *China* 56 H8
Bozkır *Turkey* 72 D5
Bozkurt *Turkey* 47 D11
Bozouls *France* 20 D6
Bozoum *C.A.R.* 84 C3
Bozova *Antalya, Turkey* 47 D12
Bozova *Sanliurfa, Turkey* 73 D8
Bozovici *Romania* 28 F7
Boztepe *Turkey* 70 B2
Bra *Italy* 40 D4
Braås *Sweden* 11 G9
Brabant □ *Belgium* 17 D4
Brabant L. *Canada* 103 B8

Brabrand *Denmark* **11** H4
Brač *Croatia* **41** E13
Bracadale, L. *U.K.* **13** D2
Bracciano *Italy* **41** F9
Bracciano, L. di *Italy* **41** F9
Bracebridge *Canada* **114** A5
Bracieux *France* **18** E8
Bräcke *Sweden* **10** B9
Brackettville *U.S.A.* **116** G4
Bracknell *U.K.* **15** F7
Bracknell Forest □ *U.K.* **15** F7
Brad *Romania* **28** D7
Brádano → *Italy* **43** B9
Bradenton *U.S.A.* **117** H13
Bradford *Canada* **114** B5
Bradford *U.K.* **14** D6
Bradford *Pa., U.S.A.* **114** E6
Bradford *Vt., U.S.A.* **115** C12
Bradley *Ark., U.S.A.* **116** E8
Bradley *Calif., U.S.A.* **110** K6
Bradley Institute *Zimbabwe* **87** F3
Brady *U.S.A.* **116** F5
Brædstrup *Denmark* **11** J3
Braeside *Canada* **115** A8
Braga *Portugal* **36** D2
Braga □ *Portugal* **36** D2
Bragadiru *Romania* **29** G10
Bragado *Argentina* **126** D3
Bragança *Brazil* **125** D9
Bragança *Portugal* **36** D4
Bragança □ *Portugal* **36** D4
Bragança Paulista *Brazil* **127** A6
Brahmanbaria *Bangla.* **67** H17
Brahmani → *India* **67** J15
Brahmapur *India* **67** K14
Brahmaputra → *Asia* **69** H13
Braich-y-pwll *U.K.* **14** E3
Braidwood *Australia* **95** F4
Brăila *Romania* **29** E12
Brăila □ *Romania* **29** E12
Brainerd *U.S.A.* **112** B6
Braintree *U.K.* **15** F8
Braintree *U.S.A.* **115** D14
Brak → *S. Africa* **88** D3
Brake *Germany* **24** B4
Brakel *Germany* **24** D5
Brakna □ *Mauritania* **82** B2
Bräkne-Hoby *Sweden* **11** H9
Brakwater *Namibia* **88** C2
Brålanda *Sweden* **11** F6
Bramberg *Germany* **25** E6
Bramdrupdam *Denmark* **11** J3
Bramming *Denmark* **11** J2
Brämön *Sweden* **10** B11
Brampton *Canada* **114** C5
Brampton *U.K.* **14** C5
Bramsche *Germany* **24** C3
Bramton I. *Australia* **94** J7
Branco → *Brazil* **124** D6
Brandberg *Namibia* **88** C1
Brandberg △ *Namibia* **88** C1
Brande *Denmark* **11** J3
Brandenburg =
    Neubrandenburg
    Germany **24** B9
Brandenburg *Germany* **24** C8
Brandenburg □ *Germany* **24** C9
Brandfort *S. Africa* **88** D4
Brando *France* **21** F13
Brandon *Canada* **103** D9
Brandon *U.S.A.* **115** C11
Brandon B. *Ireland* **12** D1
Brandon Mt. *Ireland* **12** D1
Brandsen *Argentina* **126** D4
Brandvlei *S. Africa* **88** E3
Brandýs nad Labem
    Czech Rep. **26** A7
Brăneşti *Romania* **29** F11
Branford *U.S.A.* **115** E12
Braniewo *Poland* **30** D6
Bransfield Str. *Antarctica* **5** C18
Brańsk *Poland* **31** F9
Branson *U.S.A.* **112** G7
Brantford *Canada* **114** C4
Brantôme *France* **20** C4
Branzi *Italy* **40** B6
Bras d'Or L. *Canada* **105** C7
Brasher Falls *U.S.A.* **115** B10
Brasil = Brazil ■ *S. Amer.* **125** F9
Brasil, Planalto *Brazil* **122** E6
Brasiléia *Brazil* **124** F5
Brasília *Brazil* **125** G9
Brasília Legal *Brazil* **125** D7
Braslaw *Belarus* **32** E4
Braslovče *Slovenia* **41** B12
Braşov *Romania* **29** E10
Braşov □ *Romania* **29** E10
Brass *Nigeria* **83** E6
Brass → *Nigeria* **83** E6
Brassac-les-Mines *France* **20** C7
Brasschaat *Belgium* **17** C4
Brassey, Banjaran *Malaysia* **62** D5
Brassey Ra. *Australia* **93** E3
Brasstown Bald *U.S.A.* **117** D13
Brastad *Sweden* **11** F5
Brastavăţu *Romania* **29** G9

Bratan = Morozov *Bulgaria* **45** D9
Brateş *Romania* **29** E11
Bratislava *Slovak Rep.* **27** C10
Bratislava M.R. Stefanik ✈
    (BTS) *Slovak Rep.* **27** C10
Bratislavský □ *Slovak Rep.* **27** C10
Bratsigovo *Bulgaria* **45** D8
Bratsk *Russia* **53** D11
Brattleboro *U.S.A.* **115** D12
Bratunac *Bos.-H.* **28** F4
Braunau *Austria* **26** C6
Braunschweig *Germany* **24** C6
Braunton *U.K.* **15** F3
Brava *C. Verde Is.* **78** b
Bravicea *Moldova* **29** C13
Bråviken *Sweden* **11** F10
Bravo del Norte, Rio =
    Grande, Rio → *N. Amer.* **116** J6
Brawley *U.S.A.* **111** N11
Bray *Ireland* **12** C5
Bray, Mt. *Australia* **94** A1
Bray-sur-Seine *France* **19** D10
Brazeau → *Canada* **102** C5
Brazil *Italy* **112** F10
Brazil ■ *S. Amer.* **125** F9
Brazilian Highlands =
    Brasil, Planalto *Brazil* **122** E6
Brazo Sur → *S. Amer.* **126** B4
Brazos → *U.S.A.* **116** G7
Brazzaville *Congo* **84** E3
Brčko *Bos.-H.* **28** F3
Brda → *Poland* **31** E5
Brdy *Czech Rep.* **26** B6
Breaden, L. *Australia* **93** E4
Breaksea Sd. *N.Z.* **91** F1
Bream B. *N.Z.* **91** A5
Bream Hd. *N.Z.* **91** A5
Breas *Chile* **126** B1
Breaza *Romania* **29** E10
Brebes *Indonesia* **63** G13
Brechin *Canada* **114** B5
Brechin *U.K.* **13** E6
Brecht *Belgium* **17** C4
Břeclav *Czech Rep.* **27** C9
Brecon *U.K.* **15** F4
Brecon Beacons *U.K.* **15** F4
Brecon Beacons △ *U.K.* **15** F4
Breda *Neths.* **17** C4
Bredaryd *Sweden* **11** G7
Bredasdorp *S. Africa* **88** E3
Bredbo *Australia* **95** F4
Bredebro *Denmark* **11** J2
Bredstedt *Germany* **24** A4
Bree *Belgium* **17** C5
Bregalnica → *Macedonia* **44** E6
Bregenz *Austria* **26** D2
Bregovo *Bulgaria* **44** B6
Bréhal *France* **18** D5
Bréhat, Î. de *France* **18** D4
Breiðafjörður *Iceland* **8** D2
Breil-sur-Roya *France* **21** E11
Breisach *Germany* **25** G3
Brejo *Brazil* **125** D10
Bremen *Germany* **24** B4
Bremen □ *Germany* **24** B4
Bremer Bay *Australia* **93** F2
Bremer I. *Australia* **94** A2
Bremerhaven *Germany* **24** B4
Bremerton *U.S.A.* **110** C4
Bremervörde *Germany* **24** B5
Brenes *Spain* **37** H5
Brenham *U.S.A.* **116** F6
Brenne *France* **20** B5
Brenne △ *France* **20** B5
Brennerpass *Austria* **26** D4
Breno *Italy* **40** C7
Brent *U.S.A.* **117** E11
Brenta → *Italy* **41** C9
Brentwood *U.K.* **15** F8
Brentwood *Calif., U.S.A.* **110** H5
Brentwood *N.Y., U.S.A.* **115** F11
Bréscia *Italy* **40** C7
Breskens *Neths.* **17** C3
Breslau = Wrocław *Poland* **31** G4
Bresle → *France* **18** B8
Bressanone *Italy* **41** B8
Bressay *U.K.* **13** A7
Bresse *France* **19** F12
Bressuire *France* **18** F6
Brest *Belarus* **23** B12
Brest *France* **18** D2
Brest □ *Belarus* **33** F4
Brest-Litovsk = Brest
    Belarus **23** B12
Bretagne □ *France* **18** D3
Bretçu *Romania* **29** D11
Bretenoux *France* **20** D5
Breteuil, Eure, *France* **18** D7
Breteuil, Oise, *France* **19** C9
Breton *Canada* **102** C6
Breton, Pertuis *France* **20** B2
Breton Sd. *U.S.A.* **117** G10
Brett, C. *N.Z.* **91** A5
Bretten *Germany* **25** F4
Breuil-Cervínia *Italy* **40** C4

Brevard *U.S.A.* **117** D13
Breves *Brazil* **125** D8
Brewarrina *Australia* **95** E4
Brewer *U.S.A.* **113** C19
Brewer, Mt. *U.S.A.* **110** J8
Brewerville *Liberia* **82** D2
Brewster *N.Y., U.S.A.* **115** E11
Brewster *Ohio, U.S.A.* **114** F3
Brewster *Wash., U.S.A.* **108** B4
Brewster, Kap =
    Kangikajik *Greenland* **4** B6
Brewton *U.S.A.* **117** F11
Breyten *S. Africa* **89** D5
Breza *Bos.-H.* **28** F3
Brežice *Slovenia* **41** C12
Breznik *Bulgaria* **44** D7
Brezno *Slovak Rep.* **27** C12
Brezoi *Romania* **29** E9
Brezovica *Serbia* **44** D5
Brezovo *Bulgaria* **45** D9
Bria *C.A.R.* **84** C4
Briançon *France* **21** D10
Briare *France* **19** E9
Briático *Italy* **43** D9
Bribie I. *Australia* **95** D5
Bribri *Costa Rica* **120** E3
Bricenì *Moldova* **29** B12
Bricquebec *France* **18** C5
Bridgefield *Barbados* **121** g
Bridgehampton *U.S.A.* **115** F12
Bridgend *U.K.* **15** F4
Bridgend □ *U.K.* **15** F4
Bridgenorth *Canada* **114** B6
Bridgeport *Calif., U.S.A.* **110** G7
Bridgeport *Conn., U.S.A.* **115** E11
Bridgeport *N.Y., U.S.A.* **115** C9
Bridgeport *Nebr., U.S.A.* **112** E2
Bridgeport *Tex., U.S.A.* **116** E6
Bridger *U.S.A.* **108** D9
Bridgeton *U.S.A.* **113** F16
Bridgetown *Australia* **93** F2
Bridgetown *Barbados* **121** g
Bridgetown *Canada* **105** D6
Bridgewater *Australia* **95** G4
Bridgewater *Canada* **105** D7
Bridgewater *Mass., U.S.A.* **115** E14
Bridgewater *N.Y., U.S.A.* **115** D9
Bridgewater, C. *Australia* **95** F3
Bridgnorth *U.K.* **15** E5
Bridgton *U.S.A.* **115** B14
Bridgwater *U.K.* **15** F5
Bridgwater B. *U.K.* **15** F4
Bridlington *U.K.* **14** C7
Bridlington B. *U.K.* **14** C7
Bridport *Australia* **95** G4
Bridport *U.K.* **15** G5
Brie, C.A.R.
Brielle *Neths.* **17** C4
Brienne-le-Château *France* **19** D11
Brienon-sur-Armançon
    France **19** E10
Brienz *Switz.* **25** J4
Brienzersee *Switz.* **25** J3
Brière △ *France* **18** E4
Brig *Switz.* **25** J3
Brigg *U.K.* **14** D7
Brigham City *U.S.A.* **108** F7
Bright *Australia* **95** F4
Brighton *Australia* **95** F2
Brighton *Canada* **114** B7
Brighton *Trin. & Tob.* **125** K15
Brighton *U.K.* **15** G7
Brighton *U.S.A.* **114** C7
Brightside *U.S.A.* **115** A8
Brignogan-Plage *France* **18** D2
Brignoles *France* **21** E10
Brihuega *Spain* **38** E2
Brikama *Gambia* **82** C1
Brilliant *U.S.A.* **114** F4
Brilon *Germany* **24** D4
Bríndisi *Italy* **43** B10
Brinje *Croatia* **41** D12
Brinkley *U.S.A.* **116** D9
Brinnon *U.S.A.* **110** C4
Brion, Î. *Canada* **105** C7
Brionne *France* **18** C7
Brionski *Croatia* **41** D10
Brioude *France* **20** C7
Briouze *France* **18** D6
Brisay *Canada* **105** B5
Brisbane *Australia* **95** D5
Brisbane → *Australia* **95** D5
Brisighella *Italy* **41** D8
Bristol *U.K.* **15** F5
Bristol *Conn., U.S.A.* **115** E12
Bristol *Pa., U.S.A.* **115** F10
Bristol *R.I., U.S.A.* **115** E13
Bristol *Tenn., U.S.A.* **117** C13
Bristol *Vt., U.S.A.* **115** B11
Bristol, City of □ *U.K.* **15** F5
Bristol B. *U.S.A.* **106** a
Bristol Channel *U.K.* **15** F3
Bristol I. *Antarctica* **5** B1
Bristol L. *U.S.A.* **109** J6
Bristow *U.S.A.* **116** D6
Britain = Great Britain *Europe* **6** E5
British Columbia □ *Canada* **102** C3
British Indian Ocean Terr.
    = Chagos Arch. ☒ *Ind. Oc.* **50** J9

British Isles *Europe* **16** D5
British Virgin Is. ☒ *W. Indies* **121** e
Brits *S. Africa* **89** D4
Britstown *S. Africa* **88** E3
Britt *Canada* **104** C3
Brittany = Bretagne □
    France **18** D3
Britton *U.S.A.* **112** C5
Brive-la-Gaillarde *France* **20** C5
Briviesca *Spain* **36** C7
Brixen = Bressanone *Italy* **41** B8
Brixham *U.K.* **15** G4
Brnaze *Croatia* **41** E13
Brněnský □ *Czech Rep.* **27** B9
Brno *Czech Rep.* **27** B9
Broach = Bharuch *India* **66** J8
Broad → *U.S.A.* **117** D14
Broad Arrow *Australia* **93** F3
Broad B. *U.K.* **13** C2
Broad Haven *Ireland* **12** B2
Broad Law *U.K.* **13** F5
Broad Pk. = Faichan
    Kangri *India* **69** B7
Broad Sd. *Australia* **94** C4
Broadalbin *U.S.A.* **115** C10
Broadback → *Canada* **104** B4
Broadhurst Ra. *Australia* **93** D3
Broads, The *U.K.* **14** E9
Broadus *U.S.A.* **108** D11
Broager *Denmark* **11** K3
Broby *Sweden* **11** H8
Brocēni *Latvia* **30** B9
Brochet *Canada* **103** B8
Brochet, L. *Canada* **103** B8
Brock I. *Canada* **101** B8
Brocken *Germany* **24** D6
Brockport *U.S.A.* **114** C7
Brockton *U.S.A.* **115** D13
Brockville *Canada* **115** B9
Brockway *Mont., U.S.A.* **108** C11
Brockway *Pa., U.S.A.* **114** E6
Brocton *U.S.A.* **114** D5
Brod *Macedonia* **44** E5
Brodarevo *Serbia* **44** C3
Brodeur Pen. *Canada* **101** B11
Brodick *U.K.* **13** F3
Brodnica *Poland* **31** E6
Brody *Ukraine* **23** C13
Brogan *U.S.A.* **108** D5
Broglie *France* **18** C7
Brok *Poland* **31** F8
Broken Arrow *U.S.A.* **116** C7
Broken Bow *Nebr., U.S.A.* **112** E4
Broken Bow *Okla., U.S.A.* **116** D7
Broken Bow Lake *U.S.A.* **116** D7
Broken Hill *Australia* **95** E3
Broken Ridge *Ind. Oc.* **96** L1
Broken River Ra. *Australia* **94** K6
Brokind *Sweden* **11** F9
Bromley □ *U.K.* **15** F8
Bromo *Indonesia* **63** G15
Bromölla *Sweden* **11** H8
Bromsgrove *U.K.* **15** E5
Brønderslev *Denmark* **11** G3
Brong-Ahafo □ *Ghana* **82** D4
Broni *Italy* **40** C6
Brønnøysund *Norway* **8** D15
Bronte *Italy* **43** E7
Brook Park *U.S.A.* **114** E4
Brookhaven *U.S.A.* **117** F9
Brookings *Oreg., U.S.A.* **108** E1
Brookings *S. Dak., U.S.A.* **112** C5
Brooklin *Canada* **114** C6
Brooklyn Park *U.S.A.* **112** C7
Brooks *Canada* **102** C6
Brooks Range *U.S.A.* **106** a
Brooksville *U.S.A.* **117** G13
Brookton *Australia* **93** F2
Brookville *U.S.A.* **114** E6
Broom, L. *U.K.* **13** D3
Broome *Australia* **92** C3
Broons *France* **18** D4
Brora *U.K.* **13** C5
Brora → *U.K.* **13** C5
Brørup *Denmark* **11** J2
Brösarp *Sweden* **11** J8
Brosna → *Ireland* **12** C4
Broşteni *Mehedinţi, Romania* **28** F7
Broşteni *Suceava, Romania* **29** C10
Brothers *U.S.A.* **108** E3
Brou *France* **18** D8
Brouage *France* **20** C2
Brough *U.K.* **14** C5
Brough Hd. *U.K.* **13** B5
Broughton Island =
    Qikiqtarjuaq *Canada* **101** C13
Broumov *Czech Rep.* **27** A9
Brovary *Ukraine* **23** C16
Brovst *Denmark* **11** G3
Brown, L. *Australia* **93** F2
Brown, Pt. *Australia* **95** E1
Brown City *U.S.A.* **114** C2
Brown Willy *U.K.* **15** G3
Brownfield *U.S.A.* **116** E3
Browning *U.S.A.* **108** B7
Brownsville *Oreg., U.S.A.* **108** D2
Brownsville *Pa., U.S.A.* **114** F5
Brownsville *Tenn., U.S.A.* **117** D10

Brownsville *Tex., U.S.A.* **116** J6
Brownville *U.S.A.* **115** C9
Brownwood *U.S.A.* **116** F5
Browse I. *Australia* **92** B3
Bruas *Malaysia* **65** K3
Bruay-la-Buissière *France* **19** B9
Bruce, Mt. *Australia* **92** D2
Bruce Pen. *Canada* **114** B3
Bruce Peninsula △ *Canada* **114** A3
Bruce Rock *Australia* **93** F2
Bruche → *France* **19** D14
Bruchsal *Germany* **25** F4
Bruck an der Leitha *Austria* **27** C9
Bruck an der Mur *Austria* **26** D8
Brue → *U.K.* **15** F5
Bruges = Brugge *Belgium* **17** C3
Brugg *Switz.* **25** H4
Brugge *Belgium* **17** C3
Bruin *U.S.A.* **114** E5
Brûk, W. el → *Egypt* **74** E2
Brûlé *Canada* **102** C5
Brûlé, L. *Canada* **105** B7
Brûlon *France* **18** E6
Brumado *Brazil* **125** F10
Brumath *France* **19** D14
Brumunddal *Norway* **8** F14
Bruneau *U.S.A.* **108** E6
Bruneau → *U.S.A.* **108** E6
Bruneck = Brunico *Italy* **41** B8
Brunei = Bandar Seri
    Begawan *Brunei* **62** D5
Brunei ■ *Asia* **62** D5
Brunflo *Sweden* **10** A8
Brunico *Italy* **41** B8
Brunna *Sweden* **10** E11
Brunnen *Switz.* **25** J4
Brunner, L. *N.Z.* **91** E3
Brunsbüttel *Germany* **24** B5
Brunssum *Neths.* **17** D5
Brunswick =
    Braunschweig *Germany* **24** C6
Brunswick *Ga., U.S.A.* **117** F14
Brunswick *Maine, U.S.A.* **113** D19
Brunswick *Md., U.S.A.* **113** F15
Brunswick *Mo., U.S.A.* **112** F7
Brunswick *Ohio, U.S.A.* **114** E3
Brunswick, Pen. de *Chile* **128** G2
Brunswick B. *Australia* **92** C3
Brunswick Junction
    Australia **93** F2
Brunt Ice Shelf *Antarctica* **5** D2
Bruntál *Czech Rep.* **27** B10
Brus Laguna *Honduras* **120** C3
Brusartsi *Bulgaria* **44** C7
Brush *U.S.A.* **108** F12
Brushton *U.S.A.* **115** B10
Brusio *Switz.* **25** J6
Brusque *Brazil* **127** B6
Brussel *Belgium* **17** D4
Brussel ✈ (BRU) *Belgium* **17** D5
Brussels = Brussel *Belgium* **17** D4
Brussels *Canada* **114** C3
Brusy *Poland* **30** E4
Bruthen *Australia* **95** F4
Bruxelles = Brussel *Belgium* **17** D4
Bruyères *France* **19** D13
Bruz *France* **18** D5
Brwinów *Poland* **31** F7
Bryagovo *Bulgaria* **45** E9
Bryan *Ohio, U.S.A.* **113** E11
Bryan *Tex., U.S.A.* **116** F6
Bryan, Mt. *Australia* **95** E2
Bryanka *Ukraine* **33** H10
Bryansk *Bryansk, Russia* **33** F8
Bryansk *Dagestan, Russia* **35** H8
Bryansk □ *Russia* **33** F7
Bryanskoye = Bryansk
    Russia **35** H8
Bryce Canyon △ *U.S.A.* **109** H7
Bryne *Norway* **9** G11
Bryson City *U.S.A.* **117** D13
Bryukhovetskaya *Russia* **33** K10
Brza Palanka *Serbia* **44** B6
Brzeg *Poland* **31** H4
Brzeg Dolny *Poland* **31** G3
Brześć Kujawski *Poland* **31** F5
Brzesko *Poland* **31** J7
Brzeziny *Poland* **31** G6
Brzozów *Poland* **31** J9
Bsharri *Lebanon* **74** A5
Bū Baqarah *U.A.E.* **71** E8
Bu Craa *W. Sahara* **78** C3
Bū Ḩasā *U.A.E.* **71** F7
Bua *Fiji* **91** a
Bua *Sweden* **11** G6
Bua Yai *Thailand* **64** E4
Buan *S. Korea* **57** G14
Buapinang *Indonesia* **63** E6
Buba *Guinea-Biss.* **82** C2
Bubanza *Burundi* **86** C2
Bubaque *Guinea-Biss.* **82** C1
Bube *Ethiopia* **81** F4
Bubi → *Zimbabwe* **87** G3
Buca *Fiji* **91** a
Buca *Turkey* **47** C9
Bucak *Turkey* **47** D12
Bucaramanga *Colombia* **124** B4
Bucas Grande I. *Phil.* **61** G6

Bucasia *Australia* **94** K7
Buccaneer Arch. *Australia* **92** C3
Buccino *Italy* **43** B8
Buccoo Reef *Trin. & Tob.* **125** J16
Bucecea *Romania* **29** C11
Bucegi △ *Romania* **29** E10
Buchach *Ukraine* **23** D13
Buchan *U.K.* **13** D6
Buchan Ness *U.K.* **13** D7
Buchanan *Canada* **103** C8
Buchanan *Liberia* **82** D2
Buchanan, L. *Queens.,*
    Australia **94** C4
Buchanan, L. *W. Austral.,*
    Australia **93** E3
Buchanan, L. *U.S.A.* **116** F5
Buchanan Cr. → *Australia* **94** B2
Buchans *Canada* **105** C8
Bucharest = Bucureşti
    Romania **29** F11
Buchen *Germany* **25** F5
Bucheon *S. Korea* **57** F14
Buchholz *Germany* **24** B5
Buchloe *Germany* **25** G6
Buchon, Pt. *U.S.A.* **110** K6
Buciumi *Romania* **28** C8
Buck Hill Falls *U.S.A.* **115** E9
Bückeburg *Germany* **24** C5
Buckeye Lake *U.S.A.* **114** G2
Buckhannon *U.S.A.* **113** F13
Buckhaven *U.K.* **13** E5
Buckhorn L. *Canada* **114** B6
Buckie *U.K.* **13** D6
Buckingham *Canada* **104** C4
Buckingham *U.K.* **15** E7
Buckingham B. *Australia* **94** A2
Buckinghamshire □ *U.K.* **15** F7
Buckle Hd. *Australia* **92** B4
Buckleboo *Australia* **95** E2
Buckley *U.K.* **14** D4
Buckley → *Australia* **94** C2
Bucklin *U.S.A.* **112** G4
Bucks L. *U.S.A.* **110** F5
Bucquoy *France* **19** B9
Bucureşti *Romania* **29** F11
Bucureşti Otopeni ✈ (OTP)
    Romania **29** F11
Bucyrus *U.S.A.* **113** E12
Budacu, Vf. *Romania* **29** C10
Budalin *Burma* **67** H19
Budaörs *Hungary* **28** C3
Budapest *Hungary* **28** C4
Budapest ✈ (BUD) *Hungary* **28** C4
Budaun *India* **69** E8
Budd Coast *Antarctica* **5** C8
Buddusò *Italy* **42** B2
Bude *U.K.* **15** G3
Budennovsk *Russia* **35** H7
Budeşti *Romania* **29** F11
Budeyi *Ukraine* **29** B14
Budge Budge = Baj Baj
    India **69** H13
Budgewoi *Australia* **95** E5
Budia *Spain* **38** E2
Büdingen *Germany* **25** E5
Budjala *Dem. Rep. of the Congo* **84** D3
Budoni *Italy* **42** B2
Búdrio *Italy* **41** D8
Budva *Montenegro* **44** D2
Budzyń *Poland* **31** F3
Buea *Cameroon* **83** E6
Buellton *U.S.A.* **111** L6
Buena Esperanza *Argentina* **126** C2
Buena Park *U.S.A.* **111** M9
Buena Vista *Colo., U.S.A.* **108** G10
Buena Vista *Va., U.S.A.* **113** G14
Buena Vista Lake Bed
    U.S.A. **111** K7
Buenaventura *Colombia* **124** C3
Buenaventura *Mexico* **118** B3
Buendía, Embalse de *Spain* **38** E2
Buenos Aires *Argentina* **126** C4
Buenos Aires *Costa Rica* **120** E3
Buenos Aires □ *Argentina* **126** D4
Buenos Aires, L. *Argentina* **128** F2
Buffalo *Mo., U.S.A.* **112** G7
Buffalo *N.Y., U.S.A.* **114** D6
Buffalo *Okla., U.S.A.* **116** C5
Buffalo *S. Dak., U.S.A.* **112** C2
Buffalo *Wyo., U.S.A.* **108** D10
Buffalo → *Canada* **102** A5
Buffalo → *S. Africa* **89** D5
Buffalo △ *U.S.A.* **116** D8
Buffalo Head Hills *Canada* **102** B5
Buffalo L. *Alta., Canada* **102** C6
Buffalo L. *N.W.T., Canada* **102** A5
Buffalo Narrows *Canada* **103** B7
Buffalo Springs → *Kenya* **86** B4
Buffels → *S. Africa* **88** D2
Buford *U.S.A.* **117** D12
Bug = Buh → *Ukraine* **33** J6
Bug → *Poland* **31** F8
Buga *Colombia* **124** C3
Bugala I. *Uganda* **86** C3
Buganda *Uganda* **86** C3
Buganga *Uganda* **86** C3
Bugasong *Phil.* **61** F5
Bugeat *France* **20** C5

Bugel, Tanjung *Indonesia* 63 G14
Búger *Spain* 48 B9
Bugojno *Bos.-H.* 28 F2
Bugsuk I. *Phil.* 62 C5
Buguma *Nigeria* 83 E6
Bugun Shara *Mongolia* 60 B5
Bugungu *Uganda* 86 B3
Buguruslan *Russia* 52 D6
Buh *Ukraine* 33 J6
Buharkent *Turkey* 47 D10
Buheirat-Murrat-el-Kubra *Egypt* 80 H8
Buhera *Zimbabwe* 89 B5
Bühl *Germany* 25 G4
Buhl *U.S.A.* 108 E6
Buhuşi *Romania* 29 D11
Bui △ *Ghana* 82 D4
Builth Wells *U.K.* 15 E4
Buinsk *Russia* 34 C9
Buir Nur *Mongolia* 60 B6
Buis-les-Baronnies *France* 21 D9
Buitrago del Lozoya *Spain* 36 E7
Bujalance *Spain* 37 H6
Bujanovac *Serbia* 44 D5
Bujaraloz *Spain* 38 D4
Buje *Croatia* 41 C10
Bujumbura *Burundi* 86 C2
Bük *Hungary* 28 C1
Buk *Poland* 31 F3
Bukachacha *Russia* 53 D12
Bukama *Dem. Rep. of the Congo* 87 D2
Bukavu *Dem. Rep. of the Congo* 86 C2
Bukene *Tanzania* 86 C3
Bukhara = Buxoro *Uzbekistan* 52 F7
Bukhoro = Buxoro *Uzbekistan* 52 F7
Bukima *Tanzania* 86 C3
Bukit Badung *Indonesia* 63 K18
Bukit Kerajaan *Malaysia* 65 c
Bukit Mertajam *Malaysia* 65 c
Bukit Ni *Malaysia* 65 c
Bukit Panjang *Singapore* 65 d
Bukit Tengah *Malaysia* 65 c
Bukittinggi *Indonesia* 62 E2
Bükk *Hungary* 28 B5
Bükki △ *Hungary* 28 B5
Bukoba *Tanzania* 86 C3
Bukum, Pulau *Singapore* 65 d
Bukuru *Nigeria* 83 D6
Bukuya *Uganda* 86 B3
Būl, Kuh-e *Iran* 71 D7
Bula *Guinea-Biss.* 82 C1
Bula *Indonesia* 63 E8
Bülach *Switz.* 25 H4
Bulahdelah *Australia* 95 E5
Bulan *Phil.* 61 E5
Bulancak *Turkey* 73 B8
Bulandshahr *India* 68 E7
Bulanık *Turkey* 73 C10
Bûlâq *Egypt* 80 B3
Bulawayo *Zimbabwe* 87 G2
Buldan *Turkey* 47 C10
Bulgar *Russia* 34 C9
Bulgaria ■ *Europe* 45 D9
Bulghera, Monte *Italy* 43 B8
Bulgurca *Turkey* 47 D9
Buli, Teluk *Indonesia* 63 D7
Buliluyan, C. *Phil.* 61 G2
Bulim *Singapore* 65 d
Bulki *Ethiopia* 81 F4
Bulkley *Canada* 102 B3
Bull Shoals L. *U.S.A.* 116 C8
Bullaque *Spain* 37 G6
Bullas *Spain* 39 G3
Bulle *Switz.* 25 J3
Bulleringa △ *Australia* 94 B3
Bullhead City *U.S.A.* 111 K12
Bullock Creek *Australia* 94 B3
Bulloo *Australia* 95 D3
Bulloo L. *Australia* 95 D3
Bulls *N.Z.* 91 D5
Bully-les-Mines *France* 19 B9
Bulman *Australia* 94 A1
Bulnes *Chile* 126 D1
Bulqizë *Albania* 44 E4
Bulsar = Valsad *India* 66 J8
Bultfontein *S. Africa* 88 D4
Bulukumba *Indonesia* 63 F6
Bulun *Russia* 53 B13
Bumba *Dem. Rep. of the Congo* 84 D4
Bumbah, Khalīj *Libya* 79 B10
Bumbești-Jiu *Romania* 29 E8
Bumbiri I. *Tanzania* 86 C3
Bumbuna *S. Leone* 82 D2
Bumhpa Bum *Burma* 67 F20
Bumi *Zimbabwe* 87 F2
Buna *Kenya* 86 B4
Bunaken *Indonesia* 63 D6
Bunawan *Phil.* 61 G6
Bunazi *Tanzania* 86 C3
Bunbury *Australia* 93 F2
Bunclody *Ireland* 12 D5
Buncrana *Ireland* 12 A4
Bundaberg *Australia* 95 C5
Bünde *Germany* 24 C4

Bundey *Australia* 94 C2
Bundi *India* 68 G6
Bundjalung △ *Australia* 95 D5
Bundoran *Ireland* 12 B3
Bundukia *Sudan* 81 F3
Bung Kan *Thailand* 64 C4
Bunga *Nigeria* 83 C6
Bungay *U.K.* 15 E9
Bungil Cr. *Australia* 95 D4
Bungle Bungle = Purnululu △ *Australia* 92 C4
Bungo-Suidō *Japan* 55 H6
Bungoma *Kenya* 86 B3
Bungotakada *Japan* 55 H5
Bungu *Tanzania* 86 D4
Bunia *Dem. Rep. of the Congo* 86 B3
Bunji *Pakistan* 69 B6
Bunkie *U.S.A.* 116 F8
Bunnell *U.S.A.* 117 G14
Buñol *Spain* 39 F4
Bunsuru *Nigeria* 83 C5
Buntok *Indonesia* 62 E4
Bununu Dass *Nigeria* 83 C6
Bununu Kasa *Nigeria* 83 D6
Bunya Mts. △ *Australia* 95 D5
Bünyan *Turkey* 72 C6
Bunyola *Spain* 48 B9
Bunyu *Indonesia* 62 D5
Bunza *Nigeria* 83 C5
Buol *Indonesia* 63 D6
Buon Brieng *Vietnam* 64 F7
Buon Ma Thuot *Vietnam* 64 F7
Buong Long *Cambodia* 64 F6
Buorkhaya, Mys *Russia* 53 B14
Buqayq *Si. Arabia* 71 E6
Buqbuq *Egypt* 80 A2
Bur Acaba = Buurhakaba *Somali Rep.* 75 G3
Bûr Fuad *Egypt* 80 H8
Bûr Safâga *Egypt* 70 E2
Bûr Sa'îd *Egypt* 80 H8
Bûr Sûdân *Sudan* 80 D4
Bûr Taufiq *Egypt* 80 J8
Bura *Kenya* 86 C4
Burakin *Australia* 93 F2
Buram *Sudan* 81 E2
Burao = Burco *Somali Rep.* 75 F4
Burāq *Syria* 74 B5
Buraydah *Si. Arabia* 70 E4
Burbank *U.S.A.* 111 L8
Burco *Somali Rep.* 75 F4
Burda *India* 68 G6
Burdekin *Australia* 94 B4
Burdur *Turkey* 47 D12
Burdur □ *Turkey* 47 D12
Burdur Gölü *Turkey* 47 D12
Burdwan = Barddhaman *India* 69 H12
Bure *Gojam, Ethiopia* 81 E4
Bure *Ilubabor, Ethiopia* 81 F4
Bure *U.K.* 14 E9
Büren *Germany* 24 D4
Bureya *Russia* 53 E13
Burford *Canada* 114 C4
Burg *Germany* 24 C7
Burg auf Fehmarn *Germany* 24 A7
Burg el Arab *Egypt* 80 H6
Burg et Tuyur *Sudan* 80 C2
Burg Stargard *Germany* 24 B9
Burgas *Bulgaria* 45 D11
Burgas □ *Bulgaria* 45 D10
Burgaski Zaliv *Bulgaria* 45 D11
Burgdorf *Germany* 24 C6
Burgdorf *Switz.* 25 H3
Burgenland □ *Austria* 27 D9
Burgeo *Canada* 105 C8
Burgersdorp *S. Africa* 88 E4
Burgess, Mt. *Australia* 93 F3
Burghausen *Germany* 25 G8
Burghead *U.K.* 13 D5
Búrgio *Italy* 42 E6
Burglengenfeld *Germany* 25 F8
Burgohondo *Spain* 36 E6
Burgos *Spain* 36 C7
Burgos □ *Spain* 36 C7
Burgstädt *Germany* 24 E8
Burgsvik *Sweden* 11 G12
Burguillos del Cerro *Spain* 37 G4
Burgundy = Bourgogne □ *France* 19 F11
Burhaniye *Turkey* 47 B8
Burhanpur *India* 66 J10
Burhi Gandak *India* 69 G12
Burhner *India* 69 H9
Buri Pen. *Eritrea* 81 D4
Burias I. *Phil.* 61 E4
Burica, Pta. *Costa Rica* 120 E3
Burien *U.S.A.* 110 C4
Burigi, L. *Tanzania* 86 C3
Burigi △ *Tanzania* 86 C3
Burin *Canada* 105 C8
Buriram *Thailand* 64 E4
Burji *Ethiopia* 81 F4
Burkburnett *U.S.A.* 116 D5
Burke *U.S.A.* 112 D5
Burke Chan. *Canada* 102 C3
Burketown *Australia* 94 B2
Burkina Faso ■ *Africa* 82 C4
Burk's Falls *Canada* 104 C4

Burlada *Spain* 38 C3
Burleigh Falls *Canada* 114 B6
Burley *U.S.A.* 108 E7
Burlingame *U.S.A.* 110 H4
Burlington *Canada* 114 C5
Burlington *Colo., U.S.A.* 108 G12
Burlington *Iowa, U.S.A.* 112 E8
Burlington *Kans., U.S.A.* 112 F6
Burlington *N.C., U.S.A.* 117 C15
Burlington *N.J., U.S.A.* 115 F10
Burlington *Vt., U.S.A.* 115 B11
Burlington *Wash., U.S.A.* 110 B4
Burlington *Wis., U.S.A.* 112 D9
Burma ■ *Asia* 67 J20
Burnaby I. *Canada* 102 C2
Burnet *U.S.A.* 116 F5
Burney *U.S.A.* 108 F3
Burnham *U.S.A.* 114 F7
Burnham-on-Sea *U.K.* 15 F5
Burnie *Australia* 95 G4
Burnley *U.K.* 14 D5
Burns *U.S.A.* 108 E4
Burns Junction *U.S.A.* 108 E5
Burns Lake *Canada* 102 C3
Burnside *Canada* 100 C9
Burnside, L. *Australia* 93 E3
Burnsville *U.S.A.* 112 C7
Burnt River *Canada* 114 B6
Burntwood *Canada* 103 B9
Burntwood L. *Canada* 103 B8
Burqān *Kuwait* 70 D5
Burra *Australia* 95 E2
Burra *Nigeria* 83 C6
Burray *U.K.* 13 C6
Burrel *Albania* 44 E4
Burren *Ireland* 12 C2
Burren △ *Ireland* 12 C3
Burren Junction *Australia* 95 E4
Burriana *Spain* 38 F4
Burrinjuck Res. *Australia* 95 F4
Burro, Serranías del *Mexico* 118 B4
Burrow Hd. *U.K.* 13 G4
Burruyacú *Argentina* 126 B3
Burry Port *U.K.* 15 F3
Bursa *Turkey* 45 F13
Bursa □ *Turkey* 72 B3
Burseryd *Sweden* 11 G7
Burstall *Canada* 103 C7
Burton *Ohio, U.S.A.* 114 E3
Burton *S.C., U.S.A.* 117 E14
Burton, L. *Canada* 104 B4
Burton upon Trent *U.K.* 14 E6
Buru *Indonesia* 63 E7
Burullus, Bahra el *Egypt* 80 H7
Burûn, Râs *Egypt* 74 D2
Bururi *Burundi* 86 C2
Burutu *Nigeria* 83 D6
Burwell *U.S.A.* 112 E4
Burwick *U.K.* 13 C5
Bury *U.K.* 14 D5
Bury St. Edmunds *U.K.* 15 E8
Buryatia □ *Russia* 53 D12
Buryn *Ukraine* 33 G7
Burzenin *Poland* 31 G5
Busalla *Italy* 40 D5
Busan *S. Korea* 57 G15
Busango Swamp *Zambia* 87 E2
Buşayrah *Syria* 73 E9
Busca *Italy* 40 D4
Bushat *Albania* 44 E3
Büshehr *Iran* 71 D6
Büshehr □ *Iran* 71 D6
Bushenyi *Uganda* 86 C3
Bushire = Büshehr *Iran* 71 D6
Bushtyna *Ukraine* 29 B8
Busie *Ghana* 82 C4
Businga *Dem. Rep. of the Congo* 84 D4
Büsingen *Germany* 25 H4
Busko-Zdrój *Poland* 31 H7
Busovača *Bos.-H.* 28 F2
Buşra ash Shām *Syria* 74 C5
Busselton *Australia* 93 F2
Busseri *Sudan* 81 F2
Busseto *Italy* 40 D7
Bussière-Badil *France* 20 C4
Bussolengo *Italy* 40 C7
Bussum *Neths.* 17 B5
Busto, C. *Spain* 36 B4
Busto Arsízio *Italy* 40 C5
Busu Djanoa *Dem. Rep. of the Congo* 84 D4
Busuanga I. *Phil.* 61 E4
Büsum *Germany* 24 A4
Busungbiu *Indonesia* 63 J17
Buta *Dem. Rep. of the Congo* 86 B1
Butare *Rwanda* 86 C2
Butaritari *Kiribati* 96 G9
Bute *U.K.* 13 F3
Bute Inlet *Canada* 102 C4
Butemba *Uganda* 86 B3
Butembo *Dem. Rep. of the Congo* 86 B2
Buteni *Romania* 28 D7
Butera *Italy* 43 E7
Butere *Kenya* 86 B3

Butha Qi *China* 60 B7
Butiaba *Uganda* 86 B3
Butler *Mo., U.S.A.* 112 F6
Butler *Pa., U.S.A.* 114 F5
Buton *Indonesia* 63 F6
Butte *Mont., U.S.A.* 108 C7
Butte *Nebr., U.S.A.* 112 D4
Butte Creek *U.S.A.* 110 F5
Butterworth = Gcuwa *S. Africa* 89 E4
Butterworth *Malaysia* 65 c
Buttevant *Ireland* 12 D3
Buttfield, Mt. *Australia* 93 D4
Button B. *Canada* 103 B10
Buttonwillow *U.S.A.* 111 K7
Butty Hd. *Australia* 93 F3
Butuan *Phil.* 61 G6
Butuku-Luba *Eq. Guin.* 83 E6
Butung = Buton *Indonesia* 63 F6
Buturlinovka *Russia* 34 E5
Butzbach *Germany* 25 E4
Bützow *Germany* 24 B7
Buurhakaba *Somali Rep.* 75 G3
Buxa Duar *India* 69 F13
Buxar *India* 69 G10
Buxoro *Uzbekistan* 52 F7
Buxtehude *Germany* 24 B5
Buxton *U.K.* 14 D6
Buxy *France* 19 F11
Buy *Russia* 34 A5
Buyant-Uhaa *Mongolia* 60 B6
Buynaksk *Russia* 35 J8
Buyo *Ivory C.* 82 D3
Buyo, L. de *Ivory C.* 82 D3
Büyük Menderes *Turkey* 47 D9
Büyükçekmece *Turkey* 45 E12
Büyükkariştıran *Turkey* 45 E11
Büyükkemikli Burnu *Turkey* 45 F10
Büyükorhan *Turkey* 47 B10
Büyükyoncalı *Turkey* 45 E11
Buzançais *France* 18 F8
Buzău *Romania* 29 E11
Buzău □ *Romania* 29 E11
Buzău *Romania* 29 E12
Buzău, Pasul *Romania* 29 E11
Buzen *Japan* 55 H5
Buzet *Croatia* 41 C10
Buziaş *Romania* 28 E6
Büzmeýin *Turkmenistan* 71 B8
Buzuluk *Russia* 52 D6
Buzuluk *Russia* 34 E6
Buzzards Bay *U.S.A.* 115 E14
Bwana Mkubwe *Dem. Rep. of the Congo* 87 E2
Bwindi △ *Uganda* 86 C2
Byala *Ruse, Bulgaria* 45 C9
Byala *Varna, Bulgaria* 45 D11
Byala Slatina *Bulgaria* 44 C7
Byarezina *Belarus* 23 B16
Byaroza *Belarus* 33 F3
Bychawa *Poland* 31 G9
Byczyna *Poland* 31 G5
Bydgoszcz *Poland* 31 E5
Byelorussia = Belarus ■ *Europe* 23 B14
Byers *U.S.A.* 108 G2
Byesville *U.S.A.* 114 G3
Byfield △ *Australia* 94 C5
Bykhaw *Belarus* 23 B16
Bykhov = Bykhaw *Belarus* 23 B16
Bykovo *Russia* 34 F7
Bylas *U.S.A.* 109 K8
Bylot *Canada* 103 B10
Bylot I. *Canada* 101 B12
Byrd, C. *Antarctica* 5 C17
Byrock *Australia* 95 E4
Byron, C. *Australia* 95 D5
Byron Bay *Australia* 95 D5
Byrranga, Gory *Russia* 53 B11
Byrranga Mts. = Byrranga, Gory *Russia* 53 B11
Byrum *Denmark* 11 G5
Byske *Sweden* 8 D19
Byskeälven *Sweden* 8 D19
Bystrytsya *Ukraine* 29 B9
Bystrzyca *Dolnośląskie, Poland* 31 H3
Bystrzyca *Lubelskie, Poland* 31 G9
Bystrzyca Kłodzka *Poland* 31 H3
Bytča *Slovak Rep.* 27 B11
Bytkiv *Ukraine* 29 B9
Bytom *Poland* 31 H5
Bytom Odrzański *Poland* 31 G2
Bytów *Poland* 30 D4
Byumba *Rwanda* 86 C3
Bzenec *Czech Rep.* 27 C10
Bzura *Poland* 31 F7

C

C.W. McConaughy, L. *U.S.A.* 112 E3
Ca *Vietnam* 64 C5
Ca Mau *Vietnam* 65 H5
Ca Mau, Mui *Vietnam* 65 H5
Ca Na *Vietnam* 65 G7

Caacupé *Paraguay* 126 B4
Caaguazú △ *Paraguay* 127 B4
Caála *Angola* 85 G3
Caamaño Sd. *Canada* 102 C3
Caazapá *Paraguay* 126 B4
Caazapá □ *Paraguay* 127 B4
Cabadbaran *Phil.* 61 G6
Cabalian = San Juan *Phil.* 61 F6
Caballeria, C. de *Spain* 48 A11
Cabana de Bergantiños *Spain* 36 B2
Cabañaquinta *Spain* 36 B5
Cabanatuan *Phil.* 61 D4
Cabañeros △ *Spain* 37 F6
Cabanes *Spain* 38 E5
Cabano *Canada* 105 C6
Čabar *Croatia* 41 C11
Cabazon *U.S.A.* 111 M10
Cabedelo *Brazil* 125 E12
Cabeza del Buey *Spain* 37 G5
Cabezón de la Sal *Spain* 36 B6
Cabildo *Chile* 126 C1
Cabimas *Venezuela* 124 A4
Cabinda *Angola* 84 F2
Cabinda □ *Angola* 84 F2
Cabinet Mts. *U.S.A.* 108 B6
Cabo Blanco *Argentina* 128 F3
Cabo de Gata-Níjar △ *Spain* 39 J2
Cabo Frio *Brazil* 127 A7
Cabo Pantoja *Peru* 124 D3
Cabo San Lucas *Mexico* 118 C3
Cabo Verde = Cape Verde Is. ■ *Atl. Oc.* 78 b
Cabonga, Réservoir *Canada* 104 C4
Cabool *U.S.A.* 112 G7
Caboolture *Australia* 95 D5
Cabora Bassa Dam = Cahora Bassa, Lago de *Mozam.* 87 F3
Caborca *Mexico* 118 A2
Cabot, Mt. *U.S.A.* 115 B13
Cabot Hd. *Canada* 114 A3
Cabot Str. *Canada* 105 C8
Cabra *Spain* 37 H6
Cabra del Santo Cristo *Spain* 37 H7
Cábras *Italy* 42 C1
Cabrera *Spain* 48 B9
Cabrera, Sierra *Spain* 36 C4
Cabrera △ *Spain* 39 F7
Cabri *Canada* 103 C7
Cabriel *Spain* 39 F3
Cabugao *Phil.* 61 C4
Cacabelos *Spain* 36 C4
Caçador *Brazil* 127 B5
Čačak *Serbia* 44 C4
Caçapava do Sul *Brazil* 127 C5
Cáccamo *Italy* 42 E6
Cacém *Portugal* 37 G1
Cáceres *Brazil* 124 G7
Cáceres *Spain* 37 F4
Cáceres □ *Spain* 36 F5
Cache Bay *Canada* 104 C4
Cache Cr. *U.S.A.* 110 G5
Cache Creek *Canada* 102 C4
Cacheu *Guinea-Biss.* 82 C1
Cachi *Argentina* 126 B2
Cachimbo, Serra do *Brazil* 125 E7
Cachinal de la Sierra *Chile* 126 A2
Cachoeira *Brazil* 125 F11
Cachoeira do Sul *Brazil* 127 C5
Cachoeiro de Itapemirim *Brazil* 127 A7
Cachopo *Portugal* 37 H3
Cacine *Guinea-Biss.* 82 C1
Cacólo *Angola* 84 G3
Caconda *Angola* 85 G3
Cader Idris *U.K.* 15 E4
Cadereyta de Jiménez *Mexico* 118 B5
Cadí, Sierra del *Spain* 38 C6
Cadí-Moixeró △ *Spain* 38 C3
Cadibarrawirracanna, L. *Australia* 95 D2
Cadillac *France* 20 D3
Cadillac *U.S.A.* 113 C11
Cadiz *Phil.* 61 F5
Cádiz *Spain* 37 J4
Cadiz *Calif., U.S.A.* 111 L11
Cadiz *Ohio, U.S.A.* 114 F4
Cádiz □ *Spain* 37 J5
Cádiz, G. de *Spain* 37 J3
Cadiz L. *U.S.A.* 109 J6
Cadney Park *Australia* 95 D1
Cadomin *Canada* 102 C5
Cadotte Lake *Canada* 102 B5
Cadours *France* 20 E5
Cadoux *Australia* 93 F2
Caen *France* 18 C6
Caernarfon *U.K.* 14 D3
Caernarfon B. *U.K.* 14 D3
Caernarvon = Caernarfon *U.K.* 14 D3
Caerphilly *U.K.* 15 F4
Caerphilly □ *U.K.* 15 F4
Caesarea *Israel* 74 C3

Caetité *Brazil* 125 F10
Cafayate *Argentina* 126 B2
Cafu *Angola* 88 B2
Cagayan *Phil.* 61 B4
Cagayan de Oro *Phil.* 61 G6
Cagayan Is. *Phil.* 61 G4
Cagayan Sulu I. *Phil.* 61 H3
Cagli *Italy* 41 E9
Cágliari *Italy* 42 C2
Cágliari, G. di *Italy* 42 C2
Cagnano Varano *Italy* 41 G12
Cagnes-sur-Mer *France* 21 E11
Caguán *Colombia* 124 C3
Caguas *Puerto Rico* 121 d
Caha Mts. *Ireland* 12 E2
Cahama *Angola* 88 B1
Caher *Ireland* 12 D4
Cahersiveen *Ireland* 12 E1
Cahora Bassa, L. de *Mozam.* 87 F3
Cahora Bassa, Lago de *Mozam.* 87 F3
Cahore Pt. *Ireland* 12 D5
Cahors *France* 20 D5
Cahul *Moldova* 29 E13
Cai Bau, Dao *Vietnam* 58 G6
Cai Nuoc *Vietnam* 65 H5
Caia *Mozam.* 87 F4
Caianda *Angola* 87 E1
Caibarién *Cuba* 120 B4
Caibiran *Phil.* 61 F6
Caicara *Venezuela* 124 B5
Caicó *Brazil* 125 E11
Caicos Is. *Turks & Caicos* 121 B5
Caicos Passage *W. Indies* 121 B5
Caidian *China* 59 B10
Caiguna *Australia* 93 F4
Căinari *Moldova* 29 D14
Caird Coast *Antarctica* 5 D1
Cairn Gorm *U.K.* 13 D5
Cairngorm Mts. *U.K.* 13 D5
Cairngorms △ *U.K.* 13 D5
Cairnryan *U.K.* 13 G3
Cairns *Australia* 94 B4
Cairns L. *Canada* 103 C10
Cairo = El Qâhira *Egypt* 80 H7
Cairo *Ga., U.S.A.* 117 F12
Cairo *Ill., U.S.A.* 112 G9
Cairo *N.Y., U.S.A.* 115 D10
Cairo Montenotte *Italy* 40 D5
Caithness *U.K.* 13 C5
Caithness, Ord of *U.K.* 13 C5
Caja de Muertos, I. *Puerto Rico* 121 d
Cajamarca *Peru* 124 E3
Cajarc *France* 20 D5
Cajazeiras *Brazil* 125 E11
Čajetina *Serbia* 44 C3
Çakırgol *Turkey* 73 B8
Çakırlar *Turkey* 47 E12
Čakovec *Croatia* 41 B13
Çal *Turkey* 47 C11
Cala *Spain* 37 H4
Cala *Spain* 37 H4
Cala Cadolar, Punta de = Rotja, Pta. *Spain* 39 G6
Cala d'Or *Spain* 48 B10
Cala en Porter *Spain* 48 B11
Cala Figuera *Spain* 48 B10
Cala Figuera, C. de *Spain* 48 B9
Cala Forcat *Spain* 48 B10
Cala Major *Spain* 48 B9
Cala Mezquida = Sa Mesquida *Spain* 48 B11
Cala Millor *Spain* 48 B10
Cala Murada *Spain* 48 B10
Cala Ratjada *Spain* 48 B10
Cala Santa Galdana *Spain* 48 B10
Calabanga *Phil.* 61 E5
Calabar *Nigeria* 83 E6
Calabogie *Canada* 115 A8
Calabozo *Venezuela* 124 B5
Calábria □ *Italy* 43 C9
Calábria △ *Italy* 43 C9
Calaburras, Pta. de *Spain* 37 J6
Calaceite *Spain* 38 D5
Calacuccia *France* 21 F13
Calafat *Romania* 28 G7
Calafell *Spain* 38 D6
Calahorra *Spain* 38 C3
Calais *France* 19 B8
Calais *U.S.A.* 113 C20
Calakmul △ *Mexico* 119 D7
Calalaste, Cord. de *Argentina* 126 B2
Calama *Brazil* 124 E6
Calama *Chile* 126 A2
Calamar *Colombia* 124 A4
Calamian Group *Phil.* 61 F3
Calamocha *Spain* 38 E3
Calamonte *Spain* 37 G4
Călan *Romania* 28 E7
Calañas *Spain* 37 H4
Calanda *Spain* 38 E4
Calang *Indonesia* 62 D1
Calangiánus *Italy* 42 B2
Calanscio, Sarîr *Libya* 79 C10
Calapan *Phil.* 61 E4
Călărași *Moldova* 29 C13

Călăraşi *Romania* **29** F12
Călăraşi □ *Romania* **29** F12
Calasparra *Spain* **39** G3
Calatafimi *Italy* **42** E5
Calatayud *Spain* **38** D3
Călăţele *Romania* **28** D8
Calato = Kalathos *Greece* **47** E10
Calauag *Phil.* **61** E5
Calavà, C. *Italy* **43** D7
Calavite, C. *Phil.* **61** E4
Calayan *Phil.* **61** B4
Calbayog *Phil.* **61** E6
Calca *Peru* **124** F4
Calcasieu L. *U.S.A.* **116** G8
Calcium *U.S.A.* **115** B9
Calcutta = Kolkata *India* **69** H13
Calcutta *U.S.A.* **114** F4
Caldaro *Italy* **41** B8
Caldas da Rainha *Portugal* **37** F1
Caldas de Reis *Spain* **36** C2
Calder → *U.K.* **14** D6
Caldera *Chile* **126** B1
Caldera de Taburiente △
    Canary Is. **48** F2
Caldwell *Idaho, U.S.A.* **108** E5
Caldwell *Kans., U.S.A.* **112** G5
Caldwell *Tex., U.S.A.* **116** F6
Caledon *Canada* **114** C5
Caledon *S. Africa* **88** E2
Caledon → *S. Africa* **88** E4
Caledon B. *Australia* **94** A2
Caledonia *Canada* **114** C5
Caledonia *U.S.A.* **114** D7
Calella *Spain* **38** D7
Calemba *Angola* **88** B2
Calen *Australia* **94** J6
Calenzana *France* **21** F12
Caletones *Chile* **126** C1
Calexico *U.S.A.* **111** N11
Calf of Man *I. of Man* **14** C3
Calgary *Canada* **102** C6
Calheta *Madeira* **48** D2
Calhoun *U.S.A.* **117** D12
Cali *Colombia* **124** C3
Calicut *India* **66** P9
Caliente *U.S.A.* **109** H6
California *Mo., U.S.A.* **112** F7
California, Pa., U.S.A. **114** F5
California □ *U.S.A.* **110** H7
California, Baja, T.N. =
    Baja California □ *Mexico* **118** B2
California, Baja, T.S. =
    Baja California Sur □
    Mexico **118** B2
California, G. de *Mexico* **118** B2
California City *U.S.A.* **111** K9
California Hot Springs
    U.S.A. **111** K8
Călilabad *Azerbaijan* **73** C13
Calilegua △ *Argentina* **126** B3
Călimăneşti *Romania* **29** E9
Călimani, Munţii *Romania* **29** C10
Calingasta *Argentina* **126** C2
Calipatria *U.S.A.* **111** M11
Calistoga *U.S.A.* **110** G4
Calitri *Italy* **43** B8
Calitzdorp *S. Africa* **88** E3
Callabonna, L. *Australia* **95** D3
Callac *France* **18** D3
Callan *Ireland* **12** D4
Callander *U.K.* **13** E4
Callao *Peru* **124** F3
Callicoon *U.S.A.* **115** E9
Calling Lake *Canada* **102** B6
Calliope *Australia* **94** C5
Callosa de Segura *Spain* **39** G4
Callosa d'En Sarrià *Spain* **39** G4
Calma, Costa de la *Spain* **48** B9
Calne *U.K.* **15** F6
Calola *Angola* **88** B2
Calolbon = San Andres *Phil.* **61** E6
Calonge *Spain* **38** D8
Caloocan *Phil.* **61** D4
Calore → *Italy* **43** A7
Caloundra *Australia* **95** D5
Calpe *Spain* **39** G5
Calpella *U.S.A.* **110** F3
Calpine *U.S.A.* **110** F6
Calstock *Canada* **104** C3
Caltabellotta *Italy* **42** E6
Caltagirone *Italy* **43** E7
Caltanissetta *Italy* **43** E7
Çaltılıbük *Turkey* **45** G12
Caluire-et-Cuire *France* **19** G11
Calulo *Angola* **84** G2
Caluso *Italy* **40** C4
Calvados □ *France* **18** C6
Calvert → *Australia* **94** B2
Calvert I. *Canada* **102** C3
Calvert Ra. *Australia* **92** D3
Calvi *France* **21** F12
Calvià *Spain* **48** B9
Calvillo *Mexico* **118** C4
Calvinia *S. Africa* **88** E2
Calvo, Mte. *Italy* **41** G12
Calwa *U.S.A.* **110** J7
Calzada Almuradiel =
    Almuradiel *Spain* **37** G7

Calzada de Calatrava *Spain* **37** G7
Cam → *U.K.* **15** E8
Cam Lam *Vietnam* **65** G7
Cam Pha *Vietnam* **58** B6
Cam Ranh *Vietnam* **65** G7
Cam Xuyen *Vietnam* **64** C6
Camabatela *Angola* **84** F3
Camacha *Madeira* **48** D3
Camacupa *Angola* **85** G3
Camagüey *Cuba* **120** B4
Camaiore *Italy* **40** E7
Camaná *Peru* **124** G4
Camanche Res. *U.S.A.* **110** G6
Camaquã *Brazil* **127** C5
Camaquã → *Brazil* **127** C5
Câmara de Lobos *Madeira* **48** D3
Camarat, C. *France* **21** E10
Camarès *France* **20** E6
Camaret-sur-Mer *France* **18** D2
Camargo *Mexico* **119** B5
Camargue *France* **21** E8
Camargue △ *France* **21** E8
Camarillo *U.S.A.* **111** L7
Camariñas *Spain* **36** B1
Camas *Spain* **37** H4
Camas *U.S.A.* **110** E4
Camas Valley *U.S.A.* **108** E2
Camballin *Australia* **92** C3
Cambará *Brazil* **127** A5
Cambay = Khambhat *India* **68** H5
Cambay, G. of =
    Khambhat, G. of *India* **66** J8
Cambil *Spain* **37** H7
Cambo-les-Bains *France* **20** E2
Cambodia ■ *Asia* **64** F5
Camborne *U.K.* **15** G2
Cambrai *France* **19** B10
Cambre *Spain* **36** B2
Cambria *U.S.A.* **110** K5
Cambrian Mts. *U.K.* **15** E4
Cambridge *Canada* **114** C4
Cambridge *Jamaica* **120** a
Cambridge *N.Z.* **91** B5
Cambridge *U.K.* **15** E8
Cambridge *Mass., U.S.A.* **115** D13
Cambridge *Minn., U.S.A.* **112** C7
Cambridge *N.Y., U.S.A.* **115** C11
Cambridge *Nebr., U.S.A.* **112** E3
Cambridge *Ohio, U.S.A.* **114** F3
Cambridge Bay =
    Ikaluktutiak *Canada* **100** C9
Cambridge G. *Australia* **92** B4
Cambridge Springs *U.S.A.* **114** E4
Cambridgeshire □ *U.K.* **15** E7
Cambrils *Spain* **38** D6
Cambuci *Brazil* **127** A7
Cambundi-Catembo *Angola* **84** G3
Camden *Australia* **95** B5
Camden *Ala., U.S.A.* **117** F11
Camden *Ark., U.S.A.* **116** E8
Camden *Maine, U.S.A.* **113** C19
Camden *N.J., U.S.A.* **115** G9
Camden *N.Y., U.S.A.* **115** C9
Camden *S.C., U.S.A.* **117** D14
Camdenton *U.S.A.* **112** F7
Camden Sd. *Australia* **92** C3
Camelford *U.K.* **15** G3
Çameli *Turkey* **47** D11
Camenca *Moldova* **29** B13
Camerino *Italy* **41** E10
Cameron *Ariz., U.S.A.* **109** J8
Cameron *La., U.S.A.* **116** G8
Cameron *Mo., U.S.A.* **112** F6
Cameron *Tex., U.S.A.* **116** F6
Cameron Highlands
    Malaysia **65** K3
Cameron Hills *Canada* **102** B5
Cameroon ■ *Africa* **79** G7
Camerota *Italy* **43** B8
Cameroun → *Cameroon* **83** E6
Cameroun, Mt. *Cameroon* **83** E6
Cametá *Brazil* **125** D9
Çamiçi Gölü *Turkey* **47** D9
Camiguin □ *Phil.* **61** G6
Camiguin I. *Phil.* **61** B4
Camiling *Phil.* **61** D4
Camilla *U.S.A.* **117** F12
Caminha *Portugal* **36** D2
Camino *U.S.A.* **110** G6
Camira Creek *Australia* **95** D5
Cammal *U.S.A.* **114** E7
Cammarata *Italy* **42** E6
Camocim *Brazil* **125** D10
Camooweal *Australia* **94** B2
Camooweal Caves △
    Australia **94** C2
Camopi *Fr. Guiana* **125** C8
Camotes Is. *Phil.* **61** F6
Camotes Sea *Phil.* **61** F6
Camp Hill *U.S.A.* **114** F8
Camp Nelson *U.S.A.* **111** J8
Camp Pendleton *U.S.A.* **111** M9
Camp Verde *U.S.A.* **109** J8
Camp Wood *U.S.A.* **116** G4

Campagna *Italy* **43** B8
Campana *Argentina* **126** C4
Campana, I. *Chile* **128** F1
Campanário *Madeira* **48** D2
Campanario *Spain* **37** G5
Campanet *Spain* **48** B9
Campánia □ *Italy* **43** B7
Campbell *S. Africa* **88** D3
Campbell *Calif., U.S.A.* **110** H5
Campbell *Ohio, U.S.A.* **114** E4
Campbell I. *Pac. Oc.* **96** N8
Campbell L. *Canada* **103** A7
Campbell Plateau *S. Ocean* **5** A11
Campbell River *Canada* **102** C3
Campbell Town *Australia* **95** G4
Campbellford *Canada* **114** B7
Campbellpur *Pakistan* **68** C5
Campbellsville *U.S.A.* **113** G11
Campbellton *Canada* **105** C6
Campbelltown *Australia* **95** E5
Campbeltown *U.K.* **13** F3
Campeche *Mexico* **119** D6
Campeche □ *Mexico* **119** D6
Campeche, Golfo de *Mexico* **119** D6
Câmpeni *Romania* **28** D8
Camperdown *Australia* **95** F3
Camperville *Canada* **103** C8
Campi Salentina *Italy* **43** B11
Campidano *Italy* **42** C1
Câmpia Turzii *Romania* **29** D8
Campíglia Maríttima *Italy* **40** E7
Campillo de Altobuey *Spain* **39** F3
Campillos *Spain* **37** H6
Câmpina *Romania* **29** E10
Campina Grande *Brazil* **125** E11
Campinas *Brazil* **127** A6
Campione *Italy* **21** C12
Campli *Italy* **41** F10
Campo *Spain* **38** C5
Campo de Criptana *Spain* **37** F7
Campo de Gibraltar *Spain* **37** J5
Campo Grande *Brazil* **125** H8
Campo Maior *Brazil* **125** D10
Campo Maior *Portugal* **37** F3
Campo Mourão *Brazil* **127** A5
Campo Túres *Italy* **41** B8
Campobasso *Italy* **43** A7
Campobello di Licata *Italy* **42** E6
Campobello di Mazara *Italy* **42** E5
Campofelice di Roccella *Italy* **42** E6
Campomarino *Italy* **41** G12
Camporeale *Italy* **42** E6
Camporrobles *Spain* **38** F3
Campos *Brazil* **127** A7
Campos *Spain* **48** B10
Campos Belos *Brazil* **125** F9
Campos del Paraíso =
    Carrascosa del Campo
    Spain **38** E2
Campos Novos *Brazil* **127** B5
Camprodon *Spain* **38** C7
Camptonville *U.S.A.* **110** F5
Camptown *U.S.A.* **115** E8
Câmpulung *Argeş, Romania* **29** E10
Câmpulung *Suceava,
    Romania* **29** C10
Câmpuri *Romania* **29** D11
Camrose *Canada* **102** C6
Camsell Portage *Canada* **103** B7
Çamyuva *Turkey* **47** E12
Çan *Turkey* **45** F11
Can Clavo *Spain* **48** C7
Can Creu *Spain* **48** C7
Can Gio *Vietnam* **65** G6
Can Pastilla *Spain* **48** B9
Can Tho *Vietnam* **65** G5
Canaan *U.S.A.* **115** D11
Canada ■ *N. Amer.* **100** D10
Canada Abyssal Plain *Arctic* **4** B18
Canada Basin *Arctic* **4** B18
Cañada de Gómez *Argentina* **126** C3
Canadian *U.S.A.* **116** D4
Canadian → *U.S.A.* **116** D7
Canadian Shield *Canada* **98** D12
Canajoharie *U.S.A.* **115** D10
Çanakkale *Turkey* **45** F10
Çanakkale □ *Turkey* **45** F10
Çanakkale Boğazı *Turkey* **45** F10
Canal Flats *Canada* **102** C5
Canalejas *Argentina* **126** D2
Canals *Argentina* **126** C3
Canals *Spain* **39** G4
Canandaigua *U.S.A.* **114** D7
Canandaigua L. *U.S.A.* **114** D7
Cananea *Mexico* **118** A2
Canarias, Is. *Atl. Oc.* **48** F4
Canaries *St. Lucia* **121** f
Canarreos, Arch. de los
    Cuba **120** B3
Canary Is. = Canarias, Is.
    Atl. Oc. **48** F4
Canaseraga *U.S.A.* **114** D7
Canatlán *Mexico* **118** C4
Canaveral, C. *U.S.A.* **117** G14
Canaveral △ *U.S.A.* **117** G14
Canaveieiras *Brazil* **125** G11
Canberra *Australia* **95** F4
Canby *Calif., U.S.A.* **108** F3

Canby *Minn., U.S.A.* **112** C5
Canby *Oreg., U.S.A.* **110** E4
Cancale *France* **18** D5
Canche → *France* **19** B8
Cancún *Mexico* **119** C7
Candanchú *Spain* **38** C4
Çandarlı *Turkey* **47** C8
Çandarlı Körfezi *Turkey* **47** C8
Candás *Spain* **36** B5
Candé *France* **18** E5
Candela *Italy* **43** A8
Candelaria *Argentina* **127** B4
Candelaria *Canary Is.* **48** F3
Candelaria → *Spain* **36** E5
Candelo *Australia* **95** F4
Candeleda *Spain* **36** E5
Candi Dasa *Indonesia* **63** J18
Candia = Iraklio *Greece* **49** D7
Candia, Sea of = Crete, Sea
    of *Greece* **47** E7
Candle L. *Canada* **103** C7
Candlemas I. *Antarctica* **5** B1
Cando *U.S.A.* **112** A4
Candon *Phil.* **61** C4
Canea = Chania *Greece* **49** D6
Canelli *Italy* **40** D5
Canelones *Uruguay* **127** C4
Canet-Plage *France* **20** F7
Cañete *Chile* **126** D1
Cañete *Spain* **38** E3
Cañete de las Torres *Spain* **37** H6
Cangas *Spain* **36** C2
Cangas de Onís *Spain* **36** B5
Cangas del Narcea *Spain* **36** B4
Cangnan *China* **59** D13
Canguaretama *Brazil* **125** E11
Canguçu *Brazil* **127** C5
Canguçu, Serra do *Brazil* **127** C5
Cangwu *China* **59** F8
Cangxi *China* **58** B5
Cangyuan *China* **58** F2
Cangzhou *China* **56** E9
Caniapiscau → *Canada* **105** A6
Caniapiscau, L. *Canada* **105** B6
Canicattì *Italy* **42** E6
Canicattini Bagni *Italy* **43** E8
Caniles *Spain* **37** H8
Canim Lake *Canada* **102** C4
Canindeyu □ *Paraguay* **127** A5
Canino *Italy* **41** F8
Canisteo *U.S.A.* **114** D7
Canisteo → *U.S.A.* **114** D7
Cañitas de Felipe Pescador
    Mexico **118** C4
Cañizal *Spain* **36** D5
Canjáyar *Spain* **37** H8
Çankırı *Turkey* **72** B5
Çankırı □ *Turkey* **72** B5
Cankuzo *Burundi* **86** C3
Canmore *Canada* **102** C5
Cann River *Australia* **95** F4
Canna *U.K.* **13** D2
Cannanore *India* **66** P9
Cannes *France* **21** E11
Canning Town = Port
    Canning *India* **69** H13
Cannington *Canada* **114** B5
Cannóbio *Italy* **40** B5
Cannock *U.K.* **15** E5
Cannonball → *U.S.A.* **112** B3
Cannondale Mt. *Australia* **94** D4
Cannonsville Res. *U.S.A.* **115** D9
Cannonvale *Australia* **94** J6
Canoas *Brazil* **127** B5
Canoe L. *Canada* **103** B7
Cañon City *U.S.A.* **108** G11
Cañón de Rio Blanco △
    Mexico **119** D5
Cañón del Río Lobos △ *Spain* **36** D7
Cañón del Sumidero △
    Mexico **119** D5
Canonniers Pt. *Mauritius* **85** d
Canora *Canada* **103** C8
Canosa di Púglia *Italy* **43** A9
Canowindra *Australia* **95** E4
Canso *Canada* **105** C7
Cantabria □ *Spain* **36** B7
Cantabria, Sierra de *Spain* **38** C2
Cantabrian Mts. =
    Cantábrica, Cordillera
    Spain **36** C5
Cantábrica, Cordillera *Spain* **36** C5
Cantal □ *France* **20** C6
Cantal, Plomb du *France* **20** C6
Cantanhede *Portugal* **36** E2
Cantavieja *Spain* **38** E4
Čantavir *Serbia* **28** E4
Cantemir *Moldova* **29** D13
Canterbury *Australia* **94** D3
Canterbury *U.K.* **15** F9
Canterbury Bight *N.Z.* **91** F3
Canterbury Plains *N.Z.* **91** E3
Cantil *U.S.A.* **111** K9
Cantillana *Spain* **37** H5
Canton = Guangzhou *China* **59** F9
Canton *Ga., U.S.A.* **117** D12
Canton *Ill., U.S.A.* **112** E8
Canton *Miss., U.S.A.* **117** E9

Canton *Mo., U.S.A.* **112** E8
Canton *N.Y., U.S.A.* **115** B9
Canton *Ohio, U.S.A.* **114** F3
Canton *Pa., U.S.A.* **114** E8
Canton *S. Dak., U.S.A.* **112** D5
Canton L. *U.S.A.* **116** C5
Canudos *Brazil* **124** E7
Canumã → *Brazil* **124** D7
Canutama *Brazil* **124** E6
Canutillo *U.S.A.* **116** F1
Canvey *U.K.* **15** F8
Canyon *U.S.A.* **116** D4
Canyon De Chelly △ *U.S.A.* **109** H9
Canyonlands △ *U.S.A.* **109** G9
Canyons of the Ancients △
    U.S.A. **109** H9
Canyonville *U.S.A.* **108** E2
Cao Bang *Vietnam* **58** F6
Cao He → *China* **57** D13
Cao Lanh *Vietnam* **65** G5
Cao Xian *China* **56** G8
Cáorle *Italy* **41** C9
Cap-aux-Meules *Canada* **105** C7
Cap-Chat *Canada* **105** C6
Cap-de-la-Madeleine
    Canada **104** C5
Cap-Haïtien *Haiti* **121** C5
Cap Pt. *St. Lucia* **121** f
Capac *U.S.A.* **114** C2
Capanaparo → *Venezuela* **124** B5
Capánnori *Italy* **40** E7
Capbreton *France* **20** E2
Capdenac *France* **20** D6
Capdepera *Spain* **38** F8
Cape → *Australia* **94** C4
Cape Arid △ *Australia* **93** F3
Cape Barren I. *Australia* **95** G4
Cape Breton Highlands △
    Canada **105** C7
Cape Breton I. *Canada* **105** C7
Cape Charles *U.S.A.* **113** G15
Cape Coast *Ghana* **83** D4
Cape Cod △ *U.S.A.* **113** E18
Cape Coral *U.S.A.* **117** H14
Cape Crawford *Australia* **94** B2
Cape Dorset = Kingait
    Canada **101** C12
Cape Fear → *U.S.A.* **117** E15
Cape Girardeau *U.S.A.* **112** G9
Cape Hatteras △ *U.S.A.* **117** D17
Cape Le Grand △ *Australia* **93** F3
Cape Lookout △ *U.S.A.* **117** D16
Cape May *U.S.A.* **113** F16
Cape May Point *U.S.A.* **113** F16
Cape Melville △ *Australia* **94** A3
Cape Mount △ *Liberia* **82** D2
Cape Peninsula △ *S. Africa* **88** E2
Cape Range △ *Australia* **92** D1
Cape St. George *Canada* **105** C8
Cape Tormentine *Canada* **105** C7
Cape Town *S. Africa* **88** E2
Cape Tribulation △ *Australia* **94** B4
Cape Verde Is. ■ *Atl. Oc.* **78** b
Cape Vincent *U.S.A.* **115** B8
Cape York Peninsula
    Australia **94** A3
Capela *Brazil* **125** F11
Capella *Australia* **94** C4
Capendu *France* **20** E6
Capestang *France* **20** E7
Capesterre-Belle-Eau
    Guadeloupe **120** b
Capesterre-de-Marie-
    Galante *Guadeloupe* **120** b
Capim → *Brazil* **125** D9
Capistrello *Italy* **41** G10
Capitan *U.S.A.* **109** K11
Capitán Arturo Prat
    Antarctica **5** C17
Capitol Reef △ *U.S.A.* **109** G8
Capitola *U.S.A.* **110** J5
Capizzi *Italy* **43** E7
Capoche → *Mozam.* **87** F3
Capodichino, Nápoli ✈
    (NAP) *Italy* **43** B7
Capoterra *Italy* **42** C1
Cappadocia *Turkey* **72** C6
Capraia *Italy* **40** E6
Capraprara, Pta. *Italy* **42** A1
Caprara, Pta. *Italy* **42** A1
Caprarola *Italy* **41** F9
Capreol *Canada* **104** C3
Caprera *Italy* **42** A2
Capri *Italy* **43** B7
Capricorn Coast *Australia* **94** C5
Capricorn Group *Australia* **94** C5
Capricorn Ra. *Australia* **92** D2
Caprino Veronese *Italy* **40** C7
Caprivi Game △ *Namibia* **88** B3
Caprivi Strip *Namibia* **88** B3
Caps et Marais d'Opale △
    France **19** B9
Captain's Flat *Australia* **95** F4
Captieux *France* **20** D3
Capulin Volcano △ *U.S.A.* **116** C3
Caquetá → *Colombia* **124** D5

Caracal *Romania* **29** F9
Caracas *Venezuela* **124** A5
Caracol *Belize* **120** C2
Caracol *Mato Grosso do Sul,
    Brazil* **126** A4
Caracol *Piauí, Brazil* **125** E10
Caráglio *Italy* **40** D4
Caraguatatuba *Brazil* **125** E8
Carajás *Brazil* **125** E8
Carajás, Serra dos *Brazil* **125** E8
Carangola *Brazil* **127** A7
Caransebeş *Romania* **28** E7
Carantec *France* **18** D3
Caraquet *Canada* **105** C6
Caras Severin □ *Romania* **28** E7
Caraşova *Romania* **28** E6
Caratasca, L. de *Honduras* **120** C3
Caratinga *Brazil* **125** G10
Caraúbas *Brazil* **125** E11
Caravaca de la Cruz *Spain* **39** G3
Caravággio *Italy* **40** C6
Caravela *Guinea-Biss.* **82** C1
Caravelas *Brazil* **125** G11
Caravelí *Peru* **124** G4
Caravelle, Presqu'île de la
    Martinique **120** c
Caraz *Peru* **124** E3
Carazinho *Brazil* **127** B5
Carballino = O Carballiño
    Spain **36** C2
Carballo *Spain* **36** B2
Carberry *Canada* **103** D9
Carbó *Mexico* **118** B2
Carbonara, C. *Italy* **42** C2
Carbondale *Colo., U.S.A.* **108** G10
Carbondale *Ill., U.S.A.* **112** G9
Carbondale *Pa., U.S.A.* **115** E9
Carbonear *Canada* **105** C9
Carboneras *Spain* **39** J3
Carboneras de Guadazaón
    Spain **38** F3
Carbónia *Italy* **42** C1
Carcabuey *Spain* **37** H6
Carcagente = Carcaixent
    Spain **39** F4
Carcaixent *Spain* **39** F4
Carcajou *Canada* **102** B5
Carcarana → *Argentina* **126** C3
Carcasse, C. *Haiti* **121** C5
Carcassonne *France* **20** E6
Carcross *Canada* **102** A2
Çardak *Çanakkale, Turkey* **45** F10
Çardak *Denizli, Turkey* **47** D11
Cardamon Hills *India* **66** Q10
Cardamom Mts. =
    Kravanh, Chuor Phnum
    Cambodia **65** G4
Cardeña *Spain* **37** G6
Cárdenas *Cuba* **120** B3
Cárdenas *San Luis Potosí,
    Mexico* **119** C5
Cárdenas *Tabasco, Mexico* **119** D6
Cardener → *Spain* **38** D6
Cardenete *Spain* **38** F3
Cardiff *U.K.* **15** F4
Cardiff □ *U.K.* **15** F4
Cardiff-by-the-Sea *U.S.A.* **111** M9
Cardigan *U.K.* **15** E3
Cardigan B. *U.K.* **15** E3
Cardinal *Canada* **115** B9
Cardona *Spain* **38** D6
Cardona *Uruguay* **126** C4
Cardoso, Ilha do *Brazil* **127** B5
Cardston *Canada* **102** D6
Cardwell *Australia* **94** B4
Careen L. *Canada* **103** B7
Carei *Romania* **28** C7
Careme = Ciremay
    Indonesia **63** G13
Carentan *France* **18** C5
Carey *U.S.A.* **108** E7
Carey, L. *Australia* **93** E3
Carey L. *Canada* **103** A8
Careysburg *Liberia* **82** D2
Cargèse *France* **21** F12
Carhaix-Plouguer *France* **18** D3
Carhué *Argentina* **126** D3
Caria *Turkey* **47** D10
Cariacica *Brazil* **125** H10
Cariati *Italy* **43** C9
Caribbean Sea *W. Indies* **121** D5
Cariboo Mts. *Canada* **102** C4
Caribou *U.S.A.* **113** B19
Caribou → *Man., Canada* **103** B10
Caribou → *N.W.T., Canada* **102** A3
Caribou I. *Canada* **104** C2
Caribou Is. *Canada* **102** A6
Caribou L. *Man., Canada* **103** B9
Caribou L. *Ont., Canada* **104** B2
Caribou Mts. *Canada* **102** B5
Caribou River △ *Canada* **103** B9
Caribrod = Dimitrovgrad
    Serbia **44** C6
Carichíc *Mexico* **118** B3
Carigara *Phil.* **61** F6
Carignan *France* **19** C12
Carignano *Italy* **40** D4
Carinda *Australia* **95** E4

Cariñena *Spain* **38** D3
Carinhanha *Brazil* **125** F10
Carinhanha → *Brazil* **125** F10
Carini *Italy* **42** D6
Cariño *Spain* **36** B3
Carinola *Italy* **42** A6
Carinthia = Kärnten □
 Austria **26** E6
Caripito *Venezuela* **124** A6
Carlet *Spain* **39** F4
Carleton, Mt. *Canada* **105** C6
Carleton Place *Canada* **115** A8
Carletonville *S. Africa* **88** D4
Cârlibaba *Romania* **29** C10
Carlin *U.S.A.* **108** F5
Carlingford L. *U.K.* **12** B5
Carlinville *U.S.A.* **112** F9
Carlisle *U.K.* **14** C5
Carlisle *U.S.A.* **114** F7
Carlisle B. *Barbados* **121** g
Carlisle I. *Australia* **94** J7
Carlit, Pic *France* **20** F5
Carloforte *Italy* **42** C1
Carlos Casares *Argentina* **126** D3
Carlos Tejedor *Argentina* **126** D3
Carlow *Ireland* **12** D5
Carlow □ *Ireland* **12** D5
Carlsbad *Calif., U.S.A.* **111** M9
Carlsbad *N. Mex., U.S.A.* **109** K11
Carlsbad Caverns △ *U.S.A.*
 109 K11
Carluke *U.K.* **13** F5
Carlyle *Canada* **103** D8
Carmacks *Canada* **100** C6
Carmagnola *Italy* **40** D4
Carman *Canada* **103** D9
Carmarthen *U.K.* **15** F3
Carmarthen B. *U.K.* **15** F3
Carmarthenshire □ *U.K.* **15** F3
Carmaux *France* **20** D6
Carmel *U.S.A.* **115** E11
Carmel-by-the-Sea *U.S.A.* **110** J5
Carmelo *Uruguay* **126** C4
Carmen *Paraguay* **127** B4
Carmen → *Mexico* **118** A3
Carmen, I. *Mexico* **118** B2
Carmen de Patagones
 Argentina **128** E4
Cármenes *Spain* **36** C5
Carmensa *Argentina* **126** D2
Carmi *Canada* **102** D5
Carmi *U.S.A.* **112** F9
Carmichael *U.S.A.* **110** G5
Carmila *Australia* **94** C4
Carmona *Costa Rica* **120** E2
Carmona *Spain* **37** H5
Carn Ban *U.K.* **13** D4
Carn Eige *U.K.* **13** D3
Carnac *France* **18** E3
Carnamah *Australia* **93** E2
Carnarvon *Australia* **93** D1
Carnarvon *Canada* **114** A6
Carnarvon *S. Africa* **88** E3
Carnarvon △ *Australia* **94** C4
Carnarvon Ra. *Queens.,*
 Australia **94** D4
Carnarvon Ra. *W. Austral.,*
 Australia **93** E3
Carnation *U.S.A.* **110** C5
Carncastle *U.K.* **12** B6
Carndonagh *Ireland* **12** A4
Carnduff *Canada* **103** D8
Carnegie *U.S.A.* **114** F4
Carnegie, L. *Australia* **93** E3
Carnegie Ridge *Pac. Oc.* **97** H19
Carnic Alps = Karnische
 Alpen *Europe* **26** E6
Carniche Alpi = Karnische
 Alpen *Europe* **26** E6
Carnot *C.A.R.* **84** D3
Carnot, C. *Australia* **95** E2
Carnot B. *Australia* **92** C3
Carnoustie *U.K.* **13** E6
Carnsore Pt. *Ireland* **12** D5
Caro *U.S.A.* **113** D12
Caroga Lake *U.S.A.* **115** C10
Carol City *U.S.A.* **117** J14
Carolina *Brazil* **125** E9
Carolina *Puerto Rico* **121** d
Carolina *S. Africa* **89** D5
Caroline I. *Kiribati* **97** H12
Caroline Is. *Micronesia* **96** G6
Caroni → *Trin. & Tob.* **125** K15
Caroní → *Venezuela* **124** B6
Caronie = Nébrodi, Monti
 Italy **43** E7
Caroona *Australia* **95** E5
Carpathians *Europe* **23** D11
Carpaţii Meridionali
 Romania **29** E9
Carpentaria, G. of *Australia* **94** A2
Carpentras *France* **21** D9
Carpi *Italy* **40** D7
Cărpineni *Moldova* **29** D13
Carpinteria *U.S.A.* **111** L7
Carpio *Spain* **36** D5
Carr Boyd Ra. *Australia* **92** C4

Carra, L. *Ireland* **12** C2
Carrabelle *U.S.A.* **117** G12
Carral *Spain* **36** B2
Carranza, Presa V. *Mexico* **118** B4
Carrara *Italy* **40** D7
Carrascal *Phil.* **61** G6
Carrascosa del Campo *Spain* **38** E2
Carrauntoohill *Ireland* **12** D2
Carrick-on-Shannon *Ireland* **12** C3
Carrick-on-Suir *Ireland* **12** D4
Carrickfergus *U.K.* **12** B6
Carrickmacross *Ireland* **12** C5
Carrieton *Australia* **95** E2
Carrillo *Mexico* **118** B3
Carrington *U.S.A.* **112** B4
Carrión → *Spain* **36** D6
Carrión de los Condes *Spain* **36** C6
Carrizal Bajo *Chile* **126** B1
Carrizalillo *Chile* **126** B1
Carrizo Cr. → *U.S.A.* **109** H12
Carrizo Plain △ *U.S.A.* **110** K7
Carrizo Springs *U.S.A.* **116** G5
Carrizozo *U.S.A.* **109** K11
Carroll *U.S.A.* **112** D6
Carrollton *Ga., U.S.A.* **117** E12
Carrollton *Ill., U.S.A.* **112** F8
Carrollton *Ky., U.S.A.* **113** F11
Carrollton *Mo., U.S.A.* **112** F7
Carrollton *Ohio, U.S.A.* **114** F3
Carron → *U.K.* **13** D4
Carron, L. *U.K.* **13** D3
Carrot → *Canada* **103** C8
Carrot River *Canada* **103** C8
Carrouges *France* **18** D6
Carrù *Italy* **40** D4
Carruthers *Canada* **103** C7
Carsa Dek *Ethiopia* **81** F4
Çarşamba *Turkey* **72** B7
Carsóli *Italy* **41** F10
Carson *Calif., U.S.A.* **111** M8
Carson *N. Dak., U.S.A.* **112** B3
Carson → *U.S.A.* **110** F8
Carson City *U.S.A.* **110** F7
Carson Sink *U.S.A.* **108** G4
Cartagena *Colombia* **124** A3
Cartagena *Spain* **39** H4
Cartago *Colombia* **124** C3
Cartago *Costa Rica* **120** E3
Cártama *Spain* **37** J6
Cartaxo *Portugal* **37** F2
Cartaya *Spain* **37** H3
Cartersville *U.S.A.* **117** D12
Carterton *N.Z.* **91** D5
Carthage *Tunisia* **42** F3
Carthage *Ill., U.S.A.* **112** E8
Carthage *Mo., U.S.A.* **112** G6
Carthage *N.Y., U.S.A.* **113** D16
Carthage *Tex., U.S.A.* **116** E7
Cartier I. *Australia* **92** B3
Cartwright *Canada* **105** B8
Caruaru *Brazil* **125** E11
Carúpano *Venezuela* **124** A6
Caruthersville *U.S.A.* **112** G9
Carvin *France* **19** B9
Carvoeiro *Brazil* **124** D6
Carvoeiro, C. *Portugal* **37** F1
Cary *U.S.A.* **117** D15
Casa, Pas de la = Envalira,
 Port d' *Europe* **38** C6
Casa Branca *Portugal* **37** G2
Casa de Piedra *Argentina* **126** D2
Casa de Piedra, Embalse
 Argentina **126** D2
Casa Grande *U.S.A.* **109** K8
Casa Nova *Brazil* **125** E10
Casablanca *Chile* **126** C1
Casablanca *Morocco* **78** B4
Casacalenda *Italy* **41** G11
Casalbordino *Italy* **41** F11
Casale Monferrato *Italy* **40** C5
Casalmaggiore *Italy* **40** D7
Casalpusterlengo *Italy* **40** C6
Casamance → *Senegal* **82** C1
Casarano *Italy* **43** B11
Casares *Spain* **37** J5
Casas Ibáñez *Spain* **39** F3
Casasimarro *Spain* **39** F2
Casatejada *Spain* **36** F5
Casavieja *Spain* **36** E6
Cascada de Basaseachic △
 Mexico **118** B3
Cascade *Seychelles* **85** b
Cascade *Idaho, U.S.A.* **108** D5
Cascade *Mont., U.S.A.* **108** C8
Cascade Locks *U.S.A.* **110** E5
Cascade Ra. *U.S.A.* **110** D5
Cascade Res. *U.S.A.* **108** D5
Cascades, Pte. des *Réunion* **85** c
Cascais *Portugal* **37** G1
Cascavel *Brazil* **127** A5
Cáscina *Italy* **40** E7
Casco B. *U.S.A.* **113** D19
Caselle Torinese *Italy* **40** C4
Caserta *Italy* **43** A7
Casey *Antarctica* **5** C8
Caseyr, Raas = Asir, Ras
 Somali Rep. **75** E5
Cashel *Ireland* **12** D4

Casiguran *Phil.* **61** C5
Casilda *Argentina* **126** C3
Casimcea *Romania* **29** F13
Casino *Australia* **95** D5
Casiquiare → *Venezuela* **124** C5
Čáslav *Czech Rep.* **26** B8
Casma *Peru* **124** E3
Casmalia *U.S.A.* **111** L6
Cásola Valsénio *Italy* **41** D8
Cásoli *Italy* **41** F11
Caspe *Spain* **38** D4
Casper *U.S.A.* **108** E10
Caspian Depression *Eurasia* **35** G9
Caspian Sea *Eurasia* **52** E6
Cass City *U.S.A.* **114** C1
Cass Lake *U.S.A.* **112** B6
Cassà de la Selva *Spain* **38** D7
Cassadaga *U.S.A.* **114** D5
Cassano allo Iónio *Italy* **43** C9
Cassel *France* **19** B9
Casselman *Canada* **115** A9
Casselton *U.S.A.* **112** B5
Cassiar Mts. *Canada* **102** B2
Cassino *Italy* **42** A6
Cassis *France* **21** E9
Cassville *U.S.A.* **112** G7
Castagneto Carducci *Italy* **40** E7
Castaic *U.S.A.* **111** L8
Castalia *U.S.A.* **114** E2
Castanhal *Brazil* **125** D9
Castara *Trin. & Tob.* **125** J16
Castéggio *Italy* **40** C6
Castejón de Monegros *Spain* **38** D4
Castèl di Sangro *Italy* **41** G11
Castèl San Giovanni *Italy* **40** C6
Castèl San Pietro Terme
 Italy **41** D8
Castelbuono *Italy* **43** E7
Castelfidardo *Italy* **41** E10
Castelfiorentino *Italy* **40** E7
Castelfranco Emília *Italy* **40** D8
Castelfranco Véneto *Italy* **41** C8
Casteljaloux *France* **20** D4
Castellabate *Italy* **43** B7
Castellammare, G. di *Italy* **42** D5
Castellammare del Golfo
 Italy **42** D5
Castellammare di Stábia
 Italy **43** B7
Castellamonte *Italy* **40** C4
Castellane *France* **21** E10
Castellaneta *Italy* **43** B9
Castelli *Argentina* **126** D4
Castelló de la Plana *Spain* **38** F4
Castellón de la Plana □
 Spain **38** E4
Castellote *Spain* **38** E4
Castelmáuro *Italy* **41** G11
Castelnau-de-Médoc *France* **20** C3
Castelnau-Magnoac *France* **20** E4
Castelnaudary *France* **20** E5
Castelnovo ne' Monti *Italy* **40** D7
Castelnuovo di Val di
 Cécina *Italy* **40** E7
Castelo *Brazil* **127** A7
Castelo Branco *Portugal* **36** F3
Castelo Branco □ *Portugal* **36** F3
Castelo de Paiva *Portugal* **36** D2
Castelo de Vide *Portugal* **37** F3
Castelsardo *Italy* **42** B1
Castelsarrasin *France* **20** D5
Casteltérmini *Italy* **42** E6
Castelvetrano *Italy* **42** E5
Casterton *Australia* **95** F3
Castets *France* **20** E2
Castiglion Fiorentino *Italy* **41** E8
Castiglione del Lago *Italy* **41** E9
Castiglione della Pescáia
 Italy **40** F7
Castiglione delle Stiviere
 Italy **40** C7
Castilblanco *Spain* **37** F5
Castile *U.S.A.* **114** D6
Castilla, Playa de *Spain* **37** J4
Castilla-La Mancha □ *Spain* **37** F7
Castilla y Leon □ *Spain* **36** D6
Castillo de Locubín *Spain* **37** H7
Castillon-en-Couserans
 France **20** F5
Castillonès *France* **20** D4
Castillos *Uruguay* **127** C5
Castle Dale *U.S.A.* **108** G8
Castle Douglas *U.K.* **13** G5
Castle Rock *Colo., U.S.A.* **108** G11
Castle Rock *Wash., U.S.A.* **110** D4
Castlebar *Ireland* **12** C2
Castleblaney *Ireland* **12** B5
Castlederg *U.K.* **12** B4
Castleford *U.K.* **14** D6
Castlegar *Canada* **102** D5
Castlemaine *Australia* **95** F3
Castlemaine *Ireland* **12** D2
Castlepollard *Ireland* **12** C4
Castlerea *Ireland* **12** C3
Castlereagh → *Australia* **95** E4
Castlereagh B. *Australia* **94** A2
Castleton *U.S.A.* **115** C11

Castleton-on-Hudson
 U.S.A. **115** D11
Castletown *I. of Man* **14** C3
Castletown Bearhaven
 Ireland **12** E2
Castor *Canada* **102** C6
Castor → *Canada* **104** B4
Castorland *U.S.A.* **115** C9
Castres *France* **20** E6
Castricum *Neths.* **17** B4
Castries *St. Lucia* **121** f
Castril *Spain* **37** H8
Castro *Brazil* **127** A6
Castro *Chile* **128** E2
Castro Alves *Brazil* **125** F11
Castro del Río *Spain* **37** H6
Castro-Urdiales *Spain* **36** B7
Castro Valley *U.S.A.* **110** H4
Castro Verde *Portugal* **37** H2
Castrojeriz *Spain* **36** C6
Castropol *Spain* **36** B4
Castroreale *Italy* **43** D8
Castrovíllari *Italy* **43** C9
Castroville *U.S.A.* **110** J5
Castuera *Spain* **37** G5
Cat Ba, Dao *Vietnam* **64** B6
Cat Ba △ *Vietnam* **64** B6
Cat I. *Bahamas* **121** B4
Cat L. *Canada* **104** B1
Cat Lake *Canada* **104** B1
Cat Tien △ *Vietnam* **65** G6
Catacamas *Honduras* **120** D2
Cataguases *Brazil* **127** A7
Çatak *Turkey* **73** C10
Çatalağzı *Turkey* **72** B4
Catalão *Brazil* **125** G9
Çatalca *Turkey* **45** E12
Catalina *Canada* **105** C9
Catalina *Chile* **126** B2
Catalina *U.S.A.* **109** K8
Catalonia = Cataluña □
 Spain **38** D6
Cataluña □ *Spain* **38** D6
Çatalzeytin *Turkey* **72** B6
Catamarca *Argentina* **126** B2
Catamarca □ *Argentina* **126** B2
Catanauan *Phil.* **61** E5
Catanduanes □ *Phil.* **61** E6
Catanduva *Brazil* **127** A6
Catánia *Italy* **43** E8
Catánia, G. di *Italy* **43** E8
Catanzaro *Italy* **43** D9
Catarman *Phil.* **61** E6
Catatumbo-Bari △ *Colombia* **121** E5
Catbalogan *Phil.* **61** F6
Catchacoma *Canada* **114** B6
Cateel *Phil.* **61** H7
Catembe *Mozam.* **89** D5
Caterham *U.K.* **15** F7
Cathcart *S. Africa* **88** E4
Cathedral City *U.S.A.* **111** M10
Cathlamet *U.S.A.* **110** D3
Catio *Guinea-Biss.* **82** C1
Catlettsburg *U.S.A.* **113** F12
Çatma Dağı *Turkey* **47** C11
Catoche, C. *Mexico* **119** C7
Catriló *Argentina* **126** D3
Catrimani *Brazil* **124** C6
Catrimani → *Brazil* **124** C6
Catskill *U.S.A.* **115** D11
Catskill △ *U.S.A.* **115** D10
Catskill Mts. *U.S.A.* **115** D10
Catt, Mt. *Australia* **94** A1
Cattaraugus *U.S.A.* **114** D6
Catterick *U.K.* **14** C6
Cáttolica *Italy* **41** E9
Cáttolica Eraclea *Italy* **42** E6
Catuala *Angola* **88** B2
Catuane *Mozam.* **89** D5
Catur *Mozam.* **87** E4
Cauca → *Colombia* **124** B4
Caucaia *Brazil* **125** D11
Caucasus Mountains *Eurasia* **35** J7
Caucete *Argentina* **126** C2
Caudete *Spain* **39** G3
Caudry *France* **19** B10
Caulnes *France* **18** D4
Caulónia *Italy* **43** D9
Caungula *Angola* **84** F3
Cauquenes *Chile* **126** D1
Caura → *Venezuela* **124** B6
Cauresi → *Mozam.* **87** F3
Căuşani *Moldova* **29** D14
Causapscal *Canada* **105** C6
Caussade *France* **20** D5
Causse-Méjean *France* **20** D7
Causses du Quercy → *France* **20** D5
Cauterets *France* **20** F3
Cauvery → *India* **66** P11
Caux, Pays de *France* **18** C4
Cava de' Tirreni *Italy* **43** B7
Cávado → *Portugal* **36** D2
Cavagrande del Cassibile △
 Italy **43** F8
Cavaillon *France* **21** E9

Cavalaire-sur-Mer *France* **21** E10
Cavalese *Italy* **41** B8
Cavalier *U.S.A.* **112** A5
Cavalla = Cavally → *Africa* **82** E3
Cavalla △ *Liberia* **82** D3
Cavallo, Î. de *France* **21** G13
Cavally → *Africa* **82** E3
Cavan *Ireland* **12** B4
Cavan □ *Ireland* **12** C4
Cavárzere *Italy* **41** C9
Cave City *U.S.A.* **113** G11
Cavenagh Ra. *Australia* **93** E4
Cavendish *Australia* **95** F3
Caviana, I. *Brazil* **125** C8
Cavite *Phil.* **61** D4
Cavnic *Romania* **29** C8
Cavour *Italy* **40** D4
Cavtat *Croatia* **44** D2
Cawndilla L. *Australia* **95** E3
Cawnpore = Kanpur *India* **69** F9
Caxias *Brazil* **125** D10
Caxias do Sul *Brazil* **127** B5
Çay *Turkey* **72** C4
Cay Sal Bank *Bahamas* **120** B4
Cayambe *Ecuador* **124** C3
Çaycuma *Turkey* **72** B5
Çayeli *Turkey* **73** B9
Cayenne *Fr. Guiana* **125** B8
Cayey *Puerto Rico* **121** d
Caygören Baraji *Turkey* **47** B10
Cayiralan *Turkey* **72** C6
Caylus *France* **20** D5
Cayman Brac *Cayman Is.* **120** C4
Cayman Is. ☑ *W. Indies* **120** C3
Cayman Trough *Caribbean* **98** H11
Cayres *France* **20** D7
Cayuga *Canada* **114** D5
Cayuga *U.S.A.* **115** D8
Cayuga Heights *U.S.A.* **115** D8
Cayuga L. *U.S.A.* **115** D8
Cazalla de la Sierra *Spain* **37** H5
Căzăneşti *Romania* **29** F12
Cazaubon *France* **20** E3
Cazaux et de Sanguinet,
 Étang de *France* **20** D2
Cazenovia *U.S.A.* **115** D9
Cazères *France* **20** E5
Cazin *Bos.-H.* **41** D12
Čazma *Croatia* **41** C13
Cazombo *Angola* **85** G4
Cazorla *Spain* **37** H7
Cazorla, Sierra de *Spain* **37** G8
Cea → *Spain* **36** C5
Ceamurlia de Jos *Romania* **29** F13
Ceanannus Mor *Ireland* **12** C5
Ceará = Fortaleza *Brazil* **125** D11
Ceará □ *Brazil* **125** D11
Ceará-Mirim *Brazil* **125** E11
Ceauru, L. *Romania* **29** F8
Cébaco, I. de Panama *128* D7
Cebollar *Argentina* **126** B2
Cebollera, Sierra de *Spain* **38** D2
Cebreros *Spain* **36** E6
Cebu *Phil.* **61** F5
Čečava *Bos.-H.* **28** F2
Ceccano *Italy* **42** A6
Cece *Hungary* **28** D3
Cechi *Ivory C.* **82** D4
Cecil Plains *Australia* **95** D5
Cécina *Italy* **40** E7
Cécina → *Italy* **40** E7
Ceclavín *Spain* **36** F4
Cedar → *U.S.A.* **112** E9
Cedar City *U.S.A.* **109** H7
Cedar Creek Res. *U.S.A.* **116** E6
Cedar Falls *Iowa, U.S.A.* **112** D7
Cedar Falls *Wash., U.S.A.* **110** C5
Cedar Key *U.S.A.* **117** G13
Cedar L. *Canada* **103** C9
Cedar Park *U.S.A.* **116** F6
Cedar Rapids *U.S.A.* **112** E8
Cedarvale *Canada* **102** B3
Cedarville *S. Africa* **89** E4
Cedeira *Spain* **36** B2
Cedral *Mexico* **118** C4
Cedro *Brazil* **125** E11
Cedros, I. *Mexico* **118** B1
Cedros B. *Trin. & Tob.* **125** K15
Ceduna *Australia* **95** E1
Cedynia *Poland* **31** F1
Cée *Spain* **36** C1
Ceeldheere *Somali Rep.* **75** G4
Ceerigaabo *Somali Rep.* **75** E4
Cefalù *Italy* **43** D7
Cega → *Spain* **36** D6
Cegléd *Hungary* **28** C4
Céglie Messápico *Italy* **43** B10
Cehegín *Spain* **39** G3
Cehu-Silvaniei *Romania* **29** C8

Cekik *Indonesia* **63** J17
Čelákovice *Czech Rep.* **26** A7
Celano *Italy* **41** F10
Celanova *Spain* **36** C3
Celaque △ *Honduras* **120** D2
Celaya *Mexico* **118** C4
Celebes = Sulawesi *Indonesia* **63** E6
Celebes Sea *Indonesia* **63** D6
Čelić *Bos.-H.* **28** F3
Celina *U.S.A.* **113** E11
Celinac *Bos.-H.* **28** F2
Celje *Slovenia* **41** B12
Celldömölk *Hungary* **28** C2
Celle *Germany* **24** C6
Celorico da Beira *Portugal* **36** E3
Celtic Sea *Atl. Oc.* **16** F2
Çeltikçi *Turkey* **47** D12
Çemişgezek *Turkey* **73** C8
Cenderwasih, Teluk
 Indonesia **63** E9
Cengong *China* **58** D7
Ceno → *Italy* **40** D7
Centallo *Italy* **40** D4
Centelles *Spain* **38** D7
Center *N. Dak., U.S.A.* **112** B3
Center *Tex., U.S.A.* **116** F7
Centerburg *U.S.A.* **114** F2
Centerville *Calif., U.S.A.* **110** J7
Centerville *Iowa, U.S.A.* **112** E7
Centerville *Pa., U.S.A.* **114** F5
Centerville *Tenn., U.S.A.* **117** D11
Centerville *Tex., U.S.A.* **116** F7
Cento *Italy* **41** D8
Central = Tsentralnyy □
 Russia **34** D4
Central □ *Ghana* **83** D4
Central □ *Kenya* **86** C4
Central □ *Malawi* **87** E3
Central □ *Zambia* **87** E2
Central, Cordillera *Colombia* **124** C4
Central, Cordillera
 Costa Rica **120** D3
Central, Cordillera
 Dom. Rep. **121** C5
Central, Cordillera *Phil.* **61** C4
Central, Cordillera
 Puerto Rico **121** d
Central African Rep. ■
 Africa **79** G9
Central America *America* **98** H11
Central Butte *Canada* **103** C7
Central City *Colo., U.S.A.* **108** G11
Central City *Ky., U.S.A.* **112** G10
Central City *Nebr., U.S.A.* **112** E4
Central I. *Kenya* **86** B4
Central Island △ *Kenya* **86** B4
Central Kalahari △
 Botswana **88** C3
Central Makran Range
 Pakistan **66** F4
Central Pacific Basin
 Pac. Oc. **96** G10
Central Patricia *Canada* **104** B1
Central Point *U.S.A.* **108** E2
Central Russian Uplands
 Europe **6** E13
Central Siberian Plateau
 Russia **50** B12
Central Square *U.S.A.* **115** C8
Centralia *Canada* **114** C3
Centralia *Ill., U.S.A.* **112** F9
Centralia *Mo., U.S.A.* **112** F7
Centralia *Wash., U.S.A.* **110** D4
Centre □ *Cameroon* **83** E7
Centre de Flacq *Mauritius* **85** d
Centreville *N.Y., U.S.A.* **114** D6
Centreville *Pa., U.S.A.* **114** F5
Cenxi *China* **59** F8
Čeotina → *Bos.-H.* **44** C2
Cephalonia = Kefalonia
 Greece **46** C2
Čepin *Croatia* **28** E3
Ceprano *Italy* **42** A6
Ceptura *Romania* **29** E11
Cepu *Indonesia* **63** G14
Ceram = Seram *Indonesia* **63** E7
Ceram Sea = Seram Sea
 Indonesia **63** E7
Cerbère *France* **20** F7
Cerbicales, Îs. *France* **21** G13
Cercal *Portugal* **37** H2
Cerdaña *Spain* **38** C6
Cère → *France* **20** D5
Cerea *Italy* **41** C8
Ceredigion □ *U.K.* **15** E3
Ceres *Argentina* **126** B3
Ceres *S. Africa* **88** E2
Ceres *U.S.A.* **110** H6
Céret *France* **20** F6
Cerf *Seychelles* **85** b
Cergy *France* **19** C9
Cerignola *Italy* **43** A8
Cerigo = Kythira *Greece* **46** E5
Cérilly *France* **19** F9
Cerisiers *France* **19** D10
Cerizay *France* **18** F6
Çerkeş *Turkey* **72** B5
Çerkezköy *Turkey* **45** E12

Cerknica *Slovenia* **41** C11
Cerkovica *Bulgaria* **45** C8
Cermerno *Serbia* **44** C4
Çermik *Turkey* **73** C8
Cerna *Romania* **29** E13
Cerna → *Romania* **29** F8
Cernavodă *Romania* **29** F13
Cernay *France* **19** E14
Cernik *Croatia* **28** E2
Cernavoda *Italy* **40** E8
Cerralvo, I. *Mexico* **118** C3
Cërrik *Albania* **44** E3
Cerritos *Mexico* **118** C4
Cerro Chato *Uruguay* **127** C4
Cerro Cofre de Perote △
  Mexico **119** D5
Cerro Corá △ *Paraguay* **127** A4
Cerro el Copey △ *Venezuela* **121** D7
Cerro Hoya △ *Panama* **120** E3
Cerro Saroche △ *Venezuela* **121** D6
Certaldo *Italy* **40** E8
Cervaro → *Italy* **43** A8
Cervati, Monte *Italy* **43** B8
Cerventes *Australia* **93** F2
Cervera *Spain* **38** D6
Cervera de Pisuerga *Spain* **36** C6
Cervera del Río Alhama
  Spain **38** C3
Cervéteri *Italy* **41** F9
Cérvia *Italy* **41** D9
Cervignano del Friuli *Italy* **41** C10
Cervinara *Italy* **43** A7
Cervione *France* **21** F13
Cervo *Spain* **36** B3
Cesarò *Italy* **43** E7
Cesena *Italy* **41** D9
Cesenático *Italy* **41** D9
Cēsis *Latvia* **32** D3
Česká Lípa *Czech Rep.* **26** A7
Česká Rep. = Czech Rep. ■
  Europe **26** B8
Česká Třebová *Czech Rep.* **27** B9
České Budějovice *Czech Rep.* **26** C7
České Velenice *Czech Rep.* **26** C7
Českobudějovický □
  Czech Rep. **26** B7
Českomoravská Vrchovina
  Czech Rep. **26** B8
Český Brod *Czech Rep.* **26** A7
Český Krumlov *Czech Rep.* **26** C7
Český Těšín *Czech Rep.* **27** B11
Česma → *Croatia* **41** C13
Çeşme *Turkey* **47** C8
Cessnock *Australia* **95** E5
Cesson-Sévigné *France* **18** D5
Cestas *France* **20** D3
Cestos → *Liberia* **82** D3
Cestos Sehnkwehn △ *Liberia* **82** D3
Cetate *Romania* **28** F8
Cetin Grad *Croatia* **41** C12
Cetina → *Croatia* **41** E13
Cetinje *Montenegro* **44** D2
Cetraro *Italy* **43** C8
Ceva *Italy* **40** D5
Cévennes *France* **20** D7
Cévennes △ *France* **20** D7
Ceyhan *Turkey* **72** D6
Ceyhan → *Turkey* **72** D6
Ceylanpınar *Turkey* **73** D9
Ceylon = Sri Lanka ■ *Asia* **66** R12
Cèze → *France* **21** D8
Cha-am *Thailand* **64** F2
Chabanais *France* **20** C4
Chabeuil *France* **21** D9
Chablais *France* **21** F13
Chablis *France* **19** E10
Chacabuco *Argentina* **126** C3
Chachapoyas *Peru* **124** E3
Chachoengsao *Thailand* **64** F3
Chachran *Pakistan* **68** E4
Chachro *Pakistan* **68** G4
Chaco □ *Argentina* **126** B3
Chaco □ *Paraguay* **126** B4
Chaco → *U.S.A.* **109** H9
Chaco △ *Argentina* **126** B4
Chaco Austral *S. Amer.* **128** B4
Chaco Boreal *S. Amer.* **124** H6
Chaco Central *S. Amer.* **128** A4
Chaco Culture △ *U.S.A.* **109** H10
Chacon, C. *U.S.A.* **102** C2
Chad ■ *Africa* **79** F8
Chad, L. = Tchad, L. *Chad* **79** F8
Chadileuvú → *Argentina* **126** D2
Chadiza *Zambia* **87** E3
Chadron *U.S.A.* **112** D2
Chadyr-Lunga =
  Ciadâr-Lunga *Moldova* **29** D13
Chae Hom *Thailand* **64** C2
Chae Son △ *Thailand* **64** C2
Chaem → *Thailand* **64** C2
Chaeryŏng *N. Korea* **57** E13
Chafe *Nigeria* **83** C6
Chagai Hills = Chāh Gay
  Hills *Afghan.* **66** E3
Chagda *Russia* **53** D14
Chaghcharān *Afghan.* **66** B4
Chagny *France* **19** F11
Chagoda *Russia* **32** C8

Chagos Arch. ☑ *Ind. Oc.* **50** J9
Chagres △ *Panama* **120** E4
Chaguanas *Trin. & Tob.* **125** K15
Chāh Akhvor *Iran* **71** C8
Chāh Bahar *Iran* **71** E9
Chāh-e Kavīr *Iran* **71** C8
Chāh Gay Hills *Afghan.* **66** E3
Chahar Borj *Iran* **73** D11
Chahār Borjak *Afghan.* **66** D3
Chahār Mahāll va
  Bakhtīārī □ *Iran* **71** C6
Chai Badan *Thailand* **64** E3
Chaibasa *India* **69** H11
Chaillé-les-Marais *France* **20** B2
Chainat *Thailand* **64** E3
Chaiya *Thailand* **65** H2
Chaiyaphum *Thailand* **64** E4
Chaj Doab *Pakistan* **68** C5
Chajari *Argentina* **126** C4
Chak Amru *Pakistan* **68** C6
Chaka *Sudan* **81** G3
Chakar → *Pakistan* **68** E3
Chakari *Zimbabwe* **89** B4
Chake Chake *Tanzania* **86** D4
Chakhānsūr *Afghan.* **66** D3
Chakradharpur *India* **69** H11
Chakrata *India* **68** D7
Chakwal *Pakistan* **68** C5
Chala *Peru* **124** G4
Chalais *France* **20** C4
Chalchihuites *Mexico* **118** C4
Chalcis = Halkida *Greece* **46** C5
Châlette-sur-Loing *France* **19** D9
Chaleur B. *Canada* **105** C6
Chalfant *U.S.A.* **110** H8
Chalhuanca *Peru* **124** F4
Chaliki *Greece* **46** B4
Chalindrey *France* **19** E12
Chaling *China* **59** D9
Chalisgaon *India* **66** J9
Chalk River *Canada* **104** C4
Chalkar, Ozero = Shalkar
  Köli *Kazakhstan* **34** E10
Chalky Inlet *N.Z.* **91** G1
Challans *France* **18** F5
Challapata *Bolivia* **124** G5
Challawa Gorge Res. *Nigeria* **83** C6
Challenger Deep *Pac. Oc.* **96** F6
Challenger Fracture Zone
  Pac. Oc. **97** L17
Challis *U.S.A.* **108** D6
Chalmette *U.S.A.* **117** G10
Chalon-sur-Saône *France* **19** F11
Chalong *Thailand* **65** a
Chalonnes-sur-Loire *France* **18** E6
Châlons-en-Champagne
  France **19** D11
Chálten, Cerro = Fitz Roy,
  Cerro *Argentina* **128** F2
Châlus *France* **20** C4
Chālūs *Iran* **71** B6
Cham *Germany* **25** F8
Cham, Cu Lao *Vietnam* **64** E7
Chama *U.S.A.* **109** H10
Chamaicó *Argentina* **126** D3
Chaman *Pakistan* **66** D5
Chamba *India* **68** C7
Chamba *Tanzania* **87** E4
Chambal → *India* **69** F8
Chamberlain *U.S.A.* **112** D4
Chamberlain → *Australia* **92** C4
Chamberlain L. *U.S.A.* **113** B19
Chambers *U.S.A.* **109** J9
Chambersburg *U.S.A.* **113** F15
Chambéry *France* **21** C9
Chambeshi → *Zambia* **84** G6
Chambly *Canada* **115** A11
Chambord *Canada* **105** C5
Chamboulive *France* **20** C5
Chamchamal *Iraq* **73** E11
Chamela *Mexico* **118** D3
Chamical *Argentina* **126** C2
Chamkar Luong *Cambodia* **65** G4
Chamoli *India* **69** D8
Chamonix-Mont Blanc
  France **21** C10
Chamouchuane =
  Ashuapmushuan →
  Canada **104** C5
Champa *India* **69** H10
Champagne *Canada* **102** A1
Champagne *France* **19** D11
Champagnole *France* **19** F12
Champaign *U.S.A.* **112** E9
Champassak *Laos* **64** E5
Champaubert *France* **19** D10
Champawat *India* **69** E9
Champdeniers-St-Denis
  France **20** B3
Champdoré, L. *Canada* **105** A6
Champeix *France* **20** C7
Champion *U.S.A.* **114** E4
Champlain *U.S.A.* **115** B11
Champlain, L. *U.S.A.* **115** B11
Champlitte *France* **19** E12
Champotón *Mexico* **119** D6
Champua *India* **69** H11

Chamusca *Portugal* **37** F2
Chana *Thailand* **65** J3
Chañaral *Chile* **126** B1
Chanārān *Iran* **71** B8
Chanasma *India* **68** H5
Chancery Lane *Barbados* **121** g
Chanco *Chile* **126** D1
Chand *India* **69** J8
Chandan *India* **69** G12
Chandan Chauki *India* **69** E9
Chandannagar *India* **69** H13
Chandausi *India* **69** E8
Chandeleur Is. *U.S.A.* **117** G10
Chandeleur Sd. *U.S.A.* **117** G10
Chandigarh *India* **68** D7
Chandil *India* **69** H12
Chandler *Australia* **95** D1
Chandler *Canada* **105** C7
Chandler *Ariz., U.S.A.* **109** K8
Chandler *Okla., U.S.A.* **116** D6
Chandod *India* **68** J5
Chandpur *Bangla.* **67** H17
Chandra → *India* **69** C7
Chandrapur *India* **66** K11
Chānf *Iran* **71** E9
Chang, Ko *Thailand* **65** G4
Chang, Ko *Thailand* **65** G4
Chang'an = Chang
  Jiang → *China* **59** B13
Chang Jiang → *China* **59** B13
Chang-won *S. Korea* **57** G15
Changa *China* **69** C7
Changanacheri *India* **66** Q10
Changane → *Mozam.* **89** C5
Changbai *China* **57** D15
Changbai Shan *China* **57** C15
Changchiak'ou =
  Zhangjiakou *China* **56** D8
Ch'angchou = Changzhou
  China **59** B12
Changchun *China* **57** C13
Changchunling *China* **57** B13
Changde *China* **59** C8
Changdo-ri *N. Korea* **57** E14
Changfeng *China* **59** A11
Changhai = Shanghai
  China **59** B13
Changhua *China* **59** B12
Changhua *Taiwan* **59** E13
Changhŭngni *N. Korea* **57** D15
Changi *Singapore* **65** d
Changi, Singapore ✈ (SIN)
  Singapore **65** M4
Changjiang *China* **64** C7
Changjin *N. Korea* **57** D14
Changjin-ho *N. Korea* **57** D14
Changle *China* **59** E12
Changli *China* **57** E10
Changling *China* **57** B12
Changlun *Malaysia* **65** J3
Changning *Hunan, China* **59** D9
Changning *Sichuan, China* **58** C5
Changning *Yunnan, China* **58** E2
Changping *China* **56** D9
Changsha *China* **59** C9
Changshan *China* **59** C12
Changshan Qundao *China* **57** E12
Changshu *China* **59** B13
Changshun *China* **58** D6
Changtai *China* **59** E11
Changting *China* **59** E11
Changuinola *Panama* **120** E3
Changwu *China* **56** G4
Changxing *China* **59** B12
Changyang *China* **59** B8
Changyi *China* **57** F10
Changyŏn *N. Korea* **57** E13
Changyuan *China* **56** G8
Changzhi *China* **56** F7
Changzhou *China* **59** B12
Chanhanga *Angola* **88** B1
Chania *Greece* **49** D6
Chania → *Greece* **49** D6
Chanion, Kolpos *Greece* **49** D5
Chanlar = Xanlar *Azerbaijan* **35** K8
Channapatna *India* **66** N10
Channel Is. *U.K.* **15** H5
Channel Is. *U.S.A.* **111** M7
Channel Islands △ *U.S.A.* **111** L7
Channel-Port aux Basques
  Canada **105** C8
Channel Tunnel *Europe* **15** F9
Channing *U.S.A.* **116** D3
Chantada *Spain* **36** C3
Chanthaburi *Thailand* **64** F4
Chantilly *France* **19** C9
Chantonnay *France* **18** F5
Chantrey Inlet *Canada* **100** C10
Chanute *U.S.A.* **112** G6
Chanza → *Spain* **37** H3
Chao Hu *China* **59** B11
Chao Phraya → *Thailand* **64** F3
Chao Phraya Lowlands
  Thailand **64** E3
Chaocheng *China* **56** F8
Chaohu *China* **59** B11
Chaoyang *Guangdong, China* **59** F11
Chaoyang *Liaoning, China* **57** D11

Chaozhou *China* **59** F11
Chapaev *Kazakhstan* **34** E10
Chapais *Canada* **104** C5
Chapala *Mexico* **118** C4
Chapala, L. de *Mexico* **118** C4
Chapayevsk *Russia* **34** D9
Chapecó *Brazil* **127** B5
Chapel Hill *U.S.A.* **117** D15
Chapleau *Canada* **104** C3
Chaplin *Canada* **103** C7
Chaplin L. *Canada* **103** C7
Chaplino *Ukraine* **33** H9
Chaplygin *Russia* **32** F11
Chappell *U.S.A.* **112** E2
Chapra = Chhapra *India* **69** G11
Chaqābel *Iran* **73** F12
Chara *Russia* **53** D12
Charadai *Argentina* **126** B4
Charagua *Bolivia* **124** G6
Charakas *Greece* **49** D7
Charambirá, Punta
  Colombia **124** C3
Charaña *Bolivia* **124** G5
Charantsavan *Armenia* **35** K7
Charanwala *India* **68** F5
Charata *Argentina* **126** B3
Charcas *Mexico* **118** C4
Charcot I. *Antarctica* **5** C17
Chard *U.K.* **15** G5
Chardon *U.S.A.* **114** E3
Chardzhou =
  Türkmenabat
  Turkmenistan **71** B9
Charente □ *France* **20** C4
Charente → *France* **20** C2
Charente-Maritime □
  France **20** C3
Charenton-du-Cher *France* **19** F9
Chari → *Chad* **79** F8
Chārīkār *Afghan.* **66** B6
Chariton *U.S.A.* **112** E7
Chariton → *U.S.A.* **112** F7
Chärjew = Türkmenabat
  Turkmenistan **71** B9
Charkhari *India* **69** G8
Charkhi Dadri *India* **68** E7
Charleroi *Belgium* **17** D4
Charleroi *U.S.A.* **114** F5
Charles, C. *U.S.A.* **113** G16
Charles City *U.S.A.* **112** D8
Charles de Gaulle, Paris ✈
  (CDG) *France* **19** D9
Charles L. *Canada* **103** B6
Charles Town *U.S.A.* **113** F15
Charlesbourg *Canada* **113** B18
Charleston *Ill., U.S.A.* **112** F9
Charleston *Miss., U.S.A.* **117** D9
Charleston *Mo., U.S.A.* **112** G9
Charleston *S.C., U.S.A.* **117** E15
Charleston *W. Va., U.S.A.* **113** F13
Charleston L. *Canada* **115** B9
Charleston Peak *U.S.A.* **111** J11
Charlestown *Ireland* **12** C3
Charlestown *S. Africa* **89** D4
Charlestown *Ind., U.S.A.* **113** F11
Charlestown *N.H., U.S.A.* **115** C12
Charlestown of Aberlour
  U.K. **13** D5
Charleville = Rath Luirc
  Ireland **12** D3
Charleville *Australia* **95** D4
Charleville-Mézières *France* **19** C11
Charlevoix *U.S.A.* **113** C11
Charlieu *France* **19** F11
Charlotte *Mich., U.S.A.* **113** D11
Charlotte *N.C., U.S.A.* **117** D14
Charlotte *Vt., U.S.A.* **115** B11
Charlotte Amalie
  U.S. Virgin Is. **121** e
Charlotte Harbor *U.S.A.* **117** H13
Charlotte L. *Canada* **102** C3
Charlottenberg *Sweden* **10** E6
Charlottesville *U.S.A.* **113** F14
Charlottetown *Nfld. & L.,
  Canada* **105** B8
Charlottetown *P.E.I.,
  Canada* **105** C7
Charlotteville *Trin. & Tob.* **125** J16
Charlton *Australia* **95** F3
Charlton I. *Canada* **104** B4
Charmes *France* **19** D13
Charny *Canada* **105** C5
Charnyany *Belarus* **31** G11
Charolles *France* **19** F11
Chârost *France* **19** F9
Charre *Mozam.* **87** F4
Charrouх *France* **20** B4
Charsadda *Pakistan* **68** B4
Charters Towers *Australia* **94** C4
Chartres *France* **18** D8
Chascomús *Argentina* **126** D4
Chase *Canada* **102** C5
Chasefu *Zambia* **87** E3
Chashma Barrage *Pakistan* **68** C4
Chassenenuil-sur-
  Bonnieure *France* **20** C4

Chât *Iran* **71** B7
Chatal Balkan = Udvoy
  Balkan *Bulgaria* **45** D10
Château-Arnoux-St-
  Auban *France* **21** D10
Château-Chinon *France* **19** E10
Château-d'Olonne *France* **20** B2
Château-du-Loir *France* **18** E7
Château-Gontier *France* **18** E6
Château-la-Vallière *France* **18** E7
Château-Landon *France* **19** D9
Château-Renard *France* **19** D9
Château-Renault *France* **18** E7
Château-Salins *France* **19** D13
Château-Thierry *France* **19** C10
Châteaubourg *France* **18** D5
Châteaubriant *France* **18** E5
Châteaudun *France* **18** D8
Châteaugay *U.S.A.* **115** B10
Châteaugiron *France* **18** D5
Châteauguay, L. *Canada* **105** A5
Châteaulin *France* **18** D2
Châteaumeillant *France* **19** F9
Châteauneuf-du-Faou
  France **18** D3
Châteauneuf-sur-Charente
  France **20** C3
Châteauneuf-sur-Cher
  France **19** F9
Châteauneuf-sur-Loire
  France **19** E9
Châteaurenard *France* **21** E8
Châteauroux *France* **19** F8
Châteauvillain *France* **19** D11
Châteaux, Pte. des
  Guadeloupe **120** b
Châtelaillon-Plage *France* **20** B2
Châtelguyon *France* **20** C7
Châtellerault *France* **18** F7
Châtelus-Malvaleix *France* **19** F9
Châtillon *Italy* **40** C4
Châtillon-Coligny *France* **19** E9
Châtillon-en-Diois *France* **21** D9
Châtillon-sur-Indre *France* **18** F8
Châtillon-sur-Loire *France* **19** E9
Châtillon-sur-Seine *France* **19** E11
Chatmohar *Bangla.* **69** G13
Chatra *India* **69** G11
Chatrapur *India* **67** K14
Chats, L. des *Canada* **115** A8
Chatsu *India* **68** F6
Chatsworth *Canada* **114** B4
Chatsworth *Zimbabwe* **87** F3
Châttagâm = Chittagong
  Bangla. **67** H17
Chattahoochee *U.S.A.* **117** F12
Chattahoochee → *U.S.A.* **117** F12
Chattanooga *U.S.A.* **117** D12
Chatteris *U.K.* **15** E8
Chatturat *Thailand* **64** E3
Chau Doc *Vietnam* **65** G5
Chaudes-Aigues *France* **20** D7
Chauffailles *France* **19** F11
Chaukan Pass *Burma* **67** F20
Chaumont *France* **19** D12
Chaumont *U.S.A.* **115** B8
Chaumont-en-Vexin *France* **19** C8
Chaumont-sur-Loire *France* **18** E8
Chaunay *France* **20** B4
Chauny *France* **19** C10
Chausey, Îs. *France* **18** D5
Chaussin *France* **19** F12
Chautauqua L. *U.S.A.* **114** D5
Chauvigny *France* **18** F7
Chauvin *Canada* **103** C6
Chavanges *France* **19** D11
Chaves *Brazil* **125** D9
Chaves *Portugal* **36** D3
Chawang *Thailand* **65** H2
Chazelles-sur-Lyon *France* **21** C8
Chazy *U.S.A.* **115** B11
Cheb *Czech Rep.* **26** A5
Cheboksarskoye Vdkhr.
  Russia **34** B8
Cheboksary *Russia* **34** B8
Cheboygan *U.S.A.* **113** C11
Chebsara *Russia* **32** C10
Chech, Erg *Africa* **78** D5
Chechelnyk *Ukraine* **29** B14
Chechen, Ostrov *Russia* **35** H8
Chechenia □ *Russia* **35** J7
Checheno-Ingush Republic
  = Chechenia □ *Russia* **35** J7
Chechnya = Chechenia □
  Russia **35** J7
Chęciny *Poland* **31** H7
Checotah *U.S.A.* **116** D7
Cheduba I. *Burma* **67** K18
Cheepie *Australia* **95** D4

Cheepie *Australia* **95** D4
Chef-Boutonne *France* **20** B3
Chegdomyn *Russia* **53** D14
Chegga *Mauritania* **78** C4
Chegutu *Zimbabwe* **87** F3
Chehalis *U.S.A.* **110** D4
Chehalis → *U.S.A.* **110** D3
Cheile Nerei-Beusnita △
  Romania **28** F6
Cheiron, Mt. *France* **21** E10
Cheju = Jeju *S. Korea* **57** H14
Cheju-do = Jeju-do *S. Korea* **57** H14
Chekalin *Russia* **32** E9
Chekhovo *Russia* **30** D7
Chekiang = Zhejiang □
  China **59** C13
Chel = Kuru, Bahr el →
  Sudan **81** F2
Chela, Sa. da *Angola* **88** B1
Chelan *U.S.A.* **108** C3
Chelan, L. *U.S.A.* **108** B3
Cheleken = Hazar
  Turkmenistan **52** F6
Cheleken Yarymadasy
  Turkmenistan **71** B7
Chelforó *Argentina* **128** D3
Chelkar = Shalqar
  Kazakhstan **52** E6
Chella *Ethiopia* **81** F4
Chelles *France* **19** D9
Chełm *Poland* **31** G10
Chełmno *Poland* **31** E5
Chelmsford *U.K.* **15** F8
Chełmża *Poland* **31** E5
Chelsea *Australia* **95** F4
Chelsea *U.S.A.* **115** C12
Cheltenham *U.K.* **15** F5
Chelva *Spain* **38** F4
Chelyabinsk *Russia* **52** D7
Chelyuskin, C. =
  Chelyuskin, Mys *Russia* **53** B11
Chelyuskin, Mys *Russia* **53** B11
Chemainus *Canada* **110** B3
Chemba *Mozam.* **85** H6
Chembar = Belinskiy *Russia* **34** D6
Chemillé *France* **18** E6
Chemin Grenier *Mauritius* **85** d
Chemnitz *Germany* **24** E8
Chemult *U.S.A.* **108** E4
Chen, Gora *Russia* **53** C15
Chenab → *Pakistan* **68** D5
Chenab Nagar *Pakistan* **68** D5
Chenango Forks *U.S.A.* **115** D9
Chencha *Ethiopia* **81** F4
Chenchiang = Zhenjiang
  China **59** A12
Cheney *U.S.A.* **108** C5
Cheng Xian *China* **56** H3
Chengbu *China* **59** D8
Chengcheng *China* **56** G5
Chengchou = Zhengzhou
  China **56** G7
Chengde *China* **57** D9
Chengdong Hu *China* **59** A11
Chengdu *China* **58** B5
Chenggong *China* **58** E4
Chenggu *China* **56** H4
Chenghai *China* **59** F11
Chengjiang *China* **58** E4
Chengkou *China* **58** B7
Chengmai *China* **64** C7
Ch'engtu = Chengdu *China* **58** B5
Chengwu *China* **56** G8
Chengxi Hu *China* **59** A11
Chengyang *China* **57** F11
Chenjiagang *China* **57** G10
Chennai *India* **66** N12
Chenôve *France* **19** E12
Chenxi *China* **59** C8
Chenzhou *China* **59** E9
Cheò, Eilean a' = Skye *U.K.* **13** D2
Cheom Ksan *Cambodia* **64** E5
Cheonan *S. Korea* **57** F14
Cheongdo *S. Korea* **57** G15
Cheongju *S. Korea* **57** F14
Cheorwon *S. Korea* **57** E14
Chepelare *Bulgaria* **45** E8
Chepén *Peru* **124** E3
Chepes *Argentina* **126** C2
Chepo *Panama* **120** E4
Chepstow *U.K.* **15** F5
Chequamegon B. *U.S.A.* **112** B8
Cher □ *France* **19** E9
Cher → *France* **18** E7
Chéradi *Italy* **43** B10
Cherasco *Italy* **40** D4
Cheraw *U.S.A.* **117** D15
Cherbourg *France* **18** C5
Cherdakly *Russia* **34** C9
Cherdyn *Russia* **52** C6
Cheremkhovo *Russia* **53** D11
Cherepovets *Russia* **32** C9
Chergui, Chott ech *Algeria* **78** B6
Cherikov = Cherykaw
  Belarus **23** B16
Cherkasy *Ukraine* **33** H7
Cherkasy □ *Ukraine* **33** H6
Cherkessk *Russia* **35** H6

Cherlak *Russia* **52** D8
Chernaya *Russia* **53** B9
Chernelytsya *Ukraine* **29** B10
Cherni *Bulgaria* **44** D7
Chernigov = Chernihiv
  Ukraine **33** G6
Chernigovka *Russia* **54** B6
Chernihiv *Ukraine* **33** G6
Chernihiv □ *Ukraine* **33** G7
Chernivtsi *Chernivtsi,*
  Ukraine **29** B10
Chernivtsi *Vinnyts'ka,*
  Ukraine **29** B13
Chernivtsi □ *Ukraine* **29** B10
Chernobyl = Chornobyl
  Ukraine **23** C16
Chernogorsk *Russia* **53** D10
Chernomorskoye =
  Chornomorske *Ukraine* **33** K7
Chernovtsy = Chernivtsi
  Ukraine **29** B10
Chernyakhovsk *Russia* **30** D8
Chernyanka *Russia* **33** G9
Chernysheyskiy *Russia* **53** C12
Chernnye Zemli *Russia* **35** H8
Cherokee *Iowa, U.S.A.* **112** D6
Cherokee *Okla., U.S.A.* **116** C5
Cherokee Village *U.S.A.* **116** C9
Cherokees, Grand Lake O'
  The *U.S.A.* **116** C7
Cherrapunji *India* **67** G17
Cherry Valley *U.S.A.* **115** D10
Cherskiy *Russia* **53** C17
Cherskogo Khrebet *Russia* **53** C15
Chersonisos *Greece* **49** D7
Chersonisos Akrotiri *Greece* **49** D6
Chertkovo *Russia* **33** H11
Cherven *Belarus* **23** B15
Cherven-Bryag *Bulgaria* **45** C8
Chervonoarmiyske *Ukraine* **29** E13
Chervonohrad *Ukraine* **23** C13
Cherwell → *U.K.* **15** F6
Cherykaw *Belarus* **23** B16
Chesapeake *U.S.A.* **113** G15
Chesapeake B. *U.S.A.* **113** F14
Cheshire □ *U.K.* **14** D5
Cheshskaya Guba *Russia* **52** C5
Cheshunt *U.K.* **15** F7
Chesil Beach *U.K.* **15** G5
Chesley *Canada* **114** B3
Cheste *Spain* **39** F4
Chester *U.K.* **14** D5
Chester *Calif., U.S.A.* **108** F3
Chester *Ill., U.S.A.* **112** G9
Chester *Mont., U.S.A.* **108** B8
Chester *Pa., U.S.A.* **113** F16
Chester *S.C., U.S.A.* **117** D14
Chester *Vt., U.S.A.* **115** C12
Chester *W. Va., U.S.A.* **114** F4
Chester-le-Street *U.K.* **14** C6
Chesterfield *U.K.* **14** D6
Chesterfield, Îs. *N. Cal.* **90** C8
Chesterfield Inlet *Canada* **100** C10
Chesterton Ra. *Australia* **95** D4
Chesterton Range △
  Australia **95** D4
Chestertown *U.S.A.* **115** C11
Chesterville *Canada* **115** A9
Chesuncook L. *U.S.A.* **113** C19
Chéticamp *Canada* **105** C7
Chetrosu *Moldova* **29** B12
Chetumal *Mexico* **119** D7
Chetumal, B. de *Cent. Amer.* **119** D7
Chetwynd *Canada* **102** B4
Chevanceaux *France* **20** C3
Cheviot, The *U.K.* **14** B5
Cheviot Hills *U.K.* **14** B5
Cheviot Ra. *Australia* **94** D3
Chew Bahir *Ethiopia* **81** G4
Chewelah *U.S.A.* **108** B5
Chewore △ *Zimbabwe* **87** F2
Cheyenne *Okla., U.S.A.* **116** D5
Cheyenne *Wyo., U.S.A.* **108** F11
Cheyenne → *U.S.A.* **112** C3
Cheyenne Wells *U.S.A.* **108** G12
Cheyne B. *Australia* **93** F2
Chhabra *India* **68** G7
Chhaktala *India* **68** H6
Chhapra *India* **69** G11
Chhata *India* **68** F7
Chhatarpur *Jharkhand, India* **69** G11
Chhatarpur *Mad. P., India* **69** G8
Chhattisgarh □ *India* **69** J10
Chhep *Cambodia* **64** F5
Chhindwara *Mad. P., India* **69** H8
Chhindwara *Mad. P., India* **69** H8
Chhlong *Cambodia* **65** F5
Chhota Tawa → *India* **68** H7
Chhoti Kali Sindh → *India* **68** G6
Chhuk *Cambodia* **65** G5
Chi → *Thailand* **64** E5
Chiai *Taiwan* **59** F13
Chiali *Taiwan* **59** F13
Chiamboni *Somali Rep.* **84** E8
Chianciano Terme *Italy* **41** E8
Chiang Dao *Thailand* **64** C2
Chiang Kham *Thailand* **64** C3

Chiang Khan *Thailand* **64** D3
Chiang Khong *Thailand* **58** G3
Chiang Mai *Thailand* **64** C2
Chiang Rai *Thailand* **64** C2
Chiang Saen *Thailand* **58** G3
Chianti *Italy* **41** E8
Chiapa → *Mexico* **119** D6
Chiapa de Corzo *Mexico* **119** D6
Chiapas □ *Mexico* **119** D6
Chiapas, Sa. Madre de
  Mexico **119** D6
Chiaramonte Gulfi *Italy* **43** E7
Chiaravalle *Italy* **41** E10
Chiaravalle Centrale *Italy* **43** D9
Chiari *Italy* **40** C6
Chiatura *Georgia* **35** J6
Chiautla de Tapia *Mexico* **119** D5
Chiávari *Italy* **40** D6
Chiba *Japan* **55** G10
Chiba □ *Japan* **55** G10
Chibabava *Mozam.* **89** C5
Chibemba *Cunene, Angola* **85** H2
Chibemba *Huila, Angola* **88** B2
Chibi *Zimbabwe* **89** C5
Chibia *Angola* **85** H2
Chibougamau *Canada* **104** C5
Chibougamau, L. *Canada* **104** C5
Chibuk *Nigeria* **83** C7
Chibuto *Mozam.* **89** C5
Chic-Chocs, Mts. *Canada* **105** C6
Chicacole = Srikakulam
  India **67** K13
Chicago *U.S.A.* **112** E10
Chicago Heights *U.S.A.* **112** E10
Chichagof I. *U.S.A.* **100** D6
Chichaoua *Morocco* **78** B4
Chichawatni *Pakistan* **68** D5
Chichén-Itzá *Mexico* **119** C7
Chicheng *China* **56** D8
Chichester *U.K.* **15** G7
Chichester Ra. *Australia* **92** D2
Chichibu *Japan* **55** F9
Chichibu-Tama △ *Japan* **55** G9
Ch'ich'ihaerh = Qiqihar
  China **53** E13
Chicholi *India* **68** H8
Chickasaw △ *U.S.A.* **116** D6
Chickasha *U.S.A.* **116** D6
Chiclana de la Frontera
  Spain **39** J4
Chiclayo *Peru* **124** E3
Chico *U.S.A.* **110** F5
Chico → *Chubut, Argentina* **128** E3
Chico → *Santa Cruz,*
  Argentina **128** E3
Chicomo *Mozam.* **89** C5
Chicomostoc *Mexico* **118** C4
Chicontepec *Mexico* **119** C5
Chicopee *U.S.A.* **115** D12
Chicoutimi *Canada* **105** C5
Chicualacuala *Mozam.* **89** C5
Chidambaram *India* **66** P11
Chidenguele *Mozam.* **89** C5
Chidley, C. *Canada* **101** C13
Chiducuane *Mozam.* **89** C5
Chiede *Angola* **88** B2
Chiefs Pt. *Canada* **114** B3
Chiem Hoa *Vietnam* **64** A5
Chiemsee *Germany* **25** H8
Chiengi *Zambia* **87** D2
Chiengmai = Chiang Mai
  Thailand **64** C2
Chienti → *Italy* **41** E10
Chieri *Italy* **40** C4
Chiers → *France* **19** C11
Chiesa in Valmalenco *Italy* **40** B6
Chiese → *Italy* **40** C7
Chieti *Italy* **41** F11
Chifeng *China* **57** C10
Chigirin *Ukraine* **33** H7
Chignecto B. *Canada* **105** C7
Chiguana *Bolivia* **126** A2
Chigwell *U.K.* **15** F8
Chihli, G. of = Bo Hai *China* **57** E10
Chihuahua *Mexico* **118** B3
Chihuahua □ *Mexico* **118** B3
Chiili = Shīeli *Kazakhstan* **52** E7
Chik Bollapur *India* **66** N10
Chikmagalur *India* **66** N9
Chikwawa *Malawi* **87** F3
Chilanga *Zambia* **87** F2
Chilapa *Mexico* **119** D5
Chilas *Pakistan* **69** B6
Chilaw *Sri Lanka* **66** R11
Chilcotin → *Canada* **102** C4
Childers *Australia* **95** D5
Childress *U.S.A.* **116** D4
Chile ■ *S. Amer.* **128** D2
Chile Rise *Pac. Oc.* **97** L18
Chilecito *Argentina* **126** B2
Chilete *Peru* **124** E3
Chilia, Braţul → *Romania* **29** E14
Chililabombwe *Zambia* **87** E2
Chilim *Pakistan* **69** B6
Chilin = Jilin *China* **57** C14
Chiliomodi *Greece* **46** D4
Chilka L. *India* **67** K14

Chilko → *Canada* **102** C4
Chilko L. *Canada* **102** C4
Chillagoe *Australia* **94** B3
Chillán *Chile* **126** D1
Chillicothe *Ill., U.S.A.* **112** E9
Chillicothe *Mo., U.S.A.* **112** F7
Chillicothe *Ohio, U.S.A.* **113** F12
Chilliwack *Canada* **102** D4
Chilo *India* **68** F5
Chiloane, I. *Mozam.* **89** C5
Chiloé, I. de *Chile* **128** E2
Chilpancingo *Mexico* **119** D5
Chiltern Hills *U.K.* **15** F7
Chilton *U.S.A.* **112** C9
Chilubi *Zambia* **87** E2
Chilubula *Zambia* **87** E3
Chilumba *Malawi* **87** E3
Chilung *Taiwan* **59** E13
Chilwa, L. *Malawi* **87** F4
Chimaltitán *Mexico* **118** C4
Chimán *Panama* **120** E4
Chimanimani *Zimbabwe* **89** B5
Chimay *Belgium* **17** D4
Chimayo *U.S.A.* **109** J11
Chimbas *Argentina* **126** C2
Chimborazo *Ecuador* **124** D3
Chimbote *Peru* **124** E3
Chimkent = Shymkent
  Kazakhstan **52** E7
Chimoio *Mozam.* **87** F3
Chimpembe *Zambia* **87** D2
Chin □ *Burma* **67** J18
Chin Hills *Burma* **67** H18
Chin Ling Shan = Qinling
  Shandi *China* **56** H5
China *Mexico* **119** B5
China ■ *Asia* **60** D6
China, Great Plain of *Asia* **50** E13
China Lake *U.S.A.* **111** K9
Chinan = Jinan *China* **56** F9
Chinandega *Nic.* **120** D2
Chinati Peak *U.S.A.* **116** G2
Chincha Alta *Peru* **124** F3
Chinchaga → *Canada* **102** B5
Chinchilla *Australia* **95** D5
Chinchilla de Monte
  Aragón *Spain* **39** G3
Chinchorro, Banco *Mexico* **119** D7
Chinchou = Jinzhou *China* **57** D11
Chincoteague *U.S.A.* **113** G16
Chinde *Mozam.* **87** F4
Chindwin → *Burma* **67** J19
Chineni *India* **69** C6
Chinga *Mozam.* **87** F4
Chingola *Zambia* **87** E2
Chingole *Malawi* **87** E3
Ch'ingtao = Qingdao *China* **57** F11
Chinguetti *Mauritania* **78** D3
Chingune *Mozam.* **89** C5
Chinhanguanine *Mozam.* **89** D5
Chinhoyi *Zimbabwe* **87** F3
Chini *India* **68** D8
Chiniot *Pakistan* **68** D5
Chínipas *Mexico* **118** B3
Chinji *Pakistan* **68** C5
Chinju = Jinju *S. Korea* **57** G15
Chinko → *C.A.R.* **84** D4
Chinle *U.S.A.* **109** H9
Chinmen *Taiwan* **59** E13
Chinmen Tao *Taiwan* **59** E12
Chinnampo = Namp'o
  N. Korea **57** E13
Chino *Japan* **55** G9
Chino *U.S.A.* **111** L9
Chino Valley *U.S.A.* **109** J7
Chinon *France* **18** E7
Chinook *U.S.A.* **108** B9
Chinook Trough *Pac. Oc.* **96** C10
Chinsali *Zambia* **87** E3
Chióggia *Italy* **41** C9
Chíos = Hios *Greece* **47** C8
Chipata *Zambia* **87** E3
Chiperceni *Moldova* **29** C13
Chipindo *Angola* **85** G3
Chipinge *Zimbabwe* **87** G3
Chipinge △ *Zimbabwe* **87** G3
Chipiona *Spain* **37** J4
Chipley *U.S.A.* **117** F12
Chipman *Canada* **105** C6
Chipoka *Malawi* **87** E3
Chippenham *U.K.* **15** F5
Chippewa → *U.S.A.* **112** C7
Chippewa Falls *U.S.A.* **112** C8
Chipping Norton *U.K.* **15** F6
Chiprovtsi *Bulgaria* **44** C7
Chiputneticook Lakes
  N. Amer. **113** C20
Chiquián *Peru* **124** F3
Chiquibul △ *Belize* **120** C2
Chiquimula *Guatemala* **120** D2
Chiquinquira *Colombia* **124** B4
Chir → *Russia* **35** F6
Chirala *India* **66** M12
Chiramba *Mozam.* **87** F3
Chirawa *India* **68** E6
Chirchiq *Uzbekistan* **52** E7
Chiredzi *Zimbabwe* **89** C5
Chirfa *Niger* **79** D8
Chiricahua △ *U.S.A.* **109** K9

Chiricahua Peak *U.S.A.* **109** L9
Chiriquí, G. de *Panama* **120** E3
Chiriquí, L. de *Panama* **120** E3
Chirisa △ *Zimbabwe* **87** F2
Chirivira Falls *Zimbabwe* **87** G3
Chirmiri *India* **69** H10
Chirnogi *Romania* **29** F11
Chirpan *Bulgaria* **45** D9
Chirripó Grande, Cerro
  Costa Rica **120** E3
Chirundu *Zimbabwe* **89** B4
Chisamba *Zambia* **87** E2
Chisapani *Nepal* **69** E9
Chisasibi *Canada* **104** B4
Chishui *China* **58** C5
Chishui He → *China* **58** C5
Chisholm *Canada* **102** C6
Chisholm *U.S.A.* **112** B7
Chishtian Mandi *Pakistan* **68** E5
Chishui *China* **58** C5
Chishui He → *China* **58** C5
Chisimaio = Kismaayo
  Somali Rep. **75** H3
Chisimba Falls *Zambia* **87** E3
Chişinău *Moldova* **29** C13
Chişinău ✈ (KIV) *Moldova* **29** C13
Chişineu Criş *Romania* **28** D2
Chisone → *Italy* **40** D4
Chisos Mts. *U.S.A.* **116** G3
Chistopol *Russia* **34** C10
Chita *Russia* **53** D12
Chitipa *Malawi* **87** D3
Chitose *Japan* **54** C10
Chitral *Pakistan* **66** B7
Chitré *Panama* **120** E3
Chittagong *Bangla.* **67** H17
Chittagong □ *Bangla.* **67** G17
Chittaurgarh *India* **68** G6
Chittoor *India* **66** N11
Chitungwiza *Zimbabwe* **87** F3
Chiusi *Italy* **41** E8
Chiva *Spain* **39** F4
Chivasso *Italy* **40** C4
Chivhu *Zimbabwe* **87** F3
Chivilcoy *Argentina* **126** C4
Chiwanda *Tanzania* **87** E3
Chixi *China* **59** G9
Chizarira *Zimbabwe* **87** F2
Chizarira △ *Zimbabwe* **87** F2
Chizela *Zambia* **87** E2
Chkalov = Orenburg *Russia* **52** D6
Chkolovsk *Russia* **34** B6
Chloride *U.S.A.* **111** K12
Chlumec nad Cidlinou
  Czech Rep. **26** A8
Chmielnik *Poland* **31** H7
Chmielnik *Poland* **31** H7
Cho Bo *Vietnam* **58** G5
Cho-do *N. Korea* **57** E13
Cho Phuoc Hai *Vietnam* **65** G6
Choa Chu Kang *Singapore* **65** d
Choba *Kenya* **86** B4
Chobe △ *Botswana* **88** B4
Chocianów *Poland* **31** G2
Chociwel *Poland* **31** B2
Chocolate Mts. *U.S.A.* **111** M11
Choctawhatchee → *U.S.A.*
  117 F11
Chodecz *Poland* **31** F6
Chodov *Czech Rep.* **26** A5
Chodziez *Poland* **31** F3
Choele Choel *Argentina* **128** D3
Choiseul *St. Lucia* **121** f
Choiseul *Solomon Is.* **90** B8
Choix *Mexico* **118** B3
Chojna *Poland* **31** F1
Chojnice *Poland* **30** E4
Chojnów *Poland* **31** G2
Chok Chai *Thailand* **64** E4
Chōkai-San *Japan* **54** E10
Choke Canyon Res. *U.S.A.* **116** G5
Choke Mts. *Ethiopia* **81** E4
Chokurdakh *Russia* **53** B15
Cholame *U.S.A.* **110** K6
Cholet *France* **18** E6
Cholguan *Chile* **126** D1
Choloma *Honduras* **120** C2
Choluteca *Honduras* **120** D2
Choluteca → *Honduras* **120** D2
Chom Bung *Thailand* **64** F2
Chom Thong *Thailand* **64** C2
Choma *Zambia* **87** F2
Chomolungma = Everest,
  Mt. *Nepal* **69** E12
Chomun *India* **68** F6
Chomutov *Czech Rep.* **26** A6
Chon Buri *Thailand* **64** F3
Chon Thanh *Vietnam* **65** G6
Chone *Ecuador* **124** D2
Chong Kai *Cambodia* **64** F4
Chong Mek *Thailand* **64** E5
Chong Phangan *Thailand* **65** b
Chong Samui *Thailand* **65** b
Chongde *China* **59** B13
Chongging *N. Korea* **57** D14
Chŏngju *N. Korea* **57** E13
Chongli *China* **56** D8
Chongming *China* **59** B13
Chongming Dao *China* **59** B13
Chongqing *Chongqing, China* **58** C6

Chongqing *Sichuan, China* **58** B4
Chongqing Shi □ *China* **58** C6
Chongren *China* **59** D11
Chonguene *Mozam.* **89** C5
Chongyi *China* **59** E10
Chongzuo *China* **58** F6
Chonogi *Romania* **29** F11
Chonos, Arch. de los *Chile* **128** F2
Chop *Ukraine* **28** B7
Chopim → *Brazil* **127** B5
Chor *Pakistan* **68** G3
Chora *Greece* **49** D3
Chora Sfakion *Greece* **49** D6
Chorbat La *India* **69** B7
Chorley *U.K.* **14** D5
Chorna *Ukraine* **29** C14
Chornobyl *Ukraine* **23** C16
Chornomorske *Ukraine* **33** K7
Chorolque, Cerro *Bolivia* **126** A2
Choroszcz *Poland* **31** E9
Chorregon *Australia* **94** C3
Chorro el Indio △ *Venezuela* **121** E5
Chortkiv *Ukraine* **23** D13
Chorzele *Poland* **31** E7
Chorzów *Poland* **31** H5
Chos-Malal *Argentina* **126** D1
Ch'osan *N. Korea* **57** D13
Choszczno *Poland* **31** E2
Choteau *U.S.A.* **108** C7
Chotěboř *Czech Rep.* **26** B8
Chotila *India* **68** H4
Chotta Udepur *India* **68** H6
Chowchilla *U.S.A.* **110** H6
Choybalsan *Mongolia* **60** B6
Choyr *Mongolia* **53** E11
Christchurch *N.Z.* **91** F4
Christchurch *U.K.* **15** G6
Christian I. *Canada* **114** B4
Christiana *S. Africa* **88** D4
Christiansfeld *Denmark* **11** J3
Christiansted *U.S. Virgin Is.* **121** C7
Christie B. *Canada* **103** A6
Christina → *Canada* **103** B6
Christmas Cr. → *Australia* **92** C4
Christmas I. = Kiritimati
  Kiribati **97** G12
Christmas I. *Ind. Oc.* **96** J2
Christopher, L. *Australia* **93** D4
Chrudim *Czech Rep.* **26** B8
Chrzanów *Poland* **31** H6
Chtimba *Malawi* **87** E3
Chū = Shū *Kazakhstan* **52** E8
Chūbu □ *Japan* **55** G8
Chubu-Sangaku △ *Japan* **55** F8
Chubut → *Argentina* **128** E3
Chuchi L. *Canada* **102** B4
Chuda *India* **68** H4
Chudovo *Russia* **32** C6
Chudskoye, Ozero *Russia* **32** C4
Chūgoku □ *Japan* **55** G6
Chūgoku-Sanchi *Japan* **55** G6
Chuguyev = Chuhuyiv
  Ukraine **33** H9
Chuhuyiv *Ukraine* **33** H9
Chuka *Kenya* **86** C4
Chukchi Plateau *Arctic* **4** B17
Chukchi Sea *Russia* **53** C19
Chukotskoye Nagorye
  Russia **53** C18
Chula Vista *U.S.A.* **111** N9
Chulucanas *Peru* **124** E2
Chulym → *Russia* **52** D9
Chum Phae *Thailand* **64** D4
Chum Saeng *Thailand* **64** E3
Chumar *India* **69** C8
Chumbicha *Argentina* **126** B2
Chumerna *Bulgaria* **45** D9
Chumikan *Russia* **53** D14
Chumphon *Thailand* **65** G2
Chumuare *Mozam.* **87** E3
Chuna → *Russia* **53** D10
Chun'an *China* **59** C12
Chuncheon *S. Korea* **57** F14
Chunchura *India* **69** H13
Chunga *Zambia* **87** F2
Chunggang-ŭp *N. Korea* **57** D14
Chunghwa *N. Korea* **57** E13
Chungju *S. Korea* **57** F14
Chungking = Chongqing
  China **58** C6
Chungli *Taiwan* **59** E13
Chungt'iaoshan =
  Zhongtiao Shan *China* **56** G6
Chungyang Shanmo
  Taiwan **59** F13
Chunian *Pakistan* **68** D6
Chunya *Tanzania* **87** D3
Chunyang *China* **57** C15
Chupara Pt. *Trin. & Tob.* **125** K15
Chuquibamba *Peru* **124** G4

Chuquicamata *Chile* **126** A2
Chur *Switz.* **25** J5
Churachandpur *India* **67** G18
Church Stretton *U.K.* **15** E5
Churchill *Canada* **103** B10
Churchill → *Man., Canada* **103** B10
Churchill → *Nfld. & L.,*
  Canada **105** B7
Churchill, C. *Canada* **103** B10
Churchill Falls *Canada* **105** B7
Churchill L. *Canada* **103** B7
Churchill Pk. *Canada* **102** B3
Churki *India* **69** H10
Churu *India* **68** E6
Churún Merú = Angel
  Falls *Venezuela* **124** B6
Chushal *India* **69** C8
Chuska Mts. *U.S.A.* **109** H9
Chusovoy *Russia* **52** D6
Chute-aux-Outardes
  Canada **105** C6
Chuuk = Truk *Micronesia* **96** G7
Chuvash Republic =
  Chuvashia □ *Russia* **34** C8
Chuvashia □ *Russia* **34** C8
Chuwārtah *Iraq* **73** E11
Chuxiong *China* **58** E3
Chuy *Uruguay* **127** C5
Chuzhou *China* **59** A12
Chynadiyeve *Ukraine* **28** B7
Ci Xian *China* **56** F8
Ciacova *Romania* **28** E6
Ciadâr-Lunga *Moldova* **29** D13
Ciamis *Indonesia* **63** G13
Cianjur *Indonesia* **63** G12
Cianorte *Brazil* **127** A5
Cibola *U.S.A.* **111** M12
Cibuta *Mexico* **118** A2
Cicero *U.S.A.* **112** E10
Cicia *Fiji* **91** a
Cidacos → *Spain* **38** C3
Cide *Turkey* **72** B5
Ciéagas del Catatumbo △
  Venezuela **121** E5
Ciechanów *Poland* **31** F7
Ciechanowiec *Poland* **31** F9
Ciechocinek *Poland* **31** F5
Ciego de Ávila *Cuba* **120** B4
Ciénaga *Colombia* **124** A4
Cienfuegos *Cuba* **120** B3
Cierp-Gaud *France* **20** F4
Cíes, Is. *Spain* **36** C2
Cieszanów *Poland* **31** H10
Cieszyn *Poland* **31** J5
Cieza *Spain* **39** G3
Çifteler *Turkey* **72** C4
Cifuentes *Spain* **38** E2
Cihanbeyli *Turkey* **72** C5
Cihuatlán *Mexico* **118** D4
Cijara, Embalse de *Spain* **37** F6
Cijara △ *Spain* **37** F6
Cijulang *Indonesia* **63** G13
Cilacap *Indonesia* **63** G13
Çıldır *Turkey* **73** B10
Çıldır Gölü *Turkey* **73** B10
Cilento e Vallo di Diano △
  Italy **43** B8
Cili *China* **59** C8
Cilibia *Romania* **29** E12
Cilicia *Turkey* **72** D5
Cill Chainnigh = Kilkenny
  Ireland **12** D4
Cilo Dağı *Turkey* **73** D10
Cima *U.S.A.* **111** K11
Cimarron *Kans., U.S.A.* **112** G3
Cimarron *N. Mex., U.S.A.* **109** H11
Cimarron → *U.S.A.* **116** C6
Cimişlia *Moldova* **29** D13
Cimone, Mte. *Italy* **40** D7
Çınar *Turkey* **73** D9
Çınarcık *Turkey* **45** F13
Cinca → *Spain* **38** D5
Cincar *Bos.-H.* **28** G2
Cincinnati *U.S.A.* **113** F11
Cincinnatus *U.S.A.* **115** D9
Çine *Turkey* **47** D10
Ciney *Belgium* **17** D5
Cingoli *Italy* **41** E10
Cinigiano *Italy* **41** F8
Cinto, Mte. *France* **21** F12
Cintruénigo *Spain* **38** C3
Ciocile *Romania* **29** F12
Ciolăneşti din Deal *Romania* **29** F10
Ciorani *Romania* **29** F11
Čiovo *Croatia* **41** E13
Circeo, Mte. *Italy* **42** A6
Circle *Alaska, U.S.A.* **106** a
Circle *Mont., U.S.A.* **108** C11
Circleville *U.S.A.* **113** F12
Cirebon *Indonesia* **63** G13
Ciremay *Indonesia* **63** G13
Cirencester *U.K.* **15** F6
Cireşu *Romania* **28** F7
Cirey-sur-Vezouze *France* **19** D13
Ciriè *Italy* **40** C4
Cirium *Cyprus* **49** E11
Cirò *Italy* **43** C10

Cirò Marina *Italy* **43** C10
Ciron → *France* **20** D3
Cisco *U.S.A.* **116** E5
Cislău *Romania* **29** E11
Cisna *Poland* **31** J9
Cisnădie *Romania* **29** E9
Cisterna di Latina *Italy* **42** A5
Cisternino *Italy* **43** B10
Cistierna *Spain* **36** C5
Citeli-Ckaro =
　Tsiteli-Tsqaro *Georgia* **35** K8
Citlaltépetl = Orizaba, Pico
　de *Mexico* **119** D5
Citrus Heights *U.S.A.* **110** G5
Citrusdal *S. Africa* **88** E2
Città del Vaticano =
　Vatican City ■ *Europe* **41** G9
Città della Pieve *Italy* **41** F9
Città di Castello *Italy* **41** E9
Città Sant' Angelo *Italy* **41** F11
Cittadella *Italy* **41** C8
Cittaducale *Italy* **41** F9
Cittanova *Italy* **43** D9
Ciuc, Munţii *Romania* **29** D11
Ciucaş, Vf. *Romania* **29** E10
Ciucea *Romania* **28** D7
Ciuciulea *Moldova* **29** C12
Ciuciuleni *Moldova* **29** C13
Ciudad Acuña *Mexico* **118** B4
Ciudad Altamirano *Mexico* **118** D4
Ciudad Anáhuac *Mexico* **118** B4
Ciudad Bolívar *Venezuela* **124** B6
Ciudad Camargo *Mexico* **118** B3
Ciudad Cortés *Costa Rica* **120** E3
Ciudad de México *Mexico* **119** D5
Ciudad de Valles *Mexico* **119** C5
Ciudad del Carmen *Mexico* **119** D6
Ciudad del Este *Paraguay* **127** B5
Ciudad Delicias = Delicias
　Mexico **118** B3
Ciudad Frontera *Mexico* **118** B4
Ciudad Guayana *Venezuela* **124** B6
Ciudad Guerrero *Mexico* **118** B3
Ciudad Guzmán *Mexico* **118** D4
Ciudad Juárez *Mexico* **118** A3
Ciudad Lerdo *Mexico* **118** B4
Ciudad Madero *Mexico* **119** C5
Ciudad Mante *Mexico* **119** C5
Ciudad Obregón *Mexico* **118** B3
Ciudad Real *Spain* **37** G7
Ciudad Real □ *Spain* **37** G7
Ciudad Rodrigo *Spain* **36** E4
Ciudad Victoria *Mexico* **119** C5
Ciudadela *Spain* **48** B10
Ciulniţa *Romania* **29** F12
Ciumeghiu *Romania* **28** D6
Ciuperceni *Romania* **28** E6
Civa Burnu *Turkey* **72** B7
Cividale del Friuli *Italy* **41** B10
Civita Castellana *Italy* **41** F9
Civitanova Marche *Italy* **41** E10
Civitavécchia *Italy* **41** F8
Civray *France* **20** B4
Çivril *Turkey* **47** C11
Cixerri → *Italy* **42** C1
Cixi *China* **59** B13
Cizre *Turkey* **73** D10
Clackmannanshire □ *U.K.* **13** E5
Clacton-on-Sea *U.K.* **15** F9
Clain → *France* **18** F7
Claire, L. *Canada* **102** B6
Clairton *U.S.A.* **114** F5
Clairvaux-les-Lacs *France* **19** F12
Claise → *France* **20** B5
Clallam Bay *U.S.A.* **110** B2
Clamecy *France* **19** E10
Clanton *U.S.A.* **117** E11
Clanwilliam *S. Africa* **88** E2
Clara *Ireland* **12** C4
Claraville *U.S.A.* **111** K8
Clare *Australia* **95** E2
Clare *U.S.A.* **113** D11
Clare □ *Ireland* **12** D3
Clare → *France* **12** C2
Clare I. *Ireland* **12** C1
Claremont *Calif., U.S.A.* **111** L9
Claremont *N.H., U.S.A.* **115** C12
Claremont Pt. *Australia* **94** A3
Claremore *U.S.A.* **116** C7
Claremorris *Ireland* **12** C3
Clarence → *Australia* **95** D5
Clarence → *N.Z.* **91** E4
Clarence, I. *Chile* **128** G2
Clarence I. *Antarctica* **5** C18
Clarence Str. *Australia* **92** B5
Clarence Town *Bahamas* **121** B5
Clarendon *Pa., U.S.A.* **114** E5
Clarendon *Tex., U.S.A.* **116** D4
Clarenville *Canada* **105** C9
Claresholm *Canada* **102** D6
Clarie Coast *Antarctica* **5** C9
Clarinda *U.S.A.* **112** E6
Clarington *Canada* **114** C6
Clarion *Iowa, U.S.A.* **112** D7
Clarion *Pa., U.S.A.* **114** E5
Clarion → *U.S.A.* **114** E5
Clarion Fracture Zone
　Pac. Oc. **98** H7

Clark *U.S.A.* **112** C5
Clark, Pt. *Canada* **114** B3
Clark Fork *U.S.A.* **108** B5
Clark Fork → *U.S.A.* **108** B5
Clarkdale *U.S.A.* **109** J7
Clarke City *Canada* **105** B6
Clarke I. *Australia* **95** G4
Clarke Ra. *Australia* **94** J6
Clarks Fork
　Yellowstone → *U.S.A.* **108** D9
Clark's Harbour *Canada* **105** D6
Clarks Hill L. = J. Strom
　Thurmond L. *U.S.A.* **117** E13
Clarks Summit *U.S.A.* **115** E9
Clarksburg *U.S.A.* **113** F13
Clarkston *U.S.A.* **108** C5
Clarksdale *U.S.A.* **117** D9
Clarksville *Ark., U.S.A.* **116** D8
Clarksville *Tenn., U.S.A.* **117** C11
Clarksville *Tex., U.S.A.* **116** E7
Clatskanie *U.S.A.* **110** D3
Claude *U.S.A.* **116** D4
Claveria *Phil.* **61** B4
Clay *U.S.A.* **110** G5
Clay Center *U.S.A.* **112** F5
Claypool *U.S.A.* **109** K8
Claysburg *U.S.A.* **114** F6
Claysville *U.S.A.* **114** F4
Clayton *Canada* **115** A8
Clayton *N. Mex., U.S.A.* **109** H12
Clayton *N.Y., U.S.A.* **115** B8
Clear, C. *Ireland* **12** E2
Clear, L. *Canada* **114** A7
Clear Hills *Canada* **102** B5
Clear I. *Ireland* **12** E2
Clear L. *U.S.A.* **110** F4
Clear Lake *Iowa, U.S.A.* **112** D7
Clear Lake *S. Dak., U.S.A.* **112** C5
Clear Lake Res. *U.S.A.* **108** F3
Clearfield *Pa., U.S.A.* **114** E6
Clearfield *Utah, U.S.A.* **108** F7
Clearlake *U.S.A.* **110** G4
Clearwater *Canada* **102** C4
Clearwater *U.S.A.* **117** H13
Clearwater → *Alta., Canada* **102** C6
Clearwater → *Alta., Canada* **103** B6
Clearwater L. *Canada* **103** C9
Clearwater Lake △ *Canada* **103** C8
Clearwater Mts. *U.S.A.* **108** C6
Clearwater River △ *Canada* **103** B7
Cleburne *U.S.A.* **116** E6
Clee Hills *U.K.* **15** E5
Cleethorpes *U.K.* **14** D7
Cleeve Cloud *U.K.* **15** F6
Clelles *France* **21** D9
Clemson *U.S.A.* **117** D13
Clerke Reef *Australia* **92** C2
Clermont *Australia* **94** C4
Clermont *France* **19** C9
Clermont *U.S.A.* **117** G14
Clermont-en-Argonne
　France **19** C12
Clermont-Ferrand *France* **20** C7
Clermont-l'Hérault *France* **20** E7
Clerval *France* **19** E13
Clervaux *Lux.* **17** D6
Cles *Italy* **40** B8
Clevedon *U.K.* **15** F5
Cleveland *Miss., U.S.A.* **117** E9
Cleveland *Ohio, U.S.A.* **114** E3
Cleveland *Okla., U.S.A.* **116** C6
Cleveland *Tenn., U.S.A.* **117** D12
Cleveland *Tex., U.S.A.* **116** F7
Cleveland, C. *Australia* **94** B4
Cleveland, Mt. *U.S.A.* **108** B7
Cleveland Heights *U.S.A.* **114** E3
Clevelândia *Brazil* **127** B5
Clew B. *Ireland* **12** C2
Clewiston *U.S.A.* **117** H14
Clifden *Ireland* **12** C1
Clifden *N.Z.* **91** G1
Cliffdell *U.S.A.* **110** D5
Cliffy Hd. *Australia* **93** G2
Clifton *Australia* **95** D5
Clifton *Ariz., U.S.A.* **109** K9
Clifton *Colo., U.S.A.* **108** G9
Clifton *Tex., U.S.A.* **116** F6
Clifton Beach *Australia* **94** B4
Clinch → *U.S.A.* **117** D12
Clingmans Dome *U.S.A.* **117** D13
Clint *U.S.A.* **116** F1
Clinton *B.C., Canada* **102** C4
Clinton *Ont., Canada* **114** C3
Clinton *N.Z.* **91** G2
Clinton *Ark., U.S.A.* **116** D8
Clinton *Conn., U.S.A.* **115** E12
Clinton *Ill., U.S.A.* **112** E9
Clinton *Ind., U.S.A.* **112** F10
Clinton *Iowa, U.S.A.* **112** E8
Clinton *Mass., U.S.A.* **115** D13
Clinton *Miss., U.S.A.* **117** E9
Clinton *Mo., U.S.A.* **112** F7
Clinton *N.C., U.S.A.* **117** D15
Clinton *Okla., U.S.A.* **116** D5
Clinton *S.C., U.S.A.* **117** D14
Clinton *Tenn., U.S.A.* **117** C12
Clinton *Wash., U.S.A.* **110** C4
Clinton C. *Australia* **94** C5

Clinton Colden L. *Canada* **100** C9
Clintonville *U.S.A.* **112** C9
Clipperton, I. *Pac. Oc.* **97** F17
Clipperton Fracture Zone
　Pac. Oc. **97** G16
Clisham *U.K.* **13** D2
Clisson *France* **18** E5
Clitheroe *U.K.* **14** D5
Clo-oose *Canada* **110** B2
Cloates, Pt. *Australia* **92** D1
Clocolan *S. Africa* **89** D4
Clodomira *Argentina* **126** B3
Clogher Hd. *Ireland* **12** C5
Clonakilty *Ireland* **12** E3
Clonakilty B. *Ireland* **12** E3
Cloncurry *Australia* **94** C3
Cloncurry *U.S.A.* **117** C4
Cloncurry → *Australia* **94** B3
Clondalkin *Ireland* **12** C5
Clones *Ireland* **12** B4
Clonmel *Ireland* **12** D4
Cloppenburg *Germany* **24** C4
Cloquet *U.S.A.* **112** B7
Cloud Bay *Canada* **104** C2
Cloud Peak *U.S.A.* **108** D10
Cloudcroft *U.S.A.* **109** K11
Cloverdale *U.S.A.* **110** G4
Clovis *Calif., U.S.A.* **110** J7
Clovis *N. Mex., U.S.A.* **109** J12
Cloyes-sur-le-Loir *France* **18** E8
Cloyne *Canada* **114** B7
Cluj □ *Romania* **29** D8
Cluj-Napoca *Romania* **29** D8
Clunes *Australia* **95** F3
Cluny *France* **19** F11
Cluses *France* **19** F13
Clusone *Italy* **40** C6
Clutha → *N.Z.* **91** G2
Clwyd → *U.K.* **14** D4
Clyde *Canada* **102** C6
Clyde *N.Z.* **91** F2
Clyde *U.S.A.* **114** C8
Clyde → *U.K.* **13** F4
Clyde, Firth of *U.K.* **13** F3
Clyde Muirshiel △ *U.K.* **13** F4
Clyde River *Canada* **101** B13
Clydebank *U.K.* **13** F4
Clymer *N.Y., U.S.A.* **114** D5
Clymer *Pa., U.S.A.* **114** D5
Ćmielów *Poland* **31** H8
Côa → *Portugal* **36** D3
Coachella *U.S.A.* **111** M10
Coachella Canal *U.S.A.* **111** N12
Coahoma *U.S.A.* **116** E4
Coahuayana → *Mexico* **118** D4
Coahuila □ *Mexico* **118** B4
Coal → *Canada* **102** B3
Coalane *Mozam.* **87** F4
Coalcomán *Mexico* **118** D4
Coaldale *Canada* **102** D6
Coalgate *U.S.A.* **116** D6
Coalinga *U.S.A.* **110** J6
Coalisland *U.K.* **12** B5
Coalville *U.K.* **14** E6
Coalville *U.S.A.* **108** F8
Coamo *Puerto Rico* **121** d
Coari *Brazil* **124** D6
Coast □ *Kenya* **86** C4
Coast Mts. *Canada* **102** C3
Coast Ranges *U.S.A.* **110** G4
Coatbridge *U.K.* **13** F4
Coatepec *Mexico* **119** D5
Coatepeque *Guatemala* **120** D1
Coatesville *U.S.A.* **113** F16
Coaticook *Canada* **115** A13
Coats I. *Canada* **101** C11
Coats Land *Antarctica* **5** D1
Coatzacoalcos *Mexico* **119** D6
Cobá *Mexico* **119** C7
Cobadin *Romania* **29** F13
Cobalt *Canada* **104** C4
Cobán *Guatemala* **120** C1
Çobanlar *Turkey* **47** C12
Cobar *Australia* **95** E4
Cóbh *Ireland* **12** E3
Cobija *Bolivia* **124** F5
Cobleskill *U.S.A.* **115** D10
Coboconk *Canada* **114** B6
Cobourg *Canada* **114** C6
Cobourg Pen. *Australia* **92** B5
Cobram *Australia* **95** F4
Cóbué *Mozam.* **87** E3
Coburg *Germany* **25** E6
Coca *Spain* **36** D6
Cocanada = Kakinada
　India **67** L3
Cocentaina *Spain* **39** G4
Cochabamba *Bolivia* **124** G5
Cochem *Germany* **25** E3
Cochemane *Mozam.* **87** F3
Cochin *India* **66** Q10
Cochin China =
　Nam-Phan *Vietnam* **65** G6
Cochran *U.S.A.* **117** E13
Cochrane *Alta., Canada* **102** C6
Cochrane *Ont., Canada* **104** C3
Cochrane *Chile* **128** F2

Cochrane → *Canada* **103** B8
Cochrane, L. *Chile* **128** F2
Cochranton *U.S.A.* **114** E4
Cockburn *Australia* **95** E3
Cockburn, Canal *Chile* **128** G2
Cockburn I. *Canada* **104** C3
Cockburn Ra. *Australia* **92** C4
Cockermouth *U.K.* **14** C4
Cockpit Country, The
　Jamaica **120** a
Coco → *Cent. Amer.* **120** D3
Coco, I. del *Pac. Oc.* **97** G19
Cocoa *U.S.A.* **117** G14
Cocobeach *Gabon* **84** D1
Cocora *Romania* **29** F12
Cocos B. *Trin. & Tob.* **125** K15
Cocos Is. *Ind. Oc.* **96** J1
Cocos Ridge *Pac. Oc.* **97** G19
Cod, C. *U.S.A.* **113** D18
Codajás *Brazil* **124** D6
Codigoro *Italy* **41** D9
Codlea *Romania* **29** E10
Codó *Brazil* **125** D10
Codogno *Italy* **40** C6
Codróipo *Italy* **41** C10
Codru, Munţii *Romania* **28** D7
Cody *U.S.A.* **108** D9
Coe Hill *Canada* **114** B7
Coelemu *Chile* **126** D1
Coen *Australia* **94** A3
Coesfeld *Germany* **24** D3
Coeur d'Alene *U.S.A.* **108** C5
Coeur d'Alene L. *U.S.A.* **108** C5
Coevorden *Neths.* **17** B6
Cofete *Canary Is.* **48** F5
Coffeyville *U.S.A.* **112** G6
Coffin B. *Australia* **95** E2
Coffin Bay *Australia* **95** E2
Coffin Bay △ *Australia* **95** E2
Coffin Bay Peninsula
　Australia **95** E2
Coffs Harbour *Australia* **95** E5
Cofrentes *Spain* **39** F3
Cogalnic → *Moldova* **29** E14
Cogealac *Romania* **29** F13
Coghinas → *Italy* **42** B1
Coghinas, L. del *Italy* **42** B2
Cognac *France* **20** C3
Cogne *Italy* **40** C4
Cogolin *France* **21** E10
Cogolludo *Spain* **38** E1
Cohocton *U.S.A.* **114** D7
Cohocton → *U.S.A.* **114** D7
Cohoes *U.S.A.* **115** D11
Cohuna *Australia* **95** F3
Coiba, I. de *Panama* **120** E3
Coig → *Argentina* **128** G3
Coigeach, Rubha *U.K.* **13** C3
Coihaique *Chile* **128** F2
Coimbatore *India* **66** P10
Coimbra *Brazil* **124** G7
Coimbra *Portugal* **36** E2
Coimbra □ *Portugal* **36** E2
Coín *Spain* **37** J6
Coipasa, Salar de *Bolivia* **124** G5
Cojimies *Ecuador* **124** C3
Cojocna *Romania* **29** D8
Cojutepeque *El Salv.* **120** D2
Coka *Serbia* **28** E5
Cokeville *U.S.A.* **108** E8
Colac *Australia* **95** F3
Colatina *Brazil* **125** G10
Colbeck, C. *Antarctica* **5** D13
Colborne *Canada* **114** C7
Colby *U.S.A.* **112** F3
Colca → *Peru* **124** G4
Colchester *U.K.* **15** F8
Colchester *U.S.A.* **115** E12
Cold L. *Canada* **103** C7
Cold Lake *Canada* **103** C6
Coldstream *Canada* **102** C5
Coldstream *U.K.* **13** F6
Coldwater *Canada* **114** B5
Coldwater *Kans., U.S.A.* **112** G4
Coldwater *Mich., U.S.A.* **113** E11
Colebrook *U.S.A.* **115** B13
Coleman *Canada* **102** D6
Coleman *U.S.A.* **116** F5
Coleman → *Australia* **94** B3
Colenso *S. Africa* **89** D4
Coleraine *Australia* **95** F3
Coleraine *U.K.* **12** A5
Coleridge, L. *N.Z.* **91** E3
Colesberg *S. Africa* **88** E4
Coleville *U.S.A.* **110** G7
Colfax *Calif., U.S.A.* **110** F6
Colfax *La., U.S.A.* **116** F8
Colfax *Wash., U.S.A.* **108** C5
Colhué Huapi, L. *Argentina* **128** F3
Colibaşi *Moldova* **29** E13
Colibaşi *Romania* **29** F9
Cólico *Italy* **40** B6
Coligny *France* **19** F12
Coligny *S. Africa* **89** D4
Colima *Mexico* **118** D4
Colima □ *Mexico* **118** D4
Colima, Nevado de *Mexico* **118** D4

Colina *Chile* **126** C1
Colina do Norte *Guinea-Biss.* **82** C2
Colinas *Brazil* **125** E10
Colindres *Spain* **36** B7
Coll *U.K.* **13** E2
Collahuasi *Chile* **126** A2
Collarada, Peña *Spain* **38** C4
Collarenebri *Australia* **95** D4
Colle di Val d'Elsa *Italy* **40** E8
Collécchio *Italy* **40** D7
Colleen Bawn *Zimbabwe* **87** G2
College Park *U.S.A.* **117** E12
College Station *U.S.A.* **116** F6
Collesalvetti *Italy* **40** E7
Colli Euganei △ *Italy* **41** C8
Collie *Australia* **93** F2
Collier B. *Australia* **92** C3
Collier Ra. *Australia* **93** D2
Collier Range △ *Australia* **93** D2
Collierville *U.S.A.* **117** D10
Collina, Passo di *Italy* **40** D7
Collingwood *Canada* **114** B4
Collingwood *N.Z.* **91** D4
Collins *Canada* **104** B2
Collins Bay *Canada* **115** B8
Collinsville *Australia* **94** C4
Collipulli *Chile* **126** D1
Collooney *Ireland* **12** B3
Colmar *France* **19** D14
Colmars *France* **21** D10
Colmenar *Spain* **37** J6
Colmenar de Oreja *Spain* **36** E7
Colmenar Viejo *Spain* **36** E7
Colo → *Australia* **95** E5
Cologne = Köln *Germany* **24** E2
Colom, I. d'en *Spain* **48** B11
Coloma *U.S.A.* **110** G6
Colomb-Béchar = Béchar
　Algeria **78** B5
Colombey-les-Belles *France* **19** D12
Colombey-les-Deux-Églises
　France **19** D11
Colombia ■ *S. Amer.* **124** C4
Colombian Basin *S. Amer.* **98** H12
Colombo *Sri Lanka* **66** R11
Colomiers *France* **20** E5
Colón *B. Aires, Argentina* **126** C3
Colón *Entre Ríos, Argentina* **126** C4
Colón *Cuba* **120** B3
Colón *Panama* **120** E4
Colón, Arch. de *Ecuador* **122** D1
Colonia del Sacramento
　Uruguay **126** C4
Colonia Dora *Argentina* **126** B3
Colonial Beach *U.S.A.* **113** F15
Colonie *U.S.A.* **115** D11
Colonna, C. *Italy* **43** C10
Colonsay *Canada* **103** C7
Colonsay *U.K.* **13** E2
Colorado □ *U.S.A.* **108** G11
Colorado → *Argentina* **128** D4
Colorado → *N. Amer.* **109** L6
Colorado → *U.S.A.* **116** G7
Colorado City *U.S.A.* **116** E4
Colorado Plateau *U.S.A.* **109** H8
Colorado River Aqueduct
　U.S.A. **111** L12
Colorado Springs *U.S.A.* **108** G11
Colorno *Italy* **40** D7
Colotlán *Mexico* **118** C4
Colstrip *U.S.A.* **108** D10
Colton *U.S.A.* **115** B10
Columbia *Ky., U.S.A.* **113** G11
Columbia *La., U.S.A.* **116** E8
Columbia *Miss., U.S.A.* **117** F10
Columbia *Mo., U.S.A.* **112** F7
Columbia *Pa., U.S.A.* **115** F8
Columbia *S.C., U.S.A.* **117** D14
Columbia *Tenn., U.S.A.* **117** D11
Columbia → *N. Amer.* **110** D2
Columbia, C. *Canada* **101** A11
Columbia, District of □
　U.S.A. **113** F15
Columbia, Mt. *Canada* **102** C5
Columbia Basin *U.S.A.* **108** C4
Columbia Falls *U.S.A.* **108** B6
Columbia Mts. *Canada* **102** C5
Columbia Plateau *U.S.A.* **108** E5
Columbiana *U.S.A.* **114** F4
Columbretes, Is. *Spain* **38** F5
Columbus *Ga., U.S.A.* **117** E12
Columbus *Ind., U.S.A.* **113** F11
Columbus *Kans., U.S.A.* **112** G6
Columbus *Miss., U.S.A.* **117** E10
Columbus *Mont., U.S.A.* **108** D9
Columbus *N. Mex., U.S.A.* **109** L10
Columbus *Nebr., U.S.A.* **112** E5
Columbus *Ohio, U.S.A.* **113** F12
Columbus *Tex., U.S.A.* **116** G6
Colunga *Spain* **36** B5
Colusa *U.S.A.* **110** F4
Colville *U.S.A.* **108** B5
Colville → *U.S.A.* **106** a
Colville, C. *N.Z.* **91** B5
Colwood *Canada* **110** B3
Colwyn Bay *U.K.* **14** D4
Coma *Ethiopia* **81** F4

Comácchio *Italy* **41** D9
Comalcalco *Mexico* **119** D6
Comallo *Argentina* **128** E2
Comana *Romania* **29** F11
Comanche *U.S.A.* **116** F5
Comandante Ferraz
　Antarctica **5** C18
Comăneşti *Romania* **29** D11
Comarnic *Romania* **29** E10
Comayagua *Honduras* **120** D2
Combahee → *U.S.A.* **117** E14
Combarbalá *Chile* **126** C1
Combe Martin *U.K.* **15** F3
Combermere *Canada* **114** A7
Comblain-au-Pont *Belgium* **17** D5
Combourg *France* **18** D5
Combrailles *France* **19** F9
Combronde *France* **20** C7
Comeragh Mts. *Ireland* **12** D4
Comet *Australia* **94** C4
Comilla *Bangla.* **67** H17
Comino *Malta* **49** C1
Comino, C. *Italy* **42** B2
Cómiso *Italy* **43** F7
Comitán de Domínguez
　Mexico **119** D6
Commentry *France* **19** F9
Commerce *Ga., U.S.A.* **117** D13
Commerce *Tex., U.S.A.* **116** E7
Commercy *France* **19** D12
Committee B. *Canada* **101** C11
Commodore, C. *Canada* **114** B4
Commonwealth B. *Antarctica* **5** C10
Commoron Cr. → *Australia* **95** D5
Communism Pk. = imeni
　Ismail Samani, Pik
　Tajikistan **52** F8
Como *Italy* **40** C6
Como, Lago di *Italy* **40** B6
Comodoro Rivadavia
　Argentina **128** F3
Comoé △ *Ivory C.* **82** D4
Comorâşte *Romania* **28** E6
Comorin, C. =
　Kanyakumari *India* **66** Q10
Comoros ■ *Ind. Oc.* **85** a
Comox *Canada* **102** D4
Compiègne *France* **19** C9
Comporta *Portugal* **37** G2
Compostela *Mexico* **118** C4
Comprida, I. *Brazil* **127** A6
Compton *Canada* **115** A13
Compton *U.S.A.* **111** M8
Comrat *Moldova* **29** D13
Con Cuong *Vietnam* **64** C5
Con Dao △ *Vietnam* **65** H6
Con Son *Vietnam* **65** H6
Conakry *Guinea* **82** D2
Conara *Australia* **95** G4
Concarneau *France* **18** E3
Conceição *Mozam.* **87** F4
Conceição da Barra *Brazil* **125** G11
Conceição do Araguaia
　Brazil **125** E9
Concepción *Argentina* **126** B2
Concepción *Bolivia* **124** G6
Concepción *Chile* **126** D1
Concepción *Mexico* **119** D6
Concepción *Paraguay* **126** A4
Concepción □ *Chile* **126** D1
Concepción → *Mexico* **118** A2
Concepción, Est. de *Chile* **128** G2
Concepción, L. *Bolivia* **124** G6
Concepción, Pta. *Mexico* **118** B2
Concepción del Oro *Mexico* **118** C4
Concepción del Uruguay
　Argentina **126** C4
Conception, Pt. *U.S.A.* **111** L6
Conception B. *Canada* **105** C9
Conception B. *Namibia* **88** C1
Conception I. *Bahamas* **121** B4
Concession *Zimbabwe* **87** F3
Conchas Dam *U.S.A.* **109** J11
Conches-en-Ouche *France* **18** D4
Concho *U.S.A.* **109** J9
Concho → *U.S.A.* **116** F5
Conchos → *Chihuahua,*
　Mexico **118** B4
Conchos → *Chihuahua,*
　Mexico **118** B3
Conchos → *Tamaulipas,*
　Mexico **119** B5
Concord *Calif., U.S.A.* **110** H4
Concord *N.C., U.S.A.* **117** D14
Concord *N.H., U.S.A.* **115** C13
Concórdia *Antarctica* **5** D17
Concordia *Argentina* **126** C4
Concórdia *Brazil* **124** D5
Concórdia *Brazil* **127** B5
Concordia *Mexico* **118** C3
Concórdia *U.S.A.* **112** F5
Concrete *U.S.A.* **108** B3
Condamine *Australia* **95** D5
Condat *France* **20** C6
Conde *U.S.A.* **112** C4

Condé-sur-Noireau *France* **18** D6
Condeúba *Brazil* **125** F10
Condobolin *Australia* **95** E4
Condom *France* **20** E4
Condon *U.S.A.* **108** D3
Conegliano *Italy* **41** C9
Conejera, I. = Conills, I. des
  Spain **48** B9
Conejos *Mexico* **118** B4
Conemaugh → *U.S.A.* **114** F5
Conero △ *Italy* **41** E10
Confolens *France* **20** B4
Confuso → *Paraguay* **126** B4
Congaz *Moldova* **29** D13
Conghua *China* **59** F9
Congjiang *China* **58** E7
Congleton *U.K.* **14** D5
Congo (Brazzaville) =
  Congo ■ *Africa* **84** E3
Congo (Kinshasa) =
  Congo, Dem. Rep. of
  the ■ *Africa* **84** E4
Congo ■ *Africa* **84** E3
Congo → *Africa* **84** F2
Congo, Dem. Rep. of the ■
  Africa **84** E4
Congo Basin *Africa* **84** E4
Congonhas *Brazil* **127** A7
Congress *U.S.A.* **109** J7
Conil de la Frontera *Spain* **37** J4
Conills, I. des *Spain* **48** B9
Coniston *Canada* **104** C3
Conjeeveram =
  Kanchipuram *India* **66** N11
Conklin *Canada* **103** B6
Conklin *U.S.A.* **115** D9
Conn, L. *Ireland* **12** B2
Connacht □ *Ireland* **12** C2
Conneaut *U.S.A.* **114** E4
Conneautville *U.S.A.* **114** E4
Connecticut □ *U.S.A.* **115** E12
Connecticut → *U.S.A.* **115** E12
Connell *U.S.A.* **108** C4
Connellsville *U.S.A.* **114** F5
Connemara *Ireland* **12** C2
Connemara △ *Ireland* **12** C2
Connerré *France* **18** D7
Connersville *U.S.A.* **113** F11
Connors Ra. *Australia* **94** C4
Conoename → *Suriname* **125** B7
Conques *France* **20** D6
Conquest *Canada* **103** C7
Conrad *U.S.A.* **108** B8
Conrad Rise △ *S. Ocean* **5** B5
Conran, C. *Australia* **95** F4
Conroe *U.S.A.* **116** G7
Consecon *Canada* **114** C7
Conselheiro Lafaiete *Brazil* **127** A7
Consell *Spain* **48** B9
Conselve *Italy* **41** C8
Consett *U.K.* **14** C6
Consort *Canada* **103** C6
Constance = Konstanz
  Germany **25** H5
Constance, L. = Bodensee
  Europe **25** H5
Constanţa *Romania* **29** F13
Constanţa □ *Romania* **29** F13
Constantina *Spain* **37** H5
Constantine *Algeria* **78** A7
Constitución *Chile* **126** D1
Constitución *Uruguay* **126** C4
Constitución de 1857 △
  Mexico **118** A1
Consuegra *Spain* **37** F7
Consul *Canada* **103** D7
Contact *U.S.A.* **108** F6
Contai *India* **69** J12
Contamana *Peru* **124** E4
Contarina *Italy* **41** C9
Contas → *Brazil* **125** F11
Contes *France* **21** E11
Contoocook *U.S.A.* **115** C13
Contra Costa *Mozam.* **89** D5
Contres *France* **18** E8
Contrexéville *France* **19** D12
Contwoyto L. *Canada* **100** C8
Conversano *Italy* **43** B10
Conway = Conwy *U.K.* **14** D4
Conway = Conwy → *U.K.* **14** D4
Conway *Australia* **94** J6
Conway *Canada* **114** B8
Conway *Ark., U.S.A.* **116** D8
Conway *N.H., U.S.A.* **115** C13
Conway *S.C., U.S.A.* **117** E15
Conway, C. *Australia* **94** J6
Conway, L. *Australia* **95** D2
Conwy *U.K.* **14** D4
Conwy □ *U.K.* **14** D4
Conwy → *U.K.* **14** D4
Coober Pedy *Australia* **95** D1
Cooch Behar = Koch Bihar
  India **67** F16
Cooinda *Australia* **92** B5
Cook *Australia* **93** F5
Cook *U.S.A.* **112** B7
Cook, B. *Chile* **128** H3
Cook, C. *Canada* **102** C3

Cook, Mt. = Aoraki Mount
  Cook *N.Z.* **91** E3
Cook Inlet *U.S.A.* **100** D4
Cook Is. *Pac. Oc.* **97** J12
Cook Strait *N.Z.* **91** D5
Cookeville *U.S.A.* **117** C12
Cookhouse *S. Africa* **88** E4
Cooks Harbour *Canada* **105** B8
Cookshire *Canada* **115** A13
Cookstown *Canada* **114** B5
Cookstown *U.K.* **12** B5
Cooksville *Canada* **114** C5
Cooktown *Australia* **94** B4
Coolabah *Australia* **95** E4
Cooladdi *Australia* **95** D4
Coolah *Australia* **95** E4
Coolamon *Australia* **95** E4
Coolangatta *Australia* **95** D5
Coolgardie *Australia* **93** F3
Coolidge *U.S.A.* **109** K8
Coolidge Dam *U.S.A.* **109** K8
Cooma *Australia* **95** F4
Coon Rapids *U.S.A.* **112** C7
Coonabarabran *Australia* **95** E4
Coonamble *Australia* **95** E4
Coonana *Australia* **93** F3
Coondapoor *India* **66** N9
Cooninnie, L. *Australia* **95** D2
Cooper *U.S.A.* **116** E7
Cooper Cr. → *Australia* **95** D2
Cooper Ridge *Pac. Oc.* **97** G12
Cooperstown *N. Dak., U.S.A.* **112** B4
Cooperstown *N.Y., U.S.A.* **115** D10
Coorabie *Australia* **93** F5
Coorow *Australia* **93** E2
Cooroy *Australia* **95** D5
Coos Bay *U.S.A.* **108** E1
Coosa → *U.S.A.* **117** E11
Cootamundra *Australia* **95** E4
Cootehill *Ireland* **12** B4
Copahue Paso *Argentina* **126** D1
Copainalá *Mexico* **119** D6
Copake *U.S.A.* **115** D11
Copalnic Mănăştur *Romania* **29** C8
Copán *Honduras* **120** D2
Cope *U.S.A.* **108** G12
Cope, C. *Spain* **39** H3
Copenhagen = København
  Denmark **11** J6
Copenhagen *U.S.A.* **115** C9
Copertino *Italy* **43** B11
Copiapó *Chile* **126** B1
Copiapó → *Chile* **126** B1
Coplay *U.S.A.* **115** F9
Copo △ *Argentina* **126** B3
Copp L. *Canada* **102** A6
Copparo *Italy* **41** D8
Copper Canyon =
  Barranca del Cobre △
  Mexico **118** B3
Copper Harbor *U.S.A.* **112** B10
Copper Queen *Zimbabwe* **87** F2
Copperas Cove *U.S.A.* **116** F6
Copperbelt □ *Zambia* **87** E2
Coppermine = Kugluktuk
  Canada **100** C8
Coppermine → *Canada* **100** C8
Copperopolis *U.S.A.* **110** H6
Copşa Mică *Romania* **29** D9
Coquet → *U.K.* **14** B6
Coquille *U.S.A.* **108** E1
Coquimbo *Chile* **126** C1
Coquimbo □ *Chile* **126** C1
Coquitlam *Canada* **102** D4
Corabia *Romania* **29** G9
Coracora *Peru* **124** G4
Coraki *Australia* **95** D5
Coral *U.S.A.* **114** F5
Coral Bay *Australia* **92** D1
Coral Gables *U.S.A.* **117** J14
Coral Harbour *Canada* **101** C11
Coral Sea *Pac. Oc.* **90** C4
Coral Sea Basin *Pac. Oc.* **96** J7
Coral Sea Islands Terr. □
  Australia **90** C8
Coral Springs *U.S.A.* **117** H14
Coraopolis *U.S.A.* **114** F4
Corato *Italy* **43** A9
Corbeil-Essonnes *France* **19** D9
Corbett △ *India* **69** E8
Corbie *France* **19** C9
Corbières *France* **20** F6
Corbigny *France* **19** E10
Corbin *U.S.A.* **113** G11
Corbones → *Spain* **37** H5
Corby *U.K.* **15** E7
Corcaigh = Cork *Ireland* **12** E3
Corcoran *U.S.A.* **110** J7
Corcovado △ *Costa Rica* **120** E3
Cordele *U.S.A.* **117** F13
Cordell *U.S.A.* **116** D5
Cordenòns *Italy* **41** C9
Córdoba *Argentina* **126** C3
Córdoba *Mexico* **119** D5
Córdoba *Spain* **37** H6
Córdoba □ *Argentina* **126** C3

Córdoba □ *Spain* **37** G6
Córdoba, Sierra de
  Argentina **126** C3
Cordon *Phil.* **61** C4
Cordova *U.S.A.* **100** C5
Corella *Spain* **38** C3
Corella → *Australia* **94** B3
Corfield *Australia* **94** C3
Corfu = Kerkyra *Greece* **49** A3
Corfu *U.S.A.* **114** D6
Corfu ✈ (CFU) *Greece* **46** B1
Corfu, Str. of = Kerkyras,
  Notio Steno *Greece* **49** A4
Corgo = O Corgo *Spain* **36** C3
Cori *Italy* **42** A5
Coria *Spain* **36** F4
Coria del Río *Spain* **37** H4
Corigliano Cálabro *Italy* **43** C9
Coringa Is. *Australia* **94** B4
Çorlu *Turkey* **45** E11
Corleone *Italy* **42** E6
Corleto Perticara *Italy* **43** B9
Çorlu *Turkey* **45** E11
Cormack L. *Canada* **102** A4
Cormòns *Italy* **41** C10
Cormorant *Canada* **103** C8
Cormorant L. *Canada* **103** C8
Corn Is. = Maíz, Is. del *Nic.* **120** D3
Cornalvo △ *Spain* **36** B3
Cornélio Procópio *Brazil* **127** A5
Corner Brook *Canada* **105** C8
Corneşti *Moldova* **29** C13
Corníglio *Italy* **40** D7
Corning *Ark., U.S.A.* **117** C9
Corning *Calif., U.S.A.* **108** G2
Corning *Iowa, U.S.A.* **112** E6
Corning *N.Y., U.S.A.* **114** D7
Corno Grande *Italy* **41** F10
Cornwall *Canada* **115** A10
Cornwall *U.S.A.* **115** F8
Cornwall □ *U.K.* **15** G3
Cornwall I. *Canada* **101** B10
Cornwallis I. *Canada* **101** B10
Corny Pt. *Australia* **95** E2
Coro *Venezuela* **124** A5
Coroatá *Brazil* **125** D10
Corocoro *Bolivia* **124** G5
Coroico *Bolivia* **124** G5
Coromandel *N.Z.* **91** B5
Coromandel Coast *India* **66** N12
Corona *Calif., U.S.A.* **111** M9
Corona *N. Mex., U.S.A.* **109** J11
Coronado *U.S.A.* **111** N9
Coronado, B. de *Costa Rica* **120** E3
Coronados, Is. Los *Mexico* **111** N9
Coronation *Canada* **102** C6
Coronation Gulf *Canada* **100** C9
Coronation I. *Antarctica* **5** C18
Coronation Is. *Australia* **92** B3
Coronda *Argentina* **126** C3
Coronel *Chile* **126** D1
Coronel Bogado *Paraguay* **126** B4
Coronel Dorrego *Argentina* **126** D3
Coronel Oviedo *Paraguay* **126** B4
Coronel Pringles *Argentina* **126** D3
Coronel Suárez *Argentina* **126** D3
Coronel Vidal *Argentina* **126** D4
Coropuna, Nevado *Peru* **124** G4
Çorovodë *Albania* **44** F4
Corowa *Australia* **95** F4
Corozal □ *Belize* **119** D7
Corozal Pt. *Trin. & Tob.* **125** K15
Corps *France* **21** D9
Corpus *Argentina* **127** B4
Corpus Christi *U.S.A.* **116** H6
Corpus Christi, L. *U.S.A.* **116** G6
Corral de Almaguer *Spain* **36** F7
Corralejo *Canary Is.* **48** F6
Corraun Pen. *Ireland* **12** C2
Corréggio *Italy* **40** D7
Correntes, C. das *Mozam.* **89** C6
Corrib, L. *Ireland* **12** C2
Corridónia *Italy* **41** E10
Corrientes *Argentina* **126** B4
Corrientes □ *Argentina* **126** B4
Corrientes → *Argentina* **126** C4
Corrientes → *Peru* **124** D4
Corrientes, C. *Colombia* **124** B3
Corrientes, C. *Cuba* **120** B3
Corrientes, C. *Mexico* **118** C3
Corrigan *U.S.A.* **116** F7
Corrigin *Australia* **93** F2
Corriverton *Guyana* **124** B7
Corry *U.S.A.* **114** E5

Corse □ *France* **21** G13
Corse, C. *France* **21** E13
Corse △ *France* **21** F13
Corse-du-Sud □ *France* **21** G13
Corsica = Corse □ *France* **21** G13
Corsicana *U.S.A.* **116** E6
Corte *France* **21** F13
Corte Pinto *Portugal* **37** H3
Cortés, Mar de =
  California, G. de *Mexico* **118** B2
Cortez *U.S.A.* **109** H9
Cortina d'Ampezzo *Italy* **41** B9
Cortland *N.Y., U.S.A.* **115** D8
Cortland *Ohio, U.S.A.* **114** E4
Cortona *Italy* **41** E8
Coruche *Portugal* **37** G2
Corubal → *Guinea-Biss.* **82** C2
Çoruh → *Turkey* **35** K5
Çorum *Turkey* **72** B6
Çorum □ *Turkey* **72** B6
Corumbá *Brazil* **124** G7
Corund *Romania* **29** D10
Corunna = A Coruña *Spain* **36** B2
Corvallis *U.S.A.* **108** D2
Corvette, L. de la *Canada* **104** B5
Corvo *Azores* **78** a
Corydon *U.S.A.* **112** E7
Cosalá *Mexico* **118** C3
Cosamaloapan de Carpio
  Mexico **119** D5
Cosenza *Italy* **43** C9
Coşereni *Romania* **29** F11
Cosmo Newberry *Australia* **93** E3
Cosmonaut Sea *S. Ocean* **5** C5
Cosne-Cours-sur-Loire
  France **19** E9
Coso Junction *U.S.A.* **111** J9
Coso Pk. *U.S.A.* **111** J9
Cospeito *Spain* **36** B3
Cosquín *Argentina* **126** C3
Cossato *Italy* **40** C5
Cossé-le-Vivien *France* **18** E6
Cosson → *France* **18** E8
Costa Blanca *Spain* **39** G4
Costa Brava *Spain* **38** D8
Costa Daurada *Spain* **38** D6
Costa del Sol *Spain* **37** J6
Costa de los Pins *Spain* **48** B10
Costa Mesa *U.S.A.* **111** M9
Costa Rica ■ *Cent. Amer.* **120** E3
Costa Smeralda *Italy* **42** A2
Costeşti *Romania* **29** F9
Costigliole d'Asti *Italy* **40** D5
Cosumnes → *U.S.A.* **110** G5
Coswig *Sachsen,* *Germany* **24** D9
Coswig *Sachsen-Anhalt,*
  Germany **24** D8
Cotabato *Phil.* **61** H6
Cotagaita *Bolivia* **126** A2
Côte d'Azur *France* **21** E11
Côte-d'Ivoire = Ivory
  Coast ■ *Africa* **82** D4
Côte d'Or *France* **19** E11
Côte-d'Or □ *France* **19** E11
Coteau des Prairies *U.S.A.* **112** C5
Coteau du Missouri *U.S.A.* **112** B4
Cotentin *France* **18** C5
Côtes-d'Armor □ *France* **18** D4
Côtes de Meuse *France* **19** C12
Côtes-du-Nord =
  Côtes-d'Armor □ *France* **18** D4
Cotiella *Spain* **38** C5
Cotillo *Canary Is.* **48** F5
Cotiujeni *Moldova* **29** C13
Cotonou *Benin* **83** D5
Cotopaxi *Ecuador* **124** D3
Cotronei *Italy* **43** C9
Cotswold Hills *U.K.* **15** F5
Cottage Grove *U.S.A.* **108** E2
Cottam *Canada* **114** D2
Cottbus *Germany* **24** D10
Cottonwood *U.S.A.* **109** J7
Cotulla *U.S.A.* **116** G5
Coubre, Pte. de la *France* **20** C2
Couches *France* **19** F11
Couço *Portugal* **37** G2
Coudersport *U.S.A.* **114** E6
Coudedic, C. du *Australia* **95** F2
Couëron *France* **18** E5
Couesnon → *France* **18** D5
Couhé *France* **20** B4
Coulanges-sur-Yonne
  France **19** E10
Coulee City *U.S.A.* **108** C4
Coulee Dam Nat. Recr.
  Area = Lake
  Roosevelt △ *U.S.A.* **108** B4
Coulman I. *Antarctica* **5** D11
Coulommiers *France* **19** D10
Coulon → *France* **21** E9
Coulonge → *Canada* **104** C4
Coulonges-sur-l'Autize
  France **20** B3
Coulounieix-Chamiers
  France **20** C4
Coulterville *U.S.A.* **110** H6

Council *U.S.A.* **108** D5
Council Bluffs *U.S.A.* **112** E6
Council Grove *U.S.A.* **112** F5
Coupeville *U.S.A.* **110** B4
Courantyne → *S. Amer.* **124** B7
Courcelles *Belgium* **17** D4
Courchevel *France* **21** C10
Courçon *France* **20** B3
Couronne, C. de *France* **21** E9
Cours-la-Ville *France* **19** F11
Coursan *France* **20** E7
Courseulles-sur-Mer *France* **18** C6
Courtenay *Canada* **102** D4
Courtenay *France* **19** D10
Courtland *Canada* **114** D4
Courtland *U.S.A.* **110** G5
Courtrai = Kortrijk *Belgium* **17** D3
Courtright *Canada* **114** D2
Coushatta *U.S.A.* **116** E8
Coutances *France* **18** C5
Coutras *France* **20** C3
Coutts Crossing *Australia* **95** D5
Couva *Trin. & Tob.* **125** K15
Couvin *Belgium* **17** D4
Covarrubias *Spain* **36** C7
Covasna *Romania* **29** E11
Covasna □ *Romania* **29** E10
Cove I. *Canada* **114** A3
Coventry *U.K.* **15** E6
Covilhã *Portugal* **36** E3
Covington *Ga., U.S.A.* **117** E13
Covington *Ky., U.S.A.* **113** F11
Covington *Tenn., U.S.A.* **117** D10
Covington *Va., U.S.A.* **113** G14
Cowal, L. *Australia* **95** E4
Cowan, L. *Australia* **93** F3
Cowan, L. *Canada* **103** C7
Cowangie *Australia* **95** F3
Cowansville *Canada* **115** A12
Coward Springs *Australia* **95** D2
Cowcowing Lakes *Australia* **93** F2
Cowdenbeath *U.K.* **13** E5
Cowell *Australia* **95** E2
Cowes *U.K.* **15** G6
Cowichan L. *Canada* **110** B2
Cowlitz → *U.S.A.* **110** D4
Cowra *Australia* **95** E4
Cox *Spain* **39** G4
Cox's Bazar *Bangla.* **67** J17
Coxim *Brazil* **125** G8
Coxilha Grande *Brazil* **127** B5
Coyote Wells *U.S.A.* **111** N11
Coyuca de Benitez *Mexico* **119** D4
Coyuca de Catalán *Mexico* **118** D4
Cozad *U.S.A.* **112** E4
Cozes *France* **20** C3
Cozumel *Mexico* **119** C7
Cozumel, Isla *Mexico* **119** C7
Crab Hill *Barbados* **121** g
Cracow = Kraków *Poland* **31** H11
Cracow *Australia* **95** D5
Cradle Mt.-Lake St. Clair △
  Australia **95** G4
Cradock *Australia* **95** E2
Cradock *S. Africa* **88** E4
Craig *U.S.A.* **108** F10
Craigavon *U.K.* **12** B5
Craigmore *Zimbabwe* **87** G3
Craik *Canada* **103** C7
Crailsheim *Germany* **25** F6
Craiova *Romania* **29** F8
Cramsie *Australia* **94** C3
Cranberry L. *U.S.A.* **115** B10
Cranberry Portage *Canada* **103** C8
Cranbrook *Australia* **93** F2
Cranbrook *Canada* **102** D5
Crandon *U.S.A.* **112** C9
Crane *Oreg., U.S.A.* **108** E4
Crane *Tex., U.S.A.* **116** F3
Crane, The *Barbados* **121** g
Cranston *U.S.A.* **115** E13
Craon *France* **18** E6
Craonne *France* **19** C10
Craponne-sur-Arzon *France* **20** C7
Crasna *Romania* **29** D12
Crasna → *Romania* **28** C7
Crasnei, Munţii *Romania* **29** C8
Crater L. *U.S.A.* **108** E2
Crater Lake △ *U.S.A.* **108** E2
Craters of the Moon △
  U.S.A. **108** E7
Crateús *Brazil* **125** E10
Crati → *Italy* **43** C9
Crato *Brazil* **125** E11
Crato *Portugal* **37** F3
Craven, L. *Canada* **104** B4
Crawford *U.S.A.* **112** D2
Crawfordsville *U.S.A.* **112** E10
Crawley *U.K.* **15** F7
Crazy Mts. *U.S.A.* **108** C8
Crean L. *Canada* **103** C7
Crécy-en-Ponthieu *France* **18** B8
Crediton *Canada* **114** C3
Crediton *U.K.* **15** G4
Cree → *Canada* **103** B7
Cree → *U.K.* **13** G4
Cree L. *Canada* **103** B7

Creede *U.S.A.* **109** H10
Creekside *U.S.A.* **114** F5
Creemore *Canada* **114** B4
Creighton *Canada* **103** C8
Creighton *U.S.A.* **112** D5
Creil *France* **19** C9
Crema *Italy* **40** C6
Cremona *Italy* **40** C7
Crepaja *Serbia* **28** E5
Crépy *France* **19** C10
Crépy-en-Valois *France* **19** C9
Cres *Croatia* **41** D11
Crescent City *U.S.A.* **108** F1
Crescentino *Italy* **40** C5
Crespo *Argentina* **126** C3
Cresson *U.S.A.* **114** F6
Crest *France* **21** D9
Cresta, Mt. *Phil.* **61** C5
Crestline *Calif., U.S.A.* **111** L9
Crestline *Ohio, U.S.A.* **114** F2
Creston *Canada* **102** D5
Creston *Calif., U.S.A.* **110** K6
Creston *Iowa, U.S.A.* **112** E6
Crestview *Calif., U.S.A.* **110** H8
Crestview *Fla., U.S.A.* **117** F11
Crêt de la Neige *France* **19** F12
Crete = Kriti *Greece* **49** D7
Crete *U.S.A.* **112** E5
Crete, Sea of *Greece* **47** E7
Créteil *France* **19** D9
Creus, C. de *Spain* **38** C8
Creuse □ *France* **19** F9
Creuse → *France* **20** B4
Creutzwald *France* **19** C13
Creuzburg *Germany* **24** D6
Crèvecoeur-le-Grand *France* **19** C9
Crevillent *Spain* **39** G4
Crewe *U.K.* **14** D5
Crewkerne *U.K.* **15** G5
Crianlarich *U.K.* **13** E4
Criciúma *Brazil* **127** B6
Cricova *Moldova* **29** C13
Crieff *U.K.* **13** E5
Crikvenica *Croatia* **41** C11
Crimea □ *Ukraine* **33** K8
Crimean Pen. = Krymskyy
  Pivostriv *Ukraine* **33** K8
Crimmitschau *Germany* **24** E8
Cristuru Secuiesc *Romania* **29** D10
Crişul Alb → *Romania* **28** D6
Crişul Negru → *Romania* **28** D6
Crişul Repede → *Romania* **28** D5
Criuleni *Moldova* **29** C14
Crivitz *Germany* **24** B7
Crna → *Macedonia* **44** E5
Crna Gora =
  Montenegro ■ *Europe* **44** D3
Crna Gora *Macedonia* **44** D5
Crna Reka = Crna →
  Macedonia **44** E5
Crna Trava *Serbia* **44** D6
Crni Drim → *Macedonia* **44** E4
Crni Timok → *Serbia* **44** C6
Crnoljeva Planina *Serbia* **44** D5
Črnomelj *Slovenia* **41** C12
Croagh Patrick *Ireland* **12** C2
Croatia ■ *Europe* **41** C13
Crocker, Banjaran *Malaysia* **62** C5
Crockett *U.S.A.* **116** F7
Crocodile = Umgwenya →
  Mozam. **89** D5
Crocodile Is. *Australia* **94** A1
Crocq *France* **20** C6
Crodo *Italy* **40** B5
Crohy Hd. *Ireland* **12** B3
Croisette, C. *France* **21** E9
Croisic, Pte. du *France* **18** E4
Croix, L. la *Canada* **104** C1
Croker, C. *Australia* **92** B5
Croker, C. *Canada* **114** B4
Croker I. *Australia* **92** B5
Cromarty *U.K.* **13** D4
Cromer *U.K.* **14** E9
Cromwell *N.Z.* **91** F2
Cromwell *U.S.A.* **115** E12
Cronat *France* **19** F10
Crook *U.K.* **14** C6
Crooked → *Canada* **102** C4
Crooked → *U.S.A.* **108** D3
Crooked I. *Bahamas* **121** B5
Crooked Island Passage
  Bahamas **121** B5
Crookston *Minn., U.S.A.* **112** B5
Crookston *Nebr., U.S.A.* **112** D3
Crookwell *Australia* **95** E4
Cropane-Micone △ *Italy* **43** D9
Crosby *U.K.* **14** D4
Crosby *N. Dak., U.S.A.* **112** A2
Crosby *Pa., U.S.A.* **114** E6
Crosbyton *U.S.A.* **116** E4
Crosía *Italy* **43** C9
Cross → *Nigeria* **83** D6
Cross City *U.S.A.* **117** G13
Cross L. *Canada* **103** C9
Cross Lake *Canada* **103** C9
Cross Fell *U.K.* **14** C5
Cross River □ *Nigeria* **83** D6

Cross River △ *Nigeria* **83 D6**
Cross Sound *U.S.A.* **100 D6**
Crossett *U.S.A.* **116 E9**
Crosshaven *Ireland* **12 E3**
Crossmaglen *U.K.* **12 B5**
Crossville *U.S.A.* **117 D12**
Croswell *U.S.A.* **114 C2**
Croton-on-Hudson *U.S.A.* **115 E11**
Crotone *Italy* **43 C10**
Crow → *Canada* **102 B4**
Crow Agency *U.S.A.* **108 D10**
Crow Hd. *Ireland* **12 E1**
Crowell *U.S.A.* **116 E5**
Crowley *U.S.A.* **116 F8**
Crowley, L. *U.S.A.* **110 H8**
Crown Point *Ind., U.S.A.* **112 E10**
Crown Point *N.Y., U.S.A.* **115 C11**
Crown Pt. *Trin. & Tob.* **125 J16**
Crownpoint *U.S.A.* **109 J9**
Crows Landing *U.S.A.* **110 H5**
Crows Nest *Australia* **95 D5**
Crowsnest Pass *Canada* **102 D6**
Croydon *Australia* **94 B3**
Croydon □ *U.K.* **15 F7**
Crozet, Is. *Ind. Oc.* **3 G12**
Crozon *France* **18 D2**
Crusheen *Ireland* **12 D3**
Cruz, C. *Cuba* **120 C4**
Cruz Alta *Brazil* **127 B5**
Cruz del Eje *Argentina* **126 C3**
Cruzeiro *Brazil* **127 A7**
Cruzeiro do Oeste *Brazil* **127 A5**
Cruzeiro do Sul *Brazil* **124 E4**
Cry L. *Canada* **102 B3**
Crystal Bay *U.S.A.* **110 F7**
Crystal Brook *Australia* **95 E2**
Crystal City *U.S.A.* **116 G5**
Crystal Falls *U.S.A.* **112 B9**
Crystal River *U.S.A.* **117 G13**
Crystal Springs *U.S.A.* **117 F9**
Csenger *Hungary* **28 C7**
Csongrád *Hungary* **28 D5**
Csongrád □ *Hungary* **28 D5**
Csorna *Hungary* **28 C2**
Csurgo *Hungary* **28 D2**
Cu Lao Hon *Vietnam* **65 G7**
Cua Rao *Vietnam* **64 C5**
Cuácua → *Mozam.* **87 F4**
Cuamato *Angola* **88 B3**
Cuamba *Mozam.* **87 E4**
Cuando → *Angola* **85 H4**
Cuando Cubango □ *Angola* **88 B3**
Cuangar *Angola* **88 B2**
Cuango = Kwango →
  Dem. Rep. of the Congo **84 E3**
Cuanza → *Angola* **84 F2**
Cuarto → *Argentina* **126 C3**
Cuatrociénegas *Mexico* **118 B4**
Cuauhtémoc *Mexico* **118 B3**
Cuba *Portugal* **37 G3**
Cuba *N. Mex., U.S.A.* **109 H10**
Cuba *N.Y., U.S.A.* **114 D6**
Cuba ■ *W. Indies* **120 B4**
Cubango → *Africa* **88 B3**
Çubuk *Turkey* **72 B5**
Cuc Phuong △ *Vietnam* **64 B5**
Cuchumatanes, Sierra de
  los *Guatemala* **120 C1**
Cuckfield *U.K.* **15 F7**
Cucuí *Brazil* **124 C5**
Cucurpé *Mexico* **118 A2**
Cúcuta *Colombia* **124 B4**
Cudalbi *Romania* **29 E12**
Cuddalore *India* **66 P11**
Cuddapah *India* **66 M11**
Cuddapan, L. *Australia* **94 D3**
Cudillero *Spain* **36 B2**
Cue *Australia* **93 E2**
Cuéllar *Spain* **36 D6**
Cuenca *Ecuador* **124 D3**
Cuenca *Spain* **38 E2**
Cuenca □ *Spain* **38 F3**
Cuenca, Serranía de *Spain* **38 F3**
Cuenca Alta del
  Manzanares △ *Spain* **36 E7**
Cuerda del Pozo, Embalse
  de la *Spain* **38 D2**
Cuernavaca *Mexico* **119 D5**
Cuero *U.S.A.* **116 G6**
Cuers *France* **21 E10**
Cueva de la Quebrada del
  Toro △ *Venezuela* **121 D6**
Cuevas del Almanzora *Spain* **39 H3**
Cuevo *Bolivia* **124 H6**
Cugir *Romania* **29 E8**
Cugnaux *France* **20 E5**
Cuhai-Bakony → *Hungary* **28 C2**
Cuiabá *Brazil* **125 G7**
Cuiabá → *Brazil* **125 G7**
Cuijk *Neths.* **17 C5**
Cuilco *Guatemala* **120 C1**
Cuillin Hills *U.K.* **13 D2**
Cuillin Sd. *U.K.* **13 D2**
Cuilo = Kwilu →
  Dem. Rep. of the Congo **84 E3**
Cuiseaux *France* **19 F12**

Cuito → *Angola* **88 B3**
Cuitzeo, L. de *Mexico* **118 D4**
Cujmir *Romania* **28 F7**
Cukai *Malaysia* **65 K4**
Çukurca *Turkey* **73 D10**
Culbertson *U.S.A.* **108 B11**
Culcairn *Australia* **95 F4**
Culebra *Puerto Rico* **121 d**
Culebra, Sierra de la *Spain* **36 D4**
Culfa *Azerbaijan* **73 C11**
Culgoa → *Australia* **95 D4**
Culgoa Flood Plain △
  Australia **95 D4**
Culiacán *Mexico* **118 C3**
Culiacán → *Mexico* **118 C3**
Culik *Indonesia* **63 J18**
Culion *Phil.* **61 F4**
Cúllar *Spain* **37 H8**
Cullarin Ra. *Australia* **95 E4**
Cullen *U.K.* **13 D6**
Cullen Pt. *Australia* **94 A3**
Cullera *Spain* **39 F4**
Cullman *U.S.A.* **117 D11**
Cullompton *U.K.* **15 G4**
Culoz *France* **21 C9**
Culpeper *U.S.A.* **113 F14**
Culuene → *Brazil* **125 F8**
Culver, Pt. *Australia* **93 F3**
Culverden *N.Z.* **91 E4**
Cumaná *Venezuela* **124 A6**
Cumaovası *Turkey* **47 C9**
Cumberland *B.C., Canada* **102 D4**
Cumberland *Ont., Canada* **115 A9**
Cumberland *U.S.A.* **113 F14**
Cumberland → *U.S.A.* **112 G9**
Cumberland, L. *U.S.A.* **113 G11**
Cumberland Gap △ *U.S.A.* **113 G12**
Cumberland I. *U.S.A.* **117 F14**
Cumberland Is. *Australia* **94 J7**
Cumberland Island △
  U.S.A. **117 F14**
Cumberland L. *Canada* **103 C8**
Cumberland Pen. *Canada* **101 C13**
Cumberland Plateau *U.S.A.*
  117 D12
Cumberland Sd. *Canada* **101 C13**
Cumbernauld *U.K.* **13 F5**
Cumborah *Australia* **95 D4**
Cumbres de Majalca △
  Mexico **118 B3**
Cumbres de Monterrey △
  Mexico **118 B4**
Cumbres Mayores *Spain* **37 G4**
Cumbria □ *U.K.* **14 C5**
Cumbrian Mts. *U.K.* **14 C5**
Cumbum *India* **66 M11**
Cuminá → *Brazil* **125 D7**
Cummings Mt. *U.S.A.* **111 K8**
Cummins *Australia* **95 E2**
Cumnock *Australia* **95 E4**
Cumnock *U.K.* **13 F4**
Cumpas *Mexico* **118 B3**
Cumplida, Pta. *Canary Is.* **48 F2**
Çumra *Turkey* **72 D5**
Cunco *Chile* **128 D2**
Cuncumén *Chile* **126 C1**
Cunderdin *Australia* **93 F2**
Cunene → *Angola* **88 B1**
Cúneo *Italy* **40 D4**
Çüngüş *Turkey* **70 B3**
Cunillera, I. = Sa Conillera
  Spain **48 C7**
Cunlhat *France* **20 C7**
Cunnamulla *Australia* **95 D4**
Cuorgnè *Italy* **40 C4**
Cupar *Canada* **103 C8**
Cupar *U.K.* **13 E5**
Cupcini *Moldova* **29 B12**
Cupertino *U.S.A.* **110 H4**
Cupica, G. de *Colombia* **124 B3**
Čuprija *Serbia* **44 C5**
Curaçao *Neth. Ant.* **121 D6**
Curanilahue *Chile* **126 D1**
Curaray → *Peru* **124 D4**
Cure → *France* **19 E10**
Curepipe *Mauritius* **85 d**
Curepto *Chile* **126 D1**
Curiapo *Venezuela* **124 B6**
Curicó *Chile* **126 C1**
Curieuse *Seychelles* **85 b**
Curinga *Italy* **43 D9**
Curitiba *Brazil* **127 B6**
Curitibanos *Brazil* **127 B5**
Currabubula *Australia* **95 E5**
Currais Novos *Brazil* **125 E11**
Curral Velho *C. Verde Is.* **78 b**
Curralinho *Brazil* **125 D9**
Currane, L. *Ireland* **12 E1**
Currant *U.S.A.* **108 G6**
Currawinya △ *Australia* **95 D3**
Current → *U.S.A.* **116 C9**
Currie *Australia* **95 F3**
Currie *U.S.A.* **108 F6**
Curtea de Argeş *Romania* **29 E9**
Curtici *Romania* **28 D6**
Curtin Springs *Australia* **93 E5**
Curtis *U.S.A.* **112 E3**
Curtis Group *Australia* **95 F4**

Curtis I. *Australia* **94 C5**
Curuápanema → *Brazil* **125 D7**
Curuçá *Brazil* **125 D9**
Curuguaty *Paraguay* **127 A4**
Curup *Indonesia* **62 E2**
Cururupu *Brazil* **125 D10**
Curuzú Cuatiá *Argentina* **126 B4**
Curvelo *Brazil* **125 G10**
Cusco = Cuzco *Peru* **124 F4**
Cushendall *U.K.* **12 A5**
Cushing *U.S.A.* **116 D6**
Cushing, Mt. *Canada* **102 B3**
Cusihuiriáchic *Mexico* **118 B3**
Cusna, Mte. *Italy* **40 D7**
Cusset *France* **19 F10**
Custer *U.S.A.* **112 D2**
Cut Bank *U.S.A.* **108 B7**
Cuthbert *U.S.A.* **117 F12**
Cutler *U.S.A.* **110 J7**
Cutro *Italy* **43 C9**
Cuttaburra → *Australia* **95 D3**
Cuttack *India* **67 J14**
Cuvier, C. *Australia* **93 D1**
Cuvier I. *N.Z.* **91 B5**
Cuxhaven *Germany* **24 B4**
Cuyahoga Falls *U.S.A.* **114 E3**
Cuyahoga Valley △ *U.S.A.* **114 E3**
Cuyapo *Phil.* **61 D4**
Cuyo *Phil.* **61 F4**
Cuyo East Pass *Phil.* **61 F4**
Cuyo West Pass *Phil.* **61 F4**
Cuyuni → *Guyana* **124 B7**
Cuzco *Bolivia* **124 H5**
Cuzco *Peru* **124 F4**
Čvrsnica *Bos.-H.* **28 G2**
Cwmbran *U.K.* **15 F4**
Cyangugu *Rwanda* **86 C2**
Cybinka *Poland* **31 F1**
Cyclades *Greece* **46 E6**
Cyclades □ *Greece* **46 D6**
Cygnet *Australia* **95 G4**
Cynthiana *U.S.A.* **113 F11**
Cypress Hills *Canada* **103 D7**
Cypress Hills △ *Canada* **103 D7**
Cyprus ■ *Asia* **49 E12**
Cyrenaica = Barqa *Libya* **79 C10**
Cyrene *Libya* **79 B10**
Czaplinek *Poland* **30 E3**
Czar *Canada* **103 C6**
Czarna → *Łódzkie, Poland* **31 G6**
Czarna → *Świętokrzyskie,*
  Poland **31 H8**
Czarna Białostocka *Poland* **31 E10**
Czarna Woda *Poland* **30 E5**
Czarne *Poland* **30 E3**
Czarnków *Poland* **31 F3**
Czech Rep. ■ *Europe* **26 B8**
Czechowice-Dziedzice *Poland* **31 J5**
Czempiń *Poland* **31 F3**
Czeremcha *Poland* **31 F10**
Czerniejewo *Poland* **31 F4**
Czersk *Poland* **30 E4**
Czerwieńsk *Poland* **31 F2**
Czerwionka-Leszczyny
  Poland **31 H5**
Częstochowa *Poland* **31 H6**
Człopa *Poland* **31 E3**
Człuchów *Poland* **30 E4**
Czyżew-Osada *Poland* **31 F9**

D

Da → *Vietnam* **58 G5**
Da Hinggan Ling *China* **60 B7**
Da Lat *Vietnam* **65 G7**
Da Nang *Vietnam* **64 D7**
Da Qaidam *China* **60 C4**
Da Yunhe → *Hopei, China* **57 E9**
Da Yunhe → *Jiangsu, China* **57 G11**
Da'an *China* **57 B13**
Daan Viljoen △ *Namibia* **88 C2**
Dab'a, Ras el *Egypt* **80 H6**
Daba Shan *China* **58 B7**
Dabai *Nigeria* **83 C6**
Dabakala *Ivory C.* **82 D4**
Dabas *Hungary* **28 C4**
Dabat *Ethiopia* **81 E4**
Dabbagh, Jabal *Si. Arabia* **70 E2**
Dabhoi *India* **68 H5**
Dąbie *Poland* **31 F5**
Dabnou *Niger* **83 C6**
Dabo = Pasirkuning
  Indonesia **62 E2**
Dabola *Guinea* **82 C2**
Dabou *Ivory C.* **82 D4**
Daboya *Ghana* **83 D4**
Dabravolya *Belarus* **31 F10**
Dąbrowa Białostocka
  Poland **30 E10**
Dąbrowa Górnicza *Poland* **31 H6**
Dąbrowa Tarnowska *Poland* **31 H7**
Dabu *China* **59 E11**
Dabung *Malaysia* **65 K4**
Dabus → *Ethiopia* **81 E4**
Dacato → *Ethiopia* **81 F5**

Dacca = Dhaka *Bangla.* **69 H14**
Dacca = Dhaka □ *Bangla.* **69 G14**
Dachau *Germany* **25 G7**
Dachigam △ *India* **68 B6**
Dachstein, Hoher *Austria* **26 D6**
Dačice *Czech Rep.* **26 B8**
Dacre *Canada* **114 A8**
Dadanawa *Guyana* **124 C7**
Daday *Turkey* **72 B5**
Dade City *U.S.A.* **117 G13**
Dadhar *Pakistan* **68 E2**
Dadiya *Nigeria* **83 D7**
Dadra & Nagar Haveli □
  India **66 J8**
Dadri = Charkhi Dadri *India* **68 E7**
Dadu *Pakistan* **68 F2**
Dadu He → *China* **58 C4**
Daegu *S. Korea* **57 G15**
Daejeon *S. Korea* **57 F14**
Daejeong *S. Korea* **57 H14**
Daet *Phil.* **61 D5**
Dafang *China* **58 D5**
Dafnes *Greece* **49 D7**
Dafni *Greece* **46 D4**
Dağ *Turkey* **47 D12**
Dagana *Senegal* **82 B1**
Dagash *Sudan* **80 D3**
Dagestan □ *Russia* **35 J8**
Dagestanskiye Ogni *Russia* **35 J9**
Daggett *U.S.A.* **111 L10**
Daghestan Republic =
  Dagestan □ *Russia* **35 J8**
Daghfeli *Sudan* **80 D3**
Dağlıq Qarabağ =
  Nagorno-Karabakh □
  Azerbaijan **73 C12**
Dago = Hiiumaa *Estonia* **32 C2**
Dagu *China* **57 E9**
Daguan *China* **58 D4**
Dagupan *Phil.* **61 C4**
Daguragu *Australia* **92 C5**
Dahab *Egypt* **70 D2**
Dahlak Kebir *Eritrea* **81 D5**
Dahlak Marine △ *Eritrea* **81 D5**
Dahlenburg *Germany* **24 B6**
Dahlonega *U.S.A.* **117 D13**
Dahme *Germany* **24 D9**
Dahod *India* **68 H6**
Dahong Shan *China* **59 B9**
Dahongliutan *China* **69 B8**
Dahra *Libya* **79 C9**
Dahra *Senegal* **82 B1**
Dahshûr *Egypt* **80 J7**
Dahūk *Iraq* **73 D10**
Dahūk □ *Iraq* **73 D10**
Dai Hao *Vietnam* **64 C6**
Dai-Sen *Japan* **55 G6**
Dai Shan *China* **59 B14**
Dai Xian *China* **56 E7**
Daicheng *China* **56 E9**
Daikondi = Day Kundī □
  Afghan. **66 C5**
Daimiel *Spain* **37 F7**
Daingean *Ireland* **12 C4**
Dainkog *China* **58 A1**
Daintree *Australia* **94 B4**
Daintree △ *Australia* **94 B4**
Daiō-Misaki *Japan* **55 G8**
Dair, J. ed *Sudan* **81 E3**
Dairût *Egypt* **80 B3**
Daisen-Oki △ *Japan* **55 G6**
Daisetsu-Zan *Japan* **54 C11**
Daisetsu-Zan △ *Japan* **54 C11**
Dajarra *Australia* **94 C2**
Dajiawa *China* **57 F10**
Dajin Chuan → *China* **58 B3**
Dak Dam *Cambodia* **64 F6**
Dak Nhe *Vietnam* **64 E6**
Dak Pek *Vietnam* **64 E6**
Dak Sui *Vietnam* **64 E6**
Dakar *Senegal* **82 C1**
Dakhla *W. Sahara* **78 D2**
Dakhla, El Wâhât el *Egypt* **80 B2**
Dakingari *Nigeria* **83 C5**
Dakor *India* **68 H5**
Dakoro *Niger* **83 C6**
Dakota City *U.S.A.* **112 D5**
Đakovica *Croatia* **28 E3**
Đakovo *Croatia* **28 E3**
Dalai Nur *China* **56 C9**
Dālakī *Iran* **71 D6**
Dalälven → *Sweden* **10 D10**
Dalaman *Turkey* **47 E10**
Dalaman → *Turkey* **47 E10**
Dalandzadgad *Mongolia* **56 C3**
Dalap-Uliga-Darrit =
  Majuro *Marshall Is.* **96 G9**
Dalarna *Sweden* **10 D8**
Dalarnas län □ *Sweden* **10 C8**
Dālbandīn *Pakistan* **66 E4**
Dalbeattie *U.K.* **13 G5**
Dalbeg *Australia* **94 C4**
Dalbosjön *Sweden* **11 F6**

Dalby *Australia* **95 D5**
Dalby *Sweden* **11 J7**
Dalby Söderskog △ *Sweden* **11 J7**
Dale City *U.S.A.* **113 F15**
Dale Hollow L. *U.S.A.* **117 C12**
Dalga *Egypt* **80 B3**
Dalgán *Iran* **71 E8**
Dalhart *U.S.A.* **116 C3**
Dalhousie *Canada* **105 C6**
Dalhousie *India* **68 C6**
Dali *Shaanxi, China* **56 G5**
Dali *Yunnan, China* **58 E3**
Dalian *China* **57 E11**
Daliang Shan *China* **58 D4**
Daling He → *China* **57 D11**
Dāliyat el Karmel *Israel* **74 C4**
Dalj *Croatia* **28 E3**
Dalkeith *U.K.* **13 F5**
Dallas *Oreg., U.S.A.* **108 D2**
Dallas *Tex., U.S.A.* **116 E6**
Dalles, The *U.S.A.* **108 D3**
Dallol *Ethiopia* **81 E5**
Dalmā *U.A.E.* **71 E7**
Dalmacija *Croatia* **41 E13**
Dalmas, L. *Canada* **105 B5**
Dalmatia = Dalmacija
  Croatia **41 E13**
Dalmau *India* **69 F9**
Dalmellington *U.K.* **13 F4**
Dalnegorsk *Russia* **54 B7**
Dalnerechensk *Russia* **54 B6**
Dalnevostochnyy □ *Russia* **53 C14**
Daloa *Ivory C.* **82 D3**
Dalou Shan *China* **58 C6**
Dalry *U.K.* **13 F4**
Dalrymple, L. *Australia* **94 C4**
Dalrymple, Mt. *Australia* **94 K6**
Dals Långed *Sweden* **11 F6**
Dalsjöfors *Sweden* **11 G7**
Dalsland *Sweden* **11 F6**
Daltenganj *India* **69 H11**
Dalton, Ga., U.S.A. **117 D12**
Dalton *Mass., U.S.A.* **115 D11**
Dalton *Nebr., U.S.A.* **112 E2**
Dalton-in-Furness *U.K.* **14 C4**
Dalupiri I. *Phil.* **61 B4**
Dalvík *Iceland* **8 D4**
Dálvvadis = Jokkmokk
  Sweden **8 C18**
Dalwallinu *Australia* **93 F2**
Daly → *Australia* **92 B5**
Daly City *U.S.A.* **110 H4**
Daly L. *Canada* **103 B7**
Daly River *Australia* **92 B5**
Daly Waters *Australia* **94 B1**
Dalyan *Turkey* **47 E10**
Dam Doi *Vietnam* **65 H5**
Dam Ha *Vietnam* **64 B6**
Damachova *Belarus* **31 G10**
Daman *India* **66 J8**
Dāmaneh *Iran* **71 C6**
Damanhûr *Egypt* **80 H7**
Damant L. *Canada* **103 A7**
Damanzhuang *China* **56 E9**
Damaq *Iran* **73 E13**
Damar *Indonesia* **63 F7**
Damara *C.A.R.* **84 D3**
Damaraland *Namibia* **88 C2**
Damascus = Dimashq *Syria* **74 B5**
Damasi *Greece* **46 B4**
Damaturu *Nigeria* **83 C7**
Damāvand *Iran* **71 C7**
Damāvand, Qolleh-ye *Iran* **71 C7**
Damba *Angola* **84 F3**
Damboa *Nigeria* **83 C7**
Dâmbovița □ *Romania* **29 F10**
Dâmbovița → *Romania* **29 F11**
Dâmbovnic → *Romania* **29 F10**
Dame Marie *Haiti* **121 C5**
Dāmghān *Iran* **71 B7**
Dămienesti *Romania* **29 D11**
Damietta = Dumyât *Egypt* **80 H7**
Daming *China* **56 F8**
Damīr Qābū *Syria* **73 D10**
Damme *Germany* **24 C4**
Damodar → *India* **69 H12**
Damoh *India* **69 H8**
Dampier *Australia* **92 D2**
Dampier, Selat *Indonesia* **63 E8**
Dampier Arch. *Australia* **92 D2**
Damrei, Chuor Phnum
  Cambodia **65 G4**
Damvillers *France* **19 C12**
Damyang *S. Korea* **57 G14**
Dan-Gulbi *Nigeria* **83 C6**
Dan-Sadau *Nigeria* **83 C6**
Dana *Indonesia* **63 F6**
Dana *Jordan* **74 E4**
Dana, L. *Canada* **104 B4**
Dana, Mt. *U.S.A.* **110 H7**
Danakil Desert *Ethiopia* **81 E5**
Danao *Phil.* **61 F6**
Danau Poso *Indonesia* **63 E6**

Danba *China* **58 B3**
Danbury *U.S.A.* **115 E11**
Danby L. *U.S.A.* **109 J6**
Dand *Afghan.* **68 D1**
Dande △ *Zimbabwe* **87 F3**
Dandeldhura *Nepal* **69 E9**
Dandeli *India* **66 M9**
Dandenong *Australia* **95 F4**
Dandī *Iran* **73 D12**
Dandîl *Egypt* **80 J7**
Dandong *China* **57 D13**
Danfeng *China* **56 H6**
Dangan Liedao *China* **59 F10**
Dangé-St-Romain *France* **20 B4**
Dângeni *Romania* **29 C11**
Danger Is. = Pukapuka
  Cook Is. **97 J11**
Danger Pt. *S. Africa* **88 E2**
Danginpuri *Indonesia* **63 K18**
Dangla *Ethiopia* **81 E4**
Dangla Shan = Tanggula
  Shan *China* **60 C4**
Dangora *Nigeria* **83 C6**
Dangouadougou
  Burkina Faso **82 D4**
Dangrek, Phnom *Thailand* **64 E5**
Dangriga *Belize* **119 D7**
Dangshan *China* **56 G9**
Dangtu *China* **59 B12**
Dangyang *China* **59 B8**
Daniel *U.S.A.* **108 E8**
Daniel's Harbour *Canada* **105 B8**
Danielskuil *S. Africa* **88 D3**
Danielson *U.S.A.* **115 E13**
Danilov *Russia* **32 C11**
Danilovgrad *Montenegro* **44 D3**
Danilovka *Russia* **34 E7**
Daning *China* **56 F6**
Danja *Nigeria* **83 C6**
Danjiangkou *China* **59 A8**
Danjiangkou Shuiku *China* **59 A8**
Dank *Oman* **71 F8**
Dankalwa *Nigeria* **83 C7**
Dankama *Nigeria* **83 C6**
Dankhar Gompa *India* **68 C8**
Dankov *Russia* **32 F10**
Danleng *China* **58 B4**
Danlí *Honduras* **120 D2**
Danmark = Denmark ■
  Europe **11 J3**
Dannemora *U.S.A.* **115 B11**
Dannenberg *Germany* **24 B7**
Dannevirke *N.Z.* **91 C6**
Dannhauser *S. Africa* **89 D5**
Dansville *U.S.A.* **114 D7**
Danta *India* **68 G5**
Dantan *India* **69 J12**
Danube = Dunărea →
  Europe **29 E14**
Danvers *U.S.A.* **115 D14**
Danville *Ill., U.S.A.* **112 E10**
Danville *Ky., U.S.A.* **113 G11**
Danville *Pa., U.S.A.* **115 F8**
Danville *Va., U.S.A.* **113 G14**
Danville *Vt., U.S.A.* **115 B12**
Danyang *China* **59 B12**
Danzhai *China* **58 D6**
Danzhou *China* **64 C7**
Danzig = Gdańsk *Poland* **30 D5**
Dão → *Portugal* **36 E2**
Dao Xian *China* **59 E8**
Daocheng *China* **58 C3**
Daoukro *Ivory C.* **82 D4**
Dapaong *Togo* **83 C5**
Dapchi *Nigeria* **83 C7**
Dapitan *Phil.* **61 G5**
Daqing Shan *China* **56 D6**
Daqq-e Sorkh, Kavīr *Iran* **71 C7**
Daqu Shan *China* **59 B14**
Dar Banda *Africa* **76 F6**
Dar el Beida = Casablanca
  Morocco **78 B4**
Dar es Salaam *Tanzania* **86 D4**
Dar Mazār *Iran* **71 D8**
Dar'ā *Syria* **74 C5**
Dar'ā □ *Syria* **74 C5**
Dārāb *Iran* **71 D7**
Daraban *Pakistan* **68 D4**
Darabani *Romania* **29 B11**
Daraina *Madag.* **89 A8**
Daraj *Libya* **79 B8**
Dārān *Iran* **71 C6**
Daravica *Serbia* **44 D4**
Daraw *Egypt* **80 C3**
Dārayyā *Syria* **74 B5**
Darazo *Nigeria* **83 C7**
Darband *Pakistan* **68 B5**
Darband, Kūh-e *Iran* **71 D8**
Darbhanga *India* **69 F11**
D'Arcy *Canada* **102 C4**
Darda *Croatia* **28 E3**
Dardanelle *Ark., U.S.A.* **116 D8**
Dardanelle *Calif., U.S.A.* **110 G7**
Dardanelles = Çanakkale
  Boğazı *Turkey* **45 F10**
Dare → *Ethiopia* **81 F5**
Darende *Turkey* **72 C7**
Dārestān *Iran* **71 D8**

Darfo *Italy* 40 C7
Dârfûr *Sudan* 79 F10
Dargai *Pakistan* 68 B4
Dargaville *N.Z.* 91 A4
Dargol *Niger* 83 C5
Darhan *Mongolia* 60 B5
Darhan Muminggan
    Lianheqi *China* 56 D6
Dari *Sudan* 81 F3
Darıca *Turkey* 72 B3
Darién, G. del *Colombia* 124 B3
Darién △ *Panama* 120 E4
Dariganga = Ovoot *Mongolia* 56 B7
Darjeeling = Darjiling *India* 69 F13
Darjiling *India* 69 F13
Darkan *Australia* 93 F2
Darkhana *Pakistan* 68 D5
Darkhazîneh *Iran* 71 D6
Darkot Pass *Pakistan* 69 A5
Darling → *Australia* 95 E3
Darling Downs *Australia* 95 D5
Darling Ra. *Australia* 93 F2
Darlington *U.K.* 14 C6
Darlington *U.S.A.* 117 D15
Darlington □ *U.K.* 14 C6
Darlington, L. *S. Africa* 88 E4
Darlot, L. *Australia* 93 E3
Darlowo *Poland* 30 D3
Dărmănești *Bacău, Romania* 29 D11
Dărmănești *Suceava,
    Romania* 29 C11
Darmstadt *Germany* 25 F4
Darnah *Libya* 79 B10
Darnall *S. Africa* 89 D5
Darney *France* 19 D13
Darnley, C. *Antarctica* 5 C6
Darnley B. *Canada* 100 C7
Daroca *Spain* 38 D3
Darou-Mousti *Senegal* 82 B1
Darr → *Australia* 94 C3
Darra Pezu *Pakistan* 68 C4
Darrequeira *Argentina* 126 D3
Darrington *U.S.A.* 108 B3
Darreh Shahr *Iran* 73 F12
Darrsser Ort *Germany* 24 A8
Dart → *U.K.* 15 G4
Dart, C. *Antarctica* 5 D14
Dartford *U.K.* 15 F8
Dartmoor *U.K.* 15 G4
Dartmoor △ *U.K.* 15 G4
Dartmouth *Canada* 105 D7
Dartmouth *U.K.* 15 G4
Dartmouth Res. *Australia* 95 D4
Dartuch, C. = Artrutx, C.
    de *Spain* 48 B10
Daruvar *Croatia* 28 E2
Darvaza *Turkmenistan* 52 E6
Darvel, Teluk = Lahad
    Datu, Telok *Malaysia* 63 D5
Darwen *U.K.* 14 D5
Darwendale *Zimbabwe* 89 B5
Darwha *India* 66 J10
Darwin *Australia* 92 B5
Darwin *U.S.A.* 111 J9
Darya Khan *Pakistan* 68 D4
Daryācheh-ye Bakhtegān
    Iran 71 D7
Daryoi Amu =
    Amudarya → *Uzbekistan* 52 E6
Dās *U.A.E.* 71 E7
Dashen, Ras *Ethiopia* 81 E4
Dashetai *China* 56 D5
Dashkesan = Daşkäsän
    Azerbaijan 35 K7
Dashköpri *Turkmenistan* 71 B9
Dashoguz *Turkmenistan* 52 E6
Dasht → *Pakistan* 66 G2
Daska *Pakistan* 68 C6
Daşkäsän *Azerbaijan* 35 K7
Dassa *Benin* 83 D5
Dasuya *India* 68 D6
Datça *Turkey* 47 E9
Datia *India* 69 G8
Datian *China* 59 E11
Datong *Anhui, China* 59 B11
Datong *Shanxi, China* 56 D7
Dattakhel *Pakistan* 68 C3
Datteln *Germany* 24 D3
Datu, Tanjung *Indonesia* 62 D3
Datu Piang *Phil.* 61 H6
Datuk, Tanjong = Datu,
    Tanjung *Indonesia* 62 D3
Daua = Dawa → *Africa* 81 G5
Daud Khel *Pakistan* 68 C4
Daudnagar *India* 69 G11
Daugava → *Latvia* 32 D3
Daugavpils *Latvia* 32 E4
Daulpur *India* 68 F7
Daun *Germany* 25 E2
Dauphin *Canada* 103 C8
Dauphin *U.S.A.* 114 F8
Dauphin L. *Canada* 103 C9
Dauphiné *France* 21 D9
Daura *Borno, Nigeria* 83 C7
Daura *Katsina, Nigeria* 83 C6
Dausa *India* 68 F7
Dāväçi *Azerbaijan* 35 K9
Davangere *India* 66 M9

Davao *Phil.* 61 H6
Davao G. *Phil.* 61 H6
Dāvar Panāh = Sarāvān
    Iran 71 E9
Davenport *Calif., U.S.A.* 110 H4
Davenport *Iowa, U.S.A.* 112 E8
Davenport *Wash., U.S.A.* 108 C4
Davenport Ra. *Australia* 94 C1
Davenport Range △
    Australia 94 C1
Daventry *U.K.* 15 E6
David *Panama* 120 E3
David City *U.S.A.* 112 E5
David Glacier *Antarctica* 5 D21
David Gorodok = Davyd
    Haradok *Belarus* 23 B14
Davidson *Canada* 103 C7
Davis *Antarctica* 5 C6
Davis *U.S.A.* 110 G5
Davis Dam *U.S.A.* 111 K12
Davis Inlet *Canada* 105 A7
Davis Mts. *U.S.A.* 116 F3
Davis Sea *Antarctica* 5 C7
Davis Str. *N. Amer.* 98 C14
Davlos *Cyprus* 49 D12
Davo → *Ivory C.* 82 D3
Davos *Switz.* 25 J5
Davutlar *Turkey* 47 D9
Davy L. *Canada* 103 B7
Davyd Haradok *Belarus* 23 B14
Dawa → *Australia* 81 G5
Dawaki *Bauchi, Nigeria* 83 D6
Dawaki *Kano, Nigeria* 83 C6
Dawei = Tavoy *Burma* 64 E2
Dawes Ra. *Australia* 94 C5
Dawlish *U.K.* 15 G4
Dawna Ra. *Burma* 64 D2
Dawros Hd. *Ireland* 12 B3
Dawson *U.S.A.* 117 F12
Dawson, I. *Chile* 128 G2
Dawson B. *Canada* 103 C8
Dawson City *Canada* 100 C6
Dawson Creek *Canada* 102 B4
Dawson Inlet *Canada* 103 A10
Dawson Ra. *Australia* 94 C4
Dawu *Hubei, China* 59 B9
Dawu *Sichuan, China* 58 B3
Dax *France* 20 E2
Daxian *China* 58 B6
Daxin *China* 58 F6
Daxindian *China* 57 F11
Daxinggou *China* 57 C15
Daxue Shan *Sichuan, China* 58 B3
Daxue Shan *Yunnan, China* 58 F2
Day Kundī □ *Afghan.* 66 C5
Dayao *China* 58 E3
Daye *China* 59 B10
Dayet en Naharat *Mali* 82 B4
Dayi *China* 58 B4
Daylesford *Australia* 95 F3
Dayr az Zawr *Syria* 73 E9
Dayr az Zawr □ *Syria* 73 E9
Daysland *Canada* 102 C6
Dayton *Nev., U.S.A.* 110 F7
Dayton *Ohio, U.S.A.* 113 F11
Dayton *Pa., U.S.A.* 114 F5
Dayton *Tenn., U.S.A.* 117 D12
Dayton *Wash., U.S.A.* 108 C5
Dayton *Wyo., U.S.A.* 108 D10
Daytona Beach *U.S.A.* 117 G14
Dayu *China* 59 E10
Dayville *U.S.A.* 108 D4
Dazhu *China* 58 B6
Dazkırı *Turkey* 47 D11
Dazu *China* 58 C5
De Aar *S. Africa* 88 E3
De Biesbosch △ *Neths.* 17 C4
De Funiak Springs *U.S.A.* 117 F11
De Grey → *Australia* 92 D2
De Haan *Belgium* 17 C3
De Hoge Veluwe △ *Neths.* 17 B5
De Hoop △ *S. Africa* 88 E3
De Kalb Junction *U.S.A.* 115 B9
De Kennemerduinen △
    Neths. 17 B4
De Land *U.S.A.* 117 G14
De Leon *U.S.A.* 116 E5
De Panne *Belgium* 17 C2
De Pere *U.S.A.* 112 C9
De Queen *U.S.A.* 116 D7
De Quincy *U.S.A.* 116 F8
De Ruyters *U.S.A.* 115 D9
De Smet *U.S.A.* 112 C5
De Soto *U.S.A.* 112 F8
De Tour Village *U.S.A.* 113 B12
De Witt *U.S.A.* 116 D8
Dead Sea *Asia* 74 D4
Deadwood *U.S.A.* 112 C2
Deadwood L. *Canada* 102 B3
Deal *U.K.* 15 F9
Deal I. *Australia* 95 F4
Dealesville *S. Africa* 88 D4
De'an *China* 59 C10
Dean → *Canada* 102 C3
Dean, Forest of *U.K.* 15 F5
Dean Chan. *Canada* 102 C3
Deán Funes *Argentina* 126 C3

Dease → *Canada* 102 B3
Dease L. *Canada* 102 B2
Dease Lake *Canada* 102 B2
Death Valley *U.S.A.* 111 J10
Death Valley △ *U.S.A.* 111 J9
Death Valley Junction
    U.S.A. 111 J10
Deauville *France* 18 C7
Deba *Spain* 38 B2
Deba Habe *Nigeria* 83 C7
Debagram *India* 69 H14
Debao *China* 58 F6
Debar *Macedonia* 44 E4
Debark *Ethiopia* 81 E4
Debden *Canada* 103 C7
Dębica *Poland* 31 H8
Dęblin *Poland* 31 G8
Dębno *Poland* 31 F1
Débo, L. *Mali* 82 B4
DeBolt *Canada* 102 B5
Deborah East, L. *Australia* 93 F2
Deborah West, L. *Australia* 93 F2
Debre Birhan *Ethiopia* 81 F4
Debre Markos *Ethiopia* 81 E4
Debre May *Ethiopia* 81 E4
Debre Sina *Ethiopia* 81 F4
Debre Tabor *Ethiopia* 81 E4
Debre Zebit *Ethiopia* 81 E4
Debre Zeyit *Ethiopia* 81 F4
Debrecen *Hungary* 28 C6
Debrzno *Poland* 30 E4
Dečani *Serbia* 44 D4
Decatur *Ala., U.S.A.* 117 D11
Decatur *Ga., U.S.A.* 117 E12
Decatur *Ill., U.S.A.* 112 F9
Decatur *Ind., U.S.A.* 113 E11
Decatur *Tex., U.S.A.* 116 E6
Decazeville *France* 20 D6
Deccan *India* 66 L11
Deception Bay *Australia* 95 D5
Deception I. *Antarctica* 5 C17
Deception L. *Canada* 103 B8
Dechang *China* 58 D4
Dechhu *India* 68 F5
Děčín *Czech Rep.* 26 A7
Decize *France* 19 F10
Deckerville *U.S.A.* 114 C2
Decollatura *Italy* 43 C9
Decorah *U.S.A.* 112 D8
Deda *Romania* 29 D9
Dedéagach =
    Alexandroupoli *Greece* 45 F9
Deder *Ethiopia* 81 F5
Dedham *U.S.A.* 115 D13
Dedoplis Tskaro =
    Tsiteli-Tsqaro *Georgia* 35 K8
Dédougou *Burkina Faso* 82 C4
Dedovichi *Russia* 32 D5
Dedza *Malawi* 87 E3
Dee → *Aberds., U.K.* 13 D6
Dee → *Dumf. & Gall., U.K.* 13 G4
Dee → *Wales, U.K.* 14 D4
Deep B. *Canada* 102 A5
Deepwater *Australia* 95 D5
Deer → *Canada* 103 B10
Deer L. *Canada* 103 C10
Deer Lake *Nfld. & L., Canada* 105 C8
Deer Lake *Ont., Canada* 103 C10
Deer Lodge *U.S.A.* 108 C7
Deer Park *U.S.A.* 108 C5
Deer River *U.S.A.* 112 B7
Deeragun *Australia* 94 B4
Deerdepoort *S. Africa* 88 C4
Defiance *U.S.A.* 113 E11
Degana *India* 68 F6
Dêgê *China* 58 B2
Degebe → *Portugal* 37 G3
Degeberga *Sweden* 11 J8
Dégelis *Canada* 105 C6
Degema *Nigeria* 83 E6
Degerfors *Sweden* 10 E8
Degerhamn *Sweden* 11 H10
Deggendorf *Germany* 25 G8
Degh → *Pakistan* 68 D5
Değirmendere *Turkey* 45 F13
Degirmenlik = Kythréa
    Cyprus 49 D12
Deh Bīd *Iran* 71 D7
Deh Dasht *Iran* 71 D6
Deh-e Shīr *Iran* 71 D7
Dehaj *Iran* 71 D7
Dehak *Iran* 71 E9
Dehdez *Iran* 71 D6
Dehej *India* 68 J5
Dehestān *Iran* 71 D7
Dehgolān *Iran* 73 E12
Dehibat *Tunisia* 79 B8
Dehlorān *Iran* 73 F12
Dehnow-e Kūhestān *Iran* 71 E8
Dehra Dun *India* 68 D8
Dehri *India* 69 G11
Dehua *China* 59 E12
Dehui *China* 57 B13
Deim Zubeir *Sudan* 81 F2
Deinze *Belgium* 17 D3
Dej *Romania* 29 C8

Deje *Sweden* 10 E7
Dejiang *China* 58 C7
Deka → *Zimbabwe* 88 B4
DeKalb *U.S.A.* 112 E9
Dekemhare *Eritrea* 81 D4
Dekese *Dem. Rep. of the Congo* 84 E4
Del Mar *U.S.A.* 111 N9
Del Norte *U.S.A.* 109 H10
Del Rio *U.S.A.* 116 G4
Delai *Sudan* 80 D4
Delambre I. *Australia* 92 D2
Delami *Sudan* 81 E3
Delano *U.S.A.* 111 K7
Delano Peak *U.S.A.* 108 G7
Delareyville *S. Africa* 88 D4
Delaronde L. *Canada* 103 C7
Delavan *U.S.A.* 112 D9
Delaware *U.S.A.* 113 E12
Delaware □ *U.S.A.* 113 F16
Delaware → *U.S.A.* 115 G9
Delaware B. *U.S.A.* 113 F16
Delaware Water Gap △
    U.S.A. 115 E10
Delay → *Canada* 105 A5
Delbrück *Germany* 24 D4
Delčevo *Macedonia* 44 E5
Delegate *Australia* 95 F4
Delémont *Switz.* 25 H3
Delevan *U.S.A.* 114 D6
Delft *Neths.* 17 B4
Delfzijl *Neths.* 17 A6
Delgado, C. *Mozam.* 87 E5
Delgerhet *Mongolia* 56 B6
Delgo *Sudan* 80 C3
Delhi *Canada* 114 D4
Delhi *India* 68 E7
Delhi *La., U.S.A.* 116 E9
Delhi *N.Y., U.S.A.* 115 D10
Deli Jovan *Serbia* 44 B6
Delia *Canada* 102 C6
Delice *Turkey* 72 C6
Delicias *Mexico* 118 B3
Delījān *Iran* 71 C6
Déline *Canada* 100 C7
Delisle *Canada* 103 C7
Delitzsch *Germany* 24 D8
Dell City *U.S.A.* 116 F2
Dell Rapids *U.S.A.* 112 D5
Delle *France* 19 E14
Delmar *U.S.A.* 115 D11
Delmenhorst *Germany* 24 B4
Delnice *Croatia* 41 C11
Delonga, Ostrova *Russia* 53 B15
Deloraine *Australia* 95 G4
Deloraine *Canada* 103 D8
Delphi *Greece* 46 C4
Delphi *U.S.A.* 112 E10
Delphos *U.S.A.* 113 E11
Delportshoop *S. Africa* 88 D3
Delray Beach *U.S.A.* 117 H14
Delta *Colo., U.S.A.* 108 G9
Delta *Utah, U.S.A.* 108 G7
Delta □ *Nigeria* 83 D6
Delta del Ebre △ *Spain* 38 E5
Delta del Po △ *Italy* 41 D9
Delta du Saloum △ *Senegal* 82 C1
Delta Dunărea △ *Romania* 29 E14
Delta Junction *U.S.A.* 100 C5
Deltona *U.S.A.* 117 G14
Delungra *Australia* 95 D5
Delvada *India* 68 J4
Delvinaki *Greece* 46 B2
Delvinë *Albania* 46 B2
Delyatyn *Ukraine* 29 B9
Demak *Indonesia* 63 G14
Demanda, Sierra de la *Spain* 38 C2
Demavend = Damāvand,
    Qolleh-ye *Iran* 71 C7
Dembecha *Ethiopia* 81 E4
Dembi *Ethiopia* 81 F4
Dembia *Dem. Rep. of the Congo* 86 B2
Dembidolo *Ethiopia* 81 F3
Demchok *India* 69 C8
Demer → *Belgium* 17 D4
Demetrias *Greece* 46 B5
Demidov *Russia* 32 E6
Deming *N. Mex., U.S.A.* 109 K10
Deming *Wash., U.S.A.* 110 B4
Demini → *Brazil* 124 D6
Demirci *Turkey* 47 B10
Demirköprü Baraji *Turkey* 47 C10
Demirköy *Turkey* 45 E11
Demmin *Germany* 24 B9
Demonte *Italy* 40 D4
Demopolis *U.S.A.* 117 E11
Dempo *Indonesia* 62 E2
Demyansk *Russia* 32 D7
Den Bosch =
    's-Hertogenbosch *Neths.* 17 C5
Den Burg *Neths.* 17 A4
Den Chai *Thailand* 64 D3
Den Haag =
    's-Gravenhage *Neths.* 17 B4
Den Helder *Neths.* 17 B4
Den Oever *Neths.* 17 B5
Denain *France* 19 B10
Denair *U.S.A.* 110 H6

Denali = McKinley, Mt.
    U.S.A. 106 a
Denau *Uzbekistan* 52 F7
Denbigh *Canada* 114 A7
Denbigh *U.K.* 14 D4
Denbighshire □ *U.K.* 14 D4
Dendang *Indonesia* 62 E3
Dendermonde *Belgium* 17 C4
Deneba *Ethiopia* 81 F4
Denezhkin Kamen, Gora...
Dengchuan *China* 58 E3
Denge *Nigeria* 83 C6
Dengfeng *China* 56 G7
Dengi *Nigeria* 83 D6
Dengkou *China* 56 D4
Dengzhou *China* 59 A9
Denham *Australia* 93 E1
Denham, Mt. *Jamaica* 120 a
Denham Ra. *Australia* 94 C4
Denham Sd. *Australia* 93 E1
Denholm *Canada* 103 C7
Denia *Spain* 39 G5
Denial B. *Australia* 95 E1
Deniliquin *Australia* 95 F3
Denison *Iowa, U.S.A.* 112 D6
Denison *Tex., U.S.A.* 116 E6
Denison Plains *Australia* 92 C4
Denizli *Turkey* 47 D11
Denizli □ *Turkey* 47 D11
Denman Glacier *Antarctica* 5 C7
Denmark *Australia* 93 F2
Denmark ■ *Europe* 11 J3
Denmark Str. *Atl. Oc.* 98 C17
Dennery *St. Lucia* 121 f
Dennison *U.S.A.* 114 F3
Denny *U.K.* 13 E5
Denpasar *Indonesia* 63 K18
Denpasar ✈ (DPS) *Indonesia* 63 K18
Denton *Mont., U.S.A.* 108 C9
Denton *Tex., U.S.A.* 116 E6
D'Entrecasteaux, Pt.
    Australia 93 F2
D'Entrecasteaux △ *Australia* 93 F2
D'Entrecasteaux Is.
    Papua N. G. 90 B8
Denu *Ghana* 83 D5
Denver *Colo., U.S.A.* 108 G11
Denver *Pa., U.S.A.* 115 F8
Denver City *U.S.A.* 116 E3
Deoband *India* 68 E7
Deogarh *India* 69 G12
Deoghar *India* 69 G12
Deolali *India* 66 K8
Deoli = Devli *India* 68 G6
Deoli *India* 68 F4
Deori *India* 69 G8
Deoria *India* 69 F10
Deosai Mts. *Pakistan* 69 B6
Deosri *India* 69 F14
Depalpur *India* 68 H6
Deping *China* 57 F9
Deposit *U.S.A.* 115 D9
Depuch I. *Australia* 92 D2
Deputatskiy *Russia* 53 C14
Dera Ghazi Khan *Pakistan* 68 D4
Dera Ismail Khan *Pakistan* 68 D4
Derabugti *Pakistan* 68 E3
Derawar Fort *Pakistan* 68 E4
Derbent *Russia* 35 J9
Derbent *Turkey* 47 C10
Derby *Australia* 92 C3
Derby *U.K.* 14 E6
Derby *Conn., U.S.A.* 115 E11
Derby *Kans., U.S.A.* 112 G5
Derby *N.Y., U.S.A.* 114 D6
Derby City □ *U.K.* 14 E6
Derby Line *U.S.A.* 115 B12
Derbyshire □ *U.K.* 14 D6
Đerdap △ *Serbia* 44 B5
Derdepoort *S. Africa* 88 C4
Derecske *Hungary* 28 C6
Dereham *U.K.* 15 E8
Dereköy *Turkey* 45 E11
Dereli *Turkey* 73 B8
Derg → *U.K.* 12 B4
Derg, L. *Ireland* 12 D3
Dergachi = Derhaci *Ukraine* 33 G9
Derhaci *Ukraine* 33 G9
DeRidder *U.S.A.* 116 F8
Derik *Turkey* 73 D9
Derinkuyu *Turkey* 72 C6
Dermantsi *Bulgaria* 45 C8
Dermott *U.S.A.* 116 E9
Dêrong *China* 58 C2
Derry = Londonderry *U.K.* 12 B4
Derry = Londonderry □
    U.K. 12 B4
Derry *N.H., U.S.A.* 115 D13
Derry *Pa., U.S.A.* 114 F5
Derryveagh Mts. *Ireland* 12 B3
Derudub *Sudan* 80 D4
Derval *France* 18 E5
Derveni *Greece* 46 C4
Derventa *Bos.-H.* 28 F2
Derwent → *Cumb., U.K.* 14 C4
Derwent → *Derby, U.K.* 14 E6

Derwent → *N. Yorks., U.K.* 14 D7
Derwent Water *U.K.* 14 C4
Des Moines *Iowa, U.S.A.* 112 E7
Des Moines *N. Mex., U.S.A.* 109 H12
Des Moines *Wash., U.S.A.* 110 C4
Des Moines → *U.S.A.* 112 E8
Desa *Romania* 28 G8
Desaguadero → *Argentina* 126 C2
Desaguadero → *Bolivia* 124 G5
Desantne *Ukraine* 29 E14
Desar *Malaysia* 65 d
Descanso, Pta. *Mexico* 111 N9
Descartes *France* 20 B4
Deschaillons-sur-St-
    Laurent *Canada* 105 C5
Deschambault L. *Canada* 103 C8
Deschutes → *U.S.A.* 108 D3
Dese *Ethiopia* 81 E4
Desenzano del Garda *Italy* 40 C7
Deseado → *Argentina* 128 F3
Deseronto *Canada* 114 B7
Desert Center *U.S.A.* 111 M11
Desert Hot Springs *U.S.A.* 111 M10
Desfina *Greece* 46 C4
Deshnok *India* 68 F5
Desierto Central de Baja
    California △ *Mexico* 118 B2
Deskati *Greece* 44 E4
Desna → *Ukraine* 23 C16
Desnătui → *Romania* 29 G8
Desolación, I. *Chile* 128 G2
Despeñaperros, Paso *Spain* 37 G7
Despeñaperros △ *Spain* 37 G7
Despotiko *Greece* 46 E6
Despotovac *Serbia* 44 B5
Dessau *Germany* 24 D8
Dessye = Dese *Ethiopia* 81 E4
D'Estrees B. *Australia* 95 F2
Desuri *India* 68 G5
Desvres *France* 19 B8
Det Udom *Thailand* 64 E5
Deta *Romania* 28 E6
Dete *Zimbabwe* 88 B4
Đetinja → *Serbia* 44 C4
Detmold *Germany* 24 D4
Detour, Pt. *U.S.A.* 112 C10
Detroit *U.S.A.* 114 D1
Detroit Lakes *U.S.A.* 112 B6
Detva *Slovak Rep.* 27 C12
Deua △ *Australia* 95 F4
Deurne *Neths.* 17 C5
Deutsch-
    Luxemburgischer △
    Germany 25 F2
Deutsche Bucht *Germany* 24 A4
Deutschland =
    Germany ■ *Europe* 24 E6
Deutschlandsberg *Austria* 26 E8
Deux-Sèvres □ *France* 18 F6
Deva *Romania* 28 E7
Devakottai *India* 66 Q11
Devaprayag *India* 69 D8
Dévaványa *Hungary* 28 C5
Deveci Dağları *Turkey* 72 B7
Devecikonağı *Turkey* 45 G12
Devecser *Hungary* 28 C2
Develi *Turkey* 72 C6
Deventer *Neths.* 17 B6
Deveron → *U.K.* 13 D6
Devesel *Romania* 28 F7
Devgadh Bariya *India* 68 H5
Devikot *India* 68 F4
Devils Den *U.S.A.* 110 K7
Devils Hole = Death
    Valley △ *U.S.A.* 111 J9
Devils Lake *U.S.A.* 112 A4
Devils Paw *Canada* 102 B2
Devils Postpile △ *U.S.A.* 110 H7
Devils Tower *U.S.A.* 108 D11
Devils Tower △ *U.S.A.* 108 D11
Devin *Bulgaria* 45 E8
Devine *U.S.A.* 116 G5
Devizes *U.K.* 15 F6
Devli *India* 68 G6
Devnya *Bulgaria* 45 C11
Devoll → *Albania* 44 F4
Devon *Canada* 102 C6
Devon □ *U.K.* 15 G4
Devon I. *Canada* 101 B11
Devonport *Australia* 95 G4
Devonport *N.Z.* 91 B5
Devrek *Turkey* 72 B4
Devrekâni *Turkey* 72 B5
Devrez → *Turkey* 72 B6
Dewas *India* 68 H7
Dewetsdorp *S. Africa* 88 D4
Dewey *Puerto Rico* 121 d
Dexing *China* 59 C11
Dexter *Maine, U.S.A.* 113 C19
Dexter *Mo., U.S.A.* 112 G9
Dexter *N. Mex., U.S.A.* 109 K11
Dey-Dey, L. *Australia* 93 E5
Deyang *China* 58 B5
Deyhūk *Iran* 71 C8
Deyyer *Iran* 71 E6
Dez → *Iran* 73 F13
Dezadeash L. *Canada* 102 A1
Dezfûl *Iran* 73 F13

Dezhneva, Mys *Russia* 53 C19
Dezhou *China* 56 F9
Dhadhar → *India* 69 G11
Dhahabān *Si. Arabia* 80 C4
Dhahiriya = Aẕ Ẕāhirīyah
  West Bank 74 D3
Dhahran = Aẕ Ẕahrān
  Si. Arabia 71 E6
Dhak *Pakistan* 68 C5
Dhaka *Bangla.* 69 H14
Dhaka □ *Bangla.* 69 G14
Dhali *Cyprus* 49 D12
Dhamār *Yemen* 75 E3
Dhampur *India* 69 E8
Dhamtari *India* 67 J12
Dhanbad *India* 69 H12
Dhangarhi *Nepal* 69 E9
Dhankuta *Nepal* 69 F12
Dhanpuri *India* 69 H9
Dhar *India* 68 H6
Dharampur *India* 68 H6
Dharamsala = Dharmsala
  India 68 C7
Dharan *Nepal* 69 F12
Dhariwal *India* 68 D6
Dharla → *Bangla.* 69 G13
Dharmapuri *India* 66 N11
Dharmjaygarh *India* 69 H10
Dharmsala *India* 68 C7
Dharni *India* 68 J7
Dharwad *India* 66 M9
Dhasan → *India* 69 G8
Dhaulagiri *Nepal* 69 E10
Dhebar, L. *India* 68 G6
Dheftera *Cyprus* 49 D12
Dhenkanal *India* 67 J14
Dherinia *Cyprus* 49 D12
Dheskáti = Deskati *Greece* 44 G5
Dhī Qār □ *Iraq* 70 D5
Dhiārrizos → *Cyprus* 49 E11
Dhībān *Jordan* 74 D4
Dhilwan *India* 68 D6
Dhimarkhera *India* 69 H9
Dhodhekánisos =
  Dodecanese *Greece* 47 E8
Dholka *India* 68 H5
Dhomokós = Domokos
  Greece 46 B4
Dhoraji *India* 68 J4
Dhragonísi = Tragonhsi
  Greece 47 D7
Dhrangadhra *India* 68 H4
Dhrol *India* 68 H4
Dhuburi *India* 67 F16
Dhule *India* 66 J9
Di-ib, W. → *Sudan* 80 C4
Di Linh *Vietnam* 65 G7
Di Linh, Cao Nguyen
  Vietnam 65 G7
Dia *Greece* 49 D7
Diabakania *Guinea* 82 C2
Diablo Range *U.S.A.* 110 J5
Diafarabé *Mali* 82 C4
Diala *Mali* 82 C3
Dialakoro *Mali* 82 C3
Dialakoto *Senegal* 82 C2
Diallassagou *Mali* 82 C4
Diamante *Argentina* 126 C3
Diamante *Italy* 43 C8
Diamante → *Argentina* 126 C2
Diamantina *Brazil* 125 G10
Diamantina → *Australia* 95 D2
Diamantina △ *Australia* 94 C3
Diamantino *Brazil* 125 F7
Diamond Bar *U.S.A.* 111 L9
Diamond Harbour *India* 69 H13
Diamond Is. *Australia* 94 B5
Diamond Mts. *U.S.A.* 108 G6
Diamond Springs *U.S.A.* 110 G6
Dian Chi *China* 58 E4
Dianalund *Denmark* 11 J5
Dianbai *China* 59 G8
Diancheng *China* 59 G8
Dianjiang *China* 58 B6
Diano Marina *Italy* 40 E5
Dianra *Ivory C.* 82 D3
Diaoyu Tai = Senkaku-
  Shotō *E. China Sea* 55 M1
Diapaga *Burkina Faso* 83 C5
Diapangou *Burkina Faso* 83 C5
Diariguila *Guinea* 82 C2
Dībā *U.A.E.* 71 E8
Dibagah *Iraq* 73 E10
Dibai *India* 68 E8
Dibaya *Dem. Rep. of the Congo* 84 F4
Dibaya-Lubue
  Dem. Rep. of the Congo 84 E3
Dibbeen △ *Jordan* 74 C4
D'Iberville, Lac *Canada* 104 A5
Dibete *Botswana* 88 C4
Dibrugarh *India* 67 F19
Dickens *U.S.A.* 116 E4
Dickinson *U.S.A.* 112 B2
Dickson *U.S.A.* 117 C11
Dickson City *U.S.A.* 115 E9
Dicle Barajı *Turkey* 73 D9
Dicle Nehri → *Turkey* 73 D9
Dicomano *Italy* 41 E8

Didesa, W. → *Ethiopia* 81 E4
Didi *Sudan* 81 F3
Didiéni *Mali* 82 C3
Didimoticho *Greece* 45 E10
Didsbury *Canada* 102 C6
Didwana *India* 68 F6
Die *France* 21 D9
Diébougou *Burkina Faso* 82 C4
Diecke *Guinea* 82 D3
Diefenbaker, L. *Canada* 103 C7
Diego de Almagro *Chile* 126 B1
Diego Suarez =
  Antsiranana *Madag.* 89 A8
Diekirch *Lux.* 17 E6
Diéma *Mali* 82 C3
Diembéring *Senegal* 82 C1
Diemelsee △ *Germany* 24 D4
Dien Ban *Vietnam* 64 E7
Dien Bien *Vietnam* 58 G4
Dien Khanh *Vietnam* 65 F7
Diepholz *Germany* 24 C4
Dieppe *France* 18 C8
Dierks *U.S.A.* 116 D7
Diest *Belgium* 17 D5
Dietikon *Switz.* 25 H4
Dieulefit *France* 21 D9
Dieuze *France* 19 D13
Dif *Somali Rep.* 75 G3
Diffa □ *Niger* 83 B7
Differdange *Lux.* 17 E5
Dig *India* 68 F7
Digba *Dem. Rep. of the Congo* 86 B2
Digby *Canada* 105 D6
Diggi *India* 68 F6
Dighinala *Bangla.* 67 H18
Dighton *U.S.A.* 112 F3
Digna *Mali* 82 C3
Digne-les-Bains *France* 21 D10
Digoin *France* 19 F11
Digor *Turkey* 73 B10
Digos *Phil.* 61 H6
Digranes *Iceland* 8 C6
Digul → *Indonesia* 63 F9
Digya △ *Ghana* 83 D5
Dihang = Brahmaputra →
  Asia 69 H13
Dijlah, Nahr → *Asia* 70 D5
Dijon *France* 19 E12
Dikhil *Djibouti* 81 E5
Dikili *Turkey* 47 B8
Dikirnis *Egypt* 80 H7
Dikodougou *Ivory C.* 82 D3
Diksmuide *Belgium* 17 C2
Dikson *Russia* 52 B9
Dikti Oros *Greece* 49 D7
Dikwa *Nigeria* 83 C7
Dila *Ethiopia* 81 F4
Dilek Yarimadisi △ *Turkey* 47 D9
Dili *E. Timor* 63 F7
Dilijan *Armenia* 35 K7
Dilinata *Greece* 46 C2
Dilizhan = Dilijan *Armenia* 35 K7
Dilj *Croatia* 28 E3
Dillenburg *Germany* 24 E4
Dilley *U.S.A.* 116 G5
Dilli = Delhi *India* 68 E7
Dilling *Sudan* 81 E2
Dillingen *Bayern, Germany* 25 G6
Dillingen *Saarland, Germany* 25 F2
Dillingham *U.S.A.* 106 a
Dillon *Canada* 103 B7
Dillon *Mont., U.S.A.* 108 D7
Dillon *S.C., U.S.A.* 117 D15
Dillon → *Canada* 103 B7
Dillsburg *U.S.A.* 114 F7
Dilly *Mali* 82 C3
Dilolo *Dem. Rep. of the Congo* 84 G4
Dilos *Greece* 47 D7
Dilove *Ukraine* 29 C9
Dimas *Mexico* 118 C3
Dimashq *Syria* 74 B5
Dimashq □ *Syria* 74 B5
Dimbaza *S. Africa* 89 E4
Dimbokro *Ivory C.* 82 D4
Dimboola *Australia* 95 F3
Dîmbovița =
  Dâmbovița → *Romania* 29 F11
Dimbulah *Australia* 94 B4
Dimitrovgrad *Bulgaria* 45 D9
Dimitrovgrad *Russia* 34 C9
Dimitrovgrad *Serbia* 44 C6
Dimitrovo = Pernik *Bulgaria* 44 D7
Dimitsana *Greece* 46 D4
Dimmitt *U.S.A.* 116 D3
Dimo *Sudan* 81 F2
Dimona *Israel* 74 D4
Dimovo *Bulgaria* 44 C6
Dinagat *Phil.* 61 F6
Dinajpur *Bangla.* 67 G16
Dinan *France* 18 D4
Dīnān Āb *Iran* 71 C8
Dinant *Belgium* 17 D4
Dinapur *India* 69 G11
Dinar *Turkey* 47 C12
Dīnār, Kūh-e *Iran* 71 D6
Dinara Planina *Croatia* 41 D13
Dinard *France* 18 D4

Dinaric Alps = Dinara
  Planina *Croatia* 41 D13
Dindanko *Mali* 82 C3
Dinder, Nahr ed → *Sudan* 81 E3
Dinder △ *Sudan* 81 E4
Dindigul *India* 66 P11
Dindori *India* 69 H9
Ding Xian = Dingzhou *China* 56 E8
Dinga *Pakistan* 68 G2
Dingalan *Phil.* 61 D4
Ding'an *China* 64 C8
Dingbian *China* 56 F4
Dingelstädt *Germany* 24 D6
Dingle *Ireland* 12 D1
Dingle *Sweden* 11 F5
Dingle B. *Ireland* 12 D1
Dingmans Ferry *U.S.A.* 115 E10
Dingnan *China* 59 E10
Dingo *Australia* 94 C4
Dingolfing *Germany* 25 G8
Dingtao *China* 56 G8
Dinguira *Mali* 82 C2
Dinguiraye *Guinea* 82 C2
Dingwall *U.K.* 13 D4
Dingxi *China* 56 G3
Dingxiang *China* 56 E7
Dingyuan *China* 59 A11
Dingzhou *China* 56 E8
Dinh, Mui *Vietnam* 65 G7
Dinh Lap *Vietnam* 58 G6
Dinin → *Ireland* 12 D4
Dinira △ *Venezuela* 121 E6
Dinokwe *Botswana* 88 C4
Dinorwic *Canada* 103 D10
Dinosaur *Canada* 102 C6
Dinosaur △ *U.S.A.* 108 F9
Dinuba *U.S.A.* 110 J7
Diö *Sweden* 11 H8
Dioïla *Mali* 82 C3
Dioka *Mali* 82 C2
Diongoï *Mali* 82 C3
Dionisades *Greece* 49 D8
Diósgyör *Hungary* 28 B5
Diosig *Romania* 28 C7
Diouani *Mali* 82 C4
Diouloulou *Senegal* 82 C1
Dioura *Mali* 82 C3
Diourbel *Senegal* 82 C1
Diourbel □ *Senegal* 82 C1
Dipalpur *India* 68 D5
Dipkarpaz = Rizokarpaso
  Cyprus 49 D13
Diplo *Pakistan* 68 G3
Dipolog *Phil.* 61 G5
Dipperu △ *Australia* 94 C4
Dir *Pakistan* 66 B7
Diré *Mali* 82 B4
Dire Dawa *Ethiopia* 81 F5
Dirfis Oros *Greece* 46 C5
Diriamba *Nic.* 120 D2
Dirk Hartog I. *Australia* 93 E1
Dirranbandi *Australia* 95 D4
Disa *India* 68 G5
Disa *Sudan* 81 E3
Disappointment, C. *U.S.A.* 108 C1
Disappointment, L. *Australia* 92 D3
Disaster B. *Australia* 95 F4
Discovery B. *Australia* 95 F3
Disentis Muster *Switz.* 25 J4
Dishna *Egypt* 80 B3
Disina *Nigeria* 83 C6
Disko = Qeqertarsuaq
  Greenland 98 C14
Disna = Dzisna → *Belarus* 32 E5
Disney Reef *Tonga* 91 c
Diss *U.K.* 15 E9
Disteghil Sar *Pakistan* 69 A6
District of Columbia □
  U.S.A. 113 F15
Distrito Federal □ *Brazil* 125 G9
Distrito Federal □ *Mexico* 119 D5
Disûq *Egypt* 80 H7
Diu *India* 68 J4
Dīvāndarreh *Iran* 73 E12
Dives → *France* 18 C6
Dives-sur-Mer *France* 18 C6
Divichi = Dǝvǝçi *Azerbaijan* 35 K9
Divide *U.S.A.* 108 D7
Dividing Ra. *Australia* 93 E2
Divinópolis *Brazil* 125 H10
Divjake *Albania* 44 F3
Divnoye *Russia* 35 H6
Divo *Ivory C.* 82 D3
Divriği *Turkey* 73 C8
Dīwāl Kol *Afghan.* 68 B2
Dixie Mt. *U.S.A.* 110 F6
Dixon *Calif., U.S.A.* 110 G5
Dixon *Ill., U.S.A.* 112 E9
Dixville *Canada* 115 A13
Dixon Entrance *U.S.A.* 100 D6

Djamba *Angola* 88 B1
Djambala *Congo* 84 E2
Djanet *Algeria* 78 D7
Djawa = Jawa *Indonesia* 62 F3
Djelfa *Algeria* 78 B6
Djema *C.A.R.* 86 A2
Djenné *Mali* 82 C4
Djerba, Î. de *Tunisia* 79 B8
Djerid, Chott *Tunisia* 78 B7
Djibo *Burkina Faso* 83 C4
Djibouti *Djibouti* 81 E5
Djibouti ■ *Africa* 81 E5
Djolu *Dem. Rep. of the Congo* 84 D4
Djougou *Benin* 83 D5
Djoum *Cameroon* 84 D2
Djourab, Erg du *Chad* 79 E9
Djugu *Dem. Rep. of the Congo* 86 B3
Djukbinj △ *Australia* 92 B5
Djúpivogur *Iceland* 8 D6
Djurås *Sweden* 10 D9
Djurö △ *Sweden* 11 F7
Djursland *Denmark* 11 H4
Dmitriya Lapteva, Proliv
  Russia 53 B15
Dmitriyev Lgovskiy *Russia* 33 F8
Dmitrov *Russia* 32 D9
Dmitrovsk-Orlovskiy *Russia* 33 F8
Dnepr = Dnipro → *Ukraine* 33 J7
Dneprodzerzhinsk =
  Dniprodzerzhynsk
  Ukraine 33 H8
Dneprodzerzhinskoye
  Vdkhr. =
  Dniprodzerzhynske
  Vdskh. *Ukraine* 33 H8
Dnepropetrovsk =
  Dnipropetrovsk *Ukraine* 33 H8
Dneprorudnoye =
  Dniprorudne *Ukraine* 33 J8
Dnestr = Dnister → *Europe* 23 E16
Dnieper = Dnipro →
  Ukraine 33 J7
Dniester = Dnister →
  Europe 23 E16
Dnipro → *Ukraine* 33 J7
Dniprodzerzhynsk *Ukraine* 33 H8
Dniprodzerzhynske Vdskh.
  Ukraine 33 H8
Dnipropetrovsk *Ukraine* 33 H8
Dniprorudne *Ukraine* 33 J8
Dnister → *Europe* 23 E16
Dnistrovskyy Lyman
  Ukraine 33 J6
Dno *Russia* 32 D5
Dnyapro = Dnipro →
  Ukraine 33 J7
Do Gonbadān =
  Gachsārān *Iran* 71 D6
Doaktown *Canada* 105 C6
Doan Hung *Vietnam* 58 G5
Doany *Madag.* 89 A8
Doba *Chad* 79 G9
Dobandi *Pakistan* 68 D2
Dobbiaco *Italy* 41 B9
Dobbyn *Australia* 94 B3
Dobczyce *Poland* 31 J7
Dobele *Latvia* 30 B10
Dobele □ *Latvia* 30 B10
Döbeln *Germany* 24 D9
Doberai, Jazirah *Indonesia* 63 E8
Dobiegniew *Poland* 31 F2
Doblas *Argentina* 126 D3
Dobo *Indonesia* 63 F8
Doboj *Bos.-H.* 28 F3
Dobra *Wielkopolskie, Poland* 31 G5
Dobra *Zachodnio-Pomorskie,
  Poland* 30 E2
Dobra *Dâmbovita, Romania* 29 F10
Dobra *Hunedoara, Romania* 28 E7
Dobre Miasto *Poland* 30 E7
Dobrești *Romania* 28 D7
Dobrich *Bulgaria* 45 C11
Dobrinishta *Bulgaria* 44 E7
Dobříš *Czech Rep.* 26 B7
Dobrodzień *Poland* 31 H5
Dobromyl *Ukraine* 31 J9
Dobron *Ukraine* 28 B7
Dobropole *Ukraine* 33 H9
Dobrovolsk *Russia* 30 D9
Dobruja *Europe* 29 F13
Dobrush *Belarus* 23 B16
Dobrzany *Poland* 30 E2
Dobrzyń nad Wisłą *Poland* 31 F6
Doc, Mui *Vietnam* 64 D6
Docker River =
  Kaltukatjara *Australia* 93 D4
Docksta *Sweden* 10 A12
Doctor Arroyo *Mexico* 118 C4
Doctor Pedro P. Peña
  Paraguay 126 A3
Doda *India* 69 C6
Doda, L. *Canada* 104 C4
Dodecanese *Greece* 47 E8
Dodekanisa = Dodecanese
  Greece 47 E8
Dodekanisa □ *Greece* 47 E8
Dodge City *U.S.A.* 112 G3

Dodge L. *Canada* 103 B7
Dodgeville *U.S.A.* 112 D8
Dodo *Cameroon* 83 D7
Dodo *Sudan* 81 F2
Dodola *Ethiopia* 81 F4
Dodoma *Tanzania* 86 D4
Dodoma □ *Tanzania* 86 D4
Dodori △ *Kenya* 86 C5
Dodsland *Canada* 103 C7
Dodson *U.S.A.* 108 B9
Dodurga *Turkey* 47 B11
Doesburg *Neths.* 17 B6
Doetinchem *Neths.* 17 C6
Dog Creek *Canada* 102 C4
Dog L. *Man., Canada* 103 C9
Dog L. *Ont., Canada* 104 C2
Doğanşehir *Turkey* 72 C7
Dogliani *Italy* 40 D4
Dogondoutchi *Niger* 83 C5
Dogran *Pakistan* 68 D5
Doğubayazıt *Turkey* 73 C11
Doguéraoua *Niger* 83 C6
Doha = Ad Dawḥah *Qatar* 71 E6
Dohazari *Bangla.* 67 H18
Dohrighat *India* 69 F10
Doi *Indonesia* 63 D7
Doi Inthanon △ *Thailand* 64 C2
Doi Khuntan △ *Thailand* 64 C2
Doi Luang *Thailand* 64 C3
Doi Luang △ *Thailand* 64 C2
Doi Saket *Thailand* 64 C2
Doi Suthep △ *Thailand* 64 C2
Dois Irmãos, Sa. *Brazil* 125 E10
Dojransko Jezero *Macedonia* 44 E6
Dokkum *Neths.* 17 A5
Dokos *Greece* 46 D5
Dokri *Pakistan* 68 F3
Dokuchayevsk *Ukraine* 33 J9
Dol-de-Bretagne *France* 18 D5
Dolac *Serbia* 44 D4
Dolak, Pulau *Indonesia* 63 F9
Dolbeau *Canada* 105 C5
Dole *France* 19 E12
Doleib, Wadi → *Sudan* 81 E3
Dolenji Logatec *Slovenia* 41 C11
Dolgellau *U.K.* 14 E4
Dolgelley = Dolgellau *U.K.* 14 E4
Dolhasca *Romania* 29 C11
Doliana *Greece* 46 B2
Dolianova *Italy* 42 C2
Dolinsk *Russia* 53 E15
Dolinskaya = Dolynska
  Ukraine 33 H7
Dolj □ *Romania* 29 F8
Dolna Banya *Bulgaria* 44 D7
Dolni Chiflik *Bulgaria* 45 D11
Dolni Dŭbnik *Bulgaria* 45 C8
Dolnośląskie □ *Poland* 31 G3
Dolný Kubín *Slovak Rep.* 27 B12
Dolo *Ethiopia* 81 G5
Dolo *Italy* 41 C9
Dolomites = Dolomiti *Italy* 41 B8
Dolomiti *Italy* 41 B8
Dolomiti Bellunesi △ *Italy* 41 B9
Dolores *Argentina* 126 D4
Dolores *Uruguay* 126 C4
Dolores *U.S.A.* 109 H9
Dolores → *U.S.A.* 108 G9
Dolovo *Serbia* 28 F5
Dolsk *Poland* 31 G4
Dolyna *Ukraine* 29 B9
Dolynska *Ukraine* 33 H7
Dolynske *Ukraine* 29 C14
Dolzhanskaya *Russia* 33 J9
Dom Pedrito *Brazil* 127 C5
Doma *Nigeria* 83 D6
Doma △ *Zimbabwe* 87 F3
Domaniç *Turkey* 47 B11
Domariaganj → *India* 69 F10
Domasi *Malawi* 87 F4
Domažlice *Czech Rep.* 26 B5
Dombarovskiy *Russia* 52 D6
Dombås *Norway* 8 C15
Dombasle-sur-Meurthe
  France 19 D13
Dombes *France* 21 C9
Dombóvár *Hungary* 28 D3
Dombrád *Hungary* 28 B6
Dome Argus *Antarctica* 5 E12
Dome C. *Antarctica* 5 D17
Dome Fuji *Antarctica* 5 D5
Domel I. = Letsôk-aw
  Kyun *Burma* 65 G2
Domérat *France* 19 F9
Domeyko *Chile* 126 B1
Domeyko, Cordillera *Chile* 126 A2
Domfront *France* 18 D6
Dominador *Chile* 126 A2
Dominica ■ *W. Indies* 121 C7
Dominica Passage *W. Indies* 121 C7
Dominican Rep. ■
  W. Indies 121 C5
Dömitz *Germany* 24 B7

Domme *France* 20 D5
Domnești *Romania* 29 E9
Domodóssola *Italy* 40 B5
Dompaire *France* 19 D13
Dompierre *France* 19 D13
Dompierre-sur-Besbre
  France 19 F10
Dompim *Ghana* 82 D4
Domrémy-la-Pucelle *France*
  19 D12
Domvena *Greece* 46 C4
Domville, Mt. *Australia* 95 D5
Domžale *Slovenia* 41 B11
Don → *Russia* 33 J9
Don → *Aberds., U.K.* 13 D6
Don → *S. Yorks., U.K.* 14 D7
Don, C. *Australia* 92 B5
Don Benito *Spain* 37 G5
Don Figuero Mts. *Jamaica* 120 a
Don Sak *Thailand* 65 b
Dona Ana = Nhamaabué
  Mozam. 87 F4
Doña Mencía *Spain* 37 H6
Donaghadee *U.K.* 12 B6
Donaghmore *Ireland* 12 D4
Donald *Australia* 95 F3
Donaldsonville *U.S.A.* 116 F9
Donalsonville *U.S.A.* 117 F12
Doñana △ *Spain* 37 J4
Donau = Dunărea →
  Europe 29 E14
Donau → *Austria* 27 C10
Donau Auen △ *Austria* 27 C9
Donaueschingen *Germany* 25 H4
Donauwörth *Germany* 25 G6
Doncaster *U.K.* 14 D6
Dondo *Angola* 84 F2
Dondo *Mozam.* 87 F3
Dondo, Teluk *Indonesia* 63 D6
Dondra Head *Sri Lanka* 66 S12
Dondușeni *Moldova* 29 B12
Donegal *Ireland* 12 B3
Donegal □ *Ireland* 12 B4
Donegal B. *Ireland* 12 B3
Donets → *Russia* 35 G5
Donets Basin *Ukraine* 6 F13
Donetsk *Ukraine* 33 J9
Donetsk □ *Ukraine* 33 J9
Dong Ba Thin *Vietnam* 65 F7
Dong Dang *Vietnam* 58 G6
Dong Giam *Vietnam* 64 C5
Dong Ha *Vietnam* 64 D6
Dong Hene *Laos* 64 D5
Dong Hoi *Vietnam* 64 D6
Dong Jiang → *China* 59 F10
Dong Khe *Vietnam* 64 A6
Dong Ujimqin Qi *China* 56 B9
Dong Van *Vietnam* 64 A5
Dong Xoai *Vietnam* 65 G6
Donga *Nigeria* 83 D7
Donga → *Nigeria* 83 D7
Dong'an *China* 59 D8
Dongara *Australia* 93 E1
Dongbei *China* 54 A5
Dongchuan *China* 58 D4
Dongco *China* 67 C14
Donges *France* 18 E4
Dongfang *China* 64 C7
Dongfeng *China* 57 C13
Donggala *Indonesia* 63 E5
Donggan *China* 58 F5
Donggang *China* 57 E13
Dongguan *China* 59 F9
Dongguang *China* 56 F9
Donghae *S. Korea* 57 F15
Donghai Dao *China* 59 G8
Dongjingcheng *China* 57 B15
Dongkou *China* 59 D8
Donglan *China* 58 E6
Dongliu *China* 59 B11
Dongmen *China* 58 F6
Dongnae *S. Korea* 57 G15
Dongning *China* 57 B16
Dongnyi *China* 58 C3
Dongola *Sudan* 80 D3
Dongping *China* 56 G9
Dongsha Dao *China* 59 G11
Dongshan *China* 59 F11
Dongsheng *China* 56 E6
Dongtai *China* 57 H11
Dongting Hu *China* 59 C9
Dongtou *China* 59 D13
Dongxiang *China* 59 C11
Dongxing *China* 58 G7
Dongyang *China* 59 C13
Dongzhi *China* 59 B11

Donnelly's Crossing *N.Z.* **91** A4
Donnybrook *Australia* **93** F2
Donnybrook *S. Africa* **89** D4
Donora *U.S.A.* **114** F5
Donostia = Donostia-San
  Sebastián *Spain* **38** B3
Donostia-San Sebastián
  Spain **38** B3
Donousa *Greece* **47** D7
Donskoy *Russia* **32** F10
Donsol *Phil.* **61** E5
Donwood *Canada* **114** B6
Donzère *France* **21** D8
Donzy *France* **19** E10
Doon ➤ *U.K.* **13** F4
Dora, L. *Australia* **92** D3
Dora Báltea ➤ *Italy* **40** C5
Dora Ripária ➤ *Italy* **40** C4
Doran L. *Canada* **103** A7
Dorchester *U.K.* **15** G5
Dorchester, C. *Canada* **101** C12
Dordabis *Namibia* **88** C2
Dordogne □ *France* **20** C4
Dordogne ➤ *France* **20** C3
Dordrecht *Neths.* **17** C4
Dordrecht *S. Africa* **88** E4
Dore ➤ *France* **20** C7
Dore, Mts. *France* **20** C6
Doré L. *Canada* **103** C7
Dorfen *Germany* **25** G8
Dorgali *Italy* **42** B2
Dori *Burkina Faso* **83** C4
Doring ➤ *S. Africa* **88** E2
Doringbos *S. Africa* **88** E2
Dorking *U.K.* **15** F7
Dormaa-Ahenkro *Ghana* **82** D4
Dormans *France* **19** C10
Dormo, Ras *Eritrea* **81** E5
Dornbirn *Austria* **26** D2
Dornes *France* **19** F10
Dorneşti *Romania* **29** C11
Dornie *U.K.* **13** D3
Dornoch *Canada* **114** B4
Dornoch *U.K.* **13** D4
Dornoch Firth *U.K.* **13** D4
Dornogovi □ *Mongolia* **56** C6
Doro *Mali* **83** B4
Doro, Kavo *Greece* **46** C6
Dorog *Hungary* **28** C3
Dorogobuzh *Russia* **32** E7
Dorohoi *Romania* **29** C11
Döröö Nuur *Mongolia* **60** B4
Dorr *Iran* **71** C6
Dorre I. *Australia* **93** E1
Dorrigo *Australia* **95** E5
Dorris *U.S.A.* **108** F3
Dorset *Canada* **114** A6
Dorset *Ohio, U.S.A.* **114** E4
Dorset *Vt., U.S.A.* **115** C11
Dorset □ *U.K.* **15** G5
Dorsten *Germany* **24** D2
Dortmund *Germany* **24** D3
Dortmund-Ems-Kanal ➤
  Germany **24** D3
Dörtyol *Turkey* **72** D7
Dorum *Germany* **24** B4
Doruma
  Dem. Rep. of the Congo **86** B2
Dorüneh *Iran* **71** C8
Dos Bahías, C. *Argentina* **128** E3
Dos Hermanas *Spain* **37** H5
Dos Palos *U.S.A.* **110** J6
Döşemealtı *Turkey* **47** D12
Dosso *Niger* **83** C5
Dosso □ *Niger* **83** C5
Dosso △ *Niger* **83** C5
Dothan *U.S.A.* **117** F12
Doty *U.S.A.* **110** D3
Douai *France* **19** B10
Douako *Guinea* **82** D2
Douala *Cameroon* **83** E6
Douarnenez *France* **18** D2
Doubabougou *Mali* **82** C3
Double Island Pt. *Australia* **95** D5
Double Mountain Fork ➤
  U.S.A. **116** E4
Doubrava ➤ *Czech Rep.* **26** A8
Doubs □ *France* **19** E13
Doubs ➤ *France* **19** F12
Doubtful Sd. *N.Z.* **91** F1
Doubtless B. *N.Z.* **91** A4
Doudeville *France* **18** C7
Doué-la-Fontaine *France* **18** E6
Douentza *Mali* **82** B4
Douentza △ *Mali* **82** B4
Douglas *Canada* **114** A8
Douglas *I. of Man* **14** C3
Douglas *S. Africa* **88** D3
Douglas *Ariz., U.S.A.* **109** L9
Douglas *Ga., U.S.A.* **117** F13
Douglas *Wyo., U.S.A.* **108** E11
Douglas Apsley △ *Australia* **95** G4
Douglas Chan. *Canada* **102** C3
Douglas Pt. *Canada* **114** B3
Douglasville *U.S.A.* **117** E12
Doukaton, Akra *Greece* **46** C2
Doulevant-le-Château
  France **19** D11

Doullens *France* **19** B9
Doumen *China* **59** F9
Douna *Mali* **82** C3
Dounreay *U.K.* **13** C5
Dourada, Serra *Brazil* **125** F9
Dourados *Brazil* **127** A5
Dourados ➤ *Brazil* **127** A5
Dourados, Serra dos *Brazil* **127** A5
Dourdan *France* **19** D9
Douro ➤ *Europe* **36** D2
Douvaine *France* **19** F13
Douvres-la-Délivrande
  France **18** C6
Douze ➤ *France* **20** E3
Dove ➤ *U.K.* **14** E6
Dove Creek *U.S.A.* **109** H9
Dover *Australia* **95** G4
Dover *U.K.* **15** F9
Dover *Del., U.S.A.* **113** F16
Dover *N.H., U.S.A.* **115** C14
Dover *N.J., U.S.A.* **115** F10
Dover *Ohio, U.S.A.* **114** F3
Dover, Pt. *Australia* **93** F4
Dover, Str. of *Europe* **15** G9
Dover-Foxcroft *U.S.A.* **113** C19
Dover Plains *U.S.A.* **115** E11
Dovey = Dyfi ➤ *U.K.* **15** E3
Dovhe *Ukraine* **29** B8
Dovrefjell *Norway* **8** E13
Dow Rūd *Iran* **71** C6
Dowa *Malawi* **87** E3
Dowagiac *U.S.A.* **112** E10
Dowerin *Australia* **93** F2
Dowgha'i *Iran* **71** B8
Dowlatābād *Kermān, Iran* **71** D8
Dowlatābād *Khorāsān, Iran* **71** C8
Down □ *U.K.* **12** B5
Downey *Calif., U.S.A.* **111** M8
Downey *Idaho, U.S.A.* **108** E7
Downham Market *U.K.* **15** E8
Downieville *U.S.A.* **110** F6
Downpatrick *U.K.* **12** B6
Downpatrick Hd. *Ireland* **12** B2
Downsville *U.S.A.* **115** D10
Downton, Mt. *Canada* **102** C4
Dowsārī *Iran* **71** D8
Doxato *Greece* **45** E8
Doyle *U.S.A.* **110** E6
Doylestown *U.S.A.* **115** F9
Dozois, Rés. *Canada* **104** C4
Dra Khel *Pakistan* **68** F2
Drâa, C. *Morocco* **78** C3
Drâa, Oued ➤ *Morocco* **78** C3
Drac ➤ *France* **21** C9
Drachten *Neths.* **17** A6
Drăgănești *Moldova* **29** C13
Drăgănești-Olt *Romania* **29** F9
Drăgănești-Vlașca *Romania* **29** F10
Dragaš *Serbia* **44** D4
Drăgăşani *Romania* **29** F9
Dragichyn *Belarus* **23** B13
Dragocvet *Serbia* **44** C5
Dragon's Mouths = Bocas
  del Dragón *Venezuela* **125** K15
Dragovishtitsa *Bulgaria* **44** D6
Draguignan *France* **21** E10
Drahove *Ukraine* **29** B8
Drain *U.S.A.* **108** E2
Drake *U.S.A.* **112** B3
Drake Passage *S. Ocean* **5** B17
Drakensberg *S. Africa* **89** D4
Drama *Greece* **45** E8
Drama □ *Greece* **45** E8
Drammen *Norway* **9** G14
Drangajökull *Iceland* **8** C2
Dranov, Ostrov *Romania* **29** F14
Dras *India* **69** B6
Drastis, Akra *Greece* **49** A3
Drau = Drava ➤ *Croatia* **28** E3
Drava ➤ *Croatia* **28** E3
Dravograd *Slovenia* **41** B12
Drawa ➤ *Poland* **31** E2
Drawieński △ *Poland* **31** E2
Drawno *Poland* **31** E2
Drawsko Pomorskie *Poland* **30** E2
Drayton *Canada* **114** C4
Drayton Valley *Canada* **102** C6
Dreieich *Germany* **25** E4
Dren *Serbia* **44** C4
Drenthe □ *Neths.* **17** B6
Drepano, Akra *Greece* **49** D6
Drepanum, C. *Cyprus* **49** E11
Dresden *Canada* **114** D2
Dresden *Germany* **24** D9
Dresden *U.S.A.* **113** C13
Dreux *France* **18** D8
Drezdenko *Poland* **31** F2
Driffield *U.K.* **14** C7
Driftwood *U.S.A.* **114** E6
Driggs *U.S.A.* **108** E8
Drin ➤ *Albania* **44** C4
Drin i Zi ➤ *Albania* **44** E4
Drina ➤ *Bos.-H.* **44** B3
Drincea ➤ *Romania* **28** F7
Drinjača ➤ *Bos.-H.* **28** F4
Driopida *Greece* **46** D6

Drissa =
  Vyerkhnyadzvinsk
  Belarus **32** E4
Drniš *Croatia* **41** E13
Drøbak *Norway* **9** G14
Drobeta-Turnu Severin
  Romania **28** F7
Drobin *Poland* **31** F6
Drochia *Moldova* **29** B12
Drogheda *Ireland* **12** C5
Drogichin = Dragichyn
  Belarus **23** B13
Drogobych = Drohobych
  Ukraine **31** J10
Drohiczyn *Poland* **31** F9
Drohobych *Ukraine* **31** J10
Droichead Atha =
  Drogheda *Ireland* **12** C5
Droichead Nua *Ireland* **12** C5
Droitwich *U.K.* **15** E5
Drôme □ *France* **21** D9
Drôme ➤ *France* **21** D8
Dromedary, C. *Australia* **95** F5
Dromore *U.K.* **12** B4
Dromore West *Ireland* **12** B3
Dronero *Italy* **40** D4
Dronfield *U.K.* **14** D6
Dronne ➤ *France* **20** C3
Dronning Maud Land
  Antarctica **5** D3
Dronninglund *Denmark* **11** G4
Dronten *Neths.* **17** B5
Dropt ➤ *France* **20** D3
Drosendorf *Austria* **26** C8
Droué *France* **18** D8
Druk Yul = Bhutan ■ *Asia* **67** F17
Drumbo *Canada* **114** C4
Drumcliff *Ireland* **12** B3
Drumheller *Canada* **102** C6
Drummond *U.S.A.* **108** C7
Drummond I. *U.S.A.* **113** B12
Drummond Pt. *Australia* **95** E2
Drummond Ra. *Australia* **94** C4
Drummondville *Canada* **104** C5
Drumright *U.S.A.* **116** D6
Druskininkai *Lithuania* **32** E2
Drut ➤ *Belarus* **23** B16
Druya *Belarus* **32** E4
Druzhba *Bulgaria* **45** C12
Druzhina *Russia* **53** C15
Drvar *Bos.-H.* **41** D13
Drvenik *Croatia* **41** E13
Drwęca ➤ *Poland* **31** E5
Dry Harbour Mts. *Jamaica* **120** a
Dry Tortugas *U.S.A.* **117** F13
Dryanovo *Bulgaria* **45** D9
Dryden *Canada* **103** D10
Dryden *U.S.A.* **115** D8
Drygalski I. *Antarctica* **5** C7
Drygalski Ice Tongue
  Antarctica **5** D21
Drysdale ➤ *Australia* **92** B4
Drysdale I. *Australia* **94** A2
Drysdale River △ *Australia* **92** B4
Dschang *Cameroon* **83** D7
Du Gué ➤ *Canada* **104** A5
Du He *China* **59** A9
Du Quoin *U.S.A.* **112** F9
Du'an *China* **58** F7
Duanesburg *U.S.A.* **115** D10
Duaringa *Australia* **94** C4
Duarte, Pico *Dom. Rep.* **121** D5
Dubai = Dubayy *U.A.E.* **71** E7
Dubǎsari *Moldova* **29** C14
Dubǎsari Vdkhr. *Moldova* **29** C13
Dubawnt ➤ *Canada* **103** A8
Dubawnt L. *Canada* **103** A8
Dubayy *U.A.E.* **71** E7
Dubbo *Australia* **95** E4
Dubele *Dem. Rep. of the Congo* **86** B2
Dübendorf *Switz.* **25** H4
Dubica *Croatia* **41** C13
Dublin *Ireland* **12** C5
Dublin *Ga., U.S.A.* **117** E13
Dublin *Tex., U.S.A.* **116** E5
Dublin □ *Ireland* **12** C5
Dublin ✈ (DUB) *Ireland* **12** C5
Dubna *Russia* **32** D9
Dubnica nad Váhom
  Slovak Rep. **27** C11
Dubno *Ukraine* **23** C13
Dubois *Idaho, U.S.A.* **108** D7
Dubois *Pa., U.S.A.* **114** E6
Dubossary = Dubǎsari
  Moldova **29** C14
Dubossary Vdkhr. =
  Dubǎsari Vdkhr. *Moldova* **29** C13
Dubove *Ukraine* **29** B8
Dubovka *Russia* **35** F7
Dubovskoye *Russia* **35** G6
Dubrajpur *India* **69** H12
Dubréka *Guinea* **82** D2
Dubrovitsa = Dubrovytsya
  Ukraine **23** C14
Dubrovnik *Croatia* **44** D2

Dubrovytsya *Ukraine* **23** C14
Dubuque *U.S.A.* **112** D8
Dubysa ➤ *Lithuania* **30** C10
Duchang *China* **59** C11
Duchesne *U.S.A.* **108** F8
Duchess *Australia* **94** C2
Ducie I. *Pac. Oc.* **97** K15
Duck ➤ *U.S.A.* **117** H2
Duck Cr. ➤ *Australia* **92** D2
Duck Lake *Canada* **103** C7
Duck Mountain △ *Canada* **103** C8
Duckwall, Mt. *U.S.A.* **110** H6
Duderstadt *Germany* **24** D6
Dudhi *India* **69** G10
Dudinka *Russia* **53** C9
Dudley *U.K.* **15** E5
Dudwa *India* **69** E9
Dudwa △ *India* **69** E9
Duékoué *Ivory C.* **82** D3
Dueñas *Spain* **36** D6
Duero = Douro ➤ *Europe* **36** D2
Dufftown *U.K.* **13** D5
Dufourspitz *Switz.* **25** K3
Dugi Otok *Croatia* **41** D11
Dugo Selo *Croatia* **41** C13
Duisburg *Germany* **24** D2
Duiwelskloof =
  Modjadjiskloof *S. Africa* **89** C5
Dujiangyan *China* **58** B4
Duk Fadiat *Sudan* **81** F3
Duk Faiwil *Sudan* **81** F3
Dukat *Albania* **44** F3
Dūkdamīn *Iran* **71** C8
Dukelský Průsmyk
  Slovak Rep. **27** B14
Dukhān *Qatar* **71** E6
Dukhovshchina *Russia* **32** E7
Duki *Pakistan* **68** D6
Dukla *Poland* **31** J8
Duku *Bauchi, Nigeria* **83** C7
Duku *Sokoto, Nigeria* **83** C5
Dulag *Phil.* **61** F6
Dulce *U.S.A.* **109** H10
Dulce ➤ *Argentina* **126** C3
Dulce, G. *Costa Rica* **120** E3
Dulf *Iraq* **70** C5
Dŭlgopol *Bulgaria* **45** C11
Duliu *China* **56** E9
Dullewala *Pakistan* **68** D4
Dullstroom *S. Africa* **89** D5
Dülmen *Germany* **24** D3
Dulovo *Bulgaria* **45** C11
Duluth *U.S.A.* **112** B7
Dum Dum *India* **69** H13
Dum Duma *India* **67** F19
Dūmā *Syria* **74** B5
Dumaguete *Phil.* **61** G5
Dumai *Indonesia* **62** D2
Dumaran *Phil.* **61** F3
Dumas *Ark., U.S.A.* **116** E9
Dumas *Tex., U.S.A.* **116** D4
Dumayr *Syria* **74** B5
Dumbarton *U.K.* **13** F4
Dumbleyung *Australia* **93** F2
Dumbrăveni *Romania* **29** D9
Dumfries *U.K.* **13** F5
Dumfries & Galloway □
  U.K. **13** F5
Dumitreşti *Romania* **29** E11
Dumka *India* **69** G12
Dumlupınar *Turkey* **47** C12
Dümmer *Germany* **24** C4
Dümmer △ *Germany* **24** C4
Dumoine ➤ *Canada* **104** C4
Dumoine, L. *Canada* **104** C4
Dumont d'Urville *Antarctica* **5** C10
Dumont d'Urville Sea
  S. Ocean **5** C9
Dumraon *India* **69** G11
Dumyât *Egypt* **80** H7
Dumyât, Masabb *Egypt* **80** H7
Dún Dealgan = Dundalk
  Ireland **12** B5
Dún Laoghaire *Ireland* **12** C5
Dun-le-Palestel *France* **19** F8
Dun-sur-Auron *France* **19** F9
Dun-sur-Meuse *France* **19** C12
Duna = Dunărea ➤ *Europe* **29** E14
Duna-Drava △ *Hungary* **28** D3
Duna-völgyi-főcsatorna
  Hungary **28** D4
Dunaföldvár *Hungary* **28** D3
Dunagiri *India* **69** D8
Dunaj = Dunărea ➤
  Europe **29** E14
Dunajec ➤ *Poland* **31** H7
Dunajská Streda *Slovak Rep.* **27** C10
Dunakeszi *Hungary* **28** C4
Dunapataj *Hungary* **28** D4
Dunărea ➤ *Europe* **29** E14
Dunaszekcső *Hungary* **28** D3
Dunaújváros *Hungary* **28** D3
Dunav = Dunărea ➤
  Europe **29** E14
Dunavaţu de Jos *Romania* **29** F14
Dunavtsi *Bulgaria* **44** C6

Dunay *Russia* **54** C6
Dunayivtsi *Ukraine* **29** B11
Dunback *N.Z.* **91** F3
Dunbar *U.K.* **13** E6
Dunblane *U.K.* **13** E5
Duncan *Canada* **110** B3
Duncan *Ariz., U.S.A.* **109** K9
Duncan *Okla., U.S.A.* **116** H6
Duncan, L. *Canada* **104** B4
Duncan L. *Canada* **102** A6
Duncan Town *Bahamas* **120** B4
Duncannon *U.S.A.* **114** F7
Duncansby Head *U.K.* **13** C5
Duncansville *U.S.A.* **114** F6
Dundaga *Latvia* **30** A9
Dundalk *Canada* **114** B4
Dundalk *Ireland* **12** B5
Dundalk *U.S.A.* **113** F15
Dundalk Bay *Ireland* **12** C5
Dundas *Canada* **114** C5
Dundas, L. *Australia* **93** F3
Dundas I. *Canada* **102** C2
Dundas Str. *Australia* **92** B5
Dundee *S. Africa* **89** D5
Dundee *U.K.* **13** E6
Dundee *U.S.A.* **114** D8
Dundee City □ *U.K.* **13** E6
Dundgovĭ □ *Mongolia* **56** B4
Dundrum *U.K.* **12** B6
Dundrum B. *U.K.* **12** B6
Dunedin *N.Z.* **91** F3
Dunedin *U.S.A.* **117** G13
Dunfanaghy *Ireland* **12** A4
Dunfermline *U.K.* **13** E5
Dungannon *Canada* **114** C3
Dungannon *U.K.* **12** B5
Dungarpur *India* **68** H5
Dungarvan *Ireland* **12** D4
Dungarvan Harbour *Ireland* **12** D4
Dungeness *U.K.* **15** G8
Dunglow *Ireland* **12** B3
Dungo, L. do *Angola* **88** B2
Dungog *Australia* **95** E5
Dungu *Dem. Rep. of the Congo* **86** B2
Dungun *Malaysia* **65** K4
Dungunâb *Sudan* **80** C4
Dungunâb, Khalig *Sudan* **80** C4
Dunhua *China* **57** C15
Dunhuang *China* **60** B4
Dunk I. *Australia* **94** B4
Dunkassa *Benin* **83** C5
Dunkeld *Australia* **95** E4
Dunkeld *U.K.* **13** E5
Dunkerque *France* **19** A9
Dunkery Beacon *U.K.* **15** F4
Dunkirk = Dunkerque
  France **19** A9
Dunkirk *U.S.A.* **114** D5
Dunkuj *Sudan* **81** E3
Dunkwa *Central, Ghana* **82** D4
Dunkwa *Central, Ghana* **83** D4
Dúnleary = Dún
  Laoghaire *Ireland* **12** C5
Dunleer *Ireland* **12** C5
Dunmanus B. *Ireland* **12** E2
Dunmanway *Ireland* **12** E2
Dunmarra *Australia* **94** B1
Dunmore *U.S.A.* **115** E9
Dunmore East *Ireland* **12** D5
Dunmore Hd. *Ireland* **12** D1
Dunmore Town *Bahamas* **120** A4
Dunn *U.S.A.* **117** D15
Dunnellon *U.S.A.* **117** G13
Dunnet Hd. *U.K.* **13** C5
Dunning *U.S.A.* **112** E3
Dunnville *Canada* **114** D5
Dunolly *Australia* **95** F3
Dunoon *U.K.* **13** F4
Dunqul *Egypt* **80** C3
Duns *U.K.* **13** F6
Dunseith *U.S.A.* **112** A3
Dunshaughlin *Ireland* **12** C5
Dunsmuir *U.S.A.* **108** F2
Dunstable *U.K.* **15** F7
Dunstan Mts. *N.Z.* **91** F2
Dunster *Canada* **102** C5
Dunvegan *U.K.* **13** D2
Dunvegan L. *Canada* **103** A7
Duolun *China* **56** C9
Duong Dong *Vietnam* **65** G4
Dupree *U.S.A.* **112** C3
Dupuyer *U.S.A.* **108** B7
Duque de Caxias *Brazil* **127** A7
Durack ➤ *Australia* **92** C4
Durack Ra. *Australia* **92** C4
Durağan *Turkey* **72** B6
Durak *Turkey* **47** B10
Đurakovac *Serbia* **44** D4
Durance ➤ *France* **21** E8
Durand *U.S.A.* **112** C8
Durango *Mexico* **118** C4
Durango □ *Mexico* **118** C4
Durango *U.S.A.* **109** H10
Durankulak *Bulgaria* **45** C12
Durant *Miss., U.S.A.* **117** E10
Durant *Okla., U.S.A.* **116** E6

Duratón ➤ *Spain* **36** D6
Durazno *Uruguay* **126** C4
Durazzo = Durrës *Albania* **44** E3
Durban *France* **20** F6
Durban *S. Africa* **89** D5
Durbuy *Belgium* **17** D5
Dúrcal *Spain* **37** J7
Đurđevac *Croatia* **28** D2
Düren *Germany* **24** E2
Durg = Bhilainagar-Durg
  India **67** J12
Durgapur *India* **69** H12
Durham *Canada* **114** B4
Durham *U.K.* **14** C6
Durham *Calif., U.S.A.* **110** F5
Durham *N.C., U.S.A.* **117** D15
Durham *N.H., U.S.A.* **115** C14
Durham □ *U.K.* **14** C6
Durleşti *Moldova* **29** C13
Đurmanec *Si. Arabia* **70** E5
Durmitor *Montenegro* **44** C2
Durmitor △ *Serbia* **44** C3
Durness *U.K.* **13** C4
Durrow *Ireland* **12** D4
Dursey I. *Ireland* **12** E1
Dursley *U.K.* **15** F5
Dursunbey *Turkey* **47** B10
Durtal *France* **18** E6
Duru *Dem. Rep. of the Congo* **86** B2
Duru Gölü *Turkey* **45** E12
Durusu *Turkey* **45** E12
Duruz, Jabal ad *Jordan* **74** C5
D'Urville, Tanjung *Indonesia* **63** E9
D'Urville I. *N.Z.* **91** D4
Duryea *U.S.A.* **115** E9
Dûsh *Egypt* **80** C3
Dushak *Turkmenistan* **71** B9
Dushan *China* **58** E6
Dushanbe *Tajikistan* **52** F7
Dusheti *Georgia* **35** J7
Dushore *U.S.A.* **115** E8
Dusky Sd. *N.Z.* **91** F1
Dussejour, C. *Australia* **92** B4
Düsseldorf *Germany* **24** D2
Düsseldorf Rhein-Ruhr ✈
  (DUS) *Germany* **24** D2
Duszniki-Zdrój *Poland* **31** H3
Dutch Harbor *U.S.A.* **106** a
Dutlwe *Botswana* **88** C3
Dutsan Wai *Nigeria* **83** C6
Dutton *Canada* **114** D3
Dutton ➤ *Australia* **94** C3
Dutywa *S. Africa* **89** E4
Duved *Sweden* **10** A6
Düvertepe *Turkey* **47** B10
Duwayhin, Khawr *U.A.E.* **71** E6
Duyun *China* **58** D6
Düzağac *Turkey* **47** C12
Düzce *Turkey* **72** B4
Düzce □ *Turkey* **72** B4
Dve Mogili *Bulgaria* **45** C9
Dvina, Severnaya ➤ *Russia* **6** C14
Dvinsk = Daugavpils *Latvia* **32** E4
Dvor *Croatia* **41** C13
Dvůr Králové nad Labem
  Czech Rep. **26** A8
Dwarka *India* **68** H3
Dwellingup *Australia* **93** F2
Dwight *Canada* **114** A5
Dwight *U.S.A.* **112** E10
Dyakove *Ukraine* **28** B7
Dyatkovo *Russia* **32** F8
Dyatlovo = Dzyatlava
  Belarus **23** B13
Dyce *U.K.* **13** D6
Dyer, C. *Canada* **101** C17
Dyer Bay *Canada* **114** A3
Dyer Plateau *Antarctica* **5** D17
Dyersburg *U.S.A.* **117** C10
Dyfi ➤ *U.K.* **15** E3
Dyje ➤ *Czech Rep.* **27** C9
Dymer *Ukraine* **23** C16
Dynów *Poland* **31** J9
Dysart *Australia* **94** C4
Dyviziya *Ukraine* **29** E14
Dzaoudzi *Mayotte* **85** a
Dzerzhinsk *Russia* **34** B6
Dzhalinda *Russia* **53** D13
Dzhambul = Taraz
  Kazakhstan **52** E8
Dzhankoy *Ukraine* **33** K8
Dzhanybek = Zhänibek
  Kazakhstan **34** F8
Dzharylhach, Ostriv *Ukraine* **33** J7
Dzhezkazgan =
  Zhezqazghan *Kazakhstan* **52** E7
Dzhizak = Jizzax *Uzbekistan* **52** E7
Dzhugdzur, Khrebet *Russia* **53** D14
Dzhulynk *Ukraine* **29** B14
Dzhuryn *Ukraine* **29** B13
Dzhvari = Jvari *Georgia* **35** J6
Działdowo *Poland* **31** E7
Działoszyce *Poland* **31** H7
Działoszyn *Poland* **31** G5
Dzibilchaltún *Mexico* **119** C7
Dzierzgoń *Poland* **30** E6

Dzierżoniów *Poland* **31** H3
Dzilam de Bravo *Mexico* **119** C7
Dzisna *Belarus* **32** E5
Dzisna → *Belarus* **32** E5
Dziwnów *Poland* **30** D1
Dżūkija △ *Lithuania* **9** J21
Dzungarian Basin =
  Junggar Pendi *China* **60** B3
Dzüünmod *Mongolia* **60** B5
Dzyarzhynsk *Belarus* **23** B14
Dzyatlava *Belarus* **23** B13

E

E.C. Manning △ *Canada* **102** D4
Eabamet L. *Canada* **104** B2
Eabametoong *Canada* **104** B2
Eads *U.S.A.* **108** G12
Eagar *U.S.A.* **109** J9
Eagle *Alaska, U.S.A.* **100** C5
Eagle *Colo., U.S.A.* **108** G10
Eagle → *Canada* **105** B8
Eagle Butte *U.S.A.* **112** C3
Eagle Grove *U.S.A.* **112** D7
Eagle L. *Canada* **103** D10
Eagle L. *Calif., U.S.A.* **108** F3
Eagle L. *Maine, U.S.A.* **113** B19
Eagle Lake *Canada* **114** A6
Eagle Lake *Maine, U.S.A.* **113** B19
Eagle Lake *Tex., U.S.A.* **116** G6
Eagle Mountain *U.S.A.* **111** M11
Eagle Nest *U.S.A.* **109** H11
Eagle Pass *U.S.A.* **116** G4
Eagle Pk. *U.S.A.* **110** G7
Eagle Pt. *Australia* **92** C3
Eagle River *Mich., U.S.A.* **112** B9
Eagle River *Wis., U.S.A.* **112** C9
Eaglehawk *Australia* **95** F3
Eagles Mere *U.S.A.* **115** E8
Ealing □ *U.K.* **15** F7
Ear Falls *Canada* **103** C10
Earle *U.S.A.* **117** D9
Earlimart *U.S.A.* **111** K7
Earlville *U.S.A.* **115** D9
Earn → *U.K.* **13** E5
Earn, L. *U.K.* **13** E4
Earnslaw, Mt. *N.Z.* **91** F2
Earth *U.S.A.* **116** D3
Easley *U.S.A.* **117** D13
East Anglia *U.K.* **14** E9
East Angus *Canada* **105** C5
East Antarctica *Antarctica* **5** D7
East Aurora *U.S.A.* **114** D6
East Ayrshire □ *U.K.* **13** F4
East Bengal *Bangla.* **67** G17
East Beskids = Vychodné
  Beskydy *Europe* **27** B15
East Brady *U.S.A.* **114** F5
East Branch Clarion River
  L. *U.S.A.* **115**
East C. = Dezhneva, Mys
  Russia **53** C19
East C. *N.Z.* **91** B7
East Caroline Basin *Pac. Oc.* **96** G6
East Chicago *U.S.A.* **112** E10
East China Sea *Asia* **60** C7
East Coulee *Canada* **102** C6
East Dereham = Dereham
  U.K. **15** E8
East Dunbartonshire □ *U.K.* **13** F4
East Falkland *Falk. Is.* **128** G5
East Grand Forks *U.S.A.* **112** B5
East Greenwich *U.S.A.* **115** E13
East Grinstead *U.K.* **15** F8
East Hartford *U.S.A.* **115** E12
East Helena *U.S.A.* **108** C8
East Indies *Asia* **50** J14
East Kilbride *U.K.* **13** F4
East Lansing *U.S.A.* **113** D11
East Liverpool *U.S.A.* **114** F4
East London *S. Africa* **89** E4
East Lothian □ *U.K.* **13** F6
East Main = Eastmain
  Canada **104** B4
East Mariana Basin *Pac. Oc.* **96** F7
East Northport *U.S.A.* **115** F11
East Orange *U.S.A.* **115** F10
East Pacific Rise *Pac. Oc.* **97** J17
East Palestine *U.S.A.* **114** F4
East Pine *Canada* **102** B4
East Point *U.S.A.* **117** E12
East Pt. *Br. Virgin Is.* **121** e
East Pt. *Canada* **105** C7
East Renfrewshire □ *U.K.* **13** F4
East Retford = Retford *U.K.* **14** D7
East Riding of Yorkshire □
  U.K. **14** D7
East Rochester *U.S.A.* **114** C7
East St. Louis *U.S.A.* **112** F8
East Schelde =
  Oosterschelde → *Neths.* **17** C4
East Sea = Japan, Sea of *Asia* **54** E7
East Siberian Sea *Russia* **53** B17
East Stroudsburg *U.S.A.* **115** E9
East Sussex □ *U.K.* **15** G8
East Tasman Plateau
  Pac. Oc. **96** M7

East Tawas *U.S.A.* **113** C12
East Timor ■ *Asia* **63** F7
East Toorale *Australia* **95** E4
East Walker → *U.S.A.* **110** G7
East Windsor *U.S.A.* **115** F10
Eastbourne *N.Z.* **91** D5
Eastbourne *U.K.* **15** G8
Eastend *Canada* **103** D7
Easter Fracture Zone
  Pac. Oc. **97** K16
Easter I. = Pascua, I. de
  Chile **97** K17
Eastern □ *Ghana* **83** D4
Eastern □ *Kenya* **86** C4
Eastern □ *S. Leone* **82** D2
Eastern Cape □ *S. Africa* **88** E4
Eastern Cr. → *Australia* **94** C3
Eastern Desert = Es Sahrâ'
  Esh Sharqîya *Egypt* **80** B3
Eastern Ghats *India* **66** N11
Eastern Group = Lau
  Group *Fiji* **91** a
Eastern Group *Australia* **93** F3
Eastern Transvaal =
  Mpumalanga □ *S. Africa* **89** D5
Easterville *Canada* **103** C9
Easthampton *U.S.A.* **115** D12
Eastlake *U.S.A.* **114** E3
Eastland *U.S.A.* **116** E5
Eastleigh *U.K.* **15** G6
Eastmain *Canada* **104** B4
Eastmain → *Canada* **104** B4
Eastman *Canada* **115** A12
Eastman *U.S.A.* **117** E13
Easton *Md., U.S.A.* **113** F15
Easton *Pa., U.S.A.* **115** F9
Easton *Wash., U.S.A.* **110** C5
Eastport *U.S.A.* **113** C20
Eastsound *U.S.A.* **110** B4
Eaton *U.S.A.* **108** F11
Eatonia *Canada* **103** C7
Eatonton *U.S.A.* **117** E13
Eatontown *U.S.A.* **115** F10
Eatonville *U.S.A.* **110** C4
Eau Claire *U.S.A.* **112** C8
Eau Claire, L. à l' *Canada* **104** A5
Eauripik Rise *Pac. Oc.* **96** G6
Eauze *France* **20** E4
Eban *Nigeria* **83** D5
Ebano *Mexico* **119** C5
Ebbegebirge △ *Germany* **24** D3
Ebbw Vale *U.K.* **15** F4
Ebeltoft *Denmark* **11** H4
Ebeltoft Vig *Denmark* **11** H4
Ebenezer, Mt. *Australia* **93** E5
Ebensburg *U.S.A.* **114** F6
Ebensee *Austria* **26** D6
Eber Gölü *Turkey* **72** C4
Eberbach *Germany* **25** F4
Eberswalde-Finow *Germany* **24** C9
Ebetsu *Japan* **54** C10
Ebey's Landing △ *U.S.A.* **110** B4
Ebian *China* **58** C4
Ebingen *Germany* **25** G5
Éboli *Italy* **43** B8
Ebolowa *Cameroon* **83** E7
Ebonda *Dem. Rep. of the Congo* **84** D4
Ebonyi □ *Nigeria* **83** D6
Ebrach *Germany* **25** F6
Ebre = Ebro → *Spain* **38** E5
Ébrié, Lagune *Ivory C.* **82** D4
Ebro → *Spain* **38** E5
Ebro, Embalse del *Spain* **36** C7
Ebstorf *Germany* **24** B6
Ecatepec de Morelos *Mexico* **119** D5
Ecbatana = Hamadān *Iran* **73** E13
Eceabat *Turkey* **45** F10
Ech Chéliff *Algeria* **78** A6
Echigo-Sammyaku *Japan* **55** F9
Echinos *Greece* **45** E9
Échirolles *France* **21** C9
Echizen-Misaki *Japan* **55** G7
Echmiadzin = Yejmiadzin
  Armenia **35** K7
Echo Bay *N.W.T., Canada* **100** C8
Echo Bay *Ont., Canada* **104** C3
Echoing → *Canada* **104** B1
Echternach *Lux.* **17** E6
Echuca *Australia* **95** F3
Écija *Spain* **37** H5
Eckental *Germany* **25** F7
Eckernförde *Germany* **24** A5
Eclipse I. *Australia* **93** G2
Eclipse Is. *Australia* **92** B4
Eclipse Sd. *Canada* **101** B12
Écommoy *France* **18** E7
Écouché *France* **18** D6
Ecrins △ *France* **21** D10
Ecuador ■ *S. Amer.* **124** D3
Écueillé *France* **18** E8
 Écija *Spain* **37** H5
Ed *Sweden* **11** F5
Ed Dabbura *Sudan* **80** D3
Ed Da'ein *Sudan* **81** E2
Ed Damazin *Sudan* **79** F12
Ed Damer *Sudan* **80** D3
Ed Dar el Beida =
  Casablanca *Morocco* **78** B4

Ed Debba *Sudan* **80** D3
Ed Déffa *Egypt* **80** A2
Ed Deim *Sudan* **81** E2
Ed Dueim *Sudan* **81** E3
Edam *Canada* **103** C7
Edam *Neths.* **17** B5
Edane *Sweden* **10** E6
Eday *U.K.* **13** B6
Edd *Eritrea* **81** E5
Eddrachillis B. *U.K.* **13** C3
Eddystone *U.K.* **15** G3
Eddystone Pt. *Australia* **95** G4
Ede *Neths.* **17** B5
Ede *Nigeria* **83** D5
Édéa *Cameroon* **83** E7
Edebäck *Sweden* **10** D7
Edehon L. *Canada* **103** A9
Edekel, Adrar *Algeria* **78** D7
Edelény *Hungary* **28** B5
Eden *Australia* **95** F4
Eden *N.C., U.S.A.* **117** C15
Eden *Tex., U.S.A.* **116** F5
Eden → *U.K.* **14** C4
Edenburg *S. Africa* **88** D4
Edendale *S. Africa* **89** D5
Edenderry *Ireland* **12** C4
Edenton *U.S.A.* **117** C16
Edenville *S. Africa* **89** D4
Eder → *Germany* **24** D5
Eder-Stausee *Germany* **24** D4
Edessa *Greece* **44** F6
Edewecht *Germany* **24** B3
Edfu = Idfû *Egypt* **80** C3
Edgar *U.S.A.* **112** E5
Edgartown *U.S.A.* **115** E14
Edge Hill *U.K.* **15** E6
Edgefield *U.S.A.* **117** E14
Edgeley *U.S.A.* **112** B4
Edgemont *U.S.A.* **112** D2
Edgeøya *Svalbard* **4** B9
Édhessa = Edessa *Greece* **44** F6
Edievale *N.Z.* **91** F2
Edina *Liberia* **82** D2
Edina *U.S.A.* **112** E7
Edinboro *U.S.A.* **114** E4
Edinburg *U.S.A.* **116** H5
Edinburgh *U.K.* **13** F5
Edinburgh ✈ (EDI) *U.K.* **13** F5
Edinburgh, City of □ *U.K.* **13** F5
Edineț *Moldova* **29** B12
Edirne *Turkey* **45** E10
Edirne □ *Turkey* **45** E10
Edison *U.S.A.* **110** B4
Edithburgh *Australia* **95** F2
Edmeston *U.S.A.* **115** D9
Edmond *U.S.A.* **116** D6
Edmonds *U.S.A.* **110** C4
Edmonton *Australia* **94** B4
Edmonton *Canada* **102** C6
Edmund L. *Canada* **104** B1
Edmundston *Canada* **105** C6
Edna *U.S.A.* **116** H6
Edo □ *Nigeria* **83** D6
Edolo *Italy* **40** B7
Edremit *Turkey* **47** B9
Edremit Körfezi *Turkey* **47** B8
Edsbro *Sweden* **10** E12
Edsbyn *Sweden* **10** C9
Edson *Canada* **102** C5
Eduardo Castex *Argentina* **126** D3
Edward → *Australia* **95** F3
Edward, L. *Africa* **86** C2
Edward VII Land *Antarctica* **5** E13
Edwards *Calif., U.S.A.* **111** L9
Edwards → *U.S.A.* **115** B9
Edwards Plateau *U.S.A.* **116** F4
Edwardsville *U.S.A.* **115** E9
Edzná *Mexico* **119** D6
Edzo *Canada* **102** A5
Eeklo *Belgium* **17** C3
Eesti = Estonia ■ *Europe* **32** C3
Eferding *Austria* **26** C7
Effigy Mounds △ *U.S.A.* **112** D8
Effingham *U.S.A.* **112** F9
Eforie *Romania* **29** F13
Efxinoupoli *Greece* **46** B4
Ega → *Spain* **38** C3
Égadi, Ísole *Italy* **42** E5
Egan Range *U.S.A.* **108** G6
Eganville *Canada* **114** A7
Eger = Cheb *Czech Rep.* **26** A5
Eger *Hungary* **28** C5
Eger → *Hungary* **28** C5
Egersund *Norway* **9** G12
Egg L. *Canada* **103** B7
Eggegebirge Südlicher
  Teutoburger Wald △
  Germany **24** D4
Eggenburg *Austria* **26** C8
Eggenfelden *Germany* **25** G8
Éghezée *Belgium* **17** D4
Egina *Greece* **46** D5
Eginio *Greece* **44** F6
Egio *Greece* **46** C4
Égletons *France* **20** C6
Eglinton I. *Canada* **101** B8
Egmont *Canada* **102** D4

Egmont, C. *N.Z.* **91** C4
Egmont, Mt. = Taranaki,
  Mt. *N.Z.* **91** C5
Egmont □ *N.Z.* **91** C5
Egra *India* **69** J12
Eğridir *Turkey* **72** D4
Eğridir Gölü *Turkey* **72** D4
Egtved *Denmark* **11** J3
Egume *Nigeria* **83** D6
Egvekinot *Russia* **53** C19
Egyek *Hungary* **28** C5
Egypt ■ *Africa* **80** B3
Eha Amufu *Nigeria* **83** D6
Ehime □ *Japan* **55** H6
Ehingen *Germany* **25** G5
Ehrenberg *U.S.A.* **111** M12
Ehrwald *Austria* **26** D3
Eibar *Spain* **38** B2
Eichstätt *Germany* **25** G7
Eider → *Germany* **24** A4
Eidsvold *Australia* **95** D5
Eidsvoll *Norway* **9** F14
Eifel *Germany* **25** E2
Eiffel Flats *Zimbabwe* **87** F3
Eiger *Switz.* **40** B5
Eigg *U.K.* **13** E2
Eighty Mile Beach *Australia* **92** C3
Eil, L. *U.K.* **13** E3
Eildon, L. *Australia* **95** F4
Eilean Sar = Western
  Isles □ *U.K.* **13** D1
Eilenburg *Germany* **24** D8
Ein el Luweiqa *Sudan* **81** E3
Einasleigh *Australia* **94** B3
Einasleigh → *Australia* **94** B3
Einbeck *Germany* **24** D5
Eindhoven *Neths.* **17** C5
Einsiedeln *Switz.* **25** H4
Eire = Ireland ■ *Europe* **12** C4
Eiríksjökull *Iceland* **8** D3
Eirunepé *Brazil* **124** E5
Eiseb → *Namibia* **88** C2
Eisenach *Germany* **24** E6
Eisenberg *Germany* **24** E7
Eisenerz *Austria* **26** D7
Eisenhüttenstadt *Germany* **24** C10
Eisenkappel *Austria* **26** E7
Eisenstadt *Austria* **27** D9
Eisfeld *Germany* **25** E6
Eisleben *Germany* **24** D7
Eislingen *Germany* **25** G5
Eivissa *Spain* **48** C7
Eixe, Serra do *Spain* **36** C4
Ejea de los Caballeros *Spain* **38** C3
Ejeda *Madag.* **89** C7
Ejura *Ghana* **83** D4
Ejutla *Mexico* **119** D5
Ekalaka *U.S.A.* **108** D11
Ekaterinburg =
  Yekaterinburg *Russia* **52** D7
Ekenäs = Tammisaari
  Finland **32** B2
Ekenässjön *Sweden* **11** G9
Ekerö *Sweden* **10** E11
Eket *Nigeria* **83** E6
Eketahuna *N.Z.* **91** D5
Ekibastuz *Kazakhstan* **52** D8
Ekiti □ *Nigeria* **83** D6
Ekoli *Dem. Rep. of the Congo* **86** C1
Ekoln *Sweden* **10** E11
Ekshärad *Sweden* **10** D7
Eksjö *Sweden* **11** G8
Ekuma → *Namibia* **88** B2
Ekwan → *Canada* **104** B3
Ekwan Pt. *Canada* **104** B3
El Aaiún *W. Sahara* **78** C3
El Abanico *Chile* **126** D1
El Abbasiya *Sudan* **81** E3
El 'Agrûd *Egypt* **74** E3
El Ait *Sudan* **81** E3
El 'Aiyat *Egypt* **80** J7
El 'Alamein *Egypt* **80** A2
El 'Aqaba, W. → *Egypt* **74** E2
El 'Arag *Egypt* **80** B2
El Arīḥā *West Bank* **74** D4
El 'Arîsh *Egypt* **74** D2
El 'Arîsh, W. → *Egypt* **74** D2
El Asnam = Ech Chéliff
  Algeria **78** A6
El Astillero *Spain* **36** B7
El Badâri *Egypt* **80** B3
El Bahrein *Egypt* **80** B2
El Ballâs *Egypt* **80** B3
El Balyana *Egypt* **80** B3
El Baqeir *Sudan* **80** D3
El Barco de Ávila *Spain* **36** E5
El Barco de Valdeorras = O
  Barco *Spain* **36** C4
El Bauga *Sudan* **80** D3
El Bawiti *Egypt* **80** B2
El Bayadh *Algeria* **78** B6
El Bierzo *Spain* **36** C4
El Bluff *Nic.* **120** D3
El Bonillo *Spain* **39** G2
El Buheirat □ *Sudan* **81** F3
El Burgo de Osma *Spain* **38** D1
El Cajon *U.S.A.* **111** N10

El Calafate *Argentina* **128** G2
El Campello *Spain* **39** G4
El Campo *U.S.A.* **116** G6
El Capitan *U.S.A.* **110** H7
El Carbón *Honduras* **120** C2
El Carmen *Colombia* **124** B3
El Centro *U.S.A.* **111** N11
El Cerro *Bolivia* **124** G6
El Cerro de Andévalo *Spain* **37** H4
El Compadre *Mexico* **111** N10
El Coronil *Spain* **37** H5
El Cuy *Argentina* **128** D3
El Cuyo *Mexico* **119** C7
El Dab'a *Egypt* **80** H6
El Daheir *Egypt* **74** D3
El Deir *Egypt* **80** B3
El Descanso *Mexico* **111** N10
El Desemboque *Mexico* **118** A2
El Dilingat *Egypt* **80** H7
El Diviso *Colombia* **124** C3
El Djouf *Mauritania* **78** D4
El Dorado *Argentina* **118** C3
El Dorado *Ark., U.S.A.* **116** E8
El Dorado *Kans., U.S.A.* **112** G5
El Dorado *Venezuela* **124** B6
El Dorado Springs *U.S.A.* **112** G6
El 'Ein *Sudan* **81** D2
El Ejido *Spain* **37** J8
El Escorial *Spain* **36** E6
El Espinar *Spain* **36** D6
El Faiyûm *Egypt* **80** J7
El Fâsher *Sudan* **81** E2
El Fashn *Egypt* **80** J7
El Ferrol = Ferrol *Spain* **36** B2
El Fifi *Sudan* **81** E2
El Fuerte *Mexico* **118** B3
El Ga'a *Sudan* **81** E3
El Gal *Somali Rep.* **75** E5
El Garef *Sudan* **81** E3
El Gebir *Sudan* **81** E2
El Gedida *Egypt* **80** B2
El Geneina = Al Junaynah
  Sudan **79** F10
El Geteina *Sudan* **81** E3
El Gezira □ *Sudan* **81** E3
El Gir *Sudan* **80** D2
El Gîza *Egypt* **80** J7
El Gogorrón △ *Mexico* **118** C4
El Goléa *Algeria* **78** B6
El Golfo de Santa Clara
  Mexico **118** A2
El Grau *Spain* **39** G4
El Guácharo △ *Venezuela* **121** D7
El Guache △ *Venezuela* **121** E6
El Hagiz *Sudan* **81** D4
El Hâi *Egypt* **80** J7
El Hammam *Egypt* **80** A2
El Hawata *Sudan* **81** E3
El Heiz *Egypt* **80** B2
El Hideib *Sudan* **81** E3
El Hilla *Sudan* **81** E2
El 'Idisât *Egypt* **80** B3
El Iskandarîya *Egypt* **80** H7
El Istiwa'iya *Sudan* **79** G11
El Jadida *Morocco* **78** B4
El Jardal *Honduras* **120** D2
El Jebelein *Sudan* **81** E3
El Kab *Sudan* **80** D3
El Kafr el Sharqi *Egypt* **80** H7
El Kamlin *Sudan* **81** D3
El Karaba *Sudan* **80** D3
El Kef □ *Tunisia* **79** A7
El Kere *Ethiopia* **81** F5
El Khandaq *Sudan* **80** D3
El Khârga *Egypt* **80** B3
El Khartûm *Sudan* **81** D3
El Khartûm □ *Sudan* **81** D3
El Khartûm Bahrî *Sudan* **81** D3
El Kuntilla *Egypt* **74** E3
El Laqâwa *Sudan* **81** E2
El Leh *Ethiopia* **81** G4
El Leiya *Sudan* **81** D4
El Leoncito △ *Argentina* **126** C2
El Lucero *Mexico* **118** A3
El Maestrazgo *Spain* **38** E4
El Mafâza *Sudan* **81** E3
El Maghra *Egypt* **80** A2
El Mahalla el Kubra *Egypt* **80** H7
El Mahârîq *Egypt* **80** B3
El Maimûn *Egypt* **80** J7
El Maks el Bahari *Egypt* **80** C3
El Malpais △ *U.S.A.* **109** J10
El Manshâh *Egypt* **80** B3
El Mansûra *Egypt* **80** H7
El Manzala *Egypt* **80** H7
El Marâgha *Egypt* **80** B3
El Masid *Sudan* **81** E3
El Masnou *Spain* **38** D7
El Matarîya *Egypt* **80** H8
El Meda *Ethiopia* **81** F5
El Medano *Canary Is.* **48** F3
El Metemma *Sudan* **81** D3
El Milagro *Argentina* **126** C2
El Minyâ *Egypt* **80** B3
El Monte *U.S.A.* **111** L8
El Montseny △ *Spain* **38** D7
El Mreyye *Mauritania* **82** B3
El Niybo *Ethiopia* **81** G4

El Obeid *Sudan* **81** E3
El Odaiya *Sudan* **81** E2
El Oro *Mexico* **119** D4
El Oued *Algeria* **78** B7
El Palmar △ *Argentina* **126** C4
El Palmito, Presa *Mexico* **118** B3
El Paso *U.S.A.* **116** F1
El Pedernoso *Spain* **39** F2
El Pedroso *Spain* **37** H5
El Pinacate y Gran
  Desierto de Altar = Gran
  Desierto del Pinacate △
  Mexico **118** A2
El Pobo de Dueñas *Spain* **38** E3
El Portal *U.S.A.* **110** H7
El Porvenir *Mexico* **118** A3
El Prat de Llobregat *Spain* **38** D7
El Progreso *Honduras* **120** C2
El Pueblito *Mexico* **118** B3
El Pueblo *Canary Is.* **48** F2
El Puente del Arzobispo
  Spain **36** F5
El Puerto de Santa María
  Spain **37** J4
El Qâhira *Egypt* **80** H7
El Qantara *Egypt* **74** E1
El Qasr *Egypt* **80** B2
El Qubâbât *Egypt* **80** J7
El Queseima *Egypt* **74** E3
El Qusîya *Egypt* **80** B3
El Râshda *Egypt* **80** B2
El Real de Sta. Maria
  Panama **120** E4
El Reno *U.S.A.* **106** C7
El Rey △ *Argentina* **126** A3
El Rîdisiya *Egypt* **80** C3
El Rio *U.S.A.* **111** L7
El Ronquillo *Spain* **37** H4
El Roque, Pta. *Canary Is.* **48** F4
El Rosarito *Mexico* **118** B2
El Rubio *Spain* **37** H5
El Saff *Egypt* **80** J7
El Salto *Mexico* **118** C3
El Salvador ■ *Cent. Amer.* **120** D2
El Sauce *Nic.* **120** D2
El Saucejo *Spain* **37** H5
El Shallal *Egypt* **80** C3
El Simbillawein *Egypt* **80** H7
El Sueco *Mexico* **118** B3
El Suweis *Egypt* **80** J8
El Tabbîn *Egypt* **80** J7
El Tamarâni, W. → *Egypt* **74** E3
El Thamad *Egypt* **74** F3
El Tigre *Venezuela* **124** B6
El Tîh, Gebel *Egypt* **74** F2
El Tîna *Egypt* **80** H8
El Tofo *Chile* **126** B1
El Tránsito *Chile* **126** B1
El Turbio *Argentina* **128** G2
El Uqsur *Egypt* **80** B3
El Valle △ *Spain* **39** H3
El Vendrell *Spain* **38** D6
El Vergel *Mexico* **118** B3
El Vigía *Venezuela* **124** B4
El Viso del Alcor *Spain* **37** H5
El Wabeira *Egypt* **74** F2
El Wak *Kenya* **86** B5
El Waqf *Egypt* **80** B3
El Weguet *Ethiopia* **81** F5
El Wuz *Sudan* **81** E3
Elafonisos *Greece* **46** E4
Élancourt *France* **19** D8
Elasa *Greece* **47** F8
Elassona *Greece* **46** B4
Elat *Israel* **74** F3
Elatia *Greece* **46** C4
Elâzığ *Turkey* **73** C8
Elâzığ □ *Turkey* **73** C8
Elba *Italy* **40** F7
Elba *U.S.A.* **117** F11
Elbasan *Albania* **44** E4
Elbe *U.S.A.* **110** D4
Elbe → *Europe* **24** B4
Elbe-Seitenkanal *Germany* **24** C6
Elbert, Mt. *U.S.A.* **108** G10
Elberton *U.S.A.* **117** D13
Elbeuf *France* **18** C8
Elbing = Elbląg *Poland* **30** D6
Elbistan *Turkey* **72** C7
Elbląg *Poland* **30** D6
Elbow *Canada* **103** C7
Elbrus *Russia* **35** J6
Elbufer-Drawehn △
  Germany **24** B6
Elburz Mts. = Alborz,
  Reshteh-ye Kūhhā-ye
  Iran **71** C7
Elche *Spain* **39** G4
Elche de la Sierra *Spain* **39** G2
Elcho I. *Australia* **94** A2
Elda *Spain* **39** G4
Eldama Ravine *Kenya* **86** B4
Elde → *Germany* **24** B7
Eldon *Mo., U.S.A.* **112** F7
Eldon *Wash., U.S.A.* **110** C3
Eldora *U.S.A.* **112** D7
Eldorado *Argentina* **127** B5

Eldorado *Canada* **114** B7
Eldorado *Ill., U.S.A.* **112** G9
Eldorado *Tex., U.S.A.* **116** F4
Eldoret *Kenya* **86** B4
Eldred *U.S.A.* **114** E6
Elea, C. *Cyprus* **49** D13
Eleanora, Pk. *Australia* **93** F3
Elefantes → *Africa* **89** C5
Elefsina *Greece* **46** C5
Eleftherios Venizelos ✈
  (ATH) *Greece* **46** D5
Elektrogorsk *Russia* **32** E10
Elektrostal *Russia* **32** E10
Elele *Nigeria* **83** D6
Elemi Triangle *Africa* **81** G4
Elena *Bulgaria* **44** D7
Elephant Butte Res. *U.S.A.* **109** K10
Elephant I. *Antarctica* **5** C18
Eleshnitsa *Bulgaria* **44** E7
Eleşkirt *Turkey* **73** C10
Eleuthera *Bahamas* **120** B4
Eleutheroupoli *Greece* **45** F8
Elgin *Canada* **115** B8
Elgin *U.K.* **13** D5
Elgin *Ill., U.S.A.* **112** D9
Elgin *N. Dak., U.S.A.* **112** B3
Elgin *Oreg., U.S.A.* **108** D5
Elgin *Tex., U.S.A.* **116** F6
Elgoibar *Spain* **38** B2
Elgon, Mt. *Africa* **86** B3
Eliase *Indonesia* **63** F8
Elikonos Oros *Greece* **46** C4
Elim *Namibia* **88** B2
Elim *S. Africa* **88** E2
Elin Pelin *Bulgaria* **44** D7
Elista *Russia* **35** G7
Elizabeth *Australia* **95** E2
Elizabeth *U.S.A.* **115** F10
Elizabeth City *U.S.A.* **117** C16
Elizabethton *U.S.A.* **117** C13
Elizabethtown *Ky., U.S.A.* **113** G11
Elizabethtown *N.Y., U.S.A.* **115** B11
Elizabethtown *Pa., U.S.A.* **115** F8
Elizondo *Spain* **38** B3
Elk *Poland* **30** E9
Elk → *Canada* **102** C5
Elk → *Poland* **30** E9
Elk → *U.S.A.* **117** D11
Elk City *U.S.A.* **116** D5
Elk Creek *U.S.A.* **110** F4
Elk Grove *U.S.A.* **110** G5
Elk Island △ *Canada* **102** C6
Elk Lake *Canada* **104** C3
Elk Point *Canada* **103** C6
Elk River *Idaho, U.S.A.* **108** C5
Elk River *Minn., U.S.A.* **112** C7
Elkedra → *Australia* **94** C2
Elkhart *Ind., U.S.A.* **113** E11
Elkhart *Kans., U.S.A.* **112** G3
Elkhorn *Canada* **103** D8
Elkhorn → *U.S.A.* **112** E5
Elkhovo *Bulgaria* **45** D10
Elkin *U.S.A.* **117** C14
Elkins *U.S.A.* **113** F14
Elkland *U.S.A.* **114** E7
Elko *Canada* **102** D5
Elko *U.S.A.* **108** F6
Elkton *U.S.A.* **114** C1
Ellas = Greece ■ *Europe* **46** B3
Ellef Ringnes I. *Canada* **101** B9
Ellen, Mt. *U.S.A.* **115** B12
Ellenburg *U.S.A.* **115** B11
Ellendale *U.S.A.* **112** B4
Ellensburg *U.S.A.* **108** C3
Ellenville *U.S.A.* **115** E10
Ellerton *Barbados* **121** g
Ellery, Mt. *Australia* **95** F4
Ellesmere, L. *N.Z.* **91** G4
Ellesmere I. *Canada* **101** B12
Ellesmere Port *U.K.* **14** D5
Ellice Is. = Tuvalu ■
  Pac. Oc. **90** B10
Ellicottville *U.S.A.* **114** D6
Ellington *U.S.A.* **114** D5
Elliot *Australia* **94** B1
Elliot *S. Africa* **89** E4
Elliot Lake *Canada* **104** C3
Elliotdale = Xhora *S. Africa* **89** E4
Ellis *U.S.A.* **112** F4
Elliston *Australia* **95** E1
Ellisville *U.S.A.* **117** F10
Ellon *U.K.* **13** D6
Ellore = Eluru *India* **67** L12
Ellsworth *Kans., U.S.A.* **112** F4
Ellsworth *Maine, U.S.A.* **113** C19
Ellsworth Land *Antarctica* **5** D16
Ellsworth Mts. *Antarctica* **5** D16
Ellwangen *Germany* **25** G6
Ellwood City *U.S.A.* **114** F4
Elm *Switz.* **25** J5
Elm-Lappwald △ *Germany* **24** C6
Elma *Canada* **103** D9
Elma *U.S.A.* **110** D3
Elmadağ *Turkey* **72** C5
Elmalı *Turkey* **47** E11
Elmhurst *U.S.A.* **112** E10
Elmira *Canada* **114** C4
Elmira *U.S.A.* **114** D8

Elmira Heights *U.S.A.* **114** D8
Elmore *Australia* **95** F3
Elmshorn *Germany* **24** B5
Elmvale *Canada* **114** B5
Elne *France* **20** F6
Elora *Canada* **114** C4
Elos *Greece* **46** E4
Elounda *Greece* **49** D7
Eloy *U.S.A.* **109** K8
Éloyes *France* **19** D13
Elphin *Canada* **115** B8
Elrose *Canada* **103** C7
Elsdorf *Germany* **24** E2
Elsie *U.S.A.* **110** E3
Elsinore = Helsingør
  Denmark **11** H6
Elster → *Germany* **24** D7
Elsterwerda *Germany* **24** D9
Eltanin Fracture Zone
  System *S. Ocean* **5** B14
Eltham *N.Z.* **91** C5
Elton *Russia* **35** F8
Elton, Ozero *Russia* **35** F8
Eltville *Germany* **25** E4
Eluru *India* **67** L12
Elvas *Portugal* **37** G3
Elven *France* **18** E4
Elverum *Norway* **8** F14
Elvire → *Australia* **92** C4
Elvire, Mt. *Australia* **93** E2
Elvo → *Italy* **40** C5
Elwell, L. = Tiber Res.
  U.S.A. **108** B8
Elwood *Ind., U.S.A.* **113** E11
Elwood *Nebr., U.S.A.* **112** E4
Elx = Elche *Spain* **39** G4
Ely *U.K.* **15** E8
Ely *Minn., U.S.A.* **112** B8
Ely *Nev., U.S.A.* **108** G6
Elyria *U.S.A.* **114** E2
Elyros *Greece* **46** F5
Elz → *Germany* **25** G3
Emådalen *Sweden* **10** C8
Emāmrūd *Iran* **71** B7
Emån → *Sweden* **11** G10
Embarcación *Argentina* **126** A3
Embetsu *Japan* **54** B10
Embi *Kazakhstan* **52** E6
Embi → *Kazakhstan* **52** E6
Embonas *Greece* **49** C9
Embro *Canada* **114** C4
Embrun *France* **21** D10
Embu *Kenya* **86** C4
Emden *Germany* **24** B3
Emecik *Turkey* **47** E9
Emerald *Australia* **94** C4
Emerson *Canada* **103** D9
Emet *Turkey* **47** B11
Emi Koussi *Chad* **79** E9
Emília-Romagna □ *Italy* **40** D8
Emilius, Mte. *Italy* **40** C4
Eminabad *Pakistan* **68** C6
Emine, Nos *Bulgaria* **45** D11
Emirdağ *Turkey* **72** C4
Emissi, Tarso *Chad* **79** D9
Emlenton *U.S.A.* **114** E5
Emlichheim *Germany* **24** C2
Emmaboda *Sweden* **11** H9
Emmaus *S. Africa* **88** D4
Emmaus *U.S.A.* **115** F9
Emme → *Switz.* **25** H3
Emmeloord *Neths.* **17** B5
Emmen *Neths.* **17** B6
Emmen *Switz.* **25** H4
Emmendingen *Germany* **25** G3
Emmental *Switz.* **25** J3
Emmerich *Germany* **24** D2
Emmet *Australia* **94** C4
Emmetsburg *U.S.A.* **112** D6
Emmett *Idaho, U.S.A.* **108** E5
Emmett *Mich., U.S.A.* **114** D2
Emmonak *U.S.A.* **106** a
Emo *Canada* **103** D10
Emőd *Hungary* **28** C5
Emona *Bulgaria* **45** D11
Empalme *Mexico* **118** B2
Empangeni *S. Africa* **89** D5
Empedrado *Argentina* **126** B4
Emperor Seamount Chain
  Pac. Oc. **96** D9
Emperor Trough *Pac. Oc.* **96** C9
Empoli *Italy* **40** E7
Emporia *Kans., U.S.A.* **112** F5
Emporia *Va., U.S.A.* **113** G15
Emporium *U.S.A.* **114** E6
Empress *Canada* **103** C7
Empty Quarter = Rub' al
  Khālī *Si. Arabia* **75** D4
Ems → *Germany* **24** B3
Emsdale *Canada* **114** A5
Emsdetten *Germany* **24** C3
Emu *China* **57** C15
Emu Park *Australia* **94** C5
eMuziwezinto *S. Africa* **89** E5
'En 'Avrona *Israel* **74** F4
'En Boqeq *Israel* **74** D4
'En Gedi *Israel* **74** D4
En Nahud *Sudan* **81** E2

En Nofalab *Sudan* **81** D3
Ena *Japan* **55** G8
Enana *Namibia* **88** B2
Enånger *Sweden* **10** C11
Enard B. *U.K.* **13** C3
Enare = Inarijärvi *Finland* **8** B23
Enarotali *Indonesia* **63** E9
Encampment *U.S.A.* **108** F10
Encantadas, Serra *Brazil* **127** C5
Encarnación *Paraguay* **127** B4
Encarnación de Díaz
  Mexico **118** C4
Enchi *Ghana* **82** D4
Encinitas *U.S.A.* **111** M9
Encino *U.S.A.* **109** J11
Encounter B. *Australia* **95** F2
Encs *Hungary* **28** B6
Endako *Canada* **102** C3
Endau *Kenya* **86** C4
Endau Rompin △ *Malaysia* **65** L4
Ende *Indonesia* **63** F6
Endeavour Str. *Australia* **94** A3
Endelave *Denmark* **11** J4
Enderby *Canada* **102** C5
Enderby I. *Australia* **92** D2
Enderby Land *Antarctica* **5** C5
Enderlin *U.S.A.* **112** B5
Enderrocat, C. *Spain* **48** B9
Endicott *U.S.A.* **115** D8
Endwell *U.S.A.* **115** D8
Endyalgout I. *Australia* **92** B5
Eneabba *Australia* **93** E2
Enewetak Atoll *Marshall Is.* **96** F8
Enez *Turkey* **45** F10
Enfer, Pte. d' *Martinique* **120** c
Enfield *Canada* **105** D7
Enfield *Conn., U.S.A.* **115** E12
Enfield *N.C., U.S.A.* **117** C16
Enfield *N.H., U.S.A.* **115** C12
Engadin *Switz.* **25** J6
Engaño, C. *Dom. Rep.* **121** C6
Engaño, C. *Phil.* **63** A6
Engaru *Japan* **54** B11
Engcobo = Ngcobo *S. Africa* **89** E4
Engelberg *Switz.* **25** J4
Engels *Russia* **34** E8
Engemann L. *Canada* **103** B7
Engershatu *Eritrea* **81** D4
Enggano *Indonesia* **62** F2
England *Canada* **116** D9
England □ *U.K.* **15** E5
Englee *Canada* **105** B8
Englehart *Canada* **104** C4
Englewood *U.S.A.* **108** G11
English → *Canada* **103** C10
English Bazar = Ingraj
  Bazar *India* **69** G13
English Channel *Europe* **15** G6
English Company's Is., The
  Australia **94** A2
English River *Canada* **104** C1
Engures ezers *Latvia* **30** A10
Enguri → *Georgia* **35** J5
Enid *U.S.A.* **116** C6
Enipeas → *Greece* **46** B4
Enkhuizen *Neths.* **17** B5
Enköping *Sweden* **10** E11
Enle *China* **58** F3
Enna *Italy* **43** E7
Ennadai L. *Canada* **103** A8
Ennedi *Chad* **79** E10
Enngonia *Australia* **95** D4
Ennigerloh *Germany* **24** D4
Ennis *Ireland* **12** D3
Ennis *Mont., U.S.A.* **108** D8
Ennis *Tex., U.S.A.* **116** E6
Enniscorthy *Ireland* **12** D5
Enniskillen *U.K.* **12** B4
Ennistimon *Ireland* **12** D2
Enns *Austria* **26** C7
Enns → *Austria* **26** C7
Eno *Finland* **8** E24
Enonkoski *Finland* **8** B20
Enosburg Falls *U.S.A.* **115** B12
Enping *China* **59** F9
Enschede *Neths.* **17** B6
Ensenada *Argentina* **126** C4
Ensenada *Mexico* **118** A1
Ensenada de los Muertos
  Mexico **118** C2
Enshi *China* **58** B7
Ensiola, Pta. de n' *Spain* **48** B9
Ensisheim *France* **19** E14
Entebbe *Uganda* **86** B3
Enterprise *Canada* **102** A5
Enterprise *Ala., U.S.A.* **117** F12
Enterprise *Oreg., U.S.A.* **108** D5
Entorno de Doñana △ *Spain* **37** J4
Entraygues-sur-Truyère
  France **20** D6
Entre Ríos *Bolivia* **126** A3
Entre Ríos □ *Argentina* **126** C4
Entrepeñas, Embalse de
  Spain **38** E2
Entroncamento *Portugal* **37** F2

Enugu *Nigeria* **83** D6
Enugu □ *Nigeria* **83** D6
Enugu Ezike *Nigeria* **83** D6
Enumclaw *U.S.A.* **110** C5
Envalira, Port d' *Europe* **38** C6
Envermeu *France* **18** C8
Enviken *Sweden* **10** D9
Enying *Hungary* **28** D3
Enza → *Italy* **40** D7
Éolie, Ís. *Italy* **43** D7
Epanomi *Greece* **44** F6
Epe *Neths.* **17** B5
Epe *Nigeria* **83** D5
Épernay *France* **19** C10
Épernon *France* **19** D8
Ephesus *Turkey* **47** D9
Ephraim *U.S.A.* **108** G8
Ephrata *Pa., U.S.A.* **115** F8
Ephrata *Wash., U.S.A.* **108** C4
Epidavros Limira *Greece* **46** E5
Épila *Spain* **38** D3
Épinac *France* **19** F11
Épinal *France* **19** D13
Epiros □ *Greece* **46** B2
Episkopi *Cyprus* **49** E11
Episkopi *Greece* **49** D6
Episkopi Bay *Cyprus* **49** E11
Epitalio *Greece* **46** D3
Eppan = Appiano *Italy* **41** B8
Eppingen *Germany* **25** F4
Epsom *U.K.* **15** F7
Epukiro *Namibia* **88** C2
Equatoria = El Istiwa'iya
  Sudan **79** G11
Equatorial Guinea ■ *Africa* **84** D1
Er Hai *China* **58** E3
Er Rachidia *Morocco* **78** B5
Er Rahad *Sudan* **81** E3
Er Rif *Morocco* **78** A5
Er Rogel *Sudan* **80** D4
Er Roseires *Sudan* **81** E3
Er Rua'at *Sudan* **81** E3
Eraclea *Italy* **41** C9
Erāwadī Myit =
  Irrawaddy → *Burma* **67** M19
Erāwadī Myitwanya =
  Irrawaddy, Mouths of
  the *Burma* **67** M19
Erawan △ *Thailand* **64** E2
Erba *Italy* **40** C6
Erba *Sudan* **80** D4
Erba, J. *Sudan* **80** C4
Erbaa *Turkey* **72** B7
Erbeskopf *Germany* **25** F3
Erbil = Arbīl *Iraq* **73** D11
Erbu *Ethiopia* **81** F5
Erçek *Turkey* **70** B4
Erçiş *Turkey* **73** C10
Erçiyaş Dağı *Turkey* **70** B2
Érd *Hungary* **28** C3
Erdao Jiang → *China* **57** C14
Erdek *Turkey* **45** F11
Erdemli *Turkey* **72** D6
Erdene = Ulaan-Uul
  Mongolia **56** B5
Erdenetsogt *Mongolia* **56** C4
Erding *Germany* **25** G7
Erdre → *France* **18** E5
Erebus, Mt. *Antarctica* **5** D11
Erechim *Brazil* **127** B5
Ereğli *Konya, Turkey* **72** D6
Ereğli *Zonguldak, Turkey* **72** B4
Erei, Monti *Italy* **43** E7
Erenhot *China* **56** C7
Eresma → *Spain* **36** D6
Eresos *Greece* **47** B7
Erfelek *Turkey* **72** B6
Erfenisdam *S. Africa* **88** D4
Erfstadt *Germany* **24** E2
Erft → *Germany* **24** D2
Erfurt *Germany* **24** E7
Ergani *Turkey* **73** C8
Ergel *Mongolia* **56** C5
Ergene → *Turkey* **45** E10
Ergeni Vozvyshennost
  Russia **35** G7
Ergli *Latvia* **32** D3
Erhlin *Taiwan* **59** F13
Eria → *Spain* **36** C5
Eriba *Sudan* **81** D4
Eriboll, L. *U.K.* **13** C4
Érice *Italy* **42** D5
Erie *U.S.A.* **114** D4
Erie, L. *N. Amer.* **114** D4
Erie Canal *U.S.A.* **114** C7
Erieau *Canada* **114** D3
Erikoussa *Greece* **49** A3
Eriksdale *Canada* **103** C9
Erimanthos *Greece* **46** D3
Erimo-misaki *Japan* **54** D11
Erin *Canada* **114** C4
Erin Pt. *Trin. & Tob.* **125** K15
Erinpura *India* **68** G5
Eriskay *U.K.* **13** D1
Erithres *Greece* **46** C5
Eritrea ■ *Africa* **81** E4
Erjas → *Portugal* **36** F3
Erkelenz *Germany* **24** D2
Erkner *Germany* **24** C9

Erlangen *Germany* **25** F6
Erldunda *Australia* **94** D1
Ermelo *Neths.* **17** B5
Ermelo *S. Africa* **89** D4
Ermenek *Turkey* **72** D5
Ermil *Sudan* **81** E2
Ermioni *Greece* **46** D5
Ermones *Greece* **49** A3
Ernakulam *India* **66** Q10
Erne → *Ireland* **12** B3
Erne, Lower L. *U.K.* **12** B4
Erne, Upper L. *U.K.* **12** B4
Ernée *France* **18** D6
Ernest Giles Ra. *Australia* **93** E3
Ernstberg *Germany* **25** E2
Erode *India* **66** P10
Eromanga *Australia* **95** D3
Erongo *Namibia* **88** C2
Erquy *France* **18** D4
Erramala Hills *India* **66** M11
Errenteria *Spain* **38** B3
Errer → *Ethiopia* **81** F5
Erri-Nundra △ *Australia* **95** F4
Errigal *Ireland* **12** A3
Erris Hd. *Ireland* **12** B1
Ersekë *Albania* **44** F4
Erskine *U.S.A.* **112** B6
Erstein *France* **19** D14
Ertholmene *Denmark* **11** J9
Ertil *Russia* **34** E5
Ertis = Irtysh → *Russia* **52** C7
Ervy-le-Châtel *France* **19** D10
Erwin *U.S.A.* **117** C13
Eryuan *China* **58** D2
Erzgebirge *Germany* **24** E8
Erzin *Russia* **53** D10
Erzincan *Turkey* **73** C8
Erzincan □ *Turkey* **73** C8
Erzurum *Turkey* **73** C9
Erzurum □ *Turkey* **73** C9
Es Caló *Spain* **48** C8
Es Canar *Spain* **48** B8
Es Mercadal *Spain* **48** B11
Es Migjorn Gran *Spain* **48** B11
Es Safiya *Sudan* **81** E2
Es Sahrâ' Esh Sharqîya
  Egypt **80** B3
Es Sînâ' *Egypt* **74** F3
Es Sûkî *Sudan* **81** E3
Es Vedrà *Spain* **48** C7
Esambo *Dem. Rep. of the Congo* **86** C1
Esan-Misaki *Japan* **54** D10
Esashi *Hokkaidō, Japan* **54** B11
Esashi *Hokkaidō, Japan* **54** D10
Esbjerg *Denmark* **11** J2
Esbo = Espoo *Finland* **32** B3
Esch-sur-Alzette *Lux.* **17** E6
Eschede *Germany* **24** C6
Eschwege *Germany* **24** D6
Eschweiler *Germany* **24** E2
Escondido *U.S.A.* **111** M9
Escravos → *Nigeria* **83** D6
Escuinapa de Hidalgo
  Mexico **118** C3
Escuintla *Guatemala* **120** D1
Eséka *Cameroon* **83** E7
Eşen → *Turkey* **47** E11
Esenguly *Turkmenistan* **52** F6
Esens *Germany* **24** B3
Esenyurt *Turkey* **45** E12
Esera → *Spain* **38** C5
Eşfahān *Iran* **71** C6
Eşfahān □ *Iran* **71** C6
Esfarāyen *Iran* **71** B8
Esfideh *Iran* **71** C8
Esgueva → *Spain* **36** D6
Esh Sham = Dimashq *Syria* **74** B5
Esh Shamâlîya □ *Sudan* **80** D2
Esha Ness *U.K.* **13** A7
Eshan *China* **58** E4
Esher *U.K.* **15** F7
Eshkol △ *Israel* **74** D3
Eshowe *S. Africa* **89** D5
Esiama *Ghana* **82** E4
Esigodini *Zimbabwe* **89** C4
Esil = Ishim → *Russia* **52** D8
Esino → *Italy* **41** E10
Esira *Madag.* **89** C8
Esk → *Dumf. & Gall., U.K.* **13** G5
Esk → *N. Yorks., U.K.* **14** C7
Eskān *Iran* **71** E9
Esker Siding *Canada* **105** B6
Eskifjörður *Iceland* **8** D7
Eskilsäter *Sweden* **11** F6
Eskilstuna *Sweden* **10** E10
Eskimalatya *Turkey* **73** C8
Eskimo Point = Arviat
  Canada **103** A10
Eskişehir *Turkey* **47** B12
Eskişehir □ *Turkey* **47** B12
Esla → *Spain* **36** D5
Eslāmābād-e Gharb *Iran* **73** E12

Eslämshahr *Iran* **71** C6
Eslöv *Sweden* **11** J7
Eşme *Turkey* **47** C10
Esmeraldas *Ecuador* **124** C3
Esna = Isna *Egypt* **80** B3
Esnagi L. *Canada* **104** C3
Espalion *France* **20** D6
España = Spain ■ *Europe* **7** H5
Espanola *Canada* **104** C3
Espanola *U.S.A.* **109** J10
Esparreguera *Spain* **38** D6
Esparza *Costa Rica* **120** E3
Espelkamp *Germany* **24** C4
Esperance *Australia* **93** F3
Esperance B. *Australia* **93** F3
Esperance Harbour *St. Lucia* **121** f
Esperanza *Antarctica* **5** C18
Esperanza *Argentina* **126** C3
Esperanza *Phil.* **61** G6
Esperanza *Puerto Rico* **121** d
Espéraza *France* **20** F6
Espichel, C. *Portugal* **37** G1
Espiel *Spain* **37** G5
Espigão, Serra do *Brazil* **127** B5
Espinazo, Sierra del =
  Espinhaço, Serra do
  Brazil **125** G10
Espinhaço, Serra do *Brazil* **125** G10
Espinho *Portugal* **36** D2
Espinilho, Serra do *Brazil* **127** B5
Espinosa de los Monteros
  Spain **36** B7
Espírito Santo □ *Brazil* **125** H10
Espíritu Santo *Vanuatu* **90** C9
Espíritu Santo, B. del
  Mexico **119** D7
Espíritu Santo, I. *Mexico* **118** C2
Espita *Mexico* **119** C7
Espiye *Turkey* **73** B8
Espoo *Finland* **32** B3
Espuña, Sierra de *Spain* **39** H3
Espungabera *Mozam.* **89** C5
Esquel *Argentina* **128** E2
Esquimalt *Canada* **110** B3
Esquina *Argentina* **126** C4
Essaouira *Morocco* **78** B4
Essebie *Dem. Rep. of the Congo* **86** B3
Essen *Belgium* **17** C4
Essen *Germany* **24** D3
Essendon, Mt. *Australia* **93** E3
Essequibo → *Guyana* **124** B7
Essex *Canada* **114** D2
Essex *Calif., U.S.A.* **111** L11
Essex *N.Y., U.S.A.* **115** B11
Essex □ *U.K.* **15** F8
Essex Junction *U.S.A.* **115** B11
Esslingen *Germany* **25** G5
Essonne □ *France* **19** D9
Estaca de Bares, C. de *Spain* **36** B3
Estación Camacho *Mexico* **118** C4
Estación Simón *Mexico* **118** C4
Estadilla *Spain* **38** C5
Estados, I. de Los *Argentina* **128** G4
Estagel *France* **20** F6
Eştahbānāt *Iran* **71** D7
Estância *Brazil* **125** F11
Estancia *U.S.A.* **109** J10
Estārm *Iran* **71** D8
Estarreja *Portugal* **36** E2
Estats, Pic d' *Spain* **38** C6
Estcourt *S. Africa* **89** D4
Este *Italy* **41** C8
Este △ *Dom. Rep.* **121** C6
Estelí *Nic.* **120** D2
Estella *Spain* **38** C2
Estellencs *Spain* **48** B9
Estena → *Spain* **37** F6
Estepa *Spain* **37** H6
Estepona *Spain* **37** J5
Esterhazy *Canada* **103** C8
Esternay *France* **19** D10
Esterri d'Aneu *Spain* **38** C6
Estevan *Canada* **103** D8
Estevan Group *Canada* **102** C2
Estherville *U.S.A.* **112** D6
Estissac *France* **19** D10
Eston *Canada* **103** C7
Estonia ■ *Europe* **32** C3
Estoril *Portugal* **37** G1
Estouk *Mali* **83** B5
Estrela, Serra da *Portugal* **36** E3
Estrella *Spain* **37** G7
Estremadura *Portugal* **36** F1
Estremoz *Portugal* **37** G3
Estrondo, Serra do *Brazil* **125** E9
Esztergom *Hungary* **28** C3
Et Tîdra *Mauritania* **82** B1
Etah *India* **69** F8
Étain *France* **19** C12
Étampes *France* **19** D9
Etanga *Namibia* **88** B2
Étaples *France* **19** B8
Etawah *India* **69** F8
Etawney L. *Canada* **103** B9
Etchojoa *Mexico* **118** B3
Ete *Nigeria* **83** D6
eThekwini = Durban
  S. Africa **89** D5
Ethel *U.S.A.* **110** D4

Ethelbert *Canada* 103 C8
Ethiopia ■ *Africa* 75 F3
Ethiopian Highlands *Ethiopia* 75 F2
Etili *Turkey* 45 G10
Etive, L. *U.K.* 13 E3
Etna *Italy* 43 E7
Etoile *Dem. Rep. of the Congo* 87 E2
Etoliko *Greece* 46 C3
Etoloakarnania □ *Greece* 46 C3
Etosha △ *Namibia* 88 B2
Etosha Pan *Namibia* 88 B2
Etowah *U.S.A.* 117 D12
Étréchy *France* 19 D9
Etrek *Turkmenistan* 71 B7
Étrépagny *France* 19 C8
Étretat *France* 18 C7
Etropole *Bulgaria* 45 D8
Ettelbruck *Lux.* 17 E6
Ettlingen *Germany* 25 G4
Ettrick Water → *U.K.* 13 F6
Etuku *Dem. Rep. of the Congo* 86 C2
Etulia *Moldova* 29 E13
Etzná-Tixmucuy = Edzná
  Mexico 119 D6
Eu *France* 18 B8
Eua *Tonga* 91 c
Euboea = Evia *Greece* 46 C6
Eucla *Australia* 93 F4
Euclid *U.S.A.* 114 E3
Eucumbene, L. *Australia* 95 F4
Eudora *U.S.A.* 116 E9
Eufaula *Ala., U.S.A.* 117 F12
Eufaula *Okla., U.S.A.* 116 D7
Eufaula L. *U.S.A.* 116 D7
Eugene *U.S.A.* 108 D2
Eugowra *Australia* 95 E4
Eulo *Australia* 95 D4
Eungella △ *Australia* 94 C4
Eunice *La., U.S.A.* 116 F8
Eunice *N. Mex., U.S.A.* 109 K12
Eupen *Belgium* 17 D6
Euphrates = Furāt, Nahr
  al → *Asia* 70 D5
Eure □ *France* 18 C8
Eure → *France* 18 C8
Eure-et-Loir □ *France* 18 D8
Eureka *Canada* 101 B11
Eureka *Calif., U.S.A.* 108 F1
Eureka *Kans., U.S.A.* 112 G5
Eureka *Mont., U.S.A.* 108 B6
Eureka *Nev., U.S.A.* 108 G6
Eureka *S. Dak., U.S.A.* 112 C4
Eureka, Mt. *Australia* 93 E3
Euroa *Australia* 95 F4
Europa, Île *Ind. Oc.* 85 J8
Europa, Picos de *Spain* 36 B6
Europa, Pt. *Gib.* 37 J5
Europe 6 E10
Europoort *Neths.* 17 C4
Euskirchen *Germany* 24 E2
Eustis *U.S.A.* 117 G14
Eutin *Germany* 24 A6
Eutsuk L. *Canada* 102 C3
Evale *Angola* 88 B2
Evans *U.S.A.* 108 F11
Evans, L. *Canada* 104 B4
Evans City *U.S.A.* 114 F4
Evans Head *Australia* 95 D5
Evansburg *Canada* 102 C5
Evanston *Ill., U.S.A.* 112 D10
Evanston *Wyo., U.S.A.* 108 F8
Evansville *U.S.A.* 112 G10
Évaux-les-Bains *France* 19 F9
Evaz *Iran* 71 E7
Evciler *Afyon, Turkey* 47 C11
Evciler *Çanakkale, Turkey* 47 B8
Eveleth *U.S.A.* 112 B7
Evensk *Russia* 53 C16
Everard, L. *Australia* 95 E2
Everard Ranges *Australia* 93 E5
Everest, Mt. *Nepal* 69 E12
Everett *Pa., U.S.A.* 114 F6
Everett *Wash., U.S.A.* 110 C4
Everglades, The *U.S.A.* 117 J14
Everglades △ *U.S.A.* 117 J14
Everglades City *U.S.A.* 117 J14
Evergreen *Ala., U.S.A.* 117 F11
Evergreen *Mont., U.S.A.* 108 B6
Everöd *Sweden* 11 J8
Evertsberg *Sweden* 10 C7
Evesham *U.K.* 15 E6
Evia *Greece* 46 C6
Evia □ *Greece* 46 C5
Évian-les-Bains *France* 19 F13
Evinos → *Greece* 46 C3
Évisa *France* 21 F12
Evje *Norway* 9 G12
Évora *Portugal* 37 G3
Évora □ *Portugal* 37 G3
Évreux *France* 18 C8
Evritania □ *Greece* 46 B3
Évron *France* 18 D6
Evros □ *Greece* 45 E10
Evros → *Greece* 72 B2
Evrotas → *Greece* 46 E4
Évry *France* 19 D9
Évvoia = Evia *Greece* 46 C6
Ewe, L. *U.K.* 13 D3

Ewing *U.S.A.* 112 D4
Ewo *Congo* 84 E2
Exaltación *Bolivia* 124 F5
Excelsior Springs *U.S.A.* 112 F6
Excideuil *France* 20 C5
Exe → *U.K.* 15 G4
Exeter *Canada* 114 C3
Exeter *U.K.* 15 G4
Exeter *Calif., U.S.A.* 110 J7
Exeter *N.H., U.S.A.* 115 D14
Exmoor *U.K.* 15 F4
Exmoor △ *U.K.* 15 F4
Exmouth *Australia* 92 D1
Exmouth *U.K.* 15 G4
Exmouth G. *Australia* 92 D1
Exmouth Plateau *Ind. Oc.* 96 J3
Expedition △ *Australia* 95 D4
Expedition Ra. *Australia* 94 C4
Extremadura □ *Spain* 37 F4
Exuma Sound *Bahamas* 120 B4
Eyasi, L. *Tanzania* 86 C4
Eye Pen. *U.K.* 13 C2
Eyemouth *U.K.* 13 F6
Eygues = Aigues → *France* 21 D8
Eygurande *France* 19 G9
Eyjafjörður *Iceland* 8 C4
Eyl *Somali Rep.* 75 F4
Eymet *France* 20 D4
Eymoutiers *France* 20 C5
Eynesil *Turkey* 73 B8
Eyre (North), L. *Australia* 95 D2
Eyre (South), L. *Australia* 95 D2
Eyre, L. *Australia* 90 D6
Eyre Mts. *N.Z.* 91 F2
Eyre Pen. *Australia* 95 E2
Eysturoy *Færoe Is.* 8 E9
Eyvān *Iran* 73 F12
Eyvānkī *Iran* 71 C6
Ez Zeidab *Sudan* 80 D3
Ezcaray *Spain* 38 C1
Eżerėlis *Lithuania* 30 D10
Ezhou *China* 59 B10
Ezine *Turkey* 47 B8
Ezouza → *Cyprus* 49 E11

F

F.Y.R.O.M. =
  Macedonia ■ *Europe* 44 E5
Faaa *Tahiti* 91 d
Faaborg *Denmark* 11 J4
Faaone *Tahiti* 91 d
Fabala *Guinea* 82 D3
Fabens *U.S.A.* 116 F1
Fabero *Spain* 36 C4
Fabius *U.S.A.* 115 D9
Fabriano *Italy* 41 E9
Făcăeni *Romania* 29 F12
Fachi *Niger* 79 E8
Fada *Chad* 79 E10
Fada-n-Gourma *Burkina Faso* 83 C5
Fadd *Hungary* 28 D3
Faddeyevskiy, Ostrov
  Russia 53 B15
Faddor *Sudan* 81 F3
Fadghāmī *Syria* 73 E9
Fadlab *Sudan* 80 D3
Faenza *Italy* 41 D8
Færoe Is. = Føroyar ☑ *Atl. Oc.* 8 F9
Fafa *Mali* 83 B5
Fafe *Portugal* 36 D2
Fagam *Nigeria* 83 C7
Făgăraș *Romania* 29 E9
Făgăraș, Munții *Romania* 29 E9
Fågelmara *Sweden* 11 H9
Fagerhult *Sweden* 11 G9
Fagersta *Sweden* 10 D9
Făget *Romania* 28 E7
Făget, Munții *Romania* 29 C8
Fagnano, L. *Argentina* 128 G3
Fagnières *France* 19 D11
Faguibine, L. *Mali* 82 B4
Fahliān *Iran* 71 D6
Fahraj *Kermān, Iran* 71 D8
Fahraj *Yazd, Iran* 71 D7
Fai Tsi Long *Vietnam* 58 G6
Faial *Azores* 78 a
Faial *Madeira* 48 D3
Faichan Kangri *India* 69 B7
Fair Haven *N.Y., U.S.A.* 115 C8
Fair Haven *Vt., U.S.A.* 113 D17
Fair Hd. *U.K.* 12 A5
Fair Isle *U.K.* 16 B6
Fair Oaks *U.S.A.* 110 G5
Fairbanks *U.S.A.* 100 C5
Fairbury *U.S.A.* 112 E5
Fairfax *U.S.A.* 115 B11
Fairfield *Ala., U.S.A.* 117 E11
Fairfield *Calif., U.S.A.* 110 G4
Fairfield *Conn., U.S.A.* 115 E11
Fairfield *Idaho, U.S.A.* 108 E6
Fairfield *Ill., U.S.A.* 112 F9
Fairfield *Iowa, U.S.A.* 112 E8
Fairfield *Tex., U.S.A.* 116 F6
Fairford *Canada* 103 C9
Fairhope *U.S.A.* 117 F11
Fairlie *N.Z.* 91 F3
Fairmead *U.S.A.* 110 H6
Fairmont *Minn., U.S.A.* 112 D6

Fairmont *W. Va., U.S.A.* 113 F13
Fairmount *Calif., U.S.A.* 111 L8
Fairmount *N.Y., U.S.A.* 115 C8
Fairplay *U.S.A.* 108 G10
Fairport *U.S.A.* 114 C7
Fairport Harbor *U.S.A.* 114 E3
Fairview *Canada* 102 B5
Fairview *Mont., U.S.A.* 108 C11
Fairview *Okla., U.S.A.* 116 C5
Fairweather, Mt. *U.S.A.* 102 B1
Faisalabad *Pakistan* 68 D5
Faith *U.S.A.* 112 C2
Faizabad *India* 69 F10
Fajardo *Puerto Rico* 121 d
Fajr, W. → *Si. Arabia* 70 D3
Fakenham *U.K.* 14 E8
Faker *Sweden* 10 A8
Fakfak *Indonesia* 63 E8
Fakiya *Bulgaria* 45 D11
Fakobli *Ivory C.* 82 D3
Fakse *Denmark* 11 J6
Fakse Bugt *Denmark* 11 J6
Fakse Ladeplads *Denmark* 11 J6
Faku *China* 57 C12
Falaba *S. Leone* 82 D2
Falaise *France* 18 D6
Falaise, Mui *Vietnam* 64 C5
Falakro Oros *Greece* 44 E7
Falam *Burma* 67 H18
Falces *Spain* 38 C3
Fălciu *Romania* 29 D13
Falcó, C. des *Spain* 48 C7
Falcón, Presa *Mexico* 119 B5
Falcon Lake *Canada* 103 D10
Falcón Res. *U.S.A.* 116 H5
Falconara Maríttima *Italy* 41 E10
Falcone, C. del *Italy* 42 B1
Falconer *U.S.A.* 114 D5
Faléa *Mali* 82 C2
Falefa *Samoa* 91 b
Falelatai *Samoa* 91 b
Falelima *Samoa* 91 b
Falémé → *Senegal* 82 C2
Falerum *Sweden* 11 F10
Fălești *Moldova* 29 C12
Falfurrias *U.S.A.* 116 H5
Falher *Canada* 102 B5
Faliraki *Greece* 49 C10
Falkenberg *Germany* 24 D9
Falkenberg *Sweden* 11 H6
Falkensee *Germany* 24 C9
Falkirk *U.K.* 13 F5
Falkirk □ *U.K.* 13 F5
Falkland *U.K.* 13 E5
Falkland Is. ☑ *Atl. Oc.* 128 G5
Falkland Sd. *Falk. Is.* 128 G5
Falkonera *Greece* 46 E5
Falköping *Sweden* 11 F7
Fall River *U.S.A.* 115 E13
Fallbrook *U.S.A.* 111 M9
Fallon *U.S.A.* 108 G4
Falls City *U.S.A.* 112 E6
Falls Creek *U.S.A.* 114 E6
Falmouth *Jamaica* 120 a
Falmouth *U.K.* 15 G2
Falmouth *U.S.A.* 115 E14
Falsa, Pta. *Mexico* 118 B1
False B. *S. Africa* 88 E2
False, C. *Honduras* 120 C3
Falster *Denmark* 11 K5
Falsterbo *Sweden* 9 J15
Fălticeni *Romania* 29 C11
Falun *Sweden* 10 D9
Famagusta *Cyprus* 49 D12
Famagusta Bay *Cyprus* 49 D13
Famatina, Sierra de
  Argentina 126 B2
Famenin *Iran* 73 E13
Family L. *Canada* 103 C9
Famoso *U.S.A.* 111 K7
Fan Xian *China* 56 G8
Fana *Mali* 82 C3
Fanad Hd. *Ireland* 12 A4
Fanari *Greece* 46 B3
Fandriana *Madag.* 89 C8
Fánes-Sénnes e Braies △
  Italy 41 B9
Fang *Thailand* 58 H2
Fang Xian *China* 59 A8
Fangaga *Sudan* 80 D4
Fangak *Sudan* 81 F3
Fangchang *China* 59 B12
Fangcheng *China* 56 H7
Fangchenggang *China* 58 G7
Fangliao *Taiwan* 59 F13
Fangshan *China* 56 E6
Fangzi *China* 57 F10
Fani i Madh → *Albania* 44 E4
Fanjakana *Madag.* 89 C8
Fanjiatun *China* 57 C13
Fannich, L. *U.K.* 13 D4
Fannūj *Iran* 71 E8
Fano *Denmark* 11 J2
Fano *Italy* 41 E10
Fanshi *China* 56 E7
Fao = Al Fāw *Iraq* 71 D6
Faqirwali *Pakistan* 68 E5
Fâqûs *Egypt* 80 H7

Far East =
  Dalnevostochnyy □
  Russia 53 C14
Far East *Asia* 50 E14
Fara in Sabina *Italy* 41 F9
Faradje *Dem. Rep. of the Congo* 86 B2
Farafangana *Madag.* 89 C8
Farâfra, El Wâhât el- *Egypt* 80 B2
Farāh *Afghan.* 66 C3
Farāh □ *Afghan.* 66 C3
Farahalana *Madag.* 89 A9
Faraid, Gebel *Egypt* 80 C4
Farako *Ivory C.* 82 D4
Faramana *Burkina Faso* 82 C4
Faranah *Guinea* 82 C2
Farasān, Jazā'ir *Si. Arabia* 75 D3
Farasan Is. = Farasān,
  Jazā'ir *Si. Arabia* 75 D3
Faratsiho *Madag.* 89 B8
Fardes → *Spain* 37 H7
Fareham *U.K.* 15 G6
Farewell, C. *N.Z.* 91 D4
Farewell, C. = Nunap Isua
  Greenland 98 D15
Färgelanda *Sweden* 11 F5
Farghona *Uzbekistan* 52 E8
Fargo *U.S.A.* 112 B5
Fār'iah, W. al → *West Bank* 74 C4
Faribault *U.S.A.* 112 C7
Faridabad *India* 68 E6
Faridkot *India* 68 D6
Faridpur *Bangla.* 69 H13
Faridpur *India* 69 E8
Färila *Sweden* 10 C9
Farim *Guinea-Biss.* 82 C1
Farīmān *Iran* 71 C8
Farina *Australia* 95 E2
Fariones, Pta. *Canary Is.* 48 E6
Farmakonisi *Greece* 47 D9
Farmerville *U.S.A.* 116 E8
Farmingdale *U.S.A.* 115 F10
Farmington *Canada* 102 B4
Farmington *Calif., U.S.A.* 110 H6
Farmington *Maine, U.S.A.* 113 C18
Farmington *Mo., U.S.A.* 112 G8
Farmington *N.H., U.S.A.* 115 C13
Farmington *N. Mex., U.S.A.* 109 H9
Farmington *Utah, U.S.A.* 108 F8
Farmington → *U.S.A.* 115 E12
Farmville *U.S.A.* 113 G14
Färnäs *Sweden* 10 D8
Farne Is. *U.K.* 14 B6
Färnebofjärden △ *Sweden* 10 D10
Farnham *Canada* 115 A12
Farnham, Mt. *Canada* 102 C5
Faro *Brazil* 125 D7
Faro *Canada* 100 C6
Faro *Portugal* 37 H3
Fårö *Sweden* 9 H18
Faro □ *Portugal* 37 H2
Faro ✈ (FAO) *Portugal* 37 H3
Fårösund *Sweden* 11 G13
Farquhar, C. *Australia* 93 D1
Farrars Cr. → *Australia* 94 D3
Farrāshband *Iran* 71 D7
Farrell *U.S.A.* 114 E4
Farrokhī *Iran* 71 C8
Farruch, C. = Ferrutx, C.
  de *Spain* 48 B10
Farrukhabad *India* 69 F8
Fārs □ *Iran* 71 D7
Fārsī *Iran* 71 E6
Farsala *Greece* 46 B4
Farson *U.S.A.* 108 E9
Farsø *Denmark* 11 H3
Fartak, Rås *Si. Arabia* 70 D2
Fartak, Ra's *Yemen* 75 D5
Fârțănești *Romania* 29 E12
Fartura, Serra da *Brazil* 127 B5
Faru *Nigeria* 83 C6
Fārūj *Iran* 71 B8
Farvel, Kap = Nunap Isua
  Greenland 98 D15
Farwell *U.S.A.* 116 D3
Fāryāb □ *Afghan.* 66 B4
Fasā *Iran* 71 D7
Fasano *Italy* 43 B10
Fashoda *Sudan* 81 F3
Fassa *Mali* 82 B3
Fastiv *Ukraine* 23 C15
Fastov = Fastiv *Ukraine* 23 C15
Fatagar, Tanjung *Indonesia* 63 E8
Fatehabad *Haryana, India* 68 E6
Fatehabad *Ut. P., India* 68 F8
Fatehgarh *India* 69 F8
Fatehpur *Bihar, India* 69 G11
Fatehpur *Raj., India* 68 F6
Fatehpur *Ut. P., India* 69 F9
Fatehpur *Ut. P., India* 69 G9
Fatehpur Sikri *India* 68 F6
Fatesh *Russia* 33 F8
Fathai *Sudan* 81 F3

Fathom Five △ *Canada* 114 A3
Fatick *Senegal* 82 C1
Fatick □ *Senegal* 82 C1
Fatima *Canada* 105 C7
Fátima *Portugal* 37 F2
Fatoya *Guinea* 82 C3
Fatsa *Turkey* 72 B7
Faucille, Col de la *France* 19 F13
Faulkton *U.S.A.* 112 C4
Faulquemont *France* 19 C13
Faure I. *Australia* 93 E1
Făurei *Romania* 29 E12
Fauresmith *S. Africa* 88 D4
Fauske *Norway* 8 C16
Favara *Italy* 42 E6
Faváritx, C. de *Spain* 48 B11
Faverges *France* 21 C10
Favignana *Italy* 42 E5
Favignana, I. *Italy* 42 E5
Fawcett, Pt. *Australia* 92 B5
Fawn → *Canada* 104 A2
Fawnskin *U.S.A.* 111 L10
Faxaflói *Iceland* 8 D2
Faxälven → *Sweden* 10 A10
Faya-Largeau *Chad* 79 E9
Fayd *Si. Arabia* 70 E4
Fayence *France* 21 E10
Fayette *Ala., U.S.A.* 117 E11
Fayette *Mo., U.S.A.* 112 F7
Fayette *N.Y., U.S.A.* 115 D8
Fayetteville *Ark., U.S.A.* 116 C7
Fayetteville *N.C., U.S.A.* 117 D15
Fayetteville *N.Y., U.S.A.* 115 C9
Fayetteville *Tenn., U.S.A.* 117 D11
Fayied *Egypt* 80 H8
Fayón *Spain* 38 D5
Faylakah *Kuwait* 71 D6
Fazao-Malfakassa △ *Togo* 83 D5
Fazilka *India* 68 D6
Fazilpur *Pakistan* 68 E4
Fdérik *Mauritania* 78 D3
Feakle *Ireland* 12 D3
Feale → *Ireland* 12 D2
Fear, C. *U.S.A.* 117 E16
Feather → *U.S.A.* 108 G3
Feather Falls *U.S.A.* 110 F5
Featherston *N.Z.* 91 D5
Featherstone *Zimbabwe* 87 F3
Fécamp *France* 18 C7
Fedala = Mohammedia
  Morocco 78 B4
Federación *Argentina* 126 C4
Féderal *Argentina* 128 C5
Federal Capital Terr. □
  Nigeria 83 D6
Federal Way *U.S.A.* 110 C4
Fedeshkūh *Iran* 71 D7
Fehérgyarmat *Hungary* 28 C7
Fehmarn *Germany* 24 A7
Fehmarn Bælt = Fehmarn
  Bælt *Europe* 11 K5
Fehmarn Belt = Fehmarn
  Bælt *Europe* 11 K5
Fei Xian *China* 57 G9
Feijó *Brazil* 124 E4
Feilding *N.Z.* 91 D5
Feira de Santana *Brazil* 125 F11
Feixi *China* 59 B11
Feixiang *China* 56 F8
Fejér □ *Hungary* 28 C3
Fejø *Denmark* 11 K5
Feke *Turkey* 72 D6
Fekete → *Hungary* 28 E3
Felanitx *Spain* 48 B10
Feldbach *India* 69 F8
Feldberg
  *Mecklenburg-Vorpommern,
  Germany* 24 B9
Feldberg
  Baden-W., Germany 25 H3
Feldkirch *Austria* 26 D2
Feldkirchen *Austria* 26 E7
Félicité *Seychelles* 85 b
Felipe Carrillo Puerto
  Mexico 119 D7
Felixburg *Zimbabwe* 89 B5
Felixstowe *U.K.* 15 F9
Felletin *France* 20 C6
Fellingsbro *Sweden* 10 E9
Felton *U.S.A.* 110 H4
Feltre *Italy* 41 B8
Femer Bælt = Fehmarn
  Bælt *Europe* 11 K5
Femo *Denmark* 11 K5
Femunden *Norway* 8 E14
Fen He → *China* 56 G6
Fene *Spain* 36 B2
Fenelon Falls *Canada* 114 B6
Fener Burnu *Turkey* 47 E9
Feneroa *Ethiopia* 81 E4
Feng Xian *Jiangsu, China* 56 G9
Feng Xian *Shaanxi, China* 56 H4
Fengari *Greece* 45 F9
Fengcheng *Jiangxi, China* 59 C10
Fengcheng *Liaoning, China* 57 D13
Fengfeng *China* 56 F8
Fenggang *China* 58 D6
Fenghua *China* 59 C13
Fenghuang *China* 58 D7
Fengkai *China* 59 F8
Fengkang *Taiwan* 59 F13

Fengle *China* 59 B9
Fenglin *Taiwan* 59 F13
Fengning *China* 56 D9
Fengqing *China* 58 E2
Fengqiu *China* 56 G8
Fengrun *China* 57 E10
Fengshan *Guangxi Zhuangzu,
  China* 58 E7
Fengshan *Guangxi Zhuangzu,
  China* 58 E6
Fengshan *Taiwan* 59 F13
Fengshun *China* 59 F11
Fengtai *Anhui, China* 59 A11
Fengtai *Beijing, China* 56 E9
Fengxian *China* 59 B13
Fengxiang *China* 56 G4
Fengxin *China* 59 C10
Fengyang *China* 57 H9
Fengyi *China* 58 E3
Fengyüan *Taiwan* 59 E13
Fengzhen *China* 56 D7
Feno, C. de *France* 21 G12
Fenoarivo *Fianarantsoa,
  Madag.* 89 C8
Fenoarivo *Fianarantsoa,
  Madag.* 89 C8
Fenoarivo Afovoany *Madag.* 89 B8
Fenoarivo Atsinanana
  Madag. 89 B8
Fens, The *U.K.* 14 E7
Fensmark *Denmark* 11 J5
Fenton *U.S.A.* 113 D12
Fenxi *China* 56 F6
Fenyang *China* 56 F6
Fenyi *China* 59 D10
Feodosiya *Ukraine* 33 K8
Ferbane *Ireland* 12 C4
Ferdows *Iran* 71 C8
Fère-Champenoise *France* 19 D10
Fère-en-Tardenois *France* 19 C10
Ferentino *Italy* 41 G10
Feres *Greece* 45 F10
Ferfer *Somali Rep.* 75 F4
Fergana = Farghona
  Uzbekistan 52 E8
Fergus *Canada* 114 C4
Fergus Falls *U.S.A.* 112 B5
Feričanci *Croatia* 28 E2
Ferihegy, Budapest ✈
  (BUD) *Hungary* 28 C4
Ferkéssédougou *Ivory C.* 82 D3
Ferlach *Austria* 26 E7
Ferland *Canada* 104 B2
Ferlo, Vallée du *Senegal* 82 B2
Ferlo-Nord △ *Senegal* 82 B2
Ferlo-Sud △ *Senegal* 82 B2
Fermanagh □ *U.K.* 12 B4
Fermo *Italy* 41 E10
Fermont *Canada* 105 B6
Fermoselle *Spain* 36 D4
Fermoy *Ireland* 12 D3
Fernán Núñez *Spain* 37 H6
Fernández *Argentina* 126 B3
Fernandina Beach *U.S.A.* 117 F14
Fernando de Noronha
  Brazil 125 D12
Fernando Póo = Bioko
  Eq. Guin. 83 E6
Ferndale *Canada* 114 B3
Ferndale *U.S.A.* 110 B4
Fernie *Canada* 102 D5
Fernlees *Australia* 94 C4
Fernley *U.S.A.* 108 G4
Fernwood *U.S.A.* 115 C11
Ferozepore = Firozpur *India* 68 D6
Ferradina *Italy* 43 B9
Ferrara *Italy* 41 D8
Ferrato, C. *Italy* 42 C2
Ferreira do Alentejo *Portugal* 37 G2
Ferreñafe *Peru* 124 E3
Ferrerías *Spain* 48 B11
Ferret, C. *France* 20 D2
Ferrette *France* 19 E14
Ferriday *U.S.A.* 116 F9
Ferriere *Italy* 40 D6
Ferrières *France* 19 D9
Ferro, Capo *Italy* 42 A2
Ferrol *Spain* 36 B2
Ferron *U.S.A.* 108 G8
Ferrutx, C. de *Spain* 48 B10
Ferryland *Canada* 105 C9
Fertile *U.S.A.* 112 B5
Fertő-Hanság △ *Hungary* 28 C1
Fertőszentmiklós *Hungary* 28 C1
Fès *Morocco* 78 B5
Fessenden *U.S.A.* 112 B4
Festus *U.S.A.* 112 F8
Feté Bowé *Senegal* 82 C2
Fetești *Romania* 29 F12
Fethiye *Turkey* 47 E11
Fethiye Körfezi *Turkey* 47 E10
Fetlar *U.K.* 13 A8
Feuilles → *Canada* 101 D12
Feurs *France* 21 C8
Fez = Fès *Morocco* 78 B5
Fezzan *Libya* 79 C8
Fiambalá *Argentina* 126 B2
Fianarantsoa *Madag.* 89 C8
Fianarantsoa □ *Madag.* 89 B8

Fiche *Ethiopia* **81** F4
Fichtelgebirge *Germany* **25** E7
Fichtelgebirge △ *Germany* **25** E8
Ficksburg *S. Africa* **89** D4
Fidenza *Italy* **40** D7
Fiditi *Nigeria* **83** D5
Field ➜ *Australia* **94** C2
Field I. *Australia* **92** B5
Fieni *Romania* **29** E10
Fier *Albania* **44** F3
Fierzë *Albania* **44** D4
Fife □ *U.K.* **13** E5
Fife △ *U.K.* **13** E5
Fife Ness *U.K.* **13** E6
Figari *France* **21** G13
Figeac *France* **20** D6
Figeholm *Sweden* **11** G10
Figline Valdarno *Italy* **41** E8
Figtree *Zimbabwe* **87** G2
Figueira Castelo Rodrigo
  Portugal **36** E4
Figueira da Foz *Portugal* **36** E2
Figueiró dos Vinhos *Portugal* **36** F2
Figueres *Spain* **38** C7
Figuig *Morocco* **78** B5
Fihaonana *Madag.* **89** B8
Fiherenana *Madag.* **89** B8
Fiherenana ➜ *Madag.* **89** C7
Fiji ■ *Pac. Oc.* **91** a
Fik *Ethiopia* **81** F5
Fika *Nigeria* **83** C7
Filabres, Sierra de los *Spain* **37** H8
Filabusi *Zimbabwe* **89** C4
Filadélfia *Italy* **43** D9
Filadelfia *Paraguay* **126** A3
Fil'akovo *Slovak Rep.* **27** C12
Filchner Ice Shelf *Antarctica* **5** D1
Filey *U.K.* **14** C7
Filey B. *U.K.* **14** C7
Filfla *Malta* **49** D1
Filiaşi *Romania* **29** F8
Filiates *Greece* **46** B2
Filiatra *Greece* **46** D3
Filicudi *Italy* **43** D7
Filingué *Niger* **83** C5
Filiouri ➜ *Greece* **45** E9
Filipada *Greece* **46** B2
Filipstad *Sweden* **10** E8
Filisur *Switz.* **25** J5
Fillmore *Calif., U.S.A.* **111** L8
Fillmore *Utah, U.S.A.* **108** G7
Filotio *Greece* **47** D7
Filottrano *Italy* **41** E10
Filtu *Ethiopia* **81** F5
Fimbul Ice Shelf *S. Ocean* **5** C2
Fina △ *Mali* **82** C3
Finale Emília *Italy* **41** D8
Finale Lígure *Italy* **40** D5
Fiñana *Spain* **37** H8
Finch *Canada* **115** A9
Finch Hatton *Australia* **94** K6
Findhorn ➜ *U.K.* **13** D5
Fındıklı *Turkey* **73** B9
Findlay *U.S.A.* **113** E12
Fine *U.S.A.* **115** B9
Finger L. *Canada* **104** B1
Finger Lakes *U.S.A.* **115** D8
Fíngoè *Mozam.* **87** E3
Finike *Turkey* **47** E12
Finike Körfezi *Turkey* **47** E12
Finiq *Albania* **44** G4
Finistère □ *France* **18** D3
Finisterre = Fisterra *Spain* **36** C1
Finisterre, C. = Fisterra, C.
  Spain **36** C1
Finke *Australia* **94** D1
Finke Gorge △ *Australia* **92** D5
Finland ■ *Europe* **8** E22
Finland, G. of *Europe* **32** C3
Finlay ➜ *Canada* **102** B3
Finley *Australia* **95** F4
Finley *U.S.A.* **112** B5
Finn ➜ *Ireland* **12** B4
Finnerödja *Sweden* **11** F8
Finnigan, Mt. *Australia* **94** B4
Finniss, C. *Australia* **95** E1
Finnmark *Norway* **8** B20
Finnsnes *Norway* **8** B18
Finspång *Sweden* **11** F9
Finsteraarhorn *Switz.* **25** J4
Finsterwalde *Germany* **24** D9
Fiora ➜ *Italy* **41** F8
Fiordland △ *N.Z.* **91** F1
Fiorenzuola d'Arda *Italy* **40** D6
Fiq *Syria* **74** C4
Firat = Furât, Nahr al ➜
  Asia **70** D5
Fire Island △ *U.S.A.* **115** F11
Firebag ➜ *Canada* **103** B6
Firebaugh *U.S.A.* **110** J6
Firedrake L. *Canada* **103** A8
Firenze *Italy* **41** E8
Firenze Amerigo
  Vespucci ✈ (FLR) *Italy* **41** E8
Firenze Pisa ✈ (PSA) *Italy* **40** E7
Firenzuola *Italy* **41** D8
Firk, Sha'ib ➜ *Iraq* **70** D5
Firmi *France* **20** D6

Firminy *France* **21** C8
Firozabad *India* **69** F8
Firozpur *India* **68** D6
Firozpur-Jhirka *India* **68** F7
Fīrūzābād *Iran* **71** D7
Firvale *Canada* **102** C3
Firyal *Colombia* **124** C3
Fisciano *Italy* **43** B7
Fish ➜ *Namibia* **88** D2
Fish ➜ *S. Africa* **88** E3
Fish River Canyon *Namibia* **88** D2
Fisher B. *Canada* **103** C9
Fishers I. *U.S.A.* **115** E13
Fishguard *U.K.* **15** E3
Fishing L. *Canada* **103** C9
Fishkill *U.S.A.* **115** E11
Fisterra *Spain* **36** C1
Fisterra, C. *Spain* **36** C1
Fitchburg *Mass., U.S.A.* **115** D13
Fitchburg *Wis., U.S.A.* **112** D9
Fitz Roy *Argentina* **128** F3
Fitz Roy, Cerro *Argentina* **128** F2
Fitzgerald *Canada* **102** B6
Fitzgerald *U.S.A.* **117** F13
Fitzgerald River △ *Australia* **93** F3
Fitzmaurice ➜ *Australia* **92** B5
Fitzroy ➜ *Queens., Australia* **94** C5
Fitzroy ➜ *W. Austral.,
  Australia* **92** C3
Fitzroy Crossing *Australia* **92** C4
Fitzwilliam I. *Canada* **114** A3
Fiuggi *Italy* **41** G10
Fiume = Rijeka *Croatia* **41** C11
Fiumicino, Roma ✈ (FCO)
  Italy **41** G9
Five Points *U.S.A.* **110** J6
Fivizzano *Italy* **40** D7
Fizi *Dem. Rep. of the Congo* **86** C2
Fjällbacka *Sweden* **11** F5
Fjärdhundra *Sweden* **10** E10
Fjellerup *Denmark* **11** H4
Fjerritslev *Denmark* **11** G3
Fjugesta *Sweden* **10** E8
Flagstaff *U.S.A.* **109** J8
Flagstaff L. *U.S.A.* **115** A14
Flaherty I. *Canada* **104** A4
Flåm *Norway* **8** F12
Flambeau ➜ *U.S.A.* **112** C8
Flamborough Hd. *U.K.* **14** C7
Fläming *Germany* **24** C8
Flaming Gorge △ *U.S.A.* **108** F9
Flaming Gorge Res. *U.S.A.* **108** F9
Flamingo, Teluk *Indonesia* **63** F9
Flanders = Flandre *Europe* **19** B9
Flandre *Europe* **19** B9
Flandre-Occidentale =
  West-Vlaanderen □
  Belgium **17** D2
Flandre-Orientale = Oost-
  Vlaanderen □ *Belgium* **17** C3
Flandreau *U.S.A.* **112** C5
Flanigan *U.S.A.* **110** E7
Flannan Is. *U.K.* **13** C1
Flåsjön *Sweden* **8** D16
Flat ➜ *Canada* **102** A3
Flat I. *Mauritius* **85** d
Flathead L. *U.S.A.* **108** C6
Flattery, C. *Australia* **94** B4
Flattery, C. *U.S.A.* **110** B2
Flatwoods *U.S.A.* **113** F12
Fleetwood *U.K.* **14** D4
Fleetwood *U.S.A.* **115** F9
Flekkefjord *Norway* **9** G12
Flemington *U.S.A.* **114** E7
Flen *Sweden* **10** E10
Flensburg *Germany* **24** A5
Flers *France* **18** D6
Flesherton *Canada* **114** B4
Flesko, Tanjung *Indonesia* **63** D6
Fleurance *France* **20** E4
Fleurier *Switz.* **25** J2
Fleurieu Pen. *Australia* **95** F2
Flevoland □ *Neths.* **17** B5
Flin Flon *Canada* **103** C8
Flinders ➜ *Australia* **94** B3
Flinders B. *Australia* **93** F2
Flinders Group *Australia* **94** A3
Flinders I. *S. Austral.,
  Australia* **95** E1
Flinders I. *Tas., Australia* **95** G4
Flinders Ranges *Australia* **95** E2
Flinders Reefs *Australia* **94** B4
Flint *U.K.* **14** D4
Flint *U.S.A.* **113** D12
Flint ➜ *U.S.A.* **117** F12
Flint I. *Kiribati* **97** J12
Flintshire □ *U.K.* **14** D4
Fliseryd *Sweden* **11** G10
Flix *Spain* **38** D5
Flixecourt *France* **19** B9
Floby *Sweden* **11** F7
Floda *Sweden* **11** G6
Flodden *U.K.* **14** B5
Flogny-la-Chapelle *France* **19** E10
Floodwood *U.S.A.* **112** B7
Flora *U.S.A.* **112** F9
Florac *France* **20** D7
Florala *U.S.A.* **117** F11
Florence = Firenze *Italy* **41** E8

Florence *Ala., U.S.A.* **117** D11
Florence *Ariz., U.S.A.* **109** K8
Florence *Colo., U.S.A.* **108** G11
Florence *Oreg., U.S.A.* **108** D1
Florence *S.C., U.S.A.* **117** D15
Florence, L. *Australia* **95** D2
Florencia *Colombia* **124** C3
Florennes *Belgium* **17** D4
Florensac *France* **20** E7
Florenville *Belgium* **17** E5
Flores *Azores* **78** a
Flores *Guatemala* **120** C2
Flores *Indonesia* **63** F6
Flores I. *Canada* **102** D3
Flores Sea *Indonesia* **63** F6
Floreşti *Moldova* **29** C13
Floriano *Brazil* **125** E10
Florianópolis *Brazil* **127** B6
Florida *Cuba* **120** B4
Florida *Uruguay* **127** C4
Florida □ *U.S.A.* **117** G14
Florida, Straits of *U.S.A.* **120** B4
Florida B. *U.S.A.* **120** B3
Florida Keys *U.S.A.* **117** J14
Florídia *Italy* **43** E8
Florin *U.S.A.* **110** G5
Florina *Greece* **44** F5
Florina □ *Greece* **44** F5
Florissant *U.S.A.* **112** F8
Florø *Norway* **8** F11
Flower Station *Canada* **115** A8
Flowerpot I. *Canada* **114** A3
Floydada *U.S.A.* **116** E4
Fluk *Indonesia* **63** E7
Flúmen ➜ *Spain* **38** D4
Flumendosa ➜ *Italy* **42** C2
Fluminimaggiore *Italy* **42** C1
Flushing = Vlissingen *Neths.* **17** C3
Fluvià ➜ *Spain* **38** C8
Fly ➜ *Papua N. G.* **90** B7
Flying Fish, C. *Antarctica* **5** D15
Foa *Tonga* **91** c
Foam Lake *Canada* **103** C8
Foça *Turkey* **47** C8
Fochabers *U.K.* **13** D5
Foča *Bos.-H.* **44** C2
Focşani *Romania* **29** E12
Fodécontéa *Guinea* **82** C2
Fogang *China* **59** F9
Fóggia *Italy* **43** A8
Foggo *Nigeria* **83** C6
Foglia ➜ *Italy* **41** E9
Fogo *Canada* **105** C9
Fogo C. Verde Is. **78** b
Fogo I. *Canada* **105** C9
Fohnsdorf *Austria* **26** D7
Föhr *Germany* **24** A4
Foia *Portugal* **37** H2
Foix *France* **20** E5
Fojnica *Bos.-H.* **28** G2
Fokida □ *Greece* **46** C4
Fokino *Russia* **32** F8
Fokku *Nigeria* **83** C5
Folda *Nord-Trøndelag, Norway* **8** D14
Folda *Nordland, Norway* **8** C16
Földeák *Hungary* **28** D5
Folegandros *Greece* **46** E6
Foley *Botswana* **88** C4
Foley *U.S.A.* **117** F11
Foleyet *Canada* **104** C3
Folgefonna *Norway* **9** F12
Foligno *Italy* **41** F9
Folkestone *U.K.* **15** F9
Folkston *U.S.A.* **117** F13
Follansbee *U.S.A.* **114** F4
Follónica *Italy* **40** F7
Follónica, G. di *Italy* **40** F7
Folsom L. *U.S.A.* **110** G5
Folteşti *Romania* **29** E13
Fombeni *Comoros Is.* **85** a
Fond-du-Lac *Canada* **103** B7
Fond du Lac *U.S.A.* **112** D9
Fond-du-Lac ➜ *Canada* **103** B7
Fonda *U.S.A.* **115** D10
Fondi *Italy* **42** A6
Fonfría *Spain* **36** D4
Fongafale *Tuvalu* **90** B10
Fonni *Italy* **42** B2
Fonsagrada = A
  Fonsagrada *Spain* **36** B3
Fonseca, G. de *Cent. Amer.* **120** D2
Font-Romeu-Odeillo-Via
  France **20** F5
Fontaine-Française *France* **19** E12
Fontainebleau *France* **19** D9
Fontana *U.S.A.* **111** L9
Fontas ➜ *Canada* **102** B4
Fonte Boa *Brazil* **124** D5
Fontem *Cameroon* **83** D6
Fontenay-le-Comte *France* **20** B3
Fontenelle Res. *U.S.A.* **108** E8
Fontur *Iceland* **8** C6
Fonuafo'ou *Tonga* **91** c
Fonualei *Tonga* **90** c
Fonyód *Hungary* **28** D2
Foochow = Fuzhou *China* **59** D12
Foping *China* **56** H5
Forbach *France* **19** C13

Forbes *Australia* **95** E4
Forbesganj *India* **69** F12
Forcados *Nigeria* **83** D6
Forcados ➜ *Nigeria* **83** D6
Forcalquier *France* **21** E9
Forchheim *Germany* **25** F7
Ford City *Calif., U.S.A.* **111** K7
Ford City *Pa., U.S.A.* **114** F5
Fords Bridge *Australia* **95** D4
Fordyce *U.S.A.* **116** E8
Forécariah *Guinea* **82** D2
Forel, Mt. *Greenland* **98** C16
Foremost *Canada* **102** D6
Forest *Canada* **114** C3
Forest *U.S.A.* **117** E10
Forest City *Iowa, U.S.A.* **112** D7
Forest City *N.C., U.S.A.* **117** D14
Forest City *Pa., U.S.A.* **115** E9
Forest Grove *U.S.A.* **110** D3
Forestburg *Canada* **102** C6
Foreste Casentinesi-Monte
  Falterona-Campigna △
  Italy **41** E8
Foresthill *U.S.A.* **110** F6
Forestier Pen. *Australia* **95** G4
Forestville *Canada* **105** C6
Forestville *Calif., U.S.A.* **110** G4
Forestville *N.Y., U.S.A.* **114** D5
Forêt d'Orient △ *France* **19** D11
Forez, Mts. du *France* **20** C7
Forfar *U.K.* **13** E6
Forillon △ *Canada* **105** C7
Forks *U.S.A.* **110** C2
Forksville *U.S.A.* **115** E8
Forlì *Italy* **41** D9
Forman *U.S.A.* **112** B5
Formazza *Italy* **40** B5
Formby Pt. *U.K.* **14** D4
Formentera *Spain* **48** C7
Formentor, C. de *Spain* **48** B10
Formentor, Pen. de *Spain* **48** B10
Former Yugoslav Republic
  of Macedonia =
  Macedonia ■ *Europe* **44** E5
Fórmia *Italy* **42** A6
Formígine *Italy* **40** D7
Formosa = Taiwan ■ *Asia* **59** F13
Formosa *Argentina* **126** B4
Formosa *Brazil* **125** G9
Formosa □ *Argentina* **126** B4
Formosa, Serra *Brazil* **125** F8
Formosa B. = Ungwana B.
  Kenya **86** C5
Fornells *Spain* **48** A11
Fornos de Algodres *Portugal* **36** E3
Fornovo di Taro *Italy* **40** D7
Føroyar ☑ *Atl. Oc.* **8** F9
Forres *U.K.* **13** D5
Forrest *Australia* **93** F4
Forrest, Mt. *Australia* **93** D4
Forrest City *U.S.A.* **117** D9
Fors *Sweden* **10** D10
Forsayth *Australia* **94** B3
Forshaga *Sweden* **10** E7
Förslöv *Sweden* **11** H6
Forsmo *Sweden* **10** A11
Forssa *Finland* **32** B2
Forst *Germany* **24** D10
Forster *Australia* **95** E5
Forsvik *Sweden* **11** F8
Forsyth *U.S.A.* **108** C10
Fort Abbas *Pakistan* **68** E5
Fort Albany *Canada* **104** B3
Fort Assiniboine *Canada* **102** C6
Fort Augustus *U.K.* **13** D4
Fort Beaufort *S. Africa* **88** E4
Fort Benton *U.S.A.* **108** C8
Fort Bragg *U.S.A.* **108** G2
Fort Bridger *U.S.A.* **108** F8
Fort Chipewyan *Canada* **103** B6
Fort Clatsop △ *U.S.A.* **110** D3
Fort Collins *U.S.A.* **108** F11
Fort-Coulonge *Canada* **104** C4
Fort Covington *U.S.A.* **115** B10
Fort Dauphin = Taolanaro
  Madag. **89** D8
Fort Davis *U.S.A.* **116** F3
Fort Defiance *U.S.A.* **109** J9
Fort Dodge *U.S.A.* **112** D6
Fort Edward *U.S.A.* **115** C11
Fort Erie *Canada* **114** D6
Fort Fairfield *U.S.A.* **113** B20
Fort Frances *Canada* **103** D10
Fort Franklin = Déline
  Canada **100** C7
Fort Garland *U.S.A.* **109** H11
Fort George = Chisasibi
  Canada **104** B4
Fort Good Hope *Canada* **100** C7
Fort Hancock *U.S.A.* **116** F2
Fort Hope = Eabametoong
  Canada **104** B2
Fort Irwin *U.S.A.* **111** K10
Fort Kent *U.S.A.* **113** B19
Fort Klamath *U.S.A.* **108** E3
Fort Laramie *U.S.A.* **108** E11
Fort Lauderdale *U.S.A.* **117** H14

Fort Liard *Canada* **102** A4
Fort Liberté *Haiti* **121** C5
Fort Lupton *U.S.A.* **108** F11
Fort MacKay *Canada* **102** B6
Fort Macleod *Canada* **102** D6
Fort McMurray *Canada* **102** B6
Fort McPherson *Canada* **100** C6
Fort Madison *U.S.A.* **112** E8
Fort Meade *U.S.A.* **117** H14
Fort Morgan *U.S.A.* **108** F12
Fort Myers *U.S.A.* **117** H14
Fort Nelson *Canada* **102** B4
Fort Nelson ➜ *Canada* **102** B4
Fort Norman = Tulita
  Canada **100** C7
Fort Payne *U.S.A.* **117** D12
Fort Peck *U.S.A.* **108** B10
Fort Peck Dam *U.S.A.* **108** C10
Fort Peck L. *U.S.A.* **108** C10
Fort Pierce *U.S.A.* **117** H14
Fort Pierre *U.S.A.* **112** C3
Fort Plain *U.S.A.* **115** D10
Fort Portal *Uganda* **86** B3
Fort Providence *Canada* **102** A5
Fort Qu'Appelle *Canada* **103** C8
Fort Resolution *Canada* **102** A6
Fort Rixon *Zimbabwe* **87** G2
Fort Ross *U.S.A.* **110** G3
Fort Rupert =
  Waskaganish *Canada* **104** B4
Fort St. James *Canada* **102** C4
Fort St. John *Canada* **102** B4
Fort Saskatchewan *Canada* **102** C6
Fort Scott *U.S.A.* **112** G6
Fort Severn *Canada* **104** A2
Fort Shevchenko
  Kazakhstan **35** H10
Fort Simpson *Canada* **102** A4
Fort Smith *Canada* **102** B6
Fort Smith *U.S.A.* **116** D7
Fort Stockton *U.S.A.* **116** F3
Fort Sumner *U.S.A.* **109** J11
Fort Thompson *U.S.A.* **112** C4
Fort Union △ *U.S.A.* **109** J11
Fort Valley *U.S.A.* **117** E13
Fort Vermilion *Canada* **102** B5
Fort Walton Beach *U.S.A.* **117** F11
Fort Ware *Canada* **102** B3
Fort Wayne *U.S.A.* **113** E11
Fort William *U.K.* **13** E3
Fort Worth *U.S.A.* **116** E6
Fort Yates *U.S.A.* **112** B3
Fort Yukon *U.S.A.* **106** a
Fortaleza *Brazil* **125** D11
Forteau *Canada* **105** B8
Fortescue ➜ *Australia* **92** D2
Forth ➜ *U.K.* **13** E5
Forth, Firth of *U.K.* **13** E6
Fortín *Italy* **41** G12
Fortore ➜ *Italy* **41** G12
Fortrose *U.K.* **13** D4
Fortuna *Spain* **39** G3
Fortuna *Calif., U.S.A.* **108** F1
Fortuna *N. Dak., U.S.A.* **112** A2
Fortune *Canada* **105** C8
Fortune B. *Canada* **105** C8
Forūr *Iran* **71** E7
Fos-sur-Mer *France* **21** E8
Fosen *Norway* **8** E14
Foshan *China* **59** F9
Fosnavåg *Norway* **8** E11
Foso *Ghana* **83** D4
Fossano *Italy* **40** D4
Fossil *U.S.A.* **108** D3
Fossil Butte △ *U.S.A.* **108** F8
Fossombrone *Italy* **41** E9
Foster *Canada* **115** A12
Foster ➜ *Australia* **92** D5
Fosters Ra. *Australia* **94** C1
Fostoria *U.S.A.* **113** E12
Fotadrevo *Madag.* **89** C8
Fouesnant *France* **18** E2
Fougères *France* **18** D5
Foul Pt. *Sri Lanka* **66** Q12
Foula *U.K.* **13** A6
Foulalaba *Mali* **82** C3
Foulness I. *U.K.* **15** F8
Foulpointe *Madag.* **89** B8
Fouman *Cameroon* **83** D7
Foumbot *Cameroon* **83** D7
Foumbouni *Comoros Is.* **85** a
Foundiougne *Senegal* **82** C1
Fountain *U.S.A.* **108** G11
Fountain Hills *U.S.A.* **109** K8
Fountain Springs *U.S.A.* **111** K8
Fourchambault *France* **19** E10
Fouriesburg *S. Africa* **88** D4
Fourmies *France* **19** B11
Fourna *Greece* **46** B3
Fourni *Greece* **47** D8
Fours *France* **19** F10
Fouta Djallon *Guinea* **82** C2
Foux, Cap-à- *Haiti* **121** C5
Foveaux Str. *N.Z.* **91** G2
Fowey *U.K.* **15** G3
Fowler *Calif., U.S.A.* **110** J7
Fowler *Colo., U.S.A.* **108** G11
Fowler, Pt. *Australia* **93** F5
Fowlers B. *Australia* **93** F5

Fowman *Iran* **73** D13
Fox ➜ *Canada* **103** B10
Fox Creek *Canada* **102** C5
Fox Lake *Canada* **102** B6
Fox Valley *Canada* **103** C7
Foxboro *Canada* **114** B7
Foxboro *U.S.A.* **115** D13
Foxdale *Australia* **94** J6
Foxe Basin *Canada* **101** C12
Foxe Chan. *Canada* **101** C12
Foxe Pen. *Canada* **101** C12
Foxen *Sweden* **10** E5
Foxford *Ireland* **12** C2
Foxton *N.Z.* **91** D5
Foyle, Lough *U.K.* **12** A4
Foynes *Ireland* **12** D2
Foz *Spain* **36** B3
Foz do Cunene *Angola* **88** B1
Foz do Iguaçu *Brazil* **127** B5
Frackville *U.S.A.* **115** F8
Fraga *Spain* **38** D5
Fraile Muerto *Uruguay* **127** C5
Framingham *U.S.A.* **115** D13
Frampol *Poland* **31** H9
Franca *Brazil* **125** H9
Francavilla al Mare *Italy* **41** F11
Francavilla Fontana *Italy* **43** B10
France ■ *Europe* **7** F6
Frances *Australia* **95** F3
Frances ➜ *Canada* **102** A3
Frances L. *Canada* **102** A3
Franceville *Gabon* **84** E2
Franche-Comté □ *France* **19** F12
Francis Case, L. *U.S.A.* **112** D4
Francisco Beltrão *Brazil* **127** B5
Francisco Ignacio Madero
  Coahuila, Mexico **118** B4
Francisco Ignacio Madero
  Durango, Mexico **118** C4
Francisco Ignacio Madero,
  Presa *Mexico* **118** B3
Francistown *Botswana* **89** C4
Francofonte *Italy* **43** E7
François *Canada* **105** C8
François L. *Canada* **102** C3
Francois Peron △ *Australia* **93** E1
Francs Pk. *U.S.A.* **108** E9
Franeker *Neths.* **17** A5
Frank Hann △ *Australia* **93** F3
Frankado *Djibouti* **81** E5
Frankenberg *Germany* **24** D4
Frankenhöhe △ *Germany* **25** F6
Frankenwald *Germany* **25** E7
Frankenwald △ *Germany* **25** E7
Frankford *Canada* **114** B7
Frankfort *S. Africa* **89** D4
Frankfort *Ind., U.S.A.* **112** E10
Frankfort *Kans., U.S.A.* **112** F5
Frankfort *Ky., U.S.A.* **113** F11
Frankfort *N.Y., U.S.A.* **115** C9
Frankfurt *Brandenburg,
  Germany* **24** C10
Frankfurt *Hessen, Germany* **25** E4
Frankfurt ✈ (FRA) *Germany* **25** E4
Fränkische Alb *Germany* **25** F7
Fränkische Rezat ➜
  Germany **25** F7
Fränkische Saale ➜
  Germany **25** E5
Fränkische Schweiz
  Germany **25** E7
Fränkische
  Schweiz-Veldensteiner
  Forst △ *Germany* **25** F7
Frankland ➜ *Australia* **93** G2
Franklin *Ky., U.S.A.* **112** G10
Franklin *La., U.S.A.* **116** G9
Franklin *Mass., U.S.A.* **115** D13
Franklin *N.H., U.S.A.* **115** C13
Franklin *N.Y., U.S.A.* **115** D9
Franklin *Nebr., U.S.A.* **112** E4
Franklin *Pa., U.S.A.* **114** E5
Franklin *Va., U.S.A.* **113** G15
Franklin *W. Va., U.S.A.* **113** F14
Franklin B. *Canada* **100** C7
Franklin D. Roosevelt L.
  U.S.A. **108** B4
Franklin-Gordon Wild
  Rivers △ *Australia* **95** G4
Franklin I. *Antarctica* **5** D11
Franklin I. *Canada* **114** A4
Franklin L. *U.S.A.* **108** F6
Franklin Mts. *Canada* **100** C7
Franklin Str. *Canada* **100** B10
Franklinton *U.S.A.* **116** F9
Franklinville *U.S.A.* **114** D6
Frankston *Australia* **95** F4
Frånö *Sweden* **10** B11
Fransfontein *Namibia* **88** C2
Fränsta *Sweden* **10** B10
Frantsa Iosifa, Zemlya
  Russia **52** A6
Franz *Canada* **104** C3
Franz Josef Land = Frantsa
  Iosifa, Zemlya *Russia* **52** A6
Franz Josef Strauss ✈
  (MUC) *Germany* **25** G7
Franzburg *Germany* **24** A8
Frascati *Italy* **41** G9

Fraser *U.S.A.* **114** D2
Fraser → *B.C., Canada* **110** A3
Fraser → *Nfld. & L., Canada* **105** A7
Fraser, Mt. *Australia* **93** E2
Fraser I. *Australia* **95** D5
Fraser Lake *Canada* **102** C4
Fraserburg *S. Africa* **88** E3
Fraserburgh *U.K.* **13** D6
Fraserdale *Canada* **104** C3
Frashër *Albania* **44** F4
Frasne *France* **19** F13
Frătești *Romania* **29** G10
Frauenfeld *Switz.* **25** H4
Fray Bentos *Uruguay* **126** C4
Fray Jorge △ *Chile* **126** C1
Frechilla *Spain* **36** C6
Fredericia *Denmark* **11** J3
Frederick Md., U.S.A.* **113** F15
Frederick Okla., U.S.A.* **116** D5
Frederick S. Dak., U.S.A.* **112** C4
Fredericksburg Pa., U.S.A.* **115** F8
Fredericksburg Tex., U.S.A.* **116** F5
Fredericksburg Va., U.S.A.* **113** F15
Fredericktown Mo., U.S.A.* **112** G4
Fredericktown Ohio, U.S.A.* **114** F2
Frederico Westphalen
  Brazil **127** B5
Fredericton *Canada* **105** C6
Fredericton Junction
  Canada **105** C6
Frederikshåb = Paamiut
  Greenland **4** C5
Frederikshamn = Hamina
  Finland **32** B4
Frederikshavn *Denmark* **11** G4
Frederikssund *Denmark* **11** J6
Frederiksted *U.S. Virgin Is.* **121** C7
Frederiksværk *Denmark* **11** J6
Fredonia Ariz., U.S.A.* **109** H7
Fredonia Kans., U.S.A.* **112** G6
Fredonia N.Y., U.S.A.* **114** D5
Fredriksberg *Sweden* **10** D8
Fredrikstad *Norway* **9** G14
Free State □ *S. Africa* **88** D4
Freehold *U.S.A.* **115** F10
Freeland *U.S.A.* **115** E9
Freels, C. *Nfld. & L., Canada* **105** C9
Freels, C. *Nfld. & L., Canada* **105** C9
Freeman Calif., U.S.A.* **111** K9
Freeman S. Dak., U.S.A.* **112** D5
Freeport *Bahamas* **120** A4
Freeport Ill., U.S.A.* **112** D9
Freeport N.Y., U.S.A.* **115** F11
Freeport Ohio, U.S.A.* **114** F3
Freeport Pa., U.S.A.* **114** F5
Freeport Tex., U.S.A.* **116** G7
Freetown *S. Leone* **82** D2
Frégate, L. de la *Canada* **104** B5
Fregenal de la Sierra *Spain* **37** G4
Fregene *Italy* **41** G9
Fréhel, C. *France* **18** D4
Freiberg *Germany* **24** E9
Freibourg = Fribourg *Switz.* **25** J3
Freiburg Baden-W., Germany* **25** H3
Freiburg Niedersachsen,
  Germany **24** B5
Freilassing *Germany* **25** H8
Freire *Chile* **128** D2
Freirina *Chile* **126** B1
Freising *Germany* **25** G7
Freistadt *Austria* **26** C7
Freital *Germany* **24** D9
Fréjus *France* **21** E10
Fremantle *Australia* **93** F2
Fremont Calif., U.S.A.* **110** H4
Fremont Mich., U.S.A.* **113** D11
Fremont Nebr., U.S.A.* **112** E5
Fremont Ohio, U.S.A.* **113** E12
Fremont → *U.S.A.* **108** G8
French Camp *U.S.A.* **110** H5
French Cays = Plana Cays
  Bahamas **121** B5
French Creek → *U.S.A.* **114** E5
French Guiana ☑ *S. Amer.* **125** C8
French Polynesia ☑ *Pac. Oc.* **97** J13
Frenchman Cr. → *N. Amer.*
  108 B10
Frenchman Cr. → *U.S.A.* **112** E3
Frenštát pod Radhoštěm
  Czech Rep. **27** B11
Fresco *Ivory C.* **82** D3
Fresco → *Brazil* **125** E8
Freshfield, C. *Antarctica* **5** C10
Fresnay-sur-Sarthe *France* **18** D7
Fresnillo *Mexico* **118** C4
Fresno *U.S.A.* **110** J7
Fresno Alhándiga *Spain* **36** E5
Fresno Res. *U.S.A.* **108** B9
Freudenstadt *Germany* **25** G4
Frévent *France* **19** B9
Frew → *Australia* **94** C2
Frewsburg *U.S.A.* **114** D5
Freycinet △ *Australia* **95** G4
Freycinet Pen. *Australia* **95** G4
Freyming-Merlebach
  France **19** C13
Freyung *Germany* **25** G9
Fria *Guinea* **82** C2

Fria, C. *Namibia* **88** B1
Friant *U.S.A.* **110** J7
Frías *Argentina* **126** B2
Fribourg *Switz.* **25** J3
Fribourg □ *Switz.* **25** J3
Fridafors *Sweden* **11** H8
Friday Harbor *U.S.A.* **110** B3
Friedberg Bayern, Germany* **25** G6
Friedberg Hessen, Germany* **25** E4
Friedens *U.S.A.* **114** F6
Friedland *Germany* **24** B9
Friedrichshafen *Germany* **25** H5
Friedrichskoog *Germany* **24** A4
Friedrichstadt *Germany* **24** A5
Friendship *U.S.A.* **114** D6
Friesach *Austria* **26** E7
Friesack *Germany* **24** C8
Friesland □ *Neths.* **17** A5
Friesoythe *Germany* **24** B3
Frigate *Seychelles* **85** b
Friggesund *Sweden* **10** C10
Frillesås *Sweden* **11** G6
Frinnaryd *Sweden* **11** G8
Frio → *U.S.A.* **116** G5
Frio, C. *Brazil* **122** F6
Friol *Spain* **36** B3
Friona *U.S.A.* **116** D3
Fristad *Sweden* **11** G6
Fritch *U.S.A.* **116** D4
Fritsla *Sweden* **11** G6
Fritzlar *Germany* **24** D5
Friuli-Venézia Giulia □ *Italy* **41** B9
Frobisher B. *Canada* **101** C13
Frobisher Bay = Iqaluit
  Canada **101** C13
Frobisher L. *Canada* **103** B7
Frohavet *Norway* **8** E13
Frohnleiten *Austria* **26** D8
Frolovo *Russia* **34** F6
Frombork *Poland* **30** D6
Frome *U.K.* **15** F5
Frome → *U.K.* **15** G5
Frome, L. *Australia* **95** E2
Frómista *Spain* **36** C6
Front Range *U.S.A.* **106** C5
Front Royal *U.S.A.* **113** F14
Fronteira *Portugal* **37** F3
Frontenac → *Canada* **115** B8
Frontera *Canary Is.* **48** G2
Frontera *Mexico* **119** D6
Fronteras *Mexico* **118** A3
Frontignan *France* **20** E7
Frosinone *Italy* **42** A6
Frostburg *U.S.A.* **113** F14
Frostisen *Norway* **8** B17
Frouard *France* **19** D13
Frövi *Sweden* **10** E9
Frøya *Norway* **8** E13
Frumoasa *Romania* **29** D10
Frunze = Bishkek *Kyrgyzstan* **52** E8
Frunzivka *Ukraine* **29** C14
Fruška Gora *Serbia* **28** E4
Fruška Gora △ *Serbia* **44** A3
Frutal *Brazil* **125** H9
Frutigen *Switz.* **25** J3
Frýdek-Místek *Czech Rep.* **27** B11
Frýdlant *Czech Rep.* **26** A8
Fryeburg *U.S.A.* **115** B14
Fryvaldov = Jeseník
  Czech Rep. **27** A10
Fthiotida □ *Greece* **46** C4
Fu Jiang → *China* **58** C6
Fu Xian = Wafangdian
  China **57** E11
Fu Xian *China* **56** G5
Fu'an *China* **59** D12
Fubian *China* **58** B4
Fucécchio *Italy* **40** E7
Fucheng *China* **56** F9
Fuchou = Fuzhou *China* **59** D12
Fuchū *Japan* **55** G6
Fuchuan *China* **59** E8
Fuchun Jiang → *China* **59** B13
Fúcino, Piana del *Italy* **41** F10
Fuding *China* **59** D13
Fuencaliente *Canary Is.* **48** F2
Fuencaliente *Spain* **37** G6
Fuencaliente, Pta. *Canary Is.* **48** F2
Fuengirola *Spain* **37** J6
Fuenlabrada *Spain* **36** E7
Fuensalida *Spain* **36** E6
Fuente-Álamo *Spain* **39** G3
Fuente Álamo de Murcia
  Spain **39** H3
Fuente de Cantos *Spain* **37** G4
Fuente del Maestre *Spain* **37** G4
Fuente el Fresno *Spain* **37** F7
Fuente Obejuna *Spain* **37** G5
Fuente Palmera *Spain* **37** H5
Fuentes de Andalucía *Spain* **37** H5
Fuentes de Ebro *Spain* **38** D4
Fuentes de León *Spain* **37** G4
Fuentes de Oñoro *Spain* **36** E4
Fuentesaúco *Spain* **36** D5
Fuerte → *Mexico* **118** B3
Fuerte Olimpo *Paraguay* **126** A4
Fuerteventura *Canary Is.* **48** F6
Fuerteventura ✈ (FUE)
  Canary Is. **48** F6

Fufeng *China* **56** G5
Fuga I. *Phil.* **61** B4
Fugō *China* **56** G8
Fugu *China* **56** E6
Fuhai *China* **60** B3
Fuḥaymī *Iraq* **73** E10
Fuhlsbüttel, Hamburg ✈
  (HAM) *Germany* **24** B5
Fuji *Japan* **55** G9
Fuji-Hakone-Izu △ *Japan* **55** G9
Fuji-San *Japan* **55** G9
Fuji-Yoshida *Japan* **55** G9
Fujian □ *China* **59** E12
Fujinomiya *Japan* **55** G9
Fujisawa *Japan* **55** G9
Fujiyama, Mt. = Fuji-San
  Japan **55** G9
Fukagawa *Japan* **54** C11
Fukien = Fujian □ *China* **59** E12
Fukuchiyama *Japan* **55** G7
Fukue-Shima *Japan* **55** H4
Fukui *Japan* **55** F8
Fukui □ *Japan* **55** G8
Fukuoka *Japan* **55** H5
Fukuoka □ *Japan* **55** H5
Fukushima *Japan* **54** F10
Fukushima □ *Japan* **54** F10
Fukuyama *Japan* **55** G6
Fulacunda *Guinea-Biss.* **82** C1
Fulaga *Fiji* **91** a
Fulda *Germany* **24** E5
Fulda → *Germany* **24** D5
Fulford Harbour *Canada* **110** B3
Fuliang *China* **59** C11
Fullerton Calif., U.S.A.* **111** M9
Fullerton Nebr., U.S.A.* **112** E5
Fulongquan *China* **57** B13
Fulton Mo., U.S.A.* **112** F8
Fulton N.Y., U.S.A.* **115** C8
Fuluälven → *Sweden* **10** C7
Fulufjället *Sweden* **10** C6
Fumay *France* **19** C5
Fumel *France* **20** D4
Fumin *China* **58** E4
Funabashi *Japan* **55** G10
Funafuti = Fongafale
  Tuvalu **90** B10
Fundación *Colombia* **124** A4
Fundão *Portugal* **36** E3
Fundu Moldovei *Romania* **29** C10
Fundulea *Romania* **29** F11
Fundy, B. of *Canada* **105** D6
Fundy △ *Canada* **105** C6
Funhalouro *Mozam.* **89** C5
Funing Hebei, China* **57** E10
Funing Jiangsu, China* **57** H10
Funing Yunnan, China* **58** F5
Funiu Shan *China* **56** H7
Funsi *Ghana* **82** C4
Funtua *Nigeria* **83** C6
Fuping Hebei, China* **56** E8
Fuping Shaanxi, China* **56** G5
Fuqing *China* **59** E12
Fuquan *China* **58** D6
Furano *Japan* **54** C11
Furāt, Nahr al → *Asia* **70** D5
Furmanov *Russia* **34** B5
Furnás *Spain* **48** B8
Furnas, Represa de *Brazil* **127** A6
Furneaux Group *Australia* **95** G4
Furqlus *Syria* **74** A6
Fürstenau *Germany* **24** C3
Fürstenberg *Germany* **24** B9
Fürstenfeld *Austria* **26** D9
Fürstenfeldbruck *Germany* **25** G7
Fürstenwalde *Germany* **24** C10
Fürth *Germany* **25** F6
Fürth im Wald *Germany* **25** F8
Furtwangen *Germany* **25** G4
Furudal *Sweden* **10** C9
Furukawa *Japan* **54** E10
Furulund *Sweden* **11** J7
Fury and Hecla Str. *Canada*
  101 C11
Fusagasugá *Colombia* **124** C4
Fuscaldo *Italy* **43** C9
Fushan Shandong, China* **57** F11
Fushan Shanxi, China* **56** G6
Fushë Arrëz *Albania* **44** D4
Fushë Krujë *Albania* **44** E3
Fushun Liaoning, China* **57** D12
Fushun Sichuan, China* **58** C5
Füssen *Germany* **25** H6
Fustic *Barbados* **121** g
Fusui *China* **58** F6
Futog *Serbia* **28** E4
Fuwa *Egypt* **80** H7
Fuxian Hu *China* **58** E4
Fuxin *China* **57** C11
Fuyang Anhui, China* **56** H8
Fuyang Zhejiang, China* **59** B12
Fuyang He → *China* **56** E9

Fuying Dao *China* **59** D13
Fuyu Heilongjiang, China* **53** E13
Fuyu Jilin, China* **57** B13
Fuyuan *China* **58** D4
Fuzhou *China* **59** D12
Füzesgyarmat *Hungary* **28** C6
Füzuli *Azerbaijan* **73** C12
Fylde *U.K.* **14** D5
Fyn *Denmark* **11** J4
Fyne, L. *U.K.* **13** F3
Fynshav *Denmark* **11** K3

G

Ga *Ghana* **82** D4
Gaalkacyo *Somali Rep.* **75** F4
Gaanda *Nigeria* **83** C7
Gabarin *Nigeria* **83** C7
Gabas → *France* **20** E3
Gabela *Angola* **84** G2
Gabès *Tunisia* **79** B8
Gabès, G. de *Tunisia* **79** B8
Gabgaba, W. → *Egypt* **80** C3
Gabia la Grande *Spain* **37** H7
Găbin *Poland* **31** F6
Gabon ■ *Africa* **84** E2
Gaborone *Botswana* **88** C4
Gabriels *U.S.A.* **115** B10
Găbrīk *Iran* **71** E8
Gabrovo *Bulgaria* **45** D9
Gacé *France* **18** D7
Găch Sār *Iran* **71** B6
Gachsārān *Iran* **71** D6
Gacko *Bos.-H.* **44** C2
Gadag *India* **66** M9
Gadamai *Sudan* **81** D4
Gadap *Pakistan* **68** G2
Gadarwara *India* **69** H8
Gadebusch *Germany* **24** B7
Gadein *Sudan* **81** F2
Gadhada *India* **68** J4
Gadra *Pakistan* **68** G4
Gadsden *U.S.A.* **117** D11
Gadwal *India* **66** L10
Gadyach = Hadyach *Ukraine* **33** G8
Găești *Romania* **29** F10
Gaeta *Italy* **42** A6
Gaeta, G. di *Italy* **42** A6
Gaffney *U.S.A.* **117** D14
Gafsa *Tunisia* **78** B7
Gagarawa *Nigeria* **83** C6
Gagaria *India* **68** G4
Gagarin *Russia* **32** E8
Găgăuzia □ *Moldova* **29** D13
Gaggenau *Germany* **25** G4
Gaghamni *Sudan* **81** E2
Gagino *Russia* **34** C7
Gagliano del Capo *Italy* **43** C11
Gagnef *Sweden* **10** D9
Gagnoa *Ivory C.* **82** D3
Gagnon *Canada* **105** B6
Gagnon, L. *Canada* **103** A6
Gagra *Georgia* **35** J5
Gahini *Rwanda* **86** C3
Gahmar *India* **69** G10
Gai Xian = Gaizhou *China* **57** D12
Gaïdouronísi *Greece* **49** E7
Gail → *U.S.A.* **116** E4
Gail → *Austria* **26** E6
Gaillac *France* **20** E5
Gaillimh = Galway *Ireland* **12** C2
Gaillon *France* **18** C8
Gaines *U.S.A.* **114** E7
Gainesville Fla., U.S.A.* **117** G13
Gainesville Ga., U.S.A.* **117** D13
Gainesville Mo., U.S.A.* **112** G7
Gainesville Tex., U.S.A.* **116** E6
Gainsborough *U.K.* **14** D7
Gairdner, L. *Australia* **95** E2
Gairloch *U.K.* **13** D3
Gairloch, L. *U.K.* **13** D3
Gaizhou *China* **57** D12
Gaj *Croatia* **28** E2
Gaj → *Pakistan* **68** F2
Gakuch *Pakistan* **69** A5
Galâla, Gebel el *Egypt* **80** J8
Galán, Cerro *Argentina* **126** B2
Galana → *Kenya* **86** C5
Galanta *Slovak Rep.* **27** C10
Galapagar *Spain* **36** E7
Galápagos = Colón, Arch.
  de *Ecuador* **122** D1
Galapagos Fracture Zone
  Pac. Oc. **97** G17
Galapagos Rise *Pac. Oc.* **97** J18
Galashiels *U.K.* **13** F6
Galatas *Greece* **46** D5
Galateia *Cyprus* **49** D13
Galați *Romania* **29** E13
Galați □ *Romania* **29** E12
Galatia *Turkey* **72** C5
Galatina *Italy* **43** B11
Galátone *Italy* **43** B11
Galax *U.S.A.* **113** G13
Galaxidi *Greece* **46** C4
Galcaio = Gaalkacyo
  Somali Rep. **75** F4
Galdhøpiggen *Norway* **8** F13

Galeana Chihuahua, Mexico* **118** A3
Galeana Nuevo León, Mexico* **118** A3
Galega *Sudan* **81** E4
Galela *Indonesia* **63** D7
Galena *U.S.A.* **106** a
Galeota Pt. *Trin. & Tob.* **125** K16
Galera *Spain* **39** H2
Galera Pt. *Trin. & Tob.* **121** D7
Galesburg *U.S.A.* **112** E8
Galestan △ *Iran* **71** B8
Galeton *U.S.A.* **114** E7
Galga *Ethiopia* **81** F4
Gali *Georgia* **35** J5
Galicea Mare *Romania* **29** F8
Galich *Russia* **34** A6
Galiche *Bulgaria* **44** C7
Galicia □ *Spain* **36** C3
Galičica △ *Macedonia* **44** E4
Galilee = Hagalil *Israel* **74** C4
Galilee, L. *Australia* **94** C4
Galilee, Sea of = Yam
  Kinneret *Israel* **74** C4
Galim *Cameroon* **83** D7
Galina Pt. *Jamaica* **120** a
Galinoporni *Cyprus* **49** D13
Galion *U.S.A.* **114** F2
Galiuro Mts. *U.S.A.* **109** K8
Galiwinku *Australia* **94** A2
Gallabat *Sudan* **81** E4
Gallan Hd. *U.K.* **13** C1
Gallarate *Italy* **40** C5
Gallatin *U.S.A.* **117** C11
Galle *Sri Lanka* **66** R12
Gállego → *Spain* **38** D4
Gallegos → *Argentina* **128** G3
Galletti → *Ethiopia* **81** F5
Galley Hd. *Ireland* **12** E3
Galliate *Italy* **40** C5
Gallinas, Pta. *Colombia* **124** A4
Gallipoli = Gelibolu *Turkey* **45** F10
Gallípoli *Italy* **43** B10
Gallipolis *U.S.A.* **113** F12
Gällivare *Sweden* **8** C19
Gallneukirchen *Austria* **26** C7
Gallo, C. *Italy* **42** D6
Gallocanta, L. de *Spain* **38** E3
Galloo I. *U.S.A.* **115** C8
Galloway *U.K.* **13** F4
Galloway, Mull of *U.K.* **13** G4
Galloway △ *U.K.* **13** F4
Gallup *U.S.A.* **109** J9
Galong *Australia* **95** E4
Galoya *Sri Lanka* **66** Q12
Galt *U.S.A.* **110** G5
Galtee Mts. *Ireland* **12** D3
Galten *Denmark* **11** H3
Galtür *Austria* **26** E3
Galty Mts. *Ireland* **12** D3
Galtymore *Ireland* **12** D3
Galva *U.S.A.* **112** E8
Galve de Sorbe *Spain* **38** D1
Galveston *U.S.A.* **116** G7
Galveston B. *U.S.A.* **116** G7
Gálvez *Argentina* **126** C3
Galway *Ireland* **12** C2
Galway □ *Ireland* **12** C2
Galway B. *Ireland* **12** C2
Gam → *Vietnam* **64** B5
Gamagōri *Japan* **55** G8
Gamari, L. *Ethiopia* **81** E5
Gamawa *Nigeria* **83** C7
Gamay *Phil.* **61** E6
Gambaga *Ghana* **83** C4
Gambat *Pakistan* **68** F3
Gambela *Ethiopia* **81** F3
Gambela ☑ *Ethiopia* **81** F3
Gambela Hizboch □ *Ethiopia* **81** F3
Gambhir → *India* **68** F6
Gambia ■ *W. Afr.* **82** C1
Gambia → *W. Afr.* **82** C1
Gambier *U.S.A.* **114** F2
Gambier, C. *Australia* **92** B5
Gambier, Îs.
  French Polynesia **97** K14
Gambier Is. *Australia* **95** F2
Gambo *Canada* **105** C9
Gamboli *Pakistan* **68** E3
Gamboma *Congo* **84** E3
Gamka → *S. Africa* **88** E3
Gamkab → *Namibia* **88** D2
Gamla Uppsala *Sweden* **10** E11
Gamlakarleby = Kokkola
  Finland **8** E20
Gamleby *Sweden* **11** G10
Gammon → *Canada* **103** C9
Gammon Ranges △ *Australia* **95** E2
Gamo-Gofa *Ethiopia* **81** F4
Gamou *Niger* **83** C6
Gamtoos → *S. Africa* **88** E4
Gan *France* **20** E3
Gan Goriama, Mts.
  Cameroon **83** D7
Gan Jiang → *China* **59** C11
Ganado *U.S.A.* **109** J9
Gananita *Sudan* **80** D3
Gananoque *Canada* **115** B8
Ganāveh *Iran* **71** D6
Gäncä *Azerbaijan* **35** K8

Gancheng *China* **64** C7
Gand = Gent *Belgium* **17** C3
Ganda *Angola* **85** G2
Gandajika
  Dem. Rep. of the Congo **84** F4
Gandak → *India* **69** G11
Gandava *Pakistan* **68** E2
Gander *Canada* **105** C9
Gander L. *Canada* **105** C9
Ganderkesee *Germany* **24** B4
Ganderowe Falls *Zimbabwe* **87** F2
Gandesa *Spain* **38** D5
Gandhi Sagar *India* **68** G6
Gandhinagar *India* **68** H5
Gandi *Nigeria* **83** C6
Gandia *Spain* **39** G4
Gandino *Italy* **40** C6
Gando, Pta. *Canary Is.* **48** G4
Gandole *Nigeria* **83** D7
Gâneb *Mauritania* **82** B2
Ganedidalem = Gani
  Indonesia **63** E7
Ganetti *Sudan* **80** D3
Ganga → *India* **69** H14
Ganga Sagar *India* **69** J13
Gangafani *Mali* **82** C4
Gangan → *India* **69** E8
Ganganagar *India* **68** E5
Gangapur *India* **68** F7
Gangara *Niger* **83** C6
Gangaw *Burma* **67** H19
Gangdisê Shan *China* **69** D9
Ganges = Ganga → *India* **69** H14
Ganges *Canada* **102** D4
Ganges *France* **20** E7
Ganges, Mouths of the *India* **69** J14
Ganggyeong *S. Korea* **57** F14
Gânghester *Sweden* **11** G7
Ganghwa *S. Korea* **57** F14
Gangi *Italy* **43** E7
Gângiova *Romania* **29** G8
Gangneung *S. Korea* **57** F15
Gangoh *India* **68** E7
Gangotri *India* **69** D8
Gangotri △ *India* **69** D8
Gangseong *S. Korea* **57** E15
Gangtok *India* **67** F16
Gangu *China* **56** G3
Gangyao *China* **57** B14
Gani *Indonesia* **63** E7
Ganj *India* **69** F9
Ganluc *China* **58** C4
Gannat *France* **19** F10
Gannett Peak *U.S.A.* **108** E9
Ganquan *China* **56** F5
Gänserndorf *Austria* **27** C9
Ganshui *China* **58** C6
Gansu □ *China* **56** G3
Ganta *Liberia* **82** D3
Gantheaume, C. *Australia* **95** F2
Gantheaume B. *Australia* **93** E1
Gantsevichi = Hantsavichy
  Belarus **23** B14
Ganye *Nigeria* **83** D7
Ganyem = Genyem
  Indonesia **63** E10
Ganyu *China* **57** G10
Ganyushkino *Kazakhstan* **35** G9
Ganzhou *China* **59** E10
Gao *Mali* **83** B4
Gao Xian *China* **58** C5
Gao'an *China* **59** C10
Gaohe *China* **59** F9
Gaohebu *China* **59** B11
Gaolan Dao *China* **59** G9
Gaokeng *China* **59** D9
Gaoligong Shan *China* **58** E2
Gaomi *China* **57** F10
Gaoping *China* **56** G7
Gaotang *China* **56** F9
Gaoua *Burkina Faso* **82** C4
Gaoual *Guinea* **82** C2
Gaoxiong = Kaohsiung
  Taiwan **59** F13
Gaoyang *China* **56** E8
Gaoyao *China* **59** F9
Gaoyou *China* **59** A12
Gaoyou Hu *China* **57** H10
Gaoyuan *China* **57** F9
Gaozhou *China* **59** G8
Gap *France* **21** D10
Gapan *Phil.* **61** D4
Gapat → *India* **69** G10
Gapuwiyak *Australia* **94** A2
Gar *China* **60** D2
Gara, L. *Ireland* **12** C3
Garāb *Iran* **73** F12
Garabogazköl Aylagy
  Turkmenistan **52** E6
Garachico *Canary Is.* **48** F3
Garachiné *Panama* **120** E4
Garafia *Canary Is.* **48** F2
Garagum *Turkmenistan* **71** B8
Garah *Australia* **95** D4
Garajonay *Canary Is.* **48** F2
Garamba △
  Dem. Rep. of the Congo **86** B2
Garango *Burkina Faso* **83** C4

Garanhuns Brazil 125 E11
Garautha India 69 G8
Garawe Liberia 82 E3
Garba Tula Kenya 86 B4
Garberville U.S.A. 108 F2
Garbsen Germany 24 C5
Gard □ France 21 D8
Gard → France 21 E8
Garda, L. di Italy 40 C7
Gardabani Georgia 35 K7
Gårdby Sweden 11 H10
Garde L. Canada 103 A7
Gardelegen Germany 24 C7
Garden City Ga., U.S.A. 117 E14
Garden City Kans., U.S.A. 112 G3
Garden City Tex., U.S.A. 116 F4
Garden Grove U.S.A. 111 M9
Gardēz Afghan. 68 C3
Gardiki Greece 46 C3
Gardiner Maine, U.S.A. 113 C19
Gardiner Mont., U.S.A. 108 D8
Gardiners I. U.S.A. 115 E12
Gardner U.S.A. 115 D13
Gardner Canal Canada 102 C3
Gardnerville U.S.A. 110 G7
Gardno, Jezioro Poland 30 D4
Gardo = Qardho Somali Rep. 75 F4
Gardone Val Trómpia Italy 40 C7
Gárdony Hungary 28 C3
Gares = Puente la Reina
  Spain 38 C3
Garešnica Croatia 41 C13
Garéssio Italy 40 D5
Garey U.S.A. 111 L6
Garfield U.S.A. 108 C5
Garforth U.K. 14 D6
Gargaliani Greece 46 D3
Gargan, Mt. France 20 C5
Gargano △ Italy 41 G12
Gargantua, C. Canada 113 B11
Gargett Australia 94 K6
Gargouna Mali 83 B5
Gargždai Lithuania 30 C8
Garibaldi △ Canada 102 D4
Gariep, L. S. Africa 88 E4
Garies S. Africa 88 E2
Garig Gunak Barlu △
  Australia 92 B5
Garigliano → Italy 42 A6
Garissa Kenya 86 C4
Garkida Nigeria 83 C7
Garko Nigeria 83 C6
Garland Tex., U.S.A. 116 E6
Garland Utah, U.S.A. 108 F7
Garlasco Italy 40 C5
Garlin France 20 E3
Garmāb Semnān, Iran 71 C8
Garmāb Zanjān, Iran 73 E13
Garmisch-Partenkirchen
  Germany 25 H7
Garmsār Iran 71 C7
Garner U.S.A. 112 D7
Garnett U.S.A. 112 F6
Garo Hills India 69 G14
Garoe = Garoowe Somali Rep. 75 F4
Garonne → France 20 C3
Garonne, Canal Latéral à
  la France 20 D4
Garoowe Somali Rep. 75 F4
Garot India 68 G6
Garou, L. Mali 82 B4
Garoua Cameroon 83 D7
Garpenberg Sweden 10 D10
Garphyttan Sweden 10 E8
Garrauli India 69 G8
Garrel Germany 24 C4
Garrigues France 20 E7
Garrison Mont., U.S.A. 108 C7
Garrison N. Dak., U.S.A. 112 B3
Garrison Res. =
  Sakakawea, L. U.S.A. 112 B3
Garron Pt. U.K. 12 A6
Garrovillas de Alconétar
  Spain 37 F4
Garrucha Spain 39 H3
Garry → U.K. 13 E5
Garry, L. Canada 100 C9
Garrygala Turkmenistan 71 B8
Garsen Kenya 86 C5
Gärsnäs Sweden 11 J8
Garson L. Canada 103 B6
Garstang U.K. 14 D5
Gartempe → France 20 B4
Gartz Germany 24 B10
Garu Ghana 83 C4
Garu India 69 H11
Garub Namibia 88 D2
Garut Indonesia 63 G12
Garvão Portugal 37 H2
Garvie Mts. N.Z. 91 F2
Garwa = Garoua Cameroon 83 D7
Garwa India 69 G10
Garwolin Poland 31 G8
Gary U.S.A. 112 E10
Garz Germany 24 A9
Garzê China 58 B3

Garzón Colombia 124 C3
Gas-San Japan 54 E10
Gasan Kuli = Esenguly
  Turkmenistan 52 F6
Gascogne France 20 E4
Gascogne, G. de Europe 20 E2
Gascony = Gascogne France 20 E4
Gascoyne → Australia 93 D1
Gascoyne Junction Australia 93 E2
Gascueña Spain 38 E2
Gash, Wadi → Ethiopia 81 D4
Gash Setit △ Eritrea 81 D4
Gashagar Nigeria 83 C7
Gashaka Nigeria 83 D7
Gashaka-Gumti △ Nigeria 83 D7
Gasherbrum Pakistan 69 B7
Gashua Nigeria 83 C7
Gaspé Canada 105 C7
Gaspé, C. de Canada 105 C7
Gaspé Pen. = Gaspésie,
  Pén. de la Canada 105 C6
Gaspésie, Pén. de la Canada 105 C6
Gaspésie △ Canada 105 C6
Gassan Burkina Faso 82 C4
Gassol Nigeria 83 D7
Gasteiz = Vitoria-Gasteiz
  Spain 38 C2
Gastonia U.S.A. 117 D14
Gastouni Greece 46 D3
Gastouri Greece 46 B1
Gastre Argentina 128 E3
Gästrikland Sweden 10 D10
Gata, C. Cyprus 49 E12
Gata, C. de Spain 39 J2
Gata, Sierra de Spain 36 E4
Gataga → Canada 102 B3
Gătaia Romania 28 E6
Gatchina Russia 32 C6
Gatehouse of Fleet U.K. 13 G4
Gates U.S.A. 114 C7
Gateshead U.K. 14 C6
Gatesville U.S.A. 116 F6
Gateway △ U.S.A. 115 F11
Gaths Zimbabwe 87 G3
Gâtinais France 19 D9
Gâtine, Hauteurs de France 20 B3
Gatineau Canada 115 A9
Gatineau → Canada 104 C4
Gatineau △ Canada 104 C4
Gattaran Phil. 61 B4
Gattinara Italy 40 C5
Gatton Australia 95 D5
Gatún, L. Panama 120 E4
Gatwick, London ✈ (LGW)
  U.K. 15 F7
Gatyana S. Africa 89 E4
Gau Fiji 91 a
Gaucín Spain 37 J5
Gauer L. Canada 103 B9
Gauhati = Guwahati India 67 F17
Gauja → Latvia 30 A11
Gaujas △ Latvia 30 H21
Gaula → Norway 8 E14
Gauri Phanta India 69 E9
Gaustatoppen Norway 9 G13
Gauteng □ S. Africa 89 D4
Gāv Koshī Iran 71 D8
Gävakān Iran 71 D7
Gavarnie France 20 F3
Gavāter Iran 71 E9
Gāvbandī Iran 71 E7
Gavdopoúla Greece 49 E6
Gávdos Greece 49 E6
Gavi Italy 40 D5
Gavião Portugal 37 F3
Gaviota U.S.A. 111 L6
Gávkhūnī, Bāţlāq-e Iran 71 C7
Gävle Sweden 10 D11
Gävleborgs län □ Sweden 10 C10
Gävlebukten Sweden 10 D11
Gavorrano Italy 40 F7
Gavray France 18 D5
Gavrilov Yam Russia 32 D10
Gavrio Greece 46 D6
Gawachab Namibia 88 D2
Gawilgarh Hills India 66 J10
Gawler Australia 95 E2
Gawler Ranges Australia 95 E2
Gawu Nigeria 83 D6
Gaxun Nur China 60 B5
Gaya India 69 G11
Gaya Niger 83 C5
Gaya Nigeria 83 C6
Gayéri Burkina Faso 83 C5
Gaylord U.S.A. 113 C11
Gayndah Australia 95 D5
Gaysin = Haysyn Ukraine 29 B14
Gayvoron = Hayvoron
  Ukraine 29 B14
Gaza Gaza Strip 74 D3
Gaza □ Mozam. 89 C5
Gaza Strip ■ Asia 74 D3
Gazanjyk = Bereket
  Turkmenistan 71 B7
Gazaoua Niger 83 C6
Gāzbor Iran 71 D8
Gazi Dem. Rep. of the Congo 86
Gaziantep Turkey 72 D7

Gaziantep □ Turkey 72 D7
Gazimağusa = Famagusta
  Cyprus 49 D12
Gazipaşa Turkey 72 D5
Gbarnga Liberia 82 D3
Gbekebo Nigeria 83 D5
Gboko Nigeria 83 D6
Gbongan Nigeria 83 D5
Gcoverega Botswana 88 B3
Gcuwa S. Africa 89 E4
Gdańsk Poland 30 D5
Gdańsk ✈ (GDN) Poland 30 D5
Gdańska, Zatoka Poland 30 D6
Gdov Russia 32 C4
Gdynia Poland 30 D5
Geba → Guinea-Biss. 82 C1
Gebe Indonesia 63 D7
Gebeciler Turkey 47 C12
Gebeit Mine Sudan 80 C4
Gebel Abyad Sudan 80 D2
Gebel Iweibid Egypt 80 H8
Gebze Turkey 45 F13
Gecha Ethiopia 81 F4
Gedaref Sudan 81 E4
Gedaref □ Sudan 81 E4
Gediz Turkey 47 B11
Gediz → Turkey 47 C8
Gedo Ethiopia 81 F4
Gèdre France 20 F4
Gedser Denmark 11 K5
Gedung, Pulau Malaysia 65 c
Geegully Cr. → Australia 92 C3
Geel Belgium 17 C4
Geelong Australia 95 F3
Geelvink B. =
  Cenderwasih, Teluk
  Indonesia 63 E9
Geelvink Chan. Australia 93 E1
Geesthacht Germany 24 B6
Geidam Nigeria 83 C7
Geikie → Canada 103 B8
Geikie Gorge △ Australia 92 C4
Geilenkirchen Germany 24 E2
Geili Sudan 81 D3
Geisingen Germany 25 H4
Geislingen Germany 25 G5
Geistown U.S.A. 114 F6
Geita Tanzania 86 C3
Gejiu China 58 F4
Gel → Sudan 81 F2
Gel, Meydān-e Iran 71 D7
Gel River Sudan 81 F2
Gela Italy 43 F7
Gela, G. di Italy 43 F7
Gelahun Liberia 82 D2
Gelang Patah Malaysia 65 d
Gelderland □ Neths. 17 B6
Geldern Germany 24 D2
Geldrop Neths. 17 C5
Geleen Neths. 17 D5
Gelehun S. Leone 82 D2
Gelembe Turkey 47 B9
Gelemso Ethiopia 81 F5
Gelendost Turkey 72 C4
Gelendzhik Russia 33 K10
Gelib = Jilib Somali Rep. 75 G3
Gelibolu Turkey 45 F10
Gelibolu Yarımadası Turkey 45 F10
Gelidonya Burnu Turkey 72 D4
Gelnhausen Germany 25 E5
Gelnica Slovak Rep. 27 C13
Gelsenkirchen Germany 24 D3
Gelting Germany 24 A5
Gelugur Malaysia 65 c
Gemas Malaysia 65 L4
Gembloux Belgium 17 D4
Gembu Nigeria 83 D7
Gemena
  Dem. Rep. of the Congo 84 D3
Gemerek Turkey 72 C7
Gemla Sweden 11 H8
Gemlik Turkey 45 F13
Gemlik Körfezi Turkey 45 F12
Gemona del Friuli Italy 41 B10
Gemsa Egypt 80 B3
Gemsbok △ Botswana 88 D3
Gemünden Germany 25 E5
Genadi Greece 49 C9
Genale → Ethiopia 81 F4
Genç Turkey 73 C9
Gençay France 20 B4
Geneina, Gebel Egypt 80 B3
General Acha Argentina 126 D3
General Alvear B. Aires,
  Argentina 126 D4
General Alvear Mendoza,
  Argentina 126 D2
General Artigas Paraguay 126 B4
General Belgrano Argentina 126 D4
General Bernardo
  O'Higgins Antarctica 5 C18
General Cabrera Argentina 126 C3
General Cepeda Mexico 118 B4
General Guido Argentina 126 D4
General Juan Madariaga
  Argentina 126 D4
General La Madrid
  Argentina 126 D3
General MacArthur Phil. 61 F6

General Martin Miguel de
  Güemes Argentina 126 A3
General Pico Argentina 126 D3
General Pinedo Argentina 126 B3
General Pinto Argentina 126 C3
General Roca Argentina 128 D3
General Santos Phil. 61 H6
General Toshevo Bulgaria 45 C12
General Treviño Mexico 119 B5
General Trías Mexico 118 B3
General Viamonte
  Argentina 126 D3
General Villegas Argentina 126 D3
Genesee Idaho, U.S.A. 108 C5
Genesee Pa., U.S.A. 114 E7
Genesee → U.S.A. 114 C7
Geneseo Ill., U.S.A. 112 E8
Geneseo N.Y., U.S.A. 114 D7
Geneva = Genève Switz. 25 J2
Geneva Ala., U.S.A. 117 F12
Geneva N.Y., U.S.A. 114 D8
Geneva Nebr., U.S.A. 112 E6
Geneva Ohio, U.S.A. 114 E4
Geneva, L. = Léman, L.
  Europe 19 F13
Genève Switz. 25 J2
Gengenbach Germany 25 G4
Gengma China 58 F2
Genichesk = Henichesk
  Ukraine 33 J8
Genil → Spain 37 H5
Genisea Greece 45 E8
Genk Belgium 17 D5
Genlis France 19 E12
Gennargentu, Mti. del Italy 42 B2
Gennes France 18 E6
Genoa = Génova Italy 40 D5
Genoa Australia 95 F4
Genoa N.Y., U.S.A. 115 D8
Genoa Nebr., U.S.A. 112 E5
Genoa Nev., U.S.A. 110 F7
Génova Italy 40 D5
Génova ✈ (GOA) Italy 40 D5
Génova, G. di Italy 40 E6
Genriyetty, Ostrov Russia 53 B16
Gent Belgium 17 C3
Genteng Bali, Indonesia 63 J17
Genteng Jawa Barat,
  Indonesia 63 G12
Genthin Germany 24 C8
Genyem Indonesia 63 E10
Genzano di Lucánia Italy 43 B9
Genzano di Roma Italy 41 G9
Geoagiu Romania 29 E8
Geographe B. Australia 93 F2
Geographe Chan. Australia 93 D1
Geokchay = Göyçay
  Azerbaijan 35 K8
Georga, Zemlya Russia 52 A5
George S. Africa 88 E3
George → Canada 105 A6
George, L. N.S.W., Australia 95 F4
George, L. S. Austral.,
  Australia 95 F3
George, L. W. Austral.,
  Australia 92 D3
George, L. Uganda 86 B3
George, L. Fla., U.S.A. 117 G14
George, L. N.Y., U.S.A. 115 C11
George Gill Ra. Australia 92 D5
George Pt. Australia 94 J6
George River =
  Kangiqsualujjuaq Canada
  101 D13
George Sound N.Z. 91 F1
George Town Australia 95 G4
George Town Bahamas 120 B4
George Town Cayman Is. 120 C3
George Town Malaysia 65 c
George V Land Antarctica 5 C10
George VI Sound Antarctica 5 D17
George West U.S.A. 116 G5
Georgetown =
  Janjanbureh Gambia 82 C2
Georgetown Australia 94 B3
Georgetown Ont., Canada 114 C5
Georgetown P.E.I., Canada 105 C7
Georgetown Guyana 124 B7
Georgetown Calif., U.S.A. 110 G6
Georgetown Colo., U.S.A. 108 G11
Georgetown Ky., U.S.A. 113 F11
Georgetown N.Y., U.S.A. 115 D9
Georgetown Ohio, U.S.A. 113 F12
Georgetown S.C., U.S.A. 117 E15
Georgetown Tex., U.S.A. 116 F6
Georgia □ U.S.A. 117 E13
Georgia ■ Asia 35 J6
Georgia, Str. of N. Amer. 110 A3
Georgian B. Canada 114 A4
Georgian Bay Islands △
  Canada 114 B5
Georgiyevka Kazakhstan 52 E9
Georgina → Australia 94 C2
Georgina I. Canada 114 B5
Georgioupoli Greece 49 D6
Georgiyevsk Russia 35 H6
Georgsmarienhütte Germany 24 C4

Gera Germany 24 E8
Geraardsbergen Belgium 17 D3
Geraki Greece 46 D4
Geral, Serra Brazil 127 B6
Geral de Goiás, Serra Brazil 125 F9
Geraldine U.S.A. 108 C8
Geraldton Australia 93 E1
Geraldton Canada 104 C2
Gérardmer France 19 D13
Gercüş Turkey 73 D9
Gerede Turkey 72 B5
Gereshk Afghan. 66 D4
Gerês, Sierra do Portugal 36 D3
Geretsried Germany 25 H7
Gérgal Spain 39 H2
Gerik Malaysia 65 K3
Gering U.S.A. 112 E2
Gerlach U.S.A. 108 F4
Gerlachovský štit
  Slovak Rep. 27 B13
German Bight = Deutsche
  Bucht Germany 24 A4
German Planina Macedonia 44 D6
Germansen Landing Canada
  102 B4
Germantown U.S.A. 117 D10
Germany ■ Europe 24 E6
Germencik Turkey 47 D9
Germering Germany 25 G7
Germersheim Germany 25 F4
Germī Iran 73 C13
Germiston S. Africa 89 D4
Gernsheim Germany 25 F4
Gero Japan 55 G8
Gerokgak Indonesia 63 J17
Gerolzhofen Germany 25 F6
Gerona = Girona Spain 38 D7
Geropotamos → Greece 49 D6
Gerrard Canada 102 C5
Gers □ France 20 E4
Gers → France 20 D4
Gersfeld Germany 24 E5
Gersthofen Germany 25 G6
Gertak Sanggul Malaysia 65 c
Gertak Sanggul, Tanjung
  Malaysia 65 c
Gerung Indonesia 63 K19
Gerzat France 20 C7
Gerze Turkey 72 B6
Geseke Germany 24 D4
Geser Indonesia 63 E8
Gesso → Italy 40 D4
Gestro, Wabi → Ethiopia 81 G5
Getafe Spain 36 E7
Getinge Sweden 11 H6
Gettysburg Pa., U.S.A. 113 F15
Gettysburg S. Dak., U.S.A. 112 C4
Getxo Spain 38 B2
Getz Ice Shelf Antarctica 5 D14
Gevaş Turkey 73 C10
Gévaudan France 20 D7
Gevgelija Macedonia 44 E6
Gévora → Spain 37 G4
Gex France 19 F13
Geyikli Turkey 47 B8
Geyser U.S.A. 108 C8
Geyserville U.S.A. 110 G4
Geyve Turkey 72 B4
Ghâbat el Arab = Wang
  Kai Sudan 81 F2
Ghabeish Sudan 81 E2
Ghadaf, W. al → Iraq 73 F10
Ghadāmis Libya 79 B8
Ghaggar → India 68 E6
Ghaghara → India 69 G11
Ghaghat → Bangla. 69 G13
Ghagra India 69 H11
Ghagra → India 69 F9
Ghalla, Wadi → Sudan 81 E2
Ghallamane Mauritania 78 D4
Ghana ■ W. Afr. 83 D4
Ghansor India 69 H9
Ghanzi Botswana 88 C3
Gharb Bahr el Ghazâl □
  Sudan 81 F2
Gharb el Istiwa'iya □ Sudan 81 G3
Gharb Kordofân □ Sudan 81 E2
Gharbîya, Es Sahrâ el Egypt 80 B2
Ghardaïa Algeria 78 B6
Ghârib, G. Egypt 80 B3
Gharig Sudan 81 E2
Gharm Tajikistan 52 F8
Gharyān Libya 79 B8
Ghat Libya 79 D8
Ghatal India 69 H12
Ghatampur India 69 F9
Ghats, Eastern India 66 N11
Ghats, Western India 66 N9
Ghatsila India 69 H12
Ghaţţī Si. Arabia 70 D3
Ghawdex = Gozo Malta 49 C1
Ghazal, Bahr el → Chad 79 F9
Ghazâl, Bahr el → Sudan 81 F3
Ghaziabad India 68 E7
Ghazipur India 69 G10
Ghaznī Afghan. 66 C3
Ghaznī □ Afghan. 66 C3

Ghedi Italy 40 C7
Ghelari Romania 28 E7
Ghent = Gent Belgium 17 C3
Gheorghe Gheorghiu-
  Dej = Oneşti Romania 29 D11
Gheorgheni Romania 29 D10
Gherla Romania 29 C8
Ghidigeni Romania 29 D12
Ghilarza Italy 42 B1
Ghimeş-Făget Romania 29 D11
Ghīnah, Wādī al →
  Si. Arabia 70 D3
Ghisonaccia France 21 F13
Ghisoni France 21 F13
Ghizar → Pakistan 69 A5
Ghot Ogrein Egypt 80 A2
Ghotaru India 68 F4
Ghotki Pakistan 68 E3
Ghowr □ Afghan. 66 C4
Ghughri India 69 H9
Ghugus India 66 K11
Ghulam Mohammad
  Barrage Pakistan 68 G3
Ghūrīān Afghan. 66 B2
Gia Dinh Vietnam 65 G6
Gia Lai = Plei Ku Vietnam 64 F7
Gia Nghia Vietnam 65 G6
Gia Ngoc Vietnam 64 E7
Gia Vuc Vietnam 64 E7
Giali Greece 47 E9
Gialtra Greece 46 C4
Giamama = Jamaame
  Somali Rep. 75 G3
Gianitsa Greece 44 F6
Giannutri Italy 40 F8
Giant Forest U.S.A. 110 J8
Giant Mts. = Krkonoše
  Czech Rep. 26 A8
Giant Sequoia △ U.S.A. 110 K8
Giants Causeway U.K. 12 A5
Gianyar Indonesia 63 K18
Giarabub = Al Jaghbūb
  Libya 79 C10
Giaros Greece 46 D6
Giarre Italy 43 E8
Giaveno Italy 40 C4
Gibara Cuba 120 B4
Gibb River Australia 92 C4
Gibbon U.S.A. 112 E4
Gibe → Ethiopia 81 F4
Gibellina Nuova Italy 42 E5
Gibeon Namibia 88 D2
Gibraleón Spain 37 H4
Gibraltar ☑ Europe 37 J5
Gibraltar, Str. of Medit. S. 37 K5
Gibraltar Range △ Australia 95 D5
Gibson Desert Australia 92 D4
Gibsons Canada 102 D4
Gibsonville U.S.A. 110 F6
Giddings U.S.A. 116 F6
Gidole Ethiopia 81 F4
Giebnegáisi = Kebnekaise
  Sweden 8 C18
Gien France 19 E9
Giengen Germany 25 G6
Giessen Germany 24 E4
Gifan Iran 71 B8
Gifatin, Geziret Egypt 80 B3
Gifhorn Germany 24 C6
Gift Lake Canada 102 B5
Gifu Japan 55 G8
Gifu □ Japan 55 G8
Gigant Russia 35 G5
Giganta, Sa. de la Mexico 118 B2
Gigen Bulgaria 45 C8
Gigha U.K. 13 F3
Gíglio Italy 40 F7
Gignac France 20 E7
Gigüela → Spain 37 F7
Gijón Spain 36 B5
Gil I. Canada 102 C3
Gila → U.S.A. 109 K6
Gila Bend U.S.A. 109 K7
Gila Bend Mts. U.S.A. 109 K7
Gila Cliff Dwellings △
  U.S.A. 109 K9
Gīlān □ Iran 71 B6
Gīlān-e Gharb Iran 73 E11
Gîlău Romania 29 D8
Gilbert → Australia 94 B3
Gilbert Is. Kiribati 90 A10
Gilbert River Australia 94 B3
Gilbert Seamounts Pac. Oc. 4 D18
Gilead U.S.A. 115 B14
Gilf el Kebîr, Hadabat el
  Egypt 80 C2
Gilford I. Canada 102 C3
Gilgandra Australia 95 E4
Gilgil Kenya 86 C4
Gilgit India 69 B6
Gilgit → Pakistan 69 B6
Gili △ Mozam. 87 F4
Gilimanuk Indonesia 63 J17
Giljeva Planina Europe 44 C3
Gillam Canada 103 B10
Gilleleje Denmark 11 H6
Gillen, L. Australia 93 E3
Gilles, L. Australia 95 E2
Gillette U.S.A. 108 D11

Gilliat *Australia* **94** C3
Gillingham *U.K.* **15** F8
Gilmer *U.S.A.* **116** E7
Gilmore, L. *Australia* **93** F3
Gilmour *Canada* **114** B7
Gilo → *Ethiopia* **81** F3
Gilort → *Romania* **29** F8
Gilroy *U.S.A.* **110** H5
Gimbi *Ethiopia* **81** F4
Gimcheon *S. Korea* **57** F15
Gimhae *S. Korea* **57** G15
Gimhwa *S. Korea* **57** E14
Gimie, Mt *St. Lucia* **121** f
Gimje *S. Korea* **57** G14
Gimli *Canada* **103** C9
Gimo *Sweden* **10** D12
Gimone → *France* **20** E5
Gimont *France* **20** E4
Gin Gin *Australia* **95** D5
Ginâh *Egypt* **80** B3
Gineifa *Egypt* **80** H8
Gingin *Australia* **93** F2
Gingindlovu *S. Africa* **89** D5
Gingoog *Phil.* **61** G6
Ginir *Ethiopia* **81** F5
Ginosa *Italy* **43** B9
Ginzo de Limia = Xinzo de
   Limia *Spain* **36** C3
Giofyros → *Greece* **49** D7
Gióia, G. di *Italy* **43** D8
Gióia del Colle *Italy* **43** B9
Gióia Táuro *Italy* **43** D8
Gioiosa Iónica *Italy* **43** D9
Gioiosa Marea *Italy* **43** D7
Giona, Oros *Greece* **46** C4
Giovi, Passo dei *Italy* **40** D5
Giovinazzo *Italy* **43** A9
Gir △ *India* **68** J4
Gir Hills *India* **68** J4
Girab *India* **68** F4
Girâfi, W. → *Egypt* **74** F3
Giraltovce *Slovak Rep.* **27** B14
Girard *St. Lucia* **121** f
Girard *Kans., U.S.A.* **112** G6
Girard *Ohio, U.S.A.* **114** E4
Girard *Pa., U.S.A.* **114** E4
Girdle Ness *U.K.* **13** D6
Giresun *Turkey* **73** B8
Giresun □ *Turkey* **73** B8
Girga *Egypt* **80** B3
Giri → *India* **68** D7
Giridih *India* **69** G12
Girifalco *Italy* **43** D9
Giriftu *Kenya* **86** B4
Giriyondo *S. Africa* **89** C5
Girne = Kyrenia *Cyprus* **49** D12
Giro *Nigeria* **83** C5
Giromagny *France* **19** E13
Giron = Kiruna *Sweden* **8** C19
Girona *Spain* **38** D7
Girona □ *Spain* **38** C7
Gironde □ *France* **20** D3
Gironde → *France* **20** C2
Gironella *Spain* **38** C6
Girraween △ *Australia* **95** D5
Girrigun △ *Australia* **94** B4
Giru *Australia* **94** B4
Girvan *U.K.* **13** F4
Gisborne *N.Z.* **91** C7
Gisenyi *Rwanda* **86** C2
Gislaved *Sweden* **11** G7
Gisors *France* **19** C8
Gitega *Burundi* **86** C2
Githio *Greece* **46** B6
Giuba = Juba → *Somali Rep.* **75** G3
Giugliano in Campania *Italy* **43** B7
Giulianova *Italy* **41** F10
Giura *Greece* **46** B6
Giurgeni *Romania* **29** F12
Giurgiu *Romania* **29** G10
Giurgiu □ *Romania* **29** F10
Giurgiuleşti *Moldova* **29** E13
Give *Denmark* **11** J3
Givet *France* **19** B11
Givors *France* **21** C8
Givry *France* **19** F11
Giyon *Ethiopia* **81** F4
Giza = El Gîza *Egypt* **80** J7
Giza Pyramids *Egypt* **80** J7
Gizab *Afghan.* **68** C1
Gizhiga *Russia* **53** C17
Gizhiginskaya Guba *Russia* **53** C16
Giżycko *Poland* **30** D8
Gizzeria *Italy* **43** D9
Gjalicë e Lumës, Mal.
   Albania **44** D4
Gjegjan *Albania* **44** E4
Gjirokastër *Albania* **44** F4
Gjoa Haven *Canada* **100** C10
Gjøvik *Norway* **8** F14
Gjuhës, Kep i *Albania* **44** F3
Glace Bay *Canada* **105** C8
Glacier △ *Canada* **102** C5
Glacier △ *U.S.A.* **108** B7
Glacier Bay △ *U.S.A.* **102** B1
Glacier Peak *U.S.A.* **108** B3
Gladewater *U.S.A.* **116** E7
Gladstone *Queens., Australia* **94** C5

Gladstone *S. Austral.,
   Australia* **95** E2
Gladstone *Canada* **103** C9
Gladstone *U.S.A.* **112** C10
Gladwin *U.S.A.* **113** D11
Glafsfjorden *Sweden* **10** E6
Glagah *Indonesia* **63** J17
Głagów Małopolski *Poland* **31** H8
Glåma = Glomma →
   Norway **9** G14
Gláma *Iceland* **8** D2
Glamis *U.S.A.* **111** N11
Glamoč *Bos.-H.* **41** D13
Glamorgan, Vale of □ *U.K.* **15** F4
Glamsbjerg *Denmark* **11** J4
Glarus *Switz.* **25** H5
Glarus □ *Switz.* **25** J5
Glasco *Kans., U.S.A.* **112** F5
Glasco *N.Y., U.S.A.* **115** D11
Glasgow *U.K.* **13** F4
Glasgow *Ky., U.S.A.* **113** G11
Glasgow *Mont., U.S.A.* **108** B10
Glasgow, City of □ *U.K.* **13** F4
Glasgow Int. ✈ (GLA) *U.K.* **13** F4
Glaslyn *Canada* **103** C7
Glastonbury *U.K.* **15** F5
Glastonbury *U.S.A.* **115** E12
Glauchau *Germany* **24** E8
Glava *Sweden* **10** E6
Glavice *Croatia* **41** E13
Glazov *Russia* **34** A11
Gleichen *Canada* **102** C6
Gleisdorf *Austria* **26** D8
Gleiwitz = Gliwice *Poland* **31** H5
Glen *U.S.A.* **115** B13
Glen Affric *U.K.* **13** D3
Glen Canyon *U.S.A.* **109** H8
Glen Canyon △ *U.S.A.* **109** H8
Glen Canyon Dam *U.S.A.* **109** H8
Glen Coe *U.K.* **13** E3
Glen Cove *U.S.A.* **115** F11
Glen Garry *U.K.* **13** D3
Glen Innes *Australia* **95** D5
Glen Lyon *U.S.A.* **115** E8
Glen Mor *U.K.* **13** D4
Glen More △ *U.K.* **13** D5
Glen Moriston *U.K.* **13** D4
Glen Robertson *Canada* **115** A10
Glen Spean *U.K.* **13** E4
Glen Ullin *U.S.A.* **112** B3
Glenallen *U.S.A.* **100** C5
Glénan, Îs. de *France* **18** E3
Glenariff △ *Ireland* **12** A5
Glenbeigh *Ireland* **12** D2
Glencoe *Canada* **114** D3
Glencoe *S. Africa* **89** D5
Glencoe *U.S.A.* **112** C6
Glencolumbkille *Ireland* **12** B3
Glendale *Ariz., U.S.A.* **109** K7
Glendale *Calif., U.S.A.* **111** L8
Glendale *Zimbabwe* **87** F3
Glendive *U.S.A.* **108** C11
Glendo *U.S.A.* **108** E11
Glenelg → *Australia* **95** F3
Glenfield *U.S.A.* **112** B5
Glengad Hd. *Ireland* **12** A4
Glengarriff *Ireland* **12** E2
Glenmont *U.S.A.* **114** F2
Glenmorgan *Australia* **95** D4
Glenn *U.S.A.* **110** F4
Glennamaddy *Ireland* **12** C3
Glenns Ferry *U.S.A.* **108** E6
Glenora *Canada* **114** B7
Glenorchy *Australia* **95** G4
Glenore *Australia* **94** B3
Glenreagh *Australia* **95** E5
Glenrock *U.S.A.* **108** E11
Glenrothes *U.K.* **13** E5
Glens Falls *U.S.A.* **115** C11
Glenside *U.S.A.* **115** F9
Glenties *Ireland* **12** B3
Glenveagh △ *Ireland* **12** A3
Glenville *U.S.A.* **113** F13
Glenwood *Canada* **105** C9
Glenwood *Ark., U.S.A.* **116** D8
Glenwood *Iowa, U.S.A.* **112** E6
Glenwood *Minn., U.S.A.* **112** C6
Glenwood *Wash., U.S.A.* **110** D5
Glenwood Springs *U.S.A.* **108** G10
Glettinganes *Iceland* **8** D7
Glifada *Greece* **46** D5
Glimåkra *Sweden* **11** H8
Glin *Ireland* **12** D2
Glina *Croatia* **41** C13
Glinojeck *Poland* **31** F7
Gliwice *Poland* **31** H5
Globe *U.S.A.* **109** K8
Glodeanu Siliştea *Romania* **29** F11
Glodeni *Moldova* **29** C12
Glödnitz *Austria* **26** E7
Gloggnitz *Austria* **26** D8
Głogów *Poland* **31** G3
Głogówek *Poland* **31** H4
Glomma → *Norway* **9** G14
Glorieuses, Îs. *Ind. Oc.* **89** A8
Glosa *Greece* **46** B5
Glossop *U.K.* **14** D6
Gloucester *Australia* **95** E5
Gloucester *U.K.* **15** F5

Gloucester *U.S.A.* **115** D14
Gloucester I. *Australia* **94** J6
Gloucester Island △ *Australia* **94** J6
Gloucester Point *U.S.A.* **113** G15
Gloucestershire □ *U.K.* **15** F5
Gloversville *U.S.A.* **115** C10
Glovertown *Canada* **105** C9
Głowno *Poland* **31** G6
Głubczyce *Poland* **31** H4
Głubokiy *Russia* **35** F5
Glubokoye = Hlybokaye
   Belarus **32** E4
Głuchołazy *Poland* **31** H4
Glücksburg *Germany* **24** A5
Glückstadt *Germany* **24** B5
Golchikha *Russia* **4** B12
Glukhov = Hlukhiv *Ukraine* **33** G7
Glusk *Belarus* **23** B15
Głuszyca *Poland* **31** H3
Glyngore *Denmark* **11** H2
Gmünd *Kärnten, Austria* **26** E6
Gmünd *Niederösterreich,
   Austria* **26** C8
Gmunden *Austria* **26** D6
Gnarp *Sweden* **10** B11
Gnesta *Sweden* **10** E11
Gniew *Poland* **30** E5
Gniewkowo *Poland* **31** F5
Gniezno *Poland* **31** F4
Gnjilane *Serbia* **44** D5
Gnoien *Germany* **24** B8
Gnosjö *Sweden* **11** G7
Gnowangerup *Australia* **93** F2
Go Cong *Vietnam* **65** G6
Gō-no-ura *Japan* **55** H4
Goa *India* **66** M8
Goa □ *India* **66** M8
Goalen Hd. *Australia* **95** F5
Goalpara *India* **67** F17
Goaltor *India* **69** H12
Goalundo Ghat *Bangla.* **69** H13
Goaso *Ghana* **82** D4
Goat Fell *U.K.* **13** F3
Goba *Ethiopia* **81** F4
Goba *Mozam.* **89** D5
Gobabis *Namibia* **88** C2
Göbel *Turkey* **45** F12
Gobi *Asia* **56** C6
Gobō *Japan* **55** H7
Gobo *Sudan* **81** F3
Goce *Greece* **46** B3
Göçbeyli *Turkey* **47** B9
Gochas *Namibia* **88** C2
Goch *Germany* **24** D2
Gochas *Namibia* **88** C2
Godavari → *India* **67** L13
Godavari Pt. *India* **67** L13
Godbout *Canada* **105** C6
Godda *India* **69** G12
Godech *Bulgaria* **44** C7
Goderich *Canada* **114** D3
Goderville *France* **18** C7
Godfrey Ra. *Australia* **93** D2
Godhavn = Qeqertarsuaq
   Greenland **4** C5
Godhra *India* **68** H5
Gödöllő *Hungary* **28** C4
Godoy Cruz *Argentina* **126** C2
Gods → *Canada* **104** A1
Gods L. *Canada* **104** B1
Gods River *Canada* **103** C10
Godthåb = Nuuk *Greenland* **99** C14
Goeie Hoop, Kaap die =
   Good Hope, C. of *S. Africa* **88** E2
Goéland, L. au *Canada* **104** C4
Goélands, L. aux *Canada* **105** A7
Goeree *Neths.* **17** C3
Goes *Neths.* **17** C3
Goffstown *U.S.A.* **115** C13
Gogama *Canada* **104** C3
Gogebic, L. *U.S.A.* **112** B9
Goggetti *Ethiopia* **81** F4
Gogolin *Poland* **31** H5
Gogonou *Benin* **83** C5
Gogra = Ghaghara → *India*
   69 G11
Gogriâl *Sudan* **81** F2
Gogti *Ethiopia* **81** E5
Gohana *India* **68** E7
Goharganj *India* **68** H7
Goi → *India* **68** H6
Goiânia *Brazil* **125** D11
Goiás *Brazil* **125** G8
Goiás □ *Brazil* **125** G8
Goio-Erê *Brazil* **127** A5
Góis *Portugal* **36** E2
Gojam *Ethiopia* **81** E4
Gojra *Pakistan* **68** D5
Gökçeada *Turkey* **45** F9
Gökçedağ *Turkey* **47** B10
Gökçeören *Turkey* **47** C10
Gökçeyazı *Turkey* **47** B9
Gökırmak → *Turkey* **72** B6
Gökova *Turkey* **47** E9
Gökova Körfezi *Turkey* **47** E9
Göksu → *Turkey* **72** D6
Göksun *Turkey* **72** C7
Gokteik *Burma* **67** H20

Göktepe *Turkey* **47** D10
Gokurt *Pakistan* **68** E2
Gokwe *Zimbabwe* **89** B4
Gola *India* **69** E9
Golakganj *India* **69** F13
Golan Heights = Hagolan
   Syria **74** C4
Gołańcz *Poland* **31** F4
Golāshkerd *Iran* **71** E8
Golaya Pristen = Hola
   Pristan *Ukraine* **33** J7
Gölbaşı *Adiyaman, Turkey* **72** D7
Gölbaşı *Ankara, Turkey* **72** C5
Golconda *U.S.A.* **108** F5
Gölcük *Kocaeli, Turkey* **45** F13
Gölcük *Niğde, Turkey* **72** C6
Gold *U.S.A.* **114** E7
Gold Beach *U.S.A.* **108** E1
Gold Coast *W. Afr.* **83** E4
Gold Hill *U.S.A.* **108** E2
Gold River *Canada* **102** D3
Goldap *Poland* **30** D9
Goldberg *Germany* **24** B8
Golden *Canada* **102** C5
Golden B. *N.Z.* **91** D4
Golden Gate *U.S.A.* **109** H2
Golden Gate Highlands △
   S. Africa **89** D4
Golden Hinde *Canada* **102** D3
Golden Lake *Canada* **114** A7
Golden Spike △ *U.S.A.* **108** F7
Golden Vale *Ireland* **12** D3
Goldendale *U.S.A.* **108** D3
Goldfield *U.S.A.* **109** H5
Goldsand L. *Canada* **103** B8
Goldsboro *U.S.A.* **117** D16
Goldsmith *U.S.A.* **116** F3
Goldthwaite *U.S.A.* **116** F5
Golegã *Portugal* **37** F2
Goleniów *Poland* **30** E1
Golestān □ *Iran* **71** B7
Golestānak *Iran* **71** D7
Goleta *U.S.A.* **111** L7
Golfito *Costa Rica* **120** E3
Golfo Aranci *Italy* **42** B2
Golfo di Oroséi e del
   Gennargentu △ *Italy* **42** B2
Gölgeli Dağları *Turkey* **47** D10
Gölhisar *Turkey* **47** E12
Goliad *U.S.A.* **116** G6
Golija *Montenegro* **44** C2
Golija *Serbia* **44** C4
Golina *Poland* **31** F5
Gölköy *Turkey* **72** B7
Golo → *France* **21** F13
Gólova *Turkey* **47** E12
Golpāyegān *Iran* **71** C6
Gölpazarı *Turkey* **72** B4
Golra *Pakistan* **68** C5
Golspie *U.K.* **13** D5
Golub-Dobrzyń *Poland* **31** E6
Golubac *Serbia* **44** B5
Golyam Perelik *Bulgaria* **45** E8
Golyama Kamchiya →
   Bulgaria **45** C11
Goma *Dem. Rep. of the Congo* **86** C2
Gomal Pass *Pakistan* **68** D3
Gomati → *India* **69** G10
Gombari
   Dem. Rep. of the Congo **86** B2
Gombe *Nigeria* **83** C7
Gömbe *Turkey* **47** E11
Gombe □ *Nigeria* **83** C7
Gombe → *Tanzania* **86** C3
Gombi *Nigeria* **83** C7
Gomel = Homyel *Belarus* **23** B16
Gomera *Canary Is.* **48** F2
Gómez Palacio *Mexico* **118** B4
Gomfi *Greece* **46** B3
Gomīshān *Iran* **71** B7
Gommern *Germany* **24** C7
Gomogomo *Indonesia* **63** F8
Gomoh *India* **69** H12
Gomotarsti *Bulgaria* **44** B6
Gompa = Ganta *Liberia* **82** D3
Gonābād *Iran* **71** C8
Gonaïves *Haiti* **121** C5
Gonarezhou △ *Zimbabwe* **87** G3
Gonâve, G. de la *Haiti* **121** C5
Gonâve, Île de la *Haiti* **121** C5
Gonbad-e Kāvūs *Iran* **71** B7
Gönc *Hungary* **28** B6
Gonda *India* **69** F9
Gonder *Ethiopia* **81** E4
Gondia *India* **66** J12
Gondola *Mozam.* **87** F3
Gondomar *Portugal* **36** D2
Gondrecourt-le-Château
   France **19** D12
Gönen *Balıkesir, Turkey* **45** F11
Gönen *Isparta, Turkey* **47** D12
Gönen → *Turkey* **45** F11
Gong Xian *China* **58** C5
Gong'an *China* **59** B9
Gongcheng *China* **59** E8

Gongga Shan *China* **58** C3
Gongguan *China* **58** G7
Gonghe *China* **60** C5
Gongju *S. Korea* **57** F14
Gongola → *Nigeria* **83** D7
Gongolgon *Australia* **95** E4
Gongshan *China* **58** D2
Gongtan *China* **58** C7
Gongzhuling *China* **57** C13
Goni *Greece* **46** B4
Gonjo *China* **58** B1
Gonnesa *Italy* **42** C1
Gonnosfanádiga *Italy* **42** C1
Gonzaga *Phil.* **61** B5
Gonzales *Calif., U.S.A.* **110** J5
Gonzales *Tex., U.S.A.* **116** G6
González *Mexico* **119** C5
Good Hope, C. of *S. Africa* **88** E2
Gooderham *Canada* **114** B6
Goodhouse *S. Africa* **88** D2
Gooding *U.S.A.* **108** E6
Goodland *U.S.A.* **112** F3
Goodlands *Mauritius* **85** d
Goodlow *Canada* **102** B4
Goodooga *Australia* **95** D4
Goodsprings *U.S.A.* **111** K11
Goole *U.K.* **14** D7
Goolgowi *Australia* **95** E4
Goomalling *Australia* **93** F2
Goomeri *Australia* **95** D5
Goonda *Mozam.* **87** F3
Goondiwindi *Australia* **95** D5
Goongarrie, L. *Australia* **93** F3
Goongarrie △ *Australia* **93** F3
Goonyella *Australia* **94** C4
Goose → *Canada* **105** B7
Goose Creek *U.S.A.* **117** E14
Goose L. *U.S.A.* **108** F3
Gop *India* **68** H3
Gopalganj *India* **69** F11
Göppingen *Germany* **25** G5
Gor *Spain* **37** H8
Góra *Dolnośląskie, Poland* **31** G3
Góra *Mazowieckie, Poland* **31** F7
Góra Kalwaria *Poland* **31** G8
Gorakhpur *India* **69** F10
Goražde *Bos.-H.* **28** G3
Gorda, Pta. *Canary Is.* **48** F2
Gorda, Pta. *Nic.* **120** D3
Gordan B. *Australia* **92** B5
Gördes *Turkey* **47** C10
Gordon *U.S.A.* **112** D2
Gordon → *Australia* **95** G4
Gordon Bay *Canada* **114** A5
Gordon L. *Alta., Canada* **103** B6
Gordon L. *N.W.T., Canada* **102** A6
Gordonvale *Australia* **94** B4
Goré *Chad* **79** G9
Gore *Ethiopia* **81** F4
Gore *N.Z.* **91** G2
Gore Bay *Canada* **104** C3
Görele *Turkey* **73** B8
Goreme *Turkey* **72** C6
Gorey *Ireland* **12** D5
Gorg *Iran* **71** D8
Gorgān *Iran* **71** B7
Gorgol □ *Mauritania* **82** B2
Gorgona *Italy* **40** E6
Gorgona, I. *Colombia* **124** C3
Gorgora *Ethiopia* **81** E4
Gorham *U.S.A.* **115** B13
Gori *Georgia* **35** J7
Goriganga → *India* **69** E9
Gorinchem *Neths.* **17** C4
Goris *Armenia* **73** C12
Goritsy *Russia* **32** B9
Gorízia *Italy* **41** C10
Gorj □ *Romania* **29** E8
Gorki = Horki *Belarus* **32** E6
Gorkiy = Nizhniy
   Novgorod *Russia* **34** B7
Gorkovskoye Vdkhr. *Russia* **34** B6
Gorleston *U.K.* **15** E10
Gorlice *Poland* **31** J8
Görlitz *Germany* **24** C10
Gorlovka = Horlivka
   Ukraine **33** H10
Gorna Dzhumayo =
   Blagoevgrad *Bulgaria* **44** D7
Gorna Oryakhovitsa
   Bulgaria **45** C9
Gornja Radgona *Slovenia* **41** B13
Gornja Tuzla *Bos.-H.* **28** F3
Gornji Grad *Slovenia* **41** B11
Gornji Milanovac *Serbia* **44** B4
Gornji Vakuf *Bos.-H.* **28** G2
Gorno Ablanovo *Bulgaria* **45** C9
Gorno-Altay □ *Russia* **52** D9
Gorno-Altaysk *Russia* **52** D9
Gor, zavodsk *Russia* **53** E15
Gor, zatskiy *Russia* **35** F5

Gornyy *Saratov, Russia* **34** E9
Gornyy *Sib., Russia* **54** B6
Gorodenka = Horodenka
   Ukraine **29** B10
Gorodets *Russia* **34** B6
Gorodishche =
   Horodyshche *Ukraine* **33** H6
Gorodishche *Russia* **34** D7
Gorodnya = Horodnya
   Ukraine **33** G6
Gorodok = Haradok *Belarus* **32** E6
Gorodok = Horodok
   Ukraine **23** D13
Gorodovikovsk *Russia* **35** G5
Gorokhov = Horokhiv
   Ukraine **23** C13
Gorokhovets *Russia* **34** B6
Gorom Gorom *Burkina Faso* **83** C4
Goromonzi *Zimbabwe* **87** F3
Gorong, Kepulauan
   Indonesia **63** E8
Gorongosa *Mozam.* **89** B5
Gorongose → *Mozam.* **89** C5
Gorongoza *Mozam.* **87** F3
Gorongoza, Sa. da *Mozam.* **87** F3
Gorontalo *Indonesia* **63** D6
Gorontalo □ *Indonesia* **63** D6
Goronyo *Nigeria* **83** C6
Górowo Iławeckie *Poland* **30** D7
Gorron *France* **18** D6
Gorshechnoye *Russia* **33** G10
Gort *Ireland* **12** C3
Gortis *Greece* **49** D6
Góry Bystrzyckie *Poland* **31** H3
Goryachiy Klyuch *Russia* **35** H4
Goryeong *S. Korea* **57** G15
Gorzkowice *Poland* **31** G6
Górzno *Poland* **31** E6
Gorzów Śląski *Poland* **31** G5
Gorzów Wielkopolski *Poland* **31** F2
Gosford *Australia* **95** E5
Goshen *Calif., U.S.A.* **110** J7
Goshen *Ind., U.S.A.* **113** E11
Goshen *N.Y., U.S.A.* **115** E10
Goshogawara *Japan* **54** D10
Goslar *Germany* **24** D6
Gospič *Croatia* **41** D12
Gosport *U.K.* **15** G6
Gossas *Senegal* **82** C1
Gosse → *Australia* **94** B1
Gossi *Mali* **83** B4
Gossinga *Sudan* **81** F2
Gostivar *Macedonia* **44** E4
Gostyń *Poland* **31** G4
Gostynin *Poland* **31** F6
Göta älv → *Sweden* **11** G5
Göta kanal *Sweden* **11** F9
Götaland *Sweden* **11** G8
Göteborg *Sweden* **11** G5
Götene *Sweden* **11** F7
Goteşti *Moldova* **29** D13
Gotha *Germany* **24** E6
Gothenburg = Göteborg
   Sweden **11** G5
Gothenburg *U.S.A.* **112** E3
Gothèye *Niger* **83** C5
Gotland *Sweden* **11** G12
Gotlands län □ *Sweden* **11** G12
Gotō-Rettō *Japan* **55** H4
Gotse Delchev *Bulgaria* **44** E7
Gotska Sandön *Sweden* **9** G18
Götsu *Japan* **55** G6
Góttero, Monte *Italy* **40** D6
Göttingen *Germany* **24** D5
Gottwald = Zmiyev *Ukraine* **33** H9
Gottwaldov = Zlín
   Czech Rep. **27** B10
Goubangzi *China* **57** D11
Gouda *Neths.* **17** B4
Goudiry *Senegal* **82** C2
Goudoumaria *Niger* **83** C7
Gouéké *Guinea* **82** D3
Gouin, Rés. *Canada* **104** C5
Goitafla *Ivory C.* **82** D3
Goulburn *Australia* **95** E4
Goulburn → *Australia* **95** F4
Goulburn Is. *Australia* **94** A1
Goulia *Ivory C.* **82** C3
Goulimine *Morocco* **78** C3
Goumbou *Mali* **82** B3
Goumenissa *Greece* **44** F6
Goundam *Mali* **83** B4
Goura *Greece* **46** D4
Gourbassi *Mali* **82** C2
Gourdon *France* **20** D5
Gouré *Niger* **83** C7
Gourin *France* **18** D3
Gourits → *S. Africa* **88** E3
Gourma-Rharous *Mali* **83** B4
Gournay-en-Bray *France* **19** C8
Gournes *Greece* **49** D7
Gourock *U.K.* **13** F4
Goursi *Burkina Faso* **82** C4
Gouverneur *U.S.A.* **115** B9
Gouvia *Greece* **49** A3
Gouzon *France* **19** F9
Gove Peninsula *Australia* **94** A2
Governador Valadares
   Brazil **125** G10

Governor's Harbour *Bahamas* **120** A4
Govindgarh *India* **69** G9
Gowan Ra. *Australia* **94** D4
Gowanda *U.S.A.* **114** D6
Gower *U.K.* **15** F3
Gowna, L. *Ireland* **12** C4
Goya *Argentina* **126** B4
Göyçay *Azerbaijan* **35** K8
Goyder Lagoon *Australia* **95** D2
Goyllarisquizga *Peru* **124** F3
Göynük *Antalya, Turkey* **47** E12
Göynük *Bolu, Turkey* **72** B4
Goz Beïda *Chad* **79** F10
Goz Regeb *Sudan* **81** D4
Gozdnica *Poland* **31** G2
Gozo *Malta* **49** C1
Graaff-Reinet *S. Africa* **88** E3
Grabo *Ivory C.* **82** D3
Grabow *Germany* **24** B7
Grabów nad Prosną *Poland* **31** G5
Gračac *Croatia* **41** D12
Gračanica *Bos.-H.* **28** F3
Graçay *France* **19** E8
Gracias a Dios, C. *Honduras* **120** D3
Graciosa *Azores* **78** a
Graciosa, I. *Canary Is.* **48** E6
Grad Sofiya □ *Bulgaria* **44** D7
Gradac *Montenegro* **44** C3
Gradačac *Bos.-H.* **28** F3
Gradeška Planina *Macedonia* **44** E6
Gradets *Bulgaria* **45** D10
Gradišče *Slovenia* **41** B12
Grădiştea de Munte *Romania* **29** E8
Grado *Italy* **41** C10
Grado *Spain* **36** B4
Grady *U.S.A.* **109** J12
Graeca, Lacul *Romania* **29** F11
Grafenau *Germany* **25** G9
Gräfenberg *Germany* **25** F7
Grafham Water *U.K.* **15** E7
Grafton *Australia* **95** D5
Grafton *N. Dak., U.S.A.* **112** A5
Grafton *W. Va., U.S.A.* **113** F13
Graham *Canada* **104** C1
Graham *U.S.A.* **116** E5
Graham, Mt. *U.S.A.* **109** K9
Graham Bell, Ostrov =
　Greem-Bell, Ostrov *Russia* **52** A7
Graham I. *Canada* **102** C2
Graham Land *Antarctica* **5** C17
Grahamstown *S. Africa* **88** E4
Grahamsville *U.S.A.* **115** E10
Grahovo *Montenegro* **44** D2
Graie, Alpi *Europe* **21** C11
Grain Coast *W. Afr.* **82** E3
Grajagan *Indonesia* **63** K17
Grajagan, Teluk *Indonesia* **63** K17
Grajaú *Brazil* **125** E9
Grajaú → *Brazil* **125** D10
Grajewo *Poland* **30** E9
Gramada *Bulgaria* **44** C6
Gramat *France* **20** D5
Grammichele *Italy* **43** E7
Grámmos, Óros *Greece* **44** F4
Grampian *U.S.A.* **114** F6
Grampian Highlands =
　Grampian Mts. *U.K.* **13** E5
Grampian Mts. *U.K.* **13** E5
Grampians, The *Australia* **95** F3
Gramsh *Albania* **44** F4
Gran Canaria *Canary Is.* **48** G4
Gran Chaco *S. Amer.* **126** B3
Gran Desierto del
　Pinacate △ *Mexico* **118** A2
Gran Paradiso *Italy* **40** C4
Gran Sasso d'Itália *Italy* **41** F10
Gran Sasso e Monti Della
　Laga △ *Italy* **41** F10
Granada *Nic.* **120** D2
Granada *Spain* **37** H7
Granada *U.S.A.* **108** G12
Granada □ *Spain* **37** H7
Granadilla de Abona
　Canary Is. **48** F3
Granard *Ireland* **12** C4
Granbury *U.S.A.* **116** E6
Granby *Canada* **115** A12
Granby *U.S.A.* **108** F11
Grand → *Canada* **114** D5
Grand → *Mo., U.S.A.* **112** F7
Grand → *S. Dak., U.S.A.* **112** C3
Grand Bahama I. *Bahamas* **120** A4
Grand Baie *Mauritius* **85** d
Grand Bank *Canada* **105** C8
Grand Bassam *Ivory C.* **82** D4
Grand Bend *Canada* **114** C3
Grand Béréby *Ivory C.* **82** E3
Grand-Bourg *Guadeloupe* **120** b
Grand Canal = Da
　Yunhe → *China* **57** E9
Grand Canyon *U.S.A.* **109** H7
Grand Canyon △ *U.S.A.* **109** H7
Grand Canyon-
　Parashant △ *U.S.A.* **109** H7
Grand Cayman *Cayman Is.* **120** C3
Grand Cess *Liberia* **82** E3
Grand Coulee *U.S.A.* **108** C4
Grand Coulee Dam *U.S.A.* **108** C4

Grand Erg de Bilma *Niger* **79** E8
Grand Falls *Canada* **105** C6
Grand Falls-Windsor
　Canada **105** C8
Grand Forks *Canada* **102** D5
Grand Forks *U.S.A.* **112** B5
Grand Gorge *U.S.A.* **115** D10
Grand Haven *U.S.A.* **112** D10
Grand I. *Mich., U.S.A.* **112** B10
Grand I. *N.Y., U.S.A.* **114** D6
Grand Island *U.S.A.* **112** E4
Grand Isle *La., U.S.A.* **117** G9
Grand Isle *Vt., U.S.A.* **115** B11
Grand Junction *U.S.A.* **108** G9
Grand L. *N.B., Canada* **105** C6
Grand L. *Nfld. & L., Canada* **105** B8
Grand L. *Nfld. & L., Canada* **105** B7
Grand L. *U.S.A.* **116** G8
Grand Lahou *Ivory C.* **82** D3
Grand Lake *U.S.A.* **108** F11
Grand-Lieu, L. de *France* **18** E5
Grand Manan I. *Canada* **105** D6
Grand Marais *Mich., U.S.A.*
　113 B11
Grand Marais *Minn., U.S.A.* **104** C1
Grand-Mère *Canada* **104** C5
Grand Popo *Benin* **83** D5
Grand Portage *U.S.A.* **112** B9
Grand Prairie *U.S.A.* **116** E6
Grand Rapids *Canada* **103** C9
Grand Rapids *Mich., U.S.A.* **113** D11
Grand Rapids *Minn., U.S.A.* **112** B7
Grand St-Bernard, Col du
　Europe **25** K3
Grand Staircase-
　Escalante △ *U.S.A.* **109** H8
Grand Teton *U.S.A.* **108** E8
Grand Teton △ *U.S.A.* **108** E8
Grand Union Canal *U.K.* **15** E7
Grandas de Salime *Spain* **36** B4
Grande → *Jujuy, Argentina* **126** A2
Grande → *Mendoza,*
　Argentina **126** D2
Grande → *Bolivia* **124** G6
Grande → *Bahia, Brazil* **125** F10
Grande → *Minas Gerais,*
　Brazil **125** H8
Grande, B. *Argentina* **128** G3
Grande, Rio → *N. Amer.* **116** J6
Grande Anse *Seychelles* **85** b
Grande Baleine, R. de la →
　Canada **104** A4
Grande Cache *Canada* **102** C5
Grande Casse, Pte. de la
　France **21** C10
Grande Comore *Comoros Is.* **85** a
Grande-Entrée *Canada* **105** C7
Grande Prairie *Canada* **102** B5
Grande-Rivière *Canada* **105** C7
Grande-Terre *Guadeloupe* **120** b
Grande-Vallée *Canada* **105** C6
Grande Vigie, Pte. de la
　Guadeloupe **120** b
Grandfalls *U.S.A.* **116** F3
Grândola *Portugal* **37** G2
Grandpré *France* **19** C11
Grands Causses △ *France* **20** D6
Grands-Jardins △ *Canada* **105** C5
Grandview *Canada* **103** C8
Grandview *U.S.A.* **108** C4
Grandvilliers *France* **19** C8
Graneros *Chile* **126** C1
Grangemouth *U.K.* **13** E5
Granger *U.S.A.* **108** F9
Grängesberg *Sweden* **10** D9
Grangeville *U.S.A.* **108** D5
Granisle *Canada* **102** C3
Granite City *U.S.A.* **112** F8
Granite Falls *U.S.A.* **112** C6
Granite L. *Canada* **105** C8
Granite Mt. *U.S.A.* **111** M10
Granite Pk. *U.S.A.* **108** D9
Graniteville *U.S.A.* **115** B11
Granitola, C. *Italy* **42** E5
Granity *N.Z.* **91** D3
Granja *Brazil* **125** D10
Granja de Moreruela *Spain* **36** D5
Granja de Torrehermosa
　Spain **37** G5
Gränna *Sweden* **11** F8
Granollers *Spain* **38** D7
Gransee *Germany* **24** B9
Grant *U.S.A.* **112** E3
Grant, Mt. *U.S.A.* **108** G4
Grant City *U.S.A.* **112** E6
Grant I. *Australia* **92** B5
Grant Range *U.S.A.* **108** G6
Grantham *U.K.* **14** E7
Grantown-on-Spey *U.K.* **13** D5
Grants *U.S.A.* **109** J10
Grants Pass *U.S.A.* **108** E2
Grantsville *U.S.A.* **108** F7
Granville *France* **18** D5
Granville *N. Dak., U.S.A.* **112** A3
Granville *N.Y., U.S.A.* **115** C11
Granville *Ohio, U.S.A.* **114** F2
Granville L. *Canada* **103** B8
Graskop *S. Africa* **89** C5
Gräsö *Sweden* **10** D12

Grass → *Canada* **103** B9
Grass Range *U.S.A.* **108** C9
Grass River △ *Canada* **103** C8
Grass Valley *Calif., U.S.A.* **110** F6
Grass Valley *Oreg., U.S.A.* **108** D3
Grassano *Italy* **43** B9
Grasse *France* **21** E10
Grassflat *U.S.A.* **114** E6
Grasslands △ *Canada* **103** D7
Grassy *Australia* **95** G3
Gråsten *Denmark* **11** K3
Gråstorp *Sweden* **11** F6
Gratkorn *Austria* **26** D8
Graulhet *France* **20** E5
Graus *Spain* **38** C5
Grave, Pte. de *France* **20** C2
Gravelbourg *Canada* **103** D7
Gravelines *France* **19** A9
's-Gravenhage *Neths.* **17** B4
Gravenhurst *Canada* **114** B5
Gravesend *Australia* **95** D5
Gravesend *U.K.* **15** F8
Gravina in Púglia *Italy* **43** B9
Gravois, Pointe-à- *Haiti* **121** C5
Gravone → *France* **21** G12
Gray *France* **19** E12
Grayling *U.S.A.* **113** C11
Grays *U.K.* **15** F8
Grays Harbor *U.S.A.* **108** C1
Grays L. *U.S.A.* **108** E8
Grays River *U.S.A.* **110** D3
Grayvoron *Russia* **33** G8
Graz *Austria* **26** D8
Grdelica *Serbia* **44** D6
Greasy L. *Canada* **102** A4
Great Abaco I. = Abaco I.
　Bahamas **120** A4
Great Artesian Basin
　Australia **94** C3
Great Australian Bight
　Australia **93** F5
Great Bahama Bank
　Bahamas **120** B4
Great Barrier I. *N.Z.* **91** B5
Great Barrier Reef *Australia* **94** B4
Great Barrier Reef △
　Australia **94** B4
Great Barrington *U.S.A.* **115** D11
Great Basalt Wall △
　Australia **94** B4
Great Basin *U.S.A.* **108** G5
Great Basin △ *U.S.A.* **108** G6
Great Bear → *Canada* **100** C7
Great Bear L. *Canada* **100** C8
Great Belt = Store Bælt
　Denmark **11** J4
Great Bend *Kans., U.S.A.* **112** F4
Great Bend *Pa., U.S.A.* **115** E9
Great Blasket I. *Ireland* **12** D1
Great Britain *Europe* **6** E5
Great Camanoe *Br. Virgin Is.* **121** e
Great Codroy *Canada* **105** C8
Great Divide, The = Great
　Dividing Ra. *Australia* **94** C4
Great Divide Basin *U.S.A.* **108** E9
Great Dividing Ra. *Australia* **94** C4
Great Driffield = Driffield
　U.K. **14** C7
Great Exuma I. *Bahamas* **120** B4
Great Falls *U.S.A.* **108** C8
Great Fish = Groot-Vis →
　S. Africa **88** E4
Great Guana Cay *Bahamas* **120** B4
Great Himalayan △ *India* **68** D7
Great Inagua I. *Bahamas* **121** B5
Great Indian Desert = Thar
　Desert *India* **68** F5
Great Karoo *S. Africa* **88** E3
Great Khingan Mts. = Da
　Hinggan Ling *China* **60** B7
Great Lake *Australia* **95** G4
Great Lakes *N. Amer.* **98** E11
Great Limpopo
　Transfrontier △ *Africa* **89** C5
Great Malvern *U.K.* **15** E5
Great Miami → *U.S.A.* **113** F11
Great Ormes Head *U.K.* **14** D4
Great Ouse → *U.K.* **14** E8
Great Palm I. *Australia* **94** B4
Great Pedro Bluff *Jamaica* **120** a
Great Pee Dee → *U.S.A.* **117** E15
Great Plains *N. Amer.* **98** E9
Great Ruaha → *Tanzania* **86** D4
Great Sacandaga L. *U.S.A.* **115** C10
Great Saint Bernard Pass =
　Grand St-Bernard, Col
　du *Europe* **25** K3
Great Salt Desert = Kavīr,
　Dasht-e *Iran* **71** C7
Great Salt L. *U.S.A.* **108** F7
Great Salt Lake Desert
　U.S.A. **108** F7
Great Salt Plains L. *U.S.A.* **116** C5
Great Sand Dunes △ *U.S.A.*
　109 H11
Great Sandy △ *Australia* **95** D5
Great Sandy Desert *Australia* **92** D3
Great Sandy Desert *U.S.A.* **106** B2

Great Sangi = Sangihe,
　Pulau *Indonesia* **63** D7
Great Scarcies → *S. Leone* **82** D2
Great Sea Reef *Fiji* **91** a
Great Skellig *Ireland* **12** E1
Great Slave L. *Canada* **102** A5
Great Smoky Mts. △ *U.S.A.*
　117 D13
Great Snow Mt. *Canada* **100** D7
Great Stour = Stour → *U.K.* **15** F9
Great Victoria Desert
　Australia **93** E4
Great Wall *Antarctica* **5** C18
Great Wall *China* **56** E5
Great Whernside *U.K.* **14** C6
Great Yarmouth *U.K.* **15** E9
Great Zab = Zāb al
　Kabīr → *Iraq* **73** D10
Great Zimbabwe *Zimbabwe* **87** G3
Greater Antilles *W. Indies* **121** C5
Greater London □ *U.K.* **15** F7
Greater Manchester □ *U.K.* **14** D5
Greater St. Lucia
　Wetlands → *S. Africa* **89** D5
Greater Sudbury =
　Sudbury *Canada* **104** C3
Greater Sunda Is. *Indonesia* **62** F4
Grebbestad *Sweden* **11** F5
Grebenka = Hrebenka
　Ukraine **33** G7
Greco, C. *Cyprus* **49** E13
Greco, Mte. *Italy* **41** G10
Gredos, Sierra de *Spain* **36** E6
Greece *U.S.A.* **114** C7
Greece ■ *Europe* **46** B3
Greeley *Colo., U.S.A.* **108** F11
Greeley *Nebr., U.S.A.* **112** E4
Greely Fd. *Canada* **101** A11
Greem-Bell, Ostrov *Russia* **52** A7
Green → *Ky., U.S.A.* **112** G10
Green → *Utah, U.S.A.* **108** G9
Green B. *U.S.A.* **112** C10
Green Bay *U.S.A.* **112** C9
Green C. *Australia* **95** F5
Green Cove Springs *U.S.A.* **117** G14
Green I. = Lü Tao *Taiwan* **59** F13
Green Lake *Canada* **103** C7
Green Mts. *U.S.A.* **115** C12
Green River *Utah, U.S.A.* **108** G8
Green River *Wyo., U.S.A.* **108** F9
Green Valley *U.S.A.* **109** L8
Greenbank *U.S.A.* **110** B4
Greenbush *Mich., U.S.A.* **114** B1
Greenbush *Minn., U.S.A.* **112** A5
Greencastle *U.S.A.* **112** F10
Greene *U.S.A.* **115** D9
Greeneville *U.S.A.* **117** C13
Greenfield *Calif., U.S.A.* **110** J5
Greenfield *Calif., U.S.A.* **111** K8
Greenfield *Ind., U.S.A.* **113** F11
Greenfield *Iowa, U.S.A.* **112** E6
Greenfield *Mass., U.S.A.* **115** D12
Greenfield *Mo., U.S.A.* **112** G7
Greenfield Park *Canada* **115** A11
Greenland □ *N. Amer.* **99** C15
Greenland Sea *Arctic* **4** B7
Greenock *U.K.* **13** F4
Greenore *Ireland* **12** B5
Greenore Pt. *Ireland* **12** D5
Greenough *Australia* **93** E1
Greenough → *Australia* **93** E1
Greenough Pt. *Canada* **114** B3
Greenport *U.S.A.* **115** E12
Greensboro *Ga., U.S.A.* **117** E13
Greensboro *N.C., U.S.A.* **117** C15
Greensboro *Vt., U.S.A.* **115** B12
Greensburg *Ind., U.S.A.* **113** F11
Greensburg *Kans., U.S.A.* **112** G4
Greensburg *Pa., U.S.A.* **114** F5
Greenstone Pt. *U.K.* **13** D3
Greenvale *Australia* **94** B4
Greenville *Liberia* **82** D3
Greenville *Ala., U.S.A.* **117** F11
Greenville *Calif., U.S.A.* **110** E6
Greenville *Maine, U.S.A.* **113** C19
Greenville *Mich., U.S.A.* **113** D11
Greenville *Miss., U.S.A.* **117** E9
Greenville *Mo., U.S.A.* **112** G8
Greenville *N.C., U.S.A.* **117** D16
Greenville *N.H., U.S.A.* **115** D13
Greenville *N.Y., U.S.A.* **115** D10
Greenville *Ohio, U.S.A.* **113** E11
Greenville *Pa., U.S.A.* **114** E4
Greenville *S.C., U.S.A.* **117** D13
Greenville *Tex., U.S.A.* **116** E6
Greenwater Lake △ *Canada* **103** C8
Greenwich *Conn., U.S.A.* **115** E11
Greenwich *N.Y., U.S.A.* **115** C11
Greenwich *Ohio, U.S.A.* **114** E2
Greenwich □ *U.K.* **15** F8
Greenwood *Canada* **102** D5
Greenwood *Ark., U.S.A.* **116** D7
Greenwood *Ind., U.S.A.* **112** F10
Greenwood *Miss., U.S.A.* **117** E9
Greenwood *S.C., U.S.A.* **117** D13
Greenwood, Mt. *Australia* **92** B5
Gregbe *Ivory C.* **82** D3
Gregory *U.S.A.* **112** D4
Gregory → *Australia* **94** B2

Gregory, L. *S. Austral.,*
　Australia **95** D2
Gregory, L. *W. Austral.,*
　Australia **93** E2
Gregory, L. *W. Austral.,*
　Australia **93** E2
Gregory △ *Australia* **92** C5
Gregory Downs *Australia* **94** B2
Gregory Ra. *Queens.,*
　Australia **94** B3
Gregory Ra. *W. Austral.,*
　Australia **92** D3
Greiffenberg *Germany* **24** B9
Greifswald *Germany* **24** A9
Greifswalder Bodden
　Germany **24** A9
Grein *Austria* **26** C7
Greiz *Germany* **24** E8
Gremikha *Russia* **52** C4
Grenaa *Denmark* **11** H4
Grenada *U.S.A.* **117** E10
Grenada ■ *W. Indies* **121** D7
Grenade *France* **20** E5
Grenadier I. *U.S.A.* **115** B8
Grenadines, The *St. Vincent* **121** D7
Grenchen *Switz.* **25** H3
Grenen *Denmark* **11** G4
Grenfell *Australia* **95** E4
Grenfell *Canada* **103** C8
Grenoble *France* **21** C9
Grenville, C. *Australia* **94** A3
Grenville Chan. *Canada* **102** C3
Gréoux-les-Bains *France* **21** E9
Gresham *U.S.A.* **110** E4
Gresik *Indonesia* **63** G15
Greta → *U.K.* **14** C5
Gretna *U.S.A.* **117** G9
Greve Strand *Denmark* **11** J6
Greven *Germany* **24** C3
Grevena *Greece* **44** F5
Grevená □ *Greece* **44** F5
Grevenbroich *Germany* **24** D2
Grevenmacher *Lux.* **17** E6
Grevesmühlen *Germany* **24** B7
Grey → *Canada* **105** C8
Grey → *N.Z.* **91** E3
Grey, C. *Australia* **94** A2
Grey Ra. *Australia* **95** D3
Greybull *U.S.A.* **108** D9
Greymouth *N.Z.* **91** E3
Greystones *Ireland* **12** C5
Greytown *N.Z.* **91** E5
Greytown *S. Africa* **89** D5
Gribanovskiy *Russia* **34** E5
Gribbell I. *Canada* **102** C3
Gribës, Mali i *Albania* **44** F3
Gridley *U.S.A.* **110** F5
Griekwastad *S. Africa* **88** D3
Griesheim *Germany* **25** F4
Grieskirchen *Austria* **26** C6
Griffin *U.S.A.* **117** E12
Griffith *Australia* **95** E4
Griffith *Canada* **114** A7
Griffith I. *Canada* **114** B4
Grignols *France* **20** D3
Grigoriopol *Moldova* **29** C14
Grimailov = Hrymayliv
　Ukraine **23** D14
Grimes *U.S.A.* **110** F5
Grimma *Germany* **24** D8
Grimmen *Germany* **24** A9
Grimsay *U.K.* **13** D1
Grimsby *Canada* **114** C5
Grimsby *U.K.* **14** D7
Grímsey *Iceland* **8** C5
Grimshaw *Canada* **102** B5
Grimstad *Norway* **9** G13
Grindelwald *Switz.* **25** J4
Grindsted *Denmark* **11** J2
Grindu *Romania* **29** F11
Grinnell *U.S.A.* **112** E7
Grintavec *Slovenia* **41** B11
Gris-Nez, C. *France* **19** B8
Grise Fiord *Canada* **101** B11
Grisolles *France* **20** E5
Grisons = Graubünden □
　Switz. **25** J5
Grisslehamn *Sweden* **10** D12
Grmeč Planina *Bos.-H.* **41** D13
Groais I. *Canada* **105** B8
Grobiņa *Latvia* **30** B8
Groblersdal *S. Africa* **89** D4
Grobming *Austria* **26** D6
Grocka *Serbia* **44** B4
Gródek *Poland* **31** E10
Grodków *Poland* **31** H4
Grodno = Hrodna *Belarus* **30** E10
Grodzisk Mazowiecki *Poland* **31** F7
Grodzisk Wielkopolski
　Poland **31** F3
Grodzyanka =
　Hrodzyanka *Belarus* **23** B15
Groesbeck *U.S.A.* **116** F6
Groix *France* **18** E3
Groix, Î. de *France* **18** E3
Grójec *Poland* **31** G7

Gronau *Nordrhein-Westfalen,*
　Germany **24** C3
Grong *Norway* **8** D15
Grönhögen *Sweden* **11** H10
Groningen *Neths.* **17** A6
Groningen □ *Neths.* **17** A6
Groom *U.S.A.* **116** D4
Groot → *S. Africa* **88** E3
Groot-Berg → *S. Africa* **88** E2
Groot-Brakrivier *S. Africa* **88** E3
Groot Karasberge *Namibia* **88** D2
Groot-Kei → *S. Africa* **89** E4
Groot-Vis → *S. Africa* **88** E4
Grootdrink *S. Africa* **88** D3
Groote Eylandt *Australia* **94** A2
Grootfontein *Namibia* **88** B2
Grootlaagte → *Africa* **88** C3
Grootvloer → *S. Africa* **88** E3
Gros C. *Canada* **102** A6
Gros Islet *St. Lucia* **121** f
Gros Morne △ *Canada* **105** C8
Gros Piton *St. Lucia* **121** f
Gros Piton Pt. *St. Lucia* **121** f
Grósio *Italy* **40** B7
Grosne → *France* **19** F11
Grossa, Pta. *Spain* **48** B8
Grosse Point *U.S.A.* **114** D2
Grossenbrode *Germany* **24** A7
Grossenhain *Germany* **24** D9
Grosser Arber *Germany* **25** F9
Grosser Plöner See *Germany* **24** A6
Grosseto *Italy* **41** F8
Grossgerungs *Austria* **26** C7
Grossglockner *Austria* **26** D5
Groswater B. *Canada* **105** B8
Groton *Conn., U.S.A.* **115** E12
Groton *N.Y., U.S.A.* **115** D8
Groton *S. Dak., U.S.A.* **112** C4
Grottáglie *Italy* **43** B10
Grottaminarda *Italy* **43** A8
Grottammare *Italy* **41** F10
Grouard Mission *Canada* **102** B5
Grouin, Pte. du *France* **18** D5
Groundhog → *Canada* **104** C3
Grouw *Neths.* **17** A5
Grove City *U.S.A.* **114** E4
Grove Hill *U.S.A.* **117** F11
Groveland *U.S.A.* **110** H6
Grover Beach *U.S.A.* **111** K6
Groves *U.S.A.* **116** G8
Groveton *U.S.A.* **115** B13
Grožnjan *Croatia* **41** C10
Groznyy *Russia* **35** J7
Grubišno Polje *Croatia* **28** E2
Grudusk *Poland* **31** E7
Grudziądz *Poland* **30** E5
Gruinard B. *U.K.* **13** D3
Gruissan *France* **20** E7
Grumo Áppula *Italy* **43** A9
Grums *Sweden* **10** E7
Grünberg *Germany* **24** E4
Gründau *Germany* **25** E5
Grundy Center *U.S.A.* **112** D7
Grünstadt *Germany* **25** F4
Gruppo di Tessa △ *Italy* **40** B8
Gruvberget *Sweden* **10** C10
Gruver *U.S.A.* **116** C4
Gruyères *Switz.* **25** J3
Gruža *Serbia* **44** C4
Gryazi *Russia* **33** F10
Gryazovets *Russia* **32** C11
Grybów *Poland* **31** J7
Grycksbo *Sweden* **10** D9
Gryfice *Poland* **30** E2
Gryfino *Poland* **31** E1
Gryfów Śląski *Poland* **31** G2
Grythyttan *Sweden* **10** E8
Grytviken *S. Georgia* **128** G9
Gstaad *Switz.* **25** J3
Gua *India* **69** H11
Gua Musang *Malaysia* **65** K3
Guacanayabo, G. de *Cuba* **120** B4
Guachípas → *Argentina* **126** B2
Guadajoz → *Spain* **37** H6
Guadalajara *Mexico* **118** C4
Guadalajara *Spain* **38** E1
Guadalajara □ *Spain* **38** E2
Guadalcanal *Solomon Is.* **90** B9
Guadalcanal *Spain* **37** G5
Guadalcanal □ *Spain* **37** G5
Guadalén → *Spain* **37** G7
Guadales *Argentina* **126** C2
Guadalete → *Spain* **37** J4
Guadalimar → *Spain* **37** G7
Guadalmena → *Spain* **37** G8
Guadalmez → *Spain* **37** G5
Guadalope → *Spain* **38** D4
Guadalquivir → *Spain* **37** J4
Guadalupe =
　Guadeloupe ☑ *W. Indies* **120** b
Guadalupe *Mexico* **111** N10
Guadalupe *Zacatecas, Mexico* **118** C4
Guadalupe *Spain* **37** F5
Guadalupe *U.S.A.* **111** L6
Guadalupe → *Mexico* **111** N10
Guadalupe → *U.S.A.* **116** G6
Guadalupe, Sierra de *Spain* **37** F5
Guadalupe Bravos *Mexico* **118** A3
Guadalupe I. *Pac. Oc.* **98** G8

Guadalupe Mts. △ *U.S.A.* **116** F2
Guadalupe Peak *U.S.A.* **116** F2
Guadalupe y Calvo *Mexico* **118** B3
Guadarrama, Sierra de *Spain* **36** E7
Guadeloupe ☑ *W. Indies* **120** b
Guadeloupe △ *Guadeloupe* **120** b
Guadeloupe Passage
  W. Indies **121** C7
Guadiamar ➤ *Spain* **37** J4
Guadiana ➤ *Portugal* **37** H3
Guadiana Menor ➤ *Spain* **37** H7
Guadiaro ➤ *Spain* **37** J5
Guadiato ➤ *Spain* **37** H5
Guadiela ➤ *Spain* **38** E2
Guadix *Spain* **37** H7
Guafo, Boca del *Chile* **128** E2
Guaico *Trin. & Tob.* **125** K15
Guainía ➤ *Colombia* **124** C5
Guaíra *Brazil* **127** A5
Guaíra ☐ *Paraguay* **126** B4
Guaitecas, Is. *Chile* **128** E2
Guajará-Mirim *Brazil* **124** F5
Guajira, Pen. de la *Colombia* **124** A4
Gualán *Guatemala* **120** C2
Gualdo Tadino *Italy* **41** E9
Gualeguay *Argentina* **126** C4
Gualeguaychú *Argentina* **126** C4
Gualeguay ➤ *Argentina* **126** C4
Guam ☑ *Pac. Oc.* **96** F6
Guaminí *Argentina* **126** D3
Guamúchil *Mexico* **118** B3
Guana I. *Br. Virgin Is.* **121** e
Guanabacoa *Cuba* **120** B3
Guanacaste, Cordillera de
  Costa Rica **120** D2
Guanacaste △ *Costa Rica* **120** D2
Guanaceví *Mexico* **118** B3
Guanahani = San
  Salvador I. *Bahamas* **121** B5
Guanaja *Honduras* **120** C2
Guanajay *Cuba* **120** B3
Guanajuato *Mexico* **118** C4
Guanajuato ☐ *Mexico* **118** C4
Guandacol *Argentina* **126** B2
Guane *Cuba* **120** B3
Guang'an *China* **58** B6
Guangchang *China* **59** D11
Guangde *China* **59** B12
Guangfeng *China* **59** C12
Guanghan *China* **58** B5
Guangnan *China* **58** E5
Guangning *China* **59** F9
Guangrao *China* **57** F10
Guangshui *China* **59** B9
Guangshun *China* **58** D6
Guangwu *China* **56** F3
Guangxi Zhuangzu
  Zizhiqu ☐ *China* **58** F7
Guangyuan *China* **58** A5
Guangze *China* **59** D11
Guangzhou *China* **59** F9
Guanica *Puerto Rico* **121** d
Guanipa ➤ *Venezuela* **124** B6
Guanling *China* **58** E5
Guannan *China* **57** G10
Guantánamo *Cuba* **121** B4
Guantánamo B. *Cuba* **121** C4
Guantao *China* **56** F8
Guanyang *China* **59** E8
Guanyun *China* **57** G10
Guapay = Grande ➤
  Bolivia **124** G6
Guápiles *Costa Rica* **120** D3
Guapo B. *Trin. & Tob.* **125** K15
Guaporé *Brazil* **127** B5
Guaporé ➤ *Brazil* **124** F5
Guaqui *Bolivia* **124** G5
Guara, Sierra de *Spain* **38** C4
Guaramacal △ *Venezuela* **121** E5
Guarapari *Brazil* **127** A7
Guarapuava *Brazil* **127** B5
Guaratinguetá *Brazil* **127** A6
Guaratuba *Brazil* **127** B6
Guarda *Portugal* **36** E3
Guarda ☐ *Portugal* **36** E3
Guardafui, C. = Asir, Ras
  Somali Rep. **75** E5
Guardamar del Segura *Spain* **39** G4
Guardavalle *Italy* **43** D9
Guárdia Sanframondi *Italy* **43** A7
Guardiagrele *Italy* **41** F11
Guardo *Spain* **36** C6
Guareña *Spain* **37** G4
Guareña ➤ *Spain* **36** D5
Guárico ☐ *Venezuela* **124** B5
Guarujá *Brazil* **127** A6
Guarulhos *Brazil* **127** A6
Guasave *Mexico* **118** B3
Guasdualito *Venezuela* **124** B4
Guastalla *Italy* **40** D7
Guatemala *Guatemala* **120** D1
Guatemala ■ *Cent. Amer.* **120** C1
Guatemala Basin *Pac. Oc.* **97** F18
Guatemala Trench *Pac. Oc.* **98** H10
Guatopo ☐ *Venezuela* **124** B5
Guatuaro Pt. *Trin. & Tob.* **125** K16
Guaviare ➤ *Colombia* **124** C5

Guaxupé *Brazil* **127** A6
Guayaguayare *Trin. & Tob.* **125** K15
Guayama *Puerto Rico* **121** d
Guayaquil *Ecuador* **124** D3
Guayaquil *Mexico* **118** B1
Guayaquil, G. de *Ecuador* **124** D2
Guaymas *Mexico* **118** B2
Guba *Dem. Rep. of the Congo* **87** E2
Guba *Ethiopia* **81** E4
Gûbâl, Madîq *Egypt* **80** B3
Gubat *Phil.* **61** E6
Gúbbio *Italy* **41** E9
Guben *Germany* **24** D10
Gubin *Poland* **31** G1
Gubio *Nigeria* **83** C7
Gubkin *Russia* **33** G9
Gubkinskiy *Russia* **52** C8
Guča *Serbia* **44** C4
Gucheng *China* **59** A8
Gudbrandsdalen *Norway* **8** F14
Guddu Barrage *Pakistan* **68** E3
Gudená ➤ *Denmark* **11** H4
Gudermes *Russia* **35** J8
Gudhjem *Denmark* **11** J8
Gudur *India* **66** M11
Guebwiller *France* **19** E14
Guecho = Getxo *Spain* **38** B2
Guékédou *Guinea* **82** D2
Guéle Mendouka *Cameroon* **83** E7
Guelmine = Goulimine
  Morocco **78** C3
Guelph *Canada* **114** C4
Guéméné-Penfao *France* **18** E5
Guéméné-sur-Scorff *France* **18** D3
Guéné *Benin* **83** C5
Guer *France* **18** E4
Guérande *France* **18** E4
Guerara *Algeria* **78** B6
Guéret *France* **19** F8
Guérigny *France* **19** E10
Guerneville *U.S.A.* **110** G4
Guernica = Gernika-Lumo
  Spain **38** B2
Guernsey *U.K.* **15** H5
Guernsey *U.S.A.* **108** E11
Guerrero ☐ *Mexico* **119** D5
Guessou-Sud *Benin* **83** C5
Gueugnon *France* **19** F11
Guéyo *Ivory C.* **82** D3
Gughe *Ethiopia* **81** F4
Gügher *Iran* **71** D8
Guglionesi *Italy* **41** G11
Guhakolak, Tanjung
  Indonesia **63** G11
Gui Jiang ➤ *China* **59** F8
Guia *Canary Is.* **48** F4
Guia de Isora *Canary Is.* **48** F3
Guia Lopes da Laguna
  Brazil **127** A4
Guiana Highlands *S. Amer.* **122** C4
Guibéroua *Ivory C.* **82** D3
Guichi *China* **59** B11
Guider *Cameroon* **83** D7
Guidiguir *Niger* **83** C6
Guidimaka ☐ *Mauritania* **82** B2
Guidimouni *Niger* **83** C6
Guiding *China* **58** D6
Guidong *China* **59** D9
Guidónia-Montecélio *Italy* **41** F9
Guiers, L. de *Senegal* **82** B1
Guigang *China* **58** F7
Guiglo *Ivory C.* **82** D3
Guihulñgan *Phil.* **61** F5
Guijá *Mozam.* **89** C5
Guijuelo *Spain* **36** E5
Guildford *U.K.* **15** F7
Guilford *U.S.A.* **115** E12
Guilin *China* **59** E8
Guillaume-Delisle, L.
  Canada **104** A4
Guillaumes *France* **21** D10
Guillestre *France* **21** D10
Guilvinec *France* **18** E2
Güimar *Canary Is.* **48** F3
Guimarães *Portugal* **36** D2
Guimaras ☐ *Phil.* **61** F5
Guinda *U.S.A.* **110** G4
Guinea *Africa* **76** F4
Guinea ■ *W. Afr.* **82** C2
Guinea, Gulf of *Atl. Oc.* **83** E5
Guinea-Bissau ■ *Africa* **82** C2
Güines *Cuba* **120** B3
Guingamp *France* **18** D3
Guinguinéo *Senegal* **82** C1
Guipavas *France* **18** D2
Guiping *China* **59** F8
Guipúzcoa ☐ *Spain* **38** B2
Guir *Mali* **82** B4
Guirel *Mauritania* **82** B3
Güiria *Venezuela* **124** B6
Guiscard *France* **19** C10
Guise *France* **19** C10
Guitiriz *Spain* **36** B3
Guitri *Ivory C.* **82** D3
Guiuan *Phil.* **61** F6
Guixi *China* **59** C11
Guiyang *Guizhou, China* **58** D6
Guiyang *Hunan, China* **59** E9

Guizhou ☐ *China* **58** D6
Gujan-Mestras *France* **20** D2
Gujar Khan *Pakistan* **68** C5
Gujarat ☐ *India* **68** H4
Gujiang *China* **59** D10
Gujranwala *Pakistan* **68** C6
Gujrat *Pakistan* **68** C6
Gukovo *Russia* **35** F5
Gukuu = Mnenia *Tanzania* **87** D3
Gulbarga *India* **66** L10
Gulbene *Latvia* **32** D4
Gulf, The = Persian Gulf
  Asia **71** E6
Gulf Islands △ *U.S.A.* **117** F11
Gulfport *U.S.A.* **117** F10
Gulgong *Australia* **95** E4
Gulin *China* **58** C5
Gulistan *Pakistan* **68** D2
Gulja = Yining *China* **52** E9
Gull Lake *Canada* **103** C7
Gullbrandstorp *Sweden* **11** H6
Gullspång *Sweden* **11** F8
Güllük *Turkey* **47** D9
Güllük Dağı △ *Turkey* **47** E12
Güllük Körfezi *Turkey* **47** D9
Gulma *Nigeria* **83** C5
Gulmarg *India* **69** B6
Gülnar *Turkey* **72** D5
Gülpınar *Turkey* **47** B8
Gülşehir *Turkey* **72** C6
Gülshat *Kazakhstan* **52** C8
Gulu *Uganda* **86** B3
Gülübovo *Bulgaria* **45** D9
Gulud, J. *Sudan* **81** E2
Gulwe *Tanzania* **86** D4
Gulyaypole = Hulyaypole
  Ukraine **33** J9
Gumal ➤ *Pakistan* **68** D4
Gumbaz *Pakistan* **68** D3
Gumel *Nigeria* **83** C6
Gumi *S. Korea* **57** F15
Gumiel de Hizán *Spain* **36** D7
Gumla *India* **69** H11
Gumlu *Australia* **94** B4
Gumma ☐ *Japan* **55** F9
Gummersbach *Germany* **24** D3
Gummi *Nigeria* **83** C6
Gümüldür *Turkey* **47** C9
Gümüşçay *Turkey* **45** F11
Gümüşhacıköy *Turkey* **72** B6
Gümüşhane *Turkey* **73** B8
Gümüşsu *Turkey* **47** C11
Gumzai *Indonesia* **63** F8
Guna *Ethiopia* **81** F4
Guna *India* **68** G7
Gunbalanya *Australia* **92** B5
Gundabooka △ *Australia* **95** E4
Gundelfingen *Germany* **25** G6
Güney *Burdur, Turkey* **47** D11
Güney *Denizli, Turkey* **47** C11
Güney *Denizli, Turkey* **72** C3
Güneydoğu Toroslar *Turkey* **73** C9
Gunisao ➤ *Canada* **103** C9
Gunisao L. *Canada* **103** C9
Gunjyal *Pakistan* **68** C4
Günlüce *Turkey* **47** E10
Gunnarskog *Sweden* **10** E6
Gunnbjørn Fjeld *Greenland* **4** C6
Gunnebo *Sweden* **11** G10
Gunnedah *Australia* **95** E5
Gunnewin *Australia* **95** D4
Gunningbar Cr. ➤ *Australia* **95** E4
Gunnison *Colo., U.S.A.* **108** G10
Gunnison *Utah, U.S.A.* **108** G8
Gunnison ➤ *U.S.A.* **108** G9
Gunpowder *Australia* **94** B2
Gunsan *S. Korea* **57** G14
Guntakal *India* **66** M10
Gunter *Canada* **114** B7
Guntersville *U.S.A.* **117** D11
Guntong *Malaysia* **65** K3
Guntur *India* **67** L12
Gunungapi *Indonesia* **63** F7
Gunungsitoli *Indonesia* **62** D1
Günz ➤ *Germany* **25** G6
Gunza *Angola* **84** G2
Günzburg *Germany* **25** G6
Gunzenhausen *Germany* **25** F6
Guo He ➤ *China* **57** H9
Guoyang *China* **56** H9
Gupis *Pakistan* **69** A5
Gura Humorului *Romania* **29** C10
Gura-Teghii *Romania* **29** E11
Gurag *Ethiopia* **81** F4
Gurahonț *Romania* **28** D7
Gurbantünggüt Shamo
  China **60** B3
Gurdaspur *India* **68** C6
Gurdon *U.S.A.* **116** E8
Güre *Balıkesir, Turkey* **47** B8
Güre *Uşak, Turkey* **47** C11
Gurgaon *India* **68** E7
Gürgentepe *Turkey* **72** B7
Gurghiu, Munții *Romania* **29** D10
Gurgueia ➤ *Brazil* **125** E10
Gurha *India* **68** G4
Guri, Embalse de *Venezuela* **124** B6
Gurin *Nigeria* **83** D7
Gurjaani *Georgia* **35** K7
Gurk ➤ *Austria* **26** E7

Gurkha *Nepal* **69** E11
Gurla Mandhata =
  Naimona'nyi Feng *Nepal* **69** D9
Gurley *Australia* **95** D4
Gurnet Point *U.S.A.* **115** D14
Guro *Mozam.* **87** F3
Gürpınar *Istanbul, Turkey* **45** F12
Gürpınar *Van, Turkey* **73** C10
Gürsu *Turkey* **45** F13
Gürün *Turkey* **72** C7
Gurupá *Brazil* **125** D8
Gurupá, I. Grande de *Brazil* **125** D8
Gurupi *Brazil* **125** F9
Gurupi ➤ *Brazil* **125** D9
Guruwe *Zimbabwe* **89** B5
Gürün *Turkey* **72** C7
Gusau *Nigeria* **83** C6
Gusev *Russia* **30** D9
Gushan *China* **57** E12
Gushgy = Serhetabat
  Turkmenistan **71** C9
Gushi *China* **59** A10
Gushiago *Ghana* **83** D4
Gusinje *Montenegro* **44** D3
Gusinoozersk *Russia* **53** D11
Güspini *Italy* **42** C1
Güssing *Austria* **27** D9
Gustavsberg *Sweden* **10** E12
Gustavus *U.S.A.* **102** B1
Güstrow *Germany* **24** B8
Gusum *Sweden* **11** F10
Guta = Kolárovo
  Slovak Rep. **27** D10
Gütersloh *Germany* **24** D4
Gutha *Australia* **93** E2
Guthalungra *Australia* **94** B4
Guthrie *Canada* **114** B5
Guthrie *Okla., U.S.A.* **116** D6
Guthrie *Tex., U.S.A.* **116** E4
Gutian *China* **59** D12
Guttenberg *U.S.A.* **112** D8
Gutu *Zimbabwe* **89** B5
Guwahati *India* **67** F17
Guy Fawkes River △
  Australia **95** D5
Guyana ■ *S. Amer.* **124** C7
Guyane française = French
  Guiana ☑ *S. Amer.* **125** C8
Guyang *China* **56** D6
Guyenne *France* **20** D4
Guymon *U.S.A.* **116** G4
Guyra *Australia* **95** E5
Guyuan *Hebei, China* **56** D8
Guyuan *Ningxia Huizu, China* **56** G4
Güzelbahçe *Turkey* **47** C8
Güzelyurt *Cyprus* **49** D11
Guzhang *China* **58** C7
Guzhen *China* **57** H9
Guzmán, L. de *Mexico* **118** A3
Gvardeysk *Russia* **30** D9
Gvardeyskoye *Ukraine* **33** K8
Gwa *Burma* **67** L19
Gwaai *Zimbabwe* **87** F2
Gwaai ➤ *Zimbabwe* **87** F2
Gwabegar *Australia* **95** E4
Gwadabawa *Nigeria* **83** C6
Gwādar *Pakistan* **66** G3
Gwagwada *Nigeria* **83** C6
Gwalior *India* **68** F8
Gwanara *Nigeria* **83** D5
Gwanda *Zimbabwe* **87** G2
Gwandu *Nigeria* **83** C5
Gwane *Dem. Rep. of the Congo* **86** B2
Gwangju *S. Korea* **57** G14
Gwanju = Gwangju
  S. Korea **57** G14
Gwaram *Nigeria* **83** C7
Gwarzo *Nigeria* **83** C6
Gwasero *Nigeria* **83** D5
Gwda ➤ *Poland* **31** E3
Gweebarra B. *Ireland* **12** B3
Gweedore *Ireland* **12** A3
Gweru *Zimbabwe* **87** F2
Gwi *Nigeria* **83** D6
Gwinn *U.S.A.* **112** B10
Gwio Kura *Nigeria* **83** C7
Gwoza *Nigeria* **83** C7
Gwydir ➤ *Australia* **95** D4
Gwynedd ☐ *U.K.* **14** E3
Gyandzha = Gäncä
  Azerbaijan **35** K8
Gyaring Hu *China* **60** C4
Gydanskiy Poluostrov
  Russia **52** C8
Gyeongju *S. Korea* **57** G15
Gympie *Australia* **95** D5
Gyomaendrőd *Hungary* **28** D5
Gyöngyös *Hungary* **28** C4
Győr *Hungary* **28** C3
Győr-Moson-Sopron ☐
  Hungary **28** C2
Gypsum Pt. *Canada* **102** A6
Gypsumville *Canada* **103** C9
Gyaring Hu *China* **60** C4

Gyueshevo *Bulgaria* **44** D6
Gyula *Hungary* **28** D6
Gyumri *Armenia* **35** K6
Gyzylarbat = Serdar
  Turkmenistan **71** B8
Gyzyletrek = Etrek
  Turkmenistan **71** B7
Gzhatsk = Gagarin *Russia* **32** E8

H

Ha 'Arava ➤ *Israel* **74** E4
Ha Coi *Vietnam* **58** G6
Ha Dong *Vietnam* **58** G5
Ha Giang *Vietnam* **58** F5
Ha Karmel △ *Israel* **74** C4
Ha Long, Vinh *Vietnam* **64** B6
Ha Tien *Vietnam* **65** G5
Ha Tinh *Vietnam* **64** C5
Ha Trung *Vietnam* **64** C5
Haaksbergen *Neths.* **17** B6
Ha'ano *Tonga* **91** c
Ha'apai Group *Tonga* **91** c
Haapiti *Moorea* **91** d
Haapsalu *Estonia* **32** C2
Haarby *Denmark* **11** J4
Haarlem *Neths.* **17** B4
Haast *N.Z.* **91** E2
Haast ➤ *N.Z.* **91** E2
Haast Bluff *Australia* **92** D5
Hab ➤ *Pakistan* **68** G3
Hab Nadi Chauki *Pakistan* **68** G2
Habahe *China* **60** B3
Habaswein *Kenya* **86** B4
Habay *Canada* **102** B5
Ḥabbānīyah *Iraq* **73** F10
Ḥabbānīyah, Hawr al *Iraq* **73** F10
Habichtswald △ *Germany* **24** D5
Habo *Sweden* **11** G8
Haboro *Japan* **54** B10
Habshān *U.A.E.* **71** F7
Hachenburg *Germany* **24** E3
Hachijō-Jima *Japan* **55** H9
Hachinohe *Japan* **54** D10
Hachiōji *Japan* **55** G9
Hacı Zeynalabdin *Azerbaijan*
  73 B13
Hacıbektaş *Turkey* **72** C6
Hacılar *Turkey* **72** C6
Hackås *Sweden* **10** B8
Hackensack *U.S.A.* **115** F10
Hackettstown *U.S.A.* **115** F10
Hadali *Pakistan* **68** C5
Hadarba, Ras *Sudan* **80** C4
Hadarom ☐ *Israel* **74** E4
Ḥadd, Ra's al *Oman* **75** C6
Haddington *U.K.* **13** F6
Hadejia *Nigeria* **83** C7
Hadejia ➤ *Nigeria* **83** C7
Hadera *Israel* **74** C3
Hadera, N. ➤ *Israel* **74** C3
Haderslev *Denmark* **11** J3
Hadhramaut =
  Ḥaḍramawt *Yemen* **75** D4
Hadībōh *Yemen* **75** E5
Hadim *Turkey* **72** D5
Hadong *S. Korea* **57** G14
Ḥaḍramawt *Yemen* **75** D4
Ḥadrānīyah *Iraq* **70** C4
Hadrian's Wall *U.K.* **14** B5
Hadsten *Denmark* **11** H4
Hadsund *Denmark* **11** H4
Hadyach *Ukraine* **33** G8
Hae, Ko *Thailand* **65** a
Haeju *N. Korea* **57** E13
Haenam *S. Korea* **57** G14
Haenertsburg *S. Africa* **89** C4
Haerhpin = Harbin *China* **57** B14
Hafar al Bāṭin *Si. Arabia* **70** D5
Hafik *Turkey* **72** C7
Ḥafīrat al 'Aydā *Si. Arabia* **70** E3
Ḥafit *Oman* **71** F7
Hafizabad *Pakistan* **68** C5
Haflong *India* **67** G18
Haft Gel *Iran* **71** D6
Hagalil *Israel* **74** C4
Hagby *Sweden* **11** H10
Hagen *Germany* **24** D3
Hagenow *Germany* **24** B7
Hagerman *U.S.A.* **109** K11
Hagerman Fossil Beds △
  U.S.A. **108** E6
Hagerstown *U.S.A.* **113** F15
Hagersville *Canada* **114** D4
Hagetmau *France* **20** E3
Hagfors *Sweden* **10** D7
Hagi *Japan* **55** G5
Hagolan *Syria* **74** C4
Hagondange *France* **19** C13
Hags Hd. *Ireland* **12** D2
Hague, C. de la *France* **18** C5
Hague, The =
  's-Gravenhage *Neths.* **17** B4
Haguenau *France* **19** D14
Hai Duong *Vietnam* **58** G6
Hai'an *Guangdong, China* **59** G8
Hai'an *Jiangsu, China* **59** A13
Haicheng *Fujian, China* **59** E11
Haicheng *Liaoning, China* **57** D12
Haidar Khel *Afghan.* **68** C3

Haidarâbâd = Hyderabad
  India **66** L11
Haidargarh *India* **69** F9
Haifa = Ḥefa *Israel* **74** C4
Haifeng *China* **59** F10
Haiger *Germany* **24** E4
Haikou *China* **64** B8
Ḥā'il *Si. Arabia* **70** E4
Hailar *China* **60** B6
Hailey *U.S.A.* **108** E6
Haileybury *Canada* **104** C4
Hailin *China* **57** B15
Hailing Dao *China* **59** G8
Hailuoto *Finland* **8** D21
Haimen *Guangdong, China* **59** F11
Haimen *Jiangsu, China* **59** B13
Hainan ☐ *China* **64** C7
Hainan Dao *China* **64** C7
Hainan Str. = Qiongzhou
  Haixia *China* **59** E12
Hainaut ☐ *Belgium* **17** D4
Hainburg *Austria* **27** C9
Haines *Alaska, U.S.A.* **102** B1
Haines *Oreg., U.S.A.* **108** D5
Haines City *U.S.A.* **117** G14
Haines Junction *Canada* **102** A1
Hainfeld *Austria* **26** C8
Haining *China* **59** B13
Haiphong *Vietnam* **58** G6
Haitan Dao *China* **59** E12
Haiti ■ *W. Indies* **121** C5
Haiya *Sudan* **80** D4
Haiyan *China* **59** B13
Haiyang *China* **57** F11
Haiyuan *Guangxi Zhuangzu,*
  China **58** F6
Haiyuan *Ningxia Huizu, China* **56** F3
Haizhou *China* **57** G10
Haizhou Wan *China* **57** G10
Haj Ali Qoli, Kavīr *Iran* **71** C7
Hajdú-Bihar ☐ *Hungary* **28** C6
Hajdúböszörmény *Hungary* **28** C6
Hajdúdorog *Hungary* **28** C6
Hajdúhadház *Hungary* **28** C6
Hajdúnánás *Hungary* **28** C6
Hajdúsámson *Hungary* **28** C6
Hajdúszoboszló *Hungary* **28** C6
Haji Ibrahim *Iraq* **73** D11
Ḥājīābād *Iran* **71** C9
Hajipur *India* **69** G11
Ḥajjah *Yemen* **75** D3
Ḥājjī Muḥsin *Iraq* **70** C5
Ḥājjīābād *Iran* **71** D7
Ḥājjīābād-e Zarrīn *Iran* **71** C7
Hajnówka *Poland* **31** F10
Hakansson, Mts.
  Dem. Rep. of the Congo **87** D2
Hakkâri *Turkey* **73** D10
Hakkâri ☐ *Turkey* **73** D10
Hakkâri Dağları *Turkey* **73** C10
Hakken-Zan *Japan* **55** G7
Hakodate *Japan* **54** D10
Hakos *Namibia* **88** C2
Håksberg *Sweden* **10** D9
Haku-San *Japan* **55** F8
Haku-San △ *Japan* **55** F8
Hakui *Japan* **55** F8
Hala *Pakistan* **68** G3
Ḥalab *Syria* **72** D7
Ḥalab ☐ *Syria* **72** D7
Ḥalabjah *Iraq* **73** E11
Halaib *Sudan* **80** C4
Halaib Triangle *Africa* **80** C4
Halasa *Sudan* **81** E3
Ḥalāt 'Ammār *Si. Arabia* **70** D3
Halbā *Lebanon* **74** A5
Halberstadt *Germany* **24** D7
Halcombe *N.Z.* **91** D5
Halcon *Phil.* **63** B6
Halde Fjäll = Haltiatunturi
  Finland **8** B19
Halden *Norway* **9** G14
Haldensleben *Germany* **24** C7
Haldia *Bangla.* **69** H13
Haldwani *India* **69** E8
Hale ➤ *Australia* **94** C2
Halesowen *U.K.* **15** E5
Halesworth *U.K.* **15** E9
Haleyville *U.S.A.* **117** D11
Half Assini *Ghana* **82** D4
Half Dome *U.S.A.* **110** H7
Halfeti *Turkey* **72** D7
Halfmoon Bay *N.Z.* **91** G2
Halfway ➤ *Canada* **102** B4
Halia *India* **69** G10
Haliburton *Canada* **114** A6
Halifax *Australia* **94** B4
Halifax *Canada* **105** D7
Halifax *U.K.* **14** D6
Halifax *U.S.A.* **114** F8
Halifax B. *Australia* **94** B4
Halifax I. *Namibia* **88** D2
Halīl ➤ *Iran* **71** E8
Halki *Greece* **47** E9
Halkida *Greece* **46** C5
Halkidiki ☐ *Greece* **44** F7
Halkirk *U.K.* **13** C5
Hall Beach = Sanirajak
  Canada **101** C11

Hall in Tirol *Austria* **26** D4
Hall Pen. *Canada* **101** C13
Hallabro *Sweden* **11** H9
Halland *Sweden* **9** H15
Hallands Väderö *Sweden* **11** H6
Hallands län □ *Sweden* **11** H6
Hallandsås *Sweden* **11** H7
Hallasan *S. Korea* **57** H14
Hällbybrunn *Sweden* **10** E10
Halle *Belgium* **17** D4
Halle *Nordrhein-Westfalen, Germany* **24** C4
Halle *Sachsen-Anhalt, Germany* **24** D7
Hällefors *Sweden* **10** E8
Hälleforsnäs *Sweden* **10** E10
Hallein *Austria* **26** D6
Hällekis *Sweden* **11** F7
Hallen *Sweden* **10** A8
Hallett *Australia* **95** E2
Hallettsville *U.S.A.* **116** G6
Halley *Antarctica* **5** D1
Hallim *S. Korea* **57** H14
Hallingdalselva → *Norway* **8** F13
Hallock *U.S.A.* **112** A5
Halls Creek *Australia* **92** C4
Halls Gap *Australia* **95** F3
Halls Lake *Canada* **114** A6
Hallsberg *Sweden* **10** E9
Hallstahammar *Sweden* **10** E10
Hallstatt *Austria* **26** D6
Hallstavik *Sweden* **10** D12
Hallstead *U.S.A.* **115** E9
Halmahera *Indonesia* **63** D7
Halmeu *Romania* **28** C8
Halmstad *Sweden* **11** H6
Hals *Denmark* **11** H4
Hälsingborg = Helsingborg *Sweden* **11** H6
Hälsingland *Sweden* **10** C10
Halstead *U.K.* **15** F8
Haltern *Germany* **24** D3
Haltiatunturi *Finland* **8** B19
Halton □ *U.K.* **14** D5
Haltwhistle *U.K.* **14** C5
Ḥalūl *Qatar* **71** E7
Halvad *India* **68** H4
Ham *France* **19** C10
Ham Tan *Vietnam* **65** G6
Ham Yen *Vietnam* **64** A5
Hamab *Namibia* **88** D2
Hamad *Sudan* **81** D3
Hamada *Japan* **55** G6
Hamadān *Iran* **73** E13
Hamadān □ *Iran* **71** C6
Ḥamāh *Syria* **72** E7
Ḥamāh □ *Syria* **72** E7
Hamamatsu *Japan* **55** G8
Hamar *Norway* **8** F14
Hamâta, Gebel *Egypt* **70** E2
Hambantota *Sri Lanka* **66** R12
Hamber △ *Canada* **102** C5
Hamburg *Germany* **24** B5
Hamburg *Ark., U.S.A.* **116** E9
Hamburg *N.Y., U.S.A.* **114** D6
Hamburg *Pa., U.S.A.* **115** F9
Hamburg □ *Germany* **24** B5
Hamburg Fuhlsbüttel ✈ (HAM) *Germany* **24** B5
Ḥamḍ, W. al → *Si. Arabia* **70** E3
Hamden *U.S.A.* **115** E12
Hamdibey *Turkey* **47** B9
Häme *Finland* **32** B2
Hämeenlinna *Finland* **32** B3
Hamélé *Ghana* **82** C4
Hamelin Pool *Australia* **93** E1
Hameln *Germany* **24** C5
Hamerkaz □ *Israel* **74** C3
Hamersley Ra. *Australia* **92** D2
Hamhŭng *N. Korea* **57** E14
Hami *China* **60** B4
Hamili *Greece* **47** F8
Hamilton *Australia* **95** F3
Hamilton *Canada* **114** C5
Hamilton *N.Z.* **91** B5
Hamilton *U.K.* **13** F4
Hamilton *Ala., U.S.A.* **117** D11
Hamilton *Mont., U.S.A.* **108** C6
Hamilton *N.Y., U.S.A.* **115** D9
Hamilton *Ohio, U.S.A.* **113** F11
Hamilton *Tex., U.S.A.* **116** F5
Hamilton → *Queens., Australia* **94** C2
Hamilton → *S. Austral., Australia* **95** D2
Hamilton City *U.S.A.* **110** F4
Hamilton I. *Australia* **94** J6
Hamilton Inlet *Canada* **105** B8
Hamina *Finland* **32** B3
Hamirpur *H.P., India* **68** D7
Hamirpur *Ut. P., India* **69** G9
Hamitabat *Turkey* **45** E11
Hamju *N. Korea* **57** E14
Hamlet *U.S.A.* **117** D15
Hamley Bridge *Australia* **95** E2
Hamlin = Hameln *Germany* **24** C5

Hamlin *N.Y., U.S.A.* **114** C7
Hamlin *Tex., U.S.A.* **116** E4
Hamm *Germany* **24** D3
Hammām al Alīl *Iraq* **73** D10
Hammarstrand *Sweden* **10** A10
Hammelburg *Germany* **25** E5
Hammeren *Denmark* **11** J8
Hammerfest *Norway* **8** A20
Hammerum *Denmark* **11** H3
Hamminkeln *Germany* **24** D2
Hammond *Ind., U.S.A.* **112** E10
Hammond *La., U.S.A.* **117** F9
Hammond *N.Y., U.S.A.* **115** B9
Hammondsport *U.S.A.* **114** D7
Hammonton *U.S.A.* **113** F16
Hamneda *Sweden* **11** H7
Hamoyet, Jebel *Sudan* **80** D4
Hampden *N.Z.* **91** F3
Hampshire □ *U.K.* **15** F6
Hampshire Downs *U.K.* **15** F6
Hampton *N.B., Canada* **105** C6
Hampton *Ont., Canada* **114** C6
Hampton *Ark., U.S.A.* **116** E8
Hampton *Iowa, U.S.A.* **112** D7
Hampton *N.H., U.S.A.* **115** D14
Hampton *S.C., U.S.A.* **117** E14
Hampton *Va., U.S.A.* **113** G15
Hampton Bays *U.S.A.* **115** F12
Hampton Tableland *Australia* **93** F4
Hamra *Sweden* **10** C8
Hamrat esh Sheykh *Sudan* **81** E2
Ḥamrīn, Jabal *Iraq* **73** E11
Hamur *Turkey* **73** C10
Hamyang *S. Korea* **57** G14
Han i Hotit *Albania* **44** D3
Han Jiang → *China* **59** F11
Han Shui → *China* **59** B10
Hanak *Si. Arabia* **70** E3
Hanak *Turkey* **73** B10
Hanamaki *Japan* **54** E10
Hanang *Tanzania* **86** C4
Hanau *Germany* **25** E4
Hanbogd = Ihbulag *Mongolia* **56** C4
Hançalar *Turkey* **47** C11
Hâncești *Moldova* **29** D13
Hancheng *China* **56** G6
Hanchuan *China* **59** B9
Hancock *Mich., U.S.A.* **112** B9
Hancock *N.Y., U.S.A.* **115** E9
Hancock *Vt., U.S.A.* **115** C12
Handa *Japan* **55** G8
Handa I. *U.K.* **13** C3
Handan *China* **56** F8
Handeni *Tanzania* **86** D4
Handlová *Slovak Rep.* **27** C11
Handub *Sudan* **80** D4
Handwara *India* **69** B6
Hanegev *Israel* **74** E4
Hanford *U.S.A.* **110** J7
Hanford Reach △ *U.S.A.* **108** C4
Hang Chat *Thailand* **64** C2
Hang Dong *Thailand* **64** C2
Hangang → *S. Korea* **57** F14
Hangayn Nuruu *Mongolia* **60** B4
Hangchou = Hangzhou *China* **59** B13
Hanggin Houqi *China* **56** D4
Hanggin Qi *China* **56** E5
Hangu *China* **57** E9
Hangzhou *China* **59** B13
Hangzhou Wan *China* **59** B13
Hanh *Mongolia* **53** D11
Hanhongor *Mongolia* **56** C3
Hani *Turkey* **73** C9
Hania = Chania *Greece* **49** D6
Haria *Canary Is.* **48** E6
Haridwar *India* **68** E8
Harim, Jabal al *Oman* **71** E8
Hanīdh *Si. Arabia* **71** E6
Ḥanīsh *Yemen* **75** E3
Haniska *Slovak Rep.* **27** C14
Hanjiang *China* **59** E12
Hankinson *U.S.A.* **112** B5
Hanko *Finland* **32** C2
Hanksville *U.S.A.* **108** G8
Hanle *India* **69** C8
Hanmer Springs *N.Z.* **91** E4
Hann → *Australia* **92** C4
Hann, Mt. *Australia* **92** C4
Hanna *Canada* **102** C6
Hanna *U.S.A.* **108** F10
Hannah B. *Canada* **104** B4
Hannibal *Mo., U.S.A.* **112** F8
Hannibal *N.Y., U.S.A.* **115** C8
Hannik *Sudan* **80** D3
Hannover *Germany* **24** C5
Hanö *Sweden* **11** H8
Hanöbukten *Sweden* **11** J8
Hanoi *Vietnam* **58** G5
Hanover = Hannover *Germany* **24** C5
Hanover *Canada* **114** B3
Hanover *S. Africa* **88** E3
Hanover *N.H., U.S.A.* **115** C12
Hanover *Ohio, U.S.A.* **114** F2
Hanover *Pa., U.S.A.* **113** F15
Hanover, I. *Chile* **128** G2
Hans Lollik I. *U.S. Virgin Is.* **121** e

Hansdiha *India* **69** G12
Hanshou *China* **59** C8
Hansi *H.P., India* **68** C7
Hansi *Haryana, India* **68** E6
Hanson, L. *Australia* **95** E2
Hanstholm *Denmark* **11** G2
Hantsavichy *Belarus* **23** B14
Hanumangarh *India* **68** E6
Hanyin *China* **58** A7
Hanyuan *China* **58** C5
Hanzhong *China* **56** H4
Hanzhuang *China* **57** G9
Haora *India* **69** H13
Haoxue *China* **59** B9
Haparanda *Sweden* **8** D21
Happy *U.S.A.* **116** D4
Happy Camp *U.S.A.* **108** F2
Happy Valley-Goose Bay *Canada* **105** B7
Hapsu *N. Korea* **57** D15
Hapur *India* **68** E7
Ḥaql *Si. Arabia* **74** F3
Har *Indonesia* **63** F8
Har-Ayrag *Mongolia* **56** B5
Har Hu *China* **60** C4
Har Us Nuur *Mongolia* **60** B4
Har Yehuda *Israel* **74** D3
Ḥaraḍ *Si. Arabia* **75** C4
Haradok *Belarus* **32** E6
Härädsbäck *Sweden* **11** H8
Haramosh *Pakistan* **69** B6
Haranomachi *Japan* **54** F10
Harare *Zimbabwe* **87** F3
Harat *Eritrea* **81** D4
Harazé *Chad* **79** G10
Harbin *China* **57** B14
Harbiye *Turkey* **72** D7
Harbo *Sweden* **10** D11
Harboøre *Denmark* **11** H2
Harbor Beach *U.S.A.* **114** C2
Harborcreek *U.S.A.* **114** D5
Harbour Breton *Canada* **105** C8
Harbour Deep *Canada* **105** B8
Harburg *Germany* **24** B5
Harburger Berge △ *Germany* **24** B5
Harda *India* **68** H7
Hardangerfjorden *Norway* **9** F12
Hardangervidda *Norway* **8** F12
Hardap △ *Namibia* **88** C2
Hardap Dam *Namibia* **88** C2
Hardenberg *Neths.* **17** B6
Harderwijk *Neths.* **17** B5
Hardey → *Australia* **92** D2
Hardin *U.S.A.* **108** D10
Harding *S. Africa* **89** E4
Harding Ra. *Australia* **92** C3
Hardisty *Canada* **102** C6
Hardoi *India* **69** F9
Hardwar = Haridwar *India* **68** E8
Hardwick *U.S.A.* **115** B12
Hardwood Lake *Canada* **114** A7
Hardy, Pen. *Chile* **128** H3
Hardy, Pte. *St. Lucia* **121** f
Hare B. *Canada* **105** B8
Hareid *Norway* **8** E12
Haren *Germany* **24** C3
Harer *Ethiopia* **81** F5
Harerge *Ethiopia* **81** F5
Hareto *Ethiopia* **81** F4
Harfleur *France* **18** C7
Hargeisa = Hargeysa *Somali Rep.* **75** F3
Harghita □ *Romania* **29** D10
Harghita, Munţii *Romania* **29** D10
Hargshamn *Sweden* **10** D12
Hari → *Indonesia* **62** E2
Haria *Canary Is.* **48** E6
Haridwar *India* **68** E8
Harim, Jabal al *Oman* **71** E8
Haringhata → *Bangla.* **67** J16
Harīr, W. al → *Syria* **74** C4
Harīrūd → *Asia* **71** B9
Härjedalen *Sweden* **10** B7
Harlan *Iowa, U.S.A.* **112** E7
Harlan *Ky., U.S.A.* **113** G12
Hârlău *Romania* **29** C11
Harlech *U.K.* **14** E3
Harlem *U.S.A.* **108** B9
Harlingen *Neths.* **17** A5
Harlingen *U.S.A.* **116** H6
Harlow *U.K.* **15** F8
Harlowton *U.S.A.* **108** C9
Harmancık *Turkey* **47** B11
Harmånger *Sweden* **10** C11
Harmil *Eritrea* **81** D5
Harnai *Pakistan* **68** D2
Harney Basin *U.S.A.* **108** E4
Harney L. *U.S.A.* **108** E4
Harney Peak *U.S.A.* **112** D2
Härnön *Sweden* **10** B12
Härnösand *Sweden* **10** B11
Haro *Spain* **38** C2
Haroldswick *U.K.* **13** A8
Harp L. *Canada* **105** A7
Harper *Liberia* **82** E3
Harplinge *Sweden* **11** H6
Harr *Mauritania* **82** B2
Harrai *India* **69** H8
Harrand *Pakistan* **68** E4

Ḥarrat Khaybar *Si. Arabia* **80** B5
Ḥarrat Nawāṣīf *Si. Arabia* **80** C5
Harricana → *Canada* **104** B4
Harriman *U.S.A.* **117** D12
Harrington Harbour *Canada* **105** B8
Harris *U.K.* **13** D2
Harris, L. *Australia* **95** E2
Harris, Sd. of *U.K.* **13** D1
Harris Pt. *Canada* **114** C2
Harrisburg *Ill., U.S.A.* **112** G9
Harrisburg *Nebr., U.S.A.* **112** E2
Harrisburg *Pa., U.S.A.* **114** F8
Harrismith *S. Africa* **89** D4
Harrison *Ark., U.S.A.* **116** C8
Harrison *Maine, U.S.A.* **115** B14
Harrison *Nebr., U.S.A.* **112** D2
Harrison, C. *Canada* **105** B8
Harrison L. *Canada* **102** D4
Harrisonburg *U.S.A.* **113** F14
Harrisonville *U.S.A.* **112** F6
Harriston *Canada* **114** C4
Harrisville *Mich., U.S.A.* **114** B1
Harrisville *N.Y., U.S.A.* **115** B9
Harrisville *Pa., U.S.A.* **114** E5
Harrodsburg *U.S.A.* **113** G11
Harrogate *U.K.* **14** C6
Harrow *Canada* **114** D2
Harrow □ *U.K.* **15** F7
Harrowsmith *Canada* **115** B8
Harry S. Truman Res. *U.S.A.* **112** F7
Harsefeld *Germany* **24** B5
Harsewinkel *Germany* **24** D4
Harsīn *Iran* **73** E12
Hârşova *Romania* **29** F12
Harstad *Norway* **8** B17
Harsud *India* **68** H7
Hart *U.S.A.* **112** D10
Hart, L. *Australia* **95** E2
Hartbees → *S. Africa* **88** D3
Hartberg *Austria* **26** D8
Hartford *Conn., U.S.A.* **115** E12
Hartford *Ky., U.S.A.* **112** G10
Hartford *S. Dak., U.S.A.* **112** D5
Hartford *Vt., U.S.A.* **115** C12
Hartford *Wis., U.S.A.* **112** D9
Hartford City *U.S.A.* **113** E11
Hartland *Canada* **105** C6
Hartland Pt. *U.K.* **15** F3
Hartlepool *U.K.* **14** C6
Hartlepool □ *U.K.* **14** C6
Hartley Bay *Canada* **102** C3
Hartmannberge *Namibia* **88** B1
Hartney *Canada* **103** D8
Hârtop *Moldova* **29** D13
Harts → *S. Africa* **88** D3
Harts Range *Australia* **94** C1
Hartselle *U.S.A.* **117** D11
Hartshorne *U.S.A.* **116** D7
Hartstown *U.S.A.* **114** E4
Hartsville *U.S.A.* **117** D14
Hartswater *S. Africa* **88** D3
Hartwell *U.S.A.* **117** D13
Harunabad *Pakistan* **68** E5
Harvand *Iran* **71** D7
Harvey *Australia* **93** F2
Harvey *Ill., U.S.A.* **112** E10
Harvey *N. Dak., U.S.A.* **112** B4
Harwich *U.K.* **15** F9
Haryana □ *India* **68** E7
Haryn → *Belarus* **23** B14
Harz *Germany* **24** D6
Harz △ *Germany* **24** D6
Harzgerode *Germany* **24** D7
Hasa *Si. Arabia* **71** E6
Ḥasā, W. al → *Jordan* **74** D4
Hasaheisa *Sudan* **81** E3
Hashimoto *Japan* **55** G7
Hashtjerd *Iran* **71** C6
Hashtpur = Tālesh *Iran* **73** D13
Hashtrud *Iran* **73** D12
Haskell *U.S.A.* **116** E5
Haskovo = Khaskovo *Bulgaria* **45** E9
Hasköy *Turkey* **45** E10
Haslach *Germany* **25** G4
Hasle *Denmark* **11** J8
Haslemere *U.K.* **15** F7
Haslev *Denmark* **11** J5
Hasparren *France* **20** E2
Hassa *Turkey* **72** D7
Hassberge △ *Germany* **25** E6
Hassela *Sweden* **10** B10
Hasselt *Belgium* **17** D5
Hassfurt *Germany* **25** E6
Hassi Messaoud *Algeria* **78** B7
Hässleholm *Sweden* **11** H7
Hassloch *Germany* **25** F4
Hastholmen *Sweden* **11** F8
Hastings *N.Z.* **91** C6
Hastings *U.K.* **15** G8
Hastings *Mich., U.S.A.* **113** D11
Hastings *Minn., U.S.A.* **112** C7

Hastings *Nebr., U.S.A.* **112** E4
Hastings Ra. *Australia* **95** E5
Hästveda *Sweden* **11** H7
Hat *Canada* **105** C5
Hat Yai *Thailand* **65** J3
Hatanbulag = Ergel *Mongolia* **56** C5
Hatay *Turkey* **72** D7
Hatay □ *Turkey* **72** D7
Hatch *U.S.A.* **109** K10
Hatchet L. *Canada* **103** B8
Haţeg *Romania* **28** E7
Hateruma-Shima *Japan* **55** M1
Hatfield P.O. *Australia* **95** E3
Hatgal *Mongolia* **60** A5
Hathras *India* **68** F8
Hatia *Bangla.* **67** H17
Hatta *India* **69** G8
Hatta *U.A.E.* **71** E8
Hattah *Australia* **95** E3
Hattah Kulkyne △ *Australia* **95** E3
Hatteras, C. *U.S.A.* **117** D17
Hattiesburg *U.S.A.* **117** F10
Hatvan *Hungary* **28** C4
Hau Duc *Vietnam* **64** E7
Haugesund *Norway* **9** G11
Haukipudas *Finland* **8** D21
Haultain → *Canada* **103** B7
Hauraki G. *N.Z.* **91** B5
Hausruck *Austria* **26** C6
Haut Atlas *Morocco* **78** B4
Haut-Jura △ *France* **19** F9
Haut-Languedoc △ *France* **20** E6
Haut-Niger △ *Guinea* **82** C2
Haut-Rhin □ *France* **19** E14
Haute-Corse □ *France* **21** F13
Haute-Garonne □ *France* **20** E5
Haute-Loire □ *France* **20** C7
Haute-Marne □ *France* **19** D12
Haute-Normandie □ *France* **18** C7
Haute-Saône □ *France* **19** E13
Haute-Savoie □ *France* **21** C10
Haute-Vienne □ *France* **20** C5
Hautes-Alpes □ *France* **21** D10
Hautes Fagnes = Hohes Venn *Belgium* **17** D6
Hautes-Pyrénées □ *France* **20** F4
Hauteville-Lompnès *France* **21** C9
Hautmont *France* **19** B10
Hauts-de-Seine □ *France* **19** D9
Hauts Plateaux *Algeria* **78** B6
Hauzenberg *Germany* **25** G9
Havana = La Habana *Cuba* **120** B3
Havana *U.S.A.* **112** E8
Havant *U.K.* **15** G7
Havârna *Romania* **29** B11
Havasu, L. *U.S.A.* **111** L12
Havdhem *Sweden* **11** G12
Havel → *Germany* **24** C8
Havelian *Pakistan* **68** B5
Havelock *Canada* **114** B7
Havelock *N.Z.* **91** D4
Havelock *U.S.A.* **117** D16
Haverfordwest *U.K.* **15** F3
Haverhill *U.K.* **15** E8
Haverhill *U.S.A.* **115** D13
Haverstraw *U.S.A.* **115** E11
Håverud *Sweden* **11** F6
Havirga *Mongolia* **56** B6
Havířov *Czech Rep.* **27** B11
Havlíčkův Brod *Czech Rep.* **26** B8
Havneby *Denmark* **11** J2
Havøysund *Norway* **8** A21
Havran *Turkey* **47** B9
Havre *U.S.A.* **108** B9
Havre-Aubert *Canada* **105** C7
Havre-St.-Pierre *Canada* **105** B7
Havsa *Turkey* **45** E10
Havza *Turkey* **72** B6
Haw → *U.S.A.* **117** D15
Hawai'i *U.S.A.* **106** b
Hawai'i □ *U.S.A.* **106** b
Hawaiian Is. *Pac. Oc.* **106** b
Hawaiian Ridge *Pac. Oc.* **97** E11
Hawarden *U.S.A.* **112** D5
Hawea, L. *N.Z.* **91** F2
Hawera *N.Z.* **91** C5
Hawick *U.K.* **13** F6
Hawk Junction *Canada* **104** C3
Hawke B. *N.Z.* **91** C6
Hawker *Australia* **95** E2
Hawke's Bay *Canada* **105** B8
Hawkesbury *Canada* **104** C5
Hawkesbury I. *Canada* **102** C3
Hawkesbury Pt. *Australia* **94** A1
Hawkinsville *U.S.A.* **117** E13
Hawley *Minn., U.S.A.* **112** B5
Hawley *Pa., U.S.A.* **115** E9
Ḥawrān, W. → *Iraq* **73** F10
Hawsh Mūssá *Lebanon* **74** B4
Hawthorne *U.S.A.* **108** G4
Hay *Australia* **95** E3
Hay → *Australia* **94** C2
Hay → *Canada* **102** A5
Hay, C. *Australia* **92** B4
Hay I. *Canada* **114** B4
Hay L. *Canada* **102** B5

Hay-on-Wye *U.K.* **15** E4
Hay River *Canada* **102** A5
Hay Springs *U.S.A.* **112** D2
Haya = Tehoru *Indonesia* **63** F7
Hayachine-San *Japan* **54** E10
Hayange *France* **19** C13
Hayastan = Armenia ■ *Asia* **35** K7
Haydān, W. al → *Jordan* **74** D4
Haydarlı *Turkey* **47** C12
Hayden *U.S.A.* **108** F10
Haydon *Australia* **94** B3
Hayes *U.S.A.* **112** C3
Hayes → *Canada* **104** A1
Hayes Creek *Australia* **92** B5
Hayle *U.K.* **15** G2
Hayling I. *U.K.* **15** G7
Haymana *Turkey* **72** C5
Haymen I. *Australia* **94** J6
Hayrabolu *Turkey* **45** E11
Hays *Canada* **102** C6
Hays *U.S.A.* **112** F4
Haysyn *Ukraine* **29** B14
Hayvoron *Ukraine* **29** B14
Hayward *Calif., U.S.A.* **110** H4
Hayward *Wis., U.S.A.* **112** B8
Haywards Heath *U.K.* **15** G7
Hazafon □ *Israel* **74** C4
Hazar *Turkmenistan* **52** F6
Hazārān, Kūh-e *Iran* **71** D8
Hazard *U.S.A.* **113** G12
Hazaribag *India* **69** H11
Hazaribag Road *India* **69** G11
Hazebrouck *France* **19** B9
Hazelton *Canada* **102** B3
Hazelton *U.S.A.* **112** B3
Hazen *U.S.A.* **112** B3
Hazlehurst *Ga., U.S.A.* **117** F13
Hazlehurst *Miss., U.S.A.* **117** F9
Hazlet *U.S.A.* **115** F10
Hazleton *U.S.A.* **115** F9
Hazro *Turkey* **70** B4
He Xian *Anhui, China* **59** B12
He Xian *Guangxi Zhuangzu, China* **59** E8
Head of Bight *Australia* **93** F5
Headlands *Zimbabwe* **87** F3
Healdsburg *U.S.A.* **110** G4
Healdton *U.S.A.* **116** D6
Healesville *Australia* **95** F4
Heany Junction *Zimbabwe* **89** C4
Heard I. *Ind. Oc.* **3** G13
Hearne *U.S.A.* **116** F6
Hearst *Canada* **104** C3
Heart → *U.S.A.* **112** B3
Heart's Content *Canada* **105** C9
Heath, Pte. *Canada* **105** C7
Heathrow, London ✈ (LHR) *U.K.* **15** F7
Heavener *U.S.A.* **116** D7
Hebbronville *U.S.A.* **116** H5
Hebei □ *China* **56** E9
Hebel *Australia* **95** D4
Heber *U.S.A.* **111** N11
Heber Springs *U.S.A.* **116** D8
Hebgen L. *U.S.A.* **108** D8
Hebi *China* **56** G8
Hebrides *U.K.* **6** D4
Hebrides, Sea of the *U.K.* **13** D2
Hebron = Al Khalīl *West Bank* **74** D4
Hebron *Canada* **101** D13
Hebron *N. Dak., U.S.A.* **112** B2
Hebron *Nebr., U.S.A.* **112** E5
Heby *Sweden* **10** E10
Hecate Str. *Canada* **102** C2
Heceta I. *U.S.A.* **102** B2
Hechi *China* **58** E7
Hechingen *Germany* **25** G4
Hechuan *China* **58** B6
Hecla *U.S.A.* **112** C4
Hecla I. *Canada* **103** C9
Hedal *Norway* **10** D3
Hédé *France* **18** D5
Hede *Sweden* **10** B7
Hedemora *Sweden* **10** D9
Hedensted *Denmark* **11** J3
Hedesunda *Sweden* **10** D10
Heerde *Neths.* **17** B6
Heerenveen *Neths.* **17** B5
Heerhugowaard *Neths.* **17** B4
Heerlen *Neths.* **17** D5
Ḥefa *Israel* **74** C4
Ḥefa □ *Israel* **74** C4
Hefei *China* **59** B11
Hefeng *China* **59** C8
Hegalig *Sudan* **81** E3
Hegang *China* **60** B8
Heiban *Sudan* **81** E3
Heichengzhen *China* **56** F4
Heide *Germany* **24** A5
Heidelberg *Germany* **25** F4
Heidelberg *S. Africa* **88** E3
Heidenau *Germany* **24** E9
Heidenheim *Germany* **25** G6
Heihe *China* **53** D13
Heijing *China* **58** E3
Heilbad Heiligenstadt *Germany* **24** D6

Heilbron *S. Africa* **89** D4
Heilbronn *Germany* **25** F5
Heiligenblut *Austria* **26** D5
Heiligenhafen *Germany* **24** A6
Heilongjiang □ *China* **60** B7
Heilunkiang =
　Heilongjiang □ *China* **60** B7
Heimaey *Iceland* **8** E3
Heinola *Finland* **32** B4
Heinsberg *Germany* **24** D2
Heinze Kyun *Burma* **64** E1
Heishan *China* **57** D12
Heishui *Liaoning, China* **57** C10
Heishui *Sichuan, China* **58** A4
Hejaz = Ḥijāz *Si. Arabia* **70** E3
Hejian *China* **56** E9
Hejiang *China* **58** C5
Hejin *China* **56** G6
Hekimhan *Turkey* **72** C7
Hekla *Iceland* **8** E4
Hekou *Guangdong, China* **59** F9
Hekou *Yunnan, China* **58** F4
Hel *Poland* **30** D5
Helagsfjället *Sweden* **10** B6
Helan Shan *China* **56** E3
Helechosa de los Montes
　Spain **37** F6
Helen Atoll *Pac. Oc.* **63** D8
Helena *Ark., U.S.A.* **117** D9
Helena *Mont., U.S.A.* **108** C7
Helendale *U.S.A.* **111** L9
Helensburgh *U.K.* **13** E4
Helensville *N.Z.* **91** B5
Helenvale *Australia* **94** B4
Helgasjön *Sweden* **11** H8
Helgeland *Norway* **8** C15
Helgeland *Germany* **24** A3
Heligoland = Helgoland
　Germany **24** A3
Heligoland B. = Deutsche
　Bucht *Germany* **24** A4
Heliopolis = Masr el
　Gedida *Egypt* **80** H7
Hell Hole Gorge △ *Australia* **94** D3
Hella *Iceland* **8** E3
Hellas = Greece ■ *Europe* **46** B3
Hellertown *U.S.A.* **115** F9
Hellespont = Çanakkale
　Boğazı *Turkey* **45** F10
Hellevoetsluis *Neths.* **17** C4
Hellín *Spain* **39** G3
Hells Canyon △ *U.S.A.* **108** D5
Hell's Gate △ *Kenya* **86** C4
Helmand □ *Afghan.* **66** D4
Helmand → *Afghan.* **66** D2
Helme → *Germany* **24** D7
Helmeringhausen *Namibia* **88** D2
Helmond *Neths.* **17** C5
Helmsdale *U.K.* **13** C5
Helmsdale → *U.K.* **13** C5
Helmstedt *Germany* **24** C7
Helong *China* **57** C15
Helper *U.S.A.* **108** G8
Helsingborg *Sweden* **11** H6
Helsinge *Denmark* **11** H6
Helsingfors = Helsinki
　Finland **32** B3
Helsingør *Denmark* **11** H6
Helsinki *Finland* **32** B3
Helska, Mierzeja *Poland* **30** D5
Helston *U.K.* **15** G2
Helvellyn *U.K.* **14** C4
Helwân *Egypt* **80** J7
Hemel Hempstead *U.K.* **15** F7
Hemet *U.S.A.* **111** M10
Hemingford *U.S.A.* **112** D2
Hemis △ *India* **68** B7
Hemmingford *Canada* **115** A11
Hempstead *N.Y., U.S.A.* **115** F11
Hempstead *Tex., U.S.A.* **116** F6
Hemse *Sweden* **11** G12
Hemsön *Sweden* **10** B12
Henán *Sweden* **11** F5
Henan □ *China* **56** H8
Henares → *Spain* **36** E7
Hendaye *France* **20** E2
Hendek *Turkey* **72** B4
Henderson *Argentina* **126** D3
Henderson *Ky., U.S.A.* **112** G10
Henderson *N.C., U.S.A.* **117** C15
Henderson *N.Y., U.S.A.* **115** C8
Henderson *Nev., U.S.A.* **111** J12
Henderson *Tenn., U.S.A.* **117** D10
Henderson *Tex., U.S.A.* **116** E7
Henderson I. *Pac. Oc.* **97** K15
Hendersonville *N.C., U.S.A.*
　117 D13
Hendersonville *Tenn., U.S.A.*
　117 C11
Hendījān *Iran* **71** D6
Hendorābī *Iran* **71** E7
Heng Jiang *China* **58** C5
Heng Xian *China* **58** F7
Hengcheng *China* **56** E4
Hëngch'un *Taiwan* **59** F13
Hengdaohezi *China* **57** B15
Hengelo *Neths.* **17** B6
Hengfeng *China* **59** C10

Hengshan *Hunan, China* **59** D9
Hengshan *Shaanxi, China* **56** F5
Hengshui *China* **56** F8
Hengyang *China* **59** D9
Henichesk *Ukraine* **33** J8
Hénin-Beaumont *France* **19** B9
Henley-on-Thames *U.K.* **15** F7
Henlopen, C. *U.S.A.* **113** F16
Hennan *Sweden* **10** B9
Hennebont *France* **18** E3
Hennenman *S. Africa* **88** D4
Hennessey *U.S.A.* **116** C6
Hennigsdorf *Germany* **24** C9
Henri Pittier △ *Venezuela* **121** D6
Henrietta *N.Y., U.S.A.* **114** C7
Henrietta *Tex., U.S.A.* **116** E5
Henrietta, Ostrov =
　Genriyetty, Ostrov *Russia*
　53 B16
Henrietta Maria, C. *Canada* **104** A3
Henry *U.S.A.* **112** E9
Henryetta *U.S.A.* **116** D7
Henryville *Canada* **115** A11
Hensall *Canada* **114** C3
Henstedt-Ulzburg *Germany* **24** B6
Hentiesbaai *Namibia* **88** C1
Hentiyn Nuruu *Mongolia* **60** B5
Henty *Australia* **95** F4
Henzada *Burma* **67** L19
Hephaestia *Greece* **47** B7
Heping *China* **59** E10
Heppner *U.S.A.* **108** D4
Hepu *China* **58** G7
Hepworth *Canada* **114** B3
Heqing *China* **58** D3
Hequ *China* **56** E6
Héraðsflói *Iceland* **8** D6
Héraðsvötn → *Iceland* **8** D4
Heraklion = Iraklio *Greece* **49** D7
Herald Cays *Australia* **94** B4
Herāt *Afghan.* **66** B3
Herāt □ *Afghan.* **66** B3
Hérault □ *France* **20** E7
Hérault → *France* **20** E7
Herbault *France* **18** E8
Herbert *Canada* **103** C7
Herbert → *Australia* **94** B4
Herberton *Australia* **94** B4
Herbertsdale *S. Africa* **88** E3
Herbignac *France* **18** E4
Herborn *Germany* **24** E4
Herby *Poland* **31** H5
Herceg-Novi *Montenegro* **44** D2
Herchmer *Canada* **103** B10
Herðubreið *Iceland* **8** D5
Hereford *U.K.* **15** E5
Hereford *U.S.A.* **116** D3
Herefordshire □ *U.K.* **15** E5
Hereke *Turkey* **45** F13
Herencia *Spain* **37** F7
Herentals *Belgium* **17** C4
Herford *Germany* **24** C4
Héricourt *France* **19** E13
Herington *U.S.A.* **112** F5
Heris *Iran* **73** C12
Herisau *Switz.* **25** H5
Hérisson *France* **19** F9
Herkimer *U.S.A.* **115** D10
Herlong *U.S.A.* **110** E6
Herm *U.K.* **15** H5
Hermakivka *Ukraine* **29** B11
Hermann *U.S.A.* **112** F8
Hermannsburg *Australia* **92** D5
Hermannsburg *Germany* **24** C6
Hermanus *S. Africa* **88** E2
Hermidale *Australia* **95** E4
Hermiston *U.S.A.* **108** D4
Hermon *Canada* **114** A7
Hermon *U.S.A.* **115** B8
Hermon, Mt. = Shaykh, J.
　ash *Lebanon* **74** B4
Hermosillo *Mexico* **118** B2
Hernád → *Hungary* **28** C6
Hernandarias *Paraguay* **127** B5
Hernandez *U.S.A.* **110** J6
Hernando *Argentina* **126** C3
Hernando *U.S.A.* **117** D10
Hernani *Spain* **38** B3
Herndon *U.S.A.* **114** F8
Herne *Germany* **17** C7
Herne Bay *U.K.* **15** F9
Herning *Denmark* **11** H2
Heroica Caborca =
　Caborca *Mexico* **118** A2
Heroica Nogales = Nogales
　Mexico **118** A2
Heron Bay *Canada* **104** C2
Heron I. *Australia* **94** C5
Herradura, Pta. de la
　Canary Is. **48** F5
Herreid *U.S.A.* **112** C3
Herrenberg *Germany* **25** G4
Herrera *Spain* **37** H6
Herrera de Alcántara *Spain* **37** F3
Herrera de Pisuerga *Spain* **36** C6
Herrera del Duque *Spain* **37** F5
Herrestad *Sweden* **11** F5
Herrin *U.S.A.* **112** G9

Herriot *Canada* **103** B8
Herrljunga *Sweden* **11** F7
Hersbruck *Germany* **25** F7
Herschel I. *Canada* **4** C1
Hershey *U.S.A.* **115** F8
Herso *Greece* **44** E6
Herstal *Belgium* **17** D5
Hertford *U.K.* **15** F7
Hertfordshire □ *U.K.* **15** F7
's-Hertogenbosch *Neths.* **17** C5
Hertsa *Ukraine* **29** B11
Hertzogville *S. Africa* **88** D4
Hervás *Spain* **36** E5
Hervey B. *Australia* **94** C5
Herzberg *Brandenburg,*
　Germany **24** D9
Herzberg *Niedersachsen,*
　Germany **24** D6
Herzliyya *Israel* **74** C3
Herzogenburg *Austria* **26** C8
Ḩeşār *Fārs, Iran* **71** D6
Ḩeşār *Markazī, Iran* **71** C6
Hesdin *France* **19** B9
Heshan *China* **58** F7
Heshui *China* **56** G5
Heshun *China* **56** F7
Hesperia *U.S.A.* **111** L9
Hesse = Hessen □ *Germany* **24** E4
Hessen □ *Germany* **24** E4
Hessenreuther und
　Manteler Wald △
　Germany **25** F8
Hestra *Sweden* **11** G7
Hetauda *Nepal* **68** F11
Hetch Hetchy Aqueduct
　U.S.A. **110** H5
Hettinger *U.S.A.* **112** B2
Hettstedt *Germany* **24** D7
Heuksando *S. Korea* **57** G13
Heunghae *S. Korea* **57** F15
Heuvelton *U.S.A.* **115** B9
Heves *Hungary* **28** C5
Heves □ *Hungary* **28** C5
Hewitt *U.S.A.* **116** F6
Hexham *U.K.* **14** C5
Hexi *Yunnan, China* **58** E4
Hexi *Zhejiang, China* **59** D12
Hexigten Qi *China* **57** C9
Ḩeydarābād *Iran* **71** D7
Heysham *U.K.* **14** C5
Heyuan *China* **59** F10
Heywood *Australia* **95** F3
Heze *China* **56** G8
Hezhang *China* **58** D5
Hi Vista *U.S.A.* **111** L9
Hialeah *U.S.A.* **117** J14
Hiawatha *U.S.A.* **112** F6
Hibbing *U.S.A.* **112** B7
Hibbs B. *Australia* **95** G4
Hibernia Reef *Australia* **92** B3
Hickman *U.S.A.* **112** G9
Hickory *U.S.A.* **117** D14
Hicks, Pt. *Australia* **95** F4
Hicks L. *Canada* **103** A9
Hicksville *U.S.A.* **115** F11
Hida *Romania* **29** C8
Hida-Gawa → *Japan* **55** G8
Hida-Sammyaku *Japan* **55** F8
Hidaka-Sammyaku *Japan* **54** C11
Hidalgo *U.S.A.* **116** H5
Hidalgo □ *Mexico* **119** C5
Hidalgo, Presa M. *Mexico* **118** B3
Hidalgo del Parral *Mexico* **118** B3
Hiddensee *Germany* **24** A9
Hieflau *Austria* **26** D7
Hiendelaencina *Spain* **38** D2
Hierro *Canary Is.* **48** G1
Higashiajima-San *Japan* **54** F10
Higashiōsaka *Japan* **55** G7
Higgins *U.S.A.* **116** C4
Higgins Corner *U.S.A.* **110** F5
High Bridge *U.S.A.* **115** F10
High Level *Canada* **102** B5
High Point *U.S.A.* **117** D15
High Prairie *Canada* **102** B5
High River *Canada* **102** C6
High Tatra = Tatry
　Slovak Rep. **27** B13
High Veld *Africa* **76** J6
High Wycombe *U.K.* **15** F7
Highland □ *U.K.* **13** D4
Highland Park *U.S.A.* **112** D10
Highmore *U.S.A.* **112** C4
Highrock L. *Canada* **103** B8
Higüey *Dom. Rep.* **121** C6
Hihya *Egypt* **80** H7
Hiiumaa *Estonia* **32** C2
Ḩijar *Spain* **38** D4
Ḩijāz *Si. Arabia* **70** E3
Hijo = Tagum *Phil.* **61** H6
Hikari *Japan* **55** H5
Hikmak, Ras el *Egypt* **80** A2
Hiko *U.S.A.* **110** H11
Hikone *Japan* **55** G8
Hikurangi *Gisborne, N.Z.* **91** C6
Hikurangi *Northland, N.Z.* **91** A5
Hildburghausen *Germany* **24** E6
Hildesheim *Germany* **24** C5
Hill → *Australia* **93** E2
Hill City *Idaho, U.S.A.* **108** E6

Hill City *Kans., U.S.A.* **112** F4
Hill City *Minn., U.S.A.* **112** B7
Hill City *S. Dak., U.S.A.* **112** D2
Hill Island L. *Canada* **103** A7
Hillaby, Mt. *Barbados* **121** g
Hillared *Sweden* **11** G7
Hillcrest *Barbados* **121** g
Hillcrest Center *U.S.A.* **111** K8
Hillegom *Neths.* **17** B4
Hillerød *Denmark* **11** J6
Hillerstorp *Sweden* **11** G7
Hillsboro *Kans., U.S.A.* **112** F5
Hillsboro *N. Dak., U.S.A.* **112** B5
Hillsboro *Ohio, U.S.A.* **113** F12
Hillsboro *Oreg., U.S.A.* **110** E4
Hillsboro *Tex., U.S.A.* **116** E6
Hillsborough *Grenada* **121** D7
Hillsborough *U.S.A.* **115** C13
Hillsborough Channel
　Australia **94** J7
Hillsdale *Mich., U.S.A.* **113** E11
Hillsdale *N.Y., U.S.A.* **115** D11
Hillsport *Canada* **104** C2
Hillston *Australia* **95** E4
Hilo *U.S.A.* **106** b
Hilton *U.S.A.* **114** C7
Hilton Head Island *U.S.A.* **117** E14
Hilvan *Turkey* **73** D8
Hilversum *Neths.* **17** B5
Himachal Pradesh □ *India* **68** D7
Himalaya *Asia* **69** E11
Himalchuli *Nepal* **69** E11
Himamaylan *Phil.* **61** F5
Himarë *Albania* **44** F3
Himatnagar *India* **68** H5
Himeji *Japan* **55** G7
Himi *Japan* **55** F8
Himmerland *Denmark* **11** H3
Ḩimş *Syria* **74** A5
Ḩimş □ *Syria* **74** A6
Hinche *Haiti* **121** C5
Hinchinbrook I. *Australia* **94** B4
Hinchinbrook Island △
　Australia **94** B4
Hinckley *U.K.* **15** E6
Hinckley *U.S.A.* **112** B7
Hindaun *India* **68** F7
Hindmarsh, L. *Australia* **95** F3
Hindsholm *Denmark* **11** J4
Hindu Bagh *Pakistan* **68** D2
Hindu Kush *Asia* **66** B7
Hindupur *India* **66** N10
Hines Creek *Canada* **102** B5
Hinesville *U.S.A.* **117** F14
Hinganghat *India* **66** J11
Hingham *U.S.A.* **108** B8
Hingir *India* **69** J10
Hingoli *India* **66** K10
Hinigaran *Phil.* **61** F5
Hinis *Turkey* **73** C9
Hinna = Imi *Ethiopia* **81** F5
Hinna *Nigeria* **83** C7
Hinnerup *Denmark* **11** H4
Hinnøya *Norway* **8** B16
Hinojosa del Duque *Spain* **37** G5
Hinsdale *U.S.A.* **115** D12
Hinterrhein → *Switz.* **25** J5
Hinthada = Henzada
　Burma **67** L19
Hinton *Canada* **102** C5
Hinton *U.S.A.* **113** G13
Hios *Greece* **47** C8
Hios □ *Greece* **47** C8
Hirado *Japan* **55** H4
Hirakud Dam *India* **67** J13
Hiran → *India* **69** H8
Hirapur *India* **69** G8
Hirara *Japan* **55** M2
Hiratsuka *Japan* **55** G9
Hirfanlı Barajı *Turkey* **72** C5
Hiroo *Japan* **54** C11
Hirosaki *Japan* **54** D10
Hiroshima *Japan* **55** G6
Hiroshima □ *Japan* **55** G6
Hirson *France* **19** C11
Hirtshals *Denmark* **11** G3
Hisar *India* **68** E6
Hisarcık *Turkey* **47** B11
Hisaria *Bulgaria* **45** D8
Hisb, Sha'ib → *Iraq* **70** D5
Ḩismá *Si. Arabia* **70** D3
Ḩīt *Iraq* **73** F10
Hita *Japan* **55** H5
Hitachi *Japan* **55** F10
Hitchin *U.K.* **15** F7
Hitiaa *Tahiti* **91** d
Hitoyoshi *Japan* **55** H5
Hitra *Norway* **8** E13
Hitzacker *Germany* **24** B7
Hiva Oa *French Polynesia* **97** H14
Hixon *Canada* **102** C4
Ḩiyyon, N. → *Israel* **74** E4
Hjalmar L. *Canada* **103** A7
Hjälmaren *Sweden* **10** E9
Hjältevad *Sweden* **11** G9
Hjo *Sweden* **11** F8
Hjørring *Denmark* **11** G3

Hjort Trench *S. Ocean* **5** B10
Hjortkvarn *Sweden* **11** F9
Hkakabo Razi *Burma* **67** E20
Hlinsko *Czech Rep.* **26** B8
Hlobane *S. Africa* **89** D5
Hlohovec *Slovak Rep.* **27** C10
Hluhluwe *S. Africa* **89** D5
Hluhluwe △ *S. Africa* **89** C5
Hlukhiv *Ukraine* **33** G7
Hlyboka *Ukraine* **29** B10
Hlybokaye *Belarus* **32** E4
Hnúšťa *Slovak Rep.* **27** C12
Ho *Ghana* **83** D5
Ho Chi Minh City = Thanh
　Pho Ho Chi Minh *Vietnam* **65** G6
Ho Thuong *Vietnam* **64** C5
Hoa Binh *Vietnam* **58** G5
Hoa Da *Vietnam* **65** G7
Hoa Hiep *Vietnam* **65** G5
Hoai Nhon *Vietnam* **64** E7
Hoang Lien Son *Vietnam* **58** F4
Hoanib → *Namibia* **88** B2
Hoare B. *Canada* **101** C13
Hoarusib → *Namibia* **88** B2
Hobart *Australia* **95** G4
Hobart *U.S.A.* **116** D5
Hobbs *U.S.A.* **109** K12
Hobbs Coast *Antarctica* **5** D14
Hobe Sound *U.S.A.* **117** H14
Hoboken *U.S.A.* **115** F10
Hobro *Denmark* **11** H3
Hoburgen *Sweden* **11** H12
Hobyo *Somali Rep.* **75** F4
Hocalar *Turkey* **47** C11
Hochfeld *Namibia* **88** C2
Hochharz △ *Germany* **24** D6
Hochschwab *Austria* **26** D8
Höchstadt *Germany* **25** F6
Hochtaunus △ *Germany* **25** E4
Hockenheim *Germany* **25** F9
Hodaka-Dake *Japan* **55** F8
Hodeida = Al Ḩudaydah
　Yemen **75** E3
Hodgeville *Canada* **103** C7
Hodgson *Canada* **103** C9
Hodh El Gharbi □
　Mauritania **82** B3
Hódmezővásárhely *Hungary* **28** D5
Hodna, Chott el *Algeria* **78** A6
Hodonín *Czech Rep.* **27** C9
Hœdic, Î. de *France* **18** E4
Hoek van Holland *Neths.* **17** C4
Hoengseong *S. Korea* **57** F14
Hoeryong *N. Korea* **57** C15
Hoeyang *N. Korea* **57** E14
Hof *Germany* **25** E7
Hofgeismar *Germany* **24** D5
Hofheim *Germany* **25** E4
Hofmeyr *S. Africa* **88** E4
Höfn *Iceland* **8** D6
Hofors *Sweden* **10** D10
Hofsjökull *Iceland* **8** D4
Hōfu *Japan* **55** G5
Hogan Group *Australia* **95** F4
Höganäs *Sweden* **11** H6
Hogarth, Mt. *Australia* **94** C2
Hoge Kempen △ *Belgium* **17** C5
Hoge Veluwe △ *Neths.* **17** B5
Hoggar = Ahaggar *Algeria* **78** D7
Högsäter *Sweden* **11** F6
Högsby *Sweden* **11** G10
Högsjö *Sweden* **10** E9
Hogsty Reef *Bahamas* **121** B5
Hoh → *U.S.A.* **110** C2
Hohd ech Chargui □
　Mauritania **82** B3
Hohe Acht *Germany* **25** E3
Hohe Tauern *Austria* **26** D5
Hohe Tauern △ *Austria* **26** D5
Hohenau *Austria* **27** C9
Hohenems *Austria* **26** D2
Hohenloher Ebene *Germany* **25** F5
Hohenwald *U.S.A.* **117** D11
Hohenwestedt *Germany* **24** A5
Hoher Rhön = Rhön
　Germany **24** E5
Hoher Vogelsberg △
　Germany **24** D5
Hohes Venn *Belgium* **17** D6
Hohes Venn-Eifel △ *Europe* **24** E2
Hohhot *China* **56** D6
Hohoe *Ghana* **83** D5
Hoi An *Vietnam* **64** E7
Hoi Xuan *Vietnam* **58** G5
Hoisington *U.S.A.* **112** F4
Højer *Denmark* **11** K2
Højō *Japan* **55** G6
Hok *Sweden* **11** G8
Hökensås *Sweden* **11** G8
Hökerum *Sweden* **11** G7
Hokianga Harbour *N.Z.* **91** A4
Hokitika *N.Z.* **91** E3
Hokkaidō □ *Japan* **54** C11
Hol-Hol *Djibouti* **81** E5
Hola *Kenya* **86** B4
Hola Pristan *Ukraine* **33** J7
Holakas *Greece* **49** D9
Holbæk *Denmark* **11** J5
Holbrook *Australia* **95** F4
Holbrook *U.S.A.* **109** J8

Holcomb *U.S.A.* **114** D7
Holden *U.S.A.* **108** G7
Holdenville *U.S.A.* **116** D6
Holdrege *U.S.A.* **112** E4
Holešov *Czech Rep.* **27** B10
Holetown *Barbados* **121** g
Holguín *Cuba* **120** B4
Holíč *Slovak Rep.* **27** C10
Holice *Czech Rep.* **26** A8
Höljes *Sweden* **10** D6
Hollabrunn *Austria* **26** C9
Hollams Bird I. *Namibia* **88** C1
Holland = Netherlands ■
　Europe **17** C5
Holland *Mich., U.S.A.* **112** D10
Holland *N.Y., U.S.A.* **114** D6
Holland Centre *Canada* **114** B4
Holland Patent *U.S.A.* **115** C9
Hollandale *U.S.A.* **117** E9
Holley *U.S.A.* **114** C6
Hollfeld *Germany* **25** F7
Hollidaysburg *U.S.A.* **114** F6
Hollis *U.S.A.* **116** D5
Hollister *Calif., U.S.A.* **110** J5
Hollister *Idaho, U.S.A.* **108** E6
Höllviken = Höllviksnäs
　Sweden **11** J6
Höllviksnäs *Sweden* **11** J6
Holly Hill *U.S.A.* **117** G14
Holly Springs *U.S.A.* **117** D10
Hollywood *U.S.A.* **117** J14
Holman *Canada* **100** B8
Hólmavík *Iceland* **8** D3
Holmen *U.S.A.* **112** D8
Holmes Reefs *Australia* **94** B4
Holmsjö *Sweden* **11** H9
Holmsjön *Västernorrland,*
　Sweden **10** B10
Holmsjön *Västernorrland,*
　Sweden **10** B9
Holmslands Klit *Denmark* **11** J2
Holmsund *Sweden* **8** E19
Holod *Romania* **28** D7
Holovne *Ukraine* **31** G11
Holozubyntsi *Ukraine* **29** B11
Holroyd → *Australia* **94** A3
Holstebro *Denmark* **11** H2
Holsteinische Schweiz △
　Germany **24** A6
Holsworthy *U.K.* **15** G3
Holton *Canada* **105** B8
Holton *U.S.A.* **112** F6
Holtville *U.S.A.* **111** N11
Holwerd *Neths.* **17** A5
Holy I. *Anglesey, U.K.* **14** D3
Holy I. *Northumberland, U.K.* **14** B6
Holyhead *U.K.* **14** D3
Holyoke *Colo., U.S.A.* **108** F12
Holyoke *Mass., U.S.A.* **115** D12
Holyrood *Canada* **105** C9
Holzkirchen *Germany* **25** H7
Holzminden *Germany* **24** D5
Homa Bay *Kenya* **86** C3
Homalin *Burma* **67** G19
Homand *Iran* **71** C8
Homathko → *Canada* **102** C4
Homberg *Germany* **24** D5
Hombori *Mali* **83** B4
Hombori Tondo *Mali* **83** B4
Homburg *Germany* **25** F3
Home B. *Canada* **101** C13
Home Hill *Australia* **94** B4
Home Reef *Tonga* **91** c
Homedale *U.S.A.* **108** E5
Homer *Alaska, U.S.A.* **100** D9
Homer *La., U.S.A.* **116** E8
Homer *N.Y., U.S.A.* **115** D8
Homer City *U.S.A.* **114** F5
Homert △ *Germany* **24** D4
Homestead *Australia* **94** C4
Homestead *U.S.A.* **117** J14
Homestead △ *U.S.A.* **112** E5
Homoine *Mozam.* **89** C6
Homoljske Planina *Serbia* **44** B5
Homorod *Romania* **29** D10
Homs = Ḩimş *Syria* **74** A5
Homyel *Belarus* **23** B16
Homyel □ *Belarus* **33** F6
Hon Chong *Vietnam* **65** G5
Hon Hai *Vietnam* **65** H7
Hon Me *Vietnam* **64** C5
Honan = Henan □ *China* **56** H8
Honaz *Turkey* **47** D11
Honbetsu *Japan* **54** C11
Honcut *U.S.A.* **110** F5
Honda, Bahía *Cuba* **120** B3
Honda Bay *Phil.* **61** G3
Hondarribia *Spain* **38** B3
Hondeklipbaai *S. Africa* **88** E2
Hondo *Japan* **55** H5
Hondo *U.S.A.* **116** G5
Hondo, Río → *Belize* **119** D7
Honduras ■ *Cent. Amer.* **120** D2
Honduras, G. de *Caribbean* **120** C2
Hønefoss *Norway* **9** F14
Honesdale *U.S.A.* **115** E9
Honey Harbour *Canada* **114** B5
Honey L. *U.S.A.* **110** E6
Honfleur *France* **18** C7

Høng *Denmark* **11** J5
Hong Gai *Vietnam* **58** G6
Hong Hu *China* **59** C9
Hong He ➤ *China* **56** H8
Hong Kong □ *China* **59** F10
Hong'an *China* **59** B10
Hongcheon *S. Korea* **57** F14
Honghai Wan *China* **59** F10
Honghe *China* **58** F4
Hongjiang *China* **59** C9
Hongjiang *China* **58** D7
Hongliu He ➤ *China* **56** F5
Hongor *Mongolia* **56** B7
Hongsa *Laos* **64** C3
Hongseong *S. Korea* **57** F14
Hongshui He ➤ *China* **58** F7
Hongtong *China* **56** F6
Honguedo, Détroit d'
  Canada **105** C7
Hongwon *N. Korea* **57** E14
Hongya *China* **58** C4
Hongyuan *China* **58** A4
Hongze Hu *China* **57** H10
Honiara *Solomon Is.* **90** B8
Honiton *U.K.* **15** G4
Honjō *Japan* **54** E10
Honkoráb, Ras *Egypt* **80** C4
Honningsvåg *Norway* **8** A21
Hönö *Sweden* **11** G5
Honolulu *U.S.A.* **106** b
Honshū *Japan* **54** F9
Hontoria del Pinar *Spain* **38** D1
Hood, Mt. *U.S.A.* **108** D3
Hood, Pt. *Australia* **93** F2
Hood River *U.S.A.* **108** D3
Hoodsport *U.S.A.* **110** C3
Hooge *Germany* **24** A4
Hoogeveen *Neths.* **17** B6
Hoogezand-Sappemeer
  Neths. **17** A6
Hooghly = Hugli ➤ *India* **69** J13
Hooghly-Chinsura =
  Chunchura *India* **69** H13
Hook Hd. *Ireland* **12** D5
Hook I. *Australia* **94** J6
Hook of Holland = Hoek
  van Holland *Neths.* **17** C4
Hooker *U.S.A.* **116** C4
Hooker Creek = Lajamanu
  Australia **92** C4
Hoonah *U.S.A.* **102** B1
Hooper Bay *U.S.A.* **106** a
Hoopeston *U.S.A.* **112** E10
Hoopstad *S. Africa* **88** D4
Hoorn *Neths.* **17** B5
Hoover *U.S.A.* **117** E11
Hoover Dam *U.S.A.* **111** K12
Hooversville *U.S.A.* **114** F6
Hop Bottom *U.S.A.* **115** E9
Hopa *Turkey* **73** B9
Hope *Canada* **102** D4
Hope, Ariz., *U.S.A.* **111** M13
Hope, Ark., *U.S.A.* **116** E8
Hope, L. S. Austral., *Australia* **95** D2
Hope, L. W. Austral., *Australia* **93** F3
Hope, Pt. *U.S.A.* **98** C3
Hope I. *Canada* **114** B4
Hope Town *Bahamas* **120** A4
Hope Vale *Australia* **94** B4
Hopedale *Canada* **105** A4
Hopedale *U.S.A.* **115** D13
Hopefield *S. Africa* **88** E2
Hopei = Hebei □ *China* **56** E9
Hopelchén *Mexico* **119** D7
Hopetoun *Vic., Australia* **95** F3
Hopetoun *W. Austral.,*
  Australia **93** F3
Hopetown *S. Africa* **88** D3
Hopewell *U.S.A.* **113** G15
Hopfgarten *Austria* **26** D5
Hopkins, L. *Australia* **92** D4
Hopkinsville *U.S.A.* **112** G10
Hopland *U.S.A.* **110** G3
Hoquiam *U.S.A.* **110** D3
Hora Hoverla *Ukraine* **29** B9
Horasan *Turkey* **73** B10
Horažďovice *Czech Rep.* **26** B6
Horb *Germany* **25** G4
Hörby *Sweden* **11** J7
Horcajo de Santiago *Spain* **38** F1
Hordern Hills *Australia* **92** D5
Horezu *Romania* **29** E8
Horgen *Switz.* **25** H4
Horgoš *Serbia* **28** D4
Hořice *Czech Rep.* **26** A8
Horinchove *Ukraine* **29** B8
Horinger *China* **56** D6
Horizontina *Brazil* **127** B5
Horki *Belarus* **32** E6
Horlick Mts. *Antarctica* **5** E15
Horlivka *Ukraine* **33** H10
Hormak *Iran* **71** D9
Hormoz *Iran* **71** E7
Hormoz, Jaz.-ye *Iran* **71** E8
Hormozgān □ *Iran* **71** E8
Hormuz, Kūh-e *Iran* **71** E7
Hormuz, Str. of *The Gulf* **71** E8
Horn *Austria* **26** C8

Horn *Sweden* **11** G9
Horn ➤ *Canada* **102** A5
Horn, Cape = Hornos, C. de
  Chile **128** H3
Horn Head *Ireland* **12** A3
Horn I. *Australia* **94** A3
Horn Plateau *Canada* **102** A5
Hornachuelos *Spain* **37** H5
Hornavan *Sweden* **8** C17
Hornbeck *U.S.A.* **116** F8
Hornbrook *U.S.A.* **108** F2
Hornburg *Germany* **24** C6
Horncastle *U.K.* **14** D7
Horndal *Sweden* **10** D10
Hornell *U.S.A.* **114** D7
Hornell L. *Canada* **102** A4
Hornepayne *Canada* **104** C3
Horní Planá *Czech Rep.* **26** C7
Hornings Mills *Canada* **114** B4
Hornitos *U.S.A.* **110** H6
Hornos, C. de *Chile* **128** H3
Hornoy-le-Bourg *France* **19** C8
Hornsby *Australia* **95** B5
Hornsea *U.K.* **14** D7
Hornslandet *Sweden* **10** C11
Hörnum *Germany* **24** A4
Horobetsu = Noboribetsu
  Japan **54** C10
Horodenka *Ukraine* **29** B10
Horodnya *Ukraine* **33** G6
Horodok *Khmelnytskyy,*
  Ukraine **23** D14
Horodok *Lviv, Ukraine* **23** D12
Horodyshche *Ukraine* **33** H6
Horokhiv *Ukraine* **23** C13
Horovice *Czech Rep.* **26** B6
Horqin Youyi Qianqi *China* **57** A12
Horqueta *Paraguay* **126** A4
Horred *Sweden* **11** G6
Horse Cr. ➤ *U.S.A.* **108** F12
Horse I. *Canada* **103** C9
Horse Is. *Canada* **105** B8
Horsefly L. *Canada* **102** C4
Horseheads *U.S.A.* **114** D8
Horsens *Denmark* **11** J3
Horseshoe Lake *Canada* **114** A5
Horsham *Australia* **95** F3
Horsham *U.K.* **15** F7
Horšovský Týn *Czech Rep.* **26** B5
Horta *Azores* **78** a
Horten *Norway* **9** G14
Hortobágy ➤ *Hungary* **28** C6
Hortobágyi △ *Hungary* **28** C6
Horton *U.S.A.* **112** F6
Horton ➤ *Canada* **100** C7
Horwood L. *Canada* **104** C3
Hosaina *Ethiopia* **81** F4
Hoseynābād *Khuzestan, Iran* **71** C6
Hoseynābād *Kordestan, Iran* **73** E12
Hoshangabad *India* **68** H7
Hoshiarpur *India* **68** D6
Hospet *India* **66** M10
Hoste, I. *Chile* **128** H3
Hostens *France* **20** D3
Hot *Thailand* **64** C2
Hot Creek Range *U.S.A.* **108** G5
Hot Springs *Ark., U.S.A.* **116** D8
Hot Springs *S. Dak., U.S.A.* **112** D2
Hot Springs △ *U.S.A.* **116** D8
Hotagen *Sweden* **8** E16
Hotan *China* **60** C2
Hotazel *S. Africa* **88** D3
Hotchkiss *U.S.A.* **108** G10
Hotham, C. *Australia* **92** B5
Hoting *Sweden* **8** D17
Hotolisht *Albania* **44** E4
Hotte, Massif de la *Haiti* **121** C5
Hottentotsbaai *Namibia* **88** D1
Houat, Î. de *France* **18** E4
Houdan *France* **19** D8
Houei Sai *Laos* **58** G3
Houeillès *France* **20** D4
Houffalize *Belgium* **17** D5
Houghton *Mich., U.S.A.* **112** B9
Houghton *N.Y., U.S.A.* **114** D6
Houghton L. *U.S.A.* **113** C11
Houghton-le-Spring *U.K.* **14** C6
Houhora Heads *N.Z.* **91** A4
Houlton *U.S.A.* **113** B20
Houma *U.S.A.* **117** G9
Houndé *Burkina Faso* **82** C4
Hourtin *France* **20** C2
Hourtin-Carcans, Étang d'
  France **20** C2
Housatonic ➤ *U.S.A.* **115** E11
Houston *Canada* **102** C3
Houston *Mo., U.S.A.* **112** G8
Houston *Tex., U.S.A.* **116** G7
Hout = Mogwadi ➤
  S. Africa **89** C4
Houtkraal *S. Africa* **88** E3
Houtman Abrolhos *Australia* **93** E1
Hov □ *Mongolia* **60** B4
Hove *U.K.* **15** G7
Hovedstaden □ *Denmark* **11** J6
Hoveyzeh *Iran* **71** D6
Hovmantorp *Sweden* **11** H9
Hövsgöl *Mongolia* **56** C5

Hövsgöl Nuur *Mongolia* **60** A5
Hovsta *Sweden* **10** E9
Howakil *Eritrea* **81** D5
Howar, Wadi ➤ *Sudan* **81** D2
Howard *Australia* **95** D5
Howard *Pa., U.S.A.* **114** F7
Howard *S. Dak., U.S.A.* **112** C5
Howe *U.S.A.* **108** E7
Howe, C. *Australia* **95** F5
Howe, West Cape *Australia* **93** G2
Howe I. *Canada* **115** B8
Howell *U.S.A.* **113** D12
Howick *Canada* **115** A11
Howick *S. Africa* **89** D5
Howick Group *Australia* **94** A4
Howitt, L. *Australia* **95** D2
Howland I. *Pac. Oc.* **96** G10
Howrah = Haora *India* **69** H13
Howth *Ireland* **12** C5
Howth Hd. *Ireland* **12** C5
Hoy *U.K.* **13** C5
Hoya *Germany* **24** C5
Høyanger *Norway* **8** F12
Hoyerswerda *Germany* **24** D10
Hoylake *U.K.* **14** D4
Hoyos *Spain* **36** E4
Hövsgöl □ *Mongolia* **56** C5
Hpa-an = Pa-an *Burma* **67** L20
Hpunan Pass *Burma* **67** F20
Hradec Králové *Czech Rep.* **26** A8
Hrádek *Czech Rep.* **27** C9
Hranice *Czech Rep.* **27** B10
Hrazdan *Armenia* **35** K7
Hrebenka *Ukraine* **33** G7
Hrisoupoli *Greece* **45** F8
Hristiana *Greece* **47** E7
Hrodna *Belarus* **30** E10
Hrodna □ *Belarus* **32** F3
Hrodzyanka *Belarus* **23** B15
Hron ➤ *Slovak Rep.* **27** D11
Hrubieszów *Poland* **31** H10
Hrubý Jeseník *Czech Rep.* **27** A10
Hrvatska = Croatia ■
  Europe **41** C13
Hrymayliv *Ukraine* **23** D14
Hrynyava *Ukraine* **29** C9
Hsenwi *Burma* **67** H20
Hsiamen = Xiamen *China* **59** E12
Hsian = Xi'an *China* **56** G5
Hsinchu *Taiwan* **59** E13
Hsinhailien =
  Lianyungang *China* **57** G10
Hsinying *Taiwan* **59** F13
Hsopket *Burma* **58** F2
Hsüchou = Xuzhou *China* **57** G9
Htapodia *Greece* **47** D7
Hu Xian *China* **56** G5
Hua Hin *Thailand* **64** F2
Hua Xian *Henan, China* **56** G8
Hua Xian *Shaanxi, China* **56** G5
Hua'an *China* **59** E11
Huab ➤ *Namibia* **88** B2
Huacheng *China* **59** E10
Huachinera *Mexico* **118** A3
Huacho *Peru* **124** F3
Huade *China* **56** D7
Huadian *China* **57** C14
Huadu *China* **59** F9
Huahine, Î. *French Polynesia* **97** J12
Huai Hat △ *Thailand* **64** D5
Huai He ➤ *China* **59** A12
Huai Nam Dang △ *Thailand* **64** C2
Huai Yot *Thailand* **65** J2
Huai'an *Hebei, China* **56** D8
Huai'an *Jiangsu, China* **57** H10
Huaibei *China* **56** G9
Huaibin *China* **59** A10
Huaide = Gongzhuling
  China **57** C13
Huaidezhen *China* **57** C13
Huaihua *China* **58** D7
Huaiji *China* **59** F9
Huainan *China* **59** A11
Huaining *China* **59** B11
Huairen *China* **56** E7
Huairou *China* **56** D9
Huaiyang *China* **56** H8
Huaiyin *China* **57** H10
Huaiyuan *Anhui, China* **57** H9
Huaiyuan
  Guangxi Zhuangzu, China **58** E7
Huajuapán de León *Mexico* **119** D5
Hualapai Peak *U.S.A.* **109** J7
Hualien *Taiwan* **59** E13
Huallaga ➤ *Peru* **124** E3
Huambo *Angola* **85** G3
Huan Jiang ➤ *China* **56** G5
Huan Xian *China* **56** F4
Huancabamba *Peru* **124** E3
Huancane *Peru* **124** G5
Huancavelica *Peru* **124** F3
Huancayo *Peru* **124** F3
Huanchaca *Bolivia* **124** H5
Huang Hai = Yellow Sea
  China **57** G12
Huang He ➤ *China* **57** F10
Huang Xian *China* **57** F11
Huangchuan *China* **59** A10
Huanggang *China* **59** B10

Huangguoshu *China* **58** E5
Huangling *China* **56** G5
Huanglong *China* **56** G5
Huanglongtan *China* **59** A8
Huangmei *China* **59** B10
Huangpi *China* **59** B10
Huangping *China* **58** D6
Huangshan *Anhui, China* **59** B12
Huangshan *Anhui, China* **59** C12
Huangshi *China* **59** B10
Huangsongdian *China* **57** C14
Huangyan *China* **59** C13
Huangyangsi *China* **59** D8
Huaning *China* **58** E4
Huanjiang *China* **58** E7
Huanren *China* **57** D13
Huantai *China* **57** F9
Huánuco *Peru* **124** E3
Huaping *China* **58** D3
Huaraz *Peru* **124** E3
Huarmey *Peru* **124** F3
Huarong *China* **59** C9
Huascarán, Nevado *Peru* **124** E3
Huasco *Chile* **126** B1
Huasco ➤ *Chile* **126** B1
Huasna *U.S.A.* **111** K6
Huatabampo *Mexico* **118** B3
Huauchinango *Mexico* **119** C5
Huautla de Jiménez *Mexico* **119** D5
Huaxi *China* **58** D6
Huayin *China* **56** G6
Huayuan *China* **58** C7
Huayun *China* **58** B6
Huazhou *China* **59** G8
Hubbard *Ohio, U.S.A.* **114** E4
Hubbard *Tex., U.S.A.* **116** F6
Hubbart Pt. *Canada* **103** B10
Hubei □ *China* **59** B9
Hubli *India* **66** M9
Huch'ang *N. Korea* **57** D14
Hucknall *U.K.* **14** D6
Huddersfield *U.K.* **14** D6
Hude *Germany* **24** B4
Hudi *Sudan* **80** D3
Hudiksvall *Sweden* **10** C11
Hudson *Canada* **104** B1
Hudson *Mass., U.S.A.* **115** D13
Hudson *N.Y., U.S.A.* **115** D11
Hudson *Wis., U.S.A.* **112** C7
Hudson *Wyo., U.S.A.* **108** E9
Hudson ➤ *U.S.A.* **115** F10
Hudson, C. *Antarctica* **5** C20
Hudson Bay *Nunavut,*
  Canada **101** D11
Hudson Bay *Sask., Canada* **103** C8
Hudson Falls *U.S.A.* **115** C11
Hudson Mts. *Antarctica* **5** D16
Hudson Str. *Canada* **101** C13
Hudson's Hope *Canada* **102** B4
Hue *Vietnam* **64** D6
Huebra ➤ *Spain* **36** D4
Huedin *Romania* **28** D8
Huehuetenango *Guatemala* **120** C1
Huejúcar *Mexico* **118** C4
Huélamo *Spain* **38** E3
Huelgoat *France* **18** D3
Huelma *Spain* **37** H7
Huelva *Spain* **37** H4
Huelva □ *Spain* **37** H4
Huelva ➤ *Spain* **37** H5
Huentelauquén *Chile* **126** C1
Huércal-Overa *Spain* **39** H3
Huerta, Sa. de la *Argentina* **126** C2
Huertas, C. de las *Spain* **39** G4
Huerva ➤ *Spain* **38** D4
Huesca *Spain* **38** C4
Huesca □ *Spain* **38** C5
Huéscar *Spain* **39** H2
Huetamo *Mexico* **118** D4
Huete *Spain* **38** E2
Hugh ➤ *Australia* **94** D1
Hughenden *Australia* **94** C3
Hughesville *U.S.A.* **115** E8
Hugli ➤ *India* **69** J13
Hugo *Colo., U.S.A.* **108** G12
Hugo *Okla., U.S.A.* **116** D7
Hugoton *U.S.A.* **112** G3
Hui Xian = Huixian *China* **56** G7
Hui Xian *China* **56** H4
Hui'an *China* **59** E12
Hui'anbu *China* **56** F4
Huichang *China* **59** E10
Huichapan *Mexico* **119** C5
Huichon *N. Korea* **57** D14
Huidong *Guangdong, China* **59** F10
Huidong *Sichuan, China* **58** D4
Huifa He ➤ *China* **57** C14
Huila, Nevado del *Colombia* **124** C3
Huilai *China* **59** F11
Huili *China* **58** D4
Huimin *China* **57** F9
Huinan *China* **57** C14
Huinca Renancó *Argentina* **126** C3
Huining *China* **56** G3
Huinong *China* **56** E4
Huishui *China* **58** D6
Huisne ➤ *France* **18** E7
Huiting *China* **56** G9
Huitong *China* **58** D7

Huixian *China* **56** G7
Huixtla *Mexico* **119** D6
Huize *China* **58** D4
Huizhou *China* **59** F10
Hukawng Valley *Burma* **67** F20
Hukou *China* **59** C11
Hukuntsi *Botswana* **88** C3
Ḥulayfā' *Si. Arabia* **70** E4
Hulin He ➤ *China* **57** B12
Hull = Kingston upon Hull
  U.K. **14** D7
Hull *Canada* **115** A9
Hull ➤ *U.K.* **14** D7
Hulst *Neths.* **17** C4
Hultsfred *Sweden* **11** G9
Hulun Nur *China* **60** B6
Hulyaypole *Ukraine* **33** J9
Huma, Tanjung *Malaysia* **65** c
Humacao *Puerto Rico* **121** d
Humahuaca *Argentina* **126** A2
Humaitá *Brazil* **124** E6
Humaitá *Paraguay* **126** B4
Humansdorp *S. Africa* **88** E3
Humara, J. *Sudan* **81** D3
Humbe *Angola* **88** B1
Humber ➤ *U.K.* **14** D7
Humboldt *Canada* **103** C7
Humboldt *Iowa, U.S.A.* **112** D7
Humboldt *Tenn., U.S.A.* **117** D10
Humboldt ➤ *U.S.A.* **108** G4
Humboldt Gletscher =
  Sermersuaq *Greenland* **4** B4
Hume *U.S.A.* **110** J8
Hume, L. *Australia* **95** F4
Humenné *Slovak Rep.* **27** C14
Hummelsta *Sweden* **10** E10
Humphreys, Mt. *U.S.A.* **110** H8
Humphreys Peak *U.S.A.* **109** J8
Humpolec *Czech Rep.* **26** B8
Humptulips *U.S.A.* **110** C3
Hūn *Libya* **79** C9
Húnaflói *Iceland* **8** D3
Hunan □ *China* **59** D9
Hunchun *China* **57** C16
Hundested *Denmark* **11** J5
Hundewali *Pakistan* **68** D5
Hundred Mile House
  Canada **102** C4
Hunedoara *Romania* **28** E7
Hunedoara □ *Romania* **28** E7
Hünfeld *Germany* **24** E5
Hung Yen *Vietnam* **58** G6
Hunga Ha'apai *Tonga* **91** c
Hungary ■ *Europe* **27** D12
Hungary, Plain of *Europe* **6** F10
Hungerford *Australia* **95** D3
Hŭngnam *N. Korea* **57** E14
Huni Valley *Ghana* **82** D4
Hunjiang *China* **57** D14
Hunneberg *Sweden* **11** F6
Hunnebostrand *Sweden* **11** F5
Hunsberge *Namibia* **88** D2
Hunsrück *Germany* **25** F3
Hunstanton *U.K.* **14** E8
Hunte ➤ *Germany* **24** B4
Hunter *U.S.A.* **115** D10
Hunter I. *Australia* **95** G3
Hunter I. *Canada* **102** C3
Hunter Ra. *Australia* **95** E5
Hunters Road *Zimbabwe* **87** F2
Hunterville *N.Z.* **91** C5
Huntingburg *U.S.A.* **112** F10
Huntingdon *U.K.* **15** E7
Huntingdon *U.S.A.* **114** F6
Huntington *Ind., U.S.A.* **113** E11
Huntington *N.Y., U.S.A.* **115** F11
Huntington *Oreg., U.S.A.* **108** D5
Huntington *Utah, U.S.A.* **108** G8
Huntington *W. Va., U.S.A.* **113** F12
Huntington Beach *U.S.A.* **111** M9
Huntly *N.Z.* **91** B5
Huntly *U.K.* **13** D6
Huntsville *Canada* **114** A5
Huntsville *Ala., U.S.A.* **117** D11
Huntsville *Tex., U.S.A.* **116** F7
Hunyani ➤ *Zimbabwe* **87** F3
Hunyuan *China* **56** E7
Hunza ➤ *India* **69** B6
Huo Xian = Huozhou *China* **56** F6
Huong Khe *Vietnam* **64** C5
Huonville *Australia* **95** G4
Huoqiu *China* **59** A11
Huoshan *Anhui, China* **59** A12
Huoshan *Anhui, China* **59** B11
Huoshao Dao = Lü Tao
  Taiwan **59** F13
Huozhou *China* **56** F6
Hupeh = Hubei □ *China* **59** B9
Ḥūr *Iran* **71** D8
Hurānd *Iran* **73** C12
Ḥuraymīla *Si. Arabia* **70** E5
Hurbanovo *Slovak Rep.* **27** D11
Hurd, C. *Canada* **114** A3
Hure *Qi China* **57** C11
Hurezani *Romania* **29** F8
Hurghada *Egypt* **80** B3

Hurley *N. Mex., U.S.A.* **109** K9
Hurley *Wis., U.S.A.* **112** B8
Huron *Calif., U.S.A.* **110** J6
Huron *Ohio, U.S.A.* **114** E2
Huron *S. Dak., U.S.A.* **112** C4
Huron, L. *U.S.A.* **114** B2
Huron East *Canada* **114** C3
Hurricane *U.S.A.* **109** H7
Hurso *Ethiopia* **81** F5
Hurungwe □ *Zimbabwe* **87** F2
Hurunui ➤ *N.Z.* **91** E4
Hurup *Denmark* **11** H2
Húsavík *Iceland* **8** C5
Huşi *Romania* **29** D13
Huskvarna *Sweden* **11** G8
Hustadvika *Norway* **8** E12
Hustontown *U.S.A.* **114** F6
Hustopeče *Czech Rep.* **27** C9
Husum *Germany* **24** A5
Husum *Sweden* **10** A13
Hutchinson *Kans., U.S.A.* **112** F5
Hutchinson *Minn., U.S.A.* **112** C6
Hutte Sauvage, L. de la
  Canada **105** A7
Hüttenberg *Austria* **26** E7
Hüttener Berge △ *Germany* **24** A5
Hutton, Mt. *Australia* **95** D4
Huwun *Ethiopia* **81** G5
Huy *Belgium* **17** D5
Huzhou *China* **59** B13
Hvalpsund *Denmark* **11** H3
Hvammstangi *Iceland* **8** D3
Hvar *Croatia* **41** E13
Hvarski Kanal *Croatia* **41** E13
Hvítá ➤ *Iceland* **8** D3
Hvizdets *Ukraine* **29** B10
Hwacheon-Cheosuji
  S. Korea **57** E14
Hwang Ho = Huang He ➤
  China **57** F10
Hwange *Zimbabwe* **87** F2
Hwange △ *Zimbabwe* **88** B4
Hyannis *Mass., U.S.A.* **113** E18
Hyannis *Nebr., U.S.A.* **112** E3
Hyargas Nuur *Mongolia* **60** B4
Hybo *Sweden* **10** C10
Hydaburg *U.S.A.* **102** B2
Hyde Park *U.S.A.* **115** E11
Hyden *Australia* **93** F2
Hyder *U.S.A.* **102** B2
Hyderabad *India* **66** L11
Hyderabad *Pakistan* **68** G3
Hydra *Greece* **46** D5
Hyères *France* **21** E10
Hyères, Îs. d' *France* **21** F10
Hyesan *N. Korea* **57** D15
Hyland ➤ *Canada* **102** B3
Hyltebruk *Sweden* **11** H7
Hymia *India* **69** C8
Hyndman Peak *U.S.A.* **108** E6
Hyōgo □ *Japan* **55** G7
Hyrum *U.S.A.* **108** F8
Hysham *U.S.A.* **108** C10
Hythe *U.K.* **15** F9
Hyūga *Japan* **55** H5
Hyvinge = Hyvinkää *Finland* **32** B3
Hyvinkää *Finland* **32** B3

I

I-n-Gall *Niger* **83** B6
I-n-Ouadî *Algeria* **83** A5
I-n-Ouzzal *Algeria* **83** A5
I-n-Tadreft *Niger* **83** B6
Iablaniţa *Romania* **28** E7
Iaco ➤ *Brazil* **124** E5
Iacobeni *Romania* **29** C10
Iakora *Madag.* **89** C8
Ialissos *Greece* **49** C10
Ialomiţa □ *Romania* **29** F12
Ialomiţa ➤ *Romania* **29** F12
Ialoveni *Moldova* **29** D13
Ialpug ➤ *Moldova* **29** E13
Ianca *Romania* **29** E12
Iara *Romania* **29** D8
Iarda *Ethiopia* **81** E4
Iargara *Moldova* **29** D13
Iaşi *Romania* **29** C12
Iaşi □ *Romania* **29** C12
Iasmos *Greece* **45** E9
Ib ➤ *India* **69** J10
Iba *Phil.* **61** D4
Ibadan *Nigeria* **83** D5
Ibagué *Colombia* **124** C3
Iballë *Albania* **44** D4
Ibănești *Botoşani, Romania* **29** B11
Ibănești *Mureş, Romania* **29** D9
Ibar ➤ *Serbia* **44** C4
Ibaraki □ *Japan* **55** F10
Ibarra *Ecuador* **124** C3
Ibb *Yemen* **75** E3
Ibba *Sudan* **81** G2
Ibba, Bahr el ➤ *Sudan* **81** F2
Ibbenbüren *Germany* **24** C3
Ibembo *Dem. Rep. of the Congo* **86** B1
Ibenga ➤ *Congo* **84** D3
Ibera, L. *Argentina* **126** B4
Iberian Peninsula *Europe* **6** H5
Iberville *Canada* **115** A11

Ibi *Nigeria* **83** D6
Ibi *Spain* **39** G4
Ibiá *Brazil* **125** G9
Ibiapaba, Sa. da *Brazil* **125** D10
Ibicuí → *Brazil* **127** B4
Ibicuy *Argentina* **126** C4
Ibiza = Eivissa *Spain* **48** C7
Ibiza ✈ (IBZ) *Spain* **39** G6
Íblei, Monti *Italy* **43** E7
Ibo *Mozam.* **87** E5
Ibonma *Indonesia* **63** E8
Ibotirama *Brazil* **125** F10
Ibrāhīm → *Lebanon* **74** A4
'Ibrī *Oman* **71** F8
İbriktepe *Turkey* **45** E10
Ibshawâi *Egypt* **80** J7
Ibu *Indonesia* **63** D7
Ibusuki *Japan* **55** J5
Ica *Peru* **124** F3
Iça → *Brazil* **124** D5
Icacos Pt. *Trin. & Tob.* **125** K15
Içana *Brazil* **124** C5
Içana → *Brazil* **124** C5
İçel *Turkey* **72** D6
İçel □ *Turkey* **72** D5
Iceland ■ *Europe* **8** D4
Iceland Basin *Atl. Oc.* **4** C7
Icelandic Plateau *Arctic* **4** C7
İçeriçumra *Turkey* **72** D5
Ich'ang = Yichang *China* **59** B8
Ichchapuram *India* **67** K14
Icheon *S. Korea* **57** F14
Ichhawar *India* **68** H7
Ichihara *Japan* **55** G10
Ichikawa *Japan* **55** G9
Ichilo → *Bolivia* **124** G6
Ichinohe *Japan* **54** D10
Ichinomiya *Japan* **55** G8
Ichinoseki *Japan* **54** E10
Ichnya *Ukraine* **33** G7
Icod *Canary Is.* **48** F3
Icy C. *U.S.A.* **98** B3
Ida Grove *U.S.A.* **112** D6
Idabel *U.S.A.* **116** E7
Idaga Hamus *Ethiopia* **81** E4
Idah *Nigeria* **83** D6
Idaho □ *U.S.A.* **108** D6
Idaho City *U.S.A.* **108** E6
Idaho Falls *U.S.A.* **108** E7
Idalia △ *Australia* **94** C4
Idanha-a-Nova *Portugal* **36** F3
Idar-Oberstein *Germany* **25** F3
Idensalmi = Iisalmi *Finland* **8** E22
Idfû *Egypt* **80** C3
Ídhra = Hydra *Greece* **46** D5
Idi *Indonesia* **62** C1
Idi, Oros = Psiloritis, Oros
 Greece **49** D6
İdil *Turkey* **73** D9
Idiofa *Dem. Rep. of the Congo* **84** E3
Idkerberget *Sweden* **10** D9
Idku, Bahra el *Egypt* **80** H7
Idlib *Syria* **72** E7
Idlib □ *Syria* **72** E7
Idre *Sweden* **10** C6
Idria *U.S.A.* **110** J6
Idrija *Slovenia* **41** C11
Idritsa *Russia* **32** D5
Idutywa = Dutywa *S. Africa* **89** E4
Ieper *Belgium* **17** D2
Ierapetra *Greece* **49** E7
Ierissos *Greece* **44** F7
Ierissou Kolpos *Greece* **44** F7
Iernut *Romania* **29** D9
Iesi *Italy* **41** E10
Iésolo *Italy* **41** C9
Ifac, Penyal d' *Spain* **39** G5
Ifakara *Tanzania* **84** F7
'Ifāl, W. al → *Si. Arabia* **70** D2
Ifanadiana *Madag.* **89** C8
Ife *Nigeria* **83** D5
Iférouâne *Niger* **83** B6
Iffley *Australia* **94** B3
Ifon *Nigeria* **83** D5
Iforas, Adrar des *Africa* **83** B5
Ifould, L. *Australia* **93** F5
Igalo *Montenegro* **44** D2
Iganga *Uganda* **86** B3
Igarapava *Brazil* **125** H9
Igarka *Russia* **52** C9
Igbetti *Nigeria* **83** D5
Igbo-Ora *Nigeria* **83** D5
Igboho *Nigeria* **83** D5
Igbor *Nigeria* **83** D6
İğdır *Turkey* **73** C11
Igelfors *Sweden* **11** F9
Iggesund *Sweden* **10** C11
Iglésias *Italy* **42** C1
Igloolik = Iglulik *Canada* **101** C11
Igluligarjuk =
 Chesterfield Inlet *Canada* **100** C10
Iglulik *Canada* **101** C11
'Igma, Gebel el *Egypt* **80** B3
Ignace *Canada* **104** C1
İğneada *Turkey* **45** E11
İğneada Burnu *Turkey* **45** E12
Igoumenitsa *Greece* **46** B2
Igra *Russia* **34** B11
Igrim *Russia* **52** C7

Iguaçu → *Brazil* **127** B5
Iguaçu, Cat. del *Brazil* **127** B5
Iguaçu △ *Brazil* **127** B5
Iguaçu Falls = Iguaçu, Cat.
 del *Brazil* **127** B5
Iguala *Mexico* **119** D5
Igualada *Spain* **38** C6
Iguassu = Iguaçu → *Brazil* **127** B5
Iguatu *Brazil* **125** E11
Iguazú → *Argentina* **127** B5
Iguidi, Erg *Africa* **78** C4
Iharana *Madag.* **89** A9
Ihbulag *Mongolia* **56** C4
Iheya-Shima *Japan* **55** L3
Ihiala *Nigeria* **83** D6
Ihosy *Madag.* **89** C8
Ihotry, Farihy *Madag.* **89** C7
Ihugh *Nigeria* **83** D6
Ii *Finland* **8** D21
Ii-Shima *Japan* **55** L3
Iida *Japan* **55** G8
Iijoki → *Finland* **8** D21
Iisalmi *Finland* **8** E22
Iiyama *Japan* **55** F9
Iizuka *Japan* **55** H5
Ijâfene *Mauritania* **78** D4
Ijebu-Igbo *Nigeria* **83** D5
Ijebu-Ode *Nigeria* **83** D5
Ijevan *Armenia* **73** B11
IJmuiden *Neths.* **17** B4
Ijo älv = Iijoki → *Finland* **8** D21
IJssel → *Neths.* **17** B5
IJsselmeer *Neths.* **17** B5
Ijuí *Brazil* **127** B5
Ijuí → *Brazil* **127** B4
Ikalamavony *Madag.* **89** C8
Ikale *Nigeria* **83** D6
Ikaluktutiak *Canada* **100** C9
Ikang *Nigeria* **83** E6
Ikanga *Kenya* **86** C4
Ikara *Nigeria* **83** C6
Ikare *Nigeria* **83** D6
Ikaria *Greece* **47** D8
Ikast *Denmark* **11** H3
Ikeda *Japan* **55** G6
Ikeja *Nigeria* **83** D5
Ikela *Dem. Rep. of the Congo* **84** E4
Ikerre-Ekiti *Nigeria* **83** D6
Ikhtiman *Bulgaria* **44** D7
Iki *Japan* **55** H4
Ikimba L. *Tanzania* **86** C3
Ikire *Nigeria* **83** D5
İkizdere *Turkey* **73** B9
Ikom *Nigeria* **83** D6
Ikongo *Madag.* **89** C8
Ikopa → *Madag.* **89** B8
Ikorongo △ *Tanzania* **86** C3
Ikot Ekpene *Nigeria* **83** D6
Ikparjuk = Arctic Bay
 Canada **101** B11
Iksan *S. Korea* **57** G14
Ikungu *Tanzania* **86** C3
Ikuntji = Haast Bluff
 Australia **92** D5
Ikurun *Nigeria* **83** D5
Ila *Nigeria* **83** D5
Ilagan *Phil.* **61** C4
Ilaka *Madag.* **89** B8
Ilām *Iran* **73** F12
Ilam *Nepal* **69** F12
Īlām □ *Iran* **70** C5
Ilan *Taiwan* **59** E13
Ilanskiy *Russia* **53** D10
Ilaro *Nigeria* **83** D5
Ilatane *Niger* **83** B5
Iława *Poland* **30** E6
Ile → *Kazakhstan* **52** E8
Île-à-la-Crosse *Canada* **103** B7
Île-à-la-Crosse, Lac *Canada* **103** B7
Île-de-France □ *France* **19** D9
Ileanda *Romania* **29** C8
Ilebo *Dem. Rep. of the Congo* **84** E4
Ilek *Russia* **52** D6
Ilero *Nigeria* **83** D5
Ilesha *Kwara, Nigeria* **83** D5
Ilesha *Oyo, Nigeria* **83** D5
Ilford *Canada* **103** B9
Ilfracombe *Australia* **94** C3
Ilfracombe *U.K.* **15** F3
Ilgaz *Turkey* **72** B5
Ilgaz Dağları *Turkey* **72** B5
Ilgın *Turkey* **72** C4
Ilha de Moçambique *Mozam.* **87** F5
Ilha Grande, Represa *Brazil* **127** A5
Ilha Grande △ *Brazil* **127** A5
Ílhavo *Portugal* **36** E2
Ilhéus *Brazil* **125** F11
Ili = Ile → *Kazakhstan* **52** E8
Ilia *Romania* **28** E7
Ilía □ *Greece* **46** D3
Iliamna L. *U.S.A.* **106** a
Ilias, Profitis *Greece* **49** C9
Iliç *Turkey* **73** C8
Ilıca *Turkey* **47** B9
Iligan *Phil.* **61** G6
Iligan Bay *Phil.* **61** G6
Ilin I. *Phil.* **61** E4
Ilion *U.S.A.* **115** D9
Ilirska-Bistrica *Slovenia* **41** C11

Ilkeston *U.K.* **14** E6
Ilkley *U.K.* **14** D6
Illampu = Ancohuma,
 Nevado *Bolivia* **124** G5
Illana B. *Phil.* **61** H5
Illapel *Chile* **126** C1
Ille-et-Vilaine □ *France* **18** D5
Ille-sur-Têt *France* **20** F6
Illéla *Niger* **83** C6
Iller → *Germany* **25** G5
Illertissen *Germany* **25** G6
Illescas *Spain* **36** E7
Illetas *Spain* **48** B9
Illichivsk *Ukraine* **33** J6
Illimani, Nevado *Bolivia* **124** G5
Illinois □ *U.S.A.* **112** E9
Illinois → *U.S.A.* **112** F8
Illizi *Algeria* **78** C7
Illkirch-Graffenstaden
 France **19** D14
Íllora *Spain* **37** H7
Ilm → *Germany* **24** D7
Ilma, L. *Australia* **93** E4
Ilmajoki *Finland* **8** E20
Ilmen, Ozero *Russia* **32** C6
Ilmenau *Germany* **24** E6
Ilnytsya *Ukraine* **28** B8
Ilo *Peru* **124** G4
Ilobu *Nigeria* **83** D5
Iloilo *Phil.* **61** F5
Ilomantsi *Finland* **8** E24
Ilora *Nigeria* **83** D5
Ilorin *Nigeria* **83** D5
Ilovatka *Russia* **34** E7
Ilovlya *Russia* **35** F7
Ilovlya → *Russia* **35** F7
Iłowa *Poland* **31** G2
Ilubabor *Ethiopia* **81** F4
Ilva Mică *Romania* **29** C9
Ilwaco *U.S.A.* **110** D2
Ilwaki *Indonesia* **63** F7
Ilyichevsk = Illichivsk
 Ukraine **33** J6
Iłża *Poland* **31** G8
Ilzanka → *Poland* **31** G8
Imabari *Japan* **55** G6
Imaloto → *Madag.* **89** C8
İmamoğlu *Turkey* **72** D6
Imandra, Ozero *Russia* **8** C25
Imanombo *Madag.* **89** C8
Imari *Japan* **55** H4
Imasa *Sudan* **80** D4
Imathia □ *Greece* **44** F6
Imatra *Finland* **32** B5
Iménas *Mali* **83** B5
imeni 26 Bakinskikh
 Komissarov = Neftçala
 Azerbaijan **73** C13
imeni 26 Bakinskikh
 Komissarov *Turkmenistan* **71** B7
imeni Ismail Samani, Pik
 Tajikistan **52** F8
Imeri, Serra *Brazil* **124** C5
Imerimandroso *Madag.* **89** B8
Imfolozi → *S. Africa* **89** D5
Imi *Ethiopia* **81** F5
Imishly = Imişli *Azerbaijan* **35** L9
Imişli *Azerbaijan* **35** L9
Imlay *U.S.A.* **108** F4
Imlay City *U.S.A.* **114** D1
Immaseri *Sudan* **81** D2
Immenstadt *Germany* **25** H6
Immingham *U.K.* **14** D7
Immokalee *U.S.A.* **117** H14
Imo □ *Nigeria* **83** D6
Imo → *Nigeria* **83** E6
Ímola *Italy* **41** D8
Imotski *Croatia* **41** E14
Imperatriz *Brazil* **125** E9
Impéria *Italy* **40** E7
Imperial *Canada* **103** C7
Imperial *Calif., U.S.A.* **111** N11
Imperial *Nebr., U.S.A.* **112** E3
Imperial Beach *U.S.A.* **111** N9
Imperial Dam *U.S.A.* **111** N12
Imperial Res. *U.S.A.* **111** N12
Imperial Valley *U.S.A.* **111** N11
Imperieuse Reef *Australia* **92** C2
Impfondo *Congo* **84** D3
Imphal *India* **67** G18
Imphy *France* **19** F10
Imranlı *Turkey* **73** C8
İmroz = Gökçeada *Turkey* **45** F9
İmroz *Turkey* **45** F9
Imst *Austria* **26** D3
Imuris *Mexico* **118** A2
Imuruan B. *Phil.* **61** F3
In Akhmed *Mali* **83** B4
In Aleï *Mali* **82** B4
In Delimane *Mali* **83** B5
In Guezzam *Algeria* **83** B6
In Koufi *Mali* **83** B5
In Salah *Algeria* **78** C6
In Tallak *Mali* **83** B5
In Tebezas *Mali* **83** B5
Ina *Japan* **55** G8
Inagua △ *Bahamas* **121** B5
Inangahua *N.Z.* **91** D3

Inanwatan *Indonesia* **63** E8
Iñapari *Peru* **124** F5
Inari *Finland* **8** B22
Inarijärvi *Finland* **8** B23
Inawashiro-Ko *Japan* **54** F10
Inca *Spain* **48** B9
Inca de Oro *Chile* **126** B2
Incahuasi *Argentina* **126** B2
Incahuasi *Chile* **126** B1
İnce Burun *Turkey* **72** A6
İncekum Burnu *Turkey* **72** D5
Incesu *Turkey* **72** C6
Incheon *S. Korea* **57** F14
Inchiri □ *Mauritania* **82** B2
Incio = A Cruz do Incio
 Spain **36** C3
İncirliova *Turkey* **47** D9
Incline Village *U.S.A.* **108** G4
Incomáti → *Mozam.* **89** D5
Incudine, Mte. *France* **21** G13
Inda Silase *Ethiopia* **81** E4
Indal *Sweden* **10** B11
Indalsälven → *Sweden* **10** B11
Indaw *Burma* **67** G20
Indbir *Ethiopia* **81** F4
Independence *Calif., U.S.A.* **110** J8
Independence *Iowa, U.S.A.* **112** D8
Independence *Kans., U.S.A.* **112** G6
Independence *Ky., U.S.A.* **113** F11
Independence *Mo., U.S.A.* **112** F6
Independence Fjord *Greenland* **4** A6
Independence Mts. *U.S.A.* **108** F5
Independenţa *Romania* **29** E12
Index *U.S.A.* **110** C5
India ■ *Asia* **66** K11
Indian → *U.S.A.* **117** H14
Indian Cabins *Canada* **102** B5
Indian Harbour *Canada* **105** B8
Indian Head *Canada* **103** C8
Indian L. *U.S.A.* **115** C10
Indian Lake *U.S.A.* **115** C10
Indian Springs *U.S.A.* **111** J11
Indiana *U.S.A.* **114** F5
Indiana □ *U.S.A.* **113** F11
Indianapolis *U.S.A.* **112** F10
Indianola *Iowa, U.S.A.* **112** E7
Indianola *Miss., U.S.A.* **117** E9
Indigirka → *Russia* **53** B15
Indija *Serbia* **28** E5
Indio *U.S.A.* **111** M10
Indira Gandhi Canal *India* **68** F5
Indira Sagar *India* **68** H7
Indo-China *Asia* **50** G12
Indonesia ■ *Asia* **62** F5
Indore *India* **68** H6
Indramayu *Indonesia* **63** G13
Indravati → *India* **67** K12
Indre □ *France* **19** F8
Indre → *France* **18** E7
Indre-et-Loire □ *France* **18** E7
Indulkana *Australia* **95** D1
Indura *Belarus* **30** E10
Indus → *Pakistan* **68** G2
Indus, Mouths of the
 Pakistan **68** H3
İnebolu *Turkey* **72** B5
İnecik *Turkey* **45** F11
İnegöl *Turkey* **45** F13
Ineu *Romania* **28** D6
Infantes = Villanueva de
 los Infantes *Spain* **37** G7
Infiernillo, Presa del *Mexico* **118** D4
Infiesto *Spain* **36** B5
Ingelstad *Sweden* **11** H8
Ingenio *Canary Is.* **48** G4
Ingenio Santa Ana
 Argentina **126** B2
Ingersoll *Canada* **114** C4
Ingham *Australia* **94** B4
Ingleborough *U.K.* **14** C5
Inglewood *Queens., Australia* **95** D5
Inglewood *Vic., Australia* **95** F3
Inglewood *N.Z.* **91** C5
Inglewood *U.S.A.* **111** M8
Ingolf Fjord *Greenland* **4** A6
Ingólfshöfði *Iceland* **8** E5
Ingolstadt *Germany* **25** G7
Ingomar *U.S.A.* **108** C10
Ingonish *Canada* **105** C7
Ingore *Guinea-Biss.* **82** C1
Ingraj Bazar *India* **69** G13
Ingrid Christensen Coast
 Antarctica **5** C6
Ingul = Inhul → *Ukraine* **33** J7
Ingulec = Inhulec *Ukraine* **33** J7
Ingulets = Inhulets →
 Ukraine **33** J7
Inguri = Enguri → *Georgia* **35** J5
Ingushetia □ *Russia* **35** J7
Ingwavuma *S. Africa* **89** D5
Inhaca *Mozam.* **89** D5
Inhafenga *Mozam.* **89** C5
Inhambane *Mozam.* **89** C6
Inhambane □ *Mozam.* **89** C5
Inhaminga *Mozam.* **87** F4
Inharrime *Mozam.* **89** C6
Inharrime → *Mozam.* **89** C6
Inhisar *Turkey* **47** A12
Inhul → *Ukraine* **33** J7
Inhulec *Ukraine* **33** J7
Inhulets → *Ukraine* **33** J7

Inhulets → *Ukraine* **33** J7
Iñapari = Ipiales → *Ukraine* **33** J7
Iniesta *Spain* **39** F3
Ining = Yining *China* **52** E9
Inirida → *Colombia* **124** C5
Inishbofin *Ireland* **12** C1
Inishfree B. *Ireland* **12** A3
Inisheer *Ireland* **12** C2
Inishfree B. *Ireland* **12** A3
Inishkea North *Ireland* **12** B1
Inishkea South *Ireland* **12** B1
Inishmaan *Ireland* **12** C2
Inishmore *Ireland* **12** C2
Inishmurray I. *Ireland* **12** B3
Inishowen Pen. *Ireland* **12** A4
Inishshark *Ireland* **12** C1
Inishturk *Ireland* **12** C1
Inishvickillane *Ireland* **12** D1
Injāna *Iraq* **73** E11
Injibara *Ethiopia* **81** E4
Injune *Australia* **95** D4
Inklin → *N. Amer.* **102** B2
Inland Kaikoura Ra. *N.Z.* **91** D4
Inland Sea = Setonaikai
 Japan **55** G6
Inle L. *Burma* **67** J20
Inlet *U.S.A.* **115** C10
Inn → *Austria* **26** C6
Innamincka *Australia* **95** D3
Inner Hebrides *U.K.* **13** E2
Inner Mongolia = Nei
 Monggol Zizhiqu □ *China* **56** D7
Inner Sound *U.K.* **13** D3
Innerkip *Canada* **114** C4
Innetalling I. *Canada* **104** A4
Innisfail *Australia* **94** B4
Innisfail *Canada* **102** C6
Innsbruck *Austria* **26** D4
Innviertel *Austria* **26** C6
Inny → *Ireland* **12** C4
Inongo *Dem. Rep. of the Congo* **84** E3
İnönü *Turkey* **47** B12
Inoucdjouac = Inukjuak
 Canada **101** D12
Inousses *Greece* **47** C8
Inowrocław *Poland* **31** F5
Inscription, C. *Australia* **93** E1
Insein *Burma* **67** L20
Insjön *Sweden* **10** D9
İnşko *Poland* **30** E2
Însurăţei *Romania* **29** F12
Inta *Russia* **52** C6
Intendente Alvear
 Argentina **126** D3
İntepe *Turkey* **47** A8
Interlaken *Switz.* **25** J3
Interlaken *U.S.A.* **115** D8
International Falls *U.S.A.* **112** A7
Intiyaco *Argentina* **126** B3
Întorsura Buzăului *Romania* **29** E11
Inukjuak *Canada* **101** D12
Inútil, B. *Chile* **128** G2
Inuvik *Canada* **100** C6
Inveraray *U.K.* **13** E3
Inverbervie *U.K.* **13** E6
Invercargill *N.Z.* **91** G2
Inverclyde □ *U.K.* **13** F4
Inverell *Australia* **95** D5
Invergordon *U.K.* **13** D4
Inverloch *Australia* **95** F4
Invermere *Canada* **102** C5
Inverness *Canada* **105** C7
Inverness *U.K.* **13** D4
Inverness *U.S.A.* **117** G13
Inverurie *U.K.* **13** D6
Investigator Group *Australia* **95** E1
Investigator Str. *Australia* **95** F2
Inya *Russia* **52** D9
Inyanga *Zimbabwe* **87** F3
Inyangani *Zimbabwe* **87** F3
Inyantue *Zimbabwe* **88** B4
Inyo Mts. *U.S.A.* **110** J9
Inyokern *U.S.A.* **111** K9
Inza *Russia* **34** D8
Inzhavino *Russia* **34** D6
Iō-Jima *Japan* **55** J5
Ioannina *Greece* **46** B2
Ioannina □ *Greece* **46** B2
Iola *U.S.A.* **112** G6
Ion Corvin *Romania* **29** F12
Iona *U.K.* **13** E2
Ione *U.S.A.* **110** G6
Ionia *U.S.A.* **113** D11
Ionian Is. = Ionioi Nisoi
 Greece **46** C2
Ionian Sea *Medit. S.* **6** H9
Ionioi Nisoi *Greece* **46** C2
Ioníou Nísoi *Greece* **46** C2
Ios *Greece* **47** E7
Iowa □ *U.S.A.* **112** D7
Iowa → *U.S.A.* **112** E8
Iowa City *U.S.A.* **112** E8
Iowa Falls *U.S.A.* **112** D7
Iowa Park *U.S.A.* **116** E5
Ipala *Tanzania* **86** C3
Ipameri *Brazil* **125** G9
Ipati *Greece* **46** C4
Ipatinga *Brazil* **125** G10
Ipatovo *Russia* **35** H6
Ipel' → *Europe* **27** D11

Ipiales *Colombia* **124** C3
Ipin = Yibin *China* **58** C5
Ipixuna *Brazil* **124** E4
Ipoh *Malaysia* **65** K3
Ippy *C.A.R.* **84** C4
İpsala *Turkey* **45** F10
Ipsario, Oros *Greece* **45** F8
Ipswich *Australia* **95** D5
Ipswich *U.K.* **15** E9
Ipswich *Mass., U.S.A.* **115** D14
Ipswich *S. Dak., U.S.A.* **112** C4
Ipu *Brazil* **125** D10
Iqaluit *Canada* **101** C13
Iquique *Chile* **124** H4
Iquitos *Peru* **124** D4
Irabu-Jima *Japan* **55** M2
Iracoubo *Fr. Guiana* **125** B8
Īrafshān *Iran* **71** E9
Irahuan *Phil.* **61** G3
Iráklia *Cyclades, Greece* **47** E7
Iraklia *Serres, Greece* **44** E7
Iraklio *Greece* **49** D7
Iraklio □ *Greece* **49** D7
Iráklion = Iraklio *Greece* **49** D7
Irakliou, Kolpos *Greece* **49** D7
Irala *Paraguay* **127** B5
Iran ■ *Asia* **71** C7
Iran, Pegunungan *Malaysia* **62** D4
Iran, Pegunungan =
 Iran, Pegunungan *Malaysia* **62** D4
Īrānshahr *Iran* **71** E9
Irapuato *Mexico* **118** C4
Iraq ■ *Asia* **73** F10
Irati *Brazil* **127** B5
Irbes saurums *Latvia* **30** A9
Irbid *Jordan* **74** C4
Irbid □ *Jordan* **74** C5
Irebu *Dem. Rep. of the Congo* **84** E3
Iregua → *Spain* **38** C7
Ireland ■ *Europe* **12** C4
Irele *Nigeria* **83** D6
Irgiz, Bolshaya → *Russia* **34** D9
Iri = Iksan *S. Korea* **57** G14
Irian Jaya = Papua □
 Indonesia **63** E9
Irian Jaya Barat □ *Indonesia* **63** E8
Irié *Guinea* **82** D3
Iriga *Phil.* **61** E5
Iringa *Tanzania* **86** D4
Iringa □ *Tanzania* **86** M1
Iriomote △ *Japan* **55** M1
Iriomote-Jima *Japan* **55** M1
Iriona *Honduras* **120** C2
Iriri → *Brazil* **125** D8
Irish Republic ■ *Europe* **12** C4
Irish Sea *Europe* **14** D3
Irkutsk *Russia* **53** D11
Irlig9anlı *Turkey* **47** D11
Irma *Canada* **103** C6
Irō-Zaki *Japan* **55** G9
Iroise, Mer d' *France* **18** D2
Iron Baron *Australia* **95** E2
Iron Gate = Portile de Fier
 Europe **28** F7
Iron Knob *Australia* **95** E2
Iron Mountain *U.S.A.* **112** C9
Iron Range △ *Australia* **94** A3
Iron River *U.S.A.* **112** B9
Irondequoit *U.S.A.* **114** C7
Ironton *Mo., U.S.A.* **112** G8
Ironton *Ohio, U.S.A.* **113** F12
Ironwood *U.S.A.* **112** B8
Ironwood Forest △ *U.S.A.* **109** K8
Iroquois *Canada* **115** B9
Iroquois Falls *Canada* **104** C3
Irosin *Phil.* **61** E6
Irpin *Ukraine* **23** C16
Irrara Cr. → *Australia* **95** D4
Irrawaddy □ *Burma* **67** L19
Irrawaddy → *Burma* **67** M19
Irrawaddy, Mouths of the
 Burma **67** M19
Irricana *Canada* **102** C6
Irshava *Ukraine* **28** B8
Irsina *Italy* **43** B9
Irtysh → *Russia* **52** C7
Irumu *Dem. Rep. of the Congo* **86** B2
Irún *Spain* **38** B3
Irunea = Pamplona-Iruña
 Spain **38** C3
Irurzun *Spain* **38** C3
Irvine *Canada* **103** D6
Irvine *U.K.* **13** F4
Irvine *Calif., U.S.A.* **111** M9
Irvine *Ky., U.S.A.* **113** G12
Irvinestown *U.K.* **12** B4
Irving *U.S.A.* **116** E6
Irvona *U.S.A.* **114** F6
Irwin → *Australia* **93** E1
Irymple *Australia* **95** E3
Is, Jebel *Sudan* **80** C4
Is-sur-Tille *France* **19** E12
Isa *Nigeria* **83** C6
Isa Khel *Pakistan* **68** C4
Isaac → *Australia* **94** C4
Isabel *U.S.A.* **112** C3
Isabel, I. *Mexico* **118** C3
Isabela *Phil.* **61** H5
Isabela *Puerto Rico* **121** d

Isabella, Cord. *Nic.* **120** D2
Isabella Ra. *Australia* **92** D3
Isaccea *Romania* **29** E13
Isachenko, Ostrov *Russia* **53** B9
Ísafjarðardjúp *Iceland* **8** C2
Ísafjörður *Iceland* **8** C2
Isagarh *India* **68** G7
Isahaya *Japan* **55** H5
Isaka *Tanzania* **86** C3
Işalniţa *Romania* **29** F8
Isalo △ *Madag.* **89** C8
Isan → *India* **69** F9
Isana = Içana → *Brazil* **124** C5
Isangano △ *Zambia* **87** E3
Isanlu Makutu *Nigeria* **83** D6
Isar → *Germany* **25** G8
Isarco → *Italy* **41** B8
Isaris *Greece* **46** D3
Íscar *Spain* **36** D6
İscehisar *Turkey* **47** C12
Íschia *Italy* **42** B6
Isdell → *Australia* **92** C3
Ise *Japan* **55** G8
Ise-Shima △ *Japan* **55** G8
Ise-Wan *Japan* **55** G8
Isefjord *Denmark* **11** J5
Isel → *Austria* **26** E5
Iseo *Italy* **40** C7
Iseo, L. d' *Italy* **40** C7
Iseramagazi *Tanzania* **86** C3
Isère □ *France* **21** C9
Isère → *France* **21** D8
Iserlohn *Germany* **24** D3
Isérnia *Italy* **43** A7
Iseyin *Nigeria* **83** D5
Isfahan = Eşfahān *Iran* **71** C6
Ishëm *Albania* **44** E3
Ishigaki *Japan* **55** M2
Ishigaki-Shima *Japan* **55** M2
Ishikari-Gawa → *Japan* **54** C10
Ishikari-Sammyaku *Japan* **54** C11
Ishikari-Wan *Japan* **54** C10
Ishikawa *Japan* **55** L3
Ishikawa □ *Japan* **55** F8
Ishim *Russia* **52** D7
Ishim → *Russia* **52** D8
Ishinomaki *Japan* **54** E10
Ishioka *Japan* **55** F10
Ishkoman *Pakistan* **69** A5
Ishpeming *U.S.A.* **112** B9
Isigny-sur-Mer *France* **18** C5
Işıklar Dağı *Turkey* **45** F11
Işıklı *Turkey* **47** C11
Isil Kul *Russia* **52** D8
Ísili *Italy* **42** C2
Isiolo *Kenya* **86** B4
Isiro *Dem. Rep. of the Congo* **86** B2
Isisford *Australia* **94** C3
İskenderun *Turkey* **72** D7
İskenderun Körfezi *Turkey* **72** D6
İskilip *Turkey* **72** B6
Iskŭr → *Bulgaria* **45** C8
Iskŭr, Yazovir *Bulgaria* **44** D7
Iskut → *Canada* **102** B2
Isla → *U.K.* **13** E5
Isla Coiba △ *Panama* **120** E3
Isla Cristina *Spain* **37** H3
Isla de Salamanca △
  Colombia **121** D5
Isla Gorge △ *Australia* **94** D4
Isla Isabel △ *Mexico* **118** C3
Isla Tiburón y San
  Esteban △ *Mexico* **118** B2
Isla Vista *U.S.A.* **111** L7
Íslâhiye *Turkey* **72** D7
Islam Headworks *Pakistan* **68** E5
Islamabad *Pakistan* **68** C5
Islamgarh *Pakistan* **68** F4
Islamkot *Pakistan* **68** G4
Islampur *India* **69** F13
Islampur *Bihar, India* **69** G11
Island = Iceland ■ *Europe* **8** D4
Island L. *Canada* **103** C10
Island Lagoon *Australia* **95** E2
Island Pond *U.S.A.* **115** B13
Islands, B. of *Canada* **105** C8
Islands, B. of *N.Z.* **91** A5
Islay *U.K.* **13** F2
Isle → *France* **20** D3
Isle aux Morts *Canada* **105** C8
Isle of Wight □ *U.K.* **15** G6
Isle Royale △ *U.S.A.* **112** B9
Isleton *U.S.A.* **110** G5
Ismail = Izmayil *Ukraine* **29** E13
Ismâ'iliya *Egypt* **80** H8
Ismaning *Germany* **25** G7
Isna *Egypt* **80** B3
Isoanala *Madag.* **89** C8
Isogstalo *India* **69** B8
Ísola del Liri *Italy* **41** G10
Ísola della Scala *Italy* **40** C7
Ísola di Capo Rizzuto *Italy* **43** D10
Ísparta *Turkey* **47** D12
Ísparta □ *Turkey* **72** D4
Isperikh *Bulgaria* **45** C10
Íspica *Italy* **43** F7
İspir *Turkey* **73** B9
Israel ■ *Asia* **74** D3
Isratu *Eritrea* **81** D4

Issakly *Russia* **34** C10
Issia *Ivory C.* **82** D3
Issoire *France* **20** C7
Issoudun *France* **19** F8
Issyk-Kul, Ozero =
  Ysyk-Köl *Kyrgyzstan* **52** E8
Ist *Croatia* **41** D11
Istállós-kő *Hungary* **28** B5
İstanbul *Turkey* **45** E12
İstanbul □ *Turkey* **45** E12
İstanbul ✈ (IST) *Turkey* **45** F12
İstanbul Boğazı *Turkey* **45** E13
Istiea *Greece* **46** C5
Istok *Serbia* **44** D4
Istokpoga, L. *U.S.A.* **117** H14
Istra *Croatia* **41** C10
Istres *France* **21** E8
Istria = Istra *Croatia* **41** C10
Itá *Paraguay* **126** B4
Itaberaba *Brazil* **125** F10
Itabira *Brazil* **125** G10
Itabirito *Brazil* **127** A7
Itabuna *Brazil* **125** F11
Itacaunas → *Brazil* **125** E9
Itacoatiara *Brazil* **124** D7
Itaipú, Represa de *Brazil* **127** B5
Itaituba *Brazil* **125** D7
Itajaí *Brazil* **127** B6
Itajubá *Brazil* **127** A6
Itaka *Tanzania* **87** D3
Itala △ *S. Africa* **89** D5
Italy ■ *Europe* **7** C5
Itamaraju *Brazil* **125** G11
Itampolo *Madag.* **89** C7
Itandrano *Madag.* **89** C8
Itapecuru Mirim *Brazil* **125** D10
Itaperuna *Brazil* **127** A7
Itapetininga *Brazil* **127** A6
Itapeva *Brazil* **127** A6
Itapicuru → *Bahia, Brazil* **125** F11
Itapicuru → *Maranhão,
  Brazil* **125** D10
Itapipoca *Brazil* **125** D11
Itapuá □ *Paraguay* **127** B4
Itaquari *Brazil* **127** A7
Itaquí *Brazil* **126** B4
Itararé *Brazil* **127** A6
Itarsi *India* **68** H7
Itatí *Argentina* **126** B4
Itatiaia △ *Brazil* **127** A7
Itbayat *Phil.* **61** A4
Itchen → *U.K.* **15** G6
Itea *Greece* **46** C4
Itezhi Tezhi, L. *Zambia* **87** F2
Ithaca = Ithaki *Greece* **46** C2
Ithaca *U.S.A.* **115** D8
Ithaki *Greece* **46** C2
Iti △ *Greece* **46** C4
Itiquira → *Brazil* **125** G7
Itiyuro → *Argentina* **126** A3
Itō *Japan* **55** G9
Itoigawa *Japan* **55** F8
Iton → *France* **18** C8
Itonamas → *Bolivia* **124** F6
Itri *Italy* **42** A6
Itsa *Egypt* **80** J7
Íttiri *Italy* **42** B1
Ittoqqortoormiit *Greenland* **4** B6
Itu *Brazil* **127** A6
Itu *Nigeria* **83** D6
Itu Aba I. *S. China Sea* **62** B4
Ituiutaba *Brazil* **125** G9
Itumbiara *Brazil* **125** G9
Ituna *Canada* **103** C8
Itunge Port *Tanzania* **87** D3
Iturbe *Argentina* **126** A2
Iturup, Ostrov *Russia* **53** E15
Ituxi → *Brazil* **124** E6
Itzehoe *Germany* **24** B5
Ivahona *Madag.* **89** C8
Ivaí → *Brazil* **127** A5
Ivalo *Finland* **8** B22
Ivalojoki → *Finland* **8** B22
Ivanava *Belarus* **23** B13
Ivančice *Czech Rep.* **27** B9
Ivane-Puste *Ukraine* **29** B11
Ivangorod *Russia* **32** C5
Ivanhoe *Australia* **95** E3
Ivanhoe *Canada* **114** B4
Ivanhoe *Calif., U.S.A.* **110** J7
Ivanhoe *Minn., U.S.A.* **112** C6
Ivanhorod *Ukraine* **29** B14
Ivanić Grad *Croatia* **41** C13
Ivanjica *Serbia* **44** C4
Ivanjska *Bos.-H.* **28** F2
Ivankoyskoye Vdkhr.
  Russia **32** D9
Ivano-Frankivsk *Ukraine* **29** B9
Ivano-Frankivsk □ *Ukraine* **29** B9
Ivanovo = Ivanava *Belarus* **23** B13
Ivanovo *Russia* **32** D11
Ivanovo □ *Russia* **34** B5
Ivato *Madag.* **89** C8
Ivatsevichy *Belarus* **23** B13
Ivaylovgrad *Bulgaria* **45** E10
Ivinheima → *Brazil* **127** A5

Ivinhema *Brazil* **127** A5
Ivohibe *Madag.* **89** C8
Ivory Coast *W. Afr.* **82** E4
Ivory Coast ■ *Africa* **82** D4
Ivösjön *Sweden* **11** H8
Ívrea *Italy* **40** C4
Ívrindi *Turkey* **47** B9
Ivujivik *Canada* **101** C12
Ivybridge *U.K.* **15** G4
Iwaizumi *Japan* **54** E10
Iwaki *Japan* **55** F10
Iwakuni *Japan* **55** G6
Iwamizawa *Japan* **54** C10
Iwanai *Japan* **54** C10
Iwata *Japan* **55** G8
Iwate □ *Japan* **54** E10
Iwate-San *Japan* **54** E10
Iwo *Nigeria* **83** D5
Iwŏn *N. Korea* **57** D15
Iwonicz-Zdrój *Poland* **31** J8
Ixiamas *Bolivia* **124** F5
Ixopo *S. Africa* **89** E5
Ixtepec *Mexico* **119** D5
Ixtlán del Río *Mexico* **118** C4
Iyal Bakhit *Sudan* **81** E2
Iyo *Japan* **55** H6
Izabal, L. de *Guatemala* **120** C2
Izamal *Mexico* **119** C7
Izberbash *Russia* **35** J8
Izbica *Poland* **31** H10
Izbica Kujawska *Poland* **31** F5
Izbiceni *Romania* **29** F8
Izena-Shima *Japan* **55** L3
Izgrev *Bulgaria* **45** C10
Izhevsk *Russia* **34** B10
Izmayil *Ukraine* **29** E13
İzmir *Turkey* **47** C9
İzmir □ *Turkey* **47** C9
İzmir Adnan Menderes ✈
  (ADB) *Turkey* **47** C9
İzmir Körfezi *Turkey* **47** C8
İzmit = Kocaeli *Turkey* **45** F13
Iznájar *Spain* **37** H6
Iznalloz *Spain* **37** H7
İznik *Turkey* **72** B3
İznik Gölü *Turkey* **45** F13
Izobíl'nyy *Russia* **35** H5
Izola *Slovenia* **41** C10
Izra *Syria* **74** C5
Iztochni Rodopi *Bulgaria* **45** E9
Izu-Shotō *Japan* **55** G10
Izúcar de Matamoros
  Mexico **119** D5
Izumi-Sano *Japan* **55** G7
Izumo *Japan* **55** G6
Izyaslav *Ukraine* **23** C14
Izyum *Ukraine* **33** H9

J

J.F.K. Int. ✈ (JFK) *U.S.A.* **115** F11
J. Strom Thurmond L.
  U.S.A. **117** E13
Jaba *Ethiopia* **81** F4
Jabal at Ţā'ir *Red Sea* **81** D5
Jabalón → *Spain* **37** G6
Jabalpur *India* **69** H8
Jabbūl *Syria* **70** B3
Jabiru *Australia* **92** B5
Jablah *Syria* **72** E6
Jablanac *Croatia* **41** D11
Jablanica *Bos.-H.* **28** G2
Jablonec nad Nisou
  Czech Rep. **26** A8
Jablonica *Slovak Rep.* **27** C10
Jablonowo Pomorskie
  Poland **30** E6
Jablunkov *Czech Rep.* **27** B11
Jaboatão *Brazil* **125** E11
Jaboticabal *Brazil* **127** A6
Jabukovac *Serbia* **44** B6
Jaca *Spain* **38** C4
Jacareí *Brazil* **127** A6
Jacarèzinho *Brazil* **127** A6
Jack River △ *Australia* **94** A3
Jackman *U.S.A.* **113** C18
Jacksboro *U.S.A.* **116** E5
Jackson *Barbados* **121** g
Jackson *Ala., U.S.A.* **117** F11
Jackson *Calif., U.S.A.* **110** G6
Jackson *Ky., U.S.A.* **113** G12
Jackson *Mich., U.S.A.* **113** D11
Jackson *Minn., U.S.A.* **112** D6
Jackson *Miss., U.S.A.* **117** E9
Jackson *Mo., U.S.A.* **112** G9
Jackson *N.H., U.S.A.* **115** B13
Jackson *Ohio, U.S.A.* **113** F12
Jackson *Tenn., U.S.A.* **117** D10
Jackson *Wyo., U.S.A.* **108** E8
Jackson B. *N.Z.* **91** E3
Jackson L. *U.S.A.* **108** E8
Jacksons *N.Z.* **91** E3
Jackson's Arm *Canada* **105** C8
Jacksonville *Ala., U.S.A.* **117** E12
Jacksonville *Ark., U.S.A.* **116** D8
Jacksonville *Calif., U.S.A.* **110** H6
Jacksonville *Fla., U.S.A.* **117** F14
Jacksonville *Ill., U.S.A.* **112** F8
Jacksonville *N.C., U.S.A.* **117** D16

Jacksonville *Tex., U.S.A.* **116** F7
Jacksonville Beach *U.S.A.* **117** F14
Jacmel *Haiti* **121** C5
Jacob Lake *U.S.A.* **109** H7
Jacobabad *Pakistan* **68** E3
Jacobina *Brazil* **125** F10
Jacques-Cartier, Dét. de
  Canada **105** C7
Jacques-Cartier, Mt. *Canada* **105** C6
Jacques-Cartier △ *Canada* **105** C5
Jacqueville *Ivory C.* **82** D4
Jacuí → *Brazil* **127** C5
Jacumba *U.S.A.* **111** N10
Jacundá → *Brazil* **125** D8
Jade *Germany* **24** B4
Jade City *Canada* **102** B3
Jade Mt. = Yü Shan *Taiwan* **59** F13
Jadebusen *Germany* **24** B4
Jadovnik *Serbia* **44** C3
Jadraque *Spain* **38** E2
Jaén *Peru* **124** E3
Jaén *Spain* **37** H7
Jaén □ *Spain* **37** H7
Jafarabad *India* **68** J4
Jaffa = Tel Aviv-Yafo *Israel* **74** C3
Jaffa, C. *Australia* **95** F2
Jaffna *Sri Lanka* **66** Q12
Jaffrey *U.S.A.* **115** D12
Jagadhri *India* **68** D7
Jagadishpur *India* **69** G11
Jagdalpur *India* **67** K13
Jagersfontein *S. Africa* **88** D4
Jaghīn → *Iran* **71** E8
Jagodina *Serbia* **44** B5
Jagraon *India* **68** D6
Jagtial *India* **66** K11
Jaguariaíva *Brazil* **127** A6
Jaguaribe → *Brazil* **125** D11
Jagüey Grande *Cuba* **120** B3
Jahanabad *India* **69** G11
Jahazpur *India* **68** G6
Jahrom *Iran* **71** D7
Jaijon *India* **68** D7
Jailolo *Indonesia* **63** D7
Jailolo, Selat *Indonesia* **63** D7
Jaipur *India* **68** F6
Jais *India* **69** F9
Jaisalmer *India* **68** F4
Jaisinghnagar *India* **69** H8
Jaitaran *India* **68** F5
Jaithari *India* **69** H8
Jājarm *Iran* **71** B8
Jajce *Bos.-H.* **28** F2
Jakam → *India* **68** H6
Jakarta *Indonesia* **63** G12
Jakhal *India* **68** E6
Jakhau *India* **68** H3
Jakobstad = Pietarsaari
  Finland **8** E20
Jakupica *Macedonia* **44** E5
Jal *U.S.A.* **109** K12
Jalājil *Si. Arabia* **70** E5
Jalālābād *Afghan.* **68** B4
Jalalabad *India* **69** F8
Jalalpur Jattan *Pakistan* **68** C6
Jalama *U.S.A.* **111** L6
Jalapa *Guatemala* **120** D2
Jalapa Enríquez = Xalapa
  Mexico **119** D5
Jalasjärvi *Finland* **8** E20
Jalaun *India* **69** F8
Jalesar *India* **68** F8
Jaleswar *Nepal* **69** F11
Jalgaon *India* **66** J9
Jalibah *Iraq* **70** D5
Jalingo *Nigeria* **83** D7
Jalisco □ *Mexico* **118** D4
Jalkot *Pakistan* **69** B5
Jalna *India* **66** K9
Jalón → *Spain* **38** D3
Jalor *India* **68** G5
Jalpa *Mexico* **118** C4
Jalpaiguri *India* **67** F16
Jalpan *Mexico* **119** C5
Jaluit I. *Marshall Is.* **96** G8
Jalūlā *Iraq* **73** E11
Jamaame *Somali Rep.* **75** G3
Jamaari *Nigeria* **83** C6
Jamaica ■ *W. Indies* **120** a
Jamalpur *Bangla.* **67** G16
Jamalpur *India* **69** G12
Jamalpurganj *India* **69** H13
Jamanxim → *Brazil* **125** D7
Jambewangi *Indonesia* **63** J17
Jambi *Indonesia* **62** E2
Jambi □ *Indonesia* **62** E2
Jambongan, Pulau *Malaysia* **62** C5
Jambongon *Phil.* **61** H2
Jambusar *India* **68** H5
James → *S. Dak., U.S.A.* **112** D5
James → *Va., U.S.A.* **113** G15
James B. *Canada* **104** B3
James Ranges *Australia* **92** D5
James Ross I. *Antarctica* **5** C18
Jamestown *Australia* **95** E2
Jamestown *S. Africa* **88** E4

Jamestown *N. Dak., U.S.A.* **112** B4
Jamestown *N.Y., U.S.A.* **114** D5
Jamestown *Pa., U.S.A.* **114** E4
Jamīlābād *Iran* **71** C6
Jamira → *India* **69** J13
Jämjö *Sweden* **11** H9
Jamkhandi *India* **66** L9
Jammerbugten *Denmark* **11** G3
Jammu *India* **68** C6
Jammu & Kashmir □ *India* **69** B7
Jamnagar *India* **68** H4
Jamni → *India* **69** G8
Jampur *Pakistan* **68** E4
Jamrud *Pakistan* **68** C4
Jämsä *Finland* **32** B3
Jamshedpur *India* **69** H12
Jamtara *India* **69** H12
Jämtland *Sweden* **8** E16
Jämtlands län □ *Sweden* **10** B7
Jan L. *Canada* **103** B8
Jan Mayen *Arctic* **4** B7
Janakkala *Finland* **32** B3
Janaúba *Brazil* **125** G10
Jand *Pakistan* **68** C5
Jandaq *Iran* **71** C7
Jandía *Canary Is.* **48** F5
Jandía, Pta. de *Canary Is.* **48** F5
Jandía △ *Canary Is.* **48** F5
Jandola *Pakistan* **68** C4
Jandowae *Australia* **95** D5
Jándula → *Spain* **37** G6
Janesville *U.S.A.* **112** D9
Janga *Ghana* **83** C4
Jangamo *Mozam.* **89** C6
Janghai *India* **69** G10
Jangheung *S. Korea* **57** G14
Janikowo *Poland* **31** F5
Janin = Ioannina □ *Greece* **46** B2
Janja *Bos.-H.* **28** F3
Janjanbureh *Gambia* **82** C2
Janjevo *Serbia* **44** D5
Janjgir *India* **69** J10
Janjina *Croatia* **41** F14
Janjina *Madag.* **89** C8
Janos *Mexico* **118** A3
Jánoshalma *Hungary* **28** D4
Jánosháza *Hungary* **28** C2
Jánossomorja *Hungary* **28** C2
Janów *Poland* **31** H6
Janów Lubelski *Poland* **31** H9
Janów Podlaski *Poland* **31** F10
Janowiec Wielkopolski
  Poland **31** F4
Januária *Brazil* **125** G10
Janub □ *Sudan* **81** F2
Janub Dârfûr □ *Sudan* **81** E2
Janub Kordofân □ *Sudan* **81** E3
Janûb Sînî □ *Egypt* **74** F2
Janubio *Canary Is.* **48** F6
Janville *France* **19** D8
Janzé *France* **18** E5
Jaora *India* **68** H6
Japan ■ *Asia* **55** G8
Japan, Sea of *Asia* **54** E7
Japan Trench *Pac. Oc.* **96** D6
Japen = Yapen *Indonesia* **63** E9
Japla *India* **69** G11
Japurá → *Brazil* **124** D5
Jaquarão *Brazil* **127** C5
Jaqué *Panama* **120** E4
Jarābulus *Syria* **73** D8
Jaraicejo *Spain* **37** F5
Jaraíz de la Vera *Spain* **36** E5
Jarama → *Spain* **36** E7
Jaramānah *Syria* **72** F7
Jarandilla de la Vera *Spain* **36** E5
Jaranwala *Pakistan* **68** D5
Jarash *Jordan* **74** C4
Jarash □ *Jordan* **74** C4
Jardim *Brazil* **126** A4
Jardín → *Spain* **39** G2
Jardín América *Argentina* **127** B4
Jardine River △ *Australia* **94** A3
Jardines de la Reina, Arch.
  de los *Cuba* **120** B4
Jargalang *China* **57** C12
Jari → *Brazil* **125** D8
Jarīr, W. al → *Si. Arabia* **70** E4
Jarmen *Germany* **24** B9
Järna *Dalarna, Sweden* **10** D8
Järna *Stockholm, Sweden* **10** E11
Jarnac *France* **20** C3
Jarny *France* **19** C12
Jarocin *Poland* **31** G4
Jaroměř *Czech Rep.* **26** A8
Jarosław *Poland* **31** H9
Järpås *Sweden* **11** F6
Järpen *Sweden* **10** A7
Jarrahdale *Australia* **93** F2
Jarrahi → *Iran* **71** D6
Jarres, Plaine des *Laos* **64** C4
Jarso *Ethiopia* **81** F4
Jartai *China* **56** E3
Jarud Qi *China* **57** B11
Jarvis *Canada* **114** D4

Jarvis I. *Pac. Oc.* **97** H12
Jarvorník *Czech Rep.* **27** A10
Järvsö *Sweden* **10** C10
Jarwa *India* **69** F10
Jaša Tomić *Serbia* **28** E5
Jasdan *India* **68** H4
Jashpurnagar *India* **69** H11
Jasidih *India* **69** G12
Jasień *Poland* **31** G2
Jāsimīyah *Iraq* **73** F11
Jasin *Malaysia* **65** L4
Jāsk *Iran* **71** E8
Jasło *Poland* **31** J8
Jasmund *Germany* **24** A9
Jasmund △ *Germany* **24** A9
Jaso *India* **69** G9
Jasper *Alta., Canada* **102** C5
Jasper *Ont., Canada* **115** B9
Jasper *Ala., U.S.A.* **117** E11
Jasper *Fla., U.S.A.* **117** F13
Jasper *Ind., U.S.A.* **112** F10
Jasper *Tex., U.S.A.* **116** F7
Jasper △ *Canada* **102** C5
Jasrasar *India* **68** F5
Jassän *Iraq* **73** F11
Jastarnia *Poland* **30** D5
Jastrebarsko *Croatia* **41** C12
Jastrowie *Poland* **30** E3
Jastrzębie Zdrój *Poland* **31** J5
Jász-Nagykun-Szolnok □
  Hungary **28** C5
Jászapáti *Hungary* **28** C5
Jászárokszállás *Hungary* **28** C4
Jászberény *Hungary* **28** C4
Jászkisér *Hungary* **28** C5
Jászladány *Hungary* **28** C5
Jataí *Brazil* **125** G8
Jati *India* **68** G3
Jatibarang *Indonesia* **63** G13
Jatiluwih *Indonesia* **63** J18
Jatinegara *Indonesia* **63** G12
Játiva = Xàtiva *Spain* **39** G4
Jättendal *Sweden* **10** C11
Jaú *Brazil* **127** A6
Jauja *Peru* **124** F3
Jaunpur *India* **69** G10
Java = Jawa *Indonesia* **62** F3
Java Sea *Indonesia* **62** E3
Java Trench *Ind. Oc.* **62** F3
Javalambre, Sa. de *Spain* **38** E4
Javānrūd *Iran* **73** E12
Jávea *Spain* **39** G5
Jawa *Indonesia* **62** F3
Jawa Barat □ *Indonesia* **63** G12
Jawa Tengah □ *Indonesia* **63** G14
Jawa Timur □ *Indonesia* **63** G15
Jawad *India* **68** G6
Jawhar *Somali Rep.* **75** G4
Jawor *Poland* **31** G3
Jaworzno *Poland* **31** H6
Jaworzyna Śląska *Poland* **31** H3
Jay Peak *U.S.A.* **115** B12
Jaya, Puncak *Indonesia* **63** E9
Jayanti *India* **67** F16
Jayapura *Indonesia* **63** E10
Jayawijaya, Pegunungan
  Indonesia **63** E9
Jaynagar *India* **69** F12
Jayrūd *Syria* **72** F7
Jayton *U.S.A.* **116** E4
Jāz Mūrīān, Hāmūn-e *Iran* **71** E8
Jazīreh-ye Shīf *Iran* **71** D6
Jazminal *Mexico* **118** C4
Jazzīn *Lebanon* **74** B4
Jean *U.S.A.* **111** K11
Jean Marie River *Canada* **102** A4
Jean-Rabel *Haiti* **121** C5
Jeanerette *U.S.A.* **116** G9
Jeanette, Ostrov =
  Zhannetty, Ostrov *Russia* **53** B16
Jeannette *U.S.A.* **114** F5
Jebäl Bārez, Kūh-e *Iran* **71** D8
Jebba *Nigeria* **83** D5
Jebel, Bahr el → *Sudan* **81** F3
Jebel Ali = Minā' Jabal 'Alī
  U.A.E. **71** E7
Jebel Dud *Sudan* **81** E3
Jebel Qerri *Sudan* **81** D3
Jecheon *S. Korea* **57** F15
Jedburgh *U.K.* **13** F6
Jedda = Jiddah *Si. Arabia* **75** C2
Jeddore L. *Canada* **105** C8
Jedlicze *Poland* **31** J8
Jędrzejów *Poland* **31** H7
Jedwabne *Poland* **30** E9
Jeetzel → *Germany* **24** B7
Jefferson *Iowa, U.S.A.* **112** D6
Jefferson *Ohio, U.S.A.* **114** E4
Jefferson *Tex., U.S.A.* **116** E7
Jefferson, Mt. *Nev., U.S.A.* **108** G5
Jefferson, Mt. *Oreg., U.S.A.* **108** D3
Jefferson City *Mo., U.S.A.* **112** F7
Jefferson City *Tenn., U.S.A.* **117** C13
Jeffersontown *U.S.A.* **113** F11
Jeffersonville *U.S.A.* **113** F11
Jeffrey City *U.S.A.* **108** E10
Jega *Nigeria* **83** C5
Jeju *S. Korea* **57** H14
Jeju-do *S. Korea* **57** H14

Jēkabpils *Latvia* **32** D3
Jekyll I. *U.S.A.* **117** F14
Jelcz-Laskowice *Poland* **31** G4
Jelenia Góra *Poland* **31** H2
Jelgava *Latvia* **30** B10
Jelgava □ *Latvia* **30** B10
Jelica *Serbia* **44** C4
Jelli *Sudan* **81** F3
Jemaja *Indonesia* **65** L5
Jemaluang *Malaysia* **65** L4
Jember *Indonesia* **63** H15
Jena *Germany* **24** E7
Jena *U.S.A.* **116** F8
Jenbach *Austria* **26** D4
Jenin *West Bank* **74** C4
Jenkins *U.S.A.* **113** G12
Jenner *U.S.A.* **110** G3
Jennings *U.S.A.* **116** F8
Jeong-eup *S. Korea* **57** G14
Jeonju *S. Korea* **57** G14
Jepara *Indonesia* **63** G14
Jeparit *Australia* **95** F3
Jequié *Brazil* **125** F10
Jequitinhonha *Brazil* **125** G10
Jequitinhonha → *Brazil* **125** G11
Jerada *Morocco* **78** B5
Jerantut *Malaysia* **65** L4
Jerejak, Pulau *Malaysia* **65** c
Jérémie *Haiti* **121** C5
Jerez, Pta. *Mexico* **119** C5
Jerez de García Salinas
  Mexico **118** C4
Jerez de la Frontera *Spain* **37** J4
Jerez de los Caballeros *Spain* **37** G4
Jericho = El Arīḥā *West Bank* **74** D4
Jericho *Australia* **94** C4
Jerichow *Germany* **24** C8
Jerid, Chott el = Djerid,
  Chott *Tunisia* **78** B7
Jerilderie *Australia* **95** F4
Jermyn *U.S.A.* **115** E9
Jerome *U.S.A.* **108** E6
Jerramungup *Australia* **93** F2
Jersey *U.K.* **15** H5
Jersey City *U.S.A.* **115** F10
Jersey Shore *U.S.A.* **114** E7
Jerseyville *U.S.A.* **112** F8
Jerusalem *Israel/West Bank* **74** D4
Jervis B. *Australia* **95** F5
Jervis Inlet *Canada* **102** C4
Jerzu *Italy* **42** C2
Jesenice *Slovenia* **41** B11
Jeseník *Czech Rep.* **27** A10
Jesenké *Slovak Rep.* **27** C13
Jesi = Iesi *Italy* **41** E10
Jessnitz *Germany* **24** D8
Jessore *Bangla.* **67** H16
Jesup *U.S.A.* **117** F14
Jesús Carranza *Mexico* **119** D5
Jesús María *Argentina* **126** C3
Jetmore *U.S.A.* **112** F4
Jetpur *India* **68** J4
Jeumont *France* **19** B11
Jevnaker *Norway* **9** F14
Jewett *U.S.A.* **114** F3
Jewett City *U.S.A.* **115** E13
Jeyḥūnābād *Iran* **71** C6
Jeypore *India* **67** K13
Jeziorak, Jezioro *Poland* **30** E6
Jeziorany *Poland* **30** E7
Jeziorka → *Poland* **31** F8
Jha Jha *India* **69** G12
Jhaarkand = Jharkhand □
  India **69** H11
Jhabua *India* **68** H6
Jhajjar *India* **68** E7
Jhal *Pakistan* **68** E2
Jhal Jhao *Pakistan* **66** F4
Jhalawar *India* **68** G7
Jhalida *India* **69** H11
Jhalrapatan *India* **68** G7
Jhang Maghiana *Pakistan* **68** D5
Jhansi *India* **69** G8
Jhargram *India* **69** H12
Jharia *India* **69** H12
Jharkhand □ *India* **69** H11
Jharsuguda *India* **67** J14
Jhelum *Pakistan* **68** C5
Jhelum → *Pakistan* **68** D5
Jhilmilli *India* **69** H10
Jhudo *Pakistan* **68** G3
Jhunjhunu *India* **68** E6
Ji-Paraná *Brazil* **124** F6
Ji Xian *Hebei, China* **56** F8
Ji Xian *Henan, China* **56** G8
Ji Xian *Shanxi, China* **56** F6
Jia Xian *Henan, China* **56** H7
Jia Xian *Shaanxi, China* **56** E6
Jiading *China* **59** B13
Jiahe *China* **59** D9
Jiaji = Qionghai *China* **64** C8
Jialing Jiang → *China* **58** C6
Jiamusi *China* **60** B8
Ji'an *Jiangxi, China* **59** D10
Ji'an *Jilin, China* **57** D14
Jianchang *China* **57** D11
Jianchangying *China* **57** D10
Jianchuan *China* **58** D2

Jiande *China* **59** C12
Jiang'an *China* **58** C5
Jiangbei *China* **58** C6
Jiangcheng *China* **58** F3
Jiangchuan *China* **58** E4
Jiangdi *China* **58** D4
Jiangdu *China* **59** A12
Jiange *China* **58** A5
Jianghua *China* **59** E8
Jiangjin *China* **58** C6
Jiangkou *China* **58** D7
Jiangle *China* **59** D11
Jiangling *China* **59** B9
Jiangmen *China* **59** F9
Jiangning *China* **59** B12
Jiangshan *China* **59** C12
Jiangsu □ *China* **57** H11
Jiangxi □ *China* **59** D11
Jiangyan *China* **59** A13
Jiangyin *China* **59** B13
Jiangyong *China* **59** E8
Jiangyou *China* **58** B5
Jianhe *China* **58** D7
Jianli *China* **59** C9
Jianning *China* **59** D11
Jian'ou *China* **59** D12
Jianshi *China* **58** B7
Jianshui *China* **58** E4
Jianyang *Fujian, China* **59** D12
Jianyang *Sichuan, China* **58** B5
Jiao Xian = Jiaozhou *China* **57** F11
Jiaohe *Hebei, China* **56** E9
Jiaohe *Jilin, China* **57** C14
Jiaojiang *China* **59** C13
Jiaoling *China* **59** E11
Jiaozhou *China* **57** F11
Jiaozhou Wan *China* **57** F11
Jiaozuo *China* **56** G7
Jiashan *China* **59** B13
Jiawang *China* **57** G9
Jiaxiang *China* **56** G9
Jiaxing *China* **59** B13
Jiayi = Chiai *Taiwan* **59** F13
Jiayu *China* **59** C9
Jibiya *Nigeria* **83** C6
Jibou *Romania* **29** C8
Jibuti = Djibouti ■ *Africa* **81** E5
Jicarón, I. *Panama* **120** E3
Jičín *Czech Rep.* **26** A8
Jiddah *Si. Arabia* **75** C2
Jido *India* **67** E19
Jieshou *China* **56** H8
Jiexiu *China* **56** F6
Jieyang *China* **59** F11
Jigalong *Australia* **92** D3
Jigawa □ *Nigeria* **83** C6
Jigni *India* **69** G8
Jihlava *Czech Rep.* **26** B8
Jihlava → *Czech Rep.* **27** C9
Jihlavský □ *Czech Rep.* **26** B8
Jihočeský □ *Czech Rep.* **26** B7
Jihomoravský □ *Czech Rep.* **27** B9
Jijiga *Ethiopia* **75** F3
Jikamshi *Nigeria* **83** C6
Jikau *Sudan* **81** F3
Jilib *Somali Rep.* **75** G3
Jilin *China* **57** C14
Jilin □ *China* **57** C14
Jiloca → *Spain* **38** D3
Jilong = Chilung *Taiwan* **59** E13
Jim Thorpe *U.S.A.* **115** F9
Jima *Ethiopia* **81** F4
Jimbaran, Teluk *Indonesia* **63** K18
Jimbolia *Romania* **28** E5
Jimena de la Frontera *Spain* **37** J5
Jiménez *Mexico* **118** B4
Jimo *China* **57** F11
Jin Jiang → *China* **59** C10
Jin Xian = Jinzhou *Hebei,
  China* **56** E8
Jin Xian = Jinzhou *Liaoning,
  China* **57** E11
Jinan *China* **56** F9
Jinchang *China* **60** C5
Jincheng *China* **56** G7
Jinchuan *China* **58** B4
Jind *India* **68** E7
Jindabyne *Australia* **95** F4
Jindo *S. Korea* **57** G14
Jindřichův Hradec *Czech Rep.* **26** B8
Jing He → *China* **56** G5
Jing Shan *China* **59** B8
Jing Xian *China* **59** B12
Jing'an *China* **59** C10
Jingbian *China* **56** F5
Jingchuan *China* **56** G4
Jingde *China* **59** B12
Jingdezhen *China* **59** C11
Jingdong *China* **58** E3
Jinggangshan *China* **59** D10
Jinggu *China* **58** F3
Jinghai *China* **56** E9
Jinghong *China* **58** G3
Jingjiang *China* **59** A13
Jingle *China* **56** E6
Jingmen *China* **59** B9
Jingpo Hu *China* **57** C15
Jingshan *China* **59** B9

Jingtai *China* **56** F3
Jingxi *China* **58** F6
Jingxing *China* **56** E8
Jingyang *China* **56** G5
Jingyu *China* **57** C14
Jingyuan *China* **56** F3
Jingzhou *China* **58** D7
Jingziguan *China* **56** H6
Jinhua *China* **59** C12
Jining *Nei Monggol Zizhiqu,
  China* **56** D7
Jining *Shandong, China* **56** G9
Jinja *Uganda* **86** B3
Jinjang *Malaysia* **65** L3
Jinji *China* **56** F4
Jinjiang *Fujian, China* **59** E12
Jinjiang *Yunnan, China* **58** D3
Jinjini *Ghana* **82** D4
Jinju *S. Korea* **57** G15
Jinkou *China* **59** B10
Jinkouhe *China* **58** C4
Jinmen Dao *China* **59** E12
Jinning *China* **58** E4
Jinotega *Nic.* **120** D2
Jinotepe *Nic.* **120** D2
Jinping *Guizhou, China* **58** D7
Jinping *Yunnan, China* **58** F4
Jinsha *China* **58** D6
Jinsha Jiang → *China* **58** C5
Jinshan *China* **59** B13
Jinshi *China* **59** C8
Jintan *China* **59** B12
Jinxi *Jiangxi, China* **59** D11
Jinxi *Liaoning, China* **57** D11
Jinxian *China* **59** C11
Jinxiang *China* **56** G9
Jinyang *China* **58** D4
Jinyun *China* **59** C13
Jinzhai *China* **59** B10
Jinzhou *Hebei, China* **56** E8
Jinzhou *Liaoning, China* **57** D11
Jiparaná → *Brazil* **124** E6
Jipijapa *Ecuador* **124** D2
Jiquilpan *Mexico* **118** D4
Jirisan *S. Korea* **57** G14
Jishan *China* **56** G6
Jishou *China* **58** C7
Jishui *China* **59** D10
Jisr ash Shughūr *Syria* **72** E7
Jitarning *Australia* **93** F2
Jitra *Malaysia* **65** J3
Jiu → *Romania* **29** G8
Jiudengkou *China* **56** E4
Jiujiang *Guangdong, China* **59** F9
Jiujiang *Jiangxi, China* **59** C10
Jiuling Shan *China* **59** C10
Jiulong = Kowloon *China* **59** F10
Jiulong *China* **58** C3
Jiutai *China* **57** B13
Jiuxincheng *China* **56** E8
Jiuyuhang *China* **59** B12
Jiwani *Pakistan* **66** G2
Jixi *Anhui, China* **59** B12
Jixi *Heilongjiang, China* **57** B16
Jiyang *China* **57** F9
Jiyuan *China* **56** G7
Jīzān *Si. Arabia* **75** D3
Jize *China* **56** F8
Jizera → *Czech Rep.* **26** A7
Jizl, Wādī al → *Si. Arabia* **70** E3
Jizō-Zaki *Japan* **55** G6
Jizzax *Uzbekistan* **52** E7
Joaçaba *Brazil* **127** B5
Joal Fadiout *Senegal* **82** C1
João Pessoa *Brazil* **125** E12
Joaquín V. González
  Argentina **126** B3
Jobat *India* **68** H6
Jobourg, Nez de *France* **18** C5
Jódar *Spain* **37** H7
Jodhpur *India* **68** F5
Jodiya *India* **68** H4
Joensuu *Finland* **8** E23
Joeuf *France* **19** C12
Jofane *Mozam.* **89** C5
Jogbani *India* **69** F12
Jõgeva *Estonia* **32** C4
Jogjakarta = Yogyakarta
  Indonesia **63** G14
Johannesburg *S. Africa* **89** D4
Johannesburg *U.S.A.* **111** K9
Johansfors *Sweden* **11** H9
Johilla → *India* **69** H9
John Crow Mts. *Jamaica* **120** a
John Day *U.S.A.* **108** D4
John Day → *U.S.A.* **108** D3
John Day Fossil Beds △
  U.S.A. **108** D4
John D'or Prairie *Canada* **102** B5
John H. Kerr Res. *U.S.A.* **117** G15
John o' Groats *U.K.* **13** C5
Johnnie *U.S.A.* **111** J10
John's Ra. *Australia* **94** C1
Johnson *U.S.A.* **113** B12
Johnson City *Kans., U.S.A.* **112** G3
Johnson City *N.Y., U.S.A.* **115** D9

Johnson City *Tenn., U.S.A.* **117** C13
Johnson City *Tex., U.S.A.* **116** F5
Johnsonburg *U.S.A.* **114** E6
Johnsondale *U.S.A.* **111** K8
Johnsons Crossing *Canada* **102** A2
Johnston, L. *Australia* **93** F3
Johnston Falls =
  Mambilima Falls *Zambia* **87** E2
Johnston I. *Pac. Oc.* **97** F11
Johnstone Str. *Canada* **102** C3
Johnstown *Ireland* **12** D4
Johnstown *N.Y., U.S.A.* **115** C10
Johnstown *Ohio, U.S.A.* **114** F2
Johnstown *Pa., U.S.A.* **114** F6
Johor, Selat *Asia* **65** d
Johor Bahru *Malaysia* **65** d
Jōhvi *Estonia* **32** C4
Joigny *France* **19** E10
Joinville *Brazil* **127** B6
Joinville *France* **19** D12
Joinville I. *Antarctica* **5** C18
Jojutla *Mexico* **119** D5
Jokkmokk *Sweden* **8** C18
Jökulsá á Bru → *Iceland* **8** D6
Jökulsá á Fjöllum → *Iceland* **8** C5
Jolfā *Āzarbājān-e Sharqī, Iran* **73** C11
Jolfā *Eşfahan, Iran* **71** C6
Joliet *U.S.A.* **112** E9
Joliette *Canada* **104** C5
Jolo *Phil.* **61** J4
Jolon *U.S.A.* **110** K5
Jomalig I. *Phil.* **61** D5
Jombang *Indonesia* **63** G15
Jomda *China* **58** B2
Jonava *Lithuania* **32** E3
Jones Sound *Canada* **101** B11
Jonesboro *Ark., U.S.A.* **117** D9
Jonesboro *La., U.S.A.* **116** E8
Jong → *S. Leone* **82** D2
Jonglei *Sudan* **81** F3
Jonglei □ *Sudan* **81** F3
Joniškis *Lithuania* **30** B10
Jönköping *Sweden* **11** G8
Jönköpings län □ *Sweden* **11** G8
Jonquière *Canada* **105** C5
Jonsered *Sweden* **11** G6
Jonzac *France* **20** C3
Joplin *U.S.A.* **112** G6
Jordan *Mont., U.S.A.* **108** C10
Jordan *N.Y., U.S.A.* **115** C8
Jordan ■ *Asia* **74** E5
Jordan → *Asia* **74** D4
Jordan Valley *U.S.A.* **108** E5
Jordanów *Poland* **31** J6
Jorhat *India* **67** F19
Jori → *Norway* **10** B3
Jorm *Afghan.* **66** B7
Jörn *Sweden* **8** D19
Jorong *Indonesia* **62** E4
Jørpeland *Norway* **9** G12
Jorquera → *Chile* **126** B2
Jos *Nigeria* **83** D6
Jos Plateau *Nigeria* **83** D6
Jošanička Banja *Serbia* **44** C4
José Batlle y Ordóñez
  Uruguay **127** C4
José de San Martín
  Argentina **128** D2
Joseni *Romania* **29** D10
Joseph, L. *Canada* **114** A5
Joseph Bonaparte G.
  Australia **92** B4
Joseph L. *Canada* **105** B6
Joshinath *India* **69** D8
Joshinetsu-Kōgen △ *Japan* **55** F9
Joshua Tree *U.S.A.* **111** L10
Joshua Tree △ *U.S.A.* **111** M10
Josselin *France* **18** E4
Jost Van Dyke I. *Br. Virgin Is.* **121** e
Jostedalsbreen *Norway* **8** F12
Jostedalsbreen *Norway* **8** F12
Jotunheimen *Norway* **8** F13
Joubertberge *Namibia* **88** B1
Joué-lès-Tours *France* **18** E7
Jourdanton *U.S.A.* **116** G5
Joutseno *Finland* **32** B5
Jovellanos *Cuba* **120** B3
Jowkār *Iran* **73** E13
Joyeuse *France* **21** D8
Józefów *Lubelskie, Poland* **31** H10
Józefów *Mazowieckie, Poland* **31** F8
Ju Xian *China* **59** B12
Juan Aldama *Mexico* **118** C4
Juan Bautista Alberdi
  Argentina **126** C3
Juan de Fuca, Str of.
  N. Amer. **110** B3
Juán de Nova *Ind. Oc.* **89** B7
Juan Fernández, Arch. de
  Pac. Oc. **122** G2
Juan José Castelli *Argentina* **126** B3
Juan L. Lacaze *Uruguay* **126** C4
Juankoski *Finland* **8** E23
Juárez *Mexico* **111** N11
Juárez *Coahuila, Mexico* **118** B4
Juárez, Sierra de *Mexico* **118** A1
Juàzeiro *Brazil* **125** E10
Juàzeiro do Norte *Brazil* **125** E11
Jûbâ *Sudan* **81** G3
Juba → *Somali Rep.* **75** G3
Jubany *Antarctica* **5** C18
Jubany → *China* **56** G9
Jubayl *Lebanon* **74** A4

Jubbah *Si. Arabia* **70** D4
Jubbal *India* **68** D7
Jubbulpore = Jabalpur *India* **69** H8
Jübek *Germany* **24** A5
Jubga *Russia* **35** H4
Jubilee L. *Australia* **93** E4
Juby, C. *Morocco* **78** C3
Júcar = Xúquer → *Spain* **39** F4
Júcaro *Cuba* **120** B4
Juchitán de Zaragoza
  Mexico **119** D5
Judea = Har Yehuda *Israel* **74** D3
Judenburg *Austria* **26** D7
Judith → *U.S.A.* **108** C9
Judith, Pt. *U.S.A.* **115** E13
Judith Gap *U.S.A.* **108** C9
Juelsminde *Denmark* **11** J4
Jugoslavia = Serbia ■
  Europe **44** C4
Juigalpa *Nic.* **120** D2
Juillac *France* **20** C5
Juist *Germany* **24** B2
Juiz de Fora *Brazil* **127** A7
Jujuy □ *Argentina* **126** A2
Julesburg *U.S.A.* **108** F12
Juli *Peru* **124** G5
Julia Cr. → *Australia* **94** C3
Julia Creek *Australia* **94** C3
Juliaca *Peru* **124** G4
Julian *U.S.A.* **111** M10
Julian, L. *Canada* **104** B4
Julian Alps = Julijske Alpe
  Slovenia **41** B11
Julianatop *Suriname* **125** C7
Julianehåb = Qaqortoq
  Greenland **4** C5
Jülich *Germany* **24** E2
Julijske Alpe *Slovenia* **41** B11
Julimes *Mexico* **118** B3
Jullundur *India* **68** D6
Julu *China* **56** F8
Jumbo *Zimbabwe* **87** F3
Jumbo Pk. *U.S.A.* **111** J12
Jumentos Cays *Bahamas* **120** B4
Jumilla *Spain* **39** G3
Jumla *Nepal* **69** E10
Jumna = Yamuna → *India* **69** G9
Jumunjin *S. Korea* **57** F15
Junagadh *India* **68** J4
Junction *Tex., U.S.A.* **116** F5
Junction *Utah, U.S.A.* **109** G7
Junction B. *Australia* **94** A1
Junction City *Kans., U.S.A.* **112** F5
Junction City *Oreg., U.S.A.* **108** D2
Junction Pt. *Australia* **94** A1
Jundah *Australia* **94** C3
Jundiaí *Brazil* **127** A6
Juneau *U.S.A.* **102** B2
Junee *Australia* **95** E4
Jungfrau *Switz.* **25** J3
Junggar Pendi *China* **60** B3
Jungshahi *Pakistan* **68** G2
Juniata → *U.S.A.* **114** F7
Junín *Argentina* **126** C3
Junín de los Andes
  Argentina **128** D2
Jūniyah *Lebanon* **74** B4
Junlian *China* **58** C5
Juntas *Chile* **126** B2
Juntura *U.S.A.* **108** E4
Jur, Nahr el → *Sudan* **81** F2
Jura = Jura, Mts. du *Europe* **19** F13
Jura = Schwäbische Alb
  Germany **25** G5
Jura *U.K.* **13** F3
Jura □ *France* **19** F12
Jura □ *Switz.* **25** H3
Jūra → *Lithuania* **30** C9
Jura, Mts. du *Europe* **19** F13
Jura, Sd. of *U.K.* **13** F3
Jurbarkas *Lithuania* **30** C9
Jurien Bay *Australia* **93** F2
Jurilovca *Romania* **29** F13
Jūrmala *Latvia* **30** B10
Jurong *China* **59** B12
Jurong *Singapore* **65** d
Juruá → *Brazil* **124** D5
Juruena *Brazil* **124** F7
Juruena → *Brazil* **124** E7
Juruti *Brazil* **125** D7
Jussey *France* **19** E12
Justo Daract *Argentina* **126** C2
Jutaí → *Brazil* **124** D5
Jüterbog *Germany* **24** D9
Juticalpa *Honduras* **120** D2
Jutland = Jylland *Denmark* **11** H3
Juuka *Finland* **8** E23
Juventud, I. de la *Cuba* **120** B3
Juvigny-sous-Andaine
  France **18** D6
Jüy Zar *Iran* **73** F12
Juye *China* **56** G9
Juzennecourt *France* **19** D11
Jvari *Georgia* **35** J6
Jwaneng *Botswana* **85** J4
Jyderup *Denmark* **11** J5
Jylland *Denmark* **11** H3
Jyväskylä *Finland* **32** A3

K

K2 *Pakistan* **69** B7
Ka → *Nigeria* **83** C5
Kaakha = Kaka
  Turkmenistan **71** B8
Kaap Plateau *S. Africa* **88** D3
Kaapkruis *Namibia* **88** C1
Kaapstad = Cape Town
  S. Africa **88** E2
Kaba *Guinea* **82** C2
Kabaena *Indonesia* **63** F6
Kabala *S. Leone* **82** D2
Kabale *Uganda* **86** C3
Kabalo *Dem. Rep. of the Congo* **86** D2
Kabambare
  Dem. Rep. of the Congo **86** C2
Kabango
  Dem. Rep. of the Congo **87** D2
Kabanjahe *Indonesia* **62** D1
Kabankalan *Phil.* **61** G5
Kabara *Fiji* **91** a
Kabara *Mali* **82** B4
Kabardinka *Russia* **33** K10
Kabardino-Balkar
  Republic = Kabardino-
  Balkaria □ *Russia* **35** J6
Kabardino-Balkaria □
  Russia **35** J6
Kabarega Falls =
  Murchison Falls *Uganda* **86** B3
Kabarnet *Kenya* **86** B4
Kabasalan *Phil.* **61** H5
Kabat *Indonesia* **63** J17
Kabba *Nigeria* **83** D6
Kabi *Niger* **83** C7
Kabin Buri *Thailand* **64** F3
Kabinakagami L. *Canada* **104** C3
Kabinda
  Dem. Rep. of the Congo **84** F4
Kabna *Sudan* **80** D3
Kabompo *Zambia* **87** E1
Kabompo → *Zambia* **85** G4
Kabondo
  Dem. Rep. of the Congo **87** D2
Kabongo
  Dem. Rep. of the Congo **86** D2
Kabot *Guinea* **82** C2
Kabou *Togo* **83** D5
Kabr *Sudan* **81** E2
Kabrît, G. el *Egypt* **74** F2
Kabrousse *Senegal* **82** C1
Kabūd Gonbad *Iran* **71** B8
Kabudar Ahang *Iran* **73** E13
Kabugao *Phil.* **61** B4
Kābul *Afghan.* **68** B3
Kābul □ *Afghan.* **66** B6
Kābul → *Pakistan* **68** C5
Kabunga
  Dem. Rep. of the Congo **86** C2
Kaburuang *Indonesia* **63** D7
Kabushiya *Sudan* **81** D3
Kabwe *Zambia* **87** E2
Kačanik *Serbia* **44** D5
Kačerginė *Lithuania* **30** D10
Kachchh, Gulf of *India* **68** H3
Kachchh, Rann of *India* **68** H4
Kachchhidhana *India* **69** J8
Kachebera *Zambia* **87** E3
Kachia *Nigeria* **83** D6
Kachikau *Botswana* **88** B3
Kachin □ *Burma* **58** D1
Kachira, L. *Uganda* **86** C3
Kachīry *Kazakhstan* **52** D8
Kachisi *Ethiopia* **81** F4
Kachnara *India* **68** H6
Kachot *Cambodia* **65** G4
Kaçkar *Turkey* **73** B9
Kadam, Mt. *Uganda* **86** B3
Kadan *Czech Rep.* **26** A6
Kadan Kyun *Burma* **64** F2
Kadanai → *Afghan.* **68** D1
Kadarkút *Hungary* **28** D2
Kadavu *Fiji* **91** a
Kadavu Passage *Fiji* **91** a
Kade *Ghana* **83** D4
Kadhimain = Al
  Kāzimīyah *Iraq* **73** F11
Kadi *India* **68** H5
Kadina *Australia* **95** E2
Kadınhanı *Turkey* **72** C5
Kadiolo *Mali* **82** C4
Kadipur *India* **69** F10
Kadirli *Turkey* **72** D7
Kadiyevka = Stakhanov
  Ukraine **33** H10
Kadodo *Sudan* **81** E2
Kadoka *U.S.A.* **112** D3
Kadom *Russia* **34** C6
Kadoma *Zimbabwe* **87** F2
Kâdugli *Sudan* **81** E2
Kaduna *Nigeria* **83** C6
Kaduna □ *Nigeria* **83** C6
Kaduna → *Nigeria* **83** D6
Kaduy *Russia* **32** C9
Kaédi *Mauritania* **82** B2
Kaélé *Cameroon* **83** C7
Kaeng Khoï *Thailand* **64** E3

Kaeng Krachan △ *Thailand* 64 F2
Kaeng Tana △ *Thailand* 64 E5
Käf *Si. Arabia* 70 D3
Kafan = Kapan *Armenia* 73 C12
Kafanchan *Nigeria* 83 D6
Kafareti *Nigeria* 83 C7
Kaffrine *Senegal* 82 C1
Kafin *Nigeria* 83 D6
Kafin Madaki *Nigeria* 83 C6
Kafinda *Zambia* 87 E3
Kafr el Battikh *Egypt* 80 H7
Kafr el Dauwâr *Egypt* 80 H7
Kafr el Sheikh *Egypt* 80 H7
Kafue *Zambia* 87 F2
Kafue → *Zambia* 85 H5
Kafue △ *Zambia* 87 F2
Kafue Flats *Zambia* 87 F2
Kafulwe *Zambia* 87 D2
Kaga *Afghan.* 68 B4
Kaga Bandoro *C.A.R.* 84 C3
Kagarko *Nigeria* 83 D6
Kagawa □ *Japan* 55 G7
Kagera □ *Tanzania* 86 C3
Kagera → *Uganda* 86 C3
Kağızman *Turkey* 73 B10
Kagmar *Sudan* 81 E3
Kagoshima *Japan* 55 J5
Kagoshima □ *Japan* 55 J5
Kagul = Cahul *Moldova* 29 E13
Kahak *Iran* 71 B6
Kahama *Tanzania* 86 C3
Kahan *Pakistan* 68 E3
Kahang *Malaysia* 65 L4
Kahayan → *Indonesia* 62 E4
Kahe *Tanzania* 86 C4
Kahemba
  Dem. Rep. of the Congo 84 F3
Kahnūj *Iran* 71 E8
Kahoka *U.S.A.* 112 F9
Kaho'olawe *U.S.A.* 106 b
Kahramanmaraş *Turkey* 72 D7
Kahramanmaraş □ *Turkey* 72 D7
Kâhta *Turkey* 73 D8
Kahul, Ozero *Ukraine* 29 E13
Kahului *U.S.A.* 106 b
Kahurangi △ *N.Z.* 91 D4
Kahuta *Pakistan* 68 C5
Kahuzi-Biega △
  Dem. Rep. of the Congo 86 C2
Kai, Kepulauan *Indonesia* 63 F8
Kai Besar *Indonesia* 63 F8
Kai Is. = Kai, Kepulauan
  Indonesia 63 F8
Kai Kecil *Indonesia* 63 F8
Kai Xian *China* 58 B7
Kaiama *Nigeria* 83 D5
Kaiapoi *N.Z.* 91 E4
Kaieteur Falls *Guyana* 124 B7
Kaifeng *China* 56 G8
Kaihua *China* 59 C12
Kaijiang *China* 58 B6
Kaikohe *N.Z.* 91 A4
Kaikoura *N.Z.* 91 E4
Kailahun *S. Leone* 82 D2
Kailash = Kangrinboqe
  Feng *China* 69 D9
Kaili *China* 58 D6
Kailu *China* 57 C11
Kailua *U.S.A.* 106 b
Kaimaktsalan Oros =
  Voras Oros *Greece* 44 F5
Kaimana *Indonesia* 63 E8
Kaimanawa Mts. *N.Z.* 91 C5
Kaimganj *India* 69 F8
Kaimur Hills *India* 69 G10
Kainab → *Namibia* 88 D2
Kainji Dam *Nigeria* 83 D5
Kainji Lake △ *Nigeria* 83 C5
Kainji Res. *Nigeria* 83 C5
Kainuu *Finland* 8 D23
Kaipara Harbour *N.Z.* 91 B5
Kaiping *China* 59 F9
Kaipokok B. *Canada* 105 B8
Kaira *India* 68 H5
Kairana *India* 68 E7
Kaironi *Indonesia* 63 E8
Kairouan *Tunisia* 79 A8
Kaiserslautern *Germany* 25 F3
Kaiserstuhl *Germany* 25 G3
Kaitaia *N.Z.* 91 A4
Kaitangata *N.Z.* 91 G2
Kaithal *India* 68 E7
Kaitu → *Pakistan* 68 C4
Kaiyang *China* 58 D6
Kaiyuan *Liaoning, China* 57 C13
Kaiyuan *Yunnan, China* 58 F4
Kajaani *Finland* 8 D22
Kajabbi *Australia* 94 C3
Kajana = Kajaani *Finland* 8 D22
Kajang *Malaysia* 65 L3
Kajaran *Armenia* 73 C12
Kajiado *Kenya* 86 C4
Kajo Kaji *Sudan* 81 G3
Kajuru *Nigeria* 83 C6
Kaka *Sudan* 81 E3
Kaka *Turkmenistan* 71 B8
Kakabeka Falls *Canada* 104 C2
Kakadu △ *Australia* 92 B5

Kakamas *S. Africa* 88 D3
Kakamega *Kenya* 86 B3
Kakanj *Bos.-H.* 28 F3
Kakanui Mts. *N.Z.* 91 F3
Kakata *Liberia* 82 D2
Kakdwip *India* 69 J13
Kake *Japan* 55 G6
Kake *U.S.A.* 102 B2
Kakegawa *Japan* 55 G9
Kakeroma-Jima *Japan* 55 K4
Kākhak *Iran* 71 C8
Kakhib *Russia* 35 J8
Kakhovka *Ukraine* 33 J7
Kakhovske Vdskh. *Ukraine* 33 J7
Kakinada *India* 67 L13
Kakisa *U.S.A.* 113 C11
Kakisa → *Canada* 102 A5
Kakisa L. *Canada* 102 A5
Kakogawa *Japan* 55 G7
Kakum △ *Ghana* 83 D4
Kakuma *Kenya* 86 B3
Kakwa → *Canada* 102 C5
Kāl Gūsheh *Iran* 71 D8
Kal Sefīd *Iran* 73 E12
Kala → *Nigeria* 83 C7
Kalaallit Nunaat =
  Greenland ☑ *N. Amer.* 99 C15
Kalabagh *Pakistan* 68 C4
Kalabahi *Indonesia* 63 F6
Kalabana *Mali* 82 C3
Kalach *Russia* 34 E5
Kalach na Donu *Russia* 35 F6
Kaladan → *Burma* 67 J18
Kaladar *Canada* 114 B7
Kalahari *Africa* 88 C3
Kalahari Gemsbok △
  S. Africa 88 D3
Kalajoki *Finland* 8 D21
Kalakamati *Botswana* 89 C4
Kalakan *Russia* 53 D12
K'alak'unlun Shank'ou =
  Karakoram Pass *Asia* 69 B7
Kalam *Pakistan* 69 B5
Kalama *Dem. Rep. of the Congo* 86 C2
Kalama *U.S.A.* 110 E4
Kalamaria *Greece* 44 F6
Kalamata *Greece* 46 D4
Kalamazoo *U.S.A.* 113 D11
Kalamazoo → *U.S.A.* 112 D10
Kalambaka *Greece* 46 B3
Kalambo Falls *Tanzania* 87 D3
Kalamos *Attiki, Greece* 46 C5
Kalamos *Lefkada, Greece* 46 C2
Kalan *Turkey* 70 B3
Kalankalan *Guinea* 82 C3
Kalannie *Australia* 93 F2
Kalāntarī *Iran* 71 C7
Kalao *Indonesia* 63 F6
Kalaotoa *Indonesia* 63 F6
Kälarne *Sweden* 10 B10
Kalasin *Thailand* 64 D4
Kālat *Iran* 71 B8
Kalat *Pakistan* 66 E5
Kalāteh *Iran* 71 B7
Kalāteh-ye Ganj *Iran* 71 E8
Kalathos *Greece* 47 E10
Kalavrita *Greece* 46 C4
Kalbā *U.A.E.* 71 E7
Kalbarri *Australia* 93 E1
Kalbarri △ *Australia* 93 E1
Kalce *Slovenia* 22 F8
Kalecik *Turkey* 72 B5
Kalegauk Kyun *Burma* 64 E1
Kalehe *Dem. Rep. of the Congo* 86 C2
Kalema *Tanzania* 86 C3
Kalemie
  Dem. Rep. of the Congo 86 D2
Kalety *Poland* 31 H5
Kalewa *Burma* 67 H19
Kaleybar *Iran* 73 C12
Kalgoorlie-Boulder *Australia* 93 F3
Kali → *India* 69 F8
Kali Sindh → *India* 68 G6
Kaliakra, Nos *Bulgaria* 45 C12
Kalianda *Indonesia* 62 F3
Kalibo *Phil.* 61 F5
Kalima *Dem. Rep. of the Congo* 86 C2
Kalimantan *Indonesia* 62 E4
Kalimantan Barat □
  Indonesia 62 E4
Kalimantan Selatan □
  Indonesia 62 E5
Kalimantan Tengah □
  Indonesia 62 E4
Kalimantan Timur □
  Indonesia 62 D5
Kálimnos *Greece* 47 D8
Kalimpong *India* 69 F13
Kaliningrad *Russia* 30 D7
Kaliningrad ✈ (KGD) *Russia* 30 D7
Kalininsk *Russia* 34 E7
Kalinkavichy *Belarus* 23 B15
Kalinkovichi =
  Kalinkavichy *Belarus* 23 B15
Kalinovik *Bos.-H.* 44 C2
Kalipetrovo *Bulgaria* 45 B11

Kalirachi *Greece* 45 F8
Kaliro *Uganda* 86 B3
Kalispell *U.S.A.* 108 B6
Kalisz *Poland* 31 G5
Kalisz Pomorski *Poland* 31 E2
Kalithea *Greece* 46 D5
Kaliua *Tanzania* 86 D3
Kalivia Thorikou *Greece* 46 D5
Kalix = Kalixälven →
  Sweden 8 D20
Kalix *Sweden* 8 D20
Kalixälven → *Sweden* 8 D20
Kalka *India* 68 D7
Kalkan *Turkey* 47 E11
Kalkarindji *Australia* 92 C5
Kalkaska *U.S.A.* 113 C11
Kalkfeld *Namibia* 88 C2
Kalkfontein *Botswana* 88 C3
Kalkrand *Namibia* 88 C2
Kallavesi *Finland* 8 E22
Källby *Sweden* 11 F7
Kållered *Sweden* 11 G6
Kallimasia *Greece* 47 C8
Kallinge *Sweden* 11 H9
Kallmet *Albania* 44 E3
Kallsjön *Sweden* 8 E15
Kalmalo *Nigeria* 83 C6
Kalmar *Sweden* 11 H10
Kalmar län □ *Sweden* 11 G10
Kalmar sund *Sweden* 11 H10
Kalmyk Republic =
  Kalmykia □ *Russia* 35 G8
Kalmykia □ *Russia* 35 G8
Kalna *India* 69 H13
Kalnai *India* 69 H10
Kalo Nero *Greece* 46 D3
Kalocsa *Hungary* 28 D4
Kalofer *Bulgaria* 45 D8
Kalokhorio *Cyprus* 49 E12
Kaloko *Dem. Rep. of the Congo* 86 D2
Kalol *Gujarat, India* 68 H5
Kalol *Gujarat, India* 68 H5
Kalolimnos *Greece* 47 D9
Kalomo *Zambia* 87 F2
Kaloni *Greece* 47 B8
Kaloni, Kolpos *Greece* 47 B8
Kalpi *India* 69 F8
Kaltern = Caldaro *Italy* 41 B8
Kaltukatjara *Australia* 93 D4
Kaltungo *Nigeria* 83 D7
Kalu *Pakistan* 68 G2
Kaluga *Russia* 32 E9
Kaluga □ *Russia* 32 E8
Kalulushi *Zambia* 87 E2
Kalumburu *Australia* 92 B4
Kalundborg *Denmark* 11 J5
Kalush *Ukraine* 23 D13
Kałuszyn *Poland* 31 F8
Kalutara *Sri Lanka* 66 R12
Kalvarija *Lithuania* 30 D10
Kalyan *India* 66 K8
Kalyazin *Russia* 32 D9
Kam Albania* 44 D4
Kam → *Nigeria* 83 D7
Kama *Dem. Rep. of the Congo* 86 C2
Kama → *Russia* 6 D16
Kamachumu *Tanzania* 86 C3
Kamaishi *Japan* 54 E10
Kamalia *Pakistan* 68 D5
Kaman *India* 68 F6
Kaman *Turkey* 72 C5
Kamanjab *Namibia* 88 B2
Kamapanda *Zambia* 87 E1
Kamarān *Yemen* 75 D3
Kamativi *Zimbabwe* 88 B4
Kamba *Nigeria* 83 C5
Kambalda West *Australia* 93 F3
Kambar *Pakistan* 68 F3
Kambia *S. Leone* 82 D2
Kambolé *Togo* 83 D5
Kambolé *Zambia* 87 D3
Kambos *Cyprus* 49 D11
Kambove
  Dem. Rep. of the Congo 87 E2
Kamchatka, Poluostrov
  Russia 53 D17
Kamchatka Pen. =
  Kamchatka, Poluostrov
  Russia 53 D17
Kamchiya → *Bulgaria* 45 C11
Kame Ruins *Zimbabwe* 87 G2
Kamen *Russia* 52 D8
Kamen-Rybolov *Russia* 54 B6
Kamenica *Serbia* 44 C6
Kamenica *Serbia* 44 B3
Kamenice nad Lipou
  Czech Rep. 26 B8
Kamenjak, Rt *Croatia* 41 D10
Kamenka = Kaminka
  Ukraine 33 H7
Kamenka *Kazakhstan* 34 E10
Kamenka *Penza, Russia* 34 D6
Kamenka *Voronezh, Russia* 33 G10
Kamenka Bugskaya =
  Kamyanka-Buzka
  Ukraine 23 C13

Kamenka Dneprovskaya
  = Kamyanka-
  Dniprovska *Ukraine* 33 J8
Kamennomostskiy *Russia* 35 H5
Kameno *Bulgaria* 45 D11
Kamenolomni *Russia* 35 G5
Kamensk-Shakhtinskiy
  Russia 35 F5
Kamensk Uralskiy *Russia* 52 D7
Kamenskiy *Russia* 34 E7
Kamenskoye *Russia* 53 C17
Kamenyak *Bulgaria* 45 C10
Kamenz *Germany* 24 D10
Kameoka *Japan* 55 G7
Kamet *India* 69 D8
Kamiah *U.S.A.* 108 B5
Kamień Krajeński *Poland* 30 E4
Kamień Pomorski *Poland* 30 E1
Kamienna → *Poland* 31 G8
Kamienna Góra *Poland* 31 H3
Kamieńsk *Poland* 31 G6
Kamieskroon *S. Africa* 88 E2
Kamilukuak L. *Canada* 103 A8
Kamin-Kashyrskyy *Ukraine*
  23 C13
Kamina
  Dem. Rep. of the Congo 87 D2
Kaminak L. *Canada* 103 A10
Kaministiquia *Canada* 104 C1
Kaminka *Ukraine* 33 H7
Kaminoyama *Japan* 54 E10
Kamiros *Greece* 49 C9
Kamituga
  Dem. Rep. of the Congo 86 C2
Kamla → *India* 69 G12
Kamloops *Canada* 102 C4
Kamnik *Slovenia* 41 B11
Kamo *Armenia* 35 K7
Kamo *Japan* 54 F9
Kamoke *Pakistan* 68 C6
Kampala *Uganda* 86 B3
Kampar *Malaysia* 65 K3
Kampar → *Indonesia* 62 D2
Kampen *Neths.* 17 B5
Kampene
  Dem. Rep. of the Congo 84 E5
Kamphaeng Phet *Thailand* 64 D2
Kampinoski △ *Poland* 31 F7
Kampolombo, L. *Zambia* 87 E2
Kampong Chhnang
  Cambodia 65 F5
Kampong Pengerang
  Malaysia 65 d
Kampong Punggai *Malaysia* 65 d
Kampong Saom *Cambodia* 65 G4
Kampong Saom, Chaak
  Cambodia 65 G4
Kampong Tanjong
  Langsat *Malaysia* 65 d
Kampong Telok Ramunia
  Malaysia 65 d
Kampot *Cambodia* 65 G5
Kampti *Burkina Faso* 82 C4
Kampuchea =
  Cambodia ■ *Asia* 64 F5
Kampung Air Putih
  Malaysia 65 K4
Kampung Jerangau
  Malaysia 65 K4
Kampung Raja *Malaysia* 65 K4
Kampungbaru = Tolitoli
  Indonesia 63 D6
Kamrau, Teluk *Indonesia* 63 E8
Kamsack *Canada* 103 C8
Kamsai *Guinea* 82 C2
Kamskoye Ustye *Russia* 34 C9
Kamuchawie L. *Canada* 103 B8
Kamuela *U.S.A.* 106 b
Kamui-Misaki *Japan* 54 C10
Kamyanets-Podilskyy
  Ukraine 29 B11
Kamyanka-Buzka *Ukraine* 23 C13
Kamyanka-Dniprovska
  Ukraine 33 J8
Kamyanyets *Belarus* 31 F10
Kamyanyuki *Belarus* 31 F10
Kāmyārān *Iran* 73 E12
Kamyshin *Russia* 34 E7
Kamyzyak *Russia* 35 G9
Kan *Sudan* 81 F3
Kanaaupscow *Canada* 101 D12
Kanaaupscow → *Canada* 104 B4
Kanab *U.S.A.* 109 H7
Kanab Cr. → *U.S.A.* 109 H7
Kanacea *Lau Group, Fiji* 91 a
Kanacea *Taveuni, Fiji* 91 a
Kanagi *Japan* 54 D10
Kanairiktok → *Canada* 105 A7
Kanalia *Greece* 46 B4
Kananga
  Dem. Rep. of the Congo 84 F4
Kanash *Russia* 34 C8
Kanaskat *U.S.A.* 110 C5
Kanastraíon, Ákra =
  Paliouri, Akra *Greece* 44 G7
Kanawha → *U.S.A.* 113 F12
Kanazawa *Japan* 55 F8
Kanchanaburi *Thailand* 64 E2

Kanchenjunga *Nepal* 69 F13
Kanchipuram *India* 66 N11
Kańczuga *Poland* 31 J9
Kandaghat *India* 68 D7
Kandahār *Afghan.* 66 D4
Kandahār □ *Afghan.* 66 D4
Kandalaksha *Russia* 8 C25
Kandangan *Indonesia* 62 E5
Kandanghaur *Indonesia* 63 G13
Kandanos *Greece* 49 D5
Kandava *Latvia* 30 A9
Kandavu = Kadavu *Fiji* 91 a
Kandavu Passage =
  Kadavu Passage *Fiji* 91 a
Kandhkot *Pakistan* 68 E3
Kandhla *India* 68 E7
Kandi *Benin* 83 C5
Kandi *India* 69 H13
Kandiaro *Pakistan* 68 F3
Kandila *Greece* 46 D4
Kandıra *Turkey* 72 B4
Kandla *India* 68 H4
Kandos *Australia* 95 E4
Kandreho *Madag.* 89 B8
Kandy *Sri Lanka* 66 R12
Kane *U.S.A.* 114 E6
Kane Basin *Greenland* 98 B12
Käne'ohe *U.S.A.* 106 b
Kanevskaya *Russia* 35 G4
Kanfanar *Croatia* 41 C10
Kang *Botswana* 88 C3
Kang Krung △ *Thailand* 65 H2
Kangaba *Mali* 82 C3
Kangal *Turkey* 72 C7
Kangān *Fārs, Iran* 71 E7
Kangān *Hormozgān, Iran* 71 E8
Kangar *Malaysia* 65 J3
Kangaré *Mali* 82 C3
Kangaroo I. *Australia* 95 F2
Kangaroo Mts. *Australia* 94 C3
Kangasala *Finland* 32 B3
Kangāvar *Iran* 73 E12
Kangding *China* 58 B3
Kangdong *N. Korea* 57 E14
Kangean, Kepulauan
  Indonesia 62 F5
Kangean Is. = Kangean,
  Kepulauan *Indonesia* 62 F5
Kangen → *Sudan* 81 F3
Kanggye *N. Korea* 57 D14
Kangikajik *Greenland* 4 B6
Kangiqliniq = Rankin Inlet
  Canada 100 C10
Kangiqsualujjuaq *Canada* 101 D13
Kangiqsujuaq *Canada* 101 C12
Kangiqtugaapik = Clyde
  River *Canada* 101 B13
Kangirsuk *Canada* 101 D13
Kangkar Chemaran *Malaysia* 65 d
Kangkar Sungai Tiram
  Malaysia 65 d
Kangkar Teberau *Malaysia* 65 d
Kangping *China* 57 C12
Kangra *India* 68 C7
Kangrinboqe Feng *China* 69 D9
Kangto *China* 67 F18
Kanha △ *India* 69 H9
Kanhar → *India* 69 G10
Kani *Ivory C.* 82 D3
Kaniama
  Dem. Rep. of the Congo 86 D1
Kaniapiskau =
  Caniapiscau → *Canada* 105 A6
Kaniapiskau, L. =
  Caniapiscau, L. *Canada* 105 B6
Kanin, Poluostrov *Russia* 6 B14
Kanin Nos, Mys *Russia* 52 C5
Kanin Pen. = Kanin,
  Poluostrov *Russia* 6 B14
Kaninë *Albania* 44 F3
Kaniva *Australia* 95 F3
Kanjiža *Serbia* 28 D5
Kanjut Sar *Pakistan* 69 A6
Kankaanpää *Finland* 32 B3
Kankakee *U.S.A.* 112 E10
Kankakee → *U.S.A.* 112 E9
Kankan *Guinea* 82 C3
Kankendy = Xankändi
  Azerbaijan 73 C12
Kanker *India* 67 J12
Kankossa *Mauritania* 82 B2
Kankroli *India* 68 G5
Kannapolis *U.S.A.* 117 D14
Kannauj *India* 69 F8
Kannod *India* 66 H10
Kano *Nigeria* 83 C6
Kano □ *Nigeria* 83 C6
Kan'onji *Japan* 55 G6
Kanonorba *Ivory C.* 82 D3
Kanowit *Malaysia* 62 D4
Kanoya *Japan* 55 J5
Kanpetlet *Burma* 67 J18
Kanpur *India* 69 F9
Kansas □ *U.S.A.* 112 F4
Kansas → *U.S.A.* 112 F6
Kansas City *Kans., U.S.A.* 112 F6
Kansas City *Mo., U.S.A.* 112 F6

Kansenia
  Dem. Rep. of the Congo 87 E2
Kansk *Russia* 53 D10
Kansu = Gansu □ *China* 56 G3
Kantaphor *India* 68 H7
Kantchari *Burkina Faso* 83 C5
Kantché *Niger* 83 C6
Kanté *Togo* 83 D5
Kantemirovka *Russia* 33 H10
Kantharalak *Thailand* 64 E5
Kantli → *India* 68 E6
Kantō □ *Japan* 55 F9
Kantō-Sanchi *Japan* 55 G9
Kanturk *Ireland* 12 D3
Kanuma *Japan* 55 F9
Kanus *Namibia* 88 D2
Kanyakumari *India* 66 Q10
Kanye *Botswana* 88 C4
Kanzenze
  Dem. Rep. of the Congo 87 E2
Kanzi, Ras *Tanzania* 86 D4
Kao *Tonga* 91 c
Kao Phara *Thailand* 65 a
Kaohsiung *Taiwan* 59 F13
Kaokoveld *Namibia* 88 B1
Kaolack *Senegal* 82 C1
Kaolack □ *Senegal* 82 C1
Kaoshan *China* 57 B13
Kapaa *U.S.A.* 106 b
Kapadvanj *India* 68 H5
Kapaklı *Turkey* 45 E11
Kapan *Armenia* 73 C12
Kapanga
  Dem. Rep. of the Congo 84 F4
Kapchagai = Qapshaghay
  Kazakhstan 52 E8
Kapedo *Kenya* 86 B4
Kapela = Velika Kapela
  Croatia 41 C12
Kapelo, Akra *Greece* 46 E5
Kapema
  Dem. Rep. of the Congo 87 E2
Kapenguria *Kenya* 86 B4
Kapfenberg *Austria* 26 D8
Kapı Dağı *Turkey* 45 F11
Kapiri Mposhi *Zambia* 87 E2
Kāpīsā □ *Afghan.* 66 B6
Kapiskau → *Canada* 104 B3
Kapit *Malaysia* 62 D4
Kapiti I. *N.Z.* 91 D5
Kaplan *U.S.A.* 116 F8
Kaplice *Czech Rep.* 26 C7
Kapoe *Thailand* 65 H2
Kapoeta *Sudan* 81 G3
Kápolnásnyék *Hungary* 28 C3
Kapos → *Hungary* 28 D3
Kaposvár *Hungary* 28 D2
Kapowsin *U.S.A.* 110 D4
Kappeln *Germany* 24 A5
Kappelshamn *Sweden* 11 G12
Kapps *Namibia* 88 C2
Kaprije *Croatia* 41 E12
Kapsabet *Kenya* 86 B4
Kapsan *N. Korea* 57 D15
Kapsukas = Marijampolė
  Lithuania 30 D10
Kaptai L. *Bangla.* 67 H18
Kapuas → *Indonesia* 62 E3
Kapuas Hulu,
  Pegunungan *Malaysia* 62 D4
Kapuas Hulu Ra. =
  Kapuas Hulu,
  Pegunungan *Malaysia* 62 D4
Kapulo *Dem. Rep. of the Congo* 87 D2
Kapunda *Australia* 95 E2
Kapuni *N.Z.* 91 C5
Kapurthala *India* 68 D6
Kapuskasing *Canada* 104 C3
Kapuskasing → *Canada* 104 C3
Kapustin Yar *Russia* 35 F7
Kaputar, Mt. *Australia* 95 E5
Kapuvár *Hungary* 28 C2
Kara *Russia* 52 C7
Karā, W. → *Si. Arabia* 80 C5
Kara Ada *Turkey* 47 E9
Kara Bogaz Gol, Zaliv =
  Garabogazköl Aylagy
  Turkmenistan 52 E6
Kara Burun *Turkey* 47 E9
Kara-Kala = Garrygala
  Turkmenistan 71 B8
Kara Kalpak Republic =
  Qoraqalpoghiston □
  Uzbekistan 52 E6
Kara Kum = Garagum
  Turkmenistan 71 B8
Kara Sea *Russia* 52 B7
Karaadilli *Turkey* 47 C12
Karabiğa *Turkey* 45 F11
Karabük *Turkey* 72 B5
Karaburun *Albania* 44 F3
Karaburun *Turkey* 47 C8
Karabutak = Qarabutaq
  Kazakhstan 52 E7
Karacabey *Turkey* 45 F12
Karacakılavuz *Turkey* 45 E11
Karacaköy *Turkey* 45 E12

Karacasu *Turkey* 47 D10
Karachala = Qaraçala *Azerbaijan* 35 L9
Karachayevsk *Russia* 35 J5
Karachev *Russia* 33 F8
Karachey-Cherkessia □ *Russia* 35 J5
Karachi *Pakistan* 68 G2
Karad *India* 66 L9
Karadirek *Turkey* 47 C12
Karaga *Ghana* 83 D4
Karaganda = Qaraghandy *Kazakhstan* 52 E8
Karagayly = Qaraghayly *Kazakhstan* 52 E8
Karaginskiy, Ostrov *Russia* 53 D17
Karagola Road *India* 69 G12
Karagüney Dağları *Turkey* 72 B6
Karahallı *Turkey* 47 C11
Karaikal *India* 66 P11
Karaikkudi *India* 66 P11
Karaisali *Turkey* 72 D6
Karaj *Iran* 71 C6
Karak *Malaysia* 65 L4
Karakalpakstan = Qoraqalpoghistan □ *Uzbekistan* 52 E6
Karakaya Barajı *Turkey* 73 C8
Karakelong *Indonesia* 63 D7
Karakitang *Indonesia* 63 D7
Karakoçan *Turkey* 73 C9
Karakol *Kyrgyzstan* 52 E8
Karakoram Pass *Asia* 69 B7
Karakoram Ra. *Pakistan* 69 B7
Karakurt *Turkey* 73 B10
Karakuwisa *Namibia* 88 B2
Karalon *Russia* 53 D12
Karama *Jordan* 74 D4
Karaman *Balıkesir, Turkey* 47 B9
Karaman *Konya, Turkey* 72 D5
Karamanlı *Turkey* 47 D11
Karamay *China* 60 B3
Karambu *Indonesia* 62 E5
Karamea Bight *N.Z.* 91 D3
Karamnasa → *India* 69 G10
Karamürsel *Turkey* 45 F13
Karān *Si. Arabia* 71 E6
Karand *Iran* 73 E12
Karangana *Mali* 82 C3
Karanganyar *Indonesia* 63 G13
Karangasem *Indonesia* 63 J18
Karanjia *India* 69 J11
Karankasso *Burkina Faso* 82 C4
Karaova *Turkey* 47 D9
Karapınar *Turkey* 72 D5
Karasburg *Namibia* 88 D2
Karasino *Russia* 52 C9
Karasjok *Norway* 8 B21
Karasu *Turkey* 72 B4
Karasu → *Turkey* 47 E12
Karasuk *Russia* 52 D8
Karasuyama *Japan* 55 F10
Karataş *Adana, Turkey* 72 D6
Karataş *Manisa, Turkey* 47 C10
Karataş Burnu *Turkey* 72 D6
Karatau, Khrebet = Qarataū *Kazakhstan* 52 E7
Karatoprak *Turkey* 47 D9
Karatsu *Japan* 55 H5
Karaul *Russia* 52 B9
Karauli *India* 68 F7
Karavastasë, L. e *Albania* 44 F3
Karavia *Greece* 46 E5
Karavostasi *Cyprus* 49 D11
Karawang *Indonesia* 63 G12
Karawanken *Europe* 26 E7
Karayazı *Turkey* 73 C10
Karazhal = Qarazhal *Kazakhstan* 52 E8
Karbalā' *Iraq* 73 F11
Karbalā' □ *Iraq* 73 F10
Kårböle *Sweden* 10 C9
Karcag *Hungary* 28 C5
Karcha → *Pakistan* 69 B7
Karchana *India* 69 G9
Karczew *Poland* 31 F8
Kardam *Bulgaria* 45 C12
Kardamila *Greece* 47 C8
Kardamili *Greece* 46 E4
Kardeljovo = Ploče *Croatia* 41 E14
Karditsa *Greece* 46 B3
Karditsa □ *Greece* 46 B3
Kärdla *Estonia* 32 C2
Kareeberge *S. Africa* 88 E3
Kareha → *India* 69 G12
Kareima *Sudan* 80 D3
Karelia □ *Russia* 8 D25
Karelian Republic = Karelia □ *Russia* 8 D25
Karera *India* 68 G8
Kārevāndar *Iran* 71 E9
Kargasok *Russia* 52 D9
Kargat *Russia* 52 D9
Kargi *Kenya* 86 B4
Kargı *Turkey* 72 B6
Kargil *India* 69 B7
Kargopol *Russia* 32 B10
Kargowa *Poland* 31 F2
Karguéri *Niger* 83 C7
Karhal *India* 69 F8
Karia *Greece* 46 C2
Karīān *Iran* 71 E8
Karianga *Madag.* 89 C8
Kariba *Zimbabwe* 87 F2
Kariba, L. *Zimbabwe* 87 F2
Kariba Dam *Zimbabwe* 87 F2
Kariba Gorge *Zambia* 87 F2
Karibib *Namibia* 88 C2
Karies *Greece* 45 F8
Karijini △ *Australia* 92 D2
Karimata, Kepulauan *Indonesia* 62 E3
Karimata, Selat *Indonesia* 62 E3
Karimata Is. = Karimata, Kepulauan *Indonesia* 62 E3
Karimnagar *India* 66 K11
Karimun Kecil, Pulau *Indonesia* 65 d
Karimunjawa, Kepulauan *Indonesia* 62 F4
Karin *Somali Rep.* 75 E4
Karistos *Greece* 46 C6
Karīt *Iran* 71 C8
Kariya *Japan* 55 G8
Kariyangwe *Zimbabwe* 89 B4
Karjala *Finland* 32 A5
Karkaralinsk = Qarqaraly *Kazakhstan* 52 E8
Karkheh → *Iran* 70 D5
Karkinitska Zatoka *Ukraine* 33 K7
Karkinitskiy Zaliv = Karkinitska Zatoka *Ukraine* 33 K7
Karkuk = Kirkūk *Iraq* 73 E11
Karkur Tohl *Egypt* 80 C2
Karl Liebknecht *Russia* 33 G8
Karla, L. = Volvi, L. *Greece* 44 F7
Karleby = Kokkola *Finland* 8 E20
Karlholmsbruk *Sweden* 10 D11
Karlino *Poland* 30 D2
Karlıova *Turkey* 73 C9
Karlivka *Ukraine* 33 H8
Karlobag *Croatia* 41 D12
Karlovac *Croatia* 41 C12
Karlovarský □ *Czech Rep.* 26 A5
Karlovasi *Greece* 47 D8
Karlovka = Karlivka *Ukraine* 33 H8
Karlovo *Bulgaria* 45 D8
Karlovy Vary *Czech Rep.* 26 A5
Karlsbad = Karlovy Vary *Czech Rep.* 26 A5
Karlsborg *Sweden* 11 F8
Karlsena, Mys *Russia* 52 B7
Karlshamn *Sweden* 11 H8
Karlskoga *Sweden* 10 E8
Karlskrona *Sweden* 11 H9
Karlsruhe *Germany* 25 F4
Karlstad *Sweden* 10 E7
Karlstad *U.S.A.* 112 A5
Karlstadt *Germany* 25 F5
Karma *Niger* 83 C5
Karmėlava *Lithuania* 30 D11
Karmi'el *Israel* 74 C4
Karnak *Egypt* 80 B3
Karnal *India* 68 E7
Karnali → *Nepal* 69 E9
Karnaphuli Res. = Kaptai L. *Bangla.* 67 H18
Karnaprayag *India* 69 D8
Karnataka □ *India* 66 N10
Karnes City *U.S.A.* 116 G6
Karnische Alpen *Europe* 26 E6
Karnobat *Bulgaria* 45 D10
Kärnten □ *Austria* 26 E6
Karo *Mali* 82 C4
Karoi *Zimbabwe* 87 F2
Karon, Ao *Thailand* 65 a
Karonga *Malawi* 87 D3
Karoo △ *S. Africa* 88 E3
Karoonda *Australia* 95 F2
Karor *Pakistan* 68 D4
Karora *Sudan* 80 D4
Karounga *Mali* 82 B3
Karousades *Greece* 46 B1
Karpacz *Poland* 31 H2
Karpasia *Cyprus* 49 D13
Karpathos *Greece* 47 F9
Karpathos, Stenon *Greece* 47 F9
Karpatsky △ *Ukraine* 29 B9
Karpenisi *Greece* 46 C3
Karpuz Burnu = Apostolos Andreas, C. *Cyprus* 49 D13
Karpuzlu *Turkey* 47 D9
Karratha *Australia* 92 D2
Kars *Turkey* 73 B10
Kars □ *Turkey* 73 B10
Karsakpay *Kazakhstan* 52 E7
Karsha *Kazakhstan* 34 F10
Karshi = Qarshi *Uzbekistan* 52 F7
Karsiyang *India* 69 F13
Karsog *India* 68 D7
Karst = Kras *Croatia* 41 C10
Kartal *Turkey* 45 F13
Kartala *Comoros Is.* 85 a
Kartaly *Russia* 52 D7
Kartapur *India* 68 D6
Karthaus *U.S.A.* 114 E6
Kartuzy *Poland* 30 D5
Karufa *Indonesia* 63 E8
Karuma ⌓ *Uganda* 86 B3
Karumba *Australia* 94 B3
Karumo *Tanzania* 86 C3
Karumwa *Tanzania* 86 C3
Kārūn → *Iran* 71 D6
Karungu *Kenya* 86 C3
Karup *Denmark* 11 H3
Karviná *Czech Rep.* 27 B11
Karwan → *India* 68 F8
Karwar *India* 66 M9
Karwendel ⌓ *Austria* 26 D4
Karwi *India* 69 G9
Karymskoye *Russia* 53 D12
Kaş *Turkey* 47 E11
Kasaba *Turkey* 47 E11
Kasache *Malawi* 87 E3
Kasai → *Dem. Rep. of the Congo* 84 E3
Kasai-Oriental □ *Dem. Rep. of the Congo* 86 D1
Kasaji *Dem. Rep. of the Congo* 87 E1
Kasama *Zambia* 87 E3
Kasan *N. Korea* 57 D14
Kasandra *Greece* 44 F7
Kasandra Kolpos *Greece* 44 F7
Kasandras, Akra *Greece* 44 G7
Kasane *Namibia* 88 B3
Kasanga *Tanzania* 87 D3
Kasanka △ *Zambia* 87 E3
Kasar, Ras *Sudan* 80 D4
Kasaragod *India* 66 N9
Kasba L. *Canada* 103 A8
Kāseh Garān *Iran* 70 C5
Kasempa *Zambia* 87 E2
Kasenga *Dem. Rep. of the Congo* 87 E2
Kasese *Uganda* 86 B3
Kasewa *Zambia* 87 E2
Kasganj *India* 69 F8
Kashabowie *Canada* 104 C1
Kashaf *Iran* 71 C9
Kāshān *Iran* 71 C6
Kashechewan *Canada* 104 B3
Kashgān → *Iran* 73 F12
Kashgar = Kashi *China* 60 C2
Kashi *China* 60 C2
Kashimbo *Dem. Rep. of the Congo* 87 E2
Kashin *Russia* 32 D9
Kashipur *India* 69 E8
Kashira *Russia* 32 E10
Kashiwazaki *Japan* 55 F9
Kashk-e Kohneh *Afghan.* 66 B3
Kashksaray *Iran* 73 C11
Kashkū'īyeh *Iran* 71 D7
Kāshmar *Iran* 71 C8
Kashmir *Asia* 69 C7
Kashmor *Pakistan* 68 E3
Kashpirovka *Russia* 34 D9
Kashun Noerh = Gaxun Nur *China* 60 B5
Kasiari *India* 69 H12
Kasimov *Russia* 34 C5
Kasinge *Dem. Rep. of the Congo* 86 D2
Kasiruta *Indonesia* 63 E7
Kaskaskia → *U.S.A.* 112 G9
Kaskattama → *Canada* 103 B10
Kaskinen *Finland* 8 E19
Kaskö = Kaskinen *Finland* 8 E19
Kaslo *Canada* 102 D5
Kasmere L. *Canada* 103 B8
Kasongo *Dem. Rep. of the Congo* 86 C2
Kasongo Lunda *Dem. Rep. of the Congo* 84 F3
Kasos *Greece* 47 F8
Kasos, Stenon *Greece* 47 F8
Kaspi *Georgia* 35 K7
Kaspichan *Bulgaria* 45 C11
Kaspiysk *Russia* 35 J8
Kaspiyskiy *Russia* 35 H8
Kassab ed Doleib *Sudan* 81 E3
Kassaba *Egypt* 80 C2
Kassalâ *Sudan* 81 D4
Kassalâ □ *Sudan* 81 D4
Kassandrino *Greece* 44 F7
Kassel *Germany* 24 D5
Kassinger *Sudan* 80 D3
Kassiopi *Greece* 49 A3
Kasson *U.S.A.* 112 C7
Kastamonu *Turkey* 72 B5
Kastamonu □ *Turkey* 72 B5
Kastav *Croatia* 41 C11
Kasteli *Greece* 49 D5
Kastelli *Greece* 49 D7
Kastellórizon = Megisti *Greece* 47 E11
Kastelo, Akra *Greece* 47 F9
Kasterlee *Belgium* 17 C4
Kastlösa *Sweden* 11 H10
Kastoria *Greece* 44 F5
Kastoria □ *Greece* 44 F5
Kastorias, L. *Greece* 44 F5
Kastorio *Greece* 46 D4
Kastornoye *Russia* 33 G10
Kastos *Greece* 46 C2
Kastrosikia *Greece* 46 B2
Kastrup, København ✈ **(CPH)** *Denmark* 11 J6
Kastsyukovichy *Belarus* 32 F7
Kasulu *Tanzania* 86 C3
Kasumi *Japan* 55 G7
Kasumkent *Russia* 35 K9
Kasungu *Malawi* 87 E3
Kasungu △ *Malawi* 87 E3
Kasur *Pakistan* 68 D6
Kata, Ao *Thailand* 65 J2
Kata Archanes *Greece* 49 D7
Kata Tjuta *Australia* 93 E5
Kataba *Zambia* 87 F2
Katagum *Nigeria* 83 C7
Katahdin, Mt. *U.S.A.* 113 C19
Katako Kombe *Dem. Rep. of the Congo* 86 C1
Katakolo *Greece* 46 D3
Katale *Tanzania* 86 C3
Katanda *Katanga, Dem. Rep. of the Congo* 86 D1
Katanda *Nord-Kivu, Dem. Rep. of the Congo* 86 C2
Katanga □ *Dem. Rep. of the Congo* 86 D2
Katangi *India* 66 J11
Katanning *Australia* 93 F2
Katastari *Greece* 46 D2
Katavi △ *Tanzania* 86 D3
Katavi Swamp *Tanzania* 86 D3
Katerini *Greece* 44 F6
Katghora *India* 69 H10
Katha *Burma* 67 G20
Katherîna, Gebel *Egypt* 70 D2
Katherine *Australia* 92 B5
Katherine Gorge *Australia* 92 B5
Kathi *India* 68 J6
Kathiawar *India* 68 H4
Kathikas *Cyprus* 49 E11
Kathmandu = Katmandu *Nepal* 69 F11
Kathua *India* 68 C6
Kati *Mali* 82 C3
Katihar *India* 69 G12
Katima Mulilo *Namibia* 88 B3
Katimbira *Malawi* 87 E3
Katingan = Mendawai → *Indonesia* 62 E4
Katiola *Ivory C.* 82 D3
Katlabukh, Ozero *Ukraine* 29 E14
Katlanovo *Macedonia* 44 E5
Katmandu *Nepal* 69 F11
Katni *India* 69 H9
Kato Achaia *Greece* 46 C3
Kato Chorio *Greece* 49 D7
Kato Korakiana *Greece* 49 A3
Káto Pyrgos *Cyprus* 49 D11
Katochi *Greece* 46 C3
Katompe *Dem. Rep. of the Congo* 86 D2
Katong *Singapore* 65 d
Katonga → *Uganda* 86 B3
Katoomba *Australia* 95 E5
Katouna *Greece* 46 C3
Katowice *Poland* 31 H6
Katrancı Dağı *Turkey* 47 D12
Katrine, L. *U.K.* 13 E4
Katrineholm *Sweden* 10 E10
Katsepe *Madag.* 89 B8
Katsina *Nigeria* 83 C6
Katsina □ *Nigeria* 83 C6
Katsina Ala *Nigeria* 83 D6
Katsina Ala → *Nigeria* 83 D6
Katsumoto *Japan* 55 H4
Katsuura *Japan* 55 G10
Katsuyama *Japan* 55 F8
Kattavia *Greece* 49 D9
Kattegat *Denmark* 11 H5
Katthammarsvik *Sweden* 11 G12
Katul, J. *Sudan* 81 E2
Katumba *Dem. Rep. of the Congo* 86 D2
Katwa *India* 69 H13
Katwijk *Neths.* 17 B4
Kąty Wrocławskie *Poland* 31 G3
Kaua'i *U.S.A.* 106 b
Kauai Channel *U.S.A.* 106 b
Kaub *Germany* 25 E3
Kaudom ⌓ *Namibia* 88 B3
Kaufbeuren *Germany* 25 H6
Kaufman *U.S.A.* 116 E6
Kauhajoki *Finland* 8 E20
Kaukauna *U.S.A.* 112 C9
Kaukauveld *Namibia* 88 C3
Kaunakakai *U.S.A.* 106 b
Kaunas *Lithuania* 30 D10
Kaunas ✈ **(KUN)** *Lithuania* 30 D11
Kaunia *Bangla.* 69 G13
Kaunos *Turkey* 47 E10
Kaura Namoda *Nigeria* 83 C6
Kauru *Nigeria* 83 C6
Kautokeino *Norway* 8 B20
Kauwapur *India* 69 F10
Kavacha *Russia* 53 C17
Kavadarci *Macedonia* 44 E6
Kavajë *Albania* 44 E3
Kavak *Turkey* 72 B7
Kavak Dağı *Turkey* 47 D10
Kavaklı *Turkey* 45 E11
Kavaklıdere *Turkey* 47 D10
Kavala *Greece* 45 F8
Kavala □ *Greece* 45 E8
Kavala Kolpos *Greece* 45 F8
Kavalerovo *Russia* 54 B7
Kavali *India* 66 M12
Kavār *Iran* 71 D7
Kavarna *Bulgaria* 45 C12
Kavi *India* 68 H5
Kavimba *Botswana* 88 B3
Kavīr, Dasht-e *Iran* 71 C7
Kavīr △ *Iran* 71 C7
Kavkaz *Russia* 33 K9
Kävlinge *Sweden* 11 J7
Kavos *Greece* 49 B4
Kavousi *Greece* 47 F7
Kaw *Fr. Guiana* 125 C8
Kawa *Sudan* 81 E3
Kawagama L. *Canada* 114 A6
Kawagoe *Japan* 55 G9
Kawaguchi *Japan* 55 G9
Kawambwa *Zambia* 87 D2
Kawanoe *Japan* 55 G6
Kawardha *India* 69 J9
Kawasaki *Japan* 55 G9
Kawasi *Indonesia* 63 E7
Kawawachikamach *Canada* 105 B6
Kawerau *N.Z.* 91 C6
Kawhia *N.Z.* 91 C5
Kawhia Harbour *N.Z.* 91 C5
Kawio, Kepulauan *Indonesia* 63 D7
Kawthaung *Burma* 65 H2
Kawthoolei = Kayin □ *Burma* 67 L20
Kawthule = Kayin □ *Burma* 67 L20
Kaxholmen *Sweden* 11 G8
Kaya *Burkina Faso* 83 C4
Kayah □ *Burma* 67 K20
Kayalıköy Barajı *Turkey* 45 E11
Kayan → *Indonesia* 62 D5
Kaycee *U.S.A.* 108 E10
Kayeli *Indonesia* 63 E7
Kayenta *U.S.A.* 109 H8
Kayes *Mali* 82 C2
Kayes □ *Mali* 82 C2
Kayı *Turkey* 47 B12
Kayima *S. Leone* 82 D2
Kayin □ *Burma* 67 L20
Kaymakçı *Turkey* 47 C10
Kayoa *Indonesia* 63 D7
Kayomba *Zambia* 87 E1
Kaysatskoye *Russia* 34 F8
Kayseri *Turkey* 72 C6
Kayseri □ *Turkey* 72 C7
Kaysville *U.S.A.* 108 F8
Kaz Dağı *Turkey* 47 B8
Kazachye *Russia* 53 B14
Kazakhstan ■ *Asia* 52 E8
Kazan *Russia* 34 C9
Kazan → *Canada* 103 A9
Kazan-Rettō *Pac. Oc.* 96 E6
Kazanlŭk *Bulgaria* 45 D9
Kazanskaya *Russia* 34 F5
Kazatin = Kozyatyn *Ukraine* 23 D15
Kazaure *Nigeria* 83 C6
Kazbek *Russia* 35 J7
Kāzerūn *Iran* 71 D6
Kazi Magomed = Qazımämmäd *Azerbaijan* 35 K9
Kazimierz Dolny *Poland* 31 G8
Kazimierza Wielka *Poland* 31 H7
Kazincbarcika *Hungary* 28 B5
Kazlų Rūda *Lithuania* 30 D10
Kaztalovka *Kazakhstan* 34 F9
Kazuma Pan △ *Zimbabwe* 87 F2
Kazuno *Japan* 54 D10
Kazym → *Russia* 52 C7
Kcynia *Poland* 31 F4
Ké-Macina *Mali* 82 C3
Kea *Greece* 46 D6
Keady *U.K.* 12 B5
Kearney *U.S.A.* 112 E4
Kearny *U.S.A.* 109 K8
Kearsarge, Mt. *U.S.A.* 115 C13
Keban *Turkey* 73 C8
Keban Barajı *Turkey* 73 C8
Kebbi □ *Nigeria* 83 C5
Kébi *Ivory C.* 82 D3
Kebnekaise *Sweden* 8 C18
Kebri Dehar *Ethiopia* 75 F3
Kebumen *Indonesia* 63 G13
Kecel *Hungary* 28 D4
Kechika → *Canada* 102 B3
Keçiborlu *Turkey* 47 D12
Kecskemét *Hungary* 28 D4
Kedada *Ethiopia* 81 F4
Kėdainiai *Lithuania* 30 C11
Kedarnath *India* 69 D8
Kedgwick *Canada* 105 C6
Kediri *Indonesia* 63 G15
Kedjebi *Ghana* 83 D5
Kédougou *Senegal* 82 C2
Kedros Oros *Greece* 49 D6
Kędzierzyn-Koźle *Poland* 31 H5
Keeler *U.S.A.* 110 J9
Keeley L. *Canada* 103 C7
Keeling Is. = Cocos Is. *Ind. Oc.* 96 J1
Keelung = Chilung *Taiwan* 59 E13
Keene *Canada* 114 B6
Keene *Calif., U.S.A.* 111 K8
Keene *N.H., U.S.A.* 115 D12
Keene *N.Y., U.S.A.* 115 B11
Keep River △ *Australia* 92 C4
Keeper Hill *Ireland* 12 D3
Keerweer, C. *Australia* 94 A3
Keeseville *U.S.A.* 115 B11
Keetmanshoop *Namibia* 88 D2
Keewatin *Canada* 103 D10
Keewatin → *Canada* 103 B8
Kefa *Ethiopia* 81 F4
Kefalonia *Greece* 46 C2
Kefalonia □ *Greece* 46 C2
Kefalos *Greece* 47 E8
Kefamenanu *Indonesia* 63 F6
Kefar Sava *Israel* 74 C3
Keffi *Nigeria* 83 D6
Keffin Hausa *Nigeria* 83 C6
Keflavík *Iceland* 8 D2
Keftya *Ethiopia* 81 E4
Keg River *Canada* 102 B5
Kegaska *Canada* 105 B7
Kehancha *Kenya* 86 C3
Keheili *Sudan* 80 D3
Kehl *Germany* 25 G3
Keighley *U.K.* 14 D6
Keila *Estonia* 32 C3
Keimoes *S. Africa* 88 D3
Keita *Niger* 83 C6
Keitele *Finland* 8 E22
Keith *Australia* 95 F3
Keith *U.K.* 13 D6
Keiyasi *Fiji* 91 a
Keizer *U.S.A.* 108 D2
Kejimkujik △ *Canada* 105 D6
Kejserr Franz Joseph Fd. *Greenland* 4 B6
Kekri *India* 68 G6
Kelam *Ethiopia* 81 G4
Kelamet *Eritrea* 81 D4
Kelan *China* 56 E6
Kelang = Klang *Malaysia* 65 L3
Kelantan → *Malaysia* 65 J4
Këlcyrë *Albania* 44 F4
Kelekçi *Turkey* 47 D11
Keles *Turkey* 45 G13
Keleti-főcsatorna *Hungary* 28 C6
Kelheim *Germany* 25 G7
Kelkit *Turkey* 73 B8
Kelkit → *Turkey* 72 B7
Kellerberrin *Australia* 93 F2
Kellett, C. *Canada* 101 B7
Kelleys I. *U.S.A.* 114 E2
Kellogg *U.S.A.* 108 C5
Kells = Ceanannus Mor *Ireland* 12 C5
Kelmė *Lithuania* 30 C9
Kelmentsi *Ukraine* 29 B11
Kélo *Chad* 79 G9
Kelokedhara *Cyprus* 49 E11
Kelowna *Canada* 102 D5
Kelsey Creek *Australia* 94 J6
Kelseyville *U.S.A.* 110 G4
Kelso *N.Z.* 91 F2
Kelso *U.K.* 13 F6
Kelso *U.S.A.* 110 D4
Keluang = Kluang *Malaysia* 65 L4
Kelvington *Canada* 103 C8
Kem *Russia* 52 C4
Kema *Indonesia* 63 D7
Kemah *Turkey* 73 C8
Kemaliye *Erzincan, Turkey* 73 C8
Kemaliye *Manisa, Turkey* 47 C10
Kemalpaşa *Turkey* 47 C9
Kemaman *Malaysia* 65 K4
Kemano *Canada* 102 C3
Kemasik *Malaysia* 65 K4
Kembolcha *Ethiopia* 81 E4
Kemer *Antalya, Turkey* 47 E12
Kemer *Burdur, Turkey* 47 D12
Kemer *Muğla, Turkey* 47 E11
Kemer Barajı *Turkey* 47 D10
Kemerovo *Russia* 52 D9
Ķemeru △ *Latvia* 30 B10
Kemi *Finland* 8 D21
Kemi älv = Kemijoki → *Finland* 8 D21
Kemi träsk = Kemijärvi *Finland* 8 C22
Kemijärvi *Finland* 8 C22
Kemijoki → *Finland* 8 D21
Kemmerer *U.S.A.* 108 F8
Kemmuna = Comino *Malta* 49 C1
Kemp, L. *U.S.A.* 116 E5
Kemp Land *Antarctica* 5 C5
Kempas *Malaysia* 65 d
Kempsey *Australia* 95 E5
Kempt, L. *Canada* 104 C5
Kempten *Germany* 25 H6
Kempton *Australia* 95 G4
Kemptville *Canada* 115 B9
Ken → *India* 69 G9
Kenai *U.S.A.* 100 C4
Kendai *India* 69 H10

Kendal *Indonesia* 63 G14
Kendal *U.K.* 14 C5
Kendall *Australia* 95 E5
Kendall *U.S.A.* 117 J14
Kendall → *Australia* 94 A3
Kendallville *U.S.A.* 113 E11
Kendari *Indonesia* 63 E6
Kendawangan *Indonesia* 62 E4
Kende *Nigeria* 83 C5
Kendi, Pulau *Malaysia* 65 c
Kendrapara *India* 67 J15
Kendrew *S. Africa* 88 E3
Kene Thao *Laos* 64 D3
Kenedy *U.S.A.* 116 G6
Kenema *S. Leone* 82 D2
Keng Kok *Laos* 64 D5
Keng Tawng *Burma* 67 J21
Keng Tung *Burma* 58 G2
Kengeja *Tanzania* 86 D4
Kenhardt *S. Africa* 88 D3
Kéniéba *Mali* 82 C2
Kenitra *Morocco* 78 B4
Kenli *China* 57 F10
Kenmare *Ireland* 12 E2
Kenmare *U.S.A.* 112 A2
Kenmare River *Ireland* 12 E2
Kennebago Lake *U.S.A.* 115 A14
Kennebec *U.S.A.* 112 D4
Kennebec → *U.S.A.* 113 D19
Kennebunk *U.S.A.* 115 C14
Kennedy *Zimbabwe* 88 B4
Kennedy Ra. *Australia* 93 D2
Kennedy Range △ *Australia* 93 D2
Kenner *U.S.A.* 117 G9
Kennet → *U.K.* 15 F7
Kenneth Ra. *Australia* 93 D2
Kennett *U.S.A.* 112 G8
Kennewick *U.S.A.* 108 C4
Kennisis Lake *Canada* 114 A6
Kenogami → *Canada* 104 B3
Kenogamissi L. *Canada* 104 B3
Kenora *Canada* 103 D10
Kenosha *U.S.A.* 112 D10
Kensington *Canada* 105 C7
Kent *Ohio, U.S.A.* 114 E3
Kent *Tex., U.S.A.* 116 F2
Kent *Wash., U.S.A.* 110 C4
Kent □ *U.K.* 15 F8
Kent Group *Australia* 95 F4
Kent Pen. *Canada* 100 C9
Kentaū *Kazakhstan* 52 E7
Kentland *U.S.A.* 112 E10
Kenton *U.S.A.* 113 E12
Kentucky □ *U.S.A.* 113 G11
Kentucky → *U.S.A.* 113 F11
Kentucky L. *U.S.A.* 112 G9
Kentville *Canada* 105 C7
Kentwood *U.S.A.* 117 F9
Kenya ■ *Africa* 86 B4
Kenya, Mt. *Kenya* 86 C4
Kenyir, Tasik *Malaysia* 65 K4
Keo Neua, Deo *Vietnam* 64 C5
Keokuk *U.S.A.* 112 E8
Keoladeo △ *India* 68 F7
Keonjhargarh *India* 69 J11
Kep *Cambodia* 65 G5
Kep *Vietnam* 64 B6
Kepala Batas *Malaysia* 65 c
Kepez *Turkey* 45 F10
Kepi *Indonesia* 63 F9
Kępice *Poland* 30 D3
Kępno *Poland* 31 G4
Kepsut *Turkey* 47 B10
Kerala □ *India* 66 P10
Kerama-Rettō *Japan* 55 L3
Keran *Pakistan* 69 B5
Keran △ *Togo* 83 C5
Kerang *Australia* 95 F3
Keranyo *Ethiopia* 81 F4
Kerao → *Sudan* 81 E3
Keratea *Greece* 46 D5
Keraudren, C. *Australia* 92 C2
Kerava *Finland* 32 B3
Kerch *Ukraine* 33 K9
Kerchenskiy Proliv *Black Sea* 33 K9
Kerchoual *Mali* 83 B5
Kerempe Burnu *Turkey* 72 A5
Keren *Eritrea* 81 D4
Kerewan *Gambia* 82 C1
Kerguelen *Ind. Oc.* 3 G13
Keri *Greece* 46 D2
Keri Kera *Sudan* 81 E3
Kericho *Kenya* 86 C4
Kerinci *Indonesia* 62 E2
Kerki = Atamyrat
  Turkmenistan 52 F7
Kerkini, L. *Greece* 44 E7
Kerkouane *Tunisia* 42 F4
Kerkrade *Neths.* 17 D6
Kerkyra *Greece* 49 A3
Kerkyra □ *Greece* 46 B1
Kerkyra ✈ (CFU) *Greece* 46 B1
Kerkyras, Notio Steno
  Greece 49 A4
Kerma *Sudan* 80 D3
Kermadec Is. *Pac. Oc.* 90 E11
Kermadec Trench *Pac. Oc.* 96 L10
Kermān *Iran* 71 D8
Kerman *U.S.A.* 110 J6

Kermān □ *Iran* 71 D8
Kermān, Bīābān-e *Iran* 71 D8
Kermānshāh *Iran* 73 E12
Kermānshāh □ *Iran* 70 C5
Kermen *Bulgaria* 45 D10
Kermit *U.S.A.* 116 F3
Kern → *U.S.A.* 111 K7
Kernhof *Austria* 26 D8
Kernow = Cornwall □ *U.K.* 15 G3
Kernville *U.S.A.* 111 K8
Keroh *Malaysia* 65 K3
Keros *Greece* 47 E7
Kérou *Benin* 83 C5
Kérouane *Guinea* 82 D3
Kerpen *Germany* 24 E2
Kerrera *U.K.* 13 E3
Kerrobert *Canada* 103 C7
Kerrville *U.S.A.* 116 F5
Kerry □ *Ireland* 12 D2
Kerry Hd. *Ireland* 12 D2
Kersa *Ethiopia* 81 F5
Kerulen → *Asia* 60 B6
Kervo = Kerava *Finland* 32 B3
Kerzaz *Algeria* 78 C5
Kesagami → *Canada* 104 B4
Kesagami L. *Canada* 104 B3
Keşan *Turkey* 45 F10
Kesennuma *Japan* 54 E10
Keshāvar *Iran* 73 D12
Keshit *Iran* 71 D8
Keşiş Dağ *Turkey* 73 C8
Keskin *Turkey* 72 C5
Kestell *S. Africa* 89 D4
Kestenga *Russia* 8 D24
Keswick *U.K.* 14 C4
Keszthely *Hungary* 28 D2
Ket → *Russia* 52 D9
Keta *Ghana* 83 D5
Keta Lagoon *Ghana* 83 D5
Ketapang *Bali, Indonesia* 63 J17
Ketapang *Kalimantan,
  Indonesia* 62 E4
Ketchenery *Russia* 35 G7
Ketchikan *U.S.A.* 102 B2
Ketchum *U.S.A.* 108 E6
Ketef, Khalig Umm el *Egypt* 70 F2
Keti Bandar *Pakistan* 68 G2
Kétou *Benin* 83 D5
Ketri *India* 68 E6
Kętrzyn *Poland* 30 D8
Kettering *U.K.* 15 E7
Kettering *U.S.A.* 113 F11
Kettle → *Canada* 103 B11
Kettle Falls *U.S.A.* 108 B4
Kettle Point *Canada* 114 C2
Kettle Pt. *Canada* 114 C2
Kettleman City *U.S.A.* 110 J7
Kęty *Poland* 31 J6
Keuka L. *U.S.A.* 114 D7
Keuruu *Finland* 32 A3
Kevelaer *Germany* 24 D2
Kewanee *U.S.A.* 112 E9
Kewaunee *U.S.A.* 112 C10
Keweenaw B. *U.S.A.* 112 B9
Keweenaw Pen. *U.S.A.* 112 B9
Keweenaw Pt. *U.S.A.* 112 B10
Key, L. *Ireland* 12 C3
Key Lake Mine *Canada* 103 B7
Key Largo *U.S.A.* 117 J14
Key West *U.S.A.* 120 B3
Keyala *Sudan* 81 G3
Keynsham *U.K.* 15 F5
Keyser *U.S.A.* 113 F14
Kezhma *Russia* 53 D11
Kezi *Zimbabwe* 89 C4
Kežmarok *Slovak Rep.* 27 B13
Kgalagadi Transfrontier △
  Africa 88 D3
Khabarovsk *Russia* 53 E14
Khabr *Iran* 71 D8
Khābūr → *Syria* 73 E9
Khachmas = Xaçmaz
  Azerbaijan 35 K9
Khachrod *India* 68 H6
Khadari, W. el → *Sudan* 81 E2
Khadro *Pakistan* 68 F3
Khadyzhensk *Russia* 35 H4
Khadzhilyangar =
  Dahongliutan *China* 69 B8
Khaga *India* 69 G9
Khagaria *India* 69 G12
Khaipur *Pakistan* 68 E5
Khair *India* 68 F7
Khairabad *India* 69 F9
Khairagarh *India* 69 J9
Khairpur *Pakistan* 68 F3
Khairpur Nathan Shah
  Pakistan 68 F2
Khairwara *India* 68 H5
Khaisor → *Pakistan* 68 D3
Khajuri Kach *Pakistan* 68 C3
Khakassia □ *Russia* 52 D9
Khakhea *Botswana* 88 C3
Khalafābād *Iran* 71 D6
Khalilabad *India* 69 F10
Khalīlī *Iran* 71 E7
Khalkhāl *Iran* 73 D13
Khalkís = Halkida *Greece* 46 C5

Khalmer Yu *Russia* 52 C7
Khalūf *Oman* 75 C6
Kham Keut *Laos* 64 C5
Khamaria *India* 69 H9
Khambhaliya *India* 68 H3
Khambhat *India* 68 H5
Khambhat, G. of *India* 66 J8
Khamir *Iran* 71 E7
Khamir *Yemen* 75 D3
Khamsa *Egypt* 74 E1
Khan → *Namibia* 88 C2
Khān Abū Shāmat *Syria* 74 B5
Khān al Baghdādī *Iraq* 73 D10
Khān al Ḥammād *Iraq* 73 G11
Khān Azād *Iraq* 70 C5
Khān Mujiddah *Iraq* 70 C4
Khān Shaykhūn *Syria* 72 E7
Khān Yūnis *Gaza Strip* 74 D3
Khanai *Pakistan* 68 D2
Khānaqīn *Iraq* 73 E11
Khānbāghī *Iran* 71 B7
Khandwa *India* 66 J10
Khandyga *Russia* 53 C14
Khanewal *Pakistan* 68 D4
Khangah Dogran *Pakistan* 68 D5
Khaniá = Chania *Greece* 49 D6
Khaniadhana *India* 68 G8
Khanka, L. *Asia* 54 B6
Khankendy = Xankändi
  Azerbaijan 73 C12
Khanna *India* 68 D7
Khanozai *Pakistan* 68 D2
Khanpur *Pakistan* 68 E4
Khanty-Mansiysk *Russia* 52 C7
Khao Laem △ *Thailand* 64 E2
Khao Laem Res. *Thailand* 64 E2
Khao Lak △ *Malaysia* 65 H2
Khao Luang △ *Thailand* 65 H2
Khao Phlu *Thailand* 65 b
Khao Pu-Khao Ya △
  Thailand 65 J2
Khao Sam Roi Yot △
  Thailand 65 F2
Khao Sok △ *Thailand* 65 H2
Khao Yai △ *Thailand* 64 E3
Khaoen Si Nakarin △
  Thailand 64 E2
Khapalu *Pakistan* 69 B7
Khapcheranga *Russia* 53 E12
Khaptao △ *Nepal* 69 E9
Kharabali *Russia* 35 G8
Kharagauli *Georgia* 35 J6
Kharaghoda *India* 68 H4
Kharagpur *India* 69 H12
Kharan Kalat *Pakistan* 66 E4
Kharānaq *Iran* 71 C7
Kharda *India* 66 K9
Khardung La *India* 69 B7
Kharg = Khārk, Jazīreh-ye
  Iran 71 D6
Khârga, El Wâhât el *Egypt* 80 B3
Khargon *India* 66 J9
Khari → *India* 68 G6
Kharian *Pakistan* 68 C5
Kharit, Wadi el → *Egypt* 80 C3
Khārk, Jazīreh-ye *Iran* 71 D6
Kharkiv *Ukraine* 33 H9
Kharkiv □ *Ukraine* 33 H9
Kharkov = Kharkiv *Ukraine* 33 H9
Kharmanli *Bulgaria* 45 E9
Kharovsk *Russia* 32 C11
Kharsawangarh *India* 69 H11
Kharta *Turkey* 72 B3
Khartoum = El Khartûm
  Sudan 81 D3
Khartum *Canada* 114 A7
Khasan *Russia* 54 C5
Khasavyurt *Russia* 35 J8
Khāsh *Iran* 71 D9
Khashm el Girba *Sudan* 81 E4
Khashum *Sudan* 81 E2
Khashuri *Georgia* 35 J6
Khaskovo *Bulgaria* 45 E9
Khaskovo □ *Bulgaria* 45 E9
Khatanga *Russia* 53 B11
Khatanga → *Russia* 53 B11
Khatauli *India* 68 E7
Khatra *India* 69 H12
Khātūnābād *Iran* 71 D7
Khatyrka *Russia* 53 C18
Khavda *India* 68 H3
Khawr Fakkān *U.A.E.* 71 E8
Khay' *Si. Arabia* 80 D5
Khaybar, Ḥarrat *Si. Arabia* 70 E4
Khāzimiyah *Iraq* 70 C4
Khazzân Jabal al Awliyâ
  Sudan 81 D3
Khe Bo *Vietnam* 64 C5
Khe Long *Vietnam* 64 B5
Khe Sanh *Vietnam* 64 D6
Khed Brahma *India* 68 G5
Khekra *India* 68 E7
Khemarak Phouminville =
  Krong Kaoh Kong
  Cambodia 65 G4
Khemisset *Morocco* 78 B4
Khemmarat *Thailand* 64 D5

Khenāmān *Iran* 71 D8
Khenchela *Algeria* 78 A7
Khersān → *Iran* 71 D6
Kherson *Ukraine* 33 J7
Kherson □ *Ukraine* 33 J7
Kheta → *Russia* 53 B11
Khewari *Pakistan* 68 F3
Khilchipur *India* 68 G7
Khilok *Russia* 53 D12
Khimki *Russia* 32 E9
Khíos = Hios *Greece* 47 C8
Khirsadoh *India* 69 H8
Khiuma = Hiiumaa *Estonia* 32 C2
Khiva *Uzbekistan* 52 E7
Khlebarovo *Bulgaria* 45 C10
Khlong Khlung *Thailand* 64 D2
Khmelnik *Ukraine* 23 D14
Khmelnytskyy *Ukraine* 23 D14
Khmelnytskyy □ *Ukraine* 33 H4
Khmer Rep. =
  Cambodia ■ *Asia* 64 F5
Khoai, Hon *Vietnam* 65 H5
Khodoriv *Ukraine* 23 D13
Khodzent = Khŭjand
  Tajikistan 52 E7
Khojak Pass *Afghan.* 68 D2
Khok Kloi *Thailand* 65 a
Khok Pho *Thailand* 65 J3
Kholm *Russia* 32 D6
Kholmsk *Russia* 53 E15
Khomārlu *Iran* 73 C12
Khomas Hochland *Namibia* 88 C2
Khomeyn *Iran* 71 C6
Khomeynī Shahr *Iran* 71 C6
Khomodino *Botswana* 88 C3
Khon Kaen *Thailand* 64 D4
Khong → *Cambodia* 64 F5
Khong Sedone *Laos* 64 E5
Khonuu *Russia* 53 C15
Khoper → *Russia* 34 F6
Khor el 'Atash *Sudan* 81 E3
Khorāsān □ *Iran* 71 C8
Khorat = Nakhon
  Ratchasima *Thailand* 64 E4
Khorat, Cao Nguyen
  Thailand 64 E4
Khorixas *Namibia* 88 C1
Khorol *Ukraine* 33 H7
Khorramābād *Khorāsān, Iran* 71 C8
Khorramābād *Lorestān, Iran* 73 F13
Khorramdarreh *Iran* 73 D13
Khorrāmshahr *Iran* 71 D6
Khorugh *Tajikistan* 52 F8
Khosravī *Iran* 71 D6
Khosrowābād *Khuzestān,
  Iran* 71 D6
Khosrowābād *Kordestān,
  Iran* 73 E12
Khost *Pakistan* 68 D2
Khosūyeh *Iran* 71 D7
Khotyn *Ukraine* 29 B11
Khouribga *Morocco* 78 B4
Khowst *Afghan.* 68 C3
Khowst □ *Afghan.* 66 C6
Khoyniki *Belarus* 23 C15
Khrami → *Georgia* 35 K7
Khrenovoye *Russia* 34 E5
Khrysokhou B. *Cyprus* 49 D11
Khu Khan *Thailand* 64 E5
Khuan Wa *Thailand* 65 a
Khudzhand = Khŭjand
  Tajikistan 52 E7
Khuff *Si. Arabia* 70 E5
Khūgīānī *Afghan.* 68 D2
Khuis *Botswana* 88 D3
Khuiyala *India* 68 F4
Khujner *India* 68 H7
Khulna *Bangla.* 67 H16
Khulna □ *Bangla.* 67 H16
Khulo *Georgia* 35 K6
Khumago *Botswana* 88 C3
Khunjerab △ *Pakistan* 69 A6
Khunjerab Pass = Kinjirap
  Daban *Asia* 66 A9
Khūnsorkh *Iran* 71 E8
Khūr *Iran* 71 C8
Khurai *India* 68 G8
Khurayş *Si. Arabia* 71 E6
Khurja *India* 68 E7
Khūrmāl *Iraq* 73 E12
Khurr, Wādī al *Iraq* 70 C4
Khūsf *Iran* 71 C8
Khushab *Pakistan* 68 C5
Khust *Ukraine* 29 B8
Khutse △ *Botswana* 88 C3
Khuzdar *Pakistan* 68 F2
Khūzestān □ *Iran* 71 D6
Khvāf *Iran* 71 C9
Khvājeh *Iran* 70 B5
Khvānsār *Iran* 71 D7
Khvatovka *Russia* 34 D8
Khvor *Iran* 71 C7
Khvormūj *Iran* 71 E8
Khvorgū *Iran* 71 E8

Khvormūj *Iran* 71 D6
Khvoy *Iran* 73 C11
Khvoynaya *Russia* 32 C8
Khyber Pass *Afghan.* 68 B4
Khyriv *Ukraine* 31 J9
Kia *Fiji* 91 a
Kiabukwa
  Dem. Rep. of the Congo 87 D1
Kiama *Australia* 95 E5
Kiamba *Phil.* 61 H6
Kiambi *Dem. Rep. of the Congo* 86 D2
Kiambu *Kenya* 86 C4
Kiang West △ *Gambia* 82 C1
Kiangara *Madag.* 89 B8
Kiangsi = Jiangxi □ *China* 59 D11
Kiangsu = Jiangsu □ *China* 57 H11
Kiato *Greece* 46 C4
Kibæk *Denmark* 11 H2
Kibale △ *Uganda* 86 B3
Kibanga Port *Uganda* 86 B3
Kibara *Tanzania* 86 C3
Kibare, Mts.
  Dem. Rep. of the Congo 86 D2
Kibombo
  Dem. Rep. of the Congo 86 C2
Kibondo *Tanzania* 86 C3
Kibre Mengist *Ethiopia* 81 F4
Kıbrıs = Cyprus ■ *Asia* 49 E12
Kibumbu *Burundi* 86 C2
Kibuye *Burundi* 86 C2
Kibuye *Rwanda* 86 C2
Kibwesa *Tanzania* 86 D2
Kibwezi *Kenya* 86 C4
Kicasalih *Turkey* 45 E10
Kičevo *Macedonia* 44 E4
Kichha *India* 69 E8
Kichha → *India* 69 E8
Kicking Horse Pass *Canada* 102 C5
Kidal *Mali* 83 B5
Kidal □ *Mali* 83 B5
Kidapawan *Phil.* 61 H6
Kidderminster *U.K.* 15 E5
Kidepo Valley △ *Uganda* 86 B3
Kidete *Tanzania* 86 D4
Kidira *Senegal* 82 C2
Kidnappers, C. *N.Z.* 91 C6
Kidsgrove *U.K.* 14 D5
Kidston *Australia* 94 B3
Kidugallo *Tanzania* 86 D4
Kiel *Germany* 24 A6
Kiel Canal = Nord-Ostsee-
  Kanal *Germany* 24 A5
Kielce *Poland* 31 H7
Kielder Water *U.K.* 14 B5
Kieler Bucht *Germany* 24 A6
Kiembara *Burkina Faso* 82 C4
Kien Binh *Vietnam* 65 H5
Kien Tan *Vietnam* 65 G5
Kienge *Dem. Rep. of the Congo* 87 E2
Kiessé *Niger* 83 C5
Kiev = Kyyiv *Ukraine* 23 C16
Kifaya *Guinea* 82 C2
Kiffa *Mauritania* 82 B2
Kifisos → *Greece* 46 C5
Kifissia *Greece* 46 C5
Kifrī *Iraq* 73 E11
Kigali *Rwanda* 86 C3
Kigarama *Tanzania* 86 C3
Kigelle *Sudan* 81 F3
Kigezi △ *Uganda* 86 C2
Kiği *Turkey* 73 C9
Kigoma □ *Tanzania* 86 D3
Kigoma-Ujiji *Tanzania* 86 C2
Kigomasha, Ras *Tanzania* 86 C4
Kığzı *Turkey* 70 B4
Kihnu *Estonia* 32 C3
Kii-Sanchi *Japan* 55 G8
Kii-Suidō *Japan* 55 H7
Kiira Dam *Uganda* 86 B3
Kikaiga-Shima *Japan* 55 K4
Kikinda *Serbia* 28 E5
Kikládhes = Cyclades *Greece* 46 E6
Kikwit *Dem. Rep. of the Congo* 84 F3
Kil *Sweden* 10 E7
Kilafors *Sweden* 10 C10
Kilar *India* 68 C7
Kīlauea Caldera *U.S.A.* 106 b
Kilbeggan *Ireland* 12 C4
Kilbrannan Sd. *U.K.* 13 F3
Kilchu *N. Korea* 57 D15
Kilcoy *Australia* 95 D5
Kildare *Ireland* 12 C5
Kildare □ *Ireland* 12 C5
Kildinstroy *Russia* 8 B25
Kilfinnane *Ireland* 12 D3
Kilgarvan *Ireland* 12 E2
Kilgore *U.S.A.* 116 E7
Kilgoris *Kenya* 86 C3
Kilibo *Benin* 83 D5
Kilifi *Kenya* 86 C4
Kilimanjaro *Tanzania* 86 C4
Kilimanjaro □ *Tanzania* 86 C4
Kilimli *Turkey* 72 B4
Kilindini *Kenya* 86 C4
Kilis *Turkey* 72 D7
Kilis □ *Turkey* 72 D7

Kiliya *Ukraine* 29 E14
Kilkee *Ireland* 12 D2
Kilkeel *U.K.* 12 B5
Kilkenny *Ireland* 12 D4
Kilkenny □ *Ireland* 12 D4
Kilkieran B. *Ireland* 12 C2
Kilkis *Greece* 44 F6
Kilkís □ *Greece* 44 E6
Killala *Ireland* 12 B2
Killala B. *Ireland* 12 B2
Killaloe *Canada* 114 A7
Killaloe *Ireland* 12 D3
Killarney *Australia* 95 D5
Killarney *Canada* 103 D9
Killarney *Ireland* 12 D2
Killarney △ *Ireland* 12 D2
Killary Harbour *Ireland* 12 C2
Killdeer *U.S.A.* 112 B2
Killeen *U.S.A.* 116 F6
Killin *U.K.* 13 E4
Killiney *Ireland* 12 C5
Killington Pk. *U.S.A.* 115 C12
Killíni = Kyllíni *Greece* 46 D3
Killini *Greece* 46 D4
Killorglin *Ireland* 12 D2
Killybegs *Ireland* 12 B3
Kilmarnock *U.K.* 13 F4
Kilmez *Russia* 34 B10
Kilmez → *Russia* 34 B10
Kilmore *Australia* 95 F3
Kilmore Quay *Ireland* 12 D5
Kilondo *Tanzania* 87 D3
Kilosa *Tanzania* 86 D4
Kilrush *Ireland* 12 D2
Kilwa Kisiwani *Tanzania* 87 D4
Kilwa Kivinje *Tanzania* 87 D4
Kilwa Masoko *Tanzania* 87 D4
Kilwinning *U.K.* 13 F4
Kim *U.S.A.* 109 H12
Kim → *Cameroon* 83 D7
Kimaam *Indonesia* 63 F9
Kimamba *Tanzania* 86 D4
Kimba *Australia* 95 E2
Kimball *Nebr., U.S.A.* 112 E2
Kimball *S. Dak., U.S.A.* 112 D4
Kimberley *Australia* 92 C4
Kimberley *B.C., Canada* 102 D5
Kimberley *Ont., Canada* 114 B4
Kimberley *S. Africa* 88 D3
Kimberly *U.S.A.* 108 E6
Kimch'aek *N. Korea* 57 D15
Kimhae = Gimhae *S. Korea* 57 G15
Kimi *Greece* 46 C6
Kimmirut *Canada* 101 C13
Kimolos *Greece* 46 E6
Kimovsk *Moskva, Russia* 32 E9
Kimovsk *Tula, Russia* 32 E10
Kimparana *Mali* 82 C4
Kimpese
  Dem. Rep. of the Congo 84 F2
Kimry *Russia* 32 D9
Kimstad *Sweden* 11 F9
Kinabalu, Gunung *Malaysia* 62 C5
Kinango *Kenya* 86 C4
Kinaros *Greece* 47 E8
Kinaskan L. *Canada* 102 B2
Kinbasket L. *Canada* 102 C5
Kincardine *Canada* 114 B3
Kincolith *Canada* 102 C3
Kinda *Dem. Rep. of the Congo* 87 D2
Kindberg *Austria* 26 D8
Kinde *U.S.A.* 114 C2
Kinder Scout *U.K.* 14 D6
Kindersley *Canada* 103 C7
Kindia *Guinea* 82 D2
Kindu *Dem. Rep. of the Congo* 86 C2
Kinel *Russia* 34 D10
Kineshma *Russia* 34 B6
Kinesi *Tanzania* 86 C3
King, L. *Australia* 93 F2
King, Mt. *Australia* 94 D4
King City *U.S.A.* 110 J5
King Cr. → *Australia* 94 C2
King Edward → *Australia* 92 B4
King Edward Point
  S. Georgia 128 G9
King Frederik VI Land =
  Kong Frederik VI Kyst
  Greenland 4 C5
King George B. *Falk. Is.* 128 G4
King George I. *Antarctica* 5 C18
King George Is. *Canada* 101 D11
King George Sd. *Australia* 93 G2
King I. = Kadan Kyun
  Burma 64 F2
King I. *Australia* 95 F3
King I. *Canada* 102 C3
King Khalid Military
  City = Madinat al Malik
  Khālid al Askarīyah
  Si. Arabia 70 E5
King Leopold Ranges
  Australia 92 C4
King of Prussia *U.S.A.* 115 F9
King Sd. *Australia* 92 C3
King Sejong *Antarctica* 5 C18
King William I. *Canada* 100 C10

King William's Town
  S. Africa **88** E4
Kingait *Canada* **101** C12
Kingaok = Bathurst Inlet
  Canada **100** C9
Kingaroy *Australia* **95** D5
Kingfisher *U.S.A.* **116** D6
Kingirbān *Iraq* **70** C5
Kingisepp = Kuressaare
  Estonia **32** C2
Kingisepp *Russia* **32** C5
Kingman *Ariz., U.S.A.* **111** K12
Kingman *Kans., U.S.A.* **112** G4
Kingoonya *Australia* **95** E2
Kingri *Pakistan* **68** D3
Kings → *U.S.A.* **110** J7
Kings Canyon *Australia* **92** D5
Kings Canyon △ *U.S.A.* **110** J8
King's Lynn *U.K.* **14** E8
Kings Park *U.S.A.* **115** F11
Kings Peak *U.S.A.* **108** F8
Kingsbridge *U.K.* **15** G4
Kingsburg *U.S.A.* **110** J7
Kingscote *Australia* **95** F2
Kingscourt *Ireland* **12** C5
Kingsford *U.S.A.* **112** C9
Kingsland *U.S.A.* **117** F14
Kingsport *U.S.A.* **117** C13
Kingston *Canada* **115** B8
Kingston *Jamaica* **120** a
Kingston *N.Z.* **91** F2
Kingston *N.H., U.S.A.* **115** D13
Kingston *N.Y., U.S.A.* **115** E11
Kingston *Pa., U.S.A.* **115** E9
Kingston *R.I., U.S.A.* **115** E13
Kingston Pk. *U.S.A.* **111** K11
Kingston South East
  Australia **95** F2
Kingston upon Hull *U.K.* **14** D7
Kingston upon Hull □ *U.K.* **14** D7
Kingston-upon-Thames □
  U.K. **15** F7
Kingstown *St. Vincent* **121** D7
Kingstree *U.S.A.* **117** E15
Kingsville *Canada* **114** D2
Kingsville *U.S.A.* **116** H6
Kingussie *U.K.* **13** D4
Kingwood *U.S.A.* **116** F7
Kınık *Antalya, Turkey* **47** E11
Kınık *İzmir, Turkey* **47** B9
Kinistino *Canada* **103** C7
Kinjirap Daban *Asia* **66** A9
Kinkala *Congo* **84** E2
Kinki □ *Japan* **55** H8
Kinleith *N.Z.* **91** C5
Kinlochleven *U.K.* **13** E4
Kinmount *Canada* **114** B6
Kinna *Sweden* **11** G6
Kinnairds Hd. *U.K.* **13** D6
Kinnared *Sweden* **11** G7
Kinnarp *Sweden* **11** F7
Kinneviken *Sweden* **11** F7
Kino Nuevo *Mexico* **118** B2
Kinoje → *Canada* **104** B3
Kinomoto *Japan* **55** G8
Kinoni *Uganda* **86** C3
Kinoosao *Canada* **103** B8
Kinross *U.K.* **13** E5
Kinsale *Ireland* **12** E3
Kinsale, Old Hd. of *Ireland* **12** E3
Kinsha = Chang Jiang →
  China **59** B13
Kinshasa
  Dem. Rep. of the Congo **84** E3
Kinsley *U.S.A.* **112** G4
Kinsman *U.S.A.* **114** E4
Kinston *U.S.A.* **117** D16
Kintamani *Indonesia* **63** J18
Kintampo *Ghana* **83** D4
Kintore *U.K.* **13** D6
Kintore Ra. *Australia* **92** D4
Kintyre *U.K.* **13** F3
Kintyre, Mull of *U.K.* **13** F3
Kinushseo → *Canada* **104** A3
Kinuso *Canada* **102** B5
Kinvarra *Ireland* **12** C3
Kinyangiri *Tanzania* **86** C3
Kinyeti *Sudan* **81** G3
Kinzig → *Germany* **25** G3
Kinzua *U.S.A.* **114** E6
Kioni *Greece* **46** C2
Kiosk *Canada* **104** C4
Kiowa *Kans., U.S.A.* **112** G4
Kiowa *Okla., U.S.A.* **116** D7
Kipahigan L. *Canada* **103** B8
Kipanga *Tanzania* **86** D4
Kiparissia *Greece* **46** D3
Kiparissiakos Kolpos *Greece* **46** D3
Kipawa, L. *Canada* **104** C4
Kipembawe *Tanzania* **86** D3
Kipengere Ra. *Tanzania* **87** D3
Kipili *Tanzania* **86** D3
Kipini *Kenya* **86** C5
Kipling *Canada* **103** C8
Kippure *Ireland* **12** C5
Kipushi *Dem. Rep. of the Congo* **87** E2
Kira Panagia *Greece* **46** B6
Kirane *Mali* **82** B2
Kiranomena *Madag.* **89** B8

Kiraz *Turkey* **47** C10
Kırazlı *Turkey* **45** F10
Kirchhain *Germany* **24** E4
Kirchheim *Germany* **25** G5
Kirchheimbolanden
  Germany **25** F3
Kirchschlag *Austria* **27** D9
Kireç *Turkey* **47** B10
Kirensk *Russia* **53** D11
Kirghizia = Kyrgyzstan ■
  Asia **52** E8
Kiribati ■ *Pac. Oc.* **90** B10
Kırıkhan *Turkey* **72** D7
Kırıkkale *Turkey* **72** C5
Kirillov *Russia* **32** C10
Kirin = Jilin *China* **57** C14
Kirinyaga = Kenya, Mt.
  Kenya **86** C4
Kirirom △ *Cambodia* **65** G5
Kirishi *Russia* **32** C7
Kirishima Yaku △ *Japan* **55** J5
Kiritimati *Kiribati* **97** G12
Kırka *Turkey* **47** B11
Kirkağaç *Turkey* **47** B9
Kirkby *U.K.* **14** D5
Kirkby-in-Ashfield *U.K.* **14** D6
Kirkby Lonsdale *U.K.* **14** C5
Kirkby Stephen *U.K.* **14** C5
Kirkcaldy *U.K.* **13** E5
Kirkcudbright *U.K.* **13** G4
Kirkee *India* **66** K8
Kirkenes *Norway* **8** B24
Kirkfield *Canada* **114** B6
Kirkintilloch *U.K.* **13** F4
Kirkjubæjarklaustur *Iceland* **8** E4
Kirkkonummi *Finland* **32** B3
Kirkland *U.S.A.* **110** C4
Kirkland Lake *Canada* **104** C3
Kırklareli *Turkey* **45** E11
Kırklareli □ *Turkey* **45** E11
Kirksville *U.S.A.* **112** E7
Kirkūk *Iraq* **73** E11
Kirkwall *U.K.* **13** C6
Kirkwood *S. Africa* **88** E4
Kirn *Germany* **25** F3
Kirov *Kaluga, Russia* **32** E8
Kirov *Kirov, Russia* **52** D5
Kirovabad = Gäncä
  Azerbaijan **35** K8
Kirovograd = Kirovohrad
  Ukraine **33** H7
Kirovohrad *Ukraine* **33** H7
Kirovohrad □ *Ukraine* **33** H6
Kirovskiy *Astrakhan, Russia* **35** H9
Kirovskiy *Kamchatka, Russia* **53** D16
Kirovskiy *Primorsk, Russia* **54** B6
Kirriemuir *U.K.* **13** E5
Kirsanov *Russia* **34** D6
Kırşehir *Turkey* **72** C5
Kirtachi *Niger* **83** C5
Kirthar △ *Pakistan* **68** F2
Kirthar Range *Pakistan* **68** F2
Kirtland *U.S.A.* **109** H9
Kiruna *Sweden* **8** C19
Kirundu
  Dem. Rep. of the Congo **86** C2
Kirya *Russia* **34** C8
Kiryū *Japan* **55** F9
Kisa *Sweden* **11** G9
Kisaga *Tanzania* **86** C3
Kisalföld *Hungary* **28** C2
Kisanga
  Dem. Rep. of the Congo **86** D2
Kisangani
  Dem. Rep. of the Congo **86** B2
Kisar *Indonesia* **63** F7
Kisarawe *Tanzania* **86** D4
Kisarazu *Japan* **55** G9
Kisbér *Hungary* **28** C3
Kiselevsk *Russia* **52** D9
Kishanganga → *Pakistan* **69** B5
Kishanganj *India* **69** F13
Kishangarh *Raj., India* **68** F6
Kishangarh *Raj., India* **68** F4
Kishi *Nigeria* **83** D5
Kishinev = Chişinău
  Moldova **29** C13
Kishiwada *Japan* **55** G7
Kishtwar *India* **68** C6
Kisielice *Poland* **30** E6
Kisigo → *Tanzania* **86** D3
Kisii *Kenya* **86** C3
Kisiju *Tanzania* **86** D4
Kisir *Turkey* **73** B10
Kisizi *Uganda* **86** C2
Kiskomárom = Zalakomár
  Hungary **28** D2
Kisköre-víztároló *Hungary* **28** C5
Kiskőrös *Hungary* **28** D4
Kiskundorozsma *Hungary* **28** D5
Kiskunfélegyháza *Hungary* **28** D4
Kiskunhalas *Hungary* **28** D4
Kiskunmajsa *Hungary* **28** D4
Kiskunsági △ *Hungary* **28** D4
Kislovodsk *Russia* **35** J6
Kismaayo *Somali Rep.* **75** H3
Kiso-Gawa → *Japan* **55** G8
Kiso-Sammyaku *Japan* **55** G8
Kisofukushima *Japan* **55** G8

Kisoro *Uganda* **86** C2
Kissamos = Kasteli *Greece* **49** D5
Kissamos, Kolpos *Greece* **49** D5
Kissidougou *Guinea* **82** D2
Kissimmee *U.S.A.* **117** G14
Kissimmee → *U.S.A.* **117** H14
Kississing L. *Canada* **103** B8
Kissónerga *Cyprus* **49** E11
Kissu, J. *Sudan* **80** C2
Kistanje *Croatia* **41** E12
Kisújszállás *Hungary* **28** C5
Kisumu *Kenya* **86** C3
Kisvárda *Hungary* **28** B7
Kiswani *Tanzania* **86** C4
Kiswere *Tanzania* **87** D4
Kit Carson *U.S.A.* **108** G12
Kita *Mali* **82** C3
Kitaibaraki *Japan* **55** F10
Kitakami *Japan* **54** E10
Kitakami-Gawa → *Japan* **54** E10
Kitakami-Sammyaku *Japan* **54** E10
Kitakata *Japan* **54** F9
Kitakyūshū *Japan* **55** H5
Kitale *Kenya* **86** B4
Kitami *Japan* **54** C11
Kitami-Yamachi *Japan* **54** B11
Kitangiri, L. *Tanzania* **86** C3
Kitaya *Tanzania* **87** E5
Kitchener *Canada* **114** C4
Kitee *Finland* **32** A6
Kitega = Gitega *Burundi* **86** C2
Kitengo *Dem. Rep. of the Congo* **86** D1
Kitgum *Uganda* **86** B3
Kithira = Kythira *Greece* **46** E5
Kithnos *Greece* **46** D6
Kiti *Cyprus* **49** E12
Kiti, C. *Cyprus* **49** E12
Kitimat *Canada* **102** C3
Kitinen → *Finland* **8** C22
Kitiyab *Sudan* **81** D3
Kitros *Greece* **44** F6
Kitsman *Ukraine* **29** B10
Kitsuki *Japan* **55** H5
Kittakittaooloo, L. *Australia* **95** D2
Kittanning *U.S.A.* **114** F5
Kittatinny Mt. *U.S.A.* **115** F10
Kittery *U.S.A.* **115** C14
Kittilä *Finland* **8** C21
Kitui *Kenya* **86** C4
Kitwanga *Canada* **102** B3
Kitwe *Zambia* **87** E2
Kitzbühel *Austria* **26** D5
Kitzbühler Alpen *Austria* **26** D5
Kitzingen *Germany* **25** F6
Kivarli *India* **68** G5
Kivertsi *Ukraine* **23** C13
Kividhes *Cyprus* **49** E11
Kivik *Sweden* **11** J8
Kivotos *Greece* **44** F5
Kivu, L. *Dem. Rep. of the Congo* **86** C2
Kiwirrkurra *Australia* **92** D4
Kiyev = Kyyiv *Ukraine* **23** C16
Kiyevskoye Vdkhr. =
  Kyyivske Vdskh. *Ukraine* **23** C16
Kıyıköy *Turkey* **45** E12
Kizhi, Ostrov *Russia* **32** A8
Kiziguru *Rwanda* **86** C3
Kızıl Adalar *Turkey* **45** F13
Kızıl Irmak → *Turkey* **72** B6
Kizil Jilga *China* **69** B8
Kizil Yurt *Russia* **35** J8
Kızılcabölük *Turkey* **47** D11
Kızılcadağ *Turkey* **47** D11
Kızılcahamam *Turkey* **72** B5
Kızıldağ △ *Turkey* **70** B1
Kızılhisar *Turkey* **72** D3
Kızılırmak *Turkey* **72** B6
Kızılkaya *Turkey* **47** D12
Kızılören *Turkey* **47** C12
Kızıltepe *Turkey* **73** D9
Kizimkazi *Tanzania* **86** D4
Kizlyar *Russia* **35** J8
Kizyl-Arvat = Serdar
  Turkmenistan **71** B8
Ko Kha *Thailand* **64** C2
Ko Tarutao △ *Thailand* **65** J2
Ko Yao *Thailand* **65** a
Koartac = Quaqtaq *Canada*
  101 C13
Koba *Indonesia* **63** F8
Kobarid *Slovenia* **41** B10
Kobayashi *Japan* **55** J5
Kōbe *Japan* **55** G7
Kobelyaky *Ukraine* **33** H8
København *Denmark* **11** J6
København ✈ (CPH)
  Denmark **11** J6
Kobenni *Mauritania* **82** B3
Kōbi-Sho *Japan* **55** M1
Koblenz *Germany* **25** E3
Kobo *Ethiopia* **81** E4
Kobryn *Belarus* **23** B13
Kobuleti *Georgia* **35** K5
Kobylin *Poland* **31** G4
Kobyłka *Poland* **31** F8
Kobylkino *Russia* **34** C6
Koca *Ivory C.* **82** D3
Kocaali *Turkey* **45** F11
Kocaba *Turkey* **47** D11
Kocaeli *Turkey* **45** F13
Kocaeli □ *Turkey* **45** F13
Kočane *Serbia* **44** C5

Kleczew *Poland* **31** F5
Kleena Kleene *Canada* **102** C4
Klein-Karas *Namibia* **88** D2
Klekovača *Bos.-H.* **41** D13
Klembivka *Ukraine* **29** B13
Klenoec *Macedonia* **44** E4
Klenovec *Slovak Rep.* **27** C12
Kleszczele *Poland* **31** F10
Kletnya *Russia* **32** F7
Kletsk = Klyetsk *Belarus* **23** B14
Kletskiy *Russia* **35** F6
Kleve *Germany* **24** D2
Klickitat *U.S.A.* **108** D3
Klickitat → *U.S.A.* **110** E5
Klidhes *Cyprus* **49** D13
Klimovichi *Belarus* **32** F6
Klin *Russia* **32** D9
Klina *Serbia* **44** D4
Klinaklini → *Canada* **102** C3
Klintehamn *Sweden* **11** G12
Klintsy *Russia* **33** F7
Klip → *S. Africa* **89** D4
Klipdale *S. Africa* **88** E2
Klippan *Sweden* **11** H7
Klipplaat *S. Africa* **88** E3
Klishkivtsi *Ukraine* **29** B11
Klisura *Bulgaria* **45** D8
Kljajićevo *Serbia* **28** E4
Ključ *Bos.-H.* **41** D13
Klobuck *Poland* **31** H5
Klockestrand *Sweden* **10** B11
Klodawa *Poland* **31** F5
Kłodzko *Poland* **31** H3
Klong Wang Chao △
  Thailand **64** D2
Klos *Albania* **44** E4
Klötze *Germany* **24** C7
Klouto *Togo* **83** D5
Kluane *Canada* **102** A1
Kluane L. *Canada* **100** C6
Kluang *Malaysia* **65** L4
Kluczbork *Poland* **31** H5
Klukwan *U.S.A.* **102** B1
Klungkung *Indonesia* **63** K18
Klutina → *Canada* **102** C3
Klyetsk *Belarus* **23** B14
Klyuchevskaya, Gora
  Russia **53** D17
Klyuchi *Russia* **53** D17
Knäred *Sweden* **11** H7
Knaresborough *U.K.* **14** C6
Knee L. *Man., Canada* **104** A1
Knee L. *Sask., Canada* **103** B7
Knezha *Bulgaria* **45** C8
Knight Inlet *Canada* **102** C3
Knighton *U.K.* **15** E4
Knights Ferry *U.S.A.* **110** H6
Knights Landing *U.S.A.* **110** G5
Knin *Croatia* **41** D13
Knislinge *Sweden* **11** H8
Knittelfeld *Austria* **26** D7
Knivsta *Sweden* **10** E11
Knjaževac *Serbia* **44** C6
Knob, C. *Australia* **93** F2
Knock *Ireland* **12** C3
Knockmealdown Mts.
  Ireland **12** D4
Knokke-Heist *Belgium* **17** C3
Knossós *Greece* **49** D7
Knowlton *Canada* **115** A12
Knox *U.S.A.* **112** E10
Knox Coast *Antarctica* **5** C8
Knoxville *Iowa, U.S.A.* **112** E7
Knoxville *Pa., U.S.A.* **114** E7
Knoxville *Tenn., U.S.A.* **117** D13
Knud Rasmussen Land
  Greenland **4** A5
Knysna *S. Africa* **88** E3
Knyszyn *Poland* **30** E9
Ko Kha *Thailand* **65** a
Koartac = Quaqtaq *Canada*
Kolachi → *Pakistan* **68** F2
Kolahoi *India* **69** B6
Kolahun *Liberia* **82** D2
Kolaka *Indonesia* **63** E6
Kolar *India* **66** N11
Kolar Gold Fields *India* **66** N11
Kolaras *India* **68** G6
Kolari *Finland* **8** C20
Kolárovo *Slovak Rep.* **27** D10
Kolašin *Montenegro* **44** D3
Kolayat *India* **68** F5
Kolbäck *Sweden* **10** E10
Kolbäcksån → *Sweden* **10** E10
Kolbermoor *Germany* **25** H8
Kolbuszowa *Poland* **31** H8
Kolchugino *Russia* **32** D10
Kolda *Senegal* **82** C2
Kolda □ *Senegal* **82** C2
Koldegi *Sudan* **81** F3
Kolding *Denmark* **11** J3
Kolepom = Dolak, Pulau
  Indonesia **63** F9
Kolguyev, Ostrov *Russia* **52** C5
Kolhapur *India* **66** L9
Kolia *Ivory C.* **82** D3
Kolimbia *Greece* **49** C10
Kolín *Czech Rep.* **26** A8
Kolind *Denmark* **11** H4
Kolkas rags *Latvia* **30** A9

Kočani *Macedonia* **44** E6
Koçarlı *Turkey* **47** D9
Koceljevo *Serbia* **44** B3
Kočevje *Slovenia* **41** C11
Koch Bihar *India* **67** F16
Koch Bihar □ *India* **67** F16
Kochas *India* **69** G10
Kochi = Cochin *India* **66** Q10
Kōchi *Japan* **55** H6
Kōchi □ *Japan* **55** H6
Kochiu = Gejiu *China* **58** F4
Kochubey *Russia* **35** H8
Kock *Poland* **31** G9
Kodarma *India* **69** G11
Kode *Sweden* **11** G5
Kodiak *U.S.A.* **106** a
Kodiak I. *U.S.A.* **106** a
Kodinar *India* **68** J4
Kodinsk *Russia* **53** D10
Kodok *Sudan* **81** F3
Kodyma *Ukraine* **29** B14
Kodori → *Georgia* **35** J5
Koedoesberge *S. Africa* **88** E3
Koes *Namibia* **88** D2
Kofçaz *Turkey* **45** E11
Koffiefontein *S. Africa* **88** D4
Kofiau *Indonesia* **63** E7
Köflach *Austria* **26** D8
Koforidua *Ghana* **83** D4
Kōfu *Japan* **55** G9
Koga *Japan* **55** F9
Kogaluc → *Canada* **105** A7
Køge *Denmark* **11** J6
Køge Bugt *Denmark* **11** J6
Kogi □ *Nigeria* **83** D6
Kogin Baba *Nigeria* **83** D7
Kogon *Uzbekistan* **52** F7
Koh-i-Khurd *Afghan.* **68** C1
Koh-i-Maran *Pakistan* **68** E2
Kohat *Pakistan* **68** C4
Kohima *India* **67** G19
Kohkīlūyeh va Būyer
  Aḥmadi □ *Iran* **71** D6
Kohler Ra. *Antarctica* **5** D15
Kohlu *Pakistan* **68** E3
Kohtla-Järve *Estonia* **32** C4
Kohylnyk → *Ukraine* **29** E14
Koi Sanjaq *Iraq* **73** D11
Koillismaa *Finland* **8** D23
Koin *N. Korea* **57** D14
Koinare *Bulgaria* **45** C8
Koindu *S. Leone* **82** D2
Kojetín *Czech Rep.* **27** B10
Kojō *N. Korea* **57** E14
Kojonup *Australia* **93** F2
Kojūr *Iran* **71** B6
Koka *Sudan* **80** C3
Kokand = Qŭqon *Uzbekistan* **52** E8
Kokas *Indonesia* **63** E8
Kokava *Slovak Rep.* **27** C12
Kokchetav = Kökshetaŭ
  Kazakhstan **52** D7
Kokemäenjoki → *Finland* **32** B1
Kokhma *Russia* **34** B5
Koki *Senegal* **82** B1
Kokkola *Finland* **8** E20
Koko *Nigeria* **83** C5
Koko Kyunzu *Burma* **67** M18
Kokolopozo *Ivory C.* **82** D3
Kokomo *U.S.A.* **112** E10
Kokoro *Niger* **83** C5
Koksan *N. Korea* **57** E14
Kökshetaŭ *Kazakhstan* **52** D7
Koksoak → *Canada* **101** D13
Kokstad *S. Africa* **89** E4
Kokubu *Japan* **55** J5
Kola *Indonesia* **63** F8
Kola *Russia* **8** B25
Kola Pen. = Kolskiy
  Poluostrov *Russia* **6** B13
Kolachi → *Pakistan* **68** F2

Kolkata *India* **69** H13
Kollam = Quilon *India* **66** Q10
Kölleda *Germany* **24** D7
Kollum *Neths.* **17** A6
Kolmanskop *Namibia* **88** D2
Köln *Germany* **24** E2
Kolno *Poland* **30** E8
Koło *Poland* **31** F5
Kołobrzeg *Poland* **30** D2
Kolochava *Ukraine* **29** B8
Kolokani *Mali* **82** C3
Koloko *Burkina Faso* **82** C3
Kololo *Ethiopia* **81** F5
Kolomna *Russia* **32** E10
Kolomyya *Ukraine* **29** B10
Kolondiéba *Mali* **82** C3
Kolonodale *Indonesia* **63** E6
Kolonowskie *Poland* **31** H5
Kolosib *India* **67** G18
Kolpashevo *Russia* **52** D9
Kolpino *Russia* **32** C6
Kolpny *Russia* **33** F9
Kolskiy Poluostrov *Russia* **6** B13
Kolskiy Zaliv *Russia* **8** B26
Kolsva *Sweden* **10** E9
Kolubara → *Serbia* **44** B4
Koluszki *Poland* **31** G6
Kolwezi *Dem. Rep. of the Congo* **87** E2
Kolyma → *Russia* **53** C17
Kolymskoye Nagorye
  Russia **53** C16
Kôm Hamâda *Egypt* **80** H7
Kôm Ombo *Egypt* **80** C3
Komadugu Gana → *Nigeria* **83** C7
Komandorskiye Is. =
  Komandorskiye Ostrova
  Russia **53** D17
Komandorskiye Ostrova
  Russia **53** D17
Komárno *Slovak Rep.* **27** D11
Komarnyky *Ukraine* **29** B8
Komárom *Hungary* **28** C3
Komárom-Esztergom □
  Hungary **28** C3
Komatipoort *S. Africa* **89** D5
Komatou Yialou *Cyprus* **49** D13
Komatsu *Japan* **55** F8
Komatsushima *Japan* **55** H7
Kombissiri *Burkina Faso* **83** C4
Kombori *Burkina Faso* **82** C4
Komboti *Greece* **46** B3
Komen *Slovenia* **41** C10
Komenda *Ghana* **83** D4
Komi *Cyprus* **49** D13
Komi □ *Russia* **52** C6
Komiža *Croatia* **41** E13
Komló *Hungary* **28** D3
Kommunarsk = Alchevsk
  Ukraine **33** H10
Kommunizma, Pik =
  imeni Ismail Samani,
  Pik *Tajikistan* **52** F8
Komodo *Indonesia* **63** F5
Komoé → *Ivory C.* **82** D4
Komoran, Pulau *Indonesia* **63** F9
Komoro *Japan* **55** F9
Komotini *Greece* **45** E9
Komovi *Montenegro* **44** D3
Kompasberg *S. Africa* **88** E3
Kompong Cham *Cambodia* **65** G5
Kompong Chhnang =
  Kampong Chhnang
  Cambodia **65** F5
Kompong Chikreng
  Cambodia **64** F5
Kompong Kleang *Cambodia* **64** F5
Kompong Luong *Cambodia* **65** G5
Kompong Pranak *Cambodia* **64** F5
Kompong Som =
  Kampong Saom *Cambodia* **65** G4
Kompong Som, Chhung =
  Kampong Saom, Chaak
  Cambodia **65** G4
Kompong Speu *Cambodia* **65** G5
Kompong Sralau *Cambodia* **64** E5
Kompong Thom *Cambodia* **64** F5
Kompong Trabeck *Cambodia* **65** G5
Kompong Trabeck *Cambodia* **64** F5
Kompong Trach *Cambodia* **65** G5
Kompong Tralach *Cambodia* **65** G5
Komrat = Comrat *Moldova* **29** D13
Komsberg *S. Africa* **88** E3
Komsomolets, Ostrov
  Russia **53** A10
Komsomolsk *Russia* **32** D11
Komsomolsk-na-Amure
  Russia **53** D14
Komsomolskiy *Russia* **34** C7
Kömür Burnu *Turkey* **47** C8
Kon Tum *Vietnam* **64** E7
Kon Tum, Plateau du
  Vietnam **64** E7
Kona *Mali* **82** C4
Konakovo *Russia* **32** D9
Konar □ *Afghan.* **66** B7
Konārī *Iran* **71** D6
Konch *India* **69** G8
Konde *Tanzania* **86** C4
Kondias *Greece* **47** B7

Kondinin *Australia* **93** F2
Kondoa *Tanzania* **86** C4
Kondopaga *Russia* **32** A8
Kondratyevo *Russia* **53** D10
Kondrovo *Russia* **32** E8
Konduga *Nigeria* **83** C7
Köneürgench *Turkmenistan* **52** E6
Konevo *Russia* **32** A10
Kong = Khong ➤ *Cambodia* **64** F5
Kong *Ivory C.* **82** D4
Kong, Koh *Cambodia* **65** G4
Kong Christian IX Land
  Greenland **4** C6
Kong Christian X Land
  Greenland **4** B6
Kong Frederik IX Land
  Greenland **4** C5
Kong Frederik VI Kyst
  Greenland **4** C5
Kong Frederik VIII Land
  Greenland **4** B6
Kong Oscar Fjord *Greenland* **4** B6
Kongeå ➤ *Denmark* **11** J2
Kongerslev *Denmark* **11** H4
Konglu *Burma* **67** F20
Kongola *Namibia* **88** B3
Kongolo *Kasai-Or.,*
  Dem. Rep. of the Congo **86** D1
Kongolo *Katanga,*
  Dem. Rep. of the Congo **86** D2
Kongor *Sudan* **81** F3
Kongoussi *Burkina Faso* **83** C4
Kongsberg *Norway* **9** G13
Kongsvinger *Norway* **9** F15
Kongwa *Tanzania* **86** D4
Koni *Dem. Rep. of the Congo* **87** E2
Koni, Mts.
  Dem. Rep. of the Congo **87** E2
Koniakari *Mali* **82** C2
Koniecpol *Poland* **31** H6
Königs Wusterhausen
  Germany **24** C9
Königsbrunn *Germany* **25** G6
Königslutter *Germany* **24** C6
Konin *Poland* **31** F5
Konispol *Albania* **44** G4
Konitsa *Greece* **46** A2
Konjic *Bos.-H.* **28** F2
Konkiep *Namibia* **88** D2
Konkouré ➤ *Guinea* **82** D2
Könnern *Germany* **24** D7
Kono *S. Leone* **82** D2
Konongo *Ghana* **83** D4
Konosha *Russia* **32** B11
Kōnosu *Japan* **55** F9
Konotop *Ukraine* **33** G7
Konsankoro *Guinea* **82** D3
Końskie *Poland* **31** G7
Konstancin-Jeziorna *Poland* **31** F8
Konstantinovka =
  Kostyantynivka *Ukraine* **33** H9
Konstantinovsk *Russia* **35** G5
Konstantynów Łódzki
  Poland **31** G6
Konstanz *Germany* **25** H5
Kont *Iran* **71** E9
Kontagora *Nigeria* **83** C6
Kontcha *Cameroon* **83** D7
Kontiolahti *Finland* **8** E23
Kontokali *Greece* **49** A3
Konya *Turkey* **72** D5
Konya □ *Turkey* **72** D5
Konya Ovası *Turkey* **72** C5
Konz *Germany* **25** F2
Konza *Kenya* **86** C4
Koocanusa, L. *Canada* **108** B6
Kookynie *Australia* **93** E3
Koolyanobbing *Australia* **93** F2
Koorawatha *Australia* **95** E4
Koorda *Australia* **93** F2
Kooskia *U.S.A.* **108** C6
Kootenay ➤ *U.S.A.* **102** D5
Kootenay △ *Canada* **102** C5
Kootenay L. *Canada* **108** B5
Kootjieskolk *S. Africa* **88** E3
Kopanovka *Russia* **35** G8
Kopaonik *Serbia* **44** C4
Kopaonik △ *Serbia* **44** C4
Kópavogur *Iceland* **8** D3
Kopayhorod *Ukraine* **29** B12
Koper *Slovenia* **41** C10
Kopervik *Norway* **9** G11
Kopet Dagh *Asia* **71** B8
Kopi *Australia* **95** E2
Köping *Sweden* **10** E10
Köpingsvik *Sweden* **11** H10
Kopište *Croatia* **41** F13
Koplik *Albania* **44** D3
Köpmanholmen *Sweden* **10** A12
Kopparberg *Sweden* **10** E9
Koppeh Dāgh = Kopet
  Dagh *Asia* **71** B8
Koppies *S. Africa* **89** D4
Koppom *Sweden* **10** E6
Koprivnica *Croatia* **41** B13
Kopřivnice *Czech Rep.* **27** B11
Koprivshtitsa *Bulgaria* **45** D8

Köprübaşı *Turkey* **47** C10
Köprülü △ *Turkey* **70** B1
Kopychyntsi *Ukraine* **23** D13
Kora △ *Kenya* **86** C4
Korab *Macedonia* **44** E4
Koral *India* **68** J5
Korarou, L. *Mali* **82** B4
Korba *India* **69** H10
Korbach *Germany* **24** D4
Korça *Albania* **44** F4
Korça □ *Albania* **44** F4
Korčula *Croatia* **41** F13
Korčulanski Kanal *Croatia* **41** E13
Kord Kūy *Iran* **71** B7
Kord Sheykh *Iran* **71** D7
Kordestan = Kurdistan
  Asia **73** D10
Kordestān □ *Iran* **70** C5
Kordofân *Sudan* **79** F11
Koré Mayroua *Niger* **83** C5
Korea, North ■ *Asia* **57** E14
Korea, South ■ *Asia* **57** G15
Korea Bay *Asia* **57** E13
Korea Strait *Asia* **57** H15
Korem *Ethiopia* **81** E4
Korenevo *Russia* **33** G8
Korenovsk *Russia* **35** H4
Korets *Ukraine* **23** C14
Korfantów *Poland* **31** H4
Korgan *Turkey* **72** B7
Korgus *Sudan* **80** D3
Korhogo *Ivory C.* **82** D3
Koribundu *S. Leone* **82** D2
Korienzé *Mali* **82** B4
Korinthia □ *Greece* **46** D4
Korinthiakos Kolpos *Greece* **46** C4
Korinthos *Greece* **46** D4
Korioumé *Mali* **82** B4
Korissia, L. *Greece* **49** B3
Kōriyama *Japan* **54** F10
Korkuteli *Turkey* **47** D12
Körmend *Hungary* **28** C1
Kormor *Iraq* **73** E11
Kornat *Croatia* **41** E12
Kornat △ *Croatia* **41** E12
Korneshty = Corneşti
  Moldova **29** C10
Korneuburg *Austria* **27** C9
Kórnik *Poland* **31** F4
Koro *Fiji* **91** a
Koro *Ivory C.* **82** D3
Koro *Mali* **82** C4
Koro Sea *Fiji* **91** a
Korocha *Russia* **33** G9
Köroğlu Dağları *Turkey* **72** B5
Korogwe *Tanzania* **86** D4
Koroleve *Ukraine* **29** B8
Korolevu *Fiji* **91** a
Koronadal *Phil.* **61** H6
Koroni *Greece* **46** E3
Koronia, L. *Greece* **44** F7
Koronos *Greece* **47** D7
Koronowo *Poland* **31** E4
Koropets *Ukraine* **29** B10
Koror *Palau* **96** G5
Körös ➤ *Hungary* **28** D5
Körös Maros △ *Hungary* **28** C5
Köröstarcsa *Hungary* **28** D6
Korosten *Ukraine* **23** C15
Korostyshev *Ukraine* **23** C15
Korotoyak *Russia* **33** G10
Korovou *Fiji* **91** a
Koroyanitu △ *Fiji* **91** a
Korraraika, Helodranon' i
  Madag. **89** B7
Korsakov *Russia* **53** E15
Korsberga *Sweden* **11** G9
Korshiv *Ukraine* **29** B10
Korshunovo *Russia* **53** D12
Korsør *Denmark* **11** J5
Korsun Shevchenkovskiy
  Ukraine **33** H6
Korsze *Poland* **30** D8
Korti *Sudan* **80** D3
Kortrijk *Belgium* **17** D3
Korucu *Turkey* **47** B9
Korwai *India* **68** G8
Koryakskoye Nagorye
  Russia **53** C18
Koryukovka *Ukraine* **33** G7
Kos *Greece* **47** E9
Kosa *Ethiopia* **81** F4
Kosan *N. Korea* **57** E14
Kosaya Gora *Russia* **32** E9
Kościan *Poland* **31** F3
Kosciusko *U.S.A.* **117** E10
Kosciuszko, Mt. *Australia* **95** F4
Kősély ➤ *Hungary* **28** C6
Kosha *Sudan* **80** C3
Koshava *Bulgaria* **44** B7
K'oshih = Kashi *China* **60** C2
Koshim = Kushum ➤
  Kazakhstan **34** F10
Kosi *India* **68** F7
Kosi ➤ *India* **69** E8
Košice *Slovak Rep.* **27** C14
Košický □ *Slovak Rep.* **27** C14

Kosiv *Ukraine* **29** B10
Kosjerić *Serbia* **44** B3
Köşk *Turkey* **47** D10
Koskinou *Greece* **49** C10
Koslan *Russia* **52** C5
Kosmach *Ukraine* **29** B9
Kosovo ■ *Serbia* **44** D4
Kosovo Polje *Serbia* **44** D5
Kosovska Kamenica *Serbia* **44** D5
Kosovska Mitrovica *Serbia* **44** D4
Kossou, L. de *Ivory C.* **82** D3
Kosta *Sweden* **11** H9
Kostajnica *Croatia* **41** C13
Kostanjevica *Slovenia* **41** C12
Kostenets *Bulgaria* **44** D7
Koster *S. Africa* **88** D4
Kôstî *Sudan* **81** E3
Kostinbrod *Bulgaria* **44** D7
Kostolac *Serbia* **44** B5
Kostopil *Ukraine* **23** C14
Kostroma *Russia* **32** D11
Kostromo □ *Russia* **34** A6
Kostromskoye Vdkhr.
  Russia **32** D11
Kostrzyn *Lubuskie, Poland* **31** F1
Kostrzyn *Wielkopolskie, Poland* **31** F4
Kostyantynivka *Ukraine* **33** H9
Koszalin *Poland* **30** D3
Kőszeg *Hungary* **28** C1
Kot Addu *Pakistan* **68** D4
Kot Kapura *India* **68** D6
Kot Moman *Pakistan* **68** C5
Kot Sultan *Pakistan* **68** D4
Kota *India* **68** G6
Kota Barrage *India* **68** G6
Kota Belud *Malaysia* **62** C5
Kota Bharu *Malaysia* **65** J4
Kota Kinabalu *Malaysia* **62** C5
Kota Tinggi *Malaysia* **65** M4
Kotaagung *Indonesia* **62** F3
Kotabaru *Indonesia* **62** E5
Kotabumi *Indonesia* **62** E2
Kotamobagu *Indonesia* **63** D6
Kotapinang *Indonesia* **65** M3
Kotcho L. *Canada* **102** B4
Kotdwara *India* **68** E8
Kotel *Bulgaria* **45** D10
Kotelnich *Russia* **34** A9
Kotelnikovo *Russia* **35** G6
Kotelnyy, Ostrov *Russia* **53** B14
Kothari ➤ *India* **68** G6
Köthen *Germany* **24** D7
Kothi *Chhattisgarh, India* **69** H10
Kothi *Mad. P., India* **69** G9
Kotiro *Pakistan* **68** F2
Kotka *Finland* **32** B4
Kotlas *Russia* **52** C5
Kotlenska Planina *Bulgaria* **45** D10
Kotli *Pakistan* **68** C5
Kotma *India* **69** H9
Koton-Karifi *Nigeria* **83** D6
Kotonkoro *Nigeria* **83** C6
Kotor *Montenegro* **44** D2
Kotor Varoš *Bos.-H.* **28** F2
Kotoriba *Croatia* **41** B13
Kotovo *Russia* **34** E7
Kotovsk *Russia* **34** D5
Kotovsk *Ukraine* **23** E15
Kotputli *India* **68** F7
Kotri *Pakistan* **68** G3
Kotronas *Greece* **46** E4
Kötschach-Mauthen *Austria* **26** E6
Kotto ➤ *C.A.R.* **84** D4
Kotturu *India* **66** M10
Kotu Group *Tonga* **91** c
Kotuy ➤ *Russia* **53** B11
Kotyuzhany *Ukraine* **29** B12
Kotzebue *U.S.A.* **106** a
Kotzebue Sound *U.S.A.* **98** C3
Kouchibouguac △ *Canada* **105** C6
Koudougou *Burkina Faso* **82** C4
Koufonisi *Iraklio, Greece* **49** E8
Koufonisi *Notio Aigaio, Greece* **47** E7
Kougaberge *S. Africa* **88** E3
Kouibli *Ivory C.* **82** D3
Kouilou ➤ *Congo* **84** E2
Koula *Greece* **45** E8
Koula Moutou *Gabon* **84** E2
Koulen = Kulen *Cambodia* **64** F5
Koulikoro *Mali* **82** C3
Koulikoro □ *Mali* **82** C3
Kouloura *Greece* **49** A3
Koumala *Australia* **94** C4
Koumankou *Mali* **82** C3
Koumbia *Burkina Faso* **82** C4
Koumbia *Guinea* **82** C2
Koumboum *Guinea* **82** C2
Koumpenntoum *Senegal* **82** C2
Koumra *Chad* **79** G9
Koun-Fao *Ivory C.* **82** D4
Koundara *Guinea* **82** C2
Koundian *Guinea* **82** C3
Koungheul *Senegal* **82** C2
Kountze *U.S.A.* **116** F7
Koupéla *Burkina Faso* **83** C4

Kourémalé *Mali* **82** C3
Kouris ➤ *Cyprus* **49** E11
Kourou *Fr. Guiana* **125** B8
Kourouba *Mali* **82** C2
Kouroukoto *Mali* **82** C2
Kourouma *Burkina Faso* **82** C4
Kouroussa *Guinea* **82** C3
Koussanar *Senegal* **82** C2
Koussané *Mali* **82** C2
Koussane *Senegal* **82** C2
Kousseri *Cameroon* **79** F8
Koutiala *Mali* **82** C3
Kouto *Ivory C.* **82** D3
Kouvé *Togo* **83** D5
Kouvola *Finland* **32** B4
Kovačica *Serbia* **28** E5
Kovdor *Russia* **8** C24
Kovel *Ukraine* **23** C13
Kovin *Serbia* **28** F5
Kovrov *Russia* **34** B5
Kowal *Poland* **31** F6
Kowalewo Pomorskie
  Poland **31** E5
Kowanyama *Australia* **94** B3
Kowloon *China* **59** F10
Kowōn *N. Korea* **57** E14
Koyampattur =
  Coimbatore *India* **66** P10
Köyceğiz *Turkey* **47** E10
Köyceğiz Gölü *Turkey* **47** E10
Koyukuk ➤ *U.S.A.* **98** C4
Koyulhisar *Turkey* **72** B7
Koyunyeri *Turkey* **45** F10
Koza = Okinawa *Japan* **55** L3
Kozak *Turkey* **47** B9
Kozaklı *Turkey* **72** C6
Kozan *Turkey* **72** D6
Kozani *Greece* **44** F5
Kozani □ *Greece* **44** F5
Kozara *Bos.-H.* **41** D14
Kozara △ *Bos.-H.* **28** F2
Kozarac *Bos.-H.* **41** D13
Kozelets *Ukraine* **33** G6
Kozelsk *Russia* **32** E8
Kozhikode = Calicut *India* **66** P9
Koziegłowy *Poland* **31** H6
Kozienice *Poland* **31** G8
Kozje *Slovenia* **41** B12
Kozloduy *Bulgaria* **44** C7
Kozlovets *Bulgaria* **45** C9
Kozlovka *Russia* **34** C9
Kozlu *Turkey* **72** B4
Kozluk *Turkey* **73** C9
Koźmin *Poland* **31** G4
Kozmodemyansk *Russia* **34** B8
Kożuchów *Poland* **31** G2
Kozyatyn *Ukraine* **23** D15
Kozyrevsk *Russia* **53** D16
Kpabia *Ghana* **83** D4
Kpalimé *Togo* **83** D5
Kpandae *Ghana* **83** D4
Kpessi *Togo* **83** D5
Kra, Isthmus of = Kra,
  Kho Khot *Thailand* **65** G2
Kra, Kho Khot *Thailand* **65** G2
Kra Buri *Thailand* **65** G2
Kraai ➤ *S. Africa* **88** E4
Krabi *Thailand* **65** H2
Kracheh *Cambodia* **64** F6
Kragan *Indonesia* **63** G14
Kragerø *Norway* **9** G13
Kragujevac *Serbia* **44** B4
Krajenka *Poland* **31** E3
Krakatau = Rakata, Pulau
  Indonesia **62** F3
Krakatoa = Rakata, Pulau
  Indonesia **62** F3
Krakor *Cambodia* **64** F5
Kraków *Poland* **31** H6
Kraków ✈ (KRK) *Poland* **31** H6
Kralanh *Cambodia* **64** F4
Králíky *Czech Rep.* **27** A9
Kraljevo *Serbia* **44** C4
Kralovéhradecký □
  Czech Rep. **26** A8
Královský Chlmec
  Slovak Rep. **27** C14
Kralupy nad Vltavou
  Czech Rep. **26** A7
Kramatorsk *Ukraine* **33** H9
Kramfors *Sweden* **10** B11
Krania *Greece* **44** G5
Krania Elasonas *Greece* **46** B4
Kranidi *Greece* **46** D5
Kranj *Slovenia* **41** B11
Kranjska Gora *Slovenia* **41** B10
Krankskop *S. Africa* **89** D5
Krapina *Croatia* **41** B12
Krapina ➤ *Croatia* **41** C12
Krapkowice *Poland* **31** H4
Kras *Croatia* **41** C11
Kraskino *Russia* **54** C5
Kraslava *Latvia* **32** E4
Kraslice *Czech Rep.* **26** A5
Krasnaya Gorbatka *Russia* **34** C5
Krasnaya Polyana *Russia* **35** J5
Krasne *Ukraine* **29** D14
Krasni Okny *Ukraine* **29** C14

Krasnik *Poland* **31** H9
Krasnoarmeisk *Ukraine* **33** H9
Krasnoarmeysk *Russia* **34** E7
Krasnoarmeyskiy *Russia* **35** G6
Krasnobrod *Poland* **31** H10
Krasnodar *Russia* **35** H4
Krasnodar □ *Russia* **35** G4
Krasnodarskoye Vdkhr.
  Russia **35** H4
Krasnodon *Ukraine* **33** H10
Krasnogorskiy *Russia* **34** B9
Krasnograd = Krasnohrad
  Ukraine **33** H8
Krasnogvardeysk *Ukraine* **33** K8
Krasnogvardeyskoye *Russia* **35** H5
Krasnohrad *Ukraine* **33** H8
Krasnokamensk *Russia* **53** D12
Krasnokutsk *Ukraine* **33** G8
Krasnolesnyy *Russia* **33** G10
Krasnoperekopsk *Ukraine* **33** J7
Krasnorechenskiy *Russia* **54** B7
Krasnoselkup *Russia* **52** C9
Krasnoslobodsk *Mordvinia,*
  Russia **34** C6
Krasnoslobodsk *Volgograd,*
  Russia **35** F7
Krasnoturinsk *Russia* **52** D7
Krasnoufimsk *Russia* **52** D6
Krasnouralsk *Russia* **52** D7
Krasnovishersk *Russia* **52** C6
Krasnoye *Russia* **32** E6
Krasnoyilsk *Ukraine* **29** C10
Krasnozavodsk *Russia* **32** D10
Krasnoyarsk *Russia* **53** D10
Krasnoyarskoye *Russia* **30** D8
Krasnoye = Krasnyy *Russia* **32** E6
Krasny Sulin *Russia* **33** J11
Krasnystaw *Poland* **31** H10
Krasnyy *Russia* **32** E6
Krasnyy Kholm *Russia* **32** C9
Krasnyy Kut *Russia* **34** E8
Krasnyy Liman *Ukraine* **33** H9
Krasnyy Luch *Ukraine* **33** H10
Krasnyy Profintern *Russia* **32** D11
Krasnyy Yar *Astrakhan,*
  Russia **35** G9
Krasnyy Yar *Samara, Russia* **34** D10
Krasnyy Yar *Volgograd,*
  Russia **34** E7
Krasnyye Baki *Russia* **34** B7
Krasnyyoskolske Vdskh.
  Ukraine **33** H9
Kratie = Kracheh *Cambodia* **64** F6
Kratovo *Macedonia* **44** D6
Krau *Indonesia* **63** E10
Kravanh, Chuor Phnum
  Cambodia **65** G4
Krefeld *Germany* **24** D2
Kremaston, L. *Greece* **46** C3
Kremen *Croatia* **41** D12
Kremenchuk *Ukraine* **33** H7
Kremenchuksk Vdskh.
  Ukraine **33** H7
Kremenets *Ukraine* **23** C13
Kremennaya *Ukraine* **33** H10
Kremges = Svitlovodsk
  Ukraine **33** H7
Kremmen *Germany* **24** C9
Kremmling *U.S.A.* **108** F10
Kremnica *Slovak Rep.* **27** C11
Krems *Austria* **26** C8
Kremsmünster *Austria* **26** C7
Krenstena *Greece* **46** D3
Kretinga *Lithuania* **30** C8
Krettsy *Russia* **32** C7
Kreuzberg *Germany* **25** E5
Kreuztal *Germany* **24** E4
Kria Vrisi *Greece* **44** F6
Kribi *Cameroon* **83** E6
Krichem *Bulgaria* **45** D8
Krichev = Krychaw *Belarus* **23** B16
Kril'on, Mys *Russia* **54** B11
Krim *Slovenia* **41** C11
Krios, Akra *Greece* **49** D5
Krishna ➤ *India* **67** M12
Krishnanagar *India* **69** H13
Kristdala *Sweden* **11** G10
Kristiansand *Norway* **9** G13
Kristianstad *Sweden* **11** H8
Kristiansund *Norway* **8** E12
Kristiinankaupunki *Finland* **8** E19
Kristinehamn *Sweden* **10** E8
Kristinestad =
  Kristiinankaupunki
  Finland **8** E19
Kriti *Greece* **49** D7
Kritsa *Greece* **49** D7
Kriva ➤ *Macedonia* **44** D5
Kriva Palanka *Macedonia* **44** D6
Krivaja ➤ *Bos.-H.* **28** F3
Krivelj *Serbia* **44** B5
Křivoklátsko △ *Czech Rep.* **26** A6
Krivoy Rog = Kryvyy Rih
  Ukraine **33** J7
Križevci *Croatia* **41** B13
Krk *Croatia* **41** C11
Krka *Slovenia* **41** C12
Krka ➤ *Croatia* **41** E12
Krkonoše *Czech Rep.* **26** A8
Krkonoše △ *Czech Rep.* **26** A8
Krnov *Czech Rep.* **27** A10

Krobia *Poland* **31** G3
Krokees *Greece* **46** E4
Krokek *Sweden* **11** F10
Krokodil = Umgwenya ➤
  Mozam. **89** D5
Krokom *Sweden* **10** A8
Krokowa *Poland* **30** D5
Krolevets *Ukraine* **33** G7
Kroměříž *Czech Rep.* **27** B10
Krompachy *Slovak Rep.* **27** C13
Kromy *Russia* **33** F8
Kronach *Germany* **25** E7
Krong Kaoh Kong *Cambodia* **65** G4
Kronobergs län □ *Sweden* **11** H8
Kronprins Olav Kyst
  Antarctica **5** C5
Kronprinsesse Märtha
  Kyst *Antarctica* **5** D2
Kronshtadt *Russia* **32** C5
Kroonstad *S. Africa* **88** D4
Kröpelin *Germany* **24** A7
Kropotkin *Russia* **35** H5
Kropp *Germany* **24** A5
Krosna *Lithuania* **30** D10
Krośniewice *Poland* **31** F6
Krosno *Poland* **31** J8
Krosno Odrzańskie *Poland* **31** F2
Krotoszyn *Poland* **31** G4
Krotovka *Russia* **34** D10
Krousonas *Greece* **49** D6
Krrabë *Albania* **44** E3
Krško *Slovenia* **41** C12
Krstača *Serbia* **44** D4
Kruger △ *S. Africa* **89** C5
Krugersdorp *S. Africa* **89** D4
Kruisfontein *S. Africa* **88** E3
Krujë *Albania* **44** E3
Krulevshchina =
  Krulyewshchyna *Belarus* **32** E4
Krulyewshchyna *Belarus* **32** E4
Krumbach *Germany* **25** G6
Krumë *Albania* **44** D4
Krumovgrad *Bulgaria* **45** E9
Krung Thep = Bangkok
  Thailand **64** F3
Krupanj *Serbia* **44** B3
Krupina *Slovak Rep.* **27** C12
Krupinica ➤ *Slovak Rep.* **27** C11
Krupki *Belarus* **23** A15
Kruševac *Serbia* **44** C5
Kruševo *Macedonia* **44** E5
Krushelnyksya *Ukraine* **31** J10
Kruszwica *Poland* **31** F5
Krychaw *Belarus* **23** B16
Krymsk *Russia* **33** K10
Krymskiy Poluostrov =
  Krymskyy Pivostriv
  Ukraine **33** K8
Krymskyy Pivostriv *Ukraine* **33** K8
Krynica *Poland* **31** J7
Krynica Morska *Poland* **30** D6
Krynki *Poland* **31** E10
Krynychne *Ukraine* **29** E13
Kryvyy Rih *Ukraine* **33** J7
Kryzhopil *Ukraine* **29** B13
Krzepice *Poland* **31** H5
Krzeszów *Poland* **31** H9
Krzna ➤ *Poland* **31** F10
Krzywiń *Poland* **31** G3
Krzyż Wielkopolski *Poland* **31** F3
Ksar el Kebir *Morocco* **78** B4
Ksar es Souk = Er Rachidia
  Morocco **78** B5
Książ Wielkopolski *Poland* **31** F4
Kstovo *Russia* **34** B7
Ku, W. el ➤ *Sudan* **81** E2
Kuah *Malaysia* **65** J2
Kuala Belait *Malaysia* **62** D4
Kuala Berang *Malaysia* **65** K4
Kuala Dungun = Dungun
  Malaysia **65** K4
Kuala Kangsar *Malaysia* **65** K3
Kuala Kelawang *Malaysia* **65** L4
Kuala Kerai *Malaysia* **65** K4
Kuala Kerian *Malaysia* **65** c
Kuala Kubu Bharu *Malaysia* **65** L3
Kuala Lipis *Malaysia* **65** K4
Kuala Lumpur *Malaysia* **65** L3
Kuala Nerang *Malaysia* **65** J3
Kuala Pilah *Malaysia* **65** L4
Kuala Rompin *Malaysia* **65** L4
Kuala Selangor *Malaysia* **65** L3
Kuala Sepetang *Malaysia* **65** K3
Kuala Terengganu *Malaysia* **65** K4
Kualajelai *Indonesia* **62** E4
Kualakapuas *Indonesia* **62** E4
Kualakurun *Indonesia* **62** E4
Kualapembuang *Indonesia* **62** E4
Kualasimpang *Indonesia* **62** D1
Kuancheng *China* **57** D10
Kuandang *Indonesia* **63** D6
Kuandian *China* **57** D13
Kuangchou = Guangzhou
  China **59** F9
Kuanshan *Taiwan* **59** F13
Kuantan *Malaysia* **65** L4
Kuba = Quba *Azerbaijan* **35** K9
Kuban ➤ *Russia* **33** K9

Kuban Depression =
Prikubanskaya
Nizmennost *Russia* **35** H4
Kubaysah *Iraq* **73** G10
Kubenskoye, Ozero *Russia* **32** C10
Kubokawa *Japan* **55** H6
Kubu *Indonesia* **63** J18
Kubutambahan *Indonesia* **63** J18
Kucar, Tanjung *Indonesia* **63** K18
Kučevo *Serbia* **44** B5
Kuchaman *India* **68** F6
Kuchinda *India* **69** J11
Kuchenspitze *Austria* **26** D3
Kuchino-eruba-Jima *Japan* **55** J5
Kuchino-Shima *Japan* **55** K4
Kuchinotsu *Japan* **55** H5
Kuchl *Austria* **26** D6
Kuchurhan → *Ukraine* **29** D14
Kucing = Kuching *Malaysia* **62** D4
Kuçovë *Albania* **44** F3
Küçükbahçe *Turkey* **47** C8
Küçükköy *Turkey* **47** B8
Küçükkuyu *Turkey* **47** B8
Küçükmenderes → *Turkey* **47** D9
Kud → *Pakistan* **68** F2
Kuda *India* **68** H4
Kudat *Malaysia* **62** C5
Kudirkos Naumiestis
Lithuania **30** D9
Kudowa-Zdrój *Poland* **31** H3
Kudus *Indonesia* **63** G14
Kudymkar *Russia* **52** D6
Kueiyang = Guiyang *China* **58** D6
Kufra Oasis = Al Kufrah
Libya **79** D10
Kufstein *Austria* **26** D5
Kugaaruk = Pelly Bay
Canada **101** C11
Kugluktuk *Canada* **100** C8
Kugong I. *Canada* **104** A4
Kŭh Dasht *Iran* **73** F12
Kŭh-e-Jebāl Bārez *Iran* **71** D8
Kŭhak *Iran* **71** E9
Kuhan *Pakistan* **68** E2
Kūhbonān *Iran* **71** D8
Kūhestak *Iran* **71** E8
Kuhin *Iran* **71** B6
Kūhīrī *Iran* **71** E9
Kuhmo *Finland* **8** D23
Kuhnsdorf *Austria* **26** E7
Kūhpāyeh *Eşfahan, Iran* **71** C7
Kūhpāyeh *Kermān, Iran* **71** D8
Kūhrān, Kūh-e *Iran* **71** E8
Kui Buri *Thailand* **65** F2
Kuiseb → *Namibia* **88** C1
Kuito *Angola* **85** G3
Kuiu I. *U.S.A.* **102** B2
Kujang *N. Korea* **57** E14
Kujawsko-Pomorskie □
Poland **30** E5
Kuji *Japan* **54** D10
Kujū-San *Japan* **55** H5
Kukava *Ukraine* **29** B12
Kukavica *Serbia* **44** D5
Kukawa *Nigeria* **83** C7
Kukës *Albania* **44** D4
Kukmor *Russia* **34** B10
Kukup *Malaysia* **65** d
Kukup, Pulau *Malaysia* **65** d
Kukvidze *Russia* **34** E6
Kula *Bulgaria* **44** C6
Kula *Serbia* **28** E4
Kula *Turkey* **47** C10
Kulachi *Pakistan* **68** D4
Kulai *Malaysia* **65** M4
Kulaly, Ostrov = Kulaly
Aral *Kazakhstan* **35** H10
Kulaly Aral *Kazakhstan* **35** H10
Kulasekarappattinam *India* **66** Q11
Kulautuva *Lithuania* **30** D10
Kuldīga *Latvia* **30** B8
Kuldīga □ *Latvia* **30** B8
Kuldu *Sudan* **81** E2
Kulebaki *Russia* **34** C6
Kulen *Cambodia* **64** F5
Kulen Vakuf *Bos.-H.* **41** D13
Kulgam *India* **69** C6
Kulgera *Australia* **94** D1
Kulim *Malaysia* **65** K3
Kulin *Australia* **93** F2
Kulkayu = Hartley Bay
Canada **102** C3
Kullen *Sweden* **11** H6
Kullu *India* **68** D7
Kulmbach *Germany* **25** E7
Kŭlob *Tajikistan* **52** F7
Kulp *Turkey* **73** C9
Kulpawn → *Ghana* **83** D4
Kulsary = Qulsary
Kazakhstan **52** E6
Kulti *India* **69** H12
Kulu *Turkey* **72** C5
Kulunda *Russia* **52** D8
Kulungar *Afghan.* **68** C3
Kulvand *Iran* **71** D7
Kulwin *Australia* **95** F3
Kulyab = Kŭlob *Tajikistan* **52** F7

Kuma → *Russia* **35** H8
Kumafşarı *Turkey* **47** D11
Kumaganum *Nigeria* **83** C7
Kumagaya *Japan* **55** F9
Kumai *Indonesia* **63** J18
Kumalar Dağı *Turkey* **47** C12
Kumamba, Kepulauan
Indonesia **63** E9
Kumamoto *Japan* **55** H5
Kumamoto □ *Japan* **55** H5
Kumanovo *Macedonia* **44** D5
Kumara *N.Z.* **91** E3
Kumarina Roadhouse
Australia **93** D2
Kumasi *Ghana* **82** D4
Kumba *Cameroon* **83** E6
Kumbağ *Turkey* **45** F11
Kumbakonam *India* **66** P11
Kumbarilla *Australia* **95** D5
Kumbhraj *India* **68** G7
Kumbia *Australia* **95** D5
Kumbo *Cameroon* **83** D7
Kŭmch'ŏn *N. Korea* **57** E14
Kumdok *India* **69** C8
Kume-Shima *Japan* **55** L3
Kumeny *Russia* **34** A9
Kumharsain *India* **68** D7
Kumi *Uganda* **86** B3
Kumkale *Turkey* **45** G10
Kumla *Sweden* **10** E9
Kumluca *Turkey* **47** E12
Kummerower See *Germany* **24** B8
Kumo *Nigeria* **83** C7
Kumo älv =
Kokemäenjoki → *Finland* **32** B1
Kumon Bum *Burma* **67** F20
Kumylzhenskaya *Russia* **34** F6
Kunágota *Hungary* **28** D6
Kunashir, Ostrov *Russia* **53** E15
Kunda *Estonia* **32** C4
Kunda *India* **69** G9
Kundar → *Pakistan* **68** D3
Kundelungu △
Dem. Rep. of the Congo **87** E2
Kundelungu Ouest △
Dem. Rep. of the Congo **87** D2
Kundian *Pakistan* **68** C4
Kundla *India* **68** J4
Kung, Ao *Thailand* **65** a
Kunga → *Bangla.* **69** J13
Kungälv *Sweden* **11** G6
Kunghit I. *Canada* **102** C2
Kungrad = Qŭnghirot
Uzbekistan **52** E6
Kungsängen *Sweden* **10** E11
Kungsbacka *Sweden* **11** G6
Kungsgården *Sweden* **10** D10
Kungshamn *Sweden* **11** F5
Kungsör *Sweden* **10** E10
Kungur *Russia* **52** D6
Kungurri *Australia* **94** K6
Kunhar → *Pakistan* **69** B5
Kunhegyes *Hungary* **28** C5
Kuningan *Indonesia* **63** G13
Kunlong *Burma* **58** F2
Kunlun Shan *Asia* **60** C3
Kunmadaras *Hungary* **28** C5
Kunming *China* **58** E4
Kunów *Poland* **31** H8
Kunshan *China* **59** B13
Kunszentmárton *Hungary* **28** D5
Kunszentmiklós *Hungary* **28** C4
Kuntaur *Senegal* **82** C1
Kununurra *Australia* **92** C4
Kunwari → *India* **69** F8
Kunya-Urgench =
Köneürgench
Turkmenistan **52** E6
Künzelsau *Germany* **25** F5
Kuopio *Finland* **8** E22
Kupa → *Croatia* **41** C13
Kupang *Indonesia* **63** K18
Kupreanof I. *U.S.A.* **102** B2
Kupres *Bos.-H.* **28** G2
Kupyansk *Ukraine* **33** H9
Kupyansk-Uzlovoi *Ukraine* **33** H9
Kuqa *China* **60** B3
Kür → *Azerbaijan* **73** C13
Kür Dili *Azerbaijan* **73** C13
Kura = Kür → *Azerbaijan* **73** C13
Kuranda *Australia* **94** B4
Kuranga *India* **68** H3
Kurashiki *Japan* **55** G6
Kurayn *Si. Arabia* **71** E6
Kurayoshi *Japan* **55** G6
Kŭrchatov *Kazakhstan* **52** D8
Kürdämir *Azerbaijan* **35** K9
Kurdistan *Asia* **73** D10
Kŭrdzhali *Bulgaria* **45** E9
Kure *Japan* **55** G6
Küre *Turkey* **72** B5
Küre Dağları *Turkey* **72** B6
Kuressaare *Estonia* **32** C2
Kurgan *Russia* **52** D7
Kurganinsk *Russia* **35** H5
Kurgannaya =
Kurganinsk *Russia* **35** H5
Kuri *India* **68** F4

Kuria Maria Is. =
Hallāniyat, Jazā'ir al
Oman **75** D6
Kuridala *Australia* **94** C3
Kurigram *Bangla.* **67** G16
Kurikka *Finland* **8** E20
Kuril Basin *Pac. Oc.* **4** E15
Kuril Is. = Kurilskiye
Ostrova *Russia* **53** E16
Kuril-Kamchatka Trench
Pac. Oc. **96** C7
Kurilsk *Russia* **53** E15
Kurilskiye Ostrova *Russia* **53** E16
Kurino *Japan* **55** J5
Kurinskaya Kosa = Kür
Dili *Azerbaijan* **73** C13
Kurkur *Egypt* **80** C3
Kurlovskiy *Russia* **34** C5
Kurmuk *Sudan* **81** E3
Kurnool *India* **66** M11
Kuro-Shima *Kagoshima, Japan* **55** J4
Kuro-Shima *Okinawa, Japan* **55** M2
Kuror, J. *Sudan* **80** C3
Kurow *N.Z.* **91** F3
Kurów *Poland* **31** G9
Kurram → *Pakistan* **68** C4
Kurri Kurri *Australia* **95** E5
Kurrimine *Australia* **94** B4
Kursavka *Russia* **35** H6
Kurshskaya Kosa △ *Russia* **30** C7
Kurshskiy Zaliv *Russia* **30** C8
Kuršių Nerijos △ *Lithuania* **30** C8
Kursk *Russia* **33** G9
Kursk □ *Russia* **33** G9
Kuršumlija *Serbia* **44** C5
Kuršumlijska Banja *Serbia* **44** C5
Kurşunlu *Bursa, Turkey* **45** F13
Kurşunlu *Çankırı, Turkey* **72** B5
Kurtalan *Turkey* **73** D9
Kurtbey *Turkey* **45** E10
Kuru *Sudan* **81** F2
Kuru, Bahr el → *Sudan* **81** F2
Kurucaşile *Turkey* **72** B5
Kuruçay *Turkey* **70** B3
Kuruktag *China* **60** B3
Kuruman *S. Africa* **88** D3
Kuruman → *S. Africa* **88** D3
Kurume *Japan* **55** H5
Kurun → *Sudan* **81** F3
Kurunegala *Sri Lanka* **66** R12
Kurya *Russia* **52** C6
Kus Gölü *Turkey* **45** F11
Kuşadası *Turkey* **72** D2
Kuşadası Körfezi *Turkey* **47** D8
Kusamba *Indonesia* **63** K18
Kusatsu *Japan* **55** F9
Kusawa L. *Canada* **102** A1
Kushaka *Nigeria* **83** D6
Kushalgarh *India* **68** H6
Kushchevskaya *Russia* **35** G4
Kusheriki *Nigeria* **83** C6
Kushikino *Japan* **55** J5
Kushima *Japan* **55** J5
Kushimoto *Japan* **55** H7
Kushiro *Japan* **54** C12
Kushiro-Gawa → *Japan* **54** C12
Kushiro Shitsugen △ *Japan* **54** C12
Kŭshk *Iran* **71** D8
Kushka = Serhetabat
Turkmenistan **71** D9
Kushnytsya *Ukraine* **29** B8
Kushol *India* **69** C7
Kushtia *Bangla.* **67** H16
Kuskokwim → *U.S.A.* **98** C3
Kuskokwim B. *U.S.A.* **106** a
Kusmi *India* **69** H10
Kusŏng *N. Korea* **57** E13
Kussharo-Ko *Japan* **54** C12
Kustanay = Qostanay
Kazakhstan **52** D7
Kut, Ko *Thailand* **65** G4
Kuta *Indonesia* **63** K18
Kütahya *Turkey* **47** B12
Kütahya □ *Turkey* **47** B11
Kutaisi *Georgia* **35** J6
Kutaraja = Banda Aceh
Indonesia **62** C1
Kutch, Gulf of = Kachchh,
Gulf of *India* **68** H3
Kutch, Rann of =
Kachchh, Rann of *India* **68** H4
Kutina *Croatia* **41** C13
Kutiyana *India* **68** J4
Kutjevo *Croatia* **28** E2
Kutkashen *Azerbaijan* **35** K8
Kutná Hora *Czech Rep.* **26** B8
Kutno *Poland* **31** F6
Kutse *Botswana* **88** C3
Kuttabul *Australia* **94** K6
Kutu *Dem. Rep. of the Congo* **84** E3
Kutum *Sudan* **81** E1
Kuty *Slovak Rep.* **27** C10
Kuty *Ukraine* **29** B10
Kuujjuaq *Canada* **101** D13
Kuujjuarapik *Canada* **104** A4
Kuusamo *Finland* **8** D23
Kuusankoski *Finland* **32** B4
Kuvshinovo *Russia* **32** D8

Kuwait = Al Kuwayt *Kuwait* **70** D5
Kuwait ■ *Asia* **70** D5
Kuwana *Japan* **55** G8
Kuwana → *India* **69** F10
Kuybyshev = Samara
Russia **34** D10
Kuybyshev *Russia* **52** D8
Kuybyshevo *Ukraine* **33** J9
Kuybyshevskoye Vdkhr.
Russia **34** C9
Kuye He → *China* **56** E6
Kūyeh *Iran* **70** B5
Kuyto, Ozero *Russia* **8** D24
Kuyucak *Turkey* **47** D10
Kuyumba *Russia* **53** C10
Kuzey Anadolu Dağları
Turkey **72** B7
Kuzmin *Serbia* **28** E4
Kuznetsk *Russia* **34** D8
Kuzomen *Russia* **52** C4
Kvænangen *Norway* **8** A19
Kværndrup *Denmark* **11** J4
Kvaløya *Norway* **8** B18
Kvänum *Sweden* **11** F7
Kvareli = Qvareli *Georgia* **35** K7
Kvarner *Croatia* **41** D11
Kvarnerič *Croatia* **41** D11
Kvicksund *Sweden* **10** E10
Kvillsfors *Sweden* **11** G9
Kvismare kanal *Sweden* **10** E9
Kvissleby *Sweden* **10** B11
Kwabhaca *S. Africa* **89** E4
Kwajalein *Marshall Is.* **96** G8
Kwakhanai *Botswana* **88** C3
Kwakoegron *Suriname* **125** B7
Kwale *Kenya* **86** C4
Kwale *Nigeria* **83** D6
KwaMashu *S. Africa* **89** D5
Kwando → *Africa* **88** B3
Kwangchow = Guangzhou
China **59** F9
Kwango →
Dem. Rep. of the Congo **84** E3
Kwangsi-Chuang =
Guangxi Zhuangzu
Zizhiqu □ *China* **58** F7
Kwangtung =
Guangdong □ *China* **59** F9
Kwara □ *Nigeria* **83** D6
Kwataboahegan → *Canada* **104** B3
Kwatisore *Indonesia* **63** E8
KwaZulu Natal □ *S. Africa* **89** D5
Kweichow = Guizhou □
China **58** D6
Kwekwe *Zimbabwe* **87** F2
Kwidzyn *Poland* **30** E5
Kwiha *Ethiopia* **81** E4
Kwilu →
Dem. Rep. of the Congo **84** E3
Kwinana *Australia* **93** F2
Kwisa → *Poland* **31** G2
Kwoka *Indonesia* **63** E8
Kwolla *Nigeria* **83** D6
Kyabra Cr. → *Australia* **95** D3
Kyabram *Australia* **95** F4
Kyaikto *Burma* **64** D1
Kyakhta *Russia* **53** D11
Kyambura → *Uganda* **86** C3
Kyancutta *Australia* **95** E2
Kyaukpadaung *Burma* **67** J19
Kyaukpyu *Burma* **67** K18
Kyaukse *Burma* **67** J20
Kyburz *U.S.A.* **110** G6
Kyelang *India* **68** C7
Kyenjojo *Uganda* **86** B3
Kyjov *Czech Rep.* **27** B10
Kyle *Canada* **103** C7
Kyle Dam *Zimbabwe* **87** G3
Kyle of Lochalsh *U.K.* **13** D3
Kyll → *Germany* **25** F2
Kyllburg *Germany* **25** E2
Kyllini *Greece* **46** D3
Kymijoki → *Finland* **32** B4
Kymmene älv =
Kymijoki → *Finland* **32** B4
Kyneton *Australia* **95** F3
Kynuna *Australia* **94** C3
Kyō-ga-Saki *Japan* **55** G7
Kyoga, L. *Uganda* **86** B3
Kyogle *Australia* **95** D5
Kyom → *Sudan* **81** F2
Kyŏngju = Gyeongju
S. Korea **57** G15
Kyŏngsŏng *N. Korea* **57** D15
Kyonpyaw *Burma* **67** L19
Kyōto *Japan* **55** G7
Kyōto □ *Japan* **55** G7
Kyparissovouno *Cyprus* **49** D12
Kyperounda *Cyprus* **49** E11
Kypros = Cyprus ■ *Asia* **49** E12
Kyrenia *Cyprus* **49** D12
Kyritz *Germany* **24** C8
Kyrkhult *Sweden* **11** H8
Kyrnasivka *Ukraine* **29** B13
Kyrnychky *Ukraine* **29** E14
Kyro älv = Kyrönjoki →
Finland **8** E19

Kyrönjoki → *Finland* **8** E19
Kystatyam *Russia* **53** C13
Kysucké Nové Mesto
Slovak Rep. **27** B11
Kytay, Ozero *Ukraine* **29** E14
Kythira *Greece* **46** E5
Kythréa *Cyprus* **49** D12
Kyunhla *Burma* **67** H19
Kyuquot Sound *Canada* **102** D3
Kyurdamir = Kürdämir
Azerbaijan **35** K9
Kyūshū *Japan* **55** H5
Kyūshū □ *Japan* **55** H5
Kyushu-Palau Ridge *Pac. Oc.* **96** E5
Kyūshū-Sanchi *Japan* **55** H5
Kyustendil *Bulgaria* **44** D6
Kyusyur *Russia* **53** B13
Kyyiv *Ukraine* **23** C16
Kyyiv □ *Ukraine* **33** G6
Kyyivske Vdskh. *Ukraine* **23** C16
Kyzyl *Russia* **53** D10
Kyzyl Kum *Uzbekistan* **52** E7
Kyzyl Kyya *Kyrgyzstan* **52** E8
Kyzyl Orda = Qyzylorda
Kazakhstan **52** E7

L

La Albuera *Spain* **37** G4
La Alcarria *Spain* **38** E2
La Almarcha *Spain* **38** F2
La Almunia de Doña
Godina *Spain* **38** D3
La Amistad △ *Cent. Amer.* **120** E3
La Asunción *Venezuela* **124** A6
La Baie *Canada* **105** C5
La Banda *Argentina* **126** B3
La Bañeza *Spain* **36** C5
La Barca *Mexico* **118** C4
La Barge *U.S.A.* **108** E8
La Barra *Nic.* **120** D3
La Bastide-Puylaurent
France **20** D7
La Baule *France* **18** E4
La Belle *U.S.A.* **117** H14
La Biche → *Canada* **102** B4
La Biche, L. *Canada* **102** C6
La Bisbal d'Empordà *Spain* **38** D8
La Brea *Trin. & Tob.* **125** K15
La Brède *France* **20** D3
La Bresse *France* **19** D13
La Bureba *Spain* **36** C7
La Calera *Chile* **126** C1
La Campana △ *Chile* **126** C1
La Campiña *Spain* **37** H6
La Canal = Sa Canal *Spain* **48** C7
La Cañiza = A Cañiza *Spain* **36** C2
La Canourgue *France* **20** D7
La Capelle *France* **19** C10
La Carlota *Argentina* **126** C3
La Carlota *Phil.* **61** F5
La Carlota *Spain* **37** H6
La Carolina *Spain* **37** G7
La Cavalerie *France* **20** D7
La Ceiba *Honduras* **120** C2
La Chaise-Dieu *France* **20** C7
La Chapelle d'Angillon
France **19** E9
La Chapelle-St-Luc *France* **19** D11
La Chapelle-sur-Erdre *France* **18** E5
La Charité-sur-Loire *France* **19** E10
La Chartre-sur-le-Loir *France* **18** E7
La Châtaigneraie *France* **20** B3
La Châtre *France* **19** F9
La Chaux-de-Fonds *Switz.* **25** H2
La Chorrera *Panama* **120** E4
La Ciotat *France* **21** E9
La Clayette *France* **19** F11
La Cocha *Argentina* **126** B2
La Concepción *Panama* **120** E3
La Concordia *Mexico* **119** D6
La Coruña = A Coruña *Spain* **36** B2
La Côte-St-André *France* **21** C9
La Courtine *France* **20** C6
La Crau *Bouches-du-Rhône,
France* **21** E8
La Crau *Var, France* **21** E10
La Crescent *U.S.A.* **112** D8
La Crete *Canada* **102** B5
La Crosse *Kans., U.S.A.* **112** F4
La Crosse *Wis., U.S.A.* **112** D8
La Cruz *Costa Rica* **120** D2
La Cruz *Mexico* **118** C3
La Désirade *Guadeloupe* **120** b
La Digue *Seychelles* **85** b
La Esperanza *Argentina* **95** F3
La Esperanza *Honduras* **120** D2
La Estrada = A Estrada *Spain* **36** C2
La Faouët *France* **18** D3
La Fayette *U.S.A.* **117** D12
La Fère *France* **19** C10
La Fé *Cuba* **120** B3
La Ferté-Bernard *France* **18** D7
La Ferté-Gaucher *France* **19** D10
La Ferté-Macé *France* **18** D6
La Ferté-St-Aubin *France* **19** E8
La Ferté-sous-Jouarre
France **19** D10
La Ferté-Vidame *France* **18** D7

Kyrönjoki → *Finland* **8** E19
La Flèche *France* **18** E6
La Follette *U.S.A.* **117** C12
La Fregeneda *Spain* **36** E4
La Fuente de San Esteban
Spain **36** E4
La Gacilly *France* **18** E4
La Gineta *Spain* **39** F2
La Grand'Combe *France* **21** D8
La Grande *U.S.A.* **108** D4
La Grande → *Canada* **104** B5
La Grande 3, Rés. *Canada* **104** B4
La Grande 4, Rés. *Canada* **104** B5
La Grande-Motte *France* **21** E8
La Grange *Calif., U.S.A.* **110** H6
La Grange *Ga., U.S.A.* **117** E12
La Grange *Ky., U.S.A.* **113** F11
La Grange *Tex., U.S.A.* **116** G6
La Grave *France* **21** C10
La Guaira *Venezuela* **124** A5
La Guardia = A Guarda
Spain **36** D2
La Gudiña = A Gudiña *Spain* **36** C3
La Guerche-de-Bretagne
France **18** E5
La Guerche-sur-l'Aubois
France **19** F9
La Habana *Cuba* **120** B3
La Haute Vallée de
Chevreuse △ *France* **19** D8
La Haye-du-Puits *France* **18** C5
La Horra *Spain* **36** D7
La Independencia *Mexico* **119** D6
La Isabela *Dom. Rep.* **121** C5
La Jonquera *Spain* **38** C7
La Junta *U.S.A.* **108** H12
La Laguna *Canary Is.* **48** F3
La Libertad = Puerto
Libertad *Mexico* **118** B2
La Libertad *Guatemala* **120** C1
La Ligua *Chile* **126** C1
La Línea de la Concepción
Spain **37** J5
La Loche *Canada* **103** B7
La Londe-les-Maures
France **21** E10
La Lora *Spain* **36** C7
La Loupe *France* **18** D8
La Louvière *Belgium* **17** D4
La Lune *Trin. & Tob.* **125** K15
La Machine *France* **19** F10
La Maddalena *Italy* **42** A2
La Malbaie *Canada* **105** C5
La Malinche △ *Mexico* **119** D5
La Mancha *Spain* **39** F2
La Mariña *Spain* **36** B3
La Martre, L. *Canada* **102** A5
La Mesa *Mexico* **111** N10
La Mesa *U.S.A.* **111** N9
La Mesilla *U.S.A.* **109** K10
La Misión *Mexico* **118** A1
La Mothe-Achard *France* **18** F5
La Motte-Chalançon *France* **21** D9
La Motte-du-Caire *France* **21** D10
La Motte-Servolex *France* **21** C9
La Moure *U.S.A.* **112** B4
La Muela *Spain* **38** D3
La Mure *France* **21** D9
La Negra *Chile* **126** A1
La Oliva *Canary Is.* **48** F6
La Orotava *Canary Is.* **48** F3
La Oroya *Peru* **124** F3
La Pacaudière *France* **19** F10
La Palma *Canary Is.* **48** F2
La Palma *Panama* **120** E4
La Palma del Condado *Spain* **37** H4
La Paloma *Chile* **126** C1
La Pampa □ *Argentina* **126** D2
La Paragua *Venezuela* **124** B6
La Paz *Entre Ríos, Argentina* **126** C4
La Paz *San Luis, Argentina* **126** C2
La Paz *Bolivia* **124** G5
La Paz *Honduras* **120** D2
La Paz *Mexico* **118** C2
La Paz *Phil.* **61** F5
La Paz Centro *Nic.* **120** D2
La Pedrera *Colombia* **124** D5
La Pérade *Canada* **105** C5
La Perla *Mexico* **118** B4
La Perouse Str. *Asia* **54** B11
La Pesca *Mexico* **119** C5
La Piedad *Mexico* **118** C4
La Pine *U.S.A.* **108** E3
La Plata *Argentina* **126** D4
La Pobla de Lillet *Spain* **38** C6
La Pobla de Segur *Spain* **38** C5
La Pocatière *Canada* **105** C5
La Pola de Gordón *Spain* **36** C5
La Porta *France* **21** F13
La Porte *France* **21** F13
La Presanella *Italy* **40** B7
La Puebla = Sa Pobla *Spain* **38** F8
La Puebla de Cazalla *Spain* **37** H5
La Puebla de los Infantes
Spain **37** H5
La Puebla de Montalbán
Spain **36** F6
La Puebla del Río *Spain* **37** H4
La Puerta de Segura *Spain* **37** G8
La Purísima *Mexico* **118** B2

La Push *U.S.A.* **110** C2
La Quiaca *Argentina* **126** A2
La Réole *France* **20** D3
La Restinga *Canary Is.* **48** G2
La Rioja *Argentina* **126** B2
La Rioja □ *Argentina* **126** B2
La Rioja □ *Spain* **38** C2
La Robla *Spain* **36** C5
La Roche-Bernard *France* **18** E4
La Roche-Canillac *France* **20** C5
La Roche-en-Ardenne
   Belgium **17** D5
La Roche-sur-Foron *France* **19** F13
La Roche-sur-Yon *France* **18** F5
La Rochefoucauld *France* **20** C4
La Rochelle *France* **20** B2
La Roda *Spain* **39** F2
La Roda de Andalucía *Spain* **37** H6
La Romaine *Canada* **105** B7
La Romana *Dom. Rep.* **121** C6
La Ronge *Canada* **103** B7
La Rumorosa *Mexico* **111** N10
La Sabina = Sa Savina *Spain* **48** C7
La Sagra *Spain* **39** H2
La Salle *U.S.A.* **112** E9
La Sanabria *Spain* **36** C4
La Santa *Canary Is.* **48** E6
La Sarre *Canada* **104** C4
La Scie *Canada* **105** C8
La Selva *Spain* **38** C7
La Selva Beach *U.S.A.* **110** J5
La Selva del Camp *Spain* **38** D6
La Serena *Chile* **126** B1
La Serena *Spain* **37** G5
La Seu d'Urgell *Spain* **38** C6
La Seyne-sur-Mer *France* **21** E9
La Sila *Italy* **43** C9
La Solana *Spain* **37** G7
La Soufrière *St. Vincent* **121** D7
La Souterraine *France* **19** F8
La Spézia *Italy* **40** D6
La Suze-sur-Sarthe *France* **18** E7
La Tagua *Colombia* **124** C4
La Teste-de-Buch *France* **20** D2
La Tortuga *Venezuela* **121** D6
La Tour-du-Pin *France* **21** C9
La Tranche-sur-Mer *France* **18** F5
La Tremblade *France* **20** C2
La Trinité *Martinique* **120** c
La Tuque *Canada* **104** C5
La Unión *Chile* **128** E2
La Unión *El Salv.* **120** D2
La Unión *Mexico* **118** D4
La Unión *Spain* **39** H4
La Urbana *Venezuela* **124** B5
La Vache Pt. *Trin. & Tob.* **125** K15
La Vall d'Uixó *Spain* **38** F4
La Vecilla *Spain* **36** C5
La Vega *Dom. Rep.* **121** C5
La Vela de Coro *Venezuela* **124** A5
La Veleta *Spain* **37** H7
La Venta *Mexico* **119** D6
La Vergne *U.S.A.* **117** C11
La Villa Joiosa =
   Villajoyosa *Spain* **39** G4
La Voulte-sur-Rhône *France* **21** D8
Laa an der Thaya *Austria* **27** C9
Laaber, Grosse → *Germany* **25** G8
Laage *Germany* **24** B8
Laascaanood *Somali Rep.* **75** F4
Laatzen *Germany* **24** C5
Laba → *Russia* **35** H4
Labasa *Fiji* **91** a
Labason *Phil.* **61** G5
Labastide-Murat *France* **20** D5
Labastide-Rouairoux *France* **20** E6
Labbézenga *Mali* **83** B5
Labdah = Leptis Magna
   Libya **79** B8
Labe = Elbe → *Europe* **24** B4
Labé *Guinea* **82** C2
Laberge, L. *Canada* **102** A1
Labin *Croatia* **41** C11
Labinsk *Russia* **35** H5
Labis *Malaysia* **65** L4
Łabiszyn *Poland* **31** F4
Labo *Phil.* **61** D5
Laboe *Germany* **24** A6
Laborec → *Slovak Rep.* **27** C14
Laborie *St. Lucia* **121** f
Labouheyre *France* **20** D3
Laboulaye *Argentina* **126** C3
Labrador *Canada* **105** B7
Labrador City *Canada* **105** B6
Labrador Sea *Atl. Oc.* **101** D14
Lábrea *Brazil* **124** E6
Labruguière *France* **20** E6
Labuan *Malaysia* **62** C5
Labuan, Pulau *Malaysia* **62** C5
Labuha *Indonesia* **63** E7
Labuhan *Indonesia* **63** G11
Labuhanbajo *Indonesia* **63** F6
Labuhanbilik *Indonesia* **65** L3
Labuk, Telok *Malaysia* **62** C5
Labyrinth, L. *Australia* **95** E2
Labytnangi *Russia* **52** C7
Laç *Albania* **44** E3
Lac-Bouchette *Canada* **105** C5
Lac Brochet *Canada* **103** B8

Lac Édouard *Canada* **104** C5
Lac La Biche *Canada* **102** C6
Lac la Martre = Wha Ti
   Canada **100** C8
Lac La Ronge △ *Canada* **103** B7
Lac-Mégantic *Canada* **105** C5
Lac Thien *Vietnam* **64** F7
Lacanau *France* **20** D2
Lacanau, Étang de *France* **20** D2
Lacantún → *Mexico* **119** D6
Lácara → *Spain* **37** G4
Lacaune *France* **20** E6
Lacaune, Mts. de *France* **20** E6
Laccadive Is. =
   Lakshadweep Is. *India* **3** D13
Lacepede B. *Australia* **95** F2
Lacepede Is. *Australia* **92** C3
Lacerdónia *Mozam.* **87** F4
Lacey *U.S.A.* **110** C4
Lachania *Greece* **49** D9
Lachhmangarh *India* **68** F6
Lachi *Pakistan* **68** C4
Lachine *Canada* **104** C5
Lachlan → *Australia* **95** E3
Lachute *Canada* **104** C5
Lackagh Hills *Ireland* **12** B3
Lackawanna *U.S.A.* **114** D6
Lackawaxen *U.S.A.* **115** E10
Lacolle *Canada* **115** A11
Lacombe *Canada* **102** C6
Lacona *U.S.A.* **115** C8
Láconi *Italy* **42** C2
Laconia *U.S.A.* **115** C13
Lacq *France* **20** E3
Ladakh Ra. *India* **69** C8
Ładek-Zdrój *Poland* **31** H3
Lâdik *Turkey* **72** B6
Ladismith *S. Africa* **88** E3
Ladíspoli *Italy* **41** G9
Lâdīz *Iran* **71** D9
Ladnun *India* **68** F6
Ladoga, L. = Ladozhskoye
   Ozero *Russia* **32** B6
Ladonas → *Greece* **46** D3
Ladozhskoye Ozero *Russia* **32** B6
Ladushkin *Russia* **30** D7
Lady Elliott I. *Australia* **94** C5
Lady Grey *S. Africa* **88** E4
Ladybrand *S. Africa* **88** D4
Ladysmith *Canada* **110** B3
Ladysmith *S. Africa* **89** D4
Ladysmith *U.S.A.* **112** C8
Ladyzhyn *Ukraine* **29** B14
Lae *Papua N. G.* **90** B7
Laem Hin Khom *Thailand* **65** b
Laem Khat *Thailand* **65** a
Laem Nga *Thailand* **65** a
Laem Ngop *Thailand* **65** F4
Laem Phan Wa *Thailand* **65** a
Laem Pho *Thailand* **65** J3
Laem Phrom Thep *Thailand* **65** a
Laem Riang *Thailand* **65** a
Laem Sam Rong *Thailand* **65** a
Laem Son *Thailand* **65** a
Laem Yamu *Thailand* **65** a
Laerma *Greece* **49** C9
Læsø *Denmark* **11** G5
Læsø Rende *Denmark* **11** G4
Lafayette *Ind., U.S.A.* **112** E10
Lafayette *La., U.S.A.* **116** F8
Lafayette *Tenn., U.S.A.* **117** C11
Laferte → *Canada* **102** A5
Lafia *Nigeria* **83** D6
Lafiagi *Nigeria* **83** D6
Lafkos *Greece* **46** B5
Lafleche *Canada* **103** D7
Lafon *Sudan* **81** F3
Lagan *Sweden* **11** H7
Lagan → *Sweden* **11** H6
Lagan → *U.K.* **12** B6
Lagarfljót → *Iceland* **8** D6
Lagdo, Rés. de *Cameroon* **79** G8
Lage *Germany* **24** D4
Lågen → *Oppland, Norway* **8** F14
Lågen → *Vestfold, Norway* **9** G14
Lägerdorf *Germany* **24** B5
Lages *Brazil* **127** B5
Laghouat *Algeria* **78** B6
Lagnieu *France* **21** C9
Lagny-sur-Marne *France* **19** D9
Lago *Italy* **43** C9
Lago de Sanabria y
   Entorno △ *Spain* **36** C4
Lagôa *Portugal* **37** H2
Lagoa do Peixe △ *Brazil* **127** C5
Lagoa Vermelha *Brazil* **127** B5
Lagoaça *Portugal* **36** D4
Lagodekhi *Georgia* **35** K8
Lagónegro *Italy* **43** B8
Lagonoy G. *Phil.* **61** E5
Lagos *Greece* **45** E9
Lagos *Nigeria* **83** D5
Lagos *Portugal* **37** H2
Lagos □ *Nigeria* **83** D5
Lagos de Moreno *Mexico* **118** C4
Lagrange = Bidyadanga
   Australia **92** C3
Lagrange B. *Australia* **92** C3
Laguardia *Spain* **38** C2

Laguépie *France* **20** D5
Laguna *Brazil* **127** B6
Laguna *U.S.A.* **109** J10
Laguna, Sa. de la *Mexico* **118** C3
Laguna Beach *U.S.A.* **111** M9
Laguna de Duera *Spain* **36** D6
Laguna de la Restinga △
   Venezuela **121** D6
Laguna de Lachuá △
   Guatemala **120** C1
Laguna del Laja △ *Chile* **126** D1
Laguna del Tigre △
   Guatemala **120** C1
Laguna Limpia *Argentina* **126** B4
Lagunas *Chile* **126** A2
Lagunas *Peru* **124** E3
Lagunas de Chacahua △
   Mexico **119** D5
Lagunas de Montebello △
   Mexico **119** D6
Lagunas de Ruidera △ *Spain* **39** G2
Lahad Datu *Malaysia* **63** D5
Lahad Datu, Telok *Malaysia* **63** D5
Lahan Sai *Thailand* **64** E4
Lahanam *Laos* **64** D5
Lahar *India* **69** F8
Laharpur *India* **69** F9
Lahat *Indonesia* **62** E2
Lahewa *Indonesia* **62** D1
Lāhījān *Iran* **71** B6
Lahn → *Germany* **25** E3
Lahnstein *Germany* **25** E3
Laholm *Sweden* **11** H7
Laholmsbukten *Sweden* **11** H6
Lahore *Pakistan* **68** D6
Lahr *Germany* **25** G3
Lahri *Pakistan* **68** E3
Lährūd *Iran* **73** C12
Lahti *Finland* **32** B3
Lahtis = Lahti *Finland* **32** B3
Laï *Chad* **79** G9
Lai Chau *Vietnam* **58** F4
Lai'an *China* **59** A12
Laibin *China* **58** F7
Laifeng *China* **58** C7
L'Aigle *France* **18** D7
Laignes *France* **19** E11
L'Aiguillon-sur-Mer *France* **20** B2
Laila = Layla *Si. Arabia* **75** C4
Laingsburg *S. Africa* **88** E3
Lainioälven → *Sweden* **8** C20
Lairg *U.K.* **13** C4
Laisamis *Kenya* **86** B4
Laishui *China* **56** E8
Laissac *France* **20** D6
Láives *Italy* **41** B8
Laiwu *China* **57** F9
Laixi *China* **57** F11
Laiyang *China* **57** F11
Laiyuan *China* **56** E8
Laizhou *China* **57** F10
Laizhou Wan *China* **57** F10
Laja → *Mexico* **118** C4
Lajamanu *Australia* **92** C5
Lajere *Nigeria* **83** C7
Lajkovac *Serbia* **44** B4
Lajosmizse *Hungary* **28** C4
Lak Sao *Laos* **64** C5
Lakaband *Pakistan* **68** D3
Lakamané *Mali* **82** C3
Lake *U.S.A.* **108** D8
Lake Alpine *U.S.A.* **110** G7
Lake Andes *U.S.A.* **112** D4
Lake Arthur *U.S.A.* **116** F8
Lake Bindegolly △ *Australia* **95** D3
Lake Cargelligo *Australia* **95** E4
Lake Charles *U.S.A.* **116** F8
Lake City *Colo., U.S.A.* **108** G10
Lake City *Fla., U.S.A.* **117** F13
Lake City *Mich., U.S.A.* **113** C11
Lake City *Minn., U.S.A.* **112** C7
Lake City *Pa., U.S.A.* **114** D4
Lake City *S.C., U.S.A.* **117** E15
Lake Cowichan *Canada* **102** D4
Lake District △ *U.K.* **14** C4
Lake Elsinore *U.S.A.* **111** M9
Lake Eyre △ *Australia* **95** D2
Lake Gairdner △ *Australia* **95** E2
Lake George *U.S.A.* **115** C11
Lake Grace *Australia* **93** F2
Lake Harbour = Kimmirut
   Canada **101** C13
Lake Havasu City *U.S.A.* **111** L12
Lake Hughes *U.S.A.* **111** L8
Lake Isabella *U.S.A.* **111** K8
Lake Jackson *U.S.A.* **116** G7
Lake King *Australia* **93** F2
Lake Lenore *Canada* **103** C8
Lake Louise *Canada* **102** C5
Lake Malawi △ *Malawi* **87** E3
Lake Mburo △ *Uganda* **86** C3
Lake Mead △ *U.S.A.* **111** K12
Lake Meredith △ *U.S.A.* **116** D4
Lake Mills *U.S.A.* **112** D7
Lake Nakura △ *Kenya* **86** C4
Lake Placid *U.S.A.* **115** B11
Lake Pleasant *U.S.A.* **115** C10
Lake Providence *U.S.A.* **116** E9
Lake Roosevelt △ *U.S.A.* **108** B4

Lake St. Peter *Canada* **114** A6
Lake Superior △ *Canada* **104** C3
Lake Torrens △ *Australia* **95** E2
Lake Village *U.S.A.* **116** E9
Lake Wales *U.S.A.* **117** H14
Lake Worth *U.S.A.* **117** H14
Lakeba *Fiji* **91** a
Lakeba Passage *Fiji* **91** a
Lakefield *Canada* **114** B6
Lakefield △ *Australia* **94** B3
Lakehurst *U.S.A.* **115** F10
Lakeland *Australia* **94** B3
Lakeland *U.S.A.* **117** G14
Lakemba = Lakeba *Fiji* **91** a
Lakeport *Calif., U.S.A.* **110** F4
Lakeport *Mich., U.S.A.* **114** C2
Lakes Entrance *Australia* **95** F4
Lakeside *Calif., U.S.A.* **111** N10
Lakeside *Nebr., U.S.A.* **112** D2
Lakeview *U.S.A.* **108** E3
Lakeville *U.S.A.* **112** C7
Lakewood *Colo., U.S.A.* **108** G11
Lakewood *N.J., U.S.A.* **115** F10
Lakewood *N.Y., U.S.A.* **114** D5
Lakewood *Ohio, U.S.A.* **114** E3
Lakewood *Wash., U.S.A.* **110** C4
Lakha *India* **68** F4
Lakhimpur *India* **69** F9
Lakhisarai *India* **69** G12
Lakhnadon *India* **69** H8
Lakhnau = Lucknow *India* **69** F9
Lakhonpheng *Laos* **64** E5
Lakhpat *India* **68** H3
Läki *Azerbaijan* **35** K8
Lakin *U.S.A.* **112** G3
Lakitusaki → *Canada* **104** B3
Lakki *Greece* **49** D5
Lakki *Pakistan* **68** C4
Lakonia □ *Greece* **46** E4
Lakonikos Kolpos *Greece* **46** E4
Lakor *Indonesia* **63** F7
Lakota *Ivory C.* **82** D3
Lakota *U.S.A.* **112** A4
Laksar *India* **68** E8
Laksefjorden *Norway* **8** A22
Lakselv *Norway* **8** A21
Lakshadweep Is. *India* **3** D13
Lakshmanpur *India* **69** H10
Lakshmikantapur *India* **69** H13
Lala Musa *Pakistan* **68** C5
Lalaghat *India* **67** G18
Lalago *Tanzania* **86** C3
Lalapanzi *Zimbabwe* **87** F3
Lalapaşa *Turkey* **45** E10
Lalbenque *France* **20** D5
L'Albufera △ *Spain* **39** F4
L'Alcora *Spain* **38** E4
L'Alfàs del Pi *Spain* **39** G4
Lalganj *India* **69** G11
Lalgola *India* **69** G13
Lālī *Iran* **71** C6
Lalibela *Ethiopia* **81** E4
Lalin *China* **57** B14
Lalín *Spain* **36** C2
Lalin He → *China* **57** B13
Lalinde *France* **20** D4
Lalitapur *Nepal* **69** F11
Lalitpur *India* **69** G8
Lalkua *India* **69** E8
Lalsot *India* **68** F7
Lam Pao Res. *Thailand* **64** D4
Lama Kara *Togo* **83** D5
Lamae *Malaysia* **65** H2
Lamaing *Burma* **64** E1
Lamar *Colo., U.S.A.* **108** G12
Lamar *Mo., U.S.A.* **112** G6
Lamas *Peru* **124** E3
Lamastre *France* **21** D8
Lamayuru *India* **69** B7
Lamayuru
   Jammu & Kashmir, India **69** B7
Lambach *Austria* **26** C6
Lamballe *France* **18** D4
Lambaréné *Gabon* **84** E2
Lambasa = Labasa *Fiji* **91** a
Lambay I. *Ireland* **12** C5
Lambert's Bay *S. Africa* **88** E2
Lambesc *France* **21** E9
Lambeth *Canada* **114** D3
Lambia *Greece* **46** D3
Lambomakondro *Madag.* **89** C7
Lambro → *Italy* **40** C6
Lambton Shores *Canada* **114** C3
Lame *Nigeria* **83** C6
Lame Deer *U.S.A.* **108** D10
Lamego *Portugal* **36** D3
Lamèque *Canada* **105** C7
Lameroo *Australia* **95** F3
Lamesa *U.S.A.* **116** E4
Lamia *Greece* **46** C4
Lamington △ *Australia* **95** D5
Lamitan *Phil.* **61** H5
Lammermuir Hills *U.K.* **13** F6
Lammhult *Sweden* **11** G8
Lamoille *U.S.A.* **115** B11
Lamon B. *Phil.* **61** D5
Lamont *Canada* **102** C6
Lamont *Calif., U.S.A.* **111** K8
Lamont *Wyo., U.S.A.* **108** E10

Lamotte-Beuvron *France* **19** E9
Lampa *Peru* **124** G4
Lampang *Thailand* **64** C2
Lampasas *U.S.A.* **116** F5
Lampazos de Naranjo
   Mexico **118** B4
Lampedusa *Italy* **79** A7
Lampertheim *Germany* **25** F4
Lampeter *U.K.* **15** E3
Lampman *Canada* **103** D8
Lamprechtshausen *Austria* **26** D5
Lampung □ *Indonesia* **62** F2
Lamta *India* **69** H9
Lamu *Kenya* **86** C5
Lamy *U.S.A.* **109** J11
Lan Xian *China* **56** E6
Lan Yü *Taiwan* **59** F13
Lanak La *China* **69** B8
Lanak'o Shank'ou =
   Lanak La *China* **69** B8
Lanao, L. *Phil.* **61** H6
Lanark *Canada* **115** A8
Lanark *U.K.* **13** F5
Lanbi Kyun *Burma* **65** G2
Lancang *China* **58** G3
Lancang Jiang → *China* **58** G3
Lancashire □ *U.K.* **14** D5
Lancaster *Canada* **115** A10
Lancaster *U.K.* **14** C5
Lancaster *Calif., U.S.A.* **111** L8
Lancaster *Ky., U.S.A.* **113** G11
Lancaster *N.H., U.S.A.* **115** B13
Lancaster *Ohio, U.S.A.* **113** F12
Lancaster *Pa., U.S.A.* **115** F8
Lancaster *S.C., U.S.A.* **117** D14
Lancaster *Wis., U.S.A.* **112** D8
Lancaster Sd. *Canada* **101** B11
Lancelin *Australia* **93** F2
Lanchow = Lanzhou *China* **56** F2
Lanchyn *Ukraine* **29** B9
Lancun *China* **57** F11
Łańcut *Poland* **31** H9
Land Between the Lakes △
   U.S.A. **117** C11
Landau *Bayern, Germany* **25** G8
Landau *Rhld-Pfz., Germany* **25** F4
Landeck *Austria* **26** D3
Lander *U.S.A.* **108** E9
Lander → *Australia* **92** D5
Landerneau *France* **18** D2
Landeryd *Sweden* **11** G7
Landes □ *France* **20** D3
Landes □ *France* **20** E3
Landes de Gascogne △
   France **20** D3
Landete *Spain* **38** F3
Landi Kotal *Pakistan* **68** B4
Landisburg *U.S.A.* **114** F7
Landivisiau *France* **18** D2
Landmannalaugar *Iceland* **8** E4
Landquart *Switz.* **25** J5
Landrecies *France* **19** B10
Land's End *U.K.* **15** G2
Landsberg *Germany* **25** G6
Landsborough Cr. →
   Australia **94** C3
Landsbro *Sweden* **11** G8
Landshut *Germany* **25** G8
Landskrona *Sweden* **11** J6
Landstuhl *Germany* **25** F3
Landvetter *Sweden* **11** G6
Lanesboro *U.S.A.* **115** E9
Lanester *France* **18** E3
Lanett *U.S.A.* **117** E12
Lang Shan *China* **56** D4
Lang Son *Vietnam* **58** G6
Lang Suan *Thailand* **65** H2
Langå *Denmark* **11** H3
La'nga Co *China* **69** D9
Langadás *Greece* **44** F7
Langadia *Greece* **46** D4
Långan → *Sweden* **10** A8
Langano, L. *Ethiopia* **81** F4
Langar *Iran* **71** C9
Langara I. *Canada* **102** C2
Langarūd *Iran* **71** B6
Långås *Sweden* **11** H6
Langdai *China* **58** D5
Langdon *U.S.A.* **112** A4
Långe Jan = Ölands södra
   udde *Sweden* **11** H10
Langeac *France* **20** C7
Langeais *France* **18** E7
Langeb Baraka → *Sudan* **80** D4
Langeberg *S. Africa* **88** E3
Langeberge *S. Africa* **88** D3
Langeland *Denmark* **11** K4
Langelands Bælt *Denmark* **11** K4
Langen *Hessen, Germany* **25** F4
Langen *Niedersachsen,*
   Germany **24** B4
Langenburg *Canada* **103** C8
Langeneß *Germany* **24** A4
Langenlois *Austria* **26** C8
Langeoog *Germany* **24** B3
Langeskov *Denmark* **11** J4
Längenhem *Sweden* **11** G7
Langhirano *Italy* **40** D7

Langholm *U.K.* **13** F5
Langjökull *Iceland* **8** D3
Langkawi, Pulau *Malaysia* **65** J2
Langkon *Malaysia* **62** C5
Langley *Canada* **110** A4
Langnau *Switz.* **25** J3
Langogne *France* **20** D7
Langon *France* **20** D3
Langøya *Norway* **8** B16
Langreo *Spain* **36** B5
Langres *France* **19** E12
Langres, Plateau de *France* **19** E12
Langsa *Indonesia* **62** D1
Långsele *Sweden* **10** A11
Langshyttan *Sweden* **10** D10
Langtang △ *Nepal* **69** E11
Langtry *U.S.A.* **116** G4
Langu *Thailand* **65** J2
Langue de Barbarie △
   Senegal **82** C1
Languedoc *France* **20** E7
Languedoc-Roussillon □
   France **20** E7
Langxi *China* **59** B12
Langxiangzhen *China* **56** E9
Langzhong *China* **58** B5
Lanigan *Canada* **103** C7
Lankao *China* **56** G8
Länkäran *Azerbaijan* **73** C13
Lanmeur *France* **18** D3
Lannemezan *France* **20** E4
Lannilis *France* **18** D2
Lannion *France* **18** D3
L'Annonciation *Canada* **104** C5
Lanouaille *France* **20** C5
Lanping *China* **58** D2
Lansdale *U.S.A.* **115** F9
Lansdowne *Australia* **95** E5
Lansdowne *Canada* **115** B8
Lansdowne *India* **69** E8
Lansdowne House =
   Neskantaga *Canada* **104** B2
L'Anse *U.S.A.* **112** B9
L'Anse au Loup *Canada* **105** B8
L'Anse aux Meadows
   Canada **105** B8
L'Anse la Raye *St. Lucia* **121** f
Lansford *U.S.A.* **115** F9
Lanshan *China* **59** E9
Lansing *U.S.A.* **113** D11
Lanslebourg-Mont-Cenis
   France **21** C10
Lanta Yai, Ko *Thailand* **65** J2
Lantewa *Nigeria* **83** C7
Lantian *China* **56** G5
Lanus *Argentina* **126** C4
Lanusei *Italy* **42** C2
Lanuza *Phil.* **61** G7
Lanxi *China* **59** C12
Lanzarote *Canary Is.* **48** F6
Lanzarote ✈ (ACE) *Canary Is.* **48** F6
Lanzhou *China* **56** F2
Lanzo Torinese *Italy* **40** C4
Lao → *Italy* **43** C8
Lao Bao *Laos* **64** D6
Lao Cai *Vietnam* **58** F4
Laoag *Phil.* **61** B4
Laoang *Phil.* **61** E6
Laoha He → *China* **57** C11
Laohekou *China* **59** A8
Laois □ *Ireland* **12** D4
Laon *France* **19** C10
Laona *U.S.A.* **112** C9
Laos ■ *Asia* **64** D5
Lapa *Brazil* **127** B6
Lapai *Nigeria* **83** D6
Lapalisse *France* **19** F10
Lapeer *U.S.A.* **113** D12
Lapeyrade *France* **20** D3
Lapithos *Cyprus* **49** D12
Lapland = Lappland *Europe* **8** B21
LaPorte *Ind., U.S.A.* **112** E10
Laporte *U.S.A.* **115** E8
Lapovo *Serbia* **44** B5
Lappeenranta *Finland* **32** B5
Lappland *Europe* **8** B21
Lappo = Lapua *Finland* **8** E20
Laprida *Argentina* **126** D3
Lâpseki *Turkey* **45** F10
Laptev Sea *Russia* **53** B13
Lapua *Finland* **8** E20
Lăpuş → *Romania* **29** C8
Lăpuş, Munţii *Romania* **29** C8
Lăpuşna *Moldova* **29** D13
Łapy *Poland* **31** F9
Laqiya Arba'in *Sudan* **80** C2
Laqiya Umran *Sudan* **80** D2
L'Áquila *Italy* **41** F10
Lär *Iran* **71** E7
Larabanga *Ghana* **82** D4
Laragne-Montéglin *France* **21** D9
Laramie *U.S.A.* **108** F11
Laramie Mts. *U.S.A.* **108** F11
Laranjeiras do Sul *Brazil* **127** B5
Larantuka *Indonesia* **63** F6
Larat *Indonesia* **63** F8
L'Arbresle *France* **21** C8
Lärbro *Sweden* **11** G12

Larde *Mozam.* **87** F4
Larder Lake *Canada* **104** C4
Lardos *Greece* **49** C10
Lardos, Akra = Líndos,
  Akra *Greece* **49** C10
Lardos, Ormos *Greece* **49** C10
Lare *Kenya* **86** C4
Laredo *Spain* **36** B7
Laredo *U.S.A.* **116** H5
Laredo Sd. *Canada* **102** C3
Largentière *France* **21** D8
L'Argentière-la-Bessée
  France **21** D10
Largo *U.S.A.* **117** H13
Largs *U.K.* **13** F4
Lari *Italy* **40** E7
Lariang *Indonesia* **63** E5
Larimore *U.S.A.* **112** B5
Larino *Italy* **41** G11
Larisa *Greece* **46** B4
Larissas □ *Greece* **46** B4
Larkana *Pakistan* **68** F3
Larnaca *Cyprus* **49** E12
Larnaca Bay *Cyprus* **49** E12
Larne *U.K.* **12** B6
Larned *U.S.A.* **112** F4
Laroquebrou *France* **20** D6
Larose *U.S.A.* **117** G9
Larrimah *Australia* **92** C5
Larsen Ice Shelf *Antarctica* **5** C17
Laruns *France* **20** F3
Larvik *Norway* **9** G14
Larzac, Causse du *France* **20** E7
Las Alpujarras *Spain* **39** J1
Las Animas *U.S.A.* **108** G12
Las Anod = Laascaanood
  Somali Rep. **75** F4
Las Arenas *Spain* **36** B6
Las Batuecas △ *Spain* **36** E4
Las Brenãs *Argentina* **126** B3
Las Cabezas de San Juan
  Spain **37** J5
Las Cañadas del Teide △
  Canary Is. **48** F3
Las Cejas *Argentina* **128** B4
Las Chimeneas *Mexico* **111** N10
Las Cruces *U.S.A.* **109** K10
Las Flores *Argentina* **126** D4
Las Gabias = Gabia la
  Grande *Spain* **37** H7
Las Heras *Argentina* **126** C2
Las Lajas *Argentina* **128** D2
Las Lomitas *Argentina* **126** A3
Las Marismas *Spain* **37** H4
Las Minas *Spain* **39** G3
Las Navas de la
  Concepción *Spain* **37** H5
Las Navas del Marqués *Spain* **36** E6
Las Palmas *Argentina* **126** B4
Las Palmas *Canary Is.* **48** F4
Las Palmas → *Mexico* **111** N10
Las Palmas ✈ (LPA)
  Canary Is. **48** G4
Las Pedroñas *Spain* **39** F2
Las Piedras *Uruguay* **127** C4
Las Pipinas *Argentina* **126** D4
Las Plumas *Argentina* **128** E3
Las Rosas *Argentina* **126** C3
Las Rozas *Spain* **36** E7
Las Tablas *Panama* **120** E3
Las Toscas *Argentina* **126** B4
Las Truchas *Mexico* **118** D4
Las Tunas *Cuba* **120** B4
Las Varillas *Argentina* **126** C3
Las Vegas *N. Mex., U.S.A.* **109** J11
Las Vegas *Nev., U.S.A.* **111** J11
Las Vegas McCarran Int. ✈
  (LAS) *U.S.A.* **111** J11
Lasarte-Oria *Spain* **38** B2
Lascano *Uruguay* **127** C5
Lash-e Joveyn *Afghan.* **66** D2
Lashburn *Canada* **103** C7
Lashio *Burma* **67** H20
Lashkar *India* **68** F8
Łasin *Poland* **30** E6
Lasithi *Greece* **49** D7
Lasithi □ *Greece* **49** D7
Lāsjerd *Iran* **71** C7
Lask *Poland* **31** G6
Łaskarzew *Poland* **31** G8
Laško *Slovenia* **41** B12
Lassay-les-Châteaux *France* **18** D6
Lassen Pk. *U.S.A.* **108** F3
Lassen Volcanic △ *U.S.A.* **108** F3
Last Mountain L. *Canada* **103** C7
Lastchance Cr. → *U.S.A.* **110** E5
Lastoursville *Gabon* **84** E2
Lastovo *Croatia* **41** F13
Lastovski Kanal *Croatia* **41** F14
Lat Yao *Thailand* **64** E2
Latacunga *Ecuador* **124** D3
Latakia = Al Lādhiqīyah
  Syria **72** E6
Latchford *Canada* **104** C4
Late *Tonga* **91** c
Latehar *India* **69** H11
Laterza *Italy* **43** B9
Latham *Australia* **93** E2
Lathen *Germany* **24** C3

Lathi *India* **68** F4
Lathrop Wells *U.S.A.* **111** J10
Latiano *Italy* **43** B10
Latina *Italy* **42** A5
Latisana *Italy* **41** C10
Latium = Lazio □ *Italy* **41** F9
Laton *U.S.A.* **110** J7
Latorytsya → *Slovak Rep.* **27** C14
Latouche Treville, C.
  Australia **92** C3
Latrobe *Australia* **95** G4
Latrobe *U.S.A.* **114** F5
Latrónico *Italy* **43** B9
Latvia ■ *Europe* **32** D2
Lau *Nigeria* **83** D7
Lau Group *Fiji* **91** a
Lauchhammer *Germany* **24** D9
Lauda-Königshofen *Germany* **25** F5
Lauenburg *Germany* **24** B6
Lauenburgische Seen △
  Germany **24** B6
Lauf *Germany* **25** F7
Laughlin *U.S.A.* **109** J6
Laujar de Andarax *Spain* **39** H2
Laukaa *Finland* **8** E21
Launceston *Australia* **95** G4
Launceston *U.K.* **15** G3
Laune → *Ireland* **12** D2
Launglon Bok *Burma* **64** F1
Laupheim *Germany* **25** G5
Laura *Australia* **94** B3
Laureana di Borrello *Italy* **43** D9
Laurel *Miss., U.S.A.* **117** F10
Laurel *Mont., U.S.A.* **108** D9
Laurel Hill *U.S.A.* **114** F5
Laurencekirk *U.K.* **13** E6
Laurens *U.S.A.* **117** D13
Laurentian Plateau *Canada* **105** B6
Lauria *Italy* **43** B8
Laurie L. *Canada* **103** B8
Laurinburg *U.S.A.* **117** D15
Laurium *U.S.A.* **112** B9
Lausanne *Switz.* **25** J2
Laut *Indonesia* **62** D3
Laut, Pulau *Indonesia* **62** E5
Laut Kecil, Kepulauan
  Indonesia **62** E5
Lauterbach *Germany* **24** E5
Lauterecken *Germany* **25** F3
Lautoka *Fiji* **91** a
Lauzès *France* **20** D5
Lava → *Russia* **30** D8
Lava Beds △ *U.S.A.* **108** F3
Lavagh More *Ireland* **12** B3
Lavagna *Italy* **40** D6
Laval *France* **18** D6
Laval-des-Rapides *Canada* **104** C5
Lavalle *Argentina* **126** B2
Lāvān *Iran* **71** E7
Lavant *Canada* **115** A8
Lavara *Greece* **45** E10
Lavardac *France* **20** D4
Lavaur *France* **20** E5
Lavelanet *France* **20** F5
Lavello *Italy* **43** A8
Laverton *Australia* **93** E3
Lavis *Italy* **40** B8
Lavos *Portugal* **36** E2
Lavradio *Portugal* **37** G1
Lavras *Brazil* **127** A7
Lavre *Portugal* **37** G2
Lavrio *Greece* **46** D6
Lavris *Greece* **49** D6
Lavumisa *Swaziland* **89** D5
Lavushi Manda △ *Zambia* **87** E3
Lawaki *Fiji* **91** a
Lawas *Malaysia* **62** D5
Lawele *Indonesia* **63** F6
Lawn Hill =
  Boodjamulla △ *Australia* **94** B2
Lawqah *Si. Arabia* **70** D4
Lawra *Ghana* **82** C4
Lawrence *N.Z.* **91** F2
Lawrence *Ind., U.S.A.* **112** F10
Lawrence *Kans., U.S.A.* **112** F6
Lawrence *Mass., U.S.A.* **115** D13
Lawrenceburg *Ind., U.S.A.* **113** F11
Lawrenceburg *Tenn., U.S.A.*
  117 D11
Lawrenceville *Ga., U.S.A.* **117** E13
Lawrenceville *Pa., U.S.A.* **114** E7
Laws *U.S.A.* **110** H8
Lawton *U.S.A.* **116** D5
Lawu *Indonesia* **63** G14
Lawz, J. al *Si. Arabia* **80** B4
Laxå *Sweden* **11** F8
Laxford, L. *U.K.* **13** C3
Laxou *France* **19** D13
Lay → *France* **20** B2
Layla *Si. Arabia* **75** C4
Laylān *Iraq* **70** D5
Layon → *France* **18** E6
Layton *U.S.A.* **108** F8
Laytonville *U.S.A.* **108** G2
Lazarev *Russia* **53** D15
Lazarev Sea *S. Ocean* **5** C2
Lazarevac *Serbia* **44** B4
Lazarevskoye *Russia* **35** J4

Lazarivo *Madag.* **89** C8
Lázaro Cárdenas *Mexico* **118** D4
Lazdijai *Lithuania* **30** D10
Lazio □ *Italy* **41** F9
Lazo *Moldova* **29** C13
Lazo *Russia* **54** C6
Le Beausset *France* **21** E9
Le Bic *Canada* **105** C6
Le Blanc *France* **20** B5
Le Bleymard *France* **20** D7
Le Bourgneuf-la-Fôret
  France **18** D6
Le Bugue *France* **20** D4
Le Cateau Cambrésis *France* **19** B10
Le Caylar *France* **20** E7
Le Chambon-Feugerolles
  France **21** C8
Le Châtelet *France* **19** F9
Le Chesne *France* **19** C11
Le Cheylard *France* **21** D8
Le Conquet *France* **18** D2
Le Creusot *France* **19** F11
Le Croisic *France* **18** E4
Le Donjon *France* **19** F10
Le Dorat *France* **20** B5
Le François *France* **120** c
Le Gosier *Guadeloupe* **120** b
Le Grand-Lucé *France* **18** E7
Le Grand-Pressigny *France* **18** F7
Le Grand-Quevilly *France* **18** C8
Le Gris Gris *Mauritius* **85** d
Le Havre *France* **18** C7
Le Lamentin *Martinique* **120** c
Le Lavandou *France* **21** E10
Le Lion-d'Angers *France* **18** E6
Le Louroux-Béconnais
  France **18** E6
Le Luc *France* **21** E10
Le Lude *France* **18** E7
Le Marin *Martinique* **120** c
Le Mans *France* **18** E7
Le Mars *U.S.A.* **112** D5
Le Mayet-de-Montagne
  France **19** F10
Le Mêle-sur-Sarthe *France* **18** D7
Le Monastier-sur-Gazeille
  France **20** D7
Le Monêtier-les-Bains
  France **21** D10
Le Mont-Dore *France* **20** C6
Le Mont-St-Michel *France* **18** D5
Le Moule *Guadeloupe* **120** b
Le Moyne, L. *Canada* **105** A6
Le Muy *France* **21** E10
Le Palais *France* **18** E3
Le Perthus *France* **20** F6
Le Port *Réunion* **85** c
Le Prêcheur *Martinique* **120** c
Le Puy-en-Velay *France* **20** C7
Le Raysville *U.S.A.* **115** E8
Le Robert *Martinique* **120** c
Le Roy *U.S.A.* **114** D7
Le St-Esprit *Martinique* **120** c
Le Sueur *U.S.A.* **112** C7
Le Tampon *Réunion* **85** c
Le Teil *France* **21** D8
Le Teilleul *France* **18** D6
Le Theil *France* **18** D7
Le Thillot *France* **19** E13
Le Thuy *Vietnam* **64** D6
Le Touquet-Paris-Plage
  France **19** B8
Le Tréport *France* **18** B8
Le Val-d'Ajol *France* **19** E13
Le Verdon-sur-Mer *France* **20** C2
Le Vigan *France* **20** E7
Lea → *U.K.* **15** F8
Leach *Cambodia* **65** F4
Lead *U.S.A.* **112** C2
Leader *Canada* **103** C7
Leadville *U.S.A.* **108** G10
Leaf → *U.S.A.* **117** F10
Leaf Rapids *Canada* **103** B9
Leamington *Canada* **114** D2
Leamington *U.S.A.* **108** G7
Leamington Spa = Royal
  Leamington Spa *U.K.* **15** E6
Le'an *China* **59** D10
Leandro Norte Alem
  Argentina **127** B4
Leane, L. *Ireland* **12** D2
Learmonth *Australia* **92** D1
Leask *Canada* **103** C7
Leatherhead *U.K.* **15** F7
Leavenworth *Kans., U.S.A.* **112** F6
Leavenworth *Wash., U.S.A.* **108** C3
Leawood *U.S.A.* **112** F6
Łeba *Poland* **30** D4
Łeba → *Poland* **30** D4
Lebach *Germany* **25** F2
Lebak *Phil.* **61** H6
Lebam *U.S.A.* **110** D3
Lebane *Serbia* **44** D5
Lebanon *Ind., U.S.A.* **112** E10
Lebanon *Kans., U.S.A.* **112** F4
Lebanon *Ky., U.S.A.* **113** G11
Lebanon *Mo., U.S.A.* **112** G7
Lebanon *N.H., U.S.A.* **115** C12
Lebanon *Oreg., U.S.A.* **108** D2

Lebanon *Pa., U.S.A.* **115** F8
Lebanon *Tenn., U.S.A.* **117** C11
Lebanon ■ *Asia* **74** B5
Lebec *U.S.A.* **111** L8
Lebedyan *Russia* **33** F10
Lebedyn *Ukraine* **33** G8
Lebel-sur-Quévillon *Canada* **104** C4
Lebomboberge *S. Africa* **89** C5
Lębork *Poland* **30** D4
Lebrija *Spain* **37** J4
Lebu *Chile* **126** D1
Leca da Palmeira *Portugal* **36** D2
Lecce *Italy* **43** B11
Lecco *Italy* **40** C6
Lecco, L. di *Italy* **40** C6
Lécera *Spain* **38** D4
Lech *Austria* **26** D3
Lech → *Germany* **25** G6
Lechang *China* **59** E9
Lechena *Greece* **46** D3
Lechtaler Alpen *Austria* **26** D3
Lecontes Mills *U.S.A.* **114** E6
Lectoure *France* **20** E4
Ledesma *Spain* **36** D5
Ledong *China* **64** C7
Leduc *Canada* **102** C6
Lee *U.S.A.* **115** D11
Lee → *Ireland* **12** E3
Lee Vining *U.S.A.* **110** H7
Leech L. *U.S.A.* **112** B6
Leechburg *U.S.A.* **114** F5
Leeds *U.K.* **14** D6
Leeds *U.S.A.* **117** E11
Leek *Neths.* **17** A6
Leek *U.K.* **14** D5
Leeman *Australia* **93** E1
Leeper *U.S.A.* **114** E5
Leer *Germany* **24** B3
Leesburg *U.S.A.* **117** G14
Leeton *Australia* **95** E4
Leetonia *U.S.A.* **114** F4
Leesville *U.S.A.* **116** F8
Leeu Gamka *S. Africa* **88** E3
Leeuwarden *Neths.* **17** A5
Leeuwin, C. *Australia* **93** F2
Leeuwin Naturaliste △
  Australia **93** F2
Leeward Is. *Atl. Oc.* **121** C7
Lefka *Cyprus* **49** D11
Lefkada *Greece* **46** C2
Lefkimi *Greece* **49** B4
Lefkimis, Akra *Greece* **49** B4
Lefkoniko *Cyprus* **49** D12
Lefroy *Canada* **114** B5
Lefroy, L. *Australia* **93** F3
Łeg → *Poland* **31** H8
Leganés *Spain* **36** E7
Legazpi *Phil.* **61** E5
Lège-Cap-Ferret *France* **20** D2
Lege Hida *Ethiopia* **81** F5
Legendre I. *Australia* **92** D2
Leghorn = Livorno *Italy* **40** E7
Legionowo *Poland* **31** F7
Legnago *Italy* **41** C8
Legnano *Italy* **40** C5
Legnica *Poland* **31** G3
Legrad *Croatia* **41** B13
Leh *India* **69** B7
Lehigh Acres *U.S.A.* **117** H14
Lehighton *U.S.A.* **115** F9
Lehliu *Romania* **29** F11
Leho *Sudan* **81** F3
Lehrte *Germany* **24** C5
Lehututu *Botswana* **88** C3
Lei Shui → *China* **59** D9
Leiah *Pakistan* **68** D4
Leibnitz *Austria* **26** E8
Leibo *China* **58** C4
Leicester *U.K.* **15** E6
Leicester City □ *U.K.* **15** E6
Leicestershire □ *U.K.* **15** E6
Leichhardt → *Australia* **94** B2
Leichhardt Ra. *Australia* **94** C4
Leiden *Neths.* **17** B4
Leie → *Belgium* **17** C3
Leifers = Láives *Italy* **41** B8
Leimen *Germany* **25** F4
Leimus *Nic.* **120** D3
Leine → *Germany* **24** C5
Leinefelde *Germany* **24** D6
Leinster *Australia* **93** E3
Leinster □ *Ireland* **12** C4
Leinster, Mt. *Ireland* **12** D5
Leipalingis *Lithuania* **30** D10
Leipzig *Germany* **24** D8
Leiria *Portugal* **36** F2
Leiria □ *Portugal* **36** F2
Leirvik *Norway* **9** G11
Leishan *China* **58** D7
Leisler, Mt. *Australia* **92** D4
Leith *U.K.* **13** F5
Leith Hill *U.K.* **15** F7
Leitha → *Europe* **27** D10
Leitrim *Ireland* **12** B3
Leitrim □ *Ireland* **12** B4
Leitza *Spain* **38** B3

Leiyang *China* **59** D9
Leizhou *China* **59** G8
Leizhou Bandao *China* **58** G7
Leizhou Wan *China* **59** G8
Lek → *Neths.* **17** C4
Leka *Norway* **8** D14
Lekani *Greece* **45** E8
Lekbibaj *Albania* **44** D3
Lekeitio *Spain* **38** B2
Lekoui *Burkina Faso* **82** C4
Leland *Mich., U.S.A.* **113** C11
Leland *Miss., U.S.A.* **117** E9
Leláng *Sweden* **10** E6
Leleque *Argentina* **128** E2
Lélouma *Guinea* **82** C2
Lelystad *Neths.* **17** B5
Lem *Denmark* **11** H2
Lema *Nigeria* **83** C5
Lema Shilindi *Ethiopia* **81** G5
Lembar *Indonesia* **63** K19
Lembuak *Indonesia* **63** K19
Lemera *Dem. Rep. of the Congo* **86** C2
Lemery *Phil.* **61** E4
Lemhi Ra. *U.S.A.* **108** D7
Lemmer *Neths.* **17** B5
Lemmon *U.S.A.* **112** C2
Lemon Grove *U.S.A.* **111** N9
Lemoore *U.S.A.* **110** J7
Lempdes *France* **20** C7
Lemvig *Denmark* **11** H2
Lena → *Russia* **53** B13
Lenadoon Pt. *Ireland* **12** B2
Lengerich *Germany* **24** C3
Lenggong *Malaysia* **65** K3
Lenggries *Germany* **25** H7
Lengshuijiang *China* **59** D8
Lengshuitan *China* **59** D8
Lengua de Vaca, Pta. *Chile* **126** C1
Lengwe △ *Malawi* **87** F3
Lengyeltóti *Hungary* **28** D2
Lenhovda *Sweden* **11** H9
Lenina, Kanal → *Russia* **35** J7
Leningrad □ *Russia* **32** C7
Lenino *Ukraine* **33** K8
Leninogorsk *Kazakhstan* **52** D9
Leninsk *Russia* **35** F8
Leninsk-Kuznetskiy *Russia* **52** D9
Leninskoye *Russia* **34** A8
Lenk *Switz.* **25** J3
Lenkoran = Länkäran
  Azerbaijan **73** C13
Lenmalu *Indonesia* **63** E8
Lenne → *Germany* **24** D3
Lennestadt *Germany* **24** D4
Lennox *U.S.A.* **112** D5
Lennoxville *Canada* **115** A13
Leno *Italy* **40** C7
Lenoir *U.S.A.* **117** D14
Lenoir City *U.S.A.* **117** D12
Lenore L. *Canada* **103** C8
Lenox *U.S.A.* **115** D11
Lens *France* **19** B9
Lensahn *Germany* **24** A6
Lensk *Russia* **53** C12
Lentas *Greece* **49** E6
Lenti *Hungary* **28** D1
Lentini *Italy* **43** E8
Lenwood *U.S.A.* **111** L9
Lenya *Burma* **65** G2
Lenzen *Germany* **24** B7
Léo *Burkina Faso* **82** C4
Leoben *Austria* **26** D8
Leodhas = Lewis *U.K.* **13** C2
Leola *U.S.A.* **112** C4
Leominster *U.K.* **15** E5
Leominster *U.S.A.* **115** D13
Léon *France* **20** E2
León *Mexico* **118** C4
León *Nic.* **120** D2
León *Spain* **36** C5
León *U.S.A.* **112** E7
Leon □ *Spain* **36** C5
Leon → *U.S.A.* **116** F6
León, Montes de *Spain* **36** C4
Leonardo da Vinci,
  Roma ✈ (FCO) *Italy* **41** G9
Leonardtown *U.S.A.* **113** F15
Leonberg *Germany* **25** G5
Leonding *Austria* **26** C7
Leone *Amer. Samoa* **91** b
Leonessa *Italy* **41** F9
Leonforte *Italy* **43** E7
Leongatha *Australia* **95** F4
Leonidio *Greece* **46** D4
Leonora *Australia* **93** E3
Leopoldina *Brazil* **127** A7
Leopoldsburg *Belgium* **17** C5
Leoti *U.S.A.* **112** F3
Leova *Moldova* **29** D13
Leoville *Canada* **103** C7

Lepe *Spain* **37** H3
Lepel = Lyepyel *Belarus* **32** E5
Lepenou *Greece* **46** C3
Leping *China* **59** C11
Lépo, L. do *Angola* **88** B2
Lepontine, Alpi *Italy* **40** B5
Leppävirta *Finland* **8** E22
Lepsény *Hungary* **28** D3
Leptis Magna *Libya* **79** B8
Lequeitio = Lekeitio *Spain* **38** B2
Lercara Friddi *Italy* **42** E6
Léré *Chad* **83** D7
Léré *Mali* **82** B4
Lere *Bauchi, Nigeria* **83** D6
Lere *Kaduna, Nigeria* **83** C6
Leribe *Lesotho* **89** D4
Lérici *Italy* **40** D6
Lérida = Lleida *Spain* **38** D5
Lerma *Spain* **36** C7
Léros *Greece* **47** D8
Lérouville *France* **19** D12
Lerum *Sweden* **11** G6
Lerwick *U.K.* **13** A7
Leş *Romania* **28** D6
Les Abrets *France* **21** C9
Les Andelys *France* **18** C8
Les Borges Blanques *Spain* **38** D5
Les Cayes *Haiti* **121** C5
Les Coteaux *Canada* **115** A10
Les Escoumins *Canada* **105** C6
Les Essarts *France* **18** F5
Les Herbiers *France* **18** F5
Les Minquiers, Plateau des
  Chan. Is. **18** D4
Les Pieux *France* **18** C5
Les Ponts-de-Cé *France* **18** E6
Les Riceys *France* **19** E11
Les Sables-d'Olonne *France* **20** B2
Les Vans *France* **21** D8
Lesbos *Greece* **47** B8
L'Escala *Spain* **38** C8
Leshan *China* **58** C4
Leshwe →
  Dem. Rep. of the Congo **87** E2
Lésina *Italy* **41** G12
Lésina, L. di *Italy* **41** G12
Lesjöfors *Sweden* **10** E8
Lesko *Poland* **31** J9
Leskov I. *Antarctica* **5** B1
Leskovac *Serbia* **44** C5
Leskovik *Albania* **44** C5
Leśna *Poland* **31** G2
Lesneven *France* **18** D2
Leśnica *Poland* **31** H5
Lešnica *Serbia* **44** B3
Lesnoye *Russia* **32** C8
Lesopilnoye *Russia* **54** A7
Lesotho ■ *Africa* **89** D4
Lesozavodsk *Russia* **54** B6
Lesparre-Médoc *France* **20** C3
L'Espluga de Francolí *Spain* **38** D6
Lessay *France* **18** C5
Lesse → *Belgium* **17** D4
Lesse et Lomme △ *Belgium* **17** D5
Lessebo *Sweden* **11** H9
Lesser Antilles *W. Indies* **121** D7
Lesser Slave L. *Canada* **102** B5
Lesser Sunda Is. *Indonesia* **63** F6
Lessines *Belgium* **17** D3
Lester B. Pearson Int.,
  Toronto ✈ (YYZ) *Canada* **114** C5
Lestock *Canada* **103** C8
Lesueur I. *Australia* **92** B4
Lesueur △ *Australia* **93** F2
Lésvos = Lesbos *Greece* **47** B8
Leszno *Poland* **31** G3
Letaba *S. Africa* **89** C5
Létavértes *Hungary* **28** C6
Letchworth *U.K.* **15** F7
Letea, Ostrov *Romania* **29** E14
Lethbridge *Canada* **102** D6
Lethem *Guyana* **124** C7
Leti, Kepulauan *Indonesia* **63** F7
Leti Is. = Leti, Kepulauan
  Indonesia **63** F7
Letiahau → *Botswana* **88** C3
Leticia *Colombia* **124** D5
Leting *China* **57** E10
Letjiesbos *S. Africa* **88** E3
Letlhakane *Botswana* **88** C4
Letlhakeng *Botswana* **88** C3
Letpadan *Burma* **67** L19
Letpan *Burma* **67** K19
Letsôk-aw Kyun *Burma* **65** G2
Letterkenny *Ireland* **12** B4
Leu *Romania* **29** F9
Leucadia *U.S.A.* **111** M9
Leucate *France* **20** F7
Leucate, Étang de *France* **20** F7
Leuchars *U.K.* **13** E6
Leuk *Switz.* **25** J3
Leuseni *Moldova* **29** D13
Leuser, G. *Indonesia* **62** D1
Leutkirch *Germany* **25** H6
Leuven *Belgium* **17** D4
Leuze-en-Hainaut *Belgium* **17** D3
Lev Tolstoy *Russia* **32** F10

Levan *Albania* **44** F3
Levanger *Norway* **8** E14
Levant, Î. du *France* **21** E10
Lévanto *Italy* **40** D6
Levanzo *Italy* **42** D5
Levelland *U.S.A.* **116** E3
Leven *U.K.* **13** E6
Leven, L. *U.K.* **13** E5
Leven, Toraka *Madag.* **89** A8
Leveque C. *Australia* **92** C3
Leverano *Italy* **43** B10
Leverkusen *Germany* **24** D3
Levice *Slovak Rep.* **27** C11
Lévico Terme *Italy* **41** C8
Levie *France* **21** G13
Levier *France* **19** F13
Levin *N.Z.* **91** D5
Lévis *Canada* **105** C5
Levis, L. *Canada* **102** A5
Levitha *Greece* **47** D8
Levittown *N.Y., U.S.A.* **115** F11
Levittown *Pa., U.S.A.* **115** F10
Levka *Bulgaria* **45** E10
Levka Oros *Greece* **49** D6
Levkada □ *Greece* **46** C2
Levkás = Lefkada *Greece* **46** C2
Levkôsia = Nicosia *Cyprus* **49** D12
Levoča *Slovak Rep.* **27** B13
Levroux *France* **19** F8
Levski *Bulgaria* **45** C9
Levskigrad = Karlovo
  Bulgaria **45** D8
Levuka *Fiji* **91** a
Lewes *U.K.* **15** G8
Lewes *U.S.A.* **113** F16
Lewin Brzeski *Poland* **31** H4
Lewis *U.K.* **13** C2
Lewis → *U.S.A.* **110** E4
Lewis, Butt of *U.K.* **13** C2
Lewis Ra. *Australia* **92** D4
Lewis Range *U.S.A.* **108** B7
Lewis Run *U.S.A.* **114** E6
Lewisburg *Pa., U.S.A.* **114** F8
Lewisburg *Tenn., U.S.A.* **117** D11
Lewisburg *W. Va., U.S.A.* **113** G13
Lewisporte *Canada* **105** C8
Lewiston *Idaho, U.S.A.* **108** C5
Lewiston *Maine, U.S.A.* **113** C18
Lewiston *N.Y., U.S.A.* **114** C5
Lewistown *Mont., U.S.A.* **108** C9
Lewistown *Pa., U.S.A.* **114** F7
Lexington *Ill., U.S.A.* **112** E9
Lexington *Ky., U.S.A.* **113** F11
Lexington *Mich., U.S.A.* **114** C2
Lexington *Mo., U.S.A.* **112** F7
Lexington *N.C., U.S.A.* **117** D14
Lexington *N.Y., U.S.A.* **115** D10
Lexington *Nebr., U.S.A.* **112** E4
Lexington *Ohio, U.S.A.* **114** F2
Lexington *Tenn., U.S.A.* **117** D10
Lexington *Va., U.S.A.* **113** G14
Lexington Park *U.S.A.* **113** F15
Leyburn *U.K.* **14** C6
Leye *China* **58** E6
Leyland *U.K.* **14** D5
Leyre → *France* **20** D2
Leyte □ *Phil.* **61** F6
Leyte Gulf *Phil.* **61** F6
Leżajsk *Poland* **31** H9
Lezay *France* **20** B3
Lezhë *Albania* **44** E3
Lezhi *China* **58** B5
Lézignan-Corbières *France* **20** E6
Lezoux *France* **20** C7
Lgov *Russia* **33** G8
Lhasa *China* **60** D4
Lhazê *China* **60** D3
L'Hermite, I. *Chile* **128** H3
Lhokkruet *Indonesia* **62** D1
Lhokseumawe *Indonesia* **62** C1
L'Hospitalet de Llobregat
  Spain **38** D7
Li *Thailand* **64** D2
Li Jiang → *China* **59** E8
Li Shui → *China* **59** C9
Li Xian *Gansu, China* **56** G3
Li Xian *Hebei, China* **56** E8
Li Xian *Hunan, China* **59** C8
Liadi *Greece* **47** E9
Liancheng *China* **59** E11
Liancourt Rocks = Tokdo
  Asia **55** F5
Lianga *Phil.* **61** G7
Liangcheng
  Nei Monggol Zizhiqu, China **56** D7
Liangcheng *Shandong, China* **57** G10
Liangdang *China* **56** H4
Lianghe *China* **58** E2
Lianghekou *China* **58** C7
Liangping *China* **58** B6
Liangpran *Indonesia* **62** D4
Lianhua *China* **59** D9
Lianjiang *Fujian, China* **59** D12
Lianjiang *Guangdong, China* **59** G8
Lianping *China* **59** E10
Lianshan *China* **59** E9
Lianshanguan *China* **57** D12
Lianshui *China* **57** H10
Lianyuan *China* **59** D8

Lianyungang *China* **57** G10
Lianzhou *China* **59** E9
Liao He → *China* **57** D11
Liaocheng *China* **56** F8
Liaodong Bandao *China* **57** E12
Liaodong Wan *China* **57** D11
Liaoning □ *China* **57** D12
Liaotung, G. of = Liaodong
  Wan *China* **57** D11
Liaoyang *China* **57** D12
Liaoyuan *China* **57** C13
Liaozhong *China* **57** D12
Liapades *Greece* **49** A3
Liard → *Canada* **102** A4
Liard River *Canada* **102** B3
Liari *Pakistan* **68** G2
Libau = Liepāja *Latvia* **30** B8
Libby *U.S.A.* **108** B6
Libenge *Dem. Rep. of the Congo* **84** D3
Liberal *U.S.A.* **112** G3
Liberec *Czech Rep.* **26** A8
Liberecký □ *Czech Rep.* **26** A8
Liberia *Costa Rica* **120** D2
Liberia ■ *W. Afr.* **82** D3
Libertador □ *Chile* **126** C1
Liberty *Mo., U.S.A.* **112** F6
Liberty *N.Y., U.S.A.* **115** E10
Liberty *Pa., U.S.A.* **114** E7
Liberty *Tex., U.S.A.* **116** F7
Liberty-Newark Int. ✈
  (EWR) *U.S.A.* **115** F10
Libiąż *Poland* **31** H6
Lîbîya, Sahrâ' *Africa* **79** C10
Libo *China* **58** E6
Libobo, Tanjung *Indonesia* **63** E7
Libode *S. Africa* **89** E4
Libohovë *Albania* **44** F4
Libong, Ko *Thailand* **65** J2
Libourne *France* **20** D3
Libramont *Belgium* **17** E5
Librazhd *Albania* **44** E4
Libreville *Gabon* **84** D1
Libya ■ *N. Afr.* **79** C9
Libyan Desert = Lîbîya,
  Sahrâ' *Africa* **79** C10
Libyan Plateau = Ed Déffa
  Egypt **80** A2
Licantén *Chile* **126** D1
Licata *Italy* **42** F6
Licheng *China* **56** F7
Lichfield *U.K.* **15** E6
Lichinga *Mozam.* **87** E4
Lichtenburg *S. Africa* **88** D4
Lichtenfels *Germany* **25** E7
Lichuan *Hubei, China* **58** B7
Lichuan *Jiangxi, China* **59** D11
Licking → *U.S.A.* **113** F11
Licosa, Punta *Italy* **43** B7
Licungo → *Mozam.* **87** F4
Lida *Belarus* **23** B13
Liden *Sweden* **10** B10
Lidhult *Sweden* **11** H7
Lidköping *Sweden* **11** F7
Lido *Italy* **41** C9
Lido *Niger* **83** C5
Lido di Roma = Ôstia, Lido
  di *Italy* **41** G9
Lidoriki *Greece* **46** C4
Lidzbark *Poland* **31** E6
Lidzbark Warmiński *Poland* **30** D7
Liebenwalde *Germany* **24** C9
Lieberose *Germany* **24** D10
Liebig, Mt. *Australia* **92** D5
Liebling *Romania* **28** E6
Liechtenstein ■ *Europe* **25** H5
Liège *Belgium* **17** D5
Liège □ *Belgium* **17** D5
Liegnitz = Legnica *Poland* **31** G3
Lieksa *Finland* **8** E24
Lienart *Dem. Rep. of the Congo* **86** B2
Lienyünchiangshih =
  Lianyungang *China* **57** G10
Lienz *Austria* **26** E5
Liepāja *Latvia* **30** B8
Liepāja □ *Latvia* **30** B8
Liepājas ezers *Latvia* **30** B8
Lier *Belgium* **17** C4
Liernais *France* **19** E11
Liești *Romania* **29** E12
Lietuva = Lithuania ■
  Europe **32** E2
Liévin *France* **19** B9
Lièvre → *Canada* **104** C4
Liezen *Austria* **26** D7
Liffey → *Ireland* **12** C5
Lifford *Ireland* **12** B4
Liffré *France* **18** D5
Lifudzin *Russia* **54** B7
Ligao *Phil.* **61** E5
Lightning Ridge *Australia* **95** D4
Lignano Sabbiadoro *Italy* **41** C10
Ligny-en-Barrois *France* **19** D12
Ligonha → *Mozam.* **87** F4
Ligonier *U.S.A.* **114** F5
Ligueil *France* **18** E7
Liguria □ *Italy* **40** D5
Ligurian Sea *Medit. S.* **40** E5

Lihou Reefs and Cays
  Australia **94** B5
Lihue *U.S.A.* **106** b
Lihué Calel △ *Argentina* **126** D2
Lijiang *China* **58** D3
Likasi *Dem. Rep. of the Congo* **87** E2
Likenäs *Sweden* **10** D7
Likhoslavl *Russia* **32** D8
Likhovskoy *Russia* **33** H11
Likoma I. *Malawi* **87** E3
Likumburu *Tanzania* **87** D4
Lille *Europe* **44** C4
L'Île-Bouchard *France* **18** E7
L'Île-Rousse *France* **21** F12
Liling *China* **59** D9
Lilla Edet *Sweden* **11** F6
Lille *France* **19** B10
Lille Bælt *Denmark* **11** J3
Lillebonne *France* **18** C7
Lillehammer *Norway* **8** F14
Lillesand *Norway* **9** G13
Lillhärdal *Sweden* **10** C8
Lillian Pt. *Australia* **93** E4
Lillo *Spain* **36** F7
Lillooet *Canada* **102** C4
Lillooet → *Canada* **102** D4
Lilongwe *Malawi* **87** E3
Liloy *Phil.* **63** C6
Lim → *Europe* **44** C3
Lim Chu Kang *Singapore* **65** d
Lima *Indonesia* **63** E7
Lima *Peru* **124** F3
Lima *Mont., U.S.A.* **108** D7
Lima *N.Y., U.S.A.* **114** D7
Lima *Ohio, U.S.A.* **113** E11
Lima → *Portugal* **36** D2
Limanowa *Poland* **31** J7
Limassol *Cyprus* **49** E12
Limavady □ *U.K.* **12** A5
Limay → *Argentina* **128** D3
Limay Mahuida *Argentina* **126** D2
Limbach-Oberfrohna
  Germany **24** E8
Limbang *Brunei* **62** D5
Limbara, Mte. *Italy* **42** B2
Limbaži *Latvia* **32** D3
Limbdi *India* **68** H4
Limbe *Cameroon* **83** E6
Limburg *Germany* **25** E4
Limburg □ *Belgium* **17** C5
Limburg □ *Neths.* **17** C5
Limeira *Brazil* **127** A6
Limenaria *Greece* **45** F8
Limenas Chersonisou *Greece* **47** F7
Limerick *Ireland* **12** D3
Limerick *U.S.A.* **115** C14
Limerick □ *Ireland* **12** D3
Limestone *U.S.A.* **114** D6
Limestone → *Canada* **103** B10
Limfjorden *Denmark* **11** H3
Limia = Lima → *Portugal* **36** D2
Limingen *Norway* **8** D15
Limmared *Sweden* **11** G7
Limmen Bight *Australia* **94** A2
Limmen Bight → *Australia* **94** B2
Limni *Greece* **46** C5
Limnos *Greece* **47** B7
Limoges *Canada* **115** A9
Limoges *France* **20** C5
Limón *Costa Rica* **120** E3
Limon *U.S.A.* **108** G3
Limone Piemonte *Italy* **40** D4
Limousin □ *France* **20** C5
Limousin, Plateaux du
  France **20** C5
Limoux *France* **20** E6
Limpopo □ *S. Africa* **89** C4
Limpopo → *Africa* **89** D5
Limuru *Kenya* **86** C4
Lin Xian *China* **56** F6
Lin'an *China* **59** B12
Linapacan I. *Phil.* **61** F3
Linapacan Str. *Phil.* **61** F3
Linares *Chile* **126** D1
Linares *Mexico* **119** C5
Linares *Spain* **37** G7
Linaro, Capo *Italy* **41** F8
Línas Mte. *Italy* **42** C1
Linate, Milano ✈ (LIN) *Italy* **40** C6
Lincang *China* **58** F3
Lincheng *China* **56** F8
Linchuan *China* **59** D11
Lincoln = Beamsville
  Canada **114** C5
Lincoln *Argentina* **126** C3
Lincoln *N.Z.* **91** E4
Lincoln *U.K.* **14** D7
Lincoln *Calif., U.S.A.* **110** G5
Lincoln *Ill., U.S.A.* **112** E9
Lincoln *Kans., U.S.A.* **112** F4
Lincoln *Maine, U.S.A.* **113** C19
Lincoln *N.H., U.S.A.* **115** B13
Lincoln *N. Mex., U.S.A.* **109** K11
Lincoln *Nebr., U.S.A.* **112** E5
Lincoln City *U.S.A.* **108** D1
Lincoln Hav = Lincoln Sea
  Arctic **98** A14

Lincoln Sea *Arctic* **98** A14
Lincolnshire □ *U.K.* **14** D7
Lincolnshire Wolds *U.K.* **14** D7
Lincolnton *U.S.A.* **117** D14
Lind *U.S.A.* **108** C4
Linda *U.S.A.* **110** F5
Lindau *Germany* **25** H5
Lindeman I. *Australia* **94** J7
Linden *Guyana* **124** B7
Linden *Ala., U.S.A.* **117** E11
Linden *Calif., U.S.A.* **110** G5
Linden *Tex., U.S.A.* **116** E7
Lindenhurst *U.S.A.* **115** F11
Lindesberg *Sweden* **10** E9
Lindesnes *Norway* **9** H12
Lindi *Tanzania* **87** D4
Lindi □ *Tanzania* **87** D4
Lindi →
  Dem. Rep. of the Congo **86** B2
Lindley *U.S.A.* **114** D7
Lindö *Sweden* **11** F10
Lindome *Sweden* **11** G6
Lindos *Greece* **49** C10
Lindos, Akra *Greece* **49** C10
Lindoso *Portugal* **36** D2
Lindow *Germany* **24** C8
Lindsay *Canada* **114** B6
Lindsay *Calif., U.S.A.* **110** J7
Lindsay *Okla., U.S.A.* **116** D6
Lindsborg *U.S.A.* **112** F5
Lindsdal *Sweden* **11** H10
Line Islands *Pac. Oc.* **97** H12
Linfen *China* **56** F6
Ling Xian *Hunan, China* **59** D9
Ling Xian *Shandong, China* **56** F9
Lingao *China* **64** C7
Lingayen *Phil.* **63** A6
Lingayen G. *Phil.* **61** C4
Lingbi *China* **57** H9
Lingbo *Sweden* **10** C10
Lingchuan
  Guangxi Zhuangzu, China **59** E8
Lingchuan *Shanxi, China* **56** G7
Lingen *Germany* **24** C3
Lingga *Indonesia* **62** E2
Lingga, Kepulauan *Indonesia* **62** E2
Lingga Arch. = Lingga,
  Kepulauan *Indonesia* **62** E2
Linghem *Sweden* **11** F9
Lingle *U.S.A.* **108** E11
Lingqiu *China* **56** E8
Lingshan *China* **58** F7
Lingshi *China* **56** F6
Lingshou *China* **56** E8
Lingshui *China* **64** C8
Lingtai *China* **56** G4
Linguère *Senegal* **82** B1
Lingui *China* **59** E8
Lingwu *China* **56** E4
Lingyuan *China* **57** D10
Lingyun *China* **58** E6
Linhai *China* **59** C13
Linhares *Brazil* **125** G10
Linhe *China* **56** D4
Linjiang *China* **57** D14
Linköping *Sweden* **11** F9
Linkou *China* **57** B16
Linli *China* **59** C8
Linnhe, L. *U.K.* **13** E3
Linqi *China* **56** G7
Linqing *China* **56** F8
Linqu *China* **57** F10
Linru *China* **56** G7
Lins *Brazil* **127** A6
Linshui *China* **58** B6
Linstead *Jamaica* **120** a
Linta → *Madag.* **89** D7
Linth → *Switz.* **25** H5
Linthal *Switz.* **25** J5
Linton *Ind., U.S.A.* **112** F10
Linton *N. Dak., U.S.A.* **112** B3
Lintong *China* **56** G5
Linwood *Canada* **114** C4
Linwu *China* **59** E9
Linxi *China* **57** C10
Linxia *China* **60** C5
Linxiang *China* **59** C9
Linyanti → *Africa* **88** B4
Linyi *China* **57** G10
Linz *Austria* **26** C7
Linz *Germany* **24** E3
Linzhenzhen *China* **56** F5
Linzi *China* **57** F10
Lion, G. du *France* **20** E7
Lionárisso *Cyprus* **49** D13
Lioni *Italy* **43** B8
Lions, G. du = Lion, G. du
  France **20** E7
Lion's Den *Zimbabwe* **87** F3
Lion's Head *Canada* **114** B3
Liozno = Lyozna *Belarus* **32** E6
Lipa *Phil.* **61** E4
Lipali *Mozam.* **87** F4
Lípari *Italy* **43** D7
Lípari, I. *Italy* **43** D7
Lípari, Is. = Eólie, Ís. *Italy* **43** D7
Lipcani *Moldova* **29** B11

Liperi *Finland* **8** E23
Lipetsk *Russia* **33** F10
Lipetsk □ *Russia* **34** D4
Lipiany *Poland* **31** E1
Liping *China* **58** D7
Lipisi *Greece* **47** D8
Lipkany = Lipcani *Moldova* **29** B11
Lipljan *Serbia* **44** D5
Lipník nad Bečvou
  Czech Rep. **27** B10
Lipno *Poland* **31** F6
Lipova *Romania* **28** D6
Lipovets *Ukraine* **23** D15
Lippe → *Germany* **24** D2
Lippstadt *Germany* **24** D4
Lipscomb *U.S.A.* **116** C4
Lipsk *Poland* **30** E10
Lipsko *Poland* **31** G8
Liptovský Hrádok
  Slovak Rep. **27** B12
Liptovský Mikuláš
  Slovak Rep. **27** B12
Liptrap, C. *Australia* **95** F4
Lipu *China* **59** E8
Lira *Uganda* **86** B3
Liri → *Italy* **42** A6
Liria = Lliria *Spain* **39** F4
Lisala *Dem. Rep. of the Congo* **84** D4
Lisboa *Portugal* **37** G1
Lisboa □ *Portugal* **37** F1
Lisboa ✈ (LIS) *Portugal* **37** G1
Lisbon = Lisboa *Portugal* **37** G1
Lisbon *N. Dak., U.S.A.* **112** B5
Lisbon *N.H., U.S.A.* **115** B13
Lisbon *N.Y., U.S.A.* **115** B9
Lisbon *Ohio, U.S.A.* **114** F4
Lisbon Falls *U.S.A.* **113** D18
Lisburn *U.K.* **12** B5
Lisburne, C. *U.S.A.* **4** C17
Liscannor B. *Ireland* **12** D2
Liscia → *Italy* **42** A2
Lisdoonvarna *Ireland* **12** C2
Lishe Jiang → *China* **58** E3
Lishi *China* **56** F6
Lishu *China* **57** C13
Lishui *Jiangsu, China* **59** B12
Lishui *Zhejiang, China* **59** C12
Lisianski I. *U.S.A.* **96** E10
Lisichansk = Lysychansk
  Ukraine **33** H10
Lisieux *France* **18** C7
Liski *Russia* **33** G10
L'Isle-Jourdain *Gers, France* **20** E5
L'Isle-Jourdain *Vienne, France* **20** B4
L'Isle-sur-la-Sorgue *France* **21** E9
Lisle-sur-Tarn *France* **20** E5
Lismore *Australia* **95** D5
Lismore *Ireland* **12** D4
Lissos → *Greece* **45** E9
Lista *Norway* **9** G12
Lister, Mt. *Antarctica* **5** D11
Liston *Australia* **95** D5
Listowel *Canada* **114** C4
Listowel *Ireland* **12** D2
Lit *Sweden* **10** A8
Lit-et-Mixe *France* **20** D2
Litang *Guangxi Zhuangzu,
  China* **58** F7
Litang *Sichuan, China* **58** B3
Litang Qu → *China* **58** C3
Litani → *Lebanon* **74** B4
Litchfield *Calif., U.S.A.* **110** E6
Litchfield *Conn., U.S.A.* **115** E11
Litchfield *Ill., U.S.A.* **112** F9
Litchfield *Minn., U.S.A.* **112** C6
Litchfield △ *Australia* **92** B5
Liteni *Romania* **29** C11
Lithgow *Australia* **95** E5
Lithino, Akra *Greece* **49** E6
Lithuania ■ *Europe* **32** E2
Litija *Slovenia* **41** B11
Lititz *U.S.A.* **115** F8
Litochoro *Greece* **44** F6
Litoměřice *Czech Rep.* **26** A7
Litomyšl *Czech Rep.* **27** B9
Litschau *Austria* **26** C8
Little Abaco *Bahamas* **120** A4
Little Barrier I. *N.Z.* **91** B5
Little Belt Mts. *U.S.A.* **108** C8
Little Bighorn Battlefield △
  U.S.A. **108** D10
Little Blue → *U.S.A.* **112** F5
Little Buffalo → *Canada* **102** A6
Little Cayman *Cayman Is.* **120** C3
Little Churchill → *Canada* **103** B9
Little Colorado → *U.S.A.* **109** H8
Little Current *Canada* **104** C3
Little Current → *Canada* **104** B3
Little Falls *Minn., U.S.A.* **112** C6
Little Falls *N.Y., U.S.A.* **115** C10
Little Fork → *U.S.A.* **112** A7
Little Grand Rapids *Canada* **103** C9
Little Humboldt → *U.S.A.* **108** F5
Little Inagua I. *Bahamas* **121** B5
Little Karoo *S. Africa* **88** E3
Little Khingan Mts. = Xiao
  Hinggan Ling *China* **60** B7
Little Lake *U.S.A.* **111** K9

Little Laut Is. = Laut Kecil,
  Kepulauan *Indonesia* **62** E5
Little Mecatina = Petit-
  Mécatina → *Canada* **105** B8
Little Minch *U.K.* **13** D2
Little Missouri → *U.S.A.* **112** B2
Little Ouse → *U.K.* **15** E9
Little Rann *India* **68** H4
Little Red → *U.S.A.* **116** D9
Little River *N.Z.* **91** E4
Little Rock *U.S.A.* **116** D8
Little Ruaha → *Tanzania* **86** D4
Little Sable Pt. *U.S.A.* **112** D2
Little Scarcies → *S. Leone* **82** D2
Little Sioux → *U.S.A.* **112** E5
Little Smoky → *Canada* **102** C5
Little Snake → *U.S.A.* **108** F9
Little Tobago *Trin. & Tob.* **125** J16
Little Valley *U.S.A.* **114** D6
Little Wabash → *U.S.A.* **112** G9
Little White → *U.S.A.* **112** D3
Little Zab = Zâb aş
  Şaghîr → *Iraq* **73** E10
Littlefield *U.S.A.* **116** E3
Littlehampton *U.K.* **15** G7
Littleton *U.S.A.* **115** B13
Littoral □ *Cameroon* **83** E7
Litvinov *Czech Rep.* **26** A6
Liu He → *China* **57** D11
Liu Jiang → *China* **58** F7
Liuba *China* **56** H4
Liucheng *China* **58** E7
Liuhe *China* **57** C13
Liuheng Dao *China* **59** C14
Liujiang *China* **58** E7
Liukang Tenggaja =
  Sabalana, Kepulauan
  Indonesia **63** F5
Liuli *Tanzania* **87** E3
Liupanshui *China* **58** D5
Liuwa Plain *Zambia* **85** G4
Liuyang *China* **59** C9
Liuzhou *China* **58** E7
Liuzhuang *China* **57** H11
Livada *Romania* **28** D7
Livadero *Greece* **44** F5
Livadhia *Cyprus* **49** E12
Livadi *Greece* **46** A4
Livadia *Greece* **46** C4
Livarot *France* **18** D7
Live Oak *Calif., U.S.A.* **110** D5
Live Oak *Fla., U.S.A.* **117** F13
Lively *Canada* **113** B13
Liveras *Cyprus* **49** D11
Livermore *U.S.A.* **110** H5
Livermore, Mt. *U.S.A.* **116** F2
Livermore Falls *U.S.A.* **113** C18
Liverpool *Australia* **95** B5
Liverpool *Canada* **105** D7
Liverpool *U.K.* **14** D4
Liverpool *U.S.A.* **115** C8
Liverpool Bay *U.K.* **14** D4
Liverpool Ra. *Australia* **95** E5
Livigno *Italy* **40** B7
Livingston *Guatemala* **120** C2
Livingston *U.K.* **13** F5
Livingston *Ala., U.S.A.* **117** E10
Livingston *Calif., U.S.A.* **110** H6
Livingston *Mont., U.S.A.* **108** D8
Livingston *S.C., U.S.A.* **117** E14
Livingston *Tenn., U.S.A.* **117** C12
Livingston *Tex., U.S.A.* **116** F7
Livingston, L. *U.S.A.* **116** F7
Livingston Manor *U.S.A.* **115** E10
Livingstone *Zambia* **87** F2
Livingstone Mts. *Tanzania* **87** D3
Livingstonia *Malawi* **87** E3
Livno *Bos.-H.* **28** G2
Livny *Russia* **33** F9
Livonia *Mich., U.S.A.* **113** D12
Livonia *N.Y., U.S.A.* **114** D7
Livorno *Italy* **40** E7
Livradois-Forez △ *France* **20** E7
Livramento *Brazil* **127** C4
Livron-sur-Drôme *France* **21** D8
Livyntsi *Ukraine* **29** B11
Liwale *Tanzania* **87** D4
Liwiec → *Poland* **31** F8
Lixi *China* **58** D3
Lixian *China* **58** B4
Lixouri *Greece* **46** C2
Liyang *China* **59** B12
Lizard I. *Australia* **94** A4
Lizard Pt. *U.K.* **15** H2
Lizarra = Estella *Spain* **38** C2
Lizzano *Italy* **43** B10
Ljig *Serbia* **44** B4
Ljubija *Bos.-H.* **41** D13
Ljubinje *Bos.-H.* **44** D2
Ljubišnja *Europe* **44** C3
Ljubljana *Slovenia* **41** B11
Ljubljana ✈ (LJU) *Slovenia* **41** B11
Ljubno *Slovenia* **41** B11
Ljubovija *Serbia* **44** B3
Ljugarn *Sweden* **11** G12
Ljung *Sweden* **11** G7
Ljungan → *Sweden* **10** B11

Ljungaverk *Sweden* **10** B10
Ljungby *Sweden* **11** H7
Ljungdalen *Sweden* **10** B6
Ljungsbro *Sweden* **11** F9
Ljusdal *Sweden* **10** C10
Ljusfallshammar *Sweden* **11** F9
Ljusnan → *Sweden* **10** C11
Ljusne *Sweden* **10** C11
Ljutomer *Slovenia* **41** B13
Llagostera *Spain* **38** D7
Llancanelo, Salina
 Argentina **126** D2
Llandeilo *U.K.* **15** F4
Llandovery *U.K.* **15** F4
Llandrindod Wells *U.K.* **15** E4
Llandudno *U.K.* **14** D4
Llanelli *U.K.* **15** F3
Llanes *Spain* **36** B6
Llangollen *U.K.* **14** E4
Llanidloes *U.K.* **15** E4
Llano *U.S.A.* **116** F5
Llano → *U.S.A.* **116** F5
Llano Estacado *U.S.A.* **116** E3
Llanos *S. Amer.* **124** C4
Llanos de Challe △ *Chile* **126** B1
Llanquihue, L. *Chile* **128** E1
Llanwrtyd Wells *U.K.* **15** E4
Llebeig, C. des *Spain* **48** B9
Lleida *Spain* **38** D5
Lleida □ *Spain* **38** C6
Llentrisca, C. *Spain* **48** C7
Llera de Canales *Mexico* **119** C5
Llerena *Spain* **37** G4
Lleyn Peninsula *U.K.* **14** E3
Llico *Chile* **126** C1
Lliria *Spain* **39** F4
Llívia *Spain* **20** F5
Llobregat → *Spain* **38** D7
Llodio *Spain* **38** B2
Lloret de Mar *Spain* **38** D7
Lloseta *Spain* **48** B9
Lloyd B. *Australia* **94** A3
Lloyd L. *Canada* **103** B7
Lloydminster *Canada* **103** C7
Llubí *Spain* **48** B10
Llucena del Cid *Spain* **38** E4
Llucmajor *Spain* **48** B9
Llullaillaco, Volcán
 S. Amer. **126** A2
Llullaillaco △ *Chile* **126** A2
Lo → *Vietnam* **64** B5
Loa *U.S.A.* **108** G8
Loa → *Chile* **126** A1
Loaita I. *S. China Sea* **62** B4
Loange →
 Dem. Rep. of the Congo **84** E4
Loano *Italy* **40** D5
Lobatse *Botswana* **88** D4
Löbau *Germany* **24** D10
Lobenstein *Germany* **24** E7
Lobería *Argentina* **126** D4
Löberöd *Sweden* **11** J7
Łobez *Poland* **30** E2
Lobito *Angola* **85** G2
Lobo → *Ivory C.* **82** D3
Lobos *Argentina* **126** D4
Lobos, I. *Mexico* **118** B2
Lobos, I. de *Canary Is.* **48** F6
Łobżenica *Poland* **31** E4
Loc Binh *Vietnam* **64** B6
Loc Ninh *Vietnam* **65** G6
Locarno *Switz.* **25** J4
Loch Baghasdail =
 Lochboisdale *U.K.* **13** D1
Loch Garman = Wexford
 Ireland **12** D5
Loch Lomond and the
 Trossachs △ *U.K.* **13** E4
Loch Nam Madadh =
 Lochmaddy *U.K.* **13** D1
Lochaber □ *U.K.* **13** E3
Locharbriggs *U.K.* **13** F5
Lochboisdale *U.K.* **13** D1
Loche, L. La *Canada* **103** B7
Lochem *Neths.* **17** B6
Loches *France* **18** E7
Lochgilphead *U.K.* **13** E3
Lochinvar △ *Zambia* **87** F2
Lochinver *U.K.* **13** C3
Lochmaddy *U.K.* **13** D1
Lochnagar *Australia* **94** C4
Lochnagar *U.K.* **13** E5
Łochów *Poland* **31** F8
Lochy, L. *U.K.* **13** E4
Lock *Australia* **95** E2
Lock Haven *U.S.A.* **114** E7
Lockeford *U.S.A.* **110** G5
Lockerbie *U.K.* **13** F5
Lockhart *U.S.A.* **116** G6
Lockhart, L. *Australia* **93** F2
Lockhart River *Australia* **94** A3
Lockney *U.S.A.* **116** D4
Lockport *U.S.A.* **114** C6
Locminé *France* **18** E4
Locri *Italy* **43** D9
Locronan *France* **18** D2

Lod *Israel* **74** D3
Lodeinoye Pole *Russia* **32** B7
Lodève *France* **20** E7
Lodge Bay *Canada* **105** B8
Lodge Grass *U.S.A.* **108** D10
Lodhran *Pakistan* **68** E4
Lodi *Italy* **40** C6
Lodi *Calif., U.S.A.* **110** G5
Lodi *Ohio, U.S.A.* **114** E3
Lodja *Dem. Rep. of the Congo* **86** C1
Lodosa *Spain* **38** C2
Lödöse *Sweden* **11** F6
Lodwar *Kenya* **86** B4
Łódź *Poland* **31** G6
Łódzkie □ *Poland* **31** G6
Loei *Thailand* **64** D3
Loengo *Dem. Rep. of the Congo* **86** C2
Loeriesfontein *S. Africa* **88** E2
Lofa → *Liberia* **82** D2
Lofa Mano △ *Liberia* **82** D2
Lofer *Austria* **26** D5
Lofoten *Norway* **8** B16
Lofsdalen *Sweden* **10** B7
Lofsen → *Sweden* **10** B7
Loftahammar *Sweden* **11** G10
Loga *Niger* **83** C5
Logan *Iowa, U.S.A.* **112** E6
Logan *Ohio, U.S.A.* **113** F12
Logan *Utah, U.S.A.* **108** F8
Logan *W. Va., U.S.A.* **113** G13
Logan, Mt. *Canada* **100** C5
Logandale *U.S.A.* **111** J12
Logansport *Ind., U.S.A.* **112** E10
Logansport *La., U.S.A.* **116** F8
Logirim *Sudan* **81** G3
Logo *Sudan* **81** F3
Logone → *Chad* **79** F9
Logroño *Spain* **38** C2
Logrosán *Spain* **37** F5
Løgstør *Denmark* **11** H3
Løgumkloster *Denmark* **11** J2
Lohals *Denmark* **11** J4
Lohardaga *India* **69** H11
Loharia *India* **68** H6
Loharu *India* **68** E6
Lohja *Finland* **32** B3
Löhne *Germany* **24** C4
Lohr *Germany* **25** F5
Lohri Wah → *Pakistan* **68** F2
Loi-kaw *Burma* **67** K20
Loimaa *Finland* **32** B2
Loir → *France* **18** E6
Loir-et-Cher □ *France* **18** E8
Loire □ *France* **21** C8
Loire → *France* **18** E4
Loire Anjou Touraine △
 France **18** E6
Loire-Atlantique □ *France* **18** E5
Loiret □ *France* **19** E9
Loitz *Germany* **24** B9
Loja *Ecuador* **124** D3
Loja *Spain* **37** H6
Loji = Kawasi *Indonesia* **63** E7
Lojo = Lohja *Finland* **32** B3
Lojung *China* **58** E7
Loka *Sudan* **81** G3
Lokandu
 Dem. Rep. of the Congo **86** C2
Lokeren *Belgium* **17** C3
Lokgwabe *Botswana* **88** C3
Lokhvitsa *Ukraine* **33** G7
Lokichar *Kenya* **86** B4
Lokichokio *Kenya* **86** B3
Lokitaung *Kenya* **86** B4
Lokkan tekojärvi *Finland* **8** C22
Løkken *Denmark* **11** G3
Loknya *Russia* **32** D6
Loko *Nigeria* **83** D6
Lokoja *Nigeria* **83** D6
Lokolo →
 Dem. Rep. of the Congo **84** E3
Lokot *Russia* **33** F8
Lol → *Sudan* **81** F2
Lola *Guinea* **82** D3
Lola, Mt. *U.S.A.* **110** F6
Lolgorien *Kenya* **86** C3
Lolibai, Gebel *Sudan* **81** G3
Lolimi *Sudan* **81** G3
Loliondo *Tanzania* **86** C4
Lolland *Denmark* **11** K5
Lollar *Germany* **24** E4
Lolo *U.S.A.* **108** C6
Lolodorf *Cameroon* **83** E7
Lom *Bulgaria* **44** C7
Lom → *Bulgaria* **44** C7
Lom Kao *Thailand* **64** D3
Lom Sak *Thailand* **64** D3
Loma *U.S.A.* **108** C8
Loma Linda *U.S.A.* **111** L9
Loma Mansa *S. Leone* **82** D2
Loma Mts. *S. Leone* **82** D2
Lomaloma *Fiji* **91** a
Lomami →
 Dem. Rep. of the Congo **86** B1
Lomas de Zamora *Argentina* **126** C4
Lombadina *Australia* **92** C3
Lombárdia □ *Italy* **40** C6

Lombardy = Lombárdia □
 Italy **40** C6
Lombez *France* **20** E4
Lomblen *Indonesia* **63** F6
Lombok *Indonesia* **62** F5
Lombok, Selat *Indonesia* **63** K18
Lomé *Togo* **83** D5
Lomela *Dem. Rep. of the Congo* **84** E4
Lomela →
 Dem. Rep. of the Congo **84** E4
Lomianki *Poland* **31** F7
Lomma *Sweden* **11** J7
Lommel *Belgium* **17** C5
Lomond *Canada* **102** C6
Lomond, L. *U.K.* **13** E4
Lomonosov Ridge *Arctic* **4** A
Lomphat *Cambodia* **64** F6
Lompobatang *Indonesia* **63** F5
Lompoc *U.S.A.* **111** L6
Łomża *Poland* **31** E9
Lon, Ko *Thailand* **65** a
Loncoche *Chile* **128** D2
Londa *India* **66** M9
Londiani *Kenya* **86** C4
Londinières *France* **18** C8
London *Canada* **114** D3
London *U.K.* **15** F7
London *Ky., U.S.A.* **113** G11
London *Ohio, U.S.A.* **113** F12
London, Greater □ *U.K.* **15** F7
London Gatwick ✈ (LGW)
 U.K. **15** F7
London Heathrow ✈
 (LHR) *U.K.* **15** F7
London Stansted ✈ (STN)
 U.K. **15** F8
Londonderry *U.K.* **12** B4
Londonderry □ *U.K.* **12** B4
Londonderry, C. *Australia* **92** B4
Londonderry, I. *Chile* **128** H2
Londres *Argentina* **126** B2
Londrina *Brazil* **127** A5
Lone Pine *U.S.A.* **110** J8
Lonely Mine *Zimbabwe* **89** B4
Long B. *U.S.A.* **117** E15
Long Beach *Calif., U.S.A.* **111** M8
Long Beach *N.Y., U.S.A.* **115** F11
Long Beach *Wash., U.S.A.* **110** D2
Long Branch *U.S.A.* **115** F11
Long Creek *U.S.A.* **108** D4
Long Eaton *U.K.* **14** E6
Long I. *Australia* **94** J6
Long I. *Bahamas* **121** B4
Long I. *Canada* **104** B4
Long I. *Ireland* **12** E2
Long I. *U.S.A.* **115** F11
Long Island Sd. *U.S.A.* **115** E12
Long L. *Canada* **104** C2
Long L. *U.S.A.* **115** C10
Long Lake *U.S.A.* **115** C10
Long Point *Canada* **114** D4
Long Point B. *Canada* **114** D4
Long Prairie *U.S.A.* **112** C6
Long Prairie → *U.S.A.* **112** B6
Long Pt., Ont., *Canada* **114** D4
Long Pt., Ont., *Canada* **115** C8
Long Range Mts. *Canada* **105** C8
Long Reef *Australia* **92** B4
Long Sault *Canada* **115** A10
Long Str. = Longa, Proliv
 Russia **53** C18
Long Thanh *Vietnam* **65** G6
Long Xian *China* **56** G4
Long Xuyen *Vietnam* **65** G5
Longa *Greece* **46** E3
Longa, Proliv *Russia* **53** C18
Long'an *China* **58** F6
Longarone *Italy* **41** B9
Longbenton *U.K.* **14** B6
Longboat Key *U.S.A.* **117** H13
Longchang *China* **58** C5
Longchi *China* **58** C4
Longchuan *Guangdong,
 China* **59** E10
Longchuan *Yunnan, China* **58** E1
Longde *China* **56** G4
Longeau *France* **19** E12
Longford *Australia* **95** G4
Longford *Ireland* **12** C4
Longford □ *Ireland* **12** C4
Longhai *China* **59** E11
Longhua *China* **57** D9
Longhui *China* **59** D8
Longido *Tanzania* **86** C4
Longiram *Indonesia* **62** E5
Longkou *Jiangxi, China* **59** D10
Longkou *Shandong, China* **57** F11
Longlac *Canada* **104** C2
Longli *China* **58** D6
Longlin *China* **58** E5
Longling *China* **58** E2
Longmeadow *U.S.A.* **115** D12
Longmen *China* **59** F10
Longming *China* **58** F6
Longmont *U.S.A.* **108** F11
Longnan *China* **59** E10
Longnawan *Indonesia* **62** D4
Longobucco *Italy* **43** C9
Longquan *China* **59** C12

Longreach *Australia* **94** C3
Longshan *China* **58** C7
Longsheng *China* **59** E8
Longué-Jumelles *France* **18** E6
Longueau *France* **19** C9
Longueuil *Canada* **115** A11
Longuyon *France* **19** C12
Longvic *France* **19** E12
Longview *Tex., U.S.A.* **116** E7
Longview *Wash., U.S.A.* **110** D4
Longwy *France* **19** C12
Longxi *China* **56** G3
Longyan *China* **59** E11
Longyearbyen *Svalbard* **4** B8
Longyou *China* **59** C12
Longzhou *China* **58** F6
Lonigo *Italy* **41** C8
Löningen *Germany* **24** C3
Lonja → *Croatia* **41** C13
Lonoke *U.S.A.* **116** D9
Lonquimay *Chile* **128** D2
Lons-le-Saunier *France* **19** F12
Lönsboda *Sweden* **11** H8
Looe *U.K.* **15** G3
Lookout, C. *Canada* **104** A3
Lookout, C. *U.S.A.* **117** D16
Loolmalasin *Tanzania* **86** C4
Loon → *Alta., Canada* **102** B5
Loon → *Man., Canada* **103** B8
Loon Lake *Canada* **103** C7
Loongana *Australia* **93** F4
Loop Hd. *Ireland* **12** D2
Lop Buri *Thailand* **64** E3
Lop Nor = Lop Nur *China* **60** B4
Lop Nur *China* **60** B4
Lopare *Bos.-H.* **28** F3
Lopatin *Russia* **35** J8
Lopatina, Gora *Russia* **53** D15
Lopatka, Mys *Russia* **53** D16
Lopaye *Sudan* **81** F3
Lopez *Phil.* **61** E5
Lopez *U.S.A.* **115** E8
Lopez, C. *Gabon* **84** E1
Lopphavet *Norway* **8** A19
Lora → *Afghan.* **66** D4
Lora, Hāmūn-i- *Pakistan* **66** E4
Lora Cr. → *Australia* **95** D2
Lora del Río *Spain* **37** H5
Lorain *U.S.A.* **114** E2
Loralai *Pakistan* **68** D3
Lorca *Spain* **39** H3
Lord Howe I. *Pac. Oc.* **90** L7
Lord Howe Rise *Pac. Oc.* **96** L8
Lordsburg *U.S.A.* **109** K9
Lorestān □ *Iran* **71** C6
Loreto *Brazil* **125** E9
Loreto *Italy* **41** E10
Loreto *Mexico* **118** B2
Lorgues *France* **21** E10
Lorhosso *Burkina Faso* **82** C4
Lorient *France* **18** E3
Lőrinci *Hungary* **28** C4
Lorn *India* **69** H9
Lorn *U.K.* **13** E3
Lorn, Firth of *U.K.* **13** E3
Lorne *Australia* **95** F3
Loronyo *Sudan* **81** G3
Lorovouno *Cyprus* **49** D11
Lörrach *Germany* **25** H3
Lorraine □ *France* **19** D13
Lorraine □ *France* **19** D12
Los *Sweden* **10** C9
Los, Îles de *Guinea* **82** D2
Los Alamos *Calif., U.S.A.* **111** L6
Los Alamos *N. Mex., U.S.A.* **109** J10
Los Alcornocales △ *Spain* **37** J5
Los Altos *U.S.A.* **110** H4
Los Andes *Chile* **126** C1
Los Angeles *Chile* **126** D1
Los Angeles *U.S.A.* **111** M8
Los Angeles, Bahia de
 Mexico **118** B2
Los Angeles Aqueduct
 U.S.A. **111** K9
Los Angeles Int. ✈ (LAX)
 U.S.A. **111** M8
Los Banos *U.S.A.* **110** H6
Los Barrios *Spain* **37** J5
Los Blancos *Argentina* **126** A3
Los Cardones △ *Argentina* **126** B2
Los Chiles *Costa Rica* **120** D3
Los Corrales de Buelna *Spain* **36** B6
Los Cristianos *Canary Is.* **48** F3
Los Gallardos *Spain* **39** H3
Los Gatos *U.S.A.* **110** H5
Los Haïtises △ *Dom. Rep.* **121** C6
Los Hermanos Is. *Venezuela* **121** D7
Los Islotes *Canary Is.* **48** E6
Los Llanos de Aridane
 Canary Is. **48** F2
Los Loros *Chile* **126** B1
Los Lunas *U.S.A.* **109** J10
Los Mochis *Mexico* **118** B3
Los Monegros *Spain* **38** D4
Los Nietos *Spain* **39** H4
Los Olivos *U.S.A.* **111** L6
Los Palacios *Cuba* **120** B3
Los Palacios y Villafranca
 Spain **37** H5

Los Queñes *Chile* **126** D1
Los Reyes de Salgado
 Mexico **118** D4
Los Roques Is. *Venezuela* **121** D6
Los Santos de Maimona
 Spain **37** G4
Los Teques *Venezuela* **124** A5
Los Testigos, Is. *Venezuela* **124** A6
Los Vilos *Chile* **126** C1
Los Yébenes *Spain* **37** F7
Losar Dam *S. Africa* **89** D4
Loskop Dam *S. Africa* **89** D4
Løsning *Denmark* **11** J3
Lossiemouth *U.K.* **13** D5
Lossen → *Sweden* **10** B6
Lostwithiel *U.K.* **15** G3
Lot □ *France* **20** D5
Lot → *France* **20** D4
Lot-et-Garonne □ *France* **20** D4
Lota *Chile* **126** D1
Lotagipi Swamp *Sudan* **81** G3
Lotfābād *Iran* **71** B8
Lothair *S. Africa* **89** D5
Lotorp *Sweden* **11** F9
Lotung *Taiwan* **59** E13
Lotta → *Europe* **8** B24
Löttorp *Sweden* **11** G11
Lotung *Taiwan* **59** E13
Loubomo *Congo* **84** E2
Loudéac *France* **18** D4
Loudi *China* **59** D8
Loudonville *U.S.A.* **114** F2
Loudun *France* **18** E7
Loue → *France* **19** E12
Louga *Senegal* **82** B1
Louga □ *Senegal* **82** B1
Loughborough *U.K.* **14** E6
Loughrea *Ireland* **12** C3
Loughros More B. *Ireland* **12** B3
Louhans *France* **19** F12
Louis Trichardt *S. Africa* **89** C4
Louis XIV, Pte. *Canada* **104** B4
Louisa *U.S.A.* **113** F12
Louisbourg *Canada* **105** C8
Louisburgh *Ireland* **12** C1
Louise I. *Canada* **102** C2
Louiseville *Canada* **104** C5
Louisiade Arch. *Papua N. G.* **90** C8
Louisiana *U.S.A.* **112** F6
Louisiana □ *U.S.A.* **116** F9
Louisville *Ky., U.S.A.* **113** F11
Louisville *Miss., U.S.A.* **117** E10
Louisville *Ohio, U.S.A.* **114** F3
Louisville Ridge *Pac. Oc.* **96** L10
Loulay *France* **20** B3
Loulé *Portugal* **37** H3
Louny *Czech Rep.* **26** A6
Loup City *U.S.A.* **112** E4
Loups Marins, Lacs des
 Canada **104** A5
Lourdes *France* **20** E3
Lourdes-de-Blanc-Sablon
 Canada **105** B8
Lourinhã *Portugal* **37** F1
Louroujina *Cyprus* **49** E12
Lousã *Portugal* **36** E2
Louta *Burkina Faso* **82** C4
Louth *Australia* **95** E4
Louth *Ireland* **12** C5
Louth *U.K.* **14** D7
Louth □ *Ireland* **12** C5
Loutra Edipsou *Greece* **46** C5
Loutraki *Greece* **46** D4
Loutropoli Thermis *Greece* **47** B8
Louvain = Leuven *Belgium* **17** D4
Louviers *France* **18** C8
Louwsburg *S. Africa* **89** D5
Lovat → *Russia* **32** C6
Lovćen *Montenegro* **44** D2
Lovćen △ *Montenegro* **44** D2
Lovech *Bulgaria* **45** C8
Lovech □ *Bulgaria* **45** C8
Loveland *U.S.A.* **108** F11
Lovell *U.S.A.* **108** D9
Lovelock *U.S.A.* **108** F4
Lóvere *Italy* **40** C7
Løvstabruk *Sweden* **10** D11
Lövstabruk *Sweden* **10** D11
Low, L. *Canada* **104** B4
Low Pt. *Australia* **93** F4
Low Tatra = Nízké Tatry
 Slovak Rep. **27** C12
Lowa *Dem. Rep. of the Congo* **86** C2
Lowa →
 Dem. Rep. of the Congo **86** C2
Lowell *U.S.A.* **115** D13
Lowellville *U.S.A.* **114** E4
Löwen → *Namibia* **88** D2
Lower Alkali L. *U.S.A.* **108** F3

Lower Arrow L. *Canada* **102** D5
Lower Austria =
 Niederösterreich □
 Austria **26** C8
Lower California = Baja
 California *Mexico* **118** A1
Lower Hutt *N.Z.* **91** D5
Lower Lake *U.S.A.* **110** G4
Lower Manitou L. *Canada* **103** D10
Lower Post *Canada* **102** B3
Lower Red L. *U.S.A.* **112** B6
Lower Saxony =
 Niedersachsen □ *Germany* **24** C4
Lower Tunguska =
 Tunguska,
 Nizhnyaya → *Russia* **53** C9
Lower Zambezi △ *Zambia* **87** F2
Lowestoft *U.K.* **15** E9
Lowgar □ *Afghan.* **66** B6
Łowicz *Poland* **31** F6
Lowville *U.S.A.* **115** C9
Loxton *Australia* **95** E3
Loxton *S. Africa* **88** E3
Loyalton *U.S.A.* **110** F6
Loyalty Is. = Loyauté, Îs.
 N. Cal. **90** D9
Loyang = Luoyang *China* **56** G7
Loyauté, Îs. *N. Cal.* **90** D9
Loyev = Loyew *Belarus* **23** C16
Loyew *Belarus* **23** C16
Loyoro *Uganda* **86** B3
Lož *Slovenia* **41** C11
Loznica *Serbia* **44** B3
Lozova *Ukraine* **33** H9
Lozère □ *France* **20** D7
Lü Shan *China* **59** C11
Lü Tao *Taiwan* **59** F13
Luachimo *Angola* **84** F4
Luajan → *India* **69** G11
Lualaba →
 Dem. Rep. of the Congo **86** B2
Luampa *Zambia* **87** F1
Lu'an *China* **59** B11
Luan Chau *Vietnam* **58** G4
Luan He → *China* **57** E10
Luan Xian *China* **57** E10
Luancheng
 Guangxi Zhuangzu, China **58** F7
Luancheng *Hebei, China* **56** F8
Luanco *Spain* **36** B5
Luanda *Angola* **84** F2
Luang, Thale *Thailand* **65** J3
Luang Prabang *Laos* **58** H4
Luangwa *Zambia* **87** F3
Luangwa → *Zambia* **87** E3
Luangwa Valley *Zambia* **87** E3
Luanne *China* **57** D9
Luanping *China* **57** D9
Luanshya *Zambia* **87** E2
Luapula □ *Zambia* **87** E2
Luapula → *Africa* **87** D2
Luarca *Spain* **36** B4
Luashi *Dem. Rep. of the Congo* **87** E1
Luau *Angola* **84** G4
Lubaczów *Poland* **31** H10
Lubań *Poland* **31** G2
Lubana, Ozero = Lubānas
 Ezers *Latvia* **32** D4
Lubānas Ezers *Latvia* **32** D4
Lubang *Phil.* **61** E4
Lubang Is. *Phil.* **63** B6
Lubango *Angola* **85** G2
Lubao *Dem. Rep. of the Congo* **86** D2
Lubartów *Poland* **31** G9
Lubawa *Poland* **30** E6
Lübbecke *Germany* **24** C4
Lübben *Germany* **24** D9
Lübbenau *Germany* **24** D9
Lubbock *U.S.A.* **116** E4
Lübeck *Germany* **24** B6
Lübecker Bucht *Germany* **24** A6
Lubefu *Dem. Rep. of the Congo* **86** C1
Lubefu →
 Dem. Rep. of the Congo **86** C1
Lubelskie □ *Poland* **31** G9
Lubero = Luofu
 Dem. Rep. of the Congo **86** C2
Luberon △ *France* **21** E9
Lubersac *France* **20** C5
Lubicon L. *Canada* **102** B5
Lubień Kujawski *Poland* **31** F6
Lubilash →
 Dem. Rep. of the Congo **84** F4
Lubin *Poland* **31** G3
Lublin *Poland* **31** G9
Lubliniec *Poland* **31** H5
Lubnān = Lebanon ■ *Asia* **74** B5
Lubnān, Jabal *Lebanon* **74** B4
Lubniewice *Poland* **31** F2
Lubny *Ukraine* **33** G7
Lubomierz *Poland* **31** G2
Luboń *Poland* **31** F3
Lubongola
 Dem. Rep. of the Congo **86** C2
L'ubotín *Slovak Rep.* **27** B13
Lubraniec *Poland* **31** F5
Lubsko *Poland* **31** G1
Lübtheen *Germany* **24** B7
Lubuagan *Phil.* **61** C4

Lubudi *Dem. Rep. of the Congo* **84** F5
Lubudi →
  Dem. Rep. of the Congo **87** D2
Lubuklinggau *Indonesia* **62** E2
Lubuksikaping *Indonesia* **62** E2
Lubumbashi
  Dem. Rep. of the Congo **87** E2
Lubunda
  Dem. Rep. of the Congo **86** D2
Lubungu *Zambia* **87** E2
Lubuskie □ *Poland* **31** F2
Lubutu *Dem. Rep. of the Congo* **86** C2
Luc An Chau *Vietnam* **64** A5
Luc-en-Diois *France* **21** D9
Lucan *Canada* **114** C3
Lucania, Mt. *Canada* **100** C5
Lucas Channel = Main
  Channel *Canada* **114** A3
Lucban *Phil.* **61** D4
Lucca *Italy* **40** E7
Lucé *France* **18** D7
Luce Bay *U.K.* **13** G4
Lucea *Jamaica* **120** a
Lucedale *U.S.A.* **117** F10
Lucena *Phil.* **61** E4
Lucena *Spain* **37** H6
Lučenec *Slovak Rep.* **27** C12
Lucera *Italy* **43** A8
Lucerne = Luzern *Switz.* **25** H4
Lucerne *U.S.A.* **110** F4
Lucerne Valley *U.S.A.* **111** L10
Lucero *Mexico* **118** A3
Luchena → *Spain* **39** H3
Lucheng *China* **56** F7
Lucheringo → *Mozam.* **87** E4
Lüchow *Germany* **24** C7
Luchuan *China* **59** F8
Lucia *U.S.A.* **110** J5
Lucinda *Australia* **94** B4
Luckau *Germany* **24** D9
Luckenwalde *Germany* **24** C9
Luckhoff *S. Africa* **88** D3
Lucknow *Canada* **114** C3
Lucknow *India* **69** F9
Luçon *France* **20** B2
Lüda = Dalian *China* **57** E11
Luda Kamchiya →
  Bulgaria **45** C11
Ludbreg *Croatia* **41** B13
Lüdenscheid *Germany* **24** D3
Lüderitz *Namibia* **88** D2
Lüderitzbaai *Namibia* **88** D2
Ludhiana *India* **68** D6
Ludian *China* **58** D4
Luding Qiao *China* **58** C4
Lüdinghausen *Germany* **24** D3
Ludington *U.S.A.* **112** D10
Ludlow *U.K.* **15** E5
Ludlow *Calif., U.S.A.* **111** L10
Ludlow *Pa., U.S.A.* **114** E6
Ludlow *Vt., U.S.A.* **115** C12
Ludus *Romania* **29** D9
Ludvika *Sweden* **10** D9
Ludwigsburg *Germany* **25** G5
Ludwigsfelde *Germany* **24** C9
Ludwigshafen *Germany* **25** F4
Ludwigslust *Germany* **24** B7
Ludza *Latvia* **32** D4
Lueki *Dem. Rep. of the Congo* **86** C2
Luena *Dem. Rep. of the Congo* **87** D2
Luena *Zambia* **87** E3
Luena Flats *Zambia* **85** G4
Luenha = Ruenya → *Africa* **87** F3
Lüeyang *China* **56** H4
Lufeng *Guangdong, China* **59** F10
Lufeng *Yunnan, China* **58** E4
Lufira →
  Dem. Rep. of the Congo **87** D2
Lufkin *U.S.A.* **116** F7
Lufupa *Dem. Rep. of the Congo* **87** E1
Luga *Russia* **32** C5
Luga → *Russia* **32** C5
Lugano *Switz.* **25** J4
Lugano, L. di *Switz.* **40** C6
Lugansk = Luhansk
  Ukraine **33** H10
Lugard's Falls *Kenya* **86** C4
Lugela *Mozam.* **87** F4
Lugenda → *Mozam.* **87** E4
Lugh Ganana = Luuq
  Somali Rep. **75** G3
Lugnaquillia *Ireland* **12** D5
Lugo *Italy* **41** D8
Lugo *Spain* **36** B3
Lugo □ *Spain* **36** C3
Lugoj *Romania* **28** E6
Lugovoy = Qulan *Kazakhstan* **52** E8
Luhansk *Ukraine* **33** H10
Luhansk □ *Ukraine* **33** H10
Luhe *China* **59** A12
Luhe → *Germany* **24** B6
Luhuo *China* **58** B3
Lui → *Angola* **84** F3
Luiana *Angola* **88** B3
Luiana → *Angola* **85** H4
Luichow Pen. = Leizhou
  Bandao *China* **58** G7
Luimneach = Limerick
  Ireland **12** D3

Luing *U.K.* **13** E3
Luino *Italy* **40** C5
Luís Correia *Brazil* **125** D10
Luitpold Coast *Antarctica* **5** D1
Luiza *Dem. Rep. of the Congo* **84** F4
Luizi *Dem. Rep. of the Congo* **86** D2
Luján *Argentina* **126** C4
Lujiang *China* **59** B11
Lukang *Taiwan* **59** E13
Lukanga Swamp *Zambia* **87** E2
Lukavac *Bos.-H.* **28** F3
Lukenie →
  Dem. Rep. of the Congo **84** E3
Lŭki *Bulgaria* **45** E8
Lukolela
  Dem. Rep. of the Congo **86** D1
Lukosi *Zimbabwe* **87** F2
Lukovë *Albania* **44** G3
Lukovit *Bulgaria* **45** C8
Łuków *Poland* **31** G9
Lukoyanov *Russia* **34** C7
Lukusuzi △ *Zambia* **87** E3
Luleå *Sweden* **8** D20
Luleälven → *Sweden* **8** D20
Lüleburgaz *Turkey* **45** E11
Luliang *China* **58** E4
Luling *U.S.A.* **116** G6
Lulong *China* **57** E10
Lulonga →
  Dem. Rep. of the Congo **84** D3
Lulua →
  Dem. Rep. of the Congo **84** E4
Luma *Amer. Samoa* **91** b
Lumajang *Indonesia* **63** H15
Lumār *Iran* **73** F12
Lumbala N'guimbo *Angola* **85** G4
Lumberton *U.S.A.* **117** D15
Lumsden *Canada* **103** C8
Lumsden *N.Z.* **91** F2
Lumut *Malaysia* **65** K3
Lumut, Tanjung *Indonesia* **62** E3
Luna *India* **68** H3
Lunan *China* **58** E4
Lunavada *India* **68** H5
Lunca *Romania* **29** C10
Lunca Corbului *Romania* **29** F9
Lund *Sweden* **11** J7
Lundazi *Zambia* **87** E3
Lunderskov *Denmark* **11** J3
Lundi → *Zimbabwe* **87** G3
Lundu *Malaysia* **62** D3
Lundy *U.K.* **15** F3
Lune → *U.K.* **14** C5
Lüneburg *Germany* **24** B6
Lüneburg Heath =
  Lüneburger Heide
  Germany **24** B6
Lüneburger Heide *Germany* **24** B6
Lunel *France* **21** E8
Lünen *Germany* **24** D3
Lunenburg *Canada* **105** D7
Lunéville *France* **19** D13
Lunga → *Zambia* **87** E2
Lunga Lunga *Kenya* **86** C4
Lungi Airport *S. Leone* **82** D2
Lunglei *India* **67** H18
Luni *India* **68** G5
Luni → *India* **68** G4
Luninets = Luninyets
  Belarus **23** B14
Luning *U.S.A.* **108** G4
Lunino *Russia* **34** D7
Luninyets *Belarus* **23** B14
Lunkaransar *India* **68** E5
Lunsemfwa → *Zambia* **87** E3
Lunsemfwa Falls *Zambia* **87** E2
Luo He → *China* **56** G6
Luocheng *China* **58** E7
Luochuan *China* **56** G5
Luoci *China* **58** E4
Luodian *China* **58** E6
Luoding *China* **59** F8
Luofu *Dem. Rep. of the Congo* **86** C2
Luohe *China* **56** H8
Luojiang *China* **58** B5
Luonan *China* **56** G6
Luoning *China* **56** G6
Luoshan *China* **59** A10
Luotian *China* **59** B10
Luoxiao Shan *China* **59** D10
Luoyang *China* **56** G7
Luoyuan *China* **59** D12
Luozigou *China* **57** C16
Lupeni *Romania* **29** E8
Lupilichi *Mozam.* **87** E4
Łupków *Poland* **31** J9
Lupoing *China* **58** E5
Luquan *China* **58** E4
Luque *Paraguay* **126** B4
Luquillo, Sierra de
  Puerto Rico **121** d
Lúras *Italy* **42** B2
Luray *U.S.A.* **113** F14
Lure *France* **19** E13
Lurgan *U.K.* **12** B5
Lusaka *Zambia* **87** F2
Lusaka □ *Zambia* **87** F2
Lusambo
  Dem. Rep. of the Congo **86** C1

Lusangaye
  Dem. Rep. of the Congo **86** C2
Luseland *Canada* **103** C7
Lusenga Plain △ *Zambia* **87** D2
Lushan *Henan, China* **56** H7
Lushan *Sichuan, China* **58** B4
Lushi *China* **56** G6
Lushnjë *Albania* **44** F3
Lushoto *Tanzania* **86** C4
Lushui *China* **58** E2
Lüshun *China* **57** E11
Lusignan *France* **20** B4
Lusigny-sur-Barse *France* **19** D11
Lusk *U.S.A.* **108** E11
Lussac-les-Châteaux *France* **20** B4
Lustenau *Austria* **26** D2
Lūt, Dasht-e *Iran* **71** D8
Lutherstadt Wittenberg
  Germany **24** D8
Luton *U.K.* **15** F7
Luton □ *U.K.* **15** F7
Lutsel K'e *Canada* **103** A6
Lutsk *Ukraine* **23** C13
Lutto = Lotta → *Europe* **8** B24
Lützow Holmbukta *Antarctica* **5** C4
Lutzputs *S. Africa* **88** D3
Luuq *Somali Rep.* **75** G3
Luverne *Ala., U.S.A.* **117** F11
Luverne *Minn., U.S.A.* **112** D5
Luvua *Dem. Rep. of the Congo* **87** D2
Luvua →
  Dem. Rep. of the Congo **86** D2
Luvuvhu → *S. Africa* **89** C5
Luwegu → *Tanzania* **87** D4
Luwuk *Indonesia* **63** E6
Luxembourg *Lux.* **17** E6
Luxembourg □ *Belgium* **17** E5
Luxembourg ■ *Europe* **17** E5
Luxembourg ✈ (LUX) *Lux.* **17** E6
Luxeuil-les-Bains *France* **19** E13
Luxi *Hunan, China* **59** C8
Luxi *Yunnan, China* **58** E4
Luxi *Yunnan, China* **58** E2
Luxor = El Uqsur *Egypt* **80** B3
Luy-de-Béarn → *France* **20** E3
Luy-de-France → *France* **20** E3
Luz-St-Sauveur *France* **20** F4
Luzern *Switz.* **25** H4
Luzern □ *Switz.* **25** H3
Luzhai *China* **58** E7
Luzhany *Ukraine* **29** B10
Luzhi *China* **58** D5
Luzhou *China* **58** C5
Luziânia *Brazil* **125** G9
Lužnice → *Czech Rep.* **26** B7
Luzon *Phil.* **61** D4
Luzon Strait *Asia* **59** G13
Luzy *France* **19** F10
Luzzi *Italy* **43** C9
Lviv *Ukraine* **23** D13
Lviv □ *Ukraine* **33** H2
Lvov = Lviv *Ukraine* **23** D13
Lwówek *Poland* **31** F3
Lwówek Śląski *Poland* **31** G2
Lyakhavichy *Belarus* **23** B14
Lyakhovskiye, Ostrova
  Russia **53** B15
Lyaki = Läki *Azerbaijan* **35** K8
Lyal I. *Canada* **114** B3
Lyaskovets *Bulgaria* **45** C9
Lyasnaya *Belarus* **31** F10
Lybster *U.K.* **13** C5
Lycaonia *Turkey* **72** D5
Lychen *Germany* **24** B9
Lychkova *Russia* **32** D7
Lycia *Turkey* **47** E11
Lycksele *Sweden* **8** D18
Lycosura *Greece* **46** D4
Lydda = Lod *Israel* **74** D3
Lyddan I. *Antarctica* **5** D2
Lydenburg *S. Africa* **89** D5
Lydia *Turkey* **47** C10
Lydynia → *Poland* **31** F7
Lyell *N.Z.* **91** D4
Lyell I. *Canada* **102** C2
Lyepyel *Belarus* **32** E5
Lygnern *Sweden* **11** G6
Lykens *U.S.A.* **115** F8
Lyman *Ukraine* **29** E14
Lyman *U.S.A.* **108** F8
Lymanske *Ukraine* **29** D14
Lyme Regis *U.K.* **15** G5
Lymington *U.K.* **15** G6
Lyna → *Poland* **30** D8
Lynchburg *U.S.A.* **113** G14
Lynd → *Australia* **94** B3
Lynd Ra. *Australia* **94** C5
Lynden *Canada* **114** C4
Lynden *U.S.A.* **110** B4
Lyndhurst *Australia* **95** E2
Lyndon → *Australia* **93** D1
Lyndonville *N.Y., U.S.A.* **114** C6
Lyndonville *Vt., U.S.A.* **115** B12
Lyngen *Norway* **8** B19
Lynher Reef *Australia* **92** C3

Lynn *U.S.A.* **115** D14
Lynn Haven *U.S.A.* **117** F12
Lynn Lake *Canada* **103** B8
Lynnwood *U.S.A.* **110** C4
Lynton *U.K.* **15** F4
Lyntupy *Belarus* **32** E4
Lynx L. *Canada* **103** A7
Lyon *France* **21** C8
Lyon St-Exupery ✈ (LYS)
  France **21** C9
Lyonnais *France* **21** C8
Lyons = Lyon *France* **21** C8
Lyons *Ga., U.S.A.* **117** F13
Lyons *Kans., U.S.A.* **112** F5
Lyons *N.Y., U.S.A.* **114** C8
Lyons → *Australia* **93** E2
Lyons Falls *U.S.A.* **115** C9
Lyozna *Belarus* **32** E6
Lys = Leie → *Belgium* **17** C3
Lysá nad Labem *Czech Rep.* **26** A7
Lysekil *Sweden* **11** F5
Lysi *Cyprus* **49** D12
Lyskovo *Russia* **34** B7
Lysva *Russia* **52** C6
Lysvik *Sweden* **10** D7
Lysychansk *Ukraine* **33** H10
Lytham St. Anne's *U.K.* **14** D4
Lyttelton *N.Z.* **91** E4
Lytton *Canada* **102** C4
Lyuban *Russia* **32** C6
Lyubertsy *Russia* **32** E9
Lyubim *Russia* **32** C11
Lyubimets *Bulgaria* **45** E10
Lyuboml *Ukraine* **31** G11
Lyubotyn *Ukraine* **33** H8
Lyubytino *Russia* **32** C7
Lyudinovo *Russia* **32** F8

M

M.R. Stefanik,
  Bratislava ✈ (BTS)
  Slovak Rep. **27** C10
Ma → *Vietnam* **58** H5
Ma'adaba *Jordan* **74** E4
Maamba *Zambia* **87** F2
Ma'ān *Jordan* **74** E4
Ma'ān □ *Jordan* **74** F5
Maanselkä *Finland* **9** F18
Ma'anshan *China* **59** B12
Maarianhamina =
  Mariehamn *Finland* **9** F18
Ma'arrat an Nu'mān *Syria* **72** E7
Maas → *Neths.* **17** C4
Maaseik *Belgium* **17** C5
Maasin *Phil.* **63** B6
Maastricht *Neths.* **17** D5
Maave *Mozam.* **89** C5
Mababe Depression
  Botswana **88** B3
Mabalane *Mozam.* **89** C5
Mabel L. *Canada* **102** C5
Mabenge
  Dem. Rep. of the Congo **86** B1
Maberly *Canada* **115** B8
Mabian *China* **58** C4
Mabil *Ethiopia* **81** F4
Mablethorpe *U.K.* **14** D8
Mably *France* **19** F11
Maboma
  Dem. Rep. of the Congo **86** B2
Mabonto *S. Leone* **82** D2
Mabrouk *Mali* **83** B4
Mabuasehube △ *Botswana* **88** D3
Mac Bac *Vietnam* **65** H6
Macachín *Argentina* **126** D3
Macaé *Brazil* **127** A7
Macael *Spain* **39** H2
Macamic *Canada* **104** C4
Macao = Macau *China* **59** F9
Macão *Portugal* **37** F3
Macapá *Brazil* **125** C8
Macarao △ *Venezuela* **121** D6
McArthur → *Australia* **94** B2
McArthur, Port *Australia* **94** B2
Macau *Brazil* **125** E11
Macau *China* **59** F9
McBride *Canada* **102** C4
McCall *U.S.A.* **108** D5
McCamey *U.S.A.* **116** F3
McCammon *U.S.A.* **108** E7
McCarran Int., Las
  Vegas ✈ (LAS) *U.S.A.* **111** J11
McCauley I. *Canada* **102** C2
McCleary *U.S.A.* **110** C3
Macclenny *U.S.A.* **117** F13
Macclesfield *U.K.* **14** D5
M'Clintock Chan. *Canada* **100** B9
McClintock Ra. *Australia* **92** C4
McCloud *U.S.A.* **108** F2
McCluer I. *Australia* **94** B5
McClure *U.S.A.* **114** F7
McClure, L. *U.S.A.* **110** H6
M'Clure Str. *Canada* **101** B8
McClusky *U.S.A.* **112** B3
McComb *U.S.A.* **117** F9

McCook *U.S.A.* **112** E3
McCreary *Canada* **103** C9
McCullough Mt. *U.S.A.* **111** K11
McCusker → *Canada* **103** B7
McDermitt *U.S.A.* **108** F5
McDonald *U.S.A.* **114** F4
Macdonald, L. *Australia* **92** D4
McDonald Is. *Ind. Oc.* **3** G13
MacDonnell Ranges
  Australia **92** D5
MacDowell L. *Canada* **104** B1
Macduff *U.K.* **13** D6
Maceda *Spain* **36** C3
Macedonia *U.S.A.* **114** E3
Macedonia ■ *Europe* **44** E5
Maceió *Brazil* **125** E11
Maceira *Portugal* **36** F2
Macenta *Guinea* **82** D3
Macerata *Italy* **41** E10
McFarland *U.S.A.* **111** K7
McFarlane → *Canada* **103** B7
Macfarlane, L. *Australia* **95** E2
McGehee *U.S.A.* **116** E9
McGill *U.S.A.* **108** G6
Macgillycuddy's Reeks
  Ireland **12** E2
McGraw *U.S.A.* **115** D8
McGregor *U.S.A.* **112** D8
McGregor Ra. *Australia* **95** D3
McGuire, Mt. *Australia* **94** J6
Mach *Pakistan* **68** E2
Māch Kowr *Iran* **71** E9
Machado = Jiparaná →
  Brazil **124** E6
Machagai *Argentina* **126** B3
Machakos *Kenya* **86** C4
Machala *Ecuador* **124** D3
Machanga *Mozam.* **89** C6
Machattie, L. *Australia* **94** C2
Machault *France* **19** C11
Machava *Mozam.* **89** D5
Machece *Mozam.* **87** F4
Machecoul *France* **18** F5
Macheke *Zimbabwe* **89** B5
Macheng *China* **59** B10
Machero *Spain* **37** F6
Machhu → *India* **68** H4
Machiara △ *Pakistan* **68** B5
Machias *Maine, U.S.A.* **113** C20
Machias *N.Y., U.S.A.* **114** D6
Machichi → *Canada* **103** B10
Machico *Madeira* **48** D3
Machilipatnam *India* **67** L12
Machiques *Venezuela* **124** A4
Machu Picchu *Peru* **124** F4
Machynlleth *U.K.* **15** E4
Macia *Mozam.* **89** D5
Maciejowice *Poland* **31** G8
Măcin *Romania* **29** E13
Macina *Mali* **82** C4
McInnes L. *Canada* **103** C10
McIntosh *U.S.A.* **112** C3
McIntosh L. *Canada* **103** B8
Macintosh Ra. *Australia* **93** E4
Macintyre → *Australia* **95** D5
Macizo Galaico *Spain* **36** C3
Maçka *Turkey* **73** B8
Mackay *Australia* **94** K7
Mackay *U.S.A.* **108** E7
MacKay → *Canada* **102** B6
Mackay, L. *Australia* **92** D4
McKay Ra. *Australia* **92** D3
McKeesport *U.S.A.* **114** F5
McKellar *Canada* **114** A5
McKenna *U.S.A.* **110** D4
Mackenzie *Canada* **102** B4
McKenzie *U.S.A.* **117** C10
Mackenzie → *Australia* **94** C4
Mackenzie → *Canada* **100** C6
McKenzie → *U.S.A.* **108** D2
Mackenzie Bay *Canada* **98** C6
Mackenzie City = Linden
  Guyana **124** B7
Mackenzie King I. *Canada* **101** B8
Mackenzie Mts. *Canada* **100** C7
Mackinaw City *U.S.A.* **113** C11
McKinlay *Australia* **94** C3
McKinlay → *Australia* **94** C3
McKinley, Mt. *U.S.A.* **106** a
McKinley Sea *Arctic* **4** A7
McKinney *U.S.A.* **116** E6
Mackinnon Road *Kenya* **86** C4
McKittrick *U.S.A.* **111** K7
Macklin *Canada* **103** C7
Macksville *Australia* **95** E5
McLaughlin *U.S.A.* **112** C3
Maclean *Australia* **95** D5
McLean *U.S.A.* **116** D4
McLeansboro *U.S.A.* **112** F9
Maclear *S. Africa* **89** E4
Maclear, C. *Malawi* **87** E3
Macleay → *Australia* **95** E5
McLennan *Canada* **102** B5
McLeod → *Canada* **102** C5
McLeod, L. *Australia* **93** D1
MacLeod B. *Canada* **103** A7
McLeod L. *Canada* **102** C4
MacLeod Lake *Canada* **102** C4
McLoughlin, Mt. *U.S.A.* **108** E2

McMechen *U.S.A.* **114** G4
McMinnville *Oreg., U.S.A.* **108** D2
McMinnville *Tenn., U.S.A.* **117** D12
McMurdo *Antarctica* **5** D11
McMurdo Sd. *Antarctica* **5** D11
McMurray = Fort
  McMurray *Canada* **102** B6
McMurray *U.S.A.* **110** B4
Macodoene *Mozam.* **89** C6
Macomb *U.S.A.* **112** E9
Macomer *Italy* **42** B1
Mâcon *France* **19** F11
Macon *Ga., U.S.A.* **117** E13
Macon *Miss., U.S.A.* **117** E10
Macon *Mo., U.S.A.* **112** F8
Macossa *Mozam.* **87** F3
Macoun L. *Canada* **103** B8
Macovane *Mozam.* **89** C6
McPherson *U.S.A.* **112** F6
McPherson Pk. *U.S.A.* **111** L7
McPherson Ra. *Australia* **95** D5
Macquarie → *Australia* **95** E4
Macquarie Harbour
  Australia **95** G4
Macquarie Is. *Pac. Oc.* **96** N7
Macquarie Ridge *S. Ocean* **5** B10
MacRobertson Land
  Antarctica **5** D6
Macroom *Ireland* **12** E3
MacTier *Canada* **114** A5
Macubela *Mozam.* **87** F4
Macugnaga *Italy* **40** C4
Macuira △ *Colombia* **121** D5
Macuiza *Mozam.* **87** F3
Macumba → *Australia* **95** D2
Macuro *Venezuela* **125** K15
Macusani *Peru* **124** F4
Macuse *Mozam.* **87** F4
Macuspana *Mexico* **119** D6
Macusse *Angola* **88** B3
Mada → *Nigeria* **83** D6
Ma'dabā □ *Jordan* **74** D4
Madadeni *S. Africa* **89** D5
Madagali *Nigeria* **83** C7
Madagascar ■ *Africa* **89** C8
Madā'in Sālih *Si. Arabia* **70** E3
Madama *Niger* **79** D8
Madame, I. *Canada* **105** C7
Madan *Bulgaria* **45** E8
Madang *Papua N. G.* **90** B7
Madaoua *Niger* **83** C6
Madara *Nigeria* **83** C7
Madaripur *Bangla.* **67** H17
Madauk *Burma* **67** L20
Madawaska *Canada* **114** A7
Madawaska → *Canada* **114** A7
Madaya *Burma* **67** H20
Madbar *Sudan* **81** F3
Maddalena *Italy* **42** A2
Maddaloni *Italy* **43** A7
Madeira *Atl. Oc.* **48** D3
Madeira → *Brazil* **124** D7
Madeleine, Îs. de la *Canada* **105** C7
Maden *Turkey* **73** C8
Madera *Mexico* **118** B3
Madera *Calif., U.S.A.* **110** J6
Madera *Pa., U.S.A.* **114** F6
Madha *India* **66** L9
Madhavpur *India* **68** J3
Madhepura *India* **69** F12
Madhubani *India* **69** F12
Madhupur *India* **69** G12
Madhya Pradesh □ *India* **68** J8
Madidi → *Bolivia* **124** F5
Madikeri *India* **66** N9
Madikwe △ *S. Africa* **89** D5
Madill *U.S.A.* **116** D6
Madimba
  Dem. Rep. of the Congo **84** E3
Ma'din *Syria* **73** E8
Madina *Mali* **82** C3
Madinani *Ivory C.* **82** D3
Madinat al Malik Khālid al
  Askarīyah *Si. Arabia* **70** E5
Madīnat ath Thawrah *Syria* **73** E8
Madingou *Congo* **84** E2
Madirovalo *Madag.* **89** B8
Madison *Calif., U.S.A.* **110** G5
Madison *Fla., U.S.A.* **117** F13
Madison *Ind., U.S.A.* **113** F11
Madison *Nebr., U.S.A.* **112** E5
Madison *Ohio, U.S.A.* **114** E3
Madison *S. Dak., U.S.A.* **112** C5
Madison *Wis., U.S.A.* **112** D9
Madison → *U.S.A.* **108** D8
Madison Heights *U.S.A.* **113** G14
Madisonville *Ky., U.S.A.* **112** G10
Madisonville *Tex., U.S.A.* **116** F7
Madista *Botswana* **88** C4
Madiun *Indonesia* **63** G14
Mado Gashi *Kenya* **86** B4
Madoc *Canada* **114** B7
Madol *Sudan* **81** F2
Madon → *France* **19** D13
Madona *Latvia* **32** D4
Madonie *Italy* **42** E6
Madonna di Campíglio *Italy* **40** B7
Madra Daği *Turkey* **47** B9
Madrakah, Ra's al *Oman* **75** D6

Madras = Chennai *India* 66 N12
Madras = Tamil Nadu □
 India 66 P10
Madras *U.S.A.* 116 J6
Madre, L. *U.S.A.* 116 J6
Madre, Sierra *Phil.* 61 C5
Madre de Dios → *Bolivia* 124 F5
Madre de Dios, I. *Chile* 128 G1
Madre del Sur, Sierra
 Mexico 119 D5
Madre Occidental, Sierra
 Mexico 118 B3
Madre Oriental, Sierra
 Mexico 118 C5
Madri *India* 68 G5
Madrid *Spain* 36 E7
Madrid *U.S.A.* 115 B9
Madrid □ *Spain* 36 E7
Madrid Barajas ✈ (MAD)
 Spain 36 E7
Madridejos *Spain* 37 F7
Madrigal de las Altas
 Torres *Spain* 36 D6
Madrona, Sierra *Spain* 37 G6
Madroñera *Spain* 37 F5
Madu *Sudan* 81 E2
Madura *Australia* 93 F4
Madura *Indonesia* 63 G15
Madura, Selat *Indonesia* 63 G15
Madurai *India* 66 Q11
Madurantakam *India* 66 N11
Madzhalis *Russia* 35 J8
Mae Chan *Thailand* 64 B2
Mae Hong Son *Thailand* 64 C2
Mae Khlong → *Thailand* 64 F3
Mae Phrik *Thailand* 64 D2
Mae Ping △ *Thailand* 64 D2
Mae Ramat *Thailand* 64 D2
Mae Rim *Thailand* 64 C2
Mae Sai *Thailand* 58 G2
Mae Sot *Thailand* 64 D2
Mae Suai *Thailand* 58 H2
Mae Tha *Thailand* 64 C2
Mae Wong △ *Thailand* 64 E2
Mae Yom △ *Thailand* 64 C3
Maebashi *Japan* 55 F9
Maella *Spain* 38 D5
Maestra, Sierra *Cuba* 120 B4
Maevatanana *Madag.* 89 B8
Mafeking = Mafikeng
 S. Africa 88 D4
Mafeking *Canada* 103 C8
Maféré *Ivory C.* 82 D4
Mafeteng *Lesotho* 88 D4
Maffra *Australia* 95 F4
Mafia I. *Tanzania* 86 D4
Mafikeng *S. Africa* 88 D4
Mafra *Brazil* 127 B6
Mafra *Portugal* 37 G1
Mafungabusi Plateau
 Zimbabwe 87 F2
Magadan *Russia* 53 D16
Magadi *Kenya* 86 C4
Magadi, L. *Kenya* 86 C4
Magaliesburg *S. Africa* 89 D4
Magallanes, Estrecho de
 Chile 128 G2
Magaluf *Spain* 39 F7
Magangué *Colombia* 124 B4
Magaria *Niger* 83 C6
Magburaka *S. Leone* 82 D2
Magdagachi *Russia* 53 D13
Magdalen Is. = Madeleine,
 Îs. de la *Canada* 105 C7
Magdalena *Argentina* 126 D4
Magdalena *Bolivia* 124 F6
Magdalena *U.S.A.* 109 J10
Magdalena → *Colombia* 124 A4
Magdalena → *Mexico* 118 A2
Magdalena, B. *Mexico* 118 C2
Magdalena, I. *Mexico* 118 C2
Magdalena, Llano de
 Mexico 118 C2
Magdalena de Kino *Mexico* 118 A2
Magdeburg *Germany* 24 C7
Magdelaine Cays *Australia* 94 B5
Magdub *Sudan* 81 E2
Magee *U.S.A.* 117 F10
Magelang *Indonesia* 63 G14
Magellan's Str. =
 Magallanes, Estrecho de
 Chile 128 G2
Magenta *Italy* 40 C5
Magenta, L. *Australia* 93 F2
Mageroya *Norway* 8 A21
Maggia → *Switz.* 25 J4
Maggiorasca, Mte. *Italy* 40 D6
Maggiore, Lago *Italy* 40 B5
Maggotty *Jamaica* 120 a
Maghâgha *Egypt* 80 B3
Maghama *Mauritania* 82 B2
Maghera *U.K.* 12 B5
Magherafelt *U.K.* 12 B5
Maghreb *N. Afr.* 78 B5
Magione *Italy* 41 E9
Magistralnyy *Russia* 53 D11
Maglaj *Bos.-H.* 28 F3
Magliano in Toscana *Italy* 41 F8
Máglie *Italy* 43 B11

Magnac-Laval *France* 20 B5
Magnetic Pole (North)
 Canada 101 B9
Magnetic Pole (South)
 Antarctica 5 C9
Magnisía □ *Greece* 46 B5
Magnitogorsk *Russia* 52 D6
Magnolia *Ark., U.S.A.* 116 E8
Magnolia *Miss., U.S.A.* 117 F9
Magny-en-Vexin *France* 19 C8
Mago *Fiji* 91 a
Mago △ *Ethiopia* 81 F4
Magog *Canada* 115 A12
Magoro *Uganda* 86 B3
Magoša = Famagusta
 Cyprus 49 D12
Magoulades *Greece* 49 A3
Magoye *Zambia* 87 F2
Magpie, L. *Canada* 105 B7
Magrath *Canada* 102 D6
Magre → *Spain* 39 F4
Magrur *Sudan* 81 E3
Magrur, Wadi → *Sudan* 81 D2
Magta Lahjar *Mauritania* 82 B2
Maguan *China* 58 F5
Maguarinho, C. *Brazil* 125 D9
Magude *Mozam.* 89 D5
Magurski □ *Poland* 31 J8
Magvana *India* 68 H3
Magwe *Burma* 67 J19
Magwe Sudan* 81 G3
Magyarorszag =
 Hungary ■ *Europe* 27 D12
Maha Sarakham *Thailand* 64 D4
Mahābād *Iran* 73 D11
Mahabharat Lekh *Nepal* 69 E10
Mahabo *Madag.* 89 C7
Mahadeo Hills *India* 69 H8
Mahaffey *U.S.A.* 114 F6
Mahagi *Dem. Rep. of the Congo* 86 B3
Mahajamba → *Madag.* 89 B8
Mahajamba, Helodranon' i
 Madag. 89 B8
Mahajan *India* 68 E5
Mahajanga *Madag.* 89 B8
Mahajanga □ *Madag.* 89 B8
Mahajilo → *Madag.* 89 B8
Mahakam → *Indonesia* 62 E5
Mahalapye *Botswana* 88 C4
Mahale Mts. *Tanzania* 86 D3
Mahale Mts. △ *Tanzania* 86 D2
Mahallāt *Iran* 71 C6
Māhān *Iran* 71 D8
Mahan → *India* 69 H10
Mahanadi → *India* 67 J15
Mahananda → *India* 69 G12
Mahanoro *Madag.* 89 B8
Mahanoy City *U.S.A.* 115 F8
Maharashtra □ *India* 66 J9
Mahasham, W. → *Egypt* 74 E3
Mahasoa *Madag.* 89 C8
Mahasolo *Madag.* 89 B8
Mahattat ash Shīdīyah
 Jordan 74 F4
Mahattat 'Unayzah *Jordan* 74 E4
Mahavavy → *Madag.* 89 B8
Mahaxay *Laos* 64 D5
Mahbubnagar *India* 66 L10
Maḥdah *Oman* 71 E7
Mahdia *Tunisia* 79 A8
Mahe *India* 69 C9
Mahé *Seychelles* 85 b
Mahé ✈ (SEZ) *Seychelles* 85 b
Mahébourg *Mauritius* 85 d
Mahendragarh *India* 68 E7
Mahendranagar *Nepal* 69 E9
Mahenge *Tanzania* 87 D4
Maheno *N.Z.* 91 F3
Mahesana *India* 68 H5
Maheshwar *India* 68 H6
Mahgawan *India* 69 F8
Mahi → *India* 68 H5
Mahia Pen. *N.Z.* 91 C6
Mahilyow *Belarus* 23 B16
Mahilyow □ *Belarus* 23 B16
Mahina *Tahiti* 91 d
Mahinerangi, L. *N.Z.* 91 F2
Mahmiya *Sudan* 81 D3
Mahmud Kot *Pakistan* 68 D4
Mahmudia *Romania* 29 E14
Mahmudkhan *Turkey* 44 E9
Mahmutbey *Turkey* 45 E12
Māhneshān *Iran* 73 D12
Mahnomen *U.S.A.* 112 B6
Mahoba *India* 69 G8
Mahón = Maó *Spain* 48 B11
Mahon, Menorca ✈
 (MAH) *Spain* 38 F9
Mahone Bay *Canada* 105 D7
Mahopac *U.S.A.* 115 E11
Mahuta *Nigeria* 83 C5
Mahuva *India* 68 J4
Mahya Daği *Turkey* 45 E11
Mai-Ndombe, L.
 Dem. Rep. of the Congo 84 E3

Mai Thon, Ko *Thailand* 65 a
Maia *Portugal* 36 D2
Maials *Spain* 38 D5
Maîche *France* 19 E13
Maicuru → *Brazil* 125 D8
Maidan Khula *Afghan.* 68 C3
Maidenhead *U.K.* 15 F7
Maidstone *Canada* 103 C7
Maidstone *U.K.* 15 F8
Maiduguri *Nigeria* 83 C7
Maiella △ *Italy* 41 F11
Māieruș *Romania* 29 E10
Maigatari *Nigeria* 83 C6
Maigo *Phil.* 61 G5
Maigudo *Ethiopia* 81 F4
Maihar *India* 69 G9
Maijdi *Bangla.* 67 H17
Maikala Ra. *India* 67 J12
Maiko △
 Dem. Rep. of the Congo 86 C2
Mailani *India* 69 E9
Maillezais *France* 20 B3
Mailsi *Pakistan* 68 E5
Main → *Germany* 25 E4
Main → *U.K.* 12 B5
Main Channel *Canada* 114 A3
Main Range △ *Australia* 95 D5
Main Ridge *Trin. & Tob.* 125 J16
Mainburg *Germany* 25 G7
Maine *France* 18 D6
Maine □ *U.S.A.* 113 C19
Maine → *France* 18 E6
Maine, G. of *U.S.A.* 113 D19
Maine-et-Loire □ *France* 18 E6
Maïne-Soroa *Niger* 83 C7
Maingkwan *Burma* 67 F20
Mainit, L. *Phil.* 61 G6
Mainland *Orkney, U.K.* 13 C5
Mainland *Shet., U.K.* 13 A7
Mainoru *Australia* 94 A1
Mainpuri *India* 69 F8
Maintal *Germany* 25 E4
Maintenon *France* 19 D8
Maintirano *Madag.* 89 B7
Mainz *Germany* 25 E4
Maio *C. Verde Is.* 78 b
Maipú *Argentina* 126 D4
Maiquetía *Venezuela* 124 A5
Máira → *Italy* 40 D7
Mairabari *India* 67 F18
Maisí *Cuba* 121 B5
Maisí, Pta. de *Cuba* 121 B5
Maitland *N.S.W., Australia* 95 E5
Maitland *S. Austral., Australia* 95 E2
Maitland → *Canada* 114 C3
Maitri *Antarctica* 5 D3
Maiyema *Nigeria* 83 C5
Maiyuan *China* 59 E11
Maíz, Is. del *Nic.* 120 D3
Maizuru *Japan* 55 G7
Majalengka *Indonesia* 63 G13
Majene *Indonesia* 63 E5
Majete △ *Malawi* 87 F3
Majevica *Bos.-H.* 28 F3
Maji *Ethiopia* 81 F4
Majiang *China* 58 D6
Majorca = Mallorca *Spain* 48 B10
Majuro *Marshall Is.* 96 G9
Maka *Senegal* 82 C2
Makaha *Zimbabwe* 89 B5
Makak *Cameroon* 83 E7
Makalamabedi *Botswana* 88 C3
Makale *Indonesia* 63 E5
Makalu-Barun △ *Nepal* 69 F12
Makamba *Burundi* 86 C2
Makari *Cameroon* 83 C7
Makarikari =
 Makgadikgadi Salt Pans
 Botswana 88 C4
Makarov Basin *Arctic* 4 A
Makarovo *Russia* 53 D11
Makarska *Croatia* 41 E14
Makaryev *Russia* 34 B6
Makasar = Ujung
 Pandang *Indonesia* 63 F5
Makasar, Selat *Indonesia* 63 E5
Makasar, Str. of =
 Makasar, Selat *Indonesia* 63 E5
Makat = Maqat *Kazakhstan* 52 E6
Makedonija =
 Macedonia ■ *Europe* 44 E5
Makeni *S. Leone* 82 D2
Makeyevka = Makiyivka
 Ukraine 33 H9
Makgadikgadi △ *Botswana* 88 C3
Makgadikgadi Salt Pans
 Botswana 88 C4
Makhachkala *Russia* 35 J8
Makhado = Louis
 Trichardt *S. Africa* 89 C4
Makham, Ao *Thailand* 65 a
Makharadze = Ozurgeti
 Georgia 35 K5
Makhfar al Buşayyah *Iraq* 70 D5
Makhmūr *Iraq* 73 E10
Makian *Indonesia* 63 D7
Makindu *Kenya* 86 C4

Makīnsk *Kazakhstan* 52 D8
Makira = San Cristóbal
 Solomon Is. 90 C9
Makiv *Ukraine* 29 B11
Makiyivka *Ukraine* 33 H9
Makkah *Si. Arabia* 80 C4
Makkovik *Canada* 105 A8
Makó *Hungary* 28 D5
Mako *Senegal* 82 C2
Makokou *Gabon* 84 D2
Makongo
 Dem. Rep. of the Congo 86 B2
Makoro *Dem. Rep. of the Congo* 86 B2
Maków Mazowiecki *Poland* 31 F8
Maków Podhalański *Poland* 31 J6
Makra *Greece* 47 E7
Makrai *India* 68 H7
Makran Coast Range
 Pakistan 66 G4
Makrana *India* 68 F6
Makrany *Belarus* 31 G11
Makri *Greece* 45 F9
Makrigialos *Greece* 49 D7
Mākū *Iran* 73 C11
Makunda *Botswana* 88 C3
Makung *Taiwan* 59 F12
Makurazaki *Japan* 55 J5
Makurdi *Nigeria* 83 D6
Makūyeh *Iran* 71 D7
Makwassie *S. Africa* 88 D4
Makwiro *Zimbabwe* 89 B5
Mâl *Mauritania* 82 B2
Mal B. *Ireland* 12 D2
Mala, Pta. *Panama* 120 E3
Mala Belozërka *Ukraine* 33 J8
Malá Fatra △ *Slovak Rep.* 27 B12
Mala Kapela *Croatia* 41 D12
Mala Panew → *Poland* 31 H4
Mala Vyska *Ukraine* 33 H6
Malabang *Phil.* 61 H6
Malabar Coast *India* 66 P9
Malabon *Phil.* 61 D4
Malabu *Nigeria* 83 D7
Malacca, Straits of *Indonesia* 65 L3
Malacky *Slovak Rep.* 27 C10
Malad City *U.S.A.* 108 E7
Maladeta *Spain* 38 C5
Maladzyechna *Belarus* 23 A14
Málaga *Spain* 37 J6
Málaga □ *Spain* 37 J6
Malagarasi *Tanzania* 86 D3
Malagarasi → *Tanzania* 86 D2
Malagasy Rep. =
 Madagascar ■ *Africa* 89 C8
Malagón *Spain* 37 F7
Malagón → *Spain* 37 H3
Malahide *Ireland* 12 C5
Malaimbandy *Madag.* 89 C8
Malaita *Solomon Is.* 90 B9
Malakâl *Sudan* 81 F3
Malakand *Pakistan* 68 B4
Malakula *Vanuatu* 90 C9
Malakwal *Pakistan* 68 C5
Malamala *Indonesia* 63 E6
Malanda *Australia* 94 B4
Malang *Indonesia* 63 G15
Malanga *Mozam.* 87 E4
Malangen *Norway* 8 B18
Malanje *Angola* 84 F3
Mälaren *Sweden* 10 E11
Malargüe *Argentina* 126 D2
Malartic *Canada* 104 C4
Malaryta *Belarus* 31 G11
Malatya *Turkey* 73 C8
Malatya □ *Turkey* 72 C7
Malawi ■ *Africa* 87 E3
Malawi, L. *Africa* 87 E3
Malay Pen. *Asia* 65 J3
Malaya Belozërka = Mala
 Belozërka *Ukraine* 33 J8
Malaya Vishera *Russia* 32 C7
Malaya Viska = Mala
 Vyska *Ukraine* 33 H6
Malaybalay *Phil.* 61 G6
Malāyer *Iran* 73 E13
Malaysia ■ *Asia* 65 K4
Malazgirt *Turkey* 73 C10
Malbaza *Niger* 83 C6
Malbon *Australia* 94 C3
Malbork *Poland* 30 D6
Malcésine *Italy* 40 C7
Malchin *Germany* 24 B8
Malchow *Germany* 24 B8
Malcolm *Australia* 93 E3
Malcolm, Pt. *Australia* 93 F3
Malczyce *Poland* 31 G3
Maldah *India* 69 G13
Maldegem *Belgium* 17 C3
Malden *Mass., U.S.A.* 115 D13
Malden *Mo., U.S.A.* 112 G9
Malden I. *Kiribati* 97 H12
Maldives ■ *Ind. Oc.* 50 H9
Maldon *U.K.* 15 F8
Maldonado *Uruguay* 127 C5
Maldonado, Pta. *Mexico* 119 D5
Malè *Italy* 40 B7
Malé *Maldives* 50 H9
Malé Karpaty *Slovak Rep.* 27 C10

Maleas, Akra *Greece* 46 E5
Malebo, Pool *Africa* 84 E3
Malegaon *India* 66 J9
Malei *Mozam.* 87 F4
Malek *Sudan* 81 F3
Malek Kandī *Iran* 73 D12
Malela *Dem. Rep. of the Congo* 86 C2
Malema *Mozam.* 87 E4
Maleme *Greece* 49 D5
Malendok *Greece* 49 D7
Males *Greece* 49 D7
Malesherbes *France* 19 D9
Malesina *Greece* 46 C5
Malestroit *France* 18 E4
Malfa *Italy* 43 D7
Malgobek *Russia* 35 J7
Malgomaj *Sweden* 8 D17
Malgrat de Mar *Spain* 38 D7
Malha *Sudan* 81 D2
Malhargarh *India* 68 G6
Malheur → *U.S.A.* 108 D5
Malheur L. *U.S.A.* 108 E4
Mali *Guinea* 82 C2
Mali ■ *Africa* 82 B4
Mali → *Burma* 67 G20
Mali Kanal *Serbia* 28 E4
Mali Kyun *Burma* 64 F2
Malia *Greece* 49 D7
Malia, Kolpos *Greece* 49 D7
Malibu *U.S.A.* 111 L8
Maliku *Indonesia* 63 E6
Malili *Indonesia* 63 E6
Mālilla *Sweden* 11 G9
Malimba, Mts.
 Dem. Rep. of the Congo 86 D2
Malin Hd. *Ireland* 12 A4
Malin Pen. *Ireland* 12 A4
Malindi *Kenya* 86 C5
Malino *Indonesia* 63 D6
Malinyi *Tanzania* 87 D4
Malipo *China* 58 F5
Maliq *Albania* 44 F4
Malita *Phil.* 63 C7
Maliwun *Burma* 65 G2
Maliya *India* 68 H4
Maljenik *Serbia* 44 C5
Malka Mari △ *Kenya* 86 B5
Malkara *Turkey* 45 F10
Malkinia Górna *Poland* 31 F9
Malko Tŭrnovo *Bulgaria* 45 E11
Mallacoota Inlet *Australia* 95 F4
Mallaig *U.K.* 13 D3
Mallaoua *Niger* 83 C6
Mallawan *India* 69 F9
Mallawi *Egypt* 80 B3
Mallemort *France* 21 E9
Málles Venosta *Italy* 40 B7
Mallicolo = Malakula
 Vanuatu 90 C9
Mallorca *Spain* 48 B10
Mallorytown *Canada* 115 B9
Mallow *Ireland* 12 D3
Malmbäck *Sweden* 11 G8
Malmberget *Sweden* 8 C19
Malmédy *Belgium* 17 D6
Malmesbury *S. Africa* 88 E2
Malmivaara =
 Malmberget *Sweden* 8 C19
Malmköping *Sweden* 10 E10
Malmö *Sweden* 11 J7
Malmslätt *Sweden* 11 F9
Malmyzh *Russia* 34 B10
Malnaş *Romania* 29 D10
Malo Konare *Bulgaria* 45 D8
Maloarkhangelsk *Russia* 33 F9
Malolo *Fiji* 91 a
Malolos *Phil.* 61 D4
Malolotja △ *Swaziland* 89 D5
Malombe L. *Malawi* 87 E4
Malomice *Poland* 31 G2
Malomir *Bulgaria* 45 D10
Malone *U.S.A.* 115 B10
Malong *China* 58 E4
Małopolskie □ *Poland* 31 J7
Malorad *Bulgaria* 44 C7
Måløy *Norway* 8 F11
Maloyaroslovets *Russia* 32 E9
Malpartida de Cáceres *Spain* 37 F4
Malpaso *Canary Is.* 48 G1
Malpaso, Presa =
 Netzahualcóyotl, Presa
 Mexico 119 D6
Malpelo, I. de *Colombia* 124 C2
Malpica de Bergantiños
 Spain 36 B2
Malpur *India* 68 H5
Malpura *India* 68 F6
Mals = Málles Venosta *Italy* 40 B7
Malta *Idaho, U.S.A.* 108 E7
Malta *Mont., U.S.A.* 108 B10
Malta ■ *Europe* 49 D2
Maltahöhe *Namibia* 88 C2
Maltepe *Turkey* 45 F13
Malton *Canada* 114 C5
Malton *U.K.* 14 C7
Maluku *Indonesia* 63 E7

Maluku □ *Indonesia* 63 E7
Maluku Sea = Molucca
 Sea *Indonesia* 63 E6
Malumfashi *Nigeria* 83 C6
Malung *Sweden* 10 D7
Malungsfors *Sweden* 10 D7
Maluwe *Ghana* 82 D4
Malvan *India* 66 L8
Malvern *U.S.A.* 116 D8
Malvern Hills *U.K.* 15 E5
Malvinas, Is. = Falkland
 Is. ☑ *Atl. Oc.* 128 G5
Malý Dunaj → *Slovak Rep.* 27 D11
Malya *Tanzania* 86 C3
Malyn *Ukraine* 23 C15
Malyy Lyakhovskiy,
 Ostrov *Russia* 53 B15
Malyy Taymyr, Ostrov
 Russia 53 B11
Mama *Russia* 53 D12
Mamadysh *Russia* 34 C10
Mamanguape *Brazil* 125 E11
Mamanuca Group *Fiji* 91 a
Mamarr Mitlā *Egypt* 74 E1
Mamasa *Indonesia* 63 E5
Mambasa
 Dem. Rep. of the Congo 86 B2
Mamberamo → *Indonesia* 63 E9
Mambilima Falls *Zambia* 87 E2
Mambirima
 Dem. Rep. of the Congo 87 E2
Mambo *Tanzania* 86 C4
Mambrui *Kenya* 86 C5
Mamburao *Phil.* 61 E4
Mamedkala *Russia* 73 A13
Mameigwess L. *Canada* 104 B2
Mamers *France* 18 D7
Mamfé *Cameroon* 83 D6
Mammoth *U.S.A.* 109 K8
Mammoth Cave △ *U.S.A.* 112 G10
Mamonovo *Russia* 30 D6
Mamoré → *Bolivia* 124 F5
Mamou *Guinea* 82 C2
Mamoudzou *Mayotte* 85 a
Mampatá *Guinea-Biss.* 82 C2
Mampikony *Madag.* 89 B8
Mampong *Ghana* 83 D4
Mamry, Jezioro *Poland* 30 D8
Mamuju *Indonesia* 63 E5
Mamuno *Botswana* 88 C3
Mamuras *Albania* 44 E3
Man *Ivory C.* 82 D3
Man, I. of *U.K.* 14 C3
Man-Bazar *India* 69 H12
Man Na *Burma* 67 H20
Mana → *Fr. Guiana* 125 B8
Mana Pools △ *Zimbabwe* 87 F2
Manaar, G. of = Mannar,
 G. of *Asia* 66 Q11
Manacapuru *Brazil* 124 D6
Manacor *Spain* 48 B10
Manado *Indonesia* 63 D6
Managua *Nic.* 120 D2
Managua, L. de *Nic.* 120 D2
Manakara *Madag.* 89 C8
Manali *India* 68 C7
Manama = Al Manāmah
 Bahrain 71 E6
Manambao → *Madag.* 89 B7
Manambato *Madag.* 89 A8
Manambolo → *Madag.* 89 B7
Manambolosy *Madag.* 89 B8
Mananara → *Madag.* 89 C8
Mananara *Madag.* 89 B8
Mananara △ *Madag.* 89 B8
Mananjary *Madag.* 89 C8
Manankoro *Mali* 82 C3
Manantali, L. de *Mali* 82 C2
Manantenina *Madag.* 89 C8
Manaos = Manaus *Brazil* 124 D6
Manapire → *Venezuela* 124 B5
Manapouri *N.Z.* 91 F1
Manapouri, L. *N.Z.* 91 F1
Manaqil *Sudan* 81 E3
Manār, Jabal *Yemen* 75 E3
Manaravolo *Madag.* 89 C8
Manas *China* 60 B3
Manas → *India* 67 F17
Manaslu *Nepal* 69 E11
Manasquan *U.S.A.* 115 F10
Manassa *U.S.A.* 109 H11
Manatí *Puerto Rico* 121 d
Manaung *Burma* 67 K18
Manaus *Brazil* 124 D6
Manavgat *Turkey* 72 D4
Manawan L. *Canada* 103 B8
Manay *Phil.* 61 H7
Manbij *Syria* 72 D7
Mancha Real *Spain* 37 H7
Manche □ *France* 18 C5
Manchegorsk *Russia* 52 C4
Manchester *U.K.* 14 D5
Manchester *Calif., U.S.A.* 110 G3
Manchester *Conn., U.S.A.* 115 E12
Manchester *Ga., U.S.A.* 117 E12
Manchester *Iowa, U.S.A.* 112 D8
Manchester *Ky., U.S.A.* 113 G12

Manchester *N.H., U.S.A.* **115** D13
Manchester *N.Y., U.S.A.* **114** D7
Manchester *Pa., U.S.A.* **115** F8
Manchester *Tenn., U.S.A.* **117** D11
Manchester *Vt., U.S.A.* **115** C11
Manchester Int. ✕ (MAN)
  U.K. **14** D5
Manchester L. *Canada* **103** A7
Manchhar L. *Pakistan* **68** F2
Manchuria = Dongbei *China* **54** A5
Manchurian Plain *China* **50** D14
Manciano *Italy* **41** F8
Mancifa *Ethiopia* **81** F5
Mand → *India* **69** J10
Mand → *Iran* **71** D7
Manda *Ludewe, Tanzania* **87** E3
Manda *Mbeya, Tanzania* **86** D3
Manda *Mbeya, Tanzania* **87** D3
Mandabé *Madag.* **89** C7
Mandaguari *Brazil* **127** A5
Mandah = Töhöm *Mongolia* **56** B5
Mandal *Norway* **9** G12
Mandala, Puncak *Indonesia* **63** E10
Mandale = Mandalay
  Burma **67** J20
Mandalay *Burma* **67** J20
Mandalgarh *India* **68** G6
Mandalgovĭ *Mongolia* **56** B4
Mandalī *Iraq* **73** F11
Mandan *U.S.A.* **112** B3
Mandaon *Phil.* **61** E5
Mandar, Teluk *Indonesia* **63** E5
Mándas *Italy* **42** C2
Mandaue *Phil.* **61** F5
Mandelieu-la-Napoule
  France **21** E10
Mandera *Kenya* **86** B5
Mandeville *Jamaica* **120** a
Mandi *India* **68** D7
Mandi Burewala *Pakistan* **68** D5
Mandi Dabwali *India* **68** E6
Mandiana *Guinea* **82** C3
Mandimba *Mozam.* **87** E4
Mandioli *Indonesia* **63** E7
Mandla *India* **69** H9
Mandø *Denmark* **11** J2
Mandorah *Australia* **92** B5
Mandoto *Madag.* **89** B8
Mandoudi *Greece* **46** C5
Mandra *Greece* **46** C5
Mandra *Pakistan* **68** C5
Mandraki *Greece* **47** E9
Mandrare → *Madag.* **89** D8
Mandritsara *Madag.* **89** B8
Mandronarivo *Madag.* **89** C8
Mandsaur *India* **68** G6
Mandurah *Australia* **93** F2
Mandúria *Italy* **43** B10
Mandvi *India* **68** H3
Mandya *India* **66** N10
Mandzai *Pakistan* **68** D2
Mané *Burkina Faso* **83** C4
Maneh *Iran* **71** B8
Manengouba, Mts. *Cameroon* **83** E6
Manera *Madag.* **89** C7
Manérbio *Italy* **40** C7
Maneroo Cr. → *Australia* **94** C3
Manfalût *Egypt* **80** B3
Manfredónia *Italy* **41** G12
Manfredónia, G. di *Italy* **41** G13
Manga *Burkina Faso* **83** C4
Manga *Niger* **83** C7
Mangabeiras, Chapada das
  Brazil **125** F9
Mangaia *Cook Is.* **97** K12
Mangalia *Romania* **29** G13
Mangalore *India* **66** N9
Mangan *India* **69** F13
Mangawan *India* **69** G9
Mangaweka *N.Z.* **91** C5
Manggar *Indonesia* **62** E3
Manggawitu *Indonesia* **63** E8
Mangghystaū Tübegi
  Kazakhstan **52** E6
Manggis *Indonesia* **63** J18
Mangindrano *Madag.* **89** A8
Mangkalihat, Tanjung
  Indonesia **63** D5
Mangla *Pakistan* **68** C5
Mangla Dam *Pakistan* **69** C5
Manglaur *India* **68** E7
Manglisi *Georgia* **35** K7
Mangnai *China* **60** C4
Mango *Togo* **83** C5
Mango *Tonga* **91** c
Mangoche *Malawi* **87** E4
Mangoky → *Madag.* **89** C7
Mangole *Indonesia* **63** E6
Mangombe
  Dem. Rep. of the Congo **86** C2
Mangonui *N.Z.* **91** A4
Mangoro → *Madag.* **89** B8
Mangrol *Mad. P., India* **68** J4
Mangrol *Raj., India* **68** G6
Mangualde *Portugal* **36** E3
Mangueira, L. da *Brazil* **127** C5
Mangum *U.S.A.* **116** D5
Manguri *Australia* **95** A1

Mangyshlak, Poluostrov =
  Mangghystaū Tübegi
  Kazakhstan **52** E6
Manhattan *U.S.A.* **112** F5
Manhiça *Mozam.* **89** D5
Mania → *Madag.* **89** B8
Maniago *Italy* **41** B9
Manica *Mozam.* **89** B5
Manica □ *Mozam.* **89** B5
Manicaland □ *Zimbabwe* **87** F3
Manicoré *Brazil* **124** E6
Manicouagan → *Canada* **105** C6
Manicouagan, Rés. *Canada* **105** B6
Maniema □
  Dem. Rep. of the Congo **86** C2
Manīfah *Si. Arabia* **71** E6
Manifold, C. *Australia* **94** C5
Maniganggo *China* **58** B2
Manigotagan *Canada* **103** C9
Manigotagan → *Canada* **103** C9
Manihari *India* **69** G12
Manihiki *Cook Is.* **97** J11
Manihiki Plateau *Pac. Oc.* **97** J11
Manika, Plateau de la
  Dem. Rep. of the Congo **87** E2
Manikpur *India* **69** G9
Manila *Phil.* **61** D4
Manila *U.S.A.* **108** F9
Manila B. *Phil.* **61** D4
Manilla *Australia* **95** E5
Manimpé *Mali* **82** C3
Maningrida *Australia* **94** A1
Maninian *Ivory C.* **82** C3
Manipur □ *India* **67** G19
Manipur → *Burma* **67** H19
Manisa *Turkey* **47** C9
Manisa □ *Turkey* **47** C9
Manistee *U.S.A.* **112** C10
Manistee → *U.S.A.* **112** C10
Manistique *U.S.A.* **112** C10
Manitoba □ *Canada* **103** B9
Manitoba, L. *Canada* **103** C9
Manitou *Canada* **103** D9
Manitou, L. *Canada* **105** B6
Manitou Is. *U.S.A.* **113** C10
Manitou L. *Canada* **104** C1
Manitou Springs *U.S.A.* **108** G11
Manitoulin I. *Canada* **104** C3
Manitouwadge *Canada* **104** C2
Manitowoc *U.S.A.* **112** C10
Manizales *Colombia* **124** B3
Manja *Madag.* **89** C7
Manjacaze *Mozam.* **89** C5
Manjakandriana *Madag.* **89** B8
Manjhand *Pakistan* **68** G3
Manjimup *Australia* **93** F2
Manjra → *India* **66** K10
Mankato *Kans., U.S.A.* **112** F4
Mankato *Minn., U.S.A.* **112** C6
Mankayane *Swaziland* **89** D5
Mankera *Pakistan* **68** D4
Mankim *Cameroon* **83** D7
Mankono *Ivory C.* **82** D3
Mankota *Canada* **103** D7
Manlay = Üydzin *Mongolia* **56** B4
Manlleu *Spain* **38** C7
Manmad *India* **66** J9
Mann Ranges *Australia* **93** E5
Manna *Indonesia* **62** E2
Mannahill *Australia* **95** E3
Mannar *Sri Lanka* **66** Q11
Mannar, G. of *Asia* **66** Q11
Mannar I. *Sri Lanka* **66** Q11
Mannheim *Germany* **25** F4
Manning *Canada* **102** B5
Manning *Oreg., U.S.A.* **110** E3
Manning *S.C., U.S.A.* **117** E14
Mannu → *Italy* **42** C2
Mannu, C. *Italy* **42** B1
Mannum *Australia* **95** E2
Mano *S. Leone* **82** D2
Mano → *Liberia* **82** D2
Mano River *Liberia* **82** D2
Manoharpur *India* **69** H11
Manokwari *Indonesia* **63** E8
Manolada *Greece* **46** D3
Manombo *Madag.* **89** C7
Manono
  Dem. Rep. of the Congo **86** D2
Manono *Samoa* **91** b
Manoppello *Italy* **41** F11
Manorhamilton *Ireland* **12** B3
Manosque *France* **21** E9
Manotick *Canada* **115** A9
Manouane *Canada* **105** C5
Manouane, L. *Canada* **105** B5
Manp'o *N. Korea* **57** D14
Manpojin = Manp'o
  N. Korea **57** D14
Manpur *Chhattisgarh, India* **69** H10
Manpur *Mad. P., India* **68** H6
Manresa *Spain* **38** D6
Mansa *Gujarat, India* **68** H5
Mansa *Punjab, India* **68** E6
Mansa *Zambia* **87** E2
Mânsåsen *Sweden* **10** A8
Mansehra *Pakistan* **68** B5
Mansel I. *Canada* **101** C12
Mansfield *Australia* **95** F4

Mansfield *U.K.* **14** D6
Mansfield *La., U.S.A.* **116** E8
Mansfield *Mass., U.S.A.* **115** D13
Mansfield *Ohio, U.S.A.* **114** F2
Mansfield *Pa., U.S.A.* **114** E7
Mansfield *Tex., U.S.A.* **116** E6
Mansfield, Mt. *U.S.A.* **115** B12
Mansilla de las Mulas *Spain* **36** C5
Mansle *France* **20** C4
Mansoa *Guinea-Biss.* **82** C1
Manson Creek *Canada* **102** B4
Manta *Ecuador* **124** D2
Mantadia △ *Madag.* **89** B8
Mantare *Tanzania* **86** C3
Manteca *U.S.A.* **110** H5
Manteo *U.S.A.* **117** D17
Mantes-la-Jolie *France* **19** D8
Manthani *India* **66** K11
Manti *U.S.A.* **108** G8
Mantiqueira, Serra da
  Brazil **127** A7
Manton *U.S.A.* **113** C11
Mantorp *Sweden* **11** F9
Mántova *Italy* **40** C7
Mantua = Mántova *Italy* **40** C7
Manturovo *Russia* **34** A7
Manu *Peru* **124** F4
Manú → *Peru* **124** F4
Manu'a Is. *Amer. Samoa* **91** b
Manuel Alves → *Brazil* **125** F9
Manui *Indonesia* **63** E6
Manukau *N.Z.* **91** B5
Manuripi → *Bolivia* **124** F5
Manyani *Kenya* **86** C4
Manyara, L. *Tanzania* **86** C4
Manyas *Turkey* **45** F11
Manyava *Ukraine* **29** B9
Manych → *Russia* **35** G5
Manych-Gudilo, Ozero
  Russia **35** G6
Manyonga → *Tanzania* **86** C3
Manyoni *Tanzania* **86** D3
Manzai *Pakistan* **68** C4
Manzala, Bahra el *Egypt* **80** H7
Manzanar △ *U.S.A.* **110** J7
Manzanares *Spain* **37** F7
Manzaneda *Spain* **36** C3
Manzanillo *Cuba* **120** B4
Manzanillo *Mexico* **118** D4
Manzanillo, Pta. *Panama* **120** E4
Manzano Mts. *U.S.A.* **109** J10
Manzariyeh *Iran* **71** C6
Manzhouli *China* **60** B6
Manzini *Swaziland* **89** D5
Manzur Vadisi △ *Turkey* **70** B3
Mao *Chad* **79** F9
Maó *Spain* **48** B11
Maoke, Pegunungan
  Indonesia **63** E9
Maolin *China* **57** C12
Maoming *China* **59** G8
Maopi T'ou *China* **59** G13
Maoxian *China* **58** B4
Maoxing *China* **57** B13
Mapam Yumco *China* **69** D9
Mapastepec *Mexico* **119** D6
Maphrao, Ko *Thailand* **65** a
Mapia, Kepulauan *Indonesia* **63** D8
Mapimí *Mexico* **118** B4
Mapimí, Bolsón de *Mexico* **118** B4
Maping *China* **59** B9
Mapinga *Tanzania* **86** D4
Mapinhane *Mozam.* **89** C6
Maple Creek *Canada* **103** D7
Maple Valley *U.S.A.* **110** C4
Mapleton *U.S.A.* **108** D2
Mapuera → *Brazil* **124** D7
Mapulanguene *Mozam.* **89** C5
Mapungubwe △ *S. Africa* **87** G2
Maputo *Mozam.* **89** D5
Maputo □ *Mozam.* **89** D5
Maputo, B. de *Mozam.* **89** D5
Maputo △ *Mozam.* **89** D5
Maqat *Kazakhstan* **52** E6
Maqiaohe *China* **57** B16
Maqnā *Si. Arabia* **70** D2
Maqteïr *Mauritania* **78** D3
Maquan He =
  Brahmaputra → *Asia* **69** H13
Maqueda *Spain* **36** E6
Maquela do Zombo *Angola* **84** F3
Maquinchao *Argentina* **128** E3
Maquoketa *U.S.A.* **112** D8
Mar *Canada* **114** B3
Mar, Serra do *Brazil* **127** B6
Mar Chiquita, L. *Argentina* **126** C3
Mar del Plata *Argentina* **126** D4
Mar Menor *Spain* **39** H4
Mara *Tanzania* **86** C3
Mara □ *Tanzania* **86** C3
Maraã *Brazil* **124** D5
Maraä *Tahiti* **91** d
Marabá *Brazil* **125** E9
Maraboon, L. *Australia* **94** C4
Maracá, I. de *Brazil* **125** C8

Maracaibo *Venezuela* **124** A4
Maracaibo, L. de *Venezuela* **124** B4
Maracaju *Brazil* **127** A4
Maracas Bay Village
  Trin. & Tob. **125** K15
Maracay *Venezuela* **124** A5
Maracena *Spain* **37** H7
Marādah *Libya* **79** C9
Maradi *Niger* **83** C6
Maradi □ *Niger* **83** C6
Marāgheh *Iran* **73** D12
Marāh *Si. Arabia* **70** E5
Marahoue △ *Ivory C.* **82** D3
Marais du Cotentin et du
  Bessin △ *France* **18** C5
Marais Poitevin, Val de
  Sèvre et Vendée △ *France* **20** B3
Marajó, I. de *Brazil* **125** D9
Marākand *Iran* **70** B5
Marakele △ *S. Africa* **89** E4
Maralal *Kenya* **86** B4
Maralinga *Australia* **93** F5
Maramaraereğlisi *Turkey* **45** F11
Marambio *Antarctica* **5** C18
Marampa *S. Leone* **82** D2
Maramureş □ *Romania* **29** C9
Maran *Malaysia* **65** L4
Marana *U.S.A.* **109** K8
Maranboy *Australia* **92** B5
Maranchón *Spain* **38** D2
Marand *Iran* **73** C11
Marang *Malaysia* **65** K4
Maranguape *Brazil* **125** D11
Maranhão = São Luís
  Brazil **125** D10
Maranhão □ *Brazil* **125** E9
Marano, L. di *Italy* **41** C10
Maranoa → *Australia* **95** D4
Marañón → *Peru* **124** D4
Marão *Mozam.* **89** C5
Maraş = Kahramanmaraş
  Turkey **72** D7
Mărăşeşti *Romania* **29** E12
Maratea *Italy* **43** C8
Marateca *Portugal* **37** G2
Marathasa *Cyprus* **49** E11
Marathokambos *Greece* **47** D8
Marathon *Australia* **94** C3
Marathon *Canada* **104** C2
Marathon *N.Y., U.S.A.* **115** D8
Marathon *Tex., U.S.A.* **116** F3
Marathónas *Greece* **46** C5
Marathóvouno *Cyprus* **49** D12
Maratua *Indonesia* **63** D5
Maraval *Trin. & Tob.* **125** K15
Maravatío *Mexico* **118** D4
Marawi City *Phil.* **61** H6
Marāwih *U.A.E.* **71** E7
Marazliyivka *Ukraine* **29** D15
Marbella *Spain* **37** J6
Marble Bar *Australia* **92** D2
Marble Falls *U.S.A.* **116** F5
Marblehead *Mass., U.S.A.* **115** D14
Marblehead *Ohio, U.S.A.* **114** E2
Marburg *Germany* **24** E4
Marca, Pta. Da *Angola* **85** H2
Marcal → *Hungary* **28** C2
Marcali *Hungary* **28** D2
Marcaria *Italy* **40** C7
Mărcăuţi *Moldova* **29** B12
March *U.K.* **15** E8
Marche *France* **20** B5
Marche □ *Italy* **41** E10
Marche-en-Famenne
  Belgium **17** D5
Marchena *Spain* **37** H5
Marches = Marche □ *Italy* **41** E10
Marchesale △ *Italy* **43** D9
Marciana Marina *Italy* **40** F7
Marcianise *Italy* **43** A7
Marcigny *France* **19** F11
Marcillat-en-Combraille
  France **19** F9
Marck *France* **19** B8
Marckolsheim *France* **19** D14
Marco Island *U.S.A.* **117** J14
Marcos Juárez *Argentina* **126** C3
Mărculeşti *Moldova* **29** C13
Marcus I. = Minami-Tori-
  Shima *Pac. Oc.* **96** E7
Marcy, Mt. *U.S.A.* **115** B11
Mardan *Pakistan* **68** B5
Mardarivka *Ukraine* **29** C14
Mardin *Turkey* **73** D9
Mårdsjö *Sweden* **10** A9
Marécchia → *Italy* **41** D9
Maree, L. *U.K.* **13** D3
Mareeba *Australia* **94** B4
Mareetsane *S. Africa* **88** D4
Maremma *Italy* **41** F8
Maremma △ *Italy* **40** F8
Maréna *Kayes, Mali* **82** C2
Maréna *Koulikouro, Mali* **82** C3
Marengo *U.S.A.* **112** E8
Marennes *France* **20** C2
Marerano *Madag.* **89** C7
Maréttimo *Italy* **42** E5
Mareuil *France* **20** C4
Marfa *U.S.A.* **116** F2

Marfa Pt. *Malta* **49** D1
Marganets = Marhanets
  Ukraine **33** J8
Margaret → *Australia* **92** C4
Margaret Bay *Canada* **102** C3
Margaret L. *Canada* **102** B5
Margaret River *Australia* **93** F2
Margarita, I. de *Venezuela* **124** A6
Margariti *Greece* **46** B2
Margaritovo *Russia* **54** C7
Margate *S. Africa* **89** E5
Margate *U.K.* **15** F9
Margeride, Mts. de la *France* **20** D7
Margherita di Savóia *Italy* **43** A9
Margherita Pk. *Uganda* **86** B3
Marghilon *Uzbekistan* **52** E8
Marghita *Romania* **28** C7
Margonin *Poland* **31** F4
Margow, Dasht-e *Afghan.* **66** D3
Marguerite *Canada* **102** C4
Marhanets *Ukraine* **33** J8
Mari El □ *Russia* **34** B8
Mari Indus *Pakistan* **68** C4
Mari Republic = Mari El □
  Russia **34** B8
María, Sa. de *Spain* **39** H2
María de la Salut *Spain* **48** B10
María Elena *Chile* **126** A2
María Grande *Argentina* **126** C4
Maria I. *N. Terr., Australia* **94** A2
Maria I. *Tas., Australia* **95** G4
Maria Island △ *Australia* **95** G4
Maria van Diemen, C. *N.Z.* **91** A4
Mariager *Denmark* **11** H3
Mariager Fjord *Denmark* **11** H4
Mariakani *Kenya* **86** C4
Mariala △ *Australia* **95** D4
Marian *Australia* **94** K6
Marian L. *Canada* **102** A5
Mariana Trench *Pac. Oc.* **96** F6
Marianna *Ark., U.S.A.* **117** D9
Marianna *Fla., U.S.A.* **117** F12
Mariannelund *Sweden* **11** G9
Mariánské Lázně *Czech Rep.* **26** B5
Marías, Islas *Mexico* **118** C3
Mariato, Punta *Panama* **120** E3
Mariazell *Austria* **26** D8
Maribo *Denmark* **11** K5
Maribor *Slovenia* **41** B12
Marico → *S. Africa* **88** C4
Maricopa *Ariz., U.S.A.* **109** K7
Maricopa *Calif., U.S.A.* **111** K7
Marīdī *Sudan* **81** G2
Marīdī, Wadi → *Sudan* **81** F2
Marié → *Brazil* **124** D5
Marie Byrd Land *Antarctica* **5** D14
Marie-Galante *Guadeloupe* **120** b
Mariecourt =
  Kangiqsujuaq *Canada* **101** C12
Mariefred *Sweden* **10** E11
Mariehamn *Finland* **9** F18
Marieholm *Sweden* **11** J7
Mariembourg *Belgium* **17** D4
Marienbad = Mariánské
  Lázně *Czech Rep.* **26** B5
Marienberg *Germany* **24** E9
Mariental *Namibia* **88** C2
Marienville *U.S.A.* **114** E5
Mariestad *Sweden* **11** F7
Marietta *Ga., U.S.A.* **117** E12
Marietta *Ohio, U.S.A.* **113** F13
Marieville *Canada* **115** A11
Mariga → *Nigeria* **83** C6
Marignane *France* **21** E9
Marihatag *Phil.* **61** G7
Mariinsk *Russia* **52** D9
Mariinskiy Posad *Russia* **34** B8
Marijampolė *Lithuania* **30** D10
Marijampolė □ *Lithuania* **30** D10
Marília *Brazil* **127** A6
Marín *Spain* **36** C2
Marina *U.S.A.* **110** J5
Marinduque *Phil.* **61** B6
Marine City *U.S.A.* **114** D2
Marineo *Italy* **42** E6
Marinette *U.S.A.* **112** C10
Maringá *Brazil* **127** A5
Marinha Grande *Portugal* **36** F2
Marino *Italy* **41** G9
Marion *Ala., U.S.A.* **117** E11
Marion *Ill., U.S.A.* **112** G9
Marion *Ind., U.S.A.* **113** C11
Marion *Iowa, U.S.A.* **112** D8
Marion *Kans., U.S.A.* **112** F5
Marion *N.C., U.S.A.* **117** D13
Marion *S.C., U.S.A.* **117** D15
Marion *Va., U.S.A.* **113** G13
Marion, L. *U.S.A.* **117** E14
Mariposa *U.S.A.* **110** H7
Mariscal Estigarribia
  Paraguay **126** A3
Maritime Alps =
  Maritimes, Alpes *Europe* **21** D11
Maritimes, Alpes *Europe* **21** D11
Maritsa = Évros → *Greece* **72** B2
Maritsa *Greece* **49** C10

Mariupol *Ukraine* **33** J9
Mariusa △ *Venezuela* **121** E7
Marīvān *Iran* **73** E12
Marj 'Uyūn *Lebanon* **74** B4
Marka *Si. Arabia* **80** D5
Marka *Somali Rep.* **75** G3
Markam *China* **58** C3
Markaryd *Sweden* **11** H7
Markdale *Canada* **114** B4
Marked Tree *U.S.A.* **117** D9
Markelsdorfer Huk *Germany* **24** A7
Market Drayton *U.K.* **14** E5
Market Harborough *U.K.* **15** E7
Market Rasen *U.K.* **14** D7
Markham *Canada* **114** C5
Markham, Mt. *Antarctica* **5** E11
Marki *Poland* **31** F8
Märkische Schweiz △
  Germany **24** C10
Markkleeberg *Germany* **24** D8
Markleeville *U.S.A.* **110** G7
Markopoulo *Greece* **46** D5
Markovac *Serbia* **44** B5
Markovo *Russia* **53** C17
Markoye *Burkina Faso* **83** C5
Marks *Russia* **34** E8
Marksville *U.S.A.* **116** F8
Markt Schwaben *Germany* **25** G7
Marktoberdorf *Germany* **25** H6
Marktredwitz *Germany* **25** E8
Marl *Germany* **24** D3
Marla *Australia* **95** D1
Marlbank *Canada* **114** B7
Marlboro *U.S.A.* **115** C11
Marlborough *Australia* **94** C4
Marlborough *U.K.* **15** F6
Marlborough □ *N.Z.* **91** D13
Marlborough Downs *U.K.* **15** F6
Marle *France* **19** C10
Marlin *U.S.A.* **116** F6
Marlow *Germany* **24** A8
Marlow *U.K.* **15** F7
Marlow *U.S.A.* **116** D6
Marmagao *India* **66** M8
Marmande *France* **20** D4
Marmara *Turkey* **45** F11
Marmara, Sea of =
  Marmara Denizi *Turkey* **45** F12
Marmara Denizi *Turkey* **45** F12
Marmara Gölü *Turkey* **47** C10
Marmaris *Turkey* **47** E10
Marmaris Limanı *Turkey* **47** E10
Marmion, Mt. *Australia* **93** E2
Marmion L. *Canada* **104** C1
Marmolada, Mte. *Italy* **41** B8
Marmolejo *Spain* **37** G6
Marmora *Canada* **114** B7
Mármora, La *Italy* **42** C2
Marnay *France* **19** E12
Marne *Germany* **24** B5
Marne □ *France* **19** D11
Marne → *France* **19** D9
Marneuli *Georgia* **35** K7
Maroala *Madag.* **89** B8
Maroantsetra *Madag.* **89** B8
Maroelaboom *Namibia* **88** B2
Marofandilia *Madag.* **89** C7
Marojejy △ *Madag.* **89** B8
Marolambo *Madag.* **89** C8
Maromandia *Madag.* **89** A8
Maromokotro *Madag.* **89** A8
Marondera *Zimbabwe* **87** F3
Maroni → *Fr. Guiana* **125** B8
Maronia *Greece* **45** F9
Maronne → *France* **20** C5
Maroochydore *Australia* **95** D5
Maroona *Australia* **95** F3
Maros → *Hungary* **28** D5
Marosakoa *Madag.* **89** B8
Maroseranana *Madag.* **89** B8
Maróstica *Italy* **41** C8
Marotandrano *Madag.* **89** B8
Marotaolano *Madag.* **89** A8
Maroua *Cameroon* **83** C7
Marovato *Madag.* **89** B8
Marovoay *Madag.* **89** B8
Marquard *S. Africa* **88** D4
Marquesas Fracture Zone
  Pac. Oc. **97** H15
Marquesas Is. =
  Marquises, Îs.
  French Polynesia **97** H14
Marquette *U.S.A.* **112** B10
Marquis *St. Lucia* **121** f
Marquise *France* **19** B8
Marquises, Îs.
  French Polynesia **97** H14
Marra, Djebel *Sudan* **79** F10
Marra, Gebel *Sudan* **81** F2
Marracuene *Mozam.* **89** D5
Marradi *Italy* **41** D8
Marrawah *Australia* **95** G3
Marratxí *Spain* **38** F7
Marrawah *Australia* **95** G3
Marree *Australia* **95** D2
Marrero *U.S.A.* **117** G9
Marrimane *Mozam.* **89** C5
Marromeu *Mozam.* **89** B6
Marromeu △ *Mozam.* **89** B6

Marroquí, Punta Spain 37 K5
Marrowie Cr. → Australia 95 E4
Marrubane Mozam. 87 F4
Marrúbiu Italy 42 C1
Marrupa Mozam. 87 E4
Mars Hill U.S.A. 113 B20
Marsá 'Alam Egypt 80 B3
Marsá Matrûh Egypt 80 A2
Marsá Sha'b Sudan 80 C4
Marsá Susah Libya 79 B10
Marsabit Kenya 86 B4
Marsabit △ Kenya 86 B4
Marsala Italy 42 E5
Marsalforn Malta 49 C1
Mârşani Romania 29 F9
Marsberg Germany 24 D4
Marsciano Italy 41 F9
Marsden Australia 95 E4
Marseillan France 20 E7
Marseille France 21 E9
Marseille-Marignane ✈ (MRS) France 21 E9
Marseilles = Marseille France 21 E9
Marsh I. U.S.A. 116 G9
Marshall Liberia 82 D2
Marshall Ark., U.S.A. 116 D8
Marshall Mich., U.S.A. 113 D11
Marshall Minn., U.S.A. 112 C6
Marshall Mo., U.S.A. 112 F7
Marshall Tex., U.S.A. 116 E7
Marshall → Australia 94 C2
Marshall Is. ■ Pac. Oc. 90 A10
Marshalltown U.S.A. 112 D7
Marshbrook Zimbabwe 89 B5
Marshfield Mo., U.S.A. 112 G7
Marshfield Vt., U.S.A. 115 B12
Marshfield Wis., U.S.A. 112 C8
Marshūn Iran 71 B6
Mársico Nuovo Italy 43 B8
Märsta Sweden 10 E11
Marstal Denmark 11 K4
Marstrand Sweden 11 G5
Mart U.S.A. 116 F6
Marta → Italy 41 F8
Martaban Burma 67 L20
Martaban, G. of Burma 67 L20
Martano Italy 43 B11
Martapura Kalimantan, Indonesia 62 E4
Martapura Sumatera, Indonesia 62 E2
Marte Nigeria 83 C7
Marte R. Gómez, Presa Mexico 119 B5
Martel France 20 D5
Martelange Belgium 17 E5
Martellago Italy 41 C9
Martés, Sierra Spain 39 F4
Martfű Hungary 28 C5
Martha's Vineyard U.S.A. 115 E14
Martigné-Ferchaud France 18 E4
Martigny Switz. 25 J3
Martigues France 21 E9
Martin Slovak Rep. 27 B11
Martin S. Dak., U.S.A. 112 D3
Martin Tenn., U.S.A. 117 C10
Martín → Spain 38 D4
Martin L. U.S.A. 117 E12
Martina Franca Italy 43 B10
Martinborough N.Z. 91 D5
Martinez Calif., U.S.A. 110 G4
Martinez Ga., U.S.A. 117 E13
Martinique ☑ W. Indies 120 c
Martinique Passage W. Indies 121 C7
Martino Greece 46 C5
Martinópolis Brazil 127 A5
Martin's Bay Barbados 121 g
Martins Ferry U.S.A. 114 F4
Martinsberg Austria 26 C8
Martinsburg Pa., U.S.A. 114 F6
Martinsburg W. Va., U.S.A. 113 F15
Martinsicuro Italy 41 F10
Martinsville Ind., U.S.A. 112 F10
Martinsville Va., U.S.A. 113 G14
Marton N.Z. 91 D5
Martorell Spain 38 D6
Martos Spain 37 H7
Martuni Armenia 35 K7
Maru Nigeria 83 C6
Marudi Malaysia 62 D4
Maruf Afghan. 66 D5
Marugame Japan 55 G6
Marunga Angola 88 B3
Marungu, Mts. Dem. Rep. of the Congo 86 D3
Marv Dasht Iran 71 D7
Marvast Iran 71 D7
Marvejols France 20 D7
Marvel Loch Australia 93 F2
Marwar India 68 G5
Mary Turkmenistan 71 B9
Maryborough = Port Laoise Ireland 12 C4
Maryborough Queens., Australia 95 D5
Maryborough Vic., Australia 95 F3
Maryfield Canada 103 D8

Maryland ☐ U.S.A. 113 F15
Maryland Junction Zimbabwe 87 F3
Maryport U.K. 14 C4
Mary's Harbour Canada 105 B8
Marystown Canada 105 C8
Marysville Calif., U.S.A. 110 F5
Marysville Kans., U.S.A. 112 F6
Marysville Mich., U.S.A. 114 D2
Marysville Ohio, U.S.A. 113 E12
Marysville Wash., U.S.A. 110 B4
Maryville Mo., U.S.A. 112 E6
Maryville Tenn., U.S.A. 117 D13
Marzūq Libya 79 C8
Marzūq, Idehān Libya 79 D8
Masada Israel 74 D4
Masahunga Tanzania 86 C3
Masai Malaysia 65 d
Masai Mara △ Kenya 86 C4
Masai Steppe Tanzania 86 C4
Masaka Uganda 86 C3
Mãsãl Iran 73 D12
Masalembo, Kepulauan Indonesia 62 F4
Masalima, Kepulauan Indonesia 62 F5
Masallı Azerbaijan 73 C13
Masamba Indonesia 63 E6
Masan S. Korea 57 G15
Masandam, Ra's Oman 71 E8
Masasi Tanzania 87 E4
Masaya Nic. 120 D2
Masba Nigeria 83 C7
Masbate Phil. 61 E5
Máscali Italy 43 E8
Mascara Algeria 78 A6
Mascota Mexico 118 C4
Masela Indonesia 63 F7
Maseru Lesotho 88 D4
Mashaba Zimbabwe 87 G3
Mashābih Si. Arabia 70 E3
Mashan China 58 F7
Mashar Sudan 81 F2
Mashatu △ Botswana 89 C4
Mashegu Nigeria 83 D6
Masherbrum Pakistan 69 B7
Mashhad Iran 71 B8
Mashi Nigeria 83 C6
Mashīz Iran 71 D8
Mãshkel, Hãmũn-i- Pakistan 71 D9
Mashki Chāh Pakistan 66 E3
Mashonaland Zimbabwe 85 H6
Mashonaland Central ☐ Zimbabwe 89 B5
Mashonaland East ☐ Zimbabwe 89 B5
Mashonaland West ☐ Zimbabwe 89 B4
Mashrakh India 69 F11
Mashtaga = Maştağa Azerbaijan 35 K10
Masi Manimba Dem. Rep. of the Congo 84 E3
Masindi Uganda 86 B3
Masindi Port Uganda 86 B3
Maşīrah Oman 75 C6
Maşīrah, Khalīj Oman 75 C6
Masisi Dem. Rep. of the Congo 86 C2
Masjed Soleyman Iran 71 D6
Mask, L. Ireland 12 C2
Maskin Oman 71 F8
Maslen Nos Bulgaria 45 D11
Maslinica Croatia 41 E13
Masnou = El Masnou Spain 38 D7
Masoala, Tanjon' i Madag. 89 B9
Masoala △ Madag. 89 B9
Masoarivo Madag. 89 C7
Masohi = Amahai Indonesia 63 E7
Masomeloka Madag. 89 C8
Mason Nev., U.S.A. 110 G4
Mason Tex., U.S.A. 116 F5
Mason City U.S.A. 112 D7
Maspalomas Canary Is. 48 G4
Maspalomas, Pta. Canary Is. 48 G4
Masqat Oman 75 C6
Masr el Gedida Egypt 80 H7
Massa Italy 40 D7
Massa Maríttima Italy 40 E7
Massachusetts ☐ U.S.A. 115 D13
Massachusetts B. U.S.A. 115 D14
Massafra Italy 43 B10
Massakory Chad 79 F9
Massanella Spain 48 B9
Massangena Mozam. 89 C5
Massango Angola 84 F3
Massat France 20 F5
Massawa = Mitsiwa Eritrea 81 D4
Massena U.S.A. 115 B10
Massénya Chad 79 F9
Masset Canada 102 C2
Masseube France 20 E4
Massiac France 20 C7
Massiah Street Barbados 121 g
Massif Central France 20 D7
Massif des Bauges △ France 19 G13
Massigui Mali 82 C3
Massillon U.S.A. 114 F3
Massinga Mozam. 89 C6
Massingir Mozam. 89 C5
Masson-Angers Canada 115 A9

Masson I. Antarctica 5 C7
Mastanli = Momchilgrad Bulgaria 45 E9
Masterton N.Z. 91 D5
Mastic U.S.A. 115 F12
Mastuj Pakistan 69 A5
Mastung Pakistan 66 E5
Mastūrah Si. Arabia 80 C4
Masty Belarus 23 B13
Masuda Japan 55 G5
Masurian Lakes = Mazurski, Pojezierze Poland 30 E7
Masvingo Zimbabwe 87 G3
Masvingo ☐ Zimbabwe 87 G3
Maswa △ Tanzania 86 C3
Maşyāf Syria 72 E7
Maszewo Poland 30 E2
Mat → Albania 44 E3
Matabeleland Zimbabwe 85 H5
Matabeleland North ☐ Zimbabwe 87 F2
Matabeleland South ☐ Zimbabwe 87 G2
Matachel → Spain 37 G4
Matachewan Canada 104 C3
Matadi Dem. Rep. of the Congo 84 F2
Matagalpa Nic. 120 D2
Matagami Canada 104 C4
Matagami, L. Canada 104 C4
Matagorda B. U.S.A. 116 G6
Matagorda I. U.S.A. 116 G6
Mataiea Tahiti 91 d
Matak Indonesia 62 D3
Matala Greece 49 E6
Matam Senegal 82 B2
Matam ☐ Senegal 82 B2
Matameye Niger 83 C6
Matamoros Campeche, Mexico 119 D6
Matamoros Coahuila, Mexico 118 B4
Matamoros Tamaulipas, Mexico 119 B5
Ma'ţan as Sarra Libya 79 D10
Matandu → Tanzania 87 D3
Matane Canada 105 C6
Matang China 58 F5
Matankari Niger 83 C5
Matanomadh India 68 H3
Matanzas Cuba 120 B3
Matapa Botswana 88 C3
Matapan, C. = Tenaro, Akra Greece 46 E4
Matapédia Canada 105 C6
Matapo △ Zimbabwe 87 G2
Matara Sri Lanka 66 S12
Mataram Indonesia 63 K19
Matarani Peru 124 G4
Mataranka Australia 92 B5
Matarma, Râs Egypt 74 E1
Mataró Spain 38 D7
Matarraña → Spain 38 D5
Mataruška Banja Serbia 44 C4
Matatiele S. Africa 89 E4
Mataura N.Z. 91 G2
Matavai, B. de Tahiti 91 d
Matehuala Mexico 118 C4
Mateke Hills Zimbabwe 87 G3
Matelot Trin. & Tob. 125 K15
Matera Italy 43 B9
Matese, Monti del Italy 43 A7
Matese → Italy 43 A7
Mátészalka Hungary 28 C7
Matetsi Zimbabwe 87 F2
Matfors Sweden 10 B11
Matha France 20 C3
Matheniko △ Uganda 86 B3
Mathis U.S.A. 116 G6
Mathraki Greece 49 A3
Mathura India 68 F7
Mati Phil. 61 H7
Matiakoali Burkina Faso 83 C5
Matiali India 69 F13
Matías Romero Mexico 119 D5
Matibane Mozam. 87 E5
Matiri Ra. N.Z. 91 D4
Matjiesfontein S. Africa 88 E3
Matla → India 69 J13
Matlamanyane Botswana 88 B4
Matli Pakistan 68 G3
Matlock U.K. 14 D6
Matna Sudan 81 E4
Mato Grosso ☐ Brazil 125 F8
Mato Grosso, Planalto do Brazil 125 G8
Mato Grosso do Sul ☐ Brazil 125 G8
Matobo = Matapo △ Zimbabwe 87 G2
Matochkin Shar Russia 52 B6
Matochkin Shar, Proliv Russia 52 B6
Matopo Hills Zimbabwe 87 G2
Matopos Zimbabwe 87 G2
Matosinhos Portugal 36 D2
Matour France 19 F11
Matroosberg S. Africa 88 E2

Maţruḥ Oman 75 C6
Matsena Nigeria 83 C7
Matsesta Russia 35 J4
Matsu Tao Taiwan 59 E13
Matsue Japan 55 G6
Matsum, Ko Thailand 65 b
Matsumae Japan 54 D10
Matsumoto Japan 55 F9
Matsusaka Japan 55 G8
Matsuura Japan 55 H4
Matsuyama Japan 55 H6
Mattagami → Canada 104 B3
Mattancheri India 66 Q10
Mattawa Canada 104 C4
Matterhorn Switz. 25 K3
Mattersburg Austria 27 D9
Matthew Town Bahamas 121 C5
Matthews Ridge Guyana 124 B6
Mattice Canada 104 C3
Mattituck U.S.A. 115 F12
Mattō Japan 55 F8
Mattoon U.S.A. 112 F9
Matuba Mozam. 89 C5
Matucana Peru 124 F3
Matuku Fiji 91 a
Matūn = Khowst Afghan. 68 C3
Matura B. Trin. & Tob. 125 K15
Maturín Venezuela 124 B6
Matusadona △ Zimbabwe 87 F2
Matveyev Kurgan Russia 33 J10
Matxitxako, C. Spain 38 B2
Mau Mad. P., India 69 F8
Mau Ut. P., India 69 G10
Mau Ut. P., India 69 G9
Mau Escarpment Kenya 86 C4
Mau Ranipur India 69 G8
Maua Kenya 86 C4
Maubeuge France 19 B10
Maubin Burma 67 L19
Maubourguet France 20 E4
Maud, Pt. Australia 92 D1
Maud Rise S. Ocean 5 C3
Maude Australia 95 E3
Maudin Sun Burma 67 M19
Maués Brazil 124 D7
Mauganj India 69 G9
Maughold Hd. I. of Man 14 C3
Mauguio France 20 E7
Maui U.S.A. 106 b
Maulamyaing = Moulmein Burma 67 L20
Maule ☐ Chile 126 D1
Mauléon-Licharre France 20 E3
Maumee U.S.A. 113 E12
Maumee → U.S.A. 113 E12
Maumere Indonesia 63 F6
Maumusson, Pertuis de France 20 C2
Maun Botswana 88 C3
Mauna Kea U.S.A. 106 b
Mauna Loa U.S.A. 106 b
Maungan Kyunzu Burma 64 E1
Maungu Kenya 86 C4
Maupin U.S.A. 108 D3
Maure-de-Bretagne France 18 E5
Maurepas, L. U.S.A. 117 F9
Maures France 21 E10
Mauriac France 20 C6
Maurice, L. Australia 93 E5
Mauricie △ Canada 104 C5
Maurienne France 21 C10
Mauritania ■ Africa 78 E3
Mauritius ■ Ind. Oc. 85 d
Mauron France 18 D4
Maurs France 20 D6
Mauston U.S.A. 112 D8
Mauterndorf Austria 26 D6
Mauthen Austria 26 E6
Mauvezin France 20 E4
Mauzé-sur-le-Mignon France 20 B3
Mavli India 68 G5
Mavrovë Albania 44 F3
Mavrovo △ Macedonia 44 E4
Mavuradonha Mts. Zimbabwe 87 F3
Mawa Dem. Rep. of the Congo 86 B2
Mawai India 69 H9
Mawana India 68 E7
Mawand Pakistan 68 E3
Mawat Iraq 73 E11
Mawjib, W. al → Jordan 74 D4
Mawk Mai Burma 67 J20
Mawlaik Burma 67 H19
Mawlamyine = Moulmein Burma 67 L20
Mawqaq Si. Arabia 70 E4
Mawson Base Antarctica 5 C6
Mawson Coast Antarctica 5 C6
Max U.S.A. 112 B3
Maxcanú Mexico 119 C6
Maxesibeni S. Africa 89 E4
Maxhamish L. Canada 102 B4
Maxixe Mozam. 89 C6
Maxville Canada 115 A10
Maxwell U.S.A. 110 F4
Maxwelton Australia 94 C3
May, C. U.S.A. 113 F16

May Pen Jamaica 120 a
Maya → Russia 53 D14
Maya Mts. Belize 119 D7
Mayaguana Bahamas 121 B5
Mayagüez Puerto Rico 121 d
Mayahi Niger 83 C6
Mayaky Ukraine 29 C14
Mayals = Maials Spain 38 D5
Mayámey Iran 71 B7
Mayang China 58 D7
Mayanup Australia 93 F2
Mayapán Mexico 119 C7
Mayarí Cuba 121 B4
Mayaro B. Trin. & Tob. 125 K16
Maybell U.S.A. 108 F9
Maybole U.K. 14 F4
Maychew Ethiopia 81 E4
Maydan Iraq 73 E11
Maydan Iran 29 B8
Maydena Australia 95 G4
Maydī Yemen 81 D5
Mayen Germany 25 E3
Mayenne France 18 D6
Mayenne ☐ France 18 D6
Mayenne → France 18 E6
Mayer U.S.A. 109 J7
Mayerthorpe Canada 102 C5
Mayfield Ky., U.S.A. 112 G9
Mayfield N.Y., U.S.A. 115 C10
Mayhill U.S.A. 109 K11
Maykop Russia 35 H5
Maymyo Burma 64 A1
Maynard Mass., U.S.A. 115 D13
Maynard Wash., U.S.A. 110 C4
Maynard Hills Australia 93 E2
Mayne → Australia 94 C3
Maynooth Canada 114 A7
Maynooth Ireland 12 C5
Mayo Canada 100 C6
Mayo ☐ Ireland 12 C2
Mayo → Ireland 12 C2
Mayo Daga Nigeria 83 D7
Mayo Faran Nigeria 83 D7
Mayon Volcano Phil. 61 E5
Mayor I. N.Z. 91 B6
Mayorga Spain 36 C5
Mayotte ☑ Ind. Oc. 85 a
Mayraira Pt. Phil. 61 B4
Maysān ☐ Iraq 70 D5
Mayskiy Russia 35 J7
Maysville U.S.A. 113 F12
Mayu Indonesia 63 D7
Mayville N. Dak., U.S.A. 112 B6
Mayville N.Y., U.S.A. 114 D5
Mazabuka Zambia 87 F2
Mazagán = El Jadida Morocco 78 B4
Mazagão Brazil 125 D8
Mazamet France 20 E6
Mazán Peru 124 D4
Mãzandarãn ☐ Iran 71 B7
Mazapil Mexico 118 C4
Mazara del Vallo Italy 42 E5
Mazarrón Spain 39 H3
Mazarrón, G. de Spain 39 H3
Mazaruni → Guyana 124 B7
Mazatán Mexico 118 B3
Mazatenango Guatemala 120 D1
Mazatlán Mexico 118 C3
Mažeikiai Lithuania 30 B9
Mãzhãn Iran 71 C8
Mazinãn Iran 71 B8
Mazoe Mozam. 87 F3
Mazoe → Mozam. 87 F3
Mazowe Zimbabwe 87 F3
Mazowieckie ☐ Poland 31 F8
Mazrûb Sudan 81 E2
Mazu Dao China 59 D12
Mazurski, Pojezierze Poland 30 E7
Mazyr Belarus 23 B15
Mba Fiji 91 a
Mbaba Senegal 82 C1
Mbabane Swaziland 89 D5
Mbagne Mauritania 82 B2
M'bahiakro Ivory C. 82 D4
Mbaïki C.A.R. 84 D3
Mbala Zambia 87 D3
Mbale Uganda 86 B3
Mbalmayo Cameroon 83 E7
Mbam → Cameroon 83 E7
Mbamba Bay Tanzania 87 E3
Mbandaka Dem. Rep. of the Congo 84 D3
Mbanga Cameroon 83 E6
Mbanza Congo Angola 84 F2
Mbanza Ngungu Dem. Rep. of the Congo 84 F2
Mbarangandu Tanzania 87 D4
Mbarara Uganda 86 C3
Mbatto Ivory C. 82 D4
Mbengga = Beqa Fiji 91 a
Mbenkuru → Tanzania 87 D4
Mberengwa Zimbabwe 87 G2
Mberengwa, Mt. Zimbabwe 87 G2
Mberubu Nigeria 83 D6
Mbesuma Zambia 87 E3
Mbeya Tanzania 87 D3
Mbeya ☐ Tanzania 86 D3

Mbhashe → S. Africa 89 E4
M'bili Sudan 81 F2
Mbinga Tanzania 87 E4
Mbini = Río Muni ☐ Eq. Guin. 84 D2
Mboki C.A.R. 81 F2
M'bonge Cameroon 83 E6
Mboro Senegal 82 B1
M'boukou, Rés. de Cameroon 83 D7
Mboune Senegal 82 C2
Mboune Senegal 82 C1
Mbout Mauritania 82 B2
Mbuji-Mayi Dem. Rep. of the Congo 86 D1
Mbulu Tanzania 86 C4
Mburucuyá Argentina 126 B4
Mburucuyá △ Argentina 126 B4
Mchinja Tanzania 87 D4
Mchinji Malawi 87 E3
Mdantsane S. Africa 89 E4
Mead, L. U.S.A. 111 J12
Meade U.S.A. 112 G4
Meadow Lake Canada 103 C7
Meadow Lake △ Canada 103 C7
Meadow Valley Wash → U.S.A. 111 J12
Meadville U.S.A. 114 E4
Meaford Canada 114 B4
Mealhada Portugal 36 E2
Mealpaeg L. Canada 105 C8
Mealy Mts. Canada 105 B8
Meander River Canada 102 B5
Meares, C. U.S.A. 108 D1
Mearim → Brazil 125 D10
Meath ☐ Ireland 12 C5
Meath Park Canada 103 C7
Meaulne France 19 F9
Meaux France 19 D9
Mebechi-Gawa → Japan 54 D10
Mebulu, Tanjung Indonesia 63 K18
Mecanhelas Mozam. 87 F4
Mecca = Makkah Si. Arabia 80 C4
Mecca U.S.A. 111 M10
Mechanicsburg U.S.A. 114 F8
Mechanicville U.S.A. 115 D11
Mechara Ethiopia 81 F5
Mechelen Belgium 17 C4
Mecheria Algeria 78 B5
Mechernich Germany 24 E2
Mechetinskaya Russia 35 G5
Mecidiye Turkey 45 F10
Mecitözü Turkey 72 B6
Mecklenburg Germany 22 B7
Mecklenburg-Vorpommern ☐ Germany 24 B8
Mecklenburger Bucht Germany 24 A7
Meconta Mozam. 87 E4
Mecsek Hungary 28 D3
Meda Portugal 36 E3
Medan Indonesia 62 D1
Médanos de Coro △ Venezuela 121 D6
Medanosa, Pta. Argentina 128 F3
Mede Italy 40 C5
Médéa Algeria 78 A6
Mededa Bos.-H. 28 G4
Medellín Colombia 124 B3
Medelpad Sweden 10 B10
Medemblik Neths. 17 B5
Mederdra Mauritania 82 B1
Medford Mass., U.S.A. 115 D13
Medford Oreg., U.S.A. 108 E2
Medford Wis., U.S.A. 112 C8
Medgidia Romania 29 F13
Medi Sudan 81 F3
Media Agua Argentina 126 C2
Media Luna Argentina 126 C2
Medianeira Brazil 127 B5
Medias Romania 29 D9
Medicina Italy 41 D8
Medicine Bow U.S.A. 108 F10
Medicine Bow Mts. U.S.A. 108 F10
Medicine Bow Pk. U.S.A. 108 F10
Medicine Hat Canada 103 D6
Medicine Lake U.S.A. 108 B11
Medicine Lodge U.S.A. 112 G4
Medina = Al Madīnah Si. Arabia 70 E3
Medina N. Dak., U.S.A. 112 B4
Medina N.Y., U.S.A. 114 C6
Medina Ohio, U.S.A. 114 E3
Medina → U.S.A. 116 G5
Medina de Pomar Spain 36 C7
Medina de Ríoseco Spain 36 D5
Medina del Campo Spain 36 D6
Medina L. U.S.A. 116 G5
Medina Sidonia Spain 37 J5
Medinaceli Spain 38 D2
Medinipur India 69 H12
Mediterranean Sea Europe 6 H7
Médoc France 20 C3
Medulin Croatia 41 D10
Medveda Serbia 44 D5
Medvedevo Russia 34 B8
Medveditsa → Tver, Russia 32 D9
Medveditsa → Volgograd, Russia 34 F6
Medvedok Russia 34 B10

Medvezhi, Ostrava *Russia* **53** B17
Medvezhyegorsk *Russia* **52** C4
Medway □ *U.K.* **15** F8
Medway → *U.K.* **15** F8
Medzev *Slovak Rep.* **27** C13
Medzilaborce *Slovak Rep.* **27** B14
Medžitlija *Macedonia* **44** F5
Meekatharra *Australia* **93** E2
Meeker *U.S.A.* **108** F10
Meersburg *Germany* **25** H5
Meerut *India* **68** E7
Meeteetse *U.S.A.* **108** D9
Mega *Ethiopia* **81** G4
Megalo Horio *Greece* **47** E9
Megalonisos *Greece* **46** D6
Megalopoli *Greece* **46** D4
Meganisi *Greece* **46** C2
Megara *Greece* **46** D5
Megasini *India* **69** J12
Megdovas = Tavropos →
  Greece **46** B3
Megève *France* **21** C10
Meghalaya □ *India* **67** G17
Meghezez *Ethiopia* **81** F4
Meghna → *Bangla.* **67** H17
Megion *Russia* **52** C8
Mégiscane, L. *Canada* **104** C4
Megiste *Greece* **47** E11
Megisti *Greece* **47** E11
Megra *Russia* **32** B9
Mehadia *Romania* **28** F7
Meharry, Mt. *Australia* **92** D2
Mehedeby *Sweden* **10** D11
Mehedinți □ *Romania* **28** F7
Meheisa *Sudan* **80** D3
Mehlville *U.S.A.* **112** F8
Mehndawal *India* **69** F10
Mehr Jān *Iran* **71** C7
Mehrābād *Iran* **73** D12
Mehrābān *Iran* **73** C12
Mehrān *Iran* **73** F12
Mehrān → *Iran* **71** E7
Mehrgarh *Pakistan* **68** E2
Mehrīz *Iran* **71** D7
Mehun-sur-Yèvre *France* **19** E9
Mei Jiang → *China* **59** E11
Mei Xian *China* **56** G4
Meicheng *China* **59** C12
Meichengzhen *China* **59** C8
Meichuan *China* **59** B10
Meigu *China* **58** C4
Meihekou *China* **57** C13
Meiktila *Burma* **67** J19
Meinerzhagen *Germany* **24** D3
Meiningen *Germany* **24** E6
Meira, Serra de *Spain* **36** B3
Meiringen *Switz.* **25** J4
Meishan *China* **58** B4
Meissen *Germany* **24** D9
Meissner *Germany* **24** D5
Meissner-Kaufunger
  Wald △ *Germany* **24** D5
Meitan *China* **58** D6
Meizhou *China* **59** E11
Meja *India* **69** G10
Mejillones *Chile* **126** A1
Mekdela *Ethiopia* **81** E4
Mekele *Ethiopia* **81** E4
Mekerghene, Sebkra *Algeria* **78** C6
Mekhtar *Pakistan* **66** D6
Meknès *Morocco* **78** B4
Meko *Nigeria* **83** D5
Mekong → *Asia* **65** H6
Mekongga *Indonesia* **63** E6
Mekrou → *Benin* **83** C5
Mekvari = Kür →
  Azerbaijan **73** C13
Mel *Italy* **41** B9
Melagiri Hills *India* **66** N10
Melaka *Malaysia* **65** L4
Melalap *Malaysia* **62** C5
Melambes *Greece* **49** D6
Melaya *Indonesia* **63** J17
Melbourne *Australia* **95** F4
Melbourne *U.S.A.* **117** G14
Melchor Múzquiz *Mexico* **118** B4
Melchor Ocampo *Mexico* **118** C4
Méldola *Italy* **41** D9
Meldorf *Germany* **24** A5
Melegnano *Italy* **40** C6
Melenci *Serbia* **28** E5
Melenki *Russia* **34** C5
Mélèzes → *Canada* **104** A5
Melfi *Italy* **43** B8
Melfort *Canada* **103** C8
Melfort *Zimbabwe* **87** F3
Melgaço *Portugal* **36** C2
Melgar de Fernamental
  Spain **36** C6
Melhus *Norway* **8** E14
Melide *Spain* **36** C2
Meligales *Greece* **46** D3
Melilli *Italy* **43** E8
Melipilla *Chile* **126** C1
Melissa *Canada* **114** A5

Melissa, Akra *Greece* **49** D6
Melissa Oros *Greece* **47** D8
Melita *Canada* **103** D8
Mélito di Porto Salvo *Italy* **43** E8
Melitopol *Ukraine* **33** J8
Melk *Austria* **26** C8
Mellan Fryken *Sweden* **10** E7
Mellansel *Sweden* **8** E18
Melle *France* **20** B3
Melle *Germany* **24** C4
Mellen *U.S.A.* **112** B8
Mellerud *Sweden* **11** F6
Mellette *U.S.A.* **112** C4
Mellid = Melide *Spain* **36** C2
Mellieha *Malta* **49** D1
Mellit *Sudan* **81** E2
Mellrichstadt *Germany* **24** E6
Melnik *Bulgaria* **44** E7
Mělník *Czech Rep.* **26** A7
Melnytsya Podilska *Ukraine* **29** B11
Melo *Uruguay* **127** C5
Melolo *Indonesia* **63** F6
Melouprey *Cambodia* **64** F5
Melrhir, Chott *Algeria* **78** B7
Melrose *Australia* **95** E4
Melrose *U.K.* **13** F6
Melrose *Minn., U.S.A.* **112** C6
Melrose *N. Mex., U.S.A.* **109** J12
Melstone *U.S.A.* **108** C10
Melsungen *Germany* **24** D5
Melton Mowbray *U.K.* **14** E7
Melun *France* **19** D9
Melut *Sudan* **81** E3
Melville *Canada* **103** C8
Melville, C. *Australia* **94** A3
Melville, L. *Canada* **105** B8
Melville B. *Australia* **94** A2
Melville I. *Australia* **92** B5
Melville I. *Canada* **101** B2
Melville Pen. *Canada* **101** C11
Melvin, Lough *Ireland* **12** B3
Mélykút *Hungary* **28** D4
Memaliaj *Albania* **44** F3
Memba *Mozam.* **87** E5
Memboro *Indonesia* **63** F5
Membrilla *Spain* **37** G7
Memel = Klaipėda *Lithuania* **30** C8
Memel *S. Africa* **89** D4
Memmingen *Germany* **25** H6
Mempawah *Indonesia* **62** D3
Memphis *Egypt* **80** J7
Memphis *Mich., U.S.A.* **114** D2
Memphis *Tenn., U.S.A.* **117** D9
Memphis *Tex., U.S.A.* **116** D4
Memphrémagog, L.
  N. Amer. **115** B12
Mena *Ukraine* **33** G7
Mena *U.S.A.* **116** D7
Mena → *Ethiopia* **81** F5
Menai Strait *U.K.* **14** D3
Ménaka *Mali* **83** B5
Menan = Chao Phraya →
  Thailand **64** F3
Menarandra → *Madag.* **89** D7
Menard *U.S.A.* **116** F5
Menard Fracture Zone
  Pac. Oc. **97** M18
Menawashei *Sudan* **81** E1
Mendaña Fracture Zone
  Pac. Oc. **97** J18
Mendawai → *Indonesia* **62** E4
Mende *France* **20** D7
Mendebo Mts. *Ethiopia* **81** F4
Mendeleyev Ridge *Arctic* **4** B17
Menden *Germany* **24** D3
Menderes *Turkey* **47** C9
Mendhar *India* **69** C6
Mendi *Ethiopia* **81** F4
Mendip Hills *U.K.* **15** F5
Mendocino *U.S.A.* **108** G2
Mendocino, C. *U.S.A.* **108** F1
Mendocino Fracture Zone
  Pac. Oc. **97** D13
Mendota *Calif., U.S.A.* **110** J6
Mendota *Ill., U.S.A.* **112** E9
Mendoyo *Indonesia* **63** J17
Mendoza *Argentina* **126** C2
Mendoza □ *Argentina* **126** C2
Mene Grande *Venezuela* **124** B4
Menemen *Turkey* **47** C9
Menen *Belgium* **17** D3
Menfi *Italy* **42** E5
Mengdingjie *China* **58** F2
Mengë *Slovenia* **41** B11
Menggala *Indonesia* **62** E3
Menghai *China* **58** G3
Mengíbar *Spain* **37** H7
Mengjin *China* **56** G7
Mengla *China* **58** G3
Menglian *China* **58** F2
Mengshan *China* **59** E8
Mengyin *China* **57** G9
Mengzhe *China* **58** G3
Mengzi *China* **58** F4
Menihek *Canada* **105** B6
Menihek L. *Canada* **105** B6
Menin = Menen *Belgium* **17** D3
Menindee *Australia* **95** E3
Menindee L. *Australia* **95** E3

Menindee L. *Australia* **95** E3
Meningie *Australia* **95** F2
Menjangan, Pulau
  Indonesia **63** J17
Menlo Park *U.S.A.* **110** H4
Menominee *U.S.A.* **112** C10
Menominee → *U.S.A.* **112** C10
Menomonie *U.S.A.* **112** C10
Menongue *Angola* **85** G3
Menorca *Spain* **48** B11
Menorca ✈ (MAH) *Spain* **38** F9
Mentakab *Malaysia* **65** L4
Mentawai, Kepulauan
  Indonesia **62** E1
Menton *France* **21** E11
Mentor *U.S.A.* **114** E3
Menzies *Australia* **93** E3
Meob B. *Namibia* **88** C1
Me'ona *Israel* **74** B4
Meoqui *Mexico* **118** B3
Mepaco *Mozam.* **87** F3
Meppel *Neths.* **17** B6
Meppen *Germany* **24** C3
Mequinenza *Spain* **38** D5
Mequinenza, Embalse de
  Spain **38** D5
Mer *France* **18** E8
Merak *Indonesia* **63** F12
Meramangye, L. *Australia* **93** E5
Meran = Merano *Italy* **41** B8
Merano *Italy* **41** B8
Merate *Italy* **40** C6
Merauke *Indonesia* **63** F10
Merbein *Australia* **95** E3
Merbuk, Gunung *Indonesia* **63** J17
Merca = Marka *Somali Rep.* **75** G3
Mercantour △ *France* **21** D10
Mercato Saraceno *Italy* **41** E9
Merced *U.S.A.* **110** H6
Merced → *U.S.A.* **110** H6
Mercedes *B. Aires, Argentina* **126** C4
Mercedes *Corrientes,*
  Argentina **126** B4
Mercedes *San Luis, Argentina* **126** C2
Mercedes *Uruguay* **126** C4
Merceditas *Chile* **126** B1
Mercer *N.Z.* **91** B5
Mercer *U.S.A.* **114** E4
Mercer Island *U.S.A.* **110** C4
Mercury *U.S.A.* **111** J11
Mercy, C. *Canada* **101** C13
Merdignac *France* **18** D4
Mere *U.K.* **15** F5
Meredith, C. *Falk. Is.* **128** G4
Meredith, L. *U.S.A.* **116** D4
Merefa *Ukraine* **33** H9
Merei *Romania* **29** E11
Merga = Nukheila *Sudan* **80** D2
Mergui *Burma* **64** F2
Mergui Arch. = Myeik
  Kyunzu *Burma* **65** G1
Méribel-les-Allues *France* **21** C10
Meriç *Turkey* **45** E10
Meriç → *Turkey* **45** F10
Mérida *Mexico* **119** C7
Mérida *Spain* **37** G4
Mérida *Venezuela* **124** B4
Mérida, Cord. de *Venezuela* **124** B4
Meriden *U.K.* **15** E6
Meriden *U.S.A.* **115** E12
Meridian *Calif., U.S.A.* **110** F5
Meridian *Idaho, U.S.A.* **108** E5
Meridian *Miss., U.S.A.* **117** E10
Mérignac *France* **20** D3
Mérinaghène *Senegal* **82** B1
Merinda *Australia* **94** C4
Mering *Germany* **25** G6
Meringa *Nigeria* **83** C7
Merir *Pac. Oc.* **63** D8
Merirumā *Brazil* **125** C8
Merkel *U.S.A.* **116** E4
Mermaid Reef *Australia* **92** C2
Merowe *Sudan* **80** D3
Merowe Dam *Sudan* **80** D3
Merredin *Australia* **93** F2
Merrick *U.K.* **13** F4
Merrickville *Canada* **115** B9
Merrill *Oreg., U.S.A.* **108** E3
Merrill *Wis., U.S.A.* **112** C9
Merriman *U.S.A.* **112** D3
Merritt *Canada* **102** C4
Merritt Island *U.S.A.* **117** G14
Merriwa *Australia* **95** E5
Merry I. *Canada* **104** A4
Merryville *U.S.A.* **116** F8
Mersa Fatma *Eritrea* **81** E5
Mersch *Lux.* **17** E6
Merse → *Italy* **41** E8
Mersea I. *U.K.* **15** F8
Merseburg *Germany* **24** D7
Mersey → *U.K.* **14** D4
Merseyside □ *U.K.* **14** D4
Mersin = İçel *Turkey* **72** D6
Mersing *Malaysia* **65** L4
Merta *India* **68** F6
Merta Road *India* **68** F5
Merthyr Tydfil *U.K.* **15** F4

Merthyr Tydfil □ *U.K.* **15** F4
Merti *Kenya* **86** B4
Mértola *Portugal* **37** H3
Mertzon *U.S.A.* **116** F4
Méru *France* **19** C9
Meru *Kenya* **86** B4
Meru *Tanzania* **86** C4
Meru △ *Kenya* **86** B4
Merville *France* **19** B9
Méry-sur-Seine *France* **19** D10
Merzig *Germany* **25** F2
Mesa *U.S.A.* **109** K8
Mesa Verde △ *U.S.A.* **109** H9
Mesagne *Italy* **43** B10
Mesanagros *Greece* **49** C9
Mesaoría *Cyprus* **49** D12
Meschede *Germany* **24** D4
Mescit *Turkey* **73** B9
Mesfinto *Ethiopia* **81** E4
Mesgouez, L. *Canada* **104** B5
Meshed = Mashhad *Iran* **71** B8
Meshgīn Shahr *Iran* **73** C12
Meshoppen *U.S.A.* **115** E8
Meshra er Req *Sudan* **81** F2
Mesilinka → *Canada* **102** B4
Meslay-du-Maine *France* **18** E6
Mesocco *Switz.* **25** J5
Mesologi *Greece* **46** C3
Mesongi *Greece* **49** B3
Mesopotamia = Al Jazirah
  Iraq **73** E10
Mesopotamia *U.S.A.* **114** E4
Mesopotamo *Greece* **46** B2
Mesoraca *Italy* **43** C9
Mésou Volímais = Volimes
  Greece **46** D2
Mesquite *U.S.A.* **109** H6
Messaad *Algeria* **78** B6
Messac *France* **18** E5
Messalo → *Mozam.* **87** E4
Méssaména *Cameroon* **83** E7
Messara, Kolpos *Greece* **49** D6
Messina = Musina *S. Africa* **89** C5
Messina *Italy* **43** D8
Messina, Str. di *Italy* **43** D8
Messini *Greece* **46** D4
Messinia □ *Greece* **46** D3
Messiniakos Kolpos *Greece* **46** E4
Messkirch *Germany* **25** H5
Messlingen *Sweden* **10** B6
Mesta → *Bulgaria* **44** E7
Mesta, Akra *Greece* **47** C7
Mestanza *Spain* **37** G6
Mestre *Italy* **41** C9
Meta □ *S. Amer.* **124** C4
Meta Incognita Pen. *Canada*
  101 C13
Metabetchouan *Canada* **105** C5
Metairie *U.S.A.* **117** G9
Metalici, Munții *Romania* **28** D7
Metaline Falls *U.S.A.* **108** B5
Metallifere, Colline *Italy* **40** E8
Metán *Argentina* **126** B3
Metangula *Mozam.* **87** E3
Metauro → *Italy* **41** E10
Metcalfe *Canada* **115** A9
Metema *Ethiopia* **81** E4
Metengobalame *Mozam.* **87** E3
Methana *Greece* **46** D5
Methoni *Greece* **46** E3
Methven *N.Z.* **91** E3
Metil *Mozam.* **87** F4
Metina → *Greece*
Metkovets *Bulgaria* **44** C7
Metković *Croatia* **41** E14
Metlakatla *U.S.A.* **100** D6
Metlika *Slovenia* **41** C12
Metropolis *U.S.A.* **112** G9
Metropolitana □ *Chile* **126** C1
Metsovo *Greece* **46** B3
Metu *Ethiopia* **81** F4
Metz *France* **19** C13
Metzingen *Germany* **25** G5
Meulaboh *Indonesia* **62** D1
Meulewit *Indonesia* **62** C1
Meung-sur-Loire *France* **19** E8
Meureudu *Indonesia* **62** C1
Meurthe → *France* **19** D13
Meurthe-et-Moselle □
  France **19** D13
Meuse □ *France* **19** C12
Meuse → *Europe* **17** D5
Meuselwitz *Germany* **24** D8
Mexia *U.S.A.* **116** F6
Mexiana, I. *Brazil* **125** D9
Mexicali *Mexico* **111** N11
Mexican Plateau *Mexico* **98** G9
Mexican Water *U.S.A.* **109** H9
México *Mexico* **119** D5
Mexico *Maine, U.S.A.* **115** B14
Mexico *Mo., U.S.A.* **112** F8
Mexico *N.Y., U.S.A.* **115** C8
México □ *Mexico* **119** D5
Mexico ■ *Cent. Amer.* **118** C4
México, Ciudad de *Mexico* **119** D5
Mexico, G. of *Cent. Amer.* **119** C7
Mexico B. *U.S.A.* **115** C8
Meydān-e Naftūn *Iran* **71** D6

Meydani, Ra's-e *Iran* **71** E8
Meyenburg *Germany* **24** B8
Meyers Chuck *U.S.A.* **102** B2
Meymac *France* **20** C6
Meymaneh *Afghan.* **66** B4
Meyrueis *France* **20** D7
Meyssac *France* **20** C5
Meyzieu *France* **21** C8
Mèze *France* **20** E7
Mezen *Russia* **52** C5
Mezen → *Russia* **6** B14
Mézenc, Mt. *France* **21** D8
Mezdra *Bulgaria* **44** C7
Mézidon-Canon *France* **18** C6
Mézières-en-Brenne *France* **20** B5
Mézilhac *France* **21** D8
Mézin *France* **20** D4
Mezőberény *Hungary* **28** D6
Mezőfalva *Hungary* **28** D3
Mezőhegyes *Hungary* **28** D5
Mezőkovácsháza *Hungary* **28** D5
Mezőkövesd *Hungary* **28** C5
Mézos *France* **20** D2
Meztúr *Hungary* **28** C5
Mezha → *Russia* **32** E6
Mezhdurechensk *Russia* **52** D9
Mezhdurechenskiy *Russia* **52** D7
Mezhdurechye *Russia* **52** D7
Mezquital *Mexico* **118** C4
Mezzolombardo *Italy* **40** B8
Mfolozi → *S. Africa* **89** D5
Mgeta *Tanzania* **87** D4
Mglin *Russia* **33** F7
Mhlaba Hills *Zimbabwe* **87** F3
Mhow *India* **68** H6
Miahuatlán *Mexico* **119** D5
Miajadas *Spain* **37** F5
Miami *Fla., U.S.A.* **117** J14
Miami *Okla., U.S.A.* **116** C7
Miami *Tex., U.S.A.* **116** D4
Miami Beach *U.S.A.* **117** J14
Mian Xian *China* **56** H4
Mianchi *China* **56** G6
Miāndarreh *Iran* **71** C7
Miandrivazo *Madag.* **89** B8
Miāneh *Iran* **73** D12
Mianning *China* **58** C4
Mianwali *Pakistan* **68** C4
Mianyang *China* **58** B5
Miaoli *Taiwan* **59** E13
Miarinarivo *Antananarivo,*
  Madag. **89** B8
Miarinarivo *Toamasina,*
  Madag. **89** B8
Miariravaratra *Madag.* **89** C8
Miass *Russia* **52** D7
Miasteczko Krajeńskie
  Poland **31** E4
Miastko *Poland* **30** E3
Mica *S. Africa* **89** C5
Micăsasa *Romania* **29** D9
Michalovce *Slovak Rep.* **27** C14
Michigan □ *U.S.A.* **113** C11
Michigan, L. *U.S.A.* **112** D10
Michigan City *U.S.A.* **112** E10
Michika *Nigeria* **83** C7
Michipicoten I. *Canada* **104** C2
Michoacán □ *Mexico* **118** D4
Michurin *Bulgaria* **45** D11
Michurinsk *Russia* **34** D5
Micoud *St. Lucia* **121** f
Micronesia *Pac. Oc.* **96** G7
Micronesia, Federated
  States of ■ *Pac. Oc.* **90** A8
Mid-Pacific Seamounts
  Pac. Oc. **96** F10
Midai *Indonesia* **62** D3
Midale *Canada* **103** D8
Middelburg *Neths.* **17** C3
Middelburg *Eastern Cape,*
  S. Africa **88** E4
Middelburg *Mpumalanga,*
  S. Africa **89** D4
Middelfart *Denmark* **11** J3
Middelpos *S. Africa* **88** E3
Middelwit *S. Africa* **88** C4
Middle Alkali L. *U.S.A.* **108** F3
Middle America Trench =
  Guatemala Trench
  Pac. Oc. **98** H10
Middle Bass I. *U.S.A.* **114** E2
Middle East *Asia* **50** E5
Middle Fork Feather →
  U.S.A. **110** F5
Middle I. *Australia* **93** F3
Middle Loup → *U.S.A.* **112** E4
Middleboro *U.S.A.* **115** E14
Middleburg *Fla., U.S.A.* **117** F14
Middleburg *Pa., U.S.A.* **114** F7
Middleburgh *U.S.A.* **115** D10
Middlebury *U.S.A.* **115** B11
Middlefield *U.S.A.* **114** E3
Middlemount *Australia* **94** C4
Middleport *N.Y., U.S.A.* **114** C6
Middleport *Ohio, U.S.A.* **113** F12
Middlesboro *U.S.A.* **113** G12
Middlesbrough *U.K.* **14** C6

Middlesbrough □ *U.K.* **14** C6
Middlesex *Belize* **120** C2
Middlesex *N.J., U.S.A.* **115** F10
Middlesex *N.Y., U.S.A.* **114** D7
Middleton *Australia* **94** C3
Middleton *Canada* **105** D6
Middleton Cr. → *Australia* **94** C3
Middletown *U.K.* **12** B5
Middletown *Calif., U.S.A.* **110** G4
Middletown *Conn., U.S.A.* **115** E12
Middletown *N.Y., U.S.A.* **115** E10
Middletown *Ohio, U.S.A.* **113** F11
Middletown *Pa., U.S.A.* **115** F8
Midge Point *Australia* **94** J6
Midhurst *Canada* **114** B5
Midhurst *U.K.* **15** G7
Midi, Canal du → *France* **20** E5
Midi d'Ossau, Pic du *France* **20** F3
Midi-Pyrénées □ *France* **20** E5
Midland *Australia* **93** F2
Midland *Canada* **114** B5
Midland *Calif., U.S.A.* **111** M12
Midland *Mich., U.S.A.* **113** D11
Midland *Pa., U.S.A.* **114** F4
Midland *Tex., U.S.A.* **116** F3
Midlands □ *Zimbabwe* **87** F3
Midleton *Ireland* **12** E3
Midlothian □ *U.K.* **13** F5
Midongy,
  Tangorombohitr' i *Madag.* **89** C8
Midongy Atsimo *Madag.* **89** C8
Midou → *France* **20** E3
Midouze → *France* **20** E3
Midsayap *Phil.* **61** H6
Midtjylland □ *Denmark* **11** H2
Midu *China* **58** E3
Midway Is. *Pac. Oc.* **96** E10
Midway Wells *U.S.A.* **111** N11
Midwest *U.S.A.* **107** B9
Midwest *Wyo., U.S.A.* **108** E10
Midwest City *U.S.A.* **116** D6
Midyat *Turkey* **73** D9
Midzŏr *Bulgaria* **44** C6
Mie □ *Japan* **55** G8
Miechów *Poland* **31** H7
Miedwie, Jezioro *Poland* **31** E1
Międzybórz *Poland* **31** G4
Międzychód *Poland* **31** F2
Międzylesie *Poland* **31** H3
Międzyrzec Podlaski *Poland* **31** G9
Międzyrzecz *Poland* **31** F2
Międzyzdroje *Poland* **30** E1
Miejska Górka *Poland* **31** G3
Miélan *France* **20** E4
Mielec *Poland* **31** H8
Mienga *Angola* **88** B2
Miercurea-Ciuc *Romania* **29** D10
Miercurea Sibiului *Romania* **29** E8
Mieres *Spain* **36** B5
Mieroszów *Poland* **31** H3
Mieso *Ethiopia* **81** F5
Mieszkowice *Poland* **31** F1
Mifflintown *U.S.A.* **114** F7
Mifraz Ḥefa *Israel* **74** C4
Migennes *France* **19** E10
Migliarino *Italy* **41** D8
Migliarino-San Rossore-
  Massaciuccoli △ *Italy* **40** E7
Migori *Kenya* **86** C3
Miguel Alemán, Presa
  Mexico **119** D5
Miguelturra *Spain* **37** G7
Mihăileni *Romania* **29** C11
Mihăilești *Romania* **29** F10
Mihailovca *Moldova* **29** D13
Mihalgazi *Turkey* **47** A12
Mihaliçcik *Turkey* **72** C4
Mihara *Japan* **55** G6
Miheșu de Câmpie *Romania* **29** D9
Mijas *Spain* **37** J6
Mikese *Tanzania* **86** D4
Mikha-Tskhakaya =
  Senaki *Georgia* **35** J6
Mikhailovka =
  Mykhaylivka *Ukraine* **33** J8
Mikhaylov *Russia* **32** E10
Mikhaylovgrad =
  Montana *Bulgaria* **44** C7
Mikhaylovka *Russia* **34** E6
Mikhnevo *Russia* **32** E9
Mikines *Greece* **46** D4
Mikkeli *Finland* **32** B4
Mikkwa → *Canada* **102** B6
Míkonos = Mykonos *Greece* **47** D7
Mikri Prespa, L. *Greece* **44** F5
Mikro Derio *Greece* **45** E10
Mikstat *Poland* **31** G4
Mikulov *Czech Rep.* **27** C9
Mikumi *Tanzania* **86** D4
Mikumi △ *Tanzania* **86** D4
Milaca *U.S.A.* **112** C7
Milagro *Ecuador* **124** D3
Milagros *Phil.* **61** E5
Milan = Milano *Italy* **40** C6
Milan *Mo., U.S.A.* **112** E7
Milan *Tenn., U.S.A.* **117** D10
Milange *Mozam.* **87** F4

Milano *Italy* **40** C6
Milano Linate ✈ (LIN) *Italy* **40** C6
Milanoa *Madag.* **89** A8
Milâs *Turkey* **47** D9
Milazzo *Italy* **43** D8
Milbank *U.S.A.* **112** C5
Milden *Canada* **103** C7
Mildenhall *U.K.* **15** E8
Mildmay *Canada* **114** B3
Mildura *Australia* **95** E3
Mile *China* **58** E4
Miles *Australia* **95** D5
Miles City *U.S.A.* **108** C11
Mileşti *Moldova* **29** C13
Mileto *Italy* **43** D9
Miletto, Mte. *Italy* **43** A7
Miletus *Turkey* **47** D9
Milevsko *Czech Rep.* **26** B7
Milford *Calif., U.S.A.* **110** E6
Milford *Conn., U.S.A.* **115** E11
Milford *Del., U.S.A.* **113** F16
Milford *Mass., U.S.A.* **115** D13
Milford *N.H., U.S.A.* **115** D13
Milford *N.Y., U.S.A.* **115** D10
Milford *Pa., U.S.A.* **115** E10
Milford *Utah, U.S.A.* **108** G7
Milford Haven *U.K.* **15** F2
Milford Sd. *N.Z.* **91** F1
Milford Sound *N.Z.* **91** F1
Milḥ, Baḥr al = Razāzah,
    Buḥayrat ar *Iraq* **73** F10
Milicz *Poland* **31** G4
Milies *Greece* **46** B5
Milikapiti *Australia* **92** B5
Miling *Australia* **93** F2
Militello in Val di Catánia
    Italy **43** E7
Milk, Wadi el → *Sudan* **80** D3
Milk River *Canada* **102** D6
Mill → *U.S.A.* **114** D1
Mill I. *Antarctica* **5** C8
Mill Valley *U.S.A.* **110** H4
Millárs → *Spain* **38** F4
Millau *France* **20** D7
Millbridge *Canada* **114** B7
Millbrook *Canada* **114** B6
Millbrook *Ala., U.S.A.* **117** E11
Millbrook *N.Y., U.S.A.* **115** E11
Mille Lacs, L. des *Canada* **104** C1
Mille Lacs L. *U.S.A.* **112** B7
Milledgeville *U.S.A.* **117** E13
Millen *U.S.A.* **117** E14
Millennium I. = Caroline I.
    Kiribati **97** H12
Miller *U.S.A.* **112** C4
Miller Lake *Canada* **114** A3
Millerovo *Russia* **35** F5
Millersburg *Ohio, U.S.A.* **114** F3
Millersburg *Pa., U.S.A.* **114** F8
Millerton *U.S.A.* **115** E11
Millerton L. *U.S.A.* **110** J7
Millet *St. Lucia* **121** f
Millevaches, Plateau de
    France **20** C6
Millheim *U.S.A.* **114** F7
Millicent *Australia* **95** F3
Millington *U.S.A.* **117** D10
Millinocket *U.S.A.* **113** C19
Millmerran *Australia* **95** D5
Millom *U.K.* **14** C4
Mills L. *Canada* **102** A5
Millsboro *U.S.A.* **114** G5
Millstream Chichester △
    Australia **92** D2
Millstreet *Ireland* **12** D2
Milltown Malbay *Ireland* **12** D2
Millville *N.J., U.S.A.* **113** F16
Millville *Pa., U.S.A.* **115** E8
Millwood L. *U.S.A.* **116** E8
Milna *Croatia* **41** E13
Milne → *Australia* **94** C2
Milo *U.S.A.* **113** C19
Milon, Akra *Greece* **49** C10
Milos *Greece* **46** E6
Miłosław *Poland* **31** F4
Milot *Albania* **44** E3
Milparinka *Australia* **95** D3
Milpitas *U.S.A.* **110** H5
Miltenberg *Germany* **25** F5
Milton *N.S., Canada* **105** D7
Milton *Ont., Canada* **114** C5
Milton *N.Z.* **91** G2
Milton *Calif., U.S.A.* **110** G6
Milton *Fla., U.S.A.* **117** F11
Milton *Pa., U.S.A.* **114** F8
Milton *Vt., U.S.A.* **115** B11
Milton-Freewater *U.S.A.* **108** D4
Milton Keynes *U.K.* **15** E7
Milton Keynes □ *U.K.* **15** E7
Miluo *China* **59** C9
Milverton *Canada* **114** C4
Milwaukee *U.S.A.* **112** D10
Milwaukee Deep *Atl. Oc.* **121** C6
Milwaukie *U.S.A.* **110** E4
Mim *Ghana* **82** D4
Mimizan *France* **20** D2

Mimoň *Czech Rep.* **26** A7
Min Jiang → *Fujian, China* **59** E12
Min Jiang → *Sichuan, China* **58** C5
Min Xian *China* **56** G3
Minā' Jabal 'Alī *U.A.E.* **71** E7
Mina Pirquitas *Argentina* **126** A2
Mīnā Su'ud *Si. Arabia* **71** D6
Mīnā'al Aḥmadī *Kuwait* **71** D6
Minago → *Canada* **103** C9
Minaki *Canada* **103** D10
Minamata *Japan* **55** H5
Minami-Arapusa △ *Japan* **55** G9
Minami-Tori-Shima *Pac. Oc.* **96** E7
Minas *Uruguay* **127** C4
Minas, Sierra de las
    Guatemala **120** C2
Minas Basin *Canada* **105** C7
Minas de Riotinto *Spain* **37** H4
Minas Gerais □ *Brazil* **125** G9
Minatitlán *Mexico* **119** D6
Minbu *Burma* **67** J19
Minchinabad *Pakistan* **68** D5
Mincio → *Italy* **40** C7
Minčol *Slovak Rep.* **27** B13
Mindanao *Phil.* **61** H6
Mindanao Sea = Bohol Sea
    Phil. **63** C6
Mindanao Trench *Pac. Oc.* **61** F7
Mindel → *Germany* **25** G6
Mindelheim *Germany* **25** G6
Mindelo *C. Verde Is.* **78** b
Minden *Canada* **114** B6
Minden *Germany* **24** C4
Minden *La., U.S.A.* **116** E8
Minden *Nev., U.S.A.* **110** G7
Mindibungu = Billiluna
    Australia **92** C4
Mindiptana *Indonesia* **63** F10
Mindoro *Phil.* **61** E4
Mindoro Str. *Phil.* **61** E4
Mine *Japan* **55** G5
Minehead *U.K.* **15** F4
Mineola *N.Y., U.S.A.* **115** F11
Mineola *Tex., U.S.A.* **116** E7
Mineral King *U.S.A.* **110** J8
Mineral Wells *U.S.A.* **116** E5
Mineralnyye Vody *Russia* **35** H6
Miners Bay *Canada* **114** B6
Minersville *U.S.A.* **115** F8
Minerva *N.Y., U.S.A.* **115** C11
Minerva *Ohio, U.S.A.* **114** F3
Minervino Murge *Italy* **43** A9
Minetto *U.S.A.* **115** C8
Mingäçevir *Azerbaijan* **35** K8
Mingäçevir Su Anbarı
    Azerbaijan **35** K8
Mingan *Canada* **105** B7
Mingechaur = Mingäçevir
    Azerbaijan **35** K8
Mingechaurskoye
    Vdkhr. = Mingäçevir Su
    Anbarı *Azerbaijan* **35** K8
Mingela *Australia* **94** B4
Mingenew *Australia* **93** E2
Mingera Cr. → *Australia* **94** C2
Minggang *China* **59** A10
Mingguang *China* **59** A13
Mingin *Burma* **67** H19
Mingir *Moldova* **29** D13
Minglanilla *Spain* **39** F3
Minglun *China* **58** E7
Mingo Junction *U.S.A.* **114** F4
Mingora *Pakistan* **68** B5
Mingorría *Spain* **36** E6
Mingshan *China* **58** B4
Mingteke Daban =
    Mintaka Pass *Pakistan* **69** A6
Mingxi *China* **59** D11
Mingyuegue *China* **57** C15
Minhou *China* **59** E12
Miniçevo *Serbia* **28** G7
Minidoka *U.S.A.* **108** E7
Minigwal, L. *Australia* **93** E3
Minilya → *Australia* **93** D1
Minilya Roadhouse *Australia* **93** D1
Minipi L. *Canada* **105** B7
Mink L. *Canada* **102** A5
Minkammen *Sudan* **81** F3
Minna *Nigeria* **83** D6
Minneapolis *Kans., U.S.A.* **112** F5
Minneapolis *Minn., U.S.A.* **112** C7
Minnedosa *Canada* **103** C9
Minnesota □ *U.S.A.* **112** B6
Minnesota → *U.S.A.* **112** C7
Minnewaukan *U.S.A.* **112** A4
Minnipa *Australia* **95** E1
Minnitaki L. *Canada* **104** C1
Mino *Japan* **55** G8
Miño *Spain* **36** B2
Miño → *Spain* **36** D2
Minoa *Greece* **47** F7
Minorca = Menorca *Spain* **48** B11
Minot *U.S.A.* **112** A3
Minqin *China* **56** E2
Minqing *China* **59** D12
Minsen *Germany* **24** B5
Minsk *Belarus* **23** B14
Minsk □ *Belarus* **32** F4

Mińsk Mazowiecki *Poland* **31** F8
Mintabie *Australia* **95** D1
Mintaka Pass *Pakistan* **69** A6
Minto *Canada* **105** C6
Minto, L. *Canada* **104** A5
Minton *Canada* **103** D8
Minturn *U.S.A.* **108** G10
Minturno *Italy* **42** A6
Minudasht *Iran* **71** B8
Minûf *Egypt* **80** H7
Minusinsk *Russia* **53** D10
Minutang *India* **67** E20
Minvoul *Gabon* **84** D2
Minya el Qamh *Egypt* **80** H7
Minya Konka = Gongga
    Shan *China* **58** C3
Mionica *Bos.-H.* **28** F3
Mionica *Serbia* **44** B4
Miquelon *Canada* **104** C4
Miquelon *St-P. & M.* **105** C8
Mir *Niger* **83** C7
Mīr Kūh *Iran* **71** E8
Mīr Shahdād *Iran* **71** E8
Mira *Italy* **41** C9
Mira *Portugal* **36** E2
Mira → *Portugal* **37** H2
Mira por vos Cay *Bahamas* **121** B5
Mirabella Eclano *Italy* **43** A7
Mirabello, Kolpos *Greece* **49** D7
Mirador-Río Azul △
    Guatemala **120** C2
Miraj *India* **66** L9
Miram Shah *Pakistan* **68** C4
Miramar *Argentina* **126** D4
Miramar *Mozam.* **89** C6
Miramas *France* **21** E8
Mirambeau *France* **20** C3
Miramichi *Canada* **105** C6
Miramichi B. *Canada* **105** C7
Miramont-de-Guyenne
    France **20** D4
Miranda *Brazil* **125** H7
Miranda → *Brazil* **124** G7
Miranda de Ebro *Spain* **38** C2
Miranda do Corvo *Portugal* **36** E2
Miranda do Douro *Portugal* **36** D4
Mirande *France* **20** E4
Mirandela *Portugal* **36** D3
Mirandola *Italy* **40** D8
Mirandópolis *Brazil* **127** A5
Mirango *Malawi* **87** E3
Mirani *Australia* **94** K6
Mirano *Italy* **41** C9
Miras *Albania* **44** F4
Mirassol *Brazil* **127** A6
Mirbāṭ *Oman* **75** D5
Mirear *Egypt* **80** C4
Mirebeau *France* **18** F7
Mirebeau-sur-Bèze *France* **19** E12
Mirecourt *France* **19** D13
Mires *Greece* **49** D6
Mirgorod = Myrhorod
    Ukraine **33** H7
Miri *Malaysia* **62** D4
Miriam Vale *Australia* **94** C5
Miribel *France* **19** G11
Mirim, L. *S. Amer.* **127** C5
Mirnyy *Antarctica* **5** C14
Mirnyy *Russia* **53** C12
Miroč *Serbia* **44** B6
Mirokhan *Pakistan* **68** F3
Mirond L. *Canada* **103** B8
Mirosławiec *Poland* **30** E3
Mirpur *Pakistan* **69** C5
Mirpur Batoro *Pakistan* **68** G3
Mirpur Bibiwari *Pakistan* **68** E2
Mirpur Khas *Pakistan* **68** G3
Mirpur Sakro *Pakistan* **68** G2
Mirria *Niger* **83** C6
Mirsk *Poland* **31** H2
Mirtağ *Turkey* **70** B4
Mirtoo Sea *Greece* **46** D5
Miryang *S. Korea* **57** G15
Mirzaani *Georgia* **35** K8
Mirzapur *India* **69** G10
Mirzapur-cum-
    Vindhyachal =
    Mirzapur *India* **69** G10
Misantla *Mexico* **119** D5
Misawa *Japan* **54** D10
Miscou I. *Canada* **105** C7
Mish'āb, Ra's al *Si. Arabia* **71** D6
Mishan *China* **54** B5
Mishawaka *U.S.A.* **112** E10
Mishbih, Gebel *Egypt* **80** C3
Mishima *Japan* **55** G9
Misión *Mexico* **111** N10
Misiones □ *Argentina* **127** B5
Misiones □ *Paraguay* **126** B4
Miskah *Si. Arabia* **70** E4
Miskitos, Cayos *Nic.* **120** D3
Miskolc *Hungary* **28** B5
Misool *Indonesia* **63** E8
Misr = Egypt ■ *Africa* **80** B3
Miṣrātah *Libya* **79** B9
Missanabie *Canada* **104** C3
Missinaibi → *Canada* **104** B3

Missinaibi L. *Canada* **104** C3
Mission *Canada* **102** D4
Mission *S. Dak., U.S.A.* **112** D4
Mission *Tex., U.S.A.* **116** H5
Mission Beach *Australia* **94** B4
Mission Viejo *U.S.A.* **111** M9
Missirah *Senegal* **82** C1
Missisa L. *Canada* **104** B2
Missisicabi → *Canada* **104** B4
Mississagi → *Canada* **104** C3
Mississauga *Canada* **114** C5
Mississippi □ *U.S.A.* **117** E10
Mississippi → *U.S.A.* **117** G10
Mississippi L. *Canada* **115** A8
Mississippi River Delta
    U.S.A. **117** G10
Mississippi Sd. *U.S.A.* **117** F10
Missoula *U.S.A.* **108** C6
Missouri □ *U.S.A.* **112** F7
Missouri → *U.S.A.* **112** F8
Missouri City *U.S.A.* **116** G7
Missouri Valley *U.S.A.* **112** E6
Mist *U.S.A.* **110** E3
Mistake B. *Canada* **103** A10
Mistassibi → *Canada* **105** B5
Mistassini → *Canada* **105** C5
Mistassini, L. *Canada* **104** B5
Mistastin L. *Canada* **105** A7
Mistelbach *Austria* **27** C9
Misterbianco *Italy* **43** E8
Mistinibi, L. *Canada* **105** A7
Mistissini *Canada* **105** C5
Mistretta *Italy* **43** E7
Misty L. *Canada* **103** B8
Misurata = Miṣrātah *Libya* **79** B9
Mît Ghamr *Egypt* **80** H7
Mitatib *Sudan* **81** D4
Mitchell *Australia* **95** D4
Mitchell *Canada* **114** C3
Mitchell *Nebr., U.S.A.* **112** E2
Mitchell *Oreg., U.S.A.* **108** D4
Mitchell *S. Dak., U.S.A.* **112** D4
Mitchell → *Australia* **94** B3
Mitchell, Mt. *U.S.A.* **117** D13
Mitchell-Alice Rivers △
    Australia **94** B3
Mitchell Ra. *Australia* **94** A2
Mitchelstown *Ireland* **12** D3
Mitha Tiwana *Pakistan* **68** C5
Mithi *Pakistan* **68** G3
Mithimna *Greece* **47** B8
Mithrao *Pakistan* **68** F3
Mitilini *Greece* **47** B8
Mitilinii *Greece* **47** D8
Mitla Pass = Mamarr
    Mitlā *Egypt* **74** E1
Mito *Japan* **55** F10
Mitrofanovka *Russia* **33** H10
Mitrovica = Kosovska
    Mitrovica *Serbia* **44** D4
Mitsamiouli *Comoros Is.* **85** a
Mitsinjo *Madag.* **89** B8
Mitsiwa *Eritrea* **81** D5
Mitsiwa Channel *Eritrea* **81** D5
Mitsukaidō *Japan* **55** F9
Mitsiwa *Eritrea* **81** D5
Mittagong *Australia* **95** E5
Mittelberg *Austria* **26** D3
Mittelfranken □ *Germany* **25** F6
Mittellandkanal → *Germany* **24** C4
Mittenwalde *Germany* **24** C9
Mittersill *Austria* **26** D5
Mitterteich *Germany* **25** F8
Mittimatalik = Pond Inlet
    Canada **101** B12
Mittweida *Germany* **24** E8
Mitú *Colombia* **124** C3
Mitumba *Tanzania* **86** D3
Mitumba, Mts.
    Dem. Rep. of the Congo **86** D2
Mitwaba
    Dem. Rep. of the Congo **87** D2
Mityana *Uganda* **86** B3
Mixteco → *Mexico* **119** D5
Miyagi □ *Japan* **54** E10
Miyāh, W. el → *Egypt* **80** C3
Miyāh, W. el → *Syria* **70** C3
Miyake-Jima *Japan* **55** G9
Miyako *Japan* **54** E10
Miyako-Jima *Japan* **55** M2
Miyako-Rettō *Japan* **55** M2
Miyakonojō *Japan* **55** J5
Miyani *India* **68** J3
Miyanoura-Dake *Japan* **55** J5
Miyazaki *Japan* **55** J5
Miyazaki □ *Japan* **55** H5
Miyazu *Japan* **55** G7
Miyet, Bahr el = Dead Sea
    Asia **74** D4
Miyi *China* **58** D4
Miyoshi *Japan* **55** G6
Miyun *China* **56** D9
Miyun Shuiku *China* **57** D9
Mizan Teferi *Ethiopia* **81** F4
Mizdah *Libya* **79** B8
Mizen Hd. *Cork, Ireland* **12** E2
Mizen Hd. *Wicklow, Ireland* **12** D5
Mizhhirya *Ukraine* **29** B8
Mizhi *China* **56** F6

Mizil *Romania* **29** F11
Mizoram □ *India* **67** H18
Mizpe Ramon *Israel* **74** E3
Mizuho *Antarctica* **5** D5
Mizusawa *Japan* **54** E10
Mjällby *Sweden* **11** H8
Mjöbäck *Sweden* **11** G6
Mjölby *Sweden* **11** F9
Mjörn *Sweden* **11** G6
Mjøsa *Norway* **8** F14
Mkata *Tanzania* **86** D4
Mkhaya △ *Swaziland* **89** D5
Mkhuze → *S. Africa* **89** D4
Mkokotoni *Tanzania* **86** D4
Mkomazi *Tanzania* **86** C4
Mkomazi △ *S. Africa* **89** E5
Mkomazi △ *Tanzania* **86** C3
Mkulwe *Tanzania* **87** D3
Mkumbi, Ras *Tanzania* **86** D4
Mkushi *Zambia* **87** E2
Mkushi River *Zambia* **87** E2
Mkuze *S. Africa* **89** D5
Mladá Boleslav *Czech Rep.* **26** A7
Mladenovac *Serbia* **44** B4
Mlala Hills *Tanzania* **86** D3
Mlange = Mulanje, Mt.
    Malawi **87** F4
Mlava → *Serbia* **44** B5
Mława *Poland* **31** E7
Mlawula △ *Swaziland* **89** D5
Mlinište *Bos.-H.* **41** D13
Mljet *Croatia* **41** F14
Mljet △ *Croatia* **41** F14
Mljetski Kanal *Croatia* **41** F14
Młynary *Poland* **30** D6
Mmabatho *S. Africa* **88** D4
Mme *Cameroon* **83** D7
Mnichovo Hradiště
    Czech Rep. **26** A7
Mo i Rana *Norway* **8** C16
Moa *Cuba* **121** B4
Moa *Indonesia* **63** F7
Moa → *S. Leone* **82** D2
Moab *U.S.A.* **108** G9
Moala *Fiji* **91** a
Moama *Australia* **95** F3
Moamba *Mozam.* **89** D5
Moapa *U.S.A.* **111** J12
Moate *Ireland* **12** C4
Moba *Dem. Rep. of the Congo* **86** D2
Mobārakābād *Iran* **71** D7
Mobaye *C.A.R.* **84** D4
Mobayi *Dem. Rep. of the Congo* **84** D4
Moberly *U.S.A.* **112** F7
Moberly Lake *Canada* **102** B4
Mobile *U.S.A.* **117** F10
Mobile B. *U.S.A.* **117** F11
Mobridge *U.S.A.* **112** C4
Moc Chau *Vietnam* **64** B5
Moc Hoa *Vietnam* **65** G5
Mocabe Kasari
    Dem. Rep. of the Congo **87** D2
Moçambique =
    Mozambique ■ *Africa* **87** F4
Moçambique *Mozam.* **87** F5
Mocanaqua *U.S.A.* **115** E8
Moce *Fiji* **91** a
Mochima △ *Venezuela* **121** D7
Mochos *Greece* **49** D7
Mochudi *Botswana* **88** C4
Mocimboa da Praia *Mozam.* **87** E5
Mociu *Romania* **29** D9
Möckeln *Sweden* **11** H8
Mockfjärd *Sweden* **10** D8
Moclips *U.S.A.* **110** C2
Mocoa *Colombia* **124** C3
Mococa *Brazil* **127** A6
Mocorito *Mexico* **118** B3
Moctezuma *Mexico* **118** B3
Moctezuma → *Mexico* **119** C5
Mocuba *Mozam.* **87** F4
Modane *France* **21** C10
Modasa *India* **68** H5
Modder → *S. Africa* **88** D3
Modderrivier *S. Africa* **88** D3
Módena *Italy* **40** D7
Modena *U.S.A.* **109** H7
Modesto *U.S.A.* **110** H6
Módica *Italy* **43** F7
Modimolle *S. Africa* **89** C4
Modjadjiskloof *S. Africa* **89** C5
Mödling *Austria* **27** C9
Modo *Sudan* **81** F3
Modra *Slovak Rep.* **27** C10
Modriča *Bos.-H.* **28** F3
Moe *Australia* **95** F4
Moebase *Mozam.* **87** F4
Moëlan-sur-Mer *France* **18** E3
Moengo *Suriname* **125** B8
Moffat *U.K.* **13** F5
Moga *India* **68** D6
Mogadishu = Muqdisho
    Somali Rep. **75** G4
Mogador = Essaouira
    Morocco **78** B4
Mogadouro *Portugal* **36** D4
Mogalakwena → *S. Africa* **89** C4
Mogami-Gawa → *Japan* **54** E10
Mogán *Canary Is.* **48** G4

Mogaung *Burma* **67** G20
Mogente = Moixent *Spain* **39** G4
Mogho *Ethiopia* **81** G5
Mogi das Cruzes *Brazil* **127** A6
Mogi-Guaçu → *Brazil* **127** A6
Mogi-Mirim *Brazil* **125** H9
Mogielnica *Poland* **31** G7
Mogige *Ethiopia* **81** F4
Mogilev = Mahilyow
    Belarus **23** B16
Mogilev-Podolskiy =
    Mohyliv-Podilskyy
    Ukraine **29** B12
Mogilno *Poland* **31** F4
Mogincual *Mozam.* **87** F5
Mogliano Véneto *Italy* **41** C9
Mogocha *Russia* **53** D12
Mogok *Burma* **67** H20
Mogollon Rim *U.S.A.* **109** J8
Mógoro *Italy* **42** C1
Mograt *Sudan* **80** D3
Moguer *Spain* **37** H4
Mogumber *Australia* **93** F2
Mogwadi → *S. Africa* **89** C4
Mohács *Hungary* **28** E4
Mohales Hoek *Lesotho* **88** E4
Mohall *U.S.A.* **112** A3
Moḥammadābād *Iran* **71** B8
Mohammedia *Morocco* **78** B4
Mohana → *India* **69** G11
Mohanlalganj *India* **69** F9
Mohave, L. *U.S.A.* **111** K12
Mohawk → *U.S.A.* **115** D11
Moheda *Sweden* **11** G8
Mohéli *Comoros Is.* **85** a
Mohenjodaro *Pakistan* **68** F3
Moher, Cliffs of *Ireland* **12** D2
Mohicanville Res. *U.S.A.* **114** F2
Möhne → *Germany* **24** D3
Mohns Ridge *Arctic* **4** B7
Mohoro *Tanzania* **86** D4
Mohsenābād *Iran* **71** B8
Mohyliv-Podilskyy *Ukraine* **29** B12
Moia *Sudan* **81** F2
Moidart, L. *U.K.* **13** E3
Moineşti *Romania* **29** D11
Moira → *Canada* **114** B7
Moirans *France* **21** C9
Moirans-en-Montagne
    France **19** F12
Moisaküla *Estonia* **32** C3
Moisie *Canada* **105** B6
Moisie → *Canada* **105** B6
Moissac *France* **20** D5
Moita *Portugal* **37** G2
Moixent *Spain* **39** G4
Möja *Sweden* **10** E12
Mojácar *Spain* **39** H3
Mojados *Spain* **36** D6
Mojave *U.S.A.* **111** K8
Mojave △ *U.S.A.* **111** K11
Mojave Desert *U.S.A.* **111** L10
Mojiang *China* **58** F3
Mojjo → *Ethiopia* **81** F5
Mojkovac *Montenegro* **44** D3
Mojo *Bolivia* **126** A2
Mojo *Ethiopia* **81** F4
Mojokerto *Indonesia* **63** G15
Mokai *N.Z.* **91** C5
Mokambo
    Dem. Rep. of the Congo **87** E2
Mokameh *India* **69** G11
Mokau *N.Z.* **91** C5
Mokelumne → *U.S.A.* **110** G5
Mokelumne Hill *U.S.A.* **110** G6
Mokhotlong *Lesotho* **89** D4
Möklinta *Sweden* **10** D10
Mokokchung *India* **67** F19
Mokolo *Cameroon* **83** C7
Mokolo → *S. Africa* **89** C4
Mokopane *S. Africa* **89** C4
Mokpo *S. Korea* **57** G14
Mokra Gora *Europe* **44** D4
Mokronog *Slovenia* **41** C12
Moksha → *Russia* **34** C6
Mokshan *Russia* **34** D7
Mokwa *Nigeria* **83** D6
Mol *Belgium* **17** C5
Mola di Bari *Italy* **43** A10
Molai *Greece* **46** E4
Molale *Ethiopia* **81** E4
Molara *Italy* **42** B2
Molat *Croatia* **41** D11
Molchanovo *Russia* **52** D9
Mold *U.K.* **14** D4
Moldava nad Bodvou
    Slovak Rep. **27** C14
Moldavia = Moldova ■
    Europe **29** C13
Moldavia *Romania* **29** D12
Molde *Norway* **8** E12
Moldova ■ *Europe* **29** C13
Moldova Nouă *Romania* **28** F6
Moldoveanu, Vf. *Romania* **29** E9
Moldoviţa *Romania* **29** C10
Mole → *U.K.* **15** F7
Mole △ *Ghana* **83** D4
Mole Creek *Australia* **95** G4
Molepolole *Botswana* **88** C4

Molfetta *Italy* **43** A9
Molina de Aragón *Spain* **38** E3
Molina de Segura *Spain* **39** G3
Moline *U.S.A.* **112** E8
Molinella *Italy* **41** D8
Molinos *Argentina* **126** B2
Moliro *Dem. Rep. of the Congo* **86** D3
Moliterno *Italy* **43** B8
Molkom *Sweden* **10** E7
Mölle *Sweden* **11** H6
Molledo *Spain* **36** B6
Mollendo *Peru* **124** G4
Mollerin, L. *Australia* **93** F2
Mollerussa *Spain* **38** D5
Mollina *Spain* **37** H6
Mölln *Germany* **24** B6
Mölltorp *Sweden* **11** F8
Mölnlycke *Sweden* **11** G6
Molo *Kenya* **86** C4
Molochansk *Ukraine* **33** J8
Molochnoye, Ozero *Ukraine* **33** J8
Molodechno =
    Maladzyechna *Belarus* **23** A14
Molodezhnaya *Antarctica* **5** C9
Molodove *Ukraine* **29** D14
Moloka'i *U.S.A.* **106** b
Molokai Fracture Zone
    Pac. Oc. **97** E15
Molong *Australia* **95** E4
Molopo → *Africa* **88** D3
Molos *Greece* **46** C4
Molsheim *France* **19** D14
Molson L. *Canada* **103** C9
Molteno *S. Africa* **88** E4
Molu *Indonesia* **63** F8
Molucca Sea *Indonesia* **63** E6
Moluccas = Maluku
    Indonesia **63** E7
Moma *Dem. Rep. of the Congo* **86** C1
Moma *Mozam.* **87** F4
Mombasa *Kenya* **86** C4
Mombetsu *Japan* **54** B11
Mombuey *Spain* **36** C4
Momchilgrad *Bulgaria* **45** E9
Momi *Dem. Rep. of the Congo* **86** C2
Mompós *Colombia* **124** B4
Møn *Denmark* **11** K6
Mon □ *Burma* **67** L20
Mona, Canal de la = Mona
    Passage *W. Indies* **121** C6
Mona, Isla *Puerto Rico* **121** C6
Mona, Pta. *Costa Rica* **120** E3
Mona Passage *W. Indies* **121** C6
Monaca *U.S.A.* **114** F4
Monaco ■ *Europe* **21** E11
Monadhliath Mts. *U.K.* **13** D4
Monadnock, Mt. *U.S.A.* **115** D12
Monaghan *Ireland* **12** B5
Monaghan □ *Ireland* **12** B5
Monahans *U.S.A.* **116** F3
Monapo *Mozam.* **87** E5
Monar, L. *U.K.* **13** D3
Monarch Mt. *Canada* **102** C3
Monashee Mts. *Canada* **102** C5
Monasterevin *Ireland* **12** C4
Monastir = Bitola *Macedonia* **44** E5
Monastir *Tunisia* **79** A8
Moncada *Phil.* **61** D4
Moncalieri *Italy* **40** D4
Moncalvo *Italy* **40** C5
Monção *Portugal* **36** C2
Moncarapacho *Portugal* **37** H3
Moncayo, Sierra del *Spain* **38** D3
Monchegorsk *Russia* **8** C25
Mönchengladbach *Germany* **24** D2
Monchique *Portugal* **37** H2
Moncks Corner *U.S.A.* **117** E14
Monclova *Mexico* **118** B4
Moncontour *France* **18** D4
Moncton *Canada* **105** C7
Mondariz *Spain* **36** C2
Mondego → *Portugal* **36** E2
Mondego, C. *Portugal* **36** E2
Mondeodo *Indonesia* **63** E6
Mondeville *France* **18** C6
Mondolfo *Italy* **41** E10
Mondoñedo *Spain* **36** B3
Mondovì *Italy* **40** D4
Mondragon = Arrasate
    Spain **38** B2
Mondragon *Phil.* **61** E6
Mondragone *Italy* **42** A6
Mondrain I. *Australia* **93** F3
Moneague *Jamaica* **120** a
Monemvasia *Greece* **46** E5
Moneron, Ostrov *Russia* **54** A10
Monessen *U.S.A.* **114** F5
Monesterio *Spain* **37** G4
Monestier-de-Clermont
    France **21** D9
Monett *U.S.A.* **112** G7
Moneymore *U.K.* **12** B5
Monfalcone *Italy* **41** C10
Monflanquin *France* **20** D4
Monforte *Portugal* **37** F3
Monforte de Lemos *Spain* **36** C3
Mong Cai *Vietnam* **64** B6
Mong Hsu *Burma* **58** G2
Mong Kung *Burma* **67** J20

Mong Nai *Burma* **67** J20
Mong Pawk *Burma* **67** H21
Mong Ping *Burma* **58** G2
Mong Ton *Burma* **67** J22
Mong Wa *Burma* **67** J22
Mong Yai *Burma* **67** H21
Mongalla *Sudan* **81** F3
Mongers, L. *Australia* **93** E2
Monghyr = Munger *India* **69** G12
Mongibello = Etna *Italy* **43** E7
Mongo *Chad* **79** F9
Mongo → *S. Leone* **82** D2
Mongolia ■ *Asia* **53** E10
Mongolia, Plateau of *Asia* **50** D12
Mongonu *Nigeria* **83** C7
Mongu *Zambia* **85** H4
Môngua *Angola* **88** B2
Monifieth *U.K.* **13** E6
Monistrol-sur-Loire *France* **21** C8
Monkey Bay *Malawi* **87** E4
Monkey Mia *Australia* **93** E1
Monkey River *Belize* **119** D7
Mońki *Poland* **30** E9
Monkland *Canada* **115** A10
Monkoto
    Dem. Rep. of the Congo **84** E4
Monkton *Canada* **114** C3
Monmouth *U.K.* **15** F5
Monmouth *Ill., U.S.A.* **112** E8
Monmouth *Oreg., U.S.A.* **108** D2
Monmouthshire □ *U.K.* **15** F5
Mono, Pta. *Nic.* **120** D3
Mono L. *U.S.A.* **110** H7
Monolith *U.S.A.* **111** K8
Monolithos *Greece* **49** C9
Monongahela *U.S.A.* **114** F5
Monópoli *Italy* **43** B10
Monor *Hungary* **28** C4
Monóvar *Spain* **39** G4
Monreal del Campo *Spain* **38** E3
Monreale *Italy* **42** D6
Monroe *Ga., U.S.A.* **117** E13
Monroe *La., U.S.A.* **116** E8
Monroe *Mich., U.S.A.* **113** E12
Monroe *N.C., U.S.A.* **117** D14
Monroe *N.Y., U.S.A.* **115** E10
Monroe *Utah, U.S.A.* **108** G7
Monroe *Wash., U.S.A.* **110** C5
Monroe *Wis., U.S.A.* **112** D9
Monroe City *U.S.A.* **112** F8
Monroeton *U.S.A.* **115** E8
Monroeville *Ala., U.S.A.* **117** F11
Monroeville *Pa., U.S.A.* **114** F5
Monrovia *Liberia* **82** D2
Mons *Belgium* **17** D3
Møns Klint *Denmark* **11** K6
Monse *Indonesia* **63** E6
Monségur *France* **20** D4
Monsélice *Italy* **41** C8
Mönsterås *Sweden* **11** G10
Mont Cenis, Col du *France* **21** C10
Mont-de-Marsan *France* **20** E3
Mont-Joli *Canada* **105** C6
Mont-Laurier *Canada* **104** C4
Mont-Louis *Canada* **105** C6
Mont Peko △ *Ivory C.* **82** D3
Mont-roig del Camp *Spain* **38** D5
Mont-St-Michel, Le *France* **18** D5
Mont Sangbé △ *Ivory C.* **82** D3
Mont-Tremblant △ *Canada* **104** C5
Montabaur *Germany* **24** E3
Montagnac *France* **20** E7
Montagnana *Italy* **41** C8
Montagne d'Ambre △
    Madag. **89** A8
Montagne de Reims △
    France **19** C11
Montagu *S. Africa* **88** E3
Montagu I. *Antarctica* **5** B1
Montague *Canada* **105** C7
Montague, I. *Mexico* **118** A2
Montague Ra. *Australia* **93** E2
Montague Sd. *Australia* **92** B4
Montaigu *France* **18** F5
Montalbán *Spain* **38** E4
Montalbano Iónico *Italy* **43** B9
Montalbo *Spain* **38** F2
Montalcino *Italy* **41** E8
Montalegre *Portugal* **36** D3
Montalto *Italy* **43** E8
Montalto di Castro *Italy* **41** F8
Montalto Uffugo *Italy* **43** C9
Montalvo *U.S.A.* **111** L7
Montamarta *Spain* **36** D5
Montana *Bulgaria* **44** C7
Montana *Peru* **124** E4
Montana □ *Bulgaria* **44** C7
Montana □ *U.S.A.* **108** C9
Montaña Clara, I. *Canary Is.* **48** E6
Montañas de Malaga △
    Spain **37** J6
Montánchez *Spain* **37** F4
Montargil *Portugal* **37** F2
Montargis *France* **19** E9
Montauban *France* **20** D5
Montauk *U.S.A.* **115** E13
Montauk Pt. *U.S.A.* **115** E13

Montbard *France* **19** E11
Montbarrey *France* **19** E12
Montbéliard *France* **19** E13
Montblanc *Spain* **38** D6
Montbrison *France* **21** C8
Montceau-les-Mines *France* **19** F11
Montcenis *France* **21** B8
Montclair *U.S.A.* **115** F10
Montcornet *France* **19** C10
Montcuq *France* **20** D5
Montdidier *France* **19** C9
Monte Albán *Mexico* **119** D5
Monte Alegre *Brazil* **125** D8
Monte Azul *Brazil* **125** G10
Monte-Carlo *Monaco* **21** E11
Monte Caseros *Argentina* **126** C4
Monte Comán *Argentina* **126** C2
Monte Crísti *Dom. Rep.* **121** C5
Monte Cucco △ *Italy* **41** E9
Monte Lindo → *Paraguay* **126** A4
Monte Patria *Chile* **126** C1
Monte Quemado *Argentina* **126** B3
Monte Redondo *Portugal* **36** F2
Monte Rio *U.S.A.* **110** G4
Monte San Giovanni
    Campano *Italy* **42** A6
Monte San Savino *Italy* **41** E8
Monte Sant' Ángelo *Italy* **41** G12
Monte Santu, C. di *Italy* **42** B2
Monte Sibillini △ *Italy* **41** F10
Monte Subasio △ *Italy* **41** E9
Monte Vista *U.S.A.* **109** H10
Monteagudo *Argentina* **127** B5
Montealegre del Castillo
    Spain **39** G3
Montebello *Canada* **104** C5
Montebello Iónico *Italy* **43** E8
Montebello Is. *Australia* **92** D2
Montebelluna *Italy* **41** C9
Montebourg *France* **18** C5
Montecarlo *Argentina* **127** B5
Montecastrilli *Italy* **41** F9
Montecatini Terme *Italy* **40** E7
Montecito *U.S.A.* **111** L7
Montecristo *Italy* **40** F7
Montefalco *Italy* **41** F9
Montefiascone *Italy* **41** F9
Montefrío *Spain* **37** H7
Montegiórgio *Italy* **41** E10
Montego Bay *Jamaica* **120** a
Montehermoso *Spain* **36** E4
Montejícar *Spain* **37** H7
Montélimar *France* **21** D8
Montella *Italy* **43** B8
Montellano *Spain* **37** J5
Montello *U.S.A.* **112** D9
Montemor-o-Novo *Portugal* **37** G2
Montemor-o-Velho *Portugal* **36** E2
Montemorelos *Mexico* **119** B5
Montendre *France* **20** C3
Montenegro *Brazil* **127** B5
Montenegro ■ *Europe* **44** D3
Montenero di Bisáccia *Italy* **41** G11
Montepuez *Mozam.* **87** E4
Montepuez → *Mozam.* **87** E5
Montepulciano *Italy* **41** E8
Montereale *Italy* **41** F10
Montereau-Faut-Yonne
    France **19** D9
Monterey *U.S.A.* **110** J5
Monterey B. *U.S.A.* **110** J5
Montería *Colombia* **124** B3
Monteros *Argentina* **126** B2
Monterotondo *Italy* **41** F9
Monterrey *Mexico* **118** B4
Montes Azules △ *Mexico* **119** D6
Montes Claros *Brazil* **125** G10
Montesano *U.S.A.* **110** D3
Montesano sulla
    Marcellana *Italy* **43** B8
Montesárchio *Italy* **43** A7
Montescaglioso *Italy* **43** B9
Montesilvano *Italy* **41** F11
Montesinho △ *Portugal* **36** D4
Montevarchi *Italy* **41** E8
Montevideo *Uruguay* **127** C4
Montevideo *U.S.A.* **112** C6
Montezuma *U.S.A.* **112** E7
Montezuma Castle △
    U.S.A. **109** J8
Montfaucon *France* **18** E5
Montfaucon-d'Argonne
    France **19** C12
Montfaucon-en-Velay
    France **21** C8
Montfort-le-Gesnois *France* **18** D7
Montfort-sur-Meu *France* **18** D5
Montfragüe △ *Spain* **36** F5
Montgenèvre *France* **21** D10
Montgomery *U.K.* **15** E4
Montgomery *Ala., U.S.A.* **117** E11
Montgomery *Pa., U.S.A.* **114** E8
Montgomery *W. Va., U.S.A.*
    113 F13
Montgomery City *U.S.A.* **112** F8
Montguyon *France* **20** C3
Monthermé *France* **19** C11
Monthey *Switz.* **25** J2

Monthois *France* **19** C11
Monti *Italy* **42** B2
Monti Lucrétili □ *Italy* **41** F9
Monti Picentini □ *Italy* **43** B8
Monti Simbruini □ *Italy* **41** G10
Monticelli d'Ongina *Italy* **40** C6
Monticello *Ark., U.S.A.* **116** E9
Monticello *Fla., U.S.A.* **117** F13
Monticello *Ind., U.S.A.* **112** E10
Monticello *Iowa, U.S.A.* **112** D9
Monticello *Ky., U.S.A.* **113** G11
Monticello *Minn., U.S.A.* **112** C7
Monticello *Miss., U.S.A.* **117** F9
Monticello *N.Y., U.S.A.* **115** E10
Monticello *Utah, U.S.A.* **109** H9
Montichiari *Italy* **40** C7
Montier-en-Der *France* **19** D11
Montignac *France* **20** C5
Montigny-les-Metz *France* **19** C13
Montigny-sur-Aube *France* **19** E11
Montijo *Portugal* **37** G2
Montijo *Spain* **37** G4
Montilla *Spain* **37** H6
Montivilliers *France* **18** C7
Montluçon *France* **19** F9
Montmagny *Canada* **105** C5
Montmarault *France* **19** F9
Montmartre *Canada* **103** C8
Montmédy *France* **19** C12
Montmélian *France* **21** C10
Montmirail *France* **19** D10
Montmoreau-St-Cybard
    France **20** C4
Montmorillon *France* **20** B4
Montmort-Lucy *France* **19** D10
Monto *Australia* **94** C5
Montoire-sur-le-Loir *France* **18** E7
Montongbuwoh *Indonesia* **63** K19
Montoro *Spain* **37** G6
Montour Falls *U.S.A.* **114** D8
Montoursville *U.S.A.* **114** E8
Montpelier *Idaho, U.S.A.* **108** E8
Montpelier *Vt., U.S.A.* **115** B12
Montpellier *France* **20** E7
Montpezat-de-Quercy
    France **20** D5
Montpon-Ménestérol *France* **20** D4
Montréal *Canada* **115** A11
Montréal *Aude, France* **20** E6
Montréal *Gers, France* **20** E4
Montreal → *Canada* **104** C3
Montréal L. *Canada* **103** C7
Montreal Lake *Canada* **103** C7
Montredon-Labessonnié
    France **20** E6
Montrésor *France* **18** E8
Montret *France* **19** F12
Montreuil *Pas-de-Calais,
    France* **19** B8
Montreuil *Seine-St-Denis,
    France* **19** D9
Montreuil-Bellay *France* **18** E6
Montreux *Switz.* **25** J2
Montrevel-en-Bresse *France* **19** F12
Montrichard *France* **18** E8
Montrose *U.K.* **13** E6
Montrose *Colo., U.S.A.* **108** G10
Montrose *Pa., U.S.A.* **115** E9
Monts, Pte. des *Canada* **105** C6
Montsalvy *France* **20** D6
Montsant, Serra de *Spain* **38** D6
Montsauche-les-Settons
    France **19** E11
Montsec, Serra del *Spain* **38** C5
Montseny △ *Spain* **38** D2
Montserrat △ *Spain* **38** D6
Montserrat ☑ *W. Indies* **121** C7
Montuenga *Spain* **36** D6
Montuiri *Spain* **48** B9
Monywa *Burma* **67** H19
Monza *Italy* **40** C6
Monze *Zambia* **87** F2
Monze, C. *Pakistan* **68** G2
Monzón *Spain* **38** D5
Mooers *U.S.A.* **115** B11
Mooi → *S. Africa* **89** D5
Mooi River *S. Africa* **89** D4
Moomba *Australia* **95** A3
Moonah → *Australia* **94** C2
Moonda, L. *Australia* **94** D3
Moonie *Australia* **95** D5
Moonie → *Australia* **95** D4
Moora *Australia* **93** F2
Moorcroft *U.S.A.* **108** D11
Moore → *Australia* **93** F2
Moore, L. *Australia* **93** E2
Moore Falls *Canada* **114** B6
Moore Park *Australia* **94** C5
Moore Res. *U.S.A.* **115** B13
Moore River △ *Australia* **93** F2
Moorea *French Polynesia* **91** d
Moorefield *U.S.A.* **113** F14
Moorfoot Hills *U.K.* **13** F5
Moorhead *U.S.A.* **112** B5
Moormerland *Germany* **24** B3
Moorpark *U.S.A.* **111** L8
Moorreesburg *S. Africa* **88** E2

Moorrinna △ *Australia* **94** C3
Moosburg *Germany* **25** G7
Moose → *Canada* **104** B3
Moose → *U.S.A.* **115** C9
Moose Creek *Canada* **115** A10
Moose Factory *Canada* **104** B3
Moose Jaw *Canada* **103** C7
Moose Jaw → *Canada* **103** C7
Moose Lake *Canada* **103** C8
Moose Lake *U.S.A.* **112** B7
Moose Mountain △ *Canada* **103** D8
Moosehead L. *U.S.A.* **113** C19
Mooselookmeguntic L.
    U.S.A. **115** B14
Moosilauke, Mt. *U.S.A.* **115** B13
Moosomin *Canada* **103** C8
Moosonee *Canada* **104** B3
Moosup *U.S.A.* **115** E13
Mopane *S. Africa* **89** C4
Mopeia Velha *Mozam.* **87** F4
Mopipi *Botswana* **88** C3
Mopoi *C.A.R.* **86** A2
Mopti *Mali* **82** C4
Mopti □ *Mali* **82** C4
Moqatta *Sudan* **81** E3
Moqor *Afghan.* **68** C2
Moquegua *Peru* **124** G4
Mór *Hungary* **28** C3
Mora *Cameroon* **83** C7
Mora *Portugal* **37** G2
Mora *Spain* **37** F7
Mora *Sweden* **10** C8
Mora *Minn., U.S.A.* **112** C7
Mora *N. Mex., U.S.A.* **109** J11
Mora de Rubielos *Spain* **38** E4
Móra d'Ebre *Spain* **38** D5
Mora la Nova *Spain* **38** D5
Morača → *Montenegro* **44** D3
Moradabad *India* **69** E8
Morafenobe *Madag.* **89** B7
Morąg *Poland* **30** E6
Moral de Calatrava *Spain* **37** G7
Moraleja *Spain* **36** E4
Moramanga *Madag.* **89** B8
Moran *Kans., U.S.A.* **112** G6
Moran *Wyo., U.S.A.* **108** E8
Moranbah *Australia* **94** C4
Morano Cálabro *Italy* **43** C9
Morant Bay *Jamaica* **120** a
Morant Cays *Jamaica* **120** C4
Morant Pt. *Jamaica* **120** a
Morar *India* **68** F8
Morar, L. *U.K.* **13** E3
Moratalla *Spain* **39** G3
Moratuwa *Sri Lanka* **66** R11
Morava → *Slovak Rep.* **27** C9
Morava → *Serbia* **44** C4
Moravia *U.S.A.* **115** D8
Moravian Hts. =
    Českomoravská
    Vrchovina *Czech Rep.* **26** B8
Moravica → *Serbia* **44** C4
Moraviţa *Romania* **28** E6
Moravská Třebová
    Czech Rep. **26** B9
Moravské Budějovice
    Czech Rep. **26** B8
Morawa *Australia* **93** E2
Morawhanna *Guyana* **124** B7
Moray □ *U.K.* **13** D5
Moray Firth *U.K.* **13** D5
Morbach *Germany* **25** F3
Morbegno *Italy* **40** B6
Morbi *India* **68** H4
Morbihan □ *France* **18** E4
Mörbylånga *Sweden* **11** H10
Morcenx *France* **20** D3
Morcone *Italy* **43** A7
Mordelles *France* **18** D5
Morden *Canada* **103** D9
Mordoğan *Turkey* **47** C8
Mordovian Republic =
    Mordvinia □ *Russia* **34** C7
Mordovo *Russia* **34** D5
Mordvinia □ *Russia* **34** C7
Mordy *Poland* **31** F9
Moreau → *U.S.A.* **112** C3
Morebeng *S. Africa* **89** C4
Morecambe *U.K.* **14** C5
Morecambe B. *U.K.* **14** C5
Moree *Australia* **95** D4
Morehead *U.S.A.* **113** F12
Morehead City *U.S.A.* **117** D16
Morel → *India* **68** F7
Morelia *Mexico* **118** D4
Morella *Australia* **94** C3
Morella *Spain* **38** E4
Morelos *Mexico* **118** B3
Morelos □ *Mexico* **119** D5
Moremi △ *Botswana* **88** B3
Morena *India* **68** F8
Morena, Sierra *Spain* **37** G7
Moreni *Romania* **29** F10
Moreno Valley *U.S.A.* **111** M10
Moresby I. *Canada* **102** C2
Morestel *France* **21** C9
Moreton I. *Australia* **95** D5
Moreton Island △ *Australia* **95** D5
Moreuil *France* **19** C9
Morez *France* **19** F13

Morgan *U.S.A.* **108** F8
Morgan City *U.S.A.* **116** G9
Morgan Hill *U.S.A.* **110** H5
Morganfield *U.S.A.* **112** G10
Morganton *U.S.A.* **117** D14
Morgantown *U.S.A.* **113** F14
Morgenzon *S. Africa* **89** D4
Morges *Switz.* **25** J2
Morghak *Iran* **71** D8
Morgongåva *Sweden* **10** E10
Morhange *France* **19** D13
Morhar → *India* **69** G11
Mori *Italy* **40** C7
Mori *Japan* **54** C10
Moriarty *U.S.A.* **109** J10
Moribaya *Guinea* **82** D3
Morice L. *Canada* **102** C3
Moriki *Nigeria* **83** C6
Morinville *Canada* **102** C6
Morioka *Japan* **54** E10
Moris *Mexico* **118** B3
Morlaàs *France* **20** E3
Morlanwelz *France* **18** D3
Morlaix *France* **18** D3
Mörlunda *Sweden* **11** G9
Mormanno *Italy* **43** C8
Mormant *France* **19** D9
Mornington *Australia* **95** F4
Mornington, I. *Chile* **128** F1
Mornington I. *Australia* **94** B2
Mornos → *Greece* **46** C3
Moro *Cameroon* **83** C7
Moro *Sudan* **81** E3
Moro → *Pakistan* **68** E2
Moro G. *Phil.* **61** H5
Morocco ■ *N. Afr.* **78** B4
Morogoro *Tanzania* **86** D4
Morogoro □ *Tanzania* **86** D4
Moroleón *Mexico* **118** C4
Morombe *Madag.* **89** C7
Moron *Argentina* **126** C4
Morón *Cuba* **120** B4
Mörön *Mongolia* **53** E11
Morón de Almazán *Spain* **38** D2
Morón de la Frontera *Spain* **37** H5
Morona → *Peru* **124** D3
Morondava *Madag.* **89** C7
Morondo *Ivory C.* **82** D3
Morongo Valley *U.S.A.* **111** L10
Moroni *Comoros Is.* **85** a
Moroni *U.S.A.* **108** G8
Moronou *Ivory C.* **82** D4
Morotai *Indonesia* **63** D7
Moroto *Uganda* **86** B3
Moroto, Mt. *Uganda* **86** B3
Morozov *Bulgaria* **45** D9
Morozovsk *Russia* **35** F5
Morpeth *Canada* **114** D3
Morpeth *U.K.* **14** B6
Morphou =
    Güzelyurt
    Cyprus **49** D11
Morphou Bay *Cyprus* **49** D11
Morrilton *U.S.A.* **116** D8
Morrinhos *Brazil* **125** G9
Morrinsville *N.Z.* **91** B5
Morris *Canada* **103** D9
Morris *Ill., U.S.A.* **112** E9
Morris *Minn., U.S.A.* **112** C6
Morris *N.Y., U.S.A.* **115** D9
Morris *Pa., U.S.A.* **114** E7
Morris, Mt. *Australia* **93** E5
Morris Jesup, Kap *Greenland* **98** A16
Morrisburg *Canada* **115** B9
Morristown *Ariz., U.S.A.* **109** K7
Morristown *N.J., U.S.A.* **115** F10
Morristown *N.Y., U.S.A.* **115** B9
Morristown *Tenn., U.S.A.* **117** C13
Morrisville *N.Y., U.S.A.* **115** D9
Morrisville *Pa., U.S.A.* **115** F10
Morrisville *Vt., U.S.A.* **115** B12
Morro, Pta. *Chile* **126** B1
Morro Bay *U.S.A.* **110** K6
Morro del Jable *Canary Is.* **48** F5
Morro Jable, Pta. de
    Canary Is. **48** F5
Morrocoy △ *Venezuela* **121** D6
Morrosquillo, G. de
    Colombia **120** E4
Mörrum *Sweden* **11** H8
Morrumbene *Mozam.* **89** C6
Mörrumsån → *Sweden* **11** H8
Mors *Denmark* **11** H2
Morshansk *Russia* **34** D5
Mörsil *Sweden* **10** A7
Mortagne → *France* **19** D13
Mortagne-au-Perche *France* **18** D7
Mortagne-sur-Gironde
    France **20** C3
Mortagne-sur-Sèvre *France* **18** F6
Mortain *France* **18** D6
Mortara *Italy* **40** C5
Morteau *France* **19** E13
Morteros *Argentina* **126** C3
Mortlach *Canada* **103** C7
Mortlake *Australia* **95** F3
Morton *Tex., U.S.A.* **116** E3
Morton *Wash., U.S.A.* **110** D4
Moruga *Trin. & Tob.* **125** K15
Morundah *Australia* **95** E4
Moruya *Australia* **95** F5

Morvan *France* **19** E11
Morvan △ *France* **19** E11
Morven *Australia* **95** D4
Morvern *U.K.* **13** E3
Morwell *Australia* **95** F4
Moryń *Poland* **31** F1
Morzine *France* **19** F13
Mosalsk *Russia* **32** E8
Mosbach *Germany* **25** F5
Mošćenice *Croatia* **41** C11
Mosciano Sant' Ángelo
  Italy **41** F10
Moscos Is. *Burma* **64** F1
Moscow = Moskva *Russia* **32** E9
Moscow *Idaho, U.S.A.* **108** C5
Moscow *Pa., U.S.A.* **115** E9
Mosel → *Europe* **19** B14
Moselle = Mosel → *Europe* **19** B14
Moselle □ *France* **19** D13
Moses Lake *U.S.A.* **108** C4
Mosgiel *N.Z.* **91** F3
Moshaweng → *S. Africa* **88** D3
Moshchnyy, Ostrov *Russia* **32** B4
Moshi *Tanzania* **86** C4
Moshupa *Botswana* **88** C4
Mosina *Poland* **31** F3
Mosjøen *Norway* **8** D15
Moskenesøya *Norway* **8** C15
Moskenstraumen *Norway* **8** C15
Moskva *Russia* **32** E9
Moskva □ *Russia* **32** D9
Moskva → *Russia* **32** E10
Moslavačka Gora *Croatia* **41** C13
Mosomane *Botswana* **88** C4
Mosonmagyaróvár *Hungary* **28** C2
Mošorin *Serbia* **28** E5
Mospino *Ukraine* **33** J9
Mosquera *Colombia* **124** C3
Mosquero *U.S.A.* **109** J12
Mosqueruela *Spain* **38** E4
Mosquitia *Honduras* **120** C3
Mosquito Coast =
  Mosquitia *Honduras* **120** C3
Mosquito Creek L. *U.S.A.* **114** E4
Mosquito L. *Canada* **103** A8
Mosquitos, G. de los
  Panama **120** E4
Moss *Norway* **9** G14
Moss Vale *Australia* **95** E5
Mossaka *Congo* **84** E3
Mossbank *Canada* **103** D7
Mossburn *N.Z.* **91** F2
Mosselbaai *S. Africa* **88** E3
Mossendjo *Congo* **84** E2
Mossgiel *Australia* **95** E3
Mossingen *Germany* **25** G5
Mossman *Australia* **94** B4
Mossoró *Brazil* **125** E11
Mossuril *Mozam.* **87** E5
Most *Czech Rep.* **26** A6
Mosta *Malta* **49** D1
Mostaganem *Algeria* **78** A6
Mostar *Bos.-H.* **28** G2
Mostardas *Brazil* **127** C5
Mostiska = Mostyska
  Ukraine **31** J10
Móstoles *Spain* **36** E7
Mosty = Masty *Belarus* **23** B13
Mostyska *Ukraine* **31** J10
Mosul = Al Mawşil *Iraq* **73** D10
Mota *Ethiopia* **81** E4
Mota del Cuervo *Spain* **39** F2
Mota del Marqués *Spain* **36** D5
Motagua → *Guatemala* **120** C2
Motala *Sweden* **11** F9
Motaze *Mozam.* **89** C5
Moţca *Romania* **29** C11
Moth *India* **69** G8
Motherwell *U.K.* **13** F5
Motihari *India* **69** F11
Motilla del Palancar *Spain* **39** F3
Motnik *Slovenia* **41** B11
Motovun *Croatia* **41** C10
Motozintla de Mendoza
  Mexico **119** D6
Motril *Spain* **37** J7
Motru *Romania* **28** F7
Motru → *Romania* **29** F8
Mott *U.S.A.* **112** B2
Móttola *Italy* **43** B10
Motueka *N.Z.* **91** D4
Motueka → *N.Z.* **91** D4
Motul *Mexico* **119** C7
Mouchalagane → *Canada* **105** B6
Mouding *China* **58** E3
Moudjeria *Mauritania* **82** B2
Moudon *Switz.* **25** J2
Moudros *Greece* **47** B7
Mouila *Gabon* **84** E2
Moulamein *Australia* **95** F3
Moule à Chique, C. *St. Lucia* **121** f
Mouliana *Greece* **49** D7
Moulins *France* **19** F10
Moulmein *Burma* **67** L20
Moulouya, O. → *Morocco* **78** B5
Moultrie *U.S.A.* **117** F13
Moultrie, L. *U.S.A.* **117** E14
Mound City *Mo., U.S.A.* **112** E6
Mound City *S. Dak., U.S.A.* **112** C3

Moundou *Chad* **79** G9
Moundsville *U.S.A.* **114** G4
Moung *Cambodia* **64** F4
Mount Airy *U.S.A.* **117** C14
Mount Albert *Canada* **114** B5
Mount Aspiring △ *N.Z.* **91** F2
Mount Barker *S. Austral.,
  Australia* **95** F2
Mount Barker *W. Austral.,
  Australia* **93** F2
Mount Bellew Bridge *Ireland* **12** C3
Mount Brydges *Canada* **114** D3
Mount Burr *Australia* **95** F3
Mount Carmel = Ha
  Karmel △ *Israel* **74** C4
Mount Carmel *Ill., U.S.A.* **112** F10
Mount Carmel *Pa., U.S.A.* **115** F8
Mount Clemens *U.S.A.* **114** D2
Mount Coolon *Australia* **94** C4
Mount Darwin *Zimbabwe* **87** F3
Mount Desert I. *U.S.A.* **113** C19
Mount Dora *U.S.A.* **117** G14
Mount Edziza △ *Canada* **102** B2
Mount Elgon △ *E. Afr.* **86** B3
Mount Field △ *Australia* **95** G4
Mount Fletcher *S. Africa* **89** E4
Mount Forest *Canada* **114** C4
Mount Frankland △
  Australia **92** F2
Mount Gambier *Australia* **95** F3
Mount Garnet *Australia* **94** B4
Mount Holly *U.S.A.* **115** G10
Mount Holly Springs *U.S.A.* **114** F7
Mount Hope *N.S.W.,
  Australia* **95** E4
Mount Hope *S. Austral.,
  Australia* **95** E2
Mount Isa *Australia* **94** C2
Mount Jewett *U.S.A.* **114** E6
Mount Kaputar △ *Australia* **95** E5
Mount Kenya △ *Kenya* **86** C4
Mount Kilimanjaro △
  Tanzania **86** C4
Mount Kisco *U.S.A.* **115** E11
Mount Laguna *U.S.A.* **111** N10
Mount Larcom *Australia* **94** C5
Mount Lofty Ranges
  Australia **95** E2
Mount Magnet *Australia* **93** E2
Mount Maunganui *N.Z.* **91** B6
Mount Molloy *Australia* **94** B4
Mount Morgan *Australia* **94** C5
Mount Morris *U.S.A.* **114** D7
Mount Pearl *Canada* **105** C9
Mount Penn *U.S.A.* **115** F9
Mount Perry *Australia* **95** D5
Mount Pleasant *Iowa,
  U.S.A.* **112** E8
Mount Pleasant *Mich.,
  U.S.A.* **113** D11
Mount Pleasant *Pa., U.S.A.* **114** F5
Mount Pleasant *S.C., U.S.A.*
  117 E15
Mount Pleasant *Tenn.,
  U.S.A.* **117** D11
Mount Pleasant *Tex., U.S.A.* **116** E7
Mount Pleasant *Utah,
  U.S.A.* **108** G8
Mount Pocono *U.S.A.* **115** E9
Mount Rainier △ *U.S.A.* **110** D5
Mount Revelstoke △
  Canada **102** C5
Mount Robson △ *Canada* **102** C5
Mount St. Helens △ *U.S.A.* **110** D4
Mount Selinda *Zimbabwe* **89** C5
Mount Shasta *U.S.A.* **108** F2
Mount Signal *U.S.A.* **111** N11
Mount Sterling *Ill., U.S.A.* **112** F8
Mount Sterling *Ky., U.S.A.* **113** F12
Mount Surprise *Australia* **94** B3
Mount Union *U.S.A.* **114** F7
Mount Upton *U.S.A.* **115** D9
Mount Vernon *Ill., U.S.A.* **112** F9
Mount Vernon *Ind., U.S.A.* **112** G10
Mount Vernon *N.Y., U.S.A.*
  115 F11
Mount Vernon *Ohio, U.S.A.* **114** F2
Mount Vernon *Wash.,
  U.S.A.* **110** B4
Mount William △ *Australia* **95** G4
Mounta, Akra *Greece* **46** C2
Mountain Ash *U.K.* **15** F4
Mountain Center *U.S.A.* **111** M10
Mountain City *Nev., U.S.A.* **108** F6
Mountain City *Tenn., U.S.A.*
  117 C14
Mountain Dale *U.S.A.* **115** E10
Mountain Grove *U.S.A.* **112** G7
Mountain Home *Ark.,
  U.S.A.* **116** C8
Mountain Home *Idaho,
  U.S.A.* **108** E6
Mountain Iron *U.S.A.* **112** B7
Mountain Pass *U.S.A.* **111** K11
Mountain View *Ark., U.S.A.* **116** D8
Mountain View *Calif.,
  U.S.A.* **110** H4
Mountain View *Hawai'i,
  U.S.A.* **106** b

Mountain Zebra △ *S. Africa* **88** E4
Mountainair *U.S.A.* **109** J10
Mountlake Terrace *U.S.A.* **110** C4
Mountmellick *Ireland* **12** C4
Mountrath *Ireland* **12** D4
Moura *Australia* **94** C4
Moura *Brazil* **124** D6
Moura *Portugal* **37** G3
Mourão *Portugal* **37** G3
Mourdi, Dépression du
  Chad **79** D9
Mourdiah *Mali* **82** C3
Mourenx *France* **20** E3
Mouri *Ghana* **83** D4
Mourilyan *Australia* **94** B4
Mourmelon-le-Grand
  France **19** C11
Mourne → *U.K.* **12** B4
Mourne Mts. *U.K.* **12** B5
Mournies *Greece* **49** D6
Mouscron *Belgium* **17** D3
Moussoro *Chad* **79** F9
Mouthe *France* **19** F13
Moutier *Switz.* **25** H3
Moûtiers *France* **21** C10
Moutong *Indonesia* **63** D6
Mouy *France* **19** C9
Mouzaki *Greece* **46** B3
Mouzon *France* **19** C12
Movas *Mexico* **118** B3
Moville *Ireland* **12** A4
Mowandjum *Australia* **92** C3
Moy → *Ireland* **12** B2
Moya *Comoros* *Is.* **85** a
Moyale *Kenya* **81** G4
Moyamba *S. Leone* **82** D2
Moyen Atlas *Morocco* **78** B4
Moyo *Indonesia* **63** D6
Moyobamba *Peru* **124** E3
Moyyero → *Russia* **53** C11
Moyynqum *Kazakhstan* **52** E8
Moyynty *Kazakhstan* **52** E8
Mozambique =
  Moçambique *Mozam.* **87** F5
Mozambique ■ *Africa* **87** F4
Mozambique Chan. *Africa* **89** B7
Mozdok *Russia* **35** J7
Mozdūrān *Iran* **71** B9
Mozhaysk *Russia* **32** E9
Mozhga *Russia* **34** B11
Mozhnābād *Iran* **71** C9
Mozirje *Slovenia* **41** B11
Mozyr = Mazyr *Belarus* **23** B15
Mpanda *Tanzania* **86** D3
Mpésoba *Mali* **82** C3
Mphoengs *Zimbabwe* **89** C4
Mpika *Zambia* **87** E3
Mpulungu *Zambia* **87** D3
Mpumalanga *S. Africa* **89** D5
Mpumalanga □ *S. Africa* **89** D5
Mpwapwa *Tanzania* **86** D4
Mqanduli *S. Africa* **89** E4
Mqinvartsveri = Kazbek
  Russia **35** J7
Mramor *Serbia* **44** C5
Mrkonjić Grad *Bos.-H.* **28** F2
Mrkopalj *Croatia* **41** C11
Mrocza *Poland* **31** E4
Msaken *Tunisia* **79** A8
Msambansovu *Zimbabwe* **87** F3
M'sila → *Algeria* **78** A6
Msoro *Zambia* **87** E3
Msta → *Russia* **32** C6
Mstislavl = Mstsislaw
  Belarus **23** A16
Mstsislaw *Belarus* **23** A16
Mszana Dolna *Poland* **31** J7
Mszczonów *Poland* **31** G7
Mtama *Tanzania* **87** E4
Mtamvuna →
  Mthamvuna → *S. Africa* **89** E5
Mthamvuna → *S. Africa* **89** E5
Mthatha *S. Africa* **89** E4
Mtilikwe → *Zimbabwe* **87** G3
Mtsensk *Russia* **32** F9
Mtskheta *Georgia* **35** K7
Mtubatuba *S. Africa* **89** D5
Mtwalume *S. Africa* **89** E5
Mtwara-Mikindani *Tanzania* **87** E5
Mu Gia, Deo *Vietnam* **64** D5
Mu Ko Chang △ *Thailand* **65** G4
Mu Us Shamo *China* **56** E5
Muang Chiang Rai =
  Chiang Rai *Thailand* **58** H2
Muang Khong *Laos* **64** E5
Muang Lamphun *Thailand* **64** C2
Muang Mai *Thailand* **65** a
Muang Pak Beng *Laos* **58** H3
Muar *Malaysia* **65** L4
Muarabungo *Indonesia* **62** E2
Muaraenim *Indonesia* **62** E2
Muarajuloi *Indonesia* **62** E4
Muarakaman *Indonesia* **62** E5
Muaratebo *Indonesia* **62** E2
Muaratembesi *Indonesia* **62** E2
Muaratewe *Indonesia* **62** E4
Mubarakpur *India* **69** F10

Mubarraz = Al Mubarraz
  Si. Arabia **71** E6
Mubende *Uganda* **86** B3
Mubi *Nigeria* **83** C7
Mucajaí → *Brazil* **124** C6
Mücheln *Germany* **24** D7
Muchachos, Roque de los
  Canary Is. **48** F2
Muchinga Mts. *Zambia* **87** E3
Muchkapskiy *Russia* **34** E6
Muchuan *China* **58** C5
Muck *U.K.* **13** E2
Muckadilla *Australia* **95** D4
Muckle Flugga *U.K.* **13** A8
Mucur *Turkey* **72** C6
Mucuri *Brazil* **125** G11
Mucusso *Angola* **88** B3
Muda → *Canary Is.* **48** F6
Mudanjiang *China* **57** B15
Mudanya *Turkey* **45** F12
Muddy Cr. → *U.S.A.* **108** G8
Mudgee *Australia* **95** E4
Mudjatik → *Canada* **103** B7
Mudurnu *Turkey* **72** B4
Mueda *Mozam.* **87** E4
Muecate *Mozam.* **87** E4
Mueller Ranges *Australia* **92** C4
Muende *Mozam.* **87** E3
Muerto, Mar *Mexico* **119** D6
Mufu Shan *China* **59** C10
Mufulira *Zambia* **87** E2
Mufumbiro Range *Africa* **86** C2
Mugardos *Spain* **36** B2
Muge → *Portugal* **37** F2
Múggia *Italy* **41** C10
Mughal Sarai *India* **69** G10
Mughayrā' *Si. Arabia* **70** D3
Mugi *Japan* **55** H7
Mugia = Muxía *Spain* **36** B1
Mugila, Mts.
  Dem. Rep. of the Congo **86** D2
Muğla *Turkey* **47** D10
Muğla □ *Turkey* **47** D10
Muglad *Sudan* **81** E2
Müglizh *Bulgaria* **45** D9
Mugu *Nepal* **69** E10
Muhammad, Râs *Egypt* **70** E2
Muhammad Qol *Sudan* **80** C4
Muhammadabad *India* **69** F10
Muhesi → *Tanzania* **86** D4
Mühi → *Tanzania* **86** C3
Mühlacker *Germany* **25** G4
Mühldorf *Germany* **25** G8
Mühlhausen *Germany* **24** D6
Mühlig Hofmann fjell
  Antarctica **5** D3
Mühlviertel *Austria* **26** C7
Muhos *Finland* **8** D21
Muhu *Estonia* **32** C2
Muhutwe *Tanzania* **86** C3
Muine Bheag *Ireland* **12** D5
Muir, L. *Australia* **93** F2
Muir of Ord *U.K.* **13** D4
Mujeres, I. *Mexico* **120** B2
Mujnak = Muynak
  Uzbekistan **52** E6
Muka, Tanjung *Malaysia* **65** c
Mukacheve *Ukraine* **28** B7
Mukachevo = Mukacheve
  Ukraine **28** B7
Mukah *Malaysia* **62** D4
Mukandwara *India* **68** G6
Mukawwa, Geziret *Egypt* **70** F2
Mukawwar *Sudan* **80** C4
Mukdahan *Thailand* **64** D5
Mukden = Shenyang *China* **57** D12
Mukerian *India* **68** D6
Mukhavyets *Belarus* **31** F10
Mukhtolovo *Russia* **34** C6
Mukinbudin *Australia* **93** F2
Mukishi
  Dem. Rep. of the Congo **87** D1
Mukomuko *Indonesia* **62** E2
Mukomwenze
  Dem. Rep. of the Congo **86** D2
Muktsar *India* **68** D6
Mukur = Mokor *Afghan.* **68** C2
Mukutuwa → *Canada* **103** C9
Mukwela *Zambia* **87** F2
Mula *Spain* **39** G3
Mula → *Pakistan* **68** F2
Mulange
  Dem. Rep. of the Congo **86** C2
Mulanje, Mt. *Malawi* **87** F4
Mulchén *Chile* **126** D1
Mulde → *Germany* **24** D8
Mule Creek Junction *U.S.A.*
  108 E11
Muleba *Tanzania* **86** C3
Mulegé *Mexico* **118** B2
Muleshoe *U.S.A.* **116** D3
Muletta, Gara *Ethiopia* **81** F5
Mulgrave *Canada* **105** C7
Mulhacén *Spain* **37** H7
Mülheim *Germany* **24** D2
Mulhouse *France* **19** E14
Muli *China* **58** D3
Mulifanua *Samoa* **91** b
Muling *China* **57** B16
Mull *U.K.* **13** E3

Mull, Sound of *U.K.* **13** E3
Mullaittivu *Sri Lanka* **66** Q12
Mullen *U.S.A.* **112** D3
Mullens *U.S.A.* **113** G13
Muller, Pegunungan
  Indonesia **62** D4
Mullet Pen. *Ireland* **12** B1
Mullewa *Australia* **93** E2
Mülheim *Germany* **25** H3
Mulligan → *Australia* **94** D2
Mullingar *Ireland* **12** C4
Mullins *U.S.A.* **117** D15
Mullsjö *Sweden* **11** G7
Mullumbimby *Australia* **95** D5
Mulobezi *Zambia* **87** F2
Mulonga Plain *Zambia* **85** H4
Mulroy B. *Ireland* **12** A4
Multan *Pakistan* **68** D4
Mulumbe, Mts.
  Dem. Rep. of the Congo **87** D2
Mulungushi Dam *Zambia* **87** E2
Mulvane *U.S.A.* **112** G5
Mulwad *Sudan* **80** D3
Mumbai *India* **66** K8
Mumbwa *Zambia* **87** F2
Mumias *Kenya* **86** C4
Mumra *Russia* **35** H8
Mun → *Thailand* **64** E5
Muna *Indonesia* **63** F6
Munabao *India* **68** G4
Munamagi *Estonia* **32** D4
Muncan *Indonesia* **63** K18
Muncar *Indonesia* **63** J17
Münchberg *Germany* **25** E7
Müncheberg *Germany* **24** C10
München *Germany* **25** G7
München Franz Josef
  Strauss Int. ✈ (MUC)
  Germany **25** G7
Munchen-Gladbach =
  Mönchengladbach
  Germany **24** D2
Muncho Lake *Canada* **102** B3
Munch'ŏn *N. Korea* **57** E14
Muncie *U.S.A.* **113** E11
Muncoonie L. West *Australia* **94** D2
Mundabbera *Australia* **95** D5
Munday *U.S.A.* **116** E5
Münden *Germany* **24** D5
Mündö → *Tanzania* **86** D3
Mundiwindi *Australia* **92** D3
Mundo → *Spain* **39** G2
Mundo Novo *Brazil* **125** F10
Mundra *India* **68** H3
Mundrabilla *Australia* **93** F4
Munera *Spain* **39** F2
Mungallala *Australia* **95** D4
Mungallala Cr. → *Australia* **95** D4
Mungana *Australia* **94** B3
Mungaoli *India* **68** G8
Mungari *Mozam.* **87** F3
Mungbere
  Dem. Rep. of the Congo **86** B2
Mungeli *India* **69** H9
Munger *India* **69** G12
Mungeranie *Australia* **95** A2
Mungkan Kandju △
  Australia **94** A3
Munich = München
  Germany **25** G7
Munising *U.S.A.* **112** B10
Munka-Ljungby *Sweden* **11** H6
Munkebo *Denmark* **11** J4
Munkedal *Sweden* **11** F5
Munkfors *Sweden* **10** E7
Munku-Sardyk *Russia* **53** D11
Münnerstadt *Germany* **25** E6
Munnsville *U.S.A.* **115** D9
Muñoz Gamero, Pen. *Chile* **128** G2
Munroe L. *Canada* **103** B9
Munsan *S. Korea* **57** F14
Munster *France* **19** D14
Münster *Niedersachsen,
  Germany* **24** C6
Münster
  *Nordrhein-Westfalen,
  Germany* **24** D3
Munster □ *Ireland* **12** D3
Muntadgin *Australia* **93** F2
Muntele Mare, Vf. *Romania* **29** D8
Muntok *Indonesia* **62** E3
Munyama *Zambia* **87** F2
Munzur Dağları *Turkey* **73** C8
Muong Beng *Laos* **58** G3
Muong Boum *Vietnam* **58** F4
Muong Et *Laos* **64** B5
Muong Hai *Laos* **58** G3
Muong Hiem *Laos* **58** G4
Muong Houn *Laos* **58** G3
Muong Hung *Vietnam* **58** G4
Muong Kau *Laos* **64** E5
Muong Khao *Laos* **64** C4
Muong Khoua *Laos* **58** G4
Muong Liep *Laos* **64** C4
Muong May *Laos* **64** E6
Muong Ngeun *Laos* **58** G3
Muong Ngoi *Laos* **58** G4
Muong Nhie *Vietnam* **58** F4
Muong Nong *Laos* **64** D6

Muong Ou Tay *Laos* **58** F3
Muong Oua *Laos* **64** C3
Muong Peun *Laos* **58** G4
Muong Phalane *Laos* **64** D5
Muong Phieng *Laos* **64** C3
Muong Phine *Laos* **64** D6
Muong Sai *Laos* **58** G3
Muong Saiapoun *Laos* **64** C3
Muong Sen *Vietnam* **64** C5
Muong Sing *Laos* **58** G3
Muong Son *Laos* **58** G4
Muong Soui *Laos* **64** C4
Muong Va *Laos* **58** G4
Muong Xia *Vietnam* **64** B5
Muonio *Finland* **8** C20
Muonio älv →
  Muonionjoki → *Finland* **8** C20
Muonioälven =
  Muonionjoki → *Finland* **8** C20
Muonionjoki → *Finland* **8** C20
Muping *China* **57** F11
Mupoi *Sudan* **81** F2
Muqaddam, Wadi → *Sudan* **80** D3
Muqdisho *Somali Rep.* **75** G4
Mur → *Austria* **27** E9
Mûr-de-Bretagne *France* **18** D4
Muradiye *Manisa, Turkey* **47** C9
Muradiye *Van, Turkey* **73** C10
Murakami *Japan* **54** E9
Murallón, Cerro *Chile* **128** F2
Muranda *Rwanda* **86** C2
Murang'a *Kenya* **86** C4
Murashi *Russia* **52** D5
Murat *France* **20** C6
Murat → *Turkey* **73** C9
Murat Dağı *Turkey* **47** C11
Muratlı *Turkey* **45** E11
Murato *France* **21** F13
Murau *Austria* **26** D7
Murava *Belarus* **31** F11
Muravera *Italy* **42** C2
Murayama *Japan* **54** E10
Murça *Portugal* **36** D3
Murchison → *Australia* **93** E1
Murchison, Mt. *Antarctica* **5** D11
Murchison Falls *Uganda* **86** B3
Murchison Falls △ *Uganda* **86** B3
Murchison Ra. *Australia* **94** C1
Murchison Rapids *Malawi* **87** F3
Murchison Roadhouse
  Australia **93** E1
Murcia *Spain* **39** G3
Murcia □ *Spain* **39** H3
Murdo *U.S.A.* **112** D3
Murdoch Pt. *Australia* **94** A3
Mürefte *Turkey* **45** F11
Mureş □ *Romania* **29** D9
Mureş → *Romania* **28** D5
Mureşul = Mureş →
  Romania **28** D5
Muret *France* **20** E5
Murewa *Zimbabwe* **89** B5
Murfreesboro *N.C., U.S.A.* **117** C16
Murfreesboro *Tenn., U.S.A.* **117** D11
Murgab = Murghob *Tajikistan* **52** F8
Murgap → *Turkmenistan* **71** B9
Murgenella *Australia* **92** B5
Murgeni *Romania* **29** D13
Murgha Kibzai *Pakistan* **68** D3
Murghob = Murgap
  Tajikistan **52** F8
Murgon *Australia* **95** D5
Muri *India* **69** H11
Muria *Indonesia* **63** G14
Muriaé *Brazil* **127** A7
Müritz *Germany* **24** B8
Müritz △ *Germany* **24** B8
Murliganj *India* **69** G12
Murmansk *Russia* **8** B25
Murmashi *Russia* **8** B25
Murnau *Germany* **25** H7
Muro *France* **21** F12
Muro *Spain* **48** B10
Muro, C. de *France* **21** G12
Muro de Alcoy *Spain* **39** G4
Muro Lucano *Italy* **43** B8
Murom *Russia* **34** C6
Muroran *Japan* **54** C10
Muros *Spain* **36** C1
Muros e Noya, Ría de →
  Spain **36** C1
Muroto *Japan* **55** H7
Muroto-Misaki *Japan* **55** H7
Murovani Kurylivtsi
  Ukraine **29** B12
Murowana Gošlina *Poland* **31** F3
Murphy *U.S.A.* **108** E5
Murphys *U.S.A.* **110** G6
Murrat *Sudan* **80** D2
Murrat Wells *Sudan* **80** C3
Murray *Ky., U.S.A.* **112** G9
Murray *Utah, U.S.A.* **108** F8
Murray → *Australia* **95** F2
Murray, L. *U.S.A.* **117** D14
Murray Bridge *Australia* **95** F2
Murray Fracture Zone
  Pac. Oc. **97** D14

Murray Harbour *Canada* **105** C7
Murray River △ *Australia* **95** E3
Murraysburg *S. Africa* **88** E3
Murree *Pakistan* **68** C5
Murrieta *U.S.A.* **111** M9
Murro di Porco, Capo *Italy* **43** F8
Murrumbidgee → *Australia* **95** E3
Murrumburrah *Australia* **95** E4
Murrurundi *Australia* **95** E5
Murshid *Sudan* **80** C3
Murshidabad *India* **69** G13
Murska Sobota *Slovenia* **41** B13
Murtle L. *Canada* **102** C5
Murtoa *Australia* **95** F3
Murtosa *Portugal* **36** E2
Murungu *Tanzania* **86** C3
Mururoa *French Polynesia* **97** K14
Murwara *India* **69** H9
Murwillumbah *Australia* **95** D5
Mürz → *Austria* **26** D8
Mürzzuschlag *Austria* **26** D8
Muş *Turkey* **73** C9
Muş □ *Turkey* **73** C9
Mûsa, Gebel *Egypt* **70** D2
Musa Khel *Pakistan* **68** D3
Mûsa Qal'eh *Afghan.* **66** C4
Musafirkhana *India* **69** F9
Musā'idah *Iraq* **73** H12
Musala *Bulgaria* **44** D7
Musala *Indonesia* **62** D1
Musan *N. Korea* **57** C15
Musangu =
    Dem. Rep. of the Congo **87** E1
Musasa *Tanzania* **86** C3
Musay'īd *Qatar* **71** E6
Muscat = Masqat *Oman* **75** C6
Muscatine *U.S.A.* **112** E8
Muscle Shoals *U.S.A.* **117** D11
Musengezi =
    Unsengedsi → *Zimbabwe* **87** F3
Musgrave Harbour *Canada* **105** C9
Musgrave Ranges *Australia* **93** E5
Mushie *Dem. Rep. of the Congo* **84** E3
Mushin *Nigeria* **83** D5
Musi → *Indonesia* **62** E2
Musina *S. Africa* **89** C5
Muskeg → *Canada* **102** A4
Muskegon *U.S.A.* **112** D10
Muskegon → *U.S.A.* **112** D10
Muskegon Heights *U.S.A.* **112** D10
Muskogee *U.S.A.* **116** D7
Muskoka, L. *Canada* **114** B5
Muskoka Falls *Canada* **114** B5
Muskwa → *Canada* **102** B4
Muslimiyah *Syria* **70** B3
Musmar *Sudan* **80** D2
Musofu *Zambia* **87** E2
Musoma *Tanzania* **86** C3
Musquaro, L. *Canada* **105** B7
Musquodoboit Harbour
    Canada **105** D7
Musselburgh *U.K.* **13** F5
Musselshell → *U.S.A.* **108** C10
Mussende *Angola* **84** G3
Mussidan *France* **20** C4
Mussomeli *Italy* **42** E6
Mussoorie *India* **68** D8
Mussuco *Angola* **88** B2
Mustafakemalpaşa *Turkey* **45** F12
Mustang *Nepal* **69** E10
Musters, L. *Argentina* **128** F3
Musudan *N. Korea* **57** D15
Muswellbrook *Australia* **95** E5
Muszyna *Poland* **31** J7
Mût *Egypt* **80** B2
Mut *Turkey* **72** D5
Mutanda *Mozam.* **89** C5
Mutanda *Zambia* **87** E2
Mutare *Zimbabwe* **87** F3
Mutawintji △ *Australia* **95** E3
Mutha *Kenya* **86** C4
Muting *Indonesia* **63** F10
Mutki = Mirtağ *Turkey* **70** B4
Mutoko *Zimbabwe* **89** B5
Mutomo *Kenya* **86** C4
Mutoray *Russia* **53** C11
Mutsamudu *Comoros Is.* **85** a
Mutshatsha
    Dem. Rep. of the Congo **87** E1
Mutsu *Japan* **54** D10
Mutsu-Wan *Japan* **54** D10
Muttaburra *Australia* **94** C3
Muttalip *Turkey* **47** B12
Mutuáli *Mozam.* **87** E4
Mutum Biyu *Nigeria* **83** D7
Muweilih *Egypt* **74** E3
Muxía *Spain* **36** B1
Muy Muy *Nic.* **120** D2
Muyinga *Burundi* **86** C3
Muynak *Uzbekistan* **52** E6
Muyunkum, Peski =
    Moyynqum *Kazakhstan* **52** E8
Muzaffarabad *Pakistan* **69** B5
Muzaffargarh *Pakistan* **68** D4
Muzaffarnagar *India* **68** E7
Muzaffarpur *India* **69** F11
Muzaffirpur *Pakistan* **68** D3
Muzhi *Russia* **52** C7

Muzillac *France* **18** E4
Muzūra *Egypt* **80** J7
Mvôlô *Sudan* **81** F2
Mvuma *Zimbabwe* **87** F3
Mvurwi *Zimbabwe* **87** F3
Mwabvi △ *Malawi* **87** F3
Mwadui *Tanzania* **86** C3
Mwali = Mohéli *Comoros Is.* **85** a
Mwambo *Tanzania* **87** E5
Mwandi *Zambia* **87** F1
Mwanza
    Dem. Rep. of the Congo **86** D2
Mwanza *Tanzania* **86** C3
Mwanza *Zambia* **87** F1
Mwanza □ *Tanzania* **86** C3
Mwaya *Tanzania* **87** E3
Mweelrea *Ireland* **12** C2
Mweka *Dem. Rep. of the Congo* **84** E4
Mwene-Ditu
    Dem. Rep. of the Congo **84** F4
Mwenezi *Zimbabwe* **87** G3
Mwenezi → *Mozam.* **87** G3
Mwenga
    Dem. Rep. of the Congo **86** C2
Mweru, L. *Zambia* **87** D2
Mweru Wantipa △ *Zambia* **87** D2
Mweza Range *Zimbabwe* **87** G3
Mwilambwe
    Dem. Rep. of the Congo **86** D2
Mwimbi *Tanzania* **87** D3
Mwingi *Kenya* **86** C4
Mwinilunga *Zambia* **87** E1
My Tho *Vietnam* **65** G6
Myajlar *India* **68** F4
Myanaung *Burma* **67** K19
Myaungmya *Burma* **67** L19
Myanmar = Burma ■ *Asia* **67** J20
Myebon *Burma* **67** J19
Myedna *Belarus* **31** G10
Myeik Kyunzu *Burma* **65** G1
Myerstown *U.S.A.* **115** F8
Myingyan *Burma* **67** J19
Myitkyina *Burma* **67** G20
Myjava *Slovak Rep.* **27** C10
Mykhaylivka *Ukraine* **33** J8
Mykines *Færoe Is.* **8** E9
Mykolayiv *Ukraine* **33** J7
Mykolayiv □ *Ukraine* **33** J6
Mykonos *Greece* **47** D7
Mymensingh *Bangla.* **67** G17
Mynydd Du *U.K.* **15** F4
Mynköw *Poland* **31** H6
Myrdalsjökull *Iceland* **8** E4
Myrhorod *Ukraine* **33** H7
Myrtle Beach *U.S.A.* **117** E15
Myrtle Creek *U.S.A.* **108** E2
Myrtle Point *U.S.A.* **108** E1
Myrtou *Cyprus* **49** D12
Mysia *Turkey* **45** G11
Myślenice *Poland* **31** J6
Myślibórz *Poland* **31** F1
Mysłowice *Poland* **31** H6
Mysore = Karnataka □
    India **66** N10
Mysore *India* **66** N10
Mystic *U.S.A.* **115** E13
Myszków *Poland* **31** H6
Myszyniec *Poland* **30** E8
Mytishchi *Russia* **32** E9
Mývatn *Iceland* **8** D5
Mže → *Czech Rep.* **26** B6
Mzimba *Malawi* **87** E3
Mzimkulu → *S. Africa* **89** E5
Mzimvubu → *S. Africa* **89** E4
Mzuzu *Malawi* **87** E3

N

Na Hearadh = Harris *U.K.* **13** D2
Na Noi *Thailand* **64** C3
Na Phao *Laos* **64** D5
Na Sam *Vietnam* **58** F6
Na San *Vietnam* **64** B5
Na Thon *Thailand* **65** b
Naab → *Germany* **25** F8
Na'am *Sudan* **81** F2
Na'am → *Sudan* **81** F2
Naantali *Finland* **32** B1
Naas *Ireland* **12** C5
Nababeep *S. Africa* **88** D2
Nabadwip = Navadwip
    India **69** H13
Nabawa *Australia* **93** E1
Nabberu, L. *Australia* **93** E3
Nabburg *Germany* **25** F8
Naberezhnyye Chelny
    Russia **34** C11
Nabeul *Tunisia* **79** A8
Nabha *India* **68** D7
Nabid *Iran* **71** D8
Nabire *Indonesia* **63** E9
Nabisar *Pakistan* **68** G3
Nabisipi → *Canada* **105** B7
Nabiswera *Uganda* **86** B3
Nabadwip → *India* **69** F9
Nabeul → *India* **69** D9
Nain *Canada* **105** A7
Nã'īn *Iran* **71** C7
Naini Tal *India* **69** E8
Nainpur *India* **69** H9
Naintré *France* **18** F7
Nainwa *India* **68** G6
Nairn *U.K.* **13** D5
Nairobi *Kenya* **86** C4
Nairobi △ *Kenya* **86** C4
Nairai *Fiji* **91** a
Naissaar *Estonia* **32** C3
Nābulus *West Bank* **74** C4

Nacala-Velha *Mozam.* **87** E5
Nacaome *Honduras* **120** D2
Nacaroa *Mozam.* **87** E4
Naches *U.S.A.* **108** C3
Naches → *U.S.A.* **110** D6
Nachicapau, L. *Canada* **105** A6
Nachingwea *Tanzania* **87** E4
Nachna *India* **68** F4
Náchod *Czech Rep.* **26** A9
Nacimiento, L. *U.S.A.* **110** K6
Naco *Mexico* **118** A3
Nacogdoches *U.S.A.* **116** F7
Nácori Chico *Mexico* **118** B3
Nacozari de García *Mexico* **118** A3
Nacula *Fiji* **91** a
Nådendal = Naantali *Finland* **32** B1
Nadi *Fiji* **91** a
Nadi *Sudan* **80** D3
Nadiad *India* **68** H5
Nădlac *Romania* **28** D5
Nador *Morocco* **78** B5
Nadur *Malta* **49** C1
Nadūshan *Iran* **71** C7
Nadvirna *Ukraine* **29** B9
Nadvornaya = Nadvirna
    Ukraine **29** B9
Nadym *Russia* **52** C8
Nadym → *Russia* **52** C8
Nærbø *Norway* **9** G11
Næstved *Denmark* **11** J5
Nafada *Nigeria* **83** C7
Nafpaktos *Greece* **46** C3
Nafplio *Greece* **46** D4
Naft-e Safid *Iran* **71** D6
Naftshahr *Iran* **73** E11
Nafud Desert = An Nafūd
    Si. Arabia **70** D4
Nag Hammâdi *Egypt* **80** B3
Naga *Phil.* **61** E5
Nagagami *Canada* **104** B3
Nagahama *Japan* **55** G8
Nagai *Japan* **54** E10
Nagaland □ *India* **67** G19
Nagano *Japan* **55** F9
Nagano □ *Japan* **55** F9
Nagaoka *Japan* **55** F9
Nagappattinam *India* **66** P11
Nagar → *Bangla.* **69** G13
Nagar Parkar *Pakistan* **68** G4
Nagasaki *Japan* **55** H4
Nagasaki □ *Japan* **55** H4
Nagato *Japan* **55** G5
Nagaur *India* **68** F5
Nagda *India* **68** H6
Nagercoil *India* **66** Q10
Nagina *India* **68** E8
Nagîneh *Iran* **71** C8
Nagir *Pakistan* **69** A6
Naglarby *Sweden* **10** D9
Nagod *India* **69** G9
Nagold *Germany* **25** G4
Nagold → *Germany* **25** G4
Nagoorin *Australia* **94** C5
Nagorno-Karabakh □
    Azerbaijan **73** C12
Nagornyy *Russia* **53** D13
Nagoya *Japan* **55** G8
Nagpur *India* **66** J11
Nagua *Dom. Rep.* **121** C6
Naguabo *Puerto Rico* **121** d
Nagyatád *Hungary* **28** D2
Nagyecsed *Hungary* **28** C7
Nagykálló *Hungary* **28** C6
Nagykanizsa *Hungary* **28** D2
Nagykáta *Hungary* **28** C4
Nagykőrös *Hungary* **28** C4
Naha *Japan* **55** L3
Nahan *India* **68** D7
Nahanni △ *Canada* **102** A4
Nahanni Butte *Canada* **102** A4
Nahargarh *Mad. P., India* **68** G6
Nahargarh *Raj., India* **68** G7
Nahariyya *Israel* **72** F6
Nahāvand *Iran* **73** E13
Nahe → *Germany* **25** F3
Nahirne *Ukraine* **29** E13
Nahîya, W. → *Egypt* **80** B3
Nahuel Huapi, L. *Argentina* **128** E2
Nahuelbuta △ *Chile* **126** D1
Nai Yong *Thailand* **65** a
Naicá *Mexico* **118** B3
Naicam *Canada* **103** C8
Naikoon △ *Canada* **102** C2
Naila *Germany* **25** E7
Naimisharanya *India* **69** F9
Naimona'nyi Feng *Nepal* **69** D9
Nain *Canada* **105** A7
Nã'īn *Iran* **71** C7
Naini Tal *India* **69** E8
Nainpur *India* **69** H9
Naintré *France* **18** F7
Nainwa *India* **68** G6
Nairn *U.K.* **13** D5
Nairobi *Kenya* **86** C4
Nairobi △ *Kenya* **86** C4
Nairai *Fiji* **91** a
Naissaar *Estonia* **32** C3

Naita, Mt. *Ethiopia* **81** F4
Naitaba *Fiji* **91** a
Naivasha *Kenya* **86** C4
Naivasha, L. *Kenya* **86** C4
Najac *France* **20** D5
Najaf = An Najaf *Iraq* **73** G11
Najafābād *Iran* **71** C6
Najd *Si. Arabia* **75** B3
Nájera *Spain* **38** C2
Najerilla → *Spain* **38** C2
Najibabad *India* **68** E8
Najin *N. Korea* **57** C16
Najmah *Si. Arabia* **71** E6
Najrān *Si. Arabia* **75** D3
Naju *S. Korea* **57** G14
Nakadōri-Shima *Japan* **55** H4
Nakalagba
    Dem. Rep. of the Congo **86** B2
Nakaminato *Japan* **55** F10
Nakamura *Japan* **55** H6
Nakano *Japan* **55** F9
Nakano-Shima *Japan* **55** K4
Nakashibetsu *Japan* **54** C12
Nakfa *Eritrea* **81** D4
Nakfa △ *Eritrea* **81** D4
Nakha Yai, Ko *Thailand* **65** a
Nakhichevan = Naxçıvan
    Azerbaijan **73** C11
Nakhichevan Rep. =
    Naxçıvan □ *Azerbaijan* **73** C11
Nakhl *Egypt* **74** F2
Nakhl-e Taqī *Iran* **71** E7
Nakhodka *Russia* **54** C6
Nakhon Nayok *Thailand* **64** E3
Nakhon Pathom *Thailand* **64** F3
Nakhon Phanom *Thailand* **64** D5
Nakhon Ratchasima
    Thailand **64** E4
Nakhon Sawan *Thailand* **64** E3
Nakhon Si Thammarat
    Thailand **65** H3
Nakhon Thai *Thailand* **64** D3
Nakhtarana *India* **68** H3
Nakina *Canada* **104** B2
Naklo nad Notecią *Poland* **31** E4
Nako *Burkina Faso* **82** C4
Nakodar *India* **68** D6
Naksov *Denmark* **11** K5
Naktong → *S. Korea* **57** G15
Nakuru *Kenya* **86** C4
Nakuru, L. *Kenya* **86** C4
Nakusp *Canada* **102** C5
Nal *Pakistan* **68** F2
Nal → *Pakistan* **68** G1
Nalázi *Mozam.* **89** C5
Nalchik *Russia* **35** J6
Nalęczów *Poland* **31** G9
Nalerigu *Ghana* **83** C4
Nalgonda *India* **66** L11
Nalhati *India* **69** G12
Naliya *India* **68** H3
Nallamalai Hills *India* **66** M11
Nallıhan *Turkey* **72** B4
Nalón → *Spain* **36** B4
Nalubaale Dam *Uganda* **86** B3
Nam Can *Vietnam* **65** H5
Nam-ch'on *N. Korea* **57** E14
Nam Co *China* **60** C4
Nam Dinh *Vietnam* **58** G6
Nam Du, Hon *Vietnam* **65** H5
Nam Nao △ *Thailand* **64** D3
Nam Ngum Res. *Laos* **64** C4
Nam-Phan *Vietnam* **65** G6
Nam Phong *Thailand* **64** D4
Nam Tha *Laos* **58** G3
Nam Tok *Thailand* **64** E2
Namacunde *Angola* **88** B2
Namacurra *Mozam.* **89** B6
Namak, Daryācheh-ye *Iran* **71** C7
Namak, Kavir-e *Iran* **71** C8
Namakzār, Daryācheh-ye
    Iran **71** C9
Namaland *Namibia* **88** C2
Namanga *Kenya* **86** C4
Namangan *Uzbekistan* **52** E8
Namapa *Mozam.* **87** E4
Namaqualand *S. Africa* **88** E2
Namasagali *Uganda* **86** B3
Namber *Indonesia* **63** E8
Nambour *Australia* **95** D5
Nambouwalu =
    Nabouwalu *Fiji* **91** a
Nambucca Heads *Australia* **95** E5
Nambung △ *Australia* **93** F2
Namche Bazar *Nepal* **69** F12
Namchonjŏm =
    Nam-ch'on *N. Korea* **57** E14
Namecunda *Mozam.* **87** E4
Namenalala *Fiji* **91** a
Nameponda *Mozam.* **87** F4
Náměšt' nad Oslavou
    Czech Rep. **27** B9
Nametil *Mozam.* **87** F4
Namew L. *Canada* **103** C8
Namgia *India* **68** D8
Namhkam *Burma* **58** E1
Namib Desert *Namibia* **88** C2
Namib-Naukluft △ *Namibia* **88** C2

Namibe *Angola* **85** H2
Namibe □ *Angola* **88** B1
Namibia ■ *Africa* **88** C2
Namibwoestyn = Namib
    Desert *Namibia* **88** C2
Namīn *Iran* **73** C13
Namlea *Indonesia* **63** E7
Najd *Si. Arabia* **75** B3
Namoi → *Australia* **95** E4
Nampa *U.S.A.* **108** E5
Nampala *Mali* **82** B3
Namp'o *N. Korea* **57** E13
Nampō-Shotō *Japan* **55** J10
Nampula *Mozam.* **87** F4
Namrole *Indonesia* **63** E7
Namse Shankou *China* **69** E10
Namsen → *Norway* **8** D14
Namsos *Norway* **8** D14
Namtok Chat Trakan △
    Thailand **64** D3
Namtok Mae Surin △
    Thailand **64** C2
Namtsy *Russia* **53** C13
Namtu *Burma* **67** H20
Namtumbo *Tanzania* **87** E4
Namu *Canada* **102** C3
Namuka-i-Lau *Fiji* **91** a
Namur *Belgium* **17** D4
Namur □ *Belgium* **17** D4
Namuruputh *Kenya* **86** B4
Namutoni *Namibia* **88** B2
Namwala *Zambia* **87** F2
Namwon *S. Korea* **57** G14
Namyang *N. Korea* **57** C15
Namysłów *Poland* **31** G4
Nan *Thailand* **64** C3
Nan → *Thailand* **64** E3
Nan-ch'ang = Nanchang
    China **59** C10
Nan Ling *China* **59** E8
Nan Xian *China* **59** C9
Nana *Romania* **29** F11
Nana Kru *Liberia* **82** E3
Nanaimo *Canada* **102** D4
Nanam *N. Korea* **57** D15
Nanan *China* **59** E12
Nanango *Australia* **95** D5
Nan'ao *China* **59** F11
Nanao *Japan* **55** F8
Nanbu *China* **58** B6
Nanchang *China* **59** C10
Nancheng *China* **59** D11
Nanching = Nanjing *China* **59** A12
Nanchong *China* **58** B6
Nanchuan *China* **58** C6
Nancy *France* **19** D13
Nanda Devi *India* **69** D8
Nanda Devi △ *India* **69** D8
Nanda Kot *India* **69** D9
Nandan *China* **58** E6
Nandan *Japan* **55** G7
Nanded *India* **68** K10
Nandewar Ra. *Australia* **95** E5
Nandi = Nadi *Fiji* **91** a
Nandigram *India* **69** H12
Nandurbar *India* **68** J9
Nandyal *India* **66** M11
Nanfeng *Guangdong, China* **59** F8
Nanfeng *Jiangxi, China* **59** D11
Nang Rong *Thailand* **64** E4
Nanga-Eboko *Cameroon* **83** E7
Nanga Parbat *Pakistan* **69** B6
Nangade *Mozam.* **87** E4
Nangapinoh *Indonesia* **62** E4
Nangarhār □ *Afghan.* **66** B7
Nangatayap *Indonesia* **62** E4
Nangeya Mts. *Uganda* **86** B3
Nangis *France* **19** D10
Nangong *China* **56** F8
Nanhua *China* **58** E3
Nanhuang *China* **57** F11
Nanhui *China* **59** B13
Nanjeko *Zambia* **87** F1
Nanji Shan *China* **59** D13
Nanjian *China* **58** E3
Nanjiang *China* **58** A6
Nanjing *Fujian, China* **59** E11
Nanjing *Jiangsu, China* **59** A12
Nanjirinji *Tanzania* **87** D4
Nankana Sahib *Pakistan* **68** D5
Nankang *China* **59** E10
Nanking = Nanjing *China* **59** A12
Nankoku *Japan* **55** H6
Nanling *China* **59** B12
Nanning *China* **58** F7
Nannup *Australia* **93** F2
Nanpan Jiang → *China* **58** E6
Nanpara *India* **69** F9
Nanpi *China* **56** E9
Nanping *Fujian, China* **59** D12
Nanping *Henan, China* **59** C9
Nanri Dao *China* **59** E12
Nanripe *Mozam.* **87** E4
Nansei-Shotō =
    Ryūkyū-rettō *Japan* **55** M3
Nansen Basin *Arctic* **4** A10
Nansen Sd. *Canada* **101** A10
Nanshan I. *S. China Sea* **62** B5
Nansio *Tanzania* **86** C3
Nant *France* **20** D7

Nanterre *France* **19** D9
Nantes *France* **18** E5
Nanticoke *U.S.A.* **115** E8
Nanton *Canada* **102** C6
Nantong *China* **59** A13
Nant'ou *Taiwan* **59** F13
Nantua *France* **19** F12
Nantucket *U.S.A.* **113** E18
Nantucket I. *U.S.A.* **113** E18
Nantwich *U.K.* **14** D5
Nanty Glo *U.S.A.* **114** F6
Nanuku Passage *Fiji* **91** a
Nanuque *Brazil* **125** G10
Nanusa, Kepulauan
    Indonesia **63** D7
Nanutarra Roadhouse
    Australia **92** D2
Nanxi *China* **58** C5
Nanxiong *China* **59** E10
Nanyang *China* **56** H7
Nanyi Hu *China* **59** B12
Nanyuki *Kenya* **86** B4
Nanzhang *China* **59** B8
Nao, C. de la *Spain* **39** G5
Naococane, L. *Canada* **105** B5
Naoussa *Cyclades, Greece* **47** D7
Naoussa *Imathia, Greece* **44** F6
Naozhou Dao *China* **59** G8
Napa *U.S.A.* **110** G4
Napa → *U.S.A.* **110** G4
Napanee *Canada* **114** B8
Napanoch *U.S.A.* **115** E10
Nape *Laos* **64** C5
Nape Pass = Keo Neua,
    Deo *Vietnam* **64** C5
Napier *N.Z.* **91** C6
Napier Broome B. *Australia* **92** B4
Napier Pen. *Australia* **94** A2
Napierville *Canada* **115** A11
Naples = Nápoli *Italy* **43** B7
Naples *U.S.A.* **117** H14
Napo *China* **58** F5
Napo → *Peru* **124** D4
Napoleon *N. Dak., U.S.A.* **112** B4
Napoleon *Ohio, U.S.A.* **113** E11
Nápoli *Italy* **43** B7
Nápoli, G. di *Italy* **43** B7
Nápoli Capodichino ✈
    (NAP) *Italy* **43** B7
Napopo *Dem. Rep. of the Congo* **86** B2
Naqâda *Egypt* **80** B3
Naqadeh *Iran* **73** D11
Naqb, Ra's an *Jordan* **74** F4
Naqqāsh *Iran* **71** C6
Nara *Japan* **55** G7
Nara □ *Japan* **55** G7
Nara *Mali* **82** B3
Nara Canal *Pakistan* **68** G3
Nara Visa *U.S.A.* **109** J12
Naracoorte *Australia* **95** F3
Naradhan *Australia* **95** E4
Naraini *India* **69** G9
Naranjos *Mexico* **119** C5
Narasapur *India* **67** L12
Narathiwat *Thailand* **65** J3
Narayanganj *Bangla.* **67** H17
Narayanpet *India* **66** L10
Narberth *U.K.* **15** F3
Narbonne *France* **20** E7
Narcea → *Spain* **36** B4
Nardīn *Iran* **71** B7
Nardò *Italy* **43** B11
Narembeen *Australia* **93** F2
Narendranagar *India* **68** D8
Nares Str. *Arctic* **98** A13
Naretha *Australia* **93** F3
Narew → *Poland* **31** F7
Nari → *Pakistan* **68** F2
Narin *Afghan.* **66** A6
Narindra, Helodranon' i
    Madag. **89** A8
Narita *Japan* **55** G10
Nariva Swamp *Trin. & Tob.* **125** K15
Närke *Sweden* **10** E8
Narmada → *India* **68** J5
Narman *Turkey* **73** B9
Narnaul *India* **68** E7
Narni *Italy* **41** F9
Naro *Ghana* **82** C4
Naro Fominsk *Russia* **32** E9
Narodnaya *Russia* **6** B17
Narok *Kenya* **86** C4
Narón *Spain* **36** B2
Narooma *Australia* **95** F5
Narowal *Pakistan* **68** C6
Narrabri *Australia* **95** E4
Narran → *Australia* **95** D4
Narrandera *Australia* **95** E4
Narrogin *Australia* **93** F2
Narromine *Australia* **95** E4
Narrow Hills △ *Canada* **103** C8
Narsimhapur *India* **69** H8
Narsinghgarh *India* **68** H7
Nartes, L. e *Albania* **44** D3
Nartkala *Russia* **35** J6
Naruto *Japan* **55** G7
Narva *Estonia* **32** C5
Narva → *Russia* **32** C4

Narva Bay = Narva Laht *Estonia* 9 G22
Narva Laht *Estonia* 9 G22
Narvik *Norway* 8 B17
Narvskoye Vdkhr. *Russia* 32 C5
Narwana *India* 68 E7
Narwiański △ *Poland* 31 F9
Naryan-Mar *Russia* 52 C6
Narym *Russia* 52 D9
Naryn *Kyrgyzstan* 52 E8
Naryn Qum *Kazakhstan* 35 G9
Nasa *Norway* 8 C16
Nasau *Fiji* 91 a
Năsăud *Romania* 29 C9
Nasca = Nazca *Peru* 124 F4
Naseby *N.Z.* 91 F3
Naselle *U.S.A.* 110 D3
Naser, Buheirat en *Egypt* 80 C3
Nashua *Mont., U.S.A.* 108 B10
Nashua *N.H., U.S.A.* 115 D13
Nashville *Ark., U.S.A.* 116 E8
Nashville *Ga., U.S.A.* 117 F13
Nashville *Tenn., U.S.A.* 117 C11
Našice *Croatia* 28 E3
Nasielsk *Poland* 31 F7
Nasik *India* 66 K8
Nasipit *Phil.* 61 G6
Nasir *Sudan* 81 F3
Nasirabad *India* 68 F6
Nasirabad *Pakistan* 68 E3
Nasiri = Ahvāz *Iran* 71 D6
Nasiriyah = An Nāşirīyah *Iraq* 70 D5
Naskaupi → *Canada* 105 B7
Naso *Italy* 43 D7
Naşrābād *Iran* 71 C6
Naşriān-e Pā'īn *Iran* 70 C5
Nass → *Canada* 102 C3
Nassarawa *Nigeria* 83 D6
Nassarawa □ *Nigeria* 83 D6
Nassau *Bahamas* 120 A4
Nassau *U.S.A.* 115 D11
Nassau, B. *Chile* 128 H3
Nasser, L. = Naser, Buheirat en *Egypt* 80 C3
Nassian *Ivory C.* 82 D4
Nässjö *Sweden* 11 G8
Nastapoka → *Canada* 104 A4
Nastapoka, Is. *Canada* 104 A4
Nasugbu *Phil.* 61 D4
Näsum *Sweden* 11 H8
Näsviken *Sweden* 10 C10
Nata *Botswana* 88 C4
Nata → *Botswana* 88 C4
Natal *Brazil* 125 E11
Natal *Indonesia* 62 D1
Natal Drakensberg △ *S. Africa* 89 D4
Natalinci *Serbia* 28 F5
Naţanz *Iran* 71 C6
Natashquan *Canada* 105 B7
Natashquan → *Canada* 105 B7
Natchez *U.S.A.* 116 F9
Natchitoches *U.S.A.* 116 F8
Natewa B. *Fiji* 91 a
Nathalia *Australia* 95 F4
Nathdwara *India* 68 G5
Nati, Pta. *Spain* 48 A10
Natimuk *Australia* 95 F3
Nation → *Canada* 102 B4
National City *U.S.A.* 111 N9
Natitingou *Benin* 83 C5
Natividad, I. *Mexico* 118 B1
Natkyizin *Burma* 64 E1
Natron, L. *Tanzania* 86 C4
Natrona Heights *U.S.A.* 114 F5
Natrûn, W. el → *Egypt* 80 H7
Nättraby *Sweden* 11 H9
Natukanaoka Pan *Namibia* 88 B2
Natuna Besar, Kepulauan *Indonesia* 62 D3
Natuna Is. = Natuna Besar, Kepulauan *Indonesia* 62 D3
Natuna Selatan, Kepulauan *Indonesia* 62 D3
Natural Bridge *U.S.A.* 115 B9
Natural Bridges △ *U.S.A.* 109 H9
Naturaliste, C. *Tas., Australia* 95 G4
Naturaliste, C. *W. Austral., Australia* 93 F2
Naturaliste Plateau *Ind. Oc.* 96 L3
Nau Qala *Afghan.* 68 B3
Naucelle *France* 20 D6
Nauders *Austria* 26 E3
Nauen *Germany* 24 C8
Naugatuck *U.S.A.* 115 E11
Naujaat = Repulse Bay *Canada* 101 C11
Naujoji Akmenė *Lithuania* 30 B9
Naumburg *Germany* 24 D7
Nauru ■ *Pac. Oc.* 90 B9
Naushahra = Nowshera *Pakistan* 66 C8
Naushahro *Pakistan* 68 F3
Naushon I. *U.S.A.* 115 E14
Nausori *Fiji* 91 a
Nauta *Peru* 124 D4
Nautanwa *India* 69 F10

Naute △ *Namibia* 88 D2
Nautla *Mexico* 119 C5
Nava *Mexico* 118 B4
Nava *Spain* 36 B5
Nava del Rey *Spain* 36 D5
Navadwip *India* 69 H13
Navahermosa *Spain* 37 F6
Navahrudak *Belarus* 23 B13
Navajo Res. *U.S.A.* 109 H10
Navalcarnero *Spain* 36 E7
Navalmoral de la Mata *Spain* 36 F5
Navalvillar de Pela *Spain* 37 F5
Navan = An Uaimh *Ireland* 12 C5
Navapolatsk *Belarus* 32 E5
Navarin, Mys *Russia* 53 C18
Navarino, I. *Chile* 128 H3
Navarra □ *Spain* 38 C3
Navarre *U.S.A.* 114 F3
Navarro → *U.S.A.* 110 F3
Navas de San Juan *Spain* 37 G7
Navasota *U.S.A.* 116 F6
Navassa I. *W. Indies* 121 C5
Nävekvarn *Sweden* 11 F10
Naver → *U.K.* 13 C4
Navia *Spain* 36 B4
Navia → *Spain* 36 B4
Navia de Suarna = A Pobre *Spain* 36 C3
Navibandar *India* 68 J3
Navidad *Chile* 126 C1
Naviraí *Brazil* 127 A5
Naviti *Fiji* 91 a
Navlakhi *India* 68 H4
Navlya *Russia* 33 F8
Năvodari *Romania* 29 F13
Navoi = Navoiy *Uzbekistan* 52 E7
Navojoa *Mexico* 118 B3
Navolato *Mexico* 118 C3
Navrongo *Ghana* 83 C4
Navsari *India* 66 J8
Navua *Fiji* 91 a
Nawa Kot *Pakistan* 68 E4
Nawab Khan *Pakistan* 68 D3
Nawabganj *Ut. P., India* 69 F9
Nawabganj *Ut. P., India* 69 E8
Nawabshah *Pakistan* 68 F3
Nawada *India* 69 G11
Nawakot *Nepal* 69 F11
Nawalgarh *India* 68 F6
Nawanshahr *India* 69 C6
Nawar, Dasht-i- *Afghan.* 68 C3
Nawi *Sudan* 80 D3
Nawoiy = Navoi *Uzbekistan* 52 E7
Naxçıvan *Azerbaijan* 73 C11
Naxçıvan □ *Azerbaijan* 73 C11
Naxos *Greece* 47 D7
Nay *France* 20 E3
Nay, Mui *Vietnam* 62 B3
Nāy Band *Būshehr, Iran* 71 E7
Nāy Band *Khorāsān, Iran* 71 C8
Nayakhan *Russia* 53 C16
Nayarit □ *Mexico* 118 C4
Nayau *Fiji* 91 a
Nayé *Senegal* 82 C2
Nayong *China* 58 D5
Nayoro *Japan* 54 C11
Naypyidaw *Burma* 64 C1
Nayyāl, W. → *Si. Arabia* 70 D3
Nazar Kahrizi *Iran* 73 D12
Nazaré *Brazil* 125 F11
Nazaré *Portugal* 37 F1
Nazareth = Nazerat *Israel* 74 C4
Nazareth *U.S.A.* 115 F9
Nazarovo *Russia* 53 D10
Nazas *Mexico* 118 B4
Nazas → *Mexico* 118 B4
Nazca *Peru* 124 F4
Nazca Ridge *Pac. Oc.* 97 K19
Naze *Japan* 55 K4
Naze, The *U.K.* 15 F9
Nazerat *Israel* 74 C4
Nāzīk *Iran* 73 C11
Nazilli *Turkey* 47 D10
Nazko *Canada* 102 C4
Nazko → *Canada* 102 C4
Nāzlu *Iran* 73 D11
Nazret *Ethiopia* 81 F4
Nchanga *Zambia* 87 E2
Ncheu *Malawi* 87 E3
Ndala *Tanzania* 86 C3
Ndalatando *Angola* 84 F2
Ndali *Benin* 83 D5
Ndareda *Tanzania* 86 C4
Ndélé *C.A.R.* 84 C4
Ndiael *Senegal* 82 B1
Ndikinimeki *Cameroon* 83 E7
N'Dioum *Senegal* 82 B2
Ndjamena *Chad* 79 F8
Ndola *Zambia* 87 E2
Ndomo → *S. Africa* 89 D5
Ndoto Mts. *Kenya* 86 B4
Nduguti *Tanzania* 86 C3
Nea Alikarnassos *Greece* 47 F7
Nea Anchialos *Greece* 46 B4
Nea Epidavros *Greece* 46 D5
Nea Ionia *Greece* 46 B4
Nea Kalikratia *Greece* 44 F7
Nea Makri *Greece* 46 C5
Nea Moudania *Greece* 44 F7

Nea Peramos *Attiki, Greece* 46 C5
Nea Peramos *Kavala, Greece* 45 F8
Nea Visa *Greece* 45 E10
Nea Zichni *Greece* 44 E7
Neagh, Lough *U.K.* 12 B5
Neah Bay *U.S.A.* 110 B2
Neale → *Australia* 92 D5
Neales → *Australia* 95 D2
Neamţ □ *Romania* 29 C11
Neapoli *Kozani, Greece* 44 F5
Neapoli *Kriti, Greece* 49 D7
Neapoli *Lakonia, Greece* 46 E5
Near Is. *U.S.A.* 106 a
Neath *U.K.* 15 F4
Neath Port Talbot □ *U.K.* 15 F4
Nebbou *Burkina Faso* 82 C4
Nebelat el Hagana *Sudan* 81 E2
Nebine Cr. → *Australia* 95 D4
Nebitdag = Balkanabat *Turkmenistan* 71 B7
Nebo *Australia* 94 C4
Nebolchy *Russia* 32 C7
Nebraska □ *U.S.A.* 112 E4
Nebraska City *U.S.A.* 112 E6
Nechako → *Canada* 102 C4
Neches → *U.S.A.* 116 G8
Nechisar △ *Ethiopia* 81 F4
Neckar → *Germany* 25 F4
Neckartal-Odenwald △ *Germany* 25 F4
Necochea *Argentina* 126 D4
Necedah *U.S.A.* 112 C8
Neda *Spain* 36 B2
Neda → *Greece* 46 D3
Nedelino *Bulgaria* 45 E9
Nedelišće *Croatia* 41 B13
Nederland *Netherlands* ■ *Europe* 17 C5
Nedoboyivtsi *Ukraine* 29 B11
Needles *Canada* 102 D5
Needles *U.S.A.* 111 L12
Needles, The *U.K.* 15 G6
Neembucú □ *Paraguay* 126 B4
Neenah *U.S.A.* 112 C9
Neepawa *Canada* 103 C9
Neftçala *Azerbaijan* 73 C13
Neftegorsk *Krasnodar, Russia* 35 H4
Neftegorsk *Sakhalin, Russia* 53 D15
Neftekumsk *Russia* 35 H7
Neftyugansk *Russia* 52 C8
Nefyn *U.K.* 14 E3
Négala *Mali* 82 C3
Negapatam = Nagappattinam *India* 66 P11
Negara *Indonesia* 63 J17
Negaunee *U.S.A.* 112 B10
Negele *Ethiopia* 81 F4
Negoiul, Vf. *Romania* 29 E9
Negombo *Sri Lanka* 66 R11
Negotin *Serbia* 44 B6
Negotino *Macedonia* 44 E6
Negra, Peña *Spain* 36 C4
Negra, Pta. *Mauritania* 78 D2
Negra, Pta. *Peru* 124 E2
Negrais, C. = Maudin Sun *Burma* 67 M19
Negreşti *Romania* 29 D12
Negreşti-Oaş *Romania* 29 C8
Negril *Jamaica* 120 a
Negro → *Argentina* 128 E4
Negro → *Brazil* 124 D7
Negro → *Uruguay* 126 C4
Negros *Phil.* 61 G5
Negru Vodă *Romania* 29 G13
Neguac *Canada* 105 C6
Nehalem → *U.S.A.* 110 E3
Nehāvand *Iran* 71 C6
Nehbandān *Iran* 71 D9
Nehoiu *Romania* 29 E11
Nei Monggol Zizhiqu □ *China* 56 D7
Neiafu *Tonga* 91 c
Neiges, Piton des *Réunion* 85 c
Neijiang *China* 58 C5
Neillsville *U.S.A.* 112 C8
Neilton *U.S.A.* 110 C2
Neiqiu *China* 56 F8
Neiva *Colombia* 124 C3
Neixiang *China* 56 H6
Nejanilini L. *Canada* 103 B9
Nejd = Najd *Si. Arabia* 75 B3
Nejo *Ethiopia* 81 F4
Nekā *Iran* 71 B7
Nekemte *Ethiopia* 81 F4
Nêkheb *Egypt* 80 B3
Neksø *Denmark* 11 J9
Nelas *Portugal* 36 E3
Nelia *Australia* 94 C3
Nelidovo *Russia* 32 D7
Neligh *U.S.A.* 112 D4
Nelkan *Russia* 53 D14
Nellore *India* 66 M11
Nelson *Canada* 102 D5
Nelson *N.Z.* 91 D4
Nelson *U.K.* 14 D5

Nelson *Ariz., U.S.A.* 109 J7
Nelson *Nev., U.S.A.* 111 K12
Nelson → *Canada* 103 C9
Nelson, C. *Australia* 95 F3
Nelson, Estrecho *Chile* 128 G2
Nelson Forks *Canada* 102 B4
Nelson House *Canada* 103 B9
Nelson L. *Canada* 103 B8
Nelson Lakes △ *N.Z.* 91 D4
Nelspoort *S. Africa* 88 E3
Nelspruit *S. Africa* 89 D5
Néma *Mauritania* 82 B3
Neman → *Lithuania* 30 C8
Neman *Russia* 30 C9
Nemea *Greece* 46 D4
Nemeiben L. *Canada* 103 B7
Nemërçkë, Mal *Albania* 44 F4
Nemira, Vf. *Romania* 29 D11
Nemiscau *Canada* 104 B4
Nemiscau, L. *Canada* 104 B4
Nemours *France* 19 D9
Nemrut Daği △ *Turkey* 73 C8
Nemšová *Slovak Rep.* 27 C11
Nemunas → *Lithuania* 30 C8
Nemuro *Japan* 54 C12
Nemuro-Kaikyō *Japan* 54 C12
Nemyriv *Ukraine* 29 B9
Nen Jiang → *China* 57 B13
Nenagh *Ireland* 12 D3
Nenasi *Malaysia* 65 L4
Nene → *U.K.* 15 E8
Nenjiang *China* 60 B7
Neno *Malawi* 87 F3
Neo Chori *Greece* 46 C3
Neochori *Greece* 46 B2
Neodesha *U.S.A.* 112 G6
Neon Petritsi *Greece* 44 E7
Neora Valley △ *India* 69 F13
Neosho *U.S.A.* 112 G6
Neosho → *U.S.A.* 116 C7
Nepal ■ *Asia* 69 F11
Nepalganj *Nepal* 69 E9
Nepalganj Road *India* 69 E9
Nephi *U.S.A.* 108 G8
Nephin *Ireland* 12 B2
Nephin Beg Range *Ireland* 12 C2
Nepi *Italy* 41 F9
Nepomuk *Czech Rep.* 26 B6
Neptune *U.S.A.* 115 F10
Neqāb *Iran* 71 B8
Nera → *Italy* 41 F9
Nera → *Romania* 28 F6
Nérac *France* 20 D4
Nerang *Australia* 95 D5
Nerastro, Sarīr *Libya* 79 D10
Neratovice *Czech Rep.* 26 A7
Nerchinsk *Russia* 53 D12
Nereju *Romania* 29 E11
Nerekhta *Russia* 32 B5
Neresnytsya *Ukraine* 29 B8
Néret, L. *Canada* 105 B5
Neretvanski Kanal *Croatia* 41 E14
Neringa *Lithuania* 30 C8
Neris → *Lithuania* 32 C3
Nerja *Spain* 37 J7
Nerl → *Russia* 32 D11
Nerpio *Spain* 39 G2
Nerva *Spain* 37 H4
Nervi *Italy* 40 D6
Neryungri *Russia* 53 D13
Nescopeck *U.S.A.* 115 E8
Nesebŭr *Bulgaria* 45 D11
Neskantaga *Canada* 104 B2
Ness, L. *U.K.* 13 D4
Ness City *U.S.A.* 112 F4
Nesterov *Russia* 30 D9
Nesterov *Ukraine* 23 C12
Nestorio *Greece* 44 F5
Nestos → *Greece* 45 E8
Nesvady *Slovak Rep.* 27 D11
Nesvizh = Nyasvizh *Belarus* 23 B14
Netanya *Israel* 74 C3
Netarhat *India* 69 H11
Nete → *Belgium* 17 C4
Netherdale *Australia* 94 K6
Netherlands ■ *Europe* 17 C5
Netherlands Antilles ☑ *W. Indies* 124 A5
Neto → *Italy* 43 C10
Netrang *India* 68 J6
Nettancourt *France* 19 D11
Nettetal *Germany* 24 D2
Nettilling L. *Canada* 101 C12
Nettuno *Italy* 42 A5
Netzahualcóyotl, Presa *Mexico* 119 D6
Neu-Isenburg *Germany* 25 E4
Neu-Ulm *Germany* 25 G6
Neubrandenburg *Germany* 24 B9
Neubukow *Germany* 24 A7
Neuburg *Germany* 25 G7
Neuchâtel *Switz.* 25 J2
Neuchâtel □ *Switz.* 25 J2
Neuchâtel, Lac de *Switz.* 25 J2
Neudau *Austria* 26 D9
Neuenhagen *Germany* 24 C9
Neuenhaus *Germany* 24 C2

Neuf-Brisach *France* 19 D14
Neufahrn *Bayern, Germany* 25 G8
Neufahrn *Bayern, Germany* 25 G7
Neufchâteau *Belgium* 17 E5
Neufchâteau *France* 19 D13
Neufchâtel-en-Bray *France* 18 C8
Neufchâtel-sur-Aisne *France* 19 C11
Neuhaus *Germany* 24 B6
Neuillé-Pont-Pierre *France* 18 E7
Neuilly-St-Front *France* 19 C10
Neukalen *Germany* 24 B8
Neumarkt *Germany* 25 F7
Neumayer *Antarctica* 5 D17
Neumünster *Germany* 24 A5
Neunkirchen *Austria* 26 D9
Neunkirchen *Germany* 25 F3
Neuquén *Argentina* 128 D3
Neuquén □ *Argentina* 126 D2
Neuruppin *Germany* 24 C8
Neusäss *Germany* 25 G6
Neuse → *U.S.A.* 117 D16
Neusiedl *Austria* 27 D9
Neusiedler See *Austria* 27 D9
Neusiedler See-Seewinkel △ *Austria* 27 D9
Neuss *Germany* 24 D2
Neussargues-Moissac *France* 20 C7
Neustadt *Bayern, Germany* 25 F8
Neustadt *Bayern, Germany* 25 G7
Neustadt *Bayern, Germany* 25 F6
Neustadt *Bayern, Germany* 25 E7
Neustadt *Brandenburg, Germany* 24 C8
Neustadt *Hessen, Germany* 24 E5
Neustadt *Niedersachsen, Germany* 24 C5
Neustadt *Rhld-Pfz., Germany* 25 F4
Neustadt *Sachsen, Germany* 24 D10
Neustadt *Schleswig-Holstein, Germany* 24 A6
Neustadt *Thüringen, Germany* 24 E7
Neustrelitz *Germany* 24 B9
Neuvic *France* 20 C6
Neuville-sur-Saône *France* 21 C8
Neuvy-le-Roi *France* 18 E7
Neuvy-St-Sépulchre *France* 19 F8
Neuvy-sur-Barangeon *France* 19 E9
Neuwerk *Germany* 24 B4
Neuwied *Germany* 24 E3
Neva → *Russia* 32 C6
Nevada *Iowa, U.S.A.* 112 D7
Nevada *Mo., U.S.A.* 112 G6
Nevada □ *U.S.A.* 108 G5
Nevada City *U.S.A.* 110 F6
Nevado, Cerro *Argentina* 126 D2
Nevado de Colima = Volcán de Colima △ *Mexico* 118 D4
Nevado de Tres Cruces △ *Chile* 126 B2
Nevel *Russia* 32 D5
Nevelsk *Russia* 53 E15
Nevers *France* 19 F10
Nevertire *Australia* 95 E4
Nevesinje *Bos.-H.* 44 C2
Neville *Canada* 103 D7
Nevinnomyssk *Russia* 35 H6
Nevis *St. Kitts & Nevis* 121 C7
Nevrokop = Gotse Delchev *Bulgaria* 44 E7
Nevşehir *Turkey* 72 C6
Nevşehir □ *Turkey* 72 C6
Nevskoye *Russia* 30 D9
New → *U.S.A.* 113 F13
New Aiyansh *Canada* 102 B3
New Albany *Ind., U.S.A.* 113 F11
New Albany *Miss., U.S.A.* 117 D10
New Albany *Pa., U.S.A.* 115 E8
New Amsterdam *Guyana* 124 B7
New Angledool *Australia* 95 D4
New Baltimore *U.S.A.* 114 D2
New Bedford *U.S.A.* 115 E14
New Berlin *N.Y., U.S.A.* 115 D9
New Berlin *Pa., U.S.A.* 114 F8
New Bern *U.S.A.* 117 D16
New Bethlehem *U.S.A.* 114 F5
New Bight *Bahamas* 121 B4
New Bloomfield *U.S.A.* 114 F7
New Boston *U.S.A.* 116 E7
New Braunfels *U.S.A.* 116 G5
New Brighton *N.Z.* 91 E4
New Brighton *U.S.A.* 114 F4
New Britain *Papua N. G.* 90 B8
New Britain *U.S.A.* 115 E12
New Brunswick *U.S.A.* 115 F10
New Brunswick □ *Canada* 105 C6
New Bussa *Nigeria* 83 D5
New Caledonia ☑ *Pac. Oc.* 90 D9
New Caledonia Trough *Pac. Oc.* 96 L8
New Castile = Castilla-La Mancha □ *Spain* 37 F7
New Castle *Ind., U.S.A.* 113 F11
New Castle *Pa., U.S.A.* 114 F4
New City *U.S.A.* 115 E11
New Concord *U.S.A.* 114 G3

New Cumberland *U.S.A.* 114 F4
New Cuyama *U.S.A.* 111 L7
New Delhi *India* 68 E7
New Denver *Canada* 102 D5
New Don Pedro Res. *U.S.A.* 110 H6
New England *U.S.A.* 107 B12
New England *N. Dak., U.S.A.* 112 B2
New England Ra. *Australia* 95 E5
New Forest △ *U.K.* 15 G6
New Galloway *U.K.* 13 F4
New Glasgow *Canada* 105 C7
New Guinea *Oceania* 90 B6
New Hamburg *Canada* 114 C4
New Hampshire □ *U.S.A.* 115 C9
New Hampton *U.S.A.* 112 D7
New Hanover *S. Africa* 89 D5
New Hartford *U.S.A.* 115 C9
New Haven *Conn., U.S.A.* 115 E12
New Haven *Mich., U.S.A.* 114 D4
New Haven *N.Y., U.S.A.* 115 C8
New Hazelton *Canada* 102 B3
New Hebrides = Vanuatu ■ *Pac. Oc.* 90 C9
New Holland *U.S.A.* 115 F8
New Iberia *U.S.A.* 116 F9
New Ireland *Papua N. G.* 90 B8
New Jersey □ *U.S.A.* 113 F16
New Kensington *U.S.A.* 114 F5
New Lexington *U.S.A.* 113 F12
New Liskeard *Canada* 104 C4
New London *Conn., U.S.A.* 115 E12
New London *Ohio, U.S.A.* 114 E2
New London *Wis., U.S.A.* 112 C9
New Madrid *U.S.A.* 112 G9
New Martinsville *U.S.A.* 113 F13
New Meadows *U.S.A.* 108 D5
New Melones L. *U.S.A.* 110 H6
New Mexico □ *U.S.A.* 109 J11
New Milford *Conn., U.S.A.* 115 E11
New Milford *Pa., U.S.A.* 115 E9
New Moore I. *Ind. Oc.* 69 J13
New Norcia *Australia* 93 F2
New Norfolk *Australia* 95 G4
New Orleans *U.S.A.* 117 G9
New Philadelphia *U.S.A.* 114 F3
New Plymouth *N.Z.* 91 C5
New Plymouth *U.S.A.* 108 E5
New Port Richey *U.S.A.* 117 G13
New Providence *Bahamas* 120 A4
New Quay *U.K.* 15 E3
New Radnor *U.K.* 15 E4
New Richmond *Canada* 105 C6
New Richmond *U.S.A.* 112 C7
New River Gorge △ *U.S.A.* 113 G13
New Roads *U.S.A.* 116 F9
New Rochelle *U.S.A.* 115 F11
New Rockford *U.S.A.* 112 B4
New Romney *U.K.* 15 G8
New Ross *Ireland* 12 D5
New Salem *U.S.A.* 112 B3
New Scone = Scone *U.K.* 13 E5
New Siberian I. = Novaya Sibir, Ostrov *Russia* 53 B16
New Siberian Is. = Novosibirskiye Ostrova *Russia* 53 B15
New Smyrna Beach *U.S.A.* 117 G14
New South Wales □ *Australia* 95 E4
New Tecumseth = Alliston *Canada* 114 B5
New Town *U.S.A.* 112 B2
New Tredegar *U.K.* 15 F4
New Ulm *U.S.A.* 112 C6
New Waterford *Canada* 105 C7
New Westminster *Canada* 110 A4
New York *U.S.A.* 115 F11
New York □ *U.S.A.* 115 D9
New York J.F. Kennedy Int. ✈ (JFK) *U.S.A.* 115 F11
New Zealand ■ *Oceania* 91 D6
Newaj → *India* 68 G7
Newala *Tanzania* 87 E4
Newark *Del., U.S.A.* 113 F16
Newark *N.J., U.S.A.* 115 F10
Newark *N.Y., U.S.A.* 114 C7
Newark *Ohio, U.S.A.* 114 F2
Newark Liberty Int. ✈ (EWR) *U.S.A.* 115 F10
Newark Valley *U.S.A.* 115 D8
Newark-on-Trent *U.K.* 14 D7
Newberg *U.S.A.* 108 D2
Newberry *Mich., U.S.A.* 113 B11
Newberry *S.C., U.S.A.* 117 D14
Newberry Springs *U.S.A.* 111 L10
Newboro L. *Canada* 115 B8
Newbridge = Droichead Nua *Ireland* 12 C5
Newburgh *Canada* 114 B8
Newburgh *U.S.A.* 115 E10
Newbury *U.K.* 15 F6
Newbury *N.H., U.S.A.* 115 B12
Newbury *Vt., U.S.A.* 115 B12
Newburyport *U.S.A.* 115 D14
Newcastle *Australia* 95 E5
Newcastle *N.B., Canada* 105 C6
Newcastle *Ont., Canada* 104 D4
Newcastle *S. Africa* 89 D4

Newcastle U.K. 12 B6
Newcastle Calif., U.S.A. 110 G5
Newcastle Wyo., U.S.A. 108 E11
Newcastle Emlyn U.K. 15 E3
Newcastle Ra. Australia 92 C5
Newcastle-under-Lyme U.K. 14 D5
Newcastle-upon-Tyne U.K. 13 C6
Newcastle Waters Australia 94 B1
Newcastle West Ireland 12 D2
Newcomb U.S.A. 115 C10
Newcomerstown U.S.A. 114 F3
Newdegate Australia 93 F2
Newell Australia 94 B4
Newell U.S.A. 112 C2
Newfane U.S.A. 114 C6
Newfield U.S.A. 115 D8
Newfound L. U.S.A. 115 C13
Newfoundland Canada 105 C8
Newfoundland U.S.A. 115 E9
Newfoundland & Labrador □ Canada 105 B8
Newhaven U.K. 15 G8
Newkirk U.S.A. 116 C6
Newlyn U.K. 15 G2
Newman Australia 92 D2
Newman U.S.A. 110 H5
Newmarket Canada 114 B5
Newmarket Ireland 12 D2
Newmarket U.K. 15 E8
Newmarket U.S.A. 115 C14
Newnan U.S.A. 117 E12
Newport I. of W., U.K. 15 G6
Newport Newport, U.K. 15 F5
Newport Ark., U.S.A. 116 D9
Newport Ky., U.S.A. 113 F11
Newport N.H., U.S.A. 115 C12
Newport N.Y., U.S.A. 115 C9
Newport Oreg., U.S.A. 108 D1
Newport Pa., U.S.A. 114 F7
Newport R.I., U.S.A. 115 E13
Newport Tenn., U.S.A. 117 D13
Newport Vt., U.S.A. 115 B12
Newport Wash., U.S.A. 108 B5
Newport □ U.K. 15 F4
Newport Beach U.S.A. 111 M9
Newport News U.S.A. 113 G15
Newport Pagnell U.K. 15 E7
Newquay U.K. 15 G2
Newry U.K. 12 B5
Newton Ill., U.S.A. 112 F9
Newton Iowa, U.S.A. 112 E7
Newton Kans., U.S.A. 112 F5
Newton Mass., U.S.A. 115 D13
Newton Miss., U.S.A. 117 E10
Newton N.C., U.S.A. 117 D14
Newton N.J., U.S.A. 115 E10
Newton Tex., U.S.A. 116 F8
Newton Abbot U.K. 15 G4
Newton Aycliffe U.K. 14 C6
Newton Falls N.Y., U.S.A. 115 B10
Newton Falls Ohio, U.S.A. 114 E4
Newton Stewart U.K. 13 G4
Newtonmore U.K. 13 D4
Newtown U.K. 15 E4
Newtownabbey U.K. 12 B6
Newtownards U.K. 12 B6
Newtownbarry = Bunclody Ireland 12 D5
Newtownstewart U.K. 12 B4
Newville U.S.A. 114 F7
Nexon France 20 C5
Neya Russia 34 A6
Neyrīz Iran 71 D7
Neyshābūr Iran 71 B8
Nezhin = Nizhyn Ukraine 33 G6
Nezperce U.S.A. 108 C5
Nezvysko Ukraine 29 B10
Ngabang Indonesia 62 D3
Ngabordamlu, Tanjung Indonesia 63 F8
N'Gage Angola 84 F3
Ngala Nigeria 83 C7
Ngambé Centre, Cameroon 83 D7
Ngambé Littoral, Cameroon 83 E7
Ngami Depression Botswana 88 C3
Ngamo Zimbabwe 87 F2
Nganbéto, L. de Togo 83 D5
Ngangala Sudan 81 G3
Nganglong Kangri China 69 C9
Ngao Thailand 64 C2
Ngaoundéré Cameroon 84 C2
Ngapara N.Z. 91 F3
Ngara Tanzania 86 C3
Ngawi Indonesia 63 G14
Ngcobo S. Africa 89 E4
Nghia Lo Vietnam 58 G5
Ngoboli Sudan 81 G3
Ngoma Malawi 87 E3
Ngomahura Zimbabwe 87 G3
Ngomba Tanzania 87 D3
Ngomeni, Ras Kenya 86 C5
Ngong Kenya 86 C4
Ngop Sudan 81 F3
Ngorkou Mali 82 B4
Ngoring Hu China 60 C4
Ngorongoro Tanzania 86 C4
Ngorongoro △ Tanzania 86 C4
Ngozi Burundi 86 C2

Ngudu Tanzania 86 C3
Nguigmi Niger 79 F8
Nguila Cameroon 83 E7
Nguiu Australia 92 B5
Ngukurr Australia 94 A1
Ngunga Tanzania 86 C3
Nguru Nigeria 83 C7
Nguru Mts. Tanzania 86 D4
Ngusi Malawi 87 E3
Nguyen Binh Vietnam 58 F5
Nha Trang Vietnam 65 F7
Nhacoongo Mozam. 89 C6
Nhamaabué Mozam. 87 F4
Nhangulaze, L. Mozam. 89 C5
Nhill Australia 95 F3
Nho Quan Vietnam 58 G5
Nhulunbuy Australia 94 A2
Nia-nia Dem. Rep. of the Congo 86 B2
Niafounké Mali 82 B4
Niagara Falls Canada 114 C5
Niagara Falls U.S.A. 114 C6
Niagara-on-the-Lake Canada 114 C5
Niah Malaysia 62 D4
Niamey Niger 83 C5
Niandan-Koro Guinea 82 C3
Nianforando Guinea 82 D2
Niangara Dem. Rep. of the Congo 86 B2
Niangay, L. Mali 82 B4
Niangbo Ivory C. 82 D3
Niangoloko Burkina Faso 82 C4
Niantic U.S.A. 115 E12
Niaro Sudan 81 E3
Nias Indonesia 62 D1
Niassa □ Mozam. 87 E4
Niassa □ Mozam. 87 E4
Nibāk Si. Arabia 71 E7
Nibe Denmark 11 H3
Nicaragua ■ Cent. Amer. 120 D2
Nicaragua, L. de Nic. 120 D2
Nicastro Italy 43 D9
Nice France 21 E11
Nice-Côte-d'Azur ✈ (NCE) France 21 E11
Niceville U.S.A. 117 F11
Nichicun, L. Canada 105 B5
Nichinan Japan 55 J5
Nicholás, Canal W. Indies 120 B3
Nicholasville U.S.A. 113 G11
Nichols U.S.A. 115 D8
Nicholson Australia 92 C4
Nicholson U.S.A. 115 E9
Nicholson ➜ Australia 94 B2
Nicholson L. Canada 103 A8
Nicholson Ra. Australia 93 E2
Nicholville U.S.A. 115 B10
Nicobar Is. Ind. Oc. 51 H11
Nicola Canada 102 C4
Nicolls Town Bahamas 120 A4
Nicosia Cyprus 49 D12
Nicosia Italy 43 E7
Nicótera Italy 43 D8
Nicoya Costa Rica 120 D2
Nicoya, G. de Costa Rica 120 E3
Nicoya, Pen. de Costa Rica 120 E2
Nida Lithuania 30 C8
Nidd ➜ U.K. 14 D6
Nidda Germany 25 E5
Nidda ➜ Germany 25 E4
Nidwalden □ Switz. 25 J4
Nidzica Poland 31 E7
Niebüll Germany 24 A4
Nied ➜ Germany 19 C13
Niederaula Germany 24 E5
Niederbayern □ Germany 25 G8
Niederbronn-les-Bains France 19 D14
Niedere Tauern Austria 26 D7
Niederlausitz Germany 24 D9
Niederösterreich □ Austria 26 C8
Niedersachsen □ Germany 24 C4
Niedersächsisches Wattenmeer △ Germany 24 B3
Niekerkshoop S. Africa 88 D3
Niellé Ivory C. 82 C3
Niemba Dem. Rep. of the Congo 86 D2
Niemen = Nemunas ➜ Lithuania 30 C10
Niemodlin Poland 31 H4
Nienburg Germany 24 C5
Niepołomice Poland 31 H7
Niers ➜ Germany 24 D1
Niesky Germany 24 D10
Nieszawa Poland 31 F5
Nieu Bethesda S. Africa 88 E3
Nieuw Amsterdam Suriname 125 B7
Nieuw Nickerie Suriname 125 B7
Nieuwoudtville S. Africa 88 E2
Nieuwpoort Belgium 17 C2
Nieves, Pico de las Canary Is. 48 G4
Nièvre □ France 19 E10
Niga Mali 82 C3
Niğde Turkey 72 D6
Niğde □ Turkey 72 D6
Nigel S. Africa 89 D4
Niger □ Nigeria 83 D6

Niger ■ W. Afr. 83 B7
Niger ➜ W. Afr. 83 D6
Niger Delta Africa 83 E6
Nigeria ■ W. Afr. 83 D6
Nighasin India 69 E9
Nightcaps N.Z. 91 F2
Nigrita Greece 44 F7
Nihon = Japan ■ Asia 55 G8
Nii-Jima Japan 55 G9
Niigata Japan 54 F9
Niigata □ Japan 55 F9
Niihama Japan 55 H6
Ni'ihau U.S.A. 106 b
Niimi Japan 55 G6
Niitsu Japan 54 F9
Níjar Spain 39 J2
Nijil Jordan 74 E4
Nijkerk Neths. 17 B5
Nijmegen Neths. 17 C5
Nijverdal Neths. 17 B6
Nīk Pey Iran 73 D13
Nike Nigeria 83 D6
Nikel Russia 8 B24
Nikiniki Indonesia 63 F6
Nikisiani Greece 45 F8
Nikiti Greece 44 F7
Nikki Benin 83 D5
Nikkō Japan 55 F9
Nikkō △ Japan 55 F9
Nikolayev = Mykolayiv Ukraine 33 J7
Nikolayevsk Russia 34 E7
Nikolayevsk-na-Amur Russia 53 D15
Nikolsk Russia 34 D8
Nikolskoye Russia 53 D17
Nikopol Bulgaria 45 C8
Nikopol Ukraine 33 J8
Nikopolis Greece 46 B2
Niksar Turkey 72 B7
Nīkshahr Iran 71 E9
Nikšić Montenegro 44 D2
Nîl, Nahr en ➜ Africa 80 H7
Nîl el Abyad ➜ Sudan 81 E3
Nîl el Azraq ➜ Sudan 81 D3
Nila Indonesia 63 F7
Niland U.S.A. 111 M11
Nile = Nîl, Nahr en ➜ Africa 80 H7
Nile Delta Egypt 80 H7
Niles Mich., U.S.A. 112 E10
Niles Ohio, U.S.A. 114 E4
Nilüfer ➜ Turkey 45 F12
Nim Ka Thana India 68 F6
Nimach India 68 G6
Nimba, Mts. Guinea 82 D3
Nimbahera India 68 G6
Nîmes France 21 E8
Nimfaíon, Ákra = Pines, Akra Greece 45 F8
Nimmitabel Australia 95 F4
Nimule Sudan 81 G3
Nimule △ Sudan 81 G3
Nin Croatia 41 D12
Nīnawā Iraq 73 D10
Nīnawā □ Iraq 73 D10
Nindigully Australia 95 D4
Nineveh = Nīnawā Iraq 73 D10
Ning Xian China 56 G4
Ning'an China 57 B15
Ningaloo △ Australia 92 D1
Ningbo China 59 C13
Ningcheng China 57 D10
Ningde China 59 D12
Ningdu China 59 D10
Ninggang China 59 D9
Ningguo China 59 B12
Ninghai China 59 C13
Ninghua China 59 D11
Ningi Nigeria 83 C6
Ningjin China 56 F8
Ningjing Shan China 58 C2
Ninglang China 58 D3
Ningling China 56 G8
Ningming China 58 F6
Ningnan China 58 D4
Ningpo = Ningbo China 59 C13
Ningqiang China 56 H4
Ningshan China 56 H5
Ningsia Hui A.R. = Ningxia Huizu Zizhiqu □ China 56 F4
Ningwu China 56 E7
Ningxia Huizu Zizhiqu □ China 56 F4
Ningxiang China 59 C9
Ningyang China 56 G9
Ningyuan China 59 E8
Ninh Binh Vietnam 58 G5
Ninh Giang Vietnam 64 B6
Ninh Hoa Vietnam 64 F7
Ninh Ma Vietnam 64 F7
Nini-Suhien △ Ghana 82 D4
Ninove Belgium 17 D4
Nioaque Brazil 127 A4
Niobrara U.S.A. 112 D4
Niobrara ➜ U.S.A. 112 D4
Niokolo-Koba △ Senegal 82 C2
Niono Mali 82 C3
Nionsamoridougou Guinea 82 D3

Nioro du Rip Senegal 82 C1
Nioro du Sahel Mali 82 B3
Niort France 20 B3
Nipawin Canada 103 C8
Nipigon Canada 104 C2
Nipigon, L. Canada 104 C2
Nipishish L. Canada 105 B7
Nipissing, L. Canada 104 C4
Nipomo U.S.A. 111 K6
Nipton U.S.A. 111 K11
Niquelândia Brazil 125 F9
Nīr Iran 73 C12
Nirasaki Japan 55 G9
Nirmal India 66 K11
Nirmali India 69 F12
Niš Serbia 44 C5
Nisa Portugal 37 F3
Niṣāb Si. Arabia 70 D5
Niṣāb Yemen 75 E4
Niscemi Italy 43 E7
Nishinomiya Japan 55 G7
Nishino'omote Japan 55 J5
Nishiwaki Japan 55 G7
Niška Banja Serbia 44 C6
Niškibi ➜ Canada 104 A2
Nisko Poland 31 H9
Nisporeni Moldova 29 C13
Nisqually ➜ U.S.A. 110 C4
Nissaki Greece 49 A3
Nissan ➜ Sweden 11 H6
Nissum Bredning Denmark 11 H2
Nissum Fjord Denmark 11 H2
Nistru = Dnister ➜ Europe 23 E16
Nisutlin ➜ Canada 102 A2
Nitchequon Canada 105 B5
Niterói Brazil 127 A7
Nith ➜ Canada 114 C4
Nith ➜ U.K. 13 F5
Nitmiluk △ Australia 92 B5
Nitra Slovak Rep. 27 D10
Nitra ➜ Slovak Rep. 27 D11
Nitriansky □ Slovak Rep. 27 C11
Nittenau Germany 25 F8
Niue Pac. Oc. 97 J11
Niulan Jiang ➜ China 58 D4
Niut Indonesia 62 D4
Niutou Shan China 59 C13
Niuzhuang China 57 D12
Nivala Finland 8 E21
Nivelles Belgium 17 D4
Nivernais France 19 E10
Niverville Canada 103 D9
Niwas India 69 H9
Nixa U.S.A. 112 G7
Nixon U.S.A. 116 G6
Nizamabad India 66 K11
Nizamghat India 67 E19
Nizhne Kolymsk Russia 53 C17
Nizhnegorskiy = Nyzhnohirskyy Ukraine 33 K8
Nizhnekamsk Russia 34 C10
Nizhneudinsk Russia 53 D10
Nizhnevartovsk Russia 52 C8
Nizhniy Bestyakh Russia 53 C13
Nizhniy Chir Russia 35 F6
Nizhniy Lomov Russia 34 D6
Nizhniy Novgorod Russia 34 B7
Nizhniy Novgorod □ Russia 34 B7
Nizhniy Tagil Russia 52 D6
Nizhyn Ukraine 33 G6
Nizina Mazowiecka Poland 31 F8
Nizip Turkey 72 D7
Nízké Tatry Slovak Rep. 27 C12
Nízke Tatry △ Slovak Rep. 27 C12
Nízký Jeseník Czech Rep. 27 B10
Nizwá Oman 75 C6
Nizza Monferrato Italy 40 D5
Njakwa Malawi 87 E3
Njanji Zambia 87 E3
Njazidja = Grande Comore Comoros Is. 85 a
Njegoš Montenegro 44 D2
Njinjo Tanzania 87 D4
Njombe Tanzania 87 D3
Njombe ➜ Tanzania 87 D4
Njurundabommen Sweden 10 B11
Nkambe Cameroon 83 D7
Nkana Zambia 87 E2
Nkandla S. Africa 89 D5
Nkawkaw Ghana 83 D4
Nkayi Zimbabwe 87 F2
Nkhotakota Malawi 87 E3
Nkhotakota △ Malawi 87 E3
Nkongsamba Cameroon 83 E6
Nkurenkuru Namibia 88 B2
Nkwanta Ghana 82 D4
Nmai ➜ Burma 67 F20
Noakhali = Maijdi Bangla. 67 H17
Nobel Canada 114 A4
Nobeoka Japan 55 H5
Noblejas Spain 36 F7
Noblesville U.S.A. 112 E10
Noboribetsu Japan 54 C10
Noccundra Australia 95 D3
Noce ➜ Italy 40 B8

Nocera Inferiore Italy 43 B7
Nocera Umbra Italy 41 E9
Noci Italy 43 B10
Nocona U.S.A. 116 E6
Nocrich Romania 29 D10
Noda Japan 55 G9
Nogales Mexico 118 A2
Nogales U.S.A. 109 L8
Nogaro France 20 E3
Nogat ➜ Poland 30 D6
Nōgata Japan 55 H5
Nogent France 19 D12
Nogent-le-Rotrou France 18 D7
Nogent-sur-Seine France 19 D10
Noggara Ethiopia 81 E4
Noggerup Australia 93 F2
Noginsk Moskva, Russia 32 E10
Noginsk Tunguska, Russia 53 C10
Nogliki Russia 53 D15
Nogoa ➜ Australia 94 C4
Nogoyá Argentina 126 C4
Nógrád □ Hungary 28 C3
Noguera Pallaresa ➜ Spain 38 D5
Noguera Ribagorçana ➜ Spain 38 D5
Nohar India 68 E6
Nohfelden Germany 25 F3
Nohta India 69 H8
Noia Spain 36 C2
Noire, Montagne France 20 E6
Noires, Mts. France 18 D3
Noirétable France 20 C7
Noirmoutier, Î. de France 18 F4
Noirmoutier-en-l'Île France 18 F4
Nojane Botswana 88 C3
Nojima-Zaki Japan 55 G9
Nok Kundi Pakistan 66 E3
Nok Ta Phao, Ko Thailand 65 b
Nokaneng Botswana 88 B3
Nokia Finland 32 B2
Nokomis Canada 103 C8
Nokomis L. Canada 103 B8
Nola C.A.R. 84 D3
Nola Italy 43 B7
Nolay France 19 F11
Noli, C. di Italy 40 D5
Nolinsk Russia 34 B9
Noma Omuramba ➜ Namibia 88 B3
Nombre de Dios Panama 120 E4
Nome U.S.A. 106 a
Nomo-Zaki Japan 55 H4
Nomuka Tonga 91 c
Nomuka Group Tonga 91 c
Nonacho L. Canada 103 A7
Nonancourt France 18 D8
Nonda Australia 94 C3
None Italy 40 D4
Nong Chang Thailand 64 E2
Nong Het Laos 64 C4
Nong Khai Thailand 64 D4
Nong'an China 57 B13
Nongoma S. Africa 89 D5
Nongsa Indonesia 65 d
Nonoava Mexico 118 B3
Nonsan S. Korea 57 F14
Nonthaburi Thailand 64 F3
Nontron France 20 C4
Nonza France 21 F13
Noonamah Australia 92 B5
Noondie, L. Australia 93 E2
Noord Brabant □ Neths. 17 C5
Noord Holland □ Neths. 17 B4
Noordbeveland Neths. 17 C3
Noordoostpolder Neths. 17 B5
Noordwijk Neths. 17 B4
Noosa Heads Australia 95 D5
Nootka I. Canada 102 D3
Nopiming △ Canada 103 C9
Nora Eritrea 81 D5
Nora Sweden 10 E9
Noralee Canada 102 C3
Noranda = Rouyn-Noranda Canada 104 C4
Norberg Sweden 10 D9
Nórcia Italy 41 F10
Norco U.S.A. 111 M9
Nord □ Cameroon 83 D7
Nord □ France 19 B10
Nord-Kivu □ Dem. Rep. of the Congo 86 C2
Nord-Ostsee-Kanal Germany 24 A5
Nord-Ouest □ Cameroon 83 D7
Nord-Pas-de-Calais □ France 19 B9
Nordaustlandet Svalbard 4 B9
Nordborg Denmark 11 J3
Nordby Denmark 11 J2
Norddeich Germany 24 B3
Norden Germany 24 B3
Nordenham Germany 24 B4
Norderney Germany 24 B3
Norderstedt Germany 24 B6
Nordfjord Norway 8 F11
Nordfriesische Inseln Germany 24 A4
Nordhausen Germany 24 D6
Nordhorn Germany 24 C3
Norðoyar Færoe Is. 8 E9

Nördinge-Nol Sweden 11 G6
Nordingrå Sweden 10 B12
Nordjylland □ Denmark 11 G3
Nordkapp Norway 8 A21
Nordkapp Svalbard 4 A9
Nordkinnhalvøya Norway 8 A22
Nördlicher Teutoburger Wald-Wiehengebirge △ Germany 24 C4
Nördlingen Germany 25 G6
Nordrhein-Westfalen □ Germany 24 D3
Nordstrand Germany 24 A4
Nordvik Russia 53 B12
Nore ➜ Ireland 12 D4
Noreland Canada 114 B6
Norfolk = Simcoe Canada 114 D4
Norfolk N.Y., U.S.A. 115 B10
Norfolk Nebr., U.S.A. 112 D5
Norfolk Va., U.S.A. 113 G15
Norfolk □ U.K. 15 E8
Norfolk Broads △ U.K. 15 E9
Norfolk I. Pac. Oc. 90 D9
Norfolk Ridge Pac. Oc. 96 K8
Norfork L. U.S.A. 116 C8
Norge = Norway ■ Europe 8 E14
Norilsk Russia 53 C9
Norma, Mt. Australia 94 C3
Normal U.S.A. 112 E9
Norman U.S.A. 116 D6
Norman ➜ Australia 94 B3
Norman Wells Canada 100 C7
Normanby ➜ Australia 94 A3
Normandie-Maine △ France 18 D6
Normandin Canada 104 C5
Normanhurst, Mt. Australia 93 E3
Normanton Australia 94 B3
Normétal Canada 104 C4
Norquay Canada 103 C8
Norquinco Argentina 128 E2
Norra Dellen Sweden 10 C10
Norra Kvill △ Sweden 11 G9
Norra Ulvön Sweden 10 A12
Norrahammar Sweden 11 G8
Norrbottens län □ Sweden 8 C19
Nørre Åby Denmark 11 J3
Nørre Alslev Denmark 11 K5
Nørresundby Denmark 11 G3
Norrhult-Klavreström Sweden 11 G9
Norris Point Canada 105 C8
Norristown U.S.A. 115 F9
Norrköping Sweden 11 F10
Norrland Sweden 8 E16
Norrsundet Sweden 10 D11
Norrtälje Sweden 10 E12
Norseman Australia 93 F3
Norsk Russia 53 D14
Norte, Pta. del Canary Is. 48 G2
Norte, Serra do Brazil 124 F7
North, C. Canada 105 C7
North Adams U.S.A. 115 D11
North America 98 F10
North Arm Canada 102 A5
North Augusta U.S.A. 117 E14
North Australian Basin Ind. Oc. 96 J3
North Ayrshire □ U.K. 13 F4
North Bass I. U.S.A. 114 E2
North Battleford Canada 103 C7
North Bay Canada 104 C4
North Belcher Is. Canada 104 A4
North Bend Oreg., U.S.A. 108 E1
North Bend Pa., U.S.A. 114 E7
North Bend Wash., U.S.A. 110 C5
North Bennington U.S.A. 115 D11
North Berwick U.K. 13 E6
North Berwick U.S.A. 115 C14
North Bruce Canada 114 B3
North C. Canada 105 C7
North C. N.Z. 91 A4
North Canadian ➜ U.S.A. 116 D7
North Canton U.S.A. 114 F3
North Cape = Nordkapp Norway 8 A21
North Caribou L. Canada 104 B1
North Carolina □ U.S.A. 117 D15
North Cascades △ U.S.A. 108 B3
North Channel Canada 104 C3
North Channel U.K. 13 F3
North Charleston U.S.A. 117 E15
North Chicago U.S.A. 112 D10
North Collins U.S.A. 114 D6
North Creek U.S.A. 115 C11
North Dakota □ U.S.A. 112 B3
North Downs U.K. 15 F8
North East U.S.A. 114 D5
North East Frontier Agency = Arunachal Pradesh □ India 67 F19
North East Lincolnshire □ U.K. 14 D7
North Eastern □ Kenya 86 B5
North Esk ➜ U.K. 13 E6
North European Plain Europe 6 E10
North Foreland U.K. 15 F9
North Fork U.S.A. 110 H7
North Fork American ➜ U.S.A. 110 G5

North Fork Feather ➤ U.S.A. **110** F5
North Fork Grand ➤ U.S.A. **112** C2
North Fork Red ➤ U.S.A. **116** D5
North Frisian Is. = Nordfriesische Inseln Germany **24** A4
North Gower Canada **115** A9
North Hd. Australia **93** F1
North Henik L. Canada **103** A9
North Highlands U.S.A. **110** G5
North Horr Kenya **86** B4
North I. Kenya **86** B4
North I. N.Z. **91** C5
North I. N.Z. **91** b
North Kingsville U.S.A. **114** E4
North Kitui △ Kenya **86** C4
North Knife ➤ Canada **103** B10
North Koel ➤ India **69** G10
North Korea ■ Asia **57** E14
North Lakhimpur India **67** F19
North Lanarkshire □ U.K. **13** F5
North Las Vegas U.S.A. **111** J11
North Lincolnshire □ U.K. **14** D7
North Little Rock U.S.A. **116** H8
North Loup ➤ U.S.A. **112** E4
North Luangwa △ Zambia **87** E3
North Magnetic Pole Canada **101** B9
North Mankato U.S.A. **112** C6
North Minch U.K. **13** C3
North Moose L. Canada **103** C8
North Myrtle Beach U.S.A. **117** E15
North Nahanni ➤ Canada **102** A4
North Olmsted U.S.A. **114** E3
North Ossetia □ Russia **35** J7
North Pagai, I. = Pagai Utara, Pulau Indonesia **62** E2
North Palisade U.S.A. **110** H8
North Platte U.S.A. **112** E3
North Platte ➤ U.S.A. **112** E3
North Pole Arctic **4** A
North Portal Canada **103** D8
North Powder U.S.A. **108** D5
North Pt. Barbados **121** g
North Pt. Trin. & Tob. **125** J16
North Pt. U.S.A. **114** A1
North Rhine Westphalia = Nordrhein-Westfalen □ Germany **24** D3
North River Canada **105** B8
North Ronaldsay U.K. **13** B6
North Saskatchewan ➤ Canada **103** C7
North Sea Europe **6** D6
North Seal ➤ Canada **103** B9
North Somerset □ U.K. **15** F5
North Sydney Canada **105** C7
North Syracuse U.S.A. **115** C8
North Taranaki Bight N.Z. **91** C5
North Thompson ➤ Canada **102** C4
North Tonawanda U.S.A. **114** C6
North Troy U.S.A. **115** B12
North Twin I. Canada **104** B4
North Tyne ➤ U.K. **14** B5
North Uist U.K. **13** D1
North Vancouver Canada **110** A3
North Vernon U.S.A. **113** F11
North Wabasca L. Canada **102** B6
North Walsham U.K. **14** E9
North West = Severo-Zapadnyy □ Russia **52** C4
North-West □ S. Africa **88** D4
North West C. Australia **92** D1
North West Frontier □ Pakistan **68** C4
North West Highlands U.K. **13** D4
North West River Canada **105** B7
North Western □ Zambia **87** E2
North Wildwood U.S.A. **113** F16
North York Moors U.K. **14** C7
North York Moors △ U.K. **14** C7
North Yorkshire □ U.K. **14** C6
Northallerton U.K. **14** C6
Northam Australia **93** F2
Northam S. Africa **88** C4
Northampton Australia **93** E1
Northampton U.K. **15** E7
Northampton Mass., U.S.A. **115** D12
Northampton Pa., U.S.A. **115** F9
Northamptonshire □ U.K. **15** E7
Northbridge U.S.A. **115** D13
Northbrook Canada **114** B7
Northcliffe Australia **93** F2
Northeast Pacific Basin Pac. Oc. **97** D13
Northeast Providence Chan. W. Indies **120** A4
Northeim Germany **24** D6
Northern = Limpopo □ S. Africa **89** C4
Northern □ Ghana **83** D4
Northern □ Malawi **87** E3
Northern □ S. Leone **82** D2
Northern □ Zambia **87** E3
Northern Areas □ Pakistan **69** A5

Northern Cape □ S. Africa **88** D3
Northern Circars India **67** L13
Northern Indian L. Canada **103** B9
Northern Ireland □ U.K. **12** B5
Northern Lau Group Fiji **91** a
Northern Light L. Canada **104** C1
Northern Marianas ☑ Pac. Oc. **96** F6
Northern Province □ S. Africa **89** C4
Northern Range Trin. & Tob. **125** K15
Northern Sporades Greece **46** B5
Northern Territory □ Australia **92** D5
Northfield Minn., U.S.A. **112** C7
Northfield Vt., U.S.A. **115** B12
Northgate Canada **103** D8
Northland □ N.Z. **91** A4
Northome U.S.A. **112** B6
Northport Ala., U.S.A. **117** E11
Northport Wash., U.S.A. **108** B5
Northumberland □ U.K. **14** B6
Northumberland, C. Australia **95** F3
Northumberland Is. Australia **94** C4
Northumberland Str. Canada **105** C7
Northville U.S.A. **115** C10
Northwest Pacific Basin Pac. Oc. **96** D3
Northwest Providence Channel W. Indies **120** A4
Northwest Territories □ Canada **100** C8
Northwich U.K. **14** D5
Northwood Iowa, U.S.A. **112** D7
Northwood N. Dak., U.S.A. **112** B5
Norton U.S.A. **112** F4
Norton Zimbabwe **87** F3
Norton Sd. U.S.A. **106** a
Nortorf Germany **24** A5
Norwalk Calif., U.S.A. **111** M8
Norwalk Conn., U.S.A. **115** E11
Norwalk Iowa, U.S.A. **112** E7
Norwalk Ohio, U.S.A. **114** E2
Norway Maine, U.S.A. **113** C18
Norway Mich., U.S.A. **112** C10
Norway ■ Europe **8** E14
Norway House Canada **103** C9
Norwegian B. Canada **101** B11
Norwegian Basin Atl. Oc. **4** C2
Norwegian Sea Atl. Oc. **6** B6
Norwich Canada **114** D4
Norwich U.K. **15** E9
Norwich Conn., U.S.A. **115** E12
Norwich N.Y., U.S.A. **115** D9
Norwood Canada **114** B7
Norwood U.S.A. **115** B10
Nosappu-Misaki Japan **54** C12
Noshiro Japan **54** D10
Nosivka Ukraine **33** G6
Nosovka = Nosivka Ukraine **33** G6
Noṣratābād Iran **71** D8
Noss Hd. U.K. **13** C5
Nossebro Sweden **11** F6
Nossob ➤ S. Africa **88** D3
Nossombougou Mali **82** C3
Nosy Barren Madag. **85** H8
Nosy Bé Madag. **85** G9
Nosy Boraha Madag. **89** B8
Nosy Lava Madag. **89** A8
Nosy Varika Madag. **89** C8
Noteć ➤ Poland **31** F2
Notikewin ➤ Canada **102** B5
Notio Aigaio □ Greece **47** E7
Notios Aiyaíon = Notio Aigaio □ Greece **47** E7
Notios Evvoikos Kolpos Greece **46** C5
Noto Italy **43** F8
Noto, G. di Italy **43** F8
Notodden Norway **9** G13
Notre Dame B. Canada **105** C8
Notre-Dame-de-Koartac = Quaqtaq Canada **101** C13
Notre-Dame-des-Bois Canada **115** A13
Notre-Dame-d'Ivugivic = Ivujivik Canada **101** C12
Notre-Dame-du-Nord Canada **104** C4
Notsé Togo **83** D5
Nottawasaga B. Canada **114** B4
Nottaway ➤ Canada **104** B4
Nottingham U.K. **14** E6
Nottingham I. Canada **101** C12
Nottingham, City of □ U.K. **14** E6
Nottinghamshire □ U.K. **14** D6
Notwane ➤ Botswana **88** C4
Nouâdhibou Mauritania **78** D2
Nouâdhibou, Râs Mauritania **78** D2
Nouakchott Mauritania **82** B1
Nouâmghâr Mauritania **82** B1
Nouméa N. Cal. **90** D9
Nouna Burkina Faso **82** C4
Noupoort S. Africa **88** E3

Nouveau Comptoir = Wemindji Canada **104** B4
Nouvelle Amsterdam, Î. Ind. Oc. **3** F13
Nouvelle-Calédonie = New Caledonia ☑ Pac. Oc. **90** D9
Nouzonville France **19** C11
Nová Baňa Slovak Rep. **27** C11
Nová Bystřice Czech Rep. **26** B8
Nova Esperança Brazil **127** A5
Nova Friburgo Brazil **127** A7
Nova Gorica Slovenia **41** C10
Nova Gradiška Croatia **28** E2
Nova Iguaçu Brazil **127** A7
Nova Iorque Brazil **125** E10
Nova Kakhovka Ukraine **33** J7
Nova Lamego Guinea-Biss. **82** C2
Nova Lima Brazil **125** G10
Nova Lusitânia Mozam. **87** F3
Nova Mambone Mozam. **89** C6
Nova Odesa Ukraine **33** J6
Nová Paka Czech Rep. **26** A8
Nova Pavova Serbia **28** F5
Nova Scotia □ Canada **105** C7
Nova Siri Italy **43** B9
Nova Sofala Mozam. **89** C5
Nova Ushytsya Ukraine **29** B12
Nova Varoš Serbia **44** C3
Nova Venécia Brazil **125** G10
Nova Zagora Bulgaria **45** D10
Novaci Macedonia **44** E5
Novaci Romania **29** E8
Novaféltria Italy **41** E9
Novannenski = Novoannenskiy Russia **34** E6
Novar Canada **114** A5
Novara Italy **40** C5
Novato U.S.A. **110** G4
Novaya Kakhovka = Nova Kakhovka Ukraine **33** J7
Novaya Kazanka = Zhangaqala Kazakhstan **35** F9
Novaya Ladoga Russia **32** B5
Novaya Lyalya Russia **52** D7
Novaya Sibir, Ostrov Russia **53** B16
Novaya Zemlya Russia **52** B6
Nové Město Slovak Rep. **27** C10
Nové Město na Moravě Czech Rep. **26** B9
Nové Město nad Metují Czech Rep. **26** A9
Nové Zámky Slovak Rep. **27** C11
Novelda Spain **39** G4
Novellara Italy **40** D7
Noventa Vicentina Italy **41** C8
Novgorod Russia **32** C6
Novgorod □ Russia **32** C7
Novgorod-Severskiy = Novhorod-Siverskyy Ukraine **33** G7
Novhorod-Siverskyy Ukraine **33** G7
Novi Bečej Serbia **28** E5
Novi Iskar Bulgaria **44** D7
Novi Kneževac Serbia **28** D5
Novi Lígure Italy **40** D5
Novi Pazar Bulgaria **45** C11
Novi Pazar Serbia **44** C4
Novi Sad Serbia **28** E4
Novi Slankamen Serbia **28** E5
Novi Travnik Bos.-H. **28** F2
Novi Vinodolski Croatia **41** C11
Novigrad Istra, Croatia **41** C10
Novigrad Zadar, Croatia **41** D12
Novigradsko More Croatia **41** D12
Novo Hamburgo Brazil **127** B5
Novo Ivanivka Ukraine **29** E14
Novo Mesto Slovenia **41** C12
Novo Miloševo Serbia **28** E5
Novoaleksandrovsk Russia **35** H5
Novoaleksandrovskaya = Novoaleksandrovsk Russia **35** H5
Novoaltaysk Russia **52** D9
Novoannenskiy Russia **34** E6
Novoazovsk Ukraine **33** J10
Novocheboksarsk Russia **34** B8
Novocherkassk Russia **35** G5
Novodevichye Russia **34** D9
Novodvinsk Russia **52** C5
Novogrudok = Navahrudak Belarus **23** B13
Novohrad-Volynskyy Ukraine **23** C14
Novokachalinsk Russia **54** B5
Novokhopersk Russia **34** E5
Novokuybyshevsk Russia **34** D9
Novokuznetsk Russia **52** D9
Novolazarevskaya Antarctica **5** D3
Novomirgorod Ukraine **33** H6
Novomoskovsk Russia **32** E10
Novomoskovsk Ukraine **33** H8
Novopolotsk = Navapolatsk Belarus **32** E5
Novorossiysk Russia **33** K9
Novorybnoye Russia **53** B11
Novorzhev Russia **32** D5
Novosej Albania **44** E4
Novoselytsya Ukraine **29** B11
Novoshakhtinsk Russia **33** J10

Novosibirsk Russia **52** D9
Novosibirskiye Ostrova Russia **53** B15
Novosil Russia **33** F9
Novosokolniki Russia **32** D6
Novotitarovskaya Russia **35** H4
Novotroitsk Russia **52** D6
Novoukrayinka Ukraine **33** H6
Novouljanovsk Russia **34** C9
Novouzensk Russia **34** E9
Novovolynsk Ukraine **31** H11
Novovoronezhskiy Russia **33** G10
Novoyavoriske Ukraine **31** J10
Novozybkov Russia **33** F6
Novska Croatia **41** C14
Novvy Urengoy Russia **52** C8
Nový Bor Czech Rep. **26** A7
Novy Bug = Novyy Buh Ukraine **33** J7
Nový Bydžov Czech Rep. **26** A8
Novy Dvor Belarus **31** F11
Novy Dwór Mazowiecki Poland **31** F7
Nový Jičín Czech Rep. **27** B11
Novyy Afon Georgia **35** J5
Novyy Buh Ukraine **33** J7
Novyy Oskol Russia **33** G9
Novyy Port Russia **52** C8
Nowa Deba Poland **31** H8
Nowa Ruda Poland **31** H3
Nowa Sarzyna Poland **31** H9
Nowa Sól Poland **31** G2
Nowata U.S.A. **116** C7
Nowbarān Iran **71** C6
Nowe Poland **30** E5
Nowe Miasteczko Poland **31** G2
Nowe Miasto Poland **31** G7
Nowe Miasto Lubawskie Poland **30** E6
Nowe Skalmierzyce Poland **31** G4
Nowe Warpno Poland **30** E1
Nowgong Assam, India **67** F18
Nowgong Mad. P., India **69** G8
Nowogard Poland **30** E2
Nowogród Poland **31** E8
Nowogród Bobrzanski Poland **31** G2
Nowogrodziec Poland **31** G2
Nowra Australia **95** E5
Nowshera Pakistan **66** C8
Nowy Dwór Gdański Poland **30** D6
Nowy Sącz Poland **31** J7
Nowy Staw Poland **30** D6
Nowy Targ Poland **31** J7
Nowy Tomyśl Poland **31** F3
Nowy Wiśnicz Poland **31** J7
Noxen U.S.A. **115** E8
Noyabr'sk Russia **52** C8
Noyant France **18** E7
Noyers France **19** E10
Noyon France **19** C9
Noyon Mongolia **56** C2
Nozay France **18** E5
Nqutu S. Africa **89** D5
Nsanje Malawi **87** F4
Nsawam Ghana **83** D4
Nsomba Zambia **87** E2
Nsukka Nigeria **83** D6
Ntui Cameroon **83** E7
Nu Jiang ➤ China **58** E2
Nu Shan China **58** E2
Nuba Mts. = Nubah, Jibalan Sudan **81** E3
Nubah, Jibalan Sudan **81** E3
Nubia Africa **76** D7
Nubian Desert = Nûbîya, Es Sahrâ en Sudan **80** C3
Nûbîya, Es Sahrâ en Sudan **80** C3
Nubledo Spain **36** B5
Nuboai Indonesia **63** E9
Nucet Romania **28** D7
Nueces ➤ U.S.A. **116** H6
Nueltin L. Canada **103** A9
Nuestra Señora del Rosario de Caá-Catí Argentina **126** B4
Nueva Carteya Spain **37** H6
Nueva Ciudad Guerrero Mexico **119** B5
Nueva Gerona Cuba **120** B3
Nueva Palmira Uruguay **126** C4
Nueva Rosita Mexico **118** B4
Nueva San Salvador El Salv. **120** D2
Nueva Tabarca Spain **39** G4
Nuéve de Julio Argentina **126** D3
Nuevitas Cuba **120** B4
Nuevo, G. Argentina **128** E4
Nuevo Casas Grandes Mexico **118** A3
Nuevo Laredo Mexico **119** B5
Nuevo León □ Mexico **118** C5
Nuevo Rocafuerte Ecuador **124** D3
Nugget Pt. N.Z. **91** G2
Nugrus, Gebel Egypt **80** C3
Nuhaka N.Z. **91** C6
Nuits-St-Georges France **19** E11
Nukey Bluff Australia **95** E2

Nukhayb Iraq **73** F10
Nukheila Sudan **80** D2
Nuku Hiva French Polynesia **97** H13
Nuku'alofa Tonga **91** c
Nukus Uzbekistan **52** E6
Nules Spain **38** F4
Nullagine Australia **92** D3
Nullagine ➤ Australia **92** D3
Nullarbor Australia **93** F5
Nullarbor △ Australia **93** F2
Nullarbor Plain Australia **93** F4
Numalla, L. Australia **95** D3
Numan Nigeria **83** D7
Numata Japan **55** F9
Numatinna ➤ Sudan **81** F2
Numaykoos Lake △ Canada **103** B9
Numazu Japan **55** G9
Numbulwar Australia **94** A2
Numfoor Indonesia **63** E8
Numurkah Australia **95** F4
Nunaksaluk I. Canada **105** A7
Nunap Isua Greenland **98** D15
Nunavut □ Canada **101** C11
Nunda U.S.A. **114** D7
Nuneaton U.K. **15** E6
Nungarin Australia **93** F2
Nungo Mozam. **87** E4
Nungwe Tanzania **86** C3
Nunivak I. U.S.A. **106** a
Nunkun India **69** C7
Núoro Italy **42** B2
Nūr Iran **71** B7
Nūrābād Hormozgän, Iran **71** E8
Nūrābād Lorestān, Iran **73** E12
Nure ➤ Italy **40** C6
Nuremberg = Nürnberg Germany **25** F7
Nuri Mexico **118** B3
Nuri Sudan **80** D3
Nuriootpa Australia **95** E2
Nuristan □ Afghan. **66** B7
Nurlat Russia **34** C10
Nurmes Finland **8** E23
Nürnberg Germany **25** F7
Nurpur Pakistan **68** D4
Nurra, La Italy **42** B1
Nurran, L. = Terewah, L. Australia **95** D4
Nurrari Lakes Australia **93** E5
Nurri Italy **42** C2
Nürtingen Germany **25** G5
Nurzec ➤ Poland **31** F9
Nus Italy **40** C4
Nusa Barung Indonesia **63** H15
Nusa Dua Indonesia **63** K18
Nusa Kambangan Indonesia **63** G13
Nusa Tenggara Barat □ Indonesia **62** F5
Nusa Tenggara Timur □ Indonesia **63** F6
Nusaybin Turkey **73** D9
Nushki Pakistan **68** E2
Nuuk Greenland **99** C14
Nuupere, Pte. Moorea **91** d
Nuwakot Nepal **69** E10
Nuwayb'ī, W. an ➤ Si. Arabia **74** F3
Nuweiba' Egypt **70** D2
Nuwerus S. Africa **88** E2
Nuweveldberge S. Africa **88** E3
Nuyts, Pt. Australia **93** G2
Nuyts Arch. Australia **95** E1
Nxai Pan △ Botswana **88** B3
Nxau-Nxau Botswana **88** B3
Nyaake Liberia **82** E3
Nyabing Australia **93** F2
Nyack U.S.A. **115** E11
Nyagan Russia **52** C7
Nyahanga Tanzania **86** C3
Nyahua Tanzania **86** D3
Nyahururu Kenya **86** B4
Nyainqêntanglha Shan China **60** C4
Nyakanazi Tanzania **86** C3
Nyakrom Ghana **83** D4
Nyâlâ Sudan **81** E1
Nyamandhlovu Zimbabwe **87** F2
Nyambiti Tanzania **86** C3
Nyamira Kenya **86** C3
Nyamlell Sudan **81** F2
Nyamwaga Tanzania **86** C3
Nyandekwa Tanzania **86** C3
Nyanding ➤ Sudan **81** F3
Nyandoma Russia **32** B7
Nyanga △ Zimbabwe **87** F3
Nyangana Namibia **88** B3
Nyanguge Tanzania **86** C3
Nyankpala Ghana **83** D4
Nyanza Rwanda **86** C2
Nyanza □ Kenya **86** C3
Nyanza-Lac Burundi **86** C2
Nyaponges Sudan **81** F3
Nyasa, L. = Malawi, L. Africa **87** E3
Nyasvizh Belarus **23** B14
Nyazura Zimbabwe **87** F3
Nyazwidzi ➤ Zimbabwe **87** G3
Nyborg Denmark **11** J4
Nybro Sweden **11** H9

Nyda Russia **52** C8
Nyeri Kenya **86** C4
Nyerol Sudan **81** F3
Nyhammar Sweden **10** D8
Nyika △ Malawi **87** E3
Nyinahin Ghana **82** D4
Nyíradony Hungary **28** C6
Nyirbátor Hungary **28** C7
Nyíregyháza Hungary **28** C6
Nyiru, Mt. Kenya **86** B4
Nykarleby = Uusikaarlepyy Finland **8** E20
Nykøbing Nordjylland, Denmark **11** H2
Nykøbing Sjælland, Denmark **11** K5
Nykøbing Sjælland, Denmark **11** J5
Nyköping Sweden **11** F11
Nykroppa Sweden **10** E8
Nykvarn Sweden **10** E11
Nyland Sweden **10** A11
Nylstroom = Modimolle S. Africa **89** C4
Nymagee Australia **95** E4
Nymboida △ Australia **95** D5
Nymburk Czech Rep. **26** A8
Nynäshamn Sweden **11** F11
Nyngan Australia **95** E4
Nyoma Rap India **69** C8
Nyoman = Nemunas ➤ Lithuania **30** C8
Nyon Switz. **25** J2
Nyong ➤ Cameroon **83** E6
Nyons France **21** D9
Nyou Burkina Faso **83** C4
Nýrsko Czech Rep. **26** B6
Nysa Poland **31** H4
Nysa ➤ Europe **24** C10
Nysa Kłodzka ➤ Poland **31** H4
Nysäter Sweden **10** E6
Nyslott = Savonlinna Finland **32** B5
Nyssa U.S.A. **108** E5
Nystad = Uusikaupunki Finland **32** B1
Nysted Denmark **11** K5
Nyunzu Dem. Rep. of the Congo **86** D2
Nyurba Russia **53** C12
Nyzhankovychi Ukraine **31** J9
Nyzhnohirskyy Ukraine **33** K8
Nyzhny Vorota Ukraine **28** B8
Nzébéla Guinea **82** D3
Nzega Tanzania **86** C3
Nzérékoré Guinea **82** D3
Nzeto Angola **84** F2
Nzilo, Chutes de Dem. Rep. of the Congo **87** E2
N'zo ➤ Ivory C. **82** D3
N'zo △ Ivory C. **82** D3
Nzubuka Tanzania **86** C3
Nzwani = Anjouan Comoros Is. **85** a

O

O Barco Spain **36** C4
O Carballiño Spain **36** C2
O Corgo Spain **36** C3
O Le Pupū Pu'e △ Samoa **91** b
O Pino Spain **36** C2
O Porriño Spain **36** C2
Ō-Shima Hokkaidō, Japan **54** D9
Ō-Shima Shizuoka, Japan **55** G9
Oa, Mull of U.K. **13** F2
Oacoma U.S.A. **112** D5
Oahe, L. U.S.A. **112** C3
Oahe Dam U.S.A. **112** C3
O'ahu U.S.A. **106** b
Oak Harbor U.S.A. **110** B4
Oak Hill U.S.A. **113** G13
Oak Island U.S.A. **117** E15
Oak Ridge U.S.A. **117** C12
Oak View U.S.A. **111** L7
Oakan-Dake Japan **54** C12
Oakdale Calif., U.S.A. **110** H6
Oakdale La., U.S.A. **116** F8
Oakes U.S.A. **112** B4
Oakesdale U.S.A. **108** C5
Oakey Australia **95** D5
Oakfield U.S.A. **114** C6
Oakham U.K. **15** E7
Oakhurst U.S.A. **110** H7
Oakland Calif., U.S.A. **110** H4
Oakland Ore., U.S.A. **115** F9
Oakley Idaho, U.S.A. **108** E7
Oakley Kans., U.S.A. **112** F3
Oakover ➤ Australia **92** D3
Oakridge U.S.A. **108** E2
Oakville Canada **114** C5
Oakville U.S.A. **110** D3
Oamaru N.Z. **91** F3
Oancea Romania **29** E12
Oasi Faunistica di Vendicari △ Italy **43** F8
Oasis Calif., U.S.A. **110** H9
Oasis Calif., U.S.A. **111** M10
Oates Land Antarctica **5** C11
Oatlands Australia **95** G4
Oatman U.S.A. **111** K12
Oaxaca Mexico **119** D5

Oaxaca □ Mexico 119 D5
Ob → Russia 52 C7
Oba Canada 104 C3
Obala Cameroon 83 E7
Obama Japan 55 G7
Oban Nigeria 83 D6
Oban U.K. 13 E3
Oberá Argentina 127 B4
Oberammergau Germany 25 H7
Oberasbach Germany 25 F6
Oberbayern □ Germany 25 G7
Oberdrauburg Austria 26 E5
Obere Donau → Germany 25 G5
Oberer Bayerischer
  Wald △ Germany 25 F8
Oberfranken □ Germany 25 H6
Oberhausen Germany 24 D2
Oberkirch Germany 25 G4
Oberlausitz Germany 24 D10
Oberlin Kans., U.S.A. 112 F3
Oberlin La., U.S.A. 116 F8
Oberlin Ohio, U.S.A. 114 E2
Obernai France 19 D14
Oberndorf Germany 25 G4
Oberon Australia 95 E4
Oberösterreich □ Austria 26 C7
Oberpfalz □ Germany 25 F8
Oberpfälzer Wald Germany 25 F8
Oberpfälzer Wald △
  Germany 25 F8
Oberstdorf Germany 25 H6
Obertyn Ukraine 29 B10
Oberursel Germany 25 E4
Oberwart Austria 27 D9
Obi, Kepulauan Indonesia 63 E7
Óbidos Brazil 125 D7
Óbidos Portugal 37 F1
Obihiro Japan 54 C11
Obilatu Indonesia 63 E7
Obilnoye Russia 35 G7
Obing Germany 25 G8
Objat France 20 C5
Obluchye Russia 53 E14
Obninsk Russia 32 E9
Obo C.A.R. 86 A2
Obock Djibouti 81 E5
Obodivka Ukraine 29 B14
Oborniki Poland 31 F3
Oborniki Śląskie Poland 31 G3
Oboyan Russia 33 G9
Obozerskaya = Obozerskiy
  Russia 52 C5
Obozerskiy Russia 52 C5
Obrenovac Serbia 44 B4
Obrovac Croatia 41 D12
Obruk Turkey 72 C5
Obrzycko Poland 31 F3
Observatory Inlet Canada 102 B3
Obshchi Syrt Russia 6 E16
Obskaya Guba Russia 52 C8
Obuasi Ghana 83 D4
Obubra Nigeria 83 D6
Obudu Nigeria 83 D6
Obwalden □ Switz. 25 J4
Obzor Bulgaria 45 D11
Ocala U.S.A. 117 G13
Ocampo Chihuahua, Mexico 118 B3
Ocampo Tamaulipas, Mexico 119 C5
Ocaña Spain 36 F7
Occidental, Cordillera
  Colombia 124 C3
Occidental, Grand Erg
  Algeria 78 B6
Ocean City Md., U.S.A. 113 F16
Ocean City N.J., U.S.A. 113 F16
Ocean City Wash., U.S.A. 110 C2
Ocean Falls Canada 102 C3
Ocean I. = Banaba Kiribati 96 H8
Ocean Park U.S.A. 110 D2
Oceano U.S.A. 111 K6
Oceanport U.S.A. 115 F10
Oceanside U.S.A. 111 M9
Ochagavía Spain 38 C3
Ochakiv Ukraine 33 J6
Ochamchira Georgia 35 J5
Ochi, Óros Greece 46 C6
Ochil Hills U.K. 13 E5
Ocho Rios Jamaica 120 a
Ochsenfurt Germany 25 F6
Ochsenhausen Germany 25 G5
Ocilla U.S.A. 117 F13
Ockelbo Sweden 10 D10
Ocmulgee → U.S.A. 117 F13
Ocna Mureş Romania 29 D8
Ocna Sibiului Romania 29 D9
Ocnele Mari Romania 29 E9
Ocniţa Moldova 29 B12
Oconee → U.S.A. 117 F13
Oconomowoc U.S.A. 112 D9
Oconto U.S.A. 112 C10
Oconto Falls U.S.A. 112 C9
Ocosingo Mexico 119 D6
Ocotal Nic. 120 D2
Ocotlán Jalisco, Mexico 118 C4
Ocotlán Oaxaca, Mexico 119 D5
Ocreza → Portugal 37 F3
Ócsa Hungary 28 C4
Octeville France 18 C5

Oda Ghana 83 D4
Ōda Japan 55 G6
Oda, J. Sudan 80 C4
Ódáðahraun Iceland 8 D5
Ódaejin N. Korea 54 D4
Ódákra Sweden 11 H6
Odate Japan 54 D10
Odawara Japan 55 G9
Odda Norway 9 F12
Odder Denmark 11 J4
Odei → Canada 103 B9
Odemira Portugal 37 H2
Odemiş Turkey 47 C9
Odendaalsrus S. Africa 88 D4
Odensbacken Sweden 10 E9
Odense Denmark 11 J4
Odenwald = Neckartal-
  Odenwald △ Germany 25 F5
Odenwald Germany 25 F5
Oder → Europe 24 B10
Oder-Havel Kanal Germany 24 C10
Oderzo Italy 41 C9
Odesa Ukraine 33 J6
Odesa □ Ukraine 33 J5
Odeshög Sweden 11 F8
Odessa = Odesa Ukraine 33 J6
Odessa Canada 115 B8
Odessa Tex., U.S.A. 116 F3
Odessa Wash., U.S.A. 108 C4
Odiakwe Botswana 88 C4
Odiel → Spain 37 H4
Odienné Ivory C. 82 D3
Odintsovo Russia 32 E9
Odiongan Phil. 61 E4
Odobeşti Romania 29 E12
Odolanów Poland 31 G4
O'Donnell U.S.A. 116 E4
O'Donnell Pt. Canada 114 A4
Odorheiu Secuiesc Romania 29 D10
Odoyevo Russia 32 F9
Odra = Oder → Europe 24 B10
Odra → Spain 36 C6
Odžaci Serbia 28 E4
Odžak Bos.-H. 28 E3
Odzi Zimbabwe 89 B5
Odzi → Zimbabwe 89 B5
Oebisfelde Germany 24 C6
Oeiras Brazil 125 E10
Oeiras Portugal 37 G1
Oelrichs U.S.A. 112 D2
Oelsnitz Germany 25 E8
Oelwein U.S.A. 112 D8
Oeno I. Pac. Oc. 97 K14
Oenpelli = Gunbalanya
  Australia 92 B5
Oetz Austria 26 D3
Of Turkey 73 B9
Ofanto → Italy 43 A9
Offa Nigeria 83 D5
Offaly □ Ireland 12 C4
Offenbach Germany 25 E4
Offenburg Germany 25 G3
Officer Cr. → Australia 93 E5
Offida Italy 41 F10
Offidousa Greece 47 E8
Ofolanga Tonga 91 c
Ofotfjorden Norway 8 B17
Ofu Amer. Samoa 91 b
Ōfunato Japan 54 E10
Oga Japan 54 E9
Oga-Hantō Japan 54 E9
Ogaden Ethiopia 75 F3
Ōgaki Japan 55 G8
Ogallala U.S.A. 112 E3
Ogasawara Gunto Pac. Oc. 51 F16
Ogbomosho Nigeria 83 D5
Ogden U.S.A. 108 F8
Ogdensburg U.S.A. 115 B9
Ogeechee → U.S.A. 117 F14
Ogilby U.S.A. 111 N12
Oglio → Italy 40 C7
Óglio Nord △ Italy 40 C6
Óglio Sud △ Italy 40 C7
Ogmore Australia 94 C4
Ognon → France 19 E12
Ogoja Nigeria 83 D6
Ogoki Canada 104 B2
Ogoki → Canada 104 B2
Ogoki L. Canada 104 B2
Ogoki Res. Canada 104 B2
Ogooué → Gabon 84 E1
Ogosta → Bulgaria 44 C7
Ogowe → Gabon 84 E1
Ograźden Macedonia 44 E6
Ogre Latvia 32 D3
Ogrein Sudan 80 D3
Ogulin Croatia 41 C12
Ogun □ Nigeria 83 D5
Ogurchinskiy, Ostrov
  Turkmenistan 71 B7
Ōguta Nigeria 83 D6
Oguzeli Turkey 72 D7
Ogwashi-Uku Nigeria 83 D6
Ogwe Nigeria 83 E6
Ohai N.Z. 91 F2
Ohakune N.Z. 91 C5

Ohata Japan 54 D10
Ohau, L. N.Z. 91 F2
Ohio □ U.S.A. 114 F2
Ohio → U.S.A. 112 G9
Ohře → Czech Rep. 26 A7
Ohre → Germany 24 C7
Ohrid Macedonia 44 E4
Ohridsko Jezero Macedonia 44 E4
Ohrigstad S. Africa 89 C5
Ōhringen Germany 25 F5
Oi Qu China 58 C2
Oikou China 57 E9
Oil City U.S.A. 114 E5
Oil Springs Canada 114 D2
Oildale U.S.A. 111 K7
Oinousa = Inousses Greece 47 C8
Oise □ France 19 C9
Oise → France 19 C9
Oiseaux du Djoudj △ Senegal 82 B1
Oistins Barbados 121 g
Oistins B. Barbados 121 g
Ōita Japan 55 H5
Ōita □ Japan 55 H5
Oiticica Brazil 125 E10
Ojai U.S.A. 111 L7
Ojcowski △ Poland 31 H6
Ojinaga Mexico 118 B4
Ojiya Japan 55 F9
Ojo Caliente Mexico 118 C4
Ojos del Salado, Cerro
  Argentina 126 B2
Oka → Russia 34 B7
Okaba Indonesia 63 F9
Okahandja Namibia 88 C2
Okanagan L. Canada 102 D5
Okandja Gabon 84 E2
Okanogan U.S.A. 108 B4
Okanogan → U.S.A. 108 B4
Okanogan Range N. Amer. 102 D5
Okány Hungary 28 D6
Okapi △
  Dem. Rep. of the Congo 86 B2
Okaputa Namibia 88 C2
Okara Pakistan 68 D5
Okaukuejo Namibia 88 B2
Okavango Delta Botswana 88 B3
Okavango Swamp =
  Okavango Delta Botswana 88 B3
Okaya Japan 55 F9
Okayama Japan 55 G6
Okayama □ Japan 55 G6
Okazaki Japan 55 G8
Oke-Iho Nigeria 83 D5
Okeechobee U.S.A. 117 H14
Okeechobee, L. U.S.A. 117 H14
Okefenokee △ U.S.A. 117 F13
Okefenokee Swamp U.S.A.
  117 F13
Okehampton U.K. 15 G4
Okene Nigeria 83 D6
Oker → Germany 24 C6
Okha India 68 H3
Okha Russia 53 D15
Okhotsk Russia 53 D15
Okhotsk, Sea of Asia 53 D15
Okhotskiy Perevoz Russia 53 C14
Okhtyrka Ukraine 33 G8
Oki-Shotō Japan 55 F6
Okiep S. Africa 88 D2
Okigwi Nigeria 83 D6
Okija Nigeria 83 D6
Okinawa Japan 55 L3
Okinawa □ Japan 55 L4
Okinawa-Guntō Japan 55 L4
Okinawa-Jima Japan 55 L4
Okino-erabu-Shima Japan 55 L4
Okitipupa Nigeria 83 D5
Oklahoma □ U.S.A. 116 D6
Oklahoma City U.S.A. 116 D6
Okmulgee U.S.A. 116 D7
Oknitsa = Ocniţa Moldova 29 B12
Oko, W. → Sudan 80 C4
Okola Cameroon 83 E7
Okolo Uganda 86 B3
Okolona U.S.A. 117 E10
Okombahe Namibia 88 C2
Okonek Poland 30 E3
Okotoks Canada 102 C6
Okrika Nigeria 83 E6
Oksibil Indonesia 63 E10
Oktyabrsk
  Qandyaghash Kazakhstan 52 E6
Oktyabrsk Russia 34 D9
Oktyabrskiy =
  Aktsyabrski Belarus 23 B15
Oktyabrskiy Rostov, Russia 35 G5
Oktyabrskoy Revolyutsii,
  Ostrov Russia 53 B10
Oktyabrskoye =
  Zhovtneve Ukraine 33 J7
Okulovka Russia 32 C7
Okuru N.Z. 91 E2
Okushiri-Tō Japan 54 C9
Okuta Nigeria 83 D5
Okwa → Botswana 88 C3
Ola Russia 53 D16

Ola U.S.A. 116 D8
Ólafsfjörður Iceland 8 C4
Ólafsvík Iceland 8 D2
Olaine Latvia 30 B10
Olancha U.S.A. 111 J8
Olancha Pk. U.S.A. 111 J8
Olanchito Honduras 120 C2
Öland Sweden 11 H10
Ölands norra udde Sweden 11 G11
Ölands södra udde Sweden 11 H10
Olargues France 20 E6
Olary Australia 95 E3
Olascoaga Argentina 126 D3
Olathe U.S.A. 112 F6
Olavarría Argentina 126 D3
Oława Poland 31 H4
Olbernhau Germany 24 E9
Ólbia Italy 42 B2
Ólbia, G. di Italy 42 B2
Olching Germany 25 G7
Olcott U.S.A. 114 C6
Old Bahama Chan. =
  Bahama, Canal Viejo de
  W. Indies 120 B4
Old Baldy Pk. = San
  Antonio, Mt. U.S.A. 111 L9
Old Bridge U.S.A. 115 F10
Old Castile = Castilla y
  Leon □ Spain 36 D6
Old Crow Canada 100 C6
Old Dale U.S.A. 111 L11
Old Forge N.Y., U.S.A. 115 C10
Old Forge Pa., U.S.A. 115 E9
Old Perlican Canada 105 C9
Old Shinyanga Tanzania 86 C3
Old Speck Mt. U.S.A. 115 B14
Old Town U.S.A. 113 C19
Old Washington U.S.A. 114 F3
Old Wives L. Canada 103 C7
Oldbury U.K. 15 F5
Oldcastle Ireland 12 C4
Oldeani Tanzania 86 C4
Oldenburg Niedersachsen,
  Germany 24 B4
Oldenburg
  Schleswig-Holstein, Germany 24 A6
Oldenzaal Neths. 17 B6
Oldham U.K. 14 D5
Oldman → Canada 102 D6
Oldmeldrum U.K. 13 D6
Olds Canada 102 C6
Olduvai Gorge Tanzania 86 C4
Oldziyt Mongolia 56 B5
Olean U.S.A. 114 D6
Olecko Poland 30 D9
Oléggio Italy 40 C5
Oleiros Portugal 36 F3
Oleiros Spain 36 B2
Olekma → Russia 53 C13
Olekminsk Russia 53 C13
Oleksandriya Kirovohrad,
  Ukraine 33 H7
Oleksandriya Rivne, Ukraine 23 C14
Oleksandrovka Ukraine 33 H7
Olema U.S.A. 110 G4
Olenegorsk Russia 8 B25
Olenek Russia 53 C12
Olenek → Russia 53 B13
Olenino Russia 32 D7
Oléron, Î. d' France 20 C2
Olesk Ukraine 31 G11
Oleśnica Poland 31 G4
Olesno Poland 31 H5
Olevsk Ukraine 23 C14
Olga, L. Canada 104 C4
Olgas, The = Kata Tjuta
  Australia 93 E5
Ólgiy Mongolia 52 E9
Ølgod Denmark 11 J2
Olhão Portugal 37 H3
Olhopil Ukraine 29 B14
Olhovatka Russia 30 D9
Olib Croatia 41 D11
Oliena Italy 42 B2
Oliete Spain 38 D4
Olifants = Elefantes →
  Africa 89 C5
Olifants → Namibia 88 C2
Olifantshoek S. Africa 88 D3
Ólimbos Greece 47 F9
Ólimbos, Óros = Olympos
  Oros Greece 44 F6
Olímpia Brazil 127 A6
Olimpos-Beydağları △
  Turkey 47 E12
Olinda Brazil 125 E12
Olite Spain 38 C3
Oliva Argentina 126 C3
Oliva Spain 39 G4
Oliva, Punta del Spain 36 B5
Oliva de la Frontera Spain 37 G4
Olivares, Cerro los
  Argentina 126 C2
Olivares de Júcar Spain 38 F2
Olive Branch U.S.A. 117 D10
Olivehurst U.S.A. 110 F5
Oliveira de Azeméis Portugal 36 E2
Oliveira do Douro Portugal 36 D2
Olivenza Spain 37 G3

Oliver Canada 102 D5
Oliver L. Canada 103 B8
Olivet France 19 E8
Olkhovka Russia 34 F7
Olkusz Poland 31 H6
Ollagüe Chile 126 A2
Olmedo Spain 36 D6
Olmeto France 21 G12
Olmos Peru — (not visible)
Olney Ill., U.S.A. 112 F10
Olney Tex., U.S.A. 116 E5
Olofström Sweden 11 H8
Olomane → Canada 105 B7
Olomouc Czech Rep. 27 B10
Olomoucký □ Czech Rep. 27 B10
Olonets Russia 32 B7
Olongapo Phil. 61 D4
Olonne-sur-Mer France 20 B2
Oloron, Gave d' → France 20 E2
Oloron-Ste-Marie France 20 E3
Olosega Amer. Samoa 91 b
Olosenga = Swains I.
  Amer. Samoa 97 J11
Olot Spain 38 C7
Olovo Bos.-H. 28 F3
Olovyannaya Russia 53 D12
Oloy → Russia 53 C16
Olsberg Germany 24 D4
Olshammar Sweden 11 F8
Olshanka Ukraine 33 H6
Olshany Ukraine 33 G8
Olsztyn Poland 30 E7
Olsztynek Poland 30 E7
Olt □ Romania 29 F9
Olt → Romania 29 G9
Olten Switz. 25 H3
Olteniţa Romania 29 F11
Olton U.S.A. 116 D3
Oltu Turkey 73 B9
Oluan Pi Taiwan 59 G13
Olula del Rio Spain 39 H2
Olur Turkey 73 B10
Olutanga Phil. 61 H5
Olvega Spain 38 D2
Olvera Spain 37 J5
Olymbos Cyprus 49 D12
Olympos Oros Greece 44 F6
Olympia Greece 46 D3
Olympia U.S.A. 110 D4
Olympic △ U.S.A. 110 C3
Olympic Dam Australia 95 E2
Olympic Mts. U.S.A. 110 C3
Olympus Cyprus 49 E11
Olympus, Mt. = Olymbos
  Oros Greece 44 F6
Olympus, Mt. = Uludağ
  Turkey 45 F13
Olympus, Mt. U.S.A. 110 C3
Olyphant U.S.A. 115 E9
Olyutorskiy, Mys Russia 53 D18
Om → Russia 52 D8
Om Hajer Eritrea 81 E4
Om Koi Thailand 64 C2
Ōma Japan 54 D10
Ōmachi Japan 55 F8
Omae-Zaki Japan 55 G9
Ōmagari Japan 54 E10
Omagh U.K. 12 B4
Omagh □ U.K. 12 B4
Omaha U.S.A. 112 E6
Omak U.S.A. 108 B4
Omak L. U.S.A. 108 B4
Oman ■ Asia 75 C6
Oman, G. of Asia 71 E8
Omaruru Namibia 88 C2
Omaruru → Namibia 88 C1
Omate Peru 124 G4
Ombai, Selat Indonesia 63 F6
Omboué Gabon 84 E1
Ombrone → Italy 40 F8
Omdurmân Sudan 81 D3
Omegna Italy 40 C5
Omemee Canada 114 B6
Omeonga
  Dem. Rep. of the Congo 86 C1
Ometepe, I. de Nic. 120 D2
Ometepec Mexico 119 D5
Ominato Japan 54 D10
Omineca → Canada 102 B4
Omineca Mts. Canada 102 B3
Omiš Croatia 41 E13
Omišalj Croatia 41 C11
Omitara Namibia 88 C2
Ōmiya = Saitama Japan 55 G9
Omme Å → Denmark 11 J2
Ommen Neths. 17 B6
Ömnögovĭ □ Mongolia 56 C3
Omo → Ethiopia 81 F4
Omo △ Ethiopia 81 F4
Omo Valley Ethiopia 81 F4
Omodeo, L. Italy 42 B1
Omodhos Cyprus 49 E11
Omoko Nigeria 83 D6
Omono-Gawa → Japan 54 E10
Omolon → Russia 53 C16
Omolon Canada 115 B8
Ompha Canada 115 B8
Omsk Russia 52 D8

Omsukchan Russia 53 C16
Ōmu Japan 54 B11
Omul, Vf. Romania 29 E10
Omulew → Poland 31 E8
Ōmura Japan 55 H4
Omuramba Omatako →
  Namibia 88 B2
Omuramba Ovambo →
  Namibia 88 B2
Omurtag Bulgaria 45 C10
Ōmuta Japan 55 H5
Oña Spain 36 C7
Onaga U.S.A. 112 F5
Onalaska U.S.A. 112 D8
Onancock U.S.A. 113 G16
Onang Indonesia 63 E5
Onangue, L. Gabon 84 E2
Onaping L. Canada 104 C3
Oñati Spain 38 B2
Onavas Mexico 118 B3
Onawa U.S.A. 112 D5
Oncócua Angola 88 B1
Onda Spain 38 F4
Ondangwa Namibia 88 B2
Ondarroa Spain 38 B2
Ondava → Slovak Rep. 27 C14
Ondjiva Angola 88 B2
Ondo Nigeria 83 D5
Ondo □ Nigeria 83 D6
Öndörshil Mongolia 56 B5
Öndverðarnes Iceland 8 D2
One Tree Australia 95 E3
Oneata Fiji 91 a
Onega Russia 52 C4
Onega → Russia 6 C13
Onega, L. = Onezhskoye
  Ozero Russia 32 B8
Oneida U.S.A. 115 C9
Oneida L. U.S.A. 115 C9
O'Neill U.S.A. 112 D4
Onekotan, Ostrov Russia 53 E16
Onema Dem. Rep. of the Congo 86 C1
Oneonta U.S.A. 115 D9
Oneşti Romania 29 D11
Onezhskoye Ozero Russia 32 B8
Ongarue N.Z. 91 C5
Ongerup Australia 93 F2
Ongjin N. Korea 57 F13
Ongkharak Thailand 64 E3
Ongniud Qi China 57 C10
Ongole India 66 M12
Ongon = Havirga Mongolia 56 B7
Oni Georgia 35 J6
Onida U.S.A. 112 C4
Onilahy → Madag. 89 C7
Onitsha Nigeria 83 D6
Ono Fiji 91 a
Onoda Japan 55 G5
Ons, I. de Spain 36 C2
Onsala Sweden 11 G6
Onslow Australia 92 D2
Onslow B. U.S.A. 117 D16
Ontake-San Japan 55 G8
Ontario Calif., U.S.A. 111 L9
Ontario Oreg., U.S.A. 108 D5
Ontario □ Canada 104 B2
Ontario, L. N. Amer. 114 C7
Ontinyent Spain 39 G4
Ontonagon U.S.A. 112 B9
Ontur Spain 39 G3
Onyx U.S.A. 111 K8
Oodnadatta Australia 95 D2
Ooldea Australia 93 F5
Oombulgurri Australia 92 C4
Oorindi Australia 94 C3
Oost-Vlaanderen □ Belgium 17 C3
Oostende Belgium 17 C2
Oosterhout Neths. 17 C4
Oosterschelde → Neths. 17 C3
Oosterwolde Neths. 17 B6
Ootacamund =
  Udagamandalam India 66 P10
Ootsa L. Canada 102 C3
Op Luang △ Thailand 64 C2
Opaka Bulgaria 45 C10
Opala Dem. Rep. of the Congo 86 C1
Opalenica Poland 31 F3
Opan Bulgaria 45 D9
Opanake Sri Lanka 66 R12
Opasatika Canada 104 C3
Opasquia △ Canada 104 B1
Opatija Croatia 41 C11
Opatów Poland 31 H8
Opava Czech Rep. 27 B10
Opelika U.S.A. 117 E12
Opelousas U.S.A. 116 F8
Opémisca, L. Canada 104 C5
Opheim U.S.A. 108 B10
Ophthalmia Ra. Australia 92 D2
Opi Nigeria 83 D6
Opinaca → Canada 104 B4
Opinaca, Rés. Canada 104 B4
Opinnagau → Canada 104 B3
Opiscotéo, L. Canada 105 B6
Opobo Nigeria 83 E6

Opochka *Russia* **32 D5**
Opoczno *Poland* **31 G7**
Opol *Phil.* **61 G6**
Opole *Poland* **31 H4**
Opole Lubelskie *Poland* **31 G8**
Opolskie □ *Poland* **31 H5**
Oponono L. *Namibia* **88 B2**
Oporto = Porto *Portugal* **36 D2**
Opotiki *N.Z.* **91 C6**
Opp *U.S.A.* **117 F11**
Oppdal *Norway* **8 E13**
Óppido Mamertina *Italy* **43 D8**
Opportunity *U.S.A.* **108 C5**
Oprișor *Romania* **28 F8**
Oprtalj *Croatia* **41 C10**
Opua *N.Z.* **91 A5**
Opunake *N.Z.* **91 C4**
Opuwo *Namibia* **88 B1**
Opuzen *Croatia* **41 E14**
Ora *Cyprus* **49 E12**
Oracle *U.S.A.* **109 K8**
Oradea *Romania* **28 C6**
Öræfajökull *Iceland* **8 D5**
Orahovac *Serbia* **44 D4**
Orahovica *Croatia* **28 E2**
Orai *India* **69 G8**
Oraison *France* **21 E9**
Oral = Zhayyq ➤
  Kazakhstan **6 F16**
Oral *Kazakhstan* **34 E10**
Oran *Algeria* **78 A5**
Orange *Australia* **95 E4**
Orange *France* **21 D8**
Orange *Calif., U.S.A.* **111 M9**
Orange *Mass., U.S.A.* **115 D12**
Orange *Tex., U.S.A.* **116 F8**
Orange *Va., U.S.A.* **113 F14**
Orange ➤ *S. Africa* **88 D2**
Orange, C. *Brazil* **125 C8**
Orange Cove *U.S.A.* **110 J7**
Orange Free State = Free
  State □ *S. Africa* **88 D4**
Orange Grove *U.S.A.* **116 H6**
Orange Walk *Belize* **119 D7**
Orangeburg *U.S.A.* **117 E14**
Orangeville *Canada* **114 C4**
Orango *Guinea-Biss.* **82 C1**
Orani *Phil.* **61 D4**
Oranienburg *Germany* **24 C9**
Oranje = Orange ➤
  S. Africa **88 D2**
Oranjemund *Namibia* **88 D2**
Oranjerivier *S. Africa* **88 D3**
Oranjestad *Aruba* **121 D5**
Orapa *Botswana* **85 J5**
Orarak *Sudan* **81 F3**
Oras *Phil.* **61 E6**
Orașje *Bos.-H.* **28 E3**
Orăștie *Romania* **29 E8**
Orava ➤ *Slovak Rep.* **27 B12**
Orava, Vodna nádríž
  Slovak Rep. **27 B12**
Oravița *Romania* **28 E6**
Orb ➤ *France* **20 E7**
Orba ➤ *Italy* **40 D5**
Ørbæk *Denmark* **11 J4**
Orbe *Switz.* **25 J2**
Orbec *France* **18 C7**
Orbetello *Italy* **41 F8**
Órbigo ➤ *Spain* **36 C5**
Orbisonia *U.S.A.* **114 F7**
Orbost *Australia* **95 F4**
Örbyhus *Sweden* **10 D11**
Orcadas *Antarctica* **5 C18**
Orcas I. *U.S.A.* **110 B4**
Orce *Spain* **39 H2**
Orce ➤ *Spain* **39 H2**
Orchard City *U.S.A.* **108 G10**
Orchard Homes *U.S.A.* **108 C6**
Orchid I. = Lan Yü *Taiwan* **59 F13**
Orchies *France* **19 B10**
Orchila, I. *Venezuela* **121 D6**
Orchilla, Pta. *Canary Is.* **48 G1**
Órcia ➤ *Italy* **41 F8**
Orco ➤ *Italy* **40 C4**
Orcutt *U.S.A.* **111 L6**
Ord *U.S.A.* **112 E4**
Ord ➤ *Australia* **92 C4**
Ord, Mt. *Australia* **92 C4**
Ord Mts. *U.S.A.* **111 L10**
Ordenes = Ordes *Spain* **36 B2**
Orderville *U.S.A.* **109 H7**
Ordes *Spain* **36 B2**
Ordesa y Monte Perido △
  Spain **38 C4**
Ording = St-Peter-Ording
  Germany **24 A4**
Ordos = Mu Us Shamo *China* **56 E5**
Ordu *Turkey* **72 B7**
Ordu □ *Turkey* **72 B7**
Ordubad *Azerbaijan* **73 C12**
Orduña *Álava, Spain* **38 C2**
Orduña *Granada, Spain* **37 H7**
Ordway *U.S.A.* **108 G12**
Ordzhonikidze *Ukraine* **33 J8**
Ore *Dem. Rep. of the Congo* **86 B2**
Ore Mts. = Erzgebirge
  Germany **24 E8**
Orebić *Croatia* **41 F14**

Örebro *Sweden* **10 E9**
Örebro län □ *Sweden* **10 E8**
Orecchiella *Italy* **40 D7**
Oregon *U.S.A.* **112 D10**
Oregon □ *U.S.A.* **108 E3**
Oregon City *U.S.A.* **110 E4**
Oregon Dunes △ *U.S.A.* **108 E1**
Öregrund *Sweden* **10 D12**
Öregrundsgrepen *Sweden* **10 D12**
Orekhov = Orikhiv *Ukraine* **33 J8**
Orekhovo-Zuyevo *Russia* **32 E10**
Orel *Russia* **33 F9**
Orel □ *Russia* **33 F9**
Orel ➤ *Ukraine* **33 H8**
Orellana, Canal de *Spain* **37 F5**
Orellana, Embalse de *Spain* **37 F5**
Orellana la Vieja *Spain* **37 F5**
Orem *U.S.A.* **108 F8**
Ören *Turkey* **47 D9**
Orenburg *Russia* **52 D6**
Örencik *Turkey* **47 B11**
Orense = Ourense *Spain* **36 C3**
Orepuki *N.Z.* **91 G1**
Orestes Pereyra *Mexico* **118 B3**
Orestiada *Greece* **45 E10**
Oristano *Italy* **42 C1**
Oristano, G. di *Italy* **42 C1**
Orizaba *Mexico* **119 D5**
Orizaba, Pico de *Mexico* **119 D5**
Orizare *Bulgaria* **45 D11**
Orjen *Bos.-H.* **44 D2**
Orjiva *Spain* **37 H7**
Orkanger *Norway* **8 E13**
Örkelljunga *Sweden* **11 H7**
Örken *Sweden* **11 G9**
Örkény *Hungary* **28 C4**
Orkla ➤ *Norway* **8 E13**
Orkney *S. Africa* **88 D4**
Orkney □ *U.K.* **13 B5**
Orkney Is. *U.K.* **13 B6**
Orland *U.S.A.* **110 F4**
Orlando *U.S.A.* **117 G14**
Orlando, C. d' *Italy* **43 D7**
Orléanais *France* **19 E8**
Orléans *France* **19 E8**
Orleans *U.S.A.* **115 B12**
Orléans, Î. d' *Canada* **105 C5**
Orlice ➤ *Czech Rep.* **26 A8**
Orlivka *Ukraine* **29 E13**
Orlov *Slovak Rep.* **27 B13**
Orlov Gay *Russia* **34 E9**
Orlová *Czech Rep.* **27 B11**
Orlovat *Serbia* **28 E5**
Orly, Paris ✈ (ORY) *France* **19 D9**
Ormara *Pakistan* **66 G4**
Ormea *Italy* **40 D4**
Ormília *Greece* **44 F7**
Ormoc *Phil.* **61 F6**
Ormond *N.Z.* **91 C6**
Ormond Beach *U.S.A.* **117 G14**
Ormož *Slovenia* **41 B13**
Ormskirk *U.K.* **14 D5**
Ormstown *Canada* **115 A11**
Ornans *France* **19 E13**
Orne □ *France* **18 D7**
Orne ➤ *France* **18 C6**
Orneta *Poland* **30 D7**
Ørnö *Sweden* **10 E12**
Örnsköldsvik *Sweden* **10 A12**
Oro *N. Korea* **57 D14**
Oro ➤ *Mexico* **118 B3**
Oro Grande *U.S.A.* **111 L9**
Oro Valley *U.S.A.* **109 K8**
Orobie, Alpi *Italy* **40 B6**
Orobie Bergamasche *Italy* **40 C6**
Orobie Valtellinesi *Italy* **40 B6**
Orocué *Colombia* **124 C4**

Orodara *Burkina Faso* **82 C4**
Orodo *Nigeria* **83 D6**
Orofino *U.S.A.* **108 C5**
Orohena, Mt. *Tahiti* **91 d**
Orol Dengizi = Aral Sea *Asia* **52 E7**
Oromía □ *Ethiopia* **81 F5**
Oromocto *Canada* **105 C14**
Oron *Nigeria* **83 E6**
Orono *Canada* **114 C6**
Orono *U.S.A.* **113 C19**
Oronsay *U.K.* **13 E2**
Oropesa *Spain* **36 F5**
Oroquieta *Phil.* **61 G5**
Orosei *Italy* **42 B2**
Orosei, G. di *Italy* **42 B2**
Orosháza *Hungary* **28 D5**
Oroszlány *Hungary* **28 C3**
Orotukan *Russia* **53 C16**
Oroville *Calif., U.S.A.* **110 F5**
Oroville *Wash., U.S.A.* **108 B4**
Oroville, L. *U.S.A.* **110 F5**
Orrefors *Sweden* **11 H9**
Orroroo *Australia* **95 E2**
Orrviken *Sweden* **10 A8**
Orrville *U.S.A.* **114 F3**
Orsa *Sweden* **10 C8**
Orsara di Púglia *Italy* **43 A8**
Orsasjön *Sweden* **10 C8**
Orsha *Belarus* **32 E6**
Örsjö *Sweden* **11 H9**
Orsk *Russia* **52 D6**
Orșova *Romania* **28 F7**
Ørsted *Denmark* **11 H4**
Örsundsbro *Sweden* **10 E11**
Orta *Turkey* **72 B5**
Orta, L. d' *Italy* **40 C5**
Orta Nova *Italy* **43 A8**
Ortaca *Turkey* **47 E10**
Ortakent *Turkey* **47 D9**
Ortaklar *Turkey* **47 D9**
Ortaköy *Çorum, Turkey* **72 B6**
Ortaköy *Niğde, Turkey* **72 C6**
Orte *Italy* **41 F9**
Ortegal, C. *Spain* **36 B3**
Orthez *France* **20 E3**
Ortigueira *Spain* **36 B3**
Orting *U.S.A.* **110 C4**
Ortisei *Italy* **41 B8**
Ortles *Italy* **40 B7**
Ortón ➤ *Bolivia* **124 F5**
Ortona *Italy* **41 F11**
Ortonville *U.S.A.* **112 C5**
Orūmīyeh *Iran* **73 D11**
Orūmīyeh, Daryācheh-ye
  Iran **73 D11**
Orune *Italy* **42 B2**
Oruro *Bolivia* **124 G5**
Orust *Sweden* **11 F5**
Oruzgān □ *Afghan.* **66 C5**
Orvault *France* **18 E5**
Orvieto *Italy* **41 F9**
Orwell *N.Y., U.S.A.* **115 C9**
Orwell *Ohio, U.S.A.* **114 E4**
Orwell ➤ *U.K.* **15 F9**
Orwigsburg *U.S.A.* **115 F8**
Oryakhovo *Bulgaria* **44 C7**
Orynyn *Ukraine* **29 B11**
Orzinuovi *Italy* **40 C6**
Orzyc ➤ *Poland* **31 F8**
Orzysz *Poland* **30 E8**
Osa ➤ *Poland* **30 E5**
Osa, Pen. de *Costa Rica* **120 E3**
Osage *U.S.A.* **112 D7**
Osage ➤ *U.S.A.* **112 F8**
Osage City *U.S.A.* **112 F6**
Ōsaka *Japan* **55 G7**
Osan *S. Korea* **57 F14**
Osawatomie *U.S.A.* **112 F6**
Osborne *U.S.A.* **112 F4**
Osby *Sweden* **11 H7**
Osceola *Ark., U.S.A.* **117 D10**
Osceola *Iowa, U.S.A.* **112 E7**
Oschatz *Germany* **24 D9**
Oschersleben *Germany* **24 C7**
Óschiri *Italy* **42 B2**
Oscoda *U.S.A.* **114 B1**
Osečina *Serbia* **44 B3**
Ösel = Saaremaa *Estonia* **32 C2**
Osery *Russia* **32 E10**
Osgoode *Canada* **115 A9**
Osh *Kyrgyzstan* **52 E8**
Oshakati *Namibia* **85 H3**
Oshawa *Canada* **114 C6**
Oshigambo *Namibia* **88 B2**
Oshkosh *Nebr., U.S.A.* **112 E2**
Oshkosh *Wis., U.S.A.* **112 C9**
Oshmyany = Ashmyany
  Belarus **23 A13**
Oshnovīyeh *Iran* **73 D11**
Oshogbo *Nigeria* **83 D5**
Oshtorīnān *Iran* **73 E13**
Oshwe *Dem. Rep. of the Congo* **84 E3**
Osi *Nigeria* **83 D6**
Osieczna *Poland* **31 G3**
Osijek *Croatia* **28 E3**
Ósilo *Italy* **42 B1**
Ósimo *Italy* **41 E10**
Osintorf *Belarus* **32 E6**
Osipovichi = Asipovichy
  Belarus **23 B15**

Osiyan *India* **68 F5**
Osizweni *S. Africa* **89 D5**
Oskaloosa *U.S.A.* **112 E7**
Oskarshamn *Sweden* **11 G10**
Oskarström *Sweden* **11 H6**
Oskélanéo *Canada* **104 C4**
Oskemen *Kazakhstan* **52 E9**
Oskol ➤ *Ukraine* **33 H9**
Oslo *Norway* **9 G14**
Oslob *Phil.* **61 G5**
Oslofjorden *Norway* **9 G14**
Osmanabad *India* **66 K10**
Osmancık *Turkey* **72 B6**
Osmaniye *Turkey* **72 D7**
Osmanlı *Turkey* **45 E10**
Ösmo *Sweden* **10 F11**
Osnabrück *Germany* **24 C4**
Ośno Lubuskie *Poland* **31 F1**
Osoblaha *Czech Rep.* **27 A10**
Osogovska Planina
  Macedonia **44 B1**
Osor *Italy* **41 D11**
Osório *Brazil* **127 B5**
Osorno *Chile* **128 E2**
Osorno *Spain* **36 C6**
Osorno, Vol. *Chile* **128 D2**
Osoyoos *Canada* **102 D5**
Osoyro *Norway* **9 F11**
Ospika ➤ *Canada* **102 B4**
Osprey Reef *Australia* **94 A4**
Oss *Neths.* **17 C5**
Ossa, Mt. *Australia* **95 G4**
Ossa, Oros *Greece* **46 B4**
Ossa de Montiel *Spain* **39 G2**
Ossabaw I. *U.S.A.* **117 F14**
Osse ➤ *France* **20 D4**
Osse ➤ *Nigeria* **83 D6**
Ossi *Italy* **42 B1**
Ossining *U.S.A.* **115 E11**
Ossipee *U.S.A.* **115 C13**
Ossokmanuan L. *Canada* **105 B7**
Ossora *Russia* **53 D17**
Ostashkov *Russia* **32 D7**
Östavall *Sweden* **10 B9**
Oste ➤ *Germany* **24 B5**
Ostend = Oostende *Belgium* **17 C2**
Oster *Ukraine* **23 C16**
Österbotten = Pohjanmaa
  Finland **8 E20**
Osterburg *Germany* **24 C7**
Osterburg *U.S.A.* **114 F6**
Osterburken *Germany* **25 F5**
Österbybruk *Sweden* **10 D11**
Österbymo *Sweden* **11 G9**
Österdalälven *Sweden* **10 C9**
Österdalen *Norway* **10 C4**
Österfärnebo *Sweden* **10 D10**
Österforse *Sweden* **10 A11**
Östergötlands län □ *Sweden* **11 F9**
Osterholz-Scharmbeck
  Germany **24 B4**
Østerild *Denmark* **11 G2**
Östermyra = Seinäjoki
  Finland **8 E20**
Osterode *Germany* **24 D6**
Östersund *Sweden* **10 A8**
Östervåla *Sweden* **10 D11**
Ostfriesische Inseln *Germany* **24 B3**
Ostfriesland *Germany* **24 B3**
Östhammar *Sweden* **10 D12**
Óstia, Lido di *Italy* **41 G9**
Ostíglia *Italy* **41 C8**
Östmark *Sweden* **10 D6**
Östra Husby *Sweden* **11 F10**
Ostrava *Czech Rep.* **27 B11**
Ostravský □ *Czech Rep.* **27 B10**
Ostróda *Poland* **30 E6**
Ostrogozhsk *Russia* **33 G10**
Ostroh *Ukraine* **23 C14**
Ostrołęka *Poland* **31 E8**
Ostrov *Bulgaria* **45 C8**
Ostrov *Czech Rep.* **26 A5**
Ostrov *Romania* **29 F12**
Ostrov *Russia* **32 D5**
Ostrów Lubelski *Poland* **31 G9**
Ostrów Mazowiecka *Poland* **31 F8**
Ostrów Wielkopolski *Poland* **31 G4**
Ostrowiec-Świętokrzyski
  Poland **31 H8**
Ostrožac *Bos.-H.* **28 G2**
Ostrzeszów *Poland* **31 G4**
Ostseebad Kühlungsborn
  Germany **24 A7**
Osttirol □ *Austria* **26 E5**
Ostuni *Italy* **43 B10**
Osum ➤ *Albania* **44 F4**
Osŭm ➤ *Bulgaria* **45 C8**
Ōsumi-Kaikyō *Japan* **55 J5**
Ōsumi-Shotō *Japan* **55 J5**
Osun □ *Nigeria* **83 D5**
Osuna *Spain* **37 H5**
Oswegatchie ➤ *U.S.A.* **115 B9**
Oswego *U.S.A.* **115 C8**
Oswego ➤ *U.S.A.* **115 C8**
Oswestry *U.K.* **14 E4**
Oświęcim *Poland* **31 H6**

Otaci *Moldova* **29 B12**
Otago □ *N.Z.* **91 F2**
Otago Harbour *N.Z.* **91 F3**
Otaheite B. *Trin. & Tob.* **125 K15**
Ōtake *Japan* **55 G6**
Otaki *N.Z.* **91 D5**
Otaru *Japan* **54 C10**
Otaru-Wan =
  Ishikari-Wan *Japan* **54 C10**
Otavalo *Ecuador* **124 C3**
Otavi *Namibia* **88 B2**
Otchinjau *Angola* **88 B1**
Otego *U.S.A.* **115 D9**
Otelec *Romania* **28 E5**
Otelnuk, L. *Canada* **105 A6**
Oțelu Roșu *Romania* **28 E7**
Otero de Rey = Outeiro de
  Rei *Spain* **36 B3**
Othello *U.S.A.* **108 C4**
Othoni *Greece* **46 B1**
Othris, Oros *Greece* **46 B4**
Oti ➤ *Africa* **83 D5**
Oti △ *Togo* **83 C5**
Otineppu *Japan* **54 B11**
Otjiwarongo *Namibia* **88 C2**
Otmuchów *Poland* **31 H4**
Oto Tolu Group *Tonga* **91 c**
Otočac *Croatia* **41 D12**
Otok *Croatia* **41 E13**
Otopeni, București ✈
  (OTP) *Romania* **29 F11**
Otorohanga *N.Z.* **91 C5**
Otoskwin ➤ *Canada* **104 B2**
Otra ➤ *Norway* **9 G13**
Otradnyy *Russia* **34 D10**
Otranto *Italy* **43 B11**
Otranto, C. d' *Italy* **43 B11**
Otranto, Str. of *Italy* **43 B11**
Otrokovice *Czech Rep.* **27 B10**
Otse *S. Africa* **88 D4**
Otsego L. *U.S.A.* **115 D10**
Ōtsu *Japan* **55 G7**
Ōtsuki *Japan* **55 G9**
Ottawa *Canada* **115 A9**
Ottawa *Ill., U.S.A.* **112 E9**
Ottawa *Kans., U.S.A.* **112 F6**
Ottawa ➤ = Outaouais ➤
  Canada **104 C5**
Ottawa Is. *Canada* **101 D11**
Ottélé *Cameroon* **83 E7**
Ottensheim *Austria* **26 C7**
Otter Cr. ➤ *U.S.A.* **115 B11**
Otter Lake *Canada* **114 A5**
Otterndorf *Germany* **24 B4**
Otterup *Denmark* **11 J4**
Otterville *Canada* **114 D4**
Ottery St. Mary *U.K.* **15 G4**
Otto Beit Bridge *Zimbabwe* **87 F2**
Ottosdal *S. Africa* **88 D4**
Ottumwa *U.S.A.* **112 E7**
Otu *Nigeria* **83 D5**
Otukpa *Nigeria* **83 D6**
Oturkpo *Nigeria* **83 D6**
Otway, B. *Chile* **128 G2**
Otway, C. *Australia* **95 F3**
Otwock *Poland* **31 F8**
Otyniya *Ukraine* **29 B9**
Ötztaler Ache ➤ *Austria* **26 D3**
Ötztaler Alpen *Austria* **26 E3**
Ou ➤ *Laos* **64 B4**
Ou Neua *Laos* **58 B3**
Ou-Sammyaku *Japan* **54 E10**
Ouachita ➤ *U.S.A.* **116 F9**
Ouachita, L. *U.S.A.* **116 D8**
Ouachita Mts. *U.S.A.* **116 D7**
Ouagadougou *Burkina Faso* **83 C4**
Ouahigouya *Burkina Faso* **82 C4**
Ouahran = Oran *Algeria* **78 A5**
Oualâta *Mauritania* **82 B3**
Ouallam *Niger* **83 C5**
Ouallene *Algeria* **78 D6**
Ouarâne *Mauritania* **78 D3**
Ouargaye *Burkina Faso* **83 C5**
Ouargla *Algeria* **78 B7**
Ouarkoye *Burkina Faso* **82 C4**
Ouarra ➤ *C.A.R.* **84 C4**
Ouarzazate *Morocco* **78 B4**
Ouassouas *Mali* **83 B5**
Ouatagouna *Mali* **83 B5**
Oubangi ➤
  Dem. Rep. of the Congo **84 E3**
Ouche ➤ *France* **19 E12**
Ouddorp *Neths.* **17 C3**
Oude Rijn ➤ *Neths.* **17 B4**
Oudeïka *Mali* **83 B4**
Oudenaarde *Belgium* **17 D3**
Oudon ➤ *France* **18 E6**
Oudtshoorn *S. Africa* **88 E3**
Ouellé *Ivory C.* **82 D4**
Ouéme ➤ *Benin* **83 D5**
Ouessa *Burkina Faso* **82 C4**
Ouessant, Î. d' *France* **18 D1**
Ouesso *Congo* **84 D3**
Ouest □ *Cameroon* **83 D7**
Ouest, Pte. de l' *Canada* **105 C7**
Ouezzane *Morocco* **78 B4**
Ougarou *Burkina Faso* **83 C5**

Oughter, L. *Ireland* **12 B4**
Oughterard *Ireland* **12 C2**
Ouidah *Benin* **83 D5**
Ouidi *Niger* **83 C7**
Ouistreham *France* **18 C6**
Oujda *Morocco* **78 B5**
Oujeft *Mauritania* **82 A2**
Oulainen *Finland* **8 D21**
Ould Yenjé *Mauritania* **82 B2**
Oullins *France* **21 C8**
Oulu *Finland* **8 D21**
Oulujärvi *Finland* **8 D22**
Oulujoki ➤ *Finland* **8 D21**
Oulx *Italy* **40 C3**
Oum Chalouba *Chad* **79 E10**
Oum Hadjer *Chad* **79 F9**
Oumé *Ivory C.* **82 D3**
Ounasjoki ➤ *Finland* **8 C21**
Ounguati *Namibia* **88 C2**
Ounianga Kébir *Chad* **79 E10**
Our ➤ *Lux.* **17 E6**
Oura, Akra *Greece* **47 C8**
Ouranoupoli *Greece* **44 F7**
Ourârene *Niger* **83 B6**
Ouray *U.S.A.* **109 G10**
Ourense *Spain* **36 C3**
Ourense □ *Spain* **36 C3**
Ouricuri *Brazil* **125 E10**
Ourinhos *Brazil* **127 A6**
Ourique *Portugal* **37 H2**
Ouro Fino *Brazil* **127 A6**
Ouro-Ndia *Mali* **82 B4**
Ouro Prêto *Brazil* **127 A7**
Ouro Sogui *Senegal* **82 B2**
Oursi *Burkina Faso* **83 C4**
Ourthe ➤ *Belgium* **17 D5**
Ouse ➤ *E. Sussex, U.K.* **15 G8**
Ouse ➤ *N. Yorks., U.K.* **14 D7**
Oust *France* **20 D5**
Oust ➤ *France* **18 E4**
Outamba-Kilimi △ *S. Leone* **82 D2**
Outaouais ➤ *Canada* **104 C5**
Outardes ➤ *Canada* **105 C6**
Outeiro de Rei *Spain* **36 B3**
Outer Hebrides *U.K.* **13 D1**
Outes = A Serra de Outes
  Spain **36 C2**
Outjo *Namibia* **88 C2**
Outlook *Canada* **103 C7**
Outokumpu *Finland* **8 E23**
Outreau *France* **19 B8**
Ouvèze ➤ *France* **21 D9**
Ouyen *Australia* **95 F3**
Ouzouer-le-Marché *France* **19 E8**
Ovada *Italy* **40 D5**
Ovalau *Fiji* **91 a**
Ovalle *Chile* **126 C1**
Ovamboland *Namibia* **88 B2**
Ovar *Portugal* **36 E2**
Overath *Germany* **24 E3**
Overflakkee *Neths.* **17 C4**
Overijssel □ *Neths.* **17 B6**
Overland Park *U.S.A.* **112 F6**
Overton *U.S.A.* **111 J12**
Övertorneå *Sweden* **8 C20**
Överum *Sweden* **11 F10**
Ovid *U.S.A.* **115 D8**
Ovidiopol *Ukraine* **33 J6**
Ovidiu *Romania* **29 F13**
Oviedo *Spain* **36 B5**
Oviksfjällen *Sweden* **10 A7**
Ovišı *Latvia* **30 A3**
Ovoot *Mongolia* **56 B7**
Övör Hangay □ *Mongolia* **56 B2**
Ovoro *Nigeria* **83 D6**
Øvre Årdal *Norway* **8 F12**
Øvre Fryken *Sweden* **10 E7**
Ovruch *Ukraine* **23 C15**
Owaka *N.Z.* **91 G2**
Owambo = Ovamboland
  Namibia **88 B2**
Owasco L. *U.S.A.* **115 D8**
Owase *Japan* **55 G8**
Owatonna *U.S.A.* **112 C7**
Owbeh *Afghan.* **66 B3**
Owego *U.S.A.* **115 D8**
Owen Falls Dam =
  Nalubaale Dam *Uganda* **86 B3**
Owen Sound *Canada* **114 B4**
Owen Stanley Ra.
  Papua N. G. **90 B7**
Oweniny ➤ *Ireland* **12 B2**
Owens ➤ *U.S.A.* **110 J9**
Owens L. *U.S.A.* **111 J9**
Owensboro *U.S.A.* **112 G10**
Owerri *Nigeria* **83 D6**
Owl ➤ *Canada* **103 B10**
Owo *Nigeria* **83 D6**
Owosso *U.S.A.* **113 D11**
Owyhee *U.S.A.* **108 F5**
Owyhee ➤ *U.S.A.* **108 E5**
Owyhee, L. *U.S.A.* **108 E5**
Ox Mts. = Slieve Gamph
  Ireland **12 B3**
Öxarfjörður *Iceland* **8 C5**
Oxbow *Canada* **103 D8**
Oxelösund *Sweden* **11 F11**
Oxford *N.Z.* **91 E4**

Oxford *U.K.* **15** F6
Oxford *Mass., U.S.A.* **115** D13
Oxford *Miss., U.S.A.* **117** D10
Oxford *N.C., U.S.A.* **117** C15
Oxford *N.Y., U.S.A.* **115** D9
Oxford *Ohio, U.S.A.* **113** F11
Oxford L. *Canada* **103** C9
Oxfordshire □ *U.K.* **15** F6
Oxia *Greece* **46** C3
Oxie *Sweden* **11** J7
Oxilithos *Greece* **46** C6
Oxnard *U.S.A.* **111** L7
Oxsjövälen *Sweden* **10** B7
Oxus = Amudarya ➜
  Uzbekistan **52** E6
Oya *Burkina Faso* **82** C4
Oyama *Japan* **55** F9
Oyambre △ *Spain* **36** B6
Oyem *Gabon* **84** D2
Oyen *Canada* **103** C6
Oykel ➜ *U.K.* **13** D4
Oymyakon *Russia* **53** C15
Oyo *Nigeria* **83** D5
Oyo □ *Nigeria* **83** D5
Oyonnax *France* **19** F12
Oyster Bay *U.S.A.* **115** F11
Ōyūbari *Japan* **54** C11
Özalp *Turkey* **73** C10
Ozamiz *Phil.* **61** G5
Ozark *Ala., U.S.A.* **117** F12
Ozark *Ark., U.S.A.* **116** D8
Ozark *Mo., U.S.A.* **112** G7
Ozark Plateau *U.S.A.* **112** G8
Ozarks, L. of the *U.S.A.* **112** F7
Ożarów *Poland* **31** H8
Ózd *Hungary* **28** B5
Ozernovskiy *Russia* **53** D16
Ozernoye *Russia* **34** E10
Ozero Svityaz *Ukraine* **31** G10
Ozersk *Russia* **30** D8
Ozette, L. *U.S.A.* **110** B2
Ozieri *Italy* **42** B2
Ozimek *Poland* **31** H5
Ozinki *Russia* **34** E9
Ozona *U.S.A.* **116** F4
Ozorków *Poland* **31** G6
Ozren *Bos.-H.* **28** G7
Ozuluama *Mexico* **119** C5
Ozun *Romania* **29** E10
Ozurgeti *Georgia* **35** K5

P

Pa *Burkina Faso* **82** C4
Pa-an *Burma* **67** L20
Pa Mong Dam *Thailand* **64** D4
Pa Sak ➜ *Thailand* **64** E3
Paamiut *Greenland* **4** C5
Paar ➜ *Germany* **25** G7
Paarl *S. Africa* **88** E2
Pabbay *U.K.* **13** D1
Pabianice *Poland* **31** G6
Pabna *Bangla.* **67** G16
Pabo *Uganda* **86** B3
Pacaja ➜ *Brazil* **125** D8
Pacaraima, Sa. *S. Amer.* **124** C6
Pacasmayo *Peru* **124** E3
Paceco *Italy* **42** E5
Pachia *Greece* **47** E7
Pachino *Italy* **43** F8
Pachitea ➜ *Peru* **124** E4
Pachmarhi *India* **69** H8
Pachnes *Greece* **49** D6
Pachpadra *India* **68** G5
Pachuca *Mexico* **119** C5
Pacific Antarctic Ridge
  Pac. Oc. **5** B13
Pacific Grove *U.S.A.* **110** J5
Pacific Ocean **97** G14
Pacific Rim △ *Canada* **110** B2
Pacifica *U.S.A.* **110** H4
Pacitan *Indonesia* **63** H14
Packwood *U.S.A.* **110** D5
Pacov *Czech Rep.* **26** B8
Pacy-sur-Eure *France* **18** C8
Padaido, Kepulauan
  Indonesia **63** E9
Padang *Indonesia* **65**
Padang Endau *Malaysia* **65** L4
Padangpanjang *Indonesia* **62** E2
Padangsidempuan *Indonesia* **62** D1
Padborg *Denmark* **11** K3
Paddle Prairie *Canada* **102** B5
Paderborn *Germany* **24** D4
Padeș, Vf. *Romania* **28** E7
Padina *Romania* **29** F12
Padma *India* **69** G11
Pádova *Italy* **41** C8
Padra *India* **68** H5
Padrauna *India* **69** F10
Padre I. *U.S.A.* **116** H6
Padre Island △ *U.S.A.* **116** H6
Padrón *Spain* **36** C2
Padstow *U.K.* **15** G3
Padua = Pádova *Italy* **41** C8
Paducah *Ky., U.S.A.* **112** G9
Paducah *Tex., U.S.A.* **116** D4
Padul *Spain* **37** H7

Paea *Tahiti* **91** d
Paeroa *N.Z.* **91** B5
Paesana *Italy* **40** D4
Pafúri *Mozam.* **89** C5
Pag *Croatia* **41** D12
Paga *Ghana* **83** C4
Pagadian *Phil.* **61** H5
Pagai Selatan, Pulau
  Indonesia **62** E2
Pagai Utara, Pulau *Indonesia* **62** E2
Pagalu = Annobón *Atl. Oc.* **77** G4
Pagara *India* **69** G9
Pagastikos Kolpos *Greece* **46** B5
Pagatan *Indonesia* **62** E5
Page *U.S.A.* **109** H8
Pagégiai *Lithuania* **30** C8
Paget, Mt. *S. Georgia* **128** G9
Pago Pago *Amer. Samoa* **91** b
Pagosa Springs *U.S.A.* **109** H10
Pagwa River *Canada* **104** B2
Pāhala *U.S.A.* **106** b
Pahang □ *Malaysia* **65** L4
Pahiatua *N.Z.* **91** D5
Pahokee *U.S.A.* **117** H14
Pahrump *U.S.A.* **111** J11
Pahute Mesa *U.S.A.* **110** H10
Pai *Thailand* **64** C2
Paicines *U.S.A.* **110** J5
Paide *Estonia* **32** C3
Paignton *U.K.* **15** G4
Paiho *Taiwan* **59** F13
Päijänne *Finland* **32** B3
Pailani *India* **69** G9
Pailin *Cambodia* **64** F4
Paimpol *France* **18** D3
Painan *Indonesia* **62** E2
Painesville *U.S.A.* **114** E3
Paint Hills = Wemindji
  Canada **104** B4
Paint L. *Canada* **103** B9
Painted Desert *U.S.A.* **109** H8
Paintsville *U.S.A.* **113** G12
País Vasco □ *Spain* **38** C2
Paisley *Canada* **114** B3
Paisley *U.K.* **13** F4
Paisley *U.S.A.* **108** E3
Paita *Peru* **124** E2
Paiva ➜ *Portugal* **36** D2
Paizhou *China* **59** B9
Pajares *Spain* **36** B5
Pajares, Puerto de *Spain* **36** C5
Pajęczno *Poland* **31** G5
Pak Lay *Laos* **64** C3
Pak Phanang *Thailand* **65** H3
Pak Sane *Laos* **64** C4
Pak Song *Laos* **64** E6
Pak Suong *Laos* **58** H4
Pakaur *India* **69** G12
Pakch'ŏn *N. Korea* **57** E13
Pakenham *Canada* **115** A8
Pakhuis *S. Africa* **88** E2
Pakistan ■ *Asia* **68** E4
Pakkading *Laos* **64** C4
Paklenica △ *Croatia* **41** D12
Pakokku *Burma* **67** J19
Pakość *Poland* **31** F5
Pakowki L. *Canada* **103** D6
Pakpattan *Pakistan* **68** D5
Pakrac *Croatia* **28** E2
Pakruojis *Lithuania* **30** C10
Paks *Hungary* **28** D3
Paktīā □ *Afghan.* **66** C6
Paktīkā □ *Afghan.* **66** C6
Pakwach *Uganda* **86** B3
Pakxe *Laos* **64** E5
Pal Lahara *India* **69** J11
Pala *Chad* **79** G9
Pala *Dem. Rep. of the Congo* **86** D2
Pala *U.S.A.* **111** M9
Palabek *Uganda* **86** B3
Palacios *U.S.A.* **116** G6
Palafrugell *Spain* **38** D8
Palagiano *Italy* **43** B10
Palagonía *Italy* **43** E7
Palagruža *Croatia* **41** F13
Palaiseau *France* **19** D9
Palam *India* **66** K10
Palamás *Greece* **46** B4
Palamós *Spain* **38** D8
Palampur *India* **68** C7
Palamut *Turkey* **47** C9
Palana *Australia* **95** F4
Palana *Russia* **53** D16
Palanan *Phil.* **61** C5
Palandri *Pakistan* **69** C5
Palanga *Lithuania* **30** C8
Palangkaraya *Indonesia* **62** E4
Palani Hills *India* **66** P10
Palanpur *India* **68** G5
Palapye *Botswana* **88** C4
Palas *Pakistan* **69** B5
Palas de Rei *Spain* **36** C3
Palasponga *India* **69** J11
Palatka *Russia* **53** C16
Palatka *U.S.A.* **117** G14
Palau *Italy* **42** A2
Palau ■ *Palau* **90** A6
Palauk *Burma* **64** F2

Palawan *Phil.* **61** G3
Palayankottai *India* **66** Q10
Palazzo, Pte. *France* **21** F12
Palazzo San Gervásio *Italy* **43** B8
Palazzolo Acréide *Italy* **43** E7
Paldiski *Estonia* **32** C3
Pale *Bos.-H.* **28** G3
Palekastro *Greece* **49** D8
Paleleh *Indonesia* **63** D6
Palembang *Indonesia* **62** E2
Palencia *Spain* **36** C6
Palencia □ *Spain* **36** C6
Palenque *Mexico* **119** D6
Paleochora *Greece* **49** D5
Paleokastritsa *Greece* **49** A3
Paleometokho *Cyprus* **49** D12
Palermo *Italy* **42** D6
Palermo *U.S.A.* **108** G3
Palermo ✈ (PMO) *Italy* **42** D6
Paleros *Greece* **46** C2
Palestina *Chile* **128** A3
Palestine *Asia* **74** D4
Palestine *U.S.A.* **116** F7
Palestrina *Italy* **41** G9
Paletwa *Burma* **67** J18
Palghat *India* **66** P10
Palgrave, Mt. *Australia* **92** D2
Pali *India* **68** G5
Palikir *Micronesia* **96** G7
Palinuro *Italy* **43** B8
Palinuro, C. *Italy* **43** B8
Paliouri, Akra *Greece* **44** G7
Palisades Res. *U.S.A.* **108** E8
Paliseul *Belgium* **17** E5
Palitana *India* **68** J4
Palizada *Mexico* **119** D6
Palk Bay *Asia* **66** Q11
Palk Strait *Asia* **66** Q11
Palkānah *Iraq* **70** C5
Palkot *India* **69** H11
Pallanza = Verbánia *Italy* **40** C5
Pallarenda *Australia* **94** B4
Pallasovka *Russia* **34** E8
Pallës, Bishti i *Albania* **44** E3
Pallinup ➜ *Australia* **93** F2
Pallisa *Uganda* **86** B3
Pallu *India* **68** E6
Palm Bay *U.S.A.* **117** G14
Palm Beach *U.S.A.* **117** H14
Palm Coast *U.S.A.* **117** G14
Palm Desert *U.S.A.* **111** M10
Palm Is. *Australia* **94** B4
Palm Springs *U.S.A.* **111** M10
Palma *Mozam.* **87** E5
Palma, B. de *Spain* **48** B9
Palma de Mallorca *Spain* **48** B9
Palma de Mallorca ✈
  (PMI) *Spain* **39** F7
Palma del Río *Spain* **37** H5
Palma di Montechiaro *Italy* **42** E6
Palma Nova = Palmanova
  Spain **48** B9
Palma Soriano *Cuba* **120** B4
Palmanova *Spain* **48** B9
Palmares *Brazil* **125** E11
Palmarola *Italy* **42** B5
Pálmas, C. *Liberia* **82** E3
Pálmas, G. di *Italy* **42** D1
Palmdale *U.S.A.* **111** L8
Palmeira das Missões *Brazil* **127** B5
Palmeira dos Índios *Brazil* **125** E11
Palmela *Portugal* **37** G2
Palmer *Antarctica* **5** C17
Palmer *U.S.A.* **100** C5
Palmer ➜ *Australia* **94** B3
Palmer Arch. *Antarctica* **5** C17
Palmer Lake *U.S.A.* **108** G11
Palmer Land *Antarctica* **5** D18
Palmerston *Australia* **92** B5
Palmerston *Canada* **114** C4
Palmerston *N.Z.* **91** F3
Palmerston North *N.Z.* **91** D5
Palmerton *U.S.A.* **115** F9
Palmetto *U.S.A.* **117** H13
Palmi *Italy* **43** D8
Palmira *Argentina* **126** C2
Palmira *Colombia* **124** C3
Palmyra = Tudmur *Syria* **73** E8
Palmyra *Mo., U.S.A.* **112** F8
Palmyra *N.J., U.S.A.* **115** F9
Palmyra *N.Y., U.S.A.* **114** C7
Palmyra *Pa., U.S.A.* **115** F8
Palmyra Is. *Pac. Oc.* **97** G11
Palo Alto *U.S.A.* **110** H4
Palo Seco *Trin. & Tob.* **125** K15
Palo Verde *U.S.A.* **111** M12
Palo Verde △ *Costa Rica* **120** D2
Paloich *Sudan* **81** E3
Palomar Mt. *U.S.A.* **111** M10
Palompon *Phil.* **61** F6
Palopo *Indonesia* **63** E6
Palos, C. de *Spain* **39** H4
Palos de la Frontera *Spain* **37** H4
Palos Verdes, Pt. *U.S.A.* **111** M8
Palos Verdes Estates *U.S.A.* **111** M8
Pålsboda *Sweden* **10** E9
Palu *Indonesia* **63** E5
Palu *Turkey* **73** C9

Paluke *Liberia* **82** D3
Paluzza *Italy* **41** B10
Palwal *India* **68** E7
Pama *Burkina Faso* **83** C5
Pama △ *Burkina Faso* **83** C5
Pamanukan *Indonesia* **63** G12
Pamekasan *Indonesia* **63** G15
Pamenang *Indonesia* **63** J19
Pamiers *France* **20** E5
Pamir *Tajikistan* **52** F8
Pamlico ➜ *U.S.A.* **117** D16
Pamlico Sd. *U.S.A.* **117** D17
Pampa *U.S.A.* **116** D4
Pampa de las Salinas
  Argentina **126** C2
Pampanua *Indonesia* **63** E6
Pampas *Argentina* **126** D3
Pampas *Peru* **124** F4
Pamphylia *Turkey* **72** D4
Pamplona *Colombia* **124** B4
Pamplona-Iruña *Spain* **38** C3
Pampoenpoort *S. Africa* **88** E3
Pamukçu *Turkey* **47** B9
Pamukkale *Turkey* **47** D11
Pan de Azúcar *Chile* **126** B1
Pan de Azúcar △ *Chile* **126** B1
Pan Xian *China* **58** E5
Pana *U.S.A.* **112** F10
Panabo *Phil.* **61** H6
Panaca *U.S.A.* **109** H6
Panagyurishte *Bulgaria* **45** D8
Panaitan *Indonesia* **63** G11
Panaji *India* **66** M8
Panamá *Panama* **120** E4
Panama ■ *Cent. Amer.* **120** E4
Panamá, G. de *Panama* **120** E4
Panama, Isthmus of
  Cent. Amer. **98** J12
Panama Basin *Pac. Oc.* **97** G19
Panama Canal *Panama* **120** E4
Panama City *U.S.A.* **117** F12
Panamint Range *U.S.A.* **111** J9
Panamint Springs *U.S.A.* **111** J9
Panão *Peru* **124** E3
Panaon I. *Phil.* **61** F6
Panare *Thailand* **65** J3
Panarea *Italy* **43** D8
Panaro ➜ *Italy* **41** D8
Panay *Phil.* **61** F5
Panay G. *Phil.* **63** B6
Panayarvi △ *Russia* **8** C24
Pančevo *Serbia* **28** F5
Panch'iao *Taiwan* **59** E13
Panciu *Romania* **29** E12
Pancorbo, Desfiladero *Spain* **36** C7
Pâncota *Romania* **28** D5
Panda *Mozam.* **89** C5
Pandan *Malaysia* **65** d
Pandan *Antique, Phil.* **61** F5
Pandan *Catanduanes, Phil.* **61** D6
Pandan, Selat *Singapore* **65** d
Pandan Tampoi = Tampoi
  Malaysia **65** d
Pandegelang *Indonesia* **63** G12
Pandhana *India* **68** J7
Pandharpur *India* **66** L9
Pando *Uruguay* **127** C4
Pando, L. = Hope, L.
  Australia **95** D2
Pandokratoras *Greece* **49** A3
Pandora *Costa Rica* **120** E3
Pandrup *Denmark* **11** G3
Panevéggio-Pale di San
  Martino △ *Italy* **41** B8
Panevėžys *Lithuania* **32** E3
Panfilovo *Russia* **34** E6
Pang-Long *Burma* **67** H21
Pang Sida △ *Thailand* **64** E4
Pang-Yang *Burma* **67** H21
Panga *Dem. Rep. of the Congo* **86** B2
Pangaíon Óros *Greece* **45** F8
Pangalanes, Canal des =
  Ampangalana,
  Lakandranon' *Madag.* **89** C8
Pangani *Tanzania* **86** D4
Pangani ➜ *Tanzania* **86** D4
Pangar Djérem ➜ *Cameroon* **83** D7
Pangfou = Bengbu *China* **57** H9
Pangil *Dem. Rep. of the Congo* **86** C2
Pangkah, Tanjung
  Indonesia **63** G15
Pangkajene *Indonesia* **63** E5
Pangkalanbrandan
  Indonesia **62** D1
Pangkalanbuun *Indonesia* **62** E4
Pangkalpinang *Indonesia* **62** E3
Pangkor, P. *Malaysia* **65** K3
Pangnirtung *Canada* **101** C13
Pangody *Russia* **52** C8
Panguitch *U.S.A.* **109** H7
Pangutaran Group *Phil.* **61** H4
Panhandle *U.S.A.* **116** D4
Pani Mines *India* **68** H5
Pania-Mutombo
  Dem. Rep. of the Congo **86** D1
Panikota I. *India* **68** J4
Panipat *India* **68** E7
Panjal Range = Pir Panjal
  Range *India* **68** C7

Panjang, Hon *Vietnam* **65** H4
Panjgur *Pakistan* **66** F4
Panjin *China* **57** D12
Panjnad ➜ *Pakistan* **68** E4
Panjnad Barrage *Pakistan* **68** E4
Panjwai *Afghan.* **68** D1
Pankshin *Nigeria* **83** D6
Panmunjŏm *N. Korea* **57** F14
Panna *India* **69** G9
Panna △ *India* **69** G8
Panna Hills *India* **69** G9
Pannawonica *Australia* **92** D2
Pannga, Tanjung *Indonesia* **63** K19
Pannirtuuq =
  Pangnirtung *Canada* **101** C13
Pano Akil *Pakistan* **68** F3
Pano Lefkara *Cyprus* **49** E12
Pano Panayia *Cyprus* **49** E11
Panorama *Brazil* **127** A5
Panormos *Greece* **49** D6
Panshan = Panjin *China* **57** D12
Panshi *China* **57** C14
Pantanal *Brazil* **124** H7
Pantanos de Centla △
  Mexico **119** D6
Pantar *Indonesia* **63** F6
Pante Macassar *E. Timor* **63** F6
Pantelleria *Italy* **42** F4
Pantón *Spain* **36** C3
Pánuco *Mexico* **119** C5
Panyam *Nigeria* **83** D6
Panyu *China* **59** F9
Panzhihua *China* **58** D3
Páola *Italy* **43** C9
Paola *Malta* **49** D2
Paola *U.S.A.* **112** F6
Paonia *U.S.A.* **108** G10
Paopao *Moorea* **91** d
Paoting = Baoding *China* **56** E8
Paot'ou = Baotou *China* **56** D6
Paoua *C.A.R.* **84** C3
Pápa *Hungary* **28** C2
Papa Stour *U.K.* **13** A7
Papa Westray *U.K.* **13** B6
Papagayo ➜ *Mexico* **119** D5
Papagayo, G. de *Costa Rica* **120** D2
Papakura *N.Z.* **91** B5
Papantla *Mexico* **119** C5
Papar *Malaysia* **62** C5
Papara *Tahiti* **91** d
Paparoa △ *N.Z.* **91** E3
Papas, Akra *Greece* **46** C3
Papeete *Tahiti* **91** d
Papenburg *Germany* **24** B3
Papenoo *Tahiti* **91** d
Papenoo ➜ *Tahiti* **91** d
Papetoai *Moorea* **91** d
Paphlagonia *Turkey* **72** B5
Paphos *Cyprus* **49** E11
Papikio Oros *Greece* **45** E9
Papoose *Chile* **126** B1
Papoutsa *Cyprus* **49** E12
Papua □ *Indonesia* **63** E9
Papua, G. of *Papua N. G.* **90** B7
Papua New Guinea ■
  Oceania **90** B7
Papudo *Chile* **126** C1
Papuk *Croatia* **28** E2
Papun *Burma* **67** K20
Papunya *Australia* **92** D5
Pará = Belém *Brazil* **125** D9
Pará □ *Brazil* **125** D8
Paraburdoo *Australia* **92** D2
Paracale *Phil.* **61** D5
Paracatu *Brazil* **125** G9
Paracel Is. *S. China Sea* **62** A4
Parachilna *Australia* **95** E2
Parachinar *Pakistan* **68** C4
Paracín *Serbia* **44** C5
Paradas *Spain* **37** H5
Paradela *Spain* **36** C3
Paradip *India* **67** J15
Paradise *Calif., U.S.A.* **110** F5
Paradise *Nev., U.S.A.* **111** J11
Paradise ➜ *Canada* **105** B8
Paradise Hill *Canada* **103** C7
Paradise River *Canada* **105** B8
Paradise Valley *U.S.A.* **108** F5
Paradisi *Greece* **49** C10
Parado *Indonesia* **63** F5
Paragould *U.S.A.* **117** C9
Paragua ➜ *Venezuela* **124** B6
Paraguaçu ➜ *Brazil* **125** F11
Paraguaçu Paulista *Brazil* **127** A5
Paraguaná, Pen. de
  Venezuela **124** A5
Paraguarí *Paraguay* **126** B4
Paraguarí □ *Paraguay* **126** B4
Paraguay ■ *S. Amer.* **126** A4
Paraguay ➜ *Paraguay* **126** B4
Paraíba = João Pessoa
  Brazil **125** E12
Paraíba □ *Brazil* **125** E11
Paraíba do Sul ➜ *Brazil* **127** A7
Parainen *Finland* **32** B2
Paraíso *Mexico* **119** D6
Parak *Iran* **71** E7

Parakhino Paddubye *Russia* **32** C7
Parakou *Benin* **83** D5
Paralimni *Cyprus* **49** D12
Paralio Astros *Greece* **46** D4
Paramaribo *Suriname* **125** B7
Paramithia *Greece* **46** B2
Páramos del Batallón y La
  Negra △ *Venezuela* **121** E5
Paramushir, Ostrov *Russia* **53** D16
Paran ➜ *Israel* **74** E4
Paraná *Argentina* **126** C3
Paraná *Brazil* **125** F9
Paraná □ *Brazil* **127** A5
Paraná ➜ *Argentina* **126** C4
Paranaguá *Brazil* **127** B6
Paranaíba *Brazil* **125** G8
Paranaíba ➜ *Brazil* **125** H8
Paranapanema ➜ *Brazil* **127** A5
Paranapiacaba, Serra do
  Brazil **127** A6
Paranas *Phil.* **61** F6
Paranavaí *Brazil* **127** A5
Parang *Maguindanao, Phil.* **63** C6
Parang *Sulu, Phil.* **61** J4
Parângul Mare, Vf. *Romania* **29** E8
Paraparaumu *N.Z.* **91** D5
Paraspori, Akra *Greece* **47** F9
Paray-le-Monial *France* **19** F11
Parbati ➜ *Mad. P., India* **68** G7
Parbati ➜ *Raj., India* **68** F7
Parbhani *India* **66** K10
Parchim *Germany* **24** B7
Parczew *Poland* **31** G9
Pardes Hanna-Karkur *Israel* **74** C3
Pardilla *Spain* **36** D7
Pardo ➜ *Bahia, Brazil* **125** G11
Pardo ➜ *Mato Grosso, Brazil* **127** A5
Pardoo Roadhouse *Australia* **92** D2
Pardubice *Czech Rep.* **26** A8
Pardubický □ *Czech Rep.* **26** B8
Pare *Indonesia* **63** G15
Pare Mts. *Tanzania* **86** C4
Parecis, Serra dos *Brazil* **124** F7
Paredes de Nava *Spain* **36** C6
Paren *Russia* **53** C17
Parent *Canada* **104** C5
Parent, L. *Canada* **104** C4
Parentis-en-Born *France* **20** D2
Parepare *Indonesia* **63** E5
Parfino *Russia* **32** D6
Parga *Greece* **46** B2
Pargas = Parainen *Finland* **32** B2
Pargo, Pta. do *Madeira* **48** D2
Parham *Canada* **115** B8
Paria ➜ *U.S.A.* **109** H8
Paria, G. de *Venezuela* **125** K14
Pariaguán *Venezuela* **124** B6
Paricutín, Cerro *Mexico* **118** D4
Parigi *Indonesia* **63** E6
Parika *Guyana* **124** B7
Parikia *Greece* **47** D7
Parikkala *Finland* **32** B5
Parima, Serra *Brazil* **124** C6
Parinari *Peru* **124** D4
Pariñas, Pta. *S. Amer.* **122** D2
Parincea *Romania* **29** D12
Parintins *Brazil* **125** D7
Pariparit Kyun *Burma* **67** M18
Paris *Canada* **114** C4
Paris *France* **19** D9
Paris *Idaho, U.S.A.* **108** E8
Paris *Ky., U.S.A.* **113** F11
Paris *Tenn., U.S.A.* **117** C10
Paris *Tex., U.S.A.* **116** E7
Paris, Ville de □ *France* **19** D9
Paris Charles de Gaulle ✈
  (CDG) *France* **19** D9
Paris Orly ✈ (ORY) *France* **19** D9
Parish *U.S.A.* **115** C8
Parishville *U.S.A.* **115** B10
Park *U.S.A.* **110** B4
Park City *U.S.A.* **112** G5
Park Falls *U.S.A.* **112** C8
Park Head *Canada* **114** B3
Park Hills *U.S.A.* **112** G8
Park Range *U.S.A.* **108** F10
Park Rapids *U.S.A.* **112** B6
Park River *U.S.A.* **112** A6
Park Rynie *S. Africa* **89** E5
Parkā Bandar *Iran* **71** E8
Parkano *Finland* **32** A2
Parker *Ariz., U.S.A.* **111** L12
Parker *Pa., U.S.A.* **114** E5
Parker Dam *U.S.A.* **111** L12
Parkersburg *U.S.A.* **113** F13
Parkes *Australia* **95** E4
Parkfield *U.S.A.* **110** K6
Parkhill *Canada* **114** C3
Parkland *U.S.A.* **110** C4
Parkston *U.S.A.* **112** D5
Parksville *Canada* **102** D3
Parkway *U.S.A.* **110** G5
Parla *Spain* **36** E7
Pârlița *Moldova* **29** C12
Parma *Italy* **40** D7
Parma *Idaho, U.S.A.* **108** E5
Parma *Ohio, U.S.A.* **114** E3
Parma ➜ *Italy* **40** D7
Parnaguá *Brazil* **125** F10

Parnaíba *Brazil* **125** D10
Parnaíba → *Brazil* **125** D10
Parnassos *Greece* **46** C4
Parnitha *Greece* **46** C5
Parnitha △ *Greece* **46** C5
Parnonas Oros *Greece* **46** D4
Pärnu *Estonia* **32** C3
Paro Dzong *Bhutan* **69** F13
Paroo → *Australia* **95** E3
Paroo-Darling △ *Australia* **95** E3
Paros *Greece* **47** D7
Parowan *U.S.A.* **109** H7
Parpaillon *France* **21** D10
Parral *Chile* **126** D1
Parramatta *Australia* **95** B5
Parras *Mexico* **118** B4
Parrett → *U.K.* **15** F4
Parris I. *U.S.A.* **117** E14
Parrsboro *Canada* **105** C7
Parry I. *Canada* **114** A4
Parry Is. *Canada* **101** B9
Parry Sound *Canada* **114** A5
Parsābād *Iran* **73** C13
Parsaloi *Kenya* **86** B4
Parsberg *Germany* **25** F7
Parsęta → *Poland* **30** D2
Parsnip → *Canada* **102** B4
Parsons *U.S.A.* **113** G7
Parsons Ra. *Australia* **94** A2
Partanna *Italy* **42** E5
Partenio △ *Italy* **43** B7
Parthenay *France* **18** F6
Partinico *Italy* **42** D6
Partizansk *Russia* **54** C6
Partizánske *Slovak Rep.* **27** C11
Partridge I. *Canada* **104** A2
Partry Mts. *Ireland* **12** C2
Paru → *Brazil* **125** D8
Parvān □ *Afghan.* **66** B6
Parvatipuram *India* **67** K13
Parvatsar *India* **68** F6
Påryd *Sweden* **11** H9
Parys *S. Africa* **88** D4
Pas, Pta. des *Spain* **48** C7
Pas, The *Canada* **103** C8
Pas-de-Calais □ *France* **19** B9
Pasada *Spain* **36** B5
Pasadena *Canada* **105** C8
Pasadena *Calif., U.S.A.* **111** L8
Pasadena *Tex., U.S.A.* **116** G7
Pasaje → *Argentina* **126** B3
Pașalimanı *Turkey* **45** F11
Pasar *Indonesia* **63** J17
Pasay *Phil.* **61** D4
Pascagoula *U.S.A.* **117** F10
Pascagoula → *U.S.A.* **117** F10
Pașcani *Romania* **29** C11
Pasco *U.S.A.* **108** C4
Pasco, Cerro de *Peru* **124** F3
Pasco I. *Australia* **92** D2
Pascoag *U.S.A.* **115** E13
Pascua, I. de *Chile* **97** K17
Pasewalk *Germany* **24** B9
Pasfield L. *Canada* **103** B7
Pasha → *Russia* **32** B7
Pasinler *Turkey* **73** C9
Pasir Mas *Malaysia* **65** J4
Pasir Panjang *Singapore* **65** d
Pasir Putih *Malaysia* **65** K4
Pasirian *Indonesia* **63** H15
Pasirkuning *Indonesia* **62** E2
Påskallavik *Sweden* **11** G10
Paskūh *Iran* **71** E9
Pasłęk *Poland* **30** D6
Pasłęka → *Poland* **30** D6
Pasley, C. *Australia* **93** F3
Pašman *Croatia* **41** E12
Pasni *Pakistan* **66** G3
Paso Bravo △ *Paraguay* **126** A4
Paso Cantinela *Mexico* **111** N11
Paso de Indios *Argentina* **128** E3
Paso de los Libres *Argentina* **126** B4
Paso de los Toros *Uruguay* **126** C4
Paso Robles *U.S.A.* **110** K6
Paspébiac *Canada* **105** C6
Pasrur *Pakistan* **68** C6
Passage East *Ireland* **12** D5
Passage West *Ireland* **12** E3
Passaic *U.S.A.* **115** F10
Passau *Germany* **25** G9
Passero, C. *Italy* **43** F8
Passo Fundo *Brazil* **127** B5
Passos *Brazil* **125** H9
Passow *Germany* **24** B10
Passy *France* **21** C10
Pastavy *Belarus* **32** E4
Pastaza → *Peru* **124** D3
Pasto *Colombia* **124** C3
Pastrana *Spain* **38** E2
Pasym *Poland* **30** E7
Pásztó *Hungary* **28** C4
Patagonia *Argentina* **128** F3
Patagonia *U.S.A.* **109** L8
Patambar *Iran* **71** D9
Patan = Lalitapur *Nepal* **69** F11
Patan *India* **68** H5
Patani *Indonesia* **63** D7
Pătârlagele *Romania* **29** E11

Pataudi *India* **68** E7
Patchewollock *Australia* **95** F3
Patchogue *U.S.A.* **115** F11
Pate *Kenya* **86** C5
Pate Kenya *86* C5
Patea *N.Z.* **91** C5
Pategi *Nigeria* **83** D6
Patensie *S. Africa* **88** E3
Paterna *Spain* **39** F4
Paternion *Austria* **26** E6
Paternò *Italy* **43** E7
Pateros *U.S.A.* **108** B4
Paterson *U.S.A.* **115** F10
Paterson Ra. *Australia* **92** D3
Pathankot *India* **68** C6
Pathein = Bassein *Burma* **67** L19
Pathfinder Res. *U.S.A.* **108** E10
Pathiu *Thailand* **65** G2
Pathum Thani *Thailand* **64** E3
Pati *Indonesia* **63** G14
Patía → *Colombia* **124** C3
Patiala *Punjab, India* **68** D7
Patiala *Ut. P., India* **69** F8
Patine Kouka *Senegal* **82** C2
Patitiri *Greece* **46** B5
Patkai Bum *India* **67** F19
Patmos *Greece* **47** D8
Patna *India* **69** G11
Patnos *Turkey* **73** C10
Pato Branco *Brazil* **127** B5
Patong, Ao *Thailand* **65** a
Patonga *Uganda* **86** B3
Patos *Albania* **44** F3
Patos *Brazil* **125** E11
Patos, L. dos *Brazil* **127** C5
Patos, Río de los →
  Argentina **126** C2
Patos de Minas *Brazil* **125** G9
Patquía *Argentina* **126** C2
Patra *Greece* **46** C3
Patraikos Kolpos *Greece* **46** C3
Patras = Patra *Greece* **46** C3
Patriot Hills *Antarctica* **5** E16
Patrocínio *Brazil* **125** G9
Pattada *Italy* **42** B2
Pattani *Thailand* **65** J3
Pattaya *Thailand* **64** F3
Patten *U.S.A.* **113** B19
Patterson *Calif., U.S.A.* **110** H5
Patterson *La., U.S.A.* **116** G9
Patterson, Mt. *U.S.A.* **110** G7
Patti *Punjab, India* **68** D6
Patti *Ut. P., India* **69** G10
Patti *Italy* **43** D7
Pattoki *Pakistan* **68** D5
Patton *U.S.A.* **114** F6
Patuakhali *Bangla.* **67** H17
Patuanak *Canada* **103** B7
Patuca → *Honduras* **120** C3
Patuca, Punta *Honduras* **120** C3
Patuca △ *Honduras* **120** D2
Pătulele *Romania* **28** F7
Patvinsuo △ *Finland* **8** E24
Pátzcuaro *Mexico* **118** D4
Pau *France* **20** E3
Pau, Gave de → *France* **20** E2
Paudash *Canada* **114** B7
Pauillac *France* **20** D3
Pauk *Burma* **67** J19
Paul I. *Canada* **105** A7
Paul Smiths *U.S.A.* **115** B10
Paulatuk *Canada* **100** C7
Paulhan *France* **20** E7
Paulistana *Brazil* **125** E10
Paulo Afonso *Brazil* **125** E11
Paulpietersburg *S. Africa* **89** D5
Pauls Valley *U.S.A.* **116** D6
Pauma Valley *U.S.A.* **111** M10
Pauri *India* **69** D8
Pāveh *Iran* **73** E12
Pavelets *Russia* **32** F10
Pavia *Italy* **40** C6
Pavilion *U.S.A.* **114** D6
Pavilly *France* **18** C7
Pāvilosta *Latvia* **30** B8
Pavlikeni *Bulgaria* **45** C9
Pavlodar *Kazakhstan* **52** D8
Pavlograd = Pavlohrad
  Ukraine **33** H8
Pavlohrad *Ukraine* **33** H8
Pavlovo *Russia* **34** C6
Pavlovsk *Russia* **34** E5
Pavlovskaya *Russia* **35** G4
Pavlovskiy-Posad *Russia* **32** E10
Pavullo nel Frignano *Italy* **40** D7
Pawai, Pulau *Singapore* **65** d
Pawayan *India* **69** E9
Pawhuska *U.S.A.* **116** C6
Pawling *U.S.A.* **115** E11
Pawnee *U.S.A.* **116** C6
Pawnee City *U.S.A.* **112** E5
Pawtucket *U.S.A.* **115** E13
Paxi *Greece* **46** B2
Paximadia *Greece* **49** E6
Paxton *U.S.A.* **112** E9
Payakumbuh *Indonesia* **62** E2
Payerne *Switz.* **25** J2
Payette *U.S.A.* **108** D5
Paymogo *Spain* **37** H3

Payne Bay = Kangirsuk
  Canada **101** D13
Payne L. *Canada* **101** D12
Paynes Find *Australia* **93** E2
Paynesville *Liberia* **82** D2
Paynesville *U.S.A.* **112** C6
Pays de la Loire □ *France* **18** E6
Paysandú *Uruguay* **126** C4
Payson *Ariz., U.S.A.* **109** J8
Payson *Utah, U.S.A.* **108** F8
Paz → *Guatemala* **120** D1
Paz, B. de la *Mexico* **118** C2
Pāzanān *Iran* **71** D6
Pazar *Turkey* **73** B9
Pazarcık *Turkey* **72** D7
Pazardzhik *Bulgaria* **45** D8
Pazarköy *Turkey* **47** B9
Pazarlar *Turkey* **47** C11
Pazaryeri *Turkey* **47** B11
Pazaryolu *Turkey* **73** B9
Pazin *Croatia* **41** C10
Pčinja → *Macedonia* **44** E5
Pe Ell *U.S.A.* **110** D3
Peabody *U.S.A.* **115** D14
Peace → *Canada* **102** B6
Peace Point *Canada* **102** B6
Peace River *Canada* **102** B5
Peach Springs *U.S.A.* **109** J7
Peachland *Canada* **102** D5
Peachtree City *U.S.A.* **117** E12
Peak, The = Kinder Scout
  U.K. **14** D6
Peak Charles △ *Australia* **93** F3
Peak District △ *U.K.* **14** D6
Peak Hill *N.S.W., Australia* **95** E4
Peak Hill *W. Austral.,
  Australia* **93** E2
Peak Ra. *Australia* **94** C4
Peake Cr. → *Australia* **95** D2
Peal de Becerro *Spain* **37** H7
Peale, Mt. *U.S.A.* **108** G9
Pearblossom *U.S.A.* **111** L9
Pearl → *U.S.A.* **117** F10
Pearl City *U.S.A.* **106** b
Pearl Harbor *U.S.A.* **106** b
Pearl River = Zhu Jiang →
  China **59** F9
Pearl River *U.S.A.* **115** E10
Pearsall *U.S.A.* **116** G5
Pearson Int. Toronto ✈
  (YYZ) *Canada* **114** C5
Peary Land *Greenland* **4** A6
Pease → *U.S.A.* **116** D5
Peawanuck *Canada* **104** A2
Pebane *Mozam.* **87** F4
Pebas *Peru* **124** D4
Pebble Beach *U.S.A.* **110** J5
Peć *Serbia* **44** D4
Péccioli *Italy* **40** E7
Pechea *Romania* **29** E12
Pechenga *Russia* **8** B24
Pechenizhyn *Ukraine* **29** B9
Pechiguera, Pta. *Canary Is.* **48** F6
Pechnezhskoye Vdkhr.
  Ukraine **33** G8
Pechora *Russia* **52** C6
Pechora → *Russia* **6** B16
Pechorskaya Guba *Russia* **52** C6
Pechory *Russia* **32** D4
Pecica *Romania* **28** D6
Pecka *Serbia* **44** B3
Pécora, C. *Italy* **42** C1
Pecos *N. Mex., U.S.A.* **109** J11
Pecos *Tex., U.S.A.* **116** F3
Pecos → *U.S.A.* **116** G4
Pécs *Hungary* **28** D3
Pedasí *Panama* **120** E3
Pedder, L. *Australia* **95** G4
Peddie *S. Africa* **89** E4
Pedernales *Dom. Rep.* **121** C5
Pedieos → *Cyprus* **49** D12
Pedirka *Australia* **95** D2
Pedirka Desert *Australia* **95** A1
Pedra Azul *Brazil* **125** G10
Pedra Lume *C. Verde Is.* **78** b
Pedreguer *Spain* **39** G5
Pedreiras *Brazil* **125** D10
Pedro Afonso *Brazil* **125** E9
Pedro Cays *Jamaica* **120** D4
Pedro de Valdivia *Chile* **126** A2
Pedro Juan Caballero
  Paraguay **127** A4
Pedro Muñoz *Spain* **37** F8
Pedrógão Grande *Portugal* **36** F2
Pee Dee = Great Pee
  Dee → *U.S.A.* **117** E15
Peebinga *Australia* **95** E3
Peebles *U.K.* **13** F5
Peekskill *U.S.A.* **115** E11
Peel *I. of Man* **14** C3
Peel → *Australia* **95** E5
Peel → *Canada* **100** C6
Peel Sd. *Canada* **100** B10
Peene → *Germany* **24** B9
Peera Peera Poolanna L.
  Australia **95** D2
Peerless Lake *Canada* **102** B6
Peers *Canada* **102** C5
Pegasus Bay *N.Z.* **91** E4

Peggau *Austria* **26** D8
Pegnitz *Germany* **25** F7
Pegnitz → *Germany* **25** F6
Pego *Spain* **39** G4
Pegu *Burma* **67** L20
Pegu Yoma *Burma* **67** K20
Pehčevo *Macedonia* **44** E6
Pehlivanköy *Turkey* **45** E10
Pehuajó *Argentina* **126** D3
Pei Xian = Pizhou *China* **56** G9
Peikang *Taiwan* **59** F13
Peine *Chile* **126** A2
Peine *Germany* **24** C6
Peip'ing = Beijing *China* **56** E9
Peipus, L. = Chudskoye,
  Ozero *Russia* **32** C4
Peissenberg *Germany* **25** H7
Peitz *Germany* **24** D10
Peixe *Brazil* **125** F9
Peixe → *Brazil* **125** H8
Pek → *Serbia* **44** B5
Pekalongan *Indonesia* **63** G13
Pekan *Malaysia* **65** L4
Pekan Nenas *Malaysia* **65** d
Pekanbaru *Indonesia* **62** D2
Pekin *U.S.A.* **112** E9
Peking = Beijing *China* **56** E9
Pekutatan *Indonesia* **63** J17
Pela *Greece* **44** F6
Péla *Guinea* **82** D3
Pelabuhan Klang *Malaysia* **65** L3
Pelabuhan Ratu, Teluk
  Indonesia **63** G12
Pelabuhanratu *Indonesia* **63** G12
Pélagos = Kira Panagia
  Greece **46** B6
Pelaihari *Indonesia* **62** E4
Pelat, Mt. *France* **21** D10
Pelczyce *Poland* **31** E2
Peleaga, Vf. *Romania* **28** E7
Pelée, Mt. *Martinique* **120** c
Pelee, Pt. *Canada* **104** D3
Pelee I. *Canada* **114** E2
Pelekech *Kenya* **86** B4
Peleng *Indonesia* **63** E6
Pelentong *Malaysia* **65** d
Pélézi *Ivory C.* **82** D3
Pelhřimov *Czech Rep.* **26** B8
Pelican *U.S.A.* **102** B1
Pelican L. *Canada* **103** C8
Pelican Narrows *Canada* **103** B8
Pelister △ *Macedonia* **44** F5
Pelješac *Croatia* **41** F14
Pelkosenniemi *Finland* **8** C22
Pella *S. Africa* **88** D2
Pella *U.S.A.* **112** E7
Pella □ *Greece* **44** F6
Pello *Finland* **8** C20
Pellworm *Germany* **24** A4
Pelly → *Canada* **102** A1
Pelly Bay *Canada* **101** C11
Peloponnese □ *Greece* **46** D4
Peloritani, Monti *Italy* **43** D8
Pelorus Sd. *N.Z.* **91** D4
Pelotas *Brazil* **127** C5
Pelotas → *Brazil* **127** B5
Pelovo *Bulgaria* **45** C8
Pelplin *Poland* **30** E5
Pelvoux, Massif du *France* **21** D10
Pemalang *Indonesia* **63** G13
Pemanggil, Pulau *Malaysia* **65** L5
Pematangsiantar *Indonesia* **62** D1
Pemba *Mozam.* **87** E5
Pemba *Zambia* **87** F2
Pemba Channel *Tanzania* **86** D4
Pemba I. *Tanzania* **86** D4
Pemberton *Australia* **93** F2
Pemberton *Canada* **102** C4
Pembina → *Canada* **102** C6
Pembroke *Canada* **104** C4
Pembroke *U.K.* **15** F3
Pembrokeshire □ *U.K.* **15** F3
Pembrokeshire Coast △
  U.K. **15** F2
Pen-y-Ghent *U.K.* **14** C5
Peña, Sierra de la *Spain* **38** C4
Peña de Francia, Sierra de
  la *Spain* **36** E4
Peñafiel *Portugal* **36** D2
Peñafiel *Spain* **36** D6
Peñaflor *Spain* **37** H5
Penal *Trin. & Tob.* **125** K15
Peñalara *Spain* **36** E7
Penamacôr *Portugal* **36** E3
Penang = Pinang *Malaysia* **65** c
Penápolis *Brazil* **127** A6
Peñaranda de Bracamonte
  Spain **36** E5
Peñarroya *Spain* **38** E4
Peñarroya-Pueblonuevo
  Spain **37** G5
Penarth *U.K.* **15** F4
Peñas, C. de *Spain* **36** B5
Peñas de San Pedro *Spain* **39** G3
Peñas del Chache *Canary Is.* **48** E6
Peñausende *Spain* **36** D5
Pench △ *India* **69** J8
Pench'i = Benxi *China* **57** D12

Pend Oreille → *U.S.A.* **108** B5
Pend Oreille, L. *U.S.A.* **108** B5
Pendalofos *Greece* **44** F5
Pendembu *Eastern, S. Leone* **82** D2
Pendembu *Northern, S. Leone* **82** D2
Pender B. *Australia* **92** C3
Pendik *Turkey* **45** F13
Pendjari → *Benin* **83** C5
Pendjari △ *Benin* **83** C5
Pendleton *U.S.A.* **108** D4
Pendra *India* **69** H9
Peneda-Gerês △ *Portugal* **36** D2
Penedo *Brazil* **125** F11
Penelokan *Indonesia* **63** J18
Penetanguishene *Canada* **114** B5
Penfield *U.S.A.* **114** E6
Pengalengan *Indonesia* **63** G12
Penge *Kasai-Or.,
  Dem. Rep. of the Congo* **86** D1
Penge *Sud-Kivu,
  Dem. Rep. of the Congo* **86** C2
P'enghu Ch'üntou *Taiwan* **59** F12
Penglai *China* **57** F11
Pengshan *China* **58** B4
Pengshui *China* **58** C7
Penguin *Australia* **95** G4
Pengxi *China* **58** B5
Pengze *China* **59** C11
Penhalonga *Zimbabwe* **87** F3
Peniche *Portugal* **37** F1
Penicuik *U.K.* **13** F5
Penida, Nusa *Indonesia* **63** K18
Peninnes, Alpes =
  Pennine, Alpi *Alps* **25** J3
Peninsular Malaysia □
  Malaysia **65** L4
Peñíscola *Spain* **38** E5
Penitente, Serra do *Brazil* **125** E9
Pēnjwīn *Iraq* **73** E11
Penkridge *U.K.* **14** E5
Penmarch *France* **18** E2
Penmarch, Pte. de *France* **18** E2
Penn Hills *U.S.A.* **114** F2
Penn Yan *U.S.A.* **114** D7
Penna, Punta della *Italy* **41** F11
Penne *France* **21** D10
Penne *Italy* **41** F10
Penner → *India* **66** M12
Pennine, Alpi *Alps* **25** J3
Pennines *U.K.* **14** C5
Pennington *U.S.A.* **110** F5
Pennington → *Nigeria* **83** E6
Pennino, Mte. *Italy* **41** F9
Pennsburg *U.S.A.* **115** F9
Pennsylvania □ *U.S.A.* **113** E15
Penny *Canada* **102** C4
Penny Str. *Canada* **101** B8
Peno *Russia* **32** D7
Penobscot → *U.S.A.* **113** C19
Penobscot B. *U.S.A.* **113** C19
Penola *Australia* **95** F3
Penong *Australia* **93** F5
Penonomé *Panama* **120** E3
Penrhyn *Cook Is.* **97** H12
Penrith *Australia* **95** E5
Penrith *U.K.* **14** C5
Penryn *U.K.* **15** G2
Pensacola *U.S.A.* **117** F11
Pensacola Mts. *Antarctica* **5** E1
Pense *Canada* **103** C8
Penshurst *Australia* **95** F3
Penticton *Canada* **102** D5
Pentland *Australia* **94** C4
Pentland Firth *U.K.* **13** C5
Pentland Hills *U.K.* **13** F5
Pentland Hills △ *U.K.* **13** F5
Penza *Russia* **34** D7
Penza □ *Russia* **34** D7
Penzance *U.K.* **15** G2
Penzberg *Germany* **25** H7
Penzhino *Russia* **53** C17
Penzhinskaya Guba *Russia* **53** C17
Penzhou *China* **58** B4
Penzlin *Germany* **24** B9
Peoria *Ariz., U.S.A.* **109** K7
Peoria *Ill., U.S.A.* **112** E9
Pepacton Res. *U.S.A.* **115** D10
Pepani → *S. Africa* **88** D3
Pepel *S. Leone* **82** D2
Peqin *Albania* **44** E3
Pera Hd. *Australia* **94** A3
Perabumulih *Indonesia* **62** E2
Perachora *Greece* **46** C4
Perak → *Malaysia* **65** K3
Perales del Alfambra *Spain* **38** E4
Perales del Puerto *Spain* **36** E4
Perama *Kerkyra, Greece* **49** A3
Perama *Kriti, Greece* **49** D6
Perancak *Indonesia* **63** J17
Peräpohjola *Finland* **8** C22
Perast *Montenegro* **44** D2
Percé *Canada* **105** C7
Perche *France* **18** D8
Perche → *France* **21** D8
Perchtoldsdorf *Austria* **27** C9
Percival Lakes *Australia* **92** D4
Percy *France* **18** D5
Percy Is. *Australia* **94** C5
Perdido, Mte. *Spain* **38** C5

Perdu, Mt. = Perdido, Mte.
  Spain **38** C5
Perechyn *Ukraine* **28** B7
Perehinske *Ukraine* **29** B9
Pereira *Colombia* **124** C3
Perelazovskiy *Russia* **35** F6
Perenjori *Australia* **93** E2
Peresecina *Moldova* **29** C13
Pereslavl-Zalesskiy *Russia* **32** D10
Peretu *Romania* **29** F10
Pereyaslav-Khmelnytskyy
  Ukraine **33** G6
Pereyma *Ukraine* **29** B14
Pérez, I. *Mexico* **119** C7
Perg *Austria* **26** C7
Pergamino *Argentina* **126** C3
Pergau → *Malaysia* **65** K3
Pérgine Valsugana *Italy* **41** B8
Pérgola *Italy* **41** E9
Perham *U.S.A.* **112** B6
Perhentian, Kepulauan
  Malaysia **65** K4
Peri → *Turkey* **73** C8
Periam *Romania* **28** D5
Péribonka → *Canada* **105** C5
Péribonka, L. *Canada* **105** B5
Perico *Argentina* **126** A2
Pericos *Mexico* **118** B3
Périers *France* **18** C5
Périgord *France* **20** D4
Périgord-Limousin △ *France* **20** C4
Périgueux *France* **20** C4
Perijá, Sierra de *Colombia* **124** B4
Perijá △ *Venezuela* **121** E5
Peristera *Greece* **46** B5
Peristerona → *Cyprus* **49** D12
Perito Moreno *Argentina* **128** F2
Perivol = Dragovishtitsa
  Bulgaria **44** D6
Perkasie *U.S.A.* **115** F9
Perković *Croatia* **41** E13
Perlas, Arch. de las *Panama* **120** E4
Perlas, Punta de Nic. **120** D3
Perleberg *Germany* **24** B7
Perlez *Serbia* **28** E5
Perm *Russia* **52** D6
Përmet *Albania* **44** F4
Pernambuco = Recife
  Brazil **125** E12
Pernambuco □ *Brazil* **125** E11
Pernatty Lagoon *Australia* **95** E2
Pernik *Bulgaria* **44** D7
Peron Is. *Australia* **92** B5
Peron Pen. *Australia* **93** E1
Péronne *France* **19** C9
Perosa Argentina *Italy* **40** D4
Perow *Canada* **102** C3
Perpignan *France* **20** F6
Perris *U.S.A.* **111** M9
Perros-Guirec *France* **18** D3
Perry *Fla., U.S.A.* **117** F13
Perry *Ga., U.S.A.* **117** E13
Perry *Iowa, U.S.A.* **112** E6
Perry *N.Y., U.S.A.* **114** D7
Perry *Okla., U.S.A.* **116** C6
Perryton *U.S.A.* **116** C4
Perryville *U.S.A.* **112** G9
Persan *France* **19** C9
Persberg *Sweden* **10** E8
Perşembe *Turkey* **72** B7
Persepolis *Iran* **71** D7
Pershotravensk *Ukraine* **23** C14
Persia = Iran ■ *Asia* **71** C7
Persian Gulf *Asia* **71** E6
Perstorp *Sweden* **11** H7
Pertek *Turkey* **73** C8
Perth *Australia* **93** F2
Perth *Canada* **115** B8
Perth *U.K.* **13** E5
Perth & Kinross □ *U.K.* **13** E5
Perth Amboy *U.S.A.* **115** F10
Perth-Andover *Canada* **105** C6
Perth Basin *Ind. Oc.* **96** L2
Pertuis *France* **21** E9
Pertusato, C. *France* **21** G13
Peru *Ind., U.S.A.* **112** E10
Peru *N.Y., U.S.A.* **115** B11
Peru ■ *S. Amer.* **124** D4
Peru Basin *Pac. Oc.* **97** J18
Peru-Chile Trench *Pac. Oc.* **124** G3
Perúgia *Italy* **41** E9
Perušić *Croatia* **41** D12
Pervomaysk *Russia* **34** C6
Pervomaysk *Ukraine* **33** H6
Pervouralsk *Russia* **52** D6
Pésaro *Italy* **41** E9
Pescadores = P'enghu
  Ch'üntou *Taiwan* **59** F12
Pescara *Italy* **41** F11
Pescara → *Italy* **41** F11
Peschanokopskoye *Russia* **35** G5
Péscia *Italy* **40** E7
Peshawar *Pakistan* **68** B4
Peshkopi *Albania* **44** E4
Peshtera *Bulgaria* **45** D8
Peshtigo *U.S.A.* **112** C10
Peski *Russia* **34** E5
Pêso da Régua *Portugal* **36** D3

Pesqueira Brazil 125 E11
Pessac France 20 D3
Pest □ Hungary 28 C4
Pestovo Russia 32 C8
Pestravka Russia 34 D9
Petah Tiqwa Israel 74 C3
Petalidi Greece 46 E3
Petaling Jaya Malaysia 65 L3
Petaloudes Greece 49 C10
Petaluma U.S.A. 110 G4
Pétange Lux. 17 E5
Petaro Pakistan 68 G3
Petas Greece 46 B3
Petatlán Mexico 118 D4
Petauke Zambia 87 E3
Petawawa Canada 104 C4
Petén Itzá, L. Guatemala 120 C2
Peter I. Br. Virgin Is. 121 e
Peter I. Øy Antarctica 5 C16
Peter Pond L. Canada 103 B7
Peterbell Canada 104 C3
Peterborough Australia 95 E2
Peterborough Canada 114 B6
Peterborough U.K. 15 E7
Peterborough U.S.A. 115 D13
Peterborough □ U.K. 15 E7
Peterculter U.K. 13 D6
Peterhead U.K. 13 D7
Peterlee U.K. 14 C6
Petermann Ranges Australia 93 E5
Petersburg Alaska, U.S.A. 100 D6
Petersburg Pa., U.S.A. 114 F6
Petersburg Va., U.S.A. 113 G15
Petersburg W. Va., U.S.A. 113 F14
Petersfield U.K. 15 F7
Petershagen Germany 24 C4
Petília Policastro Italy 43 C9
Petit Goâve Haiti 121 C5
Petit Lac Manicouagan Canada 105 B6
Petit-Mécatina → Canada 105 B8
Petit-Mécatina, Î. du Canada 105 B8
Petit Piton St. Lucia 121 f
Petit-Saguenay Canada 105 C5
Petit Saint Bernard, Col du Italy 21 C10
Petitcodiac Canada 105 C6
Petite Terre, Îles de la Guadeloupe 120 b
Petitot → Canada 102 A4
Petitsikapau L. Canada 105 B6
Petlad India 68 H5
Peto Mexico 119 C7
Petone N.Z. 91 D5
Petorca Chile 126 C1
Petoskey U.S.A. 113 C11
Petra Jordan 74 E4
Petra Spain 48 B10
Petra, Ostrova Russia 53 B12
Petra Velikogo, Zaliv Russia 54 C6
Petre, Pt. Canada 114 C7
Petrel = Petrer Spain 39 G4
Petrella, Monte Italy 42 A6
Petrer Spain 39 G4
Petreto-Bicchisano France 21 G12
Petrich Bulgaria 44 E7
Petrified Forest △ U.S.A. 109 J9
Petrijanec Croatia 41 B13
Petrikov = Pyetrikaw Belarus 23 B15
Petrila Romania 29 E8
Petrinja Croatia 41 C13
Petrodvorets Russia 32 C5
Petrolândia Brazil 125 E11
Petrolia Canada 114 D2
Petrolina Brazil 125 E10
Petropavl Kazakhstan 52 D7
Petropavlovsk = Petropavl Kazakhstan 52 D7
Petropavlovsk-Kamchatskiy Russia 53 D16
Petropavlovskiy = Akhtubinsk Russia 35 F8
Petrópolis Brazil 127 A7
Petroşani Romania 29 E8
Petrova Gora Croatia 41 C12
Petrovac Montenegro 44 D2
Petrovac Serbia 44 B5
Petrovaradin Serbia 28 E4
Petrovsk Russia 34 D7
Petrovsk-Zabaykalskiy Russia 53 D11
Petrovskaya Russia 33 K9
Petrozavodsk Russia 32 B8
Petrus Steyn S. Africa 89 D4
Petrusburg S. Africa 88 D4
Petzeck Austria 26 E5
Peumo Chile 126 C1
Peureulak Indonesia 62 D1
Pevek Russia 53 C18
Peveragno Italy 40 D4
Peyrehorade France 20 E2
Peyruis France 21 D9
Pézenas France 20 E7
Pezinok Slovak Rep. 27 C10
Pfaffenhofen Germany 25 G7
Pfälzerwald △ Germany 25 F5

Pfarrkirchen Germany 25 G8
Pfeffenhausen Germany 25 G7
Pforzheim Germany 25 G4
Pfullendorf Germany 25 H5
Pfungstadt Germany 25 F4
Pha Taem △ Thailand 64 E5
Phaestos Greece 49 D6
Phagwara India 68 D6
Phala Botswana 88 C4
Phalera = Phulera India 68 F6
Phalodi India 68 F5
Phalsbourg France 19 D14
Phaluai, Ko Thailand 65 b
Phan Thailand 64 C2
Phan Rang Vietnam 65 G7
Phan Ri = Hoa Da Vietnam 65 G7
Phan Si Pan Vietnam 64 A4
Phan Thiet Vietnam 65 G7
Phanae Greece 47 C7
Phanat Nikhom Thailand 64 F3
Phangan, Ko Thailand 65 H3
Phangnga Thailand 65 H2
Phangnga, Ao Thailand 65 a
Phanom Sarakham Thailand 64 F3
Phaphund India 69 F8
Pharenda India 69 F10
Pharr U.S.A. 116 H5
Phatthalung Thailand 65 J3
Phayao Thailand 64 C2
Phelps U.S.A. 114 D7
Phelps L. Canada 103 B8
Phenix City U.S.A. 117 E12
Phet Buri Thailand 64 F2
Phetchabun Thailand 64 D3
Phetchabun, Thiu Khao Thailand 64 E3
Phetchaburi = Phet Buri Thailand 64 F2
Phi Phi, Ko Thailand 65 J2
Phiafay Laos 64 E6
Phibun Mangsahan Thailand 64 E5
Phichai Thailand 64 D3
Phichit Thailand 64 D3
Philadelphia Miss., U.S.A. 117 E10
Philadelphia N.Y., U.S.A. 115 B9
Philadelphia Pa., U.S.A. 115 G9
Philip U.S.A. 112 C3
Philippi Greece 45 E8
Philippi U.S.A. 113 F13
Philippi L. Australia 94 C2
Philippine Basin Pac. Oc. 96 F5
Philippine Sea Pac. Oc. 61 C6
Philippine Trench = Mindanao Trench Pac. Oc. 61 F7
Philippines ■ Asia 61 F5
Philippolis S. Africa 88 E4
Philippopolis = Plovdiv Bulgaria 45 D8
Philipsburg Canada 115 A11
Philipsburg Mont., U.S.A. 108 C7
Philipsburg Pa., U.S.A. 114 F6
Philipstown = Daingean Ireland 12 C4
Philipstown S. Africa 88 E3
Phillip I. Australia 95 F4
Phillips U.S.A. 112 C8
Phillipsburg Kans., U.S.A. 112 F4
Phillipsburg N.J., U.S.A. 115 F9
Philmont U.S.A. 115 D11
Philomath U.S.A. 108 D2
Phimai Thailand 64 E4
Phitsanulok Thailand 64 D3
Phnom Dangrek Thailand 64 E5
Phnom Kulen △ Cambodia 64 F5
Phnom Penh Cambodia 65 G5
Phnum Penh = Phnom Penh Cambodia 65 G5
Phoenicia U.S.A. 115 D10
Phoenix Mauritius 85 d
Phoenix Ariz., U.S.A. 109 K7
Phoenix N.Y., U.S.A. 115 C8
Phoenix Is. Kiribati 96 H10
Phoenixville U.S.A. 115 F9
Phon Thailand 64 E4
Phon Tiou Laos 64 D5
Phong → Thailand 64 D4
Phong Saly Laos 58 G4
Phong Tho Vietnam 64 A4
Phonhong Laos 64 C4
Phonum Thailand 65 H2
Phosphate Hill Australia 94 C2
Photharam Thailand 64 F2
Phra Nakhon Si Ayutthaya Thailand 64 E3
Phra Thong, Ko Thailand 65 H2
Phrae Thailand 64 C3
Phrom Phiram Thailand 64 D3
Phrygia Turkey 72 C4
Phu Bia Laos 64 C4
Phu Chong-Na Yoi △ Thailand 64 E5
Phu Dien Vietnam 64 C5
Phu Hin Rang Kla △ Thailand 64 D3
Phu Kradung △ Thailand 64 D3
Phu Loi Laos 64 B4
Phu Luang △ Thailand 64 D3
Phu Ly Vietnam 58 G5

Phu Phan △ Thailand 64 D4
Phu Quoc, Dao Vietnam 65 G4
Phu Tho Vietnam 58 G5
Phu Wiang △ Thailand 64 D4
Phuc Yen Vietnam 58 G5
Phuket Thailand 65 a
Phuket, Ko Thailand 65 a
Phul India 68 D6
Phulad India 68 G5
Phulchari Bangla. 69 G13
Phulera India 68 F6
Phulpur India 69 G10
Phun Phin Thailand 65 H2
Phuntsholing Bhutan 69 F13
Piacenza Italy 40 C6
Piai, Tanjung Malaysia 65 d
Pian Cr. → Australia 95 E4
Pian-Upe △ Uganda 86 B3
Piana France 21 F12
Pianella Italy 41 F11
Pianosa Puglia, Italy 41 F12
Pianosa Toscana, Italy 40 F7
Piapot Canada 103 D7
Pias Portugal 37 G3
Piaseczno Poland 31 F8
Piaski Poland 31 G9
Piastów Poland 31 F7
Piatra Romania 29 G10
Piatra Craiului △ Romania 29 E10
Piatra Neamţ Romania 29 D11
Piatra Olt Romania 29 F9
Piauí □ Brazil 125 E10
Piauí → Brazil 125 E10
Piave → Italy 41 C9
Piazza Ármerina Italy 43 E7
Pibor → Sudan 81 F3
Pibor Post Sudan 81 F3
Picardie □ France 19 C10
Picardie, Plaine de France 19 C9
Picardy = Picardie □ France 19 C10
Picayune U.S.A. 117 F10
Picerno Italy 43 B8
Pichhor India 69 G8
Pichilemu Chile 126 C1
Pichor India 68 G8
Pickerel L. Canada 104 C1
Pickering U.K. 14 C7
Pickering, Vale of U.K. 14 C7
Pickle Lake Canada 104 B1
Pickwick L. U.S.A. 117 D10
Pico Azores 78 a
Pico Bonito △ Honduras 120 C2
Pico Truncado Argentina 128 F3
Picos Brazil 125 E10
Picos de Europa △ Spain 36 B6
Picton Australia 95 E5
Picton Canada 114 B7
Picton N.Z. 91 D5
Pictou Canada 105 C7
Picture Butte Canada 102 D6
Pictured Rocks △ U.S.A. 112 B10
Picún Leufú Argentina 128 D3
Pidbuzh Ukraine 31 J10
Pidurutalagala Sri Lanka 66 R12
Piechowice Poland 31 H2
Piedimonte Matese Italy 43 A7
Piedmont = Piemonte □ Italy 40 D5
Piedmont Ala., U.S.A. 117 E12
Piedmont S.C., U.S.A. 107 D10
Piedra → Spain 38 D3
Piedrabuena Spain 37 G6
Piedrahita Spain 36 E5
Piedralaves Spain 36 E6
Piedras Blancas Spain 36 B5
Piedras Negras Mexico 118 B4
Piekary Śląskie Poland 31 H5
Pieksämäki Finland 8 E22
Pielinen Finland 8 E23
Piemonte □ Italy 40 D5
Pienaarsrivier S. Africa 89 D4
Pieniężno Poland 30 D7
Pieninský △ Europe 27 B13
Pieńsk Poland 31 G2
Pierceland Canada 103 C7
Pieria □ Greece 44 F6
Pierpont U.S.A. 114 E4
Pierre U.S.A. 112 C3
Pierre-Buffière France 20 C5
Pierre-de-Bresse France 19 F12
Pierrefonds Canada 115 A11
Pierrefontaine-les-Varans France 19 E13
Pierrefort France 20 D6
Pierrelatte France 21 D8
Pierreville Trin. & Tob. 125 K16
Piešťany Slovak Rep. 27 C10
Piesting → Austria 27 C9
Pieszyce Poland 31 H3
Piet Retief S. Africa 89 D5
Pietarsaari Finland 8 E20
Pietermaritzburg S. Africa 89 D5
Pietersburg = Polokwane S. Africa 89 C4
Pietragalla Italy 43 B8
Pietrasanta Italy 40 E7
Pietroşiţa Romania 29 E10

Pietrosul, Vf. Maramureş, Romania 29 C9
Pietrosul, Vf. Suceava, Romania 29 C9
Pieve di Cadore Italy 41 B9
Pieve di Teco Italy 40 D4
Pievepélago Italy 40 D7
Pigadítsa Greece 44 G5
Pigeon L. Canada 114 B6
Piges Greece 46 B3
Piggott U.S.A. 117 C9
Pigna Italy 40 E4
Pigüe Argentina 126 D3
Pihani India 69 F9
Pihlajavesi Finland 32 B5
Pijijiapan Mexico 119 D6
Pikalevo Russia 32 C8
Pikangikum Canada 103 C10
Pikes Peak U.S.A. 108 G11
Piketberg S. Africa 88 E2
Pikeville U.S.A. 113 G12
Pikou China 57 E12
Pikwitonei Canada 103 B9
Piła Poland 31 E3
Pila Spain 39 G3
Pilanesberg △ S. Africa 88 D4
Pilani India 68 E6
Pilar Paraguay 126 B4
Pilar de la Horadada Spain 39 H4
Pilas → Poland 31 E4
Pilawa Poland 31 G8
Pilaya → Bolivia 124 H6
Pilbara Australia 92 D2
Pilcomayo → Paraguay 126 B4
Pilea Greece 44 F6
Pilgrim's Rest S. Africa 89 C5
Pilgrimstad Sweden 10 B9
Pili Greece 47 E9
Pilibhit India 69 E8
Pilica → Poland 31 G8
Pilío, Óros Greece 46 B5
Pilipinas = Philippines ■ Asia 61 F5
Pilis Hungary 28 C4
Pilisvörösvár Hungary 28 C3
Pilkhawa India 68 E7
Pilliga Australia 95 E4
Pilos Greece 46 E3
Pilot Mound Canada 103 D9
Pilot Point U.S.A. 116 E6
Pilot Rock U.S.A. 108 D4
Pilštanj Slovenia 41 B12
Piltene Latvia 30 A8
Pilzno Poland 31 J8
Pima U.S.A. 109 K9
Pimba Australia 95 E2
Pimenta Bueno Brazil 124 F6
Pimentel Peru 124 E3
Pin Valley △ India 68 D7
Pinang Malaysia 65 c
Pinar, C. des Spain 48 B10
Pinar del Río Cuba 120 B3
Pınarbaşı Çanakkale, Turkey 47 B8
Pınarbaşı Kayseri, Turkey 72 C7
Pınarhisar Turkey 45 E11
Pinatubo, Mt. Phil. 61 D4
Pinawa Canada 103 C9
Pincehely Hungary 28 D3
Pinchang China 58 B6
Pincher Creek Canada 102 D6
Pinchi L. Canada 102 C4
Pinckneyville U.S.A. 112 F9
Pińczów Poland 31 H7
Pindar Australia 93 E2
Pindi Gheb Pakistan 68 C5
Pindiga Nigeria 83 D7
Pindos □ Greece 46 B3
Pindos Oros Greece 46 B3
Pindus Mts. = Pindos Oros Greece 46 B3
Pine → B.C., Canada 102 B4
Pine → Sask., Canada 103 B7
Pine Bluff U.S.A. 116 D8
Pine Bluffs U.S.A. 108 F11
Pine City U.S.A. 112 C7
Pine Cr. → U.S.A. 114 E7
Pine Creek Australia 92 B5
Pine Falls Canada 103 C9
Pine Flat L. U.S.A. 110 J7
Pine Grove U.S.A. 115 F8
Pine Hill Australia 94 C4
Pine Pass Canada 102 B4
Pine Point Canada 102 A6
Pine Ridge U.S.A. 112 D2
Pine River Canada 103 C8
Pine River U.S.A. 112 B6
Pine Valley U.S.A. 111 N10
Pinecrest U.S.A. 110 G6
Pineda de Mar Spain 38 D7
Pinedale Calif., U.S.A. 110 J7
Pinedale Wyo., U.S.A. 108 E9
Pinega → Russia 52 C5
Pinehouse L. Canada 103 B7
Pineimuta → Canada 104 B1
Pinerolo Italy 40 D4
Pines, Akra Greece 45 F8

Pineto Italy 41 F11
Pinetop-Lakeside U.S.A. 109 J9
Pinetown S. Africa 89 D5
Pineville U.S.A. 116 F8
Piney France 19 D11
Ping → Thailand 64 E3
Pingaring Australia 93 F2
Pingba China 58 D6
Pingbian China 58 F4
Pingchuan China 58 D7
Pingding China 56 F7
Pingdingshan China 56 H7
Pingdong = Pingtung Taiwan 59 F13
Pingdu China 57 F10
Pingelly Australia 93 F2
Pingguo China 58 F6
Pinghe China 59 E11
Pingjiang China 59 C9
Pingle China 59 E8
Pingli China 58 A7
Pingliang China 56 G4
Pinglu China 56 E7
Pingluo China 56 E4
Pingnan Fujian, China 59 D12
Pingnan Guangxi Zhuangzu, China 59 F8
Pingquan China 57 D10
Pingrup Australia 93 F2
Pingshan China 58 C5
Pingtan China 59 E12
Pingtang China 58 E6
P'ingtung Taiwan 59 F13
Pingwu China 56 H3
Pingxiang Guangxi Zhuangzu, China 58 F6
Pingxiang Jiangxi, China 59 D9
Pingyao China 56 F7
Pingyi China 57 G9
Pingyin China 56 F9
Pingyuan Guangdong, China 59 E10
Pingyuan Shandong, China 56 F9
Pingyuanjie China 58 F4
Pinhal Brazil 127 A6
Pinhal Novo Portugal 37 G2
Pinheiro Brazil 125 D9
Pinheiro Machado Brazil 127 C5
Pinhel Portugal 36 E3
Pini Indonesia 62 D1
Pinios → Ilia, Greece 46 D3
Pinios → Trikala, Greece 46 B4
Pinjarra Australia 93 F2
Pink Mountain Canada 102 B4
Pinkafeld Austria 27 D9
Pinnacles △ U.S.A. 110 J5
Pinnaroo Australia 95 F3
Pinneberg Germany 24 B5
Pinon Hills U.S.A. 111 L9
Pinos Mexico 118 C4
Pinos, Mt. U.S.A. 111 L7
Pinos Pt. U.S.A. 109 H3
Pinos Puente Spain 37 H7
Pinrang Indonesia 63 E5
Pins, Pte. aux Canada 114 D3
Pinsk Belarus 23 B14
Pintados Chile 124 H5
Pinyang China 59 D13
Pinyug Russia 52 C5
Pioche U.S.A. 109 H6
Piombino Italy 40 F7
Piombino, Canale di Italy 40 F7
Pioner, Ostrov Russia 53 B10
Pionerskiy Russia 30 D7
Pionki Poland 31 G8
Piopiotaki = Milford Sd. N.Z. 91 F1
Piorini, L. Brazil 124 D6
Piotrków Trybunalski Poland 31 G6
Piove di Sacco Italy 41 C9
Pip Iran 71 E9
Pipar India 68 F5
Pipar Road India 68 F5
Piparia Mad. P., India 68 H8
Piparia Mad. P., India 68 J7
Piperi Greece 46 B6
Pipestone U.S.A. 112 D5
Pipestone → Canada 104 B2
Pipestone Cr. → Canada 103 D8
Piplan Pakistan 68 C4
Piploda India 68 H6
Pipmuacan, Rés. Canada 105 C5
Pippingarra Australia 92 D2
Pipriac France 18 E5
Piqua U.S.A. 113 E11
Piquiri → Brazil 127 A5
Pir Panjal Range India 68 C7
Pīr Sohrāb Iran 71 E9
Pira Benin 83 D5
Piracicaba Brazil 127 A6
Piracuruca Brazil 125 D10
Pirae Tahiti 91 d
Piræus = Pireas Greece 46 D5
Piraiévs = Pireas Greece 46 D5
Pirajuí Brazil 127 A6
Piram I. India 68 J5
Pirané Argentina 126 B4
Pirano = Piran Slovenia 41 C10
Pīrānshahr Iran 73 D11

Pirapora Brazil 125 G10
Pirawa India 68 G7
Pirdop Bulgaria 45 D8
Pireas Greece 46 D5
Pirgi Greece 47 C7
Pirgos Ilia, Greece 46 D3
Pirgos Kriti, Greece 47 C9
Pirgovo Bulgaria 45 C9
Piribebuy Paraguay 126 B4
Pirimapun Indonesia 63 F9
Pirin △ Bulgaria 44 E7
Pirin Planina Bulgaria 44 E7
Pírineos = Pyrénées Europe 20 F4
Piripiri Brazil 125 D10
Pirlangimpi Australia 92 B5
Pirmasens Germany 25 F3
Pirna Germany 24 E9
Pirot Serbia 44 C6
Piru Indonesia 63 E7
Piru U.S.A. 111 L8
Piryatin = Pyryatyn Ukraine 33 G7
Pisa Italy 40 E7
Pisa → Poland 31 E8
Pisa, Firenze ✈ (PSA) Italy 40 E7
Pisagne Italy 40 D7
Pisagua Chile 124 G4
Pisarovina Croatia 41 C12
Pisco Peru 124 F3
Piscu Romania 29 E12
Písek Czech Rep. 26 B7
Pishan China 60 C2
Pishcha Ukraine 31 G10
Pishchanka Ukraine 29 B13
Pīshīn Iran 71 E9
Pishin Pakistan 68 D2
Pishin Lora → Pakistan 68 E1
Pisidia Turkey 72 D4
Pising Indonesia 63 F6
Pismo Beach U.S.A. 111 K6
Piso, L. Liberia 82 D2
Pissila Burkina Faso 83 C4
Pissis, Cerro Argentina 126 B2
Pissos France 20 D3
Pissouri Cyprus 49 E11
Pisticci Italy 43 B9
Pistóia Italy 40 E7
Pistol B. Canada 103 A10
Pisuerga → Spain 36 D6
Pisz Poland 30 E8
Pita Guinea 82 C2
Pitarpanga L. Australia 95 E3
Pitcairn I. Pac. Oc. 97 K14
Pitch L. Trin. & Tob. 125 K15
Piteå Sweden 8 D19
Piteälven → Sweden 8 D19
Piterka Russia 34 E8
Piteşti Romania 29 F9
Pithapuram India 67 L13
Pithara Australia 93 F2
Pithio Greece 45 E10
Pithiviers France 19 D9
Pithoragarh India 69 E9
Pithoro Pakistan 68 G3
Pitigliano Italy 41 F8
Pitkyaranta Russia 32 B6
Pitlochry U.K. 13 E5
Pitsilia Cyprus 49 E12
Pitt I. Canada 102 C3
Pittsburg Calif., U.S.A. 110 G5
Pittsburg Kans., U.S.A. 112 G6
Pittsburg Tex., U.S.A. 116 E7
Pittsburgh U.S.A. 114 F5
Pittsfield Ill., U.S.A. 112 F8
Pittsfield Maine, U.S.A. 113 C19
Pittsfield Mass., U.S.A. 115 D11
Pittsfield N.H., U.S.A. 115 C13
Pittston U.S.A. 115 E9
Pittsworth Australia 95 D5
Pituri → Australia 94 C2
Piura Peru 124 E2
Piva → Montenegro 44 C2
Piwniczna Poland 31 J7
Pixley U.S.A. 110 K7
Pizarra Spain 37 J6
Pizhou China 56 G9
Pizzo Italy 43 D9
Placentia Canada 105 C9
Placentia B. Canada 105 C9
Placer Masbate, Phil. 61 F5
Placer Surigao N., Phil. 61 G6
Placerville U.S.A. 110 G6
Placetas Cuba 120 B4
Plačkovica Macedonia 44 E6
Plainfield N.J., U.S.A. 115 F10
Plainfield Ohio, U.S.A. 114 F3
Plainfield Vt., U.S.A. 115 B12
Plains Mont., U.S.A. 108 C6
Plains Tex., U.S.A. 116 E3
Plainview Nebr., U.S.A. 112 D5
Plainview Tex., U.S.A. 116 D4
Plainwell U.S.A. 113 D11
Plaisance France 20 E4
Plaistow U.S.A. 115 D13
Plaka Greece 47 B7
Plaka, Akra Greece 49 D8
Plakenska Planina Macedonia 44 E5
Planá Czech Rep. 26 B5

Plana Cays *Bahamas* **121** B5
Planada *U.S.A.* **110** H6
Plancoët *France* **18** D4
Plandište *Serbia* **28** E6
Plano *U.S.A.* **116** E6
Plant City *U.S.A.* **117** G13
Plaquemine *U.S.A.* **116** F9
Plasencia *Spain* **36** E4
Plaški *Croatia* **41** C12
Plaster City *U.S.A.* **111** N11
Plaster Rock *Canada* **105** C6
Plastun *Russia* **54** B8
Plasy *Czech Rep.* **26** B6
Plata, Río de la → *S. Amer.* **126** C4
Plátani → *Italy* **42** E6
Platanos *Greece* **49** D5
Plateau □ *Nigeria* **83** D6
Platte *U.S.A.* **112** D4
Platte → *Mo., U.S.A.* **112** F6
Platte → *Nebr., U.S.A.* **112** E6
Platteville *U.S.A.* **112** D8
Plattling *Germany* **25** G8
Plattsburgh *U.S.A.* **115** B11
Plattsmouth *U.S.A.* **112** E6
Plau *Germany* **24** B8
Plauen *Germany* **24** E8
Plauer See *Germany* **24** B8
Plav *Montenegro* **44** D3
Plavinas *Latvia* **32** D3
Plavnica *Montenegro* **44** D3
Plavno *Croatia* **41** D13
Plavsk *Russia* **32** F9
Playa Blanca *Canary Is.* **48** F6
Playa Blanca Sur *Canary Is.* **48** F6
Playa de las Americas
    Canary Is. **48** F3
Playa de Mogán *Canary Is.* **48** G4
Playa del Carmen *Mexico* **119** C7
Playa del Inglés *Canary Is.* **48** G4
Playa Esmerelda *Canary Is.* **48** F5
Playgreen L. *Canada* **103** C9
Pleasant Bay *Canada* **105** C7
Pleasant Hill *U.S.A.* **110** H4
Pleasant Mount *U.S.A.* **115** E9
Pleasanton *Calif., U.S.A.* **110** H5
Pleasanton *Tex., U.S.A.* **116** G5
Pleasantville *N.J., U.S.A.* **113** F16
Pleasantville *Pa., U.S.A.* **114** E5
Pléaux *France* **20** C6
Plei Ku *Vietnam* **64** F7
Plélan-le-Grand *France* **18** D4
Pléneuf-Val-André *France* **18** D4
Pleniţa *Romania* **29** F8
Plenty → *Australia* **94** C2
Plenty, B. of *N.Z.* **91** B6
Plentywood *U.S.A.* **108** B11
Plérin *France* **18** D4
Plessisville *Canada* **105** C5
Plestin-les-Grèves *France* **18** D3
Pleszew *Poland* **31** G4
Pleternica *Croatia* **28** E2
Plétipi, L. *Canada* **105** B5
Pleven *Bulgaria* **45** C8
Plevlja *Montenegro* **44** C3
Plevna *Canada* **114** B8
Plitvička Jezera △ *Croatia* **41** D12
Plješevica *Croatia* **41** D12
Ploaghe *Italy* **42** B1
Ploče *Croatia* **41** E14
Plock *Poland* **31** F6
Plöckenpass *Italy* **41** B9
Plöckenstein *Germany* **25** G9
Ploemeur *France* **18** E3
Ploërmel *France* **18** E4
Ploieşti *Romania* **29** F11
Plomari *Greece* **47** E6
Plombières-les-Bains *France* **19** E13
Plomin *Croatia* **41** C11
Plön *Germany* **24** A6
Plonge, Lac la *Canada* **103** B7
Płońsk *Poland* **31** F7
Plopeni *Romania* **29** F11
Plopişului, Munţii *Romania* **28** C7
Płoty *Poland* **30** E2
Plouaret *France* **18** D3
Plouay *France* **18** E3
Ploučnice → *Czech Rep.* **26** A7
Ploudalmézeau *France* **18** D2
Plouescat *France* **18** D2
Plougasnou *France* **18** D3
Plougastel-Daoulas *France* **18** D2
Plouguerneau *France* **18** D2
Plouha *France* **18** D4
Plouhinec *France* **18** E2
Plovdiv □ *Bulgaria* **45** D8
Plovdiv ■ *Bulgaria* **45** D8
Plum *U.S.A.* **114** F5
Plum I. *U.S.A.* **115** E12
Plumas *U.S.A.* **110** F6
Plummer *U.S.A.* **108** C5
Plumtree *Zimbabwe* **87** G2
Plungė *Lithuania* **30** C8
Plužine *Montenegro* **44** C2
Plymouth *Trin. & Tob.* **125** J16
Plymouth *U.K.* **15** G3
Plymouth *Calif., U.S.A.* **110** G6
Plymouth *Ind., U.S.A.* **112** E10
Plymouth *Mass., U.S.A.* **115** E14

Plymouth *N.C., U.S.A.* **117** D16
Plymouth *N.H., U.S.A.* **115** C13
Plymouth *Pa., U.S.A.* **115** E9
Plymouth *Wis., U.S.A.* **112** D10
Plympton-Wyoming =
    Wyoming *Canada* **114** D2
Plynlimon = Pumlumon
    Fawr *U.K.* **15** E4
Plyusa *Russia* **32** C5
Plyusa → *Russia* **32** C5
Plzeň *Czech Rep.* **26** B6
Plzeňský □ *Czech Rep.* **26** B6
Pniewy *Poland* **31** F3
Pô *Burkina Faso* **83** C4
Po → *Italy* **41** D9
Po, Foci del *Italy* **41** D9
Po Hai = Bo Hai *China* **57** E10
Pobé *Benin* **83** D5
Pobé *Burkina Faso* **83** C4
Pobeda *Russia* **53** C15
Pobedy, Pik *Kyrgyzstan* **52** E8
Pobiedziska *Poland* **31** F4
Pobladura del Valle *Spain* **36** C5
Pobra de Trives *Spain* **36** C3
Pocahontas *Ark., U.S.A.* **117** C9
Pocahontas *Iowa, U.S.A.* **112** D6
Pocatello *U.S.A.* **108** E7
Počátky *Czech Rep.* **26** B8
Pochep *Russia* **33** F7
Pochinki *Russia* **34** C7
Pochinok *Russia* **32** E7
Pöchlarn *Austria* **26** C8
Pocking *Germany* **25** G9
Pocomoke City *U.S.A.* **113** F16
Poços de Caldas *Brazil* **127** A6
Podbořany *Czech Rep.* **26** A6
Poddębice *Poland* **31** G5
Podensac *France* **20** D3
Podenzano *Italy* **40** D6
Podgorač *Croatia* **28** E3
Podgorica *Montenegro* **44** D3
Podgorie *Albania* **44** F4
Podilska Vysochyna
    Ukraine **29** B13
Podkarpackie □ *Poland* **31** H9
Podkova *Bulgaria* **45** E9
Podlapača *Croatia* **41** D12
Podlaskie □ *Poland* **31** E10
Podoleni *Romania* **29** D11
Podolínec *Slovak Rep.* **27** B13
Podolsk *Russia* **32** E9
Podor *Senegal* **82** B1
Podporozhye *Russia* **32** B8
Podu Iloaiei *Romania* **29** C12
Podu Turcului *Romania* **29** D12
Podujevo *Serbia* **44** D5
Podyji △ *Czech Rep.* **26** C8
Poel *Germany* **24** B6
Pofadder *S. Africa* **88** D2
Poggiardo *Italy* **43** B11
Poggibonsi *Italy* **40** E8
Póggio Mirteto *Italy* **41** F9
Pogoanele *Romania* **29** F12
Pogorzela *Poland* **31** G4
Pogradec *Albania* **44** F4
Pogranichnyy *Russia* **54** B5
Poh *Indonesia* **63** E6
Pohang *S. Korea* **57** F15
Pohjanmaa *Finland* **8** E20
Pohnpei *Micronesia* **96** G7
Pohorelá *Slovak Rep.* **27** C13
Pohořelice *Czech Rep.* **27** C9
Pohorje *Slovenia* **41** B12
Pohri *India* **68** G6
Poiana Mare *Romania* **28** G8
Poiana Ruscăi, Munţii
    Romania **28** E7
Poiana Stampei *Romania* **29** C10
Poinsett, C. *Antarctica* **5** C8
Point Arena *U.S.A.* **110** G3
Point Baker *U.S.A.* **102** B2
Point Fortin *Trin. & Tob.* **125** K15
Point Hope *U.S.A.* **106** a
Point L. *Canada* **100** C8
Point Lisas Industrial
    Estate *Trin. & Tob.* **125** K15
Point Pedro *Sri Lanka* **66** Q12
Point Pelee △ *Canada* **114** E2
Point Pleasant *N.J., U.S.A.* **115** F10
Point Pleasant *W. Va.,
    U.S.A.* **113** F12
Point Reyes △ *U.S.A.* **110** G2
Pointe-à-Pitre *Guadeloupe* **120** b
Pointe-au-Pic = La
    Malbaie *Canada* **105** C5
Pointe-Claire *Canada* **115** A11
Pointe-Gatineau *Canada* **115** A9
Pointe-Noire *Congo* **84** E2
Pointe-Noire *Guadeloupe* **120** b
Poio *Spain* **36** C2
Poipet *Cambodia* **64** F4
Poirino *Italy* **40** D4
Poisonbush Ra. *Australia* **92** D3
Poissonnier Pt. *Australia* **92** C2
Poitiers *France* **18** F7
Poitou *France* **20** B3
Poitou-Charentes □ *France* **20** B4

Poix-de-Picardie *France* **19** C8
Poix-Terron *France* **19** C11
Pojoaque *U.S.A.* **109** J10
Pokaran *India* **68** F4
Pokataroo *Australia* **95** D4
Pokhara *Nepal* **69** E10
Pokhvistnevo *Russia* **34** D11
Poko *Dem. Rep. of the Congo* **86** B2
Poko *Sudan* **81** F3
Pokrov *Russia* **32** E10
Pokrovsk *Russia* **53** C13
Pokrovskoye *Russia* **33** J10
Pol-e Dokhtar *Iran* **73** F12
Pol-e Zahāb *Iran* **73** E11
Pola = Pula *Croatia* **41** D10
Pola *Russia* **32** D7
Pola de Allande *Spain* **36** B4
Pola de Lena *Spain* **36** B5
Pola de Siero *Spain* **36** B5
Pola de Somiedo *Spain* **36** B4
Polacca *U.S.A.* **109** J8
Polan *Iran* **71** E9
Pol'ana *Slovak Rep.* **27** C12
Poland *U.S.A.* **115** C9
Poland ■ *Europe* **31** G3
Polanica-Zdrój *Poland* **31** H3
Połaniec *Poland* **31** H8
Polanów *Poland* **30** D3
Polar Bear △ *Canada* **104** A2
Polatlı *Turkey* **72** C5
Polatsk *Belarus* **32** E5
Polcura *Chile* **126** D1
Polczyn-Zdrój *Poland* **30** E3
Polemi *Cyprus* **49** E11
Police *Poland* **30** E1
Police, Pte. *Seychelles* **85** b
Polichnitos *Greece* **47** B8
Polička *Czech Rep.* **27** B9
Policoro *Italy* **43** B9
Poliegos *Greece* **46** E6
Poligiros *Greece* **44** F7
Polignano a Mare *Italy* **43** A9
Poligny *France* **19** F12
Polillo Is. *Phil.* **61** D5
Polillo Strait *Phil.* **61** D5
Polis *Cyprus* **49** D11
Polístena *Italy* **43** D9
Polk *U.S.A.* **114** E5
Polkowice *Poland* **31** G3
Polla *Italy* **43** B8
Pollachi *India* **66** P10
Pollença *Spain* **48** B10
Pollença, B. de *Spain* **48** B10
Póllica *Italy* **43** B8
Pollino, Mte. *Italy* **43** C9
Pollino △ *Italy* **43** C9
Polna *Russia* **32** C5
Polnovat *Russia* **52** C7
Pology *Ukraine* **33** J9
Polokwane *S. Africa* **89** C4
Polokwane → *S. Africa* **89** C5
Polonne *Ukraine* **23** C14
Polonnoye = Polonne
    Ukraine **23** C14
Polski Trŭmbesh *Bulgaria* **45** C9
Polsko Kosovo *Bulgaria* **45** C9
Polson *U.S.A.* **108** C6
Poltár *Slovak Rep.* **27** C12
Poltava *Ukraine* **33** H8
Poltava □ *Ukraine* **33** G7
Põltsamaa *Estonia* **32** C4
Polunochnoye *Russia* **52** C7
Põlva *Estonia* **32** C4
Polyana *Ukraine* **28** B7
Polyarny *Russia* **8** B25
Polyarnyye Zori *Russia* **8** C25
Polynesia *Pac. Oc.* **97** F11
Polynésie française =
    French Polynesia ☑
    Pac. Oc. **97** J13
Pomarance *Italy* **40** E7
Pombal *Portugal* **36** F2
Pombia *Greece* **49** E6
Pomene *Mozam.* **89** C6
Pomeroy *Ohio, U.S.A.* **113** F12
Pomeroy *Wash., U.S.A.* **108** C5
Pomézia *Italy* **42** A5
Pomichna *Ukraine* **33** H6
Pomona *Australia* **95** D5
Pomona *U.S.A.* **111** L9
Pomorie *Bulgaria* **45** D11
Pomorskie □ *Poland* **30** D5
Pomorskie, Pojezierze *Poland* **30** E3
Pomos *Cyprus* **49** D11
Pomos, C. *Cyprus* **49** D11
Pompano Beach *U.S.A.* **117** H14
Pompei *Italy* **43** B7
Pompey *France* **19** D13
Pompeys Pillar *U.S.A.* **108** D10
Pompeys Pillar △ *U.S.A.* **108** D10
Pompton Lakes *U.S.A.* **115** F10
Ponape = Pohnpei
    Micronesia **96** G7

Ponask L. *Canada* **104** B1
Ponca *U.S.A.* **112** D5
Ponca City *U.S.A.* **116** C6
Ponce *Puerto Rico* **121** d
Ponchatoula *U.S.A.* **117** F9
Poncheville, L. *Canada* **104** B4
Pond *U.S.A.* **111** K7
Pond Inlet *Canada* **101** B12
Pondicherry = Puducherry
    India **66** P11
Ponds, I. of *Canada* **105** B8
Ponferrada *Spain* **36** C4
Pongo, Wadi → *Sudan* **81** F2
Ponikva *Slovenia* **41** B12
Ponnani *India* **66** P9
Ponoka *Canada* **102** C6
Ponorogo *Indonesia* **63** G14
Pons = Ponts *Spain* **38** D6
Pons *France* **20** C3
Ponsul → *Portugal* **36** F3
Pont-à-Mousson *France* **19** D13
Pont-Audemer *France* **18** C7
Pont-Aven *France* **18** E3
Pont Canavese *Italy* **40** C4
Pont-de-Roide *France* **19** E13
Pont-de-Salars *France* **20** D6
Pont-de-Vaux *France* **19** F11
Pont-de-Veyle *France* **19** F11
Pont-du-Château *France* **19** G10
Pont-l'Abbé *France* **18** E2
Pont-l'Évêque *France* **18** C7
Pont-St-Esprit *France* **21** D8
Pont-St-Martin *Italy* **40** C4
Pont-Ste-Maxence *France* **19** C9
Pont-sur-Yonne *France* **19** D10
Ponta Delgada *Azores* **78** a
Ponta do Sol *Madeira* **48** D3
Ponta Grossa *Brazil* **127** B5
Ponta Porã *Brazil* **127** A4
Pontacq *France* **20** E3
Pontailler-sur-Saône *France* **19** E12
Pontarlier *France* **19** F13
Pontassieve *Italy* **41** E8
Pontaumur *France* **20** C6
Pontcharra *France* **21** C10
Pontchartrain, L. *U.S.A.* **117** F9
Pontchâteau *France* **18** E4
Ponte da Barca *Portugal* **36** D2
Ponte de Sor *Portugal* **37** F2
Ponte dell'Ólio *Italy* **40** D6
Ponte di Legno *Italy* **40** B7
Ponte do Lima *Portugal* **36** D2
Ponte do Pungué *Mozam.* **87** F3
Ponte-Leccia *France* **21** F13
Ponte nelle Alpi *Italy* **41** B9
Ponte Nova *Brazil* **127** A7
Ponteareas *Spain* **36** C2
Pontebba *Italy* **41** B10
Ponteceso *Spain* **36** B2
Pontecorvo *Italy* **42** A6
Pontedeume *Spain* **36** B2
Pontedera *Italy* **40** E7
Ponteix *Canada* **103** D7
Pontevedra *Spain* **36** C2
Pontevedra □ *Spain* **36** C2
Pontevedra, R. de → *Spain* **36** C2
Pontevico *Italy* **40** C7
Pontiac *Ill., U.S.A.* **112** E9
Pontiac *Mich., U.S.A.* **113** D12
Pontian Kechil *Malaysia* **65** d
Pontianak *Indonesia* **62** E3
Pontine Is. = Ponziane,
    Ísole *Italy* **42** B5
Pontine Mts. = Kuzey
    Anadolu Dağları *Turkey* **72** B7
Pontínia *Italy* **42** A6
Pontivy *France* **18** D4
Pontoise *France* **19** C9
Ponton → *Canada* **102** B5
Pontorson *France* **18** D5
Pontrémoli *Italy* **40** D6
Pontrieux *France* **18** D3
Ponts *Spain* **38** D6
Pontypool *Canada* **114** B6
Pontypool *U.K.* **15** F4
Ponza *Italy* **42** B5
Ponziane, Ísole *Italy* **42** B5
Poochera *Australia* **95** E1
Poole *U.K.* **15** G6
Poole □ *U.K.* **15** G6
Poona = Pune *India* **66** K8
Pooncarie *Australia* **95** E3
Poopelloe L. *Australia* **95** E3
Poopó, L. de *Bolivia* **124** G5
Popayán *Colombia* **124** C3
Poperinge *Belgium* **17** D2
Popiltah L. *Australia* **95** E3
Popina *Bulgaria* **45** B10
Popio L. *Australia* **95** E3
Poplar *U.S.A.* **108** B11
Poplar → *Canada* **103** C9
Poplar Bluff *U.S.A.* **112** G8
Poplarville *U.S.A.* **117** F10
Popocatépetl, Volcán
    Mexico **119** D5
Popokabaka
    Dem. Rep. of the Congo **84** F3

Pópoli *Italy* **41** F10
Popovača *Croatia* **41** C13
Popovo *Bulgaria* **45** C10
Poppberg *Germany* **25** F7
Poppi *Italy* **41** E8
Poprad *Slovak Rep.* **27** B13
Poprad → *Slovak Rep.* **27** B13
Porali → *Pakistan* **68** G2
Porbandar *India* **68** J3
Porcher I. *Canada* **102** C2
Porcuna *Spain* **37** H6
Porcupine → *Canada* **103** B8
Porcupine → *Canada* **106** B5
Porcupine Gorge △ *Australia* **94** C3
Pordenone *Italy* **41** C9
Pordim *Bulgaria* **45** C8
Poreč *Croatia* **41** C10
Poretskoye *Russia* **34** C8
Pori *Finland* **32** B1
Pori *Greece* **46** F5
Porkhov *Russia* **32** D5
Porlamar *Venezuela* **124** A6
Porlezza *Italy* **40** B6
Porma → *Spain* **36** C5
Pornic *France* **18** E4
Poronaysk *Russia* **53** E15
Poroshiri-Dake *Japan* **54** C11
Poroszló *Hungary* **28** C6
Poroto Mts. *Tanzania* **87** D3
Porpoise B. *Antarctica* **5** C9
Porquerolles, Î. de *France* **21** F10
Porrentruy *Switz.* **25** H3
Porres *Spain* **48** C5
Porsangerfjorden *Norway* **8** A21
Porsgrunn *Norway* **9** G13
Port Alberni *Canada* **102** D4
Port Alfred *S. Africa* **88** E4
Port Alice *Canada* **102** C3
Port Allegany *U.S.A.* **114** E6
Port Allen *U.S.A.* **116** F9
Port Alma *Australia* **94** C5
Port Alma *Canada* **114** D2
Port Angeles *U.S.A.* **110** B3
Port Antonio *Jamaica* **120** a
Port Aransas *U.S.A.* **116** H6
Port Arthur *Australia* **95** G4
Port Arthur *U.S.A.* **116** G8
Port au Choix *Canada* **105** B8
Port au Port B. *Canada* **105** C8
Port-au-Prince *Haiti* **121** C5
Port Augusta *Australia* **95** E2
Port Austin *U.S.A.* **114** B2
Port Bell *Uganda* **86** B3
Port Bergé Vaovao *Madag.* **89** B8
Port Blandford *Canada* **105** C9
Port-Bouët *Ivory C.* **82** D4
Port Bradshaw *Australia* **94** A2
Port Broughton *Australia* **95** E2
Port Bruce *Canada* **114** D4
Port Burwell *Canada* **114** D4
Port Canning *India* **69** H13
Port Carling *Canada* **114** A5
Port-Cartier *Canada* **105** B6
Port Chalmers *N.Z.* **91** F3
Port Charlotte *U.S.A.* **117** H13
Port Chester *U.S.A.* **115** F11
Port Clements *Canada* **102** C2
Port Clinton *U.S.A.* **113** E12
Port Colborne *Canada* **114** D5
Port Coquitlam *Canada* **110** A4
Port Credit *Canada* **114** C5
Port-Cros △ *France* **21** F10
Port Curtis *Australia* **94** C5
Port d'Alcúdia *Spain* **48** B10
Port d'Andratx *Spain* **48** B9
Port Darwin *Australia* **92** B5
Port Darwin *Falk. Is.* **128** G5
Port Davey *Australia* **95** G4
Port-de-Bouc *France* **21** E8
Port-de-Paix *Haiti* **121** C5
Port de Pollença *Spain* **48** B10
Port de Sóller *Spain* **48** B9
Port Dickson *Malaysia* **65** L3
Port Douglas *Australia* **94** B4
Port Dover *Canada* **114** D4
Port Edward *Canada* **102** C2
Port Elgin *Canada* **114** B3
Port Elizabeth *S. Africa* **88** E4
Port Ellen *U.K.* **13** F2
Port-en-Bessin-Huppain
    France **18** C6
Port Erin *I. of Man* **14** C3
Port Essington *Australia* **92** B5
Port Ewen *U.S.A.* **115** E11
Port Fairy *Australia* **95** F3
Port Fouâd = Bûr Fuad
    Egypt **80** H8
Port Gamble *U.S.A.* **110** C4
Port-Gentil *Gabon* **84** E1
Port Germein *Australia* **95** E2
Port Ghalib *Egypt* **70** E2
Port Gibson *U.S.A.* **116** F9
Port Glasgow *U.K.* **13** F4
Port Harcourt *Nigeria* **83** E6
Port Hardy *Canada* **102** C3
Port Harrison = Inukjuak
    Canada **101** D12

Port Hawkesbury *Canada* **105** C7
Port Hedland *Australia* **92** D2
Port Henry *U.S.A.* **115** B11
Port Hood *Canada* **105** C7
Port Hope *Canada* **114** C6
Port Hope *U.S.A.* **114** C2
Port Hope Simpson *Canada* **105** B8
Port Hueneme *U.S.A.* **111** L7
Port Huron *U.S.A.* **114** D2
Port İliç *Azerbaijan* **73** C13
Port Jefferson *U.S.A.* **115** F11
Port Jervis *U.S.A.* **115** E10
Port-Joinville *France* **18** F4
Port Katon *Russia* **33** J10
Port Kelang = Pelabuhan
    Klang *Malaysia* **65** L3
Port Kenny *Australia* **95** E1
Port-la-Nouvelle *France* **20** E7
Port Lairge = Waterford
    Ireland **12** D4
Port Laoise *Ireland* **12** C4
Port Lavaca *U.S.A.* **116** G6
Port Leyden *U.S.A.* **115** C9
Port Lincoln *Australia* **95** E2
Port Loko *S. Leone* **82** D2
Port Louis *France* **18** E3
Port-Louis *Guadeloupe* **120** b
Port Louis *Mauritius* **85** d
Port MacDonnell *Australia* **95** F3
Port McNeill *Canada* **102** C3
Port Macquarie *Australia* **95** E5
Port Maria *Jamaica* **120** a
Port Matilda *U.S.A.* **114** F6
Port McNicoll *Canada* **114** B5
Port Mellon *Canada* **102** D4
Port-Menier *Canada* **105** C7
Port Moody *Canada* **110** A4
Port Morant *Jamaica* **120** a
Port Moresby *Papua N. G.* **90** B7
Port Musgrave *Australia* **94** A3
Port-Navalo *France* **18** E4
Port Neches *U.S.A.* **116** G8
Port Nolloth *S. Africa* **88** D2
Port Nouveau-Québec =
    Kangiqsualujjuaq *Canada*
    101 D13
Port of Climax *Canada* **103** D7
Port of Coronach *Canada* **103** D7
Port of Spain *Trin. & Tob.* **121** D7
Port Orange *U.S.A.* **117** G14
Port Orchard *U.S.A.* **110** C4
Port Orford *U.S.A.* **108** E1
Port Pegasus *N.Z.* **91** G1
Port Perry *Canada* **114** B6
Port Phillip B. *Australia* **95** F3
Port Pirie *Australia* **95** E2
Port Renfrew *Canada* **110** B2
Port Roper *Australia* **94** A2
Port Rowan *Canada* **114** D4
Port Safaga = Bûr Safâga
    Egypt **70** E2
Port Said = Bûr Sa'îd *Egypt* **80** H8
Port St. Joe *U.S.A.* **117** G12
Port St. Johns =
    Umzimvubu *S. Africa* **89** E4
Port-St-Louis-du-Rhône
    France **21** E8
Port St. Lucie *U.S.A.* **117** H14
Port-Ste-Marie *France* **20** D4
Port Sanilac *U.S.A.* **114** C2
Port Severn *Canada* **114** B5
Port Shepstone *S. Africa* **89** E5
Port Simpson *Canada* **102** C2
Port Stanley = Stanley
    Falk. Is. **128** G5
Port Stanley *Canada* **114** D3
Port Sudan = Bûr Sûdân
    Sudan **80** D4
Port Sulphur *U.S.A.* **117** G10
Port-sur-Saône *France* **19** E13
Port Talbot *U.K.* **15** F4
Port Taufiq = Bûr Taufiq
    Egypt **80** J8
Port Townsend *U.S.A.* **110** B4
Port-Vendres *France* **20** F7
Port Vila *Vanuatu* **90** C9
Port Vladimir *Russia* **8** B25
Port Wakefield *Australia* **95** E2
Port Washington *U.S.A.* **112** D10
Porta Orientalis *Romania* **23** F12
Portacloy *Ireland* **12** B1
Portadown *U.K.* **12** B5
Portaferry *U.K.* **12** B6
Portage *Pa., U.S.A.* **114** F6
Portage *Wis., U.S.A.* **112** D9
Portage la Prairie *Canada* **103** D9
Portageville *U.S.A.* **112** G9
Portalegre *Portugal* **37** F3
Portalegre □ *Portugal* **37** F3
Portales *U.S.A.* **109** J12
Portarlington *Ireland* **12** C4
Portbou *Spain* **38** C8
Portel *Portugal* **37** G3
Portela, Lisboa ✈ (LIS)
    Portugal **37** G1
Porter L. *N.W.T., Canada* **103** A7
Porter L. *Sask., Canada* **103** B7
Porterville *S. Africa* **88** E2
Porterville *U.S.A.* **110** J8

Portes-lès-Valence France 21 D8
Porthcawl U.K. 15 F4
Porthill U.S.A. 108 B5
Porthmadog U.K. 14 E3
Portile de Fier Europe 28 F7
Portishead U.K. 15 F5
Portiței, Gura Romania 29 F14
Portknockie U.K. 13 D6
Portland N.S.W., Australia 95 E5
Portland Vic., Australia 95 F3
Portland Canada 115 B8
Portland Conn., U.S.A. 115 E12
Portland Maine, U.S.A. 113 D18
Portland Mich., U.S.A. 113 D11
Portland Oreg., U.S.A. 110 E4
Portland Pa., U.S.A. 115 F9
Portland Tex., U.S.A. 116 H6
Portland, I. of U.K. 15 G5
Portland B. Australia 95 F3
Portland Bight Jamaica 120 a
Portland Bill U.K. 15 G5
Portland Canal U.S.A. 102 B2
Portland Int. ✈ (PDX)
  U.S.A. 110 E4
Portland Pt. Jamaica 120 a
Portmadoc = Porthmadog
  U.K. 14 E3
Portmore Jamaica 120 a
Porto France 21 F12
Porto Portugal 36 D2
Porto □ Portugal 36 D2
Porto, G. de France 21 F12
Pôrto Alegre Brazil 127 C5
Porto Azzurro Italy 40 F7
Porto Colom Spain 48 B10
Porto Cristo Spain 48 B10
Porto de Moz Brazil 125 D8
Porto Empédocle Italy 42 F6
Porto Esperança Brazil 124 G7
Porto Franco Brazil 125 E9
Porto Inglês C. Verde Is. 78 b
Porto Mendes Brazil 127 A5
Porto Moniz Madeira 48 D2
Porto Murtinho Brazil 124 H7
Porto Nacional Brazil 125 F9
Porto-Novo Benin 83 D5
Porto Primavera, Represa
  Brazil 127 A5
Porto San Giórgio Italy 41 E10
Porto Sant' Elpídio Italy 41 E10
Porto Santo, I. de Madeira 78 B2
Porto Santo Stéfano Italy 40 F8
Porto São José Brazil 127 A5
Porto Seguro Brazil 125 G11
Porto Tolle Italy 41 D9
Porto Tórres Italy 42 B1
Porto União Brazil 127 B5
Pôrto Velho Brazil 124 E6
Porto Walter Brazil 124 E4
Portobelo Panama 120 E4
Portoferráio Italy 40 F7
Portogruaro Italy 41 C9
Portola U.S.A. 110 F6
Portomaggiore Italy 41 D8
Portopetro Spain 48 B10
Portoscuso Italy 42 C1
Portovénere Italy 40 D6
Portoviejo Ecuador 124 D2
Portpatrick U.K. 13 G3
Portree U.K. 13 D2
Portrush U.K. 12 A5
Portsmouth Dominica 121 C7
Portsmouth U.K. 15 G6
Portsmouth N.H., U.S.A. 115 C14
Portsmouth Ohio, U.S.A. 113 F12
Portsmouth R.I., U.S.A. 115 E13
Portsmouth Va., U.S.A. 113 G15
Portsmouth □ U.K. 15 G6
Portsoy U.K. 13 D6
Portstewart U.K. 12 A5
Porttipahdan tekojärvi
  Finland 8 B22
Portugal ■ Europe 36 F3
Portugalete Spain 38 B1
Portumna Ireland 12 C3
Portville U.S.A. 114 D6
Porvenir Chile 128 G2
Porvoo Finland 32 B3
Porzuna Spain 37 F6
Posada Italy 42 B2
Posada → Italy 42 B2
Posadas Argentina 127 B4
Posadas Spain 37 H5
Poschiavo Switz. 25 J6
Posets Spain 38 C5
Posht-e Badam Iran 71 C7
Posidónio Greece 47 F9
Poso Indonesia 63 E6
Posof Turkey 73 B10
Posse Brazil 125 F9
Possession I. Antarctica 5 D11
Pössneck Germany 24 E7
Possum Kingdom L. U.S.A. 116 E5
Post U.S.A. 116 E4
Post Falls U.S.A. 108 C5
Postavy = Pastavy Belarus 32 E4
Poste-de-la-Baleine =
  Kuujjuarapik Canada 104 A4

Postmasburg S. Africa 88 D3
Postojna Slovenia 41 C11
Poston U.S.A. 111 M12
Postville Canada 105 B8
Posyet Russia 54 C5
Potamos Antikythira, Greece 46 F5
Potamos Kythira, Greece 46 F5
Potchefstroom S. Africa 88 D4
Potcoava Romania 29 F9
Poteau U.S.A. 116 D7
Poteet U.S.A. 116 G5
Potenza Italy 43 B8
Potenza → Italy 41 E10
Potenza Picena Italy 41 E10
Poteriteri, L. N.Z. 91 G1
Potgietersrus = Mokopane
  S. Africa 89 C4
Poti Georgia 35 J5
Potiskum Nigeria 83 C7
Potlogi Romania 29 F10
Potomac → U.S.A. 113 F14
Potosí Bolivia 124 G5
Potosi Mt. U.S.A. 111 K11
Pototan Phil. 61 F5
Potrerillos Chile 126 B2
Potsdam Germany 24 C9
Potsdam U.S.A. 115 B10
Pottenstein Germany 25 F7
Pottersville U.S.A. 115 C11
Pottstown U.S.A. 115 F9
Pottsville U.S.A. 115 F8
Pottuvil Sri Lanka 66 R12
Pouancé France 18 E5
Pouce Coupé Canada 102 B4
Poughkeepsie U.S.A. 115 E11
Pouilly-sur-Loire France 19 E9
Poulaphouca Res. Ireland 12 C5
Poulsbo U.S.A. 110 C4
Poultney U.S.A. 115 C11
Poulton-le-Fylde U.K. 14 D5
Pouso Alegre Brazil 127 A6
Pout Senegal 82 C1
Pouthisat Cambodia 64 F4
Pouzauges France 18 F6
Pova de Santa Iria Portugal 37 G1
Povážská Bystrica
  Slovak Rep. 27 B11
Poverty B. N.Z. 91 C7
Povlen Serbia 44 B4
Póvoa de Lanhosa Portugal 36 D2
Póvoa de Varzim Portugal 36 D2
Povorino Russia 34 E6
Povorotnyy, Mys Russia 54 C6
Povungnituk = Puvirnituq
  Canada 101 C12
Powassan Canada 104 C4
Poway U.S.A. 111 N9
Powder → U.S.A. 108 C11
Powder River U.S.A. 108 E10
Powell U.S.A. 108 D9
Powell, L. U.S.A. 109 H8
Powell River Canada 102 D4
Powers U.S.A. 112 C10
Pownal U.S.A. 115 D11
Powys □ U.K. 15 E4
Poyang Hu China 59 C11
Poyarkovo Russia 53 E13
Poysdorf Austria 27 C9
Poza de la Sal Spain 36 C7
Poza Rica Mexico 119 C5
Pozanti Turkey 72 D6
Požarevac Serbia 44 B5
Pozazal, Puerto Spain 36 C6
Požega Croatia 28 E2
Požega Serbia 44 C4
Poznań Poland 31 F3
Poznań ✈ (POZ) Poland 31 F3
Pozo U.S.A. 111 K6
Pozo Alcón Spain 37 H8
Pozo Almonte Chile 124 H5
Pozo Colorado Paraguay 126 A4
Pozoblanco Spain 37 G6
Pozzallo Italy 43 F7
Pozzomaggiore Italy 42 B1
Pozzuoli Italy 43 B7
Pra → Ghana 83 D4
Prabuty Poland 30 E6
Prača Bos.-H. 28 G3
Prachatice Czech Rep. 26 B6
Prachin Buri Thailand 64 F3
Prachuap Khiri Khan
  Thailand 65 G2
Pradelles France 20 D7
Prades France 20 F6
Prado Brazil 125 G11
Prado del Rey Spain 37 J5
Præstø Denmark 11 J6
Pragersko Slovenia 41 B12
Prague = Praha Czech Rep. 26 A7
Praha Czech Rep. 26 A7
Praha ✈ (PRG) Czech Rep. 26 A7
Prahecq France 20 B3
Prahova □ Romania 29 F10
Prahova → Romania 29 F10
Prahovo Serbia 44 B6
Praia C. Verde Is. 78 b
Praia a Mare Italy 43 C8
Praid Romania 29 D10

Prainha Brazil 125 D8
Prainha Nova Brazil 124 E6
Prairie Australia 94 C3
Prairie City U.S.A. 108 D4
Prairie Dog Town Fork
  Red → U.S.A. 116 D5
Prairie du Chien U.S.A. 112 D8
Prairies, L. of the Canada 103 C8
Pramanda Greece 46 B3
Prampram Ghana 83 D5
Pran Buri Thailand 64 F2
Prang Ghana 83 D4
Prapat Indonesia 62 D1
Praslin Seychelles 85 b
Prasonisi, Akra Greece 49 D9
Prästmon Sweden 10 A11
Praszka Poland 31 G5
Prata Brazil 125 G9
Pratapgarh Raj., India 68 G6
Pratapgarh Ut. P., India 69 G9
Pratas Is. = Dongsha Dao
  China 59 G11
Prato Italy 40 E8
Prátola Peligna Italy 41 F10
Prats-de-Mollo-la-Preste
  France 20 F6
Pratt U.S.A. 112 G4
Prattville U.S.A. 117 E11
Pravdinsk Kaliningrad, Russia 30 D8
Pravdinsk Nizhniy Novgorod,
  Russia 34 B6
Pravets Bulgaria 44 D7
Pravia Spain 36 B4
Praya Indonesia 62 F5
Pré-en-Pail France 18 D6
Preble U.S.A. 115 D8
Precipice △ Australia 95 D5
Precordillera Argentina 126 C2
Predáppio Italy 41 D8
Predazzo Italy 41 B8
Predeal Romania 29 E10
Predejane Serbia 44 D6
Preeceville Canada 103 C8
Preetz Germany 24 A6
Pregolya → Russia 30 D7
Pregrada Croatia 41 B12
Preiļi Latvia 32 D4
Preko Croatia 41 D12
Prelog Croatia 41 B13
Prémery France 19 E10
Premià de Mar Spain 38 D7
Premont U.S.A. 116 H5
Premuda Croatia 41 D11
Prentice U.S.A. 112 C8
Prenzlau Germany 24 B9
Přerov Czech Rep. 27 B10
Prescott Canada 115 B9
Prescott Ariz., U.S.A. 109 J7
Prescott Ark., U.S.A. 116 E8
Prescott Valley U.S.A. 109 J7
Preservation Inlet N.Z. 91 G1
Preševo Serbia 44 D5
Presho U.S.A. 112 D3
Presicce Italy 43 C11
Presidencia de la Plaza
  Argentina 126 B4
Presidencia Roque Saenz
  Peña Argentina 126 B3
Presidente Epitácio Brazil 125 H8
Presidente Hayes □
  Paraguay 126 A4
Presidente Prudente Brazil 127 A5
Presidio Mexico 118 B4
Presidio U.S.A. 116 G2
Preslav Bulgaria 45 C10
Preslavska Planina
  Bulgaria 45 C10
Prešov Slovak Rep. 27 B14
Prešovský □ Slovak Rep. 27 B13
Prespa, L. = Prespansko
  Jezero Macedonia 44 F5
Prespa □ Greece 44 F5
Prespansko Jezero Macedonia 44 F5
Presque I. U.S.A. 114 D4
Presque Isle U.S.A. 113 B19
Prestatyn U.K. 14 D4
Prestea Ghana 82 D4
Presteigne U.K. 15 E5
Přeštice Czech Rep. 26 B6
Preston Canada 114 C4
Preston U.K. 14 D5
Preston Idaho, U.S.A. 108 E8
Preston Minn., U.S.A. 112 D7
Preston, C. Australia 92 D2
Prestonburg U.S.A. 113 G12
Prestranda Norway 10 E3
Prestwick U.K. 13 F4
Pretoria S. Africa 89 D4
Preuilly-sur-Claise France 18 F7
Preveza Greece 46 C2
Préveza □ Greece 46 B2
Prey Veng Cambodia 65 G5

Priazovskoye Ukraine 33 J8
Pribilof Is. U.S.A. 106 a
Priboj Serbia 44 C3
Příbram Czech Rep. 26 B7
Price U.S.A. 108 G8
Price I. Canada 102 C3
Prichard U.S.A. 117 F10
Priego Spain 38 E2
Priego de Córdoba Spain 37 H6
Priekule Latvia 30 B8
Priekule Lithuania 30 C8
Prien Germany 25 H8
Prieska S. Africa 88 D3
Priest → U.S.A. 108 B5
Priest L. U.S.A. 108 B5
Priest Valley U.S.A. 110 J6
Prievidza Slovak Rep. 27 C11
Prijedor Bos.-H. 41 D13
Prijepolje Serbia 44 C3
Prikaspiyskaya
  Nizmennost = Caspian
  Depression Eurasia 35 G9
Prikro Ivory C. 82 D4
Prikubanskaya
  Nizmennost Russia 35 H4
Prilep Macedonia 44 E5
Priluki = Pryluky Ukraine 33 G7
Prime Seal I. Australia 95 G4
Primo Tapia Mexico 111 N10
Primorsk Kaliningrad, Russia 30 D6
Primorsk St. Petersburg,
  Russia 32 B5
Primorskiy Kray □ Russia 54 B7
Primorsko Bulgaria 45 D11
Primorsko-Akhtarsk
  Russia 33 J10
Primorskoye Ukraine 33 J9
Primrose L. Canada 103 C7
Prince Albert Canada 103 C7
Prince Albert S. Africa 88 E3
Prince Albert △ Canada 103 C7
Prince Albert Mts. Antarctica 5 D11
Prince Albert Pen. Canada 100 B8
Prince Albert Sd. Canada 100 B8
Prince Alfred, C. Canada 101 B7
Prince Charles I. Canada 101 C12
Prince Charles Mts. Antarctica 5 D6
Prince Edward Fracture
  Zone Ind. Oc. 5 A4
Prince Edward I. □ Canada 105 C7
Prince Edward Is. Ind. Oc. 3 G11
Prince George Canada 102 C4
Prince Gustaf Adolf Sea
  Canada 101 B9
Prince of Wales, C. U.S.A. 98 C3
Prince of Wales I. Australia 94 A3
Prince of Wales I. Canada 100 B10
Prince of Wales I. U.S.A. 100 D6
Prince Patrick I. Canada 4 B2
Prince Regent Inlet Canada 4 B3
Prince Rupert Canada 102 C2
Princes Town Trin. & Tob. 125 K15
Princess Charlotte B.
  Australia 94 A3
Princess Elizabeth Trough
  S. Ocean 5 C7
Princess May Ranges
  Australia 92 C4
Princess Royal I. Canada 102 C3
Princeton Canada 102 D4
Princeton Calif., U.S.A. 110 F4
Princeton Ill., U.S.A. 112 E9
Princeton Ind., U.S.A. 112 F10
Princeton Ky., U.S.A. 112 G10
Princeton Mo., U.S.A. 112 E7
Princeton N.J., U.S.A. 115 F10
Princeton W. Va., U.S.A. 113 G13
Príncipe São Tomé & Príncipe 76 F4
Principe da Beira Brazil 124 F6
Prineville U.S.A. 108 D3
Prins Harald Kyst Antarctica 5 D4
Prinsesse Astrid Kyst
  Antarctica 5 D3
Prinsesse Ragnhild Kyst
  Antarctica 5 D4
Prinzapolca Nic. 120 D3
Prior, C. Spain 36 B2
Priozersk Russia 32 B6
Pripet = Prypyat → Europe 23 C16
Pripet Marshes Europe 23 B15
Pripyat Marshes = Pripet
  Marshes Europe 23 B15
Pripyats = Prypyat →
  Europe 23 C16
Prislop, Pasul Romania 29 C9
Pristen Russia 33 G9
Priština Serbia 44 D5
Pritzwalk Germany 24 B8
Privas France 21 D8
Priverno Italy 42 A6
Privolzhsk Russia 34 B5
Privolzhskaya
  Vozvyshennost Russia 34 E7
Privolzhskiy Russia 34 E8
Privolzhskiy = Privolzhsk Russia 34 B10
Privolzhye Russia 34 D9
Priyutnoye Russia 35 G6

Prizren Serbia 44 D4
Prizzi Italy 42 E6
Prnjavor Bos.-H. 28 E7
Probolinggo Indonesia 63 G15
Prochowice Poland 31 G3
Proctor U.S.A. 115 C11
Proddatur India 66 M11
Prodhromos Cyprus 49 E11
Proença-a-Nova Portugal 36 F3
Profilia Greece 49 C9
Progreso Coahuila, Mexico 118 B4
Progreso Yucatán, Mexico 119 C7
Progress Antarctica 5 C12
Progress Russia 53 E13
Prokhladnyy Russia 35 J7
Prokletije Albania 44 D3
Prokopyevsk Russia 52 D9
Prokuplje Serbia 44 C5
Proletarsk Russia 35 G5
Proletarskaya = Proletarsk
  Russia 35 G5
Prome Burma 67 K19
Prophet → Canada 102 B4
Prophet River Canada 102 B4
Propriá Brazil 125 F11
Propriano France 21 G12
Proserpine Australia 94 J6
Prosna → Poland 31 F4
Prosna Poland 31 F4
Prospect U.S.A. 115 C9
Prosser U.S.A. 108 C4
Prostějov Czech Rep. 27 B10
Prostki Poland 30 E9
Proston Australia 95 D5
Proszowice Poland 31 H7
Proti Greece 46 D3
Provadiya Bulgaria 45 C11
Provence France 21 E9
Provence-Alpes-Côte
  d'Azur □ France 21 D10
Providence Ky., U.S.A. 112 G10
Providence R.I., U.S.A. 115 E13
Providence Bay Canada 104 C3
Providence Mts. U.S.A. 111 K11
Providencia, I. de Colombia 120 D3
Provideniya Russia 53 C19
Provincetown U.S.A. 113 D18
Provins France 19 D10
Provo U.S.A. 108 F8
Provost Canada 103 C6
Prozor Bos.-H. 28 G2
Prudentópolis Brazil 29 F11
Prudhoe Bay U.S.A. 106 a
Prudhoe I. Australia 94 C4
Prud'homme Canada 103 C7
Prudnik Poland 31 H4
Prüm Germany 25 E2
Prundu Romania 29 F11
Pruszcz Gdański Poland 30 D5
Pruszków Poland 31 F7
Prut → Romania 29 E14
Pruzhany Belarus 23 B13
Prvič Croatia 41 D11
Prydz B. Antarctica 5 C6
Pryluky Ukraine 33 G7
Pryor U.S.A. 116 C7
Prypyat → Europe 23 C16
Przasnysz Poland 31 E7
Przedbórz Poland 31 G6
Przedecz Poland 31 F5
Przemków Poland 31 G2
Przemyśl Poland 31 J9
Przeworsk Poland 31 H9
Przewóz Poland 31 G1
Przhevalsk = Karakol
  Kyrgyzstan 52 E8
Przysucha Poland 31 G7
Psachna Greece 46 C5
Psara Greece 47 C7
Psathoura Greece 46 B6
Psel → Ukraine 33 H7
Pserimos Greece 47 E9
Psiloritis, Oros Greece 49 D6
Psira Greece 49 D7
Pskov Russia 32 D5
Pskov □ Russia 32 D5
Pskovskoye, Ozero Russia 32 D5
Psunj Croatia 28 E2
Pteleos Greece 46 B4
Ptich = Ptsich → Belarus 23 B15
Ptichia = Vidos Greece 49 A3
Ptolemaida Greece 44 F5
Ptsich → Belarus 23 B15
Ptuj Slovenia 41 B12
Ptujska Gora Slovenia 41 B12
Pu Xian China 56 F6
Pua Thailand 64 C3
Puán Argentina 126 D3
Pu'an China 58 E5
Pu'apu'a Samoa 91 b
Pubei China 58 F7
Pucallpa Peru 124 E4
Pucheng China 59 D12
Pucheni Romania 29 E10
Puchheim Germany 25 G7
Puch'on = Bucheon
  S. Korea 57 F14
Púchov Slovak Rep. 27 B11
Pucioasa Romania 29 E10

Pučišća Croatia 41 E13
Puck Poland 30 D5
Pucka, Zatoka Poland 30 D5
Puçol Spain 39 F4
Pudasjärvi Finland 8 D22
Puding China 58 D5
Pudozh Russia 32 B9
Puducherry India 66 P11
Pudukkottai India 66 P11
Puebla Mexico 119 D5
Puebla □ Mexico 119 D5
Puebla de Alcocer Spain 37 G5
Puebla de Don Fadrique
  Spain 39 H2
Puebla de Don Rodrigo Spain 37 F6
Puebla de Guzmán Spain 37 H3
Puebla de la Calzada Spain 37 G4
Puebla de Sanabria Spain 36 C4
Puebla de Trives = Pobra
  de Trives Spain 36 C3
Pueblo U.S.A. 108 G11
Puelches Argentina 126 D2
Puelén Argentina 126 D2
Puente Alto Chile 126 C1
Puente-Genil Spain 37 H6
Puente la Reina Spain 38 C3
Puente San Miguel Spain 36 B6
Puenteareas = Ponteareas
  Spain 36 C2
Puentedeume =
  Pontedeume Spain 36 B2
Puentes de Garcia
  Rodriguez = As Pontes
  de García Rodríguez Spain 36 B3
Pu'er China 58 F3
Puerca, Pta. Puerto Rico 121 d
Puerco → U.S.A. 109 J10
Puerto Aisén Chile 128 F2
Puerto Ángel Mexico 119 D5
Puerto Arista Mexico 119 D6
Puerto Armuelles Panama 120 E3
Puerto Ayacucho Venezuela 124 B5
Puerto Barrios Guatemala 120 C2
Puerto Bermejo Argentina 126 B4
Puerto Bermúdez Peru 124 F4
Puerto Bolívar Ecuador 124 D2
Puerto Cabello Venezuela 124 A5
Puerto Cabezas Nic. 120 D3
Puerto Cabo Gracias á Dios
  Nic. 120 D3
Puerto Carreño Colombia 124 B5
Puerto Castilla Honduras 120 C2
Puerto Chicama Peru 124 E3
Puerto Coig Argentina 128 G3
Puerto Cortés Honduras 120 C2
Puerto Cumarebo Venezuela 124 A5
Puerto de Alcudia = Port
  d'Alcúdia Spain 48 B10
Puerto de Cabrera Spain 48 B9
Puerto de Gran Tarajal
  Canary Is. 48 F5
Puerto de la Cruz Canary Is. 48 F3
Puerto de los Angeles △
  Mexico 118 B3
Puerto de Mazarrón Spain 39 H3
Puerto de Pozo Negro
  Canary Is. 48 F6
Puerto de Sóller = Port de
  Sóller Spain 48 B9
Puerto de Somosierra Spain 36 D7
Puerto del Carmen Canary Is. 48 F6
Puerto del Rosario Canary Is. 48 F6
Puerto Deseado Argentina 128 F3
Puerto Escondido Mexico 119 D5
Puerto Heath Bolivia 124 F5
Puerto Inírida Colombia 124 C5
Puerto Juárez Mexico 119 C7
Puerto La Cruz Venezuela 124 A6
Puerto Leguízamo Colombia 124 D4
Puerto Lempira Honduras 120 C3
Puerto Libertad Mexico 118 B2
Puerto Limón Colombia 124 C4
Puerto Lobos Argentina 128 E3
Puerto Lumbreras Spain 39 H3
Puerto Madryn Argentina 128 E3
Puerto Maldonado Peru 124 F5
Puerto Manatí Cuba 120 B4
Puerto Montt Chile 128 E2
Puerto Morazán Nic. 120 D2
Puerto Morelos Mexico 119 C7
Puerto Natales Chile 128 G2
Puerto Oscuro Chile 126 C1
Puerto Padre Cuba 120 B4
Puerto Páez Venezuela 124 B5
Puerto Peñasco Mexico 118 A2
Puerto Pinasco Paraguay 126 A4
Puerto Plata Dom. Rep. 121 C5
Puerto Pollensa = Port de
  Pollença Spain 48 B10
Puerto Princesa Phil. 61 G3
Puerto Quepos Costa Rica 120 E3
Puerto Real Spain 37 J4
Puerto Rico Canary Is. 48 G4
Puerto Rico ☑ W. Indies 121 d
Puerto Rico Trench Atl. Oc. 121 C6
Puerto San Julián Argentina 128 F3
Puerto Santa Cruz
  Argentina 128 G3
Puerto Sastre Paraguay 126 A4

Puerto Serrano *Spain* **37 J5**
Puerto Suárez *Bolivia* **124 G7**
Puerto Vallarta *Mexico* **118 C3**
Puerto Varas *Chile* **128 E2**
Puerto Wilches *Colombia* **124 B4**
Puertollano *Spain* **37 G6**
Pueu *Tahiti* **91 a**
Pueyrredón, L. *Argentina* **128 F2**
Púez Odle *Italy* **41 B8**
Puffin I. *Ireland* **12 E1**
Pugachev *Russia* **34 D9**
Pugal *India* **68 E5**
Puge *China* **58 D4**
Puge *Tanzania* **86 C3**
Puget Sound *U.S.A.* **108 C2**
Puget-Théniers *France* **21 E10**
Púglia □ *Italy* **43 A9**
Pugŏdong *N. Korea* **57 C16**
Pugu *Tanzania* **86 D4**
Pügünzī *Iran* **71 E8**
Pui *Romania* **28 E8**
Puieşti *Romania* **29 D12**
Puig Major *Spain* **48 B9**
Puigcerdà *Spain* **38 C6**
Puigmal *Spain* **38 C7**
Puigpunyent *Spain* **48 B9**
Puijiang *China* **58 B4**
Puisaye, Collines de la *France* **19 E10**
Puiseaux *France* **19 D9**
Pujehun *S. Leone* **82 D2**
Pujiang *China* **59 C12**
Pujols *France* **20 D3**
Pujon-ho *N. Korea* **57 D14**
Pukaki, L. *N.Z.* **91 F3**
Pukapuka *Cook Is.* **97 J11**
Pukaskwa △ *Canada* **104 C2**
Pukatawagan *Canada* **103 B8**
Pukchin *N. Korea* **57 D13**
Pukch'ŏng *N. Korea* **57 D15**
Pukë *Albania* **44 D3**
Pukekohe *N.Z.* **91 B5**
Pukhrayan *India* **69 F8**
Pukou *China* **59 A12**
Pula *Croatia* **41 D10**
Pula *Italy* **42 C1**
Pulacayo *Bolivia* **124 H5**
Pulai *Malaysia* **65 d**
Pulandian *China* **57 E11**
Pulaski *N.Y., U.S.A.* **115 C8**
Pulaski *Tenn., U.S.A.* **117 D11**
Pulaski *Va., U.S.A.* **113 G13**
Pulau → *Indonesia* **63 F9**
Puławy *Poland* **31 G8**
Pulga *U.S.A.* **110 F5**
Pulicat L. *India* **66 N12**
Pullman *U.S.A.* **108 C5**
Pulog, Mt. *Phil.* **61 C4**
Pultusk *Poland* **31 F8**
Pülümür *Turkey* **73 C8**
Pumlumon Fawr *U.K.* **15 E4**
Puná, I. *Ecuador* **124 D2**
Punaauia *Tahiti* **91 d**
Punakaiki *N.Z.* **91 E3**
Punakha Dzong *Bhutan* **67 F16**
Punasar *India* **68 F5**
Punata *Bolivia* **124 G5**
Punch *India* **69 C6**
Punch → *Pakistan* **68 C5**
Punda Maria *S. Africa* **89 C5**
Pune *India* **66 K8**
P'ungsan *N. Korea* **57 D15**
Pungue, Ponte de *Mozam.* **87 F3**
Puning *China* **59 F11**
Punjab □ *India* **68 D7**
Punjab □ *Pakistan* **68 E6**
Puno *Peru* **124 G4**
Punpun → *India* **69 G11**
Punta, Cerro de *Puerto Rico* **121 d**
Punta Alta *Argentina* **128 D4**
Punta Arenas *Chile* **128 G2**
Punta del Díaz *Chile* **126 B1**
Punta del Hidalgo *Canary Is.* **48 F3**
Punta Gorda *Belize* **119 D7**
Punta Gorda *U.S.A.* **117 H13**
Punta Prieta *Mexico* **118 B2**
Punta Prima *Spain* **48 B11**
Punta Umbría *Spain* **37 H4**
Puntarenas *Costa Rica* **120 E3**
Puntland *Somali Rep.* **75 F4**
Punto Fijo *Venezuela* **124 A4**
Punxsatawney *U.S.A.* **114 F6**
Pupuan *Indonesia* **63 J18**
Puqi *China* **59 C9**
Puquio *Peru* **124 F4**
Pur → *Russia* **52 C8**
Puracé, Vol. *Colombia* **124 C3**
Puračić *Bos.-H.* **28 F3**
Puralia = Puruliya *India* **69 H12**
Puranpur *India* **69 E9**
Purbeck, Isle of *U.K.* **15 G5**
Purcell *U.S.A.* **116 D6**
Purcell Mts. *Canada* **102 D5**
Purdy *Canada* **114 A7**
Puri *India* **67 K14**
Purmerend *Neths.* **17 B4**
Purnia *India* **69 G12**
Purnululu △ *Australia* **92 C4**
Pursat = Pouthisat *Cambodia* **64 F4**

Purukcahu *Indonesia* **62 E4**
Puruliya *India* **69 H12**
Purus → *Brazil* **124 D6**
Puruvesi *Finland* **32 B5**
Purvis *U.S.A.* **117 F10**
Purwa *India* **69 F9**
Purwakarta *Indonesia* **63 G12**
Purwo, Tanjung *Indonesia* **63 K18**
Purwodadi *Indonesia* **63 G14**
Purwokerto *Indonesia* **63 G13**
Puryŏng *N. Korea* **57 C15**
Pusa *India* **69 G11**
Pusan = Busan *S. Korea* **57 G15**
Pushkin *Russia* **32 C6**
Pushkino *Moskva, Russia* **32 D9**
Pushkino *Saratov, Russia* **34 E8**
Püspökladány *Hungary* **28 C6**
Pustoshka *Russia* **32 D5**
Puszczykowo *Poland* **31 F3**
Put-in-Bay *U.S.A.* **114 E2**
Putahow L. *Canada* **103 B8**
Putao *Burma* **67 F20**
Putararu *N.Z.* **91 C5**
Putbus *Germany* **24 A9**
Putian *China* **59 E12**
Putignano *Italy* **43 B10**
Puting, Tanjung *Indonesia* **62 E4**
Putlitz *Germany* **24 B8**
Putna *Romania* **29 C10**
Putna → *Romania* **29 E12**
Putnam *U.S.A.* **115 E13**
Putnok *Hungary* **28 B5**
Putorana, Gory *Russia* **53 C10**
Putrajaya *Malaysia* **65 L3**
Puttalam *Sri Lanka* **66 Q11**
Puttgarden *Germany* **24 A7**
Püttlingen *Germany* **25 F2**
Putumayo → *S. Amer.* **124 D5**
Putuo *China* **59 C14**
Putussibau *Indonesia* **62 D4**
Putyla *Ukraine* **29 D14**
Puvirnituq *Canada* **101 C12**
Puy-de-Dôme *France* **20 C6**
Puy-de-Dôme □ *France* **20 C7**
Puy-l'Évêque *France* **20 D5**
Puyallup *U.S.A.* **110 C4**
Puyang *China* **56 G8**
Puylaurens *France* **20 E6**
Püzeh Rīg *Iran* **71 E8**
Puzhaykove *Ukraine* **29 B14**
Pwani □ *Tanzania* **86 D4**
Pweto *Dem. Rep. of the Congo* **87 D2**
Pwllheli *U.K.* **14 E3**
Pyana → *Russia* **34 C8**
Pyaozero, Ozero *Russia* **8 C24**
Pyapon *Burma* **67 L19**
Pyasina → *Russia* **53 B9**
Pyatigorsk *Russia* **35 H6**
Pyatykhatky *Ukraine* **33 H7**
Pydna *Greece* **44 F6**
Pyè = Prome *Burma* **67 K19**
Pyeongtaek *S. Korea* **57 F14**
Pyetrikaw *Belarus* **23 B15**
Pyhäjoki *Finland* **8 D21**
Pyinmana *Burma* **67 K20**
Pyla, C. *Cyprus* **49 E12**
Pyŏktong *N. Korea* **57 D13**
Pyŏnggang *N. Korea* **57 E14**
P'yŏngsong *N. Korea* **57 E13**
P'yŏngyang *N. Korea* **57 E13**
Pyote *U.S.A.* **116 F3**
Pyramid L. *U.S.A.* **108 F4**
Pyramid Pk. *U.S.A.* **111 J10**
Pyramids *Egypt* **80 J7**
Pyrénées *Europe* **20 F4**
Pyrénées△ *France* **20 F4**
Pyrénées-Atlantiques □ *France* **20 E3**
Pyrénées-Orientales □ *France* **20 F6**
Pyryatyn *Ukraine* **33 G7**
Pyrzyce *Poland* **31 E1**
Pyskowice *Poland* **31 H5**
Pytalovo *Russia* **32 D4**
Pyu *Burma* **67 K20**
Pyzdry *Poland* **31 F4**

Q

Qaanaaq *Greenland* **4 B4**
Qabirri → *Azerbaijan* **35 K8**
Qachasnek *S. Africa* **89 E4**
Qādisiyah, Buhayrat al *Iraq* **73 E10**
Qa'el Jafr *Jordan* **74 E5**
Qa'emābād *Iran* **71 D9**
Qā'emshahr *Iran* **71 B7**
Qagan Nur *China* **56 B9**
Qahar Youyi Zhongqi *China* **56 D7**
Qahremānshahr = Kermānshāh *Iran* **73 E12**
Qaidam Pendi *China* **60 C4**
Qaiyara *Iraq* **73 E10**
Qajarīyeh *Iran* **71 D6**
Qala, Ras il *Malta* **49 C1**
Qala-i-Jadid = Spīn Būldak *Afghan.* **68 D2**
Qala Point = Qala, Ras il *Malta* **49 C1**

Qala Viala *Pakistan* **68 D2**
Qala Yangi *Afghan.* **68 B2**
Qal'at al Akhḍar *Si. Arabia* **70 E3**
Qal'at Bīshah *Si. Arabia* **80 D5**
Qal'at Dīzah *Iraq* **73 D11**
Qal'at Şāliḥ *Iraq* **70 D5**
Qal'at Sukkar *Iraq* **73 G12**
Qalyûb *Egypt* **80 H7**
Qamani'tuaq = Baker Lake *Canada* **100 C10**
Qamdo *China* **58 B1**
Qamea *Fiji* **91 a**
Qamruddin Karez *Pakistan* **68 D3**
Qandahār = Kandahār *Afghan.* **66 D4**
Qandahār = Kandahār □ *Afghan.* **66 D4**
Qandyaghash *Kazakhstan* **52 E6**
Qapān *Iran* **71 B7**
Qapshaghay *Kazakhstan* **52 E8**
Qaqortoq *Greenland* **4 C5**
Qâra *Egypt* **80 B2**
Qara Dāgh *Iraq* **73 E11**
Qara Qash → *China* **69 B8**
Qarabutaq *Kazakhstan* **52 E7**
Qaraçala *Azerbaijan* **35 L9**
Qaraghandy *Kazakhstan* **52 E8**
Qaraghayly *Kazakhstan* **52 E8**
Qārah *Si. Arabia* **70 D4**
Qarah Āghāj *Iran* **73 D12**
Qaraqosh *Iraq* **73 D10**
Qarataū *Kazakhstan* **52 E7**
Qarataū *Zhambyl, Kazakhstan* **52 E8**
Qarazhal *Kazakhstan* **52 E8**
Qardho *Somali Rep.* **75 F4**
Qardud *Sudan* **81 E2**
Qareh → *Iran* **73 C12**
Qareh Tekān *Iran* **71 B6**
Qarnein *U.A.E.* **71 E7**
Qarqan → *China* **60 C3**
Qarqaraly *Kazakhstan* **52 E8**
Qarrasa *Sudan* **81 E3**
Qarshi *Uzbekistan* **52 F7**
Qartabā *Lebanon* **74 A4**
Qārūh *Kuwait* **71 D6**
Qaryat al Gharab *Iraq* **70 D5**
Qaryat al 'Ulyā *Si. Arabia* **70 E5**
Qasr 'Amra *Jordan* **70 D3**
Qaşr-e Qand *Iran* **71 E9**
Qaşr-e Shīrīn *Iran* **73 E11**
Qasr Farâfra *Egypt* **80 B2**
Qatanā *Syria* **74 B5**
Qatar ■ *Asia* **71 E6**
Qatlīsh *Iran* **71 B8**
Qattâra *Egypt* **80 A2**
Qattâra, Munkhafed el *Egypt* **80 B2**
Qattâra Depression = Qattâra, Munkhafed el *Egypt* **80 B2**
Qausiuittuq = Resolute *Canada* **101 B10**
Qawām al Ḥamzah = Al Ḥamzah *Iraq* **70 D5**
Qāyen *Iran* **71 C8**
Qazaqstan = Kazakhstan ■ *Asia* **52 E8**
Qazax *Azerbaijan* **35 K7**
Qazımämmäd *Azerbaijan* **35 K9**
Qazvīn *Iran* **71 B6**
Qazvīn □ *Iran* **71 B6**
Qeissan *Sudan* **81 E3**
Qena *Egypt* **80 B3**
Qena, W. → *Egypt* **80 B3**
Qeqertarsuaq *Greenland* **4 C5**
Qeqertarsuaq *Greenland* **98 C14**
Qeshlāq *Iran* **73 E12**
Qeshm *Iran* **71 E8**
Qeydār *Iran* **73 D13**
Qeys *Iran* **71 E7**
Qezel Owzen → *Iran* **71 B6**
Qezi'ot *Israel* **74 E3**
Qi Xian *China* **56 G8**
Qian Gorlos *China* **57 B13**
Qian Xian *China* **56 G5**
Qiancheng *China* **58 D7**
Qianjiang *Guangxi Zhuangzu, China* **58 F7**
Qianjiang *Hubei, China* **59 B9**
Qianjiang *Sichuan, China* **58 C7**
Qianshan *China* **59 B11**
Qianwei *China* **58 C4**
Qianxi *China* **58 D6**
Qianyang *Hunan, China* **59 D8**
Qianyang *Shaanxi, China* **56 G4**
Qianyang *Zhejiang, China* **59 B12**
Qiaojia *China* **58 D4**
Qichun *China* **59 B10**
Qidong *Hunan, China* **59 D9**
Qidong *Jiangsu, China* **59 B13**
Qijiang *China* **58 C6**
Qikiqtarjuaq *Canada* **101 C13**
Qilian Shan *China* **60 C4**
Qimen *China* **59 C11**
Qin He → *China* **56 G7**
Qin Jiang → *Guangxi Zhuangzu, China* **58 F7**
Qin Jiang → *Jiangxi, China* **59 D10**

Qin Ling = Qinling Shandi *China* **56 H5**
Qin'an *China* **56 G3**
Qing Xian *China* **56 E9**
Qingcheng *China* **57 F9**
Qingdao *China* **57 F11**
Qingfeng *China* **56 G8**
Qinghai □ *China* **60 C4**
Qinghai Hu *China* **60 C5**
Qinghecheng *China* **57 D13**
Qinghemen *China* **57 D11**
Qingjian *China* **56 F6**
Qingjiang = Huaiyin *China* **57 H10**
Qingliu *China* **59 D11**
Qinglong *China* **58 E5**
Qingping *China* **58 D6**
Qingpu *China* **59 B13**
Qingshui *China* **56 G4**
Qingshuihe *China* **56 E6**
Qingtian *China* **59 C13**
Qingtongxia Shuiku *China* **56 F3**
Qingxi *China* **58 D7**
Qingxu *China* **56 F7**
Qingyang *Anhui, China* **59 B11**
Qingyang *Gansu, China* **56 F4**
Qingyi Jiang → *China* **58 C4**
Qingyuan *Guangdong, China* **59 F9**
Qingyuan *Liaoning, China* **57 C13**
Qingyuan *Zhejiang, China* **59 D12**
Qingyun *China* **57 F9**
Qingzhen *China* **58 D6**
Qinhuangdao *China* **57 E10**
Qinling Shandi *China* **56 H5**
Qinshui *China* **56 G7**
Qinyang = Jiyuan *China* **56 G7**
Qinyuan *China* **56 F7**
Qinzhou *China* **58 G7**
Qionghai *China* **64 C8**
Qionglai *China* **58 B4**
Qionglai Shan *China* **58 B4**
Qiongzhou Haixia *China* **64 B8**
Qiqihar *China* **53 E13**
Qiraîya, W. → *Egypt* **74 E3**
Qiryat Ata *Israel* **74 C4**
Qiryat Gat *Israel* **74 D3**
Qiryat Mal'akhi *Israel* **74 D3**
Qiryat Shemona *Israel* **74 B4**
Qiryat Yam *Israel* **74 C4**
Qishan *China* **56 G4**
Qitai *China* **60 B3**
Qitaihe *China* **54 B5**
Qiubei *China* **58 E5**
Qixia *China* **57 F11**
Qiyang *China* **59 D8**
Qızılağac Körfäzi *Azerbaijan* **73 C13**
Qojūr *Iran* **70 B5**
Qom *Iran* **71 C6**
Qom □ *Iran* **71 C6**
Qomolangma Feng = Everest, Mt. *Nepal* **69 E12**
Qomsheh *Iran* **71 D6**
Qoqek = Tacheng *China* **60 B3**
Qoqon = Qŭqon *Uzbekistan* **52 E8**
Qoraqalpoghistan □ *Uzbekistan* **52 E6**
Qorveh *Iran* **73 E12**
Qostanay *Kazakhstan* **52 D7**
Qoţūr *Iran* **73 C11**
Qu Jiang → *China* **58 B6**
Qu Xian *China* **58 B6**
Quabbin Res. *U.S.A.* **115 D12**
Quairading *Australia* **93 F2**
Quakenbrück *Germany* **24 C3**
Quakertown *U.S.A.* **115 F9**
Qualicum Beach *Canada* **102 D4**
Quambatook *Australia* **95 F3**
Quambone *Australia* **95 E4**
Quamby *Australia* **94 C3**
Quan Long = Ca Mau *Vietnam* **65 H5**
Quanah *U.S.A.* **116 D5**
Quang Ngai *Vietnam* **64 E7**
Quang Tri *Vietnam* **64 D6**
Quang Yen *Vietnam* **58 G6**
Quannan *China* **59 E10**
Quanzhou *Fujian, China* **59 E12**
Quanzhou *Guangxi Zhuangzu, China* **59 E8**
Qu'Appelle → *Canada* **103 C8**
Quaqtaq *Canada* **101 C13**
Quaraí *Brazil* **126 C4**
Quarré-les-Tombes *France* **19 E11**
Quarteira *Portugal* **37 H2**
Quartu Sant'Élena *Italy* **42 C2**
Quartzsite *U.S.A.* **111 M12**
Quatre Bornes *Mauritius* **85 d**
Quatsino Sd. *Canada* **102 C3**
Quba *Azerbaijan* **35 K9**
Qūchān *Iran* **71 B8**
Queanbeyan *Australia* **95 F4**
Québec *Canada* **105 C5**
Québec □ *Canada* **105 C6**
Quebrada del Condorito △ *Argentina* **126 C3**
Quedlinburg *Germany* **24 D7**
Queen Alexandra Ra. *Antarctica* **5 E11**
Queen Charlotte City *Canada* **102 C2**

Queen Charlotte Is. *Canada* **102 C2**
Queen Charlotte Sd. *Canada* **102 C3**
Queen Charlotte Strait *Canada* **102 C3**
Queen Elizabeth △ *Uganda* **86 C3**
Queen Elizabeth △ *U.K.* **13 E4**
Queen Elizabeth Is. *Canada* **101 B10**
Queen Mary Land *Antarctica* **5 D7**
Queen Maud G. *Canada* **100 C9**
Queen Maud Land = Dronning Maud Land *Antarctica* **5 D3**
Queen Maud Mts. *Antarctica* **5 E13**
Queens Channel *Australia* **92 C4**
Queenscliff *Australia* **95 F3**
Queensland □ *Australia* **94 C3**
Queenstown *Australia* **95 G4**
Queenstown *N.Z.* **91 F2**
Queenstown *Singapore* **65 d**
Queenstown *S. Africa* **88 E4**
Queets *U.S.A.* **110 C2**
Queguay Grande → *Uruguay* **126 C4**
Queimadas *Brazil* **125 F11**
Quelimane *Mozam.* **87 F4**
Quellón *Chile* **128 E2**
Queluz *Portugal* **37 G1**
Quemado *N. Mex., U.S.A.* **109 J9**
Quemado *Tex., U.S.A.* **116 G4**
Quemoy = Chinmen *Taiwan* **59 E13**
Quemú-Quemú *Argentina* **126 D3**
Quequén *Argentina* **126 D4**
Querétaro *Mexico* **118 C4**
Querétaro □ *Mexico* **118 C5**
Querfurt *Germany* **24 D7**
Quérigut *France* **20 F6**
Querqueville *France* **18 C5**
Quesada *Spain* **37 H7**
Quesnel *Canada* **102 C4**
Quesnel → *Canada* **102 C4**
Quesnel L. *Canada* **102 C4**
Questa *U.S.A.* **109 H11**
Questembert *France* **18 E4**
Quetico △ *Canada* **104 C1**
Quetta *Pakistan* **68 D2**
Queyras *France* **21 D10**
Quezaltenango *Guatemala* **120 D1**
Quezon City *Phil.* **61 D4**
Qufār *Si. Arabia* **70 E4**
Qui Nhon *Vietnam* **64 F7**
Quibala *Angola* **84 G2**
Quibaxe *Angola* **84 F2**
Quibdó *Colombia* **124 B3**
Quiberon *France* **18 E3**
Quiberon, Presqu'île de *France* **18 E3**
Quickborn *Germany* **24 B5**
Quiet L. *Canada* **102 A2**
Quiindy *Paraguay* **126 B4**
Quilá *Mexico* **118 C3**
Quilán, C. *Chile* **128 E2**
Quilcene *U.S.A.* **110 C4**
Quilimarí *Chile* **126 C1**
Quilino *Argentina* **126 C3**
Quillabamba *Peru* **124 F4**
Quillagua *Chile* **126 A2**
Quillan *France* **20 F6**
Quillota *Chile* **126 C1**
Quilmes *Argentina* **126 C4**
Quilon *India* **66 Q10**
Quilpie *Australia* **95 D3**
Quilpué *Chile* **126 C1**
Quilua *Mozam.* **87 F4**
Quimilí *Argentina* **126 B3**
Quimper *France* **18 E2**
Quimperlé *France* **18 E3**
Quinault *U.S.A.* **110 C2**
Quincy *Calif., U.S.A.* **110 F6**
Quincy *Fla., U.S.A.* **117 F12**
Quincy *Ill., U.S.A.* **112 F8**
Quincy *Mass., U.S.A.* **115 D14**
Quincy *Wash., U.S.A.* **108 C4**
Quines *Argentina* **126 C2**
Quinga *Mozam.* **87 F5**
Quingey *France* **19 E12**
Quintana de la Serena *Spain* **37 G5**
Quintana Roo □ *Mexico* **119 D7**
Quintanar de la Orden *Spain* **37 F7**
Quintanar de la Sierra *Spain* **38 D2**
Quintanar del Rey *Spain* **39 F3**
Quintero *Chile* **126 C1**
Quintin *France* **18 D3**
Quinto *Spain* **38 D4**
Quípar → *Spain* **39 G3**
Quirihue *Chile* **126 D1**
Quirimbas △ *Mozam.* **87 E5**
Quirindi *Australia* **95 E5**
Quirinópolis *Brazil* **125 G8**
Quiroga *Spain* **36 C3**
Quissac *France* **21 E8**
Quissanga *Mozam.* **87 E5**
Quissico *Mozam.* **89 C6**
Quitilipi *Argentina* **126 B3**
Quitman *U.S.A.* **117 F13**
Quito *Ecuador* **124 D3**
Quixadá *Brazil* **125 D11**

Quixaxe *Mozam.* **87 F5**
Qujing *China* **58 E4**
Qulan *Kazakhstan* **52 E8**
Qul'ân, Jazâ'ir *Egypt* **70 E2**
Qulsary *Kazakhstan* **52 E6**
Qumbu *S. Africa* **89 E4**
Quneitra *Syria* **74 B4**
Qŭnghirot *Uzbekistan* **52 E6**
Qu'nyido *China* **58 B2**
Quoin I. *Australia* **92 B4**
Quoin Pt. *S. Africa* **88 E2**
Quorn *Australia* **95 E2**
Qŭqon *Uzbekistan* **52 E8**
Qurein *Sudan* **81 E3**
Qurnat as Sawdâ' *Lebanon* **74 A5**
Qûs *Egypt* **80 B3**
Qusar *Azerbaijan* **35 K9**
Quşaybā' *Si. Arabia* **70 E4**
Quşaybah *Iraq* **73 E9**
Quseir *Egypt* **70 E2**
Qūshchī *Iran* **73 D11**
Quthing *Lesotho* **89 E4**
Qūţīābād *Iran* **73 E13**
Quwo *China* **56 G6**
Quyang *China* **56 E8**
Quynh Nhai *Vietnam* **64 B4**
Quyon *Canada* **115 A8**
Quzhou *China* **59 C12**
Quzi *China* **56 F4**
Qvareli *Georgia* **35 K7**
Qyzylorda *Kazakhstan* **52 E7**

R

Ra, Ko *Thailand* **65 H2**
Raab *Austria* **26 C6**
Raahe *Finland* **8 D21**
Raalte *Neths.* **17 B6**
Raasay *U.K.* **13 D2**
Raasay, Sd. of *U.K.* **13 D2**
Rab *Croatia* **41 D11**
Raba *Indonesia* **63 F5**
Rába → *Hungary* **28 C3**
Raba → *Poland* **31 H7**
Rabaçal → *Portugal* **36 D3**
Rabah *Nigeria* **83 C6**
Rabai *Kenya* **86 C4**
Rabak *Sudan* **81 E3**
Rabastens *France* **20 E5**
Rabastens-de-Bigorre *France* **20 E4**
Rabat = Victoria *Malta* **49 C1**
Rabat *Malta* **49 D1**
Rabat *Morocco* **78 B4**
Rabaul *Papua N. G.* **90 B8**
Rabbit Flat *Australia* **92 D5**
Rabbit Lake Mine *Canada* **103 B8**
Rabi *Fiji* **91 a**
Rābigh *Si. Arabia* **75 C2**
Rabka *Poland* **31 J6**
Râbniţa *Moldova* **29 C14**
Rābor *Iran* **71 D8**
Rabwah = Chenab Nagar *Pakistan* **68 D5**
Rača *Serbia* **44 B4**
Răcăciuni *Romania* **29 D11**
Răcăşdia *Romania* **28 F6**
Racconigi *Italy* **40 D4**
Race, C. *Canada* **105 C9**
Rach Gia *Vietnam* **65 G5**
Rachid *Mauritania* **82 B2**
Raciąż *Poland* **31 F7**
Racibórz *Poland* **31 H5**
Racichy *Belarus* **30 E10**
Racine *U.S.A.* **112 D10**
Rackerby *U.S.A.* **110 F5**
Radama, Nosy *Madag.* **89 A8**
Radama, Saikanosy *Madag.* **89 A8**
Radan *Serbia* **44 D5**
Rădăuţi *Romania* **29 C10**
Rădăuţi-Prut *Romania* **29 B11**
Radbuza → *Czech Rep.* **26 B6**
Radcliff *U.S.A.* **113 G11**
Radeberg *Germany* **24 D9**
Radebeul *Germany* **24 D9**
Radeče *Slovenia* **41 B12**
Radekhiv *Ukraine* **23 C13**
Radekhov = Radekhiv *Ukraine* **23 C13**
Radenthein *Austria* **26 E6**
Radew → *Poland* **30 D2**
Radford *U.S.A.* **113 G13**
Radhanpur *India* **68 H4**
Radhwa, Jabal *Si. Arabia* **70 E4**
Radika → *Macedonia* **44 E4**
Radisson *Qué., Canada* **104 B3**
Radisson *Sask., Canada* **103 C7**
Radium Hot Springs *Canada* **102 C5**
Radlje ob Dravi *Slovenia* **41 B12**
Radnevo *Bulgaria* **45 D9**
Radnice *Czech Rep.* **26 B6**
Radnor Forest *U.K.* **15 E4**
Radolfzell *Germany* **25 H4**
Radom *Poland* **31 G8**
Radomir *Bulgaria* **44 D7**
Radomka → *Poland* **31 G8**
Radomsko *Poland* **31 G6**
Radomyshl *Ukraine* **23 C15**
Radomyśl Wielki *Poland* **31 H8**
Radoszyce *Poland* **31 G7**

Radoviš *Macedonia* **44** E6
Radovljica *Slovenia* **41** B11
Radstadt *Austria* **26** D6
Radstock, C. *Australia* **95** E1
Răducăneni *Romania* **29** D12
Raduša *Macedonia* **44** D5
Raduzhnyy *Russia* **52** C8
Radvanichy *Belarus* **31** F11
Radviliškis *Lithuania* **30** C10
Radville *Canada* **103** D8
Raḍwá, J. *Si. Arabia* **80** C4
Radymno *Poland* **31** J9
Radzanów *Poland* **31** F7
Radziejów *Poland* **31** F5
Radzyń Chełmiński *Poland* **30** E5
Radzyń Podlaski *Poland* **31** G9
Rae *Canada* **102** A5
Rae Bareli *India* **69** F9
Rae Isthmus *Canada* **101** C11
Raeren *Belgium* **17** D6
Raeside, L. *Australia* **93** E3
Raetihi *N.Z.* **91** C5
Rafaela *Argentina* **126** C3
Rafah *Gaza Strip* **74** D3
Rafai *C.A.R.* **86** B1
Raffadali *Italy* **42** E6
Raffili *Sudan* **81** F2
Rafḥā *Si. Arabia* **70** D4
Rafsanjān *Iran* **71** D8
Raft Pt. *Australia* **92** C3
Râgâ *Sudan* **81** F2
Raga → *Sudan* **81** F2
Ragachow *Belarus* **23** B16
Ragag *Sudan* **81** F1
Ragama *Sri Lanka* **66** R11
Ragged, Mt. *Australia* **93** F3
Ragged Pt. *Barbados* **121** g
Raghunathpalli *India* **69** H11
Raghunathpur *India* **69** H12
Raglan *N.Z.* **91** B5
Ragusa *Italy* **43** F7
Raha *Indonesia* **63** E6
Rahad, Nahr ed → *Sudan* **81** E3
Rahaeng = Tak *Thailand* **64** D2
Rahat, Ḥarrat *Si. Arabia* **80** C5
Rahatgarh *India* **69** H8
Rahden *Germany* **24** C4
Raheita *Eritrea* **81** E5
Rahimyar Khan *Pakistan* **68** E4
Rāhjerd *Iran* **71** C6
Rahon *India* **68** D7
Raiatéa, Î. *French Polynesia* **97** J12
Raichur *India* **66** L10
Raiganj *India* **69** G13
Raigarh *India* **67** J13
Raijua *Indonesia* **63** F6
Raikot *India* **68** D6
Railton *Australia* **95** G4
Rainbow Bridge △ *U.S.A.* **109** H8
Rainbow Lake *Canada* **102** B5
Rainier *U.S.A.* **110** D4
Rainier, Mt. *U.S.A.* **110** D5
Rainy, L. *Canada* **103** D10
Rainy River *Canada* **103** D10
Raippaluoto *Finland* **8** E19
Raipur *India* **67** J12
Ra'is *Si. Arabia* **80** C4
Raisen *India* **68** H8
Raisio *Finland* **32** B2
Raj Nandgaon *India* **67** J12
Raj Nilgiri *India* **69** J12
Raja, Ujung *Indonesia* **62** D1
Raja Ampat, Kepulauan *Indonesia* **63** E8
Rajahmundry *India* **67** L12
Rajaji △ *India* **68** D8
Rajang → *Malaysia* **62** D4
Rajanpur *Pakistan* **68** E4
Rajapalaiyam *India* **66** Q10
Rajasthan □ *India* **68** F5
Rajasthan Canal = Indira Gandhi Canal *India* **68** F5
Rajauri *India* **69** C6
Rajgarh *Mad. P., India* **68** G7
Rajgarh *Raj., India* **68** F7
Rajgarh *Raj., India* **68** E6
Rajgir *India* **69** G11
Rajgród *Poland* **30** E9
Rajkot *India* **68** H4
Rajmahal Hills *India* **69** G12
Rajpipla *India* **66** J8
Rajpur *India* **68** H6
Rajpura *India* **68** D7
Rajshahi *Bangla.* **67** G16
Rajshahi □ *Bangla.* **69** G13
Rajula *India* **68** J4
Rakaia *N.Z.* **91** E4
Rakaia → *N.Z.* **91** E4
Rakan, Ra's *Qatar* **71** E6
Rakaposhi *Pakistan* **69** A6
Rakata, Pulau *Indonesia* **62** F3
Rakhiv *Ukraine* **29** B9
Rakhni *Pakistan* **68** D3
Rakhni → *Pakistan* **68** E3
Rakhny-Lisovi *Ukraine* **29** B13
Rakiraki *Fiji* **91** a
Rakitnoye *Russia* **54** B7

Rakitovo *Bulgaria* **45** E8
Rakiura △ *N.Z.* **91** G1
Rakoniewice *Poland* **31** F3
Rakops *Botswana* **88** C3
Rakovica *Croatia* **41** D12
Rakovník *Czech Rep.* **26** A6
Rakovski *Bulgaria* **45** D8
Rakvere *Estonia* **32** C4
Raleigh *U.S.A.* **117** D15
Ralik Chain *Pac. Oc.* **96** G8
Ralja *Serbia* **44** B4
Ralls *U.S.A.* **116** E4
Ralston *U.S.A.* **114** E8
Ram → *Canada* **102** A4
Rām Allāh *West Bank* **74** D4
Rama *Nic.* **120** D3
Ramacca *Italy* **43** E7
Ramakona *India* **69** J8
Ramales de la Victoria *Spain* **36** B7
Rāmallāh = Rām Allāh *West Bank* **74** D4
Raman *Thailand* **65** J3
Ramanathapuram *India* **66** Q11
Ramanetaka, B. de *Madag.* **89** A8
Ramanujganj *India* **69** H10
Ramat Gan *Israel* **74** C3
Ramatlhabama *S. Africa* **88** D4
Ramban *India* **69** C6
Rambervillers *France* **19** D13
Rambi = Rabi *Fiji* **91** a
Rambipuji *Indonesia* **63** H15
Rambouillet *France* **19** D8
Rame Hd. *Australia* **95** F4
Ramechhap *Nepal* **69** F12
Ramenskoye *Russia* **32** E10
Ramganga → *India* **69** F8
Ramgarh *Jharkhand, India* **69** H11
Ramgarh *Raj., India* **68** F6
Ramgarh *Raj., India* **68** F4
Rāmhormoz *Iran* **71** D6
Ramīān *Iran* **71** B7
Ramingining *Australia* **94** A2
Ramla *Israel* **74** D3
Ramlu *Eritrea* **81** E5
Ramm = Rum *Jordan* **74** F4
Ramm, Jabal *Jordan* **74** F4
Râmna → *Romania* **29** E12
Ramnad = Ramanathapuram *India* **66** Q11
Ramnagar *Jammu & Kashmir, India* **69** C6
Ramnagar *Uttarakhand, India* **69** E8
Ramnäs *Sweden* **10** E10
Râmnicu Sărat *Romania* **29** E12
Râmnicu Vâlcea *Romania* **29** E9
Ramnous *Greece* **46** C6
Ramon *Russia* **33** G10
Ramona *U.S.A.* **111** M10
Ramonville-St-Agne *France* **20** E5
Ramore *Canada* **104** C3
Ramos → *Nigeria* **83** D6
Ramotswa *Botswana* **88** C4
Rampur *H.P., India* **68** D7
Rampur *Mad. P., India* **68** H5
Rampur *Ut. P., India* **69** E8
Rampur Hat *India* **69** G12
Rampura *India* **68** G6
Ramrama Tola *India* **69** J8
Ramree I. *Burma* **67** K19
Rāmsar *Iran* **71** B6
Ramsey *I. of Man* **14** C3
Ramsey *U.S.A.* **115** E10
Ramsey L. *Canada* **104** C3
Ramsgate *U.K.* **15** F9
Ramsjö *Sweden* **10** B9
Ramstein *Germany* **25** F3
Ramtek *India* **66** J11
Ramu *Kenya* **86** B5
Ramvik *Sweden* **10** B11
Rana Pratap Sagar Dam *India* **68** G6
Ranaghat *India* **69** H13
Ranahu *Pakistan* **68** G3
Ranau *Malaysia* **62** C5
Rancagua *Chile* **126** C1
Rance → *France* **18** D5
Rancheria → *Canada* **102** A3
Ranchester *U.S.A.* **108** D10
Ranchi *India* **69** H11
Rancho Cordova *U.S.A.* **110** G5
Rancho Cucamonga *U.S.A.* **111** L9
Randalstown *U.K.* **12** B5
Randan *France* **19** F10
Randazzo *Italy* **43** E7
Randers *Denmark* **11** H4
Randers Fjord *Denmark* **11** H4
Randfontein *S. Africa* **89** D4
Randle *U.S.A.* **110** D4
Randolph *Mass., U.S.A.* **115** D13
Randolph *N.Y., U.S.A.* **114** D6
Randolph *Utah, U.S.A.* **108** F8
Randolph *Vt., U.S.A.* **115** C12
Randsburg *U.S.A.* **111** K9
Rånessälven → *Sweden* **8** D20
Rangae *Thailand* **65** J3
Rangaunu B. *N.Z.* **91** A4
Range, The *Zimbabwe* **87** F3
Rangeley *U.S.A.* **115** B14
Rangeley L. *U.S.A.* **115** B14

Rangely *U.S.A.* **108** F9
Ranger *U.S.A.* **116** E5
Rangia *India* **67** F17
Rangiora *N.Z.* **91** E4
Rangitaiki → *N.Z.* **91** B6
Rangitata → *N.Z.* **91** E3
Rangitoto ke te tonga = D'Urville I. *N.Z.* **91** D4
Rangkasbitung *Indonesia* **63** G12
Rangon → *Burma* **67** L20
Rangoon *Burma* **67** L20
Rangpur *Bangla.* **67** G16
Rangsang *Indonesia* **65** M4
Rangsit *Thailand* **64** F3
Ranibennur *India* **66** M9
Raniganj *Ut. P., India* **69** F9
Raniganj *W. Bengal, India* **67** H15
Ranikhet *India* **69** E8
Raniwara *India* **68** G5
Rāniyah *Iraq* **73** D11
Ranka *India* **69** H10
Ranken → *Australia* **94** C2
Rankin *U.S.A.* **116** F4
Rankin Inlet *Canada* **100** C10
Rankins Springs *Australia* **95** E4
Rankweil *Austria* **26** D2
Rannoch, L. *U.K.* **13** E4
Rannoch Moor *U.K.* **13** E4
Ranobe, Helodranon' i *Madag.* **89** C7
Ranohira *Madag.* **89** C8
Ranomafana *Toamasina, Madag.* **89** B8
Ranomafana *Toliara, Madag.* **89** C8
Ranomafana △ *Madag.* **89** C8
Ranomena *Madag.* **89** C8
Ranong *Thailand* **65** H2
Ranotsara Nord *Madag.* **89** C8
Rānsa *Iran* **71** C6
Ransiki *Indonesia* **63** E8
Rantabe *Madag.* **89** B8
Rantauprapat *Indonesia* **62** D1
Rantemario *Indonesia* **63** E5
Ranthambore △ *India* **68** F7
Rantoul *U.S.A.* **112** E9
Ranum *Denmark* **11** H3
Ranyah, W. → *Si. Arabia* **80** C5
Raohe *China* **54** A7
Raon l'Étape *France* **19** D13
Raoping *China* **59** F11
Raoyang *China* **56** E8
Rap, Ko *Thailand* **65** b
Rapa *French Polynesia* **97** K13
Rapa Nui = Pascua, I. de *Chile* **97** K17
Rapallo *Italy* **40** D6
Rapar *India* **68** H4
Rāpch *Iran* **71** E8
Rapel, Lago *Chile* **126** C1
Raper, C. *Canada* **101** C13
Rapid City *U.S.A.* **112** C2
Rapid River *U.S.A.* **112** C10
Rapla *Estonia* **32** C3
Rapti → *India* **69** F10
Rapu Rapu I. *Phil.* **61** E6
Raqaba ez Zarqa → *Sudan* **81** F2
Raquette → *U.S.A.* **115** B10
Raquette Lake *U.S.A.* **115** C10
Rara △ *Nepal* **69** E10
Rarotonga *Cook Is.* **97** K12
Ra's al 'Ayn *Syria* **73** D9
Ra's al Khaymah *U.A.E.* **71** E7
Ra's at Tib *Tunisia* **76** C1
Râs el Mâ *Mali* **82** B4
Rás Ghârib *Egypt* **80** B3
Râs Mallap *Egypt* **80** B3
Rás Muhammad △ *Egypt* **80** B3
Râs Sudr *Egypt* **80** B3
Rasa, Pta. *Argentina* **126** E4
Rasca, Pta. de la *Canary Is.* **48** G3
Rășcani *Moldova* **29** C12
Raseiniai *Lithuania* **30** C10
Rashad *Sudan* **81** E3
Rashîd *Egypt* **80** H7
Rashîd, Masabb *Egypt* **80** H7
Rashmi *India* **68** G6
Rasht *Iran* **73** D13
Rasi Salai *Thailand* **64** E5
Raška *Serbia* **44** C4
Râsnov *Romania* **29** E10
Rason L. *Australia* **93** E3
Rașova *Romania* **29** F12
Rasovo *Bulgaria* **44** C7
Rasra *India* **69** G10
Rasskazovo *Russia* **34** D5
Rast *Romania* **29** G8
Rastatt *Germany* **25** G4
Rastede *Germany* **24** B4
Răstolița *Romania* **29** D9
Rasul *Pakistan* **68** C5
Raszków *Poland* **31** G4
Rat → *Canada* **103** D9
Rat Buri *Thailand* **64** F2
Rat Islands *U.S.A.* **106** a
Rat L. *Canada* **103** B9
Ratak Chain *Pac. Oc.* **96** G8
Rătan *Sweden* **10** B9
Ratangarh *India* **68** E6
Raṭāwī *Iraq* **70** D5

Rath *India* **69** G8
Rath Luirc *Ireland* **12** D3
Rathangan *Ireland* **12** C4
Rathdrum *Ireland* **12** D5
Rathenow *Germany* **24** C8
Rathkeale *Ireland* **12** D3
Rathlin I. *U.K.* **12** A5
Rathmelton *Ireland* **12** A4
Ratibor = Racibórz *Poland* **31** H5
Ratlam *India* **68** H6
Ratnagiri *India* **66** L8
Ratodero *Pakistan* **68** F3
Raton *U.S.A.* **109** H11
Rattaphum *Thailand* **65** J3
Ratten *Austria* **26** D8
Rattray Hd. *U.K.* **13** D7
Rättvik *Sweden* **10** D9
Ratz, Mt. *Canada* **102** B2
Raub *Malaysia* **65** L3
Rauch *Argentina* **126** D4
Raudales *Mexico* **119** D6
Raufarhöfn *Iceland* **8** C6
Raufoss *Norway* **8** F14
Raukumara Ra. *N.Z.* **91** C6
Rauma *Finland* **32** B1
Raumo = Rauma *Finland* **32** B1
Raung, Gunung *Indonesia* **63** J17
Raurkela *India* **69** H11
Rausu-Dake *Japan* **54** B12
Rava-Ruska *Ukraine* **31** H10
Rava Russkaya = Rava-Ruska *Ukraine* **31** H10
Ravalli *U.S.A.* **108** C6
Ravānsar *Iran* **73** E12
Ravanusa *Italy* **42** E6
Rāvar *Iran* **71** D8
Ravena *U.S.A.* **115** D11
Ravenna *Italy* **41** D9
Ravenna *Nebr., U.S.A.* **112** E4
Ravenna *Ohio, U.S.A.* **114** E3
Ravensburg *Germany* **25** H5
Ravenshoe *Australia* **94** B4
Ravensthorpe *Australia* **93** F3
Ravenswood *Australia* **94** C4
Ravenswood *U.S.A.* **113** F13
Ravi → *Pakistan* **68** D4
Ravna Gora *Croatia* **41** C11
Ravna Reka *Serbia* **44** B5
Ravne na Koroškem *Slovenia* **41** B11
Rawa Mazowiecka *Poland* **31** G7
Rawalpindi *Pakistan* **68** C5
Rawang *Malaysia* **65** L3
Rawene *N.Z.* **91** A4
Rawicz *Poland* **31** G3
Rawka → *Poland* **31** F7
Rawlinna *Australia* **93** F4
Rawlins *U.S.A.* **108** F10
Rawlinson Ra. *Australia* **93** D4
Rawson *Argentina* **128** E3
Raxaul *India* **69** F11
Ray *U.S.A.* **112** A2
Ray, C. *Canada* **105** C8
Raya Ring, Ko *Thailand* **65** a
Rayadurg *India* **66** M10
Rayagada *India* **67** K13
Raychikhinsk *Russia* **53** E13
Rāyen *Iran* **71** D8
Rayleigh *U.K.* **15** F8
Raymond *Canada* **102** D6
Raymond *Calif., U.S.A.* **110** H7
Raymond *N.H., U.S.A.* **115** C13
Raymond *Wash., U.S.A.* **110** D3
Raymondville *U.S.A.* **116** H6
Raymore *Canada* **103** C8
Rayón *Mexico* **118** B2
Rayong *Thailand* **64** F3
Raystown L. *U.S.A.* **114** F6
Rayville *U.S.A.* **116** E9
Raz, Pte. du *France* **18** D2
Razan *Iran* **73** E13
Razana *Serbia* **44** B3
Ražanj *Serbia* **44** C5
Razāzah, Buḥayrat ar *Iraq* **73** F10
Razāzah, L. = Razāzah, Buḥayrat ar *Iraq* **73** F10
Razdelna *Bulgaria* **45** C11
Razdel'naya = Rozdilna *Ukraine* **29** D15
Razdolnoye *Russia* **54** C5
Razdolnoye *Ukraine* **33** K7
Razeh *Iran* **71** C6
Razgrad *Bulgaria* **45** C10
Razim, Lacul *Romania* **29** F14
Razlog *Bulgaria* **44** E7
Razmak *Pakistan* **68** C3
Ré, Cu Lao *Vietnam* **64** E7
Ré, Î. de *France* **20** B2
Reading *U.K.* **15** F7
Reading *U.S.A.* **115** F9
Reading □ *U.K.* **15** F7
Realicó *Argentina* **126** D3
Réalmont *France* **20** E6
Ream *Cambodia* **65** G4
Ream △ *Cambodia* **65** G4

Reay Forest *U.K.* **13** C4
Rebais *France* **19** D10
Rebecca, L. *Australia* **93** F3
Rebi *Indonesia* **63** F8
Rebiana *Libya* **79** D10
Rebiana, Sahrâ' *Libya* **79** D10
Reboly *Russia* **8** E24
Rebun-Tō *Japan* **54** B10
Recanati *Italy* **41** E10
Recaş *Romania* **28** E6
Recco *Italy* **40** D6
Recherche, Arch. of the *Australia* **93** F3
Rechna Doab *Pakistan* **68** D5
Rechytsa *Belarus* **23** B16
Recife *Brazil* **125** E12
Recife *Seychelles* **85** b
Recklinghausen *Germany* **17** C7
Reconquista *Argentina* **126** B4
Recreo *Argentina* **126** B2
Recz *Poland* **31** E2
Red → *U.S.A.* **116** F9
Red Bank *U.S.A.* **115** F10
Red Bay *Canada* **105** B8
Red Bluff *U.S.A.* **108** F2
Red Bluff Res. *U.S.A.* **109** L12
Red Cliffs *Australia* **95** E3
Red Cloud *U.S.A.* **112** E4
Red Creek *U.S.A.* **115** C8
Red Deer *Canada* **102** C6
Red Deer → *Alta., Canada* **103** C7
Red Deer → *Man., Canada* **103** C8
Red Deer L. *Canada* **103** C8
Red Hook *U.S.A.* **115** E11
Red Indian L. *Canada* **105** C8
Red L. *Canada* **103** C10
Red Lake *Canada* **103** C10
Red Lake Falls *U.S.A.* **112** B5
Red Lake Road *Canada* **103** C10
Red Lodge *U.S.A.* **108** D9
Red Mountain *U.S.A.* **111** K9
Red Oak *U.S.A.* **112** E6
Red River of the North → *N. Amer.* **112** A5
Red Rock *Canada* **104** C2
Red Rock, L. *U.S.A.* **112** E7
Red Rocks Pt. *Australia* **93** F4
Red Sea *Asia* **75** C2
Red Slate Mt. *U.S.A.* **110** H8
Red Sucker L. *Canada* **104** B1
Red Tower Pass = Turnu Roşu, P. *Romania* **29** E9
Red Wing *U.S.A.* **112** C7
Reda *Poland* **30** D5
Redang *Malaysia* **65** K4
Redange *Lux.* **17** E5
Redcar *U.K.* **14** C6
Redcar & Cleveland □ *U.K.* **14** C7
Redcliff *U.S.A.* **108** A8
Redcliffe *Australia* **95** D5
Redcliffe, Mt. *Australia* **93** E3
Reddersburg *S. Africa* **88** D4
Redding *U.S.A.* **108** F2
Redditch *U.K.* **15** E6
Redfield *U.S.A.* **112** C4
Redford *U.S.A.* **115** B11
Redhead *Trin. & Tob.* **125** K16
Redkino *Russia* **32** D9
Redlands *U.S.A.* **111** M9
Redmond *Oreg., U.S.A.* **108** D3
Redmond *Wash., U.S.A.* **110** C4
Redon *France* **18** E4
Redonda *Antigua & B.* **121** C7
Redondela *Spain* **36** C2
Redondo *Portugal* **37** G3
Redondo Beach *U.S.A.* **111** M8
Redruth *U.K.* **15** G2
Redvers *Canada* **103** D8
Redwater *Canada* **102** C6
Redwood *U.S.A.* **115** B9
Redwood △ *U.S.A.* **108** F1
Redwood City *U.S.A.* **110** H4
Redwood Falls *U.S.A.* **112** C6
Ree, L. *Ireland* **12** C3
Reed City *U.S.A.* **113** D11
Reed L. *Canada* **103** C8
Reedley *U.S.A.* **110** J7
Reedsburg *U.S.A.* **112** D8
Reedsport *U.S.A.* **108** E1
Reedsville *U.S.A.* **114** F7
Reefton *N.Z.* **91** E3
Rees *Germany* **24** D2
Reese → *U.S.A.* **108** F5
Refahiye *Turkey* **73** C8
Reftele *Sweden* **11** G7
Refugio *U.S.A.* **116** G6
Rega → *Poland* **30** D2
Regalbuto *Italy* **43** E7
Regana, C. de *Spain* **48** B9
Regen *Germany* **25** G9
Regen → *Germany* **25** F8
Regensburg *Germany* **25** F8
Regenstauf *Germany* **25** F8
Reggâne = Zaouiet Reggâne *Algeria* **78** C6
Réggio di Calábria *Italy* **43** D8
Réggio nell'Emília *Italy* **40** D7
Reghin *Romania* **29** D9

Regina *Canada* **103** C8
Regina Beach *Canada* **103** C8
Registro *Brazil* **127** A6
Reguengos de Monsaraz *Portugal* **37** G3
Rehar → *India* **69** H10
Rehli *India* **69** H8
Rehoboth *Namibia* **88** C2
Rehovot *Israel* **74** D3
Reichenbach *Germany* **24** E8
Reid *Australia* **93** F4
Reidsville *U.S.A.* **117** C15
Reigate *U.K.* **15** F7
Reillo *Spain* **38** F3
Reims *France* **19** C11
Reina Adelaida, Arch. *Chile* **128** G2
Reina Sofía, Tenerife ✈ (TFS) *Canary Is.* **48** F3
Reinbek *Germany* **24** B6
Reindeer → *Canada* **103** B8
Reindeer I. *Canada* **103** C9
Reindeer L. *Canada* **103** B8
Reinga, C. *N.Z.* **91** A4
Reinosa *Spain* **36** B6
Reitz *S. Africa* **89** D4
Reivilo *S. Africa* **88** D3
Rejaf *Sudan* **81** G3
Rejmyre *Sweden* **11** F9
Rejowiec Fabryczny *Poland* **31** G10
Reka → *Slovenia* **41** C11
Rekovac *Serbia* **44** C5
Reliance *Canada* **103** A7
Rémalard *France* **18** D7
Remanso *Brazil* **125** E10
Remarkable, Mt. *Australia* **95** E2
Rembang *Indonesia* **63** G14
Remedios *Panama* **120** E3
Remeshk *Iran* **71** E9
Remetea *Romania* **29** D10
Remich *Lux.* **17** E6
Remiremont *France* **19** D13
Remo *Ethiopia* **81** F5
Remontnoye *Russia* **35** G6
Remoulins *France* **21** E8
Remscheid *Germany* **17** C7
Ren Xian *China* **56** F8
Rendang *Indonesia* **63** J18
Rende *Italy* **43** C9
Rendina *Greece* **46** B3
Rendsburg *Germany* **24** A5
Renfrew *Canada* **115** A8
Renfrew □ *U.K.* **13** F4
Renfrewshire □ *U.K.* **13** F4
Rengat *Indonesia* **62** E2
Rengo *Chile* **126** C1
Renhua *China* **59** E9
Renhuai *China* **58** D6
Reni *Ukraine* **29** E13
Renk *Sudan* **81** E3
Renmark *Australia* **95** E3
Rennell Sd. *Canada* **102** C2
Renner Springs *Australia* **94** B1
Rennes *France* **18** D5
Rennick Glacier *Antarctica* **5** D21
Rennie L. *Canada* **103** A7
Reno *U.S.A.* **110** F7
Reno → *Italy* **41** D9
Renovo *U.S.A.* **114** E7
Renqiu *China* **56** E9
Rens *Denmark* **11** K3
Renshou *China* **58** C5
Rensselaer *Ind., U.S.A.* **112** E10
Rensselaer *N.Y., U.S.A.* **115** D11
Renton *U.S.A.* **110** C4
Réo *Burkina Faso* **82** C4
Reocín = Puente San Miguel *Spain* **36** B6
Reotipur *India* **69** G10
Répcelak *Hungary* **28** C2
Republic *Mo., U.S.A.* **112** G7
Republic *Wash., U.S.A.* **108** B4
Republican → *U.S.A.* **112** F5
Repulse B. *Australia* **94** b4
Repulse Bay *Canada* **101** C11
Requena *Peru* **124** E4
Requena *Spain* **39** F3
Réquista *France* **20** D6
Reşadiye *Muğla, Turkey* **47** E9
Reşadiye *Tokat, Turkey* **72** B7
Reşadiye Yarımadası *Turkey* **47** E9
Resavica *Serbia* **44** B5
Resen *Macedonia* **44** E5
Reserve *U.S.A.* **109** K9
Resht = Rasht *Iran* **73** D13
Resistencia *Argentina* **126** B4
Reşiţa *Romania* **28** E6
Resko *Poland* **30** E2
Reso = Raisio *Finland* **32** B2
Resolute *Canada* **101** B10
Resolution I. *Canada* **101** C13
Resolution I. *N.Z.* **91** F1
Ressano Garcia *Mozam.* **89** D5
Reston *Canada* **103** D8
Reszel *Poland* **30** D8
Retalhuleu *Guatemala* **120** D1
Retenue, L. de *Dem. Rep. of the Congo* **87** E2
Retezat, Munţii *Romania* **28** E8
Retezat △ *Romania* **28** E7
Retford *U.K.* **14** D7

Rethel *France* **19** C11
Rethem *Germany* **24** C5
Rethimno *Greece* **49** D6
Rethimno □ *Greece* **49** D6
Reti *Pakistan* **68** E3
Retiche, Alpi *Switz.* **25** J6
Retiers *France* **18** E5
Retortillo *Spain* **36** E4
Retournac *France* **21** C8
Rétság *Hungary* **28** C4
Réunion ☑ *Ind. Oc.* **85** c
Reus *Spain* **38** D6
Reuterstadt Stavenhagen
  Germany **24** B8
Reutlingen *Germany* **25** G5
Reutte *Austria* **26** D3
Reval = Tallinn *Estonia* **32** C3
Revel *France* **20** E6
Revelganj *India* **69** G11
Revelstoke *Canada* **102** C5
Reventazón *Peru* **124** E3
Revigny-sur-Ornain *France* **19** D11
Revillagigedo, Is. de *Pac. Oc.*
  118 D2
Revin *France* **19** C11
Revúca *Slovak Rep.* **27** C13
Revuè → *Mozam.* **87** F3
Rewa *India* **69** G9
Rewari *India* **68** E7
Rexburg *U.S.A.* **108** E8
Rey *Iran* **71** C6
Rey, I. del *Panama* **120** E4
Rey, L. del *Mexico* **118** B4
Rey Malabo *Eq. Guin.* **83** E6
Reyðarfjörður *Iceland* **8** D6
Reyes, Pt. *U.S.A.* **110** H3
Reyhanlı *Turkey* **72** D7
Reykjahlið *Iceland* **8** D5
Reykjanes *Iceland* **8** D2
Reykjavík *Iceland* **8** D3
Reynolds Ra. *Australia* **92** D5
Reynoldsville *U.S.A.* **114** E6
Reynosa *Mexico* **119** B5
Rēzekne *Latvia* **32** D4
Rezina *Moldova* **29** C13
Rezovo *Bulgaria* **45** D12
Rezvān *Iran* **71** E8
Rezvānshahr *Iran* **73** D13
Rgotina *Serbia* **44** B6
Rhayader *U.K.* **15** E4
Rheda-Wiedenbrück
  Germany **24** D4
Rhede *Germany* **24** D2
Rhein → *Europe* **17** C6
Rhein-Main-Donau-Kanal
  Germany **25** F7
Rhein-Ruhr, Düsseldorf ✈
  (DUS) *Germany* **24** D2
Rhein-Taunus △ *Germany* **25** E4
Rhein-Westerwald △
  Germany **24** E3
Rheinbach *Germany* **24** E2
Rheine *Germany* **24** C3
Rheinfelden *Germany* **25** H3
Rheinhessen-Pfalz □
  Germany **25** F3
Rheinland-Pfalz □ *Germany* **25** E2
Rheinsberg *Germany* **24** B8
Rhin = Rhein → *Europe* **17** C6
Rhine = Rhein → *Europe* **17** C6
Rhinebeck *U.S.A.* **115** E11
Rhineland-Palatinate =
  Rheinland-Pfalz □
  Germany **25** E2
Rhinelander *U.S.A.* **112** C9
Rhinns Pt. *U.K.* **13** F2
Rhino Camp *Uganda* **86** B3
Rhir, Cap *Morocco* **78** B4
Rho *Italy* **40** C6
Rhode Island □ *U.S.A.* **115** E13
Rhodes *Greece* **49** C10
Rhodes ✈ (RHO) *Greece* **47** E10
Rhodope Mts. = Rhodopi
  Planina *Bulgaria* **45** E8
Rhodopi Planina *Bulgaria* **45** E8
Rhön *Germany* **24** E5
Rhondda *U.K.* **15** F4
Rhondda Cynon Taff □ *U.K.* **15** F4
Rhône □ *France* **21** C8
Rhône → *France* **21** E8
Rhône-Alpes □ *France* **21** C9
Rhum *U.K.* **13** E2
Rhyl *U.K.* **14** D4
Ri-Aba *Eq. Guin.* **83** E6
Ria Formosa △ *Portugal* **37** H3
Riachão *Brazil* **125** E9
Riangnom *Sudan* **81** F3
Riaño *Spain* **36** C6
Rians *France* **21** E9
Riansáres → *Spain* **37** F7
Riasi *India* **69** C6
Riau □ *Indonesia* **62** E2
Riau, Kepulauan *Indonesia* **62** D2
Riau Arch. = Riau,
  Kepulauan *Indonesia* **62** D2
Riaza *Spain* **36** D7
Riaza → *Spain* **36** D7
Riba de Saelices *Spain* **38** E2
Riba-roja de Túria *Spain* **39** F4

Ribadavia *Spain* **36** C2
Ribadeo *Spain* **36** B3
Ribadesella *Spain* **36** B5
Ribado *Nigeria* **83** D7
Ribao *Cameroon* **83** D7
Ribas = Ribes de Freser
  Spain **38** C7
Ribas do Rio Pardo *Brazil* **125** H8
Ribauè *Mozam.* **87** E4
Ribble → *U.K.* **14** D5
Ribe *Denmark* **11** J2
Ribeauvillé *France* **19** D14
Ribécourt-Dreslincourt
  France **19** C9
Ribeira = Santa Uxía de
  Ribeira *Spain* **36** C2
Ribeira Brava *Madeira* **48** D2
Ribeira Grande *C. Verde Is.* **78** b
Ribeirão Prêto *Brazil* **127** A6
Ribemont *France* **19** C10
Ribera *Italy* **42** E6
Ribérac *France* **20** C4
Ribes de Freser *Spain* **38** C7
Ribnica *Slovenia* **41** C11
Ribnitz-Damgarten *Germany* **24** A8
Ričany *Czech Rep.* **26** B7
Riccarton *N.Z.* **91** E4
Riccia *Italy* **43** A7
Riccione *Italy* **41** E9
Rice *U.S.A.* **111** L12
Rice L. *Canada* **114** B6
Rice Lake *U.S.A.* **112** C8
Rich, C. *Canada* **114** B4
Richard Toll *Senegal* **82** B1
Richards Bay *S. Africa* **89** D5
Richardson → *Canada* **103** B6
Richardson Lakes *U.S.A.* **113** C18
Richardson Springs *U.S.A.* **110** F5
Riche, C. *Australia* **93** F2
Richelieu *France* **18** E7
Richey *U.S.A.* **108** C11
Richfield *U.S.A.* **108** G7
Richfield Springs *U.S.A.* **115** D10
Richford *U.S.A.* **115** B12
Richibucto *Canada* **105** C7
Richland *Ga., U.S.A.* **117** E12
Richland *Wash., U.S.A.* **108** C4
Richland Center *U.S.A.* **112** D8
Richlands *U.S.A.* **113** G13
Richmond *Australia* **94** C3
Richmond *N.Z.* **91** D4
Richmond *U.K.* **14** C6
Richmond *Calif., U.S.A.* **110** H4
Richmond *Ind., U.S.A.* **113** F11
Richmond *Ky., U.S.A.* **113** G11
Richmond *Mich., U.S.A.* **114** D2
Richmond *Mo., U.S.A.* **112** F7
Richmond *Tex., U.S.A.* **116** G7
Richmond *Utah, U.S.A.* **108** F8
Richmond *Va., U.S.A.* **113** G15
Richmond *Vt., U.S.A.* **115** B12
Richmond Hill *Canada* **114** C5
Richmond Ra. *Australia* **95** D5
Richmondville *U.S.A.* **115** D10
Richtersveld △ *S. Africa* **88** D2
Richville *U.S.A.* **115** B9
Richwood *U.S.A.* **113** F13
Ricla *Spain* **38** D3
Ridder = Leninogorsk
  Kazakhstan **52** D9
Riddlesburg *U.S.A.* **114** F6
Ridgecrest *U.S.A.* **111** K9
Ridgefield *Conn., U.S.A.* **115** E11
Ridgefield *Wash., U.S.A.* **110** E4
Ridgeland *Miss., U.S.A.* **117** E9
Ridgeland *S.C., U.S.A.* **117** E14
Ridgetown *Canada* **114** D3
Ridgewood *U.S.A.* **115** F10
Ridgway *U.S.A.* **114** E6
Riding Mountain △ *Canada* **103** C9
Ridley, Mt. *Australia* **93** F3
Riebeek-Oos *S. Africa* **88** E4
Ried *Austria* **26** C6
Riedlingen *Germany* **25** G5
Riedstadt *Germany* **25** F4
Rienza → *Italy* **41** B8
Riesa *Germany* **24** D9
Riesi *Italy* **43** E7
Riet → *S. Africa* **88** D3
Rietavas *Lithuania* **30** C8
Rietbron *S. Africa* **88** E3
Rietfontein *Namibia* **88** C3
Rieti *Italy* **41** F9
Rieupeyroux *France* **20** D6
Riez *France* **21** E10
Rif = Er Rif *Morocco* **78** A5
Riffe L. *U.S.A.* **110** D4
Rifle *U.S.A.* **108** G10
Rift Valley *Africa* **76** G7
Rift Valley □ *Kenya* **86** B4
Rīga *Latvia* **30** B11
Rīga ✈ (RIX) *Latvia* **30** B10
Riga, G. of *Latvia* **30** D6
Rigacikun *Nigeria* **83** C6
Rīgān *Iran* **71** D8
Rīgas Jūras Līcis = Riga, G.
  of *Latvia* **30** A10
Rigaud *Canada* **115** A10

Rigby *U.S.A.* **108** E8
Rigestān *Afghan.* **66** D4
Riggins *U.S.A.* **108** D5
Rignac *France* **20** D6
Rigolet *Canada* **105** B8
Rihand Dam *India* **69** G10
Riihimäki *Finland* **32** B3
Riiser-Larsen-halvøya
  Antarctica **5** D4
Riiser-Larsen Ice Shelf
  S. Ocean **5** D2
Riiser-Larsen Sea *S. Ocean* **5** C4
Rijau *Nigeria* **83** C6
Rijeka *Croatia* **41** C11
Rijeka Crnojevića
  Montenegro **44** D3
Rijssen *Neths.* **17** B6
Rika → *Ukraine* **29** B8
Rike *Ethiopia* **81** E4
Rikuchū-Kaigan △ *Japan* **54** E11
Rikuzentakada *Japan* **54** E10
Rila *Bulgaria* **44** D7
Rila Planina *Bulgaria* **44** D7
Riley *U.S.A.* **108** E4
Rima → *Nigeria* **83** C6
Rimah, Wadi ar → *Si. Arabia* **70** E4
Rimau, Pulau *Malaysia* **65** c
Rimbey *Canada* **102** C6
Rimbo *Sweden* **10** E12
Rimersburg *U.S.A.* **114** E5
Rimforsa *Sweden* **11** F9
Rimi *Nigeria* **83** C6
Rímini *Italy* **41** D9
Rimouski *Canada* **105** C6
Rimrock *U.S.A.* **110** C3
Rinca *Indonesia* **63** F5
Rincón de la Victoria *Spain* **37** J6
Rincón de Romos *Mexico* **118** C4
Rinconada *Argentina* **126** A2
Rind → *India* **69** G9
Ringarum *Sweden* **11** F10
Ringas *India* **68** F6
Ringe *Denmark* **11** J4
Ringgold Is. *Fiji* **91** a
Ringim *Nigeria* **83** C6
Ringkøbing *Denmark* **11** H2
Ringkøbing Fjord *Denmark* **11** H2
Ringsjön *Sweden* **11** J7
Ringsted *Denmark* **11** J5
Ringvassøya *Norway* **8** B18
Ringwood *U.S.A.* **115** E10
Rinia *Greece* **47** D7
Rinjani *Indonesia* **62** F5
Rinteln *Germany* **24** C5
Río, Punta del *Spain* **39** J2
Rio Branco *Brazil* **124** E5
Río Branco *Uruguay* **127** C5
Río Bravo *Mexico* **119** B5
Río Bravo → *Mexico* **118** B4
Río Bravo del Norte →
  Mexico **119** B5
Rio Brilhante *Brazil* **127** A5
Rio Claro *Brazil* **127** A6
Rio Claro *Trin. & Tob.* **121** D7
Río Colorado *Argentina* **128** D4
Río Cuarto *Argentina* **126** C3
Rio das Pedras *Mozam.* **89** C6
Rio de Janeiro *Brazil* **127** A7
Rio de Janeiro □ *Brazil* **127** A7
Rio do Sul *Brazil* **127** B6
Río Dulce △ *Guatemala* **120** C2
Río Gallegos *Argentina* **128** G3
Río Grande *Argentina* **128** G3
Rio Grande *Brazil* **127** C5
Río Grande *Mexico* **118** C4
Río Grande *Puerto Rico* **121** d
Rio Grande → *N. Amer.* **116** J6
Rio Grande City *U.S.A.* **116** H5
Río Grande de Santiago →
  Mexico **118** C3
Rio Grande do Norte □
  Brazil **125** E11
Rio Grande do Sul □ *Brazil* **127** C5
Río Hato *Panama* **120** E3
Río Lagartos *Mexico* **119** C7
Rio Largo *Brazil* **125** E11
Rio Maior *Portugal* **37** F2
Rio Marina *Italy* **40** F7
Río Mulatos *Bolivia* **124** G5
Río Muni □ *Eq. Guin.* **84** D2
Rio Negro *Brazil* **127** B6
Rio Pardo *Brazil* **127** C5
Río Pilcomayo △ *Argentina* **126** B4
Río Platano △ *Honduras* **120** C3
Rio Rancho *U.S.A.* **109** J10
Río Segundo *Argentina* **126** C3
Rio Tercero *Argentina* **126** C3
Rio Tinto *Portugal* **36** D2
Rio Verde *Brazil* **125** G8
Río Verde *Mexico* **119** C5
Rio Vista *U.S.A.* **110** G5
Ríobamba *Ecuador* **124** D3
Ríohacha *Colombia* **124** A4
Riom *France* **20** C7
Riom-ès-Montagnes *France* **20** C6
Rion-des-Landes *France* **20** E3
Rionero in Vúlture *Italy* **43** B8

Rioni → *Georgia* **35** J5
Ríos *Spain* **36** D3
Ríosucio *Colombia* **124** B3
Riou L. *Canada* **103** B7
Ripatransone *Italy* **41** F10
Ripley *Canada* **114** B3
Ripley *Calif., U.S.A.* **111** M12
Ripley *N.Y., U.S.A.* **114** D5
Ripley *Tenn., U.S.A.* **117** D10
Ripley *W. Va., U.S.A.* **113** F13
Ripoll *Spain* **38** C7
Ripon *U.K.* **14** C6
Ripon *Calif., U.S.A.* **110** H5
Ripon *Wis., U.S.A.* **112** D9
Riposto *Italy* **43** E8
Risan *Montenegro* **44** D2
Riscle *France* **20** E3
Rishā', W. ar → *Si. Arabia* **70** E5
Rishiri-Rebun-
  Sarobetsu △ *Japan* **54** B10
Rishiri-Tō *Japan* **54** B10
Rishon le Ziyyon *Israel* **74** D3
Risle → *France* **18** C7
Risnjak △ *Croatia* **41** C11
Rison *U.S.A.* **116** E8
Risør *Norway* **9** G13
Rita Blanca Cr. → *U.S.A.* **116** D3
Riti *Nigeria* **83** D6
Ritter, Mt. *U.S.A.* **110** H7
Rittman *U.S.A.* **114** F3
Ritzville *U.S.A.* **108** C4
Riva del Garda *Italy* **40** C7
Riva Lígure *Italy* **40** D7
Rivadavia *B. Aires, Argentina*
  126 D3
Rivadavia *Mendoza,
  Argentina* **126** C2
Rivadavia *Salta, Argentina* **126** A3
Rivadavia *Chile* **126** B1
Rivarolo Canavese *Italy* **40** C4
Rivas *Nic.* **120** D2
Rivash *Iran* **71** C8
Rive-de-Gier *France* **21** C8
River Cess *Liberia* **82** D3
River Jordan *Canada* **110** B2
Rivera *Argentina* **126** D3
Rivera *Uruguay* **127** C4
Riverbank *U.S.A.* **110** H6
Riverdale *U.S.A.* **110** J7
Riverhead *U.S.A.* **115** F12
Riverhurst *Canada* **103** C7
Rivers *Canada* **103** C8
Rivers □ *Nigeria* **83** E6
Rivers Inlet *Canada* **102** C3
Riversdale *Canada* **114** B3
Riversdale *S. Africa* **88** E3
Riverside *U.S.A.* **111** M9
Riverton *Australia* **95** E2
Riverton *Canada* **103** C9
Riverton *N.Z.* **91** G2
Riverton *U.S.A.* **108** E9
Rives *France* **21** C9
Rivesaltes *France* **20** F6
Riviera *U.S.A.* **111** K12
Riviera di Levante *Italy* **40** D6
Riviera di Ponente *Italy* **40** D5
Rivière-au-Renard *Canada* **105** C7
Rivière-du-Loup *Canada* **105** C6
Rivière-Pentecôte *Canada* **105** C6
Rivière-Pilote *Martinique* **120** c
Rivière St-Paul *Canada* **105** B8
Rivière-Salée *Martinique* **120** c
Rivne *Odesa, Ukraine* **29** D14
Rivne *Rivne, Ukraine* **23** C14
Rivne □ *Ukraine* **33** G4
Rívoli *Italy* **40** C4
Rivoli B. *Australia* **95** F3
Rixheim *France* **19** E14
Riyadh = Ar Riyāḍ *Si. Arabia* **70** E5
Riyadh al Khabrā' *Si. Arabia* **70** E4
Riza *Greece* **44** F7
Rize *Turkey* **73** B9
Rize □ *Turkey* **73** B9
Rizhao *China* **57** G10
Rizokarpaso *Cyprus* **49** D13
Rizzuto, C. *Italy* **43** D10
Rjukan *Norway* **9** G13
Ro *Greece* **47** E11
Roa *Spain* **36** D7
Road Town *Br. Virgin Is.* **121** e
Roan Plateau *U.S.A.* **108** G9
Roanne *France* **19** F11
Roanoke *Ala., U.S.A.* **117** E12
Roanoke *Va., U.S.A.* **113** G14
Roanoke → *U.S.A.* **117** D16
Roanoke I. *U.S.A.* **117** D17
Roanoke Rapids *U.S.A.* **117** C16
Roatán *Honduras* **120** C2
Robāt *Iran* **73** E12
Robāt Sang *Iran* **71** C8
Robāṭkarīm *Iran* **71** C6
Robbins I. *Australia* **95** G4
Róbbio *Italy* **40** C5
Robe → *Australia* **92** D2
Röbel *Germany* **24** B8
Robert Bourassa, Rés.
  Canada **104** B4
Robert Lee *U.S.A.* **116** F4

Robertsdale *U.S.A.* **114** F6
Robertsganj *India* **69** G10
Robertson *S. Africa* **88** E2
Robertson I. *Antarctica* **5** C18
Robertson Ra. *Australia* **92** D3
Robertsport *Liberia* **82** D2
Robertstown *Australia* **95** E2
Roberval *Canada* **105** C5
Robeson Chan. *N. Amer.* **4** A4
Robesonia *U.S.A.* **115** F8
Robi *Ethiopia* **81** F4
Robinson *U.S.A.* **112** F10
Robinson → *Australia* **94** B2
Robinson Crusoe I. *Pac. Oc.* **122** F2
Robinson Ra. *Australia* **93** E2
Robinvale *Australia* **95** E3
Robledo *Spain* **39** G2
Roblin *Canada* **103** C8
Roboré *Bolivia* **124** G7
Robson, Mt. *Canada* **102** C5
Robstown *U.S.A.* **116** H6
Roca, C. da *Portugal* **37** G1
Roca Partida, I. *Mexico* **118** D2
Rocamadour *France* **20** D5
Rocas, I. *Brazil* **125** C12
Rocca San Casciano *Italy* **41** D8
Roccadáspide *Italy* **43** B8
Roccastrada *Italy* **41** F8
Roccella Iónica *Italy* **43** D9
Rocciamelone, Monte =
  Roche Melon *Italy* **21** C11
Rocha *Uruguay* **127** C5
Rochdale *U.K.* **14** D5
Roche Melon *Italy* **21** C11
Rochechouart *France* **20** C4
Rochefort *Belgium* **17** D5
Rochefort *France* **20** C3
Rochefort-en-Terre *France* **18** E4
Rochelle *U.S.A.* **112** E9
Rocher River *Canada* **102** A6
Rocheservière *France* **18** F5
Rochester *U.K.* **15** F8
Rochester *Ind., U.S.A.* **112** E10
Rochester *Minn., U.S.A.* **112** C8
Rochester *N.H., U.S.A.* **115** C14
Rochester *N.Y., U.S.A.* **114** C7
Rociu *Romania* **29** F10
Rock → *Canada* **102** A3
Rock, The *Australia* **95** F5
Rock Creek *U.S.A.* **114** E4
Rock Falls *U.S.A.* **112** E9
Rock Hill *U.S.A.* **117** D14
Rock Island *U.S.A.* **112** E8
Rock Port *U.S.A.* **112** E6
Rock Rapids *U.S.A.* **112** D5
Rock Sound *Bahamas* **120** B4
Rock Springs *Mont., U.S.A.* **108** C10
Rock Springs *Wyo., U.S.A.* **108** F9
Rock Valley *U.S.A.* **112** D5
Rockall *Atl. Oc.* **6** D3
Rockdale *Tex., U.S.A.* **116** F6
Rockdale *Wash., U.S.A.* **110** C5
Rockeby = Mungkan
  Kandju △ *Australia* **94** A3
Rockefeller Plateau
  Antarctica **5** E14
Rockford *U.S.A.* **112** D9
Rockglen *Canada* **103** D7
Rockhampton *Australia* **94** C5
Rockingham *Australia* **93** F2
Rockingham *N.C., U.S.A.* **117** D15
Rockingham *Vt., U.S.A.* **115** C12
Rockingham B. *Australia* **94** B4
Rocklake *U.S.A.* **112** A4
Rockland *Canada* **115** A9
Rockland *Idaho, U.S.A.* **108** E7
Rockland *Maine, U.S.A.* **113** C19
Rockland *Mich., U.S.A.* **112** B9
Rockly B. *Trin. & Tob.* **125** J16
Rockmart *U.S.A.* **117** D12
Rockport *Mass., U.S.A.* **115** D14
Rockport *Tex., U.S.A.* **116** G6
Rocksprings *U.S.A.* **116** F4
Rockville *Conn., U.S.A.* **115** E12
Rockville *Md., U.S.A.* **113** F15
Rockwall *U.S.A.* **116** E6
Rockwood *Canada* **114** C4
Rockwood *Maine, U.S.A.* **113** C19
Rockwood *Tenn., U.S.A.* **117** D12
Rocky Ford *U.S.A.* **108** G12
Rocky Gully *Australia* **93** F2
Rocky Harbour *Canada* **105** C8
Rocky Island L. *Canada* **104** C3
Rocky Lane *Canada* **102** B5
Rocky Mount *U.S.A.* **117** D16
Rocky Mountain △ *U.S.A.* **108** F11
Rocky Mountain House
  Canada **102** C6
Rocky Mts. *N. Amer.* **108** B6
Rocky Point *Namibia* **88** B2
Rocroi *France* **19** C11
Rod *Pakistan* **68** E3
Roda *Greece* **49** A3
Ródb *Denmark* **11** K5
Rødbyhavn *Denmark* **11** K5
Roddickton *Canada* **105** B8
Rødding *Denmark* **11** J3

Rödeby *Sweden* **11** H9
Rødekro *Denmark* **11** J3
Rodenkirchen *Germany* **24** B4
Rodez *France* **20** D6
Ródhos = Rhodes *Greece* **49** C10
Rodi Gargánico *Italy* **41** G12
Rodia *Greece* **49** D7
Rodna *Romania* **29** C9
Rodnei, Munţii *Romania* **29** C9
Rodney *Canada* **114** D3
Rodney, C. *N.Z.* **91** B5
Rodniki *Russia* **34** B7
Rodolivos *Greece* **44** F7
Rodopi □ *Greece* **45** E9
Rodopos *Greece* **49** D5
Rodriguez *Ind. Oc.* **3** E13
Roe → *U.K.* **12** A5
Roebling *U.S.A.* **115** F10
Roebourne *Australia* **92** D2
Roebuck B. *Australia* **92** C3
Roermond *Neths.* **17** C6
Roes Welcome Sd. *Canada* **101** C11
Roeselare *Belgium* **17** D3
Rogachev = Ragachow
  Belarus **23** B16
Rogagica *Serbia* **44** B3
Rogagua, L. *Bolivia* **124** F5
Rogaška Slatina *Slovenia* **41** B12
Rogatec *Slovenia* **41** B12
Rogatica *Bos.-H.* **28** G4
Rogatyn *Ukraine* **23** D13
Rogers *U.S.A.* **116** C7
Rogers City *U.S.A.* **113** C12
Rogersville *Canada* **105** C6
Roggan → *Canada* **104** B4
Roggan L. *Canada* **104** B4
Roggeveen Basin *Pac. Oc.* **97** L18
Roggeveldberge *S. Africa* **88** E3
Roggiano Gravina *Italy* **43** C9
Rogliano *France* **21** F13
Rogliano *Italy* **43** C9
Rogoaguado, L. *Bolivia* **124** F5
Rogojampi *Indonesia* **63** J17
Rogoźno *Poland* **31** F3
Rogue → *U.S.A.* **108** E1
Rohan *France* **18** D4
Rohri *Pakistan* **68** F3
Rohri Canal *Pakistan* **68** F3
Rohtak *India* **68** E7
Roi Et *Thailand* **64** D4
Roja *Latvia* **30** A9
Rojas *Argentina* **126** C3
Rojişte *Romania* **29** F8
Rojo, C. *Mexico* **119** C5
Rokan → *Indonesia* **62** D2
Rokel → *S. Leone* **82** D2
Rokiškis *Lithuania* **32** E3
Rokitno *Russia* **33** G8
Rokycany *Czech Rep.* **26** B6
Rolândia *Brazil* **127** A5
Rolla *Mo., U.S.A.* **112** G8
Rolla *N. Dak., U.S.A.* **112** A4
Rolleston *Australia* **94** C4
Rollingstone *Australia* **94** B4
Rom *Sudan* **81** F3
Roma *Australia* **95** D4
Roma *Italy* **41** G9
Roma *Sweden* **11** G12
Roma Fiumicino ✈ (FCO)
  Italy **41** G9
Roma-Los Saenz *U.S.A.* **116** H5
Romain, C. *U.S.A.* **117** E15
Romaine → *Canada* **105** B7
Roman *Bulgaria* **44** C7
Roman *Romania* **29** D11
Roman-Kosh, Gora *Ukraine* **33** K8
Romanche → *France* **21** C9
Romang *Indonesia* **63** F7
Români *Egypt* **74** E1
Romania ■ *Europe* **29** D10
Romanija *Bos.-H.* **28** G4
Romano, Cayo *Cuba* **120** B4
Romans-sur-Isère *France* **21** C9
Romanshorn *Switz.* **25** H5
Rombari *Sudan* **81** G3
Romblon *Phil.* **61** E5
Rome = Roma *Italy* **41** G9
Rome *Ga., U.S.A.* **117** D12
Rome *N.Y., U.S.A.* **115** C9
Rome *Pa., U.S.A.* **115** E8
Rometta *Italy* **43** D8
Romilly-sur-Seine *France* **19** D10
Romney *U.S.A.* **113** F14
Romney Marsh *U.K.* **15** F8
Romny *Ukraine* **33** G7
Rømø *Denmark* **11** J2
Romodan *Ukraine* **33** G7
Romodanovo *Russia* **34** C7
Romont *Switz.* **25** J2
Romorantin-Lanthenay
  France **19** E8
Romsdalen *Norway* **8** E12
Romsey *U.K.* **15** G6
Ron *Vietnam* **64** D6
Rona *U.K.* **13** D3
Ronan *U.S.A.* **108** C6
Roncador, Cayos *Colombia* **120** D3

Roncador, Serra do *Brazil* **125** F8
Ronciglione *Italy* **41** F9
Ronco → *Italy* **41** D9
Ronda *Spain* **37** J5
Ronda, Serranía de *Spain* **37** J5
Rondane *Norway* **8** F13
Rondônia □ *Brazil* **124** F6
Rondonópolis *Brazil* **125** G8
Rondu *Pakistan* **69** B6
Rong, Koh *Cambodia* **65** G4
Rong Jiang → *China* **58** E7
Rong Xian
   Guangxi Zhuangzu, China **59** F8
Rong Xian *Sichuan, China* **58** C5
Rong'an *China* **58** E7
Rongchang *China* **58** C5
Ronge, L. la *Canada* **103** B7
Rongjiang *China* **58** E7
Rongshui *China* **58** E7
Rønne *Denmark* **11** J8
Ronne Ice Shelf *Antarctica* **5** D18
Ronneby *Sweden* **11** H9
Ronnebyån → *Sweden* **11** H9
Ronsard, C. *Australia* **93** D1
Ronse *Belgium* **17** D3
Roodepoort *S. Africa* **89** D4
Roof Butte *U.S.A.* **109** H9
Rooiboklaagte → *Namibia* **88** C3
Rooniu, Mt. *Tahiti* **91** d
Roorkee *India* **68** E7
Roosendaal *Neths.* **17** C4
Roosevelt *U.S.A.* **108** F9
Roosevelt → *Brazil* **124** E6
Roosevelt, Mt. *Canada* **102** B3
Roosevelt I. *Antarctica* **5** D12
Ropczyce *Poland* **31** H8
Roper → *Australia* **94** A2
Roper Bar *Australia* **94** A1
Roque Pérez *Argentina* **126** D4
Roquefort *France* **20** D3
Roquemaure *France* **21** D8
Roquetas de Mar *Spain* **39** J2
Roquetes *Spain* **38** E5
Roquevaire *France* **21** E9
Roraima □ *Brazil* **124** C6
Roraima, Mt. *Venezuela* **124** B6
Røros *Norway* **8** E14
Rorschach *Switz.* **25** H5
Rosa *Zambia* **87** D3
Rosa, Monte *Europe* **40** C4
Rosal de la Frontera *Spain* **37** H3
Rosalia *U.S.A.* **108** C5
Rosamond *U.S.A.* **111** L8
Rosans *France* **21** D9
Rosário *Argentina* **126** C3
Rosário *Brazil* **125** D10
Rosario *Baja Calif., Mexico* **118** B1
Rosario *Sinaloa, Mexico* **118** C3
Rosario *Paraguay* **126** A4
Rosario de la Frontera
   Argentina **126** B3
Rosario de Lerma *Argentina* **126** A2
Rosario del Tala *Argentina* **126** C4
Rosário do Sul *Brazil* **127** C5
Rosarito *Mexico* **111** N9
Rosarno *Italy* **43** D8
Rosas = Roses *Spain* **38** C8
Roscoe *U.S.A.* **115** E10
Roscoff *France* **18** D3
Roscommon *Ireland* **12** C3
Roscommon □ *Ireland* **12** C3
Roscrea *Ireland* **12** D4
Rose → *Australia* **94** A2
Rose, L. *Bahamas* **121** B5
Rose Belle *Mauritius* **85** d
Rose Blanche *Canada* **105** C8
Rose Hill *Mauritius* **85** d
Rose Pt. *Canada* **102** C2
Rose Valley *Canada* **103** C8
Roseau *Dominica* **121** C7
Roseau *U.S.A.* **112** A6
Rosebery *Australia* **95** G4
Rosebud *S. Dak., U.S.A.* **112** D3
Rosebud *Tex., U.S.A.* **116** F6
Roseburg *U.S.A.* **108** E2
Rosedale *U.S.A.* **117** E9
Rosehearty *U.K.* **13** D6
Roseires Res. *Sudan* **79** F12
Roseland *U.S.A.* **110** G4
Rosemary *Canada* **102** C6
Rosenberg *U.S.A.* **116** G7
Rosendaël *France* **19** A9
Rosenheim *Germany* **25** H8
Roses *Spain* **38** C8
Roses, G. de *Spain* **38** C8
Roseto degli Abruzzi *Italy* **41** F11
Rosetown *Canada* **103** C7
Rosetta = Rashîd *Egypt* **80** H7
Roseville *Calif., U.S.A.* **110** G5
Roseville *Mich., U.S.A.* **114** D2
Roseville *Pa., U.S.A.* **115** E8
Rosewood *Australia* **95** D5
Roshkhvār *Iran* **71** C8
Rosières-en-Santerre *France* **19** C9
Rosignano Maríttimo *Italy* **40** E7
Rosignol *Guyana* **124** B7
Roşiori de Vede *Romania* **29** F10
Rositsa *Bulgaria* **45** C11

Rositsa → *Bulgaria* **45** C9
Roskilde *Denmark* **11** J6
Roskovec *Albania* **44** F3
Roslavl *Russia* **32** F7
Rosmaninhal *Portugal* **36** F3
Rosmead *S. Africa* **88** E4
Røsnæs *Denmark* **11** J4
Rosolini *Italy* **43** F7
Rosporden *France* **18** E3
Ross *Australia* **95** G4
Ross *N.Z.* **91** E3
Ross Béthio *Mauritania* **82** B1
Ross Dependency *Antarctica* **5** D12
Ross I. *Antarctica* **5** D11
Ross Ice Shelf *Antarctica* **5** E12
Ross L. *U.S.A.* **108** B3
Ross-on-Wye *U.K.* **15** F5
Ross River *Australia* **94** C1
Ross River *Canada* **102** A2
Ross Sea *Antarctica* **5** D11
Rossall Pt. *U.K.* **14** D4
Rossan Pt. *Ireland* **12** B3
Rossano *Italy* **43** C9
Rossburn *Canada* **103** C8
Rosseau *Canada* **114** A5
Rosseau, L. *Canada* **114** A5
Rosses, The *Ireland* **12** A3
Rossignol, L. *Canada* **114** B5
Rossignol L. *Canada* **105** D6
Rossiya = Russia ■ *Eurasia* **53** C11
Rossland *Canada* **102** D5
Rosslare *Ireland* **12** D5
Rosslare Harbour *Ireland* **12** D5
Rosslau *Germany* **24** D8
Rossmore *Canada* **114** B7
Rosso *Mauritania* **82** B1
Rosso, C. *France* **21** F12
Rossosh *Russia* **33** G10
Røssvatnet *Norway* **8** D16
Røst *Norway* **8** C15
Rosthern *Canada* **103** C7
Rostock *Germany* **24** A8
Rostov *Don, Russia* **33** J10
Rostov *Yaroslavl, Russia* **32** D10
Rostov □ *Russia* **35** F5
Rostrenen *France* **18** D3
Roswell *Ga., U.S.A.* **117** D12
Roswell *N. Mex., U.S.A.* **109** K11
Rota *Spain* **37** J4
Rotan *U.S.A.* **116** E4
Rotenburg *Hessen, Germany* **24** E5
Rotenburg *Niedersachsen,*
   Germany **24** B5
Roth *Germany* **25** F7
Rothaargebirge *Germany* **24** D4
Rothaargebirge △ *Germany* **24** E4
Rothenburg ob der Tauber
   Germany **25** F6
Rother → *U.K.* **15** G8
Rothera *Antarctica* **5** C17
Rotherham *U.K.* **14** D6
Rothes *U.K.* **13** D5
Rothesay *Canada* **105** C6
Rothesay *U.K.* **13** F3
Roti *Indonesia* **63** F6
Rotja, Pta. *Spain* **39** G6
Roto *Australia* **95** E4
Rotondo, Mte. *France* **21** F13
Rotoroa, L. *N.Z.* **91** D4
Rotorua *N.Z.* **91** C6
Rotorua, L. *N.Z.* **91** C6
Rott → *Germany* **25** G9
Rottenburg *Germany* **25** G4
Rottenmann *Austria* **26** D7
Rotterdam *Neths.* **17** C4
Rotterdam *U.S.A.* **115** D10
Rottne *Sweden* **11** G8
Rottnest I. *Australia* **93** F2
Rottumeroog *Neths.* **17** A6
Rottweil *Germany* **25** G4
Rotuma *Fiji* **90** C10
Roubaix *France* **19** B9
Roudnice nad Labem
   Czech Rep. **26** A7
Rouen *France* **18** C8
Rouergue *France* **20** D5
Rouillac *France* **20** C3
Rouleau *Canada* **103** C8
Round I. *Mauritius* **85** d
Round Mountain *U.S.A.* **108** G5
Round Mt. *Australia* **95** E5
Round Rock *U.S.A.* **116** F6
Roundup *U.S.A.* **108** C9
Rousay *U.K.* **13** B5
Rouses Point *U.S.A.* **115** B11
Rousesville *U.S.A.* **114** E5
Rousse = Ruse *Bulgaria* **45** C9
Roussennski Lom → *Bulgaria* **45** C9
Roussillon *Isère, France* **21** C8
Roussillon *Pyrénées-Or.,*
   France **20** F6
Rouxville *S. Africa* **88** E4
Rouyn-Noranda *Canada* **104** C4
Rovaniemi *Finland* **8** C21
Rovato *Italy* **40** C7
Rovenki *Ukraine* **33** H10
Rovereto *Italy* **40** C8
Rovigo *Italy* **41** C8
Rovinj *Croatia* **41** C10

Rovno = Rivne *Ukraine* **23** C14
Rovnoye *Russia* **34** E8
Rovuma = Ruvuma →
   Tanzania **87** E5
Row'ān *Iran* **71** C6
Rowena *Australia* **95** D4
Rowley Shoals *Australia* **92** C2
Roxa *Guinea-Biss.* **82** C1
Roxas *Capiz, Phil.* **61** F5
Roxas *Isabela, Phil.* **61** C4
Roxas *Mind. Or., Phil.* **61** E4
Roxboro *U.S.A.* **117** C15
Roxborough *Trin. & Tob.* **125** J16
Roxburgh *N.Z.* **91** F2
Roxbury *N.Y., U.S.A.* **115** D10
Roxbury *Pa., U.S.A.* **114** F7
Roxby Downs *Australia* **95** E2
Roxen *Sweden* **11** F9
Roy *Mont., U.S.A.* **108** C9
Roy *N. Mex., U.S.A.* **109** J11
Roy *Utah, U.S.A.* **108** F7
Royal Bardia △ *Nepal* **69** E9
Royal Canal *Ireland* **12** C4
Royal Chitawan △ *Nepal* **69** F11
Royal Leamington Spa *U.K.* **15** E6
Royal Natal △ *S. Africa* **89** D4
Royal Tunbridge Wells *U.K.* **15** F8
Royale, Isle *U.S.A.* **112** B9
Royan *France* **20** C2
Roye *France* **19** C9
Royston *U.K.* **15** E7
Rožaj *Montenegro* **44** D4
Różan *Poland* **31** F8
Rozay-en-Brie *France* **19** D9
Rozdilna *Ukraine* **29** D15
Rozhnyativ *Ukraine* **29** B9
Rozhyshche *Ukraine* **23** C13
Rožmitál pod Třemšínem
   Czech Rep. **26** B6
Rožňava *Slovak Rep.* **27** C13
Rozogi *Poland* **30** E8
Rozoy-sur-Serre *France* **19** C11
Roztoczański △ *Poland* **31** H10
Rozzano *Italy* **40** C6
Rrëshen *Albania* **44** E3
Rrogozhinë *Albania* **44** E3
Rtanj *Serbia* **44** C5
Rtishchevo *Russia* **34** D6
Rúa = A Rúa *Spain* **36** C3
Ruacaná *Namibia* **88** B1
Ruaha △ *Tanzania* **86** D3
Ruahine Ra. *N.Z.* **91** C6
Ruapehu *N.Z.* **91** C5
Ruapuke I. *N.Z.* **91** G2
Ruâq, W. → *Egypt* **74** F2
Rub' al Khālī *Si. Arabia* **75** D4
Rubeho Mts. *Tanzania* **86** D4
Rubezhnoye = Rubizhne
   Ukraine **33** H10
Rubh a' Mhail *U.K.* **13** F2
Rubha Hunish *U.K.* **13** D2
Rubha Robhanais = Lewis,
   Butt of *U.K.* **13** C2
Rubí → *Spain* **38** D7
Rubicon → *U.S.A.* **110** G5
Rubicone → *Italy* **41** D9
Rubik *Albania* **44** E3
Rubino *Ivory C.* **82** D4
Rubio *Venezuela* **124** B4
Rubizhne *Ukraine* **33** H10
Rubondo △ *Tanzania* **86** C3
Rubtsovsk *Russia* **52** D9
Ruby L. *U.S.A.* **108** F6
Ruby Mts. *U.S.A.* **108** F6
Rubyvale *Australia* **94** C4
Rucheng *China* **59** E9
Ruciane-Nida *Poland* **30** E8
Rūd Sar *Iran* **71** B6
Ruda *Sweden* **11** H9
Ruda Śląska *Poland* **31** H5
Rudall *Australia* **95** E2
Rudall → *Australia* **92** D3
Rudall River △ *Australia* **92** D3
Rudbar *Iran* **71** B6
Rüdersdorf *Germany* **24** C9
Rudewa *Tanzania* **87** E3
Rudkøbing *Denmark* **11** K4
Rudky *Ukraine* **31** J10
Rudna *Poland* **31** G3
Rudnik *Bulgaria* **45** D11
Rudnik *Poland* **31** H9
Rudnik *Serbia* **44** C4
Rudnya *Russia* **32** E6
Rudnytsya *Ukraine* **29** B13
Rudnyy *Kazakhstan* **52** D7
Rudo *Bos.-H.* **28** G4
Rudolfa, Ostrov *Russia* **52** A6
Rudolstadt *Germany* **24** E7
Rudong *China* **59** A13
Rudozem *Bulgaria* **45** E8
Rudyard *U.S.A.* **113** B11
Rue *France* **19** B8
Ruenya → *Africa* **87** F3
Rufa'a *Sudan* **81** E3
Ruffling Pt. *Br. Virgin Is.* **121** e
Rufiji → *Tanzania* **86** D4
Rufino *Argentina* **126** C3
Rufisque *Senegal* **82** C1
Rufunsa *Zambia* **87** F2

Rugao *China* **59** A13
Rugby *U.K.* **15** E6
Rugby *U.S.A.* **112** A4
Rügen *Germany* **24** A9
Rügen △ *Germany* **24** A9
Rugles *France* **18** D7
Ruhengeri *Rwanda* **86** C2
Ruhla *Germany* **24** E6
Ruhland *Germany* **24** D9
Ruhnu *Estonia* **30** A10
Ruhr → *Germany* **24** D2
Ruhuhu → *Tanzania* **87** E3
Rui'an *China* **59** D13
Ruichang *China* **59** C10
Ruidoso *U.S.A.* **109** K11
Ruijin *China* **59** E10
Ruili *China* **58** E1
Ruivo, Pico *Madeira* **48** D3
Ruj *Bulgaria* **44** D6
Rujen *Macedonia* **44** D6
Rujm Tal'at al Jamā'ah
   Jordan **74** E4
Ruk *Pakistan* **68** F3
Rukhla *Pakistan* **68** C4
Ruki →
   Dem. Rep. of the Congo **84** E3
Rukwa □ *Tanzania* **86** D3
Rukwa, L. *Tanzania* **86** D3
Rulhieres, C. *Australia* **92** B4
Rum = Rhum *U.K.* **13** E2
Rum *Jordan* **74** F4
Rum Cay *Bahamas* **121** B5
Rum Jungle *Australia* **92** B5
Ruma *Serbia* **28** E4
Ruma △ *Kenya* **86** C3
Rumāḥ *Si. Arabia* **70** E5
Rumania = Romania ■
   Europe **29** D10
Rumaylah *Iraq* **70** D5
Rumbêk *Sudan* **81** F2
Rumburk *Czech Rep.* **26** A7
Rumford *U.S.A.* **115** B14
Rumia *Poland* **30** D5
Rumilly *France* **21** C9
Rumoi *Japan* **54** C10
Rumonge *Burundi* **86** C2
Rumson *U.S.A.* **115** F11
Rumuruti *Kenya* **86** B4
Runan *China* **56** H8
Runanga *N.Z.* **91** E3
Runaway, C. *N.Z.* **91** B6
Runaway Bay *Jamaica* **120** a
Runcorn *U.K.* **14** D5
Rundu *Namibia* **88** B2
Rungwa *Tanzania* **86** D3
Rungwa → *Tanzania* **86** D3
Rungwa △ *Tanzania* **86** D3
Rungwe *Tanzania* **87** D3
Rungwe, Mt. *Tanzania* **84** F6
Runka *Nigeria* **83** C6
Runn *Sweden* **10** D9
Runton Ra. *Australia* **92** D3
Ruokolahti *Finland* **32** B5
Ruoqiang *China* **60** C3
Rupa *India* **67** F18
Rupar *India* **68** D7
Rupat *Indonesia* **62** D2
Rupea *Romania* **29** D10
Rupen → *India* **68** H4
Rupert *U.S.A.* **108** E7
Rupert → *Canada* **104** B4
Rupert B. *Canada* **104** B4
Rupert House =
   Waskaganish *Canada* **104** B4
Rupsa *India* **69** J12
Rur → *Europe* **24** D1
Rurrenabaque *Bolivia* **124** F5
Rus → *Spain* **39** F2
Rusambo *Zimbabwe* **87** F3
Rusape *Zimbabwe* **87** F3
Ruschuk = Ruse *Bulgaria* **45** C9
Ruse *Bulgaria* **45** C9
Ruse □ *Bulgaria* **45** C10
Ruşeţu *Romania* **29** F12
Rush *Ireland* **12** C5
Rushan *China* **57** F11
Rushden *U.K.* **15** E7
Rushmore, Mt. *U.S.A.* **112** D2
Rushville *Ill., U.S.A.* **112** E8
Rushville *Ind., U.S.A.* **113** F11
Rushville *Nebr., U.S.A.* **112** D2
Russas *Brazil* **125** D11
Russell *Canada* **103** C8
Russell *Kans., U.S.A.* **112** F4
Russell *N.Y., U.S.A.* **115** B9
Russell *Pa., U.S.A.* **114** E5
Russell Cave △ *U.S.A.* **117** D12
Russell I. *Man., Canada* **103** B8
Russell L. *N.W.T., Canada* **102** A5
Russellkonda *India* **67** K14
Russellville *Ala., U.S.A.* **117** D11
Russellville *Ark., U.S.A.* **116** D8
Russellville *Ky., U.S.A.* **112** G10
Rüsselsheim *Germany* **25** F4
Russi *Italy* **41** D9
Russia ■ *Eurasia* **53** C11
Russian → *U.S.A.* **110** G3
Russkoye Ustye *Russia* **4** B15
Rust *Austria* **27** D9

Rustam *Pakistan* **68** B5
Rustam Shahr *Pakistan* **68** F2
Rustenburg *S. Africa* **88** D4
Ruston *U.S.A.* **116** E8
Rutana *Burundi* **86** C3
Rute *Spain* **37** H6
Ruteng *Indonesia* **63** F6
Rutherford *U.S.A.* **110** G4
Rutland *U.S.A.* **115** C12
Rutland □ *U.K.* **15** E7
Rutland Water *U.K.* **15** E7
Rutledge → *Canada* **103** A6
Rutledge L. *Canada* **103** A6
Rutqa, W. → *Syria* **73** E9
Rutshuru
   Dem. Rep. of the Congo **86** C2
Ruvo di Púglia *Italy* **43** A9
Ruvu *Tanzania* **86** D4
Ruvu → *Tanzania* **86** D4
Ruvuma □ *Tanzania* **87** E4
Ruvuma → *Tanzania* **87** E5
Ruwais *U.A.E.* **71** E7
Ruwenzori *Africa* **86** B2
Ruwenzori △ *Uganda* **86** B2
Ruya → *Zimbabwe* **87** F3
Ruyigi *Burundi* **86** C3
Ruyuan *China* **59** E9
Ruzayevka *Russia* **34** C7
Ruzhevo Konare *Bulgaria* **45** D8
Ružomberok *Slovak Rep.* **27** B12
Ruzyne, Praha × (PRG)
   Czech Rep. **26** A7
Rwanda ■ *Africa* **86** C3
Ryakhovo *Bulgaria* **45** C10
Ryan, L. *U.K.* **13** G3
Ryazan *Russia* **32** E10
Ryazan □ *Russia* **34** D7
Ryazhsk *Russia* **32** F11
Rybachiy *Russia* **30** C7
Rybachiy Poluostrov *Russia* **8** B25
Rybinsk *Russia* **32** C10
Rybinskoye Vdkhr. *Russia* **32** C10
Rybnik *Poland* **31** H5
Rybnitsa = Râbniţa
   Moldova **29** C14
Rybnoye *Russia* **32** E10
Rychwał *Poland* **31** F5
Rychnov nad Kněžnou
   Czech Rep. **27** A9
Rycroft *Canada* **102** B5
Ryd *Sweden* **11** H8
Rydaholm *Sweden* **11** H8
Ryde *U.K.* **15** G6
Ryderwood *U.S.A.* **110** D3
Rydzyna *Poland* **31** G3
Rye *U.K.* **15** G8
Rye → *U.K.* **14** C7
Rye Bay *U.K.* **15** G8
Rye Patch Res. *U.S.A.* **108** F4
Ryegate *U.S.A.* **108** C9
Ryki *Poland* **31** G8
Ryley *Canada* **102** C6
Rylsk *Russia* **33** G8
Rylstone *Australia* **95** E4
Rymanów *Poland* **31** J8
Ryn *Poland* **30** E8
Ryn Peski = Naryn Qum
   Kazakhstan **35** G9
Ryōtsu *Japan* **54** E9
Rypin *Poland* **31** E6
Ryssby *Sweden* **11** H8
Rysy *Europe* **27** B13
Ryūgasaki *Japan* **55** G10
Ryukyu Is. =
   Ryūkyū-rettō *Japan* **55** M3
Ryūkyū-rettō *Japan* **55** M3
Rzepin *Poland* **31** F1
Rzeszów *Poland* **31** H8
Rzhev *Russia* **32** D8

S

Sa *Thailand* **64** C3
Sa Cabaneta *Spain* **48** B9
Sa Canal *Spain* **48** C7
Sa Conillera *Spain* **48** C7
Sa Dec *Vietnam* **65** G5
Sa Dragonera *Spain* **48** B9
Sa Kaeo *Thailand* **64** F4
Sa Mesquida *Spain* **48** B11
Sa Pa *Vietnam* **58** F4
Sa Pobla *Spain* **38** F8
Sa Savina *Spain* **48** C7
Sa'ādatābād *Fārs, Iran* **71** D7
Sa'ādatābād *Hormozgān, Iran* **71** D7
Sa'ādatābād *Kermān, Iran* **71** D7
Saale → *Germany* **24** D7
Saaler Bodden *Germany* **24** A8
Saalfeld *Germany* **24** E7
Saalfelden *Austria* **26** D5
Saane → *Switz.* **25** J2
Saanich *Canada* **110** B3
Saar → *Europe* **17** E6
Saar-Hunsrück △ *Germany* **25** F3
Saarbrücken *Germany* **25** F2
Saarburg *Germany* **25** F2

Saaremaa *Estonia* **32** C2
Saarijärvi *Finland* **8** E21
Saariselkä *Finland* **8** B23
Saarland □ *Germany* **25** F2
Saarlouis *Germany* **25** F2
Saatlı *Azerbaijan* **73** C13
Sab 'Ābar *Syria* **72** F7
Saba *W. Indies* **121** C7
Šabac *Serbia* **44** B3
Sabadell *Spain* **38** D7
Sabah □ *Malaysia* **62** C5
Sabak *Malaysia* **65** L3
Sabalān, Kūhhā-ye *Iran* **73** C12
Sabalana, Kepulauan
   Indonesia **63** F5
Sábana de la Mar *Dom. Rep.* **121** C6
Sábanalarga *Colombia* **124** A4
Sabang *Indonesia* **62** C1
Şabanözü *Turkey* **72** B5
Săbăoani *Romania* **29** C11
Sabará *Brazil* **125** G10
Sabarmati → *India* **68** H5
Sabattis *U.S.A.* **115** B10
Sabáudia *Italy* **42** A6
Saberania *Indonesia* **63** E9
Sabhā *Libya* **79** C8
Sabi → *India* **68** E7
Sabidana, J. *Sudan* **80** D4
Sabie *S. Africa* **89** D5
Sabinal *Mexico* **118** A3
Sabinal *U.S.A.* **116** G5
Sabiñánigo *Spain* **38** C4
Sabinas *Mexico* **118** B4
Sabinas → *Mexico* **118** B4
Sabinas Hidalgo *Mexico* **118** B4
Sabine → *U.S.A.* **116** G8
Sabine L. *U.S.A.* **116** G8
Sabine Pass *U.S.A.* **116** G8
Sabinov *Slovak Rep.* **27** B14
Sabirabad *Azerbaijan* **35** K9
Sablayan *Phil.* **61** E4
Sable *Canada* **105** A6
Sable, C. *Canada* **105** D6
Sable, C. *U.S.A.* **120** A3
Sable I. *Canada* **105** D8
Sablé-sur-Sarthe *France* **18** E6
Sabonkafi *Niger* **83** C6
Sabor → *Portugal* **36** D3
Sabou *Burkina Faso* **82** C4
Sabres *France* **20** D3
Sabrina Coast *Antarctica* **5** C9
Sabugal *Portugal* **36** E3
Sabulubbek *Indonesia* **62** E1
Sabuncu *Turkey* **47** B12
Sabzevār *Iran* **71** B8
Sabzvārān *Iran* **71** D8
Sac City *U.S.A.* **112** D6
Sacedón *Spain* **38** E2
Săcele *Romania* **29** E10
Sacheon *S. Korea* **57** G15
Sachigo → *Canada* **104** A2
Sachigo, L. *Canada* **104** B1
Sachimbo *Angola* **84** F4
Sachkhere *Georgia* **35** J6
Sachsen □ *Germany* **24** E9
Sachsen-Anhalt □ *Germany* **24** D7
Sächsische Schweiz △
   Germany **24** E10
Sacile *Italy* **41** C9
Sackets Harbor *U.S.A.* **115** C8
Sackville *Canada* **105** C7
Saco *Maine, U.S.A.* **115** C14
Saco *Mont., U.S.A.* **108** B10
Sacramento *U.S.A.* **110** G5
Sacramento → *U.S.A.* **110** G5
Sacramento Mts. *U.S.A.* **109** K11
Sacramento Valley *U.S.A.* **110** G5
Sacratif, C. *Spain* **37** J7
Săcueni *Romania* **28** C7
Sada *Spain* **36** B2
Sada-Misaki *Japan* **55** H6
Sádaba *Spain* **38** C3
Sadabad *India* **68** F8
Sadani *Tanzania* **86** D4
Sadao *Thailand* **65** J3
Saddl el Aali *Egypt* **80** C3
Saddle Mt. *U.S.A.* **110** E3
Sade *Nigeria* **83** C7
Sadimi *Dem. Rep. of the Congo* **87** D1
Sadiola *Mali* **82** C2
Sa'dīyah, Hawr as *Iraq* **73** F12
Sado *Japan* **54** F9
Sado → *Portugal* **37** G2
Sadon *Burma* **35** J6
Sadovoye *Russia* **35** G7
Sadra *India* **68** H5
Sadri *India* **68** G5
Sæby *Denmark* **11** G4
Saegertown *U.S.A.* **114** E4
Saelices *Spain* **38** F2
Safaalan *Turkey* **45** E12
Safaga *Egypt* **80** B3
Şafājah *Si. Arabia* **70** E4
Šafárikovo = Tornaľa
   Slovak Rep. **27** C13
Safata B. *Samoa* **91** b
Säffle *Sweden* **11** F6
Safford *U.S.A.* **109** K9

Saffron Walden *U.K.* **15** E8
Safi *Morocco* **78** B4
Şafiābād *Iran* **71** B8
Safid Dasht *Iran* **71** C6
Safid Kūh *Afghan.* **66** B3
Safid Rūd → *Iran* **71** B6
Safipur *India* **69** F9
Şāfītā *Syria* **72** E7
Safonovo *Russia* **32** E7
Safranbolu *Turkey* **72** B5
Saft Rashīn *Egypt* **80** J7
Safune *Samoa* **91** b
Şafwān *Iraq* **70** D5
Sag Harbor *U.S.A.* **115** F12
Saga *Japan* **55** H5
Saga □ *Japan* **55** H5
Sagae *Japan* **54** E10
Sagaing *Burma* **67** J19
Sagala *Mali* **82** C3
Sagamore *U.S.A.* **114** F5
Saganaga L. *Canada* **112** A8
Sagar *Karnataka, India* **66** M9
Sagar *Mad. P., India* **69** H8
Sagara, L. *Tanzania* **86** D3
Sagarejo *Georgia* **35** K7
Sagarmatha = Everest, Mt.
  Nepal **69** E12
Sagarmatha △ *Nepal* **69** F12
Sagay *Phil.* **61** F5
Saginaw *U.S.A.* **113** D12
Saginaw B. *U.S.A.* **113** D12
Sagleipie *Liberia* **82** D3
Saglouc = Salluit *Canada* **101** C12
Sagone *France* **21** F12
Sagone, G. de *France* **21** F12
Sagres *Portugal* **37** J2
Sagua la Grande *Cuba* **120** B3
Saguache *U.S.A.* **108** G10
Saguaro △ *U.S.A.* **109** K8
Saguenay → *Canada* **105** C5
Sagunt *Spain* **38** F4
Sagunto = Sagunt *Spain* **38** F4
Sagwara *India* **68** H6
Sahaba *Sudan* **80** D3
Sahagún *Spain* **36** C5
Saḥam al Jawlān *Syria* **74** C4
Sahamandrevo *Madag.* **89** C8
Sahand, Kūh-e *Iran* **73** D12
Sahara *Africa* **78** D6
Saharan Atlas = Saharien,
  Atlas *Algeria* **78** B6
Saharanpur *India* **68** E7
Saharien, Atlas *Algeria* **78** B6
Saharsa *India* **69** G12
Sahasinaka *Madag.* **89** C8
Sahaswan *India* **69** E8
Saheira, W. el → *Egypt* **74** E2
Sahel *Africa* **78** E5
Sahel, Canal du *Mali* **82** C3
Sahibganj *India* **69** G12
Sāḥilīyah *Iraq* **73** F10
Sahiwal *Pakistan* **68** D5
Şahneh *Iran* **73** E12
Sahrawi = Western
  Sahara ■ *Africa* **78** D3
Sahuaripa *Mexico* **118** B3
Sahuarita *U.S.A.* **109** L8
Sahuayo de Díaz *Mexico* **118** C4
Şahy *Slovak Rep.* **27** C11
Sai → *India* **69** G10
Sai Buri *Thailand* **65** J3
Sai Twong △ *Thailand* **64** E3
Sai Yok △ *Thailand* **64** E2
Sa'id Bundâs *Sudan* **79** G10
Sa'īdābād = Sīrjān *Iran* **71** D7
Sa'īdābād *Iran* **71** B7
Sa'īdīyeh *Iran* **71** B6
Saidpur *Bangla.* **67** G16
Saidpur *India* **69** G10
Saidu Sharif *Pakistan* **69** B5
Saignes *France* **20** C6
Saigō *Japan* **55** F6
Saigon = Thanh Pho Ho
  Chi Minh *Vietnam* **65** G6
Saijō *Japan* **55** H6
Saikai △ *Japan* **55** H4
Saikanosy Masoala *Madag.* **89** B9
Saikhoa Ghat *India* **67** F19
Saiki *Japan* **55** H5
Şā'īl *Si. Arabia* **70** E4
Sailana *India* **68** H6
Saillans *France* **21** D9
Sailolof *Indonesia* **63** E8
Saimaa *Finland* **32** B5
Saimbeyli *Turkey* **72** D7
Saimen = Saimaa *Finland* **32** B5
Şa'in Dezh *Iran* **73** D12
St. Abb's Head *U.K.* **13** F6
St-Affrique *France* **20** E6
St-Agrève *France* **21** C8
St-Aignan *France* **18** E8
St. Alban's *Canada* **105** C8
St. Albans *U.K.* **15** F7
St. Albans *Vt., U.S.A.* **115** B11
St. Albans *W. Va., U.S.A.* **113** F13
St. Alban's Head *U.K.* **15** G5
St. Albert *Canada* **102** C6
St-Amand-en-Puisaye
  France **19** E10

St-Amand-les-Eaux *France* **19** B10
St-Amand-Montrond *France* **19** F9
St-Amarin *France* **19** E14
St-Amour *France* **19** F12
St-André *Réunion* **85** c
St-André-de-Cubzac *France* **20** D3
St-André-les-Alpes *France* **21** E10
St. Andrew's *Canada* **105** C8
St. Andrews *U.K.* **13** E6
St-Anicet *Canada* **115** A10
St. Annes *Canada* **103** D9
St. Anns B. *Canada* **105** C7
St. Ann's Bay *Jamaica* **120** a
St. Anthony *Canada* **105** B8
St. Anthony *U.S.A.* **108** E8
St-Antoine *Canada* **105** C7
St-Antonin-Noble-Val
  France **20** D5
St. Arnaud *Australia* **95** F3
St-Astier *France* **20** C4
St-Aubin-du-Cormier *France* **18** D5
St-Augustin *Canada* **105** B8
St-Augustin → *Canada* **105** B8
St. Augustine *U.S.A.* **117** G14
St-Aulaye *France* **20** C4
St. Austell *U.K.* **15** G3
St-Avold *France* **19** C13
St. Barbe *Canada* **105** B8
St-Barthélemy *W. Indies* **121** C7
St-Béat *France* **20** F4
St. Bees *U.K.* **14** C4
St. Bees I. *Australia* **94** J7
St-Benoît *Réunion* **85** c
St-Benoît-du-Sault *France* **20** B5
St-Bonnet-en-Champsaur
  France **21** D10
St-Brevin-les-Pins *France* **18** E4
St-Brice-en-Coglès *France* **18** D5
St. Bride's *Canada* **105** C9
St. Brides B. *U.K.* **15** F2
St-Brieuc *France* **18** D4
St-Calais *France* **18** E7
St-Cast-le-Guildo *France* **18** D4
St. Catharines *Canada* **114** C5
St. Catherines I. *U.S.A.* **117** F14
St. Catherine's Pt. *U.K.* **15** G6
St-Céré *France* **20** D5
St-Cergue *Switz.* **25** J2
St. Cernin *France* **20** C6
St-Chamond *France* **21** C8
St. Charles *Ill., U.S.A.* **112** E9
St. Charles *Md., U.S.A.* **113** F15
St. Charles *Mo., U.S.A.* **112** F8
St. Charles *Va., U.S.A.* **113** G12
St-Chély-d'Apcher *France* **20** D7
St-Chinian *France* **20** E6
St. Christopher-Nevis = St.
  Kitts & Nevis ■ *W. Indies* **121** C7
St-Ciers-sur-Gironde *France* **20** C3
St. Clair *Mich., U.S.A.* **114** D2
St. Clair *Pa., U.S.A.* **115** F8
St. Clair → *U.S.A.* **114** D2
St. Clair, L. *N. Amer.* **114** D2
St. Clairsville *U.S.A.* **114** F4
St-Claud *France* **20** C4
St. Claude *Canada* **103** D9
St-Claude *France* **19** F12
St. Clears *U.K.* **15** F3
St-Clet *Canada* **115** A10
St. Cloud *Fla., U.S.A.* **117** G14
St. Cloud *Minn., U.S.A.* **112** C6
St-Cricq, C. *Australia* **93** E1
St. Croix *U.S. Virgin Is.* **121** C7
St. Croix → *U.S.A.* **112** C7
St. Croix Falls *U.S.A.* **112** C7
St-Cyprien *France* **20** F7
St-Cyr-sur-Mer *France* **21** E9
St. David's *Canada* **105** C8
St. David's *U.K.* **15** F2
St. David's Head *U.K.* **15** F2
St-Denis *France* **19** D9
St-Denis *Réunion* **85** c
St-Denis ✈ (RUN) *Réunion* **85** c
St-Dié *France* **19** D13
St-Dizier *France* **19** D11
St-Égrève *France* **21** C9
St-Élie *France* **115** B12
St. Elias, Mt. *U.S.A.* **100** C5
St. Elias Mts. *N. Amer.* **102** A1
St-Eloy-les-Mines *France* **19** F9
St-Émilion *France* **20** D3
St-Étienne *France* **21** C8
St-Étienne-de-Tinée *France* **21** D10
St-Étienne-du-Rouvray
  France **18** C8
St. Eugène *Canada* **115** A10
St. Eustatius *W. Indies* **121** C7
St-Exupery, Lyon ✈ (LYS)
  France **19** C11
St-Fargeau *France* **19** E10
St-Félicien *Canada* **104** C5
St-Florent *France* **21** F13
St-Florent, G. de *France* **21** F13
St-Florent-sur-Cher *France* **19** F9
St-Florentin *France* **19** E10
St-Flour *France* **20** C7
St. Francis *U.S.A.* **112** F3
St. Francis → *U.S.A.* **117** D9
St. Francis, C. *S. Africa* **88** E3
St. Francisville *U.S.A.* **116** F9

St-François, L. *Canada* **115** A10
St-Fulgent *France* **18** F5
St-Gabriel *Canada* **104** C5
St-Galmier *France* **19** G11
St-Gaudens *France* **20** E4
St-Gaultier *France* **18** F8
St-Gengoux-le-National
  France **19** F11
St-Geniez-d'Olt *France* **20** D6
St. George *Australia* **95** D4
St. George *Canada* **105** C6
St. George *Ont., Canada* **114** C4
St. George *S.C., U.S.A.* **117** E14
St. George *Utah, U.S.A.* **109** H7
St. George, C. *Canada* **105** C8
St. George, C. *U.S.A.* **117** G12
St. George Ra. *Australia* **92** C4
St. George's *Canada* **105** C8
St-Georges *Canada* **105** C5
St. George's *Grenada* **121** D7
St. George's B. *Canada* **105** C8
St. Georges Basin *N.S.W.,
  Australia* **95** F5
St. Georges Basin
  W. Austral., Australia **92** C4
St. George's Channel *Europe* **12** E6
St. Georges Hd. *Australia* **95** F5
St-Georges-lès-
  Baillargeaux *France* **20** B4
St-Germain-de-Calberte
  France **20** D7
St-Germain-en-Laye *France* **19** D9
St-Germain-Lembron *France* **20** C7
St-Gervais-d'Auvergne
  France **19** F9
St-Gervais-les-Bains *France* **21** C10
St-Gildas, Pte. de *France* **18** E4
St-Gilles *France* **21** E8
St-Girons *Ariège, France* **20** F5
St-Girons *Landes, France* **20** E2
St. Gotthard P. = San
  Gottardo, P. del *Switz.* **25** J4
St. Helena *Atl. Oc.* **76** H3
St. Helena *U.S.A.* **108** G2
St. Helena, Mt. *U.S.A.* **110** G4
St. Helena B. *S. Africa* **88** E2
St. Helens *Australia* **95** G4
St. Helens *U.K.* **14** D5
St. Helens *U.S.A.* **110** E4
St. Helens, Mt. *U.S.A.* **110** D4
St. Helier *U.K.* **15** H5
St-Herblain *France* **18** E5
St-Hilaire-du-Harcouët
  France **18** D5
St-Hippolyte *France* **19** E13
St-Hippolyte-du-Fort *France* **20** E7
St-Honoré-les-Bains *France* **19** F10
St-Hubert *Belgium* **17** D5
St-Hubert *Canada* **115** A11
St-Hyacinthe *Canada* **104** C5
St. Ignace *U.S.A.* **113** C11
St. Ignace I. *Canada* **104** C2
St. Ignatius *U.S.A.* **108** C6
St-Imier *Switz.* **25** H2
St. Ives *Cambs., U.K.* **15** E7
St. Ives *Corn., U.K.* **15** G2
St-James *France* **18** D5
St. James *U.S.A.* **112** D6
St-Jean → *Canada* **105** B7
St-Jean, L. *Canada* **105** C5
St-Jean-d'Angély *France* **20** C3
St-Jean-de-Braye *France* **19** E8
St-Jean-de-Luz *France* **20** E2
St-Jean-de-Maurienne
  France **21** C10
St-Jean-de-Monts *France* **18** F4
St-Jean-du-Gard *France* **20** D7
St-Jean-en-Royans *France* **21** C9
St-Jean-Pied-de-Port *France* **20** E2
St-Jean-Port-Joli *Canada* **105** C5
St-Jean-sur-Richelieu
  Canada **115** A11
St-Jérôme *Canada* **104** C5
St. John *Canada* **105** C6
St. John *U.S.A.* **112** F4
St. John → *Liberia* **82** D2
St. John → *N. Amer.* **113** C20
St. John, C. *Canada* **105** C8
St. John I. *U.S. Virgin Is.* **121** e
St. John's *Antigua & B.* **121** C7
St. John's *Canada* **105** C9
St. Johns *Ariz., U.S.A.* **109** J9
St. Johns *Mich., U.S.A.* **113** D11
St. Johns → *U.S.A.* **117** F14
St. John's Pt. *Ireland* **12** B3
St. Johnsbury *U.S.A.* **115** B12
St. Johnsville *U.S.A.* **115** C10
St. Joseph *Canada* **114** C3
St-Joseph *Martinique* **120** c
St-Joseph *Réunion* **85** c
St. Joseph *La., U.S.A.* **116** F9
St. Joseph *Mo., U.S.A.* **112** F6
St. Joseph → *U.S.A.* **112** D10
St. Joseph, I. *Canada* **104** C3
St. Joseph, L. *Canada* **104** B1
St-Jovite *Canada* **104** C5
St-Juéry *France* **20** E6

St-Julien-Chapteuil *France* **21** C8
St-Julien-de-Vouvantes
  France **18** E5
St-Julien-en-Genevois
  France **19** F13
St-Junien *France* **20** C4
St-Just-en-Chaussée *France* **19** C9
St-Just-en-Chevalet *France* **20** C7
St. Kilda *N.Z.* **16** C2
St. Kitts & Nevis ■
  W. Indies **121** C7
St. Laurent *Canada* **103** C9
St-Laurent-de-la-Salanque
  France **20** F6
St-Laurent-du-Pont *France* **21** C9
St-Laurent-en-Grandvaux
  France **19** F12
St-Laurent-Médoc *France* **20** C3
St. Lawrence *Australia* **94** C4
St. Lawrence *Canada* **105** C8
St. Lawrence → *Canada* **105** C6
St. Lawrence, Gulf of
  Canada **105** C7
St. Lawrence I. *U.S.A.* **106** a
St. Lawrence Islands △
  Canada **115** B9
St. Léonard *Canada* **105** C6
St-Léonard-de-Noblat *France* **20** C5
St-Leu *Réunion* **85** c
St. Lewis → *Canada* **105** B8
St-Lô *France* **18** C5
St-Louis *France* **19** E14
St-Louis *Guadeloupe* **120** b
St-Louis *Réunion* **85** c
St. Louis *Senegal* **82** B1
St. Louis *U.S.A.* **112** F8
St. Louis □ *U.S.A.* **112** B7
St. Louis → *U.S.A.* **112** B7
St. Sebastien, Tanjon' i
  Madag. **89** A8
St-Seine-l'Abbaye *France* **19** E11
St-Sernin-sur-Rance *France* **20** E6
St-Sever *France* **20** E3
St-Siméon *Canada* **105** C6
St. Simons I. *U.S.A.* **117** F14
St. Simons Island *U.S.A.* **117** F14
St. Stephen *Canada* **105** C6
St-Sulpice *France* **20** E5
St-Sulpice-Laurière *France* **20** B5
St-Sulpice-les-Feuilles *France* **20** B5
St-Syprien = St-Cyprien
  France **20** F7
St-Thégonnec *France* **18** D3
St. Thomas *Canada* **114** D3
St. Thomas I. *U.S. Virgin Is.* **121** e
St-Tite *Canada* **104** C5
St-Tropez *France* **21** E10
St-Troud = St. Truiden
  Belgium **17** D5
St. Truiden *Belgium* **17** D5
St-Vaast-la-Hougue *France* **18** C5
St-Valery-en-Caux *France* **18** C7
St-Valéry-sur-Somme *France* **19** B8
St-Vallier *France* **19** F11
St-Vallier-de-Thiey *France* **21** E10
St-Varent *France* **18** F6
St-Vaury *France* **20** B5
St. Vincent = São Vicente
  C. Verde Is. **78** b
St. Vincent *Italy* **40** C4
St. Vincent, G. *Australia* **95** F2
St. Vincent & the
  Grenadines ■ *W. Indies* **121** D7
St-Vincent-de-Tyrosse
  France **20** E2
St. Vincent Passage
  W. Indies **121** D7
St-Vith *Belgium* **17** D6
St-Vivien-de-Médoc *France* **20** C2
St. Walburg *Canada* **103** C7
St-Yrieix-la-Perche *France* **20** C5
Ste-Adresse *France* **18** C7
Ste-Agathe-des-Monts
  Canada **104** C5
Ste-Anne *Guadeloupe* **120** b
Ste-Anne, L. *Canada* **105** B6
Ste-Anne-des-Monts
  Canada **105** C6
Ste-Croix *Switz.* **25** J2
Ste-Énimie *France* **20** D7
Ste-Foy-la-Grande *France* **20** D4
Ste. Genevieve *U.S.A.* **112** G8
Ste-Hermine *France* **20** B2
Ste-Livrade-sur-Lot *France* **20** D4
Ste-Marguerite → *Canada* **105** B6
Ste-Marie *Canada* **105** C5
Ste-Marie *Martinique* **120** c
Ste-Marie *Réunion* **85** c
Ste-Marie, Ile = Nosy
  Boraha *Madag.* **89** B8
Ste-Marie-aux-Mines
  France **19** D14
Ste-Maxime *France* **21** E10
Ste-Menehould *France* **19** C11
Ste-Mère-Église *France* **18** C5
Ste-Rose *Guadeloupe* **120** b
Ste. Rose du Lac *Canada* **103** C9
Ste-Savine *France* **19** D11

St. Petersburg =
  Sankt-Peterburg *Russia* **32** C6
St. Petersburg *U.S.A.* **117** H13
St-Philbert-de-Grand-Lieu
  France **18** E5
St-Philippe *Réunion* **85** c
St-Pie *Canada* **115** A12
St-Pierre *Martinique* **120** c
St-Pierre *Réunion* **85** c
St-Pierre *St-P. & M.* **105** C8
St-Pierre, L. *Canada* **104** C5
St-Pierre-d'Oléron *France* **20** C2
St-Pierre-en-Port *France* **18** C7
St-Pierre-et-Miquelon ☒
  N. Amer. **105** C8
St-Pierre-le-Moûtier *France* **19** F10
St-Pierre-sur-Dives *France* **18** C6
St-Pol-de-Léon *France* **18** D3
St-Pol-sur-Mer *France* **19** A9
St-Pol-sur-Ternoise *France* **19** B9
St-Pons *France* **20** E6
St-Pourçain-sur-Sioule
  France **19** F10
St-Priest *France* **21** C8
St-Quay-Portrieux *France* **18** D4
St-Quentin *Canada* **105** C6
St-Quentin *France* **19** C10
St-Rambert-d'Albon *France* **21** C8
St-Raphaël *France* **21** E10
St. Regis *U.S.A.* **108** C6
St. Regis Falls *U.S.A.* **115** B10
St-Renan *France* **18** D2
St-Saëns *France* **18** C8
St-Savin *France* **20** B4
St-Savinien *France* **20** C3
St. Louis *U.S.A.* **112** F8
St. Louis □ *U.S.A.* **112** B7
St. Louis → *U.S.A.* **112** B7

Ste-Sigolène *France* **21** C8
Saintes *France* **20** C3
Saintes, Îs. des *Guadeloupe* **120** b
Stes-Maries-de-la-Mer
  France **21** E8
Saintfield *U.K.* **12** B6
Saintonge *France* **20** C3
Saipan *N. Marianas* **96** F6
Sairang *India* **67** H18
Sairecábur, Cerro *Bolivia* **126** A2
Saitama *Japan* **55** G9
Saitama □ *Japan* **55** F9
Saiteli = Kadınhanı *Turkey* **72** C5
Saiţi *Moldova* **29** D14
Saiyid *Pakistan* **68** C5
Saja-Besaya △ *Spain* **36** B6
Sajama *Bolivia* **124** G5
Sajan *Serbia* **28** E5
Sajó → *Hungary* **28** C6
Sajószentpéter *Hungary* **28** B5
Sajum *India* **69** C8
Sak → *S. Africa* **88** E3
Saka *Kenya* **86** B4
Sakaba *Nigeria* **83** C6
Sakai *Japan* **55** G7
Sakaide *Japan* **55** G6
Sakaiminato *Japan* **55** G6
Sakākah *Si. Arabia* **70** D4
Sakakawea, L. *U.S.A.* **112** B3
Sakami → *Canada* **104** B4
Sakami, L. *Canada* **104** B4
Sâkâne, 'Erg i-n *Mali* **83** A4
Sakania
  Dem. Rep. of the Congo **87** E2
Sakaraha *Madag.* **89** C7
Sakartvelo = Georgia ■ *Asia* **35** J6
Sakarya *Turkey* **72** B4
Sakarya □ *Turkey* **72** B4
Sakarya → *Turkey* **72** B4
Sakashima-Guntō *Japan* **55** M2
Sakata *Japan* **54** E9
Sakchu *N. Korea* **57** D13
Sakeny → *Madag.* **89** C8
Sakété *Benin* **83** D5
Sakha □ *Russia* **53** C14
Sakhalin *Russia* **53** D15
Sakhalinskiy Zaliv *Russia* **53** D15
Şaki *Azerbaijan* **35** K8
Šakiai *Lithuania* **30** D10
Sakon Nakhon *Thailand* **64** D5
Sakrand *Pakistan* **68** F3
Sakri *India* **69** F12
Sakrivier *S. Africa* **88** E3
Saksköbing *Denmark* **11** K5
Sakti *India* **69** H10
Sakuma *Japan* **55** G8
Sakurai *Japan* **55** G7
Saky *Ukraine* **33** K7
Sal *C. Verde Is.* **78** b
Sal → *Russia* **35** G5
Sal Rei *C. Verde Is.* **78** b
Sala *Eritrea* **81** D4
Šaľa *Slovak Rep.* **27** C10
Sala *Sweden* **10** E10
Sala → *Eritrea* **81** D4
Sala Consilina *Italy* **43** B8
Sala-y-Gómez *Pac. Oc.* **97** K17
Sala y Gómez Ridge *Pac. Oc.* **97** K18
Salaberry-de-Valleyfield
  Canada **115** A10
Salacgrīva *Latvia* **30** A11
Salada, L. *Mexico* **109** K6
Saladas *Argentina* **126** B4
Saladillo *Argentina* **126** D4
Salado → *B. Aires, Argentina*
  126 D4
Salado → *La Pampa,
  Argentina* **128** D3
Salado → *Santa Fe,
  Argentina* **126** C3
Salado → *Mexico* **116** H5
Salaga *Ghana* **83** D4
Şalāḥ *Syria* **74** C4
Şalāḥ ad Dīn □ *Iraq* **70** C4
Sălaj □ *Romania* **28** C8
Salakos *Greece* **49** C9
Salala *Liberia* **82** D2
Salala *Sudan* **80** C4
Salālah *Oman* **75** D5
Salamanca *Chile* **126** C1
Salamanca *Spain* **36** E5
Salamanca □ *Spain* **36** E5
Salamanca *U.S.A.* **114** D6
Salamanca □ *Spain* **36** E5
Salāmatābād *Iran* **70** C5
Salamina *Greece* **46** D5
Salamis *Cyprus* **49** D12
Salar de Atacama *Chile* **126** A2
Salar de Uyuni *Bolivia* **124** H5
Sălard *Romania* **28** C7
Salas *Spain* **36** B4
Salas de los Infantes *Spain* **36** C7
Salatiga *Indonesia* **63** G14
Salaverry *Peru* **124** E3
Salawati *Indonesia* **63** E8
Salaya *India* **68** H3
Salayar *Indonesia* **63** F6
Salazar → *Spain* **38** C3
Salbris *France* **19** E9

S'Albufera *Spain* **48** B10
Salcia *Romania* **29** G9
Sălciua *Romania* **29** D8
Salcombe *U.K.* **15** G4
Saldaña *Spain* **36** C6
Saldanha *S. Africa* **88** E2
Saldanha B. *S. Africa* **88** E2
Saldus *Latvia* **30** B9
Saldus □ *Latvia* **30** B9
Sale *Australia* **95** F4
Sale *Italy* **40** D5
Salé *Morocco* **78** B4
Sale *U.K.* **14** D5
Salekhard *Russia* **52** C7
Salelologa *Samoa* **91** b
Salem *India* **66** P11
Salem *Ill., U.S.A.* **112** F9
Salem *Ind., U.S.A.* **112** F10
Salem *Mass., U.S.A.* **115** D14
Salem *Mo., U.S.A.* **112** G8
Salem *N.H., U.S.A.* **115** D13
Salem *N.J., U.S.A.* **113** F16
Salem *N.Y., U.S.A.* **115** C11
Salem *Ohio, U.S.A.* **114** F4
Salem *Oreg., U.S.A.* **108** D2
Salem *S. Dak., U.S.A.* **112** D5
Salem *Va., U.S.A.* **113** G13
Salemi *Italy* **42** E5
Sälen *Sweden* **10** C7
Salernes *France* **21** E10
Salerno *Italy* **43** B7
Salerno, G. di *Italy* **43** B7
Salford *U.K.* **14** D5
Salgir ➔ *Ukraine* **33** K8
Salgótarján *Hungary* **28** B4
Salgueiro *Brazil* **125** E11
Salibabu *Indonesia* **63** D7
Salibea = Salybia
  Trin. & Tob. **125** K15
Salida *U.S.A.* **106** C5
Salies-de-Béarn *France* **20** E3
Salihli *Turkey* **72** C3
Salihorsk *Belarus* **23** B14
Salima *Malawi* **85** G6
Salina *Italy* **43** D7
Salina *Kans., U.S.A.* **112** F5
Salina *Utah, U.S.A.* **108** G8
Salina Cruz *Mexico* **119** D5
Salina di Margherita di
  Savoia *Italy* **43** A9
Salinas *Brazil* **125** G10
Salinas *Ecuador* **124** D2
Salinas *U.S.A.* **110** J5
Salinas ➔ *Guatemala* **119** D6
Salinas ➔ *U.S.A.* **110** J5
Salinas, B. de *Nic.* **120** D2
Salinas, Pampa de las
  Argentina **126** C2
Salinas Ambargasta
  Argentina **126** B3
Salinas de Hidalgo *Mexico* **118** C4
Salinas Grandes *Argentina* **126** C3
Salinas Pueblo Missions △
  U.S.A. **109** J10
Salinas Valley *U.S.A.* **110** J5
Saline ➔ *Ark., U.S.A.* **116** E8
Saline ➔ *Kans., U.S.A.* **112** F5
Saline di Trapani e
  Paceco △ *Italy* **42** E5
Salines, C. de ses *Spain* **48** B10
Salinópolis *Brazil* **125** D9
Salins-les-Bains *France* **19** F12
Salir *Portugal* **37** H2
Salisbury *Australia* **95** E2
Salisbury *U.K.* **15** F6
Salisbury *Md., U.S.A.* **113** F16
Salisbury *N.C., U.S.A.* **117** D14
Salisbury I. *Canada* **101** C12
Salisbury Plain *U.K.* **15** F6
Săliște *Romania* **29** E8
Salka *Nigeria* **83** C5
Salkhad *Syria* **74** C5
Salkove *Ukraine* **29** B14
Salla *Finland* **8** C23
Sallanches *France* **21** C10
Sallent *Spain* **38** D6
Salles *France* **20** D3
Salles-Curan *France* **20** D6
Salling *Denmark* **11** H2
Salliq = Coral Harbour
  Canada **101** C11
Sallisaw *U.S.A.* **116** D7
Sallom *Sudan* **80** D4
Salluit *Canada* **101** C12
Salmān Pak *Iraq* **73** G11
Salmás *Iran* **73** C11
Salmerón *Spain* **38** E2
Salmo *Canada* **102** D5
Salmon *U.S.A.* **108** D7
Salmon ➔ *Canada* **102** C4
Salmon ➔ *U.S.A.* **108** D5
Salmon Arm *Canada* **102** C5
Salmon Gums *Australia* **93** F3
Salmon Pt. *Canada* **114** C7
Salmon River Mts. *U.S.A.* **108** D6
Salmon River Res. *U.S.A.* **115** C9
Salo *Finland* **32** B2
Salò *Italy* **40** C7
Salobreña *Spain* **37** J7

Salome *U.S.A.* **111** M13
Salon *India* **69** F9
Salon-de-Provence *France* **21** E9
Salonica = Thessaloniki
  Greece **44** F6
Salonta *Romania* **28** D6
Salor ➔ *Spain* **37** F3
Salou *Spain* **38** D6
Salou, C. de *Spain* **38** D6
Salpausselkä *Finland* **32** B4
Salsacate *Argentina* **126** C2
Salses *France* **20** F6
Salsk *Russia* **35** G5
Salso ➔ *Italy* **42** E6
Salsomaggiore Terme *Italy* **40** D6
Salt *Spain* **38** D7
Salt ➔ *Canada* **102** B6
Salt ➔ *U.S.A.* **109** K7
Salt Fork Red ➔ *U.S.A.* **116** D5
Salt L. *Australia* **95** E3
Salt Lake City *U.S.A.* **108** F8
Salt Range *Pakistan* **68** C5
Salta *Argentina* **126** A2
Salta □ *Argentina* **126** A2
Saltara *Italy* **41** E9
Saltash *U.K.* **15** G3
Saltburn by the Sea *U.K.* **14** C7
Saltcoats *U.K.* **13** F4
Saltee Is. *Ireland* **12** D5
Saltfjellet *Norway* **8** C16
Saltfjorden *Norway* **8** C16
Saltholm *Denmark* **11** J6
Saltillo *Mexico* **118** B4
Salto *Argentina* **126** C3
Salto *Uruguay* **126** C4
Salto del Guaíra *Paraguay* **127** A5
Salton City *U.S.A.* **111** M11
Salton Sea *U.S.A.* **111** M11
Saltpond *Ghana* **83** D4
Saltsburg *U.S.A.* **114** F5
Saluda ➔ *U.S.A.* **117** D14
Salûm *Egypt* **80** A2
Salûm, Khâlig el *Egypt* **80** A2
Salur *India* **67** K13
Saluzzo *Italy* **40** D4
Salvador *Brazil* **125** F11
Salvador *Canada* **103** C7
Salvador, El ■ *Cent. Amer.* **120** D2
Salvador, L. *U.S.A.* **117** G9
Salvaterra de Magos
  Portugal **37** F2
Sálvora, I. de *Spain* **36** C2
Salween ➔ *Burma* **67** L20
Salyan *Azerbaijan* **73** C13
Salybia *Trin. & Tob.* **125** K15
Salza ➔ *Austria* **26** D7
Salzach ➔ *Austria* **26** C5
Salzburg *Austria* **26** D6
Salzburg □ *Austria* **26** D6
Salzgitter *Germany* **24** C6
Salzkotten *Germany* **24** D4
Salzwedel *Germany* **24** C7
Sam *India* **68** F4
Sam Neua *Laos* **58** G5
Sam Ngao *Thailand* **64** D2
Sam Rayburn Res. *U.S.A.* **116** F7
Sam Son *Vietnam* **64** C5
Sam Teu *Laos* **64** C5
Sama de Langreo =
  Langreo *Spain* **36** B5
Samagaltay *Russia* **53** D10
Samales Group *Phil.* **61** J5
Samālût *Egypt* **80** B3
Samana *India* **68** D7
Samana Cay *Bahamas* **121** B5
Samandağ *Turkey* **72** D6
Samandıra *Turkey* **45** F13
Samanga *Tanzania* **87** D4
Samangán □ *Afghan.* **66** B5
Samangwa
  Dem. Rep. of the Congo **86** C1
Samani *Japan* **54** C11
Samanli Dağları *Turkey* **45** F13
Samar *Phil.* **61** F6
Samara *Russia* **34** D10
Samara ➔ *Russia* **34** D10
Samara ➔ *Ukraine* **33** H8
Samaria = Shōmrōn
  West Bank **74** C4
Samaria △ *Greece* **46** F5
Samaria △ *Kriti, Greece* **49** D5
Samarinda *Indonesia* **62** E5
Samarkand = Samarqand
  Uzbekistan **52** F7
Samarqand *Uzbekistan* **52** F7
Sāmarrā' *Iraq* **73** E10
Samastipur *India* **69** G11
Şamaxı *Azerbaijan* **35** K9
Samba *Dem. Rep. of the Congo* **86** C2
Samba *India* **69** C6
Sambalpur *India* **67** J14
Sambar, Tanjung *Indonesia* **62** E4
Sambas *Indonesia* **62** D3
Sambava *Madag.* **89** A9
Sambawizi *Zimbabwe* **87** F2
Sambhal *India* **69** E8
Sambhar *India* **68** F6

Sambhar L. *India* **68** F6
Sambiase *Italy* **43** D9
Sambir *Ukraine* **31** J10
Sambor *Cambodia* **64** F6
Samborombón, B. *Argentina* **126** D4
Sambuca di Sicília *Italy* **42** E6
Samburu □ *Kenya* **86** B4
Samcheok *S. Korea* **57** F15
Same *Tanzania* **86** C4
Samer *France* **19** B8
Samfya *Zambia* **87** E2
Sami *Greece* **46** C2
Şamkir *Azerbaijan* **35** K8
Şamlı *Turkey* **47** B9
Samnah *Si. Arabia* **70** E3
Samnu *Libya* **79** C8
Samo Alto *Chile* **126** C1
Samoa ■ *Pac. Oc.* **91** b
Samobor *Croatia* **41** C12
Samoëns *France* **19** F13
Samokov *Bulgaria* **44** D7
Samorogouan *Burkina Faso* **82** C4
Samos *Greece* **47** D8
Samoš *Serbia* **28** E5
Samos *Spain* **36** C3
Samos □ *Greece* **47** D8
Samothráki = Mathraki
  Greece **49** A3
Samothraki *Greece* **45** F9
Samoylovka *Russia* **34** E6
Sampa *Ghana* **82** D4
Sampacho *Argentina* **126** C3
Sampalan *Indonesia* **63** K18
Sampang *Indonesia* **63** G15
Samper de Calanda *Spain* **38** D4
Sampéyre *Italy* **40** D4
Sampit *Indonesia* **62** E4
Sampit, Teluk *Indonesia* **62** E4
Samrong *Cambodia* **64** E4
Samrong *Thailand* **64** E3
Samsø *Denmark* **11** J4
Samsun *Turkey* **72** B7
Samsun □ *Turkey* **72** B7
Samsø Bælt *Denmark* **11** J4
Samtredia *Georgia* **35** J6
Samu *Russia* **35** K9
Samui, Ko *Thailand* **65** b
Samur ➔ *Russia* **35** K9
Samurskiy Khrebet *Russia* **35** K8
Samusole
  Dem. Rep. of the Congo **87** E1
Samut Prakan *Thailand* **64** F3
Samut Songkhram *Thailand* **64** F3
Samwari *Pakistan* **68** E2
San *Mali* **82** C4
San ➔ *Cambodia* **64** F5
San ➔ *Poland* **31** H8
San Adrián *Spain* **38** C3
San Adrián, C. de *Spain* **36** B2
San Agustín *C. Rica* **61** H7
San Agustín de Valle Fértil
  Argentina **126** C2
San Ambrosio *Pac. Oc.* **122** F3
San Andreas *U.S.A.* **110** G6
San Andres *Phil.* **61** E6
San Andrés, I. de *Caribbean* **120** D3
San Andrés del Rabanedo
  Spain **36** C5
San Andres Mts. *U.S.A.* **109** K10
San Andrés Tuxtla *Mexico* **119** D5
San Angelo *U.S.A.* **116** F4
San Anselmo *U.S.A.* **110** H4
San Antonio *Belize* **119** D7
San Antonio *Chile* **126** C1
San Antonio *Phil.* **61** D4
San Antonio *N. Mex., U.S.A.*
  109 K10
San Antonio *Tex., U.S.A.* **116** G5
San Antonio ➔ *U.S.A.* **116** G6
San Antonio, C. *Argentina* **126** D4
San Antonio, C. de *Cuba* **120** B3
San Antonio, C. de *Spain* **39** G5
San Antonio, Mt. *U.S.A.* **111** L9
San Antonio de los Baños
  Cuba **120** B3
San Antonio de los Cobres
  Argentina **126** A2
San Antonio Oeste
  Argentina **128** E4
San Arcángelo *Italy* **43** B9
San Ardo *U.S.A.* **110** J6
San Augustín *Canary Is.* **48** G4
San Augustine *U.S.A.* **116** F7
San Bartolomé *Canary Is.* **48** F6
San Bartolomé de Tirajana
  Canary Is. **48** G4
San Bartolomeo in Galdo
  Italy **43** A8
San Benedetto del Tronto
  Italy **41** F10
San Benedetto Po *Italy* **40** C7
San Benedicto, I. *Mexico* **118** D2
San Benito *U.S.A.* **116** H6
San Benito ➔ *U.S.A.* **110** J5
San Benito Mt. *U.S.A.* **110** J6
San Bernardino *U.S.A.* **111** L9
San Bernardino Mts. *U.S.A.*
  111 L10
San Bernardino Str. *Phil.* **61** E6
San Bernardo *Chile* **126** C1

San Bernardo, I. de
  Colombia **124** B3
San Blas *Mexico* **118** B3
San Blas, Arch. de *Panama* **120** E4
San Blas, C. *U.S.A.* **117** G12
San Bonifacio *Italy* **41** C8
San Borja *Bolivia* **124** F5
San Buenaventura =
  Ventura *U.S.A.* **111** L7
San Buenaventura *Mexico* **118** B4
San Carlos = Sant Carles
  Spain **48** B8
San Carlos *Argentina* **126** C2
San Carlos *Chile* **126** D1
San Carlos *Baja Calif. S.,
  Mexico* **118** C2
San Carlos *Coahuila, Mexico* **118** B4
San Carlos *Nic.* **120** D3
San Carlos *Neg. Occ., Phil.* **61** F5
San Carlos *Pangasinan, Phil.* **61** D4
San Carlos *Uruguay* **127** C5
San Carlos *U.S.A.* **109** K8
San Carlos *Venezuela* **124** B5
San Carlos de Bariloche
  Argentina **128** E2
San Carlos de Bolívar
  Argentina **126** D3
San Carlos de Bolívar
  Argentina **126** D4
San Carlos de la Rápita =
  Sant Carles de la Ràpita
  Spain **38** E5
San Carlos del Zulia
  Venezuela **124** B4
San Carlos L. *U.S.A.* **109** K8
San Cataldo *Italy* **42** E6
San Celoni = Sant Celoni
  Spain **38** D7
San Clemente *Chile* **126** D1
San Clemente *Spain* **39** F2
San Clemente *U.S.A.* **111** M9
San Clemente I. *U.S.A.* **111** N8
San Cristóbal = Es Migjorn
  Gran *Spain* **48** B11
San Cristóbal *Argentina* **126** C3
San Cristóbal *Dom. Rep.* **121** C5
San Cristóbal *Solomon Is.* **90** C9
San Cristóbal *Venezuela* **124** B4
San Cristóbal de las Casas
  Mexico **119** D6
San Damiano d'Asti *Italy* **40** D5
San Daniele del Friuli *Italy* **41** B10
San Diego *Tex., U.S.A.* **116** H5
San Diego, C. *Argentina* **128** G3
San Diego de la Unión
  Mexico **118** C4
San Diego Int. ✈ (SAN)
  U.S.A. **111** N9
San Dimitri, Ras *Malta* **49** C1
San Dimitri Point = San
  Dimitri, Ras *Malta* **49** C1
San Donà di Piave *Italy* **41** C9
San Esteban de Gormaz
  Spain **38** D1
San Felice Circeo *Italy* **42** A6
San Felice sul Panaro *Italy* **41** D8
San Felipe *Chile* **126** C1
San Felipe *Mexico* **118** A2
San Felipe *Venezuela* **124** A5
San Felipe ➔ *U.S.A.* **111** M11
San Félix *Chile* **126** B1
San Félix *Pac. Oc.* **122** F2
San Fernando = Sant
  Ferran *Spain* **48** C7
San Fernando *Chile* **126** C1
San Fernando *Mexico* **119** C5
San Fernando *La Union, Phil.* **61** C4
San Fernando *Pampanga,
  Phil.* **61** D4
San Fernando *Spain* **37** J4
San Fernando *Trin. & Tob.* **121** D7
San Fernando *U.S.A.* **111** L8
San Fernando de Apure
  Venezuela **124** B5
San Fernando de Atabapo
  Venezuela **124** C5
San Fernando di Púglia *Italy* **43** A9
San Francisco *Argentina* **126** C3
San Francisco *U.S.A.* **110** H4
San Francisco ➔ *U.S.A.* **109** K9
San Francisco, C. de
  Colombia **122** C3
San Francisco, Paso de
  S. Amer. **126** B2
San Francisco de Macorís
  Dom. Rep. **121** C5
San Francisco del Monte
  de Oro *Argentina* **126** C2
San Francisco del Oro
  Mexico **118** B3
San Francisco Int. ✈ (SFO)
  U.S.A. **110** H4
San Francisco Javier =
  Sant Francesc de
  Formentera *Spain* **48** C7
San Fratello *Italy* **43** D7
San Gabriel *Chile* **126** C1

San Gabriel Chilac *Mexico* **119** D5
San Gabriel Mts. *U.S.A.* **111** L9
San Gavino Monreale *Italy* **42** C1
San German *Puerto Rico* **121** d
San Gimignano *Italy* **40** E8
San Giórgio di Nogaro *Italy* **41** C10
San Giórgio Iónico *Italy* **43** B10
San Giovanni Bianco *Italy* **40** C6
San Giovanni in Fiore *Italy* **43** C9
San Giovanni in Persiceto
  Italy **41** D8
San Giovanni Rotondo
  Italy **41** G12
San Giovanni Valdarno *Italy* **41** E8
San Giuliano Terme *Italy* **40** E7
San Gorgonio Mt. *U.S.A.* **111** L10
San Gottardo, P. del *Switz.* **25** J4
San Gregorio *Uruguay* **127** C4
San Gregorio *U.S.A.* **110** H4
San Guillermo △ *Argentina* **126** B2
San Guiseppe Jato *Italy* **42** E6
San Ignacio *Belize* **119** D7
San Ignacio *Bolivia* **124** G6
San Ignacio *Mexico* **118** B2
San Ignacio *Paraguay* **126** B4
San Ignacio, L. *Mexico* **118** B2
San Ildefonso, C. *Phil.* **61** D5
San Isidro *Argentina* **126** C4
San Isidro *Phil.* **61** H7
San Jacinto *U.S.A.* **111** M10
San Jaime = Sant Jaume
  Spain **48** B11
San Javier *Misiones,
  Argentina* **127** B4
San Javier *Santa Fe,
  Argentina* **126** C4
San Javier *Bolivia* **124** G6
San Javier *Chile* **126** D1
San Javier *Spain* **39** H4
San Jerónimo Taviche
  Mexico **119** D5
San Joaquin *U.S.A.* **110** J6
San Joaquin ➔ *U.S.A.* **110** G5
San Joaquin Valley *U.S.A.* **110** J6
San Jon *U.S.A.* **109** J12
San Jordi = Sant Jordi *Spain* **48** B9
San Jorge *Argentina* **126** C3
San Jorge, B. *Mexico* **118** A2
San Jorge, G. *Argentina* **128** F3
San José = San Josep *Spain* **48** C7
San José *Argentina* **126** C4
San José *Costa Rica* **120** E3
San José *Guatemala* **120** D1
San Jose *Mind. Occ., Phil.* **61** E4
San Jose *Nueva Ecija, Phil.* **61** D4
San Jose *U.S.A.* **110** H5
San José, I. *Mexico* **118** C2
San Jose ➔ *U.S.A.* **109** J10
San Jose de Buenavista *Phil.* **63** B6
San José de Chiquitos
  Bolivia **124** G6
San José de Feliciano
  Argentina **126** C4
San José de Jáchal *Argentina* **126** C2
San José de Mayo *Uruguay* **126** C4
San José del Cabo *Mexico* **118** C3
San José del Guaviare
  Colombia **124** C4
San Josep *Spain* **48** C7
San Juan *Argentina* **126** C2
San Juan *Phil.* **61** F6
San Juan *Puerto Rico* **121** d
San Juan *Trin. & Tob.* **125** K15
San Juan □ *Argentina* **126** C2
San Juan ➔ *Argentina* **126** C2
San Juan ➔ *Nic.* **120** D3
San Juan ➔ *U.S.A.* **109** H8
San Juan Bautista = Sant
  Joan de Labritja *Spain* **48** B8
San Juan Bautista *Paraguay* **126** B4
San Juan Bautista *Spain* **48** B8
San Juan Bautista *U.S.A.* **110** J5
San Juan Capistrano *U.S.A.*
  111 M9
San Juan Cr. ➔ *U.S.A.* **110** J5
San Juan de Guadalupe
  Mexico **118** C4
San Juan de la Costa *Mexico*
  118 C2
San Juan de los Lagos
  Mexico **118** C4
San Juan de los Morros
  Venezuela **124** B5
San Juan del Norte *Nic.* **120** D3
San Juan del Norte, B. de
  Nic. **120** D3
San Juan del Río *Mexico* **119** C5
San Juan del Sur *Nic.* **120** D2
San Juan I. *U.S.A.* **110** B3
San Juan Island △ *U.S.A.* **110** B3
San Juan Mts. *U.S.A.* **109** H10
San Just, Sierra de *Spain* **38** E4
San Justo *Argentina* **126** C3
San Kamphaeng *Thailand* **64** C2
San Lázaro, C. *Mexico* **118** C2
San Leandro *U.S.A.* **110** H4
San Leonardo de Yagüe
  Spain **38** D1
San Lorenzo = Sant
  Llorenç des Cardassar
  Spain **48** B10

San Lorenzo *Argentina* **126** C3
San Lorenzo *Ecuador* **124** C3
San Lorenzo *Paraguay* **126** B4
San Lorenzo ➔ *Mexico* **118** C3
San Lorenzo, I. *Mexico* **118** B2
San Lorenzo, Mte. *Argentina* **128** F2
San Lorenzo de la Parrilla
  Spain **38** E2
San Lorenzo de Morunys =
  Sant Llorenç de
  Morunys *Spain* **38** C6
San Lucas = Cabo San
  Lucas *Mexico* **118** C3
San Lucas *Bolivia* **124** H5
San Lucas *Mexico* **118** C3
San Lucas *U.S.A.* **110** J5
San Lucas, C. *Mexico* **118** C3
San Lúcido *Italy* **43** C9
San Luis *Argentina* **126** C2
San Luis *Cuba* **120** B3
San Luis *Guatemala* **120** C2
San Luis *Ariz., U.S.A.* **109** K6
San Luis *Colo., U.S.A.* **109** H11
San Luis □ *Argentina* **126** C2
San Luis, I. *Mexico* **118** B2
San Luis, Sierra de
  Argentina **126** C2
San Luis de la Paz *Mexico* **118** C4
San Luis Obispo *U.S.A.* **111** K6
San Luis Potosí *Mexico* **118** C4
San Luis Potosí □ *Mexico* **118** C4
San Luis Res. *U.S.A.* **110** H5
San Luis Río Colorado
  Mexico **118** A2
San Manuel *U.S.A.* **109** K8
San Marco, C. *Italy* **42** C1
San Marco Argentano *Italy* **43** C9
San Marco in Lámis *Italy* **41** G12
San Marcos *Guatemala* **120** D1
San Marcos *Calif., U.S.A.* **111** M9
San Marcos *Tex., U.S.A.* **116** G6
San Marcos, I. *Mexico* **118** B2
San Marino *San Marino* **41** E9
San Marino ■ *Europe* **41** E9
San Martín *Antarctica* **5** C17
San Martín *Argentina* **126** C2
San Martín ➔ *Bolivia* **124** F6
San Martín, L. *Argentina* **128** F2
San Martín de la Vega *Spain* **36** E7
San Martín de los Andes
  Argentina **128** E2
San Martín de
  Valdeiglesias *Spain* **36** E6
San Mateo = Sant Mateu
  Baleares, Spain **48** B7
San Mateo = Sant Mateu
  Valencia, Spain **38** E5
San Mateo *Phil.* **61** C4
San Mateo *U.S.A.* **110** H4
San Matías *Bolivia* **124** G7
San Matías, G. *Argentina* **128** E4
San Miguel = Sant Miquel
  Spain **48** B7
San Miguel *El Salv.* **120** D2
San Miguel *Panama* **120** E4
San Miguel *U.S.A.* **110** K6
San Miguel ➔ *Bolivia* **124** F6
San Miguel de Tucumán
  Argentina **126** B2
San Miguel del Monte
  Argentina **126** D4
San Miguel I. *U.S.A.* **111** L6
San Miniato *Italy* **40** E7
San Nicolás *Canary Is.* **48** G4
San Nicolas *Phil.* **61** B4
San Nicolás de los Arroyos
  Argentina **126** C3
San Nicolas I. *U.S.A.* **111** M7
San Onofre *U.S.A.* **111** M9
San Pablo *Bolivia* **126** A2
San Pablo *Phil.* **61** D4
San Pablo *U.S.A.* **110** H4
San Páolo di Civitate *Italy* **41** G12
San Pedro *B. Aires, Argentina*
  126 C4
San Pedro *Misiones,
  Argentina* **127** B5
San Pedro *Chile* **126** C1
San Pedro *Ivory C.* **82** E3
San Pedro *Mexico* **118** C3
San Pedro □ *Paraguay* **126** A4
San Pedro ➔ *Chihuahua,
  Mexico* **118** B3
San Pedro ➔ *Nayarit,
  Mexico* **118** C3
San Pedro ➔ *U.S.A.* **109** K8
San Pedro, Pta. *Chile* **126** B1
San Pedro, Sierra de *Spain* **37** F4
San Pedro Channel *U.S.A.* **111** M8
San Pedro de Atacama
  Chile **126** A2
San Pedro de Jujuy
  Argentina **126** A3
San Pedro de las Colonias
  Mexico **118** B4
San Pedro de Macorís
  Dom. Rep. **121** C6
San Pedro del Norte *Nic.* **120** D3
San Pedro del Paraná
  Paraguay **126** B4

San Pedro del Pinatar *Spain* **39** H4
San Pedro Mártir, Sierra *Mexico* **118** A1
San Pedro Mártir △ *Mexico* **118** A1
San Pedro Ocampo = Melchor Ocampo *Mexico* **118** C4
San Pedro Pochutla *Mexico* **119** D5
San Pedro Sula *Honduras* **120** C2
San Pedro Tututepec *Mexico* **119** D5
San Pietro *Italy* **42** C1
San Pietro Vernótico *Italy* **43** B11
San Rafael *Argentina* **126** C2
San Rafael *Calif., U.S.A.* **110** H4
San Rafael *N. Mex., U.S.A.* **109** J10
San Rafael Mt. *U.S.A.* **111** L7
San Rafael Mts. *U.S.A.* **111** L7
San Ramón de la Nueva Orán *Argentina* **126** A3
San Remo *Italy* **40** E4
San Roque *Argentina* **126** B4
San Roque *Spain* **37** J5
San Rosendo *Chile* **126** D1
San Saba *U.S.A.* **116** F5
San Salvador *El Salv.* **120** D2
San Salvador de Jujuy *Argentina* **126** A3
San Salvador I. *Bahamas* **121** B5
San Salvo *Italy* **41** F11
San Sebastián = Donostia-San Sebastián *Spain* **38** B3
San Sebastián *Argentina* **128** G3
San Sebastián *Puerto Rico* **121** d
San Sebastián de la Gomera *Canary Is.* **48** F2
San Serra = Son Serra *Spain* **48** B10
San Serverino Marche *Italy* **41** E10
San Severo *Italy* **41** G12
San Simeon *U.S.A.* **110** K5
San Simon *U.S.A.* **109** K9
San Stéfano di Cadore *Italy* **41** B9
San Stino di Livenza *Italy* **41** C9
San Telmo = Sant Elm *Spain* **48** B9
San Telmo *Mexico* **118** A1
San Tiburcio *Mexico* **118** C4
San Valentin, Mte. *Chile* **128** F2
San Vicente de Alcántara *Spain* **37** F3
San Vicente de Cañete *Peru* **124** F3
San Vicente de la Barquera *Spain* **36** B6
San Vincenzo *Italy* **40** E7
San Vito *Costa Rica* **120** E3
San Vito *Italy* **42** C2
San Vito, C. *Italy* **42** D5
San Vito al Tagliamento *Italy* **41** C9
San Vito Chietino *Italy* **41** F11
San Vito dei Normanni *Italy* **43** B10
Sana' *Yemen* **75** D3
Sana → *Bos.-H.* **41** C13
Sanaba *Burkina Faso* **82** C4
Sanae IV *Antarctica* **5** D2
Şanâfir *Si. Arabia* **80** B3
Sanaga → *Cameroon* **83** E6
Sanaloa, Presa *Mexico* **118** C3
Sanana *Indonesia* **63** E7
Sanand *India* **68** H5
Sanandaj *Iran* **73** E12
Sanandita *Bolivia* **126** A3
Sanary-sur-Mer *France* **21** E9
Sanawad *India* **68** H7
Sancellas = Sencelles *Spain* **48** B9
Sancergues *France* **19** E9
Sancerre *France* **19** E9
Sancerrois, Collines du *France* **19** E9
Sancha He → *China* **58** D6
Sanchahe *China* **57** B14
Sánchez *Dom. Rep.* **121** C6
Sanchor *India* **68** G4
Sancoins *France* **19** F9
Sancti Spíritus *Cuba* **120** B4
Sancy, Puy de *France* **20** C6
Sand = Polokwane → *S. Africa* **89** C5
Sand Hills *U.S.A.* **112** D3
Sand Lakes ⌂ *Canada* **103** B9
Sand Springs *U.S.A.* **116** C6
Sanda *Japan* **55** G7
Sandakan *Malaysia* **62** C5
Sandan = Sambor *Cambodia* **64** F6
Sandanski *Bulgaria* **44** E7
Sandaré *Mali* **82** C2
Sandared *Sweden* **11** G6
Sandarne *Sweden* **10** C11
Sanday *U.K.* **13** B6
Sande *Norway* **10** E4
Sandefjord *Norway* **9** G14
Sanders *U.S.A.* **109** J9
Sanderson *U.S.A.* **116** F3
Sandersville *U.S.A.* **117** E13
Sandfire Roadhouse *Australia* **92** C3
Sandfly L. *Canada* **103** B7
Sandfontein *Namibia* **88** C2

Sandheads, The *India* **69** J13
Sandía *Peru* **124** F5
Sandıklı *Turkey* **47** C12
Sandila *India* **69** F9
Sandnes *Norway* **9** G11
Sandnessjøen *Norway* **8** C15
Sandoa *Dem. Rep. of the Congo* **84** F4
Sandomierz *Poland* **31** H8
Sândominic *Romania* **29** D10
Sandover → *Australia* **94** C2
Sandoway = Thandwe *Burma* **67** K19
Sandoy *Færoe Is.* **8** F9
Sandpoint *U.S.A.* **108** B5
Sandray *U.K.* **13** E1
Sandringham *U.K.* **14** E8
Sandstone *Australia* **93** E2
Sandu *China* **58** E6
Sandusky *Mich., U.S.A.* **114** C2
Sandusky *Ohio, U.S.A.* **114** E2
Sandveld *Namibia* **88** C3
Sandvig *Denmark* **11** J8
Sandviken *Sweden* **10** D10
Sandwich, C. *Australia* **94** B4
Sandwich B. *Canada* **105** B8
Sandwich B. *Namibia* **88** C1
Sandy *Oreg., U.S.A.* **110** E4
Sandy *Pa., U.S.A.* **114** E6
Sandy *Utah, U.S.A.* **108** F8
Sandy Bay *Canada* **103** B8
Sandy Bight *Australia* **93** F3
Sandy C. *Queens., Australia* **94** C5
Sandy C. *Tas., Australia* **95** G3
Sandy Cay *Bahamas* **121** B4
Sandy Cr. → *U.S.A.* **108** F9
Sandy Creek *U.S.A.* **115** C8
Sandy L. *Canada* **104** B1
Sandy Lake *Canada* **104** B1
Sandy Valley *U.S.A.* **111** K11
Sânfjällets ⌂ *Sweden* **10** B7
Sanford *Fla., U.S.A.* **117** G14
Sanford *Maine, U.S.A.* **115** C14
Sanford *N.C., U.S.A.* **117** D15
Sanford → *Australia* **93** E2
Sanford, Mt. *U.S.A.* **100** C5
Sang-i-Masha *Afghan.* **68** C2
Sanga → *Congo* **84** E3
Sangamner *India* **66** K9
Sangān *Iran* **71** C9
Sanganeb Atoll △ *Sudan* **80** D4
Sangar *Afghan.* **68** C1
Sangar *Russia* **53** C13
Sangar Sarai *Afghan.* **68** B4
Sangaredi *Guinea* **82** C2
Sangarh → *Pakistan* **68** D4
Sangasso *Mali* **82** C3
Sangatte *France* **19** B8
Sangāw *Iraq* **73** E11
Sangay *Ecuador* **124** D3
Sange *Dem. Rep. of the Congo* **86** D2
Sangeang *Indonesia* **63** F5
Sângeorz-Băi *Romania* **29** C9
Sanger *U.S.A.* **110** J7
Sângera *Moldova* **29** D13
Sangerhausen *Germany* **24** D7
Sanggan He → *China* **56** E9
Sanggau *Indonesia* **62** D4
Sanghar *Pakistan* **68** F3
Sangihe, Kepulauan *Indonesia* **63** D7
Sangihe, Pulau *Indonesia* **63** D7
Sangju *S. Korea* **57** F15
Sangkapura *Indonesia* **62** F4
Sangkhla Buri *Thailand* **64** E2
Sangkulirang *Indonesia* **62** D5
Sangla *Pakistan* **68** D5
Sangli *India* **66** L9
Sangmélima *Cameroon* **83** E7
Sangod *India* **68** G7
Sangre de Cristo Mts. *U.S.A.* **109** H11
Sangre Grande *Trin. & Tob.* **125** K15
Sangro → *Italy* **41** F11
Sangrur *India* **68** D6
Sangudo *Canada* **102** C6
Sangue → *Brazil* **124** F7
Sangüesa *Spain* **38** C3
Sangzhi *China* **59** C8
Sanhala *Ivory C.* **82** C3
Sanibel *U.S.A.* **117** H13
Sanikluaq *Canada* **104** A4
Sanin-Kaigan △ *Japan* **55** G7
Sanirajak *Canada* **101** C11
Sanjawi *Pakistan* **68** D3
Sanje *Uganda* **86** C3
Sanjiang *China* **58** E7
Sanjo *Japan* **54** F9
Sankh → *India* **69** H11
Sankt Andrä *Austria* **26** E7
Sankt Anton *Austria* **25** H6
Sankt Augustin *Germany* **24** E3
Sankt Blasien *Germany* **25** H4
Sankt Gallen *Switz.* **25** H5
Sankt Gallen □ *Switz.* **25** H5
Sankt Goar *Germany* **25** E3
Sankt Ingbert *Germany* **25** F3
Sankt Johann im Pongau *Austria* **26** D6

Sankt Johann in Tirol *Austria* **26** D5
Sankt Michel = Mikkeli *Finland* **32** B11
Sankt Moritz *Switz.* **25** J5
Sankt-Peterburg *Russia* **32** C6
Sankt Pölten *Austria* **26** C8
Sankt Ulrich = Ortisei *Italy* **41** B8
Sankt Valentin *Austria* **26** C7
Sankt Veit an der Glan *Austria* **26** E7
Sankt Wendel *Germany* **25** F3
Sankt Wolfgang *Austria* **26** D6
Sankuru → *Dem. Rep. of the Congo* **84** E4
Sanliurfa *Turkey* **73** D8
Sanliurfa □ *Turkey* **73** D8
Sanlúcar de Barrameda *Spain* **37** J4
Sanluri *Italy* **42** C1
Sânmartin *Romania* **29** D10
Sanmen *China* **59** C13
Sanmenxia *China* **56** G6
Sanming *China* **59** D11
Sannicandro Gargánico *Italy* **41** E9
Sânnicolau Mare *Romania* **28** D5
Sannieshof *S. Africa* **88** D4
Sannin, J. *Lebanon* **74** B4
Sannûr, W. → *Egypt* **80** B3
Sanok *Poland* **31** J9
Sanquhar *U.K.* **13** F5
Sans Souci *Trin. & Tob.* **125** K16
Sansanding *Mali* **82** C3
Sansepolcro *Italy* **41** E9
Sansha *China* **59** D13
Sanshui *China* **59** F9
Sanski Most *Bos.-H.* **41** D13
Sansui *China* **58** D7
Sant Antoni de Portmany *Spain* **48** C7
Sant Boi de Llobregat *Spain* **38** D7
Sant Carles *Spain* **48** C7
Sant Carles de la Ràpita *Spain* **38** E5
Sant Celoni *Spain* **38** D7
Sant Elm *Spain* **48** B9
Sant Feliu de Guíxols *Spain* **38** D8
Sant Feliu de Llobregat *Spain* **38** D7
Sant Ferran *Spain* **48** C7
Sant Francesc de Formentera *Spain* **48** C7
Sant Jaume *Spain* **48** B11
Sant Joan *Spain* **48** B10
Sant Joan d'Alacant *Spain* **39** G4
Sant Joan de Labritja *Spain* **48** B8
Sant Jordi *Ibiza, Spain* **48** C7
Sant Jordi *Mallorca, Spain* **48** B9
Sant Jordi, G. de *Spain* **38** E6
Sant Llorenç de Morunys *Spain* **38** C6
Sant Llorenç del Munt y l'Obac ⌂ *Spain* **38** D3
Sant Llorenç des Cardassar *Spain* **48** B10
Sant Mateu *Baleares, Spain* **48** B7
Sant Mateu *Valencia, Spain* **38** E5
Sant Miquel *Spain* **48** B7
Sant Salvador *Spain* **48** B10
Sant Vicent del Raspeig *Spain* **39** G4
Sant' Ágata Militello *Italy* **43** D7
Sant Agnès *Spain* **48** B7
Santa Ana *Bolivia* **124** F5
Santa Ana *El Salv.* **120** D2
Santa Ana *Mexico* **118** A2
Santa Ana *U.S.A.* **111** M9
Sant' Ángelo Lodigiano *Italy* **40** C6
Sant' Antíoco *Italy* **42** C1
Santa Bárbara *Chile* **126** D1
Santa Bárbara *Honduras* **120** D2
Santa Bárbara *Mexico* **118** B3
Santa Bárbara *Spain* **38** E5
Santa Barbara *U.S.A.* **111** L7
Santa Bárbara, Mt. *Spain* **39** H2
Santa Barbara Channel *U.S.A.* **111** L7
Santa Barbara I. *U.S.A.* **111** M7
Santa Catalina, Gulf of *U.S.A.* **111** N9
Santa Catalina, I. *Mexico* **118** B2
Santa Catalina I. *U.S.A.* **111** M8
Santa Catarina □ *Brazil* **127** B6
Santa Catarina, I. de *Brazil* **127** B6
Santa Caterina di Pittinuri *Italy* **42** B1
Santa Caterina Villarmosa *Italy* **43** E7
Santa Cecília *Brazil* **127** B5
Santa Clara *Cuba* **120** B4
Santa Clara *Calif., U.S.A.* **110** H5
Santa Clara *N.Y., U.S.A.* **115** B10
Santa Clara *Utah, U.S.A.* **109** H7
Santa Clara de Olimar *Uruguay* **127** C5
Santa Clara Valley *U.S.A.* **110** J5
Santa Clarita *U.S.A.* **111** L8

Santa Clotilde *Peru* **124** D4
Santa Coloma de Farners *Spain* **38** D7
Santa Coloma de Gramenet *Spain* **38** D7
Santa Comba *Spain* **36** B2
Santa Croce Camerina *Italy* **43** F7
Santa Croce di Magliano *Italy* **41** G11
Santa Cruz *Bolivia* **124** G6
Santa Cruz *Chile* **126** C1
Santa Cruz *Costa Rica* **120** D2
Santa Cruz *Madeira* **48** D3
Santa Cruz *Phil.* **61** D4
Santa Cruz *U.S.A.* **110** J4
Santa Cruz → *Argentina* **128** G3
Santa Cruz de la Palma *Canary Is.* **48** F2
Santa Cruz de la Palma ✈ (SPC) *Canary Is.* **48** F2
Santa Cruz de Mudela *Spain* **37** G7
Santa Cruz de Tenerife *Canary Is.* **48** F3
Santa Cruz del Norte *Cuba* **120** B3
Santa Cruz del Retamar *Spain* **36** E6
Santa Cruz del Sur *Cuba* **120** B4
Santa Cruz do Rio Pardo *Brazil* **127** A6
Santa Cruz do Sul *Brazil* **127** B5
Santa Cruz I. *U.S.A.* **111** M7
Santa Cruz Is. *Solomon Is.* **90** C9
Santa Cruz Mts. *Jamaica* **120** a
Santa Domingo, Cay *Bahamas* **120** B4
Sant' Egídio alla Vibrata *Italy* **41** F10
Santa Elena *Argentina* **126** C4
Santa Elena, C. *Costa Rica* **120** D2
Sant' Eufémia, G. di *Italy* **43** D9
Santa Eulària des Riu *Spain* **48** C8
Santa Fé *Argentina* **126** C3
Santa Fe *Spain* **37** H7
Santa Fe *U.S.A.* **109** J11
Santa Fé □ *Argentina* **126** C3
Santa Fé do Sul *Brazil* **125** H8
Santa Filomena *Brazil* **125** E9
Santa Fiora *Italy* **41** F8
Santa Gertrudis *Spain* **48** C7
Santa Giustina *Italy* **41** B9
Santa Inês *Brazil* **125** F11
Santa Inés *Spain* **37** G5
Santa Inés, I. *Chile* **128** G2
Santa Isabel *Argentina* **126** D2
Santa Isabel do Morro *Brazil* **125** F8
Santa Lucía *Corrientes, Argentina* **126** B4
Santa Lucía *San Juan, Argentina* **126** C2
Santa Lucía *Spain* **39** H4
Santa Lucia *Uruguay* **126** C4
Santa Lucia Range *U.S.A.* **110** K5
Santa Luzia *C. Verde Is.* **78** b
Santa Margalida *Spain* **48** B10
Santa Margarita *Argentina* **126** D3
Santa Margarita *U.S.A.* **110** K6
Santa Margarita, I. *Mexico* **118** C2
Santa Margherita *Italy* **42** D1
Santa Margherita Ligure *Italy* **40** D6
Santa María *Argentina* **126** B2
Santa Maria *Azores* **78** a
Santa Maria *Brazil* **127** B5
Santa Maria *C. Verde Is.* **78** b
Santa Maria *Phil.* **61** C4
Santa María *U.S.A.* **111** L6
Santa María → *Mexico* **118** A3
Santa Maria, B. de *Mexico* **118** B3
Santa Maria, C. de *Portugal* **37** J3
Santa Maria Cápua Vétere *Italy* **43** A7
Santa Maria da Feira *Portugal* **36** E2
Santa Maria da Vitória *Brazil* **125** F10
Santa María del Camí *Spain* **48** B9
Santa María di Léuca, C. *Italy* **43** C11
Santa María la Real de Nieva *Spain* **36** D6
Santa Marinella *Italy* **41** F8
Santa Marta *Colombia* **124** A4
Santa Marta, Sierra Nevada de *Colombia* **124** A4
Santa Marta de Tormes *Spain* **36** E5
Santa Marta Grande, C. *Brazil* **127** B6
Santa Marta Ortigueira, Ría de *Spain* **36** B3
Santa Maura = Lefkada *Greece* **46** C2
Santa Monica *U.S.A.* **111** M8
Santa Monica Mts. ⌂ *U.S.A.* **111** L8
Santa Olalla *Spain* **36** E6
Santa Olalla del Cala *Spain* **37** H4

Santa Paula *U.S.A.* **111** L7
Santa Pola *Spain* **39** G4
Santa Ponça *Spain* **48** B9
Santa Rosa *La Pampa, Argentina* **126** D3
Santa Rosa *San Luis, Argentina* **126** C2
Santa Rosa *Calif., U.S.A.* **110** G4
Santa Rosa *N. Mex., U.S.A.* **109** J11
Santa Rosa *Brazil* **127** B5
Santa Rosa and San Jacinto Mts. ⌂ *U.S.A.* **111** M10
Santa Rosa de Copán *Honduras* **120** D2
Santa Rosa de Río Primero *Argentina* **126** C3
Santa Rosa del Sara *Bolivia* **124** G6
Santa Rosa I. *Calif., U.S.A.* **111** M6
Santa Rosa I. *Fla., U.S.A.* **117** F11
Santa Rosa Range *U.S.A.* **108** F5
Santa Rosalía *Mexico* **118** B2
Santa Sylvina *Argentina* **126** B3
Santa Tecla = Nueva San Salvador *El Salv.* **120** D2
Santa Teresa *Argentina* **126** C3
Santa Teresa *Australia* **94** C1
Santa Teresa *Mexico* **119** B5
Santa Teresa △ *Uruguay* **127** C5
Santa Teresa di Riva *Italy* **43** E8
Santa Teresa Gallura *Italy* **42** A2
Santa Teresita *Argentina* **126** D4
Santa Uxía de Ribeira *Spain* **36** C2
Santa Vitória do Palmar *Brazil* **127** C5
Santa Ynez → *U.S.A.* **111** L6
Santa Ynez Mts. *U.S.A.* **111** L6
Santa Ysabel *U.S.A.* **111** M10
Santadi *Italy* **42** C1
Santaella *Spain* **37** H6
Santai *China* **58** B5
Santana *Madeira* **48** D3
Sântana *Romania* **28** D6
Santana, Coxilha de *Brazil* **127** C4
Santana do Livramento *Brazil* **127** C4
Santander *Spain* **36** B7
Santander Jiménez *Mexico* **119** C5
Santanilla, Is. *Honduras* **120** C3
Santanyí *Spain* **48** B10
Santaquin *U.S.A.* **108** G8
Santarcángelo di Romagna *Italy* **41** D9
Santarém *Brazil* **125** D8
Santarém *Portugal* **37** F2
Santarém □ *Portugal* **37** F2
Santaren Channel *W. Indies* **120** B4
Santee *U.S.A.* **111** N10
Santee → *U.S.A.* **117** E15
Santéramo in Colle *Italy* **43** B9
Santerno → *Italy* **41** D8
Santhià *Italy* **40** C5
Santi-Quaranta = Sarandë *Albania* **44** G3
Santiago = Río Grande de Santiago → *Mexico* **118** C3
Santiago = São Tiago *C. Verde Is.* **78** b
Santiago *Brazil* **127** B5
Santiago *Canary Is.* **48** F2
Santiago *Chile* **126** C1
Santiago *Panama* **120** E3
Santiago *Phil.* **61** C4
Santiago → *Peru* **124** D3
Santiago, Punta de *Eq. Guin.* **83** E6
Santiago de Compostela *Spain* **36** C2
Santiago de Cuba *Cuba* **120** C4
Santiago de los Caballeros *Dom. Rep.* **121** C5
Santiago del Estero *Argentina* **126** B3
Santiago del Estero □ *Argentina* **126** B3
Santiago del Teide *Canary Is.* **48** F3
Santiago do Cacém *Portugal* **37** G2
Santiago Ixcuintla *Mexico* **118** C3
Santiago Jamiltepec *Mexico* **119** D5
Santiago Papasquiaro *Mexico* **118** C3
Santiago Pinotepa Nacional *Mexico* **119** D5
Santiaguillo, L. de *Mexico* **118** C4
Santiguila *Mali* **82** C3
Santillana del Mar *Spain* **36** B6
Santisteban del Puerto *Spain* **37** G7
Santo Amaro *Brazil* **125** F11
Santo Anastácio *Brazil* **127** A5
Santo André *Brazil* **127** A6
Santo Ângelo *Brazil* **127** B5
Santo Antão *C. Verde Is.* **78** b
Santo Antônio do Içá *Brazil* **124** D5
Santo Antônio do Leverger *Brazil* **125** G7
Santo Domingo *Dom. Rep.* **121** C6
Santo Domingo *Baja Calif., Mexico* **118** A1
Santo Domingo *Baja Calif. S., Mexico* **118** B2
Santo Domingo *Nic.* **120** D3

Santo Domingo de la Calzada *Spain* **38** C2
Santo Domingo de los Colorados *Ecuador* **124** D3
Santo Domingo Pueblo *U.S.A.* **109** J10
Santo Stéfano di Camastro *Italy* **43** D7
Santo Tirso *Portugal* **36** D2
Santo Tomás *Mexico* **118** A1
Santo Tomás *Peru* **124** F4
Santo Tomé *Argentina* **127** B4
Santo Tomé de Guayana = Ciudad Guayana *Venezuela* **124** B6
Santomera *Spain* **39** G3
Santoña *Spain* **36** B7
Santorini *Greece* **47** E7
Santos *Brazil* **127** A6
Santos, Sierra de los *Spain* **37** G5
Santos Dumont *Brazil* **127** A7
Santuario de Aves Laguna Colorada △ *Bolivia* **126** A2
Sanur *Indonesia* **63** K18
Sanwer *India* **68** H6
Sanxenxo *Spain* **36** C2
Sanya *China* **64** C7
Sanyuan *China* **56** G5
São Bartolomeu de Messines *Portugal* **37** H2
São Bernardo do Campo *Brazil* **127** A6
São Borja *Brazil* **127** B4
São Brás de Alportel *Portugal* **37** H3
São Carlos *Brazil* **127** A6
São Cristóvão *Brazil* **125** F11
São Domingos *Brazil* **125** F9
São Domingos *Guinea-Biss.* **82** C1
São Filipe *C. Verde Is.* **78** b
São Francisco *Brazil* **125** G10
São Francisco → *Brazil* **125** F11
São Francisco do Sul *Brazil* **127** B6
São Gabriel *Brazil* **127** C5
São Gonçalo *Brazil* **127** A7
Sao Hill *Tanzania* **87** D4
São João *Guinea-Biss.* **82** C1
São João da Boa Vista *Brazil* **127** A6
São João da Madeira *Portugal* **36** E2
São João da Pesqueira *Portugal* **36** D3
São João do Araguaia *Brazil* **125** E9
São João do Piauí *Brazil* **125** E10
São João do Rei *Brazil* **127** A7
São Joaquim *Brazil* **127** B6
São Joaquim △ *Brazil* **127** B6
São Jorge *Azores* **78** a
São Jorge, Pta. de *Madeira* **48** D3
São José *Brazil* **127** B5
São José do Norte *Brazil* **127** C5
São José do Rio Preto *Brazil* **127** A6
São José dos Campos *Brazil* **127** A6
São Leopoldo *Brazil* **127** B5
São Lourenço *Brazil* **127** A6
São Lourenço → *Brazil* **125** G7
São Lourenço, Pta. de *Madeira* **48** D3
São Lourenço do Sul *Brazil* **127** C5
São Luís *Brazil* **125** D10
São Luís Gonzaga *Brazil* **127** B5
São Marcos → *Brazil* **125** G9
São Marcos, B. de *Brazil* **125** D10
São Martinho da Cortiça *Portugal* **36** E2
São Mateus *Brazil* **125** G11
São Mateus do Sul *Brazil* **127** B5
São Miguel *Azores* **78** a
São Miguel do Oeste *Brazil* **127** B5
São Nicolau *C. Verde Is.* **78** b
São Paulo *Brazil* **127** A6
São Paulo □ *Brazil* **127** A6
São Paulo de Olivença *Brazil* **124** D5
São Pedro do Sul *Portugal* **36** E2
São Roque *Madeira* **48** D3
São Roque, C. de *Brazil* **125** E11
São Sebastião, I. de *Brazil* **127** A6
São Sebastião do Paraíso *Brazil* **127** A6
São Teotónio *Portugal* **37** H2
São Tiago *C. Verde Is.* **78** b
São Tomé *São Tomé & Príncipe* **76** F4
São Tomé, C. de *Brazil* **127** A7
São Tomé & Príncipe ■ *Africa* **77** F4
São Vicente *Brazil* **127** A6
São Vicente *C. Verde Is.* **78** b
São Vicente *Madeira* **48** D2
São Vicente, C. de *Portugal* **37** H1
Saona → I. *Dom. Rep.* **121** C6
Saône → *France* **19** G11
Saône-et-Loire □ *France* **19** F11
Saonek *Indonesia* **63** E8
Sapam, Ao *Thailand* **65** a
Sapanca *Turkey* **72** B4
Saparua *Indonesia* **63** E7
Sapele *Nigeria* **83** D6

Sapelo I. *U.S.A.* **117** F14
Sapes *Greece* **45** E9
Şaphane *Turkey* **47** B11
Sapi *Zimbabwe* **87** F2
Sapienza *Greece* **46** E3
Sapo △ *Liberia* **82** D3
Sapone *Burkina Faso* **83** C4
Saposoa *Peru* **124** E3
Sapotskina *Belarus* **30** E10
Sapouy *Burkina Faso* **83** C4
Sapozhok *Russia* **34** D5
Sapphire *Australia* **94** C4
Sappho *U.S.A.* **110** B2
Sapporo *Japan* **54** C10
Sapri *Italy* **43** B8
Sapulpa *U.S.A.* **116** D6
Saqqez *Iran* **73** D12
Sar Dasht
  Āzarbāyjān-e Gharbī, Iran **73** D11
Sar Dasht *Khuzestān, Iran* **71** C6
Sar-e Pol □ *Afghan.* **66** B4
Sar Gachīneh = Yāsūj *Iran* **71** D6
Sar Planina *Macedonia* **44** E4
Sara *Burkina Faso* **82** C4
Sara *Phil.* **61** F5
Šara △ *Serbia* **44** D5
Sara Buri = Saraburi
  Thailand **64** E3
Sarāb *Iran* **73** D12
Sarābleh *Iran* **73** F12
Saraburi *Thailand* **64** E3
Saradiya *India* **68** J4
Saraféré *Mali* **82** B4
Saragossa = Zaragoza *Spain* **38** D4
Saraguro *Ecuador* **124** D3
Sarahs *Turkmenistan* **71** B9
Sarai Naurang *Pakistan* **68** C4
Saraikela *India* **69** H11
Saraiu *Romania* **29** F13
Sarajevo *Bos.-H.* **28** G3
Sarakhs = Sarahs
  Turkmenistan **71** B9
Saran, Gunung *Indonesia* **62** E4
Saranac Lake *U.S.A.* **115** B10
Saranac Lakes *U.S.A.* **115** B10
Saranda *Tanzania* **86** D3
Sarandë *Albania* **44** G3
Sarandí del Yí *Uruguay* **127** C4
Sarandí Grande *Uruguay* **126** C4
Sarangani B. *Phil.* **61** J6
Sarangani Is. *Phil.* **61** J6
Sarangarh *India* **67** J13
Saransk *Russia* **34** C7
Sarapul *Russia* **52** D6
Sarasota *U.S.A.* **117** H13
Sarata *Ukraine* **29** D14
Sarata → *Ukraine* **29** E14
Saratoga *Calif., U.S.A.* **110** H4
Saratoga *Wyo., U.S.A.* **108** F10
Saratoga △ *U.S.A.* **115** D11
Saratoga L. *U.S.A.* **115** C11
Saratoga Springs *U.S.A.* **115** C11
Saratok *Malaysia* **62** D4
Saratov *Russia* **34** E7
Saratov □ *Russia* **34** E8
Sarāvān *Iran* **71** E9
Saravane *Laos* **64** E6
Sarawak □ *Malaysia* **62** D4
Saray Tekirdağ, *Turkey* **45** E11
Saray *Van, Turkey* **73** C11
Saraya *Senegal* **82** C2
Saraycık *Turkey* **47** B11
Sarayköy *Turkey* **47** D10
Saraylar *Turkey* **45** F11
Sarayönü *Turkey* **72** C5
Sarbāz *Iran* **71** E9
Sarbīsheh *Iran* **71** C8
Sárbogárd *Hungary* **28** D3
Sarca → *Italy* **40** C7
Sarcelles *France* **19** D9
Sarda → *India* **69** F9
Sardarshahr *India* **68** E6
Sardegna □ *Italy* **42** B1
Sardhana *India* **68** E7
Sardina, Pta. *Canary Is.* **48** F4
Sardinia = Sardegna □ *Italy* **42** B1
Sardis *Turkey* **47** C10
Sārdūīyeh = Dar Mazār *Iran* **71** D8
Saren *Indonesia* **63** J18
S'Arenal *Spain* **48** B9
Sarentino *Italy* **41** B8
Sarera, G. of *Indonesia* **90** B6
Saréyamou *Mali* **82** B4
Sargasso Sea *Atl. Oc.* **98** G13
Sargodha *Pakistan* **68** C5
Sarh *Chad* **79** G9
Sarhala *Ivory C.* **82** D3
Sārī *Iran* **71** B7
Sari d'Orcino *France* **21** F12
Saria *Greece* **47** F9
Saria *India* **69** J10
Sariab *Pakistan* **68** D2
Sarıbeyler *Turkey* **47** B9
Sarıgöl *Turkey* **47** C9
Sarıkamış *Turkey* **73** B10
Sarıkaya *Turkey* **72** C6
Sarikei *Malaysia* **62** D4
Sarıköy *Turkey* **45** F11

Sarila *India* **69** G8
Sarina *Australia* **94** C4
Sariñena *Spain* **38** D4
Sarıoğlan *Turkey* **72** C6
Sarita *U.S.A.* **116** H6
Sariwŏn *N. Korea* **57** E13
Sarıyar Barajı *Turkey* **72** B4
Sarıyer *Turkey* **45** E13
Sarju → *India* **69** F9
Sark *U.K.* **15** H5
Sarkad *Hungary* **28** D6
Sarkari Tala *India* **68** F4
Şarkışla *Turkey* **72** C7
Şarköy *Turkey* **45** F11
Sarlat-la-Canéda *France* **20** D5
Sărmăşag *Romania* **28** C7
Sărmaşu *Romania* **29** D9
Sarmi *Indonesia* **63** E9
Sarmiento *Argentina* **128** F3
Sarmizegetusa *Romania* **28** E7
Särna *Sweden* **10** C7
Sarnano *Italy* **41** E10
Sarnen *Switz.* **25** J4
Sarnia *Canada* **114** D2
Sarno *Italy* **43** B7
Sarnthein = Sarentino *Italy* **41** B8
Särö *Sweden* **11** G5
Sarolangun *Indonesia* **62** E2
Saronikos Kolpos *Greece* **46** D5
Saronno *Italy* **40** C6
Saros Körfezi *Turkey* **45** F10
Sárospatak *Hungary* **28** B6
Sarpsborg *Norway* **9** G14
Sarqan *Kazakhstan* **52** E8
Sarracín *Spain* **36** C7
Sarralbe *France* **19** D14
Sarre = Saar → *Europe* **17** E6
Sarre *Italy* **40** C7
Sarre-Union *France* **19** D14
Sarrebourg *France* **19** D14
Sarreguemines *France* **19** C14
Sarria *Spain* **36** C3
Sarrión *Spain* **38** E4
Sarro *Mali* **82** C3
Sarsing *Iraq* **73** D10
Sarstedt *Germany* **24** C5
Sartène *France* **21** G12
Sarthe □ *France* **18** D7
Sarthe → *France* **18** E6
Sartilly *France* **18** D5
Saruhanlı *Turkey* **47** C9
Sărulești *Romania* **29** F11
Saruna → *Pakistan* **68** F2
Sārūr *Azerbaijan* **73** C11
Sárvár *Hungary* **28** C1
Sarvar *India* **68** F6
Sarvestān *Iran* **71** D7
Särvfjället *Sweden* **10** B7
Sárvíz → *Hungary* **28** D3
Sary-Tash *Kyrgyzstan* **52** F8
Sarych, Mys *Ukraine* **33** K7
Saryshaghan *Kazakhstan* **52** E8
Sarzana *Italy* **40** D6
Sarzeau *France* **18** E4
Sasan Gir *India* **68** J4
Sasaram *India* **69** G11
Sasebo *Japan* **55** H4
Saser Kangri *India* **69** B7
Saskatchewan □ *Canada* **103** C7
Saskatchewan → *Canada* **103** C8
Saskatoon *Canada* **103** C7
Saskylakh *Russia* **53** B12
Saslaya △ *Nic.* **120** D2
Sasolburg *S. Africa* **89** D4
Sason *Turkey* **73** C9
Sasovo *Russia* **34** C5
Sassandra *Ivory C.* **82** E3
Sassandra → *Ivory C.* **82** E3
Sássari *Italy* **42** B1
Sassnitz *Germany* **24** A9
Sasso Marconi *Italy* **41** D8
Sassocorvaro *Italy* **41** E9
Sassoferrato *Italy* **41** E9
Sasstown *Liberia* **82** E3
Sassuolo *Italy* **40** D7
Sástago *Spain* **38** D4
Sasyk, Ozero *Ukraine* **29** E14
Sata-Misaki *Japan* **55** J5
Satadougou *Mali* **82** C2
Satakunda = Satakunta
  Finland **32** B2
Satakunta *Finland* **32** B2
Satama-Soukoura *Ivory C.* **82** D4
Satara *India* **66** L8
Satara *S. Africa* **89** C5
Satbarwa *India* **69** H11
Säter *Sweden* **10** D9
Satevó *Mexico* **118** B3
Satilla → *U.S.A.* **117** F14
Satmala Hills
  Andhra Pradesh, India **66** K11
Satmala Hills *Maharashtra,
  India* **66** J9
Satna *India* **69** G9
Šator *Bos.-H.* **41** D13
Sátoraljaújhely *Hungary* **28** B6
Satpura △ *India* **68** H8

Satpura Ra. *India* **66** J10
Satrup *Germany* **24** A5
Satsuna-Shotō *Japan* **55** K5
Sattahip *Thailand* **64** F3
Satu Mare *Romania* **28** C7
Satu Mare □ *Romania* **28** C8
Satui *Indonesia* **62** E5
Satun *Thailand* **65** J3
Satupa'itea *Samoa* **91** b
Saturnina → *Brazil* **124** F7
Sauce *Argentina* **126** C4
Sauceda *Mexico* **118** B4
Saucillo *Mexico* **118** B3
Sauda *Norway* **9** G12
Sauðarkrókur *Iceland* **8** D4
Saudi Arabia ■ *Asia* **70** B3
Sauerland *Germany* **22** C4
Saugeen → *Canada* **114** B3
Saugerties *U.S.A.* **115** D11
Saugues *France* **20** D7
Saujon *France* **20** D3
Sauk Centre *U.S.A.* **112** C6
Sauk Rapids *U.S.A.* **112** C6
Saulgau *Germany* **25** G5
Saulieu *France* **19** E11
Sault *France* **21** D9
Sault Ste. Marie *Canada* **104** C3
Sault Ste. Marie *U.S.A.* **113** B11
Saumlaki *Indonesia* **63** F8
Saumur *France* **18** E6
Saunders, C. *N.Z.* **91** F3
Saunders I. *Antarctica* **5** B1
Saunders Pt. *Australia* **93** E4
Sauri *Nigeria* **83** C6
Saurimo *Angola* **84** F4
Sausalito *U.S.A.* **110** H4
Sava *Italy* **43** B10
Sava → *Serbia* **28** F5
Savá *Honduras* **120** C2
Savage *U.S.A.* **108** C2
Savage I. = Niue *Pac. Oc.* **97** J11
Savage River *Australia* **95** G4
Savai'i *Samoa* **91** b
Savalou *Benin* **83** D5
Savane *Mozam.* **87** F4
Savanna *U.S.A.* **112** D8
Savanna-la-Mar *Jamaica* **120** a
Savannah *Ga., U.S.A.* **117** E14
Savannah *Mo., U.S.A.* **112** F6
Savannah *Tenn., U.S.A.* **117** D10
Savannah → *U.S.A.* **117** E14
Savannakhet *Laos* **64** D5
Savant L. *Canada* **104** B1
Savant Lake *Canada* **104** B1
Săvârşin *Romania* **28** D7
Savaştepe *Turkey* **47** B9
Savé *Benin* **83** D5
Save → *France* **20** E5
Save → *Mozam.* **89** C5
Sāveh *Iran* **71** C6
Savelugu *Ghana* **83** D4
Savenay *France* **18** E5
Săveni *Romania* **29** C11
Saverdun *France* **20** E5
Saverne *France* **19** D14
Savigliano *Italy* **40** D4
Savigny-sur-Braye *France* **18** E7
Sávio → *Italy* **41** D9
Šavnik *Montenegro* **44** D3
Savo *Finland* **8** E22
Savoie □ *France* **21** C10
Savolax = Savo *Finland* **8** E22
Savona *Italy* **40** D5
Savonlinna *Finland* **32** B5
Savoy = Savoie □ *France* **21** C10
Savşat *Turkey* **73** B10
Sävsjö *Sweden* **11** G8
Savur *Turkey* **70** B4
Savusavu *Fiji* **91** a
Savusavu B. *Fiji* **91** a
Sawahlunto *Indonesia* **62** E2
Sawai *Indonesia* **63** E7
Sawai Madhopur *India* **68** G7
Sawaleke *Fiji* **91** a
Sawang Daen Din *Thailand* **64** D4
Sawankhalok *Thailand* **64** D2
Sawara *Japan* **55** G10
Sawatch Range *U.S.A.* **108** G10
Sawel Mt. *U.K.* **12** B4
Sawi *Thailand* **65** G2
Sawla *Ghana* **82** D4
Sawmills *Zimbabwe* **87** F2
Sawtooth △ *U.S.A.* **108** D6
Sawtooth Range *U.S.A.* **108** D6
Sawu *Indonesia* **63** F6
Sawu Sea *Indonesia* **63** F6
Saxby → *Australia* **94** B3
Saxmundham *U.K.* **15** E9
Saxony = Sachsen □
  Germany **24** D9
Saxony, Lower =
  Niedersachsen □ *Germany* **24** C4
Saxton *U.S.A.* **114** F6
Say *Mali* **82** C4
Say *Niger* **83** C5

Saya *Nigeria* **83** D5
Sayabec *Canada* **105** C6
Sayaboury *Laos* **64** C3
Sayán *Peru* **124** F3
Sayan, Vostochnyy *Russia* **53** D10
Sayan, Zapadnyy *Russia* **53** D10
Sayanogorsk *Russia* **53** D10
Saydā *Lebanon* **74** B4
Sayhandulaan = Oldziyt
  Mongolia **56** B5
Sayhūt *Yemen* **75** D5
Saykhin *Kazakhstan* **35** F8
Saylac *Somali Rep.* **75** E3
Saynshand =
  Buyant-Uhaa *Mongolia* **60** B6
Sayre *Okla., U.S.A.* **116** D5
Sayre *Pa., U.S.A.* **115** E8
Sayreville *U.S.A.* **115** F10
Sayula *Mexico* **118** D4
Sayward *Canada* **102** C3
Sazanit *Albania* **44** F3
Sázava → *Czech Rep.* **26** B7
Sazin *Pakistan* **69** B5
Sazlika → *Bulgaria* **45** E9
Scaër *France* **18** D3
Scafell Pike *U.K.* **14** C4
Scalea *Italy* **43** C8
Scalloway *U.K.* **13** A7
Scalpay *U.K.* **13** D3
Scandia *Canada* **102** C6
Scandiano *Italy* **40** D7
Scandicci *Italy* **41** E8
Scandinavia *Europe* **8** E15
Scansano *Italy* **41** F8
Scapa Flow *U.K.* **13** C5
Scappoose *U.S.A.* **110** E4
Scarámia, Capo *Italy* **43** F7
Scarba *U.K.* **13** E3
Scarborough *Trin. & Tob.* **121** D7
Scarborough *U.K.* **14** C7
Scariff I. *Ireland* **12** E1
Scarp *U.K.* **13** C1
Scarpe-Escaut △ *France* **19** B10
Scebeli = Shabeelle →
  Somali Rep. **75** G3
Šćedro *Croatia* **41** E13
Schaal See *Germany* **24** B6
Schaalsee △ *Germany* **24** B6
Schaffhausen *Switz.* **25** H4
Schagen *Neths.* **17** B4
Schaghticoke *U.S.A.* **115** D11
Schärding *Austria* **26** C6
Scharhörn *Germany* **24** B4
Scheessel *Germany* **24** B5
Schefferville *Canada* **105** B6
Scheibbs *Austria* **26** C8
Schelde → *Belgium* **17** C4
Schell Creek Ra. *U.S.A.* **108** G6
Schellsburg *U.S.A.* **114** F6
Schenectady *U.S.A.* **115** D11
Schenevus *U.S.A.* **115** D10
Scherfede *Germany* **24** D5
Schesslitz *Germany* **25** F7
Schiedam *Neths.* **17** C4
Schiermonnikoog *Neths.* **17** A6
Schiltigheim *France* **19** D14
Schinousa *Greece* **47** E7
Schio *Italy* **41** C8
Schiphol, Amsterdam ✈
  (AMS) *Neths.* **17** B4
Schladming *Austria* **26** D6
Schlanders = Silandro *Italy* **40** B7
Schlei → *Germany* **24** A5
Schleiden *Germany* **24** E2
Schleiz *Germany* **24** E7
Schleswig *Germany* **24** A5
Schleswig-Holstein □
  Germany **24** A5
Schlüchtern *Germany* **25** E5
Schmalkalden *Germany* **24** E6
Schmölln *Germany* **24** E8
Schneeberg *Austria* **26** D8
Schneeberg *Germany* **24** E8
Schneverdingen *Germany* **24** B5
Schœlcher *Martinique* **120** c
Schoharie *U.S.A.* **115** D10
Schoharie Cr. → *U.S.A.* **115** D10
Scholls *U.S.A.* **110** E4
Schönberg
  *Mecklenburg-Vorpommern,
  Germany* **24** B6
Schönberg
  Schleswig-Holstein, Germany **24** A6
Schönbuch △ *Germany* **25** G5
Schönebeck *Germany* **24** C7
Schongau *Germany* **25** H6
Schöningen *Germany* **24** C6
Schopfheim *Germany* **25** H3
Schorndorf *Germany* **25** G5
Schortens *Germany* **24** B3
Schouten, I. *Australia* **95** G4
Schouten Is. = Supiori
  Indonesia **63** E9
Schouwen *Neths.* **17** C3
Schramberg *Germany* **25** G4
Schrankogel *Austria* **26** D4
Schreiber *Canada* **104** C2
Schrems *Austria* **26** C8
Schrobenhausen *Germany* **25** G7

Schroffenstein *Namibia* **88** D2
Schroon Lake *U.S.A.* **115** C11
Schruns *Austria* **26** D2
Schuler *Canada* **103** C6
Schumacher *Canada* **104** C3
Schurz *U.S.A.* **108** G4
Schuyler *U.S.A.* **112** E5
Schuylerville *U.S.A.* **115** C11
Schuylkill → *U.S.A.* **115** G9
Schuylkill Haven *U.S.A.* **115** F8
Schwabach *Germany* **25** F7
Schwaben □ *Germany* **25** G6
Schwäbisch-Fränkischer
  Wald △ *Germany* **25** G5
Schwäbisch Gmünd
  Germany **25** G5
Schwäbisch Hall *Germany* **25** F5
Schwäbische Alb *Germany* **25** G5
Schwabmünchen *Germany* **25** G6
Schwalmstadt *Germany* **24** E5
Schwandorf *Germany* **25** F8
Schwaner, Pegunungan
  Indonesia **62** E4
Schwanewede *Germany* **24** B4
Schwarmstedt *Germany* **24** C5
Schwarze Elster → *Germany* **24** D8
Schwarzenberg *Germany* **24** E8
Schwarzrand *Namibia* **88** D2
Schwarzwald *Germany* **25** G4
Schwaz *Austria* **26** D4
Schwechat *Austria* **27** C9
Schwechat, Wien ✈ (VIE)
  Austria **27** C9
Schwedt *Germany* **24** B10
Schweinfurt *Germany* **25** E6
Schweizer-Reneke *S. Africa* **88** D4
Schwenningen =
  Villingen-
  Schwenningen *Germany* **25** G4
Schwerin *Germany* **24** B7
Schweriner See *Germany* **24** B7
Schwetzingen *Germany* **25** F4
Schwyz *Switz.* **25** H4
Schwyz □ *Switz.* **25** H4
Sciacca *Italy* **42** E6
Scicli *Italy* **43** F7
Sciliar △ *Italy* **41** B8
Scilla *Italy* **43** D8
Scilly, Isles of *U.K.* **15** H1
Ścinawa *Poland* **31** G3
Scione *Greece* **44** G7
Scioto → *U.S.A.* **113** F12
Scituate *U.S.A.* **115** D14
Scobey *U.S.A.* **108** B11
Scone *Australia* **95** E5
Scone *U.K.* **13** E5
Scordia *Italy* **43** E7
Scoresbysund =
  Ittoqqortoormiit *Greenland* **4** B6
Scornicești *Romania* **29** F9
Scotia *Calif., U.S.A.* **108** F1
Scotia *N.Y., U.S.A.* **115** D11
Scotia Sea *Antarctica* **5** B18
Scotland *Canada* **114** C4
Scott *Antarctica* **5** D11
Scott, C. *Australia* **92** B4
Scott City *U.S.A.* **112** F3
Scott Glacier *Antarctica* **5** C8
Scott I. *Antarctica* **5** C11
Scott L. *Canada* **103** B7
Scott Reef *Australia* **92** B3
Scottburgh *S. Africa* **89** E5
Scottdale *U.S.A.* **114** F5
Scottish Borders □ *U.K.* **13** F6
Scotts Valley *U.S.A.* **110** H4
Scottsbluff *U.S.A.* **112** E2
Scottsboro *U.S.A.* **117** D11
Scottsburg *U.S.A.* **113** F11
Scottsdale *Australia* **95** G4
Scottsdale *U.S.A.* **109** K8
Scottsville *Ky., U.S.A.* **112** G10
Scottsville *N.Y., U.S.A.* **114** C7
Scottville *U.S.A.* **112** D10
Scranton *U.S.A.* **115** E9
Scugog, L. *Canada* **114** B6
Sculeni *Moldova* **29** C12
Scunthorpe *U.K.* **14** D7
Scuol Schuls *Switz.* **25** J6
Scutari = Shkodër *Albania* **44** D3
Scutari = Üsküdar *Turkey* **45** F13
Sea Is. *U.S.A.* **117** F14
Seabrook, L. *Australia* **93** F2
Seaford *U.K.* **15** G8
Seaford *U.S.A.* **113** F16
Seaforth *Australia* **94** J6
Seaforth *Canada* **114** C3
Seaforth, L. *U.K.* **13** D2
Seagraves *U.S.A.* **116** E3
Seaham *U.K.* **14** C6
Seal → *Canada* **103** B10
Seal L. *Canada* **105** B7
Sealy *U.S.A.* **116** G6
Searchlight *U.S.A.* **111** K12
Searcy *U.S.A.* **116** D9
Searles L. *U.S.A.* **111** K9

Seascale *U.K.* **14** C4
Seaside *Calif., U.S.A.* **110** J5
Seaside *Oreg., U.S.A.* **110** E3
Seaspray *Australia* **95** F4
Seattle *U.S.A.* **110** C4
Seattle-Tacoma Int. ✈
  (SEA) *U.S.A.* **110** C4
Seaview Ra. *Australia* **94** B4
Sebago L. *U.S.A.* **115** C14
Sebago Lake *U.S.A.* **115** C14
Sebastián Vizcaíno, B.
  Mexico **118** B2
Sebastopol = Sevastopol
  Ukraine **33** K7
Sebastopol *U.S.A.* **110** G4
Sebba *Burkina Faso* **83** C5
Sebderat *Eritrea* **81** D4
Sébékoro *Mali* **82** C3
Seben *Turkey* **72** B4
Sebeş *Romania* **29** E8
Sebeşului, Munţii *Romania* **29** E8
Sebewaing *U.S.A.* **113** D12
Sebezh *Russia* **32** D5
Sebha = Sabhā *Libya* **79** C8
Sébi *Mali* **82** B4
Şebinkarahisar *Turkey* **73** B8
Sebiş *Romania* **28** D7
Sebnitz *Germany* **24** E10
Sebring *Fla., U.S.A.* **117** H14
Sebring *Ohio, U.S.A.* **114** F3
Sebringville *Canada* **114** C3
Sebta = Ceuta *N. Afr.* **78** A4
Sebuku *Indonesia* **62** E5
Sebuku, Teluk *Malaysia* **62** D5
Sečanj *Serbia* **28** E5
Secchia → *Italy* **40** C8
Sechelt *Canada* **102** D4
Sechura, Desierto de *Peru* **124** E2
Seclin *France* **19** B10
Secondigny *France* **18** F6
Sečovce *Slovak Rep.* **27** C14
Secretary I. *N.Z.* **91** F1
Secunderabad *India* **66** L11
Security *U.S.A.* **108** G11
Sedalia *U.S.A.* **112** F7
Sedan *France* **19** C11
Sedan *U.S.A.* **112** G5
Sedano *Spain* **36** C7
Sedbergh *U.K.* **14** C5
Seddon *N.Z.* **91** D5
Seddonville *N.Z.* **91** D4
Sedé Boqér *Israel* **74** E3
Sedeh *Fārs, Iran* **71** D7
Sedeh *Khorāsān, Iran* **71** C8
Séderon *France* **21** D9
Sederot *Israel* **74** D3
Sédhiou *Senegal* **82** C1
Sedico *Italy* **41** B9
Sedlčany *Czech Rep.* **26** B7
Sedley *Canada* **103** C8
Sedona *U.S.A.* **109** J8
Sedova, Pik *Russia* **52** B6
Sedro-Woolley *U.S.A.* **110** B4
Šeduva *Lithuania* **30** C10
Sędziszów *Poland* **31** H7
Sędziszów Małopolski *Poland* **31** H8
Seebad Ahlbeck *Germany* **24** B10
Seefeld in Tirol *Austria* **26** D4
Seehausen *Germany* **24** C7
Seeheim *Namibia* **88** D2
Seeheim-Jugenheim
  Germany **25** F4
Seeis *Namibia* **88** C2
Seekoei → *S. Africa* **88** E4
Seeley's Bay *Canada* **115** B8
Seelow *Germany* **24** C10
Sées *France* **18** D7
Seesen *Germany* **24** D6
Seevetal *Germany* **24** B6
Seewinkel = Neusiedler
  See-Seewinkel △ *Austria* **27** D9
Şefaatli *Turkey* **72** C6
Sefadu *S. Leone* **82** D2
Seferihisar *Turkey* **47** C8
Séféto *Mali* **82** C3
Sefwi Bekwai *Ghana* **82** D4
Segamat *Malaysia* **65** L4
Şegarcea *Romania* **29** F8
Ségbana *Benin* **83** C5
Segbwema *S. Leone* **82** D2
Segesta *Italy* **42** E5
Seget *Indonesia* **63** E8
Segezha *Russia* **32** C4
Segonzac *France* **20** C3
Segorbe *Spain* **38** F4
Ségou *Mali* **82** C3
Ségou □ *Mali* **82** C3
Segovia = Coco →
  Cent. Amer. **120** D3
Segovia *Spain* **36** E6
Segovia □ *Spain* **36** E6
Segré *France* **18** E6
Segre → *Spain* **38** D5
Séguéla *Ivory C.* **82** D3
Séguénéga *Burkina Faso* **83** C4
Seguin *U.S.A.* **116** G6
Segundo → *Argentina* **126** C3
Segura → *Spain* **39** G4
Segura, Sierra de *Spain* **39** G2
Seh Konj, Kūh-e *Iran* **71** D8

Seh Qal'eh *Iran* **71** C8
Sehitwa *Botswana* **88** C3
Sehlabathebe △ *Lesotho* **89** D4
Sehore *India* **68** H7
Sehwan *Pakistan* **68** F2
Şeica Mare *Romania* **29** D9
Seikan Tunnel *Japan* **54** D10
Seil *U.K.* **13** E3
Seiland *Norway* **8** A20
Seilhac *France* **20** C5
Seiling *U.S.A.* **116** C5
Seille → *Moselle, France* **19** C13
Seille → *Saône-et-Loire, France* **19** F11
Sein, Î. de *France* **18** D2
Seinäjoki *Finland* **8** E20
Seine → *France* **18** C7
Seine, B. de la *France* **18** C6
Seine-et-Marne □ *France* **19** D10
Seine-Maritime □ *France* **18** C7
Seine-St-Denis □ *France* **19** D9
Seini *Romania* **29** C8
Seirijai *Lithuania* **30** D10
Seistan = Sīstān *Asia* **71** D9
Seistan, Daryācheh-ye = Sīstān, Daryācheh-ye *Iran* **71** D9
Sejerø *Denmark* **11** J5
Sejerø Bugt *Denmark* **11** J5
Sejny *Poland* **30** D10
Seka *Ethiopia* **81** F4
Sekayu *Indonesia* **62** E2
Seke *Tanzania* **86** C3
Sekenke *Tanzania* **86** C3
Seki *Turkey* **47** E11
Sekondi-Takoradi *Ghana* **82** E4
Sekota *Ethiopia* **81** E4
Seksna *Russia* **32** C10
Sekudai *Malaysia* **65** d
Sekuma *Botswana* **88** C3
Selah *U.S.A.* **108** C3
Selama *Malaysia* **65** K3
Selárgius *Italy* **42** C2
Selaru *Indonesia* **63** F8
Selatan, Selat *Malaysia* **65** c
Selb *Germany* **25** E8
Selby *U.K.* **14** D6
Selby *U.S.A.* **112** C3
Selca *Croatia* **41** E13
Selçuk *Turkey* **47** D9
Selden *U.S.A.* **112** F3
Sele → *Italy* **43** B7
Selebi-Phikwe *Botswana* **89** C4
Selemdzha → *Russia* **53** D13
Selendi *Manisa, Turkey* **47** C10
Selendi *Manisa, Turkey* **47** C9
Selenga = Selenge Mörön → *Asia* **60** A5
Selenge Mörön → *Asia* **60** A5
Selenicë *Albania* **44** F3
Selenter See *Germany* **24** A6
Sélestat *France* **19** D14
Seletan, Tanjung *Indonesia* **62** E4
Selevac *Serbia* **44** B4
Sélibabi *Mauritania* **82** B2
Seliger, Ozero *Russia* **32** D7
Seligman *U.S.A.* **109** J7
Şelim *Turkey* **73** B10
Selîma, El Wâhât el *Sudan* **80** C2
Selîma, El Wâhât el *Sudan* **79** D11
Selimiye *Turkey* **47** D9
Selinda Spillway → *Botswana* **88** B3
Sélingué, L. de *Mali* **82** C3
Selinsgrove *U.S.A.* **114** F8
Selizharovo *Russia* **32** D7
Selkirk *Man., Canada* **103** C9
Selkirk *Ont., Canada* **114** D5
Selkirk *U.K.* **13** F6
Selkirk I. = Horse I. *Canada* **103** C9
Selkirk Mts. *Canada* **100** D8
Sellafield *U.K.* **14** C4
Sellama *Sudan* **81** E2
Sellia *Greece* **49** D6
Sellières *France* **19** F12
Sells *U.S.A.* **109** L8
Sellye *Hungary* **28** E2
Selma *Ala., U.S.A.* **117** E11
Selma *Calif., U.S.A.* **110** J7
Selma *N.C., U.S.A.* **117** D15
Selmer *U.S.A.* **117** D10
Selongey *France* **19** E12
Selous △ *Tanzania* **87** D4
Selowandoma Falls *Zimbabwe* **87** G3
Selpele *Indonesia* **63** E8
Selsey Bill *U.K.* **15** G7
Seltso *Russia* **32** F8
Seltz *France* **19** D15
Selu *Indonesia* **63** F8
Sélune → *France* **18** D5
Selva = La Selva del Camp *Spain* **38** D6
Selva *Argentina* **126** B3
Selva *Spain* **48** B9
Selva Lancandona = Montes Azules △ *Mexico* **119** D6
Selvagens, Ilhas *Madeira* **78** B2
Selvas *Brazil* **124** E5

Selwyn L. *Canada* **103** B8
Selwyn Mts. *Canada* **100** C6
Selwyn Ra. *Australia* **94** C3
Selyatyn *Ukraine* **29** C10
Seman → *Albania* **44** F3
Semarang *Indonesia* **63** G14
Sembabule *Uganda* **86** C3
Sembawang *Singapore* **65** d
Sembung *Indonesia* **63** J18
Şemdinli *Turkey* **73** D11
Sémé *Senegal* **82** B2
Semeih *Sudan* **81** E3
Semenanjung Blambangan *Indonesia* **63** K17
Semenov *Russia* **34** B7
Semenovka *Chernihiv, Ukraine* **33** F7
Semenovka *Kremenchuk, Ukraine* **33** H7
Semeru *Indonesia* **63** H15
Semey *Kazakhstan* **52** D9
Semikarakorskiy *Russia* **35** G5
Semiluki *Russia* **33** G10
Seminoe Res. *U.S.A.* **108** E10
Seminole *Okla., U.S.A.* **116** D6
Seminole *Tex., U.S.A.* **116** E3
Seminole Draw → *U.S.A.* **116** E3
Semipalatinsk = Semey *Kazakhstan* **52** D9
Semirara Is. *Phil.* **61** F4
Semitau *Indonesia* **62** D4
Semmering P. *Austria* **26** D8
Semnān *Iran* **71** C7
Semnān □ *Iran* **71** C7
Semporna *Malaysia* **63** D5
Semuda *Indonesia* **62** E4
Semur-en-Auxois *France* **19** E11
Sen → *Cambodia* **64** F5
Sen → *Cambodia* **64** F5
Senā *Iran* **71** D6
Sena *Mozam.* **87** F4
Sena Madureira *Brazil* **124** E5
Senador Pompeu *Brazil* **125** E11
Senaki *Georgia* **35** J6
Senanga *Zambia* **85** H4
Senatobia *U.S.A.* **117** D10
Sencelles *Spain* **48** B9
Sendafa *Ethiopia* **81** F4
Sendai *Kagoshima, Japan* **55** J5
Sendai *Miyagi, Japan* **54** E10
Sendai-Wan *Japan* **54** E10
Senden *Bayern, Germany* **25** G6
Senden *Nordrhein-Westfalen, Germany* **24** D3
Sendhwa *India* **68** J6
Sene → *Ghana* **83** D4
Senec *Slovak Rep.* **27** C10
Seneca *U.S.A.* **117** D13
Seneca Falls *U.S.A.* **115** D8
Seneca L. *U.S.A.* **114** D8
Senecaville L. *U.S.A.* **114** G3
Senegal ■ *W. Afr.* **82** C2
Sénégal → *W. Afr.* **82** B1
Senegambia *Africa* **76** E2
Senekal *S. Africa* **89** D4
Senftenberg *Germany* **24** D10
Senga Hill *Zambia* **87** D3
Senge Khambab = Indus → *Pakistan* **68** G2
Sengiley *Russia* **34** D9
Sengua → *Zimbabwe* **87** F2
Senhor-do-Bonfim *Brazil* **125** F10
Senica *Slovak Rep.* **27** C10
Senigállia *Italy* **41** E10
Senj *Croatia* **41** D11
Senja *Norway* **8** B17
Senkaku-Shotō *E. China Sea* **55** M1
Senkuang *Indonesia* **65** d
Senlis *France* **19** C9
Senmonorom *Cambodia* **64** F6
Sennâr *Sudan* **81** E3
Sennâr □ *Sudan* **81** E3
Senneterre *Canada* **104** C4
Senno *Belarus* **32** E5
Sénnori *Italy* **42** B1
Seno *Laos* **64** D5
Senonches *France* **18** D8
Senorbì *Italy* **42** C2
Senožeče *Slovenia* **41** C11
Sens *France* **19** D10
Senta *Serbia* **28** E5
Sentani *Indonesia* **63** E10
Sentery = Lubao *Dem. Rep. of the Congo* **86** D2
Sentinel *U.S.A.* **109** K7
Šentjur *Slovenia* **41** B12
Sentosa *Singapore* **65** d
Senya Beraku *Ghana* **83** D4
Seo de Urgel = La Seu d'Urgell *Spain* **38** C6
Seogwipo *S. Korea* **57** H14
Seohara *India* **69** E8
Seonath → *India* **69** J10
Seondha *India* **69** F8
Seongnam *S. Korea* **57** F14

Seoni *India* **69** H8
Seoni Malwa *India* **68** H8
Seonsan *S. Korea* **57** F15
Seosan *S. Korea* **57** F14
Seoul *S. Korea* **57** F14
Sepīdān *Iran* **71** D7
Sepo'o *N. Korea* **57** E14
Sepone *Laos* **64** D6
Sepopol *Poland* **30** D8
Sept-Îles *Canada* **105** B6
Sepúlveda *Spain* **36** D7
Sequeros *Spain* **36** E4
Sequim *U.S.A.* **110** B3
Sequoia △ *U.S.A.* **110** J8
Serafimovich *Russia* **34** F6
Seraing *Belgium* **17** D5
Serakhis → *Cyprus* **49** D11
Seram *Indonesia* **63** E7
Seram Sea *Indonesia* **63** E7
Serang *Indonesia* **63** G12
Serangoon *Singapore* **65** d
Serasan *Indonesia* **62** D3
Seravezza *Italy* **40** E7
Şerbettar *Turkey* **45** E10
Serbia *Serbia* **44** C5
Serbia ■ *Europe* **44** C4
Şercaia *Romania* **29** E10
Serdar *Turkmenistan* **71** B8
Serdo *Ethiopia* **81** E5
Serdobsk *Russia* **34** D7
Seredka *Russia* **32** C5
Serednye *Ukraine* **28** B7
Sereflikoçhisar *Turkey* **72** C5
Seregno *Italy* **40** C6
Seremban *Malaysia* **65** L3
Serengeti △ *Tanzania* **86** C3
Serengeti Plain *Tanzania* **86** C4
Serenje *Zambia* **87** E3
Seret → *Ukraine* **29** B10
Sereth = Siret → *Romania* **29** E12
Sergach *Russia* **34** C7
Sergen *Turkey* **45** E11
Sergeya Kirova, Ostrova *Russia* **53** B10
Sergino *Russia* **52** C7
Sergipe □ *Brazil* **125** F11
Sergiyev Posad *Russia* **32** D10
Seria *Brunei* **62** D4
Serian *Malaysia* **62** D4
Seriate *Italy* **40** C6
Seribu, Kepulauan *Indonesia* **62** F3
Sericho *Kenya* **86** B4
Sérifontaine *France* **19** C8
Serifos *Greece* **46** D6
Sérignan *France* **20** E7
Sérigny → *Canada* **105** A6
Serik *Turkey* **72** D4
Seringapatam Reef *Australia* **92** B3
Serinhisar *Turkey* **47** D11
Seririt *Indonesia* **63** J18
Serishābād *Iran* **73** E12
Sermaize-les-Bains *France* **19** D11
Sermata *Indonesia* **63** F7
Sermersuaq *Greenland* **4** B4
Sérmide *Italy* **41** D8
Sermata *Russia* **34** D10
Sernur *Russia* **34** B9
Serock *Poland* **31** F8
Serón *Spain* **39** H2
Seròs *Spain* **38** D5
Serov *Russia* **52** D7
Serowe *Botswana* **88** C4
Serpa *Portugal* **37** H3
Serpeddì, Punta *Italy* **42** C2
Serpentara *Italy* **42** C2
Serpentine Lakes *Australia* **93** E4
Serpent's Mouth = Sierpe, Bocas de la *Venezuela* **125** L15
Serpis → *Spain* **39** G4
Serpneve *Ukraine* **29** D14
Serpukhov *Russia* **32** E9
Serra da Estrela △ *Portugal* **36** E3
Serra do Navio *Brazil* **125** C8
Serra San Bruno *Italy* **43** D9
Serradilla *Spain* **36** F4
Serramanna *Italy* **42** C1
Serranía San Luís △ *Paraguay* **126** A4
Serranía San Rafael △ *Paraguay* **127** B4
Serras d'Aire e Candeeiros △ *Portugal* **37** F2
Serravalle Scrivia *Italy* **40** D5
Serre-Ponçon, L. de *France* **21** D10
Serres *France* **21** D9
Serres *Greece* **44** E7
Serres □ *Greece* **44** E7
Serrezuela *Argentina* **126** C2
Serrinha *Brazil* **125** F11
Sersale *Italy* **43** C9
Sertã *Portugal* **36** F2
Sertânia *Brazil* **125** E11
Sertanópolis *Brazil* **127** A5
Sêrtar *China* **58** A3
Serua *Indonesia* **63** F8

Serui *Indonesia* **63** E9
Serule *Botswana* **88** C4
Servia *Greece* **44** F6
Serzedelo *Portugal* **36** D2
Ses Salines *Spain* **48** B10
Sese Is. *Uganda* **86** C3
Sesepe *Indonesia* **63** E7
Sesfontein *Namibia* **88** B1
Sésia → *Italy* **40** C5
Sesheke *Zambia* **88** B3
Sesimbra *Portugal* **37** G1
S'Espalmador *Spain* **48** C7
S'Espardell *Spain* **48** C7
Sessa Aurunca *Italy* **42** A6
S'Estanyol *Spain* **48** B9
Sestao *Spain* **38** B2
Sesto Calende *Italy* **40** C5
Sesto San Giovanni *Italy* **40** C6
Sestri Levante *Italy* **40** D6
Sestriere *Italy* **40** D3
Sestroretsk *Russia* **32** B6
Sestrunj *Croatia* **41** D11
Sestu *Italy* **42** C2
Sète *France* **20** E7
Sete Lagoas *Brazil* **125** G10
Sétif *Algeria* **78** A7
Seto *Japan* **55** G8
Setonaikai *Japan* **55** G6
Setonaikai △ *Japan* **55** G6
Settat *Morocco* **78** B4
Séttimo Torinese *Italy* **40** C4
Setting L. *Canada* **103** C9
Settle *U.K.* **14** C5
Settlement, The *Br. Virgin Is.* **121** e
Settlers *S. Africa* **89** C4
Setúbal *Portugal* **37** G2
Setúbal □ *Portugal* **37** G2
Setúbal, B. de *Portugal* **37** G2
Seugne → *France* **20** C3
Seul, Lac *Canada* **104** B1
Seurre *France* **19** F12
Sevan *Armenia* **35** K7
Sevan, Ozero = Sevana Lich *Armenia* **35** K7
Sevana Lich *Armenia* **35** K7
Sevastopol *Ukraine* **33** K7
Seven Sisters *Canada* **102** C3
Sever → *Spain* **37** F3
Sévérac-le-Château *France* **20** D7
Severn → *Canada* **104** A2
Severn → *U.K.* **15** F5
Severnaya Zemlya *Russia* **53** B11
Severo-Kurilsk *Russia* **53** D16
Severo-Yeniseyskiy *Russia* **53** C10
Severo-Zapadnyy □ *Russia* **52** C4
Severobaykalsk *Russia* **53** D11
Severočeský □ *Czech Rep.* **26** A7
Severodonetsk = Syeverodonetsk *Ukraine* **33** H10
Severodvinsk *Russia* **52** C4
Severomoravský □ *Czech Rep.* **27** B10
Severomorsk *Russia* **8** B25
Seversk *Russia* **52** D9
Sevier → *U.S.A.* **108** G7
Sevier Desert *U.S.A.* **108** G7
Sevier L. *U.S.A.* **108** G7
Sevilla *Spain* **37** H5
Sevilla □ *Spain* **37** H5
Seville = Sevilla *Spain* **37** H5
Sevlievo *Bulgaria* **45** C9
Sevnica *Slovenia* **41** B12
Sèvre-Nantaise → *France* **18** E5
Sèvre-Niortaise → *France* **20** B3
Sevsk *Russia* **33** F8
Sewa → *S. Leone* **82** D2
Sewani *India* **68** E6
Seward *Alaska, U.S.A.* **100** B5
Seward *Nebr., U.S.A.* **112** E5
Seward *Pa., U.S.A.* **114** F5
Seward Peninsula *U.S.A.* **106** a
Sewell *Chile* **126** C1
Sewer *Indonesia* **63** F8
Sewickley *U.S.A.* **114** F4
Sexsmith *Canada* **102** B5
Seychelles ■ *Ind. Oc.* **85** b
Seyðisfjörður *Iceland* **8** D7
Seydişehir *Turkey* **72** D5
Seydvān *Iran* **73** C11
Seyhan → *Turkey* **72** D6
Seyhan Baraji *Turkey* **72** D6
Seyitgazi *Turkey* **47** B12
Seyitömer *Turkey* **47** B11
Seym → *Ukraine* **33** G7
Seymen *Turkey* **45** E11
Seymour *Australia* **95** F4
Seymour *S. Africa* **89** E4
Seymour *Conn., U.S.A.* **115** E11
Seymour *Ind., U.S.A.* **113** F11
Seymour *Tex., U.S.A.* **116** J5
Seyne *France* **21** D10
Seyssel *France* **21** C9
Sézanne *France* **19** D10
Sezze *Italy* **42** A5
Sfântu Gheorghe *Covasna, Romania* **29** E10
Sfântu Gheorghe *Tulcea, Romania* **29** F14

Sfântu Gheorghe, Brațul → *Romania* **29** F14
Sfax *Tunisia* **79** B8
Sha Xi → *China* **59** D12
Sha Xian *China* **59** D11
Shaanxi □ *China* **56** G5
Shaba = Katanga □ *Dem. Rep. of the Congo* **86** D2
Shaba △ *Kenya* **86** B4
Shabeelle → *Somali Rep.* **75** G3
Shabestar *Iran* **73** C11
Shabla *Bulgaria* **45** C12
Shabogamo L. *Canada* **105** B6
Shabunda *Dem. Rep. of the Congo* **86** C2
Shache *China* **56** D2
Shackleton Fracture Zone *S. Ocean* **5** B18
Shackleton Ice Shelf *Antarctica* **5** C8
Shackleton Inlet *Antarctica* **5** E11
Shādegān *Iran* **71** D6
Shadi *China* **59** D10
Shadi *India* **69** C7
Shadrinsk *Russia* **52** D7
Shadyside *U.S.A.* **114** G4
Shaffa *Nigeria* **83** C7
Shafter *U.S.A.* **111** K7
Shaftesbury *U.K.* **15** F5
Shaftsbury *U.S.A.* **115** D11
Shagamu *Nigeria* **83** D5
Shagram *Pakistan* **69** A5
Shāh Alam *Malaysia* **65** L3
Shah Alizai *Pakistan* **68** E2
Shah Bunder *Pakistan* **68** G2
Shahabad *Punjab, India* **68** D7
Shahabad *Raj., India* **68** G7
Shahabad *Ut. P., India* **69** F8
Shahadpur *Pakistan* **68** G3
Shahba' *Syria* **74** C5
Shahdād *Iran* **71** D8
Shahdād, Namakzār-e *Iran* **71** D8
Shahdadkot *Pakistan* **68** F2
Shahdol *India* **69** H9
Shahe *China* **56** F8
Shahganj *India* **69** F10
Shahgarh *India* **68** F3
Shahjahanpur *India* **69** F8
Shahpur *Salmās = Iran* **73** C11
Shahpur *India* **68** H7
Shahpur *Baluchistan, Pakistan* **68** E3
Shahpur *Punjab, Pakistan* **68** C5
Shahpur Chakar *Pakistan* **68** F3
Shahpura *Mad. P., India* **69** H9
Shahpura *Raj., India* **68** G6
Shahr-e Bābak *Iran* **71** D7
Shahr-e Kord *Iran* **71** C6
Shahrezā = Qomsheh *Iran* **71** D6
Shahrig *Pakistan* **68** D2
Shāhrud = Emāmrūd *Iran* **71** B7
Shahukou *China* **56** D7
Shaikhabad *Afghan.* **68** B3
Shajapur *India* **68** H7
Shakargarh *Pakistan* **68** C6
Shakawe *Botswana* **88** B3
Shaker Heights *U.S.A.* **114** E3
Shakhtersk *Russia* **53** E15
Shakhty *Russia* **35** G5
Shakhunya *Russia* **34** B8
Shaki *Nigeria* **83** D5
Shākir *Egypt* **80** B3
Shaksam Valley *Asia* **69** A7
Shala, L. *Ethiopia* **81** F4
Shali *Russia* **35** J7
Shalkar Köli *Kazakhstan* **34** E10
Shallow Lake *Canada* **114** B3
Shalqar *Kazakhstan* **52** E6
Shaluli Shan *China* **58** B2
Shām *Iran* **71** E8
Shām, Bādiyat ash *Asia* **70** C3
Shamāl Bahr el Ghazal □ *Sudan* **81** F2
Shamāl Dârfûr □ *Sudan* **81** E2
Shamāl Kordofân □ *Sudan* **81** E3
Shamāl Sînî □ *Egypt* **74** E2
Shamattawa *Canada* **104** A1
Shamattawa → *Canada* **104** A2
Shambe *Sudan* **81** F3
Shambe △ *Sudan* **81** F3
Shambu *Ethiopia* **81** F4
Shamil *Iran* **71** E8
Shamli *India* **68** E7
Shammar, Jabal *Si. Arabia* **70** E4
Shamo = Gobi *Asia* **56** C6
Shamo, L. *Ethiopia* **81** F4
Shamokin *U.S.A.* **115** F8
Shamrock *Canada* **115** A3
Shamrock *U.S.A.* **116** D4
Shamva *Zimbabwe* **87** F3
Shan □ *Burma* **67** J21
Shan Xian *China* **56** G9
Shanan → *Ethiopia* **81** F5
Shanchengzhen *China* **57** C13
Shāndak *Iran* **71** D9

Shandon *U.S.A.* **110** K6
Shandong □ *China* **57** G10
Shandong Bandao *China* **57** F11
Shandur Pass *Pakistan* **69** A5
Shang Xian = Shangzhou *China* **56** H5
Shangalowe *Dem. Rep. of the Congo* **87** E2
Shangani *Zimbabwe* **89** B4
Shangani → *Zimbabwe* **87** F2
Shangbancheng *China* **57** D10
Shangcheng *China* **59** B10
Shangchuan Dao *China* **59** G9
Shangdu *China* **56** D7
Shanggao *China* **59** C10
Shanghai *China* **59** B13
Shanghai Shi □ *China* **59** B13
Shanghang *China* **59** E11
Shanghe *China* **57** F9
Shanglin *China* **58** F7
Shangnan *China* **56** H6
Shangqiu *China* **56** G8
Shangrao *China* **59** C11
Shangshui *China* **60** C6
Shangsi *China* **58** F6
Shangyou *China* **59** E10
Shangyu *China* **59** B13
Shangzhi *China* **57** B14
Shangzhou *China* **56** H5
Shani *Nigeria* **83** C7
Shānidar *Iraq* **73** D11
Shanklin *U.K.* **15** G6
Shannon *N.Z.* **91** D5
Shannon → *Ireland* **12** D2
Shannon ✈ (SNN) *Ireland* **12** D2
Shannon, Mouth of the *Ireland* **12** D2
Shannonbridge *Ireland* **12** C3
Shansi = Shanxi □ *China* **56** F7
Shantar, Ostrov Bolshoy *Russia* **53** D14
Shantipur *India* **69** H13
Shantou *China* **59** F11
Shantung = Shandong □ *China* **57** G10
Shanwei *China* **59** F10
Shanxi □ *China* **56** F7
Shanyang *China* **56** H5
Shanyin *China* **56** E7
Shaodong *China* **59** D8
Shaoguan *China* **59** E9
Shaoshan *China* **59** D9
Shaowu *China* **59** D11
Shaoxing *China* **59** C13
Shaoyang *Hunan, China* **59** D8
Shaoyang *Hunan, China* **59** D8
Shap *U.K.* **14** C5
Shapinsay *U.K.* **13** B6
Shaqq el Gi'eifer → *Sudan* **81** D2
Shaqra' *Si. Arabia* **70** E5
Shaqra' *Yemen* **75** E4
Sharafa *Sudan* **81** E2
Sharafkhāneh *Iran* **73** C11
Sharashova *Belarus* **31** F11
Sharbot Lake *Canada* **115** B8
Sharhorod *Ukraine* **29** B13
Shari *Japan* **54** C12
Sharjah = Ash Shāriqah *U.A.E.* **71** E7
Shark B. *Australia* **93** E1
Shark Bay △ *Australia* **93** E1
Sharm el Sheikh *Egypt* **80** B3
Sharon *Canada* **114** B5
Sharon *Mass., U.S.A.* **115** D13
Sharon *Pa., U.S.A.* **114** E4
Sharon Springs *Kans., U.S.A.* **112** F3
Sharon Springs *N.Y., U.S.A.* **115** D10
Sharp Pt. *Australia* **94** A3
Sharpe L. *Canada* **104** B1
Sharpsville *U.S.A.* **114** E4
Sharqi, Al Jabal ash *Lebanon* **74** B5
Sharya *Russia* **34** A7
Shasha *Ethiopia* **81** F4
Shashemene *Ethiopia* **81** F4
Shashi *Botswana* **89** C4
Shashi *China* **59** B9
Shashi → *Africa* **87** G2
Shasta, Mt. *U.S.A.* **108** F2
Shasta L. *U.S.A.* **108** F2
Shatawi *Sudan* **81** E3
Shatsk *Russia* **34** C5
Shatsk *Ukraine* **31** G10
Shatsky Rise *Pac. Oc.* **96** D7
Shatskyi △ *Ukraine* **31** G10
Shatt al Arab = Arab, Shatt al → *Asia* **71** D6
Shatura *Russia* **32** E10
Shaumyani = Shulaveri *Georgia* **35** K7
Shaunavon *Canada* **103** D7
Shaver L. *U.S.A.* **110** H7
Shaw → *Australia* **92** D2
Shaw I. *Australia* **94** J7
Shawanaga *Canada* **114** A4

Shawangunk Mts. *U.S.A.* **115** E10
Shawano *U.S.A.* **112** C9
Shawinigan *Canada* **104** C5
Shawmari, J. ash *Jordan* **74** E5
Shawnee *U.S.A.* **116** D6
Shay Gap *Australia* **92** D3
Shayang *China* **59** B9
Shaybārā *Si. Arabia* **70** E3
Shayib el Banat, Gebel *Egypt* **80** B3
Shaykh, J. ash *Lebanon* **74** B4
Shaykh Miskīn *Syria* **74** C5
Shaykh Sa'd *Iraq* **73** F12
Shāzand *Iran* **71** C6
Shchekino *Russia* **32** E9
Shchigry *Russia* **33** G9
Shchors *Ukraine* **33** G6
Shchūchīnsk *Kazakhstan* **52** D8
She Xian *Anhui, China* **59** C12
She Xian *Hebei, China* **56** F7
Shebekino *Russia* **33** G9
Shebele = Shabeelle ➔
  Somali Rep. **75** G3
Sheboygan *U.S.A.* **112** D10
Shebshi Mts. *Nigeria* **83** D7
Shediac *Canada* **105** C7
Sheelin, L. *Ireland* **12** C4
Sheep Haven *Ireland* **12** A4
Sheep Range *U.S.A.* **111** J11
Sheerness *U.K.* **15** F8
Sheet Harbour *Canada* **105** D7
Sheffield *U.K.* **14** D6
Sheffield *Ala., U.S.A.* **117** D11
Sheffield *Mass., U.S.A.* **115** D11
Sheffield *Pa., U.S.A.* **114** E5
Shehojele *Ethiopia* **81** E4
Shehong *China* **58** B5
Sheikh Idris *Sudan* **81** E3
Sheikh Zayed Canal *Egypt* **80** C3
Sheikhpura *India* **69** G11
Shek Hasan *Ethiopia* **81** E4
Shekhupura *Pakistan* **68** D5
Sheki = Şaki *Azerbaijan* **35** K8
Shelburne *N.S., Canada* **105** D6
Shelburne *Ont., Canada* **114** B4
Shelburne *U.S.A.* **115** B11
Shelburne B. *Australia* **94** A3
Shelburne Falls *U.S.A.* **115** D12
Shelby *Mich., U.S.A.* **112** D10
Shelby *Miss., U.S.A.* **117** E9
Shelby *Mont., U.S.A.* **108** B8
Shelby *N.C., U.S.A.* **117** D14
Shelby *Ohio, U.S.A.* **114** F2
Shelbyville *Ill., U.S.A.* **112** F9
Shelbyville *Ind., U.S.A.* **113** F11
Shelbyville *Ky., U.S.A.* **113** F11
Shelbyville *Tenn., U.S.A.* **117** D11
Sheldon *U.S.A.* **112** D6
Sheldrake *Canada* **105** B7
Shelengo, Khawr ➔ *Sudan* **81** E2
Shell Lakes *Australia* **93** E4
Shellbrook *Canada* **103** C7
Shellharbour *Australia* **95** E5
Shelon ➔ *Russia* **32** C6
Shelter I. *U.S.A.* **115** E12
Shelton *Conn., U.S.A.* **115** E11
Shelton *Wash., U.S.A.* **110** C3
Shemakha = Şamaxı
  Azerbaijan **35** K9
Shëmri *Albania* **44** D4
Shemsi *Sudan* **80** D2
Shen Xian *China* **56** F8
Shenandoah *Iowa, U.S.A.* **112** E6
Shenandoah *Pa., U.S.A.* **115** F8
Shenandoah *Va., U.S.A.* **113** F14
Shenandoah ➔ *U.S.A.* **113** F15
Shenandoah △ *U.S.A.* **113** F14
Shenchi *China* **56** E7
Shendam *Nigeria* **83** D6
Shendī *Sudan* **81** D3
Shenge *S. Leone* **82** D2
Shengfang *China* **56** E9
Shëngjergj *Albania* **44** E4
Shëngjin *Albania* **44** E3
Shengzhou *China* **59** C13
Shenjingzi *China* **57** B13
Shenmu *China* **56** E6
Shennongjia *China* **59** B8
Shenqiu *China* **56** H8
Shensi = Shaanxi □ *China* **56** G5
Shenyang *China* **57** D12
Shenzhen *China* **59** F10
Sheo *India* **68** F4
Sheopur Kalan *India* **68** G7
Shepetivka *Ukraine* **23** C14
Shepparton *Australia* **95** F4
Sheppey, I. of *U.K.* **15** F8
Shepton Mallet *U.K.* **15** F5
Sheqi *China* **56** H7
Sherab *Sudan* **81** E1
Sherborne *U.K.* **15** G5
Sherbro ➔ *S. Leone* **82** D2
Sherbro I. *S. Leone* **82** D2
Sherbrooke *N.S., Canada* **105** C7
Sherbrooke *Qué., Canada* **115** A13
Sherburne *U.S.A.* **115** D9
Shereik *Sudan* **80** D3
Shergarh *India* **68** F5

Sherghati *India* **69** G11
Sheridan *Ark., U.S.A.* **116** D8
Sheridan *Wyo., U.S.A.* **108** D10
Sheringham *U.K.* **14** E9
Sherkin I. *Ireland* **12** E2
Sherkot *India* **69** E8
Sherlovaya Gora *Russia* **53** D12
Sherman *N.Y., U.S.A.* **114** D5
Sherman *Tex., U.S.A.* **116** E6
Sherpur *India* **69** G10
Sherridon *Canada* **103** B8
Sherwood Forest *U.K.* **14** D6
Sherwood Park *Canada* **102** C6
Sheslay ➔ *Canada* **102** B2
Shethanei L. *Canada* **103** B9
Shetland □ *U.K.* **13** A7
Shetland Is. *U.K.* **13** A7
Shetrunji ➔ *India* **68** J5
Shevchenkovo *Ukraine* **29** E14
Shevisheh *Iran* **73** E12
Shewa *Ethiopia* **81** F4
Shewa Gimira *Ethiopia* **81** F4
Shey-Phoksundo △ *Nepal* **69** E10
Sheyenne ➔ *U.S.A.* **112** B5
Shiashkotan, Ostrov *Russia* **53** E16
Shibām *Yemen* **75** D4
Shibata *Japan* **54** F9
Shibecha *Japan* **54** C12
Shibetsu *Japan* **54** B11
Shibín el Kôm *Egypt* **80** H7
Shibín el Qanâtir *Egypt* **80** H7
Shibing *China* **58** D7
Shibogama L. *Canada* **104** B2
Shibushi *Japan* **55** J5
Shicheng *China* **59** D11
Shickshinny *U.S.A.* **115** E8
Shickshock Mts. =
  Chic-Chocs, Mts. *Canada* **105** C6
Shidao *China* **57** F12
Shidian *China* **58** E2
Shido *Japan* **55** G7
Shiel, L. *U.K.* **13** E3
Shield, C. *Australia* **94** A2
Shieli *Kazakhstan* **52** E7
Shifang *China* **58** B5
Shiga □ *Japan* **55** G8
Shigu *China* **58** D2
Shiguaigou *China* **56** D6
Shihchiachuang =
  Shijiazhuang *China* **56** E8
Shihezi *China* **60** B3
Shijak *Albania* **44** E3
Shijiazhuang *China* **56** E8
Shijiu Hu *China* **59** B12
Shikarpur *India* **68** E8
Shikarpur *Pakistan* **68** F3
Shikohabad *India* **69** F8
Shikoku □ *Japan* **55** H6
Shikoku-Sanchi *Japan* **55** H6
Shikotan, Ostrov *Asia* **53** E15
Shikotsu-Ko *Japan* **54** C10
Shikotsu-Tōya △ *Japan* **54** C10
Shiliguri *India* **67** F16
Shiliu = Changjiang *China* **64** C7
Shilka *China* **53** D12
Shilka ➔ *Russia* **53** D13
Shillelagh *Ireland* **12** D5
Shillington *U.S.A.* **115** F9
Shillong *India* **67** G17
Shilo *West Bank* **74** C4
Shilong *China* **59** F9
Shilou *China* **56** F6
Shilovo *Russia* **34** C5
Shimabara *Japan* **55** H5
Shimada *Japan* **55** G9
Shimane □ *Japan* **55** G6
Shimanovsk *Russia* **53** D13
Shimba Hills △ *Kenya* **86** C4
Shimen *China* **59** C8
Shimenjie *China* **59** C11
Shimian *China* **58** C4
Shimizu *Japan* **55** G9
Shimla *India* **68** D7
Shimodate *Japan* **55** F9
Shimoga *India* **66** N9
Shimoni *Kenya* **86** C4
Shimonoseki *Japan* **55** H5
Shimpuru Rapids *Namibia* **88** B2
Shimsk *Russia* **32** C6
Shin, L. *U.K.* **13** C4
Shinano-Gawa ➔ *Japan* **55** F9
Shināş *Oman* **71** E8
Shīndand *Afghan.* **66** C3
Shinglehouse *U.S.A.* **114** E6
Shingū *Japan* **55** H7
Shingwidzi *S. Africa* **89** C5
Shinjō *Japan* **54** E10
Shinkafe *Nigeria* **83** C6
Shinkolobwe
  Dem. Rep. of the Congo **84** G5
Shinshār *Syria* **74** A5
Shinyanga *Tanzania* **86** C3
Shinyanga □ *Tanzania* **86** C3
Shio-no-Misaki *Japan* **55** H7
Shiogama *Japan* **54** E10
Shiojiri *Japan* **55** F8
Shipchenski Prokhod
  Bulgaria **45** D9

Shiping *China* **58** F4
Shippagan *Canada* **105** C7
Shippensburg *U.S.A.* **114** F7
Shippenville *U.S.A.* **114** E5
Shiprock *U.S.A.* **109** H9
Shiqian *China* **58** D7
Shiqma, N. ➔ *Israel* **74** D3
Shiquan *China* **56** H5
Shiquan He = Indus ➔
  Pakistan **68** G5
Shīr Kūh *Iran* **71** D7
Shiragami-Misaki *Japan* **54** D10
Shirakawa *Fukushima, Japan* **55** F10
Shirakawa *Gifu, Japan* **55** F8
Shirane-San *Gumma, Japan* **55** F9
Shirane-San *Yamanashi,*
  Japan **55** G9
Shiraoi *Japan* **54** C10
Shīrāz *Iran* **71** D7
Shirbīn *Egypt* **80** H7
Shire ➔ *Africa* **87** F4
Shiretoko-Misaki *Japan* **54** B12
Shirinab ➔ *Pakistan* **68** D2
Shiriya-Zaki *Japan* **54** D10
Shiroishi *Japan* **54** E10
Shiroro Res. *Nigeria* **83** D6
Shīrvān *Iran* **71** B8
Shirwa, L. = Chilwa, L.
  Malawi **87** F4
Shishi *China* **59** E12
Shishou *China* **59** C9
Shitai *China* **59** B11
Shithāthah *Iraq* **73** G10
Shivpuri *India* **68** G7
Shixian *China* **57** C15
Shixing *China* **59** E10
Shiyan *China* **59** A8
Shiyata *Egypt* **80** B2
Shizhu *China* **58** C7
Shizong *China* **58** E5
Shizuishan *China* **56** E4
Shizuoka *Japan* **55** G9
Shizuoka □ *Japan* **55** G9
Shkhara *Georgia* **73** A10
Shklov = Shklow *Belarus* **23** A16
Shklow *Belarus* **23** A16
Shkodër *Albania* **44** D3
Shkumbini ➔ *Albania* **44** E3
Shmidta, Ostrov *Russia* **53** A10
Shō-Gawa ➔ *Japan* **55** F8
Shoal L. *Canada* **103** D9
Shoal Lake *Canada* **103** C8
Shōdo-Shima *Japan* **55** G7
Sholapur = Solapur *India* **66** L9
Shōmrōn *West Bank* **74** C4
Shoreham *U.S.A.* **115** C11
Shoreham by Sea *U.K.* **15** G7
Shori ➔ *Pakistan* **68** E3
Shorkot *Pakistan* **68** D5
Shorkot Road *Pakistan* **68** D5
Shoshone *Calif., U.S.A.* **111** K10
Shoshone *Idaho, U.S.A.* **108** E6
Shoshone L. *U.S.A.* **108** D8
Shoshone Mts. *U.S.A.* **108** G5
Shoshong *Botswana* **88** C4
Shoshoni *U.S.A.* **108** E9
Shostka *Ukraine* **33** G7
Shot *Iran* **73** C11
Shou Xian *China* **59** A11
Shouchang *China* **59** C12
Shouguang *China* **57** F10
Shouning *China* **59** D12
Shouyang *China* **56** F7
Show Low *U.S.A.* **109** J8
Shpola *Ukraine* **33** H6
Shpykiv *Ukraine* **29** B13
Shqipëria = Albania ■
  Europe **44** E4
Shreveport *U.S.A.* **116** E8
Shrewsbury *U.K.* **15** E5
Shri Mohangarh *India* **68** F4
Shrirampur *India* **69** H13
Shropshire □ *U.K.* **15** E5
Shū *Kazakhstan* **52** E8
Shuangbai *China* **58** E3
Shuangcheng *China* **57** B14
Shuangfeng *China* **59** D9
Shuanggou *China* **57** G9
Shuangjiang *China* **58** F2
Shuangliao *China* **57** C12
Shuangshanzi *China* **57** D10
Shuangyang *China* **57** C13
Shuangyashan *China* **60** B8
Shubrâ el Kheima *Egypt* **80** H7
Shubrâ Khit *Egypt* **80** H7
Shucheng *China* **59** B11
Shugozero *Russia* **32** C8
Shuguri Falls *Tanzania* **87** D4
Shuiji *China* **59** D12
Shuiye *China* **56** F8
Shujalpur *India* **68** H7
Shukpa Kunzang *India* **69** B8
Shulan *China* **57** B14
Shulaveri *Georgia* **35** K7
Shule *China* **60** C2
Shumagin Is. *U.S.A.* **106** a
Shumen *Bulgaria* **45** C10
Shumerlya *Russia* **34** C8

Shumikha *Russia* **52** D7
Shunchang *China* **59** D11
Shunde *China* **59** F9
Shungay *Kazakhstan* **35** F8
Shuo Xian = Shuozhou
  China **56** E7
Shuozhou *China* **56** E7
Shūr ➔ *Fārs, Iran* **71** D7
Shūr ➔ *Kermān, Iran* **71** D8
Shūr ➔ *Yazd, Iran* **71** D7
Shūr Āb *Iran* **71** C6
Shūr Gaz *Iran* **71** D8
Shūrāb *Iran* **71** C8
Shūrjestān *Iran* **71** D7
Shurugwi *Zimbabwe* **87** F3
Shūsf *Iran* **71** D9
Shūsh *Iran* **73** F13
Shūshtar *Iran* **71** D6
Shuswap L. *Canada* **102** C5
Shuya *Russia* **34** B5
Shuyang *China* **57** G10
Shūzū *Iran* **71** D7
Shwebo *Burma* **67** H19
Shwegu *Burma* **67** G20
Shweli ➔ *Burma* **67** H20
Shymkent *Kazakhstan* **52** E7
Shyok *India* **69** B8
Shyok ➔ *Pakistan* **69** B6
Shyroke *Odesa, Ukraine* **29** E15
Shyroke *Ternopil, Ukraine* **28** B8
Si Kiang = Xi Jiang ➔ *China* **59** F9
Si Lanna △ *Thailand* **64** C2
Si Nakarin Res. *Thailand* **64** E2
Si-ngan = Xi'an *China* **56** G5
Si Prachan *Thailand* **64** E3
Si Racha *Thailand* **64** F3
Si Xian *China* **57** H9
Siachen Glacier *Asia* **69** B7
Sīah Chashmeh *Iran* **73** C11
Siahaf ➔ *Pakistan* **68** E3
Siahan Range *Pakistan* **66** F4
Siaksriindrapura *Indonesia* **62** D2
Sialkot *Pakistan* **68** C6
Siam = Thailand ■ *Asia* **64** E4
Sian = Xi'an *China* **56** G5
Sian Ka'an △ *Mexico* **119** D7
Sianów *Poland* **30** D3
Siantan *Indonesia* **62** D3
Sīārēh *Iran* **71** D9
Siargao I. *Phil.* **61** G7
Siari *Pakistan* **69** B7
Siasi *Phil.* **63** C6
Siasi I. *Phil.* **61** J4
Siatista *Greece* **44** F5
Siau *Indonesia* **63** D7
Šiauliai *Lithuania* **30** C10
Šiauliai □ *Lithuania* **30** C10
Siazan = Siyäzän *Azerbaijan* **35** K9
Sibâi, Gebel el *Egypt* **70** E2
Sibang *Indonesia* **63** K18
Sibayi, L. *S. Africa* **89** D5
Sibdu *Sudan* **81** E2
Šibenik *Croatia* **41** E12
Siberia = Sibirskiy ➔ *Russia* **53** D10
Siberia *Russia* **4** D13
Siberut *Indonesia* **62** E1
Sibi *Pakistan* **68** E2
Sibil = Oksibil *Indonesia* **63** E10
Sibiloi △ *Kenya* **86** B4
Sibirskiy ➔ *Russia* **53** D10
Sibirtsevo *Russia* **54** B5
Sibiti *Congo* **84** E2
Sibiu *Romania* **29** E9
Sibiu □ *Romania* **29** E9
Sibley *U.S.A.* **112** D6
Sibolga *Indonesia* **62** D1
Siborongborong *Indonesia* **65** L2
Sibsagar *India* **67** F19
Sibu *Malaysia* **62** D4
Sibuco *Phil.* **61** H5
Sibuguey B. *Phil.* **61** H5
Sibut *C.A.R.* **84** C3
Sibutu *Phil.* **63** D5
Sibutu Group *Phil.* **61** J3
Sibutu Passage *E. Indies* **61** J4
Sibuyan I. *Phil.* **61** E5
Sibuyan Sea *Phil.* **61** E5
Sic *Romania* **29** D8
Sicamous *Canada* **102** C5
Siccus ➔ *Australia* **95** E2
Sichon *Thailand* **65** H2
Sichuan □ *China* **58** B5
Sichuan Pendi *China* **58** B5
Sicilia *Italy* **43** E7
Sicily = Sicilia *Italy* **43** E7
Sicily, Str. of *Medit. S.* **42** E4
Sico ➔ *Honduras* **120** C3
Sicuani *Peru* **124** F4
Šid *Serbia* **28** E4
Sidamo *Ethiopia* **81** G4
Sidaouet *Niger* **83** B6
Sidari *Greece* **49** A3
Siddhapur *India* **68** H5
Siddipet *India* **66** K11
Sidensjö *Sweden* **10** A12
Sidéradougou *Burkina Faso* **82** C4
Siderno *Italy* **43** D9
Sideros, Akra *Greece* **49** D8
Sidhauli *India* **69** F9

Sidhi *India* **69** G9
Sîdi Abd el Rahmân *Egypt* **80** A2
Sîdi Barrâni *Egypt* **80** A2
Sidi-bel-Abbès *Algeria* **78** A5
Sîdi Haneish *Egypt* **80** A2
Sîdi Omar *Egypt* **80** A1
Sidikalang *Indonesia* **65** L2
Sidirokastro *Greece* **44** E7
Sidlaw Hills *U.K.* **13** E5
Sidley, Mt. *Antarctica* **5** D14
Sidmouth *U.K.* **15** G4
Sidmouth, C. *Australia* **94** A3
Sidney *Canada* **110** B3
Sidney *Mont., U.S.A.* **108** C11
Sidney *N.Y., U.S.A.* **115** D9
Sidney *Nebr., U.S.A.* **112** E3
Sidney *Ohio, U.S.A.* **113** E11
Sidney Lanier, L. *U.S.A.* **117** D12
Sido *Mali* **82** C3
Sidon = Saydā *Lebanon* **74** B4
Sidra, G. of = Surt, Khalīj
  Libya **79** B9
Siedlce *Poland* **31** F9
Sieg ➔ *Germany* **24** E3
Siegburg *Germany* **24** E3
Siegen *Germany* **24** E4
Siem Pang *Cambodia* **64** E6
Siem Reap = Siemreab
  Cambodia **64** F4
Siemiatycze *Poland* **31** F9
Siemreab *Cambodia* **64** F4
Siena *Italy* **41** E8
Sieniawa *Poland* **31** H9
Sieradz *Poland* **31** G5
Sieraków *Poland* **31** F3
Sierck-les-Bains *France* **19** C13
Sierning *Austria* **26** C7
Sierpc *Poland* **31** F6
Sierpe, Bocas de la
  Venezuela **125** L15
Sierra Blanca *U.S.A.* **116** F2
Sierra Blanca Peak *U.S.A.* **109** K11
Sierra City *U.S.A.* **110** F6
Sierra Colorada *Argentina* **128** E3
Sierra de Agalta △
  Honduras **120** C2
Sierra de Aracena y Picas
  de Aroche △ *Spain* **37** H4
Sierra de Bahoruco △
  Dom. Rep. **121** C5
Sierra de Baza △ *Spain* **39** H2
Sierra de Castril △ *Spain* **39** H2
Sierra de Espuña △ *Spain* **39** H3
Sierra de Grazalema △ *Spain* **37** J5
Sierra de Gredos △ *Spain* **36** E5
Sierra de Hornachuelos △
  Spain **37** H5
Sierra de Huétor △ *Spain* **37** H7
Sierra de La Culata △
  Venezuela **121** E5
Sierra de Lancandón △
  Guatemala **120** C1
Sierra de las Nieves △ *Spain* **37** J6
Sierra de las Quijadas △
  Argentina **126** C2
Sierra de María-Los
  Vélez △ *Spain* **39** H2
Sierra de San Luis △
  Venezuela **121** D6
Sierra de San Pedro Mártir,
  Parque Nacional △
  Mexico **118** A1
Sierra de Yeguas *Spain* **37** H6
Sierra del São Mamede △
  Portugal **37** F3
Sierra Gorda *Chile* **126** A2
Sierra Leone ■ *W. Afr.* **82** D2
Sierra Madre *Mexico* **119** D6
Sierra Madre Occidental
  Mexico **118** B3
Sierra Madre Oriental
  Mexico **118** C5
Sierra Mágina △ *Spain* **37** H7
Sierra Mojada *Mexico* **118** B4
Sierra Nevada *Spain* **37** H7
Sierra Nevada *U.S.A.* **110** H8
Sierra Nevada △ *Venezuela* **121** E5
Sierra Nevada de Santa
  Marta △ *Colombia* **121** D5
Sierra Norte de Sevilla △
  Spain **37** H5
Sierra Subbéticas △ *Spain* **37** H6
Sierra Vista *U.S.A.* **109** L8
Sierras de Cardeña y
  Montoro △ *Spain* **37** G6
Sierras de Cazorla, Segura
  y las Villas △ *Spain* **39** J2
Sierraville *U.S.A.* **110** F6
Sierre *Switz.* **25** J3
Sifani *Ethiopia* **81** E5
Sifié *Ivory C.* **82** D3
Sifnos *Greece* **46** E6
Sifton *Canada* **103** C8
Sifton Pass *Canada* **102** B3
Sig *Algeria* **78** A5
Sigatoka *Fiji* **91** a

Sigean *France* **20** E6
Sighetu-Marmaţiei *Romania* **29** C8
Sighişoara *Romania* **29** D9
Sigli *Indonesia* **62** C1
Siglufjörður *Iceland* **8** C4
Sigmaringen *Germany* **25** G5
Signa *Italy* **40** E8
Signakhi = Tsnori *Georgia* **35** K7
Signal de Botrang *Belgium* **17** D6
Signal Pk. *U.S.A.* **111** M12
Signy I. *Antarctica* **5** C18
Signy-l'Abbaye *France* **19** C11
Sígsig *Ecuador* **124** D3
Sigüenza *Spain* **38** D2
Siguiri *Guinea* **82** C3
Sigulda *Latvia* **32** D3
Sihora *India* **69** H9
Sihui *China* **59** F9
Siikajoki ➔ *Finland* **8** D21
Siilinjärvi *Finland* **8** E22
Siirt *Turkey* **73** D9
Siirt □ *Turkey* **73** D9
Sijarira Ra. = Chizarira
  Zimbabwe **87** F2
Sika *India* **68** H3
Sikanni Chief ➔ *Canada* **102** B4
Sikao *Thailand* **65** J2
Sikar *India* **68** F6
Sikasso *Mali* **82** C3
Sikasso □ *Mali* **82** C3
Sikeston *U.S.A.* **112** G9
Sikhote Alin, Khrebet *Russia* **54** B8
Sikhote Alin Ra. = Sikhote
  Alin, Khrebet *Russia* **54** B8
Sikia *Greece* **44** F7
Sikinos *Greece* **47** E7
Sikkim □ *India* **67** F16
Siklós *Hungary* **28** E3
Sil ➔ *Spain* **36** C3
Silacayoapan *Mexico* **119** D5
Šilalė *Lithuania* **30** C9
Silandro *Italy* **40** B7
Silawad *India* **68** J6
Silay *Phil.* **61** F5
Silba *Croatia* **41** D11
Silchar *India* **67** G18
Šile *Turkey* **45** E13
Siler City *U.S.A.* **117** D15
Silesia = Śląsk *Poland* **22** C9
Silgarhi Doti *Nepal* **69** E9
Silghat *India* **67** F18
Silhouette *Seychelles* **85** b
Sili *Burkina Faso* **82** C4
Silifke *Turkey* **72** D5
Siliguri = Shiliguri *India* **67** F16
Siling Co *China* **60** C3
Silistea Nouă *Romania* **29** F10
Silistra *Bulgaria* **45** B11
Silivri *Turkey* **45** E12
Siljan *Sweden* **10** D8
Siljansnäs *Sweden* **10** D8
Silkeborg *Denmark* **11** H3
Silkwood *Australia* **94** B4
Silla *Spain* **39** F4
Sillajhuay, Cordillera *Chile* **124** G5
Sillamäe *Estonia* **32** C4
Sillé-le-Guillaume *France* **18** D6
Silleda *Spain* **36** C2
Silloth *U.K.* **14** C4
Silo *Greece* **45** E9
Siloam Springs *U.S.A.* **116** C7
Silopi *Turkey* **73** D10
Silsbee *U.S.A.* **116** F7
Siluko *Nigeria* **83** D6
Šilutė *Lithuania* **30** C8
Silvan *Turkey* **73** D9
Silvani *India* **69** H8
Silver City *U.S.A.* **109** K9
Silver Cr. ➔ *U.S.A.* **108** E4
Silver Creek *U.S.A.* **114** D5
Silver L. *U.S.A.* **110** G6
Silver Lake *Calif., U.S.A.* **111** K10
Silver Lake *Oreg., U.S.A.* **108** E3
Silverdalen *Sweden* **11** G9
Silvermine Mts. *Ireland* **12** D3
Silverton *Colo., U.S.A.* **109** H10
Silverton *Tex., U.S.A.* **116** D4
Silves *Portugal* **37** H2
Silvi Marina *Italy* **41** F11
Silvies ➔ *U.S.A.* **108** E4
Silvrettahorn *Switz.* **40** B7
Silwa Bahari *Egypt* **80** C3
Silz *Austria* **26** D3
Simaltala *India* **69** G12
Simanggang = Sri Aman
  Malaysia **62** D4
Simao *China* **58** F3
Simard, L. *Canada* **104** C4
Şīmareh ➔ *Iran* **73** F12
Simav *Turkey* **47** B10
Simav ➔ *Turkey* **45** F12
Simav Dağları *Turkey* **47** B10
Simba *Tanzania* **86** C4
Simbach *Germany* **25** G8
Simbirsk = Ulyanovsk
  Russia **34** C9
Simbo *Tanzania* **86** C2
Simbach *Germany* **25** G8
Simcoe *Canada* **114** D4
Simcoe, L. *Canada* **114** B5

Simdega *India* **69** H11
Simeonovgrad *Bulgaria* **45** D9
Simeria *Romania* **28** E8
Simeto ➤ *Italy* **43** E8
Simeulue *Indonesia* **62** D1
Simferopol *Ukraine* **33** K8
Simi *Greece* **47** E9
Simi Valley *U.S.A.* **111** L8
Simien Mts. △ *Ethiopia* **81** E4
Simikot *Nepal* **69** E9
Simineh ➤ *Iran* **73** D11
Simitli *Bulgaria* **44** E7
Simla = Shimla *India* **68** D7
Simlångsdalen *Sweden* **11** H7
Simleu-Silvaniei *Romania* **28** C7
Simlipal △ *India* **69** J12
Simmern *Germany* **25** F3
Simmie *Canada* **103** D7
Simmler *U.S.A.* **111** K7
Simnas *Lithuania* **30** D10
Simo älv = Simojoki ➤
  Finland **8** D21
Simojoki ➤ *Finland* **8** D21
Simojovel *Mexico* **119** D6
Simonette ➤ *Canada* **102** B5
Simonstown *S. Africa* **88** E2
Simontornya *Hungary* **28** D3
Simpang Empat *Malaysia* **65** c
Simplonpass *Switz.* **25** J4
Simplontunnel *Switz.* **25** J4
Simpson Desert *Australia* **94** D5
Simpson Desert △ *Australia* **94** C2
Simpson Pen. *Canada* **101** C11
Simrishamn *Sweden* **11** J8
Simsbury *U.S.A.* **115** E12
Simushir, Ostrov *Russia* **53** E16
Sin Cowe I. *S. China Sea* **62** C4
Sina Dhago *Somali Rep.* **75** F4
Sinabang *Indonesia* **62** D1
Sinai = Es Sînâ' *Egypt* **74** F3
Sinai, Mt. = Mûsa, Gebel
  Egypt **70** D2
Sinaia *Romania* **29** E10
Sinaloa □ *Mexico* **118** C3
Sinaloa de Leyva *Mexico* **118** B3
Sinalunga *Italy* **41** E8
Sinan *China* **58** D7
Sînandrei *Romania* **28** E6
Sincan *Turkey* **72** B5
Sincanlı *Turkey* **47** C12
Sincelejo *Colombia* **124** B3
Sinch'ang *N. Korea* **57** D15
Sinch'ŏn *N. Korea* **57** E13
Sinclair *U.S.A.* **108** F10
Sinclair Mills *Canada* **102** C4
Sinclair's B. *U.K.* **13** C5
Sinclairville *U.S.A.* **114** D5
Sincorá, Sa. do *Brazil* **125** F10
Sind = Sindh □ *Pakistan* **68** G3
Sind ➤ *Jammu & Kashmir,
  India* **69** B6
Sind ➤ *Mad. P., India* **69** F8
Sind Sagar Doab *Pakistan* **68** D4
Sindal *Denmark* **11** G4
Sindangan *Phil.* **61** G5
Sindangbarang *Indonesia* **63** G12
Sinde *Zambia* **87** F2
Sindelfingen *Germany* **25** G4
Sindh = Indus ➤ *Pakistan* **68** G2
Sindh □ *Pakistan* **68** G3
Sındırgı *Turkey* **47** B10
Sindou *Burkina Faso* **82** C3
Sindri *India* **69** H12
Sine ➤ *Senegal* **82** C1
Sinegorskiy *Russia* **35** G5
Sinekli *Turkey* **45** E12
Sinelnikovo =
  Synelnykove *Ukraine* **33** H8
Sinendé *Benin* **83** C5
Sines *Portugal* **37** H2
Sines, C. de *Portugal* **37** H2
Sineu *Spain* **48** B10
Sinfra *Ivory C.* **82** D3
Sing Buri *Thailand* **64** E3
Singa *Sudan* **81** E3
Singalila △ *India* **69** F13
Singapore ■ *Asia* **65** d
Singapore, Straits of *Asia* **65** d
Singapore Changi ✈ (SIN)
  Singapore **65** M4
Singaraja *Indonesia* **63** J18
Singatoka = Sigatoka *Fiji* **91** a
Singen *Germany* **25** H4
Singida *Tanzania* **86** C3
Singida □ *Tanzania* **86** D3
Singkaling Hkamti *Burma* **67** G19
Singkang *Indonesia* **63** E6
Singkawang *Indonesia* **62** D3
Singkep *Indonesia* **62** E2
Singkil *Indonesia* **65** L1
Singleton *Australia* **95** E5
Singleton, Mt. *N. Terr.,
  Australia* **92** D5
Singleton, Mt. *W. Austral.,
  Australia* **93** E2
Singö *Sweden* **10** D12
Singoli *India* **68** G6
Singora = Songkhla *Thailand* **65** J3

Sinhüng *N. Korea* **57** D14
Siniscóla *Italy* **42** B2
Sinj *Croatia* **41** E13
Sinjai *Indonesia* **63** F6
Sinjajevina *Montenegro* **44** D3
Sinjār *Iraq* **73** D9
Sinjār, Jabal *Iraq* **73** D9
Sinkat *Sudan* **80** D4
Sinkiang = Xinjiang Uygur
  Zizhiqu □ *China* **60** B3
Sinmak *N. Korea* **57** E14
Sinmi-do *N. Korea* **57** E13
Sînnai *Italy* **42** C2
Sinnamary *Fr. Guiana* **125** B8
Sinni ➤ *Italy* **43** B9
Sinnuris *Egypt* **80** J7
Sinoie, Lacul *Romania* **29** F13
Sinop *Turkey* **72** A6
Sinop □ *Turkey* **72** B6
Sinor *India* **68** J5
Sinp'o *N. Korea* **57** E15
Sinsheim *Germany* **25** F4
Sinsk *Russia* **53** C13
Sintang *Indonesia* **62** D4
Sinton *U.S.A.* **116** G6
Sintra *Portugal* **37** G1
Sintra-Cascais △ *Portugal* **37** G1
Sinŭiju *N. Korea* **57** D13
Sinyukha ➤ *Ukraine* **33** H6
Sinzig *Germany* **24** E3
Sio ➤ *Hungary* **28** D3
Siocon *Phil.* **61** H5
Siófok *Hungary* **28** D3
Sion *Switz.* **25** J3
Sion Mills *U.K.* **12** B4
Sioux Center *U.S.A.* **112** D5
Sioux City *U.S.A.* **112** D5
Sioux Falls *U.S.A.* **112** D5
Sioux Lookout *Canada* **104** B1
Sioux Narrows *Canada* **103** D10
Sipadan *Malaysia* **63** D5
Sipalay *Phil.* **61** G5
Šipan *Croatia* **44** D1
Siparia *Trin. & Tob.* **125** K15
Sipil Daği △ *Turkey* **47** C9
Siping *China* **57** C13
Sipiwesk L. *Canada* **103** B9
Siple *Antarctica* **5** D7
Šipovo *Bos.-H.* **28** F2
Sipra ➤ *India* **68** H6
Sipura *Indonesia* **62** E1
Siquia ➤ *Nic.* **120** D3
Siquijor *Phil.* **61** G5
Siquirres *Costa Rica* **120** D3
Şīr Abū Nu'ayr *U.A.E.* **71** E7
Şīr Banī Yās *U.A.E.* **71** E7
Sir Edward Pellew Group
  Australia **94** B2
Sir Graham Moore Is.
  Australia **92** B4
Sir James MacBrien, Mt.
  Canada **100** C7
Sira ➤ *Norway* **9** G12
Siracusa *Italy* **43** E8
Sirajganj *Bangla.* **69** G13
Sirakoro *Mali* **82** C3
Şiran *Turkey* **73** B8
Sirasso *Ivory C.* **82** D3
Sirathu *India* **69** G9
Sīrdān *Iran* **73** D13
Sire *Ethiopia* **81** F4
Siren *U.S.A.* **112** C7
Sirente-Velino △ *Italy* **41** F10
Sirer *Spain* **48** C7
Siret *Romania* **29** C11
Siret ➤ *Romania* **29** E12
Sirghāyā *Syria* **74** B5
Şiria *Romania* **28** D6
Sirinat △ *Thailand* **65** a
Sirino, Mte. *Italy* **43** B8
Sîrjān *Iran* **71** D7
Sirmaur *India* **69** G9
Sirna *Greece* **47** E8
Şırnak *Turkey* **73** D10
Sirohi *India* **68** G5
Sironj *India* **68** G7
Síros = Syros *Greece* **46** D6
Sirr, Nafud as *Si. Arabia* **70** E5
Sīrrī *Iran* **71** E7
Sirsa *India* **68** E6
Sirsa ➤ *India* **69** F8
Siruela *Spain* **37** G5
Sirvän ➤ *Iran* **73** E12
Sisak *Croatia* **41** C13
Sisaket *Thailand* **64** E5
Sisante *Spain* **39** F2
Sisargas, Is. *Spain* **36** B2
Sishen *S. Africa* **88** D3
Sishui *Henan, China* **56** G7
Sishui *Shandong, China* **57** G9
Sisian *Armenia* **73** C12
Sisipuk L. *Canada* **103** B8
Sisophon *Cambodia* **64** F4
Sisseton *U.S.A.* **112** C5
Sissonne *France* **19** C10
Sīstān *Asia* **71** D9
Sīstān, Daryācheh-ye *Iran* **71** D9
Sīstān va Balūchestān □
  Iran **71** E9

Sisteron *France* **21** D9
Sisters *U.S.A.* **108** D3
Sisters, The *Seychelles* **85** b
Siswa Bazar *India* **69** F10
Sitakili *Mali* **82** C2
Sitamarhi *India* **69** F11
Sitampiky *Madag.* **89** B8
Sitapur *India* **69** F9
Siteki *Swaziland* **89** D5
Sitges *Spain* **38** D6
Sithonia *Greece* **44** F7
Sitia *Greece* **49** D8
Sitito-Ozima Ridge *Pac. Oc.* **96** E6
Sitka *U.S.A.* **102** B1
Sitoti *Botswana* **88** C3
Sitra *Egypt* **80** B2
Sittang Myit ➤ *Burma* **67** L20
Sittard *Neths.* **17** C5
Sittensen *Germany* **24** B5
Sittingbourne *U.K.* **15** F8
Sittona *Eritrea* **81** E4
Sittoung = Sittang Myit ➤
  Burma **67** L20
Sittwe *Burma* **67** J18
Situbondo *Indonesia* **63** G16
Si'umu *Samoa* **91** b
Siuna *Nic.* **120** D3
Siuri *India* **69** H12
Siutghiol, Lacul *Romania* **29** F13
Sivand *Iran* **71** D7
Sivas *Turkey* **72** C7
Sivas □ *Turkey* **72** C7
Sivaslı *Turkey* **47** C11
Siverek *Turkey* **73** D8
Sivrihisar *Turkey* **72** C4
Siwa *Egypt* **80** B2
Sîwa, El Wâhât es *Egypt* **80** B2
Siwa Oasis = Sîwa, El
  Wâhât es *Egypt* **80** B2
Siwalik Range *Nepal* **69** F10
Siwan *India* **69** F11
Siwana *India* **68** G5
Six Cross Roads *Barbados* **121** g
Sixmilebridge *Ireland* **12** D3
Sixth Cataract *Sudan* **81** D3
Siyah Kuh, Kavīr-e *Iran* **71** C7
Siyäl, Jazā'ir *Egypt* **80** C4
Siyäzän *Azerbaijan* **35** K9
Siziwang Qi *China* **56** D6
Sjælland *Denmark* **11** J5
Sjælland □ *Denmark* **11** J5
Sjællands Odde *Denmark* **11** J5
Sjenica *Serbia* **44** C3
Sjöbo *Sweden* **11** J7
Sjötofta *Sweden* **11** G7
Sjötorp *Sweden* **11** F8
Sjumen = Shumen *Bulgaria* **45** C10
Sjuntorp *Sweden* **11** F6
Skadarsko Jezero *Europe* **44** D3
Skadarsko Jezero △
  Montenegro **44** D3
Skadovsk *Ukraine* **33** J7
Skælskør *Denmark* **11** J5
Skærbæk *Denmark* **11** J2
Skaftafell *Iceland* **8** D5
Skaftafell △ *Iceland* **8** D5
Skagafjörður *Iceland* **8** D4
Skagastølstindane *Norway* **8** F12
Skagaströnd *Iceland* **8** D3
Skagen *Denmark* **11** G4
Skagern *Sweden* **10** E8
Skagerrak *Denmark* **11** G2
Skagit ➤ *U.S.A.* **110** B4
Skagway *U.S.A.* **100** D6
Skala-Podilska *Ukraine* **29** B11
Skalat *Ukraine* **23** D13
Skalbmierz *Poland* **31** H7
Skálderviken *Sweden* **11** H6
Skalica *Slovak Rep.* **27** C10
Skallingen *Denmark* **11** J2
Skalni Dol = Kamenyak
  Bulgaria **45** C10
Skanderborg *Denmark* **11** H3
Skåne *Sweden* **11** J7
Skåne län □ *Sweden* **11** H7
Skaneateles *U.S.A.* **115** D8
Skaneateles L. *U.S.A.* **115** D8
Skänninge *Sweden* **11** F9
Skånör med Falsterbo
  Sweden **11** J6
Skantzoura *Greece* **46** B6
Skara *Sweden* **11** F7
Skärblacka *Sweden* **11** F9
Skärdu *Pakistan* **69** B6
Skärhamn *Sweden* **11** G5
Skärszewy *Poland* **30** D5
Skaryszew *Poland* **31** G8
Skarżysko-Kamienna
  Poland **31** G7
Skattkärr *Sweden* **10** E9
Skattungbyn *Sweden* **10** C8
Skawina *Poland* **31** J6
Skebobruk *Sweden* **10** E12
Skeena ➤ *Canada* **102** C2
Skeena Mts. *Canada* **102** B3
Skegness *U.K.* **14** D8
Skeldon = Corriverton
  Guyana **124** B7

Skeleton Coast *Namibia* **85** J2
Skeleton Coast △ *Namibia* **88** C1
Skellefteå *Sweden* **8** D19
Skellefteälven ➤ *Sweden* **8** D19
Skelleftehamn *Sweden* **8** D19
Skerries, The *U.K.* **14** D3
Skhidnytsya *Ukraine* **31** J10
Skhíza *Greece* **46** E3
Ski *Norway* **9** G14
Skiathos *Greece* **46** B5
Skibbereen *Ireland* **12** E2
Skiddaw *U.K.* **14** C4
Skidegate *Canada* **102** C2
Skidra *Greece* **44** F6
Skien *Norway* **9** G13
Skierniewice *Poland* **31** G7
Skíhist, Mt. *Canada* **102** C4
Skikda *Algeria* **78** A7
Skillingaryd *Sweden* **11** G8
Skillinge *Sweden* **11** J8
Skilloura *Cyprus* **49** D12
Skinari, Akra *Greece* **46** D2
Skinnskatteberg *Sweden* **10** E9
Skipton *U.K.* **14** D5
Skíring, C. *Senegal* **82** C1
Skirmish Pt. *Australia* **94** A1
Skiropoula *Greece* **46** C6
Skiros *Greece* **46** C6
Skivarp *Sweden* **11** J7
Skive *Denmark* **11** H3
Skjálfandafljót ➤ *Iceland* **8** D5
Skjálfandi *Iceland* **8** C5
Skjern *Denmark* **11** J2
Skoczów *Poland* **31** J5
Škofja Loka *Slovenia* **41** B11
Skoghall *Sweden* **10** E7
Skogstorp *Sweden* **10** E10
Skoki *Poland* **31** F4
Skole *Ukraine* **23** D12
Skopelos *Greece* **46** B5
Skopi *Greece* **49** D8
Skopin *Russia* **32** F10
Skopje *Macedonia* **44** E5
Skopje ✈ (SKP) *Macedonia* **44** E5
Skórcz *Poland* **30** E5
Skørping *Denmark* **11** H3
Skövde *Sweden* **11** F7
Skovorodino *Russia* **53** D13
Skowhegan *U.S.A.* **113** C19
Skradin *Croatia* **41** E12
Skrea *Sweden* **11** H6
Skrunda *Latvia* **30** B9
Skrwa ➤ *Poland* **31** F6
Skuleskogen △ *Sweden* **10** A12
Skull *Ireland* **12** E2
Skultorp *Sweden* **11** F7
Skultuna *Sweden* **10** E10
Skunk ➤ *U.S.A.* **112** E9
Skuodas *Lithuania* **30** B8
Skurup *Sweden* **11** J7
Skutskär *Sweden* **10** D11
Skvyra *Ukraine* **23** D15
Skwierzyna *Poland* **31** F2
Skye *U.K.* **13** D2
Skykomish *U.S.A.* **108** C3
Skyros = Skiros *Greece* **46** C6
Skyttorp *Sweden* **10** D11
Slade Pt. *Australia* **94** K7
Slættaratindur *Færoe Is.* **8** E9
Slagelse *Denmark* **11** J5
Slamet *Indonesia* **63** G13
Slane *Ireland* **12** C5
Slaney ➤ *Ireland* **12** D5
Slangberge *S. Africa* **88** E3
Slănic *Romania* **29** E10
Slano *Croatia* **44** D1
Slantsy *Russia* **32** C5
Slaný *Czech Rep.* **26** A7
Śląsk *Poland* **22** C9
Śląskie □ *Poland* **31** H6
Slätbaken *Sweden* **11** F10
Slate Is. *Canada* **104** C2
Slatina *Croatia* **28** E2
Slatina *Romania* **29** F9
Slatina Timiş *Romania* **28** E7
Slatington *U.S.A.* **115** F9
Slaton *U.S.A.* **116** E4
Slave ➤ *Canada* **102** A6
Slave Coast *W. Afr.* **83** D5
Slave Lake *Canada* **102** B6
Slave Pt. *Canada* **102** A5
Slavgorod *Russia* **52** D8
Slavinja *Serbia* **44** C6
Slavkov u Brna *Czech Rep.* **27** B9
Slavkovský Les △ *Czech Rep.* **26** A5
Slavonija *Europe* **28** E2
Slavonski Brod *Croatia* **28** E3
Slavsk *Russia* **30** D8
Slavska *Ukraine* **29** B8
Slavskoye *Russia* **30** D7
Slavuta *Ukraine* **23** C14
Slavyanka *Russia* **54** C5
Slavyanovo *Bulgaria* **45** C8
Slavyansk = Slovyansk
  Ukraine **33** H9
Slavyansk-na-Kubani
  Russia **33** K10

Slawharad *Belarus* **23** B16
Sławno *Poland* **30** D3
Sławoborze *Poland* **30** E2
Sleaford *U.K.* **14** D7
Sleaford B. *Australia* **95** E2
Sleat, Sd. of *U.K.* **13** D3
Sleeper Is. *Canada* **101** D11
Sleeping Bear Dunes △
  U.S.A. **112** C10
Sleepy Eye *U.S.A.* **112** C6
Slemon L. *Canada* **102** A5
Slide Mt. *U.S.A.* **115** E10
Slidell *U.S.A.* **117** F10
Slieve Aughty *Ireland* **12** C3
Slieve Bloom *Ireland* **12** C4
Slieve Donard *U.K.* **12** B6
Slieve Gamph *Ireland* **12** B3
Slieve Gullion *U.K.* **12** B5
Slieve League *Ireland* **12** B3
Slieve Mish *Ireland* **12** D2
Slievenamon *Ireland* **12** D4
Sligeach = Sligo *Ireland* **12** B3
Sligo *Ireland* **12** B3
Sligo *U.S.A.* **114** E5
Sligo □ *Ireland* **12** B3
Sligo B. *Ireland* **12** B3
Slippery Rock *U.S.A.* **114** E4
Slite *Sweden* **11** G12
Slīteres △ *Latvia* **30** A9
Sliven *Bulgaria* **45** D10
Slivnitsa *Bulgaria* **44** D7
Sljeme *Croatia* **41** C12
Sloan *U.S.A.* **111** K11
Sloansville *U.S.A.* **115** D10
Slobidka *Ukraine* **29** C14
Slobozia *Moldova* **29** C14
Slobozia *Argeş, Romania* **29** F10
Slobozia *Ialomiţa, Romania* **29** F12
Slocan *Canada* **102** D5
Slomniki *Poland* **31** H7
Slonim *Belarus* **23** B13
Slough *U.K.* **15** F7
Slough □ *U.K.* **15** F7
Sloughhouse *U.S.A.* **110** G5
Slovak Rep. ■ *Europe* **27** C13
Slovakia = Slovak Rep. ■
  Europe **27** C13
Slovakian Ore Mts. =
  Slovenské Rudohorie
  Slovak Rep. **27** C12
Slovenia ■ *Europe* **41** C11
Slovenija = Slovenia ■
  Europe **41** C11
Slovenj Gradec *Slovenia* **41** B12
Slovenska = Slovak
  Rep. ■ *Europe* **27** C13
Slovenska Bistrica *Slovenia* **41** B12
Slovenské Konjice *Slovenia* **41** B12
Slovenské Rudohorie
  Slovak Rep. **27** C12
Slovenský Raj △ *Slovak Rep.* **27** C13
Slovyansk *Ukraine* **33** H9
Słowiński △ *Poland* **30** D4
Słubice *Poland* **31** F1
Sluch ➤ *Ukraine* **23** C14
Sluis *Neths.* **17** C3
Slŭnchev Bryag *Bulgaria* **45** D11
Slunj *Croatia* **41** C12
Słupca *Poland* **31** F4
Słupia ➤ *Poland* **30** D3
Słupsk *Poland* **30** D4
Slurry *S. Africa* **88** D4
Slutsk *Belarus* **23** B14
Slyne Hd. *Ireland* **12** C1
Slyudyanka *Russia* **53** D11
Småland *Sweden* **11** G9
Smålandsfarvandet *Denmark* **11** J5
Smålandsstenar *Sweden* **11** G7
Smalltree L. *Canada* **103** A8
Smallwood Res. *Canada* **105** B7
Smarhon *Belarus* **23** A14
Smarje *Slovenia* **41** B12
Smartt Syndicate Dam
  S. Africa **88** E3
Smartville *U.S.A.* **110** F5
Smeaton *Canada* **103** C8
Smedby *Sweden* **11** H10
Smederevo *Serbia* **44** B4
Smederevska Palanka *Serbia* **44** B4
Smedjebacken *Sweden* **10** D9
Smela = Smila *Ukraine* **33** H6
Smerwick Harbour *Ireland* **12** D1
Smethport *U.S.A.* **114** E6
Smidovich *Russia* **53** E14
Śmigiel *Poland* **31** F3
Smila *Ukraine* **33** H6
Smilyan *Bulgaria* **45** E8
Smith *Canada* **102** B6
Smith Center *U.S.A.* **112** F4
Smith River *U.S.A.* **108** F2
Smithburne ➤ *Australia* **94** B3
Smithers *Canada* **102** C3
Smithfield *S. Africa* **89** E4
Smithfield *N.C., U.S.A.* **117** D15
Smithfield *Utah, U.S.A.* **108** F8
Smiths Falls *Canada* **115** B9
Smithton *Australia* **95** G4

Smithville *Canada* **114** C5
Smithville *U.S.A.* **116** F6
Smoke Creek Desert *U.S.A.* **108** F4
Smoky ➤ *Canada* **102** B5
Smoky Bay *Australia* **95** E1
Smoky Hill ➤ *U.S.A.* **112** F5
Smoky Hills *U.S.A.* **112** F4
Smoky Lake *Canada* **102** C6
Smøla *Norway* **8** E13
Smolensk *Russia* **32** E7
Smolensk □ *Russia* **32** E7
Smolikas, Oros *Greece* **44** F4
Smolník *Slovak Rep.* **27** C13
Smolyan *Bulgaria* **45** E8
Smooth Rock Falls *Canada* **104** C3
Smoothstone L. *Canada* **103** C7
Smorgon = Smarhon
  Belarus **23** A14
Smotrych *Ukraine* **29** B11
Smotrych ➤ *Ukraine* **29** B11
Smulţi *Romania* **29** E12
Smyadovo *Bulgaria* **45** C11
Smygehamn *Sweden* **11** J7
Smyrna = İzmir *Turkey* **47** C9
Smyrna *U.S.A.* **113** F16
Snæfell *Iceland* **8** D6
Snaefell *I. of Man* **14** C3
Snæfellsjökull *Iceland* **8** D2
Snake ➤ *U.S.A.* **108** C4
Snake I. *Australia* **95** F4
Snake Range *U.S.A.* **108** G6
Snake River Plain *U.S.A.* **108** E7
Snasahögarna *Sweden* **10** A6
Snåsavatnet *Norway* **8** D15
Sneek *Neths.* **17** A5
Sneem *Ireland* **12** E2
Sneeuberge *S. Africa* **88** E3
Snejbjerg *Denmark* **11** H2
Snelling *U.S.A.* **110** H6
Snezhnoye *Ukraine* **33** J10
Sněžka *Europe* **30** A8
Snežnik *Slovenia* **41** C11
Śniadowo *Poland* **31** E8
Sniardwy, Jezioro *Poland* **30** E8
Śnieżka *Europe* **26** A8
Snigirevka = Snihurivka
  Ukraine **33** J7
Snihurivka *Ukraine* **33** J7
Snina *Slovak Rep.* **27** C15
Snizort, L. *U.K.* **13** D2
Snøhetta *Norway* **8** E13
Snohomish *U.S.A.* **110** C4
Snoqualmie Pass *U.S.A.* **110** C5
Snoul *Cambodia* **65** F6
Snover *U.S.A.* **114** C2
Snow Hill *U.S.A.* **113** F16
Snow Lake *Canada* **103** C8
Snow Mt. *Calif., U.S.A.* **110** F4
Snow Mt. *Maine, U.S.A.* **115** A14
Snow Shoe *U.S.A.* **114** E7
Snowbird L. *Canada* **103** A8
Snowdon *U.K.* **14** D3
Snowdonia △ *U.K.* **14** D4
Snowdrift = Łutsel K'e
  Canada **103** A6
Snowdrift ➤ *Canada* **103** A6
Snowflake *U.S.A.* **109** J8
Snowshoe Pk. *U.S.A.* **108** B6
Snowtown *Australia* **95** E2
Snowville *U.S.A.* **108** F7
Snowy ➤ *Australia* **95** F4
Snowy Mt. *U.S.A.* **115** C10
Snowy Mts. *Australia* **95** F4
Snug Corner *Bahamas* **121** B5
Snug Harbour *Canada* **114** A4
Snyatyn *Ukraine* **29** B10
Snyder *Okla., U.S.A.* **116** D5
Snyder *Tex., U.S.A.* **116** E4
Soahanina *Madag.* **89** B7
Soalala *Madag.* **89** B8
Soaloka *Madag.* **89** B8
Soamanonga *Madag.* **89** C7
Soan ➤ *Pakistan* **68** C4
Soanierana-Ivongo *Madag.* **89** B8
Soanindrariny *Madag.* **89** B8
Şoarş *Romania* **29** E9
Soavina *Madag.* **89** C8
Soavinandriana *Madag.* **89** B8
Sob ➤ *Ukraine* **29** B14
Soba *Nigeria* **83** C6
Sobat, Nahr ➤ *Sudan* **81** F3
Soběslav *Czech Rep.* **26** B7
Sobhapur *India* **68** H8
Sobinka *Russia* **32** E11
Sóbótka *Poland* **31** H3
Sobra *Croatia* **41** F14
Sobradinho, Represa de
  Brazil **125** E10
Sobral *Brazil* **125** D10
Sobrance *Slovak Rep.* **27** C15
Sobreira Formosa *Portugal* **36** F3
Soc Giang *Vietnam* **58** F6
Soc Trang *Vietnam* **65** H5
Soča ➤ *Europe* **26** E6
Socastee *U.S.A.* **117** E15
Sochaczew *Poland* **31** F7
Soch'e = Shache *China* **60** C2
Sochi *Russia* **35** J4

Sochos *Greece* 44 F7
Société, Îs. de la
  French Polynesia 97 J12
Society Is. = Société, Îs. de
  la *French Polynesia* 97 J12
Socompa, Portezuelo de
  Chile 126 A2
Socorro *N. Mex., U.S.A.* 109 J10
Socorro *Tex., U.S.A.* 116 F1
Socorro, I. *Mexico* 118 D2
Socotra *Yemen* 75 E5
Socovos *Spain* 39 G3
Socuéllamos *Spain* 39 F2
Soda L. *U.S.A.* 109 J5
Soda Plains *India* 69 B8
Soda Springs *U.S.A.* 108 E8
Sodankylä *Finland* 8 C22
Soddy-Daisy *U.S.A.* 117 D12
Söderala *Sweden* 10 C10
Söderåsen △ *Sweden* 11 H7
Söderbärke *Sweden* 10 D9
Söderfors *Sweden* 10 D11
Söderhamn *Sweden* 10 C11
Söderköping *Sweden* 11 F10
Södermanland *Sweden* 9 G17
Södermanlands län □
  Sweden 10 E10
Södertälje *Sweden* 10 E11
Sodiri *Sudan* 81 E2
Sodo *Ethiopia* 81 F4
Södra Dellen *Sweden* 10 C10
Södra Finnskoga *Sweden* 10 D6
Södra Sandby *Sweden* 11 J7
Södra Ulvön *Sweden* 10 B12
Södra Vi *Sweden* 11 G9
Sodražica *Slovenia* 41 C11
Sodus *U.S.A.* 114 C7
Sodwana Bay △ *S. Africa* 89 D5
Soekmekaar = Morebeng
  S. Africa 89 C4
Soest *Germany* 24 D4
Soest *Neths.* 17 B5
Sofades *Greece* 46 B4
Sofala □ *Mozam.* 89 B5
Sofara *Mali* 82 C4
Sofia = Sofiya *Bulgaria* 44 D7
Sofia → *Madag.* 89 B8
Sofievka *Ukraine* 33 H7
Sofiko *Greece* 46 D5
Sofiya *Bulgaria* 44 D7
Sofiya □ *Bulgaria* 44 D7
Sofiya ✈ (SOF) *Bulgaria* 44 D7
Sofrana *Greece* 47 E8
Sōfu-Gan *Japan* 55 K10
Sogakofe *Ghana* 83 D5
Sogamoso *Colombia* 124 B4
Sogār *Iran* 71 E8
Sögel *Germany* 24 C3
Sogndalsfjøra *Norway* 8 F12
Søgne *Norway* 9 G12
Sognefjorden *Norway* 8 F11
Söğüt *Bilecik, Turkey* 47 B12
Söğüt *Burdur, Turkey* 47 D11
Söğüt Dağı *Turkey* 47 D11
Söğütköy *Turkey* 47 E10
Soh *Iran* 71 C6
Sohâg *Egypt* 80 B3
Sohagpur *India* 68 H8
Soignies *Belgium* 17 D4
Soin *Burkina Faso* 82 C4
Soira *Eritrea* 81 E4
Soissons *France* 19 C10
Sōja *Japan* 55 G6
Sojat *India* 68 G5
Sok → *Russia* 34 D10
Sokal *Ukraine* 23 C13
Sokcho *S. Korea* 57 E15
Söke *Turkey* 47 D9
Sokelo *Dem. Rep. of the Congo* 87 D1
Sokhumi *Georgia* 35 J5
Soko Banja *Serbia* 44 C5
Sokodé *Togo* 83 D5
Sokol *Russia* 32 C11
Sokolac *Bos.-H.* 28 G3
Sokółka *Poland* 30 E10
Sokolo *Ségou, Mali* 82 C3
Sokolo *Sikasso, Mali* 82 C3
Sokolov *Czech Rep.* 26 A5
Sokołów Małpolski *Poland* 31 H9
Sokołów Podlaski *Poland* 31 F9
Sokoły *Poland* 31 F9
Sokoto *Nigeria* 83 C6
Sokoto □ *Nigeria* 83 C6
Sokoto → *Nigeria* 83 C5
Sokyrnytsya *Ukraine* 29 B8
Sokyryany *Ukraine* 29 B12
Sol Iletsk *Russia* 52 D6
Sola → *Poland* 31 H6
Solai *Kenya* 86 B4
Solan *India* 68 D7
Solana Beach *U.S.A.* 111 N9
Solander I. *N.Z.* 91 G1
Solano *Phil.* 61 C4
Solapur *India* 66 L9
Solca *Romania* 29 C10
Solda Gölü *Turkey* 47 D11
Soldănești *Moldova* 29 C13
Soldeu *Andorra* 38 C6
Soldotna *U.S.A.* 100 C4

Soléa *Cyprus* 49 D12
Solec Kujawski *Poland* 31 E5
Soledad *Colombia* 124 A4
Soledad *U.S.A.* 110 J5
Soledad *Venezuela* 124 B6
Solent, The *U.K.* 15 G6
Solenzara *France* 21 G13
Solesmes *France* 19 B10
Solfonttaggen *Norway* 9 F12
Solhan *Turkey* 73 C9
Soligorsk = Salihorsk
  Belarus 23 B14
Solihull *U.K.* 15 E6
Solikamsk *Russia* 52 D6
Solila *Madag.* 89 C8
Solimões = Amazonas →
  S. Amer. 125 D8
Solin *Croatia* 41 E13
Solingen *Germany* 24 D3
Söll *Austria* 25 H8
Sollebrunn *Sweden* 11 F6
Sollefteå *Sweden* 10 A11
Sollentuna *Sweden* 10 E11
Sóller *Spain* 48 B9
Sollerön *Sweden* 10 D8
Solling *Germany* 24 D5
Solling-Vogler △ *Germany* 24 D5
Solnechnogorsk *Russia* 32 D9
Solo → *Indonesia* 63 G15
Solofra *Italy* 43 B7
Sologne *France* 19 E8
Solok *Indonesia* 62 E2
Sololá *Guatemala* 120 D1
Sololo *Kenya* 86 B4
Solomon, N. Fork → *U.S.A.* 112 F4
Solomon, S. Fork → *U.S.A.* 112 F4
Solomon Is. ■ *Pac. Oc.* 90 B8
Solomon Rise *Pac. Oc.* 96 G7
Solon *China* 60 B7
Solon Springs *U.S.A.* 112 B8
Solor *Indonesia* 63 F6
Solotcha *Russia* 32 E10
Solothurn *Switz.* 25 H3
Solothurn □ *Switz.* 25 H3
Solotvyn *Ukraine* 29 B9
Solsona *Spain* 38 C6
Solt *Hungary* 28 D4
Šolta *Croatia* 41 E13
Soltāu *Germany* 24 C5
Soltsy *Russia* 32 C6
Solunska Glava *Macedonia* 44 E5
Solvang *U.S.A.* 111 L6
Solvay *U.S.A.* 115 C8
Sölvesborg *Sweden* 11 H8
Solway Firth *U.K.* 14 C4
Solwezi *Zambia* 87 E2
Sōma *Japan* 54 F10
Soma *Turkey* 47 B9
Somabhula *Zimbabwe* 89 B4
Somali Pen. *Africa* 76 F8
Somali Rep. ■ *Africa* 75 F4
Somalia = Somali Rep. ■
  Africa 75 F4
Somaliland □ *Somali Rep.* 75 F4
Sombernon *France* 19 E11
Sombor *Serbia* 28 E4
Sombra *Canada* 114 D2
Sombrerete *Mexico* 118 C4
Sombrero *Anguilla* 121 C7
Şomcuta Mare *Romania* 29 C8
Somdari *India* 68 G5
Somers *U.S.A.* 108 B6
Somerset *Ky., U.S.A.* 113 G11
Somerset *Mass., U.S.A.* 115 E13
Somerset *Pa., U.S.A.* 114 F5
Somerset □ *U.K.* 15 F5
Somerset East *S. Africa* 88 E4
Somerset I. *Canada* 100 B10
Somerset West *S. Africa* 88 E2
Somersworth *U.S.A.* 115 C14
Somerton *U.S.A.* 109 K6
Somerville *U.S.A.* 115 F10
Someș → *Romania* 28 C7
Someșul Mare → *Romania* 29 C8
Somme □ *France* 19 C9
Somme → *France* 19 B8
Somme, B. de la *France* 18 B8
Sommen *Jönköping, Sweden* 11 F8
Sommen *Östergötland, Sweden* 11 F9
Sommepy-Tahure *France* 19 C11
Sömmerda *Germany* 24 D7
Sommesous *France* 19 D11
Sommières *France* 21 E8
Somnath *India* 68 J4
Somogy □ *Hungary* 28 D2
Somogyszob *Hungary* 28 D2
Somosomo *Fiji* 91 a
Somosomo Str. *Fiji* 91 a
Somoto *Nic.* 120 D2
Sompolno *Poland* 31 F5
Somport, Puerto de =
  Somport, Tunnel de *Spain* 38 C4
Somport, Tunnel de *Spain* 38 C4
Son → *India* 69 G11
Son Ha *Vietnam* 64 E7
Son Hoa *Vietnam* 64 F7

Son La *Vietnam* 58 G4
Son Morrell *Spain* 48 B10
Son Rapinya *Spain* 48 B9
Son Sardina *Spain* 48 B9
Son Serra *Spain* 48 B10
Son Servera *Spain* 38 F8
Son Tay *Vietnam* 58 G5
Soná *Panama* 120 E3
Sonamarg *India* 69 B6
Sonamukhi *India* 69 H12
Sonar → *India* 69 G8
Sönch'ŏn *N. Korea* 57 E13
Sondags → *S. Africa* 88 E4
Sóndalo *Italy* 40 B7
Sondar *India* 69 C6
Sønder Felding *Denmark* 11 J2
Sønder Omme *Denmark* 11 J2
Sønderborg *Denmark* 11 K3
Sondershausen *Germany* 24 D6
Sóndrio *Italy* 40 B6
Sone *Mozam.* 87 F3
Sonepur *India* 67 J13
Song *Nigeria* 83 D7
Song *Thailand* 64 C3
Song Cau *Vietnam* 64 F7
Song Hong → *Vietnam* 58 F5
Song Xian *China* 56 G7
Songan *Indonesia* 63 J18
Songea *Tanzania* 87 E4
Songeons *France* 19 C8
Songhua Hu *China* 57 C14
Songhua Jiang → *China* 60 B8
Songjiang *China* 59 B13
Songjiang *China* 58 A4
Songnim *N. Korea* 57 E13
Songo *Mozam.* 87 F3
Songo *Sudan* 79 G10
Songpan *China* 58 A4
Songtao *China* 58 C7
Songwe *Dem. Rep. of the Congo* 86 C2
Songwe → *Africa* 87 D3
Songxi *China* 59 D12
Songzi *China* 59 B8
Sonhat *India* 69 H10
Sonid Youqi *China* 56 C7
Sonipat *India* 68 E7
Sonkach *India* 68 H7
Sonkovo *Russia* 32 C9
Sonmiani *Pakistan* 68 G2
Sonmiani B. *Pakistan* 68 G2
Sonnino *Italy* 42 A6
Sono → *Brazil* 125 E9
Sonoma *U.S.A.* 110 G4
Sonora *Calif., U.S.A.* 110 H6
Sonora *Tex., U.S.A.* 116 F4
Sonora □ *Mexico* 118 B2
Sonora → *Mexico* 118 B2
Sonoran Desert *U.S.A.* 111 L12
Sonoyta *Mexico* 118 A2
Sonqor *Iran* 73 E12
Sonseca *Spain* 37 F7
Sonsonate *El Salv.* 120 D2
Sonstorp *Sweden* 11 F9
Sonthofen *Germany* 25 H6
Soochow = Suzhou *China* 59 B13
Sooke *Canada* 110 B3
Soomaaliya = Somali
  Rep. ■ *Africa* 75 F4
Sop Hao *Laos* 58 G5
Sop Prap *Thailand* 64 D2
Sopelana *Spain* 38 B2
Sopi *Indonesia* 63 D7
Sopo, Nahr → *Sudan* 81 F2
Sopot *Bulgaria* 45 D8
Sopot *Poland* 30 D5
Sopot *Serbia* 44 B4
Sopotnica *Macedonia* 44 E5
Sopron *Hungary* 28 C1
Sopur *India* 69 B6
Sør-Rondane *Antarctica* 5 D4
Sora *Italy* 41 G10
Sorah *Pakistan* 68 F3
Söråker *Sweden* 10 B11
Sorano *Italy* 41 F8
Soraon *India* 69 G9
Sorbas *Spain* 39 H2
Sörbygden *Sweden* 10 B10
Sore *France* 20 D3
Sorel *Canada* 104 C5
Soresina *Italy* 40 C6
Sörforsa *Sweden* 10 C10
Sórgono *Italy* 42 B2
Sorgues *France* 21 D8
Sorgun *Turkey* 72 C6
Soria *Spain* 38 D2
Soria □ *Spain* 38 D2
Soriano *Uruguay* 126 C4
Soriano nel Cimino *Italy* 41 F9
Sorkh, Kuh-e *Iran* 71 C8
Sørø *Denmark* 11 J5
Soro *Guinea* 82 C3
Soroca *Moldova* 29 B13
Sorocaba *Brazil* 127 A6
Soroki = Soroca *Moldova* 29 B13

Sorong *Indonesia* 63 E8
Soroni *Greece* 49 C10
Soroti *Uganda* 86 B3
Sørøya *Norway* 8 A20
Sørøysundet *Norway* 8 A20
Sorraia → *Portugal* 37 G2
Sorrell *Australia* 95 G4
Sorrento *Italy* 43 B7
Sorsele *Sweden* 8 D17
Sörsjön *Sweden* 10 C7
Sorso *Italy* 42 B1
Sorsogon *Phil.* 61 E6
Sortavala *Russia* 32 B6
Sortino *Italy* 43 E8
Sortland *Norway* 8 B16
Sorvizhi *Russia* 34 B9
Sos del Rey Católico *Spain* 38 C3
Soscumica, L. *Canada* 104 B4
Sösdala *Sweden* 11 H7
Sosna → *Russia* 33 F10
Sosnovka *Kirov, Russia* 34 B10
Sosnovka *Tambov, Russia* 34 D5
Sosnovyy Bor *Russia* 32 C5
Sosnowiec *Poland* 31 H6
Sospel *France* 21 E11
Sossus Vlei *Namibia* 88 C2
Šoštanj *Slovenia* 41 B12
Sôsura *N. Korea* 57 C16
Sot → *India* 69 F8
Sotik *Kenya* 86 C4
Sotkamo *Finland* 8 D23
Soto del Barco *Spain* 36 B4
Soto la Marina *Mexico* 119 C5
Soto la Marina → *Mexico* 119 C5
Soto y Amío *Spain* 36 C5
Sotrondio *Spain* 36 B5
Sotuta *Mexico* 119 C7
Souanké *Congo* 84 D2
Soubré *Ivory C.* 82 D3
Souda *Greece* 49 D6
Soudas, Ormos *Greece* 49 D6
Souderton *U.S.A.* 115 F9
Soufi *Greece* 45 E10
Soufrière *Guadeloupe* 120 b
Soufrière *St. Lucia* 121 f
Soufrière Bay *Dominica* 121 f
Souillac *France* 20 D5
Souilly *France* 19 C12
Soukhouma *Laos* 64 E5
Sŏul = Seoul *S. Korea* 57 F14
Soulac-sur-Mer *France* 20 C2
Soulougou *Burkina Faso* 83 C5
Soultz-sous-Forêts *France* 19 D14
Sound, The = Øresund
  Europe 11 J6
Sound, The *U.K.* 15 G6
Sounion, Akra *Greece* 46 D6
Sources, Mt. aux *Lesotho* 89 D4
Soure *Brazil* 125 D9
Soure *Portugal* 36 E2
Souris *Man., Canada* 103 D8
Souris *P.E.I., Canada* 105 C7
Souris → *N. Amer.* 112 A4
Sourou → *Africa* 82 C4
Sourpi *Greece* 46 B4
Sousa *Brazil* 125 E11
Sousel *Portugal* 37 G3
Sousse *Tunisia* 79 A8
Soustons *France* 20 E2
Sout → *S. Africa* 88 E2
South Africa ■ *Africa* 88 E3
South America 122 E5
South Aulatsivik I. *Canada* 105 A7
South Australia □ *Australia* 95 E2
South Australian Basin
  Ind. Oc. 96 L4
South Ayrshire □ *U.K.* 13 F4
South Baldy Pk. *U.S.A.* 109 J10
South Bass I. *U.S.A.* 114 E2
South Bend *Ind., U.S.A.* 112 E10
South Bend *Wash., U.S.A.* 110 D3
South Boston *U.S.A.* 113 G14
South Branch *Canada* 105 C8
South Brook *Canada* 105 C8
South Bruny I. *Australia* 95 G4
South Carolina □ *U.S.A.* 117 E14
South Charleston *U.S.A.* 113 F13
South China Sea *Asia* 62 C4
South Cumberland Is. △
  Australia 94 J7
South Dakota □ *U.S.A.* 112 C4
South Dayton *U.S.A.* 114 D5
South Deerfield *U.S.A.* 115 D12
South Downs *U.K.* 15 G7
South East C. *Australia* 95 G4
South East Is. *Australia* 93 F3
South Esk → *U.K.* 13 E6
South Fiji Basin *Pac. Oc.* 96 K9
South Foreland *U.K.* 15 F9
South Fork American →
  U.S.A. 110 G5
South Fork Feather →
  U.S.A. 110 F5
South Fork Grand →
  U.S.A. 112 C2
South Fork Milk → *U.S.A.* 108 B10
South Fork Republican →
  U.S.A. 112 E3

South Georgia *Antarctica* 128 G9
South Gloucestershire □
  U.K. 15 F5
South Hadley *U.S.A.* 115 D12
South Haven *U.S.A.* 112 D10
South Henik L. *Canada* 103 A9
South Horr *Kenya* 86 B4
South I. *Kenya* 86 B4
South I. *N.Z.* 91 F3
South Indian Lake *Canada* 103 B9
South Invercargill *N.Z.* 91 G2
South Island △ *Kenya* 86 B4
South Kitui △ *Kenya* 86 C4
South Knife → *Canada* 103 B10
South Koel → *India* 69 H11
South Korea ■ *Asia* 57 G15
South Lake Tahoe *U.S.A.* 110 G6
South Lanarkshire □ *U.K.* 13 F5
South Loup → *U.S.A.* 112 E5
South Luangwa △ *Zambia* 87 E3
South Magnetic Pole
  Antarctica 5 C9
South Milwaukee *U.S.A.* 112 D10
South Molton *U.K.* 15 F4
South Moose L. *Canada* 103 C8
South Nahanni → *Canada* 102 A4
South Nation → *Canada* 115 A9
South Natuna Is. =
  Natuna Selatan,
  Kepulauan *Indonesia* 62 D3
South Negril Pt. *Jamaica* 120 a
South Orkney Is. *Antarctica* 5 C18
South Ossetia □ *Georgia* 35 J7
South Otselic *U.S.A.* 115 D9
South Pagai, I. = Pagai
  Selatan, Pulau *Indonesia* 62 E2
South Paris *U.S.A.* 115 B14
South Pittsburg *U.S.A.* 117 D12
South Platte → *U.S.A.* 112 E3
South Pole *Antarctica* 5 E
South Porcupine *Canada* 104 C3
South Portland *U.S.A.* 113 D18
South Pt. *Barbados* 121 g
South Pt. *U.S.A.* 114 B1
South River *Canada* 104 C4
South River *U.S.A.* 115 F10
South Ronaldsay *U.K.* 13 C6
South Sandwich Is. *Antarctica* 5 B1
South Sandwich Trench
  Atl. Oc. 5 B1
South Saskatchewan →
  Canada 103 C7
South Seal → *Canada* 103 B9
South Shetland Is. *Antarctica* 5 C18
South Shields *U.K.* 14 C6
South Sioux City *U.S.A.* 112 D6
South Sister *U.S.A.* 108 D3
South Talipatti = New
  Moore *I. Ind. Oc.* 69 J13
South Taranaki Bight *N.Z.* 91 C5
South Tasman Rise *S. Ocean* 5 A10
South Thompson →
  Canada 102 C4
South Twin I. *Canada* 104 B4
South Tyne → *U.K.* 14 C5
South Uist *U.K.* 13 D1
South Valley *U.S.A.* 109 J10
South Wellesley Is. *Australia* 94 B2
South West C. *Australia* 95 G4
South West N.Z. *N.Z.* 91 G1
South Williamsport *U.S.A.* 114 E8
South Yorkshire □ *U.K.* 14 D6
Southampton *Canada* 114 B3
Southampton *U.K.* 15 G6
Southampton *U.S.A.* 115 F12
Southampton □ *U.K.* 15 G6
Southampton I. *Canada* 101 C11
Southaven *U.S.A.* 117 D9
Southbank *Canada* 102 C3
Southbridge *N.Z.* 91 E4
Southbridge *U.S.A.* 115 D12
Southend *Canada* 103 B8
Southend-on-Sea *U.K.* 15 F8
Southend-on-Sea □ *U.K.* 15 F8
Southern □ *Malawi* 87 F4
Southern □ *S. Leone* 82 D2
Southern □ *Zambia* 87 F2
Southern Alps *N.Z.* 91 E3
Southern Cross *Australia* 93 F2
Southern Indian L. *Canada* 103 B9
Southern Lau Group *Fiji* 91 a
Southern Ocean *Antarctica* 5 C6
Southern Pines *U.S.A.* 117 D15
Southern Uplands *U.K.* 13 F5
Southington *U.S.A.* 115 E12
Southland □ *N.Z.* 91 F1
Southold *U.S.A.* 115 E12
Southport *Australia* 95 D5
Southport *U.K.* 14 D4
Southport *U.S.A.* 114 D8
Southwest △ *Australia* 95 G4
Southwest Pacific Basin
  Pac. Oc. 5 A12

Southwold *U.K.* 15 E9
Southwood △ *Australia* 95 D5
Soutpansberg *S. Africa* 89 C4
Souvigny *France* 19 F10
Sovata *Romania* 29 D10
Soverato *Italy* 43 D9
Sovetsk *Kaliningrad, Russia* 30 C8
Sovetsk *Kirov, Russia* 34 B9
Sovetskaya Gavan *Russia* 53 E15
Sovicille *Italy* 41 E8
Soweto *S. Africa* 89 D4
Sowma'eh Sarā *Iran* 73 D13
Sōya-Kaikyō = La Perouse
  Str. *Asia* 54 B11
Sōya-Misaki *Japan* 54 B10
Soyaux *France* 20 C4
Soyo *Angola* 84 F2
Sozh → *Belarus* 23 B16
Sozopol *Bulgaria* 45 D11
Spa *Belgium* 17 D5
Spain ■ *Europe* 7 H5
Spalding *Australia* 95 E2
Spalding *U.K.* 14 E7
Spanaway *U.S.A.* 110 C4
Spangler *U.S.A.* 114 F6
Spanish *Canada* 104 C3
Spanish Fork *U.S.A.* 108 F8
Spanish Town *Br. Virgin Is.* 121 e
Spanish Town *Jamaica* 120 a
Sparks *U.S.A.* 110 F7
Sparreholm *Sweden* 10 E10
Sparta = Sparti *Greece* 46 D4
Sparta *Mich., U.S.A.* 113 D11
Sparta *N.J., U.S.A.* 115 E10
Sparta *Wis., U.S.A.* 112 D8
Spartanburg *U.S.A.* 117 D14
Sparti *Greece* 46 D4
Spartivento, C. *Calabria, Italy* 43 E9
Spartivento, C. *Sard., Italy* 42 D1
Sparwood *Canada* 102 D6
Spas-Demensk *Russia* 32 E9
Spas-Klepiki *Russia* 32 E11
Spassk Dalniy *Russia* 54 B6
Spassk-Ryazanskiy *Russia* 32 E11
Spatha, Akra *Greece* 49 D5
Spatsizi → *Canada* 102 B3
Spatsizi Plateau
  Wilderness △ *Canada* 102 B3
Spean → *U.K.* 13 E4
Spearfish *U.S.A.* 112 C2
Spearman *U.S.A.* 116 C4
Speculator *U.S.A.* 115 C10
Speia *Moldova* 29 C14
Speightstown *Barbados* 121 g
Speke Gulf *Tanzania* 86 C3
Spello *Italy* 41 F9
Spence Bay = Taloyoak
  Canada 100 C10
Spencer *Idaho, U.S.A.* 108 D7
Spencer *Iowa, U.S.A.* 112 D6
Spencer *N.Y., U.S.A.* 115 D8
Spencer *Nebr., U.S.A.* 112 D4
Spencer, C. *Australia* 95 F2
Spencer B. *Namibia* 88 D1
Spencer G. *Australia* 95 E2
Spencerville *Canada* 115 B9
Spences Bridge *Canada* 102 C4
Spennymoor *U.K.* 14 C6
Spenser Mts. *N.Z.* 91 E4
Spentrup *Denmark* 11 H4
Sperchios → *Greece* 46 C4
Sperrin Mts. *U.K.* 12 B5
Spessart *Germany* 25 F5
Spetses *Greece* 46 D5
Spey → *U.K.* 13 D5
Speyer *Germany* 25 F4
Spezand *Pakistan* 68 E2
Spezzano Albanese *Italy* 43 C9
Spiddle *Ireland* 12 C2
Spiekeroog *Germany* 24 B3
Spiez *Switz.* 25 J3
Spili *Greece* 49 D6
Spilimbergo *Italy* 41 B9
Spīn Būldak *Afghan.* 68 D2
Spinalonga *Greece* 49 D7
Spinazzola *Italy* 43 B9
Spineni *Romania* 29 F9
Spirit Lake *U.S.A.* 110 D4
Spirit River *Canada* 102 B5
Spiritwood *Canada* 103 C7
Spišská Nová Ves
  Slovak Rep. 27 C13
Spišské Podhradie
  Slovak Rep. 27 B13
Spital *Austria* 26 D7
Spithead *U.K.* 15 G6
Spittal an der Drau *Austria* 26 E6
Spitzbergen = Svalbard *Arctic* 4 B8
Spjelkavik *Norway* 8 E12
Split *Croatia* 41 E13
Split ✈ (SPU) *Croatia* 41 E13
Split L. *Canada* 103 B9
Split Lake *Canada* 103 B9
Splitski Kanal *Croatia* 41 E13
Splügenpass *Switz.* 25 J5
Spofford *U.S.A.* 116 G4
Spokane *U.S.A.* 108 C5
Spoleto *Italy* 41 F9
Spooner *U.S.A.* 112 C8

Sporyy Navolok, Mys *Russia* **52** B7
Sprague *U.S.A.* **108** C5
Spratly I. *S. China Sea* **62** C4
Spratly Is. *S. China Sea* **62** C4
Spray *U.S.A.* **108** D4
Spreča → *Bos.-H.* **28** F3
Spree → *Germany* **24** C9
Spreewald *Germany* **24** D9
Spremberg *Germany* **24** D10
Sprengisandur *Iceland* **8** D4
Spring City *U.S.A.* **115** F9
Spring Creek *U.S.A.* **108** F6
Spring Garden *U.S.A.* **110** F6
Spring Hall *Barbados* **121** g
Spring Hill *U.S.A.* **117** G13
Spring Mts. *U.S.A.* **111** J11
Spring Valley *Calif., U.S.A.* **111** N10
Spring Valley *Nev., U.S.A.* **111** J11
Springbok *S. Africa* **88** D2
Springboro *U.S.A.* **114** E4
Springdale *Canada* **105** C8
Springdale *U.S.A.* **116** C7
Springe *Germany* **24** C5
Springer *U.S.A.* **109** H11
Springerville *U.S.A.* **109** J9
Springfield *Canada* **114** D4
Springfield *N.Z.* **91** E3
Springfield *Colo., U.S.A.* **109** H12
Springfield *Ill., U.S.A.* **112** F9
Springfield *Mass., U.S.A.* **115** D12
Springfield *Mo., U.S.A.* **112** G7
Springfield *Ohio, U.S.A.* **113** F12
Springfield *Oreg., U.S.A.* **108** D2
Springfield *Tenn., U.S.A.* **117** C11
Springfield *Vt., U.S.A.* **115** C12
Springfontein *S. Africa* **88** E4
Springhill *Canada* **105** C7
Springhill *U.S.A.* **116** E8
Springhouse *Canada* **102** C4
Springs *S. Africa* **89** D4
Springsure *Australia* **94** C4
Springvale *U.S.A.* **115** C14
Springville *Calif., U.S.A.* **110** J8
Springville *N.Y., U.S.A.* **114** D6
Springville *Utah, U.S.A.* **108** F8
Springwater *U.S.A.* **114** D7
Spruce-Creek *U.S.A.* **114** F6
Spruce Knob-Seneca
  Rocks △ *U.S.A.* **113** F14
Spruce Mt. *U.S.A.* **115** B12
Sprucedale *Canada* **114** A5
Spur *U.S.A.* **116** E4
Spurn Hd. *U.K.* **14** D8
Spuž *Montenegro* **44** D3
Spuzzum *Canada* **102** D4
Squam L. *U.S.A.* **115** C13
Squamish *Canada* **102** D4
Square Islands *Canada* **105** B8
Squillace, G. di *Italy* **43** D9
Squinzano *Italy* **43** B11
Squires, Mt. *Australia* **93** E4
Srbac *Bos.-H.* **28** E2
Srbica *Serbia* **44** D4
Srbija = Serbia ■ *Europe* **44** C4
Srbobran *Serbia* **28** E4
Sre Ambel *Cambodia* **65** G4
Sre Khtum *Cambodia* **65** F6
Sre Umbell = Sre Ambel
  Cambodia **65** G4
Srebrenica *Bos.-H.* **28** F4
Sredinny Ra. = Sredinnyy
  Khrebet *Russia* **53** D17
Sredinnyy Khrebet *Russia* **53** D17
Središče *Slovenia* **41** B13
Sredna Gora *Bulgaria* **45** D8
Srednekolymsk *Russia* **53** C16
Sredni Rodopi *Bulgaria* **45** E8
Srednogorie *Bulgaria* **45** D8
Šrem *Poland* **31** F4
Sremska Mitrovica *Serbia* **28** F4
Sremski Karlovci *Serbia* **28** E4
Srepok → *Cambodia* **64** F6
Sretensk *Russia* **53** D12
Sri Aman *Malaysia* **62** D4
Sri Lanka ■ *Asia* **66** R12
Srikakulam *India* **67** K13
Srinagar *India* **69** B6
Środa Śląska *Poland* **31** G3
Środa Wielkopolski *Poland* **31** F4
Srono *Indonesia* **63** J17
Srpska Crnja *Serbia* **28** E5
Srpski Itebej *Serbia* **28** E5
Staaten → *Australia* **94** B3
Staaten River △ *Australia* **94** B3
Staberhuk *Germany* **24** A7
Stade *Germany* **24** B5
Stadskanaal *Neths.* **17** A6
Stadtallendorf *Germany* **24** E5
Stadthagen *Germany* **24** C5
Stadtlohn *Germany* **24** D2
Stadtroda *Germany* **24** E7
Staffa *U.K.* **13** E2
Staffanstorp *Sweden* **11** J7
Stafford *U.K.* **14** E5
Stafford *U.S.A.* **112** G4
Stafford Springs *U.S.A.* **115** E12
Staffordshire □ *U.K.* **14** E5
Stagnone *Italy* **42** E5
Stagnone di Marsala △ *Italy* **42** E5

Staines *U.K.* **15** F7
Stainz *Austria* **26** E8
Stakhanov *Ukraine* **33** H10
Stalać *Serbia* **44** C5
Stalida *Greece* **49** D7
Stallarholmen *Sweden* **10** E11
Ställdalen *Sweden* **10** E8
Stalowa Wola *Poland* **31** H9
Stalybridge *U.K.* **14** D5
Stamford *Australia* **94** C3
Stamford *U.K.* **15** E7
Stamford *Conn., U.S.A.* **115** E11
Stamford *N.Y., U.S.A.* **115** D10
Stamford *Tex., U.S.A.* **116** E5
Stampriet *Namibia* **88** C2
Stamps *U.S.A.* **116** E8
Stančevo = Kalipetrovo
  Bulgaria **45** B11
Standerton *S. Africa* **89** D4
Standish *U.S.A.* **113** D12
Stanford *S. Africa* **88** E2
Stanford *U.S.A.* **108** C8
Stånga *Sweden* **11** G12
Stanger *S. Africa* **89** D5
Stängselåsen =
  Salpausselkä *Finland* **32** B4
Stanišić *Serbia* **28** E4
Stanislaus → *U.S.A.* **110** H5
Stanisławów *Poland* **31** F8
Stanley *Australia* **95** G4
Stanley *Falk. Is.* **128** G5
Stanley *U.K.* **14** C6
Stanley *Idaho, U.S.A.* **108** D6
Stanley *N. Dak., U.S.A.* **112** A2
Stanley *N.Y., U.S.A.* **114** D7
Stanley Mission *Canada* **103** B8
Stannards *U.S.A.* **114** D7
Stanovoy Khrebet *Russia* **53** D14
Stanovoy Ra. = Stanovoy
  Khrebet *Russia* **53** D14
Stansmore Ra. *Australia* **92** D4
Stansted, London ✈ (STN)
  U.K. **15** F8
Stanthorpe *Australia* **95** D5
Stanton *U.S.A.* **116** E4
Stanwood *U.S.A.* **110** B4
Staples *Canada* **114** D2
Staples *U.S.A.* **112** B6
Stapleton *U.S.A.* **112** E3
Stąporków *Poland* **31** G7
Star City *Canada* **103** C8
Star Lake *U.S.A.* **115** B9
Stará Ľubovňa *Slovak Rep.* **27** B13
Stara Moravica *Serbia* **28** E4
Stara Pazova *Serbia* **28** F5
Stara Planina *Bulgaria* **44** C7
Stara Sil *Ukraine* **31** J9
Stará Turá *Slovak Rep.* **27** C10
Stara Ushytsya *Ukraine* **29** B12
Stara Zagora *Bulgaria* **45** D9
Starachowice *Poland* **31** G8
Staraya Russa *Russia* **32** D6
Starbuck I. *Kiribati* **97** H12
Starchiojd *Romania* **29** E11
Starcke △ *Australia* **94** C4
Stargard Szczeciński *Poland* **30** E2
Stari Bar *Montenegro* **44** D3
Stari Trg *Slovenia* **41** C12
Staritsa *Russia* **32** D8
Starke *U.S.A.* **117** G13
Starkville *U.S.A.* **117** E10
Starnberg *Germany* **25** H7
Starnberger See *Germany* **25** H7
Starobilsk *Ukraine* **33** H10
Starodub *Russia* **33** F7
Starogard Gdański *Poland* **30** E5
Starokonstantinov =
  Starokonstyantyniv
  Ukraine **23** D14
Starokonstyantyniv
  Ukraine **23** D14
Starokozache *Ukraine* **29** D14
Starominskaya *Russia* **33** J10
Staroshcherbinovskaya
  Russia **33** J10
Start Pt. *U.K.* **15** G4
Stary Sącz *Poland* **31** J7
Staryy Biryuzyak *Russia* **35** H8
Staryy Chartoriysk *Ukraine* **23** C13
Staryy Krym *Ukraine* **33** K8
Staryy Oskol *Russia* **33** G9
Staryy Sambir *Ukraine* **31** J9
Stassfurt *Germany* **24** D7
Staszów *Poland* **31** H8
State College *U.S.A.* **114** F7
Stateline *U.S.A.* **110** G7
Staten, I. = Estados, I. de
  Los *Argentina* **128** G4
Staten I. *U.S.A.* **115** F10
Statesboro *U.S.A.* **117** E14
Statesville *U.S.A.* **117** D14
Statia = St. Eustatius
  W. Indies **121** C7
Stauffer *U.S.A.* **111** L7
Staunton *Ill., U.S.A.* **112** F9
Staunton *Va., U.S.A.* **113** F14
Stavanger *Norway* **9** G11
Staveley *N.Z.* **91** E3
Stavelot *Belgium* **17** D5

Stavern *Norway* **9** G14
Stavoren *Neths.* **17** B5
Stavropol *Russia* **35** H6
Stavropol *Serbia* **35** G6
Stavros *Cyprus* **49** D11
Stavros *Kriti, Greece* **49** D6
Stavros *Thessaloniki, Greece* **44** F7
Stavros, Akra *Greece* **49** D6
Stavroupoli *Greece* **45** E8
Stawell *Australia* **95** F3
Stawell → *Australia* **94** C3
Stawiski *Poland* **30** E9
Stawiszyn *Poland* **31** G5
Stayner *Canada* **114** B4
Stayton *U.S.A.* **108** D2
Steamboat Springs *U.S.A.* **108** F10
Steblevë *Albania* **44** E4
Steele *U.S.A.* **112** B4
Steelton *U.S.A.* **114** F8
Steen River *Canada* **102** B5
Steens Mt. *U.S.A.* **108** E4
Steenwijk *Neths.* **17** B6
Steep Pt. *Australia* **93** E1
Steep Rock *Canada* **103** C9
Ştefan Vodă *Moldova* **29** D14
Stefanie L. = Chew Bahir
  Ethiopia **81** G4
Stefansson Bay *Antarctica* **5** C5
Stefánesti *Romania* **29** C12
Ştefănesti *Romania* **29** C12
Stege *Denmark* **11** K6
Şteı *Romania* **28** D7
Steiermark □ *Austria* **26** D8
Steigerwald *Germany* **25** F6
Steigerwald △ *Germany* **25** F6
Steilacoom *U.S.A.* **110** C4
Steilrandberge *Namibia* **88** B1
Steinbach *Canada* **103** D9
Steinfurt *Germany* **24** C3
Steinhausen *Namibia* **88** C2
Steinheim *Germany* **24** D5
Steinhuder Meer *Germany* **24** C5
Steinhuder Meer △ *Germany* **24** C5
Steinkjer *Norway* **8** D14
Steinkopf *S. Africa* **88** D2
Steinwald △ *Germany* **25** F8
Stellarton *Canada* **105** C7
Stellenbosch *S. Africa* **88** E2
Stelvio, Paso dello *Italy* **40** B7
Stenay *France* **19** C12
Stendal *Germany* **24** C7
Stende *Latvia* **30** A9
Stenhamra *Sweden* **10** E11
Stenshuvud △ *Sweden* **11** J8
Stenstorp *Sweden* **11** F7
Stenungsund *Sweden* **11** F5
Steornabhaigh =
  Stornoway *U.K.* **13** C2
Stepanakert = Xankändi
  Azerbaijan **73** C12
Stepanavan *Armenia* **35** K7
Stephens Creek *Australia* **95** E3
Stephens I. *Canada* **102** C2
Stephens L. *Canada* **103** B9
Stephenville *Canada* **105** C8
Stephenville *U.S.A.* **116** E5
Stepnica *Poland* **30** E1
Steppe *Asia* **50** C7
Sterea Ellas □ *Greece* **46** C4
Sterkstroom *S. Africa* **88** E4
Sterling *Colo., U.S.A.* **108** F12
Sterling *Ill., U.S.A.* **112** E9
Sterling *Kans., U.S.A.* **112** F4
Sterling City *U.S.A.* **116** F4
Sterling Heights *U.S.A.* **113** D12
Sterling Run *U.S.A.* **114** E6
Sterlitamak *Russia* **52** D6
Sternberg *Germany* **24** B7
Šternberk *Czech Rep.* **27** B10
Sternes *Greece* **49** D6
Sterzing = Vipiteno *Italy* **41** B8
Stettin = Szczecin *Poland* **30** E1
Stettiner Haff *Germany* **24** B10
Stettler *Canada* **102** C6
Steubenville *U.S.A.* **114** F4
Stevenage *U.K.* **15** F7
Stevens Point *U.S.A.* **112** C9
Stevenson *U.S.A.* **110** E5
Stevenson → *Australia* **95** D2
Stevenson L. *Canada* **103** C9
Stevensville *U.S.A.* **108** C6
Stevns Klint *Denmark* **11** J6
Stewart *Canada* **102** B3
Stewart *U.S.A.* **110** F7
Stewart → *Canada* **100** C6
Stewart, C. *Australia* **94** A1
Stewart, I. *Chile* **128** G2
Stewart I. *N.Z.* **91** G1
Stewarts Point *U.S.A.* **110** G3
Stewartville *U.S.A.* **112** D7
Steynsburg *S. Africa* **88** E4
Steyr *Austria* **26** C7
Steyr → *Austria* **26** C7
Steytlerville *S. Africa* **88** E3
Stia *Italy* **41** E8
Stigler *U.S.A.* **116** D7
Stigliano *Italy* **43** B9
Stigtomta *Sweden* **11** F10

Stikine → *Canada* **102** B2
Stilfontein *S. Africa* **88** D4
Stilida *Greece* **46** C4
Stillwater *N.Z.* **91** E3
Stillwater *N.Y., U.S.A.* **115** D11
Stillwater *Okla., U.S.A.* **116** C6
Stillwater Range *U.S.A.* **108** G4
Stillwater Res. *U.S.A.* **115** C9
Stilo, Pta. *Italy* **43** D9
Stilwell *U.S.A.* **116** D7
Stînga Nistrului □ *Moldova* **29** C14
Štip *Macedonia* **44** E6
Stira *Greece* **46** C6
Stirling *Canada* **114** B7
Stirling *U.K.* **13** E5
Stirling □ *U.K.* **13** E4
Stirling Ra. *Australia* **93** F2
Stirling Range △ *Australia* **93** F2
Stittsville *U.S.A.* **115** A9
Stjernøya *Norway* **8** A20
Stjørdalshalsen *Norway* **8** E14
Stockach *Germany* **25** H5
Stockaryd *Sweden* **11** G8
Stockerau *Austria* **27** C9
Stockholm *Sweden* **10** E12
Stockholm Arlanda ✈
  (ARN) *Sweden* **10** E11
Stockholms län □ *Sweden* **10** E12
Stockport *U.K.* **14** D5
Stocksbridge *U.K.* **14** D6
Stockton *Calif., U.S.A.* **110** H5
Stockton *Kans., U.S.A.* **112** F4
Stockton *Mo., U.S.A.* **112** G7
Stockton-on-Tees *U.K.* **14** C6
Stockton-on-Tees □ *U.K.* **14** C6
Stockton Plateau *U.S.A.* **116** F3
Stoczek Łukowski *Poland* **31** G9
Stöde *Sweden* **10** B10
Stoeng Treng *Cambodia* **64** F5
Stoer, Pt. of *U.K.* **13** C3
Stogovo *Macedonia* **44** E4
Stoholm *Denmark* **11** H3
Stoke-on-Trent *U.K.* **14** D5
Stoke-on-Trent □ *U.K.* **14** D5
Stokes △ *Australia* **93** F3
Stokes Bay *Canada* **114** B3
Stokes Pt. *Australia* **95** G3
Stokes Ra. *Australia* **92** C5
Stokksnes *Iceland* **8** D6
Stokmarknes *Norway* **8** B16
Stolac *Bos.-H.* **44** C1
Stolberg *Germany* **24** E2
Stolbovoy, Ostrov *Russia* **53** B14
Stolbtsy = Stowbtsy *Belarus* **23** B14
Stolin *Belarus* **23** C14
Stollberg *Germany* **24** E8
Stöllet *Sweden* **10** D7
Stolnici *Romania* **29** F8
Stomio *Greece* **49** D5
Ston *Croatia* **41** F14
Stone *U.K.* **14** E5
Stoneboro *U.S.A.* **114** E4
Stonehaven *U.K.* **13** E6
Stonehenge *Australia* **94** C3
Stonehenge *U.K.* **15** F6
Stonewall *Canada* **103** C9
Stony I. *U.S.A.* **115** C8
Stony L. *Man., Canada* **103** B9
Stony L. *Ont., Canada* **114** B6
Stony Point *U.S.A.* **115** E11
Stony Pt. *U.S.A.* **115** C8
Stony Rapids *Canada* **103** B7
Stony Tunguska =
  Tunguska,
  Podkamennaya →
  Russia **53** C10
Stonyford *U.S.A.* **110** F4
Stopnica *Poland* **31** H7
Storå *Sweden* **10** E9
Storå → *Denmark* **11** H2
Stora Gla *Sweden* **10** E6
Stora Le *Sweden* **10** E5
Stora Lulevatten *Sweden* **8** C18
Storavan *Sweden* **8** D18
Stord *Norway* **9** G11
Store Bælt *Denmark* **11** J4
Store Heddinge *Denmark* **11** J6
Store Mosse △ *Sweden* **11** G7
Storebro *Sweden* **11** G9
Storfors *Sweden* **10** E8
Storlien *Sweden* **10** A6
Storm B. *Australia* **95** G4
Storm Lake *U.S.A.* **112** D6
Stormberge *S. Africa* **88** E4
Stormsrivier *S. Africa* **88** E3
Stornoway *U.K.* **13** C2
Storo *Italy* **40** C7
Storozhinets =
  Storozhynets *Ukraine* **29** B10
Storozhynets *Ukraine* **29** B10
Storrs *U.S.A.* **115** E12
Storsjön *Gävleborg, Sweden* **10** D10
Storsjön *Jämtland, Sweden* **10** B7
Storsjön *Jämtland, Sweden* **10** A8
Storuman *Sweden* **8** D17
Storuman *Sweden* **8** D17
Storvätteshågna *Sweden* **10** B6
Storvik *Sweden* **10** D10
Storvreta *Sweden* **10** E11
Stouffville *Canada* **114** C5

Stoughton *Canada* **103** D8
Stour → *Dorset, U.K.* **15** G6
Stour → *Kent, U.K.* **15** F9
Stour → *Suffolk, U.K.* **15** F9
Stourbridge *U.K.* **15** E5
Stout L. *Canada* **103** C10
Stove Pipe Wells Village
  U.S.A. **111** J9
Støvring *Denmark* **11** H3
Stow *U.S.A.* **114** E3
Stowbtsy *Belarus* **23** B14
Stowmarket *U.K.* **15** E9
Strabane *U.K.* **12** B4
Stracin *Macedonia* **44** D6
Stradella *Italy* **40** C6
Strahan *Australia* **95** G4
Strajitsa *Bulgaria* **45** C9
Strakonice *Czech Rep.* **26** B6
Straldzha *Bulgaria* **45** D10
Stralsund *Germany* **24** A9
Strand *S. Africa* **88** E2
Stranda *Møre og Romsdal,
  Norway* **8** E12
Stranda *Nord-Trøndelag,
  Norway* **8** D14
Strandby *Denmark* **11** G4
Strangford L. *U.K.* **12** B6
Strängnäs *Sweden* **10** E11
Stranorlar *Ireland* **12** B4
Stranraer *U.K.* **13** G3
Strasbourg *Canada* **103** C8
Strasbourg *France* **19** D14
Strasburg *Germany* **24** B9
Strășeni *Moldova* **29** C13
Stråssa *Sweden* **10** E9
Stratford *Canada* **114** C4
Stratford *N.Z.* **91** C5
Stratford *Calif., U.S.A.* **110** J7
Stratford *Conn., U.S.A.* **115** E11
Stratford *Tex., U.S.A.* **116** C3
Stratford-upon-Avon *U.K.* **15** E6
Strath Spey *U.K.* **13** D5
Strathalbyn *Australia* **95** F2
Strathaven *U.K.* **13** F4
Strathcona △ *Canada* **102** D3
Strathmore *Canada* **102** C6
Strathmore *U.K.* **13** E5
Strathmore *U.S.A.* **110** J7
Strathnaver *Canada* **102** C4
Strathpeffer *U.K.* **13** D4
Strathroy *Canada* **114** D3
Strathy Pt. *U.K.* **13** C4
Strattanville *U.S.A.* **114** E5
Stratton *U.S.A.* **115** A14
Stratton Mt. *U.S.A.* **115** C12
Straubing *Germany* **25** G8
Straumnes *Iceland* **8** C2
Strausberg *Germany* **24** C9
Strawberry → *U.S.A.* **108** F8
Strážnice *Czech Rep.* **27** C10
Streaky B. *Australia* **95** E1
Streaky Bay *Australia* **95** E1
Streator *U.S.A.* **112** E9
Středočeský □ *Czech Rep.* **26** B7
Streetsboro *U.S.A.* **114** E3
Streetsville *Canada* **114** C5
Strehaia *Romania* **29** F8
Strelcha *Bulgaria* **45** D8
Streng → *Cambodia* **64** F4
Stresa *Italy* **40** C5
Streymoy *Færoe Is.* **8** E9
Strezhevoy *Russia* **52** C8
Stříbro *Czech Rep.* **26** A6
Strilky *Ukraine* **31** J9
Strimonas → *Greece* **44** F7
Strofades *Greece* **46** D3
Strokestown *Ireland* **12** C3
Stroma *U.K.* **13** C5
Stromberg-Heuchelberg △
  Germany **25** F4
Strómboli *Italy* **43** D8
Stromeferry *U.K.* **13** D3
Stromness *U.K.* **13** C5
Strömsbruk *Sweden* **10** C11
Strömsbro *U.S.A.* **112** E5
Strömsnäsbruk *Sweden* **11** H7
Strömstad *Sweden* **11** F5
Strömsund *Sweden* **8** E16
Strongili *Greece* **47** E11
Stróngoli *Italy* **43** C10
Strongsville *U.S.A.* **114** E3
Stronie Śląskie *Poland* **31** H3
Stronsay *U.K.* **13** B6
Stroud *U.K.* **15** F5
Stroud Road *Australia* **95** E5
Stroudsburg *U.S.A.* **115** F9
Struer *Denmark* **11** H2
Struga *Macedonia* **44** E4
Strugi Krasnye *Russia* **32** C5
Strumica *Macedonia* **44** E6
Strumica → *Europe* **44** E7
Strumok *Ukraine* **29** E14
Struthers *U.S.A.* **114** E4
Stryama *Bulgaria* **45** D8
Stryker *U.S.A.* **108** B6
Stryków *Poland* **31** G6
Stryy *Ukraine* **23** D12

Strzegom *Poland* **31** H3
Strzelce Krajeńskie *Poland* **31** F2
Strzelce Opolskie *Poland* **31** H5
Strzelecki Cr. → *Australia* **95** D2
Strzelecki Desert *Australia* **95** D3
Strzelin *Poland* **31** H4
Strzelno *Poland* **31** F5
Strzybnica *Poland* **31** H5
Strzyżów *Poland* **31** J8
Stuart *Fla., U.S.A.* **117** H14
Stuart *Nebr., U.S.A.* **112** D4
Stuart → *Canada* **102** C4
Stuart Bluff Ra. *Australia* **92** D5
Stuart L. *Canada* **102** C4
Stuart Ra. *Australia* **95** D1
Stubbekøbing *Denmark* **11** K6
Stuben *Austria* **26** D3
Studen Kladenets, Yazovir
  Bulgaria **45** E9
Studenka *Czech Rep.* **27** B11
Stugun *Sweden* **10** A9
Stuhr *Germany* **24** B4
Stull L. *Canada* **104** B1
Stung Treng = Stoeng
  Treng *Cambodia* **64** F5
Stupart → *Canada* **104** A1
Stupava *Slovak Rep.* **27** C10
Stupino *Russia* **32** E10
Sturgeon B. *Canada* **103** C9
Sturgeon Bay *U.S.A.* **112** C10
Sturgeon Falls *Canada* **104** C4
Sturgeon L. *Alta., Canada* **102** B5
Sturgeon L. *Ont., Canada* **104** C1
Sturgeon L. *Ont., Canada* **114** B6
Sturgis *Canada* **103** C8
Sturgis *Mich., U.S.A.* **113** E11
Sturgis *S. Dak., U.S.A.* **112** C2
Sturkö *Sweden* **11** H9
Štúrovo *Slovak Rep.* **27** D10
Sturt △ *Australia* **95** D3
Sturt Cr. → *Australia* **92** C4
Sturt Stony Desert *Australia* **95** D3
Stutterheim *S. Africa* **88** E4
Stuttgart *Germany* **25** G5
Stuttgart *U.S.A.* **116** D9
Stuttgart Echterdingen ✈
  (STR) *Germany* **25** G5
Stuyvesant *U.S.A.* **115** D11
Stykkishólmur *Iceland* **8** D2
Styria = Steiermark □
  Austria **26** D8
Styrsö *Sweden* **11** G5
Su Xian = Suzhou *China* **56** H9
Suakin *Sudan* **80** D4
Suakin Archipelago *Sudan* **80** D4
Suan *N. Korea* **57** E14
Suar *India* **69** E8
Subang *Indonesia* **63** G12
Subansiri → *India* **67** F18
Subarnarekha → *India* **69** H12
Subay', 'Urūq *Si. Arabia* **80** C5
Subayhah *Si. Arabia* **70** D3
Subcetate *Romania* **28** E8
Subi *Indonesia* **62** D3
Subiaco *Italy* **41** G10
Subic B. *Phil.* **61** D4
Subotica *Serbia* **28** D4
Suca *Ethiopia* **81** F4
Suceava *Romania* **29** C11
Suceava □ *Romania* **29** C10
Suceava → *Romania* **29** C11
Sucha-Beskidzka *Poland* **31** J6
Suchan = Partizansk *Russia* **54** C7
Suchań *Poland* **31** E2
Suchedniów *Poland* **31** G7
Suchil *Mexico* **118** C4
Suchou = Suzhou *China* **59** B13
Süchow = Xuzhou *China* **57** G9
Suchowola *Poland* **30** E10
Suck → *Ireland* **12** C3
Sucre *Bolivia* **124** G5
Sućuraj *Croatia* **41** E14
Sucuriú → *Brazil* **125** H8
Sud □ *Cameroon* **83** E7
Sud, Pte. du *Canada* **105** C7
Sud-Kivu □
  Dem. Rep. of the Congo **86** C2
Sud-Ouest □ *Cameroon* **83** D6
Sud-Ouest, Pte. *Canada* **105** C7
Sud Ouest, Pte. *Mauritius* **85** d
Suda → *Russia* **32** C9
Sudak *Ukraine* **33** K8
Sudan *U.S.A.* **116** D3
Sudan ■ *Africa* **81** E3
Sudbury *Canada* **104** C3
Sudbury *U.K.* **15** E8
Sûdd *Sudan* **81** F3
Sudeifel = Deutsch-
  Luxemburgischer △
  Germany **25** F2
Süderbrarup *Germany* **24** A5
Süderlügum *Germany* **24** A4
Süderoogsand *Germany* **24** A4
Sudeten Mts. = Sudety
  Europe **27** A9
Sudety *Europe* **27** A9
Südheide △ *Germany* **24** C6
Suðuroy *Færoe Is.* **8** F9

Sudi *Tanzania* **87** E4
Sudirman, Pegunungan *Indonesia* **63** E9
Sudiţi *Romania* **29** F12
Sudogda *Russia* **34** C5
Sudong, Pulau *Singapore* **65** d
Sudova Vyshnya *Ukraine* **31** J10
Sudzha *Russia* **33** G8
Sue ⟶ *Sudan* **81** F2
Sueca *Spain* **39** F4
Sŭedinenie *Bulgaria* **45** D8
Suemez I. *U.S.A.* **102** B2
Suez = El Suweis *Egypt* **80** J8
Suez, G. of = Suweis, Khalig el *Egypt* **80** J8
Suez Canal = Suweis, Qanâ es *Egypt* **80** H8
Suffield *Canada* **102** C6
Suffolk *U.S.A.* **113** G15
Suffolk □ *U.K.* **15** E9
Şufiān *Iran* **73** C11
Şugag *Romania* **29** E8
Sugar Grove *U.S.A.* **114** E5
Sugarcreek *U.S.A.* **114** E5
Sugarive ⟶ *India* **69** F12
Suğla Gölü *Turkey* **72** D5
Sugluk = Salluit *Canada* **101** C12
Suhaia, Lacul *Romania* **29** G10
Şuḥār *Oman* **71** E8
Sühbaatar □ *Mongolia* **56** B8
Suhl *Germany* **24** E6
Şuhut *Turkey* **47** C12
Sui *Pakistan* **68** E3
Sui Xian *China* **56** G8
Šuica *Bos.-H.* **28** G2
Suichang *China* **59** C12
Suichuan *China* **59** D10
Suide *China* **56** F6
Suifenhe *China* **57** B16
Suihua *China* **53** E13
Suijiang *China* **58** C4
Suining *Hunan, China* **59** D8
Suining *Jiangsu, China* **57** H9
Suining *Sichuan, China* **58** B5
Suiping *China* **56** H7
Suippes *France* **19** C11
Suir ⟶ *Ireland* **12** D4
Suisse = Switzerland ■ *Europe* **25** J4
Suisun City *U.S.A.* **110** G4
Suixi *China* **59** G8
Suiyang *Guizhou, China* **58** D6
Suiyang *Heilongjiang, China* **57** B16
Suizhong *China* **57** D11
Suizhou *China* **59** B9
Sujangarh *India* **68** F6
Sukabumi *Indonesia* **63** G12
Sukadana *Indonesia* **62** E4
Sukagawa *Japan* **55** F10
Sukaraja *Indonesia* **62** E4
Sukawati *Indonesia* **63** K18
Sukch'ŏn *N. Korea* **57** E13
Sukhindol *Bulgaria* **45** C9
Sukhinichi *Russia* **32** E8
Sukhona ⟶ *Russia* **52** D4
Sukhothai *Thailand* **64** D2
Sukhumi = Sokhumi *Georgia* **35** J5
Sukkur *Pakistan* **68** F3
Sukkur Barrage *Pakistan* **68** F3
Sukovo *Serbia* **44** C6
Sukri ⟶ *India* **68** G4
Sukumo *Japan* **55** H6
Sukunka ⟶ *Canada* **102** B4
Sula *Ukraine* **33** H7
Sula, Kepulauan *Indonesia* **63** E7
Sula ⟶ *Russia* **52** A6
Sulaco ⟶ *Honduras* **120** C2
Sulaiman Range *Pakistan* **68** D3
Sulak ⟶ *Russia* **35** J8
Sulakyurt *Turkey* **72** B5
Sūlār *Iran* **71** D6
Sulawesi *Indonesia* **63** E6
Sulawesi Barat □ *Indonesia* **63** E5
Sulawesi Sea = Celebes Sea *Indonesia* **63** D6
Sulawesi Selatan □ *Indonesia* **63** E6
Sulawesi Tengah □ *Indonesia* **63** E6
Sulawesi Tenggara □ *Indonesia* **63** E6
Sulawesi Utara □ *Indonesia* **63** D6
Sulechów *Poland* **31** F2
Sulęcin *Poland* **31** F2
Sulejów *Poland* **31** G6
Sulejówek *Poland* **31** F8
Süleymanlı *Turkey* **47** C9
Sulima *S. Leone* **82** D2
Sulina *Romania* **29** E14
Sulina, Braţul ⟶ *Romania* **29** E14
Sulingen *Germany* **24** C4
Suliţa *Romania* **29** C11
Sulitjelma *Norway* **8** C17
Sułkowice *Poland* **31** J6
Sullana *Peru* **124** D2
Süller *Turkey* **47** C11
Sullivan *Ill., U.S.A.* **112** F9
Sullivan *Ind., U.S.A.* **112** F10
Sullivan *Mo., U.S.A.* **112** F8
Sullivan Bay *Canada* **102** C3
Sullivan I. = Lanbi Kyun *Burma* **65** G2

Sullom Voe *U.K.* **13** A7
Sully-sur-Loire *France* **19** E9
Sulmierzyce *Poland* **31** G4
Sulmona *Italy* **41** F10
Sulphur *La., U.S.A.* **116** F8
Sulphur *Okla., U.S.A.* **116** H6
Sulphur Pt. *Canada* **102** A6
Sulphur Springs *U.S.A.* **116** E7
Sultan *Canada* **104** C3
Sultan *U.S.A.* **110** C5
Sultan Dağları *Turkey* **72** C4
Sultan Hamud *Kenya* **86** C4
Sultanābād = Arāk *Iran* **71** C6
Sultanhisar *Turkey* **47** D10
Sultaniça *Turkey* **45** F10
Sultaniye *Turkey* **45** F12
Sultanpur *Mad. P., India* **68** H8
Sultanpur *Punjab, India* **68** D6
Sultanpur *Ut. P., India* **69** F10
Sulu Arch. *Phil.* **61** J4
Sulu Sea *E. Indies* **61** H4
Sülüklü *Turkey* **72** C5
Sululta *Ethiopia* **81** F4
Suluova *Turkey* **72** B6
Suluq *Libya* **79** B10
Sulzbach *Germany* **25** F3
Sulzbach-Rosenberg *Germany* **25** F7
Sulzberger Ice Shelf *Antarctica* **5** E13
Sumalata *Indonesia* **63** D6
Sumampa *Argentina* **126** B3
Sumatera *Indonesia* **62** D2
Sumatera Barat □ *Indonesia* **62** E2
Sumatera Utara □ *Indonesia* **62** D1
Sumatra = Sumatera *Indonesia* **62** D2
Sumava △ *Czech Rep.* **26** C6
Sumba *Indonesia* **63** F5
Sumba, Selat *Indonesia* **63** F5
Sumbawa *Indonesia* **62** F5
Sumbawa Besar *Indonesia* **62** F5
Sumbawanga □ *Tanzania* **84** F6
Sumbe *Angola* **84** G2
Sumbu △ *Zambia* **87** D3
Sumburgh Hd. *U.K.* **13** B7
Sumdeo *India* **69** D8
Sumdo *China* **69** B8
Sumedang *Indonesia* **63** G12
Sümeg *Hungary* **28** D2
Sumeih *Sudan* **81** F2
Šumen = Shumen *Bulgaria* **45** C10
Sumenep *Indonesia* **63** G15
Sumgait = Sumqayıt *Azerbaijan* **35** K9
Summer L. *U.S.A.* **108** E3
Summerland *Canada* **102** D5
Summerside *Canada* **105** C7
Summersville *U.S.A.* **113** F13
Summerville *Ga., U.S.A.* **117** D12
Summerville *S.C., U.S.A.* **117** E14
Summit Lake *Canada* **102** C4
Summit Peak *U.S.A.* **109** H10
Sumner *Iowa, U.S.A.* **112** D7
Sumner *Wash., U.S.A.* **110** C4
Sumoto *Japan* **55** G7
Šumperk *Czech Rep.* **27** B9
Sumqayıt *Azerbaijan* **35** K9
Sumter *U.S.A.* **117** E14
Sumy *Ukraine* **33** G8
Sumy □ *Ukraine* **33** G7
Sun City *S. Africa* **88** D4
Sun City *Ariz., U.S.A.* **109** K7
Sun City *Calif., U.S.A.* **111** M9
Sun City Center *U.S.A.* **117** H13
Sun Lakes *U.S.A.* **109** K8
Sun Valley *U.S.A.* **108** E6
Sunagawa *Japan* **54** C10
Sunan *N. Korea* **57** E13
Sunart, L. *U.K.* **13** E3
Sunburst *U.S.A.* **108** B8
Sunbury *Australia* **95** F3
Sunbury *U.S.A.* **115** F8
Sunchales *Argentina* **126** C3
Suncheon *S. Korea* **57** G14
Suncho Corral *Argentina* **126** B3
Sunch'on *N. Korea* **57** E13
Suncook *U.S.A.* **115** C13
Sunda, Selat *Indonesia* **62** F3
Sunda Is. *Indonesia* **96** H2
Sunda Str. = Sunda, Selat *Indonesia* **62** F3
Sunda Trench = Java Trench *Ind. Oc.* **62** F3
Sundance *Canada* **103** B10
Sundance *U.S.A.* **108** D11
Sundar Nagar *India* **68** D7
Sundarbans *Asia* **67** J16
Sundarbans △ *India* **69** J13
Sundargarh *India* **67** H14
Sundays = Sondags ⟶ *S. Africa* **88** E4
Sunderland *Canada* **114** B5
Sunderland *U.K.* **14** C6
Sundown △ *Australia* **95** D5
Sundre *Canada* **102** C6
Sunds *Denmark* **11** H3
Sundsvall *Sweden* **10** B11

Sundsvallsbukten *Sweden* **10** B11
Sung Hei *Vietnam* **65** G6
Sungai Acheh *Malaysia* **65** c
Sungai Kolok *Thailand* **65** J3
Sungai Lembing *Malaysia* **65** L4
Sungai Petani *Malaysia* **65** K3
Sungaigerong *Indonesia* **62** E2
Sungailiat *Indonesia* **62** E3
Sungaipenuh *Indonesia* **62** E2
Sungari = Songhua Jiang ⟶ *China* **60** B8
Sunghua Chiang = Songhua Jiang ⟶ *China* **60** B8
Sungikai *Sudan* **81** E2
Sungurlu *Turkey* **72** B6
Sunja *Croatia* **41** C13
Sunland Park *U.S.A.* **109** L10
Sunnansjö *Sweden* **10** D8
Sunndalsøra *Norway* **8** E13
Sunne *Sweden* **10** E7
Sunnemo *Sweden* **10** E7
Sunnyside *U.S.A.* **108** C4
Sunnyvale *U.S.A.* **110** H4
Sunrise Manor *U.S.A.* **111** J11
Suntar *Russia* **53** C12
Sunyani *Ghana* **82** D4
Suomenselkä *Finland* **8** E21
Suomi = Finland ■ *Europe* **8** E22
Suomussalmi *Finland* **8** D23
Suoyarvi *Russia* **32** A7
Supai *U.S.A.* **109** H7
Supaul *India* **69** F12
Superior *Ariz., U.S.A.* **109** K8
Superior *Mont., U.S.A.* **108** C6
Superior *Nebr., U.S.A.* **112** E4
Superior *Wis., U.S.A.* **112** B7
Superior, L. *N. Amer.* **104** C2
Supetar *Croatia* **41** E13
Suphan Buri *Thailand* **64** E3
Suphan Dağı *Turkey* **73** C10
Supiori *Indonesia* **63** E9
Supraśl *Poland* **31** E10
Supraśl ⟶ *Poland* **31** E9
Supung Shuiku *China* **57** D13
Sũq ash Shuyũkh *Iraq* **70** D5
Sũq Suwayq *Si. Arabia* **70** E3
Suqian *China* **57** H10
Suquṭrá = Socotra *Yemen* **75** E5
Sũr *Lebanon* **74** B4
Şūr *Oman* **75** C6
Sur, Pt. *U.S.A.* **110** J5
Sura ⟶ *Russia* **34** C8
Surab *Pakistan* **68** E2
Surabaja = Surabaya *Indonesia* **63** G15
Surabaya *Indonesia* **63** G15
Surahammar *Sweden* **10** E10
Suraia *Romania* **29** E12
Surakarta *Indonesia* **63** G14
Šurany *Slovak Rep.* **27** C11
Surat *Australia* **95** D4
Surat *India* **66** J8
Surat Thani *Thailand* **65** H2
Suratgarh *India* **68** E5
Suraxanı *Azerbaijan* **35** K10
Şuraymilā *Si. Arabia* **70** E5
Suraż *Poland* **31** F9
Surazh *Belarus* **32** E6
Surazh *Russia* **33** F7
Surduc *Romania* **29** C8
Surduc Pasul *Romania* **29** E8
Surdulica *Serbia* **44** D6
Surendranagar *India* **68** H4
Surf *U.S.A.* **111** L6
Surfers Paradise *Australia* **95** D5
Surgères *France* **20** B3
Surgut *Russia* **52** C8
Suriapet *India* **66** L11
Surigao *Phil.* **61** G6
Surigao Strait *Phil.* **61** F6
Surin *Thailand* **64** E4
Surin Nua, Ko *Thailand* **65** H1
Surinam = Suriname ■ *S. Amer.* **125** C7
Suriname ■ *S. Amer.* **125** C7
Suriname ⟶ *Suriname* **125** B7
Sürmaq *Iran* **71** D7
Sürmene *Turkey* **73** B9
Surovikino *Russia* **35** F6
Surrey *Canada* **110** A4
Surrey □ *U.K.* **15** F7
Sursand *India* **69** F11
Sursar ⟶ *India* **69** F12
Sursee *Switz.* **25** H4
Sursk *Russia* **34** D7
Surskoye *Russia* **34** C8
Surt *Libya* **79** B9
Surt, Khalīj *Libya* **79** B9
Surtanahu *Pakistan* **68** F4
Surte *Sweden* **11** G6
Surtsey *Iceland* **8** E3
Sürüç *Turkey* **73** D8
Suruga-Wan *Japan* **55** G9
Susa *Italy* **40** C4
Suså ⟶ *Denmark* **11** J5
Sušac *Croatia* **41** F13
Susak *Croatia* **41** D11
Susaki *Japan* **55** H6

Süsangerd *Iran* **73** G13
Susanville *U.S.A.* **108** F3
Suşehri *Turkey* **73** B8
Sušice *Czech Rep.* **26** B6
Susleni *Moldova* **29** C13
Susner *India* **68** H7
Susong *China* **59** B11
Susquehanna *U.S.A.* **115** E9
Susquehanna ⟶ *U.S.A.* **115** G8
Susques *Argentina* **126** A2
Sussex *Canada* **105** C6
Sussex *U.S.A.* **115** E10
Sussex, E. □ *U.K.* **15** G8
Sussex, W. □ *U.K.* **15** G7
Sustut ⟶ *Canada* **102** B3
Susuman *Russia* **53** C15
Susunu *Indonesia* **63** E8
Susurluk *Turkey* **47** B10
Susuz *Turkey* **73** B10
Susz *Poland* **30** E6
Sutak *India* **69** C8
Sütçüler *Turkey* **72** D4
Suţeşti *Romania* **29** E12
Sutherland *S. Africa* **88** E3
Sutherland *U.K.* **13** C4
Sutherland *U.S.A.* **112** E3
Sutherland Falls *N.Z.* **91** F1
Sutherlin *U.S.A.* **108** E2
Suthri *India* **68** H3
Sutjeska △ *Bos.-H.* **28** G3
Sutlej ⟶ *Pakistan* **68** E4
Sutter *U.S.A.* **110** F5
Sutter Buttes *U.S.A.* **110** F5
Sutter Creek *U.S.A.* **110** G6
Sutton *Canada* **115** A12
Sutton *Nebr., U.S.A.* **112** E5
Sutton *W. Va., U.S.A.* **113** F13
Sutton ⟶ *Canada* **104** A3
Sutton Coldfield *U.K.* **15** E6
Sutton in Ashfield *U.K.* **14** D6
Sutton L. *Canada* **104** B3
Suttor ⟶ *Australia* **94** C4
Suttsu *Japan* **54** C10
Suva *Fiji* **91** a
Suva Gora *Macedonia* **44** E5
Suva Planina *Serbia* **44** C6
Suva Reka *Serbia* **44** D4
Suvorov *Russia* **32** E9
Suvorov Is. = Suwarrow Is. *Cook Is.* **97** J11
Suvorove *Ukraine* **29** E13
Suvorovo *Bulgaria* **45** C11
Suwałki *Poland* **30** D9
Suwana *Indonesia* **63** K18
Suwannaphum *Thailand* **64** E4
Suwannee ⟶ *U.S.A.* **117** G13
Suwanose-Jima *Japan* **55** K4
Suwarrow Is. *Cook Is.* **97** J11
Suwayqīyah, Hawr as *Iraq* **73** G12
Suweis, Khalîg el *Egypt* **80** J8
Suweis, Qanâ es *Egypt* **80** H8
Suwon *S. Korea* **57** F14
Suzdal *Russia* **32** D11
Suzhou *Anhui, China* **56** H9
Suzhou *Jiangsu, China* **59** B13
Suzu *Japan* **55** F8
Suzu-Misaki *Japan* **55** F8
Suzuka *Japan* **55** G8
Suzzara *Italy* **40** D7
Svalbard *Arctic* **4** B8
Svalbard Radio = Longyearbyen *Svalbard* **4** B8
Svalöv *Sweden* **11** J7
Svalyava *Ukraine* **28** B7
Svaneke *Denmark* **11** J9
Svängsta *Sweden* **11** H8
Svanskog *Sweden* **10** E6
Svappavaara *Sweden* **8** C19
Svärdsjö *Sweden* **10** D9
Svartå *Sweden* **10** E8
Svartisen *Norway* **8** C15
Svartvik *Sweden* **10** B11
Svatove *Ukraine* **33** H10
Svatovo = Svatove *Ukraine* **33** H10
Svay Chek *Cambodia* **64** F4
Svay Rieng *Cambodia* **65** G5
Svealand □ *Sweden* **10** D9
Svedala *Sweden* **11** J7
Sveg *Sweden* **10** B8
Svendborg *Denmark* **11** J4
Svenljunga *Sweden* **11** G7
Svenstavik *Sweden* **10** B8
Svenstrup *Denmark* **11** H3
Sverdlovsk *Ukraine* **33** H10
Sverdrup Chan. *Canada* **101** B10
Sverdrup Is. *Canada* **101** B10
Sverige = Sweden ■ *Europe* **9** H16
Svetac *Croatia* **41** E12
Sveti Nikola, Prokhad *Europe* **44** C6
Sveti Nikole *Macedonia* **44** E5
Sveti Rok *Croatia* **41** D12
Svetlaya *Russia* **54** A9
Svetlogorsk = Svyetlahorsk *Belarus* **23** B15
Svetlogorsk *Russia* **30** D7
Svetlograd *Russia* **35** H6
Svetlovodsk = Svitlovodsk *Ukraine* **33** H7

Svetlyy *Russia* **30** D7
Svidník *Slovak Rep.* **27** B14
Svilaja Planina *Croatia* **41** E13
Svilajnac *Serbia* **44** B5
Svilengrad *Bulgaria* **45** E10
Svir ⟶ *Russia* **32** B7
Sviritsa *Russia* **32** B7
Svishtov *Bulgaria* **45** C9
Svislach *Belarus* **31** E11
Svitava ⟶ *Czech Rep.* **27** B9
Svitavy *Czech Rep.* **27** B9
Svitlovodsk *Ukraine* **33** H7
Svizzera = Switzerland ■ *Europe* **25** J4
Svobodnyy *Russia* **53** D13
Svoge *Bulgaria* **45** D7
Svolvær *Norway* **8** B16
Svratka ⟶ *Czech Rep.* **27** B9
Svrljig *Serbia* **44** C5
Svyatoy Nos, Mys *Russia* **34** D9
Svyetlahorsk *Belarus* **23** B15
Swabian Alps = Schwäbische Alb *Germany* **25** G5
Swaffham *U.K.* **15** E8
Swains I. *Amer. Samoa* **97** J11
Swainsboro *U.S.A.* **117** E13
Swakop ⟶ *Namibia* **88** C2
Swakopmund *Namibia* **88** C1
Swale ⟶ *U.K.* **14** C6
Swan ⟶ *Australia* **93** F2
Swan ⟶ *Canada* **103** C8
Swan Hill *Australia* **95** F3
Swan Hills *Canada* **102** C5
Swan Is. = Santanilla, Is. *Honduras* **120** C3
Swan L. *Man., Canada* **103** C8
Swan L. *Ont., Canada* **104** B1
Swan Ra. *U.S.A.* **108** C7
Swan River *Canada* **103** C8
Swanage *U.K.* **15** G6
Swansea *Australia* **95** G4
Swansea *Canada* **114** C5
Swansea *U.K.* **15** F4
Swansea □ *U.K.* **15** F3
Swartberge *S. Africa* **88** E3
Swartmodder *S. Africa* **88** D3
Swartnossob ⟶ *Namibia* **88** C2
Swartruggens *S. Africa* **88** D4
Swarzędz *Poland* **31** F4
Swastika *Canada* **104** C3
Swat ⟶ *Pakistan* **69** B5
Swatow = Shantou *China* **59** F11
Swaziland ■ *Africa* **89** D5
Sweden ■ *Europe* **9** H16
Swedru *Ghana* **83** D4
Sweet Grass *U.S.A.* **108** B8
Sweet Home *U.S.A.* **108** D2
Sweetwater *Nev., U.S.A.* **110** G7
Sweetwater *Tenn., U.S.A.* **117** D12
Sweetwater *Tex., U.S.A.* **116** E4
Sweetwater ⟶ *U.S.A.* **108** E10
Swellendam *S. Africa* **88** E3
Swider ⟶ *Poland* **31** F8
Świdnica *Poland* **31** H3
Świdnik *Poland* **31** G9
Świdwin *Poland* **30** E2
Świebodzice *Poland* **31** H3
Świebodzin *Poland* **31** F2
Świecie *Poland* **30** E5
Świerzawa *Poland* **31** G2
Świętokrzyski △ *Poland* **31** H7
Świętokrzyskie □ *Poland* **31** H7
Świętokrzyskie, Góry *Poland* **31** H7
Swift Current *Canada* **103** C7
Swift Current ⟶ *Canada* **103** C7
Swilly, L. *Ireland* **12** A4
Swindon *U.K.* **15** F6
Swindon □ *U.K.* **15** F6
Swinemünde = Świnoujście *Poland* **30** E1
Swinford *Ireland* **12** C3
Świnoujście *Poland* **30** E1
Switzerland ■ *Europe* **25** J4
Swords *Ireland* **12** C5
Swoyerville *U.S.A.* **115** E9
Syasstroy *Russia* **32** B7
Sychevka *Russia* **32** E8
Syców *Poland* **31** G4
Syddanmark □ *Denmark* **11** J2
Sydenham ⟶ *Canada* **114** D2
Sydney *Australia* **95** E5
Sydney *Canada* **105** C7
Sydney L. *Canada* **103** C10
Sydney Mines *Canada* **105** C7
Sydprøven = Alluitsup Paa *Greenland* **4** D5
Sydra, G. of = Surt, Khalīj *Libya* **79** B9
Syeverodonetsk *Ukraine* **33** H10
Syke *Germany* **24** C4
Sykesville *U.S.A.* **114** E6
Syktyvkar *Russia* **52** C6
Sylacauga *U.S.A.* **117** E11
Sylarna *Sweden* **8** E15
Sylhet *Bangla.* **67** G17
Sylhet □ *Bangla.* **67** G17
Sylt *Germany* **24** A4
Sylvan Beach *U.S.A.* **115** C9
Sylvan Lake *Canada* **102** C6
Sylvania *Ga., U.S.A.* **117** E14

Sylvania *Ohio, U.S.A.* **113** E12
Sylvester *U.S.A.* **117** F13
Sym *Russia* **52** C9
Synelnykove *Ukraine* **33** H8
Synevyr △ *Ukraine* **29** B8
Synevyrska Polyana *Ukraine* **29** B8
Synnot Ra. *Australia* **92** C4
Synyak *Ukraine* **28** B7
Syowa *Antarctica* **5** C5
Syracuse *Kans., U.S.A.* **112** G3
Syracuse *N.Y., U.S.A.* **115** C8
Syracuse *Nebr., U.S.A.* **112** E5
Syrdarya ⟶ *Kazakhstan* **52** E7
Syria ■ *Asia* **73** E8
Syrian Desert = Shām, Bādiyat ash *Asia* **70** C3
Syros *Greece* **46** D6
Syssleback *Sweden* **10** D6
Syzran *Russia* **34** D9
Szabolcs-Szatmár-Bereg □ *Hungary* **28** B6
Szadek *Poland* **31** G5
Szamocin *Poland* **31** E4
Szamos ⟶ *Hungary* **28** B7
Szamotuły *Poland* **31** F3
Száraz ⟶ *Hungary* **28** D5
Szarvas *Hungary* **28** D5
Százhalombatta *Hungary* **28** C3
Szczawnica *Poland* **31** J7
Szczebrzeszyn *Poland* **31** H9
Szczecin *Poland* **30** E1
Szczecinek *Poland* **30** E3
Szczeciński, Zalew = Stettiner Haff *Germany* **24** B10
Szczekociny *Poland* **31** H6
Szczucin *Poland* **31** H8
Szczuczyn *Poland* **30** E9
Szczyrk *Poland* **31** J6
Szczytna *Poland* **31** H3
Szczytno *Poland* **30** E7
Szechuan Basin = Sichuan Pendi *China* **58** B5
Szechwan = Sichuan □ *China* **58** B5
Szécsény *Hungary* **28** B4
Szeged *Hungary* **28** D5
Szeghalom *Hungary* **28** C6
Székesfehérvár *Hungary* **28** C3
Szekszárd *Hungary* **28** D3
Szendrő *Hungary* **28** B5
Szentendre *Hungary* **28** C4
Szentes *Hungary* **28** D5
Szentgotthárd *Hungary* **28** D1
Szentlőrinc *Hungary* **28** D3
Szerencs *Hungary* **28** B5
Szigetszentmiklós *Hungary* **28** C4
Szigetvár *Hungary* **28** D2
Szikszó *Poland* **28** B5
Szklarska Poreba *Poland* **31** H2
Szkwa ⟶ *Poland* **31** E8
Szlichtyngowa *Poland* **31** G3
Szob *Hungary* **28** C4
Szolnok *Hungary* **28** C5
Szombathely *Hungary* **28** C1
Szprotawa *Poland* **31** G2
Sztum *Poland* **30** E6
Sztutowo *Poland* **30** D6
Szubin *Poland* **31** E4
Szydłowiec *Poland* **31** G7
Szypliszki *Poland* **30** D10

T

Ta Khli *Thailand* **64** E3
Ta Khli Khok *Thailand* **64** E3
Ta Lai *Vietnam* **65** G6
Tab *Hungary* **28** D3
Tabacal *Argentina* **126** A3
Tabaco *Phil.* **61** E5
Tabagné *Ivory C.* **82** D4
Tābah *Si. Arabia* **70** E4
Tabanan *Indonesia* **63** K18
Tabankort *Niger* **83** B5
Ţabas *Khorāsān, Iran* **71** C9
Ţabas *Yazd, Iran* **71** C8
Tabasará, Serranía de *Panama* **120** E3
Tabasco □ *Mexico* **119** D6
Tabāsīn *Iran* **71** D8
Tabatinga, Serra da *Brazil* **125** F10
Taber *Canada* **102** D6
Taberg *Sweden* **11** G8
Tabla *Niger* **83** C5
Tablas *Phil.* **61** E5
Tablas de Daimiel △ *Spain* **37** F7
Tablas Strait *Phil.* **61** E4
Table, Pte. de la *Réunion* **85** c
Table B. *Canada* **105** B8
Table B. *S. Africa* **88** E2
Table Mt. *S. Africa* **88** E2
Table Rock L. *U.S.A.* **112** G7
Tabletop, Mt. *Australia* **94** C4
Tábor *Czech Rep.* **26** B7
Tabora *Tanzania* **86** D3
Tabora □ *Tanzania* **86** D3
Tabou *Ivory C.* **82** E3
Tabrīz *Iran* **73** C12
Tabuaeran *Kiribati* **97** G12
Tabuenca *Spain* **38** D3

Tabūk *Si. Arabia* **70 D3**
Tabūk □ *Si. Arabia* **70 E3**
Taburno-Camposauro △
Italy **43 A7**
Täby *Sweden* **10 E12**
Tacámbaro de Codallos
Mexico **118 D4**
Tacheng *China* **60 B3**
Tach'i *Taiwan* **59 E13**
Tachia *Taiwan* **59 E13**
Tach'ing Shan = Daqing
Shan *China* **56 D6**
Tachov *Czech Rep.* **26 B5**
Tácina → *Italy* **43 D9**
Tacloban *Phil.* **61 F6**
Tacna *Peru* **124 G4**
Tacoma *U.S.A.* **110 C4**
Tacuarembó *Uruguay* **127 C4**
Tademaït, Plateau du *Algeria* **78 C6**
Tadio, L. *Ivory C.* **82 D3**
Tadjoura *Djibouti* **81 E5**
Tadjoura, Golfe de *Djibouti* **81 E5**
Tadmor *N.Z.* **91 J4**
Tadoule L. *Canada* **103 B9**
Tadoussac *Canada* **105 C6**
Tadrés → *Niger* **83 B6**
Tadzhikistan =
Tajikistan ■ *Asia* **52 F8**
Taegu = Daegu *S. Korea* **57 G15**
Taegwan *N. Korea* **57 D13**
Taejŏn = Daejeon *S. Korea* **57 F14**
Taen, Ko *Thailand* **65 J3**
Tafalla *Spain* **38 C3**
Tafar *Sudan* **81 F2**
Tafelbaai = Table B. *S. Africa* **88 E2**
Tafermaar *Indonesia* **63 F8**
Tafí Viejo *Argentina* **126 B2**
Tafīhān *Iran* **71 D7**
Tafiré *Ivory C.* **82 D3**
Tafo *Ghana* **83 D4**
Tafresh *Iran* **71 C6**
Taft *Iran* **71 D7**
Taft *Phil.* **61 F6**
Taft *U.S.A.* **111 K7**
Taftan *Pakistan* **66 E2**
Taftān, Kūh-e *Iran* **71 D9**
Taga *Samoa* **91 b**
Taga Dzong *Bhutan* **67 F16**
Taganrog *Russia* **33 J10**
Taganrogskiy Zaliv *Russia* **33 J10**
Tagânt □ *Mauritania* **82 B3**
Tagatay *Phil.* **61 D4**
Tagbilaran *Phil.* **61 G5**
Tággia *Italy* **40 E4**
Tagish *Canada* **102 A2**
Tagish L. *Canada* **102 A2**
Tagliacozzo *Italy* **41 F10**
Tagliamento → *Italy* **41 C10**
Táglio di Po *Italy* **41 D9**
Tago *Phil.* **61 G7**
Tagomago *Spain* **48 B8**
Tagourâret *Mauritania* **82 B3**
Taguatinga *Brazil* **125 F10**
Tagudin *Phil.* **61 C4**
Tagum *Phil.* **61 H6**
Tagus = Tejo → *Europe* **37 F2**
Tahakopa *N.Z.* **91 G2**
Tahan, Gunung *Malaysia* **65 K4**
Tahat *Algeria* **78 D7**
Tāherī *Iran* **71 E7**
Tahiti *French Polynesia* **91 d**
Tahiti, I. *Tahiti* **91 d**
Tahlequah *U.S.A.* **116 D7**
Tahoe, L. *U.S.A.* **110 G6**
Tahoe City *U.S.A.* **110 F6**
Tahoka *U.S.A.* **116 E4**
Taholah *U.S.A.* **110 C2**
Tahoua *Niger* **83 C6**
Tahrūd *Iran* **71 D8**
Tahsis *Canada* **102 D3**
Tahta *Egypt* **80 B3**
Tahtaköprü *Turkey* **45 G13**
Tahtalı Dağları *Turkey* **72 C7**
Tahulandang *Indonesia* **63 D7**
Tahuna *Indonesia* **63 D7**
Taï *Ivory C.* **82 D3**
Taï △ *Ivory C.* **82 D3**
Tai Hu *China* **59 B12**
Tai Rom Yen △ *Thailand* **65 H2**
Tai Shan *China* **57 F9**
Tai'an *China* **57 F9**
Taiarapu, Presqu'île de *Tahiti* **91 d**
Taibei = T'aipei *Taiwan* **59 E13**
Taibique *Canary Is.* **48 G2**
Taibus Qi *China* **56 D8**
Taicang *China* **59 B13**
T'aichung *Taiwan* **59 E13**
Taieri → *N.Z.* **91 G3**
Taigu *China* **56 F7**
Taihang Shan *China* **56 G7**
Taihape *N.Z.* **91 C5**
Taihe *Anhui, China* **56 H8**
Taihe *Jiangxi, China* **59 D10**
Taihu *China* **59 B11**
Taijiang *China* **58 D7**
Taikang *China* **56 G8**
Tailem Bend *Australia* **95 F2**
Tailfingen *Germany* **25 G5**
T'ailuko *Taiwan* **59 E13**

Taimyr Peninsula =
Taymyr, Poluostrov
Russia **53 B11**
Tain *U.K.* **13 D4**
T'ainan *Taiwan* **59 F13**
Taining *China* **59 D11**
T'aipei *Taiwan* **59 E13**
Taiping *China* **59 B12**
Taiping *Malaysia* **65 K3**
Taipingzhen *China* **56 H6**
Tairbeart = Tarbert *U.K.* **13 D2**
Taishan *China* **59 F9**
Taishun *China* **59 D12**
Taita Hills *Kenya* **86 C4**
Taitao, Pen. de *Chile* **128 F2**
T'aitung *Taiwan* **59 F13**
Taivalkoski *Finland* **8 D23**
Taiwan ■ *Asia* **59 F13**
Taiwan Strait *Asia* **59 E12**
Taixing *China* **59 A13**
Taiyara *Sudan* **81 E3**
Taiyiba *Israel* **74 C4**
Taiyuan *China* **56 F7**
Taizhong = T'aichung
Taiwan **59 E13**
Taizhou *China* **59 A12**
Taizhou Liedao *China* **59 C13**
Ta'izz *Yemen* **75 E3**
Tājābād *Iran* **71 D7**
Tajima *Japan* **55 F9**
Tajo = Tejo → *Europe* **37 F2**
Tajrīsh *Iran* **71 C6**
Tak *Thailand* **64 D2**
Takāb *Iran* **73 D12**
Takachiho *Japan* **55 H5**
Takachu *Botswana* **88 C3**
Takada *Japan* **55 F9**
Takahagi *Japan* **55 F10**
Takaka *N.Z.* **91 D4**
Takamaka *Seychelles* **85 b**
Takamatsu *Japan* **55 G7**
Takaoka *Japan* **55 F8**
Takapuna *N.Z.* **91 B5**
Takasaki *Japan* **55 F9**
Takatsuki *Japan* **55 G7**
Takaungu *Kenya* **86 C4**
Takayama *Japan* **55 F8**
Take-Shima *Japan* **55 J5**
Takefu *Japan* **55 G8**
Takengon *Indonesia* **62 D1**
Takeo *Japan* **55 H5**
Takeshima = Tokdo *Asia* **55 F5**
Tåkern *Sweden* **11 F8**
Tåkestān *Iran* **71 C6**
Taketa *Japan* **55 H5**
Takev *Cambodia* **65 G5**
Takh *India* **69 C7**
Takhmau *Cambodia* **65 G5**
Takht-Sulaiman *Pakistan* **68 D3**
Takikawa *Japan* **54 C10**
Takla L. *Canada* **102 B3**
Takla Landing *Canada* **102 B3**
Takla Makan *China* **60 C3**
Taklamakan Shamo =
Takla Makan *China* **60 C3**
Taksimo *Russia* **53 D12**
Taku → *Canada* **102 B2**
Takua Pa *Thailand* **65 H2**
Takua Thung *Thailand* **65 a**
Takum *Nigeria* **83 D6**
Tal Halāl *Iran* **71 D7**
Tala *Uruguay* **127 C4**
Talachyn *Belarus* **32 E5**
Talacogan *Phil.* **61 G6**
Talagang *Pakistan* **68 C5**
Talagante *Chile* **126 C1**
Talak *Niger* **83 B6**
Talamanca, Cordillera de
Cent. Amer. **120 E3**
Talampaya △ *Argentina* **126 B2**
Talant *France* **19 E11**
Talara *Peru* **124 D2**
Talas *Kyrgyzstan* **52 E8**
Talas *Turkey* **72 C6**
Talâta *Egypt* **74 E1**
Talata Mafara *Nigeria* **83 C6**
Talaud, Kepulauan *Indonesia* **63 D7**
Talaud Is. = Talaud,
Kepulauan *Indonesia* **63 D7**
Talavera de la Reina *Spain* **36 F6**
Talavera la Real *Spain* **37 G4**
Talayan *Phil.* **61 H6**
Talayuela *Spain* **36 F5**
Talbandh *India* **69 H12**
Talbert, Sillon de *France* **18 D3**
Talbot, C. *Australia* **92 B4**
Talbragar → *Australia* **95 E4**
Talca *Chile* **126 D1**
Talcher *India* **67 J14**
Talcho *Niger* **83 C5**
Taldy Kurgan =
Taldyqorghan *Kazakhstan* **52 E8**
Taldyqorghan *Kazakhstan* **52 E8**
Tālesh *Iran* **73 D13**
Tālesh, Kūhhā-ye *Iran* **73 D13**
Talguharai *Sudan* **80 D4**
Tali Post *Sudan* **81 F3**

Taliabu *Indonesia* **63 E6**
Talibon *Phil.* **63 B6**
Talihina *U.S.A.* **116 D7**
Talisayan *Phil.* **61 G6**
Taliwang *Indonesia* **62 F5**
Tall 'Afar *Iraq* **73 D10**
Tall Kalakh *Syria* **74 A5**
Tall Kayf *Iraq* **73 D10**
Talla *Egypt* **80 B3**
Talladega *U.S.A.* **117 E11**
Tallahassee *U.S.A.* **117 F12**
Tallangatta *Australia* **95 F4**
Tallard *France* **21 D10**
Tällberg *Sweden* **10 D9**
Tallering Pk. *Australia* **93 E2**
Talli *Pakistan* **68 E3**
Tallmadge *U.S.A.* **114 E3**
Tallulah *U.S.A.* **116 E9**
Tălmaciu *Romania* **29 E9**
Talmont-St-Hilaire *France* **20 B2**
Talnakh *Russia* **53 C9**
Talne *Ukraine* **33 H6**
Talnoye = Talne *Ukraine* **33 H6**
Talodi *Sudan* **81 E3**
Talovaya *Russia* **34 E5**
Taloyoak *Canada* **100 C10**
Talpa de Allende *Mexico* **118 C4**
Talparo *Trin. & Tob.* **125 K15**
Talsi *Latvia* **30 A9**
Talsi = Latvia **30 A9**
Taltal *Chile* **126 B1**
Taltson → *Canada* **102 A6**
Talwood *Australia* **95 D4**
Talyawalka Cr. → *Australia* **95 E3**
Tam Ky *Vietnam* **64 E7**
Tam Quan *Vietnam* **64 E7**
Tama *U.S.A.* **112 E7**
Tama △ *Ethiopia* **81 F4**
Tamale *Ghana* **83 D4**
Taman *Russia* **33 K9**
Taman Negara △ *Malaysia* **65 K4**
Tamani *Mali* **82 C3**
Tamano *Japan* **55 G6**
Tamanrasset *Algeria* **78 D7**
Tamaqua *U.S.A.* **115 F9**
Tamar → *U.K.* **15 G3**
Tamarin *Mauritius* **85 d**
Tamarinda *Spain* **48 B10**
Tamarite de Litera *Spain* **38 D5**
Tamashima *Japan* **55 G6**
Tamási *Hungary* **28 D3**
Tamaské *Niger* **83 C6**
Tamatave = Toamasina
Madag. **89 B8**
Tamaulipas □ *Mexico* **119 C5**
Tamaulipas, Sierra de
Mexico **119 C5**
Tamazula *Mexico* **118 C3**
Tamazunchale *Mexico* **119 C5**
Tamba-Dabatou *Guinea* **82 C2**
Tambach *Kenya* **86 B4**
Tambacounda *Senegal* **82 C2**
Tambacounda □ *Senegal* **82 C2**
Tambelan, Kepulauan
Indonesia **62 D3**
Tambellup *Australia* **93 F2**
Tambo *Australia* **94 C4**
Tambo de Mora *Peru* **124 F3**
Tambohorano *Madag.* **89 B7**
Tambora *Indonesia* **62 F5**
Tambov *Russia* **34 D5**
Tambov □ *Russia* **34 D5**
Tambre → *Spain* **36 C2**
Tambuku *Indonesia* **63 G15**
Tamburâ *Sudan* **81 F2**
Tâmchekket *Mauritania* **82 B2**
Tâmega → *Portugal* **36 D2**
Tamenglong *India* **67 G18**
Tamgué, Massif du *Guinea* **82 C2**
Tamiahua, L. de *Mexico* **119 C5**
Tamil Nadu □ *India* **66 P10**
Tamis → *Serbia* **28 F5**
Tamluk *India* **69 H12**
Tammerfors = Tampere
Finland **32 B2**
Tammisaari *Finland* **32 B2**
Tämnaren *Sweden* **10 D11**
Tamo Abu, Banjaran
Malaysia **62 D5**
Tampa *U.S.A.* **117 H13**
Tampa, Tanjung *Indonesia* **63 K19**
Tampa B. *U.S.A.* **117 H13**
Tampere *Finland* **32 B2**
Tampico *Mexico* **119 C5**
Tampin *Malaysia* **65 L4**
Tampoi *Malaysia* **65 d**
Tamsweg *Austria* **26 D6**
Tamu *Burma* **67 G19**
Tamuja → *Spain* **37 F4**
Tamworth *Australia* **95 E5**
Tamworth *Canada* **114 B8**
Tamworth *U.K.* **15 E6**
Tan An *Vietnam* **65 G6**
Tan Chau *Vietnam* **65 G5**
Tan-Tan *Morocco* **78 C3**
Tana → *Kenya* **86 C5**
Tana → *Norway* **8 A23**
Tana, L. *Ethiopia* **81 E4**

Tana River Primate △ *Kenya* **86 C5**
Tanabe *Japan* **55 H7**
Tanafjorden *Norway* **8 A23**
Tanahbala *Indonesia* **62 E1**
Tanahgrogot *Indonesia* **62 E5**
Tanahjampea *Indonesia* **62 E1**
Tanahmasa *Indonesia* **62 E1**
Tanahmerah *Indonesia* **63 F10**
Tanakpur *India* **69 E9**
Tanakura *Japan* **55 F10**
Tanami Desert *Australia* **92 C5**
Tanami Mine *Australia* **92 C4**
Tananarive =
Antananarivo *Madag.* **89 B8**
Tánaro → *Italy* **40 D5**
Tancheng *China* **57 G10**
Tanch'ŏn *N. Korea* **57 D15**
Tanda *Ut. P., India* **69 F10**
Tanda *Ut. P., India* **69 E8**
Tanda *Ivory C.* **82 D4**
Tandag *Phil.* **61 G7**
Tandaia *Tanzania* **87 D3**
Tăndărei *Romania* **29 F12**
Tandaué *Angola* **88 B2**
Tandil *Argentina* **126 D4**
Tandil, Sa. del *Argentina* **126 D4**
Tandlianwala *Pakistan* **68 D5**
Tando Adam *Pakistan* **68 G3**
Tando Allahyar *Pakistan* **68 G3**
Tando Bago *Pakistan* **68 G3**
Tando Mohammed Khan
Pakistan **68 G3**
Tandou L. *Australia* **95 E3**
Tandoureh △ *Iran* **70 B8**
Tandragee *U.K.* **12 B5**
Tandsjöborg *Sweden* **10 C8**
Tane-ga-Shima *Japan* **55 J5**
Taneatua *N.Z.* **91 C6**
Tanen Tong Dan = Dawna
Ra. *Burma* **64 D2**
Tanew → *Poland* **31 H9**
Tanezrouft *Algeria* **78 D6**
Tang, Koh *Cambodia* **65 G4**
Tang, Ra's-e *Iran* **71 E8**
Tang Krasang *Cambodia* **64 F5**
Tanga *Tanzania* **86 D4**
Tanga □ *Tanzania* **86 D4**
Tanganyika, L. *Africa* **86 D3**
Tangaza *Nigeria* **83 C5**
Tanger *Morocco* **78 A4**
Tangerang *Indonesia* **63 G12**
Tangerhütte *Germany* **24 C7**
Tangermünde *Germany* **24 C7**
Tanggu *China* **57 E9**
Tanggula Shan *China* **60 C4**
Tanghe *China* **56 H7**
Tanghla Range =
Tanggula Shan *China* **60 C4**
Tangier = Tanger *Morocco* **78 A4**
Tangorin *Australia* **94 C3**
Tangorombohitr'i Makay
Madag. **89 C8**
Tangshan *China* **57 E10**
Tangtou *China* **57 G10**
Tanguiéta *Benin* **83 C5**
Tangxi *China* **59 C12**
Tangyan He → *China* **58 C7**
Tanimbar, Kepulauan
Indonesia **63 F8**
Tanimbar Is. = Tanimbar,
Kepulauan *Indonesia* **63 F8**
Taninthari = Tenasserim
Burma **65 F2**
Tanjay *Phil.* **61 G5**
Tanjong Malim *Malaysia* **65 L3**
Tanjong Pelepas *Malaysia* **65 d**
Tanjore = Thanjavur *India* **66 P11**
Tanjung *Indonesia* **63 J19**
Tanjung *Phil.* **62 E5**
Tanjung Tokong *Malaysia* **65 c**
Tanjungbalai *Indonesia* **62 D1**
Tanjungbatu *Indonesia* **62 D5**
Tanjungkarang
Telukbetung = Bandar
Lampung *Indonesia* **62 F3**
Tanjungpandan *Indonesia* **62 E3**
Tanjungpinang *Indonesia* **62 D2**
Tanjungredeb *Indonesia* **62 D5**
Tanjungselor *Indonesia* **62 D5**
Tank *Pakistan* **68 C4**
Tankhala *India* **68 J5**
Tankwa-Karoo △ *S. Africa* **88 E2**
Tännäs *Sweden* **10 B6**
Tannersville *U.S.A.* **115 E9**
Tannis Bugt *Denmark* **11 G4**
Tannu Ola *Asia* **53 D10**
Tannum Sands *Australia* **94 C5**
Tano → *Ghana* **82 D4**
Tanon Str. *Phil.* **61 F5**
Tanout *Niger* **83 C6**
Tanshui *Taiwan* **59 E13**
Tansilla *Burkina Faso* **82 C4**
Tanta *Egypt* **80 H7**
Tantoyuca *Mexico* **119 C5**
Tantung = Dandong *China* **57 D13**
Tanumshede *Sweden* **11 F5**
Tanunda *Australia* **95 E2**
Tanus *France* **20 D6**
Tanzania ■ *Africa* **86 D3**

Tanzilla → *Canada* **102 B2**
Tao, Ko *Thailand* **65 G2**
Tao'an = Taonan *China* **57 B12**
Tao'er He → *China* **57 B13**
Taohua Dao *China* **59 C14**
Taole *China* **56 E4**
Taolanaro *Madag.* **89 D8**
Taonan *China* **57 B12**
Taormina *Italy* **43 E8**
Taos *U.S.A.* **109 H11**
Taoudenni *Mali* **78 D5**
Taoyuan *China* **59 C8**
T'aoyüan *Taiwan* **59 E13**
Tapa *Estonia* **32 C3**
Tapa Shan = Daba Shan
China **58 B7**
Tapachula *Mexico* **119 E6**
Tapah *Malaysia* **65 K3**
Tapajós → *Brazil* **125 D8**
Tapaktuan *Indonesia* **62 D1**
Tapanahoni → *Suriname* **125 C8**
Tapanui *N.Z.* **91 F2**
Tapauá → *Brazil* **124 E6**
Tapes *Brazil* **127 C5**
Tapeta *Liberia* **82 D3**
Taphan Hin *Thailand* **64 D3**
Tapia de Casariego *Spain* **36 B4**
Tapirapecó, Serra *Venezuela* **124 C6**
Tapo-Capara △ *Venezuela* **121 E5**
Tapolca *Hungary* **28 D2**
Tapti → *India* **66 J8**
Tapuae-o-Uenuku *N.Z.* **91 E4**
Tapul Group *Phil.* **61 J4**
Tapurucuará *Brazil* **124 D5**
Taquara *Brazil* **127 B5**
Taquari → *Brazil* **124 G7**
Tara *Australia* **95 D5**
Tara *Canada* **114 B3**
Tara *Russia* **52 D8**
Tara *Zambia* **87 F2**
Tara → *Montenegro* **44 C2**
Tara △ *Serbia* **44 C3**
Taraba □ *Nigeria* **83 D7**
Taraba → *Nigeria* **83 D7**
Tarābulus *Lebanon* **74 A4**
Tarābulus *Libya* **79 B8**
Tarābulus *N. Afr.* **79 B8**
Taraclia *Taraclia, Moldova* **29 E13**
Taraclia *Tighina, Moldova* **29 D14**
Taradehi *India* **69 H8**
Tarajalejo *Canary Is.* **48 F5**
Tarakan *Indonesia* **62 D5**
Tarakit, Mt. *Kenya* **86 B4**
Tarama-Jima *Japan* **55 M2**
Taran, Mys *Russia* **30 D6**
Taranagar *India* **68 E6**
Taranaki □ *N.Z.* **91 C5**
Taranaki, Mt. *N.Z.* **91 C5**
Tarancón *Spain* **38 E1**
Tarangire △ *Tanzania* **86 C4**
Taransay *U.K.* **13 D1**
Táranto *Italy* **43 B10**
Táranto, G. di *Italy* **43 B10**
Tarapacá *Colombia* **124 D5**
Tarapacá □ *Chile* **126 A2**
Tarapoto *Peru* **124 E3**
Tarare *France* **21 C8**
Tararua Ra. *N.Z.* **91 D5**
Tarascon *France* **21 E8**
Tarascon-sur-Ariège *France* **20 F5**
Tarashcha *Ukraine* **23 D16**
Tarauacá *Brazil* **124 E4**
Tarauacá → *Brazil* **124 E5**
Taravao *Tahiti* **91 d**
Taravao, Isthme de *Tahiti* **91 d**
Taravo → *France* **21 G12**
Tarawa *Kiribati* **96 G9**
Tarawera *N.Z.* **91 C6**
Tarawera, L. *N.Z.* **91 C6**
Taraz *Kazakhstan* **52 E8**
Tarazona *Spain* **38 D3**
Tarazona de la Mancha
Spain **39 F3**
Tarbagatay, Khrebet
Kazakhstan **52 E9**
Tarbat Ness *U.K.* **13 D5**
Tarbela Dam *Pakistan* **68 B5**
Tarbert *Ireland* **12 D2**
Tarbert *Argyll & Bute, U.K.* **13 F3**
Tarbert *W. Isles, U.K.* **13 D2**
Tarbes *France* **20 E4**
Tarboro *U.S.A.* **117 D16**
Tărcău, Munţii *Romania* **29 D11**
Tarcento *Italy* **41 B10**
Tarcoola *Australia* **95 E1**
Tarcoon *Australia* **95 E4**
Tardets-Sorholus *France* **20 E3**
Tardoire → *France* **20 C4**
Taree *Australia* **95 E5**
Tarfa, W. el → *Egypt* **80 B3**
Tarfaya *Morocco* **78 C3**
Târgovişte *Romania* **29 F10**
Tárgu Bujor *Romania* **29 E12**
Tărgu Cărbuneşti *Romania* **29 E8**
Tárgu Frumos *Romania* **29 C12**
Tárgu Jiu *Romania* **29 E8**
Tárgu Lăpuş *Romania* **29 C8**
Tárgu Mureş *Romania* **29 D9**

Tárgu Neamţ *Romania* **29 C11**
Tárgu Ocna *Romania* **29 D11**
Tárgu Secuiesc *Romania* **29 E11**
Tárguşor *Romania* **29 F13**
Tărhăus, Vf. *Romania* **29 D11**
Tarif *U.A.E.* **71 E7**
Tarifa *Spain* **37 J5**
Tarija *Bolivia* **126 A3**
Tarija □ *Bolivia* **126 A3**
Tariku → *Indonesia* **63 E9**
Tarim Basin = Tarim Pendi
China **52 F9**
Tarim He → *China* **60 C3**
Tarim Pendi *China* **52 F9**
Taritatu → *Indonesia* **63 E9**
Tarka → *S. Africa* **88 E4**
Tarka La *Bhutan* **69 F13**
Tarkastad *S. Africa* **88 E4**
Tarkhankut, Mys *Ukraine* **33 K7**
Tarko Sale *Russia* **52 C8**
Tarkwa *Ghana* **82 D4**
Tarlac *Phil.* **61 D4**
Tarm *Denmark* **11 J2**
Tarma *Peru* **124 F3**
Tarmiya *Iraq* **73 D11**
Tarn □ *France* **20 E6**
Tarn → *France* **20 D5**
Tarn-et-Garonne □ *France* **20 D5**
Tarna → *Hungary* **28 C4**
Târnava Mare → *Romania* **29 D8**
Târnava Mică → *Romania* **29 D8**
Târnăveni *Romania* **29 D9**
Tarnica *Poland* **31 J9**
Tarnobrzeg *Poland* **31 H8**
Tarnogród *Poland* **31 H9**
Tarnos *France* **20 E2**
Târnova *Moldova* **29 B12**
Târnova *Romania* **28 E6**
Tarnów *Poland* **31 H8**
Tarnowskie Góry *Poland* **31 H5**
Tärnsjö *Sweden* **10 D11**
Táro → *Italy* **40 C7**
Ţārom *Iran* **71 D7**
Taroom *Australia* **95 D4**
Taroudannt *Morocco* **78 B4**
Tarp *Germany* **24 A5**
Tarpon Springs *U.S.A.* **117 G13**
Tarquínia *Italy* **41 F8**
Tarrafal *C. Verde Is.* **78 b**
Tarragona *Spain* **38 D6**
Tarragona □ *Spain* **38 D6**
Tarraleah *Australia* **95 G4**
Tarrasa = Terrassa *Spain* **38 D7**
Tàrrega *Spain* **38 D6**
Tarrytown *U.S.A.* **115 E11**
Tårs *Denmark* **11 G4**
Tarshiha = Me'ona *Israel* **74 B4**
Tarsus *Turkey* **72 D6**
Tartagal *Argentina* **126 A3**
Tártär *Azerbaijan* **35 K8**
Tártär → *Azerbaijan* **35 K8**
Tartas *France* **20 E3**
Tartu *Estonia* **32 C4**
Ţarţūs *Syria* **72 E6**
Ţarţūs □ *Syria* **72 E7**
Tarumizu *Japan* **55 J5**
Tarussa *Russia* **32 E9**
Tarutao = Ko Tarutao △
Thailand **65 J2**
Tarutao, Ko *Thailand* **65 J2**
Tarutung *Indonesia* **62 D1**
Tarutyne *Ukraine* **29 D14**
Tarvísio *Italy* **41 B10**
Taseko → *Canada* **102 C4**
Tash-Kömür *Kyrgyzstan* **52 E8**
Tash-Kumyr =
Tash-Kömür *Kyrgyzstan* **52 E8**
Tashauz = Dashoguz
Turkmenistan **52 E6**
Tashi Chho Dzong =
Thimphu *Bhutan* **67 F16**
Ţashk, Daryācheh-ye *Iran* **71 D7**
Tashkent = Toshkent
Uzbekistan **52 E7**
Tashtagol *Russia* **52 D9**
Tasiilaq *Greenland* **4 C6**
Tasik Kenyir *Malaysia* **65 K4**
Tasikmalaya *Indonesia* **63 G13**
Tåsinge *Denmark* **11 J4**
Tåsjön *Sweden* **8 D16**
Taskan *Russia* **53 C16**
Taşkent *Turkey* **72 D5**
Tasker *Niger* **83 C7**
Taşköprü *Turkey* **72 B6**
Taşlâc *Moldova* **29 C14**
Taşlıçay *Turkey* **73 C10**
Tasman □ *N.Z.* **91 D4**
Tasman Basin *Pac. Oc.* **96 M7**
Tasman Mts. *N.Z.* **91 D4**
Tasman Pen. *Australia* **95 G4**
Tasman Sea *Pac. Oc.* **90 E9**
Tasmania □ *Australia* **95 G4**
Tasmanian Wilderness
World Heritage Area △
Australia **95 G4**
Ţăşnad *Romania* **28 C7**
Taşova *Turkey* **72 B7**
Tassili n'Ajjer *Algeria* **78 C7**
Tassili-Oua-n-Ahaggar
Algeria **78 D7**

Tassili Tin-Rerhoh Algeria 83 A5
Tasuj Iran 73 C11
Tat Ton △ Thailand 64 E4
Tata Hungary 28 C3
Tata Morocco 78 C4
Tatabánya Hungary 28 C3
Tatahouine Tunisia 79 B8
Tataouine Tunisia 79 B8
Tatar Republic =
  Tatarstan □ Russia 34 C10
Tatarbunary Ukraine 29 E14
Tatarsk Russia 52 D8
Tatarstan □ Russia 34 C10
Tatarskiy Proliv Russia 53 E15
Tataran, C10
Tatatua, Pte. Tahiti 91 d
Tateyama Japan 55 G9
Tathlina L. Canada 102 A5
Tathra Australia 95 F4
Tatinnai L. Canada 103 A9
Tatla Lake Canada 102 C4
Tatlısu Turkey 45 F11
Tatnam, C. Canada 103 B10
Tatra = Tatry Slovak Rep. 27 B13
Tatranský △ Slovak Rep. 27 B13
Tatry Slovak Rep. 27 B13
Tatshenshini → Canada 102 B1
Tatsuno Japan 55 G7
Tatta Pakistan 68 G2
Tatuí Brazil 127 A6
Tatum U.S.A. 109 K12
Tat'ung = Datong China 56 D7
Tatvan Turkey 73 C10
Ta'ū Amer. Samoa 91 b
Taubaté Brazil 127 A6
Tauberbischofsheim
  Germany 25 F5
Taucha Germany 24 D8
Tauern Austria 22 E7
Tauern-tunnel Austria 26 D6
Taufikia Sudan 81 F3
Taulé France 18 D3
Taumarunui N.Z. 91 C5
Taumaturgo Brazil 124 E4
Taung S. Africa 88 D3
Taungdwingyi Burma 67 J19
Taunggyi Burma 67 J20
Taungup Burma 67 K19
Taunsa Pakistan 68 D4
Taunsa Barrage Pakistan 68 D4
Taunton U.K. 15 F4
Taunton U.S.A. 115 E13
Taunus Germany 25 E4
Taupo N.Z. 91 C6
Taupo, L. N.Z. 91 C5
Tauragė Lithuania 30 C9
Tauragė □ Lithuania 30 C9
Tauranga N.Z. 91 B6
Tauranga Harb. N.Z. 91 B6
Taureau, Rés. Canada 104 C5
Taurianova Italy 43 D9
Taurus Mts. = Toros
  Dağları Turkey 72 D5
Tauste Spain 38 D3
Tautira Tahiti 91 d
Tauyskaya Guba Russia 53 D16
Tauz = Tovuz Azerbaijan 35 K7
Tavas Turkey 47 D11
Tavastehus =
  Hämeenlinna Finland 32 B3
Tavda Russia 52 D7
Tavda → Russia 52 D7
Tavernes de la Valldigna
  Spain 39 F4
Taveta Kenya 86 C4
Taveuni Fiji 91 a
Taviano Italy 43 C11
Tavignano → France 21 F13
Tavira Portugal 37 H3
Tavistock Canada 114 C4
Tavistock U.K. 15 G3
Tavolara Italy 42 B2
Távora → Portugal 36 D3
Tavoy Burma 64 E2
Tavrichanka Russia 54 C5
Tavropos → Greece 46 B3
Tavşanlı Turkey 47 B11
Tavua Fiji 91 a
Tavuki Fiji 91 a
Taw → U.K. 15 F3
Tawa → India 68 H8
Tawas City U.S.A. 113 C12
Tawau Malaysia 62 D5
Taweisha Sudan 81 E2
Tawi-Tawi Phil. 63 C6
Tawu Taiwan 59 F13
Tāwūq Iraq 73 E11
Taxco Mexico 119 D5
Taxila Pakistan 68 C5
Tay → U.K. 13 E5
Tay, Firth of U.K. 13 E5
Tay, L. Australia 93 F3
Tay, L. U.K. 13 E4
Tay △ U.K. 13 E5
Tay Ninh Vietnam 65 G6
Tayabamba Peru 124 E3
Tayabas Bay Phil. 61 E4
Taygetos Oros Greece 46 D4
Taylakova Russia 52 D8
Taylor Canada 102 B4

Taylor Nebr., U.S.A. 112 E4
Taylor Pa., U.S.A. 115 E9
Taylor Tex., U.S.A. 116 F6
Taylor, Mt. U.S.A. 109 J10
Taylorville U.S.A. 112 F10
Taymā Si. Arabia 70 E3
Taymyr, Oz. Russia 53 B11
Taymyr, Poluostrov Russia 53 B11
Tayport U.K. 13 E6
Tayrona △ Colombia 121 D5
Tayshet Russia 53 D10
Taytay Phil. 61 F3
Taz → Russia 52 C8
Taza Morocco 78 B5
Tāza Khurmātū Iraq 73 E11
Tazawa-Ko Japan 54 E10
Tazerbo Libya 79 C10
Tazin Serbia 44 B6
Tazin → Canada 103 B7
Tazin L. Canada 103 B7
Tazovskiy Russia 52 C8
Tbilisi Georgia 35 K7
Tchad = Chad ■ Africa 79 F8
Tchad, L. Chad 79 F7
Tchaourou Benin 83 D5
Tch'eng-tou = Chengdu
  China 58 B5
Tchentlo L. Canada 102 B4
Tchetti Benin 83 D5
Tchibanga Gabon 84 E2
Tchien Liberia 82 D3
Tchin Tabaraden Niger 83 B6
Tch'ong-k'ing =
  Chongqing China 58 C6
Tczew Poland 30 D5
Te Anau, L. N.Z. 91 F1
Te Aroha N.Z. 91 B5
Te Awamutu N.Z. 91 C5
Te Ika a Maui = North I.
  N.Z. 91 C5
Te Kuiti N.Z. 91 C5
Te-n-Dghâmcha, Sebkhet
  Mauritania 82 B1
Te Puke N.Z. 91 B6
Te Waewae B. N.Z. 91 G1
Te Wai Pounamu = South
  I. N.Z. 91 F3
Teaca Romania 29 D9
Teague U.S.A. 116 F6
Teahupoo Tahiti 91 d
Teano Italy 43 A7
Teapa Mexico 119 D6
Teba Spain 37 J6
Tebakang Malaysia 62 D4
Teberda Russia 35 J5
Teberu Malaysia 65 d
Tébessa Algeria 78 A7
Tebicuary → Paraguay 126 B4
Tebingtinggi Riau, Indonesia 62 E2
Tebingtinggi
  Sumatera Utara, Indonesia 62 D1
Tebulos Georgia 35 J7
Tecate Mexico 111 N10
Tecer Dağları Turkey 72 C7
Tech → France 20 F7
Techiman Ghana 83 D4
Techirghiol Romania 29 F13
Tecka Argentina 128 E2
Tecomán Mexico 118 D4
Tecopa U.S.A. 111 K10
Tecoripa Mexico 118 B3
Tecuala Mexico 118 C3
Tecuci Romania 29 E12
Tecumseh Canada 114 D2
Tecumseh Mich., U.S.A. 113 D12
Tecumseh Okla., U.S.A. 116 D6
Tedzhen = Tejen
  Turkmenistan 52 F7
Tees → U.K. 14 C6
Tees B. U.K. 14 C6
Teeswater Canada 114 C3
Tefé Brazil 124 D6
Tefenni Turkey 47 D11
Tegal Indonesia 63 G13
Tegallalang Indonesia 63 J18
Tegalsari Indonesia 63 J17
Tegel, Berlin ✈ (TXL)
  Germany 24 C9
Tegernsee Germany 25 H7
Teggiano Italy 43 B8
Tegid, L. = Bala, L. U.K. 14 E4
Tegina Nigeria 83 C6
Tegucigalpa Honduras 120 D2
Teguidda i-n-Tessoum Niger 83 B6
Tehachapi U.S.A. 111 K8
Tehachapi Mts. U.S.A. 111 L8
Tehamiyam Sudan 80 D4
Teheran = Tehrān Iran 71 C6
Tehilla Sudan 80 D4
Téhini Ivory C. 82 D4
Tehoru Indonesia 63 E7
Tehrān Iran 71 C6
Tehrān □ Iran 71 C6
Tehri India 69 D8
Tehuacán Mexico 119 D5
Tehuantepec Mexico 119 D5
Tehuantepec, G. de Mexico 119 D5
Tehuantepec, Istmo de
  Mexico 119 D6

Teide, Pico de Canary Is. 48 F3
Teifi → U.K. 15 E3
Teign → U.K. 15 G4
Teignmouth U.K. 15 G4
Teigebyen Norway 10 D5
Teiuş Romania 29 D8
Tejakula Indonesia 63 J18
Tejam India 69 E9
Tejen Turkmenistan 52 F7
Tejen → Turkmenistan 71 B9
Tejo → Europe 37 F2
Tejon Pass U.S.A. 111 L8
Tekamah U.S.A. 112 E5
Tekapo, L. N.Z. 91 E3
Tekax Mexico 119 C7
Teke Turkey 45 E13
Tekeli Kazakhstan 52 E8
Tekeze → Ethiopia 81 E4
Tekija Serbia 44 B6
Tekirdağ Turkey 45 F11
Tekirdağ □ Turkey 45 E11
Tekirova Turkey 47 E12
Tekkali India 67 K14
Tekke Turkey 72 B7
Tekman Turkey 73 C9
Tekoa U.S.A. 108 C5
Tekong Besar, Pulau
  Singapore 65 d
Tel Aviv ✈ (TLV) Israel 74 C3
Tel Aviv-Yafo Israel 74 C3
Tel Lakhish Israel 74 D3
Tel Megiddo Israel 74 C4
Tela Honduras 120 C2
Telanaipura = Jambi
  Indonesia 62 E2
Telašćica △ Croatia 41 E12
Telavi Georgia 35 J7
Telč Czech Rep. 26 B8
Telciu Romania 29 C9
Telde Canary Is. 48 G4
Telegraph Creek Canada 102 B2
Telekhany =
  Tsyelyakhany Belarus 23 B13
Telemark Norway 9 G12
Telén Argentina 126 D2
Teleneşti Moldova 29 C13
Teleng Iran 71 E9
Teleño Spain 36 C4
Teleorman → Romania 29 G10
Teleorman → Romania 29 G10
Teles Pires → Brazil 124 E7
Telescope Pk. U.S.A. 111 J9
Teletaye Mali 83 B5
Telfer Mine Australia 92 C3
Telford U.K. 15 E5
Telford and Wrekin □ U.K. 14 E5
Telfs Austria 26 D4
Télimélé Guinea 82 C2
Teljo, J. Sudan 81 E2
Telkwa Canada 102 C3
Tell City U.S.A. 112 G10
Tellicherry India 66 P9
Telluride U.S.A. 109 H10
Teloloapán Mexico 119 D5
Telpos Iz Russia 6 C17
Telsen Argentina 128 E3
Telšiai Lithuania 30 C9
Telšiai □ Lithuania 30 C9
Teltow Germany 24 C9
Teluk Anson = Teluk
  Intan Malaysia 65 K3
Teluk Bahang Malaysia 65 c
Teluk Betung = Bandar
  Lampung Indonesia 62 F3
Teluk Intan Malaysia 65 K3
Teluk Kumbar Malaysia 65 c
Telukbutun Indonesia 62 D3
Telukdalem Indonesia 62 D1
Tema Ghana 83 D5
Temagami, L. Canada 104 C3
Temax Mexico 119 C7
Temba S. Africa 89 D4
Tembagapura Indonesia 63 E9
Tembe Dem. Rep. of the Congo 86 C2
Tembe △ S. Africa 89 D5
Tembleque Spain 36 F7
Temblor Range U.S.A. 111 K7
Teme → U.K. 15 E5
Temecula U.S.A. 111 M9
Temengor, Tasik Malaysia 65 K3
Temerloh Malaysia 65 L4
Teminabuan Indonesia 63 E8
Temir Kazakhstan 52 E6
Temirtau Russia 52 D9
Témiscaming Canada 104 C4
Témiscamingue, L. Canada 104 C4
Temnikov Russia 34 C6
Temo → Italy 42 B1
Temosachic Mexico 118 B3
Tempe U.S.A. 109 K8
Tempino U.S.A. 110 H11
Témpio Pausánia Italy 42 B2
Temple U.S.A. 116 F6
Temple B. Australia 94 A3
Templemore Ireland 12 D4
Templeton U.S.A. 110 K6
Templeton → Australia 94 C2

Templin Germany 24 B9
Tempoal de Sánchez Mexico
  119 C5
Temryuk Russia 33 K9
Temská → Serbia 44 C6
Temuco Chile 128 D2
Temuka N.Z. 91 F3
Tenabo Mexico 119 C6
Tenaha U.S.A. 116 F7
Tenakee Springs U.S.A. 102 B1
Tenali India 67 L12
Tenancingo de Degollado
  Mexico 119 D5
Tenango del Valle Mexico 119 D5
Tenaro, Akra Greece 46 E4
Tenasserim Burma 65 F2
Tenasserim □ Burma 64 F2
Tenby U.K. 15 F3
Tenda, Colle di France 21 D11
Tendaho Ethiopia 81 E5
Tende France 21 D11
Tendelti Sudan 81 E3
Tendrovskaya Kosa Ukraine 33 J6
Tendukhera India 69 H8
Tenerife Canary Is. 48 F3
Tenerife, Pico Canary Is. 48 G1
Tenerife Norte ✈ (TFN)
  Canary Is. 48 F3
Tenerife Sur ✈ (TFS)
  Canary Is. 48 F3
Teng Xian
  Guangxi Zhuangzu, China 59 F8
Teng Xian Shandong, China 57 G9
Tengah, Kepulauan
  Indonesia 62 F5
Tengchong China 58 E2
Tengchowfu = Penglai
  China 57 F11
Tenggarong Indonesia 62 E5
Tenggol, Pulau Malaysia 65 K4
Tengiz Köli Kazakhstan 52 D7
Tenhult Sweden 11 G8
Teniente Enciso △ Paraguay 126 A3
Teniente Rodolfo Marsh
  Antarctica 5 C18
Tenino U.S.A. 110 D4
Tenkasi India 66 Q10
Tenke Katanga,
  Dem. Rep. of the Congo 87 E2
Tenke Katanga,
  Dem. Rep. of the Congo 87 E2
Tenkodogo Burkina Faso 83 C4
Tenna → Italy 41 E10
Tennant Creek Australia 94 B1
Tennessee □ U.S.A. 117 D11
Tennessee → U.S.A. 117 C10
Teno, Pta. de Canary Is. 48 F3
Tenom Malaysia 62 C5
Tenosique Mexico 119 D6
Tenryū-Gawa → Japan 55 G8
Tenterden U.K. 15 F8
Tenterfield Australia 95 D5
Teo = A Ramallosa Spain 36 C2
Teófilo Otoni Brazil 125 G10
Tepa Indonesia 63 F7
Tepalcatepec → Mexico 118 D4
Tepecik Bursa, Turkey 45 F12
Tepecik Kütahya, Turkey 47 B11
Tepehuanes Mexico 118 B3
Tepelenë Albania 44 F4
Tepetongo Mexico 118 C4
Tepic Mexico 118 C4
Teplá Czech Rep. 26 B5
Teplice Czech Rep. 26 A6
Teplyk Ukraine 29 B14
Tepoca, C. Mexico 118 A2
Tequila Mexico 118 C4
Ter → Spain 38 C8
Ter Apel Neths. 17 B7
Téra Niger 83 C5
Tera → Spain 36 D5
Teraina Kiribati 97 G12
Terakeka Sudan 81 F3
Téramo Italy 41 F10
Terang Australia 95 F3
Terang, Teluk Indonesia 63 K19
Terazit, Massif de Niger 83 A6
Tercan Turkey 73 C9
Terceira Azores 78 a
Tercero → Argentina 126 C3
Terebovlya Ukraine 23 D13
Teregova Romania 28 E7
Tereida Sudan 81 E3
Terek → Russia 35 J8
Terepaima △ Venezuela 121 E6
Tereshka → Russia 34 E8
Teresina Brazil 125 E10
Terespol Poland 31 F10
Teresva → Ukraine 23 D8
Terevaka Chile 97 b
Terewah, L. Australia 95 D4
Terges → Portugal 37 H3
Tergnier France 19 C10
Teridgerie Cr. → Australia 95 E4

Terlizzi Italy 43 A9
Termas de Río Hondo
  Argentina 126 B3
Terme Turkey 72 B7
Termez = Termiz Uzbekistan 52 F7
Términi Imerese Italy 42 E6
Términos, L. de Mexico 119 D6
Termiz Uzbekistan 52 F7
Térmoli Italy 41 F12
Ternate Indonesia 63 D7
Terneuzen Neths. 17 C3
Terney Russia 54 B8
Terni Italy 41 F9
Ternitz Austria 26 D9
Ternivka Ukraine 29 B14
Ternopil Ukraine 23 D13
Ternopil □ Ukraine 33 H3
Ternopol = Ternopil
  Ukraine 23 D13
Terowie Australia 95 E2
Terpni Greece 44 F7
Terra Bella U.S.A. 111 K7
Terra Nova △ Canada 105 C9
Terrace Canada 102 C3
Terrace Bay Canada 104 C2
Terracina Italy 42 A6
Terralba Italy 42 C1
Terrasini Italy 42 D6
Terrassa Spain 38 D7
Terrasson-la-Villedieu
  France 20 C5
Terre Haute U.S.A. 112 F10
Terrebonne B. U.S.A. 117 G9
Terrecht Mali 83 B5
Terrell U.S.A. 116 E6
Terrenceville Canada 105 C9
Terry U.S.A. 108 C11
Terryville U.S.A. 115 E11
Terschelling Neths. 17 A5
Tersko-Kumskiy Kanal
  Russia 35 H7
Tertenía Italy 42 C2
Terter = Tärtär → Azerbaijan 35 K8
Teruel Spain 38 E4
Teruel □ Spain 38 E4
Tervel Bulgaria 45 C11
Tervola Finland 8 C21
Teryaweynya L. Australia 95 E3
Tešanj Bos.-H. 28 F3
Teseney Eritrea 81 D4
Tesha → Russia 34 C6
Teshio Japan 54 B10
Teshio-Gawa → Japan 54 B10
Tešica Serbia 44 C5
Tesiyn Gol → Mongolia 60 A4
Teslić Bos.-H. 28 F2
Teslin Canada 102 A2
Teslin → Canada 102 A2
Teslin L. Canada 102 A2
Tessalit Mali 83 A5
Tessaoua Niger 83 C6
Tessin Germany 24 A8
Tessit Mali 83 B5
Test → U.K. 15 G6
Testa del Gargano Italy 41 G13
Testigos, Is. Los Venezuela 121 D7
Tetachuck L. Canada 102 C3
Tetas, Pta. Chile 126 A1
Tete Mozam. 87 F3
Tete □ Mozam. 87 F3
Teterev → Ukraine 23 C16
Teterow Germany 24 B8
Teteven Bulgaria 45 D8
Tethul → Canada 102 A6
Tetiyev Ukraine 23 D15
Teton → U.S.A. 108 C8
Tétouan Morocco 78 A4
Tetovo Macedonia 44 D4
Tetufera, Mt. Tahiti 91 d
Tetyushi Russia 34 C9
Teuco → Argentina 126 B3
Teulada Italy 42 D1
Teulon Canada 103 C9
Teun Indonesia 63 F7
Teuri-Tō Japan 54 B10
Teutoburger Wald Germany 24 C4
Tevere → Italy 41 G9
Tevere △ Italy 41 F9
Teverya Israel 74 C4
Teviot → U.K. 13 F6
Tewantin Australia 95 D5
Tewkesbury U.K. 15 F5
Texada I. Canada 102 D4
Texarkana Ark., U.S.A. 116 E7
Texarkana Tex., U.S.A. 116 E7
Texas Australia 95 D5
Texas □ U.S.A. 116 F5
Texas City U.S.A. 116 G7
Texel Neths. 17 A4
Texline U.S.A. 116 C3
Texoma, L. U.S.A. 116 E6
Teyateyaneng Lesotho 85 K5
Teykovo Russia 32 D11
Teza → Russia 34 C6
Teziutlán Mexico 119 D5
Tezin Afghan. 68 B3
Tezpur India 67 F18

Tezzeron L. Canada 102 C4
Tha-anne → Canada 103 A10
Tha Deua Laos 64 D4
Tha Deua Laos 64 C3
Tha Li Thailand 64 D3
Tha Pla Thailand 64 D3
Tha Rua Thailand 64 E3
Tha Sala Thailand 65 H2
Tha Song Yang Thailand 64 D1
Thaba Putsoa Lesotho 89 D4
Thabana Ntlenyana Lesotho 89 D4
Thabazimbi S. Africa 89 C4
Thādiq Si. Arabia 70 E5
Thai Binh Vietnam 58 G6
Thai Muang Thailand 65 H2
Thai Nguyen Vietnam 58 G5
Thailand ■ Asia 64 E4
Thailand, G. of Asia 65 G3
Thakhek Laos 64 D5
Thal Pakistan 68 C4
Thal Desert Pakistan 68 D4
Thala La = Hkakabo Razi
  Burma 67 E20
Thalabarivat Cambodia 64 F5
Thallon Australia 95 D4
Thalu, Ko Thailand 65 b
Thalwil Switz. 25 H4
Thames N.Z. 91 B5
Thames → Canada 114 D2
Thames → U.K. 15 F8
Thames → U.S.A. 115 E12
Thames Estuary U.K. 15 F8
Thamesford Canada 114 C4
Thamesville Canada 114 D3
Than India 68 H4
Than Uyen Vietnam 64 B4
Thana Gazi India 68 F7
Thandla India 68 H6
Thandwe Burma 67 K19
Thane India 66 K8
Thanesar India 68 D7
Thanet, I. of U.K. 15 F9
Thangool Australia 94 C5
Thanh Hoa Vietnam 64 C5
Thanh Hung Vietnam 65 H5
Thanh Pho Ho Chi Minh
  Vietnam 65 G6
Thanh Thuy Vietnam 64 A5
Thanjavur India 66 P11
Thann France 19 E14
Thano Bula Khan Pakistan 68 G2
Thaolintoa L. Canada 103 A9
Thaon-les-Vosges France 19 D13
Thap Lan △ Thailand 64 E4
Thap Sakae Thailand 65 G2
Thap Than Thailand 64 E2
Thar Desert India 68 F5
Tharad India 68 G4
Thargomindah Australia 95 D3
Tharp Fracture Zone
  S. Ocean 5 B14
Tharrawaddy Burma 67 L19
Tharthār, Buhayrat ath
  Iraq 73 E10
Tharthar, L. = Tharthār,
  Buhayrat ath Iraq 73 E10
Tharthār, W. ath → Iraq 73 E10
Thasopoula Greece 45 F8
Thasos Greece 45 F8
That Khe Vietnam 58 F6
Thatcher Ariz., U.S.A. 109 K9
Thatcher Colo., U.S.A. 109 H11
Thaton Burma 67 L20
Thau, Bassin de France 20 E7
Thaungdut Burma 67 G19
Thayer U.S.A. 112 G8
Thayetmyo Burma 67 K19
Thazi Burma 67 J20
Thbeng Meanchey Cambodia 64 F5
The Broads U.K. 14 E9
The Everglades U.S.A. 117 J14
The Gulf = Persian Gulf Asia 71 E6
The Hague =
  's-Gravenhage Neths. 17 B4
The Pas Canada 103 C8
The Wash U.K. 14 E8
The Weald U.K. 15 F8
Thebes = Thiva Greece 46 C5
Thebes Egypt 80 B3
Thedford U.S.A. 112 E3
Theebine Australia 95 D5
Thekulthili L. Canada 103 A7
Thelon → Canada 103 A8
Thénezay France 18 F6
Thenon France 20 C5
Theodore Australia 94 C5
Theodore Canada 103 C8
Theodore U.S.A. 117 F10
Theodore Roosevelt △
  U.S.A. 112 B2
Theodore Roosevelt L.
  U.S.A. 109 K8
Thepha Thailand 65 J3
Thérain → France 19 C9
Theresa U.S.A. 115 B9
Thermopolis U.S.A. 108 E9
Thermopylae Greece 46 C4
Thesprotia □ Greece 46 B2
Thessalon Canada 104 C3

Thessalonica, Gulf of =
Thessaloniki Kolpos
Greece **44** F6
Thessaloniki *Greece* **44** F6
Thessaloniki □ *Greece* **44** F7
Thessaloniki Kolpos *Greece* **44** F6
Thessaloniki ✈ (SKG) *Greece* **44** F7
Thessaly □ *Greece* **46** B4
Thetford *U.K.* **15** E8
Thetford Mines *Canada* **105** C5
Theun ➤ *Laos* **64** C5
Theunissen *S. Africa* **88** D4
Thevenard *Australia* **95** E1
Thiamis ➤ *Greece* **46** B2
Thiberville *France* **18** C7
Thibodaux *U.S.A.* **117** G9
Thicket Portage *Canada* **103** B9
Thief River Falls *U.S.A.* **112** A5
Thiel Mts. *Antarctica* **5** E16
Thiene *Italy* **41** C8
Thiérache *France* **19** C10
Thiers *France* **20** C7
Thiès *Senegal* **82** C1
Thiès □ *Senegal* **82** C1
Thiesi *Italy* **42** B1
Thiet *Sudan* **81** F2
Thika *Kenya* **86** C4
Thille-Boubacar *Senegal* **82** B1
Thimphu *Bhutan* **67** F16
Thina ➤ *S. Africa* **89** E4
Þingvallavatn *Iceland* **8** D3
Thionville *France* **19** C13
Thira = Santorini *Greece* **47** E7
Thirasia *Greece* **47** E7
Third Cataract *Sudan* **80** D3
Thirsk *U.K.* **14** C6
Thiruvananthapuram =
Trivandrum *India* **66** Q10
Thisted *Denmark* **11** H2
Thistle I. *Australia* **95** F2
Thithia = Cicia *Fiji* **91** a
Thiva *Greece* **46** C5
Thiviers *France* **20** C4
Thizy *France* **19** F11
Þjórsá ➤ *Iceland* **8** E3
Thlewiaza ➤ *Canada* **103** A10
Thmar Puok *Cambodia* **64** F4
Tho Vinh *Vietnam* **64** C5
Thoa ➤ *Canada* **103** A7
Thoen *Thailand* **64** D2
Thoeng *Thailand* **64** C3
Thohoyandou *S. Africa* **85** J6
Tholdi *Pakistan* **69** B7
Thomas *U.S.A.* **116** D5
Thomas, L. *Australia* **95** D2
Thomaston *U.S.A.* **117** E12
Thomasville *Ala., U.S.A.* **117** F11
Thomasville *Ga., U.S.A.* **117** F13
Thomasville *N.C., U.S.A.* **117** D14
Thompson *Canada* **103** B9
Thompson *U.S.A.* **115** E9
Thompson ➤ *Canada* **102** C4
Thompson ➤ *U.S.A.* **112** F7
Thompson Falls *U.S.A.* **108** C6
Thompson Pk. *U.S.A.* **108** F2
Thompson Springs *U.S.A.* **108** G9
Thompsontown *U.S.A.* **114** F7
Thomson *U.S.A.* **117** E13
Thomson ➤ *Australia* **94** C3
Thônes *France* **21** C10
Thong Yang *Thailand* **65** b
Thonon-les-Bains *France* **19** F13
Thorez *Ukraine* **33** H10
Þórisvatn *Iceland* **8** D4
Thornaby on Tees *U.K.* **14** C6
Thornbury *Canada* **114** B4
Thorne *U.K.* **14** D7
Thornton *Canada* **114** B5
Thornton *U.S.A.* **108** G11
Thorold *Canada* **114** C5
Þórshöfn *Iceland* **8** C6
Thouarcé *France* **18** E6
Thouars *France* **18** F6
Thouet ➤ *France* **18** E6
Thouin, C. *Australia* **92** D2
Thousand Islands *U.S.A.* **115** B9
Thousand Oaks *U.S.A.* **111** L8
Thrace *Turkey* **45** F10
Thrace, Sea of *Greece* **45** F8
Three Forks *U.S.A.* **108** D8
Three Gorges Dam *China* **59** B8
Three Hills *Canada* **102** C6
Three Hummock I. *Australia* **95** G3
Three Pagodas Pass *Asia* **64** E2
Three Points, C. *Ghana* **82** E4
Three Rivers *Calif., U.S.A.* **110** J8
Three Rivers *Tex., U.S.A.* **116** G5
Three Springs *Australia* **93** E2
Throssell, L. *Australia* **93** E3
Throssell Ra. *Australia* **92** D3
Thrushton △ *Australia* **95** D4
Thua ➤ *Kenya* **86** C4
Thuan Hoa *Vietnam* **65** H5
Thubun Lakes *Canada* **103** A6
Thueyts *France* **21** D8
Thuin *Belgium* **17** D4
Thuir *France* **20** F6
Thule = Qaanaaq *Greenland* **4** B4
Thule Air Base =
Uummannaq *Greenland* **4** B4

Thun *Switz.* **25** J3
Thunder B. *U.S.A.* **114** B1
Thunder Bay *Canada* **104** C2
Thunersee *Switz.* **25** J3
Thung Salaeng Luang △
Thailand **64** D3
Thung Song *Thailand* **65** H2
Thunkar *Bhutan* **67** F17
Thuong Tra *Vietnam* **64** D6
Thur ➤ *Switz.* **25** H5
Thurgau □ *Switz.* **25** H5
Thüringen □ *Germany* **24** D6
Thüringer Wald *Germany* **24** E6
Thurles *Ireland* **12** D4
Thurn P. *Austria* **26** D5
Thurrock □ *U.K.* **15** F8
Thursday I. *Australia* **94** A3
Thurso *Canada* **104** C4
Thurso *U.K.* **13** C5
Thurso ➤ *U.K.* **13** C5
Thurston I. *Antarctica* **5** D16
Thury-Harcourt *France* **18** D6
Thutade L. *Canada* **102** B3
Thy *Denmark* **11** H2
Thyborøn *Denmark* **11** H2
Thyolo *Malawi* **87** F4
Ti-n-Amzi ➤ *Niger* **83** B5
Ti-n-Barraouene, O. ➤
Africa **83** B5
Ti-n-Zaouatene *Algeria* **83** B5
Ti-Tree *Australia* **94** C1
Tiadiaye *Senegal* **82** C1
Tian Shan *Asia* **60** B3
Tianchang *China* **59** A12
Tiandeng *China* **58** F6
Tiandong *China* **58** F6
Tian'e *China* **58** E6
Tianhe *China* **58** E7
Tianjin *China* **57** E9
Tianjin *China* **57** E9
Tiankoura *Burkina Faso* **82** C4
Tianlin *China* **58** E6
Tianmen *China* **59** B9
Tianquan *China* **58** B4
Tianshifu *China* **57** D13
Tianshui *China* **56** G3
Tiantai *China* **59** C13
Tianyang *China* **58** F6
Tianyar *Indonesia* **63** J18
Tianzhen *China* **56** D8
Tianzhu *China* **58** D6
Tianzhuangtai *China* **57** D12
Tiarei *Tahiti* **91** d
Tiaret *Algeria* **78** A6
Tiassalé *Ivory C.* **82** D4
Tibagi *Brazil* **127** A5
Tibagi ➤ *Brazil* **127** A5
Tibastī, Sarīr *Libya* **79** D9
Tibati *Cameroon* **83** D7
Tibe *Ethiopia* **81** F4
Tiber = Tevere ➤ *Italy* **41** G9
Tiber Res. *U.S.A.* **108** B8
Tiberias = Teverya *Israel* **74** C4
Tiberias, L. = Yam
Kinneret *Israel* **74** C4
Tibesti *Chad* **79** D9
Tibet = Xizang Zizhiqu □
China **60** C3
Tibet, Plateau of *Asia* **50** E10
Tibiao *Phil.* **61** F5
Tibiri *Niger* **83** C6
Tibnī *Syria* **73** E8
Tibooburra *Australia* **95** D3
Tibro *Sweden* **11** F8
Tiburón, I. *Mexico* **118** B2
Ticao I. *Phil.* **61** E5
Tîchît *Mauritania* **82** B3
Ticho *Ethiopia* **81** F4
Ticino □ *Switz.* **25** J4
Ticino ➤ *Italy* **25** J4
Ticleni *Romania* **29** F8
Ticonderoga *U.S.A.* **115** C11
Ticul *Mexico* **119** C7
Tidaholm *Sweden* **11** F7
Tidan *Sweden* **11** F8
Tiddim *Burma* **67** H18
Tidioute *U.S.A.* **114** E5
Tidjikja *Mauritania* **82** B2
Tidore *Indonesia* **63** D7
Tiébissou *Ivory C.* **82** D3
Tiefa *China* **57** C12
Tiel *Neths.* **17** C5
Tiel *Senegal* **82** C1
Tieling *China* **57** C12
Tielt *Belgium* **17** C3
Tien Shan = Tian Shan *Asia* **60** B3
Tien-tsin = Tianjin *China* **57** E9
Tien Yen *Vietnam* **64** B6
Tienching = Tianjin *China* **57** E9
Tienen *Belgium* **17** D4
Tiénigbé *Ivory C.* **82** D3
Tientsin = Tianjin *China* **57** E9
Tieri *Australia* **94** C4
Tierp *Sweden* **10** D11
Tierra Amarilla *Chile* **126** B1
Tierra Amarilla *U.S.A.* **109** H10
Tierra Colorada *Mexico* **119** D5
Tierra de Barros *Spain* **37** G4

Tierra de Campos *Spain* **36** C6
Tierra del Fuego, I. Grande
de *Argentina* **128** G3
Tiétar ➤ *Spain* **36** F4
Tietê ➤ *Brazil* **127** A5
Tiffin *U.S.A.* **113** E12
Tifton *U.S.A.* **117** F13
Tifu *Indonesia* **63** E7
Tiga Res. *Nigeria* **83** C6
Tighina *Moldova* **29** D14
Tigil *Russia* **53** D16
Tignish *Canada* **105** C7
Tigray □ *Ethiopia* **81** E4
Tigre ➤ *Peru* **124** D4
Tigre ➤ *Venezuela* **124** B6
Tigris = Dijlah, Nahr ➤
Asia **70** D5
Tigveni *Romania* **29** E9
Tigyaing *Burma* **67** H20
Tîh, Gebel el *Egypt* **80** B3
Tihāmah *Asia* **75** D3
Tijara *India* **68** F7
Tijuana *Mexico* **111** N9
Tikal *Guatemala* **120** C2
Tikal △ *Guatemala* **120** C2
Tikamgarh *India* **69** G8
Tikaré *Burkina Faso* **83** C4
Tikhoretsk *Russia* **35** H5
Tikhvin *Russia* **32** C7
Tikirarjuaq = Whale Cove
Canada **103** A10
Tikmehdāsh *Iran* **73** D12
Tiko *Cameroon* **83** E6
Tikrīt *Iraq* **73** E10
Tiksi *Russia* **53** B13
Tilamuta *Indonesia* **63** D6
Tilburg *Neths.* **17** C5
Tilbury *Canada* **114** D2
Tilbury *U.K.* **15** F8
Tilcara *Argentina* **126** A2
Tilden *U.S.A.* **112** D5
Tilemses *Niger* **83** B5
Tilemsi, Vallée du *Mali* **83** B5
Tilhar *India* **69** F8
Tilichiki *Russia* **53** C17
Tilissos *Greece* **49** D7
Till ➤ *U.K.* **14** B5
Tillabéri *Niger* **83** C5
Tillamook *U.S.A.* **108** D2
Tillberga *Sweden* **10** E10
Tillia *Niger* **83** B5
Tillsonburg *Canada* **114** D4
Tillyeria *Cyprus* **49** D11
Tilogne *Senegal* **82** B2
Tilos *Greece* **47** E9
Tilpa *Australia* **95** E3
Tilt ➤ *U.K.* **13** E5
Tilton *U.S.A.* **115** C13
Tiltonsville *U.S.A.* **114** F4
Tim *Denmark* **11** H2
Timanfaya △ *Canary Is.* **48** F6
Timaru *N.Z.* **91** F3
Timashevo *Russia* **34** D10
Timashevsk *Russia* **35** H4
Timau *Kenya* **86** B4
Timbaki *Greece* **49** D6
Timbedgha *Mauritania* **82** B3
Timber Creek *Australia* **92** C5
Timber Lake *U.S.A.* **112** C3
Timber Mt. *U.S.A.* **110** H10
Timbo *Guinea* **82** C2
Timbo *Liberia* **82** D3
Timbuktu = Tombouctou
Mali **82** B4
Timeiaouine *Algeria* **83** A5
Timétrine *Mali* **83** B4
Timétrine, Mts. *Mali* **83** B4
Timfi Oros *Greece* **46** B2
Timfristos, Oros *Greece* **46** C3
Timi *Cyprus* **49** E11
Tîmia *Niger* **83** B6
Timimoun *Algeria* **78** C6
Timiris, Râs *Mauritania* **82** B1
Timiş = Tamiš ➤ *Serbia* **28** F5
Timiş □ *Romania* **28** E6
Timiskaming, L. =
Témiscamingue, L.
Canada **104** C4
Timişoara *Romania* **28** E6
Timmersdala *Sweden* **11** F7
Timmins *Canada* **104** C3
Timok ➤ *Serbia* **44** B6
Timoleague *Ireland* **12** E3
Timor *Asia* **63** F7
Timor Leste = East
Timor ■ *Asia* **63** F7
Timor Sea *Ind. Oc.* **92** B4
Timrå *Sweden* **10** B11
Tin Can Bay *Australia* **95** D5
Tin Ethisane *Mali* **83** B4
Tin Gornai *Mali* **83** B4
Tin Mt. *U.S.A.* **110** J9
Tina = Thina ➤ *S. Africa* **89** E4
Tîna, Khalîg el *Egypt* **74** D1
Tinaca Pt. *Phil.* **61** J6
Tinajo *Canary Is.* **48** F6
Tinca *Romania* **28** D6
Tindal *Australia* **92** B5
Tindouf *Algeria* **78** C4

Tinée ➤ *France* **21** E11
Tineo *Spain* **36** B4
Tinfunque △ *Paraguay* **126** A3
Ting Jiang ➤ *China* **59** E11
Tinggi, Pulau *Malaysia* **65** L5
Tingi Mts. *S. Leone* **82** D2
Tinglev *Denmark* **11** K3
Tingo María *Peru* **124** E3
Tingrela *Ivory C.* **82** C3
Tingsryd *Sweden* **11** H9
Tingstäde *Sweden* **11** G12
Tinh Bien *Vietnam* **65** G5
Tinian *N. Marianas* **96** F6
Tinnevelly = Tirunelveli
India **66** Q10
Tinogasta *Argentina* **126** B2
Tinos *Greece* **47** D7
Tiñoso, C. *Spain* **39** H3
Tinpahar *India* **69** G12
Tintina *Argentina* **126** B3
Tintinara *Australia* **95** F3
Tintioulé *Guinea* **82** C3
Tinto ➤ *Spain* **37** H4
Tioga *N. Dak., U.S.A.* **112** A2
Tioga *Pa., U.S.A.* **114** E7
Tioman, Pulau *Malaysia* **65** L5
Tione di Trento *Italy* **40** B7
Tionesta *U.S.A.* **114** E5
Tior *Sudan* **81** F3
Tipperary *Ireland* **12** D3
Tipperary □ *Ireland* **12** D4
Tipton *Calif., U.S.A.* **110** J7
Tipton *Iowa, U.S.A.* **112** E8
Tipton Mt. *U.S.A.* **111** K12
Tiptonville *U.S.A.* **117** C10
Tīrān *Iran* **71** C6
Tīrān *Si. Arabia* **80** B3
Tirana = Tiranë *Albania* **44** E3
Tiranë *Albania* **44** E3
Tiranë ✈ (TIA) *Albania* **44** E3
Tirano *Italy* **40** B7
Tirari Desert *Australia* **95** D2
Tiraspol *Moldova* **29** D14
Tirdout *Mali* **83** B4
Tire *Turkey* **47** C9
Tirebolu *Turkey* **73** B8
Tiree *U.K.* **13** E2
Tiree, Passage of *U.K.* **13** E2
Tîrgovişte = Târgovişte
Romania **29** F10
Tîrgu Jiu = Târgu Jiu
Romania **29** E8
Tîrgu Mureş = Târgu
Mureş *Romania* **29** E8
Tirich Mir *Pakistan* **66** A7
Tiriolo *Italy* **43** D9
Tiriro *Guinea* **82** C3
Tiritiri o te Moana =
Southern Alps *N.Z.* **91** E3
Tirnavos *Greece* **46** B4
Tirodi *India* **66** J11
Tirol □ *Austria* **26** D3
Tirschenreuth *Germany* **25** F8
Tirso ➤ *Italy* **42** C1
Tirstrup *Denmark* **11** H4
Tiruchchirappalli *India* **66** P11
Tirunelveli *India* **66** Q10
Tirupati *India* **66** N11
Tiruppur *India* **66** P10
Tiruvannamalai *India* **66** N11
Tisa ➤ *India* **68** C7
Tisa ➤ *Serbia* **28** E5
Tisdale *Canada* **103** C8
Tishomingo *U.S.A.* **116** D6
Tisjön *Sweden* **10** D7
Tisnaren *Sweden* **11** F9
Tišnov *Czech Rep.* **27** B9
Tisovec *Slovak Rep.* **27** C12
Tisza = Tisa ➤ *Serbia* **28** E5
Tiszaföldvár *Hungary* **28** D5
Tiszafüred *Hungary* **28** C5
Tiszalök *Hungary* **28** B6
Tiszavasvári *Hungary* **28** C6
Tit-Ary *Russia* **53** B13
Titaguas *Spain* **38** F3
Titao *Burkina Faso* **83** C4
Titel *Serbia* **28** E5
Tithwal *Pakistan* **69** B5
Titicaca, L. *S. Amer.* **124** G5
Titisee *Germany* **25** H4
Titiwa *Nigeria* **83** C7
Tito *Italy* **43** B8
Titova Korenica *Croatia* **41** D12
Titu *Romania* **29** F10
Titule *Dem. Rep. of the Congo* **86** B2
Titusville *Fla., U.S.A.* **117** G14
Titusville *Pa., U.S.A.* **114** E5
Tivaouane *Senegal* **82** C1
Tivat *Montenegro* **44** D2
Tivedens △ *Sweden* **11** F8
Tiverton *Canada* **114** B3
Tiverton *U.K.* **15** G4
Tívoli *Italy* **41** G9
Tiyo *Eritrea* **81** E5
Tizi-Ouzou *Algeria* **78** A6
Tizimín *Mexico* **119** C7
Tiznit *Morocco* **78** C4
Tjæreborg *Denmark* **11** J2
Tjeggelvas *Sweden* **8** C17
Tjeggelvas = Tjeggelvas
Sweden **8** C17
Tjirebon = Cirebon
Indonesia **63** G13
Tjluring *Indonesia* **63** J17
Tjörn *Sweden* **11** F5
Tkibuli = Tqibuli *Georgia* **35** J6
Tkvarcheli = Tqvarcheli
Georgia **35** J5
Tlacotalpan *Mexico* **119** D5
Tlahualilo de Zaragoza
Mexico **118** B4
Tlaquepaque *Mexico* **118** C4
Tlaxcala *Mexico* **119** D5
Tlaxcala □ *Mexico* **119** D5
Tlaxiaco *Mexico* **119** D5
Tlemcen *Algeria* **78** B5
Tlumach *Ukraine* **29** B10
Tluszcz *Poland* **31** F8
Tlyarata *Russia* **35** J8
To Bong *Vietnam* **64** F7
Toa Payoh *Singapore* **65** d
Toad ➤ *Canada* **102** B4
Toad River *Canada* **102** B3
Toamasina *Madag.* **89** B8
Toamasina □ *Madag.* **89** B8
Toay *Argentina* **126** D3
Toba *China* **58** B1
Toba *Japan* **55** G8
Toba, Danau *Indonesia* **62** D1
Toba Kakar *Pakistan* **68** D3
Toba Tek Singh *Pakistan* **68** D5
Tobago *Trin. & Tob.* **121** D7
Tobarra *Spain* **39** G3
Tobelo *Indonesia* **63** D7
Tobermory *Canada* **114** A3
Tobermory *U.K.* **13** E2
Tobi *Pac. Oc.* **63** D8
Tobi-Shima *Japan* **54** D9
Tobin, L. *Australia* **92** D4
Tobin, L. *Canada* **103** C8
Toblach = Dobbiaco *Italy* **41** B9
Toboali *Indonesia* **62** E3
Tobol ➤ *Russia* **52** D7
Toboli *Indonesia* **63** E6
Tobolsk *Russia* **52** D7
Tobor *Senegal* **82** C1
Tobruk = Tubruq *Libya* **79** B10
Tobyhanna *U.S.A.* **115** E9
Tobyl = Tobol ➤ *Russia* **52** D7
Tocantinópolis *Brazil* **125** E9
Tocantins □ *Brazil* **125** F9
Tocantins ➤ *Brazil* **125** D9
Toccoa *U.S.A.* **117** D13
Toce ➤ *Italy* **40** C5
Tochi ➤ *Pakistan* **68** C4
Tochigi *Japan* **55** F9
Tochigi □ *Japan* **55** F9
Tocina *Spain* **37** H5
Töcksfors *Sweden* **10** E5
Toco *Trin. & Tob.* **125** K16
Toconao *Chile* **126** A2
Tocopilla *Chile* **126** A1
Tocumwal *Australia* **95** F4
Tocuyo ➤ *Venezuela* **124** A5
Todd ➤ *Australia* **94** C2
Todeli *Indonesia* **63** E6
Todenyang *Kenya* **86** B4
Todgarh *India* **68** G5
Todi *Italy* **41** F9
Todos os Santos, B. de
Brazil **125** F11
Todos Santos *Mexico* **118** C2
Todtnau *Germany* **25** H3
Toe Hd. *U.K.* **13** D1
Toecé *Burkina Faso* **83** C4
Tofield *Canada* **102** C6
Tofino *Canada* **102** D3
Töfsingdalens △ *Sweden* **10** B6
Tofua *Tonga* **91** c
Tōgane *Japan* **55** G10
Togba *Mauritania* **82** B2
Togian, Kepulauan *Indonesia* **63** E6
Togliatti *Russia* **34** D9
Togo ■ *W. Afr.* **83** D5
Togtoh *China* **56** D6
Tohiea, Mt. *Moorea* **91** d
Tohma ➤ *Turkey* **72** C8
Tōhoku □ *Japan* **54** E10
Töhöm *Mongolia* **56** B5
Toinya *Sudan* **81** F2
Toiyabe Range *U.S.A.* **108** G5
Tojikiston = Tajikistan ■
Asia **52** F8
Tojo *Indonesia* **63** E6
Tōjō *Japan* **55** G6
Tok *U.S.A.* **100** C5
Tokachi-Dake *Japan* **54** C11
Tokachi-Gawa ➤ *Japan* **54** C11
Tokaj *Hungary* **28** B6
Tokala *Indonesia* **63** E6
Tōkamachi *Japan* **55** F9
Tokanui *N.Z.* **91** G2
Tokar *Sudan* **80** D4
Tokara-Rettō *Japan* **55** K4
Tokarahi *N.Z.* **91** F3
Tokashiki-Shima *Japan* **55** L3
Tokat *Turkey* **72** B7
Tokat □ *Turkey* **72** B7

Tŏkch'ŏn *N. Korea* **57** E14
Tokdo *Asia* **55** F5
Tokeland *U.S.A.* **110** D3
Tokelau Is. *Pac. Oc.* **96** H10
Tokmak *Kyrgyzstan* **52** E8
Tokmak *Ukraine* **33** J8
Toko Ra. *Australia* **94** C2
Tokoro-Gawa ➤ *Japan* **54** B12
Toku *Tonga* **91** c
Tokuno-Shima *Japan* **55** L4
Tokushima *Japan* **55** G7
Tokushima □ *Japan* **55** H7
Tokuyama *Japan* **55** G5
Tōkyō □ *Japan* **55** G9
Tolaga Bay *N.Z.* **91** C7
Tolbukhin = Dobrich
Bulgaria **45** C11
Toledo *Brazil* **127** A5
Toledo *Spain* **36** F6
Toledo *Ohio, U.S.A.* **113** E12
Toledo *Oreg., U.S.A.* **108** D2
Toledo *Wash., U.S.A.* **108** C2
Toledo, Montes de *Spain* **37** F6
Toledo Bend Res. *U.S.A.* **116** F8
Tolentino *Italy* **41** E10
Tolfa *Italy* **41** F8
Tolga *Australia* **94** B4
Toliara *Madag.* **89** C7
Toliara □ *Madag.* **89** C8
Tolima *Colombia* **124** C3
Tolitoli *Indonesia* **63** D6
Tolkmicko *Poland* **30** D6
Tollarp *Sweden* **11** J7
Tollensesee *Germany* **24** B9
Tollhouse *U.S.A.* **110** H7
Tolmachevo *Russia* **32** C4
Tolmezzo *Italy* **41** B10
Tolmin *Slovenia* **40** B10
Tolna *Hungary* **28** D3
Tolna □ *Hungary* **28** D3
Tolo, Teluk *Indonesia* **63** E6
Tolochin = Talachyn *Belarus* **32** E5
Tolosa *Spain* **38** B2
Tolox *Spain* **37** J6
Toluca *Mexico* **119** D5
Tom Burke *S. Africa* **89** C4
Tom Price *Australia* **92** D2
Toma *Burkina Faso* **82** C4
Tomah *U.S.A.* **112** D8
Tomahawk *U.S.A.* **112** C9
Tomai *Moldova* **29** D13
Tomakomai *Japan* **54** C10
Tomales *U.S.A.* **110** G4
Tomales B. *U.S.A.* **110** G3
Tomanivi *Fiji* **91** a
Tomar *Portugal* **37** F2
Tomaros, Oros *Greece* **46** B2
Tomarza *Turkey* **72** C6
Tomashevka *Belarus* **31** G10
Tomashpil *Ukraine* **29** B13
Tomaszów Lubelski *Poland* **31** H10
Tomaszów Mazowiecki
Poland **31** G7
Tomatlán *Mexico* **118** D3
Tombadonkéa *Guinea* **82** C2
Tombador, Serra do *Brazil* **124** F7
Tombe *Sudan* **81** F3
Tombigbee ➤ *U.S.A.* **117** F11
Tombouctou *Mali* **82** B4
Tombouctou □ *Mali* **82** B4
Tombstone *U.S.A.* **109** L8
Tombua *Angola* **88** B1
Tomé *Chile* **126** D1
Tomelilla *Sweden* **11** J7
Tomelloso *Spain* **37** F7
Tomini *Indonesia* **63** D6
Tomini, Teluk *Indonesia* **63** E6
Tominian *Mali* **82** C4
Tomiño *Spain* **36** D2
Tomintoul *U.K.* **13** D5
Tomislavgrad *Bos.-H.* **28** G2
Tomkinson Ranges *Australia* **93** E4
Tommot *Russia* **53** D13
Tomnop Ta Suos *Cambodia* **65** G5
Tomo ➤ *Colombia* **124** B5
Toms Place *U.S.A.* **110** H8
Toms River *U.S.A.* **115** G10
Tomsk *Russia* **52** D9
Tomtabacken *Sweden* **11** G8
Tona *Spain* **38** D7
Tonalá *Chiapas, Mexico* **119** D6
Tonalá *Jalisco, Mexico* **118** C4
Tonale, Passo del *Italy* **40** B7
Tonantins *Brazil* **124** D5
Tonasket *U.S.A.* **108** B4
Tonawanda *U.S.A.* **114** D6
Tonb *Iran* **71** E7
Tonbridge *U.K.* **15** F8
Tondano *Indonesia* **63** D6
Tondela *Portugal* **36** E2
Tønder *Denmark* **11** K2
Tondi Kiwindi *Niger* **83** C5
Tondibi *Mali* **83** B4
Tondoro *Namibia* **88** B2
Tone ➤ *Australia* **93** F2
Tone-Gawa ➤ *Japan* **55** F9
Tonekābon *Iran* **71** B6
Tong Xian *China* **56** E9
Tong-Yeong *S. Korea* **57** G15

Tôngâ *Sudan* 81 F3
Tonga ■ *Pac. Oc.* 91 c
Tonga Trench *Pac. Oc.* 96 J10
Tongaat *S. Africa* 89 D5
Tong'an *China* 59 E12
Tongareva = Penrhyn
  Cook Is. 97 H12
Tongariro △ *N.Z.* 91 C5
Tongatapu *Tonga* 91 c
Tongatapu Group *Tonga* 91 c
Tongbai *China* 59 A9
Tongcheng *Anhui, China* 59 B11
Tongcheng *Hubei, China* 59 C9
Tongchuan *China* 56 G5
Tongdao *China* 58 D7
Tongeren *Belgium* 17 D5
Tonggu *China* 59 C10
Tongguan *China* 56 G6
Tonghai *China* 58 E4
Tonghua *China* 57 D13
Tongjiang *China* 58 B6
Tongjosŏn Man *N. Korea* 57 E15
Tongking, G. of = Tonkin,
  G. of *Asia* 64 C7
Tongliang *China* 58 C6
Tongliao *China* 57 C12
Tongling *China* 59 B11
Tonglu *China* 59 C12
Tongnan = Anyue *China* 58 B5
Tongobory *Madag.* 89 C7
Tongoy *Chile* 126 C1
Tongren *China* 58 D7
Tongres = Tongeren
  Belgium 17 D5
Tongsa Dzong *Bhutan* 67 F17
Tongshi *China* 64 C7
Tongue *U.K.* 13 C4
Tongue → *U.S.A.* 108 C11
Tongwei *China* 56 G3
Tongxiang *China* 59 B13
Tongxin *China* 56 F4
Tongyang *N. Korea* 57 E14
Tongyu *China* 57 B12
Tongzi *China* 58 C6
Tonj *Sudan* 81 F2
Tonj → *Sudan* 81 F2
Tonk *India* 68 F6
Tonkawa *U.S.A.* 116 C6
Tonkin = Bac Phan *Vietnam* 58 G5
Tonkin, G. of *Asia* 64 C7
Tonle Sap *Cambodia* 64 F5
Tonnay-Charente *France* 20 C3
Tonneins *France* 20 D4
Tonnerre *France* 19 E10
Tönning *Germany* 24 A4
Tono *Japan* 54 E10
Tonopah *U.S.A.* 109 G5
Tonosí *Panama* 120 E3
Tons → *Haryana, India* 68 D7
Tons → *Ut. P., India* 69 F10
Tønsberg *Norway* 9 G14
Tonto △ *U.S.A.* 109 K8
Tonumea *Tonga* 91 c
Tonya *Turkey* 73 B8
Toobanna *Australia* 94 B4
Toodyay *Australia* 93 F2
Tooele *U.S.A.* 108 F7
Toompine *Australia* 95 D3
Toora *Australia* 95 F4
Toora-Khem *Russia* 53 D10
Toowoomba *Australia* 95 D5
Top Springs *Australia* 92 C5
Topalu *Romania* 29 F13
Topaz *U.S.A.* 110 G7
Topeka *U.S.A.* 112 F6
Topl'a → *Slovak Rep.* 27 C14
Topley *Canada* 102 C3
Toplica → *Serbia* 44 C5
Topliţa *Romania* 29 D10
Topocalma, Pta. *Chile* 126 C1
Topock *U.S.A.* 111 L12
Topola *Serbia* 44 B4
Topolčani *Macedonia* 44 E5
Topol'čany *Slovak Rep.* 27 C11
Topolnitsa → *Bulgaria* 45 D8
Topolobampo *Mexico* 118 B3
Topoloveni *Romania* 29 E9
Topolovgrad *Bulgaria* 45 D10
Topolváţu Mare *Romania* 28 E6
Topozero, Ozero *Russia* 8 D25
Toppenish *U.S.A.* 108 C3
Topraisar *Romania* 29 F13
Topusko *Croatia* 41 C12
Torà *Spain* 38 D6
Tora Kit *Sudan* 81 E3
Toraka Vestale *Madag.* 89 B7
Torata *Peru* 124 G4
Torbalı *Turkey* 47 C9
Torbat-e Heydārīyeh *Iran* 71 C8
Torbat-e Jām *Iran* 71 C9
Torbay *Canada* 105 C9
Torbay △ *U.K.* 15 G4
Torbjörntorp *Sweden* 11 F7
Tordesillas *Spain* 36 D6
Töreboda *Sweden* 11 F8
Torekov *Sweden* 11 H6
Torellò *Spain* 38 C7
Toreno *Spain* 36 C4
Torfaen □ *U.K.* 15 F4

Torgau *Germany* 24 D8
Torgelow *Germany* 24 B10
Torhamn *Sweden* 11 H9
Torhout *Belgium* 17 C3
Torhovytsya *Ukraine* 29 B10
Tori *Ethiopia* 81 F3
Tori-Shima *Japan* 55 J10
Torigni-sur-Vire *France* 18 C6
Torija *Spain* 38 E1
Torino *Italy* 40 C4
Torit *Sudan* 81 G3
Torkamān *Iran* 73 D12
Torkovichi *Russia* 32 C6
Tormac *Romania* 28 E6
Tormes → *Spain* 36 D4
Tornado Mt. *Canada* 102 D6
Tornal'a *Slovak Rep.* 27 C13
Torneå = Tornio *Finland* 8 D21
Torneälven → *Europe* 8 D21
Torneträsk *Sweden* 8 B18
Tornio *Finland* 8 D21
Tornionjoki =
  Torneälven → *Europe* 8 D21
Tornquist *Argentina* 126 D3
Toro *Baleares, Spain* 48 B11
Toro *Zamora, Spain* 36 D5
Torö *Sweden* 11 F11
Toro, Cerro del *Chile* 126 B2
Toro △ *Uganda* 86 C3
Toro Pk. *U.S.A.* 111 M10
Törökszentmiklós *Hungary* 28 C5
Toronto *Canada* 114 C5
Toronto *U.S.A.* 114 F4
Toronto Lester B. Pearson
  Int. ✈ (YYZ) *Canada* 114 C5
Toropets *Russia* 32 D6
Tororo *Uganda* 86 B3
Toros Dağları *Turkey* 72 D5
Torpa *India* 69 H11
Torquay *U.K.* 15 G4
Torquemada *Spain* 36 C6
Torrance *U.S.A.* 111 M8
Torrão *Portugal* 37 G2
Torre Annunziata *Italy* 43 B7
Torre de Moncorvo *Portugal* 36 D3
Torre del Campo *Spain* 37 H7
Torre del Greco *Italy* 43 B7
Torre del Mar *Spain* 37 J6
Torre-Pacheco *Spain* 39 H4
Torre Péllice *Italy* 40 D4
Torreblanca *Spain* 38 E5
Torrecampo *Spain* 37 G6
Torrecilla en Cameros *Spain* 38 C2
Torredembarra *Spain* 38 D6
Torredonjimeno *Spain* 37 H7
Torrejón de Ardoz *Spain* 36 E7
Torrejoncillo *Spain* 36 F4
Torrelaguna *Spain* 36 E7
Torrelavega *Spain* 36 B6
Torremaggiore *Italy* 41 G12
Torremolinos *Spain* 37 J6
Torrens, L. *Australia* 95 E2
Torrens Cr. → *Australia* 94 C4
Torrens Creek *Australia* 94 C4
Torrent *Spain* 39 F4
Torrenueva *Spain* 37 G7
Torreón *Mexico* 118 B4
Torreperogil *Spain* 37 G7
Torres *Brazil* 127 B5
Torres *Mexico* 118 B2
Torres Novas *Portugal* 37 F2
Torres Strait *Australia* 90 B7
Torres Vedras *Portugal* 37 F1
Torrevieja *Spain* 39 H4
Torrey *U.S.A.* 108 G8
Torridge → *U.K.* 15 G3
Torridon, L. *U.K.* 13 D3
Torrijos *Spain* 36 F6
Torring *Denmark* 11 J3
Torrington *Conn., U.S.A.* 115 E11
Torrington *Wyo., U.S.A.* 108 E11
Torroella de Montgrí *Spain* 38 C8
Torrox *Spain* 37 J7
Torsås *Sweden* 11 H9
Torsby *Sweden* 10 D6
Torshälla *Sweden* 10 E10
Tórshavn *Færoe Is.* 8 E9
Torslanda *Sweden* 11 G5
Torsö *Sweden* 11 F7
Tortola *Br. Virgin Is.* 121 e
Tórtoles de Esgueva *Spain* 36 D6
Tortolì *Italy* 42 C2
Tortona *Italy* 40 D5
Tortorici *Italy* 43 D7
Tortosa *Spain* 38 E5
Tortosa, C. *Spain* 38 E5
Tortosendo *Portugal* 36 E3
Tortue, Î. de la *Haiti* 121 B5
Tortuguero △ *Costa Rica* 120 D3
Tortum *Turkey* 73 B9
Torūd *Iran* 71 C7
Torul *Turkey* 73 B8
Toruń *Poland* 31 E5
Torun *Ukraine* 29 B8
Tory Hill *Canada* 114 B6
Tory I. *Ireland* 12 A3
Torysa → *Slovak Rep.* 27 C14
Torzhok *Russia* 32 D8
Torzym *Poland* 31 F2

Tosa *Japan* 55 H6
Tosa-Shimizu *Japan* 55 H6
Tosa-Wan *Japan* 55 H6
Toscana □ *Italy* 40 E8
Toscano, Arcipelago *Italy* 40 F7
Toshka *Egypt* 80 C3
Toshka Lakes *Egypt* 80 C3
Toshkent *Uzbekistan* 52 E7
Tosno *Russia* 32 C6
Tossa de Mar *Spain* 38 D7
Tösse *Sweden* 11 F6
Tostado *Argentina* 126 B3
Tostedt *Germany* 24 B5
Tostón, Pta. de *Canary Is.* 48 F5
Tosu *Japan* 55 H5
Tosya *Turkey* 72 B6
Toszek *Poland* 31 H5
Totana *Spain* 39 H3
Totebo *Sweden* 11 G10
Toteng *Botswana* 88 C3
Tôtes *France* 18 C8
Tótkomlós *Hungary* 28 D5
Totma *Russia* 52 D5
Totnes *U.K.* 15 G4
Totness *Suriname* 125 B7
Toto *Nigeria* 83 D6
Totonicapán *Guatemala* 120 D1
Totoya, I. *Fiji* 91 a
Totten Glacier *Antarctica* 5 C8
Tottenham *Australia* 95 E4
Tottenham *Canada* 114 B5
Tottori *Japan* 55 G7
Tottori □ *Japan* 55 G7
Touaret *Niger* 83 A6
Touba *Ivory C.* 82 D3
Touba *Senegal* 82 C1
Toubkal, Djebel *Morocco* 78 B4
Toucy *France* 19 E10
Tougan *Burkina Faso* 82 C4
Touggourt *Algeria* 78 B7
Tougouri *Burkina Faso* 83 C4
Tougué *Guinea* 82 C2
Toukoto *Mali* 82 C3
Toul *France* 19 D12
Toulepleu *Ivory C.* 82 D3
Touliu *Taiwan* 59 F13
Toulon *France* 21 E9
Toulouse *France* 20 E5
Toulouse Blagnac ✈ (TLS)
  France 20 E5
Toummo *Niger* 79 D8
Toumodi *Ivory C.* 82 D3
Tounan *Taiwan* 59 F13
Toungo *Nigeria* 83 D7
Toungoo *Burma* 67 K20
Touques → *France* 18 C7
Touraine *France* 18 E7
Tourcoing *France* 19 B10
Touriñán, C. *Spain* 36 B1
Tournai *Belgium* 17 D3
Tournan-en-Brie *France* 19 D9
Tournay *France* 20 E4
Tournon-St-Martin *France* 18 F7
Tournon-sur-Rhône *France* 21 C8
Tournus *France* 19 F11
Tours *France* 18 E7
Toussoro, Mt. *C.A.R.* 84 C4
Touws → *S. Africa* 88 E3
Touwsrivier *S. Africa* 88 E3
Tovarkovskiy *Russia* 32 F10
Tovste *Ukraine* 29 B10
Tovuz *Azerbaijan* 35 K7
Towada *Japan* 54 D10
Towada-Hachimantai △
  Japan 54 D10
Towada-Ko *Japan* 54 D10
Towanda *U.S.A.* 115 E8
Tower *U.S.A.* 112 B7
Towerhill Cr. → *Australia* 94 C3
Towner *U.S.A.* 112 A3
Townsend *U.S.A.* 108 C8
Townshend I. *Australia* 94 C5
Townsville *Australia* 94 B4
Towraghondī *Afghan.* 66 B3
Towson *U.S.A.* 113 F15
Towuti, Danau *Indonesia* 63 E6
Toya-Ko *Japan* 54 C10
Toyama *Japan* 55 F8
Toyama □ *Japan* 55 F8
Toyama-Wan *Japan* 55 F8
Toyapakeh *Indonesia* 63 K18
Toyohashi *Japan* 55 G8
Toyokawa *Japan* 55 G8
Toyonaka *Japan* 55 G7
Toyooka *Japan* 55 G7
Toyota *Japan* 55 G8
Tozeur *Tunisia* 78 B7
Tqibuli *Georgia* 35 J6
Tqvarcheli *Georgia* 35 J5
Trá Li = Tralee *Ireland* 12 D2
Tra On *Vietnam* 65 H5
Trabancos → *Spain* 36 D5
Traben-Trarbach *Germany* 25 F3
Trabzon *Turkey* 73 B8
Trabzon □ *Turkey* 73 B8
Tracadie *Canada* 105 C7
Tracy *Canada* 104 C5
Tracy *Calif., U.S.A.* 110 H5
Tracy *Minn., U.S.A.* 112 C6

Tradate *Italy* 40 C5
Trade Town *Liberia* 82 D3
Trafalgar, C. *Spain* 37 J4
Tragonhsi *Greece* 47 D7
Traian *Brăila, Romania* 29 E12
Traian *Tulcea, Romania* 29 E13
Trail *Canada* 102 D5
Trainor L. *Canada* 102 A4
Trakai △ *Lithuania* 9 J21
Trákhonas *Cyprus* 49 D12
Tralee *Ireland* 12 D2
Tralee B. *Ireland* 12 D2
Tramore *Ireland* 12 D4
Tramore B. *Ireland* 12 D4
Tramuntana, Serra de *Spain* 48 B9
Tran Ninh, Cao Nguyen
  Laos 64 C4
Tranås *Sweden* 11 F8
Tranbjerg *Denmark* 11 H4
Trancas *Argentina* 126 B2
Trancoso *Portugal* 36 E3
Tranebjerg *Denmark* 11 J4
Tranemo *Sweden* 11 G7
Trang *Thailand* 65 J2
Trangahy *Madag.* 89 B7
Trangan *Indonesia* 63 F8
Trangie *Australia* 95 E4
Trångsviken *Sweden* 10 A7
Trani *Italy* 43 A9
Tranoroa *Madag.* 89 C8
Tranqueras *Uruguay* 127 C4
Transantarctic Mts.
  Antarctica 5 E12
Transcarpathia =
  Zakarpattya □ *Ukraine* 29 B8
Transilvania *Romania* 29 D9
Transilvanian Alps =
  Carpaţii Meridionali
  Romania 29 E9
Transnistria = Stînga
  Nistrului □ *Moldova* 29 C14
Transtrand *Sweden* 10 C7
Transtrandsfjällen *Sweden* 10 C6
Transylvania =
  Transilvania *Romania* 29 D9
Trápani *Italy* 42 D5
Trapper Pk. *U.S.A.* 108 D6
Traralgon *Australia* 95 F4
Trarza □ *Mauritania* 82 B2
Trasacco *Italy* 41 G10
Trăscău, Munţii *Romania* 29 D8
Trasimeno, L. *Italy* 41 E9
Träslövsläge *Sweden* 11 G6
Trasvase Tajo-Segura,
  Canal de *Spain* 38 E2
Trat *Thailand* 65 F4
Tratani → *Pakistan* 68 E3
Traun *Austria* 26 C7
Traunreut *Germany* 25 H8
Traunsee *Austria* 26 D6
Traunstein *Germany* 25 H8
Travellers L. *Australia* 95 E3
Travemünde *Germany* 24 B6
Travers, Mt. *N.Z.* 91 E4
Traverse City *U.S.A.* 113 C11
Travis, L. *U.S.A.* 116 F6
Travnik *Bos.-H.* 28 F2
Trawbreaga B. *Ireland* 12 A4
Trbovlje *Slovenia* 41 B12
Trebišnjica → *Bos.-H.* 44 D2
Trebel → *Germany* 24 B9
Trébeurden *France* 18 D3
Trebević △ *Bos.-H.* 28 G3
Třebíč *Czech Rep.* 26 B8
Trebinje *Bos.-H.* 44 D2
Trebisacce *Italy* 43 C9
Trebišnjica → *Bos.-H.* 44 D2
Trebišov *Slovak Rep.* 27 C14
Trebižat → *Bos.-H.* 41 E14
Trebnje *Slovenia* 41 C12
Třeboň *Czech Rep.* 26 B7
Trebonne *Australia* 94 B4
Třeboňsko △ *Czech Rep.* 26 B7
Trebujena *Spain* 37 J4
Trecate *Italy* 40 C5
Tregaron *U.K.* 15 E4
Tregnago *Italy* 41 C8
Tregrosse Is. *Australia* 94 B5
Tréguier *France* 18 D3
Trégunc *France* 18 E3
Treherne *Canada* 103 D9
Tréia *Italy* 41 E10
Treignac *France* 20 C5
Treinta y Tres *Uruguay* 127 C5
Treis-karden *Germany* 25 E3
Treklyano *Bulgaria* 44 D6
Trelawney *Zimbabwe* 89 B5
Trélazé *France* 18 E6
Trelew *Argentina* 128 E3
Trélissac *France* 20 C4
Trelleborg *Sweden* 11 J7
Tremadog Bay *U.K.* 14 E3
Trémiti *Italy* 41 F12
Tremonton *U.S.A.* 108 F7
Tremp *Spain* 38 C5
Trenche → *Canada* 104 C5
Trenčiansky □ *Slovak Rep.* 27 C11
Trenčín *Slovak Rep.* 27 C11
Trenggalek *Indonesia* 63 H14

Trenque Lauquen *Argentina* 126 D3
Trent → *Canada* 114 B7
Trent → *U.K.* 14 D7
Trentino-Alto Adige □ *Italy* 41 B8
Trento *Italy* 40 B8
Trenton *Canada* 114 B7
Trenton *Mo., U.S.A.* 112 E7
Trenton *N.J., U.S.A.* 115 F10
Trenton *Nebr., U.S.A.* 112 E3
Trepassey *Canada* 105 C9
Trepuzzi *Italy* 43 B11
Tres Arroyos *Argentina* 126 D3
Três Corações *Brazil* 127 A6
Três Lagoas *Brazil* 125 H8
Tres Lomas *Argentina* 126 D3
Tres Montes, C. *Chile* 128 F1
Tres Pinos *U.S.A.* 110 J5
Três Pontas *Brazil* 127 A6
Tres Puentes *Chile* 126 B1
Tres Puntas, C. *Argentina* 128 F3
Três Rios *Brazil* 127 A7
Tres Valles *Mexico* 119 D5
Tresco *U.K.* 15 H1
Treska → *Macedonia* 44 E5
Treskavica *Bos.-H.* 28 G3
Trespaderne *Spain* 36 C7
Tresticklan △ *Sweden* 11 F5
Trets *France* 21 E9
Treuchtlingen *Germany* 25 G6
Treuenbrietzen *Germany* 24 C8
Trevi *Italy* 41 F9
Treviglio *Italy* 40 C6
Trevínca, Peña *Spain* 36 C4
Treviso *Italy* 41 C9
Trévoux *France* 21 C8
Trgovište *Serbia* 44 D6
Triabunna *Australia* 95 G4
Trianda *Greece* 49 C10
Triangle *Zimbabwe* 89 C5
Triaucourt-en-Argonne
  France 19 D12
Tribal Areas □ *Pakistan* 68 C4
Tribsees *Germany* 24 A8
Tribulation, C. *Australia* 94 B4
Tribune *U.S.A.* 112 F3
Tricárico *Italy* 43 B9
Tricase *Italy* 43 C11
Trichinopoly =
  Tiruchchirappalli *India* 66 P11
Trichonida, L. *Greece* 46 C3
Trichur *India* 66 P10
Trida *Australia* 95 E4
Trier *Germany* 25 F2
Trieste *Italy* 41 C10
Trieste, G. di *Italy* 41 C10
Trieux → *France* 18 D3
Triggiano *Italy* 43 A9
Triglav *Slovenia* 41 B10
Triglavski △ *Slovenia* 41 B10
Trigno → *Italy* 41 F11
Trigueros *Spain* 37 H4
Trikala *Greece* 46 B3
Trikala □ *Greece* 46 B3
Trikeri *Greece* 46 B5
Trikomo *Cyprus* 49 D12
Trikora, Puncak *Indonesia* 63 E9
Trilj *Croatia* 41 E13
Trillo *Spain* 38 E2
Trim *Ireland* 12 C5
Trimmu Dam *Pakistan* 68 D5
Trincomalee *Sri Lanka* 66 Q12
Trindade *Brazil* 125 G9
Trindade, I. *Atl. Oc.* 2 F8
Třinec *Czech Rep.* 27 B11
Trinidad *Bolivia* 124 F6
Trinidad *Cuba* 120 B4
Trinidad *Trin. & Tob.* 121 D7
Trinidad *Uruguay* 126 C4
Trinidad *U.S.A.* 109 H11
Trinidad → *Mexico* 119 D5
Trinidad & Tobago ■
  W. Indies 121 D7
Trinitápoli *Italy* 43 A9
Trinity *Canada* 105 C9
Trinity *U.S.A.* 116 F7
Trinity → *Calif., U.S.A.* 108 F2
Trinity → *Tex., U.S.A.* 116 G7
Trinity B. *Canada* 105 C9
Trinity Hills *Trin. & Tob.* 125 K15
Trinity Is. *U.S.A.* 106 a
Trinity Range *U.S.A.* 108 F4
Trinkitat *Sudan* 80 D4
Trino *Italy* 40 C5
Trinway *U.S.A.* 114 F2
Triolet *Mauritius* 85 d
Trionto, C. *Italy* 43 C9
Triora *Italy* 40 D4
Tripoli = Tarābulus *Lebanon* 74 A4
Tripoli = Tarābulus *Libya* 79 B8
Tripoli *Greece* 46 D4
Tripolitania = Tarābulus
  N. Afr. *79 B8*
Tripura □ *India* 67 H18
Tripylos *Cyprus* 49 E11
Trischen *Germany* 24 A4
Tristan da Cunha *Atl. Oc.* 77 K2
Trisul *India* 69 D8
Trivandrum *India* 66 Q10
Trivento *Italy* 41 G11

Trizin *Greece* 46 D5
Trnava *Slovak Rep.* 27 C10
Trnavský □ *Slovak Rep.* 27 C10
Troarn *France* 18 C6
Trochu *Canada* 102 C6
Trodely I. *Canada* 104 B4
Trogir *Croatia* 41 E13
Troglav *Croatia* 41 E13
Tróia *Italy* 43 A8
Troilus, L. *Canada* 104 B5
Troina *Italy* 43 E7
Trois-Pistoles *Canada* 105 C6
Trois-Rivières *Canada* 104 C5
Trois-Rivières *Guadeloupe* 120 b
Troisdorf *Germany* 24 E3
Troitsk *Russia* 52 D7
Troitsko Pechorsk *Russia* 52 C6
Troitskoye *Russia* 35 G7
Trölladyngja *Iceland* 8 D5
Trollhättan *Sweden* 11 F6
Trollheimen *Norway* 8 E13
Trombetas → *Brazil* 125 D7
Tromsø *Norway* 8 B18
Tron *Thailand* 64 D3
Trona *U.S.A.* 111 K9
Tronador, Mte. *Argentina* 128 E2
Trøndelag *Norway* 8 D14
Trondheim *Norway* 8 E14
Trondheimsfjorden *Norway* 8 E14
Trönninge *Sweden* 11 H6
Tronto → *Italy* 41 F10
Troodos *Cyprus* 49 E11
Troon *U.K.* 13 F4
Tropea *Italy* 43 D8
Tropic *U.S.A.* 109 H7
Tropojë *Albania* 44 D4
Trosa *Sweden* 11 F11
Trostan *U.K.* 12 A5
Trostberg *Germany* 25 G8
Trostyanets *Sumy, Ukraine* 33 G8
Trostyanets *Vinnyts'ka,
  Ukraine* 29 B14
Trou Gras Pt. *St. Lucia* 121 f
Trout → *Canada* 102 A5
Trout L. *N.W.T., Canada* 102 A4
Trout L. *Ont., Canada* 103 C10
Trout Lake *Canada* 102 B6
Trout Lake *U.S.A.* 110 E5
Trout River *Canada* 105 C8
Trout Run *U.S.A.* 114 E7
Trouville-sur-Mer *France* 18 C7
Trowbridge *U.K.* 15 F5
Troy *Turkey* 47 B8
Troy *Ala., U.S.A.* 117 F12
Troy *Kans., U.S.A.* 112 F7
Troy *Mo., U.S.A.* 112 F8
Troy *Mont., U.S.A.* 108 B6
Troy *N.Y., U.S.A.* 115 D11
Troy *Ohio, U.S.A.* 113 E11
Troy *Pa., U.S.A.* 115 E8
Troyan *Bulgaria* 45 D8
Troyes *France* 19 D11
Trpanj *Croatia* 41 E14
Trstenik *Serbia* 44 C5
Trubchevsk *Russia* 33 F7
Truchas Pk. *U.S.A.* 109 J11
Trucial States = United
  Arab Emirates ■ *Asia* 71 F7
Truckee *U.S.A.* 110 F6
Trudfront *Russia* 35 H8
Trudovoye *Russia* 54 C6
Trujillo *Honduras* 120 C2
Trujillo *Peru* 124 E3
Trujillo *Spain* 37 F5
Trujillo *U.S.A.* 109 J11
Trujillo *Venezuela* 124 B4
Truk *Micronesia* 96 G7
Trumann *U.S.A.* 117 D9
Trumansburg *U.S.A.* 115 D8
Trumbull, Mt. *U.S.A.* 109 H7
Trŭn *Bulgaria* 44 D6
Trun *France* 18 D7
Trundle *Australia* 95 E4
Trung-Phan = Annam
  Vietnam 64 E7
Truro *Canada* 105 C7
Truro *U.K.* 15 G2
Truskavets *Ukraine* 23 D12
Trŭstenik *Bulgaria* 45 C8
Trustrup *Denmark* 11 H4
Trutch *Canada* 102 B4
Truth or Consequences
  U.S.A. 109 K10
Trutnov *Czech Rep.* 26 A8
Truyère → *France* 20 D6
Tryavna *Bulgaria* 45 D9
Tryonville *U.S.A.* 114 E5
Trzcianka *Poland* 31 E3
Trzciel *Poland* 31 F2
Trzcińsko Zdrój *Poland* 31 F1
Trzebiatów *Poland* 30 D2
Trzebiez *Poland* 30 E1
Trzebnica *Poland* 31 G4
Trzemeszno *Poland* 31 F4
Tržič *Slovenia* 41 B11
Tsagan Aman *Russia* 35 G8
Tsamandas *Greece* 46 B2
Tsandi *Namibia* 88 B1
Tsaratanana *Madag.* 89 B8

Tsaratanana, Mt. de = Maromokotro *Madag.* **89** A8
Tsaratanana △ *Madag.* **89** A8
Tsarevo *Bulgaria* **45** D9
Tsaritsani *Greece* **46** B4
Tsau *Botswana* **88** C3
Tsavo *Kenya* **86** C4
Tsavo East △ *Kenya* **86** C4
Tsavo West △ *Kenya* **86** C4
Tsebrykove *Ukraine* **33** J6
Tsentralnyy □ *Russia* **34** D4
Tses *Namibia* **88** D2
Tsetserleg *Mongolia* **60** B5
Tsévié *Togo* **83** D5
Tshabong *Botswana* **88** D3
Tshane *Botswana* **88** C3
Tshela *Dem. Rep. of the Congo* **84** E2
Tshesebe *Botswana* **89** C4
Tshibeke
Dem. Rep. of the Congo **86** C2
Tshibinda
Dem. Rep. of the Congo **86** C2
Tshikapa
Dem. Rep. of the Congo **84** F4
Tshilenge
Dem. Rep. of the Congo **86** D1
Tshinsenda
Dem. Rep. of the Congo **87** E2
Tshofa *Dem. Rep. of the Congo* **86** D2
Tshwane = Pretoria *S. Africa* **89** D4
Tshwane *Botswana* **88** C3
Tsigara *Botswana* **88** C4
Tsihombe *Madag.* **89** D8
Tsiigehtchic *Canada* **100** C6
Ts'il-os △ *Canada* **102** C4
Tsimlyansk *Russia* **35** G6
Tsimlyansk Res. =
Tsimlyanskoye Vdkhr.
Russia **35** F6
Tsimlyanskoye Vdkhr.
Russia **35** F6
Tsinan = Jinan *China* **56** F9
Tsineng *S. Africa* **88** D3
Tsinghai = Qinghai □ *China* **60** C4
Tsingtao = Qingdao *China* **57** F11
Tsingy de Bemaraha △
Madag. **89** B8
Tsingy de Namoroka △
Madag. **89** B8
Tsinjoarivo *Madag.* **89** B8
Tsinjomitondraka *Madag.* **89** B8
Tsirigo = Kythira *Greece* **46** E5
Tsiroanomandidy *Madag.* **89** B8
Tsiteli-Tsqaro *Georgia* **35** K8
Tsitondroina *Madag.* **89** C8
Tsitsikamma △ *S. Africa* **88** E3
Tsivilsk *Russia* **34** C8
Tsivory *Madag.* **89** C8
Tskhinvali *Georgia* **35** J7
Tsna → *Russia* **34** C6
Tsnori *Georgia* **35** K7
Tso Moriri, L. *India* **69** C8
Tsobis *Namibia* **88** B2
Tsodilo Hill *Botswana* **88** B3
Tsogttsetsiy = Baruunsuu
Mongolia **56** C3
Tsolo *S. Africa* **89** E4
Tsomo *S. Africa* **89** E4
Tsu *Japan* **55** G8
Tsu L. *Canada* **102** A6
Tsuchiura *Japan* **55** F10
Tsuen Wan *China* **59** F10
Tsugaru-Kaikyō *Japan* **54** D10
Tsumeb *Namibia* **88** B2
Tsumis *Namibia* **88** C2
Tsuruga *Japan* **55** G8
Tsurugi-San *Japan* **55** H7
Tsuruoka *Japan* **54** E9
Tsushima *Gifu, Japan* **55** G8
Tsushima *Nagasaki, Japan* **55** G4
Tsuyama *Japan* **55** G7
Tsvetkovo *Ukraine* **33** H6
Tsyelyakhany *Belarus* **23** B13
Tua → *Portugal* **36** D3
Tual *Indonesia* **63** F8
Tualatin *U.S.A.* **110** E4
Tuam *Ireland* **12** C3
Tuamotu, Îs.
French Polynesia **97** J13
Tuamotu Arch. =
Tuamotu, Îs.
French Polynesia **97** J13
Tuamotu Ridge *Pac. Oc.* **97** K14
Tuan Giao *Vietnam* **64** B4
Tuanfeng *China* **59** B10
Tuanxi *China* **58** D6
Tuao *Phil.* **61** C4
Tuapse *Russia* **35** H4
Tuas *Singapore* **65** d
Tuatapere *N.Z.* **91** G1
Tuba City *U.S.A.* **109** H8
Tuban *Indonesia* **63** G15
Tubani *Botswana* **88** C4
Tubarão *Brazil* **127** B6
Tūbās *West Bank* **74** C4
Tubas → *Namibia* **88** C2
Tübingen *Germany* **25** G5
Tubou *Fiji* **91** a
Tubruq *Libya* **79** B10

Tubuaï, Îs. *French Polynesia* **97** K13
Tuc Trung *Vietnam* **65** G6
Tucacas *Venezuela* **124** A5
Tu'ch'ang *Taiwan* **59** E13
Tuchitua *Canada* **102** A3
Tuchodi → *Canada* **102** B4
Tuchola *Poland* **30** E4
Tuchów *Poland* **31** J8
Tuckanarra *Australia* **93** E2
Tucson *U.S.A.* **109** K8
Tucumán □ *Argentina* **126** B2
Tucumcari *U.S.A.* **109** J12
Tucupita *Venezuela* **124** B6
Tucuruí *Brazil* **125** D9
Tucuruí, Represa de *Brazil* **125** D9
Tuczno *Poland* **31** E3
Tudela *Spain* **38** C3
Tudmur *Syria* **73** E8
Tudor, L. *Canada* **105** A6
Tudora *Romania* **29** C11
Tuella → *Portugal* **36** D3
Tufanbeyli *Turkey* **72** C7
Tugela → *S. Africa* **89** D5
Tuguegarao *Phil.* **61** C4
Tugur *Russia* **53** D14
Tui *Spain* **36** C2
Tuineje *Canary Is.* **48** F5
Tukangbesi, Kepulauan
Indonesia **63** F6
Tukarak I. *Canada* **104** A4
Tukayyid *Iraq* **70** D5
Tûkh *Egypt* **80** H7
Tukhlya *Ukraine* **29** B8
Tukobo *Ghana* **82** D4
Tuktoyaktuk *Canada* **100** C6
Tukums *Latvia* **30** B10
Tukums □ *Latvia* **30** B10
Tukuyu *Tanzania* **87** D3
Tula *Hidalgo, Mexico* **119** C5
Tula *Tamaulipas, Mexico* **119** C5
Tula *Nigeria* **83** D7
Tula *Russia* **32** E9
Tula □ *Russia* **32** F9
Tulancingo *Mexico* **119** C5
Tulare *Serbia* **44** D5
Tulare *U.S.A.* **110** J7
Tulare Lake Bed *U.S.A.* **110** K7
Tularosa *U.S.A.* **109** K10
Tulbagh *S. Africa* **88** E2
Tulcán *Ecuador* **124** C3
Tulcea *Romania* **29** E13
Tulcea □ *Romania* **29** E13
Tulchyn *Ukraine* **29** B11
Tüledi Araldary *Kazakhstan* **35** H10
Tüleh *Iran* **71** C7
Tulemalu L. *Canada* **103** A9
Tulgheş *Romania* **29** D10
Tuli *Zimbabwe* **87** G2
Tulia *U.S.A.* **116** D4
Tuliszków *Poland* **31** F5
Tulita *Canada* **100** C7
Ṭūlkarm *West Bank* **74** C4
Tulla *Ireland* **12** D3
Tullahoma *U.S.A.* **117** D11
Tullamore *Australia* **95** E4
Tullamore *Ireland* **12** C4
Tulle *France* **20** C5
Tulln *Austria* **26** C9
Tullow *Ireland* **12** D5
Tullus *Sudan* **81** E1
Tully *Australia* **94** B4
Tully *U.S.A.* **115** D8
Tulnici *Romania* **29** E11
Tulovo *Bulgaria* **45** D9
Tulsa *U.S.A.* **116** C7
Tulsequah *Canada* **102** B2
Tulu Milki *Ethiopia* **81** F4
Tulu Welel *Ethiopia* **81** F3
Tuluá *Colombia* **124** C3
Tuluceşti *Romania* **29** E13
Tulun *Russia* **53** D11
Tulungagung *Indonesia* **63** H14
Tuma *Russia* **32** E11
Tuma → *Nic.* **120** D3
Tumacacori △ *U.S.A.* **109** L8
Tumaco *Colombia* **124** C3
Tumatumari *Guyana* **124** B7
Tumba *Sweden* **10** E11
Tumba, L.
Dem. Rep. of the Congo **84** E3
Tumbarumba *Australia* **95** F4
Tumbaya *Argentina* **126** A2
Tumbes *Peru* **124** D2
Tumbler Ridge *Canada* **102** B4
Tumbur *Sudan* **81** G3
Tumbwe
Dem. Rep. of the Congo **87** E2
Tumby Bay *Australia* **95** E2
Tumd Youqi *China* **56** D6
Tumen *China* **54** C4
Tumen Jiang → *China* **57** C16
Tumeremo *Venezuela* **124** B6
Tumkur *India* **66** N10
Tump *Pakistan* **66** F3
Tumpat *Malaysia* **65** J4
Tumu *Ghana* **82** C4
Tumucumaque, Serra
Brazil **125** C8
Tumut *Australia* **95** F4

Tumwater *U.S.A.* **110** C4
Tuna *India* **68** H4
Tunadal *Sweden* **10** B11
Tunapuna *Trin. & Tob.* **125** K15
Tunas de Zaza *Cuba* **120** B4
Tunbridge Wells = Royal
Tunbridge Wells *U.K.* **15** F8
Tunçbilek *Turkey* **47** B11
Tunceli *Turkey* **73** C8
Tunceli □ *Turkey* **73** C8
Tuncurry *Australia* **95** E5
Tundla *India* **68** F8
Tundubai *Sudan* **80** D2
Tunduru *Tanzania* **87** E4
Tundzha → *Bulgaria* **45** E10
Tungabhadra → *India* **66** M11
Tungaru *Sudan* **81** E3
Tungla *Nic.* **120** D3
Tungsha Tao = Dongsha
Dao → *China* **59** G11
Tungshih *Taiwan* **59** E13
Tungsten *Canada* **102** A3
Tunguska, Nizhnyaya →
Russia **53** C9
Tunguska,
Podkamennaya →
Russia **53** C10
Tunica *U.S.A.* **117** D9
Tunis *Tunisia* **78** A7
Tunis ✈ (TUN) *Tunisia* **42** F3
Tunisia ■ *Africa* **79** A7
Tunja *Colombia* **124** B4
Tunkhannock *U.S.A.* **115** E9
Tunliu *China* **56** F7
Tunnel Creek △ *Australia* **92** C4
Tunnsjøen *Norway* **8** D15
Tunø *Denmark* **11** J4
Tunungayualok I. *Canada* **105** A7
Tunuyán *Argentina* **126** C2
Tunuyán → *Argentina* **126** C2
Tuo Jiang → *China* **58** C5
Tuolumne *U.S.A.* **110** H6
Tuolumne → *U.S.A.* **110** H5
Tūp Āghāj *Iran* **73** D12
Tupã *Brazil* **127** A5
Tupelo *U.S.A.* **117** D10
Tupik *Russia* **53** D12
Tupinambarana, Ilha
Brazil **124** D7
Tupiza *Bolivia* **126** A2
Tupižnica *Serbia* **44** C6
Tupman *U.S.A.* **111** K7
Tupper *Canada* **102** B4
Tupper L. *U.S.A.* **115** B10
Tupper Lake *U.S.A.* **115** B10
Tüpqarghan Muyis
Kazakhstan **35** H10
Tupungato, Cerro *S. Amer.* **126** C2
Tuquan *China* **57** B11
Túquerres *Colombia* **124** C3
Tura *Russia* **53** C11
Turabah *Ḥā'il, Si. Arabia* **70** D4
Turabah *Makkah, Si. Arabia* **80** C5
Ṭūrān *Iran* **71** C8
Turan *Russia* **53** D10
Ṭurayf *Si. Arabia* **70** D3
Turbacz *Poland* **31** J7
Turbe *Bos.-H.* **28** F2
Türän *Iran* **71** C8
Turčianske Teplice
Slovak Rep. **27** C11
Turcoaia *Romania* **29** E13
Turda *Romania* **29** D8
Turek *Poland* **31** F5
Turén *Venezuela* **124** B5
Turfan = Turpan *China* **60** B3
Turgeon → *Canada* **104** C4
Tŭrgovishte *Bulgaria* **45** C10
Turgut *Turkey* **47** D10
Turgutlu *Turkey* **47** C9
Turgwe → *Zimbabwe* **89** C5
Turhal *Turkey* **72** B7
Turia → *Spain* **39** F4
Turiaçu *Brazil* **125** D9
Turiaçu → *Brazil* **125** D9
Turiec → *Slovak Rep.* **27** B11
Turin = Torino *Italy* **40** C4
Turka *Ukraine* **31** J10
Turkana, L. *Africa* **86** B4
Türkeli *Turkey* **45** F11
Turkestan = Türkistan
Kazakhstan **52** E7
Túrkeve *Hungary* **28** C5
Turkey ■ *Eurasia* **72** C7
Turkey Creek = Warmun
Australia **92** C4
Turki *Russia* **34** D6
Türkistan *Kazakhstan* **52** E7
Türkmenabat *Turkmenistan* **71** B9
Türkmenbashi *Turkmenistan* **71** A7
Turkmenistan ■ *Asia* **52** F6
Türkmenli *Turkey* **47** B8
Türkoğlu *Turkey* **72** D7
Twofold B. *Australia* **95** F4
Turks Island Passage
W. Indies **121** B5
Turku *Finland* **32** B2
Turkwel → *Kenya* **86** B4
Turlock *U.S.A.* **110** H6
Turnagain → *Canada* **102** B3
Turnagain, C. *N.Z.* **91** D6

Turneffe Is. *Belize* **119** D7
Turner *U.S.A.* **108** B9
Turner Pt. *Australia* **94** A1
Turner Valley *Canada* **102** C6
Turners Falls *U.S.A.* **115** D12
Turnhout *Belgium* **17** C4
Türnitz *Austria* **26** D8
Turnor L. *Canada* **103** B7
Turnov *Czech Rep.* **26** A8
Tŭrnovo = Veliko Tŭrnovo
Bulgaria **45** C9
Turnu Măgurele *Romania* **29** G9
Turnu Roşu, P. *Romania* **29** E9
Turobin *Poland* **31** H9
Turpan *China* **60** B3
Turrës, Kala e *Albania* **44** E3
Turriff *U.K.* **13** D6
Tursāq *Iraq* **73** F11
Tursi *Italy* **43** B9
Turtle Head I. *Australia* **94** A3
Turtle Is. *S. Leone* **82** D2
Turtle L. *Canada* **112** B3
Turtle Lake *U.S.A.* **112** B3
Turtleford *Canada* **103** C7
Turuépano △ *Venezuela* **121** D7
Turukhansk *Russia* **53** C9
Turzovka *Slovak Rep.* **27** B11
Tuscaloosa *U.S.A.* **117** E11
Tuscánia *Italy* **41** F8
Tuscany = Toscana □ *Italy* **40** E8
Tuscarawas → *U.S.A.* **114** F3
Tuscarora Mt. *U.S.A.* **114** F7
Tuscola *Ill., U.S.A.* **112** F9
Tuscola *Tex., U.S.A.* **116** E5
Tuscumbia *U.S.A.* **117** D11
Tuskegee *U.S.A.* **117** E12
Tuszyn *Poland* **31** G6
Tutak *Turkey* **73** C10
Tutayev *Russia* **32** D10
Tuticorin *India* **66** Q11
Tutin *Serbia* **44** D4
Tutóia *Brazil* **125** D10
Tutong *Brunei* **62** D4
Tutova → *Romania* **29** D12
Tutrakan *Bulgaria* **45** B10
Tuttle Creek L. *U.S.A.* **112** F5
Tuttlingen *Germany* **25** H4
Tutuala *E. Timor* **63** F7
Tutuila *Amer. Samoa* **91** b
Tutume *Botswana* **85** J5
Tutun *Egypt* **80** J7
Tuva □ *Russia* **53** D10
Tuvalu ■ *Pac. Oc.* **90** B10
Tuvuca *Fiji* **91** a
Tuxer Alpen *Austria* **26** D4
Tuxpan *Mexico* **119** C5
Tuxtla Gutiérrez *Mexico* **119** D6
Tuy = Tui *Spain* **36** C2
Tuy An *Vietnam* **64** F7
Tuy Duc *Vietnam* **65** F6
Tuy Hoa *Vietnam* **64** F7
Tuy Phong *Vietnam* **65** G7
Tuya L. *Canada* **102** B2
Tuyen Hoa *Vietnam* **64** D6
Tuyen Quang *Vietnam* **58** G5
Tūysarkān *Iran* **73** E13
Tuz Gölü *Turkey* **72** C5
Ṭūz Khurmātū *Iraq* **73** E11
Tuzi *Montenegro* **44** D3
Tuzigoot △ *U.S.A.* **109** J7
Tuzla *Bos.-H.* **28** F3
Tuzlov → *Russia* **33** J10
Tuzluca *Turkey* **73** B10
Tuzly *Ukraine* **29** E15
Tvååker *Sweden* **11** G6
Tvardiţa *Moldova* **29** D13
Tver *Russia* **32** D8
Tver □ *Russia* **32** D8
Tvrdošin *Slovak Rep.* **27** B12
Tvrdošovce *Slovak Rep.* **27** C11
Twain *U.S.A.* **110** E5
Twain Harte *U.S.A.* **110** G6
Twardogóra *Poland* **31** G4
Tweed → *Canada* **114** B7
Tweed → *U.K.* **13** F6
Tweed Heads *Australia* **95** D5
Tweedsmuir △ *Canada* **102** C3
Twentynine Palms *U.S.A.* **111** L10
Twillingate *Canada* **105** C9
Twin Bridges *U.S.A.* **108** C7
Twin Falls *Canada* **105** B7
Twin Falls *U.S.A.* **108** E6
Twin Valley *U.S.A.* **112** B5
Twinsburg *U.S.A.* **114** E3
Twistringen *Germany* **24** C4
Twitchell Res. *U.S.A.* **111** L6
Two Harbors *U.S.A.* **112** B8
Two Hills *Canada* **102** C6
Two Rivers *U.S.A.* **112** C10
Two Rocks *Australia* **93** F2
Twofold B. *Australia* **95** F4
Tyachiv *Ukraine* **23** D12
Tychy *Poland* **31** H5
Tyczyn *Poland* **31** J9
Tykocin *Poland* **31** E9
Tyler *Minn., U.S.A.* **112** C5
Tyler *Tex., U.S.A.* **116** E7
Tyligul → *Ukraine* **33** J6

Tymanivka *Ukraine* **29** B13
Týn nad Vltavou *Czech Rep.* **26** B7
Tynda *Russia* **53** D13
Tyndall *U.S.A.* **112** D5
Tyne → *Australia* **95** F3
Tyne → *U.K.* **14** C6
Tyne & Wear □ *U.K.* **14** B6
Tynemouth *U.K.* **14** B6
Tyre = Şūr *Lebanon* **74** B4
Tyresta → *Sweden* **11** F11
Tyringe *Sweden* **11** H7
Tyrnyauz *Russia* **35** J6
Tyrol = Tirol □ *Austria* **26** D3
Tyrone *U.S.A.* **114** F6
Tyrone □ *U.K.* **12** B4
Tyrrell → *Australia* **95** F3
Tyrrell, L. *Australia* **95** F3
Tyrrell L. *Canada* **103** A7
Tyrrhenian Sea *Medit. S.* **6** G8
Tysfjorden *Norway* **8** B17
Tysmenytsya *Ukraine* **29** B9
Tystberga *Sweden* **11** F11
Tytuvénai *Lithuania* **30** C10
Tyub Karagan, Mys =
Tüpqarghan Muyis
Kazakhstan **35** H10
Tyulenii, Ostrova = Tüledi
Araldary *Kazakhstan* **35** H10
Tyuleniy *Russia* **35** H8
Tyuleniy, Mys *Azerbaijan* **35** K10
Tyumen *Russia* **52** D7
Tywi → *U.K.* **15** F3
Tywyn *U.K.* **15** E3
Tzaneen *S. Africa* **89** C5
Tzermiado *Greece* **49** D7
Tzoumérka, Óros =
Athamanon Oros *Greece* **46** B3
Tzukong = Zigong *China* **58** C5

U

U.S.A. = United States of
America ■ *N. Amer.* **106** C7
U.S. Virgin Is. ☑ *W. Indies* **121** e
Uanle Uen = Wanleweyne
Somali Rep. **75** G3
Uatumã → *Brazil* **124** D7
Uaupés *Brazil* **124** D5
Uaupés → *Brazil* **124** C5
Uaxactún *Guatemala* **120** C2
Ub *Serbia* **44** B4
Ubá *Brazil* **127** A7
Uba *Nigeria* **83** D7
Ubaitaba *Brazil* **125** F11
Ubangi = Oubangi →
Dem. Rep. of the Congo **84** E3
Ubauro *Pakistan* **68** E3
Ubaye → *France* **21** D10
Ubayyiḍ, W. → *Iraq* **73** F10
Ube *Japan* **55** H5
Úbeda *Spain* **37** G7
Uberaba *Brazil* **125** G9
Uberlândia *Brazil* **125** G9
Überlingen *Germany* **25** H5
Ubiaja *Nigeria* **83** D6
Ubin, Pulau *Singapore* **65** d
Ubly *U.S.A.* **114** C2
Ubolratna Res. *Thailand* **64** D4
Ubombo *S. Africa* **89** D5
Ubon Ratchathani *Thailand* **64** E5
Ubondo *Dem. Rep. of the Congo* **86** C2
Ubort → *Belarus* **23** B15
Ubrique *Spain* **37** J5
Ubud *Indonesia* **63** J18
Ubundu
Dem. Rep. of the Congo **86** C2
Ucar *Azerbaijan* **73** B12
Ucayali → *Peru* **124** D4
Uchab *Namibia* **88** B2
Uchiura-Wan *Japan* **54** C10
Uchquduq *Uzbekistan* **52** E7
Uchte *Germany* **24** C4
Uchur → *Russia* **53** D14
Uckermark *Germany* **24** B9
Ucluelet *Canada* **102** D3
Uda → *Russia* **53** D14
Udachnyy *Russia* **53** C12
Udagamandalam *India* **66** P10
Udainagar *India* **68** H7
Udaipur *India* **68** G5
Udaipur Garhi *Nepal* **69** F12
Udala *India* **69** J12
Udbina *Croatia* **41** D12
Uddeholm *Sweden* **10** D7
Uddevalla *Sweden* **11** F5
Uddjaure *Sweden* **8** D17
Uden *Neths.* **17** C5
Udgir *India* **66** K10
Udhampur *India* **69** C6
Udi *Nigeria* **83** D6
Údine *Italy* **41** B10
Udintsev Fracture Zone
S. Ocean **5** B13
Udmurtia □ *Russia* **52** D6
Udon Thani *Thailand* **64** D4
Udong *Cambodia* **65** G5
Udskaya Guba *Russia* **53** D14
Udu Pt. *Fiji* **91** a
Udupi *India* **66** N9
Udvoy Balkan *Bulgaria* **45** D10
Udzungwa △ *Tanzania* **87** D4
Udzungwa Range *Tanzania* **87** D4
Ueckermünde *Germany* **24** B10
Ueda *Japan* **55** F9
Uele → *Dem. Rep. of the Congo* **84** D4
Uelen *Russia* **53** C19
Uelzen *Germany* **24** C6
Uetersen *Germany* **24** B5
Uetze *Germany* **24** C6
Ufa *Russia* **52** D6
Uffenheim *Germany* **25** F6
Ugab → *Namibia* **88** C1
Ugalla → *Tanzania* **86** D3
Ugalla River △ *Tanzania* **86** D3
Uganda ■ *Africa* **86** B3
Ugento *Italy* **43** C11
Ugep *Nigeria* **83** D6
Ughelli *Nigeria* **83** D6
Ugie → *S. Africa* **89** E4
Ugíjar *Spain* **37** J7
Ugine *France* **21** C10
Uglegorsk *Russia* **53** E15
Uglich *Russia* **32** D10
Ugljan *Croatia* **41** D12
Ugljane *Croatia* **41** E13
Ugolnye Kopi *Russia* **53** C18
Ugra → *Russia* **32** E9
Uğurchin *Bulgaria* **45** C8
Uh → *Slovak Rep.* **27** C15
Uherské Hradiště *Czech Rep.* **27** B10
Uherský Brod *Czech Rep.* **27** B10
Úhlava → *Czech Rep.* **26** B6
Uhlenhorst *Namibia* **88** C2
Uhniv *Ukraine* **31** H10
Uhrichsville *U.S.A.* **114** F3
Uíbhist a Deas = South
Uist *U.K.* **13** D1
Uíbhist a Tuath = North
Uist *U.K.* **13** D1
Uig *U.K.* **13** D2
Uíge *Angola* **84** F2
Uiha *Tonga* **91** c
Uijeongbu *S. Korea* **57** F14
Ŭiju *N. Korea* **57** D13
Uinta Mts. *U.S.A.* **108** F8
Uis *Namibia* **88** C1
Uiseong *S. Korea* **57** F15
Uitenhage *S. Africa* **88** E4
Uithuizen *Neths.* **17** A6
Ujazd *Poland* **31** H5
Újfehértó *Hungary* **28** C6
Ujh → *India* **68** C6
Ujhani *India* **69** F8
Uji-guntō *Japan* **55** J4
Ujjain *India* **68** H6
Ujście *Poland* **31** E3
Újszász *Hungary* **28** C5
Ujung Pandang *Indonesia* **63** F5
Uka *Russia* **53** D17
Ukara I. *Tanzania* **86** C3
Uke-Shima *Japan* **55** K4
Ukerewe I. *Tanzania* **86** C3
Ukholovo *Russia* **34** D5
Ukhrul *India* **67** G19
Ukhta *Russia* **52** C6
Ukiah *U.S.A.* **110** G2
Ukmergė *Lithuania* **32** E3
Ukraine ■ *Europe* **33** H7
Ukwi *Botswana* **88** C3
Ula *Turkey* **72** D3
Ulaan-Uul *Mongolia* **56** B5
Ulaanbaatar *Mongolia* **53** E11
Ulaangom *Mongolia* **60** A4
Ulaanjirem *Mongolia* **56** C6
Ulamba *Dem. Rep. of the Congo* **87** D1
Ulan Bator = Ulaanbaatar
Mongolia **53** E11
Ulan Erge *Russia* **35** G7
Ulan Khol *Russia* **35** H8
Ulan Ude *Russia* **53** D11
Ulanów *Poland* **31** H9
Ulaş *Sivas, Turkey* **72** C7
Ulaş *Tekirdağ, Turkey* **45** E11
Ulaya *Morogoro, Tanzania* **86** D4
Ulaya *Tabora, Tanzania* **86** C3
Ulcinj *Montenegro* **44** E3
Ulco *S. Africa* **88** D3
Ule älv = Oulujoki →
Finland **8** D21
Ule träsk = Oulujärvi
Finland **8** D22
Uleåborg = Oulu *Finland* **8** D21
Ulefoss *Norway* **9** G13
Ulëz *Albania* **44** E3
Ulfborg *Denmark* **11** H2
Ulhasnagar *India* **66** K8
Uliastay *Mongolia* **60** B4
Uljin *S. Korea* **57** F15
Uljma *Serbia* **28** E6
Ulla → *Spain* **36** C2
Ulladulla *Australia* **95** F5
Ullapool *U.K.* **13** D3
Ullared *Sweden* **11** G6

Ulldecona *Spain* 38 E5
Ulleungdo *S. Korea* 55 F5
Ullswater *Canada* 114 A5
Ullswater *U.K.* 14 C5
Ulm *Germany* 25 G5
Ulmarra *Australia* 95 D5
Ulmeni *Buzău, Romania* 29 E11
Ulmeni *Maramureș, Romania* 29 C8
Ulonguè *Mozam.* 87 E3
Ulricehamn *Sweden* 11 G7
Ulrika *Sweden* 11 F9
Ulsan *S. Korea* 57 G15
Ulsta *U.K.* 13 A7
Ulster □ *U.K.* 12 B5
Ulstrem *Bulgaria* 45 D10
Ulubat Gölü *Turkey* 45 F12
Ulubey *Turkey* 47 C11
Uluborlu *Turkey* 47 C12
Uluçinar *Turkey* 72 D6
Uludağ *Turkey* 45 F13
Uludağ △ *Turkey* 45 F13
Uludere *Turkey* 73 D10
Uluguru Mts. *Tanzania* 86 D4
Ulukışla *Turkey* 72 D6
Ulungur He ➔ *China* 60 B3
Uluru *Australia* 93 E5
Uluru-Kata Tjuta △ *Australia* 93 E5
Ulutau *Kazakhstan* 52 E7
Uluwatu *Indonesia* 63 K18
Ulva *U.K.* 13 E2
Ulverstone *Australia* 95 G4
Ulverston *U.K.* 14 C4
Ulya *Russia* 53 D15
Ulyanovo *Russia* 30 D9
Ulyanovsk *Russia* 34 C9
Ulyanovsk □ *Russia* 34 C9
Ulyasutay = Uliastay *Mongolia* 60 B4
Ulysses *Kans., U.S.A.* 112 G3
Ulysses *Pa., U.S.A.* 115
Ulysses, Mt. *Canada* 102 B4
Umag *Croatia* 41 C10
Umala *Bolivia* 124 G5
'Umān = Oman ■ *Asia* 75 C6
Uman *Ukraine* 23 D16
Umaria *India* 69 H9
Umarkot *Pakistan* 68 G3
Umarpada *India* 68 J5
Umatilla *U.S.A.* 108 D4
Umba *Russia* 8 B10
Umbagog L. *U.S.A.* 115 B13
Umbakumba *Australia* 94 A2
Umbértide *Italy* 41 E9
Umbrella Mts. *N.Z.* 91 F2
Umbria □ *Italy* 41 F9
Umeå *Sweden* 8 E19
Umeälven ➔ *Sweden* 8 E19
Umera *Indonesia* 63 E7
Umfuli ➔ *Zimbabwe* 87 F2
Umfurudzi △ *Zimbabwe* 87 F3
Umgusa *Zimbabwe* 87 F2
Umgwenya ➔ *Mozam.* 89 D5
Umiujaq *Canada* 104 A4
Umka *Serbia* 44 B4
Umkomaas *S. Africa* 89 E5
Umlazi *S. Africa* 85 L6
Umm ad Daraj, J. *Jordan* 74 C4
Umm al Khashab *Si. Arabia* 80 D5
Umm al Qaywayn *U.A.E.* 71 E7
Umm al Qittayn *Jordan* 74 C5
Umm Arda *Sudan* 81 D3
Umm Bāb *Qatar* 71 E6
Umm Badr *Sudan* 81 E2
Umm Baiyud *Sudan* 81 E3
Umm Bel *Sudan* 81 E2
Umm Birkah *Si. Arabia* 80 B4
Umm Boim *Sudan* 81 E2
Umm Dam *Sudan* 81 E3
Umm Debi *Sudan* 81 E3
Umm Durman = Omdurmân *Sudan* 81 D3
Umm el Fahm *Israel* 74 C4
Umm Gafala *Sudan* 81 E2
Umm Gimala *Sudan* 81 E2
Umm Inderaba *Sudan* 80 D3
Umm Keddada *Sudan* 81 E2
Umm Koweika *Sudan* 81 E3
Umm Lajj *Si. Arabia* 70 E3
Umm Merwa *Sudan* 80 D3
Umm Qantur *Sudan* 81 E3
Umm Qasr *Iraq* 70 D5
Umm Qurein *Sudan* 81 E2
Umm Ruwaba *Sudan* 81 E3
Umm Saiyala *Sudan* 81 E3
Umm Shanqa *Sudan* 81 E2
Umm Shutur *Sudan* 81 E3
Umm Sidr *Sudan* 81 E2
Umm Urūmah *Si. Arabia* 80 B4
Umm Zehetir *Egypt* 80 J8
Umnak I. *U.S.A.* 106 a
Umniati ➔ *Zimbabwe* 87 F2
Umpqua ➔ *U.S.A.* 108 E1
Umreth *India* 68 H5
Umtata = Mthatha *S. Africa* 89 E4
Umuarama *Brazil* 127 A5

Umvukwe Ra. *Zimbabwe* 87 F3
Umzimvubu *S. Africa* 89 E4
Umzingwane ➔ *Zimbabwe* 87 G2
Umzinto = eMuziwezinto *S. Africa* 89 E5
Una *India* 68 J4
Una ➔ *Bos.-H.* 41 D13
Unac ➔ *Bos.-H.* 41 D13
Unadilla *U.S.A.* 115 D9
Unalakleet *U.S.A.* 106 a
Unalaska *U.S.A.* 106 a
Unalaska I. *U.S.A.* 106 a
Ur *Iraq* 70 D5
Urad Qianqi *China* 56 D5
Urakawa *Japan* 54 C11
Ural = Uralskiy □ *Russia* 52 C7
Ural = Zhayyq ➔ *Kazakhstan* 6 F16
Ural *Australia* 95 E4
Ural Mts. = Uralskie Gory *Eurasia* 6 C17
Uralla *Australia* 95 E5
Uralsk = Oral *Kazakhstan* 34 E10
Uralskie Gory *Eurasia* 6 C17
Uralskiy □ *Russia* 52 C7
Urambo *Tanzania* 86 D3
Urandangi *Australia* 94 C2
Urandi *Brazil*
Uncastillo *Spain* 38 C3
Uncía *Bolivia* 124 G5
Uncompahgre Peak *U.S.A.* 108 G10
Uncompahgre Plateau *U.S.A.* 108 G9
Unden *Sweden* 11 F8
Underbool *Australia* 95 F3
Undersaker *Sweden* 10 A7
Underwood *Canada* 114 B3
Unecha *Russia* 33 F7
Ungarie *Australia* 95 E4
Ungarra *Australia* 95 E2
Ungava, Pén. d' *Canada* 101 D12
Ungava B. *Canada* 101 D13
Ungeny = Ungheni *Moldova* 29 C12
Unggi *N. Korea* 57 C16
Ungheni *Moldova* 29 C12
Unguala ➔ *Ethiopia* 81 F5
Ungwana B. *Kenya* 86 C5
Ungwatiri *Sudan* 81 D4
Uni *Russia* 34 B10
União da Vitória *Brazil* 127 B5
Uničov *Czech Rep.* 27 B10
Uniejów *Poland* 31 G5
Unije *Croatia* 41 D11
Unimak I. *U.S.A.* 106 a
Union *Miss., U.S.A.* 117 E10
Union *Mo., U.S.A.* 112 F8
Union *S.C., U.S.A.* 117 D14
Union City *Calif., U.S.A.* 110 H4
Union City *N.J., U.S.A.* 115 F10
Union City *Pa., U.S.A.* 114 E5
Union City *Tenn., U.S.A.* 117 C10
Union Dale *U.S.A.* 115 E9
Union Gap *U.S.A.* 108 C3
Union Springs *Ala., U.S.A.* 117 E12
Union Springs *N.Y., U.S.A.* 115 D8
Uniondale *S. Africa* 88 E3
Uniontown *U.S.A.* 113 F14
Unionville *U.S.A.* 112 E7
Unirea *Romania* 29 F12
United Arab Emirates ■ *Asia* 71 F7
United Kingdom ■ *Europe* 16 E6
United States of America ■ *N. Amer.* 106 C7
Unity *Canada* 103 C7
Universales, Mtes. *Spain* 38 E3
University Park *U.S.A.* 109 K10
University Place *U.S.A.* 110 C4
Unjha *India* 68 H5
Unna *Germany* 24 D3
Unnao *India* 69 F9
Uno, Ilha *Guinea-Biss.* 82 C1
Unsengedsi ➔ *Zimbabwe* 87 F3
Unst *U.K.* 13 A8
Unstrut ➔ *Germany* 24 D7
Unterfranken □ *Germany* 25 F5
Unterschleissheim *Germany* 25 G7
Unuk ➔ *Canada* 102 B2
Ünye *Turkey* 72 B7
Unzen-Amakusa △ *Japan* 55 H5
Unzha *Russia* 34 A7
Unzha ➔ *Russia* 34 B6
Uozu *Japan* 55 F8
Upata *Venezuela* 124 B6
Upemba, L. *Dem. Rep. of the Congo* 87 D2
Upemba △ *Dem. Rep. of the Congo* 87 D2
Upernavik *Greenland* 4 B5
Upington *S. Africa* 88 D3
Upleta *India* 68 J4
'Upolu *Samoa* 91 b
Upper □ *Ghana* 83 C4
Upper Alkali L. *U.S.A.* 108 F3
Upper Arrow L. *Canada* 102 C5
Upper Darby *U.S.A.* 113 F16
Upper Foster L. *Canada* 103 B7
Upper Hutt *N.Z.* 91 D5
Upper Klamath L. *U.S.A.* 108 E3
Upper Lake *U.S.A.* 110 F4
Upper Liard *Canada* 102 A3
Upper Manzanilla *Trin. & Tob.* 125 K15
Upper Missouri Breaks △ *U.S.A.* 108 C9
Upper Musquodoboit *Canada* 105 C7
Upper Red L. *U.S.A.* 112 A6
Upper Sandusky *U.S.A.* 113 E12
Upper Volta = Burkina Faso ■ *Africa* 82 C4

Upphärad *Sweden* 11 F6
Uppland *Sweden* 10 D12
Upplands-Väsby *Sweden* 10 E11
Uppsala *Sweden* 10 E11
Uppsala län □ *Sweden* 10 D11
Upshi *India* 69 C7
Upstart, C. *Australia* 94 B4
Upton *U.S.A.* 108 D11
Uqsuqtuuq = Gjoa Haven *Canada* 100 C10
Urad Qianqi *China* 56 D5
Urakawa *Japan* 54 C11
Ural = Uralskiy □ *Russia* 52 C7
Urbana *Ill., U.S.A.* 112 E9
Urbana *Ohio, U.S.A.* 113 E12
Urbandale *U.S.A.* 112 E7
Urbánia *Italy* 41 E9
Urbel ➔ *Spain* 36 C7
Urbino *Italy* 41 E9
Urbión, Picos de *Spain* 38 C2
Urcos *Peru* 124 F4
Urdinarrain *Argentina* 126 C4
Urdos *France* 20 F3
Ure ➔ *U.K.* 14 C6
Uren *Russia* 34 B7
Urengoy *Russia* 52 C8
Ures *Mexico* 118 B2
Urewera △ *N.Z.* 91 C6
Urfa = Sanliurfa *Turkey* 73 D8
Urganch *Uzbekistan* 52 E7
Urgench = Urganch *Uzbekistan* 52 E7
Urgüp *Turkey* 72 C6
Uri *India* 69 B6
Uri □ *Switz.* 25 J4
Uribia *Colombia* 124 A4
Uricani *Romania* 28 E8
Uriondo *Bolivia* 126 A3
Urique *Mexico* 118 B3
Urique ➔ *Mexico* 118 B3
Urk *Neths.* 17 B5
Urkiola △ *Spain* 38 B3
Urla *Turkey* 47 C8
Urlați *Romania* 29 F11
Urmia = Orūmīyeh *Iran* 73 D11
Uroševac *Serbia* 44 D5
Uroyan, Montanas de *Puerto Rico* 121 d
Urshult *Sweden* 11 H8
Uruaçu *Brazil* 125 F9
Uruapan *Mexico* 118 D4
Urubamba ➔ *Peru* 124 F4
Urucará *Brazil* 124 D7
Uruçuí *Brazil* 125 E10
Uruguai ➔ *Brazil* 127 B5
Uruguaiana *Brazil* 126 B4
Uruguay ■ *S. Amer.* 126 C4
Uruguay ➔ *S. Amer.* 126 C4
Urumchi = Ürümqi *China* 52 E9
Ürümqi *China* 52 E9
Urup ➔ *Russia* 35 H5
Urup, Ostrov *Russia* 53 E16
Uryupinsk *Russia* 34 E5
Ürzhar *Kazakhstan* 52 E9
Urzhum *Russia* 34 B9
Urziceni *Romania* 29 F11
Usa ➔ *Russia* 52 C6
Uşak *Turkey* 47 C11
Uşak □ *Turkey* 47 C11
Usakos *Namibia* 88 C2
Ušće *Serbia* 44 C4
Usedom *Germany* 24 B10
Usedom *Germany* 24 B10
Useless Loop *Australia* 93 E1
'Usfān *Si. Arabia* 80 C4
Ushakova, Ostrov *Russia* 53 A8
Ushakovo *Russia* 30 D7
Ushant = Ouessant, Î. d' *France* 18 D1
Ushashi *Tanzania* 86 C3
Ushat *Sudan* 81 F2
'Ushayrah *Ar Riyāḍ, Si. Arabia* 70 E5
'Ushayrah *Makkah, Si. Arabia* 80 C5
Ushibuka *Japan* 55 H5
Ushuaia *Argentina* 128 G3
Ushumun *Russia* 53 D13
Ushytsya ➔ *Ukraine* 29 B12
Usinsk *Russia* 52 C6
Usk ➔ *Canada* 102 C3

Usk ➔ *U.K.* 15 F5
Uska *India* 69 F10
Üsküdar *Turkey* 45 F13
Uslar *Germany* 24 D5
Usman *Russia* 33 F10
Usoke *Tanzania* 86 D3
Usolye-Sibirskoye *Russia* 53 D11
Usoro *Nigeria* 83 D6
Uspallata, P. de *Argentina* 126 C2
Ussel *France* 20 C6
Usson-du-Poitou *France* 20 B4
Ussuriysk *Russia* 54 C5
Ussurka *Russia* 54 B6
Ust-Buzulukskaya *Russia* 34 E6
Ust-Chaun *Russia* 53 C18
Ust-Chorna *Ukraine* 29 B8
Ust-Ilimsk *Russia* 53 D11
Ust-Ishim *Russia* 52 D8
Ust-Kamchatsk *Russia* 53 D17
Ust-Kamenogorsk = Öskemen *Kazakhstan* 52 E9
Ust-Khayryuzovo *Russia* 53 D16
Ust-Kut *Russia* 53 D11
Ust-Kuyga *Russia* 53 B14
Ust-Labinsk *Russia* 35 H4
Ust-Luga *Russia* 32 C5
Ust-Maya *Russia* 53 C14
Ust-Mil *Russia* 53 D14
Ust-Nera *Russia* 53 C15
Ust-Nyukzha *Russia* 53 D13
Ust-Olenek *Russia* 53 B12
Ust-Omchug *Russia* 53 C15
Ust-Port *Russia* 52 C9
Ust-Tsilma *Russia* 52 C9
Ust-Urt = Ustyurt Plateau *Asia* 52 E6
Ustaritz *France* 20 E2
Ustecký □ *Czech Rep.* 26 A7
Uster *Switz.* 25 H4
Ústí nad Labem *Czech Rep.* 26 A7
Ústí nad Orlicí *Czech Rep.* 27 B9
Ústica *Italy* 42 D6
Ustinov = Izhevsk *Russia* 52 D6
Ustka *Poland* 30 D3
Ustroń *Poland* 31 J5
Ustrzyki Dolne *Poland* 31 J9
Ustyuzhna *Russia* 32 C9
Ustyurt Plateau *Asia* 52 E6
Usu *China* 60 B3
Usuki *Japan* 55 H5
Usulután *El Salv.* 120 D2
Usumacinta ➔ *Mexico* 119 D6
Usumbura = Bujumbura *Burundi* 86 C2
Usure *Tanzania* 86 C3
Usutuo ➔ *Mozam.* 89 D5
Uta *Indonesia* 63 E9
Utah □ *U.S.A.* 108 G8
Utah L. *U.S.A.* 108 F8
Utansjö *Sweden* 11 E11
Utara, Selat *Malaysia* 65 c
Utarni *India* 68 F4
Utatlan *Guatemala* 120 C1
Ute Creek ➔ *U.S.A.* 109 J12
Utebo *Spain* 38 D3
Utena *Lithuania* 32 E7
Utete *Tanzania* 86 D4
Uthai Thani *Thailand* 64 E3
Uthal *Pakistan* 68 G2
Utiariti *Brazil* 124 F7
Utica *N.Y., U.S.A.* 115 C9
Utica *Ohio, U.S.A.* 114 F2
Utiel *Spain* 39 F3
Utikuma L. *Canada* 102 B5
Utila *Honduras* 120 C2
Utö *Sweden* 10 F12
Utopia *Australia* 94 C1
Utraula *India* 69 F10
Utrecht *Neths.* 17 B5
Utrecht *S. Africa* 89 D5
Utrecht □ *Neths.* 17 B5
Utrera *Spain* 37 H5
Utsjoki ➔ *Finland* 8 B22
Utsunomiya *Japan* 55 F9
Uttar Pradesh □ *India* 69 F9
Uttaradit *Thailand* 64 D3
Uttarakhand □ *India* 69 D8
Utterson *Canada* 114 A5
Uttoxeter *U.K.* 14 E6
Utuado *Puerto Rico* 121 d

Uwajima *Japan* 55 H6
Uwanda △ *Tanzania* 86 D3
Uweinat, Jebel *Sudan* 80 C1
Uxbridge *Canada* 114 B5
Uxin Qi *China* 56 E5
Uxmal *Mexico* 119 C7
Üydzin *Mongolia* 56 B4
Uyo *Nigeria* 83 D6
Üyüklü Tepe *Turkey* 47 D9
Uyûn Mûsa *Egypt* 74 F1
Uyuni *Bolivia* 124 H5
Uzbekistan ■ *Asia* 52 E7
Uzboy ➔ *Turkmenistan* 71 B7
Uzen, Bolshoi = Uzen, Mal ➔ *Kazakhstan* 35 F9
Uzen, Mal ➔ *Kazakhstan* 35 F9
Uzerche *France* 20 C5
Uzès *France* 21 D8
Uzh ➔ *Ukraine* 23 C16
Uzhgorod = Uzhhorod *Ukraine* 28 B7
Uzhhorod *Ukraine* 28 B7
Uzhok *Ukraine* 28 B7
Užice *Serbia* 44 C3
Uzlovaya *Russia* 32 F10
Üzümlü *Turkey* 47 E11
Uzunköprü *Turkey* 45 E10
Uzunkuyu *Turkey* 47 C8

V

Vaal ➔ *S. Africa* 88 D3
Vaal Dam *S. Africa* 89 D4
Vaalbos △ *S. Africa* 88 D3
Vaalwater *S. Africa* 89 C4
Vaasa *Finland* 8 E19
Vabre *France* 20 E6
Vacaria *Brazil* 127 B5
Vacata *Fiji* 91 a
Vacaville *U.S.A.* 110 G5
Vaccarès, Étang de *France* 21 E8
Vach = Vakh ➔ *Russia* 52 C8
Vache, Î. à *Haiti* 121 C5
Väckelsång *Sweden* 11 H8
Vacoas *Mauritius* 85 d
Väddö *Sweden* 10 D12
Vadnagar *India* 68 H5
Vado Lígure *Italy* 40 D5
Vadodara *India* 68 H5
Vadsø *Norway* 8 A23
Vadstena *Sweden* 11 F8
Vaduz *Liech.* 25 H5
Værøy *Norway* 8 C15
Vágar *Færoe Is.* 8 E9
Vaggeryd *Sweden* 11 G8
Vaghia *Greece* 46 C5
Vagia, Akra *Greece* 49 C10
Vagney *France* 19 D13
Vagnhärad *Sweden* 11 F11
Vagos *Portugal* 36 E2
Vågsfjorden *Norway* 8 B17
Váh ➔ *Slovak Rep.* 27 D11
Vahsel B. *Antarctica* 5 D1
Váhtjer = Gällivare *Sweden* 8 C19
Vaï *Greece* 49 D8
Vaiges *France* 18 D6
Vaihingen *Germany* 25 G4
Vaihiria, L. *Tahiti* 91 d
Vail *U.S.A.* 106 C5
Vailly-sur-Aisne *France* 19 C10
Vairao *Tahiti* 91 d
Vaisali ➔ *India* 69 F9
Vaison-la-Romaine *France* 21 D9
Vaitogi *Amer. Samoa* 91 b
Vakarel *Bulgaria* 44 D7
Vakfikebir *Turkey* 73 B8
Vakh ➔ *Russia* 52 C8
Vakhtan *Russia* 34 B8
Vál *Hungary* 28 C3
Val-de-Marne □ *France* 19 D9
Val-d'Isère *France* 21 C10
Val-d'Oise □ *France* 19 C9
Val-d'Or *Canada* 104 C4
Val Grande △ *Italy* 40 D5
Val Marie *Canada* 103 D7
Val Thorens *France* 21 C10
Valaam *Russia* 32 B6
Valadares *Portugal* 36 D2
Valahia *Romania* 29 F9
Valais □ *Switz.* 25 J3
Valais, Alpes du *Switz.* 25 J3
Valandovo *Macedonia* 44 E6
Valašské Meziříčí *Czech Rep.* 27 B10
Valatie *U.S.A.* 115 D11
Valaxa *Greece* 46 C6
Vålberg *Sweden* 10 E7
Valbo *Sweden* 10 D10
Valbondione *Italy* 40 B7
Vălcani *Romania* 28 D5
Vâlcea □ *Romania* 29 F9
Valcheta *Argentina* 128 E3
Valdagno *Italy* 41 C8
Valdahon *France* 19 E13
Valdai Hills = Valdayskaya Vozvyshennost *Russia* 32 D7
Valday *Russia* 32 D7

Valdayskaya Vozvyshennost *Russia* 32 D7
Valdeazogues ➔ *Spain* 37 G6
Valdecañas, Embalse de *Spain* 36 F5
Valdemarsvik *Sweden* 11 F10
Valdemoro *Spain* 36 E7
Valdepeñas *Spain* 37 G7
Valderaduey ➔ *Spain* 36 D5
Valdérice *Italy* 42 E5
Valderrobres *Spain* 38 E5
Valdés, Pen. *Argentina* 128 E4
Valdez *U.S.A.* 106 a
Valdivia *Chile* 128 D2
Valdivia Abyssal Plain *S. Ocean* 5 C6
Valdobbiádene *Italy* 41 C8
Valdosta *U.S.A.* 117 F13
Valdoviño *Spain* 36 B2
Valdres *Norway* 8 F13
Vale *Georgia* 35 K6
Vale *U.S.A.* 108 E5
Vale of Glamorgan □ *U.K.* 15 F4
Valea lui Mihai *Romania* 28 C7
Valea Mărului *Romania* 29 E12
Valemount *Canada* 102 C5
Valença *Brazil* 125 F11
Valença *Portugal* 36 C2
Valença do Piauí *Brazil* 125 E10
Valençay *France* 19 E8
Valence *France* 21 D8
Valence d'Agen *France* 20 D4
Valencia *Phil.* 61 H6
Valencia *Spain* 39 F4
Valencia *Trin. & Tob.* 125 K15
Valencia *Venezuela* 124 A5
Valencia □ *Spain* 39 F4
Valencia, G. de *Spain* 39 F5
Valencia de Alcántara *Spain* 37 F3
Valencia de Don Juan *Spain* 36 C5
Valencia I. *Ireland* 12 E1
Valenciennes *France* 19 B10
Văleni *Romania* 29 F9
Vălenii de Munte *Romania* 29 E11
Valensole *France* 21 E9
Valentigney *France* 19 E13
Valentim, Sa. do *Brazil* 125 E10
Valentin *Russia* 54 C7
Valentine *Nebr., U.S.A.* 112 D3
Valentine *Tex., U.S.A.* 116 F2
Valenza *Italy* 40 C5
Valera *Venezuela* 124 B4
Valga *Estonia* 32 D4
Valguarnera Caropepe *Italy* 43 E7
Valier *U.S.A.* 108 B7
Valinco, G. de *France* 21 G12
Valjevo *Serbia* 44 B3
Valka *Latvia* 32 D3
Valkeakoski *Finland* 32 B2
Valkenswaard *Neths.* 17 C5
Vall de Uxó = La Vall d'Uixó *Spain* 38 F4
Valla *Sweden* 10 E10
Valladolid *Mexico* 119 C7
Valladolid *Spain* 36 D6
Valladolid □ *Spain* 36 D6
Vallata *Italy* 43 A8
Valldemossa *Spain* 48 B9
Valle d'Aosta □ *Italy* 40 C4
Valle de Aran *Spain* 38 C5
Valle de la Pascua *Venezuela* 124 B5
Valle de las Palmas *Mexico* 111 N10
Valle de Santiago *Mexico* 118 C4
Valle de Zaragoza *Mexico* 118 B3
Valle del Ticino △ *Italy* 40 C6
Valle Fértil, Sierra del *Argentina* 126 C2
Valle Gran Rey *Canary Is.* 48 F2
Valle Hermoso *Mexico* 119 B5
Valle Nacional *Mexico* 119 D5
Valledupar *Colombia* 124 A4
Vallehermoso *Canary Is.* 48 F2
Vallejo *U.S.A.* 110 G4
Vallenar *Chile* 126 B1
Vallentuna *Sweden* 10 E12
Valleraugue *France* 20 D7
Vallet *France* 18 E5
Valletta *Malta* 49 D2
Valley Center *U.S.A.* 111 M9
Valley City *U.S.A.* 112 B5
Valley Falls *Oreg., U.S.A.* 108 E3
Valley Falls *R.I., U.S.A.* 115 E13
Valley of Flowers △ *India* 69 D8
Valley of the Kings *Egypt* 80 B3
Valley Springs *U.S.A.* 110 G6
Valley View *U.S.A.* 115 F8
Valley Wells *U.S.A.* 111 K11
Valleyview *Canada* 102 B5
Valli di Comácchio *Italy* 41 D9
Vallimanca, Arroyo ➔ *Argentina* 126 D4
Vallo della Lucánia *Italy* 43 B8
Vallon-Pont-d'Arc *France* 21 D8
Vallorbe *Switz.* 25 J2
Valls *Spain* 38 D6
Valmaseda = Balmaseda *Spain* 38 B1

Valmiera *Latvia* **32** D3
Valnera *Spain* **36** B7
Valognes *France* **18** C5
Valona = Vlorë *Albania* **44** F3
Valongo *Portugal* **36** D2
Valozhyn *Belarus* **23** A14
Valpaçcos *Portugal* **36** D3
Valparaíso *Chile* **126** C1
Valparaíso *Mexico* **118** C4
Valparaiso *U.S.A.* **112** E10
Valparaíso □ *Chile* **126** C1
Valpovo *Croatia* **28** E3
Valréas *France* **21** D9
Vals *Switz.* **25** J5
Vals → *S. Africa* **88** D4
Vals, Tanjung *Indonesia* **63** F9
Vals-les-Bains *France* **21** D8
Valsad *India* **66** J8
Valtellina *Italy* **40** B6
Valuyki *Russia* **33** G10
Valverde *Canary Is.* **48** G2
Valverde del Camino *Spain* **37** H4
Valverde del Fresno *Spain* **36** E4
Vama *Romania* **29** C10
Vamdrup *Denmark* **11** J3
Våmhus *Sweden* **10** C8
Vammala *Finland* **32** B2
Vamos *Greece* **49** D6
Van *Turkey* **73** C10
Van □ *Turkey* **73** C10
Van, L. = Van Gölü *Turkey* **73** C10
Van Alstyne *U.S.A.* **116** E6
Van Blommestein Meer
  Suriname **125** C7
Van Buren *Canada* **105** C6
Van Buren *Ark., U.S.A.* **116** D7
Van Buren *Maine, U.S.A.* **113** B20
Van Buren *Mo., U.S.A.* **112** G8
Van Canh *Vietnam* **64** F7
Van Diemen, C. *N. Terr.,*
  Australia **92** B5
Van Diemen, C. *Queens.,*
  Australia **94** B2
Van Diemen G. *Australia* **92** B5
Van Gölü *Turkey* **73** C10
Van Horn *U.S.A.* **116** F2
Van Ninh *Vietnam* **64** F7
Van Rees, Pegunungan
  Indonesia **63** E9
Van Wert *U.S.A.* **113** E11
Van Yen *Vietnam* **58** G5
Vanadzor *Armenia* **35** K7
Vanavara *Russia* **53** C11
Vancouver *Canada* **110** A3
Vancouver *U.S.A.* **110** E4
Vancouver, C. *Australia* **93** G2
Vancouver I. *Canada* **110** B2
Vancouver Int. ✈ (YVR)
  Canada **110** A3
Vanda = Vantaa *Finland* **32** B3
Vandalia *Ill., U.S.A.* **112** F9
Vandalia *Mo., U.S.A.* **112** F8
Vandenberg Village *U.S.A.* **111** L6
Vanderbijlpark *S. Africa* **89** D4
Vandergrift *U.S.A.* **114** F5
Vanderhoof *Canada* **102** C4
Vanderkloof Dam *S. Africa* **88** E3
Vanderlin I. *Australia* **94** B2
Vänern *Sweden* **11** F7
Vänersborg *Sweden* **11** F6
Vang Vieng *Laos* **64** C4
Vanga *Kenya* **86** C4
Vangaindrano *Madag.* **89** C8
Vanguard *Canada* **103** D7
Vanino *Russia* **53** E15
Vânju Mare *Romania* **28** F7
Vankleek Hill *Canada* **115** A10
Vännäs *Sweden* **8** E18
Vannes *France* **18** E4
Vannøya *Norway* **8** A18
Vanoise, Massif de la *France*
  21 C10
Vanrhynsdorp *S. Africa* **88** E2
Vansbro *Sweden* **10** D8
Vansittart B. *Australia* **92** B4
Vantaa *Finland* **32** B3
Vanua Balavu *Fiji* **91** a
Vanua Levu *Fiji* **91** a
Vanua Vatu *Fiji* **91** a
Vanuatu ■ *Pac. Oc.* **90** C9
Vanwyksvlei *S. Africa* **88** E3
Vanzylsrus *S. Africa* **88** D3
Vapnyarka *Ukraine* **29** B13
Var □ *France* **21** E10
Var → *France* **21** E11
Vara *Sweden* **11** F6
Varades *France* **18** E5
Varáita → *Italy* **40** D4
Varallo *Italy* **40** C5
Varāmīn *Iran* **71** C6
Varāmīn □ *Iran* **71** B6
Varanasi *India* **69** G10
Varangerfjorden *Norway* **8** A23
Varangerhalvøya *Norway* **8** A23
Varano, Lago di *Italy* **41** G12
Varaždin *Croatia* **41** B13
Varazze *Italy* **40** D5
Varberg *Sweden* **11** G6

Vardak □ *Afghan.* **66** B6
Vardar = Axios → *Greece* **44** F6
Varde *Denmark* **11** J2
Varde Å → *Denmark* **11** J2
Vardenis *Armenia* **35** K7
Vardø *Norway* **8** A24
Varel *Germany* **24** B4
Varella, Mui *Vietnam* **64** F7
Varèna *Lithuania* **32** E3
Vareš *Bos.-H.* **28** F3
Varese *Italy* **40** C5
Vårfurile *Romania* **28** D7
Varginha *Brazil* **127** A6
Vargön *Sweden* **11** F6
Varillas *Chile* **126** A1
Varkaus *Finland* **32** A4
Värmdölandet *Sweden* **10** E12
Värmeln *Sweden* **10** E6
Värmlands län □ *Sweden* **10** E6
Värmlandsbro *Sweden* **10** E7
Varna *Bulgaria* **45** C11
Varna □ *Bulgaria* **45** C11
Värnamo *Sweden* **11** G8
Varnsdorf *Czech Rep.* **26** A7
Varolles *France* **21** D10
Vars *Canada* **115** A9
Vars *France* **21** D10
Varto *Turkey* **73** C9
Varvarin *Serbia* **44** C5
Varysburg *U.S.A.* **114** D6
Varzaneh *Iran* **71** C7
Varzi *Italy* **40** D6
Varzaqān *Iran* **73** C12
Varzo *Italy* **40** B5
Varzy *France* **19** E10
Vas □ *Hungary* **28** C1
Vasa = Vaasa *Finland* **8** E19
Vasa Barris → *Brazil* **125** F11
Vásárosnamény *Hungary* **28** B7
Vascão → *Portugal* **37** H3
Vaşcău *Romania* **28** D7
Vascongadas = País
  Vasco □ *Spain* **38** C2
Vashkivtsi *Ukraine* **29** B10
Vasht = Khāsh *Iran* **71** D9
Vasilevichi *Belarus* **23** B15
Vasiliki *Greece* **46** C2
Vasiliko *Greece* **46** C2
Vasilkov = Vasylkiv
  Ukraine **23** C16
Vaslui *Romania* **29** D12
Vaslui □ *Romania* **29** D12
Väsman *Sweden* **10** D9
Vassar *Canada* **103** D9
Vassar *U.S.A.* **113** D12
Västerås *Sweden* **10** E10
Västerbotten *Sweden* **8** D19
Västerdalälven → *Sweden* **10** D8
Västergötland *Sweden* **11** F7
Västerhaninge *Sweden* **10** E12
Västervik *Sweden* **11** G10
Västmanland *Sweden* **9** G17
Västmanlands län □
  Sweden **10** E10
Vasto *Italy* **41** F11
Västra Götalands Län □
  Sweden **11** F6
Vasvár *Hungary* **28** C1
Vasylivka *Ukraine* **29** E13
Vasylkiv *Ukraine* **23** C16
Vatan *France* **19** E8
Vatersay *U.K.* **13** E1
Vathia *Greece* **46** E4
Vati *Greece* **49** C9
Vatican City ■ *Europe* **41** G9
Vaticano, C. *Italy* **43** D8
Vatili *Cyprus* **49** D12
Vatin *Serbia* **28** E6
Vatiu = Atiu *Cook Is.* **97** J12
Vatnajökull *Iceland* **8** D5
Vatolakkos *Greece* **49** D5
Vatoloha *Madag.* **89** B8
Vatomandry *Madag.* **89** B8
Vatra-Dornei *Romania* **29** C10
Vatrak → *India* **68** H5
Vättern *Sweden* **11** F8
Vatu Vara *Fiji* **91** a
Vatulele *Fiji* **91** a
Vaucluse □ *France* **21** E9
Vaucouleurs *France* **19** D12
Vaud □ *Switz.* **25** J2
Vaudreuil-Dorion *Canada* **115** A10
Vaughn *Mont., U.S.A.* **108** C8
Vaughn *N. Mex., U.S.A.* **109** J11
Vaujours L. *Canada* **104** A5
Vaupés = Uaupés → *Brazil* **124** C5
Vaupés □ *Colombia* **124** C4
Vauvert *France* **21** E8
Vauxhall *Canada* **102** C6
Vav *India* **68** G4
Vavatenina *Madag.* **89** B8
Vava'u *Tonga* **91** c
Vava'u Group *Tonga* **91** c
Vavoua *Ivory C.* **82** D3
Vawkavysk *Belarus* **23** B13

Vaxholm *Sweden* **10** E12
Växjö *Sweden* **11** H8
Våxtorp *Sweden* **11** H7
Vaygach, Ostrov *Russia* **52** C7
Veaikevárri =
  Svappavaara *Sweden* **8** C19
Vechelde *Germany* **24** C6
Vechta *Germany* **24** C4
Vechte → *Neths.* **17** B6
Vecsés *Hungary* **28** C4
Veddige *Sweden* **11** G6
Vedea → *Romania* **29** G10
Vedi *Armenia* **73** C11
Vedia *Romania* **29** F9
Vedrette di Ries-Aurina ◯
  Italy **41** B9
Vedum *Sweden* **11** F7
Veendam *Neths.* **17** A6
Veenendaal *Neths.* **17** B5
Vefsna → *Norway* **8** D15
Vega *Norway* **8** D14
Vega *U.S.A.* **116** D3
Vega Baja *Puerto Rico* **121** d
Vegadeo *Spain* **36** B3
Vegoritida, L. *Greece* **44** F5
Vegreville *Canada* **102** C6
Veinge *Sweden* **11** H7
Veisiejai *Lithuania* **30** D10
Vejbystrand *Sweden* **11** H6
Vejen *Denmark* **11** J3
Vejer de la Frontera *Spain* **37** J5
Vejle *Denmark* **11** J3
Vejle Fjord *Denmark* **11** J3
Vela Luka *Croatia* **41** F13
Velas, C. *Costa Rica* **120** D2
Velasco, Sierra de *Argentina* **126** B2
Velay, Mts. du *France* **20** D7
Velbert *Germany* **24** D3
Velddrif *S. Africa* **88** E2
Velebit ◯ *Croatia* **41** D12
Velebit Planina *Croatia* **41** D12
Velebitski Kanal *Croatia* **41** D11
Veleka → *Bulgaria* **45** D11
Velence *Italy* **40** E4
Velencei-tó *Hungary* **28** C3
Velenje *Slovenia* **41** B12
Veles *Macedonia* **44** E5
Velestino *Greece* **46** B4
Vélez-Málaga *Spain* **37** J6
Vélez Rubio *Spain* **39** H2
Velhas → *Brazil* **125** G10
Velika *Croatia* **28** E2
Velika Gorica *Croatia* **41** C13
Velika Kapela *Croatia* **41** C12
Velika Kladuša *Bos.-H.* **41** C12
Velika Kruša *Serbia* **44** D4
Velika Morava → *Serbia* **44** B5
Velika Plana *Serbia* **44** B5
Velikaya → *Russia* **32** D5
Velikaya Kema *Russia* **54** B8
Velikaya Lepetikha *Ukraine* **33** J7
Veliké Kapušany
  Slovak Rep. **27** C15
Velike Lašče *Slovenia* **41** C11
Veliki Jastrebac *Serbia* **44** C5
Veliki Kanal *Serbia* **28** E4
Veliki Popović *Serbia* **44** B5
Velikiye Luki *Russia* **32** D6
Veliko Gradište *Serbia* **44** B5
Veliko Tŭrnovo *Bulgaria* **45** C9
Velikonda Range *India* **66** M11
Vélingara *Kolda, Senegal* **82** C2
Vélingara *Louga, Senegal* **82** B2
Velingrad *Bulgaria* **44** D7
Velino, Mte. *Italy* **41** F10
Velizh *Russia* **32** E6
Velké Karlovice *Czech Rep.* **27** B11
Velké Meziříčí *Czech Rep.* **26** B9
Vel'ký Javorník *Slovak Rep.* **27** B11
Vel'ký Krtíš *Slovak Rep.* **27** C12
Vel'ký Meder *Slovak Rep.* **27** D10
Vel'ký Tríbeč *Slovak Rep.* **27** C11
Velletri *Italy* **42** A5
Vellinge *Sweden* **11** J6
Vellmar *Germany* **24** D5
Vellore *India* **66** N11
Velopoula *Greece* **46** E5
Velsen *Neths.* **17** B6
Velsk *Russia* **32** B11
Velten *Germany* **24** C9
Veluwezoom △ *Neths.* **17** B6
Velva *U.S.A.* **112** A4
Velvendos *Greece* **44** F6
Velyka Mykhaylivka
  Ukraine **29** C14
Velyki Luchky *Ukraine* **28** B7
Velykyy Berezny *Ukraine* **28** B7
Velykyy Bychkiv *Ukraine* **29** C9
Vemb *Denmark* **11** H2
Vemdalen *Sweden* **10** B7
Ven *Sweden* **11** J6
Venado *Mexico* **118** C4
Venado Tuerto *Argentina* **126** C3
Venafro *Italy* **43** A7
Venaria *Italy* **40** C4
Venaco *France* **21** F13
Venarey-les-Laumes *France* **19** E11
Venaría *Italy* **40** C4
Venčane *Serbia* **44** B4
Vence *France* **21** E11
Vendas Novas *Portugal* **37** G2

Vendée □ *France* **18** F5
Vendée → *France* **18** F5
Vendéen, Bocage *France* **20** B2
Vendeuvre-sur-Barse
  France **19** D11
Vendôme *France* **18** E8
Vendrell = El Vendrell *Spain* **38** D6
Vendsyssel *Denmark* **11** G4
Vendychany *Ukraine* **29** B12
Venelles *France* **21** E9
Véneta, L. *Italy* **41** C9
Venézia *Italy* **41** C9
Venézia, G. di *Italy* **41** C10
Véneto □ *Italy* **41** C9
Venezuela ■ *S. Amer.* **124** B5
Venezuela, G. de *Venezuela* **124** A4
Vengurla *India* **66** M8
Venice = Venézia *Italy* **41** C9
Venice *U.S.A.* **117** H13
Venissieux *France* **21** C8
Venjansjön *Sweden* **10** D8
Venkatapuram *India* **67** K12
Venlo *Neths.* **17** C6
Vennachar Junction *Canada*
  114 A7
Vennesla *Norway* **9** G12
Venosa *Italy* **43** B8
Venray *Neths.* **17** C6
Venta *Lithuania* **30** B9
Venta → *Latvia* **30** A8
Venta de Baños *Spain* **36** D6
Venta de Cardeña =
  Cardeña *Spain* **37** G6
Ventana, Punta de la
  Mexico **118** C3
Ventana, Sa. de la *Argentina* **126** D3
Ventersburg *S. Africa* **88** D4
Venterstad *S. Africa* **88** E4
Ventimíglia *Italy* **40** E4
Ventnor *U.K.* **15** G6
Ventoténe *Italy* **42** B6
Ventoux, Mt. *France* **21** D9
Ventspils *Latvia* **30** A8
Ventspils □ *Latvia* **30** A8
Ventuarí → *Venezuela* **124** C5
Ventucopa *U.S.A.* **111** L7
Ventura *U.S.A.* **111** L7
Vénus, Pte. *Tahiti* **91** d
Venus B. *Australia* **95** F4
Venustiano Carranza
  Mexico **118** A3
Vera *Argentina* **126** B3
Vera *Spain* **39** H3
Veracruz *Mexico* **119** D5
Veracruz □ *Mexico* **119** D5
Veraval *India* **68** J4
Verbánia *Italy* **40** C5
Verbicaro *Italy* **43** C8
Verbier *Switz.* **25** J3
Vercelli *Italy* **40** C5
Verchovchevo *Ukraine* **33** H8
Vercors ◯ *France* **21** D9
Verdalsøra *Norway* **8** E14
Verde → *Argentina* **128** E3
Verde → *Goiás, Brazil* **125** G8
Verde → *Mato Grosso do Sul,*
  Brazil **125** H8
Verde → *Chihuahua, Mexico* **118** B3
Verde → *Oaxaca, Mexico* **119** D5
Verde → *Veracruz, Mexico* **118** C4
Verde → *Paraguay* **126** A4
Verde → *U.S.A.* **106** D4
Verde, Cay *Bahamas* **120** B4
Verde Island Pass *Phil.* **61** E4
Verden *Germany* **24** C5
Verdi *U.S.A.* **110** F7
Verdon → *France* **21** E10
Verdon ◯ *France* **21** E10
Verdun *France* **19** C12
Verdun-sur-le-Doubs
  France **19** F12
Vereeniging *S. Africa* **89** D4
Verga, C. *Guinea* **82** C2
Vergara *Uruguay* **127** C5
Vergato *Italy* **40** D8
Vergemont Cr. → *Australia* **94** C3
Vergennes *U.S.A.* **115** B11
Vergt *France* **20** C4
Veria *Greece* **44** F5
Verín *Spain* **36** D3
Verkhnedvinsk =
  Vyerkhnyadzvinsk
  Belarus **32** E4
Verkhnetulomskoye
  Vdkhr. *Russia* **8** B24
Verkhnevilyuysk *Russia* **53** C13
Verkhniy Baskunchak
  Russia **35** F8
Verkhnyaya Russia **33** F9
Vibo Valéntia *Italy* **43** D9
Verkhovyna *Ukraine* **29** B9
Verkhoyansk *Russia* **53** C14
Verkhoyansk Ra. =
  Verkhoyanskiy Khrebet
  Russia **53** C13
Verkhoyanskiy Khrebet
  Russia **53** C13

Vermenton *France* **19** E10
Vermilion *Canada* **103** C6
Vermilion *U.S.A.* **114** E2
Vermilion → *Canada* **103** C6
Vermilion B. *U.S.A.* **116** G9
Vermilion Bay *Canada* **103** D10
Vermilion L. *U.S.A.* **112** B7
Vermillion *U.S.A.* **112** D5
Vermillion → *Canada* **104** C5
Vermont □ *U.S.A.* **115** C12
Vermosh *Albania* **44** D3
Vernadsky *Antarctica* **5** C17
Vernal *U.S.A.* **108** F9
Vernalis *U.S.A.* **110** H5
Vernazza *Italy* **40** D6
Verner *Canada* **104** C3
Verneuil-sur-Avre *France* **18** D7
Verneukpan *S. Africa* **88** E3
Vernier *Switz.* **25** J2
Vérnio *Italy* **40** D8
Vernon *Canada* **102** C5
Vernon *France* **18** C8
Vernon *U.S.A.* **116** D5
Vernonia *U.S.A.* **110** E3
Vero Beach *U.S.A.* **117** H14
Véroia = Veria *Greece* **44** F6
Véroli *Italy* **41** G10
Verona *Canada* **115** B8
Verona *Italy* **40** C7
Verrès *Italy* **40** C4
Versailles *France* **19** D9
Versmold *Germany* **24** C4
Vert, C. *Senegal* **82** C1
Vertou *France* **18** E5
Vertus *France* **19** D11
Verulam *S. Africa* **89** D5
Verviers *Belgium* **17** D5
Vervins *France* **19** C10
Verzej *Slovenia* **41** B13
Verzy *France* **19** C11
Vescovato *France* **21** F13
Veselí nad Lužnicí *Czech Rep.* **26** B7
Veselie *Bulgaria* **45** D11
Veselovskoye Vdkhr. *Russia* **35** G5
Veshenskaya *Russia* **34** F5
Vesle → *France* **19** C10
Vesoul *France* **19** E13
Vessigebro *Sweden* **11** H6
Vesterålen *Norway* **8** B16
Vestfjorden *Norway* **8** C16
Vestmannaeyjar *Iceland* **8** E3
Vestspitsbergen *Svalbard* **4** B8
Vestvågøya *Norway* **8** B15
Vesuvio *Italy* **43** B7
Vesuvius, Mt. = Vesuvio
  Italy **43** B7
Vesyegonsk *Russia* **32** C9
Veszprém *Hungary* **28** C2
Veszprém □ *Hungary* **28** C2
Vésztő *Hungary* **28** D6
Vetlanda *Sweden* **11** G9
Vetluga *Russia* **34** B7
Vetlugu → *Russia* **34** B8
Vetluzhskiy
  Kostroma, Russia **34** A7
Vetluzhskiy
  Nizhniy Novgorod, Russia **34** B7
Vetovo *Bulgaria* **45** C9
Vetralla *Italy* **41** F9
Vetren *Bulgaria* **45** D8
Vettore, Mte. *Italy* **41** F10
Veurne *Belgium* **17** C2
Veveno → *Sudan* **81** F3
Vevey *Switz.* **25** J2
Vevi *Greece* **44** F5
Veynes *France* **21** D9
Veys *Iran* **71** D6
Vézelay *France* **19** E10
Vézelise *France* **19** D13
Vézère → *France* **20** D5
Vezhen *Bulgaria* **45** D8
Vezirköprü *Turkey* **72** B6
Vezzani *France* **21** F13
Vi Thanh *Vietnam* **65** H5
Viacha *Bolivia* **124** G5
Viadana *Italy* **40** D7
Viamão *Brazil* **127** C5
Viana *Brazil* **125** D10
Viana *Spain* **38** C2
Viana do Alentejo *Portugal* **37** G3
Viana do Bolo *Spain* **36** C3
Viana do Castelo *Portugal* **36** D2
Viana do Castelo □ *Portugal* **36** D2
Vianden *Lux.* **17** E6
Viangchan = Vientiane *Laos* **64** D4
Vianópolis *Brazil* **125** G9
Vianos *Greece* **49** D7
Viar → *Spain* **37** H5
Viaréggio *Italy* **40** E7
Viaur → *France* **20** D5
Vibble *Sweden* **11** G12
Vibo Valéntia *Italy* **43** D9
Viborg *Denmark* **11** H3
Vibraye *France* **18** D7
Vic *Spain* **38** D7
Vic, Étang de *France* **20** E7
Vic-en-Bigorre *France* **20** E4
Vic-Fezensac *France* **20** E4
Vic-le-Comte *France* **19** G10

Vic-sur-Cère *France* **20** D6
Vícar *Spain* **39** J2
Vicenza *Italy* **41** C8
Vich = Vic *Spain* **38** D7
Vichada □ *Colombia* **124** C5
Vichuga *Russia* **34** B5
Vichy *France* **19** F10
Vicksburg *Ariz., U.S.A.* **111** M13
Vicksburg *Miss., U.S.A.* **117** E9
Vico *France* **21** F12
Vico, L. di *Italy* **41** F9
Vico del Gargano *Italy* **41** G12
Victor *India* **68** J4
Victor Harbor *Australia* **95** F2
Victoria *Argentina* **126** C3
Victoria *Canada* **110** B3
Victoria *Chile* **128** D2
Victoria *Guinea* **82** C2
Victoria *Malta* **49** C1
Victoria *Phil.* **61** D4
Victoria *Romania* **29** E9
Victoria *Seychelles* **85** b
Victoria *Kans., U.S.A.* **112** F4
Victoria *Tex., U.S.A.* **116** G6
Victoria □ *Australia* **95** F3
Victoria → *Australia* **92** C4
Victoria, Grand L. *Canada* **104** C4
Victoria, L. *Africa* **86** C3
Victoria, L. *Australia* **95** E3
Victoria, Mt. *Burma* **67** J18
Victoria Beach *Canada* **103** C9
Victoria de Durango =
  Durango *Mexico* **118** C4
Victoria de las Tunas = Las
  Tunas *Cuba* **120** B4
Victoria Falls *Zimbabwe* **87** F2
Victoria Harbour *Canada* **114** B5
Victoria I. *Canada* **100** B8
Victoria L. *Canada* **105** C8
Victoria Ld. *Antarctica* **5** D11
Victoria Nile → *Uganda* **86** B3
Victoria Pk. *Belize* **119** D7
Victoria River *Australia* **92** C5
Victoria Str. *Canada* **100** C9
Victoria West *S. Africa* **88** E3
Victorias *Phil.* **61** F5
Victoriaville *Canada* **105** C5
Victorica *Argentina* **126** D2
Victorville *U.S.A.* **111** L9
Vicuña *Chile* **126** C1
Vicuña Mackenna
  Argentina **126** C3
Vidal *U.S.A.* **111** L12
Vidal Junction *U.S.A.* **111** L12
Vidalia *U.S.A.* **117** E13
Vidamlya *Belarus* **31** F10
Vidauban *France* **21** E10
Videbæk *Denmark* **11** H2
Videle *Romania* **29** F10
Vidigueira *Portugal* **37** G3
Vidin *Bulgaria* **44** C6
Vidio, C. *Spain* **36** B4
Vidisha *India* **68** H7
Vidos *Greece* **49** A3
Vidra *Romania* **29** E11
Viduša *Bos.-H.* **44** D2
Vidzy *Belarus* **32** E4
Viechtach *Germany* **25** F8
Viedma *Argentina* **128** E4
Viedma, L. *Argentina* **128** F2
Vielha *Spain* **38** C5
Viella = Vielha *Spain* **38** C5
Vielsalm *Belgium* **17** D5
Vienenburg *Germany* **24** C6
Vieng Pou Kha *Laos* **58** G3
Vienna = Wien *Austria* **27** C9
Vienna *Canada* **114** D4
Vienna *Ill., U.S.A.* **112** G9
Vienna *Mo., U.S.A.* **112** F8
Vienne *France* **21** C8
Vienne □ *France* **20** B4
Vienne → *France* **18** E7
Vientiane *Laos* **64** D4
Vientos, Paso de los
  Caribbean **121** C5
Vieques *Puerto Rico* **121** d
Vierge Pt. *St. Lucia* **121** f
Viernheim *Germany* **25** F4
Viersen *Germany* **24** D2
Vierwaldstättersee *Switz.* **25** J4
Vierzon *France* **19** E9
Vieste *Italy* **41** G13
Viet Tri *Vietnam* **64** B5
Vietnam ■ *Asia* **64** C6
Vieux-Boucau-les-Bains
  France **20** E2
Vieux Fort *St. Lucia* **121** f
Vif *France* **21** C9
Vigan *Phil.* **61** C4
Vigévano *Italy* **40** C5
Vigia *Brazil* **125** D9
Viglas, Akra *Greece* **49** D9
Vignemale *France* **20** F3
Vigneulles-lès-
  Hattonchâtel *France* **19** D12
Vignola *Italy* **40** D8

Vigo *Spain* **36** C2
Vigo, Ría de *Spain* **36** C2
Vigsø Bugt *Denmark* **11** G2
Vihiers *France* **18** E6
Vihowa *Pakistan* **68** D4
Vihowa ➔ *Pakistan* **68** D4
Vijayawada *India* **67** L12
Vijosë ➔ *Albania* **44** F3
Vík *Iceland* **8** E4
Vika *Sweden* **10** D8
Vikarbyn *Sweden* **10** D9
Vikeke = Viqueque *E. Timor* **63** F7
Viken *Skåne, Sweden* **11** H6
Viken *Västra Götaland, Sweden* **11** F8
Viking *Canada* **102** C6
Vikmanshyttan *Sweden* **10** D9
Vikna *Norway* **8** D14
Vikos-Aoos △ *Greece* **46** B2
Vila da Maganja *Mozam.* **87** F4
Vila da Ribeira Brava
    C. Verde Is. **78** b
Vila de Rei *Portugal* **36** F2
Vila do Bispo *Portugal* **37** H2
Vila do Conde *Portugal* **36** D2
Vila Franca de Xira *Portugal* **37** G2
Vila Gamito *Mozam.* **87** E3
Vila Gomes da Costa *Mozam.* **89** C5
Vila Machado *Mozam.* **87** F3
Vila Mouzinho *Mozam.* **87** E3
Vila Nova de Famalicão
    Portugal **36** D2
Vila Nova de Fos Côa
    Portugal **36** D3
Vila Nova de Gaia *Portugal* **36** D2
Vila Nova de Ourém *Portugal* **36** F2
Vila Pouca de Aguiar
    Portugal **36** D3
Vila Real *Portugal* **36** D3
Vila-Real *Spain* **38** F4
Vila Real □ *Portugal* **36** D3
Vila Real de Santo António
    Portugal **37** H3
Vila-seca *Spain* **38** D6
Vila Vasco da Gama *Mozam.* **87** E3
Vila Velha *Brazil* **127** A7
Vila Viçosa *Portugal* **37** G3
Vilafranca del Maestrat
    Spain **38** E4
Vilafranca del Penedès *Spain* **38** D6
Vilagarcía de Arousa *Spain* **36** C2
Vilaine ➔ *France* **18** E4
Vilanandro, Tanjona *Madag.* **89** B7
Vilanculos *Mozam.* **89** C6
Vilanova i la Geltrú *Spain* **38** D6
Vilar Formoso *Portugal* **36** E4
Vilaseca-Salou = Vila-seca
    Spain **38** D6
Vilbjerg *Denmark* **11** H2
Vilcheka, Ostrov *Russia* **52** B6
Vilcheka, Zemlya *Russia* **4** A11
Vilches *Spain* **37** G7
Vileyka *Belarus* **23** A14
Vilhelmina *Sweden* **8** D17
Vilhena *Brazil* **124** F6
Viliya = Neris ➔ *Lithuania* **32** E3
Viljandi *Estonia* **32** C3
Vilkaviškis *Lithuania* **30** D10
Vilkija *Lithuania* **30** C10
Vilkitskogo, Proliv *Russia* **53** B11
Vilkovo = Vylkove *Ukraine* **29** E14
Villa Abecia *Bolivia* **126** A2
Villa Ana *Argentina* **126** B4
Villa Ángela *Argentina* **126** B3
Villa Bella *Bolivia* **124** F5
Villa Cañás *Argentina* **126** C3
Villa Constitución *Argentina* **126** C3
Villa de Arriaga *Mexico* **118** C4
Villa de María *Argentina* **126** B3
Villa de Méndez *Mexico* **119** B5
Villa del Rio *Spain* **37** H6
Villa Dolores *Argentina* **126** C2
Villa Frontera *Mexico* **118** B4
Villa Gesell *Argentina* **126** D4
Villa Guillermina *Argentina* **126** B4
Villa Hayes *Paraguay* **126** B4
Villa Hidalgo *Mexico* **119** C5
Villa Iris *Argentina* **126** D3
Villa María *Argentina* **126** C3
Villa Mazán *Argentina* **126** B2
Villa Minozzo *Italy* **40** D7
Villa Montes *Bolivia* **126** A3
Villa Ocampo *Argentina* **126** B4
Villa Ocampo *Mexico* **118** B3
Villa Ojo de Agua *Argentina* **126** B3
Villa San Giovanni *Italy* **43** D8
Villa San Martín *Argentina* **126** B3
Villa Santina *Italy* **41** B9
Villa Unión *Mexico* **118** C3
Villablino *Spain* **36** C4
Villacarlos *Spain* **48** B11
Villacarriedo *Spain* **36** B7
Villacarrillo *Spain* **37** G7
Villacastín *Spain* **36** E6
Villach *Austria* **26** E7
Villacidro *Italy* **42** C1
Villada *Spain* **36** C6
Villadiego *Spain* **36** C6
Villadóssola *Italy* **40** B5

Villafeliche *Spain* **38** D3
Villafranca *Spain* **38** C3
Villafranca de Bonany
    Spain **48** B10
Villafranca de los Barros
    Spain **37** G4
Villafranca de los
    Caballeros *Spain* **37** F7
Villafranca del Cid =
    Vilafranca del Maestrat
    Spain **38** E4
Villafranca del Panadés =
    Vilafranca del Penedès
    Spain **38** D6
Villafranca di Verona *Italy* **40** C7
Villafranca Tirrena *Italy* **43** D8
Villagrán *Mexico* **119** C5
Villaguay *Argentina* **126** C4
Villaharta *Spain* **37** G6
Villahermosa *Mexico* **119** D6
Villahermosa *Spain* **39** G2
Villaines-la-Juhel *France* **18** D6
Villajoyosa *Spain* **39** G4
Villalba *Spain* **36** B3
Villalba de Guardo *Spain* **36** C6
Villalón de Campos *Spain* **36** C5
Villalpando *Spain* **36** D5
Villaluenga de la Sagra
    Spain **36** E7
Villamanán *Spain* **36** C5
Villamartín *Spain* **37** J5
Villamayor de Santiago
    Spain **38** F2
Villamblard *France* **20** C4
Villanova Monteleone *Italy* **42** B1
Villanueva *U.S.A.* **109** J11
Villanueva de Castellón
    Spain **39** F4
Villanueva de Córdoba *Spain* **37** G6
Villanueva de la Fuente
    Spain **39** G2
Villanueva de la Serena
    Spain **37** G5
Villanueva de la Sierra *Spain* **36** E4
Villanueva de los
    Castillejos *Spain* **37** H3
Villanueva de los Infantes
    Spain **37** G7
Villanueva del Arzobispo
    Spain **39** G2
Villanueva del Fresno *Spain* **37** G3
Villanueva y Geltrú =
    Vilanova i la Geltrú *Spain* **38** D6
Villaputzu *Italy* **42** C2
Villaquilambre *Spain* **36** C5
Villar del Arzobispo *Spain* **38** F4
Villar del Rey *Spain* **37** F4
Villard-de-Lans *France* **21** C9
Villarramiel *Spain* **36** C6
Villarreal = Vila-Real *Spain* **38** F4
Villarrica *Chile* **128** D2
Villarrica *Paraguay* **126** B4
Villarrobledo *Spain* **39** F2
Villarroya de la Sierra *Spain* **38** D3
Villarrubia de los Ojos *Spain* **37** F7
Villars-les-Dombes *France* **19** F12
Villasayas *Spain* **38** D2
Villaseco de los Gamitos
    Spain **36** D4
Villasimíus *Italy* **42** C2
Villastar *Spain* **38** E3
Villatobas *Spain* **36** F7
Villavicencio *Argentina* **126** C2
Villavicencio *Colombia* **124** C4
Villaviciosa *Spain* **36** B5
Villazón *Bolivia* **126** A2
Ville-Marie *Canada* **104** C4
Ville Platte *U.S.A.* **116** F8
Villedieu-les-Poêles *France* **18** D5
Villefort *France* **20** D7
Villefranche-de-Lauragais
    France **20** E5
Villefranche-de-Rouergue
    France **20** D6
Villefranche-du-Périgord
    France **20** D5
Villefranche-sur-Saône
    France **21** C8
Villel *Spain* **38** E3
Villemur-sur-Tarn *France* **20** E5
Villena *Spain* **39** G4
Villenauxe-la-Grande
    France **19** D10
Villeneuve-d'Ornon *France* **20** D3
Villeneuve-d'Ascq *France* **19** B10
Villeneuve-l'Archevêque
    France **19** D10
Villeneuve-lès-Avignon
    France **21** E8
Villeneuve-sur-Allier
    France **19** F10
Villeneuve-sur-Lot *France* **20** D4
Villeneuve-sur-Yonne
    France **19** D10
Villeréal *France* **20** D4
Villers-Bocage *France* **18** C6
Villers-Cotterêts *France* **19** C10
Villers-sur-Mer *France* **18** C6

Villersexel *France* **19** E13
Villerupt *France* **19** C12
Villeurbanne *France* **21** C8
Villiers *S. Africa* **89** D4
Villingen-Schwenningen
    Germany **25** G4
Villmanstrand =
    Lappeenranta *Finland* **32** B5
Vilna *Canada* **102** C6
Vilnius *Lithuania* **32** E3
Vils *Austria* **26** D3
Vils ➔ *Bayern, Germany* **25** G9
Vils ➔ *Bayern, Germany* **25** F7
Vilshofen *Germany* **25** G9
Vilusi *Montenegro* **44** D2
Vilvoorde *Belgium* **17** D4
Vilyuchinsk *Russia* **53** D16
Vilyuy ➔ *Russia* **53** C13
Vilyuysk *Russia* **53** C13
Vimianzo *Spain* **36** B1
Vimioso *Portugal* **36** D4
Vimmerby *Sweden* **11** G9
Vimoutiers *France* **18** D7
Vimperk *Czech Rep.* **26** B6
Viña del Mar *Chile* **126** C1
Vinarós *Spain* **38** E5
Vincennes *U.S.A.* **112** F10
Vincennes Bay *S. Ocean* **5** C8
Vincent *U.S.A.* **111** L8
Vinchina *Argentina* **126** B2
Vindelälven ➔ *Sweden* **8** E18
Vindeln *Sweden* **8** D18
Vinderup *Denmark* **11** H2
Vindhya Ra. *India* **68** H7
Vineland *U.S.A.* **113** F16
Vineuil *France* **18** E8
Vinga *Romania* **28** D6
Vingåker *Sweden* **10** E9
Vinh *Vietnam* **64** C5
Vinh Linh *Vietnam* **64** D6
Vinh Long *Vietnam* **65** G5
Vinh Yen *Vietnam* **58** G5
Vinhais *Portugal* **36** D3
Vinica *Croatia* **41** B13
Vinica *Macedonia* **44** E6
Vinica *Slovenia* **41** C12
Vinita *U.S.A.* **116** C7
Vinkovci *Croatia* **28** E3
Vinnitsa = Vinnytsya
    Ukraine **23** D15
Vinnytsya *Ukraine* **23** D15
Vinnytsya □ *Ukraine* **33** H5
Vinslöv *Sweden* **11** H7
Vinson Massif *Antarctica* **5** D16
Vintjärn *Sweden* **10** D10
Vinton *Calif., U.S.A.* **110** F6
Vinton *Iowa, U.S.A.* **112** D7
Vinton *La., U.S.A.* **116** F8
Vințu de Jos *Romania* **29** D8
Viöl *Germany* **24** A5
Viotia □ *Greece* **46** C5
Vipava *Slovenia* **41** C10
Vipiteno *Italy* **41** B8
Viqueque *E. Timor* **63** F7
Vir *Croatia* **41** D12
Virac *Phil.* **61** E6
Virachey *Cambodia* **64** F6
Virachey △ *Cambodia* **64** E6
Virago Sd. *Canada* **102** C2
Viramgam *India* **68** H5
Virananşehir *Turkey* **73** D8
Virawah *Pakistan* **68** G4
Virbalis *Lithuania* **30** D9
Virden *Canada* **103** D8
Vire *France* **18** D6
Vire ➔ *France* **18** C5
Vírgenes, C. *Argentina* **128** G3
Virgin ➔ *U.S.A.* **109** H6
Virgin Gorda *Br. Virgin Is.* **121** e
Virgin Is. (British) ☑
    W. Indies **121** e
Virgin Is. (U.S.) ☑ *W. Indies* **121** e
Virgin Islands △
    U.S. Virgin Is. **121** C7
Virginia *S. Africa* **88** D4
Virginia *U.S.A.* **112** B7
Virginia □ *U.S.A.* **113** G14
Virginia Beach *U.S.A.* **113** F16
Virginia City *Mont., U.S.A.* **108** D8
Virginia City *Nev., U.S.A.* **110** F7
Virginia Falls *Canada* **102** A3
Virginiatown *Canada* **104** C4
Virje *Croatia* **41** B13
Viroqua *U.S.A.* **112** D8
Virovitica *Croatia* **28** E2
Virpazar *Montenegro* **44** D3
Virpur *India* **68** J4
Virserum *Sweden* **11** G9
Virton *Belgium* **17** E5
Virudunagar *India* **66** Q10
Virunga △
    Dem. Rep. of the Congo **86** D2
Vis *Croatia* **41** E13
Visalia *U.S.A.* **110** J7
Visayan Sea *Phil.* **61** F5
Viscount Melville Sd.
    Canada **101** B9

Visé *Belgium* **17** D5
Vise, Ostrov *Russia* **52** B8
Višegrad *Bos.-H.* **28** G4
Viseu *Brazil* **125** D9
Viseu *Portugal* **36** E3
Viseu □ *Portugal* **36** E3
Vişeu de Sus *Romania* **29** C9
Vishakhapatnam *India* **67** L13
Vişina *Romania* **29** G9
Vişineşti *Moldova* **29** D13
Visingsö *Sweden* **11** F8
Viskafors *Sweden* **11** G6
Viskan ➔ *Sweden* **11** G6
Viški Kanal *Croatia* **41** E13
Vislanda *Sweden* **11** H8
Visnagar *India* **68** H5
Višnja Gora *Slovenia* **41** C11
Viso, Mte. *Italy* **40** D4
Viso del Marqués *Spain* **37** G7
Visoko *Bos.-H.* **28** G3
Visokoi I. *Antarctica* **5** B1
Visp *Switz.* **25** J3
Vissefjärda *Sweden* **11** H9
Visselhövede *Germany* **24** C5
Vissenbjerg *Denmark* **11** J4
Vista *U.S.A.* **111** M9
Vistonida, L. *Greece* **45** E9
Vistonikos, Ormos =
    Vistonida, L. *Greece* **45** E9
Vistula = Wisła ➔ *Poland* **30** D5
Vit ➔ *Bulgaria* **45** C8
Vitanje *Slovenia* **41** B12
Vitebsk = Vitsyebsk *Belarus* **32** E6
Viterbo *Italy* **41** F9
Vitez *Bos.-H.* **28** F2
Viti Levu *Fiji* **91** a
Vitigudino *Spain* **36** D4
Vitim *Russia* **53** D12
Vitim ➔ *Russia* **53** D12
Vitina *Bos.-H.* **41** E14
Vitina *Greece* **46** D4
Vítkov *Czech Rep.* **27** B10
Vitória *Brazil* **125** H10
Vitória da Conquista *Brazil*
    125 F10
Vitória de São Antão *Brazil*
    125 E11
Vitoria-Gasteiz *Spain* **38** C2
Vitosha △ *Bulgaria* **44** D7
Vitré *France* **18** D5
Vitry-le-François *France* **19** D11
Vitry-sur-Seine *France* **19** D9
Vitsand *Sweden* **10** D7
Vitsi, Oros *Greece* **44** F5
Vitsyebsk *Belarus* **32** E6
Vitsyebsk □ *Belarus* **32** E5
Vittaryd *Sweden* **11** H7
Vitteaux *France* **19** E11
Vittel *France* **19** D12
Vittória *Italy* **43** F7
Vittório Véneto *Italy* **41** C9
Vittsjö *Sweden* **11** H7
Viveiro *Spain* **36** B3
Vivian *U.S.A.* **116** E8
Viviers *France* **21** D8
Vivonne *France* **20** B4
Viwa *Fiji* **91** a
Vizcaíno, Desierto de
    Mexico **118** B2
Vizcaíno, Sierra *Mexico* **118** B2
Vizcaya □ *Spain* **38** B2
Vize *Turkey* **45** E11
Vizianagaram *India* **67** K13
Vizille *France* **21** C9
Viziñada *Croatia* **41** C10
Viziru *Romania* **29** E12
Vizzini *Italy* **43** E7
Vlaardingen *Neths.* **17** C4
Vlachiotis *Greece* **46** E4
Vlădeasa, Vf. *Romania* **28** D7
Vladičin Han *Serbia* **44** D6
Vladikavkaz *Russia* **35** J7
Vladimir *Russia* **32** D11
Vladimir □ *Russia* **34** B5
Vladimir Volynskiy =
    Volodymyr-Volynskyy
    Ukraine **23** C13
Vladimirci *Serbia* **44** B3
Vladimirovac *Serbia* **28** E5
Vladimirovka *Russia* **35** F8
Vladimirovo *Bulgaria* **44** C7
Vladislavovka *Ukraine* **33** K8
Vladivostok *Russia* **54** C5
Vlăhița *Romania* **29** D10
Vlasenica *Bos.-H.* **28** F3
Vlašić *Bos.-H.* **28** F2
Vlašim *Czech Rep.* **26** B7
Vlasinsko Jezero *Serbia* **44** D6
Vlasotince *Serbia* **44** D6
Vlieland *Neths.* **17** A4
Vlissingen *Neths.* **17** C3
Vlorë *Albania* **44** F3
Vlorës, Gjiri i *Albania* **44** F3
Vltava ➔ *Czech Rep.* **26** A7
Vo Dat *Vietnam* **65** G6
Vobarno *Italy* **40** C7
Voćin *Croatia* **28** E2

Vodice *Croatia* **41** E12
Vodňany *Czech Rep.* **26** B7
Vodnjan *Croatia* **41** D10
Voe *U.K.* **13** A7
Vogel Pk. *Nigeria* **83** D7
Vogelkop = Doberai,
    Jazirah *Indonesia* **63** E8
Vogelsberg *Germany* **24** E5
Voghera *Italy* **40** D6
Vohibinany *Madag.* **89** B8
Vohilava *Madag.* **89** C8
Vohimarina = Iharana
    Madag. **89** A9
Vohimena, Tanjon' i *Madag.* **89** D8
Vohipeno *Madag.* **89** C8
Voi *Kenya* **86** C4
Void-Vacon *France* **19** D12
Voineşti *Iaşi, Romania* **29** C12
Voineşti *Prahova, Romania* **29** E10
Voiron *France* **21** C9
Voisey B. *Canada* **105** A7
Voitsberg *Austria* **26** D8
Vojens *Denmark* **11** J3
Vojmsjön *Sweden* **8** D17
Vojnić *Croatia* **41** C12
Vojnik *Italy* **41** B12
Vojvodina □ *Serbia* **28** E5
Vokhtoga *Russia* **32** C11
Volary *Czech Rep.* **26** C6
Volcán de Colima △ *Mexico* **118** D4
Volcano Is. = Kazan-Rettō
    Pac. Oc. **96** E6
Volcans △ *Rwanda* **86** C2
Volcans d'Auvergne △
    France **20** C6
Volchansk = Vovchansk
    Ukraine **33** G9
Volda *Norway* **8** E12
Volga = Privolzhskiy □
    Russia **34** B10
Volga *Russia* **32** C10
Volga ➔ *Russia* **35** G9
Volga Hts. =
    Privolzhskaya
    Vozvyshennost *Russia* **34** E7
Volgo-Baltiyskiy Kanal
    Russia **32** B9
Volgo-Donskoy Kanal
    Russia **35** F7
Volgodonsk *Russia* **35** G6
Volgograd *Russia* **35** F7
Volgograd □ *Russia* **34** F7
Volgogradskoye Vdkhr.
    Russia **34** E8
Volgorechensk *Russia* **34** B5
Volimes *Greece* **46** D2
Volintiri *Moldova* **29** D14
Volissos *Greece* **47** C7
Volkach *Germany* **25** F6
Völkermarkt *Austria* **26** E7
Volkhov *Russia* **32** C7
Volkhov ➔ *Russia* **32** B7
Völklingen *Germany* **25** F2
Volkovysk = Vawkavysk
    Belarus **23** B13
Volksrust *S. Africa* **89** D4
Volnansk *Ukraine* **33** H8
Volnovakha *Ukraine* **33** J9
Volochanka *Russia* **53** B10
Volodarsk *Russia* **34** B6
Volodymyr-Volynskyy
    Ukraine **23** C13
Vologda *Russia* **32** C10
Vologda □ *Russia* **32** B10
Volokolamsk *Russia* **32** D8
Volokonovka *Russia* **33** G9
Volos *Greece* **46** B4
Volosovo *Russia* **32** C5
Volovets *Ukraine* **29** B8
Volovo *Russia* **32** F10
Volozhin = Valozhyn
    Belarus **23** A14
Volsk *Russia* **34** D8
Volta □ *Ghana* **83** D5
Volta ➔ *Ghana* **83** D5
Volta, L. *Ghana* **83** D5
Volta Blanche = White
    Volta ➔ *Ghana* **83** D4
Volta Redonda *Brazil* **127** A7
Voltaire, C. *Australia* **92** B4
Volterra *Italy* **40** E7
Voltri *Italy* **40** D5
Volturno ➔ *Italy* **42** A6
Volvi, L. *Greece* **44** F7
Volyn □ *Ukraine* **33** G3
Volynë *Czech Rep.* **26** B6
Volzhsk *Russia* **34** C9
Volzhskiy *Russia* **35** F7
Vomo *Fiji* **91** a
Vondrozo *Madag.* **89** C8
Vonitsa *Greece* **46** C2
Vopnafjörður *Iceland* **8** D6
Vorarlberg □ *Austria* **26** D2
Voras Oros *Greece* **44** F5
Vorbasse *Denmark* **11** J3
Vorchdorf *Austria* **26** C6

Vorderrhein ➔ *Switz.* **25** J5
Vordingborg *Denmark* **11** J5
Vorë *Albania* **44** E3
Voreia Aigaio □ *Greece* **47** C7
Voreppe *France* **21** C9
Vori *Greece* **46** F6
Vorios Evoikos Kolpos
    Greece **46** C5
Vorkuta *Russia* **52** C7
Vormsi *Estonia* **32** C2
Vorona ➔ *Russia* **34** E6
Voronezh *Russia* **33** G10
Voronezh ➔ *Russia* **33** G7
Voronezh □ *Russia* **34** E4
Voronezh ➔ *Russia* **33** G10
Vorontsovo-
    Aleksandrovskoye =
    Zelenokumsk *Russia* **35** H6
Vorpommersche
    Boddenlandschaft △
    Germany **24** A8
Vorskla ➔ *Ukraine* **33** H8
Võrts Järv *Estonia* **32** C4
Võru *Estonia* **32** D4
Vosges *France* **19** D14
Vosges □ *France* **19** D13
Vosges du Nord △ *France* **19** D14
Voskopojë *Albania* **44** F4
Voskresensk *Russia* **32** E10
Voskresenskoye *Russia* **34** B7
Voss *Norway* **8** F12
Vostok *Antarctica* **5** D8
Vostok I. *Kiribati* **97** J12
Votice *Czech Rep.* **26** B7
Votsuri-Shima *Japan* **55** M1
Vouga ➔ *Portugal* **36** E2
Vouillé *France* **18** F7
Vouxa, Akra *Greece* **49** D5
Vouzela *Portugal* **36** E2
Vouziers *France* **19** C11
Vovchansk *Ukraine* **33** G9
Vowchyn *Belarus* **31** F10
Voyageurs △ *U.S.A.* **112** A7
Voynitsa *Russia* **8** D24
Voyvozh *Russia* **52** C6
Vozhe, Ozero *Russia* **32** B10
Vozhega *Russia* **32** B11
Voznesensk *Ukraine* **33** J6
Voznesenye *Russia* **32** B8
Vrå *Denmark* **11** G3
Vráble *Slovak Rep.* **27** C11
Vračevšnica *Serbia* **44** B4
Vrachneika *Greece* **46** C3
Vrancea □ *Romania* **29** E11
Vrancei, Munţii *Romania* **29** E11
Vrangel *Russia* **54** C6
Vranica *Bos.-H.* **28** G2
Vranje *Serbia* **44** D5
Vranjska Banja *Serbia* **44** D6
Vranov nad Topl'ou
    Slovak Rep. **27** C14
Vransko *Slovenia* **41** B11
Vransko Jezero *Croatia* **41** E12
Vrapčište *Macedonia* **44** E4
Vratsa *Bulgaria* **44** C7
Vrbas *Serbia* **28** E4
Vrbas ➔ *Bos.-H.* **28** E2
Vrbnik *Croatia* **41** C11
Vrbovec *Croatia* **41** C13
Vrbovsko *Croatia* **41** C12
Vrchlabí *Czech Rep.* **26** A8
Vrede *S. Africa* **89** D4
Vredenburg *S. Africa* **88** E2
Vredendal *S. Africa* **88** E2
Vretstorp *Sweden* **10** E8
Vrgorac *Croatia* **41** E14
Vrhnika *Slovenia* **41** C11
Vrídi *Ivory C.* **82** D4
Vrigstad *Sweden* **11** G8
Vrindavan *India* **68** F7
Vrisses *Greece* **49** D6
Vrnograč *Bos.-H.* **41** C12
Vrondados *Greece* **47** C8
Vrpolje *Croatia* **28** E3
Vršac *Serbia* **28** E6
Vrsacki Kanal *Serbia* **28** E5
Vrútky *Slovak Rep.* **27** B11
Vryburg *S. Africa* **88** D3
Vryheid *S. Africa* **89** D5
Vsetín *Czech Rep.* **27** B11
Vu Liet *Vietnam* **64** C5
Vúcha ➔ *Bulgaria* **45** D8
Vučitrn *Serbia* **44** D4
Vukovar *Croatia* **28** E3
Vuktyl *Russia* **52** C6
Vulcan *Canada* **102** C6
Vulcan *Romania* **29** E8
Vulcaneşti *Moldova* **29** E13
Vulcano *Italy* **43** D7
Vŭlchedruma *Bulgaria* **44** C7
Vulkaneshty = Vulcaneşti
    Moldova **29** E13
Vunduzi ➔ *Mozam.* **87** F3
Vung Tau *Vietnam* **65** G6
Vunidawa *Fiji* **91** a

Vunisea *Fiji* **91** a
Vŭrbitsa *Bulgaria* **45** D10
Vurshets *Bulgaria* **44** C7
Vutcani *Romania* **29** D12
Vuya *Sudan* **81** F2
Vuzlove *Ukraine* **28** B7
Vwaza △ *Malawi* **87** E3
Vyartsilya *Russia* **32** A6
Vyatka = Kirov *Russia* **52** D5
Vyatka ➤ *Russia* **34** C10
Vyatskiye Polyany *Russia* **34** B10
Vyazemskiy *Russia* **53** E14
Vyazma *Russia* **32** E8
Vyazniki *Russia* **34** B6
Vyborg *Russia* **32** B5
Vychegda ➤ *Russia* **52** C5
Vychodné Beskydy *Europe* **27** B15
Vyerkhnyadzvinsk *Belarus* **32** E4
Vyhoda *Ukraine* **29** B8
Vyksa *Russia* **34** C6
Vylkove *Ukraine* **29** E14
Vylok *Ukraine* **28** B7
Vynohradiv *Ukraine* **28** B8
Vyrnwy, L. *U.K.* **14** E4
Vyshkiv *Ukraine* **29** B8
Vyshkove *Ukraine* **29** B8
Vyshniy Volochek *Russia* **32** D8
Vyshzha = imeni 26
  Bakinskikh Komissarov
  Turkmenistan **71** B7
Vyškov *Czech Rep.* **27** B9
Vysokaye *Belarus* **31** F10
Vysoké Mýto *Czech Rep.* **27** B9
Vysokovsk *Russia* **32** D9
Vytegra *Russia* **32** B9
Vyzhnytsya *Ukraine* **29** B10
Vyzhnytsya △ *Ukraine* **29** B10

W

W du Benin △ *Benin* **83** C5
W du Burkina Faso △
  Burkina Faso **83** C4
W du Niger △ *Niger* **83** C5
W.A.C. Bennett Dam
  Canada **102** B4
Wa *Ghana* **82** C4
Waal ➤ *Neths.* **17** C5
Waalwijk *Neths.* **17** C5
Waat *Sudan* **81** F3
Wabakimi △ *Canada* **104** B2
Wabana *Canada* **105** C9
Wabasca-Desmarais
  Canada **102** B6
Wabasca ➤ *Canada* **102** B5
Wabash *U.S.A.* **113** E11
Wabash ➤ *U.S.A.* **112** G9
Wabi ➤ *Ethiopia* **81** F5
Wabigoon L. *Canada* **103** D10
Wabowden *Canada* **103** C9
Wąbrzeźno *Poland* **31** E5
Wabu Hu *China* **59** A11
Wabuk Pt. *Canada* **104** A2
Wabush *Canada* **105** B6
Wąchock *Poland* **31** G8
Wächtersbach *Germany* **25** E5
Waco *U.S.A.* **116** F6
Waconichi, L. *Canada* **104** B5
Wad Ban Naqa *Sudan* **81** D3
Wad Banda *Sudan* **81** E2
Wad el Haddad *Sudan* **81** E3
Wad en Nau *Sudan* **81** E3
Wad Hamid *Sudan* **81** D3
Wad Medanî *Sudan* **81** E3
Wad Thana *Pakistan* **68** F2
Wadai *Africa* **76** E5
Wadayama *Japan* **55** G7
Waddeneilanden *Neths.* **17** A5
Waddenzee *Neths.* **17** A5
Waddi, Chappal *Nigeria* **83** D7
Waddington *U.S.A.* **115** B9
Waddington, Mt. *Canada* **102** C3
Waddy Pt. *Australia* **95** C5
Wadebridge *U.K.* **15** G3
Wadena *Canada* **103** C8
Wadena *U.S.A.* **112** B6
Wädenswil *Switz.* **25** H4
Wadern *Germany* **25** F2
Wadeye *Australia* **92** B4
Wadhams *Canada* **102** C3
Wadhwan *India* **68** H4
Wādī as Sīr *Jordan* **74** D4
Wâdi Gemâl, J. *Egypt* **80** C4
Wadi Halfa *Sudan* **80** C3
Wadi Rum △ *Jordan* **74** F4
Wadian *China* **59** A9
Wadlew *Poland* **31** G6
Wadowice *Poland* **31** J6
Wadsworth *Nev., U.S.A.* **108** G4
Wadsworth *Ohio, U.S.A.* **114** E3
Waegwan *S. Korea* **57** G15
Wafrah *Kuwait* **70** D5
Wageningen *Neths.* **17** C5
Wager B. *Canada* **101** C11
Wagga Wagga *Australia* **95** F4
Waghete *Indonesia* **63** E9

Wagin *Australia* **93** F2
Wagner *U.S.A.* **112** D4
Wagon Mound *U.S.A.* **109** H11
Wagoner *U.S.A.* **116** D7
Wągrowiec *Poland* **31** F4
Wah *Pakistan* **68** C5
Wahai *Indonesia* **63** E7
Wahiawä *U.S.A.* **106** b
Wâhid *Egypt* **74** E1
Wahnai *Afghan.* **68** C1
Wahni *Ethiopia* **81** E4
Wahoo *U.S.A.* **112** E5
Wahpeton *U.S.A.* **112** B5
Waiau ➤ *N.Z.* **91** E4
Waibeem *Indonesia* **63** E8
Waiblingen *Germany* **25** G5
Waidhofen an der Thaya
  Austria **26** C8
Waidhofen an der Ybbs
  Austria **26** D7
Waigeo *Indonesia* **63** E8
Waihi *N.Z.* **91** B5
Waihou ➤ *N.Z.* **91** B5
Waika *Dem. Rep. of the Congo* **86** C2
Waikabubak *Indonesia* **63** F5
Waikaremoana, L. *N.Z.* **91** C6
Waikari *N.Z.* **91** E4
Waikato ➤ *N.Z.* **91** B5
Waikerie *Australia* **95** E3
Waikokopu *N.Z.* **91** C6
Waikouaiti *N.Z.* **91** F3
Wailuku *U.S.A.* **106** b
Waimakariri ➤ *N.Z.* **91** E4
Waimate *N.Z.* **91** F3
Wainganga ➤ *India* **66** K11
Waingapu *Indonesia* **63** F6
Waini ➤ *Guyana* **124** B7
Waiouru *N.Z.* **91** C5
Waipara *N.Z.* **91** E4
Waipawa *N.Z.* **91** C6
Waipiro *N.Z.* **91** C7
Waipoua Forest *N.Z.* **91** A4
Waipu *N.Z.* **91** A5
Waipukurau *N.Z.* **91** D6
Wairakei *N.Z.* **91** C6
Wairarapa, L. *N.Z.* **91** D5
Wairoa *N.Z.* **91** C6
Waitaki ➤ *N.Z.* **91** F3
Waitangi *N.Z.* **91** A5
Waitara *N.Z.* **91** C5
Waitomo Caves *N.Z.* **91** C5
Waitsburg *U.S.A.* **108** C4
Waiuku *N.Z.* **91** B5
Wajima *Japan* **55** F8
Wajir *Kenya* **86** B5
Waka *Ethiopia* **81** F4
Wakasa *Japan* **55** G7
Wakasa-Wan *Japan* **55** G7
Wakatipu, L. *N.Z.* **91** F2
Wakaw *Canada* **103** C7
Wakaya *Fiji* **91** a
Wakayama *Japan* **55** G7
Wakayama □ *Japan* **55** H7
Wake Forest *U.S.A.* **117** D15
Wake I. *Pac. Oc.* **96** F8
WaKeeney *U.S.A.* **112** F4
Wakefield *Jamaica* **120** a
Wakefield *N.Z.* **91** D4
Wakefield *U.K.* **14** D6
Wakefield *Mass., U.S.A.* **115** D13
Wakefield *Mich., U.S.A.* **112** B9
Wakkanai *Japan* **54** B10
Wakkerstroom *S. Africa* **89** D5
Wakool *Australia* **95** F3
Wakool ➤ *Australia* **95** F3
Wakre *Indonesia* **63** E8
Wakuach, L. *Canada* **105** A6
Walamba *Zambia* **87** E2
Wałbrzych *Poland* **31** H3
Walbury Hill *U.K.* **15** F6
Walcha *Australia* **95** E5
Walcheren *Neths.* **17** C3
Walcott *U.S.A.* **108** F10
Wałcz *Poland* **31** E3
Waldbröl *Germany* **24** E3
Waldburg Ra. *Australia* **93** D2
Waldeck *Germany* **24** D5
Walden *Colo., U.S.A.* **108** F10
Walden *N.Y., U.S.A.* **115** E10
Waldkirch *Germany* **25** G3
Waldkirchen *Germany* **25** G9
Waldkraiburg *Germany* **25** G8
Waldport *U.S.A.* **108** D1
Waldron *U.S.A.* **116** D7
Waldviertel *Austria* **26** C8
Walebing *Australia* **93** F2
Walembele *Ghana* **82** C4
Walensee *Switz.* **25** H5
Wales □ *U.K.* **15** E3
Walewale *Ghana* **83** C4
Walgett *Australia* **95** E4
Walgreen Coast *Antarctica* **5** D15
Walker *U.S.A.* **112** B6
Walker, L. *Canada* **105** B6
Walker L. *Canada* **103** C9
Walker L. *U.S.A.* **108** G4
Walkerston *Australia* **94** K7

Walkerton *Canada* **114** B3
Wall *U.S.A.* **112** C2
Walla Walla *U.S.A.* **108** C4
Wallace *Idaho, U.S.A.* **108** C6
Wallace *N.C., U.S.A.* **117** D16
Wallaceburg *Canada* **114** D2
Wallachia = Valahia
  Romania **29** F9
Wallal *Australia* **95** D4
Wallam Cr. ➤ *Australia* **95** D4
Wallambin, L. *Australia* **93** F2
Wallangarra *Australia* **95** D5
Wallaroo *Australia* **95** E2
Walldürn *Germany* **25** F5
Wallenhorst *Germany* **24** C4
Wallenpaupack, L. *U.S.A.* **115** E9
Wallingford, Conn., U.S.A. **115** E12
Wallingford *Vt., U.S.A.* **115** C12
Wallis & Futuna, Is.
  Pac. Oc. **90** C11
Wallowa *U.S.A.* **108** D5
Wallowa Mts. *U.S.A.* **108** D5
Walls *U.K.* **13** A7
Walls of Jerusalem △
  Australia **95** G4
Wallula *U.S.A.* **108** C4
Wallumbilla *Australia* **95** D4
Walmsley L. *Canada* **103** A7
Walney, I. of *U.K.* **14** C4
Walnut Canyon ➤ *U.S.A.* **109** J8
Walnut Creek ➤ *U.S.A.* **110** H4
Walnut Ridge *U.S.A.* **117** C9
Walpole *Australia* **93** F2
Walpole *U.S.A.* **115** D13
Walpole-Nornalup △
  Australia **93** G2
Wals *Austria* **26** D5
Walsall *U.K.* **15** E6
Walsenburg *U.S.A.* **109** H11
Walsh *U.S.A.* **109** H12
Walsh ➤ *Australia* **94** B3
Walsingham *Canada* **114** D4
Walsrode *Germany* **24** C5
Walter F. George Res.
  U.S.A. **117** F12
Walterboro *U.S.A.* **117** E14
Walters *U.S.A.* **116** D5
Waltershausen *Germany* **24** E6
Waltham *U.S.A.* **115** D13
Waltman *U.S.A.* **108** E10
Walton *U.S.A.* **115** D9
Walton-on-the-Naze *U.K.* **15** F9
Walvis Bay *Namibia* **88** C1
Walvisbaai = Walvis Bay
  Namibia **88** C1
Wamba *Dem. Rep. of the Congo* **86** B2
Wamba *Kenya* **86** B4
Wamba *Nigeria* **83** D6
Wamego *U.S.A.* **112** F5
Wamena *Indonesia* **63** E9
Wampsville *U.S.A.* **115** C9
Wamsutter *U.S.A.* **108** F10
Wamulan *Indonesia* **63** E7
Wan Xian *China* **56** E8
Wana *Pakistan* **68** C3
Wanaaring *Australia* **95** D3
Wanaka *N.Z.* **91** F2
Wanaka, L. *N.Z.* **91** F2
Wanapitei L. *Canada* **104** C3
Wandel Sea = McKinley
  Sea *Arctic* **4** A7
Wandérama *Ivory C.* **82** D4
Wanderer *Zimbabwe* **87** F3
Wandhari *Pakistan* **68** F2
Wanding *China* **58** E2
Wandoan *Australia* **95** D4
Wanfu *China* **57** D12
Wang ➤ *Thailand* **64** D2
Wang Kai *Sudan* **81** F2
Wang Noi *Thailand* **64** E3
Wang Saphung *Thailand* **64** D3
Wang Thong *Thailand* **64** D3
Wanga *Dem. Rep. of the Congo* **86** B2
Wangal *Indonesia* **63** F8
Wanganella *Australia* **95** F3
Wanganui *N.Z.* **91** C5
Wangaratta *Australia* **95** F4
Wangary *Australia* **95** E2
Wangcang *China* **58** A6
Wangcheng *China* **59** C9
Wangdu *China* **56** E8
Wangen *Germany* **25** H5
Wangerooge *Germany* **24** B3
Wangiwangi *Indonesia* **63** F6
Wangjiang *China* **59** B11
Wangmo *China* **58** E6
Wangqing *China* **57** C15
Wankaner *India* **68** H4
Wanless *Canada* **103** C8
Wanleweyne *Somali Rep.* **75** G3
Wanneroo *Australia* **93** F2
Wannian *China* **59** C11
Wanning *China* **64** C8
Wanon Niwat *Thailand* **64** D4
Wanquan *China* **56** D8
Wanrong *China* **56** G6

Wanshan *China* **58** D7
Wanshengchang *China* **58** C6
Wantage *U.K.* **15** F6
Wanxian *China* **58** B7
Wanyuan *China* **58** A7
Wanzai *China* **59** C10
Wapakoneta *U.S.A.* **113** E11
Wapato *U.S.A.* **108** C3
Wapawekka L. *Canada* **103** C8
Wapikopa L. *Canada* **104** B2
Wapiti ➤ *Canada* **102** B5
Wappingers Falls *U.S.A.* **115** E11
Wapsipinicon ➤ *U.S.A.* **112** E8
Wapusk △ *Canada* **103** B10
Warab □ *Sudan* **81** F2
Warangal *India* **66** L11
Waraseoni *India* **69** J9
Waratah *Australia* **95** G4
Waratah B. *Australia* **95** F4
Warburg *Germany* **24** D5
Warburton *Vic., Australia* **95** F4
Warburton *W. Austral.,*
  Australia **93** E4
Warburton ➤ *Australia* **95** D2
Warburton Ra. *Australia* **93** E4
Ward *N.Z.* **91** D5
Ward ➤ *Australia* **95** D4
Ward Mt. *U.S.A.* **110** H8
Wardha *India* **66** J11
Wardha ➤ *India* **66** K11
Wardsville *Canada* **114** D3
Ware *U.K.* **15** F8
Ware *U.S.A.* **115** D12
Waregem *Belgium* **17** D3
Wareham *U.S.A.* **115** E14
Waremme *Belgium* **17** D5
Waren *Germany* **24** B8
Warendorf *Germany* **24** D4
Warialda *Australia* **95** D5
Wariap *Indonesia* **63** E8
Warin Chamrap *Thailand* **64** E5
Warka *Poland* **31** G8
Warkopi *Indonesia* **63** E8
Warm Springs *U.S.A.* **109** G5
Warman *Canada* **103** C7
Warmbad = Bela Bela
  S. Africa **89** C4
Warmbad *Namibia* **88** D2
Warmińsko-Mazurskie □
  Poland **30** D8
Warminster *U.K.* **15** F5
Warminster *U.S.A.* **115** F9
Warmun *Australia* **92** C4
Warnemünde *Germany* **24** A8
Warner Mts. *U.S.A.* **108** F3
Warner Robins *U.S.A.* **117** E13
Warnow ➤ *Germany* **24** A8
Waroona *Australia* **93** F2
Warracknabeal *Australia* **95** F3
Warragul *Australia* **95** F4
Warrego ➤ *Australia* **95** E4
Warrego Ra. *Australia* **94** C4
Warren *Australia* **95** E4
Warren *Ark., U.S.A.* **116** E8
Warren *Mich., U.S.A.* **113** D12
Warren *Minn., U.S.A.* **112** A5
Warren *Ohio, U.S.A.* **114** E4
Warren *Pa., U.S.A.* **114** E5
Warrenpoint *U.K.* **12** B5
Warrensburg *Mo., U.S.A.* **112** F7
Warrensburg *N.Y., U.S.A.* **115** C11
Warrenton *S. Africa* **88** D3
Warrenton *U.S.A.* **110** D3
Warri *Nigeria* **83** D6
Warrina *Australia* **95** D2
Warrington *U.K.* **14** D5
Warrington *U.S.A.* **117** F11
Warrington □ *U.K.* **14** D5
Warrnambool *Australia* **95** F3
Warroad *U.S.A.* **112** A6
Warruwi *Australia* **94** A1
Warsa *Indonesia* **63** E9
Warsak Dam *Pakistan* **68** B4
Warsaw = Warszawa *Poland* **31** F8
Warsaw *Ind., U.S.A.* **113** E11
Warsaw *N.Y., U.S.A.* **114** D6
Warsaw *Ohio, U.S.A.* **114** F3
Warstein *Germany* **24** D4
Warszawa *Poland* **31** F8
Warszawa ✈ (WAW) *Poland* **31** F7
Warta *Poland* **31** G5
Warta ➤ *Poland* **31** F1
Warthe = Warta ➤ *Poland* **31** F1
Waru *Indonesia* **63** E8
Warwick *Australia* **95** D5
Warwick *U.K.* **15** E6
Warwick *N.Y., U.S.A.* **115** E10
Warwick *R.I., U.S.A.* **115** E13
Warwickshire □ *U.K.* **15** E6
Wasaga Beach *Canada* **114** B4
Wasagaming *Canada* **103** C9
Wasatch Ra. *U.S.A.* **108** F8
Wasbank *S. Africa* **89** D5
Wasco *Calif., U.S.A.* **111** K7
Wasco *Oreg., U.S.A.* **108** D3
Wase *Nigeria* **83** D6
Waseca *U.S.A.* **112** C7

Wasekamio L. *Canada* **103** B7
Wash, The *U.K.* **14** E8
Washago *Canada* **114** B5
Washburn *N. Dak., U.S.A.* **112** B3
Washburn *Wis., U.S.A.* **112** B8
Washim *India* **66** J10
Washington *U.K.* **14** C6
Washington *D.C., U.S.A.* **113** F15
Washington *Ga., U.S.A.* **117** E13
Washington *Ind., U.S.A.* **112** F10
Washington *Iowa, U.S.A.* **112** E9
Washington *Mo., U.S.A.* **112** F8
Washington *N.C., U.S.A.* **117** D16
Washington *N.J., U.S.A.* **115** F10
Washington *Pa., U.S.A.* **114** F4
Washington *Utah, U.S.A.* **109** H7
Washington □ *U.S.A.* **108** C3
Washington, Mt. *U.S.A.* **115** B13
Washington Court House
  U.S.A. **113** F12
Washington I. *U.S.A.* **112** C10
Washougal *U.S.A.* **110** E4
Washpool △ *Australia* **95** D5
Wasian *Indonesia* **63** E8
Wasilków *Poland* **31** E10
Wasilla *U.S.A.* **100** C5
Wasior *Indonesia* **63** E8
Wāsiţ □ *Iraq* **73** F11
Waskaganish *Canada* **104** B4
Waskaiowaka L. *Canada* **103** B9
Waskesiu Lake *Canada* **103** C7
Wasserburg *Germany* **25** G8
Wasserkuppe *Germany* **24** E5
Wassy *France* **19** D11
Waswanipi *Canada* **104** C4
Waswanipi, L. *Canada* **104** C4
Watampone *Indonesia* **63** E6
Watamu *Kenya* **86** C5
Watarrka △ *Australia* **92** D5
Water Park Pt. *Australia* **94** C5
Water Valley *U.S.A.* **117** D10
Waterberg Plateau △
  Namibia **88** C2
Waterberge *S. Africa* **89** C4
Waterbury *Conn., U.S.A.* **115** E11
Waterbury *Vt., U.S.A.* **115** B12
Waterbury L. *Canada* **103** B8
Waterdown *Canada* **114** C5
Waterford *Canada* **114** D4
Waterford *Ireland* **12** D4
Waterford *Calif., U.S.A.* **110** H6
Waterford *Pa., U.S.A.* **114** E5
Waterford □ *Ireland* **12** D4
Waterford Harbour *Ireland* **12** D5
Waterhen L. *Canada* **103** C9
Waterloo *Belgium* **17** D4
Waterloo *Ont., Canada* **114** C4
Waterloo *Qué., Canada* **115** A12
Waterloo *S. Leone* **82** D2
Waterloo *Ill., U.S.A.* **112** F8
Waterloo *Iowa, U.S.A.* **112** D8
Waterloo *N.Y., U.S.A.* **114** D8
Watermeet *U.S.A.* **112** B9
Waterton Lakes △ *Canada* **102** D6
Watertown *Conn., U.S.A.* **115** E11
Watertown *N.Y., U.S.A.* **115** C9
Watertown *S. Dak., U.S.A.* **112** C5
Watertown *Wis., U.S.A.* **112** D9
Waterval-Boven *S. Africa* **89** D5
Waterville *Canada* **115** A13
Waterville *Maine, U.S.A.* **113** C19
Waterville *N.Y., U.S.A.* **115** D9
Waterville *Pa., U.S.A.* **114** E7
Waterville *Wash., U.S.A.* **108** C3
Watervliet *U.S.A.* **115** D11
Wates *Indonesia* **63** G14
Watford *Canada* **114** D3
Watford *U.K.* **15** F7
Watford City *U.S.A.* **112** B2
Wathaman ➤ *Canada* **103** B8
Wathaman L. *Canada* **103** B8
Watheroo *Australia* **93** F2
Watheroo △ *Australia* **93** F2
Wating *China* **56** G4
Watkins Glen *U.S.A.* **114** D8
Watling I. = San Salvador
  I. *Bahamas* **121** B5
Watonga *U.S.A.* **116** D5
Watrous *Canada* **103** C7
Watrous *U.S.A.* **109** J11
Watsa *Dem. Rep. of the Congo* **86** B2
Watseka *U.S.A.* **112** E10
Watson *Canada* **103** C8
Watson Lake *Canada* **102** A3
Watsontown *U.S.A.* **114** E8
Watsonville *U.S.A.* **110** J5
Wattiwarriganna Cr. ➤
  Australia **95** D2
Wattwil *Switz.* **25** H5
Watuata = Batuata *Indonesia* **63** F6
Watubela, Kepulauan
  Indonesia **63** E8
Watubela Is. = Watubela,
  Kepulauan *Indonesia* **63** E8
Wau = Wâw *Sudan* **81** F2
Waubamik *Canada* **114** A4
Waubay *U.S.A.* **112** C5
Wauchope *N.S.W., Australia* **95** E5

Wauchope *N. Terr., Australia* **94** C1
Wauchula *U.S.A.* **117** H14
Waukarlycarly, L. *Australia* **92** D3
Waukegan *U.S.A.* **112** D10
Waukesha *U.S.A.* **112** D9
Waukon *U.S.A.* **112** D8
Waupaca *U.S.A.* **112** C9
Waupun *U.S.A.* **112** D9
Waurika *U.S.A.* **116** D6
Wausau *U.S.A.* **112** C9
Wautoma *U.S.A.* **112** C9
Wauwatosa *U.S.A.* **112** D9
Wave Hill = Kalkarindji
  Australia **92** C5
Wave Rock △ *Australia* **93** F3
Waveney ➤ *U.K.* **15** E9
Waverley *N.Z.* **91** C5
Waverly *Iowa, U.S.A.* **112** D7
Waverly *N.Y., U.S.A.* **115** E9
Wavre *Belgium* **17** D4
Wâw *Sudan* **81** F2
Wâw al Kabîr *Libya* **79** C9
Wawa *Canada* **104** C3
Wawa *Nigeria* **83** D5
Wawa *Sudan* **80** C3
Wawanesa *Canada* **103** D9
Wawona *U.S.A.* **110** H7
Waxahachie *U.S.A.* **116** E6
Way, L. *Australia* **93** E3
Waya *Fiji* **91** a
Waycross *U.S.A.* **117** F13
Wayi *Sudan* **81** F3
Wayland *U.S.A.* **114** D7
Wayne *Nebr., U.S.A.* **112** D5
Wayne *W. Va., U.S.A.* **113** F12
Waynesboro *Ga., U.S.A.* **117** E13
Waynesboro *Miss., U.S.A.* **117** F10
Waynesboro *Pa., U.S.A.* **113** F15
Waynesboro *Va., U.S.A.* **113** F14
Waynesburg *U.S.A.* **113** F13
Waynesville *U.S.A.* **117** D13
Waynoka *U.S.A.* **116** C5
Wazirabad *Pakistan* **68** C6
Wda ➤ *Poland* **30** E5
We *Indonesia* **62** C1
Weald, The *U.K.* **15** F8
Wear ➤ *U.K.* **14** C6
Weatherford *Okla., U.S.A.* **116** D5
Weatherford *Tex., U.S.A.* **116** E6
Weaverville *U.S.A.* **108** F2
Webb City *U.S.A.* **112** G6
Webequie *Canada* **104** B2
Webo = Nyaake *Liberia* **82** E3
Webster *Mass., U.S.A.* **115** D13
Webster *N.Y., U.S.A.* **114** C7
Webster *S. Dak., U.S.A.* **112** C5
Webster City *U.S.A.* **112** D7
Webster Springs *U.S.A.* **113** F13
Weda *Indonesia* **63** D7
Weda, Teluk *Indonesia* **63** D7
Weddell Abyssal Plain
  S. Ocean **5** C2
Weddell I. *Falk. Is.* **128** G4
Weddell Sea *Antarctica* **5** D1
Wedderburn *Australia* **95** F3
Wedel *Germany* **24** B5
Wedemark *Germany* **24** C5
Wedgeport *Canada* **105** D6
Wedza *Zimbabwe* **87** F3
Wee Waa *Australia* **95** E4
Weed *U.S.A.* **108** F2
Weed Heights *U.S.A.* **110** G7
Weedsport *N.Y., U.S.A.* **115** C8
Weedsport *N.Y., U.S.A.* **115** C8
Weedville *U.S.A.* **114** E6
Weenen *S. Africa* **89** D5
Weener *Germany* **24** B3
Weert *Neths.* **17** C5
Węgierska-Górka *Poland* **31** J6
Węgliniec *Poland* **31** G2
Węgorzewo *Poland* **30** D8
Węgorzyno *Poland* **30** E2
Węgrów *Poland* **31** F9
Wehda □ *Sudan* **81** F3
Wei He ➤ *Hebei, China* **56** F8
Wei He ➤ *Shaanxi, China* **56** G6
Weichang *China* **57** D9
Weichuan *China* **56** G7
Weida *Germany* **24** E8
Weiden *Germany* **25** F8
Weifang *China* **57** F10
Weihai *China* **57** F12
Weil *Germany* **25** H3
Weilburg *Germany* **24** E4
Weilheim *Germany* **25** H7
Weimar *Germany* **24** E7
Weinan *China* **56** G5
Weingarten *Germany* **25** H5
Weinheim *Germany* **25** F4
Weining *China* **58** D5
Weipa *Australia* **94** A3
Weir ➤ *Australia* **95** D4
Weir ➤ *Canada* **103** B10
Weir River *Canada* **103** B10
Weirton *U.S.A.* **114** F4
Weiser *U.S.A.* **108** D5
Weishan *Shandong, China* **57** G9
Weishan *Yunnan, China* **58** E3

Weissenburg *Germany* **25** F6
Weissenfels *Germany* **24** D7
Weisswasser *Germany* **24** D10
Wéitra *Austria* **26** C7
Weixi *China* **58** D2
Weixin *China* **58** D5
Weiyuan *China* **56** G3
Weiz *Austria* **26** D8
Weizhou Dao *China* **58** G7
Wejherowo *Poland* **30** D5
Wekusko L. *Canada* **103** C9
Welch *U.S.A.* **113** G13
Weldya *Ethiopia* **81** E4
Welega *Ethiopia* **81** F4
Welford △ *Australia* **94** D3
Welkite *Ethiopia* **81** F4
Welkom *S. Africa* **88** D4
Welland *Canada* **114** D5
Welland → *U.K.* **15** E7
Wellesley Is. *Australia* **94** B2
Wellingborough *U.K.* **15** E7
Wellington *Australia* **95** E4
Wellington *Canada* **114** C7
Wellington *N.Z.* **91** D5
Wellington *S. Africa* **88** E2
Wellington *Somst., U.K.* **15** G4
Wellington *Telford & Wrekin, U.K.* **15** E5
Wellington *Colo., U.S.A.* **108** F11
Wellington *Kans., U.S.A.* **112** G5
Wellington *Nev., U.S.A.* **110** G7
Wellington *Ohio, U.S.A.* **114** E2
Wellington *Tex., U.S.A.* **116** D4
Wellington, I. *Chile* **128** F2
Wellington, L. *Australia* **95** F4
Wellington Chan. *Canada* **101** B10
Wells *U.K.* **15** F5
Wells *Maine, U.S.A.* **115** C14
Wells *N.Y., U.S.A.* **115** C10
Wells *Nev., U.S.A.* **108** F6
Wells, L. *Australia* **93** E3
Wells, Mt. *Australia* **92** C4
Wells Gray △ *Canada* **102** C4
Wells-next-the-Sea *U.K.* **14** E8
Wells River *U.S.A.* **115** B12
Wellsboro *U.S.A.* **114** E7
Wellsburg *U.S.A.* **114** F4
Wellsville *N.Y., U.S.A.* **114** D7
Wellsville *Ohio, U.S.A.* **114** F4
Wellsville *Utah, U.S.A.* **108** F8
Wellton *U.S.A.* **109** K6
Welmel, Wabi → *Ethiopia* **81** F5
Welo *Ethiopia* **81** E4
Wels *Austria* **26** C7
Welshpool *U.K.* **15** E4
Welwyn Garden City *U.K.* **15** F7
Wem *U.K.* **14** E5
Wembere → *Tanzania* **86** C3
Wemindji *Canada* **104** B4
Wemyss *Canada* **115** B8
Wen Xian *China* **56** G7
Wenchang *China* **64** C8
Wencheng *China* **59** D13
Wenchi *Ghana* **82** D4
Wenchow = Wenzhou *China* **59** D13
Wenchuan *China* **58** B4
Wenden *U.S.A.* **111** M13
Wendeng *China* **57** F12
Wendesi *Indonesia* **63** E8
Wendo *Ethiopia* **81** F4
Wendover *U.S.A.* **108** F6
Weng'an *China* **58** D6
Wengcheng *China* **59** E9
Wengen *Switz.* **19** E14
Wengyuan *China* **59** E10
Wenling *China* **59** C13
Wenlock → *Australia* **94** A3
Wenshan *China* **58** F5
Wenshang *China* **56** G9
Wenshui *China* **56** F7
Wensleydale *U.K.* **14** C6
Wensu *China* **60** B3
Wensum → *U.K.* **14** E8
Wentworth *Australia* **95** E3
Wentzel L. *Canada* **102** B6
Wenut *Indonesia* **63** E8
Wenxi *China* **56** G6
Wenxian *China* **56** H3
Wenzhou *China* **59** D13
Weott *U.S.A.* **108** F2
Wepener *S. Africa* **88** D4
Werda *Botswana* **88** D3
Werdau *Germany* **24** E8
Werder *Germany* **24** C8
Werdohl *Germany* **24** D3
Wereilu *Ethiopia* **81** E4
Weri *Indonesia* **63** E8
Werneck *Germany* **25** F6
Wernigerode *Germany* **24** D6
Werra → *Germany* **24** D5
Werribee *Australia* **95** F3
Werrimull *Australia* **95** E3
Werris Creek *Australia* **95** E5
Wertach → *Germany* **25** G6
Wertheim *Germany* **25** F5
Wertingen *Germany* **25** G6

Wesel *Germany* **24** D2
Weser → *Germany* **24** B4
Weser-Ems □ *Germany* **24** C3
Weserbergland *Germany* **24** C5
Weserbergland Schaumburg Hameln △ *Germany* **24** C5
Wesiri *Indonesia* **63** F7
Weslaco *U.S.A.* **116** H6
Weslemkoon L. *Canada* **114** A7
Wesleyville *Canada* **105** C9
Wesleyville *U.S.A.* **114** D4
Wessel, C. *Australia* **94** A2
Wessel Is. *Australia* **94** A2
Wesselburen *Germany* **24** A4
Wessington Springs *U.S.A.* **112** C4
West *U.S.A.* **116** F6
West → *U.S.A.* **115** D12
West Allis *U.S.A.* **112** D9
West Antarctica *Antarctica* **5** D15
West Baines → *Australia* **92** C4
West Bank ■ *Asia* **74** C4
West Bend *U.S.A.* **112** D9
West Bengal □ *India* **69** H13
West Berkshire □ *U.K.* **15** F6
West Beskids = Západné Beskydy *Europe* **27** B12
West Branch *U.S.A.* **113** C11
West Branch Susquehanna → *U.S.A.* **115** F8
West Bromwich *U.K.* **15** E6
West Burra *U.K.* **13** A7
West Canada Cr. → *U.S.A.* **115** C10
West Caroline Basin *Pac. Oc.* **96** G5
West Chazy *U.S.A.* **115** B11
West Chester *U.S.A.* **115** G9
West Coast △ *Namibia* **88** C1
West Coast □ *S. Africa* **88** E2
West Columbia *U.S.A.* **116** G7
West Covina *U.S.A.* **111** L9
West Des Moines *U.S.A.* **112** E7
West Dunbartonshire □ *U.K.* **13** F4
West End *Bahamas* **120** A4
West Falkland *Falk. Is.* **128** G4
West Fargo *U.S.A.* **112** B5
West Fiji Basin *Pac. Oc.* **96** J9
West Fjord = Vestfjorden *Norway* **8** C16
West Fork Trinity → *U.S.A.* **116** E6
West Frankfort *U.S.A.* **112** G9
West Grand L. *U.S.A.* **113** C20
West Hartford *U.S.A.* **115** E12
West Haven *U.S.A.* **115** E12
West Hazleton *U.S.A.* **115** F9
West Helena *U.S.A.* **117** D9
West Hurley *U.S.A.* **115** E10
West Ice Shelf *Antarctica* **5** C7
West Indies *Cent. Amer.* **121** D7
West Jordan *U.S.A.* **108** F8
West Linn *U.S.A.* **110** E4
West Lorne *Canada* **114** D3
West Lothian □ *U.K.* **13** F5
West Lunga → *Zambia* **87** E1
West MacDonnell △ *Australia* **92** D5
West Mariana Basin *Pac. Oc.* **96** F5
West Memphis *U.S.A.* **117** D9
West Midlands □ *U.K.* **15** E6
West Mifflin *U.S.A.* **114** F5
West Milford *U.S.A.* **115** E10
West Milton *U.S.A.* **114** E8
West Monroe *U.S.A.* **116** E8
West Newton *U.S.A.* **114** F5
West Nicholson *Zimbabwe* **87** G2
West Odessa *U.S.A.* **116** F3
West Palm Beach *U.S.A.* **117** H14
West Plains *U.S.A.* **112** G8
West Point *Miss., U.S.A.* **117** E10
West Point *N.Y., U.S.A.* **115** E11
West Point *Nebr., U.S.A.* **112** E5
West Point *Va., U.S.A.* **113** G15
West Point L. *U.S.A.* **117** E12
West Pt. = Ouest, Pte. de l' *Canada* **105** C7
West Pt. *Australia* **95** F2
West Road → *Canada* **102** C4
West Rutland *U.S.A.* **115** C11
West Schelde = Westerschelde → *Neths.* **17** C3
West Seneca *U.S.A.* **114** D6
West Siberian Plain *Russia* **50** B9
West Sussex □ *U.K.* **15** G7
West-Terschelling *Neths.* **17** A5
West Valley City *U.S.A.* **108** F8
West Virginia □ *U.S.A.* **113** F13
West-Vlaanderen □ *Belgium* **17** D2
West Walker → *U.S.A.* **110** G7
West Wyalong *Australia* **95** E4
West Yellowstone *U.S.A.* **108** D8
West Yorkshire □ *U.K.* **14** D6
Westall, Pt. *Australia* **95** E1
Westbrook *U.S.A.* **113** D18
Westbury *Australia* **95** G4
Westby *U.S.A.* **108** B11
Westend *U.S.A.* **111** K9

Westerland *Germany* **24** A4
Westerly *U.S.A.* **115** E13
Western □ *Ghana* **82** D4
Western □ *Kenya* **86** B3
Western □ *S. Leone* **82** D2
Western □ *Zambia* **87** F1
Western Australia □ *Australia* **93** E2
Western Cape □ *S. Africa* **88** E3
Western Dvina = Daugava → *Latvia* **32** D3
Western Ghats *India* **66** N9
Western Isles □ *U.K.* **13** D1
Western Sahara ■ *Africa* **78** D3
Western Samoa = Samoa ■ *Pac. Oc.* **91** b
Western Sierra Madre = Madre Occidental, Sierra *Mexico* **118** B3
Westernport *U.S.A.* **113** F14
Westerschelde → *Neths.* **17** C3
Westerstede *Germany* **24** B3
Westerwald *Germany* **24** E3
Westfield *Mass., U.S.A.* **115** D12
Westfield *N.Y., U.S.A.* **114** D5
Westfield *Pa., U.S.A.* **114** E7
Westhill *U.K.* **13** D6
Westhope *U.S.A.* **112** A3
Westland △ *N.Z.* **91** E2
Westland Bight *N.Z.* **91** E3
Westlock *Canada* **102** C6
Westmar *Australia* **95** D4
Westmeath □ *Ireland* **12** C4
Westminster *Calif., U.S.A.* **111** M8
Westminster *Colo., U.S.A.* **108** G11
Westminster *Md., U.S.A.* **113** F15
Westmont *U.S.A.* **114** F6
Westmoreland *Barbados* **121** g
Westmorland *U.S.A.* **111** M11
Weston *Oreg., U.S.A.* **108** D4
Weston *W. Va., U.S.A.* **113** F13
Weston I. *Canada* **104** B4
Weston-super-Mare *U.K.* **15** F5
Westover *U.S.A.* **114** F6
Westport *Canada* **115** B8
Westport *Ireland* **12** C2
Westport *N.Z.* **91** D3
Westport *N.Y., U.S.A.* **115** B11
Westport *Oreg., U.S.A.* **110** D3
Westport *Wash., U.S.A.* **110** D2
Westray *Canada* **103** C8
Westray *U.K.* **13** B5
Westree *Canada* **104** C3
Westville *U.S.A.* **110** F6
Westwood *U.S.A.* **108** F3
Wetar *Indonesia* **63** F7
Wetaskiwin *Canada* **102** C6
Wete *Tanzania* **84** F7
Wetherby *U.K.* **14** D6
Wethersfield *U.S.A.* **115** E12
Wetteren *Belgium* **17** D3
Wetzlar *Germany* **24** E4
Wewoka *U.S.A.* **116** D6
Wexford *Ireland* **12** D5
Wexford □ *Ireland* **12** D5
Wexford Harbour *Ireland* **12** D5
Weyburn *Canada* **103** D8
Weyer Markt *Austria* **26** D7
Weyhe *Germany* **24** C4
Weyib → *Ethiopia* **81** F5
Weymouth *Canada* **105** D6
Weymouth *U.K.* **15** G5
Weymouth *U.S.A.* **115** D14
Weymouth, C. *Australia* **94** A3
Wha Ti *Canada* **100** C8
Whakaari = White I. *N.Z.* **91** B6
Whakatane *N.Z.* **91** B6
Whale → *Canada* **105** A6
Whale Cove *Canada* **103** A10
Whales, B. of *Antarctica* **5** D12
Whalsay *U.K.* **13** A8
Whangamata *N.Z.* **91** B5
Whangamomona *N.Z.* **91** C5
Whanganui △ *N.Z.* **91** C5
Whangarei *N.Z.* **91** A5
Whangarei Harb. *N.Z.* **91** A5
Wharekauri = Chatham Is. *Pac. Oc.* **96** M10
Wharfe → *U.K.* **14** D6
Wharfedale *U.K.* **14** C5
Wharton *N.J., U.S.A.* **115** F10
Wharton *Pa., U.S.A.* **114** E6
Wharton *Tex., U.S.A.* **116** G6
Wharton Basin *Ind. Oc.* **96** K1
Wheatland *Calif., U.S.A.* **110** F5
Wheatland *Wyo., U.S.A.* **108** E11
Wheatley *Canada* **114** D2
Wheaton *Md., U.S.A.* **113** F15
Wheaton *Minn., U.S.A.* **112** C5
Wheelbarrow Pk. *U.S.A.* **110** H10
Wheeler *Oreg., U.S.A.* **108** D2
Wheeler *Tex., U.S.A.* **116** D4
Wheeler → *Canada* **105** A6
Wheeler L. *U.S.A.* **117** D11
Wheeler Pk. *N. Mex., U.S.A.* **109** H11
Wheeler Pk. *Nev., U.S.A.* **108** G6
Wheeler Ridge *U.S.A.* **111** L8

Wheelersburg *U.S.A.* **113** F12
Wheeling *U.S.A.* **114** F4
Whernside *U.K.* **14** C5
Whiddy I. *Ireland* **12** E2
Whim Creek *Australia* **92** D2
Whiskey Jack L. *Canada* **103** B8
Whiskeytown-Shasta-Trinity △ *U.S.A.* **108** F2
Whistleduck Cr. → *Australia* **94** C2
Whistler *Canada* **102** C4
Whitby *Canada* **114** C6
Whitby *U.K.* **14** C7
White → *Ark., U.S.A.* **116** E9
White → *Ind., U.S.A.* **112** F10
White → *S. Dak., U.S.A.* **112** D4
White → *Tex., U.S.A.* **116** E4
White → *Utah, U.S.A.* **108** F9
White → *Vt., U.S.A.* **115** C12
White → *Wash., U.S.A.* **110** C4
White, L. *Australia* **92** D4
White B. *Canada* **105** C8
White Bird *U.S.A.* **108** D5
White Butte *U.S.A.* **112** B2
White City *U.S.A.* **108** E2
White Cliffs *Australia* **95** E3
White Hall *U.S.A.* **112** F8
White Haven *U.S.A.* **115** E9
White Horse, Vale of *U.K.* **15** F6
White I. *N.Z.* **91** B6
White L. *U.S.A.* **115** A8
White L. *Canada* **116** G8
White Lake *Canada* **115** A8
White Mountain Peak *U.S.A.* **109** H4
White Mts. *Calif., U.S.A.* **110** H8
White Mts. *N.H., U.S.A.* **115** B13
White Mts. △ *Australia* **94** C4
White Nile = Nîl el Abyad → *Sudan* **81** D3
White Nile Dam = Khazzân Jabal al Awliyâ *Sudan* **81** D3
White Otter L. *Canada* **104** C1
White Pass *U.S.A.* **110** D5
White Plains *U.S.A.* **115** E11
White River *Canada* **104** C2
White River *S. Africa* **89** D5
White River *U.S.A.* **112** D3
White Rock *Canada* **110** A4
White Rock *U.S.A.* **109** J10
White Russia = Belarus ■ *Europe* **23** B14
White Sands △ *U.S.A.* **109** K10
White Sea = Beloye More *Russia* **8** C25
White Sulphur Springs *Mont., U.S.A.* **108** C8
White Sulphur Springs *W. Va., U.S.A.* **113** G13
White Swan *U.S.A.* **110** D6
White Volta → *Ghana* **83** D4
Whitecliffs *N.Z.* **91** E3
Whitecourt *Canada* **102** C5
Whiteface Mt. *U.S.A.* **115** B11
Whitefield *U.S.A.* **115** B13
Whitefish *U.S.A.* **108** B6
Whitefish B. *U.S.A.* **104** C3
Whitefish L. *Canada* **103** A7
Whitefish Pt. *U.S.A.* **113** B11
Whitegull, L. = Goélands, L. aux *Canada* **105** A7
Whitehall *Mich., U.S.A.* **112** D10
Whitehall *Mont., U.S.A.* **108** D7
Whitehall *N.Y., U.S.A.* **115** C11
Whitehall *Wis., U.S.A.* **112** C8
Whitehaven *U.K.* **14** C4
Whitehorse *Canada* **102** A1
Whitemark *Australia* **95** G4
Whiteplains *Liberia* **82** D2
Whiteriver *U.S.A.* **109** K9
Whitesand → *Canada* **102** A5
Whitesands *S. Africa* **88** E3
Whitesboro *N.Y., U.S.A.* **115** C9
Whitesboro *Tex., U.S.A.* **116** E6
Whiteshell △ *Canada* **103** D9
Whiteville *U.S.A.* **117** D15
Whitewater *U.S.A.* **112** D9
Whitewater Baldy *U.S.A.* **109** K9
Whitewater L. *Canada* **104** B2
Whitewood *Australia* **94** C3
Whitewood *Canada* **103** C8
Whithorn *U.K.* **13** G4
Whitianga *N.Z.* **91** B5
Whitman *U.S.A.* **115** D14
Whitney *Canada* **114** A6
Whitney, Mt. *U.S.A.* **110** J8
Whitney Point *U.S.A.* **115** D9
Whitstable *U.K.* **15** F9
Whitsunday I. *Australia* **94** J7
Whitsunday Islands △ *Australia* **94** J6
Whitsunday Passage *Australia* **94** J6
Whittier *U.S.A.* **111** M8
Whittlesea *Australia* **95** F4
Wholdaia L. *Canada* **103** A8
Whyalla *Australia* **95** E2

Wiang Sa *Thailand* **64** C3
Wiarton *Canada* **114** B3
Wiawso *Ghana* **82** D4
Wiay *U.K.* **13** D1
Wiązów *Poland* **31** H4
Wibaux *U.S.A.* **108** C11
Wichian Buri *Thailand* **64** E3
Wichita *U.S.A.* **112** G5
Wichita Falls *U.S.A.* **116** E5
Wick *U.K.* **13** C5
Wickenburg *U.S.A.* **109** K7
Wickepin *Australia* **93** F2
Wickham *Australia* **92** D2
Wickham, C. *Australia* **95** F3
Wickliffe *U.S.A.* **114** E3
Wicklow *Ireland* **12** D5
Wicklow □ *Ireland* **12** D5
Wicklow Hd. *Ireland* **12** D6
Wicklow Mts. *Ireland* **12** C5
Wicklow Mts. △ *Ireland* **12** C5
Widawa → *Poland* **31** G5
Widawka → *Poland* **31** G5
Widgeegoara Cr. → *Australia* **95** D4
Widgiemooltha *Australia* **93** F3
Widnes *U.K.* **14** D5
Więcbork *Poland* **31** E4
Wiehengebirge = Nördlicher Teutoburger Wald-Wiehengebirge △ *Germany* **24** C4
Wiehl *Germany* **24** E3
Wiek *Germany* **24** A9
Wielbark *Poland* **30** E7
Wieleń *Poland* **31** F3
Wielichowo *Poland* **31** F3
Wieliczka *Poland* **31** J7
Wielkopolski △ *Poland* **31** F3
Wielkopolskie □ *Poland* **31** F4
Wieluń *Poland* **31** G5
Wien *Austria* **27** C9
Wien-Schwechat ✈ (VIE) *Austria* **27** C9
Wiener Neustadt *Austria* **27** D9
Wieprz → *Poland* **31** G8
Wieprza → *Poland* **30** D3
Wieruszów *Poland* **31** G5
Wiesbaden *Germany* **25** E4
Wiesental *Germany* **25** F4
Wiesloch *Germany* **25** F4
Wiesmoor *Germany* **24** B3
Wieżyca *Poland* **30** D5
Wigan *U.K.* **14** D5
Wiggins *Colo., U.S.A.* **108** F11
Wiggins *Miss., U.S.A.* **117** F10
Wight, I. of *U.K.* **15** G6
Wigierski △ *Poland* **30** D10
Wigry, Jezioro *Poland* **30** D10
Wigston *U.K.* **15** E6
Wigton *U.K.* **14** C4
Wigtown *U.K.* **13** G4
Wigtown B. *U.K.* **13** G4
Wil *Switz.* **25** H5
Wilamowice *Poland* **31** J6
Wilber *U.S.A.* **112** E5
Wilberforce *Canada* **114** A6
Wilberforce, C. *Australia* **94** A2
Wilburton *U.S.A.* **116** D7
Wilcannia *Australia* **95** E3
Wilcox *U.S.A.* **114** E6
Wildbad *Germany* **25** G4
Wildeshausen *Germany* **24** C4
Wildeshauser Geest △ *Germany* **24** C4
Wildon *Austria* **26** E8
Wildrose *U.S.A.* **111** J9
Wildspitze *Austria* **26** E3
Wilga → *Poland* **31** F8
Wilge → *S. Africa* **89** D4
Wilhelm II Coast *Antarctica* **5** C7
Wilhelmsburg *Austria* **26** C8
Wilhelmshaven *Germany* **24** B4
Wilhelmstal *Namibia* **88** C2
Wilkes-Barre *U.S.A.* **115** E9
Wilkes Land *Antarctica* **5** D7
Wilkie *Canada* **103** C7
Wilkinsburg *U.S.A.* **114** F5
Wilkinson Lakes *Australia* **93** E5
Willandra Creek → *Australia* **95** E4
Willapa B. *U.S.A.* **108** C1
Willapa Hills *U.S.A.* **110** D3
Willard *U.S.A.* **114** E2
Willcox *U.S.A.* **109** K9
Willemstad *Neth. Ant.* **121** D6
William → *Canada* **103** B7
William 'Bill' Dannelly Res. *U.S.A.* **117** E11
William Creek *Australia* **95** D2
Williams *Australia* **93** F2
Williams *Ariz., U.S.A.* **109** J7
Williams *Calif., U.S.A.* **110** F4
Williams Harbour *Canada* **105** B8
Williams Lake *Canada* **102** C4
Williamsburg *Ky., U.S.A.* **113** G11
Williamsburg *Pa., U.S.A.* **114** F6
Williamsburg *Va., U.S.A.* **113** G15
Williamson *N.Y., U.S.A.* **114** C7

Williamson *W. Va., U.S.A.* **113** G12
Williamsport *U.S.A.* **114** E7
Williamston *U.S.A.* **117** D16
Williamstown *Australia* **95** F3
Williamstown *Ky., U.S.A.* **113** F11
Williamstown *Mass., U.S.A.* **115** D11
Williamstown *N.Y., U.S.A.* **115** C9
Willimantic *U.S.A.* **115** E12
Willingboro *U.S.A.* **113** E16
Williston *S. Africa* **88** E3
Williston *Fla., U.S.A.* **117** G13
Williston *N. Dak., U.S.A.* **112** A2
Williston L. *Canada* **102** B4
Willits *U.S.A.* **108** G2
Willmar *U.S.A.* **112** C6
Willmore Wilderness △ *Canada* **102** C3
Willoughby *U.S.A.* **114** E3
Willow Bunch *Canada* **103** D7
Willow L. *Canada* **102** A5
Willow Wall, The *China* **57** C12
Willowick *U.S.A.* **114** E3
Willowlake → *Canada* **102** A4
Willowmore *S. Africa* **88** E3
Willows *U.S.A.* **110** F4
Willowvale = Gatyana *S. Africa* **89** E4
Wills, L. *Australia* **92** D4
Wills Cr. → *Australia* **94** C3
Willsboro *U.S.A.* **115** B11
Willunga *Australia* **95** F2
Wilmette *U.S.A.* **112** D10
Wilmington *Australia* **95** E2
Wilmington *Del., U.S.A.* **113** F16
Wilmington *N.C., U.S.A.* **117** D16
Wilmington *Ohio, U.S.A.* **113** F12
Wilmington *Vt., U.S.A.* **115** D12
Wilmslow *U.K.* **14** D5
Wilpena Cr. → *Australia* **95** E2
Wilsall *U.S.A.* **108** D8
Wilson *N.C., U.S.A.* **117** D16
Wilson *N.Y., U.S.A.* **114** C6
Wilson *Pa., U.S.A.* **115** F9
Wilson → *Australia* **92** C4
Wilson Bluff *Australia* **93** F4
Wilson Inlet *Australia* **93** G2
Wilsons Promontory *Australia* **95** F4
Wilster *Germany* **24** B5
Wilton *U.S.A.* **112** B3
Wilton → *Australia* **94** A1
Wiltshire □ *U.K.* **15** F6
Wiltz *Lux.* **17** E5
Wiluna *Australia* **93** E3
Wimborne Minster *U.K.* **15** G6
Wimereux *France* **19** B8
Wimmera → *Australia* **95** F3
Winam G. *Kenya* **86** C3
Winburg *S. Africa* **88** D4
Winchendon *U.S.A.* **115** D12
Winchester *U.K.* **15** F6
Winchester *Conn., U.S.A.* **115** E11
Winchester *Idaho, U.S.A.* **108** C5
Winchester *Ind., U.S.A.* **113** E11
Winchester *Ky., U.S.A.* **113** G11
Winchester *N.H., U.S.A.* **115** D12
Winchester *Nev., U.S.A.* **111** J11
Winchester *Tenn., U.S.A.* **117** D11
Winchester *Va., U.S.A.* **113** F14
Wind → *U.S.A.* **108** E9
Wind Cave △ *U.S.A.* **112** D2
Wind River Range *U.S.A.* **108** E9
Windau = Ventspils *Latvia* **30** A8
Windber *U.S.A.* **114** F6
Winder *U.S.A.* **117** D13
Windermere *U.K.* **14** C5
Windhoek *Namibia* **88** C2
Windischgarsten *Austria* **26** D7
Windjana Gorge △ *Australia* **92** C3
Windom *U.S.A.* **112** D6
Windorah *Australia* **94** D3
Window Rock *U.S.A.* **109** J9
Windrush → *U.K.* **15** F6
Windsor *Australia* **95** E5
Windsor *N.S., Canada* **105** D7
Windsor *Ont., Canada* **114** D2
Windsor *U.K.* **15** F7
Windsor *Calif., U.S.A.* **108** G2
Windsor *Colo., U.S.A.* **108** F11
Windsor *Conn., U.S.A.* **115** E12
Windsor *Mo., U.S.A.* **112** F7
Windsor *N.Y., U.S.A.* **115** D9
Windsor *Vt., U.S.A.* **115** C12
Windsor & Maidenhead □ *U.K.* **15** F7
Windsorton *S. Africa* **88** D3
Windward Is. *W. Indies* **121** D7
Windward Passage = Vientos, Paso de los Caribbean *Caribbean* **121** C5
Winefred L. *Canada* **103** B6
Winejok *Sudan* **81** F2
Winfield *U.S.A.* **112** G5
Wingate Mts. *Australia* **92** B5
Wingham *Australia* **95** E5
Wingham *Canada* **114** C3
Winisk → *Canada* **104** A2

Winisk L. *Canada* **104** B2
Wink *U.S.A.* **116** F3
Winkler *Canada* **103** D9
Winklern *Austria* **26** E5
Winlock *U.S.A.* **110** D4
Winneba *Ghana* **83** D4
Winnebago, L. *U.S.A.* **112** D9
Winnecke Cr. → *Australia* **92** C5
Winnemucca *U.S.A.* **108** F5
Winnemucca L. *U.S.A.* **108** F4
Winner *U.S.A.* **112** D4
Winnett *U.S.A.* **108** C9
Winnfield *U.S.A.* **116** F8
Winnibigoshish, L. *U.S.A.* **112** B6
Winnipeg *Canada* **103** D9
Winnipeg → *Canada* **103** C9
Winnipeg, L. *Canada* **103** C9
Winnipeg Beach *Canada* **103** C9
Winnipegosis *Canada* **103** C9
Winnipegosis L. *Canada* **103** C9
Winnipesaukee, L. *U.S.A.* **115** C13
Winnisquam L. *U.S.A.* **115** C13
Winnsboro *La., U.S.A.* **116** F9
Winnsboro *S.C., U.S.A.* **117** D14
Winnsboro *Tex., U.S.A.* **116** E7
Winokapau, L. *Canada* **105** B7
Winona *Minn., U.S.A.* **112** C8
Winona *Miss., U.S.A.* **117** E10
Winooski *U.S.A.* **115** B11
Winooski → *U.S.A.* **115** B11
Winschoten *Neths.* **17** A7
Winsen *Germany* **24** B6
Winsford *U.K.* **14** D5
Winslow = Bainbridge
  Island *U.S.A.* **110** C4
Winslow *U.S.A.* **109** J8
Winsted *U.S.A.* **115** E11
Winston-Salem *U.S.A.* **117** C14
Winter Garden *U.S.A.* **117** G14
Winter Haven *U.S.A.* **117** G14
Winter Park *U.S.A.* **117** G14
Winterberg *Germany* **24** D4
Winterhaven *U.S.A.* **111** N12
Winters *U.S.A.* **110** G5
Winterset *U.S.A.* **112** E6
Wintersville *U.S.A.* **114** F4
Winterswijk *Neths.* **17** C6
Winterthur *Switz.* **25** H4
Winthrop *U.S.A.* **108** B3
Winton *Australia* **94** C3
Winton *N.Z.* **91** G2
Wipper → *Germany* **24** D7
Wirrulla *Australia* **95** E1
Wisbech *U.K.* **15** E8
Wisconsin □ *U.S.A.* **112** C9
Wisconsin → *U.S.A.* **112** D8
Wisconsin Rapids *U.S.A.* **112** C9
Wisdom *U.S.A.* **108** D7
Wishaw *U.K.* **13** F5
Wishek *U.S.A.* **112** B4
Wisła *Poland* **31** J5
Wisła → *Poland* **30** D5
Wisłok → *Poland* **31** H9
Wisłoka → *Poland* **31** H8
Wismar *Germany* **24** B7
Wisner *U.S.A.* **112** E5
Wissant *France* **19** B8
Wissembourg *France* **19** C14
Wisznice *Poland* **31** G10
Witbank = eMalahleni
  S. Africa **89** D4
Witdraai *S. Africa* **88** D3
Witham *U.K.* **15** F8
Witham → *U.K.* **14** E7
Withernsea *U.K.* **14** D8
Witjira △ *Australia* **95** D2
Witkowo *Poland* **31** F4
Witless Bay *Canada* **105** C9
Witney *U.K.* **15** F6
Witnica *Poland* **31** F1
Witnossob → *Namibia* **88** D3
Wittdün *Germany* **24** A4
Witten *Germany* **24** D3
Wittenberge *Germany* **24** B7
Wittenburg *Germany* **24** B7
Wittenheim *France* **19** E14
Wittenoom *Australia* **92** D2
Wittingen *Germany* **24** C6
Wittlich *Germany* **25** F2
Wittmund *Germany* **24** B3
Wittow *Germany* **24** A9
Wittstock *Germany* **24** B8
Witu *Kenya* **86** C5
Witvlei *Namibia* **88** C2
Witzenhausen *Germany* **24** D5
Wiwon *N. Korea* **57** D14
Wkra → *Poland* **31** F7
Władysławowo *Poland* **30** D5
Wleń *Poland* **31** G2
Wlingi *Indonesia* **63** H15
Włocławek *Poland* **31** F6
Włodawa *Poland* **31** G10
Włoszczowa *Poland* **31** H6
Woburn *U.S.A.* **115** D13
Wodian *China* **56** H7
Wodonga *Australia* **95** F4
Wodzisław Śląski *Poland* **31** H5
Wœrth *France* **19** D14

Woinbogoin *China* **58** A2
Woippy *France* **19** C13
Wojcieszow *Poland* **31** H2
Wokam *Indonesia* **63** F8
Woking *U.K.* **15** F7
Wokingham *U.K.* **15** F7
Wokingham □ *U.K.* **15** F7
Wolbrom *Poland* **31** H6
Wolczyn *Poland* **31** G5
Woldegk *Germany* **24** B9
Wolf → *Canada* **102** A2
Wolf Creek *U.S.A.* **108** C7
Wolf L. *Canada* **102** A2
Wolf Point *U.S.A.* **108** B11
Wolfe I. *Canada* **115** B8
Wolfeboro *U.S.A.* **115** C13
Wolfen *Germany* **24** D8
Wolfenbüttel *Germany* **24** C6
Wolfratshausen *Germany* **25** H7
Wolfsberg *Austria* **26** E7
Wolfsburg *Germany* **24** C6
Wolgast *Germany* **24** A9
Wolhusen *Switz.* **25** H4
Wolin *Poland* **30** E1
Woliński △ *Poland* **30** E1
Wollaston, Is. *U.K.* **128** H3
Wollaston L. *Canada* **103** B8
Wollaston Lake *Canada* **103** B8
Wollaston Pen. *Canada* **100** C8
Wollongong *Australia* **95** E5
Wolmaransstad *S. Africa* **88** D4
Wolmirstedt *Germany* **24** C7
Wolomin *Poland* **31** F8
Wołów *Poland* **31** G3
Wolseley *S. Africa* **88** E2
Wolsey *U.S.A.* **112** C5
Wolstenholme, C. *Canada* **98** C12
Wolsztyn *Poland* **31** F3
Wolvega *Neths.* **17** B6
Wolverhampton *U.K.* **15** E5
Wondai *Australia* **95** D5
Wongalarroo L. *Australia* **95** E3
Wongan Hills *Australia* **93** F2
Wonju *S. Korea* **57** F14
Wonosari *Indonesia* **63** G14
Wonosobo *Indonesia* **63** G13
Wonowon *Canada* **102** B4
Wŏnsan *N. Korea* **57** E14
Wonthaggi *Australia* **95** F4
Wood Buffalo △ *Canada* **102** B6
Wood Is. *Australia* **94** A2
Wood L. *Canada* **103** B8
Woodah, I. *Australia* **94** A2
Woodbourne *U.S.A.* **115** E10
Woodbridge *Canada* **114** C5
Woodbridge *U.K.* **15** E9
Woodburn *U.S.A.* **108** D2
Woodenbong *Australia* **95** D5
Woodend *Australia* **95** F3
Woodford *Australia* **95** D5
Woodfords *U.S.A.* **110** G7
Woodlake *U.S.A.* **110** J7
Woodland *Calif., U.S.A.* **110** G5
Woodland *Maine, U.S.A.* **113** C20
Woodland *Pa., U.S.A.* **114** F6
Woodland *Wash., U.S.A.* **110** E4
Woodland Caribou △
  Canada **103** C10
Woodlands *Singapore* **65** d
Woodlands, The *U.S.A.* **116** F7
Woodonga *Australia* **95** F4
Woodridge *Canada* **103** D9
Woodroffe, Mt. *Australia* **93** E5
Woods, L. *Australia* **94** B1
Woods, L. of the *Canada* **103** D10
Woods Bay *Canada* **114** A5
Woodstock *Australia* **94** B4
Woodstock *N.B., Canada* **105** C6
Woodstock *Ont., Canada* **114** C4
Woodstock *U.K.* **15** F6
Woodstock *Ill., U.S.A.* **112** D9
Woodstock *N.Y., U.S.A.* **115** D10
Woodstock *Vt., U.S.A.* **115** C12
Woodsville *U.S.A.* **115** B13
Woodview *Canada* **114** B6
Woodville *N.Z.* **91** D5
Woodville *Miss., U.S.A.* **116** F9
Woodville *Tex., U.S.A.* **116** F7
Woodward *U.S.A.* **116** C5
Woody *U.S.A.* **111** K8
Woody → *Canada* **103** C8
Woolacombe *U.K.* **15** F3
Woolamai, C. *Australia* **95** F4
Wooler *U.K.* **14** B5
Woolgoolga *Australia* **95** E5
Woomera *Australia* **95** E2
Woonsocket *R.I., U.S.A.* **115** E13
Woonsocket *S. Dak., U.S.A.* **112** C5
Wooramel → *Australia* **93** E1
Wooramel Roadhouse
  Australia **93** E1
Wooroonooran △ *Australia* **94** B4
Wooster *U.S.A.* **114** F3
Worcester *S. Africa* **88** E2
Worcester *U.K.* **15** E5
Worcester *Mass., U.S.A.* **115** D13
Worcester *N.Y., U.S.A.* **115** D10
Worcestershire □ *U.K.* **15** E5

Wörgl *Austria* **26** D5
Workington *U.K.* **14** C4
Worksop *U.K.* **14** D6
Workum *Neths.* **17** B5
Worland *U.S.A.* **108** D10
Wormhout *France* **19** B9
Worms *Germany* **25** F4
Worsley *Canada* **102** B5
Wörth *Germany* **25** F8
Wortham *U.S.A.* **116** F6
Worth *Kenya* **86** C4
Worthing *Barbados* **121** g
Worthing *U.K.* **15** G7
Worthington *Minn., U.S.A.* **112** D6
Worthington *Pa., U.S.A.* **114** F5
Wosi *Indonesia* **63** E7
Wote *Kenya* **86** C4
Wou-han = Wuhan *China* **59** B10
Wowoni *Indonesia* **63** E6
Wrangel I. = Vrangelya,
  Ostrov *Russia* **53** B18
Wrangell *Fla., U.S.A.* **108** B2
Wrangell *Canada* **102** B2
Wrangell Mts. *U.S.A.* **100** C5
Wrath, C. *U.K.* **13** C3
Wray *U.S.A.* **108** F12
Wrekin, The *U.K.* **15** E5
Wrens *U.S.A.* **117** E13
Wrexham *U.K.* **14** D4
Wrexham □ *U.K.* **14** D5
Wriezen *Germany* **24** C10
Wright = Paranas *Phil.* **61** F6
Wright *Fla., U.S.A.* **117** F11
Wright *Wyo., U.S.A.* **108** E11
Wright Pt. *Canada* **114** C3
Wrightson, Mt. *U.S.A.* **109** L8
Wrightwood *U.S.A.* **111** L9
Wrigley *Canada* **100** C7
Wrocław *Poland* **31** G4
Wronki *Poland* **31** F3
Września *Poland* **31** F4
Wschowa *Poland* **31** G3
Wu Jiang → *China* **58** C6
Wu'an *China* **56** F8
Wubin *Australia* **93** F2
Wubu *China* **56** F6
Wuchang *China* **57** B14
Wucheng *China* **56** F9
Wuchuan *Guangdong, China* **59** G8
Wuchuan *Guizhou, China* **58** C7
Wuchuan
  Nei Monggol Zizhiqu, China **56** D6
Wudi *China* **57** F9
Wuding *China* **58** E4
Wuding He → *China* **56** F6
Wudinna *Australia* **95** E2
Wudu *China* **56** H3
Wufeng *China* **59** B8
Wugang *China* **59** D8
Wugong Shan *China* **59** D9
Wugullar = Beswick
  Australia **92** B5
Wuhan *China* **59** B10
Wuhe *China* **57** H9
Wuhsi = Wuxi *China* **59** B13
Wuhu *China* **59** B12
Wujiang *China* **59** B13
Wukari *Nigeria* **83** D6
Wulajie *China* **57** B14
Wulanbulang *China* **56** D6
Wular L. *India* **69** B6
Wulehe *Ghana* **83** D5
Wulian *China* **57** G10
Wuliang Shan *China* **58** E3
Wuliaru *Indonesia* **63** F8
Wuling Shan *China* **58** C7
Wulong *China* **58** C6
Wulumuchi = Ürümqi *China* **52** B3
Wum *Cameroon* **83** D7
Wuming *China* **58** F7
Wun Rog *Sudan* **81** F2
Wundanyi *Kenya* **86** C4
Wuning *China* **59** C10
Wunnummin L. *Canada* **104** B2
Wunsiedel *Germany* **25** E8
Wunstorf *Germany* **24** C5
Wuntho *Burma* **67** H19
Wupatki △ *U.S.A.* **109** J8
Wuping *China* **59** E11
Wuppertal *Germany* **24** D3
Wuppertal *S. Africa* **88** E2
Wuqing *China* **57** E9
Wurtsboro *U.S.A.* **115** E10
Würzburg *Germany* **25** F5
Wurzen *Germany* **24** D8
Wushan *China* **56** G3
Wushishi *Nigeria* **83** D6
Wutach → *Germany* **25** H4
Wutai *China* **56** E7
Wuting = Huimin *China* **57** F9
Wutong *China* **58** E8
Wutonghaolai *China* **57** C11
Wutongqiao *China* **58** C4
Wuwei *Anhui, China* **59** B11
Wuwei *Gansu, China* **60** C5
Wuxi *Jiangsu, China* **59** B13
Wuxi *Sichuan, China* **58** B7
Wuxiang *China* **56** F7

Wuxuan *China* **58** F7
Wuxue *China* **59** C10
Wuyang *China* **56** H7
Wuyi *Hebei, China* **56** F8
Wuyi *Zhejiang, China* **59** C12
Wuyi Shan *China* **59** D11
Wuyishan *China* **59** D12
Wuyo *Nigeria* **83** C7
Wuyuan *Jiangxi, China* **59** C11
Wuyuan
  Nei Monggol Zizhiqu, China **56** D5
Wuzhai *China* **56** E6
Wuzhi Shan *China* **64** C7
Wuzhong *China* **56** E4
Wuzhou *China* **59** F8
Wyaaba Cr. → *Australia* **94** B3
Wyalkatchem *Australia* **93** F2
Wyalusing *U.S.A.* **115** E8
Wyandotte *U.S.A.* **113** D12
Wyandra *Australia* **95** D4
Wyangala, L. *Australia* **95** E4
Wyara, L. *Australia* **95** D3
Wycheproof *Australia* **95** F3
Wycliffe Well *Australia* **94** C1
Wye → *U.K.* **15** F5
Wyemandoo *Australia* **93** E2
Wyk *Germany* **24** A4
Wymondham *U.K.* **15** E9
Wymore *U.S.A.* **112** E5
Wyndham *Australia* **92** C4
Wyndham *N.Z.* **91** G2
Wynne *U.S.A.* **117** D9
Wynyard *Australia* **95** G4
Wynyard *Canada* **103** C8
Wyola L. *Australia* **93** E5
Wyoming *Canada* **114** D2
Wyoming □ *U.S.A.* **108** E10
Wyomissing *U.S.A.* **115** F9
Wyong *Australia* **95** E5
Wyrzysk *Poland* **31** E4
Wysoka *Poland* **31** E4
Wysokie *Poland* **31** H9
Wysokie Mazowieckie
  Poland **31** F9
Wyszków *Poland* **31** F8
Wyszogród *Poland* **31** F7
Wytheville *U.S.A.* **113** G13
Wyżyna Małopolska *Poland* **31** H7

X

Xaafuun *Somali Rep.* **75** E5
Xaafuun, Ras *Somali Rep.* **75** E5
Xaçmaz *Azerbaijan* **35** K9
Xai-Xai *Mozam.* **89** D5
Xainza *China* **60** C3
Xalapa *Mexico* **119** D5
Xallas → *Spain* **36** C1
Xangongo *Angola* **88** B2
Xankändi *Azerbaijan* **73** C12
Xanlar *Azerbaijan* **35** K8
Xanten *Germany* **24** D2
Xanthi *Greece* **45** E8
Xanthi □ *Greece* **45** E8
Xanthos *Turkey* **47** E11
Xanxerê *Brazil* **127** B5
Xapuri *Brazil* **124** F5
Xar Moron He → *China* **57** C11
Xarrë *Albania* **44** G4
Xátiva *Spain* **39** G4
Xau, L. *Botswana* **88** C3
Xavantina *Brazil* **127** A5
Xenia *U.S.A.* **113** F12
Xeropotamos → *Cyprus* **49** E11
Xertigny *France* **19** D13
Xhora *S. Africa* **89** E4
Xhumo *Botswana* **88** C3
Xi Jiang → *China* **59** F9
Xi Xian *Henan, China* **59** A10
Xi Xian *Shanxi, China* **56** F6
Xia Xian *China* **56** G6
Xiachengzi *China* **57** B16
Xiachuan Dao *China* **59** G9
Xiaguan *China* **60** D5
Xiajiang *China* **59** D10
Xiajin *China* **56** F9
Xiamen *China* **59** E12
Xi'an *China* **56** G5
Xian Xian *China* **56** E9
Xianfeng *China* **58** C7
Xiang Jiang → *China* **59** C9
Xiangcheng *Henan, China* **56** H8
Xiangcheng *Henan, China* **56** H7
Xiangcheng *Sichuan, China* **58** C2
Xiangdu *China* **58** F6
Xiangfan *China* **59** A9
Xianggang = Hong
  Kong □ *China* **59** F10
Xiangning *China* **56** G6
Xiangquan *China* **56** F7
Xiangquan He = Sutlej →
  Pakistan **68** E4
Xiangshan *China* **59** C13
Xiangshui *China* **57** G10
Xiangtan *China* **59** D9
Xiangxiang *China* **59** D9

Xiangyin *China* **59** C9
Xiangyun *China* **58** E3
Xiangzhou *China* **58** F7
Xianju *China* **59** C13
Xianning *China* **59** C10
Xianshui He → *China* **58** B3
Xiantao *China* **59** B9
Xianyang *China* **56** G5
Xianyou *China* **59** E12
Xiao Hinggan Ling *China* **60** B7
Xiao Xian *China* **56** G9
Xiaofeng *China* **59** B12
Xiaogan *China* **59** B9
Xiaojin *China* **58** B4
Xiaolan *China* **59** F9
Xiaoshan *China* **59** B13
Xiaoyi *China* **56** F6
Xiapu *China* **59** D12
Xiawa *China* **57** C11
Xiayi *China* **56** G9
Xichang *China* **58** D4
Xichong *China* **58** B5
Xichou *China* **58** F5
Xichuan *China* **56** H6
Xide *China* **58** C4
Xiemahe *China* **59** B8
Xifei He → *China* **56** H9
Xifeng *Gansu, China* **56** G4
Xifeng *Guizhou, China* **58** D6
Xifeng *Liaoning, China* **57** C13
Xifengzhen = Xifeng *China* **56** G4
Xigazê *China* **60** D3
Xihe *China* **56** G3
Xihua *China* **56** H8
Xilaganni *Greece* **45** F9
Xiliao He → *China* **57** C12
Xilin *China* **58** E5
Xilinhot *China* **56** C9
Xilokastro *Greece* **46** C4
Ximana *Mozam.* **87** F3
Xime *Guinea-Biss.* **82** C2
Ximeng *China* **58** F2
Xin Jiang → *China* **59** C11
Xin Xian = Xinzhou *China* **56** E7
Xinavane *Mozam.* **89** D5
Xinbin *China* **57** D13
Xincai *China* **59** A10
Xinchang *China* **59** C13
Xincheng *Guangxi Zhuangzu, China* **58** E7
Xincheng *Jiangxi, China* **59** D10
Xincun *China* **57** E9
Xindu *China* **58** B5
Xinfeng *Guangdong, China* **59** E10
Xinfeng *Jiangxi, China* **59** D11
Xinfeng *Jiangxi, China* **59** E10
Xinfengjiang Skuiku *China* **59** F10
Xing Xian *China* **56** E6
Xing'an *Guangxi Zhuangzu, China* **59** E8
Xingan *Jiangxi, China* **59** D10
Xingcheng *China* **57** D11
Xingguo *China* **59** D10
Xinghe *China* **56** D7
Xinghua *China* **57** H10
Xinghua Wan *China* **59** E12
Xinglong *China* **57** D9
Xingning *China* **59** E10
Xingping *China* **56** G5
Xingren *China* **58** E5
Xingshan *China* **59** B8
Xingtai *China* **56** F8
Xingu  → *Brazil* **125** D8
Xingwen *China* **58** C5
Xingyang *China* **56** G7
Xinhe *China* **56** F8
Xinhua *China* **59** D8
Xinhuang *China* **58** D7
Xinhui *China* **59** F9
Xining *China* **60** C5
Xinjiang *China* **56** G6
Xinjiang *China* **56** G6
Xinjiang Uygur Zizhiqu □
  China **60** B3
Xinjie *China* **58** D3
Xinjin = Pulandian *China* **57** E11
Xinjin *China* **58** B4
Xinkai He → *China* **57** C12
Xinle *China* **56** E8
Xinlitun *China* **57** D12
Xinlong *China* **58** B3
Xinmin *China* **57** D12
Xinning *China* **59** D8
Xinping *China* **58** E3
Xinshao *China* **59** D8
Xintai *China* **57** G9
Xintian *China* **59** E9
Xinxian *China* **59** B10
Xinxiang *China* **56** G7
Xinxing *China* **59** F9
Xinyang *China* **59** A10
Xinye *China* **59** A9
Xinyi *China* **59** F8
Xinyu *China* **59** D10
Xinzhan *China* **57** C14
Xinzheng *China* **56** G7
Xinzhou *Hainan, China* **64** C7

Xinzhou *Hubei, China* **59** B10
Xinzhou *Shanxi, China* **56** E7
Xinzo de Limia *Spain* **36** C3
Xiongyuecheng *China* **57** D12
Xiping *Henan, China* **56** H8
Xiping *Henan, China* **56** H6
Xiping *Zhejiang, China* **59** C12
Xique-Xique *Brazil* **125** F10
Xisha Qundao = Paracel
  Is. *S. China Sea* **62** A4
Xishui *Guizhou, China* **58** C6
Xishui *Hubei, China* **59** B10
Xitole *Guinea-Biss.* **82** C2
Xiu Shui → *China* **59** C10
Xiuning *China* **59** C12
Xiuren *China* **59** E8
Xiushan *China* **58** C7
Xiushui *China* **59** C10
Xiuwen *China* **58** D6
Xiuyan *China* **57** D12
Xixabangma Feng *China* **69** E11
Xixia *China* **56** H6
Xixiang *China* **56** H4
Xixón = Gijón *Spain* **36** B5
Xiyang *China* **56** F7
Xizang Zizhiqu □ *China* **60** C3
Xlendi *Malta* **49** C1
Xochob *Mexico* **119** D7
Xu Jiang → *China* **59** D11
Xuan Loc *Vietnam* **65** G6
Xuan'en *China* **58** C7
Xuanhan *China* **58** B6
Xuanhua *China* **56** D8
Xuanwei *China* **58** C5
Xuanzhou *China* **59** B12
Xuchang *China* **56** G7
Xudat *Azerbaijan* **35** K9
Xuefeng Shan *China* **59** D8
Xuejiaping *China* **59** B8
Xun Jiang → *China* **59** F8
Xun Xian *China* **56** G8
Xundian *China* **58** E4
Xunwu *China* **59** E10
Xunyang *China* **56** H5
Xunyi *China* **56** G5
Xupu *China* **59** D8
Xúquer → *Spain* **39** F4
Xushui *China* **56** E8
Xuwen *China* **59** G8
Xuyen Moc *Vietnam* **65** G6
Xuyong *China* **58** C5
Xuzhou *China* **57** G9

Y

Ya Xian = Sanya *China* **64** C7
Yaamba *Australia* **94** C5
Ya'an *China* **58** C4
Yaapeet *Australia* **95** F3
Yabassi *Cameroon* **83** E6
Yabelo *Ethiopia* **81** G4
Yabelo △ *Ethiopia* **81** F4
Yablanitsa *Bulgaria* **45** C8
Yablonovyy Khrebet *Russia* **53** D12
Yablonovyy Ra. =
  Yablonovyy Khrebet
  Russia **53** D12
Yabluniv *Ukraine* **29** B9
Yablunytsya *Ukraine* **29** B9
Yabrai Shan *China* **56** E2
Yabrūd *Syria* **74** B5
Yabucoa *Puerto Rico* **121** d
Yacambú △ *Venezuela* **121** E6
Yacheng *China* **64** C7
Yacuiba *Bolivia* **126** A3
Yacuma → *Bolivia* **124** F5
Yadgir *India* **66** L10
Yadkin → *U.S.A.* **117** D14
Yadrin *Russia* **34** C8
Yadua *Fiji* **91** a
Yaeyama-Rettō *Japan* **55** M1
Yagaba *Ghana* **83** C4
Yagasa Cluster *Fiji* **91** a
Yağcılar *Turkey* **47** B10
Yagodnoye *Russia* **53** C15
Yahila *Dem. Rep. of the Congo* **86** B4
Yahk *Canada* **102** D5
Yahotyn *Ukraine* **33** G6
Yahuma
  Dem. Rep. of the Congo **84** D4
Yahyalı *Turkey* **72** C6
Yaita *Japan* **55** F9
Yaiza *Canary Is.* **48** F6
Yajiang *China* **58** B3
Yajua *Nigeria* **83** C7
Yakima *U.S.A.* **108** C3
Yakima → *U.S.A.* **108** C3
Yakishiri-Jima *Japan* **54** B10
Yako *Burkina Faso* **82** C4
Yakobi I. *U.S.A.* **102** B1
Yakoruda *Bulgaria* **44** D7
Yakovlevka *Russia* **54** B6
Yaku-Shima *Japan* **55** J5
Yakumo *Japan* **54** C10
Yakutat *U.S.A.* **100** D6
Yakutia = Sakha □ *Russia* **53** C14
Yakutsk *Russia* **53** C13

Yala *Thailand* **65** J3
Yalboroo *Australia* **94** J6
Yale *U.S.A.* **114** C2
Yalgoo *Australia* **93** E2
Yalgorup △ *Australia* **93** F2
Yalinga *C.A.R.* **84** C4
Yalkabul, Pta. *Mexico* **119** C7
Yalleroi *Australia* **94** C4
Yalobusha → *U.S.A.* **117** E9
Yalong Jiang → *China* **58** D3
Yalova *Turkey* **45** F13
Yalpuh, Ozero *Ukraine* **29** E13
Yalta *Ukraine* **33** K8
Yalu Jiang → *China* **57** E13
Yalvaç *Turkey* **72** C4
Yam Ha Melah = Dead Sea *Asia* **74** D4
Yam Kinneret *Israel* **74** C4
Yamada *Japan* **55** H5
Yamagata *Japan* **54** E10
Yamagata □ *Japan* **54** E10
Yamaguchi *Japan* **55** G5
Yamaguchi □ *Japan* **55** G5
Yamal, Poluostrov *Russia* **52** B8
Yamal Pen. = Yamal, Poluostrov *Russia* **52** B8
Yamanashi □ *Japan* **55** G9
Yamanie Falls △ *Australia* **94** B4
Yamato Ridge *Sea of Japan* **54** E7
Yamba *Australia* **95** D5
Yambarran Ra. *Australia* **92** C5
Yambéring *Guinea* **82** C2
Yâmbiô *Sudan* **81** G2
Yambol *Bulgaria* **45** D10
Yamburg *Russia* **52** C8
Yamdena *Indonesia* **63** F8
Yame *Japan* **55** H5
Yamethin *Burma* **67** J20
Yamma Yamma, L. *Australia* **95** D3
Yamoussoukro *Ivory C.* **82** D3
Yampa → *U.S.A.* **108** F9
Yampi Sd. *Australia* **92** C3
Yampil *Moldova* **23** D15
Yampol = Yampil *Moldova* **23** D15
Yamrat *Nigeria* **83** C6
Yamrukchal = Botev *Bulgaria* **45** D8
Yamuna → *India* **69** G9
Yamunanagar *India* **68** D7
Yamzho Yumco *China* **60** D4
Yan *Nigeria* **83** C7
Yana → *Russia* **53** B14
Yanagawa *Japan* **55** H5
Yanai *Japan* **55** H5
Yan'an *China* **56** F5
Yanbian *China* **58** D3
Yanbu 'al Baḥr *Si. Arabia* **70** F3
Yanchang *China* **56** F6
Yancheng *Henan, China* **56** H8
Yancheng *Jiangsu, China* **57** H11
Yanchep *Australia* **93** F2
Yanchi *China* **56** F4
Yanchuan *China* **56** F6
Yanco Cr. → *Australia* **95** F4
Yandicoogina *Australia* **92** D2
Yandoon *Burma* **67** L19
Yanfeng *China* **58** E4
Yanfolila *Mali* **82** C3
Yang Xian *China* **56** H4
Yang-yang *S. Korea* **57** E15
Yang-Yang *Senegal* **82** B1
Yangambi *Dem. Rep. of the Congo* **86** B1
Yangbi *China* **58** E2
Yangcheng *China* **56** G7
Yangch'ü = Taiyuan *China* **56** F7
Yangchun *China* **59** F8
Yanggao *China* **56** D7
Yanggu *China* **56** F8
Yangjiang *China* **59** G8
Yangliuqing *China* **57** E9
Yangon = Rangoon *Burma* **67** L20
Yangping *China* **59** B8
Yangpingguan *China* **56** H4
Yangquan *China* **56** F7
Yangshan *China* **59** E9
Yangshuo *China* **59** E8
Yangtse = Chang Jiang → *China* **59** B13
Yangtze Kiang = Chang Jiang → *China* **59** B13
Yangudi Rassa △ *Ethiopia* **81** E5
Yangxin *China* **59** C10
Yangyuan *China* **56** D8
Yangzhong *China* **59** A12
Yangzhou *China* **59** A12
Yanhe *China* **58** C7
Yanji *China* **57** C15
Yanjin *China* **58** C5
Yanjing *China* **58** C2
Yankari △ *Nigeria* **83** D7
Yankton *U.S.A.* **112** D5
Yanonge *Dem. Rep. of the Congo* **86** B1
Yanqi *China* **60** B3
Yanqing *China* **56** D8
Yanshan *Hebei, China* **57** E9
Yanshan *Jiangxi, China* **59** C11

Yanshan *Yunnan, China* **58** F5
Yanshou *China* **57** B15
Yantabulla *Australia* **95** D4
Yantai *China* **57** F11
Yantarnyy *Russia* **30** D6
Yanting *China* **58** B5
Yantra → *Bulgaria* **45** C9
Yanuca *Fiji* **91** a
Yanwa *China* **58** D2
Yanyuan *China* **58** D3
Yanzhou *China* **56** G9
Yao Noi, Ko *Thailand* **65** a
Yao Xian *China* **56** G5
Yao Yai, Ko *Thailand* **65** a
Yao'an *China* **58** E3
Yaodu *China* **58** A5
Yaoundé *Cameroon* **83** E7
Yaowan *China* **57** G10
Yapen *Indonesia* **63** E9
Yapen, Selat *Indonesia* **63** E9
Yapero *Indonesia* **63** E9
Yappar → *Australia* **94** B3
Yaqaga *Fiji* **91** a
Yaqui → *Mexico* **118** B2
Yar-Sale *Russia* **52** C8
Yaraka *Australia* **94** C3
Yaransk *Russia* **34** B8
Yarbasan *Turkey* **47** C10
Yardımcı Burnu *Turkey* **47** E12
Yare → *U.K.* **15** E9
Yaremcha *Ukraine* **29** B9
Yarensk *Russia* **52** C5
Yarfa *Si. Arabia* **80** C4
Yarí → *Colombia* **124** D4
Yarkand = Shache *China* **60** C2
Yarker *Canada* **115** B8
Yarkhun → *Pakistan* **69** A5
Yarlung Ziangbo Jiang = Brahmaputra → *Asia* **69** H13
Yarmouth *Canada* **105** D6
Yarmūk → *Syria* **74** C4
Yaroslavl *Russia* **32** D10
Yaroslavl □ *Russia* **32** C10
Yarqa, W. → *Egypt* **74** F2
Yarra Yarra Lakes *Australia* **93** E2
Yarram *Australia* **95** F4
Yarraman *Australia* **95** D5
Yarras *Australia* **95** E5
Yarrie *Australia* **92** D3
Yartsevo *Sib., Russia* **53** C10
Yartsevo *Smolensk, Russia* **32** E7
Yarumal *Colombia* **124** B3
Yasawa *Fiji* **91** a
Yasawa Group *Fiji* **91** a
Yaselda *Belarus* **23** B14
Yasen *Ukraine* **29** B9
Yashi *Nigeria* **83** C6
Yashikera *Nigeria* **83** D5
Yashkul *Russia* **35** G7
Yasin *Pakistan* **69** A5
Yasinovataya *Ukraine* **33** H9
Yasinski, L. *Canada* **104** B4
Yasinya *Ukraine* **29** B9
Yasothon *Thailand* **64** E5
Yass *Australia* **95** E4
Yāsūj *Iran* **71** D6
Yatağan *Turkey* **47** D10
Yatakala *Niger* **83** C5
Yates Center *U.S.A.* **112** G6
Yathkyed L. *Canada* **103** A9
Yatsushiro *Japan* **55** H5
Yatta Plateau *Kenya* **86** C4
Yauco *Puerto Rico* **121** d
Yavari → *Peru* **124** D4
Yávaros *Mexico* **118** B3
Yavatmal *India* **66** J11
Yavne *Israel* **74** D3
Yavoriv *Ukraine* **31** J10
Yavorov = Yavoriv *Ukraine* **31** J10
Yavuzeli *Turkey* **72** D7
Yawatahama *Japan* **55** H6
Yawri B. *S. Leone* **82** D2
Yaxi *China* **58** D6
Yaxian = Sanya *China* **64** C7
Yayladağı *Turkey* **72** E7
Yazd *Iran* **71** D7
Yazd □ *Iran* **71** D7
Yazd-e Khvāst *Iran* **71** D7
Yazıköy *Turkey* **47** E9
Yazman *Pakistan* **68** E4
Yazoo → *U.S.A.* **117** E9
Yazoo City *U.S.A.* **117** E9
Ybbs *Austria* **26** C8
Ybycuí △ *Paraguay* **126** B4
Ybytyruzú △ *Paraguay* **127** B4
Ye *Burma* **64** E1
Ye Xian *China* **56** H7
Yebyu *Burma* **64** E2
Yecheon *S. Korea* **57** F15
Yecla *Spain* **39** G3
Yécora *Mexico* **118** B3
Yedebub Biheroch Bihereseboch na Hizboch □ *Ethiopia* **81** F4
Yedintsy = Edineţ *Moldova* **29** B12
Yedseram → *Nigeria* **83** C7
Yefremov *Russia* **32** F10

Yeghegnadzor *Armenia* **73** C11
Yegorlyk → *Russia* **35** G5
Yegorlykskaya *Russia* **35** G5
Yegoryevsk *Russia* **32** E10
Yegros *Paraguay* **126** B4
Yehbuah *Indonesia* **63** J17
Yehuda, Midbar *Israel* **74** D4
Yei *Sudan* **81** G3
Yei, Nahr → *Sudan* **81** F3
Yejmiadzin *Armenia* **35** K7
Yekaterinburg *Russia* **52** D7
Yelabuga *Russia* **34** C11
Yelan *Russia* **34** E6
Yelarbon *Australia* **95** D5
Yelatma *Russia* **34** C5
Yelets *Russia* **33** F10
Yélimané *Mali* **82** B2
Yelizavetgrad = Kirovohrad *Ukraine* **33** H7
Yelizovo *Russia* **53** D16
Yell *U.K.* **13** A7
Yell Sd. *U.K.* **13** A7
Yellow = Huang He → *China* **57** G10
Yellow Sea *China* **57** G12
Yellowhead Pass *Canada* **102** C5
Yellowknife *Canada* **102** A6
Yellowknife → *Canada* **102** A6
Yellowstone → *U.S.A.* **108** C12
Yellowstone △ *U.S.A.* **108** D8
Yellowstone L. *U.S.A.* **108** D8
Yelnya *Russia* **32** E7
Yelsk *Belarus* **23** C15
Yelwa *Nigeria* **83** C5
Yemen ■ *Asia* **75** E3
Yen Bai *Vietnam* **58** G5
Yenagoa *Nigeria* **83** E6
Yenakiyeve *Ukraine* **33** H10
Yenakiyevo = Yenakiyeve *Ukraine* **33** H10
Yenangyaung *Burma* **67** J19
Yenbo = Yanbu 'al Baḥr *Si. Arabia* **70** F3
Yenda *Australia* **95** E4
Yende Millimou *Guinea* **82** D2
Yendéré *Burkina Faso* **82** C4
Yendi *Ghana* **83** D4
Yéni *Niger* **83** C5
Yeni Erenköy = Yialousa *Cyprus* **49** D13
Yenice *Ankara, Turkey* **72** C5
Yenice *Aydın, Turkey* **47** D10
Yenice *Çanakkale, Turkey* **47** B9
Yenice *Edirne, Turkey* **45** F10
Yenice → *Turkey* **72** D6
Yenifoça *Turkey* **47** C8
Yenihisar *Turkey* **47** D9
Yeniköy *Bursa, Turkey* **45** F13
Yeniköy *Çanakkale, Turkey* **47** B8
Yeniköy *Kütahya, Turkey* **47** C11
Yenipazar *Turkey* **47** D10
Yenişehir *Turkey* **45** F13
Yenisey → *Russia* **52** B9
Yeniseysk *Russia* **53** D10
Yeniseyskiy Zaliv *Russia* **52** B9
Yenne *France* **21** C9
Yenotayevka *Russia* **35** G8
Yenyuka *Russia* **53** D13
Yeo → *U.K.* **15** G5
Yeo, L. *Australia* **93** E3
Yeo I. *Canada* **114** A3
Yeoju *S. Korea* **57** F14
Yeola *India* **66** J9
Yeong-wol *S. Korea* **57** F15
Yeongcheon *S. Korea* **57** G15
Yeongdeok *S. Korea* **57** F15
Yeongdeungpo *S. Korea* **57** F14
Yeongdong *S. Korea* **57** F14
Yeongju *S. Korea* **57** F15
Yeosu *S. Korea* **57** G14
Yeovil *U.K.* **15** G5
Yepes *Spain* **36** F7
Yeppoon *Australia* **94** C5
Yerbent *Turkmenistan* **52** F6
Yerbogachen *Russia* **53** C11
Yerevan *Armenia* **35** K7
Yerington *U.S.A.* **108** G4
Yerkesik *Turkey* **47** D10
Yerköy *Turkey* **72** C6
Yermak *Kazakhstan* **52** D8
Yermo *U.S.A.* **111** L10
Yerólakkos *Cyprus* **49** D12
Yeropol *Russia* **53** C17
Yeroskipos *Cyprus* **49** E11
Yershov *Russia* **34** E9
Yerushalayim = Jerusalem *Israel/West Bank* **74** D4
Yerville *France* **18** C7
Yes Tor *U.K.* **15** G4
Yesan *S. Korea* **57** F14
Yeşilhisar *Turkey* **72** C6
Yeşilırmak → *Turkey* **72** B7
Yeşilkent *Turkey* **72** D7
Yeşilköy *Turkey* **45** F12
Yeşilova *Turkey* **47** D11
Yeşilyurt *Manisa, Turkey* **47** C10
Yeşilyurt *Muğla, Turkey* **47** D10
Yesnogorsk *Russia* **32** E9

Yeso *U.S.A.* **109** J11
Yessentuki *Russia* **35** H6
Yessey *Russia* **53** C11
Yeste *Spain* **39** G2
Yetman *Australia* **95** D5
Yeu, Î. d' *France* **18** F4
Yevlakh = Yevlax *Azerbaijan* **35** K8
Yevlax *Azerbaijan* **35** K8
Yevpatoriya *Ukraine* **33** K7
Yeya → *Russia* **33** J10
Yeysk *Russia* **33** J10
Yezd = Yazd *Iran* **71** D7
Yezerishche *Belarus* **32** E5
Yhati *Paraguay* **126** B4
Yhú *Paraguay* **127** B4
Yí → *Uruguay* **126** C4
Yi 'Allaq, G. *Egypt* **74** E2
Yi He → *China* **57** G10
Yi Xian *Anhui, China* **59** C11
Yi Xian *Hebei, China* **56** E8
Yi Xian *Liaoning, China* **57** D11
Yialiás → *Cyprus* **49** D12
Yialousa *Cyprus* **49** D13
Yibin *China* **58** C5
Yichang *China* **59** B8
Yicheng *Henan, China* **59** B9
Yicheng *Shanxi, China* **56** G6
Yichuan *China* **56** F6
Yichun *Heilongjiang, China* **60** B7
Yichun *Jiangxi, China* **59** D10
Yidu *China* **57** F10
Yidun *China* **58** B2
Yifag *Ethiopia* **81** E4
Yifeng *China* **59** C10
Yihuang *China* **59** D11
Yijun *China* **56** G5
Yiliang *Yunnan, China* **58** D5
Yiliang *Yunnan, China* **58** E4
Yilong *China* **58** B6
Yimen *China* **58** E4
Yimianpo *China* **57** B15
Yinchuan *China* **56** E4
Yindarlgooda, L. *Australia* **93** F3
Ying He → *China* **56** H9
Ying Xian *China* **56** E7
Yingcheng *China* **59** B9
Yingde *China* **59** E9
Yingjiang *China* **58** E1
Yingjing *China* **58** C4
Yingkou *China* **57** D12
Yingshan *Henan, China* **59** B9
Yingshan *Hubei, China* **59** B10
Yingshan *Sichuan, China* **58** B6
Yingshang *China* **59** A11
Yingtan *China* **59** C11
Yining *China* **52** E9
Yinjiang *China* **58** C7
Yinmabin *Burma* **67** H19
Yioúra = Giaros *Greece* **46** D6
Yipinglang *China* **58** E3
Yirba Muda *Ethiopia* **81** F4
Yirga Alem *Ethiopia* **81** F4
Yirol *Sudan* **81** F3
Yirrkala *Australia* **94** A2
Yishan *China* **58** E7
Yishui *China* **57** G10
Yishun *Singapore* **65** d
Yitong *China* **57** C13
Yiwu *China* **59** C13
Yixing *China* **59** B12
Yiyang *Henan, China* **56** G7
Yiyang *Hunan, China* **59** C9
Yiyang *Jiangxi, China* **59** C11
Yizhang *China* **59** E9
Yizheng *China* **59** A12
Yli-Kitka *Finland* **8** C23
Yliki, L. *Greece* **46** C5
Ylitornio *Finland* **8** C20
Ylivieska *Finland* **8** D21
Yngaren *Sweden* **11** F10
Yoakum *U.S.A.* **116** G6
Yob △ *Eritrea* **81** D4
Yobe □ *Nigeria* **83** C7
Yog Pt. *Phil.* **63** B6
Yogan *Togo* **83** D5
Yoğuntaş *Turkey* **45** E11
Yogyakarta *Indonesia* **63** G14
Yogyakarta □ *Indonesia* **63** G14
Yoho △ *Canada* **102** C5
Yojoa, L. de *Honduras* **120** D2
Yok Don △ *Vietnam* **64** F6
Yokadouma *Cameroon* **84** D2
Yokkaichi *Japan* **55** G8
Yoko *Cameroon* **83** D7
Yokohama *Japan* **55** G9
Yokosuka *Japan* **55** G9
Yokote *Japan* **54** E10
Yola *Nigeria* **83** D7
Yolaina, Cordillera de *Nic.* **120** D3
Yólöten *Turkmenistan* **71** B9
Yom → *Thailand* **64** E3
Yonago *Japan* **55** G6
Yonaguni-Jima *Japan* **55** M1
Yŏnan *N. Korea* **57** F14
Yonezawa *Japan* **54** F10

Yong Peng *Malaysia* **65** M4
Yong Sata *Thailand* **65** J2
Yongamp'o *N. Korea* **57** E13
Yong'an *China* **59** E11
Yongcheng *China* **56** H9
Yongchun *China* **59** E12
Yongchuan *China* **58** C5
Yongchun *China* **59** E12
Yongde *China* **58** E2
Yongdeng *China* **56** F2
Yongding *China* **59** E11
Yongfeng *China* **59** D10
Yongfu *China* **58** E7
Yonghe *China* **56** F6
Yŏnghŭng *N. Korea* **57** E14
Yongji *China* **56** G6
Yongjia *China* **59** C13
Yongkang *Yunnan, China* **58** E2
Yongkang *Zhejiang, China* **59** C13
Yongnian *China* **56** F8
Yongning *Guangxi Zhuangzu, China* **58** F7
Yongning *Ningxia Huizu, China* **56** E4
Yongping *China* **58** E2
Yongqing *China* **56** E9
Yongren *China* **58** D3
Yongshan *China* **58** C4
Yongsheng *China* **58** D3
Yongshun *China* **58** C7
Yongtai *China* **59** E12
Yongxin = Jinggangshan *China* **59** D10
Yongxing *China* **59** D9
Yongxiu *China* **59** C10
Yongzhou *China* **59** D8
Yongxin *China* **59** D10
Yonibana *S. Leone* **82** D2
Yonkers *U.S.A.* **115** F11
Yonne □ *France* **19** E10
Yonne → *France* **19** D9
York *Australia* **93** F2
York *U.K.* **14** D6
York *Ala., U.S.A.* **117** E10
York *Nebr., U.S.A.* **112** E5
York *Pa., U.S.A.* **113** F15
York, C. *Australia* **94** A3
York, City of □ *U.K.* **14** D6
York, Kap *Greenland* **4** B4
York, Vale of *U.K.* **14** C6
York Sd. *Australia* **92** C4
Yorke Pen. *Australia* **95** E2
Yorkshire Dales △ *U.K.* **14** C5
Yorkshire Wolds *U.K.* **14** C7
Yorkton *Canada* **103** C8
Yorkville *U.S.A.* **110** G3
Yoro *Honduras* **120** C2
Yoron-Jima *Japan* **55** L4
Yorosso *Mali* **82** C4
Yos Sudarso, Pulau = Dolak, Pulau *Indonesia* **63** F9
Yosemite △ *U.S.A.* **110** H7
Yosemite Village *U.S.A.* **110** H7
Yoshino-Kumano △ *Japan* **55** H8
Yoshkar Ola *Russia* **34** B8
Yotvata *Israel* **74** F4
You Jiang → *China* **58** F6
You Xian *China* **59** D9
Youbou *Canada* **110** B2
Youghal *Ireland* **12** E4
Youghal B. *Ireland* **12** E4
Youkounkoun *Guinea* **82** C2
Young *Australia* **95** E4
Young *Canada* **103** C7
Young *Uruguay* **126** C4
Younghusband, L. *Australia* **95** E2
Younghusband Pen. *Australia* **95** F2
Youngstown *Canada* **103** C6
Youngstown *N.Y., U.S.A.* **114** C5
Youngstown *Ohio, U.S.A.* **114** E4
Youngsville *U.S.A.* **114** E5
Youngwood *U.S.A.* **114** F5
Youxi *China* **59** D12
Youyang *China* **58** C7
Youyu *China* **56** D7
Yozgat *Turkey* **72** C6
Yozgat □ *Turkey* **72** C6
Ypacaraí △ *Paraguay* **126** B4
Ypané → *Paraguay* **126** A4
Ypres = Ieper *Belgium* **17** D2
Ypsingeaux *France* **21** C8
Yreka *U.S.A.* **108** F2
Yssingeaux *France* **21** C8
Ystad *Sweden* **11** J7
Ysyk-Köl *Kyrgyzstan* **52** E8
Ythan → *U.K.* **13** D7
Ytterhogdal *Sweden* **10** B8
Ytyk-Kyuyel *Russia* **53** C14
Yu Jiang → *China* **58** F7
Yü Shan *Taiwan* **59** F13
Yu Xian = Yuzhou *China* **56** G7
Yu Xian *Hebei, China* **56** E8
Yu Xian *Shanxi, China* **56** E7
Yuan Jiang → *Hunan, China* **59** C8
Yuan Jiang → *Yunnan, China* **58** F3
Yuan'an *China* **59** B8
Yuanjiang *Hunan, China* **59** C9
Yuanjiang *Yunnan, China* **58** F3
Yüanli *Taiwan* **59** E13

Yüanlin *Taiwan* **59** F13
Yuanling *China* **59** C8
Yuanmou *China* **58** E3
Yuanqu *China* **56** G6
Yuanyang *Henan, China* **56** G7
Yuanyang *Yunnan, China* **58** F4
Yuba → *U.S.A.* **110** F5
Yuba City *U.S.A.* **110** F5
Yūbari *Japan* **54** C10
Yubdo *Ethiopia* **81** F4
Yübetsu *Japan* **54** B11
Yubo *Sudan* **81** F2
Yucatán □ *Mexico* **119** C7
Yucatán, Canal de *Caribbean* **120** B2
Yucatán, Península de *Mexico* **98** H11
Yucatan Basin *Cent. Amer.* **119** D7
Yucatan Channel = Yucatán, Canal de *Caribbean* **120** B2
Yucca *U.S.A.* **111** L12
Yucca Valley *U.S.A.* **111** L10
Yucheng *China* **56** F9
Yuci *China* **56** F7
Yudu *China* **59** D10
Yuechi *China* **58** B6
Yuendumu *Australia* **92** D5
Yueqing *China* **59** C13
Yueqing Wan *China* **59** D13
Yuexi *Anhui, China* **59** B11
Yuexi *Sichuan, China* **58** C4
Yueyang *China* **59** C9
Yugan *China* **59** C11
Yugorenok *Russia* **53** D14
Yugoslavia = Serbia ■ *Europe* **44** C4
Yuhuan *China* **59** C13
Yühuan Dao *China* **59** C13
Yujiang *China* **59** C11
Yukhnov *Russia* **32** E8
Yukon □ *U.S.A.* **116** D6
Yukon → *U.S.A.* **106** a
Yukon Territory □ *Canada* **100** C6
Yüksekova *Turkey* **73** D11
Yukta *Russia* **53** C11
Yukuhashi *Japan* **55** H5
Yulara *Australia* **93** E5
Yule → *Australia* **92** D2
Yuleba *Australia* **95** D4
Yuli *Nigeria* **83** D7
Yüli *Taiwan* **59** F13
Yulin *Guangxi Zhuangzu, China* **59** F8
Yulin *Hainan, China* **64** C7
Yulin *Shaanxi, China* **56** E5
Yuma *Ariz., U.S.A.* **111** N12
Yuma *Colo., U.S.A.* **108** F3
Yuma, B. de *Dom. Rep.* **121** C6
Yumbe *Uganda* **86** B3
Yumbi *Dem. Rep. of the Congo* **86** C2
Yumen *China* **60** C4
Yumurtalık *Turkey* **72** D6
Yun Gui Gaoyuan *China* **58** E5
Yun Ling *China* **58** D2
Yun Xian *Hubei, China* **59** A8
Yun Xian *Yunnan, China* **58** E3
Yuna *Australia* **93** E2
Yunak *Turkey* **72** C4
Yunan *China* **59** F8
Yuncheng *Henan, China* **56** G8
Yuncheng *Shanxi, China* **56** G6
Yunfu *China* **59** F9
Yungas *Bolivia* **124** G5
Yungay *Chile* **126** D1
Yunhe *China* **59** C12
Yunkai Dashan *China* **59** F8
Yunlong *China* **58** E2
Yunmeng *China* **59** B9
Yunnan □ *China* **58** E4
Yunquera de Henares *Spain* **38** E1
Yunt Dağı *Turkey* **47** C9
Yunta *Australia* **95** E2
Yunxi *China* **56** H6
Yunxiao *China* **59** F11
Yupanqui Basin *Pac. Oc.* **97** J17
Yuping *China* **58** D7
Yuqing *China* **58** D6
Yuraygir △ *Australia* **95** D5
Yurga *Russia* **52** D9
Yurimaguas *Peru* **124** E3
Yurkivka *Ukraine* **29** B13
Yurubí △ *Venezuela* **121** D6
Yuryev-Polskiy *Russia* **32** D10
Yuryevets *Russia* **34** B6
Yuscarán *Honduras* **120** D2
Yûsef, Bahr → *Egypt* **80** B3
Yushan *China* **59** C12
Yushanzhen *China* **58** C7
Yushe *China* **56** F7
Yushu *Jilin, China* **57** B14
Yushu *Qinghai, China* **60** C4
Yusufeli *Turkey* **73** B9
Yutai *China* **56** G9
Yutian *China* **57** E9
Yuxari Qarabağ = Nagorno-Karabakh □ *Azerbaijan* **73** C12
Yuxi *China* **58** E4

Yuyao *China* **59** B13
Yuzawa *Japan* **54** E10
Yuzha *Russia* **34** B6
Yuzhno-Kurilsk *Russia* **53** E15
Yuzhno-Sakhalinsk *Russia* **53** E15
Yuzhno-Sukhokumsk
  Russia **35** H7
Yuzhnyy □ *Russia* **35** H5
Yuzhou *China* **56** G7
Yvelines □ *France* **19** D8
Yverdon-les-Bains *Switz.* **25** J2
Yvetot *France* **18** C7
Yzeure *France* **19** F10

Z

Zaanstad *Neths.* **17** B4
Zāb al Kabīr ➤ *Iraq* **73** D10
Zāb aş Şaghīr ➤ *Iraq* **73** E10
Žabalj *Serbia* **28** E5
Žabari *Serbia* **44** B5
Žabljak *Montenegro* **44** C3
Żabki *Poland* **31** F8
Zabłudów *Poland* **31** F9
Żabno *Poland* **31** H7
Zābol *Iran* **71** D9
Zābol □ *Afghan.* **66** D5
Zābolī *Iran* **71** E9
Zabolotiv *Ukraine* **29** B10
Zabolottya *Ukraine* **31** G11
Zabré *Burkina Faso* **83** C4
Zábřeh *Czech Rep.* **27** B9
Zabrze *Poland* **31** H5
Zabuzhzhya *Ukraine* **31** G10
Zabzuga *Ghana* **83** D5
Zacapa *Guatemala* **120** D2
Zacapu *Mexico* **118** D4
Zacatecas *Mexico* **118** C4
Zacatecas □ *Mexico* **118** C4
Zacatecoluca *El Salv.* **120** D2
Zacharo *Greece* **46** D3
Zachary *U.S.A.* **116** F9
Zachodnio-Pomorskie □
  Poland **30** D2
Zacoalco de Torres *Mexico* **118** C4
Zacualtipán *Mexico* **119** C5
Zadar *Croatia* **41** D12
Zadawa *Nigeria* **83** C7
Zadetkyi Kyun *Burma* **65** G2
Zadonsk *Russia* **33** F10
Zafarqand *Iran* **71** C7
Zafra *Spain* **37** G4
Żagań *Poland* **31** G2
Zagaoua *Chad* **79** E10
Żagarė *Lithuania* **30** B10
Zagazig *Egypt* **80** H7
Zāgheh *Iran* **71** C6
Zagnanado *Benin* **83** D5
Zagora *Greece* **46** B5
Zagorje *Slovenia* **41** B11
Zagórów *Poland* **31** F4
Zagórz *Poland* **31** J9
Zagreb *Croatia* **41** C12
Zagreb ✈ (ZAG) *Croatia* **41** C13
Zāgros, Kūhhā-ye *Iran* **71** C6
Zagros Mts. = Zāgros,
  Kūhhā-ye *Iran* **71** C6
Žagubica *Serbia* **44** B5
Zaguinaso *Ivory C.* **82** C3
Zagyva ➤ *Hungary* **28** C5
Zahamena *Madag.* **89** B8
Zāhedān *Fārs, Iran* **71** D7
Zāhedān
  Sīstān va Balūchestān, Iran **71** D9
Zahlah *Lebanon* **74** B4
Zahna *Germany* **24** D8
Záhony *Hungary* **28** B7
Zainsk *Russia* **34** C11
Zaïre = Congo ➤ *Africa* **84** F2
Zaječar *Serbia* **44** C6
Zaka *Zimbabwe* **89** C5
Zakamensk *Russia* **53** D11
Zakarpattya □ *Ukraine* **29** B8
Zakhodnaya Dzvina =
  Daugava ➤ *Latvia* **32** D3
Zākhū *Iraq* **73** D10
Zakinthos = Zakynthos
  Greece **46** D2
Zakopane *Poland* **31** J6
Zakroczym *Poland* **31** F7
Zakros *Greece* **49** D8
Zakynthos *Greece* **46** D2
Zakynthos □ *Greece* **46** D2
Zala *Ethiopia* **81** F4
Zala □ *Hungary* **28** D1
Zala ➤ *Hungary* **28** D2
Zalaegerszeg *Hungary* **28** D1
Zalakomár *Hungary* **28** D2
Zalalövő *Hungary* **28** D1
Zalamea de la Serena *Spain* **37** G5
Zalamea la Real *Spain* **37** H4
Zalari *Russia* **53** D11
Zalău *Romania* **28** C8
Žalec *Slovenia* **41** B12

Zaleshchiki = Zalishchyky
  Ukraine **29** B10
Zalesye *Russia* **30** D8
Zalew Wiślany *Poland* **30** D6
Zalewo *Poland* **30** E6
Zalingei *Sudan* **79** F10
Zalishchyky *Ukraine* **29** B10
Zama L. *Canada* **102** B5
Zambeke
  Dem. Rep. of the Congo **86** B2
Zambeze ➤ *Africa* **87** F4
Zambezi = Zambeze ➤
  Africa **87** F4
Zambezi *Zambia* **85** G4
Zambezi △ *Zimbabwe* **87** F2
Zambézia □ *Mozam.* **87** F4
Zambia ■ *Africa* **87** F2
Zamboanga *Phil.* **61** H5
Zambrów *Poland* **31** F9
Zametchino *Russia* **34** D6
Zamfara □ *Nigeria* **83** C6
Zamfara ➤ *Nigeria* **83** C5
Zamora *Mexico* **118** D4
Zamora *Spain* **36** D5
Zamora □ *Spain* **36** D5
Zamość *Poland* **31** H10
Zamtang *China* **58** A3
Zan *Ghana* **83** D4
Záncara ➤ *Spain* **39** F1
Zandvoort *Neths.* **17** B4
Zanesville *U.S.A.* **114** G2
Zangābād *Iran* **70** B5
Zangliveri *Greece* **44** F7
Zangoza = Sangüesa *Spain* **38** C3
Zangue ➤ *Mozam.* **87** F4
Zanjān *Iran* **73** D13
Zanjān □ *Iran* **71** B6
Zanjān ➤ *Iran* **71** B6
Zannone *Italy* **42** B6
Zante = Zakynthos *Greece* **46** D2
Zanthus *Australia* **93** F3
Zanzibar *Tanzania* **86** D4
Zaouiet El-Kala = Bordj
  Omar Driss *Algeria* **78** C7
Zaouiet Reggâne *Algeria* **78** C6
Zaoyang *China* **59** A9
Zaozhuang *China* **57** G9
Zap Suyu = Zāb al
  Kabīr ➤ *Iraq* **73** D10
Zapadna Morava ➤ *Serbia* **44** C5
Zapadnaya Dvina =
  Daugava ➤ *Latvia* **32** D3
Zapadnaya Dvina *Russia* **32** D7
Západné Beskydy *Europe* **27** B12
Zapadni Rodopi *Bulgaria* **44** E7
Západočeský □ *Czech Rep.* **26** B6
Zapala *Argentina* **128** D2
Zapaleri, Cerro *Bolivia* **126** A2
Zapata *U.S.A.* **116** H5
Zapatón ➤ *Spain* **37** F4
Zapolyarnyy *Russia* **8** B24
Zapopán *Mexico* **118** C4
Zaporizhzhya *Ukraine* **33** J8
Zaporizhzhya □ *Ukraine* **33** J8
Zaporozhye =
  Zaporizhzhya *Ukraine* **33** J8
Zaqatala *Azerbaijan* **35** K8
Zara *Turkey* **72** C7
Zaragoza *Coahuila, Mexico* **118** B4
Zaragoza *Nuevo León, Mexico* **119** C5
Zaragoza *Spain* **38** D4
Zaragoza □ *Spain* **38** D4
Zarand *Kermān, Iran* **71** D8
Zarand *Markazī, Iran* **71** C6
Zărandului, Munţii *Romania* **28** D7
Zaranj *Afghan.* **66** D2
Zarasai *Lithuania* **32** E4
Zárate *Argentina* **126** C4
Zarautz *Spain* **38** B2
Zaraysk *Russia* **32** E10
Zard, Kūh-e *Iran* **71** C6
Zāreh *Iran* **71** C6
Zari *Nigeria* **83** C7
Zaria *Nigeria* **83** C6
Zarineh ➤ *Iran* **73** D12
Żarki *Poland* **31** H6
Zarko *Greece* **46** B4
Zarneh *Iran* **70** C5
Żarnów *Poland* **31** H3
Zărneşti *Romania* **29** E10
Zaros *Greece* **49** D6
Żarów *Poland* **31** H3
Zarqā', Nahr az ➤ *Jordan* **74** C4
Zarrīn *Iran* **71** C7
Zarrīnābād *Iran* **73** D13
Zaruma *Ecuador* **124** D3
Żary *Poland* **31** G2
Zarza de Granadilla *Spain* **36** E4
Zarzis *Tunisia* **79** B8
Zas *Spain* **36** B2
Zaskar ➤ *India* **69** B7
Zaskar Mts. *India* **69** C7
Zastava *Ukraine* **29** B10
Zastron *S. Africa* **88** E4
Żatec *Czech Rep.* **26** A6
Zaterechnyy *Russia* **35** H7
Zator *Poland* **31** J6
Zatyshshya *Ukraine* **29** C14
Zavala *Bos.-H.* **44** D1
Zavāreh *Iran* **71** C7

Zave *Zimbabwe* **89** B5
Zavetnoye *Russia* **35** G6
Zavidovići *Bos.-H.* **28** F3
Zavitinsk *Russia* **53** D13
Zavodovski, I. *Antarctica* **5** B1
Zavolzhsk *Russia* **34** B6
Zavolzhye *Russia* **34** B6
Zawadzkie *Poland* **31** H5
Zawichost *Poland* **31** H8
Zawidów *Poland* **31** G2
Zawiercie *Poland* **31** H6
Zawiyat al Baydā = Al
  Baydā *Libya* **79** B10
Zāwyet Shammas *Egypt* **80** A2
Zâwyet Um el Rakham
  Egypt **80** A2
Zâwyet Ungeîla *Egypt* **80** A2
Zāyā *Iraq* **70** C5
Zāyandeh ➤ *Iran* **71** C7
Zaysan *Kazakhstan* **52** E9
Zaysan Köli *Kazakhstan* **52** E9
Zayü *China* **58** C1
Zazafotsy *Madag.* **89** C8
Zázrivá *Slovak Rep.* **27** B12
Zbarazh *Ukraine* **23** D13
Zbąszyń *Poland* **31** F2
Zbąszynek *Poland* **31** F2
Zblewo *Poland* **30** E5
Žďár nad Sázavou *Czech Rep.* **26** B8
Zdolbuniv *Ukraine* **23** C14
Ždrelo *Serbia* **44** B5
Zduńska Wola *Poland* **31** G5
Zduny *Poland* **31** G4
Zeballos *Canada* **102** D3
Zebediela *S. Africa* **89** C4
Zebila *Ghana* **83** C4
Zebrugge *Belgium* **17** C3
Zeehan *Australia* **95** G4
Zeeland □ *Neths.* **17** C3
Zeerust *S. Africa* **88** D4
Zefat *Israel* **74** C4
Zege *Ethiopia* **81** E4
Zeggerene, Iracher *Mali* **83** B5
Zégoua *Mali* **82** C3
Zehak *Iran* **71** D9
Zehdenick *Germany* **24** C9
Zeil, Mt. *Australia* **92** D5
Zeist *Neths.* **17** B5
Zeitz *Germany* **24** D8
Żelechów *Poland* **31** G8
Zelena *Ukraine* **29** B9
Zelengora *Bos.-H.* **44** C2
Zelenodolsk *Russia* **34** C9
Zelenogorsk *Russia* **32** B5
Zelenograd *Russia* **32** D9
Zelenogradsk *Russia* **30** D7
Zelenokumsk *Russia* **35** H6
Železná Ruda *Czech Rep.* **26** B6
Zelienople *U.S.A.* **114** F4
Želiezovce *Slovak Rep.* **27** C11
Zelina *Croatia* **41** C13
Zell *Baden-W., Germany* **25** H3
Zell *Rhld-Pfz., Germany* **25** E3
Zell am See *Austria* **26** D5
Zella-Mehlis *Germany* **24** E6
Zelów *Poland* **31** G6
Zeltweg *Austria* **26** D7
Žemaitijos □ *Lithuania* **30** B8
Zémio *C.A.R.* **86** A2
Zempléni-hegység *Hungary* **28** B6
Zemplínska šírava
  Slovak Rep. **27** C15
Zempoala *Mexico* **119** D5
Zemun *Serbia* **44** B4
Zengbé *Cameroon* **83** D7
Zengcheng *China* **59** F9
Zenica *Bos.-H.* **28** F2
Žepče *Bos.-H.* **28** F3
Zeraf, Bahr ez ➤ *Sudan* **81** F3
Zerbst *Germany* **24** D8
Żerków *Poland* **31** F4
Zermatt *Switz.* **25** J3
Zernez *Switz.* **25** J6
Zernograd *Russia* **35** G5
Zerqan *Albania* **44** E4
Zestaponi *Georgia* **35** J6
Zetel *Germany* **24** B3
Zeulenroda *Germany* **24** E7
Zeven *Germany* **24** B5
Zevenaar *Neths.* **17** C6
Zévio *Italy* **40** C8
Zeya *Russia* **53** D13
Zeya ➤ *Russia* **53** D13
Zeytinbaği *Turkey* **45** F12
Zeytindağ *Turkey* **47** C9
Zghartâ *Lebanon* **74** A4
Zgierz *Poland* **31** G6
Zgorzelec *Poland* **31** G2
Zgurița *Moldova* **29** B13
Zhabinka *Belarus* **31** F11
Zhabokrych *Ukraine* **29** B13
Zhalpaqtal *Kazakhstan* **34** F9
Zhambyl = Taraz *Kazakhstan* **52** E8
Zhangaly *Kazakhstan* **35** G10
Zhangaqala *Kazakhstan* **35** F9
Zhangaqazaly *Kazakhstan* **52** E7

Zhangbei *China* **56** D8
Zhangguangcai Ling *China* **57** B15
Zhangjiagang *China* **63** B13
Zhangjiakou *China* **56** D8
Zhangping *China* **59** E11
Zhangpu *China* **59** E11
Zhangshu *China* **59** C10
Zhangwu *China* **57** C12
Zhangye *China* **60** C5
Zhangzhou *China* **59** E11
Zhanhua *China* **57** F10
Zhänibek *Kazakhstan* **34** F8
Zhanjiang *China* **59** G8
Zhannetty, Ostrov *Russia* **53** B16
Zhanyi *China* **58** E4
Zhanyu *China* **57** B12
Zhao Xian *China* **56** F8
Zhao'an *China* **59** F11
Zhaocheng *China* **56** F6
Zhaojue *China* **58** C5
Zhaoping *China* **59** E8
Zhaoqing *China* **59** F9
Zhaotong *China* **58** D4
Zhaoyuan *Heilongjiang,
  China* **57** B13
Zhaoyuan *Shandong, China* **57** F11
Zharkent *Kazakhstan* **52** E9
Zharkovskiy *Russia* **32** E7
Zhashkiv *Ukraine* **23** D16
Zhashui *China* **56** H5
Zhayylma *Kazakhstan* **52** D7
Zhayyq ➤ *Kazakhstan* **6** F16
Zhdanov = Mariupol *Ukraine* **33** J9
Zhecheng *China* **56** G8
Zhegao *China* **59** B11
Zhejiang □ *China* **59** C13
Zheleznodorozhnyy *Russia* **30** D8
Zheleznogorsk *Russia* **33** F8
Zheleznogorsk-Ilimskiy
  Russia **53** D11
Zheltorye Vody = Zhovti
  Vody *Ukraine* **33** H7
Zhen'an *China* **56** H5
Zhenba *China* **58** A6
Zhenfeng *China* **58** E5
Zheng'an *China* **58** C6
Zhengding *China* **56** E8
Zhenghe *China* **59** D12
Zhengyang *China* **59** A10
Zhengyangguan *China* **59** A11
Zhengzhou *China* **56** G7
Zhenhai *China* **59** C13
Zhenjiang *China* **59** A12
Zhenkang *China* **58** F2
Zhenlai *China* **57** B12
Zhenning *China* **58** D5
Zhenping *Henan, China* **56** H7
Zhenping *Shaanxi, China* **58** B7
Zhenxiong *China* **58** D5
Zhenyuan *Gansu, China* **56** G4
Zhenyuan *Guizhou, China* **58** D7
Zherdevka *Russia* **34** E6
Zherebkove *Ukraine* **29** C14
Zherong *China* **59** D12
Zhetiqara *Kazakhstan* **52** D7
Zhezqazghan *Kazakhstan* **52** E7
Zhicheng *China* **59** B8
Zhidan *China* **56** F5
Zhigansk *Russia* **53** C13
Zhigulevsk *Russia* **34** D9
Zhijiang *Hubei, China* **59** B8
Zhijiang *Hunan, China* **58** D7
Zhijin *China* **58** D5
Zhilinda *Russia* **53** C12
Zhilino *Russia* **30** D8
Zhirnovsk *Russia* **34** E7
Zhitomir = Zhytomyr
  Ukraine **23** C15
Zhizdra *Russia* **32** F8
Zhlobin *Belarus* **23** B16
Zhmerynka *Ukraine* **23** D15
Zhob *Pakistan* **68** D3
Zhob ➤ *Pakistan* **68** D3
Zhodzina *Belarus* **23** A15
Zhokhova, Ostrov *Russia* **53** B16
Zhongdian *China* **58** D2
Zhongdong *China* **58** F6
Zhongdu *China* **58** E7
Zhongning *China* **56** F3
Zhongshan *Antarctica* **5** C6
Zhongshan *Guangdong, China* **59** F9
Zhongshan
  Guangxi Zhuangzu, China **59** E8
Zhongtiao Shan *China* **56** G6
Zhongwei *China* **56** F3
Zhongxiang *China* **59** B9
Zhongyang *China* **56** F6
Zhorany *Ukraine* **31** G10
Zhosaly *Kazakhstan* **52** E7
Zhoucun *China* **57** F9
Zhouning *China* **59** D12
Zhoushan *China* **59** B14
Zhoushan Dao *China* **59** C14
Zhouzhi *China* **56** G5
Zhovti Vody *Ukraine* **33** H7
Zhovtneve *Lubelskie, Ukraine* **31** H11
Zhovtneve *Mykolayiv, Ukraine* **33** J7
Zhu Jiang ➤ *China* **59** F9
Zhuanghe *China* **57** E12

Zhucheng *China* **57** G10
Zhugqu *China* **56** H3
Zhuhai *China* **59** F9
Zhuji *China* **59** C13
Zhukovka *Russia* **32** F7
Zhumadian *China* **56** H8
Zhuo Xian = Zhuozhou
  China **56** E8
Zhuolu *China* **56** D8
Zhuozhou *China* **56** E8
Zhuozi *China* **56** D7
Zhushan *China* **59** A8
Zhuxi *China* **58** A7
Zhuzhou *China* **59** D9
Zhvanets *Ukraine* **29** B11
Zhytomyr *Ukraine* **23** C15
Zhytomyr □ *Ukraine* **33** G5
Zi Shui ➤ *China* **59** C9
Žiar nad Hronom
  Slovak Rep. **27** C11
Ziarat *Pakistan* **68** D2
Zibo *China* **57** F10
Zichang *China* **56** F5
Zidarovo *Bulgaria* **45** D11
Zidi = Wandhari *Pakistan* **68** F2
Ziębice *Poland* **31** H4
Zielona Góra *Poland* **31** G2
Zierikzee *Neths.* **17** C3
Ziesar *Germany* **24** C8
Zifta *Egypt* **80** H7
Zigong *China* **58** C5
Ziguéy *Chad* **79** F9
Ziguinchor *Senegal* **82** C1
Ziguinchor □ *Senegal* **82** C1
Zihuatanejo *Mexico* **118** D4
Zijin *China* **59** F10
Zile *Turkey* **72** B6
Žilina *Slovak Rep.* **27** B11
Žilinský □ *Slovak Rep.* **27** B12
Zillah *Libya* **79** C9
Zillertaler Alpen *Austria* **26** D4
Zima *Russia* **53** D11
Zimapán *Mexico* **119** C5
Zimba *Zambia* **87** F2
Zimbabwe *Zimbabwe* **87** G3
Zimbabwe ■ *Africa* **87** F3
Zimi *S. Leone* **82** D2
Zimnicea *Romania* **29** G10
Zimovniki *Russia* **35** G6
Zinave △ *Mozam.* **89** C5
Zinder *Niger* **83** C6
Zinder □ *Niger* **83** C7
Zinga *Tanzania* **87** D4
Zingaro ○ *Italy* **42** E5
Zingst *Germany* **24** A8
Ziniaré *Burkina Faso* **83** C4
Zinnowitz *Germany* **24** A9
Zion △ *U.S.A.* **109** H7
Zirbitzkogel *Austria* **26** D7
Zirc *Hungary* **28** C2
Žiri *Slovenia* **41** B11
Žirje *Croatia* **41** E12
Zirl *Austria* **26** D4
Zirndorf *Germany* **25** F6
Ziros *Greece* **49** D8
Zirreh, Gowd-e *Afghan.* **66** E3
Zisterdorf *Austria* **27** C9
Zitácuaro *Mexico* **118** D4
Žitava ➤ *Slovak Rep.* **27** C11
Zitong *China* **58** B5
Zitsa *Greece* **46** B2
Zittau *Germany* **24** E10
Zitundo *Mozam.* **89** D5
Živinice *Bos.-H.* **28** F3
Ziwa Magharibi =
  Kagera □ *Tanzania* **86** C3
Ziway, L. *Ethiopia* **81** F4
Zixi *China* **59** D11
Zixing *China* **59** D9
Ziyang *Shaanxi, China* **56** H5
Ziyang *Sichuan, China* **58** B5
Ziyuan *China* **59** D8
Ziyun *China* **58** E6
Zizhong *China* **58** C5
Zizur Mayor *Spain* **38** C3
Zlarin *Croatia* **41** E12
Zlatar *Croatia* **41** B13
Zlatar *Serbia* **44** C3
Zlataritsa *Bulgaria* **45** C9
Zlatibor *Serbia* **44** C3
Zlatitsa *Bulgaria* **45** D8
Zlatna *Romania* **29** D8
Zlatna Panega *Bulgaria* **45** C8
Zlatni Pyasŭtsi *Bulgaria* **45** C12
Zlatograd *Bulgaria* **45** E9
Zlatoust *Russia* **52** D6
Zletovo *Macedonia* **44** E6
Zlín *Czech Rep.* **27** B10
Zlínský □ *Czech Rep.* **27** B10
Zlocienieć *Poland* **30** E3
Złoczew *Poland* **31** G5
Zlot *Serbia* **44** B5
Zlotoryja *Poland* **31** G2
Złotów *Poland* **30** E4

Znamenka = Znamyanka
  Ukraine **33** H7
Znamensk *Russia* **30** D8
Znamyanka *Ukraine* **33** H7
Żnin *Poland* **31** F4
Znojmo *Czech Rep.* **26** C9
Zobeyrī *Iran* **70** C5
Zobia *Dem. Rep. of the Congo* **86** B2
Zoetermeer *Neths.* **17** B4
Zogang *China* **58** C1
Zogno *Italy* **40** C6
Zogqên *China* **58** A2
Zohreh ➤ *Iran* **71** D6
Zolochiv *Ukraine* **33** D13
Zolotonosha *Ukraine* **33** H7
Zolotyy Potik *Ukraine* **29** B10
Zomba *Malawi* **87** F4
Zongo *Dem. Rep. of the Congo* **84** D3
Zonguldak *Turkey* **72** B4
Zonguldak □ *Turkey* **72** B4
Zongyang *China* **59** B11
Zonqor Pt. *Malta* **49** D2
Zonza *France* **21** G13
Zorgo *Burkina Faso* **83** C4
Zorita *Spain* **37** F5
Zossen *Germany* **24** C9
Zou Xiang *China* **56** G9
Zouan-Hounien *Ivory C.* **82** D3
Zouar *Chad* **79** D9
Zouérate = Zouîrât
  Mauritania **78** D3
Zouîrât *Mauritania* **78** D3
Zourika *Niger* **83** B6
Zourma *Burkina Faso* **83** C4
Zoutkamp *Neths.* **17** A6
Zrenjanin *Serbia* **28** E5
Zuarungu *Ghana* **83** C4
Zuba *Nigeria* **83** D6
Zubayr *Yemen* **81** D5
Zubtsov *Russia* **32** D8
Zuénoula *Ivory C.* **82** D3
Zuera *Spain* **38** D4
Zufār *Oman* **75** D5
Zug *Switz.* **25** H4
Zugdidi *Georgia* **35** J5
Zugersee *Switz.* **25** H4
Zugspitze *Germany* **25** H6
Zuid-Holland □ *Neths.* **17** C4
Zuidbeveland *Neths.* **17** C3
Zuidhorn *Neths.* **17** A6
Zújar *Spain* **37** H8
Zújar ➤ *Spain* **37** G5
Żukowo *Poland* **30** D5
Zula *Eritrea* **81** D4
Zülpich *Germany* **24** E2
Zumaia *Spain* **38** B2
Zumárraga *Spain* **38** B2
Zumbo *Mozam.* **87** F3
Zummo *Nigeria* **83** D7
Zumpango *Mexico* **119** D5
Zungeru *Nigeria* **83** D6
Zunhua *China* **57** D9
Zuni Pueblo *U.S.A.* **109** J9
Zunyi *China* **58** D6
Zuo Jiang ➤ *China* **58** F6
Zuozhou *China* **58** F6
Županja *Croatia* **28** E3
Žur *Serbia* **44** D4
Zurbātīyah *Iraq* **73** F12
Zürich *Switz.* **25** H4
Zürich □ *Switz.* **25** H4
Zürichsee *Switz.* **25** H4
Żuromin *Poland* **31** E6
Zut *Croatia* **41** E12
Zutphen *Neths.* **17** B6
Zuurberg △ *S. Africa* **88** E4
Zuwārah *Libya* **79** B8
Züzan *Iran* **71** C8
Zvenigorodka =
  Zvenyhorodka *Ukraine* **33** H6
Zvenyhorodka *Ukraine* **33** H6
Zvezdets *Bulgaria* **45** D11
Zvishavane *Zimbabwe* **87** G3
Zvolen *Slovak Rep.* **27** C12
Zvonce *Serbia* **44** D6
Zvornik *Bos.-H.* **28** F4
Zwedru = Tchien *Liberia* **82** D3
Zweibrücken *Germany* **25** F3
Zwenkau *Germany* **24** D8
Zwettl *Austria* **26** C8
Zwickau *Germany* **24** E8
Zwierzyniec *Poland* **31** H9
Zwiesel *Germany* **25** F8
Zwoleń *Poland* **31** G8
Zwolle *Neths.* **17** B6
Zwolle *U.S.A.* **116** F8
Žychlin *Poland* **31** F6
Żyrardów *Poland* **31** F7
Zyryan *Kazakhstan* **52** E9
Zyryanka *Russia* **53** C16
Zyryanovsk = Zyryan
  Kazakhstan **52** E9
Żywiec *Poland* **31** J6

KEY TO EUROPEAN MAP PAGES

 **Large scale maps**
(>1:2 500 000)

 **Medium scale maps**
(1:2 800 000 – 1:9 900 000)

 **Small scale maps**
(<1:10 000 000)

ICELAND

WORLD COUNTRY INDEX

Afghanistan	66
Albania	44
Algeria	78
Angola	84–85
Argentina	126, 128
Armenia	73
Australia	92–95
Austria	26–27
Azerbaijan	73
Bahamas	120–121
Bahrain	71
Bangladesh	67
Barbados	121
Belarus	32–33
Belgium	17
Belize	120
Benin	83
Bhutan	67
Bolivia	124
Bosnia-Herzegovina	41, 44
Botswana	88
Brazil	124–125, 127
Brunei	62
Bulgaria	44–45
Burkina Faso	82–83
Burma (Myanmar)	67
Burundi	86
Cambodia	64–65
Canary Is.	48
Cameroon	83, 84
Canada	100–105
Central African Republic	84
Chad	79
Chile	126, 128
China	56–60
Colombia	124
Congo	84
Congo, Dem. Rep. of the	84–85, 86–87
Costa Rica	120
Croatia	41
Cuba	120–121
Cyprus	49
Czech Republic	26–27
Denmark	11
Djibouti	81
Dominican Republic	121
East Timor	63
Ecuador	124
Egypt	80
El Salvador	120
England	14–15
Equatorial Guinea	84
Eritrea	80–81
Estonia	32
Ethiopia	75, 81
Fiji	91
Finland	8–9
France	18–21
French Guiana	125
Gabon	84
Gambia	82
Georgia	35

Germany	24–25
Ghana	82–83
Greece	44–47
Greenland	4
Guadeloupe	120
Guatemala	120
Guinea	82
Guinea-Bissau	82
Guyana	124
Haiti	121
Honduras	120
Hungary	28
Iceland	8
India	66–69
Indonesia	62–63
Iran	70–71, 73
Iraq	70–71, 73
Irish Republic	12
Israel	74
Italy	40–43
Ivory Coast	82
Jamaica	120
Japan	54–55
Jordan	74
Kazakhstan	52
Kenya	86
Korea, North	57
Korea, South	57
Kuwait	70–71
Kyrgyzstan	52
Laos	64
Latvia	32
Lebanon	74
Lesotho	89
Liberia	82
Libya	79
Lithuania	32
Luxembourg	17
Macedonia	44
Madagascar	89
Malawi	87
Malaysia	62–63, 65
Mali	78, 82–83
Malta	49
Martinique	120
Mauritania	78, 82
Mexico	118–119
Moldova	29
Mongolia	60
Montenegro	44
Morocco	78
Mozambique	87, 89
Namibia	88
Nepal	69
Netherlands	17
New Zealand	91
Nicaragua	120
Niger	78–79, 83
Nigeria	83
Northern Ireland	12
Norway	8–9
Oman	75

Pakistan	66, 68
Panama	120
Papua New Guinea	96
Paraguay	126–127
Peru	124
Philippines	61
Poland	30–31
Portugal	36–37
Puerto Rico	121
Qatar	71
Romania	28–29
Russia	32–35, 52–53
Rwanda	86
St. Lucia	121
Samoa	91
Saudi Arabia	70–71, 75
Scotland	13
Senegal	82
Serbia	28, 44
Sierra Leone	82
Singapore	65
Slovak Republic	27
Slovenia	41
Solomon Is.	96
Somali Republic	75
South Africa	88–89
Spain	36–39
Sri Lanka	66
Sudan	80–81
Suriname	124–125
Swaziland	89
Sweden	8–9
Switzerland	25
Syria	70, 72–73
Taiwan	59
Tajikistan	52
Tanzania	86–87
Thailand	64–65
Togo	83
Tonga	91
Trinidad and Tobago	125
Tunisia	78–79
Turkey	72–73
Turkmenistan	52
Uganda	86
Ukraine	33
United Arab Emirates	75
United Kingdom	12–16
USA	106–117
Uruguay	126–127
Uzbekistan	52
Vanuatu	96
Venezuela	124
Vietnam	64–65
Wales	14–15
Yemen	75
Zambia	85, 87
Zimbabwe	87

Arctic Circle

8

16 13

8

13

13

12   14

22

17

IRELAND   UNITED
KINGDOM   N

18

B

20   FRAN

36   38

ANDORRA

PORTUGAL   SPAIN   48

MOROCCO   ALG